PENGUIN HANDBOOKS

THE PENGUIN GUIDE TO COMPACT DISCS AND CASSETTES: NEW EDITION

EDWARD GREENFIELD, until his retirement in 1993, was for forty years on the staff of the *Guardian*, succeeding Neville Cardus as Music Critic in 1975. He still contributes regularly to the record column which he founded in 1954. At the end of 1960 he joined the reviewing panel of *Gramophone*, specializing in operatic and orchestral issues. He is a regular broadcaster on music and records for the BBC, not just on Radios 3 and 4 but also on the BBC World Service. In 1958 he published a monograph on the operas of Puccini. More recently he has written studies on the recorded work of Joan Sutherland and André Previn. He has been a regular juror on International Record awards and has appeared with such artists as Dame Elisabeth Schwarzkopf, Dame Joan Sutherland and Sir Georg Solti in public interviews. In October 1993 he was given a *Gramophone* Award for Special Achievement and in June 1994 received the OBE for services to music and journalism.

ROBERT LAYTON studied at Oxford with Edmund Rubbra for composition and with Egon Wellesz for the history of music. He spent two years in Sweden at the universities of Uppsala and Stockholm. He joined the BBC Music Division in 1959 and has been responsible for such programmes as *Interpretations on Record*. He has contributed a 'Quarterly Retrospect' to *Gramophone* for a number of years, and he has written books on Berwald and Sibelius and has specialized in Scandinavian music. He has written a monograph on the Dvořák symphonies and concertos for the BBC Music Guides, of which he was General Editor for many years. His translation of the first two volumes of Erik Tawastsjerna's definitive study of Sibelius was awarded the 1984 Finnish State Literary Prize. In 1987 he was awarded the Sibelius Medal and in the following year was made a Knight of the Order of the White Rose of Finland for his services to Finnish music. His recent publications have included *A Companion to the Concerto* and *A Companion to the Symphony*.

IVAN MARCH is a former professional musician. He studied at Trinity College of Music, London, and at the Royal Manchester College. After service in the Central Band of the RAF, he played the horn professionally for the BBC and travelled with the Carl Rosa and D'Oyly Carte opera companies. Now director of the Long Playing Record Library, the largest commercial lending library for classical music on compact discs in the British Isles, he is a well-known lecturer, journalist and personality in the world of recorded music. As a journalist, he contributes to a number of record-reviewing magazines, including *Gramophone*, where his regular monthly 'Collector's Corner' deals particularly with important reissues.

The Penguin Guide to Compact Discs and Cassettes
New Edition

Ivan March, Edward Greenfield and Robert Layton
Edited by Ivan March

PENGUIN BOOKS

Dedicated (without permission) with much affection and admiration to Quita Chavez,
now at three-quarters-time and still going strong.
The record scene in England would never have been quite the same without her.

PENGUIN BOOKS

Published by the Penguin Group
Penguin Books Ltd, 27 Wrights Lane, London W8 5TZ, England
Penguin Books USA Inc., 375 Hudson Street, New York, New York 10014, USA
Penguin Books Australia Ltd, Ringwood, Victoria, Australia
Penguin Books Canada Ltd, 10 Alcorn Avenue, Toronto, Ontario, Canada M4V 3B2
Penguin Books (NZ) Ltd, 182–190 Wairau Road, Auckland 10, New Zealand

Penguin Books Ltd, Registered Offices: Harmondsworth, Middlesex, England

First published 1994
10 9 8 7 6 5 4 3 2 1

Typeset, from data supplied, by Datix International Ltd, Bungay, Suffolk
Made and printed in Great Britain by Clays Ltd, St Ives plc

Contents

Editor's Note

This new edition of *The Penguin Guide to Compact Discs and Cassettes* offers a completely fresh appraisal of the current recording scene. Our previous comments have been reconsidered, pruned and sometimes rewritten in the light of newer issues. Our first choices often remain with older recordings – many of which are now less expensive than they were, and the stability of the repertoire in that respect is notable. Yet there are countless new and reissued CDs which take their place at or near the top of the list of recommendations. Among these is not only a remarkable expansion of desirable historical or 'almost historical' recordings but also a vast range of new lower-priced CDs. Bargain and super-bargain CDs of good quality from labels like Naxos proliferate in ever-increasing numbers; this challenge has been met by the major companies with the 'duo' series. Honourably pioneered by Philips, two very well-filled CDs of top-line repertoire are thus offered for the price of one, and this often brings astonishing value for money. Great recorded music has not only widened its range and coverage but is also, on average, less expensive now than it ever was. The special joys of CD hardly need restating: ease of access, great presence and clarity of the sound-image, with background noise either (as in a digital master) obliterated or greatly minimized and made unobtrusive by modern technology. It is sad that the tape cassette has now been all but superseded by the bargain-price CD. Few recordings are available on musicassettes but, where they are, we have included details. We have thought it useful to indicate recordings (or reissued recordings) which are new to the present survey by using the symbol ⊛ placed immediately before the evaluation, catalogue number and performance details.

Ivan March (Editor)

Preface

We are in the middle of an extraordinary expansion of repertoire on CD that is unprecedented in the history of recording. It is on a scale undreamed of in the previous dramatic period of growth, in the halcyon days of mono LPs. Frontiers of musical experience are being pushed back, so that the gramophone (phonograph) offers a breadth of experience far beyond that possible in live performances.

Today's record producers are no longer content to explore beyond the standard repertoire in piecemeal fashion and arbitrarily to introduce selected works from lesser-known composers. Instead, they are recording whole œuvres in a methodical order. Printed music stored in libraries and archives and in other unlikely places (even, in the case of a recently rediscovered work by Haydn, in an attic in Dublin) is being sought out solely for recording purposes.

It seems that, almost every day, a new name is coming into focus as a composer of inspired music, a source of refreshment as much for our own times as for his own period. Medieval and Renaissance vocal repertory is suddenly joining the bestseller lists. Ten volumes already exist of an exploration by the Gothic Voices into ecclesiastical and secular music of the fourteenth and fifteenth centuries. Projects are already under way to give us the complete organ music of Bach many times over, on various organs and with different players; to offer the hundred-plus Haydn symphonies and eighty or so string quartets in several alternative complete sets; to issue on CD everything Liszt wrote for the piano and Purcell for the voice, while Marco Polo – already responsible for many fascinating new discoveries – is more than halfway through a complete edition on compact disc of the dance music of Johann Strauss Junior, which (with a dozen items per CD) has already reached Volume 36. The output of father and brother Strausses is to follow! The public response in Europe has already proved that here was an untapped demand just waiting to be met.

The coverage of the works of the major composers has become so exhaustive that duplication of recordings is almost overwhelming – we lost count of the number of CDs available world-wide of the public's top favourite, Vivaldi's *Four Seasons*, long ago. It is this huge area of popular symphonic, instrumental and vocal music that presents problems for the major companies, seeking to renew the repertory with today's performers – and no less a problem for us!

Newest is no longer synonymous with best; instead, we are rediscovering our performance heritage from the earlier years of the century, and this particular exploration has coincided with a sudden and profound improvement in the technology of transferring to CD recordings dating from before the LP era. These often exist only on 78 shellac pressings and, while private collections of these records exist in fairly pristine condition, only recently has it been found possible to re-create the original sound-balance in a CD transfer.

All three authors have been avid record collectors since the era of 78s and we know how good those records sounded. Until now, however, many transfers have been a travesty of that original listening experience. Happily this is no longer the case. Led by the remarkable Dutton Laboratories in the UK, CDs are appearing which offer a pleasing and well-balanced listening experience, with the body, bloom and ambience of the originals retained and with no attempt made to achieve false brilliance.

One has only to sample, for instance, Bruno Walter's 1938 LSO recordings or Beecham's LPO records from the same period, Stokowski's early Philadelphia records of the Stravinsky ballets, or the première recording of Vaughan Williams's *Tallis fantasia* by the Boyd Neel String Orchestra, made with the composer present, to understand the scope of this technological achievement. A similar improvement is also beginning to apply to transfers made from mono LPs (and one thinks here of the Beulah transfers of the marvellous Anthony Collins Decca/London set of Sibelius symphonies from the early 1950s). Suddenly the great musicians of the past can communicate their musical insights directly to us.

Digital remastering of more recent analogue, stereo recordings, so long a source of complaint, has also greatly improved so that now they can often be judged with confidence alongside their digital competitors. In particular, BMG/RCA's team, directed by John Pfeiffer, are to be congratulated in this respect, with the Chicago recordings of Fritz Reiner from the late 1950s standing out for the vividness and richness of the stereo image, while Wilma Cozart Fine of Mercury continues to prove the worth of this company's pioneering simplicity in their microphone techniques for recording in natural stereo.

Authenticity and the playing of period instruments has moved onwards from those disagreeable early days – although there were honourable exceptions – when violins were Gillette-edged, wind and horns uncomfortably out of tune, and phrasing offered bulges not unlike traffic calmers – 'speed bumps' in American parlance. Now that baroque music can actually sound beautiful when played with authentic manners, we can properly judge the advantages of the true balance and transparency of texture that early instruments immediately bring.

And this is never truer than with a new group, Tafelmusik, directed with great sensitivity and musicianship by Bruno Weil; they have greatly impressed us in Mozart and Vivaldi concertos but most of all in the *Sturm und Drang* symphonies of Haydn, where they have had the additional advantage of H. C. Robbins Landon as their musical adviser.

Recently, the wider musical public have discovered a new self-confidence in selecting contemporary music, often rejecting the *avant-garde*, barbed-wire repertoire so long foisted on us all by the powerful musical establishment. Led by the minimalist school, composers who communicate and write recognizable melodic lines have become fashionable again, and names like John Tavener and Górecky have found a wide popular following. Suddenly dissonance is being used to heighten the effect of a tune rather than as a replacement for it. We are also rediscovering many earlier-twentieth-century composers (in America as well as in Britain and Europe) who were bypassed by atonalism; for the Editor, one of the most reassuring of recent successes has been the *Symphonic Mass* of George Lloyd, written in the composer's eightieth year, which was recorded directly after its first performance at the Brighton Festival and immediately became a CD bestseller.

Inadequate documentation remains a problem. With occasional honourable exceptions, CD presentation of background information, vocal texts and translations cannot match the finest examples from the LP era, and artwork inevitably suffers from the size of the CD package. Interestingly, BMG/RCA have recently tried to get round this problem by using larger, slimline boxes, of the kind which once packaged boxed sets of cassettes. They were used for special presentations of Tchaikovsky ballet recordings, with beautifully imaginative accompanying artwork, to entice younger listeners. We hope this experiment may lead to more lavish productions – for their parents!

In conclusion, we must unashamedly make clear that in no way is our current survey absolutely complete – nor could it be within the pages of a single volume (which is the only practicable format for such a *Guide*). What we have tried to do is to offer a balanced selection of what we see as the most desirable recordings currently before the public. It is an impossible task, but we hope it has been accomplished with honour. We know that you will write and tell us about the key records that you – our readers – have discovered and which have eluded us, and we welcome this. There is always a supplementary volume in progress and always a next time.

Edward Greenfield, Robert Layton and Ivan March

Introduction

As in previous editions, the object of the current *Penguin Guide to Compact Discs and Cassettes* is to give the serious collector a comprehensive survey of the finest recordings of permanent music on CD. As most records are issued almost simultaneously on both sides of the Atlantic and use identical international catalogue numbers, this *Guide* should be found to be equally useful in Great Britain and the USA. The internationalization of repertoire and numbers now applies to almost all CDs issued by the major international companies and by many smaller ones too, while most of the smaller European labels are imported in their original formats into both Britain and the USA.

The sheer number of records of artistic merit now available causes considerable problems in any assessment of overall and individual excellence. While in the case of a single popular repertoire work it might be ideal for the discussion to be conducted by a single reviewer, it has not always been possible for one person to have access to every version, and division of reviewing responsibility becomes inevitable. Also there are certain works and certain recorded performances for which one or another of our team has a special affinity. Such a personal identification can often carry with it a special perception too. We feel that it is a strength of our basic style to let such conveyed pleasure or admiration for the merits of an individual recording come over directly to the reader, even if this produces a certain ambivalence in the matter of choice between competing recordings. Where disagreement is more positive (and this has rarely happened), then readers will find an indication of this difference in the text. In the present edition, the Pletnev recording of the Rachmaninov *Second Symphony* is an obvious example of such divergence of views.

We have considered (and rejected) the use of initials against individual reviews, since this is essentially a team project. The occasions for disagreement generally concern matters of aesthetics, for instance in the manner of recording-balance, where a contrived effect may trouble some ears more than others, or in the matter of style, where the difference between robustness and refinement of approach appeals differently to listening sensibilities, rather than involving a question of artistic integrity. But over the years our views seem to grow closer together rather than to diverge; perhaps we are getting mellower, but we are seldom ready to offer strong disagreement following the enthusiastic reception by one of the team of a controversial recording, if the results are creatively stimulating. Our perceptions of the advantages and disadvantages of performances of early music on original (as against modern) instruments seem fairly evenly balanced; again, any strong feelings are indicated in the text.

Evaluation

Most recordings issued today by the major companies are of a high technical standard and offer performances of a quality at least as high as is experienced in the concert hall. In adopting a starring system for the evaluation of records, we have decided to make use of from one to three stars. Brackets round one or more of the stars indicate some reservations about its inclusion, and readers are advised to refer to the text. Brackets round all the stars usually indicate a basic qualification: for instance, a mono recording of a performance of artistic interest, where considerable allowances have to be made for the sound-quality, even though the recording may have been digitally remastered.

Our evaluation system may be summarized as follows:

*** An outstanding performance and recording in every way.
** A good performance and recording of today's normal high standard.
* A fair performance, reasonably well or well recorded.

Our evaluation is normally applied to the record as a whole, unless there are two main works or groups of works, and by different composers. In this case, each is dealt with separately in its appropriate place. In the case of a collection of shorter works we feel that there is little point in giving a separate starring to each item, even if their merits are uneven, since the record has to be purchased as a complete programme.

Rosettes

To a very few records we have awarded a Rosette: ❀.

Unlike our general evaluations, in which we have tried to be consistent, a Rosette is a quite arbitrary compliment by a member of the reviewing team to a recorded performance which, he finds, shows special illumination, magic, or a spiritual quality, or even outstanding production values, that places it in a very special class. Occasionally a Rosette has been awarded for an issue that seems to us to offer extraordinary value for money, but that presupposes that the performance or performances are outstanding too. The choice is essentially a personal one (although often it represents a shared view), and in some cases it is applied to an issue where certain reservations must also be mentioned in the text of the review. The Rosette symbol is placed before the usual evaluation and the record number. It is quite small – we do not mean to imply an 'Academy Award' but a personal token of appreciation for something uniquely valuable. We hope that, once the reader has discovered and perhaps acquired a 'rosetted' CD, its special qualities will soon become apparent.

Digital recordings

Nearly all new compact discs are recorded digitally, but an increasingly large number of digitally remastered, reissued analogue recordings are now appearing, and we think it important to include a clear indication of the difference:

Dig. This indicates that the master recording was digitally encoded.

Bargain and super-bargain issues

Since the publication of our last main volume we have seen a further huge expansion of the mid- and bargain-price labels from all the major companies. These are usually standard-repertoire works in excellent analogue recordings, digitally remastered. Often these reissue CDs are generous in playing time, increasing their value to the collector. There are also even cheaper classical CDs at super-bargain price, usually featuring performances by artists whose names are not internationally familiar, notably on the now rightly famous Naxos label. While many of these recordings derive from Eastern Europe, where recording costs have in the past been much lower than in the West, now this enterprising company is spreading its wings to embrace major orchestras and ensembles from Great Britain and Ireland.

A further super-bargain label, appropriately called Discover, has also appeared since our last volume. Most of these inexpensive issues are digitally encoded and some offer outstanding value, both technically and musically. The major companies have responded vigorously to this competition, not only by issuing super-bargain issues of their own (as on the DG Classikon and Polygram Belart logos) but also by the introduction of Duos and Doubles: two CDs packaged back-to-back in a single jewel-case, generously filled with top-line repertoire and offered for the cost of single premium-price CD. Thus the collector has plenty of scope in deciding how much to pay for a recorded performance, with a CD range from about £5 up to nearly three times that amount.

Our listing of each recording first indicates if it is not in fact in the premium-price category, as follows:

(M) Medium-priced label

(B) Bargain-priced label

(BB) Super-bargain label

See below for price structures for CDs and cassettes in the UK and the USA.

Layout of text

We have aimed to make our style as simple as possible, even though the catalogue numbers of recordings are no longer as straightforward as they once were. So, immediately after the evaluation and before the catalogue number, the record make is given, often in abbreviated form (a key to the abbreviations is provided on pages xxi–xxii). In the case of a set of two or more CDs, the number of units involved is given in brackets after the catalogue number. Cassette numbers are still denoted by being given in italic type.

American catalogue numbers

The numbers which follow in square brackets are US catalogue numbers, while the abbreviation [id.] indicates that the American number is identical to the European, which is increasingly becoming the case. Even BMG/RCA has recently moved over to completely identical numbers, although earlier issues have an alphabetical prefix in the UK which is not used by the Schwann catalogue in the USA.

There are certain other small differences to be remembered by American readers. For instance, a CBS/Sony number could have a completely different catalogue number on either side of the Atlantic, or it could use the same digits with different alphabetical prefixes, although this now seldom occurs. Both will be clearly indicated. EMI/Angel use extra digits for their British compact discs; thus the US number CDC 47001 becomes CDC7 47001-2 in Britain (the -2 is the European indication that this is a compact disc). We have taken care to check catalogue information as far as is possible, but as all the editorial work has been done in England there is always the possibility of error; American readers are therefore invited, when ordering records locally, to take the precaution of giving their dealer the fullest information about the music and recordings they want.

The indications (M), (B) and (BB) immediately before the starring of a disc refer only to the British record, as pricing systems are not always identical on both sides of the Atlantic.

Where no American catalogue number is given, this does not necessarily mean that a record is not available in the USA; the transatlantic issue may not have been made at the time of the publication of this *Guide*. Readers are advised to check the current *Schwann* catalogue and to consult their local record store.

Abbreviations

To save space we have adopted a number of standard abbreviations in listing orchestras and performing groups (a list is provided below), and the titles of works are often shortened, especially where they are listed several times. Artists' forenames are sometimes omitted if they are not absolutely necessary for identification purposes. Also we have not usually listed the contents of operatic highlights and collections; these can sometimes be found in *The Classical Catalogue*, published by *Gramophone* magazine (177–179, Kenton Road, Kenton, Harrow, Middlesex, HA3 0HA, England).

We have followed common practice in the use of the original language for titles where it seems sensible. In most cases, English is used for orchestral and instrumental music and the original language for vocal music and opera. There are exceptions, however; for instance, the Johann Strauss discography uses the German language in the interests of consistency.

Order of music

The order of music under each composer's name broadly follows that adopted by *The Classical Catalogue*: orchestral music, including concertos and symphonies; chamber music; solo instrumental music (in some cases with keyboard and organ music separated); vocal and choral music; opera; vocal collections; miscellaneous collections.

The Classical Catalogue now usually includes stage works alongside opera; in the main we have not followed this practice, preferring to list, say, ballet music and incidental music (where no vocal items are involved) in the general orchestral group. Within each group our listing follows an alphabetical sequence, and couplings within a single composer's output are *usually* discussed together instead of separately with cross-references. Occasionally and inevitably because of this alphabetical approach, different recordings of a given work can become separated when a record is listed and discussed under the first work of its alphabetical sequence. The Editor feels that alphabetical consistency is essential if the reader is to learn to find his or her way about.

Catalogue numbers

Enormous care has gone into the checking of CD catalogue numbers and contents to ensure that all details are correct, but the editor and publishers cannot be held responsible for any mistakes that may have crept in despite all our zealous checking. When ordering CDs, readers are urged to provide their record-dealer with full details of the music and performers, as well as the catalogue number.

Deletions

Compact discs, especially earlier, full-priced issues not too generous in musical content, are now steadily succumbing to the deletions axe, and more are likely to disappear during the lifetime of this book. Sometimes copies may still be found in specialist shops, and there remains the compensatory fact that most really important and desirable recordings are eventually reissued, usually costing less!

Of all the major international labels, EMI seems to maintain the least stable catalogue. Where companies like Chandos and Hyperion give the fullest support to their recording artists by retaining even the most esoteric repertoire on an ongoing basis, EMI often withdraws really important issues, sometimes only months after their appearance (or reappearance). Collectors must find this as frustrating as we do. In certain areas where the sudden disappearance of a valuable recording seems particularly difficult to justify, we have let the listing and review remain, in the book in the hope that the company concerned may have second thoughts. We have indicated such a withdrawal in the text.

Coverage

As the output of major and minor labels continues to expand, it will obviously be impossible for us to mention *every* CD that is available, within the covers of a single book; this is recognized as a practical limitation if we are to update our survey regularly. We have to be carefully selective in choosing the discs to be included (although on rare occasions a recording has been omitted simply because a review copy was not available);

anything which eludes us can always be included next time. However, we do welcome suggestions from readers about such omissions if they seem to be of special interest, and particularly if they are inexpensive. But borderline music on specialist labels that are not readily and reliably obtainable on both sides of the Atlantic cannot be given any kind of priority.

Acknowledgements

Our thanks, as ever, are due to Roger Wells, our copy editor, who has worked closely alongside us throughout the preparation of this book and, as a keen CD collector himself, also frequently made valuable creative suggestions. Kathleen March once again zealously checked the proofs for errors and reminded us when the text proved ambiguous, clumsily repetitive in its descriptive terminology, or just plain contradictory. Barbara Menard and Roy Randle contributed to the titling – never an easy task, and especially complicated in the many boxed anthologies involving a bouquet of different performers. Our team of Penguin proofreaders are also indispensable. Grateful thanks also go to all those readers who write to us to point out factual errors and remind us of important recordings which have escaped our notice.

Finally, we again welcome back to our cover the whimsical portrait of Nipper, the most famous dog in the world. He is associated with a deservedly world-famous trademark and reminds us that fine records have been available from this source for almost exactly one hundred years!

To American Readers

From your many letters and from visiting record stores in the USA, we know that our *Penguin Guide* is read, enjoyed and used as a tool by collectors on both sides of the Atlantic. We also know that some of you feel that our reviews are too frequently orientated towards European and British recordings and performances.

In concentrating on records which have common parlance in both Europe and the USA, we obviously give preference to the output of international companies, and in assessing both performers and performances we are concerned with only one factor: musical excellence. In a 400-year-old musical culture centred in Europe, it is not surprising that a great number of the finest interpreters should have been Europeans, and many of them have enjoyed recording in London, where there are four first-class symphony orchestras and many smaller groups at their disposal, supported by recording producers and engineers of the highest calibre.

Yet in the first half of this century the lure of the New World drew many of the top musicians across the Atlantic. America has been the home for many famous émigré instrumental soloists, of whom Horowitz, Heifetz and composer/pianist Rachmaninov (to say nothing of Stravinsky) are the most famous, and all Russian-born. Horowitz himself has no less than two special editions of recordings to himself in the Recitals section of this book, and Rachmaninov's own recordings are exhaustively covered. Heifetz is very well represented too, yet he has his own special edition due for release during the lifetime of this book and running to over 50 CDs, which we will consider next time around.

Singers jet-set all over the world and no single nation, other than their country of birth, can claim any special rights to their art. But it is the conductors who are the key figures in our musical culture, and many of the greatest have made their homes and careers in the USA. In the first half of the century.

America's great orchestras were led by giants!

Italian-born Toscanini began revolutionizing performances at the Met. as early as 1907, and it was not very long before he was also directing the New York Philharmonic. In 1936 he relinquished the NYPO and formed his own NBC Symphony – but, alas, no one was brave enough to tell him that the notorious acoustics of Studio 8H were totally unsuitable for recording, and many of his records have to be listened to with very tolerant ears.

At this point another distinguished name from the past comes into the picture: Dimitri Mitropoulos, born in Greece, who made his début with the Boston Symphony in 1936. In 1937 he moved to take charge in Minneapolis, where he stayed until 1949, at which point he took over the New York Philharmonic. His art is currently too little known, and we need more of his recordings to come back into currency.

Mitropoulos was succeeded in 1959 by Leonard Bernstein, about whom little need be said. As an inspired composer-conductor-pianist, musical scholar and lecturer with the common touch (and one of America's very greatest sons), he is generously represented in these pages.

When Mitropoulos left Minneapolis, the Hungarian, Antal Dorati, took his place. Dorati promptly put the orchestra on the recording map, beginning before the stereo era with a series of famous, first complete recordings of the major ballet scores, including those of Tchaikovsky.

Stokowski, part Polish, part British, as early as 1909 had travelled from London to Cincinnati, where he established his reputation over a period of three years. In 1912 he went to Philadelphia and built one of the finest orchestras in the world. He remained its director for three decades. Recording came abolutely naturally to Stokowski since he cared most about the quality of the sound and its balancing. Some of his early electric 78-r.p.m. records are of astonishing technical quality, notably his 1929/30 recording of Stravinsky's *Rite of spring* and the 1937 *Petrushka*, and they are now available on CD. Unlike Toscanini, Stokowski lived on into the stereo era and made many of his finest later recordings in Europe.

Stokowski's successor was another outstanding Hungarian musician, Eugene Ormandy, and the succession seemed to provide a fresh Philadelphia symbiosis between orchestra and conductor. Certainly their early records together showed real inspiration (notably a famous pioneer recording of suites from Ravel's *Daphnis and Chloé*). But Ormandy was to suffer from inadequate engineering, with recording producers determined on a brilliant, up-front sound-balance. Relatively few of his many fine records reproduce the Philadelphia sound naturally; too often those wonderful string sonorities are degraded and made to seem glossy and artificial. Even so, there are some splendid exceptions discussed in our pages. In later years Ormandy continued to make records which showed that the Philadelphia was still a great orchestra, but his interpretations at times sounded tired and even had an element of routine.

Russian-born Serge Koussevitzky, whom some would count greatest of all, had begun life as a phenomenal European virtuoso double-bass player. He soon exchanged bow for baton and conducted in Paris and London; his genius as an interpretative musician was instinctive. He was appointed Musical Director of the Boston Symphony in 1924. It was a year or two before his presence had the fullest effect, but by the early 1930s his music-making was producing electrifying results, even if his RCA recording engineers sometimes found it difficult to come to terms with the resonant acoustics of Boston's Symphony Hall, which can make a live concert there sound so glorious. Koussevitzky died in 1951, before the coming of stereo, and currently his recorded repertoire available is sadly limited.

It was left to the French conductor, Charles Munch, to continue the great orchestral tradition in Boston, which he did admirably – witness his 1955 early stereo recording of the complete *Daphnis et Chloé*, in many ways still unsurpassed for orchestral virtuosity and sensuous feeling. William Steinberg later conducted the orchestra from 1969 until 1972 with fine results.

In Chicago it was Frederick Stock, originally a bandmaster in the German army, who laid the foundations for the later supreme excellence of the Symphony Orchestra. He arrived in 1905 and had very soon established its reputation for an outstanding brass sonority which continues to the present day. But it was Fritz Reiner, another Hungarian, who created the great orchestra now so familiar to us.

After a decade as maestro at Pittsburgh (from 1938 until 1948, when his successor was Steinberg) Reiner moved, via the Metropolitan Opera, to Chicago. He took over there in 1953 and, during his tenure, Chicago's Orchestra Hall was famous for its acoustics, at that time more suitable for recording than any other concert hall in America. (Later the hall's natural ambience – so we are told – was to be adversely affected by the installation of air conditioning.)

It was the Mercury recording team who established the unique excellence of the hall by using the simplest microphone techniques for their mono and, later, stereo recordings of the 1950s, followed by the RCA engineers when that company took over the orchestra's recording contract. The story goes that the new team asked the orchestral members where the Mercury people had put their microphones! In consequence, Reiner conducted his superb orchestra in some of the most spectacular recordings made anywhere in the world during those early years of stereo, and they still sound marvellous today.

For Americans, the name of the French-born Pierre Monteux will always be associated with the San Francisco Symphony, whose musical director he became in 1936 and where he stayed for sixteen years until 1952. He conducted and made recordings world-wide (his first 78 discs were cut in the 1920s). If he had something very special to say in French repertoire (his 1961 Boston recording of the César Franck *Symphony* is still a first choice among countless versions recorded since) he refused to be musically typecast and was equally successful in the symphonies of Brahms and Beethoven. His recording career is celebrated in the present volume with his own special edition of 15 CDs.

George Szell, yet another Hungarian, made a world-wide reputation in the 1920s and '30s conducting all over Europe and also in Britain, but he too was drawn across the Atlantic – to take over (and for once this expression is used literally) the orchestra in Cleveland, Ohio, in 1946. He was an infamous martinet, but the results he gained were nothing short of extraordinary, and by the 1960s he had made the Cleveland Orchestra into one of the world's greatest virtuoso ensembles. Some would say 'the greatest' when he was at the peak of his career. Fortunately he had the excellent Severance Hall in which to make his records, and this mitigated some of the effect of the inadequately balanced engineering from which his recordings almost always suffered. Once again the CBS engineers sought a brilliant sound; their close microphones, while not negating the effect of the hall ambience, reduced the range of dynamic contrast, so that when the orchestra achieved rapt pianissimo playing it was seldom carried through to the finished record.

There are other names we do not have space to mention here, but that of Bruno Walter cannot be omitted. Like Toscanini, he was an unwitting gift of the Nazis to the USA and settled there permanently in 1939, just before the outbreak of the Second World War. His music-making was the epitome of the heart-warming pre-war Viennese tradition, as his Mahler symphony recordings readily show. How he made music in 1938 – just before he departed for the USA – is shown in a splendidly transferred Dutton Laboratories CD which contains three key recordings (of the music of Beethoven, Haydn and Schumann), made with the London Symphony Orchestra.

By one of those rare miracles of recording history, Walter had a magical Indian summer of recording in America at the end of the 1950s and the beginning of the 1960s. CBS set up two different orchestras of hand-picked players, one on the East Coast and one on the West, and well-known and established musicians 'fought' to be included in the ensembles. Walter then made a glowing series of records of music from his homeland (Beethoven, Bruckner, Mahler, Haydn, Mozart, Wagner) and somehow placed a Viennese mantle over that group of dedicated Americans, gathered together under the name, Columbia Symphony. The recordings are beautifully balanced and warm in timbre, to match the quality of the music-making, and included among them is a complete set of the Brahms Symphonies which are very special indeed. They belong to Sony now and will almost certainly reappear during the lifetime of this book.

When they died, each of these great musicians left a vacuum behind him which it has seemed almost impossible to fill. Although Bernstein continued to hold the reins in New York, he made many of his later recordings in Europe and Israel, and American orchestral managements have again looked over the seas, to the east as well as the west, to find a new generation of conducting talent. New names have been appearing, and we must mention here Gerard Schwarz in Seattle who has revealed another great orchestra in the making and is making distinguished recordings of music by the (until recently) almost forgotten generation of American composers of the inter-war years, including Creston, Diamond, Hanson and Piston.

Our performance coverage in the present volume – helped by the huge proportion of reissued older records – certainly reflects the American achievement, past and present, and with the current phenomenal improvements in transferring technology we hope that more of the early recordings made by those great names from America's musical past will enjoy the attention of the wider public.

Price Ranges – UK and USA

Price differences in the UK and USA

Compact discs and cassettes in all price ranges are more expensive in Britain and Europe than they are in the USA but, fortunately, in nearly all cases the various premium-price, mid-price, bargain and super-bargain categories are fairly consistent on both sides of the Atlantic. However, where records are imported in either direction, this can affect their domestic cost. For instance, (British) EMI's Classics for Pleasure and Eminence labels are both in the mid-price range in the USA, whereas CfP is a bargain series in the UK. Similarly Naxos, a super-bargain digital label in the UK, is a bargain label in the USA.

Vox Boxes are exceptionally good value at super-budget price in America, while in Britain they are comparable with the Duos and 'two for the price of one' series. Of course retail prices are not fixed in either country, and various stores may offer even better deals at times, so our price structure must be taken as a guideline only. One major difference in the USA is that almost all companies make a dollar surcharge (per disc) for mid-priced opera sets (to cover the cost of librettos) and Angel apply this levy to all their boxed sets. The Pickwick RPO and MCD compact disc series appear to be available only as a special import in the USA. The Vanguard CD label (except for the 8000 Series, which retails at around $15) is upper-mid-price in the USA but lower-mid-price in the UK. In *listing* records we have not used the major record companies' additional label subdivisions (like Decca/London's Ovation, DG's Galleria, EMI's Studio and Références, Philips's Concert Classics, Sony's Essential Classics and so on) in order to avoid further confusion, although these designations are sometimes referred to in the text of reviews.

Comparable prices in the UK and USA

Premium-priced CDs (although they cost less west of the Atlantic) are top-price repertoire the world over. Here are comparative details of the other price ranges:

(M) MID-PRICED SERIES (sets are multiples of these prices)
Includes: BMG/RCA; Chandos (Collect); Decca/London; DG; EMI/Angel (Studio and Références; Eminence); Erato/Warner (UK), Erato/WEA (USA); HM/BMG (UK), DHM/BMG (USA); Mercury; Philips; Saga; Sony (including Portrait and Essential Classics); Teldec/Warner (UK), Teldec/WEA (USA); Unicorn (UK only).

    UK
    CDs: under £10; more usually £8–£9
    Cassettes: around £5
    USA
    CDs: under $12
    Cassettes: $5–$6.50 – but very few are available

(B) DUOS – two CDs for the cost of one premium-priced CD which results in an 'upper' bargain price per disc, but compensates by offering exceptionally generous playing time.
Includes: EMI Rouge et Noir (CZS); Erato Bonsai Duos; Decca/London and DG Doubles; Philips Duos

(B) BARGAIN-PRICED SERIES (sets are multiples of these prices)

Includes: BMG/RCA; Decca/London; CfP (UK only); Harmonia Mundi Musique d'Abord; Hungaroton White Label; Philips; Pickwick (UK only); Sony.

UK
CDs: £5–£7.50
Cassettes: around £4
USA
CDs: under $7
Cassettes: around $4

SPECIAL SETS: Vox Boxes cost only $5 per disc in the USA, but (alongside the Turnabout Doubles) are UK imports and are priced at around £5–£6 per disc in Britain, where available. EMI CZS multiple sets are also within the bargain range in the UK but may cost rather more in the USA.

(BB) SUPER-BARGAIN SERIES – CDs

Includes: ASV (UK only); BMG/Victrola; Discover; DG Classikon; Naxos; Pickwick (PWK); Polygram Belart; Virgin (Virgo).

UK
CDs: under £5; some (including Discover) cost around £4
USA
CDs: under $5–$6

(In some cases, equivalent cassettes are available, usually costing slightly less than bargain cassettes.)

An International Mail-order Source for Recordings

Readers are urged to support a local dealer if he is prepared and able to give a proper service, and to remember that obtaining many CDs involves perseverance. If, however, difficulty is experienced locally, we suggest the following mail-order alternative, which operates world-wide:

PG Dept
Squires Gate Music Centre
Squires Gate Station Approach
Blackpool
Lancashire FY8 2SP
England
Tel.: 0253 44360 Fax: 0253 406686

This organization (which is operated under the direction of the Editor of the *Penguin Guide to Compact Discs and Cassettes: New Edition*) patiently extends compact disc orders until they finally come to hand. A full guarantee of safe delivery is made on any order undertaken. Please write for further details, enclosing a stamped and self-addressed envelope if within the UK.

Squires Gate Music Centre also offers a simple bi-monthly mailing with a hand-picked selection of current new and reissued CDs (and, where available, cassettes) chosen by the Editor of the *Penguin Guide*, Ivan March. If you would like a copy send a s.a.e. to the above address. Regular customers of Squires Gate Music Centre receive the bulletin as available, sent automatically with their purchases.

American readers seeking a domestic mail-order source may write to the following address where a comparable supply service is in operation (for both American and imported European labels). Please write for further details (enclosing a stamped, self-addressed envelope if within the USA) or send your order to:

PG Dept
Serenade Records
1713 G St, N.W.
Washington DC 20006
USA
Tel.: (202) 638-6648 Fax: (202) 783-0372
Tel.: (for US orders only) 1-800-237-2930

Availability of previous volumes of the *Penguin Guides* (in hardback format)

Many CDs issued over the years are no longer included in the current *Guide* for reasons of space, while others have been deleted. Collectors interested in buying previous editions of the *Guide* which discuss such records can obtain the following publications in hardback format at a reasonable cost, although in some cases remaining stock is well under 100 copies. Please write to either of the above addresses, stating which book(s) you need, and you will receive a quotation to include carriage.

New Penguin Guide to CDs and Cassettes (published 1988)
Penguin Guide to Compact Discs (1990)
Yearbook (1991)

Penguin Guide to CDs and Cassettes New Edition (1992)
Penguin Guide to Bargain Compact Discs (1992)
(The *Bargain Guide* is still in print in paperback format and can be readily obtained through booksellers.)

Abbreviations

AAM	Academy of Ancient Music	Hung.	Hungaroton
Ac.	Academy, Academic	L.	London
Amb. S.	Ambrosian Singers	LAPO	Los Angeles Philharmonic Orchestra
Ang.	Angel		
Ara.	Arabesque	LCO	London Chamber Orchestra
arr.	arranged		
ASMF	Academy of St Martin-in-the-Fields	LMP	London Mozart Players
		LOP	Lamoureux Orchestra of Paris
Bar.	Baroque		
Bav.	Bavarian	LPO	London Philharmonic Orchestra
BPO	Berlin Philharmonic Orchestra		
		LSO	London Symphony Orchestra
Cal.	Calliope		
Cap.	Caprice	Mer.	Meridian
CBSO	City of Birmingham Symphony Orchestra	Met.	Metropolitan
		MoC	Ministry of Culture
CfP	Classics for Pleasure	movt	movement
Ch.	Choir; Chorale; Chorus	N.	North
Chan.	Chandos	nar.	narrated
CO	Chamber Orchestra	Nat.	National
COE	Chamber Orchestra of Europe	NY	New York
		O	Orchestra, Orchestre
Col. Mus. Ant.	Musica Antiqua, Cologne	OAE	Orchestra of the Age of Enlightenment
Coll.	Collegium		
Coll. Aur.	Collegium Aureum	O-L	Oiseau-Lyre
Coll. Mus.	Collegium Musicum	Op.	Opera (in performance listings); opus (in music titles)
Concg. O	Royal Concertgebouw Orchestra of Amsterdam		
		orch.	orchestrated
cond.	conductor, conducted	ORTF	L'Orchestre de la radio et télévision française
Cons.	Consort		
DG	Deutsche Grammophon	Ph.	Philips
Dig.	digital recording	Phd.	Philadelphia
E.	England, English	Philh.	Philharmonia
ECCO	European Community Chamber Orchestra	PO	Philharmonic Orchestra
		Qt	Quartet
ECO	English Chamber Orchestra	R.	Radio
		RLPO	Royal Liverpool Philharmonic Orchestra
Ens.	Ensemble		
Fr.	French		
GO	Gewandhaus Orchestra	ROHCG	Royal Opera House, Covent Garden
HM	Harmonia Mundi France		
HM/RCA	Deutsche Harmonia Mundi	RPO	Royal Philharmonic Orchestra

RSO	Radio Symphony Orchestra	Sup.	Supraphon
		trans.	transcription, transcribed
S.	South	V.	Vienna
SCO	Scottish Chamber Orchestra	Van.	Vanguard
		VCM	Vienna Concentus Musicus
Sinf.	Sinfonietta		
SNO	Royal Scottish National Orchestra	VPO	Vienna Philharmonic Orchestra
SO	Symphony Orchestra	VSO	Vienna Symphony Orchestra
Soc.	Society		
Sol. Ven.	I Solisti Veneti	W.	West
SRO	Suisse Romande Orchestra		

Abel, Carl Friedrich (1723–87)

6 Symphonies, Op. 7.
**(*) Chan. Dig. CHAN 8648; *ABTD 1334* [id.]. Cantilena, Shepherd.

The six *Symphonies* of Op. 7 speak much the same language as J. C. Bach or early Mozart. The performances are not the last word in elegance, but they are both lively and enjoyable as well as being well recorded.

Adam, Adolphe (1803–56)

Le Corsaire (ballet; complete).
☞ *** Decca Dig. 430 286-2 (2) [id.]. ECO, Richard Bonynge.

Le Corsaire was Adam's swansong as a ballet composer and was first performed in 1856. Delibes added music for a production two decades later, notably a *Pas de fleurs* in Act III. The music is agreeably colourful and amiably melodic, but has little of the distinction of *Giselle*. Bonynge conducts it with finesse, warmth and drama, and the recording is out of Decca's top drawer, warm and vivid. But with 131 minutes of music which has a fair quotient of blandness, this recording is strictly for balletomanes.

Giselle (ballet): complete.
(M) *** Decca Dig. 433 007-2 (2) [id.]. ROHCG O, Richard Bonynge.

Giselle (1841) is the first of the great classical ballets. Bonynge's performance offers the complete original score, exactly as Adam scored it, with all repeats.

Giselle (arr. Büsser).
☞ *** Royal Opera House ROH 007; *ROHMC 007* [id.]. ROHCG O, Mark Ermler.

The alternative, nearly complete recording (74 minutes) from Mark Ermler uses the Büsser score, but few balletomanes will notice or mind the slight differences that this entails. The orchestral playing is alive and has an agreeable warmth and finesse; the string phrasing has genuine ballet grace and the brass gleam and have plenty of bite and sonority. The recording too is first class, and this can be recommended alongside the Tilson Thomas version, though not in preference to it. Generally good documentation: a synopsis is provided but is not track-related, surprising from a label specializing in complete ballet scores.

Giselle (ballet); abridged version.
*** Sony Dig. SK 42450 [id.]. LSO, Michael Tilson Thomas.
(M) **(*) Decca 417 738-2 [id.]. VPO, Karajan.

Sony offer an outstanding, modern (1986), digital recording, made – like the Bonynge set – in London's Henry Wood Hall. Nothing of consequence is omitted. The LSO playing is beautifully polished, warm, graceful and elegant.

Karajan offers sixty minutes of music: he effectively combines drama with an affectionate warmth.

Adams, John (born 1947)

Fearful symmetries; (i) The wound dresser.
*** Nonesuch/Warner Dig. 7559 79218-2 [id.]. (i) Sanford Sylvan; St Luke's O, composer.

In *The wound dresser* Adams rises well above the limitations of minimalism in one of his most moving works. *Fearful symmetries* is a characteristically strong, energetic piece, more varied in its tonal contrasts than many examples of minimalism. Excellent, well-balanced sound.

Harmonielehre; The Chairman dances; (i) 2 Fanfares: Tromba Lontana; Short ride in a fast machine.
☞ *** EMI Dig. CDC5 55051-2 [id.]. CBSO, Simon Rattle; (i) with Jonathan Holland, Wesley
   Warren.

Harmonielehre is an extraordinary, large-scale (39-minute) work in three parts. Its minimalist progress is powerfully sustained by Rattle through a very long (perhaps too long) first movement, which opens with great rhythmic and vividly coloured insistence yet produces a haunting, lyrical cantilena at its centre. The second movement, *The Amfortas wound* (which was a genital affliction), also brings a strong melodic impulse of considerable intensity, and then in the finale darkness turns to an iridescent, glimmering light, the spirits lift in a movement described as *Meister Eckhardt and Quackie* – dreamlike figures pulsing through outer space. The other works are somewhat more succinct, though (with the composer drawing on music from his opera, *Nixon in China*) *The Chairman dances* his foxtrot for a full 13 minutes, if with unabated energy. The *Two Fanfares* mystically and hauntingly pay their respects to Ives as well as Copland while the *Short* (exhilarating) *ride in a fast machine*, propelled by what sounds like bursts of rocket power, is just as described in the title and has an agreeably unstoppable momentum. Admirers of this remarkably imaginative composer, easily the most impressive of the American minimalists, will find this programme at the very least stimulating and, with a degree of patience, rewarding too. The performances bring the most persuasive advocacy and the excellent recording, clear, vivid and spacious, speaks well for the acoustics of Birmingham's Symphony Hall. The principal work was premièred on CD by Edo de Waart and the San Francisco Symphony Orchestra on Nonesuch (7559 79115-2) and that performance has the freshness of new discovery. But the Nonesuch disc is without the three extra items provided by Rattle.

Harmonium (for large orchestra and chorus).
*** ECM 821 465-2 [id.]. San Francisco SO & Ch., Edo de Waart.

Harmonium is a setting of three poems. John Donne's curiously oblique 'Negative love' opens the piece, with the orchestra lapping gently round the chorus. The other two poems are by Emily Dickinson. The magnificent, resonantly expansive 1984 analogue recording is certainly worthy of the performance; one might complain that this CD plays for only just over 32 minutes, yet for some ears it may seem longer.

Shaker loops.
☞ ❀ (M) *** Virgin/EMI CUV5 61121-2 [id.]. LCO, Warren-Green – GLASS: *Company* etc.; REICH: *8 Lines;* HEATH: *Frontier*. ***
*** Ph. 412 214-2 [id.]. San Francisco SO, De Waart – REICH: *Variations for winds*. ***

The inspired performance by Christopher Warren-Green and his London Concert Orchestra is full of imaginative intensity, and understandably it received the composer's imprimatur. Outstandingly vivid recording, and even more attractive at mid-price.

The alternative Philips version is also first rate and very well recorded, but the coupling is less generous.

The Death of Klinghoffer (complete).
☞ *** Elektra-Nonesuch/Warner Dig. 7559 79281-2 (2) [id.]. Sylvan, Maddalena, Friedman, Hammons, E. Op. Ch., Op. de Lyons, Nagano.

Of all minimalist composers the one who most strikingly rises above the obvious limitations is John Adams, showing an emotional depth rare in music that relies on the basic minimalist technique of the 'eternal um-chum' or endless ostinato. The key to that emotional impact lies in Adams's melodic gift. Far more than his minimalist colleagues he regularly has a free-flowing, beautifully shaped line soaring above the minimalist texture. That love of melody also points to his potential as an opera-composer. As in his first opera, the headline-catching *Nixon in China*, so too in *The Death of Klinghoffer* Adams has moved away from subjective expression, traditional in opera, to a stylized setting of a modern myth.

To take the painful 1985 news-story of the hijacking of the cruise liner *Achille Lauro* and the gratuitous murder by Palestinian terrorists of a helpless old man in a wheelchair, Leon Klinghoffer, was certainly bold. Dramatic treatment of an incident inspiring such natural revulsion could easily have spilled over into embarrassment. With his librettist, Alice Goodman, Adams has worked towards countering that in his stylization. He even dares to relate his opera to the Bach *Passions*, and the gravity and intensity of what he is saying is never in doubt. That brings *The Death of Klinghoffer* far closer to a dramatic oratorio than to an opera, with its lack of incident and its sequence of meditative solos and choruses of comment.

A recording loses very little, and that is particularly true in as strong a performance as this one in which Kent Nagano conducts Lyon Opéra forces with the original singers who directly inspired the composer. The treatment of the story, based on the age-old conflict between Palestinians and Jews, is conscientiously dispassionate. Even the murder of Klinghoffer and the casting of his body into the sea are merely described, not shown; yet at structured points in his broadly contemplative score Adams cleverly screws up tension with faster ostinatos and long-sustained crescendos. That leads finally at the climax of Act II to an emotional resolution on a poignant posthumous solo for Klinghoffer, set in the form of a *Gymnopédie*, with Adams echoing Satie but finding a depth far beyond his model. The closing scene brings the one solo of fully operatic intensity, the bitter concluding lament of Klinghoffer's wife, Marilyn. It is as though, after all the detachment, Adams is bringing us back finally to emotional reality, and the result is the more moving. The mezzo, Sheila Nadler, rises to the challenge superbly, and the baritone Sanford Sylvan is comparably sensitive as Klinghoffer himself, well matched by James Maddalena as the Captain, an Evangelist-like commentator, and by Thomas Hammons and Janice Felty in multiple roles. The recorded sound is excellent, but the booklet reproduces an unrevised version of the libretto.

Addinsell, Richard (1904–77)

Warsaw concerto.
(M) *** Decca Dig. 430 726-2 [id.]. Ortiz, RPO, Atzmon – GERSHWIN: *Rhapsody* **(*); GOTTSCHALK: *Grand fantasia* ***; LITOLFF: *Scherzo* ***; LISZT: *Hungarian fantasia.* ***
*** Ph. Dig. 411 123-2 [id.]. Dichter, Philh. O, Marriner (with Concert of concertante music ***).

Richard Addinsell's pastiche miniature concerto, written for the film *Dangerous Moonlight* in 1942, is perfectly crafted and its atmosphere combines all the elements of the Romantic concerto to great effect; moreover it has a truly memorable main theme.
  Cristina Ortiz offers a warmly romantic account, spacious in conception. It is also beautifully played in the Marriner recording. The sound is first rate in both versions.

Addison, John (born 1920)

Carte blanche (ballet suite).
☞ (M) (***) EMI mono CDM7 64718-2 [id.]. Pro Arte O, composer – ARNELL: *Great Detective;* ARNOLD: *A Grand Grand Overture;* BLISS: *Checkmate;* RAWSTHORNE: *Madame Chrysanthème* etc. (***)

John Addison is known mainly for his film music (including *A Taste of Honey, Reach for the Sky* and *The Charge of the Light Brigade*). The ballet, *Carte blanche*, written for Sadler's Wells, attracted the attention of Sir Thomas Beecham. It is wittily precocious writing (immediately introducing a xylophone solo in the *Prelude*), readily melodic and nicely scored. Unpretentious but entertaining, and well played and brightly recorded under the composer in 1960.

Aguado, Dionisio (1784–1849)

Adagio; Polonaise; Introduction and Rondo, Op. 2/1–3.
☞ (M) **(*) BMG/RCA Dig.09026 61607-2. Julian Bream (guitar) – SOR: *Collection.* **(*)

Aguado was a contemporary of Sor, with whom his music is coupled – the two composers played duets together in Paris. The *Adagio* is the most striking piece, serene and introspective; it might have been even more effective had Bream been slightly less deliberate and reflective and chosen to move the music on a little more. However, the other pieces have plenty of life, and all are played with Bream's characteristic feeling for colour. The New York recording is truthful and realistic.

Aho, Kalevi (born 1949)

(i) *Violin concerto; Hiljaisuus (Silence); Symphony No. 1.*
*** BIS Dig. CD 396 [id.]. (i) Manfred Gräsbeck; Lahti SO, Vänskä.

Aho's *First Symphony* betokens an impressive musical personality at work. *Silence* is an imaginative piece. It is related to (and was conceived as an introduction to) the post-expressionist and more 'radical' and trendy *Violin concerto*; it is a work of considerable resource and imaginative intensity. Good performances and recording.

Albéniz, Isaac (1860–1909)

Iberia (suite; orch. Arbós).

*** Chan. Dig. CHAN 8904; *ABTD 1513* [id.]. Philh. O, Yan Pascal Tortelier – FALLA: *Three-cornered hat.* ***

The transcriptions of five of the twelve piano pieces which make up *Iberia* were made by Albéniz's contemporary and friend, Enrique Arbós. The music itself glows and flickers with the nuances of Spanish dance-rhythms. The Philharmonia's response brings glowing woodwind colours and seductive string phrasing, well projected by the warmly resonant recording.

Suite española (arr. Frühbeck de Burgos).

(M) *** Decca 417 786-2. New Philh. O, Frühbeck de Burgos – FALLA: *El amor brujo* *** (with GRANADOS: *Goyescas: Intermezzo* ***).

Albéniz's early *Suite española* offers light music of the best kind, colourful, tuneful, exotically scored and providing orchestra and recording engineers alike with a chance to show their paces, the sound bright and glittering.

GUITAR MUSIC

Cantos de España: Córdoba, Op. 232/4; Mallorca (Barcarola), Op. 202; Piezás características: Zambra Granadina; Torre Bermaja, Op. 92/7, 12; Suite española: Granada; Sevilla; Cádiz; Asturias, Op. 47/1, 3–5.
*** Sony Dig. MK 36679 [id.]. John Williams (guitar).

Some of Albéniz's more colourful miniatures are here, and John Williams plays them most evocatively.

Cantos de España: Córdoba, Op. 232/4; Mallorca, Op. 202; Suite española, Op. 47: Cataluña; Granada; Sevilla; Cádiz.
☞ ⊛ (M) *** BMG/RCA Dig. 09026 61608-2. Julian Bream (guitar) – GRANADOS: *Collection.* *** ⊛

Julian Bream is in superb form in this splendid recital (his own favourite record), vividly recorded in the pleasingly warm acoustic of Wardour Chapel, near his home in Wiltshire. The CD is electrifying, giving an uncanny impression of the great guitarist sitting and making music just beyond the loudspeakers. The playing itself has wonderfully communicative rhythmic feeling, great subtlety of colour, and its spontaneity increases the impression that one is experiencing a 'live' recital. The performance of the haunting *Córdoba*, which ends the group, is unforgettable.

Suite española No. 1, Op. 47; Recuerdos de viaje, Op. 71.
☞ (B) ** CfP Dig. CD-CFP 4631 [id.]. Julian Byzantine (guitar).

Attractively colourful music played with agreeable intimacy and avoiding any picture-postcard overcharacterization. But many will feel that this music needs more Latin fire, although it does not lack evocative atmosphere. Julian Byzantine is most naturally recorded.

Azulejos; Cantos de España (Preludio (Asturias); Oriental; Bajo la palmera (Cuba); Córdoba; Seguidillas (Castilla)). Malagueña; Mallorca (Barcarola); La Vega; Zambra Granadina; Zaragoza.
☞ (M) *** EMI CDM7 64523-2. Alicia de Larrocha.

Dating from 1959, this recital is another stimulating example of the younger Alicia de Larrocha playing with enormous dash and a glowing palette – the famous *Córdoba* is full of atmospheric poetry, helped by the warm bass resonance of the recording. Several of the items included as separate pieces were added by the composer's publishers to fill out the *Suite española*, and the opening *Preludio (Asturias)* of the *Cantos de España* has more fire here than in the hands of Alma Petchersky. De Larrocha's glittering articulation in the *Seguidillas (Castilla)* and the brilliant *Zaragoza* is equally arresting, and the wide pianistic range of the extended *La Vega* brings playing that is both ruminative and dazzling, although the recording jangles at climaxes. Otherwise it is well focused and realistic. This CD has been withdrawn as we go to press.

Cantos de España; Suite española.
(M) *** Decca Analogue/Dig. 433 923-2 (2). Alicia de Larrocha – GRANADOS: *12 Danzas españolas* etc. ***

This is most rewarding repertoire and de Larrocha's playing is imbued with many subtle changes of colour and has refreshing vitality.

Iberia; Navarra; Suite española.
⊛ *** Decca Dig. 417 887-2 [id.]. Alicia de Larrocha.

On her digital Decca version, Alicia de Larrocha brings an altogether beguiling charm and character to these rewarding miniature tone-poems and makes light of their sometimes fiendish technical difficulties. The recording is among the most successful of piano sounds Decca has achieved.

Iberia (complete); *Suite española* (excerpts): *Granada; Cataluña; Sevilla; Cádiz; Aragon; Navarra. Pavana capricho, Op. 12; España (6 Hojas de album): Tango* (only); *Recuerdos de viaje: Rumores de la caleta; Puerta de Tierra.*
(M) *** EMI CMS7 64504-2 (2). Alicia de Larrocha.

The EMI set offers de Larrocha's earliest stereo recording of Albéniz's great piano suite, *Iberia*, made for Hispavox in 1962. The younger de Larrocha is far tougher, more daring, more fiery and if anything even more warmly expressive than she was later. The EMI discs include the haunting *Tango*, deliciously done, the most celebrated of all Albéniz's music, making this a more popular collection. Alas, this CD has also just been withdrawn by EMI.

Iberia (complete); *España (6 Hojas de album), Op. 165: Malagueña; Tango. Pavana capricho, Op. 12. Recuerdos de viaje: Puerta de Tierra; Rumores de la caleta.*
(M) *** Decca 433 926-2 (2) [id.]. Alicia de Laroccha – FALLA: *Fantasia bética* etc. ***

Alicia de Larrocha's second analogue set of *Iberia* dates from 1973. As in the earlier Hispavox version, she plays with rather more full-blooded temperament and fire than in her most recent digital set, both here and in the other colourful genre pieces included in the recital and though there are occasional touches of wilful rubato, her natural overriding spontaneity carries the day. The piano recording is excellent in its realism and range, more natural than on the EMI set.

Sonata in D.
(M) *** Decca 433 920-2 (2) [id.]. Alicia de Larrocha – GRANADOS: *Goyescas* etc. *** ⊛; SOLER: *Sonatas.* ***

Albéniz's delectably cool *Sonata*, with its obvious homage to Domenico Scarlatti, has enormous character. It is beautifully played and recorded.

Suite española, Op. 47.
☞ (BB) **(*) ASV CDQS 6079. Alma Petchersky – FALLA: *Fantasia bética* (with GRANADOS: *Allegro de concierto*). **(*)

Alma Petchersky is an Argentinian pianist, a sensitive and musical player of excellent credentials. Hers is at present the only available version of these justly popular salon pieces, and obviously she is thoroughly at home with them. She plays engagingly and with a natural spontaneity that gives pleasure. The recording is generally faithful, without being in the top bracket. At super-bargain price this is worth considering.

Albinoni, Tommaso (1671–1750)

Adagio in G min. for organ and strings (arr. Giazotto).
*** Ph. Dig. 410 606-2 [id.]. I Musici (with Baroque Concert. ***)
☞ (M) *** Virgin/EMI Dig. CUV5 61145-2 [id.]. LCO, Warren-Green – VIVALDI: *4 seasons;* PACHELBEL: *Canon.* ***
(B) *** Pickwick Dig. PCD 802; *CIMPC 802.* Scottish CO, Laredo (with String masterpieces ***).

I Musici gave the *Adagio* its CD début; collectors who have a soft spot for the piece will find this performance thoroughly recommendable. Christopher Warren-Green's version is also as impressive as any in the catalogue, opening with an attractively volatile violin solo and leading to a richly upholstered climax.

No less telling is the bargain-priced, digitally recorded Pickwick account, strongly contoured and most responsively played by the Scottish Chamber Orchestra under Jaime Laredo. Other versions are listed in the Concerts section.

12 Concerti a cinque, Op. 5.
(M) *** Ph. Dig. 422 251-2; *422 251-4* [id.]. Pina Carmirelli, I Musici.

This fine body of concertos has variety and resource to commend it. I Musici, with Pina Carmirelli as the solo player, are every bit as fresh as the music, and they are accorded altogether first-rate sound.

12 Concerti, Op. 7; Sonatas for strings a 5: in D & G min., Op. 2/5–6.
☞ *** Ph. Dig. 432 115-2 (2) [id.]. Heinz Holliger, Maurice Bourgue, I Musici.

Albinoni's Op. 7 consists of four each of solo oboe concertos, double oboe concertos and concertos for strings, with continuo. This new recording by Heinz Holliger and Maurice Bourgue and I Musici of familiar repertoire is comparatively robust in using modern instruments but is eminently stylish, the effect sunny and lively by turns, with the many fine solo movements all warmly relished. The digital recording is fresh and naturally balanced. The two *String sonatas* from Op. 2 are particularly attractive works, and here the recording is slightly closer.

Concerti a cinque, Op. 7/2, 3, 5, 6, 8, 9, 11 & 12.
(M) *** DG 427 111-2 [id.]. Holliger, Elhorst, Bern Camerata.

The playing of Heinz Holliger, Hans Elhorst and the Bern Camerata is refined, persuasive and vital, and the CD could hardly be more truthful or better detailed.

Oboe concertos, Op. 7/3, 6, 9 & 12; Op. 9/2, 5, 8 & 11.
*** Unicorn Dig. DKPCD 9088; *DKPC 9088* [id.]. Sarah Francis, L. Harpsichord Ens.

Those looking for a selection of *Oboe concertos* from both Opp. 7 and 9 will find that Sarah Francis is an immensely stylish and gifted soloist. She is accompanied with warmth and grace, and the recording is first class, transparent yet full and naturally balanced.

Concerti a cinque, Op. 9/1, 4, 6–7, 10 & 12.
(M) *** Ph. 426 080-2; *426 080-4*. Ayo, Holliger, Bourgue, Garatti, I Musici.

Concerti a cinque, Op. 9/2, 3, 5, 8, 9 & 11.
(M) *** Ph. 434 157-2; *434 157-4* [id.]. Holliger, Bourgue, I Musici.

This pair of excellent mid-priced CDs includes all the Opus 9 concertos with Heinz Holliger and Maurice Bourgue. They are played with much finesse and style and the 1966 recording is brightly remastered.

Concerti a cinque, Op. 9/1–3, 5, 6, 10 & 11.
☞ (B) *** Erato/Warner 2292 45921-1 [id.]. Pierlot, Chambon, Toso, Sol. Ven., Scimone.

Albinoni's music continues to be underrated – his best concertos are as fine as the finest Vivaldi, as this collection readily demonstrates. Pierre Pierlot, with his elegant phrasing and lovely tone, is ravishing in the slow movements of the *D minor* (particularly beautiful) and *C major* (solo) *concertos* (Op. 9, Nos. 2 and 5 respectively) and Jacques Chambon (in the *Double Oboe concerto in F*, Op. 9/3) and Piero Toso (in the two concertos for violin) also make impressive contributions. Scimone and I Solisti Veneti are also on form, and the recording is full and naturally balanced. With 71 minutes of music, this is a genuine bargain, even though this Erato Bonsai label provides no documentation about the music – except titles.

Concerti a cinque, Op. 9/2, (i) 3; 5, 8, (i) 9; 11.
☞ (BB) *** Naxos Dig. 8.550739; *4.550739* [id.]. Anthony Camden, (i) Julia Girdwood, L. Virtuosi, John Georgiadis.

The calibre of Anthony Camden's playing is shown in the *Adagio* of the *D minor Concerto*, Op. 9/5, which opens with a long, controlled crescendo on a sustained note, which is beautifully managed, but both the solo playing (with Julia Girdwood an excellent partner in the two double concertos) and the lively and sensitive accompaniments give great pleasure throughout this freshly recorded disc, another of Naxos's best bargains.

Alfvén, Hugo (1872–1960)

Symphony No. 1 in F min., Op. 7; Andante religioso; Drapa (Ballad for large orchestra); Uppsala rhapsody, Op. 24.
*** BIS Dig. CD 395 [id.]. Stockholm PO, Neeme Järvi.

Järvi's version of the *First Symphony* supersedes the earlier Westerberg version; it is superior both artistically and technically and leaves the listener more persuaded as to its merits. The *Uppsala rhapsody* is based on student songs but it is pretty thin stuff, and the *Andante religioso* is rather let down by its sugary closing pages. Drapa opens with some fanfares, full of sequential clichés and with a certain naïve pomp and splendour that verges on bombast.

Symphony No. 2 in D, Op. 11; Swedish rhapsody No. 1 (Midsummer vigil).
*** BIS Dig. CD 385 [id.]. Stockholm PO, Neeme Järvi.

Like those of its predecessor, the ideas of the *Second Symphony* are pleasing though they do not possess a particularly individual stamp. On the whole, Järvi is very persuasive in the symphony and gives a delightful performance of the popular *Midsummer vigil.*

(i) *Symphony No. 4 (Havsbandet – From the outermost skerries), Op. 29; A Legend of the Skerries, Op. 20.*
*** BIS Dig. CD 505 [id.]. Stockholm PO, Järvi, (i) with Christina Högman, Claes-Håkan Ahnsjö.

Alfvén's *Fourth Symphony* is perhaps his most ambitious work. There is a romantic programme relating to the emotions of two young lovers, whose wordless melisma is heard to excellent effect in this very fine recording. However, the results are conventionally voluptuous rather than ethereal. Alfvén's scoring is eminently resourceful, and no one with an interest in this composer will be disappointed either by the performance, which is sensitive and persuasive, or by the superbly balanced recording with its natural perspective and admirable detail.

Symphony No. 5 in A min.; The Mountain King (Bergakungen): suite; Gustav II Adolf: Elegy.
☞ *** BIS Dig. CD 585 [id.]. Royal Stockholm PO, Neeme Järvi.

The *Fifth Symphony* is a late work. Alfvén composed the long first movement in 1942 in time for his seventieth birthday. For some time it was just called 'First Movement', but during the remainder of the decade he produced the remaining three movements, which were premièred when he was eighty. It was to be his last work (the ballet score he composed in the late 1950s for *The Prodigal Son* but which he did not orchestrate is really based exclusively on folk music he had collected earlier in life). The symphony draws freely on ideas from the ballet, *The Mountain King*, whose suite completes this CD. The first movement is by far the best, despite its echoes of Wagner and Sibelius – and the second group is almost Baxian. 'Both technically and in other respects the *least* terrible thing I have produced,' the composer once said, though it does not begin to match *Midsummer Vigil (Midsommar-vaka)* or the *Third Symphony.* The second movement has some beautiful ideas but the last two movements, which became 'problem children' in his old age, are really rather feeble. *The Mountain King* is an inventive and attractive score; and both works, as well as the touching *Elegy* from the music to *Gustav II Adolf,* could hardly be more persuasively presented by Neeme Järvi and his fine orchestra. The engineering is absolutely first class. This is one of the most natural and lifelike sound recordings to have appeared in the last couple of years.

Choral music: (i) *Aftonen; Anders, han var en hurtiger dräng; Berceuse;* (ii) *Glädjens blomster. Gryning vid havet; Gustaf Frödings jordafärd; Hör I Orphei Drängar; Kulldansen;* (ii) *Lindagull (Serenade). Min kära;* (ii) *Natt. Och jungfrun hon går i ringen; Oxbergsmarschen; Papillon;* (ii) *Prövningen. Roslagsvår; Stemning; Sveriges flagga; Trindskallarna; Uti vår hage; Vaggvisa;* (ii) *Vallgossens visa;* (ii) *Värmlandsvisan.* Songs (ii; iii) *Du är stilla ro; I stilla timmar; Jag längtar dig; Saa tag mit Hjerte; Skogen sofver; Sommardofter.* (i) SODERMAN, arr. ALFVEN: *I månans skimmer.*
☞ *** BIS Dig. CD 633 [id.].(i) Orphei Drängar Ch., Robert Sund; (ii) with Claes-Håkan Ahnsjö;
   (iii) Folke Alin.

For much of his life Alfvén was director of Orphei Drängar (Sons of Orpheus), the male choir founded in 1853 and centred at Uppsala, and it achieved legendary status both in Sweden and abroad. Even now it collects reviews as the world's finest male-voice choir on account of its refined tonal balance, precision of ensemble and impeccable intonation. Some of the part-songs he composed for them are collected here and are sung to the highest standards of tonal virtuosity. Their singing is quite remarkable: wide in dynamic range and cultured in tonal blend – in terms of male choir singing, the equivalent of the Berlin Philharmonic. It is superbly recorded too. Recommended with enthusiasm even to those who find the symphonies inflated and self-indulgent.

Aliabiev, Alexander (1787–1851)

(i; ii) *Introduction and theme with variations in D min.;* (iii; ii) *Souvenir de Moscou, Op. 6;* (iv) *Piano trio in A min.;* (v) *12 Romances.*
*** Olympia OCD 181 [id.]. (i) Venyavsky; (ii) USSR Ac. SO, Verbitsky; (iii) Grauch; (iv)
   Voskresensky, Ambarpumyan, Knyasev; (v) Pluzhnikov, Mishuk.

Aliabiev's (or Alyabiev's) *Trio in A minor* is a delightful piece with something of the fluency of Weber and Mendelssohn, and it is heard to good advantage here. The *Introduction and theme with variations in D minor* is sandwiched between two groups of songs, nearly all of which have great charm and appeal. The recording of the two insubstantial pieces for violin and orchestra comes off less well. This disc almost gives the lie to the impression that Russian music begins with Glinka.

Alkan, Charles (1813–88)

Grand duo concertante in F sharp min. for piano and violin, Op. 21; Piano trio in G min., Op. 30; Sonate de concert in E for piano and cello, Op. 47.
** Marco Polo Dig. 8.223383. Trio Alkan.

This is a welcome introduction to Alkan's instrumental and chamber music. All three works have plenty of character, although the most striking is the emotionally ambitious *Grand duo concertante*. The *Piano trio*, the first work to be written, is the most conventional-sounding piece here, and these artists find the necessary bravura and flair – the violin sonata comes off best, as the cellist does not produce a very expansive tone. The recording is fully acceptable and certainly vivid, but the ear craves a little more opulence in such music.

Barcarolle; Gigue, Op. 24; Marche, Op. 37/1; Nocturne No. 2, Op. 57/1; Saltarelle, Op. 23; Scherzo diabolico, Op. 39/3; Sonatine, Op. 61.
(B) *** HM HMA 190 927 [id.]. Bernard Ringeissen.

Bernard Ringeissen could be more flamboyant but he is fully equal to the cruel technical demands of this music. The recording, from the beginning of the 1970s, is first class.

Grande sonate (Les quatre ages), Op. 33; Prelude: La chanson de la folle au bord de la mer, Op. 31/8. 12 Studies in all minor keys, Op. 39 (excerpts): Comme le vent; En rythme molossique; Scherzo diabolique; Le festin d'Ésope. 12 Studies in all major keys, Op. 35: Allegro barbaro (only).
(M) *** EMI CDM7 64280-2 [id.]. Ronald Smith.

The *Grande sonate* dates from 1847, some six years before the Liszt *Sonata*, and is a quite extraordinary piece. Its four movements describe four decades of a man's life: his twenties, thirties, forties and fifties, each getting progressively slower. Some of the other music is quite astonishing, and it goes without saying that Ronald Smith's virtuosity is remarkable and his understanding of this repertoire beyond question. The piano-sound is realistic and clean. Inadequate back-up notes.

25 Preludes, Op. 31.
*** Decca Dig. 433 055-2 [id.]. Olli Mustonen – SHOSTAKOVICH: *24 Preludes.* ***

The *Preludes* are more poetic than barnstorming and date from 1847. They go through all the major and minor keys, returning to C major in No. 25. The young Finnish pianist Olli Mustonen plays them supremely well. The recording is absolutely first class, though the pedal-stamping in the *Tenth Prelude, Dans le style fugué*, should have been curbed. Strongly recommended.

ORGAN MUSIC

8 Petites Préludes sur les huit gammes du plainchant; 13 Prières, Op. 64; Impromptu on Luther's 'Un fort rampart est notre Dieu', Op. 39.
☞ *** Nimbus Dig. NI 5089 [id.]. Kevin Bowyer (organ of Salisbury Cathedral).

One does not think of Alkan as an composer for the organ, and indeed only the eight *Little preludes on the eight modes of plainchant* were actually conceived for this instrument. They are piquant little morsels, which might almost have been written by Jean Françaix. The *Treize prières* are much more ambitious, totalling altogether 52 minutes; like the *Impromptu* they were conceived for an obsolete pedal organ (the illustration shows a baby grand with organ pedals attached under the player's stool). Their descriptive title is misleadingly eccentric. Only a few of these pieces have a genuinely prayerful mood: they are often simply innocent (*Doucement* – No. 9), at times quirky or extrovert, like the Widor-like *Tempo giusto* of No. 8, while the *Allegretto* (No. 12) is a genial march, and the finale, *Largement et majestueuse*, is distinctly celebratory. The *Impromptu* on '*A mighty fortress is our God*' is a jolly set of variations ending in florid spectacle. Kevin Bowyer is clearly a master of this repertoire and conveys his enjoyment in music which has personality and is readily melodic. Perhaps the mellow Salisbury Cathedral organ was not an ideal choice (a French instrument would have had more reedy bite), but this remains an attractive and generous (74 minutes) recital.

Allaga, Géza (1841–1913)

Concerto hongrois for (solo) *cymbalum; Etudes de concert: in A; A min. (Tempest); C; D; D min.; B flat; F (Chorale); Pizzicato and glissando;* (i) *Hungarian rhapsody for cymbalom and string quintet. arr. of Liszt: Le Dieu des Hongrois; Arrangements for flute and cymbalom:* (ii) SCHUBERT: *Ave Maria.* FIELD: *Nocturne.*
☞ (B) *** HM Dig. HMA 1903075 [id.]. Viktória Herrencsár; (i) Zsolnai, Tóth, Papp, Nagy, Tibay; (ii) Béla Drahos.

A fascinating collection. Géza Allaga founded a school for what has come to be regarded as Hungary's national instrument, the cymbalum (though it was in use in various forms for thousands of years and originated in Asia). He left a complete course of study for beginners and experts: many of these pieces obviously demand much bravura. Moreover he tried to avoid the tremolo, a very hackneyed technique, used judiciously in the *C major Etude de concert*, reminding one just a little of Tarrega's *Recuerdos*. The *Tempest study* which follows shows the instrument's more dramatic possibilities, while the *D minor study* is hauntingly romantic and the *B flat major* catchily jolly, while the *A major* brings an equally personable and busy *moto perpetuo*. Indeed Allaga's invention is always agreeable and his use of folk-tunes in the two extended works, the one solo and the other with an agreeably warm string backing, is also very pleasing. The soloist here is both a virtuoso and a sensitive musician and she demonstrates the wide range of styles possible on an instrument we so often hear played (as Allaga knew too well) with an almost abrasive tremolando. Here there is much subtlety, both of colour and of dynamic range, while Béla Drahos produces an elegant flute line in the Schubert and Field arrangements. The recording is excellent.

Allegri, Gregorio (1582–1652)

Miserere.
*** Gimell CDGIM 339; *1585-T-39* [id.]. Tallis Scholars, Phillips – MUNDY: *Vox patris caelestis;* PALESTRINA: *Missa Papae Marcelli.* ***
(M) *** Decca 421 147-2 [id.]. King's College Ch., Willcocks – PALESTRINA: *Collection.* ***
☞ (BB) ** Naxos Dig. 8.550827; *4.550827* [id.]. Oxford Camerata, Jeremy Summerly (with BACH: *Chorales: Ein feste Burg; Jesu, joy of man's desiring.* MOZART: *Ave verum corpus.* PALESTRINA: *Lesson I for Maundy Thursday.* Choruses from: BACH: *Mass in B min.* (& *Agnus Dei*); *Christmas oratorio.* HANDEL: *Messiah.* MOZART: *Requiem. Solemn Vespers: Laudate Dominum*).

Mozart was so impressed with Allegri's *Miserere* when he heard it in the Sistine Chapel (which originally claimed exclusive rights to its performance) that he wrote the music out from memory so that it could be performed elsewhere. On the much-praised Gimell version, the soaring treble solo is taken by a girl, Alison Stamp, and her memorable contribution is enhanced by the recording itself.

The famous King's performance of Allegri's *Miserere*, with its arresting treble solo so beautifully and securely sung by Roy Goodman, is now coupled with Palestrina at mid-price.

The Oxford Camerata's performance is very confident, with a full-throated solo from the treble. But he does not match the gentle soaring ecstasy of Roy Goodman's famous version. The rest of the programme is a sampler of the Naxos choral catalogue, all items enjoyable and well recorded, the only disappointment being Anna di Mauro's unmemorable account of the *Laudate Dominum* from Mozart's *Solemn Vespers*.

Alwyn, William (1905–85)

(i) *Autumn legend* (for cor anglais and string orchestra); (ii) *Lyra Angelica* (concerto for harp and string orchestra); (iii) *Pastoral fantasia* (for viola and string orchestra); *Tragic interlude.*
*** Chan. Dig. CHAN 9065 [id.]. (i) Nicholas Daniel; (ii) Rachel Masters; (iii) Stephen Tees; City of L. Sinfonia, Richard Hickox.

Autumn legend (1954) is a highly atmospheric tone-poem, very Sibelian in influence. It is beautifully played. The *Pastoral fantasia* also contains a curious Sibelius quotation – perhaps unconscious – near the beginning. Yet the piece has its own developing individuality. Again a fine performance, with Stephen Tees highly sympathetic to the music's fluid poetic line. The *Tragic interlude* is a powerful lament for the dead of wars past, written on the eve of the Second World War. But the highlight of the disc is the *Lyra Angelica*, a radiantly beautiful, extended piece (just over half an hour in length), inspired by the metaphysical poet, Giles Fletcher's '*Christ's victorie and triumph*'. The performance here is very moving, and the recording has great richness of string-tone and a delicately balanced harp texture. Rachel Masters's contribution is distinguished. This is the record to start with for those beginning to explore the music of this highly rewarding composer.

Concerti grossi Nos. 1 in B flat for chamber orchestra; 2 in G for string orchestra; 3 for woodwind, brass and strings; (i) *Oboe concerto.*
*** Chan. Dig. CHAN 8866 [id.]. (i) Daniel; City of L. Sinfonia, Hickox.

The improvisatory feeling and changing moods of the *Oboe concerto* are beautifully caught by Nicholas Daniel, with Hickox and the Sinfonia players providing admirable support. They then turn to the more extrovert and strongly contrasted *Concerti grossi*, the first a miniature concerto for orchestra, the second in the ripest tradition of English string writing. The third is a fine *in memoriam* for Sir Henry Wood. Excellent Chandos sound, gaining from the warm ambience of St Jude's in north-west London, yet with textures unclouded.

(i) *Piano concerto No. 1. Symphony No. 1.*
☞ *** Chan. Dig. CHAN 9155 [id.]. (i) Howard Shelley; LSO, Hickox.

Hickox's performance of the *First Symphony* is just as compelling as the composer's own version on Lyrita (coupled with No. 4 – SRCD 227). Its unashamed flamboyance and energy, helped by Chandos's spectacular recording, brings great vitality to the music, while the opulent textures make the very most of the composer's spacious tapestries of sound – so reminiscent of his best film music – and, if the finale nearly goes over the top, the exuberance is highly communicative. The poignant atmosphere of the *Adagio* is equally well caught. The *First Piano concerto* is also a flamboyant piece, written in 1930 for Clifford Curzon. It is in a single movement, but with four clear subsections: the toccata-like energy of the opening is only partly dispelled by the slow section, which alternates tranquillity and passion, before the joyful return of the toccata leads to a peaceful epilogue of considerable beauty. Howard Shelley is a splendid soloist, fully up to the rhetoric and touching the listener when the passion subsides, creating a haunting stillness at the very end. Again splendid recording.

(i) *Piano concerto No. 2; Sinfonietta for strings; Symphony No. 5 (Hydriotaphia).*
☞ *** Chan. Dig. CHAN 9196 [id.]. (i) Howard Shelley; LSO, Richard Hickox.

The *Piano concerto No. 2* was written in 1960 for the Dutch pianist, Cor de Groot, who became paralysed in one arm just before the planned première, which had to be cancelled. The score was saved but, before the recording, the composer's wife devised a closing section for the first movement and restored the slow movement which Alwyn had discarded. The concerto opens boldly and expansively and is romantically rhetorical, with sweeping use of the strings. The imaginative *Andante* is its highlight, but the jazzy 'fuoco' finale with its calm central section is overlong (13 minutes). Howard Shelley plays with brilliance and much sensitivity, and Alwyn admirers will be glad to have the work available on record, even if it is flawed.

The cogent *Fifth Symphony* (1973), with its dense argument distilled into one movement with four sub-sections, has a strange subtitle. It is called '*Hydriotaphia*' and the work is dedicated to the memory of physician/philosopher Sir Thomas Browne (1605–82), whose writings were always on the composer's bedside table. Browne's elegy on death was first published under this title *Hydriotaphia: Urn burial, or a Discourse of the Sepulchral Urns lately found in Norfolk.* Quotations preface each section of Alwyn's score: 'Life is a pure flame' is the inspiration of the first movement, while the *Andante* depicts 'sad and sepulchral pictures expressing old mortality'. The angry Scherzo suggests that 'iniquity comes at long strides upon us', and the ambivalent finale brings the thought that 'man is a noble animal, splendid in ashes'.

The *Sinfonietta for strings*, a much more expansive piece, is almost twice as long as the symphony. The string writing, very much in the English tradition, is vigorous in the first movement and hauntingly atmospheric, especially in the beautiful *Adagio*, desperate in its melancholy. The highly original finale is unpredictably contrapuntal, with the momentum continually fluctuating. The recordings were made in the resonant acoustic of All Saints', Tooting, which provides spectacular results although detail is not always sharply defined. But it suits the string work especially well. Hickox, who understands the composer's sound-world, is consistently sympathetic, with the structure of the symphony held in a strong grip. The LSO, clearly dedicated, play with particular eloquence in the *Sinfonietta*.

(i) *Violin concerto. Symphony No. 3.*
☞ *** Chan. Dig. CHAN 9187 [id.]. (i) Lydia Mordkovitch; LSO, Hickox.

The *Violin concerto* – so sympathetically played here by Lydia Mordkovitch – is, like the *Piano concerto No. 2*, unknown. It was turned down by the BBC (in spite of Sir Henry Wood's enthusiasm) when a wartime première was proposed at the Proms. Yet it is a very appealing work and its lyrical threnody brings a reminder of the Vaughan Williams of *The Lark ascending*, although in the second-movement *Allegretto* there are also hints of Elgar. The Vaughan Williams impression returns later, when a solo viola gently shares the closing section of the central movement with the soloist. The concerto is discursive but has moments of intense beauty, especially at the rapt closing section of the first movement, where Lydia Mordkovitch plays exquisitely. Indeed her performance is very sensitive and often touchingly beautiful.

John Ireland suggested to the composer that the *Third Symphony* is 'the finest British Symphony since the Elgar No. 2', and Hickox's reading is every bit as convincing as that of the composer on Lyrita, while the LSO again respond to a symphony that is strongly conceived, powerfully argued, consistently inventive and impressively laid out. The expansive Chandos recording suits both works admirably, and the *Violin concerto* is balanced most convincingly.

4 Elizabethan dances (from the set of 6); *Derby Day overture; Festival march; The Magic island* (symphonic prelude); *Sinfonietta for strings.*
☞ *** Lyrita SRCS 229 [id.]. LPO, composer.

An exceptionally attractive compilation and one of the composer's most successful records. Alwyn's *Elizabethan dances* are extrovert and tuneful in the Malcolm Arnold tradition (if not quite so ebullient in orchestration). The central movements have a whiff of the Constant Lambert of *Horoscope*. The second, a gentle waltz marked *Languidamente*, is delightful and the third, *Poco allegretto*, is equally winning in its lightness of touch. The final dance reminds one a little of Gershwin in its melodic sweep. Alwyn is no less successful in *Derby Day* with its pithily rhythmic main theme, and he is both poetic and romantically expansive in the Shakespearean evocation of *The Magic island*. In the *Festival march*, written for the opening of the Festival of Britain in 1951 (but never used for that occasion), while acknowledging his debt to Elgar and Walton he brings an individual, restrained nobilmente to the main lyrical tune. But the most important work here is the *Sinfonietta for strings*, written in 1970. It is expertly laid out, full of striking ideas and its central *Adagio* is hauntingly beautiful. The Lyrita recordings were made between 1972 and 1979 and show the usual engineering flair which distinguishes all issues on this label. Everything is naturally laid out and timbres are both truthful and vivid.

Film scores: *The Fallen Idol; The History of Mr Polly; Odd Man Out; The Rake's Progress: Calypso* (all restored and arr. Christopher Palmer).
☞ *** Chan. Dig. CHAN 9243; *ABTD* 1606 [id.]. LSO, Richard Hickox.

Alwyn made his name as a film composer in the days when the immediate post-war British films as often as not had a 'symphonic score'. He took his film composition as seriously as his sym-phonies and lavished great care on their invention and construction. Unfortunately the major scores were all inadvertently destroyed at Pinewood Studios, and Christopher Palmer has had to return to the composer's sketches for these recordings. The result is impressive. *Odd Man Out* (about the IRA) has the most compellingly poignant music, but the lightweight *History of Mr Polly* is charming and *The Fallen Idol* sophisticated in its delineation of action and character. The orchestral playing is both warmly committed and polished, and the recording is out of Chandos's top drawer.

Symphonies Nos. 1; 4.
*** Lyrita SRCD 227 [id.]. LPO, composer.

The first of Alwyn's symphonies dates from 1950 and is a work of considerable power and maturity. Its gestures are occasionally overblown, particularly in the finale, and offer obvious echoes of the film-scores of which Alwyn is so consummate a master. The LPO responds splendidly to the composer's direction and the Lyrita analogue recording has fine presence, body and clarity.

Symphonies Nos. 2–3; 5 (Hydriotaphia).
*** Lyrita SRCD 228 [id.]. LPO, composer.

The *Second Symphony* is a powerfully inventive work that shows an original cast of mind. Its language is not exploratory either in terms of new harmonies or of sonorities, but it is coherent and personal. The *Third Symphony* is a well-argued and imaginative score, richly coloured and at times even reminiscent of Bax. The title of the *Fifth* derives from Sir Thomas Browne, whose 'Urn Burial' or *Hydriotaphia* is its source of inspiration. However, it was Browne's magnificently flowery prose that captured the composer's imagination and is quoted to express the feeling of each of the work's four sections, within a compressed (15-minute), one-movement structure. Again the music is impressively wrought and emotionally eloquent. All three works reward the listener, and the composer's performances could hardly be more authoritative. The sound is full and naturally balanced, with fine presence and clarity.

Symphony No. 2; Derby Day overture; Fanfare for a joyful occasion; The Magic island; Overture to a masque.
☞ *** Chan. Dig. CHAN 9093 [id.]. LSO, Richard Hickox.

Hickox's account of the Sibelian *Third Symphony* is every bit as fine as the composer's own performance on Lyrita, and the modern Chandos digital recording provides even fuller and more expansive sound for brass and strings and a natural concert-hall balance. The structural grip of Hickox's reading is especially telling at the work's close when the brass climax leads to the sombre theme in the lower strings, while the *molto calmato* passage at the end of the first movement has movingly rapt concentration. However, while the composer's own Lyrita CD offers two more symphonies, Nos. 3 and 5, subtitled *Hydriotaphia*, the Chandos couplings are more lightweight. Certainly *The Magic island* is a fine piece, inspired by *The Tempest*, and Hickox's account is beautifully played and full of atmosphere. The pithy *Derby Day overture* has plenty of energy here, but the *Overture to a masque* with its 'pipe and tabor' Elizabethan flavour is comparatively slight. The brilliant *Fanfare*, appropriately dedicated to the percussion player, James Blades, ends the concert spectacularly with the bright, sonorous recording impressively wide in range.

Symphony No. 4; Elizabethan dances; Festival march.
*** Chan. Dig. CHAN 8902 [id.]. LSO, Richard Hickox.

Richard Hickox's conception of the *Fourth* is marginally more spacious than the composer's own – as the timings of the outer movements demonstrate. Yet he has a masterly grip on the score. The Chandos digital recording, made in St Jude's, in London NW 11, is superbly rich and spacious. The *Elizabethan suite* doesn't bridge the opposing styles of the times of the queens, Elizabeth I and II, too convincingly, but there is a graceful waltz, an engaging mock-morris dance and a pleasing pavane. The *Festival march* is agreeable enough, but its grand tune lacks the memorability of those by Elgar and Walton.

CHAMBER MUSIC

Concerto for flute and 8 wind instruments; Music for three players; Naiades fantasy (Sonata for flute and harp); Suite for oboe and harp; Trio for flute, cello and piano.
☞ *** Chan. Dig. CHAN 9152 [id.]. Haffner Wind Ens. of L., Daniel, with Jones, Drake.

Alwyn's part-writing, pleasing invention and skilful manipulation of colour and texture make this a particularly rewarding collection. The *Concerto for flute and eight instruments* is richly textured, yet the consistent inner movement fascinates the ear. The soloist dominates an agreeably swirling blend of colourful sonorities, the second movement, *In tempo grazioso*, is a witty and cultivated little waltz with a wry secondary theme, appealingly shared by flute and oboe. The *Andante* is gently ethereal, with its touch of melancholy released in the joyful finale following a slow fugato, begun on the bassoon and taken up by the others. The charmingly pastoral *Suite for oboe and harp* is most delectably played by Nicholas Daniel (oboe) and Ieuan Jones (harp), its closing *Jig* winningly articulated. The *Naiades fantasy for flute and harp* is a chimerical piece in six movements (alas, not cued individually). It too has an engaging waltz (somewhat Ravelian) which in the nimbly brilliant finale leads us naturally into the peaceful opening *Prelude* of the *Music for three players* (violin, clarinet and piano). Again there is a Ravelian influence in these eight vignettes, so imaginatively contrasted in mood and texture. The final work, an equally attractive two-movement *Trio*, brings a memorable cello line from Caroline Dearnley, and the combination of cello and flute with piano (Julius Drake) proves most successful. The Haffner Wind Ensemble are very impressive, both individually as solo personalities and as a team, expertly matching timbres in part-writing which always rewards their skill and musicianship. Their playing is spontaneous and conveys delight in the music, so the listener too is delighted, the more so as Alwyn's melodic facility never fails him. The recording is admirably balanced and very realistic, reflecting the usual high standards we expect from Chandos. The acoustic is particularly well judged. A concert that can be recommended with no reservations whatsoever.

(i) *Rhapsody for piano quartet. String quartet No. 3; String trio.*
*** Chan. Dig. CHAN 8440; *ABTD 1153* [id.]. (i) David Willison; Qt of London.

The *Third Quartet* is the most important work on this record; like its two predecessors, it is a concentrated and thoughtful piece of very considerable substance, elegiac in feeling. The playing of the Quartet of London throughout (and of David Willison in the *Rhapsody*) is both committed and persuasive. The recording brings the musicians vividly into one's living-room.

String quartets Nos. 1 in D min.; 2 (Spring waters).
☞ **(*) Chan. Dig. CHAN 9219 [id.]. Qt of London.

Both quartets are works of substance. The *First* comes from the mid-1950s and immediately precedes the *Third Symphony*. It has a probing, deeply felt first movement, a dancing, gossamer Scherzo and a profound, yearning *Andante*. Its companion comes 20 years later and derives its subtitle, *Spring waters*, from Turgenev: 'My careless years, my precious days, like the waters of springtime, have melted away.' Its theme is the daunting prospect of old age, and there is a note of disillusion and resignation running through its pages. Both works are well played and the performances are obviously felt and thoroughly committed. Playing of this calibre undoubtedly moves the listener, particularly in the introspective self-questioning of No. 2. The digital recording from the early 1980s has clarity and presence and sounds admirably natural in its CD format. However, the playing time is too short for a full-priced record (45 minutes).

Fantasy-waltzes; 12 Preludes.
☞ **(*) Chan. Dig. CHAN 8399 [id.]. John Ogdon.

This record has just been restored to the catalogue at full price (even though it dates from 1985) and a price reduction might have been feasible. The *Fantasy-waltzes* are highly attractive and are excellently played by John Ogdon, who is also responsible for a perceptive insert-note. The *Twelve Preludes* are equally fluent and inventive pieces that ought to be better known and well repay investigation. The recording, made at The Maltings, Snape, is first rate and carries the imprimatur of the composer in whose presence it was made. Recommended.

VOCAL MUSIC

(i) *Invocations;* (ii) *A Leave-taking* (song-cycles).
☞ *** Chan. Dig. CHAN 9220 [id.]. (i) Jill Gomez, John Constable; (ii) Anthony Rolfe Johnson, Graham Johnson.

Almost as an offshoot from his opera, *Miss Julie*, Alwyn wrote these two song-cycles for the two singers who sang the principal roles of Julie and the Gamekeeper. In each, with a distinctive and unexpected choice of poems, Alwyn shows a keen ear for matching word-movement in music with a free arioso style. Notable in the tenor cycle, *A Leave-taking* (to words by the Victorian, John Leicester Warren), is *The ocean wood*, subtly evocative in its sea inspirations. The soprano cycle (to words by Michael Armstrong) is almost equally distinguished, leading to a beautiful *Invocation to the Queen of Moonlight*, which suits Jill Gomez's sensuous high soprano perfectly. Excellent performances, not least from the accompanists, and first-rate recording, transferred most naturally to CD.

Miss Julie (complete).
☞ *** Lyrita SRCD 2218 (2) [id.]. Jill Gomez, Benjamin Luxon, Della Jones, John Mitchinson, Philh. O, Tausky.

As a highly successful film composer William Alwyn is a master of atmosphere and dramatic timing. Strindberg's chilling study of Miss Julie's sudden infatuation for her father's manservant, Jean, adapted by the composer himself, is given the punch and power of verismo opera, with much learnt from Puccini above all. Alwyn's operatic gestures are big and, though the melodies hardly match Puccini's, the score is rich and confident, passionately performed by the Philharmonia under Tausky's direction. Jill Gomez sings ravishingly as Miss Julie and Benjamin Luxon gives a most convincing characterization of the manservant lover, with roughness a part of the mixture. Della Jones's mezzo is not contrasted enough with the heroine's soprano, but she sings warmly, and it is good to have as powerful a tenor as John Mitchinson in the incidental role of Ulrik. The 1983 Lyrita recording is well up to standard, beautifully clear as well as full, and it projects the narrative evocatively and involvingly.

Anderson, Leroy (1908–75)

Belle of the ball; Blue tango; Chicken reel; China doll; Fiddle-faddle; The first day of spring; The girl in satin; Horse and buggy; Jazz legato; Jazz pizzicato; The phantom regiment; Plink, plank, plunk!; Promenade; Saraband; Scottish suite: The bluebells of Scotland. Serenata; Sleigh ride; Song of the bells; Summer skies; The syncopated clock; The typewriter; The waltzing cat. Arr. of HANDEL: *Song of Jupiter.*
(M) *** Mercury 432 013-2 [id.]. Eastman-Rochester Pops O, or O, Frederick Fennell.

Belle of the ball; Bugler's holiday; Fiddle-faddle; Forgotten dreams; Jazz pizzicato; Plink, plank, plunk!; Sandpaper ballet; Saraband; Serenata; Sleigh ride; Song of the bells; The syncopated clock; Trumpeter's lullaby; The typewriter.
(M) **(*) Van. 08.6008.71 [OVC 6008]. Utah SO, Maurice Abravanel.

The reissue of Fennell's Mercury performances is most welcome; although certain key numbers such as *Bugler's holiday, Forgotten dreams* and *A Trumpeter's lullaby* are missing; they will no doubt, arrive on a later issue. His performances have a witty precision which is most attractive. The sound throughout is truthful, if not opulent.

The collection by the Utah Symphony Orchestra under Maurice Abravanel is also very enjoyable, affectionate and polished, if not as racy as Anderson's own recordings. Some might also feel that the Utah acoustic is a bit resonant for this lightly orchestrated writing, but it does not blunt the music's wit.

Andriessen, Hendrik (1892–1981)

(i) *Chromatic variations; Variations and fugue on a theme by Kuhnau;* (ii) *Variations on a theme by Couperin;* (iii) *Fiat Domine; Magna res est amor; Miroir de Peine* (song-cycle).
☞ *** NM Classics Dig. 92023 [id.]. Netherlands R. CO, Porcelijn; with (i) Reinders, Vincken, Bosman, Ferschtman; (ii) Verhey, Stoop; (iii) Alexander.

The Dutch composer, Hendrik Andriessen, began his professional career as a journalist (while also training as an organist). When his father died in 1913, he took over the directorship of music at St Josef Church in Haarlem and – while retaining his post as music critic on the local paper – began also to study composition at the Amsterdam Conservatoire. His melodic gift is very appealing and his scoring for strings shows a remarkable grasp of sonority and textural colour: there is much imaginative and haunting writing in his three sets of variations. The Couperin set (1944) also includes some delightfully delicate scoring for flute and harp, while the *Chromatic variations* (1970), among his last works, is virtually a miniature sinfonia concertante, with felicitous interweaving of the soloists: flute, oboe, violin and cello. The vocal works are highly atmospheric and show a strong French influence, with *Magna res est amor* very operatic in its rapturous line. Roberta Alexander soars aloft with glorious tone and she is hardly less ravishing in the song-cycle, setting poems by Henri Ghéon which illustrate Christ's passion as seen through Mary's eyes. The *Portement de Croix* with its restless accompaniment leads on to the *Crucifixion*, which is sung with moving tenderness. This is very rewarding music, of much beauty. It is performed with persuasive depth of feeling and considerable subtlety too, and the glowingly warm recording increases the listener's pleasure. Very highly recommended.

d'Anglebert, Jean-Henry (1635–91)

Pièces de clavecin: Suites: in D (Tombeau de M. de Chambonnières); D min.; G; G min.
☞ (B) **(*) HM HMA 190941. Kenneth Gilbert (harpsichord) (with CHAMBONNIERES: *Chaconne in F; Rondeau in F;* DUMONT: *Pavane in D min.;* L. COUPERIN: *La Piémontoise; Passacaille in C* **(*)).

Jean-Henry d'Anglebert, along with Louis Couperin, was a pupil of Chambonnières – both represented here – and an important figure in his day. Kenneth Gilbert has recorded his music before and is an expert advocate. It is highly decorated music, and that will be the snag for some listeners. The Prelude to each of the suites (where to some extent Gilbert has had to be conjectural) seems almost to be more decoration than content. But the dances (allemande, courante, saraband and gigue) which make up the main content are certainly inventive and have no little expressive feeling. In many ways this is a specialist record, but the collector who perseveres will find much that is rewarding.

Antheil, George (1900–1959)

Symphony No. 4.
** Bay Cities BCD 1016 [id.]. LSO, Goossens – GOULD: *Formations* etc. ***

George Antheil's *Fourth Symphony* is resolutely tonal and has a directness of expression that is not unappealing. There is a lot of Shostakovich in the piece too. The transfer greatly improves (particularly in bass definition) on the 1958 Everest recording, which originally appeared on LP with Ginastera's *Estancia* as a coupling.

Arensky, Anton (1861–1906)

Silhouettes (Suite No. 2), Op. 23.
*** Chan. Dig. CHAN 8898; *ABTD 1509* [id.]. Danish Nat. RSO, Järvi – SCRIABIN: *Symphony No. 3.* ***

Arensky's *Silhouettes* have a lot of period charm – particularly *Le rêveur*, which is almost the Russian equivalent of Elgar's *Dream children*. The Danish Radio Orchestra play for Neeme Järvi with great freshness and elegance, as if they are enjoying making the acquaintance of this rarely heard music – as we did!

Symphonies Nos. 1 in B min., Op. 4; 2 in A, Op. 22; Dream on the Volga overture.
** Olympia OCD 167 [Mobile Fidelity MFCD 878 (without Overture)]. USSR Ac. SO, Svetlanov.

Arensky's *First Symphony* is beautifully put together and has considerable melodic freshness. The *Second* is the more individual of the two and is full of highly attractive ideas. The *Overture* opens bombastically but also has its attractive moments, though its inspiration is less consistent than either of the symphonies. The performances are spirited, though the brass are at times raw in climaxes.

Variations on a theme of Tchaikovsky, Op. 35a.
☞ *** Unicorn Dig. DKPCD 9134 [id.]. Primavera CO, Paul; Manley – TCHAIKOVSKY: *Andante cantabile* etc. **(*)
*** ROH ROH 304/5; *ROHMC 304/5* [id.]. ROHCG O, Ermler – TCHAIKOVSKY: *Nutcracker ballet.* **(*)

An enjoyably affectionate, polished account of Arensky's endearing Tchaikovskian tribute. The theme is a song, *Legend*, a charming carol about Jesus the child, and Arensky's treatment never forgets its composer. Manley's performance, without lacking vitality, makes the most of the work's lovely nostalgic closing section. Clearly defined recording, yet with plenty of atmosphere.

Warm and easy on the ear, particularly in this ripely recorded performance, Arensky's unpretentious string work makes an attractive fill-up for Mark Ermler's Covent Garden recording of Tchaikovsky's *Nutcracker*.

Piano trio No. 1 in D min., Op. 32.
*** CRD CRD 3409; *CRDC 3409* [id.]. Ian Brown, Nash Ens. – RIMSKY-KORSAKOV: *Quintet.* ***
*** Chan. Dig. CHAN 8477 [id.]. Borodin Trio – GLINKA: *Trio.* ***
☞ (M) ** Pickwick Dig. MCD 52 [id.]. Solomon Trio – TCHAIKOVSKY: *Piano trio.* **
☞ (BB) * Naxos Dig. 8.550467 [id.]. Stamper, Jackson, Vovka Ashkenazy – TCHAIKOVSKY: *Piano trio.* *

Arensky's delightful *D minor Piano trio* was composed a year after Tchaikovsky's death and a decade after Tchaikovsky's own contribution to the genre. The account by members of the Nash Ensemble is first class in every way. These fine players capture the Slav melancholy of the *Elegia*, and in the delightful *Scherzo* Ian Brown is both delicate and nimble-fingered. The warm, resonant 1982 analogue recording has transferred naturally to CD.

The Borodins, too, give a lively and full-blooded account of the *Trio*. The *Scherzo* comes off well, and the whole does justice to the Borodins' genial playing.

There is much to delight in the playing of Yonty Solomon, Rodney Friend and Timothy Hugh, though the piano does at times swamp the sound-picture. Not that Yonty Solomon is wanting in delicacy in the Scherzo, and all three artists are imaginative. Generally speaking though, in this particular coupling the Pickwick version, which is at the very top end of the mid-price range, does not displace its CRD rival.

Despite some good musicianship and a highly competitive price, the Naxos is not a strong recommendation. The acoustic is not ideal and the playing of Richard Stamper, Christine Jackson and Vovka Ashkenazy, though far from pedestrian, is not quite distinguished enough to warrant the permanence of recording. They despatch the Scherzo well enough, but there are some infelicitous touches and insufficient lightness of touch elsewhere.

String quartet No. 2 in A min., Op. 35.
*** Mer. Dig. CDE 84211; *KE 77211* [id.]. Arienski Ens. – BORODIN: *Sextet movements;*
TCHAIKOVSKY: *Souvenir de Florence.* **

A charming three-movement work whose middle movement, the variations on a theme of Tchaikovsky, is best known in its transcription for full strings, it has, like so much of this composer's music, real quality. The playing is very committed indeed.

Arne, Thomas (1710–78)

6 'Favourite' concertos: Nos. 1 in C for harpsichord; 2 in G for organ; 3 in A for fortepiano; 4 in B flat for organ; 5 in G min. for harpsichord; 6 in B flat for fortepiano.
☞ **(*) Hyp. Dig. CDA 66509 [id.]. Paul Nicholson, Parley of Instruments.

The Arne concertos for organ, fortepiano or harpsichord were probably composed in the 1750s and offer some of the most advanced English keyboard music of the period. They did not appear in print until 1793, fifteen years after the composer had died. They are given spirited performances here but, compared with the sounds made by the ASMF in No. 5 (see below), the Parley of Instruments, however authentic, shows less finesse. One of the problems is the resonant acoustic, which means that the relationship between the various keyboards and the orchestral group is artificial, dictated by the microphone placing, and there is still a balance problem.

Harpsichord concerto No. 5 in G min.; Overture No. 1 in E min.
☞ (M) *** Decca 440 033-2 [id.]. George Malcolm, ASMF, Marriner – C. P. E. BACH: *Harpsichord concerto in C min.;* J. C. BACH: *Harpsichord concerto in A min.;* HAYDN: *Harpsichord concerto in D* etc. ***

This is the pick of the six concertos above and a most winning example of post-Handelian concertante writing. It is part of a most attractive anthology, recorded in 1967 with the Academy under Marriner at its early peak. George Malcolm not only plays a fine solo role in the concerto but provides the continuo for the attractive *Overture*, in effect a four-part sinfonia (slow-fast-slow-fast). The harpsichord is recorded realistically and life-size, too, not overblown.

Organ concertos Nos. 1 in C; 2 in G; 3 in A; 4 in B flat; 5 in G min.; 6 in B flat.
**(*) Chan. Dig. CHAN 8604/5; *DBTD 2013* (2) [id.]. Roger Bevan Williams, Cantilena, Shepherd.

Though Arne's concertos are simpler in style and construction than those of Handel, their invention is consistently fresh. The performances here have admirable style and spirit, and the recording is ideally balanced – the organ seems perfectly chosen for this consistently engaging music. A recommendable set in every respect, except for the playing time (only 86 minutes).

8 Overtures: Nos. 1 in E min.; 2 in A; 3 in G; 4 in F; 5 in D; 6 in B flat; 7 in D; 8 in G min.
☞ ** O-L 436 859-2 [id.]. AAM, Hogwood.

Arne's *Overtures*, besides showing a pleasing individuality of invention, are formally imaginative too in not slavishly following either the traditional French or the newer Italian patterns. The performances here, recorded (in 1973) in the resonant but not inflated acoustic of All Saints', Petersham, are well made and spirited, if perhaps a little humourless. While the use of authentic instruments (especially when skilfully played) has much in its favour in this repertory, to offer an 'impossible' fanfare-like passage on open horn harmonics (as in *Overture No. 4*) seems perverse, even grotesque, when modern instruments could encompass the passage without assaulting the ears of the listener. This blemish apart, the disc makes agreeable listening and it is well documented, if expensive.

Cymon and Iphigenia; Frolic and free (cantatas); Jenny; The Lover's recantation; The Morning (cantata); Sigh no more, ladies; Thou soft flowing Avon; What tho' his guilt.
*** Hyp. Dig. CDA 66237 (id.]. Emma Kirkby, Richard Morton, Parley of Instruments, Goodman.

The present collection admirably shows the ingenuous simplicity of Arne's vocal writing, very much in the mid-eighteenth-century English pastoral school with its 'Hey down derrys'. Excellent, warm recording, with the voices naturally projected. A most entertaining concert.

Arnell, Richard (born 1917)

The Great Detective (ballet suite).

☞ (M) (***) EMI mono CDM7 64718-2 [id.]. Pro Arte O, composer – ADDISON: *Carte blanche;*
ARNOLD: *A Grand Grand Overture;* BLISS: *Checkmate;* RAWSTHORNE: *Madame Chrysanthème*
etc. (***)

The Great Detective, is of course Sherlock Holmes and Richard Arnell's ballet was written for
Sadler's Wells in 1953. Arnell described the music as 'a mixture of wit, self-importance, low cunning
and, where it depicts the fiend, animal ferocity'. The writing is engagingly lightweight and tuneful,
with a *Pas de deux for Distressed lady and a suspect* and a *Pas de trois for Doctor and Ladies*. In the
Dance of deduction Sherlock briefly plays his fiddle. The lively performance under the composer
makes for a highlight in this collection of unpretentious, well-written British music, vividly recorded.

Punch and the child (ballet), *Op. 49.*

☞ (M) (***) Sony mono SMK 46683 [id.]. RPO, Beecham – BERNERS: *The Triumph of Neptune;*
DELIUS: *Paris.* ***

Richard Arnell enjoyed something of a vogue immediately after the war. His *Fourth Symphony* scored
some success at the Cheltenham Festival in the late 1940s and his imaginative and inventive ballet,
Punch and the child, was mounted by the New York City Ballet. Yet his present representation in the
catalogue is meagre in the extreme and by no means commensurate with his gifts. Sir Thomas
Beecham recorded the *Punch and the child suite* on five 78-r.p.m. sides in 1950. Its musical inspiration
is as fresh, individual and memorable as its neglect is unaccountable. We have relished this score over
the years and its attractions remain as strong as ever in this well-transferred set. The sound is
amazingly good for 1950 – but then it was pretty much state-of-the-art at that time.

Arnold, Malcolm (born 1921)

Clarinet concertos Nos. 1, Op. 20; 2, Op. 115; Scherzetto.

☞ *** Hyp. Dig. CDA 66634 [id.]. Thea King, ECO, Wordsworth – BRITTEN: *Clarinet concerto
movement;* MACONCHY: *Concertinos.* ***

Designed in part as a tribute to the great clarinettist, Frederick Thurston, Thea King's collection of
short concertante works for clarinet makes an exceptionally attractive disc, beautifully recorded and
superbly performed. Particularly when Thea King, Thurston's widow, was also his star pupil, it
makes a splendid addition to the list of discs of English clarinet music, not just concertos, she has
recorded for Hyperion. King's ever-seductive tone, at once sensuously beautiful yet clear, perpetuates
the qualities Thurston sought to instil. The first of Arnold's concertos, like the first of Maconchy's
concertinos, was written with Thurston's playing in mind, as was the *Scherzetto*, a delightfully jaunty
piece adapted by Christopher Palmer from Arnold's music for the film, *You Know What Sailors Are.*
The other direct influence here is Benny Goodman, who not only inspired the second Arnold
concerto but also the *Concertino* movement of Britten. The Arnold brings a lusciously bluesy slow
movement which leads to riotous rag-music in the finale. Not only Thea King but the ECO (the
orchestra in which she has been a distinguished principal for many years) under Barry Wordsworth
bring out the warmth as well as the rhythmic drive.

(i) *Clarinet concerto No. 1, Op. 20;* (ii) *Flute concerto No. 1, Op. 45;* (iii) *Horn concerto No. 2, Op. 58;*
(iv) *Double violin concerto, Op. 77.*

*** Conifer Dig. CDCF 172 [id.]. (i) Collins; (ii) Jones; (iii) Watkins; (iv) Sillito and Fletcher; L.
Musici, Mark Stephenson.

These works provide outstanding examples of a genre which Arnold has cultivated with conspicuous
success and which might be described as 'the quarter-hour concerto'. On Conifer in the *Double
concerto* Kenneth Sillito and Lyn Fletcher are sweetly matched in writing which presents the most
severe demands on purity of intonation, while both Michael Collins and Karen Jones give urgent,
exhilarating readings of works which aim for brilliance above all. The horn soloist, Richard Watkins,
may not quite match the wonderfully wide tonal range that the late Alan Civil achieves on the earlier
recording, but he is weightier in the slow movement and even brisker in the finale.

(i) *Clarinet concerto No. 2, Op. 115;* (ii) *Flute concerto No. 2, Op. 111;* (iii) *Horn concerto No. 1, Op.
11;* (iv) *Concerto for piano duet and strings, Op. 32.*

☞ *** Conifer Dig. CDCF 228; *MCFC 228* [id.]. (i) Michael Collins; (ii) Karen Jones; (iii) Richard
Watkins; (iv) David Nettle & Richard Markham; London Musici, Mark Stephenson.

The brief concertos which Sir Malcolm Arnold has written for a whole range of instruments, generally inspired by particular performers, form a most attractive side of his work. This Conifer issue, superbly performed and recorded, makes the perfect complement to the earlier disc of Arnold concertos from that company, also with Mark Stephenson conducting the London Musici and with some of the same soloists. In the *Second Clarinet concerto*, written for Benny Goodman in 1974, Michael Collins (who played it at the 1993 Last Night of the Proms) is even more persuasive, more volatile than Thea King in her fine Hyperion version. The *Horn Concerto No. 1* is the earliest work here, written in 1946 for Charles Gregory, then Arnold's colleague in the London Philharmonic. It is the longest of the works included, with an extended central *Andante* with dark overtones and a hunting-rhythm finale. Richard Watkins, principal horn of the Philharmonia, plays it with great panache and glorious tone.

Karen Jones, principal flute of the Bournemouth orchestra and Shell–LSO prizewinner in 1985, is equally sympathetic in the *Flute Concerto No. 2*. In its layout this concerto, written in 1972, is the most original work on the disc, with a central Scherzo flanked by an equivocal *Allegro moderato* and a final lyrical *Allegretto*. The *Concerto for piano duet* of 1950 should not be confused with the three-handed *Concerto for two pianos* that Arnold wrote for Cyril Smith and Phyllis Sellick. In its use of block chords for the four hands at one keyboard, it is a chunkier work but is full of characteristic Arnold touches. After an emphatic first movement, a central *Passacaglia* brings craggy contrasts, leading to a jazzy finale with relaxed episodes. Nettle and Markham play as one at their single keyboard; and under Mark Stephenson the young musicians of London Musici perform throughout with the understanding and precision that have marked all their Conifer recordings.

(i) *Flute concerto No. 1, Op. 45;* (ii) *Oboe concerto, Op. 39; Sinfoniettas Nos. 1–3, Opp. 48, 65 & 81.*
*** Hyp. Dig. CDA 66332 [id.]. (i) Beckett, (ii) Messiter; L. Festival O, Ross Pople.

It makes a delightful programme having Arnold's three *Sinfoniettas* framing two wind concertos that come from the same early period, the 1950s. The performances here are all excellent, with warm, well-balanced sound.

Guitar concerto, Op. 67.
☞ (M) *** BMG/RCA 09026 61598-2. Julian Bream, Melos Ens., composer – Richard Rodney
   BENNETT: *Concerto;* RODRIGO: *Concierto de Aranjuez.* ***
☞ *** EMI Dig. CDC7 54661-2 [id.]. Julian Bream, CBSO (members), Rattle – RODRIGO:
   Concierto de Aranjuez. TAKEMITSU: *To the Edge of Dream.* ***

There are few guitar concertos to match the effectiveness of this jazz-inflected piece, written in 1957 for Julian Bream, whose first recording, made two years later with the composer directing the Melos Ensemble, is surely definitive. It was recorded by Decca engineers, so the balance is exemplary and the sound has plenty of atmosphere and the most vivid colouring. The composer makes his mark in raptly establishing the ambivalent atmosphere of the slow movement, an elegiac tribute to the jazz guitarist, Django Reinhardt, greatly admired by both Arnold and Bream. The lightening and darkening of the mood is subtly yet powerfully managed and the performance overall has that combination of intensity and spontaneity which marks the finest of recording premières, especially when the composer is an able participant. The soloist, too, is in inspirational form.

Bream's second recording, with Rattle, is also very successful indeed and gains from the modern digital sound, which is vividly focused. The delicious secondary theme which dominates the first movement melodically is presented with affectionate neatness, and the blues-inspired slow movement with its moments of darkness and fantasy is played here with natural understanding of its jazz idiom as well as characteristic virtuosity from the soloist. As with the earlier version, the work is recorded in its original chamber scoring, which is especially effective in the infectious finale.

(i) *Double violin concerto. Serenade for small orchestra, Op. 26; Sinfoniettas Nos 1–2.*
**(*) Koch Dig. 37134-2 [id.]. (i) Igor and Vesna Gruppman; San Diego CO, Barra.

These are warm-hearted performances, very well recorded, of four of Malcolm Arnold's most attractive earlier works, each in his favourite form of three compact movements. The *Serenade for small orchestra*, the first of the four, with the most ambitious orchestration, is particularly valuable, when otherwise it is unavailable on CD. The San Diego Chamber Orchestra gives a winning account, full of high spirits. Consistently the American players rise to the dashing challenge which Arnold makes in the finales of all these works, but they are less successful in evoking the Bachian overtones of the *Double Violin concerto*, with the central *Andantino* too romantic in style, and the soloists consistently adopting too heavy a vibrato, with the occasional portamento.

(i) *4 Cornish dances; 8 English dances, Sets 1, Op. 27; 2, Op. 33; 4 Scottish dances, Op. 59* (all arr. Farr); *Fantasy for brass band, Op. 114; Little suites for brass band Nos. 1, Op. 80; 2, Op. 92;* (ii) *The Padstow Lifeboat* (march), *Op. 94.*
☞ *** Conifer Dig. CDCD 222; *M CFC 222* [id.]. Grimethorpe Colliery Band, (i) Elgar Howarth;
    (ii) composer.

Sir Malcolm Arnold, who was present at the recording sessions, gave high praise to Elgar Howarth's carefully prepared yet winningly spontaneous performances, unerringly paced. The composer himself directs the final march, *The Padstow Lifeboat,* with its warning off-key foghorn (based on the pitch of the foghorn at Trevose in Cornwall). The astonishing virtuosity and the wide palette of colour achieved by the Grimethorpe Colliery Band is consistently stimulating throughout this highly enjoyable programme. The infectious ebullience of the playing is captivating in the first of the *Scottish dances* and, in the second, the 'drunken' solo bass trombone is in the best humorous tradition of Arnoldian music-making. But when the players reach the magical third *Scottish dance* (one of the composer's finest melodic inspirations) the subtlety of colouring is quite remarkable and the effect meltingly frisson-creating. The contrasting vitality of the last dance is irresistible. The *Eight English dances* are also most enjoyable, but here one misses the vivid orchestral colouring at times. However, the players do a chirpy flute/piccolo imitation in the *First Dance* in Set II by whistling the air themselves! The elegiac atmosphere of the *Cornish dances* – ideally suited for brass band transcription – is movingly caught, with their evocation of 'the deserted engine-houses of the tin and copper-mines', and echoes of sonorous Sankey and Moody hymns. The two *Little suites* and *Fantasy* (like the *Padstow* march) were original works for brass. The first brings an engaging *Siciliano* second movement and the second an exhilarating *Galop* finale, where the players really let their hair down. But the *Fantasy* is the most imaginatively inventive of all, a sequence of sharply observed vignettes including a regal opening *Prelude,* a richly sonorous and very touching *Elegy,* a wittily unbuttoned *Scherzo* and a closing *Vivace* full of zesty bravura scales. The performances are superb and the recording, made – appropriately – in Dewsbury Town Hall, Yorkshire, is completely natural and very realistically balanced, and it makes the very most of the hall's ambience without any loss of definition. This is very much in the demonstration bracket and is also a most entertaining 66 minutes of good tunes and brilliant invention, very cleverly scored.

Cornish dances, Op. 91; English dances, Set 1, Op. 27; Set 2, Op. 33; Irish dances, Op. 126; Scottish dances, Op. 59; Solitaire (ballet): *Sarabande; Polka.*
*** Lyrita SRCD 201 [id.]. LPO, composer.
*** Chan. Dig. CHAN 8867; *ABTD 1482* [id.]. Philh. O, Bryden Thomson.

Arnold's four sets of British national dances make a wonderfully varied and colourful musical entertainment. The two numbers specially written for *Solitaire* in 1956 augmented the eight *English dances,* to form the ballet of this name. The *Sarabande* has a wistful charm and the *Polka* brings characteristically witty orchestral colouring.

  Bryden Thomson has the advantage of the extra definition superb digital sound brings, with no loss of ambient feeling. The composer's tempi are usually fractionally slower than Thomson's, underlining contrasts, yet Arnold's strong rhythmic pointing brings even greater bite and thrust. Both these sets of performances are admirable in different ways, and those who choose the Chandos disc for its digital spectacle will not be disappointed.

8 English dances.
(M) (***) Decca mono 425 661-2 [id.]. LPO, Boult – WALTON: *Façade* etc. *** ⊛

Arnold's first essay in writing colourful regional pieces receives a vividly sympathetic performance under Boult, with the mono recording still sounding remarkably well.

Film music: *The Bridge on the River Kwai* (suite for large orchestra); *Hobson's Choice* (orchestral suite); *The Inn of the Sixth Happiness* (suite); *The Sound Barrier* (rhapsody), *Op. 38; Whistle Down the Wind* (small suite for small orchestra).
☞ *** Chan. Dig. CHAN 9100; *ABTD 1600* [id.]. LSO, Richard Hickox.

Malcolm Arnold wrote over 100 film scores, and it was the music for *The Bridge on the River Kwai* which – as the composer has acknowledged – put his name before the wider public. He justly won an Oscar for what in essence was the provision of an exuberant counter-melody to sail over the top of Kenneth Alford's march, *Colonel Bogey* (written as long ago as 1914, and loved ever since by British troops, not least because of the very rude words that can readily fit its main rhythmic idea). What is so exasperating is that the Alford estate refused permission for this inimitable musical amalgam to be recorded, so what we are give here is separate performances of the Alford march and Arnold's breezy counter-theme. What is so striking here and throughout this 78-minute collection is the sheer fecundity of Arnold's invention. The tunes pour out during a period (between 1953 and 1961) when few composers could write them at all. In *Kwai* Christopher Palmer, Arnold's amanuensis for this project, took various fragments and sections and reassembled them with the composer's blessing: the result is very strong. Much the same applies to the lighter score for *Hobson's Choice* (David Lean's engaging film adaptation of Harold Brighouse's play, with John Mills as the hero and the great Charles Laughton in the lead). But how charmingly melodic it is. *Whistle Down the Wind*, also set in Lancashire, is a story of three farm children who find a stranger in the barn and think he is Jesus. This touching theme, gently and sensitively handled in the movie, brings in its *Prelude* one of Arnold's most indelible ideas originally including a human whistle, which the producer, Richard Attenborough, provided in the soundtrack but which here is a piccolo. The powerful *Rhapsody*, based on the score for *The Sound Barrier*, was fashioned by Arnold himself, and its vivid use of the orchestral palette recalls the *English dances*. *The Inn of the Sixth Happiness* is more Hollywoodian in its flamboyance, but it has a charming central romantic interlude. All this music is superbly played by Hickox and the LSO (who obviously relish the often virtuoso instrumental scoring), and the recording is as lavish as anyone could wish – very much in the Chandos demonstration bracket.

A Grand Grand Overture.
☞ (M) (***) EMI mono CDM7 64718-2 [id.]. Pro Arte O, composer – ADDISON: *Carte blanche;* ARNELL: *Great Detective;* BLISS: *Checkmate;* RAWSTHORNE: *Madame Chrysanthème* etc. (***)

Malcolm Arnold's *Grand Grand overture* with its rifle-shots and parts in the score for three vacuum-cleaners and a floor-polisher, was written for the first Hoffnung Festival in 1956. It has quite a good main theme but its flagrant audacity wears a bit thin, away from the visual occasion. It is perhaps the least repeatable offering on this otherwise attractive collection of British lightweight composer-conducted music. The mono sound is vivid enough, and the rest of the compilation is recorded in stereo.

(i) *Symphony No. 1;* (ii) *Concerto for 2 pianos (3 hands), Op. 104;* (iii) *English dances Nos. 3 & 5;* (i) *Solitaire: Sarabande; Polka;* (iii) *Tam O'Shanter: overture, Op. 51.*
(M) *** EMI CDM7 64044-2. (i) Bournemouth SO; (ii) Phyllis Sellick and Cyril Smith, CBSO; (iii) Philh. O; composer.

This is a strong performance of the *First Symphony* under the composer, while the concerto is a delightful, undemanding work, superbly played by the dedicatees, which makes a good foil alongside the rumbustious overture, *Tam O'Shanter*. Finally come the two pieces Arnold added to his *English dances* for the ballet *Solitaire*, and two of the most attractive of the *Dances*.

(i) *Symphony No. 2, Op. 40;* (ii) *Symphony No. 5, Op. 74;* (i) *Peterloo: overture.*
(M) *** EMI CDM7 63368-2 [id.]. (i) Bournemouth SO, Groves; (ii) CBSO, composer.

The recoupling of two of Arnold's most impressive symphonies can be warmly welcomed. Both recordings date from the 1970s. The composer secures an excellent response from the Birmingham orchestra, as Groves, in Bournemouth, is equally dedicated. The CD transfer is outstandingly successful, and the overture makes a highly effective encore. Splendid value at mid-price.

Symphonies Nos. 3, Op. 63; 4, Op. 71.
☞ *** Chan. Dig. CHAN 9290 [id.]. LSO, Hickox.

Symphony No. 4, Op. 71.
*** Lyrita Dig. SRCD 200 [id.]. LPO, composer.

Arnold's symphonies have comparatively little of the good-natured optimism which distinguishes so many of his shorter works. The symphonies somehow mirror his experience of life in its broader context, with disappointment, frustration and even tragedy all included within the package that humanity has to accept. As it happens, the immediately communicative *Third Symphony* does have a good-natured finale; even if there is a sting at the end with a fierce, Holst-like rhythmic warning in the coda, the despair is met head on in the final few bars. The work, commissioned by the Royal Liverpool Philharmonic Society and first performed in 1957, is more notable for the long, expressively austere string-melody in the opening movement and the desolation of its *Lento* slow movement, both played with great expressive intensity under Hickox.

The *Fourth Symphony*, already recorded by the composer on Lyrita, was commissioned by the BBC and, after its broadcast first performance in 1960, Andrew Porter described it as 'a symphony for fun ... exuberant, melodious, unabashed, likeable'. The first movement is dominated by one of those entirely winning, Arnoldian lyrical tunes, even though there is jagged dissonance in the central episode, perhaps prompted by the contemporary Notting Hill race riots, which also may be the reason for the presence of Caribbean percussion instruments, often used aggressively, although the Scherzo is chimerical. The slow movement brings another long-breathed, almost Mahlerian, melodic flow, although with more overt sensuousness, and the finale, complete with fugue, has its bizarre, indeed raucous moments, including a curious march sequence. Richard Hickox has the work's full measure, and the Chandos recording is superb, full of colour and atmosphere. The composer's own performance on Lyrita inevitably has something special about it, for he was an excellent conductor, but he co-operated with Hickox for the Chandos project, and without a coupling the Lyrita CD is upstaged by the new one.

Symphony No. 6, Op. 95; (i) *Fantasy on a theme of John Field for piano and orchestra, Op. 116.*
Sweeny Todd (ballet): *concert suite, Op. 68a; Tam O'Shanter overture, Op. 51.*
☞ *** Conifer Dig. CDCF 224 [id.]. RPO, Vernon Handley, (i) with John Lill.

Written in 1967 during his unhappy Cornish period, the powerfully bleak *Sixth Symphony* brings a striking example of the darker, more troubled side of Arnold's genius. The first two of its three compact movements are equivocal in feeling, hinting at jollity quickly submerged in a mood of melancholy, always with fascinating orchestral timbres kaleidoscopically presented, not least in the elegiac central slow movement. Few will easily forget the stabbing brass of the opening movement or the haunting atmosphere of the *Lento* with its ghostly march. Yet, as Piers Burton-Page's perceptive note says, this is an economical symphony in the spareness of both the argument and the instrumentation. The work finally resolves its enigmatic despondency in the up-beat *Con fuoco* finale, a rondo based on a characteristically ebullient Arnoldian trumpet-tune, a movement somewhat Shostakovich-like in its quirkiness. The *Fantasy on a theme of John Field*, written for John Lill during the composer's Irish period, is a splendid example of the more extrovert Arnold in the bravura of the piano writing. It uses one of Field's most innocently charming nocturnes, in which John Lill revels with much delicate poetry. The 13 sections bring a characterful sequence of variants on the Field theme, with warmly tonal melodic writing periodically contradicted. The orchestra at first offers some pungent opposition, but the lovely theme regularly reasserts its charm and, after much entertaining diversity in the central variations and moments of more violent dissonance, the work ends with a grandiloquent re-presentation in the style of Rachmaninov. The *Sweeney Todd* music, drawn from a ballet score with the help of David Ellis, brings a contradiction between the grimness of the subject and the open jollity of the treatment, with cakewalks, polkas and other dance-rhythms freely used. The suite brims over with high spirits and catchy tunes, often with a music-hall flavour, even including an Offenbachian can-can. The *Tam O'Shanter overture*, the best-known item, is an idiosyncratic, rumbustious showpiece characteristic of the early Arnold. The histrionics of Tam O'Shanter's drunken encounter with a witches' sabbath, bagpipes and all, makes for a vividly exuberant closing item. The composer was present at the recording sessions, and everyone is obviously on his or her toes: the result is highly spontaneous and consistently stimulating. Handley draws colourful and committed playing from the orchestra, with John Lill a masterful, flamboyant soloist in the music written for him. First-class recording and 78 minutes of music give this issue a strong profile within the growing Arnold discography.

Symphonies Nos. 7, Op. 113; 8, Op. 124.
*** Conifer CDCF 177 [id.]. RPO, Vernon Handley.

The bitterness in the *Seventh* is inescapable. Dedicated to the composer's three children, the writing is most strongly influenced by his son Edward, tragically autistic. The *Eighth* is emotionally hardly less pungent. Handley's performances of both symphonies generate great power and depth of feeling, with the most eloquent response from the RPO players, and the recording is outstandingly real and vivid. However, neither work offers an easy listening experience.

CHAMBER MUSIC

Divertimento for flute, oboe and clarinet, Op. 37; Duo for flute and viola, Op. 10; Flute sonata, Op. 121; Oboe quartet, Op. 61; Quintet for flute, violin, viola, horn and piano, Op. 7; 3 Shanties for wind quintet, Op. 4.
*** Hyp. Dig. CDA 66173 [id.]. Nash Ens.

Duo for 2 cellos, Op. 85; Piano trio, Op. 54; Viola sonata No. 1, Op. 17; Violin sonatas Nos. 1, Op.
15; 2, Op. 43; Pieces for violin and piano, Op. 54.
*** Hyp. Dig. CDA 66171 [id.]. Nash Ens.

Clarinet sonatina, Op. 29; Fantasies for wind, Opp. 86–90; Flute sonatina, Op. 19; Oboe sonatina, Op.
28; Recorder sonatina, Op. 41; Trio for flute, bassoon and piano, Op. 6.
*** Hyp. Dig. CDA 66172 [id.]. Nash Ens.

There is much here that belies Malcolm Arnold's image as just an entertaining and genial tunesmith.
All the pieces on the first disc show conspicuous resource in the handling of the instruments. The
second disc includes two *Violin sonatas* which are cool, civilized and intelligent. The *Piano trio* of
1956 has a powerful sense of direction. The third listing concentrates on the wind music. This is
perhaps more for admirers of Arnold's music than for the generality of collectors. The playing is
brilliant and sympathetic throughout all three discs and the recording first rate.

Arriaga, Juan (1806–26)

String quartets Nos. 1 in D min.; 2 in A; 3 in E flat.
*** CRD CRD 33123 (2) [id.]. Chilingirian Qt – WIKMANSON: *String quartet No. 2.* ***

These three *Quartets* are marvellous works of great warmth and spontaneity that can hold their own
in the most exalted company. It is barely credible that a boy still in his teens could have produced
them. The Chilingirians play with both conviction and feeling.

Atterberg, Kurt (1887–1974)

Symphonies Nos. (i) *1 in B min., Op. 3;* (ii) *4 in G min. (Sinfonia piccola), Op. 14.*
☞ **(*) Complete Record Co. Sterling CDS 1010-2 [id.]. (i) Swedish RSO, Westerberg; (ii)
    Norrköping SO, Frykberg.

Although Atterberg composed nine symphonies, only the *Sixth* has made any headway abroad.
However, he had a well-stocked imagination and a good feeling for the orchestra and he deserves
wider dissemination. The *First Symphony* (1909, revised 1913) is derivative but well fashioned, and
well played too. The *Sinfonia piccola* (1922) is slight, almost sinfonietta-like; it makes extensive use of
folk material. A useful coupling, though the performance of the folksy *Sinfonia piccola* is not quite
top-drawer.

Symphony No. 6 in C, Op. 31; Ballad without words, Op. 56; A Värmland rhapsody, Op. 36.
** BIS Dig. CD 553 [id.]. Norrköping SO, Jun'ichi Hirokami.

Atterberg's *Sixth Symphony* is a colourful and inventive score which deserves wide popularity. *A*
Värmland rhapsody is, appropriately enough, strongly folkloric. The *Ballad without words* has many
imaginative touches. The Norrköping orchestra includes many sensitive players, but the string-tone
lacks weight and opulence. The recording is very clean.

Autumn ballads, Op. 15; Rondo rétrospectif, Op. 26; Trio concertante in G min./C, Op. 57; Valse
monotone in C; Violin sonata in B min., Op. 27.
☞ ** Marco Polo Dig. 8.223404 [id.]. Eszter Pérényi, András Kiss, Ilona Prunyi, Sándor Falvay,
    György Kertész, Deborah Sipkay.

The *Violin sonata* (subsequently arranged for horn – see below – and originally intended for
Atterberg's own instrument, the cello) is a well-wrought piece, which sounds better here than on the
horn. The *Autumn ballads*, however, are rather banal. The *Valse monotone* is a piano transcription of
the last movement of the *Suite for violin, viola and strings*, one of the composer's very best works. The
Rondeau rétrospectif is an entertaining piece from the 1920s for piano (four hands), much in the
irreverent spirit of the finale of the *Sixth Symphony*, and which quotes freely from various classics
including the *Pathétique Symphony* and the *Emperor concerto*. The *Trio concertante* is an arrangement
for violin, cello and harp of his *Double concerto* for violin, cello and orchestra (1960). None of this is
great music but it is well played and more than adequately recorded.

(i) *Horn sonata, Op. 27;* (ii) *Piano quintet in C, Op. 31b;* (iii) *Suite No. 1 (orientale) for 2 violins, cello*
& piano.
☞ ** Marco Polo Dig. 8.223405 [id.]. (i–iii) I. Prunyi; (i) Magyari; (ii) New Budapest Qt; (iii) Kiss,
    Balogh, G. Kertész.

Predominantly an arrangements disc. The *Piano quintet* is none other than our old friend, the '*Dollar Symphony*', which Atterberg transcribed in 1942. One or two of the effects (the percussion at the end of the finale) do not come off in transcription, and the piece as a whole makes a much stronger impact in its original form. There is a BIS recording of it (see above). The *Horn sonata* is an arrangement of the 1925 *Violin sonata* (see also above), made in the 1950s for Domenico Ceccarossi, a well-argued piece whose middle movement is folk-inspired. The *Suite orientale* is slight in both length and substance. Good performances, decent recording.

Auber, Daniel (1782–1871)

Overtures: The Bronze horse; Fra Diavolo; Masaniello.
⊛ (M) *** Mercury 434 309-2 [id.]. Detroit SO, Paray – SUPPÉ: *Overtures*. ***

Dazzling performances, full of verve and style, which will surely never be surpassed. The present recordings, made in the suitably resonant acoustic of Detroit's Old Orchestra Hall, shows Mercury engineering (1959 vintage) at its very finest.

Fra Diavolo (complete).
☞ *** EMI Dig. CDS7 54810-2 (2) [id.]. Gedda, Mesplé, Cordazza, Berbié, Dran, Bastin, Jean Laforge Ch. Ens., Monte Carlo PO, Soustrot.

With a comic English milord and two comic bandits (played by Laurel and Hardy in the Hollywood film version of 1933), *Fra Diavolo* is a delightful piece, given a sparkling performance under Marc Soustrot. Some of the patter ensembles suggest that Sullivan and maybe Gilbert too knew this comic opera. The numbers are separated by spoken French dialogue but, with a cast very much in tune with the style of the piece, it adds to the dramatic point. Though Nicolai Gedda's voice has lost its youthful sweetness and often sounds strained, he is very characterful in the title, and similarly Mady Mesplé with her typically French, tinkly soprano is very idiomatic as Zerline. The others are all excellent, and the 1984 digital sound is well balanced.

Auric, Georges (1899–1983)

L'éventail de Jeanne (complete ballet, including music by Delannoy, Ferroud, Ibert, Milhaud, Poulenc, Ravel, Roland-Manuel, Roussel, Florent Schmitt). *Les Mariés de la Tour Eiffel:* (complete ballet, including music by Honegger, Milhaud, Poulenc, Tailleferre).
⊛ *** Chan. Dig. CHAN 8356 [id.]. Philh. O, Simon.

A carefree spirit and captivating wit run through both these composite works. In fact these pieces are full of imagination and fun. Geoffrey Simon and the Philharmonia Orchestra give a very good account of themselves and the Chandos recording is little short of spectacular.

Overture.
☞ (M) *** Mercury 434 335-2 [id.]. LSO, Dorati – FETLER: *Contrasts;* FRANCAIX: *Piano concertino;* MILHAUD: *Le bœuf sur le toit;* SATIE: *Parade*. ***

Georges Auric's breezy *Overture* dates from 1938. Although it seems to use part of a theme from Debussy's *Petite suite*, the music has a predominantly Montmartre atmosphere. It is irrepressibly high-spirited and its melodic freshness and Dorati's vivacious performance help to dispel the impression that it is a shade too long for its content. Vividly clear and transparent sound from near the end of the Mercury vintage era: 1965.

Avison, Charles (1709–70)

12 Concerti grossi after Scarlatti.
☞ (B) *** Ph. Duo 438 806-2 (2) [id.]. ASMF, Marriner.

Charles Avison was born in Newcastle-upon-Tyne. During the early part of his career he went to Italy; he sojourned also in London, where he studied under the resident Italian composer, Francesco Geminini. In 1736 he returned to his home city; there, besides teaching, playing and composing, he began a series of subscription concerts, rather like Hallé was to do in Manchester more than a century later. Avison wrote in a mature baroque style and it was a brilliant idea of Marriner to delve into these endlessly refreshing concertos which Avison based on keyboard sonatas by Domenico

Scarlatti. The transcriptions for strings were attractively free (borrowing was always acceptable for composers in the eighteenth century) and he varied Scarlatti-based movements with original ones of his own. Marriner and his players bring these delightful works fully to life: the playing is both refined and resilient, with Iona Brown leading the solo group with grace and style. The beautifully balanced 1978 recording sounds most realistic in these expert CD transfers.

Bacarisse, Salvator (1898–1963)

Concertino in A min. for guitar and orchestra.
☞ (M) ** DG 439 526-2 [id.]. Narciso Yepes, Spanish R. & TV O, Alonso – RODRIGO: *Concertos.* **

Bacarisse's *Concertino* is slight but engaging. The masterly Yepes makes the very most of it, notably the hauntingly nostalgic *Adagio*, and Alonso presents the *Entrada*-like movement which opens the work with full Renaissance flavour and is similarly colourful in the linked variants of the finale. The 1972 recording sounds a bit insubstantial in presenting the orchestra, but the quality of the solo playing makes one almost forget the slightly dated sound, focused well enough in the CD transfer.

Bacewicz, Grazyna (1909–69)

(iii; v) *Concerto for orchestra;* (i; iii; vi) *Double piano concerto;* (ii; iii; vi) *Viola concerto;* (iv) *Divertimento for strings;* (iii; v) *Pensieri Notturni.*
**(*) Olympia OCD 311 [id.]. (i) Maksymiuk, Witkowski; (ii) Kamasa; (iii) Warsaw Nat. PO; (iv) Warsaw Nat. Philharmonic CO, Teutsch; (v) Rowicki; (vi) Wislocki.

Bacewicz shows a cultured and resourceful creative mind rather than a strongly individual profile: there is just a touch of general-purpose modernity about her music, but all the same it is well worth hearing and has far more substance to it than, say, Penderecki. Dedicated performances, particularly of the *Viola concerto* (1968) which is splendidly played by the dedicatee, Stefan Kamasa. Decent and eminently serviceable analogue recordings.

(i) *String quartets Nos. 4, 7;* (ii) *Piano quintet No. 1.*
**(*) Olympia OCD 310 [id.]. (i) Grazyna Bacewicz Warsaw String Qt; (ii) Warsaw Piano Quintet.

The three chamber works assembled here show much expertise in writing for the strings. Good performances, though the *Piano Quintet* recorded in 1969 is rather too closely balanced for comfort.

The Bach family, including Johann Sebastian

Johann Christoph (1642–1703)   Johann Michael (1648–94)
Johann Bernhard (1676–1749)   Johann Sebastian (1685–1750)
Johann Lorenz (1695–1773)   Johann Ernst (1722–77)

'The Bach family: Organ works': J. S. BACH: *Toccata and Fugue in D min., BWV 565; Fantasia and fugue in A min., BWV 904; Prelude and fugue in C, BWV 547; Prelude (Fantasia) and fugue in G min., BWV 542; Chorale with 6 variations on 'Wenn wir in höchsten Nöten sein', BWV Anh. 78; Capriccio in E, BWV 993.* J. L. BACH: *Prelude and fugue in D min.* J. M. BACH: Chorales: *Allein Gott in der Höh sei Ehr; Wenn wir in höchsten Nöten sein.* J. C. BACH: *Prelude and fugue in E flat;* Chorales: *Warum betrübst du dich, mein Herz; Wach auf, mein Herz, und singe; Aus meines Herzens Grunde.* J. B. BACH: *Passacaglia (Chaconne) in B flat; Partita on 'Du Friedefürst, Herr Jesu Christ'.* J. E. BACH: *Fantasia and fugue in F.*
☞ (M) *** Teldec/Warner 4505 92176 (2) [id.]. Wilhelm Krumbach (Herbst organ of the Schlosskirche, Lahm/Itzgrund, Germany).

Seven generations of Bach's family were professional or semi-professional musicians, most employed as church Kantors, which inevitably involved composing. Johann Christoph and Johann Michael Bach were distant uncles of Johann Sebastian; Johann Bernhard Bach was his first cousin once removed; Johann Lorenz was his first nephew once removed (and also his pupil); Johann Ernst was the son of Johann Bernhard. So much for the family tree, but what of the music? The whole family were – naturally enough – good at chorales, and both Johann Lorenz and Johann Christoph could write a respectable prelude and fugue. But the star here is Johann Bernhard, whose *Passacaglia in B flat* is a splendid piece, while the *Chorale partita on Du Friedefürst Herr Jesu Christ* is also very inventive. The programme ends with Johann Ernst's remarkably flamboyant *Fantasia and fugue in F*, but that is much later than the other works. Performances are first class and so is the organ. It was good to have the *Chorale variations* and *Capriccio* of Johann Sebastian as an illuminating yardstick but, had the other of his works been omitted, this programme could have fitted economically on to a single CD. Nevertheless this is a fascinating set.

Bach, Carl Philipp Emanuel (1714–88)

Cello concertos: in A min., Wq.170; in B flat, Wq.171; in A, Wq.172.
*** Virgin/EMI Dig. VC7 59541-2 [id.]. Anner Bylsma, O of Age of Enlightenment, Leonhardt.
☞ (B) **(*) HM Dig. HM 1903026 [id.]. Miklós Perényi, Liszt CO, János Rolla.

These concertos also have alternative versions for both keyboard and flute, but they suit the cello admirably. Bylsma's expressive intensity communicates strongly, without ever taking the music outside its boundaries of sensibility, and these artists convey their commitment to this music persuasively.

The Harmonia Mundi CD is warmly recorded and, though authenticists may find string textures on the ample side, others will relish János Rolla's warm phrasing. His soloist, Miklós Perényi, while not an extrovert player is a highly musical one and he plays the fine slow movements of the *B flat Concerto* and especially the lovely *Largo* of the *A major* with a touchingly restrained romantic feeling.

Cello concertos: in B flat, Wq.171; in A, Wq.172.
(B) **(*) Hung. White Label HRC 117 [id.]. Csába Onczay, Liszt CO, Rolla (with CHERUBINI: *13 Contredanses* **).

Onczay, who has a warm, well-focused tone, plays very sympathetically. The accompaniments for him are polished, elegant and alert, and the recording has a pleasing ambience.

Cello concerto in A, Wq.172.
(BB) *** Virgin/EMI Dig. VJ7 91453-2 [id.]. Caroline Dale, Scottish Ens., Jonathan Rees – J. S. BACH: *Violin concertos.* ***

Caroline Dale at a spacious *Largo* plays the slow movement of the splendid *A major Cello concerto* with full expressiveness. With vigorous outer movements, this is a valuable work to have as makeweight for three of J. S. B.'s most popular violin concertos.

Flute concertos: in D min., Wq.22; in A min., Wq.166; in B flat, Wq.167; in A, Wq.168; in G, Wq.169.
*** Capriccio Dig. 10 104 (Wq.22, 166, 168); 10 105 (Wq.167, 169) [id.]. Eckart Haupf, C. P. E. Bach CO, Haenchen.

Eckart Haupf gives lively, cleanly articulated performances of these concertos, written for the court of Frederick the Great, well supported by the strong, full-bodied and vigorous accompaniments of the C. P. E. Bach Chamber Orchestra under Hartmut Haenchen. Full, atmospheric recording from East German VEB engineers.

Flute concerto in D min., Wq.22.
(BB) **(*) ASV CDQS 6012. Dingfelder, ECO, Mackerras – HOFFMEISTER: *Concertos Nos. 6 & 9.* **(*)

Those who are interested in the Hoffmeister coupling will find Ingrid Dingfelder's playing both spirited and stylish.

Flute concertos: in A, Wq.168; in G, Wq.169; in D min. (from Harpsichord concerto).
*** BMG/RCA Dig. RD 60244 [60244-2-RC]. James Galway, Württemberg CO, Joerg Faerber.

James Galways plays these three works with his customary musicianship, virtuosity and polish. Faerber and his Württemberg orchestra accompany persuasively, with no attempt made to create 'authentic' textures. Excellent recording. Recommended, except to authenticists.

Harpsichord concerto in G min., Wq.6.
*** Capriccio Dig. 10 283 [id.]. Gerald Hambitzer, Concerto Köln – J. C. BACH: *Sinfonia;* J. C. F. BACH: *Sinfonias;* W. F. BACH: *Sinfonia* etc. ***

The *G minor Concerto*, Wq.6 (1740), is one of the most remarkable of C. P. E. Bach's early works. Gerald Hambitzer is an expert and persuasive soloist, and the performance has abundant vitality and imagination. The recording is very naturally balanced.

(i) *Harpsichord concerto in D min., Wq.23;* (i–ii) *Double harpsichord concerto in F, Wq.46;* (iii) *Oboe concerto in E flat, Wq.165.*
(M) **(*) HM/BMG GD77061 [77061-RG-2]. (i) Leonhardt, (ii) Curtis, (iii) Hucke; Coll. Aur., Maier.

The better-known *D minor Concerto*, Wq.23, receives a dashing and fiery performance from Gustav Leonhardt and the Collegium Aureum. The *Oboe concerto* is notable for its forward-looking and expressive slow movement. All these performances have a spirit and expressive vitality that are sometimes missing from more modern ensembles.

Harpsichord concerto in C min., Wq.43/4.
☞ (M) *** Decca 440 033-2 [id.]. George Malcolm, ASMF, Marriner – ARNE: *Harpsichord concerto No. 5* etc; J. C. BACH: *Harpsichord concerto in A min.;* HAYDN: *Harpsichord concerto in D* etc. ***

The *C minor Concerto* comes from Bach's Hamburg period and is highly inventive and brilliant; the structure of the piece is original: when one is expecting the recapitulation, the composer sets out on a slow movement in a remote key and completes the material of the first movement only after a minuet. The musical material is as interesting as its formal layout. The performance has splendid life and vitality, and the 1968 recording is as fresh as you could wish, with the harpsichord most naturally caught. A first-rate collection.

Double concerto in E flat for harpsichord and fortepiano; Double concerto in F for 2 harpsichords, Wq.46.
*** Erato/Warner Dig. 2292 45306-2 [id.]. Koopman, Mathot, Amsterdam Baroque O.

This spirited and delightful *E flat Concerto for harpsichord and fortepiano* comes from Bach's last year; the *F major Concerto for two harpsichords* comes from a different world: it was composed almost half a century earlier for Frederick II's court. The Erato recording is as good as the playing. The only grumble: at 43 minutes this is short measure – but what it wants in quantity it certainly makes up for in quality.

Oboe concertos: in B flat, Wq.164; in E flat, Wq.165; Sonata for oboe and continuo in G min., Wq.135.
(M) *** Erato/Warner Dig. 2292 45430-2 [id.]. Ku Ebbinge, Amsterdam Bar. O, Koopman.

C. P. E. Bach's pair of *Oboe concertos* are very appealing in their wide range of mood, and the *Largo e mesto* of Wq.164 is plaintively haunting in Ku Ebbinge's hands. Koopman provides gracefully alert accompaniments and the recording balance is fresh and realistic, with textures transparent.

Oboe concertos: in B flat, Wq.164; in E flat, Wq.165; (Unaccompanied) *Oboe sonata in A min., Wq.132.*
☞ (BB) **(*) Naxos Dig. 8.550556 [id.]. József Kiss, Ferenc Erkel CO – MARCELLO: *Concerto.* **(*)

József Kiss's account of Bach's pair of *Oboe concertos* is sensitive and musical, if without quite the individuality of Ebbinge's versions on Erato, but they are very well accompanied and beautifully recorded. The solo *Sonata* is also worth having on disc, although one might have liked more dynamic light and shade here. But with an enjoyable Marcello coupling, this is well worth its modest cost.

Organ concerto in G, Wq. 34.
☞ (B) **(*) Erato/Warner 4509 94581 [id.]. Marie-Claire Alain, Jean-François Paillard CO, Paillard – HAYDN: *Organ concertos.* ***

The *G major Organ concerto*, which also exists in a version for the flute, dates from the mid-1730s and is representative of C. P. E. Bach at something like his best. Marie-Claire Alain plays with excellent style, and the orchestra accompanies with spirit, even if ensemble is not always impeccable. The sound is not quite as rich as the original LP but is bright and generally well focused.

Organ concertos: in G; in E flat, Wq.34–5; Fantasia and fugue in C min., Wq.119/7; Prelude in D, Wq.70/7.
*** Capriccio Dig. 10 135 [id.]. Roland Munch, C. P. E. Bach CO, Haenchen.

Hartmut Haenchen and his admirable C. P. E. Bach Chamber Orchestra reinforce the lively expressiveness of the music, alongside the soloist, Roland Munch, on a Berlin baroque organ of the 1750s.

Berlin sinfonias: in C; in F, Wq.174/5; in E min.; in E flat, Wq.178/9; in F, Wq.181.
*** Capriccio Dig. 10 103 [id.]. C. P. E. Bach CO, Haenchen.

The playing of Haenchen's excellent C. P. E. Bach group is alert and vigorous, with airy textures and attractively sprung rhythms. Modern instruments are used in the best possible way. Excellent sound.

6 Hamburg sinfonias, Wq.182/1–6.
*** DG 415 300-2 [id.]. E. Concert, Pinnock.
☞ (M) *** O-L 443 192-2 [id.]. AAM, Hogwood.

The six *Hamburg string sinfonias* are magnificent examples of Bach's later style when, after the years at the Berlin court, he had greater freedom in Hamburg. The English Concert under Pinnock offers an authentic performing style which retains great concern for eighteenth-century poise and elegance. The 1960 analogue recording sounds splendidly fresh and clear.

On the other hand, the abrasiveness of the writing comes out more sharply in the kind of authenticity favoured by Hogwood's Academy of Ancient Music in 1979. They have mellowed somewhat since then, but the music-making here is typical of their earlier style and some listeners may find that their angularity, though undoubtedly stimulating, does not make for relaxed listening. No complaints about the recording, and the Oiseau-Lyre disc has a distinct price advantage.

4 Hamburg sinfonias, Wq.183/1–4.
*** Erato/Warner Dig. 2292 45430-2 [id.]. Amsterdam Bar. O, Koopman.
☞ *(*) Capriccio Dig. 10175 [id.]. C. P. E. Bach CO, Haenchen.

4 Hamburg sinfonias, Wq. 183/1–4; Sinfonia in B min., Wq. 182/5.
☞ *** Virgin/EMI Dig. VC7 59543-2 [id.]. O of Age of Enlightenment, Leonhardt.

Unlike the six *Hamburg sinfonias* which C. P. E. Bach wrote earlier for Baron von Swieten, these four later works involve wind as well as strings. The writing is just as refreshing in its unexpectedness and originality. Gustav Leonhardt's account of this second set, Wq. 183, is the one to have if you want them on period instruments. They are lively and alert, and distinguished by fine musical intelligence. This set is to be preferred, albeit by a small margin, to that by Koopman and in any case includes an extra work.

Koopman and his talented Amsterdam players also use period instruments and his performances gain from the extra transparency. He tends to favour relatively relaxed speeds, but the music-making remains very enjoyable in its easy-sounding spontaneity.

Hartmut Haenchen proves as *kapellmeisterish* here as he has been at the Royal Opera House, Covent Garden, in recent years. There is plenty of vigour but few poetic insights and little real musical imagination. Very good, well-defined recording.

CHAMBER AND INSTRUMENTAL MUSIC

Fantasia (Fantasy-sonata) in F sharp min. (Empfindungen), Wq.80; Sonatas for piano and violin in B min., Wq.76; C min., Wq.78.
*** Denon Dig. CO 72434 [id.]. Huguette Dreyfus, Eduard Melkus.

The subtitle of the *Fantasy-sonata, Empfindungen* ('The Sentiments'), gives some idea of its introspective character, which emerges immediately in the first of its twelve sections; it finds Bach at his most individual. Its two companions are less striking – though in their different way they are rewarding. They are excellently played.

Flute sonatas: in D, Wq.83; in E, Wq.84; in G, Wq.85; in G, Wq.86; in C, Wq.87.
(BB) **(*) Naxos Dig. 8.550513 [id.]. Béla Drahos, Zsuzsa Pertis (harpsichord).

These sonatas sound less exploratory in idiom and less unpredictable than is often the case with this composer in these simply stated and highly musical performances by Drahos and Pertis. They are recorded in an ecclesiastical acoustic and, although the acoustic could with advantage have been drier, the effect is natural.

Flute sonatas: in E min., Wq.124; in G; in A min.; in D, Wq.127–9; in G, Wq.133; in G, Wq.134.
*** Capriccio Dig. 10 101 [id.]. Eckart Haupf, Siegfried Pank, Armin Thalheim.

Six of the composer's eleven flute sonatas in fresh, lively performances, well recorded, ending with one written in Bach's Hamburg period, two years before he died, altogether lighter and more conventionally classical, presenting an interesting perspective on the rest.

Trio sonatas: in B min., Wq.76 (H.512); in A, Wq.146 (H.570); in D, H.585.
*** HM/BMG Dig. RD 77250 [77050-2-RC]. Les Adieux – J. C. BACH: *Quintets;* J. C. F. BACH: *Quartet.* ***

These three sonatas span three decades: between them, they give a good idea of the composer's artistic development. They are played with admirable style and no mean virtuosity by Les Adieux. Excellent recording.

Quartets (Trios) for flute, viola, fortepiano: in A min., D & G, Wq.93/5.
(M) *** HM/BMG GD 77052 [77052-2-RG]. Les Adieux.

Quartets for flute, viola, fortepiano (& optional) *cello: in A min., D & G, Wq.93/5;* (Keyboard)
Fantasy in C.
*** O-L 433 189-2 [id.]. McGegan, Mackintosh, Pleeth, Hogwood.

Although these works were designated by Bach as *Quartets*, no bass part survives. Piano, flute and viola are musically handled so equally, and everything is so minutely written out, that an added cello would always remain 'the fifth wheel on the wagon'. The playing of Les Adieux matches the music in its finish, lightness of touch and spontaneity.

In the Oiseau-Lyre performances the cello line is added judiciously where it seems useful to reinforce the texture, and the result has that bit more weight and gravitas without losing any of the charm of the writing. Christopher Hogwood uses a fortepiano rather than harpsichord and makes a good case for doing so. The playing overall is absolutely first rate; the recording is most naturally balanced and could hardly be bettered.

Sinfonia a tre voci in D; 12 Variations on La Folia, Wq.118/9; Trio sonatas: in B flat, Wq.158; in C min. (Sanguineus & Melancholicus), Wq.161/1; Viola da gamba sonata in D, Wq.137.
*** Hyp. Dig. CDA 66239 [id.]. Purcell Qt.

The *Variations on La Folia* are fresh and inventive, particularly in Robert Woolley's hands, but the remaining pieces are hardly less rewarding. The Purcell Quartet play with sensitivity and seem well attuned to the particularly individual sensibility of this composer. The Hyperion recording is well balanced, faithful and present.

KEYBOARD MUSIC

Concerto for harpsichord solo in C, Wq.112/1; 6 Prussian sonatas, Wq.48; 6 Württemberg sonatas, Wq.49.
☞ (M) *** Teldec/Warner 9031 77623-2 (3). Bob van Asperen (harpsichord).

Bach's six *Prussian sonatas* were written between 1740 and 1742; they immediately demonstrate the formal and expressive adventurousness which characterizes so much of this composer's music. Like the later *Württemberg sonatas* (so named as they are dedicated to the Duke of Württemberg), they were much admired by Haydn, who acknowledged their influence. The *Württemberg sonatas* date from 1744 and are at once even more daring and powerfully expressive than their immediate predecessors. They are arguably more suited to the clavichord than to the harpsichord (they are too early for the fortepiano) and one small criticism of Bob van Asperen's performances concerns the range of dynamic contrast he achieves: this could ideally be wider. The solo *Concerto* is a much later work, more elaborately Italianate and florid – perhaps suitable for the fortepiano, but here sounding well on the plucked instrument. Van Asperen uses a fine reproduction of a Dulcken harpsichord, and his approach throughout has a welcome rhythmic freedom, a fine sense of line and an appropriate intensity of feeling when required. He is very well recorded and, if the volume level is judiciously set, the effect brings both realism and a natural presence. These reissues from 1977/79 are part of Teldec's admirable Das Alte Werk series: this repertoire is not otherwise available on CD.

VOCAL MUSIC

Anbetung dem Erbamer (Easter cantata) Wq.243; Auf, shicke dich trecht feierlich (Christmas cantata), Wq.249; Heilig, Wq.217; Klopstocks Morgengesang am Schöpfungfeste, Wq.239.
*** Capriccio Dig. 10 208 [id.]. Schlick, Lins, Pregardien, Elliott, Varcoe, Schwarz, Rheinische Kantorei, Kleine Konzert, Hermann Max.

Klopstocks Morgengesang am Schöpfungfeste ('Klopstock's morning song on the celebration of creation') is a work of many beauties and is well performed by these artists. *Anbetung dem Erbamer* ('Worship of the merciful') is another late work, full of modulatory surprises. *Auf, shicke dich trecht feierlich* ('Up, be reconciled') and *Heilig* ('Holy') (1779) are Christmas works. A record of unusual interest, very well performed and naturally recorded.

(i) *Die Auferstehung und Himmelfahrt Jesu (The Resurrection and Ascension of Jesus), Wq.240;* (ii) *Gott hat den Herrn auferweckt (Easter cantata), Wq.244.*
*** Capriccio Dig. 10 206/7 (2) [id.]. (i) Schlick, Lins, Pregardien; (ii) Elliott, Varcoe, Schwarz; Rheinische Kantorei, Kleine Konzert, Hermann Max.

Carl Philipp Emanuel numbered *Die Auferstehung und Himmelfahrt Jesu* among his finest works. This two-CD set offers good solo singing and generally very good playing; the choral singing for the most part is respectable without being distinguished. Impressive music which no one with an interest in this composer should pass over.

Die letzten Leiden des Erlösers (The Last Sufferings of the Saviour), Wq.233.
(M) *** HM/BMG GD 77042 [77042-2-RG]. Schlick, Reyghere, Patriasz, Prégardien, Egmond, Ghent Coll. Vocale, La Petite Bande, Kuijken.

Die letzten Leiden has good claims to be considered one of Carl Philipp Emanuel's masterpieces, and it is given a first-class performance by the excellent team of soloists assembled here. Fine, well-balanced recording.

Magnificat, Wq.215.
(M) *** Decca 421 148-2. Palmer, Watts, Tear, Roberts, King's College Ch., ASMF, Ledger – J. S. BACH: *Magnificat.* ***

With vividly atmospheric recording, the performance under Philip Ledger comes electrically to life, with choir, soloists and orchestra all in splendid form. Aptly coupled with Johann Sebastian's earlier setting, this CD can be strongly recommended. It sounds extremely vivid.

Bach, Johann Christian (1735–82)

Bassoon concertos: in B flat; in E flat.
(B) ** Hung. White Label HRC 041 [id.]. Gábor Janota, Liszt CO, Rolla; or József Vajda, Budapest SO, Lehel – HUMMEL: *Bassoon concerto.* ***

Good playing from both soloists (especially from Janota in the latter) and warm, polished accompaniments.

Clavier concertos, Op. 1/1–6; Op. 7/1–6.
☞ (B) *** Ph. Duo 438 712-2 (2) [id.]. Ingrid Haebler, V. Capella Academica, Eduard Melkus.

J. C. Bach composed three sets of *Clavier concertos*, each comprising six works. The earliest set are all simple, two-movement works, except for No. 4, which has a wistful central *Andante* and jolly finale, and No. 6, which closes with some rather engaging variations on *God save the king*. Op. 7 were published in or around 1780 and were clearly designated with the option of performance on either harpsichord or fortepiano, which the composer himself played in public. Their form continues the two-part structure, again with two exceptions, Nos. 5 and 6. All the concertos here are in major keys and are attractive, well-wrought compositions. It would be difficult to find a more suitable or persuasive advocate than Ingrid Haebler, who is excellently accompanied and most truthfully recorded. Indeed the balance of the fortepiano with the small string group using modern instruments with much finesse and no lack of vitality is remarkably perfect. The sound of the fortepiano itself seems exactly right for this music. There is some delightful invention here and it is difficult to imagine it being better presented. Moreover this pair of CDs is surely inexpensive enough to tempt collectors to sample repertoire which they might otherwise pass by.

Harpsichord concerto in A min., T 297/1.
☞ (M) *** Decca 440 033-2 [id.]. George Malcolm, ASMF, Marriner – ARNE: *Harpsichord concerto No. 5* etc. C. P. E. BACH: *Harpsichord concerto in C min.;* HAYDN: *Harpsichord concerto in D.* ***

This is a delightful concerto, though its authenticity is doubtful. Whatever the source, it is a particularly happy example of the keyboard concerto of the period: the invention is fresh and engaging. The playing is extremely crisp and vital, with a sensitively shaped *Andante* which uses moments of pizzicato charmingly. The recording is a model of its kind: the harpsichord is not too forwardly balanced and sounds completely lifelike, while the string-tone is both realistic and firm. This collection is strongly recommended.

Sinfonia concertante in C for flute, oboe, violin, cello and orchestra; Sinfonias: in G min., Op. 6/6; Sinfonia for double orchestra in E flat, Op. 18/1; Sinfonia in D, Op. 18/4; Overture: Adriano in Siria.
☞ **(*) Chan. Dig. CHAN 0540 [id.]. AAM, Standage.

An enterprising and enjoyable programme. The *Sinfonia concertante* is perhaps the most conventional piece but it has a memorable finale. The *G minor Sinfonia* shows J. C. Bach's imagination at full stretch, lively and intense. The little overture is given three separate bands to show how its fast–slow–fast format was the basis of the symphony. Excellent, well-played 'authentic' performances, but the characteristic Chandos resonance prevents the crispest focus.

Sinfonia concertante in A for violin, cello and orchestra; Grand Overture in E flat.
(*) Sony MK 39964 [id.]. Yo-Yo Ma, Zukerman, St Paul CO – BOCCHERINI: *Cello concerto* (arr. Grützmacher). *

Generally this is an enjoyable pairing and the playing of the soloists in the *Sinfonia concertante* establishes a fine musical interplay, although the cadenza is over-elaborated. Good sound, with excellent stereo effects.

Sinfonias concertantes in A for violin, cello and orchestra, SC 3; E flat for 2 violins, 2 violas, cello and orchestra (MSC E flat 1); E flat for 2 clarinets, bassoon and orchestra (MSC E flat 4); G for 2 violins, cello and orchestra, SC 1.
☞ (BB) *** ASV CDQS 6138 [id.]. London Festival O, Ross Pople.

The performances here are eminently vital and enthusiastic, and the recording is very bright and present. This is an invigorating disc which can be recommended strongly, especially at super-bargain price.

6 Sinfonias, Op. 6; 6 Sinfonias, Op. 9; 6 Sinfonias, Op. 18; Overture, La calamità de cuori.
☞ (B) *** Ph. Duo 442 275-2 (2) [id.]. Netherlands CO, David Zinman.

The Philips back-catalogue is rich in repertoire of this kind. Although recorded in the 1970s, these *Sinfonias* were last reissued within a set of five LPs to mark the composer's bicentenary in 1982. Apart from Op. 3 – which were admirably performed by Marriner and the ASMF and will probably reappear during the lifetime of this book – the cream of that box appears here as a remarkable Duo bargain: two CDs for the cost of one premium-price CD. David Zinman secures good, lively playing from the Netherlanders and few (except dedicated authenticists) will quarrel with the results. A case could be made for giving some of the outer movements less elegance and greater weight. Memories of Raymond Leppard's Op. 6 set, made in the late 1960s, are not entirely banished, for he brought a greater intensity and sense of style to them. But if there are times when one feels that Zinman is too brisk, any newer versions using original instruments are likely to be brisker! Certainly Zinman gives stimulation and pleasure with the vigour of his presentation of the outer movements and the charm of the slower ones. This set has many first-class performances and, at its modest cost, would form a valuable cornerstone for any collector about to embark on this composer.

Sinfonia in G min. Op. 6/6.
*** Capriccio Dig. 10 283 [id.]. Concerto Köln – C. P. E. BACH: *Harpsichord concerto;* J. C. F. BACH: *Sinfonias;* W. F. BACH: *Sinfonia* etc. ***

This remarkable symphony, written in 1770 when Johann Christian was at the height of his fame, is altogether darker than is usual with this most gracious and genial of composers, and the Concerto Köln discover greater dramatic intensity in it than do most ensembles. It is recorded as excellently as it is played.

6 Sinfonias (Grand overtures), Op. 18.
☞ (M) *** Decca 433 730-2 [id.]. Stuttgart CO, Münchinger.
☞ **(*) Nimbus Dig. NI 5403 [id.]. E. String O, William Boughton.

During Bach's final years in London the concerts he shared with his colleague and compatriot, Carl Abel, became less and less popular, and when he died (on New Year's Day 1782) Bach left considerable debts. The *Six Sinfonias* (or 'Grand Overtures' as he called them) were published only the year before and – scored for oboes, flutes, clarinets, horns and strings – ironically they represent the composer at his orchestral peak.

Münchinger is persuasive in every way, graceful and smiling, yet vital. The first movement of Op. 18, No. 1, is made to sound almost like Mozart, and slow movements – especially that of Op. 18, No. 5 – are beautifully done. The music itself is a constant joy, full of J. C. Bach's most felicitous invention. The scoring too is remarkably forward-looking, using flutes most engagingly, oboes (the *Andante* of Op. 18, No. 2, opens with an oboe solo), horns and even clarinets. Decca's recording, made in the Schloss Ludwigsburg in 1973 and 1975, is naturally balanced with the acoustic not too resonant; the CD transfer is admirable.

Boughton's performances are appealingly warm, certainly not lacking liveliness or spontaneity; but the effect of the resonant recording is to make the orchestra, playing modern instruments, seem a shade too ample, although this music-making is easy to enjoy.

Oboe quartet in B flat, Op. 8/6.
*** Denon Dig. C37 7119 [id.]. Holliger, Salvatore Qt – M. HAYDN: *Divertimenti;* MOZART: *Adagio.*
***

The unpretentious elegance of J. C. Bach's *Oboe quartet* is beautifully caught by the incomparable Holliger and his stylish partners. An excellent coupling for even more compelling works, all vividly recorded.

Quintets: in C, Op. 11/1; in D, Op. 11/6; in D, Op. 22/1. Sextet in C.
*** DG Dig. 423 385-2 [id.]. English Concert.

This is a self-recommending collection. The music, delectably scored for unexpected combinations of instruments, is wonderfully fresh and inventive in these spirited performances.

Quintets (for flute, oboe, violin, viola & continuo) in G & F, Op. 11/2–3.
*** HM/BMG Dig. RD 77250 [77050-2-RC]. Les Adieux – C. P. E. BACH: *Trio sonatas;* J. C. F. BACH: *Quartet.* ***

The *Quintets* find Johann Christian at his most delightful; there are moments of considerable expressive poignancy, which these imaginative and elegant players make the most of. This is one of the best records devoted to the sons of Bach and the sound-quality is first class.

Bach, Johann Christoph Friedrich (1732–95)

Sinfonias Nos. 1 in F; 2 in B flat; 3 in G min.; 4 in E flat; 6 in C; 10 in E flat; 20 in B flat.
☞ ** Koch Schwann 3 1048-2 (2) [id.]. Cologne CO, Helmut Müller-Brühl.

Johann Christoph Friedrich spent the greater part of his life in relative isolation at the Court of Bückenberg. Much of his work appeared to be lost but now these seven *Sinfonias* have turned up (which include the *E flat Sinfonia* mentioned below). There were 20 altogether, and perhaps others will also be found. The first four are very conventional three-movement works, written in 1768/9. But those on the second disc are far more indebted to Carl Philip Emanuel, and No. 20 is a very attractive four-movement piece, notable for an engaging Minuet, using the woodwind to charming effect in the Trio, and a catchy Rondo finale. Performances are sound, but the recording, though warm and full, is rather over-resonant: this music would benefit from a sharper profile.

Sinfonias: in D min.; E flat, Wfv 1/3 & 10.
*** Capriccio Dig. 10 283 [id.]. Concerto Köln – C. P. E. BACH: *Harpsichord concerto;* J. C. BACH: *Sinfonia;* W. F. BACH: *Sinfonia* etc. ***

Both works recorded here are elegantly written and are well worth investigating, even if Johann Christoph Friedrich does not have the strong musical personality of his brothers. The playing of the Concerto Köln is enthusiastic, sprightly and sensitive, and they are excellently recorded.

Flute quartet No. 3 in C.
*** HM/BMG Dig. RD 77250 [77050-2-RC]. Les Adieux – C. P. E. BACH: *Trio sonatas;* J. C. BACH: *Quintets.* ***

Johann Christoph Friedrich's music is untroubled by any depths but has a genuine charm that is beautifully communicated by these accomplished players. Excellent recording.

Musikalisches Vielerley: Cello sonata in A.
*** Sony Dig. SK 45945 [id.]. Anner Bylsma, Bob van Asperen – J. S. BACH: *Viola da gamba sonatas Nos. 1–3.*

This *Sonata* is a work of slight but not negligible musical interest, and it is here played imaginatively by Anner Bylsma, using a piccolo cello, and by Bob van Asperen on a 'trunk' or chamber organ. Excellently recorded.

Bach, Johann Sebastian (1685–1750)

Brandenburg concertos Nos. 1–6, BWV 1046/51; Orchestral Suites Nos. 1–4, BWV 1066/9.
⊛ (M) (**(*)) EMI mono CHS7 64047-2 (3) [id.]. Adolf Busch Chamber Players, Busch.
☞ (M) ** HM/BMG 05472 77251-2 (3). Coll. Aur., Franzjosef Maier.

The Busch version of the *Brandenburgs* must take a special place. Although modern instruments are used, there is a greater 'authenticity' of spirit than in many rigid modern performances. Rudolf

Serkin, Busch's son-in-law, plays the piano, and the other soloists are all artists of comparable calibre, including Evelyn Rothwell on the oboe, Aubrey Brain (father of Dennis) on the horn, George Eskdale on the Bach trumpet and Marcel Moyse on the flute. Though slow movements are not sentimentalized, the phrasing has full expressive warmth, and speeds are almost always slower than we would expect today. That is also true of many of the fast movements, as in the outer movements of Nos. 1 and 6, but with such bouncy, resilient rhythms the results never drag. The *Suites* also stand up well, but there the interpretation is rather more controversial, when the slow speeds for the introductions do become very heavy without double-dotting. The sound is more than acceptable. The result is watercolour rather than a freshly cleaned oil painting, but the actual performances could hardly be more richly hued. Alas, this set has been withdrawn as we go to press, but we hope it will be reissued in a lower price-range.

Of the two early (1960s) recordings of the Bach *Brandenburgs* and *Suites*, the Collegium Aureum are generally to be preferred to the more eccentric Harnoncourt series (see below) but the styles of both now sound dated in terms of current Bach scholarship. In the *Brandenburgs* the use of older wind instruments creates some attractive sounds and No. 3 has clean string lines. No. 1 is taken rather steadily and the ear notices the occasional lapses of intonation from the hand horns. No. 4 with its bright recorders is a success, and No. 5 is also fresh, although the harpsichord contribution has a tendency to sound metronomic. In No. 2 the balance does not favour the trumpet unduly, and the colour of the other wind instruments is highly effective. The recording, made in the Cedernsaal of Schloss Kirchheim, is spacious and reverberant, and both in the *Concertos* and in the *Suites* the relatively small orchestral group is given an attractive richness and breadth. The resonant acoustic is not always caught with absolute clarity and the Collegium Aureum's approach to the *Suites* is comparatively expressive – the famous *Air* in *Suite No. 3* is restrained but is played with feeling. Tempi here are often similar to more modern practice, although the overall pulse is at times comparatively measured, and slow introductions are not as crisply dotted as we would expect today. With the early trumpets one again has to accept moments of poor intonation in the upper register. But this remains enjoyable in its mellow way, and the sound has none of the Gillette edge of certain other German baroque groups.

Brandenburg concertos Nos. 1–6, BWV 1046/51; Orchestral suites Nos. 2–3, BWV 1067/8.
☞ (B) *(*) DG Double 437 461-2 (2). BPO, Karajan.

By the time Karajan came to record the *Brandenburg concertos* in the mid-1960s his approach to Bach had been somewhat modified. Although textures are ample – to say the least – the playing is highly polished, the rythms resilient and, whatever the authenticists may say, the viola melody of the slow movement of No. 6 is a joy to the ear when played like this. There are many fresher performances on record, but these demonstrate Karajan's love of the music and that he can be lively in this repertoire. The *Orchestral Suites*, however, are very sumptuous indeed – one only has to try the opening *Overture* of No. 2 to experience the sheer amplitude of the sound. Here Karajan seems to think of Bach harmonically rather than contrapuntally, and the full-bodied textures are matched by unstylish rhythms. Although there is some superb flute playing from Karlheinz Zöller in the *B minor Suite* (particularly in the *Badinerie*), modern scholarship has remaindered these performances into the area of musical curiosities. The recorded sound, however, is as vivid as it is opulent.

Brandenburg concertos Nos. 1–6, BWV 1046/51.
☞ *** DG Dig. 410 500/1-2 [id.]. E. Concert, Trevor Pinnock.
☞ (M) *** EMI Dig. CD-EMX 2200 (*Nos. 1, 3 & 4*); CD-EMX 2201 (*Nos. 2, 5 & 6*). Hanover Band, Anthony Halstead.
*** Ph. 400 076/7-2 (2) [id.]. ASMF, Marriner.
☞ (B) *** Erato/Warner Dig. 4509 91935-2 (2) [id.]. Amsterdam Bar. O, Ton Koopman.
(B) *** Pickwick Dig. PCD 830; *CIMPC 830* (*Nos. 1–3*); PCD 845; *CIMPC 845* (*Nos. 4–6*) [id.]. ECO, Ledger.
☞ **(*) Hyp. Dig. CDA 66711/2 [id.]. Brandenburg Concert, Roy Goodman.
☞ (M) ** Teldec/Warner 9031 77611-2 (2) [id.]. VCM, Harnoncourt.

Undoubtedly Pinnock's DG set of *Brandenburgs*, played on original instruments, represents the peak of his achievement as an advocate of authentic performance with sounds that are clear and refreshing but not too abrasive. After a period when a limited edition of this set was available at mid-price, this now reverts to DG's full-price Archiv label. The recordings are, however, alternatively available on three mid-priced CDs (423 492-2) coupled with the *Orchestral Suites*, but the latter are somewhat controversial, bringing a distinct loss of breadth and grandeur.

Fortunately a recommendable new recording from Anthony Halstead and the Hanover Band has arrived on EMI Eminence which will surely meet the needs of collectors looking for a recommendable authentic mid-priced set. The playing is consistently fresh and tempi are admirably chosen to give a feeling of liveliness and a joyful alertness without pressing on too hard while, throughout, lyrical lines flow pleasingly and textures are clean and transparent. In the sparkling *Third Concerto*, one of the most stimulating performances, the lightness of the strings in the finale is an example of authenticity at its most illuminating, while there is no abrasiveness. In No. 2, Mark Bennett's trumpet timbre is bright and unthrottled, and the internal balance is excellent – as it is in the concertos featuring recorder or flute – while in the closing Minuets of No. 1 the horns and oboes are glowingly colourful. In the finale of No. 4 there is some exhilarating virtuosity from the string soloists, even including a dramatic tremolando passage, while the recorder line soars overhead. The recording was made in the Henry Wood Hall and its warm acoustic provides an admirable background ambience for the music-making.

Marriner's analogue Philips set has been remastered since it was first issued and the sound is both natural and lively. Above all, these performances communicate warmth and enjoyment; and they are strong in personality. However, this set has to face strong competition in the mid-priced range. Those wanting a first-class set using modern instruments can still rest content with Marriner – if paying a premium price is acceptable. With star soloists and beautifully sprung performances, this is very enjoyable indeed, with sound that is natural and lively.

Relaxed and intimate, Koopman's account makes a highly recommendable bargain alternative to Pinnock, for those who prefer expressive contrasts to be less sharply marked. Like Pinnock, Koopman is not afraid to read *Affetuoso* on the slow movement of No. 5 as genuinely expressive and warm, though without sentimentality. As with Pinnock, players are one to a part, with excellent British soloists included in the band. In the *Third Concerto*, Koopman effectively interpolates the *Toccata in G*, BWV 916, as a harpsichord link between the two movements. The sound on CD is immediate, but not aggressively so. Repackaged in a single jewel case in Erato's Bonsai Duo series, this digital set is second to none, except for its complete absence of documentation, apart from titles.

On Pickwick, Ledger has the advantage of fresh and detailed digital recording. He directs resilient, well-paced readings of all six concertos, lively yet never over-forced. The slow movements in particular are most beautifully done, persuasively and without mannerism. Flutes rather than recorders are used in No. 4.

On Hyperion, Roy Goodman not only directs but also plays as a string soloist. This set, too, is an attractive example of authenticism, lacking something in polish if not spirit. Again there is fine trumpet playing, from Stephen Keavy. Characterization is strong, even if slow movements are less smooth than with Halstead, and tempi of outer movements are often very brisk. The recording is bright and vivid, and there is certainly no lack of either individuality or vitality, but the end result is less naturally rewarding than the EMI Eminence set.

Harnoncourt's 1964 analogue set (recorded in the Great Hall of the Schönberg Palace) has now been reissued as part of Teldec's Das Alte Werk series. It was originally an early adventure in authenticity; it has undoubted interest but is of uneven musical appeal. The excessive closeness of the sound-picture, which is consistent throughout, means that there is nothing like a real pianissimo, and internal balances produce variable degrees of success: Nos. 2 and 5, for instance, integrate better than No. 4. Generally tempi are traditional, but here and there – as in the plodding speed for the first movement of No. 2 and the insensitively fast first movement of No. 6 – the direction is less convincing.

Brandenburg concertos 1–6, BWV 1046/51; Violin concertos Nos. (i) *1 in A min.;* (ii) *2 in E, BWV 1041/2.*
☞ (B) ** Ph. Duo 438 317-2 (2) [id.]. I Musici, with (i) Michelucci; (ii) Ayo.

Philips have reissued I Musici's earlier (1965) analogue recording of the *Brandenburgs* in their bargain-price Duo series (two CDs separately suspended back to front in a single CD pack). Although famous soloists are featured, including Maurice André, Heinz Holliger and Frans Brüggen, and the performances are dedicated and thoroughly musical, the approach is rather solid, generally slow of tempo and unresilient of rhythm. The CD transfer produces good sound, both here and in the two solo *Violin concertos*, recorded nearly a decade earlier. Here Felix Ayo, who plays the *E major*, shows rather more flair than his colleague, Roberto Michelucci, brings to the *A minor*, but the clear, unaffected approach gives pleasure; the only snag is that the acoustic is reverberant, which rarely allows the harpsichord to come through with any bite. It is a pity, too, that the slow tempi in the *Brandenburgs* mean that room could not be found for the *Double violin concerto* from the same source. The Duo series is well documented.

Brandenburg concertos Nos. 1–6; (i) *Violin concertos 1–2, BWV 1041/2;* (i; ii) *Double violin concerto in D min., BWV 1043;* (iii) *Cantata No. 170: Vergnügte Ruh', beliebte Seelenlust.*
☞ (M) * Ph. 438 507-2 (3). Netherlands CO, Goldberg; (i) Goldberg; (ii) with Magyar; (iii) Heynis.

Szyman Goldberg is celebrated here both as violin soloist and as director of the Netherlands Chamber Orchestra. Unfortunately his 1958 set of *Brandenburgs,* although they do not lack warmth, have leisured tempi and are rhythmically phlegmatic, while Janny van Wering's harpsichord solo in No. 5 is uninspiring. In the solo *Violin concertos* Goldberg's playing has much to commend it, and he is well partnered by Thomas Magyar in the *Double concerto.* But orchestral textures are inflated and at times almost overwhelm the soloist, except in slow movements. The noble-voiced Afje Heynis joins the orchestra for the cantata and gives a richly eloquent performance; but Goldberg is much better remembered by his recordings of the Mozart *Violin sonatas* with Radu Lupu on Decca.

(i) *Brandenburg concerto No. 2, BWV 1047; Clavier concerto No. 2 in E, BWV 1053;* (ii) *Triple clavier concerto in C, BWV 1064; Chromatic fantasia and fugue, BWV 903; Fantasia and fugue in A min., BWV 904; Fantasia in C min., BWV 906.*
☞ (M) (***) EMI mono CDH7 64928-2 [id.]. Edwin Fischer (piano), with (i) Harold Jackson,
    Gareth Morris, Sidney Sutcliffe, Manoug Parikian, Raymond Clare, Geraint Jones; (ii) Ronald
    Smith & Denis Matthews; Philh. O.

The *Second Brandenburg concerto* with the trumpeter Harold Jackson and the woodwind stars of the 1950s' Philharmonia is something of an exercise in nostalgia. The string-sound inclines to be opaque and the phrasing does not have the lightness that distinguished the Boyd Neel or Busch versions which preceded this set. But if this does not quite take wing, the famous set of the *Triple Concerto* with Denis Matthews and Ronald Smith is exhilarating in every way. The three stars are for this and for Fischer's magisterial accounts of the solo keyboard pieces. Very acceptable mono sound, decently transferred.

Flute concertos: in C (from *BWV 1055*); *in E min.* (from movements of *Cantata No. 35*); *in G min.* (from *BWV 1056*); *Sinfonia* (from *Cantata No. 209*).
(M) **(*) Sony Dig. MDK 46510 [id.]. Rampal, Ars Redivivia, Munclinger.

If you enjoy transcriptions of Bach for the flute – and they are easy to enjoy here – it is difficult to imagine them being played better than by Jean-Pierre Rampal. However, those who count minutes will note that there are only 42½ of them here.

Harpsichord concertos Nos. 1–7, BWV 1052/8; No. 8 in D min. (reconstructed Kipnis), *BWV 1059.*
☞ (B) *** Sony SB2K 53243 (2). Kipnis, L. Strings, Marriner.

Between 1967 and 1970 Igor Kipnis undertook a series of sessions with the London Strings (the St Martin's Academy under a pseudonym), recording not merely the well-known keyboard concertos but also the fringe works: the arrangements of the *Violin concertos* in *E* and *A minor* and of the *Fourth Brandenburg,* plus an eighth work reconstructed by Kipnis himself from a fragment of nine bars identical with the *Sinfonia* of *Cantata No. 35.* Kipnis scored that movement for concertante forces and added two other movements from the same cantata; that is typical of his eager approach to Bach. The recording was made either in EMI's No. 1 Studio at Abbey Road or at the London Olympic studios, which produce a very similar balance of sound. This is more realistic than many made by CBS records at that time and the effect on CD is full and vivid. The music-making is infectious, the accompaniments are characteristic of the vintage ASMF recordings. At budget price this can certainly be recommended.

Harpsichord concertos Nos. 1 in D min.; 2 in E; 3 in D, 4 in A; 5 in F; 6 in F; 7 in G min., BWV 1052/ 8.
*** DG Dig. 415 991-2 (*Nos. 1–3*); 415 992-2 (*Nos. 4–7*) [id.]. Pinnock, E. Concert.
*** Decca Dig. 425 676-2 (2) [id.]. András Schiff (piano), COE.

Clavier concertos Nos. 1 in D min., BWV 1052; 2 in E, BWV 1053; 3 in D, BWV 1054.
(BB) *** Naxos Dig. 8.550422; 4.550422 [id.]. Hae-won Chang (piano), Camerata Cassovia,
    Stankovsky.

Clavier concertos Nos. 4 in A, BWV 1055; 5 in F min., BWV 1056; 6 in F, BWV 1057; 7 in G min., BWV 1058.
(BB) *** Naxos Dig. 8.550423; 4.550423 [id.]. Hae-won Chang (piano), Camerata Cassovia,
    Stankovsky.

Trevor Pinnock plays with real panache, his scholarship tempered by excellent musicianship. Apart from the very quick tempi, which may strike an unsympathetic note, this set is thoroughly recommendable.

As in his solo Bach records, Schiff's control of colour and articulation never seeks to present merely a harpsichord imitation, and his shaping of Bach's lovely slow movements brings fine sustained lines and a subtle variety of touch. He directs the Chamber Orchestra of Europe from the keyboard and chooses spirited, uncontroversial tempi for allegros, at the same time providing decoration that always adds to the joy and sparkle of the music-making. This makes a clear first choice for those who, like us, enjoy Bach on the piano.

Miss Chang is a highly sympathetic Bach exponent, playing flexibly yet with strong rhythmic feeling, decorating nimbly and not fussily. Robert Stankovsky directs freshly resilient accompaniments; and both artists understand the need for a subtle gradation of light and shade. The digital recording, made in the House of Arts, Košice, is first class, with the piano balanced not too far forward.

Clavier concerto No. 1 in D min., BWV 1052.
☞ (M) (**) Sony mono SK 52686 [id.]. Glenn Gould, Leningrad Conservatoire Ac. SO, Slovák –
BEETHOVEN: *Piano concerto No. 2.* (**)

Glenn Gould was at the height of his powers in 1957 when this performance was recorded, though it must be admitted that his studio recording of the *D minor Concerto* with Leonard Bernstein is more characterful and is to be preferred. All the same, there are many felicities of articulation, particularly in the slow movement. The dryish sound calls for some tolerance. The audience is unobtrusive and Gould controls his (subsequently tiresome) propensity to vocalise.

Clavier concertos Nos. 1–5; 7, BWV 1052/6, 1058.
☞ (M) (**) Sony mono (*No. 1*)/stereo SM2K 52591 (2) [id.]. Glenn Gould (piano), Columbia SO,
Bernstein (*No. 1*) or Golschmann.

The quality is variable; the *D minor Concerto* was recorded in 1957 with Bernstein conducting, the remainder date from various times: the *F minor*, BWV 1056, in 1958; the *D major*, BWV 1054, and *G minor*, BWV 1058, in 1967 and the remaining two in 1969, all with Vladimir Golschmann conducting. The performances are strongly personal and, whether or not you like them, strangely compelling. The finale of the *A major* is very, very fast and there is some odd but not excessively intrusive vocalise.

Clavier concertos Nos. 1 in D min., BWV 1052; 2 in E, BWV 1053; 3 in D, BWV 1054; 4 in A, BWV 1055; 5 in F min., BWV 1056; 6 in F, BWV 1057; 7 in G, BWV 1058; French suite No. 5.
☞ (M) **(*) EMI Dig. CDM5 65173/4-2 [id.]. Andrei Gavrilov (piano), ASMF, Marriner.

In terms of dexterity and clarity of articulation, Andrei Gavrilov cannot be faulted and he produces some beautiful sound when his playing is lyrical and relaxed. If at times one feels he pushes on relentlessly, and his incisive touch can be a bit unremitting in some movements, there are also a lot of memorable things. Indeed in the slow movement of the *D minor* and *F minor concertos* there is playing of real poetry and delicacy – and, for that matter, in the finale of the *A major*. The recordings are excellently balanced, with the piano well integrated into the overall picture.

Clavier concertos Nos. 1 in D min., BWV 1052; 3 in D, BWV 1054; 5 in F min., BWV 1056; 6 in F, BWV 1057.
(M) *** Teldec/Warner Dig. 9031 74779-2 [id.]. Cyprien Katsaris (piano), Liszt CO, Rolla.

Cyprien Katsaris possesses the most remarkable technique and feeling for colour, which are to be heard to excellent advantage in this vividly recorded and well-filled disc. Exhilarating and imaginative performances all round.

Clavier concertos Nos. 1 in D min., BWV 1052; 4 in A, BWV 1055; 5 in F min., BWV 1056.
☞ (B) *** Erato/Warner 4509 92864-2 [id.]. Maria-João Pires (piano), Gulbenkian Foundation CO
(Lisbon), Corboz.

Maria-João Pires provides admirable bargain versions of these concertos on the piano. Her crisp and nimble fingerwork is a joy in the allegros and the orchestral strings are not too heavy, with Corboz providing plenty of lift in the allegros. The famous *Largo* of the *F minor Concerto* is beautifully serene. The sound-balance is fresh and believable. Most enjoyable.

Harpsichord concerto No. 4 in A, BWV 1055; Double harpsichord concertos Nos. 1–3, BWV 1060/62; Triple harpsichord concertos Nos. 1–2, BWV 1063/4; Triple concerto for flute, violin and harpsichord in A min., BWV 1044; Quadruple harpsichord concerto in A min., BWV 1065.
☞ (B) ** Erato Dig. 4509 91929-2 (2) [id.]. Koopman and soloists, Amsterdam Bar. O.

Reissued at bargain price in Erato's Bonsai Duo series, this set is not a first choice. Koopman is a fine player, but the performances and recording here are a disappointment. The harpsichords are made to sound unpleasantly jangly with mechanical noises intruding, while the orchestra sounds too heavy, lacking the transparency of period performances, with Koopman often failing to lift rhythms. The absence of any notes about the music presents another drawback.

Double harpsichord concertos: Nos. 1 in C min.; 2 in C; 3 in C min., BWV 1060/2.
**(*) DG Dig. 415 131-2 [id.]. Pinnock, Gilbert, E. Concert.

The combination of period instruments and playing of determined vigour certainly makes a bold impression, but the relatively unrelaxed approach to the slow movements will not appeal to all ears.

Double clavier concertos Nos. 1 in C min., BWV 1060; 2 in C, BWV 1061; Triple clavier concerto in D min., BWV 1063; Quadruple clavier concerto in A min., BWV 1065.
*** DG Dig. 415 655-2 [id.]. Eschenbach, Frantz, Oppitz, Schmidt (pianos), Hamburg PO, Eschenbach.

These concertos are presented with vigour, with slow movements correspondingly thoughtful and responsive. The recording is rather resonant, but the spirit of this record is very communicative.

Triple harpsichord concertos Nos. 1 in D min.; 2 in C, BWV 1063/4; Quadruple harpsichord concerto in A min., BWV 1065.
**(*) DG Dig. 400 041-2 [id.]. Pinnock, Gilbert, Mortensen, Kraemer, E. Concert.

Fine playing here too, but the slightly aggressive style of the music-making – everything alert, vigorously paced and forwardly projected – emphasizes the bravura of Bach's conceptions.

Oboe concertos: in A (from BWV 1055); in D min. (from BWV 1059); in F (from BWV 1053).
*** DG Dig. 429 225-2 [id.]. Douglas Boyd, COE.
*** Ph. Dig. 415 851-2 [id.]. Heinz Holliger, ASMF, Iona Brown.

Boyd's resilient and imaginative playing goes with well-sprung rhythms, bringing an infectious sense of fun. On the whole this may be preferred to Holliger, who at times leans towards Romantic expressiveness in slow movements. First-rate sound.

Oboe concerto in F (from BWV 1053); Oboe d'amore concerto in A (from BWV 1055); Triple concerto in D min. for violin, oboe, flute and strings (from BWV 1063); Triple violin concerto in D (from BWV 1064).
☞ (M) *** Decca 440 037-2 [id.]. Soloists, ASMF, Marriner.

The idea behind this reissued (Argo) disc is to present Bach harpsichord concertos in reconstructions for alternative instruments that either did exist or might have existed. Purists may throw up their hands in horror, but the sparkle, charm and sensitivity of all these performances under Marriner, with soloists from among early Academy members, should silence all but the severest Bachian, and it will certainly please those for whom three harpsichords is too much of a good thing. Indeed the *Triple harpsichord concerto in D minor* sounds wonderfully fresh, arranged for violin, oboe and flute, while its companion appears with three violins taking over the solo roles. Most beautiful is the *Oboe d'amore concerto*, arranged from the solo *Harpsichord concerto*, BWV 1055. Splendidly lively and naturally balanced recording, made in the Henry Wood Hall in 1973/4, admirably transferred to CD.

Oboe d'amore concerto in A, BWV 1055; Cantatas Nos. 12, 21 & 156: Sinfonias.
☞ (BB) *(*) Virgin/EMI Dig. VJ7 59686-2 [id.]. Ray Still, Ac. of L., Stamp – STRAUSS: *Concerto;* MARCELLO: *Concerto.* *(*)

Accomplished playing comes from this fine American player, but the performances are a little wanting in warmth; the rather stiff accompaniment from Richard Stamp and the Academy of London does not help. The sound has a little more bloom than the Strauss coupling.

Violin concertos Nos. 1 in A min., BWV 1041; 2 in E, BWV 1042.
☞ (M) **(*) Sony SBK 48273 [id.]. Zukerman, ECO – VIVALDI: *Double and solo concertos.* **(*)

Fine playing from Zukerman: the *Andante* of the *A minor Concerto* is memorably beautiful. He directs the accompanying ECO in what are in essence genial performances, warmly recorded, although the bass line in slow movements is made to sound very ample by the resonance. The Vivaldi couplings are equally successful.

Violin concertos Nos. (i) *1, BWV 1041;* (ii) *2, BWV 1042;* (iii) *Double violin concerto, BWV 1043;*
(iv) *Double concerto for violin & oboe in D min., BWV 1060.*
֎ (M) *** Ph. 420 700-2. Grumiaux; (iii) Krebbers, (iv) Holliger; (i–iii) Les Solistes Romandes, Arpad
     Gerecz; (iv) New Philh. O, Edo de Waart.

Arthur Grumiaux is joined in the *Double concerto* by Hermann Krebbers. The result is an outstanding
success. The way Grumiaux responds to the challenge of working with another great artist comes
over equally clearly in the concerto with oboe, reconstructed from the *Double harpsichord concerto in
C minor.* Grumiaux's performances of the two solo concertos are equally satisfying.

Violin concertos Nos. 1 in A min.; 2 in E; (i) *Double concerto, BWV 1041/3;* (ii) *Triple violin concerto
in D, BWV 1064* (arr. of *Triple harpsichord concerto*).
☞ *** Virgin/EMI Dig. VC7 59319-2 [id.]. Elisabeth Wallfisch; (i) Alison Bury; (ii) Pavlo Beznosiuk;
     Catherine Mackintosh, O of Age of Enlightenment.

Performances on original instruments are gradually becoming more amiable and sophisticated, with
edginess almost banished and squeezed phrasing moderated. This new Virgin collection of the Bach
Violin concertos is vigorously stimulating and does not shirk tasteful expressiveness. All the soloists
are expert and their playing has plenty of character, with felicitous, unfussy decoration; the arrangement of the *Triple harpsichord concerto* is particularly convincing. Excellent balance and believable
sound make this highly recommendable, alongside Kuijken, with the advantage of first-class modern
digital recording.

Violin concertos Nos. 1 in A min.; 2 in E; (i) *Double concerto, BWV 1041/3.*
(M) *** HM/BMG GD 77006; *GK 77006* [77006-2-RG; *77006-4-RG*]. Sigiswald Kuijken; (i) Lucy
     van Dael; La Petite Bande.

Kuijken is a fine Bach player, and these performances of the *Violin concertos* go to the top of the list
for those wanting period performances on original instruments. The slight edge on the solo timbre is
painless and La Petite Bande provide lively, resilient allegros, the playing both polished and alert.
Excellent, well-balanced, 1981 digital recording.

Violin concertos Nos. 1 in A min.; 2 in E; (i) *Double violin concerto in D, BWV 1041/3;* (ii) *Violin and
harpsichord sonata in C min., BWV 1017.*
☞ (B) ** Erato/Warner 4509 94575-2 [id.]. Gérard Jarry; (i) Pierre Amoyal; Jean-François Paillard
     CO, Paillard; (ii) Josef Suk, Zuzana Ruzickova.

On Erato Bonsai the two solo *Violin concertos* are lively and musical but rather plain; when Pierre
Amoyal joins Jarry for the *Double concerto,* however, the temperature rises and the slow movement
comes off well. In the *Violin sonata* the playing is on a higher inspirational level, and this is the most
enjoyable performance on the disc. Good sound throughout.

Violin concertos Nos. 1 in A min.; 2 in E, BWV 1041–2; in D min. (after *BWV 1052*).
☞ (M) ** Unicorn UKCD 2067 [id.]. Ruggiero Ricci, City of L. Ens.

These concertos are warmly played – no one could fail to be affected by Ricci's response to the
beautiful slow movements. But the accompaniments are heavy and show no real sense of Bach style,
so that the continuo has little impact. The *D minor Concerto* is another version of the *D minor
Harpsichord concerto.* The 1969 recording is full and well balanced.

Violin concertos Nos. 2 in E, BWV 1042; in G min. (from *BWV 1056);* (i) *Double violin concerto in D
min., BWV 1043.*
(BB) *** Virgin/EMI Dig. VJ7 91453-2 [id.]. Jonathan Rees, (i) with Jane Murdoch; Scottish Ens.,
     Jonathan Rees – C. P. E. BACH: *Cello concerto.* ***

Jonathan Rees directs the Scottish Ensemble in warm, buoyant readings of three of Bach's violin
concertos. Allegros are infectiously sprung, while slow movements are allowed full expressiveness
without sentimentality. A bargain.

Double violin concerto in D min., BWV 1043.
☞ (**) Pearl mono GEMMCDS 9996 (2) [id.]. Fritz Kreisler, Efrem Zimbalist & Qt – BEETHOVEN;
     BRAHMS; MENDELSSOHN; MOZART: *Violin concertos.* (**)

There are several quite extraordinary things about this record. First, after the first shock one scarcely
notices the absence of an orchestra, so gorgeous is Kreisler's tone – and the one-to-a-part texture is
far from out of tune with our times. Second, Efrem Zimbalist is hardly less impressive in the weight
of his sonority and the beauty of sound he produces (which will come as no surprise to those who
have heard his Rococo LP of the Brahms *Concerto* with Koussevitzky). Third – and most astonishing

– is the date given for this recording (1915), for it is only marginally less vivid than the 1926 recordings with Leo Blech. If you want to hear wonderfully musical phrasing and can tolerate low-fi and surface noise, you should investigate this performance.

Double violin concerto in D min., BWV 1043; Triple violin concerto in D, BWV 1064.
☞ (M) ** EMI CD-EMX 2205; TC-EMX 2205. Y. Menuhin, Ha Kun, Mi-Kung Li, Camerata Lysy, Gstaad – VIVALDI: *Concertos.* **

Despite the persuasive artistry of Menuhin and fresh, bouncy playing from the young orchestra, the version of the *Double Concerto* with the Camerata Lysy is disappointing, largely because of the boxy, unhelpful recording which, as well as taking bloom from string-tone, exposes flaws of ensemble. The arrangement of the delightful *C major Harpsichord concerto* for three violins makes an interesting curiosity, well played but suffering even more from edgy sound.

(i) *Double violin concerto in D min., BWV 1043. Suite in D, BWV 1068: Air* (arr. Wilhelmj).
(Unaccompanied) *Violin sonata No. 1 in G min., BWV 1001: Adagio.*
☞ (M) (***) Biddulph mono LAB 056-7[id.]. Arnold Rosé, (i) with Alma Rosé, O – BEETHOVEN: *String quartets Nos. 4, 10 & 14.* (***)

The issue is valuable in that it affords an insight into a style of playing that has long passed into history. Arnold Rosé's sonata-partner was Bruno Walter and his brother-in-law was Mahler. His daughter, Alma, with whom he is heard in a 1931 recording of the Bach *D minor Double concerto*, perished in Auschwitz. Interesting though these recordings are, the principal musical rewards in the set come from the three Beethoven quartets with which they are coupled.

The Musical Offering, BWV 1079.
*** Ph. 412 800-2 [id.]. ASMF, Marriner.

Sir Neville Marriner uses his own edition and instrumentation: strings with three solo violins, solo viola and a solo cello; flute, organ and harpsichord. The performance here is of high quality, though some of the playing is a trifle bland. It is, however, excellently recorded and overall must be numbered among the most successful accounts of the work.

The Musical Offering, BWV 1079; (i) Suite No. 2 in B min, BWV 1067.
(M) **(*) Decca 430 266-2; 430 266-4. Stuttgart CO, Münchinger, (i) with Rampal.

Münchinger's 1976 version of the *Musical Offering* offers playing of genuine breadth and eloquence, particularly in the *Trio sonata*. For the reissue, the 1962 recording of the *B minor Suite* for flute and strings has been added, the best of the set.

Orchestral suites Nos. 1–4, BWV 1066/9.
☞ (M) *** Erato/Warner Dig. 4509 91800-2 (2) [id.]. E. Bar. Soloists, Gardiner.
(M) *** Decca 430 378-2; 430 378-4 [id.]. ASMF, Marriner.
☞ (M) **(*) Teldec/Warner 4509 92174-2 (2) [id.]. VCM, Harnoncourt.

Gardiner's four Bach *Orchestral suites* at last return to the catalogue at mid-price, making a clear first recommendation for those wanting these works played on period instruments. In his characteristic manner, allegros tend to be fast and lightly sprung, with slower movements elegantly pointed. Though the edginess of baroque violins using a squeeze technique on sustained notes makes for some abrasiveness, Gardiner avoids the extremes which mark even Pinnock's English Concert version on CD (see above). Thanks to full and immediate recording, textures are fresh and clear, with trumpet and timpani biting through but not excessively. Marriner's 1970 recording, using modern instruments, remains a unique bargain on a single CD, but Gardiner's set is fully competitive with its modern, digital sound.

Marriner's 1970 recording of the Bach *Suites* with the ASMF comes on a single CD (77 minutes 48 seconds) and the remastering of the fine (originally Argo) recording is fresh and vivid. The playing throughout is expressive without being romantic, and always buoyant and vigorous. A fine bargain for those not insisting on original instruments; there is nothing remotely unstylish here.

Harnoncourt's newest, digital recording with the Vienna Concentus Musicus proved disappointingly lacking in finesse and not always convincingly balanced. Thus his earlier set, recorded in 1966, which broke new ground in its pioneering of an authentic approach, is welcome back to the catalogue at mid-price. The effect is clean and literal, the acoustic bright and somewhat hard. Slow introductions are taken fast in allemande style, minuets are taken slowly and – hardest point to accept – there is no concession to expressiveness in the famous *Air* from *Suite No. 3*. The *Sarabande* of No. 2 may sound a little disconcerting with its use of *notes inégales*, but the *Gigue* of No. 3 – and, for that matter, all the fast movements and fugues – are splendidly alive. The drawback is the prevailing *mezzo forte* of these performances; but admirers of the conductor will find his approach has all the usual hallmarks of his baroque style.

Orchestral suites Nos. 1–2, BWV 1066/7; (i) *Double harpsichord concerto No. 1 in C min., BWV 1060.*
☞ (M) *** O-L Dig. 443 181-2 [id.]. (i) Rousset, Hogwood; AAM, Hogwood.

Orchestral suites Nos. 3–4, BWV 1068/9; (i) *Double harpsichord concerto No. 3 in C min., BWV 1062.*
☞ (M) *** O-L Dig. 433 182-2 [id.]. (i) Rousset, Hogwood; AAM, Hogwood.

Hogwood's set of the Bach orchestral *Suites* illustrates how the Academy of Ancient Music has developed in refinement and purity of sound, modifying earlier abrasiveness without losing period-instrument freshness. That comes out in the famous *Air* from *Suite No. 3* where, with multiple violins and an avoidance of the old squeezed style, the tone is sweet even with little or no vibrato – a movement which in the Pinnock version on DG Archiv, for example, sounds very sour. *Allegros* tend to be on the fast side but are well sprung, not breathless. The refinement of the ensemble is enhanced by the slight distancing of the recording, giving sharper, leaner ensembles than in most rival versions but with less-defined contrasts between solo and ripieno passages. The *Concertos for two harpsichords* (a Hemsch of 1761 and a Ruckers of 1646, modified by Taskin in 1785) added for the mid-priced reissue are imaginatively played by Christopher Hogwood and Christophe Rousset. This may be didactic in purpose but the results are pleasing, particularly in view of the clean and truthful recording. Hogwood aficionados need not hesitate.

CHAMBER MUSIC

The Art of fugue, BWV 1080.
*** Sony Dig. S2K 45937 (2) [id.]. Juilliard Qt.

The Juilliard Quartet's new version has the field virtually to itself, and hearing it again in this medium gives undoubted pleasure. They play with far less vibrato than usual (at times one is tempted to feel that they are aspiring to the condition of a consort of viols) and they convey a feeling of intimacy and a clarity of the part-writing that is very satisfying. This is a very worthwhile alternative to the relatively abundant keyboard versions, and musically very satisfying.

(Unaccompanied) *Cello suites Nos. 1–6, BWV 1007/12.*
☞ *** Virgin/EMI Dig. VCD5 45086-2 (2) [id.]. Ralph Kirshbaum.
*** EMI Dig. CDS7 47471-8 (2). Heinrich Schiff.
*** BMG/RCA Dig. RD 70950 (2). Anner Bylsma.
(M) *** DG 419 359-2 (2) [id.]. Pierre Fournier.
☞ (B) *** Ph. Duo 442 293-2 (2) [id.]. Maurice Gendron.
(M) (***) EMI mono CHS7 61027-2 (2) [Ang. CDH 61028/9]. Pablo Casals.

Ralph Kirshbaum's newest set of the Bach *Cello suites* is second to none. He has the advantage of an absolutely natural recording which displays his full timbre to great advantage. He plays a Domenico Montagnana Venetian cello of 1729 and gives it a warmly vivid personality. Articulation in the dance movements is clear; expressive playing is without bulges and does not shirk a degree of vibrato. The performances have intensity, dedication, spontaneity and an intimate thoughtfulness which is genuinely moving. Strongly recommended alongside Schiff.

Strong and positive, producing a consistent flow of beautiful tone at whatever dynamic level, Schiff here establishes his individual artistry very clearly, his rhythmic pointing a delight. He is treated to an excellent recording, with the cello given fine bloom against a warm but intimate acoustic.

Using a baroque cello, Bylsma brings a vivid musical imagination and an ardent intensity to each movement. He is rhythmically flexible and always thoughtful, and he brings the music alive in an unforced, seemingly natural way. This is worth acquiring as it offers new insights.

Fournier's richly phrased and warm-toned performances carry an impressive musical conviction. Fournier can be profound and he can lift rhythms infectiously in dance movements, but above all he conveys the feeling that this is music to be enjoyed. The recording does not sound in the least dated.

No one artist holds all the secrets in this repertoire, but few succeed in producing such consistent beauty of tone as Maurice Gendron, with the digital remastering firming up the focus of what was originally an excellent and truthful analogue recording. His phrasing is unfailingly musical, and although these readings have a certain sobriety (save, perhaps, for No. 6 which has distinct flair) their restraint and fine judgement command admiration. At Philips's Duo price, they can be given a warm welcome back to the catalogue.

It was Casals who restored these pieces to the repertory after long decades of neglect. Some of the playing is far from flawless; passage-work is rushed or articulation uneven, and he is often wayward. But he brought to the *Cello suites* insights that remain unrivalled. Casals brings one closer to this music than do most (one is tempted to say, any) of his rivals. The sound is inevitably dated but still comes over well in this transfer.

Flute sonatas Nos. 1 in B min.; 2 in E flat; 3 in A; 4 in C; 5 in E min.; 6 in E, BWV 1030/35.
☞ (BB) *** ASV CDQS 6108 [id.]. William Bennett, George Malcolm, Michael Evans.

William Bennett uses a modern flute, and in the first three sonatas he and George Malcolm manage without the nicety of including a viola da gamba in the continuo. The effect is undoubtedly robust, particularly as the recording places the flute well forward. However, the harpsichord is most natural in timbre and the balance between the two instruments is very convincing. In *Sonatas Nos. 4–6* the two players are joined by Michael Evans and the bass is subtly but tangibly reinforced and filled out, though the balance remains just as impressive. The playing, as might be expected of these artists, has superb character: it is strong in personality yet does not lack finesse. Moreover it is strikingly alive and spontaneous and, since the CD transfer brings the most vivid presence without the sound being in the least overblown, this can be enthusiastically recommended at super-bargain price to all but those who demand the finer points of authenticity above all else. Bennett himself has made the reconstruction of the first movement of BWV 1032.

Flute sonatas Nos. 1–6, BWV 1030/35; in G min., BWV 1020; Partita in A min. (for solo flute), *BWV 1013.*
*** CRD CRD 3314/5 (2) [id.]. Stephen Preston, Trevor Pinnock, Dordi Savall.

Two of these *Sonatas*, BWV 1031 and 1033, are unauthenticated, but still contain attractive music. Using an authentic one-key instrument, Stephen Preston plays all six with a rare delicacy. Throughout, the continuo playing, led by Trevor Pinnock, is of the highest standard; for those willing to stretch to the expense of two premium-priced records, this is a clear first choice for this repertoire.

(i) *Flute sonatas Nos. 1–6, BWV 1030/35; in G min., BWV 1020.* (ii) *Viola da gamba sonatas Nos. 1–3, BWV 1027/29.*
☞ (B) ** Ph. Duo 438 809-2 (2) [id.]. (i) Maxence Larrieu, Rafael Puyana, Wieland Kuijken; (ii) Marçal Cervera, Puyana.

The Philips Duo set comes from 1967 and places the flute very much in the foreground, though it is otherwise well enough recorded. Maxence Larrieu plays a modern flute, Rafael Puyana an instrument modelled on a large German harpsichord of the eighteenth century, and Wieland Kuijken a seven-stringed viola da gamba from the Tyrol and probably dating from the second half of the eighteenth century. The performances are highly accomplished and often persuasive. Moreover the *G minor Sonata*, BWV 1020, is also included. There are doubts about its authenticity, but Carl Philipp Emanuel has claimed that his father wrote it; if so, it almost certainly pre-dates the other works included. Puyana has made a sensible, fairly straightforward reconstruction of the incomplete first movement of BWV 1032. The set, which is very economically priced, makes agreeable listening. The performances of the *Viola da gamba sonatas* by Marçal Cervera and Puyana are much less attractive: the balance is not entirely convincing and these works need cleaner, more stylish playing if they are not to sound muddy and dull. The recording is acceptable but not up to Philips's highest standards.

Flute sonatas Nos. 1 in B min., BWV 1030; 3 in A, BWV 1032; 5 in E, BWV 1034; 6 in E, BWV 1035; Suite (Trio) in C min. for flute, harpsichord and cello, BWV 997.
☞ ** Ph. Dig. 434 996-2 [id.]. Irena Grafenauer, Brigitte Engelhard, Joerg Baumann.

Irena Grafenauer chooses to play only the authenticated sonatas, and she plays them very well. As a bonus, she offers the *Partita in C minor*, usually heard on the lute, though also known in a harpsichord version. Here it is played as a trio sonata. However, most collectors will prefer to have all six flute sonatas, including those written by other hands. The present performances use modern instruments, but the forward flute and the backward harpsichord (much less robust than the one used by Puyana) do not make for a very convincing balance, even though the digital recording is otherwise truthful.

Lute music transcribed for guitar

Lute suites (arr. for guitar): *Nos. 1–4, BWV 995/7 and 1006a.*
*** Sony MK 42204 [id.]. John Williams (guitar).

With all four *Suites* conveniently fitted on to a single compact disc, this CBS issue offers a clear first choice in this repertoire.

(i) *Lute suites Nos. 1 in E min., BWV 996; 2 in C min., BWV 997;* (ii) *Trio sonatas Nos. 1 in E flat, BWV 525; 5 in C, BWV 529* (ed. Bream).
☞ (M) *** BMG/RCA 09026 61603-2. Julian Bream (i) (guitar); (ii) (lute), George Malcolm.

This compilation comes from records made between 1965 and 1969. The two *Lute suites* are played with great subtlety and mastery on the guitar; the *Trio sonatas* were originally written for organ; here they are heard on lute and harpsichord and are elegantly played and cleanly recorded within a convincing ambience. Perhaps the harpsichord is a little less well defined in the bass register than is ideal, but the effect is pleasingly transparent and intimate.

Other guitar transcriptions

Trio sonatas Nos. 1 in D min., 2 in C, 3 & 4 in G, BWV 1036/9.
*** HM Dig. HMC 901173; *HMC 401173* [id.]. L. Bar.

The playing of the London Baroque has great freshness and spirit, and readers wanting this repertoire need not hesitate. The recording is eminently satisfactory, too.

Viola da gamba sonatas Nos. 1–3, BWV 1027/9.
*** Sony Dig. MK 37794 [id.]. Yo-Yo Ma (cello), Kenneth Cooper.
*** DG Dig. 415 471-2 [id.]. Mischa Maisky (cello), Martha Argerich (piano).
(M) *** HM/BMG GD 77044 [77044-2-RG]. Wieland Kuijken, Gustav Leonhardt.
☞ (B) **(*) Erato/Warner Duo 4509 95359-2 (2) [id.]. Paul Tortelier, Robert Veyron-Lacroix –
    VIVALDI: *Cello sonatas.* **(*)

Yo-Yo Ma plays with great eloquence and natural feeling. His tone is warm and refined and his technical command remains, as ever, irreproachable. Kenneth Cooper is a splendid partner.

Mischa Maisky is also a highly expressive cellist and he opts for the piano – successfully, for Martha Argerich is a Bach player of the first order. In fact the sonority of the cello and the modern piano seems a happier marriage than the compromise Ma and Cooper adopt. A most enjoyable account for collectors who do not care for period instruments.

Kuijken and Leonhardt are both sensitive and scholarly musicians. This is the most authentic account to have appeared on the market in recent years and is among the most rewarding.

As the opening *Adagio* of BWV 1027 shows, Tortelier's are inspirational performances, deeply felt yet with allegros spirited and lightly articulated, by both artists. One has only to sample the rapt *Andante* of the same sonata, or the glorious (almost vocal) *Adagio* of BWV 1029, to feel the emotional strength of this music-making, and indeed the rapport between the two artists, while the finale is full of joy and easy bravura. The opening *Adagio* of BWV 1028 again brings Tortelier's searchingly restrained melodic line against Veyron-Lacroix's gentle, poised accompaniment, while the *Andante* also combines simplicity of line with much expressive warmth. Considering that Tortelier's playing is so richly timbred, the balance is remarkably successful with the less assertive keyboard instrument never masked, even in the energetic virtuoso interplay of the *Vivace* first movement of BWV 1029. It is a pity that this Erato Bonsai Duo set is not better documented but, with a fine Vivaldi coupling, it makes a very attractive bargain.

(Unaccompanied) *Violin sonatas Nos. 1–3, BWV 1001, 1003 & 1005; Violin partitas Nos. 1–3, BWV 1002, 1004 & 1006.*
⊛ *** EMI Dig. CDS7 49483-2 (2) [id.]. Itzhak Perlman.
☞ ⊛ *** Erato/Warner 2292 45805-2 (2) [id.]. Oleg Kagan.
*** ASV CDDCD 454 (2) [id.]. Oscar Shumsky.
(M) *** DG 423 294-2 (2) [id.]. Milstein.
☞ (B) *** Ph. Duo 438 736-2 (2) [id.]. Arthur Grumiaux.
(M) *** HM/BMG GD 77043 (2) [77043-2-RG]. Sigiswald Kuijken.
☞ (M) **(*) Unicorn Dig. UKCD 2053/4. Ruggiero Ricci.
☞ (B) (**) EMI mono CZS7 67810-2 (2). Yehudi Menuhin.

The range of tone in Perlman's playing adds to the power of these performances, infectiously rhythmic in dance movements but conveying the intensity of live performance in the great slow movements in hushed playing of great refinement. Some may still seek a greater sense of struggle conveyed in order to bring out the full depth of the writing, but the sense of spontaneity, of the player's own enjoyment in the music, makes this set a unique, revelatory experience.

Oleg Kagan made these recordings during live performances in the Concertgebouw in 1989. He died not long afterwards. Fortunately the CDs are a worthy memento, celebrating his wisdom and supreme musicianship. They have all the magnetism of live music-making and a serenity of spirit that is completely satisfying. As performances they are less reserved and aristocratic than those of Milstein, not as emotionally extrovert as with Perlman; technically they are almost flawless. The Concertgebouw acoustics add a warm ambience to the beautifully focused violin image and the effect is very real and vivid.

Shumsky's clean attack and tight vibrato, coupled with virtuosity of the highest order, make for strong and refreshing readings, full of flair and imagination. If you want big-scale playing of Bach, this supplies the need splendidly, though the dry, close acoustic reduces the scale and undermines tenderness.

Milstein's set from the mid-1970s remains among the most satisfying of all versions. Every phrase is beautifully shaped and there is a highly developed feeling for line. In some ways his earlier, mono set (EMI ZDMB7 64793-2) is fresher and technically more secure, sparkling and exhilarating, very much a young man's interpretation; but there is no want of virtuosity in the DG stereo version, and these performances have an aristocratic poise and a classical finesse which is very satisfying.

Arthur Grumiaux's fine performances were recorded in Berlin in 1960/61. The venue offers a pleasingly warm background ambience against which the violin is forward, recorded in strong profile with complete realism and with no microphonic exaggeration of the upper partials. He strikes just the right balance between expressive feeling and purity of style. Some may prefer a rhythmically freer, more charismatic approach, as with Perlman and Milstein for instance; but Grumiaux's simplicity of manner, without exaggerated temperament, lets the music unfold naturally, and his readings of all six works are the product of superlative technique and a refined musical intellect. At bargain price this set is very tempting.

Kuijken's accounts are as little painful or scratchy as you are ever likely to get in the authentic field.

Ricci gives good, old-fashioned readings. Speeds in movements both fast and slow are measured, the tone is romantically ripe and full, but the expressive style is not exaggerated. The readings were made without editing. Occasionally flaws occur, but they are generally balanced out by the warm concentration. Excellent recording.

Menuhin's mono recordings, made in 1956 and 1957, give far greater artistic satisfaction than the set he recorded later in stereo. They are strong, athletic performances, simply stated, without idiosyncrasy; but he has less in the way of personal insights to offer in this music than, say, Milstein or Grumiaux.

(Unaccompanied) *Violin partita No. 1 in B min., BWV 1002.*
*** Ph. Dig. 420 948-2 [id.]. Viktoria Mullova – BARTOK: *Sonata* *** (also with PAGANINI: *Introduction and variations on Nel cor più non misento* ***).

Viktoria Mullova's account of the *B minor Partita* is undeniably impressive and is in every way compelling. Good if forward recording.

(Unaccompanied) *Violin partitas Nos. 2, BWV 1004* (complete); *3 (Minuets I & II only), BWV 1006; Violin sonatas Nos. 1, BWV 1001; 3, BWV 1005* (complete); (i) *English suite No. 3 in E, BWV 808: Sarabande; Gavottes Nos. I & II.*
☞ (M) (***) EMI mono CDH7 64492-2 [id.]. Heifetz, (i) with Arpad Sándor.

In his note for this CD, Lionel Salter quotes George Bernard Shaw who, writing to the nineteen-year-old Heifetz, advised, 'If you provoke a jealous God by playing with such superhuman perfection, you will die young. I earnestly advise you to play something badly every night before going to bed, instead of saying your prayers.' Surely that was asking the impossible, and the playing here is as miraculous as ever. The three complete works were recorded with remarkable faithfulness at Abbey Road in 1935. Heifetz's Bach was by no means romantic, indeed this is thoughtfully inspirational playing, but his chimerical bowing produces more variety of timbre and subtlety of dynamic shading in the *Allemanda* and *Giga* of the *D minor Partita* than would have been likely or possible in Bach's time, while the great *Chaconne* has wonderful detail, without losing strength. Such is the spontaneity of effect that the result gives enormous pleasure, with the *Giga* running like quicksilver. Heifetz's approach is often without the puposeful onward flow of a Milstein, but the result remains immensely compelling. In his own transcription of the *Sarabanda* from the *Third English suite* (recorded a year earlier) the playing has a depth of feeling that contradicts any ideas that Heifetz's playing was cold and impersonal. The transfer is bright but truthful: the violin image is real if the volume level is not set too high.

Violin sonatas (for violin and harpsichord) *Nos. 1–6, BWV 1014/9.*
(M) *** HM/BMG GD 77170 (2) [77170-2-RG]. Sigiswald Kuijken, Gustav Leonhardt.
☞ (M) *(*) DG 439 849-2 (2) [id.]. Wolfgang Schneiderhan, Karl Richter.

Violin sonatas Nos. 1–6, BWV 1014/9; 1019a; Sonatas for violin and continuo, BWV 1020/4.
⊛ (M) *** Ph. 426 452-2; *426 452-4* (2). Arthur Grumiaux, Christiane Jaccottet, Philippe Mermoud (in *BWV 1021 & 1023*).

The Bach *Sonatas for violin and harpsichord* and for *violin and continuo* are marvellously played, with all the beauty of tone and line for which Grumiaux is renowned; they have great vitality too. His admirable partner is Christiane Jaccottet, and in BWV 1021 and 1023 Philippe Mermoud (cello) joins the continuo. There is endless treasure to be discovered here, particularly when the music-making is so serenely communicative.

Sigiswald Kuijken uses a baroque violin, and both he and Gustav Leonhardt give us playing of rare eloquence. This reissue is an admirable example of the claims of authenticity and musical feeling pulling together rather than apart. This is a wholly delightful set and the transparency of the sound is especially appealing.

Schneiderhan's classical timbre would seem custom-made for these fine works with their ready lyricism, but the snag is the reverberant (1966) Archiv recording, which has necessitated a very close, unflattering balance for the violin. The texture too is blown up. Schneiderhan's playing, it hardly needs saying, is often beautiful, but the balance helps to give a feeling of not enough light and shade, and Karl Richter's very determined account of the harpsichord part is accurate without being in any way imaginative, even if there is no lack of vitality and projection.

Violin sonatas (for violin and harpsichord) *Nos. 1 in B min.; 2 in A; 6 in G, BWV 1019.*
☞ ** Ph. Dig. 434 084-2 [id.]. Viktoria Mullova, Bruno Canino (with J. C. BACH: *Sonata in C min., Wq. 78* **).

There is nothing special here. Mullova is recorded a fraction too near the microphone and there is a hint of edginess on her tone, but Bruno Canino emerges as the stronger personality. But the performances fail to make a good case for these works to be played on violin and piano.

KEYBOARD MUSIC

Complete keyboard music

Chromatic fantasia and fugue in D min., BWV 903; Italian concerto, BWV 971; French suites Nos. 1 in D min., BWV 812; 2 in C min., BWV 813.
☞ (BB) **(*) Naxos Dig. 8.550709 [id.]. Wolfgang Rübsam (piano).

French suites Nos. 3 in B min., BWV 814; 4 in E flat, BWV 815; 5 in G, BWV 816; 6 in E, BWV 817.
☞ (BB) **(*) Naxos Dig. 8.550710 [id.]. Wolfgang Rübsam (piano).

Partitas Nos. 1 in B flat, BWV 825; 2 in C min., BWV 826; Capriccio on the departure of a beloved brother, BWV 992; Prelude and fuguetta in G, BWV 902.
☞ (BB) **(*) Naxos Dig. 8.550692 [id.]. Wolfgang Rübsam (piano).

Partitas Nos. 3 in A min., BWV 827; 4 in D, BWV 828.
☞ (BB) **(*) Naxos Dig. 8.550693 [id.]. Wolfgang Rübsam (piano).

Partitas Nos. 5 in G, BWV 829; 6 in E min., BWV 830.
☞ (BB) **(*) Naxos Dig. 8.550694 [id.]. Wolfgang Rübsam (piano).

Toccatas Nos. 1 in F sharp min.; 2 in C min.; 3 in D; 4 in D min.; 5 in E min.; 6 in G min.; 7 in G, BWV 910/916.
☞ (BB) **(*) Naxos Dig. 8.550708 [id.]. Wolfgang Rübsam (piano).

Wolfgang Rübsam is embarking on a complete survey of Bach's keyboard music on the piano for Naxos. His manner is simple and thoughtful, never inflexible, always sensing the flow of the musical line. Ornamentation is unfussy, and the only cavil is that his expressive playing brings little hesitations, which are very much part of his style and to which one adjusts, although this may trouble some listeners. Nothing here is metronomic and tempi are never pushed too hard. The *Chromatic fantasia*, brilliantly articulated as it is, is not treated as a chance for virtuoso display for its own sake and some might feel that the *Toccatas* are not flamboyant enough, but Rübsam sees them as being like sinfonias, beginning with a flourish and with the music satisfyingly brought together in the closing sections. The recording is clear and truthful.

'Bach and Tureck at home' (A birthday offering): (i) *Adagio in G, BWV 968; Aria and 10 variations in the Italian style, BWV 989; Capriccio on the departure of a beloved brother, BWV 992; Chromatic fantasia and fugue, BWV 903; Fantasia, adagio and fugue in D, BWV 912; The Well-tempered clavier, Book 1: Prelude & fugue in B flat, BWV 866.* (ii) *English suite No. 3 in G min., BWV 808; Italian concerto, BWV 971; Sonata in D min., BWV 964* (trans. from Unaccompanied *Violin sonata No. 2 in A min., BWV 1003); Well-tempered clavier, Book 1: Preludes & fugues: in C min; in C, BWV 847/8; Book 2: Preludes & fugues in C sharp, BWV 872; in G, BWV 884.* (iii) *Goldberg variations, BWV 988;* (iv) *Partitas Nos. 1 in B flat, BWV 825; 2 in C min., BWV 826; 6 in E min., BWV 830.*
⊕ *** (i) VAIA 1041; (ii) VAIA 1051; (iii) VAIA 1029; (iv) VAIA 1040 (available separately).
Rosalyn Tureck (piano).

These recordings originated in the home of William F. Buckley at Wallach's Point, Stamford, Connecticut. They were planned as an inspired birthday present by his wife, but the initial event expanded to five evenings, the first on 24 November 1979 and the last in May 1984. The result is a series of Bach programmes that have all the advantages of live music-making – notably a wonderfully spontaneous feeling of music taking wing as one listens – and none of the disadvantages.

Rosalyn Tureck's Bach playing is legendary, and the performances here show that her keyboard command and fluent sense of Bach style are as remarkable as ever. Miss Tureck uses a wide dynamic and expressive range with consummate artistry, her decoration always adds to the musical effect, and she makes us feel that Bach's keyboard music could be played in no other way than this – the hallmark of a great artist.

These recordings, originally issued on the Troy label, are now on the American VAI Audio label (158 Linwood Plaza, Suite 301, Fort Lee, New Jersey 07024, USA) and are distributed in the UK by Video Artists (c/o Club 50/50, PO Box 1277, Chippenham, Wilts, SN15 3YZ).

Aria variata in A min., BWV 989; Capriccio on the departure of a beloved brother, BWV 992; Prelude and fugue in A min., BWV 894; Toccatas: in F sharp min., BWV 910; C min., BWV 911; G min., BWV 915.
☞ **(*) DG Dig. 437 555-2 [id.]. Kenneth Gilbert (harpsichord).

These are all brilliant and colourful works, and Kenneth Gilbert plays them with panache. The recording of the Jan Couchet harpsichord in a fairly resonant acoustic makes it sound a little larger than life-size.

The Art of fugue, BWV 1080 (see also string quartet and orchestral versions).
*** HM HMC 901169/70; HMC 401169/70 [id.]. Davitt Moroney (harpsichord).

Davitt Moroney's account commands not only the intellectual side of the work but also the aesthetic, and his musicianship is second to none.

The Art of fugue, BWV 1080; 4 Duets, BWV 802/3; Musical offering, BWV 1079: 3-Part & 6-Part Ricercare.
☞ ** Hyp. Dig. CDA 66631/2 [id.]. Tatiana Nikolayeva (piano).

There are many moments of great pianistic beauty in Tatiana Nikolayeva's performance that rub shoulders with some curiously ugly playing elsewhere. It is all too uneven to be a strong recommendation.

The Art of fugue, BWV 1080; Italian concerto, BWV 971; Partita in B min., BWV 831; Prelude, fugue and allegro in E flat, BWV 998.
(M) *** HM/BMG GD 77013 (2) [77013-2-RG]. Gustav Leonhardt (harpsichord).

Under the fingers of Leonhardt every strand in the texture emerges with clarity and every phrase is allowed to speak for itself. This is a very impressive and rewarding set, well recorded and produced.

Capriccio in B flat (on the departure of a beloved brother), BWV 992; Chorale preludes: Befiehl du deine Wege, BWV 727; Es ist gewisslich an der Zeit, BWV 307 & 734; Ich ruf zu dir, Herr Jesu Christ, BWV 639; In dulci jubilo, BWV 751; Jesu, joy of man's desiring, from BWV 147; Nun komm' der Heiden Heiland, BWV 659; Wachet auf, from BWV 140; Wir danken dir, Gott, BWV 29; Harpsichord concerto in F min., BWV 1056: Largo. Flute sonata in E flat, BWV 1031: Siciliano.

English suite No. 3 in G, BWV 808; French suite No. 5 in G, BWV 816; Toccata in D, BV 912; The
Well-tempered Clavier, Book I, excerpts; Preludes and fugues Nos. 4, BWV 849; 9–14, BWV 854/9;
Book II, excerpts: Preludes Nos. 3, BWV 872; 6–7, BWV 875/6; 15, BWV 884; 24, BWV 893.
☞ (B) *** DG Double 439 672-2 (2) [id.]. Wilhelm Kempff (with GLUCK: *Orfeo ed Euridice: Ballet*
   music ***).

Wilhelm Kempff begins this two-disc recital by appropriating many of Bach's best tunes, and two
Gluck lollipops into the bargain, and, whether it be the chorale preludes, the delicious *Sicilano* from
BWV 1031 or the slow movement of the *F minor Harpsichord concerto*, he 'magics' them and makes
them completely his own. He then offers an *English suite* (sample the first *Gavotte* for elegance) and
gives an inspired account of the best-known *French suite* (with another unforgettable *Gavotte*) where
its final *Gigue* is as light as thistledown. The great German pianist then turns to the *Well-tempered*
Clavier and makes an entirely personal selection. We are told that Kempff regards these preludes and
fugues as poetic creations, no different in this respect from the piano sonatas of Beethoven. The 150-
minute recital then ends with Bach's vividly pictorial *Capriccio on the departure of a beloved brother*
(where again Kempff invests the *Adagissimo* with great poetic feeling); he then finds infinite variety of
colour and feeling in the elaborate *Toccata*, BWV 912, with its ruminating *Adagio con discrezione*
and genial, sprightly closing gigue-like fugue. Played like this, Bach is a joyful and compelling master,
far removed from the relentless plod favoured by some harpsichordists. Though Kempff was well into
his eighties when these recordings were made, his intellectual vigour, technical command and musical
feeling seem ever fresh. The sound is truthful, warm and clear, and everyone who cares about Bach
and piano playing should investigate this issue. One can only lament that, although this new Double
DG series (two CDs for the price of one) is generous value, the documentation is inadequate.

Chorale: Jesu, joy of man's desiring (arr. Hess).
☞ (M) (***) Dutton Lab. mono CDLX 7005 [id.]. Dame Myra Hess – SCHUMANN: *Piano concerto;*
   FRANCK: *Symphonic variations.* (***)

Many collectors will be glad to have Dame Myra's own recording of her famous transcription, played
simply and persuasively. The transfer (from a 78-r.p.m. shellac pressing) is immaculately done.

Chromatic fantasia and fugue in D min., BWV 903; 4 Duets, BWV 802/5; Italian concerto in F, BWV
971; Partita in B min., BWV 831.
🏵 *** O-L Dig. 433 054-2 [id.]. Christophe Rousset (harpsichord).

Christophe Rousset's playing combines the selfless authority and scholarly dedication of such artists
as Leonhardt and Gilbert with the flair and imagination of younger players, and all the performances
here have a taste and musical vitality that reward the listener. Strongly recommended.

Chromatic fantasia & fugue in D min., BWV 903; Fantasias: in C min., BWV 906; G min., BWV 917;
C min., BWV 919; Fantasia & fugue in A min., BWV 904; Preludes: in C min., BWV 921; A min.,
BWV 922; Preludes & fugues: in A min., BWV 894; F, BWV 901; G, BWV 902.
*** HM/BMG RD 77039 [RCA 77039-2-RC]. Andreas Staier (harpsichord).

What is good about Staier's playing is its air of freedom, for although he keeps a firm grip on rhythm
he is never rigid or inflexible, and his approach and registration are varied enough for his programme
to be heard at one sitting. The recording has impressive clarity and presence and is made in a
pleasingly warm acoustic. Strongly recommended.

4 Duets, BWV 802–5; Overture (Partita) in the French style, BWV 831; Italian concerto in F, BWV
971.
☞ (BB) ** HM Dig. HMA 901278 [id.]. Kenneth Gilbert (harpsichord).

Kenneth Gilbert's recital is recorded at a deafeningly high level; if it is to sound at all realistic, it
should be played at a very much lower-than-usual level setting. In the *Italian concerto* and the
Overture in the French style he uses a German harpsichord by Bernhard von Tucher, modelled on a
seventeenth-century instrument by Gräbner of Dresden, and in the *Duets* another Tucher, modelled
on Christian Vater of Hanover. Kenneth Gilbert is a scholarly guide in this repertoire and does not
have the flair or fantasy of, say, Rousset, who offers, in addition to the above, the *Chromatic fantasy*
and fugue.

English suites Nos. 1–6, BWV 806/11.
*** Decca Dig. 421 640-2 (2) [id.]. András Schiff (piano).

Schiff is straightforward, finely articulated, rhythmically supple and vital. Ornamentation is stylishly
and sensibly observed. Everything is very alive, without being in the least over-projected or exaggerated in any way. The Decca recording is altogether natural and present.

English suites Nos. 2 in A min.; 3 in G min., BWV 807/8.
*** DG Dig. 415 480-2 [id.]. Ivo Pogorelich (piano).

The young Yugoslav pianist plays both *Suites* with a welcome absence of affectation. It is all beautifully articulate and fresh. The recording is one of DG's best.

English suite No. 2 in A min., BWV 807; Partita No. 2 in C min., BWV 826; Toccata in C min., BWV 911.
(M) *** DG 423 880-2 [id.]. Martha Argerich (piano).

Martha Argerich's playing is alive and keenly rhythmic but also wonderfully flexible and rich in colour. She is very well recorded.

English suite No. 6 in D min., BWV 811; French suite No. 5 in G, BWV 816; Well-tempered Clavier: Preludes & fugues Nos. 15 in G, BWV 860; 39 in G, BWV 884.
☞ (M) ** Decca 433 901-2 [id.]. Wilhelm Backhaus – HAYDN: *Sonatas.* **(*)

Backhaus was not particularly associated with Bach and these performances, recorded in 1956, do not suggest that he feels the music very intensely; on the other hand, they are very well played – with the single reservation that the close balance presents a relatively unvarying dynamic level. But if you like clean, clinical, unemotional Bach, you will like this record. The piano timbre is truthfully transferred to CD.

French suites Nos. 1–6, BWV 812/17.
☞ *** Erato/Warner Dig. 4509 94805-2 [id.]. Ton Koopman (harpsichord).
☞ **(*) Collins Dig. 1371-2 [id.]. Joanna MacGregor (piano).

Ton Koopman fits all six *French suites* on to a single, 70-minute CD. He uses a copy of a Ruckers to admirable effect and these performances are stimulatingly rhythmic, exciting and thoughtful by turns. The best-known *Fifth suite* is especially spontaneous. The effect of the recording – not too closely balanced – is vivid and realistic. Ornaments are nicely handled and there is not a trace of pedantry here. A first choice for those not wanting the extra suites offered by Hogwood.

Like Thurston Dart before her (in the LP era) Joanna MacGregor manages to get the six *Suites* on to a single CD – though not by having to cut all the repeats, as he did. This Collins disc plays for 79 minutes 11 seconds. MacGregor's style is relatively soft-grained to which the warm acoustics of The Maltings, Snape, contribute not a little. So the effect is mellow rather than incisive, quite unlike a clavichord (as favoured by Dart) or harpsichord, and while the opening *Allemandes* flow fluidly some listeners may feel that more bite is needed in the livelier dance movements. Yet the *Gigues* are delightfully articulated, as is the lively *Air* in the *Second Suite in C minor*, the nicely pointed *Sarabande* in No. 4 and the famous *Gavotte* of No. 5. Indeed the characterization in both the *Fourth* and *Fifth suites* gives special pleasure. In spite of the hall resonance, MacGregor conveys intimacy of feeling alongside spontaneous joy in the music, and and many will enjoy this playing a lot. The disc is certainly excellent value.

French suites Nos. 1–6; Suites: in A min., BWV 818a; in E flat, BWV 819; Allemande, BWV 819a.
*** O-L Dig. 411811-2 (2) [id.]. Christopher Hogwood (harpsichord).

Christopher Hogwood's performances have both style and character and can be recommended with some enthusiasm. To the *French suites* themselves he adds the two others that Bach had obviously intended to include as Nos. 5 and 6.

6 French suites, BWV 812/17; Italian concerto in F, BWV 971; Partita in B min., BWV 831.
☞ *** Decca Dig. 433 313-2 (2). András Schiff (piano).

András Schiff has few peers in playing Bach on the piano. He continues his distinguished series with highly rewarding performances of the *French suites*, his expressive style entirely without personal indulgence, his freedom in slow movements seemingly improvisatory and spontaneous, and his faster dance movements an unqualified delight. Try the famous *Gavotte* in the *Fifth Suite* for rhythmic lift or the slow movement of the *Italian concerto* to experience his sustained line at its most beautiful. The *Partita in B minor* is slightly more severe in style than the rest of the programme. As with the rest of his series, the Decca recording is appealingly realistic and an ideal acoustic has been chosen.

Goldberg variations, BWV 988.
*** EMI Dig. CDC7 54209-2 [id.]. Bob van Asperen (harpsichord).
*** DG 415 130-2 [id.]. Trevor Pinnock (harpsichord).

☞ ⊛ *** VAI Audio VAIA 1029 [id.]. Rosalyn Tureck (piano).
*** Decca Dig. 417 116-2 [id.]. András Schiff (piano).
☞ *** Virgin/EMI Dig. VC7 59045-2 [id.]. Maggie Cole (harpsichord).
☞ (M) *(**) Sony Dig. SMK 52619 [id.] (1981 recording). Glenn Gould (piano).
☞ ** Hyp. Dig. CDA 66589 [id.]. Tatiana Nicolayeva (piano).
☞ ** DG Dig. 435 436-2 [id.]. Andrei Gavrilov (piano).

Goldberg variations, BWV 988; Well-tempered Clavier: Fugues in E, BWV 878; F sharp min., BWV 883.
☞ (M) (**(*)) Sony mono SMK 52594 [id.] (1955 recording). Glenn Gould (piano).

It becomes increasingly difficult to choose among the innumerable versions of the *Goldberg* now before the public and, given the fact that there are nearly 40 currently available, detailed exegesis of their merits or otherwise would be impossible.

Bob van Asperen is an artist of keen musical intelligence and sensitivity, whose thoughtful playing is well captured by the engineers. He does not observe every repeat but his CD accommodates 80 minutes' music.

Trevor Pinnock retains repeats in more than half the variations – which seems a good compromise, in that variety is maintained yet there is no necessity for an additional disc. The playing is eminently vital and intelligent, with alert, finely articulated rhythm. The recording is very truthful and vivid.

While this work should properly be heard on the harpsichord and Bob van Asperen and Trevor Pinnock will fully satisfy in this respect, Rosalyn Tureck's recording is very special indeed – there is no other record of Bach played on the piano quite as compelling as this, and for I. M. it would be a desert island disc. (The circumstances of this recording are discussed above under '*Bach and Tureck at home*'.)

For those who prefer Bach on the piano and want a digital recording, András Schiff's set can receive the most enthusiastic welcome, especially for those collectors who find Tureck too freely improvisational in her approach. Schiff is admirably spontaneous and the part-writing emerges with splendid definition and subtlety: Schiff does not play as if he is performing a holy ritual but with a keen sense of enjoyment of the piano's colour and sonority. The Decca recording is excellent in every way, clean and realistic.

Maggie Cole plays a copy by Andrew Warlick of an instrument by J. C. Goujon of 1749. She is recorded with great clarity; as so often, the playback level needs to be reduced if a truthful and realistic effect is to be made. Her playing is completely straightforward and she holds the listener's interest throughout.

Glenn Gould's famous (1955) mono recording runs to 38 minutes – almost exactly half that of Gavrilov's. It enjoyed cult status in its day, and its return will occasion rejoicing among his admirers. He observes no repeats and in terms of sheer keyboard wizardry commands admiration, even if you do not respond to the results. There is too much that is wilful and eccentric for this to be a straightforward recommendation, but it is a remarkable performance nevertheless.

Gould's later, stereo version was one of the last records he made. As in his earlier account, there are astonishing feats of prestidigitation and the clarity he produced in the part-writing is often little short of extraordinary. In his earlier record he made no repeats; now he repeats a section of almost half of them and also joins some pairs together (6 with 7 and 9 with 10, for example). Yet, even apart from his vocalise, he does a number of weird things – fierce staccatos, brutal accents, and so on – that inhibit one from suggesting this as a first recommendation even among piano versions. The recording is, as usual with this artist, inclined to be dry and forward (he engineered his own records and admired this kind of sound) which aids clarity. A thought-provoking rather than a satisfying reading – an award-winning disc, too; however, for all that, many readers will find the groans and croons intolerable and will be bewildered by many things he does. The withdrawn, rapt, opening *Aria* is rather beautiful – but why, one wonders, does he emphasize the third part in many of the canons? The CD has admirable presence but emphasizes the vocalise.

Tatiana Nicolayeva on Hyperion gives an account of the *Goldberg* that will appeal to those who warm to the anachronistic. Hers is not the kind of Bach playing that will appeal to purists at all, and there are times when those who welcome a romantic, nineteenth-century approach will raise their eyebrows. There are many felicities and she was, of course, an artist of strong musical personality. A qualified recommendation.

Andrei Gavrilov, too, is a player of astonishing keyboard prowess and there is much that will prompt admiration for both his integrity and articulation. All the same, he makes heavy weather of some of the variations and is, more importantly, handicapped by a less than glamorous recording. There is not enough space round the sound and the instrument is too closely balanced.

15 2-Part Inventions, BWV 772/786; 15 3-Part Inventions, BWV 787/801.
*** Capriccio Dig. 10 210 [id.] (with *6 Little preludes, BWV 933/8*). Ton Koopman (harpsichord).
**(*) Decca Dig. 411 974-2 [id.]. András Schiff (piano).

15 2-Part Inventions; 15 3-Part Inventions; Fragments of Anna Magdelena's Notebook: March in D; 3 Minuets in G; Minuet in D min.; Musette in D; 2 Polonaises in G min.
☞ (BB) **(*) Naxos Dig. 8.550679 [id.]. János Sebestyén (piano).

Ton Koopman scores over rivals in offering the *Six Little preludes* in addition to the two sets of *Inventions*, and Koopman plays with spontaneity and sparkle.

András Schiff's playing is (for this repertoire) rather generous with rubato and other expressive touches, but elegant in the articulation of part-writing. Such is his musicianship and pianistic sensitivity, however, that the overall results are likely to persuade most listeners. The recording is excellent.

János Sebestyén is by no means inflexible, but his performances are straighter than those of Schiff. They have less individuality, but this is sensitive, well-structured Bach playing, truthfully recorded, and there is the welcome bonus of eight small-scale keyboard pieces which Bach provided for his second wife.

Partitas Nos. 1–6, BWV 825/30.
☞ *** O-L Dig. 440 217-2 (2) [id.]. Christophe Rousset (harpsichord).
☞ *** EMI Dig. CDC7 54462-2 (*Nos. 1, 2 & 4*); CDC7 54464-2 (*Nos. 3, 5 & 6*). Maria Tipo (piano).
*** DG Dig. 415 493-2 (2) [id.]. Trevor Pinnock (harpsichord).
*** Decca Dig. 411 732-2 (2) [id.]. András Schiff (piano).

Bach playing doesn't come much better than it does in Christophe Rousset's two-CD set on Oiseau-Lyre. Here is an artist who wears his elegance and erudition lightly; there are none of the scholarly hang-ups that so often afflict performers of this repertoire. The playing has complete naturalness and is obviously the product of a vital musical imagination. This must now be the first recommendation in this repertoire.

Maria Tipo belongs to the old school. Like the late lamented Tatiana Nikolayeva, hers is music-making of a different age, yet it is every bit as living and vibrant as any now before the public. The part-writing and the inner voices all 'tell' and speak with great sweep and, when required, vigour. She phrases very musically; nothing is mechanical or metronomic. Her phrasing has breadth and freedom and, what is more, she is beautifully recorded. In its way this is as good as any in the current catalogue. As we go to print the set has been withdrawn, but we hope the discs may reappear at mid-price.

Trevor Pinnock's tempi are generally well judged, rhythms vital yet free, and there is little to justify the criticism that he rushes some movements. He also conveys a certain sense of pleasure that is infectious and he has great spirit.

Schiff is a most persuasive advocate of Bach on the piano. Though few will cavil at his treatment of fast movements, some may find him a degree wayward in slow movements, though the freshness of his rubato and the sparkle of his ornamentation are always winning. The sound is outstandingly fine.

Toccatas: in F sharp min.; C min.; D; D min.; E min.; G min.; G; BWV 910/16.
*** EMI Dig. CDC7 54081-2 [id.]. Bob van Asperen (harpsichord).
☞ (M) ** Sony SM2K 52612 (2). Glenn Gould (piano).

The *Toccatas* are very varied, and this distinguished Dutch player conveys their improvisatory character with great flair. This is one of the most enjoyable Bach keyboard issues of recent years.

The seven *Toccatas* offer some of Glenn Gould's finest Bach playing. They are often quite complex in structure, but Gould has their full measure. His approach combines fastidiousness and remarkable pianism with some impulsive – not to say wilful – touches. But the music is always alive; slow sections often have striking thoughtfulness and serenity, and undoubtedly this is Bach playing of distinction. The recording balance is close and rather dry but truthful and with rather more bloom than in previous incarnations. The one overriding snag is the vocalise, which is even more apparent against the quiet background. If one can accept this, there is much to admire here, with the contrapuntal strands beautifully balanced and clarified. However, when these *Toccatas* were first issued on CD (at full price), they were coupled with the *Inventions*; without them, this reissue is poor value in playing time: the first disc plays for 43 minutes, the second for merely 38.

The Well-tempered Clavier (48 Preludes & fugues), BWV 846/893.
*** DG Dig. 413 439-2 (4) [id.]. Kenneth Gilbert (harpsichord).

The Well-tempered Clavier, Book I, Preludes and fugues Nos. 1–24, BWV 846/69.
⊛ *** Decca Dig. 414 388-2 (2) [id.]. András Schiff (piano).
☞ (B) ** Erato/Warner Duo Dig. 4509 95304-2 (2) [id.]. Ton Koopman (harpsichord).

The Well-tempered Clavier, Book II, Preludes and fugues Nos. 25–48, BWV 870/93.
⊛ *** Decca Dig. 417 236-2 (2) [id.]. András Schiff (piano).
☞ (B) ** Erato/Warner Duo Dig. 4509 95305-2 (2) [id.]. Ton Koopman (harpsichord).

Gilbert has made some superb harpsichord records, but his set of the 'Forty-eight' crowns them all. By a substantial margin it now supplants all existing harpsichord versions, with readings that are resilient and individual, yet totally unmannered, although some might feel that the acoustic is just a shade too resonant.

Schiff often takes a very individual view of particular preludes and fugues, but his unexpected readings regularly win one over long before the end. Consistently he translates this music into pianistic terms, rarely if ever imitating the harpsichord, and though his very choice of the piano will rule him out with those seeking authenticity, his voyage of discovery through this supreme keyboard collection is the more riveting, when the piano is an easier instrument to listen to over long periods. First-rate sound.

Ton Koopman's keenly responsive playing has been very successful on a number of Bach records, but here some reservations have to be made. He uses a fine copy of a Rückers harpsichord and plays with consistent vitality and often with obvious thoughtfulness. But his speeds are often brisk, and at times there is a feeling that the forward momentum is pursued somewhat relentlessly. This is more striking in the first book than the second. He is well recorded, and this set is inexpensive, being offered on two Bonsai Duo issues with each of the two CDs offered for the price of one. However, the non-existent documentation and inadequate titling is characteristic of this poorly produced bargain series.

The Well-tempered Clavier (48 Preludes & fugues), Book I, Preludes & fugues Nos. 1–24, BWV 846/ 869.
☞ ** Denon Dig. CO 75638/9 [id.]. Huguette Dreyfus (harpsichord).

Huguette Dreyfus is an artist of quality whose Couperin and Bach have won much admiration – and rightly so! She plays a Hemsch of 1763 which is reproduced with excellent clarity, even if the level at which it is played back (as is so often the case these days) needs to be lower than usual if it is to produce a lifelike effect. Although there is much that is illuminating, there is more that is merely didactic and, artistically speaking, heavy-handed. No challenge to first recommendations here.

The Well-tempered Clavier, Book II, Preludes and fugues Nos. 25–48, BWV 870/93.
*** ECM Dig. 847936-2 [id.]. Keith Jarrett (harpsichord).

Keith Jarrett is a highly intelligent and musical player, whose readings can hold their own against the current opposition.

ORGAN MUSIC

Complete organ music

Wolfgang Rübsam Philips series
Volume 1. *Allabreve, BWV 589; Canzona, BWV 588; Fantasias, BWV 562 & 572; in C min.; Fugues, BWV 575, 577–9; 581; Passacaglia, BWV 582; Pedal-Exercitium, BWV 598; Prelude, adagio-trio, fantasia & fugue; Prelude, BWV 568; Preludes & fugues, 531–6; 538–9; 541; 543–550; Toccata, BWV 564; Toccatas & fugues, BWV 540, 564–566; Trios, BWV 583, 586, 1027a.* (4 discs)

Volume 2: *Canonic variations on the Christmas chorale, Vom Himmel hoch, BWV 769; Chorale partitas: Christ, du bist der helle Tag, BWV 766; O Gott, du frommer Gott, BWV 767; Sei gegrüsset, Jesu gütig, BWV 768; Ach, was soll ich Sünder machen?, BWV 770; Chorales & Chorale preludes: BWV 691a, 717, 725, 739, 745, 747; Chorale variations: Allein Gott in der Höh' sei Ehr', BWV 717; Fantasia, BWV 571; Fugue on a theme of Legrenzi, BWV 574; Orgelbüchlein, BWV 599–644; Pastorale in F, BWV 590; Trio sonatas Nos. 1–6, BWV 525/30.* (4 discs)

Volume 3: *Chorales & Chorale preludes: BWV 653b, 748–750, 754, 756, 759; Chorale: O Lamm Gottes unschuldig; 6 Schübler chorales, BWV 645–650; Clavierübung, Part III: German organ mass: (Prelude in E flat, BWV 552/1; Catechism chorales, Kyrie and Gloria BWV 669–689; Duets Nos. 1–4, BWV 802/805; Fugue in E flat, BWV 552/2). 18 Leipzig chorales, BWV 651–668; 6 Concertos after other composers, BWV 592/7; Fugue on the Magnificat, BWV 733.* (4 discs)

Volume 4: *Aria in F after Couperin, BWV 587; The Art of Fugue, BWV 1080; Chorales & Chorale preludes: BWV 668a; 690–695, 700, 705–707, 708–711, 712–715, 716, 718–720, 722–724, 726–727, 728–732, 734–736, 737, 740, 738, 741–744, 746, 751–752, 755, 757–758, 760–763, 765, 795–796; Fughettas on: Christum wir sollen loben schon, BWV 696; Gelobet seist du, Jesu Christ, BWV 697; Herr Christ, der ein'ge Gottes Sohn, BWV 698; Nun komm' der Heiden Heiland, BWV 699; Vom himmel hoch, BWV 701; Das Jesulein soll doch mein Trost, BWV 702; Gottes Sohn ist kommen, BWV 703; Lob sei dem allmächt'gen Gott, BWV 704; Allein Gott in der Höh' sei Ehr', BWV 716; Fantasia in C, BWV 570; Fantasia and fugue in A min., BWV 561; Fantasia con imitazione in B min., BWV 563; Fugues: in G, BWV 576; in D, BWV 580; Kleine harmonisches Labyrinth, BWV 591; Preludes in C, BWV 567; in A min., BWV 569; Prelude and fugue in A min., BWV 551; Trio from Cantata BWV 166, BWV 584; Trio after Fasch, BWV 585.* (4 discs)

☞ (B) *** Ph. 438 170-2 (16) [id.]. Wolfgang Rübsam (organs of Frauenfeld & Freiburg).

Wolfgang Rübsam made his highly recommendable complete survey at the beginning of the 1970s, using two organs. He recorded the bulk of the music on the fine instrument at St Nikolaus in Frauenfeld, Switzerland, which had been rebuilt by Metzler Söhne in 1969. For the chorale preludes and fughettas and a few miscellaneous works on CDs 14 and 15 he turned to the Belgian Hockhois organ at Freiburg Münster, which had also been rebuilt in the 1960s by Marcussen & Son of Denmark. Sonically the results are highly stimulating and in works calling for a wide range of colour, including the *Leipzig chorales, Orgelbüchlein,* and the chorale variants of all kinds, one could not ask for more suitable reeds or more innocent piping in flute stops, while there is plenty of supporting weight in the pedals. While the *cantus firmus* is always apparent in the chorale divisions, its prominence is never exaggerated. The *Chorale partitas* move on agreeably, if without quite the momentum displayed by Christopher Herrick. The *Schübler chorales* are most successful, with *Wachet auf* managed without the lumpy rhythmic framework affected by some players. The *Trio sonatas* are especially attractive and compare well with Simon Preston's highly praised set (see below) in both their luminous palette and their liveliness. The six solo *Concertos* based on music of others, principally Ernst and Vivaldi, are comparably successful, although here Rübsam adopts extreme tempi, with adagios very measured against sprightly allegros. The so-called *German Organ Mass,* in essence a further collection of chorales, some extensively varied but many quite simply presented, framed by the mighty *Prelude and fugue in E flat,* BWV 552, is by no means heavy-going, while in *The Art of Fugue* Rübsam generally choses a brighter, somewhat swifter (but by no means hurried) presentation of the *Contrapuncti* as compared to his more recent, Naxos set – see below. They are given in their original numbered order, followed by the *Canons* and ending with the incomplete final fugue.

But the key to the success of any Bach survey must lie with the way the performer approaches the large-scale concert pieces, notably the *Preludes and fugues* and *Toccatas and fugues,* and these are nearly all in the first volume. This opens with the most famous work of all in D minor, BWV 565, which is certainly a success. Rübsam is particularly adept with the earlier works dating from Bach's Arnstadt and Weimar periods which are attractively spirited and spontaneous. Some of these are available as a separate recital, which has been around for some time and has been highly praised by us – see below. The *Dorian Toccata,* BWV 538, which opens disc 2 is full of vigour. Certainly in these works Rübsam is consistently more vital than Rogg, and his registration often tickles the ear (as, for instance, in the *Prelude in A minor,* BWV 543, and the *A major Prelude and fugue,* BWV 536) or it can be majestic and massive without congealing (BWV 547). The *Fugue on a theme by Corelli* is a good example of how clearly inner lines emerge, while the *E major Toccata and fugue,* BWV 566, which opens disc 4, is a good example of Rübsam's apt control of tempi, and the extrovert *Pedal-Exercitium* brings a vigorously robust spirit. The famous *Toccata, adagio and fugue,* BWV 564, is equally well judged, a work that can easily become ponderous, while the *Passacaglia in C minor,* BWV 582, has a convincing forward momentum and plenty of imaginative detail. The set comes on 16 bargain-priced CDs, laid out in four boxes of four CDs within a slipcase. The documentation is excellent, far preferable to that provided with Peter Hurford's Decca survey, which is at mid-price and involves an extra CD.

Lionel Rogg Harmonia Mundi series

Volume 1: *Fugues, BWV 575, 577–9; Preludes & fugues, BWV 531–535, 539, 549, 550 & 553.* (HMX 290772)

Volume 2. *Toccatas & fugues, BWV 538 (Dorian), 540, 565–5; Toccata, adagio & fugue, BWV 564.* (HMX 290773)

Volume 3. *Allabreve, BWV 586; Canzone, BWV 588; Chorale partitas: Christ, der du bist der helle Tag, BWV 766; O Gott, du frommer Gott, BWV 767; Sei gegrüsset Jesu gütig, BWV 768; Pastorale, BWV 590.* (HMX 290774)

Volumes 4/5. *Orgelbüchlein: Chorales BWV 599–643; Chorale preludes BWV, 653b, 720, 727, 734, 736–7.* (HMX 290775/6)

Volume 6. *Fantasias, BWV 562 & 572; Fantasias & fugues, BWV 537 & 542; Fuguettas on chorales, BWV 696–9, 701, 703–4; Fugue on the Magnificat; Passacaglia and fugue, BWV 582.* (HMX 290777)

Volumes 7/8. *Leipzig chorale preludes, BWV 651–668; Chorale preludes BWV 690–1, 706, 709–713, 714, 717–718, 731, 738.* (HMX 290778/9)

Volume 9. *6 Trio Sonatas, BWV 525–530.* (HMX 290780)

Volumes 10/11. *Prelude, BWV 552; German organ mass, BWV 669–689; Fugue, BWV 552b; Canonic variations on Vom Himmel hoch, BWV 769; 6 Schübler chorales, BWV 645/50.* (HMX 290781/2)

Volume 11/12. *Preludes & fugues, BWV 536, 541, 543–548.* (HMX 290783)

☞ (BB) ** HM 290772/83 (12) [id.].

The Bach scholar, Lionel Rogg, made his second survey of Bach's organ music for Harmonia Mundi at Arlesheim in 1970 and he has provided his own extensive notes about the music and the historical and personal background against which it was written. The chosen Silberman organ is admirably suited to the repertoire and has the widest range of baroque timbre. But Rogg does not register flamboyantly. He is less concerned with colour in any orchestral sense, and the result is relatively restrained but almost always apt, and in its unostentatious fashion it serves the music well. He is at his best in the Arnstadt *Preludes and fugues* in Volume 1, early works written when the young Bach was in his teens and early twenties. Although even here Rogg is never carried away by exuberance, he registers the famous *G major Fugue* (BWV 577) and the *'Little' Fugue in G minor* brightly and effectively. The *Toccatas and fugues* are strong but not flamboyant, though not lacking tension or momentum and, like all other organists, Rogg indulges himself in piquant registration for the charming *Pastorale*, BWV 590. The *Chorale partitas* each open with a bold, fully registered presentation of the chorale, then the variations are deftly coloured in pastel shades; and Rogg, without being pedantic, is always concerned that the chorale outline is clearly defined, and this applies equally to the *Orgelbüchlein* and especially the miscellaneous chorales also included in Volume 5. In the *Fuguettas* based on chorales in Volume 6, however intricate the argument, the chorale tune can always be heard. In this respect Rogg's registration, which is never dull, is masterly. This particular volume opens with the *Passacaglia and fugue in C minor*, BWV 582, and Rogg's grave, indeed sombre, presentation establishes his seriousness of purpose which pervades the whole architecture of the 14-minute piece, the tempo held steady throughout and Rogg's eyes clearly set on the final cadence. The *Leipzig Chorale preludes* follow the established Rogg pattern of clear, mellow registration with the chorale theme kept unexaggeratedly to the fore, and they cause one to reflect that the presentation here is excessively sober and a somewhat more flamboyant approach would not be out of place. The *Trio sonatas* are in no way extrovert either. They are pleasantly registered, although a little more glowing Italianate colour might be welcome, but even the movements marked *Vivace* are relatively restrained; indeed Rogg does better with the marking *Un poco allegro* for the finale of No. 4, which is on the way to being jaunty. In the *German organ mass*, where one might have expected a more intensely expressive style, Rogg is content to let the music speak for itself. He is again at his very best in Volume 11, varying the mood and colour of the six *Schübler chorales* very tellingly (for all their relative sobriety, these are among the most individual versions available). The *Canonic variations* on the Christmas chorale, *Vom Himmel hoch*, build from the simplest opening to an exultant climax and here, for once, Rogg really lets himself go for it. The last disc offers the later *Preludes and fugues*, and they are played simply and straightforwardly. Everything is laid out clearly, with reliable architectural control, and the unforced momentum confirms that Rogg seldom seeks to achieve a cumulative emotional thrust, even at the end of the fugues. One senses that he feels that increase of tension lies in the structure of the music itself. This will please those who like their Bach straight and without any overlay of rhetoric. The recording, truthful but unspectacular, suits the manner of the music-making and the discs are inexpensive.

Kevin Bowyer Nimbus series

Aria in F (after Couperin), *BWV 587; Concerto in A min.* (after Vivaldi), *BWV 593; Fugue in G, BWV 576; Prelude and fugue in D min., BWV 539; Toccata and fugue in F, BWV 540.*
☞ *** Nimbus Dig. NI 5400 [id.]. Kevin Bowyer (Marcussen organ of Sct. Hans Kirke, Odense, Denmark).

Chorale partita: Sei gegrüsset, Jesu gütig, BWV 768; Concerto in D min. after Vivaldi, BWV 596; Preludes and fugues: in F min., BWV 534; in F min., BWV 543. ·
☞ **(*) Nimbus NI 5290 [id.]. Kevin Bowyer (Marcussen organ of Sct. Hans Kirke, Odense, Denmark).

Chorale preludes: Aus tiefer Not schrei ich zu dir, BWV 1099; Erbarm' dich mein, O Herre Gott, BWV 721; Concerto in G (after Prince Johann Ernst), *BWV 592; Fantasia and fugue in G min., BWV 542; Trio sonata No. 1 in E flat, BWV 525.*
☞ *** Nimbus Dig. NI 5280 [id.]. Kevin Bowyer (Marcussen organ of Sct. Hans Kirke, Odense, Denmark).

Kevin Bowyer is another of the younger generation of organists who is embarking on a complete Bach survey, but he has chosen to produce a series of carefully planned recitals rather than grouping works together in their respective genres. For the collector this may bring the problem of duplication unless the intention is to acquire the whole series, but the advantage is that each CD can be enjoyed as an individual recital. Characteristically, the Nimbus engineers produce a sound-image with plenty of ambience, with glowing, colourful pipings and throaty reeds, the effect often expansively grand.

The first volume in the series (NI 5280) sets the pattern by framing a collection of lighter pieces and chorale preludes with two ambitious major works. Bowyer's opening *Toccata and fugue in D minor* is second to none, the Toccata strong yet improvisational in feeling; then, after a solemn cadence, the fugue is vividly brilliant with a powerful apotheosis. The sound is magnificently rich in colour. After a mellow chorale prelude (*Aus tiefer*), the solo *Concerto*, arranged from a jolly piece by the amateur composer, Prince Ernst, and the equally diverting and Italianate *Trio sonata*, we have the charmingly registered *Pastorella*, its siciliano given varied treatment in four sections, with the final *Gigue* especially captivating. The solemn chorale prelude, *Erbarm' dich mein, O Herre Gott*, is capped by the rhythmically strong *G minor Fantasia* with its strikingly florid opening and rich closing cadence, with the following fugue vibrantly cheerful and ending simply.

Volume 3 (NI 5290) seems slightly less successful overall than some of Bowyer's collections, with a rather easy-going approach to the *Sei gegrüsset variations* and the Vivaldi concerto, too, not as sprightly as it might be. The framing *Preludes and fugues* are powerful and vigorous, especially the closing *A minor*, but the recording seems fractionally brighter than usual and the reeds just a trifle grainy.

Volume 5 in the series (NI 5400) begins with Bach's arrangement of Vivaldi, the *Concerto in A minor*, opening jauntily, and almost immediately brings some engaging fluting in the glowing registration, as does the brightly extrovert *Fugue in G*. The colouring of the chorale preludes is nicely varied, *Herr Gott, dich loben wir* suitably massive, *Christ ist erstanden* grave and darkly coloured; but the others bring more gentle contrast. The *Prelude and fugue in D minor* again has an improvisational thoughtfulness, while the closing Weimar *Toccata and fugue in F* is vigorously articulated and suitably resplendent and weighty. The expansive recording provides a broad canvas but with the lighter detail bright and clear.

Chorale preludes: Ein feste Burg ist unser Gott, BWV 720; Gelobet seist du, Jesu Christ, BWV 697 & BWV 722; In dulci jubilo, BWV 751 & BWV 729; Vom Himmel hoch, BWV 738; Fugue (Gigue) in G, BWV 577; Prelude and fugues: in D, BWV 532; in G, BWV 541; Trio sonata No. 5 in C, BWV 529.
☞ *** Nimbus Dig. NI 5289 [id.]. Kevin Bowyer (Marcussen organ of Sct. Hans Kirke, Odense, Denmark).

Fantasia & imitatio in B min., BWV 563; Fugue in C min., BWV 575; 2 Fugues on themes of Albinoni: in A & B min., BWV 950/1; 8 Short Preludes and fugues, BWV 553/60; Toccatas: in G min., BWV 915; in G, BWV 915.
☞ ⊕ *** Nimbus Dig. NI 5377 [id.]. Kevin Bowyer (Marcussen organ of Sct. Hans Kirke, Odense, Denmark).

Volume 2 of Kevin Bowyer's survey (NI 5289), a predominantly cheerful programme, brings more examples of his lively rhythmic style and the appealing colours and husky reeds of this fine Danish organ. After the spirited *G major Prelude and fugue*, the *Trio Sonata* is enjoyably light and appealing, and the dancing *G major 'Gigue' Fugue* is equally spontaneous although here the reverberation means that the focus is not absolutely sharp. The *Prelude and fugue in A* is also infectiously extrovert. The juxtaposition of the two settings both of *In dulci jubilo* and of *Gelobet seist du* in each case brings a striking contrast, with the first piquant and the second massively expansive. The closing *Prelude and fugue in D* opens with vigorous gusto and, after the enormously arresting and elaborate cadence of the prelude, the fugue itself generates great energy, with the ample Odense acoustic adding to the impact.

Volume 4 is even more stimulating, opening with the brilliantly flamboyant *Toccata in G minor* which, after its thoughtful centrepiece, encapsulates a bouncing, minor-key version of the *'Gigue' fugue*. This is marvellously played; yet the highlight of the recital is surely the set of *Short Preludes and fugues*, BWV 553/60, conceived by Bach in pedagogical style and planned in an ascending scale of major and minor keys from C major to B flat. In Bowyer's imaginative hands they burst into spontaneous life and their scholarly base merely underpins a series of pieces which seem infinitely varied in tempo and style (and, of course, registration), with the final *Prelude* producing a dazzling series of bravura pedal solos before giving forth to its vigorous fugue. Of the other items, the energetically florid *Fugue in C minor* is brightly registered and the two Albinoni-based works are very agreeable. The *Fantasia and imitatio in B minor* makes a charming interlude, again showing the organ's flutey woodwind colouring. Finally the three-part Weimar *G minor Toccata* again opens with cascading brilliance, leading to a quietly reflective arioso, then closes the programme with sprightly, dancing 6/8 exuberance (obviously G major set Bach's feet a-tapping). The bright, clear recording seems ideally judged, cleaner in focus than the earlier Nimbus CDs in this fine series. There are few more invigorating Bach organ recitals than this.

Christopher Herrick Hyperion series
Canonic variations: Vom Himmel hoch, BWV 679; Chorale partitas: Christ, der du bist der helle Tag, BWV 766; O Gott, du frommer Gott, BWV 767; Sei gegrüsset, Jesu gütig, BWV 767/768; Ach, was soll ich Sünder machen, BWV 770.
☞ *** Hyp. Dig. CDA 66455 [id.]. Christopher Herrick (organ of St Nicholas Church, Bremgarten, Switzerland).

Christopher Herrick is very much of the new generation of organists, giving equal precedence to momentum and vitality and colourful registration, alongside a feeling for the musical architecture. There is certainly no lack of momentum here, and in his hands the splendid Metzler organ at Bremgarten illuminates Bach's intricate divisions with a wide colouristic range. Herrick always keeps the music moving and in the *Chorale partitas* this is to advantage. Certainly the recording does the organ justice in vivid palette and truthful balance, and the music-making is consistently alive.

Fantasias: in C min., BWV 562; in G min., BWV 572; in C min., BWV 537; in G min., BWV 542; Preludes and fugues: in A, BWV 536; in A min., BWV 543; in B min., BWV 544; in C, BWV 545; in C min., BWV 546; in C, BWV 547; in D, BWV 532; in E min. (Wedge), BWV 548; in E flat (St Anne), BWV 552; in F min., BWV 534; in G, BWV 541.
☞ *** Hyp. Dig. CDA 66791/2 [id.]. Christopher Herrick (organ of Jesuits' Church, Lucerne).

Among all the complete sets and individual mixed recitals, this very imposing two-disc set centres on some of the most powerfully structured and intellectually cogent of all Bach's major organ works. Christopher Herrick offers a presentation which is obviously built on a background of careful preparation, with a spontaneously vivid presentation that never gives an impression of the music simply 'trundling on' and is as emotionally compelling as it is authoritative, with each fugue moving on to a gripping apotheosis. The chosen Swiss instrument seems ideal for the repertoire and it is superbly recorded, giving weight, amplitude and clarity in equal measure.

Passacaglia in C min., BWV 582; Toccatas and fugues: in D min. (Dorian), BWV 538; in D min., BWV 565; in F, BWV 540; Toccata, adagio and fugue in C, BWV 564.
☞ *** Hyp. Dig. CDA 66434 [id.]. Christopher Herrick (Metzler organ of Stadkirche, Zofingen, Switzerland).

These are all powerfully structured yet attractively lively performances. Christopher Herrick yet again is obviously determined not to get bogged down with the pedagogues, and his forward thrust is consistently impressive: the famous *D minor* work certainly sparkles yet does not lack power, while the *Fugue in C major* which follows on after the *Toccata and adagio*, BWV 564, is not too heavy.

Similarly the *Passacaglia in C minor* has gravitas without seeming too sombre and is glowingly decorated. This collection is not for those who consider that solemn consideration and architectural deliberation are a first priority in these pieces, for both BWV 582 and BWV 564 can sound more granite-like, if not more compelling in their underlying vitality. The recording has fine spectacle and realism.

Trio sonatas Nos. 1–6, BWV 525/30.
☞ *** Hyp. Dig. CDA 66390 [id.]. Christopher Herrick (Metzler organ of St Nicholas Church, Bremgarten, Switzerland).

As a recent Philips recording by Daniel Chorzempa too readily demonstrated, these works can too easily sound mellifluous and sensationally boring. But not here. Herrick's performances are comparatively relaxed, but the playing has plenty of lift and he produces colours in slow movements to charm the ear, with the lyrical lines flowing. He has an instrument well suited to this repertoire and he is in full command of its palette, with registration suited to the character of each movement and articulation that is precise without pedantry. The Hyperion recording, too, cannot be faulted, and even the order of works is chosen to make the most of their variety of style.

Peter Hurford Decca series
Volume 1: *Fantasias, BWV 562, 570, 572; Fantasias & fugues, BWV 537, 542, 561; Fugues, BWV 575/577, 579, 581, 946; Kleines harmonisches Labyrinth, BWV 591; Passacaglia & fugue, BWV 582; Pedal-Exercitium, BWV 598; Preludes & fugues, BWV 531/533, 535, 548/551; Toccata, adagio & fugue, BWV 564; Toccatas & fugues, BWV 538, 540, 565; Trios, BWV 583, 585.*
(M) *** Decca 421 337-2 (3) [id.]. Peter Hurford (organs of Ratzeburg Cathedral, Germany, Church of Our Lady of Sorrows, Toronto).

Volume 2: *Chorale preludes, BWV 672/675, 677, 681, 683, 685, 687, 689; 24 Kirnberger Chorale preludes, BWV 690/713; Clavier-Ubung, Part 3: German organ Mass (Prelude & fugue in E flat, BWV 552 & Chorale preludes, BWV 669/671, 676, 678, 680, 682, 684, 686, 688); 6 Trio sonatas, BWV 525/530.*
(M) *** Decca 421 341-2 (3) [id.]. Peter Hurford (organs of Chapels at New College, Oxford, & Knox Grammar School, Sydney; Church of Our Lady of Sorrows, Toronto; Ratzeburg Cathedral).

Volume 3: *Canonic variations: Vom Himmel hoch, BWV 769; Chorale partitas: Christ, der du bist; O Gott, du frommer Gott; Sei gegrüsset, Jesu gütig, BWV 766/768; Chorale preludes, BWV 726/740; Schübler chorale preludes, BWV 645/650; Chorale variations: Ach, was soll ich sünder machen; Allein Gott in der Höh' sei Ehr, BWV 770/771. Concertos Nos. 1–6, BWV 592/597.*
✪ (M) *** Decca 421 617-2 (3) [id.]. Peter Hurford (organs as above, & Melk Abbey, Austria, and Eton College, Windsor).

Volume 4: *35 Arnstadt chorale preludes, BWV 714, 719, 742, 957 & 1090/1120 (from Yale manuscript, copied Neumeister); 18 Leipzig chorale preludes, BWV 651/58. Chorale preludes, BWV 663/668 & BWV 714/725.*
(M) *** Decca Dig./Analogue 421 621-2 (3) [id.]. Peter Hurford (Vienna Bach organ, Augustinerkirche, Vienna, & organs of All Souls' Unitarian Church, Washington, DC, St Catharine's College Chapel, Cambridge, Ratzeburg Cathedral, Knox Grammar School, Sydney, and Eton College, Windsor).

Volume 5: *Allabreve in D, BWV 589; Aria in F, BWV 587; Canzona in D min., BWV 588; Fantasias, BWV 563 & BWV 571; Fugues, BWV 574, BWV 578 & BWV 580; Musical offering, BWV 1079: Ricercar. Pastorale, BWV 590; Preludes, BWV 567/569; Preludes & fugues, BWV 534, 535a (incomplete), BWV 536, BWV 539, BWV 541, BWV 543/547; 8 Short Preludes & fugues, BWV 553/560; Prelude, trio & fugue, BWV 545b; Toccata & fugue in E, BWV 566; Trios, BWV 584, BWV 586 & BWV 1027a.*
(M) *** Decca 425 631-2 (3). Peter Hurford (organs of the Church of Our Lady of Sorrows, Toronto; Ratzeburg Cathedral; Eton College, Windsor; St Catharine's College Chapel, Cambridge; New College, Oxford; Domkirche, St Pölten, Austria; Stiftskirche, Melk, Austria; Knox Grammar School, Sydney).

Volume 6: *Chorale preludes Nos. 1–46 (Orgelbüchlein), BWV 599/644. Chorale preludes, BWV 620a, BWV 741/748, BWV 751/2, BWV 754/5, BWV 757/763, BWV 765, BWV Anh. 55; Fugue in G min., BWV 131a.*
(M) *** Decca 425 635-2 (2) [id.]. Peter Hurford (organs of the Church of Our Lady of Sorrows, Toronto; St Catharine's College Chapel, Cambridge; Eton College, Windsor).

With the exception of the *Arnstadt chorale preludes*, which were added in 1986 (and are digital), Peter Hurford recorded his unique survey of Bach's organ music for Decca's Argo label over a period of eight years, 1974–1982. Performances are consistently fresh and engrossing in their spontaneity; there is no slackening of tension and the registration features a range of baroque colour that is almost orchestral in its diversity.

Anyone wishing to explore the huge range of this repertoire could hardly do better than begin with one of these boxes, and perhaps a good jumping-off point would be Volume 3, to which we award a token Rosette: this includes many of the *Chorale preludes* and *Chorale variations*, in particular the splendid half-dozen chorales which were published at the very end of Bach's life and which commemorate the name of an otherwise unknown music-engraver called Schübler. The only real drawback to these otherwise admirable reissues is their sparse documentation. The organ specifications are included, but too little about the music itself.

Organ collections

Adagio in C (from BWV 565); Chorales: Herzlich tut mich verlangen, BWV 727; Liebster Jesu, BWV 730; Wachet auf, BWV 645; Fantasia and fugue in G min., BWV 542; Fugue in E flat (St Anne), BWV 552; Passacaglia and fugue in C min., BWV 582; Toccata and fugue in D min., BWV 565.
(M) *** Decca 417 711-2 [id.]. Peter Hurford (various organs).

An admirable popular recital. Performances are consistently alive and the vivid recording projects them strongly. A self-recommending issue.

Allabreve in D, BWV 589; Chorale prelude: Ach Gott und Herr, BWV 714; Preludes and fugues, BWV 532 and BWV 553/560; Toccata and fugue in D min., BWV 565.
*** Mer. ECD 84081 [id.]. David Sanger (organ of St Catherine's College, Cambridge).

The organ at St Catherine's College, Cambridge, was completely rebuilt in 1978/9. The result is a great success, and its reedy clarity and brightness of timbre are especially suitable for Bach. David Sanger's playing throughout is thoughtful and well structured; registration shows an excellent sense of colour without being flamboyant.

35 Arnstadt chorale preludes, BWV 714, 719, 742, 957 & 1090/1120. Chorale prelude, BWV 639; Preludes and fugues: in C, BWV 531; in D min., BWV 549a; in G min., BWV 535; in E, BWV 566.
*** ASV Gaudeamus Dig. CD GAU 120/121 (available separately). Graham Barber (organ of St Peter Mancroft, Norwich).

33 Arnstadt chorale preludes (from Yale manuscript).
(B) *** HM Dig. HMA 905158 [id.]. Joseph Payne (organ of St Paul's, Brookline, Mass.).

Graham Barber seems ideally suited to this early Bach repertoire, with the *Preludes and fugues* used to frame two separate recitals of the *Chorales*. Barber plays these opening and closing pieces with splendid vitality and structural grip, and presents the chorale variants simply and effectively, constantly changing colours and sound-weighting. The recording is very much in the demonstration class.

Joseph Payne collects the complete set together on a single CD and is very economically priced. Now reissued on Harmonia Mundi's budget Musique d'Abord label, this is even more attractive.

The Art of fugue, BWV 1080.
☞ *** Erato/Warner Dig. 4509 91946-2 [id.]. Marie-Claire Alain (organ of Saint-Martin à Masevaux, Haut-Rhin).

The Art of fugue, BWV 1080; Chorale partita: Sei gegrüsset Jesu gütig, BWV 768; Passacaglia in C min., BWV 582.
☞ (BB) **(*) Naxos Dig. 8.550703/4 [id.]. Wolfgang Rübsam (Flenthop organ of Duke Chapel, Duke University, Durham, USA).

Marie-Claire Alain has at Saint-Martin à Masevaux an almost ideal instrument for presenting *The Art of fugue*, with a clear focus and a wide range of effective colouring. The digital recording provides an excellent focus and her performance is admirable.

Wolfgang Rübsam, too, has a fine instrument at his disposal and, excellent Bach player that he is, the work's detail is admirably displayed. Both artists alter the order of presentation of the Contrapuncti. Rübsam, of course, has the advantage of economy and offers two substantial bonuses. However, both these works are played very slowly and deliberately indeed. The timing here for the *Sei gegrüsset chorale partita* is 25 minutes (against Herrick's 16 minutes), while the *Passacaglia* is quite remorseless, and takes 19 minutes (against Herrick's 13 minutes or Rübsam's own earlier Philips version which is 12 minutes 21 seconds).

Chorale partita on Sei gegrüsset, Jesu gütig, BWV 768; Prelude and fugue in D, BWV 532; Prelude in G, BWV 568; Sonata No. 4 in E min., BWV 528.
*** Denon Dig. C37 7376 [id.]. Jacques Van Oortmerssen (organ of Waalse Kerk, Amsterdam).

The organ of the Waalse Kerk is a magnificent instrument. The playing here, always alive, is traditional in the best sense, and the CD recording is superbly realistic. A most rewarding recital.

Chorale preludes Nos. 1–45 (Orgelbüchlein), BWV 599–644 (complete).
*** DG Dig. 431 816-2 [id.]. Simon Preston (organ of Sorø Abbey, Denmark).

Simon Preston conveniently gathers all 45 chorales of the *Orgelbüchlein* on to a single (74-minute) CD and plays them with persuasive musicianship on a fine Danish organ.

Chorale preludes: Ich ruf' zu dir, Herr Jesu Christ, BWV 639; Nun komm der Heiden Heiland, BWV 659; Schübler chorale: Wachet auf, BWV 645; Fantasia and fugue in G min., BWV 542; Partita: O Gott, du frommer Gott, BWV 767; Prelude and fugue in E flat (St Anne), BWV 552; Toccata and fugue in D min., BWV 565.
*** Novalis Dig. 150 005-2 [id.]. Ton Koopman (Christian Müller organ, Waalse Kerk, Amsterdam).

Ton Koopman opens with three of Bach's most powerfully structured works for this instrument. The three chorales make a contrasting centrepiece. For the most popular of all Bach's organ pieces Ton Koopman then changes to a more flamboyant style. The organ is itself a 'co-star' of the programme, producing magnificent, unclouded sonorities. The recording is in the demonstration bracket, the microphones in exactly the right place for a proper illusion of reality.

Chorale preludes: Vater unser im Himmelreich, BWV 682; Jesu Christus, unser Heiland, BWV 688; Fantasia in G, BWV 572; Partita: Sei gegrüsset, Jesu gütig, BWV 768; Prelude and fugue in A min., BWV 543; Toccata and fugue in D min. (Dorian), BWV 538; Trio sonata in G, BWV 530.
*** Novalis Dig. 150 036-2 [id.]. Ton Koopman (organ of Grote Kerk, Leeuwarden).

Another outstanding recital, extremely well played and splendidly recorded, using an organ admirably suited to Bach's music. The programme runs for over 70 minutes and is very well laid out for continuous listening.

Concertos (for solo organ) Nos. 1 in G (after ERNST: *Concerto); 2 in A min. (after* VIVALDI: *Concerto, Op. 3/8); 3 in C (after* VIVALDI: *Concerto, Op. 7/11); 4 in C (after* ERNST: *Concerto); 5 in D min. (after* VIVALDI: *Concerto, Op. 3/11), BWV 592/6.*
*** DG Dig. 423 087-2 [id.]. Simon Preston (organ of Lübeck Cathedral).

It was Prince Johann Ernst who introduced Bach to the Italian string concertos; these are Bach's arrangements, with the music for the most part left with little alteration or embellishment. The two Ernst works show a lively and inventive if not original musicianship. The performances are first class and the recording admirably lucid and clear, yet with an attractively resonant ambience.

Fantasia in C min., BWV 562; Fantasia in G, BWV 572; Preludes and fugues: in A min., BWV 543; in D, BWV 532; Toccata, adagio and fugue in C, BWV 564. Toccatas and fugues: in D min. (Dorian), BWV 538; in D min., BWV 565.
☞ (M) *** Decca 436 225-2 [id.]. Peter Hurford (organs of Church of Our Lady of Sorrows, Toronto; Chapel of New College, Oxford; Ratzeburg Cathedral, Germany).

Another splendid recital culled from Peter Hurford's integral Bach recordings, made in the late 1970s, and, even though it duplicates the ubiquitous BWV 565, the 75-minute programme is highly recommendable for its colour, power and rhythmic felicity, which so often brings a sense almost of fantasy. The vividly projected sound is always excellent and usually on a demonstration level; there is just a hint of harshness at the opening of the *D major Prelude*.

Fantasia and fugue in G min., BWV 542; Passacaglia and fugue in C min., BWV 582; 6 Schübler chorales, BWV 645/50; Toccata, adagio and fugue in C, BWV 564; Toccata and fugue in F, BWV 540.
⊛ *** DG Dig. 435 381-2 [id.]. Simon Preston (Sauer organ in St Peter's, Waltrop, near Dortmund).

Simon Preston's recital at St Peter's, Waltrop, is a magnificent demonstration of the splendour and power of Bach's more ambitious organ statements, admirably contrasted with music which is inherently less weighty, if not less inspired. The engaging *Schübler chorales* are used to provide contrast at the centre of the 71-minute recital, and Preston chooses a lighter, more pointed style than usual. The Sauer organ in Waltrop is a modern instrument (1984) of splendid range, with a diversity of colour that is ideal for baroque repertoire and Bach in particular. There is an enormous reserve of power in the pedals, and the richer sonorities elsewhere bring no attendant clouding. This is one of the very finest Bach collections of the digital CD era.

Passacaglia and fugue in C min., BWV 582; Toccata, adagio and fugue in C, BWV 564; Toccatas and fugues: in D min., BWV 565; in E, BWV 566; 6 Schübler chorales, BWV 645.
☞ (B) ** Erato/Warner 2292 45922-2 [id.]. Marie-Claire Alain (organ).

Marie-Claire Alain's playing here is bold and secure. The organ is unnamed – the documentation in this Erato Bonsai series is totally inadequate – but the reeds have a characteristic French brightness. There is exuberance in the most famous *D minor Toccata and fugue* and a proper sense of weight and power in the great *C minor Passacaglia*; BWV 564 is also impressive. But the *Schübler chorales* have a rhythmic 'jerkiness' (especially *Wachet auf*, which is prone to such over-characterization) that is not entirely felicitous. This playing has more spontaneity than Alain's newer, digital Bach records.

8 Little Preludes and fugues, BWV 553/560; Prelude and fugue in D, BWV 532; Toccata, adagio & fugue in C, BWV 564; Trio sonata No. 1 in E flat, BWV 525.
*** ASV Novalis Dig. 150 066-2; *150 066-4* [id.]. Ton Koopman (organ of Grote Kerk, Maassluis).

Ton Koopman's continuing series never fails to stimulate, and this is one of the very finest of his recitals, demonstrating a magnificent instrument, highly suitable for Bach, of which he is completely the master. The digital recording is first rate: Bach organ records don't come any better than this.

6 Trio sonatas, BWV 525/530.
☞ *** DG Dig. 437 835-2 [id.]. Simon Preston (Klais organ in St Katharina's, Blankenburg, near Bonn).

Enjoyable as is Christopher Herrick's Hyperion recording of the *Trio Sonatas* (see above), Simon Preston's performances are even more attractive. The sounds made by the Blankenburg organ are a sheer delight, with glowing colours giving a halo-like incandescence in slow movements – the *Adagio e dolce* of No. 3 is a delightfully example – while the reeds bring a touch more baroque bite to add character to the allegros, where Preston is always buoyant. Indeed the recording is in the demonstration bracket. The six sonatas are played in numerical order to good effect.

VOCAL MUSIC

Cantatas (for Easter): *Nos. 1: Wie schön leuchtet der Morgenstern; 4: Christ lag in Todesbanden; 6: Bleib bei uns, denn es will Abend werden; 12: Weinen, Klagen, Sorgen, Zagen; 23: Du wahrer Gott und Davids Sohn; 67: Halt im Gedächtnis Jesum Christ; 87: Bisher habt ihr nichts gebeten in meinem Namen; 92: Ich habe in Gottes Herz und Sinn; 104: Du Hirte Israel, hörel; 108: Es ist euch gut, dass ich hingehe; 126: Erhalt uns, Herr, bei deinem Wort; 158: Der Friede sei mit dir; 182: Himmelskönig, wei Willkommen.*
☞ (B) ** DG 439 374-2 (5) [id.]. Edith Mathis, Anna Reynolds, Hertha Töpper, Peter Schreier, Ernst Haefliger, Dietrich Fischer-Dieskau, Theo Adam, Munich Bach Ch. & O, Karl Richter.

DG's Archiv label have currently made a major reissue from Karl Richter's series of Bach's cantata recordings, made over the years. Thanks to Karl Richter, we had the most comprehensive survey of Bach cantatas ever to be put on record before the ambitious Harnoncourt/Leonhardt venture got into its stride. The present reissues are grouped into five bargain boxes, the first three centring on the three key celebrations of the Church year and Volumes 4 and 5 covering the middle and later Sundays after Trinity. The set of thirteen cantatas in Volume 2 are all linked by the theme of Easter and the Passion. The performances are variable, some being impressive and spacious, others less sensitive. In No. 4, the chorale melody is quoted in plain or varied form in each movement and dominates proceedings. This is a cantata which, given the wrong approach, can all too readily sound dull and sombre, but Richter seems wholly in sympathy with the work and secures some splendid and dignified playing from the orchestra. The solo singing is distinguished. There is certainly a dignity about Richter's account of *Du wahrer Gott* (No. 23) but this sometimes spills over into pomposity; nor does his reading of *Bisher habt ihr nichts gebeten in meinem Namen* (No. 87) show the imagination and sympathy of which this artist at his best is capable. In spite of distinguished singing from the soloists, there is a Kapellmeisterish quality about both these readings that limits their appeal. However, No. 92 brings an impressive performance. Bach's music has some striking musical imagery and powerfully imaginative invention. Peter Schreier is in splendid form in the tenor arias, in which he defies Satan, and Fischer-Dieskau excites keen admiration in his effortless delivery of an exceptionally demanding (rather instrumentally conceived) line. *Erhalt uns, Herr, bei deinem Wort* (No. 126), on the other hand, is short and dramatic. The performance has fine spirit (the oboi d'amore are superb).

These are merely examples, and there is not space here to detail every performance. Sufficient to say that readers wanting a more vigorous and full-blooded approach to this repertoire than Harnoncourt's and Leonhardt's will find this a welcome offering, particularly as solos are reliable, as indeed is the fine obbligato playing. The digitally remastered transfers sound very good indeed, and collectors need have no worries on that score. Richter, of course, was heavy-handed at times, but he often brought a weight and dignity to this music that are sometimes missing in the more authentic versions.

Volume 1: *Cantatas Nos. 1: Wie schön leuchtet uns der Morgenstern; 2: Ach Gott, vom Himmel; 3: Ach Gott, wie manches Herzeleid; 4: Christ lag in Todesbanden.*
(M) *** Teldec/Warner 2292 42497-2 (2) [id.]. Treble soloists from V. Boys' Ch., Esswood, Equiluz, Van Egmond, V. Boys' Ch., Ch. Viennensis, VCM, Harnoncourt.

Volume 2: (i) *Cantatas Nos. 5: Wo soll ich fliehen hin; 6: Bleib bei uns;* (ii) *7: Christ unser Herr zum Jordan kam; 8: Liebster Gott.*
(M) *** Teldec/Warner 2292 42498-2 (2) [id.]. Esswood, Equiluz, Van Egmond, (i) Treble soloists from V. Boys' Ch., Ch. Viennensis, V. Boys' Ch., VCM, Harnoncourt; (ii) Regensburg treble soloists, King's College Ch., Leonhardt Cons., Leonhardt.

Volume 3: (i) *Cantatas Nos. 9: Es ist das Heil; 10: Meine Seele erhebt den Herrn;* (ii) *11: Lobet Gott in seinen Reichen.*
(M) *** Teldec/Warner 2292 42499-2 (2) [id.]. Esswood, Equiluz, Van Egmond; (i) Regensburg treble soloists, King's College Ch., Leonhardt Cons., Leonhardt; (ii) Treble soloists from V. Boys' Ch., Ch. Viennensis, V. Boys' Ch., VCM, Harnoncourt.

The remarkable Teldec project, a complete recording of all Bach's cantatas, began in the early 1970s and has now reached completion. The digital remastering has proved consistently successful. The CDs retain the English translations of the texts and excellent notes by Alfred Dürr. The authentic character of the performances means that boys replace women, not only in the choruses but also as soloists, and the size of the forces is confined to what we know Bach himself would have expected. The simplicity of the approach brings its own merits, for the imperfect yet other-worldly quality of some of the treble soloists refreshingly focuses the listener's attention on the music itself. Less appealing is the quality of the violins, which eschew vibrato – and, it would sometimes seem, any kind of timbre! Generally speaking, there is a certain want of rhythmic freedom and some expressive caution. Rhythmic accents are underlined with some regularity and the grandeur of Bach's inspiration is at times lost to view.

Cantatas Nos. (i) *4: Christ lag in Todesbanden;* (ii) *12: Weinen, Klagen, Sorgen Zagen; 51: Jauchzet Gott in allen Landen!; 54: Widerstehe doch der Sünde; 56: Ich will den Kreuzstab gerne tragen; 67: Halt im Gedächtnis Jesum Christ;* (i) *80: Ein feste Burg ist unser Gott; 82: Ich habe genug; 131: Aus der Tiefen rufe ich, Herr, zu dir; 140: Wachet auf, ruft uns die Stimme;* (ii) *143: Lobe den Herrn, meine Seele;* (i) *147: Herz und Mund und Tat und Leben;* (ii) *170: Vergnügte Ruh', beliebte Seelenlust.*
☞ (M) *** Teldec/Warner Analogue/Dig. 4509 92627-2 (4) (from above sets, with Kweksilber, Esswood, Equiluz, Van Egmond, Huttenlocher, soloists, choruses, (i) VCM, Harnoncourt; (ii) Leonhardt Consort Leonhardt).

This box of four CDs is described, fairly enough, as containing *'Favourite cantatas'* and as such makes a good sampler for the Teldec Bach series, warts and all. As it happens, the first cantata included, *Christ lag in Todesbanden*, shows some of the limitations of the 'authentic' approach. It lacks the fullest sense of scale and breadth, but No. 12, *Weinen, klagen, sorgen, zagen* ('weeping, lamenting, worrying, fearing'), has its melancholy sensitively caught; while the joyous *Jauchzet Gott* has an altogether superb soloist in Marianne Kweksilber and, with Don Smithers playing the trumpet obbligato, this is in every way outstanding. Nos. 54 and 56 are also done with distinction. No. 67 is disappointing (the dialogue between the voice of Christ and the chorus is prosaic), and neither *Ein feste Burg* nor *Ich habe genug* are among the more impressive Harnoncourt performances. On the other hand, *Aus der Tiefen rufe ich, Herr, zu dir* ('Out of the deep I have called unto thee, O Lord') is a marvellous, inspired piece whose grave beauty is eloquently conveyed. In No. 140 there are two beautiful duets between treble and bass, representing dialogues between Jesus and the human soul, which are memorably sung. In No. 147 some may be a little disconcerted by the minor swelling effect in the phrasing of *Jesu, joy of man's desiring*, but otherwise the authentic approach brings much to enjoy. Leonhardt is in charge in No. 143, *Lobe den Herrn, meine Seele*, which is unusual in having three horns. He directs with vitality and there is a particularly fine treble contribution from Roger Cericius. No. 170, *Vergnügte Ruh'*, is for alto and instruments and is without a chorus or chorale. There is a moving alto aria, eloquently sung by Paul Esswood who copes with the demanding role very impressively. With excellent sound and first-class documentation, this is well worth considering for those not collecting the series overall.

Cantatas Nos. (i) *4: Christ lag in Todesbanden;* (ii) *78: Jesu, der du meine Seele; 106: Gottes Zeit ist die allerbeste Zeit;* (i) *140: Wachet auf, ruft uns die Stimme!*.

☞ (M) ** Van. 08.9180.2 (2) [id.]. (i) Laurence Dutoit, Equiluz, Braun; (ii) Stich-Randall, Hermann, Dermota, Braun; V. State Chamber Ch. & Op. O, Prohaska.

These recordings are not of recent provenance (no dates are given on the inadequate leaflet) but they are certainly enjoyable. No. 4 has greater spontaneity and fire than the Harnoncourt, though it must of course yield to it in matters of authentic performance practice. No. 78 brings a fine duet from Teresa Stich-Randall and Dagmar Hermann and, like No. 106, has generally impressive solo contributions; No. 140 brings an appealing warmth. The choir is good, accompaniments are well managed and the transfers are fresh and full. But in playing time this is not especially generous, 97 minutes overall.

Cantatas Nos. 4: Christ lag in Todesbanden; 131: Aus der Tiefen rufe ich, Herr, zu dir.

☞ (M) **(*) Erato/Warner 2292 45988-2 [id.]. Kendall, Varcoe, Monteverdi Ch., E. Bar. Soloists, Gardiner.

These recordings, using original instruments and the style of squeezed phrasing associated with 'authenticity' in that period, first appeared in LP form in the early 1980s, linked with other cantatas and the Motets, which are now in a separate (equally desirable) box – see below. The account of one of the best-loved of all the cantatas, *Christ lag in Todesbanden*, is expressively rich, yet Gardiner's lively tempi ensure plenty of life in the music-making. Smooth, natural transfers, though the disc's timing (44 minutes) is not generous.

Cantatas (for the latter part of the Church year) *Nos. 5: Wo soll ich fliehen hin; 26: Ach wie flüchtig, ach wie nichtig; 38: Aus tiefer Not schrei ich zu dir; 55: Ich armer Mensch, ich Sündenknecht; 56: Ich will den Kreuzstab gerne tragen; 60: O Ewigkeit, du Donnerwort; 70: Wachet! betet! betet! wachet!; 80: Ein feste Burg ist unser Gott; 96: Herr Christ, der ein'ge Gottessohn; 106: Gottes Zeit ist die allerbeste Zeit (Actus tragicus); 115: Mache dich, mein Geist, bereit; 116: Du Friedefürst, Herr Jesu Christ; 130: Herr Gott, dich loben alle wir; 139: Wohl dem, der sich auf seinen Gott; 140: Wachet auf, ruft uns die Stimme; 180: Schmücke dich, O liebe Seele*.

☞ (BB) **(*) DG 439 394-2 (5) [id.]. Mathis, Buckel, Schmidt, Töpper, Schreier, Haefliger, Fischer-Dieskau, Adam, Engen, Munich Bach Ch. & O, Karl Richter.

This fifth Richter box collects cantatas that Bach composed for the last ten Sundays of Trinity, plus three others, a Reformation Festival piece (No. 80), a cantata for St Michael's Day (No. 130) and Bach's funeral cantata, *Gottes Zeit* – the so-called *Actus tragicus* (No. 106); it is given a first-rate performance, with fine solo singing and committed direction. Most of these cantatas are chorale-based and nearly all emerge with the dignity and majesty one expects from these forces. They were all recorded in the Munich Herkulessaal, for the most part in 1978, and the sound is warm and spacious. Karl Richter's heavy tread seems over the years to have moderated into a more flexible and human gait, though a certain inflexibility and lack of imagination still surface occasionally. Some of his finest performances are of little-known works. No. 26 (*Ach wie flühchtig*), for instance, has a striking opening chorus, philosophically debating the briefness of man's life-span, in which Richter is suitably spirited. Then later there is a lively tenor aria using the metaphor of a swiftly flowing stream (represented by a flute) which Haefliger manages with great agility and only a few intrusive aitches. Elsewhere there are some odd touches: for example the flute replaces the flauto piccolo in the opening of No. 96, thus diminishing the brilliance of the morning star apostrophized in the text. Richter also opted for the trumpets and drums in *Ein feste Burg* (No. 80), which these days are thought to have been added by Wilhelm Friedemann Bach. Yet the attractions of this survey far outweigh any reservations. There is a vision and breadth to offset the Teutonic heaviness, and the solo singing is a welcome change from the boys who in the rival complete set from Teldec try so manfully to cope with the cruelly demanding soprano parts. Fischer-Dieskau is perhaps too blustery at times, though there are some splendid things from him too, and he is at his most sophisticated in the *Kreuzstab Cantata* (No. 56), one of the earlier recordings, made in 1969. Edith Mathis is altogether excellent, and the

Munich Chorus and Orchestra are obviously thoroughly at home. The CD transfers are admirable.

Cantatas (for the middle Sundays after Trinity) *Nos. 8: Liebster Gott, wann werd'ich sterben?; 9: Es ist das Heil uns kommen her; 17: Wer Dank opfert, der preiset mich; 27: Wer weiss, wie nahe mir mein Ende!; 33: Allein zu dir, Herr Jesu Christ; 45: Es ist dir gesagt, Mensch, was gut ist; 51: Jauchzet Gott in allen Landen; 78: Jesu, der du meine Seele; 100: Was Gott tut, das ist wohlgetan; 102: Herr deine Augen sehen nach dem Glauben; 105: Herr, gehe nicht ins Gericht; 137: Lobe den Herren, den mächtigen König der Ehren; 148: Bringet dem Herrn Ehre seines Namens; 178: Wo Gott der Herr nicht bei uns hält; 179: Siehe zu, dass deine Gottesfurcht nicht Heuchelei sei; 187: Es wartet alles auf dich; 199: Mein Herz schwimmt im Blut.*

☞ (B) **(*) DG 439 387-2 (6) [id.]. Buckel, Mathis, Stader, Hamari, Töpper, Schreier, Haefliger, Van Kesteren, Fischer-Dieskau, Engen, Munich Bach Ch. & O, Karl Richter.

The fourth box in Richter's series runs to six CDs and offers the cantatas composed for the sixth Sunday after Trinity through to the seventeenth. Like the others, it continues the 'unauthentic' approach of Karl Richter and forms a welcome alternative to the Harnoncourt/Leonhardt venture. Again the spacious venue is the Munich Herkulessaal and most of the cantatas included were recorded in 1977, though just a few were much earlier (Nos. 45 and 51 date from 1959 and No. 78 from 1961, but the sound remains good). The chorus is probably larger than it should be, but the results are invariably musical, and Richter shows greater flexibility and imagination than often has been the case. Just occasionally his heavy touch is felt, but so much of this set is first rate that reservations can be all but overruled. The soloists are thoroughly dependable, though Fischer-Dieskau is not always on his best form. The sublime No. 8 (*Liebster Gott*), for instance, provides wonderful material for all four soloists; indeed the beautifully sung tenor (Ernst Haefliger) and bass (Kieth Engen) arias must surely be counted among the finest of Bach's meditative vocal pieces. On the other hand, No. 78, generally a distinguished account with uniformly good soloists (Buckel, Töpper, Van Kesteren and Engen), contains no really inspired singing. Whatever one's feelings about 'authentic' Bach, these performances bring to life a great deal of inspired music that at this reasonable price should enjoy the widest currency and the strongest appeal.

Cantata No. 10: Meine Seele erhebt den Herrn.

(M) *** Decca 425 650-2 [id.]. Ameling, Watts, Krenn, Rintzler, V. Ac. Ch., Stuttgart CO, Münchinger – *Easter oratorio*. ***

An excellent coupling for a first-rate account of the surprisingly little-recorded *Easter oratorio*. This fine cantata is very well sung and played, with all the performers at their best. The recording too is freshly vivid.

Cantatas (for Ascension Day; Whitsun; Trinity): *Nos. 10: Meine Seele erhebt den Herrn; 11: Lobet Gott in seinen Reichen; 21: Ich hatte viel Bekümmernis; 24: Ein ungefärbt Gemüte; 30: Freue dich, erlöste Schar; 34: O ewiges Feuer, O Ursprung der Liebe; 39: Brich dem Hungrigen dein Brot; 44: Sie werden euch in den Bann tun; 68: Also hat Gott die Welt geliebt; 76: Die Himmel erzählen die Ehre Gottes; 93: Wer nur den lieben Gott lässt walten; 129: Gelobet sei der Herr, mein Gott; 135: Ach, Herr, mich armen Sünder; 147: Herz und Mund und Tat und Leben; 175: Er rufet seinen Schafen mit Namen.*

☞ (B)**(*) DG 439 380-2 (6) [id.]. Edith Mathis, Ursula Buckel, Anna Reynolds, Hertha Töpper, Peter Schreier, Ernst Haefliger, John van Kesteren, Dietrich Fischer-Dieskau, Kurt Moll, Kieth Engen, Munich Bach Ch. & O, Karl Richter.

The first performance offered here (Volume 3 of the Richter series) is the glorious Ascension cantata, *Lobet Gott in seinen Reichen* (No. 11), which opens and closes joyfully with resplendent trumpets. All four soloists are first rate, and Anna Reynolds is especially memorable in her famous aria, *Ach, bleib doch, mein liebstes Leben,* warmly supported by the strings of the Munich ensemble. Richter's performances of Nos. 10 and 25 also have a breadth and sense of space that are really quite impressive. He makes heavy weather of *Ein ungefärbt Gemüte* (No. 24), but on the whole the dignity of these performances outweighs the occasional pedestrian moments. The festive cantata, *O ewiges Feuer* (No. 34), is finely done and brings some distinguished singing from Anna Reynolds. No. 68 (*Also hat Gott die Welt geliebt*) is another success (this is the cantata with the famous aria, *My heart ever faithful*]. *Ach, Herr, mich armen Sünder* (No. 135), based on the Hassler Passion chorale, is also impressive here, as is the Whitsun cantata (No. 175) that deserves to be far better known than it is. No. 147, *Herz und Mund und Tat und Leben,* (which includes *Jesu, joy of man's desiring*) is among the best of Richter's series. Ursula Buckel sings beautifully, as does the tenor, John van Kesteren, and the choral singing is also very good. On the whole a successful box.

Cantatas (for Advent and Christmas): *Nos. 13: Meine Seufzer, meine Tränen; 28: Gottlob! nun geht das Jahr zu Ende; 58: Ach Gott, wie manches Herzeleid; 61: Nun komm, der Heiden Heiland; 63: Christen ätzet diesen Tag; 64: Sehet, welch eine Liebe hat uns der Vater erzwiget; 65: Sie werden aus Saba alle kommen; 81: Jesus schläft, was soll ich hoffen?; 82: Ich habe genug; 111: Was mein Gott will, das g'scheh allzeit; 121: Christum wir sollen loben schon; 124: Meinen Jesum lass ich nicht; 132: Bereitet die Wege, bereitet die Bahn; 171: Gott, wie dein Name, so ist auch dein Ruhm.*

☞ (B) **(*) DG 439 369-2 (4) [id.]. Edith Mathis, Sheila Armstrong, Lotte Schädle, Anna Reynolds, Hertha Töpper, Peter Schreier, Ernst Haefliger, Dietrich Fischer-Dieskau, Theo Adam, Munich Bach Ch. & O, Karl Richter.

It is useful to have this anthology (Volume 1 in this Richter series), which collects the cantatas appropriate to the Christmas festival; though there are some reservations to be made, there need be nothing but admiration for the purpose of the enterprise. The instrumental playing is extremely fine throughout and much of the solo singing is of genuine distinction. There is a greater boldness about Richter's approach than, say, Harnoncourt's, but he is at times a little earthbound and not free from pedantry. However, it is good to hear full-bodied choral singing and warm orchestral textures. The acoustic is a pleasing one; it has warmth and clarity at the same time, considering the forces used. There is much noble music-making and much noble music in this set.

Volume 4: *Cantatas Nos. 12: Weinen, klagen, sorgen, zagen; 13: Meine Seufzer, meine Tränen; 14: Wär Gott nicht mit uns diese Zeit; 16: Herr Gott, dich loben wir.*
(M) *** Teldec/Warner 2292 42500-2 (2) [id.]. Gampert, Hinterreiter, Esswood, Equiluz, Van Altena, Van Egmond, Tölz Boys' Ch., King's Coll. Ch., Leonhardt Cons., Leonhardt.

Volume 5: *Cantatas Nos. 17: Wer Dank opfert, der preiset mich; 18: Gleichwie der Regen und Schnee vom Himmel; 19: Es erhub sich ein Streit; 20: O Ewigkeit, du Donnerwort.*
(M) *** Teldec/Warner 2292 42501-2 (2) [id.]. Treble soloists from V. Boys' Ch., Esswood, Equiluz, Van Egmond, V. Boys' Ch., Ch. Viennensis, VCM, Harnoncourt.

Volume 6: *Cantatas Nos. (i) 21: Ich hatte viel Bekümmernis; (ii) 22: Jesus nahm zu sich die Zwölfe; 23: Du wahrer Gott und Davids Sohn.*
(M) **(*) Teldec/Warner 2292 42502-2 (2) [id.]. Esswood, Equiluz; (i) Walker, Wyatt, V. Boys' Ch., Ch. Viennensis, VCM, Harnoncourt; (ii) Gampert, Van Altena, Van Egmond, King's College Ch., Leonhardt Cons., Leonhardt.

Volume 7: *Cantatas Nos. 24: Ein ungefärbt Gemüte; 25: Es ist nicht Gesundes an meinem Leibe; 26: Ach wie flüchtig, ach wie nichtig; 27: Wer weiss, wie nahe mir mein Ende!.*
(M) *** Teldec/Warner 2292 42503-2 (2). Esswood, Equiluz, Van Egmond, Nimsgern, V. Boys' Ch., Ch. Viennensis, VCM, Harnoncourt.

Cantatas Nos. 27: Wer weiss, wie nahe mir mein Ende!; 158: Der Friede sei mit dir; 198: Lass, Fürstin, lass noch einen Strahl (Trauer-Ode).
☞ (M) *** Teldec/Warner 4509 93687-2 [id.]. Rotraud Hansmann, Helen Watts, Kurt Equiluz, Max van Egmond, Hamburg Monteverdi Ch., Concerto Amsterdam, Jürgen Jürgens.

This is one of the most outstanding Bach cantata records on the market. Not only are the performances extremely sensitive yet vital, with excellent solo and choral singing as well as enthusiastic but disciplined instrumental support, but the cantatas themselves are among Bach's most inspired. No. 27 has great distinction and at times a visionary intensity that one finds only in the greatest Bach. No. 198 is not a church cantata but an ode mourning Queen Christiane Eberhardine of Saxony, whose death in 1727 caused a spontaneous outburst of public sympathy. The libretto extols the queen's character, and Bach's especially imaginative scoring suggests he too had great affection and sympathy for her. After the impressive opening chorus, the soprano, contralto and tenor each sing the queen's praises and the mood of the work at the close is happy and optimistic, the queen's translation to Heaven obviously assured. The performance here is spontaneous as if the artists were fired by such a rewarding and little-known masterpiece. The recording, too, from the mid-1960s is first rate.

Volume 8: *Cantatas Nos. 28: Gottlob! nun geht das Jahr zu Ende; 29: Wir danken dir, Gott; 30: Freue dich, erlöste Schar.*
(M) *** Teldec/Warner 2292 42504-2 (2). Esswood, Equiluz, Van Egmond, Nimsgern, V. Boys' Ch., Ch. Viennensis, VCM, Harnoncourt.

Volume 9: *Cantatas Nos. (i) 31: Der Himmel lacht! die Erde jubilieret; (ii) 32: Liebster Jesu, mein*

Verlangen; 33: Allein zu dir, Herr Jesu Christ; (i) *34: O ewiges Feuer, O Ursprung der Liebe.*
(M) *** Teldec/Warner 2292 42505-2 (2). (i) Esswood, Equiluz, Nimsgern, V. Boys' Ch., Ch.
Viennensis, VCM, Harnoncourt; (ii) Gampert, Jacobs, Van Altena, Van Egmond, Hanover
Boys' Ch., Leonhardt Cons., Leonhardt.

Volume 10: *Cantatas Nos. 35: Geist und Seele wird verwirret; 36: Schwingt freudig euch empor; 37: Wer da gläubet und getauft wird; 38: Aus tiefer Not schrei ich zu dir.*
(M) *** Teldec/Warner 2292 42506-2 (2). Esswood, Equiluz, Van der Meer, V. Boys' Ch., Ch.
Viennensis, VCM, Harnoncourt.

Volume 11: *Cantatas Nos.* (i) *39: Brich dem Hungrigen dein Brot;* (i; ii) *40: Dazu ist erschienen der Sohn Gottes;* (iii) *41: Jesu, nun sei gepreiset; 42: Am Abend aber desselbigen Sabbats.*
(M) ** Teldec/Warner 2292 42556-2 (2). (i) Jacobs, Van Egmond, Hanover Boys' Ch., Leonhardt
Cons., Leonhardt; (ii) Van Altena; (iii) Esswood, Equiluz, Van der Meer, V. Boys' Ch., Ch.
Viennensis, VCM, Harnoncourt.

Volume 12: *Cantatas Nos.* (i) *43: Gott fähret auf mit Jauchzen; 44: Sie werden euch in die Bann tun;*
(ii) *45: Es ist dir gesagt, Mensch, was gut ist; 46: Schauet doch und sehet.*
(M) *** Teldec/Warner 2292 42559-2 (2) [id.]. (i) Jelosits, Esswood, Equiluz, Van der Meer, V. Boys'
Ch., Ch. Viennensis, VCM, Harnoncourt; (ii) Jacobs, Equiluz, Kunz, Hanover Boys' Ch.,
Leonhardt Cons., Leonhardt.

Volume 13: *Cantatas Nos. 47: Wer sich selbst erhöhet; 48: Ich elender Mensch, wer wird mich erlösen;*
49: Ich geh' und suche mit Verlangen; 50: Nun ist das Heil und die Kraft.
(M) *** Teldec/Warner 2292 42560-2 (2) [id.]. Jelosits, Esswood, Equiluz, Van der Meer, V. Boys'
Ch., Ch. Viennensis, VCM, Harnoncourt.

Cantatas Nos. 50: Nun ist das Heil und die Kraft; 118: O Jesu Christ, meine Lebens Licht.
☞ (M) *** Erato/Warner 2292 45979-2 (2) [id.]. Monteverdi Ch., E. Bar. Soloists, Gardiner – *Motets.*
***

This is a superb set. The magnificent cantata movement, BWV 50, for double choir, is used as an
epilogue to the glorious *Singet dem Herrn.* Alongside this, the high point is *O Jesus Christ, meine
Lebens Licht,* given in its second version and with genuine majesty. Gardiner's tempi are often
characteristically brisk and there is no question about the vitality of the music-making, both here and
in the coupled motets. The CD transfers are vivid and immediate and make the very most of the fine
analogue recording, made in All Saints', Tooting, in 1980. The *Motets* are equally fine.

Cantata No. 51: Jauchzet Gott in allen Landen.
*** Ph. Dig. 411 458-2 [id.]. Emma Kirkby, E. Bar. Soloists, Gardiner – *Magnificat.* ***

Jauchzet Gott is one of Bach's most joyful cantatas; Emma Kirkby follows the example of the
opening trumpeting (Crispian Steele-Perkins – in excellent form) when she begins. It is a brilliantly
responsive performance, admirably accompanied and very well recorded.

Volume 14: *Cantatas Nos. 51: Jauchzet Gott in allen Landen; 52: Falsche Welt, dir trau ihr nicht; 54:
Widerstehe doch der Sünde; 55: Ich armer Mensch, ich Sündenknecht; 56: Ich will den Kreuzstab
gerne tragen.*
(M) *** Teldec/Warner 2292 42422-2 (2) [id.]. Kweksilber, Kronwitter, Esswood, Equiluz, Schopper,
Hanover Boys' Ch., Leonhardt Cons., Leonhardt.

Cantatas Nos. (i) *51: Jauchzet Gott in allen Landen;* (ii) *202: Weichet nur (Wedding cantata);* (i) *209:
Non sa che sia dolore.*
☞ (M) *** Van. 08.2028.71. (i) Teresa Stich-Randall, V. State Op. O, Anton Heiller; (ii) Anny
Felbermeyer, Bach Guild O, Felix Prohaska.

Teresa Stich-Randall, in one of her finest records, gives a glorious account of the two solo cantatas.
In *Jauchzet Gott* she is supported by an estimably brilliant trumpet soloist and in the Italian cantata
by a sensitive, if not quite so striking, flute obbligato (neither player is named in the documentation)
and Heiller provides fresh accompaniments. Anny Felbermeyer is pleasingly fresh in the *Wedding
cantata,* if perhaps not quite so distinctive, and here the 1953 recording is probably from a mono
source, disguised by the pleasing resonance. Overall a very good disc, cleanly remastered.

*Cantatas Nos. 51: Jauchzet Gott in allen Landen; 208: Was mir behagt, ist nur die muntre Jagd (Hunt
cantata).*
☞ (BB) **(*) Naxos Dig. 8.550643 [id.]. Kertesi, Pászthy, Nemeth, Mukk, Gáti, Hungarian R. Ch.,
Failoni CO, Budapest, Antál.

The Naxos accounts are not quite the 'superbargain' they first appear to be, as between them *Jauchzet Gott in allen Landen* and the so-called 'Hunt cantata', *Was mir behagt, ist nur die muntre Jagd*, add up to 49 minutes 57 seconds. All the same, they offer excellent value artistically for those who do not insist on period instrument ensembles. Ingrid Kertesi is a very good soloist in *Jauchzet Gott*, though the unnamed trumpet obbligato could do with greater zest and spirit. *Was mir behagt, ist nur die muntre Jagd* employs Wilhelm Friedemann's addition, made after Bach's death, of three trumpets and kettledrum, and flutes instead of treble recorders. Anyway the soloists are all of a high standard and, although the recorded balance is not always ideal, the sound has warmth and immediacy, and Matyás Antál gets good results from his orchestra.

Cantatas Nos. 54: Widerstehe doch der Sünde; 169: Gott soll allein; 170: Vergnügte Ruh'.
*** Hyp. Dig. CDA 66326 [id.]. James Bowman, King's Consort, King.

James Bowman is on impressive form and his admirers need not hesitate here. The present disc is very desirable and the King's Consort under Robert King give excellent support. Good recorded sound.

Volume 15: *Cantatas Nos. 57: Selig ist der Mann; 58: Ach Gott, wie manches Herzelied; 59: Wer mich liebet, der wird mein Wort halten; 60: O Ewigkeit, du Donnerwort.*
(M) **(*) Teldec/Warner 2292 42423-2 [id.]. Jelosits, Kronwitter, Esswood, Equiluz, Van der Meer, Tölz Boys' Ch., VCM, Harnoncourt.

Cantatas Nos. 57: Selig ist der Mann; 58: Ach Gott, wie manches; 59: Wer mich liebet; 152: Tritt auf die Glaubensahn.
*** Hung. Dig. HCD 12897 [id.]. Zádori, Polgár, Savaria Vocal Ens., Capella Savaria, Pál Németh.

These dialogue cantatas are well served by the Capella Savaria and the two soloists. A rewarding, well-recorded issue.

Volume 16: *Cantatas Nos. 61: Nun komm, der Heiden Heiland; 62: Nun komm, der Heiden Heiland; 63: Christen, ätzet diesen Tag; 64: Sehet, welch eine Liebe.*
(M) **(*) Teldec/Warner 2292 42565-2 (2) [id.]. Jelosits, Kronwitter, Esswood, Equiluz, Van der Meer, Tölz Boys' Ch., VCM, Harnoncourt.

Volume 17: *Cantatas Nos.* (i) 65: *Sie werden aus Saba alle kommen;* (ii) 66: *Erfreut euch, ihr Herzen;* 67: *Halt im Gedächtnis Jesum Christ;* (i) 68: *Also hat Gott die Welt geliebt.*
(M) ** Teldec/Warner 2292 42571-2 (2) [id.]. (i) Jelosits, Equiluz, Van der Meer, Tölz Boys' Ch., VCM, Harnoncourt; (ii) Esswood, Equiluz, Van Egmond, Hanover Boys' Ch., Ghent Coll. Vocale, Leonhardt Cons., Leonhardt.

Volume 18: *Cantatas Nos. 69 & 69a: Lobe den Herrn, meine Seeele; 70: Wachet! betet! betet! wachet!; 71: Gott ist mein König; 72: Alles nur nach Gottes Willen.*
(M) *** Teldec/Warner 2292 42572-2 (2) [id.]. Esswood, Equiluz, Van der Meer, Visser, Tölz Boys' Ch., VCM, Harnoncourt.

Volume 19: *Cantatas Nos. 73: Herr, wie du willt, so schicks mit mir; 74: Wer mich liebet, der wird mein Wort halten; 75: Die Elenden sollen essen.*
(M) ** Teldec/Warner 2292 42573-2 [id.]. Erler, Klein, Esswood, Equiluz, Kraus, Van Egmond, Hanover Boys' Ch., Ghent Coll. Vocale, Leonhardt Cons., Leonhardt.

Volume 20: *Cantatas Nos.* (i) 76: *Die Himmel erzählen die Ehre Gottes;* (ii) 77: *Du sollt Gott, deinen Herren, lieben;* 78: *Jesu, der du meine Seele;* (ii) 79: *Gott der Herr ist Sonn' und Schild.*
(M) **(*) Teldec/Warner 2292 42576-2 (2) [id.]. Esswood, (i) Wiedl, Equiluz, Van der Meer, Tölz Boys' Ch., VCM, Harnoncourt; (ii) Bratschke, Kraus, Van Egmond, Hanover Boys' Ch., Ghent Coll. Vocale, Leonhardt Cons., Leonhardt.

Volume 21: *Cantatas Nos. 80: Ein feste Burg; 81: Jesus schläft, was soll ich hoffen?; 82: Ich habe genug; 83: Erfreute Zeit im neuen Bunde.*
(M) *(*) Teldec/Warner 2292 42577-2 (2) [id.]. Esswood, Equiluz, Van der Meer, Huttenlocher, Van Egmond, Tölz Boys' Ch., V. Boys' Ch., Ch. Viennensis, VCM, Harnoncourt.

Cantatas Nos. 80: Ein feste Burg ist unser Gott; 140: Wachet auf, ruft uns die Stimme.
☞ (M) **(*) Decca Dig. 436 226-2 [id.]. Fontana, Hamari, Winbergh, Krause, Stuttgart Hymnus Ch., Stuttgart CO, Münchinger.

This digital coupling of two of Bach's most popular cantatas is most welcome at mid-price. Münchinger, who uses the trumpets and timpani added by Bach's eldest son, Wilhelm Friedemann, has the advantage of excellently transparent and well-detailed Decca digital recording and a fine team of soloists: both Gösta Winbergh and Tom Krause make positive contributions. Karl Münchinger does not bring quite the warmth or musicality that distinguishes the finest performances of Bach, but there is little of the pedantry that has at times afflicted his performances. On CD, extra pleasure is afforded by the attractive ambience – the concert-hall balance is expertly managed – and by the tangibility of the chorus, whose vigorous contribution is given striking body and presence. All the movements are separately banded.

Cantatas Nos. 80: Ein feste Burg ist unser Gott; 147: Herz und Mund und Tat und Leben.
☞ (BB) **(*) Naxos Dig. 8.550642 [id.]. Kertesi, Nemeth, Mukk, Gáti, Hungarian R. Ch., Failoni CO, Budapest, Antál.

Like its companion above, this Naxos disc is eminently good value at 53 minutes 48 seconds. Neither performance disappoints in any significant respect; both are reasonably spirited in direction and offer satisfactory singing. Those who do not insist on period-instrument ensembles will find a great deal to enjoy here, particularly the singing of Ingrid Kertesi. The sound has real warmth and immediacy, though detail is not always as transparent as in, say, Gardiner's Bach cantata recordings on Archiv. Nevertheless very enjoyable.

Cantata No. 82: Ich habe genug.
⊛ (M) (***) EMI CDH7 63198-2 [id.]. Hans Hotter, Philh. O, Bernard – BRAHMS: *Lieder*. (***) ⊛

One of the greatest cantata performances ever. Glorious singing from Hans Hotter and wonderfully stylish accompanying from Anthony Bernard and the Philharmonia. This 1950 mono recording was never reissued on LP, and it sounds eminently present in this fine transfer.

Cantatas Nos. (i; ii) 82: Ich habe genug; (i; iii; iv) 159: Sehet, wir gehn hinauf gen Jerusalem; (iii) 170: Vergnügte Ruh', beliebte Seelenlust.
⊛ (M) *** Decca 430 260-2; *430 260-4.* (i) Shirley-Quirk; (ii) Lord; (iii) J. Baker; (iv) Tear, St Anthony Singers; ASMF, Marriner.

John Shirley-Quirk's performance of *Ich habe genug* is much to be admired, not only for the sensitive solo singing but also for the lovely oboe obbligato of Roger Lord. But this reissue is to be prized even more for the other two cantatas. Both Dame Janet Baker and Shirley-Quirk are in marvellous voice, and *Vergnügte Ruh'* makes a worthy companion. This is among the half-dozen or so cantata records that ought to be in every collection.

Volume 22: *Cantatas Nos. (i) 84: Ich bin vergnügt mit meinem Glücke; 85: Ich bin ein guter Hirt; 86: Wahrlich, wahrlich, ich sage euch; 87: Bisher habt ihr nichts gebeten; (ii) 88: Siehe, ich will viel Fischer aussenden; 89: Was soll ich aus dir machen, Ephraim?; 90: Es reisset euch ein schrecklich Ende.*
(M) ** Teldec/Warner 2292 42578-2 (2) [id.]. Esswood, Equiluz, (i) Wiedl, Van der Meer, Tölz Boys' Ch., VCM, Harnoncourt; (ii) Klein, Van Egmond, Hanover Boys' Ch., Ghent Coll. Vocale, Leonhardt Cons., Leonhardt.

Volume 23: *Cantatas Nos. (i) 91: Gelobet seist du, Jesus Christ; 92: Ich habe in Gottes Herz und Sinn; (ii) 93: Wer nur den lieben Gott lässt walten; 94: Was frag' ich nach der Welt.*
(M) *** Teldec/Warner 2292 42582-2 (2) [id.]. Esswood, Equiluz, (i) Bratschke, Van Egmond, Hanover Boys' Ch., Ghent Coll. Vocale, Leonhardt Cons., Leonhardt; (ii) Wiedl, Van der Meer, Huttenlocher, Tölz Boys' Ch., VCM, Harnoncourt.

Volume 24: *Cantatas Nos. (i) 95: Christus, der ist mein Leben; 96: Herr Christ, der ein'ge Gottesohn; 97: In allen meinen Taten; (ii) 98: Was Gott tut, das ist wohlgetan.*
(M) **(*) Teldec/Warner 2292 42583-2 [id.]. Esswood, Equiluz, (i) Wiedl, Huttenlocher, Van der Meer, Tölz Boys' Ch., VCM, Harnoncourt; (ii) Lengert, Van Egmond, Hanover Boys' Ch., Ghent Coll. Vocale, Leonhardt Cons., Leonhardt.

Volume 25: *Cantatas Nos. (i) 99: Was Gott tut, das ist wohlgetan; (ii) 100: Was Gott tut, das ist wohlgetan; (i) 101: Nimm von uns, Herr, du treuer Gott; 102: Herr, deine Augen sehen nach dem Glauben.*
(M) **(*) Teldec/Warner 2292 42584-2 (2) [id.]. Esswood, Equiluz, (i) Wiedl, Huttenlocher, Tölz Boys' Ch., VCM, Harnoncourt; (ii) Bratschke, Van Egmond, Hanover Boys' Ch., Ghent Coll. Vocale, Leonhardt Cons., Leonhardt.

Volume 26: *Cantatas Nos. (i; ii) 103: Ihr werdet weinen und heulen; (iii; iv) 104: Du Hirte Israel, höre; (v; iv) 105: Herr, gehe nicht ins Gericht; (vi; ii) 106: Gottes Zeit ist die allerbeste Zeit (Actus tragicus).*

(M) *** Teldec/Warner 2292 42602-2 [id.]. (i) Esswood, Equiluz, Van Egmond; (ii) Hanover Boys'
   Ch., Ghent Coll. Vocale, Leonhardt Cons., Leonhardt; (iii) Esswood, Huttenlocher; (iv) Tölz
   Boys' Ch., VCM, Harnoncourt; (v) Wiedl, Equiluz, Van der Meer; (vi) Klein, Harten, Van
   Altena, Van Egmond.

Cantatas Nos. 106: Gottes Zeit ist die allerbeste Zeit; 118: O Jesu Christ, mein Lebens Licht (2nd
version); *198: Lass, Fürstin, lass noch einen Strahl.*
*** DG Dig. 429 782-2 [id.]. Argenta, Chance, Rolfe Johnson, Varcoe, Monteverdi Ch., E. Bar.
   Soloists, Eliot Gardiner.

Gardiner directs dedicated, intense performances of three of Bach's finest cantatas, all valedictory
works. The new account of No. 118 is more intimate than the 1980 version, less grandly dramatic,
more devotional; the whole record suggests a scale of performance apt for a small chapel.

Cantatas Nos. 106: Gottes Zeit ist die allerbeste Zeit; 131: Aus der Tiefen.
*** O-L Dig. 417 323-2 [id.]. Monoyios, Rickards, Brownlees, Opalach, Bach Ens., Rifkin.

Rifkin's one-voice-to-a-part principle is applied here: the opening of *Gottes Zeit* is one of the most
beautiful moments in all Bach and is beautifully done. *Aus der Tiefen* is hardly less fine, and the
singers are all first class. One feels the need for greater weight and a more full-blooded approach at
times, but this is outweighed by the sensitivity and intelligence that inform these excellently balanced
recordings.

*Cantatas Nos. 106: Gottes Zeit ist die allerbeste Zeit; 152: Tritt auf die Glaubensahn; 161: Komm du
süsse Todenstunde.*
☞ Koch Int. 37164-2 [id.]. Brandes, Minter, Sharp, American Bach Soloists, Thomas.

These are one-voice-to-a-part performances, and those allergic to them should give this disc a wide
berth. Moreover some of the singing shows distinct signs of strain, and none of it can be called really
distinguished. No stars.

Volume 27: *Cantatas Nos.* (i) *107: Wass willst du dich betrüben;* (ii) *108: Es ist euch gut, dass ich
hingehe; 109: Ich glaube, lieber Herr, hilf meinem Unglauben!; 110: Unser Mund sei voll Lachens.*
(M) *** Teldec/Warner 2292 42603-2 (2) [id.]. Equiluz, (i) Klein, Van Egmond, Hanover Boys' Ch.,
   Ghent Coll. Vocale, Leonhardt Cons., Leonhardt; (ii) Wiedl, Frangoulis, Stumpf, Lorenz,
   Esswood, Van der Meer, Tölz Boys' Ch., VCM, Harnoncourt.

Volume 28: *Cantatas Nos.* (i) *111: Was mein Gott will, das g'scheh allzeit; 112: Der Herr ist mein
getreuer Hirt;* (ii) *113: Herr Jesu Christ, du höchstes Gut; 114: Ach, lieben Christen, seid getrost.*
(M) *** Teldec/Warner 2292 42606-2 (2) [id.]. Equiluz, (i) Huber, Esswood, Van der Meer, Tölz
   Boys' Ch., VCM, Harnoncourt; (ii) Hennig, Jacobs, Van Egmond, Hanover Boys' Ch., Ghent
   Coll. Vocale, Leonhardt Cons., Leonhardt.

Volume 29: *Cantatas Nos.* (i; iii; iv) *115: Mache dich, mein Geist, bereit; 116: Du Friedefürst, Herr
Jesu Christ;* (ii; v; vi) *117: Sei Lob und Ehr dem höchsten Gut;* (i; iii; vii) *119: Preise, Jerusalem, den
Herrn.*
(M) *** Teldec/Warner 2292 42608-2 (2) [id.]. (i) Tölz Boys' Ch., VCM, Harnoncourt; (ii) Equiluz,
   Hanover Boys' Ch., Ghent Coll. Vocale, Leonhardt Cons., Leonhardt; with (iii) Huber, Esswood;
   (iv) Huttenlocher; (v) Jacobs; (vi) Van Egmond; (vii) Holl.

Volume 30: *Cantatas Nos. 120: Gott, mann lobet dich in der Stille; 121: Christum wir sollen loben;
122: Das neugebor'ne Kindelein; 123: Liebster Immanuel, Herzog der Frommen.*
(M) *** Teldec/Warner 2292 42609-2 (2) [id.]. Treble soloists from Tölz Ch., Esswood, Equiluz,
   Huttenlocher or Holl, Tölz Boys' Ch., VCM, Harnoncourt.

Volume 31: *Cantatas Nos.* (i) *124: Meinen Jesum lass ich nicht; 125: Mit Fried und Freud ich fahr
dahin; 126: Erhalt uns, Herr, bei deinem Wort;* (ii) *127: Herr Jesu Christ wahr' Mensch und Gott.*
(M) *** Teldec/Warner 2292 42615-2 [id.]. (i) Bergius, Rampf, Esswood, Equiluz, Thomaschke, Tölz
   Boys' Ch., VCM, Harnoncourt; (ii) Hennig, Van Egmond, Hanover Boys' Ch., Ghent Coll.
   Vocale, Leonhardt Cons., Leonhardt.

Volume 32: *Cantatas Nos.* (i) *128: Auf Christi Himmelfahrt allein; 129: Gelobet sei der Herr, mein
Gott;* (ii) *130: Herr Gott, dich loben alle wir; 131: Aus der Tiefen rufe ich, Herr, zu dir.*
(M) **(*) Teldec/Warner 2292 42617-2 (2) [id.]. Hennig, Bergius, Jacobs, Rampf, Equiluz, Van
   Egmond, Heldwein, Holl; (i) Hanover Boys' Ch., Ghent Coll. Vocale, Leonhardt Consort,
   Leonhardt; (ii) Tölz Boys' Ch., VCM, Harnoncourt.

Cantatas Nos. (i) *128: Auf Christi Himmelfahrt allein; 129: Gelobet sei der Herr, mein Gott;* (ii) *130: Herr Gott, dich loben alle wir.*
(M) **(*) Teldec/Warner 2292 43055-2 [id.]. (recordings as above).

Volume 33: *Cantatas Nos. 132: Bereitet die Wege, bereitet die Bahn; 133: Ich freue mich in dir; 134: Ein Herz, das seinen Jesum lebend weiss; 135: Ach Herr, mich armen Sünder.*
(M) **(*) Teldec/Warner 2292 42618-2 (2) [id.]. Hennig, Jacobs, Van Altena, Van Egmond, Hanover Boys' Ch., Ghent Coll. Vocale, Leonhardt Cons., Leonhardt.

Volume 34: *Cantatas Nos. 136: Erforsche mich, Gott, und erfahre mein Herz; 137: Lobe den Herren, den mächtigen König der Ehren; 138: Warum betrübst du dich, mein Herz?; 139: Wohl dem, der sich auf seinen Gott.*
(M) ** Teldec/Warner 2292 42619-2 [id.]. Bergius, Rampf, Esswood, Equiluz, Holl, Heldwein, Hartinger, Tölz Boys' Ch., VCM, Harnoncourt.

Volume 35: *Cantatas Nos.* (i) *140: Wachet auf, ruft uns die Stimme;* (ii) *143: Lobe den Herrn, meine Seele; 144: Nimm, was dein ist, und gehe hin;* (i) *145: Ich lebe, mein Herze, zu deinem Ergötzen; 146: Wir müssen durch viel Trübsal.*
(M) *** Teldec/Warner Dig. 2292 42630-2 (2) [id.]. Esswood, Equiluz, (i) Bergius, Hampson, Tölz Boys' Ch., VCM, Harnoncourt; (ii) Cericius, Pfeiffer, Van Egmond, Hanover Boys' Ch., Ghent Coll. Vocale, Leonhardt Cons., Leonhardt.

Cantatas Nos. 140: Wachet auf, ruft uns die Stimme; 147: Herz und Mund und Tat und Leben.
*** DG Dig. 431 809-2; *431 809-4* [id.]. Holton, Chance, Rolfe Johnson, Varcoe, Monteverdi Ch., E. Bar. Soloists, Gardiner.

Two popular Bach cantatas are coupled in highly accomplished performances under John Eliot Gardiner. The level of instrumental playing is generally more polished than in the celebrated Teldec series, and Ruth Holton, Anthony Rolfe Johnson, Michael Chance and Stephen Varcoe make equally satisfying contributions. The recordings are immediate and well balanced. A strong recommendation.

(i; ii) *Cantata No. 147: Herz und Mund und Tat und Leben;* Motets: (i) *Fürchte dich nicht, BWV 228; Der Geist hilft unsrer Schwachheit auf, BWV 226;* (i; iii) *Lobet den Herrn, BWV 230.*
☞ (M) *(*) EMI CD-EMX 2199. (i) King's College, Cambridge, Ch., Willcocks; (ii) with Ameling, J. Baker, Partridge, Shirley-Quirk, ASMF; (iii) Hall, Slatford, Hare.

This reissue from 1972 offers Bach's most popular cantata – the source of the chorale, *Jesu, joy of man's desiring,* which is the final number – in a good performance with excellent soloists. The motets are rather less successful than the cantata; they are sung unaccompanied except for *Lobet den Herrn,* which has a continuo with organ. Unfortunately the 1972 recording has not transferred very satisfactorily to CD; the cantata's opening chorus sounds woolly and the motets are ill-focused. Fortunately the famous chorale sounds well enough.

Volume 36: *Cantatas Nos.* (i) *147: Herz und Mund und Tat und Leben; 148: Bringet dem Herrn Ehre seines Namens;* (ii) *149: Man singet mit Freuden vom Sieg; 150: Nach dir, Herr, verlanget mich; 151: Süsser Trost, mein Jesus kömmt.*
(M) *** Teldec/Warner Dig. 2292 42631-2 (2) [id.]. Bergius, Hennig, Esswood, Equiluz, Hampson, Van Egmond; (i) Tölz Boys' Ch., VCM, Harnoncourt; (ii) Ghent Coll. Vocale, Leonhardt Cons., Leonhardt.

Volume 37: *Cantatas Nos. 152: Tritt auf die Glaubensahn; 153: Schau, lieber Gott, wie meine Feind; 154: Mein liebster Jesus ist verloren; 155: Mein Gott, wie lang, ach lange; 156: Ich steh' mit einem Fuss im Grabe.*
(M) **(*) Teldec/Warner Dig. 2292 42632-2 (2) [id.]. Wegmann, Bergius, Rampf, Esswood, Equiluz, Hampson, Tölz Boys' Ch., VCM, Harnoncourt.

Volume 38: *Cantatas Nos.* (i) *157: Ich lasse dich nicht, du segnest mich denn; 158: Der Friede sei mit dir; 159: Sehet, wir gehn hinauf gen Jerusalem;* (ii) *161: Komm, du süsse Todesstunde; 162: Ach! ich sehe, jetzt, da ich zur Hochzeit gehe; 163: Nur jedem das Seine.*
(M) ** Teldec/Warner Dig. 2292 42633-2 (2) [id.]. Eiwanger, Esswood, Equiluz, Van Egmond, Tölz Boys' Ch., (i) Wegmann, Ghent Coll. Vocale, Leonhardt; (ii) Iconomou, Holl, VCM, Harnoncourt.

Volume 39: *Cantatas Nos.* (i) *164: Ihr, die ihr euch von Christo nennet; 165: O heil'ges Geist und*

Wasserbad; 166: Wo gehest du hin?; (ii) *167: Ihr Menschen, rühmet Gottes Liebe; 168: Tue, Rechnung! Donnerwort; 169: Gott soll allein mein Herze haben.*
(M) ** Teldec/Warner Dig. 2292 42634-2 (2) [id.]. Esswood, Equiluz, Tölz Boys' Ch.; (i) Wegmann, Eiwanger, Van Egmond, Ghent Coll. Vocale, Leonhardt Cons., Leonhardt; (ii) Iconomou, Immler, Holl, VCM, Harnoncourt.

Volume 40: *Cantatas Nos.* (i) *170: Vergnügte Ruh', beliebte Seelenlust;* (ii) *171: Gott, wie dein Name, so ist auch dein Ruhm;* (i) *172: Erschallet, ihr Lieder;* (ii) *173: Erhöhtes Fleisch und Blut; 174: Ich liebe den Höchsten von ganzem Gemüte.*
(M) **(*) Teldec/Warner Dig. 2292 42635-2 (2) [id.]. (i) Esswood, Van Altena, Van Egmond, Hanover Boys' Ch., Ghent Coll. Vocale, Leonhardt Cons., Leonhardt; (ii) Equiluz, Holl, Tölz Boys' Ch., VCM, Harnoncourt.

Volume 41: *Cantatas Nos.* (i) *175: Er rufet seinen Schafen mit Namen; 176: Es ist ein trotzig und verzagt Ding;* (ii) *177: Ich ruf zu dir, Herr Jesu Christ; 178: Wo Gott der Herr nicht bei uns hält; 179: Siehe zu, dass deine Gottesfurcht.*
(M) ** Teldec/Warner Dig. 2292 42428-2 (2) [id.]. (i) Echternach, Esswood, Van Altena, Van Egmond, Hanover Boys' Ch., Ghent Coll. Vocale, Leonhardt Cons.; (ii) Wittek, Iconomou, Equiluz, Holl, Tölz Boys' Ch., VCM, Harnoncourt.

Volume 42: *Cantatas Nos* (i) *180: Schmücke dich, O liebe Seele; 181: Leichtgesinnte Flattergeister;* (ii) *182: Himmelskönig, sei wilkommen; 183: Sie werden euch in den Bann tun;* (i) *184: Erwunschtes Freudenlicht.*
(M) *** Teldec/Warner Dig. 2292 42738-2 (2) [id.]. (i) O'Farrell, Esswood, Equiluz, Van Egmond, Hanover Boys' Ch., Ghent Coll. Vocale, Leonhardt Cons., Leonhardt; (ii) Wittek, Holl, Hampson, Tölz Boys' Ch., VCM, Harnoncourt.

Volume 43: *Cantatas Nos.* (i) *185: Barmherziges Herze der ewigen Liebes; 186: Argre dich, O Seele, nicht;* (ii) *187: Es wartet alles auf dich;* (i) *188: Ich habe meine Zuversicht.*
(M) **(*) Teldec/Warner Dig. 2292 44179-2 (2). (i) Wittek, Equiluz, Hampson, Holl, Tölz Boys' Ch., VCM, Harnoncourt; (ii) Emmermann, Esswood, Van Egmond, Hanover Boys' Ch., Ghent Coll. Vocale, Leonhardt Cons., Leonhardt.

Volume 44: *Cantatas Nos.* (i) *192: Nun danket alle Gott;* (ii) *194: Höchsterwünschtes Freudenfest;* (iii) *195: Dem Gerechten muss das Licht immer wieder aufgehen.*
(M) **(*) Teldec/Warner Dig. 2292 44193-2 [id.]. (i) Wittek, (i; ii) Hampson, (ii) Stricker, Gienger, Equiluz, (iii) O'Farrell, Jacobs, Elwes, Van der Kamp; (i; ii) Tölz Boys' Ch., VCM, Harnoncourt; (iii) Hanover Boys' Ch., Ghent Coll. Vocale, Leonhardt Consort, Leonhardt.

Volume 45: *Cantatas Nos.* (i) *196: Der Herr denket an uns;* (ii) *197: Gott ist unsrer Zuversicht;* (iii) *198: Lass, Fürstin, lass noch einen Strahl;* (iv) *199: Mein Herze schwimmt im Blut.*
(M) ** Teldec/Warner Dig. 2292 44194-2 (2) [id.]. (i) Wittek, Equiluz, Hampson, (ii; iii) O'Farrell, Jacobs, Van der Kamp, (iii) Elwes, (iv) Bonney; (i) Tölz Boys' Ch., (ii; iii) Hanover Boys' Ch., Ghent Coll. Vocale; (i; iv) VCM, Harnoncourt; (ii; iii) Leonhardt Consort, Leonhardt.

Cantatas Nos. 202: Weichet nur, betrübte Schatten' (Wedding); 209: Non sa che sia dolore; 210: O holder Tag, erwünschte Zeit.
☞ (B) ** HM Dig. HMA 1903010 [id.]. Mária Zádori, Capella Savaria, Pál Németh.

The contents of this disc are described collectively as 'Wedding cantatas', and certainly No. 202 urges the betrothed couple 'to surrender to love and joyfully embrace' and 'let no sudden accident or thunderbolt afright the loving heart's desire!', while No. 210 convincingly argues the case that a nuptial rejoicing should not be silent: 'Nothing can give you greater pleasure than music's sweet art.' However, the valedictory No. 209, *Non sa che sia dolore* ('He knows not what pain is'), is about the loss of a friend, and its mood makes a useful contrast with the other two. Mária Zádori sings eloquently and has the full measure of the music's expressive range. Her timbre seems right for these secular expressions of joy and grief, and the Capella Savaria accompaniments are most stylish, with characterful obbligato playing from oboe and flute. The snag is that Zádori lets the music's expressive ardour affect the security of her intonation, and this is noticeable near the very opening of *Weichet nur*. This first cantata on the disc is the most affected, but the others are not completely immune. A pity, for otherwise this is most enjoyably involving singing and can still be enjoyed despite the flaws.

Cantata No. 205: Der zufriedengestellte Aolus.
(M) *** Teldec/Warner Dig. 2292 42957-2 [id.]. Kenny, Lipovšek, Equiluz, Holl, Arnold Schönberg Ch., VCM, Harnoncourt.

Bach describes this cantata as '*Dramma per musica*'. The performance is very good indeed, and the recording has a decently spacious acoustic and no lack of detail. Recommended.

Cantatas Nos. 205: Der zufriedengestellte Aolus; 214: Tönet, ihr Pauken! Erschallet, Trompeten!
☞ *** Ph. Dig. 432 161-2 [id.]. Van der Sluis, Jacobs, Prégardien, Thomas, Age of Enlightenment Ch. & O, Leonhardt.

Here are two congratulatory cantatas, the grandly scored *Der zufriedengestellte Aolus* (1725) for August Müller, a professor of botany, subsequently pressed into service for the coronation of August, the Elector of Saxony, as King of Poland in 1734, and *Tönet, ihr Pauken! Erschallet, Trompeten!*, composed in honour of his consort in 1733 and subsequently re-used in the *Christmas oratorio*. There is some fine singing from the four soloists. Muike van der Sluis is an attractive singer and reports of her vulnerable intonation are greatly exaggerated. Gustav Leonhardt gets very good playing from the Orchestra of the Age of Enlightenment, though accents are hammered home in the opening of BWV 214 in a rather pedestrian fashion. Outstanding recording.

Cantata No. 208: Was mir behagt, ist nur die muntre Jagd (Hunt cantata).
*** Hyp. Dig. CDA 66169 [id.]. Jennifer Smith, Emma Kirkby, Simon Davis, Michael George, Parley of Instruments, Goodman.

This is a cantata rich in melodic invention of the highest quality. The performance has the benefit of excellent soloists and first-class instrumental playing.

Cantatas Nos. 211: Schweigt stille, plaudert nicht (Coffee cantata); 212: Mer hahn en neue Oberkeet (Peasant cantata).
*** O-L Dig. 417 621-2 [id.]. Kirkby, Rogers, Covey-Crump, Thomas, AAM, Hogwood.
☞ (BB) **(*) Naxos Dig. 8.550642 [id.]. Kertesi, Mukk, Gáti, Failoni CO, Budapest, Mátyás Antál.

Emma Kirkby is particularly appealing in the *Coffee cantata* and her father is admirably portrayed by David Thomas. Hogwood opts for single strings, and some may find they sound thin. However, there is a corresponding gain in lightness and intimacy. The recording is altogether first class.

Very serviceable accounts on Naxos of the *Coffee* and *Peasant cantatas*, and those who appreciated Ingrid Kertesi's *Jauchzet Gott* will find her singing gives as much pleasure here. Mátyás Antál's direction is lively and, although its press has not been uniformly welcoming, this is as enjoyable an issue as the other cantatas from this source, save only for the tenor, who falls short of distinction. The recording is warm and spacious. Not necessarily a first choice, particularly not for those who are wedded to period instruments, but worth the modest sum asked for.

(i) *Cantatas Nos. 211: Schweight stille, plaudert nicht (Coffee); 212: Mer hahn en neue Oberkeet (Peasant), BWV 212.* (ii) *Masses: in A, BWV 234, in G, BWV 236.*
☞ (B) **(*) EMI Dig. CZS7 67552-2 (2) [id.]. (i) Hofmann, Reinhart; (ii) Akerlund, Sharon Weller, Varcoe, Basle Madrigalists; (i; ii) Guy de May, Linde Consort, Linde.

Bach at his most genial is presented here in authentic performances of the paired secular cantatas, which are also warmly communicative. Linde is light and lively here and, though the voices are recorded in a fairly resonant ambience, the result is intimate. The singers are all splendid at bringing out the charm and humour of both pieces with vivid painting of words. The performances of the two Lutheran cantatas are not quite on this level, but the well-balanced and lifelike sound is again a plus point. There is some good solo singing, particularly from Sharon Weller and Stephen Varcoe. Lina Akerlund phrases sensitively, but the *Qui tollis* of the *A major Mass* brings moments of insecurity and frail intonation from the flutes. The chorus sings well, however, and, although the performances are straightforward rather than individually imaginative, they are still enjoyable when the presentation on CD is so fresh and transparent.

Christmas oratorio, BWV 248.
*** DG Dig. 423 232-2 (2) [id.]. Rolfe Johnson, Argenta, Von Otter, Blochwitz, Bär, Monteverdi Ch., E. Bar. Soloists, Gardiner.
☞ (M) **(*) Teldec/Warner 9031 77610-2 (2) [id.]. Treble soloists from V. Boys' Ch., Esswood, Equiluz, Nimsgern, V. Boys' Ch., Ch. Viennensis. VCM, Harnoncourt.
☞ **(*) Collins Dig. 7028-2 (2). Russell, Padmore, Wyn-Rogers, George, The Sixteen, Christophers.
☞ (BB) ** Naxos Dig. 8.550428/30 [id.]. Kertesi, Nemeth, Mukk, Tóth, Hungarian R. Ch., Failoni CO, Géza Oberfrank.
☞ (M) ** Erato/Warner Dig. 2292 45212-2 (3) [id.]. Schlick, Watkinson, Equiluz, Nimsgern, Brodard, Lausanne Ens. & Ch., Corboz.

The freshness of the singing and playing in the DG set is a constant pleasure, with Gardiner's often brisk speeds sounding bright and eager, not breathless. Far more than usual, one registers the joyfulness of the work, from the trumpets and timpani at the start onwards. Anthony Rolfe Johnson makes a pointful and expressive Evangelist, and also outstanding is Anne Sofie von Otter with her natural gravity and exceptionally beautiful mezzo. Beauty of tone consistently marks the singing of Nancy Argenta, Hans-Peter Blochwitz and Olaf Bär. The whole oratorio is neatly contained on only two discs, with three cantatas on each instead of two. The sound is full and atmospheric.

Harnoncourt's famous pioneering 'authentic' version of the *Christmas oratorio*, made in 1971/2, has at last been reissued on a pair of mid-priced CDs in Teldec's Das Alte Werk series. Harnoncourt has rarely been more successful than here. It will not be to everyone's taste to have a boy treble and male counter-tenor instead of women soloists, but the purity of sound of these singers is most affecting. Above all, Harnoncourt in this instance never allows his pursuit of authentic sound to weigh the performance down: it has a lightness of touch which should please everyone. The sound, as usual from this source, is excellent.

Harry Christophers conducts a crisp, sympathetic reading, very well played and sung, which at speeds generally a little slower than John Eliot Gardiner's just fails to match that rival in exhilaration and intensity. He has a first-rate quartet of soloists – where Gardiner has different soloists for the arias from those for the Christmas narrative – with the tenor, Mark Padmore, particularly impressive not just in the arias but as the Evangelist. Good, atmospheric recording, with trumpets and drums dramatically prominent.

The Naxos bargain set, with many of the same performers as in their companion version of the *St Matthew Passion*, presents a performance on modern instruments that generally adopts the speeds and manner now associated with period performances. With the tenor, József Mukk, again outstanding as the Evangelist, there is a comparable dramatic tension, even though some of Oberfrank's speeds verge on the breathless, and the recording exaggerates a slight unsteadiness in the mezzo-soprano soloist, Judit Nemeth. The performance is spread on to three discs instead of two, making it less of a bargain.

Festive with trumpets, superbly played, Corboz's version begins exceptionally well, with fresh and beautifully balanced sound from chorus and orchestra. All six cantatas are presented very attractively, with bright sound set within an intimate but helpful acoustic; however, too often Corboz falls into a rhythmic jogtrot which undermines the imaginative singing and solo playing. The four soloists all have clean, very attractive voices, marred only by Michel Brodard's heavily aspirated style. Carolyn Watkinson is outstanding, but the tenderness of her singing in the *Cradle song* in the second cantata is minimized when the accompaniment is pedestrian. Although this digital set is now available at mid-price, it is put out of court by being spread over three CDs, which negates the economy.

Christmas oratorio; Magnificat, BWV 243.
(M) *** Decca 425 441-2 (3) [id.]. Ameling, Watts, Pears, Krause, Ch., Stuttgart CO, Münchinger.

Münchinger directs an admirably fresh performance of the *Christmas oratorio*, sharp in tone and bright in recording (which dates from 1967). With an excellent team of soloists and with Lübeck trebles adding to the freshness, this is a good middle-of-the-road version, representative of modern scholarship as determined in the immediate pre-authentic era. Münchinger's recording of the *Magnificat* dates from 1969 and was another of his finest Bach performances.

Christmas oratorio: Arias and choruses.
(M) *** DG Dig. 435 088-2 [id.] (from above complete recording, cond. Gardiner).
(M) *** Teldec/Warner 9031 74893-2 [id.]. Treble soloists from V. Boys' Ch., Esswood, Equiluz,
    Nimsgern, V. Boys' Ch., Ch. Viennensis, VCM, Harnoncourt.

The 70-minute selection on DG offers choruses and arias from all six cantatas and includes the *Sinfonia* to introduce the four items from Part Two.

The highlights from Harnoncourt's outstandingly spontaneous performance of the *Christmas oratorio* are equally attractive, particularly as the CD plays for nearly 78 minutes.

Easter oratorio.
(M) *** Decca 425 650-2 [id.]. Ameling, Watts, Krenn, Krause, Stuttgart CO, Münchinger – *Cantata No. 10.* ***

Münchinger is at his finest in the *Easter oratorio*, giving a spacious and impressive reading. He is well supported by his splendid team of soloists, and the Decca recording is well up to the lively standard of his Stuttgart series.

Magnificat in D, BWV 243.

*** Ph. Dig. 411 458-2 [id.]. Argenta, Kwella, Kirkby, Brett, Rolfe Johnson, David Thomas, E. Bar. Soloists, Gardiner – *Cantata No. 51.* ***

☞ *** Chan. Dig. CHAN 0518 [id.]. Kirkby, Bonner, Chance, Ainsley, Varcoe, Coll. Mus. 90, Hickox – VIVALDI: *Gloria.* ***

☞ *** EMI Dig. CDC7 54283-2 [id.]. Hendricks, Murray, Rigby, Heilmann, Hynninen, ASMF Ch. & O, Marriner – VIVALDI: *Gloria.* ***

(M) *** Decca 421 148-2. Palmer, Watts, Tear, Roberts, King's College Ch., ASMF, Ledger – C. P. E. BACH: *Magnificat.* ***

☞ (B) *** Erato/Warner 2292 45923-2 [id.]. Yakar, J. Smith, Finnilä, Rolfe Johnson, Van Dam, Lausanne Vocal and Instrumental Ens., Corbóz – VIVALDI: *Gloria & Kyrie.* ***

☞ (M) ** EMI CDM7 64634-2 [id.]; *EG 764634-4.* Popp, Pashley, J. Baker, Tear, Hemsley, Garrard, New Philh. Ch. & O, Barenboim – FAURE: *Requiem.* ***

☞ (M) ** Sony SBK 48280 [id.]. Augér, Murray, Watts, Adalbert Kraus, Huttenlocher, Schöne, Gächinger Kantorei, Stuttgart, Rilling – VIVALDI: *Beatus vir; Gloria.* *(*)

The better-known, D major version of the *Magnificat* receives an exhilarating performance from Gardiner. Tempi are consistently brisk but the vigour and precision of the chorus are such that one never has the feeling that the pacing is hurried. A splendid team of soloists, and the accompaniment and recording are nop less impressive.

Both Richard Hickox and Neville Marriner couple the *Magnificat* with the popular D major *Gloria*, RV 589, of Vivaldi, and for collectors seeking this coupling the clear choice is between period and modern instruments. Those who like the former will gravitate towards Hickox, who directs a most musical account and has the benefit of such fine singers as Emma Kirkby, Michael Chance and Stephen Varcoe, and good Chandos recording. Marriner's performance with the Academy is well paced and executed with precision and fine musical intelligence. No quarrel with the soloists either or the splendidly warm and present recording. Both can be recommended with confidence.

Philip Ledger's account, recorded by Argo in the late 1970s, is also most attractive, highly recommendable if boys' voices are preferred in the chorus, and is excellent value.

Bach's glorious *Magnificat* is well represented in the catalogue at mid-price, but this Erato coupling is the first bargain version that can be strongly recommended. The professional singers of the Lausanne choir are generally admirable and the soloists make a excellent team, with the soprano solos particularly beautiful. The music-making is spiritedly vigorous and spontaneous and the CD transfer of an excellent (1979) recording vividly managed. The Vivaldi couplings are equally recommendable and the only minus point is the absence of information about the music, characteristic of Erato's Bonsai series.

Barenboim's way with Bach in his 1968 recording of the *Magnificat* is nothing if not boisterous, and he sets a very fast tempo for the opening. But no one should miss the joyfulness of the music as presented here. The solo singing too is more imaginative than in many rival versions, and Dame Janet Baker's singing of the two mezzo arias is intensely moving. The recording – made in a fairly small South London church – was originally agreeably warm and smooth, but the CD transfer, alas, has added an artificial edge to the upper range.

Rilling includes the four interpolations for the celebration of Christmas which are found in Bach's original version, and there is some magnificent solo singing on this Sony disc. The lively contribution from the Gächinger Kantorei is also to be admired. But the recording lacks depth of perspective; both the chorus and strings are too close (the latter very noticeably so in the tenor's vibrant *Deposuit potentes*) and the close microphones rob the acoustic overall of its sense of space. A pity, as the performance is very stimulating, although the Vivaldi coupling is less recommendable.

Mass in B min., BWV 232.

*** DG Dig. 415 514-2 [id.]. Argenta, Dawson, Fairfield, Knibbs, Kwella, Hall, Nichols, Chance, Collin, Stafford, Evans, Milner, Murgatroyd, Lloyd-Morgan, Varcoe, Monteverdi Ch., E. Bar. Soloists, Gardiner.

*** EMI Dig. CDS7 47293-8 [Ang. CDCB 47292] (2). Kirkby, Van Evera, Iconomou, Immler, Kilian, Covey-Crump, David Thomas, Taverner Cons. and Players, Parrott.

☞ **(*) Chan. Dig. CHAN 0533/4 [id.]. Argenta, Denley, Tucker, Varcoe, Coll. Mus. 90, Hickox.

☞ (M) **(*) BMG/RCA GD 77040 (2). Poulenard, Laurens, Jacobs, Elwes, Van Egmond, Van der Kemp, Netherlands Bach Coll. Mus., La Petite Bande, Leonhardt.

(i) *Mass in B min., BWV 232;* (ii) *Missa brevis in F, BWV 233.*

☞ (M) **(*) Ph. Duo 438 739-2 (2) [id.]. (i) Lois Marshall, Töpper, Pears, Borg, Bav. R. Ch. & RSO, Jochum; (ii) Giebel, Litz, Prey, Lausanne Pro Arte Ch., Munich Pro Arte O, Redel.

John Eliot Gardiner gives a magnificent account of the *B minor Mass*, one which attempts to keep within an authentic scale but which also triumphantly encompasses the work's grandeur. Gardiner masterfully conveys the majesty (with bells and censer-swinging evoked) simultaneously with a crisply resilient rhythmic pulse. The choral tone is luminous and powerfully projected. The regular solo numbers are taken by choir members making a cohesive whole. The recording is warmly atmospheric but not cloudy.

Parrott, hoping to re-create even more closely the conditions Bach would have expected in Leipzig, adds to the soloists a ripieno group of five singers from the Taverner Consort for the choruses. The instrumental group is similarly augmented with the keenest discretion. Speeds are generally fast, with rhythms sprung to reflect the inspiration of dance; however, the inner darkness of the *Crucifixus*, for example, is conveyed intensely in its hushed tones, while the *Et resurrexit* promptly erupts with a power to compensate for any lack of traditional weight. Soloists are excellent, with reduction of vibrato still allowing sweetness as well as purity. If you want a performance on a reduced scale, the recording, made in St John's, Smith Square, is both realistic and atmospheric.

With an excellent chorus and a first-rate quartet of soloists, Richard Hickox conducts a period performance that emerges on a larger scale than many. This is thanks to a reverberant recording rather than to large-scale forces. His speeds are on the fast side, though never breathless-sounding, and his springing of rhythms is always infectious. With a relatively close recording-balance for the orchestra, the panoply of trumpets and drums in the more extrovert numbers comes over dramatically, and the soloists too are presented in close-up. That makes the recording of the chorus – more vital than any other element in this work – seem too distant and less involving than in such a version as Gardiner's.

Jochum's dedicated approach to Bach brings a performance which steadily gathers intensity, finding its apex in the great spacious *Sanctus*, capped by the *Osanna in excelsis*, with the *Dona nobis pacem* given a broad, satisfying finality. The early stereo is remarkably good, though not sharply defined, yet the firm, inspirational choral contribution carries its own weight and focus. Generally good solo singing, with Hertha Töpper rising to the occasion in the *Agnus Dei*, and a young, fresh-voiced Peter Pears contributing to the *Benedictus*. Redel's *F major Missa brevis* is not on this level but is acceptable enough.

Leonhardt's manner, unlike that of most advocates of period performance and authentic-sized forces, is relaxed at generally slow speeds. That underlines the devotional quality of his whole performance, its concentration. To that extent it provides a welcome alternative to brisker perform-ances, but the slackness of much of the choral singing is a shortcoming when, in this of all Bach's works, the chorus provides the central focus. The team of soloists has no weak link, and La Petite Bande once again proves itself one of the most accomplished of baroque groups. Well-balanced recording too, originally designed for broadcast transmission through the European Broadcasting Union.

Motets: *Singet dem Herrn ein Neues Lied, BWV 225; Der Geist hilft unser Schwachheit, BWV 226; Jesu meine Freude, BWV 227; Der Gerechte Kommt um Fürchte dich nicht, BWV 228; Komm, Jesu, Komm, BWV 229; Lobet den Herrn, BWV 230; Sei Lob und Preis mit Ehren, BWV 231.*

☞ (M) *** Erato/Warner 2292 45979-2 (2). Priday, Fisher, Stafford, McKenzie, Savage (soloists in BWV 227), Monteverdi Ch., E. Bar. Soloists, Gardiner – *Cantatas Nos. 50 & 118.* ***
*** Conifer Dig. CDCF 158; *MCFC 158* [id.] (without *BWV 231*). Trinity College, Cambridge, Ch., Marlow, G. Jackson and R. Pearce.

John Eliot Gardiner's set of Bach's great motets, recorded for Erato in 1980, was one of his first major Bach recordings with the Monteverdi Choir. As well as bringing exceptionally strong and stylish performances, spaciously conceived with crisp, clean, resilient rhythms, the set has the attendant advantages of including not just the six motets regularly recognized in the Bach Gesellschaft Edition but two motet-like works that have been counted as cantatas. The set also includes a rarity in *Sei Lob und Preis mit Ehren*. It makes a superb collection in such performances, beautifully recorded in the helpful acoustic of All Saints', Tooting, and vividly transferred to CD. This is a clear first choice among the recordings of the Bach motets, irrespective of the bonuses.

The Conifer issue of Bach's great motets by Richard Marlow and the Trinity College Choir brings delightfully crisp and resilient performances of the six regular motets, marked by refined ensemble and transparent textures. With discreet organ accompaniment this is a fine single-disc or -tape version, consistently stylish and set against a helpful acoustic, with plenty of presence.

St John Passion, BWV 245.
*** DG Dig. 419 324-2 (2) [id.]. Rolfe Johnson, Varcoe, Hauptmann, Argenta & soloists, Monteverdi

Ch., E. Bar. Sol., Gardiner.

☞ *(**) Ph. Dig. 434 905-2 (2) [id.]. Stumpius, Bowman, Van der Meel, Prégardien, Sigmundsson, Kooy, Netherlands Chamber Ch., O of 18th Century, Brüggen.

☞ (M) **(*) BMG/RCA GD 77041 (2) [77041-2-RG]. Prégardien, Van der Kamp, Schlick, Jacobs, Van der Meel, Van Egmond, La Petite Bande Ch. & O, Sigiswald Kuijken.

☞ (M) ** EMI CMS7 64234-2 (2) [id.]. Wunderlich, Fischer-Dieskau, Grümmer, Ludwig, St Hedwig's Cathedral Ch., Berlin SO, Karl Foster.

☞ (B) ** EMI CZS7 62592-2 (2). Altmeyer, Crass, Moll, Ameling, Fassbaender, Equiluz, Nimsgern, S. German Madrigal Ch. & Consortum Musicum, Gönnenwein.

☞ * BMG/RCA Dig. RD 60903 (2) [id.]. Ahnsjö, Prokopetz, Quasthoff, Nielsen, Stutzman, Scharinger, Swensen, Schneider, Chorgemeinschaft Neubeuern, Munich Bach Collegium, Enoch zu Guttenberg.

Gardiner conducts an exhilarating performance, so dramatic in its approach and so wide-ranging in the emotions conveyed it might be a religious opera. Speeds are regularly on the fast side but, characteristically, Gardiner consistently keeps a spring in the rhythm. Chorales are treated in contrasted ways, which may not please the more severe authenticists but, as with so much of Gardiner's work, here is a performance using authentic scale and period instruments which speaks in the most vivid way to anyone prepared to listen, not just to the specialist. Soloists – regular contributors to Gardiner's team – are all first rate. Warm and atmospheric, yet clear and detailed recording. A selection of arias and choruses is available on DG 427 319-2.

It is disappointing that the Brüggen version is so marred by the distancing of the chorus. This is particularly serious when, in contrast with the choir, the soloists as well as the players of the Orchestra of the 18th Century are very forwardly placed. When the *St John Passion* depends so much on its choruses, not just the big landmark numbers at the beginning and end but the chorales and, above all, the little 'turba' choruses of comment on the Passion story, the impact of the performance is seriously undermined. Most of the soloists are good, with a young, expressive Evangelist in Nico van der Meel and with the male alto, James Bowman, and the tenor, Christoph Prégardien, outstanding among the others.

At mid-price on BMG/Deutsche Harmonia Mundi, the Sigiswald Kuijken version offers Prégardien and van der Meel singing even better with their roles reversed; indeed Prégardien as the Evangelist provides an outstandingly beautiful and intense performance. Harry van der Kamp as Jesus also stands out with his fresh, firm and resonant bass, while Barbara Schlick is the radiant soprano. With excellent sound, the chorus sings the brief, elaborate 'turba' choruses of comment with exemplary point, and only the big choruses fall short.

The pioneering all-male Harnoncourt version of 1965 (Teldec 2292 42492-2) is also available at mid-price but, next to Kuijken, it now seems heavy, despite the agile singing of Kurt Equiluz as the Evangelist.

Among other premium-priced issues, Parrot's EMI version with the Taverner Consort and Players (EMI CDC7 54083-2), using only 11 voices in all, is an intimate, thoughtful reading, with soloists coming from the choir. Though instrumental textures are commendably clear, the choral sound is not as cleanly detailed as on many versions, and Gardiner still provides the more intense experience. Similarly Herreweghe's period-instrument account (Harmonia Mundi HMC 901264/5) is no match for Gardiner in the choral singing, which tends to be slack, although a fine team of soloists is headed by an excellent Evangelist in Howard Crook, matched by the Christus of Peter Luka. Harry Christophers' version with The Sixteen (Chandos CHAN 0507/8) was recorded during live performances and brings a period version that has both freshness and warmth. With uniquely mellifluous singing from Ian Partridge as the Evangelist, and a well-matched Jesus from David Wilson-Johnson, this is certainly enjoyable, although any recommendation must again be tempered by the backward balance of the chorus, which lacks inner clarity and bite.

Of the two much earlier EMI reissues, the Berlin recording is the more striking with its starry line-up of soloists all providing impressive contributions, while the late Karl Foster directs the St Hedwig's Choir with warmth and sensitivity. However, the Berlin acoustic is ample, which prevents the sharpest focus in those dramatic little interjections that give the work its special flavour among Bach's choral works.

At what amounts to bargain price, Gönnenwein's version of the work is fairly competitive. Theo Altmeyer's Evangelist is a fine one, and the tenor arias done by Kurt Equiluz are impressively musical. In fact there is little to fault here in the way of solo singing, and the choral and orchestral forces are expertly directed. As an account in the older German tradition, this has its place in the catalogue, and the CD transfer is satisfactory.

There is nothing special about the newest RCA digital recording, a large-scale performance with modern instruments from southern Germany. While Claes Ahnsjö is an impressive Evangelist, the other soloists are more variable; the choral singing, though dramatic, is rhythmically heavy and no special advantages obtain from the fact that the recording was made during live performances.

St Matthew Passion, BWV 244.
*** DG Dig. 427 648-2 (3) [id.]. Rolfe Johnson, Schmidt, Bonney, Monoyios, Von Otter, Chance, Crook, Bär, Hauptmann, Monteverdi Ch., E. Bar. Soloists, Gardiner.
(M) *** EMI CMS7 63058-2 (3). Pears, Fischer-Dieskau, Schwarzkopf, Ludwig, Gedda, Berry, Hampstead Parish Church Ch., Philh. Ch. & O, Klemperer.
☞ (BB) *** Naxos Dig. 8.550832/34 [id.]. József Mukk, István Gáti, Judit Németh, Ibolya Verebits, Péter Köves, Péter Cser, Ferenc Korpás, Rózsa Kiss, Agnes Csenki, Hungarian R. Children's Ch., Hungarian Festival Ch. & State SO, Géza Oberfrank.
☞ (M) **(*) DG 427 704-2 (3) [id.]. Peter Schreier, Dietrich Fischer-Dieskau, Edith Mathis, Dame Janet Baker,, Salminen, Regensburger Domspatzen, Munich Bach. Ch. & O, Karl Richter.
☞ (B) ** DG 439 338-2 (3) [id.]. Ernst Haefliger, Irmgard Seefried, Hertha Töpper, Dietrich Fischer-Dieskau, Kieth Engen, Antoine Fahlberg, Munich Bach Ch. & O with Boys' Ch., Karl Richter.
☞ (M) ** Teldec/Warner 2292 42509-2 (3) [id.]. Equiluz, Esswood, Sutcliffe, Bowman, Nigel Rogers, Ridderbusch, Van Egmond, Schopper, Regensburger Boys' Ch., King's College, Cambridge, Ch., VCM, Harnoncourt.
☞ ** Erato/Warner Dig. 2292 45814-2 (3) [id.]. De Mey, Kooy, Schlick, Wessel, Prégardien, Mertens, Netherlands Bach Boys' Ch., Breda Ch., Amsterdam Bar. O, Ton Koopman.

Gardiner's version of the *St Matthew Passion*, the culminating issue in his Bach choral series for DG Archiv, brings an intense, dramatic reading which now makes a clear first choice, not just for period-performance devotees but for anyone not firmly set against the new authenticity. The result is an invigorating, intense telling of the story, with Gardiner favouring high dynamic contrasts and generally fast speeds which are still geared to the weighty purpose of the whole work. He and his performers were recorded in what proved an ideal venue, The Maltings at Snape, where the warm acoustic gives body and allows clarity to period textures.

While it certainly will not appeal to the authentic lobby, Klemperer's 1962 Philharmonia recording of the *St Matthew Passion* represents one of his greatest achievements on record, an act of devotion of such intensity that points of style and interpretation seem insignificant. The whole cast clearly shared Klemperer's own intense feelings, and one can only sit back and share them too, whatever one's preconceptions.

At bargain price the completely new version from Naxos uses modern, not period, instruments but, following authentic trends, has brisk speeds and well-sprung rhythms. Though the performance takes no less than 35 minutes less than, say, Richter's, in its alertness it never seems rushed, with the Hungarian State Symphony Orchestra and Festival Choir on excellent form, conducted by Géza Oberfrank. A refreshingly lithe and young-sounding Evangelist, József Mukk, leads a team of Hungarian soloists with fresh, clear voices. The obbligato wind-playing is also attractive (if closely balanced) and the recording is spacious and full, and kind to voices.

Karl Richter's pioneering (1958) version for DG Archiv with Munich forces has some fine singing, both from the chorus and from the soloists, who include the young Dietrich Fischer-Dieskau as baritone soloist. Though Richter represented the authentic cause at the time, using relatively small forces, his speeds are very slow indeed by the standards of period performance today, and there was no question of his using anything but modern instruments. Though there is a glow and dedication in the music-making, with Ernst Haefliger a radiant Evangelist and Irmgard Seefried producing ravishing sounds, the performance has come to sound stodgy, not just a question of speeds but of rhythmic squareness. Vocally the disappointment is the fruity contralto, Hertha Töpper, a key soloist in this work.

This CD reissue comes at bargain price, but Richter's later (1979) version, now at mid-price, is still preferable. Richter's last major Bach recording, it too is rhythmically heavy but dedicated, with Janet Baker's singing a crowning glory, not least in *Erbarme dich*, and with the Regensburger Domspatzen 'cathedral sparrows' providing splendid treble contributions.

Harnoncourt's early-1970s set emerges as freshly in its digital remastering as the others in the series, remarkable for its daring authenticity. The vocal sound remains unique in its total reliance on male voices (including boy trebles); the choral singing is incisive and lightweight. For many, the emotional kernel of Bach's great work lies in the solo contributions; here, they are variable, with Karl Ridderbusch and Paul Esswood outstanding. Some of the other contributions are less reliable, and the use of boy trebles for the soprano arias produces a strangely detached effect, although the singing itself is usually technically good.

Koopman directs an amiable account of the *St Matthew*, generally avoiding speeds as controversially fast as some of Gardiner's. Yet the very opening (where Gardiner, even at a fast 12/8, conveys an ominous tension) finds Koopman too easy and comfortable, making you register nothing more serious than a dance. Barbara Schlick and Christoph Prégardien are excellent among the soloists, but otherwise they hardly match Gardiner's team, even Guy de Mey as the Evangelist, while the Dutch chorus sounds muddy beside Gardiner's Monteverdi Choir.

St Matthew Passion (complete; in English).
☞ (BB) ** ASV CDQSS 324 (3) [id.]. Robert Tear, John Shirley-Quirk, Felicity Lott, Alfreda Hodgson, Neil Jenkins, Stephen Roberts, Bach Ch., St Paul's Cathedral Ch. Boys, Thames CO, Willcocks.

For anyone wanting the *St Matthew Passion* in English, ASV on its super-bargain Quicksilva label offers Sir David Willcocks's traditional account, recorded in 1978 with the Bach Choir, a splendid memento for anyone who has enjoyed his annual performances at the Festival Hall in London. The outstanding soloists include Robert Tear's Evangelist and John Shirley-Quirk's Christus, with Felicity Lott as the soprano soloist and the late Alfreda Hodgson as the contralto; but Peter's denial – usually a supremely moving moment – is here less powerful than usual. Not as slow as the Richter reading, in its weighty approach with a large chorus it misses the bright intensity of the Hungarians. The pity is that this version fails to lift quite as it ought. Willcocks, most experienced of choirmasters, draws light and rhythmic singing from the chorus, and the chorales avoid heaviness. The (originally) Argo recording is clear and well balanced and has a most realistic ambience, admirably conveyed in a first-rate CD transfer.

Vocal collections

Arias: *Bist du bei mir; Cantata 202: Weichet nur, Betrubte Schatten. Cantata 209: Ricetti gramezza. St Matthew Passion: Blute nur; Ich will dir mein Herze schenken.*
**(*) Delos Dig. D/CD 3026 [id.]. Arleen Augér, Mostly Mozart O, Schwarz – HANDEL: *Arias.* **(*)

Arleen Augér's pure, sweet soprano, effortlessly controlled, makes for bright performances of these Bach arias and songs, very recommendable for admirers of this delightful singer, well coupled with Handel arias.

Arias: *Mass in B min.: Agnus dei; Qui sedes. St John Passion: All is fulfilled. St Matthew Passion: Grief for sin.*
(M) (***) Decca mono 433 474-2; *433 474-4*. Kathleen Ferrier, LPO, Boult – HANDEL: *Arias.* (***) ⊛

On 7th and 8th October 1952, Kathleen Ferrier made her last and perhaps greatest record in London's Kingsway Hall, coupling four arias each by Bach and Handel. The combined skill of John Culshaw and Kenneth Wilkinson ensured a recording of the utmost fidelity by the standards of that time. Now it re-emerges with extraordinary naturalness and presence.

Transcriptions

Transcriptions: arr. BUSONI: *Chaconne* (from *Violin Partita No. 2*); *Chorales: Ich ruf zu dir; Nun freut euch, lieben Christen; Nun komm der Heiden Heiland; Wachet auf; Toccata & fugue in D min.* arr. LISZT: *Prelude & fugue in A min.* arr. LORD BERNERS: *In dolci jubilo.* arr. MYRA HESS: *Jesu, joy of man's desiring.* arr. KEMPFF: *Siciliano.* arr. LE FLEMING: *Sheep may safely graze.* arr. RACHMANINOV: *Suite from Partita No. 3 in E.*
*** ASV Dig. CDDCA 759; *ZCDCA 759* [id.]. Gordon Fergus-Thompson (piano).

A highly entertaining collection, played with much flair and, in the case of the lyrical pieces at the centre of the recital (notably Wilhelm Kempff's delightful *Siciliano* and Dame Myra Hess's famous arrangement of *Jesu, joy of man's desiring*), stylish charm.

Arrangements: Bach–Stokowski

Adagio in C, BWV 564; Chorales: Jesus Christus Gottes Sohn (from *Easter cantata*); *Komm süsser Tod; Mein Jesu; Sheep may safely graze; Wie glauben all' an Einen Gott (Giant fugue), BWV 680. Fugue in G min. (Little), BWV 578; Passacaglia and fugue in C min., BWV 582; Suite No. 3 in D, BWV 1068: Air. Toccata and fugue in D min., BWV 565; Violin & harpsichord sonata No. 4, BWV 1017: Siciliano; Well-tempered Clavier, Book 1, Prelude No. 24.*
☞ *** Chan. Dig. CHAN 9259 [id.]. BBC PO, Matthias Bamert.

This sumptuously recorded Chandos CD brings together the dozen published Stokowski Bach transcriptions. Matthias Bamert, assistant conductor to Stokowski while he was with the American Symphony Orchestra at the end of his career, has here followed the maestro's idea of 'free-bowing' in the strings. The result certainly produces a rich patina. Bamert's warmly sympathetic readings obviously follow his mentor's way with this music, if without quite managing the naturally spontaneous rubato which was one of Stokowski's special gifts. Nor is the playing as vital and electrifying as the great conductor's own record. But the result is very enjoyable, and the Chandos stereo here is very much in the demonstration bracket.

Chorales: Jesu, joy of man's desiring; Sheep may safely graze; We all believe in one God (Fugue on *Wir glauben all' an einen Gott), BWV 680; English suite No. 2, BWV 807: Bourrée. Komm süsser Tod, BWV 478; Chaconne* (from *Partita No. 2 in B min.* for unaccompanied violin), *BWV 1004; Well-tempered Clavier,* Book 1: *Prelude in B min., BWV 869. Easter oratorio: Chorale. Toccata and fugue in D minor, BWV 565.*
⊛ (M) *** BMG/RCA mono GD 60922 [id.]. SO, Leopold Stokowski.

The *Toccata and fugue in D minor* is a mono recording made in 1947, and absolutely no technical apologies need be made for it. The sound is clear and full and has an impressively resonant bass. The violins sound more real than many stereo recordings made in America over the next two decades. The rest of the programme dates from three years later. The sobriquet, 'Symphony Orchestra', in this case describes a pick-up group of musicians drawn from the New York Philharmonic and NBC Symphony. They play marvellously. The collector's item here is the incredibly wayward account of Bach's famous *Chaconne*, with its funereal opening tempo. Milstein's account takes 14 minutes; Stokowski stretches it out to 17 minutes 22 seconds and his indulgent *espressivo* alters its character entirely.

Bach, Wilhelm Friedemann (1710–84)

Sinfonia in D, F64; Adagio & fugue in D min., F65.
*** Capriccio Dig. 10 283 [id.]. Concerto Köln – J. C. F. BACH: *Sinfonia;* C. P. E. BACH: *Harpsichord concerto;* J. C. BACH: *Sinfonia.* ***

Wilhelm Friedemann's three-movement *Sinfonia in D major* was intended for use as an introduction to the Whitsun cantata, *Dies ist der Tag.* The better-known *Adagio and fugue in D minor* is possibly the last two movements of a symphony. It is a very extraordinary and expressive piece and makes one wonder whether Wilhelm Friedemann did not possess the most powerful imagination of all the sons. It is played by this period group with great expressive vitality and is well recorded.

Fantasia in C min., F2; 8 Fugues, F11; March, F30; Prelude, F29; Sonatas: in G, F7; A min., F8; Suite in C min., K24.
☞ (B) *** HM Dig. HMA 1901305 [id.]. Christophe Rousset (harpsichord).

Here is another recital to confirm Wilhelm Friedemann's strong musical personality. The extraordinary *Fantasia in C minor* has a darkly dramatic opening, then immediately evokes memories of Johann Sebastian's *Chromatic fantasia* in its florid brilliance. But it remains very much Wilhelm's own piece. The two sonatas are also impressive works. The *A minor* has a closing Presto – a flowing *moto perpetuo* – that could almost become a lollipop if given more exposure, and the *G major* has a thoughtful *Lament* at its centre and another engaging finale, which Christophe Rousset despatches with fine dash. He was nineteen when he recorded this recital and he plays with remarkable maturity and discernment throughout. He certainly brings out the diversity of the eight succinct miniature *Fugues* which readily demonstrate Wilhelm's contrapuntal mastery.

Keyboard fantasias: Nos. 1–8 & 10, F14–21 & F23.
*** Denon Dig. CO 72588 [id.]. Huguette Dreyfus (harpsichord).

These works are engagingly unpredictable, all bringing quite bold and daring harmonic sleights of hand. So, too, is the excellent playing of Huguette Dreyfus, who has the advantage of an outstanding recording.

Baermann, Heinrich (1784–1847)

Adagio for clarinet and orchestra.
*** ASV Dig. CDDCA 559; ZCDCA 559 [id.]. Emma Johnson, ECO, Groves – CRUSELL: *Concerto No. 2* *** ⊛; ROSSINI: *Introduction, theme and variations***; WEBER: *Concertino.* ***

Heinrich Baermann's rather beautiful *Adagio*, once attributed to Wagner, is offered by a young clarinettist who plays the work warmly and sympathetically.

Bairstow, Edward (1874–1946)

Organ sonata in E flat.
☞ *** Priory Dig. PRCD 401 [id.]. John Scott (St Paul's Cathedral organ) (with William HARRIS: *Sonata* ***) – ELGAR: *Sonata No. 1.* ***

Bairstow began his professional organ-playing career in Wigan; he then moved to Leeds, before moving on to York where he remained for over 30 years. His *Organ sonata* was written in 1937 while on holiday in the Isle of Arran and its nostalic opening movement surely recalls the beauty which surrounded him. It is Elgarian in feeling and the central Scherzo produces a blaze of orchestral sound unsurpassed by Elgar in either of his works for the instrument. The performance here is admirable and the St Paul's Cathedral organ is just right for it. The third work on the disc, a much more conventional sonata by William Harris (1883–1973), at least has a rather pleasing central *Adagio*.

Anthems and choral settings: *Blessed city, heavenly Salem; Blessed Virgin's cradle song; Evening Canticles in D; If the Lord had not helped me; Jesu, grant me this I pray; Jesu, the very thought; Lamentation* (from *Jeremiah*); *Let all mortal flesh keep silence; Lord I call upon Thee; Lord thou has been our refuge; Save us O Lord.*
☞ *** Priory Dig. PRDC 365 [id.]. York Minster Ch., Philip Moore; John Scott Whiteley.

Bairstow was an energetic all-rounder: chorus master, conductor indefatigable organizer, fine teacher and composer. He is (rightly) best known for his moving and comparatively short anthem, *Let all mortal flesh keep silence*; but, as this collection shows, he wrote much else that gives full rein to his subtle understanding of choral blending and instinctive response to liturgical texts, especially those drawn from the Psalms which were one of his favourite scriptural sources. This is well demonstrated here in his rich but brief setting of Psalm 114, *When Israel came out of Egypt*. The gloriously expansive *Blessed city, heavenly Salem*, which opens the concert, makes the firmest of Christian statements and the depth of the composer's religious feeling is expressed touchingly in the poignant *Jesu, the very thought of you*. The choir excel in thrillingly ardent accounts of *Lord thou has been our refuge*, and the shorter but not less powerful *Lord I call upon Thee*, while *Save us, O Lord* brings a lovely flowing line, richly harmonized, and *The Blessed Virgin's cradle song* (given to soaring trebles) shows Bairstow's pleasingly simple melodic facility. The rhapsodic *If the Lord had not helped* brings an extraordinarily wide range of expressive feeling and the *Gloria* of the closing *Nunc Dimittis* has a resoundingly satisfying fugue. The performances here are very well prepared and excitingly committed and spontaneous. The chorus is set back in the ample and resonant Minster acoustic, which provides plenty of space for climaxes to expand gloriously, while the balance with the excellent organ accompaniments could hardly be bettered. First-rate accompanying documentation. If you enjoy fine choral music from the great tradition of English cathedral music, you will not be disappointed with this.

Balakirev, Mily (1837–1910)

Piano concertos Nos. 1 in F sharp min., Op. 1; 2 in E flat, Op. posth.
☞ *** Hyp. Dig. CDA 66640 [id.]. Malcolm Binns, E. N. Philh. O, Lloyd-Jones – RIMSKY-KORSAKOV: *Concerto.* ***

Piano concerto No. 1 in F sharp min., Op. 1.
☞ **(*) Russian Disc MK 417087 [id.]. Igor Zhukov, USSR R. & TV Large SO, Dmitriev – MEDTNER; RIMSKY-KORSAKOV: *Piano concertos.* **(*)

The one-movement *First Piano concerto* (*Youth*) comes, as its opus number shows, from the beginning of Balakirev's career: it was composed when he was eighteen and is modelled on his adored Chopin. All the same, there are some touches of individuality, and it is well served on both these recordings. Igor Zhukov's version comes from the early 1970s and is eminently satisfactory but is not really the equal of Malcolm Binns' intelligent and sensitive performance, which also has the advantage of fine orchestral support and up-to-date recording. It also has the only available account of the more characteristic *Second Concerto*, which Balakirev started in 1861 but (like the *First Symphony*) put on one side. It was left incomplete and finished after his death by Lyapounov.

Islamey (orch. Lyapunov).
** Olympia OCD 129 [id.]. USSR Ac. SO, Svetlanov – LYAPUNOV: *Hashish* etc. **

An effective performance here of Lyapunov's effective orchestration of *Islamey*. It makes a logical coupling for an interesting disc of Lyapunov's very Balakirevian orchestral music. Rough-and-ready but acceptable recording.

Symphony No. 1 in C; Islamey (orch. Lyapunov); *Tamara*.
☞ (BB) *** Naxos Dig. 8.550792 [id.]. Russian State SO, Igor Golovschin.

Symphony No. 1; Russia (symphonic poem).
**(*) Hyp. Dig. CDA 66493 [id.]. Philh. O, Svetlanov.

Symphony No. 1 in C; Tamara (symphonic poem).
(M) **(*) EMI CDM7 63375-2 [id.]. RPO, Beecham.

Balakirev's sumptuously lyrical *First Symphony* has had a chequered gramophone career. Beecham's 1955 has always been the yardstick by which other versions were judged. It has many felicities and is coupled at mid-price with *Tamara*, with the early stereo responding quite well to the CD face-lift, although the lack of amplitude in the string tone is disadvantageous. There is some disagreement among us about the Svetlanov version on Hyperion (his second stereo recording, as he did the work previously with the USSR Symphony Orchestra); but with the new Russian Naxos CD tending to sweep the board, this becomes less important.

Golovschin may not quite have the uncanny grip on the rather loose-structured first movement that Beecham found, but his reading is exciting, convincing in its pacing and control of tension. Moreover it is very well played by a Russian ensemble who have this music in their bones. After a lively Scherzo, the slow movement is glorious, with its sinuous clarinet solo immediately finding a seductive affinity with Rimsky's *Scheherazade*. The finale too has fine impetus and brilliance. The Russian brass have weight and sonority but are characteristically bright (though not blatant) and forwardly balanced in tuttis; the wind and strings play with appealing warmth and finesse. The two supporting works are hardly less successful. *Islamey* starts off with tremendous Slavonic bustle and again produces a subtly alluring oriental flavour in its central section, while *Tamara* is warmly atmospheric and held together very well, again with glowing woodwind contributions and the Eastern melodic influences deliciously caught. The 1993 recording was made at the Mosfilm Studio and is vivid and full; although the acoustic is inevitably drier and less open than the Hyperion, it is not confining and the stereo ambience brings plenty of bloom.

Svetlanov's performance brings some beautiful playing from the Philharmonia Orchestra in both works. The soaring clarinet solo at the beginning of the slow movement is ravishingly done (presumably by Michael Collins). However, there is some disagreement among us concerning Svetlanov's grip on the first three movements. R.L. finds the performance well paced and free from overheated romanticism; for E.G., the playing lacks bite and tension. Both are agreed that in the finale the emotional thrust of this music is powerfully caught, and the Hyperion recording, warm and full, deserves the highest grading. The coupling is both apt and successful in all respects.

Symphony No. 2 in D min.; Russia.
☞ (BB) *** Naxos Dig. 8.550793 [id.]. Russian State SO, Igor Golovschin.

Symphony No. 2 in D min.; Overture on 3 Russian themes; Tamara.
**(*) Hyp. Dig. CDA 66586 [id.]. Philh. O, Svetlanov.

The *Second Symphony* is a late work (although the rumbustious *Scherzo alla cossacca* is much earlier). The first movement is tautly constructed; Golovschin controls its layout impressively and at the same time provides plenty of impetus. The Scherzo has Slavonic gusto but, as with the *First Symphony*, it is the *Andante* where this very Russian performance is so telling – spacious and refined, the strings swelling out spontaneously from a romantic onward flow that is beautifully shaped. The jolly *Polacca* finale is despatched with zest without being pressed too hard, its lyrical strain ardent, and the vigorous brass injections are bright and strong without crudeness. The opening of *Russia* is warmly atmospheric and its integrated folk material again brings seductive woodwind playing and highly responsive strings; after the brass livens things up in a folk dance, Golovschin sustains a raptly beautiful close.

In the *Second Symphony* the playing of the Philharmonia is cultured and the sound pleasingly natural and well balanced. It comes with the attractive *Overture on three Russian themes* and *Tamara*, arguably Balakirev's masterpiece. Yet once again there is lack of consensus over Svetlanov's reading. R.L. enjoys its spacious breadth; however, while agreeing that it is tauter than that of the *First*, E.G.

suggests that it does little to promote a symphony which inevitably runs the risk of seeming a repetition of the earlier work. *Tamara* too – almost as extended as a one-movement symphony – needs to be stronger and more purposeful, as Beecham's version demonstrates.

Islamey (oriental fantasy).
(M) *** EMI CDM7 64329-2. Andrei Gavrilov – PROKOFIEV: *Concerto No. 1;* TCHAIKOVSKY: *Piano concerto No. 1* etc. ***

Gavrilov's dazzling account of Balakirev's fantasy is outstandingly charismatic; it is well recorded, too. It comes in harness with an equally dazzling version of Prokofiev's *First Piano concerto* and a performance of the Tchaikovsky *B flat minor Concerto* which is rather less convincing.

Piano sonata in B flat min.
**(*) Olympia OCD 354 [id.]; Archduke *MARC 2*. Donna Amato – DUTILLEUX: *Sonata.* **(*)
**(*) Kingdom Dig. KCLCD 2001 [id.]. Gordon Fergus-Thompson – SCRIABIN: *Sonata No. 3* etc. **(*)

The Balakirev is arguably the greatest Russian piano sonata of the pre-1914 era. Donna Amato gives a musicianly account of it, well paced and authoritative. The recording is very lifelike, and this is a most desirable issue, even if the playing time at 47 minutes is not particularly generous.

Gordon Fergus-Thompson, too, is fully equal to the considerable demands of the Balakirev *Sonata* and offers excellent playing, though the recording is reverberant and the piano not always dead in tune. Fergus-Thompson also includes Balakirev's arrangement of Glinka's *The Lark* as an encore.

Balfe, Michael (1808–70)

The Bohemian Girl (opera): complete.
☞ ** Argo Dig. 433 324-2; *433 324-4* (2) [id.]. Thomas, Power, Summers, Cullen, De Carlo, RTE Philharmonic Ch., Nat. SO of Ireland, Bonynge.

Sir Thomas Beecham famously revived Balfe's most celebrated opera, *The Bohemian Girl*, at the time of the Festival of Britain in 1951, but it took another four decades for a complete recording to appear. This one with a flawed cast and a lacklustre orchestra is only a stop-gap. The Irishman, Michael Balfe, was extraordinarily successful in his own day, writing no fewer than 21 English operas, three in French and four in Italian. His lyrical facility comes out at its most charming in *Bohemian Girl*, with the heroine's aria, *I dreamt that I dwelt in marble halls*, justly still popular as a separate number. Though Richard Bonynge is an ideal conductor for such a piece, with his gift for springing rhythms and moulding phrases persuasively, he is not well served either by the Irish orchestra, recorded rather dimly, or by the principal singers, most of whom sound fluttery and even uncertain, perhaps caught badly by the microphones. Patrick Power as the hero, Thaddeus, has a light, lyrical tenor which sounds well enough until it is stressed, when it acquires a throaty bleating tone on top. Nova Thomas as the heroine, Arline, is at once throaty-sounding and fluttery, yet bright on top, not helped by her curious vowel sounds. Jonathan Summers is the strongest in the cast, as Count Arnhem, but even he has sounded better-focused on disc; while the bass tones of John de Carlo as Devilshoof, King of the Gypsies, are marred by his unashamedly aspirated style in florid passages. The recording, slightly recessed, is not ideally detailed. A separate cast of actors is lined up for the spoken dialogue. A generous package, though, with 150 minutes on the two CDs.

Bantock, Granville (1868–1946)

Celtic Symphony; Hebridean Symphony; The Sea reivers; The Witch of Atlas.
*** Hyp. Dig. CDA 66450 [id.]. RPO, Handley.

Vernon Handley conducts warmly atmospheric performances of four of Bantock's Hebridean inspirations. Most ambitious is the *Hebridean Symphony* of 1913, with nature music echoing Wagner and Delius as well as Sibelius, whose music Bantock introduced into Britain. The two tone-poems are attractive too, but best of all is the *Celtic Symphony*, a late work written in 1940, which uses strings and six harps. This is in the grand string tradition of Vaughan Williams's *Tallis fantasia* and Elgar's *Introduction and allegro*, a beautiful, colourful work that deserves to be far better known. With warm, atmospheric recording to match, Handley draws committed performances from the RPO.

Fifine at the fair (tone poem No. 3).
(M) (***) EMI mono CDM7 63405-2 [id.]. RPO, Sir Thomas Beecham – BAX: *Garden of Fand;*
   BERNERS: *Triumph of Neptune.* (***)

Beecham always had a soft spot for *Fifine at the fair* and his advocacy is so persuasive that one could
wish for the piece to be restored to the repertoire. The early (1949) sound is a bit confined and
opaque, but the CD transfer makes the very most of the 78-r.p.m. master.

Pagan Symphony; Fifine at the fair; 2 Heroic ballads.
☞ *** Hyp. Dig. CDA 66630 [id.]. RPO, Handley.

A fine successor to Handley's earlier pairing of the *Celtic* and *Hebridean Symphonies*. The *Pagan
Symphony* dates from 1928, so it comes mid-way between the others, and the writing brings touches
of Elgar as well as German influences. It is tuneful and well crafted. Perhaps it isn't as individual a
work as *Fifine at the fair*, with which Beecham understandably identified; but Handley is equally at
home in this colourful tone-poem, and it is good to have it presented in stereo as vivid as this. The
two *Ballads* are rather more conventional but still make a considerable impression.

The Pierrot of the minute: overture.
☞ (M) *** Chan. CHAN 6566 [id.]. Bournemouth Sinf., Norman Del Mar – BRIDGE: *Summer* etc.;
   BUTTERWORTH: *Banks of Green Willow.* ***

Bantock's overture is concerned with Pierrot's dream, in which he falls in love with a Moon Maiden
who tells him their love must die at dawn, but he will not listen. He wakes to realize that his dream of
love lasted a mere minute. The writing is often delicate and at times Elgarian, and the piece is well
worth investigating. The 1978 recording sounds remarkably fresh.

Barber, Samuel (1910–81)

Adagio for strings, Op. 11.
*** Argo 417 818-2 [id.]. ASMF, Marriner – COPLAND: *Quiet city;* COWELL: *Hymn;* CRESTON:
   Rumor; IVES: *Symphony No. 3.* ***
(M) *** DG Dig. 427 806-2; *427 806-4.* LAPO, Bernstein – BERNSTEIN: *Overture Candide; West Side
   Story; On the Town* ***; GERSHWIN: *Rhapsody in blue.* **(*)
☞ (M) *** DG Dig. 439 528-2 [id.]. LAPO, Bernstein – COPLAND: *Appalachian spring* ***;
   GERSHWIN: *Rhapsody in blue.* **(*)
☞ *** Koch Schwann Dig. 3-7243-2 [id.]. New Zealand SO, James Sedares – DELLO JOIO: *The
   Triumph of St Joan* etc. ***
☞ (M) **(*) Sony SMK 47567 [id.]. NYPO, Bernstein – HOLST: *Planets.* *(**)

Marriner's 1976 performance of Barber's justly famous *Adagio* is arguably the most satisfying version
we have had since the war, although Bernstein's alternative has the advantage of digital recording.
The quality of sound on the remastered Argo CD retains most of the richness and body of the
analogue LP, but at the climax the brighter lighting brings a slightly sparer violin texture than on the
original LP.

Bernstein's 1971 Sony account is slow and intense, the brightly lit sound revealing all the linear
detail. The later DG recording (variously coupled), with more modern digital sound, is preferable,
but the earlier version is just as deeply felt.

The principal interest of this Koch CD is the coupled music by Norman Dello Joio, but the
programmes ends with a deeply felt account of Barber's *Adagio*, given in memory of Andrew Schenck
who conducted many of the New Zealand orchestra's earlier records on this label.

On DG, Bernstein's powerfully expressive and deeply felt reading of Barber's *Adagio* has an
expansively restrained, elegiac feeling, but his control of the climax – in what is substantially a live
recording – is unerring.

(i) *Adagio for strings;* (i; ii) *Cello concerto, Op. 22;* (ii; iii) *Cello sonata, Op. 6.*
*** Virgin/EMI Dig. VC7 59565-2 [id.]. (i) SCO; Saraste; (ii) Ralph Kirshbaum; (iii) Roger
   Vignoles.

Kirshbaum's view of the Barber *Cello concerto*, with splendid support from Saraste and the Scottish
Chamber Orchestra, is darker and spikier than those of his direct rivals, and rather more urgent in
the outer movements, yet it is just as beautifully played. He is equally convincing in Barber's other,
much rarer cello work, the *Cello sonata* of 1932. Roger Vignoles copes well with piano-writing
unhelpful to a degree surprising from a pianist-composer. The celebrated *Adagio*, coolly done, makes
a worthwhile fill-up. Spacious, well-focused recording.

Adagio for strings; (i) *Piano concerto, Op. 38; Medea's meditation and Dance of vengeance, Op. 23a.*
*** ASV Dig. CDDCA 534 [id.]. (i) Joselson; LSO, Schenck.

In Barber's *Concerto* Tedd Joselson is marvellously and dazzlingly brilliant, as well as being highly sensitive and poetic with an unforced and responsive orchestral contribution from the LSO under Andrew Schenck. The LSO also give a singularly fine account of the *Medea* excerpt (not to be confused with the Suite) and a restrained and noble one of the celebrated *Adagio.*

Adagio for strings, Op. 11; Essays Nos. 1, Op. 12; 2, Op. 17; Music for a scene from Shelley, Op. 7; Overture, The School for Scandal, Op. 5; Symphony No. 1, Op. 9.
☞ *** Argo Dig. 436 288 [id.]. Baltimore SO, Zinman.

In the last edition of the *CD Guide* we recommended Leonard Slatkin's RCA disc of the *First Symphony* as an excellent entry-point into Barber's world. This Argo disc, which also concentrates on his early music, would serve equally well as a visiting card for this most musical of American composers who has now come back into his own. The performances are very alert and vital, particularly that of the *First Symphony,* which is as good as any now available; the recording has superb presence and detail. Apart from the first two *Essays* for orchestra, Zinman's disc includes the more rarely heard *Music for a scene from Shelley,* a sumptuously scored and gloriously atmospheric work inspired by lines from *Prometheus Unbound.* This is the best account of it since Golschmann's from the late 1960s, and adds greatly to the attractions of an already desirable issue. Zinman and his excellent orchestra play the *Overture* to Sheridan's *The School for Scandal,* Barber's celebrated graduation exercise on leaving the Curtis Institute, with equal commitment. Strongly recommended.

(i) *Adagio for strings;* (ii) *Essay No. 2 for orchestra; Music for a scene from Shelley; Serenade for strings, Op. 1;* (ii; iii) *A Stopwatch and an ordnance map, Op. 15;* (iv) *Chorus: Let down the bars, O Death!* (ii; v) *A Hand of bridge* (chamber opera), *Op. 35.*
(M) *** Van. 08.4016.71 [OVC 4016]. (i) I Solisti di Zagreb, Antonio Janigro; (ii) Symphony of the Air, Golschmann; (iii) with Robert De Cormier Chorale; (v) with Neway, Alberts, Lewis, Maero; (iv) Washington Cathedral Ch., Callaway.

An admirable and highly rewarding anthology of works by a composer whose *Adagio for strings* has wrongly overshadowed his achievement elsewhere. Excellent singing and playing throughout.

Adagio for strings, Op. 11. Medea: Medea's Meditation and Dance of vengeance, Op. 23a.
☞ (M) *** BMG/RCA 09026 61424-2 [id.]. Boston SO, Munch – ELGAR: *Introduction and allegro* **; TCHAIKOVSKY: *Serenade.* **(*)

Munch's performance of the *Adagio* has a spacious nobility and generates great passion and ardour at the climax. It is marvellously played, and the playing in the excerpts from *Medea* is equally electrifying. The 1957 recording now sounds fuller and much more realistic than on LP: indeed the CD remastering is remarkably convincing.

Cave of the heart (original version of *Medea*).
*** Koch Dig. 3-7019-2; *2-7019-4* [id.]. Atlantic Sinf., Schenck – COPLAND: *Appalachian spring.* ***

The original version of *Medea* was entitled *Cave of the heart;* in this original form it sounds much darker in feeling and harder-edged, and it has stronger Stravinskian overtones. The effect in this full-blooded, vividly present recording is, if anything, brawnier than the more sumptuous revision. A most interesting and stimulating score.

Cello concerto, Op. 22.
*** Chan. Dig. CHAN 8322; *ABTD 1085* [id.]. Wallfisch, ECO, Simon – SHOSTAKOVICH: *Cello concerto No. 1.* ***

Wallfisch gives an impressive and eloquent reading, and the elegiac slow movement is especially fine. Wallfisch is forwardly balanced, but otherwise the recording is truthful; the orchestra is vividly detailed.

(i; ii) *Piano concerto, Op. 38;* (ii) *Symphony No. 1, Op. 9;* (i; iii) *Souvenirs, Op. 28* (arr. piano, 4 hands); *Canzone.*
*** BMG/RCA Dig. RD 60732 [60732-2-RC]. (i) John Browning; (ii) St Louis SO, Leonard Slatkin; (iii) Slatkin (piano).

In his version of Samuel Barber's *Symphony No. 1,* Slatkin has an obvious advantage. At the very start, the tautness of attack by the St Louis players immediately commands attention, while Järvi (see below) builds tension more gradually. Though Järvi's sense of spontaneity gives extra warmth at times, Slatkin secures ensemble a degree crisper. The coupling will be the decisive point for many, and on RCA it is good to have a new recording of the *Piano concerto* by John Browning, the pianist for whom Barber originally wrote this formidable half-hour work. As an exceptionally generous make-weight Slatkin joins Browning in a piano duo playing Barber's two-piano piece, *Souvenirs*, as Browning points out a work of 'pure nostalgia', played here with winning lightness.

Violin concerto, Op. 14.
(M) *** EMI Dig. CDM7 64305-2 [id.]. Elmar Oliveira, St Louis SO, Slatkin – COPLAND: *Clarinet concerto* ***; GERSHWIN: *Concerto in F.* **
☞ ** EMI Dig. CD7 54314-2 [id.]. Salerno-Sonnenberg, LSO, M. Shostakovich – SHOSTAKOVICH: *Violin concerto No. 1.* **

Anyone who enjoys Barber's *Adagio for strings* must respond to the *Violin concerto.* Elmar Oliveira's version reacts to the nostalgia of the *Andante* with a vein of bitter-sweet yearning that is most affecting. It is a fine performance overall, with a brilliantly played finale, and is warmly and realistically recorded, with Slatkin directing an entirely sympathetic accompaniment. Rich, atmospheric sound.

Nadja Salerno-Sonnenberg enjoys a wide popular following in the USA, and if this CD introduces the wider public to two relatively unfamiliar masterpieces it will serve its purpose. Certainly it does this artist credit that she is not ploughing more commercially obvious furrows. Her performance of the Barber *Violin concerto* emphasizes its warmth and romanticism. Those who don't respond to this kind of approach may find it over-lush. Even the opening idea suffers from expressive exaggeration and the soloist certainly wears her heart on her sleeve. Not everyone will warm to her rather gushing slow movement, and greater restraint would have yielded greater artistic rewards. The LSO give good support under Maxim Shostakovich's baton, and the recording is very good indeed. Not a first choice; however, notwithstanding these reservations, there are some lovely touches.

Essays Nos. 1, Op. 12; 2, Op. 17; 3, Op. 47.
*** Chan. Dig. CHAN 9053; *ABTD 1589* [id.]. Detroit SO, Järvi – IVES: *Symphony No. 1.* ***

Both in terms of sonority and approach, Neeme Järvi's account of these appealing works differs from their American predecessors. The strings have a lightness and subtlety and are highly responsive. The recording is very natural and present, and beautifully balanced.

Essay for orchestra No. 3, Op. 47; Fadograph of a Yestern Scene, Op. 44; Medea: suite, Op. 23.
*** Koch Dig. 3-7010-2; *2-7010-4* [id.]. New Zealand SO, Andrew Schenck.

A welcome recording of two Barber rarities from the 1970s in sympathetic performances by the New Zealand orchestra under Andrew Schenck. The recording has outstanding clarity and definition, but the acoustic has the very slightly dry quality of a studio rather than the expansiveness of a concert hall.

Medea (ballet): suite.
(M) *** Mercury 462 016-2 [id.]. Eastman-Rochester O, Howard Hanson – GOULD: *Fall River legend* etc. ***

Hanson's performance is both polished and dramatic, and the brilliant 1959 Mercury recording has astonishing clarity and vivid presence.

Medea's meditation and dance of vengeance, Op. 23a; Music for a scene from Shelley, Op. 7; Vanesssa: 2 excerpts.
☞ *** Chan. Dig. CHAN 9253 [id.]. Detroit SO, Järvi – CHADWICK: *Symphony No. 3.* ***

Music for a scene from Shelley is an early work, written at about the same time as his graduation overture, *School for Scandal*, and just as inspired. It is a powerfully atmospheric, rich and haunting score, already available on the Argo disc from Zinman and the Baltimore orchestra (as well as Golschmann's version from the 1970s), but this proves to be as appealing an alternative. The two excerpts (the vocal line being taken by solo instruments) from *Vanessa* are captivating; the celebrated dance from *Medea* comes off splendidly under Neeme Järvi and the recording is absolutely state-of-the-art.

Souvenirs.
*** Koch Dig. 3-7005-2; *2-7005-4* [id.]. New Zealand SO, Schenck – MENOTTI: *Amahl* etc. ***

Souvenirs is an absolutely enchanting score which has bags of charm and, unlike the delightful Menotti with which it is coupled, every idea is so memorable that it instantly replaces the one that came before. It is very well played here by the New Zealand Symphony Orchestra under Andrew Schenck and is eminently well recorded too. Strongly recommended.

Symphony No. 1 (in one movement), *Op. 9; Essays for Orchestra Nos. 1, Op. 12; 2, Op. 17; Night flight, Op. 19a.*
(M) *** Unicorn UKCD 2046 [id.]. LSO, David Measham.

Symphony No. 1; The School for scandal: Overture, Op. 5.
*** Chan. Dig. CHAN 8958; *ABTD 1550* [id.]. Detroit SO, Järvi – BEACH: *Symphony in E min.* ***

Neeme Järvi's account of Barber's *First Symphony* is broader than usual and gains enormously in symphonic coherence. Barber's youthful *Overture* to *The School for scandal* with its marvellously fresh and lyrical second theme is equally well served. Good playing from the Detroit orchestra and very good recorded sound.

David Measham also proves a splendid advocate of Barber's *First Symphony*, securing a passionately committed performance and bringing out its (at times) somewhat Waltonian manner. Those looking for a mid-priced version should be well pleased, for the first two *Essays for orchestra* are very well played, as is the hauntingly evocative movement, *Night flight*, all that the composer wanted to survive from his *Symphony No. 2.*

Symphony No. 2, Op. 19; Adagio for strings, Op. 11.
☞ *** Chan. Dig. CHAN 9169 [id.]. Detroit SO, Järvi – BRISTOW: *Symphony No. 2.* ***

Symphony No. 2; Adagio for strings; Overture to a School for Scandal; Essay No. 1; Music for a scene from Shelley.
☞ **(*) Koch Stradivari Dig. SCD-8012 [id.]. New Zealand SO, Andrew Schenck.

The *Second Symphony* enjoys the unusual distinction of being dedicated to the United States Army Air Force, or perhaps that should be the other way round; in any event, there cannot be many other symphonies sharing this peculiarity. Samuel Barber recorded the piece himself on a 10-inch Decca LP in the early 1950s (there was an abrupt drop in pitch in the finale), but its few public performances prompted doubts and in a fit of depression he withdrew it, save for the slow movement which he retitled *Night Music*. Fortunately there has been renewed interest in the piece, which is a powerful work with a strong first movement. There is a particularly beguiling second group which has some of the innocence and warmth of the second theme from the *School for Scandal* Overture. Of the two performances now available, Neeme Järvi on Chandos is the one to have: the Detroit orchestra turn in the more polished playing and the Chandos recording is richer and more vivid than the New Zealand alternative under Andrew Schenck. Taken in isolation, this is still very recommendable, particularly if you want the *Music for a scene from Shelley* and the *School for Scandal* Overture.

CHAMBER MUSIC

String quartet, Op. 11.
☞ *** ASV Dig. CDDCA 825 [id.]. Lindsay Qt – A. TCHAIKOVSKY: *String quartet No. 2;* WIREN: *String quartet No. 3;* WOOD: *String quartet No. 3.* ***
☞ *** BMG/RCA Dig. 09026 61387-2 [id.]. Tokyo Qt – BRITTEN: *Quartet No. 2;* TAKEMITSU: *A Way A Lone.* ***
☞ **(*) DG Dig. 435 864-2 [id.]. Emerson Qt – IVES: *Quartets 1–2.*
☞ ** Collins Dig. 1386-2 [id.]. Duke Qt – DVORAK: *Quartet No. 12* **(*); GLASS: *Quartet No. 1.* **

Samuel Barber's early *String quartet* (1936) is a short work whose *Adagio* Toscanini made famous in its transcription for full strings. Despite the enormous popularity of the *Adagio* in particular and of its composer in general, the quartet has rather languished on the edges of the repertory. The Lindsays give the more humane and deeply felt account, and no one wanting to add the piece to their collection is likely to be disappointed. Their performance comes from a broadcast given in 1987 and so has the feel of live music-making. Their coupling blends enterprise and interest, offering quartets by André Tchaikovsky, better known during his lifetime as an accomplished pianist, Hugh Wood and Dag Wirén.

The Tokyo Quartet's account of the Barber is hard to beat. They produce a sumptuous and beautifully blended sonority and they play with feeling. Choice will no doubt be affected by the coupling, but there is no doubt that theirs is very remarkable playing, and no one wanting the coupling should hesitate.

The Emerson Quartet play with all the brilliance and technical expertise with which one associates them, but there is something rather soulless about them. The tone is rich, their tonal blend immaculate and their ensemble impeccable – indeed nothing can be faulted; but their expressive eloquence sounds over-rehearsed as if the feeling is painted on afterwards. All the same, it is in its way stunningly played and those who admire their brilliance and tonal sheen will find it eminently well captured by the DG engineers. Given this level of accomplishment, it would be curmudgeonly to deny them a strong recommendation.

A rather upfront balance diminishes enthusiasm for the very well-played Duke Quartet account, coupled with Dvořák and Glass. A very musical performance that can hold its own with most competition but that is not superior to the front-runners. If the hybrid coupling appeals, it is worth considering.

Summer music.
*** Crystal CD 750 [id.]. Westwood Wind Quintet – CARLSSON: *Nightwings;* LIGETI: *Bagatelles;*
    MATHIAS: *Quintet.* ***
(M) **(*) Sony SMK 46250 [id.]. Members of the Marlboro Festival – NIELSEN: *Woodwind quintet;*
    HINDEMITH: *Octet.* **

Samuel Barber's *Summer music* is an evocative mood-picture of summer, a gloriously warm and lyrical piece whose neglect on record is difficult to understand. The Crystal CD offers superbly committed and sensitive playing and vivid, warm recording.

Barber's delightful *Summer music* is also sensitively played by the artists at the Marlboro Festival, who capture its air of tenderness and melancholy very well. The 1981 sound-quality is very acceptable and the coupling valuable.

PIANO MUSIC

Ballade, Op. 46; 4 Excursions, Op. 20; Nocturne (Homage to John Field), Op. 33; Sonata, Op. 26.
**(*) Hyp. CDH 88016 [id.]. Angela Brownridge.

This CD accommodates Barber's entire output for the piano. Angela Brownridge gives a good account of herself in the dazzling *Sonata*. The recording is not first class; the resonant acoustic makes the piano sound slightly unfocused, though the ear soon adjusts.

Piano sonata, Op. 26.
☞ (M) (***) BMG/RCA mono GD 60377 [60377-2-RG]. Vladimir Horowitz (with FAURE: *Nocturne
    No. 13;* POULENC: *Presto ***) – KABALEVSKY; PROKOFIEV: *Sonatas etc.* (***)
(M) **(*) BMG/RCA GD 60415 [60415-2-RG]. Van Cliburn (with DEBUSSY: *Estampes: Soirée dans
    Grenade; Jardins sous la pluie; Etude No. 5; Images, Book I: Reflets dans l'eau; Préludes, Book 2:
    La terrasse des audiences du clair de lune; Feux d'artifice **; MOZART: Piano sonata No. 10 **).*

Horowitz gave the première of Barber's *Sonata* and his performance has never been surpassed. It is a remarkable work and, in Horowitz's hands, completely riveting: sample his playing in the quicksilver Scherzo or the articulation of the spirited closing *Fuga*. The 1950 sound is confined but fully acceptable. Of the encores, the scintillating Poulenc *Presto* shows the great pianist at his most dazzling.

Van Cliburn's recording is pretty masterly and, although the sound could be more ingratiating and have a warmer ambience, it is still acceptable.

VOCAL MUSIC

Agnus Dei.
*** Hyp. Dig. CDA 66129 [id.]. Corydon Singers, Matthew Best – BERNSTEIN: *Chichester Psalms;*
    COPLAND: *In the beginning etc.* ***

Barber's *Agnus Dei* is none other than our old friend the *Adagio*, arranged for voices by the composer in 1967. Matthew Best's fine performance moves spaciously and expansively to an impressive climax.

Choral music: *Agnus Dei; Heaven-Haven; Let down the bars, O Death; The monk and his cat;
Reincarnations (Mary Hynes; Anthony O. Daly; The coolin). A Stopwatch and an ordnance map; Sure
on this shining night; To be sung on the water; Twelfth night; The Virgin martyrs. (Opera
arrangements): Anthony and Cleopatra: On the death of Anthony; On the death of Cleopatra. Vanessa:
Under the willow tree.*
☞ *** Gamut Dig. GAMCD 535 [id.]. Cambridge University Chamber Ch., Timothy Brown.

Apart from the *Agnus Dei* (our old friend, the *Adagio*, arranged for chorus and sung gently and without the degree of passion at the climax of the version for strings), the most striking piece here is *A Stopwatch and an ordnance map*, a starkly dramatic Stephen Spender setting about sudden death on the battlefield, opening with side drum snares and punctuated by the timpani. Yet the opening Irish trilogy (words by the blind folk poet, Anthony Raferty) has all the lyrical softness and open beauty of the countryside in County Mayo. The excerpts from the aborted opera *Anthony and Cleopatra* are choral arrangements of two key Cleopatra arias and, with piano accompaniment, are less than completely effective, in spite of the passion of the singing at the closing climax of the heroine's death scene. But the Laurie Lee poem, *Twelfth night*, 'No night could be darker than this night' is extremely vivid. *The monk and his cat* (W. H. Auden) with its tripping piano obbligato is delightful, and the gently ecstatic *Sure on this shining night* (James Agee) is matched by the spiritual simplicity of the novice nun's song, *Heaven-Haven*. The closing item is well chosen when the soaring line of *To be sung on the water* then fades into the distance as if carried away by the stream. Any minor reservations do not detract from the value or appeal of this 50-minute programme overall, persuasively performed by a well-rehearsed and well-balanced choir and excellently recorded in a warm but not clouding acoustic.

(i) *Andromache's farewell;* (ii) *Dover Beach;* (iii) *Hermit songs;* (iv) *Knoxville: summer of 1915.*
(M) (***) Sony mono/stereo MPK 46727 [id.]. (i) Arroyo, NYPO, Schippers; (ii) Fischer-Dieskau, Juilliard Qt; (iii) Leontyne Price, composer; (iv) Eleanor Steber, Dumbarton Oaks O, William Strickland.

This collection of vintage recordings makes a splendid mid-priced Barber compendium, representing four of his finest vocal works, all in superb performances. Excellent CD transfers. No texts are provided but words are exceptionally clear.

Despite and still (song-cycle), *Op. 41; 10 Hermit songs* (to poems translated from anonymous Irish texts of 8th to 13th centuries), *Op. 29; Mélodies passagères, Op. 27: (Puisque tout passe; Un cygne; Tombeau dans une pare; Le clocher chante); 3 Songs, Op. 2 (The daisies; With rue my heart is laden; Bessie Bobtail); 3 Songs, Op. 10 (Rain has fallen; Sleep now; I hear an army); 4 Songs, Op. 13 (A nun takes the veil; The secrets of the old; Sure on this shining night; Nocturne); 2 Songs, Op. 18 (The Queen's face on the summary coin; Monks and raisins); 3 Songs, Op. 45 (Now I have fed and eaten up the rose; A green lowland of pianos; O boundless, boundless evening); Beggar's song; Dover Beach; In the dark pinewood; Love at the door; Love's caution; Night wanderers; Nuvoletta; Of that so sweet imprisonment; Serenades; A slumber song of the Madonna; Strings in the earth and air; There's nae lark.*
☞ *** DG Dig. 435 867-2 (2) [id.]. Cheryl Studer, Thomas Hampson, John Browning; Emerson Quartet.

Samuel Barber wrote songs throughout his composing career. The first included here – *A slumber song of the Madonna* – was one of the 10 previously unpublished ones revived specially for this recording. It dates from 1925 when Barber was fifteen and was composed for his aunt, the celebrated contralto, Louise Homer. The last three, Opus 45, were written in 1972 for Dietrich Fischer-Dieskau; in between, Barber's style, easily lyrical, sensitively responding to the cadences of English verse, remained remarkably consistent. Barber had no special wish to write American songs, and very few of the poems he set are by his compatriots. Rather he chose to set British – and particularly Irish – poets, with whom he felt a special affinity, notably James Joyce. The longest cycle is the sequence of *Hermit songs*, written to translations of lines by medieval Irish monks. W. H. Auden contributes two of the most striking translations, including *The monk and his cat*, which inspires Barber to write a catchy tune. Barber's sense of humour frequently emerges, as in the setting of Joyce's *Solitary hotel* in the Op. 41 group, *Despite and still*, written in 1968–9. It is marked to be performed 'like a rather fast tango in 2'. Cheryl Studer sings beautifully in the *Hermit songs*, but it is Thomas Hampson who establishes the full flavour of the collection, which includes a sprinkling of vigorous, extrovert songs. He is particularly fine in Barber's best-known song, the extended *Dover Beach*, a setting of Matthew Arnold, written early in Barber's career. In that Hampson is accompanied immaculately by the Emerson Quartet. Otherwise it is John Browning – a pianist specially associated with Barber's music and the prime mover behind this recording project – who sharpens the focus and heightens the fantasy in deeply sympathetic accompaniments. Excellent, natural recording, first-class documentation and full texts.

(i) *Hermit songs, Op. 29;* (ii) *Knoxville: Summer of 1915* (cantata); (i) Songs: *The Daisies; Nocturne; Nuvoletta; Sleep now.* (ii) *Antony and Cleopatra* (opera): scenes: *Give me some music; Give me my robe.*
☞ (M) (***) BMG/RCA mono/stereo 09026 61983-2 [id.]. Leontyne Price, with (i) composer (piano); (ii) New Philh. O, Schippers.

This mid-priced CD offers all the recordings of Barber made by Leontyne Price, long associated with his music. The evocative cantata to words by James Agee, *Knoxville: Summer of 1915*, has never been done more hauntingly and, as on LP, is well coupled with the heroine's arias from the opera, *Antony and Cleopatra*, the role she created in the original Met. production. Far rarer is the private recording from the Library of Congress of the very first performance in October 1953 of the *Hermit songs*, also specially written for her. Accompanied by the composer, she is more rugged than Studer in the collected song edition, but just as intense. The mono sound is very limited but conveys the atmosphere of a historic occasion. Otherwise good stereo sound.

The Lovers, Op. 43. Prayers of Kierkegaard, Op. 30.
*** Koch Dig. 3-7125-2. Dale Duesing, Sarah Reese, Chicago Ch. & SO, Andrew Schenck.

The Lovers, written in 1971, was Barber's last major work, a substantial choral cantata setting nine erotic poems by the Chilean, Pablo Neruda. It is music of heartwarming richness, here given a splendid first recording, taken from live performances given in Chicago in October 1991. The nine songs, varied in mood and length, follow the development of a love affair from first passion past various states of ecstasy through to the sadness and disillusion of lost love. It makes a moving sequence, with the soloist, Dale Duesing, matching the responsiveness of the outstanding Chicago Symphony Chorus. *The Prayers of Kierkegaard*, written in 1952, is a tougher, more uncompromising work, but approachable too, again with magnificent writing for chorus. Schenck's colourful performances bring a timely memorial for a fine conductor who died early in 1992.

Vanessa (opera): complete.
(M) *** BMG/RCA GD 87899 (2) [7899-2-RG]. Steber, Elias, Resnik, Gedda, Tossi, Met. Op. Ch. & O, Mitropoulos.

Vanessa inhabits much the same civilized world as Strauss or Henry James. Although it has not held the stage, its melodic freshness and warmth will ensure a reversal of its fortunes some day. This, its only recording so far, was made at the time of its first performance in 1958, but no apologies are needed for its quality; it stands the test of time as well as does the opera itself.

Bargiel, Woldemar (1828–97)

Octet in C min. for strings, Op. 15a.
*** Hyp. Dig. CDA 66356 [id.]. Divertimenti – MENDELSSOHN: *Octet.* ***

What strikes one about this music is its independence of outlook and dignity. Indeed it is something of a discovery; the delightful scherzo-like section embedded in the slow movement is particularly felicitous. Divertimenti play it with real feeling and conviction and are excellently recorded.

Barrios, Agustin (1885–1944)

Aconquija; Aire de Zamba; Le catedral; Cueca; Estudio; Una limosna por el amor de Dios; Madrigal (Gavota); Maxixa; Mazurka appassionata; Minuet; Preludio; Un sueño en la floresta; Valse No. 3; Vallancico de Navidad.
(M) *** Sony SBK 47669 [id.]. John Williams – PONCE: *Folia de España.* ***

In the expert hands of John Williams this collection provides a very entertaining recital, ideal for late-evening listening. The recording is excellent. The remarkable extended set of Ponce *Variations* added for the CD reissue brings the total playing time up to 77 minutes.

Bartók, Béla (1881–1945)

Concerto for orchestra.
(M) *** Decca 417 754-2 [id.]. Chicago SO, Solti – MUSSORGSKY: *Pictures.* ***
(*) Decca Dig. 425 694-2 [id.]. Cleveland O, Dohnányi – LUTOSLAWSKI: *Concerto for orchestra.* *
☞ (M) **(*) Telarc Dig. CD 82010 [id.]. Los Angeles PO, André Previn – JANACEK: *Sinfonietta.* **(*)

Solti gave Bartók's *Concerto for orchestra* its compact disc début. The upper range is very brightly lit indeed, which brings an aggressive feeling to the upper strings. This undoubtedly suits the reading, fierce and biting on the one hand, exuberant on the other. Superlative playing from Solti's own Chicago orchestra, and given vivid sound.

Dohnányi's brings an even fuller, richer sound than Solti's with the Chicago orchestra or Dutoit's with the Montreal Symphony. Dohnányi's reading is relatively straight – the night music of the third movement lacks mystery, and the humour of the fourth-movement trio is a little stiff – but, with ensemble even crisper than on either rival disc, the bite and power of much of the playing is sharply contrasted with the extreme refinement and delicacy of the string articulation, as in the scurrying main theme of the finale.

Previn and the Los Angeles Philharmonic give a comfortable, relaxed reading of Bartók's *Concerto*. Previn is at his best in the fun of the couple-play in the second movement or the Shostakovich parody of the fourth movement. For him, it is above all a work of fun, although there is no lack of excitement in the finale. The Telarc recording captures the full bloom of the orchestra as few recordings from Los Angeles have. The coupling is unique. Those seeking a relatively mellow account of the Bartók *Concerto* will certainly not be disappointed in the spectacular sound, and this is certainly competitive on Telarc's new Bravo! mid-priced label.

(i) *Concerto for orchestra;* (ii) *Piano concertos Nos. 1–3;* (i; iii) *Violin concerto No. 2 in B min.*
☞ (B) *** Ph. Duo 438 812-2 (2) [id.]. (i) Concg. O, Haitink; (ii) Kovacevich, LSO or BBC SO (in *No. 2*), Sir Colin Davis; (iii) Szeryng.

This is as enticing a bargain Bartók collection as you could find. Not unexpectedly in Haitink's 1960 *Concerto for orchestra*, the orchestral playing is of the highest quality and the recording is both atmospheric and clear. The performance is more subtle, less tense than Solti's mid-priced version, although the element of dramatic contrast is not missing. Haitink's touch of restraint brings a gentle character to the *Elegy* and the close of the *Allegretto*. Thus the contrasts of the furious bravura of the opening of the finale and the splendour of the work's closing pages are the more telling. Szeryng joins Haitink for the *B minor Violin concerto* with equally satisfying artistic results. The balance is not absolutely ideal (the solo violin is placed somewhat forward in relation to the orchestra), but such is the conviction of the playing that reservations pale. Haitink keeps a firm grip on proceedings and there is a genuine sense of momentum and impetus about the performance that is really exciting. The Concertgebouw Orchestra play with their accustomed panache and brilliance, yet there is no lack of mystery in the more reflective passages of the first movement or in the marvellously poetic *Andante tranquillo*. The 1969 recording is vivid, and firmly and realistically focused. Kovacevich's direct, concentrated readings of the three *Piano concertos* are hardly less persuasive. Sir Colin Davis accompanies sensitively and vigorously. Kovacevich seems intent on countering the idea that No. 3 is a facile work, with the central *Adagio religioso* played with hushed dedication between spiky outer movements, giving concentrated intensity to compare with late Beethoven. No complaints about the bright, full recording.

(i) *Concerto for orchestra;* (ii) *Dance suite; 2 Portraits, Op. 5; Mikrokosmos* (orch. Serly): *Bourrée; From the diary of a fly.*
(M) *** Mercury 432 017-2 [id.]. (i) LSO; (ii) Philharmonia Hungarica, Dorati.

Dorati secures outstandingly brilliant and committed playing from the LSO. The recording, made in Wembley Town hall, shows characteristic expertise of balance. The rest of the programme was recorded in 1958 in the Grosse Saal of the Vienna Konzerthaus, which affords Dorati's fine orchestra of Hungarian émigrés plenty of body without blurring outlines.

Concerto for orchestra; Kossuth (symphonic poem); *The Miraculous Mandarin*: suite.
☞ (B) ** Pickwick Dig. PCD 1013; *PK 515*. Hungarian Nat. PO, Tobor Ferenc.

The main interest on the bargain Pickwick CD is *Kossuth*, an early symphonic poem first performed in 1904, representing the national hero of the 1848 Hungarian uprising, Lajos Kossuth, and written under the influence of Richard Strauss's *Ein Heldenleben*. The ambitiously scored piece quotes irreverently from Haydn's famous Austrian national anthem in the battle sequence and involves plenty of somewhat crude melodrama but ends in disconsolate mourning. It is hardly a lost masterpiece but is surely of interest to Bartókians, even if neither performance nor recording is specially well focused. The orchestra is obviously more familiar with the other two orchestral showpieces and, if the playing is red-blooded rather than refined, both pieces are involving and make plenty of impact.

(i) *Concerto for orchestra;* (ii) *The Miraculous Mandarin: suite.*
☞ **(*) Nimbus Dig. NI 5229 [id.]. Hungarian State SO, Adám Fischer.
☞ (M) ** DG 437 247-2 [id.]. Boston SO, (i) Kubelik; (ii) Ozawa.
☞ *(*) Sony Dig. SK 45748 [id.]. BPO, Mehta.

Concerto for orchestra; The Miraculous Mandarin: suite; 2 Pictures, Op. 10.
☞ (B) *(**) Sony SBK 48263 [id.]. Phd. O, Ormandy.

The Philadelphia *Concerto for orchestra* is superbly played and there is plenty of panache in
Ormandy's reading. The snag is that, even with careful digital remastering, the upper strings are
inclined to be a bit shrill. Predictably, Ormandy also draws a brilliant, polished performance from his
orchestra in *The Miraculous Mandarin,* not as committed as Solti's, nor as flexible, but still enjoyable,
even with the usual close-up sound-picture favoured by CBS in the 1960s. Even Bartók enthusiasts
must often have confused the *2 Pictures for orchestra,* Op. 10, with the *Two Portraits,* Op. 5. Opus 10
has an uninhibitedly romantic piece, fittingly labelled *In full bloom* (cue for the full Philadelphia
sound), and a *Village dance,* fairly easy-going by Bartókian standards. A generous triptych (74
minutes) and it is a pity there have to be reservations about the recording, which certainly does not
lack vividness.

The Nimbus recording is full of atmosphere, and both works are characterized powerfully and
Slavonically and are strongly played with obvious idiomatic feeling. There is no lack of tension, but
in the last resort Adám Fischer's readings, though never dull, are too waywardly individual to give
the music the strength of profile of the finest Western versions.

Kubelik gives a relatively relaxed performance of the *Concerto for orchestra.* He certainly yields
points to Solti in biting excitement, but the way he brings out the Shostakovich parody in the fourth
movement is delectable, and in the slow movement he provides added atmospheric evocation, if
without the clean precision of the Hungarian conductor. The Boston sound adds allure here,
although in Ozawa's coupling of the *Suite* from *The Miraculous Mandarin* the acoustic of Symphony
Hall is hardly recognizable. The balance is aggressively close, with comparatively little sense of space.
It might be argued that aggressive sound is appropriate for this particularly vehement orchestral
writing, and the playing has much force and bravura, often creating a bizarre pungency.

Mehta gets a superb response from the BPO but the end result is curiously negative. This is
virtuoso playing, and there is no lack of physical excitement and orchestral spectacle but nothing to
give these readings any kind of memorability. Recordings are good, the *Concerto* the more atmospheric, the *Miraculous Mandarin* the more sharply defined in detail.

Concerto for orchestra; Music for strings, percussion and celesta.
*** EMI Dig. CDC7 54070-2; *EL 754070-4* [id.]. Oslo PO, Jansons.
*** Decca Dig. 421 443-2 [id.]. Montreal SO, Dutoit.
☞ (B) ** DG 439 402-2 [id.]. (i) BPO, Maazel; (ii) Boston SO, Ozawa.

Jansons and the Oslo Philharmonic give outstanding performances of both works, making this by a
small margin a first recommendation in this now-favourite coupling of two Bartók masterpieces. The
Oslo orchestra plays with unfailingly crisp ensemble, and the sound is excellent too, full and open.

Helped by warm and atmospheric recording, Dutoit conducts performances of both these
masterpieces which convey the message that Bartók is a composer of warmth and refinement rather
than of barbarism. Dutoit is particularly successful in bringing out the vein of humour, too, not only
in the *Concerto* but also in the *Music for strings, percussion and celesta.*

Maazel's reading of the *Concerto,* exciting and very well played, has warmth as well as bite, but it
lacks wit in such a movement as the 'Play of the couples'. The recording, made in the Berlin Jesus-
Christus-Kirche in 1979, is spectacularly full and wide-ranging, and is vividly transferred to CD,
although for some reason the trumpet is backwardly balanced. The coupling of Ozawa's 1980 *Music
for strings, percussion and celesta* is less recommendable. The Boston playing is often impressive, yet
the brilliant second and fourth movements sound relatively slack, and Reiner creates far more tension
in the first and third. The microphones have been placed close and, while the range of dynamic is
wider than in the Chicago recording, the Boston violins are made to sound somewhat aggressive in
fortissimo, with the spacious Boston ambience partly cancelled out by the multi-track recording
technique.

Concerto for orchestra; Music for strings, percussion and celesta; Hungarian sketches.
☞ (M) *** BMG/RCA 09026 61504-2 [id.]. Chicago SO, Fritz Reiner.

Reiner's version of the *Concerto for orchestra* was recorded in 1955 but in its latest CD format the
sound approaches demonstration standard in its spacious warmth, clarity and impact. The perform-

ance is most satisfying, surprisingly straightforward from one brought up in central Europe, but with plenty of cutting edge. The *Music for strings, percussion and celesta*, recorded three years later, suffers from a forward balance which prevents a true pianissimo, yet the concentration of the playing at the hushed opening of the first and third movements all but overcomes this defect, and the folk-based set of five *Hungarian sketches*, which completes the programme, is utterly seductive when played and recorded with such vividness of colour and a natural understanding of the music's rhythmic impetus.

Concerto for orchestra; 4 Orchestral pieces, Op. 12.
☞ **(*) DG Dig. 437 826-2 [id.]. Chicago SO, Boulez.

Boulez's is a strong and perceptively detailed account of the *Concerto for orchestra*. He secures brilliant playing from the Chicago orchestra, but they are able to relax in the central movements – which is just as well, for the finale is very powerfully driven indeed. The *Four Orchestral Pieces* was the nearest Bartók came to writing a symphony, complete with Scherzo and melancholy slow movement. The present account is powerfully characterized and makes the piece seem more symphonic than ever. Boulez has recorded both these works before with the NYPO, and if his earlier version of Op. 12 is marginally superseded by this new performance, the *Concerto for orchestra*, for all its excitement, is preferable to the earlier CBS version only in terms of its recorded sound. That New York version somehow had a greater degree of idiosyncrasy.

Piano concertos Nos. 1–3.
☞ *** EMI Dig. CDC7 54871-2 [id.]. Peter Donohoe, CBSO, Rattle.

Peter Donohoe and Sir Simon Rattle give first-class accounts of all three Bartók concertos and they have the advantage of equally impressive sound. Given the advances in technology, all three can now be accommodated on one CD. The keenest competition comes from Stephen Kovacevich and Sir Colin Davis (Philips), also accommodated on one CD and now available in one of Philips's Duo couplings, along with Szeryng's account of the 1938 *Violin concerto* and the *Concerto for orchestra*, all at the same price (see above). At the same time, taken in isolation and purely on its own merits, this EMI CD is a highly recommendable issue which offers thoroughly idiomatic playing.

Piano concertos Nos. 1–3; Music for strings, percussion & celesta; Rhapsody for piano and orchestra; Scherzo for piano and orchestra.
*** Ph. Dig. 416 831-2 (3) [id.]. Kocsis, Budapest Festival O, Fischer.

(i) *Piano concertos Nos. 1–3; Rhapsody for piano and orchestra; Concerto for orchestra.*
(M) *** DG 427 410-2 (2) [id.]. (i) Géza Anda, Berlin RSO, Fricsay.

(i) *Piano concertos Nos. 1–3;* (ii) *Sonata for 2 pianos and percussion.*
(M) *** Decca Dig./Analogue 425 573-2 (2) [id.]. Vladimir Ashkenazy; (i) LPO, Solti; (ii) Vovka Ashkenazy, D. Corkhill, Andrew Smith.

This Philips set remains fairly competitive in this repertoire and the *Third* is superbly done, to make it perhaps the finest on record. The inclusion of the *Music for strings, percussion and celesta* may be counted a disadvantage by some, particularly as the resonant acoustic and rather forward balance prevent an absolute pianissimo and detract from the feeling of mystery; but this is still an exciting and involving performance. The full-bodied recording with a rich, tangible piano-image is very satisfying.

Ashkenazy's versions of both the *First Concerto* and the *Sonata* (with his son, Vovka) are tough, even aggressive performances, biting, never relaxing, spectacularly caught in (1984) digital sound with the widest range of dynamics. The *Second* and *Third Concertos*, recorded four years earlier, are analogue, but the recording, although reverberant, is comparably vivid and present.

Anda's recordings of the Bartók *Concertos* and the *Rhapsody*, which is attractively volatile, have acquired classic status. The performances are refined yet urgent, incisive but red-blooded too. Fricsay's *Concerto for orchestra* was recorded in 1957 and is a first-class example of DG's expertise in the pre-stereo era.

Piano concertos Nos. 1 in A; 2 in G.
*** DG 415 371-2 [id.]. Pollini, Chicago SO, Abbado.

The DG issue forms an exuberant partnership between two of the most distinguished Italian musicians of the day. Virtuosity goes with a sense of spontaneity. The Chicago orchestra, vividly recorded, is in superb form and the CD gives a new lease of life to the 1979 analogue recording.

Concerto for 2 pianos, percussion and celesta.
*** Ph. Dig. 416 378-2 [id.]. Freire, Argerich, L. and J. Pustjens, Concg. O, Zinman – KODALY: *Dances of Galánta.* ***

Martha Argerich with Stephen Kovacevich recorded a fierily vibrant performance of the *Sonata*, and there is much of the same high-voltage electricity in her recording of the orchestral version with Nelson Freire. The recording with pianos placed relatively close is well detailed but lacks something in mystery.

Viola concerto (ed. Tibor Serly).
☞ *** EMI Dig. CDC7 54101-2 [id.]. Tabea Zimmermann, Bav. RSO, David Shallon – HINDEMITH: *Der Schwanendreher.* ***

The *Viola concerto* comes from the very end of Bartók's career, and it was Tibor Serly, who had worked closely with the composer, who turned the sketches which the composer had left into the present finished work. This new EMI version, coupled with Hindemith, offers merely 47 minutes 40 seconds playing time, not exactly generous value these days for full-price CDs. All the same, Tabea Zimmermann and the Orchestra of Bayerischen Rundfunks are strongly recommendable if artistic considerations are paramount. This is playing of great eloquence and taste, and the balance is much finer than that offered by the DG engineers on their newest version – see below. The soloist is helped, but she is not so forward as to mask orchestral detail, which is wonderfully present and beautifully placed. If you do not recoil at the prospect of paying full price for the disc, you will at least be well rewarded in terms of excellent artistry and outstanding recorded quality.

Viola concerto; Violin concerto No. 1; (i) Rhapsodies Nos. 1–2.
(M) *** EMI CDM7 63985-2 [id.]. Sir Yehudi Menuhin, New Philh. O, Dorati; (i) BBC SO, Boulez.

Menuhin with his strongly creative imagination plays these concertos with characteristic nobility of feeling, and he and Dorati make much of the Hungarian dance rhythms. There is a comparably earthy, peasant manner in Menuhin's playing of the two *Rhapsodies*, and it is matched by Boulez's approach, warm and passionate rather than clinical. The soloist is rather close. However, the balance responds to the controls, and this remains one of Menuhin's most worthwhile reissues.

Viola concerto; Violin concerto No. 2.
*** BMG/RCA Dig. RD 60749 [60749-2-RC]. Zukerman, St Louis SO, Slatkin.

Pinchas Zukerman gives an attractively lively account of the Bartók *Violin concerto No. 2*, aptly coupled with the *Viola concerto*, with Zukerman once again demonstrating his supreme mastery on the bigger string instrument. Fine orchestral playing and excellent sound.

(i) *Viola concerto* (ed. Tibor Serly); *Music for strings, percussion and celesta.*
☞ **(*) DG Dig. 437 993-2 [id.]. (i) Wolfram Christ, BPO, Ozawa.

The DG recording offers 52 minutes 26 seconds, and as such is better value in playing time than the EMI version above, but it is still not exactly generous and, good though these performances are, some readers will be forgiven if they understandably gravitate to the alternative versions of both works. In the 1989 DG account of the *Viola concerto* the soloist is very forward; the recording is multi-mike rather than a natural concert-hall balance and there is often a two-dimensional effect with little back-to-front perspective. All the same, Wolfram Christ plays marvellously and in view of its artistic excellence it would be curmudgeonly to deny a third star. Ozawa's dramatic and highly charged account of the *Music for strings, percussion and celesta* is first rate and there is more air round the sound. Recorded at a concert in 1993, the audience is impressively silent.

Violin concertos Nos. 1 and 2.
(M) *** Decca Dig./Analogue 425 015-2 [id.]. Kyung Wha Chung, Chicago SO or LPO, Solti.
☞ *** Nimbus Dig. NI 5333 [id.]. Gerhart Hetzel, Hungarian State SO, Adám Fischer.

Though on Decca the soloist is rather forwardly balanced, the hushed intensity of the writing, as well as bitingly Hungarian flavours, is caught superbly, thanks to the conductor as well as to the soloist. The expressive warmth behind Bartók's writing is fully brought out, and there is no sentimental lingering. This leads the field in both works.

Gerhart Hetzel is a relatively infrequent visitor to the recording studios and is little known as a soloist in the UK. At the time these recordings were made he was chief concertmaster of the Vienna Philharmonic. To judge from these performances of the Bartók concertos the loss is ours, for he plays both concertos with great feeling and understanding. He brings us into a wholly different world from the superficial razzle-dazzle and ego-centred account DG issued some time ago with Mutter and

Ozawa. There is no want of virtuosity, but nor is there virtuosity for its own sake (or, rather, that of the soloist's ego). Ideas are fashioned with great sensitivity and, although dynamic nuances are scrupulously observed, there is none of the exaggeration which draws attention to the soloist rather than to Bartók. The variations in the slow movement of the 1938 concerto are beautifully shaped by conductor and soloist alike. These are performances of strong but unintrusive personality. Both concertos are very well recorded, with a natural, excellent balance which helps the soloist to just the right extent, and it must rank among the very best now available.

Violin concerto No. 2.
☞ (M) (**(*)) BMG/RCA mono 09026 61395-2 [id.]. Menuhin, Dallas SO, Dorati (with ELGAR: *Salut d'amour;* DEBUSSY: *Prélude: La fille aux cheveux de lin;* LALO: *Symphonie espagnole* (**(*))).

It was in Menuhin's première recording of the Bartók *Violin concerto* that many collectors will have first encountered the piece. As so often with first recordings, it has an immediacy and freshness that neither of his later records (with Furtwängler and, in the mid-1960s, Dorati again) surpassed. There is a strong sense of atmosphere and colour here (the texture is generally lighter and more transparent than it is in the Furtwängler/Philharmonia issue, though that was superb in other ways). The transfers sound as if they are made from commercial pressings rather than masters, though this comment is conjectural; however, one can imagine another team making a more expert job of it. Artistically this still remains a very strong account. The Lalo coupling is an admirable 1945 performance, with the San Francisco Symphony under Monteux, which has never been released before.

Violin concerto No. 2; 2 Rhapsodies for violin and orchestra.
☞ *** EMI Dig. CDC7 54211-2 [id.]. Kyung Wha Chung, CBSO, Rattle.
☞ *** BMG/RCA Dig. 09026 61675-2 [id.]. Takezawa, LSO, Tilson Thomas.

Kyung Wha Chung in her EMI version gives a commanding, inspired performance, full of fire and imagination, helped by the inspirational accompaniment of Rattle and the Birmingham orchestra. Where in her earlier recording with Solti for Decca Chung was above all powerful, matching the conductor's Hungarian bite, here she delves deeper, finding extra mystery in the first two movements, both in their way elusive, as well as more fire. In the scherzando passages her playing has a mercurial quality that gives an infectious lift to Hungarian rhythms, and she is well matched by her accompanists. The same qualities come out just as vividly in the two flamboyant *Rhapsodies*, each in two nicely contrasted movements.

Takezawa's recording with the LSO was linked to the television performance she gave in Tilson Thomas's 'Concerto' series of programmes. It is a powerful performance in which a young virtuoso is fearlessly note-perfect. Well recorded, with fine playing from the LSO, it would have been even more welcome had it not appeared simultaneously with the more searching, more imaginative Chung reading on EMI, offering the same coupling.

Divertimento for strings.
☞ (M) *** EMI CDM5 65079-2 [id.]. ECO, Daniel Barenboim – HINDEMITH: *Trauermusik;* SCHOENBERG: *Verklaerte Nacht.* ***

Barenboim's passionate earthiness makes this a very strong account of the *Divertimento*. Ensemble may be slightly on the wild side, but the rapt pianissimo at the opening of the *Molto adagio* is to lead to a searing climax, and the result is red-bloodedly involving, with a vigorous communication of high spirits in the finale. The work is, of course, in concerto grosso style and here the solo quartet is a distinguished one (José-Luis Garcia, John Tunnel, Cecil Aronowitz and Adrian Beers). The 1969 Abbey Road recording brings admirably full string textures. With excellent couplings this makes a first-rate triptych.

Divertimento for strings; Music for strings, percussion and celesta.
*** Hung. Dig. HCD 12531 [id.]. Liszt CO, Rolla.

Divertimento for string orchestra; Music for strings, percussion and celesta; (i) *2 Portraits.*
☞ (M) (***) DG mono 437 675-2 [id.]. (i) Rudolf Schulz; Berlin RIAS SO, Fricsay.

Divertimento for strings; Music for strings, percussion and celesta; (i) *2 Portraits, Op. 5; The Wooden Prince* (suite), *Op. 13.*
☞ *(*) Nimbus Dig. NI 5362/3 [id.]. (i) Gerhart Herzel; Hungarian State SO, Adám Fischer.

On Hungaroton both performances are expert and distil a powerful atmosphere in the slow movements of each piece. They command beautifully rapt *pianissimo* tone and keen intensity. The sound is less reverberant than some rivals, but there is no lack of ambience.

There is something special about Ferenc Fricsay's Bartók: a total identification with the idiom and an authentic sense of pace and atmosphere. Both the *Music for strings, percussion and celesta* and the *Divertimento* were recorded in 1953, and the *Two Portraits* in the previous year; few allowances need be made for the quality (except perhaps for the string timbre above the stave in louder passages). Rudolf Schulz plays with great eloquence in the *Portraits*.

For a start, the first record of this Nimbus set has a playing time of only 39 minutes 25 seconds and the second (at 57 minutes 10 seconds) hardly compensates. There is nothing special about the performances of either the *Divertimento* or the *Music for strings, percussion and celesta*, although the *Wooden Prince suite*, atmospherically and vividly recorded, is much more successful and Gerhart Herzel (leader of the VPO) makes a persuasive contribution to the *Two Portraits*.

Hungarian sketches; Romanian folk dances.
(M) *** Mercury 432 005-2 [id.]. Minneapolis SO, Dorati – KODALY: *Dances; Háry János*. ***

Dorati, himself a Hungarian, provided the pioneer stereo recording of these works, yet the 1956 sound is vivid and full and wears its years very lightly indeed. The Minneapolis orchestra, on top form, provides plenty of ethnic feeling and colour.

The Miraculous Mandarin (complete ballet), *Op. 19*.
(*) Delos Dig. DE 3083 [id.]. Seattle SO, Gerard Schwarz – KODALY: *Háry János; Galánta dances*. *

Gerard Schwarz directs the Seattle orchestra in a powerfully atmospheric account of Bartók's malignant ballet score, not as idiomatically aggressive as some, but with plenty of grip and excitement at the climax. Aptly and generously coupled with Kodály, this can be strongly recommended.

The Miraculous Mandarin (suite); *Music for strings, percussion and celesta.*
☞ (M) **(*) EMI CDC5 65175-2 [id.]. Phd. O, Ormandy – HINDEMITH: *Symphonic metamorphoses*. **(*)

This (1978) EMI version of *The Miraculous Mandarin*, recorded in the Old Met., does greater justice to the body of the Philadelphia strings and the sonorities of their cellos and basses than the earlier, Sony/CBS recording. The playing here is dazzling; the only reservations concern the *Music for strings, percussion and celesta*, where greater mystery is needed (at least in the first and third movements). There is no want of eloquence and passion, but the dynamic range at the bottom end of the spectrum leaves something to be desired. That said, there is much to enjoy here: the orchestral playing is of the very first order.

4 Orchestral pieces, Op. 12; (i) *The Miraculous Mandarin* (complete ballet), *Op. 19;* (ii) *3 Village scenes.*
(M) *** Sony SMK 45837 [id.]. (i) Schola Cantorum; (ii) Camerata Singers; NYPO, Pierre Boulez.

Boulez proves a strong and sympathetic advocate in all this music, and his approach is surprisingly warm. This is even more striking in *The Miraculous Mandarin*. The New York orchestra responds with deeply expressive playing and, with spacious recording, many will prefer it on that account.

The Wooden prince (ballet), *Op. 13* (complete); *Hungarian pictures.*
*** Chan. Dig. CHAN 8895; *ABTD 1506* [id.]. Philh. O, Järvi.

Järvi's red-blooded performance relates the work to romantic sources, even to Wagner's *Rheingold* at the very start. The drama of the fairy story is told in glowing colours and, unlike most rivals, Järvi ignores the many little cuts that the composer sanctioned, reluctantly or not, over the years. The opulent playing of the Philharmonia is greatly enhanced by the full, vivid Chandos recording. The suite, *Hungarian pictures*, drawn from various folk-based piano pieces, provides a colourful if trivial makeweight.

CHAMBER AND INSTRUMENTAL MUSIC

Contrasts for clarinet, violin and piano.
*** Delos Dig. D/CD 3043 [id.]. Shifrin, Bae, Lash – MESSIAEN: *Quatuor*. ***

David Shifrin and his colleagues from Chamber Music Northwest admirably capture the diverse moods of Bartók's triptych, including the mordant wit and vitality of the outer sections and the dark colouring of the centrepiece. They are very well recorded in an agreeable acoustic.

(i) *Contrasts. Mikrokosmos*: excerpts.

(M) (***) Sony mono MPK 47676 [id.]. Composer; (i) with Joseph Szigeti, Benny Goodman.

Contrasts was commissioned by Benny Goodman. In 1940 Bartók added a further movement, and it was in this form that the three artists made their recording. That same year Bartók recorded 31 pieces from *Mikrokosmos* and these performances are indicative of the wide range and delicacy of keyboard colour that Bartók commanded. The sound is surprisingly good, given that it is over half a century old! An indispensable issue.

(i) *7 Hungarian Folk tunes; 6 Romanian folk dances* (both arr. Szigeti). *Allegro barbaro; Bagatelle No. 2; Burlesque No. 2; Easy pieces Nos. 5 & 10; Mikrokosmos: Staccato, Ostinato. Romanian dance No. 1; Suite, Op. 14.* (ii) *5 Hungarian folksongs;* (iii) *8 Hungarian folksongs* (without No. 4).

☞ (M) (***) EMI mono CDC5 55031-2 [id.]. Composer (piano), with (i) Joseph Szigeti; (ii) Vilma Medgyaszay; (iii) Mária Basildes (*Nos. 1, 2, 3 & 5*), Ferenc Székelyhidy (*Nos. 6–8*) – DOHNÁNYI: *Variations.* (***)

The majority of these performances were recorded in Budapest in 1929 and the remainder at various times between 1928 and 1937. They sound remarkably good for their period and the special character of Bartók's playing comes over with great clarity. There is in all 50 minutes of him, either as a brilliant and subtle soloist or accompanying the three singers listed above and, of course, Szigeti who, incidentally, plays wonderfully but not quite with the same rapture as the young Menuhin. The 'Composers in Person' series enjoys extensive and perceptive documentation, nowhere more so than in Zoltán Kocsis's notes to this disc.

Sonata for 2 pianos and percussion.

*** Sony Dig. MK 42625 [id.]. Perahia, Solti, Corkhill, Glennie – BRAHMS: *Variations on a theme by Haydn.* ***

An unexpected and highly creative partnership produces a vivid and strongly characterized performance. The recording is vivid to match, giving the players great presence.

(i) *Sonata for 2 pianos and percussion;* (ii) (Solo) *Violin sonata.*

*** Accord Dig. 149047. (i) Janka and Jurg Wyttenbach, Schmid, Huber; (ii) Schneeberger.

Hans-Heinz Schneeberger is obviously an accomplished artist and his account can withstand comparison with most if not all rivals. The *Sonata for 2 pianos and percussion* receives an exhilarating performance, and the CD recording is astonishingly good and also very natural.

String quartets Nos. 1–6.

☞ (M) *** DG 445 241-2 (3). Tokyo Qt.

*** DG Dig. 423 657-2 (2) [id.]. Emerson Qt.

**(*) EMI Dig. CDS7 47720-8 (3) [Ang. CDCC 47720]. Alban Berg Qt.

(**(*)) ASV Dig. CDDCS 301 (3) [id.]. Lindsay Qt.

☞ (B) **(*) Ph. Duo 442 284-2 (2) [id.]. Novák Qt.

☞ ** Hyp. Dig. CDA 66581/2 [id.]. New Budapest Qt.

☞ * Canyon Classics Dig. 3698-2 (3). Bartók Qt.

The performances by the Tokyo Quartet bring an almost ideal combination of fire and energy with detailed point and refinement. The readings are consistently satisfying, outshining even the Emersons. Though the polish is high, the sense of commitment and seeming spontaneity are greater too. So the range of expression includes in the fullest measure not only the necessary Bartókian passion but the sparkle and wit, each interpretative problem closely considered and solved with finesse and assurance. The *pesante* idea that opens the main section of the *Sixth Quartet* is a typical example of their full sonority, combined with a naturally expressive eloquence in which they are preferable to the Emersons. Unlike that other DG set, the layout of the Tokyo performance is on three discs, but they are offered at mid-price and the splendid recording is admirably transferred to CD.

The Emerson Quartet's set comes on only two CDs. They project very powerfully and, in terms of virtuosity, finesse and accuracy, outstrip most of their rivals. If at times their projection and expressive vehemence are a bit too much of a good thing, these are concentrated and brilliant performances that are very well recorded.

The Alban Berg Quartet's are very impressive performances indeed, technically almost in a class of their own. They are very well recorded too, but at times they appear to treat this music as a vehicle for their own supreme virtuosity.

The Lindsay performances, searching, powerful and expressive, are now reissued together. The digital recording, though first class, occupies three discs which, like the Alban Berg set, places it at a distinct disadvantage to the DG Emerson version.

The Novák Quartet, a fine Czech group, bring plenty of grip to their performances and there is certainly no lack of fire and expressive intensity. If not as polished as the Tokyo versions, they have the advantage of being complete on a pair of Duo CDs, which Philips offer for the cost of one premium-price disc. So there is no question of their bargain status, as the recording is firm and well balanced.

Like the Emersons, the New Budapest Quartet enjoy an advantage in accommodating all six *Quartets* on two CDS (odd numbers on the first CD and even numbers on its companion). The performances are generally very good, though they are not as imaginative or as compelling as the Tokyo, Lindsay or Alban Berg Quartets. Nor does the recording have the tonal richness and bloom of the Alban Berg or Tokyo Quartet on DG.

The eponymous Bartók Quartet gives a serviceable rather than distinguished account of the cycle that in no way represents a challenge to existing recommendations, though it is not, of course, without merit. However, although these performances, recorded in Tokyo, would pass muster in concert, they are of insufficient stature to prompt collectors to return to them very often.

String quartets Nos. 1, Op. 7; 5.
☞ *** Collins Dig. 1279-2 [id.]. Talich Qt.

No need for reservations about the Talich Quartet, who are completely inside this music. These performances will prove ideal for those who seek a less aggressive approach than is offered by the much-praised Emerson complete set, with its vehement dynamic contrasts (DG 423 657-2), and they are without the self-conscious virtuosity of the Alban Berg recordings on EMI (CDS7 47720-8). Instead, there is plenty of that kind of atmosphere that comes from within. The opening movement of the *First Quartet* and the second and fourth movements of the *Fifth* have just the right air of mystery, and the Talich pianissimo tone has a rapt quality that seems just right. These are finely argued, marvellously played and splendidly and truthfully recorded versions that can be recommended without any serious qualification.

String quartet No. 2.
☞ ** BMG/RCA Dig. 09026 61185 [id.]. Vogler Qt – BEETHOVEN: *String quartet No. 9.* **

In a sense the Vogler Quartet start with a competitive handicap. Most collectors tend to find multi-composer CDs less attractive than single-composer collections – and understandably so. A reader wanting the Bartók may not be overjoyed at the prospect of duplicating the *C major Rasumovsky*, and vice versa. The Vogler are an excellent group who play with great expertise and considerable musical feeling. Their account of the Bartók *Second Quartet* does not displace existing recommendations all the same: more inwardness of feeling and greater scrupulousness in observing *pp* markings would not come amiss. For all its good qualities, in this repertoire their new (and well-recorded) performance is not a first choice.

Violin sonata No. 1.
*** DG Dig. 427 351-2 [id.]. Gidon Kremer, Martha Argerich – JANACEK: *Sonata* **(*); MESSIAEN: *Theme and variations.* ***

The *First Violin sonata* is played with great expressive intensity, enormous range of colour and effortless virtuosity by Gidon Kremer and Martha Argerich; indeed it would be difficult to improve on their performance or the excellent DG recording.

Violin sonatas Nos. 1 and 2.
**(*) Hung. HCD 11655-2. Kremer, Smirnov.

Kremer and Smirnov play with total commitment and their performances can only be described as masterly. The recording (from the early 1970s) is rather closely balanced and the acoustic somewhat drier than is ideal.

(Solo) Violin sonata.
*** Ph. Dig. 420 948-2 [id.]. Viktoria Mullova – BACH: *Partita No. 1 in B min.* *** (with PAGANINI: *Introduction and variations on Nel cor più non misento* ***).

Viktoria Mullova's account of the Bartók *Sonata* is undoubtedly one of the best now before the public. She brings keener musical insights and more finesse to this remarkable score than Kennedy on EMI (CDC7 47621-2). She is much closer to Bartók's own timing, too, and has the benefit of excellent recording.

(Solo) Violin sonata; Violin sonata No. 2; Rhapsody No. 1; Rumanian folk dances.

☞ *** ASV Dig. CDDCA 852 [id.]. Susanne Stanzeleit, Gusztáv Fenyö.

The young German-born violinist Susanne Stanzeleit studied with Kogan, Parachkevov, Yfrah Neaman, Milstein, Végh and practically every great violinist or violin teacher you care to name. She certainly plays the *Solo sonata*, written for Menuhin, and the *Second Sonata* for violin and piano (1922) with uncommon authority. She and her partner, Gustáv Fenyö, are completely inside the idiom (not altogether surprising, since the sleeve-note tells us that the latter is related to Jelly d'Arányi, for whom Bartók composed the sonatas, and can trace his ancestry to Joachim). At the time of its first appearance, ASV were loud in trumpeting the praises of this issue, and one can see why. This is totally committed playing – and the performances are as good as any you can find in the current catalogue. The recording, too, is altogether first rate.

PIANO MUSIC

Allegro barbaro; Andante; 3 Burlesques; 10 Easy pieces; 3 Rondos on folk tunes; Rumanian folk dances; 2 Rumanian dances.
*(**) ASV Dig. CDDCA 687 [id.]. Peter Frankl.

Peter Frankl plays with splendid fire and spirit, and with no lack of sensitivity. He is totally inside this music and is wholly persuasive, but he is let down by a rather unflattering and not fully focused recording balance.

Allegro barbaro; 6 Dances in Bulgarian rhythm; 3 Hungarian folksongs from the Csik District; 15 Hungarian peasant songs; Mikrokosmos (excerpts); 3 Rondos on Slovak folktunes; Sonatina.
☞ (BB) **(*) Naxos Dig. 8.550451 [id.]. Balázs Szokolay.

Balázs Szokolay has a good musical pedigree (his father is the composer of the opera, *Blood Wedding*) and his Bartók recital is highly idiomatic and keenly alive. His performances deserve the highest recommendation and, were his recording just a little less forward, this would have been worth a full three-star grading. However, the recording is perfectly acceptable and the disc will surely meet a need.

14 Bagatelles, Op. 6; 2 Elegies, Op. 8b; 3 Hungarian folk tunes; 6 Rumanian folk tunes; Sonatina.
☞ ⊛ *** Ph. Dig. 434 104-2 [id.]. Zoltán Kocsis.

In our 1982 edition we called Zoltán Kocsis's Bartók LP 'a marvellous record with playing of exceptional sensitivity and range', and much the same could be said of this new (1992) recording. Since this new issue says 'Works for Piano Solo – 1', it presumably heralds a complete cycle which, if it is as good as this, will be hard to beat. Earlier surveys by Andor Foldes in the 1950s and by György Sandor have carried the authenticity of close association with the composer, but this has the advantage not only of state-of-the-art recording quality but of playing that is far more subtle and imaginative than Foldes'. When the latter played one of his pieces to Bartók, the composer reproached him for being too percussive ('Why are you so Bartókish?'). Kocsis can produce power and drama when required, but he also commands a wide-ranging palette and a marvellously controlled vitality. The sound is never beautified but is also never aggressive; indeed his playing calls to mind Bartók's own injunction that performances must be 'beautiful but true'. Bartók playing doesn't come much better than this.

Dance suite; Hungarian peasant songs; 3 Rondos on folk tunes; Rumanian dances.
*** Denon Dig. C37 7092 [id.]. András Schiff (piano).

András Schiff's range of mood, tone and expression brings vivid colouring and these *Rumanian dances* have rarely been played with such infectious rhythms. The piano sound is first rate, with plenty of bite, and losing inner clarity only with the heaviest textures of the *Dance suite*.

6 Dances in Bulgarian Rhythm; Out of doors: suite.
☞ ** Collins Dig. 1404-2 [id.]. Joanna MacGregor – DEBUSSY: *Etudes;* RAVEL: *Valses nobles.* **

Joanna MacGregor's Bartók is first rate, though she does not enjoy as good recorded sound as Philips give Zoltán Kocsis. The sound is a bit thick at the bottom end of the register and too closely balanced, but she produces highly intelligent and atmospheric sounds in *Night music*. Her mixed programme is obviously conceived with admirers of the artist in mind rather than the needs of the catalogue.

For Children (Books 1–4) complete; Mikrokosmos (Books 1–6) complete.
(M) *** Teldec/Warner 9031 76139-2 (3). Dezsö Ránki.

Dezsö Ránki here shows his musicianship and plays all 85 pieces with the utmost persuasion and with the art that conceals art, for the simplicity of some of these pieces is deceptive; darker currents lurk beneath their surface. He gives us the composer's original edition of 1908–9. Ránki also plays the *Mikrokosmos* with an effortless eloquence and a welcome straightforwardness. He is very clearly if forwardly recorded, and he is given a realistic presence.

For children, Volumes I & II (revised version); *15 Hungarian peasant songs; Mikrokosmos: 6 Bulgarian dances. 10 easy pieces; 6 Rumanian popular dances; A simple air; Sonata; Sonatine.*
☞ (B) *** EMI CZS5 68101-2 (2) [id.]. Michel Béroff.

Bartók's pieces for children are a collection of Hungarian (Book I) and Slovak (Book II) folksongs which possess a beguiling simplicity and (when taken in small doses) unfailing musical interest. Choice between Michel Béroff and Dezsö Ránki is simplified by the fact that Béroff records the revised score and Ránki gives us the original edition of 1908/9. Moreover Ránki's set is coupled with *Mikrokosmos*, whereas Béroff offers a number of Bartók's other major piano works. Béroff's playing has an unaffected eloquence that is touching, and the recording is very good.

Mikrokosmos (complete).
☞ (M) (***) Sony mono MP2K 52528 (2) [id.]. György Sándor.
(B) **(*) HM HMA 90968/9 [id.]. Claude Helffer (with Haakon Austbö).

Bartók originally intended the piano pieces he began composing in 1926 as a pedagogic exercise with his young son Péter in mind. He began work on them in earnest in the summer of 1932 and finished the last and most technically demanding Sixth Book in 1939. There are some 157 pieces in all, though the first three books are intended for the practice room rather than the concert hall. Bartók himself never performed any of the First Book and only a handful of the Second and Third. György Sándor was closely associated with Bartók and older collectors will recall that he made the pioneering post-war recording of the *Third Piano concerto* with Ormandy and the Philadelphia Orchestra. And it is naturally of great value to hear so authentic a voice in this repertoire, though to record the complete set may be taking comprehensiveness a bit too far. Music-lovers will be concentrating on the second of these CDs. The sound is monochrome but not too dry and lends the set a certain period flavour.

Claude Helffer gives an intelligent account of all six Books of Bartók's *Mikrokosmos*, though at times he tends to invest detail with rather more expressive emphasis than this most simple of music can bear. The piano recording is realistic and naturally remastered. Even though the cueing is ungenerous (there are only twelve bands to cover 153 pieces), this is good value in the bargain range.

OPERA

Bluebeard's Castle (sung in Hungarian).
*** Sony Dig. MK 44523 [id.]. Marton, Ramey, Hungarian State O, Adám Fischer.
(M) *** Decca 433 082-2 [id.]. Kovats, Sass, Sztankay (speaker), LPO, Solti.
☞ (M) **(*) Mercury Dig. 434 325-2 [id.]. Mihály Székely, Olga Szönyi, LSO, Dorati – BERG:
   Wozzeck (excerpts). **(*)

The glory of the CBS version is the magnificent singing of Samuel Ramey in the title-role. Eva Marton, also Hungarian-born, may lack the vulnerability as well as the darker tone-colours of the ideal Judith but, with more than a touch of abrasiveness in the voice, she still gives a powerful reading. The recording brings full and brilliant sound, well balanced and clear. The single CD comes with libretto in a separate box.

Solti directs a richly atmospheric reading, not as searingly dramatic as one might have expected but with analogue recording of spectacular range. The Hungarian soloists are tangily authentic, though their voices are not always perfectly steady, but Sylvia Sass with her exquisite pianissimo singing is more appealing than Eva Marton on CBS. The resulting effect is more romantic than usual, even revealing an affinity with Richard Strauss. With full libretto included, this makes a fine mid-priced alternative to the CBS/Sony version, dominated by Samuel Ramey.

Antal Dorati, drawing brilliant playing from the LSO, recorded in vivid, immediate Mercury sound, finds power rather than mystery in Bartók's unique one-Acter. It is a positive and often urgent reading of a work which, with its absence of action, in the wrong hands can seem to meander. The abrasiveness of the vision is enhanced by having two Hungarian soloists. Székely as Bluebeard is taut and intense, using his characterful bass imaginatively. Olga Szönyi is more uneven, strong and incisive but with squally moments. Though rival versions are more atmospheric than this, Dorati relates the work more clearly to later Bartók. The CD transfer is very vivid, though tape-hiss is quite high. As a practical advantage, the disc not only comes at mid-price but also it uniquely offers a generous coupling, an equally positive account of the three concert-excerpts from Berg's *Wozzeck*. There are adequate notes, but no libretto.

Bax, Arnold (1883–1953)

(i) *Christmas eve; Dance of Wild Irravel; Festival overture; Nympholet; Paean;* (ii) *Tintagel.*
☞ **(*) Chan. Dig. CHAN 9168 [id.]. (i) LPO; (ii) Ulster O, Bryden Thomson.

These shorter works were originally used as fillers for the separate issues of the symphonies, and it might have been more generous of Chandos to reissue them at mid-price. Apart from *Tintagel, Nympholet* is probably the most interesting piece. The *Paean* and the *Dance of Wild Irravel* may strain the allegiance of some. Performances and recordings give absolutely no cause for complaint.

(i) *Cello concerto; Cortège; Mediterranean; Northern Ballad No. 3; Overture to a picaresque comedy.*
*** Chan. Dig. CHAN 8494; *ABTD 1204* [id.]. (i) Wallfisch; LPO, Bryden Thomson.

The *Cello concerto* is rhapsodic in feeling and Raphael Wallfisch plays it with marvellous sensitivity and finesse, given splendid support by the LPO under Bryden Thomson. The other pieces are of mixed quality: in the *Overture to a picaresque comedy* Bryden Thomson sets rather too measured a pace for it to sparkle as it should. The recording maintains the high standards of the Bax Chandos series.

(i) *Violin concerto. Golden Eagle* (incidental music): *suite; A Legend; Romantic overture.*
*** Chan. Dig. CHAN 9003 [id.]. (i) Lydia Mordkovitch; LPO, Bryden Thomson.

The *Violin concerto* is full of good, easily remembered tunes, yet there is a plangent, bitter-sweet quality about many of its ideas and an easygoing Mediterranean-like warmth that is very appealing. Lydia Mordkovitch plays it with commitment and conviction. The *Romantic overture* is for chamber orchestra and has a prominent role for the piano. All this music is new to the catalogue and the concerto deserves to be popular.

The Garden of Fand (symphonic poem).
(M) (***) EMI mono CDM7 63405-2 [id.]. RPO, Sir Thomas Beecham – BANTOCK: *Fifine at the fair;* BERNERS: *Triumph of Neptune.* (***)

The Garden of Fand found a ready advocate in Sir Thomas Beecham, who related its atmospheric feeling to the music of Delius. It is played superbly here, although the 1947 recording is a bit confined and two-dimensional; it is very well transferred to CD, however.

The Garden of Fand; The happy forest; November woods; Summer music.
*** Chan. Dig. CHAN 8307 [id.]. Ulster O, Bryden Thomson.

The Celtic twilight in Bax's music is ripely and sympathetically caught in the first three items, while *Summer music*, dedicated to Sir Thomas Beecham and here given its first ever recording, brings an intriguing kinship with the music of Delius. The Chandos recording is superb.

The Garden of Fand (symphonic poem); *Mediterranean; Northern ballad No. 1; November Woods; Tintagel* (symphonic poems).
☞ *** Lyrita SRCD 231 [id.]. LPO, Boult.

It says a great deal for Lyrita engineering that these recordings, made in the late 1960s, are of such exceptional clarity and refinement in their new CD format. Even the violins, though not quite as sumptuous as we would now expect, are remarkably full, and the brass sounds splendid. Sir Adrian Boult's recording of *The Garden of Fand* is full of poetry and almost erases memories of Beecham's magical account. *Tintagel* is no less involving and beguiling and, though not as uninhibited as Barbirolli's, is equally valid. The *Northern ballad No. 1*, though less memorable than either *Fand* or *Tintagel*, is well worth having, as is *November Woods*, a lush, romantic score. *Mediterranean*, a Spanish picture postcard and almost a waltz, has an endearing touch of vulgarity uncharacteristic of its composer.

In the faery hills; Into the twilight; Rosc-Catha; The tale the pine-trees knew.
*** Chan. Dig. CHAN 8367 [id.]. Ulster O, Bryden Thomson.

The tale the pine-trees knew is here done with total sympathy. The other three tone-poems form an Irish trilogy. The performances and recording are well up to the high standard of this series.

Malta G.C. (complete); *Oliver Twist: suite* (film-scores).
(M) *** ASV Dig. CDWHL 2058. RPO, Kenneth Alwyn – ARNOLD: *The Sound Barrier.* ***

Both these film-scores are in the form of a series of miniatures; on the whole, *Oliver Twist* stands up more effectively without the visual imagery. Kenneth Alwyn conducts the RPO with fine flair and commitment.

On the sea-shore.
*** Chan. Dig. CHAN 8473; *ABTD 1184* [id.]. Ulster O, Handley – BRIDGE: *The Sea;* BRITTEN:
  Sea interludes. ***

Bax's Prelude, *On the sea-shore*, makes a colourful and atmospheric companion to the masterly
Bridge and Britten pieces on the disc, played and recorded with similar warmth and brilliance.

Phantasy for viola and orchestra.
**(*) Conifer Dig. CDCF 171; *MCFC 171* [id.]. Golani, RPO, Handley – ELGAR: *Concerto* etc. **

Bax's *Phantasy* is in effect a three-movement viola concerto, drawing heavily on his Irish vein in its
use of folk-material. For all Vernon Handley's devoted advocacy, the piece sounds flabby next to the
Elgar with which it is coupled. Excellent recorded sound.

3 Pieces for small orchestra: Evening piece; Irish landscape; Dance in the sunlight.
☞ (M) *** EMI Dig. CDM7 64200-2 [id.]. ECO, Jeffrey Tate – BRIDGE: *There is a willow* **(*);
  BUTTERWORTH: *Banks of green willow* etc. **(*); MOERAN: *2 Pieces.* ***

The three Bax *Pieces* as attractive rarities make a welcome appearance in Tate's English recital. The
first two are characteristically evocative, while the third is in Bax's brightest, most extrovert vein.
Refined performances, warmly recorded, with the CD bringing good detail and presence without loss
of atmosphere.

Spring fire; Northern ballad No. 2; Symphonic scherzo.
*** Chan. Dig. CHAN 8464; *ABTD 1180* [id.]. RPO, Vernon Handley.

Highly idiomatic playing from Vernon Handley and the RPO, and a thoroughly lifelike and
characteristically well-detailed recording from Chandos.

Symphonic variations for piano and orchestra; Morning Song (Maytime in Sussex).
*** Chan. Dig. CHAN 8516; *ABTD 1226* [id.]. Margaret Fingerhut, LPO, Bryden Thomson.

Margaret Fingerhut reveals the *Symphonic variations* as a work of considerable substance with some
sinewy, powerful writing in the more combative variations, thoughtful and purposeful elsewhere. This
CD is in the demonstration class.

Symphonies 1–7.
(M) *** Chan. Dig. CHAN 8906/10 [id.]. LPO or Ulster O, Bryden Thomson.

Chandos have repackaged the cycle of seven symphonies and it makes better sense for those primarily
interested in these richly imaginative symphonies to pay for five rather than seven CDs. The
recordings continue to make a strong impression. For those who prefer to have the symphonies
separately and with their original couplings, and for tape collectors, we list below full details.

Symphony No. 1 in E flat; Christmas Eve.
☞ *** Chan. Dig. CHAN 8480; *ABTD 1192* [id.]. LPO, Bryden Thomson.

Symphonies Nos. 1 in E flat; 7 in A flat.
☞ *** Lyrita SRCD 232 [id.]. LPO, (i) Fredman; (ii) Leppard.

Symphony No. 2; Nympholept.
*** Chan. Dig. CHAN 8493; *ABTD 1203* [id.]. LPO, Bryden Thomson.

Symphony No. 3; Paean; The Dance of Wild Irravel.
*** Chan. Dig. CHAN 8454; *ABTD 1165* [id.]. LPO, Bryden Thomson.

Symphony No. 4; Tintagel.
*** Chan. Dig. CHAN 8312; *ABTD 1091* [id.]. Ulster O, Bryden Thomson.

Symphony No. 5; Russian suite.
*** Chan. Dig. CHAN 8669; *ABTD 1356* [id.]. LPO, Bryden Thomson.

Symphony No. 6; Festival overture.
*** Chan. Dig. CHAN 8586; *ABTD 1278* [id.]. LPO, Bryden Thomson.

Symphony No. 7 in A flat; (i) 4 Songs: Eternity; Glamour; Lyke-wake; Slumber song.
*** Chan. Dig. CHAN 8628; *ABTD 1317* [id.]. (i) Martyn Hill; LPO, Bryden Thomson.

Bax's symphonies remain controversial and some listeners find their quality of invention and
argument less intensely sustained than the composer's shorter orchestral tone-poems. Nevertheless
they have a breadth of imagination which the smaller structures do not always carry. The *First*

Symphony began life originally as a piano sonata. Bax wrote it in 1921–2, and the music has a certain Russian quality (Bax had been to Russia in 1910), especially noticeable in the finale. The Lyrita coupling is particularly generous (78 minutes) and the performances by Myer Fredman and Raymond Leppard respectively are powerful and finely shaped and can well hold their own with the later, Chandos digital versions. The Lyrita 1970s analogue sound, too, is vivid and clear, wide in range and with both richness and depth to commend it.

The Chandos couplings have their own interest. *Christmas Eve* is an early work, coming from the Edwardian era, and it displays a less developed idiom than the symphonies. The four songs offer great contrasts of manner and style, and Martyn Hill presents them very sensitively.

Symphony No. 3.
(M) (***) EMI mono CDH7 63910-2. Hallé O, Barbirolli – IRELAND: *Forgotten rite* etc. (***)

Barbirolli's account of the *Third* was the first Bax symphony ever to be recorded and, though the 1944 sound is obviously limited in frequency range, remarkably few allowances need be made for this transfer. There is an authentic feel to Barbirolli's performance which successfully captures the epic quality of this symphony and does justice to the composer's imaginative vision.

The Truth about the Russian dancers (incidental music); *From dusk till dawn* (ballet).
*** Chan. Dig. CHAN 8863; *ABTD 1478* [id.]. LPO, Bryden Thomson.

The Truth about the Russian dancers is vintage Bax, full of characteristic writing decked out in attractive orchestral colours. *From dusk till dawn* has many evocative ideas with some impressionistic orchestral touches. Not top-drawer Bax but often delightful, and very well played by the London Philharmonic under Bryden Thomson, and splendidly recorded.

Winter Legends; Saga fragment.
*** Chan. Dig. CHAN 8484; *ABTD 1195* [id.]. Margaret Fingerhut, LPO, Bryden Thomson.

The *Winter Legends*, for piano and orchestra, comes from much the same time as the *Third Symphony*, to which at times its world seems spiritually related. The soloist proves an impressive and totally convincing advocate for the score and it would be difficult to imagine the balance between soloist and orchestra being more realistically judged. The companion piece is a transcription of his one-movement *Piano quartet* of 1922. A quite outstanding disc.

CHAMBER AND INSTRUMENTAL MUSIC

Cello sonata in E flat; Cello sonatina in D; Legend sonata in F sharp min.; Folk tale.
☞ ** ASV Dig. CDDCA 896 [id.]. Bernard Gregor-Smith, Yolande Wrigley.

This disc collects all of Bax's music for cello and piano and will be required listening for Baxians, even though not all of it is Bax at his best. The *Cello sonata* (1923) is a big piece, lasting over half an hour; it has many characteristic touches and an imaginative slow movement. Bernard Gregor-Smith and Yolande Wrigley are both highly sensitive and responsive players who command a wide dynamic range and variety of colour. In the *Sonata* the recording does not give quite enough back-to-front depth and there is a touch of glassiness about the sound. Things are a bit better in the *Folk-Tale* (1920), but the recording is sufficiently wanting in bloom to inhibit a three-star recommendation.

Clarinet sonata.
**(*) Chan. CHAN 8683; *ABTD 1078* [id.]. Janet Hilton, Keith Swallow – BLISS: *Clarinet quintet;*
    VAUGHAN WILLIAMS: *6 Studies.* ***

Bax's *Clarinet sonata* opens most beguilingly, and Janet Hilton's phrasing is quite melting. Moreover the Bliss coupling is indispensable.

(i) *Harp quintet;* (ii) *Piano quartet; String quartet No. 1.*
*** Chan. Dig. CHAN 8391; *ABTD 1113* [id.]. (i) Skaila Kanga, (ii) John McCabe; English Qt.

The *First String quartet* is music with a strong and immediate appeal. The *Harp quintet* is more fully characteristic and has some evocative writing to commend it, alongside the *Piano quartet*, with its winning lyricism. These may not be Bax's most important scores, but they are rewarding; and the performances are thoroughly idiomatic and eminently well recorded.

Oboe quintet.
*** Chan. Dig. CHAN 8392; *ABTD 1114* [id.]. Sarah Francis, English Qt – HOLST: *Air & variations,* etc.; MOERAN: *Fantasy quartet;* JACOB: *Quartet.* ***

Bax's *Oboe quintet* is a confident, inventive piece. Sarah Francis proves a most responsive soloist –

though she is balanced too close; in all other respects the recording is up to Chandos's usual high standards, and the playing of the English Quartet is admirable.

(i) *Piano quintet in G min.; String quartet No. 2.*
**(*) Chan. Dig. CHAN 8795; *ABTD 1427* [id.]. Mistry Qt; (i) with David Owen Norris.

The *Piano quintet* is symphonic in scale. The playing of the Mistry Quartet is dedicated and David Owen Norris is the excellent and sensitive pianist. The *Second Quartet* is tauter and more powerful. The performance has plenty of feeling and the recording is excellent.

Piano trio in B flat.
**(*) Chan. Dig. CHAN 8495; *ABTD 1205* [id.]. Borodin Trio – BRIDGE: *Trio No. 2.* **(*)

Even if this is not Bax at his best, it is most welcome, particularly in view of the excellence of both performance and recording.

Rhapsodic Ballad (for solo cello).
*** Chan. Dig. CHAN 8499 [id.]. Raphael Wallfisch – BRIDGE: *Cello sonata;* DELIUS: *Cello sonata;* WALTON: *Passacaglia.* ***

The *Rhapsodic Ballad* for cello alone is a freely expressive piece, played with authority and dedication by Raphael Wallfisch. The recording has plenty of warmth and range.

Violin sonatas Nos. 1 in E; 2 in D.
*** Chan. Dig. CHAN 8845; *ABTD 1462* [id.]. Erich Gruenberg, John McCabe.

The *Second* is the finer of the two sonatas and is thematically linked with *November woods.* Rhapsodic and impassioned, this is music full of temperament. Erich Gruenberg is a selfless and musicianly advocate and John McCabe makes an expert partner.

PIANO MUSIC

Apple-blossom time; Burlesque; The maiden with the daffodil; Nereid; O dame get up and bake your pies (Variations on a north country Christmas carol); On a May evening; The princess's rose-garden (Nocturne); Romance; 2 Russian tone pictures: Nocturne (May night in the Ukraine; Gopak); Sleepy-head.
**(*) Chan. Dig. CHAN 8732; *ABTD 1372* [id.]. Eric Parkin.

The smaller pieces are not among Bax's most important works, but in Eric Parkin's hands they certainly sound pleasingly spontaneous.

Piano sonatas Nos. 1 in E flat; 2 in G; Legend.
☞ *** Continuum Dig. CCD 1045 [id.]. John McCabe.

Bax's *First Piano sonata* was some years in gestation and was finally completed in 1921. The *Second,* which appeared first, dates from two years earlier. It is obviously the more pianistic of the two, written in a single movement but in seven varying moods or sections. It is dedicated to Harriet Cohen, who was the composer's mistress as well as his finest pianistic advocate. It was she who decided that the *First sonata* had better be a symphony and so it was (*No. 1 in E flat*), all but the slow movement *Lento con molto espressione* which Bax found untranscribable, so he wrote a completely new slow movement for the orchestral work. It is therefore not surprising that the *Lento* is the most pianistic part of the sonata; but much of the rest of it is convincing in John McCabe's hands – in fact, more convincing than the *Legend,* written for an Australian pianist, John Simons, in the mid-1930s but not performed by its dedicatee until 1969. A thoroughly enterprising issue, excellently recorded.

Piano sonatas Nos. 1 & 2; Country Tune; Lullaby (Berceuse); Winter waters.
**(*) Chan. Dig. CHAN 8496; *ABTD 1206* [id.]. Eric Parkin (piano).

Piano sonatas Nos. 3 in G sharp min.; 4 in G; A Hill tune; In a vodka shop; Water music.
**(*) Chan. Dig. CHAN 8497; *ABTD 1207* [id.]. Eric Parkin.

These *Sonatas* are grievously neglected in the concert hall. Eric Parkin proves a sympathetic guide in this repertoire. The recording is on the resonant side, but the playing is outstandingly responsive.

Beach, Amy (1867–1944)

Symphony in E min. (Gaelic).
*** Chan. Dig. CHAN 8958; *ABTD 1550* [id.]. Detroit SO, Järvi – BARBER: *Symphony No. 1* etc.
***

Amy Beach is a rather more remarkable figure than she is given credit for. She was largely self-taught. Her *Symphony in E minor* operates at a high level of accomplishment and has a winning charm, particularly its delightful and inventive second movement. Once heard, this haunting movement is difficult to exorcize from one's memory. A very persuasive performance by the Detroit orchestra under Neeme Järvi, and good recorded sound.

Beethoven, Ludwig van (1770–1827)

Piano concertos Nos. 1–5.
(M) *** Sony M3K 44575 (3) [id.]. Perahia, Concg. O, Haitink.
☞ *** DG Dig. 435 467-2 (3) [id.]. Krystian Zimerman, VPO (*Nos. 3–5* cond. Bernstein).
☞ (M) (**) Sony SM3K 52632 (3) [id.]. Glenn Gould; Columbia SO, Golschmann (*No. 1*); Columbia SO, Bernstein (*Nos. 2–3*); NYPO, Bernstein (*No. 4*); American SO, Stokowski (*No. 5*).

Perahia brings us as close to the heart of this music as any. These are masterly performances, and it is good that their more competitive price will bring them within the reach of an even wider audience. The sound is full and well balanced.

Krystian Zimerman, a thinker and poet among pianists, recorded the last three Beethoven concertos with Leonard Bernstein, less than a year before the conductor died. It was a challenging, sympathetic partnership, with Bernstein responding to the varying needs of his soloist in each concerto, leading through the poetry of No. 4 to the elemental power of the *Emperor*. Significantly, Bernstein seems more concerned than most to be consistent over tempo in tuttis. Zimerman then completed the cycle, after Bernstein died, directing from the keyboard in light, crisp performances. The recording of the piano is on the bright side, not always allowing a full pianissimo. Not a first choice, then, but a stimulating alternative view.

The merits of Glenn Gould's Beethoven concertos are well known, as is the excellence of Sony's 20-bit technology. It needs to be to deal with the strident, papery quality of some of the originals. The *Second Piano concerto*, recorded in mono in New York in 1957, precedes the Leningrad account discussed below and is one of his finest and most enduring performances. The remainder are all stereo: No. 1, recorded with Vladimir Golschmann the following year, is first class, and so, too, is the *C minor*, recorded with Bernstein, which is impressive. However, his 1966 *Emperor* with Stokowski still sounds insufferably slow and mannered. The *G major Concerto* with Bernstein is far more acceptable, but the signs of eccentricity that became more pronounced later on are already in evidence: humming and muttering, albeit far less obtrusively than in later years. The undoubted insights Gould brought to his playing would not lead one to prefer him to such of his contemporaries as Arrau, Leon Fleisher, Katchen or Kempff, all on the market in the 1960s. All the same, this is still worth considering for Nos. 1–3.

(i) *Piano concertos Nos. 1–5;* (ii) *Triple concerto for violin, cello and piano, Op. 56.*
(M) *** Sony SB3K 48397 (3) [id.]. (i) Fleisher, Cleveland O, Szell; (ii) Stern, Rose, Istomin, Phd. O, Ormandy.

Apart from No. 4, which was recorded first in 1959 (and is the finest performance of the set), Fleisher made his series with Szell during 1961. Throughout their musical partnership was at its peak, and these performances are uncommonly rewarding. The remastering has greatly improved the recording, flattering the piano more than it did on LP, while the orchestra gains from the Severance Hall ambience.

Piano concertos Nos. 1–5; Rondos, Op. 51/1–2.
(M) (***) DG mono 435 744-2 (3) [id.]. Wilhelm Kempff, BPO, Van Kempen.

There is a mood of carefree delight running through this, the earlier of Kempff's two cycles of the Beethoven *Piano concertos*. Even more than his stereo cycle, this one, recorded in mono in 1953, finds Kempff at his most individual, turning phrases and pointing ornamentation with a sparkle and sense of fun to have you smiling in response. Kempff is often idiosyncratic, as in his decision in the first four concertos to play his own cadenzas, making them sound like spontaneous improvisations. This is a classic recording guaranteed to give delight, which has been transferred to CD in full, immediate, well-detailed sound.

(i) *Piano concertos Nos. 1–5. Piano sonata No. 18 in E flat, Op. 31/2.*
☞ (M) ** BMG/RCA stereo/mono 09026 61260-2 (3) [id.]. Artur Rubinstein; (i) Symphony of the Air, Josef Krips.

Rubinstein's set of the Beethoven concertos with Josef Krips was among the very first to be recorded in stereo, in 1956. In our original reviews in the very first *Stereo Record Guide*, we greeted the performances with mixed enthusiasm: at times the partnership between pianist and conductor fails to generate the kind of electricity that makes the finest studio recordings lift off. The *First Concerto* is certainly successful. Here Krips and his charismatic soloist seem to be at one over questions of style and tempo; the slow movement has fine depth of expression and the finale is joyously witty. The result is more imaginative in detail than with Backhaus. No. 2 goes well, too, though perhaps the last degree of spontaneity is missing here, and Backhaus is preferable. But the *Third* has a rather subdued opening tutti from the orchestra and, though this is a good, direct account and contains accurate and understanding interplay and ensemble, overall it is unmemorable. In the *Fourth Concerto* the easy, warm, lyrical style in the outer movements brings an appealing, glowing lyricism but, at the famous opening of the *Andante*, Krips, maintaining this mood, is curiously unassertive. Rubinstein's poetry later more than makes amends. The *Emperor*, as almost always, brings the best from conductor and pianist alike. Rubinstein's performance is masterly in its power and controlled brilliance. His boldly flamboyant playing of the opening is matched by crystal-clear passage-work, while the slow movement shows him at the height of his powers. Here one would have liked a rather fuller sonority from the piano, but throughout the set the orchestral recording is remarkably full-bodied for its period, although the multi-miked tuttis are opaque and not always refined in focus. The balance overall, if artificially contrived, is quite good and the piano timbre is generally clear and faithful in the transatlantic manner of the time. The *Sonata* is given a characteristically mercurial performance, and the 1954 mono recording (again closely balanced) compares favourably with the stereo quality of the concertos.

(i) *Piano concertos Nos. 1–5; Piano sonata No. 32 in C min., Op. 111.*
(B) *** DG 427 237-2 (3) [id.]. Kempff; (i) BPO, Leitner.

Kempff's stereo accounts all come from the early 1960s and still sound remarkably good for their age, and the wisdom Kempff dispensed is as fresh as ever.

(i) *Piano concertos Nos. 1–5. Bagatelles* (complete).
☞ **(*) Chan. Dig. CHAN 9084-6 (3) [id.]. John Lill, (i) CBSO, Walter Weller.

John Lill gives strong, generally direct and superbly articulated performances of the five concertos. Concentrated power rather than poetry is the keynote. With Weller conducting the Birmingham orchestra in warm, sympathetic accompaniments, not always ideally taut but ripely recorded, it makes a viable set, if you want the complete Beethoven *Bagatelles* as fill-up, an extra hour of music.

(i) *Piano concertos Nos. 1–5. Diabelli variations, Op. 120.*
☞ (M) **(*) Decca 433 891-2 (3) [id.]. Wilhelm Backhaus; (i) VPO, Schmidt-Isserstedt.

Backhaus recorded the Beethoven concertos in 1958/9 when he was in his mid-seventies (the *Diabelli variations* date from 1955). His bold style, sometimes lacking in grace and wit, yet had remarkable authority, and now these early stereo recordings emerge with remarkable freshness. For every moment of wilfulness there is a balancing sense of spontaneity; if charm and subtlety of touch are not his strong points, the composer's spirit is ever present. In the early concertos, and especially in the *B flat major* (No. 2), the Mozartian heritage is clear, and the classical underpinning is tangible, especially in the cool, poised slow movements, which are undoubtedly moving in their serene containment. No. 3 is one of the finest of the set. Backhaus is magisterial and direct, and there is both power and intensity in the first movement. No. 4, among the first to be recorded, is notable for breadth of style rather than the kind of melting poetry which Kempff for one brings to it, yet the command and flow of the music-making (as in No. 3) are compelling. Not surprisingly, it is the *Emperor* which shows the pianist at his most commanding. Backhaus is in excellent form and gives a vigorous and forthright performance. The outer movements have all the power and drive they need; the *Adagio* too is impressive, even if there is not the variety of colour some artists provide. Throughout the set Schmidt-Isserstedt directs accompaniments of a high standard and the VPO playing is flexible, but ensemble is excellent. The recordings, made in the Sofiensaal, are amazingly good and the digital remastering brings a full, atmospheric sound-picture, without edginess, and a very truthful piano image. The effect is remarkably satisfying. In the *Diabelli variations* the moments of brusqueness are much more apparent and the close balance prevents a real pianissimo. There is magnetism here and the impulse of the playing never flags, but ideally one requires more light and shade in the earlier variations and rather more of a sense of repose.

Piano concertos Nos. 1–5; (i) Choral Fantasia, Op. 80.
*** EMI Dig. CDC7 54063-2 (3) [Ang. CDCC 54063]. Melvyn Tan, L. Classical Players, Norrington.
(M) *** EMI CMS7 63360-2 (3) [Ang. CDMC 63360]. Daniel Barenboim, New Philh. O, Klemperer, (i) with John Alldis Ch.

Those wanting a complete set of the Beethoven Concertos on period instruments need look no further than this fine EMI three-CD set. The Tan–Norrington partnership has great spontaneity and Melvyn Tan has a flair and poetic feeling that is rather special.

The earlier combination of Barenboim and Klemperer, recording together in 1967/8, is nothing if not stimulating and, for every wilfulness of a measured Klemperer, there is a youthful spark from the spontaneously combusting Barenboim. The concentration is formidable and especially compelling in the slow movements. The Choral Fantasia too is given an inspired performance. The remastered sound is vivid and clear and quite full.

Piano concertos Nos. 1 in C, Op. 15; 2 in B flat, Op. 19.
*** Sony Dig. MK 42177 [id.]. Perahia, Concg. O, Haitink.
*** EMI Dig. CDC7 49509-2 [id.]. Tan (fortepiano), L. Classical Players, Norrington.
(B) *** Ph. 422 968-2 [id.]. Kovacevich, BBC SO, Sir Colin Davis.
☞ *** DG Dig. 437 545-2 [id.]. Krystian Zimerman, VPO.
☞ (BB) **(*) Discover DICD 920104. Jasminka Stancul, Slovak R. New PO, Rahbari.
☞ (M) ** Decca Dig. 430 750-2 [id.]. Ashkenazy, VPO, Mehta.

Murray Perahia's coupling of Nos. 1 and 2 brings strong and thoughtful performances very characteristic of this pianist, which yet draw a sharp distinction between the two works. No. 2, the earlier, brings a near-Mozartian manner in the first movement, but then rightly a deep and measured account of the slow movement takes Beethoven into another world, hushed and intense. The First Concerto finds Perahia taking a fully Beethovenian view from the start. Bernard Haitink proves a lively and sympathetic partner, with the Concertgebouw playing superbly. The recording sets the orchestra in a pleasingly warm acoustic.

Melvyn Tan's coupling of the first two concertos, using a fortepiano, brings performances of natural, unselfconscious expressiveness which will delight those looking for versions on period instruments. Even when Tan's speeds for slow movements are very fast indeed, his ease of expression makes them very persuasive, avoiding breathlessness while simultaneously conveying more gravity than you might expect.

These first two works, ideally coupled, bring characteristically crisp and refreshing readings from Stephen Kovacevich with Sir Colin Davis, which convey their conviction with no intrusive idiosyncrasies. That these model performances and recordings come on the cheapest Philips label is something to marvel at.

Zimerman, completing the cycle he began with Bernstein, directs the Vienna Philharmonic in bright, elegant, often witty performances that bring home that these are early works. Bright recording.

Jasminka Stancul gives fleet, sparklingly articulated performances of both concertos, brightly accompanied and warmly recorded in a reverberant acoustic. A fair recommendation at super-bargain price, though Kovacevich on Philips is even finer.

Ashkenazy's 1983 performances stay essentially within the brief of early Beethoven. The opening movement of the C major is light and relaxed, with a tactful accompaniment from Mehta, the slow movement thoughtful in an unmannered way. No. 2 is at once restrained and sparkling, thoughtful in the amazingly prophetic quasi-recitative which closes the Adagio, yet keeping the whole work within an apt scale. Excellent recording, made in the Sofiensaal, bright and atmospheric, but in the last resort this is not a distinctive coupling and the effect is rather cool.

Piano concerto No. 2 in B flat, Op. 19.
☞ (**) Sony mono SK 52686 [id.]. Glenn Gould, Leningrad Conservatoire Ac. SO, Ladislav Slovák
   – BACH: Concerto No. 1. (**)

Glenn Gould was at the height of his powers in 1957 when this performance was recorded, long before his irritating vocalization had got out of hand. Here he leaves everything to his fingers, and his performance is eminently sensitive and alive, perhaps less expansive than his version with Bernstein, recorded in the same year, but every bit as well recorded.

Piano concertos Nos. 2; 4
(M) *** Sony SBK 48165 [id.]. Fleisher, Cleveland O, Szell.

This coupling by Leon Fleisher and George Szell brings masterly examples of their inspired artistry. No. 2 receives a powerful, intense, spontaneous-sounding performance, giving weight to early Beethoven. In No. 4 Fleisher and Szell are even more searching, with the soloist's refreshingly imaginative playing matched by glorious sounds from the Cleveland Orchestra. The bright, forward recordings, both made in Severance Hall, have been transferred with satisfying fullness and body.

Piano concertos Nos. 3 in C min., Op. 37; 4 in G, Op. 58.
*** Sony Dig. MK 39814 [id.]. Murray Perahia, Concg. O, Haitink.
*** EMI Dig. CDC7 49815-2 [id.]. Melvyn Tan (fortepiano), L. Classical Players, Norrington.
(B) *** Ph. 426 062-2 [id.]. Kovacevich, BBC SO, Sir Colin Davis.
☞ *** DG Dig. 429 749-2 [id.]. Krystian Zimerman, VPO, Bernstein.
☞ (BB) ** Discover DICD 920 121. Jasminka Stancul, Slovak R. New PO, Rahbari.
☞ (**) Testament mono SBT 1021 [id.]. Artur Schnabel, Philh. O, Issay Dobrowen.

Perahia gives readings that are at once intensely poetic and individual, but also strong, with pointing and shading of passage-work that consistently convey the magic of the moment caught on the wing, helped by fine, spacious and open recorded sound.

With the fortepiano balanced naturally against the orchestra of period instruments, not at all spotlit, Melvyn Tan gives fresh and individual performances of both concertos that will delight those who want to hear Beethoven in period style. Tan's individual expressiveness comes over naturally and unforcedly, to make these readings characterful without unwanted wilfulness. Naturally balanced, undistracting sound-quality.

The Philips versions of Nos. 3 and 4 from Kovacevich and Sir Colin Davis would be top recommendations even if they cost far more. In both works the playing of the soloist has a depth and thoughtful intensity that have rarely been matched. The refined Philips recording has transferred admirably to CD: the balance is altogether excellent.

Zimerman finds the vein of poetry not only in No. 4, but in the much earlier No. 3, very sympathetically accompanied by Bernstein, who exactly matches his soloist in the thoughtful dialogue of the central *Andante* of No. 4. Bright sound that yet does not allow a full pianissimo. But this is refreshing music-making that consistently rewards the listener.

As in Nos. 1 and 2, Jasminka Stancul gives bright, sparkling performances of both concertos, expressive in slow movements but never letting them linger. Though warmly recorded, her accompanists are not as sharp or alert as in the earlier concertos.

There is a certain fierceness in the treble of the present transfer which is well worth putting up with for the sake of Schnabel's very special insights. The *G major Concerto* was recorded in 1946 and the *C minor* the following year at the Abbey Road Studios. They are classic accounts, and these transfers sound better than the earlier, Arabesque attempt to rejuvenate them.

(i) *Piano concerto No. 3; Andante favori in F, WoO 57; Für Elise; 6 Bagatelles, Op. 26.*
☞ (M) *** Decca Dig. 436 471-2 [id.]. Ashkenazy; (i) VPO, Mehta.

Ashkenazy's performance of the *Third Piano concerto* is enjoyably relaxed, much more so than in his earlier, Chicago version with Solti. The first movement is noticeably slower and less forceful. It sounds engagingly spontaneous, and Beethoven's big cadenza is also presented in a relaxed way rather than as a fireworks display. The slow movement is more easily lyrical than before, the finale lighter, more sparkling and with plenty of charm. Although tuttis are strong, Mehta relaxes too and, with its generous solo fill-ups, coming from earlier sessions and equally successful, this makes an admirable choice for those just wanting the *Third Concerto* alone. The Decca recording, made in the Sofiensaal, is first class in every way.

(i) *Piano concerto No. 3 in C min. Piano sonata No. 18 in E flat, Op. 31/3.*
☞ (M) *** Ph. 434 168-2 [id.]. Clara Haskil; (i) LOP, Markevitch.

Clara Haskil, in a clean, strongly classical style, gives a most refreshing performance, one of her relatively rare records, made in 1959 not long before she died. Her first entry establishes that feminine delicacy is not her style. Intellectual concentration married to sharp articulation (most remarkable in the left hand) characterizes a performance where even the delicate pianissimos at the end of the slow movement convey concentration. The recording is completely undated, one of Philips's best, with full, bold piano timbre and an excellent balance with the orchestra. The *Sonata* has comparable appeal in its direct spontaneity and is also realistically recorded. Admirers of this fine artist should note that this is a limited edition, not likely to be available beyond the lifetime of this book.

Piano concerto No. 4 in G, Op. 58.

(M) *** Sony MYK 44832 [MYK 37762]. Leon Fleisher, Cleveland O, Szell – MOZART: *Piano concerto No. 25.* ***

Fleisher's is a magical performance, memorable in every bar. The 1959 CBS recording has been skilfully remastered for CD and can be made to sound well.

Piano concertos Nos. 4 in G; 5 (Emperor), Op. 73.

☞ (M) **(*) O-L Dig. 443 186-2 [id.]. Steven Lubin, AAM, Hogwood.

☞ (BB) ** ASV Dig. CDQS 6129 [id.]. Osorio, RPO, Bátiz.

☞ (M) (**) BMG/RCA mono 09026 61393-2 [id.]. Artur Schnabel, Chicago SO, Frederick Stock.

Lubin uses a Graf fortepiano in both works, but in the *Emperor* it was 're-voiced' in order to brighten the treble; opportunely, the première of this work came at the same time as the availability of Graf's instruments in Vienna. In No. 4 the performance seems to miniaturize Beethoven, partly a question of balance, and here the *Andante* dialogue is disappointing. The *Emperor* sounds far fuller, providing overall weight and the necessary flair to the opening flourishes. Speeds are brisk, but not uncomfortably so, and Hogwood accompanies effectively. The recording is certainly vivid. An interesting experiment.

This ASV record with a Mexican pianist and conductor brings the rare and generous coupling of the last and greatest two concertos, well recorded in modern digital sound. Jorge Federico Osorio conveys no great new insights but his performances are intelligent, well sprung and cleanly articulated, with speeds generally on the spacious side. If there is a weakness, it lies in the occasionally dull orchestral playing, as in the pedestrian account of the opening tutti of No. 4. All in all, this cannot compare with the very finest versions of either work.

Schnabel's wartime performances of the *G major* and *Emperor concertos* in Chicago never quite enjoyed the celebrity of either his post-war set with Dobrowen and the Philharmonia or his cycle with Sargent from the 1930s. But on the other hand, they have never been heard to such good effect as here on this new transfer. RCA transfers of historic material vary in quality; some, like the bulk of Reiner's records with this orchestra or Pfeiffer's Rachmaninov set, are marvellous; others are indifferent. The present transfer produces cleaner and more 'present' detail and altogether more comfortable sound than earlier LP issues did. We praised the performances in the 1970s: the *G major* has great beauty and, in addition to the breadth and majesty that his studio accounts of the *Emperor* commanded, this has something of the impetuous and instinctive feeling that live music-making communicates. Well worth investigating.

(i) *Piano concertos Nos. 4–5. Für Elise; Piano sonatas Nos. 6 (Pathétique); 14 (Moonlight); 23 (Appassionata).*

☞ (B) **(*) Decca 436 380-2 (2) [id.]. Ashkenazy; (i) Chicago SO, Solti.

Ashkenazy's account of the *G major* (No. 4) is one of the finest performances of his cycle with Solti, most striking in the interplay of the *Andante* where Solti's gruff boldness contrasts so tellingly with Ashkenazy's melting response. The *Emperor* is an excitingly dramatic performance on the largest possible scale, yet one which is consistently imbued with poetry. Unfortunately the digital remastering of both concertos is fierce and not quite comfortable at fortissimo level. Of the solo sonatas the *Pathétique* is the most successful as a recording. In the opening of the *Moonlight* Ashkenazy does not find the depths that distinguish the very finest accounts; in every other respect this is formidable playing, and the *Appassionata* is admirable. The analogue recordings have been satisfactorily if not outstandingly transferred. *Für Elise* is digital and makes a delightful introduction to the second CD. The two CDs are offered for the price of one and come in a normal jewel-case, ingeniously hinged from the centre.

Piano concerto No. 5 in E flat (Emperor), Op. 73.

*** Ph. Dig. 416 215-2 [id.]. Arrau, Dresden State O, Sir Colin Davis.

☞ *** DG Dig. 429 748-2 [id.]. Krystian Zimerman, VPO, Bernstein.

*** Sony Dig. MK 42330 [id.]. Perahia, Concg. O, Haitink.

☞ (M) *** BMG/RCA 09026 61961-2 [id.]. Van Cliburn, Chicago SO, Reiner – TCHAIKOVSKY: *Piano concerto No. 1.* ***

Piano concerto No. 5 in E flat (Emperor); Grosse Fuge in B flat, Op. 133.

⊛ (M) *** EMI Dig. CD-EMX 2184. Stephen Kovacevich, Australian CO.

(i) *Piano concerto No. 5 in E flat (Emperor); Piano sonata No. 30 in E, Op. 109.*
(B) *** Ph. 422 482-2. Kovacevich; (i) LSO, C. Davis.

Kovacevich is unsurpassed today as an interpreter of this most magnificent of concertos. His superb account for Philips, now on Concert Classics, has set a model for everyone and, with its sonata coupling, remains highly recommendable. This new Eminence version, with the soloist directing from the keyboard, is recognizably from the same inspired artist, though speeds are consistently faster and the manner is sharper and tauter. The piano sound on the digital recording is aptly brighter and more faithful than on the Philips, making this a first choice for this much-recorded work, even with no allowance for price. For fill-up, Kovacevich conducts a comparably electrifying account of the *Grosse Fuge*.

On Philips, with alert, sharp-edged accompaniment from Sir Colin Davis, Kovacevich gives a clean, dynamic performance of the outer movements, then in the central slow movement finds a depth of intensity that completely explodes any idea of this as a lighter central resting-point. The 1969 sound begins to show its age, with the bass a little boomy and the piano rather clattery on fortissimos, though well defined. For coupling there is one of the most deeply perceptive performances of a late Beethoven sonata on record.

The wonder is that Arrau, for long an inhibited artist in the studio, should in his *Emperor* recording, made when he was over eighty, sound so carefree. There are technical flaws, and the digital recording is rather resonant in bass, but with Sir Colin Davis and the Dresden State Orchestra as electrifying partners, the voltage is even higher than in his earlier versions of the mid-1960s. This is a thrillingly expansive *Emperor* which will give much satisfaction.

Zimerman reserves for the *Emperor* his most powerful playing, and Bernstein sensitively encourages him into spontaneous-sounding expressiveness, turning phrases with consistent imagination.

Perahia's account of the *Emperor*, strong and thoughtful yet with characteristic touches of poetry, rounds off an outstanding cycle of the Beethoven concertos. The approach is spacious, and with Bernard Haitink and the Concertgebouw Orchestra firm, responsive partners, each movement immediately takes wing, though a touch of bass-heaviness in the recording needs correcting.

Van Cliburn creates much excitement and intensity in the outer movements, with powerful support from Reiner. It is an individual but satisfying reading, with the slow movement a little restrained in the phrasing but poised in its beauty, and this effectively offsets the virtuosity of the outer movements. The finale is by no means driven too hard; if anything it is slower than usual but has a fine lilt and genuine bravura. The remastered recording sounds very well indeed, with the small reservation that the very upper notes of the piano bring a fractional discrepancy in tuning, noticeable only momentarily in the *Adagio*. This might disturb some ears but most will not be bothered by a phenomenon not at all unusual at live performances.

(i) *Piano concerto No. 5 in E flat (Emperor);* (ii) *Triple concerto for violin, cello and piano in C, Op. 56.*
(M) *** Sony SBK 46549 [id.]. (i) Leon Fleisher, Cleveland O, Szell; (ii) Stern, Rose, Istomin, Phd. O, Ormandy.
☞ (M) **(*) EMI CDM7 67796-2 [id.]. (i) Gieseking, Philh. O, Galliera; (ii) Oborin, D. Oistrakh, Knushevitsky, Philh. O, Sargent.

Leon Fleisher is a pianist who worked with special understanding in the Szell regime at Cleveland, and by any count his reading of the *Emperor* is impressive for its youthful dramatic vigour. For the coupling, Stern, Rose and Istomin – three friends who invariably reveal their personal joy in making music together – make a wonderful trio of soloists. Unfortunately the CBS balance, as usual, favours the soloists so that the contrast of their soft playing is endangered; but the performance as a whole is so compelling that it would take a much more serious recording fault to undermine the concentration.

The Gieseking stereo recording of the *Emperor* comes from the late 1950s and the sound is remarkably good if orchestrally a bit dry. However, Gieseking's incandescently bright timbre is captured truthfully, while the orchestra is well detailed. The performance is admirably fresh and imbued with classical feeling. Gieseking's playing is appealingly spontaneous and the slow movement is impressively poised. Admirers of this artist should not be disappointed. The coupling also dates from the earliest days of stereo, yet the balance (with Walter Legge producing) is among the most successful the *Triple concerto* has received on record. Sargent is authoritative and musical and the soloists make a good team as well as displaying plenty of individual personality. The slow movement is strikingly eloquent and the finale spirited. The CD transfer is clear and clean rather than opulent.

(i) *Piano concerto No. 5 (Emperor). Polonaise in C, Op. 89;* (ii) *Choral Fantasia in C min., Op. 80.*
☞ (M) ** BMG/RCA 09026 61213-2 [id.]. Emanuel Ax; (i) RPO, Previn; (ii) NY Choral Artists, NYPO, Mehta.

Emanuel Ax gives a thoughtful rather than a forceful reading of the *Emperor*, sympathetically supported by Previn and the RPO. The relaxed quality in his playing makes this a less bitingly compelling version than many, with the first movement less of a contest than it can be, while the flowing speed for the slow movement and the scherzando quality in the finale make it less weighty than usual, powerful as Ax's articulation is. Unexceptionable recording, rather thin on piano tone. The *Polonaise*, a comparative rarity, makes a lively encore, but the *Choral Fantasia* – recorded live – springs fully to life only at the choral entry. It is well recorded.

Piano concerto No. 5 (Emperor); (i) *Choral Fantasia, Op. 80.*
⊛ *** EMI Dig. CDC7 49965-2; *EL 749965-4.* Melvyn Tan, (i) Schütz Ch.; L. Classical Players, Roger Norrington.

Melvyn Tan plays with real flair and musical imagination. He has a poetic fire and brilliance all his own. The disc conveys the feeling of a live performance rather than an academic exercise, and the artists follow Czerny's brisk (and authoritative) tempo markings. The inspiriting account of the *Choral Fantasia* possesses a mercurial quality and a panache that show this sometimes underrated work in a most positive light. Norrington and the chorus and orchestra are no less persuasive. A splendidly natural recording completes the attractiveness of this fine disc.

Violin concerto in D, Op. 61.
*** EMI Dig. CDC7 54072-2 [id.]; *EL 754072-4.* Kyung Wha Chung, Concg. O, Tennstedt –
  BRUCH: *Violin concerto No. 1.* ***
☞ **(*) EMI Dig. CDC7 54574-2; *EL 754574-4* [id.]. Kennedy, N. German RSO, Tennstedt (with
  BACH: (Unaccompanied) *Violin Sonatas and Partitas*).
☞ **(*) Trittico Dig. 27103 [id.]. Vanessa-Mae, LSO, Bakels – TCHAIKOVSKY: *Violin concerto.* **(*)
☞ (M) ** Decca Dig. 430 752-2 [id.]. Kyung Wha Chung, VPO, Kondrashin – MENDELSSOHN:
  Concerto. ***
☞ (**) Pearl mono GEMMCDS 9996 (2) [id.]. Fritz Kreisler, Berlin State Op. O, Leo Blech –
  BACH: *Double violin concerto;* BRAHMS; MENDELSSOHN; MOZART: *Violin concertos.* (**)
☞ (**) Pearl mono GEMMCD 9345 [id.]. Joseph Szigeti, British SO, Bruno Walter – BRAHMS:
  Violin concerto. (**)
☞ (M) (*(*)) Teldec/Warner mono 9031 76443-2 [id.]. Georg Kulenkampff, BPO, Schmidt-Isserstedt
  – BRUCH: *Concerto No. 1.* (***)

(i) *Violin concerto in D;* (ii) *Romances Nos. 1 in G, Op. 40; 2 in F, Op. 50.*
☞ ⊛ *** Teldec/Warner Dig. 9031 74881-2 [id.]. Kremer, COE, Harnoncourt.
*** EMI Dig. CDC7 49567-2 [id.]. Perlman, BPO, Barenboim.
⊛ (B) *** DG 427 197-2 [id.]. (i) Schneiderhan, BPO, Jochum; (ii) D. Oistrakh, RPO, Goossens.
(BB) *** Naxos Dig. 8.550149; *4550149* [id.]. Takako Nishizaki, Slovak PO (Bratislava), Kenneth
  Jean.
☞ **(*) Virgin/EMI Dig. VC5 45001-2 [id.]. Dmitry Sitkovetsky, ASMF, Marriner.
☞ (M) ** EMI Dig. CD-EMX 2217 [id.]. Monica Huggett, O of Age of Enlightenment, Mackerras
  – MENDELSSOHN: *Concerto.* **
☞ ** Cala Dig. CACD 1013. Stephanie Chase, Hanover Band, Goodman.
☞ (B) ** Hung. White Label HRC 147. Dénes Kovács; (i) Hungarian State O, Ferencsik; (ii)
  Budapest SO, Lehel.
☞ (M) *(*) EMI CDM7 64324-2 [id.]. Y. Menuhin; (i) New Philh. O, Klemperer; (ii) Philh. O,
  Pritchard.

(i) *Violin concerto in D;* (ii) *Violin sonata No. 5 in F (Spring).*
☞ (M) (**) Sony mono MPK 52536 [id.]. Joseph Szigeti; (i) NYPO, Walter; (ii) Horszowski.

(i) *Violin concerto in D;* (ii) *Violin sonata No. 10 in G, Op. 96.*
☞ **(*) BMG/RCA 09026 61219-2 [id.]. Zukerman, (i) LAPO, Mehta; (ii) Marc Neikrug.

Gidon Kremer's Teldec account of Beethoven's *Violin concerto* was taken from performances with Nikolaus Harnoncourt and the COE in Graz in July 1992, and offers one of his most commanding recordings, both polished and full of flair, magnetically spontaneous from first to last, with tone ravishingly pure. Harnoncourt's contribution as conductor is vital too, for, as in his records of the Beethoven symphonies, also with the COE, he applies lessons he learnt over his years as a pioneer of period performance. If Kremer regularly has you registering new detail in the solo part, the orchestral writing too is superbly realized, with magical sounds in the slow movement in particular. It is particularly refreshing that Kremer takes a relatively urgent view of the first movement, strong yet never wilful or perfunctory. After a thoughtful and dedicated, slightly understated reading of the slow movement, he and Harnoncourt round the performance off magically with a finale that skips along the more infectiously thanks to light, clean articulation and textures. Traditional performances seem heavyweight by comparison. The controversial point for some will be the cadenza in the first movement. It is described as by 'Beethoven/Kremer', for (like Wolfgang Schneiderhan in his classic DG recording) he uses a transcription of the big cadenza which Beethoven wrote for his piano arrangement of the work. But where Schneiderhan had the solo violin backed up by only the timpani (just as Beethoven does), Kremer introduces a piano as well. It makes a very long cadenza indeed – 5 minutes exactly – but he can quote Beethoven in his support. He also plays violin versions of the other cadenzas and flourishes that punctuate Beethoven's piano version – many more than in normal performances. Altogether one of the most refreshing versions of the concerto ever put on disc, backed up by crisp, unsentimental readings of the two *Romances*, with the first of the two flowing faster and more freshly than we are used to.

Perlman's Berlin recording was made at a live performance in the Philharmonie in Berlin in 1986. The live occasion prompts the soloist to play with extra flair and individuality, spontaneous in imagination, with depth of insight married to total technical command. Though (as always with Perlman) the solo violin is balanced well forward, the sound is not overbearing. Anyone wanting an uncontroversial, modern, digital version cannot do better than opt for this. The two *Romances*, recorded by the same performers in the studio, are just as persuasive.

Kyung Wha Chung's EMI performance, recorded live in the Concertgebouw, is searching and intense. Next to Perlman on another live recording from EMI, Chung is lighter and more mercurial. The element of vulnerability in Chung's reading adds to the emotional weight, above all in the slow movement, which in its wistful tenderness is among the most beautiful on record, while the outer movements are full of flair. The recording, with the soloist not balanced too close, is remarkably full and atmospheric for one made live.

Schneiderhan's stereo version of the *Violin concerto* is among the greatest recordings of this work: the serene spiritual beauty of the slow movement, and the playing of the second subject in particular, have never been surpassed on record; the orchestra under Jochum provides a background tapestry of breadth and dignity. As an added point of interest, Schneiderhan uses cadenzas that were provided for the transcription of the work for piano and orchestra. David Oistrakh's accounts of the *Romances* are of high quality too, and the remastering is well managed.

Those looking for a super-bargain, digital version will find that Nishizaki's highly spontaneous performance can measure up to many accounts by more famous names. Helped by a strongly sympathetic backing from the excellent Slovak Philharmonic under Kenneth Jean, her playing is individual yet unselfconscious and has a fresh simplicity of approach which is consistently appealing. The *Larghetto* is poised and serene, and the finale is nicely buoyant. The two *Romances* are also very well played. The digital recording, made in the Reduta Concert Hall in Bratislava, is first class, the violin well forward but with the resonantly full orchestral tapestry spaciously caught.

Compared with Zukerman's spacious reading from the late 1970s with Daniel Barenboim and the Chicago Symphony Orchestra, his new RCA version has an extra depth. If in the earlier version the characteristic warmth of Zukerman's tone marked the whole performance, this one brings greater emphasis on purity and refinement. The violin-sound has less fat on it, and in this work that helps to convey an extra inner intensity. Zukerman is also stricter with himself over maintaining steady speeds, again purifying his concept. The result may be more disciplined, but never too rigid, with even the opening of the finale on the main rondo theme given a sense of gentle communing, not as outward-going as before. The recording helps, with the solo violin less forwardly balanced. It makes an apt and surprisingly unusual coupling to have the concerto presented alongside the last and most elusive of the Beethoven *Violin sonatas*, taken from Zukerman's complete cycle with the pianist Marc Neikrug, who sadly fails to match the violinist in imagination.

Nigel Kennedy's performance was recorded live, not by editing various performances together (the general practice) but taken from a single performance in Lubeck, presented complete with encores (movements from the solo Bach *Sonatas* and *Partitas*). The snag is that many minutes of tuning up and applause have also been included. Like his interpretation of the Brahms, issued a year earlier, Kennedy's reading of the Beethoven is in principle wilfully slow but, far more than in that studio recording of the Brahms, the sense of spontaneity carries persuasion even when, after the big Kreisler cadenza in the first movement, he and Tennstedt threaten to come to a dead halt. The cadenza in the finale brings the most controversial point: Kennedy's own protracted improvisation which, towards the end, lapses into quarter-tones and hints of the twentieth century. Whatever the hype surrounding him these days, Kennedy here still produces much magical playing, but this well-recorded performance will not be to all tastes.

The thirteen-year-old Vanessa-Mae refreshingly adopts speeds markedly faster than have latterly become common in the first two movements. Her first entry brings a sourness happily not typical of the whole, for her lightness and agility in passage-work are most winning, and her hushed trills are particularly beautiful, as in the poised moment before the second subject. Neither the coda nor the slow movement brings really hushed playing, and the finale finds her occasionally rushing rhythms. Yet the impetuosity is very winning. The recording is full and bright, making this a formidable, generous coupling, one not otherwise listed.

With his bright, rather than warm tone, Sitkovetsky gives a clean-cut reading, matched by the fresh and straightforward accompaniment of Sir Neville Marriner and the Academy. Next to the very strong, positive readings of Perlman and Kremer, both of them recorded live, Sitkovetsky's may seem rather small-scale, but there is a place for his direct approach, with measured speeds generally kept steady and with impulsive rubato generally avoided. It is a reading that tends to linger rather than press on, though Sitkovetsky's disciplined control readily holds the long first movement together, helped by crisply dramatic tutti in which Marriner, following convention, does tend to press ahead of the basic tempo. The two *Romances*, with Sitkovetsky offering pure, sweet tone, also effectively sustain speeds on the slow side.

The opening timpani strokes are not very arresting in Monica Huggett's 'authentic' version, although, later, Mackerras achieves incisive enough orchestral tuttis. Yet overall this is not a performance that convinces by either its emotional power or its serenity in the slow movement, which is comparatively uninvolving.

Stephanie Chase in her period performance aptly takes the first movement rather fast, using a pleasantly pure tone. The playing of the Hanover Band and the recorded sound are outstanding, but the soloist on her first entry in the *Concerto* totally fails to convey any sense of command. Only after a minute or so does she seem to relax, and then the purity and the directness of the reading begin to add up, not just in the first movement but throughout, with clean attack from the orchestra as well as the soloist. This version will perhaps suit those who want directness above all in a period performance.

A fine, fresh account of the *Violin concerto* from Dénés Kovács, well accompanied and given full, clear sound. But there is nothing special here and, with Schneiderhan and Grumiaux available at bargain price in the same coupling, this Hungaroton reissue is not really competitive.

Menuhin's 1966 recording with Klemperer is disappointing. The two artists do not bring out the best in each other and there is no feeling of incandescence. Moreover the soloist's timbre is often not very ingratiating, and the remastered recording makes it sound thinner still, while orchestral tuttis are fierce. The two *Romances*, which come first on the record and were recorded earlier in 1960, are smoother and more pleasing.

In the days of 78-r.p.m. shellac discs it was one of the marks of the real gramophone connoisseur to prefer the Kulenkampff Telefunken set of the Beethoven *Violin concerto* to such popular (and easily obtained) versions as Heifetz's or Kreisler's. It was not just snobbery (scoff though some did), for even before the war Telefunken had achieved a sound-quality that in its range and immediacy sounds remarkably faithful even today. Added to that, Kulenkampff brought thoughtfulness and relaxation to a performance that in no way inhibited its spontaneity. His pianissimo tone above the stave could be fabulously pure and thus created a serenity which was to be passed on to future generations of interpreters, notably Schneiderhan and Grumiaux. There are shortcomings, too, including moments when solo intonation is not always quite secure. Above all, this is a performance of enormous individuality and Hans Schmidt-Isserstedt's accompaniment has great verve, with the finale scintillating in the spirit of the dance. Even with the removal of inhibition brought about by tape techniques, few violinists have approached Kulenkampff on record in sense of freedom and spaciousness, and for that alone this CD is invaluable. The Bruch coupling is hardly less remarkable. A word of warning, however: the transfer is of very poor quality and, as anyone who heard them will know, does scant justice to the original 78-r.p.m. discs, which were very good indeed for the period. The sound here is scrawny and unnatural, though you can still hear enough to recognize Kulenkampff's artistry.

Kyung Wha Chung's 1979 Decca performance is now totally superseded by her later (1990) EMI version with Tennstedt. The earlier account, measured and thoughtful, lacks the compulsion one would have predicted, largely due to the often prosaic conducting of Kondrashin. There is poetry in individual movements – the minor-key episode of the finale, for example, which alone justifies the unusually slow tempo – but, with too little of the soloist's natural electricity conveyed and none of her volatile imagination, it must be counted a disappointment despite the first-class digital sound. The Mendelssohn coupling is a different matter.

When Kreisler recorded the Beethoven concerto with Barbirolli he was in his sixties, and this 1926 account with Leo Blech, which sonically was quite good for its period, shows his wonderful tone and consummate artistry to better advantage. However, those who have the earlier LP transfer (EMI HLM 7016), with which we compared this, will probably be better satisfied with the smoother, warmer sound on the HMV LP. The Pearl transfer has greater presence and detail, but there is some roughness and a lot more hiss.

The two Szigeti recordings come from different periods in his career, but both have the advantage of Bruno Walter's conducting: the first and more celebrated is with the British Symphony Orchestra and was made at Westminster Central Hall in 1932; the second comes from New York and 1947. In some respects the earlier version remains artistically stronger in that the disturbing vibrato and occasional vinegary tone which troubled this great violinist in the last decade of his career had already begun to surface. Of course, the conception remains much the same, and there are notable couplings which make choice difficult. In the Pearl CD we have the Brahms *Concerto* with Sir Hamilton Harty and the Hallé Orchestra, albeit in 1928 sound, and on the Sony CD a lovely (1953) account of the *Spring sonata* with Horszowski which finds both artists in very good form.

Konzertsatz (Concerto movement) in C, WoO 5; Romance No. 1 in G, Op.40.
(M) *** DG 431 168-2 [id.]. Kremer, LSO, Tchakarov – SCHUBERT: *Konzertstück* etc. ***

The early *Concerto movement in C* is performed in a completion by Wilfried Fischer that is effective enough; and the mixed bag of Schubert which acts as coupling is certainly apt. All the music is beautifully played by Kremer; the 1978 recording, made in the London Sir Henry Wood Hall, has transferred splendidly to CD.

Triple concerto for violin, cello and piano in C, Op. 56.
☞ (M) *** EMI CDM7 64744-2 [id.]. D. Oistrakh, Rostropovich, S. Richter, BPO, Karajan – BRAHMS: *Double concerto*. ***
(B) *** Pickwick Dig. PCD 917; *IMPC 917*. Trio Zingara, ECO, Heath – BOCCHERINI: *Concerto No. 7*. ***

(i) *Triple concerto, Op. 56;* (ii) *Symphony No. 10: First movement* (realized & completed Cooper).
(M) *** Chan. Dig. CHAN 6501 [id.]. (i) Kalichstein–Laredo–Robinson Trio, ECO, Gibson; (ii) CBSO, Weller.

The star-studded cast on the EMI recording makes a breathtaking line-up. The results are predictably arresting, with Beethoven's priorities among the soloists well preserved in the dominance of Rostropovich over his colleagues. This is warm, expansive music-making that confirms even more clearly than before the strength of the piece. The resonant recording suffers from loss of focus in some climaxes, but this is not too serious. The new transfer is remarkably vivid and has firmed up the orchestral tuttis most satisfactorily. Now recoupled with a similarly commanding account of the Brahms *Double concerto*, this is an irresistible mid-priced bargain.

The 1984 Chandos version of the *Triple concerto* with three young American soloists is exceptionally well recorded. Sharon Robinson, the cellist, takes the lead with pure tone and fine intonation, though both her partners are by nature more forceful artists. A clean-cut, often refreshing view of the work, it is now reissued coupled with Weller's strong version of Barry Cooper's completion of the first movement of Beethoven's projected *Tenth Symphony*, also very well recorded.

On Pickwick, Felix Schmidt, who is also the cello soloist in the Boccherini, plays with consistently beautiful, firm and clean tone, well matched by his two partners, creating the illusion of live performance, full of bounce and vigour. At bargain price, in full and vivid digital sound, it makes an excellent recommendation.

(i) *Triple concerto, Op. 56;* (ii) *Choral Fantasia* (for piano, chorus & orchestra), *Op. 80.*
☞ *** Ph. Dig. 438 005-2 [id.]. (i) Beaux Arts Trio; (ii) Menahem Pressler, Mid-German R. Ch.; Leipzig GO, Masur.

Since the Beaux Arts Trio last recorded Beethoven's *Triple concerto* in 1977, two of its personnel have changed, leaving Menahem Pressler, now in his seventies, as the ever-lively survivor. Not only does Pressler's playing sparkle even more brightly in the concerto than before, he is an inspired protagonist in the *Choral Fantasia*, setting the pattern of joyfulness in this performance from his opening improvisation-like solo onwards. The other prime mover is Kurt Masur, who has rarely conducted more electrifying Beethoven performances on disc. What marks this performance out, distinguishing it not just from the previous Beaux Arts one but from most others, is its exhilarating urgency, quicker in its speeds than most rivals. The evenness and clarity of Pressler's articulation in scales and passage-work is a delight. As for the brief central meditation, led – like most main themes in this work – by the cello, it flows very warmly and naturally, with Peter Wiley finding an even wider dynamic range than his Beaux Arts predecessor. The soloists are well focused in the front, with the orchestra warm and full behind – though, in a way typical of Leipzig sound, the bass is at times boomy and thick. The performance of the *Choral Fantasia* is most persuasive too, largely because it takes the work less seriously than most, with witty pointing of the variations. It is rather like having the choral finale of the *Ninth Symphony* anticipated with tongue in cheek. The soloists and chorus are set behind the orchestra, and if the initial impression is that the soloists are too distant, the focus is so crisp and clear that one quickly accepts them (rightly) as part of the chorus.

12 Contredanses, WoO 14; 12 German dances, WoO 8; 12 Minuets, WoO 7; 11 Mödlinger dances, WoO 17.
(BB) *** Naxos 8.550433 [id.]. Capella Istropolitana, Oliver Dohnányi.

It is always a delight to catch Beethoven relaxing and showing how warmly he felt towards the Viennese background in which he lived. The excellent Capella Istropolitana group used for the recording seems to be of exactly the right size, and they play the music with light rhythmic feeling, yet with plenty of spirit. Dipped into, this will give pleasure.

12 Contretänze, WoO 14; (i) 2 Romances for violin and orchestra, Opp. 40 & 50. Mödlinger Tänze, WoO 17.
☞ (M) **(*) Decca 436 782-2 [id.]. V. Mozart Ens., Willi Boskovsky, (i) with Boskovsky (violin) – MOZART: *Les Petits Riens: Overture and ballet music.* ***

Beethoven's scoring produces an uncharacteristic sound-world at times, yet one to tickle the ear: the use of lead clarinet in the *Mödlinger Tänze*, plus genial horn writing, is delightfully colourful. Boskovsky and his players interpret these unpretentious dances to the manner born, and the remastered recording, from the late 1960s, is wonderfully vivid. However, Boskovsky's tone in the two *Romances* is lean and uningratiating and it is a pity that an outside virtuoso was not brought in.

The Creatures of Prometheus: Overture and ballet music, Op. 43 (complete).
*** DG Dig. 419 608-2 [id.]. Orpheus CO.

As this splendid recording demonstrates, there is much to admire in this lesser-known Beethoven score, often anticipating later, greater works in sudden flashes, with moods varying widely from tragedy to country-dance felicity. The very talented conductorless orchestra plays most stylishly, helped by bright, clean recording.

OVERTURES

Overtures: The Consecration of the house, Op. 124; Coriolan, Op. 62; The Creatures of Prometheus, Op. 43; Egmont, Op. 84; Fidelio, Op. 72c; King Stephen, Op. 117; Leonora Nos. 1–3, Opp. 138; 72a; 72b; The Ruins of Athens, Op. 113; Zur Namensfeier, Op. 115.
(M) *** DG 427 256-2 (2) [id.]. BPO, Karajan.

Karajan's set of overtures was recorded in the mid- and late 1960s. They are impressive performances that have stood the test of time. They show an imposing command of structure and detail as well as the customary virtuosity one expects from this conductor and the Berlin Philharmonic. The sound is fresh and bright.

(i) *Overtures: The Consecration of the house, Op. 124; Coriolan, Op. 62; The Creatures of Prometheus, Op. 43; Egmont, Op. 84; Fidelio, Op. 72c; King Stephen, Op. 117; Leonora Nos. 1–3, Opp. 138, 72 a–b; The Ruins of Athens, Op. 113; Zur Namensfeier, Op. 115;* (ii) *12 Contredanses, WoO 14; 12 German dances, WoO 8; 12 Minuets, WoO 7.*
☞ (B) *** Ph. Duo 438 706-2 (2) [id.]. (i) Leipzig GO, Masur; (ii) ASMF, Marriner.

Masur's performances of the *Overtures* are more direct than those of Karajan and they are wholly satisfying in their strong motivation and lack of mannerism. The Philips recording from the early 1970s is of high quality, and the remastering has enhanced its vividness and impact, although the characteristic Leipzig resonance remains. To complete the second CD, Marriner and the Academy offer a splendid foil with the dance music. Even as a composer of light music Beethoven was a master, and this collection, beautifully played and recorded (in 1978), can be equally warmly recommended though, again, the acoustic is perhaps slightly over-resonant.

Overtures: The Consecration of the house, Op. 124; Coriolan, Op. 62; The Creatures of Prometheus, Op. 43; Egmont, Op. 84; Fidelio, Op. 72c; King Stephen, Op. 117; Leonora No. 2, Op. 72a; The Ruins of Athens, Op. 113.
**(*) Nimbus NI 5205 [id.]. Hanover Band, Roy Goodman or Monica Huggett.

Recorded at various periods in conjunction with the Hanover Band's other Beethoven recordings for Nimbus, this compilation makes a generous and attractive collection. Anyone who wants the principal Beethoven overtures played on period instruments will be well pleased.

SYMPHONIES

Symphonies Nos. 1–9.
☞ *** DG Dig. 439 900-2 (5) [id.]. O Révolutionnaire et Romantique, Gardiner (with Orgonasova, Von Otter, Rolfe Johnson, Cachemaille, Monteverdi Ch. in *No. 9*).
*** Teldec/Warner Dig. 2292 46452-2 (5) [id.]. COE, Harnoncourt (with Margiono, Remmert, Schasching, Holl, Arnold Schoenberg Ch. in *No. 9*).
(B) *** DG 429 036-2 (5) [id.]. BPO, Karajan (with Janowitz, Rössel-Majdan, Kmentt, Berry, V. Singverein in *No. 9*).
☞ *(*) Ph. Dig. 426 290-2 (5) [id.]. Leipzig GO, Masur (with Sylvia McNair, Jard van Nes, Uwe Heilmann, Bernd Weikl, Leipzig GO Ch. in *No. 9*).

Symphonies Nos. 1–9; Overtures: Coriolan; Creatures of Prometheus; Egmont.
☞ (M) **(*) EMI CMS5 65184-2 (6) [id.]. L. Classical Players, Norrington (with Yvonne Kenny, Sarah Walker, Patrick Power, Petteri Salomaa, L. Schütz Ch. in *No. 9*).

Symphonies Nos. 1–9; Overtures: Coriolan; Egmont.
**(*) O-L Dig. 425 696-2 (6) [id.]. AAM, Hogwood (with Augér, Robbin, Rolfe Johnson, Reinhard, London Symphony Ch. in *No. 9*).

Symphonies Nos. 1–9; Overtures: Coriolan; Egmont; Fidelio; Leonora No. 3.
☞ **(*) DG Dig. Gold 439 200-2 (6) [id.]. BPO, Karajan (with Perry, Baltsa, Cole, Van Dam, V. Singverein in *No. 9*).

Symphonies Nos. 1–9; Overtures: Egmont; Fidelio; King Stephen.
(M) **(*) Sony SB5K 48396 (5). Cleveland O, George Szell (with Addison, Hobson, Lewis, Bell, Cleveland Ch. in *No. 9*).

Symphonies Nos. 1–9; Overture Leonora No. 3.
(M) (***) BMG/RCA mono GD 60324 (5) [60324-2-RG]. NBC SO, Toscanini (with Farrell, Merriman, Peerce, Scott, Shaw Chorale in *No. 9*).

Symphonies Nos. 1–9; 10 (realized Cooper): *1st movt; Overtures: Coriolan; The Creatures of Prometheus* (with rehearsals of *Symphonies Nos. 6 & 10*).
*** Chan. CHAN 8712/7; *DBTD 6001* (6) [id.]. CBSO, Weller (with Barstow, Finnie, Rendall, Tomlinson, CBSO Ch. in *No. 9*).

As we go to press, Gardiner's long-promised cycle arrives as a clear first choice for those wanting period performances. With sound that is warmer and weightier than in the first generation of such versions, yet still transparent, and with Gardiner himself acknowledging the influence of Harnoncourt's cycle, it can also be recommended strongly to those who would normally opt for modern instruments. These are exhilarating performances which have bite and imagination and a sense of spontaneity, reflecting the shrewd programme of recording, linked to live performances. Like Norrington, Gardiner observes Beethoven's own fast metronome markings, but less rigidly, so that he allows himself a degree more expansion in the slow movements of the *Eroica* and the *Ninth*. By contrast, his speeds for the opening *Allegros* of both these key symphonies are even faster than Norrington's, yet more resilient. Significant among Gardiner's many corrections of traditional scores – with Jonathan Del Mar a scholarly helper – is his amendment of the marking for the Turkish March in the finale of the *Ninth*, twice as brisk as Norrington and leading logically into the fugue. This inspired account of the *Ninth* – recorded immediately after live performances in Britain and Japan – crowns the whole cycle, as it should. The set, given full, luminous sound, is complete on only five discs, with a sixth containing an illustrated talk by Gardiner in three languages.

Harnoncourt's cycle with the Chamber Orchestra of Europe, presented convincingly on a biggish chamber scale, is among the most refreshing of any and deservedly won the *Gramophone* Orchestral Award for 1992. Reflecting his work as a period-performance pioneer, Harnoncourt makes rhythms light and textures clean and with sparing vibrato. Periodically, as in the opening movement of the *Eroica*, he adopts a hectically fast tempo, but that is the exception. More usually, his choice of speeds is regularly geared to bringing out the rhythmic and expressive finesse characteristic of this brilliant young orchestra. That the performances so consistently display the joy in Beethoven, his natural exuberance, reflects the way they were made, done live over an intensive period in Graz in the summer of 1990. The *Ninth* was recorded almost a year after the rest and equally refreshingly reflects the lessons of period performance, though the dry manner in the great *Adagio*, taken at a flowing speed, underplays the emotional depth. Excellent sound. Admirers of Harnoncourt need not hesitate. The records comprising this set are also available separately, with the symphonies coupled as follows: Nos. 1 and 3 (9031 75708-2), Nos. 2 and 5 (9031 75712-2), Nos. 4 and 7 (9031 75714-2), Nos. 6 and 8 (9031 75709-2), No. 9 (9031 75713-2).

Of Karajan's four recorded cycles, the 1961–2 set is the most consistent and in many ways the most compelling, combining high polish with a biting sense of urgency and spontaneity. There is one major disappointment, in the over-taut reading of the *Pastoral*, which in addition omits the vital repeat in the scherzo. Otherwise these are incandescent performances, superbly played. On CD the sound is still excellent, the best-balanced in any of his Beethoven series and on five CDs at bargain price, this makes outstanding value for money.

Walter Weller's Beethoven cycle for Chandos is by far his finest achievement on record. Although this is the City of Birmingham Symphony Orchestra, there is a warm, refined, Viennese quality in the playing and interpretation, to remind you that this conductor started his career as concertmaster of the Vienna Philharmonic. The Chandos sound is full and glowing to match, by far the finest to date given to any conductor in a collected Beethoven cycle. The sixth (supplementary) disc brings Dr Barry Cooper's re-creation of the first movement of No. 10, plus substantial extracts of rehearsal and two overtures.

Repackaged at mid-price, Norrington's set with the London Classical Players makes a strong recommendation for a period-performance cycle, though these studio recordings often lack some of the bounce and energy that so marked his live performances and those in his television series. His determination to observe Beethoven's metronome markings regularly leads to refreshing results, though some of the more extreme speeds come to sound wilful, especially in the *Choral Symphony* where the slow movement becomes a sweet interlude rather than a meditation, far shorter than the other movements. The male soloists, too, leave much to be desired. Hogwood is to be preferred here, as he is in the *Pastoral*, although Norrington scores in the *Eroica*, a very convincing and powerful performance. The recording, made in Abbey Road, is faithful and well balanced, though not always as full and immediate as it might be.

Of the Beethoven cycles on period instruments, Hogwood's with the Academy of Ancient Music is recorded very vividly. His pointing of rhythms is not always as alert or imaginative as that of his direct rivals; as a whole, the cycle may lack something in individual moments of insight but, with clean and generally well-disciplined playing, it is consistently satisfying.

Szell's compellingly strong, direct view of Beethoven brings much to stimulate. The marvellously polished and always responsive Cleveland playing never brings a suspicion of routine, but reservations must be made about the close CBS sound-balance which prevents a real pianissimo from registering, even though the ear readily senses when the orchestra is playing gently.

In Karajan's last, digital set, the recording seems to have been affected by the need to make a version on video at the same sessions. The gain is that these performances have keener spontaneity, the loss that they often lack the brilliant, knife-edged precision of ensemble one has come to regard as normal with Karajan. Though there is relatively little homing-in of microphones to spotlight individual detail, the sound too often grows thick and congested in big fortissimo tuttis. However, with the earlier recordings now issued at mid-price or less, the attractions of this digital box are much reduced even if, with speeds generally a little less extreme, there are a number of movements which sound more persuasive than before. The six discs are now remastered to Digital Gold standards – for comments see the individual issues below – and are offered at a slightly reduced price for the set: six CDs for the price of five.

The NBC Toscanini versions are faster and more tense than the earlier Beethoven readings that he committed to records, but they are far from rigid or unloving, and they are crowned by performances of breathtaking power in the *Eroica* and the *Ninth*. Listening to this Beethoven is never a relaxing experience, but it is a uniquely involving one.

It is disappointing that this digitally recorded Beethoven *Symphony* cycle from Kurt Masur and the Leipzig Gewandhaus Orchestra on Philips contains too many performances where conductor and players seem to be on automatic pilot. Their earlier cycle from 1975 has been a steady and reliable standby, clean-cut and unidiosyncratic; though the new one improves on the old in observing more of the marked repeats, and though occasionally Masur has revised his ideas on tempo to give sharper results, as in the first movement of No. 7, there are many more minuses than pluses.

Symphonies Nos. 1–9 (arr. Liszt).
**(*) Teldec/Warner Dig. 9031 71619-2 (6) [id.]. Cyprien Katsaris (piano).

In Cyprien Katsaris's cycle of the Liszt/Beethoven transcriptions the sound generally speaking is a bit synthetic; but in the *Eroica*, the *Eighth* and the *Choral*, the playing is really quite astonishing, not only in purely pianistic terms and in a feeling for texture but also for architecture. The *Fifth* is the only real let-down.

Symphonies Nos. 1 in C, Op. 21; 2 in D, Op. 36.
☞ **(*) DG Dig. Gold 439 001-2 [id.]. BPO, Karajan.

Karajan's digital Beethoven series brings some surprisingly slack ensemble in the recording of the first two symphonies. The performances are relaxed in good ways too, with Karajan's flair and control of rhythm never leading to breathless speeds. Not unexpectedly, there are moments when detail is perceptively revealed, but the heavy reverberation of the recording makes the result arguably too weighty for these works and pianissimos are rarely gentle enough. (The 1977 versions are more satisfying, both as performances and as recordings.) This reissue, like the other Beethoven symphonies from Karajan's 1984 set, has been remastered for the Karajan Gold series, by a system called Original-image-bit processing. Outlines are firmer, and the sound is cleaner in focus, but this is by no means demonstration sound-quality.

Symphonies Nos. 1 and 2 (trans. Liszt).
*** Teldec/Warner Dig. 2292 43661-2 [id.]. Cyprien Katsaris (piano).

Transcendental technique and a fine musical intelligence are the distinguishing features of these performances, which remain without peer in the Beethoven–Liszt discography.

Symphonies Nos. 1–2; 4–5.
☞ (B) **(*) DG Double 439 681-2 (2) [id.]. VPO, Karl Boehm.

Boehm's performances come from his Vienna cycle of the early 1970s, centrally satisfying readings (especially Nos. 2 and 4), smoothly yet vividly recorded, with a good deal of resonance in the lower range to add weight without clouding the upper range. The performances are mature and completely reliable and surely represent an admirable first way to come to terms with these four masterpieces. What the readings lack is the sort of sharp idiosyncrasy which makes for dramatic individuality. So the first movement of No. 1 is spacious and mellow; the *Andante* is beautifully played, and the remaining movements have both character and vitality, although there is comparatively little extrovert excitement. Equally in No. 2, after a brisk and dramatic reading of the first movement (not quite as fast as Karajan in the *Allegro*), Boehm gives genial accounts of the remaining movements, affectionately expansive in the slow movement, joyful and weighty in the Scherzo and finale. In the *Fourth* Boehm's approach notes the kinship with the *Pastoral Symphony*. The *Allegro vivace* is relatively easy-going but with big, satisfying contrasts; the slow movement is warmly lyrical and the last two movements bounce along joyfully. If Boehm misses some of the tensions, there is no lack of weight or strength. Boehm's account of the *Fifth* may not be the most powerful available, but the excellent playing and the rich weightiness of the recording, with plenty of liveliness on top, make it a good version to live with. With this pair of CDs on a desert island one would certainly sense the presence of Beethoven. The transfers to CD retain the full character of the original sound.

Symphonies Nos. 1 in C; 3 in E flat (Eroica), Op. 55.
☞ *** Teldec/Warner Dig. 9031 75708-2 [id.]. COE, Harnoncourt.
(M) **(*) Sony SMK 47514 [id.]. NYPO, Bernstein.
(M) (***) BMG/RCA mono GD 60252 [60252-2-RG]. NBC O, Toscanini.
☞ ** (M) ** BMG/RCA mono/stereo 09026 61399-2 [id.]. Boston SO, Munch.

Harnoncourt's *Eroica* brings an extremely fast tempo in the first movement, and his austere view of the great *Funeral march* is chillingly intense. The result is as individual as it is powerful. No. 1, too, is splendidly alive.

Bernstein's *First* receives a well-shaped reading, with no lack of momentum and pace (first-movement exposition repeat included). The reading clearly looks forward to the coupled, electrically intense *Eroica*, also dating from 1964. The *Funeral march* is darkly tragic, and the reading as a whole has great power. The bright yet full sound offers dramatic projection.

Toscanini's are performances which convey breathtaking power, notably the magnificent account of the *Eroica*, never comfortable but far from rigid or unloving.

Munch's *Eroica* comes from 1957 and is tautly held together and very well played. In fact, heard after Paul van Kempen's 1954 Berlin recording, it sounds a bit hard-driven and wanting in spaciousness. In actual time there is only a few seconds between the two accounts of the first movement, but there is a world of difference in their perception of its space. In the Scherzo the second repeat marking is not observed. The *First Symphony* comes from 1950 but sounds very good for its age. Again it is a highly disciplined but less driven account than the *Eroica*.

Symphonies Nos. 1 in C; 4 in B flat, Op. 60; Egmont overture.
(M) *** DG 419 048-2; *419 048-4* [id.]. BPO, Karajan.

Karajan's 1977 version of No. 1 is exciting, polished and elegant; in No. 4 the balance is closer, exposing every flicker of tremolando. Yet the body and ambience of the recording combine to give a realistic presence, and overall this is very impressive.

Symphonies Nos. 1 in C; 6 in F (Pastoral), Op. 68.
(M) *** BMG/RCA GD 60002 [60002-2-RG]. Chicago SO, Reiner.

Symphonies Nos. 1 in C; 6 in F (Pastoral), Op. 68; Overture Egmont, Op. 84.
(M) **(*) Sony SBK 46532 [id.]. Cleveland O, Szell.

In its newly remastered form, Reiner's 1961 *Pastoral* sounds wonderfully warm and full. The performance too is among the finest ever recorded, outstandingly fresh and enjoyable. The *First Symphony* is weighty and direct, less incandescent but still a considerable account.

Szell's dynamic performance of the *First Symphony* makes up for any absence of charm. In the *Pastoral* Szell is subtle in his control of phrasing, for all the firmness of his style. However, it is a pity that the close-up sound robs the slow movement of much of its gentleness and delicacy of atmosphere. The finale, by contrast, is attractively relaxed.

Symphonies Nos. 1; 7 in A, Op. 92.
☞ *** Sony Dig. SK 48236 [id.]. La Scala PO, Giulini.
(BB) **(*) ASV CDQS 6066. N. Sinfonia of England, Richard Hickox.
(M) **(*) EMI CDM7 63354-2 [id.]. Philh. O, Klemperer.

Giulini in his late seventies takes a more expansive view of both symphonies than almost any predecessor. This was the first disc in his projected cycle of the symphonies with the La Scala Philharmonic, an orchestra drawn not just from the opera-house but from other leading Italian orchestras too. With sympathetic players he finds a rare lyricism, moulding phrases persuasively, but without making them seem mannered. And his gift of springing rhythms prevents the result from stagnating. Warm, if not ideally clear, sound.

Hickox's view of both works is unaffected and direct and so gets the best of both worlds: finely detailed yet substantial; and the very lack of idiosyncrasy makes for easy listening. The CD transfer is full and agreeable but provides a rather resonant bass.

With Klemperer the slow speeds and heavyweight manner in both works will for many get in the way of enjoyment. That said, the compulsion of Klemperer in Beethoven remains strong, with rhythmic pointing consistently preventing stagnation.

Symphonies Nos. 2 in D; 4 in B flat, Op. 60.
(M) *** EMI CDM7 63355-2 [id.]. Philh. O, Klemperer.

The coupling for CD emphasizes the consistency of Klemperer's approach to Beethoven, with both the *Second* and *Fourth* symphonies sounding the more powerful through weighty treatment. The *Fourth* brings one of the most compelling performances of all. The sound is fresh yet full.

Symphonies Nos. 2 in D; 5 in C min., Op. 67.
☞ *** Teldec/Warner Dig. 9031 75712-2 [id.]. COE, Harnoncourt.
(M) **(*) Sony SBK 47651 [id.]. Cleveland O, George Szell.

Harnoncourt's exuberance does not mean a lack of weight in the *Fifth*, while the slow movement is particularly fine and the finale grows seamlessly out of the Scherzo. This Teldec record makes a clear first choice in this coupling. The orchestral playing has splendid bite and lift.

There is some marvellously clean articulation from the strings in the first movement of Szell's No. 2 and the adrenalin runs free; yet here, as in the similarly brilliant account of No. 5, Szell understands the need to give full scope to the lyrical elements.

Symphonies Nos. 2 in D; 7 in A, Op. 92.
(M) *** DG 419 050-2; *419 050-4* [id.]. BPO, Karajan.
(M) **(*) Sony SMK 47515 [id.]. NYPO, Bernstein.

In Karajan's *Second*, the firm lines give the necessary strength. The *Seventh* is tense and exciting, with the conductor emphasizing the work's dramatic rather than its dance-like qualities.

In Bernstein's No. 2 the NYPO play as if their very lives depended on it. The *Seventh* is hardly less vital, with the *Allegretto* bringing an intense climax and the finale very exciting without being overdriven. In both symphonies the 1964 sound is a bit fierce on top but has plenty of underlying body.

Symphonies Nos. 2; 8 in F, Op. 93.
*** EMI Dig. CDC7 47698-2 [id.]. L. Classical Players, Norrington.
(BB) **(*) ASV CDQS 5067. N. Sinfonia, Hickox.
☞ **(*) Sony Dig. SK 48238 [id.]. La Scala PO, Giulini.

The coupling of Nos. 2 and 8 was the first of Norrington's Beethoven series and showed the London Classical Players as an authentic group with a distinctive sound, sweeter and truer in the string section than most, generally easier on non-specialist ears. In following Beethoven's own metronome markings for both symphonies the results are exhilarating, never merely breathless, bringing far more than proof of an academic theory.

Richard Hickox directs his chamber-scale orchestra in fresh, warm and relaxed readings of these two even-numbered symphonies. Playing is refined and rhythms resilient. The scale is well established by the slightly backward balance of the modest string section, with the focus rather sharper in No. 8 than in No. 2.

Predictably spacious readings from Giulini of both symphonies, the expansiveness working better in the glowing account of No. 2 than in No. 8 which lacks mercurial feeling; yet the purposeful strength of this reading remains impressive. Playing is excellent; the sound is good, better in No. 2 than in No. 8, which is not quite as full or as vivid.

Symphony No. 3 in E flat (Eroica), Op. 55.
(M) (***) BMG/RCA mono GD 60271 [60271-2-RG]. NBC SO, Toscanini – MOZART: *Symphony No. 40.* (**)
☞ (M) **(*) Ph. 438 277-2 [id.]. Concg. O, Kondrashin.

Symphony No. 3 (Eroica); Grosse Fuge, Op. 133.
(M) *** EMI CDM7 63356-2 [id.]. Philh. O, Klemperer.

Symphony No. 3 (Eroica); Overture, Coriolan.
(B) *** Pickwick Dig. PCD 900; *CIMPC 900* [id.]. LSO, Wyn Morris.

Symphony No. 3 (Eroica); Overtures: Coriolan; Fidelio.
☞ (M) **(*) BMG/RCA 09026 60962-2 [id.]. Chicago SO, Reiner.

Symphony No. 3 (Eroica); Creatures of Prometheus: Overture.
*** EMI Dig. CDC7 49101-2. L. Classical Players, Norrington.

Symphony No. 3 (Eroica); Overture Egmont, Op. 84.
☞ *** Ph. Dig. 434 120-2 [id.]. Dresden State O, Sir Colin Davis.
☞ **(*) DG Dig. Gold 439 002-2 [id.]. BPO, Karajan.

Symphony No. 3 (Eroica); Overtures: Leonora Nos. 2 & 3.
(M) (***) EMI mono CDM7 63855-2 [id.]. Philh. O, Klemperer.

(i) *Symphony No. 3 (Eroica);* (ii) *Serenade in D, for string trio, Op. 8.*
(BB) *** Virgin/EMI Dig. VJ7 91567-2 [id.]. (i) Scottish CO, Saraste; (ii) Sitkovetsky, Caussé, Geringas.

With the Dresden Staatskapelle, Sir Colin Davis conducts a splendid account of the *Eroica* that masterfully sustains spaciousness and expansive speeds. Davis is electrifying in the great build-up of the development, leading to grinding dissonances. Equally, the hushed intensity of Davis's slow, concentrated reading of the *Funeral march* has rarely been matched on disc, helped by superb sound. It is good to have a fresh, new *Eroica* to take its place comfortably at the top of the list.

The digital remastering of Klemperer's spacious 1961 version of the *Eroica* reinforces its magnificence, keenly concentrated to sustain speeds slower than in his earlier, mono account. That alternative, mono version by Klemperer was among the very first records he made with the Philharmonia for EMI, but the success of these first Beethoven works revealed his full strength. This *Eroica* is one of his supreme achievements.

Saraste directs the Scottish Chamber Orchestra in one of the most compelling of modern *Eroicas*, the first one fully to present the work satisfyingly on a chamber scale, thanks to the relatively intimate recording. The coupling is generous and unusual: a well-characterized and stylish account of the Opus 8 *Serenade for string trio*. At super-bargain price, this is an outstanding issue in every way.

Norrington's account of the *Eroica* is consistently even faster than his closest period-performance rivals, yet one quickly forgets any feeling of haste when rhythms are so crisp and supple in their spring, and the great *Funeral march* has natural gravity.

Wyn Morris on the Pickwick label conducts a taut reading of the *Eroica*, dark and intense, with allegros consistently urgent, and the LSO responds with both bite and refinement. An excellent bargain.

Toscanini's version has a far keener emotional intensity than the studio recording which appeared earlier as part of his Beethoven cycle in the BMG Toscanini series. Toscanini had a special insight into this of all Beethoven's symphonies, making this disc a valuable addition to his discography.

The gain in Karajan's digital version of the *Eroica* over his previous recordings lies most of all in the *Funeral march*, very spacious and intense, with dynamic contrasts intensified. Here, and even more noticeably in the allegros, the playing is marginally less polished than before, lacking something of the knife-edged bite associated with Karajan. The recording, remastered for the Karajan Gold series, now sounds cleaner and firmer, but there is still a degree of congestion in big tuttis. Nevertheless, the power and concentration make it an epic reading.

Reiner's is undoubtedly a compulsive *Eroica*, big-boned and spectacular in its epic qualities, but the first movement does not maintain an unerring single sweep forward, and the *Funeral march* is majestic and not greatly touched by tragedy. Characteristically full, late-1950s Chicago sound.

Kirill Kondrashin gives a formidable account of the *Eroica*, unaffected and with a good sense of forward movement, weighty without ever being ponderous, spontaneous, yet well thought out. Very good playing from the Concertgebouw Orchestra, recorded at a concert. Given the competition – there are well over 80 versions currently on the market – this is not a front-runner but it is well worth attention.

Symphonies Nos. 3 (Eroica); 7–8; Overture: Consecration of the house.
☞ ⊛ (M) (***) Ph. mono 438 533-2 (2) [id.]. BPO, Paul van Kempen.

Astonishingly few allowances need be made for these mono recordings by Paul van Kempen and the Berlin Philharmonic. The *Eroica* dates from 1954, a year before the conductor's death (not 1959, as stated on the sleeve and labels), and the *Seventh* and *Eighth* from 1953. These are performances of classic profile: they have grandeur, integrity and power. Both the *Eroica* and the *Eighth* are worth a Rosette, so strong is their fallout! Had van Kempen lived, no doubt he would have assumed the mantle of Furtwängler that fell instead to Klemperer. Very impressive indeed.

Symphonies Nos. 3 (Eroica); 8 in F, Op. 93.
(M) (***) BMG/RCA mono GD 60269 [60269-2-RG]. NBC SO, Toscanini.
(M) **(*) Sony SBK 46328 [id.]. Cleveland O, Szell.
☞ * Ph. Dig. 434 913-2 [id.]. Leipzig GO, Masur.

Toscanini's 1939 recording of the *Eroica*, made live, brings one of the most compelling recordings he ever made. Not only does he conduct at white heat, he is far more flexible in his musical manners than he became later, both moulding melodic lines with Italianate warmth and allowing himself far freer rubato. The *Eighth* is hard-driven and on the biggest scale (Toscanini, exceptionally for the days of 78s, observes the exposition repeat in the first movement). Yet this is a performance which sustains a satisfying power, far more persuasive in rhythm and phrasing than Toscanini's later NBC version.

Szell's is a fine performance in the Toscanini tradition, hard-driven and dramatic. The digital remastering is very successful: the sound is firm, full and brilliant. The performance of the *Eighth* is also a compelling one. The first-movement repeat is taken and the performance is not over-driven.

Even in the *Eroica*, Masur sounds bland, with little build-up of tension in the great paragraphs of the first two movements. No. 8 too lacks necessary sparkle and vigour.

Symphony No. 4 in B flat, Op. 60.
(M) ** Sony SMK 46246 [id.]. Marlboro Festival O, Casals – SCHUBERT: *Symphony No. 5.* **(*) ⊛

Casals's recording of the *Fourth Symphony* comes from the 1969 season at Marlboro. There is a real sense of mystery at the opening and Casals keeps a firm grip on proceedings, with good choice of tempi and finely judged phrasing. This is dedicated music-making which has a sense of musical purpose that puts you completely under its spell.

Symphonies Nos. 4 in B flat; 5 in C min., Op. 67.
*** EMI Dig. CDC7 49656-2 [id.]. L. Classical Players, Norrington.
*** O-L Dig. 417 615-2 [id.]. AAM, Hogwood.

(B) *** Pickwick Dig. PCD 869; *CIM PC 869* [id.]. LSO, Wyn Morris.

Symphonies Nos. 4 in B flat; 5 in C min.; Egmont: Overture.
(M) **(*) Sony SMK 47516 [id.]. NYPO, Bernstein.
☞ (B) **(*) Decca 433 600-2. VPO, Schmidt-Isserstedt.

This coupling of Nos. 4 and 5 – the same as Oiseau-Lyre offers in the rival Hogwood series – shows Norrington at his most refreshing and inspired, relishing his fast speeds; and the finale of No. 5 has infectious swagger. The sound is up to the high standard of the series.

Hogwood's generous coupling of Nos. 4 and 5 presents excellent alternative versions for anyone wanting performances on period instruments. Dramatic contrasts are strongly marked, with no feeling of miniaturization, and the clarity of textures is admirable, with natural horns in particular braying out superbly.

Wyn Morris generally adopts speeds close to those of Karajan and, though he cannot match that master in sharpness of focus or pointed intensity, his urgency goes with fine, biting strength, helped by some first-rate playing from the LSO. A bargain.

Bernstein's performance of the *Fourth* has genuine stature. Overall, this reading has splendid grip. The *Fifth* is a strong, dramatic reading, not quite as memorable as the *Eroica* but concentrated and vital, with a balancing warmth in the slow movement.

Schmidt-Isserstedt's late-1960s account of the first movement of the *Fourth* has more relaxation in it than is common these days, and the very slow *Adagio* he chooses allows Beethoven's lyricism to flower in a comparatively gentle atmosphere. This does not mean that the reading is too small-scale or wayward, but that he finds a different range of Beethoven qualities. The *Fifth* is strong and direct: the first movement – exposition repeat included – has both bite and breathing space, a nicely measured, warmly played *Andante* and a triumphant finale. Only the Scherzo offers controversy in its slow tempo. Both recordings are vivid and full; the *Fifth* has a slightly less clean transfer than the *Fourth*, which sounds excellent.

Symphonies Nos. 4 in B flat; 6 in F (Pastoral), Op. 68.
(M) (***) BMG/RCA mono GD 60254 [60254-2-RG]. NBC SO, Toscanini.

The *Pastoral* was one of Toscanini's favourite Beethoven symphonies and the performance has a natural, unforced freshness which allows the most delicate shading and persuasive moulding between sections. No. 4 is more characteristic of the later Toscanini, though the fast, fierce manner in the first movement conveys joyful exuberance, and the slow movement brings fine moulding.

Symphonies Nos. 4 in B flat; 7 in A, Op. 92.
☞ *** Teldec/Warner Dig. 9031 75714-2 [id.]. COE, Harnoncourt.
*** Chan. Dig. CHAN 8753; *ABTD 1392* [id.]. CBSO, Weller.
☞ **(*) DG Dig. Gold 439 003-2 [id.]. BPO, Karajan.

Symphonies Nos. 4 in B flat; 7 in A; King Stephen overture, Op. 117.
(M) *** Sony SBK 48158 [id.]. Cleveland O, Szell.

Brilliant, vital readings from Harnoncourt, with high contrasts in the slow movement of No. 4, bringing soaring lyricism over nagging rhythmic figures below. In the outer movements of No. 7 – wonderfully spirited – the horns shine out, adding to the joyous release after an *Allegretto* full of under-the-surface tension.

Szell is at his finest in both symphonies. Along with powerful outer movements, tense and spontaneous-sounding, go exceptional accounts of the slow movements in both symphonies and in No. 7 Szell makes the second movement a genuine *Allegretto*, taking it almost as fast as a period specialist like Roger Norrington, and with magnetic concentration.

Weller and the CBSO are at their best in both works, warm and companionable, giving the impression of live communication. Warm, full recording.

Karajan's digital coupling of the *Fourth* and *Seventh symphonies* comes from his last series of Beethoven symphony recordings. The impression is of more spontaneous, less meticulous perform-ances than in his previous versions of these works, presumably recorded this time with longer takes. The bravura is most compelling, and there is no doubt about the command of Karajan's never-routine view of Beethoven – but too much is lost. The slow movement of the *Fourth* is fresh, sweet and beautifully moulded but is never hushed; and the *Allegretto* of No. 7, taken characteristically fast, is so smooth that the dactylic rhythm at the start is almost unidentifiable. The recording – remastered for reissue in the Karajan Gold series -is resonantly full. Now generally firmer in focus, it does not avoid a degree of clouding, approaching congestion at louder climaxes.

Symphonies Nos. 4; 8 in F (trans. Liszt).
*** Teldec/Warner Dig. 2292 43259-2 [id.]. Cyprien Katsaris (piano).

Simply astonishing! Apart from his dazzling technique, Katsaris has enormous musicianship, a great range of colour and a real sense of scale. It is as if one is encountering this music for the first time.

Symphonies Nos. 5 in C min.; 6 (Pastoral).
☞ *** BMG/RCA Dig. 09026 61930-2 [id.]. N. German RSO, Wand.
☞ (B) *** DG 439 403-2 [id.]. BPO, Karajan.
☞ **(*) DG Dig. Gold 439 004-2 [id.]. BPO, Karajan.
☞ ** EMI Dig. CDC7 54504-2 [id.]. Concg. O, Sawallisch.

Recorded live in October 1992, Wand's later versions of Nos. 5 and 6 offer exceptionally sympathetic, compelling readings of both works, a generous and unusual coupling. The *Pastoral*, easy and glowing, beautifully phrased and understandingly paced, is particularly successful, leading superbly up to the final apotheosis in the last movement. The sound is warm and sympathetic, though a little distanced. A first choice in this coupling, and distinctly preferable to Masur on Philips (434 156-2).

Karajan's 1962 coupling of the *Fifth* and *Pastoral Symphonies* has been reissued on DG's Classikon bargain label. The *Fifth* is thoroughly recommendable, if anything more intense than Karajan's later (1977) version, more spacious in the *Andante* with blazing horns in the finale. The *Pastoral* is a brisk, lightweight performance, very well played, and marred only by the absence of the repeat in the Scherzo. The sound has freshness and body, and this is undoubtedly good value.

Karajan's digital versions of the *Fifth* and *Sixth* present characteristically strong and incisive readings, recorded in longer takes than previously. The sound may not be as cleanly focused as in his earlier Berlin versions, but the feeling of spontaneous performance is most compelling, so that the typically fast speed for the first movement of the *Pastoral* no longer sounds too tense. The new digital transfers offered in the Karajan Gold series have improved the sound, especially in the *Fifth*, where the power and weight of the performance come over more readily than the atmospheric poetry of the *Pastoral*, in which the storm sounds more like a tempest.

In his Beethoven series for EMI, Wolfgang Sawallisch draws consistently beautiful sounds from the Royal Concertgebouw Orchestra, a perfect match between orchestra and the magnificent building that gave it its name. Yet the mellow acoustic has encouraged Sawallisch in the *Fifth Symphony* for example into middle-aged spread. This is a performance that unashamedly adopts old-fashioned manners – notably in a lethargic account of the slow movement. The result is short on tension, until blazing brass introduces an altogether more electrifying view of the finale. A relaxed view of the *Pastoral* is more sympathetic but, with sound not ideally clear, this cannot be recommended without considerable reservations.

Symphonies Nos. 5; 7 in A, Op. 92.
☞ (M) *** EMI Dig. CD-EMX 2212; *TC-EMX 2212*. RLPO, Sir Charles Mackerras.
(M) *** Decca Dig. 430 701-2 [id.]. Philh. O, Ashkenazy.
(M) (***) EMI mono CDM7 63868-2 [id.]. Philh. O, Klemperer.

Symphonies Nos. 5; 8 in F, Op. 93.
(M) **(*) EMI CDM7 63357-2 [id.]. Philh. O, Klemperer.

Symphonies Nos. 5; 8; Fidelio: overture.
(M) *** DG 419 051-2; *419 051-4* [id.]. BPO, Karajan.

Sir Charles Mackerras and the Royal Liverpool Philharmonic give revelatory performances of both the *Fifth* and *Seventh*, following up their excellent version, also for EMI, of the *Ninth Symphony*. The speed for the first movement of the *Fifth* initially takes one's breath away, so fast is it. Yet Sir Charles – who has made some outstanding recordings using period instruments – has learnt from period practice. Here he demonstrates that fast speeds in Beethoven can go with clarity and rhythmic spring. Tempi are on the fast side in all four movements but, thanks to the rhythmic control, they never sound hectic. The dramatic contrasts in this exhilarating performance are underlined by the superb recording, both weighty and atmospheric. The coupling is generous and ideal, an equally refreshing account of the *Seventh Symphony*. Those two favourite symphonies are normally too long to fit on a single disc, if (as here) exposition repeats are observed: the brisker speeds make all the difference.

Karajan's 1977 version of the *Fifth* is magnificent in every way, tough and urgently incisive, with fast tempi bringing weight as well as excitement. The coupling is an electrically intense performance of the *Eighth* plus the *Fidelio overture*.

Ashkenazy's reading of the *Fifth* is urgent and vivid and is notable for its rich, Kingsway Hall recording. Well-adjusted speeds here, with joyful exuberance a fair substitute for grandeur. The reading of the *Seventh* is equally spontaneous. This mid-priced digital CD ranks high among records of these two symphonies, especially for those for whom outstanding recording quality is a priority.

Klemperer never surpassed these first EMI interpretations of either symphony. Though the recording is in mono only, both works have a clarity, immediacy and fidelity of balance that enhance electrifying readings, revealing Klemperer at his peak.

Klemperer's stereo renditions of Nos. 5 and 8 bring a clean and natural sound on top, notably in violin tone. The *Fifth* is plainly less electric than his earlier, mono version but, with exposition repeats observed in both outer movements, this retains its epic quality.

Symphony No. 6 in F (Pastoral), Op. 68.
☞ (B) **(*) CD-CFP 4419; *TC-CFP 4419*. Munich PO, Kempe.

Symphonies No. 6 (Pastoral); Overtures: Coriolan; Creatures of Prometheus.
(BB) *** ASV CDQS 6053. N. Sinfonia, Richard Hickox.

Symphony No. 6 (Pastoral); Overtures: Coriolan; Egmont.
☞ *** Sony Dig. SK 53974 [id.]. La Scala PO, Giulini.
*** O-L Dig. 421 416-2 [id.]. AAM, Hogwood.

Symphony No. 6 (Pastoral); Overture: The Creatures of Prometheus; (i) Egmont: Overture; Die Trommel geruhet; Freudvoll und leidvoll; Klarchens Tod, Op. 84.
(M) *** EMI CDM7 63358-2 [id.]. Philh. O, Klemperer; (i) with Birgit Nilsson.

Symphony No. 6 (Pastoral); Overture: Egmont, Op. 84.
☞ (BB) ** Tring Dig. TRP 001. RPO, Mark Ermler.

Symphony No. 6 (Pastoral); Overtures: Egmont; Leonora No. 3.
(M) *** Decca Dig. 430 721-2 [id.]. Philh. O, Vladimir Ashkenazy.

Symphony No. 6 (Pastoral); Overture: Leonora No. 2, Op. 72a.
(B) *** Sony MYK 42536 [MYK 36720]. Columbia SO, Walter.

Ashkenazy's performance has a beguiling warmth and it communicates readily. With generally spacious tempi, the feeling of lyrical ease and repose is most captivating, thanks to the response of the Philharmonia players and the richness of the recording, made in the Kingsway Hall. The two overtures make a thoroughly satisfactory makeweight.

Giulini's newest version of the *Pastoral*, measured, essentially warm and relaxed, speaks very much of the sunny Italian scene where it was recorded. Even the peasants sound Mediterranean in their robust vigour. The La Scala players are on their finest form throughout and play with great radiance in the glorious finale. The symphony is framed by the two overtures, *Coriolan* ruggedly powerful at the opening and *Egmont* highly histrionic at the somewhat manipulated climax. But the coda is strong. Excellently full recording.

Bruno Walter's is an affectionate and completely integrated performance from a master who thought and lived the work all his life. The sound is beautifully balanced.

Hickox directs a persuasively paced reading, with a small orchestra used to give a performance of high contrasts, intimate in the lighter textures but expanding dramatically in the tuttis, while the finale, fresh and pure, brings a glowing climax. With warm, analogue recording giving a fine sense of presence, this is one of the best of the Hickox Beethoven series. The two *Overtures* come in vigorously dramatic readings.

Klemperer's account of the *Pastoral* is one of the very finest of all his records. The scherzo may be eccentrically slow but, with superbly dancing rhythms, it could not be more bucolic, and it falls naturally into place within the reading as a whole. The exquisitely phrased slow movement and the final *Shepherds' hymn* bring peaks of beauty, made the more intense by the fine digital transfer, reinforcing the clarity and balance of the original sound. The *Egmont* music follows the *Symphony*, an unusual but valuable coupling with Nilsson in her prime, unexpectedly but effectively cast in the two simple songs, the first made to sound almost Mahlerian.

The clarity and vivid sense of presence in Hogwood's period performance of the *Pastoral* go with fresh, resilient playing from the Academy of Ancient Music. As in this conductor's earlier Beethoven recordings, the extra detail is presented without fussiness and this is far preferable to Norrington's version, coupled with No. 1 (EMI CDC7 49746-2).

Kempe, adopting relatively crisp speeds, gives a plain, rather unvarnished account. Yet its very directness is appealing: the brook flows agreeably yet strongly, and the incandescent energy wells up to produce radiant climaxes in the finale; then the work ends in a mood of the utmost simplicity. The Munich orchestra is very responsive and the 1974 recording, bright and clear, also has a warmly resonant bass to underpin the body of the sound.

In the Royal Philharmonic Collection at a very low budget price, Mark Ermler conducts the RPO in a comfortably relaxed account of Beethoven's *Pastoral Symphony*. Speeds are so slow that with only the *Egmont overture* for coupling the disc lasts nearly an hour, yet for E.G. Ermler sustains them very persuasively with glowing orchestral tone brightly recorded. For I.M. this is a disappointingly lethargic performance, although the RPO plays sympathetically enough.

Symphonies Nos. 6 (Pastoral), Op. 68; 8 in F, Op. 93.
☞ *** Teldec/Warner Dig. 9031 75709-2 [id.]. COE, Harnoncourt.
(M) *** EMI Dig. CDD7 63891-2 [id.]. LPO, Tennstedt.
***Chan. Dig. CHAN 8754; *ABTD 1393* [id.]. CBSO, Walter Weller.

Symphonies Nos. 6 (Pastoral); 8 in F; King Stephen: Overture.
(M) **(*) Sony SMK 47517 [id.]. NYPO, Bernstein.

There is nothing over-tense about Harnoncourt's *Pastoral*, with the brook flowing amd perhaps bubbling a little, over the stream bed; No. 8 has drama and bite and resilience too.

Tennstedt's fresh, alert and imaginative performance of the *Pastoral* comes with the *Eighth*, given an equally enjoyable reading. Well-balanced recording, bright and fresh.

Weller directs a glowing, amiable account of the *Pastoral*, one of the most treasurable performances in his cycle. Warmly atmospheric recording.

Although he chooses a joyfully buoyant tempo for the opening movement, Bernstein (as usual in Beethoven) is admirably free of undue expressive vehemence in his 1963 *Pastoral*. By contrast, the brightly lit *Eighth* is given tremendous sweep and power.

Symphony No. 7 in A, Op. 92.
☞ **(*) DG Dig. 431 768-2. Boston SO, Bernstein – BRITTEN: *Peter Grimes: Sea interludes.* **(*)

Symphony No. 7; Overtures: Coriolan; Creatures of Prometheus; Egmont.
(B) *** DG 429 509-2 [id.]. VPO, Boehm.

Symphony No. 7; Overture: The Creatures of Prometheus.
(M) *** EMI CDM7 69183-2 [id.]. Philh. O, Klemperer.

Symphony No. 7; (i) The Ruins of Athens (Overture and incidental music), Op. 113.
(M) *** EMI CDM7 69871-2. RPO, Beecham; (i) with Beecham Choral Soc.

Symphonies Nos. 7; 8 in F, Op. 93.
*** DG Dig. 423 364-2 [id.]. VPO, Abbado.
**(*) O-L Dig. 425 695-2 [id.]. AAM, Hogwood.

Boehm's 1972 recording with the VPO is excellent, full and fresh, and the whole performance has lift and spontaneity. Boehm's direct style is most satisfying: full of impetus, yet with plenty of weight. The overtures go well too, especially *Egmont*.

Klemperer's 1955 recording of the *Seventh* is among his very finest Beethoven interpretations on disc. Speeds are consistently faster, the tension more electric, with phrasing moulded more subtly, than in the later Philharmonia version.

Beecham's 1959 *Seventh* is one of the briskest accounts of the symphony ever, yet the result is exhilarating. Only the slow movement reverts to old-fashioned slow manners in what is in effect an *Andante* rather than an *Allegretto*, but Beecham's rhythmic sense and care for phrasing still avoid heaviness. The fill-up of incidental music makes a valuable and enjoyable rarity.

The *Seventh* has always been a favourite symphony with Abbado, and the main allegro of the first movement is beautifully judged, as also is the *Eighth*, which is instantly established as more than a little symphony. As in the *Seventh*, speeds are beautifully judged, and the tensions of a live occasion are vividly conveyed. A splendid coupling.

Hogwood gives clean performances of both *Symphonies*, well played and recorded, but rhythmically a degree less resilient than those of his rivals.

Leonard Bernstein, recorded live with the Boston Symphony Orchestra, at the very last concert he ever conducted in Tanglewood on 19 August 1990, takes an extraordinarily expansive view, quite different from his previous recordings. Yet, for all the slowness of the basic speeds, he consistently conveys the joy of Beethoven's inspiration while springing rhythms with characteristic infectiousness. First-rate sound, considering the problems of live recording at Tanglewood, and an unusual coupling.

Symphony No. 7 (trans. Liszt).
*** Teldec/Warner Dig. 2292 43065-2 [id.]. Cyprien Katsaris (with SCHUMANN: *Exercises on Beethoven's Seventh Symphony* **).

Cyprien Katsaris does wonders in translating Liszt's transcription into orchestral terms, providing an unexpectedly illuminating listening experience. The sound is excellent.

Symphony No. 8 in F, Op. 93; Overtures: Coriolan; Fidelio; Leonora No. 3.
☞ **(*) DG Dig. Gold 439 005-2 [id.]. BPO, Karajan.

Karajan's more relaxed view of the *Eighth* (compared with his 1977 Berlin version) is almost always pure gain. Nevertheless, Karajan's is a massive view of what has often been dubbed Beethoven's 'little symphony', taking it well into the powerful world of the nineteenth century, with fierceness part of the mixture in the outer movements. The three overtures are made massively Olympian too, with *Coriolan* especially impressive. The recording is marginally brighter and clearer than in most of the series and, although there is still a degree of congestion in fortissimos, the remastered sound is firmer than before.

Symphony No. 9 in D min. (Choral), Op. 125.
(M) *** EMI Dig. CD-EMX 2186; *TC-EMX 2186*. Joan Rodgers, Della Jones, Peter Bronder, Bryn Terfel, RLPO Ch. & O, Sir Charles Mackerras.
(M) *** DG 415 832-2; *415 832-4* [id.]. Tomowa-Sintow, Baltsa, Schreier, Van Dam, V. Singverein, BPO, Karajan.
*** DG 429 861-2 [id.]. Anderson, Walker, König, Rootering, various Chs., Bav. RSO, Dresden State O, etc., Bernstein.
☞ *** Teldec/Warner Dig. 9031 75713-2 [id.]. Margiono, Remmert, Schasching, Holl, Schoenberg Ch., COE, Harnoncourt.
(BB) *** ASV CDQS 6069 [id.]. Harper, Hodgson, Tear, Howell, Sinfonia Ch., London Symphony Ch. (members), N. Sinfonia, Hickox.
*** O-L Dig. 425 517-2 [id.]. Augér, Robbin, Rolfe Johnson, Reinhart, London Symphony Ch., AAM, Hogwood.
☞ (M) **(*) BMG/RCA 09026 61795-2 [id.]. Curtin, Kopleff, McCollum, Gramm, Chicago SO & Ch., Fritz Reiner.
☞ (BB) **(*) Discover Dig. DICD 920151 [id.]. Gauci, Van Deyck, George, Rosca, Cantores Oratorio Ch., BRTN PO, Rahbari.
☞ **(*) Ph. Dig. 438 158-2 [id.]. Lynne Dawson, Jard van Nes, Anthony Rolfe Johnson, Wilm Schulte, Gulbenkian Ch., O of 18th Century, Brüggen.
☞ **(*) DG Dig. Gold 439 006-2 [id.]. Perry, Baltsa, Cole, Van Dam, V. Singverein, BPO, Karajan.
(M) (**(*)) BMG/RCA mono GD 60256; [60256-2-RG]. Farrell, Merriman, Peerce, Scott, Shaw Ch., NBC O, Toscanini.
☞ ** Erato/Warner Dig. 4509 94353-2 [id.]. Marc, Vermillion, Jerusalem, Struckmann, Berlin State Op. Ch., BPO, Barenboim.

(i) *Symphony No. 9 (Choral), Op. 125. Overture Fidelio.*
(B) **(*) Sony SBK 46533 [id.]. Addison, Hobson, Lewis, Bell, Cleveland O Ch. & O, Szell.

Sir Charles Mackerras conducts the Royal Liverpool Philharmonic in an exceptional, inspired account of the *Ninth*, one which – more than any other with a traditional symphony orchestra – has learnt from the lessons of period performance. Articulation is light and clean, vibrato is used sparingly, making textures unusually clear; and, like Roger Norrington, Sir Charles has taken careful note of Beethoven's controversial metronome markings. The recording is among the very finest ever given to this symphony, warm yet transparent and with plenty of body; and the singing in the finale is splendid, even if the tenor, Peter Bronder, is on the strenuous side. Anyone wanting a refreshingly different version of the *Ninth*, which yet brings all the dramatic power and intensity of a more conventional reading, need not hesitate.

Of the three stereo recordings Karajan has made of the *Ninth*, his 1977 account (415 832-2/4) is the most inspired in its insight, above all in the *Adagio*, where he conveys spiritual intensity at a slower tempo than in his earlier, 1962 version (currently withdrawn). In the finale, the concluding eruption has an animal excitement rarely heard from this highly controlled conductor. The soloists make an excellent team, with contralto, tenor and bass all finer than their predecessors. The sound has tingling projection and drama.

Recorded live on the morning of Christmas Day 1989, Bernstein's Berlin version may have been issued to commemorate a particular occasion of celebration, but it is far more than just a memento of a historic event, the destruction of the Berlin Wall. It brings a performance that has something special to say, even after all the many recordings of this work, and not only because Bernstein substitutes the

word '*Freiheit*', 'Freedom', for '*Freude*', 'Joy', in the choral finale, something Beethoven himself
might well have approved of. The orchestra, drawn mainly from Germany, both East and West, the
Bavarian RSO and Dresden Staatskapelle, also included members of the Kirov Theatre Orchestra in
Leningrad, the New York Philharmonic, the Orchestre de Paris and the LSO. The choirs similarly
came from East and West Germany, while the soloists represented four countries: America (June
Anderson), Britain (Sarah Walker), Germany (Klaus König) and Holland (Jan-Hendrik Rootering).
For many, the uniqueness of this version and the emotions it conveys will make it a first choice,
despite obvious flaws.

For some listeners the fast pace of the slow movement of Harnoncourt's *Ninth* will seem a
drawback, but otherwise the performance caps the cycle splendidly, with a very compelling account of
the finale.

Hickox's performance, using an orchestra of the size Beethoven originally had, brings some of the
advantages of period performance: clarity of articulation and texture; otherwise one might not realize
that the string band is any smaller than one on a regular recording of the *Ninth*. In his pacing
throughout the work, Hickox is unerring and conveys from first to last the tension of a genuine
performance, in a way that some of his rivals among international stars do not manage. This is the
most successful issue in his Beethoven series for ASV. The performance culminates in a glowing
account of the choral finale with four excellent soloists. At super-bargain price this is very competitive
indeed.

Hogwood with his period forces is very well recorded. The ensemble is clear and well balanced
both in the instrumental movements and in the choral finale, where an apt scale is achieved, neither
too large nor too small. Hogwood has taken close note of Beethoven's controversial metronome
markings. But Hogwood's manner is not too rigorous and he scores significantly over his direct
rivals, not just in the sound-quality but in the quality of solo and choral singing. Though rhythms are
not always ideally resilient, this is the most recommendable period performance of the *Ninth* currently
available.

As bitingly dramatic as Toscanini in the first movement and electrically intense all through, Szell
directs a magnetic, seemingly inevitable account of the *Ninth* which demonstrates the glories of the
Cleveland Orchestra. The chorus sings with similarly knife-edged ensemble, set behind the orchestra
but not too distantly. The performance of the *Fidelio overture* is electrifying.

Reiner's 1961 version has returned to the catalogue in an impressively full-bodied new transfer,
although the immediacy undermines pianissimos. The choral focus could be sharper, but otherwise
the recording barely sounds its age, and both soloists and chorus are very good in the last movement,
which moves to an exciting close. Reiner's reading conveys power rather than mystery. Ensembles
have knife-edged precision, rhythms are beautifully sprung and speeds are relatively broad, not least
in the slow movement which, like the first, is presented in the full light of day. In the drum-and-fife
episode of the finale too, Reiner's speed is surprisingly slow, but there and throughout he sustains
tension magnetically, helped by the warm Chicago ambience. This is a fine example of Reiner's
mastery and well worth hearing, even if there are greater accounts of the *Ninth* on CD.

Among versions at super-bargain price, Rahbari's Brussels version, digitally recorded, makes an
excellent recommendation, consistently conveying vigour and spontaneity, as in a live, rather than a
studio performance. The first movement is strong and purposeful, the Scherzo excitingly fast, with
the slow movement sustaining measured speeds well, and the finale is helped by confident choral and
solo singing. The recording is reverberant, but not so as to muddle an involving performance.

With the Orchestra of the 18th Century, Frans Brüggen is recording a complete Beethoven
symphony cycle, providing a worthwhile alternative for those who prefer the new stimulus of period
instruments. His version of the *Ninth*, inevitably the most challenging of the series for anyone using
such forces, has points of advantage over such direct rivals as Norrington on EMI, Hogwood on
L'Oiseau-Lyre and Roy Goodman and the Hanover Band on Nimbus, notably that he is warmer and
more relaxed in his treatment of the slow movement. By traditional standards his speeds are still fast,
but there is greater expressive freedom and flexibility. The sound too has an appropriate weight,
though the acoustic of the church in Utrecht where the recording was made undermines the clarity,
notably in passages where the timpani adds a fuzz over the whole texture. In the finale, soloists are
well caught, with the soprano, Lynne Dawson, and the baritone, Eike Wilm Schulte, both outstanding.
The serious snag is that the small chorus is set too far back. It should be worth waiting for John Eliot
Gardiner's version with his Orchestre Révolutionnaire et Romantique.

The high point of Karajan's digital version of the *Ninth* is the sublime slow movement, here
exceptionally sweet and true, with the lyricism all the more persuasive in a performance recorded in a
complete take. The power and dynamism of the first two movements are also striking, but the choral
finale is flawed above all by the singing of the soprano, Janet Perry, far too thin of tone and

unreliable. The sound of the choir has plenty of body, and definition has been improved in this remastered version, reissued on the Karajan Gold label. As in the others in the series, the recording is less analytical than that usually given to Karajan, but the effect is generally convincing.

Toscanini's electrifying account of the *Ninth* is marred somewhat by the excessive treble emphasis, more noticeable than on the earlier, full-priced reissue.

Barenboim's Erato version is a disappointment. In his choice of speeds he demonstrates his devotion to Furtwängler but, unlike that master, he cannot (for example) sustain the *Adagio* so as to prevent tension from sagging at his extremely slow speeds. In the finale three of the soloists are outstanding, but the baritone, Falk Struckmann, wobbles badly, undermining the impact of his dramatic first entry. As with Furtwängler, the end of the finale is frenetic.

Symphony No. 9 (trans. Liszt).
**(*) Teldec/Warner Dig. 2292 42985-2 [id.]. Cyprien Katsaris (piano).

Cyprien Katsaris's performance is nothing short of a *tour de force*: his virtuosity is altogether remarkable and there is a demonic Beethovenian vehemence and drive. The piano is closely observed in a reverberant acoustic ambience and listeners may at times be disturbed by its somewhat jangly quality.

Symphony No. 10 in E flat: 1st movement (realized and completed by Dr Barry Cooper – includes lecture by Dr Cooper).
(B) *** Pickwick Dig. PCD 911; *CIMPC 911* [id.]. LSO, Wyn Morris.

As re-created from Beethoven's sketches by Dr Barry Cooper, this movement from what was planned as the *Tenth Symphony* is, as Dr Cooper says, no more than an 'artist's impression'. The master would have moulded this into something far greater, but it is well worth hearing music that so dwells in the mind. Wyn Morris in this first recording directs a broad, strong reading, very well played and recorded. Dr Cooper's half-hour lecture fascinatingly amplifies and illustrates his detailed notes, making clear his scholarly credentials as well as his devotion to Beethoven's plan.

Wellington's victory (Battle symphony), Op. 91.
** Telarc Dig. CD 80079 [id.]. Cincinnati SO, Kunzel – LISZT: *Hunnenschlacht.* **

With a characteristically natural overall sound-balance, Kunzel's Telarc recording is technically the most sophisticated presentation of Beethoven's 'Battle' Symphony on record, though the real musketry and cannon featured in the recording sound curiously like a fireworks display.

CHAMBER MUSIC

Cello sonatas Nos. 1–5, Op. 5/1–2; Op. 69; Op. 102/1–2.
*** Decca Dig. 417 628-2 [id.]. Lynn Harrell, Vladimir Ashkenazy.
**(*) Ph. 412 256-2 [id.]. Mstislav Rostropovich, Sviatoslav Richter.

Lynn Harrell and Vladimir Ashkenazy have the advantage of superb recording: they are sensibly balanced, neither instrument being too prominent or too reticent. Artistically, too, these performances are in the first league.

Made in the early 1960s, the classic Philips performances by Mstislav Rostropovich and Sviatoslav Richter, two of the instrumental giants of the day, have withstood the test of time astonishingly well and sound remarkably fresh in this compact disc transfer. Apart from the usual gains in continuity and freedom from background, there is so much greater presence and realism. But this should now be reissued at mid-price.

Cello sonatas Nos. 1–5; 7 Variations on 'Bei Männern' (from Mozart's Die Zauberflöte), WoO 46; 12 Variations on 'See the conqu'ring hero comes' (from Handel's Judas Maccabaeus), WoO 46; 12 Variations on 'Ein Mädchen' (from Mozart's Die Zauberflöte), Op. 66.
(M) *** EMI CMS7 63015-2 (2). Jacqueline Du Pré, Daniel Barenboim.
(M) *** DG 423 297-2 (2) [id.]. Pierre Fournier, Wilhelm Kempff.
☞ (M) *** DG 437 352-2 (2) [id.]. Pierre Fournier, Friedrich Gulda.

Cello sonatas Nos. 1 in F, Op. 5/1; 2 in G min., Op. 5/2; 7 Variations on 'Bei Männern, welche Liebe fühlen', WoO 46; 12 Variations on 'Ein Mädchen oder Weibchen', Op. 66.
☞ *** DG Dig. 431 801-2 [id.]. Mischa Maisky, Martha Argerich.

Cello sonatas Nos. 3 in A, Op. 69; 4 in C, Op. 102/1; 5 in D, Op. 102/2; 12 Variations on a theme from Handel's Judas Maccabaeus.

☞ *** DG Dig. 437 514-2 [id.]. Mischa Maisky, Martha Argerich.

The set of performances by Jacqueline Du Pré with Daniel Barenboim was recorded live for the BBC during the Edinburgh Festival of 1970. The playing may not have the final polish that studio performances would no doubt have achieved, but the concentration and intensity of the playing are wonderfully caught.

Fournier was to re-record Beethoven's complete music for cello and piano again for DG with Wilhelm Kempff, but those were 'live' performances, spontaneously fresh, yet some of the weight was missing. These earlier accounts, made in the Brahms-Saal of the Vienna Musikverein in 1959, though not less spontaneous have more gravitas. Where in that later set introductions are taken relatively fast, it is immediately noticeable that the two *Adagio* introductions to the Op. 5 *Sonatas* are rapt and thoughtful, improvisatory in feeling. Gulda's contribution is strong – he is more than a passive partner – and both artists bring a marvellous rapport to the glorious first movement of the *A major Sonata*, while Fournier's gentle opening to the *C major*, echoed by Gulda, is equally compelling. The *D major Sonata* is given a wonderfully rounded performance: the *Adagio* brings great concentration and the fugato finale has corresponding vitality without ever being heavy. The *Variations* are slight pieces, intended to divert, but once again in Fournier's hands they assume a greater significance than one might expect. The recording of both instruments is close but full and natural, beautifully balanced against an ideal acoustic.

Mischa Maisky and Martha Argerich make a strong partnership and there is enormous character about their playing here. Indeed it would be possible to feel that their readings are overcharacterized, so attentive are they to every dynamic nuance and hairpin that is marked (and plenty that aren't). Indeed by the side of, say, Rostropovich and Richter or Fournier and Kempff, their artistry is a bit intrusive, and they are certainly too fast and glitzy in the finale of Op. 5, No. 2. All the same the performances are exhilarating and will be relished by many collectors, particularly in such vivid recordings. A bit too incandescent and personal to be what is called 'a library choice', but three stars all the same.

Cello sonatas Nos. 1 in F; 2 in G min., Op. 5/1–2; 7 Variations on Mozart's 'Bei Männern', WoO 45; 12 Variations on Handel's 'See the conqu'ring hero comes', WoO 46; 12 Variations on Mozart's 'Ein Mädchen', Op. 66.

☞ (BB) ** Naxos Dig. 8.550479 [id.]. Csaba Onczay, Jenö Jandó.

Although they do not have the personality of, say, Maisky and Argerich – let alone Rostropovich and Richter – Csaba Onczay and Jenö Jandó turn in serviceable accounts of both *Sonatas*. The cellist is a little colourless and does not have quite as much fervour or character as the pianist. Decent recording.

Cello sonatas Nos. (i; ii) 1 in F; (i; iii) 2 in G min., Op. 5/1–2; 5 in D, Op. 102/2; Piano trios Nos. (i; iii; iv) 3 in C min., Op. 1/3; (i; iii; v) 5 in D (Ghost), Op. 70/1; (i; iii; iv) 7 in B flat (Archduke), Op. 97.

☞ (M) **(*) Ph. 438 520-2 (3) [id.]. (i) Casals; (ii) Kempff; (iii) Horszowski; (iv) Végh; (v) Engel.

These performances of Beethoven *Cello sonatas* and *Piano trios* featuring Pablo Casals were recorded live when he was in his eighties. When smudges and flawed intonation so disfigure the playing you have to listen with a 'creative ear', both to him and to the violinist, Sandor Végh. Great artistry is certainly there, but it is heavily obscured. What is a consistent joy is the playing of the pianist-partners, not just Wilhelm Kempff in the *Cello sonata*, Op. 5/1, but even more strikingly Mieczyslaw Horszowski in two other *Sonatas*, Op. 5/2 and Op. 102/2, as well as in the *Trios*, Op. 1/3, the *Ghost* and the *Archduke*. Horszowski may have had a gentle personality, but he is clearly the musical leader here.

Cello sonatas Nos. 3 in A, Op. 69; 5 in D, Op. 102/2.

(M) *** EMI CDM7 69179-2. Jacqueline du Pré, Kovacevich.

The Du Pré/Bishop-Kovacevich recordings of Nos. 3 and 5 come from 1966, the year after Jacqueline had made her definitive record of the Elgar *Concerto*. Du Pré's tone ranges from full-blooded fortissimo to the mere whisper of a half-tone, and these artists allow the most free range of expressive rubato. With excellent recording, these performances are most welcome on CD, sounding crisp and present in their new format.

Duo for viola and cello in E flat, WoO 32; Sextet for 2 horns, 2 violins, viola & cello, Op. 81b; String quintet in A (arr. of *Violin sonata in A, Op. 47 (Kreutzer)*).
☞ ** Sony Dig. SK 48076 [id.]. L'Archibudelli.

L'Archibudelli play on period instruments and are an accomplished group. The arrangement of the *Kreutzer sonata* is not Beethoven's but is possibly by Ferdinand Ries. There is some striking horn playing here in the *Sextet*, Op. 81b, and elsewhere some occasional moments of vulnerable intonation. Very good 20-bit recording.

(i) *Flute trio in G* (for flute, bassoon & piano), *WoO 37;* (ii–iii) *Horn sonata in F, Op. 17;* (iii; v) *Piano and wind quintet, Op. 16;* (iv) *Serenade in D for flute, violin & viola, Op. 25;* (v) *Septet, Op. 20; Sextet in E flat, Op. 81b; Wind octet in E flat, Op. 103; Wind sextet in E flat, Op. 71.*
☞ (M) *** DG 439 852-2 (3) [id.]. (i) Zöller, Thunemann, Kontarsky; (ii) Seifert; (iii) Demus; (iv) Zöller, Brandis, Ueberschaer; (v) BPO (members).

These are all beautifully alert, civilized performances and they are recorded (except perhaps for the *Trio*, WoO 37, where the effect is a shade over-reverberant) with fine clarity and definition and an appealing bloom. There are some minor reservations. There are perhaps more spontaneous accounts of the *Serenade*, Op. 25, in the catalogue (although this version is certainly most enjoyable) and more starry accounts of the *Piano and wind quintet* (although Demus and his colleagues play freshly and spontaneously). In the *Septet*, Op. 20, the Berlin players are richly mellifluous in style, especially noticeable in the Minuet. But it might be argued that, although some versions have a lighter, wittier touch, the Berliners give more cogency to the arguments in the first movement; and certainly in the Scherzo and finale they are irrepressibly fleet of foot. There is no rival compilation of this scope on the market at present and, even if there were, it is difficult to imagine it surpassing the present set (originally issued on five LPs).

Piano trios Nos 1–9; 10 (Variations on an original theme in E flat), Op. 44; 11 (Variations on 'Ich bin der Schneider Kakadu'), Op. 121a; Allegretto in E flat, Hess 48.
*** EMI Dig. CDS7 47455-8 (4) [Ang. CDCD 47455]. Ashkenazy, Perlman, Harrell.

Piano trios Nos. 1–3, Op. 1; 4 in B flat, Op. 11; 5 in D (Ghost), Op. 70/1; 6 in E flat, Op. 70/2; 7 in B flat (Archduke), Op. 97; 14 Variations on an original theme in E flat, Op. 44; 10 Variations on 'Ich bin der Schneider Kakadu', Op. 121a.
☞ (M) **(*) Teldec/Warner Dig. 9031 73281-2 (3) [id.]. Trio Fontenay.

Piano trios Nos. 1–11.
☞ (M) *** Ph. 438 948-2 (3) [id.]. Beaux Arts Trio.

Piano trios Nos. 1–11; Trio in E flat (from Septet), Op. 38; Trio in D (from *Symphony No. 2*); *Trio movement in E flat.*
(M) **(*) Ph. Analogue/Dig. 432 381-2 (5) [id.]. Beaux Arts Trio.

Piano trios Nos. 1–3; 5–7; 9–10 (Variations on an original theme in E flat); 11 (Variations on 'Ich bin der Schneider Kakadu'); Allegretto in E flat, Hess 48.
(M) **(*) EMI CMS7 63124-2 (3) [Ang. CDMC 63124]. Daniel Barenboim, Pinchas Zukerman, Jacqueline du Pré.

Piano trios Nos. 1–3; 5–7.
(M) **(*) DG 415 879-2 (3) [id.]. Kempff, Szeryng, Fournier.

Piano trios Nos. 5 in D (Ghost), Op. 70/1; 7 in B flat (Archduke), Op. 97.
(M) **(*) DG 429 712-2 [id.]. Kempff, Szeryng, Fournier.

Piano trios Nos. 7 (Archduke); 9 in B flat, WoO 39.
*** EMI Dig. CDC7 47010-2 [id.]. Ashkenazy, Perlman, Harrell.

Ashkenazy, Perlman and Harrell lead the field in this repertoire. The recordings have been made over a period of five years and at various locations, but the sound is consistently fresher, warmer, more richly detailed and more present than with most other rivals. The playing is unfailingly perceptive and full of those musical insights that make one want to return to the set. The *Archduke*, coupled with *No. 9 in B flat*, is available separately.

In their analogue set, dating from 1965, the Beaux Arts are let down a little by the ungenerous tone of their leader, Daniel Guilet; set against the refreshing spontaneity of the playing as a whole, however, this is of little moment. The pianist, Manahem Pressler, is a constant source of delight (particularly in the early *Trios*, which have never sounded more attractive on disc) and Bernard

Greenhouse's cello-line is warmly responsive. Tempi are admirably chosen (save for the *Ghost Trio*, which is very brisk; the work's drama and intensity, however, are projected to brilliant effect) and phrasing is marvellously alive. The approach to the *Archduke Trio* is not unlike that of the later version but has even more life, and the overall feeling is of lightness and grace. Ultimately the Beaux Arts score here on account of the chamber-music quality of their playing. They convey a sense of music-making in the home rather than in the concert hall, and the naturally balanced recording also has an attractive combination of warmth and intimacy. With the eleven *Trios* offered on three mid-priced CDs, this makes a very attractive alternative to the EMI set.

The Fontenay versions were recorded between 1990 and 1992 in the Teldec studios in Berlin. Alert and intelligent playing throughout, attentive phrasing and bright, well-lit recorded sound. The *Ghost* is rather closely balanced; the Op. 1 *Trios* are much better in this respect. Very good playing, without perhaps the last touch of humanity and depth, such as we find in the Beaux Arts – particularly in their earlier set from the 1960s. The *Archduke* Scherzo is really rather rushed, and there are times when they are just a little business-like rather than inspired. But although it is not a first choice, it still deserves a three-star grading – just! Exposition repeats are observed in the first movements of Op. 70, No. 1, but not in Op. 1, No. 1.

The Barenboim/Zukerman/du Pré set (by omitting Nos. 4 and 8) is fitted economically on to three mid-priced CDs. Even more than usual, the individual takes involved long spans of music, often complete movements, sometimes even a complete work. The result is music-making of rare concentration, spontaneity and warmth. The excellent recording has been freshened on CD.

The Kempff/Szeryng/Fournier team recorded their survey of the Beethoven *Trios* in the early 1970s. Wilhelm Kempff is an unfailingly interesting artist, and both Henryk Szeryng and that aristocrat of cellists, Pierre Fournier, are in impressive form throughout. The CD transfers are fresh and clear and the 1970 recording has plenty of fullness as well as a natural presence.

Unlike their earlier set, the later Beaux Arts box offers absolutely everything Beethoven composed (or arranged) for this grouping. However, five (well-filled) CDs are involved; four of the recordings are digital. The transfers are well up to the usual high Philips standard and the performances are as accomplished and musical as one would expect from this celebrated team. However, it has to be said that the earlier, analogue set had a freshness and sparkle that these new accounts do not wholly match.

Piano trios Nos. 1 in E flat; 2 in G, Op. 1/1–2.
*** Hyp. Dig. CDA 66197 [id.]. L. Fortepiano Trio.
☞ (BB) ** Naxos Dig. 8.550946 [id.]. Stuttgart Piano Trio.

The London Fortepiano Trio play with considerable virtuosity, particularly in the finales, which are taken at high speed and to considerable effect. The use of a fortepiano serves to enhance clarity of texture in this particular repertoire, and readers should make an effort to sample what one assumes will be a complete cycle.

The Stuttgart Piano Trio (Monika Leonhard, piano, Rainer Kussmaul, violin, and Claus Kanngiesser, cello) play these early works of Beethoven with pleasing simplicity. They have not quite the individuality of the Beaux Arts, yet both slow movements are eloquently sustained and finales have sparkle, especially that to the G major which is infectious. The recording is naturally balanced in a warm acoustic which provides a clean realistic focus.

Piano trios Nos. 1 in E flat, Op. 1/1; 5 in D (Ghost), Op. 70/1.
☞ ** EMI Dig. CDC7 54579-2 [id.]. Chung Trio.

One problem here (as it was to some extent in their performance of the Tchaikovsky *Trio*) is the reticence of the cellist and the dominance of the pianist. This is no doubt painting the picture in broad brush-strokes, but if you were to place one of the movements of either the *E flat Trio* or the *Geistertrio* alongside, say, the Beaux Arts recordings or the Perlman–Harrell–Ashkenazy discs, this impression would be reinforced. There is some very good and highly musical playing from these wonderful artists, and the recording is very clean, but this does not challenge any of the top recommendations.

Piano trios Nos. 3 in C min., Op,. 1/3; 8 in E flat, WoO 38; 10 (Variations in E flat), Op. 44;
Allegretto in E flat, Hess 48.
☞ (BB) **(*) Naxos Dig. 8.550947 [id.]. Stuttgart Piano Trio.

Although the first movement of Op. 1/3 is on the brisk side, it springs to life spontaneously and the variations which follow are appealingly fresh. The other early *Trio in E flat* is very persuasively done and the *Variations*, Op. 44, are hardly less successful. With excellent recording, performances on this

CD have obviously more sparkle than those on its earlier companion. Again the sound is fresh and naturally balanced.

Piano trios Nos. 5 in D (Ghost); 6 in E flat, Op. 70/1–2.
☞ *** Pickwick Dig. MCD 44 [id.]. Solomon Trio.

Two of Beethoven's greatest trios played with fine dedication and intelligence by Yonty Solomon, Rodney Friend and Timothy Hugh in a lively but not over-bright acoustic that does justice to their music-making. These artists have an excellent rapport; there is no playing to the gallery and one is left in no doubt that it is Beethoven's muse they are trying to serve rather than any corporate ego. The only real snag is the dominance in the aural picture of the pianist – up to a point understandable, since the keyboard part is so important. If the less-than-ideal perspective must be noted, it should not deny these musical and perceptive accounts their rightful place in any collection. The CD is offered at upper-mid-price.

Piano trios Nos. 5 in D (Ghost), Op. 70/1; 7 in B flat (Archduke).
☞ (B) **(*) Sony SBK 53514 [id.]. Eugene Istomin, Isaac Stern, Leonard Rose.

The playing from the Istomin/Stern/Rose trio is strong, polished and alive, with good teamwork and the individual personality of each player coming over forcefully. The *Archduke* is a very impressive performance indeed (preferable to the Beaux Arts), bold and traditional in approach and full of energy. One of the slight drawbacks of the transatlantic recording is the comparative shallowness of the piano tone and the touch of thinness on the violin timbre, but the ambience is convincing, the basic sound is warm and the balance not too close to rob the music-making of its dynamic range. An impressive coupling.

Piano trio No. 7 in B flat, Op. 97.
☞ (M) ** Ph. 438 308-2 [id.]. Beaux Arts Trio – SCHUBERT: *Piano trio No. 2.* **(*)

It was a pity that Philips chose the later (1979) Beaux Arts recording of the *Archduke* for this reissue, as it proves to be one of their least compelling recordings. The first movement at a very slow tempo sounds self-conscious and mannered; the Scherzo fails to maintain its spring, and so does the finale. The slow variations have little sense of flow. The recording quality is first rate and, as ever, the ensemble is immaculate.

Piano trios Nos. 7 (Archduke); 11 (Variations on 'Ich bin der Schneider Kakadu').
(B) *** Pickwick Dig. PCD 874; *CIMPC 874* [id.]. Kalichstein, Laredo, Robinson.

The Kalichstein/Laredo/Robinson Trio's interpretations of both the *Archduke* and the *Variations* are unaffected, supremely musicianly and thoughtful. A marvellous performance and a very good, splendidly clean recording, even if it is bright and forward.

Piano and wind quintet in E flat, Op. 16.
*** Sony Dig. MK 42099 [id.]. Perahia, members of ECO – MOZART: *Quintet.* ***
(M) *** Decca 421 151-2; *421 151-4*. Ashkenazy, L. Wind Soloists – MOZART: *Quintet.* ***

(i) *Piano and wind quintet in E flat;* (ii) *Piano quartet in E flat, Op. 16.*
☞ (B) *(*) HM Dig. HMA 1903020 [id.]. Zoltán Kocsis; (i) Budapest Wind Ens.; (ii) Keller Qt (members) – MOZART: *Piano and wind quintet.* *

First choice for Beethoven's *Piano and wind quintet* lies with Perahia's CBS version, recorded at The Maltings. The first movement is given more weight than usual, with a satisfying culmination. In the *Andante*, Perahia's playing is wonderfully poetic and serene and the wind soloists are admirably responsive. With the recording most realistically balanced, this issue can be recommended with all enthusiasm.

Ashkenazy's recording from 1966 is also in every way recommendable. The sound is first class, the balance rather forward but very vivid and real.

It was an appealing idea to offer the Beethoven *Piano and wind quintet* alongside the alternative version for piano quartet (besides the usual Mozart coupling), but in the event the performance, very much dominated by Kocsis, seems too over-stressed and forceful in the pacing of the first movement (although, curiously, the strong thrust works better in the string arrangement than it does with wind scoring). The recording is truthful, and the rest of the work goes well enough, but the coupled Mozart performance, in very much the same vein, cannot be recommended.

Septet in E flat, Op. 20.
☞ **(*) O-L Dig. 433 044-2 [id.]. AAM Chamber Ens. – WEBER: *Clarinet quintet.* ***

Septet in E flat, Op. 20; Sextet in E flat, Op. 81b.
*** Hyp. Dig. CDA 66513 [id.]. Gaudier Ens.

(i) *Septet in E flat, Op. 20;* (ii) *Duo for clarinet and bassoon in B flat, WoO 27/3.*
*** Novalis Dig. 150 021-2 [id.]. (i) Schweizer Soloists; (ii) Kurt Weber, Tomas Sosnowski.

Septet in E flat, Op. 20; String quintet in C, Op. 29.
☞ *** EMI Dig. CDC7 54656-2 [id.]. Hausmusik.

The young members of the Gaudier Ensemble give an exuberant performance of the *Septet*, bringing it home as one of the young Beethoven's most joyfully carefree inspirations. The rarer *Sextet* for two horns and string quartet makes a generous coupling. Excellent sound, with the wind well forward.

Hausmusik's version of the *Septet* is outstanding among period performances, presenting a fresh, lively view with the advantage of extra clarity in the textures and pointed rhythms. The strings are light, tangy without abrasiveness, and the wind are characterfully contrasted. The *String quintet* makes a generous and attractive coupling.

On Novalis, the splendid new digital CD, made by a young Swiss group, in almost all respects supersedes the distinguished older version on Decca. At the very outset one is struck by the freshness of their playing, by the excellent internal blending, helped by a naturally balanced recording, and by the spirit and warmth of their music-making. The *Duo* which follows is also played with much charm.

The Academy of Ancient Music give a light-textured and lively account of this genial work. Solo playing of the early instruments is impeccable, but somehow the lack of opulence of timbre is accompanied by lack of a sense of sheer infectious joy in the music. There is no absence of vivacity but other versions are more endearingly seductive. No complaints about the recording.

Serenade in D for flute, violin and viola, Op. 25.
🏵 (BB) *** Pickwick/CDI Dig. PWK 1139. Israel Flute Trio (with Recital: '*Flute Serenade*' ***).

The light and charming combination of flute, violin and viola inspired the youthful Beethoven to write in an unexpectedly carefree and undemanding way. The sequence of tuneful, unpretentious movements reminds one of Mozart's occasional music, and this delectable Israel performance brings out all its charm. Er'ella Talmi is a superb flautist and she receives admirable support from her colleagues. The recording is wonderfully natural in sound and balance: it is as if the players were making music in one's own room.

Serenade in D, Op. 8 (arr. Matiegka).
*** Mer. Dig. CDE 84199; *KE 77199* [id.]. Clive Conway, Paul Silverthorne, Gerald Garcia –
KREUTZER; MOLINO: *Trios.* ***

Beethoven's early *Serenade* for string trio was arranged for violin, viola and guitar as early as 1807 by the Bohemian composer and guitarist, Wenceslaus Matiegka. Gerald Garcia has here rearranged it for the present unusual and delightful combination, offering the violin part to the flute, and giving the guitar a more taxing contribution. As a companion-piece for the rare Kreutzer and Molino items, it makes a charming oddity in its seven brief movements, very well played and warmly recorded.

String quartets

String quartets Nos. 1–16; Grosse Fuge, Op. 133.
(M) *** Valois V 4400 (8) [id.]. Végh Qt.
*** Valois V 4401 (*Nos. 1 & 5*); V 4402 (*Nos. 2–4*); V 4403 (*Nos. 6–7*); V 4404 (*Nos. 8–9*); V 4405
    (*Nos. 10 & 12*); V 4406 (*Nos. 11 & 15*); V 4407 (*Nos. 13 & Grosse Fugue*); V 4408 (*Nos. 14 & 16*)
    [id.]. Végh Qt.
(M) (***) EMI mono CZS7 67236-2 (7). Hungarian Qt.
☞ (M) ** Praga PR 255 4009/15 (7) [id.]. (i) Vlach Qt; (ii) Janáček Qt.

The Végh performances were recorded in the mid-1970s; they have been rightly hailed for their simplicity and depth. Intonation may not always be absolutely immaculate, but flaws are few and trivial when one considers the wisdom and experience the Végh communicate. In short they are in a different league from most of their rivals: there is no cultivation of surface polish though there is both elegance and finesse. The CD transfers are successful in producing an altogether cleaner image and a slightly firmer focus than the original analogue LPs, although the imbalance towards the cello remains. The eight discs are now available together at mid-price.

The Hungarian Quartet's first recorded cycle of the Beethoven *Quartets*, with the mono sound firm and full, is superb, with tonal beauty never an end in itself. Polished ensemble goes with a sense of spontaneity in readings fresher and more direct than those of 1966. The spacious, unhurried playing of the great slow movements here has rarely been matched. Those primarily concerned with the music as opposed to sound-quality will find little difficulty in adjusting to the recording.

The present survey by the Vlach Quartet on the Praga label derives from Czech Radio performances made during the period 1960–69. Presumably no satisfactory account of Op. 130 survives since this – though not the *Grosse Fuge* – is replaced by a surprisingly hard-driven version by the Janáček Quartet. It is not altogether clear whether these are live performances or studio accounts, which would give some limited opportunities for retakes; but in any event they have the combination of concentration and spontaneity often found on radio. First-movement exposition repeats are not observed in the Op. 18 set, save for the *D major* (No. 3), so that all six can be accommodated on two CDs. Generally speaking, the performances are plain and sensible, free from any hint of narcissism. They offer no real challenge however to the Talich, Végh, Lindsay and Alban Berg Quartets in terms of insight. The recorded sound is satisfactory for its period (though very good equipment with a lot of top range reveals a certain hardness and wiriness above the stave from the leader). Seven CDs at mid-price is quite an economical package – though the Quartetto Italiano, albeit on ten mid-price CDs, are in every way superior and worth the extra outlay. All the same, this is a serviceable set that inspires a certain respect and admiration for its integrity.

String quartets Nos. 1–6, Op. 18/1–6.
*** EMI Dig. CDS7 47127-8 [Ang. CDC 47126] (3). Alban Berg Qt.
☞ (M) (***) Sony mono M2K 52531 (2) [id.]. Budapest Qt.
(M) **(*) Ph. 426 046-2 (3) [id.]. Italian Qt.

The Alban Berg undoubtedly offer polish and tonal finesse. The playing is immaculate and the sound has all the usual advantages of the medium: excellent definition, presence and body. The CDs are also available separately (CDC7 47127/8/9-2).

The celebrated set by the Budapest Quartet first appeared in the UK on the Philips label in 1956 and on Columbia in the USA. For long they were a yardstick by which newcomers were judged, and after revisiting them one is tempted to say that they remain very much in a class of their own. Unlike their 1960s re-make, which was pretty rough-and-ready, the sonority is perfectly focused and the readings have weight, animation and dedication. They have command of the music's architecture and of expressive detail that is captured in sound of outstanding fidelity, given the period. The Sony engineers have effected transfers of excellent quality which can hold their own against many later versions. These finely balanced and warmly musical readings are something special and not to be missed.

The Italian performances are in superb style. The only reservations concern Nos. 2 and 4: the latter is perhaps a little wanting in forward movement, while the conventional exchanges at the opening of No. 2 seem a shade too deliberate. The balance is truthful but the digital remastering does draw the ear to a certain thinness in the treble, slightly more noticeable in the earliest recordings.

String quartets Nos. 1–6, Op. 18/1–6; F (arr. of Piano sonata in E, Op. 14/1); (i) String quintet in C, Op. 29.
☞ *** BMG/RCA Dig. 09026 61284-2 (3) [id.]. Tokyo Qt; (i) Zukerman.

There may be some quartet groups in the world that are as fine as the Tokyo, but one is hard pushed to think of one that is finer. They produce a sumptuous, beautifully blended sonority and play with impeccable ensemble; nor are they in any way wanting in musical insight. Their account of the Op. 18 *Quartets* is surely the best to have appeared for many years; it is more imaginative than the Talich, has greater finesse than the Lindsay and can match, though not surpass, the Végh in depth. Not since the Quartetto Italiano set in the mid-1970s have we encountered a more musically satisfying or beautifully recorded set. If the playing has all the polish and technical virtuosity of a great modern ensemble, it somehow retains contact with the sensibility of the period: dynamic nuances are scrupulously observed but are not exaggerated, and tempi are consistent with horse-drawn rather than jet-propelled vehicles! First-movement exposition repeats are all observed. The three CDs offer an additional *bonne bouche* in the form of Beethoven's own transcription of the *E major Piano sonata* and the more substantial bonus of the *C major String quintet*, Op. 29, which at times almost seems to anticipate Schubert. There is plenty of space round the sound and a good back-to-front perspective. Among modern recordings this must now be a first recommendation.

String quartets Nos. 1–6, Op. 18/1–6; 10 in E flat (Harp), Op. 74; 11 in F min., Op. 95.
**(*) ASV CDDCS 305 (3) [id.]. Lindsay Qt.

The great merit of the Lindsay Quartet in Beethoven lies in the natural expressiveness of their playing, most strikingly of all in slow movements, which brings a hushed inner quality too rarely caught on record. The sense of spontaneity necessarily brings the obverse quality: these performances are not as precise as those in the finest rival sets; but there are few Beethoven quartet recordings that so convincingly bring out the humanity of the writing, its power to communicate. The recording of Op. 18, set against a fairly reverberant acoustic, is warm and realistic; the transfers reflect the fact that the recordings are more modern and rather fuller than the remastered Philips quality for the Italian group.

String quartets Nos. 1–3, Op. 18/1–3.
*** Nimbus Dig. NI 5173 [id.]. Medici Qt.

The Medici are not a jet-set ensemble; their playing is refreshingly unglamorous and yet thoroughly polished; nor do they fail to penetrate the depths. They are given a very natural and well-balanced recording, and these performances will give considerable satisfaction.

String quartets Nos. 1 in F; 2 in G, Op. 18/1–2.
☞ (BB) ** Naxos Dig. 8.550558 [id.]. Kodály Qt.

At super-bargain price, the Kodály Quartet deserve favourable consideration. They do not attempt to dress things up in the manner of jet-setting quartets and their readings of both *Quartets* are decent and straightforward, and free from idiosyncrasy. Tempi are well judged and the Naxos recordings are first rate, albeit closer than that which RCA provide for the Tokyo (see above); first-movement exposition repeats are also observed. All the same, they are at times a bit pedestrian – both the Scherzo and the finale of the *F major* fail to get very far off the ground. There is also more to the slow movement than they find.

String quartets Nos. 3 in D, Op. 18/3; 14 in C sharp min., Op. 131.
☞ ** Delos Dig. DE 3036 [id.]. Orford Qt.

Neither performance gives cause to modify the impression made by the earlier discs in this distinguished Canadian ensemble's cycle. These are well-recorded, highly polished, immaculately played and strongly projected readings, which do not, alas, penetrate far below the surface.

String quartets Nos. 4–6, Op. 18/4–6.
☞ **(*) Nimbus Dig. NI 5353 [id.]. Brandis Qt.

Nimbus for some reason have completed their set of Op. 18 (begun by the Medici Quartet) by letting the Brandis group take over. As with other CDs in their cycle, the Brandis show themselves thoughtful and musicianly. Their *C minor quartet* is dramatic without ever going into overdrive, each phrase being allowed to speak naturally; the *A major* is sweet-toned and vital, and the *B flat* excellently shaped; indeed the performance of the last of the set is particularly fine. They produce a beautiful sound; exposition repeats are observed and they scarcely put a foot wrong. Tempi are well chosen and the unanimity of ensemble is impressive. The recording is well balanced: the Nimbus acoustic is big and the sound warm, but the players seem rather too forwardly placed, with a shade of microphone brightness on the leader's tone. They do not displace the first recommendations (the Tokyo Quartet and Quartetto Italiano, among others), who are better recorded.

String quartets Nos. 4 in C min., Op. 18/4; 10 in E flat (Harp), Op. 74; 14 in C sharp min., Op. 131.
☞ (M) (***) Biddulph mono LAB 056-7 [id.]. Rosé Qt – BACH: *Double concerto* etc.

Music-making from another age and totally selfless. These performances bring us as close as we can possibly get to the kind of playing Brahms and Mahler would have heard. The first thing that strikes one about the *C minor*, Op. 18, No. 4, is the utter naturalness of the tempi: they are unhurried but not 'measured'. The *Harp quartet* is equally unhurried and totally natural, and these players all seem to think as one person. Indeed it is the sheer musical personality of the playing that is so refreshing after the relative anonymity we encounter so often today. The recordings were made in 1930 and 1932, while the *C sharp minor Quartet* dates from 1927, so allowance has to be made for pretty primitive sound. Rosé's use of expressive vibrato is very restrained; intonation, though not always perfect, is remarkable in Op. 131, a reading of enormous authority and concentration. This is a most valuable set.

String quartets Nos. 7–9 (Rasumovsky Nos. 1–3), Op. 59/1–3; 10 in E flat (Harp), Op. 74; 11 in F min., Op. 95.
(M) *** Ph. 420 797-2 (3) [id.]. Italian Qt.
*** BMG/RCA Dig. RD 60462 (3) [60462-2-RC]. Tokyo Qt.

String quartets Nos. 7–9 (Rasumovsky Nos. 1–3), Op. 59/1–3.
*** ASV Dig. CDDCS 207 (2) [id.]. Lindsay Qt.

String quartets Nos. 8 in E min.; 9 in C (Rasumovsky Nos. 2–3), Op. 59/2–3.
*** ASV Dig. CDDCA 554 [id.]. Lindsay Qt.

The Lindsay set contains performances of real stature; and though they are not unrivalled in some of their insights, among modern recordings they are not often surpassed. As a recording, this set is comparable with most of its competitors and superior to many; artistically, it can hold its own with the best. They are now placed together in a box, with some saving in cost.

The Tokyo Quartet's account of *No. 7 in F major* is one of the very finest in the catalogue. The tempi throughout are splendidly judged and the performance as a whole is beautifully proportioned. There is, however, some minor cause for reservation in Op. 59, No. 3. The fugal finale is rather too headlong in pace and there are some traces of slickness elsewhere. But for the most part this is a powerful set and its strengths far outweigh its weaknesses. The account of the *F minor*, Op. 95, is appropriately taut and concentrated. The recording is excellent, rich in sonority yet completely truthful and unglamorized.

The remastered Italian set still sounds well: there is now only a slight thinness on top to betray their age, with no lack of body and warmth in the middle range. Their superiority in terms of sheer quartet playing is still striking: purity of intonation, perfectly blended tone and superb ensemble and attack. Their tempi are perfectly judged and every phrase is sensitively shaped, and these performances remain very recommendable at mid-price.

String quartets Nos. 7 in F, Op. 59/1; 9 in C, Op. 59/3 (Rasumovsky Nos. 1 & 3).
☞ **(*) Nimbus Dig. NI 5382 [id.]. Brandis Qt.

There is much to admire in the Brandis Quartet's account of the *F major* and *C major Rasumovsky Quartets*; they are distinguished by musical phrasing, good ensemble and tonal blend, well-judged tempi and a feeling for the architecture of each piece. They are very well played indeed and are refreshingly unconcerned with outward show; yet their virtuosity in, say, the fugal finale of Op. 59/3 is not in question. The recording is acceptable but not worthy of a three-star grading; the sound is a bit hard.

String quartets Nos. 8, Op. 59/2; 10 (Harp), Op. 74.
(B) *** Hung. White Label HRC 063. Bartók Qt.

The Bartók Quartet give strong, well-paced readings of Op. 59/2 and the *Harp quartet*, with slow movements to match any rival versions at whatever price. With excellent Hungaroton recording, this is an outstanding bargain in the White Label series.

String quartet No. 9 in C (Rasumovsky), Op. 59/3.
☞ ** BMG/RCA Dig. 09026 61185 [id.]. Vogler Qt – BARTOK: *Quartet No. 2.* **

In the *C major Rasumovsky* the Vogler Quartet start at something of a disadvantage. Most collectors wanting it will first turn to a complete set of Op. 59, while a reader wanting the Bartók *Second* may not want to duplicate the *C major Quartet*. Not that the Voglers are anything other than expert and musical but, to be frank, their *C major Rasumovsky* does not go far beneath the surface. Good quartet playing, but untouched by real distinction. In spite of some good playing and equally serviceable RCA recording, it represents no real challenge.

String quartet No. 10 in E flat (Harp), Op. 74.
☞ (BB) **(*) Discover Dig. DICD 920171 [id.]. Sharon Qt – MOZART: *Quartet No. 1;* ***; RAVEL: *Quartet.* **(*)

The Sharon Quartet give a remarkably enjoyable account of the the *Harp Quartet*, expressive and sensive in the *Adagio* and perceptive in the closing *Allegretto con variazioni*. They are recorded in a Cologne church, which means that the sound is a shade reverberant (the Scherzo is affected most), but the blend is attractively full and it would be carping to complain when the playing is so well matched and responsive and gives the impression of a real performance.

String quartets Nos. 12 in E flat, Op. 127; 13 in B flat, Op. 130; 14 in C sharp min., Op. 131; 15 in A min., Op. 132; 16 in F, Op. 135.
☞ **(*) BMG/RCA Dig. RD 60975 (3) [09026 60975-2]. Tokyo Qt.

The Tokyo recordings of Op. 18 and the middle-period *Quartets* set very high standards. Late Beethoven is always better than any possible performance: the Tokyo Quartet, it must be admitted, play marvellously and on that score are a joy to listen to. They will undoubtedly be a bit too sweet-toned for some, and their readings are open to the charge of placing beauty before truth. The opening of Op. 131, for example, is a shade too expressive (the hairpins are a bit exaggerated) and there is more depth in the slow movement of Op. 127 than they discover. All the same, if they do not displace earlier recommendations (Lindsay, Végh, Quartetto Italiano, etc.), they are well worth considering as an alternative. They are superbly recorded and, although they are just too beautiful at times to be ideal in this great music, they have obviously thought long and hard about it.

String quartets Nos. 12 in E flat, Op. 127; 13 in B flat, Op. 130; 14 in C sharp min., Op. 131; 15 in A min., Op. 132; 16 in F, Op. 135; Grosse Fuge in B flat, Op. 133.
*** ASV DCS 403 (4) [id.]. Lindsay Qt.
(M) **(*) Ph. 426 050-2 (4) [id.]. Italian Qt.

The Lindsays get far closer to the essence of this great music than most of their rivals. They have the benefit of very well-balanced recording; the sound of the ASV set is admirably present. They seem to find tempi that somehow strike the listener as completely right and which enable them to convey so much of both the letter and the spirit of the music. They bring much rich musical characterization and musical strength. Taken overall, these are among the very finest versions to have been made in recent years.

The merits of the Italian Quartet's performances are considerable. The sonority that they produce is beautifully blended and splendidly focused. They do not sound as sumptuous as some modern quartet recordings and their reissue on four instead of three medium-price CDs is less competitive than it might be. However, for many the Italians' searching and thoughtful interpretations will ultimately prove most satisfying.

String quartets Nos. 12 in E flat, Op. 127; 14 in C sharp min., Op. 131.
(B) *** Hung. White Label HRC 125. Bartók Qt.

On the Bartók Quartet's very generous coupling of Opp. 127 and 131 the sweetness and purity of the string-playing matches that of any rival versions; but the sureness of control over the span of the sublime slow movements still makes this an outstanding version, even taking no account of price.

String quartets Nos. 12 in E flat, Op. 127; 16 in F, Op. 135.
☞ *** Hyp. Dig. CDA 66408 [id.]. New Budapest Qt.
(M) *** Ph. 422 840-2. Italian Qt.

The New Budapest Quartet's cycle has gone from strength to strength and has grown in stature. Their Op. 127 is very fine indeed and is distinguished by consistent (but not excessive) refinement of sonority and impeccable ensemble and intonation. It has some memorable passages (the D flat section in the second movement, a few bars before the enharmonic change to C sharp minor, is handled with great imagination) and the coda of the finale has great insight. Not everything is as successful or as full of insight, and the very opening is somewhat lacking in weight. This also applies to the *F major*, Op. 135, which is less searching than the Talich, the Lindsays or the Végh. All the same, the excellent quality of the playing and the transparent, well-balanced recorded sound make these performances very competitive indeed.

String quartet No. 13 in B flat, Op. 130; Grosse Fuge in B flat, Op. 133.
*** ASV CDDCA 602 [id.]. Lindsay Qt.

The Lindsay's account of Op. 130 includes both the *Grosse Fuge* as an ending and also the finale Beethoven substituted, so that listeners can choose for themselves.

String quartet No. 13 in B flat, Op. 130; Grosse Fuge, Op. 133.
☞ (B) **(*) Hung. White Label HRC 136 [id.]. Bartók Qt.

A strong performance of Op. 130 from the Bartók Quartet with simple intensity in the keynote *Cavatina Adagio* fifth movement and in the earlier *Andante*. As is now normal practice, they provide the replacement finale, alongside (a powerfully rugged version of) the daunting *Grosse Fuge*.

String quartet No. 14 in C sharp min., Op. 131.
*** ASV CDDCA 603 [id.]. Lindsay Qt.

The Lindsay's account of Op. 131 is as fine as any in the catalogue.

String quartets No. 14 in C sharp min., Op. 131; 16 in F, Op. 135 (versions for string orchestra).
☞ *** DG Dig.435 779-2 [id.]. VPO, Bernstein.

Not long before he died, Bernstein nominated his string-orchestra version of Op. 131 as his personal favourite among his own recordings. Basing the adaptation on one prepared by his mentor, Dmitri Mitropoulos, he draws dedicated playing from the Vienna Philharmonic, finding a concentration and an inner quality too often missing in recordings by four players alone. Significantly, he dedicated the recording to the memory of his wife. The CD version adds a similar string version of Op. 135, a work which Toscanini presented in this form a generation earlier.

String quartets Nos. 15 in A min., Op. 132; 17 in F, Op. 135.
☞ (B) *** Hung. White Label HRC 126 [id.]. Bartók Qt.

Like their companion coupling of Opp. 127 and 131, the Bartók Quartet's versions of the *A minor* and *F major Quartets* make an impressive bargain. The blending of timbre and secure intonation is matched by playing of genuine vitality, and the concentration in the *Heiliger Danksesang* of Op. 132 is matched by a comparable intensity in the *Lento assai e cantante tranquillo* of Op. 135.

String trios Nos. 1 in E flat, Op. 3; 2 in G; 3 in D; 4 in C min., Op. 9/1–3; Serenade in D (for string trio), Op. 8.
☞ ** EMI Dig. CDS7 54198-2 (2) [id.]. Perlman, Zukerman, Harrell.

String trio No. 1 in E flat, Op. 3; Serenade in D, Op. 8.
*** Unicorn Dig. DKPCD 9059 [id.]. Cummings Trio.

String trios Nos. 2 in G; 3 in D; 4 in C min., Op. 9/1–3.
*** Unicorn Dig. DKPCD 9042 [id.]. Cummings Trio.

The playing of the Cummings Trio is cultured but not overcivilized; there is an unforced naturalness about it all. These players let Beethoven speak for himself and in quieter moments there is a winning sense of repose: in short, this is real chamber-music-making, with excellent recording; indeed it is in the demonstration class.

The Perlman–Zukerman–Harrell performances were recorded at public performances in New York in 1989 and 1990, and they have won golden opinions in the press – and from reliable voices. Readers will no doubt want to give some weight to that in the light of less enthusiastic responses. No one could complain that this distinguished trio do not bring zest in plenty to their music-making, though subtlety is not always in strong supply. Dynamic markings tend to be strongly contrasted, yet the performances are in other respects surprisingly routine. Assembling glamorous names may impress the uninitiated, but it is no substitute for the artistry born of long musical association and a common musical purpose. Whatever the strengths of the Perlman–Zukerman–Harrell partnership, they are undoubtedly handicapped by the very close balance chosen by their engineers (doubtless to minimize extraneous audience-noise), which does not flatter the tone of any of the artists and which lends them an edge which would not be apparent were the listener more discreetly placed. To be frank, these performances fail to yield compellingly positive musical results, as do the Cummings, which is much to be preferred to the present version.

Violin sonatas Nos. 1–10.
(M) *** Decca 421 453-2 (4); 436 892-2 (*Nos. 1–3*), 436 893-2 (*Nos. 4–5*), 436 894-2 (*Nos. 6–8*), 436 895-2 (*Nos. 9–10*). Itzhak Perlman, Vladimir Ashkenazy.
(M) *** DG 415 874-2 (3) [id.]. Yehudi Menuhin, Wilhelm Kempff.
(M) (***) Ph. mono 422 140-2 (3). Arthur Grumiaux, Clara Haskil.

Perlman and Ashkenazy's set of the *Violin sonatas*, now reissued on four mid-priced CDs, will be difficult to surpass. These performances offer a blend of classical purity and spontaneous vitality that it is hard to resist; moreover the realism and presence of the recording in its CD format are very striking. They are also now available on four separate mid-priced CDs.

Though Menuhin and Kempff do not always offer the most immaculate performances on disc, they consistently reflect the joy and sense of wonder of pianist and violinist alike, often relaxed in tempo but magnetic from first to last, brightly transferred to CD.

Arthur Grumiaux and Clara Haskil made their celebrated recordings in 1956–7 and they sound remarkably well for their age. The performances are wonderfully civilized and aristocratic, and no one investing in them will regret it. They accommodate all ten *Sonatas* on three CDs at mid-price, as opposed to the four of Perlman and Ashkenazy.

Violin sonatas Nos. 1 in D; 2 in A; 3 in E flat, Op. 12/1–3.
*** DG Dig. 415 138-2 [id.]. Gidon Kremer, Martha Argerich.

The partnership of Kremer and Argerich, two inspirational artists, works superbly in the first three sonatas, with the to-and-fro exchanges typical of early Beethoven consistently delightful. The CD gives a keen sense of presence.

Violin sonatas Nos. 1 in D; 2 in A; 3 in E flat, Op.12/1–3.
☞ (BB) *** Naxos Dig. 8.550284 [id.]. Takako Nishizaki, Jenö Jandó.

Violin sonatas No. 4 in A min., Op. 23; 10 in G, Op. 96; 12 variations on Mozart's 'Se vuol ballare'
from 'Le nozze di Figaro', WoO 40.
☞ (BB) *** Naxos Dig. 8.550285 [id.]. Takako Nishizaki, Jenö Jandó.

Naxos are on to a winning combination here. These performances are wonderfully fresh and alive. Takako Nishizaki isn't a 'big' player but her timbre is admirably suited to Beethoven and she is clearly in complete rapport with Jandó, who is in excellent form. Just sample the spirited *Rondo* of Op. 12/1 (or indeed of Op. 13/3), its theme-and-variations central movement, the beautifully paced *Andante scherzoso* of Op. 23 or the calm *Adagio espressivo* of Op. 96 to appreciate the calibre of this music-making. The *Mozart variations*, too, are winningly done. The recording is most naturally balanced, the acoustic is spacious without in any way clouding the focus. You can't do better at twice the price!

Violin sonatas Nos. 4 in A min., Op. 23; 6 in A; 7 in C min.; 8 in G, Op. 30/1–3.
☞ (M) ** Sony MPK 52534 [id.]. Zino Francescatti, Robert Casadesus.

These performances are alive and unfailingly musical, and the closeness of the partnership is reflected by the excellent balance. There is an occasional tendency to virtuosity at the expense of the music's structure, but this may be just natural exuberance. The offering is generous (76 minutes) and this could be a good supplement for those already possessing a coupling of the *Spring* and *Kreutzer Sonatas*. However, the snag is that the dry, close recording of the violin is not altogether flattering to Francescatti's sweet but slightly febrile tone production.

Violin sonatas Nos. 5 in F (Spring), Op. 24; 7 in C min., Op. 30/2.
(M) (***) EMI CDH7 63494-2. Adolf Busch, Rudolf Serkin (with BACH: *Violin partita No. 2* (***)).

Music-making from another age, unhurried, humane and of supreme integrity. Playing of such naturalness and artistry transcends the inevitable sonic limitations.

Violin sonatas Nos. 5 in F (Spring); 8 in G, Op. 30/3; 9 in A (Kreutzer).
☞ (M) *** EMI CDM7 64631-2 [id.]; *EG 764631-4.* Pinchas Zukerman, Daniel Barenboim.
☞ (M) ** BMG/RCA 09026 61861-2 [id.]. Henryk Szeryng, Artur Rubinstein.

The Zukerman/Barenboim 1973 coupling of the *Spring* and *Kreutzer sonatas*, long a favourite recommendation, is made even more attractive by the inclusion of the *G major Sonata*, Op. 30/3, an equally memorable work, when the playing is just as disarmingly spontaneous. The CD transfer scarcely betrays its age.

The Szeryng/Rubinstein account of *No. 8 in G* is a particularly fine one and the 1961 recording, although dry, is quite full. The *Spring* and *Kreutzer sonatas* date from 1958, and the microphones are less flattering to Szeryng's timbre, which sounds slightly wiry. The *Spring sonata* is effective enough, but the *Kreutzer* is the least penetrating of the three performances.

Violin sonatas Nos. 5 in F (Spring), Op. 24; 9 in A (Kreutzer), Op. 47.
*** Decca 410 554-2 [id.]. Itzhak Perlman, Vladimir Ashkenazy.
(M) *** DG 435 101-2 [id.]. Sir Yehudi Menuhin, Wilhelm Kempff.
(BB) *** Naxos Dig. 8.550283; *4550283* [id.]. Takako Nishizaki, Jenö Jandó.
☞ **(*) BMG/RCA Dig. 09026 61561-2 [id.]. Pinchas Zukerman, Marc Neikrug.

On Decca an obvious recoupling from the Perlman/Ashkenazy series – although at full price! The dynamism is there but never becomes too extrovert, and the music unfolds naturally and spontaneously. The recording quality is excellent and has transferred smoothly to CD, though the EMI transfer of the Zukerman/Barenboim recordings is even more impressive.

There is no doubt that Menuhin and Kempff give inspirational accounts of both works, and the recording has striking presence and naturalness on CD.

Takako Nishizaki does not produce a large sound but the balance with Jandó is expertly managed, and the result is very natural and real. The performances are delightful in their fresh spontaneity. This is a bargain.

The partnership of Zukerman and Neikrug produces enjoyable but not distinctive performances. Mostly the playing is fresh and committed, but there are other even more spontaneous versions of these two favourite works. The artists have good presence, but at times the balance is not wholly natural.

Violin sonatas Nos. 6 in A; 7 in C min.; 8 in G, Op. 30/1–3.

(BB) *** Naxos Dig. 8.550286; *4.550286* [id.]. Takako Nishizaki, Jenö Jandó.

All three of the Op. 30 *Sonatas* on one CD represents very good value for money, particularly as the playing is of considerable quality.

Wind music

(Wind) *Octet in E flat, Op. 103; Quintet in E flat for oboe, 3 horns & bassoon; Rondino in E flat for wind octet, WoO 25; Sextet in E flat, Op. 71.*
*** ASV Dig. CDCOE 807 [id.]. Wind Soloists of COE.

The wind soloists of the Chamber Orchestra of Europe give strong and stylish performances of this collection of Beethoven's wind music, marked by some outstanding solo work, notably from the first oboe, Douglas Boyd. They are recorded in warm but clear sound, with good presence.

SOLO PIANO MUSIC

Piano sonatas Nos. 1–32 (complete).
⊛ (M) (***) EMI mono CHS7 63765-2 (8) [Ang. CDHH 3765]. Artur Schnabel.
(B) *** DG 429 306-2 (9) [id.]. Wilhelm Kempff.
(M) *** EMI CZS7 62863-2 (10). Daniel Barenboim.
☞ (M) **(*) Decca 433 882-2 (8). Wilhelm Backhaus.
☞ *** Elektra-Nonesuch/Warner Dig. 7559 79328-2 (10) [id.]. Richard Goode.

Piano sonatas Nos. 1–32; 6 Variations in F, Op. 43; Variations and fugue in E flat on a theme from Prometheus (Eroica), Op. 35; 32 Variations in C min., WoO 80.
(M) *** Ph. 432 301-2 (11) [id.]. Claudio Arrau.

For many music-lovers and record collectors of an older generation, Schnabel was the voice of Beethoven; returning to this pioneering set again, one realizes that his insights were deeper than those of almost anyone who followed him, though his pianism has been surpassed. This is one of the towering classics of the gramophone and, whatever other individual Beethoven sonatas you may have, this is an indispensable reference point.

Kempff's recordings, all dating from 1964/5, are to the 1960s what Schnabel's were to the pre-war years – performances that represent a yardstick by which all others are judged. Kempff's shading of pianistic colour is so imaginative that the ear readily accommodates any slight dryness in the upper range. The interpretations have a commanding stature, yet Kempff brings his own individuality to every bar and a clarity and sparkle that make you want to go on listening.

Barenboim's earlier set of the Beethoven *Sonatas*, recorded for EMI when he was in his late twenties, remains one of his very finest achievements on record. The readings are sometimes idiosyncratic, with unexpected tempi both fast and slow, but the spontaneous style is unfailingly compelling. At times Barenboim's way is mercurial, with an element of fantasy. But overall this is a keenly thoughtful musician living through Beethoven's great piano cycle with an individuality that puts him in the line of master pianists.

After years of concentrating on chamber music, the American pianist Richard Goode has emerged in his own right as one of the most searching Beethoven interpreters today. This cycle of the 32 sonatas was recorded over a period of years – the late sonatas were available earlier – and after Goode had given a number of cycles in live concert. In America, Goode has often been likened to Schnabel or Serkin, rugged Beethovenians, but that is misleading. It is not just the power of Goode's playing that singles him out, but the beauty, when he has such subtle control over a formidably wide tonal and dynamic range. Even at its weightiest, the sound is never clangorous. Particularly in the early sonatas Goode brings out the wit and parody, while slow movements regularly draw sensuously velvety legato. Helped by an unusually full and clear recording, with no haze of reverberation, the clarity of his articulation is breathtaking, as in the running semiquavers of the finale of the *Appassionata sonata*. Above all, Goode has a natural gravity which compels attention. One has to go

back to the pre-digital era to find a Beethoven cycle of comparable command and intensity – to the
earlier of Barenboim's two cycles (EMI), daringly spacious in its speeds, or to the jewelled clarity of
Wilhelm Kempff (DG).

Arrau's Beethoven cycle, recorded during the 1960s, is a survey of extreme distinction. The great
Chilean pianist possessed a quite distinctive keyboard sonority, rich and aristocratic in its finesse. The
late sonatas show his artistry at its most consummate: one of the very finest of these performances
(and one of the very finest records he ever made) is his *Hammerklavier*, which represents his art at its
most fully realized. No apologies need be made for the recordings, which belie their age.

Backhaus recorded his survey over a decade, from 1958 to 1969 (with the exception of the
Hammerklavier, which came much earlier, in 1953, and is mono). As it happens, the latter represents
the peak of the cycle, offering playing of great power and concentration. When the other records
appeared individually as LPs, they received a mixed press, and our own welcome for them was not
always enthusiastic. Now a reassessment is surely due, for Backhaus's direct, sometimes brusque
manner does not derive from any lack of feeling, rather from a determination to present Beethoven's
thoughts adorned with no idiosyncratic excrescences. At his best, as in the *Waldstein* and *Appassionata
sonatas*, the performances present a characteristic mixture of rugged spontaneity and wilfulness which
can be remarkably compelling. But there are many other examples of his positive, alert and
imaginative response which balance the apparently uncompromising wilfulness of manner. He was
less suited to the more lightweight works such as the sprightly little *G major Sonata* of Op. 14 (No.
10), and the literal manner also robs the *G minor* of Op. 49 (No. 19) of charm. Yet even here he
plainly enjoyed himself in his own way, so that his own responses are conveyed to the listener.
Generally – as with the *Hammerklavier* – the bigger the challenge for him, the more impressive the
performance. Yet he could relax, and his performance of *No. 18 in E flat*, Op. 31/3, is an almost ideal
interpretation, full of grace and poise in the first movement and never lacking brio in the finale. His
account of the *A flat Sonata*, Op. 26 (No. 12), also shows him at his finest: his way of handling the
violent rhythmic irregularities of the Scherzo, and his undeniably heroic approach to the *Marcia
funèbre* are matched by the variety of touch in the variations, and at the minor section in the finale.
His massive, rather gruff style naturally suits the later rather than the earlier sonatas, but even in Op.
101, where the challenge is greatest, the uningratiating manner will not suit all tastes, and the very
powerful accounts of Op. 109 and Op. 111 do not always leave the music quite enough space to
breathe. But overall the set is a formidable achievement and a reminder of a keyboard giant. The
recording is remarkably faithful; the only real drawback is that the close balance brings a comparative
lack of dynamic range.

Piano sonatas Nos. 1 in F min.; 2 in A; 3 in C, Op. 2/1–3.
☞ *** EMI Dig. CDC7 54657-2 [id.]. Melvyn Tan (fortepiano).
☞ *** Chan. Dig. CHAN 9212 [id.]. Louis Lortie.
(BB) **(*) Naxos Dig. 8.550150; *4550150* [id.]. Jenö Jandó.

There is an ardour and eloquence in Melvyn Tan's playing that is wholly persuasive, even for those
who do not normally respond to the fortepiano. He treats the instrument as an artist, without the
solemnity and caution of the scholar-performer. These excellent performances can be strongly
recommended.

Louis Lortie has the benefit of an immediate and truthful recording, made at The Maltings,
Snape, which greatly enhances the satisfaction his playing gives. He brings his usual refined musical
intelligence to all three of the Op. 2 *Sonatas* and gives ample evidence of his instinctive musicianship
and artistry. Lortie sustains momentum throughout and characterizes each phrase with a real sense of
the music's meaning.

Jenö Jandó's complete recording of the Beethoven *Piano sonatas* is also available in two flimsy
slip-cases, each comprising five CDs (8.505002 and 8.505003). This first CD (actually Volume 3)
establishes Jandó's credentials as a strong, unidiosyncratic Beethovenian. If there is not the individuality of a Kempff or a Barenboim, the playing is always direct and satisfying. The piano sound is real,
full and bold.

Piano sonatas Nos. 1 in F min.; 2 in A, Op. 2/1–2; 19 in G min.; 20 in G, Op. 49/1–2.
☞ (BB) **(*) ASV CDQS 6055. John Lill.

This first record of John Lill's cycle offers some of the most characteristic performances in the series.
There is a directness of utterance about Lill's Beethoven which is undoubtedly compulsive, particularly
as the recording has great presence and the tone is admirably secure and realistic. Lill brings a
formidable technique to all these sonatas and his deliberation at the opening of the *F minor Sonata*
(No. 1) gives the first movement great character. The slow movement too is eloquently played, and

the *Largo appassionato* of No. 2 also makes a strong impression, though some will feel that the fortissimo outbursts are over-characterized.The closing Rondo (*Grazioso*), however, lilts appealingly. As he shows in the two Opus 49 *Sonatas*, Lill is not strong on charm, yet there is an appealing simplicity and a strong profile. Moreover, there is an integrity about this playing that the listener cannot fail to notice.

Piano sonatas Nos. 1 in F min., Op. 2/1; 5 in C min., Op. 10/1; 8 (Pathétique); 17 (Tempest), Op. 31/2.
☞ (*) Ph. Dig. 432 137-2 [id.]. Zoltán Kocsis.

Zoltán Kocsis is among the most intelligently articulate of keyboard virtuosi and the bad press that greeted this Beethoven disc aroused scepticism. However, the fact is that the sound is every bit as dry and the playing every bit as remote and unengaged as it was said to be.

Piano sonatas Nos. 4 in E flat, Op. 7; 13 in E flat, Op. 27/1; 19 in G min., 20 in G, Op. 49/1–2; 22 in F, Op. 54.
(BB) **(*) Naxos Dig. 8.550167; 4550167 [id.]. Jenö Jandó.

The performances of both the *E flat Sonata*, Op. 7, and the *Sonata quasi una fantasia*, Op. 27/1, in which Jandó is comparably responsive to Beethoven's wide expressive range, show the continuing excellence of this series, and the three shorter works are also freshly presented.

Piano sonatas Nos. 5 in C min.; 6 in F; 7 in D, Op. 10/1–3.
☞ (BB) *(*) ASV CDQS 6057 [id.]. John Lill.

These are among the more disappointing of Lill's sonata readings, rather square and charmless. The great D major slow movement of Op. 10/3 is taken challengingly slowly, but there is little feeling of flow. Bright, realistic, well-focused recording.

Piano sonatas Nos. 5 in C min.; 6 in F; 7 in D, Op. 10/1–3; 25 in G, Op. 79.
*** EMI Dig. CDC7 54207-2 [id.]. Melvyn Tan (fortepiano).
(BB) *** Naxos Dig. 8.550161; 4.550161 [id.]. Jenö Jandó.

The young Singapore-born Melvyn Tan gives performances of the three Op. 10 *Sonatas* that have both brilliance and sensitivity in equal measure. Even collectors whose taste inclines to the modern piano rather than the fortepiano will surely find both the sounds and the musical sense well conveyed here. Recommended with enthusiasm.

The three splendid Op. 10 *Sonatas* also show Jandó at his most perceptive and unselfconscious.

Piano sonatas Nos. 5 in C min.; 10 in G, Op. 14/2; 19 in G min.; 20 in G, Op. 49/1–2.
**(*) DG Dig. 419 172-2 [id.]. Emil Gilels.

Gilels manages to make one believe that his is exactly the *tempo giusto* even when one feels tempted to question the very deliberate speed he adopts in the slow movement of the *C minor*, Op. 10, No. 1. Such is his magic that, while under his spell, doubts are silenced. He is well recorded, too.

Piano sonatas Nos. 7 in D, Op. 10/3; 18 in E flat, Op. 31/3; 15 Variations and fugue on a theme from Prometheus (Eroica variations), Op. 35.
*** DG 423 136-2 [id.]. Emil Gilels.

Gilels's account of the *Eroica variations* is masterly. In the *D major Sonata* he is hardly less impressive, though there are odd mannerisms. Op. 31, No. 3 is distinguished, too, though the recording acoustic is somewhat drier than that of its companions.

Piano sonatas Nos. 7 in D; 23 in F min. (Appassionata), Op. 57.
*** Sony Dig. MK 39344 [id.]. Murray Perahia.

Intense, vibrant playing from Perahia in the *D major Sonata*, with great range of colour and depth of thought, and the *Appassionata* is a performance of comparable stature. These are among the few interpretations to have appeared in recent years that can be recommended alongside Gilels. The recorded sound is truthful.

Piano sonatas Nos. 8 (Pathétique), Op. 13; 13; 14 (Moonlight), Op. 27/1–2.
**(*) DG Dig. 400 036-2 [id.]. Emil Gilels.

Gilels's opening movement of the *E flat Sonata* is strangely reserved, as if he feared the charge of self-indulgence or out-of-period sentiment. However, such are the strengths of this playing that few will quarrel with the magnificence of his conceptions of all three pieces. The digital recording is lifelike, although the balance is very close.

Piano sonatas Nos. 8 (Pathétique), Op. 13; 14 (Moonlight), Op. 27/2; 15 (Pastoral), Op. 28; 17
(Tempest), Op. 31/2; 21 (Waldstein), Op. 53; 23 (Appassionata), Op. 57; 26 (Les Adieux), Op. 81a.
☞ (B) *** Ph. Duo 438 730-2 [id.]. Alfred Brendel.

In offering seven of Beethoven's most popular named sonatas, this Duo set – two discs for the price
of one – is in every way an outstanding bargain, well worth having even if duplication is involved. All
the performances are undeniably impressive and the recording consistently excellent. The *Tempest*,
Op. 31/2, is finely conceived and thoroughly compelling, and the central movements of the *Pastoral*
resonate in the memory, the performance radiant and beautifully shaped, with every detail fitting in
harmoniously with the artist's conception of the whole. While Brendel's earlier *Waldstein* (on Vox/
Turnabout) has claims to be considered among the very finest on record, this is only marginally less
impressive and is certainly much better recorded.

Piano sonatas Nos. 8 in C min. (Pathétique), Op. 13; 14 in C sharp min. (Moonlight), Op. 27/2; 15 in
D (Pastoral), Op. 28; 24 in F sharp, Op. 78.
(M) *** DG 415 834-2; *415 834-4* [id.]. Wilhelm Kempff.

Kempff's masterly recordings show so well his ability to rethink Beethoven's music within the
recording studio. Everything he does has his individual stamp, and above all he never fails to convey
the deep intensity of a master in communion with Beethoven.

Piano sonatas Nos. 8 in C min. (Pathétique), Op. 13; 14 in C sharp min. (Moonlight), Op. 27/2; 17 in
D min. (Tempest), Op. 31/2; 23 in F min. (Appassionata), Op. 57.
☞ (B) ** Erato/Warner 2292 45924-2 [id.]. Maria-João Pires.

Maria-João Pires is a comparatively romantic Beethovenian, as she demonstrates in the wide range of
colour and fluctuating dynamic in the opening movement of the *Moonlight sonata* and her almost
Chopinesque rubato in the *Adagio* of the *Pathétique*. There is an appealing sense of fantasy in the
first movement of *The Tempest* and no lack of strength or virtuosity throughout, although she lets the
coda of the finale of the *Appassionata* almost run away with her. The recording is faithful, but not
flattering.

Piano sonatas Nos. 8 in C min. (Pathétique), Op. 13; 14 in C sharp min. (Moonlight), Op. 27/2; 23 in
F min. (Appassionata), Op. 57.
(BB) **(*) Naxos Dig. 8.550045; *4550045* [id.]. Jenö Jandó.

Jandó's clean, direct style and natural spontaneity are particularly admirable in the slow movements
of the *Pathétique* and *Appassionata*, warmly lyrical in feeling, yet not a whit sentimental. Only in the
coda of the finale of the *Appassionata* does one feel a loss of poise, when the closing *presto* becomes
prestissimo and the exuberance of the music-making nearly gets out of control.

Piano sonatas Nos. 8 (Pathétique); 14 (Moonlight); 23 (Appassionata); 26 (Les Adieux).
☞ ⊛ (M) *** BMG/RCA 09026 61443-2 [id.]. Artur Rubinstein.

Artur Rubinstein almost always conveys a sense of spontaneity in his recorded performances, and the
sense of a live interpretation is specially vivid here. He was not a Beethoven specialist, but it is
perhaps surprising that he had never recorded the *Moonlight* before this version (dating from 1962),
nor even played it in public. But there is a combination of freshness and maturity in his reading which
makes it stand out even among many fine recorded versions. The improvisatory feeling in the opening
movement is remarkable. The *Pathétique* has a youthful urgency in the outer movements, yet the
Adagio cantabile has a wonderful simplicity. The impulsive surge of feeling in the *Appassionata* is
equally compelling, with the finale reminding one of Richter's famous record. The exhilaration and
power of Rubinstein's playing, both here and in *Les Adieux*, are beyond praise. If he has forged a
special link with any Beethoven work, it is with Op. 81a. The recordings, made in the Manhattan
Center, New York City, sound firmer and fuller than they did on LP and reflect great credit on John
Pfeiffer's remastering for CD.

Piano sonatas Nos. 8 in C min. (Pathétique); 23 in F min. (Appassionata), Op. 57; 31 in A flat, Op.
110.
☞ ⊛ (B) *** DG Dig./Analogue 439 426-2 [id.]. Emil Gilels.

This DG Classikon reissue is a remarkable bargain. If the *Pathétique* does not rank among Gilels's
very finest Beethoven performances on record, such are the strengths of his playing that the reading
still leaves a profound impression. The account of the *Appassionata* has previously been hailed by us
as among the finest ever made and the 1973 analogue recording is both full and believably present.
Op. 110 is given a performance of real stature. Even when Gilels storms the greatest heights in the

closing fugue, no fortissimo ever sounds percussive or strained. The *Pathétique* and Op. 110 are truthful digital recordings, both made in the Berlin Jesus-Christus-Kirche; the *Pathétique*, made in 1980, has the microphones a bit close, but in No. 31 (dating from five years later) the balance is better judged. An outstanding bargain, all the same.

Piano sonatas Nos. 9 in E; 10 in G, Op. 14/1–2; 24 in F sharp, Op. 78; 27 in E min., Op. 90; 28 in A, Op. 101.
(BB) *** Naxos Dig. 8.550162; 4550162 [id.]. Jenö Jandó.

Opp. 90 and 101 show this artist at full stretch. These are demanding works and Jandó does not fall short, particularly in the slow movements, which are very eloquent indeed. The piano sound is most believable.

Piano sonatas Nos. 11 in B flat, Op. 22; 29 in B flat (Hammerklavier), Op. 106.
(BB) **(*) Naxos Dig. 8.550234; 4550234 [id.]. Jenö Jandó.

From its very opening bars, the *Hammerklavier* is commanding; there is rapt concentration in the slow movement, and the closing fugue runs its course with a powerful inevitability. Again, most realistic recording.

Piano sonata No. 12 in A flat, Op. 26; 6 Variations in F, Op. 34.
☞ (M) *** Ph. 438 306-2 [id.]. Alfred Brendel – MOZART: *Piano sonata No. 11 etc.* ***

The Op. 26 *Piano sonata* receives a surpassingly beautiful reading at Brendel's hands, and the 1977 analogue recording does full justice to the colour and refinement of his pianism. The *Variations*, recorded digitally 13 years later (with each banded separately), show his Beethovenian affinity in no way diminished – they are full of imagination and a constant pleasure to the ear. The Mozart coupling is in no way less distinguished. A treasurable reissue, immaculately transferred to CD.

Piano sonatas Nos. 12 in A flat, Op. 26; 16 in G; 18 in E flat, Op. 31/1 & 3.
(BB) **(*) Naxos Dig. 8.550166 [id.]. Jenö Jandó.

Volume 7 with its trio of middle-period sonatas can be recommended with few reservations. No. 18 is a considerable success, and there is much to stimulate the listener's interest here. Excellent sound.

Piano sonatas Nos. 14 in C sharp min. (Moonlight), Op. 27/2; 21 in C (Waldstein), Op. 53; 23 in F min. (Appassionata), Op. 57.
*** Virgin/EMI Dig. VC7 59247-2 [id.]. Mikhail Pletnev.
(M) *** Decca 417 732-2. Vladimir Ashkenazy.
(M) **(*) BMG/RCA GD 60375 [60375-2-RG]. Vladimir Horowitz.

Some will find the Pletnev *Moonlight* a bit mannered, but he has the capacity to make you listen intently – as every great pianist does, and he also finds the right depths in the slow movement and finale of the *Waldstein*. The account of the *Appassionata* is masterly. The engineering is immaculate and does justice to Pletnev's individual sound-world.

An excellent mid-priced grouping of three popular sonatas from Ashkenazy. The *Waldstein* (1975) is splendidly structured and the *Appassionata* (1973) superb, although those who feel strongly about matters of tempo may well find Ashkenazy a little too free in the first movement.

Horowitz was not thought of primarily as a Beethoven pianist, but these recordings, made in 1956 (the *Moonlight* and *Waldstein*) and 1959, show how powerful he could be in the music of this composer. His delicacy, too, is equally impressive. The sound has been improved in the remastering process; there is some hardness on top but little shallowness, and the bass sonority is telling.

Piano sonatas: No. 15 in D (Pastoral), Op. 28; (Kurfürstensonaten) in E flat, F min., D, WoO 47/1–3; in C (incomplete), WoO 51; Sonatinas: in G, F, Anh. 5/1–2.
(BB) ** Naxos Dig. 8.550255 [id.]. Jenö Jandó.

Jandó's playing is fresh, clean and intelligent and, if the two *Sonatinas* are not authentic, they make agreeable listening here. The *Pastoral sonata* is admirably done.

Piano sonatas Nos. 16 in G; 17 in D min. (Tempest); 18 in E flat, Op. 31/1–3.
*** Decca 417 663-2 [id.]. Vladimir Ashkenazy.
☞ (BB) **(*) ASV CDQS 6060 [id.]. John Lill.

The performances here are among the best of Ashkenazy's Beethoven cycle: he brings concentration of mind, together with spontaneity of feeling. The command of keyboard colour is, as always, impressive and in terms of both dramatic tension and the sense of architecture these are thoroughly satisfying performances.

This is one of the most impressive discs in John Lill's series and it is very well recorded. Obviously the Op. 31 *Sonatas* strike a spark in his consciousness and the first movement of No. 16 is keenly alive, while the slow movement is characteristically direct and there are some sensitive touches. There is no want of fire in *The Tempest*, and there is much to admire in the *E flat Sonata*, although Lill's tendency to aggressiveness brings some exaggerated sforzandos in the Scherzo. But the playing throughout is strong and keenly intelligent.

Piano sonatas Nos. 17 in D min., Op. 31/2; 18 in E flat, Op. 31/3; 26 in E flat (Les Adieux), Op. 81a.
*** Sony Dig. MK 42319 [id.]. Murray Perahia.

Wonderfully concentrated performances. All these readings have the blend of authority, finesse and poetry that distinguishes this great artist at his best.

Piano sonatas Nos. 17 in D min. (Tempest), Op. 31/2; 21 in C (Waldstein), Op. 53; 26 in E flat (Les Adieux), Op. 81a.
(BB) **(*) Naxos Dig. 8.550054 [id.]. Jenö Jandó.

Jandó offers here the other three famous named sonatas, and very enjoyable they are in their direct manner.

Piano sonatas Nos. 17 in D min. (Tempest), Op. 31/2; 29 in B flat (Hammerklavier), Op. 106.
(M) *** DG 419 857-2 [id.]. Wilhelm Kempff.

Kempff's preference for measured allegros and fastish andantes gives a different weighting to movements from the usual, but there is a profound thoughtfulness of utterance.

Piano sonatas Nos. 21 in C (Waldstein), Op. 53; 23 in F min. (Appassionata), Op. 57; 26 in E flat (Les Adieux), Op. 81a.
⊛ *** DG 419 162-2 [id.]. Emil Gilels.
*** EMI Dig. CDC7 49330-2 [id.]. Melvyn Tan (fortepiano).
(M) *** DG 419 053-2 [id.]. Wilhelm Kempff.

Gilels's account of the *Appassionata* has previously been hailed by us as among the finest ever made, and much the same must be said of the *Waldstein*. Moreover, Gilels's fastidiously sensitive yet commanding *Les Adieux* is also one of the most impressive ever committed to disc. These are all performances to relish, to study and to keep for special occasions.

Melvyn Tan offers a CD for those who are unconverted to the fortepiano and find its exponents tame. In all three sonatas he exhibits consummate artistry and real temperament and fire. Nor is there any want of poetic feeling. The EMI recording is excellent; in short, an outstanding issue.

Kempff's *Appassionata* is characteristically clear, classically straight in the same way that the *Waldstein* is cooler and fresher than usual. *Les Adieux*, like the *Appassionata*, may be less weightily dramatic than in other readings, but the concentration is irresistible.

Piano sonatas Nos. 21 in C (Waldstein), Op. 53; 23 in F min. (Appassionata), Op. 57; 27 in E min., Op. 90.
☞ *(*) BMG/RCA Dig. 09026 61280-2 [id.]. Barry Douglas.

Barry Douglas is an accomplished and intelligent player, but these performances, though fluent, assured and by no means unimaginative, leave no great lasting impression. To be competitive, given the abundance which the catalogues have to offer these days, this well-recorded disc would have to offer performances of greater artistic stature.

Piano sonatas Nos. 21 (Waldstein); 24 in F sharp, Op. 78; 31 in A flat, Op. 110.
☞ *** EMI Dig. CDC7 54896-2 [id.]. Stephen Kovacevich.

This second disc in Stephen Kovacevich's projected Beethoven cycle for EMI brings revelatory performances from one of the deepest thinkers among Beethoven pianists. Compared with Richard Goode – whose cycle has now appeared complete – Kovacevich allows himself a degree more expressive freedom, giving foretastes of romantic music to come. The *Waldstein* as well as Op. 110 has a visionary quality. As with the first disc, the piano is set at a distance in a reverberant acoustic, blurring the edges.

Piano sonata No. 23 in F min. (Appassionata), Op. 57.
(M) *** BMG/RCA GD 86518 [RCA 6518-2-RG]. Sviatoslav Richter – BRAHMS: *Piano concerto No. 2.* ***

Richter's thrilling 1960 *Appassionata* is a superb example of a studio recording sounding like a live performance, with the wide dynamic range bringing out both the drama and passion of this boldly contrasted sonata.

Piano sonatas Nos. 24 in F sharp, Op. 78; 29 in B flat (Hammerklavier), Op. 106.
☞ *** Sony SMK 52645 [id.]. Glenn Gould.

Whether or not you are a Gould devotee, no one could miss his unique magnetism in this long-buried recording of what he provocatively describes as 'the longest, most inconsiderate and probably least rewarding piece that Beethoven wrote for the piano'. He adds: 'I decided that since the piece is hopelessly unpianistic . . . I would attempt an orchestral approach.' In practice this means that in all but the second-movement Scherzo Gould takes a very broad view. The first movement must be the slowest version ever. It is not just that his basic tempo is very measured indeed, but that he takes every opportunity to linger over linking passages, coming virtually to a halt at the start of the development section. By personal magnetism the result is compelling, aptly rugged and muscular. The other movements too have their Gouldian eccentricities – quite apart from his incurable habit of singing and humming, particularly at the start of a new theme – but there the approach is rather less extreme, with the great *Adagio* no more spacious than, say, with Solomon. Gould's shading of phrase and tone is often persuasive, despite the unhelpfully dry, if full and immediate, recorded CBC sound of 1970. In the little Op. 78 *Sonata*, recorded by CBS in their New York studios almost three years earlier, Gould again consciously avoids lightness and charm, but his weighty, muscular approach to the first movement and his bright, sparky and ultimately hectoring view of the *Allegro vivace* are again magnetic.

Piano sonatas Nos. 27 in E min., Op. 90; 28 in A, Op. 101; 29 in B flat (Hammerklavier), Op. 106; 30 in E, Op. 109; 31 in A flat, Op. 110; 32 in C min., Op. 111.
☞ (B) *** Sony SB2K 53531 (2) [id.]. Charles Rosen.
☞ (B) *** Ph. Duo 438 374-2 (2) [id.]. Alfred Brendel.

Charles Rosen is one of the most commanding interpreters of Beethoven's longest and most taxing sonatas. His streak of toughness, his analytical powers (he has made a fascinating study in depth of the inner links) and his concentration make for an unforgettable experience. The first movement of the *Hammerklavier* is magnificently strong and the fast tempo – as near Beethoven's impossible metronome marking as is reasonable – makes for an absolute concentration and no sense of hastiness. The great *Adagio* (taken slower than in his first, American recording) is played with an inner depth that allows no sentimentality, and the finale has rarely if ever been played on record with such dynamic power and clarity. A performance even for those who otherwise follow Barenboim or Brendel in their Beethoven cycles. The little *E minor Sonata* begins a little gruffly, but later Rosen shows that he can encompass the softer mood of this very different work. In the visionary last two sonatas, less searingly intense than those preceding them, some may resist the uningratiating manner, but Rosen's commanding toughness compels attention, and repeated hearings are the more rewarding. The recordings, made at the EMI studios between November 1968 and July 1970, are firm and realistic, and allow a wide range of dynamic.

Reissued in Philips's Duo bargain series, this Brendel set of the late sonatas is certainly value for money. In the glorious *E minor Sonata*, Op. 90, there are some expressive rubati that may worry some listeners, but Brendel provides a thoughtful, sensitive reading of the *E major Sonata*, Op. 109. The *A major*, Op. 101, is one of the finest of his cycle, and the sheer beauty of tone in the *A flat major*, Op. 110, is most persuasive: the playing of a thoughtful dreamer. There is a tendency in the *Adagio* of Op. 111, beautifully played as it is, for the forward impulse to lose its spontaneity, and the carefully considered account of the *Hammerklavier* has not quite the fire and sense of spontaneity that marked Brendel's earlier account on Turnabout. Yet with the help of the Philips engineers the great *Adagio* has a genuinely hushed tone (which the forward balance on Turnabout prevented from registering) and this is undoubtedly a fine performance, very well recorded. Generally speaking, this is among the most distinguished Beethoven playing of the analogue era. The recordings were made in the 1970s and are most realistic and satisfying in the latest CD transfers. The documentation, too, can be commended.

Piano sonatas Nos. 27 in E min., Op. 90; 28 in A, Op. 101; 32 in C min., Op. 111.
☞ *** EMI Dig. CDC7 54599-2 [id.]. Stephen Kovacevich.

Nothing Stephen Kovacevich does is untouched by distinction and readers who recall his 1975 Beethoven LP of Opp. 110 and 111 on Philips will not be surprised to learn that this new disc of late Beethoven is very impressive indeed. Here is an artist who gets to the heart of this music, which (to quote Schnabel) is better than it can ever be played. As one would expect from this artist, it is entirely selfless and free from affectation. His Op. 90 is among the finest in the catalogue and the *A major*, Op. 101, is among the most serene since the eloquent account by Gilels on a beautifully recorded DG

LP. Its first movement has a subtlety of colour and tone that long resonates with the listener, and its short slow movement seems to commune with another world. The *C minor*, Op. 111, is a performance of stature, free from any attempt to beautify (though it is full of tonal beauties), and among the finest of this Olympian work to have appeared in recent years. The recording is excellent, and the only reservation to make is that some may be distracted by the pianist's breathing which is audible at moments of strain. This CD adds to (but does not displace) his earlier views on the work, which Philips should restore to circulation without delay.

Piano sonatas Nos. 28–32.
☞ ⊛ (M) *** EMI CDH7 64708-2 [id.]. Solomon.

EMI have been slow to reissue Solomon's classic performances of the late Beethoven *Sonatas*. His stroke prevented the great pianist from completing the cycle, but he did at least give us the last five. This is Beethoven pure and unadulterated; this music-making comes as near to the truth as any in the catalogue. They have something of the depth of Schnabel, the tonal beauty of Arrau, the selflessness and integrity of Kempff and the perfect pianism of Pollini on DG or the magisterial, early Brendel set. While Solomon has been ignored in the UK, his reputation in Germany has remained high, thanks to the advocacy of such authorities as Joachim Kayser. The *Hammerklavier sonata* is one of the greatest recordings of the work ever made (this is one of the few weaknesses in Schnabel's complete set) and few have matched – let alone surpassed – it. Opp. 109 and 111 were recorded in 1951, the *Hammerklavier* a year later; Opp. 90 and 110 in 1956, not long before he was struck down. The engineers have done wonders with the transfers. The sound emerges in startling freshness and fullness. Magisterial, thoughtful, deeply lyrical and commanding performances that make so many later versions sound quite shallow.

Piano sonata No. 29 (Hammerklavier), Op. 106.
*** DG Dig. 410 527-2 [id.]. Emil Gilels.

Gilels's *Hammerklavier* is a performance of supreme integrity, Olympian, titanic, subtle, imperious, one of the finest accounts ever recorded. However, the recording is close and bright and harder than ideal.

Piano sonatas Nos. 29 in B flat (Hammerklavier), Op. 106; 32 in C min., Op. 111.
☞ *** BBC MM 119. Edith Vogel.

This disc was offered briefly on the cover of the March 1994 edition of the BBC *Music Magazine*, and deserves to be more permanently available. Edith Vogel was a pianist inexplicably ignored by the recording world, but belatedly appreciated in the BBC. Her radio recordings of the *Hammerklavier* (done in the studio in January 1977) and of Op. 111, the last sonata of all (done live at St John's, Smith Square, in April 1985) have a power and thrusting intensity to match any, even if there is the odd smudge in the fingerwork. We hope that the disc may be taken up for separate issue. The analogue sound is naturally balanced.

Piano sonatas Nos. 30 in E, Op. 109; 31 in A flat, Op. 110.
*** DG Dig. 419 174-2 [id.]. Emil Gilels.
⊛ (M) (***) EMI mono CDH7 63787-2 [id.]. Myra Hess (with BACH: *Jesu, joy of man's desiring* and music by BEETHOVEN, BRAHMS, GRANADOS, MENDELSSOHN and D. SCARLATTI (***)).

On DG, both sonatas are given performances of stature that seek out their profoundest truths. Even when Gilels storms the greatest heights in the closing fugue of Op. 110, no fortissimo ever sounds percussive or strained.

These celebrated performances by Dame Myra Hess bring playing which is every bit as masterly and seraphic as one had remembered. At times, some might feel the need for a more firmly etched line (in the final movement of Op. 110, for instance), but most collectors will wonder at her great plasticity of touch and sheer tonal beauty. The record comes with a generous recital of encore pieces, including her famous arrangement of Bach's *Jesu, joy of man's desiring*. But it is for the Beethoven collector that these thoughtful and deeply musical performances will be essential.

Piano sonatas Nos. 30 in E, Op. 109; 31 in A flat, Op. 110; 32 in C min., Op. 111.
☞ *** MusicMasters Dig. 67098-2 [id.]. Vladimir Feltsman.
(BB) *** Naxos Dig. 8.550151 [id.]. Jenö Jandó.
☞ (BB) ** ASV CDQS 6064. John Lill.
☞ *(*) Decca Dig. 436 076-2 [id.]. Vladimir Ashkenazy.

Vladimir Feltsman, born in Moscow in 1952 and since 1987 established in the United States, demonstrates in the last three sonatas that age is not an essential even with the most searching

Beethoven works. Interestingly, Feltsman's recordings were supervised by the same recording producer as Goode's, Max Wilcox, and the clean, bright, well-focused sound reflects that. The sound underlines unexpected differences in Feltsman's approach to each of the sonatas. In the first movement of Op. 109 he is freely rhapsodic to the point of wildness, with the piano made to clatter, as it does in the central Scherzo too. The simple dedication of Feltsman's playing in the sublime last movement then takes one by surprise. Similarly, in Op. 110 too Feltsman's fresh, simple account of the measured paragraphs of the final fugue happily tends to cancel out any disappointment over the bright forcefulness earlier. Opus 111 then comes as a culmination, for here his many qualities focus splendidly, not just in the drama of the compressed first movement but in the spaciousness of the final *Arietta*.

The last three sonatas of Beethoven, offered in Naxos's Volume 4, are very imposing indeed in Jandó's hands. There is serenity and gravitas in these readings and a powerful control of structure.

In the hands of John Lill, Op. 109 is given a somewhat four-square performance, the structural freedom of the first movement underplayed and put into a strict sonata frame. Even the lyrical first movement of Op. 110, very slow and direct, keeps to the pattern of ruggedness, though the intensity of Lill's playing is never in doubt. The concentration in the *C minor* is well sustained, with the variations especially successful. The transfers to CD are expertly managed, the sound bold and realistic, if a little hard. This is Beethoven unvarnished, and the CD is worth its modest cost.

While Ashkenazy's latest thoughts on the last three Beethoven sonatas are not to be dismissed lightly, his new digital recording is not the success one might have hoped. The recording is far from ideally focused; it goes to the opposite extreme from the bright, forward image DG provide for so many of their pianists. This is not close enough, and the reverberant studio does not help. Nor are Ashkenazy's readings as fresh or thought-provoking as in his earlier disc – and there are idiosyncratic touches, too, which are unappealing (as in the slow movement of Op. 111). However, the distinctly unglamorous piano-sound is the major obstacle to a warm recommendation.

Piano sonata No. 32 in C min., Op. 111; 6 Bagatelles, Op. 126; Bagatelle in A min., 'Für Elise', WoO 59; Rondo a capriccio in G, Op. 129.
☞ * DG Dig. 435 881-2 [id.]. Anatol Ugorski.

Anatol Ugorski's Beethoven for DG has had an indifferent press so far and, as an example of the bizarre, his highly idiosyncratic account of Op. 111 far outdoes Pogorelich on the same label. He takes the best part of 40 minutes, and his changes of tempo in the variations seem guided by no real musical purpose. Undoubtedly there are some felicities in the course of this recital, but the wilfulness of this playing far offsets them. The usual, forward, clinical, DG piano balance does not enhance the attractions of this issue, which is not recommended. One star for the recording; none for the interpretation – and that is possibly erring on the generous side.

Miscellaneous piano music

Allegretto in C min., WoO 53; Andante favori, WoO 57; 'Für Elise', WoO 59; 6 Variations in F, Op. 34.
*** EMI CDC7 49793-2 [id.]. Melvyn Tan (fortepiano) – SCHUBERT: *Moments musicaux* etc. ***

Melvyn Tan is a spirited artist and an enormously persuasive exponent of the fortepiano. The *F major Variations* come off splendidly; this is a thoroughly enjoyable recital and is recorded with great realism and presence in The Maltings at Snape.

7 Bagatelles, Op. 33; 11 Bagatelles, Op. 119; 6 Bagatelles, Op. 126.
(B) *** Ph. 426 976-2. Stephen Kovacevich.
(BB) **(*) Naxos Dig. 8.550474 [id.]. Jenö Jandó.

Bagatelles, Op. 33; 119; 126; WoO 52 & 56.
☞ *** Chan. Dig. CHAN 9201 [id.]. John Lill.

Beethoven's *Bagatelles*, particularly those from Opp. 119 and 126, have often been described as chips from the master's workbench; but rarely if ever has that description seemed so apt as in these searchingly simple and completely spontaneous readings by Kovacevich.

John Lill's collection of Beethoven's *Bagatelles*, the fill-up for his fine *Concerto* cycle for Chandos, is here brought together. Characteristically he takes a serious view of these chips from the master's workbench, bringing out their relationship to some of the full masterpieces.

Jandó plays the early set of *Bagatelles*, which date from 1802, with a crisply rhythmic style, almost at times as if he was thinking of a fortepiano. Then in the later works he finds more depth of tone and is thoughtful as well as flamboyant. He has an excellent, modern, digital recording.

Bagatelles, Opp. 33 & 119; Fantasia in G min.; Variations on 'God save the King' & 'Rule Britannia'.
☞ *** EMI Dig. CDC7 54526-2. Melvyn Tan.

A recital with a difference. In 1816 Thomas Broadwood presented Beethoven with the celebrated piano for which he composed his last works, including the *Hammerklavier sonata* and the *C minor Sonata*, Op. 111. On Beethoven's death it passed into Liszt's possession and then into the collection of the Hungarian National Museum. Expert restoration work reveals an instrument that is very richly timbred and full-bodied, far more vibrant than any modern copy. Melvyn Tan plays these pieces with all the spontaneity and flair which he exhibits consistently and in the *G minor Fantasy* conveys an improvisatory quality far removed from the judicious, scholarly rectitude of so many period-instrument specialists. He could allow himself more time in some of the *Bagatelles*, but there are no real quibbles here in what is a record of enormous interest, offering refreshing insights into the sound-world with which Beethoven himself would have been familiar. The recording has great realism and presence.

7 Bagatelles, Op. 33; 6 Bagatelles, Op. 126; 6 Variations in F, Op. 34; 15 Variations with fugue in E flat (Eroica), Op. 35; 32 Variations on an original theme in C min., WoO 80.
☞ (M) *(**) Sony SM2K 52646 (2) [id.]. Glenn Gould (piano).

Glenn Gould's *Bagatelles* and *Variations* are a good deal better and less quirky than his Beethoven *Piano sonatas*, which are not competitive, given the number of great cycles in the catalogue. Gould fanatics can invest in them; others who are not converted can be assured that any eccentricity is positive and thought-provoking. Not a first choice (or anywhere near it) but deserving of a place in the catalogue.

6 Bagatelles, Op. 126; 6 Ecossaises, WoO 83; 'Für Elise', WoO 59; 15 Variations and fugue on a theme from Prometheus (Eroica variations), Op. 35.
*** Ph. 412 227-2 [id.]. Alfred Brendel.

Brendel may lack some of the sheer bravura of his own early playing in this collection of shorter pieces, but his consistent thoughtfulness and imagination bring out the truly Beethovenian qualities of even the most trivial pieces.

6 Bagatelles, Op. 126; Polonaise in C, Op. 89; Variations and fugue on a theme from Prometheus (Eroica variations), Op. 35.
*** Nimbus Dig. NIM 5017 [id.]. Bernard Roberts.

Bernard Roberts gives a characteristically fresh and forthright reading of the *Eroica variations*, recorded in exceptionally vivid sound. He may not have quite the dash of Brendel, but the crispness and clarity of his playing are most refreshing. The shorter pieces bring performances even more intense, with the *Bagatelles* for all their brevity given last-period intensity.

Variations on 'Quant'è più bello' (Paisiello), WoO 69; Variations on a Russian dance from 'Das Waldmädchen (Wranitsky), WoO 71. Variations on 'Nel cor più non mi sento' (Paisiello), WoO 70; Variations on 'Rule Britannia', WoO 79; 7 Variations on 'God Save the King', WoO 78; 32 Variations in C min., WoO 80; in F, Op. 34; 15 Variations and fugue in E flat (Eroica), Op. 35.
☞ ** Decca Dig. 436 834-2 [id.]. Olli Mustonen.

The young Finnish pianist has the benefit of excellent Decca engineering. He possesses a sophisticated keyboard palette and crisp articulation. There are many self-conscious touches, staccato endings to phrases and so on, that tend to draw attention to themselves and which many listeners will find unpleasing. There is much that is intelligent and stimulating in the course of these performances but too much that is idiosyncratic. What may stimulate when heard once in the course of a recital may prove increasingly irksome on repetition.

6 Variations in F, Op. 34; 6 Variations on 'Nel cor più non mi sento', WoO 70; 15 Variations and fugue on a theme from Prometheus in E flat (Eroica variations), Op. 35; 32 Variations in C min., WoO 80.
☞ (BB) **(*) Naxos Dig. 8.550676 [id.]. Jenö Jandó.

Jandó essays the same strong, direct style in his performances of the two major sets of variations that he does in the sonatas. Occasionally his forceful manner in Op. 35 and the *C minor Variations* reaches the point of brusqueness in its forceful accenting but no one could deny the strength of this playing. His approach is appropriately lighter in Op. 34 and the very agreeable short set based on the duet by Paisiello. Excellent recording, clear and vivid, to match the other records in his Naxos series.

6 Variations in F, Op. 34; 15 Variations and fugue on a theme from Prometheus in E flat (Eroica variations), Op. 35; 2 Rondos, Op. 51; Bagatelle: 'Für Elise', WoO 59.
*** Chan. Dig. CHAN 8616; *ABTD 1305* [id.]. Louis Lortie.

The Canadian pianist Louis Lortie is an artist of distinction; his readings have both grandeur and authority. This account of the *Eroica variations* belongs in exalted company and can be recommended alongside such magisterial accounts as that of Gilels.

6 Variations in F, Op. 34; 6 Variations in G on 'Nel cor più non mi sento', WoO 70; 5 Variations in D on 'Rule Britannia', WoO 79.
*** Ph. Dig. 432 093-2 [id.]. Alfred Brendel – SCHUMANN: *Symphonic études.* ***

This is among the best records Brendel has given us in recent years, full of intelligence and, in the *Rule Britannia* variations, wit. Exemplary recordings made in The Maltings, Snape.

6 Variations in D, Op. 76; in F, Op. 34; 15 Variations and fugue in E flat (Eroica), Op. 35.
☞ (**) Olympia stereo OCD 339 [id.]. Richter – SCHUMANN: *Etudes symphoniques.* **

Richter is Richter, but the sound here calls for lots of tolerance. The recordings emanate from the Ariolo label and were made in 1970. In the *F major Variations* the piano sounds very close and synthetic, and in the *D major*, Op. 76, this is compounded by an unacceptable degree of reverberation and shallow, clattery tone – it is quite awful. The *Eroica variations* are unflatteringly recorded and this sadly diminishes the attraction of this disc.

33 Variations on a waltz by Diabelli, Op. 120.
(B) *** Ph. 422 969-2. Stephen Kovacevich.
*** Ph. Dig. 426 232-2 [id.]. Alfred Brendel.
☞ DG Dig. 435 615-2 [id.]. Anatol Ugorski.

33 Variations on a waltz by Diabelli; 6 Bagatelles, Op. 126.
☞ (M) *** Vox Turnabout 115913-2 [id.]. Alfred Brendel.

33 Variations on a waltz by Diabelli; 32 Variations in C min.
*** ASV Dig. CDDCA 715 [id.]. Benjamin Frith.

Kovacevich gives one of the most deeply satisfying performances ever recorded. Avoiding the idiosyncrasies of most other interpreters, he may at times seem austere, but his concentration is magnetic from first to last.

Benjamin Frith gives a fresh, clear reading, tense and dedicated, which conveys Beethoven's mastery without exaggeration and no self-indulgence. Clear recording to match.

On Philips, Brendel, here working in the studio, captures the music's dynamism, the sense of an irresistible force building up this immense structure, section by section. It would be hard to imagine a more dramatic reading, sparked off by the cheeky wit of Brendel's treatment of the Diabelli theme itself. The whirlwind power of the whole performance is irresistible, and the piano sound is full and immediate.

Brendel's earlier, Vox/Turnabout recording is now available on an imported American CD. It is most realistically transferred. Although the balance is a bit close, it never sounded as real as this on LP and offers a powerful, commanding performance of Beethoven's most taxing piano work. As in his live performances, Brendel builds up the variations unerringly, but it is surprising to find to what degree he indulges in little accelerandos in each half of those variations which involve crescendos. Broadly his approach is romantic, with the *Adagio* variation, No. 29 (band 30 on the disc), made into a moving lament. Few performances of this work on record convey its continuity so convincingly. The recording is quite faithful, but not really soft enough in its pianissimos, although this comment is somewhat less applicable to the *Bagatelles*, beautifully done, which make a splendidly substantial encore, and an overall playing time of 73 minutes.

Anatol Ugorski's reading is so wilful and perverse, with speeds extreme in both directions, that any magnetism in his playing is nullified.

VOCAL MUSIC

Lieder: *Adelaide; Ich liebe Dich; Der Kuss; Resignation.*
(M) **(*) DG 429 933-2 [id.]. Fritz Wunderlich, Hubert Giesen – SCHUBERT: *Lieder;* SCHUMANN: *Dichterliebe.* ***

Wunderlich was thirty-five when he recorded these songs and the unique bloom of the lovely voice is beautifully caught. Though the accompanist is too metrical at times, the freshness of Wunderlich's singing makes one grieve again over his untimely death.

An die ferne Geliebte, Op. 98. Lieder: *Adelaide; L'amant impaziente; Es war einmal ein König; In questa tomba oscura; Maigesang; Zartliche Liebe.*
**(*) DG 415 189-2 [id.]. Dietrich Fischer-Dieskau, Joerg Demus – BRAHMS: *Lieder.* **(*)

Recorded in 1966, Fischer-Dieskau's DG Beethoven selection finds him at his vocal peak, and though Demus's accompaniment is not as imaginative as the singer received in other versions of these songs, Fischer-Dieskau's individuality is as positive as ever, with detail touched in as with no one else.

Bundeslied, Op. 122; Eligischer Gesang, Op. 118; King Stephen (incidental music), *Op. 117; Meeresstille und glückliche Fahrt (Calm sea and a prosperous voyage), Op. 112; Opferlied, Op. 121b.*
*** Sony Dig. CD 76404 [MK 33509]. Amb. S., LSO, Tilson Thomas.

Tilson Thomas's collection of Beethoven choral rarities plus the *King Stephen* incidental music makes an attractive out-of-the-way disc for Beethovenians. With excellent singing and playing, they are all enjoyable.

(i) *Choral Fantasia* (for piano, chorus & orchestra), *Op. 80;* (ii) *Missa solemnis in D, Op. 123.*
(M) *** Sony SM2K 47522 (2) [id.]. (i) Rudolf Serkin, (i; ii) Westminster Ch.; (ii) Farrell, Carol Smith, Lewis, Borg; NYPO, Bernstein – HAYDN: *Mass No. 12.* ***
☞ *(*) BMG/RCA Dig. 09026 60967-2 (2) [id.]. Orgonosova, Rappé, Heilmann, Rootering; (i) Oppitz; Bav. R. Ch. & SO, Sir Colin Davis.

Bernstein is at his most intense in this fine, dedicated account of Beethoven's supreme choral masterpiece. It is an inspirational performance, though it is a drawback that, like the Jochum set, it overlaps on to a second disc when, with an overall playing time of about 77 minutes, it could easily have been accommodated on a single CD. However, the couplings are recommendable and worth having, especially the Haydn (digital) *Theresia Mass.* Serkin's *Choral Fantasia* opens with a solo cadenza almost to rival Brendel's.
    During his years as music director of the Bavarian Radio Orchestra, Sir Colin Davis's view of Beethoven, always direct, has grown broader, not just in speeds but in manner. So both the *Kyrie* and the opening of the *Credo* are so measured, with rhythms evenly stressed, that they do not avoid stodginess. That the chorus is balanced rather distantly also mutes the impact, and the soloists do not make a perfect match, with the tenor, Uwe Heilmann, sounding fluttery. Having the *Choral Fantasia* as makeweight on the second disc is some compensation but hardly justifies a strong recommendation in a crowded marketplace.

Christus am Olberge, Op. 85.
(M) **(*) Sony MPK 45878 [id.]. Raskin, Lewis, Herbert Beattie, Temple University Choirs, Phd. O, Ormandy.
**(*) HM HMC 905181 [id.]. Pick-Hieronimi, Anderson, Von Halem, Ch. & O Nat. de Lyon, Baudo.

Ormandy is at his most purposeful and warmly understanding, and the soloists are outstandingly fine, with the pure-toned Judith Raskin very aptly cast as the Seraph and with Richard Lewis at his freshest and most expressive as Jesus.
    Monica Pick-Hieronimi, a singer of some power, brings Leonore-like qualities to her role as Seraph. Baudo directs an energetic and lively account of it which, if lacking the utmost refinement of detail, generates urgency and breadth in the fine closing section.

(i) *Egmont: Overture and incidental music* (complete), *Op. 84;* (ii) *Leonora overture No. 3.*
☞ (B) **(*) Discover Dig. DICD 920114. (i) Miriam Gauci, Dirk Schortemeier, Belgian R. & TV O; (ii) LPO; Rahbari.

On the bargain Discover label, Alexander Rahbari offers all ten movements of Beethoven's *Egmont* music, not just the selection made by Szell. Such rarities as the third and fourth entr'actes and the melodrama, *Susse Schlaf,* with Schortemeier as the speaker, are chips from the master's workbench rather than significant pieces, but together with the well-known items they present an attractive whole. Both in *Egmont* and in the *Leonora No. 3* overture (with the LPO) Rahbari conducts crisp, well-sprung, often exciting performances, with Miriam Gauci the warm-toned soprano. Atmospheric recording, pleasantly reverberant.

(i) *King Stephen* (incidental music), *Op. 117: Overture and excerpts. The Ruins of Athens* (incidental music), *Op. 113: Overture and excerpts.* (ii) *The Creatures of Prometheus overture.*
(B) *** Hung. White Label HRC 118 [id.]. (i) Hungarian R. & TV Ch., Budapest PO, Oberfrank;

(ii) Hungarian State O, Kórodi.

Beethoven's incidental music, though not always characteristic, is full of imagination and vitality. The fervour of the singing of the Hungarian Radio Chorus adds much to the sparkle of the performances, admirably conducted by Géza Oberfrank; as an apt encore, András Kórodi directs a lively account of *The Creatures of Prometheus overture.*

Mass in C, Op. 86.
(M) *** Decca 430 361-2 [id.]. Palmer, Watts, Tear, Keyte, St John's College, Cambridge, Ch., ASMF, Guest – BRUCKNER: *Motets.* ***

(i) *Mass in C, Op. 86; Meeresstille und glückliche Fahrt (Calm sea and a prosperous voyage), Op. 112.*
☞ *** DG Dig. 435 391-2 [id.]. Margiono, Robbin, Kendall, Miles, Monteverdi Ch., O Révolutionnaire et Romantique, Gardiner.
**(*) Decca Dig. 417 563-2 [id.]. (i) Dunn, Zimmermann, Beccaria, Krause; Berlin RIAS Chamber Ch. & RSO, Chailly.

(i) *Mass in C, Op. 86. The Ruins of Athens (Overture and incidental music), Op. 113.*
(M) *** EMI CDM7 64385-2 [id.]. (i) Vyvyan, Sinclair, Lewis, Nowakowski, Beecham Ch. Soc.; RPO, Beecham.

With a first-rate team of soloists and excellent choral singing, Beecham leads the field. The fill-up of incidental music is equally vibrant, and the transfer is vivid and lively with clear choral sound.

It is only in relation to the vast vision of the *Missa solemnis* that the *Mass in C* unfairly tends to be regarded as less than a masterpiece. When Beethoven in his mid-thirties was asked to write a setting of the Mass for Prince Esterhazy, as Haydn had done in his later years, the result was regarded as so new and radical that traditionalists took fright. That is a quality which Gardiner's performance brings out. With clean textures and sprung rhythms married to an expressive warmth not regularly associated with period manners, this is just as refreshing a performance as Gardiner's earlier, prize-winning account of the *Missa solemnis.* Aptly clear-toned soloists match the freshness of the Monteverdi Choir: Charlotte Margiono, Catherine Robbin, William Kendall and Alastair Miles. As an imaginatively chosen coupling Gardiner offers the dramatic soprano scena, *Ah! perfido,* with Charlotte Margiono as soloist, and the brief choral cantata, *Meeresstille und glückliche Fahrt.*

George Guest's reading is designedly intimate. Naturally, with boys' voices in the choir and a smaller band of singers, the results are less dramatic; but, with splendid recording, the scale works admirably and the result is refreshing.

The Chailly performance is on the right expansive scale. The solo team is also very good although the tenor, Bruno Beccaria, is too histrionically operatic in style. The recording has the widest dynamic range.

(i) *Mass in C, Op. 86;* (ii) *Missa solemnis, Op. 123.*
☞ (B) **(*) Ph. Duo 438 362-2 (2) [id.]. (i) Eda-Pierre, Moll; (ii) Tomowa-Simtow, Lloyd; (i; ii) Payne, Tear, L. Symphony Ch., LSO, C. Davis.

The freshness of the choral singing and the clarity of the sound make Sir Colin Davis's an outstandingly dramatic version of the *Mass in C.* The cry, *'Passus'* ('suffered'), in the *Credo* has rarely been so tellingly presented on record, and the quartet of soloists is first rate. As it is in the *Missa solemnis,* and this too is a fine performance, if not consistently generating quite the same degree of intensity: this is especially noticeable when one moves to the second disc, which opens with the *Agnus Dei* of the *Missa solemnis,* where there is a fall-off in concentration. The 1977 recording, well focused, spacious and atmospheric, is given a natural, concert-hall balance and the CD transfer is first class. Good documentation.

Missa solemnis in D, Op. 123.
☞ *** DG Dig. 435 770-2 (2) [id.]. Studer, Norman, Domingo, Moll, Leipzig R. Ch., Swedish R. Ch., VPO, Levine.
*** DG Dig. 429 779-2; *429 779-4* [id.]. Margiono, Robbin, Kendall, Miles, Monteverdi Ch., E. Bar. Soloists, Eliot Gardiner.
*** EMI Dig. CDC7 49950-2 [id.]. Vaness, Meier, Blochwitz, Tschammer, Tallis Chamber Ch., ECO, Tate.
☞ **(*) Teldec/Warner Dig. 9031 74884-2 (2). Mei, Lipovšek, Rolfe Johnson, Holl, Schoenberg Ch., COE, Harnoncourt.
☞ **(*) Erato/Warner Dig. 4509 91731-2 [id.]. Kiberg, Meier, Aler, Holl, Chicago Symphony Ch. & O, Barenboim.

(M) (**(*)) BMG/RCA mono GD 60272 (2) [60272-RG-2]. Marshall, Merriman, Conley, Hines, Robert Shaw Ch., NBC SO, Toscanini – CHERUBINI: *Requiem.* (**(*))

(i) *Missa solemnis in D;* (ii) *Choral Fantasia in C, Op. 80.*

(M) **(*) EMI CMS7 69538-2 (2) [Ang. CDMB 69538-2]. (i) Söderström, Höffgen, Kmentt, Talvela, New Philh. Ch.; (ii) Barenboim, Alldis Ch.; New Philh. O, Klemperer.

Just two years after Herbert von Karajan died, the 1991 Salzburg Festival honoured its late music director in a performance of Beethoven's *Missa solemnis.* The choice of conductor surprised many – James Levine, very much a favourite at Salzburg over Karajan's last years, but one who with his American background would not normally be counted in the central Beethovenian line represented by Karajan himself. That the quartet of soloists could not have been starrier – Cheryl Studer, Jessye Norman, Plácido Domingo and Kurt Moll – and the fact that DG recorded the two performances live may point to media hype rather than any serious devotional purpose. As the discs consistently demonstrate, the results have an incandescence that silences any doubts. In conveying the atmosphere of a great occasion, as this work should, this version has no rival, and the DG engineers have obtained the richest, weightiest sound yet on any recording made in the tricky Salzburg venue, not least from the massed choruses. The two-disc format may be extravagant, but for such an intense visionary experience, defying the conventional view of Levine, this is a version not to be missed.

Gardiner's inspired reading matches even the greatest of traditional performances on record in dramatic weight and spiritual depth, while bringing out the white heat of Beethoven's inspiration with new intensity. Though the performers are fewer in number than in traditional accounts, the Monteverdi Choir sings with bright, luminous tone, and the four soloists are excellent. The recording is vivid too. Even those who normally resist period performance will find this very compelling.

Tate, with chorus and orchestra on a modest chamber scale, gains in incisiveness and loses hardly at all in weight, with bright, fresh singing from the Tallis Chamber Choir. The soloists make an outstanding quartet, with Hans Tschammer adding to Tate's deeply devotional treatment of the *Agnus Dei.* The well-balanced recording is at rather a low level, but sounds well at full volume.

The glory of Klemperer's set is the superb choral singing of the New Philharmonia Chorus. The soloists are less happily chosen: Waldemar Kmentt seems unpleasantly hard and Elisabeth Söderström does not sound as firm as she can be. It was, however, a happy idea to include the *Choral Fantasia* as a bonus.

Like Levine's performance a year earlier, Harnoncourt's was recorded live at the Salzburg Festival but it represents the new, post-Karajan era at that grandest of music festivals. Like Harnoncourt's Beethoven symphony cycle, this performance conveys the dramatic tensions of a live occasion, with finely matched forces performing with freshness and clarity. As with Levine, the devotional element is clear, though the rather distanced sound makes the results marginally less involving than either the Levine version or John Eliot Gardiner's period-performance.

Daniel Barenboim takes a weighty view of the *Missa solemnis,* but the magnificence of the Chicago Symphony Chorus, trained as it has been for generations by Margaret Hillis, is reduced when the recording-balance sets it well behind the orchestra. As recorded in Symphony Hall, Chicago, a difficult venue, the sound is not ideally clear, and the occasional flaw in ensemble suggests a live performance, though that is not acknowledged. The two discs, at reduced price, come in a single jewel-case.

Toscanini's tensely dramatic account of the *Missa solemnis* leaves you in no doubt as to the work's magisterial power, even if the absence of a true pianissimo makes it less meditative than usual. Fine singing from choir and soloists alike, though the typical harshness of the recording is unappealing.

Fidelio (complete).

🏵 (M) *** EMI CMS7 69324-2 (2) [Ang. CDMB 69324]. Ludwig, Vickers, Frick, Berry, Crass, Philh. Ch. & O, Klemperer.

*** Ph. Dig. 426 308-2 (2) [id.]. Jessye Norman, Goldberg, Moll, Wlaschiha, Coburn, Blochwitz, Dresden State Op. Ch. & O, Haitink.

☞ (M) *** EMI mono CHS7 64901-2 (2) [id.]. Kirsten Flagstad, Julius Patzak, Paul Schoeffler, Josef Greindl, Elisabeth Schwarzkopf, Anton Dermota, V. State Op. Ch., VPO, Furtwängler.

☞ (M) (**) BMG/RCA mono GD 60273 (2) [62073-RG]. Bampton, Peerce, Laderoute, Steber, Belarsky, Janssen, Moscona, Ch., NBC SO, Toscanini.

☞ * Decca Dig. 436 627-2 (2). Schnaut, Protschka, Welker, Rydl, Ziesak, Heilmann, Krause, V. State Op. Concert Ch., VPO, Christoph von Dohnányi.

Klemperer's great set of *Fidelio* sweeps the board in its new format. Its incandescence and spiritual strength are unique, with wonderful performances from all concerned and with a final scene in which, more than in any other recording, the parallel with the finale of the *Choral Symphony* is underlined.

The unsurpassed nobility of Jessye Norman's voice is perfectly matched to this noblest of operas. In detail of characterization she may not outshine Christa Ludwig, Klemperer's firm and incisive Leonore, but her reading is consistently rich and beautiful, like those rivals bringing a new revelation. With excellent digital sound and with strong, forthright conducting from Haitink, this is the finest of modern versions, even if it does not replace Klemperer or Karajan.

Taken from performances at the Salzburg Festival in 1950, with Wilhelm Furtwängler conducting an incomparably starry cast, this should not be confused with the studio recording he made with some of the same cast two years later. This is an Austrian Radio recording, previously available in pirated versions, but here treated to sound which captures the voices on stage with astonishing vividness. The epic scale of Kirsten Flagstad's voice as Leonore sometimes blasts the microphone, but it is a joy to hear such forthright power and security in a role nowadays too often given to squally singers. Elisabeth Schwarzkopf is a delight as Marzelline, vivacious in the dialogue and masterfully sustaining Furtwängler's expansive speed for the Act I quartet. With dialogue included, this is even more compelling than Furtwängler's studio recording, also with Julius Patzak as a superb Florestan, but with Paul Schoeffler a powerful Pizarro and Josef Greindl as Rocco.

Recorded in December 1944, when victory was in sight in the Second World War, this was the first of the concert performances of complete operas that Toscanini conducted in New York. Though the sound is even drier and less helpful to voices than in his latest NBC opera-recordings, the performance is characteristically incandescent. There is no attempt at a dramatic presentation. This is just Beethoven's score with no dialogue whatever, not even in the great confrontation of the Act II quartet; but that makes one concentrate the more on the music, which is plainly what Toscanini wants. Typically his choice of soloists favours voices that are clean-cut and accurate rather than conventionally beautiful, and it is good to have Rose Bampton as a powerful Leonore, an American singer too little appreciated in Europe and too little recorded. Eleanor Steber is a weightier Marzelline than usual, but the clarity and precision are impressive, well matched by the Jaquino of Joseph Laderoute. Sidor Belarsky as Rocco is similarly clean of attack and, though Herbert Janssen is not as fresh-toned as he was earlier, this is a strong and characterful performance. As Florestan, Jan Peerce, Toscanini's favourite American tenor of the time, sings cleanly too if not with great imagination. The transfer follows the honest if unflattering pattern favoured in RCA's Toscanini Edition.

The great merit of the latest Decca version, using its magnificent studio in the Konzerthaus in Vienna, is the spectacular sound. Never has Beethoven's score glowed so richly on disc as in this opulent and beautifully balanced recording, with the Vienna Philharmonic under Christoph von Dohnányi sounding sumptuous, with incandescent singing from the Vienna State Opera Choir and vividly convincing production of the spoken dialogue. The irony is that the effort achieves so little, when this is the worst-sung *Fidelio* in years, one that does not begin to match the classic sets of the past under such conductors as Klemperer, Karajan, Furtwängler or Fricsay. The main problem is that almost all the principals are wobblers. By far the worst culprit is the Leonore of Gabriele Schnaut, alone making the set unrecommendable. Quite apart from her ill-focused wobbling, she regularly lets out painful yowls of indeterminate pitch. The great *Abscheulicher*, so far from being a vocal climax, comes to sound like a Disney farmyard, with her piercing top notes the steadiest she manages. Ruth Ziesak as Marzelline is the one principal who, with a warm, sweet tone, focuses well, singing with animation to create a rounded character. Both Hartmut Welker's Don Pizarro and Kurt Rydl's Rocco are distractingly unsteady on sustained notes, and Uwe Heilmann as Jaquino whines disagreeably, while Josef Protschka as Florestan, after starting well, also finds it hard to sing sustained notes without at least a judder. Ironically the best-sung solo passage comes in the glorious, hushed ensemble in the Act II finale, beginning with Leonore's *O Gott, welch'ein Augenblick*.

Fidelio: highlights.
(M) *** EMI CDM7 63077-2. Dernesch, Vickers, Ridderbusch, Van Dam, Kelemen, German Op. Ch., BPO, Karajan.

Those who acquire Klemperer's classic set will welcome just under an hour of well-chosen highlights from the fine alternative Karajan recording, made in 1970.

Bellini, Vincenzo (1801–35)

Beatrice di Tenda (complete); Arias: *Norma: Casta diva. I Puritani: Son vergin vezzosa; Oh rendetemi la speme. La sonnambula: Ah, non credea mirarti.*
☞ (M) *** Decca 433 706-2 (3) [id.]. Sutherland, Pavarotti, Opthof, Veasey, Ward, Amb. Op. Ch.,
   LSO, Bonynge.

Beatrice di Tenda was Bellini's last opera but one, coming after *La sonnambula* and *Norma* and before *I Puritani*. It had an unfortunate birth, for the composer had to go to the law courts to wring the libretto out of his collaborator, Romani; the result is not exactly compelling dramatically. The story involves a whole string of unrequited loves. Bellini always intended to revise the score but failed to do so before his death. As it is, the piece remains essentially a vehicle for an exceptional prima donna with a big enough voice and brilliant enough coloratura. Dame Joan Sutherland has made it her own in recent years – this recording was made in 1966 – and although here she indulges in some of the 'mooning' one hoped she had left behind, there are many dazzling examples of her art. The other star of the set is Richard Bonynge, whose powers as a Bellini conductor are most impressive. The supporting cast could hardly be better, with Pavarotti highly responsive. The recording, made in Walthamstow Assembly Hall, is of Decca's best vintage and it has transferred splendidly to CD, with vivid atmosphere and colour. Four famous arias are provided as a filler: one from Sutherland's 1964 *Norma*, two from her 1963 *I Puritani* and one from the 1962 *La sonnambula*.

Norma (complete).
(M) *** Decca 425 488-2 (3) [id.]. Sutherland, Horne, Alexander, Cross, Minton, Ward, London
   Symphony Ch., LSO, Bonynge.
**(*) Decca Dig. 414 476-2 (3) [id.]. Sutherland, Pavarotti, Caballé, Ramey, Welsh Nat. Op. Ch. &
   O, Bonynge.
(M) **(*) EMI CMS7 63000-2 (3) [Ang. CDMC 63000]. Callas, Corelli, Ludwig, Zaccharia, Ch. &
   O of La Scala, Milan, Serafin.

Norma: highlights.
(M) *** Decca 421 886-2 [id.] (from above complete recording with Sutherland, Horne; cond.
   Bonynge).
(M) **(*) EMI CDM7 63091-2 (from above complete recording with Callas, Corelli; cond. Serafin).

In her first, mid-1960s recording of *Norma*, Sutherland was joined by an Adalgisa in Marilyn Horne whose control of florid singing is just as remarkable as Sutherland's own, and who sometimes even outshines the heroine in musical imagination. The other soloists are very good indeed. Overall this is a most compelling performance, helped by the conducting of Richard Bonynge, and the Walthamstow recording is vivid but also atmospheric in its CD format.

Dame Joan Sutherland was fifty-eight when her second *Norma* recording was made. The conjunction of Sutherland with Pavarotti and Caballé does not always work easily. Though Pavarotti is in some ways the set's greatest strength, easily expressive yet powerful as Pollione, Caballé as Adalgisa seems determined to outdo Sutherland in mooning manner, cooing self-indulgently. Full, brilliant, well-balanced recording of the complete score.

By the time Callas came to record her 1960 stereo version, the tendency to hardness and unsteadiness in the voice above the stave, always apparent, had grown more serious, but the interpretation was as sharply illuminating as ever, a unique assumption, helped by Christa Ludwig as Adalgisa, while Corelli sings heroically. Serafin as ever is the most persuasive of Bellini conductors.

Il Pirata (complete).
☞ (M) ** EMI CMS7 64169-2 (2). Cappuccilli, Caballé, Martí, Raimondi, Rome R. & TV Ch. & O,
   Gavazzeni.

This is the first complete recording of *Il Pirata*, the composer's third opera, written for La Scala and first produced in 1827. In the best traditions of Italian opera, in the finale the pirate-hero is killed, his rival is condemned to death, and the heroine loses her mind. With a not very promising scenario the opera is too long for its material. Caballé is well suited to the role of the heroine, though by her finest standards there is some carelessness in her singing – clumsy changes of register and less than the expected beauty of tonal contrast. Nor is the conducting and presentation sparkling enough to mask the comparative poverty of Bellini's invention at this early stage of his career. Bernabé Martí makes a fair stab at the difficult part of the pirate. The 1970 recording flatters the voices and has plenty of atmosphere but it is not as vividly projected as the best Decca offerings from this period.

I Puritani (complete).
*** Decca 417 588-2 (3). Sutherland, Pavarotti, Ghiaurov, Luccardi, Caminada, Cappuccilli,
ROHCG Ch. & O, Bonynge.

Whereas her earlier set was recorded when Sutherland had adopted a soft-grained style, with
consonants largely eliminated and a tendency to lag behind the beat, this time her singing is fresher
and brighter. Pavarotti shows himself a remarkable Bellini stylist, Ghiaurov and Cappuccilli make up
an impressive cast, and the only disappointing contributor is Anita Caminada in the small role of
Enrichetta. Vivid, atmospheric recording.

La Sonnambula (complete).
*** Decca Dig. 417 424-2 (2) [id.]. Sutherland, Pavarotti, Della Jones, Ghiaurov, L. Op. Ch., Nat.
PO, Bonynge.
(***) EMI mono CDS7 47378-8 (2) [CDCB 47377]. Callas, Monti, Cossotto, Zaccaria, Ratti, La
Scala, Milan, Ch. and O, Votto.

Sutherland's singing here is even more affecting and more stylish than her earlier version, generally
purer and more forthright, if with diction still clouded at times. The challenge of singing opposite
Pavarotti adds to the bite of the performance, crisply and resiliently controlled by Bonynge.
   Substantially cut, the Callas version was recorded in mono in 1957, yet it gives a vivid picture of
the diva at the peak of her powers. Nicola Monti makes a strong rather than a subtle contribution
but blends well with Callas in the duets; and Fiorenza Cossotto is a good Teresa.

Ben-Haim, Paul (1897–1984)

Violin concerto.
☞ *** EMI Dig. CDC7 54296-2 [id.]. Perlman, Israel PO, Mehta – CASTELNUOVO-TEDESCO:
Concerto No. 2. ***

Perlman's coupling of concertos by Castelnuovo-Tedesco and Ben-Haim brings a heartfelt tribute to
his Jewish background. These are live recordings, made in the Mann Auditorium in Tel Aviv, happily
with the orchestral sound less brutally dry than usual, here given an acceptable bloom. Ben-Haim,
born in 1897 in Munich, started life as Paul Frankenburger, but after fleeing from Hitler and settling
in Palestine in 1933, he adopted his new Hebraic name. The Hindemithian vigour of the outer
movements of this compact work – with a march theme dominating the first movement and an even
jauntier main theme over oompah rhythm in the finale – readily gives way to Bloch-like melodic
writing, with augmented intervals reflecting the music of the synagogue. The central *Andante
affetuoso* too is a simple Jewish song, with the main melody returning at the end stratospherically
high. As in the Castelnuovo-Tedesco work, Perlman is inspired to some of his most masterly playing,
not just breathtakingly brilliant but deeply felt.

Sweet Psalmist of Israel.
(M) **(*) Sony SM2K 47533 (2). Marlowe, Stavrache, NYPO, Bernstein – BLOCH: *Sacred service;*
FOSS: *Song of songs.* ***

As the biblical King David was a versatile musician, Ben-Haim represents him here by the use of both
concertante harp and (more dubiously) harpsichord in his vividly scored triptych. The recording is
balanced very forwardly, with the microphones too close, especially to the solo instruments. However,
the early movements have a certain textural charm.

Benjamin, George (born 1960)

(i) *Ringed by the flat horizon.* (ii) *At first light. A Mind of winter.*
*** Nimbus Dig. NI 5075 [id.]. (i) BBC SO, Elder; (ii) Penelope Walmsley-Clark, L. Sinf.,
composer.

Ringed by the flat horizon is a 20-minute orchestral piece, with the big climax masterfully built. *A
Mind of winter* is a 9-minute setting of *The Snowman* by Wallace Stevens, beautifully sung by the
soprano Penelope Walmsley-Clark. Sound of great warmth and refinement to match the music make
this a collection well worth exploring.

Piano sonata.
☞ ** Nimbus Single NI 1415 [id.]. Composer.

George Benjamin is one of the most imaginative composers of the younger generation. His *Piano sonata* dates from 1978 when he was still a student at the Paris Conservatoire. The influences are predominantly Gallic, and in particular the music of Messiaen (hardly surprising, considering that he studied with both that master and Yvonne Loriod). Benjamin is also a very good pianist, but the recording, made in 1980, is not quite three-star and sounds a bit synthetic. A 'single', this runs to 22 minutes 26 seconds.

Bennett, Richard Rodney (born 1936)

Guitar concerto (for guitar and chamber ensemble).
☞ (M) *** BMG/RCA 09026 61598-2. Julian Bream, Melos Ens., Atherton – ARNOLD: *Concerto;* RODRIGO: *Concierto de Aranjuez.* ***

Bennett's concerto, written in 1970, is dedicated to Bream. It is imaginatively conceived, and its variety of texture, glittering and transparent, consistently intrigues the ear. If the work's idiom and language start out from the twelve-tone system, there is nothing difficult for the listener to assimilate. The central *Andante lento* has recognizable melody and haunting atmosphere, while Latin American percussion instruments add to the rhythmic exoticism of the infectious *Con brio* finale. The performance, like its Arnold coupling, is definitive and the 1972 recording is first class in every way.

Bennett, Robert Russell (1894–1981)

Symphonic songs for band.
(M) *** Mercury 432 009-2 [id.]. Eastman Wind Ens., Fennell – HOLST: *Hammersmith* ***; JACOB: *William Byrd suite* ***; WALTON: *Crown Imperial.* *** ⊛

Bennett's triptych, not surprisingly, relies more on colouristic manipulation and sonority than on content. Marvellous playing and Mercury's best recording. The disc also includes a *Fanfare and allegro* by Clifton Williams.

Benoit, Peter (1834–1901)

Hoogmis (High Mass).
☞ (BB) *(**) Discover Dig. DICD 920178 [id.]. Donald George, Belgian R. & TV Philharmonic Ch., Koninklijk Vlaams Antwerp Music Conservatoire Ch. & Caecilia Chorale, Gemengd Ars Musica Merksem Ch., Zingende Wandelkring Saint Norbertus Ch., Belgian R. & TV PO, Rahbari.

The bargain Discover label offers a fascinating rarity, the *Hoogmis* (*High Mass*), by the Belgian composer, Peter Benoit, a contemporary of Brahms. Alexander Rahbari's account with the BRTN Philharmonic Orchestra of Brussels and massed choirs, with the tenor, Donald George, taking the solos in the *Benedictus* and *Dona nobis pacem*, has all the thrust you need for an ambitious work lasting 55 minutes. With themes square-cut rather than individual and with crisply effective choral writing, the piece echoes Beethoven's *Missa solemnis* rather than any French model. The trouble is that the live recording, though atmospheric and full of presence, brings washy sound, and starts without warning.

Bentzon, Niels Viggo (born 1919)

Feature on René Descartes, Op. 357.
☞ **(*) BIS CD 79 [id.]. Danish Nat. R. O, Schmidt – JORGENSON: *To love music;* NORBY: *The Rainbow snake.* ***

Niels Viggo Bentzon is the most prolific living Danish composer with some 500 works to his credit, including 20 symphonies and an equal number of piano sonatas, 15 piano concertos and more than a dozen quartets. He is directly descended from the nineteenth-century Danish composer, J. P. E. Hartmann (whose daughter Sophie married Niels Gade), and his cousin, Jørgen Bentzon, was also an accomplished composer. *Krönik om René Descartes* ('Feature on René Descartes') comes from 1975, and this recording was made at its première that year. The first movement gives a 'musical version of the Cartesian vortex which refers to a medieval notion of rotating heavenly bodies moving at enormous speed'; in other movements we are at the centre of the Aristotelean storm, and the final movement addresses Descartes' celebrated proposition, *Cogito ergo sum.* There are occasional flashes during its 27-minute duration that remind one of his best and most visionary music and, although there are enough good things to make it worth investigating, it is not a recommended or even characteristic entry-point into his world. An eminently well-prepared performance and good recording.

Symphonies Nos. 3, Op. 46 (1947); 4 (Metamorphoses), Op. 55 (1949).
☞ *** Marco Polo DaCapo DCCD 9102 [id.]. Aarhus SO, Ole Schmidt.

In 1981 the Aarhus Orchestra and Ole Schmidt recorded four of Niels Viggo Bentzon's symphonies (the above two and Nos. 5 and 7). His music fuses something of the lean, rhythmic neo-classicism of Stravinsky, the contrapuntal vitality of Hindemith and the open-air diatonicism of Nielsen. Both the symphonies recorded here are teeming with invention: the pastoral opening of the *Third* unleashes a rich flow of ideas, all of memorable quality. The *Fourth* (*Metamorphoses*) is a most imaginative work, music of real vision and individuality, powerful, concentrated and inventive. It is quite unlike anything else in music and deserves the strongest recommendation. Along with the *Sixth* and *Seventh Symphonies* of Holmboe, this is arguably the finest Nordic symphony after Nielsen and Ole Schmidt, and the Aarhus orchestra play it with all the conviction and passion they can muster. Although, ideally, the acoustic of the Aarhus hall is not quite ample enough for big climaxes, the recording is very good indeed, with plenty of detail and a good balance. Two remarkable works.

Berg, Alban (1885–1935)

Chamber concerto for piano, violin & 13 wind.
*** Teldec/Warner Dig. 2292 46019-2; *2292 46019-4* [id.]. Maisenberg, COE, Holliger –
    SCHOENBERG: *Chamber symphony.* ***

(i) *Chamber concerto;* (ii) *Violin concerto.*
(M) *** Decca Analogue/Dig. 430 349-2 [id.]. (i) Pauk, Crossley, L. Sinf., Atherton; (ii) Kyung Wha
    Chung, Chicago SO, Solti.

György Pauk and Paul Crossley are outstanding soloists, the Sinfonietta plays with precision as well as commitment, and the 1980 analogue recording is excellent, cleanly detailed yet not too dry. Kyung Wha Chung's fine 1983 version of the *Violin concerto* may not be as powerful as Perlman (at full price), but her tenderness and poetry bring an added dimension to the music.

Those wanting a modern digital recording, and for whom the coupling with Schoenberg is suitable, will find the Teldec version gives every satisfaction. It observes the long repeat in the finale, which radically affects the balance of movements. Excellent recording.

(i) *Chamber concerto;* (ii) *4 Pieces for clarinet and piano, Op. 5; Piano sonata, Op. 1.*
(M) *** DG 423 237-2 [id.]. Barenboim with (i) Zukerman & Ens. InterContemporain, Boulez; (ii)
    Antony Pay.

Boulez sets brisk tempi in the *Chamber concerto*, seeking to give the work classical incisiveness. The result is characterful and convincing. In the apt coupling, Antony Pay is an outstanding soloist.

Violin concerto.
*** DG 413 725-2 [id.]. Itzhak Perlman, Boston SO, Ozawa – STRAVINSKY: *Concerto.* ***
☞ *** Teldec/Warner Dig. 2292 46449-2 [id.]. Zehetmair, Philh. O, Heinz Holliger – HARTMANN:
    Concerto funèbre; JANACEK: *Violin concerto.* ***
☞ *** DG Dig. 437 093-2 [id.]. Mutter, Chicago SO, Levine – RIHM: *Gesungene Zeit; Time
    chant.* ***
(M) *** EMI CDM7 63989-2 [id.]. Sir Yehudi Menuhin, BBC SO, Boulez – BLOCH: *Violin concerto.*
    ***
(M) *** DG 431 740-2. Szeryng, Bav. RSO, Kubelik – SCHOENBERG: *Concertos.* **(*)

The Berg *Concerto* currently must outstrip most other modern concertos, if the CD catalogues are an accurate barometer of taste. There are more than twice as many versions than of the Bartók or the Walton; only the Prokofiev *D major concerto* has comparable representation. Perlman's performance is totally commanding. The Boston orchestra accompanies superbly and, though the balance favours the soloist, the recording is excellent.

The Teldec recording by Thomas Zehetmair and the Philharmonia Orchestra under Heinz Holliger is one of the best to appear for a long time. Zehetmair plays with great sensitivity and a natural eloquence that many will prefer to the much (and rightly) admired account by Mutter on DG. That has tremendous brilliance and panache, but the glitzy elegance and slight coolness are less affecting than Zehetmair's reading. His version is less sensational and brings you closer to the heart of this poignant music. It offers more interesting couplings in the form of the Hartmann *Concerto funèbre* and the fragmentary Janáček *Concerto* of 1927-8. The recording, made at The Maltings in Snape, is of exemplary clarity and has great presence.

Anne-Sophie Mutter begins the *Concerto* with a pianissimo of such delicacy that it has one's ears pricking. She proceeds to give an intensely passionate reading, both freely expressive and intensely purposeful, with James Levine and the Chicago orchestra matching her in subtle shading. As an imaginative coupling, Mutter offers a concerto written for her by the 40-year-old German composer, Wolfgang Rihm.

Menuhin's is a warm and vibrant performance and, though technically this is not as dashing or immaculate a performance as several others on record, it is one that compels admiration on its own terms of greatness.

Henryk Szeryng, too, gives a persuasive, perceptive and sympathetic account of this fine work, and is well accompanied by the Bavarian orchestra under Kubelik.

(i) *Violin concerto;* (ii) *Lyric suite.*
☞ (***) Testament mono SBT1004 [id.]. (i) Louis Krasner, BBC SO, Anton Webern; (ii) Galimir Qt.

This CD is of enormous interest as it brings back to life a broadcast of the *Violin concerto* by Louis Krasner who commissioned it and gave its first performance (and who subsequently made the first commercial recording on 78-r.p.m. discs). Webern had been due to conduct the première of the concerto in Barcelona (in April 1936) but he never got further than the first few bars and in the end Scherchen stood in for him; to their credit, the BBC, knowing of Webern's somewhat impractical methods of rehearsing, did not cancel but allotted additional time, and the performance took place at a late-night concert at Broadcasting House the following month. This is the second performance of the work ever, given only five months after Berg's death, and it is laden with an intensity and feeling that it would be impossible for anyone else to recapture. The quality is poor (it comes from the soloist's own acetates) but the spirit is extraordinarily powerful and vibrant, and the BBC orchestra play superbly. It comes with another 1936 recording, the Galimir Quartet's pioneering Polydor 78s of the *Lyric suite* – impeccably played but recorded in a horribly dry acoustic. Never mind, the concerto is a document of quite extraordinary interest.

Lyric suite: 3 Pieces; 3 Pieces for orchestra, Op. 6.
(M) *** DG 427 424-2 (3) [id.]. BPO, Karajan – SCHOENBERG; WEBERN: *Orchestral pieces.* ***

Karajan's justly famous collection of music by the Second Viennese School is here available as a set of three mid-priced CDs. Beautiful, refined recording, admirably transferred to CD.

3 Pieces for orchestra, Op. 6.
*** DG Dig. 419 781-2 [id.]. BPO, Levine – SCHOENBERG; WEBERN: *Pieces.* ***

Levine gives a powerful, warmly emotional reading of Berg's Opus 6, though odd emphasis of individual lines is intrusive in an otherwise full and vivid recording.

3 Pieces for orchestra, Op. 6; (i) *Lulu: symphonic suite.*
(M) *** Mercury 432 006-2 [id.]. (i) Helga Pilarczyk; LSO, Dorati – SCHOENBERG; WEBERN: *Orchestral pieces.* ***

In his pioneering 1962 Mercury coupling Dorati set the pattern for later recordings of this twentieth-century orchestral triptych, none recorded more clearly or vividly. The LSO plays fluently and warmly. For the *Lulu* suite, recorded a year earlier, Helga Pilarczyk is most impressive: the murder produces the most blood-curdling scream.

3 Pieces for orchestra, Op. 6; 5 Orchestral songs, Op. 4; (i) *Lulu: symphonic suite.*
(M) *** DG 423 238-2 [id.]. (i) M. Price; LSO, Abbado.

Abbado makes it clear above all how beautiful Berg's writing is, not just in the *Lulu* excerpts but in the early Opus 4 *Songs* and the Opus 6 *Orchestral pieces.*

Piano sonata, Op. 1.
☞ ** DG Dig. 423 678-2 [id.]. Maurizio Pollini – DEBUSSY: *Etudes.* **

An impressive enough account of Berg's one-movement *Sonata*, as powerful as any on disc. But it is not helped by a clinical, rather closely balanced recording, and the Debussy *Etudes* with which it is coupled are conspicuously wanting in atmosphere and poetry.

7 Early songs (1905–8 versions).
☞ *** DG Dig. 437 515-2. Anne Sofie von Otter, Bengt Forsberg – KORNGOLD: *Lieder;* STRAUSS: *Lieder.* ***

In the seven early songs of Berg, Anne Sofie von Otter and Bengt Forsberg follow up the success of their prize-winning disc of Grieg songs with inspired playing and singing, drawing out the intensity of emotion to the full without exaggeration or sentimentality. Along with Strauss and Korngold songs, a fascinating programme, magnetically performed.

(i; ii) *7 Early songs* (1905–8 & 1928 versions); (i) *An Leukon. Schliesse mir die Augen Beide* (1st and 2nd settings). (iii) *Der Wein.*
☞ ** DG Dig./Analogue 437 719-2 [id.]. (i) Margaret Marshall, Geoffrey Parsons; (ii) Kari Lövaas, N. German RSO, Blomstedt; (iii) Sabine Hass, VSO, Rozhdestvensky.

Margaret Marshall also gives fine, rich-toned performances of 1905–8 *Early songs*, and she is very well accompanied. The contrast with the 1928 orchestral settings (each song differently scored) is apt, though here Kari Lövaas makes a less sensitive if fulsome contribution. The histrionic performance of *Der Wein* by Sabine Hass, however, is lacking in subtlety and is not helped by forwardly balanced recording.

Lulu (with orchestration of Act III completed by Friedrich Cerha).
*** DG 415 489-2 (3) [id.]. Stratas, Minton, Schwarz, Mazura, Blankenheim, Riegel, Tear, Paris Op. O, Boulez.
☞ *** EMI Dig. CDS7 54622-2 (3) [Ang. CDCC 54622]. Wise, Fassbaender, Straka, Clark, Schone, Clarey, O Nat. de France, Tate.

The full three-Act structure of Berg's *Lulu*, with Yvonne Minton singing the Countess Geschwitz's lament, is most moving, though Lulu remains to the last a repulsive heroine. Teresa Stratas's bright, clear soprano is well recorded. Altogether this is an intensely involving performance of a work which in some ways is more lyrically approachable than *Wozzeck*.

Jeffrey Tate conducts the Orchestre National and an excellent non-French cast in a live recording of the full three-Act version. It provides a welcome alternative to the pioneer DG recording from Pierre Boulez with the original Paris Opéra cast. Tate's reading is more flexible, more volatile, more emotional than Boulez's. There are stage noises and some minor flaws of ensemble, and the recording is at a relatively low level, not as satisfying as the firmer, clearer, better-balanced DG sound for Boulez, who as a Berg interpreter is forceful, direct and rugged rather than affectionate. On casting, Tate's set is marginally preferable, with Patricia Wise in the title-role more sensuous than Teresa Stratas for Boulez, and with Brigitte Fassbaender incomparable as the predatory Countess Geschwitz, spontaneously expressive for Tate. Otherwise Graham Clark is a fine match for Robert Tear in various tenor roles, and Peter Straka is a more idiomatic Alwa than the clear-toned Kenneth Riegel for Boulez.

Lulu: symphonic suite.
*** EMI Dig. CDC7 49857-2 [id.]. Arleen Augér, CBSO, Rattle – SCHOENBERG: *5 Pieces;* WEBERN: *6 Pieces.* ***

Augér's pure, true soprano in the vocal passages of the *Lulu* suite is presented as an adjunct to the orchestra, rather than as a salient solo. The sound is of demonstration quality, adding enormously to the attractiveness of the disc.

Wozzeck (complete).
*** Decca Dig. 417 348-2 (2) [id.]. Waechter, Silja, Winkler, Laubenthal, Jahn, Malta, Sramek, VPO, Dohnányi – SCHOENBERG: *Erwartung.* ***
**(*) DG 423 587-2 (2) [id.]. Grundheber, Behrens, Haugland, Langridge, Zednik, V. State Op. Ch., VPO, Abbado.

Dohnányi, with refined textures and superb playing from the Vienna Philharmonic, presents an account of *Wozzeck* that not only is more accurate than any other on record but also is more beautiful.

The Abbado version, recorded live in the opera house, is very compelling in its presentation of the drama, given extra thrust through the tensions of live performance. However, there are drawbacks, too. Not only do you get the stage noises; the voices are also set behind the orchestra, with the instrumental sound putting a gauze between listener and singers.

Wozzeck (excerpts).
☞ (M) **(*) Mercury Dig. 434 325-2 [id.]. Pilarczyk, LSO, Dorati – BARTOK: *Bluebeard's castle* (complete). **(*)

These three concert-excerpts from *Wozzeck* come as a very generous fill-up to Dorati's 1962 recording of Bartók's *Bluebeard's Castle*. The LSO play brilliantly, with the highly analytical Mercury recording bringing out both the power and the delicate poetry, even though pianissimos tend to be overamplified. The snag is the abrasive, at times under-the-note singing of Helga Pilarczyk in the brief vocal passages.

Bergman, Erik (born 1911)

Bim bam bum; Fåglarna; Hathor Suite; Nox.
*** Chan. Dig. CHAN 8478 [id.]. Walmsley-Clark, Varcoe, Potter, New London Chamber Ch., Endymion Ens., James Wood.

The Finnish composer, Erik Bergman, is at his best and most characteristic in writing for voices. All four works are well performed and recorded, and the record forms an invaluable introduction to a highly imaginative and sensitive artistic personality.

Berio, Luciano (born 1925)

A-Ronne; The Cries of London.
(M) *** Decca 425 620-2. Swingle II, composer.

A-Ronne, literally 'A–Z', is an extraordinary setting of a multilingual poem by Edoardo Sanguinetti. *The Cries of London* is almost equally surrealistic, an updating of the cries used by Elizabethan madrigal composers. The performances by Swingle II are nothing less than brilliant and they are recorded with stunning immediacy.

Différences; 2 Pieces; (i) Sequenza III; (ii) Sequenza VII; (i) Chamber music.
(M) *** Ph. 426 662-2. (i) Cathy Berberian; (ii) Heinz Holliger; Juilliard Ens. (members), composer.

The biggest work here is *Différences* for five instruments and tape; but the two virtuoso solos – *Sequenza III* for voice and *Sequenza VII* for oboe – are if anything even more striking in their extensions of technique and expressive range. First-rate sound, well transferred.

Eindrucke; Sinfonia.
*** Erato/Warner Dig. 2292 45228-2 [id.]. Pasquier, New Swingle Singers, O Nat. de France, Boulez.

It was in 1969 that Berio's *Sinfonia*, written for the New York Philharmonic, made a far wider impact on the music world than is common with an avant-garde composer. Boulez records the complete work for the first time in this fine Erato version. *Eindrucke* is another powerful work, much more compressed, bare and uncompromising in its layering of strings and wind.

Coro (revised version).
(M) *** DG 423 902-2 [id.]. Cologne R. Ch. and SO, composer.

Coro is one of the most ambitious of Berio's works, with each of forty singers paired with an instrumentalist and with folk verse on basic themes contrasted with poems of Pablo Neruda. The composer directs a committed performance here, helped by the impact of the forward sound.

Berkeley, Lennox (1903–89)

Guitar concerto.
☞ (M) *** BMG/RCA 09026 61605-2 [id.]. Julian Bream, Monteverdi O, Gardiner – BROUWER; RODRIGO: *Concertos.* ***

This is a really splendid concerto with memorable invention and elegant architecture which presents a serious as well as attractive argument and a stylish brand of guitar writing that never leans barrenly on Spanish models. The *Lento* is particularly atmospheric. Bream's performance is superb and the recording vivid. This, with the equally stimulating Brouwer, makes an attractive if out-of-the-way coupling for the most popular of all guitar concertos.

Divertimento in B flat, Op. 18; Partita for chamber orchestra, Op. 66; Serenade for strings, Op. 12; (i) *Sinfonia concertante for oboe and chamber orchestra, Op. 84: Canzonetta* (only). *Symphony No. 3 in one movement, Op. 74; Mont Juic* (with Britten), *Op. 9.*
☞ *** Lyrita SRCD 226 [id.]. LPO, composer; (i) with Roger Winfield.

A CD representation of Lennox Berkeley's orchestral music was sorely needed, and this beautifully planned Lyrita collection fills the bill admirably. It introduces some of the most elegant and enjoyable music that Berkeley wrote. The *Divertimento* is enchanting, with its four stylish and highly inventive movements, while the *String serenade*, similarly in four sections, is hardly less attractive and brings a beautiful *Lento* closing movement. In its rather weightier tone of voice the *Partita* belies that it was written originally with a youth orchestra in mind, while the fourth movement from the *Sinfonia concertante* makes a splendid interlude before the closing *Symphony No. 3*. This is a concise, one-movement work, slightly more austere in its lyricism, but with a popular element entering the finale. Here at times one has the feeling that the composer would have created an even stronger effect had he held the performance more tautly. Even so, the music's argument is not difficult to follow and the other performances could hardly be bettered. The recording, too, from the early 1970s, is first class, vividly natural in timbre (especially the strings), and the CD transfers only improve the sense of presence and realism. The programme opens with the charmingly spontaneous *Mont Juic* suite which Berkeley wrote in collaboration with Benjamin Britten. They met at the 1936 Festival of the International Society for Contemporary Music in Barcelona, and during their stay the two composers enjoyed a display of Catalan folk-dancing in the park called Mont Juic. Writing the tunes down on any scrap of paper which came to hand, they then produced the suite, two movements each (Berkeley contributing the opening pair), and the work was later published jointly as Berkeley's Op. 9 and Britten's Op. 12.

Improvisation on a theme of Falla, Op. 55/2; Mazurka, Op. 101/2; 3 Mazurkas (Hommage à Chopin), Op. 32; Paysage; 3 Pieces; Polka, Op. 5a; 6 Preludes, Op. 23; 5 Short pieces, Op. 4; Sonata, Op. 20.
**(*) Kingdom KCLCD 2012; *CKCL 2012* [id.]. Christopher Headington.

With the exception of the *Sonata*, all these pieces are miniatures, some of considerable elegance. Christopher Headington is a sympathetic exponent and he is completely attuned to the idiom. The recording is eminently serviceable and truthful.

Berkeley, Michael (born 1948)

(i; ii) *Clarinet concerto;* (i) *Flighting;* (iii; ii) *Père du doux repos (Father of sweet sleep* from *Speaking silence).*
☞ *** ASV Dig. Single CDDCB 1101 [id.]. (i) Emma Johnson; (ii) N. Sinfonia, Sian Edwards; (iii) Henry Herford.

The *Clarinet concerto*, written for Emma Johnson in 1991, represents a new generation in Michael Berkeley's work, less lyrical, more abrasive and, above all, concentrated. The single movement of 20 minutes presents a well-defined structure not unlike that of Sibelius's *Seventh Symphony*. The soloist's concentration leads one magnetically through a thicket of virtuoso writing, often marked by stratospheric shrieks, which she consistently makes compelling, thanks also to the dedicated accompaniment under Sian Edwards. A central, meditative *Adagio* leads to a climactic screech of pain, which is then released into a brief elegiac epilogue. That closing section leads logically on to the two much briefer works on the disc, what the composer describes as 'fitting pendants'. The vocal work is a setting of a sonnet by the sixteenth-century French poet, Pontus de Tyard, while the solo clarinet piece grows out of the song, bringing out the soloist's warmly lyrical side further.

Berlin, Irving (1888–1989)

Annie get your gun (musical).
⊛ *** EMI Dig. CDC7 54206-2 [id.]; *EL 754206-4*. Criswell, Hampson, Graee, Luker, Amb. Ch., L. Sinf., John McGlinn.

This is one of the most delectable of all show records. John McGlinn follows up the pattern of his best-selling set of Jerome Kern's *Show Boat* with another performance that is at once scholarly and pulsing with life. Not only is the singing strong, characterful and idiomatic, the whole performance – not least from the players of the London Sinfonietta – is full of fun. Kim Criswell as Annie with her electric personality and bitingly bright voice here confirms herself as the natural successor to Ethel Merman, the original Annie Oakley, characterizing strongly while pitching precisely. Equally remarkably, Thomas Hampson makes an ideal hero, an opera-singer with an exceptionally rich and firm baritone who naturally gets inside the idiom. First-rate, full-bodied sound.

Berlioz, Hector (1803–69)

(i) *Harold in Italy, Op. 16;* (ii) *La damnation de Faust, Op. 24: Hungarian march; Ballet des sylphes; Menuet des follets;* (iii) *Les Troyens: Trojan march;* (iv) *Royal Hunt & Storm.*
☞ (B) **(*) Sony SBK 53255 [id.]. (i) Joseph de Pasquale; (i; iii) Phd. O, Ormandy; (ii) Phd. O, Munch; (iv) O de Paris, Barenboim.

(i) *Harold in Italy, Op. 16;* (ii) *Overtures: Benvenuto Cellini, Op. 23; Les Francs-juges, Op. 3.*
☞ (M) *** EMI CDM7 64745-2 [id.]. (i) Donald McInnes, O Nat. de France, Bernstein; (ii) LSO, Previn.

(i) *Harold in Italy. Overtures: Benvenuto Cellini; Waverley, Op. 1.*
☞ ** EMI Dig. CDC7 542372 [id.]. Gérard Caussé, Toulouse Capitole O, Plasson.

(i) *Harold in Italy; Overtures: Le Corsaire, Op. 21; Rob Roy.*
**(*) Decca Dig. 421 193-2 [id.]. (i) Zukerman; Montreal SO, Dutoit.

(i) *Harold in Italy;* (ii) *Tristia: (Méditation religieuse; La mort d'Ophélie; Marche funèbre pour la dernière scène de Hamlet), Op. 18; Les Troyens à Carthage: Prelude to Act II.*
*** Ph. 416 431-2 [id.]. (i) Imai; (ii) Alldis Ch.; LSO, C. Davis.

With the understanding players of the Orchestre National, Bernstein gives a performance that is both exciting and introspective. His earlier account with his own New York Philharmonic for CBS was sharper-focused than this, thanks in part to the recording, and its tauter discipline made for a performance at once fiercer and more purposeful. But with French players Bernstein's slightly more relaxed manner is in some ways more authentic, so that the galloping rhythms of the first and third movements are more lilting, if fractionally less precise. Donald McInnes is a violist with a superbly rich and even tone. His first entry, with the phrase echoed, is a ravishing moment and he responds at all times to the conductor, yet has plenty of individuality. The 1976 recording, made in the Salle Wagram, has an opulent spread and plenty of warmth; on CD it is brighter and more firmly focused. This goes to the top of the list of available recordings of this somewhat elusive work and is certainly first choice at mid-price. It is made the more attractive by the addition of the two overtures. Under Previn, the swing-along melody of *Les Francs-juges* swaggers boldly. Again excellent transfers, with rich, deep brass.

The Philips account offers good value. In addition to a noble account of *Harold* in which Nobuko Imai is on top form, this CD offers the *Tristia*, which includes the haunting *Funeral march for the last scene of Hamlet* given with chorus, as well as the *Prelude* to the second Act of *Les Troyens*. The sound is completely natural and realistic, and has impressive transparency and detail.

Dutoit's version of *Harold in Italy* is very richly recorded. With as characterful a soloist as Zukerman, highly individual and warmly expressive, if not always at his purest, the centre of gravity of the work is shifted. Though the beauty of the writing is very satisfying, the work seems to lose some of its purpose when the soloist comes to be phased out. With the viola's contribution all but eliminated, the *Orgy* seems just a little tame, and speeds throughout tend to be on the broad side. *Rob Roy* and *Le Corsaire* make appropriate Byronic couplings.

Ormandy's 1965 recording of *Harold in Italy* with the Philadelphia Orchestra was never issued in the UK at the time, but it has a lot going for it. Joseph de Pasquale is a thoughtful and cultured soloist and he is truthfully and expertly balanced in relation to the orchestra. The performance is beautifully shaped, though the finale could perhaps do with a shade more abandon. Although the recording perspective is excellent, the sound is not as transparent as some rivals, thanks to the reverberant acoustic. For all that, this is an impressive *Harold*, not perhaps as incandescent as the pioneering Koussevitzky/Primrose, but superbly played. The three excerpts from *La damnation de Faust* were recorded in 1963, when Munch was guest conductor in Philadelphia, and they have a Beecham-like elegance. Daniel Barenboim's recording of the *Royal Hunt and Storm* from *Les Troyens* with the Orchestre de Paris comes from the mid-1970s and has the benefit of better sound; it is well enough played though it is not really in the same street as the Munch or Ormandy performances. Nevertheless this CD is eminently recommendable and very good value.

Although it is good to have a disc including the rare *Waverley overture*, Plasson's version of *Harold in Italy* is a disappointment. The performance opens atmospherically and ends with an exciting *Brigand's orgy*; the central Pilgrim evocation is much less convincing. Gérard Caussé is a fine player, but he is balanced very forwardly and dominates in an extrovert way which is out of place: this is not a concerto.

(i) *Harold in Italy, Op. 16;* (ii) *Roméo et Juliette, Op. 17.*

☞ (M) *** Decca 425 053-2 (2) [id.]. (i) Ludwig, Sénéchal, Ghiaurov, Les Solistes des Choeurs de l'ORTF, V. State Op. Ch., VPO; (ii) Robert Veyron, Cleveland O; Maazel.

(i) *Harold in Italy. Roméo et Juliette* (excerpts).

(M) (***) BMG/RCA mono GD 60275 [60275-2-RG]. (i) Carlton Cooley; NBC SO, Toscanini.

This is Maazel at his best, and the vintage Decca recording from the 1970s is very impressive in both works, with superb clarity and definition in *Romeo and Juliet* (recorded in the Sofiensaal in 1972) and a good balance in *Harold in Italy* in the flattering acoustics of Cleveland's Masonic Hall auditorium, five years later. Robert Veyron is an excellent soloist and if, in terms of imagination and insight, this does not displace the Bernstein version of *Harold in Italy* and Sir Colin Davis might be marginally preferred in *Romeo and Juliet*, this Decca set is excellent value at mid-price and readers can follow their own inclination, for there is little to choose in the latter work.

Toscanini's famous 1953 recording of *Harold in Italy* is of very high voltage, with Carlton Cooley an excellent soloist. The demonic fires glow with great intensity in the *Orgy of the Brigands*; perhaps the *Pilgrims' march* is just a shade hard driven. In spite of the sonic limitations, the excitement of the performance still comes across the decades.

Overtures: *Béatrice et Bénédict; Benvenuto Cellini; Le Carnaval romain; Le Corsaire. Roméo et Juliette: Queen Mab scherzo. Les Troyens: Royal hunt and storm.*

☞ ⊛ (M) *** BMG/RCA 9026 61400-2 [id.]. Boston SO, Munch (with SAINT-SAENS: *Le rouet d'Omphale ***).

Dazzlingly brilliant performances of four favourite overtures – the virtuosity of the Boston players, especially the violins in *Béatrice et Bénédict* and *Le Corsaire* – is breathtaking. But it is for the wonderfully poetic and thrilling account of the *Royal hunt and storm* from *Les Troyens* that this CD earns its Rosette. The horn solo is ravishing and the brass produce a riveting climax as the storm reaches its peak. Then the scene of a rain-drenched countryside is magically evoked as the horn steals back in the closing bars. The early stereo (1957/59) is remarkable: one really feels the hall ambience, and John Pfeiffer's remastering is expert. *Romeo and Juliet* was recorded in 1961, and again one marvels at the articulation of the Boston violins and horns. The Saint-Saëns bonus is the earliest recording of all (1957). It is beautifully played and, after a robust climax, has the most delicate, pianissimo ending.

Overtures: *Béatrice et Bénédict; Le Carnaval romain, Op. 9; Le Corsaire, Op. 21; Rob Roy; Le Roi Lear, Op. 4.*

**(*) Chan. Dig. CHAN 8316; *ABTD 1067* [id.]. SNO, Gibson.

Rob Roy finds Gibson and the SNO at their most dashingly committed. *King Lear*, another rarity, also comes out most dramatically, and though *Béatrice et Bénédict* is not quite so polished, the playing is generally excellent. With first-rate digital recording, this can be generally recommended.

Overtures: *Benvenuto Cellini; Le Corsaire. Roméo et Juliette*: excerpts. *Les Troyens: Royal hunt and storm.*

☞ (M) (***) Decca mono 433 405-2. Paris Conservatoire O, Charles Munch.

The *Benvenuto Cellini* overture was recorded in Walthamstow in 1946, *Le Corsaire* in 1948 and the *Roméo* excerpts and *Royal hunt and storm* the following year at the Maison de la mutualité in Paris with the young Kenneth Wilkinson responsible for the engineering! For the most part the performances are marvellous, particularly the mercurial and delicate account of the *Queen Mab Scherzo*, despite the woodwind intonation at the side-turn (still audible). These were the days of Decca *ffrr* (full frequency range recording), though those brought up on digital recording will not realize just how revolutionary it was at the time. To modern ears the *Benvenuto Cellini* overture sounds pretty muddy at the top (it is marvellously played), though the slightly later *Queen Mab* recording is much more transparent. A very faint hum is audible at times in *Le Corsaire* and in the three Romeo excerpts. Wind intonation is far from impeccable in the *Scène d'amour* and the Parisian French horns of the 1940s had a vibrato almost reminiscent of the saxophone, which is disturbing in the *Royal hunt and storm* (the Boston version is much superior). But, never mind, this is real Berlioz with all the fervour and fever that this extraordinary imagination exhibited. In a way the *Roméo* excerpts sound more thoroughly Berliozian in spirit than Munch's later recordings. Indeed his subsequent stereo RCA collection is obviously a preferable choice in this repertoire and, because of its minor flaws and acoustic limitations, this Decca CD is not recommended, perhaps, for younger collectors coming fresh to this repertoire; but lovers of Berlioz who are tolerant of 1940s sonics should not pass this over.

Overtures: *Le Carnaval romain, Op. 9; Le Corsaire, Op. 21; Les Francs-juges, Op. 3; Le Roi Lear, Op. 4; Waverley, Op. 1.*
**(*) Ph. 416 430-2. LSO, C. Davis.

This is music which ideally calls for modern digital sound; in spite of this, Sir Colin's collection can hold its own, even though it should now be in the mid-price bracket. The playing undoubtedly has fire and brilliance.

Roméo et Juliette: Queen Mab scherzo.
(M) (**) BMG/RCA mono GD 60314 [60314-2-RG]. Phd. O, Toscanini – MENDELSSOHN: *Midsummer Night's Dream.* (***)

Toscanini's quicksilver reading of this fairy scherzo has much in common with his fine Philadelphia recording of Mendelssohn's fairy music. The 1941 recording is clear.

Symphonie fantastique, Op. 14.
*** Ph. 411 425-2 [id.]. Concg. O, C. Davis.
☞ *** Ph. Dig. 434 402-2 [id.]. Orchestre Révolutionnaire et Romantique, Gardiner.
**(*) EMI Dig. CDC7 49541-2 [id.]. L. Classical Players, Norrington.

(i) *Symphonie fantastique;* (ii) *Overtures: Béatrice et Bénédict; Le Carnaval romain; Le Corsaire.*
☞ (M) **(*) EMI CDM7 64630-2 [id.]. (i) O Nat. de France, Bernstein; (ii) LSO, Previn.

Symphonie fantastique; Overtures: Béatrice et Bénédict: Le Corsaire, Op. 21.
☞ * BMG/RCA Dig. 09026 61203-2 [id.]. RPO, Temirkanov.

Symphonie fantastique; Overtures: Benvenuto Cellini; Le Carnaval romain.
☞ (B) ** Erato/Warner 2292 45925 [id.]. Strasbourg PO, Alain Lombard.

Symphonie fantastique; Overture Le Carnaval romain, Op. 9.
☞ (BB) **(*) Virgin/EMI VJ5 61100-2. RPO, Sir Yehudi Menuhin.
☞ * EMI Dig. CDC7 54479-2 [id.]. Concg. O, Jansons.

Symphonie fantastique; Overtures: Le Carnaval romain; Le Corsaire.
☞ (BB) **(*) ASV CDQS 6090. RPO, Bátiz.

Symphonie fantastique; Overtures: Le Carnaval romain; Le Corsaire; La damnation de Faust: Marche hongroise. Les Troyens: Trojan march.
☞ (M) **(*) Mercury 434 328-2 [id.]. Detroit SO, Paul Paray.

(i) *Symphonie fantastique; Overtures:* (ii) *Le Carnaval romain;* (iii) *Le Roi Lear.*
(M) (***) EMI mono CDM7 64032-2 [id.]. (i) O. Nat. de l'ORTF; (ii) LPO; (iii) RPO, Sir Thomas Beecham.

Symphonie fantastique; Overture: Le Corsaire, Op. 21.
(M) *** Pickwick/RPO Dig. CDRPO 7016; *ZCRPO 7016* [id.]. RPO, Previn.
☞ ** Chan. Dig. CHAN 9052 [id.]. Royal Stockholm PO, Rozhdestvensky.

Sir Colin Davis's 1974 Concertgebouw recording – his first with that orchestra – remains a primary recommendation. The Philips recording is very satisfying. The Concertgebouw performance has superb life and colour.

John Eliot Gardiner, with his Orchestre Révolutionnaire et Romantique, has followed Roger Norrington in recording the *Symphonie fantastique* on period instruments, and the comparisons are fascinating. Instead of working in the studio, Gardiner opted to go to the old hall of the Conservatoire in Paris, where the symphony was first heard in 1830. Gardiner wanted, like Norrington, 'to recapture the sometimes shocking originality of Berlioz's creation'. The hall is quite small, seating some 300–400, but its acoustic for a recent live piano recital with an audience present proved quite generous. So it is curious that the sound of this CD is very dry; however, Gardiner uses the extra sharpness of focus to add to the dramatic bite, without undermining the intensely atmospheric moments in this colourful programme work. Thus the opening of the second-movement waltz, the *Scene at the ball*, is more sinister than with Norrington, with the interpretation faster and more impulsive. The evocation of thunder at the end of the slow movement, the *Scene in the country*, is even more dramatic and, though the brass in the last two movements lacks the bloom given to Norrington in his EMI recording, Gardiner conducts the *March to the scaffold* and the *Witches' Sabbath* with more excitement and panache. That is largely because he modifies the surprisingly slow speeds marked for those last two movements, taking them faster than Norrington. Generally Gardiner is far less strict in observing metronome markings, both over the basic tempo and over modifying it, and, despite the unhelpful acoustic, the violins have more body than those of Norrington's London Classical Players. Gardiner's performance also gains from his more openly expressive style of phrasing, while in Berlioz's wild syncopations he is second to none in conveying the astonishing modernity of music written within three years of Beethoven's death. Some will still prefer the Norrington version for its warmer sound; but Gardiner is more electrifying, building imaginatively on similar ingredients.

Though Berlioz was writing so soon after the death of Beethoven, he represented a leap forward in the art of orchestration. The gains from using period instruments are less striking here than in Beethoven, but the rasp of heavy brass and the bite of authentic timpani stand out more vividly. As in his Beethoven, Norrington does his utmost to observe the composer's metronome markings; but where his Beethoven is consistently fast, some of these speeds are more relaxed than we are used to – as in the *March to the scaffold* and the *Ronde du sabbat*. As usual, his lifting of rhythms prevents the music from dragging, at the same time giving new transparency; and his revelations here certainly give his version a key place.

With full-ranging digital sound, well balanced with fine presence and atmosphere, André Previn conducts the RPO in a keenly dramatic reading marked by characteristically well-lifted rhythms, with dynamic contrasts powerfully underlined, which heightens the sinister side of the composer's night-mare vision. This is one of Previn's RPO recordings which matches his achievements in his vintage days with the LSO, and it makes an excellent alternative recommendation.

Bernstein directs a brilliant and understanding performance which captures more than most the wild, volatile quality of Berlioz's inspiration. Sir Colin Davis may give a clearer idea of the logic of the piece, but Bernstein (unlike Davis, omitting the exposition repeat) has even more urgency, and his reading culminates in superb accounts of the *March to the scaffold* and the *Witches' sabbath*, full of rhythmic swagger and natural flair. However, the remastering of the late-1970s analogue recording gives slight over-emphasis to the brilliance with its tendency to shrillness in the upper strings. Some weight has also been lost at the bass end, but the warm resonance of the recording retains the body of the orchestral sound. There is a successful chrome tape, not as bright as the CD on top, but well balanced. The three overtures make a fine bonus, and the 1974 recording, made at Abbey Road, offers appreciably fuller violins, while there is plenty of warmth and atmosphere. *Le Corsaire* is here less hectic than Previn has been known to present it in the concert hall, but it hardly loses from that. *Béatrice et Bénédict* fizzes with wit, and there is no lack of panache in *Le Carnaval romain*.

Bátiz's ASV CD is fully competitive in the super-bargain range. It has the advantage of an excellent digital recording, which is brilliant and well balanced. As always in the recording studio, he brings the score vividly to life, and his consistent warmth and intensity are highly persuasive. Points of detail may be less subtle than with Davis, for instance, but one has the feeling here of live music-making, and the two overtures are equally strong and spontaneous. The sound balance is more convincing than in Bernstein's remastered EMI version.

Although not a first choice, Menuhin's reading of the *Symphonie fantastique* is full of character and he brings his own humanistic insights. The neurosis is there but slightly tempered, the *Waltz* notably effective, and the bizarre power of the final two movements is relished. Yet in Menuhin's hands this is primarily a symphony. The RPO play very well for him and the recording is first class, brilliant, but with a satisfyingly full and resonant bass. The overture is enjoyable in a similar way, not just treated as a vehicle for orchestral virtuosity. A refreshing bargain alternative for those who already have Sir Colin Davis or Beecham.

The Beecham Edition version of the *Symphonie fantastique* with the Orchestre National is a mono recording, made only a short time before his stereo account. What is surprising is to discover how different the two performances are. The mono version is faster in all five movements, with an astonishing difference in overall timing of six minutes in a three-quarter-hour work. More important is the difference of tension, with the final *March to the scaffold* and *Witches' sabbath* much more exciting in the faster, mono version.

Paray's excitingly hard-pressed reading is full of passionate, mercurial neurosis. The first movement immediately spurts away, and it is only the conductor's firm grip that prevents the movement from getting out of hand. The *Waltz*, too, is fast, though not inelegant, and the *Adagio*, even though it has moments of pastoral repose, never drags its feet. The final two movements have great verve, and there are few performances that combine such a high level of tension with a true understanding of the music's inner pulse. Fine playing, of course, and brilliant recording, with a tendency to thinness in the violins. The encores are similarly exciting and vivid, and again one marvels that a stereo recording from as early as 1958/59 should sound so impressive today.

Lombard also has the measure of Berlioz's flickering neurosis, even if he is not as spontaneously mercurial as Paray, and if the *Marche au supplice* and closing *Witches' sabbath* lack something in venomous bite, they are exciting enough, and the whole performance, very well played, makes a satisfying whole. The two overtures are excitingly direct, and there are few bargain Berlioz records with a richer-bodied sound, projected from within an agreeably spacious acoustic.

There are many good things in Gennady Rozhdestvensky's account with the Royal Stockholm Philharmonic of Berlioz's masterpiece. It is an interpretation attentive to every detail, though (in what seems to be the present fashion) the introduction is very measured. The performance is eminently well prepared and there are many impressive touches, notably the Ball scene with its slight hint of menace, but elsewhere it is less well characterized, and the *Scène aux champs* is far less atmospheric than one would expect from a conductor of this stature. The Chandos recording is very fine indeed and the Stockholm orchestra responds well, but the overall impression it leaves is less strong.

Yuri Temirkanov's account of Berlioz's masterpiece is a highly self-conscious affair, full of tiresome exaggerations. The opening is terribly slow; *accelerandi* are abrupt, the *Marche au supplice* over-charged. Temirkanov approaches the work as a virtuoso orchestral showpiece rather than a poetic vision. He comes closer to Berlioz's spirit in the overture *Le Corsaire*; *Béatrice et Bénédict* could do with greater lightness of touch. In any event, given the strength of the opposition, this is not a serious contender.

Nor is Mariss Jansons's account a serious challenge, though the playing of the Royal Concertgebouw Orchestra is predictably responsive. Again the opening is measured to the point of sounding laboured, and much else in the symphony is curiously heavy-handed. A *Symphonie fantastique* wanting in atmosphere and that mercurial temperament and white-hot intensity which is such an essential ingredient in Berlioz's sensibility is a non-starter.

Symphonie fantastique, Op. 14; (i) *Lélio (Le retour à la vie), Op. 14b.*
(B) *** EMI CZS7 62739-2 (2). (i) Gedda, Burles, Van Gorp, Sendrez, Topart, Ch. of R. France; ORTF Nat. O, Martinon.

Berlioz intended *Lélio* as a sequel to the *Symphonie fantastique*, and Martinon conveniently offers the works paired at bargain price. His account of the *Symphonie* shows a unique seductiveness. Martinon gives the first-movement exposition repeat and provides the often omitted extra brass parts; though the result is brilliant, he never presses on too frenetically. But most of all this reading is outstanding for its warm shaping of phrase, even if the finale, with its tolling bells of doom, has a flamboyance and power to match any available. The 1973 sound remains remarkably vivid. *Lélio* quotes the *idée fixe* from the *Symphonie*, which helps the listener to feel at home. It is difficult to imagine this performance being bettered, and the 1974 sound is suitably atmospheric.

Symphonie fantastique, Op. 14; (i) *La mort de Cléopâtre.*
☞ (B) ** DG 434 404-2 [id.]. O de Paris, Barenboim, (i) with Jessye Norman.

Barenboim's 1978 Paris version, reissued on DG's bargain Classicon label, is disappointing, with the first movement hectic and erratic. Only in the 'March to the scaffold' and the finale does the performance suddenly acquire the necessary sharpness of focus. Jessye Norman's performance of *La Mort de Cléopâtre* hardly affects the balance of advantage.

VOCAL MUSIC

La damnation de Faust, Op. 24.
*** Ph. 416 395-2 (2) [id.]. Veasey, Gedda, Bastin, Amb. S., Wandsworth School Boys' Ch., London Symphony Ch., LSO, C. Davis.
*** Decca Dig. 414 680-2 (2) [id.]. Riegel, Von Stade, Van Dam, King, Chicago Ch. & SO, Solti.

Both Gedda as Faust and Bastin as Mephistopheles are impressive in the 1974 Philips set. The response of the chorus and orchestra is never less than intelligent and, in the quieter passages, highly sensitive and the recording perspective is outstandingly natural and realistic.

Solti's performance, searingly dramatic, is given stunning digital sound to make the *Ride to Hell* supremely exciting. But with Von Stade singing tenderly, this is a warmly expressive performance too; and the *Hungarian march* has rarely had such sparkle and swagger. The extra brightness matches the extrovert quality of the performance, less subtle than Davis's.

L'enfance du Christ, Op. 25.
**(*) Ph. 416 949-2 (2) [id.]. Baker, Tappy, Langridge, Allen, Herincx, Rouleau, Bastin, Alldis Ch., LSO, C. Davis.
**(*) Erato/Warner Dig. 2292 45275-2 (2) [id.]. Von Otter, Rolfe Johnson, Van Dam, Cachemaille, Bastin, Monteverdi Ch., Lyons Op. O, Gardiner.
☞ (M) **(*) BMG/RCA 09026 61234-2 (2) [id.]. Valletti, Kopleff, Souzay, Tozzi, New England Conservatory Ch., Boston SO, Munch – *Nuits d'été.* *

In Sir Colin Davis's second version for Philips the beautifully balanced recording intensifies the colour and atmosphere of the writing, so that for example the *Nocturnal march* in the first part is wonderfully mysterious. There is a fine complement of soloists, and though Eric Tappy's tone as narrator is not always sweet, his sense of style is immaculate. Others are not always quite so idiomatic, but Dame Janet Baker and Thomas Allen, as ever, both sing beautifully.

John Eliot Gardiner has the advantage of fine modern recording, made in the Church of Sainte-Madeleine, Pérouges, very well balanced but with the resonance bringing warm atmosphere rather than great clarity. He has some fine soloists, too. Anne Sofie von Otter's Mary is outstanding, by far the best currently on record, sung with rapt simplicity. Gardiner often – though not always – adopts brisker tempi than Davis, and his vibrancy brings a new dimension to some of the music. This is a very vivid reading, marred only by two questionable speeds. Generally, however, Davis's choice of pacing is even more apt.

Charles Munch's account of *L'enfance du Christ* comes from 1956 and makes a welcome return to circulation in the economically packaged two-CD sets that look like one. Needless to say, the performance is thoroughly idiomatic and the playing of the Boston Symphony has a splendour and sonority that the (obviously dated) recording still conveys. The line-up as far as the soloists are concerned is impressive: Florence Kopleff as Mary and Gérard Souzay, then at the height of his powers, as Joseph. The chorus is a weakness; they do not have the tenderness and flexibility to be found in either of Colin Davis's accounts, and even Munch himself must yield in that Berliozian fervour to the English conductor. Leontyne Price is gloriously full-toned in her 1963 recording of *Nuits d'été*, though in terms of characterization she is no match for Danco or Crespin. She produces much the same colour in each of the songs, but the performance is well worth having for the sake of the magical playing of the Chicago orchestra under Reiner. The transfers are excellently effected. Very recommendable indeed, though not as the only version in one's collection.

(i) *Herminie; La mort de Cléopâtre;* (ii) *La belle voyageuse;* (iii) *La captive;* (iv) *Le chasseur danois;* (v) *Le jeune pâtre breton;* (ii) *Zaïde.*
*** Ph. 416 960-2 [id.]. (i) Dame Janet Baker; (ii) Sheila Armstrong; (iii) Josephine Veasey; (iv) John Shirley-Quirk; (v) Frank Patterson; LSO, C. Davis.

Dame Janet Baker sings with passionate intensity while Sir Colin Davis draws committed playing from the LSO. Sheila Armstrong is very successful in her two songs provided as the fill-up; Josephine Veasey's contribution is also an individual one; but Frank Patterson, the weakest of the soloists, lacks the necessary charm.

Irlande, Op. 2: excerpts: *La belle voyageuse; Adieu, Bessy!; Le coucher du soleil; Elégie; L'origine de la harpe.*
☞ ⊛ *** EMI Dig. CDC5 55047-2 [id.]. Thomas Hampson, Geoffrey Parsons – LISZT; WAGNER: *Lieder.* *** ⊛

Thomas Hampson gives glowing performances of five of the nine songs, using translations from English texts by the poet Thomas Moore, which Berlioz wrote very early in his career. In their expressive warmth they make a perfect match for the fascinating selections of songs by Wagner and Liszt, with Geoffrey Parsons adding to the impact. Warm, helpful sound.

Mélodies: Aubade; La belle voyageuse; La captive; Le chasseur danois; Le jeune pâtre breton; La mort d'Ophélie; Les nuits d'été; Zaïde.
*** Erato/Warner Dig. 2292 045517-2 [id.]. Montague, Robbin, Fournier, Crook, Cachemaille, Lyon Op. O, Gardiner.

Mélodies: *La belle voyageuse; La captive; Les nuits d'été, Op. 7; Zaïde.*
☞ (M) *** Virgin/EMI Dig. CUV5 61118-2 [id.]. Dame Janet Baker, City of L. Sinfonia, Hickox –
 RESPIGHI: *La sensitiva.* ***

John Eliot Gardiner here divides the six keenly atmospheric songs of *Les nuits d'été* between four
singers, in some ways an ideal solution when each song demands such different timbre and different
tessitura. His choice of singers is inspired and the presiding genius of the conductor makes this a
memorable Berlioz disc.

Dame Janet Baker's new recording of *Les nuits d'été* also includes extra orchestral songs. Helped
by full, rich recording and a warmly sympathetic accompaniment from Hickox, the interpretation, if
anything, glows even more warmly than in Dame Janet's classic EMI reading with Barbirolli, and the
voice shows next to no sign of the passing years.

Messe solennelle; Resurrexit (revised version).
☞ *** Ph. Dig. 442 137-2 [id.]. Donna Brown, Jean-Luc Viala, Gilles Cachemaille, Monteverdi Ch.,
 O Révolutionnaire et Romantique, Gardiner.

The story of how this long-lost work was rediscovered in 1991 in the organ gallery of a Belgian
church is fascinating. The Berlioz scholar, Hugh Macdonald, confirmed the manuscript's authenticity
– Berlioz said he had destroyed it, but in fact he gave a score to a Belgian violinist friend as a
souvenir. This massive work, completed in 1824, was among the first that the young Berlioz wrote.
He was twenty and largely untrained, but both the scale of the inspiration and its actual execution are
remarkable considering that background. As John Eliot Gardiner says in his notes, 'At times
unquestionably gawky, dull here and there, the overriding impression which emerged first in rehearsal
and then in performance was of the bravado of the man.'

This performance, recorded live at the British première in Westminster Cathedral in October 1993,
amply confirms that. It is an uneven work, but the glow of inspiration shines out over any
shortcomings. Especially illuminating are the passages where Berlioz draws on themes we know from
other contexts – a *Roman carnival* theme in the vigorous *Gloria*, a *Fantastic Symphony* theme in the
Gratias, used totally differently. In 1849, 25 years after writing the Mass, Berlioz re-used the *Agnus*
with its tenor solo in his *Te Deum*. Gardiner conducts with characteristic flair and sense of drama,
bringing brilliant singing from the Monteverdi Choir, though the choral sound is backwardly
balanced. A second, modified and slightly expanded version of the violent *Resurrexit* is included as a
supplement, a revised version that Berlioz himself acknowledged.

(i) *La mort de Cléopâtre;* (ii) *Les nuits d'été, Op. 7* (see also below).
*** DG Dig. 410 966-2 [id.]. (i) Jessye Norman; (ii) Kiri Te Kanawa, O de Paris, Barenboim.

The coupling of Jessye Norman in the scena and Dame Kiri Te Kanawa in the song-cycle makes for
one of the most ravishing of Berlioz records, with each singer at her very finest.

Les nuits d'été (song-cycle), *Op. 7.*
*** Decca 417 813-2 [id.]. Régine Crespin, SRO, Ansermet (with *Recital of French songs* ***).
☞ **(*) BMG/RCA GD 60681 (2) [09026 60681-2]. De los Angeles, Boston SO, Munch – *Roméo
 et Juliette.* (***)
☞ * (M) BMG/RCA 09026 61234-2 (2) [id.]. Leontyne Price, Chicago SO, Reiner – *L'enfance du
 Christ.* **(*)

(i) *Les nuits d'été* (song-cycle), *Op. 7;* (ii) *La mort de Cléopâtre* (lyric scena); (ii; iii) *Les Troyens, Act
V, Scenes ii & iii.*
⊛ (M) *** EMI CDM7 69544-2. Dame Janet Baker, (i) New Philh. O, Barbirolli; (ii) LSO, Gibson;
 (iii) with Greevy, Erwen, Howell & Amb. Op. Ch.

The collaboration of Dame Janet Baker at the peak of her powers and Sir John Barbirolli in what is
probably the most beautiful of all orchestral song-cycles produces ravishing results.

Crespin's richness of tone and a style which has an operatic basis do not prevent her from
bringing out the subtlety of detail and, with Ansermet accompanying brilliantly, this glowing
performance is a tour de force.

Victoria de los Angeles's celebrated recording comes from 1955 and still possesses a luminous
freshness and purity that come over very well in this new transfer, where they are coupled with
Munch's *Roméo et Juliette*. This is far more beautifully characterized than Leontyne Price's account,
which suffers from rather generalized responses and little variety of colour or dynamics, though her
voice is striking enough and she is well supported by Reiner and the Chicago orchestra in its heyday.

Requiem Mass (Grande messe des morts).
☞ (B) ** EMI CZS5 68104-2 (2) [id.]. Robert Tear, CBSO Ch., CBSO, Frémaux – FAURE: *Requiem.* ***

(i) *Requiem Mass (Grande messe des morts). Overtures: Benvenuto Cellini; Le Carnaval romain; Le Corsaire.*
**(*) DG Dig. 429 724-2 (2) [id.]. (i) Pavarotti, Ernst-Senff Ch.; BPO, Levine.

(i) *Requiem Mass;* (ii) *Symphonie funèbre et triomphale, Op. 15.*
**(*) Ph. 416 283-2 (2) [id.]. (i) Dowd, Wandsworth School Boys' Ch., London Symphony Ch.; (ii) John Alldis Ch.; LSO, Sir Colin Davis.

(i) *Requiem Mass (Grande messe des morts), Op. 5;* (ii) Choral music: *Ballet des ombres; Chanson à boire; Chant des Bretons; Chant guerrier; Chant sacré; Hymn à la France; La Menace des Francs; Prière du matin; Tantum ergo; Le Temple Universel; Veni, creator.*
☞ (M) ** Decca 425 056-2 (2) [id.]. (i) Riegel, Cleveland Ch. & O, Maazel; (ii) Ryland Davies, David Thomas, Heinrich Schütz Ch. & Chorale, Norrington; Peter Smith (piano and harmonium).

For Sir Colin Davis's recording of the *Requiem* Philips went to Westminster Cathedral and, thanks to the closeness of the microphones, in many passages one can hear individual voices in the choir. However, the large-scale brass sound is formidably caught and the choral fortissimos are glorious, helped by the fresh cutting edge of the Wandsworth School Boys' Choir. The LSO provides finely incisive accompaniment, and there is no doubt that the CD remastering has added to the overall impact and tangibility. However, the *Symphonie funèbre et triomphale* needs more persuasive handling than Sir Colin's if it is not to outstay its welcome.

Levine's account of the *Requiem*, one of his Berlioz series with the Berlin Philharmonic, is the most recommendable of the modern, digitally recorded versions, though in dramatic bite it cannot quite match the vintage Colin Davis and the Ernst-Senff Choir falls short of its usual high standards in the raggedness of some of the choral entries. Having Pavarotti as a characterful, imaginatively expressive soloist in the *Sanctus* is an advantage. Levine's coupling of three of Berlioz's most popular overtures is not as unusual as Davis's *Symphonie funèbre* but works very well in these excellent performances.

With an impressively clear CD transfer, Maazel's version makes plenty of impact, but the result is strangely unatmospheric, with the choral balance less than satisfactory. The performance, too, is at times prosaic though no one could deny the impact of the *Tuba mirum*. The shorter choral pieces are rare and are well worth exploring, for they show Berlioz in an unfamiliar and often rewarding light. Here both performances and recordings are of high quality.

It is disappointing that for the Frémaux Birmingham set the EMI engineers fell into the same trap as their Philips colleagues in the Davis set, only rather more so. The choir and orchestra are recorded relatively close, to make the result seem too small-scale for such a work. Detail is clarified and there is bloom on the sound, but the absence of any true pianissimos is just as serious as the failure to expand in the big climaxes, making a potentially fine performance far less effective than it might have been. The chorus, too, is surprisingly variable.

(i) *Requiem Mass (Grande messe des morts), Op. 5;* (ii) *Harold in Italy.*
☞ (B) ** DG Double stereo/mono 439 705-2 (2) [id.]. (i) Peter Schreier, Bav. R. Ch. & O, Munch; (ii) Heinz Kirchner, BPO, Markevitch.

In many ways Munch's second attempt to record Berlioz's *Requiem* at the end of the 1960s is less successful than the first (for RCA), for the playing of the Bavarian Radio Orchestra does not match that of the Boston orchestra, and though the Bavarian Radio Chorus sings with professional precision the result is not massive enough. The recording quality, though cleaner and more precise than the earlier American one, has less atmosphere and lacks mystery. The brilliant and exciting mono recording of *Harold in Italy* by Heinz Kirchner, a first-rate soloist, with the Berlin Philharmonic under Markevitch brings a riveting final orgy but this hardly compensates, although the mono sound is remarkably good.

Roméo et Juliette, Op. 17.
☞ *** Ph. 416 962-2 (2) [id.]. Kern, Tear, Shirley-Quirk, Alldis Ch., London Symphony Ch. & LSO, C. Davis.
☞ (M) **(*) DG 437 244-2 (2) [id.]. Minton, Araiza, Bastin, Ch. & O de Paris, Barenboim – FRANCK: *Chasseur maudit* etc. **(*)
☞ (M) (***) BMG/RCA mono GD 60681 (2) [09026 60681-2]. Roggero, Chabay, Yi-Kwei-Sze,

Harvard Glee Club, Radcliffe Ch. Soc., Boston SO, Munch – *Nuits d'été.* **(*)

☞ ** Denon Dig. CO 73210/11 [id.]. Ewing, Gulyas, Denize, Cole, Lloyd, Cologne R. Ch., Stuttgart R. Ch., Berlin RIAS Chamber Ch., Frankfurt RSO, Inbal.

☞ (M) (**) BMG/RCA mono GD 60274 (2) [60274-2-RG]. Gladys Swarthout, John Garris, Nicola Moscona, NBC Ch. & SO, Toscanini (with BIZET: *L'Arlésienne & Carmen suites* **).

☞ *(*) Orfeo Dig. C 087 042 H (2) [id.]. Fassbaender, Gedda, Shirley-Quirk, ORD Ch. & O, Gardelli.

(i) *Roméo et Juliette. Symphonie funèbre et triomphale, Op. 15.*

*** Decca 417 302-2 (2) [id.]. (i) Quivar, Cupido, Krause, Tudor Singers, Montreal Ch. & SO, Dutoit.

Dutoit's is a masterly, heart-warming reading of Berlioz's curious mixture of symphony, cantata and opera, superbly recorded in richly atmospheric sound, with a triumphantly successful account of the *Symphonie funèbre et triomphale* as a generous coupling. Dutoit is here at his most uninhibited, brilliantly skirting the very edge of vulgarity in this outgoing ceremonial piece.

Colin Davis's vintage version brings a deeply perceptive reading, with finely wrought detail and brilliant playing from the LSO. It also offers an outstanding trio of soloists, with the 1968 sound still exceptionally full and well-focused. A pity it still comes uncoupled at full price.

Barenboim's Paris recording, reissued at mid-price with an unusual Franck coupling, offers the only current version with a French orchestra. It is a warmly idiomatic reading, not as brilliant as some and not always as well-played, but with a satisfying weight that relates such a sequence as the love music to Wagner's *Tristan*. The soloists are first rate and the recording is atmospheric. The Franck coupling is also successful.

Charles Munch recorded the complete *Roméo et Juliette* Symphony in 1953 only four years after his Decca recording of the three orchestral excerpts, not long after his appointment to Boston in succession to Koussevitzky. (He re-recorded it in 1961 in stereo with Rosalind Elias, Cesare Valetti and Giorgi Tozzi as the soloists.) The RCA remastering has done wonders for the sound, and in the three orchestral movements the playing of the Boston orchestra is vastly superior to that of the Paris Conservatoire, but it also occasionally sounds in its sheer brilliance (in the *Queen Mab Scherzo*, for example) as if Munch was carried away by the sheer feats of virtuosity this great orchestra could perform. This was the first recording of the whole work and the soloists, Margaret Roggero, Leslie Chabay and Yi-Kwei-Sze, are impressive. While it would be an exaggeration to call the recording boxy, the mono sound does not convey much sense of space. In no way a challenge to the Colin Davis account from the 1960s this nevertheless remains a valuable historical document and a welcome supplement. Moreover, it comes with a lovely account of *Nuits d'été* from Victoria de los Angeles at her prime.

Inbal conducts a refined account of Berlioz's great dramatic symphony which yet lacks power and necessary weight, not helped by distanced sound and speeds that often sound cautious, as in the *Queen Mab scherzo*.

Toscanini's concert performance of February 1947 brings many electrifying moments, with the melodic lines often drawn out lovingly in a Verdian way and with the virtuoso passages delivered with panache. But the sound, recorded in the notorious Studio 8H, is dry and fizzy, far less full than the RCA recording for Charles Munch in Boston, made only two years later. The Bizet coupling offers brilliant playing, but Munch is a more idiomatic Berliozian and offers a more interesting coupling in *Les nuits d'été* with Victoria de los Angeles.

Gardelli on Orfeo conducts a curiously low-powered reading. Often moulded in a Verdian way, it yet lacks brilliance despite excellent sound and three fine soloists.

Te Deum, Op. 22.

*** DG Dig. 410 696-2 [id.]. Araiza, London Symphony Ch., LPO Ch., Woburn Singers, Boys' Ch., European Community Youth O, Abbado.

The DG recording from Abbado is very impressive. The sound is wide-ranging, with striking dynamic contrasts: Abbado brings great tonal refinement and dignity to this performance, and the spacious sound helps. Francisco Araiza is altogether first class.

OPERA

Béatrice et Bénédict (complete).

*** Ph. 416 952-2 (2) [id.]. Baker, Tear, Eda-Pierre, Allen, Lloyd, Van Allan, Watts, Alldis Ch., LSO, C. Davis.

*** Erato/Warner Dig. 2292 45773-2 (2) [id.]. Graham, Viala, McNair, Robbin, Bacquier, Cachemaille, Le Texier, Lyon Opera Ch. & O, John Nelson.

Béatrice et Bénédict presents not just witty and brilliant music for the heroine and hero (Dame Janet Baker and Robert Tear at their most pointed) but sensuously beautiful passages too. First-rate solo and choral singing, brilliant playing and sound refined and clear in texture, bright and fresh, even if minimal hiss betrays an analogue source.

The Lyon Opera version conducted by John Nelson makes an excellent alternative to the vintage Colin Davis recording. In spacious, modern, digital sound it offers substantially more of the French dialogue, well spoken by actors but more dryly recorded than the musical numbers. Susan Graham is a characterful Béatrice, lighter in the big aria than Janet Baker for Davis but aptly younger-sounding. Jean-Luc Viala is a comparably light Bénédict, pointing the fun in his big aria, and Sylvia McNair and Catherine Robbin are superb as Hero and Ursule.

Les Troyens, Parts 1 & 2 (complete).
⊛ *** Ph. 416 432-2 (4) [id.]. Veasey, Vickers, Lindholm, Glossop, Soyer, Partridge, Wandsworth School Boys' Ch., ROHCG Ch. & O, C. Davis.

Throughout this long and apparently disjointed score Davis compels the listener to concentrate, to appreciate its epic logic. Only in the great love scene of *O nuit d'ivresse* would one have welcomed the more expansive hand of a Beecham. Veasey on any count, even next to Dame Janet Baker, makes a splendid Dido, singing always with fine heroic strength, with Vickers a ringing Aeneas. The Covent Garden Chorus and Orchestra excel themselves in virtuoso singing and playing, while CD brings out the superb quality of sound all the more vividly.

Les Troyens (abridged).
☞ (**) VAIA mono VAIA 1006-3 (3) [id.]. Regina Resnik, Steber, Cassilly, Singher, Sarfaty, Ch. & O, Robert Lawrence.

The sound on this 1960 live recording is very variable and always limited so that at its worst it is dim and distant. The playing of the orchestra (or orchestras, when the recordings spanned performances in both New York and Washington) is generally rough, but there is an excitement conveyed, and some of the singing is thrilling, notably from Eleanor Steber as a magnificent Cassandra, perhaps finer than any on disc yet, and Regina Resnik as Dido. Both Richard Cassilly, a clear, strong Aeneas, and Resnik sound fresher and firmer than they often have on commercial discs. Yet ensembles hardly make the impact they should in this work, and with 3¼ hours of music recorded, as against four in the complete Davis version, these concert performances involved more cuts than we should allow nowadays.

Les Troyens (highlights).
☞ (*) VAIA mono VAIA 1026 [id.]. Del Monaco, Rankin, Simionato, Ch. & O, Kubelik.

This is a curiosity, valuable chiefly for the warm, concentrated conducting of Rafael Kubelik. Otherwise there is little to applaud for, using an Italian translation, these singers have only a sketchy idea of Berlioz style, with Mario del Monaco predictably coarse even in the great love-duet nocturne. The 1960 sound is closely focused but very limited.

Berners, Lord (Gerald Tyrwhitt-Wilson) (1883–1950)

The Triumph of Neptune (ballet suite): excerpts.
(M) (***) EMI mono CDM7 63405-2 [id.]. LPO, Sir Thomas Beecham – BANTOCK: *Fifine at the fair;* BAX: *Garden of Fand.* (***)
☞ (M) (***) Sony mono SMK 46683 [id.]. Phd. O, Beecham – ARNELL: *Punch and the child;* DELIUS: *Paris.* (***)

The Triumph of Neptune was a rare example of music by an English composer being commissioned and performed by Diaghilev's Ballets Russes. The composer has often been called the English Satie, and Satie's love of circus music was echoed by Berners' taste for the music hall. The 1937 EMI excerpts include the *Scottische, Hornpipe, Polka: the sailor's return, Harlequinade, Dance of the fairy princess, Intermezzo, Sunday morning* and *Apotheosis of Neptune.* The LPO playing has all the whimsical flair one would expect, and the CD transfer by Michael Dutton and John Holland admirably retains the fullness and atmosphere of those old shellac discs. The sound may be confined but it is never thinned out or made edgy.

Sir Thomas recorded the nine excerpts with the Philadelphia Orchestra in 1952; most of them overlap with his 1937 version of the suite, an essential item in any discography, but two (*Cloudland* and *The Frozen Forest*) are not included on the earlier record. The Philadelphia Orchestra respond to this music in a brilliant if rather bemused fashion – what must they have thought of the vocal contributions they were required to add to the *Scottische*! However, they obviously enjoy the music and Sir Thomas ensures that there is no lack of suave polish and wit. The recording is remarkably good, and this disc is also a 'must' for the sake of the couplings.

The Triumph of Neptune (ballet): extended suite; *Fantaisie espagnole; Fugue in C min.; 3 Morceaux; Nicholas Nickleby* (film music).
☞ (M) *** EMI Dig. CDM5 65098-2 [id.]. RLPO, Wordsworth.

Barry Wordsworth puts us in his debt by providing a fine modern version of *The Triumph of Neptune* and giving it in more complete form. While memories of Beecham remain undimmed (in his hands, *Cloudland* and *The Frozen Forest* had a very special character and elegance that sparkled through all the surface noise), Wordsworth captures the character of this music remarkably well. Moreover we have other enjoyable (and valuable) repertoire: the *Trois morceaux* and the *Fantaisie espagnole* are new to the catalogue. They date from 1918 and are Gallic in inspiration and sympathy, as their titles suggest, and are attractively imaginative. Some commentators have drawn parallels with Satie: both were renowned eccentrics and both had an irreverent sense of humour, but Satie's vein of melancholy went deeper and his awareness of pain was more acute. The recording is good without being in the demonstration class; detail is well defined and there is plenty of body. The frontispiece of the CD gives Berners his appropriate epitaph: 'Here lies Lord Berners, one of the learners, / His great love of learning may earn him a burning, / But praise to the Lord, he seldom was bored.' Nor are we.

Bernstein, Leonard (1918–90)

(i) *Candide: overture; Facsimile* (choreographic essay); *Fancy Free* (ballet); *On the Town* (3 dance episodes); (ii) *On the Town* (musical); (i) *On the Waterfront* (symphonic suite); (iii) *Trouble in Tahiti (opera in 7 scenes);* (i) *West Side story: Symphonic dances* (orch. Sid Ramin & Irwin Kostal).
(M) *** Sony SM3K 47154 (3) [id.]. (i) NYPO; (ii) Betty Comden, Adolph Green, Nancy Walker, John Reardon, Cris Alexander, George Gaynes, Ch. & O; (iii) Nancy Williams, Julian Patrick & Vocal Trio, Columbia Wind Ens.; all cond. composer.

Candide: overture; West Side story: symphonic dances.
(M) *** Sony SMK 47529 [id.]. NYPO, composer – GERSHWIN: *American in Paris* etc. ***

Fancy free (ballet); *On the Town* (3 dance episodes); *On the Waterfront* (symphonic suite).
(M) **(*) Sony SMK 47530 [id.]. NYPO, composer.

Candide overture – placed at the beginning of Disc 2 – provides the perfect curtain-raiser for this indispensable box of Bernstein's vibrant, early recordings of his theatrical and film music. The New York Philharmonic, in cracking form, display virtuosity and tremendous spirit in the ballet music and comparable gusto in the noisily pungent film score, plus a natural command of the jazz rhythms, while the tender moments in the *West Side story* dances have great poignancy. The recordings are remarkably vivid and have been impressively remastered. Bernstein's exhilarating and definitive New York performances of his theatre music are now reissued separately as part of the Sony 'Royal Edition'.

(i) *Candide: overture;* (ii) *On the Town: 3 Dance episodes;* (i) *West Side story: Symphonic dances;* (iii) *America.*
(M) *** DG Dig. 427 806-2; *427 806-4.* (i) LAPO; (ii) Israel PO; (iii) Troyanos with O; composer – BARBER: *Adagio* ***; GERSHWIN: *Rhapsody in blue.* **(*)

In his later DG account of the *Overture* to *Candide* the composer still directs with tremendous flair, his speed a fraction slower than in his New York studio recording for CBS. The colourful and vigorous dances are given vivid if close-up digital sound, obviously more modern than in the CBS/Sony versions.

3 Meditations for cello and orchestra (from *Mass*).
☞ (B) *** DG Double 437 952-2 (2) [id.]. Rostropovich, Israel PO, composer – BOCCHERINI: *Cello concerto No. 2;* GLAZUNOV: *Chant du Ménestrel;* SHOSTAKOVICH: *Cello concerto No. 2;* TARTINI: *Cello concerto;* TCHAIKOVSKY: *Andante cantabile* etc.; VIVALDI: *Cello concertos.* ***

Bernstein's concertante piece, *Meditations for cello and orchestra*, readily reflects the poetry of

Rostropovich's art – the piece was written for him and he plays it masterfully. This is part of a remarkably generous Double DG bargain anthology.

(i) *On the Town: suite;* (ii) *7 Anniversaries.*
(M) (***) BMG/RCA mono GD 60915 [60915-2]. (i) On the Town O, Bernstein; (ii) Bernstein (piano) – COPLAND: *Billy the Kid* etc. (***)

There is always something special about first recordings. There is great vitality and swagger here and no apologies need be made for the mono recording, which though slightly shrill has great vividness. The stage music is followed by *Seven anniversaries,* a set of vignettes composed in 1943, dedicated to family and musical friends, opening with Aaron Copland and closing with William Schuman.

Prelude, fugue and riffs.
(***) Sony MK 42227 [id.]. Goodman, Columbia Jazz Combo, composer – COPLAND: *Clarinet concerto;* STRAVINSKY: *Ebony concerto;* BARTOK: *Contrasts;* GOULD: *Derivations.* (***)
☞ *** BMG/RCA Dig. 09026 61350-2 [id.]. Stolzman, LSO, Leighton Smith – COPLAND: *Concerto;* CORIGLIANO: *Concerto;* STRAVINSKY: *Ebony concerto.*

Bernstein's exuberant, sometimes wild, yet structured *Prelude, fugue and riffs* fits well within this CBS collection of jazz-inspired pieces in a vintage performance, directed by the composer. It sounds exceptionally vivid on CD.

Like Benny Goodman before him, Richard Stolzman couples Bernstein's *Prelude, fugue and riffs* with Copland's masterly concerto and Stravinsky's *Ebony concerto* and makes the most of its unbuttoned jazziness. He is better recorded than Goodman, and his record can be recommended strongly on all counts.

Symphonies Nos. (i) *1 (Jeremiah);* (ii) *2 (The age of anxiety)* for piano and orchestra; (i; iii) *3 (Kaddish): To the beloved memory of President Kennedy* (original version); (vi) *Prelude, fugue and riffs;* (iv) *Serenade after Plato's Symposium* (for solo violin, string orchestra, harp & percussion); (v) *Chichester Psalms.*
(M) *** Sony SM3K 47162 (3) [id.]. (i) Tourel; (ii) Entremont; (iii) F. Montealegre (speaker), Camerata Singers; Columbus Boychoir; (iv) Francescatti; (v) J. Bogart, Camerata Singers; (i–iv) NYPO; (vi) Benny Goodman, Columbia Jazz Combo; all cond. composer.

All three recordings were made in the Manhattan Center, New York, in the early 1960s; the acoustic is agreeably spacious, the bass resonantly full and the strings have plenty of body, so that no apologies need be made for the sound-quality. The *Chichester Psalms,* also impressively transferred to CD, was written in response to a commission from the Dean of Chichester. The *Serenade* must rank among Bernstein's most resourceful and inspired creations. Francescatti responds naturally to the Hebrew flavour of the lyrical writing but he is very closely balanced, as is the orchestra, and Bernstein's passionate climaxes are given an aggressive fierceness.

Symphonies Nos. (i) *1 (Jeremiah);* (ii) *2 (The Age of anxiety)* for piano and orchestra; (iii) *3 (Kaddish);* (iv) *Serenade after Plato's Symposium* (for solo violin, string orchestra, harp and percussion).
☞ (M) *** DG 445 245-2 (2) [id.]. Israel PO, composer; with (i) Christa Ludwig; (ii) Lukas Foss; (iii) Caballé, Wager, V. Jeunesse Ch., Berlin Boys' Ch.; (iv) Gidon Kremer.

Bernstein's three symphonies have been undervalued because of his theatre music and his willingness to draw on popular influences, but their surface facility is deceptive. The *Jeremiah Symphony* dates from the composer's early twenties and ends with a moving passage from Lamentations for the mezzo soloist – here with Christa Ludwig responding sensitively. As the title suggests, the *Second Symphony* was inspired by the poem of W. H. Auden, and the work includes a concertante piano part, admirably played by Lukas Foss. The *Third Symphony,* written in memory of John F. Kennedy, is recorded here in its revised version (with a male speaker), which concentrates the original concept of a dialogue beween man and God, a challenge from earth to heaven. The performances here are not always quite as polished or as forceful as those Bernstein recorded earlier for CBS in New York (see above), but they never fail to reflect the warmth of Bernstein's writing. The *Serenade* must rank among Bernstein's most resourceful and inspired creations, full of ideas, often thrilling and exciting, and equally often moving. Gidon Kremer has all the nervous intensity and vibrant energy to do justice to this powerful and inventive score, and throughout the playing of the Israel Philharmonic is extremely vivid. So are the CD transfers (of 1977/78) recordings throughout this thoroughly worthwhile anthology.

(i–iii) *Symphony No. 1 (Jeremiah);* (iv) *Anniversaries: In memoriam Nathalie Koussevitzky;* (ii; v) *Songfest.*

☞ (M) (***) BMG/RCA stereo/mono 09026 61581-2 [id.]. (i) Nan Merriman; (ii) St Louis SO; (iii) composer; (iv) Leonard Slatkin (piano); (v) Hohenfeld, White, Spence, Planté, Hartman, Cheek, cond. Slatkin.

Songfest, a cycle for six soloists and orchestra, celebrating all things American, finds Bernstein's inspiration focused sharply within a limited frame, and the result is one of his finest works. Specially moving, and beautifully sung by John Cheek, is the setting of a long-buried Whitman poem, celebrating male love; but each poem has been perceptively chosen to illustrate the variegated strands of American society. Leonard Slatkin's new recording hardly replaces Bernstein's own (currently withdrawn) on DG, but it offers another fine performance, recorded in a more mellow acoustic and with a warmer ensemble. In place of the *Chichester Psalms* on the DG issue comes Bernstein's own historic first recording of the *Jeremiah Symphony*, made for RCA in 1945, with Nan Merriman the clear-toned soloist. The mono sound is limited but conveys the high voltage of the performance. Between the two main works Slatkin plays the brief piano piece commemorating the first wife of Serge Koussevitzky, taken from the *Anniversaries suite.*

(i) *Symphony No. 2 (Age of anxiety); Overture Candide; Fancy Free* (ballet).

☞ (M) *** Virgin/EMI Dig. CUV5 61119-2 [id.]. (i) Kahane; Bournemouth SO, Andrew Litton.

Bernstein holds nothing back, but Litton in his less thrusting way is just as compelling and often more subtly expressive, helped by a more poetic, less muscular pianist, Jeffrey Kahane. Anyone fancying Litton's popular coupling need not hesitate.

VOCAL MUSIC

Arias and Barcarolles. On the Town: Some other time; Lonely town; Carried away; I can cook. Peter Pan: Dream with me. Songfest: Storyette, H. M.; To what you said. Wonderful Town: A little bit in love.

*** Koch International Classics Dig. 37000-2 [id.]. Judy Kaye, William Sharp; Michael Barrett, Steven Blier.

Arias and Barcarolles for two soloists and piano duet is a family charade of a work. It is a charming piece, here given – with the composer himself approving the performance – in the original version with piano and excellent, characterful soloists. The bizarre title relates to a comment made by President Eisenhower, after he had heard Bernstein play a Mozart concerto: 'I like music with a theme, not all them arias and barcarolles.' It became a Bernstein family joke. That half-hour work, very well recorded, is coupled with an equivalent collection of eight of Bernstein's most haunting songs and duets.

Chichester Psalms.

(M) *** Pickwick/RPO Dig. CDRPO 7007; ZCRPO 7007 [id.]. Aled Jones, London Symphony Ch., RPO, Hickox – FAURE: *Requiem.* ***

Chichester Psalms (reduced score).

*** Hyp. Dig. CDA 66219 [id.]. Martelli, Corydon Singers, Masters, Kettel, Trotter; Best – BARBER: *Agnus Dei;* COPLAND: *In the beginning* etc. ***

Bernstein's *Chichester Psalms* make an instant communication and respond to familiarity too, especially in Richard Hickox's fresh and colourful reading, with Aled Jones bringing an ethereal contribution to the setting of the 23rd Psalm. The recorded sound is firm and well focused.

Martin Best uses the composer's alternative reduced orchestration. The treble soloist, Dominic Martelli, cannot match Aled Jones, but his chaste contribution is persuasive and the choir scales down its pianissimos to accommodate him, with elegiac effect. Excellent sound, with the acoustic of St Jude-on-the-Hill, Hampstead, creating the right atmosphere.

(i) *Dybbuk* (ballet): complete; (ii) *Mass (for the death of President Kennedy).*

(M) *** Sony SM3K 47158 (3) [id.]. (i) David Johnson, John Ostendorf, NY City Ballet O; (ii) Alan Titus (celebrant), Scribner Ch., Berkshire Boys' Ch., Rock Band & O; composer.

Outrageously eclectic in its borrowings from pop and the avant garde, Bernstein's *Mass* presents an extraordinary example of the composer's irresistible creative energy. Bernstein's ghoulish ballet on lost spirits presents much the same happy and colourful amalgam of influences as you find in other Bernstein ballets, a touch of the *Rite of spring* here and a whiff of *West Side story* there. The vocal parts, although fairly substantial (and very well done here), are merely incidental.

Songs: *La bonne cuisine* (French and English versions); *I hate music* (cycle); *2 Love songs; Piccola serenata; Silhouette; So pretty; Mass: A simple song; I go on. Candide: It must be so; Candide's lament. 1600 Pennsylvania Ave: Take care of this house. Peter Pan: My house; Peter Pan; Who am I; Never-Never Land.*
*** Etcetera Dig. KTC 1037 [id.]. Roberta Alexander, Tan Crone.

A delightful collection, consistently bearing witness to Bernstein's flair for a snappy idea as well as his tunefulness. Roberta Alexander's rich, warm voice and winning personality are well supported by Tan Crone at the piano. The recording is lifelike and undistracting.

Stage works

Candide (musical: original Broadway production): *Overture and excerpts.*
(M) *** Sony SK 48017 [id.]. Adrian, Cook, Rounseville and original New York cast, Krachmalnick.

This exhilarating CBS record encapsulates the original 1956 Broadway production and has all the freshness of discovery inherent in a first recording, plus all the zing of the American musical theatre. The lyrics, by Richard Wilbur, give pleasure in themselves. Brilliantly lively sound.

Candide (final, revised version).
⊛ *** DG Dig. 429 734-2; *429 734-4* (2) [id.]. Hadley, Anderson, Green, Ludwig, Gedda, Della Jones, Ollmann, London Symphony Ch., LSO, composer.

Candide: highlights.
*** DG Dig. 435 487-2; *435 487-4* [id.] (from above set, cond. composer).

John Mauceri, dissatisfied with the results of his 1982 score of *Candide*, undertook yet a further revision in the mid-1980s, this time with Bernstein's collaboration. Its humour, satirically reflecting Voltaire's rubbishing of enforced establishment values, at one point draws a ready parallel between the Spanish Inquisition and Bernstein's own experience during America's darkest political era.

The result is a triumph, both in the studio recording which Bernstein made immediately after the concert performances and in the video recording of the actual concert at the Barbican. It confirms *Candide* as a classic, bringing out not just the vigour, the wit and the tunefulness of the piece more than ever before, but also an extra emotional intensity, something beyond the cynical Voltaire original. There is no weak link in the cast. Jerry Hadley is touchingly characterful as Candide, producing heady tone, and June Anderson as Cunegonde is not only brilliant in coloratura but warmly dramatic too. The character roles are brilliantly cast too. It was an inspired choice to have Christa Ludwig as the Old Woman, and equally original to choose Adolph Green, lyric writer for Broadway musicals as well as cabaret performer, for the dual role of Dr Pangloss and Martin. Nicolai Gedda also proves a winner in his series of cameo roles, and the full, incisive singing of the London Symphony Chorus adds to the weight of the performance without inflation.

What is missing in the CD set is the witty narration, prepared by John Wells and spoken by Adolph Green and Kurt Ollmann in the Barbican performance. As included on the video of the live concert (laser disc DG 072 423-1; VHS DG 072 423-3), those links leaven the entertainment delightfully. Even those with the CDs should investigate the video version, which also includes Bernstein's own moving speeches of introduction before each Act.

On the Town (complete; with narration by Comden and Green).
☞ *** DG Dig. 437 516-2; *437 516-4* [id.]. Frederica von Stade, Tyne Daly, Marie McLaughlin, Thomas Hampson, David Garrison, Kurt Ollmann, Samuel Ramey, Evelyn Lear, Adolph Green, Cleo Laine, Meriel Dickinson, LSO, Tilson Thomas.

It was bold of Michael Tilson Thomas in June 1992 to seek to follow up Leonard Bernstein's last triumph in London, his performances and recording of *Candide*, with another concert performance with the LSO at the Barbican of Bernstein's earliest musical, *On the Town*. With the librettists, Betty Comden and Adolph Green, as narrators, it was as though Bernstein himself was performing as well as providing the music, another triumph. One problem with *On the Town* is that everyone remembers the brilliant film and expects it to be the same. In fact the film, faithful enough in telling of three sailors on a day's shore-leave in wartime New York, kept remarkably few of Bernstein's numbers. If anything, the full score in the exuberance of youth is even richer in catchy tunes than *West Side story* or *Candide*. A concert performance, bringing in some of the extra numbers that were originally cut from the Broadway show for lack of time, provides the perfect formula.

As in *Candide* (if not *West Side story*), the mixing of opera stars with the Broadway tradition works like a charm. Thomas Hampson, rich and resonant, sings Gabey, the lead-sailor in search of

Miss Turnstiles, with another fine American baritone, Kurt Ollmann, as Chip and David Garrison giving authentic point to the third sailor, Ozzie. Then in opulent casting Samuel Ramey sings a series of incidental roles, including the ever-understanding Pitkin, constantly pushed aside by his man-mad girlfriend, Claire. In that role Frederica von Stade firmly establishes herself as the central star, and anyone hesitating should hear the way she leads the ensemble in the climactic nostalgia of *Some other time*. Marie McLaughlin as Ivy, Miss Turnstiles, is slightly less at home, but Tyne Daly – the Cagney of TV's 'Cagney and Lacey' – as the predatory taxi-driver, Hildy, is winningly larger-than-life. The authentic Broadway brassiness of her voice is combined with clean, pure attack. Add to that such stars as Cleo Laine and Evelyn Lear in small roles, all supported by the fizzing energy of the LSO under Tilson Thomas.

In contrast with *Candide*, the live recording has been used for both the CD and the video (072 197-3 [VHS], 072 197-1 [Laserdisc]) yet the results are startlingly different. With the CD the numbers are presented dry, as though recorded in the studio, with no linking narration and no applause. Not only that, but two of the extra numbers and several encores are omitted to keep the result on a single, well-filled CD. In recompense, an extra number, omitted from the video, *The intermission's great*, is included on the CD. As with *Candide*, the video version, over half an hour longer, proves even more enjoyable, including narration as well as extra numbers. As narrators, Comden and Green are the most winning guides, ending up by leading a final encore of the big weepy tune, *Some other time*, helping to convey the magic and electricity of a great occasion. The result is often very funny as well as moving, with the personality of each member of the cast coming over even more vividly. The video not only shows Patricia Birch's clever staging of the story (uncostumed), but punctuates it with black-and-white newsreel clips of wartime New York. So it must be the video which earns our Rosette.

A Quiet place (complete).
* DG Dig. 419 761-2 (2) [id.]. Wendy White, Chester Ludgin, Beverly Morgan, John Brandstetter, Peter Kazaras, Vocal Ens., Austrian RSO, composer.

In flashbacks in Act II of *A Quiet place*, Bernstein incorporates his 1951 score, *Trouble in Tahiti*, with its popular style set in relief against the more serious idiom adopted for the main body of the opera. Bernstein's score is full of thoughtful and warmly expressive music, but nothing quite matches the sharp, tongue-in-cheek jazz-influenced invention of *Trouble in Tahiti*. The recording was made in Vienna, with an excellent cast of American singers, and with the Austrian Radio orchestra responding splendidly on its first visit to the Vienna State Opera.

West Side story: complete recording; *On the Waterfront (Symphonic suite)*.
⊛ ***** DG Dig. 415 253-2 (2) [id.]. Te Kanawa, Carreras, Troyanos, Horne, Ollmann, Ch. and O, composer.

West Side story: highlights.
(M) **(*) DG Dig. 431 027-2; *431 027-4* (from complete recording, with Te Kanawa, Carreras, Troyanos, Horne, Ollmann; cond. composer).

Bernstein's recording of the complete score of his most popular work – the first time he had ever conducted the complete musical himself – takes a frankly operatic approach in its casting, but the result is highly successful, for the great vocal melodies are worthy of voices of the highest calibre. Tatiana Troyanos, herself brought up on the West Side, spans the stylistic dichotomy to perfection in a superb portrayal of Anita. The clever production makes the best of both musical worlds, with Bernstein's son and daughter speaking the dialogue most affectingly. Bernstein conducts a superb instrumental group of musicians 'from on and off Broadway', and they are recorded with a bite and immediacy that is captivating. The power of the music is greatly enhanced by the spectacularly wide dynamic range of the recording, with a relatively dry acoustic keeping the sound-picture within an apt scale but without losing bloom. The two-disc set includes, besides the musical, the vivid *Symphonic suite* from *On the Waterfront*.

West Side Story (film soundtrack recording).
☞ (M) **(*) Sony SK 48211 [id.]. Nixon, Bryant, Tamblyn, Wand, Chakaris, Ch. & O, Johnny Green.

Few musicals have been transferred to the screen with more success than *West Side Story*, and there are some who feel that, even though the principals' voices are ghosted, the soundtrack recording is preferable to Bernstein's own version using opera stars. The film was splendidly cast and the 'ghosts' were admirably chosen. In the romantic scenes, *Tonight* and *One hand, one heart*, the changes from sung to spoken words are completely convincing and the tragic (mostly spoken) final scene – here included on record for the first time – is very moving. Russ Tamblyn, who sings his own songs, is first class and Marni Nixon and Jim Bryant as the pair of lovers sing touchingly and with youthful freshness. The performance is vibrantly conducted by Johnny Green, and it is a pity that the CD transfer is so 'toppy', bringing a degree of edge both to voices and to the brilliant orchestral playing. Even so, the performance is very involving, and it is good that the *Overture* and End Titles sequence are included here – like the finale, for the first time on disc. The result is an essential supplement to the composer's own later version.

Bertrand, Anthoine de (1540–81)

Amours de Ronsard, Book 1; *Amours de Cassandre:* excerpts.
(B) *** HM Dig. HMA 431147 [id.]. Clément Janequin Ens.

Anthoine de Bertrand's chansons as recorded here by the Clément Janequin Ensemble show him to be, if not a great master, at least a composer of feeling and considerable resource. The performances are excellent throughout, and admirably recorded. At bargain price this is well worth trying.

Berwald, Franz (1797–1868)

(i) *Piano concerto in D;* (ii) *Violin concerto in C sharp min., Op. 2; Festival of the Bayadères; Overture: The Queen of Golconda; Serious and joyful fancies.*
☞ (M) *** EMI CDM5 65073-2 [id.]. (i) Marian Migdal; (ii) Arve Tellefsen; RPO, Björlin.

All these performances were recorded in 1976 and appeared in a four-LP set in harness with the four symphonies and the other tone-poems. This CD creams off the very best performances and makes a highly recommendable pendant to the Järvi DG set of the symphonies. The *Violin concerto* (1820) is an early work, written in the shadow of Spohr and Weber, but it has great charm and a keen melodic facility. A beautiful and elegant performance from Arve Tellefsen and the RPO under the late Ulf Björlin. The *Piano concerto* (1855) is a strange piece. The piano plays all the time without a moment's rest – indeed the score notes that the work can be performed without orchestra. There are some beautiful ideas, including the Chopinesque second group, and they are heard to splendid advantage in Marian Migdal's poetic and imaginative reading. The three shorter pieces are also delightful: the two tone-poems are vintage Berwald and come from the same period (1841–2) as the *Sinfonie sérieuse*, and it is possible that the *Queen of Golconda overture* (1862) also incorporates (either in part or in whole) a lost *Humoristisches Capriccio* written in the 1840s. Very acceptable performances of the orchestral pieces, excellent ones of the *Concertos*, and very good transfers make this a highly desirable issue, particularly at its competitive price.

Symphonies Nos. 1 in G min. (Sérieuse); 2 in D (Capricieuse); 3 in C (Singulière); 4 in E flat.
*** DG Dig. 415 502-2 (2) [id.]. Gothenburg SO, Järvi.

On DG, the orchestral playing has abundant spirit and energy; this is music that is wholly in the life-stream of the Gothenburg orchestra, and the excellent acoustic of the Gothenburg Hall shows the scores to great advantage. Neeme Järvi sets generally brisk tempi, yet the pacing feels right. The sound is altogether superb.

Symphonies Nos. 1 (Sérieuse); 3 (Singulière); Overture: Estrella de Soria (2 performances of each & rehearsal of overture).
☞ (**) Caprice mono/stereo CAP 22032 (2) [id.]. Gothenburg RSO or Stockholm PO, Tor Mann; Stockholm PO or Swedish RSO, Sten Broman.

A set of somewhat specialized appeal. It contrasts the approach of two Swedish conductors to the same Berwald symphonies. Tor Mann made more of a reputation in his day than did Sten Broman. Mann was a pupil of Schnéevoigt and Ellberg, who prepared the score of the *Sinfonie capricieuse*, Broman of Henri Marteau and Zemlinsky. Broman's account of the *Estrella overture* is imaginative and so, too, is his first movement of the *Sinfonie singulière*, much broader than conductors like Blomstedt and Järvi – and, for that matter, Tor Mann, who rushes it off its feet. Broman's performances were recorded in 1968 in Stockholm, Tor Mann's are of earlier provenance (1938–46) and his *Sinfonie sérieuse* serves as a reminder that the Gothenburg orchestra was a very different body from today's. The recordings are of acceptable quality.

Symphonies Nos. 1 (Sinfonie sérieuse); 4 in E flat (Sinfonie naïve).
☞ **(*) Decca Dig. 436 597-2 [id.]. San Francisco SO, Blomstedt.

Blomstedt gets very good playing from the San Francisco orchestra and his accounts of the *Sérieuse* and the *E flat Symphonies* are eminently civilized. *No. 4 in E flat* is the sunniest of the symphonies, though in Blomstedt's realization the sun has a rather cool pallor. Tempi are somewhat measured and there is little of the infectious sparkle that Neeme Järvi gets in his communicative and enthusiastic performances on DG, which have the advantage of the livelier, warmer acoustic of the Gothenburg hall. The Decca recording has a truthful perspective to commend it and clean, well-detailed sound, but the strings are a bit top-heavy and have a chilly timbre, doubtless induced by the acoustic. Yet these are well-shaped, highly intelligent readings that deserve a three-star recommendation, though by the side of Järvi and Ehrling they sound a bit laid back.

Symphonies Nos. 3 in C (Sinfonie singulière); No. 4 in E flat.
*** Bluebell ABD 037 [id.]. LSO, Sixten Ehrling.

Sixten Ehrling's records of Berwald's masterpiece, the *Sinfonie singulière*, and its sunny and high-spirited companion, the *Symphony No. 4 in E flat*, were made in 1967 for Decca and still sound as fresh and satisfying as ever. Although the sound is not digital, there is no reason to withhold a third star.

Grand septet in B flat.
*** CRD CRD 3344 [id.]. Nash Ens. – HUMMEL: *Septet*. ***

Berwald's only *Septet* is a work of genuine quality and deserves a secure place in the repertory instead of on its periphery. It is eminently well played by the Nash Ensemble, and finely recorded.

(i) *Piano quintet No. 1 in C min.;* (ii) *Piano trios Nos. 1 in E flat; 3 in D min.*
**(*) MS Dig. MSCD 521 [id.]. (i) Stefan Lindgren, Berwald Qt; (ii) Bernt Lysell, Ola Karlsson, Lucia Negro.

The performances of the *Trios* are very good indeed, though not necessarily superior to those of the Prunyi–Kiss–Onczay team on Marco Polo. One minor quibble: a little more space round and distance from the instruments would have shown these fine players to even greater advantage.

Piano trios Nos. 1 in E flat; 2 in F min., 3 in D min.
*** Marco Polo Dig. 8.223170 [id.]. Prunyi, Kiss, Onczay.

These Hungarian players give spirited accounts of all three recorded here and make out a persuasive case for this music. The string players (András Kiss and Czaba Onczay) are both highly accomplished; perhaps the most demanding writing is for the piano and it is a pity that Ilona Prunyi proves at times to be a little less imaginative than her companions. The recording, made at the Italian Institute in Budapest, is very good indeed, fresh and present.

Piano trios: in C (1845); No. 4 in C (1853); in C (fragment); in E flat (fragment).
☞ **(*) Marco Polo Dig. 8.223430 [id.]. Kalman Drafi, Jozsef Mondrian, György Kertész.

The *C major Trio* (1845) survives only in copies and was not published until 1981. Like its companions and the fragments recorded here, it is fresh and inventive. These performances by Kalman Drafi, Jozsef Mondrian and György Kertész are faithful and committed and are very well recorded at the Festetic Castle in Budapest. They are by no means as imaginative or brilliant as Wilhelm Walz, Jörg Metzger and Arne Torger were on the Big Ben label (572 005-2). If readers see this set (or if it becomes available again during the lifetime of this book), snap it up. Good though these are, the rival set is far more spirited.

String quartet in G min.
☞ *** CRD CRD 3361; CRDC 4061 [id.]. Chilingirian Qt – WIKMANSON: *Quartet*. ***

Berwald composed four quartets: two in 1849 after the symphonies, and two in his mid-twenties. The *G minor Quartet* and a companion in B flat which has not survived, date from 1818. This work did not appear in print until the 1940s, when the parts of the middle movements were discovered during stocktaking at the Royal Swedish Academy of Music. It is, as one would expect from an accomplished violinist, a remarkably assured piece, and the first movement is full of modulatory audacities. The thematic substance is both characterful and appealing. The trio of the Scherzo has a touching charm that is almost Schubertian, though it is impossible that Berwald could have been aware of his great contemporary. This is a highly interesting and often bold *Quartet*, and the Chilingirian players give a well-shaped and sensitive account of it. They are truthfully recorded, and the coupling – another

Swedish quartet – enhances the attractions of this issue. The CD transfer is fresh and clear, and there is an excellent cassette equivalent. Strongly recommended.

Biber, Heinrich (1644–1704)

Battalia a 10; Sonata in D min. for violins, trombone and bass viola da gamba; Sonata No. 6 in B flat (Peasants' church-going); Sonata a 8 in B flat.
☞ (M) *** DG 437 081-2. VCM, Harnoncourt – MUFFAT: *Concerto No. 1 in D min.* etc. ***

Heinrich Biber's *Battle* evocation is as spectacular as any of the baroque era. The picture of 'The dissolute company' brings a half-minute of well-organized instrumental cacophony, and the battle sequence itself has some hair-raising instrumental effects, including barbaric pizzicati representing the cannon. In the *March* there is a bizarre fife-and-drum imitation by violin and double bass. The piece closes with a *Lament of the wounded musketeers.* The *Sonatas for strings* (and, in the case of the D minor work, a virtuoso solo trombone) show this Bohemian-born, Viennese Court Kapellmeister as a resourceful and inventive musician who knew how to manage more lyrical pictorial effects as well as dramatic ones. His musical ideas are certainly attractive. The performances have great character – Nikolaus Harnoncourt was always good at explosive effects – and are very well recorded.

Harmonia Artificiosa-Ariosa (for 2 violins scordatura and continuo): Partitas III & V. Rosenkranz sonata No. 10 (for violin scordatura and continuo); Passacaglia No. 16 for solo violin; Sonata No. VI; Sonata representativa (both for violin and continuo).
☞ *** BIS Dig. CD 608 [id.]. Maria Lindal, Ens. Saga.

Heinrich Biber is fast emerging as a major personality, and this record shows that his chamber music has as much character as that of Vivaldi. The *Harmonia Artificiosa-Ariosa* are every bit as inventive as the more familiar *Rosenkranz* set (the term scordatura, incidentally, indicated a different system of tuning rather than the usual fifths) and the melancholy *Passacaglia* for solo violin is totally memorable. But the hit of the programme is the *Sonata representativa* with its bird evocations – they are more than just imitations – including the nightingale, thrush, cuckoo (a most striking approach) and cockerel. Maria Lindal is a splendid soloist, and the style of the playing here is vibrantly authentic: the ear quickly adjusts to the plangent (but in no way anaemic) timbres which suit this repertoire admirably.

Rosenkranz sonatas Nos. 1–16.
(M) **(*) HM/BMG Dig. GD 77102 (2) [77102-RG]. Franzjosef Maier, Franz Lehrndorfer, Max Engel, Konrad Junghänel.

Biber's *Sonatas* for violin and basso continuo, based on the Mysteries of the rosary, include music of great poetic feeling and sensibility. The playing here is of high quality and, although the recording could provide better internal definition, it is full and pleasing.

Sonatae tam Aris, quam Aulis servientes: Nos. 2 in D; 3 in G min.; 5 in E min.; 11 in A.
☞ **(*) HM/BMG 05472 77303-2 [id.]. Freiburg Bar. Cons. – MUFFAT: *Sonatas.* **(*)

Biber's *Sonatae tam Auris, quam Aulis servientes* were written in 1670, intended, as the title suggests, for use in church (at the altar) or court. Each is short (4–5 minutes) and structured in a single movement yet each combines both expressive elements and a rhythmic vitality deriving from the dance. They are splendidly chimerical miniatures and confirm yet again the fecundity of the composer's imagination, with sleight-of-hand changes of tempo and apt use of contrapuntal devices. The result is wittily entertaining, yet retains its propriety, with the dance elements thoroughly absorbed so as not to offend the clergy with any vulgar associations. The performances here are winningly vital (try No. 2 as a sampler as it is briefest of all) and the only drawback for some ears is the tendency in sustained, chordal writing for the well-blended 'authentic' string group to sound a bit like a harmonium. Also the playing time is not generous (59 minutes) and there would certainly have been room for a couple more of these sonatas.

Requiem a 15 in A; Vesperae a 32.
☞ *** Erato/Warner Dig.4509 91725-2 [id.]. Bongers, Grimm, Wessel, De Groot, Reyans, S. Davies, Steur, De Koning, Amsterdam Bar. Ch. & O, Koopman.

As might be expected from the major key (hardly a usual one for a post-Renaissance requiem) Biber's A major setting is more robust than its companion in F minor. It is a gloriously exultant piece. Here death has very little sting, with the promises of forgiveness and heaven to come, and Biber immediately in the opening *Introitus* uses rich brass sonorities and his combined forces of singers in the grandest manner. In the Salzburg Court Cathedral of his day it was possible to place soloists, brass and choral groups in five different places. Here the polyphonic and polychoral writing is spread across a wide proscenium with brass and voices echoing each other ambitiously in overlapping phrases. There is plenty of vitality in the writing: the *Sequenz* ('Day of wrath!') bursts with energy from all concerned and the *Offertorium* moves along strongly to deliver sinners from the pains of hell. The *Sanctus* gives the soloists a chance to shine vivaciously, while in the *Agnus Dei* they echo each other in radiant lyricism. The closing *Communio* joyfully and expressively draws all the participants together and the work ends in gentle solemnity. The *Vespers* is in two parts, consisting of a *Dixit Dominus* and *Magnificat*. Although its polyphony is hardly less complex and its writing equally inventive, this work depends more on continual contrast to makes its effect, with the soloists consistently used in alternation with the more massive choral and brass outbursts. It has some splendid moments. The *Magnificat* brings a fine flowing fugato and, after much interplay between the solo group and the others, ends with a very positive closing *Amen*. The performances here are inspired with the most glorious sounds coming from all concerned, and the solo team matching voices and singing splendidly together. Very highly recommended.

Requiem in F min.
☞ **(*) HM/BMG Dig. 05472 77277-2 [id.]. Piau, Van der Sluis, Lettinga, Elwes, Van der Kamp, Netherlands Bach Festival Bar. Ch. & O, Leonhardt – VALLS: *Missa Scala Aretina.* **(*)

(i) *Requiem in F min.;* (ii) *Serenada 'Der Nachtwächter'; Balletae à 4; Battalia à 10; Sonata à 6 in B (Die Pauern Kirchfarht genandt).*
☞ *** O-L Dig. 436 460-2. (i) Catherine Bott, Tessa Bonner, Christopher Robson, John Mark Ainsley, Michael George; (ii) Simon Grant; New L. Cons., Pickett.

Biber is a rewarding, inventive figure – and, as the instrumental pieces show, a delightful one too. Philip Pickett calls the *Serenada* (in which Simon Grant participates characterfully, and the sonata, *Die Pauern Kirchfarht genandt*, 'a programmatic *tour de force*', and they are both quite astonishingly vivid pieces. In the *Requiem in F minor* Pickett lays out his forces as they would have been positioned in Salzburg Cathedral in the 1690s, 'recreating the spatial polychoral effects which the surviving performance parts suggest'. The piece is powerful and makes a stronger effect than in the 1968 Harnoncourt performance, coupled with the *St Polycarpi sonata* and the *Cantata, Laetatus sum*, which we much admired in its day. Fine singing, remarkable music and excellent recording.

Leonhardt's performance, too, is a fine one and he has good soloists. He is committed and the reading has genuine spontaneity and fervour; moreover it is richly recorded. However, this version is not quite so distinctive nor the music so imaginatively realized as on the Oiseau-Lyre CD and its coupling, although enterprising, is less attractive.

Birtwistle, Harrison (born 1934)

Carmen Arcadiae mechanicae perpetuum; Secret theatre; Silbury air.
*** Etcetera Dig. KTC 1052 [id.]. L. Sinf., Elgar Howarth.

Silbury air is one of Birtwistle's 'musical landscapes', bringing ever-changing views and perspectives on the musical material and an increasing drawing-out of melody. With melody discarded, *Carmen Arcadiae mechanicae perpetuum* (*The perpetual song of Mechanical Arcady*) superimposes different musical mechanisms to bring a rhythmic kaleidoscope of textures and patterns. The title of *Secret theatre* is taken from a poem by Robert Graves which refers to 'an unforeseen and fiery entertainment', and there is no doubting the originality of the writing, utterly typical of the composer. Howarth and the Sinfonietta could hardly be more convincing advocates, recorded in vivid, immediate sound.

Earth dances.
*** Collins Dig. Single 2001-2. BBC SO, Eötvös.

This is a characteristically rugged and characterful piece by Birtwistle, recorded live at the Proms in 1991 in spectacular sound. It is a generally slow-moving ritual, brilliantly written for the orchestra. Unfortunately, there are no separate tracks for the individual sections.

(i; iii) *Melencolia I;* (ii; iii) *Meridian;* (iii) *Ritual Fragment.*
☞ *** NMC Dig. NMCD 009 [id.]. (i) Antony Pay; (ii) Mary King, Michael Thompson, Christopher van Kampen; L. Sinf. Voices; (iii) L. Sinf. (members); Oliver Knussen.

The NMC Birtwistle disc has the London Sinfonietta under Oliver Knussen in three works revealing the composer at his most uncompromising. *Ritual Fragment* was inspired by the death of Michael

Vyner, the dynamic and influential artistic director of London Sinfonietta. It was perhaps the most moving of the pieces specially written for the Vyner memorial concert at Covent Garden. Just as dark and even more obsessive are the two longer works on the disc, *Melencolia I* and *Meridian*, that last the grimmest of love-songs.

Punch and Judy (opera) complete.
☞ *** Etcetera KTC 2014 (2) [id.]. Roberts, DeGaetani, Bryn-Julson, Langridge, Wilson-Johnson, Tomlinson, L. Sinf., David Atherton.

Punch and Judy is a brutal, ritualistic piece, 'the first modern English opera', as it was called when it first appeared at the Aldeburgh Festival in 1968. In setting the traditional puppet story, Birtwistle has characteristically adopted a sharp, abrasive style, the more angular because Stephen Pruslin's libretto has a stylized patterning based on nursery rhymes and children's games. It may not make easy listening, but nor is it easy to forget for, behind the aggressiveness, Birtwistle's writing has a way of touching an emotional chord, just as Stravinsky's so often does. Heard on record, Punch's war-cry and first murder (his wife Judy battered to death) have an impact that reminds one of the shower-bath murder in the film *Psycho*, itself intensified by music. Stephen Roberts is outstanding as Punch, and among others there is not a single weak link. David Atherton, conductor from the first performances, excels himself with the Sinfonietta. The clear, vivid recording, originally made by Decca for their enterprising LP Headline series, has been licensed by Etcetera.

The Triumph of Time; Gawain (opera): *Gawain's journey.*
☞ *** Collins Dig. 1387-2 [id.]. Philh. O, Elgar Howarth.

In their unmistakable power and authority, the two major works on this Collins disc are typical of the mature Birtwistle. *The Triumph of Time*, inspired by the Breughel engraving, was the piece which – with Pierre Boulez responsible for its first recording – was influential in making Birtwistle an international figure. Its power is undiminished: a grim, relentless processional. Even more welcome is *Gawain's journey*, one of Birtwistle's richest and most approachable scores, which in its 25-minute span reworks salient passages from his unforgettable Covent Garden opera, *Gawain*, first heard in 1991. Under Elgar Howarth, both works are brilliantly played by the Philharmonia and stunningly recorded.

Bizet, Georges (1838–75)

L'Arlésienne (complete incidental music; ed. Riffauld).
☞ *** EMI Dig. CDC7 47460-2 [id.]. Orféon Donstiarra, Toulouse Capitole O, Plasson.

(i) *L'Arlésienne* (complete incidental music, with spoken melodramas); *Jeux d'enfants.*
☞ (BB) *(**) Discover Dig. DICD 920115 [id.]. (i) Marcel Dossogne (reciter), Belgian R. & TV Ch. & PO, Rahbari.

The EMI recording of the complete incidental music appears to have returned to the catalogue, although it may take perseverance to obtain. The score that Michel Plasson and his excellent French forces have recorded is based on the 1872 autograph, and the singing of the Orféon Donstiarra is as excellent as the orchestral playing. The less familiar music is every bit as captivating as the suites so that the performance has great charm, and the EMI recording is very good indeed. Strongly recommended.

The alternative Discover issue is in the cheapest price-range. It is well played and recorded, with an excellent choral contribution, so that allowances can be made for its drawbacks. The reciter, Marcel Dossogne, is ever present, mostly between the numbers, but sometimes speaking over the orchestra. Those who understand French (no translation is provided) may feel that his contribution adds something to the presentation of the music, but because there are no internal cues – only one band for each of the five Acts – he is inseparable from it. The performance is sympathetic and the recording atmospheric, but Plasson's account manages admirably without the melodramas and the Toulouse playing has more character and style. For Dutch-speaking readers there is also a Flemish version (an obligation in Belgium, where it is necessary to please both racial groups), but few will think that this alternative (DICD 920116) sounds as colloquial or as effective.

L'Arlésienne (incidental music): *suites Nos. 1–2.*
*** EMI CDC7 47794-2 [id.]. RPO, Beecham – *Symphony.* ***

Beecham's magical set, dating from 1957, still sounds remarkably well. Besides the beauty and unique character of the wind solos, Beecham's deliciously sprightly *Minuet* and his affectingly gentle sense of nostalgia in the *Adagietto* (both from the first suite) are as irresistibly persuasive as the swaggering brilliance of the closing *Farandole* of the second.

L'Arlésienne: suites Nos. 1–2; Carmen: suite No. 1.
(B) *** DG 431 160-2; *431 160-4* [id.]. BPO, Karajan (with OFFENBACH: *Contes d'Hoffmann: Barcarolle; Orpheus in the Underworld: overture* **(*)).
(M) *** DG 423 472-2 [id.]. LSO, Abbado.

L'Arlésienne: suites Nos. 1 & 2; Carmen: suites Nos. 1 & 2.
*** Decca Dig. 417 839-2 [id.]. Montreal SO, Dutoit.

L'Arlésienne: suites Nos. 1 & 2; Carmen: suite No. 1; suite No. 2: excerpts; *Patrie overture.*
☞ (M) **(*) Mercury 343 321-2 [id.]. Detroit SO, Paray – THOMAS: *Overtures: Raymond; Mignon.* ***

With playing that is both elegant and vivid, and with superb, demonstration-worthy sound, Dutoit's polished yet affectionate coupling of the *L'Arlésienne* and *Carmen* suites makes a clear first choice.

The metallic clash of the cymbals for the opening *Carmen Prélude* on Karajan's 1971 disc sets the seal on the brilliance of both the orchestral playing and the recording. This version is undoubtedly fresher than Karajan's later, digital recording with the same forces. The two Offenbach encores, polished and vivacious, are welcome.

Among analogue couplings of *L'Arlésienne* and *Carmen* suites, Abbado's 1981 DG recording stands out, available at medium price on CD. The orchestral playing is characteristically refined, the wind solos cultured and eloquent, especially in *L'Arlésienne*, where the pacing of the music is nicely judged.

Another astonishing Mercury reissue of remarkable quality. The *L'Arlésienne* and *Carmen* suites were recorded as early as 1956 and, apart from some background hiss, it would be impossible to guess, so full is the sound. This was one of the first sessions in the then new Ford Auditorium in Detroit; there is a slight excess of bass resonance but otherwise the balance is admirably natural. Paray's performances are neat and polished, certainly Gallic if without quite the panache of Beecham's version, made for EMI a year later. Paray adopts a phlegmatic tempo for the famous dotted tune in *L'Arlésienne*; by the same token, his *Minuetto* in the second suite is very brisk indeed. But this music-making is attractively alive, and in the flamboyant (if slightly empty *Patrie overture*), recorded two years later in Old Orchestral Hall, the Detroit brass enjoy themselves hugely. What makes this disc especially attractive is the inclusion of the two overtures of Thomas, which are superbly done.

L'Arlésienne: suite No. 1 (with *Andante molto*); *Jeux d'enfants* (*suite*; including *Les quatre coins*); *Overture in A; Marche funèbre in B min.*
☞ *** EMI Dig. CDC7 54765-2 [id.]. Toulouse Capitole O, Michel Plasson.

L'Arlésienne: suite No. 1; Jeux d'enfants (petite suite); La jolie Fille de Perth (suite).
☞ (M) *** EMI CDM7 64869-2 [id.]. O de Paris, Barenboim.

Neither Barenboim nor Plasson offers the second *L'Arlésienne* suite, although Plasson includes the delicate *Andante molto* with its refined saxophone solo. He also offers an attractively busy extra movement (*Les quatre coins*) from *Jeux d'enfants* which the composer unaccountably discarded, even though he had reworked and extended the piano duet original. The other important novelty here is the delightful *Overture in A* which is contemporary with the *Symphony* and is equally felicitously scored. It is substantial (13 minutes) and graciously tuneful, and the vivacious finale has a whiff of Rossini. The *Marche funèbre* is in fact the relatively flamboyant *Prélude* to the discarded opera, *La Coupe du roi de Thulé*. Plasson's performances are alive and persuasive throughout and he presents the gentle *Adagietto* of *L'Arlésienne* and the *Berceuse* from *Jeux d'enfants* most gracefully and affectionately. The recording, made in the Hall-aux-Grains, Toulouse, is of best EMI quality.

But then so is the analogue sound (from 1972 and 1975) of Barenboim's earlier programme, and those who want this particular grouping of works will find the mid-priced CD thoroughly recommendable. The performances are vivid and affectionate and Barenboim's winning combination of delicacy and sparkle in *La jolie fille de Perth* suggests that he has been influenced by the Beecham recordings of this music. The CD transfer is one of EMI's best in its combination of fullness and brilliance. The *Patrie overture*, which can sound over-melodramatic, is here presented most convincingly. The only snag is that incorrect cueing in the *Carmen suite* (which includes five (not six) items, as the opening of the Act I *Prélude* is placed last) means that all the following items are wrongly banded in the accompanying liner-booklet.

Carmen: suites Nos. 1–2.
☞ (BB) ** Tring Dig. TRP 002 [id.]. RPO, Mark Ermler – GRIEG: *Peer Gynt suites 1–2.* *(*)

The RPO play well enough under Mark Ermler (the trumpet soloist is striking in the *Toreador song*) and there are some good woodwind contributions. But there is little of the magic that Beecham found with the same orchestra, and the vivid, modern recording does not compensate.

Jeux d'enfants (Children's games), Op. 22.
(B) *** CfP CD-CFP 4086; *TC-CFP 40086.* SNO, Gibson – RAVEL: *Ma Mère l'Oye;* SAINT-SAENS; *Carnival.* ***

From Classics for Pleasure a fresh approach, lively orchestral playing and excellent mid-1970s sound; with excellent couplings, this is highly recommendable.

Symphony in C.
*** DG Dig. 423 624-2 [id.]. Orpheus CO – BRITTEN: *Simple symphony;* PROKOFIEV: *Symphony No. 1.* ***
*** EMI CDC7 47794-2 [id.]. French Nat. R. O, Beecham – *L'Arlésienne.* ***
☞ (M) *** Sony SBK 48264 [id.]. Nat. PO, Stokowski – MENDELSSOHN: *A Midsummer Night's Dream* ***; SMETANA: *Vltava.* ***

The freshness of the seventeen-year-old Bizet's *Symphony* is well caught by the Orpheus group who present it with all the flair and polished ensemble for which they are famous. First-rate sound, most realistic in effect.

Beecham's version from the beginning of the 1960s above all brings out its spring-like qualities. The playing of the French orchestra is not quite as polished as that of Marriner's group, but Beecham's panache more than compensates. The remastered sound is bright on top, without glare.

Stokowski's exhilaratingly polished account of the Bizet *Symphony* was recorded at Abbey Road in May/June 1977, only three months before he died; it is a superb example of his last vintage recording period, as vital and alive as anything he recorded in his youth. David Theodore's oboe solo in the *Adagio* is very elegantly done and the *moto perpetuo* finale is wonderfully light and sparkling. A fine bargain coupling, ranking alongside the top recommendations of Beecham and Marriner. The couplings, too, show Szell at his finest.

Symphony in C; L'Arlésienne (incidental music): *suites Nos. 1–2.*
☞ **(*) EMI Dig. CDC5 55118-2 [id.]. ASMF, Marriner.

Marriner's latest EMI account of Bizet's *Symphony*, which is generous with repeats in the outer movements, does not quite re-create the sparkling lightness of touch of his early Argo (now Decca) version, currently withdrawn. In the first movement there is plenty of energy, but not the same sense of complete spontaneity. The two *L'Arlésienne suites* are beautifully played, the *Adagietto* given a gossamer delicacy, and the Abbey Road recording is first class.

Jeux d'enfants, Op. 22.
*** Ph. Dig. 420 159-2 [id.]. Katia and Marielle Labèque – FAURE: *Dolly;* RAVEL: *Ma Mère l'Oye.* ***

The Labèque sisters characterize Bizet's wonderfully inventive cycle of twelve pieces with vitality, great wit and delicacy of feeling and touch. Superb recording in the best Philips tradition.

Nocturne in F; Variations chromatiques.
☞ (M) *(*) Sony SM2K 52654 (2). Glenn Gould – GRIEG: *Sonata;* SIBELIUS: *Kyllikki* etc. *(*)

The sound of these 1973 performances is much improved but it comes in a two-CD box which is really rather poor value in that the Grieg/Bizet disc runs to 45 minutes 05 seconds and the Sibelius sonatinas and *Kyllikki* takes a mere 38 minutes 35 seconds. All the same, these are interesting pieces and not easy to track down.

OPERA

Carmen (opera; complete).
*** DG Dig. 410 088-2 (3) [id.]. Baltsa, Carreras, Van Dam, Ricciarelli, Barbaux, Paris Op. Ch., Schoenberg Boys' Ch., BPO, Karajan.
(B) *** DG 427 440-2 (3) [id.]. Horne, McCracken, Krause, Maliponte, Manhattan Op. Ch., Met. Op. O, Bernstein.
(M) *** BMG/RCA GD 86199 (3) [6199-2-RG]. Leontyne Price, Corelli, Merrill, Freni, Linval, V. State Op. Ch., VPO, Karajan.

Carmen: highlights.
*** DG Dig. 413 322-2 [id.] (from above recording with Baltsa, Carreras; cond. Karajan).

Karajan's newest DG set of *Carmen* makes a clear first choice among currently available versions. In Carreras he has a Don José, lyrical and generally sweet-toned. José van Dam is incisive and virile, the public hero-figure; which leaves Agnes Baltsa as a vividly compelling Carmen, tough and vibrant, yet with tenderness under the surface.

Bernstein's 1973 *Carmen* was recorded at the New York Metropolitan Opera. Some of his slow tempi will be questioned, but what really matters is the authentic tingle of dramatic tension which permeates the whole entertainment. Marilyn Horne – occasionally coarse in expression – gives a most fully satisfying reading of the heroine's role, a great vivid characterization. The rest of the cast similarly works to Bernstein's consistent overall plan. It is very well transferred and comes on three bargain CDs.

With Karajan's RCA version, made in Vienna in 1964, much depends on the listener's reaction to the conductor's tempi and to Leontyne Price's smoky-toned Carmen. Corelli has moments of coarseness, but his is still a heroic performance. Robert Merrill sings with gloriously firm tone, while Mirella Freni is, as ever, enchanting as Micaela. With often spectacular recording, this three-disc set, now offered at mid-price, remains a keen competitor.

Carmen: highlights (sung in English).
(B) **(*) CfP CD-CFP 4596; *TC-CFP 4596*. Johnson, Smith, Herincx, Robson, Hunter, Greene, Stoddart, Moyle, Sadler's Wells Ch. & O, Sir Colin Davis.

Those who enjoy opera in English will find this a highly successful example, thanks both to the strongly animated conducting of Sir Colin Davis and to the rich-voiced, reliable singing of Patricia Johnson as Carmen.

(i) *Les pêcheurs de perles* (complete). (ii) *Ivan IV:* highlights.
** EMI Dig. CDS7 49837-2 (2) [Ang. CDCB 49837]. Hendricks, Aler, Quilico, Capitole, Toulouse, Ch. & O, Plasson.

Michel Plasson with the choir and orchestra of the Capitole, though sympathetic, fails to draw out as warmly committed a performance as he usually does in his French opera recordings. John Aler and Gino Quilico as the two fishermen sing cleanly and with lyrical freshness, but often their phrasing could be more affectionate. Barbara Hendricks is aptly alluring as Leila, beloved of both of them, but too often she attacks notes from below.

Blake, Howard (born 1938)

Clarinet concerto.
*** Hyp. Dig. CDA 66215 [id.]. Thea King, ECO, composer – LUTOSLAWSKI: *Dance preludes; SEIBER: Concertino.* ***

Howard Blake provides a comparatively slight but endearing *Clarinet concerto*, which is played here with great sympathy by Thea King, who commissioned the work.

Bliss, Arthur (1891–1975)

(i; ii) *Adam Zero* (ballet): *suite; Mêlée fantasque; Hymn to Apollo;* (i; ii; iii) *Rout for soprano and orchestra;* (i; iv; v) *Serenade for orchestra and baritone;* (i; vi; vii) *The World is charged with the grandeur of God.*
☞ *** Lyrita SRCS 225 [id.]. (i) LSO; (ii) cond. composer; (iii) with Rae Woodland; (iv) John Shirley-Quirk; (v) cond. Brian Priestman; (vi) with Amb. S.; (vii) cond. Philip Ledger.

The ballet *Adam Zero* may not show Bliss at his finest but the four excerpts here contain some attractive moments. The *Mêlée fantasque* (well named) is even more striking with strong Stravinskian influences but with a characteristic elegiac section at its centre. After the *Hymn to Apollo*, although the rest of the programme is primarily vocal, it is in fact the orchestral writing that one remembers most vividly, for the *Serenade* has two purely orchestral movements out of three. The second, *Idyll*, shows Bliss's lyrical impulse at its most eloquent. The orchestra is almost more important than the voice in *Rout*. One can see why Diaghilev admired this short cantata, for its music has a splendid vigour and spontaneity, together with a certain *chic* quality characteristic of the period during which the great ballet impresario made his reputation. The solo vocal performances throughout this CD are of high quality, and John Shirley-Quirk's swashbuckling account of the gay finale of the *Serenade* must have pleased the composer greatly. In *The World is charged with the grandeur of God*, the invention is less memorable, and it is again the orchestration that shows the composer's imagination at work, notably the atmospheric scoring for the flutes in the second section. The recordings date from the early 1970s and are of high quality. The *Serenade, Rout, Apollo* and *The World is charged* were put on LP to celebrate the composer's eightieth birthday in August 1971.

Checkmate (ballet): *5 dances.*
(M) *** Chan. CHAN 6576; *CBT 1023* [id.]. West Australian SO, Schönzeler – RUBBRA: *Symphony No. 5* ***; TIPPETT: *Little music.* **(*)

Checkmate (ballet suite).
☞ (M) (***) EMI mono CDM7 64718-2 [id.]. Pro Arte O, composer – ADDISON: *Carte blanche;* ARNELL: *The Great Detective;* ARNOLD: *A Grand Grand Overture;* RAWSTHORNE: *Madame Chrysanthème* etc. (***)

The idea of a ballet based on chess with all its opportunities for symbolism and heraldic splendour appealed to Bliss, and the score he produced remains one of his most inventive creations. The five dances on the Chandos issue are well played under Hans-Hubert Schönzeler and, with its valuable Rubbra coupling, this is welcome back in the catalogue at mid-price.

It is good to have the composer's own performance of the *Checkmate ballet suite*, admirably recorded in the Kingsway Hall in 1960. He conducts his score with obvious authority and plenty of vitality.

(i) *Cello concerto; Introduction and allegro; Meditations on a theme of John Blow.*
☞ **(*) Argo 443 170-2 [id.]. (i) Robert Cohen; RPO, Wordsworth.

Bliss wrote his *Cello concerto* for Rostropovich, who gave its première at the 1970 Aldeburgh Festival. In spite of Britten's initial championing, it is not a memorable work and is unlikely to enter the repertoire. However, its great advantage is that it gets better as it goes along. The *Larghetto* is much more attractive than the weak first movement and the finale gathers together the best of the composer's ideas, including the main theme of the opening movement. Robert Cohen gives a committed performance and he is well accompanied. The *Introduction and allegro* (1923) is flambuoyantly scored (with the Philadelphia Orchestra in mind) and has a striking lyrical idea; the *Meditations on a theme of John Blow* was written for the CBSO in 1955. It is a series of variations designed to illustrate the different verses of the 23rd Psalm. The composer thought highly of it, but it is an amiable and rather rambling piece. It is certainly well played here and the Walthamstow recording is spectacular.

(i) *Piano concerto; March of homage.*
(M) **(*) Unicorn Dig. UKCD 2029; *UKC 2029.* (i) Philip Fowke; RLPO, David Atherton.

Bliss's concerto is a work which needs a passionately committed soloist, and that is what it finds in Philip Fowke, urgent and expressive, well matched by David Atherton and the Liverpool orchestra. The occasional piece is also given a lively performance. The digital recording is full and vivid.

A Colour Symphony; Checkmate (ballet): *suite.*
*** Chan. Dig. CHAN 8503 [id.]. Ulster O, Handley.

Each of the movements of Bliss's *Colour Symphony* evokes the heraldic symbolism of four colours – purple, red, blue and green – and the quality of his invention and imagination is fresh. Vernon Handley directs with complete authority and evident enthusiasm; the *Checkmate* ballet is given with equal success. Excellent sound.

A Colour Symphony; Metamorphic variations.
*** Nimbus Dig. NI 5294; *NC 5294* [id.]. BBC Welsh SO, Wordsworth.

The title, *Metamorphic variations*, may be unattractive, but this is one of the most cogent of Bliss's mature works. *A Colour Symphony* also represents Bliss at his most immediately appealing. Wordsworth is a degree broader in his approach than Vernon Handley on the rival Chandos version, yet his control of rhythm and line makes his reading just as warm and sympathetic. As recorded, the Welsh string-tone is not quite so full and warm as that of Handley's Ulster Orchestra, but anyone who wants this exceptionally generous and apt coupling is unlikely to be disappointed.

Conversations; Madam Noy; (i; ii) *Rhapsody;* (ii) *Rout; The Women of Yueh; Oboe quintet.*
*** Hyp. CDA 66137 [id.]. Nash Ens., (i) Anthony Rolfe Johnson; (ii) Elizabeth Gale.

The predominant influence in *Rout*, for soprano and chamber orchestra, and in the *Rhapsody*, with its two wordless vocal parts, is Ravel. The *Oboe quintet* is a work of considerable quality. The music assembled here represents Bliss at his very best. A lovely disc, which can be warmly recommended, and eminently well engineered, too.

Clarinet quintet.
*** Chan. Dig. CHAN 8683; *ABTD 1078* [id.]. Hilton, Lindsay Qt – BAX: *Sonata;* VAUGHAN
   WILLIAMS: *Studies.* ***

The *Clarinet quintet* is arguably Bliss's masterpiece. These artists have the measure of its autumnal melancholy; the recording is natural and well focused, and the music-making is of the highest quality.

String quartets Nos. 1 in B flat; 2 in F min.
*** Hyp. CDA 66178 [id.]. Delmé Qt.

These performances by the Delmé Quartet are not only thoroughly committed but enormously persuasive and can be recommended even to readers not normally sympathetic to this composer. Strongly recommended.

(i) *Viola sonata;* Piano works: *2 Interludes; Masks; Toccata; Triptych.*
*** Chan. Dig. CHAN 8770; *ABTD 1408* [id.]. Kathron Sturrock, (i) with Emanuel Vardi.

Bliss once called the viola 'the most romantic of instruments, a veritable Byron in the orchestra'. His feeling for it is clearly evident in his *Sonata*. The first movement has heroic thrust, masterfully interpreted by the American viola-player, Emanuel Vardi. The broad lyricism of the slow movement and the dashing energy of the tarantella finale find him equally sympathetic, with Kathron Sturrock a powerful partner, both of them helped by the warm, forward recording. The solo piano pieces mostly date from the 1920s, when Bliss was much influenced by a prolonged stay in America. Many with their jazzy syncopations are like Gershwin with an English flavour. Sturrock is a warm and understanding interpreter.

Piano sonata; Pieces: *Bliss (One-step); Miniature scherzo; Rout trot; Study. Suite; Triptych.* Arr. of
BACH: *Das alte Jahr vergangen ist (The old year has ended).*
*** Chan. Dig. CHAN 8979; *ABTD 1567* [id.]. Philip Fowke.

The biggest work on the disc is the *Sonata*. Its neo-romantic rhetoric is less convincing than some of the earlier pieces he composed, in particular the *Suite* (1925). One of its movements is a dignified and affecting *Elegy* (Track 3), an outpouring of grief at the loss of his brother, which was to find further expression in *Morning heroes*. There are some other lighter pieces like the *The Rout trot* and *Bliss (One-step)*, written in the 1920s when his inspiration was at its freshest. Good performances and excellent recording, made in The Maltings, Snape.

VOCAL MUSIC

Lie strewn the white flocks.
*** Hyp. CDA 66175 [id.]. Shirley Minty, Judith Pierce (flute), Holst Singers & O, Hilary Davan
   Wetton – BRITTEN: *Gloriana: Choral dances;* HOLST: *Choral hymns from Rig Veda.* ***

Bliss's *Pastoral* is given a winning performance by the Holst Singers and Orchestra, with the choral sections (the greater part of the work) aptly modest in scale but powerful in impact. With glowing sound and very attractive works for coupling, this is an outstanding issue.

Morning heroes.
(M) **(*) EMI CDM7 63906-2. Westbrook (nar.), RLPO Ch. & O, Groves.

Morning heroes is an elegiac work, written as a tribute to the composer's brother and to all who fell in the First World War. This is a strong performance, even if the music itself has a curious element of complacency. Fine recording and an excellent transfer.

Bloch, Ernest (1880–1959)

Concerti grossi Nos. 1 & 2; (i) *Schelomo.*
(M) *** Mercury 432 718-2 [id.]. Eastman-Rochester O, Hanson, (i) with Miquelle.

In Bloch's two *Concerti grossi* the neo-classical style brings a piano continuo in the Baroque manner in No. 1; the second, for strings alone, is more intense in feeling. The performances here are admirable, although the violin-timbre is distinctly astringent. *Schelomo*, with Georges Miquelle its soloist, makes a useful bonus for this mid-priced reissue.

Violin concerto.
(M) *** EMI CDM7 63989-2 [id.]. Menuhin, Philh. O, Kletzki – BERG: *Violin concerto.* ***

(i) *Violin concerto. Baal Shem.*
*** ASV Dig. CDDCA 785. (i) Michael Guttman; RPO, Serebrier (with SEREBRIER: *Momento; Poema **).

Menuhin's deeply felt and finely recorded 1963 account is passionate and committed from the very first note, and any weaknesses in the score are quite lost when the playing is so compelling. Paul Kletzki accompanies with equal distinction. The 1964 Kingsway Hall recording sounds very well indeed.

The newcomer from Michael Guttman has plenty going for it: it has both fire and colour, and no attempt is made to rein in the freely rhapsodic flow of the piece. It also has well balanced modern digital recording.

Concerto symphonique for piano and orchestra.
☞ (M) (**) Van. 08.4052.71 . Marjorie Mitchell, V. State Op. O, Golschmann (with LITOLFF: *Concerto symphonique No. 4: Scherzo ***).

Bloch's *Concerto symphonique*, a late work written in 1948, is an inflated piece, the outer movements noisily rhetorical and the brass writing making the music sound as if it belongs on the soundtrack of an epic film. Even the central movement begins *Allegro vivace*, and the best part of the whole work is when it later calms down. There are one or two quite good ideas around and the excellent soloist and well-prepared, enthusiastic accompanists do their best for them, but they become buried in the musical verbiage. The Litolff *Scherzo* which acts as an encore is given a sparkling performance and is worth ten of this, but one must remember that the Litolff *Concerto symphonique No. 4* from which it is extracted is also hopelessly overblown.

From Jewish life (orch. Palmer).
☞ *** BMG/RCA Single 09026 61966-2 [id.]. Steven Isserliss, Moscow Virtuosi, Spivakov – TAVENER: *Eternal memory.* ***

Bloch's soliloquy, if more extrovert and tangible than the drifting mysticism of Tavener's *Eternal memory*, nevertheless makes an apt coupling, especially when played with poignant warmth of feeling in this judicious expansion by Christopher Palmer of the composer's original version (for cello and piano) to feature instead orchestral strings. Excellent recording.

(i) *Israel Symphony;* (ii) *Schelomo.*
(M) **(*) Van. 08 4047.71 [OVC 4047]. (i) Christensen, Basinger, Fraenkel, Politis, Heder, Watts; (ii) Nelsova; Utah SO, Abravanel.

Bloch's *Israel Symphony* is a large-scale work, but its way of anticipating the style of Hollywood film composers means that the music has something in common with the soundtracks of Hollywood's biblical epics. The performance here has the vigour and spontaneity that are characteristic of Abravanel's Utah performances, and the only snag is that the soloists, who are introduced at the end of the work, are wobbly and not especially distinguished. *Schelomo* is an appropriate coupling. The recordings were made in 1967 and are transferred to CD with great success.

Schelomo (Hebraic rhapsody) for cello and orchestra.
*** BMG/RCA Dig. RD 60757 [60757-2-RC]. Ofra Harnoy, LPO, Mackerras – BRUCH: *Adagio on Celtic themes* etc. ***
☞ (M) *** Sony SBK 48278 [id.]. Leonard Rose, Phd. O, Ormandy – FAURE: *Elégie ***; LALO: *Concerto **(*); TCHAIKOVSKY: *Rococo variations.* ***

Harnoy catches the passionate, Hebraic feeling of the melodic line and in this is matched by Mackerras, whose central climax is riveting. Fine, well-balanced and expansive sound.

A darkly passionate, rhapsodical account from Leonard Rose, with an equally strong accompaniment from Ormandy. The recording balance is close, which reduces the possible dynamic range, but the compelling power of the music-making triumphs – this very good 71-minute compilation is worthy of a fine (perhaps underrated) cellist.

Sacred service (Avodath Hakodesh).

(M) *** Sony SM2K 47533 (2) [id.]. Robert Merrill, Rabbi Juhah Cahn, Choirs of Metropolitan Synagogue & NY Community Church, NYPO, Bernstein – FOSS: *Song of songs* ***; BEN-HAIM: *Psalmist of Israel.* **(*)

Bernstein pioneered this work on record as early as 1958, but the age of the recording, made in the St George Hotel, Brooklyn, is disguised by the remastering which preserves the spaciousness and enhances the vividness of this persuasively committed performance, which has far more ardour and intensity than the more recent version on Chandos. Robert Merrill is the excellent soloist and the only possible drawback for repeated listening by the non-Jewish listener is the inclusion in the Epilogue of the spoken Kaddish Prayer and, of course, the Benediction. The documentation helpfully includes the picturesque original Hebrew, and a line-by-line translation of romanized Hebrew text. The irritating thing about this reissue in the Royal Bernstein Edition, is that the Bloch and the stimulating Foss coupling could both have been fitted on to a single CD, as their total playing time is just over 78 minutes.

Blomdahl, Karl-Birger (1916–68)

Symphonies Nos. 1–2; 3 (Facetter).

☞ *** BIS Dig. CD 611 [id.]. Swedish RSO, Segerstam.

Karl-Birger Blomdahl occupied a dominant position in Swedish musical life in the 1950s and '60s both as a teacher and as Head of Music in Swedish Radio. (Those were the days when radio stations had composers on their staffs.) His *First Symphony*, written in his mid-twenties during the war, is not particularly individual and, though more than student work, is less than a mature one. There is a certain debt to his master, Hilding Rosenberg, and, in the slow movement, Honegger. At the same time a strong symphonic impulse runs through it, even if the scoring is less expert than in *Facetter*. Blomdahl is an eclectic figure: there are echoes of Bartók, Hindemith and serial composers in the *Second* and *Third Symphonies*. The *Third* is a dark and powerful piece and though it is, as one critic put it, 'deficient in thematic vitality', there is a powerful atmosphere. Good performances by the Swedish Radio Orchestra under Segerstam and excellent BIS recording.

Blow, John (1649–1708)

Anthems: *Blessed is the man; God spake sometimes in visions.*

☞ (M) **(*) Decca 436 259-2 [id.]. King's College, Cambridge, Ch., Willcocks – HANDEL: *Ode for St Cecilia's Day.* **

Anthems: *Cry aloud, and spare not; I was glad; O sing unto the Lord.*

☞ (M) **(*) Decca 436 256-2 [id.]. King's College, Cambridge, Ch., ASMF, Willcocks – HANDEL: *Coronation anthems.* ***

John Blow, born in Newark, was one of the first choirboys in the Chapel Royal after the Restoration, and he climaxed his career by becoming official Composer to that same Chapel Royal. These anthems impress, both by their grandeur and by the confidence of the part-writing for individual solo voices, sung here by members of the choir. *O sing unto the Lord* is a particularly eloquent and expressive piece; *God spake sometimes in visions* was written for the coronation of James II in 1685, while *I was glad*, with its trumpet obbligato, was composed for the opening of the chancel of St Paul's Cathedral (all that was completed in 1697). The performances, if lacking something in robust flair, are agreeably secure, and the recording is spacious and full, even if the focus of the King's acoustic lacks something in sharpness.

(i) *Ode on the death of Mr Henry Purcell;* (ii) *Amphion Angelicus* (song collection): *Ah, heaven! What is't I hear?; Cloe found Amintas lying all in tears; Loving above himself; Shepherds deck your crooks; Why weeps Asteria? ; Epilogue: Sing, sing, ye muses.*

(M) **(*) HM/BMG GD 71962. (i) René Jacobs, James Bowman; (ii) Yamamoto, Van der Speek, Jacobs, Van Altena, Van Egmond, Ens., Leonhardt.

John Blow's *Ode on the death of Purcell*, a highly eloquent setting of an allegorical poem by John Dryden, makes a worthy memorial to the great English composer. The other items in the programme are admirably presented, especially the closing *Epilogue* for vocal quartet. Gustav Leonhardt and his chamber ensemble accompany authentically, and the 1973 recording has a good ambience and no lack of presence.

Ode on the death of Mr Henry Purcell: Mark how the lark and linnet sing. Ah, heav'n! What is't I hear?.
*** Hyp. Dig. CDA 66253; *KA 66253* [id.]. James Bowman, Michael Chance, King's Consort, King
  – PURCELL: *Collection.* ***

Where Leonhardt on RCA is spacious in his concept and more detailed in his concern for word-meanings, the result also more polished, Robert King's spontaneous style is infectious with the orchestral comments engagingly animated. Both performances are highly rewarding, and in the last resort couplings will dictate choice. The Hyperion disc is more expensive but includes a quarter of an hour more music.

Venus and Adonis.
(M) *** HM/BMG GD 77117 (2). Kirkby, Tubb, King, Wistreich, Bonner, Holden, Cass, Nichols,
  Cornwell, Müller, Consort of Musicke, Rooley – GIBBONS: *Cupid and Death.* ***
(B) *** HM Dig. HMA 90 1276 [id.]. Argenta, Dawson, Varcoe, Covey-Crump, L. Bar. & Ch.,
  Medlam.

Venus and Adonis is like a Lully opera in miniature. Rooley directs an elegant, lightly sprung performance, very well sung, recorded in good analogue sound (1984) in a warm acoustic.

Charles Medlam with London Baroque gives a period performance and takes care that the early instruments are well blended rather than edgy and the choral sound is full, bright and clean. The soloists too are all remarkable for sweetness and freshness of tone. This record is now offered at bargain price in the Musique d'Abord series.

Boccherini, Luigi (1743–1805)

Cello concerto No. 2 in D, G.479.
☞ (B) *** DG Double 437 952-2 (2) [id.]. Rostropovich, Zurich Coll. Mus., Sacher – BERNSTEIN: *3 Meditations;* GLAZUNOV: *Chant du Ménestrel;* SHOSTAKOVICH: *Cello concerto No. 2;* TARTINI: *Cello concerto;* TCHAIKOVSKY: *Andante cantabile* etc; VIVALDI: *Cello concertos.* ***

Although essentially a performance in the grand manner, Rostropovich is so compelling that reservations are swept aside. He is given an alert accompaniment by Sacher, and the recording has fine body and presence. This is now part of a self-recommending Double DG bargain anthology.

Cello concertos Nos. 4 in C, G.477; 6 in D, G.479; 7 in G, G.480; 8 in C, G.81.
☞ (M) *** Anner Bylsma, Concerto Amsterdam, Schröder.

These concertos were originally published as Nos. 1–4 but are numbered as above in the Gérard catalogue. They are scored for strings with the addition of simple horn parts in Nos. 4 and 8 and are agreeable works which sit easily between the galant and classical styles. There are few moments of routine in the writing, and it is always elegant and pleasing. *No. 6 in D major* is a particularly fine work, while the finale of No. 9 is very jolly. Anner Bylsma is a fine player and seems eminently suited to this repertoire, while Schröder's accompaniments are most stylish and full of vitality. Charm, too, is an important element and it is not missing here, while the sombre *Adagio* of No. 7 has undoubted eloquence and is ideally paced to contrast with the sprightly and tuneful finale. The 1965 recording is first class and, like so many of Teldec's *Das Alte Werk* series, the immaculate CD transfer makes the very most of the sound.

(i) *Cello concerto in B flat* (original version, revised Gendron); (ii; iii) *Flute concerto in D, Op. 27* (attrib.; now thought to be by Franz Pokorny); (iv) *Symphonies Nos. 3 in C; 5 in B flat, Op. 12/3 & 5;* (v) *Guitar quintets Nos. 4 in D (Fandango); 9 in C (La Ritirata di Madrid);* (vi) *String quartet in D, Op. 6/1;* (iii) *String quintet in E, Op. 13/5: Minuet* (only).
☞ (B) *** Ph. Duo 438 377-2 (2) [id.]. (i) Gendron, LOP, Casals; (ii) Gazzelloni; (iii) I Musici; (iv) New Philh. O, Leppard; (v) Pepe Romero, ASMF Chamber Ens.; (vi) Italian Qt.

Entitled 'The best of Boccherini including the *Minuet*', this most attractive anthology was assembled especially for the Philips Duo series. It is well documented and the famous *Minuet* could hardly be presented more winningly. It is the one digital recording here. It is good, too, that Gendron's version of the *Cello concerto* is included, for he pioneered the return of the original version (without Grützmacher's reworking), and he plays it admirably. The *Flute concerto* is a galant piece, elegantly played by Gazzelloni, and one can see why it was mistakenly attributed; Boccherini is all too readily dismissed as *la femme de Haydn*, but underneath the surface charm and elegance that one associates with him there are deeper currents and an altogether special pathos to disturb the attentive listener. This is already beginning to appear in the *Andante amoroso* of the early *Third Symphony* from Op. 12, which appeared in Paris in 1771, and again in the graceful slow movement of No. 5 from the same set. This offers some ambitious horn writing in conversation with the flutes and strings (Boccherini's use of the flutes gives his scoring a pleasing individuality). Both works are full of vitality in these excellent performances under Raymond Leppard and are very well recorded. The Italian Quartet first gave us the *D major Quartet*, Op. 6/1, in the days of 78s, and the performance here, recorded in 1976, is just as notable for its freshness and refinement. The *Guitar quintets* were arranged by Boccherini for his Spanish patron, the Marquis Benavente, even to the extent of adding a castanet part to the *Fandango* of the D major work. No. 9 takes its name from the final rondo, which imitates the ceremony of retreat (by the Night Watch) with a cleverly calculated use of crescendo and diminuendo. The guitar part was obviously intended for the Marquis to perform, so its contribution is sometimes limited to an accompanying role, but the music has considerable charm, though it is somewhat uneven. The performances are unfailingly warm and sensitive and they are well recorded too, although there is a touch of thinness on top. The set is supported with good documentation.

Cello concerto No. 7 in G, G.480.

(B) *** Pickwick Dig. PCD 917; *IMPC 917.* Felix Schmidt, ECO, Heath – BEETHOVEN: *Triple concerto.* ***

This is the concerto from which Grützmacher extracted the slow movement in his phoney, cobbled-together 'Boccherini Concerto', the movement everyone remembers. It makes an unusual but apt and attractive coupling for the Trio Zingara's excellent version of the Beethoven *Triple concerto.*

Cello concerto in B flat (arr Grützmacher).

*** Sony MK 39964 [id.]. Yo-Yo Ma, St Paul CO, Zukerman – J. C. BACH: *Sinfonia concertante* etc. **(*)

(BB) *** Naxos Dig. 8.550059; *4550059* [id.]. Ludovít Kanta, Capella Istropolitana, Peter Breiner – HAYDN: *Cello concertos Nos. 1 & 2.* ***

(*) EMI CDC7 47840-2 [id.]. Jacqueline du Pré, ECO, Barenboim – HAYDN: *Concerto in D.* *

Like Jacqueline du Pré before him, Yo-Yo Ma chooses the Grützmacher version. He plays it with taste and finesse, not wearing his heart on his sleeve as obviously as du Pré, but with his warm, if refined, timbre and style not missing the romanticism. The recording is first class.

Ludovít Kanta's playing is distinguished by imaginative and musicianly phrasing and a warm tone. The Slovak players under Peter Breiner give a good account of themselves, and this can hold its own against versions costing twice or three times as much.

Working for the first time in the recording studio with Daniel Barenboim, du Pré was inspired to some really heart-warming playing, broadly romantic in style – but then that is what Grützmacher plainly asks for.

Symphonies, Op. 12, Nos. 1 in D; 2 in E flat; 3 in C; 4 in D min.; 5 in B flat; 6 in A.

☞ (M) *** Ph. 438 314-2 (2) [id.]. New Philh. O, Leppard.

Boccherini's Op. 12 was published in 1776. The scoring is for the normal classical orchestra, including two flutes or oboes and horns, but the composer's individuality emerges in his writing for the strings – with divided cellos – which are always predominant in the main argument. Even so, there are many pleasing touches of woodwind colour, like the perky flute solo in the Trio of the Minuet of No. 1 (almost a miniature concerto). The opening *Grave* of this D major work is quite touching, with oboes strongly featured, then the allegro, starting gently, suddenly produces bursts of energy. The *Andantino* introduces a delightful and memorable cantilena, imbued with the composer's characteristically gentle pathos, and the *Presto assai* finale is full of fire. The *E flat Symphony* (No. 2) is a remarkably fine work. It has a stately and gracious opening featuring the horns, taken (elegantly) up to and even above the top of their range. The work then becomes virtually a sinfonia concertante with important bravura duets, first for two violins, then for a pair of cellos (the composer's own instrument); there is even a cadenza. The slow movement is rather beautiful, thoughtfully eloquent, and again includes important solo string passages. The easy-going finale aptly releases the tension in its often exhilarating progress. At the beginning of No. 3, the flutes immediately give the string tutti a soft inner lining, while the Trio of the Minuet of this work brings another little concerto movement, this time for a pair of violins. The *Adagio* is shared at first by flutes and horns, who are again asked to play with restrained bravura in their highest register. The other symphonies are all of comparable interest, with Boccherini's silken melancholy strongly featured in the lyrical writing. The composer's craftsmanship is as ever deft, although perhaps his attempt at cyclic construction brings a too easy solution in *No. 6 in A major* when, after the *Grave* introduction to the finale, he simply repeats the latter part of the first movement, starting at the central double bar! In short, this set of six attractive symphonies is well worth exploring, particularly as Leppard consistently secures playing from the highly alert New Philharmonia Orchestra that is polished, elegant and never superficial. The Philips 1971 recording is excellent and so is the CD transfer, losing nothing of the bloom but firming up the overall focus admirably.

Symphonies: in D; in C, Op. 12/3; in D min., Op. 12/4; in B flat, Op. 35/6; in D min., Op. 37/3; in A, Op. 37/4.
**(*) Chan. Dig. CHAN 8414/5; *DBTD 3005* (3) [id.]. Cantilena, Adrian Shepherd.

In all, Boccherini composed twenty symphonies. These are sympathetic rather than high-powered performances and will give considerable pleasure, though lacking the last ounce of finish. But there is no want of feeling for this unjustly neglected repertoire, and the symphonies are well recorded.

Symphonies: in D min. (La casa del diavolo), Op. 12/4; in A, Op. 12/6; in A, Op. 21/6.
*** Hyp. Dig. CDA 66236 [id.]. L. Festival O, Ross Pople.

Ross Pople's record duplicates only one work included in the more ambitious Chandos collection, *La casa del diavolo*, Op. 12/4; in his account the demons are certainly let loose in the finale, with the most frantically energetic playing from the strings. Elsewhere the performances are the soul of elegance; altogether this well-played and well-recorded collection can be given the warmest welcome.

CHAMBER MUSIC

Cello quintet, Op. 37/7 (Pleyel).
(b) **(*) Decca 421 637-2; *421 637-4*. ASMF – MENDELSSOHN: *Octet.* **(*)

This is an inspired piece: it would be worth getting for its own sake – and the coupled performance of the Mendelssohn *Octet* is a particularly fine one. The recording shows its age just a little in the upper range.

Guitar quintets Nos. 1–7, G.445/51; 9 (La Ritirata di Madrid), G.453.
☞ (b) *** Ph. Duo 438 769-2 (2) [id.]. Pepe Romero, ASMF Chamber Ens.

Boccherini wrote or arranged twelve *Guitar quintets*, but only the present eight have survived, plus another version of *No. 4 in D (Fandango)*, G.448. Although some of the music is bland, it is nearly all agreeably tuneful in an unostentatious way, and there are some highly imaginative touches, with attractive hints of melancholy and underlying passion. These performances by Pepe Romero (often willing to take a relatively minor role) and members of the ASMF Chamber Ensemble are wholly admirable, and Philips are especially good at balancing textures of this kind in the most natural way, the guitar able to be assertive when required without overbalancing the ensemble. The recording is slightly less smooth than the original LPs, but the CD transfer has brought greater presence and a bolder outline. This is an engagingly undemanding set to dip into in the late evening.

Guitar quintets Nos. (i) 4 in D (Fandango); 7 in E min., G.451; 9 in C (La ritirata di Madrid).
(b) *** DG 429 512-2 [id.]. Yepes, Melos Qt; (i) with Lucero Tena.

In the DG bargain compilation from 1971 the sound is very good, full yet lively and well projected. The playing is expert and, in the boisterous *Fandango* finale of No. 4, Lucero Tena makes a glittering contribution with his castanets.

Guitar quintets Nos. 1 in D min.; 2 in E; 3 in B flat, G.445/7.
☞ (bb) * Naxos Dig. 8.550551 [id.]. Zoltán Tokos, Danubius Qt.

Guitar quintets Nos. 4 in D (Fandango); 5 in D; 6 in G, G.448/450.
☞ (bb) *(*) Naxos Dig. 8.550552 [id.]. Zoltán Tokos, Danubius Qt.

(i) *Guitar quintets Nos. 7 in E min., G.451; 9 in C (La ritirata di Madrid), G.453.* (ii) *String quintet in E, G.275.*
☞ (bb) * Naxos Dig. 8.550731 [id.]. Danubius Qt, with (i) Zoltán Tokos; (ii) György Eder.

Unfortunately the Naxos recordings are made in the same Unitarian Church in Budapest to which the Kodály Quartet have recently moved to record Haydn. The result is the same: inflated textures which make the group sound almost like a string orchestra, especially in the crescendo of *La ritirata di Madrid*, which is blown up out of all proportion. The playing itself is warmly sympathetic, but the guitarist is all but buried among the strings, sounding like a barely audible continuo. The performances on the second of the three discs are the most successful: the lovely opening *Pastorale* of G.448 (No. 4) is most beautifully played and the castanets come through vigorously in the infectious finale.

6 Oboe quintets, Op. 45.
(M) *** Decca 433 173-2 [id.]. Sarah Francis, Allegri Qt.

An attractive collection, very persuasively played and recorded. These *Quintets* have a sunny grace that is altogether beguiling, and a gentle, wistful lyricism that is unfailing in its appeal.

Piano quintets: in E min., G.407; in F, G.408; in D, G.411, Op. 56/1.
☞ *** Audivis Dig. E 8518 [id.]. Patrick Cohen, Mosaïques Qt.

Piano quintets: in B flat, G.414; in E min., G.415; in C, G.418, Op. 57/2, 3 & 6.
☞ *** Audivis Dig. E 8721 [id.]. Patrick Cohen, Mosaïques Qt.

The scope of Boccherini's achievement in the field of chamber music is becoming more and more apparent. There are twelve piano quintets and Patrick Cohen and the Mosaïques Quartet are obviously embarking – so far with great success – on a complete set. There is drama and grace and warmth of feeling, balanced by elegance, in this music; and the playing here also emphasizes its vitality. Slow movements are particularly eloquent and the use of period instruments in no way inhibits the expressive range of the music.

Piano quintets: in A min., Op. 56/2, G.412; in E flat, Op. 56/3, G.410; in E min., Op. 57/3, G.415; in C, Op. 57/6, G.418.
(M) *** BMG/RCA Dig. GD 77053 [77053-2-RG]. Les Adieux.

The lovely *E minor* (Op. 57/3) which starts the disc and the *A minor* (Op. 56/2) both have those hints of beguiling, almost sultry melancholy that makes this composer's musical language so distinctive. This accomplished period-instrument group turn in performances of great finesse and charm, though the recording balance places the listener very much in the front row of the salon.

String quintets: in E, Op. 11/5, G.275; in D min., Op. 13/4, G.280; in D, Op. 39/3, G.339; in C min., Op. 51/2, G.377.
**(*) Denon Dig. CO 2199 [id.]. Berlin Philh. Ens.

The Denon disc offers music-making of great elegance and charm. There is depth and pathos in some of these *Quintets* (the *Andante* of the *D minor* or the *Andantino con innocenza* of the *C minor*, for example). These fine musicians play with dedication, though at times there is a degree of caution as if they are a little inhibited by courtly manners. Good if rather forward recording.

String sextets Nos. 1 in E flat, G.454; 2 in B flat, G.455; 5 in D, G.458, Op. 23/1–2 & 5.
☞ **(*) HM Dig. HMC 90 1478 [id.]. Ens. 415.

Boccherini's special vein of melancholy, which yet never suggests gloom and indeed refreshes the spirit, is heard at its most appealing in these works, notably the *Andantino* of the *B flat Quartet* and the *Grave* which opens the *D major*. He is never a conventional composer, and even the minuets are unpredictable (one has several trios). In short, these are very appealing works and they are played with refined polish and feeling by this sensitive ensemble, who use original instruments with much finesse. However, it must be said that the overall texture produced here is somewhat meagre, and at times one feels the need for the fuller, more robust sound of modern instruments.

Böhm, Georg (1661–1733)

Capriccio in D; Chorale partitas on 'Ach wie nichtig, ach wie flüchtig'; on 'Wer nur den lieben Gott lässt walten'; Overture in D; Praeludium in G min.; Suites in C min.; E flat; F min.
☞ *** Sony Dig. SK 53114 [id.]. Gustav Leonhardt (harpsichord/clavichord).

Böhm was one of the most interesting and influential North German precursors of Bach, and this excellent recital by Gustav Leonhardt makes a useful introduction to his art. After some years in Hamburg, where he came into contact with a wide variety of musical styles, he moved to Lüneburg, of whose Johanniskirche he was organist for more than 30 years. His chorale partitas exercised a strong influence on Bach himself and his suites are both resourceful and inventive. Leonhardt intersperses the suites with the other pieces and ensures variety of texture and colour by using both clavichord and harpsichord, the latter a copy of an early-eighteenth-century instrument from Berlin and the clavichord a modern instrument by Skowroneck of Bremen. Excellent recording, though (as is so often the case) it has to be played at a lower than normal level setting if a truthful picture of either instrument is to emerge.

Boieldieu, François (1775–1834)

Harp concerto in 3 tempi in C.
⊛ (M) *** Decca 425 723-2; *425 723-4*. Marisa Robles, ASMF, Iona Brown – DITTERSDORF;
   HANDEL: *Harp concertos* etc. *** ⊛

Boieldieu's *Harp concerto* has been recorded elsewhere but never more attractively. The (originally
Argo) recording is still in the demonstration class and very sweet on the ear. To make the reissue even
more attractive, three beguiling sets of *Variations* have been added, including music by Handel and
Beethoven and a *Theme, variations and Rondo pastorale* attributed to Mozart.

Boito, Arrigo (1842–1918)

Mefistofele (complete).
**(*) Decca Dig. 410 175-2 [id.]. Ghiaurov, Pavarotti, Freni, Caballé, L. Op. Ch., Trinity Boys' Ch.,
   Nat. PO, Fabritiis.
☞ (M) **(*) Decca 440 054-2 [id.]. Siepi, Del Monaco, Tebaldi, Cavalli, Santa Cecilia Academy,
   Rome, Ch. & O, Serafin.
☞ ** Sony Dig. S2K 44983 (2) [id.]. Domingo, Marton, Ramey, Hungarian State Op. Ch. & O,
   Giuseppe Patanè.

The modern digital recording given to the Fabritiis set brings obvious benefits in the extra weight of
brass and percussion – most importantly in the heavenly prologue. With the principal soloists all at
their best – Pavarotti most seductive, Freni finely imaginative on detail, Caballé consistently sweet
and mellifluous as Elena – this is a highly recommendable set.

On the earlier (1958) Decca Rome set, Serafin, the most persuasive Italian conductor of his day,
draws glorious sounds from his performers, even from Mario del Monaco, who is here almost sensitive. Tebaldi is a rich-toned Margherita – almost too rich-toned for so frail a heroine – and Siepi makes
an excellent Mefistofele. The Decca engineers came up trumps: the stereo remains remarkably spacious,
particularly in the Prologue, making a good mid-priced alternative to the later Decca version.

Just as Oliviero de Fabritiis died soon after making his Decca recording of this opera about
heaven and hell, so ominously did Giuseppe Patanè soon after this Sony recording. Sadly, unlike the
Decca recording, it does not do the conductor justice, for this is a stiff, rather perfunctory reading. It
is not helped by a studio acoustic which, with the chorus cleanly but unatmospherically placed, makes
it sound more like an oratorio than an opera. Plácido Domingo sings well, but there is little bloom on
the voice, and, noble and commanding as Samuel Ramey's performance is, he does not sound
sinister. The biggest snag is the singing of Eva Marton, far too heavyweight and unsteady a soprano
for Margherita, and hardly better suited to the role of Elena (Helen of Troy) which she doubles –
another drawback to the set. Its only advantage over the Decca is that it comes on two discs instead
of three.

Mefistofele: Prologue.
(M) (***) BMG/RCA mono GD 60276; *GK 60276* [60276-2-RG; *60276-4-RG*]. Moscona, Robert
   Shaw Ch., Columbus Boychoir, NBC SO, Arturo Toscanini – VERDI: *I Lombardi; Rigoletto*:
   excerpts. (**)
(M) **(*) DG 431 171-2 [id.]. Ghiaurov, V. State Op. Ch., VPO, Bernstein – R. STRAUSS: *Salome* etc.
   **(*)

The hair-raising intensity of Toscanini's performance gives Boito's multi-layered *Prologue* a cogency
never matched since on record. The dryness of sound even seems to help, when offstage choruses are
accurately focused, and the singing of the Robert Shaw Chorale has thrillingly dramatic bite.

The DG recording finds Ghiaurov in excellent form. Bernstein, too, conducts this highly
imaginative piece vividly and atmospherically. This does not quite have the electricity of Toscanini
but, for those wanting a modern version, it will serve admirably.

Nerone (complete).
**(*) Hung. Dig. HCD 12487/9-2 [id.]. Nagy, Tokody, Dene, Miller, Takács, Gregor, Hungarian R.
   and TV Ch., Hungarian State Op. O, Queler.

Eve Queler conducts a powerful and atmospheric performance of Boito's massive, uncompleted
opera, superbly performed by the company of the Hungarian State Opera, whose soloists are far less
afflicted with Slavonic wobbles than is common in Eastern Europe. The recording is of outstanding
quality, with the atmospheric perspectives demanded by the score most realistically conveyed.

Bononcini, Giovanni (1670–1747)

Cello sonata in A min.; Trio sonata for 2 violins and continuo in D min. (i) Cantatas: *Già la stagion d'amore; Lasciami un sol momento; Misero pastorello; Siedi, Amarilli mia.*
☞ *** Virgin/EMI Dig. VC5 45000-2 [id.]. Gérard Lesne, Il Seminario Musicale.

Giovanni Bononcini was a much-travelled musician. Born in Modena, he moved first to Rome then on to serve the Habsburgs in Vienna and, after a further itinerant period, he finally settled in London in 1720, where his operas – directed by Handel – were received with enthusiasm. These cantatas were also popular and were published in London in 1721. They reveal their composer to be far more than a historical figure. *Lasciami un sol momento* stands out as a particularly moving work with its melancholy opening aria ('Leave me but for one moment, O bitter memory of my betrayed love') leading to a bravura finale, *Soffro in pace* ('I bear these chains in peace'). The instrumental works are also highly inventive and characterful: the *Lento* of the lively *Trio sonata* is gently touching and its finale wonderfully spirited. All this music is worth knowing, and the advocacy of these fine artists brings it fully to life. If you believe you may not respond to four cantatas sung by a male alto, your doubts will be swept away by the vocal skill and expressive eloquence of Gérard Lesne's singing, here using the most felicitous ornamentation. The recording too is first class.

Borodin, Alexander (1833–87)

In the Steppes of Central Asia; (i) *Nocturne* (from *String quartet No. 2*) arr. for violin & orchestra by Rimsky-Korsakov; *Petite suite* (orch. Glazunov); (ii; iii) *Requiem* (orch. Stokowski, arr. Simon). *Prince Igor: Overture;* (iii) *Chorus of Polovtsian maidens. Dance of Polovtsian maidens; Polovtsian march; Polovtsian dances.*
☞ **(*) Cala Dig. CACD 1011; CAMC 1011 [id.]. Philh. O, Geoffrey Simon, with (i) Stephanie Chase; (ii) Ian Boughton; (iii) BBC SO Ch.

An interesting and valuable anthology that is recommendable, but for one curious and serious drawback. Borodin's 5½-minute piano piece called *Requiem* is played in Stokowski's flamboyantly expansive orchestration, to which Geoffrey Simon has added solo tenor and male chorus to great effect. (Borodin wrote the Latin words over the piano score and indicated the vocal possibilities.) The piece is ingeniously based on 'Chopsticks' (although Stokowski's richly sombre brass sonorities completely overcome the triviality of the source material and the theme is all but unrecognizable). It is in the form of a long crescendo and diminuendo, and the great double climax has been recorded with an exaggerated dynamic range which is ridiculously too wide. At any normal setting of the controls the pianissimo opening, played by tremolando violins, is all but inaudible. The other works are all given full-bodied sound, a shade lacking in sparkle, and a normal dynamic range. *In the Steppes of Central Asia*, rather forwardly recorded, would have been more effective with a bit more dynamic contrast. It is a warmly languorous but not distinctive performance. The excerpts from *Prince Igor* include the sinuously seductive *Chorus of Polovtsian maidens* which opens Act II of the opera and also a version of the *Polovtsian march* which includes both chorus and off-stage band. In the march and the famous *Polovtsian dances*, the singing of the BBC Chorus is of a high standard, though Geoffrey Simon's direction is lively rather than electrifying, both here and in the Overture. Rimsky-Korsakov's concertante arrangement of the famous *Nocturne* for violin and orchestra – in spite of Stephanie Chase's pleasing advocacy – gives the piece the character of a salon encore, charming but insouciant. The *Petite suite*, a set of six piano miniatures orchestrated by Glazunov, comes off very engagingly.

Petite suite (arr. Glazunov).
*** Olympia OCD 114 A/B (2) [id.]. USSR RSO, Cherkassov – MUSSORGSKY: *Sorochinsky Fair*. ***

Not long before Borodin died, he compiled a suite of piano pieces and these became the *Petite suite* which Glazunov orchestrated after Borodin's death. It is a colourful, undemanding work, very well played and recorded.

Symphonies Nos. 1 in E flat; 2 in B min.; 3 in A min. (completed Glazunov); *In the Steppes of Central Asia; Nocturne* (orchestrated Nicolai Tcherepnin); *Petite suite* (arr. Glazunov); *Prince Igor: Overture;* (i) *Polovtsian dances.*

*** DG Dig. 435 757-2 (2) [id.]. Gothenburg SO, Neeme Järvi; (i) with Gothenburg Ch.

For those wanting all three symphonies, the Järvi DG set remains recommendable. The alternative versions by Serebrier (ASV CDDCA 706) and Gunzenhauser (Naxos 8.550238) each have the advantage of being offered on a single CD, but Serebrier's performances – recorded in Rome – lack Russian feeling, and one needs a more sumptuous body of tone for this music than the Bratislava Radio Symphony Orchestra on Naxos can provide. While Gunzenhauser's accounts are fresh and pleasing and undoubtedly good value, this is not a distinctive triptych.

Järvi's *First* has plenty of individuality and colour; the slow movement is radiant, the Scherzo beautifully sprung and the finale made to anticipate the *Prince Igor overture* in its bright, rhythmic pointing. The *Second* is a strong, spacious reading, at its finest in the *Andante*, presented in a full flood of romanticism; however, alongside Ashkenazy and Tjeknavorian, the first movement is a little lacking in rhythmic bite and thrust. The *Third Symphony* (completed by Glazunov), comes off vividly, although it is not as strong a work as the other two. The other pieces are equally well played by the excellent Gothenburg orchestra, notably the *Petite suite*, although there are some reservations about Tcherepnin's very exotic orchestration of the famous *Nocturne* from the *D major String quartet*, and perhaps Järvi doesn't pull out all the stops in his undoubtedly vivid account of the *Polovtsian dances*. Yet the choral Swedish singing, if not uninhibited, is vital enough and even includes a brief solo interpolation representing the Khan. The digital recording throughout is from DG's top drawer.

Symphonies Nos. 1 in E flat; 2 in B min.; In the Steppes of Central Asia.
☞ *** Decca Dig. 436 651-2 [id.]. RPO, Ashkenazy.

Symphonies Nos. 1 in E flat; 3 in A min.; Prince Igor: overture; Polovtsian march.
☞ ** BMG/RCA Dig. 09026 61674-2 [id.]. Russian State SO, Svetlanov.

Symphony No. 2 in B min.; Petite suite.
☞ ** BMG/RCA Dig. 09026 62505-2 [id.]. Russian State SO, Svetlanov.

With the opening in octaves brisk and dramatic and with speeds throughout that never drag, Ashkenazy's Decca reading of Borodin's *Second Symphony* is exceptionally warm and brilliant, helped by full-bodied Decca recording. The RPO wind soloists are outstanding, and the horn solo in the slow movement is satisfyingly opulent. The prestissimo Scherzo of the second movement is a special delight, not just brilliant but witty, and the dashing speed for the finale is thrilling. The coupling is both apt and generous. It may not include the unfinished *Symphony No. 3* along with No. 1, as Gunzenhauser's Naxos version and Serebrier's ASV both do, but there is no doubt that the symphonic poem, *In the Steppes of Central Asia*, offered instead, is a finer example of Borodin's genius, and it is given a warmly atmospheric performance here. If in the *Symphony No. 1* Ashkenazy's performance is less high-powered than in the *Second*, its many delights come over richly, thanks not only to the quality of the RPO's playing but also to the warm recording. For these two works alone this makes a clear first choice.

Svetlanov's recordings with the Russian State Symphony orchestra were recorded on tour in France, and the sound is very good indeed, full of warmth and colour. The *Prince Igor overture* comes off well – a very romantic reading – although some might not take to the vibrato of the very responsive horn soloist. The *Polovtsian march*, however, is rather phlegmatic, and the symphonies also fail to spring fully to life. The outer movements of the *First* are curiously lacking in drive, with the *Andante* needing more fervour and impetus. The *Second Symphony* is disappointingly stodgy at slow speeds, with heavy rhythms. Only in the finale does Svetlanov burst into life. Similarly the *Petite suite* – seven genre pieces arranged from the original piano versions by Glazunov – is too heavily treated until the last movement, a sparkling Scherzo leading to a final *Nocturne*.

In the two-movement *Third Symphony* Svetlanov seems fascinated by Glazunov's delightful woodwind colouring, as well he might be, especially at the opening; and certainly the lovely string-tune in the Trio of the second-movement Scherzo blossoms in a very Russian way. But generally the relaxed playing makes the music sound more like a ballet than a symphony.

Symphony No. 2 in B min.; In the Steppes of Central Asia; Prince Igor: Overture; (i) Polovtsian march; Polovtsian dances.
(B) *** BMG/RCA VD 60535; *VK 60535* [60535-2-RV; 60535-4-RV]. Nat. PO, (i) with John Alldis Ch.; Tjeknavorian.

Tjeknavorian is an Armenian by birth and he knows what this music is about. His pacing, swift and vital, of the first movement of this most Russian of symphonies is admirably judged: the reading has a powerful rhythmic thrust, the orchestral playing is polished and full of colour. The vibrant Scherzo bursts upwards like rockets exploding in the sky, and the ardour of the slow movement brings a climax of great passion. The finale, too, has plenty of gusto. With full and spacious recording this is very involving. The fine performance of Borodin's evocative *In the Steppes of Central Asia* comes as a rich-hued interlude before vibrant accounts of the *Overture, Polovtsian march* and *Polovtsian dances* from *Prince Igor*, including the percussion-led *Dance of the Polovtsian maidens*.

Sextet (2 movements).
** Mer. Dig. CDE 84211 [id.]. Arienski Ens. – ARENSKY: *Quartet* ***; TCHAIKOVSKY: *Souvenir de Florence*. **

Borodin composed his *Sextet* on a visit to Heidelberg in 1860 but, unfortunately, only two of its movements survive. The Arienski Ensemble play with enthusiasm and conviction and are decently recorded.

String quartets Nos. 1 in A; 2 in D.
*** EMI CDC7 47795-2 [id.]. Borodin Qt.
☞ ** Olympia OCD 538 [id.]. Shostakovich Qt.

String quartet No. 2 in D.
(M) **(*) Decca 425 541-2; *425 541-4* [id.]. Borodin Qt – SHOSTAKOVICH; TCHAIKOVSKY: *Quartets*. **(*)
☞ *(*) DG Dig. 427 618-2 [id.]. Emerson Qt – TCHAIKOVSKY: *Quartet No. 1*. *(*)

The EMI performances from the eponymous Borodin Quartet are admirable in all respects. The quality achieved by the Melodiya engineers has fine clarity; on CD the focus of the first violin line is firmer than before. The ambient warmth remains.

The Borodins' first version on Decca is hardly less fine. However, the forward recording, though rich-textured, approaches fierceness in the CD transfer, and some will prefer a softer-grained effect.

The Olympia performances were recorded at the studios of Moscow Radio in 1977–8 and are thoroughly enjoyable, though they offer no real challenge to the superb EMI version with the eponymous Borodin Quartet.

Again the Emerson Quartet are unrivalled in terms of technical expertise. It seems curmudgeonly not to respond to their superlative playing, but it is all very chromium-plated. Good, if very present, DG recording.

Songs: *Arabian melody; Arrogance; The beauty no longer loves me; The false note; The fisher-maiden; From my tears; From the shores of thy far native land; Listen to my song little friend; The magic garden; The queen of the sea; The sea; The sleeping princess; Song of the dark forest; There is poison in my songs; Those people; Why art thou so early, dawn?*
(M) *** EMI CMS7 63386-2 (3) [Ang. CDMC 63386]. Christoff, Tcherepnin, Reiss, Lamoureux O, Tzipine – *Prince Igor*. **(*)

Accompanied at the piano in all but three of the songs by the composer Alexander Tcherepnin, Christoff gives glorious performances of these rare items, sung, of course, in Russian.

Prince Igor (opera) complete.
*** Sony Dig. S3K 44878 (3) [id.]. Martinovich, Evstatieva, Kaludov, Ghiuselev, Ghiaurov, Miltcheva, Sofia Nat. Op. Ch. & Festival O, Tchakarov.
(M) **(*) EMI CMS7 63386-2 (3) [Ang. CDMC 63386]. Chekerliiski, Christoff, Todorov, Sofia Nat. Theatre Op. Ch. & O, Jerzy Semkow – *Songs*. ***

Tchakarov's complete recording of *Prince Igor* fills one of the most important gaps in the catalogue. Nicola Ghiuselev as Galitzky is powerful but rather unsteady and Nicolai Ghiaurov makes a splendid Konchak. Boris Martinovich makes a firm, very virile Igor, and both the principal women have vibrantly Slavonic voices which still never distract in wobbling. The dramatic tension in this long work is held very well and its richness of invention over its very episodic span comes across vividly, notably in all its memorable melody and high colour.

In the colourful EMI recording, Act III is completely omitted, on the grounds that it was almost entirely the work of Rimsky-Korsakov and Glazunov. Boris Christoff as both Galitzky and Konchak easily outshines all rivals. Jerzy Semkow with his Sofia Opera forces is most sympathetic, but the other soloists are almost all disappointing, with the women sour-toned and the men often strained and unsteady. The sound is limited but agreeably atmospheric.

Prince Igor: Overture and Polovtsian dances.
*** EMI CDC7 47717-2 [id.]. Beecham Choral Soc., RPO, Beecham – RIMSKY-KORSAKOV:
Scheherazade.***

Prince Igor: Polovtsian dances.
(M) *** DG 419 063-2; *419 063-4* [id.]. BPO, Karajan – RIMSKY-KORSAKOV: *Scheherazade.* ***
(M) **(*) Mercury 434 308-2 [id.]. London Symphony Ch., LSO, Dorati – RIMSKY-KORSAKOV:
Capriccio espagnol etc. ***

Beecham's 1957 recording of the *Polovtsian dances* sweeps the board, even though it omits the
percussion-led opening *Dance of the Polovtsian maidens.* Beecham draws an almost Russian fervour
from his choristers. The recorded sound is little short of astonishing in its fullness, vividness and
clarity.

Karajan's Berlin Philharmonic version has great flair and excitement, though it lacks a chorus.

Dorati's Mercury recording is not among the most refined from this source, but no one could say
that effect lacks vividness or boisterous vitality, and the climax is exhilarating.

Bottesini, Giovanni (1821–89)

Gran duo concertante for violin, double-bass and orchestra; Gran concerto in F sharp min. for double-
bass; Andante sostenuto for strings; Duetto for clarinet and double-bass.
**(*) ASV Dig. CDDCA 563 [id.]. Garcia, Martin, Emma Johnson, ECO, Andrew Litton.

The ASV recording combines the *Gran duo concertante* with another *Duo for clarinet and double-bass*
which Emma Johnson ensures has plenty of personality. To be frank, none of this amiable music is
very distinctive. The recording is excellent, well balanced and truthful.

Capriccio di bravura; Elegia in Re; Fantasia on Beatrice di Tenda; Fantasia on Lucia di Lammermoor;
Grand allegro di concerto; Introduzione e Bolero; Romanza drammatica; (i) *Romanza: Une bouche*
aimée.
** ASV Dig. CDDCA 626 [id.]. Thomas Martin, Anthony Halstead; (i) with J. Fugelle.

Thomas Martin is a superb virtuoso of the double-bass, and he obviously relishes these display pieces,
but some of the high tessitura is inevitably uncomfortable. The recording is most realistic.

Boughton, Rutland (1878–1960)

(i) *Oboe concerto; Symphony No. 3 in B min.*
*** Hyp. Dig. CDA 66343 [id.]. (i) Sarah Francis; RPO, Vernon Handley.

Rutland Boughton's *Third Symphony* is old-fashioned in idiom, expertly fashioned and often imaginative, and it hardly puts a foot wrong. The *Oboe concerto* is hardly less rewarding. The recording is in
the demonstration class and the performances are totally committed, even if the strings of the RPO
are not quite on top form.

The Immortal hour (opera): complete.
*** Hyp. Dig. CDA 66101/2 [id.]. Kennedy, Dawson, Wilson-Johnson, Davies, Geoffrey Mitchell
Ch., ECO, Melville.

Analysed closely, much of *The Immortal hour* may seem like Vaughan Williams and water; but this
fine performance, conducted by a lifelong Boughton devotee, brings out the hypnotic quality which
had 1920s music-lovers attending performances many times over, entranced by its lyrical evocation of
Celtic twilight. The simple tunefulness goes with a fine feeling for atmosphere. The excellent cast of
young singers includes Anne Dawson as the heroine, Princess Etain, and Maldwyn Davies headily
beautiful in the main tenor rendering of the *Faery song.* Warm, reverberant recording, undoubtedly
enhanced in its CD format.

Boulanger, Lili (1893–1918)

(i) *Cortège; D'un matin de printemps; Nocturne* (3 pieces for violin & piano); (ii) *Du fond de l'abîme;*
(iii) *Pié Jesu;* (iv) *Psaume 24;* (v) *Psaume 129;* (vi) *Vieille prière bouddhique.*
(M) *(**) EMI mono/stereo CDM7 64281-2 [id.]. (i) Menuhin, Curzon; (ii) Dominguez, Amade; (iii)
Fauqueur; (iii; iv) Grunenwald; (iv) Sénéchal; (v) Mollet; (ii; iv–vi) Chorale Elizabeth Brasseur;

(ii–vi) LOP, Markevitch.

This is a haunting piece that quite transcends its very dated, dryish 1958 mono recording by Oralia Dominguez and the Lamoureux Orchestra of Paris under Igor Markevitch. The opening of the *Psaume 24* almost looks forward to the Honegger of *Le roi David*, and the *Vieille prière bouddhique* to Holst. The three pieces for violin and piano, *Cortège; D'un matin de printemps; Nocturne* are more Ravel-like, and are beautifully played by Yehudi Menuhin and Clifford Curzon. An altogether fascinating disc: the music deserves three stars, the recordings only one. But this disc has been withdrawn as we go to press.

Boulez, Pierre (born 1926)

Rituel: In memoriam Bruno Maderna; Eclat-Multiples.
(M) *** Sony SK 45839 [id.]. BBC SO, Ens. InterContemporain, composer.

Eclat-Multiples started (in 1964) simply as *Eclat*, a brilliant showpiece, an exuberant mosaic of sounds; but then, in 1970, it started developing from there in the pendant work, *Multiples*. *Rituel* is the most moving music that Boulez has ever written, inspired by the premature death of his friend and colleague, Bruno Maderna. This record, very well played and recorded, provides both a challenge and a reward.

Le soleil des eaux.
(M) *** EMI CDM7 63948-2 [id.]. Nendick, McDaniel, Devos, BBC Ch. & SO, composer –
   KOECKLIN: *Les Bandar-Log;* MESSIAEN: *Chronochromie* etc. ***

Boulez's cantata is best thought of initially in its atmospheric context. Josephine Nendick, the principal soloist, is breathtakingly precise and the result is far more enjoyable as a result. Both performance and recording are of a high standard and the CD transfer gives striking presence.

Boyce, William (1710–79)

Overtures Nos. 1–9.
(M) *** Chan. CHAN 6531; *MBTD 6531* [id.]. Cantilena, Adrian Shepherd.

Overtures Nos. 10–12; Concerti grossi: in B flat; in B min.; in E min.
(M) *** Chan. CHAN 6541 [id.]. Cantilena, Adrian Shepherd.

This reissue offers Cantilena's complete set of the Boyce *Overtures* and includes the three *Concerti grossi*. Though these works do not quite have the consistent originality which makes the Boyce *Symphonies* so refreshing, the energy of the writing – splendidly conveyed in these performances – is recognizably the same, with fugal passages that turn in unexpected directions. Cantilena's performances readily convey the freshness of Boyce's inspiration. The recording is oddly balanced but is both atmospheric and vivid and provides a refreshing musical experience.

Symphonies Nos. 1–8, Op. 2.
☞ *** O-L Dig. 436 761-2 [id.]. AAM, Hogwood.
*** DG Dig. 419 631-2 [id.]. E. Concert, Pinnock.
*** CRD CRD 3356 [id.]. Bournemouth Sinf., Ronald Thomas.
☞ (M) **(*) Van. 08.2037.71. I Solisti di Zagreb, Antonio Janigro.

Christopher Hogwood and the Academy of Ancient Music turn in performances that are every bit as lively and well played as Trevor Pinnock's set with the English Concert, and perhaps more sensitively shaped. By comparison, Pinnock now sounds just a bit bright and business-like. The Academy version is now a safe first choice among period-instrument versions.

Pinnock's disc of the Boyce *Symphonies* wears its scholarship very easily and in so doing brings not only lively, resilient playing but fresh revelation in the treatment of the *vivace* movements. Nicely scaled recording, bright but atmospheric.

Thomas's tempi are often brisk, and certainly swifter-paced than Pinnock's 'new look'. But even against such strong competition as this, the buoyant playing of the Bournemouth Sinfonietta still gives much pleasure by its sheer vitality. Bright, clear sound.

Janigro's set dates from the mid-1960s but serves to provide an excellent mid-priced alternative. There is an attractive freshness about the playing of the excellent I Solisti di Zagreb, who seem to relish the music's Handelian associations. They play on modern instruments, but the resilient string-playing and clear textures, with a comparatively light bass, make for less difference in sound than one would expect. When the trumpets enter in No. 5, the recording is rather less sharply defined, but the effect is suitably regal and full-blooded.

Organ voluntaries Nos. 1, 2, 4 & 10. (i) Anthems: *By the waters of Babylon; I have surely built Thee a house; O where shall wisdom be found; Turn unto me, O Lord.*
(M) *** Saga SCD 9006. Arthur Wills, (i) Ely Cathedral Ch., Gerald Clifford.

The music of Boyce is most compelling, especially when sung with such warmth. The organ voluntaries have plenty of character. This makes a most stimulating introduction to valuable and rare repertoire, and the CD transfer catches the cathedral ambience to perfection.

Solomon (serenata).
*** Hyp. Dig. CDA 66378; *KA 66378* [id.]. Bronwen Mills, Howard Crook, Parley of Instruments, Goodman.

William Boyce's *Solomon* is a totally secular piece, a dialogue between She and He, with the verses freely based on the *Song of Solomon.* As this stylish and alert period performance using young, fresh-voiced soloists makes clear, it has some delightful inspirations, less influenced by Italian models than by popular English song. First-rate sound.

Brade, William (1560–1630)

Hamburger Ratsmusik: Allemandes, Canzonas, Courantes, Galliards, Intradas (1609, 1614 & 1617 collections).
(M) *** HM/BMG Dig. GD 77168 (2) [77168-2-RG]. Hespèrion XX, Jordi Savall.

This collection of dances is absolutely delightful, varied in both content and instrumental colour, and excellently played by Hespèrion XX under Jordi Savall, while the recording, from 1981, is very good indeed.

Brahms, Johannes (1833–97)

(i) *Piano concertos Nos. 1–2. Academic festival overture; Tragic overture; Variations on a theme of Haydn.*
☞ (B) **(*) Ph. Duo 438 320-2 (2) [id.]. (i) Claudio Arrau; Concg. O, Haitink.

Arrau's readings undoubtedly have vision and power, and the *D minor Concerto* is majestic and eloquent. There is some characteristic agogic distortion that will not convince all listeners, and, by the side of Gilels, Arrau seems idiosyncratic. In the *Second Concerto* his playing has a splendid combination of aristocratic finesse and warmth of feeling, and in both concertos Haitink and the Royal Concertgebouw Orchestra give excellent support. In the *B flat Concerto* the engineers strike the right balance between the piano and the orchestra, and the orchestral texture is fuller and better-focused than in the *D minor Concerto.* The inclusion of the two overtures and *St Anthony variations*, all finely played, makes the set even more competitive. The *Academic festival overture* has a strong ending, and there is also a rush of adrenalin in the *Variations*, a beautiful and exciting reading, very well recorded. Excellent value, and the set is well documented.

(i) *Piano concertos Nos. 1–2. Ballades Op. 10; 8 Pieces, Op. 76.*
☞ *(*) BMG/RCA Dig. 09026 61620-2 (2) [id.]. Gerhard Oppitz; (i) Bav. RSO, Sir Colin Davis.

Piano concerto No. 1 in D min., Op. 15.
☞ *(*) BMG/RCA Dig. 09026 61618-2 [id.] (with *4 Ballades, Op. 10*). Oppitz, Bav. RSO, Sir Colin Davis.

Piano concerto No. 2; 8 Pieces, Op. 76.
☞ *(*) BMG/RCA Dig. 09026 61619-2 [id.]. Oppitz, Bav. RSO, Sir Colin Davis.

Gerhard Oppitz is much admired in Germany and he has the technique and dramatic power to cope with the formidable demands this concerto makes. All the same, an imaginative and poetic dimension is missing and, despite good playing from the wonderful Bavarian Radio Symphony Orchestra under Colin Davis and a warm acoustic, it offers no challenge to the even better-recorded Kovacevich and Sawallisch on EMI, or Arrau–Haitink and Gilels–Jochum at mid-price, or the many other versions with which the catalogue is endowed.

(i) *Piano concertos Nos. 1–2. 4 Ballades, Op. 10; 8 Pieces, Op. 76; Scherzo in E flat, Op. 4.*
☞ (B) *** Ph. 442 109-2 (2) [id.]. Steven Kovacevich; (i) LSO, Sir Colin Davis.

This reissue of the early recordings of the two Brahms *Piano concertos* made by Kovacevich in 1979, together with a generous and equally distinguished selection of piano music dating from 1983, makes an extraordinary bargain. The current remastering of the concertos has greatly improved the focus of the sound, especially in No. 1, and there are no complaints at all about the quality of the solo recital. In the *D minor concerto* Kovacevich plays with great tenderness and lyrical feeling. In the hushed slow movement he achieves real inwardness and poetry, and in the first movement he makes no attempt either to exaggerate or to understate the combative, leonine side of the solo part. Similarly, No. 2 combines poetic feeling and intellectual strength and reflects an unforced naturalness that compels admiration. The first movement unfolds simply without any false urgency; the second is sparkling and fresh, and in the *Adagio* there is a rapt, poetic quality that becomes magically hushed at the close. Douglas Cummings, the cello soloist, plays with gentle nobility. The finale has wit and delicacy and brings a spontaneous surge of adrenalin at the close. Sir Colin Davis provides wholly sympathetic support throughout, and this set can be spoken of alongside Gilels; the recording is less well balanced, but still full and quite satisfying. The piano music originally took up a whole LP by itself. The accounts of the *Ballades* and the Op. 76 *Klavierstücke* have both fire and tenderness and are truthfully recorded.

(i) *Piano concertos Nos. 1–2. Capriccio in B min., Op. 76/2; Intermezzi: in E, Op. 116/6; in E flat, Op. 117/1; in E min.; in C, Op. 119/2–3; Rhapsody in B min., Op. 79/1; 6 Pieces, Op. 118.*
☞ (M) **(*) Decca 433 895-2 (2) [id.]. Wilhelm Backhaus; (i) VPO, Boehm.

Backhaus recorded the *First Concerto* in 1953 and no apologies need be made for the mono recording. The acoustics of the Musikverein ensure a fine spread of sound and the performance has great impetus and authority, showing the pianist at his very finest in repertoire to which he was especially well suited. The *Second Concerto* was made in the Sofiensaal in 1967 when Backhaus was in his eighties, and the rugged strength of his conception is matched by playing of remarkable power. His is a broad, magisterial account. Tempi are inclined to be spacious but there is no great loss of momentum or of architectural grip. The recording wears its years remarkably lightly: it sounds fresh, full-bodied and is finely detailed. The solo pieces date from 1956. Backhaus is again in excellent form, though the *Intermezzi*, which are played sensitively, come in for rather more subtle treatment than the *Capriccio* and *Rhapsody*. Here the recording is good, for the most part, but not outstanding – Decca have given us better. But admirers of Backhaus will want this set even more than his Beethoven records.

Piano concerto No. 1 in D min., Op. 15.
*** Ph. Dig. 420 071-2 [id.]. Brendel, BPO, Abbado.
**(*) Decca Dig. 410 009-2 [id.]. Ashkenazy, Concg. O, Haitink.
☞ (BB) **(*) ASV CDQS 6083. John Lill, Hallé O, Loughran.

(i) *Piano concerto No. 1. Variations and fugue on a theme of Handel, Op. 24.*
(***) Testament mono SBT1041 [id.]. Solomon, (i) Philh. O, Kubelik.
(i) *Piano concerto No. 1; (ii) Variations on a theme of Haydn, Op. 56a.*
(M) *** EMI CDM7 63536-2 [id.]. (i) Barenboim, Philh. O; (ii) VPO; Barbirolli.

(i) *Piano concerto No. 1. 4 Ballades, Op. 10.*
(M) *** DG 431 595-2 [id.]. Gilels, (i) BPO, Jochum.

(i) *Piano concerto No. 1 in D min., Op. 15. Capriccio in B min., Op. 76/2; Intermezzo in E flat min., Op. 118/6; Rhapsody in B min., Op. 79/1.*
☞ (M) **(*) BMG/RCA 09026 61263-2 [id.]. Artur Rubinstein; (i) Chicago SO, Reiner.

(i) *Piano concerto No. 1 in D min., Op. 15; (ii) 2 Songs, Op. 91.*
☞ ⊛ *** EMI Dig. CDC7 54578-2. (i) Stephen Kovacevich, LPO, Sawallisch; (ii) Anne Murray, Nobuko Imai.

Stephen Kovacevich's account of the Brahms *D minor Concerto* is the finest to have appeared for many years. Noble and dedicated, this is a performance of stature which belongs in the most exalted company. It can be recommended alongside such classic accounts as the Gilels/Jochum (DG); indeed, it must now take precedence. Moreover it is accorded fine digital sound which has all the warmth and spaciousness one could ask for, together with splendid presence and detail. This is one of the outstanding records of the year and deserves the strongest recommendation. There is a welcome fill-up in the form of the two Op. 91 *Songs* with viola, admirably presented by Anne Murray and

Nobuko Imai.

Gilels's reading of the *D minor Concerto* has a magisterial strength blended with a warmth, humanity and depth that are altogether inspiring. Jochum is a superb accompanist and the remastered 1972 recording has a better focus on CD. The *Ballades* have never been played so marvellously on record, and the recording is very believable.

Brendel produces a consistently beautiful sound and balances the combative and lyrical elements of the work with well-nigh perfect judgement.

Barenboim's performance of the *First Concerto* with Barbirolli is among the most inspired ever committed to disc. The playing is heroic and marvellously spacious, and the performance is sustained by the intensity of concentration, especially in the pianissimo passages of the slow movement; the joyous finale uplifts the spirit and communicates a life-enhancing confidence. The *Variations* again show the conductor at his finest; the late-1960s recordings have transferred splendidly to CD.

Ashkenazy gives a commanding and magisterial account of the solo part that is full of poetic imagination. The performance is very impressive indeed and there is superlative playing from the Concertgebouw Orchestra. The recording is enormously vivid.

Rubinstein's Chicago recording was made in stereo as early as 1954 and the sound remains remarkably good, thanks to the sympathetic Chicago acoustics. This is a poetic and essentially lyrical reading, impulsive and intent on avoiding Brahmsian stodginess – though it is by no means without power, for Reiner's control of the orchestra, volatile and imaginative, has a spacious strength. The only snag is the forward balance of the piano, which means that (as in Rubinstein's RCA version of the *Second Concerto*) a real pianissimo fails to register, although the recording brings out the brightness of Rubinstein's tone attractively. The three solo piano pieces, now added as a bonus, are characteristically chimerical. This is a fine memento of a great artist, not the most profound version but a consistently enjoyable one.

Solomon's magisterial account with Rafael Kubelik and the Philharmonia Orchestra belongs (with Gilels, Curzon and, most recently, Kovacevich) among the greatest ever made. It has a majestic grandeur and blends the dramatic power of youth with the wisdom of old age. Of course the 1952 recording does not possess the range or bloom of subsequent versions, but the transfer succeeds in making it sound astonishingly present. Of his celebrated 1942 set of the Brahms *Handel variations*, one is tempted to say the same: that in its classic poise it must be numbered among the greatest – if not *the* greatest – recording of the work.

John Lill has the measure of the work's fire and drama, yet his playing is fundamentally classical; indeed, it is unfailingly impressive and scrupulous in its observance of every dynamic marking and expressive nuance. He is given warm and spirited support from Loughran and the Hallé – natural Brahmsians – even though woodwind intonation in one or two places is not wholly above reproach. Masterly and commanding playing, although at times there is a slightly reserved quality that inhibits unqualified recommendation. Nevertheless, with very good (1978) recording, this is well worth considering in the lowest price range.

(i) *Piano concerto No. 1 in D min. 4 Ballades Op. 10; 2 Capricii, Op. 76/1–2; Intermezzo in B flat, Op. 76/4; 2 Rhapsodies, Op. 79; Piano sonata No. 3 in F min., Op. 5; Scherzo in E flat, Op. 4.*
☞ (B) *** DG Double mono/stereo 437 374-2 (2) [id.]. Wilhelm Kempff; (i) Dresden State O, Konwitschny.

Kempff was born in 1895, two years before the death of Brahms, and the great pianist himself died in 1991. This set spans his major solo Brahms recordings, made between 1957 and 1963, and includes the mono account of the Brahms *D minor Concerto* from 1956; no complaints about the DG recording of this work. The internal orchestral balance may be less well integrated than with a stereo version, but in all other respects the sound is very good, with a full-bodied patina of strings and excellently balanced wind and the piano naturally caught and well integrated, yet able to dominate where needed. The orchestral introduction is measured and powerful and Konwitschny brings plenty of weight and thrust and no lack of warmth to outer movements. Kempff entering thoughtfully is able immediately to create rapt inner tension, yet providing the necessary bravura while investing the *Adagio* with characteristic poetry and bringing joyfully articulated vigour to the finale. In the solo items, mostly recorded in the early 1960s, Kempff more than almost any rival brings lightness and delicacy to the thick textures. In the *Capriccii* and *Rhapsodies* poetry is emphasized rather than brilliance, and the absence of extrovert virtuosity in Op. 79 does not mean that the music is without a strong impulse. The four *Ballades* emerge very much as a young man's music, full of ardour, as does the *F minor Sonata* which was released in 1958 and was discussed in our very first hardback *Stereo Record Guide*. The interpretation of the sonata could hardly be warmer or more sympathetic. Kempff was then in his middle sixties and the very fact that there are minor technical smudges underlines the massiveness of the work and its sheer physical difficulty. In the waltz-like middle movement of the five, Kempff has an engaging lilt to his playing which turns what can seem elephantine into the warm-hearted interlude that Brahms intended, while in the finale the entry of the descending chorale-like theme is a superb moment. The *Scherzo in E flat minor* – still comparatively rarely heard – makes a fine encore. We noted at the time of the LP issue that the recording was splendidly full and clear and that the acoustic of the studio seemed just about right.

Piano concerto No. 2 in B flat, Op. 83.
*** Ph. Dig. 432 975-2; *432 975-4* [id.]. Brendel, BPO, Abbado.
(M) *** BMG/RCA GD 86518 [RCA 6518-2-RG]. Sviatoslav Richter, Chicago SO, Leinsdorf –
   BEETHOVEN: *Piano sonata No. 23.* ***
(M) *** DG 431 596-2; *431 596-4* [id.]. Pollini, VPO, Abbado.
(BB) **(*) ASV CDQS 6088. John Lill, Hallé O, Loughran.
☞ (M) **(*) Sony SBK 53262 [id.]. Rudolf Serkin, Cleveland SO, Szell – R. STRAUSS: *Burleske.* *(**)
☞ (BB) ** Naxos Dig. 8.550506 [id.]. Jenö Jandó, Belgian R. & TV O, Rahbari (with SCHUMANN:
   Introduction and allegro appassionata *(*)).
☞ (M) * Teldec/Warner Dig. 9031 77599-2 [id.]. Katsaris, Philh. O, Inbal.

(i) *Piano concerto No. 2;* (ii) *Academic festival overture; Tragic overture.*
(M) *** EMI CDM7 63537-2 [id.]. (i) Barenboim, Philh. O; (ii) VPO; Barbirolli.

(i) *Piano concerto No. 2 in B flat. Variations on a theme of Haydn, Op. 56a.*
(M) *** Sony SMK 47359 [id.]. (i) André Watts; NYPO, Bernstein.

(i) *Piano concerto No. 2 in B flat. Fantasias, Op. 116.*
(M) *** DG 435 588-2 [id.]. Gilels; (i) BPO, Jochum.

(i) *Piano concerto No. 2. Intermezzi: in E min., Op. 116/5; in B flat min., Op. 117/2; Rhapsody in G min., Op. 79/2.*
☞ (M) *** BMG/RCA 09026 61442-2 [id.]. Rubinstein, (i) RCA Victor SO, Krips.

(i) *Piano concerto No. 2. Intermezzo in B flat min., Op. 117/2; in C, Op. 119/3; Rhapsody in G min., Op. 79/2.*
☞ (***) Testament mono SBT1042 [id.]. Solomon, (i) Philh. O, Dobrowen.

The partnership of Gilels and Jochum produces music-making of rare magic and the digital remastering has improved definition: the sound is full in an appropriately Brahmsian way. In the *Fantasias*, Op. 116, Gilels displays artistry of an order that silences criticism.

Brendel's new account of the concerto is massive and concentrated, and has greater depth than his earlier account with Haitink. It is a worthy successor to their *D minor*, though in terms of humanity and wisdom it does not displace the celebrated Gilels–Jochum version.

Richter's 1960 RCA performance has all the intensity of a live occasion and finds him in splendid form. It is wayward, mannered in places, but the basic structure is always kept in sight; there is impressive weight and authority as well as a warm, Brahmsian lyrical feeling.

Pollini's 1977 recording makes a good alternative choice, also at mid-price. His account is powerful, in many ways more classical in feeling than Richter's. He is given first-rate support by the Vienna Philharmonic under Abbado.

The commanding Solomon set of the *B flat Concerto* with Issay Dobrowen and the Philharmonia Orchestra comes from 1947. There is a leonine nobility about this performance and an immediacy, spontaneity and dramatic fire that sweep all before it. Like his *D minor Concerto*, this is a classic account, which no admirer of this artist (or of Brahms, for that matter) should pass over. The piano is not always perfect (the C above the stave is out of tune in one passage) but the pianist is! One soon forgets the sonic limitations and is swept along by the performance.

With Barenboim's reading with Barbirolli, the first two movements remain grandly heroic and the slow movement has something of the awed intensity you find in the middle movement of the *First Concerto*, while the finale erupts gracefully into rib-tickling humour. This is a performance to love in its glowing spontaneity. Of the fill-ups, the *Tragic overture* is a performance of considerable distinction; but the measured account of the *Academic festival overture* could do with more sparkle.

André Watts also gives a powerful and compelling performance that stands as one of the finest on record. At every point he shows deep feeling and intelligence. His Brahms style is boldly lyrical. Bernstein accompanies very positively and the only surprising element is the variably exact ensemble that he secures from the orchestra. Even so this is a very rewarding and spontaneous account and the *Haydn variations* are also characteristically alive and by no means predictable.

It is good to have John Pfeiffer's remastering of this scintillating and very involving Rubinstein performance, recorded at the Manhattan Center in New York City in 1958. The piano balance remains forward but the integration with the vividly recorded orchestra is much more realistic. The close balance means that a true pianissimo is never registered, although it is obvious that the playing of soloist and orchestra alike seeks the widest range of dynamic. Rubinstein was at his peak, and his technical mastery brings a charismatic response to the changing moods of the first movement, while the finale is a delight with its deftness of articulation and rippling lyricism. Rubinstein was lucky to have Josef Krips as his collaborator, for he brings a Viennese touch to the orchestra and matches Rubinstein's spontaneity. This is a reading which emphasizes the bright and luminous aspects of the work and is all the more refreshing for that, even if other accounts have more gravitas and weight. The three substantial encores are well chosen to make a miniature (15-minute) solo recital after the concerto; once again, the sound is realistic and the playing distinguished.

John Lill first recorded the *Second Concerto* not long after winning the Moscow Tchaikovsky competition. This newer (1982) version with the Hallé Orchestra under James Loughran is in many ways a strong account, well thought out, finely paced and without the slightest trace of self-indulgence. The opening has a powerful, masculine ring, particularly the build-up just before the orchestral tutti, and it is the space and power of Brahms's conception that are given priority, rather than his poetry. Not that the performance is wanting in feeling or imagination. There is a stronger sense of the philosopher musing than of the poet dreaming. The recorded sound is eminently well balanced and quite full, though climaxes could open out a bit more. Nevertheless in the budget range this is competitive.

As with the *First Concerto*, Serkin's recording with Szell was his third on LP, and on most counts it is the finest. There is a strength and purposefulness about all the playing; with the help of Szell, Serkin achieves an ideal balance between straightforwardness and expressiveness. In the opening cadenza, for example, he has all the weight one could ask for, but he still manages to point the dotted rhythm very winningly and achieves remarkable clarity. In the Scherzo he is again strong but manages to convey more lilt than many rivals, while the slow movement has a genuine 'inner' intensity, with some wonderfully expressive playing by the Cleveland principal cellist. Serkin chooses a comparatively slow speed for the finale, but the flow and energy of the music are not impaired and the Hungarian motifs of the second subject sparkle with point and wit. Unfortunately the piano tone is not as full as one would ideally like but, as with the *First Concerto*, the remastering produces a firm orchestral image and the hall ambience contributes to a Brahmsian sonority. The new coupling is a commanding account of the Richard Strauss *Burleske*, though here the recording is rather less flattering.

Jandó and Rahbari provide a strong, positive account of the *B flat Concerto* but not one that remains in the memory. The slow movement has warmth but not a very wide range of dynamic, and the finale lacks a sense of fantasy. The recording is spacious and full, and Jandó's playing is not wanting in bravura, although his rugged approach to the coupled Schumann piece does not endear it to the listener.

Katsaris's account, recorded as recently as 1989, has full, well-balanced sound, but the partnership with Inbal fails to strike sparks and the performance obstinately refuses to spring to life. The result is well structured but dull.

Violin concerto in D, Op. 77.
☞ (M) *** EMI Dig. CD-EMX 2203; *TC-EMX 2203* [id.]. Tasmin Little, RLPO, Handley –
SIBELIUS: *Violin concerto.* ***
☞ *** EMI Dig. CDC7 54580-2 [id.]. Itzhak Perlman, BPO, Barenboim.
*** ASV CDDCA 748 [id.]. Xue-Wei, LPO, Ivor Bolton – MENDELSSOHN: *Violin concerto.* ***
☞ (M) *** BMG/RCA 09026 61495-2. Heifetz, Chicago SO, Reiner – TCHAIKOVSKY: *Concerto.* ***
*** Chan. Dig. CHAN 8974; *ABTD 1563* [id.]. Hideko Udagawa, LSO, Mackerras – BRUCH:
   Concerto No. 1. ***
(M) (***) EMI mono CDH7 61011-2. Ginette Neveu, Philh. O, Issay Dobrowen – SIBELIUS:
   Concerto. (***)
☞ (***) Testament mono SBT 1037 [id.]. Johanna Martzy, Philh. O, Kletzki – MENDELSSOHN:
   Concerto. (***)
☞ (***) Testament mono SBT 1038 [id.]. Ida Haendel, LSO, Celibidache – TCHAIKOVSKY:
   Concerto. (***)
**(*) EMI Dig. CDC7 54187-2; *EL 754187-4* [id.]. Nigel Kennedy, LPO, Klaus Tennstedt.
☞ (M) **(*) EMI CDM7 64632-2 [id.]; *EG 764632-4*. David Oistrakh, Fr. Nat. RSO, Klemperer –
   MOZART: *Sinfonia concertante.* **

☞ (M) **(*) Teldec/Warner 4509 91443-2 [id.]. Zehetmair, Cleveland O, Dohnányi – SCHUMANN: *Fantasy*. ***

☞ (**) Pearl mono GEMMCDS 9996 (2) [id.]. Kreisler, Berlin State Op. O, Leo Blech – BACH: *Double violin concerto;* BEETHOVEN; MENDELSSOHN; MOZART: *Violin concertos.* (**)

☞ (**) Pearl mono GEMMCD 9345 [id.]. Joseph Szigeti, British SO, Bruno Walter – BEETHOVEN: *Violin concerto.* (**)

☞ (M) *(*) Mercury 434 318-2 [id.]. Szeryng, LSO, Dorati – KHACHATURIAN: *Violin concerto.* **

(i) *Violin concerto in D. Tragic overture, Op. 81.*
(B) *** Ph. 422 972-2. (i) Hermann Krebbers; Concg. O, Haitink.

(i) *Violin concerto in D;* (ii) *Piano trio No. 2 in C, Op. 87.*
☞ (M) (*(*)) Sony mono MPK 52535 [id.]. Szigeti; (i) Phd. O, Ormandy; (ii) Hess; Casals.

(i) *Violin concerto in D;* (ii) *Violin sonata No. 1 in G, Op. 78.*
☞ (B) ** DG 439 405-2 [id.]. Zukerman, (i) O de Paris, Barenboim; (ii) Barenboim (piano).

Tasmin Little gives a warmly satisfying account of the Brahms, at once brilliant and deeply felt. The rapt poetry she finds in the first two movements has rarely been matched, with powerful bravura set against yearning pianissimos. She also brings an element of fun to the Hungarian dance finale, rarely caught so winningly. Even more than in her earlier recordings, there is a dramatic thrust and intensity that mirrors live communication, strongly matched by the RLPO under Handley. At mid-price the disc is even more recommendable when it also contains an equally searching and exuberant account of the Sibelius *Violin concerto*.

Perlman's newest digital account of the Brahms finds him at his most commanding, powerful and full of nonchalant flair to a degree that no rival today can quite match. With Perlman the advantage of a live recording is that, as here, there is an extra warmth of commitment, with no sense that the performance has been too easily achieved. There is no fill-up, but few will complain with a reading that is so strong and compelling.

Hermann Krebbers, concertmaster of the Concertgebouw Orchestra, here gives one of the most deeply satisfying readings of the Brahms *Violin concerto* ever recorded: strong and urgent yet tenderly poetic too, and always full of spontaneous imagination. The total commitment behind the performance is not just the achievement of the soloist but also that of his colleagues and their conductor, who perform as at a live concert.

Xue-Wei's version of the Brahms is fresh and well-mannered. There is a degree of emotional reticence here compared with more flamboyant performers but, with Ivor Bolton drawing first-rate playing from the LPO, it is a performance to live with and can be warmly recommended. The sound is first rate too.

Heifetz's performance is both dazzling and enormously stimulating, and the new CD transfer has quite transformed the 1955 recording, making it vivid and fresh instead of harsh, while the excellent qualities of the balance in the warm acoustics of Orchestra Hall come out in full, giving a fine three-dimensional focus. The speeds for all three movements may be fast but Heifetz's ease and detailed imagination make them more than just dazzling, while the central *Andante* at a flowing speed is delectably songful. Recoupled with the Tchaikovsky *Concerto* – a work which Heifetz made his own in the 78-r.p.m. era – this is a reissue not to be missed.

Hideko Udagawa gives a powerful, persuasively spontaneous-sounding reading. Her biting attack on the most taxing passages is often thrilling, even if her violin-sound is not always the sweetest. The personality of the player and her magnetic temperament submerge reservations on detail, particularly when Mackerras draws comparably powerful playing from the LSO. Warm, full and well-balanced recording.

Ginette Neveu's is a magnificent performance, urgently electric, remarkable not just for sweetness of tone and her pinpoint intonation but also for the precision and clarity of even the most formidable passages of double stopping. The transfer from the original 78s brings satisfyingly full-bodied sound, surprisingly good on detail.

It is sad that Johanna Martzy, born in Romania in 1924 but trained in Budapest, made all her major recordings at the end of the mono era and then refused to let them be reissued. Warmly sponsored by Walter Legge, she was an outstanding artist with a gloriously sweet and true tone that is consistently and satisfyingly in the middle of the note. Her warmth of temperament is also ideal. She always sounds spontaneous in her freely flexible rubato which never falls into wilfulness or sentimentality. Hers is an exceptionally warm and persuasive account of the Brahms, marked by a very wide range of dynamic and tone. Few versions of whatever period can match the hushed tenderness of Martzy in the coda of the first movement, and so it is too in the slow movement, while the finale is played with Hungarian point and flair. Kletzki proves an ideal accompanist. The Testament reissue, superbly transferred, ideally coupled with an equally inspired account of the Mendelssohn, at last does justice to a long-underappreciated artist.

With Sergiu Celibidache making a rare appearance as conductor on disc, Ida Haendel, too, gives a powerful, full-toned reading of the Brahms. Recorded in mono in 1953, it was never reissued in the LP era, but it comes up very freshly and intensely in this superb CD transfer from Testament. With the soloist well forward, the recording does not convey a true pianissimo, but the clarity and bite of the playing, as well as its strength and nobility, are splendidly caught, confirming the mastery of a great violinist too little heard on disc. Generously coupled with a full-blooded, romantic reading of the Tchaikovsky.

Kennedy's version of the Brahms is by a fair margin the slowest ever put on disc, but Kennedy's musical personality and his devotion to the work give an intensity to sustain all the eccentricities. Tennstedt draws concentrated playing from the LPO, the whole richly recorded.

The conjunction of two such positive artists as Oistrakh and Klemperer makes for a reading characterful to the point of idiosyncrasy, monumental and strong rather than sweetly lyrical. Oistrakh sounds superbly poised and confident, and in the finale, if the tempo is a shade deliberate, the total effect is one of clear gain. The 1961 recording seems smoother than in its most recent incarnation; the CD transfer is brightly lit, but the solo violin, although sharply focused, is more naturally caught – and the orchestral violins are fuller too. EMI have now also added a sizeable Mozart bonus, if a somewhat disappointing one.

Zehetmair's is a warm and thoroughly musical account: his timbre is sweet, and both he and Dohnányi, who accompanies sympathetically, offer a good response to Brahmsian lyricism. The Cleveland orchestral playing is beyond criticism and the Teldec sound-balance impressively natural. But other versions of this work have a much stronger profile, and this performance fails to resonate in the memory. The rare Schumann coupling, however, makes this record more attractive than when first issued at full price, for the recording is first class.

Zukerman is rightly famed for his sweetness of tone, and his general approach can often seem a little bland by comparison with the greatest artists. This is a well-conceived reading that has finish and facility yet ultimately leaves the listener untouched by any feeling that he or she is in contact with great music. Zukerman is exposed to a close balance, but this does not mask the Orchestre de Paris under Barenboim, who give excellent support and receive a well-detailed recording in spite of the unrealistic perspective. The sound of the solo violin is even more present in digitally remastered format, as is the coupled *Violin sonata*, a generous bonus. For the Classikon bargain reissue, DG have changed the violin sonata coupling from *No. 2 in A major* to the *G major*, Op. 78. But both sonatas are also available separately, coupled together, a very recommendable CD.

It was with the LSO that Szeryng made his earlier version of the Brahms *Violin concerto* for RCA in the early days of stereo, but the conductor then was Monteux. That fact alone may help to explain the comparative disappointment of this 1962 Mercury account. Szeryng is rarely a forthcoming artist: he seems to require encouragement in order to give a warm performance, and here Dorati (unlike Monteux) fails to provide the right support. Tempi are relaxed and the result is generally unconvincing and often cold, even though inevitably the detail is admirably managed. The recording is not one of Mercury's most impressive efforts and is not kind to Szeryng's distinctive tone-colour, making the violin-timbre sound thin.

Kreisler's Brahms *Concerto* was made in 1926, and its lyrical fervour and warmth give it a special place in the catalogue. As a performance it rates more stars and rosettes than most versions of the CD era put together, but the untamed surfaces and edgy treble will pose a problem to all but devoted enthusiasts, even though some ears do adjust and, of course, Kreisler's commanding entry silences any criticism. He is very closely balanced indeed and one is tempted to be grateful for that. But it ought to be possible to improve greatly on this transfer with the technical facilities currently available.

There are now two accounts of the Brahms *Concerto* from Szigeti back in circulation: the first with the Hallé Orchestra under Sir Hamilton Harty, recorded in 1928, and the second with Philadelphia and Ormandy, recorded in 1945. Although, generally speaking, Szigeti's post-war tone was wirier and his vibrato wider than in the inter-war years, his artistic approach remains consistently individual and aristocratic. The 1945 Ormandy set has the advantage of superior orchestral playing and more acceptable recording, but Szigeti himself is in loftier form in the earlier version and his insights are deeper. There is much purer tone and a sense of effortlessness as well as a breadth and space about it that make its claims the stronger – or would, were the sound not a serious encumbrance. The upper strings sound distinctly acidulated in this transfer. However, it comes with the celebrated 1932 recording he made in Westminster Central Hall of the Beethoven *Concerto* with Bruno Walter and the British Symphony Orchestra.

In addition to some superb orchestral playing and a generally superior sound-quality, the 1945 version has many beautiful things, but the rougher, almost juddering tone Szigeti was beginning to produce in his last decades is discernible and, artistically, the solo playing, while of some stature, has too many rough moments. It does have the advantage of offering another legendary performance: the *C major Piano trio*, Op. 87, with Casals and Myra Hess, recorded at the 1952 Prades Festival. Low on 'fi' perhaps, but high on musicianship and humanity: a richly rewarding account that soon rises above the inevitable sonic limitations, Szigeti's moments of rough tone and Casals' groans.

Violin concerto (with cadenzas by Busoni, Joachim, Singer, Hermann, Auer, Ysaÿe, Ondricek, Kneisel, Marteau, Kreisler, Tovey, Kubelik, Busch, Heifetz, Milstein, Ricci).
*** Biddulph Dig. LAW 002 [id.]. Ruggiero Ricci, Sinf. of London, Del Mar.

The veteran Ruggero Ricci not only gives a strong, assured performance of the concerto, he adds no fewer than 16 cadenzas as well, any of which can be programmed into the main performance on CD. Though Ricci is no longer as fiery or incisive as he once was, his is an attractive performance of the concerto, well recorded.

Violin concerto in D, Op. 77; (i) *Double concerto for violin, cello and orchestra, Op. 102.*
☞ *** DG Dig. 439 007-2 [id.]. Mutter, (i) with Meneses; BPO, Karajan.
(M) **(*) Sony SBK 46335 [id.]. Stern, (i) with Rose; Phd. O, Ormandy.

This is an attractive new coupling for the Karajan Gold series, and both recordings have been remastered with the use of Original-image-bit processing. The *Double concerto* is particularly success-ful. With two young soloists Karajan conducts an outstandingly spacious and strong performance. Anne-Sophie Mutter conveys a natural authority comparable to Karajan's own, and the precision and clarity of Meneses' cello as recorded make an excellent match. The central slow movement in its spacious way has a wonderfully Brahmsian glow, and all these qualities come out vividly in the new transfer, though the relatively close balance of the soloists – particularly that of the cellist – is the more noticeable. Mutter's account of the *Violin concerto*, too, has an unforced freshness, yet has both flair and individuality. There is a lightness of touch, a gentleness in the slow movement, that is highly appealing, while in the finale the incisiveness of the solo playing is well displayed by the clear digital sound. Needless to say, Karajan's accompaniment is strong in personality and the Berlin Philharmonic play beautifully. Their opening tutti for the first movement sounds marvellous in the new transfer, and the recording has vivid presence, although the very close balance of the soloist now brings a brighter lighting of the violin timbre and emphasizes the gutsy edge of the passionate solo contribution. The performance itself represents a genuine partnership between youthful inspiration and eager experience. All in all, this is a most impressive coupling, with both performances very involving.

Stern's glorious 1959 account of the *Violin concerto* with Ormandy is now given a coupling that is both generous and suitable, the mid-1960s' collaboration with Leonard Rose in the *Double concerto*. The two soloists unfailingly match each other's playing, with Ormandy always an understanding accompanist. The forward balance of the soloists brings glorious tone, even if this means that there are no pianissimos. The CD transfers are well managed.

Double concerto for violin, cello and orchestra in A min., Op. 102.
☞ (M) *** EMI CDM7 64744-2 [id.]. D. Oistrakh, Rostropovich, Cleveland O, Szell – BEETHOVEN: *Triple concerto.* ***
*** Sony Dig. MK 42387 [id.]. Isaac Stern, Yo-Yo Ma, Chicago SO, Abbado – *Piano quartet No. 3.* **
☞ (M) (***) BMG/RCA mono 09026 61485-2 [id.]. Milstein, Piatigorsky, Robin Hood Dell O of Philadelphia, Reiner – R. STRAUSS: *Don Quixote.* (***)

Although Rostropovich has re-recorded the *Double concerto* with Perlman and Haitink, this earlier (1969) recording has claims to be regarded with equal esteem as one of the finest of all versions. The remastered sound is full and vivid and has great presence. If it places the soloists too far forward, few will grumble when the playing is so ripely, compellingly Brahmsian and the solo timbres so richly projected. The *Andante* is glorious. Szell's powerful tutti and warmly sympathetic backing keep the Cleveland Orchestra well in the picture. Coupled with an equally arresting version of Beethoven's *Triple concerto*, this reissue is a superb bargain of the first order.

The CBS version with Isaac Stern, Yo-Yo Ma and the Chicago Symphony Orchestra under Claudio Abbado is one of the more successful of recent years. The balance is well judged and the playing of both soloists and orchestra alike is glorious. The *Piano quartet* coupling, however, is rather less successful.

The Milstein–Piatigorsky–Reiner account ranks with the great performances of the *Double concerto* such as the Thibaud–Casals–Cortot, though it is much better recorded. It has warmth, vitality, nobility and power; Reiner gets some fabulous playing from his Philadelphia Orchestra. It comes with a no less remarkable *Don Quixote* from Piatigorsky which should not be missed. A very good transfer.

Hungarian dances Nos. 1–21 (complete).
❀ (BB) *** Naxos Dig. 8.550110; *4550110* (*Nos. 1–2; 4–21*). Budapest SO, István Bogár.

The Budapest recording of the Brahms *Hungarian dances* is sheer delight from beginning to end. The playing has warmth and sparkle, and the natural way the music unfolds brings a refreshing feeling of rhythmic freedom. Bogár's rubato is wholly spontaneous. The recording is warm and full, yet transparent, with just the right brilliance on top. This is an outright winner among the available versions.

Hungarian dances Nos. 1, 2, 4 & 7.
☞ *** EMI Dig. CDC7 54753-2 [id.]. Sarah Chang, Jonathan Feldman – TCHAIKOVSKY: *Violin concerto.* ***

It may be an ungenerous coupling for the Tchaikovsky *Concerto*, but Chang's performances of four of the Brahms *Hungarian dances* – recorded with Jonathan Feldman in New York – are delectable. Though her tone remains pure and unsoupy, they are marked by the sort of naughty pointing of phrase and rhythm that tickles one's musical funny-bone, just as the playing of Kreisler always did.

Hungarian dances Nos. 1, 3, 5, 10, 16 & 18–21.
☞ **(*) DG Dig. 437 506-2; *437 506-4* [id.]. N. German RSO, Gardiner – DVORAK: *Czech suite* etc.
**(*)

As an unexpected fill-up to his main Dvořák items, Gardiner offers sparkling, strongly characterized performances of these nine *Hungarian dances*, with the last four aptly coming in Dvořák's own arrangements. They are not always helped by the rather bass-heavy and reverberant sound, but form a welcome item in Gardiner's first disc with the orchestra of which he has become chief conductor.

Piano quartet in G min. (orch. Schoenberg).
*** Collins Dig. 1175-2; *1175-4* [id.]. LPO, Rozhdestvensky – RACHMANINOV: *Etudes-tableaux.* ***

Piano quartet in G min. (orch. Schoenberg); *Variations and fugue on a theme by Handel, Op. 24* (orch. Rubbra).
*** Chan. Dig. CHAN 8825; *ABTD 1450* [id.]. LSO, Järvi.

The current craze for Schoenberg's transcription of the Brahms *Piano quartet in G minor* is puzzling. Neeme Järvi's new version with the LSO is as good as any. It is performed with some enthusiasm and well recorded.

So too, for that matter, is Gennady Rozhdestvensky's account with the London Philharmonic, which makes out every bit as good a case for Schoenberg's often masterly scoring. Choice will probably depend on the coupling.

Serenades Nos. 1 in D, Op. 11; 2 in A, Op. 16.
☞ (B) **(*) Pickwick Dig. PCD 1024; *PK 515*. West German Sinf., Dirk Joeres.
(M) **(*) Ph. 432 510-2 [id.]. Concg. O, Haitink.

An excellent digital bargain-CD coupling of two of Brahms's most endearing works. The boisterous first movement of No. 1 with its exuberant horns is very jolly, and the beguilingly warm lyricism of the opening of the *A major* work is equally well conveyed. The orchestral playing is responsive and polished throughout. The resonant acoustic makes textures sound rather ample, but this is a genuine Brahmsian sound and the recording, made by West German Radio in Cologne, is naturally balanced, its richness never congealing. The charming Rondo finale of No. 2 brings some neat woodwind articulation, and again the genial horns add to the listener's pleasure.

Haitink's account of the *D major Serenade* is finely proportioned, relaxed yet vital. The *A major Serenade* has lighter scoring (the string section does without violins altogether) and, while the recording is warm, it is yet more lucid in detail. Haitink's performance is similarly sound in conception and well shaped, and the conductor's warmth is obvious. The Kertész performances have a slightly more vivid characterization and the Decca sound-quality is undoubtedly fresher.

Serenade No. 1 in D, Op. 11; Academic festival overture; Tragic overture.
*** Sony Dig. SK 45932 [id.]. LSO, Tilson Thomas.

Serenade No. 2 in A, Op. 16; Hungarian dances Nos. 1, 3, 10, 17–21; Variations on a theme of Haydn (St Antoni chorale), Op. 56a.
*** Sony Dig. SK 47195 [id.]. LSO, Tilson Thomas.

Sony missed a trick in not coupling Michael Tilson Thomas's musicianly accounts of the *Serenades* together. Most collectors will hesitate before buying two full-price discs in order to get these lovely works. All the same, Tilson Thomas gets admirable results from the LSO and the Sony engineers serve them both well.

SYMPHONIES

Symphonies Nos. 1–4.
(M) **(*) DG 429 644-2 (3) [id.]. BPO, Karajan.
☞ (B) ** Ph. Duo 438 757-2 (2) [id.]. VSO, Sawallisch.

Symphonies Nos. 1–4; Academic festival overture; Tragic overture; Hungarian dances Nos. 1, 3 & 10; Serenades Nos. 1–2; Variations on a theme of Haydn, Op. 56a.
δ☞ (B) *** Ph. 422 068-2 (4). Concg. O, Haitink.

Symphonies Nos. 1–4; Academic festival overture; Tragic overture; Variations on a theme of Haydn, Op. 56a.
☞ **(*) BMG/RCA Dig. 09026 61511-2 (4) [id.]. Bav. RSO Ch. & O, Sir Colin Davis.
☞ **(*) Erato/Warner Dig. 4509 94817-2 (4). Chicago SO, Barenboim.

Symphonies Nos. 1–4; Academic festival overture; Tragic overture; Variations on a theme of Haydn; (i) Hungarian dances Nos. 17–21.
(M) **(*) Sony SB3K 48398 (3). Cleveland O, George Szell; (i) Phd. O, Ormandy.

Symphonies Nos. 1–4; Academic festival overture; Tragic overture; Variations on a theme of Haydn, Op. 56a; (i) Alto rhapsody, Op. 53.
☞ ** Ph. Dig. 434 867-2 (4) [id.]. (i) Norman; Phd. O, Muti.

Symphonies Nos. 1–4; Academic festival overture; Variations on a theme of Haydn; (i) Song of destiny (Schicksalslied).
☞ (M) ** EMI Dig. CDM7 64519-2 (4) [id.]. (i) Amb. S.; LPO, Sawallisch.

Symphonies Nos. 1–4; Academic festival overture; Tragic overture; Variations on a theme of Haydn, Op. 56a; (i) Alto rhapsody, Op. 53; Fragment from Goethe's Hart Journey in Winter; (ii) Gesang der Parzen (Song of the Fates), Op. 89; Nänie, Op. 82; Schicksalslied, Op. 54.
☞ *** DG Dig. 435 683-2 (4) [id.]. BPO, Abbado; (i) with Marjana Lipovšek, Ernest Senf Ch.; (ii) Berlin R. Ch.

Symphonies Nos. 1–4; Tragic overture; Variations on a theme of Haydn.
**(*) DG Dig. 427 602-2 (3) [id.]. BPO, Karajan.

Abbado's is the most successful of the modern, digital cycles and makes a clear first choice, with playing at once polished and intense, glowingly recorded. Perhaps surprisingly, Abbado proves a more passionate, more romantic Brahmsian than either of his Italian rivals, Muti and Chailly, presenting the warmth of Brahms in full strength, never sentimentally. The set gains from having a generous collection of imaginatively chosen couplings: the rare, brief, choral works, as well as the usual supplements in the overtures and variations.

Broadly, Karajan's 1978 cycle shows that his readings of the Brahms *Symphonies*, with lyrical and dramatic elements finely balanced, changed little over the years. The playing of the Berlin Philharmonic remains uniquely cultivated: the ensemble is finely polished, yet can produce tremendous bravura at times. The remastering has freshened the sound: textures are clear and clean. There is less emphasis in the middle frequencies so that the Brahmsian richness is conveyed less readily.

Haitink is at his best in Nos. 1 and 3, but anyone fancying this generously full, Haitink Edition bargain box will find that all his readings are well argued and have considerable power, and the 1970s Philips sound is fresh and full.

Szell's powerful view of Brahms is consistently revealed in this masterful series of performances, recorded in the 1960s when he had made the Cleveland Orchestra America's finest. His approach is generally plain and direct, crisp and detached rather than smooth and moulded. Speeds are broad, and in the manner of the time no exposition repeats are observed, not even in No. 3. Though the sound, as transferred, is not as full as on the original LPs, it is clear and bright, with superb detail.

With variably focused sound, Karajan's last cycle of the Brahms *Symphonies* is not his finest; but he remained a natural Brahmsian to the last, and this compilation, with Nos. 2 and 3 on the second disc, and No. 4 coupled with the *Variations*, makes a better investment than the original issues, for those who must have digital sound. However, this set is at full price.

Sir Colin Davis offers clear-cut readings, beautifully played and recorded, fresh and crisp in outer movements, intense in slow movements, where he tends to adopt speeds markedly slower than usual. This is one of the most enjoyable of recent sets, but it is not preferable to Abbado.

Barenboim dons his Furtwänglerian mantle for his Erato accounts of the first two symphonies which, though very well played, suffer from his wilful flexibility and eccentric structural control: at one point in the finale of the *First Symphony*, the great Chicago orchestra is very nearly brought to a dead stop but subsequently recovers to end the work very positively. Barenboim's inspirational volatility works well in the *Third Symphony*, which does not lose its ongoing purpose and brings beautiful orchestral playing in the central movements. No. 4 is finest of all, a highly concentrated interpretation that moves forward powerfully; even though the tempo for the *Andante* is slow, it is ardently presented and capped by a gripping performance of the closing *Passacaglia*.

As a Brahmsian, Sawallisch's great strength lies in his lyrical warmth. In his EMI set, Nos. 2 and 4 are markedly more successful than Nos. 1 and 3, thanks in part to the variable sound. The playing of the LPO is not consistently polished but is warmly responsive. In a hotly competitive market, this set barely competes, even at mid-price and with its extra items, and admirers of Sawallisch will probably find his plainer Philips Duo bargain reissue a better proposition.

The Philips engineers, faced with recording in the difficult Philadelphia venue, only gradually overcame their problems. It follows that the Muti set, too, is inconsistent, generally offering crisp, beautifully played readings, which are distinguished without being strongly characterized, occasionally dull and lacking in tension. Individually, the most desirable of the four issues is of No. 3, well coupled with the *Alto rhapsody*, beautifully sung by Jessye Norman (426 253-2).

Recorded between 1959 and 1963, Wolfgang Sawallisch's early stereo Brahms cycle was made with the VSO rather than the VPO, offering playing which has generally good ensemble and commitment but which is plain-spun rather than luminous. No. 1 is the most successful, in which Sawallisch's straightforwardness is often effective, but in the slow movement and the 6/8 Trio of the Scherzo the playing could ideally have more lift. No. 2 has deliberately expressive phrasing and free speed changes, but Sawallisch appears as a not naturally romantic Brahms conductor, and too often his exaggerations lead to unwanted heaviness. In No. 3 the beat sounds curiously stiff, and that rather than the choice of speed again brings heaviness. The slow movement is taken more slowly than usual, but there is no incandescence in the VSO playing. Sawallisch's approach (a strong beat inconsistently combined with speed-changes) suits No. 4 better than Nos. 2 and 3; there is a square strength about this performance which has much to commend it, while the playing of the Vienna Symphony Orchestra comes close to the first-rate form it shows in No. 1. One listens in vain for any great revealing detail of interpretation, but the final *Passacaglia* stands up well. The recording throughout the set is clear and reasonably full (altogether better than on the original LPs) but, even with all four symphonies offered for the cost of one premium-priced CD, there are better options open in the budget range for this repertoire.

Symphonies Nos. 1–4; Academic festival overture; (i) *Double concerto in A min., Op. 102. Hungarian dances Nos. 1, 17, 20 & 21; Tragic overture; Variations on a theme of Haydn;* (ii) *Liebeslieder-Walzer, Op. 52;* (iii) *Song of the Fates (Gesang der Parzen). Op. 89.*

(M) (***) BMG/RCA mono GD 60325; *GK 60325* (4) [60325-2-RG; *60325-4-RG*]. NBC SO, Toscanini, with (i) Mischakoff, Miller; (ii) Ch., Artur Balsam, Joseph Kahn; (iii) (without O) Robert Shaw Ch.

The *First Symphony* starts very fast and intensely; but often speeds are surprisingly broad, and the *Fourth Symphony*, Toscanini's favourite, brings a magnificent performance. The soloists in the *Double concerto* were principals in the NBC orchestra, even though Toscanini allowed them less expressive freedom than they really needed. The CD transfers do everything possible for the dry and limited original sound.

Symphony No. 1 in C min., Op. 68.

(B) *** DG 431 161-2 [id.]. BPO, Karajan – SCHUMANN: *Overture, Scherzo and Finale.* ***

☞ **(*) DG Dig. 435 347-2; *435 347-4* [id.]. VPO, Giulini.

☞ (BB) **(*) ASV Dig. CDQS 6101. RLPO, Marek Janowski.

☞ ** Erato/Warner Dig. 4509 95191-2. Chicago SO, Daniel Barenboim.

Symphony No. 1; Academic festival overture, Op. 80.
(B) *** Pickwick Dig. PCD 882; *CIMPC 882* [id.]. Hallé O, Skrowaczewski.

Symphony No. 1; Academic festival overture; Tragic overture.
(M) *** EMI CDM7 69651-2 [id.]. Philh. O, Klemperer.

Symphony No. 1 in C min.; Hungarian dances Nos. 1, 3 & 10.
☞ **(*) Ph. Dig. 432 121-2 [id.]. Saito Kinen O, Seiji Ozawa.

Symphony No. 1; Serenade No. 2 in A, Op. 16.
(M) (**) BMG/RCA mono GD 60277 [60277-2-RG]. NBC SO, Toscanini.

Symphony No. 1 in C min.; Variations on a theme of Haydn, Op. 56a.
☞ *** EMI Dig. CDC7 54286-2 [id.]. L.Classical Players, Norrington.
☞ *** BMG/RCA Dig. RD 60382 [id.]. Bav. RSO, Sir Colin Davis.

(i) *Symphony No. 1; Variations on a theme of Haydn;* (ii) *Hungarian dances Nos. 17–21.*
(M) **(*) Sony SBK 46534 [id.]. (i) Cleveland O, Szell; (ii) Phd. O, Ormandy.

Symphony No. 1; (i) *Gesang der Parzen (Song of the Fates), Op. 89.*
☞ *** DG Dig. 431 790-2 [id.]. BPO, Abbado, (i) with Berlin R. Ch.

Symphony No. 1 in C min.; (i) *Schicksalslied, Op. 54.*
☞ ** EMI Dig. CDC7 54359-2 [id.]. LPO, Sawallisch, (i) with Amb. S.

After a spacious introduction, Abbado launches into a warm, dramatic reading, rhythmically well sprung and finely shaded, with the full power of the great dramatic climaxes brought out in the finale, from the rapt pianissimo of the opening onwards. The *Gesang der Parzen* makes an unusual and warmly attractive coupling, very well sung.

Norrington takes the opening introduction surprisingly fast – rather as Toscanini used to – but then adopts a relaxed tempo for the main *Allegro*, making it easy and bouncy rather than dramatic. More characteristically, he then adopts a flowing speed for the *Andante*, and in the finale the natural horn and dry timpani add to the dramatic impact. A very good recommendation, well coupled, if a period performance is wanted.

Klemperer's spacious opening with its thundering, relentless timpani strokes is as compelling as ever and the close of the work has a comparable majesty; and the reading remains unique for its feeling of authority and power, supported by consistently fine Philharmonia playing. The remastered sound has gained in clarity while retaining its fullness.

Karajan's 1978 analogue recording – his fourth – is also highly recommendable (especially at bargain price and now with its present Schumann coupling), and the sound is still remarkably good.

Sir Colin Davis is fresh and direct in his Brahmsian manners for the faster movements, with unusually brisk speeds in the first movement. He contrasts them with an exceptionally hushed and spacious reading of the second-movement *Andante*. He prefers steady speeds but builds the finale to an exciting close. Good, clean recording and beautiful playing. A good recommendation, if this coupling is acceptable.

Szell's account of No. 1 is one of the most impressive of his set. His bold, direct thrust gives the outer movements plenty of power and impetus, and the inner movements bring relaxation and a fair degree of warmth.

Skrowaczewski conducts the Hallé in a powerful performance of No. 1, both warmly sympathetic and refined, with sound which is fresh, bright and clear and with a good, open atmosphere. The first movement is ideally paced, but also without the exposition repeat. His view of the finale is big and bold, but with a rather old-fashioned slowing for the final appearance of the chorale theme in the coda. It makes an excellent bargain-price digital choice.

Janowski's plain yet sympathetic reading is greatly enhanced on a CD which is full-bodied, clearly detailed and well balanced. The added fullness is much more flattering to the orchestral timbres and makes a very satisfying sound overall. Janowski, unlike most, does observe the exposition repeat in the first movement. At super-bargain price, this is excellent value.

The Saito Kinen Orchestra plays beautifully for Ozawa and with an intensity that simulates live performance. The reading, generally unmannered, culminates in a superb account of the finale and an exciting close. One snag is the ungenerous if attractively presented coupling.

Like the others in Giulini's series with the Vienna Philharmonic, No. 1 brings speeds far slower than usual, almost eccentrically so in the *Allegro* of the first movement. Yet such is the weight and tension of the reading that the result is compelling, with the sound of the Vienna Philharmonic gloriously full and rich. However, there is no other music on this CD.

Sawallisch's lyrical approach makes for a warm, persuasive reading, lacking dramatic bite in the outer movements, not helped by rather edgy LPO violins, but with the slow movement raptly simple and direct. The *Schicksalslied* makes an attractive, unusual coupling.

Barenboim's reading is exasperatingly idiosyncratic. His pacing is spacious and measured (the recessed opening timpani strokes are unassertive), phrasing is moulded, with the tension variably controlled. The *Andante* is relaxed and songful, but there is an unexpected burst of energy in the central section of the gentle *Allegretto*. After the atmospheric opening, the finale, its big tune richly presented, gathers impetus until at the recapitulation Barenboim effects a long, sustained *rallentando* and, just before the reprise of the secondary lyrical theme (13 minutes 22 seconds) the symphony almost comes to a halt. Nevertheless the closing bars bring a powerful coda, with the Chicago brass chorale ringing out thrillingly, helped by the warm acoustics of Orchestra Hall.

The *First Symphony* is the performance Toscanini recorded in Carnegie Hall during 1941. It differs from the version he made ten years later with the same orchestra in the greater breadth of the first movement allegro, and in the tenderness he shows in the *Andante*, which at the same time remains completely unsentimental. The sound is not at all bad for the period. There is however little one can do with the 1942 broadcast – made in Studio 8-H – of the *Serenade*. The performance, too, is held together on a tight rein and sounds unrelaxed.

Symphony No. 2 in D, Op. 73.
(M) *** DG 435 067-2 [id.]. BPO, Karajan – SCHUMANN: *Symphony No. 2.* ***
☞ (***) Testament mono SBT 1015 [id.]. BBC SO, Toscanini (with MENDELSSOHN: *Midsummer Night's Dream:* excerpt; ROSSINI: *Semiramide: Overture* ***).
☞ **(*) DG Dig. 435 348-2; *435 348-4* [id.]. VPO, Giulini.
☞ ** Decca Dig. 433 549-2 [id.]. Cleveland O, Ashkenazy – DVORAK: *Serenade for strings.* **(*)

Symphony No. 2 in D; Tragic overture.
☞ **(*) EMI Dig. CDC7 54875-2 [id.]. L. Classical Players, Norrington.
☞ **(*) Ph. Dig. 432 094-2; *432 094-4* [id.]. Boston SO, Haitink.
☞ (BB) **(*) ASV Dig. CDQS 6102. RLPO, Marek Janowski.
☞ (M) ** BMG/RCA GD 60682. Boston SO, Munch – SCHUMANN: *Genoveva overture.* **
☞ ** Erato/Warner Dig. 4509 95192-2 [id.]. Chicago SO, Barenboim.

Symphony No. 2; Variations on a theme of Haydn, Op. 56a.
*** DG Dig. 423 142-2 [id.]. BPO, Karajan.

Symphony No. 2; (i) Alto rhapsody, Op. 53.
*** DG Dig. 427 643-2 [id.]. (i) Lipovšek, Senff Ch.; BPO, Abbado.
(M) *** EMI CDM7 69650-2 [id.]; *EG 769650-4.* (i) Ludwig, Philh. Ch.; Philh. O, Klemperer.

Among modern versions Abbado's now stands as an easy first choice, particularly when, with Marjana Lipovšek a radiant soloist, it also contains a gravely beautiful account of the *Alto rhapsody*. Abbado's approach to Brahms is generally direct, but his control of rhythm and phrase makes the performance instantly compelling. He observes the exposition repeat in the first movement, while in the finale, through his rhythmic control, Abbado makes a relatively measured speed sound much more exciting than it does with any of the speed-merchants. This is an outstanding version in every way.

Karajan's 1978 reading is more direct, less mellow than the earlier (1964) account – see below – and this is most striking in the third movement. The finale has even more impetus than before, its brilliant pacing challenging the Berliners to exciting virtuosity. Some will prefer the earlier version, but the coupling with Schumann is very generous.

Karajan's digital reading of the *Second Symphony* suffers less than the *First* from the thick, undifferentiated recording. It is a magnificent reading, even warmer and more glowing than his previous versions, with consistently fine playing from the Berlin Philharmonic, who approach with striking freshness a symphony which they must have played countless times. As in the *First Symphony*, Karajan omits the first-movement exposition repeat, but compensates with an appealing performance of the *Haydn variations*.

Klemperer's is also a great performance, the product of a strong and vital intelligence. He may seem a trifle severe and uncompromising, but he was at his peak in his Brahms cycle and he underlines the power of the *Symphony* without diminishing its eloquence in any way. The *Alto rhapsody*, with Klemperer at his most masterful and Ludwig on fine form, is a beautifully expressive performance. Ludwig sings gloriously in the opening section, and later her voice blends naturally with the male chorus.

Toscanini's account with the BBC Symphony Orchestra, recorded in 1938, will come as a revelation to those who view the legendary Italian as a hard-driving, demonic maestro. Tempi are relaxed, the first movement is unhurried and the mood is sunny and smiling. There is none of the hard-driven momentum and over-drilled intensity that marked his final, NBC version. Gratitude is in order that this performance has been rescued for posterity: the sound calls for tolerance but the playing is worth it.

Norrington, with his London Classical Players presenting leaner textures than usual, takes a clean, direct view, adopting speeds on the fast side in all four movements. He misses some of the work's charm but consistently makes it sound fresh and bright. A fair recommendation if you need a period performance.

Haitink directs a strong, steady reading, in which the rapt pianissimos convey tension quite as much as the dramatic outbursts. That is partly the result of the Boston sound, generally warm and full, which yet does not expand in richness for climaxes.

Janowski's plain style is least convincing in this most lyrical of symphonies, with rhythms tending to sound too rigid, whether in his metrical view of the slow movement or the rather charmless account of the third. The overture is much more successful, and the digital recording is excellently balanced: this is certainly worth considering at its super-bargain price.

Giulini takes an exceptionally spacious view of the *Second*, understandably preferring not to observe the exposition repeat in the first movement, which in his hands becomes very long, even without it. The weight and warmth of Giulini's approach go with ripe and resonant playing from the Vienna Philharmonic, richly recorded. Yet such an approach misses some of the charm of this fundamentally lyrical work.

Munch's account of the *Second Symphony* comes from December 1955 and is an eminently straightforward and powerfully argued reading. It is tautly held together but completely free from any hint of that overdriven quality that could on occasion affect his performances. As was the practice of the time, the exposition repeat in the first movement is not observed. The second group has an eloquence that is all the more telling for not being in the slightest overstated or underlined by rubati. The slow movement is on the fast side but no less affecting for that, thanks to the strong sense of line, though perhaps Munch presses ahead in the middle of the movement a bit too much. The sound is very good indeed for its period (very early stereo) though tuttis tend to sound just a shade dry. But this is an interesting reading well worth hearing, with the *Genoveva overture* as a bonus. There is a high-powered and highly dramatic account of the *Tragic overture*, too, perhaps a shade hard-driven at the opening. Munch did much to champion Brahms in France where the composer was slow to take hold, and he proves a convincing exponent.

Ashkenazy draws beautiful playing from the Cleveland Orchestra, taking a direct, unmannered view but failing to simulate the tension of a live performance. He rectifies that in the extrovert finale, which he makes exciting without any hint of hysteria. The disc's chief claim lies in having the Dvořák *String serenade* as an unusual, attractive coupling. Full, bright sound.

If only the whole symphony had been played like the finale – full of impetus, with the great second subject gloriously re-presented in the recapitulation – then Barenboim's Chicago performance would have been very highly recommendable. But having opened *sotto voce*, the first movement proceeds in its richly moulded, leisurely way and Barenboim again reduces the momentum at the horn solo towards the end. The central movements are comparably spacious, the tension not consistently maintained, and, while the warm Chicago sound suits this relaxed approach, this is too wilful a reading to be completely satisfying. The *Tragic overture*, however, responds well to Barenboim's dramatic and lyrical emphases.

Symphonies Nos. 2–3.
(B) *** DG 429 153-2; *429 153-4* [id.]. BPO, Karajan.
☞ **(*) Ph. Dig. 434 089-2 [id.]. Saito Kinen O, Ozawa.
(M) **(*) Ph. 426 632-2. Concg. O, Haitink.

Karajan's 1964 reading of the *Second* is among the sunniest and most lyrical accounts, and its sound is fully competitive even now. The companion performance of the *Third* is marginally less compelling, but still very fine. He takes the opening expansively and omits the exposition repeat. But clearly he sees the work as a whole: the third movement is also slow and perhaps slightly indulgent, but the closing pages of the finale have a memorable autumnal serenity. A bargain.

With the exposition repeat omitted in the first movement, Ozawa finds space to couple the *Second Symphony* generously with the *Third*. With intense, committed playing from the Saito Kinen Orchestra, the reading of No. 2 is warmly expressive and finely moulded without becoming mannered. The finale is particularly strong and convincing. The playing in No. 3 is not quite so alert, but

Ozawa's relatively relaxed view is still warm and persuasive, with full, warm recording, a little bass-heavy, as in the rest of the series. A fair recommendation for a digital version of this coupling.

Haitink's account of No. 2 opens soberly. The sunshine quickly breaks through, however, so that the gentle high entry of the violins is magically sweet. This is a thoughtful reading, marked by beautifully refined string playing, but in a way it is too controlled. The *Third* is much more impressive, and Haitink's firmness of grip and lyrical eloquence make this a very satisfying account. The sound is fresh yet full in the Philips manner.

Symphony No. 3 in F, Op. 90.
☞ **(*) Decca Dig. 436 466-2 [id.]. Concg. O, Chailly – SCHOENBERG: *Chamber symphony No. 1.*
**(*)

Symphony No. 3; Academic festival overture.
☞ *(*) EMI Dig. CDC7 54523-2 [id.]. LPO, Sawallisch.

Symphony No. 3 in F; Tragic overture.
☞ ** BMG/RCA Dig. RD 60118. Bav. RSO, Sir Colin Davis.

Symphony No. 3 in F; Tragic overture; (i) *Song of Destiny (Schicksalslied), Op. 54.*
*** DG Dig. 429 765-2; *429 765-4* [id.]. BPO, Abbado; (i) with Ernest-Senff Ch.

Symphony No. 3; Variations on a theme of Haydn, Op. 56a.
☞ *** DG Dig. 431 681-2 [id.]. VPO, Carlo Maria Giulini.
☞ *** Erato/Warner Dig. 4509 95193-2 [id.]. Chicago SO, Daniel Barenboim.
(B) *** Pickwick Dig. PCD 906; *CIMPC 906* [id.]. Hallé O, Skrowaczewski.
☞ (BB) *** ASV Dig. CDQS 6103; *ZCQS 6103.* RLPO, Marek Janowski.

Abbado directs a glowing, affectionate performance of No. 3, adopting generally spacious speeds and finely moulded phrasing but never sounding self-conscious, thanks to the natural tension which gives the illusion of live, spontaneous music-making. The rich, well-balanced, clean-textured recording underlines the big dramatic contrasts. This now heads the list of modern digital recordings of this symphony.

In the *Third Symphony*, unlike the rest, Giulini is recorded live. The speeds, though on the expansive side, are not so extreme, with the finale no slower than in many other versions. The result is a big-scaled, powerful reading, marked by ripe, resonant playing, given full and satisfying sound. The second-movement *Andante* is particularly beautiful. The *Variations* are similarly expansive and compelling, a welcome coupling.

Barenboim's volatile approach works much better in the *Third Symphony* than in the first two and, although there must be some minor reservations about his freely spacious treatment of both central movements, they are beautifully played and warmly lyrical. The first movement (exposition repeat very much part of the interpretation) has plenty of power and glowing lyrical feeling, ensuring that Barenboim's flexible style is convincing. The finale has exciting thrust and the valedictory ending is managed most sensitively. The *Variations*, too, are full of imaginative touches. Fine, committed orchestral playing and richly expansive sound suit the nature of the interpretation.

Skrowaczewski chooses consistently slow tempi for the central movements, yet with refined playing there is no hint of dragging. In the third movement he underlines the tender wistfulness, with a gorgeous horn solo in the reprise, full and spacious. The hush at the start of the finale then leads to a powerfully rhythmic performance, ending with a most refined account of the gentle coda. An excellent digital bargain-price version, well coupled with a fresh reading of the *Haydn variations.*

The *Third* is the finest of Janowski's Brahms cycle, with surging outer movements (exposition repeat included) and the central *Andante* and *Poco allegretto* given an appealing, unforced Brahmsian lyricism. An exciting and satisfying performance, given bright, full, digital sound, not absolutely refined on top. The *Variations* also have plenty of impetus and are strongly characterized. In its price-range this is very recommendable.

The Chailly version is distinguished by bright Decca sound which gives an edge to the Concertgebouw violins, and the inner detail is cleaner than usual in Brahms. That goes with a fresh, direct reading, not always avoiding rhythmic dullness, which culminates in a bitingly strong account of the finale. Recommended for anyone attracted by the unusual coupling of a fine, early Schoenberg work, given a strong, persuasive performance.

Sir Colin Davis gives a characteristically direct reading, but he is not quite so well served by either players or engineers in No. 3 as in the rest of his RCA series. The relative distancing of the sound intensifies a lack of tension in the performance, which goes with some rhythmic stodginess, as in the central episode of the *Andante*, which is unduly expansive.

Sawallisch is less successful in No. 3 than in the rest of his cycle, with the first two movements low on tension. The finale expands warmly, helped by fuller sound. Not a generous coupling for the shortest of the Brahms symphonies.

Symphonies Nos. (i) *3 in F, Op. 90;* (ii) *4 in E min., Op. 98.*
(M) *** EMI CDM7 69649-2 [id.]. Philh. O, Klemperer.
(M) *** DG 437 645-2 [id.]. BPO, Karajan.
☞ (M) **(*) Teldec/Warner Dig. 4509 92144-2 [id.]. Cleveland O, Dohnányi.

In No. 3, there is a severity about Klemperer's approach which may at first seem unappealing but which comes to underline the strength of the architecture. Similarly in No. 4, Klemperer's granite strength and his feeling for Brahmsian lyricism make his version one of the most satisfying ever recorded. The finale may lack something in sheer excitement, but the gravity of Klemperer's tone of voice, natural and unforced in this movement as in the others, makes for a compelling result.

In his 1978 recording Karajan gives superb grandeur to the opening of the *Third Symphony* but then characteristically refuses to observe the exposition repeat. Comparing this reading with Karajan's earlier, 1964 version (coupled with No. 2), one finds him more direct and strikingly more dynamic and compelling. In the *Fourth Symphony* Karajan refuses to overstate the first movement, starting with deceptive reticence. His easy, lyrical style, less moulded in this 1978 reading than in his 1964 account, is fresh and unaffected and highly persuasive. The scherzo, fierce and strong, leads to a clean, weighty account of the finale.

Those for whom quality of sound is of the highest consideration will certainly find Dohnányi's mid-priced Cleveland coupling tempting. The performances are clean and direct and superbly played. The fine tonal blend and balance in the *Third* means that the often thick orchestration is made clear as well as naturally weighty in a version which (exposition repeat included) emphasizes classical values. In the second-movement *Andante*, taken on the slow side, Dohnányi does not entirely avoid squareness and, although the third-movement *Allegretto* flows warmly, the horn reprise of the main theme is forthright rather than affectionate. The opening of the finale lacks mystery and the hemiola rhythms of the second subject, for all the power of the performance, fail to leap aloft. These detailed criticisms are given merely to suggest why, with such superlative playing and an irreproachably direct manner, the result finally lacks something in Brahmsian magic. The *Fourth* opens simply and seductively, a strong and finely controlled reading, lacking only occasionally in a flow of adrenalin. The slow movement is hushed and thoughtful, the third clear and fresh in its crisp articulation, while the weight of the finale is well caught – even if it is not thrust home at the close as sharply as it might be.

Symphony No. 4 in E min., Op. 98.
☞ **(*) Decca Dig. 433 151-2 [id.]. Concg. O, Chailly – SCHOENBERG: *5 Orchestral pieces.* ***
**(*) DG Dig. 400 037-2 [id.]. VPO, Carlos Kleiber.
☞ (M) ** BMG/RCA 09026 61206-2 [id.]. Boston SO, Munch – DVORAK: *Symphony No. 8.* *(*)

Symphony No. 4; Hungarian dances Nos. 1, 3 & 10.
(B) *** Pickwick Dig. PCD 897; *CIMPC 897* [id.]. Hallé O, Skrowaczewski.

Symphony No. 4; Academic festival overture.
☞ *** Erato/Warner 4509 95194-2 [id.]. Chicago SO, Barenboim.
☞ (M) *** Telarc Dig. CD 82006 [id.]. RPO, Previn.
☞ (BB) **(*) ASV Dig. CDQS 6104. RLPO, Marek Janowski.

Symphony No 4; Tragic overture, Op. 81.
*** DG Dig. 429 403-2; *429 403-4* [id.]. VPO, Giulini.

Symphony No. 4 in E min.; Variations on a theme of Haydn, Op. 56a.
☞ (B) **(*) CfP CD-CFP 4615; *TC-CFP 4615.* Hallé O, James Loughran.

Symphony No. 4; Variations on a theme of Haydn, Op. 56a; (i) *Nänie, Op. 82.*
☞ *** DG Dig. 435 349-2 [id.]. BPO, Abbado, (i) with Berlin R. Ch.

Abbado rounds off his outstanding series with an incandescent performance of the *Fourth*, marked by strong, dramatic contrasts and finely moulded phrasing. The coupling is exceptionally generous, not just the *Haydn variations* but the rare choral piece to words by Schiller, *Nänie.*

Barenboim's Chicago reading is grippingly compulsive. He opens the first movement gently and affectionately, but the performance soon develops a compulsive lyrical power. Like Solti in his account with the same orchestra, Barenboim takes the *Andante* more slowly than marked but, with a richly ardent response from the Chicago strings, the result is eloquently convincing, with much refined orchestral detail. After an excitingly ebullient Scherzo, the finale sets off with a powerful thrust that carries through to the final bar, though Barenboim's flexible style prevents any feeling of rigidity. There is a tremendous burst of energy in the coda to make the *Passacaglia*'s final apotheosis very gripping indeed. The *Academic festival overture* is unusually expansive, bringing superb playing from the Chicago brass. Throughout the sound is suitably full-bodied within the aptly resonant acoustics of Chicago's Orchestra Hall.

As the delicate opening demonstrates, Giulini's affectionate control of line completely disguises any slowness, and in the development the big, dramatic fortissimo contrasts bring a rugged manner, equally compelling. The great melody of the slow movement is rapt and refined as well as warm, and the last two movements bring satisfyingly extreme contrasts of tension and dynamic, helped by the rich and refined recording. The *Tragic overture* is given a similarly spacious and affectionate reading.

There is a Boultian directness about the opening of Previn's account, fresh and alert, which immediately commands attention, helped by naturally balanced Telarc sound, just a little distanced. The finale is similarly strong and energetic, well drawn together; only in the bold third movement does the distancing detract from the impact of the performance, while allowing some clouding of inner detail. With a good – if hardly generous – coupling and now reissued on Telarc's Bravo! mid-priced label, it is one of the best of the modern digital versions.

The refinement of the very opening in Skrowaczewski's Pickwick version leads to an exceptionally satisfying reading, outstanding in the bargain-price range and finer than many full-price versions. The phrasing is affectionate without ever sounding self-conscious, and the alertness as well as the refinement of the Hallé playing confirms the excellence; if the coupling of only three *Hungarian dances* is hardly generous, they are certainly attractively presented.

Any record from Carlos Kleiber is an event, and his is a performance of real stature. Everything is shaped with the attention to detail one would expect from this great conductor. A gripping and compelling performance. However, the limitations of the early digital recording are exposed here. The strings above the stave sound a little shrill and glassy, while there is a want of opulence in the bass.

Loughran's 1974 account, like Barbirolli's before him with the same orchestra, is outstanding. His approach is unobtrusively direct. He is rarely if ever concerned to underline interpretative points, yet as the concentration grows after the deceptively gentle start so one appreciates more and more the satisfying assurance with which he solves every problem. His tempi – except for a relatively slow account of the Scherzo – are unexceptionable and, like Barbirolli, he believes in adopting expressive phrasing within a basically steady tempo. The Hallé strings are in excellent form and the recording is of high quality; it is a pity that the CD transfer brightens the violin-timbre; most ears will need a softening of the treble response, although the sound is full enough. The *Variations* come off well to make a reasonably generous filler.

Chailly's reading is clean and direct, marked by big dynamic contrasts, generally enhanced by the bright Decca recording, though the sound is more distanced than in the rest of the series. Recommended, if the mould-breaking Schoenberg work is wanted as an unusual coupling, here given a red-blooded performance to bring out its ancestry in the romantic movement.

Following the success of the *Third*, Janowski gives a refreshingly direct reading of the *Fourth*. Speeds are unexceptionable, with the second-movement *Andante*, introduced very gently, slower than usual, but certainly expressive. The recording sounds vivid and full on CD and the weight of the final *Passacaglia* is well established. The coda of the symphony, like the overture which follows, brings real excitement.

Munch's Boston account of the *Fourth Symphony* is a bit later than his version of the *Second*, discussed above. Curiously enough, the 1958 recording is considerably more strident than in the *Second*. However, this is a performance to reckon with; it is tautly held together, indeed so much so that it comes close to being a shade driven, but there is much to admire in its splendid sense of line and firm grip. It is good value, too, in that it comes with an – albeit rather fierce – 1961 account of the Dvořák *G major Symphony*.

Variations on a theme of Haydn, Op. 56a.

☞ ** Teldec/Warner Dig. 9031 74007-2 [id.]. NYPO, Masur – IVES: *Variations on America;* REGER: *Variations and fugue on a theme of Mozart.* **

The *St Antoni Chorale variations* find Kurt Masur in a leisurely mood. Some collectors may want them to move on just a little more. This is a cultured, measured and judicious reading, and it is pleasing to find the New York Philharmonic playing with greater refinement and subtlety than they have for many years. A valid reading, but not a front-runner perhaps.

CHAMBER MUSIC

Cello sonatas Nos. 1 in E min., Op. 38; 2 in F, Op. 99.
*** DG Dig. 410 510-2 [id.]. Mstislav Rostropovich, Rudolf Serkin.
*** Decca 414 558-2. Lynn Harrell, Vladimir Ashkenazy.
*** Hyp. Dig. CDA 66159; *KA 66159* [id.]. Steven Isserlis, Peter Evans.
☞ *** Channel Classics Dig. CCS 5483 [id.]. Pieter Wispelwey, Paul Komen.
☞ (M) **(*) BMG/RCA Dig. 09026 61355-2. Yo-Yo Ma, Emanuel Ax.
☞ (BB) *(*) Discover Dig. DICD 920186 [id.]. Dmitri Yablonski, Oxana Yablonsky.

Cello sonatas Nos. 1 in E min., Op. 38; 2 in F, Op. 99; in D min., Op. 108 (arr. of *Violin sonata in D min.*).
☞ *** Sony Dig. SK 48191 [id.]. Yo-Yo Ma, Emanuel Ax.
☞ *(*) (BB) Naxos Dig. 8.550656 [id.]. Maria Kliegel, Kristin Merscher.

The partnership of the wild, inspirational Russian cellist and the veteran Brahmsian pianist on DG is a challenging one. It proves an outstanding success, with inspiration mutually enhanced, whether in the lyricism of Op. 38 or the heroic energy of Op. 99. Good if close recording.

Although with the Rostropovich/Serkin account available, Yo-Yo Ma and Emanuel Ax may not be a first choice in the Brahms *Cello sonatas*, their performances on Sony are certainly among the finest in the current lists. Both are highly responsive artists and are of one mind concerning matters of phrasing. As always, Ma produces tone of great beauty and refinement, here without excessive indulgence in the withdrawn tone that has characterized some of his recent appearances on CDs. Emmanuel Ax plays with great sensitivity, though there are times when he is in danger of overpowering his partner. In addition to the two sonatas, they add their own transcription of the *D minor Violin sonata*, perhaps an unnecessary luxury when one thinks of the abundance of cello repertoire of Brahms's period that could with advantage be explored. Distinguished playing and very good recording, even if the piano is slightly favoured.

Harrell and Ashkenazy give almost ideal performances of the two Brahms *Cello sonatas*, strong and passionate as well as poetic. However, although they are naturally recorded and well balanced, the acoustic is resonant and the imagery lacks the last degree of sharpness of focus.

Using gut strings, Isserlis produces an exceptionally warm tone, here nicely balanced in the recording against the strong and sensitive playing of his regular piano partner. In every way these perceptive and well-detailed readings stand in competition with the finest.

The Dutch partnership, Pieter Wispelwey and Paul Komen, offer something rather different. The cellist plays a nineteenth-century Bohemian cello and the pianist a Viennese period instrument: thus theirs is the only version of the sonatas to approximate to the sound Brahms himself might have heard. There is nothing anaemic or academic about their playing and no sense of scholarly inhibition. These are full-blooded performances, vivid in feeling and passionate, at no time wanting in eloquence. Good recording-quality adds to the attractions of this interesting issue.

In the alternative performances from Yo-Yo Ma and Emanuel Ax on RCA the balance favours the piano, for Ax sometimes produces too thick a sound in climaxes and Ma is, as always, sensitive and smaller in tone. Theirs is an essentially romantic view, and some might find the first movement of the *E minor Sonata* rather too wayward. They are certainly more measured in their tempi than almost any of their rivals. Yo-Yo Ma's pianissimos occasionally draw attention to themselves, though the grace and tenderness of his playing is not in question. The claims of these readings reside in their refined lyricism rather than in their muscularity, and these artists have splendid rapport. The RCA recording is very truthful, and admirers of this great cellist need not hesitate, especially now that this coupling has been reissued at mid-price.

The gifted Russian duo, Yablonski and Yablonskaya, are let down by a resonantly amorphous recording which seems to place the cello on top of the piano in a resonant acoustic. They open the *E minor Sonata* gently and meditatively and play the first movement (with its echoes of the *Horn trio*) with improvisational ardour. There is no lack of feeling in the F major work, but it is the *Adagio affettuoso* that makes the most affecting impression; elsewhere, the lack of profile to the recording detracts from the projection of the music-making.

Naxos offer two very accomplished performers and also throw in a transcription, made in the year of Brahms's death, by Paul Klengel of the *G major Violin sonata*, bringing the disc up to near maximum playing time (77 minutes). Maria Kliegel won the 1981 Rostropovich Competition; her partner, Kristin Merscher, made a strong impression at the Leeds Piano Competition in the early 1980s but is handicapped here by less than sympathetic recording. Whether or not they are a permanent partnership, the rapport between the two artists does not seem particularly strong and, in spite of some felicities, they do not really match current rivals in imagination or poetic feeling.

Clarinet quintet in B min., Op. 115.
(M) *** EMI CDM7 63116-2 [id.]. Gervase de Peyer, Melos Ens. – MOZART: *Quintet.* ***
(B) *** Pickwick Dig. PCD 883; *CIMPC 883* [id.]. Keith Puddy, Delmé Qt – DVORAK: *Quartet No. 12.* ***

(i) *Clarinet quintet in B min., Op. 115;* (ii) *Clarinet sonata No. 2 in E flat, Op. 120/2.*
(M) *** Chan. CHAN 6522; *MBTD 6522* [id.]. Janet Hilton, (i) Lindsay Qt; (ii) Peter Frankl.

(i) *Clarinet quintet in B min., Op. 115;* (ii) *Clarinet trio in A min., Op. 114.*
*** Hyp. CDA 66107 [id.]. King, (i) Gabrieli Qt; (ii) Georgian, Benson (piano).
☞ (BB) **(*) Naxos Dig. 8.550391. József Balogh, with (i) Danubius Qt; (ii) Jenö Jandó, Csaba Onczay.

Gervase de Peyer's vintage performance of the *Clarinet quintet* with the Melos Ensemble is a warmly lyrical reading, dominated by the clarinettist, who brings out wistfully autumnal overtones. The sound is full and immediate, set in a relatively dry acoustic.

Keith Puddy's warm tone is well suited to Brahms and, with spacious speeds in all four movements, this is a consistently sympathetic reading; the digital recording is equally fine, vivid and full. Excellent value.

Janet Hilton's essentially mellow performance of the *Clarinet quintet*, with the Lindsay Quartet playing with pleasing warmth and refinement, has a distinct individuality. Her lilting syncopations in the third movement are delightful. Hilton's partnership with Peter Frankl in the *E flat Clarinet sonata* is rather less idiosyncratic and individual; nevertheless this performance offers considerable artistic rewards, even if the resonance means that the aural focus is a little diffuse.

Thea King and the Gabrieli Quartet give a radiantly beautiful performance of the *Clarinet quintet*, as fine as any put on record, expressive and spontaneous-sounding, with natural ebb and flow of tension as in a live performance. The recording of the strings is on the bright side, very vivid and real.

József Balogh, principal clarinet with both the Hungarian State Opera and Radio Orchestras, is a highly sensitive player with a lovely tone. He is well supported by the Danubius Quartet and their account of the *Clarinet quintet* is a rewarding one, with warmth and atmosphere, and rising to considerable heights of intensity in the *Adagio*. The *Clarinet trio* is an enjoyably fresh account, though not quite so memorable, except in the *Andantino grazioso* which is delightfully done. Nevertheless Balogh, Jandó and Onczay are thoroughly sympathetic and, with excellent recording, this is still a worthwhile disc and inexpensive to boot.

(i) *Clarinet quintet in B min., Op. 115;* (ii) *Piano quintet in F min., Op. 34.*
☞ **(*) Gala Dig. CACD 1009; *CAMC 1011* [id.]. (i) James Campbell; (ii) Rian de Waal; Allegri Qt.
☞ ** Whitehall/Medici MQCD 8001 [id.]. (i) Jack Brymer; (ii) John Lill; Medici Qt.

A good idea to couple the two big Brahms *Quintets* on one disc – with an exceptionally long playing time. The performances on Gala are distinguished by good musicianship and attentive treatment of detail, and both James Campbell and Rian de Waal play with considerable finesse. Ultimately, however, they do not match the best versions in the catalogue in character and expressive intensity.

These Medici performances are dominated by their two guest artists. John Lill brings strength and concentration to the piano part of Op. 34 and Jack Brymer is ever seductive in Brahms's beautiful, autumnal *Clarinet quintet*, especially so in his gentle solo passage at the end of the *Adagio*. But the Medici Quartet's contribution does not offer sufficient finesse to give the finest support; their playing has more life than polish. No complaints about the recording.

(i) *Clarinet quintet in B min., Op. 115; String quartet No. 1 in C min., Op. 51/1.*
☞ (M) (**(*)) EMI mono CDH7 64932-2 [id.]. (i) Reginald Kell; Busch Qt.

(i) *Clarinet quintet in B min., Op. 115;* (ii) *Horn trio.*
☞ (**) Testament mono SBT 1001 [id.]. (i) Reginald Kell, Busch Qt; (ii) Adolf Busch; Aubrey Brain, Rudolf Serkin.

Reginald Kell's beauty of tone was legendary and his 1937 account of the *Clarinet quintet* with the Busch Quartet is among the greatest recordings of the piece (and certainly far superior to his post-war remake on the Brunswick label). Kell's vibrato was not to all tastes, but his playing here is heard at its most refined and the Busch produce a splendidly autumnal feeling in the slow movement. The *C minor Quartet*, recorded in 1932, may not be as polished as in some more recent accounts (and certainly sounds its age), but the playing is full of imagination and vitality.

On paper, the Testament version is the more logical coupling. But the *Horn Trio*, in spite of the excellence of Aubrey Brain, is not really the inspired performance these distinguished names would lead one to expect. The finale comes off best. In any case this CD is much more expensive than the EMI alternative.

(i) *Clarinet quintet in B min., Op. 115. String quintet No. 2 in G, Op. 111.*
**(*) Delos Dig. DE 3066 [id.]. (i) David Shifrin; Chamber Music NorthWest.

David Shifrin plays most beautifully in the *Clarinet quintet* and fully catches its serenity and autumnal nostalgia. He receives highly sympathetic support from Chamber Music NorthWest who find a parallel in the atmosphere of the *Adagio* of the *String quintet*, which is also played with a natural Brahmsian feeling.

Clarinet sonatas Nos. 1 in F min.; 2 in E flat, Op. 120/1–2.
*** Chan. Dig. CHAN 8563; *ABTD 1265* [id.]. Gervase de Peyer, Gwenneth Prior.

Superb performances from Gervase de Peyer and Gwenneth Prior, commanding, aristocratic, warm and full of subtleties of colour and detail. The recording too is outstandingly realistic.

(i) *Clarinet trio in A min.* (for clarinet, cello and piano), *Op. 114; Clarinet sonatas Nos. 1–2, Op., 120/ 1–2.*
☞ *** Gutman Records Dig. CD 931 [id.]. Hein Wiedijk, Frank van de Laar; (i) with Pieter Wispelwey.

It has taken a small label to provide this ideal coupling of the three major Brahms works featuring the clarinet. Hein Wiedijk is a most sensitive player, with a warm timbre and clear articulation. He can be persuasively gentle as well as ardent, and he has the full measure of Brahms's lyricism. This is playing of subtlety as well as warmth, and Frank van de Laar is an excellent partner. They are then joined by Pieter Wispelwey for an equally persuasive account of the *Clarinet trio*, full of autumnal feeling. The recording is real and vivid and well balanced in a slightly dry but not unsympathetic acoustic.

(i; ii) *Clarinet trio in A min., Op. 114;* (i; iii) *Horn trio in E flat, Op. 40;* (iv) *Piano trios Nos. 1 in B, Op. 8; 2 in C, Op. 87; 3 in C min., Op. 101.*
☞ (M) **(*) DG 437 131-2 (2) [id.]. (i) Eschenbach; (ii) Leister, Donderer; (iii) Seifert, Drolc; (iv) Trio di Trieste.

Some reservations have to be expressed about this DG set, but it generously encapsulates five major works in worthwhile performances and in natural, well-balanced recordings that have the requisite spaciousness and depth. Karl Leister and Gerd Seifert are not soloists with extrovert personalities but they are thoroughly musical and they understand Brahms. The *Clarinet trio* is mellow and beautifully played. The opening of the *Horn trio* is romantic rather than ardent (after the manner of Tuckwell, Perlman and Ashkenazy – see our main volume) but its forward impulse gathers momentum as the music unfolds. Eschenbach emerges as the strongest personality: he dominates the Scherzo and obviously exerts a strong influence on the beautiful slow movement and lively finale. The balance is more natural than in the Decca version. The Trio di Trieste bring plenty of Italian warmth to the *Piano trios* and strong characterization; No. 3 is particularly successful in this respect. These are straightforward accounts, well balanced and with a concern for detail and dynamic, and with plenty of life. They are undoubtedly enjoyable when the late-1960s sound is so pleasingly transferred to CD.

(i; ii) *Clarinet trio in A min., Op. 114;* (iii) *Horn trio in E flat, Op. 40;* (ii) *Piano trios Nos. 1 in B, Op. 8; 2 in C, Op. 87; 3 in C min., Op. 101; 4 in A, Op. posth.*
☞ (B) *** Ph. Duo 438 365-2 (2) [id.]. (i) George Pieterson; (ii) Beaux Arts Trio; (iii) Francis Orval, Arthur Grumiaux, Gyorgy Sebok.

The splendid Beaux Arts set of the *Piano trios* was originally issued on two separate, full-priced LPs at the beginning of 1978. Now they come on a pair of joined CDs at bargain price, with two other outstanding performances thrown in for good measure. George Pieterson is a first-rate artist and his account of the *Clarinet trio* with members of the Beaux Arts group offers masterly playing from all three participants and a very well-integrated recording. The balance in the *Horn trio* is even more adroitly managed, perhaps the most successful on record. The fine horn player, Francis Orval, seeks not to dominate but to be one of the group, and he achieves this without any loss of personality in his playing (note the richness of his contribution to the Trio of the Scherzo). The performance is warmly lyrical and completely spontaneous, with a racy finale to round off a particularly satisfying reading, never forced but deeply felt. Arthur Grumiaux's playing is a constant pleasure, and the pianist, Gyorgy Sebok, is hardly less admirable.

As for the *Piano trios*, the performances are splendid, with strongly paced, dramatic allegros, consistently alert and thoughtful, and with sensitive playing in slow movements. Characterization is positive (yet never over-forceful) and structural considerations are well judged: each reading has its own special individuality. The sound is first class and the resonance of Bernard Greenhouse's cello is warmly caught without any clouding of focus. The CD transfer has brightened the top a little, but not excessively. Excellent notes, too.

Horn trio in E flat, Op. 40 (see also above).

(M) *** Decca 433 695-2 [id.]. Tuckwell, Perlman, Ashkenazy – FRANCK: *Violin sonata;* SAINT-SAENS: *Romance;* SCHUMANN: *Adagio & allegro.* ***

☞ (BB) **(*) Naxos Dig. 8.550441 [id.]. Jenö Keveházi, Jenö Handó, Ildikó Hegyi (with Heinrich HERZOGENBERG: *Trio for horn, oboe & piano, Op. 61* (with József Kiss); Frédéric DUVERNOY: *Horn trio* **(*)).

☞ ** Decca Dig. 433 850-2 [id.]. Radovan Vlatkovic, Hans Maile, Vladimir Ashkenazy – SCHUMANN: *Adagio and allegro* etc. **(*)

A superb performance of Brahms's marvellous *Horn trio* from Tuckwell, Perlman and Ashkenazy. They realize to the full the music's passionate impulse, and the performance moves forward from the gentle opening, through the sparkling scherzo and the more introspective but still outgiving *Adagio*, to the gay and spirited finale. The recording is worthy of the playing, although the new ADD transfer of the 1968 recording seeks to provide a more sharply defined sound-picture than before, and the attempt to clarify its imagery brings moments when the refinement of texture slips at climaxes.

The Naxos version has plenty of vitality and romantic ardour, but rather less in the way of refinement. The excellent horn player, Jenö Keveházi, has a touch of vibrato but the ear soon adjusts, and he makes a strong, full-blooded contribution. The whole performance goes with plenty of impetus, with the *Adagio mesto* a sensitive interlude before the exuberant finale. The players are somewhat backwardly placed in the fairly resonant Unitarian Church, Budapest, but the result is convincing with a good relationship between the three instruments. The other two *Horn trios* are enjoyable but not distinctive. The oboe makes an effective substitute for the violin in the Herzogenberg piece, which cribs from the Brahms finale in its second-movement *Presto*. The Duvernoy *Trio* has two movements only, slow–fast, with the second rather jolly. They are both well played and recorded.

The new Decca digital version of the *Horn trio* again features Ashkenazy but has a relatively low level of tension. Its kernel is the slow movement, played gently and expressively, but, suprisingly the ensemble slips in the vigorously exuberant finale. This is not an easy work to balance, and here the recording is warmly atmospheric but not especially clearly defined.

(i) *Horn trio in E flat;* (ii) *Piano quintet in F min., Op. 34.*

☞ **(*) CRD Dig. CRD 3489 [id.]. Nash Ens.: (i) Frank Lloyd; (i; ii) Marcia Crayford, Ian Brown; (ii) Elizabeth Layton, Roger Chase, Christopher van Kampen.

These amiable CRD performances of two strongly characterized Brahms works may not be as high-powered as such virtuoso accounts as that with Tuckwell, Ashkenazy and Perlman on Decca (differently coupled), but the Nash Ensemble's more comfortable approach, derived from long experience performing this music in concert, provides a different view. They have extra expressive warmth at spacious speeds, firmly underpinned by the incisive playing of the pianist, Ian Brown, and this is heard at its best in the *Piano quintet*. The romanticism of the Nash approach comes out too in the opening *Andante* of the *Horn trio*, but the horn soloist, Frank Lloyd, is (for I.M.) rather too reticent here. He produces an exceptionally rich tone to remind one of Dennis Brain, but he indulges the lovely tune at the centre of the Scherzo, which is consequently somewhat lacking in momentum. He then helps the group to give a raptly beautiful account of the *Adagio*. Following these relaxed accounts of the first three movements, the galloping finale is then given with joyful panache, with the horn braying splendidly. Thanks partly to the CRD recording, the Nash performances are made to sound satisfyingly beefy, almost orchestral, though some may find the full-bodied sound a degree too reverberant, not ideally balanced in the *Horn trio* and a little lacking in sparkle in the *Piano quintet*. Yet, with both performances undoubtedly characterful and enjoyable, the disc can be recommended, particularly when this is the only issue coupling these two works.

(i) *Horn trio in E flat;* (ii) *String sextet No. 2 in G, Op. 36.*

⊛ (M) **(*) Sony SMK 46249 [id.]. (i) Myron Bloom, Michael Tree, Rudolph Serkin; (ii) Pina Carmirelli, Toth, Naegele, Caroline Levine, Arico, Reichenberger.

The performance of the *Horn trio*, recorded at the Marlboro Festival in 1960, is quite splendid. Myron Bloom's horn playing is superb, and Michael Tree matches his lyrical feeling, while Serkin holds the performance together so that, when the fervour of the music-making brings a few slips in rhythmic precision, the listener is carried along by the exhilaration of the moment. The *Trio* comes paired with another Marlboro performance, of the *G major String sextet*, by a string group led by Pina Carmirelli. Recorded in 1967, this is at an altogether lower voltage.

Piano quartets Nos. 1 in G min., Op. 25; 2 in A, Op. 26; 3 in C min., Op. 60.
*** Sony Dig.S2K 45846 (2) [id.]. Jaime Laredo, Isaac Stern, Yo Yo Ma, Emanuel Ax.
☞ (M) **(*) DG Dig. 430 856-2 (2) [id.]. Tamás Vásáry, Thomas Brandis, Wolfram Christ, Ottomar Borwitzky.

Piano quartet No. 1 in G min., Op. 25.
*** Sony Dig. MK 42361 [id.]. Murray Perahia, Amadeus Qt (members).

Piano quartets Nos. 1 in G min.; 3 in C min., Op. 60.
*** Virgin/EMI Dig. VC7 59248-2 [id.]. Domus.

The Stern–Laredo–Ma–Ax partnership produces some pretty high-voltage playing and a real sense of give-and-take. There is little sense of four stars just coming together for a recording session but more of a genuine musical rapport. The listener is placed rather closer to the artists than some readers might like. All the same, no one investing in the Sony set is likely to be in the least disappointed.

This Perahia version of the *G minor Piano quartet* has an expressive power and eloquence that silence criticism. The sound has both warmth and presence in its CD format and this is arguably the finest account of the work since Gilels recorded it with the same string group.

However, Domus offer not only the *G minor Quartet* but also the *C minor*, and they give marvellously spontaneous accounts of both works, urgent and full of warmth, yet with no lack of subtlety. The full, vivid recording can be recommended strongly.

The DG set dates from 1982 and the performances are commanding. Tamás Vásáry is particularly impressive throughout and the string playing from the three principals of the Berlin Philharmonic is hardly less magnificent. These artists have a thorough grasp of these unfailingly rich and inventive scores and penetrate their character completely. The one reservation concerns the quality of the early digital recording, made in the Berlin Jesus-Christus-Kirche. The microphones have been placed very close and the effect is artificial: the players are very forward and it is as if one were listening to them in the confines of an enclosed space, without there being sufficient room for the sound to expand. The bright, forward timbre of the strings is achieved at the expense of a natural tonal bloom which one might have expected from the ecclesiastical ambience. American readers would do better with the Vox Box [CDX 5052] by the Eastman Quartet. Their set is distinguished by some very fine playing, in particular from the pianist, Frank Glazer, whose sensitivity and imagination are always in evidence. There is nothing sensational or jet-setting about the playing and, though the 1968 sound is more forward than is ideal, it is acceptably warm and preferable to the digital DG balance. However, this Vox Box has not yet been issued in the UK.

Piano quartet No. 2 in A, Op. 26.
*** Virgin/EMI Dig. VC7 90739-2 [id.]. Domus – MAHLER: *Quartet movement.* ***

With this CD, Domus complete their set of the Brahms *Piano quartets*, and one need hardly say more than that this record is fully worthy of its companion. The disc is currently withdrawn and awaiting reissue.

Piano quartet No. 2 in A, Op. 26; Piano quintet in F min., Op. 34.
☞ (M) (**) EMI mono CDH7 64702-2 [id.]. Rudolf Serkin, Busch Qt.

Rudolf Serkin was at his most sensitive and responsive in pre-war days when he made these recordings with the Busch Quartet (in 1932 and 1938 respectively). The *F minor Quintet* is given a powerfully coherent and dramatic reading and, though allowances have to be made for the sound, the performances are full of thought-provoking touches.

Piano quartet No. 3 in C min., Op. 60.
** Sony Dig. MK 42387 [id.]. Stern, Ma, Laredo, Ax – *Double concerto.* ***

Excellent playing from all concerned on the Sony/CBS disc, even if Emanuel Ax delivers too thick a fortissimo tone at times – though he can produce beautiful pianissimo tone as well. There are pianists more sensitive in this respect on rival recordings.

Piano quintet in F min., Op. 34.
(BB) *** Naxos Dig. 8.550406; *4550406* [id.]. Jenö Jandó, Kodály Qt – SCHUMANN: *Piano quintet.*
***

Although not quite as refined as some of its full-price competitors, this fine Naxos account has a great deal going for it, even though it does not include the first-movement exposition repeat. The playing is boldly spontaneous and has plenty of fire and expressive feeling. The opening of the finale has mystery too, and overall, with full-bodied recording and plenty of presence, this makes a strong impression. It is certainly a bargain.

Piano trios Nos. 1 in B, Op. 8; 2 in C, Op. 87; 3 in C min., Op. 101; 4 in A, Op. posth.
*** Teldec/Warner Dig. 9031 76036-2 (2) [id.]. Trio Fontenay.
☞ (BB) ** Naxos Dig. 8.550746 (*Nos. 1 & 2*); 8.550747 (*Nos. 3 & 4*). Vienna Piano Trio.

Piano trio No. 1 in B, Op. 8.
*** Teldec/Warner Dig. 2292 44924-2 [id.]. Trio Fontenay – IVES: *Trio.* ***

Piano trio No. 2 in C, Op. 87.
*** Teldec/Warner Dig. 2292 44177-2 [id.]. Trio Fontenay – DVORAK: *Piano trio No. 1.* ***

Powerful, spontaneous playing with a real Brahmsian spirit, given excellent, modern recording, puts these admirable performances by the Trio Fontenay at the top of the list.

The accounts by the Vienna Piano Trio on Naxos are warm and unidiosyncratic and have no lack of vitality. Slow movements are shaped and phrased very musically and there is a Brahms feel to the stronger allegros, which are well paced. These are not distinctive performances but they are fresh and worth their modest cost. The recording in a resonant acoustic (a hall in a castle in Budapest) has brought fairly close microphones, but the presence given to the group does not sound too noticeably artificial.

Piano trios Nos. 1 in B, Op. 8; 2 in C, Op. 87.
(M) *** Decca 421 152-2; *421 152-4.* Julius Katchen, Josef Suk, Janos Starker.

Piano trios Nos. 1 in B, Op. 8; 2 in C, Op. 87; 3 in C min., Op. 101; 4 in A, Op. posth.
*** Ph. Dig. 416 838-2 (2) [id.]. Beaux Arts Trio.

The new digital recordings by the Beaux Arts Trio were made in La Chaux-de-Fonds, Switzerland, and they bring one close to the artists. The playing is always highly vital and sensitive. There is a splendid, finely projected sense of line and the delicate, sensitive playing of Menahem Pressler is always a delight.

The Katchen/Suk/Starker performances are warm, strong and characterful. The richness of the acoustics at The Maltings adds to the Brahmsian glow; and if the sound of the remastered disc is a little limited in the upper range, it provides a real Brahmsian amplitude which is very satisfying.

String quartets Nos. 1 in C min.; 2 in A min., Op. 51/1–2; 3 in B flat, Op. 67.
☞ *** EMI Dig. CDS7 54829-2 (2) [id.]. Alban Berg Qt.
☞ **(*) Claves Dig. 50-9404/5 (2) [id.]. Quartet Sine Nomine.
☞ (M) *(*) DG 437 128-2 (2) [id.]. LaSalle Qt – WOLF: *Quartet.* **

On EMI, the outer quartets, the *C minor*, Op. 51/1, and the *B flat*, Op. 67, were recorded in Switzerland (in a church) and are accommodated on the first CD; the *A minor*, Op. 51/2, is from a live performance given at the Palais Yusopov in St Petersburg and is on the second CD – rather short measure these days for a full-price CD. All the same there is nothing short-measured about the performances, which have all the finesse and attack one expects from the Alban Berg Quartet along with impeccable technical address. The *A minor* has just the right kind of dramatic intensity, and the range of colour and dynamics they produce in all three works is impressive. The EMI engineers produced well-detailed, truthful sound in the Swiss venue; the slightly greater freshness and spontaneity of the St Petersburg performance is offset by a slight loss in tonal radiance. All the same, these are all performances of quality and can be recommended even to those who find this ensemble at times a little too glossy.

The Sine Nomine Quartet are splendidly recorded in a helpful acoustic, and the effect here is just like a series of live performances. The playing, though well integrated and responsive with plenty of Brahmsian spirit, has not the degree of sophistication and finesse the Borodins display, but it does have consistent vitality and spontaneity; the *Third, B flat major Quartet* is particularly alive: it leaps out of the speakers towards the listener, and again the closing variations are a highlight of the performance. The snag here is one of economy. The set is offered on two discs, together in a single

Duo jewel-case, but there is no price reduction and the second CD has a playing time of only 34 minutes!

The LaSalle players give efficient, streamlined accounts but convey less sense of feeling or tenderness. There is no question as to the polish and expertise of these players, but these are not performances that bring one closer to the music. The 1978/9 recording sounds bright and immediate.

String quartets Nos. 1 in C min.; 2 in A min., Op. 51/1–2.
☞ *** Denon Dig. CD75756 [id.]. Carmina Qt.
*** Chan. Dig. CHAN 8562; *ABTD 1264* [id.]. Gabrieli Qt.
*** Decca Dig. 425 526-2 [id.]. Takács Qt.
☞ ** Pickwick Dig. MCD 53 [id.]. New World String Qt.

The Denon coupling of the Op. 51 *Quartets* is one of the best recent issues – and perhaps the finest since the Quartetto Italiano's account in the days of vinyl. The *A minor Quartet* is placed first, and some may find its opening a little too sweet-toned; but they have a firm grasp on the architecture of the music and convey pleasure in music-making. They are recorded with presence and body.

Richly recorded in an agreeably expansive ambience, the Gabrielis give warm, eloquent performances of both the Op. 51 *Quartets*, deeply felt and full-textured without being heavy; the *Romanze* of Op. 51, No. 1, is delightfully songful. There are both tenderness and subtlety here, and the sound is first class.

The Takács Quartet's coupling of the *C minor* and *A minor Quartets* has vitality and sensitivity, and their accounts of both works are eminently well shaped. They may be recommended alongside the Gabrielis on Chandos.

The New World Quartet have the full measure of both works and evince an admirable feeling for the architecture of both works and their sense of onward lyrical flow. There is no lack of ardour and intensity but they (and the Pickwick engineers) do not achieve the lucidity of texture of some rivals; nor does their playing, fine though it is, have quite the same spontaneity as their Hyperion rivals listed below. All the same, these are thoughtful and musicianly performances and, were the recording not quite so close and the disc more competitively priced (it is in the upper-mid-price range), it would be a three-stars-minus recommendation.

String quartets Nos. 1 in C min.; 2 in A min., Op. 51/1–2; 3 in B flat, Op. 67; (i) *Piano quintet in F min., Op. 34.*
☞ *** Hyp. Dig. CDA 66651/52 [id.]. (i) Lane; New Budapest Qt.

The New Budapest Quartet bring warmth and spontaneity to all three scores, responding to their dramatic fervour and lyrical flow in equal measure. Their intonation is altogether impeccable and they are scrupulously attentive to Brahms's dynamic markings, with pleasing results in terms of clarity and transparency. Both the *C minor* and *A minor Quartets* can so often sound opaque, and in this respect the New Budapest produce as clean and open a sonority as any. They also have plenty of character and rhythmic vitality. They enjoy two further advantages over some earlier rivals in that, first, they also offer an excellently shaped and musicianly account of the *F minor Piano quintet* with responsive playing from Piers Lane and, secondly, they are among the best and most naturally recorded to have appeared in recent years. Moreover the two CDs come separately and not as a package. But most collectors will surely want both.

String quartets Nos. 1 in C min., Op. 51/1; 3 in B flat, Op. 67.
☞ **(*) Teldec/Warner Dig. 4509 90889-2 [id.]. Borodin Qt.

Marvellously sophisticated playing from the Borodins, with wonderful tonal blending, absolute security of intonation and immaculate ensemble. The first movement of No. 1 sets off with considerable impetus, but the thoughtfulness of the performance establishes itself within a few bars, and the inner movements of this *Quartet* have much grace and delicacy of feeling, while in Op. 67 the subtle treatment of the variations which make up the last movement is a high point of the record. The digital recording is firm and truthful, if a shade close and bright; but the main reservation here is that these performances, although they offer much to admire and enjoy, lack the kind of spontaneity that really grips the listener; moreover many listeners might like their Brahms to sound rather more robust.

String quintets Nos. 1 in F, Op. 88; 2 in G, Op. 111.
(M) **(*) Ph. 426 094-2; *426 094-4.* BPO Octet (members).

Although the remastering has brought a thinner, more astringent treble response than the original LP, the performances by the Berlin Philharmonic group are searching and artistically satisfying, combining freshness with polish, warmth with well-integrated detail.

String sextets Nos. 1 in B flat, Op. 18; 2 in G, Op. 36.
*** Hyp. Dig. CDA 66276 [id.]. Raphael Ens.
☞ *** Sony Dig. S2K 45820 (2) [id.]. Stern, Lin, Ma, Robinson, Laredo, Tree.
☞ *** Chan. Dig. CHAN 9151 [id.]. ASMF Chamber Ens.

String sextets Nos. 1 in B flat, Op. 18; 2 in G, Op. 36: Scherzo only.
☞ ** EMI Dig. CDC7 54216-2 [id.]. Amadeus Ens. & Alban Berg Qt.

The *Sextets* are among Brahms's most immediately appealing chamber works. The Raphael Ensemble are fully responsive to all their subtleties as well as to their vitality and warmth. In short, these are superb performances; the recording is very vivid and immediate, although some ears might find it a shade too present.

The Sony award-winning version of the *String sextets* deserves its laurels. Names alone are not in themselves enough to ensure success, even if they are as resplendent as those of Isaac Stern, Cho-Liang Lin, Yo-Yo Ma, Jaime Laredo and so on; but the rapport and interplay so vital in chamber-music playing is in ample evidence. There is a keen feeling for the warmth and generosity of feeling, as well as for the strength and architecture of these masterpieces, and the Sony engineering is impressive. In spite of awards and razzmatazz, this is a clear first choice alongside the Raphael Ensemble (Hyperion), which have the advantage of being accommodated on one CD. The Sony issue involves two premium-priced CDs, so many may feel that the Hyperion remains 'best buy'.

The Chandos alternative is also highly recommendable, with both *Sextets* again accommodated on one CD without sacrificing the exposition repeats, so that at almost 78 minutes the Academy of St Martin-in-the-Fields offer excellent value for money. Moreover these well-prepared and musical performances are perceptive and intelligent. There are no exaggerated dynamic contrasts, in fact no exaggeration of any kind. Free from interpretative point-making, these performances are musically satisfying and are given finely detailed and present recording.

The Amadeus Ensemble and the Alban Berg Quartet were recorded at a public occasion and can be recommended mainly to their admirers. Those who find difficulties with Norbert Brainin's vibrato will probably not gravitate towards this version of the *First Sextet*, which offers only the Scherzo of the *G major Sextet* as a filler. It is decently recorded and the playing has plenty of spontaneity, even if the tonal blend is less than ideal. There is a sense of occasion here but, given the current competition, it is not the strongest contender.

Violin sonatas Nos. 1 in G, Op. 78; 2 in A, Op. 100; 3 in D min., Op. 108.
☞ *** Hyp. Dig. CDA 66465 [id.]. Krysia Osostowicz, Susan Tomes.
*** Sony Dig. SK 45819 [id.]. Itzhak Perlman, Daniel Barenboim.
(M) *** DG 431 599-2 [id.]. Pinchas Zukerman, Daniel Barenboim.
*** EMI Dig. CDC7 47403-2 [id.]. Itzhak Perlman, Vladimir Ashkenazy.
☞ *** DG Dig. 435 800-2 [id.]. Augustin Dumay, Maria João Pires.
☞ (***) Testament mono SBT 1024 [id.]. Gioconda De Vito, Edwin Fischer; Tito Aprea (in *No. 2*).
☞ *(*) Collins Dig. 1226-2 [id.]. Igor Oistrakh, Natalia Zertsalova.

Violin sonatas Nos. 1 in G, Op. 78; 2 in A, Op. 100; 3 in D min., Op. 108; Scherzo in C min.
*** Decca Dig. 430 555-2 [id.]. Pierre Amoyal, Pascal Rogé.

Krysia Osostowicz and Susan Tomes give performances of such natural musicality that criticism is almost disarmed. They phrase with great spontaneity yet with apparently effortless care and artistry, and the interplay between the two partners is instinctive. The Hyperion engineers manage the sound and balance with their customary skill, and theirs is certainly to be preferred to some of the more glamorous rivals now on the market.

Pierre Amoyal and Pascal Rogé are hardly less fine; they are unfailingly musical in their responses and they do have the advantage of offering the *C minor scherzo* movement into the bargain. These are lovely performances that can be recommended alongside the finest in the catalogue.

This Sony recording, made at a live recital in Chicago, finds Perlman in far more volatile form, more urgently persuasive with naturally flowing speeds and more spontaneous rubato than he adopts in his spacious readings with Ashkenazy on EMI. Barenboim too is less aggressive and more fanciful than he was with Zukerman on DG.

Zukerman and Barenboim are inspired to take a more expansive view of Brahms to produce songful, spontaneous-sounding performances that catch the inspiration of the moment. Compared with Perlman and Ashkenazy, the manner is warmer, less self-conscious – if at times less refined.

Perlman and Ashkenazy bring out the trouble-free happiness of these lyrical inspirations, fully involved yet avoiding underlying tensions. In their sureness and flawless confidence at generally spacious speeds, they are performances which carry you along, cocooned in rich sound.

Augustin Dumay and Maria João Pires on DG are certainly among the most interesting of the other CD couplings. They bring temperament and finesse to all three sonatas and, though there are one or two interpretative touches that may not enjoy universal appeal, these are too trifling to detail and are unlikely to inhibit pleasure. These are artists of strong personality: certainly those with a special admiration for this partnership need not hesitate, for they are very well recorded.

Gioconda De Vito made all too few records. Her accounts of the *G major* and *D minor Sonatas* with Edwin Fischer come from 1954 and show her to excellent advantage. She possessed warmth and finesse in equal measure, and her playing conveys a sense of expressive freedom which makes one regret that her recording career was so short. Fischer's playing is characteristically magisterial and the *A major Sonata*, which she recorded with her normal partner, Tito Aprea, is hardly less beautiful. This is all rather special playing, and few allowances need be made for the excellent mono recording.

Igor Oistrakh and Natalia Zertsalova on Collins are quite simply not in this league either technically or artistically, though they are well enough recorded, even if the violin is too up front. Oistrakh wears his heart on his sleeve, and with the best will in the world in no way does the son challenge memories of his father in this repertoire. Zertsalova is a supportive accompanist but does not possess the subtlety or finesse of the front-runners in this field.

Viola sonatas Nos. 1 in F min.; 2 in E flat, Op. 120/1–2.
☞ ⊛ *** Virgin/EMI Dig. VC7 59309-2 [id.]. Lars Anders Tomter, Leif Ove Andsnes – SCHUMANN: *Märchenbilder.* ***

Viola sonatas Nos. 1 in F min.; 2 in E flat, Op. 120/1–2; F.A.E. Sonata: Scherzo.
**(*) Chan. Dig. CHAN 8550; *ABTD 1256* [id.]. Nobuko Imai, Roger Vignoles – SCHUMANN: *Märchenbilder.* **(*)
☞ (M) **(*) DG 437 248-2 [id.]. Pinchas Zukerman, Daniel Barenboim.

(i) *Viola sonatas Nos. 1 in F min.; 2 in E flat, Op. 120/1–2;* (ii) *2 Songs for contralto, viola and piano, Op. 91.*
☞ *(*) BMG/RCA Dig. 09026 61276-2 [id.]. Pinchas Zukerman, with (i) Mark Neikrug; (ii) Horne, Katz.

This young Norwegian partnership gives us the best account of these sonatas in their viola form now on CD. Theirs is playing of great sensitivity and imagination. Lars Anders Tomter and Leif Ove Andsnes bring a wide range of colour to this music and phrase with an unforced naturalness that is very persuasive. Very well balanced, though there is a slight bias in favour of the piano. Altogether rather special.

Nobuko Imai is an almost peerless violist and it is difficult to find a flaw in her accounts of the two Op. 120 *Sonatas* with Roger Vignoles. The reverberant acoustic does not show the piano to good advantage but, apart from that, this is an impressive issue.

Zukerman's 1975 recording with Barenboim, which we liked enough at the time to award it three stars (perhaps a bit too generously), is back in circulation on the DG Galleria label. Although it will be too sweet for some tastes, these are spontaneous-sounding performances, and the expressiveness never sounds contrived, always buoyant. After the *sonatas*, Zukerman shows his versatility by changing over to the violin for the lively *Scherzo in C minor* from the *F.A.E. Sonata*, a work composed jointly with Schumann and Albert Dietrich. The recording has good presence and it is much to be preferred to the new RCA issue.

In terms of freshness and spontaneity of feeling Zukerman's later recordings with Mark Neikrug are no match for the young Norwegian duo. Undoubtedly they play these sonatas as if they mean something, even though the sound Zukerman produces is rather too honeyed and cloying; yet neither he nor his assertive pianist is anywhere near as subtle or imaginative as Tomter and Andsnes. Marilyn Horne brings her usual artistry to the songs, but the voice now has lost much of its bloom.

Piano music, four hands

Piano music, 4 hands: *Hungarian dances Nos. 1–21; Waltzes, Op. 39.*
☞ **(*) Sony Dig. SK 53285 [id.]. Yaara Tal and Andreas Groethuysen.

The playing here has enormous verve and energy and is seemingly spontaneous in the way the two artists play as one, with considerable rubato flowing quite naturally. Their style, however, brings the very widest dynamic range and is very percussive at fortissimo level. (This is even more striking at a live recital.) So this is not intimate playing, although the *Waltzes* provide plenty of examples when the brilliance scintillates, and there is also some beguilingly gentle pianism at times, especially in the delightful closing *D minor Waltz*, better known as Brahms's *Lullaby*.

Solo piano music

Complete solo piano music: *4 Ballades, Op. 10; Fantasias, Op. 116; Gavotte by Gluck* (arrangement); *Gigues: in A min.; B min.; Hungarian dances; Kanon; Kanon* (inverted); *Kleine Klavierstücke; Pieces, Opp. 76, 117–119; 2 Rhapsodies, Op. 79; Sarabandes: in A; B min.; Sarabande & 2 Gavottes; Scherzo, Op. 4; Sonatas Nos. 1–3; Studies Nos. 1–5; Study for the left hand; Theme and variations in D min.* (from 2nd movement of *String sextet, Op.18*); *Variations on an original theme, Op. 21/1; Variations on a Hungarian song, Op. 21/2; Variations and fugue on a theme of Handel, Op. 24; Variations on a theme of Paganini, Op. 35; Variations on a theme of Schumann, Op. 9; 16 Waltzes, Op. 39.*
☞ ** Nimbus Dig. NI 1788 (6) [id.]. Martin Jones.

Familiar problems arise here. Martin Jones is a fine musician whose artistry is not in question but, as in his survey of Debussy on this label, he is placed at the far end of a large and reverberant studio so that the instrument is heard in less-than-ideal focus. The somewhat distant image and the surrounding ambient sound considerably diminish the pleasure his playing gives. In the *C major* and *F sharp minor Sonatas* he adopts a straightforward approach with sensible, well-judged tempi and there is a welcome freedom from any egocentric idiosyncrasies. There are more poetic readings of the Op. 10 *Ballades* to be found (the *Second in D major* finds him dangerously close to auto-pilot mode) but elsewhere there are perceptive touches, particularly in the late pieces. Jones takes the many technical hurdles of the *Handel* and *Paganini variations* in his stride, even if the performances would not be first recommendations. Try the Op. 116 *Fantasias*, which give a good idea of the set as a whole: his playing of the *Intermezzo*, Op. 116/4, is sensitive and imaginative; at other times he can sound less deeply involved in what he is doing. None of these performances falls below a high standard of musicianship though some, such as the *F minor Sonata*, fall short of real distinction. These are readings of integrity and sensitivity but, given the distant balance and the abundant wealth of alternatives, they can receive only a qualified recommendation.

4 Ballades, Op. 10.
*** DG Dig. 400 043-2 [id.]. Michelangeli – SCHUBERT: *Sonata No. 4.* **
*** Ph. Dig. 426 439-2 [id.]. Alfred Brendel – WEBER: *Piano sonata No. 2.* ***

Michelangeli gives the *Ballades* a performance of the greatest distinction and without the slightly aloof quality that at times disturbs his readings. He is superbly recorded.

A thoughtful (and at times self-aware) account of the Op. 10 *Ballades* by Brendel in a wonderfully clear, digital recording. This is playing of stature that should be heard by all the great pianist's admirers.

4 Ballades, Op. 10; 7 Fantasias, Op. 116; Hungarian dances Nos. 1–10; (i) Nos. 11–21. 3 Intermezzi, Op. 117; 8 Piano pieces, Op. 76; 6 Piano pieces, Op. 118; 4 Piano pieces, Op. 119; Piano sonatas Nos. 1 in C, Op. 1; 2 in F sharp min., Op. 2; 3 in F min., Op. 5; 2 Rhapsodies, Op. 79; Variations on a Hungarian song, Op. 21/2; Variations on a theme by Paganini, Op. 35; Variations and fugue on a theme by Handel, Op. 24; Variations on a theme by Schumann, Op. 9; Variations on an original theme, Op. 21/1; Waltzes, Op. 39.
(M) **(*) Decca mono/stereo 430 053-2 (6). Julius Katchen, (i) with J.-P. Marty.

Brahms often brought out the best in Katchen, and he is particularly good in the impulsive early music. If at times one could make small criticisms, the spontaneity and understanding are always there, and of course the excitement that comes when bravura is controlled by a sensitive and musical mind. Katchen's style in Brahms is distinctive: there is a boldness about it that suits some works more than others. The playing is extremely brilliant and assured. The lesser-known *Variations on a Hungarian song* and *On an original theme*, plus those *On a theme by Schumann*, are particularly successful. They are played with the utmost persuasiveness and artistry. Katchen plays Book One of the *Hungarian dances* in Brahms's later arrangement for piano solo; the remaining dances are offered in the more traditional form with Jean-Pierre Marty as Katchen's partner. On CD the recordings, made between 1962 and 1966, are remarkably realistic. The four *Ballades* are mono.

4 Ballades, Op. 10; 2 Rhapsodies, Op. 79; Variations and fugue on a theme of Handel, Op. 24.
☞ *** Decca Dig. 433 849-2 [id.]. Pascal Rogé.

Unfailing beauty of tone and very natural recorded sound that enhances the eloquence of Pascal Rogé's playing. Although the *Variations and fugue on a theme of Handel* are not new to Rogé's discography (he coupled them with the Op. 116 pieces on an earlier Decca LP), the *Four Ballades* are, and he does them full justice. It is one of those discs to which one returns with increasing satisfaction, noticing new felicities that one had missed before and relishing other insights. Rogé's refined feeling for texture is of particular value in this repertoire and, although memories of Gilels's classic set of the *Ballades* on DG are not eclipsed, Rogé's has a special distinction and finesse. With the splendid Decca recording taken into account, this becomes a first choice for this repertoire.

4 Ballades, Op. 10; Variations and fugue on a theme of Handel, Op. 24; Variations on a theme of Schumann, Op. 9.
*** ASV Dig. CDDCA 616 [id.]. Jorge-Federico Osorio.

Jorge-Federico Osorio's account of the *Variations and fugue on a theme of Handel* is tremendously impressive. He possesses an unfailing sense of the Brahms style, and this is undoubtedly his best record to date, for the Schumann set and the four *Ballades* are also played with fine sensitivity and character. ASV provide excellent, well-focused sound with plenty of depth.

Capriccio in F sharp min., Op. 76/1; 3 Intermezzi, Op. 117; Intermezzo in A, Op. 118/2; Rhapsodies, Op. 79/1–2.
☞ * DG Dig. 437 460-2 [id.]. Ivo Pogorelich.

At 53 minutes or so, Pogorelich is somewhat short on playing time but long on narcissism. The playing is eminently self-conscious throughout. Brahms's tempo markings are paid scant regard, and the scores are treated as a vehicle for this artist's considerable powers of keyboard colour. The *A major Intermezzo* of Op. 118 is unbearably slow and drawn out – as, indeed, is the *Capriccio*. The irrational lurching and dragging of such a piece as the *Rhapsody in G minor*, drawn out to absurd lengths, is totally unacceptable. This is for admirers of Pogorelich rather than for lovers of Brahms.

Fantasias, Op. 116.
☞ *** Ottavio Dig. OTRC 39027 [id.]. Imogen Cooper – SCHUMANN: *Abegg variations* etc. ***

The impulsively spontaneous flow of Imogen Cooper's stirring account of the *Capriccio* which opens the set captures the listener immediately and the variety of colour and mood gives enormous pleasure throughout. The gentle *Intermezzi* are most beautiful, for the recording does this memorable playing full justice. The listening experience here is as if one was present at a live recital.

Fantasias, Op. 116; 3 Intermezzi, Op. 117; 6 Pieces, Op. 118; 4 Pieces, Op. 119.
☞ (M) **(*) DG 437 249-2 [id.]. Wilhelm Kempff.

Kempff's style in Brahms is characteristically individual: poetry emphasized rather than brilliance, subtle timbres rather than virtuosity. It follows that Kempff shines in the gentle fancies of Brahms's last period, with his magic utterly beguiling in the *Intermezzi in A minor, E major* and *E minor* from Op. 116 and especially in the lovely *E flat major Andante* of Op. 117 that is curiously reminiscent of a famous German Christmas carol. Don't be put off by the opening *Capriccio in D minor* of Op. 116 which sounds rather hard, the piano timbre lacking sonority; at lower dynamic levels the piano colouring is exquisite.

3 Intermezzi, Op. 117; 6 Pieces, Op. 118; 4 Pieces, Op. 119; 2 Rhapsodies, Op. 79.
*** Decca 417 599-2 [id.]. Radu Lupu.

Radu Lupu's late Brahms is quite outstanding in every way. There is great intensity and inwardness when these qualities are required and a keyboard mastery that is second to none. This is undoubtedly one of the most rewarding Brahms recitals currently before the public.

Intermezzi, Op. 117; 6 Pieces, Op. 118; Variations on a theme by Paganini, Op. 35.
*** DG Dig. 431 123-2 [id.]. Lilya Zilberstein.

Lilya Zilberstein has flawless technique and keen musical instincts. The recording is marvellously present and clear.

2 Rhapsodies, Op. 79.
☞ (M) **(*) DG 437 252-2 [id.]. Martha Argerich – LISZT: *Sonata* **; SCHUMANN: *Piano sonata No. 2.* *(*)

Brahms's two *Rhapsodies* are marked *Agitato* and *Molto appassionato* respectively, and their mood suits Argerich's impetuosity. The 1960 recording too has a fuller sonority than the Liszt and Schumann couplings, made a decade later.

Piano sonatas Nos. 1 in C, Op. 1; 2 in F sharp min., Op. 2; 3 in F min., Op. 5; 4 Ballades, Op. 10;
Scherzo in E flat, Op 4.
**(*) DG 423 401-2 (2) [id.]. Krystian Zimerman.

Krystian Zimerman's account of the lesser-known *C major Sonata* is powerful and concentrated. His version of the *F minor*, Op. 5, is also particularly commanding and is worthy to stand alongside the great performances of the past. There is leonine power, tempered with poetic feeling. There is no want of tenderness as well as strength in the Op. 10 *Ballades*, although in adding presence the digital remastering has brought a degree of hardness to the upper range at higher dynamic levels.

Piano sonatas Nos. 1 in C, Op. 1; 2 in F sharp min., Op. 2.
☞ *** Decca Dig. 436 457-2 [id.]. Sviatoslav Richter.

Recorded in Mantova in February 1987, these performances show Richter at his most commanding. He makes the most heavily chordal piano writing sound totally pianistic and there is exquisite shading of tone and flawless legato. Both slow movements are most subtly coloured and the opening of the finale of the *F sharp minor Sonata* has a wonderful improvisational feeling. The playing throughout has the spontaneity of live music-making and the Decca engineers have secured most realistic sound.

Piano sonata No. 3 in F min., Op. 5; 4 Ballades, Op. 10.
☞ * Discover Dig. DICD 920123 [id.]. David Lively.

Piano sonata No. 3; 4 Ballades; Intermezzo in E, Op. 116/6; Romance in F, Op. 118/5.
☞ (M) ** BMG/RCA 09026 61862-2 [id.]. Artur Rubinstein.

Piano sonata No. 3; Capriccio in B min., Op. 76/2; Intermezzo in E flat min., Op. 118/6; Rhapsodies: in B min., Op. 79/1; E flat, Op. 119/4.
*** Sony Dig. SK 47181 [id.]; 40-47181. Murray Perahia.

Piano sonata No. 3; 2 Rhapsodies, Op. 79; Theme and variations in D min. (from *String sextet, Op. 18*).
*** Teldec/Warner Dig. 2292 44186-2 [id.]. Cyprien Katsaris.

Piano sonata No. 3; Theme and variations in D min. (from *String sextet, Op. 18*).
*** Decca Dig. 417 122-2. Radu Lupu.

Murray Perahia's account of the Brahms *Sonata in F minor* is undoubtedly the most eloquent and thoughtful (as well as beautiful) among recent recordings. Such is Perahia's artistry that all the subtle agogic shifts that arise in the course of these pieces seem completely natural and convincing. Sony particularly deserve praise for the excellence of the recorded sound they have achieved, which has naturalness and refinement. The smaller pieces are equally successful.

Noble, dignified and spacious are the adjectives that spring to mind when listening to Lupu's Op. 5. Lupu's view is inward, ruminative and always beautifully rounded. The recording is most realistic.

Cyprien Katsaris possesses a pretty breathtaking technique and his Brahms *F minor Sonata* is second to none. Katsaris takes few of the agogic liberties that have sometimes distinguished him in the romantic repertoire and this is strong, exciting playing, and the recording is excellent.

Rubinstein's impulsive way with Brahms, though arresting at the opening of the *Sonata*, is not always convincing. His comparatively fast pacing of the second and fourth movements means that he does not entirely catch the feeling of reverie in the *Andante*, suggested by Brahms's quotation from Stenau: 'The eve is falling ... the moonbeams rise,' and in the finale the entry of the chorale-like secondary theme is almost thrown away by the forward momentum. The rather hard, unexpansive (1959) recording does not help the *Sonata*; but the two shorter pieces seem to have slightly more bloom, and the *Ballades*, too, recorded in Rome in 1970, are fuller although the balance remains close and the acoustic cool. They are given a totally unsentimental approach and there are times when one feels the playing is somewhat shorn of mystery: one misses the extremes of both tension and repose. Nevertheless this is still music-making to reckon with, remarkably youthful in spirit and full of personality, even if it does not really match the poetry of some others of the Brahms/Rubinstein records, the *Second Concerto*, for instance, where the finale is an absolute delight.

David Lively's performances on the Discover bargain label are curiously relaxed and unspontaneous, as the very opening flourish of the *F minor Sonata* demonstrates. A youthful work of this nature needs above all a commanding impetuosity and, although the central movements are not without poetic feeling, the outer movements are not a success – the arrival of the great chordal chorale-like tune in the finale is distinctly lukewarm. The *Ballades* too are pale, despite piano recording which, though sonorous, has a rather bright treble.

Variations on a theme of Haydn, Op. 56a (arr. for piano duet).

*** Sony Dig. MK 42625 [id.]. Murray Perahia, Sir Georg Solti – BARTOK: *Sonata for 2 pianos and percussion.* ***

Murray Perahia and Solti bring out the fullest possible colouring in their performance, so that one hardly misses the orchestra.

ORGAN MUSIC

11 Chorale preludes, Op. 22. Chorale prelude and fugue on 'O Trauerigkeit, O Herzeleid'; Fugue in A flat min. (original and published versions); Preludes and fugues: in A min.; G min.
☞ *** Nimbus Dig. NI 5262 [id.]. Kevin Bowyer (organ of Odense Cathedral).

11 Chorale preludes, Op. 22; Chorale prelude and fugue on 'O Trauerigkeit, O Herzeleid'; Fugue in A flat min.; Preludes and fugues: in A min.; G min.
*** CRD Dig. CRD 3404; *CRDC 4104* [id.]. Nicholas Danby (organ).

Kevin Bowyer, already successful in the music of Bach, now provides an admirable Brahms survey. He has the advantage of the splendid Danish organ in Odense Cathedral which combines a full tone and a warmly coloured palette with a clear profile. Like Nicholas Danby, Bowyer is obviously at home both in the early *Preludes and fugues* in which he produces considerable bravura (helped by the fresh, bright sound of the organ) and in the very late set of *Chorale preludes*, from the period of the *Four Serious Songs*, and which are comparably mellow. He then closes the recital with Brahms's original manuscript forms of the two earliest pieces (which we have already heard in their published formats), the *Chorale prelude and fugue on 'O Trauerigkeit'* (unvarnished and about a third of the length of the final published work) and the unpolished *A flat minor fugue*. These two items are treated as appendices, and the organist suggests in his notes that, had Brahms had a say in the matter, they would not have been recorded at all! The disc is very well documented.

Nicholas Danby playing the organ of the Church of the Immaculate Conception in London, which also seems ideally suited to this repertoire, gives restrained, clean-cut readings (which yet have a strong profile) of Brahms's complete organ works. The sound of the Farm Street organ is beautifully caught by the recording. Choice between these two discs might well depend on preference for the type of organ used. The effect on CRD is rather more incisive, yet has firmness and weight of tone and certainly does not lack amplitude.

VOCAL MUSIC

Lieder: *Ach, wende diesen Blick; Die Mainacht; Heimweh; Mädchenlied; Meine Liebe ist grün; O kühler Wald; Ständchen; Unbewegte laue Luft; Von ewiger Liebe; Wie rafft' ich mich auf; Wiegenlied.*
(i) *2 Songs with viola: (Gestille Sehnsucht & Geistliches Wiegenlied), Op. 91. 3 Volkslieder: Dort in den Weiden; Sonntag; Vergebliches Ständchen. 8 Zigeunerlieder Op. 103/1–7 & 11.*
*** DG Dig. 429 727-2 [id.]. Anne Sofie von Otter, Bengt Forsberg, (i) with Nils-Erik Sparf.

Anne Sofie von Otter gives these Brahms Lieder the natural freshness of folksong, which so often they resemble, or even quote, as in the radiant melody of *Sonntag*. She phrases unerringly, holding and changing tension and mood as in a live recital. Compared with some, there is still a degree of expressive restraint, but there are few Brahms song-recital discs to match this one, and her accompanist is strongly supportive. In the Op. 91 settings they are joined by Nils-Erik Sparf, who plays with admirable taste.

Lieder: *Dein blaues Auge hält; Dort in den Weiden; Immer leiser wird mein Schlummer; Klage I & II; Liebestreu; Des Liebsten Schwur; Das Mädchen; Das Mädchen spricht; Regenlied; Romanzen und Lieder, Op. 84; Salome; Sapphische Ode, Op. 94/4; Der Schmied;* (i) *2 Songs with viola, Op. 91; Therese; Vom Strande; Wie Melodien zieht es; Zigeunerlieder, Op. 103.*
(M) *** DG Dig. 431 600-2; *431 600-4* [id.]. Jessye Norman, Daniel Barenboim; (i) Wolfram Christ.

Jessye Norman's glorious Lieder recital with Barenboim, recorded in 1981/2, is one of her finest records, while Wolfram Christ makes a distinguished contribution to Op. 91. The recording is wonderfully vivid, giving the artists a tangible presence.

Vier ernste Gesänge, Op. 121; Lieder: Auf dem Kirchhofe; Botschaft; Feldeinsamkeit; Im Waldeseinsamkeit; Minnelied III; Mondenschein; O wüsst ich doch den Weg züruck; Sapphische Ode; Sommerabend; Ständchen.
⊛ (M) (***) EMI CDH7 63198-2 [id.]. Hotter, Moore – BACH: *Cantata No. 82: Ich habe genug.* (***) ⊛

Glorious singing from Hans Hotter, wonderfully accompanied by Gerald Moore. An excellent transfer.

Lieder: *Abendregen; Alte Liebe; Feldensamkeit; Immer leiser wird mein Schlummer; Der Jäger; Liebestreu; Mädchenfluch; Mädchenlied; Das Mädchen spricht; Meine Liebe ist grün; Regenlied; Salome; Der Schmied; Sommerabend; Therese; Der Tod, das ist die kühle Nacht; Von ewiger Liebe; Vor dem Fenster; Wir wandelten.*
*** Orfeo C 058831A [id.]. Margaret Price, James Lockhart.

Margaret Price sings radiantly, with the voice ideally suited to the soaring lines of many of these songs, finely coloured over the changes of mood in a song such as *Alte Liebe*. Clean, bright recording.

Lieder: *An die Nachtigall; Botschaft; Dein blaues Auge hält so still; Feldeinsamkeit; Der Gang zum Liebchen; Geheimnis; Im Waldeseinsamkeit; Komm bald; Die Kränze; Die Mainacht; Meine Liebe ist grün; Minnelied; Nachtigall; O wüsst ich doch den Weg zurück; Sah dem edlen Bildnis; Salamander; Die Schale der Vergessenheit; Serenade; Sonntag; Ständchen; Von ewiger Liebe; Von waldbekränzter Höhe; Wie bist du, Meine Königin; Wiegenlied; Wir wandelten.*
*** Virgin/EMI Dig. VC7 91130-2; *VC 791130-4* [id.]. Thomas Allen, Geoffrey Parsons.

Thomas Allen, in one of his most successful Lieder records yet, gives fresh, virile performances of a particularly attractive collection of Brahms songs. There are many felicities here, with Geoffrey Parsons an ever-sympathetic accompanist and with sound more cleanly focused than in earlier Lieder issues from this source. This collection is currently withdrawn, awaiting reissue.

Heine Lieder: *Es liebt sich so lieblich im Lenze; Es schaunen die Blumen; Meerfahrt; Mondenschein; Sommerabend; Der Tod, das ist die kühle Nacht.* Volkslieder: *Da unten im Tale; Dort in den Weiden; Du mein einzig Licht; Gold überwiegt die Liebe; Klage; Mädchenfluch; Schwesterlein; Sehnsucht; Spannung; Ständchen; Vergebliches Ständchen; Vergangen ist mir Glück und Heil; Vor dem Fenster; Vom verwundeten Knaben. 8 Zigeunerlieder, Op. 103.*
☞ *(*) BMG/RCA Dig. 09026 60901-2 [id.]. Margaret Price, Graham Johnson.

As their Hyperion disc of Schubert shows, the Lieder partnership of Margaret Price and Graham Johnson sparks off exceptionally illuminating performances. Here, sadly, in a most attractive Brahms collection the results are marred by unhelpful recording. Not only is Price's voice caught with an edge to it, but – more seriously – Johnson's piano sounds shallow and twangy.

(i) *Alto rhapsody, Op. 53. 4 Gesänge, Op. 17.*
*** Virgin/EMI Dig. VC7 59589-2 [id.]. (i) J. Baker; London Symphony Ch., City of L. Sinfonia, Hickox – MENDELSSOHN: *Infelice* etc. ***

This is a more openly expressive and spacious reading than Dame Janet's earlier, EMI one with Boult, matching her performances in the two Mendelssohn items. The four early Brahms songs, Opus 17, for women's chorus with two horns and harp accompaniment, are delightfully done.

(i) *Alto rhapsody, Op. 53;* (ii) *German Requiem; Song of destiny (Schicksalslied), Op. 54. Academic festival overture; Tragic overture; Variations on a theme by Haydn.*
☞ (B) **(*) Ph. Duo 438 760-2 (2) [id.]. (i) Aafjé Heynis; (ii) Wilma Lipp, Franz Crass; (i; ii) V. Singverein; VSO, Sawallisch.

In the *German Requiem* Sawallisch may not penetrate the spiritual depths as deeply as a conductor like Haitink but, with a simple, dedicated manner that lets the music flow naturally and with the help of very fine choral singing and recording to point the climaxes, it is still a deeply satisfying version, with an account of the final movements both dramatic and ethereal. Franz Crass's dark bass colouring make his solos tonally distinctive, but the singing of Wilma Lipp in *Ich hab' nur Traurigkeit* is a blot, wobbly and plaintive-sounding. However, what makes this inexpensive set worth considering, even against the competition, is Aafjé Heynis's lovely singing in the *Alto rhapsody*. It is even more dedicated and 'inner' than Kathleen Ferrier's, and the tonal shading is most beautiful. The emotionally more turbulent *Song of destiny* is also a considerable success. Not all collectors will need the overtures, but they are well enough played and recorded, although the early date (1959) of the *Variations* shows in the violin timbre. Sawallisch's performance is brisk and alive, with the slower variations not quite as convincing as the quick ones.

German Requiem, Op. 45.
⊛ *** Ph. Dig. 432 140-2 [id.]. Margiono, Gilfry, Monteverdi Ch., O Révolutionnaire et Romantique, Eliot Gardiner.
(M) *** Teldec/Warner Dig. 9031 75862-2 [id.]. M. Price, Ramey, Amb. S., RPO, Previn.

*** EMI CDC7 47238-2 [id.]. Schwarzkopf, Fischer-Dieskau, Philh. Ch. & O, Klemperer.

☞ (M) **(*) BMG/RCA Dig. 09026 61349-2. Battle, Hagegård, Chicago Ch. & SO, Levine.

☞ (B) **(*) EMI Dig. CZS7 67819-2 (2) [id.]. Jessye Norman, Jorma Hynninen, LPO Ch., LPO, Tennstedt – SCHUMANN: *Requiems.* ***

☞ (M) **(*) Decca 425 042-2 [id.]. Kiri Te Kanawa, Bernd Weikl, Chicago Ch. & SO, Solti.

Gardiner's 'revolutionary' account of the *German Requiem* brings a range of choral sound even more thrilling than in the concert hall. With period instruments and following Viennese practice of the time, speeds tend to be faster than usual, though the speed for the big fugue is surprisingly relaxed. Charlotte Margiono makes an ethereal soprano soloist, while Rodney Gilfry, despite a rapid vibrato, is aptly fresh and young-sounding. One could not ask for a more complete renovation of a masterpiece often made to sound stodgy and square.

It is the seeming simplicity of Previn's dedicated approach, with radiant singing from the chorus and measured speeds held steadily, that so movingly conveys an innocence in the often square writing, both in the powerful opening choruses and in the simple, songful *Wie lieblich*. The great fugatos are then powerfully presented. Both soloists are outstanding, Margaret Price golden-toned, Samuel Ramey incisively dark. The recording is warmly set against a helpful church acoustic with the chorus slightly distanced.

Measured and monumental, Klemperer's performance defies preconceived doubts. The speeds are consistently slow – too slow in the vivace of the sixth movement, where Death has little sting – but, with dynamic contrasts underlined, the result is uniquely powerful.

Levine's version features the Chicago Symphony Chorus, which is probably the finest in America, while his two soloists both prove excellent, Kathleen Battle pure and sweetly vulnerable-sounding, Hagegård clear-cut and firm. Levine is not the most illuminating conductor in this work and his pacing is not always convincing; yet the performance is alive, with power as well as impetus, and it undoubtedly gives pleasure. The recording is not ideal, with inner textures growing cloudy in tuttis.

Tennstedt's is an unusually spacious view of the *Requiem*, with speeds slower than on any rival version. His dedication generally sustains them well, with a reverential manner always alert, never becoming merely monumental, though the choir's ensemble is not always perfect. Jorma Hynninen proves an excellent soloist. What does sound monumental rather than moving is Jessye Norman's solo, *Ihr habt nun Traurigkeit*, though the golden tone is glorious. On CD, generally fine, spacious recording which matches the spaciousness of the interpretation.

Even more strikingly than in his set of the Brahms symphonies, Solti here favours very expansive tempi, smooth lines and refined textures. There is much that is beautiful, even if the result overall is not as involving as it might be. Dame Kiri Te Kanawa sings radiantly, but Bernd Weikl with his rather gritty baritone is not ideal. Fine recording, glowing and clear.

Liebeslieder waltzes, Op. 52; New Liebeslieder waltzes, Op. 65; 3 Quartets, Op. 64.

*** DG Dig. 423 133-2 [id.]. Mathis, Fassbaender, Schreier, Fischer-Dieskau; Engel and Sawallisch (pianos).

One of the most successful recordings yet of the two seductive but surprisingly difficult sets of *Liebeslieder waltzes*. The CD has fine realism and presence.

Liebeslieder waltzes, Op. 52; New Liebeslieder waltzes, Op. 65/15.

☞ (M) (***) Decca mono 425 995-2 [id.]. Irmgaard Seefried, Kathleen Ferrier, Julius Patzak, Günter, Curzon, Gá – MAHLER: *Kindertotenlieder.* (**)

Recorded at the Edinburgh Festival in September 1952, the Decca historic performance brings a dazzling team together. Though it is not the most relaxed account, there are countless touches of imagination, not least from the very distinctive tenor, Julius Patzak, and the ever-responsive Clifford Curzon taking the upper piano part. Limited but clear sound.

Motets: *Ave Maria, Op. 12; 3 Fest- und Gedensprüche, Op. 109; Geistliche Chöre, Op. 37; Geistliches Lied, Op. 30; 2 Motets, Op. 29; 2 Motets, Op. 74; 3 Motets, Op. 110; Psalm 13, Op. 27.*

*** Conifer Dig. CDCF 178 [id.]. Trinity College, Cambridge, Ch., Richard Marlow.

Richard Marlow and his excellent Cambridge choir add to their distinguished list of records with this invaluable collection, bringing together all sixteen of the motets which Brahms wrote over the course of his long career. With superb singing recorded vividly, this is an outstanding issue.

Brian, Havergal (1876–1972)

(i) *Violin concerto; The Jolly Miller (comedy overture); Symphony No. 18.*
(**) Marco Polo Dig. 8.223479 [id.]. (i) Marat Bisengaliev, BBC Scottish SO, Lionel Friend.

Havergal Brian wrote the first draft of his *Violin concerto* in the spring of 1934, then left the manuscript on a train. It was never recovered and he had to start all over again. The result is a work on the most ambitious scale, obviously with an eye on the Elgar concerto in its use of a very large orchestra as a backcloth. While its melodic inspiration does not match Elgar's masterpiece, it has attractive and readily identifiable folksong-like ideas, notably the second subject of the first movement and the lyrical theme on which the slow movement's fifteen chimerical variations are based. The finale has an important cadenza in which the orchestra finally joins and it is the orchestra which, unusually, finishes the concerto without the soloist in a last grandiloquent treatment of a march theme which, when it first appeared, was on a much smaller scale, even nonchalant in mood. It is an impressive work and is played with much feeling by Marat Bisengaliev, who is given powerful support by the BBC Scottish Orchestra under Lionel Friend. The snag is the close-miked recording, which at times brings an edge to the solo violin timbre and makes the many passionate orchestral tuttis sound fierce and aggressive instead of opulent in an Elgarian way. It is difficult to find a volume setting at which the violin is reproduced at an acceptable level without the next vigorously loud orchestral entry making one almost wince. The concerto is prefaced by a jolly little overture introducing the folksong, *The Miller of Dee*, and is followed by a rather good small-scale symphony, with its three movements all based on march-like themes, ranging over a whole gamut of emotions and ending forcefully. There is excellent back-up documentation and, helpfully, its full analysis of the concerto's structure is matched by cues within each of the three movements to identify salient points of interest.

Symphony No. 1 (Gothic).
*** Marco Polo Dig. 8.223280/1; *4.223280/1* [id.]. Jenisová, Pecková, Dolezal, Mikulás, Slovak Philharmonic Ch., Slovak Nat. Theatre Op. Ch., Slovak Folk Ens. Ch., Lucnica Ch., Bratislava Chamber Ch. & Children's Ch., Youth Echo Ch., Czech RSO (Bratislava), Slovak PO, Ondrej Lenárd.

This first of the symphonies here receives a passionately committed performance from Slovak forces. Despite a few incidental flaws, it conveys surging excitement from first to last, helped by a rich recording which gives a thrilling impression of massed forces. The final *Te Deum*, alone lasting 72 minutes, brings fervent choral writing of formidable complexity, with the challenge superbly taken up by the Czech musicians.

Symphony No. 3 in C sharp min.
**(*) Hyp. Dig. CDA 66334. Ball, Jacobson, BBC SO, Friend.

The *Third Symphony* began life as a concerto for piano; this perhaps explains the prominent role given to two pianos in the score. The work is full of extraordinarily imaginative and original touches, but the overall lack of rhythmic variety is a handicap. The playing of the BBC Symphony Orchestra under Lionel Friend is well prepared and dedicated, but the recording does not open out sufficiently in climaxes.

Symphonies Nos. 7 in C; 31; The Tinker's wedding: comedy overture.
☞ (M) *** EMI CDM7 64717-2 [id.]. RLPO, Mackerras.

In this recording made in association with the Havergal Brian Society, Mackerras and the Royal Liverpool Philharmonic contribute the most valuable record of his music to date. The choice of symphonies from the 32 he completed is a shrewd one, bringing together the last of the expansive works, No. 7, completed in 1948, allying Brian's earlier style with the often elliptical manners of his later, more concentrated work, and the penultimate symphony of the whole series, written just 20 years later, after an amazing eruption of creative activity. The brilliant comedy overture, *The Tinker's wedding*, more conventional in its material and manner if still at times unpredictable, provides an attractive makeweight. Starting with a martial fanfare, the *Seventh Symphony* was inspired not by war but by the city of Strasbourg and its cathedral. The moderately paced second movement also features tolling bells and a fanfare; and it is the third movement, the longest of the four, combining slow movement and Scherzo, which brings weightier argument, before the finale again revolves round the bell sounds and fanfares characteristic of the work. No. 31 in a single movement starts with a jolly idea which, with its jingling, might have Christmas overtones; yet it brings a characteristic example of Brian's later, compressed style, relying on elaborate counterpoint. The unconverted may still have doubts whether Brian's music has quite the cohesion and musical strength it obviously aims at, but this collection presents him and his achievement more effectively than any other disc. Beautifully played and vividly recorded, it can be recommended to anyone fascinated by an extraordinary, offbeat composer.

Symphonies Nos. 10 in C min.; 21 in E flat.
(M) **(*) Unicorn UKCD 2027. Leicestershire Schools SO, Loughran or Pinkett.

Both these *Symphonies* are works of old age; No. 10, a powerfully wrought and original one-movement piece, is the more appealing of the two; No. 21 dates from the composer's late eighties. There need be no serious reservations about the recordings, and the performances are astonishingly accomplished.

Bridge, Frank (1879–1941)

Cherry ripe; Sir Roger de Coverley; Suite for strings; There is a willow grows aslant a brook.
☞ **(*) Koch Dig. 3-7139-2 [id.]. New Zealand CO, Nicholas Braithwaite – DELIUS: *Sonata for strings.* **(*)

A nicely played, pastel-shaded performance of Bridge's *Suite for string orchestra*, with the delicacy of feeling in the lovely, ethereal *Nocturne* making amends for any lack of robustness elsewhere. The folksong arrangements are also attractively done and, if Britten's old ECO recording of *Sir Roger de Coverley* was even wittier, the poignant 'impression' (the composer's own term), *There is a willow grows aslant a brook*, is beautifully played. The modern digital recording is both fresh and transparent.

Enter spring (rhapsody); (i) *Oration (Concerto elegiaco).*
*** Pearl SHECD 9601 [id.]. (i) Baillie; Cologne RSO, Carewe.

Oration (Concerto elegiaco) for cello and orchestra.
(M) *** EMI Dig. CDM7 63909-2. Isserlis, City of L. Sinfonia, Hickox – BRITTEN: *Symphony for cello and orchestra.* ***

Oration is in effect a massive cello concerto in nine linked sections. Though Isserlis is not always as passionate as Baillie, his focus is sharper, and with Hickox he brings out the originality of the writing all the more cleanly. It is fascinating to find some passages anticipating the more abrasive side of Britten, and specifically the *Cello symphony* with which this is coupled.

Alexander Baillie is certainly an eloquent advocate, at times wearing his heart unashamedly on his sleeve, at others more thoughtfully reticent. John Carewe matches his rhapsodic approach and secures wholly idiomatic playing from the fine Cologne orchestra, both here and in a splendidly fluid account of the expansive tone-poem, *Enter spring*, which is wholly spontaneous and generates considerable power. The studio recording is vivid and wide-ranging.

2 Entr'actes: Rosemary; Canzonetta. Heart's ease. 3 Lyrics for piano: No. 1, Heart's ease (orch. Cornford). *Norse legend;* (i) *Suite for cello and orchestra (Morning song; Elegie; Scherzo),* arr. & orch. Cornford. *Threads* (incidental music); *2 Intermezzi. 3 Vignettes de danse. The turtle's retort (one-step),* orch. Wetherell.
*** Pearl SHECD 9600 [id.]. (i) Lowri Blake; Chelsea Op. Group O, Howard Williams.

Those who enjoy Elgar's lighter music will surely find much to delight them in this diverse and very tuneful collection, even if a number of the items are arrangements by other hands. The Chelsea orchestra are a semi-professional group, but no apologies need be made for their response or their ensemble, and Howard Williams directs with spontaneous warmth and an apt sense of pacing. The recording is first rate, with plenty of colour and ambient warmth.

Phantasm for piano and orchestra.
*** Conifer Dig. CDFC 175; *MCFC 175* [id.]. Kathryn Stott, RPO, Handley – IRELAND: *Piano concerto;* WALTON: *Sinfonia concertante.* ***

Bridge's curiously titled *Phantasm* is a large-scale piano concerto, some 26 minutes long, in a single, massive movement. Kathryn Stott, most sympathetically accompanied by Vernon Handley and the RPO, proves a persuasive, committed interpreter, matching her achievement in the other two works on the disc. Warm, generally well-balanced recording.

The Sea (suite).
*** Chan. Dig. CHAN 8473; *ABTD 1184* [id.]. Ulster O, Handley – BAX: *On the sea-shore;* BRITTEN: *Sea interludes.* ***

The Sea receives a brilliant and deeply sympathetic performance from Handley and the Ulster

Orchestra, recorded with a fullness and vividness to make this a demonstration disc.

Suite for strings.
*** Chan. Dig. CHAN 8390; *ABTD 1112* [id.]. ECO, Garforth – IRELAND: *Downland suite; Holy Boy; Elegiac meditations.* ***
*** Nimbus Dig. NI 5068 [id.]. E. String O, Boughton – BUTTERWORTH: *Banks of green willow; Idylls; Shropshire lad;* PARRY: *Lady Radnor's suite.* ***

Suite for string orchestra; Summer; There is a willow grows aslant a brook.
☞ (M) *** Chan. CHAN 6566 [id.]. Bournemouth Sinf., Norman Del Mar – BANTOCK: *Pierrot of the minute;* BUTTERWORTH: *Banks of green willow.* ***

Summer is beautifully played by the Bournemouth Sinfonietta under Norman Del Mar. The same images of nature permeate the miniature tone-poem, *There is a willow grows aslant a brook*, an inspired piece, very sensitively managed. The *Suite for strings* is equally individual. Its third movement, a *Nocturne*, is lovely. The CD transfer is excellent and one can relish its fine definition and presence.

The ECO also play well for David Garforth in the *Suite for strings*. This performance is extremely committed; it is certainly excellently recorded, with great clarity and presence.

The Nimbus collection is more generous and is certainly well chosen. Here Bridge's *Suite* again receives a lively and responsive performance, from William Boughton and his excellent Birmingham-based orchestra, treated to ample, sumptuously atmospheric recording, more resonant than its competitors.

There is a willow grows aslant a brook.
☞ (M) **(*) EMI Dig. CDM7 64200-2 [id.]. ECO, Jeffrey Tate – BAX: *3 Pieces* ***; BUTTERWORTH: *Banks of green willow; Idylls* **(*); MOERAN: *2 Pieces.* ***

Bridge's 'Impression for small orchestra', *There is a willow grows aslant a brook*, is a masterpiece of evocation that yet completely avoids English cliché, bringing many indications of the composer's later development. It makes a welcome item in Tate's English collection, beautifully if not quite magically done in warm and refined sound.

CHAMBER MUSIC

Cello sonata.
*** Chan. Dig. CHAN 8499; *ABTD 1209* [id.]. Raphael and Peter Wallfisch – BAX: *Rhapsodic ballad;* DELIUS: *Sonata;* WALTON: *Passacaglia.* ***

Cello sonata; 2 Pieces: Meditation; Spring song.
**(*) ASV Dig. CDDCA 796 [id.]. Bernard Gregor-Smith, Yolande Wrigley – DEBUSSY; DOHNANYI: *Sonatas.* **(*)

It is a distinctive world that Bridge evokes in the *Cello sonata* and one to which Raphael Wallfisch and his father, Peter, are completely attuned, and they are beautifully recorded.

The ASV account by Bernard Gregor-Smith and Yolande Wrigley can hold its head high. It is played with intensity and sensitivity. The recording is a bit close, but those wanting the coupling (and the Dohnányi is an excellent piece) need not hesitate.

3 Idylls for string quartet.
*** Conifer Dig. CDCF 196. Brindisi Qt – BRITTEN: *String quartet No. 2;* Imogen HOLST: *String quartet No. 1.* ***

The *Three Idylls* are currently unrepresented in the catalogue except by this CD, and are well served by the Brindisi Quartet.

(i) *Phantasy (quartet) in F sharp min. Phantasy trio in C min.; Piano trio No. 2.*
*** Hyp. Dig. CDA 66279 [id.]. Dartington Trio; (i) with P. Ireland.

Piano trio No. 2.
(*) Chan. Dig. CHAN 8495; *ABTD 1205* [id.]. Borodin Trio – BAX: *Piano trio.* *

The playing of the *Phantasy trio* by the Dartington Trio is of exceptional eloquence and sensitivity. They are no less persuasive in the *F sharp minor Phantasy*. Their account of the visionary post-war *Piano trio No. 2* of 1929 is completely inside this score. The Hyperion recording is altogether superb, in the demonstration bracket, perfectly natural and beautifully proportioned.

The playing of the Borodin Trio is also very distinguished, if not quite as compelling as that by the Dartington group on Hyperion.

Phantasy trio in C min.
*** Gamut Dig. GAMCD 518 [id.]. Hartley Trio – CLARKE: *Piano trio;* IRELAND: *Phantasie.* ***

Bridge's *Phantasy trio*, just over 15 minutes long, is an urgent and passionate piece which richly deserves this revival, along with trios by other pupils of Stanford. Warmly persuasive playing, well recorded.

String quartet No. 3.
*** Virgin/EMI Dig. VC7 91196-2 [id.]. Endellion Qt – WALTON: *String quartet.* ***

Like the *Piano sonata*, this was a work profoundly influenced by the composer's response to the First World War and the deaths of many friends. Often bald in expression, bitter and abrasive, the three large-scale movements no longer seem disturbing in their idiom, though they are still disturbing in their emotions. The Endellion Quartet, one of our very finest, plays with polish, purpose and passion, and is very well recorded. This CD is currently withdrawn, awaiting reissue.

PIANO MUSIC

Arabesque; Capriccios Nos. 1–2; Dedication; Fairy tale suite; Gargoyle; Hidden fires; In autumn; 3 Miniatures; Pastorals, Sets 1–2; Sea idyll; 3 Improvisations for the left hand; Winter pastoral.
*** Continuum Dig. CCD 1016 [id.]. Peter Jacobs.

Berceuse; Canzonetta; 4 Characteristic pieces; Dramatic fantasia; Etude rhapsodic; Lament; Pensées fugitives; 3 Pieces; 4 Pieces; 3 Poems; Scherzettino.
*** Continuum Dig. CCD 1018 [id.]. Peter Jacobs.

Piano sonata; Graziella; The Hour-glass; 3 Lyrics; Miniature pastorals, Set 3; Miniature suite (ed. Hindmarsh); *3 Sketches.* arr. of BACH: *Chorale: Komm, süsser Tod, BWV 478.*
*** Continuum Dig. CCD 1019 [id.]. Peter Jacobs.

Peter Jacobs provides a complete survey of the piano music of Frank Bridge, and it proves an invaluable enterprise. The recorded sound is very good indeed: clean, well defined and present, and the acoustic lively. Calum MacDonald's excellent notes tracing his development over these years are worth a mention too.

Piano sonata; Capriccios Nos. 1 & 2; Ecstasy; The Hour-glass; Sea Idyll; Vignettes de Marseille.
*** Conifer Dig. CDCF 186 [id.]. Kathryn Stott.

Kathryn Stott provides a formidable and illuminating single-disc and -tape selection from the piano music of Frank Bridge, for those who are unable or unwilling to stretch to Peter Jacobs's indispensable complete survey. Kathryn Stott's recital culminates in the masterly large-scale *Sonata* that Bridge wrote in disillusion in the years after the First World War, and she gives it a powerfully concentrated account. It is arguably the greatest piano sonata ever written by a British composer. The short early pieces, brilliantly and imaginatively written, give little inkling of such a development. Kathryn Stott is responsive to every changing mood, and these are outstanding performances, very well recorded.

Bristow, George Frederick (1825–98)

Symphony in F sharp min., Op. 26.
☞ *** Chan. Dig. CHAN 9169 [id.]. Detroit SO, Järvi – BARBER: *Symphony No. 2.* ***

George Frederick Bristow was an American composer and educator, a slightly older contemporary of John Knowles Paine; for some years he was a violinist in the New York Philharmonic. Although he was a vigorous campaigner for American music, there is little distinctively American in his *Symphony in F sharp minor* (1858). Its speech is rather Mendelssohnian and, although it serves to fill in our picture of American music of the period, its claims to mastery are slim.

Britten, Benjamin (1913–76)

Clarinet concerto movement (orch. Colin Matthews).
☞ *** Hyp. Dig. CDA 66634 [id.]. Thea King, ECO, Wordsworth – ARNOLD: *Clarinet concertos* etc.; MACONCHY: *Concertinos.* ***

Benny Goodman, having commissioned Bartók to write *Contrasts*, turned in 1942 to the young

Benjamin Britten, then in the United States, to write a concerto for him. Sadly, just before Britten returned to England, Goodman suggested a delay, and the composer never even sorted out the sketches. Colin Matthews, who worked closely with Britten during his last three years, has here fathomed what Britten intended and has orchestrated the result to make a highly attractive short piece, alternately energetic and poetic, with material adroitly interchanged and with percussion used most imaginatively. Thea King, as in the rest of the disc, plays the piece most persuasively, making one regret deeply that it was never completed.

Piano concerto, Op. 13.
☞ (M) **(*) Chan. CHAN 6580 [id.]. Gillian Lin, Melbourne SO, John Hopkins – COPLAND: *Concerto.* **(*)

Gillian Lin provides a useful alternative to Richter's classic recording. Miss Lin cannot match the Soviet master in detailed imagination but, from her sharp attack on the opening motif onwards, she gives a strong and satisfying reading, well accompanied by Hopkins and the Melbourne orchestra. The 1978 recorded sound is wide-ranging and well balanced on this lively CD, which makes a useful mid-priced alternative, with its rarer Copland coupling.

(i) *Piano concerto in D, Op. 13. Paul Bunyan overture.*
*** Collins Dig. 1102-2 [id.]. (i) Joanna MacGregor; ECO, Bedford – SAXTON: *Music to celebrate the resurrection of Christ.* ***

Britten wrote his formidable *Piano concerto* for a Prom in 1938. He later rejected the slow movement and replaced it in 1945 with an *Impromptu*, simpler and more obviously apt. The characterful young Joanna MacGregor gets the best of both worlds by recording both slow movements, so that you can take your pick. With Steuart Bedford a deeply understanding conductor, this is a ripe and refreshing performance, well recorded. The brassy *Paul Bunyan overture*, never used with the operetta, has been orchestrated by Colin Matthews.

(i) *Piano concerto, Op. 13;* (ii) *Violin concerto, Op. 15.*
(M) *** Decca 417 308-2. (i) Sviatoslav Richter; (ii) Lubotsky; ECO, composer.
*** Collins Dig. 1301-2 [id.]. (i) Joanna MacGregor; (ii) Lorraine McAslan; ECO, Bedford.

Richter is incomparable in interpreting the *Piano concerto*, not only the thoughtful, introspective moments but the Liszt-like bravura passages. With its highly original sonorities the *Violin concerto* makes a splendid vehicle for another Soviet artist, Mark Lubotsky. Recorded in The Maltings, the playing of the ECO under the composer's direction matches the inspiration of the soloists.

This apt recoupling of Britten's two concertos in these outstanding Collins recordings makes an attractive disc, though the original slow movement of the *Piano concerto* has here been omitted.

Violin concerto, Op. 15.
☞ (M) *** EMI CDM7 64202-2 [id.]. Ida Haendel, Bournemouth SO, Berglund – WALTON: *Violin concerto.* ***

Ida Haendel's ravishing playing places the work firmly in the European tradition. She brings great panache and brilliance to the music, as well as great expressive warmth. This is a reading very much in the grand manner and it finds Paavo Berglund in excellent form. His support is sensitive in matters of detail and full of atmosphere. The recording is full and realistic, with a beautifully spacious perspective that creates a positively Mediterranean feeling. The soloist is balanced a little close, but the security of her technique can stand up to such a spotlight and the performance has great conviction.

(i) *Violin concerto, Op. 15. Canadian carnival overture, Op. 19; Mont Juic* (written with Lennox Berkeley).
⊛ *** Collins Dig. 1123-2 [id.]. (i) Lorraine McAslan, ECO, Steuart Bedford.

Lorraine McAslan's virtuosity is effortless and always subservient to musical ends; her artistic insights are unusually keen and she brings to the *Concerto* a subtle imagination and great emotional intensity. Steuart Bedford gets first-class playing from the English Chamber Orchestra and emphasizes the pain and poignancy underlying much of this music. The recording is remarkably well balanced, truthful and exceptionally wide-ranging and vivid. *Mont Juic* and the *Canadian carnival overture* are eminently well served by these splendid musicians and the engineers.

Diversions for piano (left hand) and orchestra.
☞ *** Sony Dig. SK 47188 [id.]. Fleisher, Boston SO, Ozawa – PROKOFIEV: *Piano concerto No. 4;* RAVEL: *Left-hand concerto.* ***

Leon Fleisher lost the use of his right hand at the height of his career and is currently engaged on an ambitious project with Sony to record repertoire for the left hand. The present issue assembles three of the most brilliant and rewarding pieces for the medium, all commissioned by Paul Wittgenstein, brother of the philosopher, who lost his right hand during the First World War. The *Diversions* is a wartime work, highly inventive and resourceful, whose neglect over the years is puzzling. Julius Katchen recorded it twice for Decca in the 1950s, since when it has been given scant attention. Fleisher gives a sensitive and intelligent account with great sympathy and skill. His playing has strong character and he receives more than decent support from Ozawa and the Boston orchestra and eminently truthful recording.

(i) *Diversions for piano (left hand) and orchestra, Op. 21;* (ii) *Sinfonia da Requiem, Op. 20;* (iii) *Young person's guide to the orchestra, Op. 34.*
☞ (M) **(*) Sony Dig./Analogue SMK 58930 [id.]. (i) Leon Fleisher, Boston SO, Ozawa; (ii) St Louis SO, Previn; (iii) LSO, Andrew Davis.

Britten's *Diversions for piano and orchestra,* written in 1940 for Paul Wittgenstein, is the most underrated of his concertante works. This recording is also available differently coupled – see above. Leon Fleisher, a superb soloist, fully realizes its delicacy, wit and robust bravura, and Ozawa accompanies perceptively. With the piano well defined by the excellent digital recording, the atmospheric Boston acoustic adds a pleasing glow to highly spontaneous music-making. The St Louis orchestra plays with great spirit in the *Sinfonia da Requiem* and Previn's performance is obviously deeply felt. If it is not quite a match for the composer's own, it has a well-detailed (1963) recording. To complete the disc, Andrew Davis directs an account of the *Young person's guide* that is bright and workmanlike, rather than one with any special flair or brilliance. But it is enjoyable enough, and the (1975) Abbey Road recording sounds well on CD. Good documentation.

(i) *Lachrymae (Reflections on a song by John Dowland), Op. 48a; Prelude and fugue for 18-part string orchestra, Op. 29; Simple Symphony, Op. 4.* PURCELL, arr. Britten: *Chacony in G min.*
**(*) Virgin/EMI Dig. VCy7 91080-2 [id.]. (i) Roger Chase; LCO, Christopher Warren-Green.

The sheer energy of the opening movement of the *Simple Symphony* is breathtaking; this is surely too fast, even for a *Boisterous bourrée,* but with bold articulation the effect is certainly exhilarating. The *Sentimental saraband,* by contrast, is very relaxed and winningly nostalgic; the incandescent energy returns in the finale. The players of the LCO obviously enjoy themselves in Britten's arrangement of the great Purcell *Chaconne,* expanded from its sparer original version into a grand – even sumptuous – affair for a full string orchestra. This CD is withdrawn and awaits reissue on Virgin's mid-price Ultraviolet label.

Matinées musicales; Soirées musicales; Variations on a theme of Frank Bridge.
☞ (B) *** CfP Dig. CD-CFP 4598. ECO, Gibson.

The ECO play very well indeed for Sir Alexander Gibson, and readers requiring this particular coupling need not hesitate on either artistic or technical grounds. Both the *Matinées musicales* and the *Soirées* – witty arrangements of Rossini that originated as film music and later became ballets – are comparative rarities in the concert hall, and their charm and high spirits are splendidly conveyed here. The *Frank Bridge variations* display strong characterization and virtuosity in equal measure. The recording is full and resonant; only the bright lighting of the violin-timbre above the stave betrays the early date of the digital recording (1982).

(i) *Matinées musicales; Soirées musicales;* (ii; iv) *Young person's guide to the orchestra;* (iii; iv) *Peter Grimes: 4 Sea interludes and Passacaglia.*
(M) *** Decca 425 659-2 [id.]. (i) Nat. PO, Bonynge; (ii) LSO; (iii) ROHCG O; (iv) composer.

Britten wrote his *Soirées musicales* for a GPO film-score in the 1930s; the *Matinées* followed in 1941 and were intended as straight ballet music. Bonynge's versions are brightly played and extremely vividly recorded in the best Decca manner. They are now reissued at mid-price, coupled with Britten's accounts of the *Young person's guide to the orchestra* and the *Sea interludes and Passacaglia.*

Prelude and fugue for 18 solo strings, Op. 29; Simple Symphony, Op. 4; Variations on a theme of Frank Bridge, Op. 10.
*** ASV Dig. CDDCA 591 [id.]. N. Sinfonia, Hickox.
☞ (M) **(*) Chan. CHAN 6592 [id.]. Bournemouth Sinf., Ronald Thomas.

The ASV issue is notable for an outstandingly fine account of the *Frank Bridge variations,* which stands up well alongside the composer's own version. Throughout, the string playing is committedly responsive, combining polish with eloquence, the rich sonorities resonating powerfully in the glowing ambience of All Saints' Quayside Church, Newcastle.

Though comparisons with Britten's own recordings of these three string works inevitably reveal felicities that are missing here, the Chandos coupling is most attractive, the performances have a natural expressive warmth which is most engaging and, not least, the recording has a ripeness and resonance which are most satisfying, particularly in the bass registers, especially telling in the *Variations* in their CD format.

The Prince of the Pagodas (complete).
🔊 *** Virgin/EMI Dig. VCD7 59578-2 (2) [id.]. L. Sinf., Knussen.

The multicoloured instrumentation – much influenced by Britten's visit to Bali – is caught with glorious richness in Oliver Knussen's really complete version. Most importantly he opens out more than 40 cuts, most of them small, which Britten sanctioned to fit his own recording on to four LP sides. The performance is outstanding and so is the recording.

(i) *The Prince of the Pagodas* (ballet), *Op. 57* (complete); (ii) *Diversions for piano (left hand) and orchestra, Op. 21.*
**(*) Decca 421 855-2 (2) [id.]. (i) ROHCG O; (ii) Julius Katchen, LSO, composer.

The composer's own recording was originally made after the first performances at Covent Garden, early in 1957, with Britten drawing playing of electric intensity and knife-edged precision from the orchestra. With Julius Katchen as soloist in the distinctive left-hand piano part, Britten conducts the LSO in an equally inspired account of the *Diversions*. This is in mono, and the quality is inevitably flatter than in the complete ballet.

Simple Symphony (for strings), Op. 4.
*** DG Dig. 423 624-2 [id.]. Orpheus CO – BIZET: *Symphony;* PROKOFIEV: *Symphony No. 1.* ***

Simple Symphony, Op. 4; Variations on a theme of Frank Bridge, Op. 10.
☞ (M) (***) Dutton mono CDAX 8007 [id.]. Boyd Neel O, Neel – VAUGHAN WILLIAMS: *Concerto accademico* etc. (***)

(i) *Simple Symphony, Op. 4; Variations on a theme of Frank Bridge, Op. 10;* (ii) *The Young person's guide to the orchestra (Variations and fugue on a theme of Purcell), Op. 34.*
☞ (M) *** Decca 440 321-2 [id.]. (i) ECO; (ii) LSO, composer (with DELIUS: (i) *2 Aquarelles;* BRIDGE: *Sir Roger de Coverley for string orchestra* ***).

Britten's three most famous orchestral works now return in Decca's series of 'British Classics', generously supplemented with warmly atmospheric accounts of the two Delius *Aquarelles* and a refreshingly lively performance of Bridge's *Sir Roger de Coverley*, which wittily interpolates *Auld lang syne*. The three Britten works are very brightly transferred with very tangible strings and great clarity and presence overall; some ears, however, might decide that the violins are too brightly lit. Britten takes a very brisk view of his *Young person's guide*, so brisk that even the LSO players cannot always quite match him. But every bar has a vigour which makes the music sound more youthful than usual, and the headlong, uninhibited account of the final fugue (trombones as vulgar as you like) is an absolute joy. In the *Frank Bridge variations* Britten goes more for half-tones and he achieves an almost circumspect coolness in the waltz-parody of the *Romance;* in the *Viennese waltz* section later, he is again subtly atmospheric; and in the *Funeral march* he is relatively solemn. The *Simple Symphony* makes a splendid foil, with its charm and high spirits; no one else has found quite the infectious bounce in the *Playful pizzicato* that the composer does, aided by the glowing resonance of The Maltings where the recording was made.

The *Simple Symphony* goes nicely alongside the Bizet and Prokofiev works, especially when played as freshly and characterfully as here by the Orpheus group. Britten himself found more fun in the *Playful pizzicato*, but the reading is all-of-a-piece and enjoyably spontaneous. Excellent, realistic sound.

The Boyd Neel String Orchestra was formed in the early 1930s and soon established itself as the premier ensemble of its kind in England. In 1937 they commissioned the 23-year-old Benjamin Britten to write a new work for them to take to that year's Salzburg Festival; the *Variations on a theme of Frank Bridge* was the result. They recorded it on three gold-label Decca 78s the following year and, although Britten's own Decca performance remains indispensable, there is something very special about this pioneering recording. The playing is full of imaginative touches and there is a poetic intensity that brings this music vividly to life. Michael Dutton has done a splendid job in restoring these discs, and those who are acquainted with or possess the originals will be astonished at his results. The same applies to the *Simple Symphony*, which the same artists recorded some months later.

Sinfonietta, Op. 1; Sinfonia da Requiem, Op. 20.
☞ ** Capriccio Dig. 10428 [id.]. Stuttgart RSO, Marriner – HONEGGER: *Symphony No. 3.* *(*)

The *Sinfonietta* is well played and recorded, and so for that matter is the *Sinfonia da Requiem*. The Stuttgart Radio Orchestra play well, though their strings are wanting in the opulence that rival orchestras possess. All the same, there is nothing really special about Marriner's reading.

Sinfonia da Requiem, Op. 20.
☞ (M) *** EMI Dig. CDM7 64870-2 [id.]. CBSO, Simon Rattle – SHOSTAKOVICH: *Symphony No. 10.* **

Rattle's passionate view of the *Sinfonia da Requiem* is unashamedly extrovert, yet it finds subtle detail too. The EMI recording is admirably vivid and clear, but the Shostakovich coupling is less convincing.

(i) *Sinfonia da Requiem, Op. 20;* (ii) *Symphony for cello and orchestra, Op. 68;* (iii) *Cantata misericordium, Op. 69.*
(M) *** Decca 425 100-2 [id.]. (i) New Philh. O; (ii) Rostropovich, ECO; (iii) Pears, Fischer-Dieskau, London Symphony Ch., LSO; composer.

All the performances here are definitive, and Rostropovich's account of the *Cello symphony* in particular is everything one could ask for. The CD transfers are admirably managed.

Sinfonia da Requiem, Op. 20; The Young person's guide to the orchestra, Op. 34; Peter Grimes: 4 Sea interludes & Passacaglia, Op. 34.
**(*) Virgin/EMI Dig. VC7 59950-2 [id.]. RLPO, Libor Pešek.

Though Pešek fails to convey the full ominous weight of the first movement of the *Sinfonia da Requiem*, he then directs a dazzling account of the central *Dies Irae scherzo*, taken breathtakingly fast, and finds an intense repose in the calm of the final *Requiem aeternam*. The *Sea interludes* sound very literal, not ideally atmospheric. The *Young person's guide* lacks a degree of tension, with the fugue not dashing enough. The recording is comfortably reverberant.

Suite on English folksongs (A time there was); Young person's guide to the orchestra, Op. 34; Peter Grimes: 4 Sea interludes and Passacaglia.
(M) **(*) Sony SMK 47541. NYPO, Leonard Bernstein.

Bernstein's charismatic account of the *Young person's guide to the orchestra* brings much exhilarating bravura from the New York soloists, notably the flutes, clarinets and trumpets. The 1961 recording, made in the New York Manhattan Center, is fuller than usual from this source. The performance of *A time there was* (its title quoting Hardy) reveals a darkness and weight of expression behind the seemingly trivial plan. For violins alone, *Hunt the squirrel* is brief, brilliant and witty. Bernstein misses a little of the wit but is warmly sympathetic, and the dramatic account of the *Grimes interludes*, with a powerful *Passacaglia*, makes a good coupling.

Symphony for cello and orchestra, Op. 68.
☞ (M) *** Sony Dig. SMK 58928 [id.]. Yo-Yo Ma, Baltimore SO, David Zinman – MAXWELL DAVIES: *Violin concerto.* ***
(M) *** EMI Dig. CDM7 63909-2. Stephen Isserlis, City of L. Sinfonia, Hickox – BRIDGE: *Oration.* ***

☞ **(*) Russian Disc RDCD 11108 [id.]. Rostropovich, Moscow PO, composer – SAUGUET: *Mélodie concertante.* ***

(i) *Symphony for cello and orchestra, Op. 68. Death in Venice: suite, Op. 88* (arr. Bedford).
*** Chan. Dig. CHAN 8363; ABTD 1126 [id.]. (i) Wallfisch; ECO, Bedford.

Sounding less improvisatory than Rostropovich, Wallfisch and Bedford give a more consistent sense of purpose, and the weight and range of the brilliant and full Chandos recording quality add to the impact, with Bedford's direction even more spacious than the composer's. Steuart Bedford's encapsulation of Britten's last opera into this rich and colourful suite makes a splendid coupling.

Yo-Yo Ma, in partnership with David Zinman, gives a superb performance of the Britten *Cello symphony*. What predominates is the wayward mystery in the first movement, rather than its more aggressive qualities, and in the Scherzo Ma is masterly in bringing out the lightness and fantasy. The third-movement *Adagio* is softer-grained than usual, with the soloist placed naturally, leading on to an account of the finale, a shade faster than usual, compellingly purposeful, which brings out the Copland-like swagger of the main passacaglia theme. The orchestra plays with brilliance and commitment in a full and well-balanced recording.

Stephen Isserlis provides a valuable mid-priced alternative to Wallfisch and Ma. With speeds generally a little slower, Isserlis is not quite as taut and electric as his rival, partly because the recording does not present the solo instrument so cleanly.

The special interest of the Russian Disc issue resides in the fact that it includes a recording of the very first performance of the *Cello Symphony* on 12 March 1964, given by its dedicatee and 'onlie begetter' with Britten himself conducting. It is not as well recorded as the version Rostropovich and Britten made for Decca not long afterwards, but there is terrific intensity and concentration here. The value of this issue is enhanced by the coupling, Sauguet's *Mélodie concertante*, also written for Rostropovich – a beautiful and thoughtful concerto that deserves to be a repertory piece.

The Young person's guide to the orchestra (Variations and fugue on a theme of Purcell), Op. 34.
(M) *** EMI Dig. CD-EMX 2165; *TC-EMX 2165* (without narration). LPO, Sian Edwards –
PROKOFIEV: *Peter and the wolf* **(*); RAVEL: *Ma Mère l'Oye.* **
☞ (M) ** EMI Dig. CDM7 64300-2 [id.]. Minnesota SO, Marriner (with PURCELL: *Abdelazar:
Rondeau:* Taverner Players, Parrott ***) – HOLST: *The Planets.* **

Sian Edwards does not press the earlier variations too hard, revelling in the colour of her wind soloists, yet the violins enter zestfully and the violas make a touching contrast. The brass bring fine bite and sonority. The fugue has plenty of vitality and the climax is spectacularly expansive in the resonant acoustics of Watford Town Hall.

Marriner's Minnesota account of the *Young person's guide* is well played but a little stiff. It has the advantage of being introduced by an authentic performance of Purcell's tune (from *Abdelazar*) on which the variations are based, from Andrew Parrott and his Taverner Players.

CHAMBER MUSIC

Alla marcia; 3 Divertimenti for string quartet; 2 Insect pieces; Phantasy oboe quartet, Op. 2; Phantasy in F min. for string quintet; Temporal variations for oboe and piano.
☞ (M) *** Unicorn Dig. UKCD 2060 [id.]. Derek Wickens, John Constable, Augmented Gabrieli Qt.

Derek Wickens, formerly principal oboe of the RPO and a consummate artist, is heard at his finest in this rewarding recital, recorded with exceptional naturalness in St Giles', Cripplegate, in 1982. Here his contributions to the *Phantasy oboe quartet* (with its passages of seeming improvisation) as well as to the two rediscovered works, the *Temporal variations* and the evocatively etched *Insect pieces*, are incisive and poised, with a most effectively restrained, lyrical feeling. The Gabrieli Quartet too play with a degree of restraint which works especially well in the two works for strings. The *Phantasy in F minor* won the Cobbett Prize in 1932 for its teenage composer. It is a finely wrought piece but not as striking as the *Phantasy oboe quartet* in its material. This ends the recital quite memorably, but there is striking material in plenty in the *Alla marcia* of 1933 and the three string *Divertimenti* of 1936, with ideas in both pointing forward to the song cycle, *Les Illuminations.* A rewarding reissue on all counts.

Cello sonata, Op. 65.
**(*) Sony Dig. MK 44980 [id.]. Yo-Yo Ma, Emanuel Ax – R. STRAUSS: *Sonata.* **(*)

Yo-Yo Ma and Emanuel Ax give an account of the *Cello sonata* which is very carefully thought out, with exaggerated pianissimi and self-conscious phrasing. The recording is very truthful.

(i) *Cello sonata in C, Op. 65;* (Unaccompanied) *Cello suites Nos. 1, Op. 72; 2, Op. 80.*
(M) *** Decca 421 859-2 [id.]. Rostropovich; (i) with composer.

This strange five-movement *Cello sonata* is coupled with two of the *Suites for unaccompanied cello.* This is rough, gritty music in Britten's latterday manner, but Rostropovich gives such inspired accounts that the music reveals more and more with repetition.

Cello suites (Suites for unaccompanied cello) Nos. 1, Op. 72; 2, Op. 80; 3, Op. 87.
*** BIS Dig. CD 446 [id.]. Torleif Thedéen.

Torleif Thedéen has magnificent tonal warmth and eloquence, and he proves a masterly advocate of these *Suites*, which sound thoroughly convincing in his hands.

Cello suite No. 3.
*** Virgin/EMI Dig. VC7 59052-2 [id.]. Steven Isserlis – TAVENER: *The Protecting veil.* ***

Steven Isserlis brings out the spiritual element in a work which draws on traditional Russian themes, including Orthodox church music, and such a performance relates well to the Tavener work with which it is coupled.

Lachrymae, Op. 48.
*** EMI Dig. CDC7 54394-2 [id.]. Tabea Zimmermann, Hartmut Höll – SHOSTAKOVICH: *Viola sonata;* STRAVINSKY: *Elégie.* ***

Tabea Zimmermann gives the moving *Lachrymae* ('Reflections on a song of John Dowland') with an altogether exemplary eloquence and is recorded with great naturalness and presence.

(i) *Sinfonietta, Op. 1;* (ii) *String quartets Nos. 2, Op. 36; 3, Op. 94.*
(M) *** Decca 425 715-2. (i) Vienna Octet; (ii) Amadeus Qt.

Britten's Opus 1 was written when he was in his teens. Its mixture of seriousness and assurance is not unappealing and its astringency is brought out well in this appropriately Viennese chamber perform-ance. The *Third Quartet*, a late work, was written for the Amadeus, who play it convincingly. The *Second* ends with a forceful *Chaconne*. The contrasts of style and mood are developed well here, in performances that could be regarded as definitive.

String quartet No. 1 in D, Op. 25a.
*** CRD CRD 3351 [id.]. Alberni Qt – SHOSTAKOVICH: *Piano quintet.* **(*)

String quartets Nos. 2 in C, Op. 36; 3, Op. 94.
*** CRD CRD 3395 [id.]. Alberni Qt.

The Alberni Quartet have good ensemble and intonation, and they play with considerable feeling; moreover the CDs are available separately. The recording is vivid and clear.

String quartet No. 2 in C.
☞ *** BMG/RCA Dig. 09026 61387-2 [id.]. Tokyo Qt – BARBER: *Quartet;* TAKEMITSU: *A Way A Lone.* ***
*** Conifer Dig. CDCF 196. Brindisi Qt – BRIDGE: *3 Idylls;* Imogen HOLST: *String quartet No. 1.* ***

In the Britten *Second Quartet*, the Tokyo Quartet are little short of superb. Their sound has consistent beauty and refinement. However, the problem with hybrid records is that those wanting the Britten will probably be tempted to the more logical coupling offered by the Alberni Quartet. However, there is no doubt that the Tokyo give a remarkable performance, arguably the best now available; and no one wanting the coupling should hesitate. The recording is as superb as the playing.

The Brindisi on Conifer give an excellent account of the *Second Quartet* which can hold its own with the best and comes with interesting couplings.

String quartet No. 3, Op. 94.
*** ASV Dig. CDDCA 608 [id.]. Lindsay Qt – TIPPETT: *Quartet No. 4.* ***

The Lindsay performance brings the most expansive and deeply expressive reading on record. The ASV recording is vivid, with fine presence; but extraneous sounds are intrusive at times: heavy breathing, snapping of strings on finger-board, etc.

(i) *Suite for harp, Op. 83;* (ii) *2 Insect pieces, for oboe & piano; 6 Metamorphoses after Ovid (for oboe solo), Op. 49.*
*** Mer. CDE 84119 [id.]. (i) Osian Ellis; (ii) Sarah Watkins; Ledger – *Tit for Tat* etc. ***.

It was for Osian Ellis that Britten wrote the *Harp suite*, and Ellis remains the ideal performer. Sarah Watkins gives biting and intense performances of the unaccompanied *Metamorphoses*, as well as the two early *Insect pieces*, with Philip Ledger. The sound is full and immediate, set convincingly in a small but helpful hall.

PIANO MUSIC

Music for 2 pianos: (i) *2 Lullabies; Mazurca elegiaca; Introduction and Rondo alla burlesca.* (Piano): *3 Character Pieces; Holiday Diary; Notturno; Sonatina romantica; 12 Variations; Five Waltzes.*
*** Virgin/EMI Dig. VC7 91203-2 [id.]. Stephen Hough, (i) with Ronan O'Hora.

Britten wrote relatively little piano music. Stephen Hough, an inspired interpreter, generously collects it all, including early pieces revived since the composer's death. Hough's love of keyboard sonorities masterfully overcomes the awkwardness of the writing. He is joined by a most sympathetic partner for the items for two pianos. Excellent sound.

VOCAL MUSIC

Advance democracy; Antiphon; The ballad of Little Musgrave and Lady Barnard; Rejoice in the Lamb;
Sacred and profane; The Sycamore tree; Te Deum; A Wedding anthem.
☞ *** Collins Dig. 1343-2 [id.]. The Sixteen, Harry Christophers.

The two main works of this third of Christophers' Britten series represent two very different periods:
the delightful cantata to words by Christopher Smart, *Rejoice in the Lamb*, dating from 1943, and
Sacred and profane, setting medieval lyrics, his last work for unaccompanied voices. Among the rest
are celebratory works like the *Te Deum* and the *Wedding anthem* for Lord Harewood and Marion
Stein. Even the anthem, *Advance democracy*, written during Britten's actively left-wing phase before
the war, transcends Randall Swingler's propagandist words in its musical imagination. Bright, clear
singing from The Sixteen with their boyish-sounding sopranos.

Blues: *Blues; Boogie-Woogie; The Clock on the wall; The Spider and the fly;* Cabaret songs (to words
of W. H. Auden): *As it is, plenty; Calypso; Funeral blues; O tell me the truth about love; Johnny;*
When you're feeling like expressing your affection.
☞ *** Unicorn Dig. DKPCD 9138 [id.]. Jill Gomez, Martin Jones, Instrumental Ens. – PORTER:
Songs. **(*)

As in her earlier recording of Schoenberg's *Brettl-lieder*, Jill Gomez finds a winning compromise
between art-song and cabaret proper. Surprisingly, Britten tends to override W. H. Auden's clear
rhythmic indications in the poems, but these are all fun-pieces, and as a bonus Jill Gomez includes the
jazzy song, *As it is, plenty*, from the cycle, *On this Island*. The accompanist, Martin Jones, is far less
helpful and more deadpan in five classic Cole Porter songs which Jill Gomez also sings. To fill the
disc, an instrumental ensemble plays Daryl Runswick's inventive arrangements of four blues numbers
by Britten, drawn from the operetta *Paul Bunyan* as well as his early incidental music for plays.

(i) *A Boy was born;* (ii) *A Ceremony of carols;* (iii) *Psalm 150; Songs from Friday afternoons.*
☞ (M) **(*) Decca stereo/mono 436 394-2 [id.]. (i) Hartnett, Purcell Singers, Boys' voices of English
Op. Group, All Saint's Ch., Margaret St; (ii) Copenhagen Boys Ch.; (iii) Downside School,
Purley; all cond. composer.

For this reissue, *A Boy was born* is presented in good, early (1957) stereo, but the *Ceremony of carols*
is mono, the composer's first LP recording dating from 1953. No complaints whatsoever about the
sound, which is both clear and atmospheric. The performance is lyrical rather than biting and not
ideally polished, but the natural enthusiasm of the singing comes over well, especially in the *Deo
gratias*, and the slight Danish accent of the singers adds a charm of its own. *A Boy was born* was
written just before Britten was twenty, but there is little hint of immaturity, and both performance
and recording are excellent. The remaining two works were recorded much later (in 1966), designed as
what the composer called a 'School concert', and the original LP also included the *Gemini variations*.
In both performances the uninhibited joy of the young artists involved suggests a school concert from
Elysium. The *Friday afternoons songs* were written for a school where Britten's brother was head-
master; the *Psalm 150* setting was done for the centenary of the composer's own former preparatory
school in Suffolk (the makeshift arrangements for the first performance involved a mouth-organ
substituting for the trumpet). The CD transfers convey the realism of the original sound-balance.

A Boy was born; 5 Flower songs; Hymn to St Cecilia; Gloriana: Choral dances.
☞ *** Collins Dig. 1286-2 [id.]. The Sixteen, Harry Christophers.

This first of Harry Christophers' Britten series for Collins sets the fine pattern for the following
issues, starting with the early cantata, *A Boy was born*, and including the brilliant Auden setting,
Hymn to St Cecilia, and the choral dances taken from the opera, *Gloriana*. Bright, fresh soprano tone,
atmospherically recorded, puts these among the finest versions of these works; if this particular
grouping is wanted, this is very recommendable.

A Boy was born, Op. 3; Festival Te Deum, Op. 32; Rejoice in the Lamb, Op. 30; A Wedding anthem,
Op. 46.
*** Hyp. CDA 66126 [id.]. Corydon Singers, Westminster Cathedral Ch., Best; Trotter (organ).

All the works included here are sharply inspired. The refinement and tonal range of the choirs could
hardly be more impressive, and the recording is refined and atmospheric to match.

The Burning fiery furnace (2nd Parable), Op. 77.

(M) *** Decca 414 663-2. Pears, Tear, Drake, Shirley-Quirk, Ch. & O of E. Op. Group, composer
and Viola Tunnard.

The story of *Burning fiery furnace* is obviously dramatic in the operatic sense, with vivid scenes like
the *Entrance of Nebuchadnezzar*, the *Raising of the Idol*, and the putting of the three Israelites into the
furnace. The performers, both singers and players, are the same hand-picked cast that participated in
the first performance at Orford Parish Church, where this record was made.

*Canticles Nos. 1, My beloved is mine, Op. 40; 2, Abraham and Isaac, Op. 51; 3, Still falls the rain, Op.
55; 4, Journey of the Magi, Op. 86; 5, Death of St Narcissus, Op. 89. A birthday hansel.* Arr. of
PURCELL: *Sweeter than roses.*

(M) *** Decca 425 716-2. Peter Pears, Hahessy, Bowman, Shirley-Quirk, Tuckwell, Ellis, composer.

This CD brings together on a single record all five of the miniature cantatas to which Britten gave the
title 'Canticle', plus the *Birthday hansel*, written in honour of the seventy-fifth birthday of Queen
Elizabeth the Queen Mother, and a Purcell song-arrangement. A beautiful collection as well as a
historical document, with recording that still sounds well.

*A Ceremony of carols, Op. 28; Festival Te Deum; Hymn of St Columba; Hymn to St Peter; Hymn to
the Virgin; Jubilate Deo; Missa brevis; Rejoice in the Lamb, Op. 30.*

(M) *** Decca 430 097-2. Tear, Forbes Robinson, St John's College Ch., Guest; Robles; Runnett.

Guest's account of the delightful *Ceremony of carols* has tingling vitality, spacious sound and a
superb contribution from Marisa Robles. The performance of *Rejoice in the Lamb* is very similar to
Britten's own, but much better recorded, and the *Missa brevis* has the same striking excellence of
style. All the shorter pieces show the choir in superb form and the Argo analogue engineering at its
most impressive.

*A Ceremony of carols; Festival Te Deum; Jubilate Deo!; A Hymn of Saint Columba; Hymn to Saint
Peter; Hymn to the Virgin; Missa brevis in D; A New Year carol; A Shepherd's carol; Sweet was the
sound.*

☞ *** Collins Dig. 1370-2 [id.]. The Sixteen, Harry Christophers.

With bright-toned sopranos taking the place of boy trebles, Harry Christophers in his Britten series
for Collins directs superbly incisive, refreshingly dramatic performances of all these works, giving
extra bite even to so well-known a piece as the *Ceremony of carols*. The delightful *Missa brevis*,
written for the boys of Westminster Cathedral, has never been more telling, and the shorter pieces all
confirm Britten's mastery in choral writing, with Christophers terracing the dynamic contrasts with
fine precision. Excellent sound, both warm and well detailed. Highly recommended.

*A Ceremony of carols; Deus in adjutorium meum; Hymn of St Columba; Hymn to the Virgin; Jubilate
Deo in E flat; Missa brevis, Op. 63.*

*** Hyp. Dig. CDA 66220 [id.]. Westminster Cathedral Ch., David Hill; (i) with S. Williams;
J. O'Donnell (organ).

Particularly impressive here is the boys' singing in the *Ceremony of carols*, where the ensemble is
superb, the solo work amazingly mature, and the range of tonal colouring a delight. Along with the
other, rarer pieces, this is an outstanding collection, beautifully and atmospherically recorded.

(i) *A Ceremony of carols, Op. 28; Hymn to St Cecilia, Op. 27;* (ii) *Jubilate Deo;* (i) *Missa brevis in D,
Op. 63;* (ii) *Rejoice in the Lamb* (Festival cantata), *Op. 30; Te Deum in C.*

☞ (M) *** EMI CDM7 64653-2 [id.]. King's College, Cambridge, Ch.; (i) Osian Ellis, Willcocks; (ii)
James Bowman, Ledger.

There was a time when Britten's insistence on an earthily boyish tone among trebles seemed at the
farthest remove from the King's tradition. But towards the end of Sir David Willcocks' stay at
Cambridge a happy accommodation was achieved not only in appearances of the choir at the
Aldeburgh Festival but also in their fine triptych of recordings from the early 1970s. The King's
trebles may still have less edge in the *Ceremony of carols* than their Cambridge rivals at St John's
College, and the *Missa brevis* can certainly benefit from a throatier sound, but the results here are
dramatic as well as beautiful. To make a generous reissue EMI have added Philip Ledger's 1974
version of the cantata, *Rejoice in the Lamb*, with timpani and percussion added to the original organ
part. Here the biting climaxes are sung with passionate incisiveness, while James Bowman is in his
element in the delightful passage which tells you that 'the mouse is a creature of great personal
valour'. The *Te Deum* setting and *Jubilate* are a bonus and are no less well sung and recorded.

4 Chansons françaises; Les illuminations; Serenade for tenor, horn and strings.
**(*) Chan. Dig. CHAN 8657; *ABTD 1343* [id.]. Felicity Lott, Anthony Rolfe Johnson, Michael Thompson, SNO, Bryden Thomson.

The *Four French songs* were written when Britten was only fourteen. Felicity Lott gives a strong and sensitive performance, as she does of the other early French cycle on the disc, *Les illuminations*, bringing out the tough and biting element rather than the sensuousness. Anthony Rolfe Johnson, soloist in the *Serenade*, gives a finely controlled performance, but Michael Thompson is not as evocative in the horn solo as his most distinguished predecessors have been. Bryden Thomson draws crisp, responsive playing from the SNO.

(i) *Children's crusade;* (ii) *The Little Sweep (Let's make an opera);* (iii) *Gemini variations.*
☞ (M) (***) Decca stereo/mono 436 393-2 [id.]. (i) Hartnett, Purcell Singers, English Op. Group Boys' Ch.; Choristers of All Saints', Margaret St, composer; (ii) Soloists, Wandsworth School Boys' Ch., Burgess; composer (piano); (iii) G. & Z. Jeney.

Britten's own mono recording of *The Little Sweep* sounds amazingly vivid, with voices in particular full and immediate. As a performance it has never been surpassed in its vigour and freshness, with David Hemmings here impressive in the title-role for treble. Others in the cast, like Jennifer Vyvyan and April Cantelo, represent the accomplished group of singers that Britten gathered for his Aldeburgh Festival performances. The choruses, usually sung by the audience, are here done by the school choir. The *Children's crusade*, written for the Save the Children Fund, is darker but equally vivid. The *Gemini variations* (interchanging flute, violin and piano) was written for the Jeney twins, who play it here.

Curlew River (1st parable for church performance).
(M) *** Decca 421 858-2 [id.]. Pears, Shirley-Quirk, Blackburn, soloists, Instrumental Ens., composer and Viola Tunnard.

Curlew River was initially inspired by Britten's recollection of a Noh-play which he saw in Japan. Harold Blackburn plays the Abbot of the monastery who introduces the drama, while John Shirley-Quirk plays the ferryman who takes people over the Curlew River and Peter Pears sings the part of the madwoman who, distracted, searches fruitlessly for her abducted child. The recording is outstanding even by Decca standards.

Folksong arrangements: *The ash grove; Avenging and bright; La belle est au jardin d'amour; The bonny Earl o' Moray; The brisk young widow; Ca' the yowes; Come you not from Newcastle?; Early one morning; The foggy, foggy dew; How sweet the answer; The last rose of summer; The Lincolnshire poacher; The miller of Dee; The minstrel boy; Oft in the stilly night; O Waly, Waly; The plough boy; Le roi s'en va-t'en chasse; Sally in our alley; Sweet Polly Oliver; Tom Bowling.*
(M) *** Decca 430 063-2 [id.]. Peter Pears, Benjamin Britten.

It is good to have the definitive Pears/Britten collaboration in the folksong arrangements. Excellent, faithful recording, well transferred to CD.

Folksong arrangements: *The ash grove; La belle est au jardin d'amour; The bonny Earl o' Moray; The brisk young widow; Ca' the yowes; Come you not from Newcastle?; The foggy, foggy dew; The Lincolnshire poacher; Little Sir William; The minstrel boy; O can ye sew cushions; Oliver Cromwell; O Waly, Waly; The plough boy; Quand j'étais chez mon père; Le roi s'en va-t'en chasse; The Salley Gardens; Sweet Polly Oliver; The trees they grow so high.*
(M) *** EMI CDM7 69423-2. Robert Tear, Philip Ledger.

Close as Robert Tear's interpretations are to those of Peter Pears, he does have a sparkle of his own, helped by resilient accompaniment from Philip Ledger. In any case, the record is a delight on its own account. Fine recording.

Folksong arrangements: *The ash grove; La belle est au jardin d'amour; Come you not from Newcastle?; Dear harp of my country; Early one morning; Fileuse; How sweet the answer; The last rose of summer; Little Sir William; O can ye sew cushions; Oft in the stilly night; Oliver Cromwell; O Waly, Waly; The plough boy; Quand j'étais chez mon père; Sweet Polly Oliver; There's none to soothe; The trees they grow so high; Voici le printemps.*
☞ (B) ** CfP Dig. CD-CFP 4638; *TC-CFP 4638*. Sarah Brightman, Geoffrey Parsons.

Sarah Brightman, a charming if slight-toned soprano in the music that Andrew Lloyd-Webber has written for her, is disappointing in these Britten folksongs, trying too hard to inject expression, often at speeds manifestly too slow (as in the first item, *Early one morning*), regularly missing the carefree sparkle. Geoffrey Parsons does his best to compensate: one hopes Miss Brightman's next such venture will prove less inhibited. The recording has fine presence on CD and chrome cassette alike.

(i) *The Golden Vanity;* (ii) *Noye's Fludde.*

(M) *** Decca 436 397-2. (i) Wandsworth School Boys' Ch., Burgess, composer (piano); (ii) Brannigan, Rex, Anthony, East Suffolk Children's Ch. & O, E. Op. Group O, Del Mar.

The Golden Vanity is a 'vaudeville' written for the Vienna Boys' Choir. The Wandsworth Boys are completely at home in the music and sing with pleasing freshness. The coupling was recorded during the 1961 Aldeburgh Festival, and not only the professional choristers but the children too have the time of their lives to the greater glory of God. All the effects have been captured miraculously here, most strikingly the entry into the Ark, while a bugle band blares out fanfares, with the stereo readily catching the sense of occasion and particularly the sound of *Eternal Father* rising above the storm at the climax of *Noye's Fludde.*

(i) *Noye's Fludde;* (ii) *Serenade for tenor, horn & strings, Op. 31.*

☞ (M) **(*) Virgin/EMI Dig. CUV5 61122-2 [id.]. (i) Maxwell, Ormiston, Pasco, Salisbury & Chester Schools Ch. & O, Coull Qt, Alley, Watson, Harwood, Endymion Ens. (members); (ii) Martyn Hill, Frank Lloyd, City of L. Sinfonia, Hickox.

On the Virgin disc the instrumental forces, including a schools' orchestra as well as professional soloists, are relatively recessed. Compare the storm sequence here with the Decca account, and the distancing undermines any feeling of threat so that the entry of the hymn, *Eternal Father,* instantly submerges the orchestral sound, instead of battling against it. Not even Donald Maxwell as Noah, strong and virile, can efface memories of the incomparable Owen Brannigan.

Holy sonnets of John Donne, Op. 35; 7 Sonnets of Michelangelo, Op. 22.

☞ (***) EMI mono CDC7 54605-2 [id.]. Peter Pears, composer – POULENC: *Songs.* (***)

Peter Pears's early EMI recordings of Britten's two sonnet-cycles, both made soon after the works had been composed, have a freshness and vigour that he did not quite recapture in his later versions for Decca. Even among the many recordings that Britten made with Pears of the works which his voice inspired, these have a special place, well transferred in the 'Composers in Person' series, and imaginatively coupled with the Bernac/Poulenc collection.

(i) *Les Illuminations* (song-cycle), *Op. 18;* (ii) *Nocturne;* (iii) *Serenade for tenor, horn and strings, Op. 31.*

☞ (M) *** Decca 436 395-2 [id.]. (i–iii) Peter Pears; (i) ECO; (ii) wind soloists; (ii; iii) LSO strings, composer; (iii) with Barry Tuckwell.

With dedicated accompaniments under the composer's direction, these Pears versions of *Les Illuminations* and the *Serenade* (with its horn obbligato superbly played by Barry Tuckwell) make a perfect coupling. For the CD release Decca have added the recording of the *Nocturne* from 1960. It is a work full – as is so much of Britten's output – of memorable moments. Each song has a different obbligato instrument (with the ensemble unified for the final Shakespeare song) and each instrument gives the song it is associated with its own individual character. Pears, as always, is the ideal interpreter, the composer a most efficient conductor, and the fiendishly difficult obbligato parts are played superbly. The recording is brilliant and clear, with just the right degree of atmosphere although, for some reason, the transfer of *Les Illuminations* is brighter than the other two works.

(i) *Our Hunting Fathers, Op. 8; Folksong arrangements: The bonny Earl o'Moray; Come you not from Newcastle?; Little Sir William; Oliver Cromwell; O Waly, Waly; The plough boy;* (ii) *Serenade for tenor, horn and strings.*

☞ (M) **(*) EMI Dig./Analogue CDM7 69522-2 [id.]. (i) Elisabeth Söderström, Welsh Nat. Op. O, Richard Armstrong; (ii) Robert Tear, Alan Civil, N. Sinfonia, Marriner.

Inexplicably, *Our Hunting Fathers* – Britten's first major work using full orchestra, written for the Norwich Festival in 1936 – was neglected by the record companies until this valuable, strongly presented interpretation appeared in 1982. W. H. Auden put together the sequence of poems on an anti-bloodsport theme, designing it to shock the Norwich audience (which it did) and providing two of the poems himself. The piece, with its obvious acerbities – like the shrieks in *Rats away* – still has the power to shock, and this performance finds Söderström a committed soloist, even if a tenor voice suits this work even more. The folksongs make an attractive bonus, and the new coupling with Robert Tear's 1970 version of the *Serenade* adds to the interest of this reissue. Tear is very much in the Aldeburgh tradition set by Pears, yet he gives a new and positive slant to each of Britten's lovely songs, with the Johnson *Hymn to Diana* given extra jollity, thanks partly to the brilliant galumphing of Alan Civil on the horn. The recording's resonance provides atmosphere without clouding.

The Prodigal Son (3rd parable), Op. 81.
(M) *** Decca 425 713-2. Pears, Tear, Shirley-Quirk, Drake, E. Op. Group Ch. & O, composer and Viola Tunnard.

The last of the parables is the sunniest and most heart-warming. Britten cleverly avoids the charge of oversweetness by introducing the Abbot, even before the play starts, in the role of Tempter, confessing he represents evil and aims to destroy contentment in the family he describes: 'See how I break it up' – a marvellous line for Peter Pears. An ideal performance is given here with a characteristically real and atmospheric Decca recording.

St Nicholas; Hymn to St Cecilia.
*** Hyp. Dig. CDA 66333 [id.]. Rolfe Johnson, Corydon Singers, St George's Chapel, Windsor, Ch., Girls of Warwick University Chamber Ch., Ch. of Christ Church, Southgate, Sevenoaks School, Tonbridge School, Penshurst Ch. Soc., Occasional Ch., Edwards, Alley, Scott, ECO, Best.

For the first time in a recording, the congregational hymns are included in Matthew Best's fresh and atmospheric account of *St Nicholas*. That adds enormously to the emotional impact of the whole cantata. Though the chorus is distanced slightly, the contrasts of timbre are caught well, with the waltz-setting of *The birth of Nicholas* and its bath-tub sequence delightfully sung by boy-trebles alone. The *Hymn to St Cecilia* is also beautifully sung, with gentle pointing of the jazzy syncopations in crisp, agile ensemble and with sweet matching among the voices.

(i) *St Nicholas, Op. 42;* (ii) *Rejoice in the Lamb, Op. 30.*
(M) (***) Decca mono 425 714-2. (i) Hemmings, Pears, St John Leman School, Beccles, Girls' Ch., Ipswich School Boys' Ch., Aldeburgh Festival Ch. & O; R. Downes; (ii) Hartnett, Steele, Todd, Francke, Purcell Singers, G. Malcolm; composer.

With rare exceptions, Britten's first recordings of his own works have a freshness and vigour unsurpassed since. Britten's performances capture the element of vulnerability, not least in the touching setting of words by the deranged poet, Christopher Smart, *Rejoice in the Lamb.*

Serenade for tenor, horn and strings.
*** ASV Dig. CDRPO 8023; *ZCRPO 8023* [id.]. Martyn Hill, Bryant, RPO, Ashkenazy – KNUSSEN: *Symphony No. 3;* WALTON: *Symphony No. 2.* ***

If it seems strange that Martyn Hill has made a second recording of this masterpiece so soon after the Virgin Classics one with Hickox, the choice of Jeffrey Bryant for the horn part brings ample justification, quite apart from Ashkenazy's red-blooded direction. The oddly balanced recording – with tenor and horn set behind the strings – hardly interferes with the compulsion of the performance.

(i) *Serenade for tenor, horn and strings, Op. 31;* (ii) *7 Sonnets of Michelangelo, Op. 22; Winter words, Op. 52.*
☞ (M) (***) Decca mono 425 996-2 [id.]. Peter Pears, (i) Dennis Brain, Boyd Neel String O, composer; (ii) composer (piano).

This compilation brings together some of Britten's historic early recordings for Decca. This first recording of the *Serenade*, though not helped by unatmospheric sound, is wonderfully intense, with Dennis Brain uniquely magnetic on the horn. The first recording of the Hardy song-cycle, *Winter words*, has never been matched by more recent recordings, an intensely evocative performance with Britten drawing magical sounds from the piano in support of Pears. This version of the *Michelangelo sonnets* is not quite as fresh-toned as the even earlier EMI one, but it still offers a searchingly intense performance. Limited but clear mono sound.

Songs and proverbs of William Blake, Op. 74; Tit for Tat; 3 Early songs: Beware that I'd ne'er been married; Epitaph; The clerk. Folksong arrangements: Bonny at morn; I was lonely; Lemady; Lord! I married me a wife!; O Waly, Waly; The Salley Gardens; She's like the swallow; Sweet Polly Oliver.
**(*) Chan. Dig. CHAN 8514; *ABTD 1224* [id.]. Benjamin Luxon, David Williamson.

Benjamin Luxon's lusty baritone gives an abrasive edge whether to early songs, folksong settings or the Blake cycle. Only rarely does he become too emphatic. Excellent, sensitive accompaniment and first-rate recording.

(i) *Songs from the Chinese, Op. 58;* Folksong arrangements: *I will give my love an apple; Master Kilby; Sailor boy; The shooting of his dear; The soldier and the sailor. Gloriana: Second lute song of the Earl of Essex. Nocturnal* (for solo guitar), *Op. 70.*

☞ (M) *** BMG/RCA 09026 61601-2 [id.]. Julian Bream (guitar); (i) Peter Pears (with FRICKER: *O Mistress mine*) – SEIBER: *French folksongs;* WALTON: *Anon in love.* ***

Nearly all the music on this record was written with Julian Bream in mind, and the *Nocturnal*, based on a tune by Dowland, was dedicated to him. Characteristically Britten exploits every nuance of expression that Bream's virtuosity makes possible and, though inevitably in so long a work (18 minutes 33 seconds) the limited texture of the instrument is exposed, the wonder is that such concentration and richness are achieved. The haunting lute song from *Gloriana* by contrast brings a remarkable Elizabethan feeling. The *Songs from the Chinese* are based on Arthur Waley's translations of Chinese poetry. The second, *The old lute,* is appropriately evocative and in the third the accompanying guitar becomes *The autumn wind.* Of the folksong arrangements, *The shooting of his dear* brings guitar gunshots, but it is *I will give my love an apple* where Pears's tender vocal-line is particularly memorable. The closing *Soldier and the sailor* has all the pay-off wit for which Britten's arrangements are famous. Peter Racine Fricker's soaring setting of *O Mistress mine* seems tailor-made for Pears, his voice at its freshest throughout. With Seiber and Walton couplings equally rewarding, this (Volume 18) is outstanding among the reissues in the Julian Bream Edition where he is joined by other artists. The recording of the songs was made by a Decca team in 1963/4, and Kenwood House provides an ideally intimate acoustic with pleasing ambience. The *Nocturnal* was recorded in Bream's favourite venue, Wardour Chapel, Wiltshire in 1966, and is equally real.

(i) *Spring symphony, Op. 44;* (ii) *Cantata academica;* (iii) *Hymn to St Cecilia.*

☞ (M) *** Decca 436 396-2 [id.]. (i; ii) Vyvyan, Pears; (i) Procter, Emanuel School, Wandsworth, Boys' Ch., ROHCG O, composer; (ii) Watts, Brannigan; (ii; iii) L. Symphony Ch.; (ii) LSO; (ii; iii) Malcolm.

(i) *Spring symphony, Op. 44; Peter Grimes: 4 Sea interludes.*

☞ (M) *** EMI CDM7 64736-2 [id.]. (i) Armstrong, J. Baker, Tear, St Clement Dane's School Boys' Ch., L. Symphony Ch.; LSO, Previn.

(i) *Spring Symphony, Op. 44;* (ii) *Welcome ode, Op. 95;* (iii) *Psalm 150, Op. 67.*

**(*) Chan. Dig. CHAN 8855; *ABTD 1472* [id.]. (i) Gale, Hodgson, Hill, Southend Boys' Ch., LSO; (ii) City of London Schools' Ch., LSO; (iii) City of London Schools' Ch. and O; Hickox.

It is the freshness of Britten's imagination in dozens of moments that makes this work as memorable as it is joyous. Who but Britten would have dared use so unexpected an effect as boys whistling? Who but he would have introduced a triumphant C major *Sumer is icumen in* at the end, the boys' voices ringing out over everything else? Here, of course, a recording helps enormously. Thanks to the Decca engineers, one hears more than is usually possible in a live performance. Jennifer Vyvyan and Peter Pears are both outstanding, and Britten shows that no conductor is more vital in his music than he himself. The Decca reissue couples the work to the *Cantata academica,* with its deft use of a 12-note row, written for Basel, and the *Hymn to St Cecilia,* an ambitious piece written just before the war, when Britten's technique was already prodigious. The setting exactly matches the imaginative, capricious words of Auden. Performances are first class and so is the CD transfer.

Like Britten, Previn makes this above all a work of exultation, a genuine celebration of spring; but here, more than in Britten's recording, the kernel of what the work has to say comes out in the longest of the solo settings, using Auden's poem *Out on the lawn I lie in bed.* With Dame Janet Baker as soloist it rises above the lazily atmospheric mood of the opening to evoke the threat of war and darkness. Perhaps surprisingly, it is Britten who generally adopts faster tempi and a sharper rhythmic style, whereas Previn is generally the more atmospheric and mysterious, grading the climaxes and shading the tones over longer spans. He also takes greater care over pointing Britten's pay-offs, often with the help of Robert Tear's sense of timing, as at the very end on *I cease.* The *Four Sea interludes,* which make a generous bonus, are presented in their concert form, with tailored endings. Previn springs the bouncing rhythms of the second interlude – the picture of Sunday morning in the Borough – even more infectiously than the composer himself in his complete recording of the opera.

With more variable soloists – the tenor Martyn Hill outstandingly fine, the soprano Elizabeth Gale often too edgy – Hickox's version of the *Spring Symphony* does not quite match the composer's own in gutsy urgency. But this CD brings the advantage of a first recording of Britten's last completed work, the *Welcome ode.* The third work, equally apt, is the boisterous setting of *Psalm 150.*

(i) *Tit for Tat;* (ii) Folksong arrangements: *Bird scarer's song; Bonny at morn; David of the White Rock; Lemady; Lord! I married me a wife!; She's like the swallow.*
*** Mer. CDE 84119; *KE 77119* [id.]. Shirley-Quirk; (i) Ledger; (ii) Ellis – *Suite for harp* etc. ***

John Shirley-Quirk was the baritone who first sang the cycle, *Tit for Tat*, with the composer at the piano, and he is still unrivalled in the sharp yet subtle way he brings out the irony in these boyhood settings of De la Mare poems. It is also good to have him singing the six late folk-settings with harp accompaniment, here played by Osian Ellis for whom (with Peter Pears) they were originally written.

War Requiem, Op. 66.
*** Decca 414 383-2 [id.]. Vishnevskaya, Pears, Fischer-Dieskau, Bach Ch., London Symphony Ch., Highgate School Ch., Melos Ens., LSO, composer.
*** EMI Dig. CDS7 47034-8 [id.]. Söderström, Tear, Allen, Trebles of Christ Church Cathedral Ch., Oxford, CBSO Ch., CBSO, Rattle.
☞ **(*) DG Dig. 437 801-2 (2) [id.]. Orgonasova, Rolfe Johnson, Skovhus, Monteverdi Ch., Tölz Boys' Ch., N. German R. Ch. & SO, Gardiner.

(i) *War Requiem;* (ii) *Ballad of heroes, Op. 14; Sinfonia da requiem, Op. 20.*
*** Chan. Dig. CHAN 8983/4; *DBTD 2032* [id.]. (i) Harper, Langridge, Shirley-Quirk, (ii) Hill; St Paul's Cathedral Choristers, London Symphony Ch., LSO & CO, Richard Hickox.

Richard Hickox's Chandos version rivals even the composer's own definitive account in its passion and perception, and must be now regarded as a first choice. Hickox thrusts home the big dramatic moments with unrivalled force, helped by the weight of the Chandos sound. The boys' chorus from St Paul's Cathedral is exceptionally fresh. Heather Harper is as golden-toned as she was at the very first Coventry performance, fearless in attack. Philip Langridge has never sung more sensitively on disc, and both he and John Shirley-Quirk bring many subtleties to their interpretations. Adding to the attractions of the set come two substantial choral works, also in outstanding performances.

Britten's own 1963 recording of the *War Requiem* comes near to the ideal, but it is a pity that Britten insisted on Vishnevskaya for the soprano solos. Having a Russian singer was emotionally right, but musically Heather Harper would have been better still. The digital remastering, as with *Peter Grimes*, brings added textural refinement and makes the recording sound newly minted; it also reveals a degree of background hiss.

With Elisabeth Söderström a far more warmly expressive soloist than the oracular Vishnevskaya, the human emotions behind the Latin text come out strongly with less distancing than from the composer. If Tear does not always match the subtlety of Pears on the original recording, Allen sounds more idiomatic than Fischer-Dieskau. Rattle's approach is warm, dedicated and dramatic, with fine choral singing (not least from the Christ Church Cathedral trebles). The various layers of perspective are impressively managed by the digital recording. Yet in its combination of imaginative flair with technical expertise, the Culshaw recording of two decades earlier is by no means surpassed.

Recorded live in Lübeck by the North German Radio Orchestra and Choir under their chief conductor, John Eliot Gardiner, this is a thoughtful rather than a dramatic reading. It is intense and compelling, as one would expect from Gardiner, but it is seriously undermined by dim, inconsistent recording, with soloists and chorus often ill-focused. In every way Richard Hickox's Chandos version is warmer and more powerful as an interpretation, as well as far better recorded. For the same price the two Chandos discs also contain the *Sinfonia da Requiem* and the early *Ballad of heroes.*

What works far better than Gardiner's CD is the video version of the same performance (LaserDisc 072 198-1; VHS 072 198-3), set in the beautiful Marienkirche. With the singers in close-up, the ear obligingly ignores bad balances to have one appreciating the firm Slavonic tang of Luba Orgonasova, the intimate intensity of Anthony Rolfe Johnson and the youthful ardour of the baritone, Boje Skovhus. Another advantage is that on a single VHS cassette there is no break in the middle.

OPERA

Albert Herring (complete).
**(*) Decca 421 849-2 (2) [id.]. Pears, Fisher, Noble, Brannigan, Cantelo, ECO, Ward, composer.

Britten's own 1964 recording of the comic opera, *Albert Herring*, is a delight. Peter Pears's portrait of the innocent Albert was caught only just before he grew too old for the role, but it is full of unique touches. Sylvia Fisher is a magnificent Lady Billows, and it is good to have so wide a range of British singers of the 1960s so characterfully presented. The recording, made in Jubilee Hall, remains astonishingly vivid.

Billy Budd (complete).

*** Decca 417 428-2 (3) [id.]. Glossop, Pears, Langdon, Shirley-Quirk, Wandsworth School Boys' Ch., Amb. Op. Ch., LSO, composer (with *Holy Sonnets of John Donne; Songs and Proverbs of William Blake* ***).

☞ (**) VAIA mono 1034-3 (3) [id.]. Pears, Uppman, Dalberg, Alan, G. Evans, Langdon, ROHCG Ch. & O, Britten.

An ideal cast, with Glossop a bluff, heroic Billy, and Langdon a sharply dark-toned Claggart, making these symbol-figures believable. Magnificent sound, and the many richly imaginative strokes – atmospheric as well as dramatic – are superbly managed. The layout on three CDs begins with the *John Donne Holy Sonnets* (sung by Pears) and the *Songs and Proverbs of William Blake* (sung by Fischer-Dieskau), with the Prologue and Act I of the opera beginning thereafter. They are equally ideal performanes.

Though the sound is very scrubby, disconcertingly so at the very start, this historic recording of the very first performance of the opera in December 1951 is doubly valuable: not only does it let us hear the fresh, youthful-sounding performance of Theodor Uppman in the title-role, as well as Peter Pears as Captain Vere, clearer and more flexible than in his studio recording of 16 years later; it also presents the original, four-Act text, with its substantial muster scene at the end of the original Act I, later cut. Other passages were also elided. Philip Reed provides a brief but informative comment on the text and the recording, but there is no libretto. Meticulously the booklet also lists seven tiny passages, never more than a few bars, that were missing from the only audio source. It is interesting that, though the orchestra sounds dim and limp at the start, Britten as conductor whips up searing tension through the opera.

Death in Venice (complete).

*** Decca 425 669-2 (2) [id.]. Pears, Shirley-Quirk, Bowman, Bowen, Leeming, E. Op. Group Ch., ECO, Bedford.

Thomas Mann's novella, which made an expansively atmospheric film, far removed from the world of Mann, here makes a surprisingly successful opera. Pears's searching performance in the central role of Aschenbach is set against the darkly sardonic singing of John Shirley-Quirk in a sequence of roles as the Dionysiac figure who draws Aschenbach to his destruction and, though Steuart Bedford's assured conducting lacks some of the punch that Britten would have brought, the whole presentation makes this a set to establish the work outside the opera house.

Gloriana (complete).

☞ *** Decca Dig. 440 213-2 (2) [id.]. Josephine Barstow, Philip Langridge, Della Jones, Jonathan Summers, WNO Ch. & O, Mackerras.

It took exactly 40 years for Britten's coronation opera, *Gloriana*, to appear in a recording, reflecting the deep disappointment, even derision, that greeted its first staging at Covent Garden in 1953 as a tribute to Queen Elizabeth II on her coronation. It was not just that the first-night audience was largely made up of notables with little musical knowledge or taste, but that its searching portrait of Queen Elizabeth I had more than its measure of darkness. If Britten, mindful of the need to celebrate a new Elizabethan Age, included pageants, processions, balls and masques, by the final Act they had faded away in favour of painful tragedy. Instead of a celebration, *Gloriana* represents a dying fall, with no happy ending, only the portrait of a lonely monarch forced to do her duty and condemn to the scaffold a man, the Earl of Essex, whom she loved more than anyone, but who had rebelled against her.

Britten wrote that central role of the Virgin Queen for his friend and collaborator, Joan Cross, and one would have thought that many more sopranos or mezzos towards the end of their careers would have jumped at such a rich acting role. There were earlier plans for recording *Gloriana* with Dame Janet Baker, first with Britten himself conducting and later with Simon Rattle, but they fell through. Without effacing memories of earlier interpreters, Josephine Barstow gives a splendid reading, tough and incisive, with the slight unevenness in the voice adding to the abrasiveness. No easy option, this one.

Only in the final scene when, after the execution of Essex, the queen muses to herself in fragments of spoken monologue does the reading lack weight. A chestier speaking voice would have helped, but just before that the final confrontation between Elizabeth and Essex brings a thrilling climax in what amounts to an 'out-of-love' duet. Elizabeth attacks her lover not for infidelity but for treason. This astonishingly original sequence, full of anger, finally resolves itself in a tender reminiscence of one of Essex's lute-songs, movingly indicating the queen's continuing love.

Philip Langridge's portrait of Essex is, if anything, even more striking. More than the original interpreter, Peter Pears, he consistently brings out the character's arrogant bravado, the quality which first attracted the queen but then finally destroyed the man. Though Langridge's voice is mellifluous and flexible in the lute songs, its bright, cutting quality helps to enhance that characterization.

The rest of the cast is equally starry, with Alan Opie as the queen's principal adviser, Sir Robert Cecil, balefully dark rather than sinister, while the warm-toned Della Jones as Essex's wife and the abrasive Yvonne Kenny as his sister, Lady Penelope Rich, both well cast, sharply draw out the opposing sides of the queen's character, when in turn they make their final pleas for Essex's life, the latter with disastrous results.

In addition, it is generous casting to have such outstanding and characterful singers as Bryn Terfel, Willard White, John Shirley-Quirk and John Mark Ainsley in tiny roles, all very well suited. Sir Charles Mackerras directs his Welsh National Opera forces in a performance that brings out the full splendour of this rich score, characteristically full of original effects, as well as boasting the colourful genre pieces that have become known separately. The Decca recording, made in Brangwyn Hall, Swansea, is comparably splendid, a crowning achievement in the complete cycle of Britten operas begun by the composer himself.

Gloriana: Choral dances.
*** Hyp. CDA 66175 [id.]. Martyn Hill, Thelma Owen, Holst Singers & O, Hilary Davan Wetton –
    BLISS: *Lie strewn the white flocks;* HOLST: *Choral hymns from the Rig Veda.* ***

The composer's own choral suite, made up of unaccompanied choral dances linked by passages for solo tenor and harp, makes an excellent coupling for the equally attractive Bliss and Holst items. Excellent, atmospheric recording.

A Midsummer Night's Dream (complete).
*** Decca 425 663-2 (2) [id.]. Deller, Harwood, Harper, Veasey, Watts, Shirley-Quirk, Brannigan,
    Downside and Emmanuel School Ch., LSO, composer.

The beauty of instrumental writing comes out in this recording even more than in the opera house, for John Culshaw, the recording manager, put an extra halo round the fairy music to act as a substitute for visual atmosphere. Britten again proves himself an ideal interpreter of his own music and draws virtuoso playing from the LSO. Peter Pears has shifted to the straight role of Lysander. The mechanicals are admirably led by Owen Brannigan as Bottom; and among the lovers Josephine Veasey (Hermia) is outstanding. Deller, with his magical male alto singing, is the eerily effective Oberon.

(i) *Owen Wingrave* (complete); (ii) *6 Hölderlin fragments, Op. 61;* (iii) *The Poet's echo, Op. 76.*
☞ *** Decca 433 200-2 (2) [id.]. (i) Pears, Fisher, Harper, Vyvyan, J. Baker, Luxon, Shirley-Quirk,
    ECO, composer; (ii) Pears, composer; (iii) Vishnevskaya, Rostropovich.

Britten's television opera marked a return after the *Church parables* to the mainstream pattern of his operatic style, with a central character isolated from society. Each of the seven characters is strongly conceived, with the composer writing specially for the individual singers in the cast. The performance is definitive and the recording very atmospheric. The set is filled out with the *Six Hölderlin fragments* and *The Poet's echo*, Russian settings of Pushkin, written for Vishnevskaya who performs them with her husband at the piano.

Paul Bunyan (complete).
⊛ *** Virgin/EMI Dig. VCD7 59249-2 (2) [id.]. James Lawless, Dan Dressen, Elisabeth Comeaux
    Nelson, soloists, Ch. & O of Plymouth Music Series, Minnesota, Philip Brunelle.

Aptly, this first recording of Britten's choral operetta comes from the state, Minnesota, where the story is set. When the principal character is a giant who can appear only as a disembodied voice, the piece works rather better on record or radio than on stage. Musically, Britten's conscious assumption of popular American mannerisms does not prevent his invention from showing characteristic originality. Recorded in clean, vivid sound, with Philip Brunelle a vigorous conductor, this excellent first recording richly deserves the prizes it won for the Virgin Classics label.

Peter Grimes (complete).
⊛ *** Decca 414 577-2 (3) [id.]. Pears, Claire Watson, Pease, Jean Watson, Nilsson, Brannigan,
    Evans, Ch. and O of ROHCG, composer.
☞ *** EMI Dig. CDC7 54832-2 (2) [id.]. Anthony Rolfe Johnson, Felicity Lott, Thomas Allen, Ch.
    & O of ROHCG, Bernard Haitink.
(M) *** Ph. 432 578-2 (2) [id.]. Vickers, Harper, Summers, Bainbridge, Cahill, Robinson, Allen,
    ROHCG Ch. & O, C. Davis.

The Decca recording of *Peter Grimes* was one of the first great achievements of the stereo era. Few opera recordings can claim to be so definitive, with Peter Pears, for whom it was written, in the name-part, Owen Brannigan (another member of the original team) and a first-rate cast. Britten conducts superbly and secures splendidly incisive playing, with the whole orchestra on its toes throughout. The recording, superbly atmospheric, has so many felicities that it would be hard to enumerate them, and the Decca engineers have done wonders in making up aurally for the lack of visual effects.

Bernard Haitink's reading of *Grimes*, after Britten's own recording of 1959 and Sir Colin Davis's of 1978, represents a third generation of interpretation which, while learning from the composer's own example, brings new vitality and renewed freshness. That is in great measure due to Haitink's inspired conducting which, with heightened contrasts – helped by one of EMI's most spectacular recordings yet – finds more light and shade in this extraordinarily atmospheric score. Haitink is not the only one who has learnt from the composer's own recording. Far more than the Philips team, the EMI engineers have followed the vivid example of the 1959 Decca recording, as when the procession marches off to Grimes's hut in Act II. The distancing on EMI, as on Decca, reflects Britten's imaginative lowering of pitch – the Doppler effect in musical terms – as the voices get further away. By comparison the Philips reminds one more clearly of the studio.

Anthony Rolfe Johnson too comes far closer to Peter Pears in the Britten recording than Jon Vickers does for Davis, with his rugged, bull-like portrait. Vickers' speeds are almost all slower, not least in the two key monologues – when in Act II Grimes sees the sea 'boiling' with fish, and when, crazed in the fog at the end of Act III, he eludes the searchers. Rolfe Johnson is the most inward of the three, singing the most beautifully, less troubled than Pears by the high tessitura. He presents Grimes as suffering from hysteria rather than outright madness, and the result is at least as touching. Felicity Lott makes a tenderly sympathetic Ellen Orford, less mature than Heather Harper for Davis, more characterful than Claire Watson for Britten.

The sharply drawn characters of the Borough are all cast from strength with portraits, where necessary, larger than life. Sarah Walker, for example, is unforgettable as Mrs Sedley, the laudanum-taking gossip, and Thomas Allen is a wise and powerful Balstrode, making the Act III duel with Ellen an emotional resolution, preparing for the final tragedy. The Covent Garden Chorus and Orchestra are used in all three recordings, outstanding in all three but with the extra range and vividness of EMI's latest digital recording adding to the impact, not least of the chorus, whether singing on stage or in evocative off-stage effects. The set has the advantage over Britten's own of coming (like the Davis) on two instead of three discs, though the three-disc format allows each Act to be offered complete on a single disc.

Sir Colin Davis takes a fundamentally darker, tougher view of *Peter Grimes* than the composer himself. Jon Vickers' heroic interpretation sheds keen new illumination on what arguably remains the greatest of Britten's operas, even if it cannot be said to supplant the composer's own version. Heather Harper as Ellen Orford is very moving, and there are fine contributions from Jonathan Summers as Captain Balstrode and Thomas Allen as Ned Keene. The recording is full and vivid, with fine balancing.

(i, ii) *Peter Grimes* (scenes); (i, iii) *The Rape of Lucretia* (abridged); (iv) French folksong arrangements: *La belle est au jardin d'amour; La fileuse; Quand j'étais chez mon père; Le roi s'en va-t'en chasse; Voici le printemps;* (v) English folksongs: *The Ash grove; The Bonny Earl o' Moray; Come you not from Newcastle?; The Foggy, foggy dew; Heigh ho, heigh hi!; The King is gone a-hunting; Little Sir William; O, Waly, Waly; Oliver Cromwell; The Plough boy; The Salley Gardens; Sweet Polly Oliver; There's none to soothe.*

☞ (M) (***) EMI mono CMS7 64727-2 (2) [id.]. (i) Joan Cross, Peter Pears; (ii) Nancy Evans, E. Op. Group Chamber O; (iii) BBC Theatre Ch., ROHCG O, Reginald Goodall; (iv) Sophie Wyss, composer; (v) Peter Pears, composer.

Both of these abridged recordings of Britten's earliest operas, made in the 1940s, have a freshness and energy that reflect the excitement they aroused at their first appearance, transforming the British musical scene. More specifically, they illustrate both the resilient energy of Peter Pears at this early stage, lighter and fresher of voice than later, and the urgent intensity of Reginald Goodall, conducting Britten in a way very different from his later, solidly weighty manner in Wagner. Though the recordings, transferred from 78s, are boxy in sound, the closeness adds to the bite and impact. So Pears's solos from *Peter Grimes*, including the Mad scene, may lack some of the atmosphere of the later complete recording of the opera, but the tension is even greater. The Act I monologue, *Now the Great Bear*, is here published for the first time. Britten originally refused to let the *Grimes* excerpts be issued, but most of them appeared on LP not long before he died. They are particularly valuable for demonstrating the character and point of Joan Cross as Ellen Orford. It was a role written for her, as indeed was the Female Chorus part in *Lucretia*. In the latter opera it is good to have Nancy Evans in the title-role, tenderly affecting, with the contrasts between the heroine's tragic grief and the beauty of the serving maids' Flower duet superbly brought out.

The recordings of folksong settings are delightful, made not just by Peter Pears for both Decca and EMI, but by Sophie Wyss (for whom *Les illuminations* was written). The wit and point of such songs as *The foggy, foggy dew* and *Little Sir William* come out even more delightfully than in later recordings, with Britten as accompanist at his most inspired.

Peter Grimes: 4 Sea interludes and Passacaglia.
*** Chan. Dig. CHAN 8473; *ABTD 1184* [id.]. Ulster O, Handley – BAX: *On the Sea-shore;*
    BRIDGE: *The Sea.* ***

Handley draws brilliant and responsive playing from the Ulster Orchestra in readings that fully capture the atmospheric beauty of the writing, helped by vivid recording of demonstration quality.

The Rape of Lucretia (complete).
☞ *** Chan. Dig. CHAN 9254/5 [id.]. Rigby, Robson, Pierard, Maxwell, Miles, Rozario, Gunson,
    City of L. Sinf., Hickox.

(i) *The Rape of Lucretia* (complete); (ii) *Phaedra, Op. 93.*
*** Decca 425 666-2 (2) [id.]. (i) Pears, Harper, Shirley-Quirk, J. Baker, Luxon, ECO, composer; (ii)
    J. Baker, ECO, Bedford.

In combining on CD *The Rape of Lucretia* with *Phaedra*, Decca celebrates two outstanding performances by Dame Janet Baker, recorded at the peak of her career. Among other distinguished vocal contributions to the opera, Peter Pears and Heather Harper stand out, while Benjamin Luxon makes the selfish Tarquinius into a living character. The seductive beauty of the writing – Britten then at his early peak – is splendidly caught, the melodies and tone-colours as ravishing as any that he ever conceived.

Richard Hickox follows up his outstanding version of Britten's *War Requiem* for Chandos, as well as his version of *A Midsummer Night's Dream* for Virgin, with this colourful and atmospheric account of *The Rape of Lucretia*. It was recorded soon after concert performances given at the Spitalfields Festival in 1993, and the interplay of voices reflects that live experience. Though Hickox's overall timings for each Act are noticeably longer than Britten's own in his superb 1970 recording (nearly five minutes in each), that extra spaciousness never brings a sense of dragging and, in at least one key moment (the lamenting cor anglais solo before the raped Lucretia sings her solo, *Flowers bring to every year*), it brings an extra poignancy. The cast is a strong one, with no weak link. Though the soloists in the Britten recording – notably Janet Baker in the title-role – are more sharply characterful and well-contrasted, the alternative views presented here are comparably convincing. Jean Rigby as Lucretia may lack the warmth and weight of Baker, but she gains from having a younger-sounding voice. Equally the timbre of Nigel Robson as the Male Chorus, rather darker than Peter Pears's, adds to the dramatic bite of his characterization, virile in attack. Catherine Pierard as the Female Chorus has a more sensuous voice than most sopranos taking this role, making it a more involved commentary. The others are comparably fresh and clear, though the recording, full and atmospheric, seems to bring out and perhaps exaggerate the vibrato in each. The digital sound is warm and glowing, fully revealing the sensuous beauty of Britten's chamber orchestration. Such sound-effects as Tarquinius's knocking on the door are even more atmospheric than in the Decca recording, though voices are not so immediate. Quite apart from its unique authority, Britten's Decca set (also at full price) comes with a valuable fill-up in *Phaedra*, the work he wrote for Janet Baker; but the Chandos rival gives an equally strong, in some ways more dramatic view of a masterly opera.

The Turn of the screw.
☞ *** Collins Dig. 7030-2 (2) [id.]. Langridge, Lott, Pay, Hulse, Cannan, Secunde, Aldeburgh
    Festival Ens., Bedford.
(M) (***) Decca mono 425 672-2 (2) [id.]. Pears, Vyvyan, Hemmings, Dyer, Cross, Mandikian, E.
    Op. Group O, composer.

When Britten's own recording of *The Turn of the screw*, powerful and intense, is in mono only, this vividly recorded, warmly atmospheric version conducted by Steuart Bedford could not be more welcome. Bedford, who took over from Britten himself when he could no longer conduct his own recordings, here presents a similarly idiomatic performance with a comparable sharpness and magnetism which, thanks to the spacious recording, brings out the eerie atmosphere of the piece, the quality which originally attracted the young Britten to Henry James's ghost story. The recording also allows one to appreciate the more the sharp originality of the instrumentation in what by any standards is the tautest of Britten's operas. The singers too have been chosen to follow the pattern set by the original performers. Langridge here, like Pears before him, takes the double role of narrator and Peter Quint, echoing Pears's inflexions but putting his own stamp on the characterization. Felicity Lott is both powerful and vulnerable as the Governess, rising superbly to the big climaxes which, thanks to the recording quality, have a chilling impact, not least at the very end. Sam Pay is a fresh-voiced Miles, less knowing than David Hemmings in the Britten set, with Eileen Hulse bright and girlish as Flora. Nadine Secunde is a strong Miss Jessel, and Phyllis Cannan even matches up to the strength of her predecessor, Joan Cross. An outstanding set, with the Aldeburgh Festival Ensemble including such outstanding artists as Jennifer Stinton on the flute, Nicholas Daniel on the oboe, Richard Watkins on the horn and the Brindisi String Quartet.

Though the recording is in mono only, the very dryness and the sharpness of focus give an extra intensity to the composer's own incomparable reading of his most compressed opera. Peter Pears as Peter Quint is superbly matched by Jennifer Vyvyan as the governess and by Joan Cross as the housekeeper, Mrs Grose. It is also fascinating to hear David Hemmings as a boy treble, already a confident actor. Excellent CD transfer.

Collection

'The world of Britten': (i; ii) *Simple Symphony;* (iii; ii) *Young person's guide to the orchestra.* (iv; v) *Folksong arrangements: Early one morning; The plough boy.* (vi) *Hymn to the Virgin.* (iv; vii; iii; ii) *Serenade for tenor, horn & strings: Nocturne.* Excerpts from: *Ceremony of carols; Noye's Fludde; Spring Symphony; Billy Budd; Peter Grimes.*

☞ (M) *** Decca 436 990-2; *436 990-4.* (i) ECO; (ii) cond. composer; (iii) LSO; (iv) Pears; (v) composer (piano); (vi) St John's College Ch., Guest; (vii) Tuckwell; & var. artists.

The Britten sampler is well worth having for the composer's own vibrant account of the *Variations on a theme of Purcell* and the *Simple Symphony,* where the *Playful pizzicato* emerges with wonderful rhythmic spring and resonance (in the warm Maltings acoustics). The Pears contributions are very enjoyable too, notably the haunting *Nocturne* from the *Serenade,* with Barry Tuckwell in splendid form. Excellent sound throughout, although the tuttis in the *Young person's guide to the orchestra* could with advantage have had a more expansive sonority.

Brouwer, Leo (born 1939)

Concerto elegiaco (Guitar concerto No. 3).
☞ (M) *** BMG/RCA 09026 61605-2 [id.]. Julian Bream, RCA Victor CO, composer – LENNOX BERKELEY; RODRIGO: *Concertos.* ***

Leo Brouwer is a Cuban composer with avant-garde credentials. However, in the present work he has blended earlier Afro-Cuban and Javanese influences with romantic feeling, even adopting a cyclic structure as 'a homage to César Franck or the leitmotif of the nineteenth century'. The result, however, is very much a twentieth-century piece, if by no means a difficult one, with a short but haunting central *Lento* and a brilliant *Toccata*-like finale which sums up the earlier lyrical ideas. Bream's performance draws the music's threads together and yet displays much bravura. He is very well recorded.

Bruch, Max (1838–1920)

Adagio on Celtic themes, Op. 56; Ave Maria, Op. 61; Canzone, Op. 55; Kol Nidrei, Op. 55.
*** BMG/RCA Dig. RD 60757 [60757-2-RC]. Ofra Harnoy, LPO, Mackerras – BLOCH: *Schelomo* etc. ***

Ofra Harnoy undoubtedly has the full measure of Bruch's sombre, Hebraic lyricism in the best-known piece here, *Kol Nidrei,* and she receives warm support from Mackerras. The rest of the programme creates a lighter mood, with the engaging *Adagio on Celtic themes* recalling the *Scottish fantasia.* An excellent recording, made in Watford Town Hall.

Double piano concerto in A flat min., Op. 88a.
☞ **(*) Ph. Dig. 432 095-2 [id.]. Katia and Marielle Labèque, Philh. O, Bychkov – MENDELSSOHN: *Double concerto.* **(*)

Bruch's *Double piano concerto* was conceived as a concertante suite for organ. It was transcribed by

Bruch for two of his students, who then purloined it, edited it out of recognition and claimed to have written it! The work finally reappeared in its original format and was given its concert première by the Cann Duo (who, one hopes, may be persuaded to record it). Bychkov makes a meal of the opening, but the contrapuntal writing for the pianos that follows is rather agreeable; one thinks of Reger. After a second movement which moves from *Andante* to *Allegro molto*, there is a romantic *Adagio* more typical of the composer. The Labèques play with bravura and panache and are given good solid support. The recording is full and resonant but lacks transparency, and the effect is surely heavier than need be.

Violin concertos Nos. 1 in G min.; 2 in D min., Op. 44; 3 in D min., Op. 58; Adagio appassionato, Op. 57; In Memoriam, Op. 65; Konzertstücke, Op. 84; Romanze, Op. 42; Serenade, Op. 75.
(M) *** Ph. 432 282-2 (3) [id.]. Salvatore Accardo, Leipzig GO, Kurt Masur.

This valuable set gathers together all Bruch's major works for violin and orchestra. Although no other piece quite matches the famous *G minor Concerto* in inventive concentration, the delightful *Scottish fantasia*, with its profusion of good tunes, comes near to doing so, and the first movement of the *Second Concerto* has two themes of soaring lyrical ardour. The *Third Concerto* brings another striking lyrical idea in the first movement and has an endearing *Adagio* and a jolly finale. The engagingly insubstantial *Serenade* was originally intended to be a fourth violin concerto. The two-movement *Konzertstück* dates from 1911 and is one of Bruch's last works. *In Memoriam* is finer still and the *Adagio appassionato* and *Romanze* are strongly characterized pieces. Throughout the set Accardo's playing is so persuasive in its restrained passion that even the less inspired moments bring pleasure. Because of the resonant Leipzig acoustics, the Philips engineers put their microphones rather too close to the soloist and there is at times a degree of shrillness on his upper range. This is most noticeable on the first disc, containing the *G minor Concerto*, but the ear adjusts; throughout the rest of the collection one's pleasure is hardly diminished, for the orchestral recording is full and spacious.

Violin concerto No. 1 in G min., Op. 26.
(M) *** Sony/CBS Dig. MDK 44902 [id.]. Cho-Liang Lin, Chicago SO, Slatkin – MENDELSSOHN: *Concerto* *** (with Sandra Rivers (piano): SARASATE: *Introduction and Tarantella* ***; KREISLER: *Liebesfreud* ***).
*** EMI Dig. CDC7 54072-2 [id.]. Kyung Wha Chung, LPO, Tennstedt – BEETHOVEN: *Concerto.* ***
*** ASV Dig. CDDCA 680. Xue Wei, Philh. O, Bakels – SAINT-SAENS: *Concerto No. 3.* ***
(B) *** CfP Dig. CD-CFP 4566; TC-CFP 4566 [Ang. CDB 62920]. Tasmin Little, RLPO, Handley – DVORAK: *Concerto.* ***
(B) *** Pickwick Dig. PCD 829; CIMPC 829 [id.]. Jaime Laredo, SCO – MENDELSSOHN: *Concerto.* ***
*** Chan. Dig. CHAN 8974; ABTD 1563 [id.]. Hideko Udagawa, LSO, Mackerras – BRAHMS: *Concerto.* ***
*** EMI Dig. CDC7 49663-2; EL 749663-4 [id.]. Nigel Kennedy, ECO, Tate – MENDELSSOHN: *Concerto;* SCHUBERT: *Rondo.* ***
☞ (M) **(*) Sony SBK 48274 [id.]. Zukerman, LAPO, Mehta – LALO: *Symphonie espagnole;* VIEUXTEMPS: *Concerto No. 5.* **(*)
☞ (**) Teldec/Warner mono 9031 76443-2 [id.]. Georg Kulenkampff, BPO, Keilberth – BEETHOVEN: *Violin concerto.* (*(*))

There have been few accounts on record of Bruch's slow movement that begin to match the raptness of Lin. He is accompanied most sensitively by Slatkin and the Chicago orchestra, and this reading is totally compelling in its combination of passion and purity, strength and dark, hushed intensity. The Kreisler and Sarasate bonuses, recorded three years earlier, are also presented with great flair. The recording is excellent.

Compared with her earlier Decca recording, Chung's expressive rubato is more marked, so that in the first movement the opening theme is more impulsive, and her freedom in the second subject vividly conveys the sort of magic you find in her live performances. The slow movement brings extreme contrasts of dynamic and expression from orchestra as well as soloist, and the finale is again impulsive in its bravura. That makes this an exceptionally attractive issue and an essential one for this much-loved violinist's admirers.

Xue Wei's approach to the concerto is at once passionately committed and refined in its delicacy of detail. Fortunately he is accompanied superbly by Kees Bakels, while Wei can equally seduce the listener with a most magical pianissimo. The slow movement is ravishing in its poetic flair, and the finale is full of fire. An outstanding début.

The movement in the Bruch where Tasmin Little's individuality comes out most clearly is the central *Adagio*, raptly done with a deceptive simplicity of phrasing, totally unselfconscious, that matches the purity of her sound. Her speeds in the outer movements are broader than those of such rivals as Lin. At full price this would be a first-rate recommendation: on CfP it is an outstanding bargain.

Jaime Laredo with consistently fresh and sweet tone gives a delightfully direct reading, warmly expressive but never for a moment self-indulgent. The orchestral ensemble is particularly impressive, when no conductor is involved. With first-rate modern digital recording, this is a highlight of the Pickwick budget-price catalogue.

Full of temperament, Hideko Udagawa gives a persuasively passionate performance of the Bruch, very well recorded, and with strong, colourful playing from the orchestra the hushed opening of the slow movement is caught beautifully.

Nigel Kennedy's masculine strength goes with a totally unsentimental view of Bruch's lyricism, as in the central slow movement. This may not have quite the individual poetry of the very finest versions; but, coupled with an outstanding account of the Mendelssohn and the rare Schubert *Rondo*, it makes an excellent recommendation. The recording is full, warm and well balanced.

Zukerman's reissued Sony triptych shows him at his finest, and it is a pity that the close-up balance brings inevitable reservations. His Bruch is a passionately extrovert performance, tempered by genuine tenderness in the slow movement. The brilliantly lit recording increases the sense of fiery energy in the outer sections and, with the excitement of the solo playing and the strongly committed accompaniment, the larger-than-life effect is almost overwhelming.

Kulenkampff made his famous recording of the Beethoven *Violin concerto*, with which this is coupled, in 1936. His recording of the Bruch concerto was less well-known in the UK than the Beethoven. The Bruch dates from the war years (1941) and is, if anything, even more riveting. The opening line of the violin entry has such character that most versions recorded since sound pale beside it, and the slow movement has a tremendously gutsy ardour. It is an unforgettable performance, and Keilberth's strong backing is worthy of the soloist. Kulenkampff was an artist of sublime refinement who possessed a tone of great purity. However, as with the latter, the transfer is poor in quality. Nevertheless this record should not be missed by anyone who cares about violin playing and the documentary history of the instrument's greatest executants.

Violin concerto No. 1 in G min., Op. 26; Scottish fantasy, Op. 46.
*** BMG/RCA RD 86214 [RCA 6214-2-RC]. Heifetz, New SO of L., Sargent – VIEUXTEMPS: *Concerto No. 5.* ***

All lovers of great violin playing should at least hear this coupling, for Heifetz's panache and the subtlety of his bowing and colour bring a wonderful freshness to Bruch's charming Scottish whimsy.

Violin concerto No. 2 in D min., Op. 44; Scottish fantasy, Op. 46.
**(*) EMI Dig. CDC7 49071-2 [id.]. Perlman, Israel PO, Mehta.

Perlman may be less intimately reflective in both works than he was when he recorded this coupling before with the New Philharmonia, but in the fast movements there are ample compensations in the sharp concentration from first to last.

Kol Nidrei, Op. 47.
*** DG Dig. 427 323-2 [id.]. Matt Haimovitz, Chicago SO, Levine – LALO: *Concerto;* SAINT-SAENS: *Concerto No. 1.* ***
(B) ** DG 429 155-2 [id.]. Fournier, LOP, Martinon – DVORAK: *Cello concerto;* BLOCH: *Schelomo.* **(*)

Matt Haimovitz, born in Israel, has a natural feeling for the piece and his performance, balancing restraint with expressive intensity, is serenely moving.

Fournier's performance, while not without feeling, is slightly lacking in romantic urgency.

Scottish fantasia for violin and orchestra, Op. 46.
*** BMG/RCA Dig. RD 60942. Anne Akiko Meyers, RPO, López-Cobos – LALO: *Symphonie espagnole.* **(*)

Anne Meyers is admirably partnered by López-Cobos and the RPO. The very opening, with its melancholy, sonorous brass, is unforgettable, and the hushed violin entry is to be matched later by most tender playing in the *Andante*, where the response of the RPO is equally warm. First-class Abbey Road recording, expansive and very well balanced.

Symphonies Nos. 1 in E flat, Op. 28; 2 in F min., Op. 36; 3 in E, Op. 51.
☞ **(*) EMI CDS5 550 046-2 (3) [id.]. Gürzenich O; Cologne PO, James Conlon.

Symphonies Nos. 1 in E flat; 2 in F min.; 3 in E; 7 Swedish dances, Op. 63.
** Ph. Dig. 420 932-2 (2) [id.]. Leipzig GO, Masur.

When the first of Bruch's three symphonies is the one that is most striking in its invention and each has its weaknesses, one has to deduce that he was more a symphonist by default than by nature. Masur's performances with the Leipzig Gewandhaus Orchestra are characteristically warm and refined, with smooth recording to match, but sparkle is largely missing.

On the whole, James Conlon's performances are more convincing, if not ideal. Both orchestras (it is not clear which plays which work, or indeed if these are two different names for the same group) emphasize the music's Brahmsian and Schumannesque derivations, and indeed a rather good case is made for the *Third Symphony* here. The romantic opening is richly done, the slow-movement variations are warmly effective and the Scherzo (which the composer regarded as the finest movement in all three works) is made to sound quite original in its scoring. Only the finale rather lets the piece down. The orchestral playing is committed throughout, but at times one feels that greater drive is needed from the conductor. There is no fill-up, and the second CD plays for only 36 minutes.

Bruckner, Anton (1824–96)

Symphonies Nos. '0'; 1–9; (i) *Helgoland;* (i; ii) *Psalm 150;* (i; iii) *Te Deum.*
☞ (M) **(*) DG Dig./Analogue 429 025-2 (10) [id.]. Chicago SO, Barenboim, (i) with Chicago SO Ch.; (ii) Ruth Welting; (iii) Jessye Norman, Yvonne Minton, David Rendall, Samuel Ramey.

Barenboim's cycle has many excellent things, not least the account of No. 8, volatile and passionate, with flexible phrasing and urgent stringendi. The *Ninth*, too, is very well done, if not a first choice. Barenboim gives us the underrated *Nullte*, a performance comparable to Chailly's, though less successful than with Haitink. Barenboim brings keener and deeper responses to No. 3, and his *Seventh* has a strongly flowing current; although these performances are not to be recommended in preference to Karajan or Jochum at their best – as in the *Eighth* – they deserve to rank alongside them, which is no mean achievement. In Nos. 1–3 and 8 (and also the *Te Deum*) Barenboim has the advantage of excellent digital sound, and the analogue recordings are spaciously transferred, though with just a hint of fierceness on Bruckner's massive fortissimos, noticeable immediately in No. 4. But no one investing in this set is likely to be greatly disappointed, and the magnificent *Te Deum* and *Psalm 150* are majestically done, though Ruth Welting is too shallow in the *Psalm* and David Rendall too tight of tone in the *Te Deum. Helgoland* is the valuable rarity.

Symphonies Nos. '0'; 1–9.
δ☞ (B) **(*) Ph. 442 040-2 (9) [id.]. Concg. O, Haitink.

Haitink's set of Bruckner symphonies (reissued as part of the Haitink Edition) has all the classic virtues: they are well shaped and free from affectation or any kind of agogic distortion. Haitink's grasp of the architecture is strong and his feeling for beauty of detail refined. He has a less developed sense of mystery and atmosphere than Jochum, whose readings have a spiritual dimension at which Haitink only hints; however, Jochum recorded the Nowak edition. Haitink's judgements on matters of text are as sound as his approach is dedicated, and he secures consistently fine playing from the Concertgebouw Orchestra. Only the *Eighth* with its generally brisk tempi is at all controversial. The CD transfers bring much more vivid sound than on LP, yet the overall balance is always convincing. The set also has the additional advantage of economy, with only No. 1 split between CDs; the other symphonies each occupy a single CD.

Symphonies Nos. 1–9.
(M) *** DG 429 648-2 (9) [id.]. BPO, Karajan.
(M) *** DG 429 079-2 (9) [id.]. BPO or Bav. RSO, Jochum.

The reappearance of Karajan's magnificent cycle, long a yardstick by which others were measured – and at mid-price, too – must be warmly welcomed. We have sung the praises of these recordings loud and long, and in their new format they are outstanding value.

Jochum's DG cycle was recorded between 1958 and 1967. It enjoys the advantage of accommodating one symphony per disc. No apology need be made for the quality of the recorded sound. Jochum still has special claims as a guide in this terrain. He communicates a lofty inspiration to his players, and many of these readings can more than hold their own with later rivals.

Symphony No. 0 in D min.; Overture in G min.
**(*) Decca Dig. 421 593-2 [id.]. Berlin RSO, Chailly.

Riccardo Chailly's account of the unnumbered *D minor* (the so-called *Die Nullte*) is eminently acceptable. The Berlin Radio Orchestra respond well to Chailly's direction and, both as a recording and as a performance, this deserves recommendation.

Symphony No. 0 in D min.; (i) Helgoland (for male chorus & orchestra); (i; ii) Psalm 150 (for soprano, chorus & orchestra).
☞ (M) **(*) DG 437 250-2 [id.]. Chicago SO, Barenboim, with (i) Chicago Symphony Ch., (ii) Ruth Welting.

Bruckner's early *D minor Symphony* contains some inspired music. Barenboim shows evident affection for it but, once again donning his Furtwänglerian mantle, he is not always content to let the music speak for itself. However, he gets a generally positive response from the Chicago Symphony, and the 1979 recording is full and spacious. In *Helgoland* the islanders pray to be spared from the marauding Romans; a storm saves them in this brief but graphic piece. The Chicago forces sing and play with heart-warming resonance in both this and the Psalm setting and, although Ruth Welting is too shallow a soloist in the *Psalm*, this disc is well worth considering.

Symphonies Nos. 0 in D min.; 8 in C min.
☞ (M) (*) Sony Dig. S2K 45864 (2) [id.]. Israel PO, Mehta.

Zubin Mehta made his LP début with a fine account of the *Ninth Symphony* on the Decca label in the late 1960s. Glimpses of that initial promise have been relatively few of late, and these accounts of the lovely unnumbered *D minor Symphony* and the mighty *Eighth* are not among them. The Israel orchestra is not strong on refinement, nor does Mehta's conception have much in the way of nobility or sensitivity.

Symphony No. 1 in C min.
*** Orfeo Dig. C 145851A [id.]. Bav. State O, Sawallisch.

Symphony No. 1 in C min.; (i) Te Deum.
(M) **(*) DG Dig. 435 068-2; *435 068-4* [id.]. Chicago SO, Barenboim; (i) with Jessye Norman, Minton, Rendall, Ramey, Chicago Symphony Ch.

Symphonies Nos. 1 in C min.; 5 in B flat.
**(*) DG 415 985-2 (2) [id.]. BPO, Karajan.

Sawallisch's interpretation of the *First* is impressive in its honesty and dignity. There is warmth and some beautiful playing from the fine Bavarian orchestra, which is recorded in a spacious, yet not over-reverberant acoustic.

Barenboim's version of the *Symphony No. 1* comes with the *Te Deum* with its starry quartet of soloists and the magnificent Chicago Symphony Chorus. In both works he directs beautifully played, spontaneous-sounding performances that mould Brucknerian lines persuasively, but in the *Symphony* the dramatic tension is less keen, lacking something in concentration. The early digital recording is good but not ideally clear, with a brightness that needs a little taming.

Karajan's No. 1 is digital (1982), but the recording is brightly lit and not always ideally expansive at the bottom end. It is still an incisive and powerful reading. Karajan, like Sawallisch, uses the revised Linz version. In the *Fifth Symphony* the ear registers a greater resonant warmth in the (1977) analogue sound. The reading is not just poised and polished; it is superbly structured on every level, clear on detail as well as on overall architecture, even if the slow movement lacks some of the simple dedication which makes Jochum's earlier version with the same orchestra so compelling.

Symphony No. 2 in C min.
☞ *** Decca Dig. 436 154-2 [id.]. Concg. O, Chailly.
☞ *** Decca Dig. 436 844-2 [id.]. Chicago SO, Solti.
*** DG Dig. 415 988-2 [id.]. BPO, Karajan.

Bruckner's *Second Symphony* is very long. Chailly uses the complete, Haas edition and his laid-back performance does not shirk that problem. It is a beautifully simple reading, with the slow-movement climax nobly graduated, a strong Scherzo without repeats (the Trio has a tuneful charm) and a finale that is not pressed forward ruthlessly but generates a positive and exciting closing section. The Decca recording is appropriately spacious and luminous, and for many this will be a first choice for the most elusive work in the Bruckner canon.

Solti, too, follows Haas. His overall momentum is characteristically more urgent than Chailly but there is no real sense of too much emotional pressure; indeed some will feel Chailly is too relaxed with his spaciously moulded paragraphs. The effect of the Chicago recording, too, is more robust and full-blooded. It is a satisfying alternative view. Solti aficionados need not hesitate.

Karajan modifies the Nowak edition by opening out some of the cuts, but by no means all. He starts reticently, only later expanding in grandeur. The scherzo at a fast speed is surprisingly lightweight, the finale relatively slow and spacious. It is a noble reading, not always helped by rather bright digital recording.

Symphony No. 3 in D min. (original, 1873 version).
☞ (M) *** Teldec/Warner Dig. 4509 91445-2 [id.]. Frankfurt RSO, Eliahu Inbal.

There are in all three versions of the *Third Symphony*: the first completed on the last day of 1873, a second which Bruckner undertook immediately after the completion of the *Fifth Symphony* in 1877, and then, after that proved unsuccessful, a third which he made in 1889. The 1873 is by far the longest version, running to nearly 66 minutes (the first movement alone lasts 24 minutes), and for those who have either of the others it will make far more than a fascinating appendix. The playing of the Frankfurt Radio Orchestra under Eliahu Inbal is very respectable indeed, with a sensitive feeling for atmosphere and refined dynamic contrasts; the recording is most acceptable without being top-drawer. Reissued at mid-price, this disc is even more tempting.

Symphony No. 3 in D min. (1877 version).
*** Ph. Dig. 422 411-2 [id.]. VPO, Bernard Haitink.
☞ * Decca Dig. 436 154-2 [id.]. Chicago SO, Solti.

Haitink gives us the 1877 version, favoured by many Bruckner scholars. Questions of edition apart, this is a performance of enormous breadth and majesty, and Philips give it a recording to match. The playing of the Vienna Philharmonic is glorious throughout, and even collectors who have alternative versions should acquire this magnificent issue.

Despite excellent Decca engineering, Solti's account with the Chicago Symphony does not begin to compete with Haitink and the Vienna Philharmonic (or, for that matter, with his earlier, Concertgebouw disc from the mid-1960s, now restored to circulation in the Haitink Edition). This is pretty crude and coarse, with little of the refinement of sonority with which collectors of Reiner's records will associate the Chicago orchestra.

Symphony No. 3 in D min. (Nowak edition).
*** DG Dig. 421 362-2 [id.]. BPO, Karajan.
☞ (M) *** Decca 425 032-2 [id.]. VPO, Karl Boehm.
☞ **(*) BMG/RCA Dig. 09026 61374-2. N. German RSO, Hamburg, Wand.

Karajan opts for the Nowak edition of 1888–9. One is awe-struck by the eloquence and beauty of the orchestral playing and the command of architecture here. Karajan achieves a sense of majesty in the opening movement and an other-worldliness and spirituality in the slow movement that cannot fail to move the listener.

There are many who admire Boehm's Bruckner, and he certainly controls the lyrical flow of this symphony convincingly, helped by fine playing from the VPO. The vintage (1970) Decca recording, made in the Sofiensaal, is excellent, with splendid detail and firm sonority, and the performance is admirably free from eccentricity. Like Karajan and Jochum, Boehm opts for the Nowak text, and if his version is less imaginative than either of theirs it has a certain magnetic quality and makes a good mid-priced alternative. The CD transfer is admirable.

As in his earlier version from 1981, made with the Cologne orchestra, Günter Wand also opts for the 1889 version. This recording was compiled from public performances given at the Hamburg Musikhalle in January 1992, and the feeling of a live occasion comes across. The new version is better played and more sumptuously recorded, even though the sound is not in the demonstration bracket. Generally speaking, Wand's overall conception of the work is largely unchanged. The only flaw in what remains an altogether compelling account is the slow movement, which some Brucknerians may find a shade brisk.

Symphonies Nos. 3 in D min.; 8 in C min.
☞ (B) *** Sony SB2K 53519 (2) [id.]. Cleveland O, Szell.

In No. 3 Szell does not indulge the listener in a gentle, moulded style and the close-up Cleveland recording adds to the tangibility of his reading. But this outstanding American orchestra – here at its peak in 1966 – under the most incisive of conductors is hard to resist. Szell uses the controversial 1889 Nowak Edition in which Bruckner was persuaded by Franz Schalk to cut large sections of the finale.

Szell himself used to argue that this revision was preferable to the original version. Not many Brucknerians will agree, but this reissue presents a marvellously strong interpretation which is well worth having in its own right. In No. 8 Szell again uses a suspect text, but here the differences between this and the Nowak edition favoured by Jochum are relatively minor. Szell's interpretation as a whole is masterly, with refinement and strength, expansiveness and drama superbly balanced, and the Cleveland Orchestra produces glorious playing, recorded, like No. 3, in the spacious acoustics of Severance Hall (in 1969). Szell finds a concentration that matches and outshines Karajan's earlier, Berlin Philharmonic version – though not his final, superb, Vienna Philharmonic recording. Szell's manner is direct and tempi are generally uncontroversial, the exception being the Scherzo where, like Klemperer, Szell favours a massively measured tempo to bring out the bell-like tolling of the ostinato figures. The last two movements are held together superbly, and in this instance there is a genuine argument in favour of keeping the cuts which Bruckner himself approved, when the Haas Edition arguably marries together two different versions of the score. The CD transfers are expertly done: the sound remains brightly lit but the dynamic range in No. 8 is wide, partly because Szell insists on real pianissimo playing.

Symphony No. 4 in E flat (Romantic) (original, 1874 version).
☞ (M) **(*) Teldec/Warner 9031 77597-2 [id.]. Frankfurt RSO, Inbal.

Like the *Third*, there are three versions of the *Romantic Symphony*, and no one has recorded the original before. The differences are most obvious in the Scherzo, a completely different and more fiery movement, but the opening of the finale is also totally different. Inbal's performance is more than adequate – indeed he has a genuine feeling for the Bruckner idiom and pays scrupulous attention to dynamic refinements. The recording is well detailed, though the climaxes almost (but not quite) reach congestion. An indispensable and fascinating issue, especially attractive at mid-price.

Symphony No. 4 in E flat (Romantic).
(B) *** DG 427 200-2 [id.]. BPO, Jochum.
☞ (M) *** DG 439 522-2 [id.]. BPO, Karajan.
☞ (M) *** Decca 425 036-2 [id.]. VPO, Karl Boehm.
*** Decca Dig. 425 613-2 [id.]. Concg. O, Riccardo Chailly.
*** Denon Dig. C37 7126 [id.]. Dresden State O, Blomstedt.
☞ (M) **(*) EMI CDM7 69006-2 [id.]. BPO, Karajan.
☞ (B) **(*) Pickwick Dig. PCD 1059 [id.]. Hallé O, Skrowaczewski.
☞ ** Teldec/Warner Dig. 9031 73272-2 [id.]. BPO, Barenboim.

Jochum's way with Bruckner is unique. So gentle is his hand that the opening of each movement or even the beginning of each theme emerges into the consciousness rather than starting normally. The purist may object that, in order to do this, Jochum reduces the speed far below what is marked, but Jochum is for the listener who wants above all to love Bruckner. The recording from the late 1960s still sounds vivid and firm.

Karajan's opening (on his DG version) also has more beauty and a greater feeling of mystery than almost anyone else on CD. As in his earlier, EMI record, Karajan brings a keen sense of forward movement to this music as well as showing a firm grip on its architecture. His slow movement is magnificent. The current remastering of the 1975 analogue recording, made in the Philharmonie, is very impressive. The sound may lack the transparency and detail of the very finest of his records, but it is full and firmly focused and there is no doubt that this is a performance of considerable stature.

Boehm's very compelling 1974 performance – even finer than that of the *Third* – is beautifully shaped, finely played and splendidly recorded. The sound on CD is very spacious and realistic, finer than Jochum's for DG, with very impressive strings and brass. At medium price it goes to the top of the list alongside Jochum and Karajan.

Chailly's new account has two things in its favour: the incomparable Concertgebouw Orchestra at their most resplendent, and a Decca recording of magnificent opulence. Chailly himself is a far from unimpressive Brucknerian, who can evoke a strong sense of atmosphere. Perhaps he does not quite match the greatest of his rivals in strength of personality, but this account has a great deal to commend it and will have a high priority with those who enjoy sound which is undoubtedly in the demonstration bracket.

Blomstedt opts for the Nowak edition, and the spacious and resonant acoustic in which his version is recorded lends it a pleasing sense of atmosphere. The performance has a certain ardour and conviction that impress. The slow movement has more feeling and poetry than one normally associates with this conductor, and the sumptuous tone produced by the Dresden orchestra is a joy in itself. This is not bright and analytical, but it is a beautiful sound and it suits Bruckner.

Karajan's earlier recording for EMI had undoubted electricity and combines simplicity and strength. The playing of the Berlin Philharmonic is very fine. The resonance means that there is a touch of harshness on the considerable fortissimos, while pianissimos are relatively diffuse. However, at mid-price this remains well worth considering.

Stanislav Skrowaczewski's reading with the Hallé Orchestra is eminently straightforward and well shaped. As one would expect from this conductor, the tempi are well judged and the concept spacious and majestic, with scrupulous attention to detail in matters of both phrasing and dynamics. The playing from the Hallé is responsive and sensitive, and there is no idiosyncrasy or self-indulgence. Overall this is a fine performance, full of perceptive touches. The recording has plenty of back-to-front perspective and no lack of atmosphere, though the acoustic does not have great warmth. There is a certain digital chill in big climaxes.

Barenboim's account with the Berlin Philharmonic is his second recording of the work. This well-recorded version is decent rather than distinguished; it is difficult to find flaws but at the same time it inspires little enthusiasm. The verdict here is: nothing special. There can be no reason to pay full price for it.

Symphony No. 5 in B flat.
☞ *** Decca Dig. 433 819-2 [id.]. Concg. O, Chailly.

Chailly gave us an outstanding Bruckner *Seventh* with the Berlin Radio Symphony Orchestra in the early days of CD which still ranks high among all the competition (though it is temporarily withdrawn). This new version of the *Fifth* is, if anything, even finer. The Royal Concertgebouw Orchestra play with sumptuous magnificence, and Chailly's overall control of a work that is notable for its diverse episodes is unerring, moving towards an overwhelming final apotheosis. The *Adagio* is very beautiful and never sounds hurried. The Decca recording is superb, very much in the demonstration bracket, with the brass attacking brilliantly, yet producing the fullest sonority, and the strings equally expansive. An easy first choice.

Symphony No. 5 in B flat; (i) *Te Deum.*
*** Ph. Dig. 422 342-2 (2) [id.]. (i) Mattilla, Mentzer, Cole, Holl, Bav. R. Ch., VPO, Haitink.

Bernard Haitink's *Fifth* is superbly recorded and the orchestral playing is predictably of the very highest quality. The only snag, perhaps, is the slow movement, which is rather on the brisk side, yet at the same time he succeeds in conveying an unhurried effect. Anyway this is a performance of nobility, and the *Te Deum* is an added inducement to invest in this set.

Symphony No. 6 in A.
☞ *** Decca Dig. 436 129-2 [id.]. San Francisco SO, Blomstedt (with WAGNER: *Siegfried Idyll ***).
*** Orfeo Dig. C 024821 [id.]. Bav. State O, Sawallisch.
(M) *** EMI CDM7 63351-2 [id.]. New Philh. O, Klemperer.
**(*) DG 419 194-2 [id.]. BPO, Karajan.
☞ (*) Telarc Dig. CD 80264 [id.]. Cincinnati SO, López-Cobos.

Blomstedt uses the Nowak edition, and in warmth and intensity the San Francisco strings readily match those of any rival, even Karajan's Berlin Philharmonic. The performance is splendidly shaped and the broad-spanned slow movement is particularly fine. Quite apart from providing a generous and beautifully played coupling (which no rival does), Decca's recording is also outstanding, at once full-bodied and warm but cleanly defined.

Sawallisch's account of the *Sixth Symphony* is beautifully shaped, spacious yet never portentous or inflated. Tempi – never too slow but never hurried – are beautifully judged, and the Bavarian State Orchestra respond splendidly to his direction. The acoustic has plenty of warmth but is not too reverberant, and the recording sounds excellent.

Klemperer directs a characteristically strong and direct reading. It is disarmingly simple rather than expressive in the slow movement (faster than usual) but is always concentrated and strong, and the finale is particularly well held together. Splendid playing from the orchestra and clear, bright recording.

Karajan is not as commanding here as in his other Bruckner recordings yet this is still a compelling performance, tonally very beautiful and with a glowing account of the slow movement that keeps it in proportion. The 1980 analogue recording might ideally have been more expansive.

Jesús López-Cobos's cycle with the Cincinnati orchestra on Telarc has so far aroused cool responses, and his *Sixth* is unlikely to prompt the pulse to run faster. This is very much *vin ordinaire*.

Symphony No. 7 in E (original version).

☞ (M) ** Teldec/Warner Dig. 4509 92686-2 [id.]. Frankfurt RSO, Inbal.

In terms of the excellence of orchestral playing and vividness of recording, Inbal's *Seventh* is well up to the standard of his Bruckner series, using the original scores; but the performance itself, although it does not lack an overall structural grip, lacks the flow of adrenalin that can make this loud symphony so compulsive, and the orgasmic climax of the slow movement is much less telling without those two famous cymbal crashes.

Symphony No. 7 in E.
(M) *** Ph. 434 155-2; *434 155-4* [id.]. Concg. O, Haitink.
(M) *** EMI CDM7 69923-2. BPO, Karajan.
*** Denon Dig. C37 7286 [id.]. Dresden State O, Blomstedt.
☞ *** DG Dig. 435 786-2 [id.]. Dresden State O, Sinopoli.
☞ *** EMI Dig. CDC7 54434-2 [id.]. LPO, Welser-Möst.
☞ **(*) Decca Dig. 430 841-2 [id.]. Cleveland O, Dohnányi.
☞ ** Teldec/Warner Dig. 9031 73243-2 [id.]. NYPO, Kurt Masur.
☞ *(*) BMG/RCA Dig. 09026 61398-2 [id.]. N. German RSO, Wand.

With our previous first choice, Chailly's highly praised Decca version, suddenly deleted just as we go to press, Haitink's 1978 version offers a fine alternative at mid-price. The recording is wide in range and refined in detail, yet retains the ambient warmth of the Concertgebouw. Haitink's reading is more searching than his earlier version, made in the 1960s. The Concertgebouw Orchestra play with their accustomed breadth of tone and marvellously blended ensemble.

Karajan's reading of No. 7 for EMI shows a superb feeling for the work's architecture, and the playing of the Berlin Philharmonic is gorgeous. The recording has striking resonance and amplitude, making a good alternative medium-price choice for this favourite Bruckner symphony, generally preferable to his later, digital recording for DG. The EMI reading has a sense of mystery that is really rather special.

A well-shaped account of the *Seventh* comes from Herbert Blomstedt and the Staatskapelle, Dresden; the beautiful playing of the orchestra and the expansive acoustic of the Lukaskirche are strong points in its favour. The reading is totally dedicated and Blomstedt has both strength and imagination to commend him.

It is not uncommon to hear Sinopoli spoken of as a 'stop-go' conductor, and it is true that he sometimes tends to cosset this or that detail and is reluctant to allow the musical argument to speak for itself. His account of the *Seventh Symphony* with the Staatskapelle, Dresden, is, however, unaffected, very well held together and beautifully played. Indeed it must be numbered among the best of Sinopoli's recordings, both artistically and technically, although Blomstedt's set with the same orchestra has greater nobility.

EMI's version with the LPO conducted by Franz Welser-Möst comes from a 1991 Prom and so enjoys a warmer ambience than most studio performances. The LPO are responsive and produce a real Bruckner sound, save perhaps at the bottom end of the aural spectrum. As one would expect from a native Austrian, Welser-Möst has a natural feel for Bruckner's spacious lyricism and there is little here to quarrel with. Audience noise is minimal, save at the very end, when it is anything but! This is among the better newer versions, though not a first recommendation.

The newest Decca Dohnányi recording of the *Seventh* sounds quite wonderful, with the rich acoustics of Severance Hall producing the most sumptuous string-tone and glorious brass sonorities. Of course, this would not be possible if the playing itself was not of the highest calibre, but ensemble here is peerless and the orchestral timbres a pleasure to the ear. The opening arching theme of the first movement is beautifully shaped and the similar string cantilena (over a sustained timpani crescendo), which leads to the coda on the brass, is as arresting as the cymbal-capped climax of the *Adagio*. The Scherzo gallumphs ebulliently and the finale has plenty of rhythmic lift and rounds the performance off without being too pontifical. This could well be a first choice for those for whom the demonstration sound-quality is a paramount consideration. Others may find that, even though the orchestral playing is thoroughly committed, Dohnányi's moulded phrasing is at times too calculated, missing that last ounce of spontaneity that gives the impression of a live performance.

Kurt Masur's account with the New York Philharmonic comes from a live concert, given in September 1991 when their relationship was in the bloom of youth and he was working hard to banish the unrefined sonority that distinguished so many of their recordings with Mehta. They certainly produce a more cultured and better-blended sound than before. His opening is very spacious and expansive with consequent accellerandi later on. The performance is arguably more characterful than his Leipzig account from the 1970s and has quite a lot going for it – albeit not quite enough to overcome the unpleasing acoustic of Avery Fisher Hall, hardly a Bruckner venue, and certainly not enough to effect a challenge to the front recommendations.

Günther Wand currently traverses Bruckner terrain for the second time but less impressively in this instance than in his fine account of the *Third*. The sound, as usual from this source, is pleasingly recessed but the performance does not add up to anything special. In fact on most counts this is not an improvement on his earlier version and certainly offers no challenge to our first recommendations.

Symphony No. 8 in C min.
ⓒ *** DG Dig. 427 611-2 (2) [id.]. VPO, Karajan.
(B) **(*) DG 431 163-2. BPO, Jochum.
☞ (M) *** EMI Dig. CDM7 64849-2 [id.]. LPO, Tennstedt.

Karajan's last version of the *Eighth Symphony* is with the Vienna Philharmonic Orchestra and is the most impressive of them all. The sheer beauty of sound and opulence of texture is awe-inspiring but never draws attention to itself: this is a performance in which beauty and truth go hand in hand. The recording is superior to either of its predecessors in terms of naturalness of detail and depth of perspective. This is quite an experience!

Jochum uses the Nowak Edition, which involves cuts in the slow movement and finale, and in addition he often presses the music on impulsively in both the outer movements and especially in his account of the *Adagio*, where the climax has great passion and thrust. The symphony fits on to a single bargain-priced CD – which is worth any Brucknerian's money.

The plainness and honesty of Tennstedt in Bruckner is heard at its finest in this impressive account of the *Eighth*. It may not have the degree of exaltation which marked the performance which he conducted with this same orchestra at the Proms just after he made this record, but the inwardness and hushed beauty of the great *Adagio* in particular are superbly projected in unforced concentration. Though Karajan conveys more of the work's visionary power, Tennstedt in his comparative reticence carries similar conviction. Where generally in the other symphonies he prefers the Haas editions to those of Nowak, here he is firmly in favour of Nowak without the additional material in the recapitulation. Fine, well-balanced recording, with the CD clarity filled out by the fullness of ambience. EMI's No. 1 Studio is made to sound like a concert hall.

Symphony No. 9 in D min. (1896 original version).
☞ (M) **(*) Teldec/Warner Dig. 4509 91446-2 [id.]. Frankfurt RSO, Eliahu Inbal.

Eliahu Inbal's reading of the *Ninth* with the Frankfurt Radio Orchestra is far from negligible, even though it may not be a performance of the highest stature. The playing is often very fine, and Inbal is scrupulously attentive to detail; however, there is not the sense of scale that is to be found in the finest of his rivals.

Symphony No. 9 in D min.
ⓒ (M) *** Sony MYK 44825 [id.]. Columbia SO, Bruno Walter.
(M) *** DG 429 904-2; *429 904-4* [id.]. BPO, Karajan.
*** Teldec/Warner Dig. 9031 72140-2 [id.]. BPO, Barenboim.
*** DG Dig. 427 345-2 [id.]. VPO, Giulini.
(B) **(*) DG 429 514-2; *429 514-4* [id.]. BPO, Jochum.
**(*) Decca Dig. 425 405-2 [id.]. Cleveland O, Dohnányi.
☞ (M) *(*) EMI CDM5 65177-2 [id.]. Chicago SO, Giulini.
☞ *(*) DG Dig. 435 350-2 [id.]. VPO, Bernstein.

Bruno Walter's 1959 recording is a superb achievement. Walter's mellow, persuasive reading leads one on through the leisurely paragraphs so that the logic and coherence seem obvious where other performances can sound aimless. Perhaps the scherzo is not vigorous enough to provide the fullest contrast – though the sound here has ample bite – yet it exactly fits the overall conception. The final slow movement has a nobility which makes one glad that Bruckner never completed the intended finale. After this, anything would have been an anticlimax.

This DG Galleria reissue offers a glorious performance of Bruckner's last and uncompleted symphony, moulded in a way that is characteristic of Karajan and displaying a simple, direct nobility that is sometimes missing in this work. Even in a competitive field, this 1966 disc stands out at mid-price, to rank alongside Bruno Walter's noble 1959 version.

Daniel Barenboim's new account has depth and strength and, of course, the advantage of superb orchestral playing. Moreover the recorded sound has splendid body and transparency and, although it does not displace the Karajan account or the old Bruno Walter, must be numbered among the strongest newer recommendations.

Giulini's *Ninth* is a performance of great stature, the product of deep thought. As always, there is the keenest feeling for texture and beauty of contour, and he distils a powerful sense of mystery from the first and third movements. The DG recording has a welcome sense of space and transparency of texture.

Jochum's reading has greater mystery than any other and the orchestral playing reaches a degree of eloquence that disarms criticism. If at times Jochum tends to phrase too affectionately so that consequently the architecture does not emerge unscathed, he is still magnetic in everything he does. The 1966 recording sounds remarkably good.

Decca provide the Cleveland Orchestra and Christoph von Dohnányi with a recording of enormous clarity and presence. Dohnányi's reading makes the most of the dramatic tensions inherent in the score – at the expense, perhaps, of its sense of mystery. It gives the impression of a newly cleaned and restored painting, with the colours in bold relief and the drama highlighted.

Giulini's earlier Chicago version is a good deal less persuasive than his later, DG recording. There is no lack of power or grandeur and, predictably, Giulini expends enormous care over detail, fashioning each phrase with thought and concern. Indeed that may lie at the heart of the problem, for in some ways the sheer mystery of this noble score seems to elude him on this occasion.

Bernstein draws some beautiful (and at times inspired) playing from the Vienna Philharmonic in his 1990 performance in the Musikverein, but his account is not consistently satisfying. The first movement periodically grinds to a halt and there is no sense of that vital current which any great symphonic performance must exhibit. The Scherzo, too, will be too measured for most tastes, but things pick up in the finale.

CHAMBER MUSIC

String quintet in F.
(M) *** Decca 430 296-2 [id.]. VPO Quintet with H. Weiss – SCHMIDT: *Piano quintet.* ***

Bruckner's beautiful *Quintet* is music of substance and depth and has not been better served on records since this account by the Vienna Philharmonic Quintet, recorded in the Sofiensaal in 1974.

VOCAL MUSIC

Helgoland (cantata).
☞ (B) *** Pickwick PCD 1042; *PK 515.* Ambrosian Male Voice Ch., L. Symphonica, Wyn Morris – WAGNER: *Liebesmahl der Apostel.* **(*)

Helgoland was written during the long-delayed composition of Bruckner's *Ninth Symphony*, and it might be regarded as a secular counterpart to the *Te Deum.* It is as well to ignore the banal words of Dr August Silberstein about the North Sea island which was successively under the crowns of Denmark and Great Britain, before being ceded to Germany. Though latterly the work was underprized, early responses were more enthusiastic than was common with Bruckner, and this recording, ardently conducted by Wyn Morris, helps to explain why. The Ambrosians sing with fervour and – despite the relatively small chorus being just a little dwarfed by the orchestra – the final climax has splendid bite and breadth. The sound is atmospheric and the CD transfer highly successful.

(i) *Masses Nos. 1 in D min.; 2 in E min.; 3 in F min.; Motets: Afferentur regi virgines; Ave Maria; Christus factus est pro nobis; Ecce sacerdos magnus; Locus iste; Os justi; Pange lingua; Tota pulchra es, Maria; Vexilla regis; Virga Jesse.* (ii) *Psalm 150; Te Deum.*
(M) **(*) DG 423 127-2 (4) [id.]. (i) Soloists, Bav. R. Ch. & SO; (ii) Soloists, Ch. of German Op., Berlin, BPO; Jochum.

Bruckner's choral music, like the symphonies, spans his musical career. With excellent soloists, including Maria Stader, Edith Mathis, Ernst Haefliger, Kim Borg and Karl Ridderbusch, the performances of the large-scale works have fine eloquence and admirable breadth and humanity and no lack of drama. The CD remastering has lost some of the atmospheric fullness, although the effect is undoubtedly fresher and brighter. The beautiful motets are particularly successful.

(i) *Mass No. 2 in E min.; Te Deum;* (ii) *Motets: Ave Maria; Christus factus est; Locus iste; Virga Jesse floruit.*
☞ (M) *(*) Decca 425 075-2 [id.]. (i) Blegen, Lilowa, Ahnsjö, Meven, V. State Op. Ch., VPO, Mehta; (ii) John Alldis Ch., Alldis.

Both the major works here are well served on CD, the *Mass* by Norrington, the *Te Deum* by Jochum and others. Even if they were not, this 1976 Mehta coupling would still have few attractions, not because the recording is lacking in realism – on the contrary, it is most vivid – but because the performances are not really idiomatic. Mehta is a shade too expressive and his chorus a little too histrionically operatic in character as well as name. (There are moments when one has an almost Slavic feeling.) The motets, however, are admirably performed by the John Alldis Choir with clean lines bringing out the devotional intensity. They too are very well recorded.

Motets: *Afferentur regi virgines; Ave Maria; Christus factus est; Ecce sacerdos magnus; Inveni David; Locus iste; Os justi; Pange lingua; Tota pulchra es, Maria; Vexilla regis; Virga Jesse.*
**(*) Hyp. CDA 66062 [id.]. Salmon, Corydon Singers, Best; Trotter (organ).

Motets: *Afferentur regi virgines; Ecce sacerdos magnus; Inveni David; Os justi; Pange lingua gloriosa.*
(M) *** Decca 430 361-2 [id.]. St John's College, Cambridge, Ch., ASMF, Guest – BEETHOVEN:
     Mass in C. ***

The Corydon Singers under Matthew Best are not quite as well blended or as homogeneous in tone as the Bavarian Radio Chorus, but Best's direction is often imaginative and he achieves a wide tonal range.
     The St John's performances are also of the highest quality and the recording is marvellously spacious.

Requiem in D min.; Psalms 112 and 114.
**(*) Hyp. CDA 66245 [id.]. Rodgers, Denley, Maldwyn Davies, George, Corydon Singers, ECO,
     Best; T. Trotter (organ).

Matthew Best here tackles the very early setting of the *Requiem* which Bruckner wrote at the age of twenty-five. The quality of the writing in the Psalm settings also varies; but with fine, strong performances from singers and players alike, including an excellent team of soloists, this is well worth investigating by Brucknerians. First-rate recording.

Bruhns, Nicolaus (1665–97)

2 Preludes in E min.; Preludes: in G ; G min.; (i) Fantasia on *'Nun komm der Heiden Heiland'.*
☞ *** Chan. Dig. CHAN 0539 [id.]. Piet Klee (organ of Roskilde Cathedral, Denmark), (i) with
     Elisabeth Rehling – BUXTEHUDE: *Chorale preludes.* ***

Nicolaus Bruhns here almost completely upstages his contemporary and teacher, Dietrich Buxtehude, who was to outlive his talented pupil. Just five Bruhns organ works survive (all included in this recital). Though he uses the term 'Praeludium', each consists of an introduction and one or two fugues, written with an eager flair that recalls the early organ works of the young Johann Sebastian, who certainly knew of this music. The spirited opening *Prelude in E minor* is striking enough, but most remarkable of all is the flamboyant G major work with its bravura writing for the pedals. It also has a jolly fugue subject. The *Fantasia on 'Nun komm der Heiden Heiland'* has its *cantus firmus* introduced by a soprano voice, and she returns to repeat the chorale (undecorated) at a central point, after three variants. The florid *Prelude in G minor* which closes the recital brings another lusty burst of pedal fireworks; again the fugal subject is genial and is worked out briefly but very satisfyingly. Piet Klee presents all this music with splendid life and colour, and his Danish organ, recently restored, brings vivid registration which is a pleasure to the ear. The recording is in the demonstration bracket. If you enjoy Bach's Arnstadt and Weimar preludes and fugues, you should certainly try this.

Brumel, Antoine (c. 1460– c. 1520)

Missa: Et ecce terrae motus; Sequentia: Dies irae, dies illa.
☞ ⊛ *** Sony/Vivarte Dig. SK 46348 [id.]. Huelgas Ens., Paul van Nevel.

Missa: Et ecce terrae motus; Lamentations. Magnificat secundi toni.
☞ *** Gimell Dig. CDGIM 026 [id.]. Tallis Scholars, Peter Phillips.

Brumel belongs to the same period as Josquin, Isaac, Pierre de la Rue and Obrecht, and was spoken of with veneration by such contemporaries as Rabelais and Glareanus. Born in Chartres, he served at Notre-Dame and at Chambéry in Savoy, before settling in Italy where he succeeded Josquin as maestro di cappella at Ferrara. Morley in his *Plaine and Easie Introduction to Practicall Musicke* wrote that 'only Josquin des Pres and Brumel were able to teach one everything about older canonic techniques'. Lassus himself prepared and took part in a performance of the twelve-part Mass, *Et ecce terrae motus*, in Munich in the 1570s, and this is the only copy of the work that survives. But it is not just the contrapuntal ingenuity of Brumel's music that impresses but the sheer beauty of sound with which we are presented. Brumel was not only one of the first to write a polyphonic *Requiem* but the very first to make a polyphonic setting of the sequence, *Dies irae, dies illa*. This is a more severe work than the glorious 12-part Mass which occupies the bulk of this CD, and it is written in a more medieval tonal language. The performances by the Huelgas Ensemble under its founder-director, Paul van Nevel, are fervent and eloquent and vividly bring this music back to life. This was its first recording, made in the ample acoustic of the Irish Chapel in Liège, and is resplendent. This will be something of a revelation to those for whom Brumel has only been a name in the history books.

The Tallis Scholars follow hot on the heels of the Sony issue and are hardly less impressive. In some respects their disc is complementary in that they opt for a different solution to the *Agnus Dei*, which is incomplete in the Munich manuscript. Nevel favours a Danish source that Phillips and his editor reject on the grounds that it uses six voices and voices of different range. The texture in their performance has greater transparency and clarity than the richer, darker sonority of the Nevel. Both can be recommended; neither should be ignored, and either or both should be acquired.

Buller, John (born 1927)

(i) *Proença (Provençal). The Theatre of memory.*
(M) *** Unicorn Dig. UKCD 1049 [id.]. (i) Sarah Walker, Timothy Walker; BBC SO, Mark Elder.

The more immediately compelling work here is *Proença*, exuberant and energetic, a sequence of settings of troubadour songs in the original Provençale. Sarah Walker is the passionately committed soloist, with Timothy Walker on the electric guitar adding a wild, amplified dimension to the sound at climactic points. Though *The Theatre of memory* is more severely controlled, less attractively wild, it too is a substantial work with a clear structure and memorable landmarks. So here seven soloists come forward in turn in front of formalized 'chorus' groups. Buller's use of an adventurous but accessible idiom in both works makes this music immediately approachable. Mark Elder, who conducted the same performers at the Proms première in 1981, here draws passionately committed playing from the BBC orchestra, vividly recorded.

Burgon, Geoffrey (born 1941)

At the round earth's imagined corners; But have been found again; Laudate Dominum; Magnificat; Nunc dimittis; A prayer to the Trinity; Short mass; This world; Two hymns to Mary.
**(*) Hyp. Dig. CDA 66123 [id.]. Chichester Cathedral Ch., Alan Thurlow.

Burgon's famous *Nunc dimittis* is well matched here with the *Magnificat* that he later wrote to complement it and a series of his shorter choral pieces, all of them revealing his flair for immediate, direct communication, and well performed. First-rate recording.

Requiem.
(M) *** Decca Dig. 430 064-2; *430 064-4* [id.]. Jennifer Smith, Murray, Rolfe Johnson, London
    Symphony Ch., Woburn Singers, City of L. Sinfonia, Hickox.

Geoffrey Burgon is best known for his incidental music to John le Carré's *Tinker Tailor Soldier Spy* and Evelyn Waugh's *Brideshead Revisited* on television. In idiom his *Requiem* owes much to Benjamin Britten and perhaps early Messiaen. The composer has shown considerable resource in his handling of texture and, though the melodic invention is unmemorable, the overall impression is quite powerful. The work enjoys committed advocacy from these artists and remarkably fine (1981) recorded quality.

Bush, Geoffrey (born 1920)

(i) *The End of love; Greek love songs;* (ii; iii) *A little love music;* (iii) *3 Songs of Ben Jonson; Songs of wonder.*
*** Chan. Dig. CHAN 8830; *ABTD 1053* [id.]. (i) Luxon; (ii) Cahil; (iii) Partridge; composer.

Geoffrey Bush has a particularly sensitive ear for the cadences of the English language and shows no lack of musical resource in their setting. The repertoire here ranges from his early Jonson settings

(1952) through to the relatively recent cycle, *A little love music* (1976), which are economical in style – the piano is silent – and touching in their directness of utterance. The *Greek love songs* obviously fire the composer with their heady passion. *The End of love* has darker imagery, and there is a touching central lament. *The Songs of wonder*, based on children's rhymes but by no means simplistic, make a happy contrast and Ian Partridge relishes their lively character. All these songs are performed with freshness and spontaneity, while the composer, who is an excellent pianist, provides admirable accompaniments.

Farewell, earth's bliss; 4 Hesperides songs; A Menagerie; (i) *A Summer serenade.*
*** Chan. Dig. CHAN 8864; *ABTD 1479* [id.]. Varcoe, Thompson, Westminster Singers, City of London Sinfonia, Hickox, (i) with Eric Parkin.

The delightful *Summer serenade* of seven song-settings, written in 1948, five years after Britten's very comparable *Serenade*, has long been Bush's most frequently performed work – a favourite with small choral groups – and this first recording glowingly brings out the sharp contrasts of mood within and between the songs. The instrumentation is just as felicitous as the choral writing, with a spiky concertante part for piano played by Eric Parkin. It is well coupled with a solo song-cycle of comparable length, *Farewell, earth's bliss*, with Stephen Varcoe the baritone soloist; four songs from Herrick's *Hesperides*, also for baritone and strings; and three for unaccompanied voices, including an insistently menacing setting of Blake's *Tyger*. The tenor, Adrian Thompson, not ideally pure-toned, contributes to only two of the *Serenade* songs; otherwise these are near-ideal performances in warm, open sound.

Busoni, Ferruccio (1866–1924)

Clarinet concertino.
☞ *** Denon Dig. CO 75289 [id.]. Paul Meyer, ECO, Zinman – COPLAND; MOZART: *Concertos.*
***

Busoni's *Concertino* (1918) lasts about ten minutes and encompasses two quite striking ideas, the first soon heard in fugato style; but this is a not-too-serious but very well-crafted rhapsodical piece that is a worthwhile addition to the repertoire. It is played with elegance and improvisational spirit by the excellent Paul Meyer, and David Zinman and the ECO provide an equally well-judged accompaniment. They are given first-rate recording within a pleasantly resonant acoustic.

Piano concerto, Op. 39.
(M) *** EMI CDM7 69850-2. John Ogdon, Alldis Ch., RPO, Revenaugh.
☞ (M) *** Telarc Dig. CD 82012 [id.]. Garrick Ohlsson, Cleveland Men's Ch., Cleveland O, Dohnányi.

Busoni's marathon *Piano concerto* is unique, running to 70 minutes, roughly the same time as Beethoven's *Choral Symphony*, with which it has another parallel in its choral finale. John Ogdon's magisterial and powerful advocacy is matched by both his brilliance and his passionate commitment, making the music surge forward, and he is well supported by Daniel Revenaugh and the RPO, with an incandescent contribution from the John Alldis Choir. The EMI recording from the late 1960s sounds bold and immediate in its CD format.

The mid-price alternative from Telarc can be warmly recommended too, even if the first-rate modern digital sound brings fewer advantages than expected, other than highlighting the solo piano. In the choral finale the John Alldis Choir on EMI has far more impact than the men of the Cleveland Orchestra Chorus, making it into a genuine culmination. With extra prominence given to the solo instrument, Garrick Ohlsson's bravura display is very exciting, and the pianist's own enjoyment in virtuosity enhances his electricity and flair.

(i) *Violin concerto, Op. 35a;* (ii) *Violin sonata No. 2 in E min., Op. 36a.*
☞ (M) (***) Sony mono MPK 52537 [id.]. Szigeti, with (i) Little O Soc., Scherman; (ii) Horszowski.

In recent years Busoni's *Piano concerto* has come in from the cold and is now represented quite generously on CD; it is puzzling that the somewhat earlier *Violin concerto* has still to be recorded in stereo. Szigeti's pioneering LP was made in 1954, when he was well past his prime. The *Concerto* has a warmth and lyricism that reflect something of Busoni's admiration for Brahms and Strauss, and yet the afterglow of romanticism is still tinged with the forward-looking Busoni to come. The opening theme is particularly memorable. It is good to have Szigeti's 1956 mono recording of the *Second*

Violin sonata, since he knew the composer. Despite the wide vibrato and slightly dry timbre Szigeti had developed by this time, the performance is well worth having – not least for the sake of Horszowski's artistry. Some allowance must be made for the sound, but the disc deserves a three-star recommendation purely on interest grounds and as the only version of a beautiful concerto.

Turandot suite, Op. 41.
☞ *** Sony Dig. SK 53280 [id.]. La Scala PO, Muti – CASELLA: *Paganiniana;* MARTUCCI: *Giga* etc.
***

Why is Busoni's *Turandot suite* neglected? It has all the ingredients of popularity: colour, a captivating lightness of spirit and vivid musical ideas presented with wonderful imagination. It ought to enjoy great success at a Prom. It is good that its CD première is so successful in every respect; with excellent playing from the La Scala Orchestra under Muti, its wit and character are splendidly conveyed. Muti conducts the 1905 version of the suite (Sir Malcolm Sargent used to omit the third movement, replacing it with one of the later numbers Busoni added in 1917). Good, well-detailed recording in a slightly dryish acoustic.

Violin sonatas Nos. 1 in E min., Op. 29; 2 in E min., Op. 36a.
*** Chan. Dig. CHAN 8868; *ABTD 1483* [id.]. Lydia Mordkovitch, Victoria Postnikova.

Busoni's two *Violin sonatas* are rarities in the concert hall. There is no current alternative to the *First*, and Lydia Mordkovitch and Victoria Postnikova are impressive advocates of this somewhat uneven piece. The *Second* is a one-movement piece, dating from 1898, with a *langsam* opening, a Presto and a most beautiful *Andante* section leading to a set of variations. Mordkovitch and her partner give a sympathetic reading and, with excellent recording, this disc should be sought out by admirers of this composer.

Fantasia contrappuntistica; Fantasia after J. S. Bach; Toccata.
**(*) Altarus AIR-2-9074. John Ogdon.

Ronald Stevenson calls Busoni's remarkable *Fantasia contrappuntistica* a masterpiece and, listening to John Ogdon's performance, one is tempted to agree. The *Fantasia after J. S. Bach* was written a year earlier and is among Busoni's most concentrated and powerful piano works. The balance places Ogdon rather far back and, as the acoustic is somewhat reverberant, the piano sounds a little clangy.

OPERA

(i) *Arlecchino* (complete); (ii) *Turandot* (complete).
☞ *** Virgin/EMI Dig. VCD 759313-2 (2) [id.]. (i) Ernst Theo Richter, Mohr, Holzmair, Huttenlocher, Dahlberg, Mentzer; (ii) Gessendorf, Selig, Dahlberg, Schäfer, Kraus, Holzmair, Struckmann, Sima, Rodde; Lyon Op. Ch. & O, Nagano.

Kent Nagano follows up the success of his previous Lyon Opéra recordings with a set which vividly illustrates the elusive genius of Busoni. *Arlecchino* ('Harlequin'), is a sparkling comedy that builds on *commedia dell'arte* conventions with a point rarely matched in opera. Busoni's writing has a rare lightness and wit, though for the non-German-speaking listener a snag of the piece is that the title-role is a speaking part. On disc, prolonged passages of spoken German give anything but an impression of frothiness, providing a deterrent to frequent repetition. Even so, it would be hard to imagine a finer performance than this, with the conductor's finesse, not least in controlling tension, matched by a brilliant German cast with no weak link.

The fascination of Busoni's *Turandot* is to compare it with Puccini's weightier opera using the same Gozzi fairy-tale. Busoni is far closer to Gozzi, evoking a fantasy fairy-tale atmosphere in a piece that is not only lighter in texture but far more compact, with motivation aptly quirky rather than realistic. In place of Puccini's Liù you have Adelma, Turandot's maidservant, and the *commedia dell'arte* element is more central than with Puccini's Ping, Pang and Pong. The surreal atmosphere is enhanced when the improbable theme for the evocative interlude before Act II (at a point after the riddles, equivalent to where Puccini put *Nessun dorma*) is not Chinese but English – *Greensleeves*. Again Nagano's conducting gives a thrusting intensity to a piece that might seem wayward, and the casting is comparably brilliant, with Mechthild Gessendorf masterly as Turandot and Stefan Dahlberg heady-toned as Kalaf. The recording is vividly atmospheric, with plenty of presence.

Doktor Faust (opera) complete.
(M) *** DG 427 413-2 (3) [id.]. Fischer-Dieskau, Kohn, Cochran, Hillebrecht, Bav. Op. Ch. & R. O, Leitner.

Busoni's epic *Doktor Faust* was left incomplete at the composer's death. Unfortunately, this recording is full of small cuts; however, with superb, fierily intense conducting from Leitner, it fully conveys the work's wayward mastery, the magnetic quality which establishes it as Busoni's supreme masterpiece, even though it was finished by another hand. The cast is dominated by Fischer-Dieskau, here in 1969 at his very finest; and the only weak link among the others is Hildegard Hillebrecht as the Duchess of Parma. Though this is a mid-price set, the documentation is generous.

Bussotti, Sylvano (born 1931)

(i) *Bergkristall; Lorenzaccio Symphony* (both for large orchestra); (ii) *Rara Requiem*.
☞ (M) (***) DG 437 739-2 (2) [id.]. (i) N. German RSO, Sinopoli; (ii) Surrat, Plantamura, Baratti, Desderi, Saarbrücken Conservatory Ch., Saarbrücken RSO, Taverna.

Bussotti's *Bergkristall* ballet and *Lorenzaccio Symphony* come in a two-disc set together with the *Rara Requiem*. It would be easy to write that Bussotti's ballet *Bergkristall* (a half-hour piece for full orchestra) and the shorter, 13-minute *Lorenzaccio Symphony* contain a mélange of fascinating, organized sounds. Indeed, in his note Josef Hausler suggests that 'the final pages of the score of *Bergkristall* contain an abundance of costume sketches, figurines and stage designs'. He may well be right, but the earlier music for *Christmas eve in the mountains, The children receive presents* and *The Christmas tree in the house of the grandparents* is singularly ugly and unevocative, though the composer is more at home with *The disaster of the baker's boy, Losing the path* and *In the regions of eternal ice*. The *Lorenzaccio Symphony* is mercifully shorter, though even more violently dissonant. It begins with a series of powerfully co-ordinated rhythmic slashes, orchestral bubblings and eruptions but finally leads to a period of relative repose, and sometimes the reflective coolness of the music here is rather impressive, with silence not far away. But the ugliness keeps spurting back. The performances are obviously expert: one cannot but admire Sinopoli's firmness of control. In the longer *Rara Requiem*, the fragmented verbal textures (which draw from Homer, Tasso, Heine, Racine, Mallarmé and others) are less obviously dissonant. The textures combine vocal, instrumental and percussive laminations (even a momentary police whistle, used without intended humour), so I shall quote the note-writer (translated by our good friend, Lionel Salter) who in turn quotes the view of Roland Barth that the composer's confrontation with an empty page is filled 'often under the impulse of a furious *horror vacu*, with a labyrinth of signs [which] tend towards an impossible mimesis of its associated sounds'. Make what you will of that! But he goes on to detail the *Rara Requiem* more succinctly as 'Seven solo voices in effective and brilliant blocks, together with a modest veil of an orchestra of wind, harp, piano and percussion . . . [which] launch the incandescent sound material . . . The entire composition is presented as a sequence of slow circular journeys which repeat *ad infinitum*'. That is not an understatement. Again the performance, by forces of the Saarbrücken Radio Orchestra and members of the Munich Conservatory Chorus, is held well together by Gianpiero Taverna, and the recording is exemplary in its atmosphere and clarity. But in the end this is the kind of 'music' which soon becomes boring and even causes one to wonder if it can all really be taken seriously. The recording is admirably transferred to CD.

Butterworth, George (1885–1916)

The banks of green willow.
☞ (M) *** Chan. CHAN 6566 [id.]. Bournemouth Sinf., Norman Del Mar – BANTOCK: *The Pierrot of the minute: overture;* BRIDGE: *Summer* etc. ***

The banks of green willow; 2 English idylls.
☞ (M) **(*) EMI Dig. CDM7 64200-2 [id.]. ECO, Jeffrey Tate – BAX: *3 Pieces* ***; BRIDGE: *There is a willow* **(*); MOERAN: *2 Pieces.* ***

The banks of green willow; 2 English idylls; A Shropshire lad (rhapsody).
☞ (M) *** Decca 440 325-2 [id.]. ASMF, Marriner – VAUGHAN WILLIAMS: *Lark ascending* etc.; WARLOCK: *Capriol suite* etc. ***
*** Nimbus Dig. NI 5068 [id.]. E. String O, Boughton – BRIDGE: *Suite;* PARRY: *Lady Radnor's suite.* ***

Reissued in Decca's 'British Classics' series, this collection of music by Butterworth, Vaughan Williams and Warlock makes an exceptionally generous anthology (74 minutes). Butterworth's *Shropshire lad* represents the English folksong school at its most captivatingly atmospheric, and the other works are in a similarly appealing pastoral vein. Marriner's performances with the Academy are stylishly beautiful, without the last degree of finesse but very fine indeed, with vivid, wide-ranging recording quality.

Boughton secures from his Birmingham-based orchestra warm and refined playing in well-paced readings. In an ample acoustic, woodwind is placed rather behind the strings.

On Chandos, Del Mar gives a glowingly persuasive performance of *The banks of green willow*, which comes as part of another highly interesting programme of English music, devoted also to Butterworth's somewhat older contemporaries, Bantock and Frank Bridge. The digital transfer of a 1979 analogue recording has the benefit of even greater clarity without loss of atmosphere.

The banks of green willow and the two *English idylls* make attractive items in Tate's recital of English pieces, but it is a pity that *A Shropshire Lad* was not also included. The playing is refined and sensitive but lacks something in magic, with slow speeds for the *Idylls* making them sound a little unspontaneous. Warm, full recording.

Love blows as the wind (3 songs).
☞ (M) *** EMI CDM7 64731-2 [id.]. Robert Tear, CBSO, Vernon Handley – ELGAR; VAUGHAN WILLIAMS: *Songs*. ***

These three charming songs (*In the year that's come and gone, Life in her creaking shoes, Coming up from Richmond*), to words by W. E. Henley, provide an excellent makeweight for a mixed bag of orchestral songs based on the first recording of Vaughan Williams's *On Wenlock Edge* in its orchestral form. The sound is clear yet enjoyably warm and atmospheric.

A Shropshire lad (song-cycle).
(M) *** Decca 430 368-2 [id.]. Benjamin Luxon, David Willison – VAUGHAN WILLIAMS: *Blake songs* etc. ***

Benjamin Luxon gives powerful, dramatic performances of songs which can take such treatment, not quite the miniatures they may sometimes seem. Well-balanced recording and an admirable coupling.

Buxtehude, Diderik (c. 1637–1707)

Trio sonatas: in G; B flat and D min., Op. 1/2, 4 & 6 (Bux WV 253, 255 & 257); in D and G min., Op. 2/2–3, (Bux WV 260–1).
*** ASV/Gaudeamus CDGAU 110. Trio Sonnerie.

Make no mistake, this is music of real quality: its invention is fertile and distinguished by a lightness of touch and colour that is quite individual; the melodic lines are vivacious and engaging, and their virtuosity inspiriting. The Trio Sonnerie show real enthusiasm and expertise, and their virtuosity is agreeably effortless and unostentatious.

Trio sonatas for violin, viola da gamba and harpsichord: in A min., Op. 1/3; in B flat, Op. 1/4; in G min., Op. 2/3; in E, Op. 2/6 (Bux WV 254–5, 261; 264).
(B) *** HM HMA 901089 [id.]. Boston Museum Trio.

The Boston Museum Trio are a highly accomplished group and display an exemplary feeling for style. The music is unfailingly inventive and, despite the obvious Italianate elements, distinctive. Not only are the playing, recording and presentation of high quality, but the cost is modest.

Canzona in E min., Bux WV 169; Canzonetta in G, Bux WV 171; Ciacona in E min., Bux WV 160; Chorales: Ach Herr, mich armen Sünder, Bux WV 178; In dulci jubilo, Bux WV 197; Komm, Heiliger Geist, Herre Gott, Bux WV 199; Vater unser im Himmelreich, Bux WV 219; Magnificat primi toni, Bux WV 203; Preludes: in C, Bux WV 137; in D, Bux WV 139.
(*) Chan. Dig. CHAN 0514; *EBT 0514* [id.]. Piet Kee (organ of St Laurent Church, Alkmaar) – SWEELINCK: *Collection*. *

Kee's performance of the opening *Magnificat primi toni* is little short of magnificent. The closing *Ciacona in E minor* is pretty impressive too, while the *Canzonetta in G* is deliciously registered, with piping flute colouring. One's reservations, however, concern the presentation of the chorales which, Kee suggests, 'require poetic expression'. Perhaps they do, but they also need to be moved on rather faster. The Chandos recording is superb.

Chorales: Auf meinen lieben Gott, Bux WV 179; Gott der Vater wohn uns bei, Bux WV 190; Nimm von uns, du treuer Gott, Bux VW 207; Nun komm der Heiden Heiland, Bux WV 211; Puer natus in Bethlehem, Bux WV 217; Von Gott will ich nicht lassen (2 settings), Bux WV 220/221.
☞ *** Chan. Dig. CHAN 0539 [id.]. Piet Klee (organ of Roskilde Cathedral, Denmark) – BRUHNS:

Preludes. ***

The restored baroque organ at Roskilde Cathedral has a palette to tempt the most jaded listener and, although Piet Klee still persists in playing these chorales and their variants rather slowly, his piquant registration is very effective, so that they serve as attractively serene interludes between the remarkably flamboyant *Preludes* by Buxtehude's precociously inspired pupil, Nicolaus Bruhns, whose genius was sadly cut short when he died before his mentor, at the early age of thirty-two. The recording is very much in the demonstration class throughout this disc.

Chorales: Christ unser Herr zum Jordan kam; Durch Adams Fall ist ganz verderbt; Ein feste Burg ist unser Gott; Erhalt uns Herr bei deinem Wort; Es ist das Heil uns kommen her; Es spricht der unweisen Mund wohl; Gelobet seist du, Jesu Christ; Gott der Vater, wohn uns bei; Magnificat primi toni; 2 Preludes and fugues in A min.; Preludes and fugues: in C; F sharp min.

(B) *** HM HMA 90942 [id.]. René Saorgin (Schnitger organ of the Church of St Michel de Zwolle, Holland).

This collection makes an admirable introduction to the organ music of a composer more written about than listened to. The Schnitger organ is sensitively and colourfully registered by Saorgin: he is particularly impressive in the serene, reflective chorales, *Durch Adams Fall* and *Es spricht der unweisen Mund wohl*, while the elaborations of the *Magnificat* are finely made. Excellent recording, vividly transferred.

Ciaconas: in C min.; E min., Bux WV 159/60; Passacaglia in D min., Bux WV 161; Preludes and fugues: in D; D min.; E; E min.; Bux WV 139/142; in F; F sharp min., Bux WV 145/146; in G min., Bux WV 149.

(M) *** DG 427 133-2. Helmut Walcha (organ of Church of SS Peter and Paul, Cappel, West Germany).

Helmut Walcha has the full measure of this repertoire and these performances on the highly suitable Arp Schnitger organ in Cappel, Lower Saxony, are authoritative and spontaneous. The 1978 recording is excellent and the disc comprises generous measure: 73 minutes.

(i) *Preludes and fugues: in G min.; F; Chorales: Herr Christ, der einig Gottes Sohn; In dulci jubilo; Lobt Gott, ihr Christen allzugleich; Chorale fantasy: Gelobet seist du, Jesu Christ. Cantatas:* (ii) *In dulci jubilo; Jubilate Domino.*

(B) **(*) HM HMA 90700 [id.]. (i) René Saorgin (organ of St Laurent, Alkmaar); (ii) Alfred Deller, Deller Cons., Perulli, Chapuis.

A good, inexpensive sampler of Buxtehude, dating from 1971. The opening *Prelude and fugue in G minor* is fully worthy of the young J. S. Bach and, like its companion, is splendidly played by René Saorgin. The chorales are more static and less interesting than Bach's treatment of the same ideas. Of the cantatas, *In dulci jubilo* is a florid piece for four voices with instrumental accompaniment, while *Jubilate Domino* is a solo cantata accompanied by viola da gamba and organ continuo. Deller is in good form throughout.

Cantatas: An Filius non est Dei, Bux WV 6; Cantata Domino, Bux WV 12; Frohlocket mit Händen, Bux WV 29; Gott fähret auf mit Jauchzen, Bux WV 33; Herr, wenn ich nur Dich habe, Bux WV 39; Heut triumphieret Gottes Sohn, Bux WV 43; Ich bin die Auferstehung, Bux WV 44; Ich habe Lust abzuscheiden, Bux WV 46; Ihr lieben Christen, Bux WV 51; In dulci jubilo, Bux WV 52; Jesus dulcis memoria, Bux WV 56; Jesu meines Lebens Leben, Bux WV 62; Jubilate Deo, Bux WV 64; Mein Gemüt erfreuet sich, Bux WV 72; Nichts soll uns scheiden, Bux WV 77; Nun danket alle Gott, Bux WV 79; Wie wird erneuet, wie wird er freuet, Bux WV 110.

*** Erato/Warner Dig. 2292 45294-2 (3) [id.]. Schlick, Frimmer, Chance, Jacobs, Prégardien, Kooy, Hannover Knabenchor, Amsterdam Bar. O, Koopman.

All the works here are of a pietist religious character, although the music readily expands into joyously extrovert expressions of praise. Some attractively combine the form of a concerto grosso, with alternating solos and tuttis, and a few are more ambitious, including chorus, trumpets and cornetts, and even trombones, and drums too. The brass writing is inevitably primitive, but highly effective in its stylized way. The solo singing is excellent, and the soloists match pleasingly when they sing in duet or trio. There is plenty to discover here for any collector who enjoys the pre-Bach era. Accompaniments are alive, textures transparent, and the recording balance is altogether excellent.

Membra Jesu nostri, Bux WV 75.

☞ *** DG Dig. 427 660-2 [id.]. Monteverdi Ch., E. Bar. Soloists, Gardiner – SCHUTZ: *O bone Jesu.*
***

Membra Jesu nostri, Bux WV 75; Heut triumphieret Gottes Sohn, Bux WV 43.
☞ **(*) HM Dig. HMC 901333 [id.]. Concerto Vocale & Instrumental Ens., Jacobs.

The *Membra Jesu nostri* is a cycle of seven cantatas, each addressed to different parts of the body of the crucified Christ, all of a simple, dignified, expressive power that, as always with this composer, make a strong impression. Of the two performances John Eliot Gardiner's is the more searching and devotional; the Concerto Vocale, though beautifully sung, is less atmospheric both as a performance and as a recording. The Harmonia Mundi is more forwardly balanced; the Gardiner has more space and the sense of one of Buxtehude's own Abendmusik. Compare the sixth of the cantatas, *Ad cor*, and the more reverential approach and feeling of the Gardiner tells. There are only a few seconds between the two, but the latter feels wonderfully spacious and unhurried. But both issues can be recommended; the impressive *Heut triumphieret Gottes Sohn* comes with the Harmonia Mundi disc and one of the Schütz *Geistliches konzert, O bone Jesu*, related in spirit, comes on the Archiv recording.

Byrd, William (1543–1623)

Complete consort music: *Christe qui lux a 4, Nos. 1–3; Christe redemptor a 4; Fantasia a 3, Nos. 1–3; Fantasia a 4, No. 1; Fantasia a 5 (Two in one); Fantasia a 6, Nos. 2–3; In nomine a 4, Nos. 1–2; In nomine a 4, Nos. 1–5; Miserere a 4; Pavan & Galliard a 5; Pavan & Galliard a 6; Prelude & Ground a 5; Sermon blande blando a 3; Sermon blando a 4, No. 1; Te lucis a 4, No. 2, verse 2.*
☞ *** Virgin/EMI Dig. VC5 45031-2 [id.]. Fretwork, with Christopher Wilson (lute).

Fretwork have now completed their survey of Byrd's consort music – part of which was originally issued coupled with Dowland's *Lachrimae* – and the complete consort music (76 minutes) is now fitted on to a single CD. The grave feeling of much of this music is apparent in the opening *Prelude and Ground a 5*; then the mood quickly lightens as the texture is woven in more swiftly moving configurations to make a typically satisfying whole. Indeed, while there is much that is austere, especially the earlier works, there is much greater variety of feeling than one might expect in music often dominated by plainsong. Not all of it, though. *Browning* has the alternative title of *The leaves be green* and consists of divisions on a popular song, while the *Fantasia a 6* which closes the concert is a masterly compression of ideas into a fluid structure as powerful as Purcell's famous *Chaconne*. Performances have consistent authority and freshness and, although the recording seems rather close, it is vivid and realistic.

My Ladye Nevells Booke, 1591 (42 keyboard pieces).
☞ ⊛ *** O-L 430 484-2 (3). Christopher Hogwood (virginal, harpsichord, chamber organ).

This collection of Byrd's music was compiled by John Baldwin of Windsor, 'a gentleman of the Chapel Royal', and must be reckoned the finest collection in Europe of keyboard writing of the sixteenth century. Christopher Hogwood rings the changes by using a variety of instruments: a virginal, two harpsichords (one Flemish and the other Italian) and a fine chamber organ, all of which he plays with sympathy and vitality. Hogwood's scholarly gifts are shown in the fine notes that accompany the set, but, more importantly, his masterly keyboard technique and artistic sensitivity are sustained throughout the three discs. The recording is exemplary, very real and in excellent perspective. A landmark in records of early keyboard music.

Pavans and galliards (collection).
*** HM HMC 901241/2 [id.]. Davitt Moroney (harpsichord).

On the first of the two discs Davitt Moroney presents the sequence of nine pavans and galliards Byrd composed in the 1570s and '80s, which come from *My Ladye Nevell's Booke* (1591), and the second creates a second cycle of pieces on the same lines. Between them, Davitt Moroney constructs a sequence of Byrd's finest late pavans, taking care to model it on the same lines of symmetry and contrast that distinguish Byrd's own. The playing is totally committed and authoritative though a trifle didactic. His recording, made on an Italian instrument of 1677, is very naturally recorded. The documentation is excellent.

VOCAL MUSIC

Motets in paired settings: *Ave verum corpus* (with PHILIPS: *Ave verum corpus*); *Haec Dies* (with PALESTRINA: *Haec Dies*); *Iustorum animae* (with LASSUS: *Iustorum animae*); *Miserere mei* (with G. GABRIELI: *Miserere mei*); *O quam gloriosum* (with VICTORIA: *O quam gloriosum*); *Tu es Petrus* (with

PALESTRINA: *Tu es Petrus*).
(B) *** CfP CD-CFP 4481; *TC-CFP 4481*. King's College, Cambridge, Ch., Sir David Willcocks.

This is an imaginatively devised programme of motets in which settings of Latin texts by Byrd are directly contrasted with settings of the same words by some of his greatest contemporaries. As was the intention, quite apart from adding variety to the programme, the juxtaposition makes one listen to the individual qualities of these polyphonic masters the more keenly, and to register their individuality. The recording emerges with remarkable freshness on CD, and the beauty of the singing is never in doubt.

Cantiones sacrae, Book 1: Aspice Domine; Domine secundum multitudinem; Domine tu iurasti; In resurrectione tua; Ne irascaris Domine; O quam gloriosum; Tristitia et anxiestas; Vide Domine afflictionem; Virgilate.
**(*) CRD Dig. CRD 3420; *CRDC 4120* [id.]. New College, Oxford, Ch., Higginbottom.

Cantiones sacrae, Book 2: Circumdederunt me; Cunctis diebus; Domine, non sum dignus; Domine, salva nos; Fac sum servo tuo; Exsurge, Domine; Haec dicit Dominus; Haec dies; Laudibus in sanctis Dominum; Miserere mei, Deus; Tribulatio proxima est.
**(*) CRD Dig. CRD 3439; *CRDC 4139* [id.]. New College, Oxford, Ch., Higginbottom.

Though the New College Choir under its choirmaster Edward Higginbottom does not sing with the variety of expression or dynamic which marks its finest Oxbridge rivals, it is impossible not to respond to the freshness of its music-making. The robust, throaty style suggests a Latin feeling in its forthright vigour, and the directness of approach in these magnificent *cantiones sacrae* is most attractive, helped by recording which is vividly projected, yet at once richly atmospheric.

The Great Service (with anthems).
*** Gimell Dig. CDGIM 011; *1585T-11* [id.]. Tallis Scholars, Phillips.
*** EMI Dig. CDC7 47771-2. King's College, Cambridge, Ch., Cleobury; Richard Farnes (organ).

Peter Phillips and the Tallis Scholars give a lucid and sensitively shaped account of Byrd's *Great Service*. Theirs is a more intimate performance than one might expect to encounter in one of the great English cathedrals; they are fewer in number and thus achieve greater clarity of texture. The recording is quite excellent: it is made in a church acoustic (the Church of St John, Hackney) and captures detail perfectly. It includes three other anthems, two of which (*O Lord make thy servant Elizabeth* and *Sing joyfully unto God our strength*) are included on the rival EMI disc. This CD will give great musical satisfaction.

Collectors wanting *The Great Service* in a cathedral acoustic will turn to the King's version, which is beautifully recorded on EMI. They have the advantages of boy trebles, a larger complement of singers who can offer more contrast between solo and full verses, and a well-played organ accompaniment, which it probably had in the 1580s. Stephen Cleobury also sets the music in a more authentic liturgical background: he offers the *Kyrie* and puts the two canticles for Evensong into their context with anthems and responses.

Mass for 3 voices.
☞ (M) *(*) DG 437 077-2. Pro Cantione Antiqua, Bruno Turner – TALLIS: *Lamentations of Jeremiah.* *(*)

There are no complaints here about the performance. It may be too overtly expressive for some tastes, but it is thoroughly convincing and superbly executed. Unfortunately, the recording resorts to multi-mike techniques that produce a sound-picture which is too close to us, and at the same time the ambience is confused.

Mass for 3 voices; Mass for 4 voices; Mass for 5 voices.
⊛ (M) *** Decca 433 675-2 [id.]. King's College, Cambridge, Ch., Willcocks.
*** Argo Dig. 430 164-2 [id.]. Winchester Cathedral Ch., David Hill.
(B) **(*) HM HMA 90211[id.]. Deller Cons.

Masses for 3, 4 and 5 voices; Ave verum corpus.
*** Gimell Dig. CDGIM 345 [id.]. Tallis Scholars, Phillips.

Although later versions of the *Mass for 5 voices* have produced singing that is more dramatic and more ardent, the serenity of the King's account with its long, flowing paragraphs remains very appealing. The performances of the *Masses for 3 and 4 voices*, dating from 1963, remain classics of the gramophone. Under Willcocks there is an inevitability of phrasing and effortless control of sonority and dynamic that completely capture the music's spiritual and emotional feeling. The Argo recording – a great tribute to the late Harley Usill – is extraordinarily real.

Peter Phillips is a master of this repertoire; undoubtedly these performances have more variety and great eloquence so that, when the drama is varied with a gentler mood, the contrast is the more striking; and certainly the sound made by the Scholars in Merton College Chapel is beautiful, both warm and fresh.

David Hill and the Choir of Winchester Cathedral can be confidently recommended for those wanting the convenience of all three together, digitally recorded. Fine performances that can rate alongside the Tallis Scholars without displacing it.

Whether or not it is historically correct for Byrd's Masses to be sung by solo voices, the great merit of these French Harmonia Mundi performances is their clarity, exposing the miracle of Byrd's polyphony, even though the tonal matching is not always flawless. The 1968 recording is clean and truthful, although it lacks something in ecclesiastical atmosphere.

Mass for 3 voices; Mass for 4 voices; Mass for 5 voices; Ave verum corpus; Infelix ego; The Great Service. Anthems: O God the Proud are risen against me; O Lord, make thy servant; Sing joyfully unto God.
☞ *** Gimell Dig. CDGIM 343/4 [id.]. Tallis Scholars, Peter Phillips.

In honour of the 450th anniversary of Byrd's birth, Gimell have reissued their key performances coupled into a two-disc set which seems no great advantage when there is no perceptible saving in cost.

Mass for 3 voices: Mass Propers for the Nativity: Puer natus est nobis; Viderunt omnes fines terrae; Dies sanctificatus; Tui sunt coeli; Viderunt omnes fines terrae. Motets: A solis ortus cardine; Christe redemptor omnium; Hodie Christus natus est; O admirabile Commertium; O magnum misterium.
☞ ** Nimbus Dig. NI 5302 [id.]. Christ Church Cathedral Ch., Stephen Darlington.

Mass for 4 voices; Mass Propers for the Feast of Corpus Christi: Cibavit eos; Oculi omnium; Lauda Sion salvatorem; Sacerdote Domini; Quotiescunque manducabitis. Motets: Ave verum corpus; O salutaris hostia; Pange lingua gloriosa.
☞ ** Nimbus Dig. NI 5287 [id.]. Christ Church Cathedral Ch., Stephen Darlington.

Mass for 5 voices; Mass Propers for All Saints' Day; Gaudeamus omnes; Timete Dominum; Justorum animae; Baeti mundo corde. Motets: Laudate Dominum; Laudate pueri Dominum; Laudibus in sanctis.
☞ ** Nimbus Dig. NI 5237 [id.]. Christ Church Cathedral Ch., Stephen Darlington.

The Christ Church recordings on Nimbus have followed the approach pioneered by Harry Christophers and The Sixteen on Virgin, in that each of the three Masses is interspersed with Mass Propers from the *Gradualia* and the performance placed at a key point in the church year. The other motets or Psalm settings included on each disc reflect that choice, so that the *Mass for three voices*, for instance, includes suitable Christmas music. This will be a drawback for collectors primarily wanting just the Masses as it means that possessing all three incurs purchasing three full-price CDs. The performances are in the traditional English cathedral manner but are of high quality, the music's flowing lines bringing poise and serenity, but they are in no way dramatic: the choir is set back and the cathedral ambience is very telling. Enjoyable, but not really distinctive.

Mass for 4 voices with Propers for the Feast of Saints Peter and Paul (Gradualia 1607); Motets: Hodie Simon Petrus; Quodcunque ligaveris; Quomodo cantabimus?; Tu es pastor omnium.
*** Virgin/EMI Dig. VC7 91133-2 [id.]. The Sixteen, Harry Christophers.

Mass for 5 voices with Propers for the Feast of All Saints (Gradualia 1605); Motets: Ad dominum cum tribularer; Diliges dominum.
*** Virgin/EMI Dig. VC7 90802-2 [id.]. The Sixteen, Harry Christophers (with: MONTE: *Super flumina Babylonis* ***).

The advantage of the two (currently withdrawn) Virgin discs by The Sixteen and Harry Christophers is that the Masses are placed in a wider musical context; the *Mass for 4 voices* is contrasted with some of the richer six-part motets from the 1607 Gradualia, including *Quomodo cantabimus?*. Suitably appended is Philippe de Monte's *Super flumina Babylonis*, which the composer had sent Byrd in 1583 and to which the *Quomodo cantabimus?* is a response.

The *Mass for 5 voices* similarly comes with the *Propers for the Feast of All Saints*, which come from the Gradualia of 1605 and includes the 8-part motet *Ad dominum cum tribularer*, notable for its rich-textured, poignant false relations. The singing is very impressive, the recording excellently focused and the acoustic appropriately spacious.

Mass for 4 voices; Mass for 5 voices; Infelix ego.
☞ (BB) *** Naxos Dig. 8.550574; *4.550574* [id.]. Oxford Camerata, Jeremy Summerly.

This new coupling from the Oxford Camerata represents one of Naxos's most enticing bargains and it is no wonder that it has already become a bestseller. The full-throated singing has spontaneous ardour but no lack of repose in the music's more serene moments. Summerly offers the motet, *Infelix ego*, as a bonus. These readings are distinctive in a different way from those by the Tallis Scholars. They are recorded outstandingly vividly, and this super-bargain coupling gives every satisfaction.

Anthems: *Praise our Lord, all ye Gentiles; Sing joyfully; Turn our captivity.* Motets: *Attolite portas; Ave verum corpus; Christus resurgens; Emendemus in melius; Gaudeamus omnes; Justorum animae; Laudibus in sanctis; Non vos relinquam; O magnum mysterium; O quam suavis; Plorans plorabit; Siderum rector; Solve iubente Deo; Veni sancte spiritus; Visita quaesumus Domine.*
*** Coll. Dig. COLCD 110; *COLC 110* [id.]. Cambridge Singers, John Rutter.

This is the first of a projected series intended to cover all Byrd's music. John Rutter brings a composer's understanding to these readings, which have a simple, direct eloquence, the music's serene spirituality movingly caught; and the atmospheric recording is very faithful, even if detail could be sharper. The programme is divided into four groups, first Anthems, and then Motets: of penitence and prayer; of praise and rejoicing; and for the Church year.

Psalmes, Sonets and Songs of sadness (1588): All as a sea; Care for thy soul; Come to me grief; If women could be fair; In fields abroad; Lullaby; The match that's made; O God give ear; O Lord how long; O that most rare breast; Susanna fair; What a pleasure to have great Princes.
☞ *** O-L 443 187-2 [id.]. Cons. of Musicke, Rooley.

Byrd's *Psalmes, Sonets and Songs of sadness* of 1588 enjoyed such popularity in their time that they were reprinted twice in the first year of publication. They are more than just a collection of madrigals, as the title suggests, and are given exemplary performances here. Anthony Rooley gives many of them as consort pieces, some with their full number of repeated stanzas, where the artists discreetly embellish. This is a first-class reissue and the excellent (1980) analogue recording sounds uncommonly real and fresh.

Cage, John (1912–92)

Sonatas and Interludes for prepared piano.
*** Denon Dig. C37 7673 [id.]. Yuji Takahashi.

The sixteen sonatas included here, each in binary form not very different from Scarlatti's, are – by Cage's standards – closely structured, and in their sequence are punctuated by four interludes, very similar in style. One can readily appreciate the attraction of an Eastern performer to this music with its pentatonic passages as well as its odd textures and unexpected sounds – induced by the insertion of bolts, screws, coins, etc., on most of the piano strings. Takahashi's commitment is reinforced by close, rather dry recording, apt for this music.

Caldara, Antonio (1670–1736)

Cantatas: *Dari; La forriera del giorno; Il Gelsomino; Lungi dall'Idol mio; Stella ria.* Madrigals: *Dell'uom la vita; De piaceri; Fra pioggie, nevi e gelo; Fugge di Lot la Moglie; Là su morbide; Vedi co'l crine sciolto.*
☞ ** Unicorn Dig. DKPCD 9130 [id.]. Wren Bar. Soloists, Elliott.

An enterprising group that is new to the *Penguin Guide* has uncovered the music of Antonio Caldara, a prolific but little-known contemporary of Vivaldi. He wrote some 300 cantatas, and those included here suggest that they were of high quality. The madrigals too are very fresh, as the opening *Fra pioggie, nevi e gelo* ('With rain, snow and ice') readily shows. The singers here share out the cantatas and their sometimes ingenuous style is pleasing if perhaps not distinctive. One of the more striking pieces is *Dario*, in which the King both laments his wife's death and almost curses the gods. It is sung by the bass, Martin Elliott, who is also the director of the group, and he is better at the lament than the cries of anger. The soprano, Nicola Jenkin, has a happier subject in *La forriera del giorno* ('The herald of the day'), while the tenor has a charming piece called 'The Jasmine' (*Il Gelsomino*). The resonant acoustic adds atmosphere and this is certainly enjoyable, even if one wonders what Emma Kirby, Hogwood and company could do with this repertoire.

Camilleri, Charles (born 1931)

Piano concertos Nos. 1 (Mediterranean); 2 (Maqam); 3 (Leningrad).
☞ **(*) Unicorn Dig. DKPCD 9150 [id.]. André de Grotte, Bournemouth SO, Michael Laus.

Charles Camirelli was born in Malta and there is an Italianate, sunny good nature about the *First Piano concerto* (1948), unashamedly popular and agreeably slight when presented with such sparkle. The *Second concerto* (1967/8) came from what is described as the composer's 'Afro-Arabic-Hindu period'. The Arabic word 'Maqam' suggests improvisation, but within a predetermined framework; its structure is not easy to fathom. There are hectic bursts of energy from orchestra and percussion interweaving with a melancholy theme in the woodwind, all of which the piano embroiders, finally ending with a flourish which all share. The even thornier *Leningrad concerto* dates from a Russian visit in 1985 and has a political inspiration and a philosophical basis. The piano takes the role of twentieth-century man, spiritually aware (there is a long central interlude of quiet calm) and struggling to come to terms with his own brutality and power-lust. Much of what goes on here is not very coherent but the work ends with a ruthless toccata that finds no solution and ends abruptly. Performances of all three works are full of vitality and the recording sharply observes and vividly details yet has plenty of atmosphere. But neither of the two later concertos is easily fathomed and the back-up notes offer the listener few guidelines.

Organ music: *L'amour de Dieu; Invocation to the creator; Morphogenesis (5 pieces); Wine of peace.*
☞ *** Unicorn Dig. DKPCD 9151 [id.]. Kevin Bowyer (organ of Ely Cathedral).

Camilleri's world of musical metaphysics is much more coherently and colourfully conveyed in these extraordinary organ pieces, written between 1976 and 1980. The influence of Messiaen is so strong that the five sections which make up *Morphogenesis*, are entitled – by a Maltese composer! – in French. The fourth, *L'activation de l'énergie humaine*, has tremendously flamboyant, aggressive vitality, while the fifth and last, *Le monde de la matière* ('The world of matter'), has a remarkable cool purity and conjures up the infinite world of outer space. *The wine of peace* has comparable serenity. Kevin Bowyer produces explosive bursts of textural grandeur and his bravura is often breathtaking, yet he achieves an almost sublime sense of stillness when the music becomes very static, with changes of colour seemingly imperceptible. Ely Cathedral with its haunting, medieval atmosphere was surely the right place to record these phantasmagorical, mystical works and the organ seems just right, with a seemingly endless palette at Bowyer's disposal. Marvellous recording.

Campra, André (1660–1744)

Cantatas: *Arion; La dispute de l'Amour et de l'Hymen; Enée et Didon; Les femmes.*
☞ (B) *** HM Dig. HMA 1901238 [id.]. Jill Feldman, Dominique Visse, Jean-François Gardeil, Les Arts Florissants, William Christie.

A particularly appealing and useful collection of four major Campra cantatas. Their influence from the world of Italian opera is as striking as their distinct French flavour, and they combine drama with fine, expressive ardour. Jill Feldman is at her most spirited and eloquent in the dramatic narrative of *Arion* (which has an effective flute obbligato) and Dominique Visse's tangy alto is equally telling in the altercation of the conflicting interests of Marriage and Love which need to be resolved harmoni-ously. In *Les Femmes* there is disillusion from a male lover who, first dolorously and then with considerable animation, laments the vagaries of the fair sex who promise much, yet are at once prudish and coquettish, jealous and capricious; his final conclusions are far from optimistic. This is sung with both feeling and sparkle by Jean-François Gardeil. The most ambitious of the four works is a brilliant duet celebrating the nuptials of Aeneas and Dido, which conveniently leaves out the unhappy ending to come later in the story. With sensitive and strongly paced accompaniments from Christie and Les Arts Florissants, it is difficult to imagine that these works could be re-created more tellingly, helped by the presence and atmosphere of the excellent recording.

Requiem Mass.
☞ (M) *** Erato/Warner 2292 45993-2 [id.]. Nelson, Harris, Orliac, Evans, Roberts, Monteverdi Ch., E. Bar. Soloists, Gardiner.
**(*) HM HMC 901251; *HMC 401251* [id.]. Baudry, Zanetti, Benet, Elwes, Varcoe, Chapelle Royale Ch. & O, Herreweghe.

The music of André Campra, who came from Provence and had Italian blood, often possesses a genial lyricism that seems essentially Mediterranean. Although he is best-known now for *L'Europe galante* and other *opéras-ballets*, he wrote a large quantity of sacred music, Psalm settings and motets. This *Requiem* is a lovely work, with luminous textures and often beguiling harmonies, and its neglect is difficult to understand. John Eliot Gardiner and his team of fine singers and players have clearly lavished much affection on this performance and they bring to it intelligence and sensitivity. Campra is one of the most delightful composers of this period, and this admirably recorded disc should go some way towards gaining him a rightful place in the repertoire. The radiance of the singing of the Monteverdi Choir is caught all the more vividly on CD, as well as the bloom on the voices of the excellent team of soloists, with the contrasted tenor timbres of the Frenchman, Jean-Claude Orliac, and of the Welsh singer, Wynford Evans, brought out the more sharply. The intimacy of the accompaniment in such a number as the *Agnus Dei*, with its delicate flute solo, is set nicely in scale, though in slow sections the strings of the English Baroque Soloists are edgier and more squeezy than they became after 1981, when this recording was made.

Herreweghe's performance, with refined solo and choral singing, makes a good alternative to John Eliot Gardiner's version, for those who prefer a cooler approach to church music of 1700. The recording is refined, to match the performance.

L'Europe galante (opera-ballet): suite.
(M) *** HM/BMG GD 77059 (2) [77059-2-RG]. Yakar, Kweksilber, René Jacobs, La Petite Bande,
    Leonhardt – LULLY: *Bourgeois gentilhomme.* ***
☞ (M) *** Decca 433 733-2 [id.]. ECO, Leppard – RAMEAU: Le *Temple de la Gloire.* ***

Like Couperin's *Les Nations*, though in a very different fashion, this enchanting divertissement attempts to portray various national characteristics: French, Spanish, Italian and Turkish. The three soloists all shine and the instrumentalists, directed by Leonhardt, are both expert and spirited. The recording too is well balanced and sounds very fresh on CD.

Campra, who was a few years older than Couperin, possessed keen melodic instincts and a genuine freshness. His work seems to be gaining a wider following now and this suite is marked by a characteristic lyrical grace. It is given a thoroughly idiomatic performance with modern instruments used to good effect, for Leppard has a fine sense of texture. The 1966 Kingsway Hall recording still sounds well, with added definition on CD.

Idomenée (tragédie lyrique).
**(*) HM HMC 901396/8 [id.]. Deletre, Piau, Zanetti, Fouchécourt, Boyer, Les Arts Florissants,
    Christie.

In this first complete recording of any opera by Campra, Christie opts for the later revision of the piece which the composer made for the revival in 1731, eliminating two incidental characters and reworking several scenes. In the manner of the time, it relies on free cantilena rather than formal numbers, with set-pieces kept short and with the chorus often contributing to such brief arias as there are. Christie with his talented Les Arts Florissants team presents the whole work with a taut feeling for its dramatic qualities, though there is nothing here to compare with the big moments in Mozart's opera. The matching of voices to character is closer here than we would conventionally expect in Mozart, and in the breadth of its span and its frequent hints as to what Purcell might have achieved, had he tackled a full-length opera, this is a fascinating work, vividly recorded.

Tancrède (opera); complete.
** Erato/Warner Dig. 2292 45001-2 (2). François Le Roux, Evangelatos, Dubosc, Le Maigat,
    Reinhart, Alliot-Lugaz, Visse, The Sixteen, La Grande Ecurie et la Chambre du Roy, Malgoire.

André Campra had an extraordinary melodic facility. *Tancrède*, the first of his *tragédies lyriques*, comes at the beginning of the eighteenth century: it is very much in the tradition of Lully but is stronger in its blend of lyricism and dance than in dramatic coherence. This recording was made at a performance in Aix-en-Provence in 1986 and, though there are stage noises and at times some less than polished playing, it is well worth investigating.

Canteloube, Marie-Joseph (1879–1957)

(i) *Chants d'Auvergne: Series 1–5* (complete); (ii) Appendix: *Chants d'Auvergne et Quercy: La Mère Antoine; Lorsque le meunier; Oh! Madelon, je dois partir; Reveillez-vous, belle endormie. Chants paysans Bearn: Rossignolet qui chants. Chants du Languedoc: La fille d'un paysan; Moi j'ai un homme; Mon père m'a plasée; O up!; Quand Marion va au moulin. Chants des Pays Basques: Allons, beau rossignole; Comment donc Savoir; Dans le tombeau; J'ai un douce amie; Le premier de tous les oiseaux.*

⊛ (M) *** Van. 08.8002.72 [OVC 8001/2]. Netania Davrath, O, (i) Pierre de la Roche; (ii) Gershon Kingsley.

It was Netania Davrath who in 1963 and 1966 – a decade before the De los Angeles selection – pioneered a complete recording of Canteloube's delightful song-settings from the Auvergne region of France. While her voice has a lovely, sweet purity and freedom in the upper range, she also brings a special kind of colour and life to these infinitely varied settings. All 30 songs from the five series are included, plus an important appendix of 15 more, collected by Canteloube and admirably scored by Gershon Kingsley, very much in the seductive manner of the others. They are quite as delightful as any of the more familiar chants, and some of them are unforgettable, providing a programme of two hours of enchanting music which, when dipped into, will give endless pleasure. The accompaniments are freshly idiomatic, warm but not over-upholstered, and the CD transfers retain all the sparkle and atmosphere of the original recordings.

Chants d'Auvergne: L'Aio dè rotso; L'Antouèno; Baïlèro; Brezairola; Malurous qu'o uno fenno; Passo pel prat; Pastourelle.
(M) *** BMG/RCA GD 87831 [7831-2-RG]. Anna Moffo, American SO, Stokowski – RACHMANINOV: *Vocalise;* VILLA-LOBOS: *Bachianas Brasileiras No. 5.* ***

Moffo gives radiant performances, helped by the sumptuous accompaniment which Stokowski provides. The result is sweet, seductively so. The recording, from the early 1960s, is opulent to match.

Chants d'Auvergne: L'Antouèno; Baïlèro; 3 Bourrées; Lou Boussu; Brezairola; Lou coucut; Chut, chut; La Délaïssádo; Lo Fïolairé; Jou l'pount d'o Mirabel; Malurous qu'o uno fenno; Passo pel prat; Pastourelle; Postouro, sé tu m'aymo; Tè, l'co, tè.
⊛ (M) *** EMI Dig. CD-EMX 9500; *TC-EMX 2075* [Ang. CDM 62010]. Jill Gomez, RLPO, Handley.

Jill Gomez's selection of these increasingly popular songs, attractively presented on a mid-price label, makes for a memorably characterful record which, as well as bringing out the sensuous beauty of Canteloube's arrangements, keeps reminding us, in the echoes of rustic band music, of the genuine folk base. An ideal purchase for the collector who wants just a selection.

Chants d'Auvergne: L'Antouèno; Baïlèro; 3 Bourrées; 2 Bourrées; Brezairola; La Délaïssádo; Lo Fïolairé; Lou Boussu; Malurous qu'o uno fenno; La pastrouletta è lou chibalie; Passo pel prat; La pastoura als camps; Pastourelle.
*** Decca Dig. 410 004-2 [id.]. Te Kanawa, ECO, Tate.

Chants d'Auvergne, 4th and 5th series (complete).
(*) Decca 411 730-2 [id.]. Te Kanawa, ECO, Tate – VILLA-LOBOS: *Bachianas Brasileiras No. 5.* *

In Dame Kiri Te Kanawa's recital the warmly atmospheric Decca recording brings an often languorous opulence to the music-making. In such an atmosphere the quick songs lose a little in bite and *Baïlèro,* the most famous, is taken extremely slowly. With the sound so sumptuous, this hardly registers and the result remains compelling, thanks in great measure to sympathetic accompaniment from the ECO under Jeffrey Tate.

Chants d'Auvergne: Baïlèro; 3 Bourrées; Brezairola; Lou Boussu; Lou coucut; Chut, chut; La Délaïssádo; Lo Fïolairé; Jou l'pount d'o Mirabel; Malurous qu'o uno fenno; Oï ayaï; Pastourelle; La pastrouletta; Postouro, sé tu m'aymo; Tè, l'co, tè; Uno jionto postouro.
☞ (M) *** Virgin/EMI Dig. CUV5 61120-2 [id.]. Arleen Augér, ECO, Yan Pascal Tortelier.

Arleen Augér's lovely soprano is ravishing in the haunting, lyrical songs like the ever-popular *Baïlèro.* In the playful items she conveys plenty of fun, and in the more boisterous numbers the recording has vivid presence.

Caplet, André (1878–1925)

La Masque de la mort rouge (Conte fantastique for harp and orchestra).
☞ (M) **(*) EMI Dig. CDM7 64687-2 [id.]. Cambreling, Monte Carlo PO, Prêtre – DEBUSSY: *Chute de la Maison Usher;* SCHMIDT: *Palais hanté.* ***

La Masque de la mort rouge (Conte fantastique); Divertissements; Les Prières; Septet; 2 Sonnets.
☞ *** HM Dig. HMC 901417 [id.]. Soloists of Ens. Musique Oblique.

André Caplet is not well represented on CD, though a Mass was recorded some years ago. Although his idiom is strongly Debussian, he possessed fastidious craftsmanship and a refined sensibility of distinctive quality. His best-known work is the *Conte fantastique* for harp and strings, based on Edgar Allan Poe's *Masque of the Red Death*, a work strong on evocative menace. This new Harmonia Mundi offers the more intimate, chamber version of the score and makes a strong challenge to the vividly recorded Virgin recording by Virginia McKeand and the Allegri (VC7 90721-2). That came in a mixed programme of French music, including Debussy and Ravel, while this new programme is admirably chosen and serves to flesh out a portrait of Caplet himself. Moreover it is better balanced than the EMI reissue, which presents the work (dating from 1908) in its original form: the composer later transcribed it for chamber forces. Here it is eminently well played by Frédérique Cambreling and the Monte Carlo orchestra under Georges Prêtre, but the placing of the harp so forwardly diminishes the sense of mystery and atmosphere. However, the EMI Debussy and Schmidt couplings are rare – the Debussy uniquely so and very desirable – and the EMI CD also has a price advantage.

5 Ballades françaises; Chanson d'automne; 3 Fables de Jean de la Fontaine; Green; Nuit d'automne; Oraison dominicale; La Part à Dieu; Pie Jesu; 3 Poèmes de Jean-Aubry; Prière Normande; Quand reverrai-je, hélas; Salutation angélique; Viens! Une flûte invisible soupire.
☞ * Unicorn Dig. DKPCD 9142 [id.]. Claudette Leblanc, Boaz Sharon.

Apart from the *Masque of the Red Death*, André Caplet is remembered for his championship of Debussy: it was he who collaborated with the latter on the scoring of *Le Martyre de Saint Sébastien*, of which he conducted the first performance, and *La boîte à joujoux*. This CD presents 21 of Caplet's songs, many of which are of great beauty. The Canadian singer, Claudette Leblanc, sings them with undoubted intelligence, but the voice has little tonal beauty or bloom and has an unpleasing vibrato. Her partner, Boaz Sharon, accompanies sensitively and they are well recorded. A disappointment.

Cardoso, Frei Manuel (c. 1566–1650)

Requiem: Magnificat; Motets, Mulier quae erat; Non mortui; Nos autem gloriari; Sitivit anima mea.
⊛ *** Gimell CDGIM 021; *1585T-21* [id.]. Tallis Scholars, Phillips.

Cardoso's *Requiem* opens in striking and original fashion. The polyphony unfolds in long-breathed phrases of unusual length and eloquence, and both the motets, *Mulier quae erat* ('A woman, a sinner in that city') and the short *Nos autem gloriari* ('Yet should we glory'), are rich in texture and have great expressive resplendence. Cardoso's use of the augmented chord at the opening of the *Requiem* gives his music some of its distinctive stamp. The Tallis Scholars sing with characteristic purity of tone and intonation, and they are splendidly recorded. A glorious issue.

Carissimi, Giacomo (1605–74)

Duos & cantatas: A piè d'un verde alloro; Bel tempo per me; Così volete, così sarà; Deh, memoria è che più chiedi; Hor che si Sirio; Il mio cor è un mar; Lungi homai deh spiega; Peregrin d'ignote sponde; Rimati in pace homai; Scrivete, occhi dolente (Lettera amorosa); Tu m'hai preso à consumare; Vaghi rai, pupille ardenti.
(B) *** HM Dig. HMA 901262; HMA 431262 [id.]. Concerto Vocale, René Jacobs.

Carissimi's achievement as a sacred composer has long overshadowed his secular music, whose riches are generously displayed here and whose inspiration and mastery are immediately evident. These are performances of great style and are beautifully recorded. A bargain.

Jepthe; Judicium Salomonis (The Judgement of Solomon); Jonas (oratorios).
*** Mer. Dig. CDE 84132; *KE 77132* [id.]. Coxwell, Hemington Jones, Harvey, Ainsley, Gabrieli
    Cons. 8 Players, Paul McCreesh.

The present disc collects three of the best known of Carissimi's chamber oratorios. *Jepthe* is affectingly presented in this well-prepared and intelligent performance, which is let down only by some vocal insecurities at the very top. The continuo part is imaginatively realized with some pleasing sonorities (organ, double harp, chitarrone, etc.). Despite some undoubted shortcomings, these are most convincing accounts of all three works.

Carlsson, Mark (born 1952)

Nightwings.
*** Crystal Dig. CD 750 [id.]. Westwood Wind Quintet – BARBER: *Summer music;* LIGETI: *Bagatelles;* MATHIAS: *Quintet.* ***

In *Nightwings* the flute assumes the persona of a dreamer, the taped music may be perceived as a dream-world, and the other four instruments appear as characters in a dream. On this evidence, however, the conception is in some respects more interesting than the piece itself. Excellent playing and recording.

Carmina Burana (c. 1300)

Carmina Burana – songs from the original manuscript.
*** O-L Dig. 417 373-2 [id.]. New L. Cons., Pickett.
**(*) HM HMC 90335 [id.]. Clemencic Cons., René Clemencic.

Carmina Burana – songs from the original manuscript, Vol. 2.
*** O-L Dig. 421 062-2 [id.]. New L. Cons., Pickett.

This was the collection on which Carl Orff drew for his popular cantata. The original manuscript comprises more than 200 pieces from many countries, dating from the late eleventh to the thirteenth century, organized according to subject-matter: love songs, moralizing and satirical songs, eating, drinking, gambling and religious texts. The performances on these well-filled Oiseau-Lyre discs have the merit of excellent singing from Catherine Bott and Michael George, and sensitive playing from the instrumentalists under Pickett.

René Clemencic's performances, recorded in 1977, have immense spirit and liveliness, and there is much character. The presentation suffers slightly in comparison with its rival from slightly over-reverberant sound, though this at times brings a gain in atmosphere.

Carter, Elliott (born 1908)

Concerto for orchestra; (i) *Violin concerto; 3 Occasions.*
*** Virgin/EMI Dig. VC7 91503 [id.]. (i) Ole Bohn; L. Sinf., Knussen.

The 1969 *Concerto for orchestra,* in four linked sections plus introduction and coda, marks a watershed in Carter's career, fully establishing his mature style, gritty and uncompromising. The other two works are much more recent and more approachable in Carter's later, more lyrical manner. All are splendidly performed. The composer himself supervised the sessions. The recording is of spectacular range and depth, bringing out the brilliance of the London Sinfonietta's playing.

(i) *Piano concerto. Variations for orchestra.*
*** New World NWCD 347 [id.]. (i) Ursula Oppens; Cincinnati SO, Gielen.

The *Concerto* is a densely argued piece, complex in its structure, with a concertino of seven instruments, surrounding the piano, who act as 'a well-meaning but impotent intermediary'. The *Variations* is an inventive and fascinating work, splendidly played by these Cincinnati forces. The recording was made at concert performances and is excellent.

Carver, Robert (c. 1484–c. 1568)

Mass: Cantate Domino for 6 voices.
☞ *** Gaudeamus/ASV Dig. CDGAU 136 [id.]. (i) Graham Lovett; David Hamilton, Cappella Nova, Alan Tavener (with: ANGUS: *All my belief;* (i) *The Song of Simeon.* ANON.: *Descendi in hortum meum.* BLACK: *Ane lesson upone the feiftie psalme; Lytill Blak.* PEEBLES: *Psalms 107; 124; Si quis diligit me* ***).

This anthology celebrates the music heard in the 1560s after the return from France of Mary, Queen of Scots. Most of the pieces, by David Peebles (who flourished 1530–76), John Black (c. 1520–87) and John Angus (fl. 1562–90), come from *Musica Britannica* Vol. XV ('Music of Scotland, 1500–1700') and appear on record for the first time. Though the authorship of the *Mass: Cantate Domino* is not definitely established, it is related to the five-part *Fera pessima* by Robert Carver and is almost certainly a re-working, possibly by Carver himself, of the earlier, five-part piece for six voices. In any event, this is a record of much interest, well sung and recorded.

10-part Mass, 'Dum sacrum mysterium'; Motets: *Gaude flore Virginali; O bone Jesu.*
*** Gaudeamus Dig. CDGAU 124; *ZCGAU 124* [id.]. Cappella Nova, Alan Tavener.

There is relatively little biographical information to be had about the Scottish composer, Robert Carver – even his dates are uncertain. The opening piece, the motet *O bone Jesu*, is in 19 parts and is of exceptional luminosity and richness. The 10-part *Mass, Dum sacrum mysterium*, was written at the beginning of the sixteenth century, and it is thought that in its final form it was performed at the coronation of the infant James V at Stirling. As the note puts it, among Carver's *Masses* this is 'undoubtedly the grandest in scope, the most extended in development and the richest in detail'. The motet, *Gaude flore Virginali* for five voices, though less sumptuous, has some adventurous modulations. The Cappella Nova under Alan Tavener give a thoroughly dedicated account of all three pieces, though the pitch drops very slightly in the *Gaude flore Virginali*. The recording is very good indeed.

Missa: L'Homme armé for 4 voices; Mass for 6 voices.
☞ *** Gaudeamus/ASV Dig. CDGAU 126; *ZCGAU 126* [id.]. Cappella Nova, Alan Tavener.

Masses: Fera pessima for 5 voices; Pater creator omnium for 4 voices.
☞ *** Gaudeamus/ASV Dig. CDGAU 127; *ZCGAU 127* [id.]. Cappella Nova, Alan Tavener.

These two CDs, together with his ten-part *Missa Dum sacrum mysterium* which is thought to have accompanied the coronation of the young King James V in Stirling in 1513, represent the complete sacred music of the early-sixteenth-century Scottish composer, Robert Carver. His long life spans the transition from the decorative, late-medieval style through to Renaissance polyphony. Those who know the first issue in the series will need no prompting to investigate the other two, for both singing and recorded sound are excellent. In the *L'Homme armé Mass* of 1520, Carver is the only British composer to make use of the French popular song which inspired so many Mass settings by continental composers, from Josquin onwards. The six-part *Mass* of 1515 is cyclic (each Mass section opens with similar music, and the presence of other common material suggests that it is a parody Mass, possibly based, it is thought, on an earlier Carver motet.

Like the *L'Homme armé*, the *Fera pessima* is another *cantus firmus* Mass (i.e. based on a recurring melody, mostly in longer notes and usually placed in the tenor) and dates from 1525; its companion, the four-part *Pater creator omnium*, comes from 1546 and reflects the changing style of the period. Much of the music Carver composed in the intervening years has been lost and the *Pater creator* survives only in incomplete form; the two missing parts in the *Kyrie* and *Gloria* have been added by Kenneth Elliott. Committed singing from the Cappella Nova and Alan Tavener, and very well recorded too. A rewarding series.

Casella, Alfredo (1883–1947)

Paganiniana, Op. 65.
☞ *** Sony Dig. SK 53280 [id.]. La Scala PO, Muti – BUSONI: *Turandot suite;* MARTUCCI: *Giga* etc. ***
☞ (M) **(*) Ph. 438 281-2 [id.]. Concg. O, Kondrashin – RAVEL: *Daphnis et Chloé.* *
☞ (***) Testament mono SBT 1017 [id.]. St Cecilia, Rome, O, Cantelli – DUKAS: *L'apprenti sorcier;*
   FALLA: *Three-cornered hat;* RAVEL: *Daphnis et Chloé: suite No. 2.* (***)

Paganiniana was commissioned by the Vienna Philharmonic to mark its centenary in 1942. It is a delightful, effervescent score whose sparkling yet dry wit and exuberance fare well in Muti's hands (as it did in Ormandy's celebrated recording with the Philadelphia Orchestra). It also has the advantage of an enterprising and imaginative coupling.

Kondrashin's account of this extremely attractive example of Casella's expert orchestral writing is unfortunately harnessed to a rather uncompetitive version of the complete *Daphnis* music. The scoring is masterly, the colours vivid and the musical ideas manipulated with great skill. There is no depth but much to divert and entertain, and Kondrashin and the Concertgebouw rise to the occasion. Good recording, too, though it is perhaps impractical, given the coupling, to recommend this.

Cantelli's pioneering record dates from 1949 and comes up sounding very well in a marvellously transferred Testament issue which also offers his 1955–6 Philharmonia recording of the *Daphnis* suite and his 1954 *Three-cornered hat*. Elegant playing.

Casken, John (born 1949)

Cello concerto.

☞ *** Collins Dig. CD single 2006-2 [id.]. N. Sinfonia, Heinrich Schiff.

Second only to the irrepressible Mstislav Rostropovich, Heinrich Schiff is a great inspirer among cellists today. It is good to find nowadays how – like Rostropovich – he can inspire with his conducting as well as with his playing. As Music Director of the Northern Sinfonia, he has brought a new driving force to music-making in Newcastle and elsewhere, as instanced in this superb disc celebrating his achievement on multiple fronts. John Casken, a Yorkshireman born in Barnsley in 1949 and now Professor of Music at Manchester University, wrote this 20-minute *Cello concerto* for Schiff and the Northern Sinfonia in a shrewdly practical way so that it does not need a separate conductor. On the Collins recording, as in his live performances, Schiff directs the orchestra from the cello, and the result is one of the richest, most powerful accounts of a new work on any recent disc.

The piece, strong, lyrical and dramatic, is in two substantial movements, with individual sections in each inspired by a cryptic five-line poem rather like a haiku. Casken, who is above all a communicator, thinks of his soloist as an individual set in a landscape; the result is a work full of movement and striking contrasts. It is hard to fathom how the line 'on folds of stone' relates to the vigorous pizzicato scherzo section at the start of the second movement, but what matters is that this is music that has inspired Schiff and his brilliant players to give a performance that is magnetic from first to last. Collins has issued it in its twentieth-century-plus series as a CD 'single', costing about £6, the sort of price to encourage anyone to experiment.

Golem (chamber opera in 2 parts).
*** Virgin/EMI Dig. VC7 91204-2 [id.]. Clarke, Hall, Robson, Music Projects London, Richard
    Bernas.

Golem is based on the well-known Jewish legend of the rabbi, the Maharal, who creates a saviour figure, a Golem, from lifeless clay. The Maharal's altruistic aims are thwarted when the Golem, developing human feelings, refuses to be controlled. Though through the Prelude and five continuous scenes the Maharal's monologues take up a disproportionate share of the whole, that matters little in a recording, particularly when the role is so confidently taken by Adrian Clarke. John Hall as the Golem is equally convincing and most striking of all is Christopher Robson in the counter-tenor role of Ometh, 'a Promethean figure of hope and conscience'.

Castelnuovo-Tedesco, Mario (1895–1968)

Guitar concertos Nos. 1 in D, Op. 99; 2 in C, Op. 160; (i) Double guitar concerto, Op. 201.
☞ ** BMG/RCA Dig. RD 60355 [60355-2-RC]. Kazuhito Yamashita; (i) with Naoko Yamashita;
    LPO, Slatkin.

It is sensible to put all three of the Castelnuovo-Tedesco *Concertos* together, even if the first is by far the best. The second opens invitingly but does not sustain its length, although the central *Sarabanda con variazione* has some nice touches of colour. The quality of invention of the *Double concerto* is unimpressive to say the least, although some might find the Mexican *mariachi* influences in the finale suitably exotic. The Yamashitas are excellent guitarists but the performances here are too cosy by half, with the mellow, over-resonant sound contributing to the enervating atmosphere. In the *First concerto* the central *Andantino alla romanza* with its theme that reminds one of a famous operetta aria is sensuously over-romanticized and indulgent. The Naxos version is infinitely fresher and more enjoyable.

Guitar concerto No. 1 in D, Op. 99.
☞ (BB) *** Naxos Dig. 8.550729 [id.]. Norbert Kraft, Northern CO, Nicholas Ward – RODRIGO;
    VILLA-LOBOS: *Concertos.* ***

On Naxos a first-class version of this slight but attractive concerto, which is well suited by the relatively intimate scale of the performance. The recording is well balanced and vivid, and this is happily coupled with enjoyable versions of two other favourite concertos. The soloist, Norbert Kraft, has plenty of personality and the accompaniment is fresh and polished. Typically excellent Naxos value.

Violin concerto No. 2 (I Profeti), Op. 66.
☞ *** EMI Dig. CDC7 54296-2 [id.]. Perlman, Israel PO, Mehta – BEN-HAIM: *Concerto.* ***

Castelnuovo-Tedesco's *Violin concerto No. 2* is the best-known of the three he wrote, a favourite of

Jascha Heifetz, who commissioned it and recorded it in 1954. Perlman is just as commanding as Heifetz himself, relishing not just the bravura of the piece but the warm lyricism. Often recalling Hollywood epic film-music, the opening orchestral motif with its parallel-fifths chords is very Bloch-like and leads on to one heart-stirring Jewish melody after another. The subtitle of this work is *I Profeti* ('The Prophets'), with the three movements devoted respectively to Isaiah, Jeremiah and Elijah. That first *Isaiah* movement, the longest, leads to an imaginative cadenza in which the soloist is accompanied by the harp. The second movement, *Jeremiah*, is a lament, gently melancholy rather than deeply sorrowful, with the warm melodies punctuated by a brass fanfare motif. The finale seems the least attuned to its subject, with a jaunty march for main theme, much brilliant passage-work for the soloist and a brassy conclusion. It hardly amounts to an apt tribute to Elijah, the thundering prophet, who prompted a far more accurate portrait from Mendelssohn. As in the Ben-Haim work, Perlman is inspired to dazzling fiddle-playing, helping to conceal any weaknesses in the episodic structure. Recorded live in the Mann Auditorium, Tel-Aviv, the sound is warmer and less aggressive than usual in this venue, with Mehta drawing committed if not always ideally polished playing from the Israel orchestra.

Catalani, Alfredo (1854–93)

La Wally (opera): complete.
(M) *** Decca 425 417-2 (2) [id.]. Tebaldi, Del Monaco, Diaz, Cappuccilli, Marimpietri, Turin Lyric Ch., Monte Carlo Op. O, Fausto Cleva.

The title-role of *La Wally* prompts Renata Tebaldi to give one of her most tenderly affecting performances on record, a glorious example of her singing late in her career. Mario del Monaco begins coarsely, but the heroic power and intensity of his singing are formidable, and it is good to have the young Cappuccilli in the baritone role of Gellner. The sound in this late-1960s recording is superbly focused and vividly real.

Cavalli, Francesco (1602–76)

La Calisto (complete version – freely arranged by Raymond Leppard).
☞ (M) *** Decca 436 216-2 (2) [id.]. Cotrubas, Trama, J. Baker, Bowman, Gottlieb, Cuénod, Hughes, Glyndebourne Festival Op. Ch., LPO, Leppard.

No more perfect Glyndebourne entertainment has been devised than this freely adapted version of an opera written for Venice in the 1650s but never heard since. It exactly relates that permissive society of the seventeenth century to our own. It is the more delectable because of the brilliant part given to the goddess, Diana, taken by Dame Janet Baker. In Leppard's version she has the dual task of portraying first the chaste goddess herself, then in the same costume switching immediately to the randy Jupiter disguised as Diana, quite a different character. The opera is splendidly cast. Parts for such singers as James Bowman draw out their finest qualities, and the result is magic. No one should miss Dame Janet's heartbreakingly intense singing of her tender aria *Amara servitù*, while a subsidiary character, Linfea, a bad-tempered, lecherous, ageing nymph, is portrayed hilariously by Hugues Cuénod. The opera has transferred admirably to a pair of CDs, with each of the two Acts offered without a break; the recording, made at Glyndebourne, is gloriously rich and atmospheric, with the Prologue in a different, more ethereal acoustic than the rest of the opera. A full libretto is provided.

Giasone (complete).
*** HM Dig. HMC 901282/4 [id.]. Chance, Schopper, Dubosc, Deletré, Mellon, Banditelli, Visse, De Mey, Concerto Vocale, Jacobs.

With the brilliant and sensitive counter-tenor, Michael Chance, in the title-role, René Jacobs's recording of Cavalli's opera is a remarkable achievement. The admixture of comedy that can be embarrassing in operas of this period is here handled splendidly. The vividly characterful Dominique Visse in particular scores a huge success in the drag-role of the nurse, Delfa, very much in the tradition of Hugues Cuénod's performances for Raymond Leppard in Cavalli at Glyndebourne. It is a pity that none of the others characterize like Visse, beautifully as they sing. Clean, well-balanced sound.

Xerse (complete).
*** HM HMC 901175/8 [id.]. René Jacobs, Nelson, Gall, Poulenard, Mellon, Feldman, Elwes, De
  Mey, Visse, Instrumental Ens., Jacobs.

'Ombra mai fù,' sings King Xerxes in the opening scene, addressing a plane tree, and most listeners
will have a double-take, remembering Handel's *Largo*, which comes from a later setting of the same
libretto. As well as directing his talented team, Jacobs sings the title-role, only one of the four
counter-tenors, nicely contrasted, who take the castrato roles. The fruity alto of Dominique Visse in a
comic servant role is particularly striking, and among the women – some of them shrill at times – the
outstanding singer, Agnès Mellon, takes the other servant role, singing delightfully in a tiny laughing
song.

Certon, Pierre (died 1572)

Chansons: *Amour a tort; Ce n'est a vous; C'est grand pityé; De tout le mal; En espérant; Entre vous
gentilz hommes; Heilas ne fringuerons nous; Je l'ay aymé; Je neveulx poinct; Martin s'en alla; Plus nu
suys; Que n'est auprès de moy; Si ta beaulté; Ung jour que Madame dormait.* Mass: *Sur le pont
d'Avignon.*
(B) *** HM HMA 190 1034 [id.]. Boston Camerata, Joel Cohen.

The Mass, *Sur le pont d'Avignon*, has genuine appeal, and the chansons also exercise a real charm
over the listener. The Mass is performed *a cappella*, and the chansons enjoy instrumental support. In
both sacred and secular works the Boston Camerata bring freshness, musical accomplishment and
stylistic understanding to bear; the recording, made in a spacious acoustic, creates the most beautiful
sounds.

Cesti, Antonio (1623–69)

Cantatas: *Amanti, io vi disfido; Pria ch'adori.*
(B) **(*) HM HMA 901011 [id.]. Concerto Vocale – D'INDIA: *Duets, Laments & Madrigals.* **(*)

Cesti's 17-minute cantata, *Pria ch'adori*, is a serenata for two voices, after the Monteverdi style,
including even a *Lamento d'Arianna* in duet form. *Amanti, io vi disfido* is a much shorter, bravura
piece. The performances by Judith Nelson and René Jacobs are certainly pleasingly fresh, and the
distinguished instrumental group includes William Christie providing the continuo.

Chabrier, Emmanuel (1841–94)

Bourrée fantasque; España (rhapsody); *Marche joyeuse; Menuet pompeux; Prélude pastorale; Suite
pastorale; Le Roi malgré lui: Danse slave; Fête polonaise.*
☞ *** EMI Dig. CDC7 49652-2. Capitole Toulouse O, Plasson.

Bourrée fantasque; España (rhapsody); *Marche joyeuse; Suite pastorale; Gwendoline: Overture. Le
Roi malgré lui: Danse slave; Fête polonaise.*
(M) *** Mercury 434 303-2 [id.]. Detroit SO, Paray – ROUSSEL: *Suite.* **(*)

Chabrier is Beecham territory and he calls for playing of elegance and charm. Michel Plasson and his
excellent Toulouse forces bring just the right note of exuberance and *joie de vivre* to this delightful
music. The recording is eminently satisfactory, though it is a shade resonant and, as a result, lacks the
last ounce of transparency. Even so, the effect suits the music, and the elegant performance of the
delightful *Suite pastorale* ensures a strong recommendation for this CD, recently restored to the EMI
catalogue, still at full price.

   The return of this finely played and idiomatically conducted Mercury collection of Chabrier's best
orchestral pieces does not disappoint. Paray's whimsically relaxed and sparkling account of *España*
gives great pleasure and his rubato in the *Fête polonaise* is equally winning. The *Suite pastorale* is a
wholly delightful account, given playing that is at once warm and polished, neat and perfectly in
scale, with the orchestra beautifully balanced. The *Marche joyeuse* was recorded in Detroit's Old
Orchestral Hall a year before the rest of the programme.

España (rhapsody); *Suite pastorale.*
*** Chan. Dig. CHAN 8852; ABTD 1469 [id.]. Ulster O, Yan Pascal Tortelier – DUKAS: *L'apprenti sorcier; La Péri.* **(*)

Yan Pascal Tortelier and the excellent Ulster Orchestra give an altogether first-rate account of Chabrier's delightful *Suite pastorale*, distinguished by an appealing charm and lightness of touch. There is a spirited account of *España*, too.

PIANO MUSIC

Bourrée fantasque; Impromptu in C; 10 Pièces pittoresques.
(M) **(*) Pianissimo Dig. PP 10792 [id.]. Richard McMahon.

Franck described Chabrier's *Dix Pièces pittoresques* as 'a bridge between our own times and those of Couperin and Rameau'. Richard McMahon's highly individual rubato catches the impulsive feeling of the opening *C major Impromptu* rather well, and he is equally free in handling the rest of the ten pieces. The *Bourrée fantasque* is played with much rhythmic vigour. Any minor reservations here are dwarfed by the interest of this attractively enterprising programme, for McMahon certainly brings all this music vividly to life. He is well recorded too.

OPERA

L'Etoile (complete).
✪ *** EMI Dig. CDS7 47889-8 (2) [Pathé id.]. Alliot-Lugaz, Gautier, Bacquier, Raphanel, Damonte, Le Roux, David, Lyon Opéra Ch. and O, Gardiner.

This fizzing operetta is a winner: the subtlety and refinement of Chabrier's score go well beyond the usual realm of operetta, and Gardiner directs a performance that from first to last makes the piece sparkle bewitchingly. Colette Alliot-Lugaz and Gabriel Bacquier are first rate and numbers such as the drunken duet between King and Astrologer are hilarious. Outstandingly good recording, with excellent access.

Le roi malgré lui (complete).
(M) *** Erato/Warner 2292 45792-2 (2) [id.]. Hendricks, Garcisanz, Quilico, Jeffes, Lafont, French R. Ch. & New PO, Dutoit.

This long-neglected opera is another Chabrier masterpiece, a modified Cinderella story, ending happily, which prompts a series of superb numbers, some *España*-like in brilliance (the well-known Waltz of Act II transformed in its choral form) and some hauntingly romantic, with even one sextet suggesting a translation of Wagner's Rhinemaiden music into waltz-time. The pity is that the linking recitatives have been completely omitted from this recording, and in addition the score has been seriously cut. But Charles Dutoit is a most persuasive advocate. Star among the singers is Barbara Hendricks as the slave-girl Cinderella figure, Minka. The recording is naturally balanced and has plenty of atmosphere.

Chadwick, George (1854–1931)

Symphony No. 2, Op. 21.
*** New World Dig. NWCD 339 [id.]. Albany SO, Julius Hegyi – PARKER: *Northern Ballad.* ***

George Chadwick's *Second Symphony* (1883–6) breathes much the same air as Brahms and Dvořák; the scoring is beautifully clean and the ideas appealing. The Scherzo is quite delightful. The symphony as a whole is cultivated, well crafted and civilized. Very natural recorded sound and an excellent performance from these New England forces. An interesting disc.

Symphony No. 3 in F.
☞ *** Chan. Dig. CHAN 9253 [id.]. Detroit SO, Järvi – BARBER: *Medea's meditation* etc. ***

Chadwick's *Third Symphony* is an attractive piece in the received idiom of the day. In 1894 it won first prize in a competition whose jury was chaired by Dvořák, and it breathes much the same air as Brahms, Dvořák and Svendsen; although its musical language is not strongly individual, it is fresh and compelling, particularly in so persuasive a performance. The *Largo* is beautifully shaped and the Scherzo delightfully light and piquant. Absolutely first-class recording too.

Serenade for strings.
*** Albany Dig. TROY 033-2 [id.]. V. American Music Ens., Hobart Earle – GILBERT: *Suite*. ***

Chadwick's *Serenade*, written in 1890, is here given its European première. This very well-crafted piece by the so-called 'Boston classicist' gives much pleasure. It is quite beautifully played by this excellent Viennese group, drawn from younger members of the Vienna Symphony Orchestra. The sound too is first rate, a successful example of a 'live recording' bringing no loss in realism and a gain in spontaneity.

Chambonnières, Jacques Champion de (*c.* 1602–72)

Pièces de clavecin, Livres I & II: Suites in A, C, D & G.
☞ *** HM/BMG Dig. 05472 77210-2. Skip Sempé (harpsichord).

Skip Sempé plays as if he had composed this music. He is able to make this repertoire sound spontaneous and vital in a way that relatively few of his colleagues can (except Andreas Staier and Melvyn Tan). Chambonnières is spoken of as the father of the French harpsichord school, but Sempé speaks of his music as 'a keyboard synthesis of the *Air de Cour* and Italian recitative, the declamation and rhetoric of Italian monody'. While retaining a feeling of dance, Sempé is able to convey an improvisatory touch that brings every piece alive. He plays a Flemish instrument of about 1680, and in four of them he is joined by Brian Feehan as theorbo continuo. Very good recording.

Chaminade, Cécile (1857–1944)

Air à danser, Op. 164; Air de ballet, Op. 30; Automne; Autrefois; Contes bleus No. 2, Op. 122; Danse créole, Op. 94; Guitare, Op. 32; La Lisonjera, Op. 50; Lolita, Op. 54; Minuetto, Op. 23; Pas des écharpes, Op. 37; Pas des sylphes: Intermezzo; Pierette, Op. 41; 3 Romances sans paroles, Op. 76/1, 3 & 6; Sérénade, Op. 29; Sous la masque, Op. 116; Toccata, Op. 39; Valse arabesque.
☞ *** Chan. Dig. CHAN 8888; *ABTD 1499* [id.]. Eric Parkin.

Autrefois; Callirhoë; Elévation in E; Etude mélodique in G flat; Etude pathétique in B min.; Etude scholastique La Lisonjera; L'Ondine; Pêcheurs de nuit; Romance; Scherzo in C; Sérénade in D; Solitude; Souvenance; Thème varié in A; Valse romantique; Waltz No. 2.
☞ *** Hyp. Dig. CDA 66584 [id.]. Peter Jacobs.

These days Chaminade occupies a more peripheral position than she did in Victorian drawing-rooms, when her piano miniatures gained wide currency. As a glance at her entry in *Grove* will show, she was enormously prolific and wrote some 350 compositions, including operas, ballets, orchestral and chamber music, as well as a hundred or so songs. (Her Op. 11 *Piano Trio in G minor* has been recorded in a box devoted to women composers; her choral symphony on the subject of the Amazons has not, but doubtless Marco Polo will rise to the challenge.) Yet it is for her piano music that she is best remembered, and both Eric Parkin and Peter Jacobs offer excellent and well-filled selections. Only a handful overlap, so both discs can be acquired without risk of much duplication. Artistically these pieces are rather stronger than one had suspected and, although they are by no means the equal of Grieg or early Fauré, they can hold their own with Saint-Saëns and are more inventive than the *Brises des Orients* of Félicien David. There is a quality of gentility that has lent a certain pallor to Chaminade's charms, but both pianists here make out a stronger case for her than most people would imagine possible. It goes without saying that neither recital should be played straight off if these pieces are not to lose something of their allure. They are, of course, stronger on surface than on substance. Both are well recorded and in this respect there is little to choose between the two. Nor is there much to choose as far as the performances are concerned; both are persuasive, though Parkin has a slight edge over his colleague in terms of elegance and finesse. Both can be recommended, with the Chandos perhaps making the better starting-point.

Charpentier, Gustave (1860–1956)

Louise (gramophone version conceived and realized by the composer).
☞ (M) (***) Nimbus mono NI 7829 [id.]. Vallin, Thill, Pernet, Lecouvreur, Gaudel, Ch. Raugel & O, Eugène Bigot.

These substantial excerpts from *Louise* were recorded in 1935 under the 75-year-old composer's supervision; they feature two ideally cast French singers as the two principals, Ninon Vallin enchanting in the title-role and the tenor, Georges Thill, heady-toned as the hero, Julien. France has produced few singers to rival them since. The original eight 78-r.p.m. records are fitted neatly on to a single CD, and – in the selection of items, made by the composer himself – just the delights and none of the *longueurs* of this nostalgically atmospheric opera are included. The voices are caught superbly in the Nimbus transfers, but their system of playing the original 78s on an acoustic horn gramophone works far less well for the orchestral sound: with an early electrical recording like this it becomes muddled. Yet even Nimbus has rarely presented voices as vividly as here.

Louise (opera): complete.
(M) *** Sony S3K 46429 (3) [id.]. Cotrubas, Berbié, Domingo, Sénéchal, Bacquier, Amb. Op. Ch.,
    New Philh. O, Prêtre.
☞ (M) **(*) Ph. 442 082-2. Monmart, Larose, Michel, Musy, Opéra-Comique Ch. & O, Jean
    Fournet.

This fine, atmospheric recording, the first in stereo, explains why *Louise* has long been a favourite opera in Paris. The love-duets are enchanting and Ileana Cotrubas makes a delightful heroine, not always flawless technically but charmingly girlish. Plácido Domingo is a relatively heavyweight Julien, and Jane Berbié and Gabriel Bacquier are excellent as the parents. Under Georges Prêtre, far warmer than usual on record, the ensemble is rich and clear, with refined recording every bit as atmospheric as one could want. A set which splendidly fills an obvious gap in the catalogue.

Dating from 1956, Fournet's version on a mid-priced Philips CD offers a keenly idiomatic performance, beautifully paced thanks to the warmly understanding direction of Fournet, a conductor too little known on disc. The Opéra-Comique cast contains no stars but relies on singers with experience of their roles in the theatre. It is hardly a direct rival to the Sony version with Cotrubas and Domingo, but with Monmart a bright-toned, very French and girlish Louise and Larose a ringing tenor, equally French in tone, the set conveys the authentic atmosphere, despite close and limited recording.

Charpentier, Marc-Antoine (1634–1704)

Concert à 4 (for viols), H.545; Musique de théâtre pour Circé et Andromède; Sonata à 8 (for 2 flutes & strings), H.548.
**(*) HM Dig. HMC 901244; *HMC 401244* [id.]. London Baroque, Medlam.

These pieces are most expertly played here by the members of London Baroque (though the string sound still does not entirely escape the faint suspicion that it has been marinaded in vinegar) and will reward investigation. The sound is excellent.

Le malade imaginaire (incidental music).
*** Erato/Warner Dig. 2292 45002-2 [id.]. Poulenard, Feldman, Ragon, Les musiciens du Louvre,
    Marc Minkowski.
*** HM Dig. HMC 90-1336; 40-1336 [id.]. Zanetti, Rime, Brua, Visse, Crook, Gardeil, Les Arts
    Florissants, Christie.

This sequence of extended prologue and three *intermèdes* tingles with energy, and is superbly realized on this first recording of the complete incidental music, much of which was lost for three centuries. Eight first-rate soloists and a lively period orchestra are spurred by the consistently animated direction of Marc Minkowski, and the vivid recording adds to the illusion of live performance.

With rather less forward and more refined sound, Christie – though he uses percussion just as dramatically as his rival – is lighter in his textures and rhythms, often opting for faster speeds. The format is cumbersome, with a single disc contained in a double jewel-case, but the libretto is far more readable.

Motets: *Alma Redemptoris; Amicus meus; Ave regina; Dialogus inter Magdalenam et Jesum; Egredimini filiae Sion; Elevations; O pretiosum; O vere, o bone, Magdalena lugens; Motet du saint sacrement; O vos omnes; Pour le passion de notre Seigneur* (2 settings); *Salve regina; Solva vivebat in antris Magdalena lugens.*
*** HM HMC 901149 [id.]. Concerto Vocale.

Half of the motets on this record are for solo voice and the others are duets. Among the best and most moving things here are the *O vos omnes* and *Amicus meus*, which are beautifully done. Another motet to note is *Magdalena lugens*, in which Mary Magdalene laments Christ's death at the foot of the Cross. Expressive singing from Judith Nelson and René Jacobs, and excellent continuo support. Worth a strong recommendation.

(i) *Beatus vir; Salve Regina* (for 3 choirs and orchestra); (ii) *Te Deum. Tenebrae factae sunt* (for bass and orchestra).

☞ (B) *** Erato/Warner 2292 45926-2 [id.]. Huttenlocher, Gulbenkian Foundation of Lisbon Ch. & O, Michel Corboz, with (i) Brunner, Vieira, Zaepffel, Ramirez; (ii) Saque, Silva, Williams, Serafim, Lopes.

A fine bargain introduction to a great French baroque master. Alas, for the newcomer there is no documentation telling of the music's glories but, such is the crass way of major companies now when reissuing high-quality material at bargain price, that such a critical comment goes unheeded. The music itself is splendid and the programme admirably conceived. The *Te Deum* is an imposingly resplendent piece, well laced with gleaming trumpets, then comes the lyrically more expressive *Beatus vir*, followed by the sumptuous *Salve regina* for three choirs, spread spaciously across the sound spectrum in front of the listener. The singing and playing of the Lisbon choir and orchestra under the excellent Michel Corboz is full of vigour and commitment. None of the soloists except Philippe Huttenlocher is well-known, and it is he who sings the closing *Tenebrae factae sunt* with tender feeling. The editions used are either by Guy Lambert or Roger Blanchard (*Beatus vir*) and, though ideas on performance practice may have changed in the last two decades, there is much pleasure to be had from this music-making. Excellent, full-bodied sound from the end of the 1970s, effectively transferred.

Caecilia, virgo et martyr; Filius prodigus (oratorios); *Magnificat.*
*** HM Dig. HMC 90066 [id.]. Grenat, Benet, Laplenie, Reinhard, Studer, Les Arts Florissants, Christie.

The music's stature and nobility are fully conveyed here. The *Magnificat* is a short piece for three voices and has an almost Purcellian flavour. One thing that will immediately strike the listener is the delicacy and finesse of the scoring. All this music is beautifully recorded; the present issues can be recommended with enthusiasm.

Elévation; In obitum augustissimae nec non piissimae gallorum Reginae lamentum; Luctus de morte augustissimae Mariae Theresiae Reginae Galliae.
(M) *** Erato/Warner Dig. 2292 45339-2 [id.]. Degelin, Verdoodt, Smolders, Crook, Vandersteene, Widmer, Namur Chamber Ch., Musica Polyphonica, Devos.

All three works here lament the death in 1683 of Queen Maria Teresa, wife of Louis XIV of France since 1660. Clearly the event moved Charpentier deeply, and each reflects the paradox of the Christian faith in contrasting grief with joy and hope in the life hereafter. The performances could hardly be bettered, bringing out all the music's drama, joy and depth of feeling. The recording, made in a spacious acoustic, is also first class in every way. Very highly recommended.

In navitatem Domini nostri Jésus Christi (canticum), H.414; Pastorale sur la naissance de notre Seigneur Jésus Christ, H.483.
*** HM HMC 901082; *HMC 401082*. Les Arts Florissants Vocal & Instrumental Ens., Christie.

This *Canticum* has much of the character of an oratorio. The invention has great appeal and variety. The *Pastorale* is a most rewarding piece, and the grace and charm of the writing continue to win one over to this eminently resourceful composer. This collection by William Christie is self-recommending, so high are the standards of performance and recording, and so fertile is Charpentier's imagination.

In navitatem Domini nostri Jésus Christi, H.416; Pastorale sur la naissance de notre Seigneur Jésus Christ.
*** HM HMC 905130 [id.]. Les Arts Florissants Vocal & Instrumental Ens., Christie.

The cantata is one of Charpentier's grandest, a finely balanced edifice in two complementary halves, separated by an instrumental section, an eloquent evocation of the night. The little pastorale was written in the tradition of the ballet de cour or divertissement. This is enchanting music, elegantly played and excellently recorded.

Leçons de ténèbres.
*** HM HMC 901005 [id.]. Jacobs, Nelson, Verkinderen, Kuijken, Christie, Junghänel.

These *Leçons de ténèbres* are eloquent and moving pieces, worthy of comparison with Purcell. René Jacobs's performance, like that of his colleagues, is so authentic in every respect that it is difficult to imagine it being surpassed. The recording is as distinguished as the performances.

Leçons de ténèbres for Good Friday.
☞ *** Virgin/EMI Dig. VC7 59295-2 [id.]. Gérard Lesne, Agnès Mellon, Ian Honeyman, Jacques
Bona, Il Seminario Musicale.

Charpentier composed a variety of settings of the *Tenebrae* lessons. The attempt to reconstruct a
Tenebrae Office for Good Friday poses many problems: although the three on this recording were all
composed for Good Friday, they were not necessarily intended for the same Good Friday. Be that as
it may, as the music unfolds, its effect is both powerful and elevating. In the context of this service,
Charpentier's music has a quiet and affecting directness as well as spirituality. Both the singing and
the instrumental playing are of the highest quality, and the recording, made at L'Abbaye Royale de
Fontrevaud, could not be bettered in terms of balance and fidelity.

Méditations pour le Carême; Le reniement de St Pierre.
*** HM Dig. HMC 905151; *HMC 405151* [id.]. Les Arts Florissants, William Christie.

Le reniement de Saint Pierre is one of Charpentier's most inspired and expressive works and its text
draws on the account in all four Gospels of St Peter's denial of Christ. The *Méditations pour le
Carême* are a sequence of three-voice motets for Lent with continuo accompaniment (organ, theorbo
and bass viol) that may not have quite the same imaginative or expressive resource but which are full
of nobility and interest. The performances maintain the high standards of this ensemble, and the
same compliment can be paid to the recording.

(i) *Messe de minuit pour Noël (Midnight Mass for Christmas Eve); (ii) Te Deum.*
(M) **(*) EMI CDM7 63135-2. (i) Cantelo, Gelmar, Partridge, Bowman, Keyte, King's College Ch.,
ECO, Willcocks; (ii) Lott, Harrhy, Brett, Partridge, Roberts, King's College Ch., ASMF,
Ledger.

There is a kinship between Charpentier's lovely *Christmas Mass* and Czech settings of the Mass that
incorporate folk material, even the *Kyrie* having a jolly quality about it. The King's performance is
warm and musical, but there isn't much Gallic flavour. The recording comes from the late 1960s and
certainly now has more bite than it did; but reservations remain about the basic style of the singing.
The coupling is the best known of the *Te Deum* settings, and this time the King's performance has a
vitality and boldness to match the music and catches also its douceur and freshness.

Miserere, H.219; Motets: *pour la seconde fois que le Saint Sacrament vien au même reposoir, H.372;
pour le Saint Sacrement au reposoir, H.346. Motet pour une longue offrande, H.434.*
*** HM Dig. HMC 901185; *HMC 401185* [id.]. Mellon, Poulenard, Ledroit, Kendall, Kooy,
Chapelle Royale, Herreweghe.

Charpentier's *Motet pour une longue offrande* is one of his most splendid and eloquent works. The
Miserere was written for the Jesuit Church on Rue Saint-Antoine, whose ceremonies were particularly
sumptuous. All four works on the disc are powerfully expressive and beautifully performed. The
recording, made in collaboration with Radio France, is most expertly balanced.

OPERA

Actéon (complete).
(B) *** HM HMA 901095; *HMA 401095* [id.]. Visse, Mellon, Laurens, Feldman, Paut, Les Arts
Florissants Vocal & Instrumental Ens., Christie.

Actéon is particularly well portrayed by Dominique Visse; his transformation in the fourth tableau
and his feelings of horror are almost as effective as anything in nineteenth-century opera! The other
singers are first rate, in particular the Diane of Agnès Mellon. Alert playing and an altogether natural
recording, as well as excellent presentation, make this a most desirable issue and a real bargain.

Les Arts Florissants (opéra et idyle en musique).
(B) *** HM HMA 901083 [id.]. Les Arts Florissants Vocal & Instrumental Ens., William Christie.

Les Arts Florissants is a short entertainment in five scenes; the libretto tells of a conflict between the
Arts who flourish under the rule of Peace, and the forces of War, personified by Discord and the
Furies. This and the little Interlude that completes the music include some invigorating and fresh
invention, performed very pleasingly indeed by this eponymous group under the expert direction of
William Christie. Period instruments are used, but intonation is always good and the sounds often
charm the ear. The recording is excellent. A bargain.

David et Jonathas (complete).
(M) *** Erato/Warner 2292 45162-2 [id.]. Esswood, Alliot-Lugaz, Huttenlocher, Soyer, David,
Jacobs, Lyon Opera Ch., E. Bar. Festival O, Corboz.
**(*) HM Dig. HMC 90 1289/90 [id.]. Lesne, Zanetti, Gardeil, Visse, Les Arts Florissants, Christie.

David et Jonathas confirms the impression, made by many other Charpentier records during the last few years, that in him France has one of her most inspired Baroque masters. The Erato performance is marked by some good singing, though there are passages which would, one feels, benefit from greater finish. But Michel Corboz gets generally excellent results from his artists and is well recorded.

Christie's version on Harmonia Mundi may not always be especially dramatic, but it has a notably sure sense of authentic Baroque style and scale, as well as fine choral singing. However, only one of Christie's soloists is really outstanding, the characterfully distinctive counter-tenor, Dominique Visse, who gives a vivid, highly theatrical performance; but those who relish authenticity above all else will clearly take to this version, very well recorded.

Medée (complete).
⊛ *** HM HMC 901139/41 [id.]. Feldman, Ragon, Mellon, Boulin, Bona, Cantor, Les Arts
Florissants Ch. & O, Christie.

Few records of early Baroque opera communicate as vividly as this, winner in 1985 of the International record critics' award and the Early Music prize in the Gramophone record awards. Despite the classical convention of the libretto and a strictly authentic approach to the performance, Christie's account has a vitality and a sense of involvement which bring out the keen originality of Charpentier's writing, his implied emotional glosses on a formal subject. This was Charpentier's only tragédie-lyrique, and richly extends our knowledge of a long-neglected composer. Les Arts Florissants, in the stylishness of its playing on period instruments, matches any such group in the world, and the soloists are all first rate. Excellent recording.

Chausson, Ernest (1855–99)

Poème for violin and orchestra.
☞ *** EMI Dig. CDC7 47725-2 [id.]. Perlman, O de Paris, Martinon – RAVEL: *Tzigane;* SAINT-
SAENS: *Havanaise* etc. ***
(M) *** Ph. Dig. 432 513-2. Kremer, LSO, Chailly (with Concert ***).
*** DG Dig. 423 063-2 [id.]. Perlman, NYPO, Mehta – RAVEL: *Tzigane;* SAINT-SAENS: *Havanaise*
etc.: SARASATE: *Carmen fantasy.* ***
☞ (M) *(*) Sony SMK 47548 [id.]. Francescatti, NYPO, Bernstein – FAURE: *Ballade* **; FRANCK:
Symphony *(*); RAVEL: *Tzigane.* *(*)

Chausson's beautiful *Poème* has been generously represented on records; Perlman's 1975 recording with the Orchestre de Paris under Jean Martinon is a classic account by which newcomers are measured. What a glorious and inspired piece it is when played with such feeling! The digital transfer exchanges some of the opulence of the original for a gain in presence (not that Perlman isn't near enough already) but still sounds full. Perlman's glorious tone is undiminished, even if now the ear perceives a slightly sharper outline to the timbre.

Kremer's poetic account of Chausson's *Poème* is part of a highly recommendable concert of French concertante works for violin and orchestra.

Perlman's 1987 digital version is a very fine one and will not disappoint. The sound is immediate and refined in detail, while the balance of the soloist is very slightly less forward.

Bernstein provides backing atmosphere but Francescatti's slightly febrile timbre will not please all tastes here, and the closely balanced 1964 recording is unflattering.

(i) *Poème for violin & orchestra;* (ii) *Poème de l'amour et de la mer.*
☞ *** Chan. Dig. CHAN 8952; *ABTD 1546.* (i) Yan Pascal Tortelier; (ii) Linda Finnie; Ulster O,
Tortelier – FAURE: *Pavane* etc. ***

No quarrels with Yan Pascal Tortelier's playing in the *Poème*, which he directs from the bow. There is consistent beauty of tone and, what is more important, refinement of feeling. In the *Poème de l'amour et de la mer* Linda Finnie can hold her own with the very best; her feeling for the idiom is completely natural and her voice is beautifully coloured. Ferrier and de los Angeles are, of course, special cases; but among newer recordings this has very strong claims. Indeed in rapport between singer and orchestra none is better.

(i) *Poème, Op. 25. Symphony in B flat, Op. 20.*
☞ (M) **(*) BMG/RCA GD 60683 [0926 60683-2]. (i) David Oistrakh; Boston SO, Munch (with
    SAINT-SAENS: *Introduction & Rondo capriccioso* ***).

Munch's 1962 account of the *Symphony in B flat* is high-powered and splendidly played. The CD
transfer has, of course, improved matters, but the orchestral texture, which is fairly thick at times, is
not perhaps as transparent as it might be. Some may also find the performance just a shade
overdriven. David Oistrakh's 1955 account of the *Poème* is masterly – and, were there nothing else
on this disc, it would still be worth buying, and the Saint-Saëns encore tops it off nicely.

Symphony in B flat, Op. 20.
*** Denon Dig. CO 73675 [id.]. Netherlands R. PO, Jean Fournet – FAURE: *Pelléas et Mélisande*.
    ***

Symphony in B flat; Soir de fête, Op. 32; The Tempest, Op. 18: 2 Scenes.
**(*) Chan. Dig. CHAN 8369; *ABTD 1135* [id.]. Radio-Télévision Belge SO, Serebrier.

Symphony in B flat; Soir de fête; Viviane, Op. 5.
☞ (M) ** EMI CDM7 64686-2 [id.]. Toulouse Capitole O, Michel Plasson.

Jean Fournet's new account of the *Symphony in B flat* is arguably the finest now on the market. Not
only is it very well shaped, but the texture in the voluptuous slow movement is heard in excellent
focus. Fournet paces all three movements well and gets sensitive results from his players. It is to be
preferred to Serebrier's account, though that is more logically coupled with other Chausson pieces,
Soir de Fête plus two scenes from the incidental music for *The Tempest*. Serebrier's account of the
Symphony has real conviction and receives good recording, but on balance Fournet is first choice.

Michel Plasson gives a sensitive account of the Chausson *Symphony* and, particularly in the
powerful introduction and the somewhat Tristanesque slow movement, secures playing of real feeling
from the Toulouse orchestra. This is an eloquent performance and, were the recording more refined,
it would be a high recommendation, particularly as the couplings are such rarities. *Soir de fête* was
written the year before the composer's death and remained unpublished for many years, as Chausson
had intended to revise it. It is the poetic middle section which finds him at his best. For the reissue
EMI have added a more recent recording (1986) of the early tone-poem, *Viviane*. The recordings
were made in the somewhat reverberant acoustic of the Halle-aux-Graines, Toulouse. Detail could be
better focused, and the digital remastering of the two analogue masters has emphasized an unpleasing
edge on the strings, though fairly acceptable results can be secured by the manipulation of the
controls.

CHAMBER MUSIC

Concert for piano, violin and string quartet, Op. 21.
**(*) Essex CDS 6044. Accardo, Canino, Levin, Batjer, Hoffman, Wiley – SAINT-SAENS: *Violin
    sonata No. 1.* ***
(*) Decca Dig. 425 860-2 [id.]. Thibaudet, Bell, Takács Qt – RAVEL: *Piano trio.* *

Concert for piano, violin and string quartet; String quartet in C min., Op. 35 (completed d'Indy).
☞ *** EMI Dig. CDC7 47548-2 [id.]. Collard, Dumay, Muir Qt.

(i) *Concert for piano, violin and string quartet;* (ii) *Pièce in C for cello and piano, Op. 39.*
☞ (B) ** HM HMP 3901135 [id.]. (i) R. Pasquier, Daugareil, Simonot, B. Pasquier; (ii) Ridoux; (i;
    ii) Pennetier.

Jean-Philippe Collard and Augustin Dumay unquestionably lead the field. These artists are completely
attuned to the sensibility of the period and they bring an impressive authority to the work. Both
Dumay and Collard are scrupulous in their observance of the dynamic markings, and there is an
authenticity of feeling that is completely involving. The *C minor String quartet* that was left
incomplete and to which Vincent d'Indy put the finishing touches provides a splendid makeweight,
and this is not otherwise available. The playing is effortless and unforced, and the recording is
extremely vivid and lifelike. Unfortunately this CD is currently withdrawn, but we hope it will
reappear during the lifetime of this book.

Salvatore Accardo and Bruno Canino and their four colleagues convey a sense of effortless music-
making and of pleasure in making music in domestic surroundings. Accardo is particularly songful in
the third movement, light and delicate elsewhere. It is a thoroughly enjoyable account, recorded in a
warm acoustic.

Decca's team comprises Joshua Bell, Jean-Yves Thibaudet and the Takács Quartet, and they give a good account of themselves. Joshua Bell is perhaps a little too forceful and thrustful in tone in the main theme of the first movement, and they are rather on the fast side in the finale and wanting in breadth. The recording is bright and well focused.

The Harmonia Mundi alternative is inexpensive and it includes also the Op. 39 *Pièce for cello and piano*. This is good value. The French team here are by no means wanting in imagination, but the effect is less poetic than the Collard/Dumay version; the HMV recording too is distinctly superior.

(i) *Concert in D for violin, piano and string quartet;* (ii) *Chanson perpetuelle;* (iii) *Poème de l'amour et de la mer.*
☞ (M) ** EMI CDM7 64368-2 [id.]. (i) Ferras; (i–ii) Barbizet, Parrenin Qt; (ii) Andrée Esposito; (iii) Victoria de los Angeles; LOP, Jacquillat.

A useful compilation for lovers of this French master, but a qualified recommendation. The major work here is the *Concert for violin, piano and string quartet*, played with fervour and intensity by Christian Ferras, Pierre Barbizet and the Parrenin Quartet. The 1970s recording, which has not been released in the UK before, is a little too forwardly balanced to be ideal. It is certainly no match for Jean-Philippe Collard, Augustin Dumay and the Muir Quartet, at present out of circulation but surely soon due for reissue. Victoria de los Angeles's 1973 account of the *Poème de l'amour et de la mer* is voluptuous and poetic, and she is well supported by the Lamoureux Orchestra under Jean-Jacques Jacquillat. Andrée Esposito is also persuasive in the familiar *Chanson perpetuelle*. Readers whose foremost priority is the *Concerto* can do better elsewhere.

Piano quartet in A, Op. 30; Piano trio in G min., Op. 3.
(B) **(*) HM HMA 901115 [id.]. Les Musiciens.

The Op. 30 *Piano quartet* of 1896 is one of Chausson's finest works. Les Musiciens comprise the Pasquier Trio and Jean-Claude Pennetier, but they are recorded rather closely, and their performance is lacking some of the subtlety and colour one knows this ensemble can command. The effect both here and in the early *G minor Trio*, Op. 3, is somewhat monochrome. However, the playing is both warm and spontaneous, and the ambience of the acoustic is pleasing.

Piano trio in G min., Op. 3.
*** Ph. Dig. 411 141-2 [id.]. Beaux Arts Trio – RAVEL: *Trio in A min.* ***

The early *G minor Trio* will come as a pleasant surprise to most collectors, for its beauties far outweigh any weaknesses. The playing of the Beaux Arts Trio is superbly eloquent and the recording is very impressive on CD.

Quelques danses, Op. 26; Paysage, Op. 38.
☞ (*) Erato/Warner Dig. 4509 92402 [id.]. Jean Hubeau – FRANCK: *Danse lente* etc. (*)

Chausson's piano music is rarely heard in the recital room – or on CD, for that matter; but it needs to be more sensitively played if it is to make its way into the repertoire. The veteran French pianist offers little in the way of keyboard finesse and subtlety here, and the rather shallow recording does not enhance the attractions of the disc as a whole.

VOCAL MUSIC

(i) *Chanson perpétuelle;* (ii) *Poème de l'amour et de la mer, Op. 19;* (iii) *5 mélodies, Op. 2/2–5 & 7*
(Le charme; Le colibri; La dernière feuille; Sérénade italienne; Les papillons).
*** Erato/Warner 2292 45368-2 [id.]. Jessye Norman, (i) Monte Carlo Qt, Dalberto; (ii) Monte Carlo PO, Jordan; (iii) Michel Dalberto.

Although Jessye Norman's account of the glorious *Poème de l'amour et de la mer* does not wholly eclipse memories of Dame Janet Baker's version, it is still very competitive in its own right. The orchestral texture is splendidly opulent and atmospheric, and Jessye Norman makes an impressive sound throughout.

Poème de l'amour et de la mer.
☞ (B) **(*) Pickwick PCD 1037; *PK 515* [id.]. Caballé, L. Symphonica, Wyn Morris – DEBUSSY: *La damoiselle elue.* **(*)

Montserrat Caballé, singing a role often taken by a mezzo-soprano, gives a warm and expressive reading – though, compared with Dame Janet Baker's version (which is currently awaiting reissue), it centres less on word-meanings and seeks instead to create an impressionistic melisma. Caballé's tone is lovely and the voice floats within the acoustic of All Saints' Church, Tooting, in the most beguilingly sensuous way, with the warm, slightly vague recording given a clearer focus on CD without loss of ambience. Anyone attracted by the reasonable price and the rare Debussy coupling will find this CD has much to offer.

Le roi Arthus (opera): complete.
(M) *** Erato/Warner Dig. 2292 45407 (3) [id.]. Zylis-Gara, Quilico, Winbergh, Massis, Fr. R. Ch. & New PO, Jordan.

This first ever recording of *Le roi Arthus* reveals it to be a powerful piece, full of overt Wagnerian echoes. Armin Jordan directs a warmly committed performance which brings out the full stature of the work. Gino Quilico in the name-part sings magnificently, and the freshness and freedom of Gösta Winbergh's tone are very apt for Lancelot's music. Teresa Zylis-Gara, though not always ideally sweet-toned, is an appealing Guinevere; the recorded sound is generally full and well balanced.

Chávez, Carlos (1899–1978)

Symphonies Nos. 1 (Sinfonia de Antigona); 4 (Sinfonia romantica).
*** ASV Dig. CDDCA 653; *ZCDCA 653* [id.]. RPO, Bátiz – REVUELTAS: *Caminos* etc. ***

The *Sinfonia de Antigona* is a primitive, highly exotic piece with plenty of colour and a large wind section; the extravagant scoring includes heckelphone, eight horns, two harps and plenty of percussion. The effect is appropriately primeval. The *Fourth Symphony* is perhaps less blatantly exotic but is full of character. Excellent playing from the RPO, offering demonstration sound of great impact, detail and presence.

Cherubini, Luigi (1760–1842)

Symphony in D; Overtures: Ali-Baba; Anacréon; Médée.
☞ (M) (***) BMG/RCA mono GD 60278 [60278-2-RG]. NBC SO, Toscanini (with CIMAROSA:
  Overtures: Il matrimonio per raggiro; Il matrimonio segreto (**)).

The Cherubini *Symphony* is rightly one of Toscanini's most famous records. It was made in the Carnegie Hall, so even the sound is good. The playing has great finesse and the performance sparkles, though some ears may find its high level of underlying intensity out of place in such repertoire. The overtures are just as characterful, *Anacréon* taken from a broadcast concert, again using Carnegie Hall. The other performances, including the brilliant – some might say hard-driven – Cimarosa items, were done in the famously dry Studio 8-H. The sheer incandescent energy of *Il matrimonio per raggiro* is remarkable and *Ali-Baba*, too, is very brisk indeed. With its 'Turkish' percussion, it sounds very piquant and the end is very like the 'chase' music in a silent movie. The transfers are first class.

String quartets Nos 1–6.
(M) *** DG 429 185-2 (3). Melos Qt.

Cherubini's melodic inspiration is often both distinguished and distinctive, although there are times when it falls short of true memorability; but a fine musical intelligence and polished craftsmanship are always in evidence. The Melos Quartet play these works with real commitment and authority, while the remastered recorded sound is well balanced and clear.

String quartet No. 1 in E flat.
*** Collins Dig. 1267-2 [id.]. Britten Qt – VERDI: *Quartet;* TURINA: *La Oración del Torero.* ***

Cherubini's early *First Quartet* (1814) apparently uses ideas borrowed from the symphonies of Méhul, but they are thoroughly absorbed, so that all four movements spring from the same basic material. This is a highly rewarding work and one cannot imagine it being better played or recorded. The sound and balance is very realistic indeed and the acoustic perfectly judged.

(i) *Coronation Mass for King Charles X; Marche religieuse.* (ii) *Requiem in C min.;* (iii) *Requiem in D min. for male voices;* (iv) *Solemn mass in G for the Coronation of Louis XVIII.*
(M) *** EMI Dig./Analogue CMS7 63161-2 (4). (i) Philh. Ch. & O; (ii) Amb. S., Philh. O; (iii) Amb. S., New Philh. O; (iv) LPO Ch., LPO; Muti.

Three of these records are digital, the *D minor Requiem* (recorded in 1975) is analogue. They come in a handsome slip-case and, at mid-price, should bring this fine repertoire to a wider audience. The *C minor Requiem*, the best known, was called by Berlioz 'the greatest of the greatest of his [Cherubini's] work', and he went on to claim that 'no other production of this great master can bear any comparison with it for abundance of ideas, fullness of form and sustained sublimity of style'. Muti directs a tough, incisive reading, underlining the drama, to remind one that this was a work also recorded by Toscanini some three decades earlier. Muti is well served both by his orchestra and by the relatively small professional choir; and the full, clear recording is most satisfying.

Requiem in C min.
☞ **(*) EMI Dig. CDC7 49678-2 [id.]. Amb. S., Philh. O, Muti.
(M) (**(*)) BMG/RCA mono GD 60272 (2) [60272-RG-2]. Marshall, Merriman, Conley, Hines, Robert Shaw Ch., NBC SO, Toscanini – BEETHOVEN: *Missa solemnis.* (**(*))

EMI have restored Muti's incisive account of the *C minor Requiem* at full price, and the disc contains only 49 minutes of music. It is a fine, dramatic performance, well recorded; but readers are referred to the four-disc set of Cherubini's *Requiems* and *Masses* (including the present disc) – see above.

Toscanini was an admirer of Cherubini's choral music, and though the start of this live performance of 1950 lacks the full Toscanini electricity, the Shaw Chorale, superbly disciplined, quickly responds to the maestro, to produce searingly incisive singing in such movements as the *Dies irae.* Characteristically dry recording.

OPERA

Lodoiska (complete).
**(*) Sony Dig. S2K 47290 (2) [id.]. Devia, Lombardo, Moser, Corbelli, Shimell, Luperi, La Scala, Milan, Ch. & O, Muti.

Muti's conviction in this live recording brings much to enjoy, suggesting that the piece is more effective on disc when the staging is left to one's imagination. The British baritone, William Shimell, is a splendid Dourlinski. As Lodoiska herself the soprano, Mariella Devia sounds sweeter and purer than when heard live, and so does Thomas Moser in the heavyweight tenor role of the Tartar chief, Titzikan. In the high tenor role of the hero, Floreski, Bernard Lombardo copes well with the high tessitura, but the voice bleats disagreeably. In the dry acoustic of La Scala the voices have been recorded close, so that there is a lack of atmosphere, and stage noises keep intruding, though the Sony engineers have done well to get such body in the sound.

Medea (complete).
*** Hung. HCD 11904/5 [id.]. Sass, Luchetti, Kováts, Takács, Kalmár, Gregor, Hungarian Radio and TV Ch., Budapest SO, Gardelli.
(M) ** EMI CMS7 63625-2 (2) [Ang. CDMB 63625]. Callas, Scotto, Pirazzini, Picchi, La Scala Ch. & O, Serafin (with BEETHOVEN: *Ah! perfido* **).

This Hungarian set, originally made in 1978 but sounding very fresh and vivid on CD, shows off the formidable strengths of the Hungarian State Opera, and in particular the artistry of Sylvia Sass, who has rarely if ever sounded as impressive on disc as here, helped by fine support from the other principals, not to mention Gardelli and the orchestra. Kolos Kováts as Creon and Klára Takács as Neris are particularly fine, and Veriano Luchetti is stronger and more individual than he has generally been on disc. Well-balanced sound, cleanly transferred.

Callas's 1957 studio recording of *Medea* is a magnificent example of the fire-eating Callas. She completely outshines any rival. A cut text is used and Italian instead of the original French, with Serafin less imaginative than he usually was; but, with a cast more than competent – including the young Renata Scotto – it is an enjoyable set. Callas's recording of the Beethoven scena, *Ah! perfido*, makes a powerful fill-up, even though in this late recording (1963/4) vocal flaws emerge the more.

Chopin, Frédéric (1810–49)

Idil Biret Complete Chopin Edition
Piano concerto No. 1, Op. 11; Andante spianato et Grande Polonaise, Op. 22; Fantasia on Polish airs, Op. 13.
☞ (BB) **(*) Naxos Dig. 8.550368; 4.550368 [id.] (with Slovak State PO, Stankovsky).

Piano concerto No. 2, Op. 21; Krakowiak, Op. 14; Variations on Mozart's 'Là ci darem la mano', Op. 2.
☞ (BB) ** Naxos Dig. 8.550369; 4.550369 [id.] (with Slovak State PO, Stankovsky).

Ballades Nos. 1–4; Berceuse, Op. 57; Cantabile; Fantaisie, Op. 49; Gallop marquis; Largo; Marche funèbre; 3 Nouvelles Etudes.
☞(BB)** Naxos Dig. 8.550508; *4.550084* [id.].

Mazurkas, Op. posth: in D; A flat; B flat; G; C; B flat; Rondos, Op. 1, Op. 16 & Op. 73; Rondo à la Mazurka, Op. 5; Souvenir de Paganini; Variations brillantes; (i) Variations for four hands; Variations on a German theme; Variations on themes from 'I Puritani' of Bellini.
☞(BB) *** Naxos Dig. 8.550367 [id.] ((i) with Martin Sauer).

Nocturnes Nos. 1–21.
☞(BB) *** Naxos Dig. 8.550356/7 [id.] (available separately).

Polonaises Nos. 1–6; 7 (Polonaise fantaisie).
☞(BB) **(*) Naxos Dig. 8.550360 [id.].

Polonaises Nos. 8–10, Op. 71; in G min.; B flat; A flat; G sharp min.; B flat min. (Adieu); G flat, all Op. posth.; Andante spianato et Grande Polonaise in E flat, Op. 22 (solo piano version).
☞(BB) **(*) Naxos Dig. 8.550361 [id.].

Piano sonatas Nos. 1, Op. 4; 2 (Funeral march); 3, Op. 58.
☞(BB) *** Naxos Dig. 8.550363; *4.550363* [id.].

Waltzes Nos. 1–19; Contredanse in G flat; 3 Ecossaises, Op. 72; Tarantelle, Op. 43.
☞(BB) ** Naxos Dig. 8.550365; *4.550365* [id.].

The Turkish pianist, Idil Biret, has recorded a Complete Chopin Edition for Naxos which has been made available as a boxed set in France but in England is steadily being issued a disc at a time. She has all the credentials for the undertaking. As a child prodigy, her studies at the Paris Conservatoire were financed by the Turkish government who had to pass a special law in order to pay for her family to accompany her and live in France. Among others, she studied with both Cortot and Wilhelm Kempff (known to her as 'Uncle Kempff') and had the teenage privilege of performing the Mozart *Double piano concerto* with the great German pianist without understanding the full implications of such an experience. She has a prodigious technique and the recordings we have heard so far suggest that overall her Chopin survey is an impressive achievement.

Her impetuous style and chimerical handling of phrasing and rubato are immediately obvious in the *First Concerto*, especially in the freely poetic account of the *Larghetto* and her very flexible rhythmic approach to the *Polacca* finale. Following Stankovsky's bold tutti, Biret makes a commanding entry in the *F minor Concerto*, then almost immediately relaxes into her limpidly flexible style. Some might feel here that she lets the momentum of the passage-work drift; in the *Larghetto*, too, the solo playing brings a gently improvisational manner, and the finale really gathers pace only at the entry of the orchestra (which is recorded rather resonantly throughout). Later there is more dash from the soloist.

Of the other short concertante pieces, the opening of the *Andante spianato* is very delicate and there is some scintillating playing in the following *Grande Polonaise* and *Fantasia on Polish airs* – and a touch of heaviness, too, in the former, but here Stankovsky and the Slovak State Philharmonic Orchestra, who are generally sympathetic in the concertos and quite strong in No. 1, take rather a back seat. The introductory *Largo* of the *Mozart variations* is a bit too dreamy and diffuse but, once the famous tune arrives, the performance springs into life, although the closing section is again a bit slow and the orchestra on the heavy side, so that this work tends to outstay its welcome. Similarly, the introduction to the charming *Krakowiak Rondo* hangs fire but again the *Rondo* sparkles, with the rhythmic rubato nicely handled, though the orchestral tuttis could ideally be firmer.

The first of the solo recordings were made in the Clara Wieck Auditorium, Heidelberg; the sound is a little studio-ish but truthful and often expands impressively in fortissimo. The *Ballades* brings impetuously romantic interpretations where the rubato at times seems mannered; in No. 2, after the gentle opening the fortissimo entry is rather aggressive. The pensive opening of *No. 4 in F minor* is seemingly spontaneous, but later there is a degree of heaviness, if also some impressive bursts of bravura. The *Berceuse* is tender and tractable, the *Fantaisie in F minor* begins rather deliberately but opens up excitingly later; though the playing is rather Schumannesque, it is also imaginative; the three *Nouvelles Etudes*, too, are attractively individual.

The disc called 'Rondos and variations' (8.550367) is worth anyone's money. Much of the music here is little known and none of it second rate. The *Rondos* are more ambitious than one would expect (Op. 16 takes 11 minutes); the six posthumously published *Mazurkas* are all engaging, and the sets of *Variations* show Biret's technique at its most prodigious and glittering, especially the twinkling upper tessitura of the *Souvenir de Paganini*. Martin Sauer, the producer, plays the second piano part in the *Four-handed Variations*.

Perhaps not surprisingly, the *Nocturnes* are a great success, the rubato simple, the playing free and often thoughtful, sometimes dark in timbre, but always spontaneous. The favourites in *E flat major*, Op. 9/1, *F sharp major*, Op. 15/2, and the melting *D flat Nocturne*, Op. 27/2, are all most sensitively played, while the *F minor*, Op. 55/1, is quite haunting. The *'Sylphides' nocturne in A flat major* opens reflectively then is off with the wind, so that the gentle nostalgia of the posthumous *C minor* which follows is all the more telling. The recording venue has now changed to the Tonstudio van Geest in Heidelberg and throughout is pleasingly full in timbre.

The seven *Polonaises* demonstrate Biret's sinewy strength: the famous *A major* is a little measured, but the *A flat* is fresh and exciting and the whole set commanding, while the *Polonaise fantaisie* shows imaginative preparation yet comes off spontaneously like the others. Nos. 8–10, published as Op. 71, are early works, written between 1825 and 1828. Biret, at her most appealing, makes all three sound mature. Then comes the first *Polonaise* of all, in G minor, written in 1817 and presented here with distinct charm. The rest are nearly all products of the 1820s and are presented here with something of a lilt, so they often sound rather like Mazurkas. The recital ends with a fine account of the solo piano version of the *Andante spianato* (quite lovely) and *Grande Polonaise*, which is more appealing than the concertante version. Throughout these two discs the piano recording is vividly present but a little hard at fortissimo level, although not too distractingly so.

The three *Sonatas* are fitted comfortably on to one CD (75 minutes) and, irrespective of cost, this represents one of the finest achievements in Idil Biret's series so far. The little-played *First Sonata* is extremely persuasive, with the *Larghetto* quite memorable, and the *Third Sonata* is a *tour de force*, with a compelling slow movement that shows a remarkable control of colour, followed by a thrillingly spontaneous finale. In Op. 58 the *Funeral march* is dark and sombre, with a dreamily poetic mood for the central section. The finale is not sharply articulated and sounds like rustling leaves. The recording is bold and clear.

The *Waltzes* brought another change of venue, to the Tonstudio in Sandhausen. The recording is bright, somewhat more resonant, and a little dry in the treble; the piano is set back a little. Idil Biret starts impetuously and immediately favours a fast tempo in the *Grande valse brillante*, Op. 18/1, which opens the recital, and even more so in the *F major*, Op. 34/4, where one notices the hardness on top. This is charismatic playing, giving opportunities for exciting bravura, but too many of these pieces are pressed on without respite, the *Waltz in A flat* for instance, or the *Waltz in E minor*. The *Ecossaises* and *Taranatelle* are also thrown off at almost breakneck speed.

(i) *Piano concertos Nos. 1–2. Andante spianato & Grande polonaise brillante; Ballades Nos. 1–4; Barcarolle* (1946 & 1962 recordings); *Berceuse* (1946 & 1962 recordings); *Boléro; Fantaisie in F min.; Impromptus Nos. 1–4; 51 Mazurkas; 19 Nocturnes; 3 Nouvelles-études; 6 Polonaises; Polonaise-Fantaisie; 24 Préludes; Scherzi Nos. 1–4; Sonata No. 2* (1946 & 1961 recordings); *Sonata No. 3; Tarantelle; 14 Waltzes.*
(M) *** BMG/RCA GD 60822 [60822-2-RG] (11). Artur Rubinstein, (i) with London New SO, Scrowaczewski; or Symphony of the Air, Wallenstein.

Rubinstein's principal Chopin œuvre is offered here on eleven CDs at mid-price. His achievement was unique in this repertoire, and for the most part the remastered recordings are almost worthy of the playing. Alternative versions are offered of several pieces, but most of the recordings listed are discussed below as individual issues, many still at full price.

(i) *Piano concertos Nos. 1 in E min., Op. 11; 2 in F min., Op. 21. Andante spianato & grande polonaise brillante, Op. 22; Barcarolle, Op. 60; Berceuse, Op. 57; Mazurkas Nos. 1–51; Nocturnes Nos. 1–19; Polonaises Nos. 1–7; Scherzi Nos. 1–4 Waltz in C sharp min., Op. 64/1.*
☞ (M) (***) EMI mono CHS7 64933-2 (5) [id.]. Rubinstein, (i) with LSO, Barbirolli.

Andante spianato & grande polonaise brillante, Op. 22; Barcarolle, Op. 60; Berceuse, Op. 57; Mazurkas Nos. 1–51; Polonaises Nos. 1–7; Scherzi Nos. 1–4; Waltz in C sharp min., Op. 64/1.
☞ (M) (***) EMI mono CHS7 64697-2 (3) [id.]. Arthur Rubinstein.

The five-CD set listed above falls into two parts, the first consisting of the two piano concertos, recorded with Barbirolli and the LSO in 1937 (*E minor*) and 1931 (*F minor*), the *C sharp minor Waltz*, recorded in 1930, and the celebrated set of the *Nocturnes* from 1936–7. The second set of three CDs comprises the *Mazurkas* (recorded in 1938), some of the most totally idiomatic Chopin playing ever committed to record, the 1932 *Scherzi* and the *Polonaises* (1934) and various other pieces. They can be bought in two separate packages or together. Quite simply, the best advice is to get both; each of the discs is packed to capacity and the transfers are excellent. Rubinstein was at the height of his powers when he made these recordings and he rarely equalled and never surpassed them in the post-war, LP era. The *Mazurkas* and *Nocturnes* have a poetic spontaneity and aristocratic finesse that are totally convincing.

Piano concertos Nos. 1 in E min., Op. 11; 2 in F min., Op. 21.
*** DG 415 970-2 [id.]. Zimerman, LAPO, Giulini.
*** Sony Dig. SK44922 [id.]. Perahia, Israel PO, Mehta.
(BB) *** Naxos Dig. 8.550123; *4550123* [id.]. István Székely, Budapest SO, Gyula Németh.
(B) *** DG 429 515-2 [id.]. Tamás Vásáry, BPO, Semkow or Kulka.
☞ **(*) Hyp. Dig. CDA 66647 [id.]. Nikolai Demidenko, Philh. O, Heinrich Schiff.
☞ (B) ** Erato/Warner 2292 45927-2 [id.]. Maria-João Pires, Monte-Carlo Opera O, Jordan.

The CD coupling of Zimerman's performances of the two Chopin *Concertos* with Giulini is hard to beat. Elegant, aristocratic, sparkling, it has youthful spontaneity and at the same time a magisterial authority, combining sensibility with effortless pianism. Both recordings are cleanly detailed.

Perahia's effortless brilliance and refinement of touch recall artists like Hoffman and Lipatti. Mehta provides a highly sensitive accompaniment once the soloist enters but is curiously offhand and matter-of-fact (indeed almost brutal) in the orchestral ritornelli. The sound is dryish and far from ideal. The three stars are for Perahia's playing, not the sound!

István Székely is particularly impressive in the *E minor Concerto*, but in both works he finds atmosphere and poetry in slow movements and an engaging dance spirit for the finales, with rhythms given plenty of character. Németh accompanies sympathetically; the orchestral contribution here is quite refined. The recording is resonantly full in the Hungarian manner, not absolutely clear on detail; but the piano image is bold and realistic. A splendid bargain in every sense of the word.

Vásáry's approach is much more self-effacing: his gentle poetry is in clear contrast with the opulent orchestral sound (especially in No. 1, where the recording is more resonantly expansive than in No. 2). Yet soloist and orchestra match their styles perfectly in both slow movements, which are played most beautifully, and the finales have no lack of character and sparkle. In their way, these performances will give considerable pleasure and, with recording that retains its depth and bloom, this makes a fine bargain coupling.

Nikolai Demidenko's recording of the two concertos can be strongly recommended to his admirers, but those who are not always persuaded by him should approach it with some caution. He produces consistent beauty of sound but his rubati can be disruptive: his slowing down for the second group of the *E minor Concerto* will not be to all tastes – certainly not ours! As in his earlier CDs, finesse and elegance are much in evidence but, if his pianistic control is not in question, it is considerably offset by moments of disturbing self-consciousness. Probably the best things are in the middle movements, though even these are not always allowed to speak for themselves. Heinrich Schiff gets an excellent response from the Philharmonia Orchestra throughout and the recording, though not top-drawer, is perfectly acceptable. For the dedicated admirer of the pianist rather than of the composer.

There is no lack of poetry from Maria-João Pires and slow movements are played with tenderness. Finales, too, have plenty of rhythmic lift, and Jordan provides accompaniments which do not flag. Good 1978 sound, well transferred. But this coupling is not distinctive.

Piano concerto No. 1.
☞ **(*) Chesky CD 93 [id.]. Earl Wild, RPO, Sargent – FAURE: *Ballade;* LISZT: *Concerto No. 1.* ***

(i) *Piano concerto No. 1. Ballade No. 1, Op. 23; Nocturnes Nos. 4 & 5, Op. 15/1–2; 7 Op. 27/1; Polonaise No. 6, Op. 53.*
(M) *** EMI CDM7 64354-2 [id.]. Pollini, (i) Philh. O, Kletzki.

Pollini's classic recording still remains the best available of the *E minor Concerto*. This is playing of such total spontaneity, poetic feeling and refined judgement that criticism is silenced. The digital remastering has been generally successful. The additional items come from Pollini's first EMI solo recital, and the playing is equally distinguished, the recording truthful.

Earl Wild offers a flamboyantly romantic account of Chopin's *E minor Concerto*, well supported by Sargent and the RPO. This was one of the RCA recordings produced for *Reader's Digest* in the mid-1960s and engineered by Decca. The vintage recording hardly sounds dated at all. A pity this has to be at full-price.

Piano concerto No. 2 in F min., Op. 21.
(M) *** Decca 417 750-2 [id.]. Ashkenazy, LSO, Zinman – TCHAIKOVSKY: *Piano concerto No. 1.* ***

Ashkenazy's 1965 recording is a distinguished performance: his sophisticated use of light and shade in the opening movement, and the subtlety of phrasing and rubato, are a constant source of pleasure. David Zinman and the LSO are obviously in full rapport with their soloist, and the vintage recording has been remastered most satisfactorily.

(i) *Piano concerto No. 2 in F min., Op. 21. Ballades Nos. 1–4; Barcarolle, Op. 60; Berceuse, Op. 57* (2 versions); *Chants polonais, Op. 74* (trans. Liszt); *Etudes, Op. 10, Nos. 1–12* (2 versions); *Op. 25, Nos. 1–12* (2 versions); *Nouvelles Etudes; Impromptus, Opp. 29, 36; Nocturnes Opp. 9/2; 15/1–2; 27/1; 55/1 & 2; 24 Preludes, Op. 28; Prelude in C sharp min., Op. 45; Piano sonatas Nos. 2 in B flat min. (Funeral march), Op. 35; 3 in B min., Op. 58; Waltzes Nos. 1–14.*
☞ (M) (***) EMI CZS7 67359-2 (6). Alfred Cortot, (i) with O, Barbirolli.

This Cortot compilation encompasses most (but not all) of the recordings he made between 1920 and 1949, arranged in roughly chronological order. His 1933 set of the *Preludes* is omitted (perhaps logically, as they appeared separately, together with the *Fantaisie-impromptu*, also omitted, some time ago). The quality of the performances is such that they would need several pages to do them justice; Cortot's spontaneity, poetic feeling and keyboard refinement are heard to prodigal effect on these six CDs. Several alternative versions (for example, both sets of the Opp. 10 and 25 *Etudes* from 1934 and 1942 are included) offer food for thought. But in any event this is playing of a quite special quality: aristocratic yet full of fire and spontaneity. The transfers are strikingly good and bring Cortot very much before one's eyes.

Les Sylphides (ballet; orch. Douglas).
☞ ⊛ (B) *** DG Double 437 404-2 (2) [id.]. BPO, Karajan – DELIBES: *Coppélia suite* ***; GOUNOD: *Faust* etc. **(*); OFFENBACH: *Gaîté parisienne;* RAVEL: *Boléro* ***; TCHAIKOVSKY: *Sleeping Beauty* (suite). **(*)
(M) *** Sony SBK 46550 [id.]. Phd. O, Ormandy – DELIBES: *Coppélia; Sylvia:* suites ***; TCHAIKOVSKY: *Nutcracker suite.* **(*)
☞ (B) **(*) Ph. Duo 438 763-2 (2) [id.]. Rotterdam PO, David Zinman – DELIBES: *Coppélia;* GOUNOD: *Faust: ballet music.* **(*)
(M) **(*) Decca Dig. 430 723-2; *430 723-4* [id.]. National PO, Bonynge – ROSSINI/RESPIGHI: *Boutique fantasque.* **(*)

Karajan conjures consistently beautiful playing with the Berlin Philharmonic Orchestra, and he evokes a delicacy of texture which consistently delights the ear. The woodwind solos are played gently and lovingly, and one can feel the conductor's touch on the phrasing. The upper register of the strings is bright, fresh and clearly focused, the recording is full and atmospheric. Within a two-disc Double DG set it is now coupled not only with the *Coppélia suite* (no longer truncated) but also with ballet music by Offenbach, Gounod and Tchaikovsky. However, the inclusion of Ravel's *Boléro*, very well played though it is, was a curious choice.

The Philadelphia strings are perfectly cast in this score and, although the CBS sound is less svelte than the DG quality for Karajan, it is still very good. Ormandy begins gently and persuasively. Later the lively sections are played with irrepressible brilliance.

David Zinman's approach is less suavely characterful than Karajan's, but he secures smoothly beautiful playing from his Rotterdam orchestra and there is no lack of vitality. Most enjoyable, when the 1980 recording is so natural and resonantly full (obviously more modern than the DG).

Bonynge's performance shows a strong feeling for the dance rhythms of the ballet, and the orchestral playing is polished and lively. Bonynge also has the advantage of excellent 1982 digital recording, made in the Kingsway Hall.

CHAMBER MUSIC

Cello sonata in G min., Op. 65.
*** Claves CD 50-703 [CD 703]. Claude Starck, Ricardo Requejo – GRIEG: *Cello sonata.* ***
(M) **(*) EMI CMS7 63184-2. Du Pré, Barenboim – FRANCK: *Cello sonata.* **(*)
(B) **(*) Hung. White Label HRC 171 [id.]. Miklós Perényi, Tibor Wehner – FAURE: *Cello sonatas.* ***

(i) *Cello sonata in G min., Op. 65; Introduction and polonaise brillante in C, Op. 3;* (ii) *Ballades Nos. 3 in A flat, Op. 47; 4 in F min., Op. 52.*
(M) *** DG 431 583-2; *431 583-4.* (i) Rostropovich, Argerich; (ii) Sviatoslav Richter.
☞ *(*) EMI Dig. CDC7 54819-2 [id.]. Gary Hoffman, Jean-Philippe Collard – RACHMANINOV: *Cello sonata.* **

With such characterful artists as Rostropovich and Argerich challenging each other, this is a memorably warm and convincing account of the *Cello sonata.* The contrasts of character between expressive cello and brilliant piano are also richly caught in the *Introduction and polonaise,* and the recording is warm to match. Richter's 1961/62 accounts of the two *Ballades* have a commanding individuality, and the recording is remarkably good throughout this disc.

The Claves performance is fluent and well characterized and the recording is eminently truthful. The playing has authority and dedication, and collectors need not hesitate to choose this version if the Grieg coupling is suitable.

The easy romanticism of the *Cello sonata* is beautifully caught by Jacqueline du Pré and Daniel Barenboim. Though the cellist phrases with all her usual spontaneous-sounding imagination, this is one of her more reticent records, while still bringing an autumnal quality to the writing which is very appealing. The recording is excellently balanced.

Though the Hungaroton performance has not the stature of the Rostropovich–Argerich account, it offers playing of quality. Miklós Perényi is not as well served by the engineers as he is in the coupled Fauré sonatas, where his tonal eloquence comes into its own, but he plays with real musical feeling and taste, and his pianist, Tibor Wehner, is excellent.

Gary Hoffman lacks the lyrical fervour for which this music (and the Rachmaninov coupling) cries out. He is an artist of great taste and refined musicianship, but his reticence, underlined by the recording balance which much favours the piano, makes for unsatisfactory listening. A keen admiration for both artists (and in particular for Jean-Philippe Collard) notwithstanding, it is difficult to recommend this.

Piano trio in G min., Op. 8.
*** Teldec/Warner Dig. 2292 43715-2 [id.]. Trio Fontenay – SMETANA: *Piano trio.* **

The Trio Fontenay give a vividly characterized and well-projected account of the Op. 8 *Trio,* written when Chopin was eighteen, and not exactly one of his greatest works. It is well worth hearing, all the same. Good clear recording.

SOLO PIANO MUSIC

Albumblatt in E; Allegro de concert, Op. 46; Barcarolle, Op. 60; Berceuse, Op. 57; Boléro, Op. 19; 2 Bourrées; Cantabile in B flat; Contredanse in G flat; 3 Ecossaises, Op. 72/3; Fugue in A min.; Galop marquis; Largo in E flat; Marche funèbre, Op. 72/2; 3 Nouvelles Etudes; Rondos, Opp. 1, 5, 16 & 73; Sonata No. 1 in C min., Op. 4; Tarantelle, Op. 43; Variations brillantes, Op. 12; Variation No. 6 from Hexameron; Variations on a German National air; Variations (Souvenir de Paganini); (i) *Variations for piano duet.* (i) *Wiosna* from *Op. 74/2.*
*** Decca 421 035-2 (2) [id.]. Vladimir Ashkenazy; (i) with Vovka Ashkenazy.

Many of the shorter pieces presented here are very early. Here as elsewhere Ashkenazy's playing is often magical, fresh and direct, full of touches of insight. But there are substantial works too, including the *Barcarolle* and *Berceuse,* both superbly done, as is the *Allegro de concert.* In the *D major Variations* Ashkenazy is joined by his son. The *C major Sonata* is not deeply characteristic, but Ashkenazy makes out a more persuasive account for it than anyone who has recorded it so far.

Andante spianato et Grande polonaise brillante, Op. 22; Barcarolle in F sharp min., Op. 60; Berceuse in D flat, Op. 57; Boléro in C, Op. 19; Impromptus Nos. 1–4; Fantaisie-impromptu, Op. 66; 3 Nouvelles études, Op. posth.; Tarantelle in A flat, Op. 43.
*** BMG/RCA RD 89911 [RCA 5617-2-RC]. Artur Rubinstein.

In Chopin piano music generally, Rubinstein has no superior. The *Andante spianato and Grande polonaise* obviously inspires him, and his clear and relaxed accounts of the *Impromptus* make most other interpretations sound forced by comparison. The magnificent *Barcarolle* and *Berceuse* contain some of Chopin's finest inspirations – and if the *Tarantelle* may appear musically less interesting and not very characteristic, in Rubinstein's hands it is a glorious piece, full of bravura.

Allegro de concert, Op. 45; Ballades Nos. 1–4; Introduction & variations on Je vends des scapulaires, Op. 12.
*** CRD CRD 3360; *CRDC 4060*. Hamish Milne.

Hamish Milne gives thoughtful and individual performances of the *Ballades*. They may initially sound understated, but in their freshness and concentration they prove poetic and compelling. Similarly he plays the two rarities with total conviction, suggesting that the *Allegro de concert* at least (originally a sketch for a third piano concerto) is most unjustly neglected. The recorded sound is first rate.

Ballades Nos. 1–4; Impromptus Nos. 1–4 (Fantaisie-impromptu); Polonaises Nos. 6–7 (Polonaise-Fantaisie); 24 Preludes, Op. 28; Preludes Nos. 25–26; Sonatas Nos. 2 (Funeral march); 3.
☞ (M) ** Erato/Warner Dig. 4509 92403-2 (3) [id.]. François-René Duchable.

This collection is a mixed success. Duchable's *G minor Ballade* is barn-storming and brilliant without being sensitive to the finer, more aristocratic side of Chopin's sensibility. Admittedly the recording is close and the instrument, a Bösendorfer, sounds thunderous. Even so, the beginning of the *A flat Ballade* leaves no doubt that tenderness is not this artist's priority in these works; indeed, those melting bars marked *sotto voce* and at one point *pianissimo* are treated in a very cavalier fashion. The *Impromptus* are more successful, but the *Preludes*, though technically proficient, are curiously square at times, the rubato seemingly calculated. The two *Polonaises* are bold enough, and the set is redeemed by the performances of the *Sonatas*, strongly impulsive and full of drama. In No. 2, the *Funeral march* is immediately compelling in its intensity, with the middle section elegiacally simple (much straighter than with Rubinstein, who still offers the yardstick by which performances of these works come to be judged). Some might find Duchable's reading of No. 3 too intensely volatile, although it is certainly eloquent – Rubinstein's performance has an aristocratic poise which is not part of Duchable's vocabulary – but his playing is commandingly spontaneous.

Ballades Nos. 1–4; Polonaises: in A flat & F sharp min. (NI 5209); *Barcarolle, Op. 60; Piano sonatas Nos. 2 (Funeral march); 3 in B min.* (NI 5038); *Berceuse, Op. 57; Fantasy in F min., Op. 49; 24 Preludes, Op. 28; Prelude in C sharp min., Op. 45* (NI 5064); *Etudes, Op. 10/1–12; Op. 25/1–12; 3 Nouvelles Etudes* (NI 5095); *Mazurkas, Op. 17/4; Op. 24/2; Op. 30/4; Op. 33/4; Op. 41/1 & 4; Op. 50/3; Op. 43; Op. 56/2–3; Op. 59/1–3; Op. 63/1–3; Op. 68/4; Scherzo No. 3, Op. 39; Tarantelle in A flat, Op. 43* (NI 5393); *Nocturnes: in B, Op. 9/3; in F, F sharp; G min. Op. 15/1–3; in C sharp min.; in D flat, Op. 27/1–2; in C min.; in F sharp min., Op. 48/1–2; in E flat, Op. 55/2; in E, Op. 62/1* (NI 5012).
☞ *(*) (M) Nimbus Dig. NI 1787 (6). Vlado Perlemuter.

Born in 1904, Vlado Perlemuter was a pupil of Moszkowski before studying with Cortot at the Paris Conservatoire, where he later became a professor. In his day he was a pianist and teacher of great distinction and particularly admired for his Chopin and Ravel. He recorded most of this repertoire for the BBC in the 1960s, but these performances, recorded when he was advanced in years, do not really do his art full justice. Of course there are many insights and evidences of fine sensibility, but in terms of neither keyboard mastery nor recorded sound do these successfully compete with other Chopin anthologies currently on offer.

Ballades Nos. 1–4; Barcarolle, Op. 60; Fantaisie in F min., Op. 49.
*** DG Dig. 423 090-2 [id.]. Krystian Zimerman.

Ballades Nos. 1–4; Scherzi Nos. 1–4.
*** BMG/RCA RD 89651 [RCD1 7156]. Artur Rubinstein.
*** Decca 417 474-2 [id.]. Vladimir Ashkenazy.

Krystian Zimerman's impressive set of the *Ballades* and the other two works on this disc are touched by distinction throughout and have spontaneity as well as tremendous concentration to commend them. Indeed, readers who elect to have only one set of the *Ballades* would find this an eminently satisfying first choice, for the modern digital recording is of fine DG quality.

Rubinstein's readings are unique and the digital remastering has been highly successful. The performances of the *Ballades* are a miracle of creative imagination, with Rubinstein at his most inspired. The *Scherzi*, which gain most of all from the improved sound (they were originally very dry), are both powerful and charismatic.

Ashkenazy's playing is full of poetry and flair, as the opening *G minor Ballade* readily demonstrates, while the *Ballade in A flat* has exceptional warmth and sonority. The *Scherzi* have characteristic panache and the whole programme is imbued with imaginative insights and a recital-like spontaneity.

*Barcarolle, Op. 60; Berceuse, Op. 57; Cantabile in B flat; Contredanse in G flat; Fantaisie in F min.,
Op. 49; Feuille d'album in E; Fugue in A min.; Funeral march in C min., Op. 72/2; Largo in E flat; 3
Nouvelles-Etudes, Op. posth; Polonaise-Fantaisie, Op. 61; Souvenie de Paganini in A (Variations).*
☞ (B) *** Sony Analogue/Dig. SBK 53515 [id.]. Fou Ts'ong.

Fou Ts'ong is a pianist of intelligence and sensibility and his admirers need not hesitate here. The
programme is enterprising – how many readers, we wonder, have heard Chopin's succinct little *Fugue
in A minor*? The smaller pieces are played with a distinction and dedication that completely win one
over, and the closing *Paganini variations* are disarmingly attractive. The recording, partly analogue,
partly digital, is good but not quite top-drawer: in general the analogue items sound best. But this 66-
minute bargain recital is well worth exploring.

*Barcarolle, Op. 60; Berceuse, Op. 57; Fantaisie in F min., Op. 49; Impromptu No. 1 in A flat, Op. 29;
Impromptu No. 2 in F sharp, Op. 36; Impromptu No. 3 in G flat, Op. 51.*
*** Sony Dig. MK 39708 [id.]. Murray Perahia.

Perahia is a Chopin interpreter of the highest order. There is an impressive range of colour and an
imposing sense of order. This is highly poetic playing and an indispensable acquisition for any
Chopin collection. The CBS recording does him justice.

Barcarolle, Op. 60; Berceuse, Op. 57; Scherzi Nos. 1–4.
**(*) DG Dig. 431 623-2; *431 623-4* [id.]. Maurizio Pollini.

Berceuse, Op. 57; Fantaisie in F min., Op. 49; Scherzi Nos. 1–4.
*** Chan. Dig. CHAN 9018 [id.]. Howard Shelley.

Howard Shelley offers much the same programme as Maurizio Pollini on DG. He emerges unscathed
from any comparison; he has the advantage of a more sympathetic recording. But there is a greater
freshness and tenderness about his approach and though he is obviously totally inside this music, he
manages to convey the feeling that he is discovering it for the first time. These are performances of no
mean quality.
   There is no want of intellectual power or command of keyboard colour in Maurizio Pollini's
accounts of the Chopin *Scherzi*. This is eminently magisterial playing with powerfully etched contours
and hard surfaces that inspires more admiration than pleasure.

*Barcarolle in F sharp, Op. 60; Berceuse in D flat, Op. 57; Fantaisie in F. min., Op. 49; Nocturne No. 4
in F, Op. 15/1; Polonaise No. 4 in C min., Op. 40/2; Sonata No. 3 in B min., Op. 58.*
(B) **(*) Pickwick Dig. PCD 834; *CIMPC 834* [id.]. John Ogdon.

John Ogdon's collection presents fresh and thoughtful performances, not as electrifying as some he
recorded earlier in his career but often bold and full of individual insights. Bright, clear, realistic
recording, giving the piano a powerful presence.

Etudes, Op. 10/1–12; Op. 25/1–12; 3 Nouvelles études.
*** Chan. Dig. CHAN 8482; *ABTD 1194* [id.]. Louis Lortie.

Etudes, Op. 10, Nos. 1–12; Op. 25, Nos. 1–12.
*** Decca 414 127-2 [id.]. Vladimir Ashkenazy.
*** DG 413 794-2 [id.]. Maurizio Pollini.

Louis Lortie's set of the 24 *Etudes* can hold its own with the best. His playing has a strong poetic
feeling and an effortless virtuosity. He is beautifully recorded at The Maltings, Snape (whose acoustic
occasionally clouds the texture).
   Ashkenazy's 1975 version sounds wonderfully vivid in its CD form, and the fine transfer that
Decca provide may well make this a first choice for some collectors.
   Pollini's record also comes from 1975 and sounds splendidly fresh in its digitally remastered form.
These are vividly characterized accounts, masterly and with the sound eminently present, although
not as full in sonority as the more recent versions.

Mazurkas Nos. 1–51.
*** BMG/RCA RD 85171 (2) [RCA 5614-2-RC]. Artur Rubinstein.
*** Decca 417 584-2 (2) [id.]. Vladimir Ashkenazy.
☞ *(*) DG Dig. 435 760-2 (2) [id.]. Jean-Marc Luisada.

Mazurkas Nos. 1–57.
☞ (B) **(*) Sony Dig. SB2K 53246 (2) [id.]. Fou Ts'ong.

Rubinstein could never play in a dull way to save his life, and in his hands these fifty-one pieces are endlessly fascinating, though on occasion in such unpretentious music one would welcome a completely straight approach. As with the *Ballades* and *Scherzi*, the digital remastering has brought a much more pleasing piano timbre.

Ashkenazy's recordings were made at various times between 1975 and 1985. His are finely articulated, aristocratic accounts and the sound is amazingly fresh and consistent, considering the time-span involved. He includes the posthumously published *Mazurkas* and the recording quality is more modern and more natural than that afforded to Rubinstein, with a believable presence.

After recording the *Nocturnes*, Fou Ts'ong went on to record all the *Mazurkas*, including two early works from 1826 in G and B flat major, another two in D and B flat (the latter dedicated to Alexandrine Wolowaska in 1832), the *Mazurkas in C* (1833) and *A flat* (1834) and the two A minor works of 1840 (*Notre temps* and *à Emile Gaillard*). Fou Ts'ong's style is distinctive and rhythmically strong but not lacking poetry. Sometimes the rubato seems a shade too impulsive, but for the most part the playing is compelling. The digital recording from 1984 is bold and clear.

The gifted Tunisian-born pianist, Jean-Marc Luisada, first came to attention when he gained a place in the finals of the 1985 Chopin Competition in Warsaw. He has considerable elegance and finesse – but, alas, like so many young pianists of his generation, he has difficulty in finding real simplicity of expression. He has the eloquence that submerges eloquence: he cannot let the composer speak for himself, and Chopin's line is so often the victim of wilful rubato. There are some good things during the course of the survey, but they are too few and far between to permit anything other than the most qualified recommendation. There are plenty of alternatives available that will give much greater musical satisfaction.

Nocturnes Nos. 1–19.
*** BMG/RCA RD 89563 (2) [RCA 5613-2-RC]. Artur Rubinstein.

Nocturnes Nos. 1–21.
*** Decca 414 564-2 (2) [id.]. Vladimir Ashkenazy.
**(*) Hyp. Dig. CDA 66341/2 [id.]. Lívia Rév.
**(*) Ph. 416 440-2 (2) [id.]. Claudio Arrau.
(M) **(*) DG Dig. 423 916-2 (2) [id.]. Daniel Barenboim.
☞ (B) **(*) Sony SB2K 53249 (2) [id.]. Fou Ts'ong.

Nocturnes Nos. 1–21; Barcarolle; Fantaisie-impromptu.
☞ **(*) Unicorn Dig. DKPCD 9147/8 [id.]. Kathryn Stott.

Rubinstein in Chopin is a magician in matters of colour; his unerring sense of nuance and the seeming inevitability of his rubato demonstrate a very special musical imagination in this repertoire. The recordings were the best he received in his Chopin series for RCA.

Ashkenazy's set includes the two posthumously published *Nocturnes*: the performances were recorded over a decade from 1975 to 1985. As always, Ashkenazy is completely attuned to Chopin's unique sound-world, though occasionally some may feel that his tone is too big in fortissimo passages for these intimate pieces – as if he is playing in a large concert hall rather than in a late-night salon.

As is immediately apparent in the *Fantaisie-impromptu* which acts an introduction to her survey, Kathryn Stott's Chopin is very romantic, seldom understated and with a wide dynamic range. Op. 48/1 (on disc 2) shows how she can change from a raptly gentle manner to passionate ardour, yet with her quiet playing of the chorale theme in Op. 37/1 she touches the listener by her very calmness. Rubato is convincing managed and overall her playing has a stronger profile than that of Lívia Rév. She is most realistically recorded.

Lívia Rév is an artist of refined musicianship and impeccable taste, selfless and unconcerned with display or self-projection. Indeed there are times when she comes too close to understatement. But still these are lovely performances and the recording has great warmth.

Arrau's approach clearly reflects his boyhood training in Germany, creating tonal warmth coupled with inner tensions of the kind one expects in Beethoven. With the *Nocturnes* it can be apt to have an element of seriousness, and this is a very compelling cycle, full of poetry, the rubato showing an individual but very communicable sensibility.

Barenboim's playing is of considerable eloquence, the phrasing beautifully moulded, and he is superbly recorded. Compared with Rubinstein (at full price), they lack a mercurial dimension. The recording is first class.

Fou Ts'ong sometimes reminds one of Solomon – and there can surely be no higher tribute. He is at his very best in the gentle, poetic pieces; in the more robust *Nocturnes* his rubato is less subtle, the style not so relaxed. But this is undoubtedly distinguished and, with good transfers of well-balanced recording from the late 1970s, this is competitive at budget price.

*Nocturnes Nos. 2 in E flat, Op. 9/2; 5 in F sharp min., Op. 15; 7 in C sharp min.; 8 in D flat, Op. 27/1–
2; 9 in B; 10 in A flat, Op. 32/1–2; 12 in G, Op. 37/2; Waltzes Nos. 1 in E flat (Grande Valse
brillante), Op. 18; 3 in A min.; 4 in F, Op. 34/2–3; 5 in A flat, Op. 42; 9 in A flat; 10 in E min., Op.
69/1–2; 11 in G flat; 12 in F min.; 13 in D flat Op. 70/1–3.*

☞ (M) *** Decca Dig. 430 751-2 [id.]. Vladimir Ashkenazy.

Ashkenazy's selection of waltzes and nocturnes is aptly chosen and felicitously arranged to make a
most satisfying programme of two groups in each genre. The *Nocturnes* are mostly reflective and
poetically create a magical atmosphere in Ashkenazy's hands. The famous *E flat*, the very beautiful *D
flat* and *B major* and the *Sylphides Nocturne in A flat*, Op. 32/2, are highlights. First-class digital
sound ensures a welcome for this reissue.

*Polonaises Nos. 1–6; 7 (Polonaise fantaisie); 8–9, 10 (2 versions), Op. 71; in G min.; B flat; A flat; G
sharp min.; B flat min. (Adieu); G flat, all Op. posth.; Andante spianato et Grande Polonaise in E flat,
Op. 22; Marche funèbre in C min., Op. 72/2 (3 versions).*

☞ *** Sony Dig. S2K 53967 [id.]. Cyprien Katsaris.

Cyprien Katsaris provides a fine new survey of the Chopin *Polonaises*, excellently recorded. We know
he can sometimes rush his fences and here in the central section of the famous *Polonaise in A flat
major* he does almost let the music run away with him in his spontaneous fervour. But the
performance is undoubtedly thrilling and we can forgive him this when for the most part there is a
strong sense of structure in these readings, a wide range of colour and plenty of flexibility. The
Andante spianato is gentle and poetic and the posthumously published early works are presented with
flair, more extrovert than Idil Biret's performances; the difference of approach of these two artists
makes a fascinatuing comparison as surely both approaches are valid. Katsaris's virtuosity, one need
hardly say, is never in doubt, indeed it is often breathtaking. A stimulating set. To tidy up properly,
he includes both the autograph and an edited version by Julian Fontana of Op. 71/3 and three
different versions of the *Marche funèbre* which the composer never finalized and which exists in a
number of differing editions.

Polonaises Nos. 1–7.
*** BMG/RCA RD 89814 [RCA 5615-2]. Artur Rubinstein.
*** DG 413 795-2 [id.]. Maurizio Pollini.

Master pianist that he was, Rubinstein seems actually to be rethinking and re-creating each piece,
even the hackneyed '*Military*' and *A flat* works, at the very moment of performance in this recording,
made in Carnegie Hall. His easy majesty and natural sense of spontaneous phrasing gives this
collection a special place in the catalogue.

   Pollini offers playing of outstanding mastery as well as subtle poetry, and the DG engineers have
made a decent job of the transfer. This is magisterial playing, in some ways more commanding than
Rubinstein (and rather better recorded) though not more memorable.

*24 Préludes, Op. 28; Prélude in C sharp min., Op. 45; Prélude in A flat, Op. posth.; Allegretto &
Mazur; Allegretto in F sharp; Boléro in C, Op. 19; 2 Bourrées; Cantabile in B flat; Contredanse in G
flat; 3 Ecossaises, Op. 72/3; Ecossaises, WN 27; Feuille d'album in E; Fugue in A min.; Galop Marquis
in A flat; Largo in E flat; Wiosna in G min., Op. 74/2.*

☞ **(*) Sony Dig. SK 53355 [id.]. Cyprien Katsaris.

One of the attractions of the Sony recital disc by Cyprien Katsaris is the inclusion of a dozen or so
miniatures, some trifles of less than a minute. His account of the *Préludes* has no want of panache or
virtuosity, though he does not perhaps match the very finest versions in terms of poetic feeling or
Lívia Rév in naturalness. There are some idiosyncratic touches (he pulls back a few bars into the very
first prelude), but to be fair his rubati are not unduly obtrusive. But if the playing is brilliant and
commanding, it is rarely touching. These matters are highly personal and readers should perhaps
investigate the set for themselves, but the overall impression of the set is a shade charmless. It is, of
course, good to have the rarities: the manuscript version of the *Ecossaises*, WN 27, and the two
Allegrettos are new to the gramophone. In some but not all of the preludes the sound is wanting in
transparency; the instrument is closely observed and the balance seems to favour the middle and bass
end of the instrument at the expense of the treble.

*24 Preludes, Op. 28; Preludes Nos. 25–26; Barcarolle, Op. 60; Polonaise No. 6 in A flat, Op. 53;
Scherzo No. 2 in B flat min., Op. 31.*

(M) **(*) DG 415 836-2; 415 836-4 [id.]. Martha Argerich.

Preludes, Op. 28; Preludes Nos. 25–26; Berceuse, Op. 57; Fantasy in F min., Op. 4.
*** Hyp. Dig. CDA 66324 [id.]. Lívia Rév.

24 Preludes, Op. 28; Preludes Nos. 25–26; Impromptus Nos. 1–4; Fantaisie-impromptu, Op. 66.
*** Decca 417 476-2 [id.]. Vladimir Ashkenazy.
(M) **(*) Ph. 426 634-2; *426 634-4.* Claudio Arrau.

24 Preludes, Op. 28; Preludes Nos. 25–26; 3 Mazurkas, Op. 59; Scherzo No. 3 in C sharp min., Op. 39.
(M) *** DG 431 584-2; *431 584-4* [id.]. Martha Argerich.

Ashkenazy's 1979 set of the *Preludes* combines drama and power with finesse and much poetic delicacy when called for. The presence of the four *Impromptus* and the *Fantaisie-impromptu* makes this CD even more attractive. There is an aristocratic quality about these excellently recorded performances that is wholly Chopinesque.

Lívia Rév's playing has an unforced naturalness that is most persuasive. She is an artist to her fingertips and, though she may not have the outsize musical personality of some great pianists, she does not have the outsize ego either. She includes not only the extra *Preludes*, but two other substantial pieces as well.

The *Preludes* show Martha Argerich at her finest, spontaneous and inspirational, though her moments of impetuosity may not appeal to all tastes. But her instinct is sure, with many poetic, individual touches. The other pieces are splendidly played.

Arrau's *Preludes* date from the mid-1970s and are much admired. Arrau's Chopin is seldom mercurial, but it is never inflexible and has its own special insights. The *Fantaisie-impromptu* is a highlight here, with the richly coloured piano timbre contributing a good deal to the character of its presentation.

Piano sonatas Nos. 1 in C min., Op. 4; 2 in B flat min., Op. 35; 3 in B min., Op. 58.
☞ *** Sony Dig. SK 48483 [id.]. Cyprien Katsaris.

Cyprien Katsaris gives highly characterized and well-thought-out readings of all three *Sonatas* and he is often challenging and thought-provoking. Ultimately, however, though less outwardly virtuosic, Leif Ove Andsnes is the more musically satisfying, and his is the preferred version.

Piano sonatas Nos. 1 in C min., Op. 4; 2 in B flat min., Op. 35; 3 in B min., Op. 58; Etudes, Op. 10/6; Op. 25/3, 4, 10 & 11; Mazurkas, Op. 17/1–4.
(B) *** Virgin/EMI Dig. VCK7 59072-2 (2) [id.]. Leif Ove Andsnes.

The young Norwegian pianist has the advantage of state-of-the-art piano-sound and his recital comes in one of these slim two-CD packs for the price of one. As such it is splendid value. Andsnes proves as idiomatic an interpreter of Chopin as he has of Grieg. He also makes out a very good case for the early *C minor Sonata,* Op. 4, which is less well represented on disc and which he plays with real conviction and flair. The other pieces generally come off well and collectors can invest in this set with complete confidence.

Piano sonata No. 2 in B flat min. (Funeral march), Op. 35; Ballades Nos. 1–4.
*** DG Dig. 435 622-2 [id.]. Andrei Gavrilov.

Piano sonatas Nos. 2 in B flat min., Op. 35; 3 in B min., Op. 58.
**(*) Ph. Dig. 420 949-2 [id.]. Mitsuko Uchida.

Gavrilov's set of the *Ballades,* coupled with the *B flat minor Sonata,* finds him in much better form than he has been for some time. Here we find finesse and control as well as real poetic feeling. It is good to be able to recommend this without any serious reservation, and to note that the DG engineers produce very good and realistic sound.

Mitsuko Uchida's Chopin is not quite as successful as her extraordinary set of the Debussy *Etudes,* though she always produces a beautiful sound and there is some particularly refined tone in the slow movements of both sonatas. A very present and realistic piano image, and plenty of sensitive touches, even if she lacks the sweep and power of many rivals.

Piano sonata No. 2; Barcarolle in F sharp, Op. 60; Polonaise No. 6 in A flat (Heroic), Op. 53; Polonaise-fantaisie in A flat, Op. 61.
(M) **(*) DG 431 582-2; *431 582-4* [id.]. Martha Argerich.

Martha Argerich's *B flat minor Sonata* was recorded in 1975 and its combination of impetuosity and poetic feeling is distinctly individual. Her brilliance is admirably suited to the two *Polonaises,* and the *Barcarolle* (the earliest recording here) is also charismatic.

Piano sonatas Nos. 2 in B flat min. (Funeral march), Op. 35; 3 in B min., Op. 58.
*** DG Dig. 415 346-2 [id.]. Maurizio Pollini.
*** Sony CD 76242 [MK 37280]. Murray Perahia.

Piano sonatas Nos. 2 (Funeral march); 3 in B min., Op. 58; Fantaisie in F min., Op. 49.
*** BMG/RCA RD 89812 [RCA 5616-2-RC]. Artur Rubinstein.
*** Decca 417 475-2 [id.]. Vladimir Ashkenazy.

Rubinstein's readings of the *Sonatas* are unsurpassed, with a poetic impulse that springs directly from the music and a control of rubato to bring many moments of magic. The sound is improved, too, though both Pollini and Ashkenazy gain in this respect.

Pollini's performances are enormously commanding; his mastery of mood and structure gives these much-played *Sonatas* added stature. The slow movement of Op. 35 has tremendous drama and atmosphere, so that the contrast of the magical central section is all the more telling. Both works are played with great distinction, but the balance is just a shade close.

Murray Perahia's technique is remarkable, but it is so natural to the player that he never uses it for mere display; always there is an underlying sense of structural purpose. The dry, unrushed account of the finale of the *B flat Sonata* is typical of Perahia's freshness, and the only pity is that the recording of the piano is rather clattery and close.

Ashkenazy's *B flat minor Sonata* is the version released in 1981. Both this and its companion are impressive, though not necessarily a first choice – if such there can be – in this field. There is a shade less tenderness and vision in the slow movement of the *B minor* than there is in some rival versions, though the *B flat minor* has wonderful panache. An authoritative account of the *F minor Fantasy* provides an excellent makeweight. The recordings still sound first class.

Piano sonata No. 3 in B min., Op. 58; Barcarolle, Op. 60; Fantaisie-impromptu, Op. 66; Impromptus Nos. 1–3, Opp. 29, 36 & 51.
☞ *** Chan. Dig. CHAN 9175 [id.]. Howard Shelley.

An outstanding Chopin recital from Howard Shelley whose interpretative powers continue to grow in stature. His playing has poetic feeling and ardent but well-controlled temperament. Very good sound.

(i) *Piano sonata No. 3 in B min., Op. 58;* (ii) *Polonaises Nos. 1 in C sharp min.; 2 in E flat min., Op. 26/1–2;* (i) *3 in A (Military); 4 in C min., Op. 40/1–2.*
(M) **(*) DG 431 587-2; *431 587-4* [id.]. (i) Emil Gilels; (ii) Lazar Berman.

Gilels's account of the *B minor Sonata* is thoughtful and ruminative, seen through a powerful mind and wholly individual fingers, and there is not a bar that does not have one thinking anew about this music. The two *Polonaises* are also superb, and the 1978 recording, made in the Berlin Jesus-Christus Kirche, is very satisfactory. For the reissue, DG have added the two Op. 26 *Polonaises*, recorded in Munich by Lazar Berman a year later. These readings possess a certain magisterial command and are also well recorded.

Scherzi Nos. 1–4; Introduction and variations on a German air; Variations on 'La ci darem la mano', Op. 2.
☞ **(*) Hyp. Dig. CDA 66514 [id.]. Nikolai Demidenko.

Nikolai Demidenko plays with magisterial keyboard authority and command of colour. There are narcissistic and idiosyncratic touches to which not all listeners will respond; all the same, there is still much that will (and does) give pleasure, but this artist does not offer the 100 per cent Chopin we get, for instance, from Kissin's recital (see below).

Waltzes Nos. 1–14.
*** BMG/RCA RD 89564 [RCD1-5492]. Artur Rubinstein.

Waltzes Nos. 1–14; Barcarolle, Op. 60; Mazurka in C sharp min., Op. 50/3; Nocturne in D flat, Op. 27/2.
⊛ (M) (***) EMI CDH7 69802-2. Dinu Lipatti.

Waltzes Nos. 1–18.
☞ ** Erato/Warner Dig. 4509 92887-2 [id.]. Jean-Bernard Pommier.

Waltzes Nos. 1–19.
*** Decca 414 600-2 [id.]. Vladimir Ashkenazy.
☞ (M) ** Ph. Dig. 438 302-2 [id.]. Zoltán Kocsis.

Lipatti's classic performances were recorded by Walter Legge in the rather dry acoustic of a Swiss

Radio studio at Geneva in the last year of Lipatti's short life, and with each LP reincarnation they seem to have grown in wisdom and subtlety. The reputation of these meticulous performances is fully deserved.

Ashkenazy's recordings were made over the best part of a decade (1977–85) but, despite the time-span, the sound is expertly matched by the engineers. There is an impressive feeling for line throughout, an ability to make these *Waltzes* seem spontaneous and yet as carefully wrought as a tone-poem.

Rubinstein's performances have a chiselled perfection, suggesting the metaphor of finely cut and polished diamonds, emphasized by the crystal-clear quality of the RCA recording. The digital remastering has softened the edges of the sound-image, and there is an illusion of added warmth.

Zoltán Kocsis is full of fire and temperament, but he is just a little too concerned to dazzle us with his superb technical prowess. Many of these are breathlessly fast and rushed, though there is no want of poetry in some of them. He includes five of the posthumous waltzes omitted by Arrau and Rubinstein. Kocsis is vividly – albeit too closely – recorded, but his playing is too eccentric and rushed to displace Alexeev and Ashkenazy.

Jean-Bernard Pommier plays with thoughtful lyrical feeling and unostentatious brilliance. He is heard at his best in the gentle Op. 69/2, although Op. 70/1 does not lack a gentle glitter, and his unexaggerated rubato in Op. 70/3 is pleasingly musical. This is not playing of the strongest profile but, with very natural recording, it is certainly agreeable.

RECITAL COLLECTIONS

Andante spianato et Grande polonaise brillante, Op. 22; Ballades Nos. 1, Op. 23; 4, Op. 52; Barcarolle, Op. 60; Etudes: in G flat, Op. 10/5; in C sharp min., Op. 25/7; Polonaise-fantaisie, Op. 61; Waltz in A flat, Op. 69/1.
(M) *** BMG/RCA GD 87752 [7752-2-RG]. Vladimir Horowitz.

All these performances derive from live recitals. The performances are fabulous; to the end of his career Horowitz's technique was transcendental and his insights remarkable. There is much excitement – but even more that is unforgettably poetic, and not a bar is predictable. With the sound so realistic, his presence is very tangible.

Ballade No. 1 in G min.; Berceuse in D flat; Etudes, Op. 10/1, 5, 6, & 12 (Revolutionary); Impromptu No. 1 in A flat, Op. 29; Mazurkas: in B flat, Op. 7/1; in C, Op. 67/3; in A min., Op. 68/2; in A flat, Op. posth.; Polonaise No. 6 in A flat, Op. 53; Scherzos No. 3 in C sharp min.; 4 in E, Op. 54; Waltzes Nos. 3 in A min., Op. 34/2; 14 in E min., Op. posth.
☞ (B) **(*) DG 439 406-2 [id.]. Tamás Vásáry.

An excellent bargain recital, compiled for DG's Classikon label from Vásáry's mid-1960s recordings. The layout is attractive, opening poetically with the *G minor Ballade* and *Berceuse*, ranging through the *Waltzes*, *Etudes*, *Scherzos* (very well done) and *Mazurkas*, and ending with the *A flat Polonaise*. But why no *Nocturnes*? The sound is a fraction dry but firm and believable. The documentation – which begins on the front of the liner-leaflet – is impressive.

Ballades Nos. 1 in G min., Op. 23; 4 in F min., Op. 52; Berceuse in D flat, Op. 57; 12 Etudes, Op. 10; Scherzo No. 4 in E, Op. 54; 3 Waltzes, Op. 64.
☞ ** EMI Dig. CDC7 54416-2 [id.]. Peter Donohoe.

In his generously filled recital Peter Donohoe enjoys recording of exemplary clarity. His playing is clean, fleet-fingered and highly accomplished, but he rarely moves the listener and there are few individual insights. In short, very good playing but untouched by distinction.

Ballade No. 3 in A flat, Op. 47; Barcarolle, Op. 60; Berceuse in D flat, Op. 57; Etudes: in E; in G flat (Black keys); in C min. (Revolutionary), Op. 10/3, 5 & 12; Fantaisie-impromptu, Op. 66; Mazurkas: in B flat, Op. 7/1; in D, Op. 33/2; Nocturnes: in E flat, Op. 9/2; in D flat, Op. 27/2; in B, Op. 32/1; in F min., Op. 55/1; Polonaises: in A, Op. 40/1; in A flat, Op. 53; Prelude in D flat (Raindrop), Op. 28/15; Scherzo No. 2 in B flat min., Op. 32; Sonata No. 2 in B flat min. (Funeral march), Op. 35. Waltzes: in E flat (Grande Valse brillante), Op. 18; in A min., Op. 34/2; in D flat (Minute); in C sharp min., Op. 64/1–2; in A flat, Op. 69/1; in G flat, Op. 70/1.
☞ (B) *** Double Decca 436 389-2 (2). Vladimir Ashkenazy.

Most music-lovers would count themselves lucky to attend a recital offering the above programme, as effectively laid out as it is on these two discs and with a total playing time of 130 minutes. The first CD opens and closes with a *Polonaise*, the second begins with the *Grande Valse brillante* and ends with the *Funeral march Sonata*, particularly well recorded at a live recital in Essex University in 1972, though the applause has been edited out. The recordings otherwsie date from between 1967 and 1984 and match up surprisingly well. Rather more than a third of them are digital. The two discs are offered for the price of one within a standard-width jewel case, centrally hinged.

Ballade No. 1 in G min., Op. 23; Barcarolle, Op. 60; Fantaisie-impromptu, Op. 66; Mazurkas: in B flat, Op. 7/1; in D, Op. 33/2; Nocturnes: in E flat, Op. 9/2; in F sharp, Op. 15/2; in D flat, Op. 27/2; in G min., Op. 37/1; Polonaises: in A (Military), Op. 40/1; in A flat, Op. 53; Waltzes: in A flat, Op. 34/ 1; in D flat (Minute); in C sharp min., Op. 64/1–2.

(M) *** BMG/RCA GD 87725 [7725-2-RG]. Artur Rubinstein.

An outstanding mid-priced recital – there is no more distinguished miscellaneous Chopin collection in the catalogue – with fourteen contrasted pieces, well programmed.

'Favourites': Ballade No. 1 in G min., Op. 23; Fantaisie-impromptu, Op. 66; Mazurkas: in B flat, Op. 7/1; in D, Op. 33/2; Nocturnes: in E flat, Op. 9/2; in F sharp, Op. 15/2; in B, Op. 32/1; Polonaise in A flat, Op. 53; Scherzo in B flat min., Op. 31; Waltzes: in E flat (Grand valse brillante), Op. 18; in A min., Op. 34/2; in A flat; B min., Op. 69/1–2; in G flat, Op. 70/1.

(M) *** Decca Dig. 417 798-2; *417 798-4*. Vladimir Ashkenazy.

An exceptionally attractive recital, with many favourites, played with Ashkenazy's customary poetic flair and easy brilliance. The digital recordings were made at various times during the early 1980s but match surprisingly well: the sound has striking realism and presence.

Ballade No. 1 in G min., Op. 23; Mazurkas Nos. 19 in B min., 20 in D flat, Op. 30/2–3; 22 in G sharp min., 25 in B min., Op. 33/1 and 4; 34 in C, Op. 56/2; 43 in G min., 45 in A min., Op. 67/2 and 4; 46 in C; 47 in A min., 49 in F min., Op. 68/1–2 and 4; Prelude No. 25 in C sharp min., Op. 45; Scherzo No. 2 in B flat min., Op. 31.

**(*) DG 413 449-2 [id.]. Arturo Benedetti Michelangeli.

Although this recital somehow does not quite add up as a whole, the performances are highly distinguished. Michelangeli's individuality comes out especially in the *Ballade* and is again felt in the *Mazurkas*, which show a wide range of mood and dynamic. The *Scherzo* is extremely brilliant, yet without any suggestion of superficiality. The piano tone is real and lifelike.

Ballade No. 3 in A flat, Op. 47; Barcarolle in F sharp, Op. 60; Fantaisie in F min., Op. 49; Fantaisie-impromptu, Op. 66; Nocturnes Nos. 2 in E flat, Op. 9/2; 5 in F sharp, Op. 15/2; Prelude in D flat, Op. 28/15; Waltzes Nos. 7 in C sharp min., Op. 64/2; 9 in A flat, Op. 69/1.

(M) *** Ph. 420 655-2 [id.]. Claudio Arrau.

A fine recital, showing both poetry and the thoughtful seriousness which distinguishes Arrau's Chopin, which is West rather than East European in spirit. The CD is admirably transferred.

Ballade No. 4 in F min., Op. 52; Berceuse, Op. 57; Etudes, Opp. 10/3, 8 & 9; 25/1–3; Fantaisie in F min., Op. 49; Mazurka in A min., Op. 68/2; Nocturnes in E flat, Op. 9/2; D flat, Op. 27/2; Polonaise in A, Op. 40/1; A flat, Op. 53; Waltzes in A flat, Op. 42; E min., Op. posth.

☞ (**(*)) Testament mono SBT 1030 [id.]. Solomon.

Although he was thought of primarily as a master of the central Viennese repertoire (and particularly Beethoven) rather than a Chopin interpreter, this anthology affords ample proof of Solomon's power to distil magic in pretty well whatever composer he touched. Most of these 78 recordings were made between 1942 and 1946; the F minor *Fantaisie* is pre-war (1932), a wonderfully searching account, and the sheer delicacy and poetry of the playing shine through the often frail recorded sound. Good transfers.

'Chopin masterpieces': (i) Etudes: Op. 10, Nos. 3 in E; 5 in G flat; 12 in C min. (Revolutionary); (ii) Op. 25, No. 9 in G flat; (iii) Fantaisie-impromptu, Op. 66; Nocturnes: Nos. 2 in E flat, Op. 9/2; (ii) 10 in A flat, Op. 32/2; (iv) Polonaises: Nos. 3 in A, Op. 40/1; (v) 6 in A flat (Heroic), Op. 53; (vi) Préludes, Op. 28, Nos. 7 in A; 20 in C min.; (vii) Waltzes Nos. 1 in E flat (Grande valse brillante), Op. 18; 6 in D flat (Minute); 7 in C sharp min., Op. 64/1–2.

(B) *** CfP CD-CFP 4501; *TC-CFP 4501* (i) Anievas; (ii) Adni; (iii) Ogdon; (iv) Ohlsson; (v) Pollini; (vi) Orozco; (vii) Malcuzynski.

EMI first made this compilation available in 1974 and it is as successful today as it was then. The programme includes many favourites and the selection has been made with skill. The recital opens and closes with a polonaise (Pollini is in splendid form in the final item). But this excellent roster of pianists never disappoints and the quality is consistently good. Malcuzynski's contribution is among the highlights: his *Grande valse brillante* has a characteristic glitter, while other attractive performances include the *Sylphides Nocturne in A flat* and Daniel Adni's *'Butterfly' Study*, which takes wing with charming grace. The transfers are all well managed.

Fantaisie in F min., Op. 49; Nocturnes in C sharp min., Op. 27/1; in D flat, Op. 27/2; in A flat, Op. 32/ 2 ; Polonaise in F sharp min., Op. 44; Scherzo No. 2 in B flat min., Op. 31; Waltzes: in A flat, Op. 34/ 1; in A min., Op. 34/2; in A flat, Op. 42.
☞ ⊛ *** BMG/RCA Dig. 09026 60445-2 [id.]. Evgeny Kissin.

Evgeny Kissin's Chopin anthology comes from a Carnegie Hall recital given early in 1993 when he was still twenty-one. His playing remains remarkably unaffected and, in the *F minor Fantasy* for example, touchingly direct. His virtuosity and brilliance are always harnessed to musical ends and there is total dedication to Chopin and no indulgence in the narcissistic idiosyncrasies that at times have afflicted such young talents as Demidenko and Pogorelich. Chopin playing of real quality and well recorded, though the sound is a bit thick in the bass.

Piano sonata No. 2 in B flat min., Op. 35; Barcarolle in F sharp, Op. 60; Nocturnes Nos. 5 in F sharp, Op. 15/2; 13 in C min., Op. 48/1; 15 in E, Op. 62/2; 20 in C sharp min., Op. posth.; Scherzo No. 2 in B flat min., Op. 31.
*(**) Virgin/EMI Dig. VC7 90738-2. Mikhail Pletnev.

Pletnev is a master pianist: in his hands the finale of the *Sonata* has a wizardry comparable only with Horowitz and Rachmaninov. However, whatever it *is*, this is not a self-effacing performance, and the expressive posturing will disappoint his growing circle of admirers. Of course there are marvellous things here – the *C minor Nocturne* is one – but on the whole this is masterly pianism first and Chopin second.

Arrangements

Arrangements by Leopold Godowsky: *Etudes, Op. 10/1, 3, 5 (2 versions), 6, 7; Op. 25/1. 3 Nouvelles études No. 1, Op. posth.; Waltzes, Op. 64/1 & 3; Op. 69/1; Op. 70/2–3; Op. 18* (concert paraphrase).
☞ (M) ** Decca 425 059-2 [id.]. Jorge Bolet.

It seems remarkable today that anyone should want to try to 'improve' Chopin, yet Leopold Godowsky (1870–1938) made transcriptions of a great deal of his music, elaborating the textures in such a way as to place the new versions beyond the reach of all but the bravest virtuosi. It must be said that these performances by Jorge Bolet show the most remarkable technical command of Godowsky's complexities, but what Bolet fails to do is convince the listener that the prodigious effort is really worth while. A degree more audacity of manner might have helped, but, brilliant though the playing is, one is not persuaded to enjoy oneself despite all preconceptions. The recording is admirably realistic.

Cilea, Francesco (1866–1950)

Adriana Lecouvreur (complete).
*** Decca Dig. 425 815-2; 425 815-4 (2) [id.]. Sutherland, Bergonzi, Nucci, d'Artegna, Ciurca, Welsh Nat. Op. Ch. & O, Bonynge.
(M) **(*) Decca 430 256-2 (2) [id.]. Tebaldi, Simionato, Del Monaco, Fioravanti, St Cecilia, Rome, Ac. Ch. & O, Capuana.

Sutherland's performance in the role of a great tragic actress could not be warmer-hearted. She impresses with her richness and opulence in the biggest test, the aria *Io son l'umile ancella*, an actress's credo, and her formidable performance is warmly backed up by the other principals, and equally by Richard Bonynge's conducting, not just warmly expressive amid the wealth of rich tunes, but light and sparkling where needed, easily idiomatic.

Tebaldi's consistently rich singing misses some of the flamboyance of Adriana's personality but in her characterization both *Io son l'umile ancella* and *Poveri fiori* are lyrically very beautiful. One wishes that Del Monaco had been as reliable as Tebaldi but, alas, there are some coarse moments among the fine, plangent top notes. Simionato is a little more variable than usual but a tower of strength nevertheless. The recording is outstanding for its time (early 1960s), brilliant and atmospheric.

Cimarosa, Domenico (1749–1801)

Il maestro di cappella (complete).
(M) *** Decca 433 036-2 (2) [id.]. Fernando Corena, ROHCG O, Argeo Quadri – DONIZETTI: *Don Pasquale.* ***
*** Hung. Dig. HCD 12573 [id.]. József Gregor, Boys of Schola Hungarica, Corelli CO, Pál – TELEMANN: *Der Schulmeister.* ***

Corena's classic assumption of the role of incompetent Kapellmeister has been out of the catalogue for too long. Corena shows complete mastery of the buffo bass style, and he is so little troubled by the florid passages that he can relax in the good humour. The vintage 1960 recording is clear and atmospheric, with the directional effects naturally conveyed.

Plainly, Gregor's performance has benefited from stage experience. Though his comic style is on the broad side, his magnetism pulls the piece together very effectively, with Tamás Pál a responsive conductor. It is aptly if ungenerously coupled with the more heavily Germanic Telemann cantata. First-rate recording.

Il pittor parigino (complete).
**(*) Hung. Dig. HCD 12972/3-2 [id.]. Szucs, Kincses, Garino, Gregor, Klietmann, Salieri CO, Pál.

Tamás Pál is an efficient conductor, himself playing harpsichord recitatives, and he draws a lively performance – using modern instruments – from the Salieri Chamber Orchestra. The cast is a strong one, using a number of soloists from the Budapest Opera who are becoming increasingly well known on record. The outstanding performance comes from the veteran buffo bass, József Gregor, brilliant as the Baron.

Clarke, Rebecca (1886–1979)

Piano trio.
*** Gamut Dig. GAMCD 518 [id.]. Hartley Trio – BRIDGE: *Phantasie trio;* IRELAND: *Phantasie.* ***

This very striking *Piano trio* shows influences from Bloch and Bartók much more than from English sources. The vehemence of the first movement gives way to mystery and melancholy in the slow movement, with the finale drawing on both those contrasting moods. The Hartley Trio gives a passionate, warmly persuasive performance, and the recording is full and forward.

Viola sonata.
☞ *** Gamut Dig. GAMCD 537 [id.]. Philip Dukes, Sophia Rahman – MACONCHY: *5 Sketches;* SHOSTAKOVICH: *Sonata.* ***

Rebecca Clarke, British-born, a viola player as well as a composer (pupil of Stanford in his later years), had great success in the United States after the First World War. Her superb *Viola sonata* vied with Bloch's *Viola suite* in a major competition. In three movements, with the first aptly named *Impetuoso* and an *Adagio* finale, it is a work that instantly communicates and becomes the more rewarding the better one gets to know it. It is given a superb performance here. Philip Dukes and Sophia Rahman have complete rapport and technical command. They play with expressive depth and have an obvious imaginative grasp of Clarke's graceful writing for their instruments. The recording is first class and the couplings are recommendable too: the miniatures of Maconchy and Shostakovich's bleak but powerful *Sonata.*

Chinese puzzle; Lullaby; Midsummer moon; A Psalm of David (for violin and piano). Songs: *As I was goin' to Ballynure; The aspidestra; The cherry blosom wand; The cloths of heaven; Come, O come, my life's delight; Cradle song; The donkey; Down by the Sally gardens; A dream; Eight o'clock; God made a tree; Greeting; Infant joy; I know my love; I know where I'm going; It was a lover and his lass; June twilight; Lethe; Phillis on the new made hay; The seal man; Shy one; The tailor and his mouse; Tears; The tiger.*
☞ *** Gamut GAMCD 534 [id.]. Patricia Wright, Jonathan Rees, Kathron Sturrock.

As we know from her *Viola sonata*, Rebecca Clarke is a true melodist and none of these delightful songs is wanting in memorability of line; indeed the second item here, *A Dream* (W. B. Yeats), displays a lovely, gentle rapture, while *Come, O come, my life's delight* (words written by the composer) pays someone a blissful compliment. The folksong settings are particularly enjoyable, notably those with violin accompaniment instead of piano: *It was a lover and his lass*, with its busy obbligato complete with telling pizzicatos, and the vigorous *Tailor and his mouse* (attributed on the listing, mistakenly, to A. E. Housman, as are the three Irish folksongs which are similarly presented). John Masefield's *The seal man* is touchingly set and William Blake's *The Tiger* is vividly pictorial. There is little quirkiness, *The Donkey* (G. K. Chesterton) being something of an exception and very strongly characterized. The pieces for violin and piano make engaging interludes; a lark appears to flit across *The Midsummer moon* (hints of Vaughan Williams, but also a chromatic ecstasy that is the composer's own); the *Lullaby* too rises to an ardent climax. Patricia Wright's fresh soprano is well suited to this repertoire: she is a committed and enticing soloist, and the contributions of Jonathan Rees (violin) and Kathron Sturrock (piano) are comparably sympathetic. Excellent recording in a pleasing acoustic, but black marks for documentation or, rather, lack of it: just a list of titles and poets, not always correctly spelt.

Clemens non Papa, Jacob (c. 1510/15–c. 1555/6)

Missa Pastores quidnam vidistis; Motets: Pastores quidnam vidistis; Ego flos campi; Pater peccavi; Tribulationes civitatum.
ⓒ *** Gimell Dig. CDGIM 013; *1585T-13* [id.]. Tallis Scholars, Peter Phillips.

This admirable disc serves as an introduction to the music of Jacob Clement or Clemens non Papa (who was jokingly known as Clemens-not-the-Pope, so as to distinguish him from either Pope Clement VII or the Flemish poet, Jacobus Papa). The beauty of line and richness of texture in the masterly *Missa Pastores quidnam vidistis* are unforgettable in this superb performance by the Tallis Scholars. The programme opens with the parody motet associated with the Mass, which has a glorious eloquence. Of the other motets, *Pater peccavi*, solemnly rich-textured, is especially memorable; but the whole programme is designed to reveal to twentieth-century ears another name hitherto known only to scholars. The recording is uncannily real and superbly balanced. It was made in the ideal acoustics of the Church of St Peter and St Paul, Salle, Norfolk.

Clementi, Muzio (1752–1832)

(i) *Piano concerto in C; Symphonies: in B flat & D, Op. 18; Nos. 1–4; Minuetto pastorale; Overtures in C & D.*
🕶 (M) ** ASV Dig. CDDCS 322 (3) [id.]. (i) Pietro Spada; Philh. O, Francesco D'Avalos.

(i) *Piano concerto in C; Symphonies in B flat & D, Op. 18; Minuetto pastorale.*
🕶 (M) **(*) ASV Dig. CDDCA 802 [id.]. (i) Pietro Spada; Philh. O, Francesco D'Avalos.

Symphonies Nos. 1 in C; 2 in D; 3 (Great National) in G; 4 in D.
🕶 (M) *** Erato/Warner 4509 92191-2 (2) Philh. O, Claudio Scimone.

Symphonies Nos. 1 in C; 3 in G (Great National); Overture in C.
🕶 ** ASV Dig. CDDCA 803 [id.]. Philh. O, Francesco D'Avalos.

Symphonies Nos. 2 in D; 4 in D; Overture in D.
🕶 ** ASV Dig. CDDCA 804 [id.]. Philh. O, Francesco D'Avalos.

Clementi, publisher as well as composer, tragically failed to put most of his symphonic output into print, and it has been left to modern scholars to unearth and, in many cases, reconstruct the works which were being performed around 1800, some of them prompted by Haydn's visits to London. Six of his 20 symphonies survive, and these are here made available thanks to the researches of Pietro Spada. The four numbered works come from the first decade of the nineteenth century. They are all scored for much larger forces than the Op. 18 set and even include trombones. Their musical content explains Clementi's high reputation in his lifetime as a composer for the orchestra, not just the piano.

If the *Great National Symphony* is the most immediately striking, with *God save the King* ingeniously worked into the third movement so that its presence does not emerge until the very end, the other works are all boldly individual. The *Larghetto cantabile* of No. 2 is surely almost worthy of Haydn, with its floating melody and attractive scoring. The *Fourth* is a remarkably powerful symphonic statement, immediately creating a concentrated intensity in the opening *Andante sostenuto*, which finds some release in the following *Allegro vivace* but which soon returns in the gracious slow movement and carries through into the Minuet. The work brings some striking modulations and there is some unexpected chromatic writing (unexpected, that is, to those who are not familiar with the famous set of the piano sonatas that Horowitz recorded).

Moreover Clementi's use of the orchestra is often very imaginative, though his indebtedness to the

Haydn of the *London Symphonies* is again very striking. But this is surely a work which makes one appreciate that Clementi was very much Beethoven's contemporary. Scimone's performances with the Philharmonia are strong and sympathetic, and the recording, made in London's Henry Wood Hall in 1978, is full, resonant and natural, bringing weight as well as freshness.

The three-disc ASV set includes also the two Op. 18 symphonies on the first disc. These were published in London in 1787 and are much indebted to Haydn, even if they want his melodic distinction and imagination; the *Piano Concerto in C*, an arrangement of a piano sonata, is a later piece with a good deal of Mozart and some Beethoven, though without their inventive fertility. Pietro Spada, who has edited all the pieces on these records, himself appears as the secure and accomplished soloist. Francesco D'Avalos gets spirited playing from the Philharmonia, though he is not strong on subtleties of phrasing; Scimone with the Philharmonia finds rather more finesse, and no less energy or commitment. There are places, too, in the ASV set where ensemble could be improved upon, and the CD coupling (the *Second* and *Fourth* together with an *Overture* thrown in for good measure) produces an hour of predominantly D major!

The ASV digital sound is bright and a bit forward, but the texture is insufficiently transparent and clean to warrant a three-star grading. The sound is certainly not preferable to the analogue quality of the Erato discs. There is some arresting music in the course of the four mature symphonies to make them worth investigating, and the reissued Erato set takes precedence for this purpose, although the first ASV disc – though it makes the least urgent claims on the collector – could be chosen as a supplement.

Symphonies: No. 1 in C, WoO 32 (reconstructed Casella); in B flat and D, Op. 18/1–2 (1787).
☞ *** Chan. Dig. CHAN 9234 [id.]. LMP, Matthias Bamert.

Bamert's performances are on a chamber scale and are refreshingly alive and polished. They are given top-class Chandos sound. If you want just one CD of Clementi symphonies, this is the one to have, and indeed the music here is rather engaging.

Piano sonatas in G min., Op. 7/3; in F min., Op. 13/6; in B flat, Op. 24/2; in F sharp min.; in D; Op. 25/5–6.
☞ **(*) D & J Athene Dig. ATH CD 4 [id.]. Peter Katin.

Peter Katin plays a square piano, built by Clementi and Company in 1832 (the year of the composer's death), which has subsequently been restored. So the sounds he creates are as authentic as one could find. The work which comes off best in his recital is the *G minor Sonata*, Op. 7/3, with its spirited opening movement, central *Cantabile e lento* and lively finale with its gruff bass figurè which sounds so effective on the fortepiano. So does the finale of the *D major*, Op. 25/5, very nicely articulated, and the *F minor Sonata*, Op. 13/6, also seems exactly suited to the instrument. The slow movement of the *F sharp minor*, Op. 25/5, sounds utterly different here from Maria Tipo's version, the playing altogether more direct, seeking no romantic overtones; generally, Peter Katin's approach is plainspun to suit the somewhat dry sonority of his instrument. He is very realistically recorded.

Piano sonatas: in G min., Op. 8/1; in F, Op. 13/6; in F sharp min., Op. 25/5; in D, Op. 40/3; Introduction, Andante grazioso, Allegretto and coda on 'Batti batti' from Mozart's Don Giovanni.
☞ **(*) EMI Dig. CDC7 54766-2 [id.]. Maria Tipo (piano).

Maria Tipo plays sensitively and musically and produces an attractive range of colour; moreover she is very realistically recorded – this is EMI's best piano-quality. She finds Clementi as essentially a romantic composer (the *Lento e patetico* of Op. 25/5, which is beautifully played, is made to sound like Schubert). Elsewhere her personal touches of rubato bring a style more appropriate for Chopin. Even so, she brings all this music to life, and she is particularly impressive in the splendid *D major Sonata*, Op. 40/3: in her hands the first movement is particularly engaging.

Piano sonatas: in F min., Op. 13/6; in B flat, Op. 24/2; in F sharp min., Op. 25/5; in G, Op. 37/1.
*** Accent ACC 67911D [id.]. Jos van Immerseel.

Very fleet and brilliant performances from Jos van Immerseel. The slow movements of these sonatas have some considerable expressive depth, and the outer ones are full of a brilliance that is well served by this eminently skilful and excellent artist.

Piano sonatas: in F min., Op. 14/3; in F sharp min., Op. 26/2; in C (quasi concerto), Op. 33/3; in G min., Op. 34/2; Rondo (from Sonata, Op. 47/2).
(M) *** BMG/RCA GD 87753 [7753-2-RC]. Vladimir Horowitz (piano).

These electrifying performances from the 1950s show a Clementi of greater substance and sterner mettle than the composer we thought we knew and, though the piano sound is shallow by the side of most up-to-date recordings, the quality is a great improvement upon either of the vinyl transfers with which we have compared it.

Piano sonatas: in E flat, Op. 24/3; in D, Op. 26/3; in C; in G, Op. 39/1-2.
(B) **(*) Hung. White Label HRC 092 [id.]. Donatella Failoni.

Donatella Failoni is a thoughtful and intelligent player, with a clean, direct style. She makes a good case for these underrated works and she is given a bold, faithful recording. This is well worth exploring at its reasonable price.

Clérambault, Louis-Nicolas (1676–1749)

(i) *Harpsichord suites Nos. 1 in C; 2 in C min.;* (ii) *Cantatas: Orphée; Médée.*
☞ (M)*** DG Dig./Analogue 437 085-2. (i) Kenneth Gilbert; (ii) Yakar, Goebel, Hazelzet, Medlam, Curtis.

The two *Harpsichord suites* recorded here represent only a fraction of Clérambault's output for the harpsichord, but all that survives. Both suites were published during his lifetime in 1702 or 1704. They have splendidly improvisatory preludes rather in the style of Louis Couperin, and are notated without barlines. Although not as distinctive or original as Clérambault's organ music, the suites have a genuine vein of lyricism, not inappropriate in a composer of so much vocal music, and they are played most persuasively and authoritatively by Kenneth Gilbert on a copy by David Rubio of a (1680) Vaudry harpsichord, held in the Victoria & Albert Museum. The recording is not balanced too closely and gives a very vivid and truthful impression.

   The two cantatas come from the first of five books of cantatas and appeared in 1910. In his day, *Orphée* was widely thought of as Clérambault's masterpiece; in the hands of these artists its attractions reside in its melodic freshness and variety of invention. Both *Orphée* and the more dramatic *Médée* make considerable demands on the soprano soloist, and Rachel Yakar rises to them with distinction. The instrumentalists use period instruments or copies and they give her excellent support. Neither cantata outstays its welcome (*Orphée* lasts less than 20 minutes) and both are very well recorded. Together with the *Harpsichord suites*, this makes an attractive and spirited introduction to a fine composer and, in the case of the vocal music, to a repertoire which, though short-lived (the cantata was virtually extinct by the middle of the eighteenth century in France), is especially well worth investigating.

Coates, Eric (1886–1958)

Ballad; By the sleepy lagoon; London suite; The Three Bears (phantasy); *The Three Elizabeths* (suite).
(M) *** ASV Dig. CDWHL 2053. East of England O, Malcolm Nabarro.

Nabarro has the full measure of Coates's leaping allegros and he plays the famous marches with crisp buoyancy. *The Three Bears* sparkles humorously, as it should; only in *By the sleepy lagoon* does one really miss a richer, more languorous string-texture. Excellent, bright recording, and the price is right.

(i) *By the sleepy lagoon;* (ii) *Calling all workers* (march); (iii) *Cinderella* (phantasy); *From meadow to Mayfair: suite; London suite; London again suite;* (i) *The Merrymakers overture;* (iii) *Music everywhere* (march); (iv) *Saxo-rhapsody;* (i) *The Three Bears* (phantasy); (ii) *The Three Elizabeths* (suite); (i) *The three men* (suite): *Man from the sea.* (iii) *Wood nymphs* (valsette).
(B) *** CfP CD-CFPD 4456 (2) [id.]. (i) LSO, Mackerras; (ii) CBSO, Kilbey; (iii) R LPO, Groves; (iv) with Jack Brymer.

This collection of the music of Eric Coates includes, besides some very lively performances from Sir Charles Mackerras, several outstanding ones from the CBSO under Reginald Kilbey, who proves the ideal Coates conductor. Although the CDs bring out the brittleness in the upper range, notably in the Groves recordings, the ambient effect helps to prevent too great an imbalance towards the treble.

Calling all workers: march; Cinderella; The Dam Busters: march; The Merrymakers: overture; London suite; London again suite; The Selfish giant.
☞ ** Marco Polo Dig. Slovak RSO, Leaper.

There is an element of disappointment here. Adrian Leaper directs this repertoire with plenty of zest and is especially good in *Cinderella* and *Calling all workers*. But he overdoes the ritenuto for the famous central melody in *The Dam Busters*, and elsewhere the Slovak Radio Orchestra produce too thin a string sonority to balance the ebullient brass; almost certainly there are too few string players. The recording is lively but a bit overbright and studio-ish. Frankly this CD is overpriced.

The 4 Centuries: suite; The Jester at the wedding: ballet suite; The 7 Dwarfs.
☞ (M) **(*) ASV Dig. CDWHL 2075 [id.]. East of England O, Malcolm Nabarro.

For their second anthology of music by Eric Coates, the orchestra based in Nottinghamshire (where the composer was born) offer a particularly delectable account of *The Jester at the wedding ballet suite*; agreeably tuneful and vivacious and scored with delicacy, its light textures are most pleasingly realized. *The Four Centuries* is a masterly and engaging pastiche of styles from four different periods, and again it receives a performance of some subtlety, although at times one wishes for a more opulent sound from the violins, and the closing jazzy evocation of the 1930s and 1940s could be more uninhibitedly rumbustious. *The Seven Dwarfs* is an early work (1930), a ballet written for a short-lived London revue. Coates later re-scored it for full orchestra and renamed it *The Enchanted Garden*. Here we have the original, lightly scored and pleasing, with the romantic sequence containing the most memorable music. It is nicely coaxed back into life and the recording is very good.

The Three Elizabeths (suite).
☞ (M) **(*) Mercury 434 330-2 [id.]. London Pops O, Fennell – GRAINGER: *Country gardens* etc. **

Fennell's performance is notable for its spirit and polish: the closing march, *The Youth of Britain*, sounds particularly fresh and alert, while the slow movement is nicely expressive. But the 1965 Mercury recording, made in Watford Town Hall, though fuller and with a more attractive ambience than the coupled Grainger items, still lacks something in expansiveness, though not clarity of detail.

VOCAL MUSIC

Songs: *Always as I close my eyes; At sunset; Bird songs at eventide; Brown eyes I love; Dinder courtship; Doubt; Dreams of London; Green hills o'Somerset; Homeward to you; I heard you singing; I'm lonely; I pitch my lonely caravan; Little lady of the moon; Reuben Ranzo; Song of summer; A song remembered; Stonecracker John; Through all the ages; Today is ours.*
☞ (M) *** ASV Dig. CDWHL 2081. Brian Rayner Cook, Raphael Terroni.

Eric Coates, as well as writing skilful orchestral music, also produced fine Edwardian ballads which in many instances transcended the limitations of the genre, with melodies of genuine refinement and imagination. Most date from earlier in his career, prior to the Second World War. Brian Rayner Cook, with his rich baritone beautifully controlled, is a superb advocate and makes a persuasive case for every one of the 19 songs included in this recital. His immaculate diction is infectiously demonstrated in the opening *Reuben Ranzo* (a would-be sailor/tailor), in which he breezily recalls the spirited projection of another famous singer of this kind of repertoire in the early days of the gramophone, Peter Dawson. The recording is admirably clear.

Colding-Jørgenson, Henrik (born 1944)

To love music.
☞ ** BIS CD 79 [id.]. Danish Nat. RO, Schmidt – BENTZON: *Feature on René Descartes* **;
   NORBY: *The Rainbow snake.* ***

Henrik Colding-Jørgenson studied with Vagn Holmboe among others and began his career as an organist and teacher; he has written a good deal of music for educational purposes. *At elske musikken* ('To love music') falls into two parts: 'To love music with the head' and, secondly, '. . . with the heart'. Its musical language is eclectic and far from inaccessible; indeed, during the course of its 26 minutes there are many moments of beauty. But while it is undeniably imaginative, it is difficult to discern any strong sense of musical purpose and organic growth. One feels that the music could stop or start anywhere and, given the thinness of some of the musical substance, it outstays its welcome. Dedicated playing from the Danish orchestra under Ole Schmidt, and a good analogue recording.

Coleridge-Taylor, Samuel (1875–1912)

(i) *Clarinet quintet in A;* (ii; iii) *Ballade in D min.* (for violin and piano); (iii) *Petite suite de concert;* arr. of spirituals: *Take Nabandji; Going up; Deep river; Run, Mary, run; Sometimes I feel like a motherless child; The Bamboula.*
** Koch Dig. 3-7056-2 [id.]. (i) Harold Wright, Hawthorne Qt; (ii) Michael Ludwig, (iii) Virginia Eskin.

Coleridge-Taylor's *Clarinet quintet* is in no way distinctive; its 12-minute first movement seems a little overlong for its material, but it has a pleasingly wistful *Larghetto affectuoso*. It is very well played here by Harold Wright, the principal clarinet of the Boston Symphony, with a quartet made up of other front-desk players from the orchestra and given a faithful if studio-ish recording. The *Ballade in D minor* is even less memorable, but is adequately presented. The CD opens with a charmless account of the *Petite suite de concert* in (presumably) a piano arrangement, which is made even less enticing by the clattery piano recording. The arrangements of the *Spirituals* are effective enough but overall this 80-minute collection is a disappointment.

Scenes from The Song of Hiawatha (complete).
*** Argo Dig. 430 356-2 (2) [id.]. Helen Field, Arthur Davies, Bryn Terfel, Welsh Nat. Op. Ch. & O, Kenneth Alwyn.

Coleridge-Taylor's choral trilogy based on Longfellow's epic poem had its first performance under the composer in the Royal Albert Hall in 1900. Part One, *Hiawatha's wedding feast*, is still regularly performed by choral societies in the north of England, and one wondered about the neglect of Parts Two and Three, *The Death of Minnehaha* and *Hiawatha's departure*. Alas, the reason is made clear: there is a distinct falling-off in the composer's inspiration, so fresh and spontaneously tuneful in Part One. Part Two has plenty of drama, and towards the end Helen Field has a memorably beautiful solo passage, which she sings radiantly, echoed by the chorus, *Wahonomin! Wahonomin! Would that I had perished for you*. Kenneth Alwyn is completely at home in this music. He directs a freshly spontaneous account and has the advantage of excellent soloists, though the Welsh Opera Choir seem less naturally at home in the idiom than Sargent's own Royal Choral Society.

Constantinescu, Paul (1909–63)

The Nativity (Byzantine Christmas oratorio).
☞ **(*) Olympia OCD 402 (2) [id.]. Emelia Petrescu, Martha Kessler, Valentin Teodorian, Helge Bömches, Bucharest Georges Enescu Ch. & PO, Mircea Basarab.

Paul Constantinescu is hardly a household name outside his native Romania, where he is the principal figure to have emerged in the generation after Enescu. Unlike his compatriot, however, he did not establish a reputation outside his country as a performer and remained for many years as head of music in Romanian Radio. His interests would seem to have largely centred on Byzantine and folk music, and his musical language draws on both. *The Nativity*, which he subtitles *Byzantine Christmas oratorio*, dates from 1947 and is an extended work of some quality in three parts: *Annunciation*, *Nativity* and *The Three Magi*. This impressive performance comes from the late 1970s and first appeared on four LPs. Apart from the exoticism of the Byzantine material and liturgical references, there are reminders of expressionism (Constantinescu studied in Vienna) and of such contemporary models as Honegger and Bartók. Constantinescu writes effectively both for the chorus and for solo voices, and his orchestration too is expert. The soloists are excellent (and in different circumstances may well have made names for themselves outside their native country) and the analogue recording is very good indeed. Readers with an interest in the exotic and a touch of enterprise are recommended to investigate this set.

Cooke, Arnold (born 1906)

Clarinet concerto.
*** Hyp. CDA 66031 [id.]. Thea King, NW CO of Seattle, Alun Francis – JACOB: *Mini-concerto;* RAWSTHORNE: *Concerto.* ***

Arnold Cooke's music contains an element of Hindemithian formalism, carefully crafted, but the slow movement of this concerto soars well beyond. Thea King makes a passionate advocate, brilliantly accompanied by the Seattle Orchestra in excellent 1982 analogue sound, faithfully transferred.

Copland, Aaron (1900–90)

Appalachian spring (ballet; complete original version)
*** Koch Dig. 3-7019-2; 2-7019-4 [id.]. Atlantic Sinf., Schenck – BARBER: *Cave of the heart.* ***

This Koch International issue offers a welcome chance to hear a modern digital recording of *Appalachian spring* in its original form for thirteen instruments and the bright, upfront recording presents the chamber version in the best possible light. This is a most interesting and stimulating issue.

Appalachian spring (ballet) *suite.*
☞ (M) *** DG Dig. 439 528-2 [id.]. LAPO, Bernstein – BARBER: *Adagio for strings* ***; GERSHWIN: *Rhapsody in blue.* **(*)

Bernstein's DG version of *Appalachian spring* was recorded at a live performance, and the conductor communicates his love for the score in a strong yet richly lyrical reading, and the compulsion of the music-making is obvious. The recording is close but not lacking in atmosphere, and it sounds extremely vivid. It is here recoupled with his rather less recommendable second recording of Gershwin's *Rhapsody in blue.*

(i) *Appalachian spring* (ballet) *suite; Billy the Kid: ballet suite;* (ii) *Clarinet concerto;* (i) *Danzón Cubano; Fanfare for the common man; John Henry; Letter from home;* (i; iv) *Lincoln portrait;* (iii) *Music for movies;* (i) *Our Town; An Outdoor overture; Quiet city; Rodeo (4 Dance episodes);* (iii) *El Salón México;* (i) *Symphony No. 3;* (v) *Las agachadas.*
(M) *** Sony SM3K 46559 (3) [id.]. (i) LSO; (ii) Benny Goodman, Columbia Symphony Strings; (iii) New Philh. O; (iv) with Henry Fonda; (v) New England Conservatory Ch.; composer.

Sony here offer a comprehensive anthology of the major orchestral works, ballet suites and film scores dating from Copland's vintage period, 1936–48. The composer directs with unrivalled insight throughout. The remastering for CD is done most skilfully, retaining the ambience of the originals, while achieving more refined detail.

(i) *Appalachian spring* (ballet) *suite; Billy the Kid* (ballet) complete; (ii) *Danzón cubano; El salón México.*
(M) *** Mercury 434 301-2 [id.]. (i) LSO; (ii) Minneapolis SO, Antal Dorati.

Dorati pioneered the first stereo recording of the complete *Billy the Kid* ballet, and the 1961 Mercury LP caused a sensation on its first appearance for its precision of detail and brilliance of colour, while the generous acoustics of Watford Town Hall added ambient warmth. The gunshots (track 13) were and remain electrifying, with their clean percussive transients, while the LSO playing combines tremendous vitality and rhythmic power with genuine atmospheric tension. For the CD, earlier (1957) Minneapolis versions of the *Danzón cubano* and *El salón México* have been added. The recording is crisp and clean to suit his approach.

Appalachian spring: ballet suite; Billy the Kid: ballet suite; Rodeo: 4 dance episodes; Symphony No. 3: Fanfare for the common man.
☞ ⊛ (M) *** Sony SMK 47543 [id.]. NYPO, Leonard Bernstein.

Bernstein's unique triptych of Copland ballet scores is now properly reissued as part of the Bernstein Edition with excellent historical documentation. He recorded these ballet scores in the early 1960s when he was at the peak of his creative tenure with the NYPO. No one – not even the composer –has approached these performances for racy rhythmic exuberance or for the tenderness and depth of nostalgia in the lyrical music, especially in the opening sequence of *Appalachian spring* and the *Corral nocturne* from *Rodeo.* The opening *Buckaroo holiday* and the final *Hoedown* from the latter ballet, taken at a tremendous pace, have an unforgettable rhythmic bite and zest, with amazing precision of ensemble from the New York players, whose adrenalin is obviously running at unprecedented levels. The evocation of *The open prairie* in *Billy the Kid* is magical and the picture of a *Street in a frontier town* has a piquant charm, while the projection of the score's more strident moments brings a characteristic pungency. The *Fanfare for the common man* is not the original, commissioned in 1942 by Eugene Goossens for the Cincinnati Orchestra, but the composer's reworking, when he introduced it as a springboard for the finale of his *Third Symphony.* There could be no finer memorial to Copland's genius or Bernstein's interpretative flair than this ballet triptych, and we are fortunate that the recordings are so good, vivid, spacious and atmospheric. *Appalachian spring* (1961) and *Rodeo* (1960) were made at the Manhattan Center (once again put to use by DG for their recordings by the Orpheus Chamber Orchestra) and *Billy the Kid* in Symphony Hall, Boston, in 1959.

Appalachian spring (ballet) *suite; Dance symphony; Fanfare for the common man; Rodeo: 4 dance episodes; El salón México.*
(M) *** Decca Dig. 430 705-2; 430 705-4 [id.]. Detroit SO, Dorati.

Dorati has the full measure of Copland's masterly *Appalachian spring* score. The 1984 Decca digital recording is impressive in its range and beauty of texture. The other works on this mid-priced CD were all digitally recorded in 1981. They are notable for their bright, extrovert brilliance and the playing demonstrates very clearly the degree of orchestral virtuosity available in Detroit.

Appalachian spring (ballet) *suite; 3 Latin-American sketches; Quiet city; Short symphony.*
*** DG 427 335-2 [id.]. Orpheus CO.

Appalachian spring (ballet) *suite; Short symphony.*
*** Pro Arte Dig. CDD 140 [id.]. St Paul CO, Russell Davies – IVES: *Symphony No. 3.* ***

With exceptionally vivid sound, bright and immediate, giving a realistic sense of presence, the Orpheus Chamber Orchestra's collection makes for a very distinctive Copland record of four works in which the composer is at his most approachable. The version of *Appalachian spring* here is the shortened text of the suite allied to the original 13-instrument ballet scoring. The performances, immaculately drilled, have a consistent sense of corporate purposefulness, of live communication made the more intense by the realism of the recording.

On Pro Arte, using a smaller ensemble than is usual, Russell Davies conducts fresh and immediate performances of both the *Short symphony* and the well-known suite from *Appalachian spring*, which was originally conceived for chamber orchestra. The recording is bright and forward to match the performances. An excellent and recommendable anthology.

Appalachian spring (ballet) *suite; The Tender Land* (opera): *suite.*
☞ (M) *** BMG/RCA 09026 61505-2 [id.]. Boston SO, composer – GOULD: *Fall River legend* etc.
***

The composer's first (1959) Boston recording of the *Appalachian spring suite* has moments of special resonance, its atmospheric feeling at times quite profound, helped by splendid orchestral playing and the warm Boston acoustic. The suite from *The Tender Land* is also well worth having. We are given the *Love duet* virtually complete, the Party music from Act II and the quintet, *The promise of living* (all, of course, without voices). The 'Living Stereo' remastering by John Pfeiffer and his team creates the most vivid and full-bodied sound-picture.

Billy the Kid (ballet): *suite; Rodeo* (ballet) *suite.*
☞ (M) **(*) BMG/RCA 09026 61667-2 [id.]. O, Morton Gould – GROFE: *Grand Canyon suite.* **(*)

Morton Gould, himself a composer, is thoroughly at home in Copland's 'Western' ballet suites and he takes the opportunity to include a genuine 'honky-tonk' piano in the *Interlude* of *Rodeo* – he was the first to do so on record. The performances are vivid and full of rhythmic vitality, yet not as electrifying as Bernstein's with the NYPO. The early stereo, made in the Manhattan Center in 1957, has just a touch of harshness on fortissimos, in spite of the enhancement of the digital remastering.

(i) *Billy the Kid* (ballet suite); (ii) *Piano sonata.*
(M) (***) BMG/RCA mono GD 60915 [60915-2]. (i) RCA Victor SO, Bernstein; (ii) Bernstein
(piano) – BERNSTEIN: *On the Town: suite* etc. (***)

Bernstein got to know the music of *Billy the Kid* by sitting with the composer and playing the full score on the piano. He also learned the formidable *Sonata* as it was being written in 1941. Both performances are full of nervous energy and must be regarded as definitive.

Ceremonial fanfare; John Henry (A railroad ballad); Jubilee variations; (i) *Lincoln portrait;* (ii) *Old American songs, set 1; An Outdoor overture; The Tender Land: The promise of living.*
*** Telarc Dig. CD 80117 [id.]. Cincinnati Pops O, Kunzel; (i) with Katharine Hepburn (nar.); (ii)
Sherrill Milnes.

Katharine Hepburn's remarkable delivery of Abraham Lincoln's words quite transcends any limitations in Copland's *Lincoln portrait* and makes it an undeniably moving experience, and Kunzel, clearly inspired by the authority of her reading, punctuates the text with orchestral comments of singular power. The shorter pieces are also given splendid life. Sherrill Milnes's highly infectious performance of the first set of *Old American songs* shows a spirited boisterousness that recalls Howard Keel in *Seven Brides for Seven Brothers*. Altogether a collection that is more than the sum of its parts, given superlative Telarc recording, highly spectacular and realistic, yet with natural balance.

Clarinet concerto.
☞ *** BMG/RCA Dig. 09026 61360-2. Stoltzman, LSO, Leighton Smith – BERNSTEIN: *Prelude,*
fugue and riffs. CORIGLIANO: *Concerto;* STRAVINSKY: *Ebony concerto.* ***
*** Sony MK 42227 [id.]. Benny Goodman, Columbia SO, composer – BERNSTEIN: *Prelude, fugue*

and riffs; GOULD: *Derivations;* STRAVINSKY: *Ebony concerto* ***; BARTOK: *Contrasts.* (***)
*** Chan. Dig. CHAN 8618; *ABTD 1307* [id.]. Janet Hilton, SNO, Bamert – NIELSEN: *Concerto;*
   LUTOSLAWSKI: *Dance preludes.* ***
*** ASV Dig. CDDCA 568 [id.]. MacDonald, N. Sinfonia, Bedford – FINZI: *Concerto;* MOURANT:
   Pied Piper. ***
☞ **(*) Denon Dig. CO 75289 [id.]. Paul Meyer, ECO, Zinman – BUSONI: *Adagio;* MOZART:
   Concerto. ***

Copland's splendid *Clarinet concerto* is at last coming into its own, on record at least. Stoltzman is effectively cool in the serene opening and catches the work's later quirky jazz elements to perfection; in this he is well matched by Lawrence Leighton Smith and the LSO players, who let their hair down without losing rhythmic sharpness or crispness of ensemble. The finale's flair is exhilarating and, with first-rate RCA recording, this bids to upstage even Benny Goodman in its combination of idiomatic understanding, natural virtuosity and superior sound. Now reissued with Stravinsky's *Ebony concerto* added to the original programme, this CD is even more attractive.

Benny Goodman gives a splendid account of the concerto he commissioned in 1947, and the recording from the early 1960s sounds admirably fresh in remastered form.

Janet Hilton's performance is softer-grained and has a lighter touch than Stolzman's, yet she finds plenty of sparkle for the finale and her rhythmic felicity is infectious. She is at her very finest, however, in the gloriously serene opening, where her tender poetic line is ravishing.

George MacDonald gives a virtuoso performance, not quite as dramatic and full of flair as that of the dedicatee, Benny Goodman, but in many ways subtler in expression and particularly impressive in the long lyrical paragraphs of the first of the two movements.

The gifted French clarinettist Paul Meyer (first prizewinner of the Concours des Jeunes Musiciens) was introduced to this concerto by its dedicatee, Benny Goodman, while he was taking a further award in New York in 1984. Meyer plays it with characteristic Gallic finesse and offers a winningly sprightly cadenza; he and Zinman wring remarkably felt intensity from the expressive opening section. Surprisingly, the popular rhythmic elements which come in the Rondo finale are presented straight, without jazzy inflexions. Fine, spacious recording.

Piano concerto.
(M) *** Van. 08.4029.71 [OVC 4029]. Earl Wild, Symphony of the Air, composer – MENOTTI: *Piano
   concerto.* **(*)
☞ (M) **(*) Chan. CHAN 6580 [id.]. Gillian Lin, Melbourne SO, John Hopkins – BRITTEN:
   Concerto. **(*)

This Vanguard record, with a supreme piano virtuoso providing a glittering account of the piano part, is very recommendable. The 1961 recording is first rate.

Gillian Lin is undoubtedly successful in the Copland *Concerto*, bringing out the jazz element in this syncopated music. Copland uses that easily imitable idiom far more imaginatively than most of his American colleagues – which helps to explain the work's continuing success – and one would hardly appreciate from the idiom alone that this is a work (written in 1926) which represents the composer before he had attained full maturity. The 1978 stereo recording is well balanced and realistically transferred to CD. A thoroughly worthwhile mid-priced coupling.

(i; ii) *Piano concerto;* (iii) *Dance symphony;* (ii) *Music for the theatre;* (iii) *2 Pieces for string
orchestra; Short symphony (Symphony No. 2); Statements; Symphonic ode;* (iv; ii) *Symphony for
organ and orchestra.*
(M) *** Sony SM2K 47232 (2) [id.]. (i) Composer (piano); (ii) NYPO, Bernstein; (iii) LSO,
   composer; (iv) with E. Power Biggs.

This second Sony Copland collection covers early orchestral and concertante music written between 1922 and 1935 and is, if anything, more valuable than the first box. The 1923 *Rondino*, the second of his *Two Pieces for string orchestra*, is the earliest work here. The *Lento* is a totally memorable piece. The *Symphony for organ and orchestra* is a powerful and strikingly innovative work, dating from 1924. It is given an extremely idiomatic and responsive performance by Power Biggs, who is fully sensitive to its atmosphere, and Bernstein balances the overall sounds with great skill and a marvellous feeling for colour. The *Piano concerto* (1927) is both abrasive and strongly jazz-influenced. The pungently flamboyant *Symphonic ode*, commissioned by the Boston Symphony, helped the orchestra to celebrate its fiftieth anniversary: it was written between 1927 and 1929. The *Dance symphony* was completed that same year. The *Short symphony* dates from 1931–3; both works are full of originality and energy and are tautly constructed. *Statements* (1934–5), as the bald title suggests, is one of Copland's less expansive works, but its six vignettes, *Militant, Cryptic, Dogmatic, Subjective,*

Jingo and *Prophetic*, reveal a compression of thought and sharpness of idea that are most refreshing. All these performances have a definitive authority combined with total spontaneity of response from the participants which makes them compelling listening, and the recordings – dating from between 1964 and 1967 – are very well engineered, extremely vivid in the excellent CD transfers.

(i) *Connotations;* (ii) *Dance panels; Down a country lane;* (i) *Inscape;* (ii) *3 Latin-American sketches; Music for a great city; Orchestral variations; Preamble for a solemn occasion; The Red Pony* (film score).
(M) *(**) Sony SM2K 47236 (2) [id.]. (i) NYPO, Bernstein; (ii) LSO or New Philh. O, composer.

This third Copland box from Sony is something of a disappointment – not the music, which is even rarer than before and of great interest. *The Red Pony* is vintage Copland, and the *Orchestral variations*, though strictly an orchestral version of the *Piano variations* of 1930, make a unique and impressive contribution to Copland's oeuvre. *Connotations* and to a lesser extent *Inscape*, the major work of the composer's final period, are serially orientated. *Dance panels* is an abstract ballet without a narrative line, and *Music for a great city*, with its jazz influences and nocturnal scene, derives from another film-score (*Something Wild*). The performances are all extremely successful, but the CD transfers are over-bright and, for all their vividness of detail, tiring to the ear, particularly the thin violins and the more pungent climaxes of the later works.

Quiet city.
*** Argo 417 818-2 [id.]. ASMF, Marriner – BARBER: *Adagio;* COWELL: *Hymn;* CRESTON: *Rumor;* IVES: *Symphony No. 3.* ***

Marriner's 1976 version is both poetic and evocative, and the playing of the trumpet and cor anglais soloists is of the highest order. The digital remastering has brought added clarity without loss of atmosphere.

Symphony No. 3.
(M) *** EMI Dig. CDM7 64304-2 [id.]. Dallas SO, Mata – HANSON: *Symphony No. 2.* ***

Symphony No. 3; Quiet city.
*** DG Dig. 419 170-2 [id.]. NYPO, Bernstein.

With Bernstein conducting Copland's *Third Symphony*, you appreciate more than with rival interpreters that this is one of the great symphonic statements of American music. The electricity of the performance is irresistible. The recording is full-bodied and bright, but its brashness is apt for the performance. The hushed tranquillity of *Quiet city*, another of Copland's finest scores, is superbly caught by Bernstein in the valuable fill-up.

Eduardo Mata and the Dallas Symphony Orchestra give a powerful, unexaggerated reading. Mata follows the composer's indications in the score, not least his often-repeated instruction, 'with simple expression', and the concentration and cohesiveness of the whole performance bear out his confidence, helped by full and well-balanced recording. This CD is currently withdrawn in the UK.

VOCAL MUSIC

(i) *In the Beginning. Help us, O Lord; Have mercy on us, O my Lord; Sing ye praises to our King.*
*** Hyp. Dig. CDA 66219; *KA 66219* [id.]. (i) Catherine Denley; Corydon Singers, Best – BARBER: *Agnus Dei;* BERNSTEIN: *Chichester Psalms.* ***

In the Beginning is a large-scale, fifteen-minute motet for unaccompanied chorus and soprano solo, written in 1947, and the long span of the work is well structured with the help of the soprano soloist, here the fresh-toned Catherine Denley. The chorus is just as clear and alert in its singing, not just in the big motet but also in the three delightful little pieces which come as an appendix. Vivid recording, full of presence.

Old American songs: Sets 1 and 2 (original versions).
*** Argo Dig. 433 027-2 [id.]. Samuel Ramey, Warren Jones – IVES: *Songs.* ***
*** Chan. Dig. CHAN 8960; *ABTD 1552* [id.]. Willard White, Graeme McNaught (with collection: '*American spirituals; Folk-songs from Barbados and Jamaica*' ***).

Both these discs of the Copland *Old American songs* offer the original versions with piano accompaniment. Samuel Ramey and his excellent accompanist treat them far more as art songs, with subtler shading of phrase and tempo, and a more extreme range of speeds within each song. Though the voice is not so smoothly caught as usual, Ramey's focus is much sharper than Willard White's, and it is only in part a question of vocal quality.

Characteristically White's opulent bass comes with a pronounced vibrato which on disc tends to get exaggerated. Yet with its helpful acoustic the Chandos recording captures the richness of his voice most attractively, very characterfully black in its evocations.

The Tender Land (opera) complete.
*** Virgin/EMI Dig. VCD7 59253-2 (2) [id.]. Comeaux, Dressen, Soloists, Ch. and O of Plymouth Music Series, Philip Brunelle.

Copland wrote as guileless an opera as could be, innocent-seeming in its diatonic harmony, sparing of dissonance, to match the rustic simplicity of the story of a farm family. The key passage is the big quintet at the end of Act I, *The promise of living*. It brings a simple tune that builds up to a memorable, moving climax. Nothing has quite the sharpness of *Appalachian spring*, but it is an amiable piece, beautifully performed here. Elizabeth Comeaux and Dan Dressen make an affecting pair of lovers, and the recording is open and atmospheric, conveying the stage picture very effectively.

Corelli, Arcangelo (1653–1713)

Concerti grossi, Op. 6/1–12.
*** BMG/RCA Dig. RD 60071 (2) [09026 60071-2]. Guildhall Ens., Robert Salter.
*** DG Dig. 423 626-2 (2) [id.]. E. Concert, Pinnock.
(BB) *** Naxos Dig. 8.550402/3 [id.]. Capella Istropolitana, Jaroslav Kr(e)chek.
(M) *** HM/BMG GD 77007 (2) [77077-2-RG]. La Petite Bande, Kuijken.

The Guildhall Ensemble and Robert Salter are very fine indeed and is probably a first choice for those who prefer modern instruments. They have the benefit of really excellent recording: immediate and present without being too forward, full-bodied and transparent in detail. The playing is really vital and imaginative and has plenty of warmth and imagination.

The DG performances bring not only an enthusiasm for this music but a sense of its spacious grandeur. The English Concert are entirely inside its sensibility, and the playing of the concertino group (Simon Standage, Micaela Comberti and Jaap Ter Linden) is wonderfully fresh-eyed and alert, yet full of colour.

At super-bargain price, the Naxos set by the Capella Istropolitana under Jaroslav Kr(e)chek represents very good value indeed. The players are drawn from the Slovak Philharmonic and have great vitality and, when necessary, virtuosity to commend them. The digital recording is clean and well lit, but not over-bright, and makes their version strongly competitive.

La Petite Bande offers a useful mid-price alternative to the Pinnock set. Authentic instruments are used to excellent effect, and the playing is always expressive and musical. The 1977 recordings were made in a highly sympathetic acoustic, that of Cedernsaal at Schloss Kirchheim; besides being splendidly lifelike, they are also impressive in conveying the nobility and grandeur of Corelli.

Concerti grossi, Op. 6/1, 3, 7, 8 (Christmas), 11 & 12.
(M) *** DG Dig. 431 706-2; 431 706-4. E. Concert, Trevor Pinnock.

At mid-price, with the *Christmas Concerto* included, this will admirably suit those collectors who want an original-instrument version and who are content with a single-disc selection.

Trio sonatas, Op. 1/1, 3, 7, 9, 11–12; Op. 2/4, 6, 9, 12.
*** DG Dig. 419 614-2 [id.]. E. Concert (members), Pinnock.

Trio sonatas, Op. 1/9, 10 & 12 (Ciacona); Op. 2/4; Op. 3/5; Op. 4/1; Violin sonata, Op. 5/3; Concerto grosso in B flat, Op. 6/5.
**(*) EMI Dig. CDC7 47965-2 [id.]. L. Baroque, Medlam.

Trio sonatas, Op. 1/9; Op. 2/4 & 12 (Ciacona); Op. 3/12; Op. 4/3; Op. 5/3, 11 & 12 (La Follia).
*** Hyp. Dig. CDA 66226 [id.]. Purcell Qt.

The quality of invention in these pieces underlines the injustice of their neglect. The players from the English Concert dispatch them with a virtuosity and panache that is inspiriting, and their evident enthusiasm for this music is infectious. This is a most impressive and rewarding issue –and excellently recorded into the bargain.

Though not lacking vitality, the London Baroque performances here are graceful and comparatively restrained, lighter in feeling and texture than Pinnock and his English Concert, and thus providing a genuine alternative approach.

The Hyperion disc is one of six designed to illustrate the widespread use in the eighteenth century of the famous *La Follia* theme. It includes a varied collection of sonate da chiesa and sonate da camera. Excellent performances from all concerned, and recording to match.

Violin sonatas, Op. 5/1, 3, 6, 11 and 12 (La Follia).
*** Accent Dig. ACC 48433D [id.]. Sigiswald & Wieland Kuijken, Robert Kohnen.

When authenticity of spirit goes hand in hand with fine musical feeling and accomplishment, the results can be impressive, as they undoubtedy are here, drawing one into the sensibility of the period. This is a thoroughly recommendable issue which deserves to reach a wider audience than early-music specialists; the recording is natural and the musicianship refined and totally at the service of Corelli.

Corigliano, John (born 1938)

Clarinet concerto.
☞ *** BMG/RCA Dig. 09026 61350-2. Stoltzman, LSO, Leighton Smith – BERNSTEIN: *Prelude, fugue and riffs;* COPLAND: *Concerto;* STRAVINSKY: *Ebony concerto.* ***

Stoltzman gives an outstanding performance of John Corigliano's attractive *Concerto*, his richly expressive treatment of the slow movement balanced by superb flair and virtuosity in the finale. Moreover his reissued CD sweeps the board in including three equally outstanding couplings.

Flute concerto (Pied Piper fantasy); Voyage.
**(*) BMG/RCA Dig. RD 86602 [6602-2-RC]. James Galway, Eastman Philh. O, David Effron.

Galway is at his inimitable best in Corigliano's *Flute concerto*. The picaresque qualities of its invention in detailing the Pied Piper narrative are spread thinly in memorability of material, although the closing section when the children are led away into the distance is right up Galway's street. The serene *Voyage* is shorter and more memorable.

(i) *Oboe concerto;* (ii; iii) *3 Irish folksong settings: The Sally Gardens; The foggy dew; She moved thro' the fair;* (ii; iv) *Poem in October.*
(M) *** BMG Analogue/Dig. GD 60395 [60395-2-RG]. (i) Humbert Lucarelli, American SO, Kazuyoshi Akiyama; (ii) Robert White; (iii) Ransom Wilson; (iv) Nyfenger, Lucarelli, Rabbai, American Qt, Peress (cond. from harpsichord).

John Corigliano's highly imaginative *Oboe concerto* opens ingeniously with the orchestra tuning up, and the music springs fairly naturally from this familiar aleatory pattern of sound. The performance here is outstanding, expert and spontaneous and very well recorded. The three *Folksong settings* are for tenor and flute; Robert White's headily distinctive light tenor gives much pleasure, as he does in the Dylan Thomas setting, *Poem in October.*

Symphony No. 1.
*** Erato/Warner Dig. 2292 45601-2 [id.]. Stephen Hough, John Sharp, Chicago SO, Barenboim.

This fine, deeply felt work is an elegy for friends of the composer, three in particular who have died of Aids. The *Symphony* opens with an expression of rage while the brief finale is an epilogue quoting all three movements. Barenboim and the Chicago orchestra bring out the full passionate intensity of the inspiration in this live recording. The sound is immediate and full-bodied, giving full scope to the colourful and often spectacular orchestral writing. This is well worth exploring and very rewarding.

Cornysh, William (c. 1468–1523)

Adieu, adieu my heartes lust; Adieu, courage; Ah Robin; Ave Maria, mater Dei; Gaude, virgo, mater Christi; Magnificat; Salve regina; Stabat Mater; Woefully arrayed.
⊛ *** Gimell Dig. CDGIM 014; *1585T-14* [id.]. Tallis Scholars, Phillips.

Cornysh's music is quite unlike much other polyphony of the time and is florid, wild, complex and, at times, grave. The Tallis Scholars give a magnificent, totally committed account of these glorious pieces – as usual their attack, ensemble and true intonation and blend are remarkable. Excellent recording.

Corrette, Michel (1709–95)

6 Organ concertos, Op. 26.
☞ (B) *** HM HMA 190 5248 [id.]. René Saorgin (organ of L'Eglise de l'Escarène, Nice), Bar.
Ens., Gilbert Bezzina.

These lively and amiable concertos from a minor eighteenth-century French composer are here given admirably spirited and buoyant performances, splendidly recorded using period instruments. The orchestral detail is well observed and René Saorgin plays vividly on an attractive organ. Michel Corrette's invention has genuine spontaneity and this makes an enjoyable collection to dip into, though not to play all at one go.

Couperin, François (1668–1733)

L'apothéose de Corelli; L'apothéose de Lully; Concert 'dans le goût théatral'.
*** Erato/Warner Dig. 2292 45011-2 [id.]. Bury, Wilcock, Campbell, E. Bar. Soloists, Gardiner.

Gardiner here presents an ideal Couperin coupling in superb performances, bringing together the two great instrumental works, both called apothéoses, celebrating first Corelli and then, even more grandly, Lully. The disc is completed with a fine *Concerto 'in the theatrical style'*, in which the instrumentation has been realized by Peter Holman. First-rate sound.

Concerts Royaux Nos. 1 in G; 2 in D; 3 in A; 4 in E min.
*** ASV Gaudeamus CDGAU 101 [id.]. Trio Sonnerie.
☞ (B) ** HM HMA 190 1151 [id.]. Robert Claire, Davitt Moroney, Jaap ter Linden, Janet See.

The *Concerts Royaux* can be performed in a variety of forms. The Trio Sonnerie give them in the most economical fashion (violin, viola da gamba and harpsichord) and the contribution of all three musicians is unfailingly imaginative. Excellent recording.

Davitt Moroney and his colleagues opt for two flute, bass viol and harpsichord in the *Concerts Royaux*. This was music intended for Louis XIV's diversion of a Sunday evening, and here the effect is just a shade wan. There is a certain uniformity of colour, and in addition their playing is just a little wanting in panache and vitality.

Les Goûts-réunis: Nouveaux concerts Nos. 8; 9 (Ritratto dell'amore).
(M) **(*) HM/BMG GD 71968. Kuijken Ens.

The Kuijken Ensemble use original instruments, and one only has to sample the *Overture* of the *Eighth Concert* to find how attractive is their sound-world. The *Ninth Concert* has a linking programme and its eight dance movements contrast the many facets of love.

Les Nations (complete).
☞ (M) *** Teldec/Warner 4509 93689-2 (2) Quadro Amsterdam (Frans Brüggen, Jaap Schröder, Anner Bysma, Gustav Leonhardt).

Couperin's *Les Nations*, published in 1726, divides into four sections, described by the composer as *ordres*, each being made up of a large-scale, many-movement trio sonata which serves as a prelude to a following suite. Couperin gave each a geographical connotation, *La Françoise*, *L'Espagnole* (where there is a touch of flamenco influence in the *Sonata*), *L'Impériale* and *La Piémontoise*, but the music itself is not really programmatic, though the invention is full of diversity and colour. The performance by the starry Quadro Amsterdam, using period instruments without any of those excesses of phrasing which sometimes affect much so-called 'authentic' music-making, is another of the treasures of the mid-1960s Telefunken Das Alte Werk catalogue. They are alive, elegant, polished and thoroughly idiomatic. Moreover they are beautifully recorded. Highly recommended.

L'apothéose de Lulli; La Parnasse ou l'apothéose de Corelli; Pièces de clavecin: 9e Ordre: Allemande à deux. 14e Ordre: La Juilliet. 15e Ordre: Muséte de Choisi; Muséte de Taverni. 16e Ordre: La Létiville.
*** HM Dig. HMC 901269; *HMC 401269* [id.]. William Christie, Christophe Rousset
(harpsichords).

Couperin's preface explains that he himself played these works on two harpsichords with members of his family and pupils; and William Christie has chosen to follow his example. Surprisingly, they sound rather more exciting in this form than in the more familiar instrumental versions, largely perhaps because of the sheer sparkle and vitality of these performers.

L'Art de toucher le clavecin: Preludes in A, C, B flat, D min., E flat, F, & G min. L'Arlequine; Les Baricades mistérieuses; Suites in C min., Ordre 3; B min., Ordre 8; Suite in A.
⊛ *** HM/BMG Dig. RD77219 [77219-2-RC]. Skip Sempé (harpsichord).

This is playing of real insight and flair, by far the best Couperin recital to have appeared in recent years and one of the most imaginative. There is expressive freedom about this playing and a poetic vitality that will persuade those who have hitherto found it difficult to come to terms with eighteenth-century French keyboard music. Sempé plays a modern copy by Bruce Kennedy of a Ruckers-Taskin and is very well recorded.

Harpsichord suites, Book 1, Ordres 1–5.
(B) *** HM HMA 190351/3 [id.]. Kenneth Gilbert.

Harpsichord suites, Book 2, Ordres 6–12.
(B) *** HM HMA 190354/6 [id.]. Kenneth Gilbert.

Harpsichord suites, Book 3, Ordres 13–19.
(B) *** HM HMA 190357/8 [id.]. Kenneth Gilbert.

Harpsichord suites, Book 4, Ordres 20–27.
(B) *** HM HMA 190359/60 [id.]. Kenneth Gilbert.

Professor Gilbert's performances are scrupulous in matters of registration, following what is known of eighteenth-century practice in France. There is no want of expressive range throughout the series and Gilbert plays with authority and taste – and, more to the point, artistry. He is also well served by the engineers.

Harpsichord suites, Book 2, Ordres 8 & 9.
*** Denon Dig. CO 1719 [id.]. Huguette Dreyfus (harpsichord).

Huguette Dreyfus plays with her customary authority and restraint. The *Huitième ordre* includes the famous *Passacaille* that Landowska played with such panache and flair. Excellent balance and recording.

Harpsichord suites, Book 2, Ordre 11; Book 3, Ordre 13.
*** Denon Dig. C37 7070 [id.]. Huguette Dreyfus (harpsichord).

For Ordres 11 and 13, Huguette Dreyfus plays a Dowd and shows herself yet again to have great understanding of this style. She is impeccably recorded.

Harpsichord suites, Book 3, Ordres 13–19; Concerts royaux Nos. 1–4.
☞ *** HM Dig. HMC 901442/4 [id.]. Christophe Rousset (with Blandine Rannou).

Harpsichord suites, Book 4, Ordres 20–27.
☞ *** HM Dig. HMC 901445/6 [id.]. Christophe Rousset (with Kaori Uemura).

The estimable Christophe Rousset is embarking on a splendid new digital recording of this engaging repertoire. In Volume Three he plays a seventeenth-century French instrument from the Villa Médici in Rome and in Volume 4 a Ruckers from the Musée d'Art d'Histoire, Neuchâtel. Both are ideally chosen and are beautifully recorded to give the most natural and intimate effect. Apart from his inherent sense of style and feeling for decoration, Rousset well understands terms like *gracieusement*, *gayement*, *très tendrement* and *agréable*, *sans lenteur*, which he realizes to perfection. The pleasures of Couperin's immensely varied and inventive series of *pièces de clavecin* are still known to only a relatively small group of music-lovers, and we hope this new Harmonia Mundi series will expand awareness of this rewarding music. The *Concerts royaux* were of course written for a small chamber group, but the composer also encouraged their performance on the keyboard alone. Rousset is joined in a very few items by Blandine Rannou on a second harpsichord; and in *La Croûilli ou la Couperinète*, from Book 4, Ordre 20, Kaori Uemura provides a vigorous basso continuo for the closing section.

Messe a l'usage ordinaire des paroisses.
(B) *** HM HMA 90714; HMA 43714 [id.]. Michel Chapuis (organ of St Mazimin-en-Var).

Couperin was an organist all his working life, but the two *Organ Masses* which constitute his entire output for the instrument were composed in 1690 when he was twenty-two. The performance has all the scholarship, authority and style one would expect from this fine player, and this makes a good bargain in the Musique d'Abord series.

3 Leçons de ténèbres.
(B) *** HM HMA 90210 [id.]. Deller, Todd, Perulli, Chapuis.

3 Leçons de ténèbres; Motet pour le jour de Pâques.
*** O-L 430 283-2 [id.]. Nelson, Kirkby, Ryan, Hogwood.

The *Trois Leçons de ténèbres* were written for performance on Good Friday and were the only ecclesiastical music Couperin published during his lifetime. Purity and restraint rather than warmth and humanity are the keynote of these Hogwood performances, but few listeners are likely to complain of the results.

Deller's account of the *Trois Leçons* is inevitably less authentic, since this music, written for a convent, did not envisage performances by male voices. In every other respect, however, it has a wonderful authenticity of feeling and a blend of scholarship and artistry that gives it a special claim on the attention of collectors.

Motets: *Domine salvum fac regem; Jacunda vox ecclesiae; Laetentur coeli; Lauda Sion salvatorem; Magnificat; O misterium ineffabile; Regina coeli; Tantum ergo sacramentum; Venite exultemus Domine; Victoria, Christo resurgenti.*
(B) *** HM HMA 901150; HMA 431150 [id.]. Feldman, Poulenard, Reinhart, Linden, Moroney.

The motets on this record cover a wider spectrum of feeling and range of expressive devices than might at first be imagined. The performances are eminently acceptable, with some particularly good singing from Jill Feldman; the recording is made in a spacious and warm acoustic.

Couperin, Louis *(c. 1626–61)*

Suites de pièces and complete harpsichord music.
(B) *** HM 901124/27 (4) [id.]. Davitt Moroney (harpsichord).

Louis Couperin was a pupil of Chambonnières, and his keyboard output comprises enough individual dance pieces to make sixteen suites, as well as other pieces. This comprehensive survey makes out a strong case for this repertoire; readers expecting it to be greatly inferior in quality to the clavecin music of François-le-Grand will be pleasantly surprised – though, of course, there is less of the poetic fantasy of his nephew at his best. The recording is eminently truthful and the CD transfer wholly natural.

Harpsichord suites: in A min.; in C; in F; Pavane in F sharp min.
(M) *** HM/BMG GD 77058 [77058-2-RG]. Gustav Leonhardt (harpsichord).

Leonhardt has such subtlety and panache that he makes the most of the grandeur and refinement of this music to whose sensibility he seems wholly attuned. This is the best introduction to Louis Couperin's keyboard suites now before the public.

Pièces de clavecin: Suites: in A min.; D; F; G min.
☞ (M) *** DG 437 084-2. Alan Curtis (harpsichord).

Alan Curtis is a fine player; he uses a period instrument from the second half of the seventeenth century, tuned to the mean-tone temperament. François Couperin's uncle is a far from negligible figure, and the four *Suites* collected here give a splendid idea of his range and personality. These scholarly performances are excellently recorded and the disc is urgently recommended to any collector wanting to investigate this original and inventive composer.

Harpsichord suites: in F; in G; in D min.; Passacaille in C; Pavane in F sharp min.
☞ *** EMI Dig. CDC7 54340-2 [id.]. Bob van Asperen.

For those whose interest extends beyond Couperin-Le-Grand to his uncle, Louis, Bob van Asperen's recital serves as an admirable introduction. He uses a Ruckers of 1624, an instrument made at the time of Couperin's birth and now in the Musée d'Unterlinden in Colmar, Alsace; it was also used by Blandine Verlet in her earlier survey on Astrée Auvidis. Bob van Asperen plays with characteristic panache and is freely expressive in the darker, slower pieces like the *Tombeau de Monsieur de Blancrocher* or the *Sarabande* from the *F major Suite* or the improvisatory *Prélude* to the *G minor*. One word of warning: the recording reproduces at a higher level than may be desirable, so if you want a realistic and truthful sound it is essential to set the volume at a low level.

Cowell, Henry (1897–1965)

Hymn and fuguing tune No. 10 for oboe and strings.
*** Argo 417 818-2 [id.]. Nicklin, ASMF, Marriner – BARBER: *Adagio;* COPLAND: *Quiet city;* CRESTON: *Rumor;* IVES: *Symphony No. 3.* ***

This likeable *Hymn and fuguing tune,* by a composer otherwise little known, is well worth having and is expertly played and recorded here. The digital remastering has slightly clarified an already excellent recording.

Cowen, Frederick (1852–1935)

Symphony No. 3 in C min. (Scandinavian); The Butterfly's ball: concert overture; Indian rhapsody.
** Marco Polo Dig. 8.220308 [id.]. Czechoslovak State PO (Košice), Adrian Leaper.

The *Symphony No. 3* (1880) shows (to borrow Hanslick's judgement) 'good schooling, a lively sense of tone painting and much skill in orchestration, if not striking originality'. But what Cowen lacks in individuality he makes up for in natural musicianship and charm. His best-known work is the *Concert overture, The Butterfly's ball* (1901), which is scored with Mendelssohnian delicacy and skill. The *Indian rhapsody* (1903) with its naïve orientalisms carries a good deal less conviction. The performances are eminently lively. The recording is pleasingly reverberant but somewhat lacking in body.

Creston, Paul (born 1906)

A Rumor.
*** Argo 417 818-2 [id.]. ASMF, Marriner – BARBER: *Adagio;* COPLAND: *Quiet city;* COWELL: *Hymn;* IVES: *Symphony No. 3.* ***

A Rumor is a witty and engaging piece and is played here with plenty of character by the Academy under Sir Neville Marriner. It completes a thoroughly rewarding and approachable disc of twentieth-century American music that deserves the widest currency. The sound is first class.

Symphony No. 2, Op. 35; Corinthians XIII, Op. 82; Walt Whitman, Op. 53.
*** Koch Dig. 37036-2 or KI 7036 [id.]. Krakow PO, David Amos.

Paul Creston's musical language is strongly influenced by French music. His orchestration is both opulent and expert, though some climaxes are overblown. The *Second Symphony* (1944) opens rather like a Roy Harris symphony but subsequently becomes highly exotic in the manner of a Roussel or a Villa-Lobos, with infectiously vital rhythms and lush textures. It is played with real enthusiasm and affection by these Polish forces and is well very recorded, even though the sound could do with greater transparency in the upper range. This should enjoy wide appeal.

Symphony No. 3 (Three Mysteries), Op. 48; Invocation and Dance; Out of the cradle; Partita for flute, violin and strings.
☞ *** Delos Dig. DEL 3114 [id.]. Seattle SO, Schwarz.

At last it would seem that Paul Creston is coming in from the cold. Since his *Second* and *Third Symphonies* were first recorded on Nixa in the early days of LP, his music has undergone a long period of neglect. His unashamedly opulent tonal palette and neo-Impressionist musical language went out of fashion in the 1960s' climate of serialism and post-serialism. But a generation force-fed on Elliott Carter and Milton Babbitt is now beginning to rediscover the American symphonic tradition of the 1940s and '50s. True, Creston's work is uneven, but the idiom is approachable, nowhere more so than in the *Third Symphony*, a work of strong invention and lyrical impulse. Incidentally, the *Three Mysteries* of the subtitle allude to the Nativity, Crucifixion and Resurrection. Gerard Schwarz gives a fervent and committed account, drawing excellent playing from his Seattle orchestra, and completely supersedes the earlier account. The exhilarating *Invocation and Dance* has also been recorded before – as, for that matter, has the *Partita*, which is somewhat more austere, or at least less opulent. All these pieces, including the less successful *Out of the cradle,* benefit not only from Schwarz's committed advocacy but also from superb engineering. The sound is in the demonstration class. If you already have the *Second Symphony,* you will need no promptings to invest in the present issue; but if you haven't, do try this warm-hearted and appealing music for yourself.

Crusell, Bernhard (1775–1838)

Clarinet concertos Nos. 1 in E flat, Op. 1; 2 in F min., Op. 5; 3 in E flat, Op. 11.
*** ASV Dig. CDDCA 784; *ZCDCA 784* [id.]. Emma Johnson, RPO/ECO, Herbig; Groves; or Schwarz.
☞ *** Virgin/EMI Dig. VC7 59287-2 [id.]. Antony Pay, O of Age of Enlightenment.
☞ *** Hyp. CDA 66708 [id.]. Thea King, LSO, Alun Francis.

Crusell, born in Finland but working in Stockholm most of his career, was himself a clarinettist and these delightful concertos demonstrate his complete understanding of the instrument. There are echoes of Mozart, Weber and Rossini in the music, with a hint of Beethoven.

No one brings out the fun in the writing quite as infectiously as Emma Johnson, and this generous recoupling (74 minutes) bringing all three together is a delight. With well-structured first movements, sensuous slow movements and exuberant finales, Johnson establishes her disc as a first choice above all others.

Pay's is the first period performance of these works. As well as directing the Orchestra of the Age of Enlightenment himself, he uses a reproduction of a nine-key clarinet as made around 1810 by Heinrich Grenser; Crusell himself is known to have used a ten-key Grenser clarinet. The slight edginess of the sound goes well with Pay's preference for fastish – often very fast – speeds which yet never get in the way of his imaginative rhythmic pointing. The results in outer movements are exhilarating, with phenomenal articulation of rapid passage-work. They sparkle with wit, while slow movements have a flowing songfulness that is comparably persuasive. The Virgin recording, made at Abbey Road studio, is clear, well balanced and atmospheric.

Thea King with her beautiful, liquid tone also makes an outstanding soloist. Her approach is often more serious, especially in the *Second Concerto*, where she brings out the Beethovenian character of the first movement, while the *Andante pastorale* slow movement is played with the widest range of tone-colour. Throughout, she is well accompanied by Alun Francis; and the resonant Hyperion recording, with the soloist balanced forward, emphasizes the feeling of added gravitas.

Clarinet concerto No. 1 in E flat, Op. 1.
☞ *** ASV Dig. CDDCA 763; *ZCDCA 763* [id.]. Emma Johnson, RPO, Herbig – KOZELUCH; KROMMER: *Concertos.* ***

Even though many collectors may prefer the CD containing all three of the Crusell concertos, Emma Johnson's version of the *First Clarinet concerto* makes a highly attractive compilation with lesser-known but enticing works by Kozeluch and Krommer, especially when her warm-toned playing is magnetically individual, and the ASV recording brings out the great range of sensuously beautiful tone-colours she produces.

Clarinet concerto No. 2 in F min., Op. 5.
⊛ *** ASV Dig. CDDCA 559; *ZCDCA 559* [id.]. Emma Johnson, ECO, Groves – BAERMANN: *Adagio;* ROSSINI: *Introduction, theme and variations;* WEBER: *Concertino.* ***

Crusell's *Second Clarinet concerto* made Emma Johnson a star, and in return she put Crusell's engagingly lightweight piece firmly on the map. Her delectably spontaneous performance is now caught on the wing and this recording sounds very like a live occasion.

Concertino for bassoon and orchestra in B flat; Introduction et air suédois for clarinet and orchestra, Op. 12; Sinfonia concertante for clarinet, horn, bassoon and orchestra, Op. 3.
*** BIS Dig. BIS CD 495 [id.]. Hara, Korsimaa-Hursti, Lanski-Otto, Tapiola Sinf., Vänskä.

The most substantial piece here is the *Sinfonia concertante, for clarinet, horn, bassoon and orchestra*. The finale is a set of variations on a chorus from Cherubini's opera, *Les deux journées*. The much later *Concertino for bassoon and orchestra* is an altogether delightful piece, which quotes at one point from Boieldieu. It is played with appropriate freshness and virtuosity by László Hara. The *Introduction et air suédois for clarinet and orchestra* is nicely done by Anna-Maija Korsimaa-Hursti. The Tapiola Sinfonietta, the orchestra of Esspoo, play with enthusiasm and spirit for Osmo Vänskä, and the BIS recording has lightness, presence and body.

Introduction, theme and variations on a Swedish air.
*** ASV Dig. CDDCA 585; *ZCDCA 585* [id.]. Emma Johnson, ECO, Yan Pascal Tortelier – DEBUSSY: *Rapsodie;* TARTINI: *Concertino;* WEBER: *Concerto No. 1.* ***

Emma Johnson, a naturally inspirational artist, skates lightly over any banalities in Crusell's *Variations*, giving a carefree performance, often witty, youthfully daring.

Clarinet quartets Nos. 1 in E flat, Op. 2; 2 in C min., Op. 4; 3 in D, Op. 7.
*** Hyp. CDA 66077; *KA 66077* [id.]. Thea King, Allegri Qt (members).

These are captivatingly sunny works, given superb performances, vivacious and warmly sympathetic. Thea King's tone is positively luscious, as recorded, and the sound is generally excellent. The CD transfer is highly successful.

Divertimento in C, Op. 9.
*** Hyp. CDA 66143 [id.]. Francis, Allegri Qt – KREUTZER: *Grand quintet;* REICHA: *Quintet.* ***

No one wanting this slight but charming piece and its companions need look further than this nicely played and well-recorded account.

Cui, César (1835–1918)

(i) *Suite concertante* (for violin & orchestra), *Op. 25. Suite miniature No. 1, Op. 20; Suite No. 3 (In modo populari), Op. 43.*
**(*) Marco Polo Dig. 8.220308 [id.]. (i) Nishizaki; Hong Kong PO, Schermerhorn.

These pieces have a faded period charm that is very appealing (try the *Petite Marche* and the equally likeable *Impromptu à la Schumann* from the *Suite miniature*) and are very well played by the Hong Kong Philharmonic. Takako Nishizaki is the expert soloist in the *Suite concertante.* An interesting issue that fills a gap in the repertoire, and very decently recorded too.

Curzon, Frederick (1899–1973)

The Boulevardier; Bravada (Paso doble); Capricante (Spanish caprice); Cascade (Waltz); Galavant; In Malaga (Spanish suite); Punchinello: Miniature overture; Pasquinade; La Peineta; Robin Hood suite; (i) *Saltarello for piano and orchestra; Simionetta (Serenade).*
☞ *** Marco Polo Dig. 8.223425 [id.]. (i) Silvia Cápová; Slovak RSO (Bratislava), Leaper.

Frederick Curzon was a professional concert (as distinct from church) organist. He began writing background music for films and then (encouraged by Sir Dan Godfrey, conductor of the Bournemouth Municipal Orchestra) progressed to the special genre of light music heard on British piers and from spa orchestras in the inter-war years. The best-known piece here is *Dance of an ostracised imp*, a droll little scherzando, much played on the radio during the Second World War. But the *Galavant* is hardly less piquant and charming, the delicious *Punchinello* sparkles with miniature vitality, and the *Simionetta* serenade is sleekly beguiling. Curzon liked to write mock Spanishry, and several pieces here have such a Mediterranean influence. Yet their slight elegance and economical scoring come from cooler climes farther north. Both *In Malaga* and the jolly *Robin Hood suite* are more frequently heard on the (military) bandstand, but their delicate central movements gain much from the more subtle orchestral scoring. The performances throughout are played with the finesse and light touch we expect from this fine Slovak series, so ably and sympathetically conducted by Adrian Leaper. The recordimg is admirable – the composer's light textures sounding colourful and vivid in the Concert Hall of Bratislava Radio.

Czerny, Karl (1791–1857)

Andante e polacca in E for horn and piano, Op. posth.; 3 Fantasias brillantes on themes of Schubert for horn and piano, Op. 339.
*** Etcetera Dig. KTC 1121 [id.]. Barry Tuckwell, David Blumenthal.

The *Andante and polacca* is a characteristically ripe piece which is enjoyable enough when played with such aplomb, but the real interest of this recital lies with the three Schubertian *Fantasias.* In effect they are pot-pourris of favourite Schubert songs, with the horn given the vocal melody against a background of glittering piano cascades. The performances could hardly be bettered; if you want Schubert Lieder without the words, then the present recording is most pleasing, the resonance flattering to both artists but the focus realistically firm.

Damase, Jean-Michel (born 1928)

Quintet for flute, harp, violin, viola & cello (1948); *Sonata for flute & harp* (1964); *Trio for flute, harp & cello* (1946); *Variations 'Early Music' for flute & harp* (1980).
☞ *** ASV Dig. CDDCA 898 [id.]. Noakes, Tingay, Friedman, Atkins, Szucs.

Jean-Michel Damase was a pupil of Alfred Cortot and Henri Büsser, and his chamber music (and in particular the *Trio for flute, harp and cello* and the *Quintet*, composed when he was eighteen and twenty respectively) was often broadcast in the early days of the Third Programme. It has a fluent, cool charm which will delight many listeners; there is little substance but it is beautifully fashioned and makes some very pleasing sounds. Those coming to it for the first time will find it very attractive. Very Gallic, with touches of Poulenc without his harmonic subtlety. It is nicely played and very well recorded.

Danzi, Franz (1763–1826)

Flute concertos Nos. 1 in G, Op. 30; 2 in D min., Op. 31; 3 in D min., Op. 42; 4 in D, Op. 43.
*** Orfeo Dig. C 00381-2H [id.]. András Adorján, Munich CO, Stadlmair.

Danzi wrote four *Flute concertos*, all included here, which suggest a style midway between eighteenth-century classicism and the more romantic manner of Weber. All four performances by András Adorján and Stadlmair with his Munich Chamber Orchestra are impeccably stylish and have plenty of vitality, and the recording is both full and transparent and is well balanced.

(i) *Piano quintet in F, Op. 53. Wind quintets, Op. 67/1–3.*
*** BIS Dig. CD 539 [id.]. (i) Love Derwinger; BPO Wind Qt.

Danzi was one of the first composers to cultivate the wind quintet. These are light, diverting pieces of no great musical substance but when played with such distinction and recorded with such great clarity and presence they offer unexpected pleasure. The *Piano quintet*, in which the Berlin quintet are joined by the young Swedish pianist, Love Derwinger, is also pretty empty-headed but rather delightful all the same.

Da Ponte, Lorenzo (1749–1838)

L'ape musicale.
**(*) Nuova Era Dig. 6845/6 (2). Scarabelli, Matteuzzi, Dara, Comencini, Teatro la Fenice Ch. & O, Vittorio Parisi.

This greatest of librettists was no composer, but he was musical enough to devise a pasticcio like *L'ape musicale* ('The musical bee') from the works of others, notably Rossini and Mozart. It makes a delightful if offbeat entertainment, generally well sung in a lively performance. The first Act – full of Rossinian passages one keeps recognizing – leads up to a complete performance of Tamino's aria, *Dies Bildnis*, sung in German at the end of the Act. Similarly, Act II culminates in an adapted version of the final cabaletta from Rossini's *Cenerentola*. The sound is dry, with the voices slightly distanced. The stage and audience noises hardly detract from the fun of the performance.

David, Félicien (1810–76)

Les brises d'Orient; Les minarets.
*(*) Marco Polo Dig. 8.223376 [id.]. Daniel Blumenthal.

The exoticism of *Les brises d'Orient* and *Les minarets* sounds very muted nowadays but they have a certain faded period charm – or would have if the rather claustrophobic acoustic in which they are recorded did full justice to Daniel Blumenthal's advocacy. Primarily of curiosity interest that is soon satisfied, though there are some pieces to which one could imagine oneself becoming attached.

Dawson, William (1899–1990)

Negro Folk Symphony.
☞ *** Chan. Dig. CHAN 9226 [id.]. Detroit SO, Neeme Järvi – STILL: *Symphony No. 2;*
    ELLINGTON: *Harlem.* ***

William Dawson began life the son of a poor Alabama labourer, yet he worked his way up to become Director of Music at the Tuskegee Institute. His *Negro Folk Symphony,* written in 1931 but revised in 1952, is designed to combine European influences and Negro folk themes. All three movements are chimerical. The first is rhapsodic with a scherzando character, interrupted by lyrical interludes. It has plenty of energy and ideas, but they are inclined to run away with their composer. The central movement is basically lyrical and passionate, opening and closing with a marching theme. The finale becomes energetic at the very close. Järvi has the advantage of excellent orchestral playing and first-class Chandos sound, and (perhaps surprisingly) he makes far more of a case for the work than did Stokowski in his pioneering stereo recording with the American Symphony Orchestra.

Debussy, Claude (1862–1918)

2 Arabesques; Clair de lune (arr. Caplet); *Estampes: Pagodes* (arr. Grainger); *La Mer; Petite suite; Prélude: La cathédrale engloutie* (arr. Stokowski); (i) *Rhapsody for clarinet and orchestra.*
*** Cala Dig. CACD 1001; *CAMC 1001* [id.]. (i) James Campbell, Philh. O, Geoffrey Simon.

Geoffrey Simon's warm, urgent reading of *La Mer,* very well recorded, comes in coupling with six items originally involving piano. Debussy did his own arrangement of the *Clarinet rhapsody* and approved André Caplet's arrangement of *Clair de lune* as well as Henri Büsser's of the *Petite suite.* Stokowski's freely imagined orchestral version of *La cathédrale engloutie* is effectively opulent, and the most fascinating instrumentation of all comes in Percy Grainger's transcription of *Pagodes,* with an elaborate percussion section simulating a Balinese gamelan.

(i) *Berceuse héroïque;* (ii; iii) *Danses sacrée et profane* (for harp and strings); (ii) *Images; Jeux; Marche écossaise; La Mer;* (ii; iv) *Nocturnes;* (ii) *Prélude à l'après-midi d'un faune;* (ii; v) *Rhapsodie for clarinet and orchestra.*
☞ ⊛ (B) *** Ph. Duo 438 742-2 (2) [id.]. Concg. O, (i) Eduard van Beinum; (ii) Bernard Haitink; with (iii) Vera Badings; (iv) women's Ch. of Coll. Mus.; (v) George Pieterson.

This must now rank as the finest Debussy collection in the CD catalogue and one of the greatest bargains that the gramophone has to offer at present – all for the cost of a single premium-priced CD. Although the programme as a whole is directed by Haitink, it is good that his distinguished predecessor, Eduard van Beinum, is remembered by the opening *Berceuse héroïque,* played with great delicacy and a real sense of mystery, with the early stereo (1957) highly effective. For the *Danses sacrée et profane* Haitink takes over, with elegant playing from the harpist, Vera Badings, who is excellently balanced. Haitink's reading of *Images* is second to none in its firmness of grip and fidelity to the score. His *Gigues* is scrupulously prepared and beautifully played by the wonderful Dutch orchestra; the sonorities are delicate and the dynamic shadings sensitively observed. Haitink's response to the atmosphere of *Ibéria* is very personal: he is positive in his evocation of *Les parfums de la nuit* (less Latin in feeling than some versions), but the subtlety of the orchestral playing is constantly telling, no more so than at the magical opening of *Le matin d'un jour de fête.* The superlative quality of the playing is matched by analogue recording of the very highest order. This applies equally to *Jeux,* where Haitink's reading is wonderfully expansive and sensitive to atmosphere and easily matches any recent rivals. Competition is even stiffer in the *Nocturnes,* but this great orchestra and conductor hold their own. The cruel vocal writing in *Sirènes* taxes the women of the Collegium Musicum Amstelodamense, but the choral balance is perfectly judged and few versions are quite as beguiling and seductive as Haitink's. Add to this an equally admirable recorded quality, with transparent textures, splendidly defined detail and truthful perspective – in short, demonstration sound – and the result is very distinguished indeed. In its original LP format the coupling of *Jeux* and *Nocturnes* received twin *Gramophone* awards for the best orchestral and the best-engineered record of 1980. Haitink's pacing of *La Mer* is comparable with Karajan's tempo in his 1964 recording. Both conductors pay close attention to dynamic gradations and both secure playing of great sensitivity and virtuosity from their respective orchestras. *De l'aube à midi sur la mer* has a special atmosphere in Haitink's hands, and the *Jeux de vagues* is no less fresh; the *Dialogue du vent et de la mer* is both fast and exciting. An interesting point is that the brief fanfares that Debussy removed, eight bars before fig. 60, are here restored (as they were by Ansermet), but Haitink gives them to horns. (Karajan, who omitted them in the first DG version, restored them in his later, EMI recording, but on trumpets.) The hazily sensuous *Prélude à l'après-midi d'un faune* and the undervalued *Clarinet rhapsody* are also played atmospherically, although the former is more overtly languorous in Karajan's hands. Again the Philips recording is truthful and natural, with beautiful perspectives and realistic colour, a marvellously refined sound. These are all, of course, analogue recordings; but the digital remastering is wholly beneficial, bringing just a little greater sense of concert-hall presence with the bass somewhat better defined.

La boîte à joujoux (orch. Caplet): complete.
*** Chan. Dig. CHAN 8711; *ABTD 1359* [id.]. Ulster O, Yan Pascal Tortelier – RAVEL: *Ma Mère l'Oye.* ***
☞ (M) **(*) Erato/Warner 2292 45819-2 [id.]. Basle SO, Armin Jordan – DUKAS: *L'apprenti sorcier* etc. **(*)

Debussy's enchanting ballet score depicts adventures in a children's box of toys, and is full of delights. It is beautifully played by the Ulster Orchestra under Yan Pascal Tortelier. The subtlety and atmosphere are captured admirably by the splendid Chandos recording, which is in the demonstration class.

Armin Jordan's account is also enjoyably atmospheric, helped by very good (1981) analogue recording. Although not distinguished by playing of the very first order, the performance is thoroughly idiomatic and sympathetic. Of the couplings, Dukas's *Polyeucte overture* is well worth having, and this is fair value at mid-price (60 minutes).

La boîte à joujoux; Jeux; Prélude à l'après-midi d'un faune.
☞ *** Sony Dig. SK 48231 [id.]. LSO, Tilson Thomas.

La boîte à joujoux is ideally suited to Michael Tilson Thomas's talents. His account is second to none and has the right lightness of touch and wistful charm. Nor will collectors be disappointed with his account of *Jeux*, which is admirably unhurried and atmospheric, or his dreamy, languorous *Prélude à l'après-midi d'un faune.* The Sony recording is first class – very natural and spacious. *Jeux* does not displace the Haitink Duo version on Philips but can be recommended alongside it.

Children's corner; Danse: Tarantelle styrienne (arr. Ravel); *Estampes: La soirée dans Grenade* (arr. Stokowski). *L'isle joyeuse; Nocturnes; Préludes: Bruyères; La fille aux cheveux de lin.*
*** Cala CACD 1002; *CAMC 1002* [id.]. Philh. O, Geoffrey Simon.

Geoffrey Simon's version of the three *Nocturnes* is colourful and atmospheric, with nothing vague in *Fêtes.* The orchestrations of piano music include Stokowski's vivid realization of *La soirée dans Grenade*, as well as Ravel's magical re-interpretation of *Danse* and André Caplet's sensitive orchestration of *Children's corner.* Full, vivid recorded sound.

Children's corner; Petite suite.
*** Chan. Dig. CHAN 8756; *ABTD 1395* [id.]. Ulster O, Yan Pascal Tortelier – RAVEL: *Le tombeau de Couperin* etc. ***

The Ulster Orchestra certainly play very well for Yan Pascal Tortelier and the recording is every bit as good as predecessors in this series.

Danse (Tarantelle styrienne); Sarabande (orch. Ravel).
(BB) *** Virgin/EMI Dig. VJ5 61104-2 [id.]. Lausanne CO, Zedda – MILHAUD: *Création du monde;* PROKOFIEV: *Sinfonietta* etc. ***

Zedda's performances with the Lausanne Chamber Orchestra are neat and polished, full of character and well recorded. But it is the couplings that make his disc specially attractive.

(i) *Danses sacrée et profane;* (ii) *Fantaisie for piano and orchestra;* (iii) *Première rhapsodie for clarinet and orchestra.*
*** Chan. Dig. CHAN 8972 [id.]. (i) Masters; (ii) Quefféléc; (iii) King, Ulster O, Y. P. Tortelier – RAVEL: *Intro & allegro* etc. **(*)

The *Fantaisie* is sensitively played by Anne Quefféléc. This is a fine performance and the *Première rhapsodie for clarinet and orchestra* is played by Christopher King with a natural unforced eloquence that is very persuasive, while the *Danses sacrée et profane* also come off well.

Images.
*** Chan. Dig. CHAN 8850; *ABTD 1467* [id.]. Ulster O, Yan Pascal Tortelier – RAVEL: *Alborada; Rapsodie espagnole.* ***
☞ (M) ** BMG/RCA mono 09026 61956-2 [id.]. Boston SO, Munch – RAVEL: *Boléro* etc. **

Images; Jeux; Le Roi Lear (incidental music).
*** EMI Dig. CDC7 49947-2. CBSO, Rattle.

Images; (i) *Nocturnes.*
*** Decca Dig. 425 502-2 [id.]. Montreal SO, Dutoit; (i) with chorus.

Rattle is just a touch more expansive than most rivals, and also more evocative, though he does not depart from the basic metronome markings. Haitink probably remains a first choice in this score, for he has atmosphere and a tauter grip on the music's flow, but Baudo's mid-priced EMI version should not be forgotten either. The *King Lear* excerpts sound splendid. First-rate recording, very vivid but beautifully balanced.

Dutoit is freer in his use of rubato, as well as in his warm, espressivo moulding of phrase. His sharp pointing of rhythm, as in the Spanish dances of *Ibéria* or the processional march in *Fêtes*, is also highly characteristic of his approach to French music. For those who like these impressionistic masterpieces to be presented in full colour, with a vivid feeling for atmosphere, this is an ideal choice.

The orchestral playing is very good indeed in Ulster under Yan Pascal Tortelier and the recorded sound is of the high quality we have come to expect of this series. It is not necessarily the best *Images* on the market, if one can speak in such crude terms, but it is certainly among the best. The *Rondes de printemps* has delicacy and freshness in their hands.

Munch's recording of the complete *Images* comes from 1956 but the recording hardly sounds its age. *Gigues* is atmospheric, as indeed is *Les parfums de la nuit* from *Ibéria* and much else in this colourful triptych, though the performances seem just a shade hard-driven. *Ibéria* is not the equal of Reiner's Chicago version from the same period. Virtuoso playing from the Boston Symphony Orchestra.

Images; (i) *Nocturnes; Le Martye de Saint Sébastien: 2 Fanfares and symphonic fragments; Printemps; Prélude à l'après-midi d'un faune;* (ii) *3 ballades de Françcois Villon;* (iii) *La Damoiselle élue.*
☞ (B) **(*) DG Double Dig./Analogue 437 934-2 (2) [id.]. O de Paris, Daniel Barenboim; with (i)
   Ch. de l'O de Paris; (ii) Dietrich Fischer-Dieskau; (iii) Barbara Hendricks.

This DG Double set includes a 72-minute single-disc collection to which we awarded a Rosette in our last volume including not only the early *Printemps* and the fragments from *Le Martyre de Saint Sébastien* but also his splendid set of *Nocturnes*. This performance, although highly individual in its control of tempo, has great fervour. Comparably in *Le Martyre* Barenboim succeeds in distilling an intense, rapt quality and brings to life its evocative atmosphere. He is no less persuasive in *Printemps*. This receives a performance as good as any in the catalogue. The 1977/8 recordings are spacious, rich in texture and well balanced, with good definition and range.

The second of the two CDs offers rather a mixed bag. The *3 Ballades de François Villon* are well sung by Dietrich Fischer-Dieskau and are valuable, as they are seldom heard in their orchestral form. Also welcome is *La Damoiselle élue*, which Barbara Hendricks sings with great sensitivity and beauty, and Barenboim draws playing of genuine atmosphere from the Orchestre de Paris. However, the other additions rather tend to dilute the appeal of this reissue. Both have a digital source. The *Prélude* brings languorous feeling which is undoubtedly telling, even if there is some lack of vitality, but there is nothing very special about the *Images*. Indeed the performances of both these works remain serviceable rather than distinguished and there is ultimately a lack of real profile: the results are curiously disappointing.

Images; Printemps; Prélude à l'après-midi d'un faune.
☞ ** DG Dig. 435 766-2; *435 766-4* [id.]. Cleveland O, Boulez.

Pierre Boulez has recorded all this repertoire before, though not with the success his DG engineers have achieved here. There is more atmosphere this time round in the *Gigues* and much to admire in the sheer beauty and finesse of the orchestral playing. *Printemps* is far more successful than before. For all that, one remains outside this music looking in admiringly; one is not drawn into its world in the same way as is the case with the greatest Debussy interpreters. Atmosphere, yes; but magic, no.

Images; (i) *Rhapsodie No. 1 for clarinet and orchestra.*
☞ (M) **(*) Sony SMK 47545 [id.]. (i) Stanley Drucker; NYPO, Bernstein – RAVEL: *Ma Mère l'Oye* etc. ***

Bernstein recorded Debussy's *Images* in 1958, and that early date shows in the upper strings, notably in the sparkling *Rondes de printemps*. But the playing has both unforced virtuosity and atmosphere, and *Gigues* has great character. In *Ibéria* the 'Perfumes of the night' are gently yet headily sensuous. This is the highlight of the performance, and at times the balmy fragrance of the nocturnal breeze is almost overwhelming, with the lead into *Le matin d'un jour de fête* exquisitely managed, bringing an explosion of colour and rhythmic energy. Debussy himself managed the orchestration for the *Clarinet rhapsody* (originally written for clarinet and piano), although this rarely played piece was not first performed until 1919, a year after the composer's death. It begins atmospherically, then subtly explores the virtuosic nature of the solo instrument. It is extremely well played here, and it is a pity that the recording – otherwise excellent – is still somewhat unflattering to the upper strings. Nevertheless these performances have great magnetism.

Images: Ibéria.
⊛ (M) *** BMG/RCA GD 60179 [60179-2-RG]. Chicago SO, Fritz Reiner – RAVEL: *Alborada* etc. *** ⊛

Fritz Reiner and the Chicago orchestra give a reading that is immaculate in execution and magical in atmosphere. This marvellously evocative performance, and the Ravel with which it is coupled, should not be overlooked, for the recorded sound with its natural concert-hall balance is greatly improved in terms of body and definition. It is amazingly realistic even without considering its vintage.

Images: Ibéria. (i) *Le Martyre de Saint-Sébastien* (incidental music, complete).
☞ (M) **(*) BMG/RCA GD 60684 [id.]. (i) Kopleff, Akos, Curtin; Boston SO, Munch.

Charles Munch's recording of the complete *Le Martyre de Saint-Sebastien* comes from 1957 and offers sumptuous orchestral sound though, Phyllis Curtin excepted, he does not have quite the same distinguished vocal line-up that Ansermet commanded on his 1954 Decca account (Suzanne Danco, Nancy Waugh and Marie-Louise Montmollin) and the recording does not have the same front-to-back depth and transparency, though it is still very good – and what magnificent playing the Boston orchestra give us! However, Munch's New England Chorus is a bit too well drilled. Unlike the Ansermet, he does give us the narration, which he speaks very expressively himself (with a slight Alsatian accent), though he is a bit too closely recorded. Ansermet's version is spread across the two discs of the Ravel operas, so anyone needing a single mid-price *Martyre* need look no further. However, Munch's version does not compete with Michael Tilson Thomas's new, sumptuously recorded, full-price version on Sony. The *Ibéria* comes from the set of *Images* Munch recorded in 1956 (see above).

Images: Ibéria. La Mer; (i) *Nocturnes.*
☞ (M) ** Decca 425 050-2 [id.]. Cleveland O, (i) with Ch.; Lorin Maazel.

The Cleveland Orchestra plays magnificently for Maazel. The performances are superbly disciplined, but there is too little magic in any of these readings. The analytical recording, though well lit and finely detailed, does not help. The performance of the *Nocturnes* is more successful than that of *La Mer*. But the wind are by no means distant enough at the opening of the *Nuages* and, although Maazel is sensitive to matters of dynamic nuance, there are inconsistencies in the observance of some of the *pianissimo* or *ppp* markings. The viola tone at Fig. 6 in *Nuages* sounds over-nourished, and in the slow movement of *Ibéria* some expressive detail is over-glamourized. This performance is taut and very well played, but it does not possess the character and sensitivity of the finest rivals, even though every detail comes over with clarity and presence in the remastering for CD.

Images: Ibéria. La Mer; Nocturnes: Nuages; Fêtes. Prélude à l'après-midi d'un faune.
(M) (**(*)) BMG/RCA mono GD 60265 [60265-2-RG]. NBC SO, Toscanini.

By emphasizing clarity, Toscanini with his electric intensity and sense of purpose consistently compels attention. One thinks of these supreme examples of musical impressionism, not as colour pieces, but as masterly structures of great originality in purely musical terms. Clean, bright transfers.

Images: Ibéria. Prélude à l'après-midi d'un faune; (i) *La damoiselle élue.*
*** DG Dig. 423 103-2 [id.]. (i) Maria Ewing, Brigitte Balleys, London Symphony Ch.; LSO, Abbado.

Maria Ewing has never sounded sweeter on record, and Brigitte Balleys, a touch raw-toned on some notes, sings with attractive freshness. The purely orchestral works bring more urgent, even impulsive performances, marked by a warmly persuasive rubato style. Though balances are not always quite natural, the ambient warmth of All Saints', Tooting, seems ideal for the music, orchestral as well as vocal, and the effect is very vivid and glowing, without loss of detail.

Jeux.
☞ (M) *(*) Decca 425 049-2 [id.]. Cleveland O, Maazel – RAVEL: *Daphnis.* **(*)

Maazel's *Jeux* is superbly disciplined but much less atmospheric than almost any other performance on record – though it must be admitted that every detail comes over with clarity and presence in the well-lit Decca recording which has transferred to CD most successfully.

Jeux; Khamma.
*** Chan. Dig. CHAN 8903; *ABTD 1512* [id.]. Ulster O, Tortelier – RAVEL: *Boléro; La valse.* ***

Yan Pascal Tortelier gets some very good playing from the Ulster Orchestra, and though this performance of *Jeux* is not to be preferred to the magical Haitink account on Philips which still sounds excellent, or either of the EMI versions (Baudo and Rattle), it remains highly competitive and desirable.

Jeux; Khamma; Prélude à l'après-midi d'un faune; Printemps.
☞ **(*) Virgin/EMI Dig. VC5 45018-2 [id.]. Finnish RSO, Saraste.

From Virgin, eminently serviceable recordings of some of Debussy's stage scores, recommendable even if there are better individual performances available elsewhere. Saraste's *Jeux* is not in the same league as the Haitink, Tilson Thomas, Baudo or Rattle. The best thing on the disc is his account of *Khamma*.

Jeux; La Mer; Nocturnes: Nuages; Fêtes (only); *Prélude à l'après-midi d'un faune.*
☞ (M) **(*) Sony SMK 47546 [id.]. NYPO, Bernstein.

These recordings were made in the Manhattan Center in 1960/61 and show Bernstein at his most charismatic. Reservations have to be expressed, for the performances undoubtedly have an air of glamour which some may find borders on excess. There is plenty to admire in the orchestral playing, however, and Bernstein has an undoubted feeling for atmosphere which he sustains even when, as in *La Mer*, the adenalin is very freely running. Both *Jeux* and the *Prélude à l'après-midi d'un faune* have more than a whiff of voluptuousness and the phrasing in the *Prélude* is self-conscious in places. But the feeling throughout is of live music-making, and such performances would receive a standing ovation at a concert. The remastered sound is remarkably convincing. The diffuse recording – though woodwind are picked out by the microphones – adds to the evocative feeling, and the remastered sound is remarkably convincing, although the balance is contrived.

Jeux; La Mer; Prélude à l'après-midi d'un faune.
⊛ (M) *** EMI Dig. CD-EMX 9502; *TC-EMX 2090* [Ang. CDM 62012]. LPO, Baudo.

Serge Baudo's version of *La Mer* is first class. The recording is beautifully natural and expertly balanced. The same may be said for his lovely account of *Prélude à l'après-midi d'un faune*, as atmospheric as any in the catalogue and more beautifully shaped than many. In the faster sections, *Jeux* is at times brisker than we are used to and well conveys the sense of the playfulness of the tennis match. Its competitive price makes it even more enticing.

La Mer.
(M) *** BMG/RCA GD 60875 [60875-2-RG]. Chicago SO, Reiner – RIMSKY-KORSAKOV: *Scheherazade.* ***
☞ (M) **(*) BMG/RCA 09026 61500-2 [id.]. Boston SO, Munch – IBERT: *Escales* ***; SAINT-SAENS: *Symphony No. 3.* *** ⊛
☞ ** Chan. Dig. CHAN 9072; *ABTD 1594* [id.]. Detroit SO, Järvi – MILHAUD: *Suite provençale;* ROUSSEL: *Sinfonietta* etc. **

La Mer; Danse (Tarantelle styrienne); (i) Nocturnes. Prélude à l'après-midi d'un faune.
☞ (M) *** Sony SBK 53266 [id.]. Phd. O, Ormandy, (i) with Temple University Womens' Ch.

La Mer; (i) Nocturnes. Prélude à l'après-midi d'un faune.
☞ (B) *** DG 439 407-2 [id.]. O de Paris, Barenboim, (i) with Ch.
(B) *** Pickwick Dig. PCD 915; *CIMPC 915*. LSO, Frühbeck de Burgos, (i) with Ch.

(i) *La Mer; (i; ii) Nocturnes; (i) Prélude à l'après-midi d'un faune; (iii) Première Rapsodie for clarinet and orchestra.*
☞ (B) ** Erato/Warner 4509 92867-2 [id.]. (i) Strasbourg PO, Lombard, (ii) with Ch. of Rhine Opéra; (iii) Antony Morf, Monte-Carlo Opéra O, Jordan.

La Mer; Prélude à l'après-midi d'un faune.
(M) *** DG 427 250-2. BPO, Karajan – RAVEL: *Boléro; Daphnis et Chloé.* ***
(M) *** EMI CDM7 64357-2 (id.]. BPO, Karajan – RAVEL: *Alborada* etc. ***
☞ ** DG Dig. 439 008-2 [id.]. BPO, Karajan – RAVEL: *Pavane; Daphnis.* **

After three decades Karajan's 1964 DG account of *La Mer* is still in a class of its own, and the performance of the *Prélude à l'après-midi d'un faune* is equally unforgettable, representing one of the maestro's finest achievements on record.

Reiner's 1960 recording has all the warmth and atmosphere that make his version of *Ibéria*, recorded at about the same time – see above – so unforgettable. Of course the marvellous acoustics of the Chicago Hall contribute to the appeal of this superbly played account: the effect is richer and fuller than in Karajan's remastered DG version, and Reiner's record gives no less pleasure.

We have not had Munch's stereo *La Mer* on CD before. It relies more on excitement than on atmosphere to make its effect but it offers marvellous Boston playing, especially from the violins, and its distinctly colloquial style places it among the more memorable versions of this much recorded piece. The 1956 recording is close and bright but sounds vastly better here than it did on LP, with the Boston ambience bringing its own particular allure.

Ormandy is a master of French repertoire, and in his 1964 set of *Nocturnes* the orchestral playing has the superb subtlety of timbre we expect from a Philadelphia performance of a great score. Ormandy's control is absolute and it is only in the last piece, *Sirènes*, where, as so often happens, the female chorus refuses to sound quite ethereal enough. Even so, Ormandy grades the dynamics of the closing pages with the same skill that he applies to the orchestral processional in *Fêtes*. The recording was made in the Philadelphia Town Hall and is quite full and atmospheric. *La Mer* has a different venue (the Broadwood Hotel) and dates from the early days of stereo (1959). It is relatively closely balanced and the dynamic range is somewhat more restricted, though not impossibly so. The orchestral playing in *Jeux de vagues* has thrilling virtuosity, and subtlety too, and the sustained gentle playing at the halfway point of the *Dialogue du vent et de la mer* means that the climax in the strings which follows seems the more ecstatic. The closing sections of both these movements show the Philadelphia bravura at its most compelling. The *Prélude à l'après-midi d'une faune* (with a fine flute solo from William Kincaid) is sensuous but refined, although the early recording date is conveyed by the timbre of the violins above the stave; the *Danse* is stunningly played, yet the conductor's touch is as light as anyone could wish. Indeed, for all the technical reservations (and the sound is not as alluringly full as on Barenboim's competing DG disc), this is one of Ormandy's most impressive Sony reissues.

Barenboim's 1978 coupling of *La Mer* and *Nocturnes*, reissued on DG's Classikon bargain label, not only offers first-class analogue recording but performances which, although highly individual in their control of tempo, have great electricity. For some ears the effect (with the wind balanced rather forward) may lack the subtlety that distinguishes Karajan's analogue version, but there is an ardour that more than compensates. The *Prélude à l'après-midi d'un faune* has comparable languor to *Sirènes*, the last of the *Nocturnes*, if not quite the same refinement of feeling. This too is very well recorded.

Although strong in Mediterranean atmosphere, Frühbeck de Burgos's account of *La Mer* has an underlying grip, helped by the wide dynamic range of the Walthamstow recording. There is much subtlety of detail, both here and in the *Nocturnes*, where textures again have the sensuousness of southern climes. The *Prélude à l'après-midi d'un faune* brings lovely delicate flute playing from Paul Edmund-Davies and a richly moulded string climax. If these are not conventional readings, they are full of impulse and superbly recorded.

Karajan's 1978 analogue re-recording of *La Mer* for EMI may not have quite the supreme refinement of his earlier DG version – partly a question of the warmer, vaguer recording – but it has a comparable concentration, with the structure persuasively and inevitably built. The *Prélude* has an appropriate languor, and there is a persuasive warmth about this performance, beautifully moulded; but again the earlier version distilled greater atmosphere and magic.

The digital remastering of Karajan's 1985 recordings is impressively clear and vivid, with the Philharmonie acoustic very well managed. But the improved sound serves only to emphasize the lack of magic in the playing compared to his earlier (1964) account. The *Prélude à l'après-midi d'un faune* is beautifully played, although the flautist has a very pronounced vibrato; and, again, the earlier version distils a more subtle fragrance.

Good, well-played performances on Erato, not without atmosphere or excitement, recorded in a warm acoustic. But there is nothing really distinctive here until the final work on the CD, a rather beautiful account of the *Clarinet rhapsody*, with a gently sensuous solo contribution from Antony Morf.

Neeme Järvi's version of *La Mer* has much going for it; it has a subtle sense of flow and a good feeling for texture. There are some oddities, though, including a slowing down in the second part of *De l'aube à midi sur la mer* some way before the passage Satie referred to as the bit he liked at about a quarter to eleven. Given the sheer quantity and quality of the competition, however, this is not really a front-runner.

La Mer; Nocturnes: Nuages; Fêtes (only); *Le Martyre de Saint-Sébastien* (symphonic fragments);
Prélude à l'après-midi d'un faune.
☞ (***) Testament mono SBT 1011. Philh. O, Guido Cantelli.

Cantelli's classic accounts have been beautifully restored and come up sounding both natural and fresh. With the exception of the two purely orchestral *Nocturnes*, which were made a year before Cantelli's death in 1956, all these performances were recorded in 1954 in the Philharmonia's heyday. Cantelli's account of the four symphonic fragments from *Le Martyre de Saint-Sébastien* is one of the most beautiful performances he ever committed to vinyl; the textures are impeccably balanced and phrases flawlessly shaped. Its atmosphere is as concentrated as that of the legendary first recording under Coppola. *La Mer* and the *Prélude à l'après-midi d'un faune* are hardly less perfect.

La Mer; Printemps.
☞ *(*) Chan. Dig. CHAN 9114 [id.]. Ulster O, Yan Pascal Tortelier – RAVEL: *Piano trio* (orch.
Tortelier). *(*)

Tortelier's account of *La Mer* is taut and held together well, though his generally brisk tempi do not always enhance the atmosphere. *Printemps* also receives an intelligently shaped reading, though the performance again is not as atmospheric or relaxed as Barenboim's, let alone the legendary Beecham set which has never been reissued but which, we hope, will be in the lifetime of this volume. The orchestration of the Ravel *Piano trio* is not the ideal makeweight.

Rhapsody for clarinet and orchestra.
*** ASV Dig. CDDCA 585; *ZCDCA 585* [id.]. Emma Johnson, ECO, Yan Pascal Tortelier –
CRUSELL: *Introduction, theme & variations;* TARTINI: *Concertino;* WEBER: *Concerto No. 1.* ***

Debussy's lovely *First Rhapsody* brings out the most persuasive qualities in Emma Johnson's artistry. The range of expression with extreme contrasts of tone and dynamic makes this an exceptionally sensuous performance, yearningly poetic, and recorded in a helpful acoustic.

Symphony in B min.
☞ ** Koch Dig. 3-7067-2 [id.]. Sinfonia O of Chicago, Barry Faldner – GOUNOD: *Petite symphonie
for winds;* MILHAUD: *Symphonies for chamber orchestra.* **

Debussy composed his *Symphony in B minor* when he was eighteen and staying in Russia with Tchaikovksy's patron, Madame von Meck. He sketched out this ten-minute piece for piano, four hands, in which form it has been recorded. To be truthful, there are few signs of the Debussy to come and much that is derivative. Barry Faldner's orchestration includes a piano so that it sounds rather like a concertante work. It is very well played but of limited musical interest. The time would have been better spent on recording all six rather than only four of the Milhaud *Petites symphonies*.

CHAMBER MUSIC

*Cello sonata; Petite pièce for clarinet and piano; Première Rapsodie for clarinet and piano; Sonata for
flute, viola and harp; Violin sonata; Syrinx for solo flute.*
*** Chan. CHAN 8385 [id.]. Athena Ens.

The most ethereal of these pieces is the *Sonata for flute, viola and harp*, whose other-worldly quality is beautifully conveyed here. In the case of the other sonatas, there are strong competitors but, as a collection, this is certainly recommendable.

Cello sonata in D min.
*** Decca 417 833-2 [id.]. Rostropovich, Britten – SCHUBERT: *Arpeggione sonata* **(*); SCHUMANN:
5 Stücke. ***
**(*) ASV Dig. CDDCA 796 [id.]. Bernard Gregor-Smith, Yolande Wrigley – BRIDGE; DOHNANYI:
Sonatas. **(*)

(i) *Cello sonata;* (ii) *Violin sonata.*
**(*) Chan. Dig. CHAN 8458; *ABTD 1170* [id.]. (i) Yuli Turovsky; (ii) Rostislav Dubinsky; Luba
Edlina – RAVEL: *Piano trio.* ***

Like Debussy's other late chamber works, the *Cello sonata* is a concentrated piece, quirkily original. The classic version by Rostropovich and Britten has a clarity and point which suit the music perfectly. The recording is first class, and if the couplings are suitable, this holds its place as first choice.

Bernard Gregor-Smith and Yolande Wrigley play with great refinement and authority, as well as much sensitivity. They are perhaps too closely balanced but this does not prevent their record being a highly desirable one.

In the *Cello sonata*, Turovsky gives a well-delineated, powerful account with Luba Edlina. In the *Violin sonata*, Rostislav Dubinsky and Luba Edlina (his wife) are in excellent form, though this is red-blooded Slavonic Debussy rather than the more ethereal, subtle playing of a Grumiaux.

(i) *Cello sonata in D min.;* (ii; iii) *Sonata for flute, viola and harp;* (iv) *Violin sonata in G min.;* (ii) *Syrinx*.
(M) *** Ph. 422 839-2. (i) Gendron, Français; (ii) Bourdin; (iii) Lequien, Challan; (iv) Grumiaux, Hajdu.

Though these excellent performances on Philips do not wholly dislodge others from one's affections, they are very fine. Gendron's version of the *Cello sonata* is most eloquent and is splendidly recorded.

Sonata for flute, viola and harp.
*** Koch Dig. 3-7016-2 [id.]. Atlantic Sinf. – JOLIVET: *Chant de Linos;* JONGEN: *Concert*. ***

The three members of the Atlantic Sinfonietta are well balanced and achieve a feeling of repose and mystery. This is the best of the recent recordings of this enormously civilized and ethereal music.

Piano trio in G.
*** Pickwick Dig. MCD 41; *MCC 41* [id.]. Solomon Trio – FAURE; RAVEL: *Piano trios*. ***

The *G major Trio* undoubtedly shows more promise than fulfilment and is almost entirely uncharacteristic. Rodney Friend, Yonty Solomon and Timothy Hugh give as good an account as any on Pickwick and are very well recorded indeed. They play with considerable finesse and sensitivity, and persuade the listener that this piece is stronger than in fact it is.

String quartet in G min.
☞ *** DG Dig. 437 836-2 (id.]. Hagen Qt – RAVEL; WEBERN: *Quartets*. ***
☞ *** Denon Dig. CO 75164 [id.]. Carmina Qt – RAVEL: *Quartet*. ***
☞ *** BMG/RCA Dig. 09026 61816-2 [id.]. Vogler Qt – JANACEK; SHOSTAKOVICH: *Quartets*. ***
☞ *** Sony Dig. SK 52554 [id.]. Juilliard Qt – DUTILLEUX; RAVEL: *Quartets*. ***
(M) *** Ph. 420 894-2 [id.]. Italian Qt – RAVEL: *Quartet*. ***
(M) *** DG 435 589-2 [id.]. LaSalle Qt – RAVEL: *Quartet*. ***
☞ (B) *** CfP Dig. CD-CFP 4652; *TC-CFP 4652* [id.]. Chilingirian Qt – RAVEL: *Quartet*. ***
(BB) **(*) Naxos Dig. 8.550249 [id.]. Kodály Qt – RAVEL: *Quartet* etc. ***
(B) **(*) Hung. White Label HRC 122 [id.]. Bartók Qt – RAVEL: *Quartet* **(*); DVORAK: *Quartet No. 12*. ***
(*) Pickwick Dig. MCD 17; *MCC 17*. New World Qt – RAVEL: *Quartet* **(*); DUTILLEUX: *Ainsi la nuit*. *
☞ *(*) Nimbus Dig. NI 5077 [id.]. Medici Qt – SHOSTAKOVICH: *String quartet No. 8*. *(*)

The Debussy and Ravel quartets are an almost mandatory coupling these days and even Dover Scores reprint the two together! For long we have recommended the Melos and Quartetto Italiano sets very highly, but the last two years have brought a number that can give them a good run for their money.

The Hagen Quartet on DG produce the greatest refinement of sound without beautifying the score; they also enjoy the benefit of superb engineering. Indeed, if pressed, this might well be a first choice, at least among recent issues.

The Carmina Denon disc can certainly be given the strongest recommendation for those willing to accept short measure, as they do not offer a third work as coupling. However, the recordings are fresh and wide-ranging (perhaps a trace fierce right at the very top) and the playing is of the highest quality. There is plenty of ardour when required and some moments of impetuousness, but in the slow movement these players achieve real repose. Dynamic contrasts are strong without being excessive, and their playing has style and finesse. This CD is not quite in the same category as the Carmina pairing of the Szymanowski quartets (see below) but it is very impressive all the same.

The Vogler on RCA offer a more unusual combination, likely to fit the needs of any collector who just happens to want the eleventh of the Shostakovich quartets and the Janáček No. 1. This kind of programming is exasperating and self-defeating. A pity, since this is an exceptionally fine account of the Debussy, fiery when required, highly sensitive to dynamic nuance and keenly atmospheric; it is as good as any now before the public. Put the Vogler slow movement, say, alongside the Juilliard, and comparison is very much to their advantage.

The Juilliard performance is impressive all the same, in spite of the wider vibrato these players employ, which one barely notices except when making a direct comparison. Their first movement is not as fresh and ardent as the Vogler, but overall this is very satisfying. They are well recorded (though the balance in the fine Dutilleux bonus is much closer than in the Debussy or Ravel).

Turning now to the mid- and bargain-priced versions, it need hardly be said that the playing of the Italian Quartet is outstanding. Perfectly judged ensemble, weight and tone still make this a most satisfying choice and, even if it is rather short measure, unlike the Denon/Carmina it is offered at mid-price. The Philips recording engineers have produced a vivid and truthful sound-picture, with plenty of impact, and the recording barely shows its age.

The LaSalle Quartet are also on top form and their reading takes a place of honour alongside – but not in preference to – the Quartetto Italiano. The 1971 recording was of high quality and the CD transfer in no way degrades its natural balance.

At bargain price the Chilingirian coupling is in every way competitive. They give a thoroughly committed account with well-judged tempi and very musical phrasing. The Scherzo is vital and spirited, and there is no want of poetry in the slow movement. The recording has plenty of body and presence and has the benefit of a warm acoustic: the sound is fuller than on the competing version by the Italian Quartet.

As we know from their Haydn recordings, the Kodály Quartet are an excellent ensemble and they give a thoroughly enjoyable account that can be recommended to those who do not want to spend that bit extra on the mid-priced Quartetto Italiano version. There are moments here (in the slow movement, for example) when the Kodály, too, are touched by distinction. This music-making has the feel of a live performance and is to be preferred to some of the glossier, mechanized accounts at full price: these players also have the benefit of a generous fill-up and very good recorded sound. Excellent value.

The account by the Bartók Quartet is full of character, and the *Andante* is certainly *doucement expressif*. The recording is good, too, and well balanced; with three quartets on offer, this record is a genuine bargain.

The New World Quartet is Harvard-based and their playing gives undoubted pleasure. The Debussy is very well played but a bit overprojected. The expressive rubato of the leader may pose problems for those with austere tastes. However, these artists add an interesting Dutilleux piece. They are very well recorded. This CD comes at slightly more than mid-price.

The Medici Quartet can be passed over. At full price and with only 46 minutes' playing time it does not offer value for money and, more to the point, is not competitive artistically.

Violin sonata in G min.
***DG Dig. 415 683–2 [id.]. Shlomo Mintz, Yefim Bronfman – FRANCK; RAVEL: *Sonatas.* ***
*** Collins Dig. 1112-2; *1112-4* [id.]. Lorraine McAslan, John Blakely – RAVEL; SAINT-SAENS: *Sonatas.* ***
** Virgin/EMI Dig. VC5 45002-2 [id.]. Dmitry Sitkovetsky, Pavel Gililov – JANACEK; R. STRAUSS: *Violin sonatas.* ***

(i) *Violin sonata in G min.;* (ii) *Sonata for flute, viola and harp.*
⊛ (M) *** Decca 421 154-2; *421 154-4.* (i) Kyung Wha Chung, Radu Lupu; (ii) Melos Ens. (members) – FRANCK: *Violin sonata;* RAVEL: *Introduction and allegro.* *** ⊛

Kyung Wha Chung plays with marvellous character and penetration, and her partnership with Radu Lupu could hardly be more fruitful. Nothing is pushed to extremes, and everything is in perfect perspective. The *Sonata for flute, viola and harp* and the Ravel *Introduction and allegro* are wonderfully sensitive and the music's ethereal atmosphere well caught. The recording sounds admirably real.

Shlomo Mintz and Yefim Bronfman give a performance that is difficult to fault and gives much pleasure. They can be recommended alongside – though not in preference to – Chung and Lupu. This is undoubtedly a magnificent account and excellently recorded, too.

Lorraine McAslan gives a very fine account of the Debussy *Sonata*, perhaps not quite as outstanding as the Ravel, where she could well be a first choice, but impressive enough in all conscience. She is well partnered by John Blakely, and the recording is very good indeed, well balanced and truthful.

Dmitry Sitkovetsky and Pavel Gililov are much stronger in the Janáček and Strauss *Sonatas* than they are in the Debussy. They give a responsive performance, but there is a change of perspective which finds the balance favouring the piano, with the result that Sitkovetsky seems all too reticent. Nor do these artists seem to have the same natural feeling for this repertoire that they have for Janáček.

PIANO MUSIC

Music for two pianos

Danses sacrée et profane; En blanc et noir; Lindaraja; Nocturnes (trans. Ravel); *Prélude à l'après-midi d'un faune.*
*** Hyp. Dig. CDA 66468 [id.]. Stephen Coombs and Christopher Scott.

Stephen Coombs and Christopher Scott made an outstanding début with this fine recording, which leads the field in this repertoire.

Solo piano music

2 Arabesques; Ballade; Danse bohémienne; Danse (Tarantelle styrienne); Images (1894); *Nocturne; Pour le piano; Rêverie; Suite bergamasque; Valse romantique.*
☞ *(**) Pickwick MCD 24; *MCC 24* [id.]. Martino Tirimo.

Tirimo's playing is distinguished and there is never any doubt as to his Debussian credentials. He plays only the two outer movements of the 1894 *Images*, arguing quite reasonably that the differences between the two versions of the *Sarabande* are very slight. But the balance is very close and the microphone even picks up the pedal mechanism (try the opening of the *Danse* on track 8) to an almost unacceptable extent. The acoustic of Rosslyn Hill Chapel, Hampstead, does permit the sound to expand – but some slight background noise from the environs (probably what was posing problems for the engineer) would be better than putting the listener virtually on the piano stool.

2 Arabesques; Children's corner; Estampes; Images, Books I–II; Mazurka; L'isle joyeuse; Pour le piano; Préludes, Books I–II.
☞ (B) **(*) Ph. Duo 438 718-2 (2) [id.]. Werner Haas.

(i) *En blanc et noir; 6 Epigraphes antiques; Lindaraja; Marche écossaise; Petite suite.* (Solo piano): *Ballade slave; Berceuse héroïque; Danse (Tarantelle styrienne); Danse bohémienne; D'un cahier d'esquisses; 12 Etudes; Hommage à Haydn; Masques; Nocturne; Le petit nègre; La plus que lente; Rêverie; Suite bergamasque; Valse romantique.*
☞ (B) *** Ph. Duo 438 721-2 (2) [id.]. Werner Haas, (i) with Noël Lee.

In the early 1960s, Werner Haas, who enjoyed an enviable reputation as an interpreter of French music, recorded (virtually) all Debussy's solo piano music, and it goes without saying that his playing never falls below a certain standard. The playing is rarely routine but at the same time does not achieve a consistently sustained level of inspiration. Book II of the *Préludes* (sample *Feux d'artifice*) and many of the pieces from Book I are very well worth having; the *Images* are pretty good too (*Reflets dans l'eau* sparkles iridescently), and many of the shorter pieces in the first listed volume are neatly and sensitively characterized. What makes this particular pair of CDs (438 721-2) indispensable is the splendid collection of Debussy's music for piano duet (four hands or two pianos), recorded a decade later, in which Haas is joined by Noël Lee. The *Petite suite* is delightfully fresh, and *En blanc et noir* and the *Six épigraphes antiques* are very distinguished indeed. The piano recording throughout is well up to Philips's high standard, and the CD transfers are first class. As usual with this bargain series, the documentation is very good.

2 Arabesques; Children's corner; Etudes: Pour les cinq doigts d'après M. Czerny; Pour les arpèges composés. Images: Poissons d'or. L'Isle joyeuse; Le petit nègre; La plus que lente; Préludes, Book I: Des pas sur la neige; Book II: Ondine; La terrasse des audiences du clair de lune; Feux d'artifice. Suite bergamasque: Prélude.
☞ (B) *** CfP Dig. CD-CFP 4653; *TC-CF 4653*. Moura Lympany.

Although it is more convenient for collectors if Debussy's piano works are assembled, like Chopin's, in genres for recording purposes, his music can be the more potent when presented in a carefully chosen recital of this kind. Dame Moura Lympany's choice cannot be faulted and this is among the finest recitals of its kind in the catalogue. The poised elegance of the opening *Prélude* from *Suite bergamasque* immediately sets the seal on playing of character and distinction: the subtle colouring of *La plus que lente* is as impressive as the power and glowing ardour of the closing *L'Isle joyeuse*. The *Arabesques* are played rhapsodically with distinct individuality and there are few finer or more imaginative performances of *Children's corner*, here presented as children's imagery seen through adult eyes. Among the *Préludes* the remarkably compelling *La terrasse des audiences du clair de lune* comes over as truly impressionistic in feeling rather than in any way pictorial. *Feux d'artifice* flashes with brilliance. The whole recital emerges as a spontaneous experience, and it is worth noting that the pianist was 76 years young when she went into EMI's Abbey Road Studio to make this record, which is very realistically recorded indeed. The notes by Peter Avis are a model of what documentation for a miscellaneous recital should be.

2 Arabesques; Children's corner; Préludes, Book 2: Feux d'artifice; Images, Books I & II; Pour le piano; Suite bergamasque: Clair de lune.
☞ (B) ** Sony SBK 48174 [id.]. Philippe Entremont.

This 73-minute recital derives from two different sources. The disc opens with a singularly angular and unevocative Clair de lune and continues with the two Arabesques from an early 1959 recital. The performances recorded then (in a New York studio) were clean and robust, but showing little delicacy of feeling and wanting in the kind of atmosphere this music ideally demands. The piano timbre was clean and clear; it was also rather hard, in the manner of CBS engineering of the early stereo era. However, Pour le piano, Images I and II and Children's corner were recorded when Entremont was in Paris in July 1963. The French ambience obviously affected him and the playing here is of an altogether different calibre; indeed the Images are remarkably evocative. The recording is still up-front but the performances triumph over the less than distinguished sound.

2 Arabesques; Images oubliées; Préludes, Book 1.
*** ASV Dig. CDDCA 720 [id.]. Gordon Fergus-Thompson.

Ballade; Berceuse héroïque; Danse; Danse bohémienne; D'un cahier d'esquisses; Elégie; Hommage à Haydn; L'isle joyeuse; Masques; Mazurka; Morceau de concours; Nocturne; Page d'album; Le petit nègre; La plus que lente; Valse romantique.
*** ASV Dig. CDDCA 711 [id.]. Gordon Fergus-Thompson.

Children's corner; Estampes; Images, I & II.
*** ASV Dig. CDDCA 695 [id.]. Gordon Fergus-Thompson.

Etudes, Books 1–2; Pour le piano.
*** ASV Dig. CDDCA 703 [id.]. Gordon Fergus-Thompson.

Préludes. Book 2; Suite bergamasque.
*** ASV Dig. CDDCA 723 [id.]. Gordon Fergus-Thompson.

Gordon Fergus-Thompson's survey maintains a consistently high standard of artistry. If one places his sets of Préludes alongside recordings by Arrau or Gieseking, then they are clearly less individually distinctive, but overall this playing shows a genuine feeling for the Debussy palette and, with fine, modern, digital sound, these records will give considerable satisfaction. The collection of shorter pieces is particularly successful.

2 Arabesques; Ballade; Danse bohémienne; Images I–II; Images (1894); Mazurka; Nocturne.
☞ (M) *** Saga EC 3376-2 [id.]. Lívia Rév.

For a long time Lívia Rév was underrated as a pianist; it was these Debussy recordings which established her reputation, receiving just acclaim when they first appeared on CD. This compilation (77 minutes 38 seconds) can hold its own with any in the catalogue. Lívia Rév has sensibility, a finely developed sense of colour, a keen awareness of atmosphere and fleet fingers. She is moreover decently recorded in a spacious acoustic, and the CD transfers are extremely successful.

2 Arabesques; Ballade; Images, Book 1; L'isle joyeuse; La plus que lente; Rêverie; Suite bergamasque.
*** Conifer Dig. CDCF 148; MCFC 148 [id.]. Kathryn Stott.

Kathryn Stott assembles an admirable recital which spans Debussy's composing career from the Deux Arabesques of 1888, through to La plus que lente (1910). She is unerringly sensitive to atmosphere, there is no lack of finesse and her impetuosity always sounds spontaneous. This is a very refreshing programme, given excellent realism and presence.

2 Arabesques; Ballade; Images, Book 1: Reflets dans l'eau; Mouvement. Book 2: Poissons d'or. L'isle joyeuse; Préludes, Book 2: Feux d'artifice. Suite bergamasque.
(M) *** EMI CD-EMX 2055-2; TC-EMX 2055. Daniel Adni.

This collection dates from 1972 and is outstanding in every way: this young Israeli pianist proves himself a Debussian of no mean order. His recital is well planned and offers playing that is as poetic in feeling as it is accomplished in technique.

2 Arabesques; Berceuse héroïque; D'un cahier d'esquisses; Hommage à Haydn; Images, Books 1 & 2; L'isle joyeuse; Page d'album; Rêverie.
⊛ *** Ph. Dig. 422 404-2 Zoltán Kocsis.

Artistically, this new recital is if anything even more distinguished in terms of pianistic finesse, sensitivity and tonal refinement than Kocsis's earlier (1983) Debussy collection – see below.

2 Arabesques; Children's corner; Images I and II; Suite bergamasque.
(M) *** Decca 417 792-2. Pascal Rogé.

Pascal Rogé's playing is distinguished by a keen musical intelligence and sympathy, as well as by a subtle command of keyboard colour. The well-defined Decca sound is most realistic.

2 Arabesques; L'isle joyeuse; Masques; La plus que lente; Pour le piano; Suite bergamasque; Tarantelle styrienne (Danse).
(B) *** DG 429 517-2 [id.]. Tamás Vásáry.

Vásáry is at his very best in the *Suite bergamasque*, and *Clair de lune* is beautifully played, as are the *Arabesques*. *La plus que lente* receives the least convincing performance. But overall this is a satisfying recital, particularly as the piano is so realistic.

Berceuse héroïque; Children's corner suite; Danse; D'un cahier d'esquisses; Mazurka; Morceau de concours; Nocturne; Le petit nègre; La plus que lente; Rêverie.
*** Denon Dig. C37 7372 [id.]. Jacques Rouvier.

An enjoyable and interesting Debussy recital from Jacques Rouvier, which has the advantage of very truthful recording. This serves as a very useful addition to the catalogue and can be thoroughly recommended.

Berceuse héroïque; D'un cahier d'esquisses; Etudes, Books 1–2; Morceau de concours; Suite bergamasque.
☞ (M) *** Saga EC 3383-2 [id.]. Lívia Rév.

Lívia Rév is consistently imaginative and her playing has considerable poetic feeling, as well as great technical accomplishment. The *Suite bergamasque* is also highly sensitive. The 1980 recording is excellent and the disc offers 75 minutes of music.

Children's corner; Elégie; Hommage à Haydn; Page d'album; Préludes, Book 1; La plus que lente; Tarantelle styrienne (Danse).
☞ (M) *** Saga EC 3377-2 [id.]. Lívia Rév.

Lívia Rév plays *Children's corner* very well, and her performance of the *Préludes* holds its own in terms of sensitivity and atmosphere. Her keyboard mastery is beyond question (just sample *La cathédrale engloutie*) and she is a fine colourist. The recording, too, is first class.

Children's corner; Images, Sets 1 & 2.
*** DG 414 372-2 [id.]. Michelangeli.

Michelangeli has made few records, but this is one of his best. It is also among the most distinguished Debussy playing in the catalogue. The remastering of the 1971 recording has been wonderfully successful.

Estampes; Images I & II; Images oubliées (1894); Pour le piano.
*** Denon Dig. CD 1411 [id.]. Jacques Rouvier.

Jacques Rouvier is very well recorded; there is plenty of atmosphere and space round the sound. His account of the *Cloche à travers les feuilles* has great poise and *Et la lune descend sur le temple qui fut* has wonderful atmosphere and repose.

Estampes; Images, Books 1–2; Préludes, Books 1–2.
(M) *** Ph. 432 304-2 (2) [id.]. Claudio Arrau.

Claudio Arrau's versions of these solo piano works by Debussy are very distinguished. The piano timbre in these 1978/9 analogue recordings has a consistent body and realism typical of this company's finest work.

Etudes, Books 1–2.
❀ *** Ph. Dig. 422 412-2 [id.]. Mitsuko Uchida.
☞ ** DG Dig. 423 678-2 [id.]. Maurizio Pollini – BERG: *Sonata, Op. 1.*

Mitsuko Uchida's remarkable account of the *Etudes* on Philips is not only one of the best Debussy piano records in the catalogue and arguably her finest recording, but also one of the best ever recordings of the instrument.

   In terms of atmosphere and poetic feeling Pollini is no match for Uchida on Philips. He offers impressive and distinguished pianisim but there is little sense of magic; no doubt the rather close and analytical recording-balance reinforces this impression. In climaxes there is also a certain hardness.

6 Etudes.
☞ ** Collins Dig. 14042 [id.]. Joanna MacGregor – BARTÓK: *6 Dances* etc.; RAVEL: *Alborada* etc. **

The claims of Joanna MacGregor's Collins discs are somewhat diminished since she gives us only six of the *Douze Etudes.* She came into prominence with the Hugh Wood *Piano concerto* some years ago and is a player of virtuosity and great tonal refinement.

Pour le piano: Sarabande. La plus que lente; Suite bergamasque; Valse romantique.
☞ ** Ph. Dig. 434 626-2 [id.]. Claudio Arrau.

Claudio Arrau's numerous admirers will want everything he recorded, and for them this CD of his final sessions, recorded in 1991 when he was eighty-eight, will be self-recommending. All the same, it must be conceded that his earlier Debussy set of the *Préludes, Estampes* and both sets of *Images* better represents him and must carry priority over the present limited edition, containing 40 minutes of Debussy – at full price. The rich Arrau sonority is still discernible, but the disc as a whole is sad: the *Suite bergamasque* is laboured, as is in particular the *Passpied.* The *Sarabande,* too, is very slow.

Préludes, Books 1–2 (complete).
⊛ (M) *** EMI mono CDH7 61004-2 [id.]. Walter Gieseking.
(M) *** Pickwick Dig. MCD 16; *M CC 16.* Martino Tirimo.
☞ *** DG Dig. 435 773-2 (2) [id.]. Krystian Zimerman.

Gieseking penetrates the atmosphere of the *Préludes* more deeply than almost any other artist. This is playing of rare distinction and great evocative quality. However, the documentation is concerned solely with the artist and gives no information about the music save the titles and the cues.

No grumbles about value for money or about quality from Martino Tirimo on Pickwick; he accommodates both Books on the same disc. His playing is very fine indeed and can withstand comparison with most of his rivals – and, apart from the sensitivity of the playing, the recording is most realistic and natural. This is first choice for those wanting a modern digital record offering the complete set.

There is no want of atmosphere or poetic feeling in Krystian Zimerman's account of the *Préludes.* This is a very distinguished performance indeed, though some may find the level of intensity too much to live with. Every note, whether the quietest of pianissimi or the strongest fortissimo, is highly charged. But if Zimerman makes a meal of every small detail, his playing is imaginative and concentrated. The DG recording is analytical, far more sensitively balanced than, say, the Pollini CD of the *Etudes,* but even so there is more than a hint of hardness in climaxes.

Préludes, Book 1; Images.
☞ * Sony. Dig. SK 52583 [id.]. Paul Crossley.

Paul Crossley has rightly excited much admiration over the years, particularly in Messiaen, Fauré, Ravel and the French repertoire, for which his fastidious temperament and finesse admirably equip him. Nor should his impressive readings of the Tippett sonatas be forgotten. It is all the more surprising, then, to find his Sony set of the First Book of *Préludes* so curiously unsatisfying. He proves in this instance to be what can euphemistically be described as an excessively attentive interpreter. Both the *Préludes* and the *Images* are marred by wilful and narcissistic rubato; rarely does he allow Debussy's muse to have its natural sway; rarely does he permit the music to flow without intrusive, agogic distortion. He produces some of the beautiful sonorities one has come to expect from such a sensitive player but, in this instance, sounds seem to matter more than musical sense. One or two pieces come off well, but that is not really good enough. Good recording.

Préludes, Book I; Images oubliées (1894).
☞ (M) **(*) Channel Classics Dig. CCS 4892 [id.]. Jos van Immerseel.

The special interest of Jos van Immerseel's recording of the first book of *Préludes* lies in his instrument, an Erard of 1897, of the kind which Debussy would have known and played. The sonority is gentle and veiled and curiously seductive except in *forte* passages; the timbre, particularly in the upper register of the instrument, is monochrome and dry, and this tells in a piece such as *La sérénade interrompue.* There is a real turn-of-the-century feel to the shadowy sound-world of *Des pas sur la neige* and the first of the *Images oubliées.* An interesting appendix for a Debussy discography, but essentially this is an issue for specialist collections.

Préludes, Book 2 (complete).
☞ (M) *** Saga EC 3347-2 [id.]. Lívia Rév.

Lívia Rév here again proves a highly sensitive and accomplished artist. Her account of Book 2 of the

Préludes has stiff competition but holds its own against all comers. She receives a very good recording, and the only disadvantage to this issue is its meagre playing time (39 minutes), although this is another case where the quality makes up for the lack of quantity. The other three CDs in her Saga series each comprise well over 70 minutes.

La demoiselle élue.

☞ (B) **(*) Pickwick PCD 1037; *PK 515* [id.]. Caballé, Coster, Ambrosian Ladies Ch., L.
  Symphonica, Wyn Morris – CHAUSSON: *Poème de l'amour et de la mer.* **(*)

Debussy's early cantata, *La damoiselle élue*, has been seriously neglected on record. It is a highly evocative setting of Rossetti in translation, using women's chorus and mezzo-soprano solo for the central role of the Blessed Damozel. This richly expressive performance is focused on Caballé's radiant account of the principal solo, with her timbre sometimes suggesting her compatriot, Victoria de Los Angeles. She produces ecstatic high pianissimos and, even if at times she allows sensuous scooping up to notes and her French enunciation is idiosyncratic, this is a beautiful and involving performance. The warmly atmospheric recording, bringing out some unexpected *Parsifal* echoes, is very well transferred to CD, and altogether this Pickwick reissue is an excellent bargain.

Le Martyre de Saint Sébastien (incidental music): complete.

☞ *** Sony Dig. SK 48240 [id.]. Leslie Caron; McNair, Murray, L. Symphony Ch., LSO, Tilson
  Thomas.
☞ (**(*)) Decca mono 423 400-2. Danco, Waugh, De Montmollin, Union Chorale de La Tour-de-
  Pielz, SRO, Ansermet – RAVEL: *L'enfant et les sortilèges; L'heure espagnole.* **(*)

It was in 1910 that Debussy was asked to provide music for the decadent drama *Le Martyre de Saint-Sébastien* by Gabriele d'Annunzio. He did it unashamedly as a rush job for money. He had to bring in as helper his friend, André Caplet, so as to meet the deadline of two months for the hour of music required – a task, he said, that would normally have taken a year. The result is a problem work, for the original entertainment lasted no less than five hours, much of it distasteful. It crudely distorts the saint's Christian message in order to fit the author's fascist philosophy of 'strength through joy', a key phrase in the full text which raises uncomfortable memories of the Nazi period. Working against the clock, Debussy produced music that is far less concentrated than in his major masterpieces, but its sweetness and simplicity often point forward to his late works. Michael Tilson Thomas here records the complete incidental music in a form that the composer approved, using a narrator, Leslie Caron, to provide the spoken links between sections. What it shows is how much richer and more varied the complete score is than the usual symphonic fragments. This is as near an ideal performance as could be imagined, with Sylvia McNair singing radiantly in the principal soprano roles, with brilliant playing from the LSO, and glorious recording which brings out the full atmospheric beauty of the choral singing, often off-stage.

  In its day Ansermet's 1954 account of *Le Martyre* was widely admired (it has the undoubted merit of fine soloists) though others have subsequently succeeded in distilling greater mystery and atmosphere. Nevertheless it has no want of style and can be recommended not only to the great Swiss conductor's many admirers but those who love this score. The work is split across two CDs so that the two Ravel operas which come with this package are heard without interruption.

OPERA

La chute de la Maison Usher (unfinished opera, arr. Blin).

☞ (M) *** EMI CDM7 64687-2 [id.]. Barbaux, Lafont, Le Roux, Le Maigat, Monte Carlo PO,
  Prêtre – CAPLET: *Masque* **(*); SCHMIDT: *Palais hanté.* ***

In the last years of his life Debussy was obsessed with the idea of writing two one-Act operas on stories by Edgar Allan Poe, a more potent force in France than in the English-speaking world, thanks above all to the superb prose translations of Poe made by Baudelaire. When Debussy died, even the sketches for his Poe project had disappeared; but in the 1970s the Chilean scholar and composer, Juan Allende Blin, put together the rediscoverd fragments of one of the two operas, *The Fall of the House of Usher*, and managed to reconstitute 400 bars of music. Debussy left the most scanty indications concerning the orchestration and the scoring is the work of Allende Blin himself. The music has extraordinary novelty, great harmonic freedom and a liberty of prosodic treatment far surpassing *Pelléas*. The music that Allende Blin rescued amounts to a little under half of the projected work, which would have taken just under an hour. The score has a great sense of mystery in the manner of *Jeux* and, perhaps, *Le martyre*, and is a real discovery. It makes, if not a full dramatic entertainment, at least a fascinating cantata, very original indeed, and very well performed here in this first commercial recording in which Jean-Philip Lafont is outstanding in the baritone role of Roderick, the doomed central character. The direction of Georges Prêtre is dedicated and the 1983 recording, although an example of early digital techniques, is reasonably atmospheric. Alas, the documentation is almost non-existent, with the libretto included with the original issue now omitted (and much more space given to the narrative background of the Caplet *Conte fantastique*). However, the fine performance and apt coupling suggest that Debussians who missed this CD first time round should snap it up now without delay.

Pelléas et Mélisande (complete).

*** DG Dig. 435 344-2 (2) [id.]. Ewing, Le Roux, Van Dam, Courtis, Ludwig, Pace, Mazzola, Vienna Konzertvereingung, VPO, Abbado.

*** Decca Dig. 430 502-2 (2) [id.]. Alliot-Lugaz, Henry, Cachemaille, Thau, Carlson, Golfier, Montreal Ch. & SO, Dutoit.

(M) **(*) Sony SM3K 47265 (3) [id.]. Shirley, Söderström, McIntyre, Ward, Minton, ROHCG Ch. & O, Boulez.

☞ (***) EMI mono CHS7 61038-2 (3). Joachim, Jansen, Etcheverry, Paris CO, Désormière (with *Mélodies*).

☞ (***) Decca mono 425 965-2 (2). Danco, Mollet, Rehfuss, SRO, Ansermet.

☞ (***) Ph. mono 434 783-2 (2). Micheau, Maurane, Roux, LOP, Fournet.

Abbado's outstanding version broadly resolves the problem of a first recommendation in this opera, which has always been lucky on record. If among modern versions the choice has been hard to make between Karajan's sumptuously romantic account, almost Wagnerian, and Dutoit's clean-cut, direct one, Abbado satisfyingly presents a performance more sharply focused than the one and more freely flexible than the other, altogether more urgently dramatic. The casting is excellent, with no weak link.

Charles Dutoit brings out the magic of Debussy's score with an involving richness typical of that venue which has played so important a part in the emergence of the Montreal orchestra into the world of international recording. This is not the dreamy reading which some Debussians might prefer, but one which sets the characters very specifically before us as creatures of flesh and blood, not mistily at one remove.

Boulez's sharply dramatic view of Debussy's atmospheric score is a performance which will probably not please the dedicated Francophile – for one thing there is not a single French-born singer in the cast – but it rescues Debussy from the languid half-tone approach which for too long has been accepted as authentic. He is supported by a strong cast; the singing is not always very idiomatic but it has the musical and dramatic momentum which stems from sustained experience on the stage. In almost every way this has the tension of a live performance.

Roger Désormière's wartime recording with Irène Joachim as Mélisande, Jacques Jansen as Pelléas and Henri-Bertrand Etcheverry's powerful Golaud is still in circulation. Made in 1942, it still has a special claim on the collector's attention in spite of its sonic limitations. Etcheverry is arguably the most strongly characterized Golaud committed to disc, and neither Joachim's Mélisande nor Jansen's Pelléas has been readily surpassed. A *Pelléas* without atmosphere is no *Pelléas*, and this classic reading puts you under its spell immediately. Perhaps wartime conditions served to heighten the special Gallic qualities one feels on encountering this. Like so many pre-war performances, it is distinguished not only by wonderful singing but also by marvellous articulation and there is a sense that every detail is in the right perspective and every nuance perfectly inflected. A further inducement for collectors is a generous selection of Debussy songs from Maggie Teyte and the celebrated recording of *Mes longs cheveux* by the original Mélisande, Mary Garden, accompanied on the piano by Debussy himself in 1904. A very special – indeed indispensable – set.

Ansermet's recording of *Pelléas* first appeared in 1952 and caused something of a stir at the time; silent surfaces – essential in this of all operas – were something of a novelty at the period. Ansermet puts us immediately under his spell and, although there are weaknesses in the Suisse Romande Orchestra (a vinegary oboe and wiry upper strings), these can easily be corrected on high-grade equipment – and in any event they are of little significance. Vocally, the set is not as striking as the Désormière, but the Mélisande of Suzanne Danco has a radiance and purity that are unforgettable. Heinz Rehfuss is a Golaud of appropriate menace and there are few real weaknesses, even if Pierre Mollet's Pelléas is not always at ease. However, this remains one of the best recordings of the opera and one of the finest performances from Ansermet's baton. The transfer comes up very well indeed.

The success of the Ansermet rather overshadowed Jean Fournet's recording, made in Paris only a year later. It had Camille Maurane at the height of his powers and a memorable Mélisande in Janine Micheau, who was a brilliant coloratura singer, if not quite as other-worldly as Danco. However, Fournet is absolutely steeped in Debussy's world and yields nothing in terms of magic or atmosphere to his rivals; and the Golaud of Michel Roux is powerful. The sound may be less finely detailed but the orchestra is better than Ansermet's Suisse Romande.

Delalande, Michel-Richard (1657–1726)

Symphonies pour les soupers du roy (complete).
*** HM Dig. HMC 901337/40; *HMC 401337/40* (4) [id.]. Ensemble La Simphonie du Marais, Reyne.

In the last years of his life, Louis XIV could choose from among a dozen suites to accompany his meal. This is the first time all have been committed to disc. Each of these four CDs contains between 36 and 45 individual movements, much of it as charming and inventive as the familiar excerpts. The young members of the Ensemble La Simphonie du Marais, led by Hugo Reyne, give thoroughly fresh and stylish accounts of them.

Confitebor tibi Domine; Super flumina Babilonis; Te Deum.
*** HM Dig. HMC 901351; *HMC 401351* [id.]. Gens, Piau, Steyer, Fouchécourt, Piolino, Corréas, Les Arts Florissants, Christie.

Confitebor tibi Domine (1699) and *Super flumina Babilonis* (1687) have much expressive writing, and the performances under William Christie are light and airy but not wanting in expressive feeling. The more familiar *Te Deum* is given as good a performance as any that has appeared in recent years. The sound is airy and spacious and the performances combine lightness and breadth.

Delibes, Léo (1836–91)

Coppélia (ballet): complete.
☞ *** Erato/Warner Dig. 4509 91730-2 (2) [id.]. Lyon Opéra O, Kent Nagano.
*** Decca Dig. 414 502-2 (2) [id.]. Nat. PO, Bonynge.
(M) *** Decca 425 472-2 (2). SRO, Richard Bonynge – MASSENET: *Le Carillon.* ***
☞ (B) **(*) Ph. 438 763-2 [id.]. Rotterdam PO, David Zinman – CHOPIN: *Les Sylphides;* GOUNOD: *Faust: ballet music.* **(*)

Delibes's delightful score for *Coppélia*, which Tchaikovsky admired so much, is available in a number of different formats, but Kent Nagano's new complete set rises fairly easily to the top of the current list of recommendations. The performance has many felicities and the Orchestre de L'Opéra de Lyon bring a sure sense of style to this elegantly crafted and engagingly tuneful music. Their playing is polished, yet warm and graceful and, under the lively yet nicely detailed direction of Kent Nagano, the spontaneity of the music-making seems to grow as the ballet proceeds. Act II, in which most of the action takes place, is full of delights, and the scene where Coppelius brings his 'daughter' to life (actually the heroine, Swanhilda, in disguise) is most evocative, with the clockwork automata deliciously caught. The ballet ends with a grand divertissement and the various dances are played with winning character, the brass and woodwind vying with each other in colour until the exhilarating closing Galop. The recording has a nicely judged acoustic, warm yet clear, full yet not too cloudily resonant but giving bloom to the violins in their many lithe and debonair turns of phrase – the *Valse de la poupée* in Act II a winning example. The set is not generous in playing time – 99 minutes overall – but every bar of the music-making is of the highest quality.

The only slight drawback to Bonynge's digital recording is the relatively modest number of violins which the clarity of the digital recording makes apparent. In moments like the delicious *Scène et valse de la poupée*, which Bonynge points very stylishly, the effect is Mozartian in its grace. But the full body of strings above the stave lacks something in amplitude, and the fortissimos bring a digital emphasis on brilliance that is not wholly natural. In all other respects the recording is praiseworthy, not only for its vividness of colour but for the balance within a concert-hall acoustic (Walthamstow Assembly Hall). Bonynge secures a high degree of polish from the Swiss Romande Orchestra, with sparkling string and wind textures and sonority and bite from the brass. The Decca recording sounds freshly minted and, with its generous Massenet bonus, little-known music of great charm, this set remains very competitive.

David Zinman's performance of *Coppélia* is beautifully played and most naturally recorded. The warm acoustic of the Rotterdam concert hall certainly suits Delibes's colourful scoring and the gracefully delicate string-playing is nicely flattered. The performance has no want of vigour or refinement and, if it is without the sheer character of Jean-Baptiste Mari's performance, it is still very enjoyable in its own right. The Chopin and Gounod couplings are similarly smooth and elegant, and all are offered at the cost of one premium-priced CD.

(i) *Coppélia* (ballet): complete; *Sylvia* (ballet): complete.
☞ (M) *** Mercury 434 313-2 (3) [id.]. (i) Minneapolis SO, Dorati; (ii) LSO, Fistoulari.

EMI passed up the opportunity to reissue Mari's fine complete recordings of these two ballets with the Paris Opéra Orchestra, and it has been left to Mercury to fill the gap, which they do admirably. Both recordings are very early stereo (*Coppélia* 1957, *Sylvia* 1958), but neither sounds its age and *Sylvia*, using the expansive acoustics of Watford Town Hall, approaches the demonstration bracket. Fistoulari was among the very greatest of ballet interpreters and this shows him at his most inspired. The conductor displays his deep affection for the ballet in every bar; his sense of delicacy and grace and his feeling for the specially French elegance of the woodwind writing are demonstrated throughout. The LSO play superbly for him, the woodwind ensemble is outstanding and the solo playing most beautiful. The principal horn in particular offers a relaxed limpidity that is strikingly lovely and he has much to play. There are some ravishing passages from the strings, especially when muted, and the luminous quality of the pianissimos is matched by the expansive, exciting climaxes.

Dorati's recording of *Coppélia* makes a lively contrast. This Minneapolis recording has never sounded better than it does here. The acoustic is rather more confined at the bottom end, but the conductor's vivid combination of energy and grace is appealing in a score that teems with bright melodies and piquant orchestral effects. The orchestral playing is less sleekly nurtured than the LSO in *Sylvia* but, with neatly pointed strings and nicely turned woodwind solos (although the oboe is small-timbred and reedy), this is very enjoyable and stimulating, a good contrast to the pastel colouring of the companion score. Highly recommended.

Coppélia: extended excerpts: Act I, Nos. 1–7; 7 bis; Act II, Nos. 11–14; 16–17; Act III, Nos. 1–10.
☞ *** ROH Dig. ROH 006; *ROMC 006* [id.]. ROHCG O, Mark Ermler.

As can be seen above, the (74 minutes) single CD selection by the Royal Opera House, Covent Garden, Orchestra under Mark Ermler is pretty comprehensive; the string playing is full of character and grace and there are delightful contributions from the woodwind soloists and horns. Those seeking modern digital sound should be well satisfied, for the recording is full and spacious, with resonant brass and an attractive ambient bloom. There are good notes, but the narrative is not related to the individual cues. However, Mari's selection is equally generous, and the Paris orchestral playing is especially seductive. The sound is marginally less opulent, but then the EMI Rouge et Noir set includes a comparable selection from *Sylvia* at the same cost – see below.

Coppélia: extended excerpts; *Sylvia:* extended excerpts.
(B) *** EMI CZS7 67208-2 (2); *EG 764265-4*. Paris Op. O, Mari.

Jean-Baptiste Mari's pair of CDs are offered for the price of one in the French Rouge et Noir series. The sound is fresh and the extra brightness of focus brings no attendant edginess. Mari uses ballet tempi throughout, yet there is never any loss of momentum, and the long-breathed string phrasing and the felicitous wind solos are a continual source of delight. Mari's natural sympathy and warmth make the very most of the less memorable parts of the score for *Sylvia* (and they are only slightly less memorable). Seventy-five minutes is offered from each ballet. The cassette gives a shorter selection but still plays for over 80 minutes.

Coppélia (ballet): suite.
☞ (B) *** DG Double 437 404-2 (2) [id.]. BPO, Karajan – CHOPIN: *Les Sylphides* *** ⊛; GOUNOD: *Faust* etc. **(*); OFFENBACH: *Gaîté parisienne;* RAVEL: *Boléro* ***; TCHAIKOVSKY: *Sleeping Beauty* (suite). **(*)

(i) *Coppélia* (ballet) suite; (ii) *Sylvia* (ballet) suite.
(M) *** Sony SBK 46550 [id.]. Phd. O, Ormandy – CHOPIN: *Les Sylphides* ***; TCHAIKOVSKY: *Nutcracker suite*. **(*)

Ormandy and the Philadelphia Orchestra are on top form here. The playing sparkles and has a fine sense of style. Both suites are done in a continuous presentation but are, unfortunately, not banded. The recording is notably full and brilliant in the CBS manner.

Karajan secures some wonderfully elegant playing from the Berlin Philharmonic Orchestra, and generally his lightness of touch is sure; the *Csárdás*, however, is played very slowly. The recording is impressive and DG have now returned the suite to its original format so that the three movements omitted on its last appearance have been restored. Other ballet music has now been added, plus Ravel's ubiquitous *Boléro*, all played with considerable panache.

Coppélia: suite; *Kassya: Trepak; Le roi s'amuse:* suite; *La Source:* suite; *Sylvia:* suite.
(BB) **(*) Naxos Dig. 8.550080; *4550080* [id.]. Slovak RSO (Bratislava), Ondrej Lenárd.

An attractive hour of Delibes, with five key items from *Coppélia*, including the *Music for the Automatons* and *Waltz*, four from *Sylvia*, not forgetting the *Pizzicato*, and four from *La Source*. Perhaps most enjoyable of all are the six pastiche ancient airs de danse, provided for a ballroom scene in Victor Hugo's play, *Le roi s'amuse*. They are played most gracefully here, and the excerpts from the major ballets are spirited and nicely turned. The brightly lit digital sound has body too, and the acoustics of the Bratislava Concert Hall are not unflattering to Delibes's vivid palette.

La Source (ballet): Act II; Act III, scene i.
*** Decca Dig. 421 431-2 (2). ROHCG O, Bonynge – MINKUS: *La Source* (Act I; Act III, scene ii); DRIGO: *La Flûte magique.* ***

The composition of the music for *La Source* was divided between two composers, the established Minkus and the younger Delibes who begins the Second Act in the elegantly lightweight style of his colleague; but soon his stronger musical personality asserts itself with a romantic horn tune and, later, an even more memorable melody in the strings. His felicitous use of the orchestral palette is readily discernible; but, even so, this is clearly a forerunner for *Coppélia* and *Sylvia* from a composer whose style is not yet fully individualized. Bonynge makes the music sparkle throughout, and the warm yet vivid sound is out of Decca's top drawer.

Sylvia (ballet): complete.
(M) *** Decca 425 475-2 (2). New Philh. O, Richard Bonynge – MASSENET: *Le Cid.* ***

Sylvia is played here with wonderful polish and affection, and the recording is full, brilliant and sparkling in Decca's best manner. The CDs offer a splendid Massenet bonus, another recording out of Decca's top drawer.

OPERA

Lakmé (complete).
(M) *** Decca 425 485-2 (2). Sutherland, Berbié, Vanzo, Bacquier, Monte Carlo Op. Ch. and O, Bonynge.

Lakmé is a strange work, not at all the piece one would expect knowing simply the famous *Bell song*. This performance seizes its opportunities with both hands. Sutherland swallows her consonants, but the beauty of her singing, with its ravishing ease and purity up to the highest register, is what matters; and she has opposite her one of the most pleasing and intelligent of French tenors, Alain Vanzo. Excellent contributions from the others too, spirited conducting and brilliant, atmospheric recording.

Delius, Frederick (1862–1934)

Air and dance for string orchestra; Fennimore and Gerda: Intermezzo. Hassan: Intermezzo and Serenade (arr. Beecham). *Irmelin: Prelude. Koanga: La Calinda. On hearing the first cuckoo in spring; Sleigh ride; A song before sunrise; Summer evening* (ed. Beecham); *Summer night on the river.*
☞ (M) *** EMI Dig. CDM5 65067-2 [id.]. N. Sinfonia, Richard Hickox.

Richard Hickox's 1985 Delius collection neatly brings together most of the shorter pieces in finely shaped, well-played readings, recorded in aptly atmospheric sound. Hickox's warm moulding of phrase goes with fine playing from the Northern Sinfonia. This is currently the best-recorded of the post-Beecham digital collections. However, Marriner's comparable analogue CD also offers lovely sound-quality and is much more generous in including also *Sea drift*.

Air and dance; Fennimore and Gerda: Intermezzo. Hassan: Intermezzo and Serenade; Koanga: La Calinda. On hearing the first cuckoo in spring; A Song before sunrise; Summer night on the river; A Village Romeo and Juliet: The Walk to the Paradise Garden. (i) *Sea Drift.*
☞ (M) *** Decca 440 323-2 [id.]. ASMF, Marriner; (ii) John Shirley-Quirk, L. Symphony Ch., RPO, Hickox.

This orchestral collection was admirably recorded in 1977, but the quality is not in the least dated. These are lovely performances, warm, tender and eloquent. They are played superbly and recorded in a flattering acoustic. The recording is beautifully balanced – the distant cuckoo is highly evocative – though, with a relatively small band of strings, the sound inevitably has less body than with a full orchestral group. *Sea Drift* was recorded (also by Argo engineers) three years later in 1980 and is a total success. Rather than lingering, Richard Hickox is urgent in his expressiveness, but there is plenty of evocative atmosphere. John Shirley-Quirk sings with characteristic sensitivity and the chorus – trained by Hickox – is outstanding. The effect of the CD transfer is most real and tangible, the chorus set back within a warm ambience.

American rhapsody (Appalachia); Norwegian suite (Folkeraadet: The Council of the people); Paa Vidderne (On the heights); Spring morning.
** Marco Polo 8.220452 [id.]. Slovak PO, Bratislava, John Hopkins.

A fascinating collection of early Delius, mostly uncharacteristic, but with pre-echoes of his later work. *Paa Vidderne*, the most substantial piece, is rather melodramatic but has a distinct melodic interest. *Spring morning* is shorter and similarly picaresque, but the *Folkeraadet suite* displays a sure orchestral touch and is most attractive in its diversity of invention. The *American rhapsody* is a concise version of *Appalachia* without the chorus, given here in its original 1896 format. John Hopkins brings a strong sympathy and understanding to this repertoire and secures a committed and flexible response from his Czech players in music which must have been wholly unknown to them.

2 Aquarelles (arr. Fenby); *Fennimore and Gerda: Intermezzo. Hassan: Intermezzo and serenade* (all arr. Beecham); *Irmelin: Prelude. Late swallows* (arr. Fenby); *On hearing the first cuckoo in spring; A Song before sunrise; Summer night on the river.*
(M) *** Chan. CHAN 6502; *MBTD 6502* [id.]. Bournemouth Sinf., Norman Del Mar.

There are few finer interpreters of Delius than the late Norman Del Mar. The 49-minute concert creates a mood of serene, atmospheric evocation – into which Eric Fenby's arrangement of *Late swallows* from the *String quartet* fits admirably – and the beauty of the 1977 analogue recording has been transferred very well to CD, with all its warmth and bloom retained.

2 Aquarelles; Fennimore and Gerda: Intermezzo. On hearing the first cuckoo in spring; Summer night on the river.
☞ (M) *** DG 439 529-2 [id.]. ECO, Barenboim – VAUGHAN WILLIAMS: *Lark ascending* etc.;
   WALTON: *Henry V.* ***

Barenboim's luxuriant performances have a gorgeous sensuousness and their warm, sleepy atmosphere should seduce many normally resistant to Delius's pastoralism. The couplings are no less enticing; indeed, some might feel that this music-making has a touch of decadence in its unalloyed appeal to the senses.

Brigg Fair; Dance rhapsody No. 2; Fennimore and Gerda: Intermezzo. Florida suite; Irmelin: Prelude. Marche-caprice; On hearing the first cuckoo in spring; Over the hills and far away; Sleigh ride; Song before sunrise; Summer evening; Summer night on the river; (i) Songs of sunset.
⊛ *** EMI CDS7 47509-8 (2) [id.]. RPO, Beecham; (i) with Forrester, Cameron, Beecham Ch. Soc.

The remastering of the complete stereo orchestral recordings of Delius's music, plus the choral *Songs of sunset*, is something of a technological miracle. Beecham's fine-spun magic, his ability to lift a phrase, is apparent throughout. In the *Songs of sunset* the choral focus is soft-grained, but the words are surprisingly audible, and the backward balance of the soloists is made to sound natural against the rich orchestral textures. The gramophone here offers music-making which is every bit as rewarding as the finest live performances.

Brigg Fair; Eventyr; In a summer garden; A Song of summer.
(B) *** CfP CD-CFP 4568; *TC-CFP 4568.* Hallé O, Vernon Handley.

Although the tempi are sometimes controversial, Handley is an understanding and exciting Delian, and these pieces are beautifully played. The digital recording is of EMI's best quality, matching clarity of definition with ambient lustre and rich colouring. A bargain.

(i) *Caprice & elegy;* (ii; iii) *Piano concerto;* (iv; v) *Violin concerto;* (vi; iii) *Hassan: Intermezzo and serenade; Koanga: La Calinda;* (v) *On hearing the first cuckoo in spring;* (vii) *Legende for violin and piano.*
☞ (***) Testament mono SBT 1014 [id.]. (i) Beatrice Harrison, CO, Eric Fenby; (ii) Moiseiwitsch,
   Philh. O; (iii) Constant Lambert; (iv) Albert Sammons; (v) Liverpool PO, Sargent; (vi) Hallé 0;
   (vii) Henry Holst, Gerald Moore.

This disc collects early, historic Delius records *not* conducted by Sir Thomas Beecham – and very good many of them are. Its greatest treasure is the first ever recording of the *Violin concerto*, made in 1944 and featuring the original soloist, Albert Sammons, arguably the most eloquent and moving account of the work ever committed to disc. The thrusting passion of the performance comes not just from Sammons but from Sargent and the Liverpool orchestra, confirming this as one of Delius's supreme masterpieces, at once warmly romantic and tautly (if unconventionally) constructed. Moiseiwitsch's recording of the *Piano concerto*, also the first ever, is hardly less powerful, making a very good case for this warm but less cogent piece. The other items range from the 1930 recording of the *Caprice and elegy* by Beatrice Harrison, the dedicatee, with suspect intonation and plentiful portamento, to Sargent's 1947 recording of the *First cuckoo*, very warm and free in its rubato. Constant Lambert is also a first-rate interpreter of Delius, as the *Hassan* and *Koanga* excerpts show. This early example of a Testament transfer has far higher surface-hiss than later issues, but the transfers are astonishingly revealing, and the disc must be as strongly recommended as the Beecham transfers from Dutton – even if these are perhaps more sophisticated.

Cello concerto.
*** BMG/RCA RD 70800. Lloyd Webber, Philh. O, Handley – HOLST: *Invocation;* VAUGHAN
   WILLIAMS: *Fantasia*. ***

Lloyd Webber is inside the idiom and plays the *Cello concerto* with total conviction. Its lyricism is beguiling enough, but the work proceeds in wayward fashion, and the soloist must play every note as if he believes in it ardently – and this Lloyd Webber and his partners do. The RCA recording conveys an almost chamber-like quality at times, with great warmth and clarity.

(i) *Cello concerto;* (ii) *Double concerto for violin and cello. Paris, the song of a great city*.
(M) *** EMI Dig. CD-EMX 2185; *TC-EMX 2185*. (i; ii) Rafael Wallfisch; (ii) Tasmin Little;
   RLPO, Mackerras.

This superb new recording of the *Double concerto*, with soloists who easily outshine their predecessors on record (however distinguished), confirms the strength of a piece which establishes its own logic, with each theme developing naturally out of the preceding one. Wallfisch is just as persuasive in the *Cello concerto*, and Mackerras proves an understanding interpreter of the composer in the big tone-poem, *Paris, the song of a great city*. The recording is comparably full and atmospheric.

Piano concerto in C min.
(B) *** Decca 433 633-2; *433 633-4*. Kars, LSO, Gibson – ELGAR: *Cello concerto* etc. ***

Jean-Rodolphe Kars proves a superb and eloquent advocate of what has previously been thought of as one of Delius's weaker pieces. The LSO under Sir Alexander Gibson provides admirable support, and the 1969 recording preserves an excellent balance between the two. Excellent value.

Violin concerto.
☞ (M) **(*) EMI CDM7 64725-2 [id.]. Sir Yehudi Menuhin, RPO, Meredith Davies – ELGAR:
   Violin concerto. ***

Violin concerto; Légende for violin and orchestra; Suite for violin and orchestra.
*** Unicorn Dig. DKPCD 9040; *DKPC 9040* [id.]. Ralph Holmes, RPO, Handley.

(i) *Violin concerto. 2 Aquarelles* (arr. Fenby); *Dance rhapsodies 1 and 2; Intermezzo from Fennimore and Gerda; Irmelin prelude; On hearing the first cuckoo in spring; Summer night on the river*.
**(*) Decca Dig. 433 704-2 [id.]. (i) Tasmin Little; Welsh Nat. Op. O, Mackerras.

(i) *Violin concerto; Dance rhapsody No. 1;* (ii) *On the mountains. Song of the high hills*.
(M) (***) EMI mono CDM7 64054-2. (i) Pougnet; (ii) Hart, L. Jones, Luton Ch. Soc.; RPO,
   Beecham.

In his intensive analysis of Delius's *Violin concerto* Deryck Cooke completely refuted the suggestion that in this superbly balanced one-movement structure Delius had no grasp of musical logic. Cooke demonstrated the inter-relationship of almost every bar. Holmes and Handley, an ideal partnership, bring out the Delian warmth in their shaping of phrase and pointing of rhythm, while keeping firm control of the overall structure. The *Légende* and the early *Suite* make ideal couplings, played with equal understanding.

Tasmin Little's shading down to hushed pianissimos is ravishing, with the close of the work bringing a moment of total repose, while Mackerras draws strong, sympathetic playing from the orchestra of WNO. The *Dance rhapsodies*, works which similarly are far from rhapsodic, here receive fresh, taut performances, but the forwardness and clarity of the recording tend to make the results less evocative than they might be.

Menuhin's performance, recorded in 1976, does not show the polish of his playing in earlier years, and the timbre is not always ideally sweet; but he gives a heartfelt performance, and the semi-improvisational freedom and radiant beauty of the writing above the stave are superbly caught.

Meredith Davies provides an accompaniment that is full of delicately sensitive detail, if not as richly expressive as Boult's partnership in the coupled Elgar *Concerto*. The Abbey Road recording is truthful, warmly atmospheric and well balanced, to make this an indispensable coupling for lovers of English music.

Glorious performances from Beecham, whose appearance in this splendidly transferred CD cannot be welcomed too warmly. Despite the limited, close-focused mono sound, they perfectly capture the mystery of Delius in these evocative works, while conveying a purposeful sense of structure. Jean Pougnet is persuasively sweet-toned in the *Violin concerto*, but it is the *Song of the high hills* that inspires Beecham to a classic performance, growing ever more sensuous in the final climactic section with wordless chorus, even though here the recording calls for more tolerance on sonic grounds than its companions. *On the Mountains* (*Paa Vidderne*), another Norwegian inspiration, is a welcome rarity.

Eventyr; Fennimore and Gerda: Intermezzo. Irmelin: prelude. Over the hills and far away; Paris, the song of a great city.
(***) Beecham Trust mono BEECHAM 2. LPO, Sir Thomas Beecham.

These recordings date from between 1935 and 1939. The transfers from the original 78 r.p.m. discs were made by the highly skilled Anthony Griffiths, and the further remastering for CD seems to have been entirely beneficial.

Eventyr; North country sketches; Over the hills and far away; (i) *Koanga: closing scene.*
☞ (M) (***) Sony mono SMK 58934 [id.]. RPO, (i) with Ch.; Sir Thomas Beecham.

A particularly valuable reissue offering very successful transfers of Beecham recordings which have not been available for some time and which have never seemed as firm and realistic as this. The orchestral playing is memorably fine, with some superbly romantic horn playing in *Over the hills and far away*. But it is the *North country sketches* that are especially valuable, with translucent sounds from the high violins in *Winter landscape* that are almost Sibelian in feeling. The woodwind shine in the closing *March of spring* and also in the capricious *Eventyr* (*Once upon a time*), where Beecham handles the rhapsodic changes of impetus and dynamic with characteristic passion and subtlety. The closing scene from *Koanga*, full of evocative feeling, makes a fascinating coda with its brief solo and choral sequence. No apologies need be made for the mono recordings – made in 1950–51 – for Beecham was a master of orchestral balance.

Fennimore and Gerda: Intermezzo. Irmelin: Prelude. Koanga: La Calinda (arr. Fenby). *On hearing the first cuckoo in spring; Sleigh ride; A Song before sunrise; Summer night on the river; A Village Romeo and Juliet: The Walk to the Paradise Garden.*
(B) *** CfP CD-CFP 4304; *TC-CFP 40304*. LPO, Vernon Handley.

Those looking for a bargain collection of Delius should find this very good value; Handley's approach to *The Walk to the Paradise Garden* is strongly emotional, closer to Barbirolli than to Beecham.

Florida suite; North Country sketches.
*** Chan. Dig. CHAN 8413; *ABTD 1150* [id.]. Ulster O, Handley.

Handley's choice of tempi is always apt and it is fascinating that in the *North Country sketches* which evoke the seasons in the Yorkshire moors a Debussian influence is revealed. Handley's refined approach clearly links the *Florida suite* with later masterpieces. The recording is superbly balanced within the very suitable acoustics of the Ulster Hall.

(i) *Koanga: La Calinda;* (ii) *Late swallows* (arr. Fenby); (iii) *A Song before sunrise;* (iv) *Cynara;* (v; iii) *Songs of Farewell;* (vi) *To be sung of a summer night on water;* (vii) *Wanderer's song;* (viii) *Margot la Rouge: Prelude. A Village Romeo and Juliet: A Walk to the Paradise Garden.*
☞ (M) *** EMI CDM7 69534-2 [id.]. (i) Philh. O, George Weldon; (ii) Hallé O, Barbirolli; (iii)
    RPO, Sargent; (iv) John Shirley-Quirk, RLPO, Groves; (v) Royal Choral Soc.; (vi) King's
    College, Cambridge, Ch., Ledger; (vii) Baccholian Singers; (viii) RPO, Meredith Davies.

An admirable 71-minute medium-priced anthology, assembled from a wide range of sources but consistently well recorded. It has been in and out of the catalogue before, so is worth snapping up before it disappears again. The programme opens with Sir Malcolm Sargent's gloriously passionate performance of the *Songs of Farewell*, settings of Walt Whitman, with the Royal Choral Society on top form (in 1964) and the RPO strings playing radiantly at the opening of the third song, *Passage to you!*. Sargent also conducts a warmly spontaneous account of *A Song before sunrise*, and Barbirolli is on hand to give a gently rapturous account of *Late swallows*. The euphoric climax of *The Walk to the*

Paradise Garden is superbly realized here under Meredith Davies; John Shirley-Quirk is at his most eloquent in the Dowson setting, *Cynara,* and the unaccompanied choral items are equally successful. The concert ends with the delectable *La Calinda.*

(i) *On hearing the first cuckoo in spring; Summer night on the river;* (ii) *Appalachia;* (iii) *Hassan: Intermezzo and Serenade; Closing Scene;* (iv) *Koanga: Closing Scene;* (v) *3 Songs: Cradle song; The Nightingale; Twilight fancies.*

☞ (M) (***) Dutton mono CDLX7011 [id.]. (i) Royal Philharmonic Soc. O; (ii) BBC Ch., LPO; (iii) Royal Op. Ch., LPO; (iv) Jan van der Gucht, London Select Ch., LPO; (v) Dora Labette; Sir Thomas Beecham (i–iv) cond.; (v) (piano).

Appalachia, subtitled *Variations on an old slave song,* is the product of Delius's years in the Deep South and this, its première recording, dating from 1938 is generally speaking the more atmospheric of the two that Beecham made. In fact all these performances (particularly the excerpts from *Hassan, On hearing the first cuckoo in spring* and *Summer night on the river*) reinforce Beecham's legendary reputation as Delius's greatest interpreter. The recordings, all pre-war, are as beautifully presented as is possible and, although their frequency-range is inevitably limited (*On hearing the first cuckoo* and *Summer night* date from 1928), they wear their years gracefully. One is unlikely ever to hear this music better played than it is here.

Paris.
☞ (M) (**) Sony mono SMK 6683 [id.]. RPO, Beecham – ARNELL: *Punch and the child;* BERNERS: *The Triumph of Neptune.* (***)

Many Delius connoisseurs prefer Sir Thomas's 1934 account of *Paris,* but to our ears there is nothing much wrong and a lot right about this 1955 version. There is plenty of atmosphere and the old Beecham magic still casts a strong spell. Music-making of stature, and an indispensable acquisition for admirers of both conductor and composer.

Sonata for strings (arr. from *String quartet* by Eric Fenby).
☞ **(*) Koch Dig. 3-7139 [id.]. New Zealand CO, Nicholas Braithwaite – BRIDGE: *Suite* etc. ***

It was Sir John Barbirolli who in 1963 commissioned Delius's amanuensis, Eric Fenby, to score the 'Late swallows' slow movement of the *String quartet* for full orchestral strings, and in 1977 he completed the arrangement of the whole work. It is arguable whether the other movements transcribe as effectively as the third (marked by the composer 'Slow and wistfully') but the performance here is persuasive, and the warm yet transparently natural sound seems right for the music.

Cello sonata.
*** Chan. Dig. CHAN 8499; *ABTD 1209* [id.]. Raphael and Peter Wallfisch – BAX: *Rhapsodic ballad;* BRIDGE: *Cello sonata;* WALTON: *Passacaglia.* ***

The Delius *Sonata* has a highly personal atmosphere, and these Chandos performers give as strong and sympathetic an account of it as is to be found. They are also excellently recorded.

String quartet.
*** ASV Dig. CDDCA 526; *ZCDCA 526* [id.]. Brodsky Qt – ELGAR: *Quartet.* ***

In this music, the ebb and flow of tension and a natural feeling for persuasive but unexaggerated rubato is vital; with fine ensemble but seeming spontaneity, the Brodsky players consistently produce that. First-rate recording.

VOCAL MUSIC

2 Aquarelles. (i) *Caprice & elegy. Fantastic dance; Irmelin: Prelude. Koanga: La Calinda. A Song of summer.* (ii) *Cynara.* (ii; iii) *Idyll.* (iv) *A late lark.* (v) *Songs of farewell.*
*** Unicorn Dig. DKPCD 9008/9 [id.]. Fenby, with (i) Lloyd Webber; (ii) Allen; (iii) Lott; (iv) Rolfe Johnson; (v) Amb. S.; RPO.

Eric Fenby draws loving, dedicated performances from the RPO. *A Song of summer* is the finest of the works which Fenby took down from the dictation of the blind, paralysed and irascible composer; but the *Songs of farewell* are most beautiful too, with Felicity Lott and Thomas Allen especially impressive in the *Idyll.* The transfer to CD is expertly managed, with Delius's comparatively thick choral textures here sounding fresh and almost transparent.

(i) *An Arabesque; Dance rhapsody No. 2; Fennimore and Gerda: Intermezzo*. (i; ii) *Songs of sunset*.
*** Unicorn Dig. DKPCD 9063; *DKPC 9063* [id.]. (i) Thomas Allen; (ii) Sarah Walker, Amb. S.,
    RPO, Fenby.

The present collection follows up Fenby's earlier two-disc set for Unicorn (see above), and brings
equally warm, well-sung and well-played performances, atmospherically recorded. What emerges as a
Delius masterpiece is *An Arabesque*. The emotional thrust of the opening sequence, superbly sung by
Thomas Allen and with passionate singing from the chorus too, subsides into characteristic Delian
reflectiveness. The *Songs of sunset* also bring ravishing sounds, with Sarah Walker as deeply
expressive as Allen. Warm, full sound, yet refined and transparent.

(i) *An Arabesque;* (ii) *Hassan* (incidental music); (iii) *Sea drift*.
(M) (*(**)) Sony mono MPK 47680 [id.]. (i) Nørby; (ii) Fry; (iii) Boyce; BBC Ch., RPO, Beecham.

It is sad that these three Delius recordings, though made between December 1954 and February 1958
after the advent of stereo, were done in mono only. Once that is said, the results are persuasive in a way
unsurpassed by any rival Delius interpreter, with the lyrical line of each passage, central to the argument, lovingly drawn out. The transfers are clear but have some roughness from the original recording.

Hassan (incidental music).
☞ (M) *** EMI CD-EMX 2207. Hill, Rayner Cook, Bournemouth Sinf. Ch. & O, Handley.

A most valuable reissue, beautifully transferred to CD. The 1979 recording, made in the Guildhall,
Southampton, is fairly immediate (some might prefer a mistier atmosphere) but the focus of chorus
and the balance of soloists is realistic and Handley is a naturally sympathetic advocate of the score,
bringing vitality and evocation in equal measure to his reading; even if memories of Beecham's briefer
selection from the incidental music are not effaced, both playing and singing are first rate and the
music springs vividly to life, including a choral version of the famous *Serenade*.

(i) *Koanga: La Calinda;* (ii) *Late swallows;* (iii; iv) *Margot La Rouge: Prelude*. (iii; v) *A Song before
sunrise;* (iii; iv) *A Village Romeo and Juliet: Walk to the Paradise Garden*. (vi) *Cynara;* (vii; iii; v)
Songs of farewell; (viii) *To be sung of a summer night on the water;* (ix) *Wanderer's song*.
☞ (M) *** EMI CD-EMX 2198; *TC-EMX 2198*. (i) Philh. O, Weldon; (ii) Hallé O, Barbirolli; (iii)
    RPO; (iv) Meredith Davies; (v) Sargent; (vi) Shirley-Quirk, RPO, Groves; (vii) Royal Choral
    Soc.; (viii) Tear, King's College Ch., Ledger; (ix) Baccholian Singers of L.

A highly successful anthology, worth any Delian's money. Only George Weldon's *La Calinda* is a
little stiff, and that comes at the very end. The programme opens with a ravishing account of the
Songs of Farewell under Sargent, who proves highly sympathetic in both the items he directs. This
was the most ambitious work the composer attempted to write after he had become blind and
paralysed. Sir Malcolm conducted the first performance in March 1932 with the Royal Choral
Society, and his presentation is committed and warm-hearted in the best tradition of Delius
recording, while the Abbey Road sound is full and sensuous. Barbirolli's *Late swallows* (another piece
in which Eric Fenby had a hand) is hardly less evocative, and John Shirley-Quirk is equally at home
in *Cynara*, a Dowson setting, while the wordless songs 'of a summer night on the water' sound
particularly well in their original *a cappella* vocal form. The transfers of recordings, all made in the
1960s – except the *Wanderer's song*, which is later – are managed most pleasingly.

(i) *A Mass of Life;* (ii) *An Arabesque;* (iii) *Songs of sunset*.
☞ (M) *** EMI CMS7 64218-2 (2) [id.]. (i) Harper, Watts, Tear, Luxon, LPO Ch., LPO; (ii) J.
    Baker, Shirley-Quirk; (ii; iii) RLPO Ch. & O; Groves.

There are few moment in Delius quite as exhilarating as the opening of his *Mass of Life* and, though
the inspiration does not remain on quite the same level of white heat throughout the work, it still
stands as one of his masterpieces. That passionate invocation to the Will (to words by Nietzsche,
taken from *Also sprach Zarathustra*) is followed by a sequence of poetic visions, superbly illustrated
by Delius. Groves inspires his performers to a magnificent account, fully worthy of the work. It is
good to have this music on CD in such fine, clearly focused sound – though, curiously, the very
mistiness of some passages in Beecham's old mono set made the results more evocative still. The
other two works are also very successful here: the *Songs of sunset*, settings of Arthur Symons that
date from 1906–7, and *An Arabesque*, a setting of Jacobsen done during the First World War. John
Shirley-Quirk does the solo part impressively and the results fall not far short of Beecham's standard,
though they lack his sense of magic. He is joined by Dame Janet Baker singing most affectingly in the
Songs of sunset. Again very good transfers of recordings made in the Philharmonic Hall, Liverpool, in
1968.

4 Old English lyrics. Songs: *I-Brasil; Indian love song; Love's philosophy; The nightingale; The nightingale has a lyre of gold; Secret love; Sweet Venevil; Twilight fancies.*
**(*) Chan. Dig. CHAN 8539; *ABTD 1247* [id.]. Benjamin Luxon, David Willison – ELGAR: *Songs.*
**(*)

This group of Delius songs draws most persuasive performances from Luxon and Willison, sadly marred by the rough tone which has latterly afflicted this fine baritone. Excellent, well-balanced recording.

Song of the high hills. Songs: *The bird's story; Le ciel est pardessus le toit; I-Brasil; Il pleure dans mon cœur; Let springtime come; La lune blanche; To daffodils; Twilight fancies; Wine roses.*
⊛ *** Unicorn Dig. DKPCD 9029; *DKPC 9029* [id.]. Lott, Sarah Walker, Rolfe Johnson, Amb. S., RPO, Fenby.

Even among Delius issues, this stands out as one of the most ravishingly beautiful of all. Eric Fenby draws a richly atmospheric performance from Beecham's old orchestra in one of the most ambitious and beautiful, yet neglected, of Delius's choral works, *Song of the high hills.* The coupling of Delius songs in beautiful, virtually unknown orchestral arrangements is ideally chosen, with all three soloists both characterful and understanding.

OPERA

A Village Romeo and Juliet (complete).
*** Argo Dig. 430 275-2 [id.]. Field, Davies, Hampson, Mora, Dean, Schoenberg Ch., Austrian RSO, Mackerras.

(i) *A Village Romeo and Juliet* (opera; complete); (ii) *Sea drift.*
(M) (***) EMI mono CMS7 64386-2 (2) [id.]. (i) Ritchie, Soames, Dowling, Sharp, Bond, Dye; (i; ii) Clinton; Ch. & RPO, Beecham.

This is one of Delius's most beautiful and heart-warming scores, and Sir Charles Mackerras – even more than Sir Charles Groves on his earlier recording – brings that out lovingly. His approach is rather broader and more affectionate, with each scene timed to convey its emotional thrust, however flimsy the story-line. The Argo cast is even finer than the EMI one, with Helen Field and Arthur Davies very sympathetic as the lovers. The spacious, atmospheric recording has the voices cleanly focused, with offstage effects beautifully caught.

Beecham made this complete recording of Delius's evocative opera in the days of 78s in 1948, and though the mono sound is limited in range, it is well focused, and Beecham's ability to mould Delius's melodic lines gives it an extra warmth and magic, even compared with later stereo recordings. It is worth any Delian getting this set for the magnificent performance of *Sea drift*, even warmer than the two other Beecham recordings, early and late, of this most moving setting of Walt Whitman, expansive but tautly held together.

Dello Joio, Norman (born 1913)

The Triumph of St Joan (Symphony); Variations, chaconne and finale.
☞ *** Koch Schwann Dig. 3-7243-2 [id.]. New Zealand SO, James Sedares – BARBER: *Adagio for strings.* ***

Norman Dello Joio is little played outside America and, apart from the *Fantasy and variations for piano and orchestra* which RCA recorded in the 1960s, his *Triumph of St Joan Symphony* from the early 1950s was for long his sole major work to reach the gramophone in one of the Louisville commission LPs. It makes a welcome CD début here and has worn well. For those who do not know it, the idiom relates loosely to early Bernstein and more closely to Hindemith, Piston and Honegger; the music is spacious, dignified and imaginative. The *Variations, chaconne and finale* is a little earlier and a good deal less convincing. It was premièred as *Three Symphonic dances* by Reiner early in 1948, and its first movement ventures almost into the realm of light music and seems ill-at-ease by the side of the more serious, portentous Hollywood-like middle movement. However, the disc is well worth investigating for the sake of the symphony (and there are good things in the companion work).

Dering, Richard (c. 1580–1630)

Motets: *Adjuro vos filiae; Ardens est cor meum; Cantate Domino; Factum est silentium; Hei mihi! Domine; Jesu decus angelicum; Jubilate Deo universa terra; O Crux ave; O vos omnes; Panis angelicus;*

Paratum cor meum; Quae est ista, quae ascendit; Quam pulchra es amica mea; Sancta et immaculata virginitas; Surge amica mea; Te laudamus . . . O Beata Trinitas; Vulnerasti cor meum.

☞ *** Gamut Dig. CD 538 [id.]. Clare College Chapel Ch., Timothy Brown; Peter Clements; Martin Pope (in *Te laudamus*).

This latest Clare College collection of Dering's motets is wholly admirable. The performances are flowing and deeply felt, at times passionate, at others rhythmically stimulating (*Adjuro vos filiae* sounds a bit like Gabrieli without the brass). Much of this music is expressively very beautiful, for instance *Hei mihi! Domine* with its soft lines and overlapping phrases, while the climax of *O Crux ave* gathers tension with its repetitions of the cry '*Dominus*'. Joyous feelings are always bubbling to the surface, and *Paratum cor meum* brings some splendid echo effects. Timothy Brown's pacing and sense of line are wholly persuasive, while the mellow resonance of St George's Church, Chesterton, seems right for the music. If you have not yet discovered Dering, this is a good place to start.

Motets: *Ardens est cor meum; Ave maria gratia plena: Ave verum corpus; Factum est silentium; Gaudent in coelis; O crux ave spes unica; O bone Jesu; O quam suavis; Quem vidistis, pastores?.*
**(*) EMI Dig. CDC7 54189-2 [id.]. King's College, Cambridge, Ch., Cleobury – PHILIPS: *Motets.* **(*)

Richard Dering and his older contemporary, Peter Philips, were Catholic expatriates who lived in the Spanish-dominated southern Netherlands. This CD contrasts and compares the two composers' settings of the same texts, drawing on Dering's *Cantiones sacrae* of 1617 and the *Cantica sacra* of 1618 and the posthumously published set of 1662. The performances are faithful though sometimes a bit stiff, and the actual sound, though good, is not ideal in focus or blend, partly perhaps but not solely due to the recording. Very recommendable all the same.

Dett, R. Nathaniel (1882–1943)

8 Bible vignettes; In the bottoms; Magnolia suite.
**(*) New World Dig. NWCD 367 [id.]. Denver Oldham.

Robert Nathaniel Dett graduated from Oberlin Conservatory in 1908, the first Negro to gain a Bachelor of Music degree. His writing is at times colourful and, though limited in its range of expressive devices, is attractive, particularly so in the suite *In the bottoms*, which evokes the moods and atmosphere of Negro life in the 'river bottoms' of the Deep South. However, this is not a disc to be taken all at once. Denver Oldham is a persuasive enough player and he is decently recorded.

Diabelli, Anton (1781–1858)

Guitar sonata in A (ed. Bream).
☞ (M) **(*) BMG/RCA 09026 61593-2. Julian Bream (guitar) – GIULIANI: *Grand overture* etc. SOR: *Grand solo Sonata in C.* **(*)

Bream combined the first two movements of Diabelli's (guitar) *Sonata in F* with the two final movements of his *Sonata in A* into a single composite work with appropriate transpositions. The result makes a quite strong (if conventional) piece, which Bream brings fully to life, even if it is perhaps a shade long for its material at 18 minutes.

Diamond, David (born 1915)

(i) *Concerto for small orchestra;* (ii) *Symphonies Nos 2; 4.*
*** Delos Dig. D/CD 3093 [id.]. (i) NY CO; (ii) Seattle SO, Gerard Schwarz.

The *Second Symphony* is a large-scale work lasting nearly three-quarters of an hour, written in 1942–3 at the height of the war, and it has great sweep and power. There is a lot of Roy Harris in the opening measures and the music unfolds with a similar sense of inevitability and purpose. The *Concerto for small orchestra* is original in form; there are two parts which open and conclude with a Fanfare with two preludes and fugues in between. The Mediterranean-like *Fourth Symphony* with its glowing, luminous textures sounds even more relaxed and lyrical in this performance than in Bernstein's account from the 1960s. Dedicated and expert performances from the Seattle Orchestra under Gerard Schwarz. The acoustic is spacious and the balance is very well judged.

(i) *Violin concerto No. 2. The Enormous room; Symphony No. 1.*
☞ *** Delos Dig. DE 3119 [id.]. (i) Ilkka Talvi; Seattle SO, Gerard Schwarz.

A further addition to Diamond's growing representation in the catalogue brings the *First Symphony*, an urbane and intelligently wrought piece which has a strong sense of both purpose and direction. Some of the material may strike the listener as a little bland, but none ever draws attention away from the music as a whole; the part is perfectly wedded to the whole. The *Second Violin concerto* is a bit Stravinskian with a dash of Walton and keeps the excellent soloist fully stretched. Not perhaps top-drawer Diamond, though *The Enormous room* shows the composer at his most imaginative. It derives its title from e. e. cummings's 'high and clear adventure'. It is rhapsodic in feeling, with orchestral textures of great luxuriance. Excellent performances from Gerard Schwarz and the Seattle orchestra, and outstanding recording.

(i) *Kaddish for cello and orchestra. Psalm; Romeo and Juliet; Symphony No. 3.*
*** Delos Dig. DE 3103 [id.]. (i) Starker; Seattle SO, Gerard Schwarz.

The *Third Symphony* is a four-movement work of no mean power. The *Romeo and Juliet* music is an inventive score, full of character and atmosphere, which shows Diamond as a real man of the orchestra; and the Seattle orchestra proves an eloquent advocate. *Kaddish* is a more recent piece and is played here by its dedicatee, János Starker.

Dibdin, Charles (1745–1814)

(i) *The Brickdust man* (musical dialogue); (ii) *The Ephesian Matron* (comic serenata); (iii) *The Grenadier* (musical dialogue).
☞ *** Hyp. Dig. CDA 66608 [id.]. (i) Barclay, West; (ii) Mills, Streeton, Padmore, Knight; (iii) Bisatt, West, Mayor; Opera Restor'd, Parley of Instruments, Holman.

Dibdin, best known as the composer of *Tom Bowling*, the song heard every year at the Last Night of the Proms, here provides three delightful pocket operas, the shorter ones officially described as musical dialogues and *The Ephesian Matron* as a comic serenata. *The Grenadier* – dating from 1773 – lasts well under a quarter of an hour, using a text that is possibly by David Garrick. The brief numbers – duets and solos – are linked by equally brief recitatives, then rounded off with a final trio. The other two pieces are just as delightful in these performances by a group that specializes in presenting just such dramatic works of this period in public. Excellent Hyperion sound.

Diepenbrock, Alphons (1862–1921)

Elektra suite; (i) *Hymn for violin & orchestra. Marsyas suite; Overture: The Birds.*
*** Chan. Dig. CHAN 8821; *ABTD 1446* [id.]. (i) Emmy Verhey; Hague Residentie O, Vonk.

The *Birds Overture*, written for a student production of Aristophanes, is rather delightful if very Straussian, with some vaguely Impressionist touches. The *Marsyas music* (1910) is expertly and delicately scored with touches of Strauss, Reger and Debussy. Good performances from the Residentie Orchestra under Hans Vonk and eminently truthful recording quality. Recommended.

(i) *Hymne an die Nacht;* (ii) *Hymne;* (i) *Die Nacht;* (iii) *Im grossen Schweigen.*
*** Chan. Dig. CHAN 8878; *ABTD 1491* [id.]. (i) Linda Finnie; (ii) Christoph Homberger; (iii) Robert Holl; Hague Residentie O, Hans Vonk.

This second volume brings four symphonic songs, all of great beauty and with an almost Straussian melancholy. There are touches of Reger and Debussy as well as Strauss, and all four pieces are expertly and delicately scored. Good performances from all three soloists and the Residentie Orchestra under Hans Vonk, and very good recording indeed.

Dittersdorf, Carl Ditters von (1739–99)

(i) *Double-bass concerto in E;* (ii) *Flute concerto in E min.;* (iii) *Symphonies in C & D.*
** Olympia OCD 405 [id.]. (i) Stefan Thomas, Arad PO, Boboc; (ii) Gavril Costea, Cluj-Napoca PO, Cristescu; (iii) Oradea Philharmonic CO, Ratiu.

The *C major* is an agreeably conventional three-movement symphony, but the *D major* is more elaborate, with an infectious opening movement, an engaging *Chanson populaire d'Elsass* for its *Andante*, a minuet with two trios and a set of variations for its modestly paced finale. Both the concertos are attractive and require considerable bravura from their soloists. The recorded sound varies somewhat but is always fully acceptable and quite well balanced.

Harp concerto in A (arr. Pilley).
⊛ (M) *** Decca 425 723-2; *425 723-4* [id.]. Marisa Robles, ASMF, Iona Brown – BOIELDIEU; HANDEL: *Harp concertos* etc. *** ⊛

Dittersdorf's *Harp concerto* is a transcription of an unfinished keyboard concerto with additional wind parts. It is an elegant piece, thematically not quite as memorable as the Boieldieu coupling, but captivating when played with such style.

6 Symphonies after Ovid's Metamorphoses.
**(*) Chan. Dig. CHAN 8564/5; *DBTD 2012* (2). Cantilena, Shepherd.

All the *Ovid symphonies* have a programmatic inspiration and relate episodes from the *Metamorphoses* of Ovid, such as *The fall of Phaeton*, which are vividly portrayed. *The rescue of Andromeda by Perseus* is a particularly effective work (it has an inspired *Adagio*) and the slow movement of the *D major*, *The petrification of Phineus and his friends*, is a delight. One well appreciates the contemporary verdict that Ditters 'spoke to the heart'. *The transformation of the Lycian peasants into frogs* could hardly be more graphic and is full of wit. This is inventive and charming music that will give much pleasure, and it is generally well served by Cantilena under Adrian Shepherd.

Dodgson, Stephen (born 1924)

(i) *Flute concerto* (for flute and strings); (ii) *Duo concertant for violin, guitar and strings;* (iii) *Last of the Leaves* (cantata for bass, clarinet and strings)
☞ *** Biddulph Dig. LAW 015 [id.]. (i) Robert Stallman; (ii) Jean-Jacques Kantorow, Anthea Gifford; (iii) Michael George, John Bradbury, N. Sinfonia, Zollman.

As Dodgson himself says in his illuminating note, 'I have developed a particular fondness for music which outwardly has the manner of a divertimento, but inwardly is quite otherwise.' All three of these works illustrate that equivocal quality in the writing, not least the *Flute concerto* which Dodgson wrote for the American flautist, Robert Stallman, who is also the fine soloist on this disc. It has the unusual layout of two preludial movements, slow leading to fast, before the main rondo-like movement, which makes up two-thirds of the work's total length. Dodgson wanted not only to draw on Stallman's agility and rhythmic flair, but on his tonal bloom and subtlety, and the performance bears that out. The *Duo Concertant*, dating from 1989, is equivocal not only in its moods but in its structure – five short movements that interlace, with thematic overlaps – and in the very forces used. With the original soloists it too receives a persuasive performance. With its hints of an English Stravinsky, this is another work that is at once thoughtful and charming. *Last of the Leaves* is a cantata for bass soloist accompanied by clarinet and strings, more consistently autumnal and elegiac, with the title taken from the longest poem, *The Leaf Burners*, by Ernest Rhys. The image of leaves being burnt is used as a metaphor for the tragic loss of life in the First World War, and the result is the more moving for its relative reticence. Framing the work are settings of poems by poets now neglected, Austin Dobson and Harold Monro, with the necessary contrast provided by the best-known poem, G. K. Chesterton's *The Donkey*, light-hearted, leading up to its surprise reference at the end to Christ's entry into Jerusalem. Though Michael George's noble bass voice is not as sweetly caught as it might be, it is a tenderly moving performance, with John Bradbury equally expressive and with the Belgian conductor, Ronald Zollman, as in the other works, a sympathetic accompanist.

Dohnányi, Ernst von (1877–1960)

Piano concertos Nos. 1 in E min., Op. 5; 2 in B min., Op. 42.
☞ *** Hyp. Dig. CDA 66684 [id.]. Martin Roscoe, BBC Scottish SO, Fedor Glushchenko.

The note provided with this coupling places Dohnányi's writing style as lying somewhere between that of Brahms and Saint-Saëns. His *Nursery-tune variations* show how good he is at pastiche over this area (and outside it), but these concertos suggest that he is hardly a musical individualist in his own right. They are well wrought, with a melodic warmth that fails to be indelible; they provide bravura for the soloist and contrast for the orchestra. The present performances are surely unlikely to be surpassed for their commitment, and the playing is finished as well as ardent; the recording, too, is excellent. But both works, ambitious as they are, are agreeable rather than distinctive.

Konzertstück for cello and orchestra, Op. 12.
*** Chan. Dig. CHAN 8662 [id.]. Wallfisch, LSO, Mackerras – DVORAK: *Cello concerto.* ***

Dohnányi's *Konzertstück* has many rich, warm ideas, not least a theme in the slow movement all too close to *Pale hands I loved beside the Shalimar*, and none the worse for that. Wallfisch's performance, as in the Dvořák, is strong, warm and committed, and the Chandos sound is first rate.

(i) *Ruralia hungarica, Op. 32b;* (i; ii) *Variations on a nursery tune, Op. 25;* (iii) *Serenade in C (for string trio), Op. 10.*
(B) *** Hung. White Label HRC 121 [id.]. (i) Budapest SO, Lehel, (ii) with István Lantos; (iii) Kovács, Bársony, Botvay.

Ruralia hungarica, although a cultivated score, still has an element of peasant earthiness. György Lehel and the Budapest orchestra successfully convey its exuberance and poetry, and the pianist in the famous *Variations*, István Lantos, is characterful as well as brilliant. The *Serenade*, Op. 10, is an expressive and inventive piece with a particularly beautiful slow movement. With excellent, well-balanced sound, this is one of the outstanding bargains on Hungaroton's White Label.

Variations on a nursery tune, Op. 25.
☞ (M) (***) EMI mono CDC5 55031-2 [id.). Composer, LSO, Lawrance Collingwood – BARTÓK: *Collection.* (***)

Dohnányi made two recordings of his celebrated *Variations on a nursery tune*, the first in 1931 with the LSO and Lawrance Collingwood and the second in 1956 with the RPO and Sir Adrian Boult (with Collingwood producing), when the composer-pianist was approaching eighty. Remarkable though the latter is, the earlier account has much greater character and more effortless virtuosity. This was its première recording and has great freshness and naturalness. The sound was always a little dry and the strings wanting in richness, but the engineers have given it a completely new lease of life.

(i) *Variations on a nursery tune, Op. 25. Capriccio in F min., Op. 28.*
*** Chesky CD-13 [id.]. Earl Wild, (i) New Philh. O, Christoph von Dohnányi – TCHAIKOVSKY: *Piano concerto No. 1.* ***

A scintillating account of the piano part from Earl Wild is matched by a witty accompaniment directed by the composer's grandson, who doesn't miss a thing. Splendid vintage analogue recording from the early 1960s. The *Capriccio*, brilliantly played, acts as an encore (before the Tchaikovsky coupling), but the recording is rather recessed.

Cello sonata in B flat min., Op. 8.
**(*) ASV Dig. CDDCA 796[id.]. Bernard Gregor-Smith, Yolande Wrigley – BRIDGE; DEBUSSY: *Sonatas.* **(*)

Like so much of Dohnányi's early music, the *Cello sonata* (1899) is very Brahmsian in feeling. There is a marvellously inventive scherzo, which leaves no doubt that it is the work of a great pianist-composer. The finale is a theme and variations and what a superb theme it is too. It is played with great expertise and fine musicianship by this excellent duo partnership. The recording is just a bit too bright and forward to be ideal but with that proviso, the disc can be cordially recommended.

(i) *Piano quintet in C min., Op. 1. String quartet No. 2 in D flat, Op. 15.*
**(*) Chan. Dig. CHAN 8718; *ABTD 1360* [id.]. (i) Wolfgang Manz; Gabrieli Qt.

Manz's performance of the Dohnányi *Quintet* lacks something in fantasy and lightness of touch. But the bigger-boned, somewhat Brahmsian effect of this performance is certainly compelling, if less strong on charm. The scherzo of the *Second Quartet* is reminiscent of the opening of *Die Walküre* and there are reminders of Dvořák and Reger as well as Brahms. It is a strong piece, splendidly played by the Gabrielis and beautifully recorded.

Donizetti, Gaetano (1797–1848)

Sinfonias (String quartets): in A; D min. (both arr. Benedek); *D* (arr. Angerer).
☞ **(*) Marco Polo Dig. 8.223577 [id.]. Failoni CO, Géza Oberfrank.

We have had the *D major Sinfonia* (arranged here by Paul Angerer) from the ASMF under Marriner. It is a delightfully spontaneous piece with a graciously beautiful *Larghetto*. The D minor work opens darkly, but the sun soon comes out and at times we are reminded of Rossini. The *Larghetto* is pensive. The *A major* has a fine, siciliano-like *Larghetto cantabile*. All this is warmly appealing music, well played and flatteringly recorded; a touch more wit and sparkle would not have come amiss, but the music is well worth having. A pity that this was not issued on the Naxos label.

Il Barcaiolo; Cor anglais concerto in G; Oboe sonata in F; (Piano) Waltz in C.
*** Mer. CDE 84147; *KE 77147* [id.]. Jeremy Polmear, Diana Ambache (with PASCULLI: *Concerto on themes from La Favorita; Fantasia on Poliuto;* LISZT: *Réminscences de Lucia di Lammermoor*).

The *Sonata in F* is an agreeable piece with a fluent *Andante* and a catchy finale; and the vignette, *Il Barcaiolo*, is even more engaging. The *Cor anglais concerto* centres on a set of variations which are not unlike the fantasias on themes from his operas by Pasculli. However, these demand the utmost bravura from the soloist. Diana Ambache proves a sympathetic partner and gives a suitably flamboyant account of Liszt's famous *Lucia paraphrase*.

String quartet No. 13 in A.
*** CRD CRD 3366; *CRDC 4066* [id.]. Alberni Qt – PUCCINI: *Crisantemi;* VERDI: *Quartet.* ***

This is an endearing work, with a scherzo echoing that in Beethoven's *Eroica*, and with many twists of argument that are attractively unpredictable. It is given a strong, committed performance and is well recorded.

Requiem.
☞ (M) ** Decca 425 043-2 [id.]. Cortez, Pavarotti, Bruson, Washington, Arena di Verona Lyric Ch. & O, Fackler.

There are many passages in Donizetti's *Requiem* which may well have influenced Verdi when he came to write his masterpiece. Donizetti's setting lasts for 65 minutes, but its inspiration is short-winded and it is not helped here by limited performance and recording, deriving from the Cime label. The singing and playing are generally indifferent. Pavarotti, recorded in 1979, is the obvious star, singing flamboyantly in his big solo, *Ingemisco*. Of curiosity value only.

OPERA

Anna Bolena (complete).
*** Decca Dig. 421 096-2 (3) [id.]. Sutherland, Ramey, Hadley, Mentzer, Welsh Nat. Op. Ch. & O, Bonynge.

In this 1987 recording of *Anna Bolena*, Sutherland crowns her long recording career with a commanding performance. Dazzling as ever in coloratura, above all exuberant in the defiant final cabaletta, she poignantly conveys the tragedy of the wronged queen's fate with rare weight and gravity. Ramey as the king is outstanding in a fine, consistent cast. Excellent recording.

L'assedio di Calais (complete).
☞ *** Opera Rara OR 9 (2) [id.]. Du Plessis, Della Jones, Focile, Serbo, Nilon, Platt, Glanville, Smythe, Treleaven, Harrhy, Bailey, Geoffrey Mitchell Ch., Philh. O, David Parry.

Donizetti's invention was at its peak in this unjustly neglected opera, written in 1839, the year following *Lucia di Lammermoor*. In *L'assedio di Calais* ('The siege of Calais'), based freely on the story of the burghers of Calais, he branched out from the Italian tradition towards French fashion, including a ballet in Act III. What above all must strike us today is the weight and intensity he gave to the big ensembles, bringing them very close not just to early but to mature Verdi. The Opera Rara set is one of the most invigorating of all the complete opera recordings made over the years by that enterprising organization. With such outstanding Opera Rara stalwarts as Della Jones and Christian du Plessis in the cast, as well as a newcomer, Nuccia Focile, as Queen Eleanor, David Parry conducts the Philharmonia in a fresh, well-sprung performance which gives a satisfying thrust to the big ensembles. The one which ends Act II, including a magnificent sextet and a patriotic prayer for the chorus, brings the opera's emotional high-point. When, in Act III, Edward III's big aria turns into a sort of jolly waltz song, the music seems less apt.

Il Campanello (complete).

*** Sony Dig. MK 38450 [id.]. Baltsa, Dara, Casoni, Romero, Gaifa, V. State Op. Ch., VSO, Bertini.

This sparkling one-Act piece is based on something like the same story which Donizetti developed later in *Don Pasquale*. Enzo Dara as the apothecary, Don Annibale, and Angelo Romero as the wag, Enrico, are delightful in their patter duet, and Agnes Baltsa is a formidable but sparkling Serafina. Gary Bertini is a sympathetic conductor who paces things well, and the *secco* recitatives – taking up rather a large proportion of the disc – are well accompanied on the fortepiano. Generally well-balanced recording.

Don Pasquale (complete).

*** EMI Dig. CDS7 47068-2 (2) [Ang. CDCB 47068]. Bruscantini, Freni, Nucci, Winbergh, Amb. Op. Ch., Philh. O, Muti.

(M) *** Decca 433 036-2 (2) [id.]. Corena, Sciutti, Oncina, Krause, V. State Op. Ch. & O, Kertész – CIMAROSA: *Il maestro di cappella.* ***

*** Erato/Warner Dig. 2292 45487-2 (2) [id.]. Bacquier, Hendricks, Canonici, Quilico, Schirrer, Lyon Opera Ch. & O, Ferro.

Muti's is a delectably idiomatic-sounding reading, one which consistently captures the fun of the piece. Freni is a natural in the role of Norina, both sweet and bright-eyed in characterization, excellent in coloratura. The buffo baritones, the veteran Bruscantini as Pasquale and the darker-toned Leo Nucci as Dr Malatesta, steer a nice course between vocal comedy and purely musical values. Muti is helped by the beautifully poised and shaded singing of Gösta Winbergh, honey-toned and stylish as Ernesto. Responsive and polished playing from the Philharmonia and excellent studio sound.

Under Kertész, Corena is an attractive *buffo*, even if his voice is not always focused well enough to sing semiquavers accurately. Juan Oncina, as often on record, sounds rather strained, but the tenor part is very small; and Krause makes an incisive Malatesta. Graziella Sciutti is charming from beginning to end, bright-toned and vivacious, and remarkably agile in the most difficult passages. The 1964 Decca recording is excellent, with plenty of atmosphere as well as sparkle.

The Erato version gains enormously from the rhythmic subtlety and affectionate phrasing encouraged by the conductor, Gabriele Ferro. This is a reading with more light and shade than Muti's or Kertész's, not so high-powered but more relaxed, genially capturing the spirit of comedy in this delightful score. Barbara Hendricks is a charming Norina with her sweet timbre, and Luca Canonici an engaging Ernesto, even if his production is not always perfectly even. The recording has fine atmosphere, though some of the vocal balances are inconsistent.

L'elisir d'amore (complete).

*** Decca 414 461-2 (2) [id.]. Sutherland, Pavarotti, Cossa, Malas, Amb. S., ECO, Bonynge.

☞ *** Erato/Warner Dig. 4509 91701-2 (2) [id.]. Devia, Alagna, Spagnoli, Praticò, Tallis Chamber Ch., ECO, Viotti.

(M) *** Sony CD 79210 (2) [M2K 34585]. Cotrubas, Domingo, Evans, Wixell, ROHCG Ch. & O, Pritchard.

☞ (B) **(*) CfP CD-CFPD 4733. Carteri, Alva, Panerai, Taddei, La Scala, Milan, Ch. & O, Serafin.

Joan Sutherland makes Adina a more substantial figure than usual, full-throatedly serious at times, at others jolly like the rumbustious Marie; and in the key role of Nemorino Luciano Pavarotti proves ideal, vividly portraying the wounded innocent. Spiro Malas is a superb Dulcamara, while Dominic Cossa is a younger-sounding Belcore, more of a genuine lover than usual. Bonynge points the skipping rhythms delectably, and the recording is sparkling to match, with striking presence.

The Erato version may offer no star names but it presents an exceptionally winning performance, in many ways the finest of all on record, with no weak link. Marcello Viotti proves an inspired Donizetti conductor, drawing playing from the ECO that sparkles consistently, with witty pointing of phrase and rhythm, subtle in rubato and finely polished. Consistently too, his timing helps the singers. This is a light, generally brisk account of the score that provides an ideal modern alternative to Richard Bonynge's version with Joan Sutherland as Adina and with the young Pavarotti. On Erato, Mariella Devia cannot match Sutherland for beauty of tone in the warmly lyrical solos, but she sparkles more, bringing out what a minx of a heroine this is. Roberto Alagna's tenor timbre is not unlike Pavarotti's, lighter if not quite so firm, and, like Devia, he delectably brings out the lightness of the writing. His performance culminates in a winningly hushed and inner account of the soaring aria, *Una furtiva lagrima*. Rounding off an excellent cast, Pietro Spagnoli is a fresh, virile Belcore, and

Bruno Praticò a clear, characterful Dr Dulcamara, an excellent *buffo* baritone, making the very most of a voice on the light side. The sound is first rate, if not as forwardly focused as the analogue Decca.

On the Sony reissue delight centres very much on the delectable Adina of Ileana Cotrubas. Plácido Domingo by contrast is a more conventional hero and less the world's fool that Nemorino should be. Sir Geraint Evans gives a vivid characterization of Dr Dulcamara, though the microphone sometimes brings out roughness of tone, and Ingvar Wixell is an upstanding Belcore. The stereo staging is effective and the remastered recording bright and immediate. This set remains at full price in the USA.

Although there are reservations, this reissued (1959) La Scala set of *L'elisir d'amore* makes a pretty good bargain; it was a fine cast in its day. Alva is a pleasantly light-voiced and engaging Nemorino with an ability to control Donizetti's florid line. Carteri's Adina ideally should be more of a minx than this, but the part is nicely sung all the same. Panerai as Belcore once again shows what a fine and musical artist he is, and Taddei is magnificent, stealing the show as any Dulcamara can and should. The drawback is Serafin's direction. The La Scala Chorus is lively enough, and it is not that the orchestral playing is slipshod: they could play Donizetti standing on their heads. Yet they provide less sparkle than they should, and in his first aria as Dr Dulcamara Taddei drives himself hard in brilliant and forceful characterization but without prodding the orchestra to follow him. However, the recording has been admirably transferred to CD. The sound is altogether fresh. The trumpet solo which herald's Dulcamara's entry is nicely distanced and reveals an attractive ambience, though the balance of the singers is close. There is a good synopsis, relating each track to the narrative. Excellent value.

L'elisir d'amore: highlights.
☞ ** DG Dig. 435 880-2. Battle, Pavarotti, Nucci, Dara, Met. Op. Ch. & O, Levine.

A good 68–minute sampler of DG's 1989 set, made at the Met., which shows neither Pavarotti nor James Levine at their best and which is most notable for Kathleen Battle's engaging Adina. Her contribution is well represented in the chosen selection; however, at premium price the disc can hardly have any kind of priority.

Emelia di Liverpool (complete). *L'eremitaggio di Liwerpool* (complete).
*** Opera Rara OR 8 (3) [id.]. Kenny, Bruscantini, Merritt, Dolton, George Mitchell Ch., Philh. O, David Parry.

The very name, *Emelia di Liverpool*, makes it hard to take this early opera of Donizetti seriously. In this set, sponsored by the Peter Moores Foundation, we have not only the original version of 1824 but also the complete reworking of four years later, which was given the revised title noted above. Such a veteran as Sesto Bruscantini makes an enormous difference in the buffo role of Don Romualdo in *Emelia*, a character who speaks in Neapolitan dialect. His fizzing duet with Federico (the principal tenor role, superbly sung by Chris Merritt) sets the pattern for much vigorous invention. With fresh, direct conducting from David Parry this is a highly enjoyable set for all who respond to this composer.

La Favorita (complete).
(M) **(*) Decca 430 038-2 (3). Cossotto, Pavarotti, Bacquier, Ghiaurov, Cotrubas, Teatro Comunale Bologna Ch. & O, Bonynge.

La Favorita may not have as many memorable tunes as the finest Donizetti operas, but red-blooded drama provides ample compensation. Fernando is strongly and imaginatively sung here by Pavarotti. The mezzo role of the heroine is taken by Fiorenza Cossotto, formidably powerful if not quite at her finest, while Ileana Cotrubas is comparably imaginative as her confidante Ines, but not quite at her peak. Bacquier and Ghiaurov make up a team which should have been even better but which will still give much satisfaction. Bright recording.

La Fille du régiment (complete).
*** Decca 414 520-2 (2) [id.]. Sutherland, Pavarotti, Sinclair, Malas, Coates, ROHCG Ch. & O, Bonynge.

It was with this cast that *La Fille du régiment* was revived at Covent Garden, and Sutherland immediately showed how naturally she takes to the role of Marie, a vivandière in the army of Napoleon. Sutherland is in turn brilliantly comic and pathetically affecting, and Pavarotti makes an engaging hero. Monica Sinclair is a formidable Countess in a fizzing performance of a delightful Donizetti romp that can be confidently recommended both for comedy and for fine singing. Recorded in Kingsway Hall, the CD sound has wonderful presence and clarity of focus.

Lucia di Lammermoor (complete).

*** Decca 410 193-2 (2) [id.]. Sutherland, Pavarotti, Milnes, Ghiaurov, Ryland Davies, Tourangeau, ROHCG Ch. & O, Bonynge.

(M) *** Decca 411 622-2 (2) [id.]. Sutherland, Cioni, Merrill, Siepi, St Cecilia Ac., Rome, Ch. & O, Pritchard.

(M) (***) EMI mono CMS7 63631-2 (2) [Ang. CDMB 63631]. Callas, Di Stefano, Panerai, Zaccaria, La Scala Ch. & O, Karajan.

☞ *** DG Dig. 435 309-2 (2) [id.]. Studer, Domingo, Pons, Ramey, Amb. Op. Ch., LSO, Marin.

(M) (***) EMI mono CMS7 69980-2 (2) [Ang. CDMB 69980]. Callas, Di Stefano, Gobbi, Arie, Ch. & O of Maggio Musicale Fiorentino, Serafin.

☞ (M) ** EMI Dig. CMS7 64622-2 (2) [Ang. CDMB 64622]. Gruberová, Kraus, Bruson, Lloyd, Amb. Op. Ch., RPO, Rescigno.

Though some of the girlish freshness of voice which marked the 1961 recording disappeared in the 1971 set, Sutherland's detailed understanding was intensified. Power is there as well as delicacy, and the rest of the cast is first rate. Pavarotti, through much of the opera not as sensitive as he can be, proves magnificent in his final scene. The sound-quality is superb on CD. In this set, unlike the earlier one, the text is absolutely complete.

The 1961 Sutherland version of *Lucia* remains an attractive proposition in the mid-price range. Though consonants were being smoothed over, the voice is obviously that of a young singer and dramatically the performance was close to Sutherland's famous stage appearances of that time, full of fresh innocence. Sutherland's coloratura virtuosity remains breathtaking, and the cast is a strong one, with Pritchard a most understanding conductor.

Recorded live in 1955, when Karajan took the company of La Scala to Berlin, for years this finest of Callas's recordings of *Lucia* was available only on pirate issues. Despite the limited sound, Callas's voice is caught with fine immediacy. Her singing is less steely than in the 1953 studio recording, and far firmer than in the 1959 one (now withdrawn).

On DG, Cheryl Studer makes an affecting heroine, singing both brilliantly and richly, and Plácido Domingo rebuts any idea that his tenor is too cumbersome for Donizetti. This is the finest version yet in digital sound, with the young Romanian, Ion Marin, drawing fresh, urgent playing from the LSO. The rest of the cast is outstandingly strong too, with Juan Pons as Lucia's brother, Enrico, and Samuel Ramey as the teacher and confidant, Raimondo, Bide-the-Bent.

Callas's earlier mono set dates from 1953. The diva is vocally better controlled than in her later stereo set (indeed some of the coloratura is excitingly brilliant in its own right), and there are memorable if not always perfectly stylish contributions from Di Stefano and Gobbi. As in the later set, the text has the usual stage cuts.

Edita Gruberová brings dramatic power as well as brilliance and flexibility to the role of Lucia and she rises well to the challenge of the Mad scene, the opera's powerful climax, where her rather overemphatic manner suits both the music and the drama best. Elsewhere a degree of gustiness in the vocal delivery – the microphones are not kind to her – and the occasional squeezed note, together with noisy breathing, detract from the purity needed. Legato lines, too, tend to be overpointed. Alfredo Kraus conceals his age astonishingly well with finely controlled singing (no problems over legato), but with an occasional over-emphasis to match his heroine. Renato Bruson and Robert Lloyd are both first rate, but Rescigno's conducting lacks point, rather matching the plainness of the recorded production. Full, natural if unremarkable 1983 digital sound: the recording was made at Abbey Road.

Lucia di Lammermoor: highlights.

(M) *** Decca 421 885-2 [id.] (from above complete recording, with Sutherland, Pavarotti; cond. Bonynge).

(M) **(*) EMI CDM7 63934-2 [id.]. Callas, Tagliavini, Cappuccilli, Ladysz, Philh. Ch. & O, Serafin.

For those who have chosen Callas or Sutherland's earlier, complete set, this 63-minute selection from her later (1971) version should be ideal.

A satisfactory hour-long selection from Callas's 1959 Kingsway Hall stereo recording, with Callas not as completely in vocal control as she was in her earlier, mono set.

Lucrezia Borgia (complete).

(M) *** Decca 421 497-2 (2) [id.]. Sutherland, Aragall, Horne, Wixell, London Op. Voices, Nat. PO, Bonynge.

Sutherland is in her element here. Aragall sings stylishly too, and though Wixell's timbre is hardly Italianate he is a commanding Alfonso. Marilyn Horne in the breeches role of Orsini is impressive in the brilliant *Brindisi* of the last Act, but earlier she has moments of unsteadiness. The recording is characteristically full and brilliant.

Maria Padilla (complete).
☞ **(*) Opera Rara ORC 6 (3) [id.]. McDonall, Della Jones, Clark, Du Plessis, Earle, Caley, Kennedy, Joan Davies, Geoffrey Mitchell Ch., LSO, Francis.

Described as a melodrama and written in 1841, *Maria Padilla* marks a return to Donizetti's Italian manner, a piece based on strong situations. It even matches *Lucia di Lammermoor* in places, with the heroine ill-used by the prince she loves, Pedro the Cruel. When the obligatory mad scene is given not to the heroine but to her father, even a tenor such as Graham Clark – future star in Bayreuth – can hardly compensate, however red-blooded the writing and strong the singing. In the title-role Lois McDonall is brightly agile, if at times a little raw. Alun Francis directs the LSO in a fresh, well-disciplined performance and, as ever with Opera Rara sets, the notes and commentary contained in the libretto are both readable and scholarly.

Maria Stuarda (complete).
(M) *** Decca 425 410-2 (2) [id.]. Sutherland, Tourangeau, Pavarotti, Ch. & O of Teatro Comunale, Bologna, Bonynge.

In Donizetti's tellingly dramatic opera on the conflict of Elizabeth I and Mary Queen of Scots, the contrast between the full soprano Maria and the dark mezzo Elisabetta is underlined by some transpositions, with Tourangeau emerging as a powerful villainess in this slanted version of the story. Pavarotti turns Leicester into a passionate Italian lover, not at all an Elizabethan gentleman. As for Sutherland, she is at her most fully dramatic too, and the great moment when she flings the insult *Vil bastarda!* at her cousin brings a superb snarl; Richard Bonynge directs an urgent account of an unfailingly enjoyable opera. Unusually for Decca, the score is slightly cut. The recording is characteristically bright and full.

Poliuto (complete).
*** Sony Dig. M2K 44821 (2) [id.]. Carreras, Ricciarelli, Pons, Polgar, V. Singakademie Ch., VSO, Oleg Caetani.

Set in Rome in the early Christian period, *Poliuto* is based on Corneille's tragedy, *Polyeucte*, a story of martyrdom. Carreras's voice is in splendid form. Ricciarelli as Paolina lacks something in dramatic bite, but she gives the heroine an inward warmth and tenderness. Pons and Polgar are also excellent and the piece is well worth investigating for one of Donizetti's most inspired ensembles in the Act II finale. The recording is clear and vivid, hardly betraying the fact that it was made live at a concert performance.

Ugo, conte di Parigi (complete).
☞ *** Opera Rara ORC1 (3) [id.]. Della Jones, Harrhy, J. Price, Kenny, Arthur, Du Plessis, Geoffrey Mitchell Ch., New Philh. O, Francis.

The 1977 recording of *Ugo, conte di Parigi* was the result of formidable detective work, revealing in this early opera of 1832 a strong plot and some fine numbers, including excellent duets. Matching such singers as Janet Price and Yvonne Kenny, Maurice Arthur sings stylishly in the title-role, with a clear-cut tenor that records well. Della Jones and Christian du Plessis, regular stalwarts of Opera Rara sets, complete a stylish cast. Reissued on CD, thanks to the Peter Moores Foundation, it offers a fresh and intelligent performance under Alun Francis, and the scholarly, readable notes and commentary, as well as libretto and translation, are models of their kind.

Dowland, John (1563–1626)

Consort music: *Captain Digorie Piper, his pavan and galliard; Fortune my foe; Lachrimae; Lady Hunsdon's almain; Lord Souch's galliard; Mistress Winter's jump; The shoemaker's wife (a toy); Sir George Whitehead's almain; Sir Henry Guildford's almain; Sir Henry Umpton's funeral; Sir John Smith's almain; Sir Thomas Collier's galliard; Suzanna.*
*** Hyp. Dig. CDA 66010 [id.]. Extempore String Ens.

The Extempore Ensemble's technique of improvising and elaborating in Elizabethan consort music is aptly exploited here in an attractively varied selection of pieces by Dowland, and on record, as in concert, the result sounds the more spontaneous. Excellent recording.

Lute music: *Almaine; Captain Digorie Piper's galliard; Dowland's first galliard; The Earl of Derby, his galliard; The Earl of Essex galliard; Frog galliard; Galliard to lachrimae; Lachrimae antiquae; Lachrimae verae; Lady Rich, her galliard; Lord De L'Isle's galliard; Melancholy galliard; Mr Langton's galliard; Mrs Vaux's gigge; My Lady Hunsdon's puffe; My Lord Chamberlain, his galliard; Piper's pavan; Resolution; Semper Dowland, semper dolens; The shoemaker's wife; Sir Henry Gifford's almaine; Sir John Smith's almaine; Sir John Souche's galliard.*

☞ (M) *** BMG/RCA 09026 61586-2. Julian Bream (lute).

Julian Bream captures the melancholy (the piece entitled *Semper Dowland, semper dolens* is certainly autobiographical) and the eloquence of these endlessly imaginative miniatures. He produces an astonishing range of colour from the lute: each phrase shows distinction, nothing is in the least routine. This mid-priced reissue in the Julian Bream Edition includes three extra items. The recordings were made over a decade between 1967 and 1976.

First Booke of Songes (1597): 1, *Unquiet thoughts;* 2, *Whoever thinks or hopes;* 3, *My thoughts are wing'd with hopes;* 4, *If my complaints;* 5, *Can she excuse my wrongs;* 6, *Now, O now I needs must part;* 7, *Dear, if you change;* 8, *Burst forth my tears;* 9, *Go crystal tears;* 10, *Think'st thou then;* 11, *Come away, come sweet love;* 12, *Rest awhile;* 13, *Sleep wayward thoughts;* 14, *All ye who love or fortune;* 15, *Wilt thou unkind;* 16, *Would my conceit;* 17, *Come again;* 18, *His golden locks;* 19, *Awake, sweet love;* 20, *Come, heavy sleep;* 21, *Away with these self-loving lads.*
*** O-L 421 653-2 [id.]. Cons. of Musicke, Rooley.

Rooley and the Consort of Musicke he directs have recorded all the contents of the *First Booke of Songes* of 1597 in the order in which they are published, varying the accompaniment between viols, lute with bass viol, voices and viols, and even voices alone. There is hardly any need to stress the beauties of the music itself, which is eminently well served by this stylish ensemble, and beautifully recorded.

Second Booke of Songes (1600): I saw my lady weep; Flow my tears; Sorrow, stay; Die not before thy day; Mourn day is with darkness fled; Time's eldest son; Then sit thee down; When others say Venite; Praise blindness eyes; O sweet words; If floods of tears; Fine knacks for ladies; Now cease my wond'ring eyes; Come, ye heavy states of night; White as lilies was her face; Woeful heart; A shepherd in a shade; Faction that ever dwells; Shall I sue; Toss not my soul; Clear or cloudy; Humour say what mak'st thou here.
*** O-L 425 889-2 [id.]. Kirkby, York Skinner, Hill, D. Thomas, Cons. of Musicke, Rooley.

The *Second Booke* contains many of Dowland's best-known songs. The solo songs are given with great restraint (sometimes perhaps rather too great) and good musical judgement, while the consort pieces receive expressive treatment. Refined intelligence is shown by all taking part. The recording is of the highest quality.

Third Booke of Songes (1603): 1, *Farewell too fair;* 2, *Time stands still;* 3, *Behold a wonder here;* 4, *Daphne was not so chaste;* 5, *Me, me and none but me;* 6, *When Phoebus first did Daphne love;* 7, *Say, Love, if ever thou didst find;* 8, *Flow not so fast, ye fountains;* 9, *What if I never speed;* 10, *Love stood amazed;* 11, *Lend you ears to my sorrow;* 12, *By a fountain where I lay;* 13, *O, what hath overwrought;* 14, *Farewell unkind;* 15, *Weep you no more sad fountains;* 16, *Fie on this feigning;* 17, *I must complain;* 18, *It was a time when silly bees;* 19, *The lowest trees;* 20, *What poor astronomers;* 21, *Come when I call.*
**(*) O-L 430 284-2 [id.]. Kirkby, Skinner, Hill, Thomas, Mackintosh, Cons. of Musicke, Rooley.

Although there are certain details with which to quarrel – a general air of sobriety and an excessive restraint in colouring words – the whole set is well worth investigation and an impressive achievement; the instrumental support is of high quality, as is the presentation. The CD transfer is absolutely refined and clear: this might almost be a digital recording.

A Pilgrim's Solace: Fourth Booke of Songes (1612): Disdain me still; Sweet stay awhile; To ask for all they love; Love, those beams that breed; Shall I strive with words to move?; Were every thought an eye; Stay, time, awhile thy flying; Tell me, true love; Go nightly cares; From silent night; Lasso vita mia; In this trembling shadow cast; If that a sinner's sighs; Thou mighty God; When David's life; When the poor cripple; Where sin sor wounding; My heart and tongue were twins; Up merry mates; Welcome black night; Cease, cease these fake sports. Mr Henry Noell Lamentations (1597): O Lord turn not away; Lord in thy wrath; O Lord consider my distress; O Lord of whom I do depend; Where righteousness doth say; Lord to thee I make my moan; Lord hear my prayer. A Prayer for the Queen's most excellent Majesty. Psalms: 38: Put me not to rebuke, O Lord; 100: All people that on earth do dwell (2 settings); *104: My soul praise the Lord; 130: Lord to thee I make my moan; 134: Behold and have regard.* 3 Sacred songs: *Sorrow come; I shame at mine unworthiness; An heart that's broken and contrite.*

☞ ***** O-L 436 188-2 (2) [id.]. Kirkby, Simpson, York Skinner, Hill, Thomas, Consort of Musicke, Rooley.

A Pilgrim's Solace, Dowland's *Fourth Booke of Songes*, appeared when he was fifty. In its Preface he dwells on the decline of his fortunes in life and love, and of the remorseless advance of age. In a collection pervaded by melancholy, variety has been achieved here by using contrasts of texture: some of the songs are performed in consort, others are given to various singers. Emma Kirkby sings with great purity and beauty of tone, though she is not always as warm or poignant as the verse and music would warrant. However, hers is a most beautiful voice, and the set also offers some perceptive singing from Martyn Hill. The pervasive melancholy, not surprisingly, persists in both *Mr Henry Noell Lamentations*, which are all sung in consort, and the three Sacred songs, two of which are part-songs, and lifts only in the Psalm settings, which are more direct and positive in their supplication. The tune for the second setting of *All people that on earth do dwell* is instantly recognizable. These motets and sacred songs are an invaluable counterpart to Dowland's better-known secular works, instrumental and vocal. Anthony Rooley's playing is accomplished and so is his direction of the proceedings, and the eloquence of this music comes over. The recording, as ever from this source, is first rate and the CD transfers immaculate. Excellent documentation.

Ayres and Lute-lessons: *Prelude and Galliard; All ye whom love; Away with these self-loving lads; Come again sweet love; Come heavy sleep; Go Christal teares; If my complaints; My thoughts are winged; Rest awhile;* (Lute): *Semper Dowland, semper dolens. A shepherd in a shade; Stay sweet awhile; Tell me, true love; What if I never speede; When Phoebus first did Daphne love; Wilt thou unkind.*

(B) **(*) HM HMA 901076 [id.]. Deller Consort, Mark Deller; Robert Spencer.

Dowland's 'ayres' were designed for a consort of singers as well as for solo singer and lute, and it is good to hear them in this form. Two of the Lute Lessons are excellently played by Robert Spencer. The performances for the most part give consistent pleasure. The sound is excellent.

Lute songs: *Awake sweet love, thou art returned; Can she excuse my wrongs?; Come again! sweet love doth now invite; Fine knacks for ladies; Flow not so fast, ye fountains; Go, crystal tears; Lady, if you so spite me; Me, me and none but me; Shall I strive with words to move?; Shall I sue?; Sorrow stay; Tell me true love; What if I never speed?; When Phoebus first did Daphne love; Lute lessons: Captain Candish's galliard; Lady Laiton's almain; Preludium and Lachrimae pavan; Semper Dowland; Semper dolens.*

(M) ***** Saga SCD 9004. James Bowman, Robert Spencer.

This record makes a fine single-disc introduction to Dowland's art. James Bowman brings sensitivity and intelligence to each song and characterizes them tellingly. The lute solos provide two central interludes. The recording is very good too, real and present.

Ayres: *Can she excuse my wrongs?; Come again, sweet love; Come heavy sleep; Flow not so fast, ye fountains; From silent night; Go nightly cares; In darkness let me dwell; I saw my lady weep; Shall I sue?.* Consort pieces: *Captain Digory Piper's pavane and galliard; The First galliard.* Lute lessons: *Melancholy galliard; Mistess White's nothing; Mistress Winter's jump; My Lady Hunsdon's puff.* Lute duets: *My Lord Chamberlain's galliard; My Lord Willoughby's welcome home.* Lute lessons: *Orlando sleepeth; Sir John Smith's almain; Tarlton's resurrection.*

* HM HMC 90245 [id.]. Alfred Deller, Consort of Six, Robert Spencer.

Ayres: *Come away, come away sweet love; Flow my tears; If my complaints could passions move; If that a sinner's sighs be angel's food; Lasso, vita mia; Me, me and none but me; O gentle Death; Say, love, if ever thou didst find; Sorrow stay; Weep you no more sad fountain; What if I never speed?; Wilt thou unkind, thus reave me.* Consort pieces: *Can she excuse galliard; Fortune my foe; The Frog galliard; Katherine Darcy's galliard; Lachrimae pavane; The Round battle galliard.* Lute lessons: *Can she excuse galliard; Galliard; The Lady Laiton's almain; Midnight; Mistress White's thing; The Shoemaker's wife (Toy).*

* HM HMC 90244. Alfred Deller, Consort of Six, Robert Spencer.

Deller's two collections are admirably planned and beautifully recorded. He is in excellent voice, while variety is provided by interweaving his solos with lute pieces and music for Elizabethan consort of six instruments (two viols, flute, lute, cittern and bandora). The recording is naturally balanced and neither of these recitals outstays its welcome.

Lachrimae, or Seaven Teares.
*** BIS Dig. CD 315 [id.]. Dowland Consort, Jakob Lindberg.

Jakob Lindberg and his consort of viols give a highly persuasive account of Dowland's masterpiece. The texture is always clean and the lute clearly present.

Lachrimae: Seven passionate pavans. Consort settings: *Captain Piper his galiard; The Earl of Essex galiard; The King of Denmarks galiard; M. Bucton his galliard; M. George Whitehead his almand. M. Giles Hoby his galiard; M. Henry Noell his galiard; M. John Langtons pavane; M. Nicholas Gryffith his galiard; M. Thomas Collier his galliard with two trebles; Mrs Nichols Almand; Semper Dowland, semper Dolens; Sir Henry Umptons funerall; Sir John Souch his galiard.*
☞ *** Virgin/EMI Dig. VC5 45005-2 [id.]. Fretwork, with Christopher Wilson.

This is a reissue of Fretwork's 1989 recording of excerpts from the *Lachrimae*, for which the 'passionate' pavans serve as introduction. Structurally they form a variation sequence, linked by a falling fourth at the opening of the first *Lachrimae antiquae* and by other common motifs of melodic line and harmony, an innovative procedure at the time. They are distinguished also by their pervading melancholy. When first issued, these excerpts were originally interspersed with consort music by Byrd. Now they are all placed together, followed by a newly recorded collection of Dowland's own galliards, so one can choose to move over to more cheerful music at any time during the separately banded *Lachrimae*. All the performances are of undoubted merit and are well recorded. However, it could be suggested that the dance music sounds even more effective on Julian Bream's lute.

Drigo, Riccardo (1846–1930)

La Flûte magique (ballet; complete).
*** Decca Dig. 421 431-2 [id.]. ROHCG O, Bonynge – DELIBES; MINKUS: *La Source.* ***

Drigo's ballet has nothing whatsoever to do with Mozart's opera, but the score is appropriately vivacious, the invention inconsequential but so prettily scored and amiably tuneful that it makes a very agreeable entertainment when played as wittily and elegantly as here. With Decca's finest sound, this cannot fail to entertain.

Dukas, Paul (1865–1935)

L'apprenti sorcier (The sorcerer's apprentice).
*** DG Dig. 419 617-2 [id.]. BPO, Levine – SAINT-SAENS: *Symphony No. 3.* ***
(*) Decca Dig. 421 527-2 [id.]. Montreal SO, Dutoit (with Concert: '*Fête à la française*' *).
(M) **(*) Chan. CHAN 6503; *MBTD 6503* [id.]. SNO, Gibson – ROSSINI/RESPIGHI: *La boutique fantasque;* SAINT-SAENS: *Danse macabre.* **(*)
☞ (***) Testament mono SBT1017 [id.]. Philh O, Cantelli – CASELLA: *Paganiniana;* FALLA: *Three-cornered hat;* RAVEL: *Daphnis et Chloé: suite No. 2.* (***)

L'apprenti sorcier; Polyeucte overture.
☞ (M) **(*) Erato/Warner Dig. 2292 45819-2 [id.]. Basle SO, Armin Jordan – DEBUSSY: *La boîte à joujoux.* ***

Levine chooses a fast basic tempo, though not as fast as Toscanini (who managed with only two 78 sides), but achieves a deft, light and rhythmic touch to make this a real orchestral scherzo. Yet the climax is thrilling, helped by superb playing from the Berlin Philharmonic. The CD has an amplitude and sparkle which are especially telling.

Dutoit does not quite match Levine's zest (nor indeed achieves the sense of calamity at the climax that the latter does), but he is genially enjoyable and is featured within a desirable collection, given demonstration-worthy recording – see our Concerts section.

Armin Jordan's account of *L'apprenti sorcier* is not without impetus but is rhythmically rather heavy. It is very well recorded, as is the *Polyeucte overture*, really a 16-minute symphonic poem after Corneille's allegorical Christian play. Although the work's melodrama shows influences of Wagner and its scoring has much in common with Lalo, the closing pages are beautiful, and are touchingly played here.

Cantelli's 1954 mono account still remains one of the very best performances ever recorded, and it is splendidly transferred.

L'apprenti sorcier; La péri.
**(*) Chan. Dig. CHAN 8852; *ABTD 1469* [id.]. Ulster O, Yan Pascal Tortelier – CHABRIER:
España etc. ***

Yan Pascal Tortelier gives a very good performance indeed of *La Péri*, with plenty of atmosphere
and feeling, and *L'apprenti sorcier* is equally successful as a performance.

Symphony in C; L'apprenti sorcier; La Péri: poème dansé (including *Fanfare*).
☞ *** Denon Dig. CO 75284 [id.]. Netherlands R. PO, Fournet.

Although there were two LP versions of the *Symphony* in the 1970s from Jean Martinon (EMI
Pathé-Marconi) and Walter Weller (Decca), this new version from the veteran Jean Fournet supersedes
both, good though they were. Along with d'Indy, Chausson and Magnard, Dukas carried the torch
for the post-Franckian symphony in France with his well-argued and imaginatively scored contribution to the genre. Its vigour and resource are bracing, particularly in such expert hands. *La Péri* is
very much to the French *art nouveau* movement in music what Balakirev's *Tamara*, whose exoticism
and atmosphere were an undoubted inspiration, was to Russian music. With its voluptuous ideas and
sumptuously scoring, full of colour, it ought to be as much a repertoire piece as Rimsky-Korsakov's
Antar or *Scheherezade*. The Fournet recording is among the best ever – and although there have been
notable interpretations from Philippe Gaubert and Ernest Ansermet onwards, this is second to none.
L'apprenti sorcier has greater competition than either of its two companions – but, even so, this is
among the best. Given the marvellously expansive yet well-focused recording, this deserves a strong
recommendation.

Ariane et Barbe-bleue (opera): complete.
(M) *** Erato/Warner Dig. 2292 45663-2 (2) [id.]. Ciesinski, Bacquier, Paunova, Schauer, Blanzat,
Chamonin, Command, Fr. R. Ch. & O, Jordan.

Ariane et Barbe-bleue is, like Debussy's *Pelléas*, set to a Maeterlinck text, but there is none of the
half-lights and the dream-like atmosphere of the latter. The performance derives from a French
Radio production and is, with one exception, well cast; its direction under the baton of Armin Jordan
is sensitive and often powerful; the recording is eminently acceptable. The complete libretto is
included, and this most enterprising and valuable reissue is strongly recommended.

Duparc, Henri (1848–1933)

Mélodies (complete): *Au pays où se fait la guerre; Chanson triste; Elégie; Extase; La fuite (duet); Le
galop; L'invitation au voyage; Lamento; Le Manoir de Rosamonde; Phidylé; Romance de Mignon;
Sérénade; Sérénade florentine; Soupir; Testament; La vague et la cloche; La vie antérieure.*
*** Hyp. Dig. CDA 66323 [id.]. Sarah Walker, Thomas Allen, Roger Vignoles.

The Hyperion issue is as near an ideal Duparc record as could be. Here are not only the thirteen
recognized songs but also four early works – three songs and a duet – which have been rescued from
the composer's own unwarranted suppression. Roger Vignoles is the ever-sensitive accompanist; and
the recording captures voices and piano beautifully, bringing out the tang and occasional rasp of
Walker's mezzo and the glorious tonal range of Allen's baritone.

Duphly, Jacques (1715–89)

*Pièces pour clavecin: La Bouchon; Courante; La Félix; La Forqueray; Les Graces; La d'Héricourt;
Légèrement; Menuets; Rondo in D; Rondeau in D min.; La Vanlo; La Victoire; La de Villeneuve.*
☞ *** Gaudeamus/ASV Dig. CDGAU 108 [id.]. Mitzi Meyerson (harpsichord).

Mitzi Meyerson's anthology is among the best records devoted to Duphly since Leonhardt's Philips
disc from the mid-1970s, though only one or two pieces overlap. These performances come from the
mid-1980s (still analogue, and none the worse for that) and are very spirited and characterful. Duphly
published four collections of harpsichord works between 1744 and 1768 and, though none of his
music can lay a claim to greatness, it has undoubted charm and grace. Mitzi Meyerson plays a Goble
harpsichord and uses no fewer than four tunings during the course of the recital. There are excellent
notes by Nicholas Anderson. Recommended.

Dupré, Marcel (1886–1971)

Symphony in G minor for organ and orchestra, Op. 25.
*** Telarc Dig. CD 80136 [id.]. Michael Murray, RPO, Ling – RHEINBERGER: *Organ concerto No. 1.* ***

If you enjoy Saint-Saëns's *Organ symphony* you'll probably enjoy this. The organ's contribution is greater, though it is not a concerto. It is a genial, extrovert piece, consistently inventive if not as memorably tuneful as its predecessor. The performance has warmth, spontaneity and plenty of flair, and the recording has all the spectacle one associates with Telarc in this kind of repertoire.

Chorale and fugue, Op. 57; 3 Esquisses, Op. 41; Preludes and fugues: in B; G min., Op. 7/1 & 3; Le tombeau de Titelouse: Te lucis ante terminum; Placare Christe servulis, Op. 38/6 & 16; Variations sur un vieux Noël, Op. 20.
*** Hyp. Dig. CDA 66205 [id.]. John Scott (St Paul's Cathedral organ).

An outstandingly successful recital, more spontaneous and convincing than many of the composer's own recordings in the past. Dupré's music is revealed as reliably inventive and with an atmosphere and palette all its own. John Scott is a splendid advocate and the St Paul's Cathedral organ is unexpectedly successful in this repertoire.

Duruflé, Maurice (born 1902)

Fugue sur la thème du Carillon des heures de la Cathédrale de Soissons; Prélude, adagio et choral varié sur la thème du Veni Creator; Prélude sur l'Introit de l'Epiphanie; Prélude et fugue sur le nom d'Alain, Op. 7; Scherzo, Op. 2; Suite, Op. 5.
**(*) Delos Dig. D/CD 3047 [id.]. Todd Wilson (Schudi organ of St Thomas Aquinas, Dallas, Texas.

The producer of this record, which contains all Duruflé's organ music, consulted the composer before choosing the present organ, and the performances of Duruflé's often powerful and always engagingly inventive music are of the highest quality. The account of the closing *Toccata* of the *Suite*, Op. 5, has breathtaking bravura and if here, as elsewhere, detail is not sharply registered, the spontaneity and power of the playing are compulsive.

Requiem, Op. 9.
☞ *** Teldec/Warner Dig. 4509 90879-2 [id.]. Jennifer Larmore, Thomas Hampson, Amb. S., Philh. O, Legrand – FAURE: *Requiem.* ***
☞ (M) *** EMI Dig. CDM7 67801-2 [id.]. Dame Janet Baker, Stephen Roberts, King's College, Cambridge, Ch., John Butt (organ), Ledger – FAURE: *Requiem.* **(*)

(i; ii; iii) *Requiem. Op. 9;* (ii) *4 Motets (Ubi Caritas et Amor; Tota pulchra es; Tu es Petrus; Tantum ergo), Op. 10;* (iii) (Organ) *Prélude et fugue sur le nom d'Alain.*
☞ (B) *** Double Decca 436 486-2 [id.]. (i) Robert King, Christopher Keyte; (ii) St John's College, Cambridge, Ch.; (iii) Stephen Cleobury (organ); George Guest – FAURE: *Requiem* etc.; POULENC: *Messe* etc. ***

Those who have sometimes regretted that the lovely Fauré *Requiem* remains unique in the output of that master of delicate inspiration should investigate this comparably evocative *Requiem* of Duruflé. The composer wrote it in 1947, overtly basing its layout and even the cut of its themes on the Fauré masterpiece. The result is far more than an imitation for (as it seems in innocence) Duruflé's inspiration is passionately committed.

On Teldec comes a splendidly vibrant new digital version. Michel Legrand uses the full orchestral version and makes the most of the passionate orchestral eruptions in the *Sanctus* and *Libera me*. He strikes a perfect balance between these sudden outbursts of agitation and the work's mysticism and warmth. The Ambrosian Choir sing ardently yet find a treble-like purity for the *Agnus Dei* and *In Paradisum*, while Jennifer Larmore gives the *Pié Jesu* more plangent feeling than its counterpart in the Fauré *Requiem*. The recording, made in Watford Town Hall, is spacious and most realistically balanced. A clear first choice.

The (originally Argo) St John's version uses boy trebles instead of women singers, even in the solo of the *Pié Jesu* – exactly parallel to Fauré's setting of those words, which was indeed first sung by a treble. The alternative organ version is used here, not so warmly colourful as the orchestral version, but very beautiful nevertheless. The 1974 recording is vividly atmospheric. To this have been added the *Four Motets* on plainsong themes, each quite short but greatly varied in character, with the final

Tantum ergo perhaps the most ambitious. They are beautifully sung here. The organ piece, another sensitive example of Duruflé's withdrawn genius, makes a further substantial bonus, especially when one realizes that this remarkably generous pair of CDs includes also the *Mass* and *Salve Regina* of Poulenc, to make an unbeatable bargain.

Philip Ledger also uses organ rather than orchestral accompaniment. Yet such is the clarity of the recording and the sense of atmosphere engendered by the performance (and enhanced by the acoustic) that one scarcely misses the orchestra. The singing is very fine and the grave beauty and emotional restraint of Duruflé's music are splendidly conveyed. John Butt's organ contribution brings an added dimension of colour in the place of the orchestra. With the obvious coupling, this is very recommendable.

Requiem, Op. 9 (3rd version); *4 Motets, Op. 10*.
*** Hyp. Dig. CDA 66191; *KA 66191* [id.]. Ann Murray, Thomas Allen, Corydon Singers, ECO, Best; Trotter (organ).

Using the chamber-accompanied version, with strings, harp and trumpet – a halfway house between the full orchestral score and plain organ accompaniment – Best conducts a deeply expressive and sensitive performance of Duruflé's lovely setting of the *Requiem*. With two superb soloists and an outstandingly refined chorus, it makes an excellent recommendation, well coupled with motets, done with similar freshness, clarity and feeling for tonal contrast. The recording is attractively atmospheric yet quite clearly focused.

Dutilleux, Henri (born 1916)

Cello concerto (Tout un monde lointain).
☞ *** EMI CDC7 49304-2 [id.]. Rostropovich, O de Paris, Baudo – LUTOSLAWSKI: *Cello concerto*.
***

Dutilleux's *Cello concerto* (whose subtitle translates as 'A whole distant world') is a most imaginative and colourful score which exerts an immediate appeal and sustains it over many hearings. Rostropovich plays it with enormous virtuosity and feeling, and the Orchestre de Paris under Serge Baudo gives splendid support. This record won the composer the 1976 Koussevitzky Award, and the 1975 recording is immensely vivid, with Rostropovich looming larger than life but given great presence. This is a straightforward full-priced reissue, retaining the original catalogue number.

Métaboles.
(M) *** Erato/Warner 2292 45689-2 [id.]. French Nat. RO, Munch – HONEGGER: *Symphony No. 4*.
***

Métaboles is a marvellously atmospheric piece, with the fastidious orchestral palette this composer commands: it has something of the rhythmic energy of Stravinsky, the evocative atmosphere of Messiaen, but is wholly individual. It is played in splendid and exhilarating fashion by the French Radio Orchestra, and the recording could have been made yesterday. Strongly recommended.

Symphony No. 1; Timbres, espace, mouvement.
*** HM Dig. HMC 905159 [id.]. O Nat. de Lyon, Serge Baudo.

In Dutilleux's *First Symphony* there is a mercurial intelligence and a vivid imagination at work, and the orchestral textures are luminous and iridescent. What is particularly impressive is its sense of forward movement: you feel that the music is taking you somewhere. *Timbres, espace, mouvement* is a more recent work, dating from 1978. Serge Baudo is an authoritative interpreter of this composer and the Lyon orchestra also serve him well. The engineering is superb: there is plenty of space round the various instruments, and the balance is thoroughly realistic.

Symphonies Nos. 1–2.
☞ ⊛ *** Chan. Dig. CHAN 9194 (id.]. BBC PO, Tortelier.
☞ ** Erato/Warner Dig. 2292-45287 (id.]. O de Paris, Barenboim.

Marvellously resourceful and inventive scores which are given vivid and persuasive performances by Tortelier and the BBC Philharmonic Orchestra. The *First Symphony* evinces a mercurial intelligence and a vivid imagination, and the orchestral textures are luminous and iridescent. There is a lot of Honegger here and in its companion from 1959, though in the latter the mantle of Stravinsky – and in particular the *Symphonies of wind instruments* – looms large. The engineers give us a splendidly detailed and refined portrayal of these complex textures – the sound is really state-of-the-art. This issue supersedes Serge Baudo's version with the Orchestre National de Lyon of the *First Symphony*, coupled with *Timbres, espace, mouvement*, and is to be preferred on all counts to the Erato alternative with the Orchestre de Paris under Barenboim. The latter also suffers from an editing slip which, as far as we know, has gone uncorrected and affects the first bars of the opening of the *First Symphony*; even putting that to one side, the Chandos is definitely the CD to have.

Symphony No. 2; Timbres, espace, mouvement (La nuit étoilée); Métaboles.
☞ *** Ph. 438 008-2 [id.]. O de Paris, Bychkov.

Magnificent orchestral playing from the Orchestre de Paris and splendidly present and clear recording, made in the Salle Pleyel; the sound has exceptional body and range. The performance has all the virtuosity and brilliance you could want, and has real fire. All the same, Tortelier and the BBC Philharmonic on Chandos have greater atmosphere and their disc of the two symphonies remains the preferred recommendation. However the *Timbres, espaces, mouvement* (*La nuit étoilée*) is available only in Serge Baudo's version, coupled with the *First Symphony*; but Tortelier and this between them supplant it. Those who do not have that or Munch's disc of the *Métaboles* might do well to consider this vividly recorded account.

String quartet (Ainsi la nuit).
☞ *** Sony Dig. SK 52554 [id.]. Juilliard Qt – DEBUSSY; RAVEL: *Quartets.* ***
*** Pickwick Dig. MCD 17; *MCC 17* [id.]. New World String Qt – DEBUSSY: *String quartet;* RAVEL: *String quartet.* **(*)

There are other versions of Dutilleux's fascinating quartet, *Ainsi la nuit*, but this impressive account from the Juilliard Quartet is a clear first choice, offering superb playing and recording. The music conjures up the moods and impressions surrounding the idea of 'night' – not night itself so much as its aura. As so often with this composer, the writing is highly imaginative.

On Pickwick, the New World Quartet offers a useful, slightly less expensive alternative, conveying the music's sense of mystery and scurrying whispers most effectively. Excellent recording too.

Piano sonata.
**(*) Olympia Dig. OCD 354 [id.]; Archduke MARC 2. Donna Amato – BALAKIREV: *Sonata.* **(*)

The Dutilleux *Sonata* has an almost symphonic breadth and sense of scale; it is tonal – the first movement is in F sharp minor and its centrepiece, a *Lied*, is finely wrought and original, and skilfully linked to the final chorale and variations. Donna Amato gives a totally committed and persuasive account of it, and the recording is very truthful.

Dvořák, Antonín (1841–1904)

Cello concerto in B min., Op. 104.
*** DG 413 819-2 [id.]. Rostropovich, BPO, Karajan – TCHAIKOVSKY: *Rococo variations.* ***
*** Chan. Dig. CHAN 8662; *ABTD 1348* [id.]. Wallfisch, LSO, Mackerras – DOHNANYI: *Konzertstück.* ***
(M) *** BMG/RCA GD 86531 (6531-2-RG]. Harrell, LSO, Levine – SCHUBERT: *Arpeggione sonata.* ***
(B) *** DG 429 155-2 [id.]. Fournier, BPO, Szell – BLOCH: *Schelomo;* BRUCH: *Kol Nidrei.* **(*)
(M) (***) EMI CDH7 63498-2 [id.]. Casals, Czech PO, Szell – ELGAR: *Concerto* (**(*)) (with BRUCH: *Kol Nidrei* (***)).
☞ (M) **(*) BMG/RCA 09026 61498-2 [id.]. Piatigorsky, Boston SO, Munch – WALTON: *Concerto.* ***
☞ **(*) Virgin/EMI Dig. VC7 59325-2 [id.]. Truls Mørk, Oslo PO, Jansons – TCHAIKOVSKY: *Rococo variations.* **(*)

If Rostropovich can sometimes sound self-indulgent in this most romantic of cello concertos, the degree of control provided by Karajan gives a firm yet supple base, and there have been few recorded accounts so deeply satisfying. The analogue recording dates from 1969 and the original sound was both rich and refined; the effect is certainly enhanced in the first-class CD transfer.

Rafael Wallfisch's is an outstanding version, strong and warmly sympathetic, masterfully played. This is a performance which, in its taut co-ordination between soloist, conductor and orchestra, far more than usual establishes the unity of the work. The excitement as well as the warmth of the piece comes over as in a live performance, and Wallfisch's tone remains rich and firm in even the most taxing passages. The orchestral playing, the quality of sound and the delightful, generous and unusual coupling all make it a recommendation which must be given the strongest advocacy.

In Lynn Harrell's first RCA recording, made in the mid-1970s, his collaboration with James Levine in Dvořák's *Cello concerto* proved a powerful and sympathetic one. Richly satisfying accounts of the first and second movements culminate in a reading of the finale which proves the most distinctive of all. The recording is bright and full and has been remastered most successfully for CD.

Fournier's reading has a sweep of conception and richness of tone and phrasing which carry the melodic lines along with exactly the mixture of nobility and tension that the work demands. The phrasing in the slow movement is ravishing, and the interpretation as a whole balances beautifully. DG's recording is forward and vivid, with a broad, warm tone for the soloist. Dating from 1962, it sounds newly minted on a single bargain-price CD and tape, coupled with Bloch and Bruch.

Casals plays with astonishing fire and the performance seems to spring to life in a way that eludes many modern artists; the rather dry acoustic of the Deutsches Haus, Prague, and the limitations of the 1937 recording are of little consequence. This disc is one of the classics of the gramophone.

When it first appeared on LP, we were inclined almost to dismiss Piatigorsky's 1960 recording because the sound was so shallow. It has been improved remarkably for this CD and, although the balance is still too close and not always flattering to the soloist, with tuttis still inclined to be somewhat two-dimensional, the quality is now fully acceptable. There is no lack of orchestral colour and the acoustic of Symphony Hall is conveyed behind the music-making. The performance is the very opposite of routine, with Piatigorsky and Munch in complete rapport, producing a consistently spontaneous melodic flow, moving from introspective thoughtfulness to expressive warmth and ardour. Tuttis blaze up in the orchestra, yet the soloist brings moments of rapt meditation; although there are also moments when intonation is less than immaculate, the inspiration of the performance carries the day.

A fine, lyrical performance from an impressive young Norwegian soloist. Truls Mørk has not the largest instrumental personality, but Jansons provides a refined orchestral introduction to set the scene for the arrival of his young soloist, who phrases both with ardour and with gently hushed tenderness when playing on a half-tone. The elegiac episode recalling earlier ideas just before the close of the finale is touchingly done. An enjoyable performance, given vivid, modern sound, but one which pales beside the glorious romanticism of the Rostropovich/Karajan partnership.

(i) *Cello concerto in B min., Op. 76;* (ii) *Rondo in G min.; Silent woods; Slavonic dance in G min., Op. 46/8.*

☞ *** Ph. Dig. 434 914-2; *434 914-4* [id.]. Heinrich Schiff, (i) VPO, Previn; (ii) Previn (piano).

Heinrich Schiff's earlier recording of Dvořák's *Cello concerto*, at once fresh, direct and warm, shone out for the fidelity with which he observed the composer's detailed markings. In this new version with André Previn and the Vienna Philharmonic, Schiff's view is very similar, but with maturity the result is even more commanding and spontaneous-sounding, as well as a degree more urgent. The passage-work is freer and more volatile, and the great second-subject melody is the more moving for its tender restraint. Unlike almost any rival, Schiff dares to play it pianissimo and at a flowing tempo, which is what the score asks for. The finale has more fun in it than before, bringing a more dramatic contrast with the meditation of the epilogue. Unlike most soloists in concerto recordings, Schiff opts for natural balance, with the instrument not spotlit. Previn, drawing ravishing sounds from the Vienna Philharmonic, particularly the brass, gives an extra lift to the Slavonic rhythms. Then at the piano Previn similarly adds sparkle to the shorter Dvořák pieces that come as encore, all of them better-known in orchestral form, but here more winning still. An ungenerous coupling, but an attractive one.

Piano concerto in G min., Op. 33.
*** BMG/RCA Dig. RD 60781 [60781-2]. Rudolf Firkušný, Czech PO, Václav Neumann – JANACEK: *Concertino; Capriccio.* ***
(*) Decca Dig. 417 802-2 [id.]. András Schiff, VPO, Dohnányi – SCHUMANN: *Introduction and allegro appassionato.* *

Firkušný has played the Dvořák *Piano concerto* in both the original version and that by Vilém Kurz, as well as a *mélange* of the two. The present recording conveys its sunny geniality to good effect, and although the great pianist was seventy-nine when this record was made, the playing still sounds both youthful and aristocratic. Firkušný now makes an admirable first choice, and his claims are enhanced by the value of the coupling, (and the 73 minutes' playing time of the CD).

Schiff's excellent performance derives from a public concert in the Musikverein, and he is given splendid support from the Vienna Philharmonic under Dohnányi. In the Decca recording, the piano is very up-front and the perspective in this respect is not wholly natural. All the same, this is an excellent performance.

Violin concerto in A min., Op. 53.

(B) *** CfP Dig. CD-CFP 4566; *TC-CFP 4566* [Ang. CDB 62920]. Tasmin Little, RLPO, Handley
– BRUCH: *Concerto No. l.* ***

(M) *** Ph. 420 895-2. Accardo, Concg. O, C. Davis – SIBELIUS: *Violin concerto.* ***

(B) *** Sup. 110601-2. Josef Suk, Czech PO, Ančerl – SUK: *Fantasy.* ***

Violin concerto in A min., Op. 53; Romance in F min., Op. 11.

*** EMI Dig. CDC7 49858-2 [id.]. Kyung Wha Chung, Phd. O, Muti.

*** EMI CDC7 47168-2 [id.]. Perlman, LPO, Barenboim.

☞ (M) **(*) Teldec/Warner Dig. 4509 91444-2 [id.]. Zehetmair, Philh. O, Inbal – SCHUMANN: *Violin concerto.* ***

Kyung Wha Chung in her first recording under her exclusive EMI contract gives a heartfelt reading of a work that can sound wayward. The partnership with Muti and the Philadelphia Orchestra is a happy one, with the sound warmer and more open than it has usually been in the orchestra's recording venue. She finds similar concentration in the *Romance*, which is also the coupling on Perlman's and Midori's versions.

Perlman and Barenboim still sound pretty marvellous and show all the warmth and virtuosity one could desire. This CD also has the eloquent and touching *F minor Romance*. Perlman is absolutely superb in both pieces: the digital remastering undoubtedly clarifies and cleans the texture, though there is a less glowing aura about the sound above the stave.

Tasmin Little brings to this concerto an open freshness and sweetness, very apt for this composer, that are extremely winning. The firm richness of her sound, totally secure on intonation up to the topmost register, goes with an unflustered ease of manner, and the recording brings little or no spotlighting of the soloist; she establishes her place firmly with full-ranging, well-balanced sound that co-ordinates the soloist along with the orchestra.

In his Philips recording, Accardo is beautifully natural and unforced, with eloquent playing from both soloist and orchestra. The engineering is altogether excellent, and in a competitive field this must rank high, especially at mid-price.

Suk's earlier performance is back in the catalogue at bargain price, effectively remastered, recoupled with the Suk *Fantasy*. Its lyrical eloquence is endearing, the work is played in the simplest possible way and Ančerl accompanies glowingly.

Thomas Zehetmair plays the concerto with brilliance and precision. He is satisfyingly clean in attack and is very sympathetic in the lovely *Romance*. He is well accomapnied by Inbal, and the Teldec recording is natural and well balanced. Even so, this is a performance in the central Viennese tradition, with Czech flavours played down and little feeling for the Czech idiom, even in the Slavonic dance of the finale. But the Schumann coupling is first class, and this generous coupling of two less familiar concertos is welcome.

(i) *Czech suite, Op. 39; Nocturne for strings in B, Op. 40; Polka for Prague students in B flat, Op. 53a; Polonaise in E flat; Prague waltzes;* (ii) *Slavonic dances Nos. 1–3; 8, Op. 46/1–3; 8; 10, Op. 72/2.*

☞ (M) *** Decca Dig. 436 476-2 [id.]. (i) Detroit SO; (ii) RPO; Antal Dorati.

A collection of Dvořák rarities, exhilaratingly performed and brilliantly recorded. The *Czech suite* can sometimes outstay its welcome – but certainly not here. The other items too have the brightness and freshness that mark out the Dvořák *Slavonic dances*, especially the *Polka* and *Polonaise*. The most charming piece of all is the set of *Waltzes*, written for balls in Prague – Viennese music with a Czech accent – while the lovely *Nocturne* with its subtle drone bass makes an apt filler. The recording has an attractive warmth and bloom to balance its brightness. On the reissued CD, the programme opens with sparkling performances by the RPO of five favourite *Slavonic dances*, and here the sound is rather more brightly lit.

Czech suite, Op. 39; Serenade for strings, Op. 22.

☞ (B) *** Erato/Warner Dig. 2292 45928-2 [id.]. Lausanne CO, Jordan (with SMETANA: *Vltava:* Strasbourg PO, Lombard *).

Jordan's bargain coupling of the *Czech suite* and *String serenade* is eminently recommendable. The performances are comparatively mellow but both works respond to this relaxed treatment, and the *Czech suite* in its undemanding, gently pastoral way becomes a charmer. First-rate playing and excellent recording. The Smetana coupling, however, is not an asset, a lifeless performance which begins too slowly and never gushes into life as a great river should.

Czech suite, Op. 39; Symphonic variations, Op. 78.
☞ **(*) DG Dig. 437 506-2; *437 506-4* [id.]. N. German RSO, Gardiner – BRAHMS: *Hungarian dances.* **(*)

John Eliot Gardiner's first recording as chief conductor of the North German Radio Orchestra amply demonstrates the responsiveness and refinement of the players as well as the conductor's imagination in what for him seems an unexpected area of the romantic orchestral repertory. His approach to this music, and to the *Symphonic variations* in particular, is unusually volatile, with subtle moulding of rhythm and phrase, and with rubato often extreme if always natural-sounding. With tempi on the brisk side and regularly getting brisker, the *Variations* have more sparkle and fun in them than usual, plus a feeling of fantasy. Gardiner's speeds are on the fast side in the *Czech suite* too. He is not only consistently brisker than Jordan on the Erato issue but is also generally lighter and more affectionate. There are passages in the *Variations* too where the results are not quite as sharply defined as one ideally wants, even if the sound is always comfortable. Whether or not recorded later, the *Czech suite* is clearer.

Overtures: *Carnival, Op. 92; Hussite, Op. 67; In nature's realm, Op. 91; My home, Op. 62; Othello, Op. 93.* Symphonic poems: *The Golden spinning wheel, Op. 109; The Noonday witch, Op. 108; The Water goblin, Op. 107; The Wood dove, Op. 110.* Symphonic variations, Op. 78.
(M) *** DG 435 074-2 (2) [id.]. Bav. RSO, Rafael Kubelik.

Kubelik's performances are among his finest on record and they are superbly played. He is splendidly dashing in *Carnival*; in the two pieces there is magic and lustre in the orchestra, and the atmospheric tension is striking. The *Symphonic variations* opens warmly and graciously, yet Kubelik is obviously determined to minimize the Brahmsian associations; his light touch and apt pacing lead on to the lively finale. The recordings, made in the Munich Hercules-Saal between 1973 and 1977, are freshly transferred to CD and generally sound excellent.

Overtures: *Carnival, Op. 92; In Nature's realm, Op. 91; Othello, Op. 93. Scherzo capriccioso, Op. 66.*
*** Chan. Dig. CHAN 8453; *ABTD 1405* [id.]. Ulster O, Handley.

Dvořák wrote this triptych immediately before his first visit to America in 1892. Handley's excellent performances put the three works in perspective. A splendid issue, superbly recorded.

Overtures: *Carnival, Op. 92; In Nature's realm, Op. 91; Othello, Op. 93. Scherzo capriccioso, Op. 66; Symphonic variations, Op. 78.*
*** ASV Dig. CDDCA 794 [id.]. RPO, Farrer.

John Farrer scores over Handley by including also the *Symphonic variations*, here given a performance of airy freshness which confounds any Brahmsian associations. The three linked overtures have comparable warmth and delicacy of colouring. There is plenty of drama too, and the only slight disappointment is that *Carnival*, while vigorous enough and with a richly hued central section, could have been even more exuberant. The *Scherzo capriccioso* is brightly vivacious. The recording, made at St Barnabas Church, Mitcham, is wide-ranging and naturally balanced.

Overture: Carnival, Op. 92; Slavonic rhapsody No. 3 in A flat, Op. 45; Symphonic variations, Op. 78;
(i) *Biblical songs, Op. 99.*
☞ **(*) Chan. Dig. CHAN 9002. SNO, Neeme Järvi; (i) with Brian Rayner Cook.

These were all fill-ups used in Järvi's set of the symphonies. An exhilarating *Carnival* is matched by a strongly characterized set of variations, with a rich lyrical emphasis, while the *Slavonic rhapsody* is done with delicious point and humour. The slight reservation concerns the ten *Biblical songs*, which Dvořák wrote in America at the same period as the *Cello concerto*. They are given positive and clean-cut performances by Brian Rayner Cook but are not very Slavonic-sounding.

Symphonic poems: *The Golden spinning wheel, Op. 109; The Noon Witch, Op. 108; The Wood dove, Op. 109.*
☞ (BB) *** Naxos Dig. 8.550598 [id.]. Polish Nat. RSO (Katowice), Stephen Gunzenhauser.

Having very successfully surveyed the Dvořák symphonies, Gunzenhauser now turns to the symphonic poems based on the sometimes horrifically melodramatic folk poems of Karel Jaromir Erben. The music itself, although often graphically descriptive, minimizes the unpleasantness. The Polish orchestra seem thoroughly at home in Dvořák's sound-world and Gunzenhauser gives warm, vivid performances and is especially evocative in the masterly *Golden spinning wheel* – a favourite of Sir Thomas Beecham – with its evocative horn-calls setting the opening hunting scene and immediately creating a romantic atmosphere. There is shapely string phrasing and a fine, sonorous contribution from the brass to illustrate a melodramatic tale about a young king and a dismembered bride-to-be, with the spinning wheel finally revealing the crime. The story ends happily with the heroine, Dornicka, put back together and restored to the arms of her beloved. Dvořák tactfully omits the final dénouement of Erben's poem, in which the wicked stepmother and her daughter (the substitute bride) are torn to pieces by wolves, and the music has a communicative optimism which is very engaging here. The concert hall of Polish Radio in Katowice has expansive acoustics – just right for the composer's colourful effects.

Overture: *Othello, Op. 93.* Symphonic poems: *The Golden spinning-wheel, Op. 109; The Water goblin, Op. 107. Scherzo capriccioso, Op. 66.*
☞ (M) **(*) Decca 425 060-2 [id.]. LSO, István Kertész.

These recordings come from a vintage Dvořák series which Kertész made for Decca in the 1960s and early 1970s. This group, coupling *The Golden spinning wheel* with its evocative horn-calls and the tale of the malignant *Water goblin*, with an outstanding version of the *Scherzo capriccioso* – considered the finest available in its day (1963) – and *Othello*, makes a most attractive anthology. Some of the richness of the original sound has been lost in the CD remastering: the violins are drier in timbre than they were on LP; but the ambient effect ensures plenty of colour. Kubelik's complete mid-priced set of the symphonic poems with the Bavarian Radio Symphony Orchestra (see above) is not displaced, but the present 73-minute collection is both generous and distinctive.

Serenade for strings in E, Op. 22.
☞ (M) **(*) Virgin/EMI Dig. CUV5 61144-2. LCO, Warren-Green – SUK: *Serenade* ***;
TCHAIKOVSKY: *Serenade.* **(*)
(BB) **(*) Naxos Dig. 8.550419 [id.]. Capella Istropolitana, Kr(e)chek – SUK: *Serenade.* ***
☞ **(*) Decca Dig. 433 549-2 [id.]. Cleveland O, Ashkenazy – BRAHMS: *Symphony No. 2.* **(*)

Serenade for strings; Romance, Op. 11.
(B) *** Pickwick Dig. PCD 928; *CIMPC 928.* Laredo, SCO, Laredo – WAGNER: *Siegfried idyll.* ***

Serenade for strings; Serenade for wind in D min., Op. 44.
*** ASV Dig. CDCOE 801 [id.]. COE, Alexander Schneider.
*** Ph. 400 020-2 [id.]. ASMF, Marriner.

Serenade for strings; Serenade for wind; Miniatures, Op. 74a.
☞ (B) *** Discover Dig. DICD 920135 [id.]. Virtuosi di Praga, Oldrich Vlcek.

The young players of the Chamber Orchestra of Europe give winningly warm and fresh performances of Dvořák's *Serenades*, vividly caught in the ASV recording.

Marriner's later, Philips performances are direct without loss of warmth, with speeds ideally chosen, refined yet spontaneous-sounding; in the *Wind serenade* the Academy produce beautifully sprung rhythms, and the recording has a fine sense of immediacy.

Laredo's performance of Dvořák's lovely *Serenade* is volatile, full of spontaneous lyrical feeling. The recording, made in City Hall, Glasgow, is admirably balanced to give a true concert-hall effect and add ambient lustre to the string timbre. As an encore Laredo takes the solo role in the *F minor Romance*, which he plays with appealing simplicity.

The wind players of the Virtuosi di Praga give a bright, idiomatic performance of Opus 44, using characteristically reedy tones. The *String serenade* is done with equal understanding, though the recording catches an edge on high violins. The opening lyrical *Moderato* and the fourth-movement *Larghetto* both bring speeds on the slow side, but the players' natural warmth sustains them without sentimentality. The rare *Miniatures* for string trio provide an attractive makeweight. An excellent bargain in full, bright sound.

Warren-Green and his excellent London Chamber Orchestra bring their characteristically fresh, spontaneous approach to the Dvořák *Serenade*. If without the winning individuality of the outstanding COE version under Schneider, this is still very enjoyable, and the Suk coupling is outstanding. Excellent sound.

Fine playing from the Capella Istropolitana on Naxos, and flexible direction from Jaroslav Kr(e)chek. His pacing is not quite as sure as in the delightful Suk coupling, and the *Adagio* could flow with a stronger current, but this is still an enjoyable and well-recorded performance.

A fresh-toned, easily lyrical (if in no way distinctive) reading, well recorded, to make an unusual but attractive coupling for Ashkenazy's Brahms.

Serenade for wind, Op. 44.
*** CRD CRD 3410; *CRDC 4110* [id.]. Nash Ens. – KROMMER: *Octet-Partita.* ***

The Nash Ensemble can hold their own with the competition in the *D minor Serenade*, and their special claim tends to be the coupling, a Krommer rarity that is well worth hearing. The CRD version of the Dvořák is very well recorded and the playing is very fine indeed, robust yet sensitive to colour, and admirably spirited.

Serenade for wind in D min., Op. 44; Hussite overture (Husitská), Op. 67; The Noonday witch, Op. 108; Symphonic variations, Op. 78.
☞ (M) *** Decca 425 061-2 [id.]. LSO, István Kertész.

Kertész gives a delightfully fresh performance of the enchanting *Wind serenade*, with excellent (1967) Decca recording clearly defining detail and providing both warmth and bloom. The *Symphonic variations* is another splendid work, still played comparatively rarely. Under Kertész its Brahmsian derivations are all but submerged by the Czech composer's freshness of spirit. Kertész is even more remarkably successful in the *Hussite overture.* This is a patriotic piece, running for nearly a quarter of an hour and including themes based on the Hussite hymn and St Wenceslas plainchant. It can too easily be made to seem rhetorical, but not here, where the drama is compellingly red-blooded. *The Noonday witch* (the traditional ogress threatened to erring children by distraught mothers) also has striking colour and warmth, and the transfers – the additional works were recorded in 1971 – are all well managed.

Slavonic dances Nos. 1–8, Op. 46; 9–16, Op. 72.
*** Decca Dig. 430 171-2 [id.]. Cleveland O, Christoph von Dohnányi.
❀ (M) *** Sony SBK 48161 [id.]. Cleveland O, George Szell.

Dohnányi's rhythmic flexibility and the ebb and flow of his rubato are a constant delight. The recording is superb, very much in the demonstration bracket, with the warm acoustics of the Cleveland Hall ideal in providing rich textures and brilliance without edge. A delightful disc.

   Szell's exuberant, elegant and marvellously played set of the *Slavonic dances* now returns to the catalogue, absolutely complete (74 minutes), newly remastered by Bejun Mehta and Christopher Herles. True, the balance is close (which means pianissimos fail to register) but the charisma of the playing is unforgettable. This is orchestral playing of extraordinary distinction, and for all the racy exuberance one senses a predominant feeling of affection and elegance. The warm acoustics of Severance Hall ensures the consistency of the orchestral sound.

(i) *Slavonic dances Nos. 1, 3, 8, Op. 46/1, 3 & 8; 9–10, Op. 72/1–2;* (ii) *Slavonic rhapsody No. 3, Op. 45/3.*
☞ (M) ** Decca 425 087-2 [id.]. (i) Israel PO, Kertész; Detroit SO, Dorati – ENESCU: *Rumanian rhapsody No. 1* ***; SMETANA: *Vltava* etc. **

As part of a generous Decca compilation of favourite Czech music Kertész offers vivacious performances of five favourite dances, and if the Israel Philharmonic was not at the time one of the world's most polished ensembles they play with plenty of spirit. However, the orchestra is not flattered by the acoustic and the violins are made to sound thin by the bright remastering of the 1962 recording. Dorati's *Slavonic rhapsody*, recorded in 1978, is another matter. Presented with sparkle and warmth, it is given the advantage of the sumptuous Detroit acoustic and makes an altogether more agreeable sonic impression.

SYMPHONIES

Symphonies Nos. 1–9.
(M) *** Chan. Dig. CHAN 9008/13 [id.]. SNO, Neeme Järvi.

Symphonies Nos. 1–9; Overtures: Carnival; In nature's realm; My home. Scherzo capriccioso.
❀ (B) *** Decca 430 046-2 (6). LSO, István Kertész.

Järvi has the advantage of outstanding, modern, digital recording, full and naturally balanced. The set is offered at upper mid-price, six CDs for the price of four. Only the *Fourth Symphony* is split centrally between discs; all the others can be heard uninterrupted. But there are no fillers, as with Kertész on Decca.

   For those not wanting to go to the expense of the digital Chandos Järvi set, Kertész's bargain box is an easy first choice among the remaining collections of Dvořák symphonies. The CD transfers are of Decca's best quality, full-bodied and vivid with a fine ambient effect. It was Kertész who first revealed the full potential of the early symphonies, and his readings gave us fresh insights into these often inspired works. To fit the symphonies and orchestral works on to six CDs some mid-work breaks have proved unavoidable; but the set remains a magnificent memorial to a conductor who died sadly young.

Symphony No. 1 in C min. (The Bells of Zlonice), Op. 3; The Hero's song, Op. 111.
*** Chan. Dig. CHAN 8597; *ABTD 1291* [id.]. SNO, Järvi.

The first of Dvořák's nine symphonies is on the long-winded side. Yet whatever its structural weaknesses, it is full of colourful and memorable ideas, often characteristic of the mature composer. Järvi directs a warm, often impetuous performance, with rhythms invigoratingly sprung in the fast movements and with the slow movement more persuasive than in previous recordings. The recording is warmly atmospheric in typical Chandos style.

Symphony No. 1 in C min. (The Bells of Zlonice), Op. 3; Legends, Op. 59/1–5.
(BB) *** Naxos Dig. 8.550266 [id.]. Slovak PO, Czecho-Slovak RSO, Gunzenhauser.

Though on a super-bargain label, this Bratislava version rivals any in the catalogue both as a performance and in sound. The ensemble of the Slovak Philharmonic is rather crisper than that on the other modern rival, Järvi's Chandos disc, and the recording, full and atmospheric, has detail less obscured by reverberation. The first five of Dvořák's ten *Legends* make a generous coupling: colourful miniatures, colourfully played.

Symphony No. 2 in B flat, Op. 4; Legends, Op. 59/6–10.
(BB) *** Naxos Dig. 8.550267 [id.]. Slovak PO, Czecho-Slovak RSO, Gunzenhauser.

With speeds more expansive than those of his Chandos rival, Neeme Järvi, Gunzenhauser gives a taut, beautifully textured account, very well played and recorded, a formidable rival in every way, even making no allowance for price. The completion of the set of *Legends* makes a very generous coupling (73 minutes).

Symphony No. 3 in E flat, Op. 10; Carnival overture; Scherzo capriccioso.
*** Virgin/EMI Dig. VC7 59257-2 [id.]. RLPO, Pešek.

Symphony No. 3 in E flat, Op. 10; Carnival overture, Op. 92; Symphonic variations, Op. 78.
*** Chan. Dig. CHAN 8575; *ABTD 1270* [id.]. SNO, Järvi.

Pešek's strong, direct manner in Dvořák here works to bring out the rhythmic freshness of the writing in a most persuasive reading. He has high concentration in sustaining a very slow speed for the central *Adagio*. The clarity of the recording, beautifully set against a believable acoustic, adds to the rhythmic freshness, not least in Pešek's account of the *Scherzo capriccioso*, in which he observes the central repeat.

Järvi's is also a highly persuasive reading, not ideally sharp of rhythm in the first movement but totally sympathetic. The recording is well up to the standards of the house and the fill-ups are particularly generous.

Symphonies Nos. 3 in E flat, Op. 10; 6 in D, Op. 60.
(BB) *** Naxos Dig. 8.550268; *4.550268* [id.]. Slovak PO, Stephen Gunzenhauser.

These exhilarating performances of the *Third* and *Sixth Symphonies* are well up to the standard of earlier records in this splendid Naxos series. Gunzenhauser's pacing is admirably judged through both works, and rhythms are always lifted. Excellent, vivid recording in the warm acoustics of the Bratislava Concert Hall.

Symphony No. 4 in D min., Op. 13; (i) Biblical songs, Op. 99.
*** Chan. Dig. CHAN 8608; *ABTD 1251* [id.]. SNO, Järvi, (i) with Brian Rayner Cook.

Järvi's affectionate reading of this early work brings out the Czech flavours in Dvořák's inspiration and makes light of the continuing Wagner influences, notably the echoes of *Tannhäuser* in the slow movement. This is a performance to win converts to an often underrated work. The recording is well up to the Chandos standard.

Symphonies Nos. 4 in D min., Op. 13; 8 in G, Op. 33.
(BB) **(*) Naxos Dig. 8.550269; *4550269* [id.]. Slovak PO, Stephen Gunzenhauser.

Gunzenhauser's *Fourth* is very convincing. In his hands the fine lyrical theme of the first movement certainly blossoms and the relative lack of weight in the orchestral textures brings distinct benefit in the Scherzo. The slow movement, too, is lyrical without too much Wagnerian emphasis. The naturally sympathetic orchestral playing helps to make the *Eighth* a refreshing experience, even though the first two movements are rather relaxed and without the impetus of the finest versions. The digital sound is excellent, vivid and full, with a natural concert-hall ambience.

Symphony No. 5 in F, Op. 76; Othello overture, Op. 93; Scherzo capriccioso, Op. 66.
🏵 *** EMI Dig. CDC7 49995-2 [id.]. Oslo PO, Jansons.

Symphony No. 5 in F, Op. 75; The water goblin, Op. 107.
*** Chan. Dig. CHAN 8552; *ABTD 1258* [id.]. SNO, Järvi.

Jansons directs a radiant account of this delectable symphony and the EMI engineers put a fine bloom on the Oslo sound. With its splendid encores, equally exuberant in performance, this is one of the finest Dvořák records in the catalogue.

Järvi is also most effective in moulding the structure, subtly varying tempo between sections to smooth over the often abrupt links. His persuasiveness in the slow movement, relaxed but never sentimental, brings radiant playing from the SNO, and Czech dance-rhythms are sprung most infectiously, leading to an exhilarating close to the whole work, simulating the excitement of a live performance.

Symphonies Nos. 5 in F, Op. 76; 7 in D min., Op. 70.
(BB) *** Naxos Dig. 8.550270; *4550270* [id.]. Slovak PO, Stephen Gunzenhauser.

Gunzenhauser's coupling is recommendable even without the price advantage. The beguiling opening of the *Fifth*, with its engaging Slovak wind solos, has plenty of atmosphere, and the reading generates a natural lyrical impulse. The *Seventh*, spontaneous throughout, brings an eloquent *Poco adagio*, a lilting scherzo, and a finale that combines an expansive secondary theme with plenty of excitement and impetus.

Symphony No. 6 in D, Op. 60.
*** Decca Dig. 430 204-2 [id.]. Cleveland O, Dohnányi – JANACEK: *Taras Bulba.* ***

Dohnányi continues his Dvořák series in Cleveland with a superb account of No. 6. With its obvious echoes of Brahms's *Symphony No. 2* (also in D major), this is a work which gains from the refinement of the playing, with the violin melody at the start of the slow movement given ethereal beauty. But in his warmth and freshness Dohnányi does not miss the earthy qualities of the writing; and the impact of the performance is greatly enhanced by the fullness and weight of the recording, one of Decca's most vivid. This easily takes precedence over the Järvi version on Chandos (CHAN 8350).

Symphonies Nos. 7 in D min., Op. 70; 8 in G, Op. 88.
(M) *** Mercury 434 312-2 [id.]. LSO, Antal Dorati.
(M) *** Decca Dig. 430 728-2 [id.]. Cleveland O, Christoph von Dohnányi.
*** Virgin/EMI Dig. VC7 59516-2 [id.]. RLPO, Pešek.

Dorati's coupling brings an extraordinary successful account of No. 7 to rank alongside Barbirolli's Hallé version in its spontaneous feel of a live performance. It is similarly enhanced by the vividly realistic concert hall balance of the (1963) Mercury recording – one of their very finest. The interpretation is free, yet Dorati's strong rhythmic grip on the first movement means that he can relax for the gentle reprise of the main theme on the horns, with a magical diminuendo. The *Poco Adagio* is similarly impulsive and the Scherzo lifts off with a sparkle. The finale has enormous energy and bite, and an exuberant thrust, leading on to a thrilling coda where the tension rises to the highest level, as Dorati broadens the few final bars. The *Eighth Symphony* was recorded four years earlier, with the acoustic of Watford Town Hall again providing a highly convincing ambience. Dorati's reading proves comparably vibrant. At the close there is another display of spontaneous combustion, when the symphony storms to its exciting close.

Dohnányi's coupling of Dvořák's *Seventh* and *Eighth Symphonies* with the Cleveland Orchestra is also very attractive indeed. Tempi are all aptly judged. The playing of the Cleveland Orchestra is so responsive that the overall impression is one of freshness, and the recording is in the demonstration class, using the acoustics of the Masonic Auditorium to give a convincingly natural balance, the internal definition achieved without any kind of digital edge.

In Pešek's *D minor*, the fresh, direct manner relates it readily to other Dvořák. The slow movement is warm and relaxed, and the scherzo becomes a happy folk-like dance, despite the minor key, while Pešek's speed in the finale also allows him to give a lift to the stamping dance-rhythms. No. 8 receives a similarly refreshing performance, persuasive in a light, relaxed way, with the folk element again brought out, above all in the middle movements. The scherzo is liltingly light; and again the performance benefits from the full, clear sound.

(i) *Symphonies Nos. 7 in D min., Op. 70; 8 in G, Op. 88;* (ii) *9 (New World);* (i) *Symphonic variations, Op. 78.*

☞ (B) *** Ph. Duo 438 347-2 (2) [id.]. (i) LSO; (ii) Concg. O, Sir Colin Davis.

Sir Colin Davis's performances of Nos. 7 and 8, with their bracing rhythmic flow and natural feeling for Dvořákian lyricism, are appealingly direct yet have plenty of life and urgency. In the famous Scherzo of No. 7 with its striking cross-rhythms, he marks the sforzandos more sharply than usual, keeping rhythms very exact. The *Adagio* of No. 8 is hardly less eloquent, and there is an engagingly zestful exuberance in the outer movements. In the *New World*, however, the very directness has its drawbacks. The cor anglais solo in the slow movement brings an appealing simplicity, yet the effect is not very resilient, and later, when the horns echo the theme at the end of the opening section, the impression is positive rather than seductively nostalgic. However, the reading is completely free from egotistical eccentricity and, with beautiful orchestral playing throughout, this is enjoyable in its way. The set is made the more attractive by the inclusion of the *Symphonic variations* – one of Dvořák's finest works, much underrated by the public – and here Davis's performance has striking freshness. The remastering of all the recordings is very successful and, with excellent notes by John Warrack, this Duo set is excellent value and will give much satisfaction.

Symphony No. 8 in G, Op. 88.
☞ (M) *(*) BMG/RCA 09026 61206-2 [id.]. Boston SO, Munch – BRAHMS: *Symphony No. 4.* **

Symphony No. 8 in G; Carnival overture; The wood dove, Op. 110.
(B) *** DG 429 518-2 [id.]. BPO or Bav. RSO, Kubelik.

Symphony No. 8 in G; Legends Nos. 4, 6 & 7, Op. 59; Scherzo capriccioso.
❀ (M) *** EMI CDM7 64193-2 [id.]. Hallé O, Sir John Barbirolli.

Symphony No. 8 in G, Op. 88; Scherzo capriccioso; Notturno for strings.
*** Telarc Dig. CD 80206 [id.]. LAPO, Previn.

Symphony No. 8 in G, Op. 88; The wood dove, Op. 110.
*** Chan. Dig. CHAN 8666; *ABTD 1352* [id.]. SNO, Järvi.

Barbirolli's account of this symphony was one of his best Pye records: the reading has immense vitality and forward impetus, the kind of spontaneous excitement that is rare in the recording studio, and yet the whole performance is imbued with a delightful, unforced lyricism. The *Scherzo capriccioso* is warm and very exciting too, and the *Legends* make a colourful bonus. This was always the finest of Barbirolli's late Dvořák symphonies technically, and the EMI documentation reveals why: it was made in 1957/8 in Manchester's recently rebuilt Free Trade Hall by the Mercury recording team, led by Wilma Cozart Fine. In remastered form it is tremendously real and vivid.

Characteristically, Previn's Dvořák style is sharply rhythmic, and his idiomatic use of rubato brings affectionate moulding of phrase and rhythm, generally kept within a steady pulse. Warmth and freshness go with the finest recorded sound yet achieved with this orchestra in Royce Hall, full and with a vivid sense of presence that allows fine inner clarity. Previn's fill-up is equally attractive, with the infectiously sprung account of the *Scherzo capriccioso* scarcely harmed by the omission of the central repeat.

Järvi's highly sympathetic account of the *Eighth* underlines the expressive lyricism of the piece, the rhapsodic freedom of invention rather than any symphonic tautness, with the SNO players reacting to his free rubato and affectionate moulding of phrase with collective spontaneity. The warm Chandos sound has plenty of bloom, with detail kept clear, and is very well balanced.

Kubelik's *Eighth* is appealingly direct, with responsive, polished playing from the Berlin Philharmonic Orchestra. For its reissue, the Bavarian Radio Orchestra provide the substantial encores, which are splendidly done.

Munch gives a strongly characterized though occasionally somewhat fierce account of one of Dvořák's most genial and sunny masterpieces. It is very firmly held together and, as always with this conductor, there is a splendid sense of line and momentum. Some might feel it a bit overdriven and at times unsmiling, though there is plenty of feeling in the slow movement. The 1961 recording is generally much superior to that of the *Fourth Symphony* of Brahms, with which it is coupled.

Symphony No. 9 in E min. (From the New World), Op. 95.
☞ (M) *** Mercury 434 317-2 [id.]. Detroit SO, Paray – SIBELIUS: *Symphony No. 2.* **
(M) (***) BMG/RCA mono GD 60279 [60279-2-RG]. NBC SO, Toscanini – KODALY: *Háry*
    János: suite (***); SMETANA: *Má Vlast: Vltava.* (**)
☞ **(*) DG Dig. 439 009-2 [id.]. VPO, Karajan – SMETANA: *Vltava.* **(*)
☞ (M) **(*) Teldec/Warner CD 82007 [id.]. St Louis SO, Leonard Slatkin.

(i) *Symphony No. 9 (New World);* (ii) *American suite, Op. 98b.*
(M) *** Decca Dig. 430 702-2 [id.]. (i) VPO, Kondrashin; (ii) RPO, Dorati.

Symphony No. 9 (New World); Carnival Overture.
☞ (B) ** Erato/Warner Dig. 4509 94576-2 [id.]. LPO, James Conlon.

Symphony No. 9 (New World); Carnival Overture; Scherzo capriccioso, Op. 66.
☞ (BB) *(*) Tring Dig. TRP 010 [id.]. RPO, Pavo Järvi.

Symphony No. 9 (New World); Carnival Overture, Op. 92; Slavonic dances Nos. 1 & 3, Op. 46/1 & 3.
☞ (M) *(*) Sony SMK 47547 [id.]. NYPO, Bernstein (with SMETANA: *Vltava* *(*)).

Symphony No. 9 (New World); My home overture, Op. 62.
*** Chan. Dig. CHAN 8510; *ABTD 1220* [id.]. SNO, Järvi.

(i) *Symphony No. 9 (New World);* (ii) *Serenade for strings.*
(M) **(*) Sony SBK 46331 [id.]. (i) LSO, Ormandy; (ii) Munich PO, Kempe.

(i) *Symphony No.9 in E min. (New World);* (ii) *Slavonic dances Nos. 1, 2, 7 & 8, Op. 46/1, 2, 7 & 8; 16, Op. 72/8.*
☞ (B) *** DG 439 436-2 [id.]. (i) BPO; (ii) Bav. RSO; Rafael Kubelik.

Symphony No. 9 (New World); Slavonic dances Nos. 1, 3 and 7, Op. 46/1, 3 & 7; 10 and 15, Op. 72/2 & 7.
(M) *** DG 435 590-2 [id.]. BPO, Karajan.

Symphony No. 9 (New World); Symphonic variations, Op. 78.
(B) *** CfP Dig. CD-CFP 9006; *TC-CFP 4382.* LPO, Macal.
☞ (M) ** Telarc Dig. 4509 91447-2 [id.]. Philh. O, Inbal.

Kondrashin's Vienna performance of the *New World Symphony* was one of Decca's first demonstration CDs, and its impact remains quite remarkable. Recorded in the Sofiensaal, the ambience of the hall prevents a clinical effect, yet every detail of Dvořák's orchestration is revealed within a highly convincing perspective. Other performances may exhibit a higher level of tension, but there is a natural spontaneity here, with the first-movement exposition repeat fitting naturally into the scheme of things. The cor anglais solo in the *Largo* is easy and songful, and the finale is especially satisfying, with the wide dynamic range adding drama and the refinement and transparency of the texture noticeably effective as the composer recalls ideas from earlier movements. This splendid disc is enhanced by the inclusion of Dorati's RPO version of the engaging *American suite*, which also has clear influences from the New World.

Macal as a Czech takes a fresh and unsentimental view of the *New World Symphony*. His inclusion of the repeat balances the structure convincingly. With idiomatic insights there is no feeling of rigidity, with the beauty of the slow movement purified, the Scherzo crisp and energetic, set against pastoral freshness in the episodes, and the finale again strong and direct, bringing a ravishing clarinet solo. The *Symphonic variations*, which acts as coupling, is less distinctive but is well characterized. A fine bargain recommendation.

Karajan's 1964 DG recording held a strong place in the catalogue for two decades, and it is certainly far preferable to his digital version. It has a powerful lyrical feeling and an exciting build-up of power in the outer movements. The *Largo* is played most beautifully, and Karajan's element of detachment lets the orchestra speak for itself, which it does, gloriously. The rustic qualities of the Scherzo are affectionately brought out, and altogether this is very rewarding. The recording is full, bright and open. This is now reissued, sounding as good as ever, coupled with five favourite *Slavonic dances*, given virtuoso performances; they remain stylish because of the superbly polished playing. In the dances the recording is overlit but can be tamed.

Kubelik's marvellously fresh Berlin Philharmonic account of the *New World*, recorded in the Berlin Jesus-Christus-Kirche in 1972, remains among the top recommendations, provided one does not mind the omission of the first movement's exposition repeat. It is brightly transferred in this Classikon reissue and is now recoupled with five sparkling *Slavonic dances*. The sound is a little dry in the bass but otherwise of vintage DG quality.

Järvi's opening introduction establishes the spaciousness of his view, with lyrical, persuasive phrasing and a very slow speed, leading into an allegro which starts relaxedly, but then develops in big dramatic contrasts. The expansiveness is underlined, when the exposition repeat is observed. The *Largo* too is exceptionally spacious, with the cor anglais player taxed to the limit but effectively supported over ravishingly beautiful string playing. The Scherzo is lilting rather than fierce, and the finale is bold and swaggering.

Paray's 1960 *New World* was very highly regarded in its day, and rightly so – it is uncommonly fresh. In the first-movement allegro he immediately sets and holds a fast, tight tempo, relaxing only slightly for the second subject, which is airy and graceful in consequence. As was the normal practice at that time, the exposition repeat is not observed, which makes the first movement sound rather brief. The *Largo*, with its poised and gentle cor anglais melody, makes a gentle contrast, and the Scherzo is admirably vivacious. The finale goes furiously and its spontaneity leaves the listener with that rare feeling that the music really has been made while he or she was listening. The recording, made in Detroit's Cass Technical High School auditorium, is well balanced in a typically natural Mercury way and adds to the freshness of effect. The Sibelius coupling is generous but the interpretation, though exciting, is rather less successful.

With speeds consistently fast and the manner clipped, Toscanini's reading of the *New World* is anything but idiomatic, but it still tells us something unique about Dvořák and his perennial masterpiece, presenting a fiery, thrilling experience. The sound is fuller than most from this source and the transfer brings that out, despite the usual dryness.

Under Ormandy the playing of the LSO has life and spontaneity, and the rhythmic freshness of the Scherzo (achieved by unforced precision) is matched by the lyrical beauty of the *Largo* and the breadth and vigour of the finale. Perhaps the reading has not the individuality of the finest versions; but the sound is full and firm in the bass to support the upper range's brilliance. For coupling, we are offered an essentially mellow account of the *String serenade*, directed by Kempe with affectionate warmth.

Karajan's digital recording of the *New World Symphony* is one of the remastered recordings reissued on the Karajan Gold label, where the improvement in the definition of the sound is most tangible. The edginess on strings and brass has been greatly mitigated, the timpani are strikingly vivid, and the focus is altogether more precise. The performance is enjoyably alive and does not lack spontaneity, although the VPO playing is less refined than on either of Karajan's analogue versions with the BPO, especially in the *Largo*. However, those wanting a Karajan performance in modern, digital sound could be well satisfied with this.

The St Louis Symphony plays for Slatkin with polish and refinement; the cor anglais solo of the slow movement is so velvety it hardly sounds like a reed instrument, and the brass which introduce the *Largo* is characteristically rich in sonority. One or two mannerisms apart, the reading is both enjoyably direct and vital, and the recording, full-bodied and naturally balanced, brings out the sweetness of the strings, even in the gentlest pianissimos. This is most enjoyable but even at mid-price (with a playing-time of only 44 minutes) remains uncompetitive without a coupling.

In spite of often beautiful playing from the Philharmonia Orchestra, especially in the *Largo*, Inbal is not a front-runner. He omits the exposition repeat in the first movement and, when the secondary theme appears, the marked relaxation of tempo does not sound entirely spontaneous. The coupling is warmly atmospheric but lacks something in red-blooded drama.

Conlon's is an essentially small-scale reading, with the refined presentation of the second subject of the first movement matched by the *Largo*, tender in its delicacy. The Scherzo and finale are robust and straightforward, but the reading overall is short on weight and power. The overture goes well and the recording is good, but there are other, preferable, bargain versions of the symphony.

Bernstein's *New World* begins well with a fresh, brilliant account of the first movement (exposition repeat included) and a beautifully played *Largo*. The third movement, however, is very fast and does not relax enough or beguile as it should. The finale is done not very imaginatively: it is just played through, with no magic when the earlier themes are recalled. The recording, made in New York's Manhattan Center in 1962, is good; Bernstein is back on form in the two *Slavonic dances*, while the *Carnival overture* is brilliant enough. *Vltava* makes a colourful encore, but here the recording of the violins in their famous lyrical melody is not very flattering.

At super-bargain price in the Royal Philharmonic Collection, Pavo Järvi conducts the *New World Symphony* with natural expressive warmth at generally expansive speeds. With glowing tone from the RPO, the result is rich and often dramatic. However, this performance is surely a collector's item for its extraordinarily indulgent treatment of the second subject of the first movement. The conductor slows right down and caresses the flute melody with an almost grotesque degree of gentle voluptuousness. This happens every time it appears (and the exposition is repeated) so that even Dvořák's lovely, fresh melody is almost made to wear out its welcome. The *Largo* is also slow, and some may find the end effect enervating. The generous coupling, *Carnival*, is lively enough, but Järvi swoons voluptuously over the lilting secondary theme of the *Scherzo capriccioso*.

CHAMBER AND INSTRUMENTAL MUSIC

Flute sonatina in G min. (trans. Galway).
*** BMG/RCA Dig. RD 87802 [7802-2-RC]. James Galway, Phillip Moll – FELD; MARTINU:
  Sonatas. ***

What the flute version of Dvořák's *Sonatina* underlines more than the violin original is how close this tuneful, unpretentious piece is to the *New World Symphony* of the same year, 1893. Well recorded, with characterful performances and an unusual and attractive coupling of two modern Czech flute works, it makes an excellent recommendation for anyone wanting a Galway record out of the ordinary.

Piano quartets Nos. 1 in D, Op. 23; 2 in E flat, Op. 87.
⊛ *** Hyp. Dig. CDA 66287 [id.]. Domus.

The Dvořák *Piano quartets* are glorious pieces, and the playing of Domus is little short of inspired. This is real chamber-music-playing: intimate, unforced and distinguished by both vitality and sensitivity. Domus are recorded in an ideal acoustic and in perfect perspective; they sound wonderfully alive and warm.

Piano quintet in A, Op. 81.
☞ *** ASV Dig. CDDCA 889 [id.]. Peter Frankl, Lindsay Qt – MARTINU: *Piano quintet No. 2.* ***
(M) *** Decca 421 153-2. Clifford Curzon, VPO Qt – FRANCK: *Quintet.* ***

This ASV account of Dvořák's glorious *Piano quintet* by the Lindsays with Peter Frankl is the finest of modern versions and can readily stand comparison with the famous early Decca account with Clifford Curzon. A highly volatile yet warmly lyrical first movement leads to playing in the central movements that is both magical and full of subtle detail. Apart from Peter Frankl's fine contribution, one especially responds to Bernard Gregor-Smith's rich cello-line. Because of the resonance, the recording is full and warm and, if there is just a hint of thinness on the violin timbre, the balance with the piano is particularly well managed.

  This wonderfully warm and lyrical (1962) performance of Dvořák's *Piano quintet* by Clifford Curzon is a classic record, one by which all later versions have come to be judged, and the CD transfer retains the richness and ambient glow of the original analogue master, yet has improved definition and presence. The piano timbre remains full and real.

Piano quintet in A, Op. 81; Piano quartet No. 2 in E flat, Op 87.
☞ **(*) DG Dig. 439 868-2 [id.]. Menahem Pressler, Emerson Quartet (augmented).

Taking temporary leave from his colleagues of the Beaux Arts Trio, Menahem Pressler joins with the Emerson Quartet in powerful, intense accounts of these two magnificent works. If the *Piano quintet*, with its wealth of memorable melody, is by far the better-known, Pressler and the Emersons demonstrate how the *Second Piano quartet*, sketched immediately after the other work and completed two years later in 1889, is just as rich in invention, in some ways even more distinctive in its thematic material. If there is one movement that above all proves a revelation, it is the *Lento* of the *Quartet*, given with a rapt, hushed concentration to put it among the very finest of Dvořák inspirations. The performance of the *Quintet* too is comparably positive in its characterization, even if many will prefer easier, even warmer readings such as that from Domus on Hyperion in the *Piano quartet*. The DG New York recording gives an unpleasant edge to high violins, making the full ensemble abrasive.

(i) *Piano quintet in A, Op. 81; String quartet No. 12 in F (American), Op. 96.*
*** BMG/RCA RD 86263 [6263-2-RC]. (i) Rubinstein; Guarneri Qt.
☞ ** Calliope Dig. CAL 9229 [id.]. (i) Kazuko Mimura; Talich Qt.

Both the RCA performances are memorably warm and spontaneous; tempi tend to be brisk, but the lyrical element always underlies the music and the playing has both great vitality and warmth. Needless to say, Rubinstein's contribution to the *Quintet* is highly distinguished. The recordings, made in April 1971 and 1972 respectively, are well balanced, detailed and fairly full, helped by the attractive studio ambience.

  The new Talich coupling, recorded in 1993, is a disappointment. The lively playing in the *Quintet* produces an athletic effect and there is less warmth and Dvořákian charm. The players are not helped by the close microphones and digital recording which combine to make climaxes sound slightly aggressive: the sparkling finale of the *American Quartet*, for instance, is articulated with commendable lightness, but the upper range is too sharply etched.

Piano trios Nos. 1 in B flat, Op. 21; 2 in G min., Op. 26; 3 in F min., Op. 65; 4 in E min. (Dumky), Op. 90.
☞ (M) *** Teldec/Warner Dig. 2292 76458-2 (2) [id.]. Trio Fontenay.

In reissuing the Trio Fontenay's set of Dvořák *Piano trios* at mid-price, Teldec tend to sweep the board. First-class playing and expertly balanced modern recording combine to make this very attractive indeed. Wolf Harden, the pianist, dominates – but only marginally so: his colleagues match him in lyrical ardour, and they are as sympathetic to Dvořák's warm lyricism as to the Czech dance characteristics of the livelier allegros.

Piano trio No. 1 in B flat, Op. 21.
*** Teldec/Warner Dig. 2292 44177-2 [id.]. Trio Fontenay – BRAHMS: *Piano trio No. 2.* ***

First-class playing and recording from the Trio Fontenay, and a useful coupling as well, of rewarding music.

Piano trios Nos. 1 in B flat min., Op. 21; 2 in G, Op. 26.
☞ *** Chan. Dig. CHAN 9172 [id.]. Borodin Trio.

We liked the Borodins' earlier recording of the *F minor Piano trio* (see below) and find much to admire in the present disc, which couples the earlier *Trios*. On one or two occasions the Borodin Trio have tended towards expressive italicization, underlining details where the music could be left to speak for itself – particularly in slow movements. But there is nothing to quarrel with here: these are spontaneous yet finely shaped performances, very well recorded.

Piano trio No. 3 in F min., Op. 65.
**(*) Chan. Dig. CHAN 8320; *ABTD 1207* [id.]. Borodin Trio.

Piano trios No. 3 in F min., Op. 65; 4 in E min. (Dumky), Op. 90.
*** Sony Dig. MK 44527 [id.]. Emanuel Ax, Young-Uck Kim, Yo-Yo Ma.
(M) **(*) Ph. 426 095-2. Beaux Arts Trio.

Piano trio No. 4 in E min. (Dumky), Op. 90.
*** Chan. Dig. CHAN 8445; *ABTD 1157* [id.]. Borodin Trio – SMETANA: *Piano trio.* ***

The *F minor Trio* is given a powerful yet sensitive performance by the Ax/Kim/Ma trio and, like the *Dumky*, it has warmth and freshness. The recording is faithful and natural.

The Beaux Arts' 1969 performances of Op. 65 and the *Dumky* still sound fresh and sparkling, though the recording on CD is a little dry in violin timbre; the *F minor*, arguably the finer and certainly the more concentrated of the two, is played with great eloquence and vitality.

The playing of the Borodin Trio in the *F minor Trio* has great warmth and fire; such imperfections as there are arise from the natural spontaneity of a live performance; however, this now seems short measure. But in the *Dumky trio* it is the spontaneous flexibility of approach to the constant mood-changes that makes the splendid Borodin performance so involving, as well as the glorious playing from each of the three soloists. The recording here is naturally balanced and the illusion of a live occasion is striking.

String quartets Nos. 1–14; Cypresses, B.152; Fragment in F, B.120; 2 Waltzes, Op. 54, B.105.
(M) *** DG 429 193-2 (9). Prague Qt.

Dvořák's *Quartets* span the whole of his creative life. The glories of the mature *Quartets* are well known, though it is only the so-called *American* which has achieved real popularity. The beauty of the present set, made in 1973–7, is that it offers more *Quartets* (not otherwise available) plus two *Quartet movements*, in *A minor* (1873) and *F major* (1881), plus two *Waltzes* and *Cypresses* for good measure, all in eminently respectable performances and decent recordings.

String quartet No. 7 in A min., Op. 16; Cypresses.
☞ **(*) Chan. Dig. CHAN 8826; *ABTD 1451* [id.]. Chilingirian Qt.

String quartets Nos. 8 in E, Op. 80; 9 in D min., Op. 34.
**(*) Chan. Dig. CHAN 8755; *ABTD 1394* [id.]. Chilingirian Qt.

String quartets Nos. 10 in E flat, Op. 51; 11 in C, Op. 61.
**(*) Chan. Dig. CHAN 8837; *ABTD 1458* [id.]. Chilingirian Qt.

Chandos provide very fine recorded sound for the Chilingirians, who play with sensitivity in all five *Quartets*. These are straightforward, well-paced readings that are eminently serviceable. Some collectors may feel, perhaps, that they fall short of the very highest distinction, but they are unfailingly musicianly and vital.

String quartet No. 12 in F (American), Op. 96.
(B) *** Pickwick Dig. PCD 883; *CIMPC 883* [id.]. Delmé Qt – BRAHMS: *Clarinet quintet.* ***

☞ *** EMI Dig. CDC7 54215-2 [id.]. Alban Berg Qt – SMETANA: *Quartet.* ***
*** Ph. Dig. 420 803-2 [id.]. Guarneri Qt – SMETANA: *String quartet No. 1.* ***
*** Ph. 420 396-2 [id.]. Orlando Qt – MENDELSSOHN: *String quartet No. 1.* ***
(B) *** Hung. White Label HRC 122 [id.]. Bartók Qt – DEBUSSY; RAVEL: *Quartets.* **(*)
☞ (M) **(*) DG 437 251-2 [id.]. Amadeus Qt. – SMETANA: *String quartet No. 1.* **(*)
☞ **(*) Collins Dig. 1386-2 [id.]. Duke Qt – BARBER: *Quartet;* GLASS: *Quartet No. 1.* **

String quartet No. 12 (American); Cypresses.
*** DG Dig. 419 601-2 [id.]. Hagen Qt – KODALY: *Quartet No. 2.* ***

The Delmé Quartet on a superbly recorded Pickwick disc at bargain price give a winningly spontaneous-sounding performance, marked by unusually sweet matching of timbre between the players, which brings out the total joyfulness of Dvořák's American inspiration.

The Hagen Quartet make an uncommonly beautiful sound and their account of this masterly score is very persuasive indeed. Their playing is superbly polished, musical and satisfying, and they play the enchanting *Cypresses*, which Dvořák transcribed from the eponymous song-cycle, with great tenderness. The recording is altogether superb, very present and full-bodied.

The Alban Berg also give a very fine account of the *F major*, Op. 96. They have their finger on the vital current that carries its musical argument forward. Phrasing is dextrously shaped and the polish and elegance of their playing are never in danger of diminishing the spontaneous-seeming character of this music. In this respect they are perhaps less successful in the Smetana coupling. Very good recording, and thoroughly recommendable to admirers of this ensemble.

The Guarneri performance is warmly romantic and in the *Largo sostenuto* one notices the rich cello line of David Soyer, within a responsive texture of finely blended lyricism. Of course there is plenty of life too, and the dance-like finale has an agreeable rhythmic lightness. The recording is full in timbre and most natural in balance and presence.

The digital remastering of the 1980 Orlando recording brings very striking presence and immediacy; it emphasizes that their approach, while still romantic, has more drama than the Guarneri account. With such realistic sound, this still ranks among the best versions of the *Quartet*.

A splendidly alive and spontaneous account from the Bartók Quartet too, polished yet with plenty of warmth and lyrical feeling, and with a dance-like sparkle in the scherzo and finale. Good sound, generous couplings and the bargain status of this issue ensure its value.

Although we have some reservations about Norbert Brainin's vibrato, which at times sounds self-conscious (especially in the slow movement), admirers of the Amadeus will certainly want their 1977 coupling of Dvořák and Smetana, recorded in Finland. This is a strongly conceived performance, full of ardour. The Scherzo and exhilarating finale show their brilliance of ensemble at its most appealing and infectious. The sound is vivid, full and immediate.

The Duke Quartet is handicapped by a curiously hybrid coupling: two American works, though it would have been better to have had a Schuman or Piston quartet along with Barber's celebrated piece rather than the empty Glass. They play the *F major Quartet* well, but not better than many rivals in the catalogue: they are very well recorded, though the balance is a bit forward.

String quartets Nos. 12 in F (American), Op. 90; 13 in G, Op. 106.
*** ASV Dig. CDDCA 797. Lindsay Qt.

In the *F major Quartet* (*American*) the Lindsays' account is certainly among the very best both in terms of performance and recording. The *G major*, Op. 106 is also very well played, with much the same dedication and sensitivity. An outstanding coupling.

String quartets Nos. 12 in F (American), Op. 96; 14 in A flat, Op. 105.
☞ **(*) Chan. Dig. CHAN 8919; *ABTD 1520* [id.]. Chilingirian Qt.

These Chilingirian performances are well up the standard of their fine series, even if their version of the *American Quartet* would not be a first choice. The recording is first class and those needing this coupling will not be disappointed.

(i) *String quartet No. 12 (American);* (ii) *String quintet in E flat, Op. 97.*
(M) *** Decca 425 537-2 [id.]. (i) Janáček Qt; (ii) Vienna Octet (members).

The Janáček performance of the *American quartet* is strikingly fresh. This is virtuosity of a high order put completely at the service of the composer, and the fine 1964 recording has depth as well as realistic definition. The coupled *E flat Quintet*, another of the greatest works of Dvořák's American period, is given a comparably eloquent and characterful performance by members of the Vienna Octet. Again the recording is full, with an attractive ambience.

String quartet No. 13 in G, Op. 106; Quartet movement in F, B.120; 2 Waltzes, Op. 54.
☞ **(*) Chan. Dig. CHAN 8874 [id.]. Chilingirian Qt.

In the last and perhaps most remarkable of Dvořák's string quartets the Chilingirians maintain the generally high quality of their cycle for Chandos. The playing has momentum and vitality and, though there are moments when they could make more of dynamic nuance, these are sympathetic and well-recorded performances. They include the *Quartet movement in F major* that Dvořák had originally intended for the piece, as well as two of the *Waltzes* Dvořák arranged from the Op. 54 piano pieces.

String quartet No. 14 in A flat, Op. 105.
☞ *** Sony Dig. SK 53282 [id.]. Artis Qt – SMETANA: *String quartet.* ***

The Artis Quartet give one of the best accounts of the *A flat Quartet*, Op. 105, to have reached the catalogue since the Smetana Quartet recorded it in the early 1970s. It is ardent and expressive without being in the least overstated, and is compelling throughout. The Sony recording is in every way first class.

String quintets: (i) *in G, Op. 77;* (ii) *in E flat, Op. 97.*
☞ *** Bayer Dig. BR 100 184CD [id.]. Stamitz Qt, with (i) Jiří Hudec; (ii) Jan Talich.

String quintets in G, Op. 77; in E flat, Op. 97; Intermezzo in B, Op. 40.
☞ *** Chan. Dig. CHAN 9046 [id.]. Chilingirian Qt.

Artistically, honours are pretty evenly divided between the Stamitz Quartet and the Chilingirians in the quintets. The *E flat String quintet*, Op. 97, which dates from his American years, is one of Dvořák's very greatest works! The Stamitz Quartet is perhaps balanced more forwardly but is pleasantly recorded, and the Chilingirian set on Chandos has more air round the sound but without any loss of focus. Both performances have the warmth and humanity that Dvořák exudes, but the Chillingirians undoubtedly score in including the beautiful *B major Intermezzo* that the composer had originally intended for the *G major Quintet* and which he subsequently expanded into an independent work for full strings, the *Nocturne*, Op. 40. This tips the balance in its favour.

String quintet in E flat, Op. 97; String sextet in A, Op. 48.
*** Hyp. Dig. CDA 66308; *KA 66308* [id.]. Raphael Ens.

The *E flat major Quintet*, Op. 97, is one of the masterpieces of Dvořák's American years, and it is most persuasively given by the Raphael Ensemble. It is also very well recorded, though we are placed fairly forward in the aural picture.

Slavonic dances Nos. 1–16, Op. 46/1–8; Op. 71/1–8.
☞ **(*) Ph. Dig. 426 264-2 [id.]. Katia & Marielle Labèque.
**(*) Ara. Dig. Z 6559 [id.]. Artur Balsam, Gena Raps (piano, four hands).

This is probably the most successful set of *Slavonic dances* in their original two-piano format now available. The playing is mercurial and does not lack imagination, although some may feel that certain of the individual nuances and the various spurts of accelerando are imposed rather arbitrarily. But the Labèque sisters obviously revel in their own cultured virtuosity and they know what they are about, so their brilliance is balanced with lyrical sensibility and a feeling for colour. However, the recording venue, an abbey, was a less than ideal choice. The engineers have put their microphones up close and, while the sound is basically natural, the resonance brings a slight preponderance of middle and bass.

Generally fine performances from Artur Balsam and Gena Raps, who respond to the music in a spirit of relaxed enjoyment, yet do not miss its brio. The recording too is well balanced in a pleasing acoustic.

VOCAL AND CHORAL MUSIC

Mass in D, Op. 86.
(M) *** Decca 430 364-2 [id.]. Ritchie, Giles, Byers, Morton, Christ Church Cathedral Ch., Preston; Cleobury (organ) – LISZT: *Missa choralis.* ***

The *Mass in D* in such a beautifully shaped reading is self-recommending, especially when coupled with a superb performance of Liszt's equally fresh *Missa choralis*. As so often, the CD remastering shows just how good was the original (Argo) recording, which is impeccably balanced.

Requiem, Op. 89.
(M) *** Decca 421 810-2 (2). Lorengar, Komlóssy, Isofalvy, Krause, Amb. S., LSO, Kertész –
  KODALY: *Hymn of Zrinyi; Psalmus Hungaricus.* ***

The *Requiem* reflects the impact on Dvořák of the English musical world of the day and has a good
deal of relatively conventional writing in it. Kertész conducts with a total commitment to the score
and secures from singers and orchestra an alert and sensitive response. The recording has a lifelike
balance and the CD remastering adds freshness and bite.

Stabat Mater, Op. 58.
☞ (B) *** DG Double 437 938-2 (2) [id.]. Mathis, Reynolds, Ochman, Shirley-Quirk, Bav. R. Ch. &
  O, Kubelik – JANACEK: *Glagolitic Mass.* **

Dvořák's devout Catholicism led him to treat this tragic religious theme with an open innocence that
avoids sentimentality. Kubelik is consistently responsive and this is a work which benefits from his
imaginative approach. The recording, made in the Munich Herkules-Saal, is of very good quality.
This set is well worth considering at this reasonable price, even though the Janáček coupling is less
magnetic.

OPERA

Rusalka (complete).
*** Sup. Dig. 10 3641-2 (3) [id.]. Beňačková-Cápová, Novak, Soukupová, Ochman, Drobkova,
  Prague Ch. & Czech PO, Neumann.

Dvořák's fairy-tale opera is given a magical performance by Neumann and his Czech forces, helped
by full, brilliant and atmospheric recording which, while giving prominence to the voices, brings out
the beauty and refinement of Dvořák's orchestration. The title-role is superbly taken by Gabriela
Beňačková-Cápová, and the famous *Invocation to the Moon* is enchanting. Vera Soukupová as the
Witch is just as characterfully Slavonic in a lower register, though not so even; while Wieslaw
Ochman sings with fine, clean, heroic tone as the Prince, with timbre made distinctive by tight
vibrato. Richard Novak brings out some of the Alberich-like overtones as the Watersprite, though
the voice is not always steady. The banding could be more generous, but a full translation is included.

Rusalka: highlights.
(B) *** Sup. Dig. 110617-2. Beňačková-Cápová, Novak, Soukupová, Ochman, Drobkova, Prague
  Ch. & Czech PO, Neumann.

This is a first-class selection, available on a bargain-priced disc and offering an hour of music,
although only a synopsis is provided.

Dyson, George (1883–1964)

At the Tabard Inn: overture; (ii) *In honour of the City;* (i; ii) *Sweet Thames run softly.*
*** Unicorn Dig. UKCD 2013 [id.]. RPO with (i) Stephen Roberts; (ii) Royal College of Music
  Chamber Ch., Willcocks.

There could hardly be a better introduction to Sir George Dyson's music than this collection, with
two vigorously sung choral pieces preceded by the overture based upon themes from his best-known
work. With Stephen Roberts an excellent baritone soloist in the more ambitious cantata, these
performances, full of life and warmth, could hardly be bettered; and the recording is first class.

(i) *Concierto leggiero* (for piano & strings); *Concerto da camera; Concerto da chiesa* (both for string
orchestra).
⊛ *** Chan. Dig. CHAN 9076 [id.]. (i) Eric Parkin; City of L. Sinfonia, Hickox.

Until now we have been inclined to think of Dyson as essentially a composer of vocal music, but this
splendid Chandos CD rights the balance and brings not only an engagingly light-textured concertante
item for piano but also two powerful and eloquent works in the great tradition of English string
music. All these pieces belong to the composer's last composing years and date from 1949/51. The
writing shows both a strongly burning creative flame as well as new influences from outside. The
performances here are wonderfully fresh and committed and the string recording has plenty of bite
and full sonority, while the balance with the piano is quite admirable. Highly recommended.

Symphony in D.
☞ *** Chan. Dig. CHAN 9200 [id.]. City of L. Sinfonia, Richard Hickox.

Dyson's *Symphony*, composed in 1937, was played in the 1940s (Felix Abrahamian took Ansermet to hear it at a performance in Southwark Cathedral) and then forgotten. Its best movement by far is the third, an attractive and diverse theme and variations (in which Ansermet justly found an affinity with ballet music). The finale is confident in its use of ideas from *The Canterbury Pilgrims* with majestic scoring for the brass, but the charming second-movement *Andante* is rather slight and the first movement, marked *Energico*, flags and fails to sustain its initial Richard Straussian momentum. An enjoyable piece, very well played and resonantly and realistically recorded, in the way of Chandos, but not an essential acquisition, except for those especially attracted to this composer.

(Organ) *Fantasia and Ground bass. 3 Choral hymns; Hierusalem; Psalm 150; 3 Songs of praise.*
*** Hyp. CDA 66150 [id.]. Vakery Hill, St Michael's Singers, Thomas Trotter, RPO, Jonathan
     Rennert.

Where the organ piece unashamedly builds on an academic model, *Hierusalem* reveals the inner man more surprisingly, a richly sensuous setting of a medieval poem inspired by the thought of the Holy City, building to a jubilant climax. It is a splendid work, and is backed here by the six hymns and the Psalm setting, all of them heartwarming products of the Anglican tradition. Performances are outstanding, with Rennert drawing radiant singing and playing from his team, richly and atmospherically recorded.

*Benedicite; Benedictus; Evening services in D; Hail, universal Lord; Live forever, glorious Lord; Te
Deum; Valour.* (i) (Organ) *Prelude; Postlude; Psalm-tune prelude (I was glad); Voluntary of praise*
(with HOWELLS: *Dyson's delight*).
*** Unicorn Dig. DKPCD 9065; *DKPC 9065* [id.]. St Catharine's College, Cambridge, Ch., Owen
     Rees; (i) Owen Rees (organ).

Sir George Dyson's writing may not always be strikingly individual, but every so often its invention soars. It is all sung with striking freshness by choristers who, young as some of them may be, seem to have its inflexions in their very being. Excellent recording too.

*The Blacksmiths. The Canterbury Pilgrims: suite. Quo vadis: Nocturne. 3 Rustic songs. Song on May
morning; Spring garland; A Summer day; To music.*
*** Unicorn Dig. DKPCD 9061; *DKPC 9061* [id.]. Neil Mackie, Royal College of Music Chamber
     Ch., RPO, Willcocks.

The Blacksmiths – done here with a reduced orchestra (two pianos, timpani, percussion and strings), as suggested by the composer – has an earthiness that sets it apart from the regular English choral tradition. *The Canterbury Pilgrims* is here represented by a suite assembled by Christopher Palmer, who also acted as record producer. The other items, most of them more conventional, make up an appealing disc, played and recorded well.

Egk, Werner (1901–83)

The Temptation of St Anthony (cantata).
(M) *** DG 429 858-2 [id.]. J. Baker, Koekert Qt, Bav. RSO (strings), composer – MARTIN:
     Everyman; The Tempest. *** ⊛

Werner Egk's song-cycle *The Temptation of St Anthony* has a certain folk-like simplicity; a modest makeweight for the Martin *Everyman* songs, it is not of comparable distinction. Dame Janet Baker was in particularly good voice at this period in her career and the recording, which dates from the mid-1960s, is very good.

Elgar, Edward (1857–1934)

(i) *Adieu; Beau Brummel: Minuet;* (ii) *3 Bavarian dances, Op. 27; Caractacus, Op. 35: Woodland
interlude. Chanson de matin; Chanson de nuit, Op. 15/1–2; Contrasts, Op. 10/3; Dream children, Op.
43; Falstaff, Op. 68: 2 Interludes. Salut d'amour; Sérénade lyrique;* (ii; iii) *Soliloquy for oboe* (orch.
Gordon Jacob); (i) *Sospiri, Op. 70; The Spanish Lady: Burlesco. The Starlight Express: Waltz.
Sursum corda, Op. 11.*
(M) *** Chan. CHAN 6544; *MBTD 6544* [id.]. Bournemouth Sinf., (i) George Hurst; (ii) Norman
     Del Mar; (iii) with Goossens.

The real treasure in this splendid collection of Elgar miniatures is the *Soliloquy* which Elgar wrote right at the end of his life for Leon Goossens. Here the dedicatee plays it with his long-recognizable tone-colour and feeling for phrase in an orchestration by Gordon Jacob. Most of the other pieces in Norman Del Mar's programme are well known but they come up with new warmth and commitment here, and the 1976 recording, made in the Guildhall, Southampton, has an appealing ambient warmth and naturalness. For the CD reissue Chandos have generously added some delightful Elgar rarities recorded by George Hurst a year earlier in Christchurch Priory. Again the recording has plenty of fullness, but the CD transfer brings more thinness to the violins than in the Del Mar recording. The disc has an overall playing time of nearly 76 minutes.

Acoustic recordings (1914–25): Abridged or excerpts: *Bavarian dances; Carillon; Carissima; Chanson de nuit; Cockaigne overture;* (i) *Cello concerto;* (ii) *Violin concerto. Enigma variations; In the South; King Olaf; Light of life; Polonia; Pomp and circumstance marches Nos. 1 & 4; Salut d'amour; The Sanguin fan; Symphony No. 2* (complete). (iii) *Fringes of the fleet;* (iv) *Sea pictures;* (iii; v) *Starlight express; Fantasia and Fugue* (Bach, arr. Elgar); *Overture* (Handel, arr. Elgar).
(M) (**(*)) Pearl GEMM CDS 9951/5 (5). (i) Beatrice Harrison; (ii) Marie Hall; (iii) Charles Mott;
    (iv) Leila Megane; (v) Agnes Nicholls; O or Royal Albert Hall O, cond. composer.

This box of five Pearl CDs gathers together all of Elgar's recordings made in the days of the acoustic gramophone. With players in limited numbers gathered round an acoustic horn, the sounds are limited but have been transferred here with astonishing fidelity. Orchestrations had to be modified to bring out the bass line, and all but the *Symphony No. 2*, among the major works, had to be cut for the medium, often drastically, as when the *Violin concerto* is reduced from 50 to 15 minutes. Speeds here are generally brisker than in his later, electrical recordings, and performances are often flawed. Marie Hall adopts an exaggeratedly portamento style in the *Violin concerto*, and Beatrice Harrison is less assured here than in her electrical recording of the full *Cello concerto*, but Leila Megane proves a formidable contralto soloist in *Sea pictures*. The sense of witnessing historic events is irresistible, with Elgar consistently hypnotic as a conductor.

3 Bavarian dances, Op. 27; 3 Characteristic pieces, Op. 10; Chanson de nuit; Chanson de matin, Op. 15/1–2; (i) *Violin concerto in B min., Op. 61. Crown of India (suite), Op. 66; Enigma variations, Op. 36; Nursery suite; Severn suite; Wand of youth suites 1–2, Op. 1a/b; The Light of Life: Meditation.* arr. of Bach: *Fantasia & fugue in C min., Op. 86;* (ii) (Choral) *The Banner of St George: It comes from the misty ages. Land of hope and glory.* Arrangements of Croft: *O God, our help in ages past. National anthem.*
☞ (***) EMI mono CDS7 54564-2 (3) [id.]. LSO, Royal Albert Hall O, New SO or LPO,
    composer, with (i) Y. Menuhin; (ii) Philharmonic Ch.

Volume 2 of the Elgar Edition centres on the two masterpieces which make up the first of the three discs: the *Enigma variations* in the 1926 recording with the Royal Albert Hall Orchestra, volatile and passionate, and the sixteen-year-old Menuhin's classic reading of the *Violin concerto*, as fresh and intense as ever. The *Wand of Youth, Nursery* and *Severn suites* make up the second disc, with Elgar sparkling as a conductor. The third disc of shorter works includes a number of rarities, all of them revealing. Excellent transfers and background notes.

Beau Brummel: minuet (2 versions); (i) *Caractacus: Woodland interlude and Triumphal march, Op. 35; Carissima;* (ii) *Cello concerto in E min, Op. 85; Cockaigne: concert overture, Op. 40* (2 versions); (iii) *Coronation march, Op. 65; Elegy, Op. 58; Falstaff: interludes, Op. 68; Froissart: concert overture, Op. 19; In the South: concert overture, Op. 50; Land of hope and glory; The Kingdom: prelude, Op. 51; May song;* (iv) *Mina* (2 versions); *Minuet, Op. 21; Pomp and circumstance marches Nos. 1–5, Op. 39* (2 versions); *Rosemary; Salut d'amour, Op. 12; Sérénade in E min., Op. 20; Sérénade lyrique;* (v) *5 Piano Improvisations.*
☞ (***) EMI mono CDS7 54568-2 (3) [id.]. LPO, Royal Albert Hall O, LSO or New SO,
    composer, with (i) Collingwood; (ii) Beatrice Harrison; (iii) Ronald; (iv) Murray, Wood; (v)
    composer (piano).

This third and last issue of EMI's Elgar Edition, like the previous volumes, demonstrates from first to last how as a conductor Elgar could electrify players, drawing from them bitingly dramatic performances that have a natural flexibility and flow unsurpassed by anyone since. The three volumes together cover the electrical recordings of most of his major works that he made between 1926 and his death in 1934; even over that brief span one notes the development in the quality of orchestral playing. The most fascinating contrast is between the two versions of the overture, *Cockaigne*, both contained in this third volume. His remake in 1933 with the recently founded BBC Symphony

Orchestra is far more polished, with portamento far less marked in the string-playing, but the earlier performance, recorded with the Royal Albert Hall Orchestra in 1926, marginally faster and at times ragged in ensemble, yet has a more intense emotional thrust. The final reprise of the big melody brings the authentic gulp such as all Elgarians will recognize in a great performance, helped by the inclusion of organ obbligato, thrillingly caught on CD.

Where the first volume centred on the *Symphonies* and *Falstaff*, and the second on the *Violin concerto* and shorter works, this third one centres on the *Cello concerto* (with Beatrice Harrison as soloist in another urgent performance) and the overtures, *Froissart* and *In the South* as well as *Cockaigne*. The incidental items are fascinating too, including multiple versions of the *Pomp and circumstance marches* and two *Caractacus* excerpts conducted by Lawrence Collingwood, which Elgar supervised by telephone from his sick-bed only a month before he died. Yet the items which give the most intimate portrait of Elgar are the five improvisations that he recorded at the piano in 1929. Musically they are of no great importance, but hearing the old man strumming to himself is extraordinarily touching. It is also good to have the soundtrack recording from the Pathé newsreel covering the opening of the Abbey Road studio. Preparing to conduct *Land of hope and glory*, Elgar asks the LSO to 'play this tune as though you've never heard it before'. Transfers are astonishingly clear and full, though at times the background hiss is higher than in previous volumes. The discs come at full not mid-price, and essays in the booklet include a fascinating one by Anthony Griffith on the practical background to recording in the days of 78.

Caractacus, Op. 35: Woodland interlude. Crown of India (suite), Op. 66; Grania and Diarmid, Op. 42: Funeral march. Light of Life, Op. 29: Meditation. Nursery suite; Severn suite, Op. 87.
(M) **(*) EMI CDM7 63280-2. RLPO, Groves.

This is all music that Groves understood warmly, and the results give much pleasure. The completely neglected *Funeral march* is a splendid piece. The CD transfer retains the bloom of the original recordings and adds to the vividness.

Cockaigne overture, Op. 40; Elegy for strings, Op. 58; Enigma variations, Op. 36; Introduction and allegro for strings, Op. 47; Pomp and circumstance march No. 1; Sospiri, Op. 70.
☞ (M) **(*) Nimbus Dig. NI 7075 [id.]. ESO, William Boughton.

Warmly affectionate performances, beautifully played and given characteristically spacious Nimbus sound, recorded in the Great Hall of Birmingham University. The resonance prevents absolute sharpness of detail, but the effect is natural. The *Introduction and allegro* has a ripely overwhelming climax, yet the fugal argument is not lost. The *Enigma variations* have many pleasingly delicate touches of colour (*Dorabella* is delightfully fey) and *Nimrod* expands spaciously from its genuine pianissimo opening to achieve a climax of dignity rather than great ardour (surely an authentic portrayal of its dedicatee, A. E. Jaeger). There are more strongly characterized versions of the work, but this performance has undoubted spontaneity and is easy to enjoy. The brass and organ make a fine effect in the finale, which brings a noble summing up. With 75 minutes of music, this is certainly excellent value.

(i) *Cockaigne overture, Op. 40;* (ii) *Elegy for strings, Op. 58;* (i) *Overture, In the South; Pomp and circumstance marches Nos. 1–5; National anthem* (arrangement).
☞ (M) *** Decca 440 317-2 [id.]. (i) LPO, Solti; (ii) ASMF, Marriner.

Solti's *Cockaigne* is sharply dramatic and exciting; his view of the *Marches* is both vigorous and refined, with sharp pointing in the outer sections, spaciousness in the great melodies. The result is both striking and satisfying. Marriner's *Elegy*, beautifully played, follows the marches as an agreeable interlude before the erupting energy of *In the South*, which is excitingly volatile rather than ripely expansive. The vivid Decca sound and bright, clean transfers match the Solti charisma.

Cockaigne overture, Op. 40; Enigma variations, Op. 36; Introduction and allegro for strings; Serenade for strings, Op. 20.
⊛ *** Teldec/Warner Dig. 9031 73279-2 [id.]. BBC SO, Andrew Davis.

Andrew Davis's collection of favourite Elgar works is electrifying. The very opening of *Cockaigne* has rarely been so light and sprightly, and it leads on to the most powerful characterization of each contrasted section. The two string works are richly and sensitively done. Similarly the big tonal contrasts in *Enigma* are dramatically brought out, notably in Davis's rapt and spacious reading of *Nimrod*, helped by the spectacular Teldec recording. This is surely a worthy successor to Barbirolli in this repertoire and is an outstanding disc in every way.

(i) *Cockaigne overture, Op. 40;* (ii) *Enigma variations;* (i) *Pomp and circumstance marches Nos. 1–5.*
☞ (M) **(*) EMI analogue/Dig. CDM7 67799-2 [id.]. LPO, (i) Boult or (ii) Mackerras.

Boult's *Cockaigne* is breezily incisive and has no lack of romantic warmth; his approach to the *Pomp and circumstance marches* is brisk and direct with an almost no-nonsense manner in places. There is not a hint of vulgarity, and the freshness is attractive, though it is a pity that he omits the repeats in the Dvořák-like No. 2. The sound is bright and quite full, but not sumptuous. Mackerras's *Enigma* is a later, digital recording, but the reading is marred by mannered and self-conscious phrasing in the opening statement of the theme and first variation as well as in *Nimrod*. However, the CD has good detail.

Cockaigne overture, Op. 40; Falstaff (symphonic study), Op. 68; Introduction and allegro for strings, Op. 47.
☞ (B) *** CfP CD-CFP 4617. LPO, Vernon Handley.

Vernon Handley directs a superb performance of *Falstaff*, one of Elgar's most difficult works; and the achievement is all the more remarkable because his tempi are unusually spacious (generally following the composer's marking), making the contrasted episodes more difficult to hold together. The playing of the LPO is warmly expressive and strongly rhythmic – the opening surges forward almost like a Richard Strauss tone-poem, and the 1978 analogue recording – made at St Augustine's Church, Kilburn – was one of the finest made by the engineer known under the pseudonym of Mr Bear, for CfP. *Cockaigne* is also given a performance that is expansive yet never hangs fire. The *Introduction and allegro* is digital and dates from 1983. It was made in Watford Town Hall, but the balance is closer, its string outline more brightly lit. The performance is direct and passionate, yet with the lyrical contrasts tenderly made. This reissue is a real bargain.

(i) *Cockaigne overture, Op. 40;* (ii) *Froissart overture, Op. 19; Pomp and circumstance marches, Op. 39, Nos* (i) *1 in D;* (ii) *2 in A min.; 3 in C min.;* (i) *4 in G;* (ii) *5 in C.*
(M) *** EMI CDM7 69563-2. (i) Philh. O; (ii) New Philh. O; Barbirolli.

It is good to have Barbirolli's ripe yet wonderfully vital portrait of Edwardian London on CD where the recording retains its atmosphere as well as its vividness. *Froissart* is very compelling too, and Barbirolli makes a fine suite of the five *Pomp and circumstance marches*, with plenty of contrast in Nos. 2 and 3 to offset the Edwardian flag-waving of Nos. 1 and 4.

Crown of India: suite, Op. 66; Enigma variations, Op. 36; Pomp and circumstance marches Nos. 1–5.
☞ (M) **(*) Sony SBK 48265 [id.]. LPO, Barenboim.

Barenboim's view of *Enigma* is full of fantasy. Its most distinctive point is its concern for the miniature element. Without belittling the delicate variations, Barenboim both makes them sparkle and gives them emotional point, while the big variations have full weight, and the finale brings the fierceness of added adrenalin at a fast tempo. Tempi are surprisingly fast in the *Pomp and circumstance marches* (though Elgar's tended to be fast too) and not all Elgarians will approve of the updating of Elgarian majesty. The rumbustious approach to the *Crown of India suite* brings this patriotic celebration of the Raj vividly to life, though here the lack of opulence in the recording is a drawback. The marches, too, could do with a more expansive middle range, though *Enigma* is fully acceptable.

Cello concerto in E min., Op. 85.
⊛ *** EMI CDC7 47329-2 [id.]; *TC-ASD 655.* Du Pré, LSO, Barbirolli – *Sea Pictures.* *** ⊛
☞ (M) *** Sony Dig. SMK 53333 [id.]. Yo-Yo Ma, LSO, Previn – WALTON: *Cello concerto.* ***
(B) *** Pickwick Dig. PCD 930; *IMPC 930* [id.]. (i) Felix Schmidt; LSO, Frühbeck de Burgos –
    VAUGHAN WILLIAMS: *Tallis fantasia; Greensleeves.* **(*)
(M) (**(*)) EMI mono CDH7 63498-2 [id.]. Casals, BBC SO, Boult – DVORAK: *Concerto* (***)
    (with BRUCH: *Kol Nidrei* (***)).

(i) *Cello concerto;* (ii) *Cockaigne overture, Op. 40; Enigma variations, Op. 36.*
*** Sony MK 76529. (i) Du Pré, Phd. O; (ii) LPO; Barenboim.

(i) *Cello concerto. Enigma variations, Op. 36.*
*** Ph. Dig. 416 354-2; *416 354-4* [id.]. (i) Julian Lloyd Webber; RPO, Menuhin.

(i) *Cello concerto;* (ii) *Introduction and allegro for strings, Op. 47.*
(B) *** Decca 433 633-2. (i) Harrell, Cleveland O, Maazel; (ii) ASMF, Marriner – DELIUS: *Piano concerto.* ***

Jacqueline du Pré was essentially a spontaneous artist. Her style is freely rhapsodic, but the result produced a very special kind of meditative feeling; in the very beautiful wlow movement, brief and concentrated, her inner intensity conveys a depth of espressivo rarely achieved by any cellist on record. Brilliant virtuoso playing too in Scherzo and finale. CD brings a subtle extra definition to heighten the excellent qualities of the 1965 recording, with the solo instrument firmly placed.

In its rapt concentration Yo-Yo Ma's recording with Previn is second to none. The first movement is lighter, a shade more urgent than the Du Pré/Barbirolli version, and in the Scherzo he finds more fun, just as he finds extra sparkle in the main theme of the finale. The key movement with Ma, as it is with du Pré, is the *Adagio*, echoed later in the raptness of the slow epilogue; there, his range of dynamic is just as daringly wide, with a thread of pianissimo at the innermost moment, poised in its intensity. Warm, fully detailed recording, finely balanced, with understanding conducting from Previn. At mid-price a splendid bargain.

The Philips coupling of the *Cello concerto* and the *Enigma variations*, the two most popular of Elgar's big orchestral works, featuring two artists inseparably associated with Elgar's music, made the disc an immediate bestseller, and rightly so. These are both warmly expressive and unusually faithful readings, the more satisfying for fidelity to the score, and Julian Lloyd Webber in his playing has never sounded warmer or more relaxed on record, well focused in the stereo spectrum.

Jacqueline du Pré's second recording of the Elgar *Cello concerto* was taken from live performances in Philadelphia in November 1970, and this is a superb picture of an artist in full flight, setting her sights on the moment in the Epilogue where the slow-movement theme returns, the work's innermost sanctuary of repose. Barenboim's most distinctive point in *Enigma* is in giving the delicate variations sparkle and emotional point, while the big variations have full weight, and the finale brings extra fierceness at a fast tempo. *Cockaigne* is comparably lively and colourful. The sound of the CBS transfer lacks something in body and amplitude.

Felix Schmidt, a young cellist with the widest expressive range, gives a bold, emotionally intense reading which finds a most satisfying middle ground between the romantic freedom typified by the unique Jacqueline du Pré and the steadier way of a Paul Tortelier. With his rich, full tone opulently recorded, his account can be recommended beside the very finest versions.

Lynn Harrell's account is here also offered with Marriner's strong but straighter performance of the *Introduction and allegro* and with an excellent account of the Delius *Piano concerto*.

Casals recorded the Elgar *Cello concerto* in London in 1946, and the fervour of his playing caused some raised eyebrows. A powerful account, not least for Sir Adrian's contribution, even though its eloquence would have been even more telling were the emotion recollected in greater tranquillity. A landmark of the gramophone all the same, and the strongly characterized Max Bruch *Kol Nidrei* makes a fine encore.

(i) *Cello concerto in E min., Op. 85;* (ii) *Violin concerto in B min., Op. 61.*
☞ (M) *** Decca 440 319-2 [id.]. (i) Lynn Harrell, Cleveland O, Maazel; (ii) Kyung Wha Chung, LPO, Solti.
(M) (***) EMI mono CDH7 69786-2. (i) Beatrice Harrison, New SO; (ii) Menuhin, LSO, composer.

This Decca reissue coupling Chung's heartfelt performance of the *Violin concerto* with Lynn Harrell's outstanding account of the *Cello concerto* on Decca offers a strong challenge. With eloquent support from Maazel and his fine orchestra (the woodwind play with appealing delicacy), this reading, deeply felt, balances a gentle nostalgia with extrovert brilliance. The slow movement is tenderly spacious, the Scherzo bursts with exuberance and, after a passionate opening, the finale is memorable for the poignantly expressive reprise of the melody from the *Adagio*, one of Elgar's greatest inspirations. In the *Violin concerto* Chung's dreamily responsive playing in the central movement is ravishing in its beauty, not least in the ethereal writing above the stave, and so too are the lyrical pages of the outer movements. Solti responds with warmth to the expressive breadth of his soloist, and no other recording brings a wider range of dynamic or tone in the soloist's playing. Both recordings are from the late 1970s and are transferred to CD with impressive body and clarity.

The 1932 Menuhin/Elgar recording of the *Violin concerto* emerges on CD with a superb sense of atmosphere and presence. As for the performance, its classic status is amply confirmed: in many ways no one has ever matched – let alone surpassed – the seventeen-year-old Menuhin in this work, even if the first part of the finale lacks something in fire. The performance of the *Cello concerto* has nothing like the same inspiration, when Beatrice Harrison's playing is at times fallible, and there are moments which seem almost perfunctory; but there is still much Elgarian feeling.

(i) *Cello concerto in E min., Op. 85. Elegy, Op. 58. Enigma variations, Op. 36; Introduction and allegro, Op. 47.*

⊛ (M) *** EMI stereo/mono CDM7 63955-2 [id.]. (i) Navarra, Hallé O, Barbirolli.

This Hallé version of the *Enigma variations* was recorded in the Manchester Free Trade Hall in 1956 by the Mercury team, Wilma Cozart and Harold Lawrence. In its new CD transfer the sound is extraordinarily good, and the performance is revealed as Barbirolli's finest account ever on record. Barbirolli generates powerful fervour and an irresistible momentum: at the very end, the organ entry brings an unforgettable, tummy-wobbling effect which engulfs the listener thrillingly. The *Introduction and allegro* is mono, and though not quite so impressively recorded, has comparable passion – the recapitulation of the big striding tune in the middle strings has superb thrust and warmth. The concert closes with a moving account of the *Elegy*, simple and affectionate. In between comes Navarra's strong and firm view of the *Cello concerto*. With his control of phrasing and wide range of tone-colour this 1957 performance culminates in a most moving account of the Epilogue.

Violin concerto in B min., Op. 61.

⊛ (M) *** EMI Dig. EMX 2058; *TC-EMX 2058.* Nigel Kennedy, LPO, Handley.

☞ (M) *** EMI CDM7 64725-2 [id.]. Sir Yehudi Menuhin, New Philh. O, Boult – DELIUS: *Violin concerto.* **(*)

(M) (***) BMG/RCA mono GD 87966 [7966-2-RG]. Heifetz, LSO, Sargent – WALTON: *Concerto.* (***)

(i) *Violin concerto in B min.; Cockaigne overture,* Op. 40.

(BB) *** Naxos Dig. 8.550489; *4.550489* [id.]. Dong-Suk Kang, Polish Nat. RSO (Katowice), Adrian Leaper.

(i) *Violin concerto; In the South (Alassio)* (concert overture).

☞ (M) *** Sony SMK 58927 [id.]. (i) Pinchas Zukerman; LPO, Barenboim.

(i) *Violin concerto. Introduction and allegro for strings, Op. 47.*

☞ ** BMG/RCA Dig. 09026 61612-2 [id.]. (i) Kyoko Takezawa; Bav. RSO, Sir Colin Davis.

(i) *Violin concerto. Salut d'amour, Op. 12.*

☞ *(*) BMG/RCA Dig. 09026 61672-2 [id.]. (i) Pinchas Zukerman; St Louis SO, Slatkin.

(i) *Violin concerto in B min.;* (ii) *Violin sonata in E min., Op. 82.*

☞ (B) *** CfP CD-CFP 4632; *TC-CFP 4632.* Hugh Bean; (i) RLPO, Groves; (ii) David Parkhouse.

This remains Nigel Kennedy's finest achievement on record, arguably even finer than the long line of versions with star international soloists either from outside or within Britain. With Vernon Handley as guide it is a truly inspired and inspiring performance and the recording is outstandingly faithful and atmospheric. At mid-price it is a supreme Elgarian bargain.

More than 30 years after the young Master Menuhin had played the solo part in this work, with the composer himself conducting (see above), he was persuaded to return to the EMI studios and do it again, this time in partnership with Sir Adrian Boult. The result is hardly less moving and inspirational. Boult directs the performance with a passionate thrust in the outer movements and the warmest Elgarian understanding in the beautiful slow movement. There is an added maturity in Menuhin's contribution to compensate for any slight loss of poise or sweetness of tone, and the finale – the most difficult movement to keep together – is stronger and more confident than it was. The long-breathed musings of the violin in the unaccompanied cadenza have a wonderful intensity, and Boult produces a superb burst of energy in the work's closing pages. Throughout, the spontaneous feeling of the music-making is never in doubt, and the (1966) Kingsway Hall recording is characteristically warm and atmospheric, yet vividly focused by the CD transfer. A record indispensable for its documentary value as well as for its musical insights.

A most successful and rewarding coupling on CfP. Hugh Bean has not the outsize personality of his most eloquent rivals, but his playing is thoroughly imbued with the English tradition and he has also given us a memorable account of Vaughan Williams's *Lark ascending*. He studied with Albert Sammons and his reading of the Elgar *Concerto* has a nobility and reticence well attuned to this composer, while his selfless artistry is wholly dedicated to the music rather than to ego projection. The introspective playing during the cadenza of the finale is particularly telling, with the secondary theme of the first movement movingly recalled; then Groves rounds off the finale with a superb flourish. The 1973 record is extremely realistic, with the balance just as in the concert hall, and its perspective seems just right for the performance. Groves is at his very finest and his understanding support is excellent in every way. The performance overall has great spontaneity and in the quieter, more reflective passages Bean has something quite special to say. The performance of the *Sonata* is dramatically alive, but ripely autumnal too, and again the (Abbey Road) recording is of high quality.

Zukerman, coming fresh to the Elgar *Violin concerto* in 1976, was inspired to give a reading which gloriously combined the virtuoso swagger of a Heifetz with the tender, heartfelt warmth of the young Menuhin, plus much individual responsiveness. In the first movement, with the command and warmth superbly established, Zukerman gives a breathtaking account of the third theme, hushed and inner as though in personal meditation. The slow movement is altogether simpler, rather less involved, while the finale in its many sections is held together masterfully, with Barenboim a splendid partner, brilliant but never breathless in the main allegro and culminating in a deeply felt rendering of the long accompanied cadenza, freely expansive yet concentrated. With full but clearly defined recording, naturally balanced, at EMI's Abbey Road studios, this is a version which all Elgarians should seek out. The coupling is an exciting and virile account of *In the South*, not quite as remarkable as the concerto but a worthwhile bonus, even if the sound is marginally less full.

Dong-Suk Kang, immaculate in his intonation, plays the Elgar with fire and urgency. This is very different from most latterday performances, with markedly faster speeds; yet those speeds relate more closely than usual to the metronome markings in the score, and they never get in the way of Kang's ability to feel Elgarian rubato naturally, guided by the warmly understanding conducting of Adrian Leaper. Irrespective of price, this is a keenly competitive version, with excellent, wide-ranging digital sound, if with rather too forward a balance for the soloist.

Heifetz's view of Elgar, with speeds unusually fast, may not be idiomatic, but this recording brings a masterly example of his artistry, demonstrating very clearly that, for all the ease and technical perfection, he is in no way a cold interpreter of romantic music. The mono recording is limited, not helped by a low hum in the transfer, and the solo instrument is balanced very close.

Kyoko Takezawa gives a fiery, passionate performance of the Elgar which is thrilling in the bravura passages, notably in the opening *Allegro* of the finale. The flaw is that Takezawa's passionate approach leads her to exaggerate her expressiveness, not only in excessive portamento – very obtrusive in both the slow movement and the epilogue – and in the use of soupy vibrato. Despite the sympathetic conducting of Davis and the fine playing of the Bavarian orchestra, the result is often vulgar. The recording is forward and full, so much so that in the *Introduction and allegro* the strings are made to sound too heavy-handed.

Sadly, Pinchas Zukerman's second recording of the *Concerto* sounds far less involved than his first, now reissued on Sony at mid-price. He tends to lack just the fiery quality so prodigally displayed by his RCA rival, Takezawa, and Slatkin's sympathetic direction of the orchestra is not helped by a recording which, though refined, lacks body, being set at a distance. The lightweight fill-up is agreeable but hardly generous.

Coronation march, Op. 65; Froissart: concert overture, Op. 19; In the South (Alassio): concert overture, Op. 50; The Light of life: Meditation, Op. 29.
*** ASV Dig. CDDCA 619 [id.]. RPO, Yondani Butt.

Yondani Butt draws warm and opulent performances from the RPO. Both overtures have splendid panache. Rich, atmospheric recording, yet with plenty of brilliance – an excellent Elgar sound, in fact.

Enigma variations (Variations on an original theme), Op. 36.
☞ (BB) *** DG 439 446-2 [id.]. LSO, Jochum – HOLST: *The Planets.* ***
☞ (M) *** EMI CDM7 64648-2 [id.]. LSO, Boult – HOLST: *Planets.* ***
(M) (***) BMG/RCA mono GD 60287 [60287-2-RG]. NBC SO, Toscanini – MUSSORGSKY:
Pictures. (**)

The DG Classikon super-bargain CD couples Steinberg's exciting and brilliantly recorded complete set of the Holst *Planets* with Eugen Jochum's inspirational reading of *Enigma*. Like others – including Elgar himself – Jochum sets a very slow *Adagio* at the start of *Nimrod*, slower than the metronome marking in the score; unlike others, he maintains that measured tempo and, with the subtlest gradations, builds an even bigger, nobler climax than you find in *accelerando* readings. It is like a Bruckner slow movement in microcosm around which the other variations revolve, all of them delicately detailed, with a natural feeling for Elgarian rubato. The playing of the LSO matches the strength and refinement of the performance. The remastered recording, however, sounds brighter and more vivid than before but has lost none of its richness.

Boult's *Enigma* comes from the beginning of the 1970s, but the recording has lost some of its amplitude in its transfer to CD: the effect is fresh, but the violins sound thinner. The reading shows this conductor's long experience of the work, with each variation growing naturally and seamlessly out of the music that has gone before. Yet the livelier variations bring exciting orchestral bravura and there is an underlying intensity of feeling that carries the performance forward.

It is a pity that Toscanini's sharply focused but warmly expressive NBC reading of *Enigma* should come in a coupling with his severe account of the Mussorgsky. The Elgar, often expansive as well as affectionately phrased, as in the statement of the theme, gives a much more sympathetic view of the taskmaster conductor than most of his late recordings. Though traditionalist Elgarians may not always approve, it makes for an electrifying experience. The transfer is clean but not too aggressive.

(i) *Enigma variations;* (ii) *Falstaff, Op. 68;* (iii) *Serenade for strings.*
☞ (M) **(*) Decca 440 326-2 [id.]. (i) Chicago SO; (ii) LPO, Solti; (iii) ASMF, Marriner.

With Solti, the *Enigma variations* becomes a dazzling showpiece. Though the charm of the work is given short measure, the structure emerges the more sharply, with the fast variations taken at breakneck speed and with the Chicago orchestra challenged to supreme virtuosity. The disappointment is *Nimrod* in which, from a basic tempo faster than usual, Solti allows himself to go faster and faster still in a style that misses the feeling of *nobilmente*. But overall it is still a gripping performance, given suitably brilliant yet warmly expansive sound. *Falstaff* is hardly a traditional view either, with the tensions too tautly held, and the effect just does not relax enough. Yet it is easy to be exhilarated by Solti's sense of momentum, and again the recording, given more weight and body on CD, is impressive. By the side of these high-powered Solti readings, Marriner's simple approach to the *Serenade* is refreshing. This performance, warm and resilient, shows this conductor at his finest.

Enigma variations, Op. 36; Grania and Diarmid (incidental music), *Op. 42; The Sanguine Fan (ballet; complete), Op. 81;* (i) *There are seven that pull the thread.*
*** Chan. Dig. CHAN 8610; *ABTD 1298* [id.]. LPO, Bryden Thomson, (i) with Jenny Miller.

Bryden Thomson conducts a broad, characterful reading of *Enigma*, warmly expressive but never mannered, leading the ear on persuasively in a purposefully structured whole. He finds all the charm of *The Sanguine Fan* ballet, characterizing it well without inflating it; while the unexpected mixture of Elgar and Celtic twilight in the *Grania and Diarmid* incidental music brings a similarly agreeable response, notably in the fine, measured *Funeral march*. The little Yeats song, *There are seven*, is warmly sung by Jenny Miller, though the microphone exaggerates her generous vibrato. First-class Chandos sound.

(i) *Enigma variations;* (ii) *Pomp and circumstance marches Nos. 1–5, Op. 39.*
(M) *** Chan. CHAN 6504; *MBTD 6504* [id.]. SNO, Sir Alexander Gibson.
(M) *** DG 429 713-2; *429 713-4* [id.]. RPO, Norman Del Mar.
(M) *** EMI CDM7 64015-2 [id.]. (i) LSO; (ii) LPO, Sir Adrian Boult.
☞ (M) **(*) Sony SMK 46684 [id.]. Philh. O, Andrew Davis.

Sir Alexander Gibson's reading of *Enigma* has stood the test of time and remains very satisfying, warm and spontaneous in feeling, with a memorable climax in *Nimrod*. The 1978 recording, made in Glasgow's City Hall, remains outstanding, with the organ sonorously filling out the bass in the finale, which has real splendour. The *Pomp and circumstance marches*, too, have fine *nobilmente* and swagger.

In the *Enigma variations* Del Mar comes closer than any other conductor to the responsive rubato style of Elgar himself, using fluctuations to point the emotional message of the work with wonderful power and spontaneity. The RPO plays superbly, both here and in the *Pomp and circumstance marches*, given Proms-style flair and urgency – although some might feel that the fast speeds miss some of the *nobilmente*. The reverberant sound here adds something of an aggressive edge to the music-making.

Boult's *Enigma* shows this conductor's long experience of the work, with each variation growing naturally and seamlessly out of the music that has gone before. Boult's approach to the *Pomp and circumstance marches* is brisk and direct, with an almost no-nonsense manner in places. There is not a hint of vulgarity and the freshness is most attractive, though it is a pity he omits the repeats in the Dvořák-like No. 2. The brightened sound brings a degree of abrasiveness to the brass.

Andrew Davis's Sony (originally CBS) version was his second stereo version of *Enigma* (the first was for Lyrita) and it brought a remarkable development in the interpretation, with the slow variations far more expansive than before. Fast variations remain crisp and incisive and the playing of the Philharmonia, well recorded, is splendid. Yet for many the reading will feel a little too plain, lacking idiosyncrasy, not quite idiomatic. The *Marches* come off splendidly, and the full-blooded

Abbey Road recording (from the beginning of the 1980s) adds to the pleasure to be had from this disc.

(i) *Enigma variations (Variations on an original theme); (ii) Pomp and circumstance marches Nos. 1–5;* (iii) *Serenade for strings.*
(B) *** Decca 433 629-2. (i) LAPO, Mehta; (ii), LSO, Bliss; (iii) ASMF, Marriner.

Sir Arthur Bliss's rumbustiously vigorous accounts of the *Pomp and circumstance marches* are worth anyone's money. Mehta proves a strong and sensitive Elgarian, and this is a highly enjoyable performance. If there are no special revelations, the transition from the nobly conceived and spacious climax of *Nimrod* to a delightfully graceful *Dorabella* is particularly felicitous. The vintage Decca recording, with the organ entering spectacularly in the finale, is outstanding in its CD transfer, and this is one of Mehta's very finest records. Marriner's elegantly played yet highly sensitive account of the *String serenade* makes a fine bonus.

Falstaff, Op. 68; Introduction and allegro for strings, Op. 47; arr. of BACH: *Fantasia and fugue in C min., Op. 86.*
(B) *** Pickwick Dig. PCD 934; *CIMPC 934* [id.]. National Youth O of Great Britain, Christopher Seaman.

These works have rarely been given such heartfelt performances as those by Christopher Seaman and the National Youth Orchestra. The weight of string sound, combined with the fervour behind the playing, makes this an exceptionally satisfying reading of the *Introduction and allegro*, while *Falstaff* demonstrates even more strikingly how, working together intensively, these youngsters have learnt to keep a precise ensemble through the most complex variations of expressive rubato. Warm, full, digital recording adds to an outstanding bargain.

Falstaff; Symphonies Nos. 1–2; (i) *Dream of Gerontius: Prelude* and excerpts. *The Music makers:* excerpts. *Civic fanfare and National anthem.*
*** EMI mono CDS7 54560-2 (3). (i) Margaret Balfour, Steuart Wilston, Herbert Heyner, Tudor Davies, Horace Stevens, Royal Ch. Soc., Three Choirs Festival Ch., LSO or Royal Albert Hall O, composer.

It is thrilling in this first volume of EMI's Elgar Edition to find that the recordings, made between 1927 and 1932, have a body and immediacy that give the most astonishing sense of presence. Elgar is with us here and now, providing in these inspired performances an insight beyond that of any other conductor of his music. Consistently these are tough performances, with rhythms pressed sharply home and with speeds generally faster than has become normal today. In addition, Elgar's sense of line, his ability to mould rhythms with natural flexibility, regularly brings an extra emotional thrust and an extra intensity. What is special is the poignancy, the vulnerability conveyed in this music even at its grandest. Most thrilling of all is the *First Symphony*, where Elgar modifies some of the markings in the score on speed-changes; and this reading of *Falstaff*, too, has never been surpassed. *Symphony No. 2* comes with fascinating supplements, including a rehearsal of the Scherzo and an alternative take of the first part of the movement. Most atmospheric of all are the live recordings of *Gerontius* and the *Music-makers* on the third disc, all recorded live at a time when recording on wax discs in short spans of under five minutes presented almost insoluble problems. The brief *Civic fanfare* is a curiosity, the only Elgar first performance preserved on record.

Introduction and allegro for strings.
☞ (M) **(*) EMI Dig. CDM7 54407-2 [id.]. City of L. Sinfonia, Hickox – VAUGHAN WILLIAMS: *Fantasia on a theme by Tallis* **(*); WALTON: *Sonata for strings.* ***
☞ (M) ** BMG/RCA 09026 61424-2 [id.]. Boston SO, Munch – BARBER: *Adagio; Medea* excerpts ***; TCHAIKOVSKY: *Serenade.* **(*)

The newest EMI recording of the *Introduction and allegro* is slightly disappointing. Hickox's athleticism is exhilarating but lacks ripeness, especially in the great surging tune on unison strings, where the playing conveys forceful brilliance rather than ripeness of feeling (like Barbirolli or Warren-Green). The recording, made in St Augustine's Church, Kilburn, is brightly lit by the close microphone placing, but does not lack weight.

A striking performance from Munch, individual in that his tempo for the big *Sul G* unison tune must be the slowest on record. In this he shows a lack of idiomatic understanding, but otherwise the performance has plenty of vitality and the 1957 recording has filled out in the excellent remastering for CD.

Introduction and allegro for strings, Op. 47; Serenade for strings in E min., Op. 20.
☞ ⊛ (M) *** Virgin/EMI Dig. CUV5 61126-2 [id.]. LCO, Christopher Warren-Green – VAUGHAN
  WILLIAMS: *Tallis fantasia* etc. *** ⊛

Repeating a coupling made famous by Sir John Barbirolli, Christopher Warren-Green, directing and leading his London Chamber Orchestra, directs the *Introduction and allegro* with tremendous ardour: the great striding theme on the middle strings is unforgettable, while the fugue has enormous bite and bravura. The whole work moves forward in a single sweep and the sense of a live performance, tingling with electricity and immediacy, is thrillingly tangible. It is very difficult to believe that the group contains only seventeen players (6-5-2-3-1), with the resonant but never clouding acoustics of All Saints' Church, Petersham, helping to create an engulfingly rich body of tone. Appropriately, the *Serenade* is a more relaxed reading yet it has plenty of affectionate warmth, with the beauty of the *Larghetto* expressively rich but not overstated.

King Arthur: suite; (i) The Starlight Express (suite), Op. 78.
☞ (M) **(*) Chan. CHAN 6582 [id.]. (i) Cynthia Glover, John Lawrenson; Bournemouth Sinf.,
  George Hurst.

The *King Arthur suite* is put together from incidental music that Elgar wrote in 1923 – well after his creative urge had fallen away – for a pageant-like play by Laurence Binyon. Though not great at all, it is full of surging, enjoyable ideas and makes an interesting novelty on record. *The Starlight Express suite* is similarly taken from music Elgar wrote in the First World War for a children's play, very much from the same world as the *Wand of Youth suites*, with a song or two included. Though the singers here are not ideal interpreters, the enthusiasm of Hurst and the Sinfonietta is conveyed well, particularly in the *King Arthur suite*. The recording is atmospheric if rather over-reverberant, but the added firmness of the CD and its refinement of detail almost make this an extra asset in providing a most evocative ambience for Elgar's music and projecting the voices of the very personable soloists, Cynthia Glover and John Lawrenson, vividly. Many Elgarians will find just about the right amount of music included here to make a well-balanced concert.

Nursery suite; Wand of Youth suites Nos. 1 and 2, Op. 1a and 1b.
*** Chan. Dig. CHAN 8318; *ABTD 1079* [id.]. Ulster O, Bryden Thomson.

The playing in Ulster is attractively spirited; in the gentle pieces (the *Sun dance, Fairy pipers* and *Slumber dance*) which show the composer at his most magically evocative, the music-making engagingly combines refinement and warmth. The *Nursery suite* is strikingly well characterized, and with first-class digital sound this is highly recommendable.

Romance for cello and orchestra, Op. 62.
☞ (M) *** EMI Dig. CDM7 64726-2 [id.]. Julian Lloyd Webber, LSO, Mackerras – SULLIVAN:
  Cello concerto etc. ***

Julian Lloyd Webber has rescued the composer's own version of the *Romance* for cello (originally for bassoon) and it provides a delightful makeweight for the Sullivan reissue, beautifully played and warmly recorded.

Serenade for strings in E min., Op. 20.
(B) *** Pickwick Dig. PCD 861; *CIMPC 861* [id.]. Serenata of London – GRIEG: *Holberg suite;*
  MOZART: *Eine kleine Nachtmusik* etc. ***

A particularly appealing account of Elgar's *Serenade*, with unforced tempi in the outer movements admirably catching its mood and atmosphere. The Serenata of London is led rather than conducted by Barry Wilde, and it is recorded with remarkable realism and naturalness.

Symphony No. 1 in A flat, Op. 55.
⊛ (B) *** Pickwick Dig. PCD 956; *CIMPC 956* [id.]. Hallé O, James Judd.
(B) *** CfP CD-CFP 9018. LPO, Vernon Handley.

(i) Symphony No. 1 in A flat; (ii) Cockaigne overture.
*** Decca Dig. 430 835-2 [id.]. LSO, Mackerras.
☞ (M) **(*) EMI CDM7 64511-2. Philh. O, Barbirolli.
☞ (BB) **(*) ASV CDQS 6082 [id.]. Hallé O, James Loughran; (ii) Philh. O, Owain Hughes.

Symphony No. 1 in A flat; Chanson de matin; Chanson de nuit; Serenade for strings, Op. 20.
(M) *** EMI CDM7 64013-2 [id.]. LPO, Sir Adrian Boult.

Symphony No. 1 in A flat; Imperial march, Op. 32.
☞ (BB) *** Naxos Dig. 8.550634 [id.]. BBC PO, George Hurst.

(i) *Symphony No. 1 in A flat;* (ii) *Introduction and allegro for strings, Op. 47; The Spanish Lady* (suite; ed. Young); *Sospiri, Op. 70.*
☞ (M) *** Decca 440 322-2 [id.]. (i) LPO, Solti; (ii) ASMF, Marriner.

Symphony No. 1 in A flat; (i) *Sea pictures, Op. 37.*
☞ (M) ** Sony SMK 58929 [id.]. LPO, Barenboim; (i) with Yvonne Minton.

James Judd, more than any rival on disc, has learnt directly from Elgar's own recording of this magnificent symphony. So the reading has extra authenticity in the many complex speed-changes (sometimes indicated confusingly in the score), in the precise placing of climaxes and in the textural balances. Above all, Judd outshines others in the pacing and phrasing of the lovely slow movement which in its natural flowing rubato has melting tenderness behind the passion, a throat-catching poignancy not fully conveyed elsewhere but very much a quality of Elgar's own reading. The refinement of the strings down to the most hushed pianissimo confirms this as the Hallé's most beautiful disc in years, recorded with warmth and opulence.

Vernon Handley directs a beautifully paced reading which can also be counted in every way outstanding. The LPO has performed this symphony many times before but never with more poise and refinement than here. It is in the slow movement above all that Handley scores, spacious and movingly expressive. With very good sound, well transferred to CD, this is a highly recommendable alternative version.

On the bargain Naxos label comes Elgar's *First Symphony* in a warmly sympathetic version from the BBC Philharmonic under George Hurst, a conductor too long neglected on record. Masterly with Elgarian rubato, he refreshingly chooses speeds faster than have become the norm, closer to those of Elgar himself. James Judd's even warmer, more tender, more ripely recorded version on Pickwick is still preferable, but no one will be disappointed with Hurst's powerful reading, well coupled with the *Imperial march*.

Mackerras's superb performance is the most bitingly passionate reading since Elgar's own, brilliantly recorded with the rasp of the brass in particular echoing the sort of sound that Elgar himself plainly preferred, and his account of the brassy final coda is the most stirring yet, a thrilling culmination. The *Cockaigne overture*, brilliantly done with high contrasts and incisive attack, makes a generous and welcome fill-up.

Solti's version of the *First Symphony* is now in Decca's 'British Classics' series, aptly recoupled with a Marriner Elgar orchestral grouping that is also not strictly idiomatic. The CD transfer brings out the fullness satisfyingly as well as the brilliance of the excellent (early 1970s) sound and, though Solti's thrusting manner will give the traditional Elgarian the occasional jolt, his clearing away of the cobwebs stems from the composer's own 78 recording. The modifications of detailed markings implicit in that are reproduced here, not with a sense of calculation but with very much the same rich, committed qualities that mark out the Elgar performance. Marriner's somewhat straight approach to the *Introduction and allegro* will not appeal to everyone, but the subtlety and strength of his unique band of string players are never in doubt. The added attraction here is the brief snippets arranged by Percy Young from Elgar's unfished opera, *The Spanish Lady*. The (1968) sound here is fresh and full – but with just a touch of astringency in the violins which adds to the bite of the *Introduction and allegro*.

Barbirolli first recorded the *A flat Symphony* in stereo for PRT in 1957 and, while this Hallé account has its moments of roughness in the playing, the first movement is far more vigorous than in Barbirolli's later (1962) Philharmonia account. With the Hallé, Barbirolli's faster tempo meant that the expansively unfolding argument carried through more convincingly, whereas on EMI there is a hint of heaviness where, after the march introduction, the music should surge along. The slow movement, too, is very slow: it is done more affectionately in the earlier version, which we hope will reappear in due course. The present transfer of a Kingsway Hall recording has lost some of the fullness in the violins; otherwise, it sounds very well. The *Cockaigne overture* is one of Barbirolli's most notable Elgar recordings. The conductor, himself a Londoner before he went to Manchester, paints a memorably vivid picture, and the recording does Elgar's richly painted canvas real justice – although again there is some slight loss of opulence in the strings.

Loughran's performance, offered in the lowest price-range, is direct and understanding, reflecting the Hallé Orchestra's long familiarity with this symphony. There is an element of reserve here, but the performance makes a strong impression, with a memorably beautiful slow movement. The 1983 analogue recording is first class, naturally balanced but vivid. James Judd's digital bargain Pickwick version, also with the Hallé, remains our primary choice in this work. Owain Arwel Hughes's version of *Cockaigne*, which is offered on ASV, is crisp and alert, but speeds are very broad, at times impairing the flow, though building to a fine, ripe climax. The sound is warm and atmospheric, but the timpani is focused imprecisely.

Boult clearly presents the *First Symphony* as a counterpart to the *Second*, with hints of reflective nostalgia amid the triumph. His EMI disc contains a radiantly beautiful performance, with no extreme tempi, richly spaced in the first movement, invigorating in the syncopated march rhythms of the Scherzo, and similarly bouncing in the Brahmsian rhythms of the finale.

Barenboim, before his 1973 interpretation, like Solti studied Elgar's own recording, and the results are certainly idiomatic, though in the long first movement Barenboim overdoes the fluctuations, thus losing momentum. The other three movements are beautifully performed, with the slow movement almost as tender as in Solti's reading. The recording is not as opulent or well balanced as Elgar's orchestration really demands. In the *Sea pictures* Yvonne Minton uses her rich tone sensitively, but there is less passion and less subtlety in her reading than in Dame Janet Baker's version and, although Barenboim is persuasive, this is not really a memorable performance.

Symphony No. 2 in E flat, Op. 63.
(B) *** CfP CD-CFP 4544. LPO, Vernon Handley.
☞ (BB) *** Naxos Dig. 8.550635 [id.]. BBC PO, Downes.

Symphony No. 2; Cockaigne overture, Op. 40.
(M) *** EMI CDM7 64014-2 [id.]. LPO, Sir Adrian Boult.

Symphony No. 2; Cockaigne overture; Imperial march.
☞ (M) **(*) Sony SMK 46682 [id.]. LPO, Daniel Barenboim.

Symphony No. 2; The Crown of India (suite), Op. 66.
(M) *** Chan. CHAN 6523; *MBTD 6523* [id.]. SNO, Gibson.

(i) *Symphony No. 2 in E flat, Op. 63;* (ii) *Elegy, Op. 58; Sospiri, Op. 70.*
☞ (M) **(*) EMI CDM7 64724-2 [id.]. (i) Hallé O; New Philh. O, Barbirolli.

Symphony No. 2 in E flat, Op. 63; In the South (Alassio), Op. 50.
☞ (B) *** Decca 436 150-2 [id.]. LPO, Solti.

(i) *Symphony No. 2 in E flat, Op. 63;* (ii) *Serenade for strings, Op. 20.*
*** BMG/RCA Dig. RD 60072 [60072-2-RC]. LPO, Slatkin.
☞ (BB) **(*) ASV Analogue/Dig. CDQS 6087. (i) Hallé O, James Loughran; (ii) ASMF, Marriner.

Handley's is the most satisfying modern version of a work which has latterly been much recorded. What Handley conveys superbly is the sense of Elgarian ebb and flow, building climaxes like a master and drawing excellent, spontaneous-sounding playing from an orchestra which, more than any other, has specialized in performing this symphony. The sound is warmly atmospheric and vividly conveys the added organ part in the bass, just at the climax of the finale, which Elgar himself suggested 'if available': a tummy-wobbling effect. This would be a first choice at full price, but as a bargain CD there are few records to match it.

George Hurst's version of Elgar's *First Symphony* with the BBC Philharmonic is followed on Naxos by an even more richly expressive and subtle account of the *Second Symphony* with the same excellent orchestra, conducted by Sir Edward Downes. Downes uses an expansive speed in the first movement to give the writing its full emotional thrust, and the hushed tension of the slow movements leads up to towering climaxes, well controlled. The Scherzo is brilliant, delicate and witty, and the finale with its sequential writing is perfectly paced. Although it has not quite the bite and thrust of Handley's version (partly the effect of the recording-balance), its valedictory feeling at the close is very moving. Indeed the only reservation is that the sound, though warm and refined, is a degree too distanced, so that the noble opening of the work does not have its full impact. This does not displace Vernon Handley, except for those needing digital recording, but it can be recommended alongside that CfP CD and is well worth having in its own right.

For his fifth recording of the *Second Symphony* Sir Adrian Boult, incomparable Elgarian, drew from the LPO the most richly satisfying performance of all. Over the years Sir Adrian's view of the glorious nobility of the first movement had mellowed a degree, but the pointing of climaxes is unrivalled. With Boult more than anyone else the architecture is clearly and strongly established, with tempo changes less exaggerated than usual. This is a version to convert new listeners to a love of Elgar, although, even more than in the *First Symphony* the ear notices a loss of opulence compared with the original LP. This is also very striking in *Cockaigne*, which opens the disc.

Gibson's recording shows his partnership with the SNO at its peak, and this performance captures all the opulent nostalgia of Elgar's masterly score. The reading of the first movement is more relaxed in its grip than Handley's, but its spaciousness is appealing and, both here and in the beautifully sustained *Larghetto*, the richly resonant acoustics of Glasgow City Hall bring out the full panoply of Elgarian sound. The finale has splendid *nobilmente*. In the *Crown of India* suite Gibson is consistently imaginative in his attention to detail, and the playing of the Scottish orchestra is again warmly responsive.

Solti's incandescent performance of Elgar's *Second Symphony* made a great impact when it first appeared in 1975, and it still thrills today. Modelled closely on the composer's own surprisingly clipped and urgent reading, it benefits from virtuoso playing from the LPO and full, well-balanced sound. Fast tempi bring searing concentration, yet the *nobilmente* element is not missed and the account of the finale presents a true climax. The effect is magnificent. *In the South*, recorded five years later, is less successful, if still exciting. But the result is nervy and tense, although the playing is excellent. Here Solti is not helped by Decca recording in which the brilliance is not quite matched by weight or body (an essential in Elgar). But the account of the symphony is well worth having, especially when the CD is so reasonably priced.

Slatkin's account of the *Second Symphony* is splendid, timed beautifully to deliver authentic frissons, and it too has extra power in the finale from the addition of pedal notes on the organ, just before the epilogue – as Elgar once suggested to Sir Adrian Boult. Previously, only Vernon Handley had included them on his equally outstanding version for CfP. Though the new Slatkin is much more expensive than that, it also includes a strong account of the *Serenade for strings*. Those looking for a first-class modern digital recording of the symphony should be well satisfied.

Even more than in his recording of No. 1, Loughran's *Second* has an element of emotional reticence. He chooses a steady pacing for the last two movements, and the finale has less exuberance than with Handley. This is still a performance of considerable character. The 1979 sound is fresh, well balanced and spacious, though the CD transfer is a little light at the bass end. Marriner's (1983) digital recording of the *Serenade* offers well-defined and cleanly focused sound; perhaps it is just a little too 'present', but the effect is truthful and never edgy. The performance adds nothing to his earlier recording, made for Argo/Decca in the late 1960s, which generates slightly greater atmosphere. All in all, however, this bargain disc is good value.

Barbirolli's 1964 Kingsway Hall recording shows its age a little in the massed violins (especially by comparison with the richer tapestry for the two short string-pieces, beautifully played, which were recorded two years later). Barbirolli's ardour is never in doubt – witness the exuberant horn-playing in the first movement and the passion of the finale – but his interpretation is a very personal one, deeply felt but with the pace of the music often excessively varied, sometimes coarsening effects which Elgar's score specifies very precisely and weakening the structure.

In 1972, having conducted this symphony all over the world, Barenboim made it his first exercise in Elgar recording for CBS. It seems as though his individual reading grew more, rather than less, idiosyncratic, after that sustained preparation. Following very much in the path set by Barbirolli, Barenboim underlines and exaggerates the contrasts of tempi, pulling the music out to the expansive limit. But given a willingness to accept an alternative viewpoint, this is still a red-blooded, passionate performance, capable of convincing, for the moment at least. All Elgarians eager to hear the work from a new standpoint should sample this. *Cockaigne* is given a warm, colourful reading, and although in neither case is the recording ideally balanced it has more body and warmth than on LP (especially in the finale of the symphony); indeed the Sony remastering brings almost an excess of bass resonance to the *Imperial march*.

CHAMBER AND INSTRUMENTAL MUSIC

Piano quintet in A min., Op. 84; String quartet in E min., Op. 83.
☞ (M) *** EMI Dig. CDM5 65099-2 [id.]. (i) Bernard Roberts; Chilingirian Qt.
**(*) Mer. ECD 84082; *KE 77082*. John Bingham, Medici Qt.

Bernard Roberts and the Chilingirian Quartet are well attuned to the Elgarian sensibility: they have dignity and restraint and they capture the all-pervading melancholy of the *Quintet*'s slow movement. In the *String quartet*, the Chilingirians are excellent too, though they do not quite match the ardour of the Medicis; indeed some people have found them too low-voltage. However, they are excellently recorded in a warm acoustic and there is plenty of space around the aural image. An impressive and rewarding issue.

John Bingham and the Medici Quartet play with a passionate dedication and bring an almost symphonic perspective to the *Piano quintet*, and there is no denying their ardour and commitment, particularly in the slow movement. They also give a fine and thoroughly considered account of the *Quartet*, and overall their reading is full of perceptive and thought-provoking touches. Unfortunately they are far too close in the *Quartet* (though less so in the *Quintet*) and it still remains difficult for a real *pp* to register, while tone tends to harden somewhat on climaxes.

(i) *Piano quintet in A min., Op. 84; String quartet in E min., Op. 83;* (ii) *La capricieuse, Op. 17;* (iii) *Serenade, Adieu* (arr. Szigeti).

☞ (M) (**) Dutton Laboratories mono CDLX 7004 [id.]. (i) Harriet Cohen, Stratton Qt; (ii) Hassid, Moore; (iii) Szigeti, Magaloff.

These pioneering records of the *Piano quintet* and the *String quartet* gave solace to the composer during the last months of his life and are obviously of historical interest. All the same, questions of sentiment apart, neither is special in quite the same way as the performances in EMI's Elgar Edition are. Harriet Cohen is neither subtle nor sensitive in the *Quintet*. The Strattons are heard to better advantage in the *Quartet*, recorded as a Christmas present to Elgar in 1933. The other odds and ends are of later provenance. Characteristically fine transfers from 78-r.p.m. shellac discs.

String quartet in E min., Op. 83.
*** Collins Dig. 1280-2 [id.]. Britten Qt – WALTON: *Quartet.* ***
*** ASV Dig. CDDCA 526 [id.]. Brodsky Qt – DELIUS: *Quartet.* ***

There is a poignancy in this late work which the beautifully matched members of the Britten Quartet capture to perfection. Not only do the Britten Quartet bring out the emotional intensity, they play with a refinement and sharpness of focus that gives superb point to the outer movements. With more portamento than one would normally expect today, the result is totally in style. Warmly expressive as the Gabrieli Quartet are in the Chandos coupling of these same works (CHAN 8474), the Brittens are even more searching.

   The young players of the Brodsky Quartet take a weightier view than usual of the central, interlude-like slow movement but amply justify it. The power of the outer movements, too, gives the lie to the idea of this as a lesser piece than Elgar's other chamber works. First-rate recording.

Violin sonata in E min., Op. 82.
**(*) ASV Dig. CDDCA 548 [id.]. Lorraine McAslan, John Blakely – WALTON: *Sonata.* **(*)

Violin sonata in E min., Op. 82; Canto popolare; Chanson de matin, Op. 15/2; Chanson de nuit, Op. 15/1; Mot d'amour, Op. 13/1; Salut d'amour, Op. 12; Sospiri, Op. 70; 6 Easy pieces in the first position.
*** Chan. Dig. CHAN 8380; *ABTD 1099* [id.]. Nigel Kennedy, Peter Pettinger.

At the start of the *Sonata*, Kennedy establishes a concerto-like scale, which he then reinforces in a fiery, volatile reading of the first movement, rich and biting in its bravura. The elusive slow movement, *Romance*, is sharply rhythmic in its weird Spanishry, while in the finale Kennedy colours the tone seductively. As a coupling, Kennedy has a delightful collection of shorter pieces, not just *Salut d'amour* and *Chanson de matin* but other rare chips off the master's bench. Kennedy is matched beautifully throughout the recital by his understanding piano partner, Peter Pettinger, and the recording is excellent.

   Though Lorraine McAslan cannot match the virtuoso command and warmth of tone of Nigel Kennedy's Chandos recording of the *Sonata*, hers is an impressive and warm-hearted version, full of natural imagination, helped by the incisive playing of John Blakely, and her coupling is more substantial. Good, forward recording, which gives the violin tone less bloom than it might.

Music for wind

Adagio cantabile (Mrs Winslow's soothing syrup); Andante con variazione (Evesham Andante); 5 Intermezzos; Harmony music No. 1.
(M) *** Chan. CHAN 6553 [id.]. Athena Ens.

4 Dances; Harmony music Nos. 2–4; 6 Promenades.
(M) *** Chan. CHAN 6554 [id.]. Athena Ens.

As a budding musician, playing not only the violin but also the bassoon, Elgar wrote a quantity of brief, lightweight pieces in a traditional style for himself and four other wind-players to perform. He called it 'Shed Music'; though there are few real signs of the Elgar style to come, the energy and inventiveness are very winning, particularly when (as here) the pieces – often with comic names – are treated to bright and lively performances. Excellent recording, with the CD transfers sounding as fresh as new paint.

PIANO MUSIC

Adieu; Carissima; Chantant; Concert allegro; Dream children, Op. 43; Griffinesque; In Smyrna; May song; Minuet; Pastorale; Presto; Rosemary; Serenade; Skizze; Sonatina.
**(*) Chan. Dig. CHAN 8438; *ABTD 1164* [id.]. Peter Pettinger.

This record includes all of Elgar's piano music. It has not established itself in the piano repertoire but, as Peter Pettinger shows, there are interesting things in this byway of English music (such as the *Skizze* and *In Smyrna*). We get both the 1889 version of the *Sonatina* and its much later revision. Committed playing from this accomplished artist, and a pleasing recording too, with fine presence on CD.

Organ sonata No. 1 in G, Op. 28.
☞ *** Priory Dig. PRDC 401 [id.]. John Scott (organ of St Paul's Cathedral) (with HARRIS: *Sonata* ***) – BAIRSTOW: *Organ sonata.* ***

Elgar's *Organ sonata* is a ripely expansive piece dating from 1895, written in the period leading up to the *Enigma variations*, a richly inspired work, more of a symphony than a sonata. John Scott gives an excitingly spontaneous performance and the St Paul's Cathedral organ seems an ideal choice, although some of the pianissimo passages become rather recessed (a feature of organ playing that works better 'live' than on a record, heard domestically). The recording has plenty of spectacle and the widest dynamic range.

VOCAL AND CHORAL MUSIC

Songs: *After; Arabian serenade; Is she not passing fair; Like to the damask rose; Oh, soft was the song; Pleading; Poet's life; Queen Mary's song; Rondel; Shepherd's song; Song of autumn; Song of flight; Through the long days; Twilight; Was it some golden star?*
**(*) Chan. Dig. CHAN 8539; *ABTD 1164* [id.]. Benjamin Luxon, David Willison – DELIUS: *Songs.* **(*)

Benjamin Luxon seemingly cannot avoid the roughness of production which has marred some of his later recordings, but gives charming freshness to this delightful selection. Brilliant and sensitive accompaniment, and a very fine recording balance.

Angelus, Op. 56/1; Ave Maria; Ave maris stella; Ave verum corpus, Op. 2; Ecce sacerdos magnus; Fear not, O land; Give unto the Lord, Op. 74; Great is the Lord, Op. 67; I sing the birth; Lo! Christ the Lord is born; O hearken thou, Op. 64; O salutaris hostia Nos. 1–3.
*** Hyp. Dig. CDA 66313 [id.]. Worcester Cathedral Ch., Donald Hunt; Adrian Partington.

Though one misses the impact of a big choir in the *Coronation anthem*, *O hearken thou*, and in the grand setting of Psalm 48, *Great is the Lord*, the refinement of Dr Hunt's singers, their freshness and bloom as recorded against a helpful acoustic, are ample compensation, particularly when the feeling for Elgarian phrasing and rubato is unerring. Vividly atmospheric recording, which still allows full detail to emerge.

The Apostles, Op. 49.
*** Chan. Dig. CHAN 8875/6; *DBTD 2024* (2) [id.]. Hargan, Hodgson, Rendall, Roberts, Terfel, Lloyd, London Symphony Ch., LSO, Hickox.
(M) *** EMI CMS7 64206-2 (2). Armstrong, Watts, Tear, Luxon, Grant, Carol Case, Downe House School Ch., LPO Ch., LPO, Boult.

Where Boult's reading has four-square nobility, Hickox is far more flexible in his expressiveness, drawing singing from his chorus which far outshines that on the earlier reading. Most of his soloists are preferable too, for example Stephen Roberts as a light-toned Jesus and Robert Lloyd characterful as Judas. Only the tenor, David Rendall, falls short, with vibrato exaggerated by the microphone. The recording, made in St Jude's, Hampstead, is among Chandos's finest, both warm and incandescent, with plenty of detail.

Boult's performance gives the closing scene great power and a wonderful sense of apotheosis, with the spacious sound-balance rising to the occasion. Generally fine singing – notably from Sheila Armstrong and Helen Watts – and a 1973/4 Kingsway Hall recording as rich and faithful as anyone could wish for. The powerfully lyrical *Meditation* from *The Light of Life* makes a suitable postlude without producing an anticlimax, again showing Boult at his most inspirational.

The Banner of St George, Op. 33; (i) *Great is the Lord (Psalm 48), Op. 67; Te Deum and Benedictus, Op. 34.*

☞ (M) *** EMI Dig. CDM5 65109-2 [id.]. L. Symphony Ch., N. Sinfonia, Hickox; (i) with Stephen Roberts.

In telling the story of St George slaying the dragon and saving the Lady Sylene, Elgar is at his most colourful, with the battle sequence leading to beautifully tender farewell music (bringing one of Elgar's most yearningly memorable melodies) and a final rousing chorus. The three motets, written at the same period, bring 'Pomp and circumstance' into church and, like the cantata, stir the blood in Hickox's strong, unapologetic performances, richly recorded.

(i) *The Black Knight* (symphony for chorus and orchestra); Part-songs: *Fly singing bird; The snow; Spanish serenade;* (ii) *Scenes from the Saga of King Olaf, Op. 30.*

☞ ❀ (M) *** EMI Dig. CMS5 65104-2 (2) [id.]. (i) RLPO Ch. & O, Groves; (ii) Cahill, Langridge, Rayner Cook, LPO Ch., LPO, Handley.

The Black Knight was Elgar's first big choral work, written just after his marriage to Alice, the woman who effectively ensured that Elgar could, against the odds, become a great composer. The happiness and confidence of the writing is what comes over with winning freshness, even though Elgarians must inevitably miss the deeper, darker, more melancholy overtones of his later, greater music. The subject, a tale of chivalry and a royal feast which brings disaster, is strikingly like that of Mahler's almost contemporary *Das klagende Lied*, but neurotic tensions are here far distant. Sir Charles Groves conducts a strong, fresh performance, not always perfectly polished in its ensemble but with bright, enthusiastic singing from the chorus. The three part-songs from the same period make an apt and attractive coupling. Clear, full recording; the CD copes admirably with the large forces.

King Olaf was the last of Elgar's works to be put on disc, and Vernon Handley, outstanding among today's Elgarians, makes it an appropriate landmark. The emotional thrust in Handley's reading confirms this as the very finest of the big works Elgar wrote before the *Enigma variations* in 1899. In its proportions it almost exactly anticipates *The Dream of Gerontius*, 90 minutes long with the first half shorter than the second, while in its big choruses its style keeps anticipating the later masterpieces, equally reflecting the influence of Wagner's *Parsifal*. The wonder is that Elgar's inspiration rises high above the doggerel of the text (Longfellow, adapted by Harry Acworth) and, though the episodic dramatic plan eventually tails off, the opposite is the case with Elgar's music, which grows even richer. Towards the end the charming 'gossip' chorus leads to the radiant pastoral duet between Olaf and Thyri, the third of his brides, followed by the exciting, dramatic chorus, *The Death of Olaf* (very Wagnerian), and finally an epilogue which transcends everything, building to a heart-tugging climax on the return of the 'Heroic Beauty' theme. Though strained at times by the high writing, Philip Langridge makes a fine, intelligent Olaf, Teresa Cahill sings with ravishing silver purity and Brian Rayner Cook brings out words with fine clarity; but it is the incandescent singing of the London Philharmonic Chorus that sets the seal on this superb set, ripely recorded, one of the finest in EMI's long Elgar history.

(i) *Caractacus, Op. 35. Severn suite* (full orchestral version).

☞ *** Chan. Dig. CHAN 9156/7; *DBTD 2004* [id.]. (i) Howarth, Wilson-Johnson, Davies, Roberts, Miles, London Symphony Ch.; LSO, Hickox.

Elgar's *Caractacus* – the nearest the composer ever got to writing an opera – draws from Hickox and his splendid LSO forces a fresh, sympathetic reading of a disconcertingly episodic piece. The oratorio is generally very well sung, with David Wilson-Johnson in the title-role, recorded in opulent Chandos sound. This is Elgar at his happiest, inspired by the countryside, and one of the high spots is a glowing duet for Eigen, Caractacus's daughter, and her lover, Orbin, sung by Judith Howarth and Arthur Davies. Much the most memorable item is the well-known *Imperial march*, introducing the final scene in Rome, made the more exciting with chorus. One even forgives the embarrassment of the concluding chorus which predicts that 'The nations all shall stand, and hymn the praise of Britain hand in hand.' The only reservation is that the earlier, EMI recording conducted by Sir Charles Groves, a sure candidate for CD, was crisper in ensemble and even better sung, with even more seductive pointing of rhythm. For coupling, Hickox has the full orchestral arrangement of Elgar's very last work, originally for brass band, the *Severn suite*.

(i) *Coronation ode, Op. 44;* (ii) *The Kingdom, Op. 51.*

☞ ❀ (M) *** EMI CMS7 64209-2 (2). (i) Lott, Hodgson, Morton, Roberts, King's College Ch., Cambridge University Musical Soc., Band of Royal Military School of Music, Kneller Hall, New

Philh. O, Ledger; (ii) M. Price, Minton, Young, Shirley-Quirk, LPO Ch., LPO, Boult.

Elgar's *Coronation ode* is far more than a jingoistic occasional piece, though it was indeed the work which first featured *Land of hope and glory*. The most tender moment of all is reserved for the first faint flickering of that second national anthem, introduced gently on the harp to clarinet accompaniment. All told, the work contains much Elgarian treasure, and Ledger is superb in capturing the necessary swagger and panache, flouting all thoughts of potentially bad taste. The choral singing, too, is memorable, more polished than in the Gibson/Chandos version (for which we have a soft spot) and as moving in the nostalgic lyrical writing (*Daughter of ancient Kings*) as in the splendidly spacious and grandiloquent ending. The 1977 recording – enhanced on CD – remains in the demonstration bracket, among the very finest ever made in King's College Chapel, and with extra brass it presents an overwhelming experience. Excellent singing and playing, though the male soloists do not quite match their female colleagues.

The coupling with Boult's 1968 recording of *The Kingdom* makes for a particularly distinguished and generous offering. Boult was devoted to this noble oratorio, openly preferring it even to *Gerontius*, and his dedication emerges clearly throughout a glorious performance. It has been suggested that the work is too static, but the Pentecost scene is intensely dramatic and the richness of musical inspiration in the remainder prevents any feeling of stagnation, certainly in a performance as inspired as this. The melody which Elgar wrote to represent the Holy Spirit is one of the noblest that even he created, and the soprano aria, *The sun goeth down* (beautifully sung by Margaret Price), leads to a deeply affecting climax. The other soloists also sing splendidly, the finest team on record. The only reservation concerns the chorus, which is not quite as disciplined as it might be and sounds a little backward for some of the massive effects which cap the power of the work, though the CD transfer has improved the clarity and presence.

(i) *Coronation ode, Op. 44; The Spirit of England, Op. 80.*
(M) *** Chan. CHAN 6574 [id.]. Cahill, SNO Ch. and O, Gibson; (i) with Anne Collins, Rolfe Johnson, Howell.

Gibson's performances combine fire and panache, and the recorded sound has an ideal Elgarian expansiveness, the choral tone rich and well focused, the orchestral brass given plenty of weight, and the overall perspective highly convincing. He is helped by excellent soloists, with Anne Collins movingly eloquent in her dignified restraint when she introduces the famous words of *Land of hope and glory* in the finale; and the choral entry which follows is truly glorious in its power and amplitude. *The Spirit of England*, a wartime cantata to words of Laurence Binyon, is in some ways even finer, with the final setting of *For the fallen* rising well above the level of his occasional music.

The Dream of Gerontius, Op. 38.
*** EMI CDS7 47208-8 (2). Helen Watts, Gedda, Lloyd, John Alldis Ch., LPO, Boult – *The Music Makers.* **(*)
*** Chan. Dig. CHAN 8641/2; *DBTD 2014* (2) [id.]. Palmer, Davies, Howell, London Symphony Ch. & LSO, Hickox – PARRY: *Anthems.* ***

(i) *The Dream of Gerontius. Organ sonata in G, Op. 28.*
☞ (M) ** EMI Dig. CD-EMXD 2500; *TC-EMXD 2500* (2). (i) Anthony Rolfe Johnson, Catherine Wyn-Rogers, Michael George, RLPO Ch., Huddersfield Ch. Soc.; RLPO, Handley.

(i) *The Dream of Gerontius. Sea pictures.*
(M) **(*) EMI CMS7 63185-2 (2). Dame Janet Baker, Hallé O, Barbirolli; (i) with Richard Lewis, Kim Borg, Hallé & Sheffield Philharmonic Ch., Amb. S.

Boult's total dedication is matched by his sense of drama. The spiritual feeling is intense, but the human qualities of the narrative are also fully realized. Boult's controversial choice of Nicolai Gedda in the role of Gerontius brings a new dimension to this characterization, and he brings the sort of echoes of Italian opera that Elgar himself – perhaps surprisingly – asked for. He is perfectly matched by Helen Watts as the Angel. It is a fascinating vocal partnership, and it is matched by the commanding manner which Robert Lloyd finds for both his roles. The orchestral playing is always responsive and often, like the choral singing, very beautiful, while the dramatic passages bring splendid incisiveness and bold assurance from the singers. The fine 1976 analogue recording is extremely well balanced and has responded admirably to its CD remastering. However, in order to make room for *The Music Makers*, a welcome enough bonus, at the end of the first disc Part I of *Gerontius* is broken immediately before the Priest's dramatic *Proficiscere, anima Christiana*, a most unfortunate choice, robbing the listener of the surprise entry of the brass.

Barbirolli's red-blooded reading of *Gerontius* is the most heart-warmingly dramatic ever recorded;

here it is offered, in a first-rate CD transfer, in coupling with one of the greatest Elgar recordings ever made: Dame Janet Baker's rapt and heartfelt account of *Sea pictures*. No one on record can match Dame Janet in this version of *Gerontius* for the fervent intensity and glorious tonal range of her singing as the Angel, one of her supreme recorded performances; and the clarity of CD intensifies the experience. In pure dedication the emotional thrust of Barbirolli's reading conveys the deepest spiritual intensity, making most other versions seem cool by comparison. The recording may have its hints of distortion, but the sound is overwhelming. Richard Lewis gives one of his finest recorded performances, searching and intense, and, though Kim Borg is unidiomatic in the bass role, his bass tones are rich in timbre, even if his projection lacks the dramatic edge of Robert Lloyd on the full-price Boult set.

Hickox's version outshines all rivals in the range and quality of its sound. Quite apart from the fullness and fidelity of the recording, Hickox's performance is deeply understanding, not always ideally powerful in the big climaxes but most sympathetically paced, with natural understanding of Elgarian rubato. The soloists make a characterful team. Arthur Davies is a strong and fresh-toned Gerontius; Gwynne Howell in the bass roles is powerful if not always ideally steady; and Felicity Palmer, though untraditionally bright of tone with her characterful vibrato, is strong and illuminating. Though on balance Boult's soloists are even finer, Hickox's reading in its expressive warmth conveys much love for this score, and the last pages with their finely sustained closing *Amen* are genuinely moving.

On EMI Eminence at mid-price Vernon Handley's version offers a modern, digital recording which captures the sound of the chorus vividly with plenty of church atmosphere. The impact of the performance is then weakened by a relatively backward placing of soloists and orchestra. One's involvement is reduced, even with Anthony Rolfe Johnson's thoughtful portrayal of Gerontius, and Catherine Wyn-Rogers as the Angel too often sounds matter-of-fact rather than dedicated. With Handley also less intense than usual, this is disappointing next to his earlier Elgar recordings, though it is welcome to have as fill-up his 1989 account of Elgar's magnificent *Organ sonata in G*, vividly orchestrated by Gordon Jacob to create what might almost be counted Elgar's 'Symphony No. 0'.

(i) *The Dream of Gerontius;* (ii) *Cello concerto.*

☞ (***) Testament mono SBT 2025 (2) [id.]. (i) Heddle Nash, Gladys Ripley, Dennis Noble, Norman Walker, Huddersfield Ch. Soc., Liverpool PO; (ii) Tortelier, BBC SO; Sargent.

It was not until the closing weeks of the Second World War in 1945 that the *Dream of Gerontius* was recorded complete for the very first time. On the eve of wartime victory, the sessions brought an atmosphere of dedication, vividly recaptured in this CD transfer of a performance that for consistency has never quite been matched since. Sir Malcolm Sargent was never finer on disc, pacing the score perfectly and drawing incandescent singing from the Huddersfield Choral Society. The soloists too, led superbly by Heddle Nash as Gerontius, have a freshness and clarity rarely matched, with Nash's ringing tenor consistently clean in attack. Though Gladys Ripley's fine contralto is caught with a hint of rapid flutter, she matches the others in forthright clarity, with Dennis Noble as the Priest and Norman Walker as the Angel of the Agony, both strong and direct. The mono recording captures detail excellently, even if inevitably the dynamic range is limited. Having the soloists balanced relatively close allows every word to be heard; in the present transfer, though the chorus lacks something in body, such a climax as *Praise to the Holiest* has thrilling bite.

The first and finest of Tortelier's three recordings of the Elgar *Cello concerto* makes an ideal coupling, emotionally intense within a disciplined frame. The third-movement *Adagio*, taken slowly at a very steady tempo, is given a rapt yet restrained performance, and the finale is strong, with the volatile element underplayed. The 1953 recording is transferred very clearly and vividly. Like all the Testament transfers of EMI material, it comes with excellent background notes.

(i) *The Kingdom* (with BACH, arr. ELGAR: *Fantasia and fugue in C min. (BWV 537), Op. 86;* HANDEL, arr. ELGAR: *Overture in D min.* from *Chandos anthem No. 2*).

*** BMG/RCA Dig. RD 87862 (2) [7862-2-RC]. (i) Kenny, Hodgson, Gillett, Luxon, LPO Ch.; LPO, Slatkin.

The Kingdom; Sursum corda; Sospiri.

*** Chan. Dig. CHAN 8788/9; *DBTD 2017* [id.]. Marshall, Palmer, Davies, Wilson-Johnson, London Symphony Ch., LSO, Hickox.

This fine Chandos version provides a strong contrast with the classic Boult recording, the first ever made and the one which, above all, brings out the oratorio's nobility. On his RCA version Slatkin, like Hickox, proves a warmly understanding Elgarian, but Hickox's manner is more ripely idiomatic.

With a more consistent team of soloists and richer recording, the Chandos is to be preferred. Hickox's soloists make a characterful quartet. Margaret Marshall is the sweet, tender soprano, rising superbly to a passionate climax in her big solo, *The sun goeth down*, and Felicity Palmer is a strong and positive – if not ideally warm-toned – Mary Magdalene. David Wilson-Johnson points the words of St Peter most dramatically, and Arthur Davies is the radiant tenor. The fill-ups are not generous: the intense little string adagio, *Sospiri*, and the early *Sursum corda*.

Slatkin sometimes jumps the gun in unleashing his forces, but he makes nonsense of any suggestion that this is an undramatic, merely meditative piece. Urgent as his view of Elgar is, Slatkin has a natural feeling for Elgarian rubato and is never rigid or breathless. When it comes to the gentler moments, he conveys a hushed dedication. The choral singing is incandescent; but sadly the set falls short in the choice of soloists. All four in varying degrees (Alfreda Hodgson less than the others) sing with uneven production and with noticeable flutter or vibrato amounting to wobble. The sound is full, rich and atmospheric, as it also is in the two ripely characteristic transcriptions of Bach and Handel that come as fill-ups.

The Light of Life (Lux Christi), Op. 29.
☞ *** Chan. Dig. CHAN 9208; *ABTD 1605* [id.]. Judith Howarth, Linda Finnie, Arthur Davies, John Shirley-Quirk, LSO Ch., LSO, Hickox.
☞ (M) *** EMI CDM7 64732-2. Marshall, Watts, Leggate, Shirley-Quirk, RLPO Ch. & O, Groves.

The Light of Life was one of the works immediately preceding the great leap forward which Elgar made with *Enigma* in 1899. The fine opening prelude, *Meditation*, is the only passage that is at all well known, but it includes some of the work's finest, most memorable motifs. Though the melodic writing too often harks back to Mendelssohn, rather than distinctively proclaiming Elgar, this hour-long oratorio, written in 1895 in the period before *Gerontius*, is full of Elgarian fingerprints, not least in the choral writing and the ripe orchestration. Notably more than Sir Charles Groves in the earlier, EMI recording, Hickox conveys the warmth of inspiration in glowing sound, with the chorus incandescent. The subject of Jesus curing the blind man is rather primly treated in the libretto, and Elgar's score inevitably suffers, but the energy and concentration of Hickox's direction prevent the mixture from seeming just sweet or bland. The solo singing is richly characterful, even if the microphone catches an unevenness in the singing of the mezzo, Linda Finnie, and of John Shirley-Quirk; nevertheless he sings nobly as Jesus in the climactic Good Shepherd solo. Arthur Davies as the blind man and the soprano, Judith Howarth, are both excellent, singing with clear, fresh tone. Warm, full, atmospheric Chandos recording adds to the impact.

Sir Charles Groves's understanding performance features four first-rate soloists and strongly involving, if not always flawless, playing and singing from the Liverpool orchestra and choir. The recording is vivid and full in EMI's recognizable Elgar manner and has been admirably transferred, with cleaner focus and no appreciable loss of amplitude.

The Music Makers, Op. 69.
(*) EMI CDS7 47208-8 (2). Dame Janet Baker, LPO Ch., LPO, Boult – *Dream of Gerontius.* *

It is some measure of the musical material in *The Music Makers* that the passages which stand out are those where Elgar used themes from his earlier works. If only the whole piece lived up to the uninhibited choral setting of the *Nimrod* variation from *Enigma*, it would be another Elgar masterpiece. Dame Janet Baker sings with dedicated mastery, though unfortunately her example is not always matched in Boult's recording by the comparatively dull-sounding choir.

3 Part-songs, Op. 18; 4 Part-songs, Op. 53; 2 Part-songs, Op. 71; 2 Part-songs, Op. 73; 5 Part-songs from the Greek Anthology, Op. 45; Death on the hills; Evening scene; Go song of mine; How calmly the evening; The Prince of Sleep; Weary wind of the West.
☞ *** Chan. Dig. CHAN 9269 [id.]. Finzi Singers, Paul Spicer.

Elgar's part-songs span virtually the whole of his creative career, and the 22 examples on the Finzi Singers' disc range from one of the most famous, *My love dwelt in a Northern land*, of 1889 to settings of Russian poems (in English translation) written during the First World War. *Death on the hills*, to words by Maikov, presents a chilling narrative about villagers on the hills being visited by the figure of Death. The basses in unison sing menacingly, representing Death, while the remaining voices sing a nagging ostinato to represent the villagers. Untypical as it is of the composer's usual style, he himself counted this motet 'one of the biggest things I have ever done'. The Finzi Singers under Paul Spicer give finely tuned, crisp and intense readings of all the pieces. The Hyperion two-disc collection also includes Elgar's ecclesiastical motets, but for the secular part-songs the Chandos performances are even finer.

4 Partsongs, Op. 53; 5 Partsongs from the Greek anthology, Op. 45. Choral songs: *Christmas greeting; Death on the hills; Evening scene; The fountain; Fly, singing bird; Goodmorrow; Go, song of mine; The herald; How calmly the evening; Love's tempest; My love dwelt; Prince of sleep; Rapid stream; Reveille; Serenade; The shower; Snow; Spanish serenade; They are at rest; The wanderer; Weary wind of the West; When swallows fly; Woodland stream; Zut! zut! zut!*

*** Hyp. Dig. CDA 66271/2 [id.]. Worcester Cathedral Ch.; Donald Hunt Singers, Hunt; K. Swallow, J. Ballard; R. Thurlby.

Though many of the partsongs, particularly the early ones, show Elgar at his most conventional, they bring many delights. The finest item is the last, in which both choirs join, the eight-part setting of *Cavalcanti* in translation by Rossetti, *Go, song of mine*. It is also fascinating to find Elgar in 1922, with all his major works completed, writing three charming songs for boys' voices to words by Charles Mackay, as refreshing as anything in the whole collection. Atmospherically recorded – the secular singers rather more cleanly than the cathedral choir – it is a delightful collection for anyone fascinated by Elgar outside the big works.

Songs: *Pleading; 3 Songs (Was it some golden star?; Oh, soft was the song; Twilight), Op. 59; 2 Songs (The torch; The river), Op. 60.*

☞ *** (M) EMI CDM7 64731-2 [id.]. Robert Tear, CBSO, Vernon Handley – BUTTERWORTH: *Songs;* VAUGHAN WILLIAMS: *On Wenlock Edge etc.* ***

At his most creative period in the early years of the century, Elgar planned another song-cycle to follow *Sea pictures*, but he completed only three of the songs, his Op. 59. The other three songs here are even more individual, a fine coupling for Vaughan Williams and Butterworth. Incisive and characterful, yet expressively sympathetic performances from Tear. The recording, well focused, is appropriately warm and atmospheric.

Sea pictures (song cycle), *Op. 37.*

⊛ *** EMI CDC7 47329-2 [id.]; *TC-ASD 655.* Dame Janet Baker, LSO, Barbirolli – *Cello concerto.* *** ⊛

(i) *Sea pictures, Op. 37. Pomp and circumstance marches Nos. 1–5, Op. 39.*

(B) *** CfP CD-CFP 9004. (i) Bernadette Greevy; LPO, Handley.

Like du Pré, Baker is an artist who has the power to convey on record the vividness of a live performance. With the help of Barbirolli she makes the cycle far more convincing than it usually seems, with often trite words clothed in music that seems to transform them. On CD, the voice is caught with extra bloom, and the beauty of Elgar's orchestration is enhanced by the subtle added definition.

Bernadette Greevy – in glorious voice – gives the performance of her recording career in an inspired partnership with Vernon Handley, whose accompaniments are no less memorable, and with the LPO players finding a wonderful rapport with the voice. In the last song Handley uses a telling *ad lib.* organ part to underline the climaxes of each final stanza. The coupled *Marches* are exhilarating, and if Nos. 2 and (especially) 3 strike some ears as too vigorously paced, comparison with the composer's own tempi reveals an authentic precedent.

Scenes from the Bavarian Highlands, Op. 27 (original version).

*** Conifer Dig. CDCF 142 [id.]. CBSO Ch, Halsey; Richard Markham – HOLST: *Dirges & Hymeneal etc.* ***

Three movements from this choral version of *Scenes from the Bavarian Highlands* were later to become the *Bavarian dances* for orchestra; but with piano accompaniment this original version is if anything even more charming, particularly when sung as freshly as by the Birmingham choir, vividly recorded.

Scenes from the Bavarian Highlands, Op. 27; Ecce sacerdos magnus; O salutaris Hostia (3 settings); Tantum ergo. The Light of Life: Doubt not thy Father's care; Light of the World.

☞ (M) **(*) Chan. CHAN 6601 [id.]. Worcester Cathedral Ch., Christopher Robinson; Frank Wibaut; Harry Bramma.

It is good to have a fine mid-priced performance of the original piano-accompanied version of the charmingly tuneful *Bavarian scenes*. Even without the orchestra, the music lifts up with remarkable freshness when the singing in Worcester is appropriately committed and spontaneous. The three versions of *O salutaris Hostia* are also worth having, the first unpublished and possibly never performed before this record was made in the late 1970s. The strong performances of *Tantum ergo* and *Ecce sacerdos magnus* add to the interest of this reissue, but, now that *The Light of Life* is available in a complete version, these two fairly brief excerpts are less valuable. Good accompaniments and fine, resonant recording, presumably made in the cathedral.

Scenes from the Bavarian Highlands, Op. 27 (orchestral version).
☞ (M) *** EMI CDM5 65129-2 [id.]. Bournemouth Ch. & SO, Del Mar – STANFORD: *Symphony No. 3.* ***

The EMI recording uses the orchestral version of the score; although the choral recording is agreeably full, balances are not always ideal, with the choral descant in the *Lullaby* outweighing the attractive orchestral detail. However, the performances are infectiously spirited, conveying warmth as well as vigour – Del Mar is a natural Elgarian. Moreover the EMI coupling of the Stanford *Third Symphony* was a happy and generous choice.

Eller, Heino (1887–1970)

Dawn (tone poem); (i) *Elegia for harp & strings; 5 pieces for strings.*
*** Chan. Dig. CHAN 8525; *ABTD 1235* [id.]. (i) Pierce; SNO, Järvi – RAID: *Symphony No. 1.* ***

Dawn is frankly romantic – with touches of Grieg and early Sibelius as well as the Russian nationalists. The *Five Pieces for strings* of 1953 are transcriptions of earlier piano miniatures and have a wistful, Grieg-like charm. The *Elegia for harp and strings* of 1931 strikes a deeper vein of feeling and has nobility and eloquence, tempered by quiet restraint; there is a beautiful dialogue involving solo viola and harp which is quite haunting. Excellent performances and recording, too. Strongly recommended.

Ellington, Edward Kennedy 'Duke' (1899–1974)

Harlem.
☞ *** Chan. Dig. CHAN 9226 [id.]. Detroit SO, Neeme Järvi – DAWSON: *Negro Folk Symphony;* STILL: *Symphony No. 2.* ***

Duke Ellington wrote *Harlem* on board the *Ile de France* in 1950. It was intended for Toscanini but the old maestro never performed it, and it was left for the composer to record it instead – a wildly exuberant but essentially optimistic picture of Harlem as it used to be before the drug age. Ellington's own programme says, 'We are strolling from 110th Street up Seventh Avenue. Everybody is nicely dressed and in a friendly mood and on their way to or from church.' He pictures a parade and a funeral, and ends with riotous exuberance. This is true written-down orchestral jazz, more authentic than Gershwin and marvellously played by musicians who know all about the Afro-American musical tradition. The trumpets are terrific. Superb recording.

Emmanuel, Maurice (1862–1938)

*Sonatine bourguignonne; Sonatine pastorale; Sonatine Nos. 3–4; Sonatine No. 5 (Alla francese);
Sonatine No. 6.*
⊛ *** Continuum CCD 1048 [id.]. Peter Jacobs.

Maurice Emmanuel was born in Burgundy and celebrated his native province in the *Sonatine bourguignonne* (1893), drawing on folk tunes as well as featuring the carillon and chimes of the cathedral at Beaune where he was a boy chorister. Later in his career he was to number Messiaen among his pupils and his *Sonatine pastorale* (1897) is inspired by the bird song which fascinated his more famous contemporary, although Emmanuel is comparatively simplistic, more atune with Satie in wittily quoting the coda from the slow movement of Beethoven's *Pastoral symphony* to conclude his portrayal of *Le Rossignol*. The later works are impressionistic, the *Third* (1920) very Debussian, then erupting into a Messiaen-like cascade of brilliance for the finale. The sinuous charms of the *Sonatine Hindous*, written in the same year, contrast with the elegant pastiche of the masterly *Sonatine alla francese* (1926), a 'French suite' in six dance movements of considerable appeal, not so far removed from Ravel's *Tombeau de Couperin*. All this music is superbly played by Peter Jacobs, whose clean articulation and vitality throughout the series afford as much pleasure as his feeling for the music's lyricism and atmosphere. Not to be missed.

Enescu, Georges (1881–1955)

Roumanian rhapsody No. 1.

(M) *** Mercury 432 015-2 [id.]. LSO, Dorati – LISZT: *Hungarian rhapsodies Nos. 1–6.* **(*)

☞ (M) *** Decca 425 087-2 [id.]. Detroit SO, Dorati – DVORAK: *Slavonic dances and rhapsody;* SMETANA: *Vltava* etc. **

☞ (M) **(*) Sony SMK 47572 [id.]. NYPO, Bernstein – LISZT: *Hungarian rhapsodies; Les Préludes.* **(*)

Enescu's chimerical *First Roumanian rhapsody* combines a string of glowing folk-derived melodies with glittering scoring to make it the finest genre piece of its kind in laminating Eastern gypsy influences under a bourgeois orchestral veneer. Dorati finds both flair and exhilaration in the closing pages, and the Mercury sound, from the early 1960s, is of a vintage standard. The coupling with the Liszt *Hungarian rhapsodies* is entirely appropriate.

Dorati's later recording was made for Decca in 1978 and the volatile Enescu piece is again done superbly; the orchestra are clearly enjoying themselves. This recording has the advantage of the warmly expansive Detroit acoustic, but the Dvořák and Smetana couplings sound less well upholstered.

Not surprisingly, Bernstein's charisma comes well to the fore in Enescu's chimerical *First Rhapsody*, a vividly individual performance gathering excitement as it proceeds. The recording does not match Dorati's Mercury version in richness of colour, but it has been effectively remastered. The Liszt couplings are impressive too, and the CD also includes a pair of Brahms *Hungarian dances*.

Symphonies Nos. 1 in E flat, Op. 13; 2 in A, Op. 17.

☞ *** EMI Dig. CDC7 54763-2 [id.]. Monte-Carlo PO, Lawrence Foster.

Enescu's creative accomplishments were long overshadowed by his career as a violinist, teacher and conductor: a fate not dissimilar to Busoni's, whose pianistic career eclipsed his music. A further handicap was that both composers divided their allegiance between two cultures: Romanian and French in Enescu's case; German and Italian in Busoni's. The *Roumanian rhapsodies* and even the visionary *Third Violin sonata* give little inkling of Enescu's stature. Now that his masterpiece, *Oedipe*, is recorded, justice is at last being done. The two symphonies recorded here are pre-First World War; No. 1 (1905) and No. 2 (1912–14) inherit the mantle of Strauss, Franck, Dukas – even Brahms – and are scored with great flair. It is true to say that they have never been played with such vigour and conviction as on this well-recorded and generously filled (77 minutes 47 seconds) disc. Lawrence Foster, who has recorded a good deal of Enescu, directs the Monte Carlo orchestra with tremendous fire and an infectious enthusiasm, and the players respond as if their lives depended on it.

Cello sonata, Op. 26/1.

** Marco Polo Dig. 8.223298 [id.]. Rebecca Rust, David Apter – VILLA-LOBOS: *Berceuse* etc. **

Despite its late opus number, the *First Cello sonata* is an early work. It reflects something of the climate of French music at the time (Franck and Fauré in particular) and, though it is well wrought and full of interesting ideas, at 37 minutes it rather outstays its welcome. However, it is admirably played by this duo, and well recorded too.

Octet in C, Op. 7.

☞ *** Chan. Dig. CHAN 9131 [id.]. ACMF Chamber Ens. – SHOSTAKOVICH: *2 Pieces for string octet;* R. STRAUSS: *Capriccio: Sextet.* ***

(i) *Octet in C, Op. 7;* (ii) *Dixtuor for winds, Op. 14.*

☞ **(*) Marco Polo Dig. 8.223147 [id.]. (i) Voces and Euterpe Qts; (ii) Winds of Iasi Moldava PO, Ion Baciu.

Enescu's *C major Octet* for strings (1900) is an amazingly accomplished piece for a nineteen-year-old, and its contrapuntal mastery says much for his studies with André Gédalge, to whom the piece is dedicated. It is a masterly and inventive score whose inspiration flows with wonderful naturalness. From the Academy of St Martin-in-the-Fields Chamber Ensemble comes a very good performance and recording.

The Marco Polo recording is less impressive and lacks the body of the Chandos. However, one can have no quarrel with the playing of the Rumanian strings, and it comes with a most valuable coupling, the *Dixtuor* or *Decet* for wind instruments of 1906, one of Enescu's best pieces, very well played by the winds of the Iasi Moldova Philharmonic under Ion Baciu. Again the recording is not top-drawer but still good enough to make this worth considering.

Violin sonatas Nos. 2–3; Torso.
**(*) Hyp. Dig. CDA 66484 [id.]. Adelina Oprean, Justin Oprean.

Enescu's *Second Violin sonata* is an early work. The *Third* (1926) is masterly and shows an altogether different personality; the difference in stylistic development could hardly be more striking. Adelina Oprean is thoroughly inside the idiom and deals with its subtle rubati and quarter-tones to the manner born. She exhibits excellent musical taste but her partner (and brother) is somewhat less scrupulous in his observance of dynamic nuance. The additional *Torso* is a sonata movement from 1911, which was published only in the 1980s.

7 Chansons de Clément Marot.
*** Unicorn Dig. DKPCD 9035; *DKPC 9035* [id.]. Sarah Walker, Roger Vignoles – DEBUSSY:
    Songs ***; ROUSSEL: *Songs.* **(*)

The set of Enescu songs, written in 1908, makes a rare, attractive and apt addition to Sarah Walker's recital of French song. As a Romanian working largely in Paris, Enescu was thinking very much in a French idiom, charming and witty as well as sweetly romantic. Ideal accompaniments and excellent recording.

Oedipe (opera) complete.
*** EMI Dig. CDS7 54011-2 (2) [Ang. CDCB 54011]. Van Dam, Hendricks, Fassbaender, Lipovšek,
    Bacquier, Gedda, Hauptmann, Quilico, Aler, Vanaud, Albert, Taillon, Orfeon Donostiarra,
    Monte Carlo PO, Lawrence Foster.

This is an almost ideal recording of a rare, long-neglected masterpiece, with a breathtaking cast of stars backing up a supremely fine performance by José van Dam in the central role of Oedipus. The idiom is tough and adventurous, as well as warmly exotic, with vivid choral effects, a revelation to anyone who knows Enescu only from his *Roumanian rhapsody*. The only reservation is that the pace tends to be on the slow side, but the incandescence of the playing of the Monte Carlo Philharmonic under Lawrence Foster and the richness of the singing and recorded sound amply compensate for that, making this a musical feast.

Englund, Einar (born 1916)

Symphonies Nos. 1 (War) (1946); 2 ('Blackbird') (1948).
**(*) Ondine Dig. ODE 751-2 [id.]. Estonian SO, Peeter Lilje.

Einar Englund's *First Symphony* is in his own words 'an expression of euphoric joy'. He has a spontaneous and natural gift, and his musical language is probably closer to Shostakovich than to anyone else. The *Second Symphony* presumably acquired its nickname from the apparent evocation of birdsong at the very opening. Englund may not be the equal of Tubin but his talents are far from negligible; he knows a thing or two about how to generate musical movement. Good performances and very acceptable (though not outstanding) recorded sound.

Symphonies Nos. 2 ('Blackbird'); (i) 4 for strings and percussion; (ii) Epinikia (Triumphal Hymn).
(M) ** Finlandia FACD 017 [id.]. Helsinki PO, Pertti Pekkanen; (ii) Berglund; (i) Espoo CO, Paavo
    Pohjola.

There is not a great deal to choose between the two versions of the *Second Symphony*; the analogue recording holds its own against its digital rival and, if anything, the Helsinki performance has the edge over the Estonian CD in terms of intensity. The *Fourth Symphony* was written in homage to Shostakovich, whose death in 1975 prompted its composition. There are some effective percussion effects, bells and ticking string pizzicati, designed – the composer says – to symbolize the brevity of existence; but for all its undoubted ingenuity, the debt to Shostakovich looms far too large. (There is also a brief allusion to *Tapiola*.)

Erkel, Ferenc (1810–93)

Hunyadi László (opera) complete.
*** Hung. HCD 12581/3 [id.]. Gulyás, Sass, Molnár, Dénes, Sólyom-Nagy, Gáti, Hungarian
    People's Army male Ch., Hungarian State Op. Ch. & O, Kovács.

Erkel's use of national music may not be as strikingly colourful as Smetana's in Czechoslovakia or Glinka's in Russia – both comparable figures – but the flavour is both distinctive and attractive, strongly illustrating a red-blooded story. Janos Kovács conducts with a vigour suggesting long experience of this work in the opera house. Denes Gulyás is a heroic, heady-toned hero, while Andras Molnár is equally effective as the villainous king, surprisingly another tenor role. Sylvia Sass is excellent as the hero's mother. First-rate sound. An excellent, unusual set, full of strong ideas, making easy listening.

Falla, Manuel de (1876–1946)

El amor brujo (original version, complete with dialogue); (i) (Piano) *Serenata; Serenata andaluza; 7 Canciones populares Españolas.*
*** Nuova Era Dig. 6809 [id.]. Martha Senn, Carme Ens., Luis Izquierdo; (i) Maria Rosa Bodini.

(i) *El amor brujo* (original version); (ii) *El corregidor y la molinara.*
☞ (M) *** Virgin/ EMI Dig. CUV5 61138-2 [id.]. (i) Claire Powell; (ii) Jill Gomez; Aquarius, Cleobury.

By including the dialogue, spoken over music, the Nuova Era issue provides the complete original conception of *El amor brujo*, rather like a one-act zarzuela, with chamber scoring and a narrative line somewhat different from the ballet we know in its full orchestral dress. Martha Senn is perfectly cast in the role of the gypsy heroine. She sings flamboyantly and often ravishingly, both here and in the delectable *Canciones populares* and the other two songs offered as coupling, and she is accompanied very sympathetically. Luis Izquierdo directs the main work atmospherically and finds plenty of gusto for the piece we know as the *Ritual fire dance*; and the recording is suitably atmospheric and vivid.

The Virgin alternative, by omitting the dialogue, finds room for the original version of the *Three-cornered hat*, also conceived for chamber orchestra, which first appeared as a mime play with music. Much is missing from the ballet we know today. Claire Powell makes an admirable gypsy in *El amor brujo*, while Jill Gomez is equally vibrant in her contributions to the companion work. Nicholas Cleobury concentrates on atmosphere rather than drama and, helped by the transluscent textures of the outstanding Virgin Classics recording, certainly seduces the ear.

El amor brujo (ballet): complete.
(M) *** Decca 417 786-2. Nati Mistral, New Philh. O, Frühbeck de Burgos – ALBENIZ: *Suite española.* ***

(i) *El amor brujo* (ballet; complete); (ii) *Nights in the gardens of Spain.*
⊛ (M) *** Decca Dig. 430 703-2; *430 703-4* [id.]. (i) Tourangeau, Montreal SO, Dutoit; (ii) De Larrocha, LPO, Frühbeck de Burgos – RODRIGO: *Concierto.* *** ⊛

Dutoit's brilliantly played *El amor brujo* has long been praised by us. With recording in the demonstration class, the performance has characteristic flexibility over phrasing and rhythm and is hauntingly atmospheric. The sound in the coupled *Nights in the gardens of Spain* is equally superb, rich and lustrous and with vivid detail. Miss de Larrocha's lambent feeling for the work's poetic evocation is matched by her brilliance in the nocturnal dance-rhythms.

Raphael Frühbeck de Burgos provides us with an alternative mid-priced version of *El amor brujo*, attractively coupled with Albéniz. The score's evocative atmosphere is hauntingly captured and, to make the most striking contrast, the famous *Ritual fire dance* blazes brilliantly. Nati Mistral has the vibrant open-throated projection of the real flamenco artist, and the whole performance is idiomatically authentic and compelling. Brilliant Decca sound to match.

(i; ii) *El amor brujo* (complete); (iii) *Nights in the gardens of Spain;* (ii) *The Three-cornered hat* (ballet): suite.
☞ (M) **(*) EMI CDM7 64746-2 [id.]. (i) De los Angeles; (ii) Philh. O, Giulini; (iii) Soriano, Paris Conservatoire O, Frühbeck de Burgos.

Giulini's performances come from the early 1960s, and the disc also includes Soriano's excellent account of *Nights in the gardens of Spain*. The Philharmonia playing is polished and responsive and Giulini produces civilized, colourful performances. The recording, too, is brightly coloured and, although noticeably resonant in *The Three-cornered hat*, the present transfers offer vivid and full-bodied sound. *El amor brujo* is not as red-blooded here as it is in the hands of Dutoit, but Victoria de los Angeles's contribution is an undoubted point in its favour.

(i) *El amor brujo* (complete); (ii) *Nights in the gardens of Spain; La vida breve: Interlude and dance.*
*** Chan. Dig. CHAN 8457; *ABTD 1169* [id.]. (i) Sarah Walker; (ii) Fingerhut, LSO, Simon.

The brightly lit Chandos recording emphasizes the vigour of Geoffrey Simon's very vital account of *El amor brujo*, and Sarah Walker's powerful vocal contribution is another asset, her vibrantly earthy singing highly involving. The Simon/Fingerhut version of *Nights in the gardens of Spain* also makes a strongly contrasted alternative to Alicia de Larrocha's much-praised reading and the effect is more dramatic, with the soloist responding chimerically to the changes of mood, playing with brilliance and power, yet not missing the music's delicacy. The *Interlude and Dance* from *La vida breve* make a very attractive encore.

El amor brujo; The Three-cornered hat (ballet): complete.
⊛ *** Decca Dig. 410 008-2 [id.]. Boky, Tourangeau, Montreal SO, Dutoit.

Dutoit provides the ideal and very generous coupling of Falla's two popular and colourful ballets, each complete with vocal parts. Few more atmospheric records have ever been made. Performances are not just colourful and brilliantly played, they have an idiomatic feeling in their degree of flexibility over phrasing and rhythm. The ideal instance comes in the tango-like seven-in-a-bar rhythms of the Pantomime section of *El amor brujo* which is lusciously seductive. The sound is among the most vivid ever; this remains in the demonstration class for its vividness and tangibility.

(i; ii) *Concierto for harpsichord, flute, oboe, clarinet, violin & cello;* (iii; iv) *El amor brujo* (ballet; complete); (v) *Nights in the gardens of Spain;* (iv; vi) *The Three-cornered hat* (ballet; complete); (iv) *La vida breve: Interlude and dance;* (vii; ii) *Psyché;* (vii; viii; ii) *El retablo de Maese Pedro (Master Peter's puppet show).*
(M) *** Decca 433 908-2 (2) [id.]. (i) John Constable; (ii) L. Sinfonia, Rattle; (iii) Marina de Gabarain; (iv) SRO, Ansermet; (v) De Larrocha, LPO, Frübeck de Burgos; (vi) Teresa Berganza; (vii) Jennifer Smith; (viii) with Oliver, Knapp.

This is a wholly recommendable set offering 140 minutes of top-quality Falla; it is worth investigating even if some duplication is involved. Ansermet's vivaciously spirited complete *Three-cornered hat* is also available coupled with Alicia de Larrocha's distinguished earlier, analogue version of *Nights in the gardens of Spain* (see below); here we are offered her later, digital account which is finer still. The surprise is the Ansermet mid-1960s *El amor brujo*, glittering with flamenco colour and with a particularly appealing soloist in the vibrant Marina de Gabarain. John Constable proves an admirable interpreter of the *Concierto* and there is no doubting the truth and subtlety of the balance or the excellence of the performance. *Psyché* is a setting of words by Jean Aubry for voice and a small instrumental grouping of the size used in the *Harpsichord concerto*. Jennifer Smith is an excellent soloist and the orchestral response in both works is thoroughly alive and characterful. *Master Peter's Puppet show* is not really an opera but a play within a play, both audience and performers being puppets. A series of tableaux is presented with The Boy (Jennifer Smith) as MC. It would be difficult to imagine The Boy being done than it is here, and the other singers are also excellent. Simon Rattle shows himself completely at home in the Spanish sunshine and the orchestral playing and recording are matchingly vivid.

(i) *Harpsichord concerto;* (ii) *Soneto a Córdoba; 7 Spanish popular songs; El amor brujo: Canción del fuego fátuo.*
☞ (M) (***) EMI mono CDC7 54836-2 [id.]. (i) Composer (harpsichord), Moyse, Bonneau, Godeau, Darrieux, Cruque; (ii) Maria Barrientos, composer (piano) – GRANADOS: *Danzas españolas* etc.; MOMPOU: *Piano pieces;* NIN: *Cantos populares españolas.* (***)

An invaluable addition to the 'Composers in Person' series which has enriched recent EMI lists. Maria Barrientos' account of the *Siete canciones populares españolas* was made in 1928 and 1930 in Paris, and it is marvellously intense from both singer and pianist; the *Asturiana* is particularly moving, as indeed are the *Canción del fuego fátuo* from *El amor brujo* ('Love the magician') and the *Sonnet to Córdoba*. The *Harpsichord concerto* was recorded in Paris in 1930 with a group of distinguished soloists, including the incomparable Marcel Moyse; and again, though one would not mistake it for a modern recording, it sounds remarkably good.

(i) *Nights in the gardens of Spain. El amor brujo: Ritual fire dance.*
☞ (M) **(*) BMG/RCA 09026 61863-2 [id.]. Rubinstein; (i) Phd. O, Ormandy – FRANCK: *Symphonic variations* ***; SAINT-SAENS: *Concerto No. 2.* **(*)

Rubinstein's version dates from 1969. His is an aristocratic reading, treating the work as a brilliantly coloured and mercurial concert-piece rather than a misty evocation, with flamenco rhythms glittering in the finale. The two encores which follow are even more arresting.

(i) *Nights in the gardens of Spain;* (ii) *The Three-cornered hat* (complete ballet).
☞ *(*) EMI Dig. CDC7 55049-2 [id.]. (i) Tzimon Barto; (ii) Ann Murray; ASMF, Marriner.

After a ferociously fast opening fanfare for *The Three-cornered hat*, it is as if the ASMF has run out of steam, and the ballet itself is a surprisingly low-key affair, with little to grip the listener apart from the vivid orchestration. *Nights in the gardens of Spain*, too, is very disappointingly lacking in allure, not the fault of the soloist.

(i) *Nights in the gardens of Spain;* (ii) *The Three-cornered hat* (ballet): complete; *La vida breve: Interlude and dance.*
(M) *** Decca 417 771-2. (i) De Larrocha, SRO, Comissiona; (ii) SRO, Ansermet.

Alicia de Larrocha's earlier (1971) recording makes an excellent mid-priced recommendation, coupled with Ansermet's lively and vividly recorded complete *Three-cornered hat*; she receives admirable support from Comissiona. The Decca analogue recording entirely belies its age. The *La vida breve* excerpts make an agreeable bonus.

The Three-cornered hat (ballet; complete).
*** Chan. Dig. CHAN 8904; *ABTD 1513* [id.]. Jill Gomez, Philh. O, Yan Pascal Tortelier –
ALBENIZ: *Iberia.* ***

Yan Pascal Tortelier is hardly less seductive than Dutoit in handling Falla's beguiling dance-rhythms. The fine Chandos recording is full and vivid, if rather reverberant, and Jill Gomez's contribution floats within the resonance; but the acoustic warmth adds to the woodwind bloom and the strings are beguilingly rich. Tortelier brings out the score's humour as well as its colour and the closing *Jota* is joyfully vigorous.

The Three-cornered hat (ballet): *3 Dances.*
☞ (***) Testament mono SBT1017 [id.]. Philh O, Cantelli – CASELLA: *Paganiniana;* DUKAS:
L'apprenti sorcier; RAVEL: *Daphnis et Chloé: suite No. 2.* (***)

It is good that Cantelli's excellent (1954) performances of these vivid dances are back in such fine transfers. Elegant, polished accounts, given very good mono sound.

PIANO MUSIC

Fantasia bética; 4 Piezas españolas.
(M) *** Decca 433 926-2 (2) [id.]. Alicia de Larrocha – ALBENIZ: *Iberia* etc. ***

These welcome and attractive couplings for Albéniz's *Iberia* are given exemplary performances and most realistic 1974 recording.

Fantasia bética; Piezas españolas (Aragonesa; Cubana; Montañesa; Andaluza); El amor brujo: Danza del terror. Three- cornered hat: 2 dances. La vida breve: Danza No. 2.
☞ (M) ** EMI CDM7 64527-2 [id.]. Alicia de Larrocha.

Another of the vibrant early recitals by the young Alicia de Larrocha, deriving from the Spanish Hispavox label, this 1958 collection is well enough recorded but offers short measure; moreover it devotes too much space to music which sounds more vivid in orchestral dress, for all the pianist's colouristic skill. The four *Piezas españolas* are another matter and are presented with great spontaneity and idiomatic feeling, with the *Montañesa* particularly haunting. The programme closes with the *Fantasia bética*, which is played with much dash and brilliance. This is more exciting than Alma Petchersky's version, but de Larrocha's impulsiveness nearly runs away with her. Unfortunately this CD has been withdrawn as we go to press.

Fantasia bética.
☞ (BB) ** ASV CDQS 6079. Alma Petchersky – ALBENIZ: *Suite española.* **(*)

Falla's masterly *Fantasia bética* calls for more dramatic fire and projection than Alma Petchersky commands. But she is a musical and neat player, the recording is very acceptable and this recital (which also includes Granados's *Allegro de concierto*) is competitively priced.

OPERA

La vida breve (complete).
**(*) DG 435 851-2 [id.]. Berganza, Nafé, Carreras, Iñigo, Ambrosian Op. Ch., LSO, Navarro.

La vida breve is a kind of Spanish *Cavalleria Rusticana* without the melodrama. Teresa Berganza may not have the light-of-eye expressiveness of her compatriot, Victoria de Los Angeles (whose version is currently withdrawn), but she gives a strong, earthy account; and it is good to have so fine a singer as José Carreras in the relatively small tenor role of Paco. With vivid performances from the Ambrosian Singers and LSO, idiomatically directed, the result here is convincing, even if the balance is not always ideal. However, while this 1978 recording comes in a box with libretto, is is ungenerously reissued at full price and so is rather uncompetitive.

Farnon, Robert (born 1917)

A la claire fontaine; Colditz march; Derby Day; Gateway to the West; How beautiful is night; 3 Impressions for orchestra: 2, In a calm; 3, Manhattan playboy. Jumping bean; Lake in the woods; Little Miss Molly; Melody fair; Peanut polka; Pictures in the fire; Portrait of a flirt; A Star is born; State occasion; Westminster waltz.
*** Marco Polo Dig. 8.223401 [id.]. Slovak RSO (Bratislava), Adrian Leaper.

Farnon's quirky rhythmic numbers, *Portrait of a flirt, Peanut polka* and *Jumping bean* have much in common with Leroy Anderson in their instant memorability; their counterpart is a series of gentler orchestral watercolours, usually featuring a wistful flute solo amid gentle washes of violins. *A la claire fontaine* is the most familiar. Then there is the film music, of which the *Colditz march* is rightly famous and the very British genre pieces, written in the 1950s. All this is played by this excellent Slovak orchestra with warmth, polish and a naturalness of idiomatic feeling that is quite astonishing. Adrian Leaper and the musicians obviously relish the atmospheric and delicately scored pastoral evocations. The recording is splendid, vivid with the orchestra set back convincingly in a concert hall acoustic.

Fauré, Gabriel (1845–1924)

Ballade for piano and orchestra, Op. 19.
*** Chan. Dig. CHAN 8773; *ABTD 1411* [id.]. Louis Lortie, LSO, Frühbeck de Burgos – RAVEL: *Piano concertos.* **(*)
☞ *** Chesky CD 93 [id.]. Earl Wild, Nat. PO, Gerhardt – CHOPIN: *Concerto No. 1* **(*); LISZT: *Concerto No. 1.* ***
☞ (M) ** Sony SMK 47548 [id.]. Casadesus, NYPO, Bernstein – FRANCK: *Symphony;* CHAUSSON: *Poème;* RAVEL: *Tzigane.* *(*)
☞ *(*) Pickwick Dig. MCD 71 [id.]. Valerie Traficante, RPO, Serebrier – D'INDY: *Symphonie;* SAINT-SAËNS: *Piano concerto No. 2.* *(*)

Louis Lortie is a thoughtful artist and his playing has both sensitivity and strength. This is as penetrating and well recorded an account of Fauré's lovely piece as any now available; however, the coupling is not one of the preferred versions of the Ravel Concertos.

A comparatively extrovert account from Earl Wild, but spontaneous and not lacking in finesse or warmth. Gerhardt accompanies positively and is also responsible for the excellent (1967) recorded quality. Admirers of this fine pianist will find this triptych very successful.

Casadesus's 1961 performance of the *Ballade* is slightly disappointing. The performance begins quite atmospherically but the elusive and delicate essence of the writing is not maintained. The recording is acceptable but not flattering to the piano.

A perfectly acceptable account from Valerie Traficante, but the rather resonant recording is less than ideal in the two companion works, although it is agreeable enough here.

(i) Berceuse, Op. 16; Violin concerto; (ii) Elégie. Masques et bergamasques: Overture, Op. 112; Pelléas et Mélisande: suite, Op. 80; Shylock: Nocturne, Op. 57.
** ASV Dig. CDDCA 686. (i) Bonucci; (ii) Ponomarev; Mexico City PO, Bátiz.

The allegro, which is all that survives of Fauré's projected *Violin concerto*, was first performed in 1880. Rodolfo Bonucci plays it with affection, as he does the charming *Berceuse* – though his tone above the stave can be a little wiry. Viocheslav Ponomarev produces a big, rich sonority in the celebrated *Elégie*, and Enrique Bátiz plays the orchestral pieces with evident feeling. Good rather than distinguished recorded sound.

Elégie in C min. (for cello and orchestra), Op. 24.
(B) *** DG 431 166-2. Heinrich Schiff, New Philh. O, Mackerras – LALO: *Cello concerto;* SAINT-

saens: *Cello concerto No. 1.* ***

☞ (m) *** Sony SBK 48278 [id.]. Leonard Rose, Phd. O, Ormandy – bloch: *Schelomo* ***; lalo: *Concerto* **(*); tchaikovsky: *Rococo variations.* ***

** Ph. Dig. 432 084-2 [id.]. Julian Lloyd Webber, ECO, Yan Pascal Tortelier – d'indy: *Lied;* honegger: *Concerto;* saint-saens: *Concerto* etc. **(*)

Heinrich Schiff gives an eloquent account of the *Elégie*, and he is finely accompanied and superbly recorded.

An ardent yet not over-pressed account from Leonard Rose of Fauré's lovely *Elégie* which admirably captures its idiom and its feeling of burgeoning yet restrained ecstasy. The recording is close, but the cello image is natural and firm. The rest of this collection is also highly recommendable.

Julian Lloyd Webber plays Fauré's *Elégie* sensitively enough. His account comes, however, on a disc of much interest in that it includes rarities by Honegger and Vincent d'Indy.

Pelléas et Mélisande (suite), Op. 80.
*** Denon Dig. CO 73675 [id.]. Netherlands R. PO, Fournet – chausson: *Symphony.* ***

The *Prélude* to *Pelléas* must be one of the most beautiful things in all music. Jean Fournet's account has a charm that is essential in this repertoire, and the Netherlands Radio Orchestra plays most sensitively throughout. They are also very well recorded.

Pelléas et Mélisande (suite), Op. 80; (i) Pavane, Op. 50.
☞ *** Chan. Dig. CHAN 8952; *ABTD 1546* [id.]. (i) Renaissance Singers; Ulster O, Y. P. Tortelier – chausson: *Poème* etc. ***

These finely finished and atmospheric performances come in harness with a fine account from the soloist-conductor of Chausson's *Poème* and a perceptive and idiomatic performance of the *Poème de la mer et de l'amour.* Very good orchestral playing and exemplary recording.

CHAMBER MUSIC

Cello sonatas Nos. 1 in D min., Op. 109; 2 in G min., Op. 117.
(b) *** Hung. White Label HRC 171 [id.]. Miklós Perényi, Loránt Szücs – chopin: *Cello sonata.* **(*)

The distinguished Hungarian cellist Miklós Perényi seems completely attuned to the elusive world of late Fauré, and in both sonatas the engineers do justice to his tone. Loránt Szücs is an excellent partner, and those who want this repertoire will find little cause for complaint. This disc is highly competitive.

Cello sonatas Nos. 1 in D min., Op. 109; 2 in G min., Op. 117; Elégie, Op. 24; Sicilienne, Op. 78.
**(*) CRD CRD 3316; *CRDC 4016* [id.]. Thomas Igloi, Clifford Benson.

Noble performances from the late Thomas Igloi and Clifford Benson that do full justice to these elusive and rewarding Fauré sonatas, and the recording is clear, if not one of CRD's finest in terms of ambient effect.

Cello sonata No. 2 in G min., Op. 117; Après un rêve, Op. 7, No. 1; Berceuse, Op. 16; Elégie, Op. 24; Papillon, Op. 77; Romance, Op. 69; Sicilienne, Op. 78.
*** Hyp. Dig. CDA 66235 [id.]. Steven Isserlis, Pascal Devoyon.

Strange that Hyperion did not record both sonatas: the *D minor* could easily have been accommodated; at under 44 minutes, this is as short on quantity as it is strong on quality! But the *G minor* is one of the most rewarding of Fauré's late works and is played with total dedication and eloquence by Steven Isserlis and Pascal Devoyon.

Piano quartets Nos. 1 in C min., Op. 15; 2 in G min., Op. 45.
⊛ *** Hyp. CDA 66166 [id.]. Domus.
☞ *** Sony Dig. SK 48066 [id.]. Ax, Stern, Laredo, Ma.

Domus have the requisite lightness of touch and subtlety, and just the right sense of scale and grasp of tempi. Their nimble and sensitive pianist, Susan Tomes, can hold her own in the most exalted company. The recording is excellent, too, though the balance is a little close, but the sound is not airless.

Sony's starry version of the two *Piano quartets* with Emanuel Ax, Isaac Stern, Jaime Laredo and Yo-Yo Ma offers the first serious challenge to the Domus account on Hyperion. The performances are of high quality and anyone could rest happy with them. But Domus convey the more idiomatic feel; theirs is domestic music-making at the highest level of accomplishment and conveys an altogether special freshness and spontaneity.

Piano quartets Nos. (i; ii) *1 in C min., Op. 15;* (i; iii) *2 in G min., Op. 45; Piano quintets Nos. 1 in C min., Op. 89; 2 in D min., Op. 115;* (iii) *String quartet in E min., Op. 121.*
(B) *** EMI CMS7 62548-2 (2). (i) Jean-Philippe Collard; (ii) Augustin Dumay, Bruno Pasquier, Frédéric Lodéon; (iii) Parrenin Qt.

The performances of the *Piano quartets* are masterly. In addition, there are authoritative and idiomatic readings of the two *Piano quintets* and other-worldly *Quartet*, Fauré's last utterance. This is enormously civilized music; however, one has to accept that, because the Paris Salle Wagram was employed for the recordings (made between 1975 and 1978), close microphones have been used to counteract the hall's resonance. The remastering has both increased the sense of presence and brought a certain dryness to the ambient effect, although the string timbres are fresh.

(i) *Piano quartet No. 1 in C min., Op. 15. Piano trio in D min., Op. 120.*
*** Ph. Dig. 422 350-2. Beaux Arts Trio, (i) with Kim Kashkashian.

Collectors of the Fauré chamber music will have to have this, even if it involves duplication. In some ways (notably in subtlety and charm) it surpasses even the Domus account on Hyperion. Theirs has the grace and lightness of youth; the Beaux Arts have the gentle wisdom of maturity. The recording is absolutely first rate.

Piano quartet No. 2 in G min., Op. 45.
☞ *** Ph. Dig. 434 071-2 [id.]. Beaux Arts Trio, Lawrence Dutton – SAINT-SAËNS: *Piano trio No. 1.* ***

Florent Schmitt called the *Second Piano quartet* 'music of the rarest fragrance', and the Beaux Arts play it with evident delight and relish. Their account can hold its own with any in the catalogue, and the Saint-Saëns coupling is delightful.

Piano quintets Nos. 1 in D min., Op. 89; 2 in C min., Op. 115.
*** Claves Dig. CD 50-8603 [id.]. Quintetto Fauré di Roma.

These two quintets are much less popular than the two piano quartets and inhabit a more private world. These artists have the measure of Fauré's subtle phrasing and his wonderfully plastic melodic lines, and their performances are hard to fault. The recording, made in a Swiss church, is warm and splendidly realistic. This music, once you get inside it, has a hypnotic effect and puts you completely under its spell.

Piano trio in D min., Op. 120.
*** Pickwick Dig. MCD 41; *MCC 41* [id.]. Solomon Trio – DEBUSSY; RAVEL: *Piano trios.* ***

The Solomon Trio's account of this subtle and rewarding score, which eludes so many artists, has great finesse and has the advantage of an excellently balanced recording. No one wanting this particular coupling is likely to be disappointed, particularly in view of the price.

Piano trio in D min., Op. 120; (i) *La bonne chanson, Op. 61.*
*** CRD CRD 3389; *CRDC 4089* [id.]. Nash Ens., (i) with Sarah Walker.

The characterful warmth and vibrancy of Sarah Walker's voice, not to mention her positive artistry, come out strongly in this beautiful reading of Fauré's early settings of Verlaine, music both tender and ardent. Members of the Nash Ensemble give dedicated performances both of that and of the late, rarefied *Piano trio*, capturing both the elegance and the restrained concentration. The atmospheric recording is well up to CRD's high standard in chamber music.

String quartet in E min., Op. 121.
☞ *(*) Nimbus Dig. NI 5114 [id.]. Medici Qt – FRANCK: *Piano quintet.* **(*)

The Fauré *Quartet* is not generously represented on CD, but while the Parrenin version of this elusive work remains available in the EMI two-CD set of Fauré's chamber music there is no need to look further. The Medici seem only intermittently at ease in its other-worldly atmosphere. The players obviously like this music, but they have yet to come fully to terms with it. They are well recorded.

Violin sonatas Nos. 1 in A, Op. 13; 2 in E min., Op. 108.
⊛ (M) *** Ph. 426 384-2. Arthur Grumiaux, Paul Crossley – FRANCK: *Sonata.* **(*)
*** Hyp. Dig. CDA 66277 [id.]. Krysia Osostowicz, Susan Tomes.

The two Fauré *Sonatas* are immensely refined and rewarding pieces, with strange stylistic affinities and disparities. Although they have been coupled before, they have never been so beautifully played or recorded as on the Philips issue. Moreover the two artists sound as if they are in the living-room; the acoustic is warm, lively and well balanced.

Both the Fauré *Sonatas* are also beautifully played by Krysia Osostowicz and Susan Tomes. There is an appealingly natural, unforced quality to their playing and they are completely persuasive, particularly in the elusive *Second Sonata*. The acoustic is a shade resonant but, such is the eloquence of these artists, the ear quickly adjusts.

PIANO MUSIC

Solo piano music

Ballade in F sharp, Op. 19; Mazurka in B flat, Op. 32; 3 Songs without words, Op. 17; Valses caprices Nos. 1–4.
*** CRD Dig. CRD 3426; *CRDC 4126* [id.]. Paul Crossley.

Crossley's playing seems to have gone from strength to strength in his series, and he is especially good in the quirky *Valses caprices*, fully equal to their many subtleties and chimerical changes of mood. He is extremely well recorded too.

Barcarolles Nos. 1–13 (complete).
*** CRD CRD 3422; *CRDC 4122* [id.]. Paul Crossley.

Barcarolles Nos. 1–13; (i) *Dolly. Impromptus Nos. 1–5; Mazurka, Op. 32; Pièces brèves Nos. 1–8, Op. 84; Romances sans paroles Nos. 1–3;* (i) *Souvenir de Bayreuth. Valses-caprices Nos. 1–4.*
(B) *** EMI CZS7 62687-2 (2) [id.]. Jean-Philippe Collard, (i) with Rigutto.

Jean-Philippe Collard has the qualities of reticence yet ardour, subtlety and poetic feeling to penetrate Fauré's intimate world but, while Collard has exceptional beauty and refinement of tone at all dynamic levels, the only regret is that full justice is not done to it by the French engineers.

Paul Crossley has a highly sensitive response to the subtleties of this repertoire and is fully equal to its shifting moods. The CRD version was made in the somewhat reverberant acoustic of Rosslyn Hill Chapel, and is more vivid than the 1971 EMI recording of Jean-Philippe Collard.

Barcarolles Nos. 1, 2, 4, Opp. 26, 41, 44; Impromptus Nos. 2 & 3, Opp. 31, 34; Nocturnes Nos. 4 & 5, Opp. 36–7; 3 Romances sans paroles, Op. 17; Valse caprice, Op. 30.
*** Decca Dig. 425 606-2. Pascal Rogé.

This CD makes an ideal introduction to Fauré's piano music. Rogé brings warmth and charm as well as all his pianistic finesse to this anthology, and his artistry is well served by the Decca engineers.

Dolly, Op. 56.
*** Ph. Dig. 420 159-2 [id.]. Katia and Marielle Labèque – BIZET: *Jeux d'enfants;* RAVEL: *Ma Mère l'Oye.* ***

The Labèque sisters give a beautiful account of Fauré's touching suite, their playing distinguished by great sensitivity and delicacy. The recording is altogether first class.

Impromptus Nos. 1–5; 9 Préludes, Op. 103; Theme and variations in C sharp min., Op. 73.
*** CRD CRD 3423; *CRDC 4123* [id.]. Paul Crossley.

The *Theme and variations in C sharp minor* is one of Fauré's most immediately attractive works; Paul Crossley plays it with splendid sensitivity and panache, so this might be a good place to start for a collector wanting to explore Fauré's special pianistic world. The recorded sound, too, is extremely well judged.

Nocturnes (complete); *Pièces brèves, Op. 84.*
**(*) CRD CRD 3406/7; *CRDC 4106/7* [id.]. Paul Crossley.

Here the recording is rather closely balanced, albeit in an ample acoustic, but the result tends to emphasize a percussive element that one does not normally encounter in this artist's playing. There is much understanding and finesse, however, and the *Pièces brèves* are a valuable fill-up.

Nocturnes Nos. 1–6; Theme and variations in C sharp min., Op. 73.
☞ (BB) ** Naxos Dig. 8.550794 [id.]. Jean Martin.

Nocturnes Nos. 7–13; Préludes, Op. 103/3 & 9; 3 Romances sans paroles, Op. 17.
☞ (BB) ** Naxos Dig. 8.550795 [id.]. Jean Martin.

This is glorious music which ranges from the gently reflective to the profoundly searching, offering a glimpse of Fauré's art at its most inward and subtle. Immensely civilized yet never aloof, the *Nocturnes* takes a greater hold of the listener at each hearing. The French pianist Jean Martin is on the teaching faculty of the Versailles Conservatoire and is obviously at home here, although he does not always catch the full delicacy of feeling, the quiet-spoken reticence which is so eloquent. He is at his best in the earlier *Nocturnes*, especially *No. 2 in B major*, Op. 33/2, while the comparatively well-known *No. 4 in E flat major* also comes off well. In the later works, notably the elusive *F sharp minor* (No. 12) and *E minor* (No. 13), his approach seems too direct and positive. The three *Songs without words* come off well, but the familiar *Theme and variations*, although strongly characterized, finds more subtlety in the hands of Collard and Ferber. Like Collard and Crossley, Martin is fairly closely recorded in the Clara Wieck Auditorium, Heidelberg, a not unsympathetic acoustic, but greater distancing aids the effect of this music.

9 Preludes, Op. 103; Theme and variations, Op. 73; Adagietto, Op. 84/5; Capriccio, Op. 84/1; Improvisation, Op. 84/4.
☞ (M) *** Saga EC 3397-2 [id.]. Albert Ferber.

This Saga disc is particularly valuable in making available, relatively inexpensively, the *Nine Preludes*, Op. 103, composed in 1909–10. These will repay the repeated attention the gramophone affords, for they are not immediately accessible yet are deeply rewarding. The *Theme and variations* is more extrovert and inventive in an instantly appealing way. It too is given a well-characterized and finely considered reading and there are some welcome smaller pieces. What a fine pianist Albert Ferber is: imaginative, poetic and content to let the music speak for itself. He is well recorded, and this is a Fauré reissue not to be missed.

VOCAL MUSIC

Après un rêve; Au bord de l'eau; Aurore; Automne; Les Berceaux; Chanson du pecheur; Clair de lune; Lydia; Mai; 5 Mélodies de Venise, Op. 58; Nell; Nocturne; Notre amour; Le papillon et la fleur; Poème d'un jour, Op. 21; Prison; Rêve d'amour; Les Roses d'Ispahan; Le secret; Soir; Spleen; Tristesse.
☞ ** BMG/RCA Dig. 09026 61439-2 [id.]. Natalie Stutzmann, Catherine Collard.

Natalie Stutzmann has a striking voice of undoubted richness and beauty. Voices are, of course, very much a matter of personal taste, and those who like her timbre will find much to enjoy. The dark colour of the voice tends to produce a rather uniform effect, and there is not quite enough variety of character; her warm vibrato strikes too matronly a note at times. The disc is also a reminder of the artistry of Catherine Collard, whose recent death will sadden all who hear this partnership. Both artists are well served by good recording and, though this would not be a first recommendation in building a Fauré song library, admirers of this remarkable artist should investigate this issue.

La chanson d'Eve, Op. 95; Mélodies: Après un rêve; Aubade; Barcarolle; Les berceaux; Chanson du pêcheur; En prière; En sourdine; Green; Hymne; Des jardins de la nuit; Mandoline; Le papillon et la fleur; Les présents; Rêve d'amour; Les roses d'Ispahan; Le secret; Spleen; Toujours!.
⊛ *** Hyp. Dig. CDA 66320 [id.]. Dame Janet Baker, Geoffrey Parsons.

Dame Janet Baker gives magical performances of a generous collection of 28 songs, representing the composer throughout his long composing career, including many of his most winning songs. Geoffrey Parsons is at his most compellingly sympathetic, matching every mood. Many will be surprised at Fauré's variety of expression over this extended span of songs.

Requiem, Op. 48.
☞ *** Teldec/Warner Dig. 4509 90879-2 [id.]. Barbara Bonnney, Thomas Hampson, Amb. S., Philh. O, Michel Legrand – DURUFLE: *Requiem.* ***
☞ (B) *** EMI CZS5 68104-2 (2) [id.]. Brian Rayner Cook, Norma Burrowes, CBSO Ch., CBSO, Frémaux – BERLIOZ: *Requiem.* **
☞ (M) **(*) EMI Dig. CDM7 67801-2 [id.]. Arleen Augér, Benjamin Luxon, King's College, Cambridge, Ch., ECO, Ledger – DURUFLE: *Requiem.* ***

Requiem; Pavane, Op. 50.
(M) *** Pickwick/RPO Dig. CDRPO 7007; *ZCRPO 7007* [id.]. Aled Jones, Stephen Roberts, London Symphony Ch., RPO, Hickox – BERNSTEIN: *Chichester Psalms.* ***
☞ (M) *** EMI CDM7 64634-2 [id.]. Sheila Armstrong, Fischer-Dieskau, Edinburgh Festival Ch., O de Paris, Barenboim – BACH: *Magnificat.* **
☞ (M) **(*) EMI CDM7 64715-2 [id.]. Chilcott, Carol Case, King's College Ch., Cambridge, New Philh. O, Willcocks.

(i; ii) *Requiem, Op. 48;* (i) *Pavane; Pelléas et Mélisande: suite, Op. 80.*
*** Decca Dig. 421 440-2 [id.]. (i) Kiri Te Kanawa, Sherrill Milnes; (ii) Montreal Philharmonic Ch.; Montreal SO, Dutoit.

Requiem, Op. 48 (1893 version). *Ave Maria, Op. 67/2; Ave verum corpus, Op. 65/1; Cantique de Jean Racine, Op. 11; Maria, Mater gratiae, Op. 47/2; Messe basse; Tantum ergo, Op. 65/2.*
*** Collegium COLCD 109 [id.]. Ashton, Varcoe, Cambridge Singers, L. Sinfonia (members), Rutter.

Requiem, Op. 48 (1893 version); *Ave verum corpus, Op. 65/1; Cantique de Jean Racine, Op. 11; Messe basse; Tantum ergo, Op. 65/2.*
*** Hyp. Dig. CDA 66292 [id.]. Mary Seers, Isabelle Poulenard, Michael George, Corydon Singers, ECO, Matthew Best.

(i) *Requiem, Op. 48;* (ii) *Cantique de Jean Racine, Op. 11;* (ii; iii) *Messe basse.*
☞ (B) *** Double Decca 436 486-2 (2) [id.]. (i) Jonathon Bond, Benjamin Luxon; (ii) Stephen Cleobury; (iii) Andrew Brunt; (i–iii) St John's College, Cambridge, Ch., Guest (i) with ASMF – FAURE: *Requiem;* POULENC: *Mass* etc. ***

(i) *Requiem; Cantique de Jean Racine;* (ii) *Messe basse;* (iii) *Pavane.*
☞ (B) *(*) Erato/Warner 4509 94579-2 [id.]. (i) Denis Thilliez, Bernard Kruysen, Philippe Caillard Ch., Monte Carlo Op. O, Frémaux; (ii) Audite Nova Vocal Ens. of Paris, Jean Sourisse; (iii) Lausanne CO, Jordan.

Requiem, Op. 48 (1894 version); *Messe des pêcheurs de Villerville.*
*** HM Dig. HMC 90 1292 [id.]. Mellon, Kooy, Audoli, Petits Chanteurs de Saint-Louis, Paris Chapelle Royale Ch., Musique Oblique Ens., Herreweghe.

John Rutter's inspired reconstruction of Fauré's original 1893 score, using only lower strings and no woodwind, opened our ears to the extra freshness of the composer's first thoughts. Rutter's fine, bright recording includes the *Messe basse* and four motets, of which the *Ave Maria* setting and *Ave verum corpus* are particularly memorable. The recording is first rate but places the choir and instruments relatively close.

Matthew Best's performance with the Corydon Singers also uses the Rutter edition but presents a choral and orchestral sound that is more refined, set against a helpful church acoustic. *In paradisum* is ethereally beautiful. Best's soloists are even finer than Rutter's, and he too provides a generous fill-up in the *Messe basse* and other motets, though two fewer than Rutter.

In many ways Philippe Herreweghe scoops both of them in his quest for authenticity, for he has had access to a score which makes use of the recently discovered instrumental parts of the original 1894 performance of the seven-movement version; unlike Rutter and Best, however, he tends to adopt speeds that are a degree slower than those marked. His soloists are more sophisticated than their British rivals, tonally very beautiful but not quite so fresh in expression. The recording has chorus and orchestra relatively close, but there is a pleasant ambience round the sound.

Michel Legrand uses the full orchestral version of 1900 in the most dramatic way possible. In the *Sanctus* the cries of '*Hosanna in excelsis*' are immensely telling, yet the delicacy of the *In Paradisum* reflects an equally sympathetic response to the gentler, mystical side of the music. Barbara Bonney's *Pié Jesu* with its simplicity and innocence is very touching. Thomas Hampson makes an eloquent contribution to the *Libera me,* and after the climax the flowing choral line shows the subtle range of colour and dynamic commanded by the Ambrosian Singers (as well as the orchestra). With superb, spacious recording this performance is very compelling indeed, and it is aptly coupled with an equally fine account of the Duruflé work which was inspired by Fauré's masterpiece.

Richard Hickox also opts for the regular full-scale text of the *Requiem,* yet at speeds rather faster than usual – no faster than those marked – he presents a fresh, easily flowing view, rather akin to John Rutter's using the original chamber scoring on his Conifer issue. Aled Jones sings very sweetly in *Pié Jesu.* With its generous and equally successful coupling, this makes a strong alternative recommendation.

Not surprisingly, the acoustics of St Eustache, Montreal, are highly suitable for recording the regular full orchestral score of Fauré's *Requiem,* and the Decca sound is superb. Dutoit's is an essentially weighty reading, matched by the style of his fine soloists, yet the performance has both freshness and warmth and does not lack transparency. There are attractive bonuses.

The St John's account has a magic that works from the opening bars onwards. Jonathon Bond and Benjamin Luxon are highly sympathetic soloists and the 1975 (originally Argo) recording is every bit as impressive as its digital competitors, while the smaller scale of the conception is probably nearer to Fauré's original conception. The Double Decca reissue offers exceptionally generous couplings, not only the Duruflé *Requiem* but other fine music by both Duruflé and Poulenc.

Frémaux's EMI version is attractively atmospheric, the recording comparatively recessed. Frémaux has a moulded style which does not spill over into too much expressiveness, and there is a natural warmth about this performance that is highly persuasive. Norma Burrowes sings beautifully, her innocent style most engaging. However, this is coupled with a much less recommendable set of the Berlioz *Requiem*.

Barenboim's 1975 recording has been splendidly remastered for its reissue on EMI's mid-priced Studio series. The recording was always first class, rich and full-bodied, and now the choral sound is firmer and better focused without loss of atmosphere: the moment when the trumpets enter in the *Sanctus* at the cry '*Hosanna in excelsis!*' is vibrant indeed. The Edinburgh Festival Chorus is freshly responsive so that, although the sound is beefier than with Rutter, the effect is never heavy and the performance is given a strong dimension of drama. Yet there is splendidly pure singing from Sheila Armstrong, and her *Pié Jesu* is even more successful here than with de los Angeles. Fischer-Dieskau is not quite as mellifluous as in his earlier account with Cluytens, but he brings a greater sense of drama. A first-rate version, including a sensitive account of the *Pavane*. It is well worth considering in the mid-price range, although the CD transfer of Bach's *Magnificat* which provides a generous coupling is less successful, with rather edgy sound.

The King's style is very much in the English cathedral tradition. On the earlier (1967) version, the solo soprano role is taken appealingly by a boy treble, Robert Chilcott. The recording, incidentally, was made in Trinity College Chapel and is very fine and splendidly remastered. The performance is eloquent and warmly moving, although some may feel its Anglican accents unidiomatic. The modest coupling is a melting version of the famous *Pavane*, with Gareth Morris playing the flute solo, given lovely, rich sound.

Ledger presents the *Requiem* on a small scale, with unusual restraint. Many will feel that this performance makes an excellent foil for the beautiful Duruflé coupling, as the digital recording allows many details of scoring to register that are normally hazed over. The singing is refreshingly direct, but anyone who warms to the touch of sensuousness in the work, its Gallic quality, may well find a degree of disappointment, though the *Sanctus* does not lack drama. This is less beautiful a performance than the earlier one, now also reissued, which was made with the same choir by Sir David Willcocks.

The bargain Erato Bonsai issue has nothing special to offer. Frémaux directs sensitively and the treble, Denis Thilliez, has a fetching innocence in the *Pié Jesu*, but Bernard Kruyson is slightly gruff. The choral singing is good but the recording is pale and not very well focused, and the bonuses are merely acceptable.

Feld, Jindrich (born 1925)

Flute sonata.
*** BMG/RCA Dig. RD 87802 [7802-2-RC]. James Galway, Phillip Moll – DVORAK: *Sonatina;* MARTINU: *Sonata.* ***

Jindrich Feld writes in a relatively conservative idiom, only occasionally betraying a specifically Czech flavour. What matters is his understanding of the flute, when it prompts Galway to play with characteristic flair. The piece makes an unusual and attractive coupling to the Dvořák and Martinů works, all of them vividly recorded in a relatively dry acoustic.

Ferguson, Howard (born 1908)

(i) *Concerto for piano and string orchestra;* (ii) *Amore langueo, Op. 18.*
☞ (M) *** EMI Dig. CDM7 64738-2 [id.]. (i) Howard Shelley; (ii) Martyn Hill, L. Symphony Ch.; City of L. Sinfonia, Hickox – FINZI: *Eclogue.* ***

This makes a substantial addition to Howard Ferguson's representation on record and should bring the composer new friends. Ferguson was a fine pianist and his concerto has something in common with the lyrical feeling of John Ireland's comparable work. At first it sounds more like a *concerto grosso*, for there is a substantial opening ritornello for the strings; but the piano makes a major contribution to the memorable theme and variations which is the work's centrepiece. As with Ireland, the finale is gay and melodically carefree. Howard Shelley's performance is admirable and Hickox secures highly sympathetic response from the City of London Sinfonia string section. *Amore langueo* is an extended cantata, lasting just over half an hour, and is based on a fifteenth-century text. Although it is subtitled *Christ's complaint to Man* and concerns Christ's spiritual love for mankind, its imagery also explicitly draws distinctly erotic associations with romantic sexual passion. To the medieval mind, spiritual and secular love were not always seen as separate experiences. The setting, for tenor solo and semi-chorus, with a strong contribution from Martyn Hill, brings a powerful response in the present performance, and Ferguson's music moves with remarkable ease from the depiction of Christ's suffering on the Cross to the sometimes even playful atmosphere of lovers in the bedchamber. An unusual and rewarding piece, recorded with great vividness on both CD and the excellent chrome-tape equivalent, but it is a pity that the separate sections of so big a work as *Amore langueo* are not individually cued on CD. This could have been put right on this reissue but it has been left unaltered.

(i) *Octet, Op. 4;* (ii; iii) *Violin sonata No. 2, Op. 10;* (iii) *5 Bagatelles.*
*** Hyp. Dig. CDA 66192 [id.]. (i) Nash Ens.; (ii) Levon Chilingirian; (iii) Clifford Benson – FINZI: *Elegy.* ***

Ferguson's *Octet* is written for the same instruments as Schubert's masterpiece, a delightful counter-part. The other works on the disc display the same gift of easy, warm communication, including the darker *Violin sonata* and Finzi's haunting *Elegy for violin and piano.*

Violin sonata No. 1, Op. 2.
(M) ** BMG/RCA GD 87872 [7872-2-RG]. Heifetz, Steuber – CASTELNUOVO-TEDESCO: *Concerto No. 2* (**); FRANCAIX: *Trio* ***; K. KHACHATURIAN: *Sonata.* **

Howard Ferguson's *First Violin sonata* is beautifully crafted and comes in a particularly enterprising compilation and is not otherwise available.

(i) *Partita for 2 pianos, Op. 56. Piano sonata in F min., Op. 8.*
*** Hyp. CDA 66130 [id.]. Howard Shelley, (i) Hilary Macnamara.

Ferguson's *Sonata* is a dark, formidable piece in three substantial movements, here given a powerful and intense performance, a work which, for all its echoes of Rachmaninov, is quite individual. The *Partita* is a large-scale piece, full of good ideas, in which Howard Shelley is joined for this two-piano version by his wife, Hilary Macnamara. Excellent, committed performances and first-rate recording, vividly transferred to CD.

Ferranti, Marco Aurelio Zani de (1801–78)

Exercice, Op. 50/14; Fantaisie variée sur le romance d'Otello (Assisa à piè), Op. 7; 4 Mélodies nocturnes originales, Op. 41a/1–4; Nocturne sur la dernière pensée de Weber, Op. 40; Ronde des fées, Op. 2.
⊛ *** Chan. Dig. CHAN 8512; ABTD 1222 [id.]. Simon Wynberg (guitar) – FERRER: *Collection.* ***
Simon Wynberg's playing fully enters the innocently compelling sound-world of this Bolognese composer; it is wholly spontaneous and has the most subtle control of light and shade. Ferranti's invention is most appealing, and this makes ideal music for late-evening reverie; moreover the guitar is most realistically recorded.

Ferrer, José (1835–1916)

Belle (Gavotte); La danse de naïades; L'étudiant de Salamanque (Tango); Vals.
*** Chan. Dig. CHAN 8512; ABTD 1222 [id.]. Simon Wynberg (guitar) – FERRANTI: *Collection.* *** ⊛

José Ferrer is a less substantial figure than Ferranti, but these four vignettes are almost as winning as that composer's music. The recording has striking realism and presence.

Fetler, Paul (born 1920)

Contrasts for orchestra.
☞ (M) *** Mercury 434 335-2 [id.]. Minneapolis SO, Dorati – AURIC: *Overture;* FRANCAIX: *Piano concertino;* MILHAUD: *Le bœuf sur le toit;* SATIE: *Parade.* ***

Paul Fetler's *Contrasts* makes a strange bedfellow for French music by members of Les Six. At the time this recording was made (1960), Fetler (American born, he had studied in Europe as well as the USA, most significantly under Paul Hindemith) was on the Faculty of Minnesota University. His four-movement sinfonietta, *Contrasts*, is based on four notes (B flat, F, C, A flat) yet is as impressive for its fine use of brass sonorities in the slow movement as for the neo-classical athleticism of the opening *Allegro* and the pervading energy of the finale where everything comes together. It is an eclectic work yet has distinct character. The performance is first rate, and so is the Mercury recording.

Fibich, Zdeněk (1850–1900)

Symphony No. 1 in F, Op. 17.
☞ *** Chan. Dig. CHAN 9230 [id.]. Detroit SO, Neeme Järvi – SMETANA: *Ma Vlast* (excerpts). ***

Fibich was almost equally attuned to the Leipzig school and the nationalism of Smetana and Dvořák. He began his *First Symphony* in 1877 and, by the time of its first performance in 1883, Dvořák had reached his *D major Symphony*. Yet there is a strong Bohemian feel to this piece and though, like so much of Fibich's music, it is a little square, such is the excellence of Neeme Järvi's performance that it doesn't feel so. This is its best performance so far on record. The coupling, two Smetana tone-poems, is unlikely to influence a collector one way or the other. It would have been more sensible to give us one of the other symphonies since there would have been plenty of room. Hybrid programmes are not always satisfactory from the collector's viewpoint, but readers should not pass this by.

(i) *Symphonies Nos. 2 in E flat, Op. 38;* (ii) *3 in E min., Op. 53.*
**(*) Sup. 11 0657-2 [id.]. Brno State PO, (i) Waldhans; (ii) Bělohlávek.

Fibich's *Second Symphony* proceeds in a somewhat predictable way, yet the *Adagio* is undoubtedly eloquent, and the Scherzo is stirring and colourful. The Brno orchestra under Jiří Waldhans give a straightforward performance and the 1976 recording is clear, with plenty of body and a convincing ambient effect. In the *Third Symphony* the invention is fresher than that of its predecessor, and the Scherzo with its catchy syncopations has great charm. The performance, directed by Jiří Bělohlávek, is sympathetic and alive.

Moods, impressions and reminiscences, Opp. 41, 44, 47 & 57; Studies of paintings, Op. 56.
☞ ** Unicorn-Kanchana Dig. DKPCD 9149 [id.]. Radoslav Kvapil.

These small vignettes are touching – they are a forerunner of Janáček's *Leaves from an overgrown path* – and spring from a love affair he had towards the end of his life. There are nearly 400 short, often poignant and always charming miniatures; a few are mere salon pieces (the famous *Poème* is one of them) but most are full of strong poetic feeling and beauty of melodic line. Readers should consult Gerald Abrahams' illuminating essay, 'An erotic diary for piano', in *Slavonic and Romantic Music* for more detailed background. They are played with great sensitivity and subtlety by Radoslav Kvapil. The music deserves three stars and a Rosette – and so does the playing, which has great sensitivity and artistry. But the recording is veiled and plummy and has no top – even electrostatic speakers fail to reveal any transparency at the treble end of the spectrum. Even so, it is worth while putting up with this for the sake of such haunting music and fine pianism.

Field, John (1782–1837)

Piano concertos Nos. 2 in A flat; 3 in E flat.
☞ ⊛ *** Telarc Dig. CD 80370 [id.]. John O'Conor, SCO, Mackerras.

John O'Conor has recorded all the John Field concertos before with the New Irish Chamber Orchestra (Onyx CD 101/3) but these Telarc versions are distinctly superior. They are beautifully recorded and the warm, naturally balanced sound gives the music the elegance it needs. The *Second Concerto* with its innocent *Adagio* based on an engaging rocking figure is delightful, and the finale – handled with much delicacy and a gentle sparkle – is equally winning. The first movement of No. 3 brings a nicely rhapsodical feeling and its *Andantino* (not a part of the original concerto) is one of the composer's daintiest *Nocturnes*, that in B flat, orchestrated to have a gentle string accompaniment. It is played with much grace and delicacy and is then followed by a Rondo, with a catchy, hopping main theme which is also one of Field's very best finales, with some exuberant bursts from the timpani to add to the geniality. O'Conor plays throughout with great distinction and always displays the lightest touch – his softly gleaming roulades are very fetching – and Mackerras accompanies with warmth and character. The recording has a somewhat resonant bass but the violins sing in an atmosphere of pleasing bloom. If the rest of the series is as good as this, then our Rosette will have to be extended to cover the whole set.

Nocturnes Nos. 1–16.
☞ **(*) Athene ATH CD 1 [id.]. Joanna Leach (fortepiano).

Joanna Leach uses three 'square' fortepianos, by Stodart and Broadwood (both from the 1820s) and a D'Almain from a decade later. The latter instrument most closely approaches the quality of a modern piano, though the Broadwood is not far behind. Joanna Leach coaxes poetic sounds from these comparatively recalcitrant instruments and plays this repertoire very sensitively. However, it cannot be denied that for most ears this music (with its remarkable anticipations of Chopin) sounds even better on a modern concert grand.

Nocturnes 1, 2, 4–6, 8–16, 18.
☞ *** Telarc Dig. CD-80199 [id.]. John O'Conor.

It would be difficult to better John O'Conor's sensitive and beautifully recorded accounts of his countryman's pioneering essays in the *Nocturne*. He captures their character to perfection, and his tonal finesse is remarkable but never self-regarding. Strongly recommended.

Piano sonatas: Nos. 1 in E flat; 2 in A; 3 in C min., Op. 1/1–3; 4 in B.
**(*) Chan. Dig. CHAN 8787; *ABTD 1422* [id.]. Míceál O'Rourke.

Míceál O'Rourke plays these two-movement *Sonatas* written by his countryman with some flair. He is particularly good in the famous *Rondo* finale of the *First Sonata*, which he plays with real Irish whimsy and sparkling touch. The *Allegretto scherzando* of No. 3 also has hit potential.

Finzi, Gerald (1901–56)

Cello concerto in A min., Op. 40.
*** Chan. Dig. CHAN 8471; *ABTD 1182* [id.]. Wallfisch, RLPO, Handley – K. LEIGHTON: *Veris gratia.* ***

Finzi's *Cello concerto* is perhaps the most searching of all his works. Wallfisch finds all the dark eloquence of the central movement, and the performance overall has splendid impetus, with Handley providing the most sympathetic backing. The Chandos recording has an attractively natural balance.

Clarinet concerto, Op. 31.
*** Hyp. CDA 66001 [id.]. Thea King, Philh. O, Francis – STANFORD: *Concerto.* ***
*** ASV Dig. CDDCA 568 [id.]. MacDonald, N. Sinfonia, Bedford – COPLAND: *Concerto;*
  MOURANT: *Pied Piper.* ***

(i) *Clarinet concerto, Op. 31;* (ii) *5 Bagatelles for clarinet and piano.*
*** ASV CDDCA 787; *ZCDCA 787* [id.]. Emma Johnson; (i) RPO, Groves; (ii) Malcolm
  Martineau – STANFORD: *Clarinet concerto* etc. ***

There is no more delightful disc of British clarinet music than this, with Emma Johnson even more warmly expressive in the concertos than Thea King on her Hyperion disc, and with Sir Charles Groves and the RPO ideally sympathetic accompanists. Finzi's sinuous melodies for the solo instrument are made to sound as though the soloist is improvising them, and with extreme daring she uses the widest possible dynamic, ranging down to a whispered pianissimo that might be inaudible in a concert-hall.

On the Hyperion label, Thea King also gives a definitive performance, strong and clean-cut. Her characterful timbre, using little or no vibrato, is highly telling against a resonant orchestral backcloth. The accompaniment of the Philharmonia under Alun Francis is highly sympathetic. With Stanford's even rarer concerto, this makes a most attractive issue, and the sound is excellent.

The coupling of Finzi and Copland makes an unexpected but attractive mix, with the Canadian clarinettist, George MacDonald, giving a brilliant and thoughtful performance, particularly impressive in the spacious, melismatic writing of the slow movement. Refined recording, with the instruments set slightly at a distance.

(i) *Clarinet concerto. Love's Labour's Lost: suite; Prelude for string orchestra; Romance for strings.*
*** Nimbus Dig. NI 5101 [id.]. (i) Alan Hacker; E. String O, Boughton.

Alan Hacker's reading of the *Concerto* is improvisatory in style and freely flexible in tempi, with the slow movement at once introspective and rhapsodic. The concert suite of incidental music for Shakespeare's *Love's Labour's Lost* is amiably atmospheric and pleasing in invention and in the colour of its scoring. The two string pieces are by no means slight and are played most expressively; the *Romance* is particularly eloquent in William Boughton's hands.

Eclogue for piano and string orchestra.
☞ (M) ******* EMI Dig. CDM7 64738-2 [id.]. Howard Shelley, City of L. Sinfonia, Hickox –
FERGUSON: *Piano concerto No. 2* etc. *******

This is the central movement of an uncompleted piano concerto which the composer decided could stand on its own. It was Howard Ferguson who edited the final manuscript and set the title, and it is appropriate that this essentially valedictory piece should be coupled with his own concerto. The mood is tranquil yet haunting, and the performance brings out all its serene lyricism. The recording is admirably realistic.

The Fall of the leaf (elegy), *Op. 20* (ed. Ferguson); *New Year music, Op. 7.*
☞ (M) ******* EMI Dig. CDM7 64721-2 [id.]. N. Sinfonia, Hickox – MOERAN: *Serenade* etc. ****(*)**

The Fall of the leaf was left by Finzi with its scoring incomplete, but Howard Ferguson finished it with such skill that no one would ever guess. This and the even more touching *New Year music* have a gentle, elegiac quality, which is well caught by the lovely playing here. The warm acoustics of All Saints', Newcastle-upon-Tyne, increase the feeling of evocation.

Grand Fantasia and Toccata (for piano and orchestra), *Op. 38;* (ii) *Intimations of Immortality, Op. 29.*
☞ (M) ******* EMI Dig. CDM7 64720-2 [id.]. (i) Philip Fowke; (ii) Philip Langridge, RLPO Ch.;
RLPO, Hickox.

This mid-priced reissue coupling Gerald Finzi's *Intimations of Immortality* and the *Grand Fantasia and Toccata* for piano and orchestra originally appeared at full price as recently as 1990. Finzi's setting of Wordsworth, which is both eclectic and Elgarian in feeling, is delightfully spontaneous. His flamboyant presentation of *Now, while the birds thus sing a joyous song* – with its exuberant syncopations – even features a xylophone solo. The rich, lyrical cantilena of this music brings constant reminders of the Elgar of *Gerontius.* The evocative orchestral introduction which sets the scene for the first poem, *There was a time when meadow, grove and stream,* is highly romantic, while the writing remains essentially within the pastoral tradition of English song-setting. The performance here is wholly committed, with the fervour of the chorus echoing the dedication of the soloist. Philip Langridge is as ardent as you could wish, although it must be conceded that his passionate line brings intrusive vibrato at times. But in moments of repose his lyrical response is very appealing. The choral recording is both spacious and brilliant. The coupling is another fascinatingly eclectic piece, this time for piano and orchestra. The Bachian·*Grand fantasia* is followed by a genial *Toccata,* fugal in style. The two parts of this concertante work were written 30 years apart, yet they join up perfectly. The piece is played compellingly by Philip Fowke, and Hickox is a fine partner. Again vividly realistic sound. Highly recommended.

Elegy for violin and piano.
*** Hyp. Dig. CDA 66192 [id.]. Chilingirian, Benson – FERGUSON: *Octet* etc. *******

Finzi's moving little *Elegy for violin and piano* makes an apt fill-up for the record of chamber music by his friend, Howard Ferguson.

(i) *Dies natalis; For St Cecilia;* (ii) *In terra pax; Magnificat.*
(M) ******* Decca 425 660-2. (i) Langridge, London Symphony Ch., LSO; (ii) Burrowes, Shirley-Quirk,
Hickox Singers, City of L. Sinfonia; Hickox.

Dies natalis is one of Finzi's most sensitive and deeply felt works. *In terra pax* is another Christmas work, this time more direct. The concert ends with the fine *Magnificat* setting from 1951, an American commission. All the performances here are both strong and convincing in their contrasting moods, taken from vintage Argo recordings made in 1978/9.

Fiorillo, Federigo (1755– after 1823)

Violin concerto No. 1 in F.
*** Hyp. Dig. CDA 66210 [id.]. Oprean, European Community CO, Faerber – VIOTTI: *Violin concerto No. 13.* ***

Fiorillo's *Concerto* is charmingly romantic. Adelina Oprean's playing can only be described as quicksilver: her lightness of bow and firm, clean focus of timbre are most appealing. She is given a warm, polished accompaniment and the recording is eminently truthful and well balanced.

Flotow, Friedrich (1812–83)

Martha (complete).
(M) *** Eurodisc 352 878 (2) [7789-2-RG]. Popp, Soffel, Jerusalem, Nimsgern, Ridderbusch, Bav. R. Ch. and O, Wallberg.

Martha is a charming opera and the Eurodisc cast is as near perfect as could be imagined. Lucia Popp is a splendid Lady Harriet, the voice rich and full yet riding the ensembles with jewelled accuracy. Doris Soffel is no less characterful as Nancy, and Siegfried Jerusalem is in his element as the hero, Lionel, singing ardently throughout. Siegmund Nimsgern is an excellent Lord Tristan, and Karl Ridderbusch matches his genial gusto. Wallberg's direction is marvellously spirited and the opera gathers pace as it proceeds. The Bavarian Radio Chorus sings with joyous precision and the orchestral playing sparkles. With first-class recording, full and vivid, this is highly recommended.

Forqueray, Antoine (1671–1745)

(i) *Pièces de viole;* (ii) *Pièces de clavecin.*
*** HM/BMG Dig. RD 77262 [77262-2]. (i) Jay Bernfeld; (ii) Skip Sempé.

Antoine Forqueray was a younger contemporary of Marin Marais and enjoyed a reputation as one of the greatest gamba players of his day. Skip Sempé's performances have all the expressive freedom and poetic feeling that the music calls for. The music has an intimacy and character that is beguiling, and Jay Bernfeld's playing has a comparable instinctive artistry. Both players are well served by the engineers who do not attempt to make either instrument larger than life.

Foss, Lucas (born 1922)

Song of Songs.
(M) *** Sony SM2K 47533 [id.]. Jennie Tourel, NYPO, Bernstein – BLOCH: *Sacred service* ***; BEN-HAIM: *Sweet Psalmist of Israel.* **(*)

This highly imaginative cantata is an attractive mixture of Copland-flavoured sonorities and a wider folk influence, not unlike that found in Canteloube's *Songs of the Auvergne*. Jennie Tourel is a strong and compelling soloist, suitably histrionic, but her lyrical singing, especially in the final song which becomes more darkly intense as it unfolds, is memorable. Bernstein secures a bravura accompaniment from his New York players, strongly involved and at their peak in 1958. Like the coupled Bloch *Sacred service*, the remastered sound is surprisingly full and graphic.

Foulds, John (1880–1939)

Dynamic triptych for piano and orchestra.
☞ *** Lyrita SRCD 211 [id.]. Howard Shelley, RPO, Handley – VAUGHAN WILLIAMS: *Piano concerto.* ***

John Foulds was working in Paris in the late 1920s when he wrote this ambitious concerto, and the profusion of memorable ideas, not always well disciplined, makes for an attractive piece, particularly so in the last of the three movements, *Dynamic rhythm*, with its extrovert references to Latin-American rhythms and the American musical. The first movement, *Dynamic mode*, using a very individual scale, is lively too, a sort of toccata; but the very scheme limits harmonic variety. The second movement, *Dynamic timbre*, brings a loosely connected sequence of evocative ideas. Played with dedication and beautifully recorded, it makes an interesting coupling for the masterly and underestimated Vaughan Williams *Piano concerto*. Howard Shelley and the RPO under Handley give a highly persuasive account of the *Triptych*, and the 1984 recording is well up to the usual high Lyrita standard.

String quartets Nos. 9 (Quartetto intimo), Op. 89; 10 (Quartetto geniale), Op. 97. Aquarelles, Op. 32.
⊛ *** Pearl SHECD 9564 [id.]. Endellion Qt.

The *Quartetto intimo*, written in 1931, is a powerful five-movement work in a distinctive idiom more advanced than that of Foulds' British contemporaries, with echoes of Scriabin and Bartók. Also on the disc is the one surviving movement of his tenth and last quartet, a dedicated hymn-like piece, as well as three slighter pieces which are earlier. Passionate performances and excellent recording, which is enhanced by the CD transfer. A uniquely valuable issue.

Françaix, Jean (born 1912)

Piano concertino.
☞ (M) *** Mercury 434 335-2 [id.].Claude Françaix, LSO, Dorati – AURIC: *Overture;* FETLER:
   Contrasts; MILHAUD: *Le bœuf sur le toit;* SATIE: *Parade.* ***

Claude Françaix, the composer's daughter and a pupil of Nadia Boulanger, partnered by Dorati made the first recommendable stereo recording of this delectable, miniature, four-movement *Concertino* in 1965. The conductor's touch is deliciously light in the outer movements and the pianist's touch is neat and accomplished. The Scherzo is also colourful but the gentle slow movement is the final test, and this is taken a fraction too fast. However, the performance is undoubtedly successful overall, and the composer's delicate effects in the winsome finale are particularly successful when the Mercury sound-picture is so lucid.

L'horloge de flore.
⊛ (M) *** BMG/RCA GD 87989 [7989-2-RG]. John de Lancie, LSO, Previn (with SATIE:
   Gymnopédies Nos. 1 & 3) – IBERT: *Symphonie concertante;* R. STRAUSS: *Oboe concerto.* ***
*** Nimbus Dig. NI 5330 [id.]. John Anderson, Philh. O, Simon Wright – MARTINU; R. STRAUSS:
   Concertos. ***

Inspired by the Linnaeus Flower Clock, *L'horloge de flore* is music of real memorability and much charm. John de Lancie, the sponsor of the piece, plays delightfully, the accompaniment is a model of felicity and good taste, and the recording is just about perfect. The Satie *Gymnopédies*, orchestrated by Debussy, which follows as an encore, are played slowly and gravely and not ineffectively.

   John Anderson's performance is hardly less enjoyable; the newer Nimbus recording is digital and has each movement separately cued.

String trio in C.
(M) *** BMG/RCA GD 87872 [7872-2-RG]. Heifetz, De Pasquale, Piatigorsky – CASTELNUOVO-
   TEDESCO: *Concerto No. 2* (**); FERGUSON: *Sonata No. 1* **; K. KHACHATURIAN: *Sonata.* **

Jean Françaix's debonair *String trio* of 1933 is a delight, full of sophistication and tenderness. All four movements are far too short, and marvellously played by Heifetz, Joseph de Pasquale and Piatigorsky.

Franchomme, Auguste (1808–84)

(i) *Air auvergnat varié, Op. 26; Air russe varié No. 2; Grande valse: Morceau de concert* (all for cello and strings); (ii) *Caprices, Op. 7/2, 4 & 7* (for 2 cellos); (iii) *Nocturne in A flat, Op. 15/2* (for cello and piano). arr. of CHOPIN: *Nocturne in G, Op. 15/1 & Op. 37/1.* FRANCHOMME/CHOPIN: *Grand duo concertante on themes from Robert le Diable* (for cello and piano).
☞ *** Sony Dig. SK 53980 [id.]. Anner Bylsma, with (i) L'Archibudelli & Smithsonian Chamber
   Players; (ii) Kenneth Slowik; (iii) Lamber Orkis (piano).

Auguste Franchomme was a Parisian cello virtuoso of great renown in his day, but he became even more famous when, as a personal friend of Chopin, they collaborated in this rather jolly *Grand duo concertante*. His own variations are effective enough when using folk themes, though his melodic facility was not really distinguished (as comparison of his own *Nocturne* with an arrangement of Chopin's readily demonstrates). But Anner Bylsma is a superb advocate and the pieces for two cellos are made attractive by his fine partnership with Kenneth Slowik. The back-up group for the amiable concertante pieces (of which the *Air auvergnat* and – especially – the *Grande valse* are the most winning) enjoy themselves playing splendid original instruments from the Smithsonian collection in Washington, DC. The result is both authentic and entertaining, and the recording could hardly be bettered. It is very well balanced and has vividness, warmth and transparency.

Franck, César (1822–90)

Le chasseur maudit; Les Eolides; Psyché (orchestral sections only).
**(*) Erato/Warner Dig. 2292 45552-2; *2292 45552-4* [id.]. Basle SO, Armin Jordan.

Jordan generates considerable excitement in *Le chasseur maudit*, one of Beecham's favourites; this is a worthy successor to his celebrated account, and both *Les Eolides* and the orchestral movements we are given from *Psyché* show real tendresse. The only thing lacking is real weight of sonority in the lower strings, but the intelligence of the playing makes up for this.

Le chasseur maudit (symphonic poem); *Rédemption (morceau symphonique);* (i) *Nocturne (O fraîche nuit).*
☞ (M) *** DG 437 244-2 (2). (i) Christa Ludwig; O de Paris, Barenboim – BERLIOZ: *Roméo et Juliette.* ***

A most attractive coupling for a highly recommendable version of Berlioz's *Roméo et Juliette. Le chasseur maudit* opens with a most evocative Sunday morning ambience; the devilish chase which follows is vividly exciting, with Franck's graphic portrayal of the accursed huntsman superbly energetic with its arresting horn calls. *Rédemption*, too, is highly convincing, again with the brass antiphonies most telling. In between comes an attractively simple but relatively brief nocturnal interlude from Christa Ludwig. Excellent mid-1970s recording, very well transferred to CD.

(i) *Les Djinns. Psyché* (orchestral sections only); *Symphony in D min.*
**(*) Decca Dig. 425 432-2 [id.]. (i) Vladimir Ashkenazy (piano/cond.), Berlin RSO.

It is good to have a fine modern recording of *Les Djinns*. The performance is first class, and Ashkenazy is equally at home in the balmy eroticism of *Psyché*. The Decca recording is suitably alluring and more transparent than Barenboim's DG version. Ashkenazy is less idiomatic in the *Symphony*, playing it with considerable fervour, in the manner of a work in the Russian tradition. The music-making is undoubtedly exciting, but the reading overall does not resonate in the memory afterwards, as does Monteux's.

Symphonic variations for piano and orchestra.
⊛ (B) *** Decca 433 628-2 [id.]. Curzon, LPO, Boult – GRIEG: *Concerto ***; SCHUMANN: *Concerto.* **(*)
☞ (M) *** BMG/RCA 09026 61863-2 [id.]. Rubinstein; Symphony of the Air, Wallenstein (with PROKOFIEV: *Love for 3 oranges: March ***) – FALLA: *Nights in the gardens of Spain* etc. SAINT-SAENS: *Concerto No. 2.* **(*)
☞ (M) (***) Dutton Lab. CDLX 7005 [id.]. Dame Myra Hess, CBSO, Basil Cameron – BACH: *Jesu, joy of man's desiring;* SCHUMANN: *Piano concerto.* (***)
☞ (BB) **(*) ASV Dig. CDQS 6092. Osorio, RPO, Bátiz – RAVEL: *Left-hand concerto ***; SAINT-SAENS: *Wedding-cake ***; SCHUMANN: *Concerto.* **(*)

Clifford Curzon's 1959 recording of the Franck *Variations* has stood the test of time; even after three decades and more there is no finer version. It is an engagingly fresh reading as notable for its impulse and rhythmic felicity as for its poetry. The vintage Decca recording is naturally balanced and has been transferred to CD without loss of bloom. The Grieg *Concerto* coupling is hardly less desirable.

Rubinstein's recording of the *Symphonic variations* was the first to appear in stereo, and it remains one of the finest available recorded performances of it. There is refinement and charm, yet his bravura tautens the structure while his warmth and freedom prevent it from seeming hard or in any way aggressive. The 1958 recording was made in the Manhattan Center, New York City, and the current remastering has brought more depth and resonance to the orchestra, while the piano has more colour and bloom than a great many of Rubinstein's early stereo recordings. A warm atmosphere in this work is far preferable to crystal clarity. The two solo encores are marvellously done, particularly the Prokofiev *March*.

Dame Myra Hess's account of the *Symphonic variations*, with the CBSO under Basil Cameron, was as celebrated in its day (1941) as Curzon's later version. It is by turns poetic, dramatic and good-humoured, and the transfer to CD from 78-r.p.m. shellac discs preserves the original quality admirably.

The ASV super-bargain disc offers fine performances of four concertante works including a really outstanding version of the Ravel *Left-hand concerto* and it adds up to more than the sum of its parts. It can receive a strong recommendation, for reservations about the Franck performance are minor. It has both poetry and impulse and lacks only a little in sparkle at the very end. It is very well recorded.

Symphony in D min.
*** Decca Dig. 430 278-2 [id.]. Montreal SO, Dutoit – D'INDY: *Symphonie sur un chant montagnard.* ***

(M) **(*) BMG/RCA GD 86805 [6805-2-RG]. Chicago SO, Monteux – D'INDY: *Symphonie sur un chant montagnard français* **(*) (with BERLIOZ: *Overture: Béatrice et Bénédict* ***).

(M) **(*) EMI CDM7 63396-2 [id.]. O Nat. de l'ORTF, Sir Thomas Beecham – LALO: *Symphony.* **(*)

☞ (M) *(*) Sony SMK 47548 [id.]. NYPO, Bernstein – FAURE: *Ballade* **; CHAUSSON: *Poème* *(*); RAVEL: *Tzigane.* *(*)

(i) *Symphony in D min.;* (iii) *Le chasseur maudit;* (iv) *Psyché: Psyché and Eros;* (ii; iii) *Symphonic variations for piano and orchestra.*
☞ *** Chesky CD 87 [id.]. (i) London O, Boult; (ii) Earl Wild; (iii) RCA Victor SO, Freccia; (iv) RPO, Prêtre.

(i) *Symphony in D min.;* (iii) *Le chasseur maudit;* (i; ii) *Symphonic variations for piano and orchestra.*
☞ (M) **(*) EMI CDM7 64747-2 [id.].(i) BPO, Karajan; (ii) with Alexis Weissenberg; (iii) Phd. O, Muti.

Symphony in D min.; Les Eolides.
☞ **(*) Teldec/Warner Dig. 9031 74863-2 [id.]. NYPO, Masur.

(i) *Symphony in D min.;* (ii) *Pièce héroïque* (orch. Charles O'Connell).
☞ ⊛ *** BMG/RCA 09026 61697-2 [id.]. (i) Chicago SO; (ii) San Francisco SO; Monteux (with (ii): D'INDY: *Istar* (***)).

Symphony in D min.; Psyché: Psyché et Eros.
☞ (M) *(*) DG Dig. 439 523-2 [id.]. BPO, Giulini.

Symphony in D min; (i) *Symphonic variations for piano and orchestra.*
(M) *** EMI Dig. CDD7 63889-2 [id.]. (i) Collard; Capitole Toulouse O, Plasson.

(i) *Symphony in D min.;* (i; ii) *Symphonic variations for piano and orchestra;* (iii) *Prélude, choral et fugue.*
☞ (B) *** Erato/Warner 4509 92871-2 [id.]. ORTF Nat. O, Martinon, (ii) with Philippe Entremont; (iii) Pascal Devoyon.

Monteux exerts a unique grip on this highly charged Romantic symphony, and his control of the continuous ebb and flow of tempo and tension is masterly, so that any weaknesses of structure in the outer movements are disguised. The splendid playing of the Chicago orchestra is ever responsive to the changes of mood, and the sound on GD 86805 is greatly improved.

However, the most recent remastering, by John Pfeifer for the Monteux Edition (fully discussed in our Concerts section, below), brings an astonishing further improvement; indeed, now the quality reflects the acoustics of Chicago's Orchestra Hall in the same way as the Reiner recordings, with textures full-bodied and glowing without loss of detail. The addition of Charles O'Donnell's orchestration of the *Pièce héroïque* is a distinct bonus. Its chromatic links with the *Symphony* are the more obvious in its orchestral format: it sounds rather like a symphonic poem with a brassy dénouement. The (1941) mono recording, although restricted, shows the excellence of the acoustics of San Francisco's War Memorial Opera House. Vincent d'Indy's *Istar* (also mono, from 1945) completes the disc. It is a colourful and increasingly energetic piece although, because of the programme, the music broadens satisfyingly at the climax. It is both a symphonic poem and a set of variations, without a theme until the very end. Istar, the Assyrian goddess of love and war, has gone in search of her slain lover, travelling through seven well-guarded gates. At each, Salome style, she is compelled to hand over a jewel or garment until the last veil is removed and her mission is triumphantly accomplished; at that moment her melody blossoms rapturously. Although the mono sound is boxy, the strings have plenty of middle sonority, and the vivid performance is unlikely to be bettered. Monteux was a friend (and pupil) of the composer and took special care with recordings of his music. This later CD is likely to be available separately by the time we are in print, but those preferring a stereo version of d'Indy's *Symphonie cévenole* as coupling can rest assured that the earlier transfer of the Franck *Symphony* still sounds very well.

Dutoit's account with the Montreal orchestra is very well proportioned, almost classical in its approach with the whole being the sum of its parts. It is magnificently played and recorded and though in terms of intensity and vision would not dislodge Monteux, it provides a good choice for those who want a more up-to-date, near-state-of-the-art recording.

Beecham is masterful in the rhythmic bite he gives to the great syncopated melodies that swagger their way through the outer movements – the second subject in the first movement and the opening theme of the finale. The recording has plenty of body, with a good sense of presence; but the transfer emphasizes an edge on top.

Martinon's 1969 reading of the *D minor Symphony* compares with Beecham in the sheer gusto with which he presents the outer movements. The effect is gripping and exhilarating: there is no indulgence or hanging about, and the chromatic second subject of the first movement emerges with real fervour. The central *Allegretto*, too, is without idiosyncrasy but has genuine eloquence. Fine playing from the ORTF National Orchestra, with the brass not shirking their rumbustious moments. Altogether a compelling account that stands high on the list of recommendations and has fuller sound than Beecham. Philippe Entremont (with *'l'aimable autorisation'* of CBS) joined the orchestra for a fresh and exciting account of the *Symphonic variations*, also well recorded. For a bonus, Pascal Devoyon provides a fine version of the *Prélude, choral et fugue*, a work strangely poised between classic form and romantic expression, between the piano and the organ loft. Here it is heard on the piano and again is convincingly recorded. A genuine bargain.

Sir Adrian Boult recorded the *Symphony in D minor* for the *Reader's Digest* record club in 1960, and the pseudonymous orchestra is almost certainly the Philharmonia at its peak. Boult's manner after the rapt and dedicated account of the slow introduction is brisk, urgent and direct, with crisply pointed rhythms preventing any feeling of breathlessness and with all sentimentality and vulgarity completely removed. This is as compelling as Monteux's famous version, yet in Sir Adrian's hands much of this music might almost be by Elgar, with nobility one of the elements. The playing is superb: the woodwind is outstandingly fine and the horn solos suggest that Alan Civil was on the roster. But it is the incisive thrust of the outer movements that is so striking. The recording, produced by Charles Gerhardt and engineered by Kenneth Wilkinson, is bright, clean and well balanced. Fortunately Earl Wild's account of the *Symphonic variations* is memorable for its gentle lyricism and poetic feeling, while Freccia ensures a vigorously buoyant closing section. He also directs a thrilling account of *The accursed huntsman* which almost goes over the top in its exuberance, and here the later recording (1968) with ripely resonant horns is very telling. Prêtre's *Psyché and Eros* is idiomatic but nothing special as either a performance or recording. But no matter, this record is highly recommendable, even at full price.

Plasson's 1985 version has conviction and genuine lyrical fervour. This may not seem as individual an account as that by Monteux, but it is certainly both exciting and satisfying, and the recording is much more modern than RCA's recording for Monteux. Jean-Philippe Collard's performance of the *Symphonic variations* is characteristically sensitive and full of imaginative colours and is touched by distinction. Those looking for a mid-priced digital version of this coupling should be well satisfied.

Bernstein's 1959 performance of the Franck *Symphony* certainly does not lack warmth or thrust, but his impulsive tempo-changes bring less than perfect orchestral discipline, especially in the finale which almost runs away with itself and coarsens. The closely balanced recording, made in the St George's Hotel, Brooklyn, is both revealing and unflattering to the timbre of the violins.

Karajan's recording of the Franck *Symphony*, made in the Salle Wagram, dates from 1969 and marked the beginning of a relatively brief recording period with EMI before he returned to DG. It is a large-scale performance, given strong projection by the CD remastering. Karajan's tempi are all on the slow side, but his control of rhythm prevents any feeling of sluggishness or heaviness. There is always energy underlying the performance, and by facing the obvious problems squarely Karajan avoids the perils. The impact of the recording, now sounding more brightly lit but with textures still full and bold, is considerable; there is potent atmosphere and the finale has both amplitude and plenty of bite. Weissenberg's account of the *Symphonic variations* has less distinction, but the poetry of the lyrical sections is not missed and Karajan ensures that the orchestral contribution is a strong one. Taken as a whole, this is spontaneous and enjoyable if not outstanding. The sound is full and clear, the balance favouring the orchestra slightly more than usual, but the pianist is realistically defined. Muti's *La chausseur maudit* is vividly dramatic and strongly presented, but there is a degree of glare on the otherwise brilliant digital recording.

Masur creates a sound-world with the New York Philharmonic which is totally different from that achieved by his predecessor, Zubin Mehta. The wind phrasing is sensitive, the brass blend more subtly and the strings produce a far more cultured sonority. Moreover the recording, too, is more sophisticated and without the brash, overlit quality we have noted in the past. The performances of both *Les Eolides* and the *Symphony* are very fine, sensitively shaped and with the architecture held together well. All the same, Masur's account of the *Symphony* does not generate quite the same excitement and blazing conviction that Monteux, Beecham or Bernstein brought to it, and does not displace existing recommendations. Moreover at full price it offers rather less than good value with playing time of only 48 minutes.

Giulini and the Berlin Philharmonic – an unexpected combination in this work – take an extremely spacious view. With textures well upholstered, the first-movement *allegro* at an extraordinarily slow speed sounds ponderous, and the scherzando element is completely missing in the contrasting passages of the central *Allegretto*, while the finale with its exhilarating main theme lacks energy. Though Giulini conducts with total dedication and the playing is superb, this is one of his less successful records.

CHAMBER MUSIC

Cello sonata in A (trans. of *Violin sonata*).
(M) **(*) EMI CDM7 63184-2. Du Pré, Barenboim – CHOPIN: *Sonata.* **(*)
**(*) CRD CRD 3391; *CRDC 4091* [id.]. Robert Cohen, Roger Vignoles (with DVORAK: *Rondo*) – GRIEG: *Cello sonata.* **(*)

Du Pré and Barenboim give a fine, mature, deeply expressive reading of a richly satisfying work. They are well balanced, but the effect of the music when transferred to the cello is inevitably mellower, less vibrant.

Cohen gives a firm and strong rendering of the Franck *Sonata* in its cello version, splendidly incisive and dashing in the second-movement *Allegro*, but the recording is more limited than one expects from CRD, a little shallow. The addition of the Dvořák *G minor Rondo*, Op. 94, makes a pleasing bonus.

Piano quintet in F min.
☞ **(*) Nimbus Dig. NI 5114 [id.]. John Bingham, Medici Qt – FAURE: *String quartet.* *(*)
(M) **(*) Decca 421 153-2. Clifford Curzon, VPO Qt – DVORAK: *Quintet.* ***

Ardent playing from the Medici and an especially imaginative contribution from their pianist, John Bingham. Artistically, this is very impressive, for the players seem more fully inside César Franck's world than they are in the Fauré coupling. In spite of somewhat excessive reverberance, there is much here that will give pleasure.

Not as seductive a performance on Decca as the glorious Dvořák coupling, partly because the sound, though basically full, has a touch of astringency on top; but Curzon and the VPO players are sensitive and firm at the same time. Curzon's playing is particularly fine.

String quartet in D.
(M) **(*) Decca 425 424-2; *425 424-4*. Fitzwilliam Qt – RAVEL: *Quartet.* **

Franck's *Quartet*, highly ambitious in its scale, contains some of the composer's most profound and compelling thought; and this magnificent performance by the Fitzwilliam Quartet completely silences any reservations. However, the CD transfer, in attempting to clarify the sound, has brought a degree of fierceness to the fortissimo violin timbre.

Violin sonata in A.
⊛ (M) *** Decca 421 154-2. Kyung Wha Chung, Radu Lupu – DEBUSSY: *Sonatas;* RAVEL: *Introduction and allegro* etc. *** ⊛
(M) *** DG 431 469-2; *431 469-4*. Kaja Danczowska, Krystian Zimerman – SZYMANOWSKI: *Mythes* etc. *** ⊛
*** DG Dig. 415 683-2 [id.]. Shlomo Mintz, Yefim Bronfman – RAVEL; DEBUSSY: *Sonatas.* ***
(M) *** Decca 433 695-2 [id.]. Itzhak Perlman, Vladimir Ashkenazy – BRAHMS: *Horn trio;* SAINT-SAENS: *Romance;* SCHUMANN: *Adagio and allegro.* ***
(M) **(*) Ph. 426 384-2. Arthur Grumiaux, György Sebok – FAURE: *Sonatas.* *** ⊛

Kyung Wha Chung and Radu Lupu give a glorious account, full of natural and not over-projected eloquence, and most beautifully recorded. The slow movement has marvellous repose and the other movements have a natural exuberance and sense of line that carry the listener with them. The 1977 recording is enhanced on CD and, with outstanding couplings, this record is in every sense a genuine bargain.

Kaja Danczowska's account of the Franck is distinguished by a fine sense of line and great sweetness of tone, and she is partnered superbly by Krystian Zimerman. Indeed, in terms of dramatic fire and strength of line, this version can hold its own alongside the finest, and it is perhaps marginally better-balanced than the Kyung Wha Chung and Radu Lupu recording.

On DG, Shlomo Mintz and Yefim Bronfman give a superbly confident account of the *Sonata*. It is impeccably played and splendidly recorded, too. This can rank alongside the best, and it has the advantage of a digital master.

With Perlman and Ashkenazy, the first movement catches the listener by the ears with the thrust of its forward impulse and the intensity of its lyrical flow. Yet there is no lack of flexibility and the sheer ardour of this interpretation makes it a genuine alternative to the Chung/Lupu account.

Grumiaux's account, if less fresh than Miss Chung's, has nobility and warmth to commend it. He is slightly let down by his partner, who is not as imaginative as Lupu in the more poetic moments, including the hushed opening bars.

ORGAN MUSIC

Andantino in E (arr. Vierne); *Cantabile; Choral Nos. 2–3; Pièce héroïque; Prélude, fugue et variation, Op. 18.*
*** Chan. Dig. CHAN 8891; *ABTD 1502* [id.]. Piet Kee (Cavaillé-Coll organ of Basilica de Santa Maria del Coro, Saint Sebastian).

The Dutch composer-organist Piet Kee omits the *Choral No. 1*, for which room could surely have been found, as the playing-time is only 61 minutes 43 seconds, but, apart from this, there can be few grumbles about his record. His interpretations strike an excellent balance between expressive freedom and scholarly rectitude.

Cantabile; Chorale No. 1; Fantaisie in C; Pièce héroïque; Prélude, fugue and variation.
**(*) Unicorn Dig. DKPCD 9013; *DKPC 9013* [id.]. Jennifer Bate.

Chorale No. 2 in B min.; Fantaisie in C, Op. 16; Grande pièce symphonique, Op. 17.
**(*) Unicorn Dig. DKPCD 9014; *DKPC 9014* [id.]. Jennifer Bate.

Jennifer Bate plays the Danion-Gonzalez organ at Beauvais Cathedral and is given the benefit of an excellent digital recording. The spacious acoustic contributes an excellent ambience to the aural image, and Miss Bate's brilliance is always put at the service of the composer. The *Pièce héroïque* seems rather well suited to the massive sounds which the Beauvais organ can command and all the music on this CD shows the instrument to good advantage.

Chorales Nos. 1–3; Pièce héroïque.
(M) *** Mercury 434 311-2 [id.]. Marcel Dupré (organ of St Thomas's Church, New York) – WIDOR: *Salve Regina* etc. ***

Dupré knows this quartet of Franck's masterpieces better than anybody, yet his interpretations remain fresh and alive from start to finish, and anyone who thinks this music is dull will surely find this CD a revelation. The great French organist exploits the Aeolian Skinner organ in St Thomas's Church on New York's Fifth Avenue, using its wonderful array of colour, with unsurpassed mastery, especially in the *A minor Chorale*, easily the finest of the three. Mercury have captured the instrument with incredible fidelity.

Fantaisie in A; Pastorale.
*** Telarc Dig. CD 80096 [id.]. Michael Murray (organ of Symphony Hall, San Francisco) – JONGEN: *Symphonie concertante*. ***

Michael Murray plays these pieces very well, although the San Francisco organ is not tailor-made for them. The Telarc recording is well up to standard.

PIANO MUSIC

Danse lente; Prélude, aria & final; Prélude, choral & fugue.
☞ (*) Erato/Warner Dig. 4509 92402 [id.]. Jean Hubeau – CHAUSSON: *Danses paysage.* (*)

Greater pianistic finesse and subtlety as well as a wider dynamic range is called for than Jean Hubeau can now offer. The close and shallow recording, made in Studio 106, Maison de la Radio in Paris, does not enhance the attractions of these performances which, alas, are really not competitive.

Prélude, choral et fugue.
*** Sony Dig. SK 47180 [id.]. Murray Perahia – LISZT: *Années de pèlerinages* etc. ***

Murray Perahia's recording of the *Prélude, choral et fugue* is in a class of its own, carefully thought out yet apparently spontaneous and highly poetic.

Frankel, Benjamin (1916–71)

Symphonies Nos. 1, Op. 33; 5, Op. 46; May Day Overture, Op. 22.
☞ *** CPO Dig. 999 240-2 [id.]. Queensland SO, Werner Andreas Albert.

Benjamin Frankel was best known as a composer of film music (he wrote the music for over 100 films, including *The Seventh Veil, The Man in the White Suit, Night of the Iguana* and *Battle of the Bulge*) and was for many years an arranger of light music, playing in the Carroll Gibbons and the Savoy Orpheans, and the Henry Hall bands. He is one of the few composers of film music, like Rawsthorne or Walton, whose personality one can place before the credit titles reach his name. His *Violin concerto*, commissioned by Max Rostal (who recorded his *Sonata for solo violin* in the days of 78s), put him firmly on the map as a composer to be reckoned with. A master of the orchestra, as one knew from his earlier scores, the *First Symphony* (1959) leaves no doubt that he was also a master symphonist. It is a powerfully concentrated and finely argued piece which has a constant feeling of onward movement. The music develops organically; Frankel has something of the strength of Sibelius combined with a Mahlerian anguish, and his serialism, like that of Frank Martin, never undermines tonal principles. This symphony withstands much repetition and reveals more on each hearing. The *Fifth Symphony* (1967), broadcast together with the *Sixth*, prompted William Mann to call him, 'doubtless our most eloquent symphonist'. It, too, is a well-argued and impressive score. The Queensland orchestra play with dedication, and the performances of both symphonies and the inventive *May Day Overture* are very well recorded too. Frankel possessed a refined imagination and a completely natural musical facility and it is good news that all eight of his symphonies are to be recorded by this orchestra and their excellent conductor.

Frescobaldi, Girolamo (1583–1643)

Il Primo Libro di Toccate (1615–37): excerpts; *Il Secondo Libro di Toccate* (1637): excerpts.
☞ *** O-L Dig. 436 197-2 (2) [id.]. Christopher Hogwood (harpsichord, virginal).

This pair of CDs covers about a third of the two books of *Toccatas* and *Partitas*, the first disc offering us two *Toccatas*, a set of variations on the *Follia* and various other pieces, while the second brings four *Toccatas* from the 1637 book and a number of other pieces, *Canzone, Gagliarde* and so on. Between them the two discs cover music suitable for the harpsichord or spinet from all periods of Frescobaldi's career, save only for the last years. Christopher Hogwood uses four instruments, all of which are reproduced pictorially in the accompanying booklet: three are from the last half of the seventeenth century, while there is an early Venetian spinet of 1540 for the *Aria detta balletto*. Frescobaldi's music is unfailingly interesting and its expressive freedom often takes the listener by surprise. Hogwood has both the artistic flair and the feeling for style to do it justice, and the clarity and presence of the recording are really beyond praise. But take care not to set the volume level too high.

Froberger, Johann (1616–67)

Canzon No. 2; Capriccio No. 10; Fantasia No. 4 sopra sollare; Lamentation faîte sur la mort très douloureuse de Sa Majesté Imperiale, Ferdinand le troisième; Ricercar No. 5; Suites Nos. 2 & 3; Suite No. 14: Lamentation sur ce que j'ay été volé. Toccatas Nos. 9, 10 & 114; Tombeau faict à Paris sur la mort de M. Blancrocher.
*** HM/BMG Dig. RD 77923 [7913-2-RC]. Gustav Leonhardt (harpsichord).

Froberger's music is highly exploratory in idiom and, in works such as the *Tombeau faict à Paris sur la mort de M. Blancrocher* and the *Plainte faite à Londres pour passer la Melancholie*, from the *Suite No. 3*, he reveals great expressive poignancy. There is space round the instrument and, heard at a low level-setting, this well-played recital produces very good results. Recommended with enthusiasm.

Harpsichord suites Nos. 1 in E min.; 2 in A; 3 in G min.; 4 in A min.; 5 in D; 6 in C. Lamentation for the death of Ferdinand III.

☞ (M) *** DG 437 080-2. Kenneth Gilbert (harpsichord).

Froberger was very highly regarded in his day, not least by Bach. His music is expressive, thoughtfully spontaneous and certainly not predictable. The reflective *Lamentation for Ferdinand III* which opens the disc (marked '*très douloureuse et se loue lentement avec discrétion*') is mirrored by the opening movement of the *Sixth suite* – the *Lamento for Ferdinand IV of Rumania* – while his musing *Sarabande* to the *Second Suite* and the melancholy opening *Allemandes* of the *Third* and *Fourth* again show the searching quality of his writing. Yet he can be infectiously jolly when writing a *gigue*. Kenneth Gilbert is completely at home in this repertoire and catches its melancholy spirit without languishing. His instrument, a Bellot le père of 1729, restored by Hubert Bédard, is beautifully recorded, and this CD can be cordially recommended.

Fuchs, Robert (1847–1927)

Cello sonatas Nos. 1 in D min., Op. 29; 2 in E flat min., Op. 83; Phantasiestücke, Op. 78.
☞ *** Marco Polo Dig. 8.223423 [id.]. Mark Drobinsky, Daniel Blumenthal.
☞ *** Biddulph Dig. LAW005 [id.]. Nancy Green, Caroline Palmer.

Many music-lovers, insofar as they think of him at all, regard Robert Fuchs as a kind of Brahms clone. He was a friend of the great composer, and the latter's influence cannot be gainsaid. In all he wrote only three pieces for cello and piano: the *First Sonata* was composed in 1881 for the celebrated Popper and, whatever the claims to the contrary, sounds very much like Brahms, who, incidentally, recommended it to the publisher, Simrock. The *Second* is much later (1908) and is, like the more Schumannesque *Phantasiestücke*, in the same conservative mould. It is well-fashioned, cultured and civilized music (no mean virtues) which may not have a strongly original profile but is well worth investigating for all that. After long neglect this music is available in two different versions. To be frank, there is not much to choose between them; both offer very good performances; both are very well recorded and deserve their three stars, so no agonies of choice are required: you can safely invest in one or the other.

Clarinet quintet, Op. 102.
*** Marco Polo Dig. 8.223282 [id.]. Rodenhäuser, Ens. Villa Musica – LACHNER: *Septet.* ***

This is beautifully crafted and speaks with the accents of Schubert and Brahms rather than with any strong individuality. It is nicely played by the Mainz-based Ensemble Villa Musica whose excellent clarinettist, Ulf Rodenhäuser, is worth a mention. A curiosity rather than a revelation then, but eminently well recorded.

Piano sonatas Nos. 1, Op. 19; 2, Op. 88.
☞ *** Marco Polo Dig. 8.223377 [id.]. Daniel Blumenthal.

Robert Fuchs is best remembered these days as the teacher of Sibelius and Mahler, Franz Schmidt and Hugo Wolf, but also for his *E minor Serenade for strings*. Yet he was a prolific composer; there are five serenades in all, three symphonies, some 40-odd chamber works and three piano sonatas. He basked in the approval of Brahms, who called his music 'beautiful, skilful and attractive'. And so it is, particularly given such masterly and persuasive advocacy as it receives at the hands of Daniel Blumenthal. The early *F minor Sonata*, Op. 19, (1877) is indeed heavily indebted to Brahms, and the rondo finale with which it concludes seems heavily indebted to the latter's *Ballades*, Op. 10. All the same it has a certain breadth and lyrical fertility that impresses. As its opus number indicates, the *Second Sonata*, Op. 88, is mature Fuchs, dating from 1910, which reflects the changed musical environment. Its invention is more chromatic and there are hints of Reger and even of Debussy and Fauré. Although Fuchs may lack a strong individual voice, he is a fine craftsman whose musical thinking has the merit of breadth and span.

Furtwängler, Wilhelm (1886–1954)

Symphony No. 2 in E min.
☞ **(*) Marco Polo Dig. 8.2234436 [id.]. BBC SO, Alfred Walter.

Furtwängler regarded himself as primarily a composer and his conducting as a secondary pursuit. Although not quite as long as its predecessor in B minor, the *Second Symphony* (1944–5) still takes over 1¼ hours to perform. The invention itself does not possess strong individuality, and the shadow of Bruckner hangs heavily over the scene. However, there is a certain nobility and majesty that are at times rather imposing. Furtwängler himself spoke of it as his spiritual testament, and if you find it convincing it is worth noting that Alfred Walter has recorded the *First* with the Košice Orchestra (Marco Polo 8.223295) and *Third* with the Brussels Radio & Televsion Orchestra (Marco Polo 8.223105); the former takes 77 minutes 50 seconds! The BBC Symphony Orchestra respond to Alfred Walter's direction with warmth and, though the acoustic of the Maida Vale studios does not allow tutti to expand as they might, the recording is expertly balanced.

Gabrieli, Andrea (1520–86)

Laudate Dominum.
(M) **(*) Decca 430 359-2. Magdalen College, Oxford, Ch., Wren O, Rose – G. GABRIELI: *Motets* **(*); PERGOLESI: *Miserere II* *** (with BASSANO: *Ave Regina* **(*)).

This fine setting of *Laudate Dominum* for two five-part choirs is most stimulating. Also included is a splendid *Ave Regina* by Andrea's contemporary, Giovanni Bassano, which is laid out for three four-part choirs and brass in a similar polychoral style. Both are are well performed, if without strong individuality, and the recording is magnificently expansive.

Gabrieli, Giovanni (1557–1612)

Canzoni e Sonate: Canzon a 5; Canzon a 6; Canzon a 7; Canzon a 8; Sonata a 4; Sonata a 8; Sonata a 15. Sacrae symphoniae: 2 Canzoni septimi toni a 8; Canzon septimi e octavio toni a 12; Sonata octavi toni a 8; Sonata piane e forte a 8.
☞ (M) **(*) DG 437 073-2. London Cornett and Sackbutt Ens., Andrew Parrott.

Using authentic instruments, Andrew Parrott and the London Cornett and Sackbutt Ensemble present stylish performances of a well-chosen collection of Gabrieli's instrumental pieces, not as dramatic or incisive as some we have heard on modern brass instruments but beautifully recorded in spacious stereo and immaculately transferred to CD. Best known is the magnificent *Sonata piane e forte*. However, this disc is not generous in content: 44 minutes.

Hodie Christus natus est; Plaudite; Virtute magna.
(M) **(*) Decca 430 359-2 [id.]. Magdalen College, Oxford, Ch., Gowman (organ), Wren O, Rose – A. GABRIELI: *Laudate Dominum* **(*); PERGOLESI: *Miserere II.* ***

The Christmas motet, *Hodie Christus natus est*, is justly the most celebrated; but the other pieces too are most beautiful, notably *Plaudite* for three separate choirs. The performances, though finely controlled, could be more positive and dramatic, but they are very well recorded.

Symphoniae sacrae II (1615): Buccinate in neomania (a 19); In ecclesiis (a 14); Jubilate Deo (a 10); Magnificat a 14; Magnificat a 17; Misericordia (a 12); Quem vidistis pastores (a 14); Suscipe a 12; Surrexit Christus (a 11).
☞ *** O-L 436 860-2 [id.]. Taverner Ch., L. Cornett and Sackbutt Ens., Parrott.

As principal composer of ceremonial music at St Mark's, Venice, the younger Gabrieli had to write all kinds of appropriate church music, and this fine collection contains some of the pieces of his later years, when – relying on instrumentalists rather than choristers – he came to include elaborate accompaniments for cornetts and sackbutts. Here, for example, six sackbuts accompany the six-part setting of *Suscipe* with glowing results; after hearing modern brass instruments and without the benefits of the St Mark's acoustics, these more authentic instruments may seem on the gentle side, with Gabrielian panoply underplayed, but the singing and playing are most stylish, helped by first-rate 1977 recording, smoothly transferred to CD.

Gade, Niels (1817–90)

Symphonies Nos. 1 in C min., Op. 5; 2 in E, Op. 10.
☞ ** Marco Polo Dacapo Dig. DCCD 9201 [id.]. Copenhagen Coll. Mus., Schønwandt.

Symphonies Nos. 4 in B flat, Op. 20; 6 in G min., Op. 32.
☞ ** Marco Polo Dacapo Dig. DCCD 9202 [id.]. Copenhagen Coll. Mus., Schønwandt.

Marco Polo have waited some time before making any challenge to Neeme Järvi's cycle with the Stockholm Sinfonietta. Michael Schønwandt gets a vital and often sensitive response from his players; no one investing in them is likely to be much disappointed on interpretative grounds, though the Swedish performances are more polished. This impression is reinforced by the rather bright, airless recording; the balance is somewhat forward and in climaxes the sound has insufficent space in which to expand, with the result that the ear tires. Comparison in each case makes one realize how much more refined and better balanced the BIS recordings for Järvi are! The recordings sound more recent than the 1988 coupling this partnership made of the *Third* and *Fifth Symphonies* (see below) but are less rather than more satisfactory.

Symphonies Nos. 1 in C min. (On Sjøland's fair plains), Op. 5; 8 in B min., Op. 47.
*** BIS Dig. CD 339 [id.]. Stockholm Sinf., Järvi.

Gade's *First Symphony* is a charming piece. Thirty years separate it from his *Eighth* and last symphony, like the *First* much indebted to Mendelssohn. Despite this debt, there is still a sense of real mastery and a command of pace. The Stockholm Sinfonietta and Neeme Järvi give very fresh and lively performances, and the recording is natural and truthful.

Symphonies Nos. 2 in E, Op. 10; 7 in F, Op. 45.
**(*) BIS Dig. CD 355 [id.]. Stockholm Sinf., Järvi.

Schumann thought No. 2 'reminiscent of Denmark's beautiful beechwoods'. The debt to Mendelssohn is still enormous here, but it is very likeable, more spontaneous than the *Seventh*, though this work has a delightful Scherzo. Splendid playing from the Stockholm Sinfonietta under Järvi, and good recording too.

Symphonies Nos. 3 in A min., Op. 15; 4 in B flat, Op. 20.
*** BIS Dig. CD 338 [id.]. Stockholm Sinf., Järvi.

Gade's *Third* has great freshness and a seemingly effortless flow of ideas and pace, and a fine sense of musical proportion. No. 4 was more generally admired in Gade's lifetime, but its companion here is the more winning. It is beautifully played and recorded.

Symphonies Nos. 3 in A min., Op. 15; (i) 5 in D min., Op. 25.
**(*) Dacapo Dig. DCCD 9004 [id.]. (i) Amalie Malling, Coll. Mus., Copenhagen, Schønwandt.

Michael Schønwandt's performances of these two Gade symphonies are most musical, and distinguished by sensitive phrasing and a fine feeling for line. In the *Fifth Symphony*, the piano is less closely observed than it is in the BIS recording. Amalie Malling is the more reticent player, too, and plays with taste and grace. However, the 1988 recording though perfectly acceptable is not as good or as fresh sounding as its BIS rival which is on balance to be preferred.

Symphonies Nos. (i) 5 in D min., Op. 35; 6 in G min., Op. 32.
*** BIS Dig. CD 356 [id.]. Stockholm Sinf., Järvi; (i) with Roland Pöntinen.

The *Fifth Symphony* is a delightfully sunny piece which lifts one's spirits; its melodies are instantly memorable, and there is a lively concertante part for the piano, splendidly played by the young Roland Pöntinen. The *Sixth Symphony* is rather more thickly scored and more academic. The recording is very good and, given the charm of the *Fifth Symphony* and the persuasiveness of the performance, this coupling must be warmly recommended.

Octet in F, Op. 17.
☞ ** Sony Dig. SK 48307 [id.]. L'Archibudelli, Smithsonian Chamber Players – MENDELSSOHN: *Octet.* *(*)

Like so much of Gade's music, the *Octet*, composed in 1848, is heavily indebted to his mentor and champion, Mendelssohn. It is well played by the combined L'Archibudelli and Smithsonian ensembles and truthfully recorded, but it is hardly a compelling piece (it does not possess a fraction of the character or inspiration of Svendsen's essay in this genre).

String quartets Nos. 1 in F min., 2 in E min., 3 in D, Op. 63.
*** BIS Dig. CD 516 [id.]. Kontra Qt.

These are pleasing works of great facility and are worth hearing, particularly in such good performances and recordings as we are given here. However, the fact remains that they show too strong a gravitational pull of Mendelssohn. Nevertheless, in terms of invention and craftsmanship, they give a certain pleasure.

Albumblad; Akvarel in A; Andantino in C sharp min.; Børnenes Jul, Op. 36; Danserinden; 4 Fantasy pieces, Op. 41; Foraarstoner (3 Pieces), Op. 2; Nye Akvareller (5 Pieces), Op. 57; Piece in B flat; Rebus (3 Pieces), Op. 2; Scherzino (Aquarel); (i) (2 pianos): *3 Characteristic pieces, Op. 18; Nordiske Tonebilleder, Op. 4.*
☞ *(*) Maro Polo Dig. DCCD 9117 [id.]. Anker Blyme, (i) with Morten Mogensen.

Some of Gade's music for piano is new to the catalogue, but it must be conceded that no masterpieces are uncovered here. This music is well-bred almost to the point of gentility, and little of it resides long in the memory. Gade never fully discharged his debt to Mendelssohn, and the mantle of the Leipzig school hangs heavily even over the folk-inspired pieces. Perhaps with more ardent and youthful performances they might be more persuasive, but Anker Blyme here sounds as if he is worthily fulfilling a duty rather than espousing a cause which he feels with every fibre of his being. Nor is the recording top-drawer either.

(i) *Efterklange af Ossian (Echoes from Ossian), Op. 1;* (ii) *Elverskud (The Elf-shot), Op. 30;* (iii) *5 Partsongs, Op. 13.*
☞ *** Chan. Dig. CHAN 9075 [id.]. (ii) Johansson, Gjevang, Elming, Danish Nat. R. Ch.; (iii) Danish Nat. R. Chamber Ch., Parkman; (i; ii) Danish Nat. RSO, Kitaienko.

Elverskud, also translated as *The Elf-king's daughter* and *The Fairy spell*, was Gade's wedding present to his wife, Sophie. It comes from the same year as his *Fifth Symphony* and is much indebted to Mendelssohn's *Die erste Valpurgisnacht*; it is certainly a work of great charm and grace. It comes here with his very first opus, the *Ossian Overture*, which drew the composer to the attention of Mendelssohn, from whose pen the second group could easily have come. A further bonus is the delightful set of *Five Partsongs, Op. 13*, beautifully sung by the Danish Radio Chamber Choir; the fourth, *Autumn song*, is particularly memorable and haunting. Gade never escapes the embrace of Mendelssohn for long; if his world is urbane, well-ordered and free from any hint of tragedy, *Elverskud*, like the *Fifth Symphony*, still gives unfailing pleasure, particularly in such a persuasive performance and excellent recording.

Korsfarerne (The Crusaders), Op. 50.
**(*) BIS Dig. CD 465 [id.]. Rorholm, Westi, Cold, Canzone Ch., Da Camera, Kor 72, Music Students' Chamber Ch., Aarhus SO, Frans Rasmussen.

Gade's *Korsfarerne* is in three sections, *In the desert*, *Armida* and *Towards Jerusalem*, and lasts the best part of an hour. The Danish forces assembled here do it proud, as do the BIS recording team, but the debt to Mendelssohn, say in the *Chorus of the Spirits of Darkness* which opens the second section, overwhelms any feeling of originality.

Gagliano, Marco da (1582–1643)

La Dafne.
☞ (M) *** DG 437 074-2. Lerer, Schlick, Kollecker, Rogers, D. Thomas, Possemeyer, Hamburg Monteverdi Ch., Camerata Academica, Jürgen Jürgens.

This delightful early opera (1608) by a little-known contemporary of Monteverdi is one of the finds of DG's 'Collectio Argentea'. Marco da Gagliano's setting of the story of the nymph Daphne who turns herself into a laurel tree in order to avoid the attentions of the god, Apollo, is arranged in a series of recitatives (which at times almost become arias), interspersed with lively choruses. The recitative is full of expressive life and the choruses comment on the action. The performance is made fresher by the delightful instrumental sounds produced by the Camerata Academica and, in the moving fifth scene where the nymphs mourn Daphne's metamorphosis, Barbara Schlick leads the chorus radiantly and touchingly with her sad lament, *Piangete, Ninfa, e con voi pianga Amore* ('Weep, o nymphs, and with you let love weep'). The whole work springs to life in this admirable performance, with Barbara Schlick doubling as Cupid, Norma Lerer as Daphne and Nigel Rogers as Apollo. The Hamburg Monteverdi Choir make a distinguished contribution and Jürgen Jürgens directs with vigour but never loses the music's Italian sunshine.

Gallo, Domenico (c. 1730– ?)

Trio sonatas: No. 2: Moderato; No. 3: Presto I; Presto II; No. 7: Allegro.

*** Decca Dig. 425 614-2 [id.]. St Paul CO, Hogwood – PERGOLESI: *Sinfonia;* STRAVINSKY: *Pulcinella* etc. ***

These tiny movements come as a valuable and delightful appendix to Hogwood's fine recording of Stravinsky's *Pulcinella*, showing how he transformed such sources as these.

Galuppi, Baldassare (1706–85)

Motets: (i) *Arripe alpestri ad vallem;* (ii) *Confitebor tibi, Domine.*
☞ ⊛ *** Virgin/EMI Dig. VC5 45030-2 [id.]. (i) Gérard Lesne, (ii) with Véronique Gens, Peter Harvey; Il Seminario Musicale.

Here is another name from the musical history books brought vividly to life by Virgin's enterprising Veritas label. Galuppi was born in Venice and eventually (in 1762) became musical director of the Doge's chapel at St Mark's. He had earlier (1740) visited London, where a number of his nearly 100 (!) operas were staged, and after that spent a period at the Russian Court in St Petersburg. He returned home in 1768 and, as the climax of his career, enlarged the orchestra at St Mark's to 35 players and augmented the choir to make a total of two dozen singers. He was a very considerable figure in his time and undoubtedly had influence on C. P. E. Bach and Haydn. So it is not before time that we are made familiar with his music. The motet, *Confitebor tibi, Domine* (praising God for his munificence), is a masterly and very beautiful piece using three soloists with a skill in its overlapping part-writing worthy of Mozart. The flowing vocal lines of the duets and trios, with their touching melancholy (*Filia omnia mandata eius*) and moving drama (*Sanctum et terribile*) and the delightfully florid *Intellectus bonus*, are consistently involving. The bass arias, the eloquent *Confessio et magnificentia* and the heroic *Redemptionem misit*, are equally memorable and are splendidly sung by Peter Harvey, while the soprano's radiant *Gloria* (Véronique Gens) is delectably decorated by a pair of flutes. Gérard Lesne, the alto, comes into his own in the coupled solo cantata, *Arripe alpestri ad vallem* ('Stop you people of the mountain tops, do not come down into the valley driving savage monsters towards me'), a metaphorical allusion to remorse for inescapable human sin. It is an extraordinary 18-minute declamation with two long arias framing a histrionic recitative ('Oh whither shall I flee') and ending with a highly individual setting of *Hallelujah.* The accompaniments from Il Seminario Musicale are refreshingly sensitive, alive and polished, and these players give splendid support to the singers while the recording has a natural presence and realism. Well worth seeking out.

Gardiner, Henry Balfour (1877–1950)

Humoresque; The joyful homecoming; Michaelchurch; Noel; 5 Pieces; Prelude; Salamanca; Shenadoah and other pieces (suite).
*** Continuum CCD 1049 [id.]. Peter Jacobs.

Balfour Gardiner was a musical contemporary of Cyril Scott, Roger Quilter and Percy Grainger. Like his musical friends he was at his finest in miniatures, and his writing has an attractive simplicity and innocence. Most of this music is slight, but its appeal is undeniable when it is presented with such authority and sympathy. It is very well recorded indeed. The source is analogue, but there is no background worth mentioning and the piano image is absolutely real, with a natural presence.

Gaubert, Philippe (1879–1941)

Music for flute and piano: *Sonatas Nos. 1–3; Sonatine. Ballade; Berceuse; 2 Esquisses; Fantaisie; Nocturne et allegro scherzando; Romance; Sicilienne; Suite; Sur l'eau.*
*** Chan. Dig. CHAN 8981/2; *DBTD 2031* [id.]. Susan Milan, Ian Brown.

Gaubert had a genuine lyrical gift and his music has an elegance and allure that will captivate. He is eminently well served by Susan Milan and Ian Brown, and they are all well balanced by the Chandos engineers. Truthful sound; civilized and refreshing music, not to be taken all at one draught but full of delight. Edward Blakeman's notes are particularly informative and interesting and there are two charming illustrations.

Gay, John (1685–1732)

The Beggar's Opera (arr. Bonynge and Gamley).
*** Decca Dig. 430 066-2 (2) [id.]. Kanawa, Sutherland, Morris, Dean, Mitchell, Hordern, Marks, Lansbury, Resnik, Rolfe Johnson, London Voices, Nat. PO, Bonynge.

This entertaining digital version of *The Beggar's Opera* creates the atmosphere of a stage musical. The musical arrangements are free – including an unashamedly jazzy sequence in Act II, complete with saxophones – but the basic musical material is of vintage quality and responds readily to a modern treatment which is always sparkling and often imaginative. The casting is imaginative too. With Alfred Marks and Angela Lansbury as Mr and Mrs Peacham a touch of humour is assured; if James Morris is not an entirely convincing Macheath, he sings nicely, and Joan Sutherland makes a spirited Lucy. Kiri Te Kanawa as Polly undoubtedly steals the show, as well she should, for it is a peach of a part. She sings deliciously and her delivery of the dialogue is hardly less memorable. The whole show is done with gusto, and the digital recording is splendid, as spacious as it is clear.

Geminiani, Francesco (1687–1762)

Concerti grossi, Op. 2/1–6; Concerti grossi after Corelli, Op. 5/3 & 5.
☞ **(*) Sony Dig. SK 48043 [id.]. Tafelmusik, Jeanne Lamon.

As with other recent recordings of the music of Geminiani, Tafelmusik's lively performances of the six concertos of Op. 2, using original instruments, shows this composer as a more considerable and innovative figure than was once supposed. Although these works are essentially *concerti grossi*, the frequent dominance of the solo violin in the concertino points the way to the solo concertos of Vivaldi. Jeanne Lamon takes this solo role and directs the performances with plenty of vitality, and the recording produces clean, full, yet transparent textures. The only drawback for some ears will be the characteristic slight swelling out of the melodic line which still characterizes such 'authentic' performances. The recording is bright and immediately balanced within the warm acoustic of Notre Dame Convent in Waterdown, Ontario, Canada.

Concerti grossi, Op. 2/5–6; Op. 3/3; Op. 7/2; in G min. (after Corelli, *Op. 5/5); in D min.* (after Corelli, *Op. 5/12); Theme & variations (La Follia).*
(M) *** BMG/RCA Dig. GD 77010 [77010-2-RG]. La Petite Bande, Sigiswald Kuijken.

The quality of invention in the Geminiani concertos recorded here rises high above the routine. There is considerable expressive depth in some of the slow movements too. La Petite Bande is incomparably superior to many of the period-instrument ensembles. Those who are normally allergic to the vinegary offerings of some rivals will find this record a joy. It is beautifully recorded too, and makes an admirable and economical introduction to this underrated and genial composer.

6 Concerti grossi, Op. 3.
☞ *** Novalis Dig. 150 083-2 [id.]. Bern Camerata, Thomas Füri.
☞ **(*) Ph. Dig. 438 145-2 [id.]. I Musici.

The Geminiani Op. 3 *Concertos* are no stranger to the catalogue and have maintained decent representation on both LP and CD. It will therefore come as a surprise to many readers that this Novalis version claims to be a first recording. Earlier recordings are of the 1733 edition, but between that time and the mid-1750s Geminiani made revisions, some quite extensive, to the six pieces; on this CD, Thomas Füri and the Bern Camerata make use of these later revisions. Their playing has the same merits of liveliness and sensitivity that have distinguished their earlier recordings of the late 1970s to early 1980s. They use modern instruments and play with a good, singing quality, consistent taste and expressive vitality. Moreover they receive eminently good recording from Novalis, well balanced and truthful.

I Musici offer a fine digital alternative, using the unrevised, 1733 edition and playing modern instruments convincingly enough, except that inevitably the harpsichord continuo is submerged under the fuller string textures. However, the playing has plenty of life and expressive warmth, and this music-making is easy to enjoy. Fairly short measure though for a 1994 issue (50 minutes).

12 Concerti grossi, Op. 5 (after Corelli).
☞ (B) *** Ph. Duo 438 766-2 (2) [id.]. Michelucci, Gallozzi, Bennici, Centurione, I Musici.

The music on which Geminiani based his Op. 5 is drawn from the splendid *Sonatas for violin and continuo* of Corelli with the same opus number. In 1726, when the Geminiani set was published in London (where Geminiani lived until he moved to Dublin in 1733), Corelli's works were very popular. Their skilful adaptation to *concerto grosso* form features a viola in the solo group as well as violins and cello. The basic musical material is unaltered in any harmonic or thematic sense, but textures are filled out and greater variety of colour is provided. The result is entirely successful. The music balances serenity and a noble expressive feeling in slow movements with vigorously spontaneous allegros. The performances by I Musici – at their very finest – are admirable in all respects, spirited and responsive, polished yet never bland. The recording is first class too, wide-ranging, full and clearly detailed. The only slight snag is that the forward balance means that there is not a great deal of dynamic contrast between the solo group and the ripieno. The CD remastering provides firm definition and added realism, and the set is well documented. Highly recommended: if you enjoy Handel's Op. 6, this inexpensive reissue is not to be missed.

Concerti grossi: in D min. (*La Folia,* from CORELLI: *Sonata in D min., Op. 5/12*); *in G min., Op. 7/2; Trio sonatas Nos. 3 in F* (from *Op. 1/9*); *5 in A min.* (from *Op. 1/11*); *6 in D min.* (from *Op. 1/12*); *Violin sonatas: in E min., Op. 1/3; in A, Op. 4/12.*
*** Hyp. Dig. CDA 66264 [id.]. Purcell Band & Qt.

This record comes from Hyperion's '*La Folia*' series, though the only piece here using that celebrated theme is the arrangement Geminiani made of Corelli's *D minor Sonata.* Apart from the *G minor Concerto,* Op. 7, No. 2, the remainder of the disc is given over to chamber works. The Purcell Quartet play with dedication and spirit and convey their own enthusiasm for this admirably inventive music to the listener.

German, Edward (1862–1936)

The Conqueror: Berceuse. Gipsy suite. Henry VII: 3 Dances. Nell Gwyn: Overture & 3 Dances. Romeo and Juliet (incidental music): *Pavane; Nocturne; Pastorale. Merrie England: 4 Dances. Tom Jones: Waltz song.*
☞ **(*) Marco Polo Dig. 8.223419 [id.]. Slovak RSO (Bratislava), Leaper.

The Edward German collection in Marco Polo's enterprising series of English light music is just a little disappointing. The Slovak Radio Orchestra play with their usual verve and Adrian Leaper is ever sympathetic. The opening *Overture* to *Nell Gwyn* introduces the folk tune, *Early one morning,* and ingeniously combines it later with German's own material. But in the series of numbers which follow, the 'Hey nonny nonny' English country-dance style becomes rhythmically rather repetitive. Moreover, it is a pity that the *Merrie England* excerpts could not have included vocalists – the *Minuet* delivers up the glorious 'With sword and buckler by my side' which cries out for a voice, as does *Sophia's waltz song* from *Tom Jones.* The most rewarding numbers are the *Berceuse* from *The Conquerer* and the three pieces written for the Forbes-Robertson production of *Romeo and Juliet* at the London Lyceum in 1895. All are charming and very nicely scored. Excellent recording.

Welsh rhapsody.
☞ (B) *** CfP CD-CFP 4635; *TC-CFP 4635.* RSNO, Gibson – HARTY: *With the wild geese;*
   MACCUNN: *Land of mountain and flood;* SMYTH: *Wreckers overture.* ***

This collection, appropriately entitled 'Music of four countries', offers first-class sound from the late 1960s, extremely well transferred to CD and, with its interesting and rare couplings, makes a highly recommendable bargain. Edward German is content not to interfere with the traditional melodies he uses, relying on his orchestral skill to retain the listener's interest, and in this he is very successful. The closing pages, based on *Men of Harlech,* are prepared in a Tchaikovskian manner to provide a rousing conclusion. The CD transfer is very well managed, though the ear perceives a slight limitation in the upper range.

Gershwin, George (1898–1937)

An American in Paris; Catfish Row (suite from Porgy and Bess); (i) Piano concerto in F. Cuban overture; 'I got rhythm' variations; Lullaby for string orchestra; Promenade; (i) Rhapsody in blue; Second Rhapsody for piano and orchestra.
(B) *** VoxBox 1154832 (2) [CDX 5007]. (i) Jeffrey Siegel; St Louis SO, Leonard Slatkin.

The orchestral playing in St Louis, projected by bold, vividly forward recording, has a tingling vitality throughout and the *Cuban overture* lifts off marvellously. The same rhythmic effervescence is no less attractive in the *Piano concerto,* a splendid performance, full of verve and colour, with an authentic atmosphere in the Andante. The *Second Rhapsody* and the delightfully witty and affectionate account of the *'I got rhythm' variations* are hardly less appealing. But above all it is the vibrancy of this music-making which is so telling, with Jeffrey Siegel not as subtle as Leonard Bernstein in the *Rhapsody in blue* but playing with genuine charisma, and Slatkin presents the central melody with an agreeable warmth. *Catfish Row*, Gershwin's own selection from *Porgy and Bess*, is strongly characterized, while Slatkin's vigorous and characterful account of *An American in Paris*, if rhythmically a little mannered at times, is no less potent than the rest of this heady transatlantic mixture. Outstanding value.

(i) *An American in Paris;* (ii) *Piano concerto in F;* (iii) *Rhapsody in blue.*
(B) *** Pickwick Dig. PCD 909; *CIMPC 909.* (ii; iii) Gwenneth Pryor; LSO, Richard Williams.
☞ (B) ** Erato/Warner 2292 45929-2 [id.]. Tachino; Monte-Carlo PO, Lawrence Foster.

An American in Paris; (i) *Piano concerto in F; Rhapsody in blue; Variations on 'I got rhythm'.*
(M) **(*) BMG/RCA GD 86519 [RCA 6519-2-RG]. (i) Earl Wild; Boston Pops O, Fiedler.

From the opening glissando swirl on the clarinet, the performance of the *Rhapsody in blue* by Gwenneth Pryor and the LSO under Richard Williams tingles with adrenalin, and the other performances are comparable. In the *Concerto*, the combination of vitality and flair and an almost voluptuous response to the lyrical melodies is very involving. *An American in Paris*, briskly paced, moves forward in an exhilarating sweep, with the big blues tune vibrant and the closing section managed to perfection. The performances are helped by superb recording, made in the EMI No. 1 Studio; but it is the life and spontaneity of the music-making that enthral the listener throughout all three works.

Earl Wild's playing is full of energy and brio, and he inspires Arthur Fiedler to a similarly infectious response. The outer movements of the *Concerto* are comparably volatile and the blues feeling of the slow movement is strong. At the end of *An American in Paris* Fiedler adds to the exuberance by bringing in a bevy of motor horns. The brightly remastered recording suits the music-making, though the resonant Boston acoustics at times prevent absolute sharpness of focus: ideally, the spectacular percussion at the beginning of the *Concerto* should sound cleaner.

The French have their own way with jazzy inflexions and these Erato performances have plenty of vitality, while the *Concerto* is placed in the mainstream of concert music. Good recording – but, though enjoyable, this is not distinctive.

An American in Paris; (i) *Rhapsody in blue.*
(M) *** Sony SMK 47529 [id.]. NYPO, Bernstein; (i) Bernstein (piano) – BERNSTEIN: *Candide overture* etc. ***

Bernstein's 1958/9 CBS (now Sony) coupling was recorded when (at the beginning of his forties) he was at the peak of his creativity, with *West Side Story* only two years behind him. This record set the standard by which all subsequent pairings of *An American in Paris* and *Rhapsody in blue* came to be judged. It still sounds astonishingly well as a recording. Bernstein's approach is inspirational, exceptionally flexible but completely spontaneous. The performance of *An American in Paris* is vividly characterized, brash and episodic; an unashamedly American view, with the great blues tune marvellously timed and phrased as only a great American orchestra can do it.

An American in Paris (revised F. Cambell-Watson); (i) *Rhapsody in blue; Girl crazy*: excerpts (arr. Leroy Anderson); *Porgy and Bess* (suite, arr. R. R. Bennett & A. Courage).
*** Ph. Dig. 426 404-2 [id.]. (i) Misha Dichter; Boston Pops O, John Williams.

John Williams is just the man for a programme like this. His touch is light and *An American in Paris* is relaxed in a most appealing way – less 'symphonic' than usual. So is the *Rhapsody in blue*, yet Misha Dichter provides plenty of bravura. The selections from *Girl crazy* (with its two big hits, *Embraceable you*, and *I got rhythm*) is infectious, and each of the eight numbers from *Porgy and Bess* is given its full individual character, rather than being streamlined into an ongoing pot-pourri. The Boston sound is first class.

Catfish Row (suite from *Porgy and Bess*).
*** Telarc Dig. CD 80086 [id.]. Tritt, Cincinnati Pops O, Kunzel – GROFE: *Grand Canyon suite.* ***

Catfish Row was arranged by the composer after the initial failure of his opera. It includes a brief piano solo, played with fine style by William Tritt in the highly sympathetic Telarc performance which is very well recorded.

Porgy and Bess: Symphonic picture (arr. Bennett).
(M) *** Decca 430 712-2 [id.]. Detroit SO, Dorati – GROFE: *Grand Canyon suite*. ***

Robert Russell Bennett's famous arrangement of Gershwin melodies has been recorded many times, but never more beautifully than on this Decca digital version from Detroit. The performance is totally memorable and the sound quite superb.

Rhapsody in blue (see also above, under *An American in Paris*).
☞ (M) **(*) DG Dig. 439 528-2 [id.]. Bernstein with LAPO – BARBER: *Adagio for strings;*
    COPLAND: *Appalachian spring*. ***

In his last recording of this work for DG, Bernstein rather goes over the top with his jazzing of the solos in Gershwin. Such rhythmic freedom was clearly the result of a live rather than a studio performance. This does not match Bernstein's inspired 1959 analogue coupling for CBS.

Song arrangements for orchestra: *Bidin' my time; But not for me; Embraceable you; Fascinating rhythm; I got rhythm; Liza; Love is sweeping the country; Love walked in; The man I love; Oh, Lady, be good; Someone to watch over me; 'S wonderful* (all arr. Ray Wright).
☞ (M) **(*) Mercury 434 327-2 [id.]. O, Frederick Fennell – PORTER: *Song arrangements*. **(*)

This is reputed to be Fennell's favourite record, and he directs every one of these famous tunes with affectionate style and a sparkling rhythmic lift. Unusually for this label, the smooth (1961) Mercury sound is multi-miked, yet it has plenty of ambience as well as both a silky lustre and a natural clarity. The orchestral playing is fully worthy of the sophistication of the scoring, and Gershwin's songs with their ripe tunefulness respond more easily than Cole Porter's to presentation without the lyrics.

Gershwin Songbook (18 songs) complete; *Impromptu in two keys; Jazzbo Brown blues; Merry Andrew; 3 Preludes; Promenade; Rialto ripples; Three-quarter blues; 2 Waltzes in C* (arr. Chaplin). *Show tunes* (arr. Bennett): *Lady be good!: Little jazz bird. Oh Kay!: Someone to watch over me. Porgy and Bess: Oh Bess.*
☞ (B) **(*) Pickwick Dig. PCD 1058 [id.]. Richard Rodney Bennett.

A generous and useful bargain anthology including all the key piano works and a *pot-pourri* of the hits in the *Gershwin Songbook* (the composer's transcriptions of 18 of his most popular numbers). Richard Rodney Bennett's own arrangements of key show tunes are effective and he plays the whole programme with lilting warmth and a genuine rhythmic understanding. Perhaps at times one thinks of the atmosphere of a piano bar, but that is no bad thing when the concert pieces are well understood, the *Three preludes* standing out from the rest. Good, truthful recording. However, this inevetably is very much a second choice after Gershwin's own recordings on Elektra/Nonesuch.

Piano arrangements of songs: *Bidin' my time; But not for me; Clap yo' hands; Do, do, do; Embraceable you; Fascinating rhythm; A foggy day; Funny face; He loves and she loves; How long has this been going on; I got rhythm; I'll build a stairway to paradise; I've got a crush on you; Let's call the whole thing off; Liza; Love is here to stay; Love is sweeping the country; Love walked in; The man I love; Maybe; Mine; Of thee I sing; Oh, Lady, be good; Somebody loves me; Someone to watch over me; Soon; Strike up the band; Swanee!; 'S wonderful; That certain feeling; They can't take that away from me; Who cares;* Excerpts from: *An American in Paris;* Themes from *Concerto in F; Piano prelude No. 2; Rhapsody in blue*: excerpts.
☞ (M) *** Van. 08.6002.71 [OVC 6002]. George Feyer (with Tommy Lucas, George Mell, Sy
    Salzberg, Edward Caccavate).

The American Hungarian émigré pianist, George Feyer, is unsurpassed in this repertory, playing all these tunes with a rhythmic lift and naturally lilting inflexions that make one almost forget that most of them also had lyrics! The rhythmic backing is first class and the 1974 recording very real. Offering some 64 minutes of marvellous melody, this CD is in a class of its own. An ideal disc to titillate the ear and senses on a late summer evening.

VOCAL MUSIC

'Kiri sings Gershwin': Boy wanted; But not for me; By Strauss; Embraceable you; I got rhythm; Love is here to stay; Love walked in; Meadow serenade; The man I love; Nice work if you can get it; Somebody loves me; Someone to watch over me; Soon; Things are looking up. Porgy and Bess: Summertime.
**(*) EMI Dig. CDC7 47454-2 [id.]; *EL 270574-4*. Kiri Te Kanawa, New Theatre O, McGlinn
    (with Chorus).

In Dame Kiri's gorgeously sung *Summertime* from *Porgy and Bess*, the distanced heavenly chorus creates the purest kitsch. But most of the numbers are done in an upbeat style. Dame Kiri is at her most relaxed and ideally there should be more variety of pacing: *The man I love* is thrown away at the chosen tempo. But for the most part the ear is seduced; however, the pop microphone techniques bring excessive sibilants in the CD format.

OPERA AND MUSICALS

Girl crazy (musical).
*** Elektra-Nonesuch/Warner Dig. 7559 79250-2. Judy Blazer, Lorna Luft, David Carroll, Eddie Korbich, O, John Mauceri.

Girl crazy with its hit numbers (*Embraceable you, I got rhythm* and *Bidin' my time*) is an escapist piece, typical of the early 1930s. The score has point and imagination from beginning to end. The casting is excellent. Judy Blazer takes the Ginger Rogers role of Kate, the post-girl, while Judy Garland's less well-known daughter, Lorna Luft, is delightful in the Ethel Merman part of the gambler's wife hired to sing in the saloon. David Carroll is the New Yorker hero, and Frank Gorshin takes the comic role of the cab-driver, Gieber Goldfarb. The whole score, 73 minutes long, is squeezed on to a single disc. The only serious reservation is that the recording is dry and brassy, aggressively so – but that could be counted typical of the period too.

Lady Be Good (musical).
☞ *** Elektra Nonesuch/Warner Dig. 7559 79308-2; *7559 79308-4* [id.]. Teeter, Morrison, Alexander, Pizzarelli, Blier, Musto, Ch. & O, Stern.

This Elektra-Nonesuch issue is the third in the series of authentic recordings of Gershwin musicals sponsored by the Library of Congress and the Gershwin estate. Happily the pursuit of authenticity under such official guidance has not in any way undermined the spontaneous energy of the piece, far from it. This charming score, dating from 1924 (just after *Rhapsody in blue*), emerges as one of the composer's freshest. Such numbers as the title-song, as well as *Fascinatin' rhythm* and the witty *Half of it, dearie, blues*, are set against such duets as *Hang on to me* and *So am I*, directly reflecting the 1920s' world that Sandy Wilson parodied so affectionately in *The Boy Friend*. *Lady Be Good* was the piece originally written for the brother-and-sister team of Fred and Adele Astaire, and the casting of the principals on the disc is first rate. These are not concert-singers but ones whose clearly projected voices are ideally suited to the repertory, including Lara Teeter and Ann Morrison in the Astaires' roles and Michael Maguire as the young millionaire whom the heroine finally marries. The score has been restored by Tommy Krasker, and an orchestra of first-rate sessions musicians is conducted by Eric Stern.

Let 'em Eat Cake; Of Thee I Sing (musicals).
*** Sony Dig. M2K 42522 (2) [id.]. Jack Gilford, Larry Kert, Maureen McGovern, Paige O'Hara, David Garrison, NY Choral Artists, St Luke's O, Tilson Thomas.

Of Thee I Sing and *Let 'em Eat Cake* are the two operettas that George Gershwin wrote in the early 1930s on a political theme, the one a sequel to the other. What the British listener will immediately register is the powerful underlying influence of Gilbert and Sullivan, not just in the plot – with Gilbertian situations exploited – but also in the music, with patter-songs and choral descants used in a very Sullivan-like manner. In every way these two very well-filled discs are a delight, offering warm and energetic performances by excellent artists under Michael Tilson Thomas. Both Larry Kert and Maureen McGovern as his wife make a strong partnership. With the recording on the dry side and well forward – very apt for a musical – the words are crystal clear.

Porgy and Bess (complete).
⊛ *** EMI Dig. CDS7 49568-2; *EX 749568-4* (3) [Ang. CDCC 49568]. Willard White, Cynthia Haymon, Harolyn Blackwell, Cynthia Clarey, Damon Evans, Glyndebourne Ch., LPO, Rattle.

Simon Rattle here conducts the same cast and orchestra as in the opera house, and the EMI engineers have done wonders in re-creating what was so powerful at Glyndebourne, establishing more clearly than ever the status of *Porgy* as grand opera, not a mere jumped-up musical or operetta. The impact of the performance is consistently heightened by the subtleties of timing that come from long experience of live performances. By comparison, Lorin Maazel's Decca version (414 559-2) sounds a degree too literal, and John DeMain's RCA set (RD 82109 [RCD3 2109]) is less subtle. More than their rivals, Rattle and the LPO capture Gershwin's rhythmic exuberance with the degree of freedom essential if jazz-based inspirations are to sound idiomatic. The chorus is the finest and most responsive of any on the three sets, and the bass line-up is the strongest. Willard White is superbly matched by the magnificent Jake of Bruce Hubbard and by the dark and resonant Crown of Gregg Baker. As Sportin' Life, Damon Evans gets nearer than any of his rivals to the original scat-song inspiration without ever short-changing on musical values. Cynthia Haymon as Bess is movingly convincing in conveying equivocal emotions, Harolyn Blackwell as Clara sensuously relishes Rattle's slow speed for *Summertime*, and Cynthia Clarey is an intense and characterful Serena. EMI's digital sound is exceptionally full and spacious.

Porgy and Bess: highlights.
*** EMI Dig. CDC7 54325-2 [id.]; *EL 754325-4* (from above recording, with White, Haymon; cond. Rattle).

Rattle's highlights disc is most generous (74 minutes) and most comprehensive. However, not all the tailoring is clean: *Summertime* ends rather abruptly and there is at least one fade.

Strike up the Band (musical).
**(*) Nonesuch/Warner Dig. 7559 79273-2; *7559 79273-4* [id.]. Barrett, Luker, Chastain, Graae, Fowler, Goff, Lambert, Lyons, Sandish, Rocco, Ch. & O, Mauceri.

Strike up the Band was the nearest that George and Ira Gershwin ever came to imitating Gilbert and Sullivan. The very subject is Gilbertian – a satirical story about the United States going to war with Switzerland over the price of cheese. Quite apart from the two undoubted hits from the show, *The man I love* and *Strike up the band*, there is a whole sequence of delightful numbers that it is good to have revived in this first really complete recording. For all its vigour, the performance lacks something of the exuberance which marks the recordings of musicals conducted by John McGlinn for EMI. It may be correct to observe the dotted rhythms of *The man I love* as precisely as this performance does, but something is lost in the flow of the music, and to latterday ears the result is less haunting than the customary reading. The singers are first rate, but they would have been helped by having at least one of their number with a more charismatic personality. The second disc includes an appendix containing seven numbers used in the abortive 1930 revival.

Gesualdo, Carlo (*c.* 1561–1613)

Ave, dulcissima Maria; Ave, regina coelorum; Maria mater gratiae; Precibus et meritus beatae Mariae (motets). *Tenebrae responsories for Holy Saturday.*
*** Gimell Dig. CDGIM 015; *1585-T-15* [id.]. Tallis Scholars, Peter Phillips.

The astonishing dissonances and chromaticisms may not be as extreme here as in some of Gesualdo's secular music but, as elaborate as madrigals, they still have a sharp, refreshing impact on the modern ear which recognizes music leaping the centuries. The Tallis Scholars give superb performances, finely finished and beautifully blended, with women's voices made to sound boyish, singing with freshness and bite to bring home the total originality of the writing with its awkward leaps and intervals. Beautifully recorded, this is another of the Tallis Scholars' ear-catching discs, powerful as well as polished.

Leçons de Ténèbres: Responsories for Maundy Thursday.
(B) *** HM HMA 190220 [id.]. Deller Cons., Deller.

The Responses for Holy Week of 1611 are as remarkable and passionately expressive as any of Gesualdo's madrigals, and in depth of feeling they should be compared only with the finest music of the age. The invention is often unpredictable and nearly always highly original. The Deller Consort bring to this music much the same approach that distinguishes their handling of the madrigal literature. The colouring of the words is a high priority, yet it never oversteps the bounds of good taste to become precious or over-expressive. The consort blends remarkably well and intonation is excellent. This is temptingly inexpensive.

Madrigals, Book 5 for 5 voices (1611).
*** O-L Dig. 410 128-2 [id.]. Kirkby, Tubb, Nichols, Cornwell, King, Wistreich, Cons. of Musicke, Rooley.

In performances with such perfect tonal blend and accurate intonation as these, the modulatory audacities and anguished suspensions of Gesualdo's music can register as they should. The documenta-tion and presentation maintain the high standards of this label, and the sound-quality is admirably balanced and truthful. Of the Gesualdo recordings released in the last decade or so, this is easily the most distinguished.

Motets for 5 voices (complete): *Ave dulcissima Maria; Ave Regina coelorum; Deus refugium et virtus; Domine ne despicias; Exaudit Deus deprecationem meam; Fignare me laudare te; Hei mihi Domine; Illumina faciem tuam; Laboravi in gemitu meo; Maria mater gratiae; O Crux benedicta; O vos omnes; Peccanteum me quotidie; Precibus et meritus beatae Mariae; Reminiscere miserationum Tuarum; Sancti Spiritus Domine; Tribularer si nescirem; Tribulationem meam; Venit lumen tuum Jerusalem.*
☞ (BB) **(*) Naxos Dig. 8.550742 [id.]. Oxford Camerata, Jeremy Summerly.

Don Carlo Gesualdo, Prince of Venosa, having murdered his wife and her lover, displayed their corpses for all to see. He remarried four years later, and his mental instability caused his second wife to seek divorce – unsuccessfully! Gesualdo's music, with its sometimes extraordinarily individual chromatic shifts, suggests a self-consciously tormented musical personality seeking penance, for much of the writing's surface serenity is prevented from being in the least bland by sudden quirks of remorse, when the text mentions tears or sorrow, or asks for pity. The dozen singers of the Oxford Camerata sing these nineteen motets with beautifully blended tone and thoughtfully moulded melodic lines. Tempi are spacious and, though not unvaried, at times perhaps rather more movement would have been advantageous. Even so, *Ave dulcissima Maria* demonstrates how well Jeremy Summerly understands Gesualdo's style, and the following, deeply felt *Domine ne despicias* is another highlight of the programme. Similarly, the flowing *Sancti Spiritus Domine* and the sustained *Hei mihi Domine* heard together show well the expressive contrast of the writing. The recordings were made in the Chapel of Hertford College, Oxford, and the choral sound has great beauty, with a finely judged balance between atmosphere and clarity. Even without texts and translations this is a stimulating and rewarding disc, and excellent value.

Motets: *Ave, dulcissima Maria; Dolcissima mia vita; Ecco, morirò dunque; Hei mihi, Domine; Moro, lasso, al mio duolo; O vos omnes.*
☞ (M) ** Decca 440 032-2 [id.]. Monteverdi Ch., John Eliot Gardiner – MONTEVERDI: *Madrigals.* **

John Eliot Gardiner, early in his recording career (1969), gives convincing and fluent performances of six Gesualdo pieces, music that is full of character even when it is not wholly convincing. The singers have excellent ensemble and intonation, though they tend to leave nothing to the listener's imagination. However, the (originally Argo) recording is particularly firm and realistic.

Getty, Gordon (20th century)

The White election (song-cycle).
*** Delos Dig. D/CD 3057 [id.]. Kaaren Erickson, Armen Guzelimian.

The simple, even primitive, yet deeply allusive poetry of Emily Dickinson is sensitively matched in the music of Gordon Getty. Here he tackles a sequence of 32 songs, building them into an extended cycle in four linked parts. Everything is aimed, in as simple a way as possible, at bringing out the meaning of the poems, which have been selected (as Getty puts it) 'to tell Emily's story in her own words'. He adds that 'The most salient features of Emily's life were taken to be the white election, with its theme of union in death, and her unsuspected poetic genius.' If at times the tinkly tunes seem to be an inadequate response to profound emotions, the total honesty of the writing disarms criticism, particularly in a performance as dedicated and sensitive as this, with Kaaren Erickson a highly expressive artist with a naturally beautiful voice. The pianist too is very responsive.

Gibbons, Christopher (1615–1676)

Cupid and Death (with Matthew Locke).
(M) *** HM/BMG GD 77117 (2). Kirkby, Tubb, King, Wistreich, Thomas, Holden, Cass, Nichols, Cornwell, King, Consort of Musicke, Rooley – BLOW: *Venus and Adonis.* ***

Cupid and Death, 'a masque in four entries', dates from 1653. Gibbons seems to have been the lesser partner in the project, with Matthew Locke providing the bulk of the music for this rustic fantasy on an ancient fable. Rooley's team consistently brings out the fresh charm of the music. For repeated listening, the spoken sections, up to ten minutes long, can easily be programmed out on CD.

Gibbons, Orlando (1583–1625)

Anthems & Verse anthems: *Almighty and Everlasting God; Hosanna to the Son of David; Lift up your heads; O Thou the central orb; See, see the word is incarnate; This is the record of John. Canticles: Short service: Magnificat and Nunc dimittis. 2nd Service; Magnificat and Nunc dimittis. Hymnes & Songs of the church: Come kiss with me those lips of thine; Now shall the praises of the Lord be sung; A song of joy unto the Lord. Organ fantasia: Fantasia for double organ; Voluntary.*
*** ASV Gaudeamus CDGAU 123 [id.]. King's College Ch., L. Early Music Group, Ledger; John Butt.

This invaluable anthology was the first serious survey of Gibbons's music to appear on CD. It contains many of his greatest pieces. Not only are the performances touched with distinction, the recording too is in the highest flight and the analogue sound has been transferred to CD with complete naturalness. Strongly recommended.

(i) Anthems: *Almighty and everlasting God; Hosanna to the Son of David; O clap your hands together – God is gone up; O Lord, increase my faith; O Lord, in thy wrath rebuke me not;* (ii) *Introit: First Song of Moses; Second setting of Preces and Proper Psalm 145 for Whit Sunday; Second Service: Voluntary I & Te Deum; Voluntary II & Jubilate. Short Service: Voluntary I & Magnificat; Voluntary II & Nunc dimittis.* Verse anthems for voices and viols: *Glorious and powerful God; See, see, the word is incarnate; This is the record of John.*
(M) **(*) Decca mono/stereo 433 677-2. King's College, Cambridge, Ch., (i) with Boris Ord; Hugh McLean (organ); (ii) with Jacobean Consort of Viols, Willcocks; Simon Preston (organ).

Of the two groups of recordings, the first (mono) was made under Boris Ord in 1955; the second (stereo) came three years later directed by David Willcocks, but with Thurston Dart lending his influence and leading the consort of viols in the verse anthems (alongside Desmond Dupré). The mono recordings have plenty of ambience to disguise their lack of antiphony. But generally the effect is remarkably real, although the consort of viols is not always very well balanced. Juxtaposing the contents of two separate LPs means that there is plenty of variety and the later stereo collection is imaginatively chosen. Gibbons is a major musical personality and it was a happy idea in each case to preface the canticles from the two *Services* with an organ voluntary; it was customary in the early seventeenth century to have such a voluntary before the reading of the first Lesson.

Gilbert, Henry (1868–1928)

Suite for chamber orchestra.
*** Albany Dig. TROY 033-2 [id.]. V. American Music Ens., Hobart Earle – CHADWICK: *Serenade for strings.* ***

Henry Gilbert belonged to a time when almost all musical influences came from Europe and the American public did not value the output of its indigenous composers. This *Suite*, which harmonically is innocuous but which has an agreeable nostalgic languor, has something in common with Delius's *Florida suite*, although Gilbert's invention is less indelible. An excellent performance here from members of the Vienna Symphony Orchestra, who are completely at home in the music, as well they might be. The recording is excellent.

Gilles, Jean (1668–1705)

Messe des morts (Requiem mass).
☞ (M) *** DG 437 087-2. Rodde, Nirouët, Hill, U. Studer, Kooy, Ghent Coll. Voc., Col. Mus. Ant., Herreweghe (with CORRETTE: *Carillon des morts* ***).

Like his English contemporary, Purcell, the Provençal Jean Gilles died sadly young. His *Requiem*, which for many years was a favourite work in France, was rejected by the two families who originally commissioned it, so Gilles decreed that it should be used for his own funeral. So great was regional pride in eighteenth-century Provence that the work was often heard alongside the *Requiem* of Campra with alternating movements from each! Gilles's rhythmic and harmonic vigour (with plentiful false relations to add tang) is well caught in this performance on original instruments, and the singers find the music's expressive style admirably. The *Carillon* was included by Michel Corrette in his own edition of the Gilles *Requiem*, printed in 1764, and is appropriately included here as a postlude.

Ginastera, Alberto (1916–83)

Harp concerto, Op. 25.
☞ *** Chan. Dig. CHAN 9094 [id.]. Rachel Masters, City of L. Sinfonia, Hickox – GLIERE:
Concertos. ***

Ginastera's 1956 *Harp concerto*, written for Nicanor Zabaleta, who also recorded it, is one of his most
attractive and frequently heard works. It is full of vivid colours and snappy, incisive rhythms and has a
highly atmospheric slow movement. All its kaleidoscopic moods are keenly projected by Rachel Masters
in this refreshing and invigorating performance. Alert playing, too, from the City of London Sinfonia
under Richard Hickox. Strongly recommended, as are the two Glière concertos with which it is coupled.

(i) *Harp concerto, Op. 25;* (ii) *Piano concerto No. 1; Estancia* (ballet suite), *Op. 89.*
*** ASV Dig. CDDCA 654 [id.]. (i) Nancy Allen; (ii) Oscar Tarrago; Mexico City PO, Bátiz.

The *Harp concerto* is a highly inventive and rewarding work whose brilliant colours are brought fully
to life here by Nancy Allen and the Mexican orchestra. *Estancia* is a comparably vivid piece of
Coplandesque macho, its character also very successfully realized. The *First Piano concerto* is mildly
serial but far from unattractive – and very brilliantly (and sensitively) played by Oscar Tarrago. An
excellent introduction to this composer.

(i) *Cello sonata, Op. 49. Danzas Argentinas, Op. 2; Estancia, Op. 8:* (i) *Pampeana No. 2, Op. 21*
(rhapsody for cello and piano). *Pequeña danza; Piano sonata No. 1, Op. 22; 5 Canciones populares
Argentinas:* (i) *Triste.* (arr. Fournier)
☞ *** ASV Dig. CDDCA 865 [id.]. Alberto Portugheis, (i) with Aurora Natola-Ginastera.

ASV are planning to record the major works of this interesting Latin-American composer. The four-
movement *Cello sonata*, ardently rhapsodic, chimerical and full of atmosphere, is dedicated to his
wife, who is the soloist here, while *Pampeana* is a rhapsody which has an Argentinian flavour without
using folk melodies. The *Piano sonata No. 1* (1952) is a powerful, integrated piece with a desolate
Adagio and a brilliant, rhythmically chimerical folk-dance finale. Alberto Portugheis is thoroughly at
home in this repertoire and plays compellingly throughout. He is well recorded.

*12 American preludes, Op. 12; Danzas argentinas, Op. 2; Rondó sobre temas infantiles Argentinos, Op.
19; Sonata; Suite de danzas Criollas, Op. 15.*
*** Globe GLO 5006 [id.]. Barbara Nissman.

Barbara Nissman packs a punch and has abundant technical resources, all of which are needed in this
high-spirited repertoire. The present disc dates from 1981 but has been digitally remastered to good
effect, though it is short on playing time.

*Canciones, Op. 3: Milonga. Malambo, Op. 7; 3 Piezas, Op. 6; Piezas infantiles; Rondo sobre temas
infantiles Argentinos, Op. 19; Sonatas Nos. 1, Op. 53; 3, Op. 58; Toccata.*
☞ *** ASV Dig. CDDCA 880 [id.]. Alberto Portugheis.

This is the record to start with if you want to explore this Argentinian composer's characterful piano
music. The pieces for children are most welcoming and are delightfully varied and intimate: the
Milonga is seductive in a Latin-American way, as are the *Three Pieces*, Op. 6. The *Sonatas* are harder
nuts to crack: the first has a formidable opening movement and a ferocious closing toccata, and the
Toccata, written for the organ and played with great bravura here, is also a piece to make one sit up.
Alberto Portugheis is a first-rate artist and his natural sympathies for the music's idiom are apparent
throughout. He is very well recorded.

Giordano, Umberto (1867–1948)

Andrea Chénier (complete).
(M) *** BMG/RCA GD 82046 (2) [RCD-2-2046]. Domingo, Scotto, Milnes, Alldis Ch., Nat. PO,
Levine.
**(*) Decca Dig. 410 117-2 (2) [id.]. Pavarotti, Caballé, Nucci, Kuhlmann, Welsh Nat. Op. Ch., Nat.
PO, Chailly.

Andrea Chénier with its defiant poet hero provides a splendid role for Domingo at his most heroic
and the former servant, later revolutionary leader, Gérard, is a character well appreciated by Milnes.
Scotto gives one of her most eloquent and beautiful performances, and Levine has rarely displayed
his powers as an urgent and dramatic opera conductor more potently on record, with the bright
recording intensifying the dramatic thrust of playing and singing.

Pavarotti may motor through the role of the poet-hero, singing with his usual fine diction; nevertheless, the red-blooded melodrama of the piece comes over powerfully, thanks to Chailly's sympathetic conducting, incisive but never exaggerated. Caballé, like Pavarotti, is not strong on characterization but produces beautiful sounds, while Leo Nucci makes a superbly dark-toned Gérard. Though this cannot replace the Levine set with Domingo, Scotto and Milnes, it is a colourful substitute with its demonstration sound.

Fedora (complete).
(M) **(*) Decca 433 033-2 (2) [id.]. Olivero, Del Monaco, Gobbi, Monte Carlo Nat. Op. Ch. & O,
    Gardelli – ZANDONAI: *Francesca da Rimini.* **(*)
☞ (M) ** Sony Dig. M2K 42181 (2). Marton, Carreras, Hungarian R. & TV Ch. & O, Patanè.

Fedora will always be remembered for one brief aria, the hero's *Amor ti vieta*; but, as this highly enjoyable recording confirms, there is much that is memorable in the score, even if nothing else quite approaches it. Meaty stuff, which brings some splendid singing from Magda Olivero and (more intermittently) from Del Monaco, with Gobbi in a light comedy part. Fine, vintage (1969), atmospheric recording.

On Sony, Eva Marton as Fedora, the Romanov princess, is more aptly cast than in the companion set from the same source of *Andrea Chénier*, also conducted by Patanè with José Carreras taking the role of hero. In a work that should sound sumptuous it is not a help that the voices are placed forwardly, with the orchestra distanced well behind. That balance exaggerates the vibrato in Marton's voice, but it is a strong, sympathetic performance; Carreras, too, responds warmly to the lyricism of the role of the hero, Loris, giving a satisfyingly forthright account of *Amor ti vieta*. The rest of the cast is unremarkable, and Patanè's direction lacks bite, again partly a question of orchestral balance.

Giuliani, Mauro (1781–1828)

Duo concertante for violin & guitar, Op. 25; Gran duetto concertante for flute & guitar, Op. 52;
Serenade for violin, cello & guitar in A, Op. 19.
**(*) BMG/RCA 09026 60237-2 [60237-2]. Swensen, Galway, Anderson, Yamashita.

Giuliani is an elegant purveyor of ingenuous, pleasing phrases, and these three works show him at his most gallantly generous. These four artists do the composer proud, playing with warmth and elegance – Joseph Swensen's timbre in the *Duo concertante* is sumptuous (almost too lush) and only in the *Serenade* is the penchant of American engineering – the recordings were made in New York City – for close balancing disturbing, when the violin catches the microphone in the galloping Scherzo. Even so, this concert is easy to enjoy.

Sonata for violin and guitar.
*** Sony MK 34508 [id.]. Itzhak Perlman, John Williams – PAGANINI: *Cantabile* etc.***

Giuliani's *Sonata* is amiable enough but hardly substantial fare; but it is played with such artistry here that it appears better music than it is. The recording is in need of more ambience, but sound is invariably a matter of taste, and there is no reason to withhold a strong recommendation. The CD transfer is admirably managed.

Grand overture, Op. 61; Rossiniana No. 3, Op. 121.
☞ (M) **(*) BMG/RCA 09026 61593-2. Julian Bream (guitar) – SOR: *Grand solo sonata* etc.;
    DIABELLI: *Sonata in A.* **(*)

The *Grand Overture* is a rather imposing piece which Bream despatches with panache, whereas Giulini's six *Rossinianae* were, as the title suggests, based on the operas of Rossini, and one might expect the music of No. 3 to be witty and memorably tuneful, but that is not so. Bream makes cuts, but the music outstays its welcome. The playing is first class, of course, and the recording exemplary.

Glass, Philip (born 1937)

Company; Façades.
☞ (M) *** Virgin/EMI Dig. CUV5 61121-2. LCO, Warren-Green – ADAMS: *Shaker loops* *** ⊛;
    REICH: *8 Lines* ***; HEATH: *Frontier.* ***

Company consists of four brief but sharply contrasted movements for strings; *Façades* offers a haunting cantilena for soprano saxophone, suspended over atmospherically undulating strings. The performances are full of intensity and are expertly played, and the recording is excellent.

Dance Pieces: Glasspieces; In the Upper Room: Dances Nos. 1, 2, 5, 8 & 9.
*** CBS Dig. MK 39539 [id.]. Ens., dir. Michael Riesman.

These two ballet scores bring typical and easily attractive examples of Glass's minimalist technique. Heard away from the stage, the music seems to have a subliminally hypnotic effect, even though rhythmic patterns often repeat themselves almost endlessly.

String quartet No. 1.
☞ ** Collins Dig. 1386-2 [id.]. Duke Qt – BARBER: *Quartet* **; DVORAK: *Quartet No. 12.* **(*)

The vogue minimalist, Philip Glass, wrote the first of his five *Quartets* in 1966. It is a short piece of meagre substance and little musical interest. The middle movement, entitled ambient pause (1 minute 54 seconds), has a separate track to itself (and would be the only one to which one might be tempted to return), but there is really nothing much to the rest of it.

Akhnaten (complete).
*** CBS M2K 42457 (2) [id.]. Esswood, Vargas, Liebermann, Hannula, Holzapfel, Hauptmann, Stuttgart State Op. Ch., Russell Davies.

Akhnaten, Glass's powerful third opera, is set in the time of Ancient Egypt. Paul Esswood in the title-role is reserved, strong and statuesque; this is an opera of historical ghosts, and its life-flow lies in the hypnotic background provided by the orchestra; indeed the work's haunting closing scene with its wordless melismas is like nothing else in music. It offers a theatrical experience appealing to a far wider public than usual in the opera house; and here the Stuttgart chorus and orchestra give the piece impressively committed advocacy.

Einstein on the beach (complete).
(***) Sony Dig. M4K 38875 (4) [id.]. Childs, Johnson, Mann, Sutton, Ch., Zukovsky (violin), Philip Glass Ens., Riesman.

In this, his first opera, Glass translated his use of slowly shifting ostinatos on to a near-epic scale. The opera takes significant incidents in Einstein's life as the basis for the seven scenes in three Acts, linked with related visual images in a dream-like way, reflecting the second half of the title, *On the Beach*, a reference to Nevil Shute's novel with its theme of nuclear apocalypse. Dedicated performances.

Satyagraha (complete).
*** Sony Dig. M3K 39672 (3) [id.]. Perry, NY City Op. Ch. and O, Keene.

The subject here is the early life of Mahatma Gandhi, pinpointing various incidents; and the text is a selection of verses from the *Bhagavadgita*, sung in the original Sanskrit and used as another strand in the complex repetitive web of sound. The result is undeniably powerful. Where much minimalist music in its shimmering repetitiveness becomes static, a good deal of this conveys energy as well as power. The writing for chorus is often thrilling, and individual characters emerge in only a shadowy way. The recording, using the device of overdubbing, is spectacular.

Glazunov, Alexander (1865–1936)

Chant du ménestrel (for cello and orchestra), Op. 71.
☞ (B) *** DG Double 437 952-2 (2) [id.]. Rostropovich, Boston SO, Ozawa – BERNSTEIN: *3 Meditations;* BOCCHERINI: *Cello concerto No. 2;* SHOSTAKOVICH: *Cello concerto No. 2;* TARTINI: *Cello concerto;* TCHAIKOVSKY: *Andante cantabile* etc.; VIVALDI: *Cello concertos.* ***
*** Chan. Dig. CHAN 8579; *ABTD 1273* [id.]. Wallfisch, LPO, Bryden Thomson – KABALEVSKY; KHACHATURIAN: *Cello concertos.* ***

Glazunov's *Chant du ménestrel* shows the nostalgic appeal of 'things long ago and far away'. It is a short but appealing piece and is splendidly played by Rostropovich within a highly recommendable Double DG anthology. Alternatively, it becomes a welcome makeweight on the Chandos CD.

Violin concerto in A min., Op. 82.
⊛ (M) (***) EMI mono CDH7 64030-2 [id.]. Heifetz, LPO, Barbirolli – SIBELIUS: *Violin concerto* (**); TCHAIKOVSKY: *Violin concerto.* (***)
*** BMG/RCA RD 87019 [RCD1-7019]. Heifetz, RCA SO, Hendl – PROKOFIEV: *Concerto No. 2;* SIBELIUS: *Violin concerto.* ***

*** EMI Dig. CDC7 49814-2 [id.]. Perlman, Israel PO, Mehta – SHOSTAKOVICH: *Violin concerto No. 1.* ***

(B) *** Pickwick Dig. PCD 966; *CIMPC 966* [id.]. Udagawa, LPO, Klein – Concert ***

Heifetz's recording of the Glazunov *Violin concerto* was made in 1934 when the composer was still alive. It has greater expressive breadth and spaciousness than his later record with Walter Hendl and the Chicago orchestra and there is great warmth. Intonation is incredibly sure and the tone sweet; generally speaking, this first Heifetz version of the concerto has never been surpassed. For those who want more modern, stereo sound, Heifetz is again incomparable; his account is the strongest and most passionate (as well as the most perfectly played) in the catalogue. The RCA orchestra under Hendl gives splendid support.

The command and panache of Perlman are irresistible in this showpiece concerto, and the whole performance, recorded live, erupts into a glorious account of the galloping final section, in playing to match that even of the supreme master in this work, Heifetz.

The Glazunov also receives a heartfelt performance from Udagawa which is just as compelling as the virtuoso stereo accounts from such master violinists as Heifetz and Perlman. In the finale she may not offer quite such bravura fireworks as they do but, with more open sound, the result is very persuasive in its lilting way.

(i) *Violin concerto. The Seasons* (ballet), *Op. 67.*
*** Chan. Dig. CHAN 8596 [id.]. (i) Oscar Shumsky; SNO, Järvi.

Neeme Järvi obtains good results from the Scottish National Orchestra in *The Seasons*, though tempi tend to be brisk. The Chandos acoustic is reverberant and the balance recessed. In the *Violin concerto*, Oscar Shumsky is perhaps wanting the purity and effortless virtuosity of Heifetz, but the disc as a whole still carries a three-star recommendation.

From the Middle Ages, Op. 79; Scènes de ballet, Op. 52.
*** Chan. Dig. CHAN 8804; *ABTD 1432* [id.]. SNO, Järvi (with LIADOV: *A musical snuffbox* ***).

Järvi makes out an excellent case for these charming Glazunov suites. Although this music is obviously inferior to Tchaikovksy, Järvi has the knack of making you think it is better than it is. The disc also includes a fine account of Liadov's delightful *A musical snuffbox*.

Raymonda (ballet), *Op. 57:* extended excerpts from Acts I & II.
*** Chan. Dig. CHAN 8447; *ABTD 1159* [id.]. SNO, Järvi.

Järvi chooses some 56 minutes of music from the first two Acts, omitting entirely the Slavic/ Hungarian Wedding *Divertissement* of the closing Act, and this contributes to the slight feeling of lassitude. But with rich Chandos recording this is a record for any balletomane to wallow in, even if a Russian performance would undoubtedly have more extrovert fire.

(i) *Les ruses d'amour* (ballet), *Op. 61;* (ii) *The Sea* (fantasy), *Op. 28;* (iii) *March on a Russian theme.*
**(*) Olympia OCD 141 [id.]. (i) USSR RSO, Ziuraitis; (ii) Provatorov; (iii) USSR Ministry of Defence O, Maltsiev.

There are some 55 minutes of ballet music here, not unlike *Raymonda. The Sea*, though not really memorable, has undoubtedly effective pictorial content; the *March* is ingenuous. All are very well played, especially the main work which reveals Algis Ziuraitis as a deft exponent of his com-patriot's music. The recording has plenty of body, along with its Russian brightness and colour.

The Sea (fantasy), *Op. 28; Spring, Op. 34.*
*** Chan. Dig. CHAN 8611; *ABTD 1299* [id.]. SNO, Järvi – KALINNIKOV: *Symphony No. 1.* ***

The tone-poem, *Spring*, was written two years after *The Sea* and is infinitely more imaginative; in fact, it is as fresh and delightful as its companion is cliché-ridden. At one point Glazunov even looks forward to *The Seasons*. Persuasive and well-recorded performances from the Scottish National Orchestra under Neeme Järvi. The spacious and vivid recording sounds well.

The Seasons (ballet) *Op. 67.*
*** Decca Dig. 433 000-2 (2) [id.]. RPO, Ashkenazy – TCHAIKOVSKY: *Nutcracker.* ***
(BB) **(*) Naxos Dig. 8.550079; *4550079* [id.]. Czech RSO (Bratislava), Ondrej Lenárd – TCHAIKOVSKY: *Sleeping Beauty suite.* **

The Seasons (ballet) complete; *Scènes de ballet, Op. 52.*
☞ *** Telarc CD Dig. CD 80347 [id.]. Minnesota O, Edo de Waart.

The Seasons and Tchaikovsky's *Nutcracker* make a perfect coupling. Both scenarios occupy a fantasy world where frost and snowflakes are glitteringly magical rather than freezing. Ashkenazy's account of Glazunov's delightful ballet is the finest it has ever received. The RPO playing is dainty and elegant, refined and sumptuous, yet the strings respond vigorously to the thrusting vitality of the Autumnal *Bacchanale*. The Decca engineers, working in Watford Town Hall, provide digital sound of great allure and warmth, very much in the demonstration bracket.

If you want *The Seasons* separately on a single CD, you will be hard put to better this Minnesota performance, elegant, polished, warm and alive, and given Telarc's top-drawer sound. The famous thrusting tune of *Autumn* is only marginally less athletic than with Ashkenazy. The *Scènes de ballet* make an ideal coupling, not quite as melodically distinctive but still very enjoyable and cosily tuneful, although the second-movement *Marionnettes* matches Delibes at his most piquant.

Ondrej Lenárd gives a pleasing bargain account of Glazunov's delightful score, finding plenty of delicacy, while the entry of Glazunov's most famous tune at the opening of the *Autumn Bacchanale* is very virile indeed. The sound is atmospheric, yet with plenty of fullness.

Stenka Razin (symphonic poem), *Op. 13*.
*** Chan. Dig. CHAN 8479; *ABTD 1199* [id.]. SNO, Järvi – RIMSKY-KORSAKOV: *Scheherazade.*
***

Stenka Razin has its moments of vulgarity – how otherwise with the *Song of the Volga Boatmen* a recurrent theme? – but it makes a generous and colourful makeweight for Järvi's fine version of *Scheherazade*. The recording is splendid.

Symphonies Nos. 1 in E, Op. 5; 5 in B flat, Op. 55.
**(*) Orfeo Dig. C 093101A [id.]. Bav. RSO, Järvi.

Symphonies Nos. 1 in E, Op. 5; 7 in F, Op. 77.
*** Olympia Dig. OCD 100 [id.]. USSR MoC SO, Rozhdestvensky.

Glazunov's prodigious *First Symphony* is not only remarkably accomplished but delightfully fresh. Rozhdestvensky's persuasive advocacy enhances the appeal of all this music. Under his direction the *First Symphony* is eloquently shaped, as is the '*Pastoral*' *Seventh*. The Scherzos, always Glazunov's best movements, are a delight. The digital recording is very bright, but full and vividly detailed.

The playing of the Bavarian Radio Symphony Orchestra under Neeme Järvi is highly sympathetic and polished. The music is made to sound cogent and civilized, if perhaps a little bland at times. The Orfeo recording lacks something in glitter, although the Scherzos remain highly effective, and in their way Järvi's versions are certainly enjoyable.

Symphony No. 2 in F sharp min., Op. 16; Concert waltz No. 1, Op. 47.
**(*) Orfeo Dig. C 148101A [id.]. Bamberg SO, Järvi.

(i) *Symphony No. 2 in F sharp min., Op. 16; Romantic intermezzo, Op. 69; Stenka Razin, Op. 13.*
**(*) Olympia Dig. OCD 119 [id.]. (i) USSR MoC SO, Rozhdestvensky; USSR RSO, Dimitriedi.

The *Second Symphony* in Rozhdestvensky's hands is played with enormous eloquence, with glowingly colourful woodwind solos from this splendid orchestra. The snag is the recording which, although it has a most attractive basic ambience, produces problems at fortissimo levels, where the brass bray fiercely and the violins above the stave lose a good deal of body and tend to shrillness. Both the *Romantic intermezzo* and *Stenka Razin*, which is very exciting indeed, are analogue recordings and have considerably more body at climaxes.

Järvi's Orfeo sound is altogether more comfortable, and the music-making is more comfortable too. However, within its boundaries, which are more inhibited than Rozhdestvensky's, this is a very good performance. The recording is naturally balanced, but could do with just a bit more brilliance.

Symphony No. 3; Concert waltz No. 2 in F, Op. 51.
*** Orfeo Dig. C 157101A [id.]. Bamberg SO, Järvi.

Symphony No. 3 in D, Op. 33; Poème lyrique, Op. 12; Solemn procession.
**(*) Olympia Dig. OCD 120 [id.]. USSR MoC SO, Rozhdestvensky.

In Järvi's hands Glazunov's *Third Symphony* is richer and more cultivated than Rozhdestvensky's version, where the Russian brass coarsens the effect; the Scherzo is delectably played. The finale has plenty of energy and almost doesn't seem too long, when the momentum is so well sustained.

In Rozhdestvensky's performance the very opening has a Mendelssohnian lightness of touch, but when the brazen Russian trombones enter, they take the music into a distinctly Slavic world and the Russian-ness of the lyricism soon asserts itself. Otherwise, the playing of the USSR Ministry of Culture Symphony Orchestra is well up to the excellent standard of this series.

Symphonies Nos. 4 in E flat, Op. 48; 5 in B flat, Op. 55.
*** Olympia Dig. OCD 101 [id.]. USSR MoC SO, Rozhdestvensky.

Symphonies Nos. 4 in E flat, Op. 48; 7 in F, Op. 77.
**(*) Orfeo C 148201A [id.]. Bamberg SO, Järvi.

Glazunov's *Fourth* is a charming and well-composed symphony, full of good things and distinctly Russian in outlook, and held together structurally by a theme which Glazunov uses in all three movements. The *Fifth* is much better known and has a particularly fine slow movement. The string playing confirms the Ministry of Culture Symphony as currently the finest Soviet orchestra. The recording is extremely vivid.

The *Seventh* also has much to attract the listener. The *Andante* is undoubtedly eloquent in Järvi's performance and the Scherzo, marked giocoso, is well up to form. The finale has plenty of bustle, even if here it sounds rather long. The sound is full and naturally balanced, lacking something in spectacle.

Symphony No. 5 in B flat, Op. 55.
☞ * Russian Disc RD CD11 165 Leningrad PO, Yevgeni Mravinsky – PROKOFIEV: *Symphony No. 5.* *

Mravinsky's performance comes from a live concert given in 1968 and is not recommendable. The recording really strains tolerance: the sound comes close to breaking up in climaxes and is unpleasant with shrill strings. It is sonically inferior to other recordings of the period such as the Honegger *Liturgique*, Hindemith's *Die Harmonie der Welt* or the Sibelius *Seventh*.

Symphony No. 6 in C min., Op. 58; Poème lyrique, Op. 12.
*** Orfeo Dig. C 157201 [id.]. Bamberg SO, Neeme Järvi.

Symphony No. 6 in C min., Op. 58; Scènes de ballet, Op. 52.
**(*) Olympia Dig. OCD 104 [id.]. USSR MoC SO or RSO, Rozhdestvensky.

Symphony No. 6 in C min., Op. 58; Serenades Nos. 1, Op. 7; 2, Op. 11; Triumphal march, Op. 40.
*** ASV Dig. CDDCA 699 [id.]. LSO or RPO, Yondani Butt.

Taken overall, Yondani Butt's is the preferred choice for Glazunov's *Sixth*, although of course couplings do come into the matter. Yet Butt's performance is marginally fresher than Järvi's, helped by the more open sound of the ASV recording, and the fine wind and brass contributions from the LSO; the brass chorale at the end of the *Variations* is effectively sonorous.

Järvi makes more than usual of the first movement of the *Sixth*, building an impressive climax. The *Theme and variations* benefits greatly from the polished playing of the Bambergers. The finale produces energy and vigour without too much bombast, for the Bamberg brass is sonorous without being blatant. The *Poème lyrique* is full of romantic atmosphere; the full yet vivid recording seems just right for the music.

Rozhdestvensky directs the work with the kind of thrust and conviction to make the very most of it, and is suitably affectionate in the *Variations*. Here, however, the brass chorale is a bit fierce as recorded, and the upper string sound could ideally be more glamorous. The *Scènes de ballet* is analogue: the recording has slightly more depth. It is characteristic of the composer's favourite genre, assured and often tuneful.

(i) *Symphony No. 8 in E flat, Op. 83; Ballade, Op. 78; Slavonic festival, Op. 26.*
*** Olympia Dig. OCD 130 [id.]. (i) USSR MoC SO, Rozhdestvensky; USSR RSO, Dimitriedi.

Symphony No. 8 in E flat, Op. 83; Overture solennelle, Op. 73; Wedding procession, Op. 21.
**(*) Orfeo C 093201A [id.]. Bav. RSO, Järvi.

Rozhdestvensky provides the most powerful advocacy. The Scherzo is splendidly played, and in the finale the brass chorale is without the blatancy one tends to expect from a Russian performance. The two bonuses are well worth having. The *Slavonic festival* is a kaleidoscope of vigorous dance-themes and sparkling orchestration. The recording throughout is more agreeable than many in Rozhdestvensky's cycle, not lacking vividness but fuller and better balanced.

As in the rest of his series, Järvi and the Bavarian players give the piece a cultivated, polished performance of the *Eighth*, thoroughly musical and undoubtedly enjoyable, with spaciousness to some extent compensating for passion, when the sound is full and pleasing.

String quartets Nos. 2 in F, Op. 10; 4 in A min., Op. 64.
* Olympia OCD 173 [id.]. Shostakovich Qt.

The *Second Quartet* is clearly indebted to Borodin; its Scherzo has lots of charm and its slow movement is really quite beautiful. The *Fourth* is far less obviously nationalistic and there are undoubted rewards. The Shostakovich Quartet play with real conviction; their 1974 recording is very good indeed.

Piano sonatas Nos. 1 in B flat min., Op. 74; 2 in E min., Op. 75; Grand concert waltz in E flat, Op. 41.
*(*) Pearl SHECD 9538 [id.]. Leslie Howard.

The Glazunov *Sonatas* are well worth investigating, particularly in performances as committed and as well recorded as these. Admirers of Glazunov's art should investigate this issue which sounds extremely impressive in its CD format.

Glebov, Yevgeni (born 1929)

Symphony No. 5 (The Seasons); The Little Prince: suite; 5 Fantastic dances.
☞ ***** Olympia OCD 552 [id.]. Byelorussian State R. & TV SO, Raisky.

Both the *Fifth Symphony* and *The Little Prince* are attractive and well fashioned but ultimately derivative. General-purpose Soviet music, heavily diluted Prokofiev–Shostakovich with little real substance to commend it – sub-Kabalevsky. The Minsk orchestra is far from negligible and they play well for Boris Raisky. The analogue recordings are undistinguished: serviceable rather than good, and generally on a par with the music. Of curiosity value but of no great artistic interest.

Glière, Reinhold (1875–1956)

(i) *Concerto for coloratura soprano, Op. 82;* (ii) *Harp concerto, Op. 74.*
☞ ******* Chan. Dig. CHAN 9094 [id.]. (i) Eileen Hulse; (ii) Rachel Masters; City of L. Sinfonia,
   Hickox – GINASTERA: *Harp Concerto.* *******

A new digital recording of Glière's lush concertos is long overdue: Dame Joan Sutherland's celebrated account on Decca (currently deleted) comes from the 1970s. However, this newcomer is highly competitive in both works and can generally be said to supersede them. The recording is suitably rich and opulent, yet every detail is audibly in place. Eileen Hulse is an impressive soloist with excellent control, well-focused tone and a good sense of line, and she is excellently supported by the City of London Sinfonia and Richard Hickox. Nor need Rachel Masters fear comparison with her predecessor, Osian Ellis; so, given such excellent sound, this is all highly self-indulgent and sybaritic.

Horn concerto in B flat, Op. 91.
☞ (M) ******* Ph. Dig. 416 380-2 [id.]. Baumann, Leipzig GO, Masur – *Collection of Horn concertos.*
   ***

Glière's *B flat Concerto* is a major find: the horn player's equivalent of the Hummel *Trumpet concerto*, it is a most attractive work, providing an infectious Russian dance finale with a catchy secondary theme that might have come from the unlikely source of Vaughan Williams's *Folksongs suite*. The eloquent first movement with its bold horn writing is very like the *First Horn concerto* of Richard Strauss, and the *Andante* has a hummable operatic melody which persists in the memory. Baumann plays the whole work with warmth, vigour and easy bravura, and the rich-textured Leipzig accompaniment is ideal. The recording is first rate and the rest of the concert is also appealing.

Symphony No. 2 in C min, Op. 25; Zaporozhy Cossacks, Op. 64.
**(*) Chan. Dig. CHAN 9071 [id.]. BBC PO, Downes.

Not even the advocacy of Sir Edward Downes with his magnificent Manchester orchestra can conceal the banality of some of the writing in this early Glière symphony – it cannot compare with Glière's later and grander *Symphony No. 3. Zaporozhy Cossacks* is less ambitious but also contains banalities. Excellent performances and outstanding recording.

Symphony No. 3 in B min. (Ilya Murometz), Op. 42.
*** Chan. Dig. CHAN 9041 [id.]. BBC PO, Sir Edward Downes.
☞ (M) ****(*)** EMI CDM7 65074-2 [id.]. Houston SO, Stokowski – LOEFFLER: *Pagan poem.* ****(*)**
☞ (BB) ****** Naxos Dig. 8.550858 [id.]. Slovak RSO, Johanos.

Downes and the BBC Philharmonic in magnificent form give an urgently passionate performance of this colourful programme piece, more convincing than any rival in what can easily seem too cumbersome a work. Downes, taut and intense, relates the writing very much to the world of Glière's close contemporary, Rachmaninov. The recording, made in the concert hall of New Broadcasting House, Manchester, is one of Chandos's finest, combining clarity and sumptuousness.

Stokowski's version dates from the earliest days of stereo (1957), and the original Capitol LP (SP 8402) was welcomed by us over 30 years ago in the very first hardback *Stereo Record Guide*. The great orchestral magician edited (and shortened) the score himself for maximum effect. His edition of the symphony (recorded in 1957) runs to 38 minutes 11 seconds, less than half the duration of the BBC version from Downes (Chandos). It almost qualifies as a highlights disc! All the same, Stokowski is Stokowski, and there are some thrilling things from the orchestra. His performance goes completely over the top, with the sheer opulence of the orchestral effects almost overwhelming yet completely carrying the day. If you enjoy an orgy of orchestral flamboyance and playing which consistently carries the highest electrical charge, this will be irresistible. In our original LP review we commented: 'There are two main provisos for a record of this sort: enthusiastic and sympathetic direction and a really good recording. Stokowski uses all his skill to provide the former and Capitol's sound is most convincing throughout. There is plenty of atmosphere and the spread and definition of the reproduction generates ample excitement.' The CD transfer finds even greater amplitude and spectacle than was present on that early stereo LP. However, because of the cuts, any recommendation must inevitably be qualified.

Naxos have acted sensibly in reducing the price of the Johanos version (originally on Marco Polo). While the Chandos alternative is well worth the extra cost, the rougher Slovak Radio performance is perfectly acceptable and will suit those who want to explore this score at little cost.

Glinka, Mikhail (1805–57)

Russlan and Ludmilla: Overture.
(M) *** BMG/RCA GD 60176 [60176-2-RG]. Chicago SO, Fritz Reiner – PROKOFIEV: *Alexander Nevsky* etc. ***

Reiner's performance is highly infectious and the (1959) Chicago sound brings plenty of colour and warmth.

Grand sextet in E flat.
*** Hyp. CDA 66163 [id.]. Capricorn – RIMSKY-KORSAKOV: *Quintet*. ***

Glinka's *Sextet* is rather engaging, particularly when played with such aplomb as it is here. The contribution of the pianist, Julian Jacobson, is brilliantly nimble and felicitous. The balance places the piano rather backwardly, but the CD provides good detail and presence.

Trio pathétique in D min.
*** Chan. Dig. CHAN 8477; *ABTD 1188* [id.]. Borodin Trio – ARENSKY: *Piano trio*. ***

Glinka's *Trio* is prefaced by a superscription; '*Je n'ai connu l'amour que par les peines qu'il cause*' ('I have known love only through the misery it causes'). It is no masterpiece – but the Borodins almost persuade one that it is. The recording is vivid and has excellent presence.

A Life for the Tsar.
☞ **(*) Sony Dig. S3K 46487 (3) [id.]. Martinovich, Pendachanska, Merritt, Toczyska, Sofia Nat. O Ch. & O, Tchakarov.

When this opera was first given in St Petersburg in November 1836 it marked a breakthrough in Russian music. Though Glinka broadly kept to a formalized layout in set numbers, as in Italian opera, he introduced Russian themes far more than his predecessors, and the subject itself reflected the nationalist fervour behind his inspiration. Even over the 70 years of the Soviet period in Russia, it was a revered masterpiece, though the text was amended (as in this present Bulgarian recording) to tone down the praise for the Tsar. There are many delightful sequences in the opera, not least the many choruses and dances, which regularly inspire the late Emil Tchakarov to spring rhythms infectiously, bringing out the peasant flavour. Against the background of a good ensemble perform-ance the soloists are more than reliable, with Boris Martinovich singing characterfully, if not always steadily. Alexandrina Pendachanska is bright and fresh as his daughter, only occasionally edgy in a Slavonic way, and Stefania Toczyaska sings beautifully as Vanya, singing this character's two arias delightfully. From outside the Slavonic area the American tenor Chris Merritt is well attuned, singing without strain. Though in its clear recording this gives little idea of a staged rather than a studio performance, it is more than a stop-gap for an essential work in the repertory.

Gluck, Christophe (1714–87)

Don Juan (complete ballet).
☞ (M) *** Decca 433 732-2 [id.]. ASMF, Marriner – HANDEL: *Ariodante* etc. ***
☞ (M) *** Erato/Warner 2292 45980-2 [id.]. E. Bar. Soloists, Gardiner.

Although some of the music is known from the French version of Orfeo, and three numbers turn up in *Iphigénie en Aulide*, *Don Juan* never maintained the popularity it enjoyed during the 1760s and 1770s, even though it possessed a narrative line with a dénouement like Mozart's *Don Giovanni*, with an earthquake added for good measure. The lack of tonal variety may worry some listeners but, for the most part, sheer delight at the quality and imaginative vitality of Gluck's invention will reward those who persevere through the 31 numbers and three-quarters of an hour of music. The ASMF playing is altogether excellent, capturing the lightness of touch and the dramatic intensity of the score. The Decca engineers in 1967 produced vivid, well-focused sound-quality, and this has been transferred very well to CD, with a substantial Handel bonus.

In many ways Gardiner is preferable to Marriner, and his 1981 recording is obviously fuller and more modern. The performance too has a cleaner and more dramatic profile, even though Marriner does not sound in the least bland. However, with his considerable Handel bonus Marriner provides much more music.

Alceste (complete).
** Orfeo Dig. C 02782 (3) [id.]. Jessye Norman, Gedda, Krause, Nimsgern, Weikl, Bav. R. Ch. and SO, Baudo.

The French version of *Alceste* in this very well-cast set has Jessye Norman commanding in the title-role, producing gloriously varied tone in every register. What is rather lacking is a fire-eating quality such as made Janet Baker's performance so memorable. That is mainly the fault of the conductor, who makes Gluck's score sound comfortable rather than tense and, as a set, this does not quite rebut the idea that in Gluck 'beautiful' means 'boring'. Good, well-focused sound.

Le Cinesi (The Chinese women).
(M) *** HM/BMG Dig. GD 77174 [77174-2-RG]. Poulenard, Von Otter, Banditelli, De Mey, Schola Cantorum Basiliensis O, Jacobs.

Gluck's hour-long opera-serenade provides a fascinating view of the composer's lighter side and, rather like Mozart in *Entführung*, Gluck uses jangling and tinkling percussion instruments in the overture to indicate an exotic setting. Otherwise the formal attitudes in Metastasio's libretto – written some twenty years before Gluck set it – are pure eighteenth century.

(i) *La Corona* (complete). (ii) *La Danza* (dramatic pastoral).
**(*) Orfeo Dig. C 135872H (2) [id.]. (i) Slowakiewicz, Gorzynska, Nowicks, Bav. R. Ch;
(ii) Ignatowicz, Myriak, Warsaw CO; Bugaj.

Hunting-calls set the scene evocatively in the three-movement sinfonia of *La Corona*, which is followed by six arias, a delightful duet and a final quartet. This performance is fresh and direct, with first-rate singing from the three sopranos. The much shorter fill-up, described as a dramatic pastoral, is less interesting and is less reliably done.

Iphigénie en Aulide (complete).
***Erato/Warner Dig. 2292 45003-2 (2). Van Dam, Anne Sofie von Otter, Dawson, Aler, Monteverdi Ch., Lyon Op. O, Gardiner.

Iphigénie en Aulide was Gluck's first piece in French and it anticipated the *Tauride* opera in its speed and directness of treatment, so different from the leisurely and expansive traditions of *opera seria*. Gardiner here eliminates the distortions of the piece which the long-established Wagner edition created and reconstructs the score as presented in the first revival of 1775; the recording conveys the tensions of a live performance without the distractions of intrusive stage noise. The darkness of the piece is established at the very start, with men's voices eliminated, and a moving portrait built up of Agamemnon, here sung superbly by José van Dam. In the title-role Lynne Dawson builds up a touching portrait of the heroine. Her sweet, pure singing is well contrasted with the positive strength of Anne Sofie von Otter as Clytemnestra, and John Aler brings clear, heroic attack to the tenor role of Achille. The performance is crowned by the superb ensemble-singing of the Monteverdi Choir in the many choruses.

Iphigénie en Tauride (complete).

⊛ *** Ph. Dig. 416 148-2 (2) [id.]. Montague, Aler, Thomas Allen, Argenta, Massis, Monteverdi Ch., Lyon Op. O, Eliot Gardiner.

☞ ** Sony Dig. S2K 52492 (2) [id.]. Vaness, Surian, Allen, Winbergh, La Scala, Milan, Ch. & O, Muti.

Gardiner's electrifying reading of *Iphigénie en Tauride* is a revelation. Though his Lyon orchestra does not use period instruments, its clarity and resilience and, where necessary, grace and delicacy are admirable. Diana Montague in the name-part sings with admirable bite and freshness, Thomas Allen is an outstanding Oreste, characterizing strongly but singing with classical precision. John Aler is a similarly strong and stylish singer, taking the tenor role of Pylade. The recording is bright and full.

Muti's set was recorded live at La Scala in March 1992, a big-scale version that provides a possible alternative to the superb Gardiner for those who insist on modern, not period, instruments. Muti's taut direction is comparably dramatic, but with its beefy orchestral sound and close-up recording it is an overweight performance that misses the essential elegance of Gluck in its lack of light and shade. Vaness's dramatic timbre is apt, but the microphone catches a flutter in the voice. Thomas Allen as Oreste is as telling as for Gardiner but, thanks to the recording, his subtler shading is missing, and Gösta Winbergh as Pylade sings with fine ringing tones yet lacks subtlety and variety.

Orfeo ed Euridice (complete).

☞ *** Ph. Dig. 434 093-2 (2) [id.]. Ragin, McNair, Sieden, Monteverdi Ch., E. Bar. Soloists, Gardiner.

*** EMI Dig. CDS7 49834-2 (2). Hendricks, Von Otter, Fournier, Monteverdi Ch., Lyon Opera O, Gardiner.

☞ (M) *** Erato/Warner Dig. 2292 45864-2 (2). J. Baker, Speiser, Gale, Glyndebourne Ch., LPO, Leppard.

**(*) Decca 417 410-2 (2) [id.]. Horne, Lorengar, Donath, ROHCG Ch. & O, Solti.

(M) **(*) BMG/RCA GD 87896 (2) [7896-2-RG]. Verrett, Moffo, Raskin, Rome Polyphonic Ch., Virtuosi di Roma, Fasano.

Gardiner's newest set for Philips could not be more sharply contrasted with the earlier recording he made for EMI in 1989. Then he was persuaded at the Lyon Opéra to record the Berlioz edition, in French, which uses a conflation of Gluck's Vienna and Paris versions of the text. But all along Gardiner has much preferred the tautness of the original, Vienna version in Italian, which here on Philips he presents with a bite and sense of drama both totally in period and deeply expressive. The element of sensuousness, not least in the beautiful singing of the counter-tenor, Derek Lee Ragin, in the title-role, contrasts strongly with the direct rival version from Sony, which under Frieder Bernius presents period instruments far more abrasively. On a smaller scale, Bernius totally misses the Elysian beauty Gardiner finds in such passages as the introduction to *Che puro ciel*. Michael Chance, as Orfeo on Sony, is firmer and more direct than Ragin but less tender. Sylvia McNair as Euridice and Cyndia Sieden as Amor complete Gardiner's outstanding solo team. One's only regret is that the set does not provide as a supplement such numbers written for Paris as *The Dance of the Blessed Spirits*.

Many will be glad to have the Berlioz edition, sung in French, which aimed at combining the best of both the Vienna and Paris versions, although once again Gardiner omits the celebratory ballet at the end of the opera. Anne Sofie von Otter is a superb Orfeo, dramatically most convincing. The masculine forthrightness of her singing matches the extra urgency of Gardiner's direction; and both Barbara Hendricks as Eurydice and Brigitte Fournier as Amour are also excellent. The chorus is Gardiner's own Monteverdi Choir, superbly clean and stylish. The recording is full and well balanced.

The Erato version of *Orfeo ed Euridice*, directly based on the Glyndebourne production in which Dame Janet Baker made her very last stage appearance in opera, was recorded in 1982, immediately after the run of live performances. That brought the advantage of the sort of dramatic commitment and spontaneity of a live performance, allied to studio precision. Leppard, abetted by the producer, Sir Peter Hall, aimed in the theatre to contrast the bitingly passionate quality in the score against the severely classical frame. Often credited with being a romanticizer of the eighteenth century, Leppard in fact presents the score with freshness and power, indeed with toughness. Nowhere is that clearer than in the great scene leading up to the aria, *Che farò*, where Dame Janet commandingly conveys the genuine bitterness and anger of Orpheus at Eurydice's death. That most famous of Gluck's arias comes over fresh and clear with no sentimentality whatever, and conversely the display aria which brings Act I to a close has passion and expressiveness even in the most elaborate coloratura.

Elisabeth Speiser as Eurydice and Elizabeth Gale as Amor are both disappointing but, as in the theatre, the result is a complete and moving experience centring round a great performance from Dame Janet. The complete ballet-postlude is included, delightful celebration music. The recording has been enhanced in the CD transfer, bright and vivid without edginess, with the modern orchestral strings sounding both fresh and warm. At mid-price this makes a clear first choice.

The surprise of the Decca set is the conducting of Georg Solti, which has a feeling for eighteenth-century idiom which is most impressive. Solti and Horne opt to conclude Act I, not as the Gluck score prescribes, but with a brilliant display aria, *Addio, o miei sospiri*, taken from the contemporary opera, *Tancredi*, by Ferdinando Bertoni. That may sound like cavalier treatment for Gluck, but stylistically Solti justifies not only that course but his whole interpretation, which combines drama with delicacy. Marilyn Horne makes a formidably strong Orfeo, with fine control of tone. Pilar Lorengar sings sweetly, but is not always steady, while Helen Donath is charming in the role of Amor. Recording quality is outstandingly fine.

Clearly, if you have a mezzo as firm and sensitive as Shirley Verrett, then everything is in favour of your using the original Italian version. Fasano also uses the right-sized orchestra (of modern instruments) and adopts an appropriately classical style. Anna Moffo and Judith Raskin match Verrett in clean, strong singing, and the Rome Polyphonic Chorus is far more incisive than most Italian choirs. The recording is vivid and atmospheric but emphasizes the music's dramatic qualities rather than its tenderness. However, this makes a good alternative mid-priced recommendation.

La rencontre imprévue (opéra-comique).
*** Erato/Warner Dig. 2292 45516-2 (2) [id.]. Lynne Dawson, Le Coz, Flechter, Dubosc, Marin-
    Degor, Guy de Mey, Viala, Lafont, Cachemaille, Dudziak, Lyon Op. O, Gardiner.

John Eliot Gardiner demonstrates here that one of Gluck's comic operas can come up as freshly as the great reform operas. It is true that *Les pèlerins de la Mecque* – as Gardiner prefers to call it, rather than using its duller, more usual title, given above – has nothing like the comic timing of Mozart. Yet all through the brisk sequence of arias and ensembles Gardiner gives the lie to the idea of the score being banal. The sweet-toned Lynne Dawson is charming as the heroine, Rezia, and Guy de Mey as the hero, Ali, is one of the few tenors who could cope effortlessly with the high tessitura. Pierre Cachemaille sings powerfully in an incidental role. The Lyon acoustic, as usual, is on the dry side, as recorded, but that has many advantages in comic opera.

Goehr, Alexander (born 1932)

Metamorphosis/Dance, Op. 36; (i) *Romanza for cello and orchestra, Op. 24.*
(M) *** Unicorn Dig. UKCD 2039. (i) Moray Welsh; RLPO, Atherton.

Moray Welsh plays the *Romanza* warmly and stylishly. *Metamorphosis/Dance*, inspired by the Circe episode in the *Odyssey*, is a sequence of elaborate variations, full of strong rhythmic interest. The performance is excellent.

Goldmark, Karl (1830–1915)

Violin concerto No. 1 in A min., Op. 28.
☞ *** EMI Dig. CDC7 47846-2 [id.]. Perlman, Pittsburgh SO, Previn – KORNGOLD: *Violin
    concerto.* ***
☞ (B) ** Hung. White Label HRC 162 [id.]. Albert Kocsis, Savaria SO, Petró – PAGANINI: *Violin
    concerto No. 1.* **

Like the *Rustic Wedding symphony* this, the first of Goldmark's two violin concertos, maintains a peripheral position in the catalogue. It is a pleasing and warm-hearted concerto in the Romantic tradition that deserves to be better known. It could not be played more beautifully than by Itzhak Perlman, whose effortless virtuosity and lyrical poise challenge even Milstein's aristocratic record of the late 1950s (now deleted). The latter was better balanced, for the EMI engineers have placed Perlman very much in the foreground – so much so that orchestral detail does not always register as it should. The sound-quality is fresher in the newer recording, and Previn accompanies sympathetically. This is very charming and likeable music, and Perlman plays it most winningly. The CD transfer is clear and refined, losing perhaps a little of the warmth of the analogue master. The present coupling with Korngold is recently restored to the EMI catalogue at full price.

Albert Kocsis offers a fine bargain alternative version. He plays expertly and, in terms of charm and romantic feeling, he is by no means completely upstaged by Perlman, even if he has not the latter's strength of personality and sheer sophistication. János Petró and the Savaria group provide good support and are spaciously recorded. The snag, however, is that the Hungaroton digital remastering has added a degree of edge to the solo violin timbre above the stave.

Rustic Wedding Symphony, Op. 26.
☞ (M) **(*) Van. 08.9051.71 [OVC 5002]. Utah SO, Abravanel.

Rustic Wedding Symphony, Op. 26; Sakuntala overture, Op. 13.
*** ASV Dig. CDDCA 791 [id.]. RPO, Yondani Butt.

'Clear-cut and faultless', Brahms called this large but consciously unpretentious programme symphony. The first movement brings not a sonata-form structure but a simple set of variations with one or two pre-echoes of Mahler in *Wunderhorn* mood. It opens with a distinctly rustic theme on the lower strings, which when taken up by the horns (with woodwind birdsong overhead) is as magical as any passage in the romantic symphonic repertory, not forgetting the beginning of Mahler's *First*. The hazily romantic evocation of a summer garden which forms the slow movement leads to a boisterous dance finale, with genial injections of fugato. Yondani Butt has the work's full measure and the RPO clearly enjoy themselves. The recording has brightly lit violins, but plenty of bloom on the woodwind, and the only miscalculation of balance concerns the trombone entry in the first movement which is too blatant and too loud. Otherwise this is in every way enjoyable. The *Overture Sakuntala* opens impressively but does not quite sustain its 18 minutes. Butt presents it with persuasive vigour and lyrical feeling, and does not shirk the melodrama.

It is good to have a recommendable mid-priced version of this highly engaging symphony – a favourite of Sir Thomas Beecham. It is beautifully recorded and, because of the pleasing Utah acoustics, one would never guess it was made nearly 30 years ago. Abravanel is affectionately straightforward: the opening variations are relaxed and there is plenty of colour in the *Bridal song* and *Serenade*, with attractive woodwind solos. The romantic ardour of *In the garden* certainly comes over and, if the reading overall is just a little undercharacterized, there is no lack of spontaneity in the playing.

Die Königin von Saba (opera).
** Hung. HCD 12179/82 [id.]. Nagy, Gregor, Kincses, Jerusalem, Miller, Takács, Hungarian State
   Op. Ch. and O, Fischer.

Klára Takács is dramatic and characterful as the Queen of Sheba while, in the tenor role of Asad, Siegfried Jerusalem gives a magnificent performance, not least in his aria, *Magische Töne*. Sándor Nagy is an impressive Solomon, and Adám Fischer draws lively performances from everyone. The recording is very acceptable, but there are many details which do not emerge as vividly as they might. The documentation, too, is poorly produced.

Goldschmidt, Berthold (born 1903)

(i) *String quartets Nos. 2–3;* (ii) *Letzte Kapitel; Belsatzar.*
*** Largo Dig. LC 8943 [id.]. (i) Mandelring Qt; (ii) Marks; Ars-Nova Ens., Berlin, Schwarz.

Berthold Goldschmidt was hounded from Nazi Germany and he settled in London. This disc collects his *Letzte Kapitel* for speaker and an instrumental ensemble, very much in the style of Kurt Weill, and the *Second Quartet*, which has something of the fluency of Hindemith. It is an excellently fashioned piece with a rather powerful slow movement, an elegy subtitled *Folia*. The CD is completed by *Belsatzar*, an *a cappella* setting of Heine, and the *Third Quartet*, a remarkable achievement for an 86-year-old, the product of a cultured and thoughtful musical mind. The performances are dedicated, the recordings satisfactory.

(i) *Der gewaltige Hahnrei* (complete); (ii) *Mediterranean songs.*
☞ *** Decca Dig. 440 850-2 (2) [id.]. (i) Alexander, Wörle, M. Kraus, Otelli, Berlin R. Ch. &
   Deutsches SO, Berlin; (ii) John Mark Ainsley, Leipzig GO, (i; ii) Zagrosek.

The opera, *Der gewaltige Hahnrei* ('The magnificent Cuckold'), was given with great success in Mannheim in 1932, but was then banned by the Nazis and forgotten. With an excellent cast, powerfully conducted and played with thrust and polish, the piece makes an invaluable addition to Decca's series of *Entartete Musik*, so-called 'decadent music', a belated recognition of a long-neglected composer exiled to Britain in 1935. The Berlin Radio Symphony Orchestra under Lothar Zagrosek brings out the point and wit of the writing from the very start. If in the ragtime rhythms of the opening there are echoes of Kurt Weill, that likeness quickly evaporates. Goldschmidt even in his twenties was less abrasive than Weill, more sweetly lyrical, less brutal in presenting a savagely ironic piece. Based on a play by Fernand Cromelynck, it is a study of a man, Bruno, whose hysterical, unfounded jealousy of his devoted wife, Stella, makes Othello look like a beginner. His ability to believe that black is white is totally bizarre. The many switches of situation in the three compact Acts have a surreal absurdity, as Bruno progressively destroys what he wants most, the love of a devoted wife. Goldschmidt deftly compresses the original play to produce a colourful, fast-moving piece, with incidental figures well characterized and with complexities both of plot and of texture skilfully clarified. One only regrets that he does not allow himself more repose, and with it a more expansive lyricism. The tenor, Robert Wörle, as Bruno, and Roberta Alexander as Stella both give rich and brilliant performances.

Dating from almost 30 years after the opera, the *Mediterranean songs* reveal Goldschmidt's lyrical gift even more richly in colourful settings of such poets as Byron, Shelley and James Elroy Flecker, all beautifully sung by John Mark Ainsley. Outstandingly vivid recording in both opera and song-cycle.

Gombert, Nicolas (c. 1495–c. 1557)

Magnificat secundi toni; Missa Tempore paschali; Marian antiphon: Regina coeli. Motets: In te Domine speravi; Media vita. Chansons: Je prens congie; Tous les regretz. Regina coeli.
☞ *** Sony Dig. SK48249 [id.]. Huelgas Ens., Paul van Nevel.

Gombert was born in southern Flanders and was probably a pupil of Josquin; he composed a *déploration* on the death of Josquin in 1545. From 1526 he was a singer at the Court of the Emperor Charles V and *maître des enfants*. In his *Practica musica* (1556) the theorist, Hermann Finck, spoke of him as an innovator showing 'the exact way to refinement and the exact imitative style ... he avoids pauses, and his work is rich with full harmonies and imitative counterpoint'. Both his sacred and secular music is often dense in texture, and both genres are represented in this beautifully sung collection, an ideal introduction to his music. There is an unusually long, scholarly note by Paul van Nevel himself.

Gordon, Gavin (1901–70)

The Rake's Progress (ballet suite).
(M) (***) EMI mono CDH7 63911-2 [id.]. ROHCG O, Constant Lambert – LAMBERT: *Horoscope* etc.; RAWSTHORNE: *Street corner.* (***)

Gavin Gordon wrote his ballet based on Hogarth for the Sadler's Wells company in 1935. In its lively English idiom it had great success. The 1946 mono recording is astonishingly vivid.

Górecki, Henryk (born 1933)

Symphony No. 3 (Symphony of Sorrowful Songs), Op. 36.
*** Elektra Nonesuch Dig. 979282-2 [id.]. Dawn Upshaw, London Sinf., David Zinman.
☞ (BB) *** Belart 450 148-2; *450 148-4*. Zofia Kilanowicz, Polish State PO (Katowice), Swoboda.

(i) *Symphony No. 3 (Symphony of Sorrowful Songs), Op. 36; 3 Pieces in the olden style.*
☞ (BB) *** Naxos Dig. 8.550822 [id.]. Zofia Kilanowicz, Polish Nat. RSO, Antoni Wit.
☞ **(*) Koch Schwann 311041 [id.]. Stefania Woytowicz, Berlin RSO, Kamirski; or Warsaw CO, Karol Teutsch;

(i) *Symphony No. 3 (Symphony of sorrowful songs)* for soprano and orchestra; (ii) *3 pieces in olden style for string orchestra;* (iii) *Amen for choir.*
☞ **(*) Olympia OCD 313 [id.]. (i) Stefania Woytowicz, Polish R. Nat. SO (Katowice), Katlewicz; (ii) Warsaw Nat. Philharmonic CO, Teutsch (iii) Poznan Boys' Ch., Kurczewski.

Scored for strings and piano with soprano solo in each of the three movements, all predominantly slow, Górecki's *Symphony No. 3* sets three laments taking the theme of motherhood. The first movement, nearly half an hour long, resolves on the central setting of a fifteenth-century text from a monastic collection. The second movement incongruously brings a switch to a sensuously beautiful idiom, with the soprano solo soaring radiantly. The third movement is the setting of a folksong with a two-chord ostinato as accompaniment, concluding in a passage of total peace. The Sinfonietta's fine performance, beautifully recorded, is crowned by the radiant singing of Dawn Upshaw.

It is good to have two excellent super-bargain versions of this moving work, its intensity of feeling carried through from the composer's unforgettable and unforgotten visit to Auschwitz when he was still quite young. Katowice was where the symphony was written and the performance by the State Philharmonic is deeply felt, the hypnotic power of the undulating, arching climax of the first movement well caught. Zofia Kilanowicz's strong, richly timbred soprano contribution is well balanced with string textures that are satisfyingly full-bodied. There could perhaps be more variety of dynamic in the second and third movements, but the effect remains hypnotic.

The Naxos alternative has the advantage of digital recording, a wider dynamic range and, of course, background silence. The sound itself is full, but not quite as lavish as the Belart; on the other hand, detail is more refined and the focus more real. By the time she had come to re-record the work, Zofia Kilanowicz had obviously become even more immersed in the word-settings (the text is given in full in the excellent Naxos documentation) and, after Antoni Wit's restrained and austerely dark opening, her entry brings a glorious expansion of feeling, while in the folk colouring of the third movement the warm vocal colouring brings voluptuous reminders of Canteloube's Auvergne settings. In the work's closing section, with its hint of a gentle but remorseless tolling bell, Wit achieves a mood of simple serenity, even forgiveness. The *Three Pieces in olden style* make a fine postlude, the second with its dance figurations, the third with its fierce tremolando violins, like shafts of bright light, suddenly resolving to a very positive ending. All in all, this seems in many ways a 'best buy'.

The performance on Olympia shares the same soloist as the Koch alternative. Stefania Woytowicz sings this very rewarding solo part beautifully and the overall performance is very satisfying. The analogue sound is full and this disc not only includes the triptych of string pieces but also a brief but rather telling choral *Amen*. Excellent value.

The Koch performance is also most eloquent, with Woytowicz again completely at home in her solo role, but it is no more moving than either of the bargain versions and the analogue recording is not appreciably finer than that offered on Belart. It does, however, include the fine triptych of old-style string pieces and, if the bargain competition were not so great, would serve as a good choice. Many will feel that any of these issues are better value than the chart-topping and digitally recorded Zinman version on Elektra/Nonesuch. Fine though that is, it is still at premium price, offers no extra music and plays for only 54 minutes.

Genesis I (Elementi per tre archi); Sonata for 2 violins, Op. 10; String quartets Nos. 1 (Already it is dusk), Op. 62; 2 (Quasi una fantasia), Op. 64.
☞ *** Olympia OCD 375 [id.]. Silesian Qt.

This record (74 minutes) contains all Górecki's chamber music written so far. As a listening experience it is certainly stimulating but hardly reassuring. Indeed one could be forgiven for thinking that the composer is very pessimistic about the human condition. The opening of the *Double violin sonata* is harsh and spiky and, although calm soon descends, it is an uneasy calm and the restlessness soon reasserts itself in a return to the frenzied opening ostinatos. The *Adagio* is weird, with curious pizzicato comments which then take over to introduce the finale, but the resolution is aggressive. Whether or not the opening of *Genesis* is meant to simulate an air-raid siren, it is an extraordinary effect. Indeed this work is full of extraordinary effects: some of the scrapings and fizzings here are remarkably imaginative. If this is the beginning of life, the bubblings and glissandi suggest a volatile primeval melting pot. The playing is skilled and powerful, and at a concert this would surely create a sensation. The *First Quartet* opens with an emphatic chord which diminuendos; then mysticism takes over, with emphatic chordal interruptions; later there is a nagging ostinato which produces a climax of considerable power. Here the sustained rhythms remind one of the Stravinsky of *The Rite of spring* and the final tableaux of *Petrushka*, but the closing section returns to spare textures drenched in mystical feeling. The *Second Quartet* begins in an atmosphere of utter desolation; the effect is of a desperate plodding journey to nowhere: the music crescendos and then falls back. This is followed by a *Deciso* second movement, where an ostinato of strong repeated chords again dissolves into a more relaxed, yet still troubled, feeling. The *Arioso* slow movement begins in a mood of piercing despair – though, to be fair, there is a warmer, calmer interlude to follow. The finale is more positive with a dance element in its main idea. Yet it moves on with a remorseless, toccata-like insistence, then the slow plodding of the work's opening reappears and, gradually becoming less insistent, returns the music to infinity. The playing throughout this collection has extraordinary power and intensity, but this is a very different musical world from that of the composer's famous *Third Symphony*. The recording is of very high quality. The composer was present and there is something special about these performances.

Gottschalk, Louis (1829–69)

(i; iii) *Grande fantaisie triomphale on the Brazilian national anthem* (arr. Adler); (i; iv) *Grande tarantelle for piano and orchestra;* (iii) *Marche solennelle* (for orchestra and bands); *Marcha triunfal y final de opera;* (iv) *Symphonies Nos. 1 (A Night in the Tropics)* (ed. Buketoff); *2 (A Montevideo);* (i; iv) *The Union: Concert paraphrase on national airs* (arr. Adler); *Variations on the Portuguese national anthem for piano and orchestra* (ed. List). (ii) *5 Pieces* (for piano, 4 hands); (iv; v) *Escenas campestres (Cuban country scenes):* opera in 1 Act.

(B) **(*) VoxBox 1154842 (2) [CDX 5009]. (i) Eugene List; (ii) Cary Lewis & Brady Millican; (iii) Berlin SO, Adler; (iv) V. State Op. O, Buketoff; (v) with Paniagua, Estevas, Garcia.

This VoxBox offers a distinguished anthology, with obvious dedication from editors and executants alike. Eugene List was just the man to choose as soloist. Whether tongue-in-cheek or not, he manages to sound stylish throughout. There is no space here to dwell on the felicities of Gottschalk's elegant vulgarity. If you want Lisztian bravura, try the concertante pieces; if you fancy romanticism mixed with popular national dance rhythms, sample the two symphonies. The solo piano pieces (very forwardly recorded) are more variable. The programme ends with some attractive vocal music (the *Escenas campestres*), which is vividly sung. The recording is not of the very best quality, yet the effect, if sometimes two-dimensional, is always vivid and sparkling, and the bright, slightly hard piano timbre is not out of place here.

(i; ii) *Grande tarantelle for piano and orchestra;* (ii) *Symphony No. 1 (A Night in the tropics);* (iii) Music for one piano, four hands: *L'étincelle; La gallina; La jota aragonesa; Marche de nuit; Orfa; Printemps d'amour; Radieuse; Réponds-moi; Ses yeux; Souvenirs d'Andalousie; Tremolo.* (2 pianos): *The Union* (concert paraphrase on national airs).

☞ (M) *** Van. 08.4051 71. (i) Reid Nibley; (ii) Utah SO, Abravanel; (iii) Eugene List with Cary Lewis or Joseph Werner.

With nearly 77 minutes of music this well-recorded Vanguard reissue makes an ideal introduction to Gottschalk's music. The *Grande tarantelle* has a very catchy main theme which keeps returning and never wears out its welcome when the performance is so vivacious. As might be expected, the two-movement *Night in the tropics* uses its title of 'symphony' very loosely. It begins somewhat soupily, then in Abravanel's hands develops a full head of emotional steam; the second movement is a kind of samba, rhythmically very winning. The music for piano, four hands, is played with flair and scintillating upper tessitura. The opening arrangement of *La jota aragonesa* heads an ear-tickling programme, with a touch of wit in the piece called *Tremolo*. When the participants move to two pianos for *The Union* concert paraphrase, the acoustic expands and the effect is properly grand, yet the balance is not too close and the players are still able to produce delicate tonal contrasts. The orchestral recordings date from 1962, the piano pieces from 1976, and the sound is excellent throughout.

Piano music for four hands

La Bananier (Chanson nègre), Op. 5; La Gallina (Danse cubaine), Op. 53; Grande Tarantelle, Op. 67; La jota aragonesa (Caprice espagnol), Op. 14; Marche de nuit, Op. 17; Ojos Criollos (Danse cubaine – Caprice brillante), Op. 37; Orfa (Grande polka), Op. 71; Printemps d'amour (Mazurka-caprice de concert), Op. 40; Réponds moi (Danse cubaine), Op. 50; Radieuse (Grand valse de concert), Op. 72; La Scintilla (L'Etincelle – Mazurka sentimentale), Op. 21; Ses yeux (Célébre polka de concert), Op. 66.
**(*) Nimbus Dig. NI 5324 [id.]. Alan Marks & Nerine Barrett (piano, 4 hands).

Alan Marks and Nerine Barrett make an effervescent Gottschalk partnership, playing this repertoire to the manner born. *La jota aragonesa* shimmers with twinkling light, while the *Grande tarantelle* makes a splendid finale. The slight snag is that they are – very realistically – recorded in an empty, resonant hall.

Solo piano music

Bamboula; Le Bananier; Le Banjo; The Dying Poet; The Last hope; The Maiden's blush; Ojos Criollos; Pasquinade; La Savane; Souvenir de Porto Rico; Suis-moi!; Tournament galop.
☞ (M) *** Van. 08.4050.71 [OVC 4050]. Eugene List.

Eugene List made this repertoire very much his own in the USA in the late 1950s and early '60s, and his performances are second to none. The glittering roulades in *Le Bananier* and *Ojos Criollos* are brought off with unaffected brilliance, and the plucking imitations at the close of *The Banjo* are

equally successful. The pieces with sentimental titles are more appealing than their names might
suggest. The *Souvenir de Porto Rico*, a set of variations, is given real substance, and the *Tournament
galop* closes the recital at an infectious canter. The recording dates from 1956 but doesn't sound its
age at all: it is very well balanced and realistic – fuller than List's Vox recordings discussed in our
main volume.

*Le Bananier; Ballad No. 6; Bamboula; Le Banjo; Danza; The dying poet; The last hope; Pasquinade;
Souvenir de Porto-Rico; Union.*
☞ ** Erato/Warner Dig. 4509 94357-2 [id.]. Noel Lee.

This music is tailored by the pianist for the Michel Deville film, *Aux petits bonheurs*. It is all played
very personably and is never sentimentalized, but other Gottschalk collections have stronger characterization. The recording, however, is excellent.

Le Banjo; Berceuse (cradle song); *The dying poet* (meditation); *Grand Scherzo; The last hope*
(religious meditation); *Mazurk; Le Mancenillier* (West Indian serenade); *Pasquinade caprice; Scherzo
romantique; Souvenirs d'Andalousie; Tournament galop; The Union: Concert paraphrase de concert on
national airs (The Star-spangled banner; Yankee Doodle; Hail Columbia).*
*** Nimbus Dig. NI 5014 [id.]. Alan Marks.

Alan Marks plays with unassuming panache: his *Souvenirs d'Andalousie* glitter with bravura, his
felicity of touch and crisp articulation bring much sparkle to the *Grand scherzo* and *Scherzo
romantique*, while he sounds like a full orchestra in the *Tournament galop*. Most importantly, he finds
simplicity and charm in the delightful *Berceuse* and *Le Mancenillier*, while there is not a hint of
sentimentality in *The last hope* or *The dying poet*. He is most realistically recorded in a fairly
reverberant acoustic, which suits the flair of his playing.

Gould, Morton (born 1913)

Derivations for clarinet and band.
*** Sony MK 42227 [id.]. Benny Goodman, Columbia Jazz Combo, composer – BARTOK: *Contrasts;*
BERNSTEIN: *Prelude, fugue and riffs;* COPLAND: *Concerto;* STRAVINSKY: *Ebony concerto.* (***)

Gould's *Derivations* is in Gershwinesque mould. Benny Goodman is in his element, and the
accompaniment under the composer is suitably improvisatory in feeling.

Fall River legend (ballet; complete).
*** Albany Dig. TROY 035 [id.]. Brock Peters, National PO, Milton Rosenstock (with recorded
conversation between Agnes de Mille and Morton Gould).

This complete recording of *Fall River legend* opens dramatically with the Speaker for the Jury reading
out the Indictment at the trial, and then the ballet tells the story in flashback. Gould's music has a
good deal in common with the folksy writing in Copland's *Appalachian spring*, and it is given a
splendidly atmospheric performance and recording by the New York orchestra under Rosenstock.
There is also a 26-minute discussion on the creation of the ballet between Agnes de Mille and the
composer.

Fall River legend (ballet): *suite. Latin-American symphonette: Tango and Guaracha.*
☞ (M) *** BMG/RCA 09026 61505-2. O, composer – COPLAND: *Appalachian spring* etc. ***

Morton Gould's own recording of the suite from *Fall River legend* is so vivid and atmospheric that at
times one almost thinks this could be Copland. The two movements from the engaging *Latin-
American symphonette* are also splendidly done. With astonishingly full and vivid recording (made in
the New York Manhattan Center in 1960), triumphantly remastered by John Pfeiffer, the irresistibly
catchy *Guaracha* is demonstration-worthy.

Fall River legend: suite; Spirituals for string choir and orchestra.
(M) *** Mercury 432 016-2 [id.]. Eastman-Rochester SO, Howard Hanson – BARBER: *Medea: suite.*
***

The composer's orchestral suite from the ballet is vividly played by the Eastman-Rochester Orchestra
under the highly sympathetic Howard Hanson, who also gives an outstandingly vibrant account of
the *Spirituals*. The 1959/60 Mercury recording has astonishing clarity, range and presence.

Formations; (i) *Spirituals.*
*** Bay Cities BCD 1016 [id.]. Knightsbridge Symphony Band, Gould; (i) LSO, Susskind –
ANTHEIL: *Symphony No. 4.* **

Morton Gould subtitled *Spirituals* 'for string choir and orchestra' because the plan was to use the
strings as if they were a vocal choir. It is an attractive, bright piece in the received Copland tradition,
very well laid out for the chosen forces and excellently played by the LSO under Walter Susskind.
Formations is a later piece (1964), commissioned for either Marching or Concert Band; exhilarating
light music and played with real spirit and enthusiasm under the composer's own baton. Good sound
too.

Gounod, Charles (1818–93)

Faust: ballet music and Waltz.
☞ (B) **(*) Ph. Duo 438 763-2 [id.]. Rotterdam PO, David Zinman – DELIBES: *Coppélia;* CHOPIN:
Les Sylphides. **(*)
☞ (B) **(*) DG Double 437 404-2 (2) [id.]. BPO, Karajan – CHOPIN: *Les Sylphides* *** ⊛; DELIBES:
Coppélia (ballet) *suite;* OFFENBACH: *Gaîté parisienne;* RAVEL: *Boléro ***;* TCHAIKOVSKY:
Sleeping Beauty (suite). **(*)

If without quite the panache of a Beecham, David Zinman's account of the *Faust ballet music* springs
readily to life: it has polish and elegance, and the *Danse de Phryné* certainly does not lack gusto. The
Waltz is taken vivaciously fast. Very good (1980) recording in a warm acoustic ensures the listener's
aural pleasure, making this collection a genuine bargain.

Brilliant orchestral playing from the Berlin Philharmonic and vivid recording, very brightly lit.
But there is a degree of streamlining and the *Waltz,* though undoubtedly exuberant, lacks something
in charm. Even so, the polish of the playing is impressive. This comes in an excellent Double DG
anthology which as a whole is very good value.

Petite symphonie for winds.
☞ ** Koch Dig. 3-7067-2 [id.]. Sinfonia O of Chicago, Barry Faldner – DEBUSSY: *Symphony in B
min,;* MILHAUD: *Symphonies for chamber orchestra.* **

A very polished and professional account of Gounod's delightful *Petite symphonie,* as one would
expect from these first-desk players of the Chicago Symphony Orchestra. It is very well recorded too,
and yields to rivals only in wanting just the last ounce of charm that is surely essential in this music.

Symphonies Nos. 1 in D; 2 in B flat.
(M) **(*) EMI CDM7 63949-2. Toulouse Capitole O, Plasson.

Gounod's two *Symphonies* sound astonishingly youthful. In No. 1, the effortless flow of first-rate
ideas and the mastery, both of the orchestra and of symphonic form, is very striking. The *Second
Symphony* is very like the *First,* and both receive decent performance from Michel Plasson. The EMI
engineers have produced fresh, warm sound.

Symphony No. 1 in D; Petite symphonie in B flat for wind instruments.
*** Decca Dig. 430 231-2 [id.]. Saint Paul CO, Hogwood – BIZET: *L'Arlésienne.* ***

Instead of the *Second Symphony,* Hogwood offers the *Petite symphonie for winds,* which is engagingly
witty and civilized. Hogwood has the full measure of the *D major Symphony* and the outer
movements are infectious in their sprung rhythms. The Saint Paul Chamber Orchestra plays on
modern instruments. In the *Petite symphonie* the matching wind timbres have lots of character and
the bright horn articulation at the opening of the Scherzo is typical of the zest of the playing.
Excellent recording and an interesting Bizet coupling.

*Mélodies and songs: L'absent; The arrow and the song; Au rossignol; Ave Maria; Boléro; Ma belle
amie est morte; La Biondina* (song-cycle); *Ce que je suis sans toi; Chanson de printemps; Clos ta
paupière; Envoi de fleurs; The fountain mingles with the river; If thou art sleeping maiden; Ilala; A lay
of the early spring; Loin du pays; Maid of Athens; Mignon; My true love hath my heart; Oh happy
home! o blessed flower!; Où voulez-vous aller?; La Pâquerette; Prière; Rêverie; Sérénade; Le soir; Le
temps des roses; Trust her not!; Venise; The worker.*
☞ *** Hyp. Dig. CDA 66801/2 [id.]. Felicity Lott, Ann Murray, Anthony Rolfe Johnson, Graham
Johnson.

As in his Schubert series, also for Hyperion, Graham Johnson here brings a revelation, thanks not only to his inspired playing but also to his devising of an enchanting programme of 41 songs. It presents the full span of Gounod's achievement not just in French mélodie (on the first of the two discs) but also in songs Gounod wrote during his extended stay in England from 1871 to 1873, an exceptionally productive, though ultimately unhappy, period. The second disc contains both songs to English words, very like the drawing-room ballads of the time but with extra refinement and subtlety, and the cycle to Italian words, *Biondina*, also written in London. The lyrical innocence of the inspiration regularly conceals both the originality of the writing and the technical problems for the performers. The soloists here, all regular contributors to Johnson's Songmakers' Almanac, are at their very finest. So on the first disc, after charming performances of the opening items from Felicity Lott, Ann Murray enters magically, totally transforming the hackneyed lines of *Ave Maria*, before tackling the most joyous of Gounod songs, the barcarolle-like *Serenade*. Rolfe Johnson is comparably perceptive in *Biondina*, bringing out the Neapolitan-song overtones, as well as in six of the English settings. As in the Schubert series, Johnson's notes are a model of scholarship, both informed and fascinating.

Mélodies: *Crépuscule; Envoi de fleurs; Hymne à la nuit; Medjé; Si la mort est le but.*
☞ **(*) EMI Dig. CDC7 54818-2 [id.]. José van Dam, Jean-Philippe Collard – MASSENET; SAINT-SAENS: *Mélodies.* **(*)

As in Massenet and Saint-Saëns, José van Dam's firm, dark tone brings out the beauty of these five Gounod songs, even though he tends to miss the subtler shades of meaning, not always helped by Collard, heavier-handed here than in his solo playing.

Messe solennelle de Saint Cécile.
*** EMI Dig. CDC7 47094-2 [id.]. Hendricks, Dale, Lafont, Ch. and Nouvel O Philharmonique of R. France, Prêtre.

Gounod's *Messe solennelle*, with its blatant march setting of the *Credo* and sugar-sweet choral writing, may not be for sensitive souls, but Prêtre here directs an almost ideal performance, vividly recorded, with glowing singing from the choir as well as the three soloists.

Faust (complete).
☞ ❀ *** Teldec/Warner Dig. 4509 90872-2 (3) [id.]. Hadley, Gasdia, Ramey, Mentzer, Agache, Fassbaender, Welsh Nat. Op. Ch. & O, Rizzi.
*** EMI Dig. CDS7 54228-2 (3) [id.]. Leech, Studer, Van Dam, Hampson, Ch. & O of Capitole de Toulouse, Plasson.
(M) **(*) EMI CMS7 69983-2 (3) [Ang. CDMC 69983]. De los Angeles, Gedda, Blanc, Christoff, Paris Nat. Op. Ch. and O, Cluytens.

Carlo Rizzi's performance is a revelation. The excessive popularity for many generations of Gounod's operatic distortion of Goethe has latterly made it hard to take the piece seriously. Yet Rizzi with an outstanding cast and vividly clear recording makes the whole score with its astonishing sequence of memorable, tuneful numbers seem totally fresh and new. In number after number one marvels at Gounod's magic touch, not just as a tune-smith, but as a master of colour and clarity in the orchestra, with Rizzi springing rhythms infectiously and drawing incisive singing from the chorus. If the EMI version under Plasson offers a beefy, thrusting performance, together with a strong cast, Rizzi reminds one, generally with more spacious speeds, that such a strikingly eventful and expressive score is not totally unworthy of Goethe.

Jerry Hadley as Faust has lyrical freshness rather than heroic power, brought out in his headily beautiful performance of *Salut! demeure*. Yet here is a positive figure and, like Rizzi's conducting, his singing has more light and shade in it than that of rivals. The tenderness as well as the bright agility of Cecilia Gasdia's singing as Marguerite brings comparable variety of expression, with the *Roi de Thule* song deliberately drained of colour to contrast with the brilliance of the *Jewel song* which follows. Her performance culminates in an angelic contribution to the final duet, with Rizzi's slow speed encouraging refinement, leading up to a shattering moment of judgement and a fine apotheosis. Alexander Agache as Valentin may be less characterful than Hampson on the EMI set, but his voice is caught more richly; but it is the commandingly demonic performance of Samuel Ramey as Mephistopheles that sets the seal on the whole set, far more sinister than José van Dam on EMI. The clarity and precision of both performance and recording, so far from blunting the power of the piece, enhance it. Like the EMI set, the Teldec offers a valuable appendix, not just the full ballet music but numbers cut from the definitive score – a drinking song for Faust and a charming aria for Siebel. EMI's supplementary items, four, all different, are more generous, but musically less interesting.

With his excellent cast headed by three American singers, Plasson comes near to providing a completely recommendable *Faust*, even if José van Dam's gloriously dark, finely focused bass-baritone does not have the heft of a full-blooded bass voice such as is associated with the role of Mephistopheles. That said, it is a masterly performance, searching and sinister, with the singer consistently exploiting his idiomatic French. Cheryl Studer conveys the girlishness of Marguerite, using the widest range of dynamic and colour. If Richard Leech's voice might in principle seem too lightweight for the role of Faust, the lyrical flow and absence of strain make his singing consistently enjoyable. As Valentin, Thomas Hampson is strongly cast, with his firm, heroic baritone. Plasson's direction is more successful than any latterday rival in giving a rhythmic lift to Gounod's score, building the final trio the more compellingly by keeping power in reserve till the final stanza. The sound has a good sense of presence, set in a pleasantly reverberant acoustic which does not obscure necessary detail. In addition to supplementary numbers, the appendix offers the complete ballet music.

In the reissued Cluytens set, the seductiveness of De los Angeles's singing is a dream and it is a pity that the recording hardens the natural timbre slightly. Christoff is magnificently Mephistophelian. Gedda, though showing some signs of strain, sings intelligently, and among the other soloists Ernest Blanc has a pleasing, firm voice, which he uses to make Valentin into a sympathetic character. Cluytens's approach is competent but somewhat workaday.

Faust (opera): highlights.
☞ (M) *** EMI CD-EMX 2215 (from above complete set, with De los Angeles, Gedda; cond. Cluytens).

The one important snag in the EMI complete set was Cluytens's rather ungracious conducting. But in this generous 75-minute set of excerpts his crisp efficiency is more than acceptable. The singing gives much pleasure, particularly that of de los Angeles and Christoff, and the choral contribution is spirited. Excellent value and an ideal way of sampling a performance which had many virtues.

Mireille (complete).
☞ (M) (**) EMI mono CMS7 64382-2 (2) [id.]. Vivalda, Gedda, Gayraud, Dens, Ignal, Aix-en-Provence Festival Ch., Paris Conservatoire O, Cluytens.

Recorded in July 1954 immediately after live performances at the Aix-en-Provence Festival, this EMI set of *Mireille* is disappointing, not only thanks to limited mono sound but also to the performance, far too rigidly conducted by Cluytens to bring out the Provençal charm of this rustic opera, with even the *Farandole chorus* sounding stiff. The piece was first heard in March 1864, exactly five years after *Faust*, but it contains too little of the fresh, memorable lyricism that marks not only *Faust* but some of the earlier Gounod operas. As Mireille, Janette Vivalda sings unimaginatively with shrill, bright tone, not helped by the recording. Happily, the other soloists are more sympathetic. The young Nicolai Gedda sings most beautifully as the hero, Vincent, and the mezzo Christiane Gayraud is comparably rich as the gypsy, Taven, with Michel Dens ringingly clear, if hardly sinister, as the villain, Ourrias.

Sapho (complete).
☞ ** Koch Dig. 3-1311-2 (2) [id.]. Command, Coste, Papis, Faury, Sarrazin, St Etienne Lyric Ch., Nouvel O de St Etienne, Fournillier.

Gounod's very first opera, dating from 1851, was a failure, but this first complete recording shows how unfair that judgement was. The piece – which was not helped at the start by trouble with the censor – contains a sequence of delightful numbers, starting with a beautiful tenor aria, *Puis-je oublier*. There follows a splendid quartet, a baritone aria, *O liberté*, which provocatively hints at the *Marseillaise*, and some magnificent solos for the mezzo taking the title-role, culminating in a sombre and spacious suicide aria. Set in Mytilene, the piece fuses together the two Sapphos of ancient Greek history, the author of the sapphic poems and the Sappho who had an ill-starred passion for Phaon. Though the Saint-Etienne orchestra under Fournillier too often sounds limp, partly thanks to the washy live recording, the solo singing is strong enough to convey both the power and the beauty of much of the writing. The rich mezzo, Michèle Command, in the title-role is well contrasted with the sweet, bright soprano, Sharon Coste, as Glycère. Christian Papis as Phaon ably uses a head-voice to cope with stratospheric notes in the tenor role, and the young baritone, Eric Faury, is fresh and confident as the rival poet to Sappho, Alcée.

Gouvy, Louis Théodore (1819–98)

Aubade, Op. 77/2; Ghiribizzi, Op. 83; 6 Morceaux, Op. 59; Scherzo, P77/1; Sonatas: in D min., Op. 36; in C min., Op. 49; in F, Op. 51.

☞ ⊛ *** Sony Dig. SK 53110 [id.]. Yaara Tal, Andreas Groethuysen.

Louis Théodore Gouvy was born near Saarbrücken and was equally at home with French and German cultures. His ambition to be a virtuoso pianist came to nothing and, after studying law in Paris, he devoted himself to composition. His output is extensive and includes symphonies, cantatas and an opera, *Der Cid*, none of which has reached the catalogue. The present well-filled CD collects three sonatas for piano, four hands, and a number of other pieces. The artists themselves say that on first hearing they noticed clear affinities with Bizet, Mendelssohn, Offenbach and Schumann before becoming conscious of 'the uniqueness of his musical language'. They also speak of falling in love with this music at first sight, and this is how the playing sounds: beautifully shaped without being in the slightest bit beautified, every shading of colour and dynamic scrupulously observed without the slightest exaggeration. As piano duet playing, it is absolutely outstanding; so, too, is the recording.

Grainger, Percy (1882–1961)

Blithe bells (Free ramble on a theme by Bach: Sheep may safely graze): Country gardens; Green bushes (Passacaglia); Handel in the Strand; Mock morris; Molly on the shore; My Robin is to the greenwood gone; Shepherd's hey; Spoon River; Walking tune; Youthful rapture.
(M) *** Chan. CHAN 6542; MBTD 6542 [id.]. Bournemouth Sinf., Montgomery.

For those wanting only a single Grainger collection, this could be first choice. Among the expressive pieces, the arrangement of *My Robin is to the greenwood gone* is highly attractive, but the cello solo in *Youthful rapture* is perhaps less effective. Favourites such as *Country gardens, Shepherd's hey, Molly on the shore* and *Handel in the Strand* all sound as fresh as new paint. The 1978 recording, made in Christchurch Priory, has retained all its ambient character in its CD transfer.

Children's march; Colonial song; Country gardens; Handel in the Strand; The immovable 'Do'; Irish tune from County Derry; Mock Morris; Molly on the shore; My Robin is to the greenwood gone; Shepherd's hey; Spoon River.
☞ (M) ** Mercury 434 330-2 [id.]. Eastman-Rochester Pops O, Fennell – COATES: *Three Elizabeths suite.* **(*)

Lively and sympathetic performances from Fennell, and good playing. But the 1959 Mercury sound here is more dated than most CDs from this source: the acoustics of the Eastman Theatre in Rochester are too dry for Grainger's more expansive string writing in the *Colonial song* and the *Irish tune from County Derry*. The pithily rhythmic pieces like *Mock Morris* come off best as the sound is always clear and clean.

Children's march; Country gardens; Over the hills and far away; Irish tune from County Derry; The Lincolnshire posy; Molly on the shore.
☞ (M) *** EMI Dig. CDM5 65122-2. Central Band of the RAF, Wing Commander Eric Banks – HOLST: *Suites;* VAUGHAN WILLIAMS: *English folksong suite.* ***

Marvellously spirited and colourful performances from the RAF Central Band under Wing Commander Banks. His sense of pacing is exhilarating, yet the band produces a fine, full sonority for the famous *Londonderry air*, thanks to the acoustics of Watford Town Hall and the excellent engineering of Brian Culverhouse. There are few military band records to match this.

Irish tune from County Derry; Lincolnshire Posy (suite); Molly on the shore; Shepherd's hey.
(M) *** ASV CDWHL 2067. L. Wind O, Wick – MILHAUD; POULENC: *Suite française.* ***

First-class playing and vivid recording, with the additional attraction of delightful couplings, make this very highly recommendable.

'Dished up for piano', Volume 1: Andante con moto; Arrival platform humlet; Bridal lullaby; Children's march; Colonial song; English waltz; Gay but wistful; The Gum-suckers' march; Handel in the Strand; Harvest hymn; The immovable 'Do'; In a Nutshell (suite); In Dahomey; Mock morris; Pastoral; Peace; Sailor's song; Saxon twi-play; To a Nordic princess; Walking tune.
*** Nimbus Dig. NI 5220 [id.]. Martin Jones.

'Dished up for piano', Volume 2: Arrangements: BACH: *Blithe bells.* BRAHMS: *Cradle song.* Chinese TRAD.: *Beautiful fresh flower.* DOWLAND: *Now, o now, I needs must part.* ELGAR: *Enigma variations: Nimrod.* Stephen FOSTER: *Lullaby; The rag-time girl.* GERSHWIN: *Love walked in; The man I love.* RACHMANINOV: *Piano concerto No. 2: Finale* (abridged). R. STRAUSS: *Der Rosenkavalier: Ramble on the last love-duet.* TCHAIKOVSKY: *Piano concerto No. 1* (opening); *Paraphrase on the Flower waltz.*
**(*) Nimbus Dig. NI 5232 [id.]. Martin Jones.

'Dished up for piano', Volume 3: Folksong arrangements: *The brisk young sailor; Bristol Town; Country gardens; Died for love; Hard-hearted Barb'ra Helen; The hunter in his career; Irish tune from County Derry; Jutish medley; Knight and shepherd's daughter; Lisbon (Dublin Bay); The merry king; Mo Ninghean Dhu; Molly on the shore; My Robin is to Greenwood gone; One more day my John* (2 versions, easy and complex); *Near Woodstock Town; The nightingale and the two sisters; O gin I were where Gowrie rins; Rimmer and goldcastle; The rival brothers; Scotch Strathspey; Shepherd's hey; Spoon River; Stalt vesselil; Sussex mummer's Christmas carol; The widow's party; Will ye gang to the Hielands, Lizzie Lindsay.*
*** Nimbus Dig. NI 5244 [id.]. Martin Jones.

Martin Jones's survey of Grainger's piano music is refreshingly lively and spontaneous. Volume 1 is particularly attractive, and that is the place to start, for there is not a dull item here. There is plenty of dash in the folksong arrangements, and charm too, and they display a much greater range than one might have expected. The transcriptions are the most fascinating of all. The opening of the Tchaikovsky *Piano concerto* – some would say the 'best bit' – is transcribed straightforwardly, with a flamboyant flourish to finish it off, and the purple patch at the end of the Rachmaninov No. 2 cannot fail to make an impact in a performance as brilliant as this. Martin Jones is equally good in the freely composed pastiche on Bach's *Sheep may safely graze (Blithe bells)*. But he plays *Nimrod* and the *Der Rosenkavalier* excerpts too slowly; such a degree of languor might come off with the orchestra, but on the piano the effect is enervating. The piano is recorded reverberantly in the Nimbus manner – but it rather suits this repertoire, and the image is absolutely truthful.

Duke of Marlborough fanfare; Green bushes (Passacaglia); Irish tune from County Derry; Lisbon; Molly on the shore; My Robin is to Greenwood gone; Shepherd's hey; Piano duet: Let's dance gay in green meadow; Vocal & choral: *Bold William Taylor; Brigg Fair; I'm seventeen come Sunday; Lord Maxwell's goodnight; The lost lady found; The pretty maid milkin' her cow; Scotch strathspey and reel; Shallow Brown; Shenandoah; The sprig of thyme; There was a pig went out to dig; Willow willow.*
(M) *** Decca 425 159-2. Pears, Shirley-Quirk, Amb. S. or Linden Singers, Wandsworth Boys' Ch., ECO, Britten or Steuart Bedford; Britten and V. Tunnard (pianos).

This is an altogether delightful anthology, beautifully played and sung by these distinguished artists. Grainger's imagination in the art of arranging folksong was prodigious. Vocal and instrumental items are felicitously interwoven, and the recording is extremely vivid, though the digital remastering has put a hint of edge on the voices.

Granados, Enrique (1867–1916)

Cuentos para la juventud, Op. 1: Dedicatoria. Danzas españolas Nos. 4 & 5, Op. 37/4–5; Tonadillas al estilo antiguo: La Maja de Goya. Valses poéticos.
☞ ⊛ (M) *** BMG/RCA Dig. 09026 61608-2. Julian Bream – ALBENIZ: *Collection.* *** ⊛

Like the Albéniz items with which these Granados pieces are coupled, these performances show Julian Bream at his most inspirational. The illusion of the guitar being in the room is especially electrifying in the middle section of the famous *Spanish dance No. 5*, when Bream achieves the most subtle pianissimo. Heard against the background silence, the effect is quite magical. But all the playing here is wonderfully spontaneous. This is one of the most impressive guitar recitals ever recorded.

12 Danzas españolas; Allegro de concierto; El Pelele.
(M) *** Decca Analogue/Dig. 433 923-2 (2) [id.]. Alicia de Larrocha – ALBENIZ: *Suite española* etc.
***

Alicia de Larrocha has an aristocratic poise to which it is difficult not to respond, and she plays with great flair and temperament. *El Pelele* is an appendix to the *Goyescas* collection and comes as one of two brilliant encores (the sparkling *Allegro de concierto* is digitally recorded). The transfer of the 1982 analogue master to CD has been very successful.

Danzas españolas: Valenciana; Danza triste. Goyescas; El pelele.

☞ (M) (***) EMI mono CDC7 54836-2 [id.]. (i) Composer – FALLA: *Harpsichord concerto* etc.;
  MOMPOU: *Piano pieces;* NIN: *Cantos populares españolas.* (***)

One of the most valuable of the marvellously documented and beautifully restored 'Composers in Person' CDs that EMI have recently published. As is obvious from his music for the instrument, Granados was a formidable pianist and it was a pity that he did not live long enough to make electric recordings. The two *Danzas españolas* and *El pelele* from the *Goyescas* were recorded in Barcelona around 1912 but the engineers have done a marvellous job in restoring them, though they have not been able to remove all the surface noise in *El pelele* and the sound remains somewhat watery but gives a good idea of what an impressive and sensitive player he must have been. An indispensable disc for those with an interest in Spanish music and the piano.

Escenas románticas; Goyescas (complete); *6 Piezas sobre cantos populares españoles.*

❀ (M) *** Decca Dig./Analogue 433 920-2 (2). Alicia de Larrocha – ALBENIZ: *Sonata;* SOLER: *8 Sonatas.* ***

Alicia de Larrocha brings special insights and sympathy to the *Goyescas* (given top-drawer Decca sound in 1977); her playing has the crisp articulation and rhythmic vitality that these pieces call for, while she is hauntingly evocative in *Quejas o la maja y el ruisñor.* The overall impression could hardly be more idiomatic in flavour nor more realistic as a recording. The subtle, expressively ambitious *Escenas románticas* again show the surprisingly wide range of Granados's piano music. They were recorded digitally in 1985, as were the *6 Piezas sobre cantos populares españoles.*

Goyescas (complete); *Escenas románticas; Seis piezas sobre cantos populares españoles; Valses poéticos.*

☞ (M) *** EMI CMS7 64524-2 (2). Alicia de Larrocha.

Like her EMI version of Albéniz's *Iberia,* Alicia de Larrocha's set of *Goyescas* derives from the Spanish Hispavox catalogue and was made in 1963, a decade before her Decca set. The performance is more impulsive, at times more intensely expressive, if less subtle in feeling than the later version, and the recording, if not as fine as the Decca, is eminently realistic. The famous *Quejas, o la maja y el ruisenor* is memorably atmospheric and *El amor y la muerte* (which opens Part 2) is no less haunting. The rest of the programme also demonstrates her youthful spontaneity and the wide range of colour she could readily command. The closing *Zapateado* of the *Cantos populares españoles* has a fire and sparkle characteristic of her playing at this stage of her career. Alas, this fine disc has been withdrawn as we go to print.

Goyescas.

☞ *(*) DG Dig. 435 787-2. Jean-Marc Luisiada.

Jean-Marc Luisiada is a gifted Tunisian-born player, who commands both sensitivity and technical accomplishment. Unfortunately he proves an intrusive interpreter who permits the music to speak for itself only intermittently. His CD is not really a satisfactory alternative to Larrocha, who brings a special authority to this repertoire.

Grechaninov, Alexander (1864–1956)

String quartet No. 1 in G, Op. 2.

☞ **(*) Olympia OCD 522 [id.]. Shostakovich Qt – TCHAIKOVSKY: *Adagio molto* etc. **(*)

Alexander Grechaninov was enormously prolific, though little of his music has gained much more than a precarious foothold on the repertoire. (There are six operas, five symphonies and four quartets.) The *First Quartet in G major* (1894) is very much in the mould of Tchaikovsky and Rubinstein, and shows little individuality. It is unmemorable but is pleasing and well fashioned – and well played, too!

Greef, Arthur de (1862–1940)

Piano concerto No. 1 in C min.

☞ (M) ** EMI CDM5 65075-2 [id.) Jean-Claude vanden Eynden, Liège PO, Pierre Bartholmée – JONGEN: *Symphonie concertante.* **

Arthur de Greef is probably better known as a celebrated virtuoso pianist in the early part of the century and as the admired interpreter of the Grieg *Piano concerto* and as friend and champion of its composer. He was himself a composer, albeit of conservative outlook, and his output includes a symphony, some tone-poems and two piano concertos. The *First Piano concerto* comes from 1914 and its ethos is clearly that of Liszt, César Franck and Saint-Saëns, to whom the piece is dedicated. Some passages call Anton Rubinstein to mind, but de Greef has both facility and fantasy. Even if he does not have a strongly individual voice, he is a civilized composer and is well served by his countrymen, Jean-Claude vanden Eynden and the Liège Philharmonic under Pierre Bartholmée. The piano writing is perhaps a little unremitting at times, but readers who enjoy the Saint-Saëns concertos will find it rewarding. The analogue recording dates from 1977 and is well balanced and spacious. For all its charms, this is not three-star music, nor is it a three star recording; the playing, on the other hand, is!

Gregorian chant

'The Tradition of Gregorian Chant': Mass Propers and chants for Christmas (Spain); *Easter and Epiphany* (Switzerland); *Good Friday with processionals* (Germany); *other Feast Days* (Italy); *and Vespers* (France).
☞ (M) *** DG 435 032-2 (4) [id.]. Various monastic choirs.

Mass Propers for Good Friday and Easter.
☞ (M) *** DG 427 120-2 [id.]. Abteikirche Münsterschwarzach, Pater Godehard Joppich.
☞ (BB) **(*) Naxos Dig. 8.550951. Nova Schola Gregoriana, Alberto Turco.

Mass Propers for the Church Year.
☞ (BB) *** Naxos Dig. 8.550711. Nova Schola Gregoriana, Alberto Turco.

'The essential Gregorian chant': Antiphons; Gradualia; Hymns; Introitus; Offertories, Processional chants and prose; Sequence for Easter Day; Versus allèluiatici.
☞ **(*) United Recordings Dig. 88035CD [id.]. Pro Cantione Antiqua (James Griffett, Ian Partridge, Gordon Jones, Stephen Roberts, Michael George), James O'Donnell.

'Gregorian chant according to the Aquitaine tradition': Mass for St John the Baptist; Mass for the Nativity of Jesus Christ.
☞ ⊛ (B) *** HM HMA 190 3031 [id.]. Schola Hungarica, Jászló Dobszay or Janka Szendrei.

The liturgy of the Catholic Church has the Mass as its central focus. The Ordinary of the Mass – those elements that are unchanging through the Church year – have been set by countless composers and include the *Kyrie* ('Lord have mercy'), the *Gloria, Credo* and *Sanctus* ('Holy, holy, holy') and the *Agnus Dei*, which is undoubtedly the most important of all for believers ('Lamb of God, who takes away the sins of the world, have mercy on us and grant us peace'). The Mass Propers are chants which change with the seasons of the year or the occasion of the celebration; they consist of Introit, Gradual, Alleluia, Tract, Offertory and Communion. These are amplified by Sequences (accretions to the liturgy) and Tropes (additions which amplify and heighten the meaning of the biblical text in prose or poetry). The changes brought about by the reforming Council of Trent in the sixteenth century removed many of these additions, but they are at the heart of medieval Church music.

To evaluate Gregorian Chant in a volume of this kind is hazardous and essentially subjective. Although this music does give much aesthetic pleasure in that these chants are of great antiquity and beauty, their purpose is devotional and the singers are not 'professional' in any normal sense of the word. The recent vogue for the two-CD EMI set by the monks of the Monasterio Benedictino de Santo Domingo de Silos (EMI CMS5 65217-2) is not directly related to its aesthetic merit, and it would be not entirely appropriate to compare their singing to that from other monasteries as if one were discussing various orchestras, instrumentalist or singers. Gregorian chant does induce a spirit of serenity and repose, but a study of its growth and interpretation is a highly specialized subject.

A useful starting-point for the lay listener might be the four-CD DG set which assembles some of the many fine recordings made by DG's Archiv label during the period 1968–77. This set, called *Die tradition des Gregorianischen Chorals*, collects chant from two Spanish monasteries, Montserrat (1973) and Silos, Burgos (1968), the Abbey of Notre-Dame de Fontgombault in France (1977), the Kloster Maria Einsiedeln in Switzerland (1972), the Cappella Musicale del Duomo di Milano from Italy (1974), and the Abteikirche Münsterschwarzach in Germany. These four CDs include examples of almost all varieties of chant, Gregorian, Ambrosian and Old Spanish. Archive also offer a number of seasonal discs, such as the Gregorian Chant for Good Friday and Easter from the Abteikirche Münsterschwarzach, led by Pater Godehard Joppich and recorded in 1981–2, while an inexpensive

Naxos disc (with full texts provided, though no translations) by the Nova Schola Gregoriana, directed by the Italian scholar, Alberto Turco, covers this same area very effectively, and this choir are recorded in the Parish Church of Quatrelle, Mantua, which provides a suitably atmospheric setting. However, this fine choral group are heard to even better effect in an excellently chosen 75-minute compilation of chants taken from different Sundays in the Church year.

The opening *Adorate Deum*, which gives the record its title, comes from the Introit of the Third Sunday after the Epiphany, and other chants derive from the Second, Fourth, Eighth and Ninth Sundays after Epiphany, while there are also Gradualia, Versus Alleluiatici, Offertoria and Communions for the Fourth, Ninth, Seventh, Eighteenth, Nineteenth and Twenty-third Sundays after Pentecost, the Fourth Sunday in Quadragesima (the last Friday before Passion Sunday), the Third and Fourth Sundays of Lent, and Sundays within the Octave of the Feast of the Sacred Heart, and the Sunday within the Octave of Corpus Christi. The singing has a firm profile and is well recorded, not seeking to create a purely atmospheric effect. It is a pity that texts and translations are not provided, but the back-up notes are very helpful. Incidentally, this CD (Naxos 8.550711) was chosen by Brian Kay of the BBC's Radio 3 as part of 'Your starter collection of CDs' and it does seem to be a distinctive and inexpensive introduction to this repertory.

United Recordings enterprisingly offer something entirely different: performances by an excellent professional group, five well-known singers brought together by James O'Donnell. They are vividly recorded in St Alban's Church, Holborn, but the effect is rather one of concert performances, though of considerable character and refinement. The collection subdivides into six sections: Advent, Christmas, Sundays after Christmas, Lent, Holy Week and Easter. The programme opens with *Rorate caeli desuper*, a comparatively late chant with a striking line, and follows it with an Advent Antiphon (a plainsong setting of words which are independent of the liturgy and which could act as an adjunct to a Psalm, acting either as prelude and postlude or as a refrain between verses). Later we are to have the *Magnificat* antiphon for Christmas Day (there is a good deal of music for the Nativity included), two processional chants for Candlemas, Chants for Holy Week and a dramatic Good Friday responsory, *Tenebrae factae sunt*. The 71-minute programme ends with a Processional hymn for Easter Day. Unfortunately, this CD, which otherwise has adequate documentation, omits texts and translations.

Finally we come a collection which can be recommended without reservation, even to a collector not normally drawn to Gregorian melisma. The Chant of the Aquitaine tradition is quite different from anything else previously discussed, not least because it moves forward at a much faster pace, but also because the performances here use a choir which includes not only men but also both boy trebles and women's voices. The writer fairly recently attended a Mass in Chartres Cathedral in which women's voices participated to considerable effect, and so the sound here is undoubtedly authentic. While the men's voices remain dark-timbred and sonorous when singing alone, the soprano line is sweet, while the trebles are frequently plangent. For example, after they and the full choir have shared a radiant dialogue in the troped *Offertorium* of the *Mass for the Nativity*, the trebles re-enter in the *Ante communio cum tropis*, enthusiastically singing *Emitte Spiritum sanctum tuum* and seeking the Holy Spirit with lusty fervour. There is a similar thrilling surge of feeling towards the end of the *Mass for St John the Baptist* when, after the flowing *Communio cum tropis* ('Praevius hic de quo pater – Tu puer propheta Altissimi') in which men's and women's voices join together in octaves, the *Benedicamen* ('Catholicorum concio') brings glowing yet simple organum harmonization, and the Mass ends with an ecstatically florid troped *Alleluja*. The performances by the Schola Hungarica have remarkable feeling and rich, clean textures. The result is totally refreshing, and the choir is beautifully recorded within an ideal ambience: the Parish Church of Sainte Famille, Zugliget, Budapest.

Grieg, Edvard (1843–1907)

Piano concerto in A min. (original 1868/72 version); *Larvikspolka* (1858); *23 Small pieces* (1859).
☞ *** BIS Dig. CD 585 [id.]. Love Derwinger, Norrköping SO, Hirokami.

In all – so Dr Allen Ho's excellent notes tell us – there have been *at least* 137 recordings of this celebrated piano concerto, but this is a version with a difference. All his life Grieg tinkered with his orchestration of the *Piano concerto* and made no fewer than seven versions of the score, the last in 1907, only a few weeks before his death. In the first version many of the familiar orchestral landmarks are absent: the lyrical second theme of the first movement appears on solo trumpet rather than the cellos; the brief dialogue between horn and cello in the *Adagio*, which Gerald Abraham called 'one of the most memorable points in the whole score', is not there, the material being allocated to the first violins. Grieg did not have the natural flair for orchestration that his countryman and contemporary, Svendsen, possessed and this release is valuable in showing how slow his orchestral skills were in developing. This CD offers us a fascinating glimpse of how the concerto must have sounded to its contemporaries, for it was this, not the familiar version, which enraptured audiences in the 1870s and '80s. Love Derwinger is the intelligent and accomplished soloist with the Norrköping orchestra, and he proves a sensitive guide in the collection of juvenilia that completes the disc. The *Larvikspolka*, written when Grieg was fifteen, is probably the very earliest of his piano pieces to survive, and the *Nine Children's Pieces* included in the set of *23 Small pieces* were written during his first months at the Leipzig conservatory. They are all very slight in substance, but they fill out the picture of the young composer and the world in which he grew up. The concerto is well balanced and Love Derwinger's solo pieces are well recorded too.

Historic recordings:
Disc 1: (i) *Piano concerto in A min., Op. 16. Album leaf, Op. 28/4; Ballade in G min., Op. 24; Lyric pieces: Op. 12/4, 5; Op. 38/1, 2, 5; Op. 43/1, 4; Op. 47/6; Op. 54/1, 3; Op. 68/5.*
☞ (*(*)) BMG/RCA mono GD 60897 [id.]. Rubinstein, (i) with Phd. O, Ormandy.

Disc 2: (i) *String quartet in G min., Op. 27;* (ii) *Violin sonata No. 3 in C min., Op. 45;* (iii) *Album leaf, Op. 28/2;* (iv) *The last spring.*
☞ (***) BMG/RCA mono 09026 61826-2. (i) Budapest Qt; (ii) Kreisler, Rachmaninov; (iii) Elman; (iv) Boston SO, Koussevitzky.

Disc 3: Songs: *And I shall have a true love; At the brook; Bilberry slopes; A Dream* (3 versions); *Eros; Good morning; Greeting; I love thee* (5 versions); *In the boat; The mother sings; The Norse people; To Norway; A swan* (3 versions); *With a primrose; With a water lily* (2 versions); *Peer Gynt: Solveig's cradle song; Solveig's song.*
☞ (**(*)) BMG/RCA mono 09026 61827-2. Björling; Crooks; Farrar; Flagstad; Frijsh; Galli-Curci; Kline; Krogh; Marsh; Melchior; Nilsson; Schumann-Heink; Traubel.
☞ (**) (M) BMG/RCA mono 09026 61879-2 (3) [id.]: Discs 1–3 complete.

The three-CD RCA set has the great advantage of being available singly. The first disc couples Rubinstein's 1942 recording of the *Piano concerto* with the Philadelphia Orchestra under Ormandy with the 1953 recordings he made in Hollywood of the *G minor Ballade* and some of the *Lyric pieces*. This account of the *Concerto* has brilliance and sensitivity but is a little wanting in spontaneity. Rubinstein does not leave you with the impression that you are hearing this familiar music for the first time, as so many performers on record, from Curzon, Lupu and Kovacevich down to the recent Andsnes, have done. The 78 surface-noise, while not disturbing, is probably more discernible than some collectors would like, and the end of the second side of the 78-r.p.m. set used for this transfer is excessively busy. Nor are the solo pieces distinguished by the poetry and freshness one might expect. The *Lyric pieces* do not begin to compare with Gilels, and both they and the *Ballade*, arguably Grieg's most deeply felt piano work, are recorded in a shallow and claustrophobic acoustic environment.

The second CD brings the famous 1928 Kreisler–Rachmaninov set of the Op. 45 *C minor Sonata*, already available in RCA's ten-CD Rachmaninov retrospective. This has been available on LP at various times, but the superb (1937) Budapest version of the *G minor String quartet* has not (to the best of our knowledge) been reissued in the UK since the days of shellac. It is a masterly performance, with splendid grip but at the same time great lyrical warmth and freshness. Whether or not it has been equalled subsequently is arguable, but it has surely not been surpassed. The eloquence of the Boston Symphony Orchestra's strings in the days of Koussevitzky was legendary and their seamless phrasing and glorious tone shine vibrantly through the years.

With such celebrated singers as Björling, Farrar, Flagstad, Galli-Curci and Melchior represented on the generously filled last disc, RCA's song compilation is self-recommending. One might regret the absence of Flagstad's earliest *Haugtussa*, particularly when there are several duplications, but no doubt it will appear in subsequent reissues. Given the quality and interest of the singing, this CD will no doubt be eagerly sought by collectors. The transfers are acceptable, though not in any way superior to the specialist issues one encounters of this repertoire on the Danacord label.

Piano concerto in A min., Op. 16.
*** Ph. 412 923-2. Kovacevich, BBC SO, Sir Colin Davis – SCHUMANN: *Piano concerto.****
*** Sony Dig. MK 44899 [id.]. Perahia, Bav. RSO, C. Davis – SCHUMANN: *Concerto.* ***
(B) *** Decca 433 628-2 [id.]. Curzon, LSO, Fjeldstad – FRANCK: *Symphonic variations* *** ⊛; SCHUMANN: *Concerto.* **(*)
☞ *** EMI Dig. CDC7 54746-2 [id.]. Lars Vogt, CBSO, Rattle – SCHUMANN: *Concerto.* ***

(B) *** CfP Dig. CD-CFP 4574 [id.]. Pascal Devoyon, LPO, Maksymiuk – SCHUMANN: *Piano concerto*. ***

☞ (B) *** EMI Dig. CDU5 65057-2 [id.]; *EU 565057-4*. Cécile Ousset, LSO, Marriner – RACHMANINOV: *Piano concerto No. 2* etc. ***

(M) **(*) Decca 417 728-2 [id.]. Radu Lupu, LSO, Previn – SCHUMANN: *Concerto*. **(*)

(M) (***) EMI mono CDH7 63497-2. Lipatti, Philh. O, Galliera – with: CHOPIN: *Piano concerto No. 1*. (**)

☞ (M) ** BMG/RCA 09026 61262-2. Artur Rubinstein, O, Wallenstein – TCHAIKOVSKY: *Piano concerto No. 1*. ***

☞ ** DG Dig. 439 015-2 [id.]. Krystian Zimerman, BPO, Karajan – SCHUMANN: *Concerto*. **(*)

☞ (B) *(*) Erato/Warner Dig. 4509 92872-2 [id.]. Duchable, Strasbourg PO, Guschlbauer – RACHMANINOV: *Piano concerto No. 2*. **(*)

Piano concerto in A min.; In autumn, Op. 11; Lyric suite, Op. 54.
☞ ** DG Dig. 437 524-2 [id.]. Lilya Zilberstein, Gothenburg SO, Neeme Järvi.

(i) *Piano concerto in A min. 6 Lyric pieces, Op. 65.*
*** Virgin/EMI Dig. VC7 59613-2 [id.]. Leif Ove Andsnes, (i) Bergen PO, Dmitri Kitaenko – LISZT: *Piano concerto No. 2*. ***

Whether in the clarity of virtuoso fingerwork or the shading of half-tone, Kovacevich is among the most illuminating of the many great pianists who have recorded the Grieg *Concerto*. He plays with bravura and refinement, the spontaneity of the music-making bringing a sparkle throughout, to balance the underlying poetry. The 1972 recording has been freshened most successfully.

Perahia revels in the bravura as well as bringing out the lyrical beauty in radiantly poetic playing. He is commanding and authoritative when required, with the blend of spontaneity, poetic feeling and virtuoso display this music calls for. He is given sympathetic support by Sir Colin Davis and the fine Bavarian Radio Symphony Orchestra, and there is no finer version of the Grieg recorded in the digital age than this.

Curzon's approach to Grieg is wonderfully poetic and this is a performance with strength and power as well as lyrical tenderness. This ranks alongside Kovacevich and Perahia and the reading is second to none in distilling the music's special atmosphere. The sound is bright and open and the recording hardly shows its age in this crisply focused CD transfer.

The young German pianist Lars Vogt made his name at the 1990 Leeds Competition when he established an obvious rapport with Simon Rattle at the final concerto round, and their partnership on CD is equally successful. He proves a highly sympathetic and imaginative interpreter who makes this familiar music sound even more fresh than it does in more routine accounts (although it seldom loses its freshness entirely; of all the famous romantic concertos it seems the most indestructible). Vogt never allows his personality to obtrude; he colours the familiar phrases with great subtlety yet without the slightest trace of narcissism. He is very well supported by Rattle and the CBSO, and excellently recorded. An unusually sensitive player, his version, with the inevitable Schumann coupling, is eminently satisfying. Curzon, Kovacevich, Lupu and Perahia are top recommendations, but among newcomers this has the strongest claims to be put among them.

Pascal Devoyon's account of the Grieg *Concerto* is characteristic of him: aristocratic without being aloof, pensive without being self-conscious, and brilliant without being flashy. He is a poetic artist whose natural musicianship shines through, and this excellent account is very competitive. This is a very fine issue, with excellent playing from the LPO under Jerzy Maksymiuk.

Ousset's is a strong, dramatic reading, not lacking in warmth and poetry but, paradoxically, bringing out what we would generally think of as the masculine qualities of power and drive. The result, with excellent accompaniment and recorded in very full sound, is always fresh and convincing. A good choice for anyone wanting this unusual coupling with the Rachmaninov *Concerto No. 2*.

Andsnes wears his brilliance lightly. There is no lack of display and bravura here, but no ostentation. Indeed he has great poetic feeling and delicacy of colour, and Grieg's familiar warhorse comes up with great freshness. His piano is in perfect condition (not always the case on records) and is excellently balanced in relation to the orchestra. This is one of the best modern accounts.

Radu Lupu's recording dates from 1974 and is now even more brightly lit than it was originally, not entirely to advantage. But the performance is a fine one; there is both warmth and poetry in the slow movement; the hushed opening is particularly telling. The orchestral contribution under Previn is a strong one.

The famous 1947 Lipatti performance remains eternally fresh, and its return to the catalogue is a cause for rejoicing, although the ear now notices a slightly drier quality and a marginal loss of bloom.

Rubinstein usually has something interesting to say about any major concerto; it is a great pity that his partner here, Alfred Wallenstein, shows little sensitivity or imagination in his handling of the light-textured but all-important orchestral contribution. Nevertheless Rubinstein produces some marvellously poetic and aristocratic playing towards the end of the slow movement, and the finale is both commanding and exciting, even if the orchestral response is aggressive. The remastering has produced a bold piano-image; the orchestral sound is bright and rather two-dimensional. The coupled Tchaikovsky *Concerto* is infinitely finer in all respects.

The digital remastering of Zimmerman's DG recording for the Karajan Gold series has greatly improved the sound: it is warm and full, and the piano image is wholly natural, forwardly balanced but not excessively so. But Zimerman and Karajan do not seem an ideal partnership here. There are, of course, many things to admire from this remarkable young pianist, but neither concerto on this CD conveys the sense that these artists are enjoying themselves very much, and there is a certain want of freshness. Judged by the standards he has set himself, Zimerman is neither as illuminating nor, indeed, quite as sensitive as one would expect in this most gentle and poetic of scores.

Lilya Zilberstein is a commanding artist with firm fingers, a good feeling for architecture and a fine musical intelligence. In the Grieg, of course, flamboyance has to go hand in hand with poetic feeling, and she has that too, though not in such strong supply as Lars Vogt. Zilberstein gives what one might call a good narrative performance – she holds your attention from moment to moment. Her playing could never be called routine, but her view is quite conventional, while Vogt brings fresh insights. Her coupling offers more Grieg, the *Lyric Suite* and the *Overture, In Autumn*, which DG released on an earlier Grieg CD. (*In Autumn* was previously coupled with the *Symphony in C minor*, and the *Lyric Suite* with the *Symphonic dances*, so that many collectors will find this involves unwelcome duplication.)

Although brilliant and even exciting, François-René Duchable's account of the Grieg *Concerto* misses almost all its gentler, tender qualities. The Rachmaninov coupling suits this soloist much better.

(i) *Piano concerto in A min.*; (ii; iii) *Holberg suite, Op. 40; Lyric suite, Op. 54*; (iv; iii) *4 Symphonic dances, Op. 64*; (ii; iii) *Peer Gynt* (incidental music): *suites Nos. 1, Op. 46; 2, Op. 55*. (v) (Piano) *Lyric pieces, Op. 12: Album leaf; Arietta; Fairy dance; National song; Norwegian melody; Popular melody; Waltz; Watchman's song; Op. 43: Butterfly; Erotikon; In my native country; Little bird; Solitary traveller; To Spring.*
☞ (M) **(*) Ph. Duo 438 380-2 (2) [id.]. (i) Kovacevich, BBC SO, C. Davis; (ii) ECO; (iii) Raymond Leppard; (iv) Philh. O; (v) Zoltán Kocsis.

Including as it does the highly praised Kovacevich/Davis account of the *Piano concerto*, so imaginatively illuminating, this bargain-priced anthology does indeed include much of 'The best of Grieg', if one leaves aside the vocal music. Leppard's performances of the two *Peer Gynt suites* are fresh, and all his performances here have an air of thoughtfulness which will appeal to many, especially as the orchestral playing is so good. However, in the slow movements of the *Holberg suite* and also occasionally in *Peer Gynt* there is just a hint of a lack of vitality. *In the hall of the Mountain King*, for instance, opens slowly then does not build up quite the head of steam one expects. The *Lyric suite*, however, is beautifully done, and the four *Symphonic dances*, recorded digitally, are also very successful with a refined response from the Philharmonia. What makes the collection especially attractive is the inclusion of 14 of the *Lyric pieces*, played by Zoltán Kocsis with much character. Perhaps he is a bit impetuous at times (as in the *Fairy dance*), but his approach certainly suits *To Spring*, his last item.

(i) *Piano concerto in A min.*; (ii) *Peer Gynt suites Nos. 1–2.*
☞ (B) **(*) DG 439 427-2 [id.]. (i) Géza Anda, BPO, Kubelik; (ii) BPO, Karajan.

Anda's account of the *Piano concerto* is more wayward than some but is strong in personality and has plenty of life. Kubelik's accompaniment is good too, and the 1963 recording sounds well. However, Karajan's analogue *Peer Gynt suites* are in a class of their own. They were also recorded – a decade later – in the Berlin Jesus-Christus-Kirche but, for some reason, the CD transfer seems very brightly lit, although the fullness and analogue ambience is retained. They are played with much expressive feeling and demonstrate superlative orchestral skill and polish, yet at the same time sound admirably fresh: they have far more character than most of their bargain competitors.

2 Elegiac melodies, Op. 34; Erotik; 2 Melodies, Op. 53; 2 Norwegian airs, Op. 63.
(BB) **(*) Naxos Dig. 8.550330; *4550330* [id.]. Capella Istropolitana, Adrian Leaper – SIBELIUS: *Andante festivo* etc. **

Adrian Leaper secures responsive and sensitive playing from the Capella Istropolitana in this Grieg collection, and the recording is very good indeed and the balance natural.

2 Elegiac melodies; Holberg suite, Op. 40.
☞ (BB) **(*) ASV CDQS 6094 Swiss CO – SUK; TCHAIKOVSKY: *String serenades.* ***

The Swiss Chamber Orchestra take the first movement of the *Holberg suite* very briskly, but it is an enjoyably spick-and-span account, with good lyrical contrast; although the *Elegiac melodies* lack opulence, these brightly recorded performances make a good bonus for outstanding versions of the Suk and Tchaikovsky *Serenades.*

2 Elegiac melodies (Heart's wounds; The last spring), Op. 34; Holberg suite, Op. 40; 2 Lyric pieces (Evening in the mountains; At the cradle); 2 Melodies (Norwegian; The first meeting), Op. 53; 2 Nordic melodies (In folk style; Cow-call), Op. 63.
☞ *** DG Dig. 437 520-2 [id.]. Gothenburg SO, Neeme Järvi.

A most attractive and well-designed anthology. The *Holberg suite,* opening athletically, has not quite the ultimate polish and charm of Karajan's version but it is presented with much character, and the other folk melodies bring some beautiful playing from the Gothenburg strings. The two lovely *Elegiac melodies* sound freshly minted and the innocent appeal of the much less familiar *Nordic melodies* is fully captured. These are all works for string orchestra, save the first of the two *Lyric pieces, Evening in the mountains,* where the effect of oboe solo – backwardly placed as the composer intended – is piquantly and engagingly managed. The following *Cradle song* is very touching. Excellent, bright, modern recording with a good ambient effect.

(i) *2 Elegiac melodies, Op. 34; Lyric suite, Op. 54: Norwegian march and Nocturne. Norwegian dance, Op. 35/2;* (i) *Peer Gynt suites Nos. 1–2 (including Solveig's lullaby);* (i) *Sigurd Jorsalfar: Homage march, Op. 56/3.*
☞ (B) *** Sony SBK 53257 [id.]. (i) Phd. O, Ormandy; (ii) Elisabeth Söderström, New Philh. O, Andrew Davis.

Andrew Davis offers freshly thought performances of the two *Peer Gynt suites,* beautifully played and warmly recorded at Abbey Road in 1976. A special attraction is the singing of Elisabeth Söderström, not only in *Solveig's song* but also in *Solveig's lullaby,* which has been added to the second suite. The Ormandy recordings date from a decade earlier but they make up a most attractive anthology. The orchestral playing is very good indeed and Ormandy's warmth is obvious. The transfers are well managed.

Holberg suite, Op. 40.
(B) *** Pickwick Dig. PCD 861; *CIMPC 861* [id.]. Serenata of London – ELGAR: *Serenade;* MOZART: *Eine kleine Nachtmusik.* ***

The performance by the Serenata of London is first class in every way, spontaneous, naturally paced and played with considerable eloquence. The digital recording is most realistic and very naturally balanced. A bargain.

Holberg suite, Op. 40; Peer Gynt suites Nos. 1 & 2.
☞ *** DG Gold Dig. 439 010-2 [id.]. BPO, Karajan – SIBELIUS: *Finlandia; Valse triste; Swan of Tuonela.* ***

This is one of the very finest of the remastered digital reissues (using Original-image-bit processing) in the Karajan Gold series. Karajan's performance of the *Holberg suite* is the finest currently available. The playing has wonderful lightness and delicacy, with cultured phrasing not robbing the music of its immediacy. There are many subtleties of colour and texture revealed here by the vividly present recording, clear and full and with a firm bass-line. The remastered *Peer Gynt suites* show an even more remarkable improvement, especially the thrillingly gusty *In the hall of the Mountain King.* Grieg's perennially fresh score is marvellously played. *Anitra* dances with elegance, and the *Death of Aase* is movingly eloquent. The digital recording now proves to be one of the best to have emerged from the Philharmonie in the early 1980s.

In Autumn overture, Op. 11; Lyric piece: Erotik, Op. 43/5; Norwegian dances, Op. 35; Old Norwegian romance with variations, Op. 51.
☞ *** Chan. Dig. CHAN 9028 (id.]. Iceland SO, Sakari (with SVENDSEN: *2 Icelandic melodies* for strings ***).

The Iceland orchestra play very responsively for their Finnish conductor, Petri Sakari, who gives very natural and straightforward accounts of this endearing music. There are no egocentric interpretative touches or unwelcome tonal sophistication; this is a kind of music-making one had thought belonged to a bygone age in these days of jet-setting virtuoso conductors. Highly musical performances, with no lack of personality, very truthfully recorded. Very recommendable.

Lyric suite, Op. 54; Norwegian dances, Op. 35; Symphonic dances, Op. 64.
*** DG Dig. 419 431-2 [id.]. Gothenburg SO, Järvi.

Excellent playing from the Gothenburg orchestra under Neeme Järvi. He secures light and transparent textures and finely balanced sonorities throughout. Very fine, wide-ranging recording, which makes excellent use of the celebrated acoustic of this orchestra's hall.

Lyric suite, Op. 54; Sigurd Jorsalfar (suite), Op. 56; Symphonic dances, Op. 64.
**(*) ASV Dig. CDDCA 722 [id.]. RPO, Yondani Butt.

The *Symphonic dances* are particularly successful here. They are not easy to bring off, yet Butt and the RPO capture their charm and energy without succumbing to melodrama in No. 4. The *Lyric suite*, too, is fresh and the trolls in the finale have an earthy pungency. However, the outer movements of *Sigurd Jorsalfar* bring an element of ponderousness. Excellent, vivid recording.

Symphonic dances, Op. 64; Sigurd Jorsalfar (suite), Op. 56; (i) Peer Gynt: Solveig's song: Solveig's lullaby. Songs: Fra Monte Pincio; En Swan; Våren; Henrik Wergeland.
☞ **(*) Chan. Dig. CHAN 9113 [id.]. (i) Solveig Kringelborn; Royal Stockholm Philh. O, Rozhdestvensky.

Like the Op. 51 variations, the *Symphonic dances*, Op. 64, began life in keyboard form; but after Grieg had scored them he wrote to his publisher that they should be performed together as a group and not separately. They certainly make a stronger impact when all four are heard together. Rozhdestvensky and his fine Swedish orchestra offer them and the popular *Sigurd Jorsalfar suite*, Op. 56, and, sandwiched in between, a group of songs with the young Norwegian soprano, Solveig Kringelborn. She has a light, pretty voice, though she is a little short on imagination; most of the songs tend to sound much the same. But the orchestral pieces are excellently done, and Chandos provide recording quality of the utmost naturalness and presence.

Symphony in C min.; In Autumn: Overture, Op. 11; Old Norwegian melody with variations, Op. 51; Funeral march in memory of Rikard Nordraak.
*** DG Dig. 427 321-2 [id.]. Gothenburg SO, Järvi.

This is the best recording of the Grieg *Symphony* to appear so far, both artistically and as a recording. Indeed Järvi produces excellent, fresh accounts of all four works on the disc. Most natural and unaffected performances, beautifully balanced.

Symphony in C min.; Symphonic dances, Op. 64.
☞ ** Virgin/EMI Dig. VC7 59301-2 [id.]. Bergen PO, Dmitri Kitaienko.
☞ * Simax Dig. PSC1091 [id.]. Lithuanian Nat. SO, Terje Mikkelsen.

Kitaienko and the Bergen Philharmonic offer a well-prepared account of the early Grieg *Symphony*, a student work which the composer disowned after he had heard the first performance of the Svendsen *D major Symphony*. It is not particularly characteristic and, though Grieg may have been unduly self-critical in condemning it to total oblivion, it does not hold a candle to the Svendsen. It is well enough recorded here, but the performance is by no means as persuasive as the earlier reading by Neeme Järvi. Nor does Kitaienko's account of the *Symphonic Dances* displace Järvi.

The enterprising Norwegian Simax label have much interesting repertoire to their credit, but their coupling of the *Symphonic dances* and the *C minor Symphony* is not really a success. The playing is not particularly distinguished and the *Symphonic dances* sound somewhat prosaic in Terje Mikkelsen's hands.

CHAMBER MUSIC

Andante con moto for piano trio.
☞ *(*) Victoria Dig. VCD 19079 [id.]. Nilsson, Kvalbein, Bratlie – MARTIN: *Trio sur des mélodies populaires irlandaises;* TCHAIKOVSKY: *Trio.* *

Grieg began a piano trio in 1878 and, like the second quartet on which he embarked in 1891, it remained unfinished. His widow Nina sent the manuscript to his life-long friend, Julius Röntgen, for comment. While the quartet was published, the *Andante con moto* remained in manuscript, despite Röntgen's positive reaction, until the appearance of the Grieg *Gesamtausgabe* in 1978. If it is not as characteristic or as individual as the two movements comprising the *Second Quartet*, it has charm and a certain eloquence. The Oslo Trio give it a persuasive and convincing performance, as they do the remainder of this well-planned disc. Unfortunately the close balance permits only a qualified recommendation and, though this is perhaps less worrying here than in the Tchaikovsky, it diminishes the attractions of this issue.

Cello sonata in A min., Op. 36.
*** Claves CD 50-703 [CD 703]. Claude Starck, Ricardo Requejo – CHOPIN: *Cello sonata.* ***
**(*) CRD CRD 3391; *CRD C 4091* [id.]. Robert Cohen, Roger Vignoles – FRANCK: *Cello sonata.* **(*)

The Grieg *Sonata* is gratefully written for both instruments and the work undoubtedly enriches the cellist's relatively small repertoire. Both Starck and his Spanish partner play with a superb and compelling artistry.

In the folk element Cohen might have adopted a more persuasive style, bringing out the charm of the music more, but certainly he sustains the sonata structures well. The recording presents the cello very convincingly. It has been most naturally transferred to CD.

Cello sonata in A min., Op. 36; Jeg elsker dig, Op. 5/3.
☞ *(*) Pickwick Dig. MCD 72 [id.]. Tim Hugh, Yonty Solomon – RACHMANINOV: *Cello sonata* etc. **

Timothy Hugh's account of the *Sonata* is full-blooded to the point of over-dramatization. He wears his heart not on his sleeve but all the way down to his cuffs. Thus much of the intimacy of Grieg's world is lost sight of, and the high emotional temperature evoked seems somehow out of keeping with his muse. Powerful playing, but open to the charge of being really a bit over-intense.

String quartet No. 1 in G min., Op. 27.
☞ *** Unicorn Dig. DKPCD 9092 [id.]. English Qt – SCHUMANN: *String quartet No. 3.* ***

String quartet No. 1 in G min., Op. 27; String quartet No. 2 in F (unfinished); Fugue (1861).
☞ *** Victoria Dig. VCD 19048 [id.]. Norwegian Qt.
☞ **(*) BIS Dig. CD 543 [id.]. Kontra Qt.

The *String quartet in G minor* served as a model for Debussy's quartet in the same key, and when Delius once declared that 'modern French music is Grieg and Grieg alone, plus the prelude to the third act of Wagner's *Tristan*', Ravel is said to have nodded in assent: '*C'est vrai. Nous sommes toujours très injuste envers Grieg.*' Grieg used his relatively recent Ibsen setting, *Spillemaend*, as a unifying figure. The Norwegian Quartet may not be as immaculate in terms of tonal blend or ensemble as their principal rival, the Guarneri on Philips, a very chromium-plated affair coupled with Sibelius's *Voces intimae*, but they do at least make it sound as if the piece is played by people. It also comes with an interesting makeweight, the two movements that survive of a second quartet which Grieg started early in 1891. Although it is not new to the catalogue, this performance is far more persuasive and reveals this attractive music at its best. Apart from the *G minor Quartet* there's an early (1861) *Fugue*, composed when Grieg was a student of seventeen. The performances are decent and have plenty of spirit, and the recorded sound is excellent.

The Kontra Quartet give us exactly the same coupling, i.e. the two movements of the *F major Quartet (1891)*, that Julius Röntgen completed from the sketches Grieg left incomplete at his death, and the early fugal exercise he wrote during his student years in Leipzig. The Kontras play with much dramatic power and invest the music with great feeling; one would hesitate to speak of unforced eloquence. In this respect the Norwegians score, for their playing is somehow truer in scale. The BIS recording is excellent and, though not perhaps a first choice artistically, the disc is perfectly recommendable.

The alternative account by the English String Quartet has a more conventional coupling in Schumann's *A major Quartet*, Op. 41, No. 1. Their playing is in some respects more impressive; they too have plenty of spirit, but there is great warmth and perhaps greater tonal refinement. They are very well recorded.

String quartets Nos. 1 in G min., Op. 27; 2 in F; (i) *Andante con moto for piano trio. Fugue in F min.*
☞ *** Olympia Dig. OCD 432 [id.]. Raphael Qt, (i) with Jet Röling.

The Raphael Quartet do not give quite as spirited an account of the *F major Quartet* as the Norwegian Quartet, but theirs is perhaps the more cultured performance. It is a question of swings and roundabouts, and their CD enjoys two points of special interest: they give us Julius Röntgen's conjectural realization of the sketches to the remaining two movements Grieg had planned for the *F major Quartet*; and they also include another rarity in the shape of the *Andante con moto* for piano trio. They are much better recorded than their Oslo rivals.

PIANO MUSIC

Agitato; Album Leaf; At the Halfdán Kjerulf Statue; 3 Pieces; 10 Norwegian melodies. Peer Gynt.
arr. of HALVORSEN: *Entry of the Boyars.*
☞ **(*) BIS Dig. CD 620 [id.]. Love Derwinger.

These are juvenilia which have never been recorded before and, although they are of interest to the Grieg specialist, they are not exactly essential listening: none of these pieces is in any sense a great discovery. The Swedish pianist, Love Derwinger, plays them sensitively and is decently recorded, and both performance and recording deserve a high rating; but it is difficult to imagine Grieg, who was fastidious in these matters, being overjoyed at seeing these slight pieces, which he chose not to publish, representing him in the catalogue.

Agitato; Album leaves, Op. 28/1 & 4; Lyric pieces, Opp. 43 & 54; Piano sonata in E min., Op. 7;
Poetic tone pieces, Op. 3/4–6.
☞ ⊛ *** Virgin/EMI Dig. VC7 59300-2 [id.]. Leif Ove Andsnes.

Being a remarkable pianist himself, Grieg naturally wrote both extensively and idiomatically for the keyboard, from his very earliest years. Oddly enough, though, his piano music has been relatively neglected in the last few years. There were LP sets of the *Lyric pieces* in the 1970s from Barenboim (DG) and Adni (HMV), as well as a complete survey of the keyboard music by the Norwegian pianist, Eva Knardal, on BIS. But the only really *great* record, the only one that counts, is the selection of the *Lyric pieces* by Emil Gilels on Deutsche Grammophon. Now, given the stimulus of the anniversary, we have some fine new CDs, most notably a recital by Grieg's countryman, Leif Ove Andsnes, which has won golden opinions – and rightly so! He includes two sets of the *Lyric pieces*, the Op. 43 which begins with the famous *Butterfly*, and the Op. 54 which Grieg later scored; there are various other short pieces, as well as the *Sonata in E minor*, Op. 7, another piece which all young students had to learn in the 1940s and '50s. Andsnes's virtuosity is always at the service of the composer, and he has that ability to make familiar music sound fresh, as if you haven't heard it before. He plays with real imagination and lightness of touch.

Album leaves, Op. 28; Ballade in the form of variations on a Norwegian melody, Op. 24; From
Holberg's time, Op. 40; Funeral march for Rikard Nordrak; Humoresques, Op. 6; Improvisations on 2
Norwegian folksongs, Op. 29; Moods, Op. 73; Nordic folksongs and dances, Op. 17; Norwegian folk-
dances, Op. 66; Norwegian peasant dances, Op. 72; 3 Piano pieces: The Dance goes on; Gnomes tune;
Piano pieces based on his own songs, Op. 52; Pictures from life in the country, Op. 17; 4 Pieces, Op. 1;
Poetic tone-pictures, Op. 3; Sonata in E min., Op. 7.
☞ * BMG/RCA Dig. 09026 61569-2 (4) [id.]. Gerhard Oppitz.

Gerhard Oppitz is hardly more persuasive in the companion set of Grieg's keyboard music than he was in the *Lyric pieces*. As you would expect from this accomplished pianist, this set is not without its merits and insights but, generally speaking, there is a certain want of grace, tenderness and poetry. His account of the *Sonata* does not begin to compare with Andsnes on Virgin in lightness of touch and spirit, and the *G minor Ballade*, Op. 24, is too prosaic. Admittedly this artist is not helped by the somewhat unglamorous quality of the recorded sound.

4 Album Leaves, Op. 28; Ballade in G min., Op. 24; 2 Elegiac melodies, Op. 34; Norwegian dances,
Op. 35.
☞ ** Victoria Dig. VCD 19027 [id.). Geir Henning Braaten.

Humoresques, Op. 6; Lyric Pieces, Op. 12; 4 Pieces, Op. 1; Poetical tone-pictures, Op. 3; Sonata in E min., Op. 7.
☞ ** Victoria Dig. VCD 19025 [id.). Geir Henning Braaten.

These CDs are part of an ambitious project by the Norwegian Victoria Record Company (distributed in the UK by Gamut) to record all Grieg's keyboard music, including his transcriptions, which will run to 12 CDs. The piano music has all been entrusted to a Norwegian artist little known outside his own country, Geir Henning Braaten. He is an accomplished player, and it goes without saying that he is completely inside the idiom. Moreover he possesses good fingers and fine musicianship. The survey is chronological and shows Grieg's growing command of the instrument. On VCD 19027 he gives us the *Ballade in G minor* that Grieg wrote in memory of his parents, arguably his finest piano work. Everything is musicianly and intelligent, though it must be said that he achieves real distinction only intermittently. There is a certain want of tenderness that may in part be the result of too close a recording-balance, which results in a rather hard quality.

(iii) *Album Leaf, Op. 28/3; Arietta, Op. 12/1;* (vi) *Ballade in G min., Op. 24;* (vii) *Cradle song, Op. 68/ 5; French serenade, Op. 62/3;* (i; ii; v) *Norwegian bridal procession, Op. 19/2;* (iv) *Piano concerto in A min., Op. 16:* (v) cadenza to 1st movt only; (i) *To spring, Op. 45/6;* (v) *Wedding day at Troldhaugen, Op. 65/6.*
☞ (*) Pearl mono GEMMCD 9933 (i) Edvard Grieg; (ii) Joanne Stockmarr; (iii) Arthur de Greef;
  (iv) Severin Eisenberger, Cincinnati Conservatoire O, Alexander von Kreisler; (v) Percy Grainger;
  (vi) Leopold Godowsky; (vii) Walter Gieseking.

Primarily a historical document, but an interesting and valuable one for all who have a special interest in this composer. It extends over a wide range of pianists associated with the great Norwegian composer. There are two of the recordings Grieg himself made in Paris in 1903, and they give some idea, albeit very faintly, of the delicacy and characterfulness of his playing. The actual sound might perhaps be said to fall short of the highest standards of 1903 and, though Pearl have done their best, use of modern technology should be able to make more of the original master. (There is a 1900 recording of Landon Ronald playing the *Norwegian bridal procession* which is even worse.) There are other performances of interest: Percy Grainger playing the cadenza of the *Piano concerto* the year after Grieg's death, not long after he had played the work to the composer; and a recently discovered (1937) recording by Severin Eisenberger, who had played the concerto in Germany under Grieg's baton. Artistically the most poetic performance is Godowsky's 1930 account of the *G minor Ballade* (which also sounds excellent), possibly the finest interpretation of this underrated piece on record. Gieseking's *French serenade*, made in 1937, is hardly less captivating and more strongly characterized than his post-war Grieg anthology on LP. The sound on some of the earlier discs varies from passable to grim; but the disc is perhaps worth the money for the Godowsky alone.

Ballade, Op. 24; 4 Lyric Pieces: March of the dwarfs; Notturno, Op. 54/3–4; Wedding day at Troldhaugen, Op. 65/6; Peace of the woods, Op. 71/4. Sonata in E min., Op. 7; arr. of songs: *Cradle song; I love thee; The princess; You cannot grasp the wave's eternal course. Peer Gynt: Solveig's song.*
**(*) Olympia OCD 197 [id.]. Peter Katin.

The *Sonata* is not one of Grieg's finest works, but it has a touching *Andante* and is agreeably inventive, if perhaps conventionally so. Katin gives it a clean, direct performance, and he is impressive in the rather dolorous set of variations which forms the *Ballade*. The song arrangements, too, come off well, and the four *Lyric pieces* are presented very appealingly.

Holberg suite, Op. 40; Lyric pieces from Opp. 12, 38, 43, 47, 54, 57, 68, 71; Norwegian dance No. 2; Peer Gynt: Morning.
☞ (M) *** Teldec/Warner Dig. 4509 92147-2 [id.]. Cyprien Katsaris.

As a glance at the above listing will show, Cyprien Katsaris draws on a wider range of Grieg's piano music than does the classic and, indeed, indispensable Gilels recital, which is drawn exclusively from the *Lyric pieces* (see below). Katsaris starts off with *Morning mood* from *Peer Gynt*; he then plays eighteen of the *Lyric pieces* (often in groups of two or three), including favourites like *At the cradle, To spring, Butterfly, Little bird, Erotik* and the *Nocturne,* Op. 54/4 (some 39 minutes of music); the rest of the recital, apart from the opening ten minutes, is devoted to the suite, *From Holberg's time,* and one of the *Norwegian dances,* Op. 35. He is moreover accorded quite outstanding recording quality; the piano sound is particularly realistic and 'present', with plenty of range and colour. He plays with character, combining both temperament and sensitivity, and is generally scrupulous in observing dynamic nuances. Of course Gilels has poetic insights and an aristocratic finesse that are special; there are occasions here when this young artist is a shade impetuous, as in Op. 54, No. 3, or in the middle section of *Home-sickness*, Op. 57, No. 6; but, for the most part, these are strong and idiomatic performances – perhaps too 'strong' in the *Holberg suite*, where he is masterful and exuberant and where more finesse could be in order. However, at mid-price this is a very attractive reissue.

Lyric pieces: Opp. 12; 38; 43; 47; 54; 57; 62; 65; 68 & 71 (complete).
(M) **(*) Unicorn Dig. UKCD 2033, *UKC 2033* (1–4); UKCD 2034, *UKC 2034* (5–7); UKCD 2035, *UKC 2035* (8–10) [id.]. Peter Katin.
☞ (*) BMG/RCA Dig. 09026 61568-2 (3) [id.]. Gerhard Oppitz.

Peter Katin is a persuasive and sensitive exponent of this repertoire, and he has the benefit of a recording of exceptional presence and clarity (though very occasionally it seems to harden in climaxes, when one notices that the microphone is perhaps a shade close). Katin has the measure of Grieg's sensibility and characterizes these pieces with real poetic feeling. His performances are by far the most sensitive and idiomatic survey of the complete set at present on offer.

Gerhard Oppitz enters a well-populated field. But even if there were no rivals to choose from, his survey would remain uncompetitive; there is little of the freshness, delicacy of feeling and innocence this music conveys. There are occasional glimpses of poetry, but Oppitz is for the most part prosaic.

Lyric pieces: Op. 12/1, 6; Op. 38/5; Op. 54/1, 4 & 5; Op. 57/4, 6; Op. 62/3, 4 & 6; Op. 65/1–4; Op. 68/ 2, 4 & 5; Op. 71/1.
☞ **(*) Naxos Dig. 8.550650 [id.]. Balázs Szokolay.

Lyric pieces: Op. 12/3, 8; Op. 38/1; Op. 43/1, 3 & 6; Op. 47/3–7; Op. 54/3, 5–6; Op. 57/1–3; Op. 62/ 1–2, 5; Op. 65/6; Op. 71/7.
☞ **(*) Naxos Dig. 8.550557 [id.]. Balázs Szokolay.

Naxos are not always lucky with their piano recordings, but the two CDs Balázs Szokolay has recorded are very good. Szokolay, who made so strong an impression in the Leeds Competition some years ago, comes from a highly musical family; his father is the composer Sandor Szokolay whose opera on Lorca's *Blood Wedding* enjoyed some success in the 1970s. Generally speaking, his playing is not as consistently subtle in colouring or as poetic in feeling as Leif Ove Andsnes, but it is pretty idiomatic. However, at super-bargain price it is really very good value indeed and the balance, though very slightly close, is not oppressively so. Both CDs give pleasure.

Lyric pieces: Op. 12/1; Op. 38/1; Op. 43/1–2; Op. 47/2–4; Op. 54/4–5; Op. 57/6; Op. 62/4 and 6; Op. 68/2, 3 and 5; Op. 71/1, 3 and 6–7.
⊛ *** DG 419 749-2 [id.]. Emil Gilels.

With Gilels we are in the presence of a great keyboard master whose characterization and control of colour and articulation are wholly remarkable. An altogether outstanding record in every way.

Lyric pieces: Op. 38/1, 3–4; Op. 47/1–2, 4, 7; Op. 54/4–5; Op. 57/2, 3 & 5; Op. 62/1 & 6; Op. 68/1–3; Op. 71/3–5.
☞ * Koch Dig. 3-7143-2 [id.]. Israela Margalit.

Artistically, Israela Margalit's Grieg recital is strong. The playing has character and refinement, but the sound is too uningratiating to invite any strong recommendation. The studio is a bit reverberant and the sound bottom-heavy.

Lyric pieces: Album leaf, Op. 47/2; Arietta, Op. 12/1; At the cradle, Op. 68/5; At your feet, Op. 68/3; Ballad, Op. 65/5; Brooklet, Op. 62/4; Butterfly, Op. 43/1; Homesickness, Op. 57/6; Cradle song, Op. 38/1; Ganger, Op. 54/2; Gone, Op. 71/6; Halling, Op. 47/4; Melody, Op. 47/3; Nocturne, Op. 54/4; Puck, Op. 71/3; Remembrances, Op. 71/7; Scherzo, Op. 54/5; Shepherd's boy, Op. 54/1; Solitary traveller, Op. 43/2; Summer's Eve, Op. 71/2.
☞ **(*) DG Dig. 437 522-2 [id.]. Andrei Gavrilov.

Andrei Gavrilov's anthology of *Lyric pieces* is virtually identical to the celebrated Gilels record, which it does not challenge in any respect. All the same, it is very well played and recorded, and there is no reason to deny it a three-star recommendation. All credit, then, to Gavrilov – but buy the Gilels!

Piano sonata in E min., Op. 7.
☞ (M) *(*) Sony SM2K 52654 [id.]. Glenn Gould – BIZET: *Nocturne* etc.; SIBELIUS: *Kyllikki* etc. *(*)

The sound of this 1973 performance is much improved but it comes in a two-CD box which is really rather poor value in that the Grieg–Bizet disc runs to 45 minutes 5 seconds and the Sibelius sonatinas and *Kyllikki* takes a mere 38 minutes 35 seconds. All except dedicated Gould followers will find Andsnes's Virgin recording (see above, under *Agitato*) more satisfying in every respect.

VOCAL MUSIC

Songs in historic performances (1888–1924): *Den første møte (First meeting); Dulgte kjaerlighed (Hidden love); En fuglevis (A Bird-Song); Eros; Fra Monte Pincio; Den gamle vise (The old song); God Morgen; Jag elsker Dig (I love thee); Jag reiste en deilig sommerkvaeld (I walked one balmy summer evening); Killingdans (Kyds' dance); Kongekvadet (The King's Song); Margaretas Vuggesang (Margareta's Cradle song); Mens jeg venter (On the water); Moderen synger (The mother's lament); Norønnafolket (The northland folk); Og jeg vil ha mig en Hjertenskaer (Midsummer Eve); Ragnhild; Solveig's Song; Solveigs vuggevise (Solveig's Cradle song); Stambogsrim (Album Lines); En Svane (A swan); Takk for dit råd (Say what you will); Eine Traume (A dream); Trudom (Faith); Våren (Spring); Vaer hilset I Damer (Greetings, fair ladies).*

☞ (*(**)) SIMAX mono PSC 1810 (3). Aino Ackté, Giuseppe Anselmi, Maria Barrientos, Borghild Bryhn-Landgaard, Otta Bronnum, Robert Burg, Eugenia Burzio, Erik Bye, Feodor Chaliapin, Edmund Clément, Peter Cornelius, Emmy Destinn, Kaia Eide, Gervase Elwes, Elisa Elizza, Geraldine Farrar, Kirsten Flagstad, John Forsell, Amelita Galli-Curci, Lucy Gates, Elena Gerhardt, Gunnar Graarud, Ellen Gulbranson, Nina Grieg, Hans Hedemark, Melitta Heim, Frida Hempel, Vilhelm Herold, Clara Hultgren, Hermann Jadlowker, Beatrice Kernic, Olive Kline, Salomea Kruszelnicka, Lilli Lehmann, Augusta Lütken, Magna Lykseth-Schjerven, Cally Monrad, Carl-Martin Ohman, Rosa Olitzka, Elisabeth Rethberg, Ernestine Schumann-Heink, Karl Scheidemantel, Leo Slezak, Greta Stückgold, Joseph Schwarz, Richard Tauber, Luisa Tetrazzini (various pianists).

As the cast-list shows, this is a veritable treasure-house of singing at the turn of the century, not only in northern Europe but elsewhere. Naturally in the early years of the gramophone singers tended to gravitate towards a handful of songs so that familiar numbers such as *Jag elsker Dig* and *En Svane* turn up in several versions, the former 11 times and the latter seven. There are no fewer than 16 different versions of *Solveig's Song*, including a few bars sung without accompaniment by Nina Grieg in 1889 when she would have been forty-four. (She stopped singing in public in the 1890s.) Grieg himself declared her to be the finest interpreter of his songs and, although she is barely audible through the deluge of background noise, the voice is obviously of great purity. Listening to her across a divide of over a century is a curiously moving experience. The roll-call is pretty dazzling, ranging as it does from big names such as Aino Ackté (for whom Sibelius composed *Luonnotar*), to Chaliapin and Emmy Destinn (the copy of her *Mens jeg venter* is unfortunately pretty rough) and there are 47 singers in all, but the less familiar names also offer valuable insights into performance practice. In all there are nearly 80 performances, and the quality of the recordings which have been subjected to the NoNoise system of reduction calls for more tolerance than many listeners will feel able to extend. This is a set for libraries, specialist collectors and students of song, and it is an invaluable resource into which to dip.

(i) *Bergliot, Op. 42;* (ii) *Den Bergtekne (The mountain thrall), Op. 32;* (iii & iv) *Foran sydens kloster (Before a Southern Convent);* (ii & iii) *7 Songs with orchestra: Den første møde; Solveigs sang; Solveigs vuggesang; Fra Monte Pincio; En svane; Våren; Henrik Wegeland.*

☞ *** DG Dig. 437 519-2 [id.]. (i) Rut Tellefsen; (ii) Håkan Hagegård; (iii & iv) Barbara Bonney; (iii) Randi Stene; Gothenburg SO, Neeme Järvi.

Some Grieg rarities here: the cantata *Foran sydens kloster* ('Before a Southern Convent') and the melodrama *Bergliot*, both to words of Bjørnstjerne Bjørnson, are hardly mainstream repertoire. Nor is *Den bergtekne* ('The Mountain Thrall') for baritone, two horns and strings, for the simple reason that performances and recordings are very rare. In fact *Before a Southern Convent* is new to the UK, though there have been two earlier recordings, one from Germany and the other from Norway. It comes on another Gothenburg record, together with seven songs with orchestra, sung by Barbara Bonney and Håkan Hagegård, as well as *The Mountain Thrall* and the melodrama *Bergliot* to words by Bjørnstjerne Bjørnson. *Before a Southern Convent* dates from 1871, three years after the *Piano concerto*, and was dedicated to Liszt. (Grieg had visited Liszt in Rome the year before and Liszt had sight-read the concerto dazzlingly.) *Before a Southern Convent* is also based on a Bjørnson poem which tells how Ingigerd, the daughter of a chieftain, has seen her father murdered by the villainous brigand, Arnljot. He was on the verge of raping her but relented and let her go. Despite what she has suffered, she feels a certain attraction for Arnljot and now seeks expiation by entering a foreign convent. The piece is in dialogue form. When she is questioned, she speaks openly to the nuns about her feelings of guilt, and the piece ends with a chorus of nuns who admit her to their number. It's not great Grieg but it has a lot going for it. It's well worth investigating, very naturally balanced with plenty of air round the sound. The singers are well placed and not right on top of you. Generally speaking, the quality on all these DG recordings is excellent – which is not surprising, as they're made by the same Gothenburg team who have recorded for the BIS label.

7 Children's songs, Op. 61; Haugtussa, Op. 67; Melodies of the heart, Op. 5; 6 Songs, Op. 4; 6 Songs, Op. 25.
☞ **(*) BIS Dig. CD 637 [id.]. Monica Groop, Love Derwinger.

The Finnish soprano, Monica Groop, possesses a striking voice of considerable colour and does not disappoint in her excellently recorded recital. All the same, her *Haugtussa* is no match for von Otter's and her recital does not possess quite the strong interpretative personality of her Swedish colleague. This is the first of a complete survey on BIS and will provide a useful alternative to the current survey on RCA from Hagegård. It deserves warm support.

Haugtussa (song-cycle), Op. 67; 6 Songs, Op. 48. Songs: Beside the stream; Farmyard song; From Monte Pincio; Hope; I love but thee; Spring; Spring showers; A Swan; Two brown eyes; While I wait; With a waterlily (sung in Norwegian).
☞ ⊛ *** DG Dig. 437 521-2 [id.]. Anne Sofie von Otter, Bengt Forsberg.

This recital of Grieg's songs by Anne Sofie von Otter and Bengt Forsberg is rather special. It begins with Grieg's most important song-cycle, *Haugtussa* ('The mountain maid'), and a generous helping of other songs includes the six songs of Op. 48. One French critic found her account of *Haugtussa* over-dramatized (*'Haugtussa souffre, hélas, d'une interpretation trop dramatisée'*); but it would be truer to describe it as strongly characterized without being over-projected. In fact it is arguably the best *Haugtussa* since Aase Nordmo Lovberg's mono Columbia LPs – and possibly even better. Anne Sofie von Otter commands an exceptionally wide range of colour and quality and in Bengt Forsberg has a highly responsive partner. Altogether a captivating recital, and beautifully recorded too.

(i) Landkjenning (Land-sighting), Op. 31; (i & ii) Olav Trygvason, Op. 50; Peer Gynt Suites Nos. 1 & 2.
☞ *** DG Dig. 437 523-2 [id.) (i) Anne Gjevang; (ii) Randi Stene; (i; ii) Håkan Hagegård; Gothenburg SO, Neeme Järvi.

The great enthusiasm which greeted *Before a Southern Convent* prompted Bjørnson to plan an opera, *Olav Trygvason. Landkjenning* ('Land-sighting') and the three scenes that survive from the opera are coupled together with the two *Peer Gynt* suites. Set in the tenth century, Bjørnson's poem tells of Olav Trygvason, the first king to convert the Norwegians to Christianity. The three tableaux that survive come closer to a cantata than an opera. In the second tableau, the role of the priestess is sung by Anne Gjevang, the Erda in the Haitink *Ring* on EMI. Some may find her vibrato a bit excessive. The other soloists, Randi Stene and Håkan Hagegård, acquit themselves well, as does the Gothenburg Orchestra and Chorus under Neeme Järvi. The *Peer Gynt* suites are not new, though two of the numbers have been re-recorded. Recommended.

Landkjenning (Land-sighting): cantata, Op. 31; Olav Trygvason (operatic fragments), Op. 50; Peer Gynt, Act V: Choral scenes.
(M) *** Unicorn UKCD 2056 [id.]. Hanssen, Hansli, Carlsen, Olso Philharmonic Ch., LSO, Per Dreier.

Neither the excerpts from *Olav Trygvason* nor *Landkjenning* is vintage Grieg, though as always there are some appealing ideas, particularly in the third scene of *Olav*. The Norwegian soloists and chorus respond in exemplary fashion to Per Dreier – indeed the choral contribution is quite thrilling in its impact, helped by the recording's dramatic range of dynamic. There is also sensitive and idiomatic playing from the LSO. The recording is naturally focused within a convincing perspective. For a bonus the CD offers three scenes from Act V of *Peer Gynt* for soprano (the admirable Toril Carlsen), chorus and orchestra. This is Grieg at his most lyrically inspired.

Melodies of the heart, Op. 5; 9 Songs, Op. 18; 6 Songs, Op. 25; The last spring, Op. 33/2; The Mountain thrall, Op. 32; Rocking, rocking on the gentles waves, Op. 49/2; Henrik Wergeland, Op. 58/3.
☞ **(*) BMG/RCA Dig. 09026 61518-2. Håkan Hagegård, Warren Jones.

Songs and ballads, Op. 9; 4 Songs, Op. 21; 5 Songs, Op. 26; Romances & songs, Op. 39; Reminiscences from mountain and flood, Op. 44.
☞ **(*) BMG/RCA Dig. 09026 61629-2. Håkan Hagegård, Warren Jones.

The centenary year has unleashed a torrent of Grieg songs which have been so grievously neglected before. Håkan Hagegård's two CDs with Warren Jones find the great Swedish baritone less than wholly persuasive. The voice is fresher than in his Stenhammar recital (Caprice) but the radiance one recalls from his stage appearances or his *Winterreise* for the Swedish Radio label (not available here) is missing. There was always then the sense of something kept in reserve and a tonal bloom that was captivating. Here there is a certain uniformity of colour and approach in many of these songs, and an occasional hardness at the tenor end of the voice. However, these discs have been widely admired and Hagegård's artistry and musical intelligence are always in evidence.

For those especially attracted to this repertory, a Simax disc by the young Norwegian baritone, Per Vollestad, is well worth looking out for. He has considerable charm and, although there is a certain hardness in the voice that at times disturbs, he is intelligently accompanied by Sigmund Hjelset and the CD includes no fewer than 34 songs (Simax PSC 1089).

Peer Gynt (incidental music), *Op. 23* (complete).
(M) *** Unicorn UKCD 2003/4 [id.]. Carlson, Hanssen, Bjørkøy, Hansli, Oslo PO Ch., LSO, Dreier.

Per Dreier achieves very spirited results from his soloists, the Oslo Philharmonic Chorus and our own LSO, with some especially beautiful playing from the woodwind; the recording is generally first class, with a natural perspective between soloists, chorus and orchestra. The Unicorn set includes 32 numbers in all, including Robert Henrique's scoring of the *Three Norwegian dances*, following the revised version of the score Grieg prepared for the 1886 production in Copenhagen. This music, whether familiar or unfamiliar, continues to astonish by its freshness and inexhaustibility.

Peer Gynt (incidental music), *Op. 23* (complete); *Sigurd Jorsalfar* (incidental music), *Op. 56* (complete).
*** DG Dig. 423 079-2 (2) [id.]. Bonney, Eklöf, Sandve, Malmberg, Holmgren; Foss, Maurstad, Stokke (speakers); Gösta Ohlin's Vocal Ens., Pro Musica Chamber Ch., Gothenburg SO, Järvi.

Neeme Järvi's recording differs from its predecessor by Per Dreier in offering the Grieg Gesamtausgabe *Peer Gynt*, which bases itself primarily on the twenty-six pieces he included in the 1875 production rather than the final published score, prepared after Grieg's death by Halvorsen. This well-documented set comes closer to the original by including spoken dialogue, as one would have expected in the theatre. The CDs also offer the complete *Sigurd Jorsalfar* score, which includes some splendid music. The performances by actors, singers (solo and choral) and orchestra alike are exceptionally vivid, with the warm Gothenburg ambience used to creative effect; the vibrant histrionics of the spoken words undoubtedly add to the drama.

Peer Gynt: extended excerpts.
*** DG Dig. 427 325-2 [id.]. Bonney, Eklöf, Malmberg, Maurstad, Foss, Gothenburg Ch. & SO, Järvi.
*** Decca Dig. 425 448-2 [id.]. Urban Malmberg, Mari-Ann Haeggander, San Francisco Ch. & SO, Blomstedt.

Neeme Järvi's disc offers more than two-thirds of the 1875 score, and the performance has special claims on the collector who wants one CD rather than two (half the second CD of the set is taken up by *Sigurd Jorsalfar*).

Decca's set of excerpts makes a useful alternative to the Järvi disc. All but about 15 minutes of the complete score is here and the spoken text is included too, all admirably performed. Perhaps the Gothenburg acoustic is to be preferred to the Davies Hall, San Francisco. However, the Decca recording approaches the demonstration class.

(i) *Peer Gynt:* excerpts. *In Autumn* (overture), *Op. 11; An Old Norwegian song with variations, Op. 51; Symphonic dance No. 2.*
☞ (M) *** EMI CDM7 64751-2 [id.]. (i) Ilse Hollweg, Beecham Ch. Soc.; RPO, Beecham.

Beecham showed a very special feeling for this score and to hear *Morning*, the gently textured *Anitra's dance* or the eloquent portrayal of the *Death of Aase* under his baton is a uniquely rewarding experience. Ilse Hollweg makes an excellent soloist. The recording dates from 1957 and, like most earlier Beecham reissues, has been enhanced by the remastering process. The most delectable of the *Symphonic dances*, very beautifully played, makes an ideal encore after *Solveig's lullaby*, affectingly sung by Hollweg. The *In Autumn* overture, not one of Grieg's finest works, is most enjoyable when Sir Thomas is so persuasive, not shirking the melodramatic moments. Finally for the present reissue, we are offered *An Old Norwegian folksong with variations* (not previously released in its stereo format). It is a piece of much colour and charm, which is fully realized here.

Peer Gynt (incidental music): *Overture; Suites 1–2. Lyric pieces: Evening in the mountain; Cradle song, Op. 68/5; Sigurd Jorsalfar: suite, Op. 56; Wedding day at Troldhaugen, Op. 65/6.*
(BB) **(*) Naxos Dig. 8.550140; *4550140* [id.]. CSSR State PO, Košice, Stephen Gunzenhauser.

A generous Grieg anthology on Naxos (70 minutes, all but 3 seconds) and the performances by the Slovak State Philharmonic Orchestra in Košice (in Eastern Slovakia) are very fresh and lively and thoroughly enjoyable. There is wide dynamic range both in the playing and in the recording, and sensitivity in matters of phrasing.

Peer Gynt: suites Nos. 1–2.
☞ (BB) *(*) Tring Dig. TRP 002 [id.]. RPO, Mark Ermler – BIZET: *Carmen suites.* **

Mark Ermler's accounts on Tring's RPO collection are well played and recorded, but there is a feeling of routine in the lyrical music and even *In the hall of the Mountain King* fails to sound really malignant.

Peer Gynt: suites Nos. 1 & 2; Holberg suite; Sigurd Jorsalfar: suite.
(M) *** DG 419 474-2; *419 474-4* [id.]. BPO, Karajan.

Karajan's analogue set remains available on a mid-priced DG CD, where the highly expressive performances were played with superlative skill and polish. There is a touch of fierceness on the *Sigurd Jorsalfar* climaxes, but otherwise these performances are given good sound.

Peer Gynt: suites Nos. 1–2; Lyric pieces: Evening in the mountains; Cradle song, Op. 68/1–2; Wedding day at Troldhaugen, Op. 65/6; Sigurd Jorsalfar suite, Op. 56.
☞ (BB) ** Naxos Dig. 8.550864 [id.]. BBC Scottish SO, Jerzy Maksymiuk.

The *Peer Gynt* music is presented with admirable simplicity by the excellent Scottish players. But although Aase's death brings a rapt closing pianissimo, *In the hall of the Mountain King* could use rather more impetus, and it is the second suite that has the greater character. What makes this disc worth considering is the very beautiful string-playing in the two *Lyric pieces* and the fine performance of the first two numbers from *Sigurd Jorsalfar*, *In the king's hall* engagingly presented and *Borghild's dream* full of atmosphere and drama. The famous *Homage march* is suitably regal but rather too slow and expansive. However, the jolly *Wedding dance* is very spirited.

Peer Gynt: suites Nos. 1, Op. 46; 2, Op. 55. Lyric suite: March of the Trolls. Norwegian dance No. 2, Op. 35.
☞ (M) ** Sony SMK 47549 [id.]. NYPO, Bernstein – SIBELIUS: *Finlandia* etc. **

These Bernstein performances are very well played and the recording is atmospheric enough, although the string tone in *Morning* lacks bloom. The slightly mannered account of *Anitra's dance*, the exotic *Arab dance* and the touch of melodrama in the second *Peer Gynt suite* add individuality to Bernstein's performances, and the famous second *Norwegian dance* is nicely managed.

(i) *Peer Gynt: suites Nos. 1–2. Lyric suite, Op. 54; Sigurd Jorsalfar: suite.*
(M) *** DG Dig. 427 807-2 [id.]. (i) Soloists, Ch.; Gothenburg SO, Järvi.

Järvi's excerpts from *Peer Gynt* and *Sigurd Jorsalfar* are extracted from his complete sets, so the editing inevitably produces a less tidy effect than normal recordings of the *Suites*. However, the performances are first class and so is the recording, and this comment applies also to the *Lyric suite*, taken from an earlier, digital orchestral collection.

4 Psalms, Op. 74.
**(*) Nimbus Dig. NI 5171 [id.]. Håkan Hagegård, Oslo Cathedral Ch., Terje Kvam –
  MENDELSSOHN: *3 Psalms.* **(*)

The *Four Psalms* are dignified, beautiful pieces, very well sung here by the choir and the Swedish baritone, Håkan Hagegård. The recording is eminently faithful, though the pauses between the Psalms are not long enough.

(i) *Sigurd Jorsalfar, Op. 22: incidental music; Funeral march in memory of Rikard Nordraak* (orch. Halvorsen); (i) *The Mountain spell, Op. 32.*
(M) *** Unicorn UKCD 2019. (i) Kåre Björköy; Oslo Philharmonic Ch., LSO, Per Dreier.

Grieg's *Sigurd Jorsalfar* comprised five movements in all, from which Grieg drew the familiar suite; but there were additional sections as well, most importantly the moving *Funeral march* in memory of Nordraak. *The Mountain spell* (or 'thrall', as it is sometimes translated) was one of Grieg's favourite pieces; it is a song of great beauty. The Oslo Philharmonic Choir give a spirited account of themselves, as do the LSO, who play sensitively for Per Dreier. Kåre Björköy is an excellent soloist with well-focused tone. The recording is very good indeed and the perspective is agreeably natural.

4 Songs, Op. 14; 6 Songs, Op. 49; Songs from Peer Gynt, Op. 55.
☞ **(*) Victoria Dig. VCD 19038 [id.]. Marianne Hirsti, Kjell Magnus Sandve, Knut Skram, Rudolf Jansen.

Although the Sibelius songs were recorded complete in the 1980s, Grieg's output for the voice, which is hardly less important, has only now been planned. The Victoria series will embrace seven CDs: they are to be shared among the soprano, Marianne Hirsti, the tenor, Kjell Magnus Sandve, and the baritone, Knut Skram. They're partnered throughout by Rudolf Jansen, one of the most imaginative accompanists of our day. Sandve made out very well in the Cardiff Singer of the World Competition some years ago when he won the Geraint Evans Mozart Prize, and he has gone on to sing at the Staatsoper in Vienna and the Deutsche Oper, Berlin: a thoroughly idiomatic and excellent interpreter. Marianne Hirsti possesses a voice of great purity; her intonation is spot-on, and the overall sound radiates a childlike innocence. She is heard at her best in, say, *Margrete's Cradlesong*, one of the four songs of Op. 15 and Grieg's very first setting of Ibsen. Characterization, on the other hand, is not always her strong suit. If you put her performance of *Forårsregn* ('Spring showers') alongside Anne Sofie von Otter's (DG), you will find much greater colour and tonal variety in the Swedish performance on DG. After prolonged exposure the ear can easily tire of this particular timbre. All the same it's a beautiful voice. Knut Skram has lost some of the bloom his voice once possessed – though none of his artistry or musical intelligence. Good recordings throughout. This should prove a rewarding series, and when it comes Hirsti's set of *Haugtussa* will be of special interest in that it will include five songs Grieg suppressed on grounds of length.

Griffes, Charles (1884–1920)

(i) *The Pleasure Dome of Kubla Khan, Op. 8;* (ii) *3 Tone pictures, Op. 5;* (ii; iii) *3 Poems of Fiona Macleod;* (iv) *4 German songs; 4 Impressions; Song of the Dagger.*
** New World NW 273/4 [id.]. (i) Boston SO; (ii) New World CO; Ozawa; (iii) with Bryn-Julson; (iv) Stapp, Milnes, Richardson, Spong.

The four *German songs* come from the early years of the century when Griffes was much influenced by Brahms; they are well sung here by Sherrill Milnes, but the four *Impressions* (1912–16) are less well served. Ozawa's performance of *The Pleasure Dome* conveys much of the work's strong atmosphere. By far the most persuasive performance comes from Phyllis Bryn-Julson in the Op. 11 settings of Fiona Macleod. The recordings date from the 1970s and are eminently acceptable.

Fantasy pieces; Legend; The Pleasure Dome of Kubla Khan; 3 Preludes; Rhapsody in B min.; Sonata; 3 Tone pictures.
** Kingdom Dig. KCLCD 2011 [id.]. James Tocco.

The *Sonata* is the most radical and expressionistic work here and *The Pleasure Dome of Kubla Khan* the best known. The three late *Preludes* have a keen sense of mystery and concentration. So, too, have the three *Tone pictures*. James Tocco plays with insight and sensitivity; he meets the virtuoso demands of the *Sonata* and is keenly responsive to the dynamic nuances of these scores. He is not well served by the acoustic, which has far too little space round the aural image. All the same, such is the interest of the music and the quality of the playing that this shortcoming should not be exaggerated.

Grofé, Ferde (1892–1972)

Grand Canyon suite.
(M) *** Decca 430 712-2; *430 712-4* [id.]. Detroit SO, Dorati – GERSHWIN: *Porgy and Bess.* ***
*** Telarc Dig. CD 80086 [id.] (with additional cloudburst, including real thunder). Cincinnati Pops O, Kunzel – GERSHWIN: *Catfish Row.* ***
☞ (M) *** BMG/RCA 09026 61667-2. O, Morton Gould – COPLAND: *Billy the Kid; Rodeo.* **(*)

Antal Dorati has the advantage of superlative Decca recording, very much in the demonstration class, with stereoscopically vivid detail. Yet the performance combines subtlety with spectacle, and this version is very much in a class of its own.

The Cincinnati performance is played with great commitment and fine pictorial splendour, although Dorati scores at *Sunrise*, where his powerful timpani strokes add to the power of the climax. What gives the Telarc CD its special edge is the inclusion of a second performance of *Cloudburst* as an appendix with a genuine thunderstorm laminated on to the orchestral recording. The result is overwhelmingly thrilling, except that in the final thunderclap God quite upstages the orchestra, who are left trying frenziedly to match its amplitude in their closing peroration.

Morton Gould gives *Grand Canyon* the full treatment, and the opulently full-blooded (1960) recording, superbly remastered by John Pfeiffer's team, ensures great washes of technicolor for Grofé's lush pictorialism. No complaints either about the spectacle of the final storm sequence with the thunderclaps on the drums impressively realistic.

Guilmant, Felix Alexandre (1837–1911)

Symphony No. 1 for organ and orchestra, Op. 42.
☞ *** Chan. Dig. CHAN 9271 [id.]. Ian Tracey (organ of Liverpool Cathedral), BBC PO, Yan Pascal Tortelier – WIDOR: *Symphony No. 5* ***; POULENC: *Organ concerto.* **(*)

This Guilmant *Symphony* (the composer's own arrangement of his *First Organ sonata*) is a real find, with all the genial vigour of the famous work of Saint-Saëns. The first movement has a gallumphing main theme and an equally pleasing secondary idea. It is followed by a tunefully idyllic Pastorale (with some delicious registration from Ian Tracey) and a rumbustiously grandiloquent finale. All great fun, and well suited to the larger-than-life resonance of Liverpool Cathedral with its long reverberation period.

Hadley, Patrick (1899–1973)

(i) *Lenten cantata. The cup of blessing; I sing of a maiden; My beloved spake; A Song for Easter.*
☞ *** ASV Dig. CDDCA 881 [id.]. (i) John Mark Ainsley, Donald Sweeney; Ch. of Gonville & Caius College, Cambridge, Geoffrey Webber; Hill or Phillips (organ) – RUBBRA: *Choral music.* ***

Patrick Hadley studied composition with Vaughan Williams and conducting with Sir Adrian Boult. Like Rubbra, he was a distinguished academic and succeeded Dent as professor of music at Cambridge. His best-known works, *The Hills* and *The Trees so high*, belong firmly in the English pastoral tradition. The most substantial piece here is the *Lenten cantata* or *Lenten meditations* for two soloists, choir and orchestra (here given in an organ transcription), composed in 1963. Not a strongly individual voice, Hadley is nevertheless a refined craftsman whose feeling for line and texture is highly developed. The performances are of high quality, and so is the recording.

Hahn, Reynaldo (1875–1947)

Le bal de Béatrice d'Este (ballet suite).
*** Hyp. Dig. CDA 66347 [id.]. New London O, Ronald Corp – POULENC: *Aubade; Sinfonietta.* ***

Le bal de Béatrice d'Este is a rather charming pastiche, dating from the early years of the century and scored for the unusual combination of wind instruments, two harps, piano and timpani. Ronald Corp and the New London Orchestra play it with real panache and sensitivity.

Songs: *A Chloris; L'Air; L'Automne; 7 Chansons Grises; La chère blessuré; D'une prison; L'enamourée; Les étoiles; Fêtes galantes; Les fontaines; L'Incrédule; Infidélité; Offrande; Quand je fus pris au pavillon; Si mes vers avaient des ailes; Tyndaris.*
**(*) Hyp. CDA 66045 [id.]. Hill, Johnson.

If Hahn never quite matched the supreme inspiration of his most famous song, *Si mes vers avaient des ailes*, the delights here are many, the charm great. Martyn Hill, ideally accompanied by Graham Johnson, gives delicate and stylish performances, well recorded.

Halévy, Jacques Fromental (1799–1862)

La juive (opera): complete.
*** Ph. Dig. 420 190-2 (3). Varady, Anderson, Carreras, Gonzalez, Furlanetto, Amb. Op. Ch., Philh.
O, Almeida.

La juive ('The Jewess') was the piece which, along with the vast works of Meyerbeer, set the pattern for the epic French opera, so popular last century. Eleazar was the last role that the great tenor, Enrico Caruso, tackled, and it was in this opera that he gave his very last performance. The greater part of the recording was completed in 1986, but that was just at the time when José Carreras was diagnosed as having leukaemia, and it was only in 1989 that he contributed his performance through 'overdubbing'. He sings astonishingly well, but the role of the old Jewish father really needs a weightier, darker voice, such as Caruso had in his last years. Julia Varady as Rachel makes that role both the emotional and the musical centre of the opera, responding both tenderly and positively. In the other soprano role, that of the Princess Eudoxia, June Anderson is not so full or sweet in tone, but she is particularly impressive in the dramatic coloratura passages, such as her Act III *Boléro*. Ferruccio Furlanetto makes a splendidly resonant Cardinal in his two big solos, and the Ambrosian Opera Chorus brings comparable bite to the powerful ensembles. Antonio de Almeida as conductor proves a dedicated advocate.

Halvorsen, Johan (1864–1935)

Air Norvégien, Op. 7; Danses Norvégiennes.
(BB) *** Naxos Dig. 8.550329 [id.]. Dong-Suk Kang, Slovak (Bratislava) RSO, Adrian Leaper –
SIBELIUS: *Violin concerto;* SINDING: *Légende;* SVENDSEN: *Romance.* ***

Dong-Suk Kang plays the attractive *Danses Norvégiennes* with great panache, character and effortless virtuosity, and delivers an equally impeccable performance of the earlier *Air Norvégien.*

Handel, George Frideric (1685–1759)

Ballet music: *Alcina: overture; Acts I & III: suites. Il pastor fido: suite. Terpsichore: suite.*
(M) *** Erato/Warner Dig. 2292 45378-2 [id.]. E. Bar. Soloists, Gardiner.

John Eliot Gardiner is just the man for such a programme. He is not afraid to charm the ear, yet allegros are vigorous and rhythmically infectious. The bright and clean recorded sound adds to the sparkle, and the quality is first class. A delightful collection, and very tuneful too.

Ariodante: Overture; Sinfonia pastorale & ballet music. Il Pastor Fido: March and Airs for the hunters I–II.
☞ (M) *** Decca 433 732-2 [id.]. ASMF, Marriner – GLUCK: *Don Juan.* ***

This is a substantial bonus for the complete recording of Gluck's *Don Juan* ballet. The music for *Ariodante* has much charm and the hunting airs from *Il Pastor Fido* have suitably effective horn parts – here despatched with aplomb. Excellent, full, spacious 1971 sound.

Concerti grossi, Op. 3/1–6.
☞ *** Sony Dig. SK 52553 [id.]. Tafelmusik, Jeanne Lamon.
*** DG 413 727-2 [id.]. E. Concert, Pinnock.
*** Ph. Dig. 411 482-2 [id.]. ASMF, Marriner.
☞ (M) **(*) Erato/Warner 2292 45981-2 [id.]. E. Bar. Soloists, Gardiner.
☞ **(*) Erato/Warner Dig. 4509 94354-2 [id.]. Les Musicians du Louvre, Marc Minkowski.

Concerti grossi, Op. 3/1–6; Overtures: Alcina; Ariodante.
(M) *** Decca 430 261-2; *430 261-4* [id.]. ASMF, Sir Neville Marriner.

Those looking for a fine, modern, digital recording of Op. 3, with its woodwind complement added to the strings and a concertante organ in No. 6, will find the Tafelmusik disc eminently satisfactory. The playing is fresh and unfussy – plainer than with Gardiner, but none the worse for that. It is alert, elegant and with plenty of warmth, and tempi are admirably judged. Original instruments are used but not flaunted too abrasively and the sound is first class, clear as well as full. Indeed the resonance ensures that the music has plenty of breadth without being muddied.

The six Op. 3 *Concertos* with their sequences of brief jewels of movements also find Pinnock and the English Concert at their freshest and liveliest, with plenty of sparkle and little of the abrasiveness associated with 'authentic' performance.

In Sir Neville Marriner's latest version with the Academy, tempi tend to be a little brisk, but the results are inspiring and enjoyable. Not unexpectedly, textures are fuller here than on Pinnock's competing Archiv recording, and the CD quality is admirably fresh.

Marriner's earlier set remains fully competitive (irrespective of price) for musical scholarship and, what is even more to the point, for musical expressiveness and spontaneity. The ASMF was in peak form when this recording was made and the sound is very well balanced and vivid. The two overtures make an acceptable bonus.

Gardiner's analogue set from 1980 has also transferred well to CD. Recorded in the Henry Wood Hall, textures are slightly more ample but still clear and admirably balanced. The starry cast-list includes Simon Standage and Roy Goodman among the violins, and there is some very lively playing here and no want of style. There is a slight lack of finish in one or two places and some poor intonation in *No. 2 in B flat* – yet there are some very good things here too, as for instance the imaginative treatment of the *Largo e staccato* of Op. 3/3 and its following *Adagio*, with Lisa Beznosiuk the engaging flute soloist.

In Minkowski's set, the original wind instruments alter the character of the tuttis, with the oboe or oboes bringing a reedy quality, and at times the wind instruments steal so much limelight from the strings that one has the impression that these are solo concertos for oboe or, in the case of No. 3, recorder and flute. In No. 6 the organ dominates. String textures are bright and transparent, with the lightest possible sonority; with brisk allegros that are always alert and vivacious, the effect here is of hearing a completely new series of works. The result is undoubtedly refreshing, but some Handelians will miss a fuller string-sound.

12 Concerti grossi, Op. 6/1–12.
⊛ *** Chan. Dig. CHAN 9004/6 [id.]. I Musici de Montréal, Yuli Turovsky.
☞ *** O-L Dig. 436 845-2 (3). Handel & Haydn Soc., Christopher Hogwood.
**(*) DG Dig. 410 897-2 (1–4); 410 898-2 (5–8); 410 899-2 (9–12) [id.]. E. Concert, Pinnock.
**(*) BMG/RCA Dig. RD 87895 [7895-2-RC] (*Nos. 1–4*); RD 87907 [7907-2-RC] (*Nos. 5–8*); RD 87921 [7921-2-RC] (*Nos. 9–12*). Guildhall String Ens., Robert Salter.

Concerti grossi, Op. 6/1–12; Concerto grosso in C (Alexander's Feast).
☞ (M) **(*) HM/BMG 05472 77267-2 (3). Coll. Aur.

A refreshing and stimulating new set of Handel's Opus 6 – the high water mark of Baroque orchestral music – from Montreal. The group uses modern instruments and Yuli Turovsky's worthy aim is to seek a compromise between modern and authentic practice, by paring down vibrato in some of the expressive music, with just a hint of squeezing on the melodic line, as when the solo group make their restrained entry in the slow movement. The pointed, almost staccato treatment of the famous *Larghetto e piano* movement of No. 12 – one of the composer's most famous tunes – might be counted controversial, but many will like Turovsky's light touch and gentle grace. The concertino, Eleonora and Natalya Turovsky and Alain Aubut, play impressively, while the main group (6.3.1.1) produces full, well-balanced tone and Handel's joyous fugues are particularly fresh and buoyant. Turovsky paces convincingly, not missing Handel's breadth of sonority and moments of expressive grandeur. This now becomes our first choice for this wonderful music.

Admirers of Hogwood's characteristically astringent rhythmic style will be well satisfied with his Op. 6. The playing has enormous vitality, with bracingly brisk tempi and emphasis on refinement and transparency of texture rather than sonority. Two harpsichords and an arch-lute are used as continuo. The playing is heard at its finest in the masterly *Fifth Concerto in D major*, with the allegros sparkling with vivacity. The sound of the solo original instruments in the lyrical writing almost suggests viols rather than violins, although the forward balance gives the concertino soloists a strikingly firm presence. Perhaps the effect is slightly too forward, producing a less than ideal dynamic contrast between concertino and ripieno, but this is always difficult for the balance engineer to get exactly right: the bright, full sound is vividly realistic. Listening to this exhilarating music-making is certainly a refreshing experience, and Hogwood is undoubtedly preferable to Pinnock, helped by the fuller, more naturally focused, Decca sound. But those who have experienced these works on modern instruments (as performed by the ASMF under Marriner or Iona Brown) will find that the music's grandeur is often understated, and clearly Hogwood feels that such an approach is inflated. The chaste presentation of the famous Handelian melody which forms the *Larghetto e piano* third movement of No. 12 is entirely indicative of his feelings in this matter. His conviction certainly carries absolute authority, even if not all ears will respond to the results.

For all its 'authenticity', Pinnock's is never unresponsive music-making, with fine solo playing set against an attractively atmospheric acoustic. Ornamentation is often elaborate – but never at the expense of line. These are performances to admire and to sample, but not everyone will warm to them. If listened through, the sharp-edged sound eventually tends to tire the ear, and there is comparatively little sense of grandeur and few hints of tonally expansive beauty. The recording is first class.

The Guildhall String Ensemble offer fresh, modestly scaled performances, with plenty of life about them. Although modern instruments are used, textures are light and transparent. The effect is very real and tangible, with the soloists nicely separated from the ripieno. Tempi are generally apt, and this music-making has a buoyantly rhythmic sparkle and a nicely balanced espressivo feeling in Handel's songful slow movements.

In Handel's Op. 6 the Collegium Aureum, led by Franzjosef Maier, use original instruments, but the effect is tempererd by the warmth of the acoustic (the Cedernsaal in the Schloss Kirchheim). There is no acid-like astringency here and phrasing in slow movements is warmly expressive and unsqueezed. Baroque oboes and bassoons are featured in Nos. 1, 2, 5 and 6 to add weight and colour within the string texture, rather than hinting at a solo role. They are fairly well submerged by the resonance. Throughout, tempi are uncontroversial and generally well judged, though the basic approach is mellow, with the famous melody in No. 12 sounding as gracious as anyone could wish. The effect is slightly old-fashioned compared to 'authentic' practices of today, but these too are undergoing change and favour warm sonorities more than they once did. The solo playing here is first class and the recorded sound is beautiful, natural in timbre and detail, allowing for reverberation. Though the continuo is often submerged, the dedication and musicianship of these accounts are never in doubt, and the breadth and variety of Handel's inspiration is consistently caught. The *Alexander's Feast concerto grosso* makes an excellent bonus.

Concerto grosso in E min., Op. 6/3: Larghetto & Polonaise; The Faithful Shepherd (ballet suite); *The Gods go a-begging* (ballet suite); *The Origin of design* (ballet suite) (all arr. Beecham); *Messiah: Pastoral Symphony. Solomon: Arrival of the Queen of Sheba.* (i) Choruses: *Israel in Egypt: Moses and the Children of Israel; But for his people; The Lord is a man of war.*
☞ (**(*)) VAI Audio mono VAIA 1045 [id.]. LPO (or SO), Beecham.

Beecham's sparkling performance of the *Arrival of the Queen of Sheba* opens this concert with pristine freshness, and so good is the transfer that it seems impossible to believe that the recording was made in 1933 (fitted in on side two of a Columbia shellac disc after Rossini's *La scala di seta overture* which Beecham cut to make room for it!). The ballet suites – Beecham's way of introducing little-known Handel, which he clearly loved, to a wider audience – are equally felicitously played, and the transfers (made in Toronto from the original 78s by David Lennick) are equally sophisticated, although there are one or two less refined moments in *The Origin of design*. The choruses from *Israel in Egypt*, recorded with the Leeds Festival Choir in 1934, are hardly an asset. For all the vigour of the singing, the original sound was poorly focused and the transfer offers a muddy effect frequently verging on distortion. It is a pity this record is at full price, but Beecham aficionados will surely want to have it.

Concerto grosso in C (Alexander's Feast); Oboe concertos Nos. 1–3; Sonata a 5 in B flat.
*** DG Dig. 415 291-2 [id.]. E. Concert, Pinnock.

Rhythms are sprightly, and Pinnock's performance of the *Alexander's Feast concerto* is as good as any now available. The *B flat Sonata* is given with great sensitivity and taste by Simon Standage and his colleagues. David Reichenberg is the excellent soloist in the *Oboe concertos*. Excellently balanced and truthful recording, but the record could have been filled more generously.

Harp concerto in B flat, Op. 4/5.
(B) *** DG 427 206-2. Zabaleta, Paul Kuentz CO – MOZART: *Flute and harp concerto;* WAGENSEIL: *Harp concerto.* ***

(i) *Harp concerto, Op. 4/6. Variations for harp.*
⊛ (M) *** Decca 425 723-2; 425 723-4. Marisa Robles, (i) ASMF, Iona Brown – BOIELDIEU; DITTERSDORF: *Harp concertos* etc. *** ⊛

Handel's Op. 4/6 is well known in both organ and harp versions. Marisa Robles and Iona Brown make an unforgettable case for the latter by creating the most delightful textures, while never letting the work sound insubstantial. The ASMF accompaniment, so stylish and beautifully balanced, is a treat in itself, and the recording is well-nigh perfect.

The DG recording sounds clear and immediate and the crystalline stream of sound is attractive. Zabaleta's approach is agreeably cool, with imaginative use of light and shade. The Privilege reissue also includes a set of variations by Spohr.

Concerto for 2 lutes in B flat, Op. 4/6.

☞ (M) **(*) BMG/RCA 09026 61588-2 [id.]. Julian Bream, Monteverdi O, Gardiner – KOHAUT; VIVALDI: *Concertos*. **(*)

Here the ever-engaging Op. 4/6 appears in Thurston Dart's reconstruction for lute and harp, which Bream has further adjusted and elaborated using a chitarrone for the slow-movement continuo. The performance is a fine one (Bream plays both solo parts) but it suffers from a forward balance for the soloists, so that their dynamic range approaches that of the orchestra with very little contrast. Delectable music-making just the same, and an immaculate CD transfer.

Oboe concertos Nos 1–3, HWV 301, 302a & 287; Concerto grosso, Op. 3/3; Hornpipe in D, HWV 356; Overture in D, HWV 337/8; Sonata a 5 in B flat, HWV 288.

(M) **(*) Ph. 426 082-2 [id.]. Heinz Holliger, ECO, Raymond Leppard.

Holliger, a masterly interpreter, does not hesitate to embellish repeats; his ornamentation may overstep the boundaries some listeners are prepared to accept. His playing and that of the other artists in this collection is exquisite, and the recording is naturally balanced.

Organ concertos, Op. 4/1–6; Op. 7/1–6.

☞ ⊛ (M) *** Erato/Warner 4509 91932-2 (2) [id.]. Ton Koopman, Amsterdam Bar. O.

☞ (M) **(*) Teldec/Warner 4509 91188-2 (2) [id.]. Herbert Tachezi, VCM, Harnoncourt.

Ton Koopman's paired sets of Opp. 4 and 7 now reappear as a remarkable bargain, complete on two CDs in Erato's Duo Bonsai series. They take precedence over all the competition, both as performances and as recordings. The playing has wonderful life and warmth, tempi are always aptly judged and, although original instruments are used, this is authenticity with a kindly presence, for the warm acoustic ambience of St Bartholomew's Church, Beek-Ubbergen, Holland, gives the orchestra a glowingly vivid coloration and the string timbre is particularly attractive. So is the organ itself, which is just right for the music. Ton Koopman plays imaginatively throughout and he is obviously enjoying himself: no single movement sounds tired and the orchestral fugues emerge with genial clarity. Koopman directs the accompanying group from the keyboard, as Handel would have done, and the interplay between soloist and ripieno is a delight. The sound is first class and the balance could hardly be better.

Herbert Tachezi also concentrates on the twelve concertos which make up Opp. 4 and 7, and Teldec have managed to fit them economically on a pair of CDs. The ornamentation provided by the soloist was achieved spontaneously at the actual recording sessions and is certainly successful, but Harnoncourt's accompaniments are straightforward, at times even seeming unadventurous and rhythmically positive. But Tachezi's registration and flourishes give constant pleasure, and the chest organ (made by Jürgen Ahrend) is very well chosen for this repertoire. The first concerto of Op. 7 exceptionally requires the use of pedals, and for this a Viennese instrument was used (built by Karl Bucklow in 1858). Both organs contrast well with Harnoncourt's authentic, chamber-sized string group, and his rhythmic pointing is always agreeably lively. Although the more robust and grander qualities of Handel's inspiration are played down somewhat, the recording is fresh, full, transparent and cleanly transferred, and there is much to enjoy here.

Organ concertos, Op. 4/1–6; Op. 7/1–6; in F (Cuckoo and nightingale), HWV 295; in A, HWV 296; in D min., HWV 304; in F, HWV 305.

☞ (M) ** HM/BMG 05472 77246-2 (3). Rudolf Ewerhart (Gabler organ in Kloster Weingarten; Baroque parish church organ, Körbecke in Westfalen; Riepp Trinity organ in Ottobeuren; or cabinet organ of Geertekerk, Utrecht), Coll. Aur., Maier.

The mid-priced Deutsche Harmonia Mundi set has the advantage of authenticity, both in the use of original instruments in the accompanying group and in the choice of three different organs, each chosen for its special range of colouring, although not all the registration is equally effective. The 1967 recording is excellent, and there is nothing pinched or abrasive about the orchestral textures. Tempi are generally rather sedate and leisurely, although individual performances are enjoyable, if without the vitality of later versions; nevertheless these recordings are likeable for the warm atmosphere of the music-making and the clear projection of the soloist.

Organ concertos, Op. 4/1–6; in A, HWV 296.

*** DG Dig. 413 465-2 (2) [id.]. Simon Preston, E. Concert, Pinnock.

Organ concertos, Op. 7/1–6; in F (The cuckoo and the nightingale); in D min., HWV 304.
*** DG Dig. 413 468-2 (2) [id.]. Simon Preston, E. Concert, Pinnock.

Organ concertos, Op. 4/1–6; in F (The cuckoo and the nightingale), HVW 295; in A, HWV 296;
Sonata in D min. (Il trionfo del tempo a del disinganno), HWV 46a.
(M) *** Decca Dig. 430 569-2 (2). Peter Hurford, Concg. CO, Joshua Rifkin.

Organ concertos, Op. 7/1–6; in D min., HWV 304; in F, HWV 305 & Appendix.
(M) *** Decca Dig. 433 176-2 (2). Peter Hurford, Concg. CO, Rifkin.

Simon Preston's set of the Handel *Organ concertos* comes in two separate packages. In the first, containing the six Op. 4 works, plus the *A major* (the old No. 14), though the balance of the solo instrument is not ideal, the playing of both Preston and the English Concert is admirably fresh and lively. Ursula Holliger is outstanding on a baroque harp in Op. 4, No. 6, and she creates some delicious sounds. The second of the two boxes, containing the six Op. 7 works, plus the *The cuckoo and the nightingale* and the old *No. 15 in D minor*, was recorded on the organ at St John's, Armitage, in Staffordshire, and is even more attractive for the warmth and assurance of the playing, which comes near the ideal for an 'authentic' performance.

Peter Hurford's 1985 Decca set also comes in two separate CD boxes and features the organ of Bethlehemkerk, Papendrecht, Holland, which has attractively fresh and bright registrations, particularly suited to the Op. 4 set. The sound is in the demonstration bracket, and this is highly recommendable. Peter Hurford's Op. 7 set has comparable sparkle, if not being quite as memorable as Op. 4.

Organ concertos, Op. 4/2; Op. 7/3–5; in F (The cuckoo and the nightingale).
(M) *** DG Dig. 431 708-2 [id.]. Simon Preston, E. Concert, Pinnock.

This is more generous than the previous (full-price) sampler from Preston's series with Pinnock; all the Op. 7 works plus the *The cuckoo and the nightingale* are recorded on the organ at St John's, Armitage, in Staffordshire, which seems particularly well suited to this repertoire. Both performances and sound are admirably fresh.

Organ concertos, Op. 4/4 & 6; Op. 7/1 & 4; in F (Cuckoo and the nightingale), HWV 295.
☞ (B) *** Erato/Warner 2922 45930-2 [id.]. Marie-Claire Alain (Kern organ of Collegiate Church, Saint-Donat, Drôme), Paillard CO, Paillard.

A French view of Handel might be expected to provide a new look, and this bargain selection from Marie-Claire Alain's highly successful (1978) Erato complete set is most enjoyable. The solo playing is consistently alert and imaginative, and the overall effect brings grandeur as well as elegance to this music. The Op. 7 works are particularly enjoyable. Op. 7/1, after an impressively regal opening, has an enchanting closing *Bourrée*. Surely the *Cuckoo and the nightingale* can never have been registered more winningly on disc, while its *Siciliano* slow movement is most graciously played. Similarly the registration at the opening of Op. 4/6 (also well known in its version for harp) is memorable. The solo playing is consistently alert and imaginative, and the CD transfers are admirable. With 71 minutes of music, this is a bargain.

Music for the Royal Fireworks (original wind scoring).
*** Telarc Dig. CD 80038 [id.]. Cleveland Symphonic Winds, Fennell – HOLST: *Military band suites.*
*** ⊛

Music for the Royal Fireworks; Concerto grosso in C (Alexander's Feast); Concerti grossi, Op. 6/1 &
6.
(M) *** DG 431 707-2. E. Concert, Trevor Pinnock.

Music for the Royal Fireworks (original version); (i) *Coronation anthems* (see also below).
*** Hyp. Dig. CDA 66350; *KA 66350* [id.]. (i) New College, Oxford, Ch.; augmented King's Consort, Robert King.

In 1978, in Severance Hall, Cleveland, Ohio, Frederick Fennell gathered together the wind and brass from the Cleveland Symphony Orchestra and recorded a performance to demonstrate spectacularly what fine playing and digital sound could do for Handel's open-air score. The overall sound-balance tends to favour the brass (and the drums), but few will grumble when the result is as overwhelming as it is on the CD, with the sharpness of focus matched by the presence and amplitude of the sound-image.

Pinnock's performance of the *Fireworks music* has tremendous zest; this is not only the safest but the best recommendation for those wanting a period-instrument version. The account of the *Alexander's Feast concerto* has both vitality and imagination and is no less recommendable.

King provides the first ever period performance of Handel's *Royal fireworks music* to use the full complement of instruments Handel demanded, assembling no fewer than 24 baroque oboists and 12 baroque bassoonists, 9 trumpeters, 9 exponents of the hand horn and 4 timpanists. It all makes for a glorious noise. King's Handel style has plenty of rhythmic bounce, and the recording in its warmly atmospheric way gives ample scale. The coupled performances of the four *Coronation anthems* are not as incisively dramatic as some but still convey the joy of the inspiration.

Music for the Royal Fireworks; Water music (complete).
☞ (B) *** Erato/Warner 2292 45931-2 [id.]. Paillard CO, Jean-François Paillard.
*** Argo 414 596-2 [id.]. ASMF, Marriner.
(BB) *** Naxos Dig. 8.550109; *4550109* [id.]. Capella Istropolitana, Bohdan Warchal.

Music for the Royal Fireworks; Water music: suites Nos. 1–3; Overture Ariodante.
☞ (M) * Sony SBK 48285 [id.]. La Grand Ecurie et la Chambre du Roy, Malgoire.

Erato offer a really first-class combination of the complete *Fireworks* and *Water music*, admirably played on modern instruments. There is both vitality and finesse, and a genuine sense of style. The *Fireworks music* is heard in its original wind scoring, and no one could complain about a lack of spectacle – the horns rasp splendidly in the *Overture*, and one can really imagine a fiery backcloth for the grand closing *Minuets*, with the exuberant horns again contrasting well with the oboes. The CD transfer of recordings made in 1973 and 1962 is admirably fresh and modern-sounding.

Marriner, using modern instruments, directs a sparkling account of the complete *Water music* plus the *Fireworks music*. Here Marriner deliberately avoids a weighty manner, even at the magisterial opening of the overture. But with full, resonant recording, this coupling makes sound sense and the remastered Argo recording still sounds both full and fresh.

Bohdan Warchal directs the Capella Istropolitana in bright and lively performances of the complete *Water music* as well as the *Fireworks music*, well paced and well scaled, with woodwind and brass aptly abrasive, and with such points as double-dotting faithfully observed. Textures are clean, with an attractive bloom on the full and immediate sound, to provide a strong bargain recommendation.

Malgoire's CD is generous in offering both the complete *Fireworks* and *Water music* plus an overture. However, although the performances are lively, apart from the robust horns the authentic textures tend to be too meagre to give real pleasure, and intonation, as so often with original instruments, is not all that could be desired.

Water music: Suites Nos. 1–3 (complete).
*** DG Dig. 410 525-2 [id.]. E. Concert, Pinnock.
*** ASV Dig. CDDCA 520 [id.]. ECO, Malcolm.

Water music (complete); *The Alchymist: Overture and suite.*
☞ *** O-L 443 177-2 [id.]. AAM, Hogwood.

Water music: suites Nos. 1–3 (complete); *Concerto grosso in C (Alexander's Feast).*
☞ (M) *** Ph. 434 729-2 [id.]. ASMF, Marriner.

The 1979 Philips version of the *Water music* brings Sir Neville Marriner's second complete recording, and characteristically he has taken the trouble to correct several tiny textural points wrongly read before. The playing, too, is even finer than on his old Argo disc, helped by full-ranging, refined recording. For anyone wanting a mid-priced version using modern instruments this is highly recommendable, and the coupled *Alexander's Feast concerto grosso* combines energy with polish. However, since this is reissued on Philips's Insignia label, no musical notes are included, only a eulogy of the performers.

To offer the *Water music* without the *Fireworks music* now seems ungenerous, but Pinnock's version on DG Archiv is very enticing. Speeds are consistently well chosen and are generally uncontroversial. One test is the famous *Air*, which here remains an engagingly gentle piece. The recording is beautifully balanced and clear.

Although Hogwood's account of the *Water music* is very attractive in its way, it does not upstage Pinnock in the authentic arena. The famous *Air* is treated briskly (some might think summarily) by Hogwood, yet it remains an engagingly gentle piece. The recording is beautifully balanced and clear, with sufficient bloom on the sound and plenty of immediacy. The added attraction – apart from the medium price on this reissue – is the inclusion of the suite from *The Alchymist*, which drew for its material on Handel's first Italian opera, *Vincer se stesso è la maggio vittorio* (later called *Rinaldo*). It was the first composition of Handel's to be performed in England, an overture and suite of eight short dance-movements, all freshly played and again given excellent recording.

Those whose taste does not extend to 'authentic' string textures should be well satisfied with George Malcolm's splendid digital recording for ASV. The playing is first class, articulation is deft and detail admirable. There is a sense of delight in the music which makes this version especially appealing.

CHAMBER MUSIC

Flute sonatas, Op. 1/1b, 5, 6, 8 & 9; & in D. Oboe sonatas Op. 1/8; in B flat (Fitzwilliam); & in F min.
(M) *** HM/BMG Dig. GD 77152 [77152-2-RG]. Camerata Köln.

Recorder sonatas, Op. 1/2, 4, 7 & 11; Recorder sonatas in B flat; in D; in G (Fitzwilliam); Trio sonata in F.
(M) *** HM/BMG Dig. GD 77104 [77104-2-RG]. Camerata Köln.

These two CDs by the Camerata Köln playing on period instruments give very satisfying accounts of this repertoire. Not only is the playing rewarding, but the quality of the 1985 sound has exemplary clarity, yet warmth too.

KEYBOARD MUSIC

Chaconne in G, HWV 435; Suites Nos. 10 in D min.; 12 in G min., 13 in B flat.
(M) **(*) Saga SCD 9028 [id.]. Robert Woolley (harpsichord).

Robert Woolley has the full measure of this repertoire. Perhaps he slightly overdoes the decoration at the very beginning of the massive *Chaconne*, which follows on effectively after the (rather similar) noble *Sarabande* with divisions, which concludes the *D minor Suite*. The *Suite in B flat* includes a splendid set of variations not unlike the famous '*Harmonious Blacksmith*' set. The theme was also used by Brahms in his Handelian variations. All in all, a rewarding disc.

Harpsichord suites Nos. 1–8.
☞ *** Erato/Warner Dig. 2292 45452-2 (2). Scott Ross (harpsichord).

Scott Ross plays a copy of a 1733 Blanchet, which suits this repertoire very well, and his performances are in exemplary style. He plays most repeats, but not all – and one wonders why, when the overall playing time is short of two hours. Still, this is a fine set, well though closely recorded.

Suites Nos. 2 in F; 3 in D min.; 5 in E; 6 in F sharp min.; 7 in G min.
**(*) HM HMC 90447 [id.]. Kenneth Gilbert (harpsichord).

Gilbert observes most first-half repeats but not the second, and he is as imaginative in the handling of decoration and ornamentation as one would expect. The recording is much better balanced and more natural than recent rivals.

VOCAL MUSIC

Acis and Galatea (masque).
*** DG 423 406-2 (2) [id.]. Burrowes, Rolfe Johnson, Martyn Hill, Willard White, E. Bar. Soloists, Gardiner.

(i) *Acis and Galatea;* (ii) *Cantata: Look down, harmonious saint.*
*** Hyp. Dig. CDA 66361/2; *KA 66361/2.* (i; ii) Ainsley; (i) McFadden, Covey-Crump, George, Harre-Jones; King's Cons., Robert King.

Robert King directs a bluff, beautifully sprung reading of *Acis and Galatea* that brings out its domestic jollity. Using the original version for five solo singers and no chorus, this may be less delicate in its treatment than John Eliot Gardiner's reading but it is, if anything, even more winning. The soloists are first rate, with John Mark Ainsley among the most stylish of the younger generation of Handel tenors, and the bass, Michael George, characterizing strongly. Claron McFadden's vibrant soprano is girlishly distinctive. This Hyperion issue provides a valuable makeweight in the florid solo cantata, thought to be originally conceived as part of *Alexander's Feast*, nimbly sung by Ainsley.

Certain of John Eliot Gardiner's tempi are idiosyncratic (some too fast, some too slow), but the scale of the performance, using original instruments, is beautifully judged, with the vocal soloists banding together for the choruses. Willard White is a fine Polyphemus. The authentic sounds of the English Baroque Soloists are finely controlled and the vibrato-less string timbre is clear and clean without being abrasive. A thoroughly rewarding pair of CDs.

(i) *Aci, Galatea e Polifemo*. (ii) *Recorder sonatas in F; C & G* (trans. to *F*).
*** HM Dig. HMC 901253/4 [id.]. (i) Kirkby, C. Watkinson, Thomas, L. Bar., Medlam; (ii) Michel
  Piquet, John Toll.

Aci, Galatea e Polifemo proves to be quite a different work from the always popular English masque,
Acis and Galatea, with only one item even partially borrowed. Charles Medlam directs London
Baroque in a beautifully sprung performance with three excellent soloists, the brightly characterful
Emma Kirkby as Aci, Carolyn Watkinson in the lower-pitched role of Galatea, and David Thomas
coping manfully with the impossibly wide range of Polifemo's part. The three recorder sonatas are
comparably delightful, a welcome makeweight. Excellent sound, full of presence.

Ah, che pur troppo è vero; Mi palpita il cor. Duets: *A miravi io son intento; Beato in ver chi può;
Conservate, raddioppiate; Fronda leggiera e mobile; Langue, geme e sospira; No, di voi non vuo fidarni;
Se tu non lasci amore; Sono liete, fortunate; Tanti strali al sen; Troppo cruda* (cantatas).
*** Hung. Dig. HCD 12564-5 [id.]. Zádori, Esswood; Falvay, Németh, Ella (cello, flute and
  harpsichord).

The two vocal soloists, the clear-voiced soprano Maria Zádori and the counter-tenor Paul Esswood,
sing delightfully throughout this generous collection of very rare Handel duet cantatas.

(i) *Alceste: Overture and incidental music;* (ii) *Comus: vocal excerpts*.
☞ (M) *** O-L 443 183-2 [id.]. Margaret Cable, David Thomas; (i) Judith Nelson, Emma Kirkby,
  Christine Pound, Margaret Cable, Catherine Denley, Paul Elliott, Rogers Covey-Crump, David
  Thomas, Christopher Keyte; (ii) Patrizia Kwella; AAM, Hogwood.

Commissioned to write incidental music for a play by Smollett (an enterprise to associate with Purcell
rather than Handel), the composer was stopped in his tracks at the abandonment of the whole
project. Nevertheless he left us much to enjoy here, with the impressively dramatic *Alceste overture* in
D minor and the *Grand entrée* for Admetus and Alceste and their wedding guests getting the
proceedings off to a fine start. There follows a series not just of solo items but also some simple
tuneful choruses, in which a small secondary vocal group participates. Hogwood draws lively
performances from his usual team and, as ever, is very well recorded. The music for *Comus* was
discovered as recently as 1969 in Manchester's Henry Watson Music Library, after research had
shown that Handel had visited Exton Hall, Leicestershire, in 1745, where he was prevailed upon by
the Earl of Gainsborough to provide a musical epilogue for a family performance of the Arne/Milton
masque, a current hit on the London stage. Though some of it was later used in the *Occasional
oratorio*, the five items offered here show how refreshing was Handel's original. The performances by
Patrizia Kwella, Margaret Cable and David Thomas with the Academy under Hogwood have all the
freshness and vigour one associates with this conductor's earlier series of Purcell theatre music. The
transfers of 1979/80 analogue recordings, made at St Jude's, London, are well up to L'Oiseau-Lyre's
usual high standard.

(i) *Alexander's Feast* (complete). (ii) *Harp concerto, Op. 4/6;* (iii) *Organ concerto, Op. 4/1*.
*** Collins Dig. 7016-2 (2). (i) Argenta, Partridge, George, The Sixteen Ch.; (ii) Lawrence-King,
  Tragicomedia; (iii) Nicholson; (i; iii) The Sixteen O, Christophers.

Alexander's Feast; Concerto grosso in C (Alexander's Feast).
**(*) Ph. Dig. 422 053-2 (2) [id.]. Carolyn Watkinson, Robson, Donna Brown, Stafford, Varcoe,
  Monteverdi Ch., E. Bar. Soloists, Eliot Gardiner.

Harry Christophers directs a lively, sympathetic account of Handel's extended cantata, very well sung
and recorded. The three soloists – Nancy Argenta, Ian Partridge and Michael George – are all first
rate, making a more consistent team than the quintet used by Gardiner. The bass, Michael George, is
satisfyingly firm and dark in the two big bass arias. Christophers also provides two of the related
Opus 4 concertos instead of Gardiner's one.
  Gardiner's version of *Alexander's Feast* was recorded live at performances given at the Göttingen
Festival. The sound is not distractingly dry, but it is still harder than usual on singers and players
alike, taking away some of the bloom. What matters is the characteristic vigour and concentration of
Gardiner's performance. Stephen Varcoe may lack the dark resonance of a traditional bass, but he
projects his voice well. Nigel Robson's tenor suffers more than do the others from the dryness of the
acoustic. The soprano, Donna Brown, sings with boyish freshness, and the alto numbers are divided
very effectively between Carolyn Watkinson and the soft-grained counter-tenor, Ashley Stafford. The
Concerto grosso in C was given with the oratorio at its first performance.

L'allegro, il penseroso, il moderato.
*** Erato/Warner 2292 45377-2 (2). Kwella, McLaughlin, Jennifer Smith, Ginn, Davies, Hill, Varcoe, Monteverdi Ch., E. Bar. Soloists, Gardiner.

Taking Milton as his starting point, Handel illustrated in music the contrasts of mood and character between the cheerful and the thoughtful. Then, prompted by his librettist, Charles Jennens, he added compromise in *Il moderato*, the moderate man. The sequence of brief numbers is a delight, particularly in a performance as exhilarating as this, with excellent soloists, choir and orchestra. The recording is first rate.

Alpestre monte; Mi palpita il cor; Tra le fiamme; Tu fedel? Tu costante? (Italian cantatas).
*** O-L Dig. 414 473-2 [id.]. Emma Kirkby, AAM, Hogwood.

The four cantatas here, all for solo voice with modest instrumental forces, are nicely contrasted, with the personality of the original singer by implication identified with *Tu fedel*, a spirited sequence of little arias rejecting a lover. Even 'a heart full of cares' in *Mi palpita il cor* inspires Handel to a pastorally charming aria, with a delectable oboe obbligato rather than anything weighty, and even those limited cares quickly disperse. Light-hearted and sparkling performances to match.

Aminta e Fillide (cantata).
*** Hyp. CDA 66118 [id.]. Fisher, Kwella, L. Handel O, Darlow.

In writing for two voices and strings, Handel presents a simple encounter in the pastoral tradition over a span of ten brief arias which, together with recitatives and final duet, last almost an hour. The music is as charming and undemanding for the listener as it is taxing for the soloists. This lively performance, beautifully recorded with two nicely contrasted singers, delightfully blows the cobwebs off a Handel work till now totally neglected.

Anthem for the Foundling Hospital; Ode for the birthday of Queen Anne.
*** O-L 421 654-2 [id.]. Nelson, Kirkby, Minty, Bowman, Hill, Thomas, Ch. of Christ Church Cathedral, Oxford, AAM, Preston – HAYDN: *Missa brevis in F.* ***

The *Ode* has its Italianate attractions, but it is the much later *Foundling Hospital anthem* which is the more memorable, not just because it concludes with an alternative version of the *Hallelujah chorus* but because the other borrowed numbers are also superb. An extra tang is given by the accompaniment on original instruments.

Apollo e Dafne (cantata).
**(*) HM HMC 905157; *HMC 405157* [id.]. Judith Nelson, David Thomas; Hayes, San Francisco Bar. O, McGegan.

Apollo e Dafne is one of Handel's most delightful cantatas, with at least two strikingly memorable numbers, a lovely siciliano for Dafne with oboe obbligato and an aria for Apollo, *Come rosa in su la spina*, with unison violins and a solo cello. Both soloists are first rate, and Nicholas McGegan is a lively Handelian, though the playing of the orchestra could be more polished and the sound more firmly focused.

Athalia (oratorio).
*** O-L Dig. 417 126-2 (2) [id.]. Sutherland, Kirkby, Bowman, Aled Jones, Rolfe Johnson, David Thomas, New College, Oxford, Ch., AAM, Hogwood.

As Queen Athalia, Dame Joan Sutherland sings boldly with a richness and vibrancy to contrast superbly with the pure silver of Emma Kirkby, not to mention the celestial treble of Aled Jones, in the role of the boy-king, Joas. That casting is perfectly designed to set the Queen aptly apart from the good Israelite characters led by the Priest, Joad (James Bowman in a castrato role), and Josabeth (Kirkby). Christopher Hogwood with the Academy brings out the speed and variety of the score that has been described as Handel's first great English oratorio. The recording is bright and clean, giving sharp focus to voices and instruments alike.

Duets: *Beato in ver; Langue, geme; Tanti strali.* Cantatas: *Parti, l'idolo mio; Sento là che ristretto.*
(B) *** HM HMA 901004; *HMA 431004* [id.]. Judith Nelson, René Jacobs, William Christie, K. Jünghanel.

These Handel duets and the two cantatas – more substantial works – contain some delightful music, Handel at his most charming. With outstanding solo singing from both Judith Nelson and René Jacobs, they are given very stylish performances, cleanly recorded. A bargain.

Belshazzar (complete).
*** DG Dig. 431 793-2 (3) [id.]. Rolfe Johnson, Augér, Robbin, Bowman, Wilson-Johnson, E.
  Concert Ch. & O, Pinnock.

Handel modified *Belshazzar* over the years, and Pinnock has opted not for the earliest but for the most striking and fully developed text. The cast is starry, with Arleen Augér at her most ravishing as the Babylonian king's mother, Nitocris, Anthony Rolfe Johnson in the title role, James Bowman as the prophet, Daniel, and Catherine Robbin as King Cyrus, all excellent. Full, well-balanced sound.

Brockes Passion.
**(*) Hung. Dig. HCD 12734/6-2 [id.]. Klietmann, Gáti, Zádori, Minter & soloists, Halle
  Stadtsingechor, Capella Savaria, McGegan.

The relatively crude Passion text by Barthold Brockes prompted a piece of some thirty or so arias, two duets and a trio, most of them brief but full of superb ideas, many of which Handel raided for his later oratorios. Nicholas McGegan with the excellent Capella Savaria using period instruments directs a lively, refreshing account of the piece that easily outshines previous versions. The team of soloists has no weak link, and the only comparative reservation concerns the singing of the chorus, fresh but less polished than the rest.

(i) *Cecilia vogi un sguardo* (cantata); *Silete venti* (motet).
*** DG Dig. 419 736-2 [id.]. Jennifer Smith, Elwes, E. Concert, Pinnock.

These two fine cantatas come from a later period than most of Handel's Italian-language works in this genre. Both reveal him at his most effervescent, a quality superbly caught in these performances with excellent singing and playing, most strikingly from Jennifer Smith whose coloratura has never been more brilliantly displayed on record. Excellent recording.

Chandos anthems Nos. 1–11 (complete).
☞ *** Chan. Dig. CHAN 0554/7 [id.]. Dawson, Kwella, Partridge, Bowman, George, The Sixteen
  Ch. & O, Harry Christophers.

It is appropriate that a record label named Chandos should record a complete set of Handel's *Chandos anthems*. This is now available on four CDs in a box (still at full price) and marks one of the most successful and worthwhile achievements of The Sixteen on CD. From the first of these fine works, which Handel based on his *Utrecht Te Deum*, to the last with its exuberant closing *Alleluja* the music is consistently inspired; it has great variety of invention and resourceful vocal scoring. The recordings are well up to the house standard.

Chandos anthems Nos. 1: O be joyful in the Lord; 2: In the Lord put I my trust; 3: Have mercy on me, HWV 246/8.
*** Chan. Dig. CHAN 8600; *ABTD 1293* [id.]. Lynne Dawson, Ian Partridge, The Sixteen Ch. &
  O, Christophers.

The impact of these performances is affected strongly by the recorded sound, set in a warm acoustic but with rather a close balance; that makes the choir sound bigger. Ian Partridge is the radiant-voiced linchpin of these performances and is superbly matched by Lynne Dawson with her gloriously pure, silvery soprano. The closeness of sound makes the instrumental sonatas which start each *Anthem* more abrasive than they might be, but not uncomfortably so.

Chandos anthems Nos. (i) *2: In the Lord put I my trust;* (ii) *10: The Lord is my light;* (iii) *11: Let God arise*.
☞ (M) *** Decca 436 258-2. (i) Langridge; (ii) Cantelo, Partridge; (iii) Vaughan, Young; King's
  College Ch., ASMF, Willcocks.

Chandos anthems Nos. (i) *5a, I will magnify Thee;* (ii) *6, As pants the heart;* (iii) *9, O praise the Lord with one consent*.
☞ (M) *** Decca 436 257-2 [id.]. (i) Friend, Langridge; (ii) Cantelo, Partridge; (iii) Vaughan, Young,
  Forbes Robinson; King's College Ch., ASMF, Willcocks.

In 1717–18 Handel wrote eleven anthems for his patron, the Duke of Chandos, to be performed at Canons, his country house near Edgware. Reflecting the period, they have grandeur, but also a direct unpretentiousness; the elements of Italianate elaboration and German fugal complexity are married in them with an assurance that only Handel could achieve. No. 6 includes a lovely *Adagio* chorus and beautiful soprano aria, while the opening line of No. 9, *O praise the Lord with one consent*, fits very nicely to the hymn tune we know as *O God our help in ages past*; but Handel helps himself to just this first line of the hymn, then weaves his own music therefrom. This is an especially impressive cantata with more than one reminder of *Messiah* (only the idiom is less grandiose), and both here and No. 11, *Let God arise*, the writing for the soloists is especially rewarding. The latter work is marginally more conventional in style but has a wonderfully imaginative chorus to the words, *Praised be the Lord*. Excellent singing from soloists and chorus alike, and stylish accompaniments. The recordings date from between 1965 and 1974, a vintage period for the Argo engineers at King's, and they are well transferred, even if the choral focus is not always absolutely sharp.

Chandos anthems Nos. 4: O sing unto the Lord a new song; 5: I will magnify thee; 6: As pants the hart for cooling streams.
*** Chan. Dig. CHAN 0504; *EBTD 0504* [id.]. Lynne Dawson, Ian Partridge, The Sixteen Ch. & O, Christophers.

The second volume of the Chandos series is hardly less appealing than the first. There are some splendidly vigorous choruses, while in No. 6 there is an equally memorable soprano aria, beautifully sung by Lynne Dawson.

Chandos anthems Nos. 7: My song shall be alway; 8: O come let us sing unto the Lord; 9: O praise the Lord.
☞ *** Chan. Dig. CHAN 0505; *EBTD 0505* [id.]. Patrizia Kwella, James Bowman, Ian Partridge, Michael George, The Sixteen Ch. & O, Christophers.

Again in this third volume there is splendid singing from the soloists, with Patrizia Kwella joining the team, and there is plenty of interest in the solo writing in these fine, contrasted works, while the choral contribution is well up to standard.

Chandos anthems Nos. 10: The Lord is my light; 11: Let God arise.
*** Chan. Dig. CHAN 0509; *EBT 0509*. Lynne Dawson, Ian Partridge, The Sixteen Ch. & O, Christophers.

The tenor soloist dominates No. 10, and Ian Partridge sings with his customary style and sweetness of timbre. Lynne Dawson makes her entry on the penultimate number. The chorus is again in exhilarating form, especially in the closing *Alleluja*. The recording is spacious while continuing to preserve the music's intimate feeling.

Coronation anthems (1. Zadok the Priest; 2. The King shall rejoice; 3. My heart is inditing; 4. Let Thy hand be strengthened).
*** DG Dig. 410 030-2 [id.]. Westminster Abbey Ch., E. Concert, Preston; Pinnock (organ).
☞ (M) *** Decca 436 259-2 [id.]. King's College Ch., ECO, Willcocks – BLOW: *Anthems.* **(*)

Coronation anthems (complete); *Judas Maccabaeus; See the conqu'ring hero comes; March; Sing unto God.*
*** Ph. Dig. 412 733-2 [id.]. ASMF Ch., ASMF, Marriner.

The extra weight of the Academy of St Martin-in-the-Fields Chorus compared with the Pinnock version seems appropriate for the splendour of music intended for the pomp of royal ceremonial occasions, and the commanding choral entry in *Zadok the Priest* is gloriously rich in amplitude, without in any way lacking incisiveness. The excerpts from *Solomon* are delightful.

Those who prefer sparer, more 'authentic' textures can choose Pinnock where, although the overall effect is less grand, the element of contrast is even more telling. To have the choir enter with such bite and impact underlines the freshness and immediacy. The use of original instruments gives plenty of character to the accompaniments. An exhilarating version.

The reissued (1961) Argo King's recording of these four anthems makes an admirable mid-priced recommendation, particularly as the extra clarity and presence given to the choir improve the balance in relation to the orchestra. The Blow *Anthems* make a fine bonus.

Dettingen Te Deum; Dettingen anthem.
*** DG Dig. 410 647-2 [id.]. Westminster Abbey Ch., E. Concert, Preston.

The *Dettingen Te Deum* is a splendidly typical work and continually reminds the listener of *Messiah*, written the previous year. Preston's Archiv performance from the English Concert makes an ideal recommendation, with its splendid singing, crisp but strong, excellent recording and a generous, apt coupling. This setting of *The King shall rejoice* should not be confused with the *Coronation anthem* of that name. It is less inspired, but has a magnificent double fugue for finale. The recording is first class.

Dixit Dominus; Nisi Dominus; Salve Regina.
*** DG Dig. 423 594-2 [id.]. Westminster Abbey Ch. & O, Simon Preston.

Dixit dominus; Nisi dominus; Silete venti.
*** Chan. Dig. CHAN 0517; *EBTD 0517* [id.]. Dawson, Russell, Brett, Partridge, George, The
Sixteen Choir & O, Harry Christophers.

On DG Archiv *Dixit Dominus* is very aptly coupled with fine performances of another – less
ambitious – Psalm setting, *Nisi Dominus*, and a votive antiphon, *Salve Regina*, which Handel
composed between the two. Preston here draws ideally luminous and resilient singing from the
Westminster Abbey Choir, with a fine team of soloists in which Arleen Augér and Diana Montague
are outstanding. The playing of the orchestra of period instrumentalists, led by Roy Goodman, in
every way matches the fine qualities of the singing.

Christophers' speeds tend to be more extreme, slow as well as fast, and the recorded sound,
though full and well detailed, is less immediate. On balance Pinnock with his rather more bouncy
rhythms remains the first choice, but the Chandos issue gains significantly from a much more
generous third item. *Silete venti* allows the silver-toned Lynne Dawson to shine even more than in the
other items, ending with a brilliant *Alleluia* in galloping compound time.

Esther (complete).
**(*) O-L Dig. 414 423-2 (2) [id.]. Kwella, Rolfe Johnson, Partridge, Thomas, Kirkby, Elliott,
Westminster Cathedral Boys' Ch., Ch. and AAM, Hogwood.

Hogwood has opted for the original 1718 score, and his rather abrasive brand of authenticity goes
well with the bright, full recorded sound which unfortunately exaggerates the choir's sibilants. The
elaborate passage-work is far too heavily aspirated, at times almost as though the singers are
laughing. The vigour of the performance is unaffected and the team of soloists is strong and
consistent, with Patrizia Kwella sounding distinctive and purposeful in the name-part.

Israel in Egypt (oratorio).
(M) **(*) DG 429 530-2 (2) [id.]. Harper, Clark, Esswood, Young, Rippon, Keyte, Leeds Festival
Ch., ECO, Mackerras.
☞ **(*) EMI Dig. CDS7 54017-2 (2) [id.]. Argenta, Van Evera, Wilson, Rolfe Johnson, Thomas,
White, Taverner Ch. & Players, Parrott.

(i) *Israel in Egypt;* (ii) *Organ concerto in F (Cuckoo and the Nightingale), HWV 295.*
☞ *(**) Collins Dig. 7035-2 (2) [id.]. (i) Nicola Jenkin, Sally Dunkley, Caroline Trevor, Neil
MacKenzie, Robert Evans, Simon Birchall, The Sixteen; (ii) Paul Nicholson; O of The Sixteen;
Harry Christophers.

(i) *Israel in Egypt; Lamentations of the Israelites for the Death of Joseph;* (ii) *The Ways of Zion do
mourn* (Funeral anthem).
☞ (M) *** Erato/Warner 2292 45399-2 (2) [id.]. (i) Knibbs, Troth, Greene, Priday, Royall, Stafford,
Gordon, Clarkson, Elliott, Kendall, Varcoe, Stewart; (ii) Burrowes, Brett, Hill, Varcoe;
Monteverdi Ch. & O, Gardiner.

Using the modern instruments of his Monteverdi Orchestra, Gardiner made his Erato recording in
1978, not long before he decided to adopt period instruments instead. His style here, crisply rhythmic,
superbly sprung, with dozens of detailed insights in bringing out word-meaning, is very much what
has since become his forte in period performances of Handel and others. The singing both of the
chorus and of the twelve soloists chosen from its members is excellent, though, like all other modern
recordings, this one slightly falls down in resonance on the most famous number, the duet for basses,
the *Lord is a Man of War*. In almost every way Gardiner gains by presenting the *Lamentations* not as
an introduction to the main oratorio – which Handel used only at the very first, unsuccessful
performance – but as a supplement, with the same music given in its original form, with text
unamended: the funeral cantata for Queen Caroline. Excellent, full-bodied, analogue sound.

Mackerras's performance represents a dichotomy of styles, using the English Chamber Orchestra
sounding crisp, stylish and lightweight and the fairly large amateur choir, impressively weighty rather
than incisive. Thus the work makes its effect by breadth and grandiloquence rather than athletic
vigour. The solo singing is distinguished, but its style is refined rather than earthy.

Parrott directs a clean-cut, well-paced reading which wears its period manners easily. This may
lack the distinctive insights of Gardiner's more sharply rhythmic version which, with modern
instruments, adopts a similar scale, but with excellent choral and solo singing the performance is
unlikely to offend anyone. Good, warm sound. Parrott follows the unique precedent of Handel's very

first performance in using as the first part of the oratorio the cantata, written on the death of Queen Caroline, *The Lamentations of the Israelites for the Death of Joseph*, with text duly adapted.

Christophers, like Parrott, uses the *Lamentations* as a first part to the oratorio, and also – another nod towards Handelian performance-practice – adds the best-known of Handel's organ concertos, the *Cuckoo and the Nightingale*, between Parts One and Two. The playing and singing are even brighter than with Parrott, but sadly the Collins recording is so reverberant that there is a serious loss of inner detail.

Jephtha.
*** Ph. Dig. 422 351-2 (3) [id.]. Robson, Dawson, Anne Sofie von Otter, Chance, Varcoe, Holton, Monteverdi Ch., E. Bar. Soloists, Gardiner.

John Eliot Gardiner's recording was made live at the Göttingen Festival in 1988 and, though the sound does not have quite the bloom of his finest studio recordings of Handel, the exhilaration and intensity of the performance come over vividly, with superb singing from both chorus and an almost ideal line-up of soloists. Nigel Robson's tenor may be on the light side for the title-role, but the sensitivity of expression are very satisfying. Lynne Dawson, with her bell-like soprano, sings radiantly as Iphis; and the counter-tenor, Michael Chance, as her beloved, Hamor, is also outstanding. Anne Sofie von Otter is powerful as Storge, and Stephen Varcoe with his clear baritone, again on the light side, is a stylish Zebul. As for the Monteverdi Choir, their clarity, incisiveness and beauty are a constant delight.

Joshua (complete).
⊛ *** Hyp. Dig. CDA 66461/2; *KA 66461/2* [id.]. Kirkby, Bowman, Ainsley, George, Oliver, New College, Oxford, Ch., King's Consort, King.

Emma Kirkby is here ideally sparkling and light in the role of Achsa, daughter of the patriarchal leader, Caleb (taken here by the bass, Michael George). Her love for Othniel, superbly sung by James Bowman, provides the romantic interest in what is otherwise a grandly military oratorio, based on the Book of Joshua. The brisk sequence of generally brief arias is punctuated by splendid choruses, with solo numbers often inspiring choral comment. The singing is consistently strong and stylish, with the clear, precise tenor, John Mark Ainsley, in the title-role giving his finest performance on record yet. Robert King and his Consort crown their achievement in other Hyperion issues, notably their Purcell series, with polished, resilient playing, and the choir of New College, Oxford, sings with ideal freshness. Warm, full sound.

Judas Maccabaeus (complete).
☞ (M) **(*) Van. 08 4072.72 (2) [OVC 4071/2]. Harper, Watts, Young, Shirley-Quirk, Amor Artis Ch., Wandsworth School Boys' Ch., ECO, Somary.

Though its popularity has been eclipsed, *Judas Maccabaeus* contains much fine and noble music, which Johannes Somary's vital performance underlines. The choruses of lamentation for the Israelites in Act I and the strong, heroic solos and choruses all through – the tenor's *Sound an alarm* typical of them – make for a work which may be long but has much to hold the attention. The solo singing is excellent, with Alexander Young a ringing tenor and Helen Watts singing the opening aria in Act III exquisitely. Very good recording – the choruses could ideally have a crisper focus, but the effect is wholly natural – and a sense of commitment throughout from all departments. The most famous chorus, *See the conqu'ring hero comes*, takes the horns up to a high G *in alt* (one note above the instrument's normal compass) and there is a famous (and true) story told about the great horn-player, Aubrey Brain (father of Dennis) who at rehearsals would wear his bowler hat and, each time he reached the high note, would raise it with one hand (and a genial smile).

Lucrezia (cantata). Arias: *Ariodante: Oh, felice mio core . . . Con l'ali do constanza; E vivo ancore? . . . Scherza infida in grembo al drudo; Dopo notte. Atalanta: Care selve. Hercules: Where shall I fly? Joshua: O had I Jubal's lyre. Rodelinda: Pompe vane di morte! . . . Dove sei, amato bene? Serse: Frondi tenere e belle . . . Ombra mai fù (Largo).*
(M) *** Ph. 426 450-2. Dame Janet Baker, ECO, Leppard.

Even among Dame Janet's most impressive records this Handel recital marks a special contribution, ranging as it does from the pure gravity of *Ombra mai fù* to the passionate virtuosity in *Dopo notte* from *Ariodante*. Leppard gives sparkling support and the whole is recorded with natural and refined balance. An outstanding disc, with admirable documentation.

Messiah (complete).

*** DG Dig. 423 630-2 (2). Augér, Anne Sofie von Otter, Chance, Crook, J. Tomlinson, E. Concert Ch., E. Concert, Pinnock.

*** Ph. Dig. 434 297-2 (2) [id.]. Marshall, Robbin, Rolfe Johnson, Brett, Hale, Shirley-Quirk, Monteverdi Ch., E. Bar. Soloists, Gardiner.

*** Hyp. Dig. CDA 66251/2; *KA 66251/2* [id.]. Lynne Dawson, Denley, Maldwyn Davies, Michael George, The Sixteen Ch. & O, Christophers.

☞ (B) *** Ph. Duo 438 356-2 (2) [id.]. Harper, Watts, Wakefield, Shirley-Quirk, L. Symphony Ch., LSO, Sir Colin Davis.

(B) *** EMI CZS7 62748-2 (2) [Ang. CDMB 62748]. Harwood, J. Baker, Esswood, Tear, Herincx, Amb. S., ECO, Mackerras.

*** Decca Dig. 414 396-2 (2) [id.]. Te Kanawa, Gjevang, Keith Lewis, Howell, Chicago Ch. & SO, Solti.

(B) **(*) CfP CD-CFPD 4718; *TC-CFPD 4718* (2) [id.]. Morison, Thomas, Lewis, Milligan, Huddersfield Ch. Soc., RLPO, Sargent.

☞ (M) **(*) EMI CMS7 63784-2 (2) Trebles from King's, Bowman, Tear, Luxon, King's College, Cambridge, Ch., ASMF, Willcocks.

☞ (BB) **(*) Naxos Dig. 8.550667/8 [id.]. Amps, Davidson, Doveton, Van Asch, Scholars Bar. Ens.

☞ (M) **(*) Erato/Warner Dig. 2292 45960-2 (2) [id.]. Kweksilber, Bowman, Elliott, Reinhardt, The Sixteen, Amsterdam Bar. O, Koopman.

☞ (M) ** Decca 433 740-2 (2) [id.]. Sutherland, Tourangeau, Krenn, Krause, Coleman, Amb. S., ECO, Bonynge.

☞ (M) * Teldec/Warner Dig. 9031 77615-2 (2) [id.]. Gale, Lipovšek, Hollweg, Kennedy, Stockholm Chamber Ch., VCM, Harnoncourt.

Pinnock presents a performance using authentically scaled forces which, without inflation, rise to grandeur and magnificence, qualities Handel himself would have relished. The fast contrapuntal choruses, such as *For unto us a Child is born*, are done lightly and resiliently in the modern manner, but there is no hint of breathlessness, and Pinnock (more than his main rivals) balances his period instruments to give a satisfying body to the sound. There is weight too in the singing of the bass soloist, John Tomlinson, firm, dark and powerful, yet marvellously agile in divisions. Arleen Augér's range of tone and dynamic is daringly wide, with radiant purity in *I know that my Redeemer liveth*. Anne Sofie von Otter sustains *He was despised* superbly with her firm, steady voice. Some alto arias are taken by the outstanding counter-tenor, Michael Chance, who in some ways is even more remarkable. The tenor, Howard Crook, is less distinctive but still sings freshly and attractively. With full, atmospheric and well-balanced recording, this is a set not to be missed, even by those who already have a favourite version of *Messiah*.

Gardiner chooses bright-toned sopranos instead of boys for the chorus and he uses, very affectingly, a solo treble to sing *There were shepherds abiding*. Speeds are fast and light, and the rhythmic buoyancy in the choruses is very striking. There is drama and boldness, too. *Why do the nations* and *The trumpet shall sound* (both sung with great authority) have seldom come over more strongly. The soloists are all first class, with the soprano Margaret Marshall finest of all, especially in *I know that my Redeemer liveth* (tastefully decorated). There are times when one craves for more expansive qualities; the baroque string sound can still give cause for doubts. Yet there are some wonderful highlights, not least Margaret Marshall's angelic version of *Rejoice greatly*, skipping along in compound time.

Christophers consistently adopts speeds more relaxed than those we have grown used to in modern performances and the effect is fresh, clear and resilient. Alto lines in the chorus are taken by male singers; a counter-tenor, David James, is also used for the *Refiner's fire*, but *He was despised* is rightly given to the contralto, Catherine Denley, warm and grave at a very measured tempo. The team of five soloists is at least as fine as that on any rival set, with the soprano, Lynne Dawson, singing with silvery purity to delight traditionalists and authenticists alike. The band of thirteen strings sounds as clean and fresh as the choir. Even the *Hallelujah chorus* – always a big test in a small-scale performance – works well, with Christophers in his chosen scale, through dramatic timpani and trumpets conveying necessary weight. The sound has all the bloom one associates with St John's recordings.

Reissued at bargain price on Philips's new Duo label, the LSO recording conducted by Sir Colin Davis has not lost its impact and sounds brightly lit and fresh in its digitally remastered format. Textures are beautifully clear and, thanks to Davis, the rhythmic bounce of such choruses as *For unto us* is really infectious. Even *Hallelujah* loses little and gains much from being performed by a chorus of this size. Excellent singing from all four soloists, particularly Helen Watts who, following early precedent, is given *For He is like a refiner's fire* to sing, instead of the bass, and produces a glorious chest register. The performance is absolutely complete and is excellent value at its new price.

The choruses on EMI have not quite the same zest as on Philips, but they have a compensating breadth and body. More than Davis, Mackerras adopted Handel's alternative versions, so the soprano aria *Rejoice greatly* is given in its optional 12/8 version, with compound time adding a skip to the rhythm. A male alto is also included, Paul Esswood, and he is given some of the bass arias as well as some of the regular alto passages. Among the soloists, Dame Janet Baker is outstanding. Her intense, slow account of *He was despised* – with decorations on the reprise – is sung with profound feeling. The recording is warm and full in ambience and, with the added brightness of CD, sounds extremely vivid.

Sir Georg Solti inspires the most vitally exciting reading on record. The Chicago Symphony Orchestra and Chorus respond to some challengingly fast but never breathless speeds, showing what lessons can be learnt from authentic performance in clarity and crispness. Yet the joyful power of *Hallelujah* and the *Amen chorus* is overwhelming. Dame Kiri Te Kanawa matches anyone on record in beauty of tone and detailed expressiveness, while the other soloists are first rate too, even if Anne Gjevang has rather too fruity a timbre. Brilliant, full sound and great tangibility, breadth and clarity on the CDs.

It is good to have Sir Malcolm Sargent's 1959 recording now restored to the catalogue in full for, apart from the pleasure given by a performance that brings out the breadth of Handel's inspiration, it provides an important corrective to misconceptions about pre-authentic practice. Sargent unashamedly fills out the orchestration (favouring Mozart's scoring where possible). By the side of Davis, his tempi are measured, but his pacing is sure and spontaneous and, with a hundred-strong Huddersfield group, no one will be disappointed with the weight or vigour of the choruses. There is some splendid singing from all four soloists, and Marjorie Thomas's *He was despised* is memorable in its moving simplicity. The success of the CD transfer is remarkable: the old analogue LPs never sounded as clear as this.

Often though *Messiah* may have been recorded, there always seems plenty of room for alternative versions, particularly those which show a new and illuminating view of the work. Willcocks's recording, made in the Chapel at King's in 1971/2, has been described as the 'all-male *Messiah*', since a counter-tenor takes over the contralto solos, and the full complement of the trebles of King's College Choir sings the soprano solos, even the florid ones like *Rejoice greatly*; the result is enchanting, often light and airy. The bigger choruses do not lack robust qualities; however, the engineers have put their microphones fairly close and the resultant added clarity loses some of the normal King's softness of focus. The sound is thus vivid as well as atmospheric, but not quite what one would encounter sitting in the Chapel. A gimmicky version, perhaps, but one that many will find refreshing and involving.

On the bargain Naxos label comes a period performance with a difference. With fresh, immediate sound adding to the impact, the Scholars Baroque Ensemble presents the oratorio on the smallest possible scale, with individual singers from the small chorus coming forward to sing the arias. In keeping with this approach, the performance is directed by one of the basses, David van Asch, and characteristically the booklet seeks as far as possible not to highlight individual contributions like his but to emphasize teamwork. At brisk speeds, with rhythms well sprung, this will please those who fancy such an approach, though the instrumental sound is abrasive in a way one associates with the earliest period performances, and none of the singers has a voice of star quality. By their own definition, these are good choristers rather than great soloists. Given that, there is much to recommend the issue, though many more than traditionalists will prefer an approach that brings out more of Handel's grandeur.

With a small choir, an authentic baroque orchestra and clear-toned, lightweight soloists, Koopman's Erato version provides an intimate view of what is usually presented with grandeur. The ease and relaxation of the approach, not at all abrasive in the way common with authentic performances, are attractive, helped by excellent recording which gives a fine sense of presence – but, inevitably, essential elements in Handel's vision are missing.

Bonynge's 1979 set offers an exuberant *Messiah*, more remarkable for brilliance and colour than for any more meditative qualities. Tempi for the choruses are often very fast and the overall result is refreshing. But as a whole the performance does not quite add up. The one serious blot is the choice of Huguette Tourangeau as contralto soloist. Hers is a remarkable voice for opera but is not suited here. Werner Krenn and Tom Krause sing neatly and enjoyably, matching the performance as a whole, while the piping tone of the treble, Dermon Coleman, adds point to a number of passages. When one expects the voice of Sutherland to enter for the first time on *There were shepherds*, you have instead this very different voice. Sutherland here is far fresher-toned than she was in 1961 (with Boult – see below), and *I know that my Redeemer liveth*, rather surprisingly, is done with no trills at all – very different from last time. First-rate analogue recording, admirably transferred.

Harnoncourt's version was originally issued on three full-priced CDs. Now it returns on two mid-priced discs as part of Teldec's Das Alte Werk series, but it is hardly more recommendable. The digital recording was compiled from two public concerts in Stockholm in 1982 with ill-balanced sound that puts the choir at a distance, making it seem even duller than it is. With the exception of Elizabeth Gale, the soloists are poor, and Harnoncourt's direction lacks vigour.

Messiah (complete; orch. Sir Eugene Goossens).
❀ (M) *** BMG/RCA GD 61266-20 (3) [61266-2]. Vyvyan, Sinclair, Vickers, Tozzi, RPO Ch. & O, Sir Thomas Beecham.

At first it sounds either shocking or exciting to hear highly anachronistic percussion (cymbals, anvil, triangle), not to mention horns and trombones and a full body of strings. But the scoring undeniably fits the sense of the words and the words come through with a remarkable clarity. This is a performance which at every point radiates the natural flair of the conductor, and Beecham is extraordinarily sensitive to Handel's rhetoric and pathos. The use of the cymbals to cap the choruses *For unto us a child is born* and *Glory to God* is unforgettable. Beecham's tempi are slower than we expect today, but given his expansive view of Handel, they are convincingly appropriate, with the possible exception of the *Hallelujah chorus*, which gathers speed exuberantly as it nears its end. Jennifer Vyvyan and Monica Sinclair both sing freshly. Jon Vickers brings to his tenor arias a heroic quality that is often welcome and effective. Giorgio Tozzi's English is sound and his management of the tricky bass arias (especially *Why do the nations*) compels admiration. But it is above all Beecham's set, and its sense of exultant glory in the riches of Handel's masterpiece.is life enhancing. The 1959 recording of the chorus and orchestra is full and expansive in its CD transfer and the soloists have remarkable presence and immediacy. The third disc with its 17-minute appendix of eight items – normally cut at the time this recording was made – comes as a bonus, as the set is priced as for two mid-range CDs.

Der Messias (sung in German, arr. Mozart): complete.
(M) **(*) DG 427 173-2 (2). Mathis, Finnilä, Schreier, Adam, Austrian R. Ch. & O, Vienna, Mackerras.

Mozart's arrangement of *Messiah* has a special fascination. It is not simply a question of trombones being added but of elaborate woodwind parts too – most engaging in a number such as *All we like sheep*, which even has a touch of humour. *The trumpet shall sound* is considerably modified and shortened. To avoid the use of a baroque instrument, Mozart shares the obbligato between trumpet and horn. Mackerras leads his fine team through a performance that is vital, not academic in the heavy sense. The remastered recording is excellent and a translation is provided.

Messiah (sung in English): highlights.
*** Ph. Dig. 412 267-2; *412 267-4* [id.] (from above set, cond. Gardiner).
*** Decca Dig. 417 449-2; *417 449-4* [id.] (from above set, cond. Solti).
(M) *** EMI CDM7 69040-2 [id.]; *EG 769040-4* (from above set, cond. Mackerras).
(B) **(*) CfP CD-CFP 9007 (from above set, cond. Sargent).
☞ (B) ** Decca 433 637-2; *433 637-4*. Sutherland, Bumbry, McKellar, Ward, London Symphony Ch., LSO, Boult.

Here Gardiner's collection reigns supreme, with the single caveat that *The trumpet shall sound* is missing. Solti's selection is undoubtedly generous, including all the key numbers and much else besides. The sound is thrillingly vivid and full. At mid-price Mackerras is first choice, while the great and pleasant surprise among the bargain selections is the Classics for Pleasure CD of highlights from Sir Malcolm Sargent's 1959 recording; no one will be disappointed with *Hallelujah*, while the closing *Amen* has a powerful sense of apotheosis.

The highlights from Decca's 1961 set provide an apt comparison with the later, Bonynge version. Here Sutherland is the only soloist among the four to pay any attention to the question of whether or not to use ornamentation in the repeats of the *da capo* arias. What she does is mostly in good taste, but her colleagues give us merely the notes as they stand. They each have their moments, but the glory of the set is the splendid singing of the London Symphony Chorus under Boult. Excellent recording.

(i) *Nell'Africaine selve; Nella stagion che, dio viole e rose* (Italian cantatas). Duets: *Quel fior che all'aba ride; No, di voi non vo' fidarmi; Tacete ohimè, tacete!;* Trio: *Se tu non lasci amore.* (ii) *The Alchymist* (incidental music): suite. Theatre songs: *Universal passion: I like the am'rous youth. The Way of the World: Love's but the frailty of the mind. The What d'ye call it: 'Twas when the seas were roaring.*

*** O-L 430 282-2 [id.]. (i) Kirkby, Nelson, Thomas; Hogwood; Sheppard; (ii) Kwella, Cable, Thomas, AAM, Hogwood.

The most ear-catching items among the Italian cantatas are those which Handel later drew on for *Messiah.* Emma Kirkby and Judith Nelson sing them brilliantly; and one of the melodically less striking pieces yet prompts an amazing virtuoso display from the bass, David Thomas, who is required to cope with an enormous range of three octaves. In the fast movements Hogwood favours breathtaking speeds (in every sense), yet the result is exciting, not too hectic, and the recording is outstanding. The coupled selection of Handel's theatre music contains more delightful rarities, and the performances by the Academy under Hogwood have all the freshness and vigour one associates with his companion set of Purcell theatre music.

Ode for the birthday of Queen Anne (Eternal source of light divine); Sing unto God (Wedding anthem); Te deum in D (for Queen Caroline).

*** Hyp. Dig. CDA 66315; *KA 66315* [id.]. Fisher, Bowman, Ainsley, George, New College, Oxford, Ch., King's Consort, Robert King.

Handel's *Birthday Ode for Queen Anne* combines Purcellian influences with Italianate writing to make a rich mixture. King's performance is richly enjoyable, with warm, well-tuned playing from the King's Consort and with James Bowman in radiant form in the opening movement. The other two items are far rarer. Warmly atmospheric recording, not ideally clear on detail.

Ode for St Cecilia's Day.

*** DG Dig. 419 220-2 [id.]. Lott, Rolfe Johnson, Ch. & E. Concert, Pinnock.

*** ASV Dig. CDDCA 512 [id.]. Gomez, Tear, King's College Ch., ECO, Ledger.

☞ (M) ** Decca 436 259-2 [id.]. Cantelo, Partridge, King's College Ch., ASMF, Willcocks – BLOW: *Anthems.* **(*)

Trevor Pinnock's account of Handel's magnificent setting of Dryden's *Ode* comes near the ideal for a performance using period instruments. Not only is it crisp and lively, it has deep tenderness too, as in the lovely soprano aria, *The complaining flute,* with Lisa Beznosiuk playing the flute obbligato most delicately in support of Felicity Lott's clear singing. Anthony Rolfe Johnson gives a robust yet stylish account of *The trumpet's loud clangour,* and the choir is excellent, very crisp of ensemble. Full, clear recording with voices vivid and immediate.

Those seeking a version with modern instruments will find Ledger's ASV version a splendid alternative. With superb soloists – Jill Gomez radiantly beautiful and Robert Tear dramatically riveting in his call to arms – this delightful music emerges with an admirable combination of freshness and weight. Ledger uses an all-male chorus; the style of the performance is totally convincing without being self-consciously authentic. The recording is first rate, rich, vivid and clear.

The CD transfer has improved the impact of what was a very fine 1967 (originally Argo) recording, but the performance is disappointing. It is not the fault of the Academy of St Martin-in-the-Fields, for the *Overture* is one of the highlights of the disc, and there is superb solo playing throughout and a notably warm contribution from the cellos. April Cantelo phrases sensitively and accurately, if with rather a white tone, but her singing seldom beguiles, and it is the tenor who brings the performance fully to life with *The trumpet's loud clangour.*

La Resurrezione.

*** O-L Dig. 421 132-2 (2) [id.]. Kirkby, Kwella, C. Watkinson, Partridge, Thomas, AAM, Hogwood.

*** Erato/Warner Dig. 2292 45617-2 [id.]. Argenta, Schlick, Laurens, De Mey, Mertens, Amsterdam Bar. O, Ton Koopman.

Hogwood directs a clean-cut, vigorous performance with an excellent cast. Emma Kirkby is at her most brilliant in the coloratura for the Angel, Patrizia Kwella sings movingly as Mary Magdalene and Carolyn Watkinson as Cleophas adopts an almost counter-tenor-like tone. Ian Partridge's tenor has a heady lightness as St John, and though David Thomas's Lucifer could have more weight, he too sings stylishly. Excellent recording.

Koopman's cast of soloists is just as strong, with Barbara Schlick as the Angel outstandingly fine and Klaus Mertens as Lucifer weightier and stronger than his opposite number. Koopman's approach is lighter and more resilient, allowing more relaxation, though the recording is less well focused, with voices less full and immediate.

Samson (complete).
☞ *** Teldec/Warner Dig. 9031 74871-2 (2) [id.]. Rolfe Johnson, Alexander, Kowalski, Scharinger, Venuti, Blasi, Arnold Schoenberg Ch., VCM, Harnoncourt.

Harnoncourt, having become an important conductor outside the period-performance field, here conducts a Handel performance very different from what one would earlier have expected with his pioneering Concentus Musicus. Abrasiveness is no longer a major element so that Handelian grandeur shines out from the opening overture with its braying horns and genially strutting dotted rhythms. He is altogether warmer than before, and a fine team of singers, led by Anthony Rolfe Johnson in the title-role, is allowed full expressiveness, with speeds in slow numbers broader than one might expect. So the blind Samson's first aria, *Total eclipse*, is very measured, with Rolfe Johnson using the widest tonal and dynamic range. Though the recording catches some flutter in Roberta Alexander's voice as Dalila, she gives a characterful performance, well contrasted with Angela Maria Blasi, her attendant, who sings the lovely aria, *With plaintive note*, most beautifully. Maria Venuti in the climactic *Let the bright seraphim* at the end is not ideally pure-toned, but she sings strongly and flexibly. Other fine singers include Alastair Miles, magnificent in the bass role of the giant, Harapha, not least in *Honour and arms*, as well as the rich-toned counter-tenor, Jochen Kowalski as Micah and Christoph Prégardien in the tenor role of the Philistine. Though the cast is less starry than the rival one on Leppard's Erato set, the singing is no less satisfying and, with the Schoenberg choir singing incisively, Harnoncourt presents the work not only with period instruments but on a more authentic scale. The clinching advantage of the Teldec set is that it comes on two instead of three CDs.

Saul (complete).
*** Ph. Dig. 426 265-2 (3) [id.]. Miles, Dawson, Ragin, Ainslie, Mackie, Monteverdi Ch., E. Bar. Soloists, Gardiner.

Gardiner's performance is typically vigorous in what represents Handel's full emergence as a great oratorio composer, with the widest range of emotions conveyed. The alternation of mourning and joy in the final sequence of numbers is startlingly effective. With Derek Lee Ragin in the counter-tenor role of David, with Alastair Miles as Saul, Lynne Dawson as Michael and John Mark Ainslie as Jonathan, it is not likely to be surpassed on disc for a long time.

Solomon.
⊛ *** Ph. Dig. 412 612-2 (2) [id.]. C. Watkinson, Argenta, Hendricks, Rolfe Johnson, Monteverdi Ch., E. Bar. Soloists, Gardiner.

This is among the very finest of all Handel oratorio recordings. With panache, Gardiner shows how authentic-sized forces can convey Handelian grandeur even with clean-focused textures and fast speeds. The choruses and even more magnificent double-choruses stand as cornerstones of a structure which may have less of a story-line than some other Handel oratorios – the Judgement apart – but which Gardiner shows has consistent human warmth. The Act III scenes between Solomon and the Queen of Sheba are given extra warmth by having in that role a singer who is sensuous in tone, Barbara Hendricks. Carolyn Watkinson's pure mezzo is very apt for Solomon himself, while Nancy Argenta is clear and sweet as his Queen, but the overriding glory of the set is the radiant singing of Gardiner's Monteverdi Choir. Its clean, crisp articulation matches the brilliant playing of the English Baroque Soloists, regularly challenged by Gardiner's fast speeds, as in the *Arrival of the Queen of Sheba*; and the sound is superb, coping thrillingly with the problems of the double choruses.

Susanna.
**(*) HM Dig. HMU 907030/2; *HMC 407030/2* [id.]. Hunt, Minter, Feldman, Parker, J & D. Thomas, U. C. Berkeley Chamber Ch., Philh. Bar. O, McGegan.

The wealth of arias and the refreshing treatment of the Apocrypha story of Susanna and the Elders make it ideal for records. McGegan's performance does not quite match those of his earlier Handel recordings, made in Budapest. This one was done live with a talented period group from Los Angeles. The main snag is that the dry acoustic brings an abrasive edge to the instrumental sound and takes away bloom from the voices. Yet with fine soloists including Lorraine Hunt (Susanna), Drew Minter (Joacim) and Jill Feldman (Daniel), this is far more than a mere stop-gap.

Theodora (complete).

☞ (M) **(*) Van. 08.4075.72 (2). Harper, Forrester, Lehane, Young, Lawrenson, Amor Artis Ch., ECO, Somary.

**(*) Teldec/Warner Dig. 2292 46447-2 (2) [id.]. Alexander, Blochwitz, Kowalski, Van Nes, Scharinger, Schönberg Ch., VCM, Harnoncourt.

Theodora was a Christian martyr, and Handel broke his normal rule in dramatic oratorios of keeping to Old Testament subjects to set this rather diffuse story involving five characters: Theodora, a princess of Antioch, and her friends on the one hand and Valens, the Roman commander, on the other. The work was first heard in 1750 and was one of the very last of Handel's oratorios, with only *Jephtha* of the major works to come. There is much fine music in Handel's score – it is said to have been his own favourite among his oratorios – and it is good to have two recordings, albeit very different in character. The reissued Vanguard account is traditional in style and is directed by an understanding and intelligent Handelian, Johannes Somary. With fresh and sympathetic singing from soloists who are stylistically at home in Handel, the result is most enjoyable. Maureen Forrester in particular sings superbly, but all the singing is at least reliable, and the recording has transferred warmly and vividly to CD.

There is much to enjoy in this lively Teldec account, with fresh, clean textures typical of the Concentus Musicus, and with Harnoncourt thrusting in manner, occasionally to the point of being heavy-handed. The solo casting is strong, though this team of international singers does not always sound at home, either stylistically or in singing English. Roberta Alexander is the finest of the soloists, with the counter-tenor Jochen Kowalski exceptionally warm of tone but hardly sounding Handelian in the role of Didymus. Jard van Nes is warm and fruity as Irene and Hans Peter Blochwitz is light and fresh as Septimius. Bright, full recording.

The Triumph of time and truth.

*** Hyp. CDA 66071/2 [id.]. Fisher, Kirkby, Brett, Partridge, Varcoe, L. Handel Ch. and O, Darlow.

Darlow's performance of Handel's very last oratorio is broader and rougher than the authentic recordings by John Eliot Gardiner, but it is hardly less enjoyable. The soloists all seem to have been chosen for the clarity of their pitching – Emma Kirkby, Gillian Fisher, Charles Brett and Stephen Varcoe, with the honey-toned Ian Partridge singing even more beautifully than the others, but with a timbre too pure quite to characterize 'Pleasure'. Good atmospheric recording.

Utrecht Te Deum and Jubilate.

☞ (M) *** O-L 443 178-2 [id.]. Kirkby, Nelson, Brett, Elliott, Covey-Crump, D. Thomas, Ch. of Christ Church Cathedral, Oxford, AAM, Simon Preston – VIVALDI: *Gloria*. ***

Using authentic instruments and an all-male choir with trebles, Preston directs a performance which is not merely scholarly but characteristically alert and vigorous, particularly impressive in the superb *Gloria* with its massive eight-part chords. With a team of soloists regularly associated with the Academy of Ancient Music, this can be confidently recommended, especially as this mid-priced reissue is now coupled with a fine account of Vivaldi's best-known *Gloria* setting.

OPERA

Agrippina (complete).

*** HM Dig. HMU 907063/65; *HMU 407063/65* (3). Bradshaw, Saffer, Minter, Hill, Isherwood, Popken, Dean, Banditelli, Sziláagi, Capella Savaria, McGegan.

Agrippina is delightfully light-hearted, magnetic in its fanciful telling of the intrigues between the Emperor Claudius, his wife Agrippina, Nero her son and Poppea, as well as Otho (Ottone) and Pallas (Pallante). Nicolas McGegan is markedly sympathetic and, with a fine bloom on voices and instruments, notably the brass, the performance is exhilaratingly fresh and alert. The cast is first rate, led by the silvery Sally Bradshaw as Agrippina, the bright Nero of Wendy Hill and the seductive Poppea of Lisa Saffer, all well contrasted in their equally stylish ways.

Alcina (complete).

*** EMI Dig. CDS7 49771-2 (3) [Ang. CDCB 49771]. Augér, Della Jones, Kuhlmann, Harrhy, Kwella, Maldwyn Davies, Tomlinson, Opera Stage Ch., City of L. Bar. Sinfonia, Hickox.

(i) *Alcina* (complete); (ii) *Giulio Cesare (Julius Caesar)*: highlights.

☞ (M) **(*) Decca 433 723-2 (3) [id.]. Sutherland, M. Sinclair, (i) Berganza, Alva, Sciutti, Freni, Flagello, LSO; (ii) Elkins, M. Horne, Conrad, New SO; Bonynge.

It would be hard to devise a septet of Handelian singers more stylish than the soloists here. Though the American, Arleen Augér, may not have the weight of Joan Sutherland, she is just as brilliant and pure-toned, singing warmly in the great expansive arias. Even next to her, Della Jones stands out in the breeches role of Ruggiero, with an extraordinary range of memorable arias, bold as well as tender. Eiddwen Harrhy as Morgana is just as brilliant in the aria, *Tornami a vagheggiar*, usually 'borrowed' by Alcina, while Kathleen Kuhlmann, Patrizia Kwella, Maldwyn Davies and John Tomlinson all sing with a clarity and beauty to make the music sparkle. Hickox underlines the contrasts of mood and speed, conveying the full range of emotion, with warm, spacious sound, recorded at EMI's Abbey Road studio. This set has been withdrawn as we go to press.

Although the 1962 Decca *Alcina* is less complete than the newer EMI set, it has the advantage of including some 50 minutes of highlights from *Giulio Cesare*, made a year later, which Sutherland did not undertake in a complete version. *Alcina*, however, represents the extreme point of what can be described as Sutherland's dreamy, droopy period. The fast arias are stupendous. Bonynge does not spare her at all, and in the brilliant Act I finale he really does rush her too fast, the result dazzling rather than musically satisfying. But anything slow and reflective, whether in recitative or aria, has Sutherland mooning about the notes, with no consonants audible at all and practically every vowel reduced to 'aw'. It is all most beautiful of course, but she could have done so much better. Of the others, Teresa Berganza is completely charming in the castrato part of Ruggiero, even if she does not manage trills very well. Monica Sinclair shows everyone up with the strength and forthrightness of her singing. Both Graziella Sciutti and Mirella Freni are delicate and clear in their two smaller parts. Richard Bonynge draws crisp, vigorous playing from the LSO. Only in those rushed showpiece arias for his wife does he sound too inflexible. The 30-year-old Walthamstow recording is vintage Decca, and the CD transfer hints at its age only in the orchestral string sound.

Not surprisingly, the *Giulio Cesare* highlights are used as a vehicle for Sutherland, and her florid elaborations of melodies turn *da capo* recitatives into things of delight and wonder. There is some marvellous singing from Marilyn Horne and Monica Sinclair too, and Bonynge conducts with a splendid sense of style. As a sample, try *V'adoro pupile* – Cleopatra's seduction aria. Full translations are provided in both works.

Alessandro (complete).
(M) **(*) HM/BMG GD 77110 (3) [77110-2-RG]. Jacobs, Boulin, Poulenard, Nirouët, Varcoe, Guy de Mey, La Petite Bande, Kuijken.

Sigiswald Kuijken directs his team of period-performance specialists in an urgently refreshing, at times sharply abrasive reading of one of Handel's key operas. As a high counter-tenor, René Jacobs copes brilliantly with the taxing role of Alexander himself. His singing is astonishingly free and agile, if too heavily aspirated. Among the others, Isabelle Poulenard at her best sounds a little like a French Emma Kirkby, though the production is not quite so pure and at times comes over more edgily. The others make a fine, consistent team, the more effective when the recording so vividly conveys a sense of presence with sharply defined directional focus.

Amadigi di Gaula (opera; complete).
☞ *** Erato/Warner Dig. 2292 45490-2 (2) [id.]. Stutzmann, Jennifer Smith, Harrhy, Fink, Musiciens du Louvre, Minkowski.

Amadigi di Gaula, dating from 1715, has suffered unjust neglect, like so many Handel operas; Minkowski's refreshing performance is one of his sharpest, dominated vocally by the magnificent young French contralto (no mere mezzo) of Nathalie Stutzmann in the title-role. She sings Amadigi's gentle arias most affectingly, notably the lovely *Sussurate, onde vezzose*, and the two women characters, Amadigi's lover Melissa and Princess Oriana, are well taken by Eiddwen Harrhy and Jennifer Smith, with the brilliant arias for Prince Dardano of Thrace superbly sung by Bernarda Fink. As in his splendid recording of Charpentier's music for *Le malade imaginaire*, Marc Minkowski directs an electrifying performance, which is given greater impact by the closeness of the recording. That also brings an abrasiveness to the period strings, but not disagreeably so; rather, the impression is of a performance on an intimate scale, and the more involving for that.

Atalanta (complete).
*** Hung. Dig. HCD 12612/4 [id.]. Farkas, Bartfai-Barta, Lax, Bandi, Gregor, Polgar, Savaria Vocal Ens. & Capella, McGegan.

This is an opera crammed with dozens of sparkling, light-hearted numbers with no flagging of the inspiration, the opposite of weighty Handel. Led by the bright-toned Katarin Farkas in the name-part, the singers cope stylishly, and the absence of Slavonic wobbles confirms the subtle difference of

Magyar voices; Joszef Gregor with his firm, dark bass is just as much in style, for example, as he regularly is in Verdi. First-rate recording.

Flavio (complete).
*** HM Dig. HMC 901312/13; *HMC 401312/13* (2) [id.]. Gall, Ragin, Lootens, Fink, *et al.*, Ens. 415, Jacobs.

Based on a staging of this unjustly neglected Handel opera at the 1989 Innsbruck Festival, René Jacobs' recording vividly captures the consistent vigour of Handel's inspiration. Handel's score was brilliantly written for some of the most celebrated singers of the time, including the castrato, Senesino. His four arias are among the highspots of the opera, all sung superbly here by the warm-toned and characterful counter-tenor, Derek Lee Ragin; almost every other aria is open and vigorous, with the whole sequence rounded off in a rousing ensemble. René Jacobs' team of eight soloists is a strong one, with only the strenuous tenor of Gianpaolo Fagotto occasionally falling short of the general stylishness. Full, clear sound.

Giulio Cesare (complete).
*** HM Dig. HMC 901385/7; *HMC 401385/7* [id.]. Larmore, Schlick, Fink, Rorholm, Ragin, Zanasi, Visse, Concerto Köln, Jacobs.

The counter-tenor, René Jacobs, now conductor of the German group, Concerto Köln, is a warmly expressive rather than a severe period performer. With a cast of consistently fresh voices, with rhythms sprung infectiously, he also allows the broadest expansion on the great reflective moments. The casting of the pure, golden-toned Barbara Schlick as Cleopatra proves outstandingly successful. Jennifer Larmore too, a fine, firm mezzo, with a touch of masculine toughness in the tone, makes a splendid Caesar. Together they crown the whole performance with the most seductive account of their final duet. Derek Lee Ragin is excellent in the sinister role of Tolomeo (Ptolemy); so are Bernarda Fink as Cornelia and Marianne Rorholm as Sesto, with the bass, Furio Zanasi, as Achille. Jacobs' expansive speeds mean that the whole opera will not fit on three CDs, but the fourth disc, at 18 minutes merely supplementary, comes free as part of the package, and includes an extra aria for the servant, Nireno, delightfully sung by the French counter-tenor, Dominique Visse. Firm, well-balanced sound.

Giulio Cesare: highlights.
☞ (M) **(*) Teldec/Warner Dig. 2292 42410 [id.]. Esswood, Alexander, Lipovšek, Murray, Schoenberg Ch., VCM, Harnoncourt.

Instead of issuing Harnoncourt's complete set on CD, Teldec offer just short of an hour of highlights. The opera is strongly cast with Marjana Lipovšek and Ann Murray both making fine contributions. Paul Esswood as Cesare sings pleasingly, especially in *Va tacito e nascosto* with its horn obbligato, but ideally one wants more striking differentiation between the voices. Roberta Alexander takes readily to Cleopatra's coloratura, although curiously she is replaced by Lucia Popp in the closing bourrée, *Ritorni omai.* Harnoncourt directs the proceedings with plenty of rhythmic spirit and makes the most of the *Sinfonia bellica.* Good, bright recording with plenty of resonant atmosphere.

Hercules (complete).
*** DG Dig. 423 137-2 (3) [id.]. Tomlinson, Sarah Walker, Rolfe Johnson, Jennifer Smith, Denley, Savidge, Monteverdi Ch., E. Bar. Soloists, Gardiner.

Gardiner's generally brisk performance of *Hercules* using authentic forces may at times lack Handelian grandeur in the big choruses, but it conveys superbly the vigour of the writing, its natural drama; and the fire of this performance is typified by the singing of Sarah Walker as Dejanira in her finest recording yet. John Tomlinson makes an excellent, dark-toned Hercules. Youthful voices consistently help in the clarity of the attack – Jennifer Smith as Iole, Catherine Denley as Lichas, Anthony Rolfe Johnson as Hyllus and Peter Savidge as the Priest of Jupiter. Refined playing and outstanding recording quality.

Orlando (complete).
*** O-L Dig. 430 845-2 (3) [id.]. Bowman, Augér, Robbin, Kirkby, D. Thomas, AAM, Hogwood.

Handel's *Orlando* was radically modified to provide suitable material for individual singers, as for example the bass role of the magician, Zoroastro, specially created for a member of Handel's company. Even so, the title-role seems to have failed to please the celebrated castrato, Senesino, for whom it was intended, probably because of Handel's breaks with tradition, notably in the magnificent mad scene which ends Act II on the aria, *Vaghe pupille*, with the simple ritornello leading to amazing inspirations. That number, superbly done here by James Bowman, with appropriate sound effects, is only one of the virtuoso vehicles for the counter-tenor. For the jewelled sequences of arias and duets, Hogwood has assembled a near-ideal cast, with Arleen Augér at her most radiant as the queen, Angelica, and Emma Kirkby characteristically bright and fresh in the lighter, semi-comic role of the shepherdess, Dorinda. Catherine Robbin assumes the role of Prince Medoro strongly and David Thomas sings stylishly as Zoroastro. This is one of Hogwood's finest achievements on record, taut, dramatic and rhythmically resilient. Vivid, open sound.

Ottone, re di Germania (complete).
☞ *** Hyp. Dig. CDA 66751/3 [id.]. Bowman, McFadden, Jennifer Smith, Denley, Visse, George, King's Consort, Robert King.
☞ **(*) HM Dig. HMU 907073/5 [id.]. Minter, Saffer, Gondek, Spence, Popken, Dean, Freiburg Bar. O, McGegan.

Ottone, one of Handel's lesser-known Italian operas for London, dates from 1722, just before *Giulio Cesare*. Previously unrecorded, it simultaneously prompted these two versions, both of which have their points of advantage. Nicholas McGegan continues his impressive Handel series for Harmonia Mundi in a recording with the Freiburg Baroque Orchestra and with Drew Minter taking the title-role, while Robert King and his King's Consort offer a version on Hyperion with James Bowman as Ottone. When the women principals in McGegan's version have purer, firmer voices than their rivals, there is a strong case for preferring his set. This is the piece – with a plot even more absurdly involved than most – which first introduced the temperamental soprano, Francesca Cuzzoni, to London, prompting the story of Handel trying to push the difficult prima donna out of the window. As the heroine, Teofane, Lisa Saffer for McGegan is markedly sweeter and clearer than Claron McFadden for King. When it comes to the key castrato roles taken by counter-tenors, it is quite different. For McGegan, Drew Minter, a stylish singer, no longer has the power to give the many bravura arias the thrust they need, whereas for King, Bowman with his far richer tone continues to sing with enormous panache and virtuoso agility. Dominique Visse as the duplicitous Adalberto on King's set tends to overcharacterize, but again the singing makes the rival version seem colourless. Add to that the extra richness and bloom on the instrumental sound in the Hyperion version, and the balance clearly goes in its favour. This may not be as distinctive as some of Handel's later Italian operas, but as ever the sequence of brief numbers has an irresistible freshness.

Partenope (complete).
(M) *** HM/BMG GD 77109 (3) [77109-2-RG]. Laki, Jacobs, York, Skinner, Varcoe, Müller-Molinari, Hill, La Petite Bande, Kuijken.

With the exception of René Jacobs, rather too mannered for Handel, the roster of soloists here is outstanding, with Krisztina Laki and Helga Müller-Molinari welcome additions to the team. Though ornamentation is sparse, the direction of Sigiswald Kuijken is consistently invigorating, as is immediately apparent in the *Overture*; the 1979 recording sounds quite marvellous in its CD format.

Il pastor fido (complete).
**(*) Hung. Dig. HCD 12912 (2) [id.]. Esswood, Farkas, Lukin, Kállay, Flohr, Gregor, Savaria Vocal Ens., Capella Savaria, McGegan.

Il pastor fido is an unpretentious pastoral piece, which charms gently rather than compelling attention. Nicholas McGegan demonstrates what talent there is in Budapest, among singers as among instrumentalists. Singers better known in much later operatic music translate well to Handel, for example the celebrated bass, József Gregor, but the most stylish singing comes from the British counter-tenor, Paul Esswood, in the castrato role of Mirtillo. Good sound and excellent documentation.

Radamisto (complete).
☞ **(*) HM Dig. HMU 907111/13 [id.]. Popken, Gondek, Saffer, Hanchard, Dean, Cavallier, Freiburger Bar. O, McGegan.

Radamisto, the first of the Italian operas Handel wrote for his opera-giving organization, the Royal Academy of Music, is a magnificent work, more appreciated nowadays in Germany than in Britain. The best-known aria, the plaintive *Ombra cara*, sung by Radamisto, leads on to a whole sequence of magnificent minor-key numbers in Act II, with some of the arias given to Zenobia, Radamisto's wife, marked by strange, sudden switches of mood. This first complete recording is very welcome in revealing much superb material, even if the period-performance manners are less sympathetic than have become common on disc. The strings of the Freiburg orchestra are very abrasive, and even under the direction of McGegan rhythms are too often square, not sprung as winningly as they might be, while recitative is on the heavy side. Nevertheless, there is some first-rate singing, with the title-role – originally written for the castrato, Senesino – strongly taken by the firm-toned counter-tenor, Ralf Popken, who projects well, even if he is occasionally hooty. It is not his fault that *Ombra cara* sounds rather stodgy, for he shades his tone most beautifully for the reprise. Juliana Gondek sings with full, warm tone as Zenobia, producing crisp trills and ornaments, though most of the others are not quite so successful. The recording, made in Göttingen after a festival production, is on the dry side but has plenty of presence.

Rodelinda, Regina de Langobardi (complete).
**(*) HM/BMG Dig. RD 771927 (3). Schlick, Schubert, Cordier, Wessel, Prégardien, Schwarz, La Stagione, Schneider.

On this German recording from Michael Schneider and La Stagione, the celebrated *Dove sei*, inaccurately translated as 'Art thou troubl'd', is tenderly sung with plaintive tone by the British counter-tenor, David Cordier, matching the rest of the excellent, otherwise all-German cast. Barbara Schlick is pure and golden in the title-role and the tenor, Christoph Prégardien, is also outstanding as the hero, Grimoaldo. Schneider is a lively and fresh Handelian not afraid of expressiveness but often adopting a clipped, abrasive manner. He encourages generous ornamentation in *da capo* repeats. First-rate, clean sound.

Semele (complete).
☞ *** DG Dig. 435 782-2 (3) [id.]. Battle, M. Horne, Ramey, Aler, McNair, Chance, Mackie, Amb. Op. Ch., ECO, John Nelson.
☞ **(*) Erato/Warner 2292 45982-2 (2). Burrowes, Della Jones, Lloyd, D. Thomas, Rolfe Johnson, Kwella, Penrose, M. Davies, Monteverdi Ch., E. Bar. Soloists, Gardiner.

DG's new digital recording of *Semele* turns away from current fashion in using modern rather than period instruments, but the balance of advantage lies very much in its favour, compared with the Erato set of Gardiner; even period fanatics may well find it the better choice. Nelson follows the rules of baroque performance as closely as most period performers, and his starry cast brings not only flair and character but a keen sense of style. Surprisingly, the Nelson performance is generally crisper and faster than Gardiner's, with rhythms sprung just as infectiously. Most importantly, he opens out the serious cuts made by Gardiner, following the old, bad tradition. If *Semele* – dating from 1744, three years after *Messiah* – is known as a rule only by its most celebrated aria, *Where'er you walk*, it contains many other superb numbers and, more than any of his other English-language works, even *Samson*, it is a genuine opera rather than an oratorio, using a witty send-up of a classical plot, based on a play by Congreve. Handel was aiming to satirize George II's mistress, Lady Yarmouth, in his portrayal of the central character of Semele – a self-regarding princess seduced by Jupiter who through him seeks to become immortal, just as Lady Yarmouth wanted to become queen. The story of *Semele* derives from Ovid's *Metamorphoses*, and Congreve's libretto was written in 1708.

Norma Burrowes for Gardiner makes the character sweetly innocent, but Kathleen Battle with alluringly rich tone is more provocative, giving the brilliant aria, *Myself I shall adore*, something of the tongue-in-cheek quality you find in the G&S heroines, notably Yum-Yum in *Mikado*. Another of Semele's arias is the celebrated *O sleep, why dost thou leave me*, which Battle sings with a sensuous beauty easily to outshine her rival. The material restored by Nelson in the opened-out cuts, so far from being dull, includes such marvellous numbers as three magnificent arias for Athamas, Semele's suitor, a counter-tenor role that is almost eliminated in the Gardiner set. On stage there is a case for such cuts, but not on disc, particularly when you have Michael Chance as the superb singer. Marilyn Horne defies the years as a fire-snorting Juno, if anything even more characterful than the splendid Della Jones for Gardiner. Though Anthony Rolfe Johnson as Jupiter for Gardiner is a more stylish, fuller-toned tenor than John Aler for Nelson, the DG cast is not only starrier but generally more consistent, to confirm a strong recommendation, whatever your preference in baroque performance.

The Erato reissue in the Libretto series of John Eliot Gardiner's 1981 version of *Semele* offers a period performance with the English Baroque Soloists using an excellent cast of British specialist singers. Very well recorded, it has the very practical advantage of coming on only two mid-price discs, and the extensive cuts which make that possible are the traditional ones, some of them sanctioned by Handel himself. Though this was an early EBS recording, not quite as polished as more recent ones, Gardiner's ability to use period performance with warmth and imagination makes it consistently compelling. Norma Burrowes is a sweet, pure Semele, and Anthony Rolfe Johnson is outstanding as Jupiter, singing *Where'er you walk* with a fine sense of line and excellent pacing

The Sorceress (pasticcio).
☞ **(*) Ph. Dig. 434 992-2 [id.]. Kiri Te Kanawa, AAM, Hogwood.

This pasticcio, with items drawn from a whole range of Handel operas (*Rinaldo, Alcina, Giulio Cesare, Ariodante, Agrippina, Admeto* and *Giustino*) was devised for a Dutch television programme. The CD – like the video version, complete with ballet interludes – is taken from the soundtrack, providing in effect a sequence of seven arias, sung with characteristic poise and sumptuous tone by Dame Kiri, spiced with instrumental pieces, mostly brief. Though the plot is broadly based on the situation in *Alcina*, only one aria is taken from that opera, *Ombre pallide*, which, preceded by an accompanied recitative, makes up by far the longest item. It is made even longer by Dame Kiri's somewhat languid performance. She is not nearly as animated as Arleen Augér was in Richard Hickox's fine complete recording of the opera. Otherwise, even with speeds on the slow side, Dame Kiri sings gloriously, with four of Cleopatra's arias from *Giulio Cesare* – including the seduction aria, *V'adoro pupille* – providing the cornerstones. Hogwood draws fresh sounds from the Academy but he might have sounded even sharper at faster speeds. Clear, well-balanced sound.

Tamerlano (complete).
(M) *** Erato/Warner Dig. 2292 45408-2 (3) [id.]. Ragin, Robson, Argenta, Chance, Findlay,
    Schirrer, E. Bar. Soloists, Gardiner.

John Eliot Gardiner's live concert performance of *Tamerlano* presents a strikingly dramatic and immediate experience. The pacing of numbers and of the recitative is beautifully thought out and the result is electrifying. Leading the cast are two outstanding counter-tenors, whose encounters provide some of the most exciting moments: Michael Chance as Andronicus, firm and clear, Derek Ragin in the name-part equally agile and more distinctive of timbre, with a rich, warm tone that avoids womanliness. Nigel Robson in the tenor role of Bajazet conveys the necessary gravity, not least in the difficult, highly original G minor aria before the character's suicide; and Nancy Argenta sings with starry purity as Asteria. The only serious snag is the dryness of the sound, which makes voices and instruments sound more aggressive on CD than they usually do in Gardiner's recordings with the English Baroque Soloists.

Teseo (opera; complete).
☞ *** Erato/Warner Dig. 2292 45806-2 (2) [id.]. James, Della Jones, Gooding, Lee Ragin, Napoli,
    Gall, Les Musiciens du Louvre, Minkowski.

Dating from December 1712, *Teseo* was only the second opera that Handel wrote for London, and the first after he had established himself here. Using an Italian translation of a French libretto originally written for Lully 40 years earlier, Handel uniquely produced a hybrid between an Italian *opera seria* and a French tragédie lyrique, with the classical story of Theseus and Medea told in a brisk sequence of short arias. Sadly, after its initial run of 13 performances *Teseo* was never produced again until the present century. The score may not contain great Handel melodies, but it is characteristically fresh and imaginative. Marc Minkowski, the liveliest of period performance specialists in France, brings out the inventiveness, helped by an excellent cast, dominated by British and American singers. These include Della Jones as Medea, Eirian James in the castrato role of Teseo, Julia Gooding as Agilea and characterful counter-tenors, Derek Lee Ragin and Jeffrey Gall, as Egeo and Arcane.

COLLECTIONS

Arias: *Aci, Galatea e Profumo: Qui l'augel di pianta in pianta. Floridante: Bramo te sola; Se dolce m'era già. Giulio Cesare in Egitto: Se in fiorito ameno prato; Va tacito. Orlando: Ah Stigie larve / Vaghe pupille; Fammi combattere. Partenope: Furibondo spira il vento. Radamisto: Ombra cara di mi sposa. Rinaldo: Cara sposa, amante cara.*
☞ *** BMG/RCA Dig. 09026 61205-2 [id.]. Nathalie Stutzmann, Hanover Band, Goodman.

Nathalie Stutzmann is both characterful and brilliant in this valuable collection of arias from ten Handel operas, recorded in London with Roy Goodman and the Hanover Band. With Stutzmann so positive a singer, each item emerges as a winner, strikingly memorable. Military rhythms are a feature in several, including the opening item, *Fammi combattere* from *Orlando*, which is like a trial run for *Let the bright Seraphim* from *Samson*. The sequence ends with the most tragic of the arias, *Ombra cara* from *Radamisto*, in which Stutzmann and her accompanists give the darkly chromatic writing the fullest expressive weight.

Arias: *Alexander's Feast: The Prince, unable to conceal his pain; Softly sweet in Lydian measures. Atalanta: Care selve. Giulio Cesare: Piangero. Messiah: Rejoice greatly; He shall feed his flock. Rinaldo: Lascia ch'io pianga. Samson: Let the bright Seraphim.*
**(*) Delos Dig. D/CD 3026 [id.]. Arleen Augér, Mostly Mozart O, Schwarz – BACH: *Arias*. **(*)

Arleen Augér's bright, clean, flexible soprano is even more naturally suited to these Handel arias than to the Bach items with which they are coupled. The delicacy with which she tackles the most elaborate divisions and points the words is a delight.

Opera arias: *Agrippina: Bel piacere. Orlando: Fammi combattere. Partenope: Funbondo spira il vento. Rinaldo: Or la tromba; Cara sposa; Venti turbini; Cor ingrato; Lascia ch'io pianga. Serse: Frondi tenere; Ombra mai fù.*
(M) **(*) Erato/Warner Dig. 2292 45186-2 [id.]. Marilyn Horne, Sol. Ven., Scimone.

Horne gives virtuoso performances. The flexibility of her voice in scales and trills and ornaments of every kind remains formidable, and the power is extraordinary down to the tangy chest register.

Arias: *Judas Maccabaeus: Father of heaven. Messiah: O Thou that tellest; He was despised. Samson: Return O God of Hosts.*
❀ (M) (***) Decca 433 474-2; *433 474-4.* Kathleen Ferrier, LPO, Boult – BACH: *Arias*. (***)

Kathleen Ferrier had a unique feeling for Handel; these performances are unforgettable for their communicative intensity and nobility of timbre and line. She receives highly sympathetic accompaniments from Boult, another natural Handelian.

Hanson, Howard (1896–1981)

(i) *Piano concerto in G, Op. 36. Mosaics; Symphonies Nos. 5 (Sinfonia sacra), Op. 43;* (ii) *7 (A Sea symphony).*
*** Delos Dig. DE 3130 [id.]. (i) Carol Rosenberger; Seattle SO, Schwarz; (ii) with Seattle Symphony Chorale.

Even if none of these works has the concentration of the early symphonies, admirers of the composer will want this collection, for all the music is given ardent advocacy and is superbly recorded. *Mosaics* is in variation form, compressed into an ongoing movement. The single-movement *Sinfonia sacra* – inspired by Christ's Passion – is also very succinct, showing the composer's Nordic inheritance. The *Sea Symphony*, a setting of Walt Whitman, contains some powerful choral writing, and the composer looks back to his most successful piece, the *Romantic Symphony*, in the finale. The four-movement *Piano concerto* (1948) is well made, and has a fine slow movement. Carol Rosenberger is an eloquent soloist.

Symphonies Nos. 1 in E min. (Nordic); 2 (Romantic); Elegy in memory of Serge Koussevitzky.
*** Delos Dig. D/CD 3073 [id.]. Seattle SO, Gerard Schwarz.

Hanson was of Swedish descent and his music has a strong individuality of idiom and colour. The *Second* is warmly appealing and melodically memorable with an indelible theme which permeates the structure. These Seattle performances have plenty of breadth and ardour, and Schwarz's feeling for the ebb and flow of the musical paragraphs is very satisfying. The recording, made in Seattle Opera House, is gloriously expansive and the balance is convincingly natural.

Symphonies Nos. 1 in E min. (Nordic), Op. 21; 2 (Romantic), Op. 30; (i) *Song of democracy.*
(M) *** Mercury 432 008-2 [id.]. Eastman-Rochester O, composer; (i) with Eastman School of Music Ch.

Hanson's own pioneering stereo recordings of his two best-known symphonies have a unique thrust and ardour. The *Song of democracy* has plenty of dramatic impact and is also very well recorded.

Symphony No. 2 (Romantic), Op. 30.
(M) *** EMI Dig. CDM7 64304-2 [id.]. St Louis SO, Slatkin – COPLAND: *Symphony No. 3.* ***

Slatkin's performance is a very satisfying one, responding to the expressive nostalgia of the slow movement and bringing an exhilarating attack to the finale – there are only three movements. The full, atmospheric recording, beautifully balanced and rich in its washes of string-tone, is a pleasure in itself.

Symphony No. 3; Elegy in memory of my friend Serge Koussevitzky, Op. 44; (i) *Lament for Beowulf.*
(M) *** Mercury 434 302-2 [id.]. Eastman-Rochester O, composer, (i) with Eastman School of Music
Ch.

For those familiar with the earlier works, the musical terrain of the *Third* is familiar: the string
threnodies surge purposefully forward, there are similar rhythmic patterns and confident rhetorical
gestures. This is highly accessible music. This applies also to the *Elegy*, while the cantata also makes
an immediate impression and is very well sung. However, here as in the orchestral works the 1958
Mercury sound is first rate.

(i) *Symphony No. 4 (Requiem), Op. 34;* (ii) *Lament for Beowulf, Op. 25; Merry Mount: suite, Op. 31;*
(iii) *Pastorale for oboe, harp and strings, Op. 38; Serenade for flute, harp and strings, Op. 35.*
*** Delos Dig. DE 3105 [id.]. (i) Seattle SO; (ii) with Symphony Chorale; (iii) NY Chamber
Symphony of 92nd Street Y; Gerard Schwarz.

Like so much of Hanson, the *Fourth Symphony* can be described as neo-Sibelian in the way that many
Swedish composers of the period such as Atterberg were. The *Lament for Beowulf* is in its way an
impressive achievement. Gerard Schwarz proves an even more eloquent exponent of the work than
the composer, who recorded it for Mercury in the 1950s but he has the benefit of a softer-grained, less
glassy recording. The *Pastorale for oboe, harp and strings* and the *Serenade for flute, harp and strings*
find Hanson at his best; they are both unpretentious and beautifully fashioned.

Harbison, John (born 1938)

(i) *Concerto for double brass choir and orchestra;* (ii) *The Flight into Egypt;* (iii) *The Natural world.*
*** New World Dig. 80395-2 [id.]. (i) LAPO, Previn; (ii) Roberta Anderson, Sanford Sylvan,
Cantata Singers & Ens., David Hoose; (iii) Janice Felty, Los Angeles Philharmonic New Music
Group, Harbison.

These three fine works provide an illuminating survey of the recent work of one of the most
communicative of American composers today. The most striking and vigorous is the concerto he
wrote as resident composer for Previn and the Los Angeles Philharmonic, and for the orchestra's
brass section in particular. The other two works reveal the more thoughtful Harbison, the one a
collection of three songs to nature poems by Wallace Stevens, Robert Bly and James Wright. *The
Flight into Egypt* is a measured and easily lyrical setting of the story of the Holy Family fleeing from
King Herod. Sanford Sylvan and the choir sing the main text, with Roberta Anderson interjecting as
the Angel. Excellent performances and recording.

Harris, Roy (1898–1979)

(i) *Violin concerto; Symphonies Nos. 1; 5.*
** Albany AR012 [id.]. (i) Gregory Fulkerston; Louisville O, Leighton Smith; Mester or Whitney.

The *First Symphony* is strong stuff, hardly less impressive than No. 3, but neither No. 5 nor the *Violin
concerto* adds greatly to our picture of its composer. Gregory Fulkerston gives a persuasive account
of the solo part, but the strings of the enterprising Louisville Orchestra are wanting in body and
lustre. The recordings are serviceable rather than distinguished.

Epilogue to profiles in courage; When Johnny comes marching home (An American overture).
** Albany TROY 027-2 [id.]. Louisville O, Jorge Mester – BECKER: *Symphonia brevis;* SCHUMAN:
Symphony No. 4 etc. **

Roy Harris's overture, *When Johnny comes marching home*, is a fresh and attractive piece and, like
most of Harris's music of the 1930s, has a vital impulse which by 1964, when he composed the
Epilogue to profiles in courage, had slackened into self-imitation. Good performances and rather good
recording too.

Symphony No. 3 in one movement.
*** DG Dig. 419 780-2 [id.]. NYPO, Bernstein – SCHUMAN: *Symphony No. 3.* ***

Roy Harris's *Third* is the archetypal American Symphony. There is a real sense of the wide open
spaces, of the abundant energy and independent nature of the American pioneers, and an instinctive
feeling for form. The music moves forward relentlessly from the very opening bars until the massive
eloquence of its coda. Bernstein gives a keenly felt but essentially softer-grained account of the work

than the famous first Koussevitzky recording. However, this is a great symphony – splendidly played and well recorded.

Hartmann, Karl Amadeus (1905–63)

Concerto funèbre (for violin and strings).
☞ *** Teldec/Warner Dig. 2292 46449-2 [id.]. Zehetmair, Philh. O, Holliger – BERG; JANACEK: *Violin concertos.* ***

As one of the two couplings for his clean-cut version of the Berg *Concerto*, Zehetmair offers this strong, intense *Concerto funèbre* for violin and strings – very much reflecting in its dark moods the troubled period, 1939, when it was written.

Harty, Hamilton (1879–1941)

(i) *Piano concerto in B min.;* (ii) *In Ireland (Fantasy for flute, harp and orchestra); With the wild geese.*
*** Chan. Dig. CHAN 8321; *ABTD 1084* [id.]. (i) Binns, (ii) Fleming, Kelly; Ulster O, Thomson.

Harty's *Piano concerto*, written in 1922, has strong Rachmaninovian influences, but the melodic freshness remains individual in this highly sympathetic performance. The *In Ireland fantasy* is full of delightful Irish melodic whimsy. Melodrama enters the scene in the symphonic poem, *With the wild geese*, but its Irishry asserts itself immediately in the opening theme. Again a splendid performance and a high standard of digital sound.

Violin concerto in D; Variations on a Dublin air.
*** Chan. CHAN 8386; *ABTD 1044* [id.]. Ralph Holmes, Ulster O, Thomson.

Though the *Violin concerto* has no strongly individual idiom, the invention is fresh and often touched with genuine poetry. Ralph Holmes gives a thoroughly committed account of the solo part and is well supported by an augmented Ulster Orchestra under Bryden Thomson. The *Variations* are less impressive though thoroughly enjoyable.

(i) *In Ireland* (fantasy for flute, harp and orchestra); *A John Field suite*. Arrangements: *Londonderry Air*. HANDEL: *Water music: suite*.
☞ (M) *** Chan. Dig./Analogue CHAN 6583 [id.]. Ulster O, Bryden Thomson; (i) with Fleming; Kelly.

Sir Hamilton Harty is better remembered as an interpreter and arranger than as a composer, but *In Ireland* is full of delightful Irish melodic whimsy, especially appealing when the playing is so winning and the digital recording so truthfully balanced. The other recordings are analogue but first rate, and these are accomplished performances. It is good to hear Harty's attractive arrangement of the John Field pieces, like the famous *Water music suite* a staple of the 78-r.p.m. catalogue.

An Irish symphony; A Comedy overture.
*** Chan. Dig. CHAN 8314; *ABTD 1027* [id.]. Ulster O, Thomson.

The *Irish symphony* has won great acclaim for its excellent scoring and good craftsmanship. The Scherzo is particularly engaging. It is extremely well played by the Ulster Orchestra under Bryden Thomson, and the overture is also successful and enjoyable. The recording is absolutely first class in every respect.

With the wild geese (symphonic poem).
☞ (B) *** CfP CD-CFP 4635; *TC-CFP 4635*. RSNO, Gibson – GERMAN: *Welsh rhapsody;* MACCUNN: *Land of Mountain and flood;* SMYTH: *Wreckers overture.* ***

With the wild geese is a melodramatic piece about the Irish soldiers fighting on the French side in the Battle of Fontenoy. The ingredients – a gay Irish theme and a call to arms among them – are effectively deployed; although the music does not reveal a strong individual personality, it is carried by a romantic sweep which is well exploited here. The 1968 recording still sounds most vivid, and this anthology makes a first-rate bargain.

VOCAL MUSIC

The Children of Lir; Ode to a nightingale.
*** Chan. Dig. CHAN 8387; *ABTD 1051* [id.]. Harper, Ulster O, Thomson.

Harty's setting of Keats's *Ode to a nightingale* is richly convincing, a piece written for his future wife, the soprano, Agnes Nicholls. The other work, directly Irish in its inspiration, evocative in an almost Sibelian way, uses the soprano in wordless melisma, here beautifully sung by Heather Harper. The performances are excellent, warmly committed and superbly recorded.

Hasse, Johann (1699–1783)

(i; ii) *Aria 'Ah Dio, ritornate'* from *La conversione di San'Agostino* for viola da gamba and harpsichord; (iii; i–ii) *Flute sonata in B min., Op. 2/6;* (ii) *Harpsichord sonata in C min. Op. 7/6;* (iv; i–iii) Cantatas: *Fille, dolce mio bene; Quel vago seno, O Fille;* Venetian ballads: *Cos e' sta Cossa?; Grazie agli inganni tuoi; No ste' a condanare; Si' la gondola avere', non crie'.*
☞ *** CRD Dig. CRD 3488 [id.]. (i) Erin Headley; (ii) Malcolm Proud; (iii) Nancy Hadden; (iv) Julianne Baird.

Johann Hasse was a remarkable example of a composer who outlived his times and was left behind by the musical course of events – the penalty of surviving until his 85th year. A member of the group of composers centred round the Court of Frederick the Great at Potsdam, his career peaked in the 1730s, although his success as an operatic composer continued on and off for another three decades. Finally in his seventies he graciously acknowledged Mozart's superiority; nevertheless he went on producing operas. The cantatas here are written in a pastoral style, with important flute obbligatos (a legacy from Frederick). They show much charm and distinct expressive feeling, and Julianne Baird has exactly the right voice for them, with a freshness of tone and purity of line matched by the right degree of ardour. The *Harpsichord sonata*, alternating fast and slow movements, is inventive and essentially good-humoured and the *Aria* for viola da gamba readily shows the composer's operatic style, while the Venetian ballads which close this elegantly performed and very well-recorded concert are also full of character, cultivated rather than folksy in their more popular idiom. Hasse may not have the strongest musical personality but everything here has a refreshing amiability.

Haydn, Josef (1732–1809)

Cello concertos in C & D, Hob XVIIb/1–2.
*** Ph. Dig. 420 923-2 [id.]. Heinrich Schiff, ASMF, Marriner.
*** O-L Dig. 414 615-2 [id.]. Christophe Coin, AAM, Hogwood.
(BB) *** Naxos Dig. 8.550059; *4550059* [id.]. Ludovít Kanta, Capella Istropolitana, Peter Breiner –
    BOCCHERINI: *Cello concerto.* ***
☞ (M) **(*) EMI Dig. CDM7 64326-2 [id.]. Lynn Harrell, ASMF, Marriner – VIVALDI: *Concertos.*
    **

Cello concerto in D, Hob VIIb/2.
*** EMI CDC7 47840-2 [id.]. Jacqueline du Pré, LSO, Barbirolli – BOCCHERINI: *Concerto.* **(*)

Heinrich Schiff produces a beautiful sound, as indeed do the Academy under Marriner. These are impressively fresh-sounding performances with lyrical and affectionate (but not too affectionate) playing from all concerned. The recording has the realistic timbre, balance and bloom one associates with Philips.

Christophe Coin, too, is a superb soloist and, provided the listener has no reservations about the use of original instruments, Hogwood's accompaniments are equally impressive. Excellent sound.

Kanta is a soloist of quality. The excellent Naxos recording is made in a bright, resonant acoustic in which every detail is clearly registered, though the players are perhaps forwardly placed. The accompaniments are alert and fresh. Kanta plays contemporary cadenzas. This record is a genuine bargain.

The attractions of Harrell's coupling are enhanced by the inclusion of two Vivaldi concertos interspersed with Haydn (although the recorded sound is strikingly different). Harrell, rather after the manner of Rostropovich, seeks to turn these elegant concertos into big, virtuoso pieces, helped by Marriner's beautifully played accompaniments. Although touches of romantic expressiveness tend to intrude, the result is enjoyable, even if cadenzas are distractingly long. The digital recording is full and vivid (the analogue Vivaldi transfers are brighter and less smooth).

With Barbirolli to partner her, Jacqueline du Pré's performance of the best-known *D major Concerto* is warmly expressive. The conviction and flair of the playing are extraordinarily compelling, and the romantic feeling is matched by an attractively full, well-balanced recording.

(i) *Cello concerto in C, Hob VIIb/1;* (ii; iv) *Horn concertos Nos. 1–2;* (iii; iv) *Trumpet concerto in D.*
(M) *** Decca 430 633-2 [id.]. (i) Rostropovich, ECO, Britten; (ii) Tuckwell; (iii) Alan Stringer; (iv) ASMF, Marriner.

Rostropovich's earlier (1964) stereo recording of the *C major Cello concerto* for Decca is undoubtedly romantic, and some may feel he takes too many liberties in the slow movement. The coupling of first-class 1966 versions of both the *Horn concertos* by Tuckwell in peak form and Stringer's 1967 account of the *Trumpet concerto* is certainly tempting.

(i) *Cello concertos: in C, Hob VIIb/1; in D, Hob VIIb/2;* (ii) *Violin concertos: in C; in A; in G, Hob VIIa/1, 3 & 4;* (ii; iii) *Double concerto for violin and harpsichord in F, Hob XVIII/6.*
☞ (B) *** Ph. Duo 438 797-2 (2) [id.]. ECO with (i) Walevska, De Waart; (ii) Accardo; (iii) Canino.

The three *Violin concertos* are all early; the *C major*, written for Tomasini, is probably the best. The other two have come into the limelight fairly recently. In the *G major* Accardo (who directs the accompaniments himself) follows the critical edition rather than the Melk autograph published by the Haydn-Mozart Presse and omits the two horns listed in the Breitkopf 1771 catalogue. Not that this is of any great importance for, although Accardo plays with great elegance and charm, it would be idle to pretend that this is great music. The same goes for the *Double Concerto for violin and harpsichord* which is of relatively slender musical interest. The soloists are perhaps a shade forward but the quality and balance are lifelike, and the 1980 recording has been well transferred. The two *Cello concertos* are, of course, much better known; Christine Walevska presents them freshly and she is well partnered by Edo de Waart and the ECO. She has a fairly small solo image and is balanced almost within the orchestra; the effect is to give a chamber-like quality to the music-making which is very agreeable, for the solo playing is not lacking in personality.

Harpsichord concerto in D, Hob XVIII/2; Overture in D, Hob Ia/7.
☞ (M) *** Decca 440 033-2 [id.]. George Malcolm, ASMF, Marriner – ARNE: *Harpsichord concerto No. 5* etc.; C. P. E. BACH: *Harpsichord concerto;* J. C. BACH: *Harpsichord concerto.* ***

This Haydn *D major Concerto* is justly well known and has never sounded better on record. It is expertly played by George Malcolm and the ASMF, both on top form, while the recording is exemplary in both tone-quality and balance. The *Overture* is an alternative finale (version B) to the *Symphony No. 53 in D* (*L'Impériale*) and is a light-hearted piece, dating from the mid-1770s. The couplings will also give much musical satisfaction, particularly given such persuasive advocacy as they are here by these artists.

Horn concerto No. 1 in D, Hob VIId/3.
(M) *** Decca 417 767-2 [id.]. Barry Tuckwell, ASMF, Marriner – MOZART: *Concertos Nos1–4.* ***

Tuckwell's playing throughout is of the highest order, and Marriner's vintage accompaniments are equally polished and full of elegance and vitality. The remastering is admirably fresh.

Horn concertos Nos. 1 in D, Hob VII/d3; 2 in D, Hob VII/d4.
(M) *** Teldec/Warner Dig. 9031 74790-2 [id.]. Dale Clevenger, Liszt CO, Rolla – M. HAYDN: *Concertino.* ***

Dale Clevenger, principal horn with the Chicago Symphony, gives superb accounts of the two *Horn concertos* attributed to Haydn (the second is of doubtful lineage). The accompaniments are supportive, polished and elegant. The Telefunken recording, made in a nicely judged and warm acoustic, is in the demonstration class.

(i) *Horn concertos Nos. 1–2;* (ii) *Trumpet concerto in E flat;* (i) *Divertimento a 3 in E flat.*
**(*) Nimbus NI 5010 [id.]. (i) Thompson; (ii) Wallace; Philh. O, Warren-Green.

Michael Thompson gives bold, confident accounts of the two concertos, with a sprinkling of decoration. John Wallace's trumpet timbre is strikingly brilliant, as recorded, and his playing in the *Trumpet concerto* is full of personality. He too likes to decorate and there are some attractive surprises in the finale. The recording was made in the resonant ambience of All Saints', Tooting.

Oboe concerto in C, Hob VIIg/C1.
*** Capriccio Dig. 10 308 [id.]. Lajos Lencsés, Stuttgart RSO, Marriner – HUMMEL: *Intro., theme &*
variations; MARTINU: *Concerto.* ***

Haydn's *Oboe concerto* in Lajos Lencsés' hands is given an almost Italianate sunny grace. Marriner is
altogether a most sympathetic accompanist. The balance is natural and the sound excellent. So are
the couplings.

3 Organ concertos in C, Hob. XVIII/1, 5 & 10.
☞ (B) *** Erato/Warner 4509 94581-2 [id.]. Marie-Claire Alain, Bournemouth Sinf., Guschlbauer –
C. P. E. BACH: *Organ concerto, Wq. 34.* **(*)

Marie-Claire Alain offers the three best-known *C major Organ concertos.* They are agreeably lively
and inventive, and the baroque orchestration with trumpets adds plenty of extra colour. It is difficult
to imagine them being presented more effectively than they are on this Erato reissue from the late
1970s. Marie-Claire Alain's registration is admirable; both solo-playing and accompaniments are
alert and sparkling. The sound is fresh and bright: the CD's treble gains from very slight paring back.
An enjoyable C. P. E. Bach concerto is offered as a bonus on this bargain-priced Bonsai reissue.

Piano concerto in D, Hob XVIII/2.
(B) **(*) Pickwick Dig. PCD 964; *IMPC 964* [id.]. Gloria d'Arti, ECCO, Aadland – BACH: *Clavier*
concerto No. 1; MOZART: *Piano concerto No. 8.* **(*)

This modern performance has plenty of vitality and is very enjoyable in its own right. It is excellently
recorded.

Piano concertos: in F, Hob. XVIII/3; in G, Hob. XVIII/4; in D, Hob. XVIII/11.
☞ *** Sony Dig. SK 48383 [id.]. Emanuel Ax, Franz Liszt CO.
☞ (B) **(*) Erato/Warner Dig 4509 94580-2 [id.]. Michèle Boegner, ECO, Garcia.

Piano concertos in G, Hob XVIII/4; in F, Hob XVIII/7; in G, Hob XVIII/9; in D, Hob XVIII/11.
☞ (BB) * Naxos Dig. 8.550713 [id.]. Hae-won Chang, Camerata Cassovia, Robert Stankovsky.

The popular *D major Concerto* comes with the *F major,* from Haydn's first years at Esterháza, and
the *G major,* which is somewhat later but still written with the harpsichord in mind. Emanuel Ax
gives them on the modern grand piano and he does so with great elegance and finesse. He evidently
enjoys a good rapport with the Franz Liszt Chamber Orchestra, who respond warmly to his
direction, and throughout all three concertos the music sounds fresh and sparkling. The quality of the
recording is outstanding; the piano sounds particularly real and lifelike, and the balance, too, is well
struck. This could well serve as the staple recommendation in this repertoire, given its artistic and
technical excellence.

   The performances by Michèle Boegner and the ECO under José-Luis Garcia are also enjoyable
and offer both modern (1991) digital recording and a very reasonable price. The accounts of the *F*
major and *G major Concertos* are fluent and musical, but the best-known *D major* (much the finest
work) springs vividly and refreshingly to life and is alone worth the price of the disc. Outer
movements sparkle and the slow movement is agreeably warm and expressive. The sound is excellent.

   Naxos offer an additional concerto and for a third of the price, so its claims appear strong. The
playing of the Camerata Cassovia under Robert Stankovsky is fresh and lively, and the recording
benefits from a warm and not excessively resonant acoustic. Unfortunately, the Korean pianist, Hae-
won Chang, is wanting in personality and her playing is colourless, primly correct and uninvolving.

Trumpet concerto in E flat.
⊛ *** Ph. Dig. 420 203-2; *420 203-4* [id.]. Håkan Hardenberger, ASMF, Marriner – HERTEL ***;
HUMMEL *** ⊛; STAMITZ: *Concertos.* ***
*** Sony CD 37846 [id.]. Marsalis, Nat. PO, Leppard – HUMMEL: *Concerto* *** (with L. MOZART:
Concerto ***).
(B) *** CfP Dig CD-CFP 4589. Ian Balmain, RLPO, Kovacevich – MOZART: *Horn concertos.* ***

Hardenberger's playing of the noble line of the *Andante* is no less telling than his fireworks in the
finale and, with Marriner providing warm, elegant and polished accompaniments throughout, this is
probably the finest single collection of trumpet concertos in the present catalogue.

   Marsalis is splendid too, his bravura no less spectacular, with the finale a tour de force, yet never
aggressive in its brilliance. His way with Haydn is eminently stylish, as is Leppard's lively and
polished accompaniment.

   With Stephen Kovacevich as conductor, Ian Balmain favours extreme speeds for Haydn's
delectable *Trumpet concerto,* playing brilliantly. It makes an apt and attractive coupling for Claire
Briggs's fine recordings of all four Mozart *Horn concertos,* very well recorded.

Violin concerto in C, Hob VIIa/1.

(M) *** Teldec/Warner Dig. 9031 74784-2 [id.]. Zehetmair, Liszt CO – M. HAYDN: *Concerto* **(*);
SIBELIUS: *Concerto.* **

Haydn's *C major Violin concerto* is given a superb performance by the young Hungarian violinist, Thomas Zehetmair, stylish, strong and resilient. He also directs the accompaniments which are alert and spirited in outer movements and responsive in the lovely *Adagio*.

Violin concertos: in C, Hob VIIa/1; in G, Hob VIIa/4.

(B) *** Ph. 426 977-2. Grumiaux, ECO or New Philh. O, Leppard – MOZART: *Adagio; Rondo;*
SCHUBERT: *Rondo.* ***

Haydn's *Violin concertos* make perfect vehicles for Grumiaux's refined classicism. Good mid-1960s sound and alert, gracious support from Leppard.

24 Minuets, Hob IX/16.

☞ (M) *** Decca 436 220-2 [id.]. Philh. Hungarica, Antal Dorati.

This collection of 24 *Minuets*, amazingly varied and imaginative, was written late in Haydn's career and, though few of them have the symphonic overtones of the minuets in the late symphonies, they represent the composer at his most inspired. It is not recommended to play them all at one sitting, but the set certainly adds point to Haydn's own definition of a good composer as 'one who can write a brand new minuet'. Dorati's performances are characteristically genial, and the excellent (1975) recording is transferred freshly and crisply, yet with plenty of weight in the orchestral sound.

The Seven Last Words of Christ on the Cross (original orchestral version).

☞ (M) ** Van. 08. 2034.71 I Solisti di Zagreb, Antonio Janigro.

It is good to have the orchestral version of Haydn's great sequence of slow movements on disc and it is played eloquently enough by Janigro and his Zagreb group and given full, realistic, late-1960s recording. However, this performance fails to move the listener as do the finest of the string quartet versions – see below.

SYMPHONIES

Symphonies Nos. 1–104; A; B.

⊛ (M) *** Decca 430 100-2 (32) [id.]. Philharmonia Hungarica, Antal Dorati.

Antal Dorati was ahead of his time as a Haydn interpreter when, in the early 1970s, he made his pioneering recording of the complete Haydn symphonies. Superbly transferred to CD in full, bright and immediate sound, the performances are a consistent delight, with brisk allegros and fast-flowing andantes, with textures remarkably clean. The slow rustic-sounding accounts of Minuets are more controversial, but the rhythmic bounce makes them very attractive too.

Another major project on Nimbus brings an ongoing series from Adám Fischer with the Austro-Hungarian Orchestra using modern instruments. This brings fresh, sympathetic, alert readings that are mellowed by the reverberant acoustic, which tends to be exaggerated by the Nimbus recording. Though the classic Dorati series is available only in boxed form – whether as a whole or in separate groups – the Decca performances and the cleanly focused sound are generally to be preferred.

Symphonies Nos. 1 in D; 2 in C; 3 in G; 4 in D; 5 in A; 6 in D (Le Matin); 7 in C (Le Midi); 8 in G (Le Soir); 9 in C; 10 in D; 11 in E flat; 12 in E; 13 in D; 14 in A; 15 in D; 16 in B flat.

(M) *** Decca 425 900-2 (4) [id.]. Philharmonia Hungarica, Antal Dorati.

These works – antedated by one or two symphonies that are later in the Breitkopf numbering – come from the early Esterházy period (1759–63) and show the young, formidably gifted composer working at full stretch. Dorati left these symphonies until well on in his great pioneering recording project, and the combination of exhilaration and stylishness is irresistible.

Symphonies Nos. 17 in F; 18 in G; 19 in D; 20 in C; 21 in A; 22 in E flat (Philosopher) (1st version); *23 in G; 24 in D; 25 in C; 26 in D min. (Lamentatione); 27 in G; 28 in A; 29 in E; 30 in C (Alleluja); 31 in D (Hornsignal); 32 in C; 33 in C.*

(M) *** Decca 425 905-2 (4) [id.]. Philharmonia Hungarica, Antal Dorati.

As in the rest of the cycle, Dorati's performances, helped by vivid recording, have you listening on from one symphony to the next, compulsively following the composer's career.

Symphonies Nos. 34 in D min.; 35 in B flat; 36 in E flat; 37 in C; 38 in C (Echo); 39 in G min.; 40 in F; 41 in C; 42 in D; 43 in E flat (Mercury); 44 in E min. (Trauer); 45 in F sharp min. (Farewell); 46 in B; 47 in G.
(M) *** Decca 425 910-2 (4) [id.]. Philharmonia Hungarica, Antal Dorati.

This particular sequence brings us to the frontier in Dorati's interpretations between those using and not using harpsichord continuo. He switches over in the middle of *No. 40 in F* – not illogically, when the finale is a fugue in which continuo would only be muddling. Unfailingly lively performances and abiding, brightly vivid sound.

Symphonies Nos. 48 in C (Maria Theresia); 49 in F min. (La Passione); 50 in C; 51 in B flat; 52 in C min.; 53 in D (L'Impériale); 54 in G; 55 in E flat (Schoolmaster); 56 in C; 57 in D; 58 in F; 59 in A (Fire).
(M) *** Decca 425 915-2 (4) [id.]. Philharmonia Hungarica, Antal Dorati.

The special value of Dorati's box is that it enables the listener to hear the ongoing sequence of nine works and to experience their historical impact in the same way as Prince Esterházy and his court must have done. The CD transfers continue to be outstandingly vivid.

Symphonies Nos. 60 in C (Il Distratto); 61 in D; 62 in D; 63 in C (La Roxolane); 64 in A; 65 in A; 66 in B flat; 67 in F; 68 in B flat; 69 in C (Laudon); 70 in D; 71 in B flat.
(M) *** Decca 425 920-2 (4) [id.]. Philharmonia Hungarica, Antal Dorati.

The only serious flaw in Dorati's interpretations – and it is something to note in a few of the symphonies in other boxes too – is his tendency to take minuets rather slowly. In many of them Haydn had already moved half-way towards a scherzo. But the Philharmonia Hungarica maintains its alertness with amazing consistency.

Symphonies Nos. 72 in D; 73 in D (La chasse); 74 in E flat; 75 in D; 76 in E flat; 77 in B flat; 78 in C min.; 79 in F; 80 in D min.; 81 in G; 82 in C (L'Ours); 83 in G min. (La Poule).
(M) *** Decca 425 925-2 (2) [id.]. Philharmonia Hungarica, Antal Dorati.

This collection – apart from No. 72, which is an earlier work, and the two *Paris Symphonies* tacked on at the end – centres on nine symphonies written more or less consecutively over a compact period of just four years (1780–84). At that time Haydn had just made contact with Mozart and though, on chronological evidence, the direct similarities can only be accidental the influence is already clear. The performances achieve an amazing degree of intensity, with alertness maintained throughout.

Symphonies Nos. 84 in E flat; 85 in B flat (La Reine); 86 in D; 87 in A (Paris Symphonies); 88 in G; 89 in F; 90 in C; 91 in E flat; 92 in G (Oxford); 93 in D; 94 in G (Surprise); 95 in C min.
(M) *** Decca 425 930-2 (4) [id.]. Philharmonia Hungarica, Antal Dorati.

It is a pity that Decca's layout in four-CD groups, and employing a consistent numerical sequence, has meant that Dorati's sets of both the six *Paris* and the first six *London Symphonies* have each had to be split over two separate CD boxes. But all are given fresh and stylish performances. Of the three *London Symphonies* included here, No. 93 brings one of the most delightful performances of Dorati's cycle, with a delectable, Ländler-like first movement.

Symphonies Nos. 96 in D (Miracle); 97 in C; 98 in B flat; 99 in E flat; 100 in G (Military); 101 in D (Clock); 102 in B flat; 103 in E flat (Drum Roll); 104 in D (London). Symphonies A in B flat; B in B flat; Sinfonia concertante in B flat (for oboe, bassoon, violin, cello & orchestra).
(M) *** Decca 425 935-2 (4) [id.]. Philharmonia Hungarica, Antal Dorati.

Dorati and the Philharmonia Hungarica completed their monumental project of recording the entire Haydn symphonic *oeuvre* with not a suspicion of routine. These final masterpieces are performed with a glowing sense of commitment, the results are authentically in scale, with individual solos emerging naturally against the glowing acoustic, and with intimacy comes extra dramatic force in sforzandos. As an appendix we are given the *Sinfonia concertante* and *Symphonies A* and *B*, presented with characteristic vitality. Dorati's account of the *Sinfonia concertante* presents the work as a further symphony with unusual scoring, rather than as a concerto-styled work.

Symphonies Nos. 1 in D min.; 2 in C; 4 in D; 5 in A; 10 in D; 11 in E flat; 18 in G; 27 in G; 32 in C; 37 in C; Symphony A (Partita) in B flat.
☞ **(*) O-L Dig. 436 428-2 (3). AAM, Hogwood.

Symphonies Nos. 3 in G; 14 in A; 15 in D; 17 in F; 19 in D; 20 in C; 25 in C; 33 in C; 36 in E flat; 108 (Partita) in B flat.
☞ **(*) O-L Dig. 436 592-2 (3) [id.]. AAM, Hogwood.

Symphonies Nos. 6 in D (Le Matin); 7 in C (Le Midi); 8 in G (Le Soir); 9 in C; 12 in E; 13 in D; 16 in B flat; 40 in F; 72 in D.
☞ **(*) O-L Dig. 433 661-2 [id.]. AAM, Hogwood.

Symphonies Nos. 21 in A; 22 in E flat (Philosopher); 23 in G; 24 in D; 28 in A; 29 in E; 30 in C (Allelujah); 31 in D (Horn signal); 34 in D min.
☞ **(*) O-L Dig. 430 082-2 (3) [id.]. AAM, Hogwood.

Symphonies Nos. 26 in D; 42 in D; 43 in E flat (Mercury); 44 in E min. (Trauer); 48 in C (Maria Theresia); 49 in F min. (La Passione).
☞ **(*) O-L Dig. 440 222-2 (3) [id.]. AAM, Hogwood.

Symphonies Nos. 35 in B flat; 38 in C; 39 in G min.; 41 in C; 58 in F; 59 in A (Fire); 65 in A.
☞ **(*) O-L Dig. 433 012-2 (3) [id.]. AAM, Hogwood.

In his Haydn series Hogwood has mellowed in period-performance manners, compared with his pioneering set of the Mozart *Symphonies*. The playing, too, is now more polished. He uses a small group of strings (about half the size of that chosen by Tafelmusik, who have the benefit of H. C. Robbins Landon's advice in this matter). In particular he avoids abrasiveness in slow movements which, though much leaner than with modern instruments, are sympathetically phrased though sometimes a little stiff. In general his direct, crisply rhythmic approach to these works tends not to convey the charm of Haydn. Even so he offers all repeats! No harpsichord continuo is employed, as in the Goodman project. The finely detailed, firmly focused recording perfectly brings out the transparency of textures, while giving body to the sound. If you are a Hogwood aficionado, these boxes can be acquired with confidence.

Symphonies Nos. 1 in D; 2 in C; 3 in G; 4 in D; 5 in A.
*** Hyp. Dig. CDA 66524 [id.]. Hanover Band, Roy Goodman.

Symphonies Nos. 6 in D (Le Matin); 7 in C (Le Midi); 8 in G (Le Soir).
*** Hyp. Dig. CDA 66523 [id.]. Hanover Band, Roy Goodman.

Symphonies Nos. 9 in C; 10 in D; 11 in E flat; 12 in E.
☞ *** Hyp. Dig. CDA 66529 [id.]. Hanover Band, Goodman.

Symphonies Nos. 13 in D; 14 in A; 15 in D; 16 in B flat.
☞ *** Hyp. Dig. CDA 66534 [id.]. Hanover Band, Goodman.

Symphonies Nos. 17 in F; 18 in G; 19 in D; 20 in C; 21 in A.
☞ *** Hyp. Dig. CDA 66533 [id.]. Hanover Band, Goodman.

Symphonies Nos. 42 in D; 43 in E flat (Mercury); 44 in E min. (Trauer).
☞ **(*) Hyp. Dig. CDA 66530 [id.]. Hanover Band, Goodman.

Symphonies Nos. 45 in F sharp min. (Farewell); 46 in B; 47 in G.
**(*) Hyp. Dig. CDA 66522 [id.]. Hanover Band, Goodman.

Symphonies Nos. 48 in C (Maria Theresia); 49 in F min. (Passione); 50 in C.
☞ **(*) Hyp. Dig. CDA 66531 [id.]. Hanover Band, Goodman.

Symphonies Nos. 70 in D, 71 in B flat, 72 in D.
*** Hyp. Dig. CDA 66526 [id.]. Hanover Band, Roy Goodman.

Symphonies Nos. 73 in D (La chasse), 74 in E flat , 75 in D.
*** Hyp. Dig. CDA 66520 [id.]. Hanover Band, Roy Goodman.

Symphonies Nos. 76 in E flat; 77 in B flat; 78 in C min.
*** Hyp. Dig. CDA 66525 [id.]. Hanover Band, Roy Goodman.

Symphonies Nos. 82 in C (The Bear); 83 in G min. (The Hen); 84 in E flat.
*** Hyp. Dig. CDA 66527; KA 66527 [id.]. Hanover Band, Goodman.

Symphonies Nos. 90 in C; 91 in E flat; 92 in G (Oxford).
*** Hyp. Dig. CDA 66521; KA 66521 [id.]. Hanover Band, Goodman.

Symphonies Nos. 93 in D; 94 in G (Surprise); 95 in C min.
☞ *** Hyp. Dig. CDA 66532 [id.]. Hanover Band, Goodman.

Symphonies Nos. 101 in D (Clock); 102 in B flat; Overture: Windsor Castle.
☞ *** Hyp. Dig. CDA 66528 [id.]. Hanover Band, Goodman.

From the very outset of his Hyperion project, Goodman, who began at the beginning with the low-numbered symphonies, established a winning manner in early Haydn and, as the series progressed, he showed that his dramatic approach (tougher than Kuijken, for instance, in his COE recordings for Virgin) was being consistently fruitful in the middle-period and later works. The performances offer consistently alert and well-sprung readings, which generally favour fast Allegros and relatively spacious slow movements which, more than in most period performances, give expressive warmth to Haydn's melodies, without overstepping the mark into romanticism. That Goodman is very much the positive director of the group is brought out by the generally close balance given to the harpsichord continuo, which is far more consistently audible than in most versions. The recording is resonant, giving bloom to the strings, yet oboes and horns (and other wind and brass, when used) come through vividly. Altogether, this Hyperion series is achieving a balance of style somewhere between the more plangent Hogwood approach and the fuller scale possible with Dorati, using modern instruments.

Other miscellaneous symphonies

Symphonies Nos. 6 in D (Le Matin); 7 in C (Le Midi); 8 in G (Le Soir).
*** DG Dig. 423 098-2 [id.]. E. Concert, Pinnock.
☞ (BB) *** Naxos Dig. 8.550722 [id.]. N. CO, Ward.
(B) *** Decca 421 627-2 [id.]. Philh. Hungarica, Dorati.

These were almost certainly the first works that Haydn composed on taking up his appointment as Kapellmeister to the Esterházys. Pinnock's performances are polished and refined, yet highly spirited, with infectious allegros and expressive feeling. There is certainly weight here, yet essentially this is a bracing musical experience with the genius of these early works fully displayed.

A splendid début in these early symphonies from the Northern Chamber Orchestra under Nicholas Ward. The 'daybreak' opening of No. 6 is nicely graduated; then the allegro sets off spiritedly, while the leader happily (and stylishly) dominates the slow movement. Throughout these works the wind players obviously relish their solos, the flute chirps merrily and the bassoon immediately has a chance to shine in the Trio of the Minuet of No. 6; even the double bass has a solo in the comparable movement of No. 7. In the *Andante* of *Le Soir* the strings create a chamber-music atmosphere, and it is the intimate scale of these performances that is so attractive. Modern instruments are used, but textures are fresh and the ambience of the Concert Hall of New Broadcasting House, Manchester, adds the right degree of warmth.

Dorati is at his finest in these relatively well-known named symphonies, with their marvellous solos for members of the Esterházy orchestra. The remastered recording sounds fresh and clear.

Symphonies Nos. 9 in C; 10 in D; 11 in E flat; 12 in E.
☞ ** Chan. Dig. CHAN 8813 [id.]. Cantilena, Adrian Shepherd.

There is a lot to be said for Adrian Shepherd's Haydn symphonies: they are musical, decently played and recorded – though wanting in the last ounce of finish – and free of any hint of affectation. Eminently serviceable accounts.

Symphonies Nos. 22 in E flat (Philosopher); 24 in D; 30 in C (Alleluja).
☞ (M) *(*) Chan. Dig CHAN 6579 [id.]. Cantilena, Adrian Shepherd.

Even in its mid-price Collect reissue this collection fails to make the grade. *The Philosopher* is not a success; the brisk tempo robs the opening of its breadth and dignity, and the minuet and Trio is pedestrian. Nos. 24 and 30 are generally more successful, with better-judged tempi and rather more polish. All these symphonies come from the mid-1760s and display characteristic musical resource. As usual from Chandos, the sound is fresh and truthful on CD.

Symphonies Nos. 22 in E flat (Philosopher); 63 in C (La Roxelane); 80 in D min.
*** DG Dig. 427 337-2 [id.]. Orpheus CO.

The Orpheus players give all three symphonies with that sense of style, polish and intelligent commitment we have come to expect from them. Pacing, suppleness of phrase and precision of ensemble again demonstrate that for them a conductor isn't necessary, and the DG sound is first class.

Symphonies Nos. 26 (Lamentatione), 35, 38–9, 41–2, 43 (Mercury), 44 (Trauer), 45 (Farewell), 46–7, 48 (Maria Theresia), 49 (La passione), 50–52, 58, 59 (Fire), 65.
(M) *** DG Dig. 435 001-2 (6). E. Concert, Trevor Pinnock.

Pinnock's forces are modest (with 6.5.2.2.1 strings), but the panache of the playing conveys any necessary grandeur. It is a new experience to have Haydn symphonies of this period recorded in relatively dry and close sound, with inner detail crystal clear (harpsichord never obscured) and made the more dramatic by the intimate sense of presence, yet with a fine bloom on the instruments. Some may find a certain lack of charm at times, and others may quarrel with the very brisk one-in-a-bar minuets and – dare one say it! – even find finales a bit rushed.

Symphonies Nos. 26 in D min. (Lamentatione); 35 in B flat; 49 in F min. (La Passione).
☞ (BB) **(*) Naxos Dig. 8.550721 [id.]. N. CO, Ward.

Although enjoyable, the second disc from Nicholas Ward and his Northern Chamber Orchestra is not quite as fresh-sounding as the first. The playing remains elegant and the horns (in B flat alto) are splendid in the Minuet of No. 35. But the opening *Allegro assai con spirito* of the *Lamentatione* could do with a shade more bite, and in the *Adagio* the warm resonance makes the finely played oboe solo almost a cor anglais and the melodic line like a Handel aria. The opening slow movement of No. 49 is not as intense as it might be, though the *Allegro di molto* which follows has plenty of energy, as does the finale, while the horns shine again in the Trio of the Minuet. The resonance of the BBC's Studio 7 in Manchester brings a pleasingly mellow sound-picture, but the string detail is not sharply defined.

ny*Symphonies Nos. 26 in D min. (Lamentatione); 44 in E min. (Trauer); 45 in F sharp min. (Farewell).*
☞ (B) ** Hung. White Label HRC 102. Hungarian CO, Vilmos Tatrai.

The Hungarian Chamber Orchestra is a first-class group of players and this is an enjoyable if not distinctive collection, played with warmth and finesse. Good but not remarkable value.

Symphonies Nos. 26 in D min. (Lamentatione); 52 in C min.; 53 in D (L'Imperiale).
*** Virgin/EMI Dig. VC7 59148-2 [id.]. La Petite Bande, Sigiswald Kuijken.

These are fresh, vital, cleanly articulated performances which wear their authenticity lightly and even indulge in speeds for slow movements that are more expansive and affectionate than many purists would allow.

Symphonies Nos. 41 in C; 42 in D; 43 in E flat (Mercury).
☞ *** Sony Dig. SK 48370 [id.]. Tafelmusik, Weil.

Symphonies Nos. 44 in E min. (Trauer); 51 in F sharp min.; 52 in C min.
☞ *** Sony Dig. SK 48371 [id.]. Tafelmusik, Weil.

Symphonies Nos. 45 in F sharp min. (Farewell); 46 in B; 47 in G.
☞ *** Sony Dig. SK 53986 [id.]. Tafelmusik, Weil.

Symphonies Nos. 50 in C; 64 in A; 65 in A.
☞ *** Sony Dig. SK 53985 [id.]. Tafelmusik, Weil.

This new series from Sony is produced with the estimable H. C. Robbins Landon as musicological and artistic consultant, and he has expressed personal pleasure with the results. In short these recordings set new standards in this repertoire. The size of the group seems just about ideal with 20 strings, 7.6.3.2.2, against which oboes and horns and sometimes trumpets are vividly balanced. There is no harpsichord continuo. All four of these records are a great success and if you want these symphonies performed on period instruments this is the way to play them. Bruno Weil's tempi are apt and Tafelmusik is sensitive to details of phrasing and dynamics and they obviously love Haydn. The effect is admirably spontaneous. The group are very well recorded, too. The sound is full yet admirably transparent. The notes are admirable and, although competing authentic performances offer different insights, the present series is surpassed by none of them.

Symphonies Nos. 43 in E flat (Mercury); 44 in E min. (Trauer); 49 in F min. (La Passione).
☞ **(*) Chan. Dig. CHAN 6590 [id.]. Cantilena, Adrian Shepherd.

Two of the symphonies (Nos. 44 and 49) offered by Adrian Shepherd's Cantilena come from the so-called *Sturm und Drang* set. This group captures their spirit effectively – particularly in the so-called *Trauer* or 'Mourning' *symphony*, in which tempi are well judged and the textures admirably clean. *La Passione* is committed enough, though the actual playing is less accomplished than in some rivals (notably the Orpheus Chamber Orchestra). The *E flat Symphony* (*Mercury*) is slightly less successful and is a bit matter-of-fact. Again the sound-quality is clean and pleasing and the balance generally well handled, and at mid-price this is now fairly competitive.

Symphony No. 44 in E min. (Trauer).
(B) *** Pickwick Dig. PCD 820; *CIMPC 820* [id.]. O of St John's, Smith Square, Lubbock –
MOZART: *Symphony No. 40.* **(*)

The Orchestra of St John's are on their toes throughout their splendidly committed account of the *Trauersymphonie*. The recording too is in the demonstration class.

Symphonies Nos. 44 in E min. (Trauer); 88 in G; 104 in D (London).
(BB) *** Naxos Dig. 8.550287; *4550287* [id.]. Capella Istropolitana, Barry Wordsworth.

Symphonies Nos. 45 in F sharp min. (Farewell); 48 in C (Maria Theresia); 102 in B flat.
(BB) *** Naxos Dig. 8.550382; *4550382* [id.]. Capella Istropolitana, Barry Wordsworth.

Symphonies Nos. 82 in C (The Bear); 96 in D (Miracle); 100 in G (Military).
(BB) *** Naxos Dig. 8.550139; *4550139* [id.]. Capella Istropolitana, Barry Wordsworth.

Symphonies Nos. 83 in G min. (The Hen); 94 in G (Surprise); 101 in D (The Clock).
(BB) *** Naxos Dig. 8.550114; *4550114* [id.]. Capella Istropolitana, Barry Wordsworth.

Symphonies Nos. 85 in B flat (La Reine); 92 in G (Oxford); 103 in E flat (Drum Roll).
(BB) *** Naxos Dig. 8.550387 [id.]. Capella Istropolitana, Barry Wordsworth.

Like Barry Wordsworth's recordings of Mozart symphonies, also with the Capella Istropolitana on the Naxos label, this Haydn collection provides a series of outstanding bargains at the lowest budget price. The sound is not quite as clean and immediate as in the Mozart series, a little boomy at times in fact, and Wordsworth's preference for relatively relaxed speeds is a little more marked here than in Mozart, but the varied choice of works on each disc is most attractive. At their modest cost, these are well worth collecting alongside Dorati's Philharmonia Hungarica boxes.

Symphonies Nos. 45 in F sharp min. (Farewell); 48 in C (Maria Theresia).
(M) *** Sony Dig. MDK 46507 [id.]. L'Estro Armonico, Derek Solomons.

Solomons keeps his ensemble of period instruments very small, with six violins but only one each of the other stringed instruments, a scale Haydn himself employed at Esterháza. Special mention must be made of the brilliant horn playing of Anthony Halstead not only in this work but also in the slow movement of No. 48, again hauntingly beautiful. The invigorating opening movement of that same work, bursting with exuberance, brings thrilling sound, and the Minuet is no less impressive.

Symphonies Nos. (i) 45 in F sharp min. (Farewell); (ii) 88 in G; (iii) 104 in D (London).
☞ (B) *** DG 439 428-2 [id.]. (i) ECO, Barenboim; (ii) VPO, Boehm; (iii) LPO, Jochum.

A highly stimulating triptych of Haydn performances by three different conductors, all of whom have something positive to say about this repertoire. Barenboim's *Farewell Symphony* has much vitality and there is sensitive playing in the remarkable *Adagio*, one of Haydn's finest. Boehm and the VPO are at their very best in No. 88, with the slow movement gravely expansive. The playing has great polish and refinement, and Boehm's touch instantly charms in the spirited finale. Jochum's is among the most musically satisfying accounts of No. 104 in the catalogue; and all three recordings (from the 1970s) sound first class in their remastered form. A genuine bargain, playing for 77 minutes.

Symphonies Nos. 53 in D (L'Impériale); 73 in D (La Chasse); 79 in F.
☞ *** DG Dig. 439 779-2 [id.]. Orpheus CO.

As with earlier issues in their Haydn symphony series, the Orpheus Chamber Orchestra turn in performances of liveliness, sensitivity and intelligence. For those who do not want period-instrument forces, they have proved a consistently reliable alternative and, despite the absence of a conductor, there is no want of personality about their readings. They are also recorded with exemplary clarity, with a comfortable halo of reverberance that lends freshness and bloom to the sound. All three symphonies are thoroughly enjoyable, and we hope the earlier issues, which were originally issued uneconomically with only two symphonies per CD, will now reappear, more generously presented.

Symphonies Nos. 59 in A (Fire); 100 in G (Military); 101 in D (Clock).
(M) *** Ph. 420 866-2 [id.]. ASMF, Marriner.

Marriner's recordings derive from the mid-1970s and the performances are very satisfactory, as is the remastering. The *Clock* is vital and intelligent, the playing of the Academy very spruce and elegant.

Symphonies Nos. 69 in C (Laudon); 89 in F; 91 in E flat.
☞ (M) **(*) Naxos Dig. 8.550769 [id.]. Budapest Nicolaus Esterházy Sinfonia, Béla Drahos.

The resonance of the Reformed Church, Budapest, prevents the sharpest definition here. The orchestra is set back and the internal balance is natural: the strings have bloom without edginess. This is alert, thoroughly musical playing with apt tempi. The *Andante con moto* of No. 89 is elegantly done, and the variations of the *Andante* of No. 91 are neatly handled (with an elegant bassoon solo). All in all this gives pleasure, but a bit more brightness on top would have been welcome.

Symphonies Nos. 80 in D min.; 87 in A; 89 in F.
*** ASV Dig. CDDCA 635 [id.]. LMP, Jane Glover.

Jane Glover conducts the reinvigorated London Mozart Players in strong and energetic performances of these three relatively rare symphonies. Though textures are not as transparent as we are beginning to demand in an age of period performance – largely a question of the ambient recorded sound – these modern-instrument performances are as winning as they are lively.

Symphonies Nos. 82 in C (The Bear); 83 in G min. (The Hen); 84 in E flat; 85 in B flat (La Reine); 86 in D; 87 in A (Paris Symphonies).
☞ (B) *** Ph. Duo 438 727-2 (2) [id.]. ASMF, Sir Neville Marriner.
☞ (M) ** Sony SM2K 47550 (2). NYPO, Bernstein.

From Marriner, spirited and well-played accounts of the *Paris Symphonies*, distinguished by excellent ensemble and keen articulation. Nos. 86 and 87 (and perhaps 84) are digital recordings, the remainder being analogue, though this is not indicated in the documentation. The playing has that touch of charm which is so essential in Haydn. It is possible to imagine performances of greater character and personality than these (in the slow movements there is a tendency to blandness) but, generally speaking, they are very lively and musical and a good alternative to the Dorati recordings. They are certainly economically priced.

Bernstein's *Paris Symphonies* are impressive. He obviously enjoys the music, and the playing of the New York Philharmonic is very alive, phrasing is sensitive and dynamic nuances are carefully attended to. The rhythmic jokiness of the finale of *The Bear* is attractively managed and the witty string writing in the first movement, which led to the christening of No. 83 as *The Hen*, is very nicely pointed. The account of *No. 84 in E flat* is particularly impressive, and the Minuets – generally more buoyant than in the *London Symphonies* – bring some delightful playing in the Trios, notably in Nos. 83, 86 and 87. In the second movement of *La Reine* Bernstein omits first-half repeats in the variations but observes those in the second. There is some delightful detail in this movement, especially from the flutes. The recordings were made in the Manhattan Center or Avery Fisher Hall between 1962 and 1967, and the CD transfers bring rather shrill violins (though there is plenty of weight), which at times makes the allegros sound a bit fierce, as in the first movements of Nos. 86 and 87; but the string ensemble is excellent and, for all one's reservations about the sound, these are performances to be reckoned with: they are eminently felt.

(Paris) Symphonies Nos. 82 in C (The Bear); 83 in G min. (The Hen); 84 in E flat.
✣ *** Virgin/EMI Dig. VC7 59263-2. O of Age of Enlightenment, Kuijken.

(Paris) Symphonies Nos. 85 in B flat (La Reine); 86 in D; 87 in A.
✣ *** Virgin/EMI Dig. VC7 59557-2. O of Age of Enlightenment, Kuijken.

These two discs, well filled, with three symphonies apiece, together present an outstanding set of Haydn's six *Paris symphonies*, between them offering among the most enjoyable period-performance recordings of Haydn ever. Above all, Kuijken and his players convey the full joy of Haydn's inspiration in every movement.

Symphony No. 88 in G.
☞ (M) **(*) Sony SM2K 47563 [id.]. NYPO, Bernstein – *Masses Nos. 10–11.* **

Like the *Paris Symphonies*, Bernstein's account of *No. 88 in G* has much to recommend it. The glorious *Largo*, taken expansively, is overtly expressive and some might feel it too heavy, but there is no mistaking Bernstein's personal warmth. The playing in the sparkling finale is most infectious. Good, well-balanced 1963 sound.

Symphonies Nos. 88 in G; 92 in G (Oxford); 95 in C min.; 98 in B flat; 100 in G (Military); 101 in D (Clock); 102 in B flat; 104 in D (London).
☞ (M) ** EMI CMS7 63667-2 (3) [id.]. Philh. O or New Philh. O, Klemperer.

Klemperer, not the likeliest conductor in Haydn, in his broad, measured view yet shows his mastery in structuring and rhythmic pointing. With good analogue sound, an interesting historical document.

Symphonies Nos. 88 in G; 95 in C min.; 101 in D (Clock).
☞ (M) **(*) BMG/RCA 09026 60729-2 [id.]. Symphony O or Chicago SO, Fritz Reiner.

Reiner's Haydn is – perhaps not surprisingly – a little Germanic: all three slow movements are measured, although Haydn's markings for both the *Clock* and No. 95 are *Andante*. The leisurely *Largo* in No. 88 is sustained by the beauty of the playing, and the spacious equivalent of No. 95 is also phrased with much care and affection. Finales, though never rushed, are nimble and sprightly. The recording – from 1960 and (in the case of the *C minor Symphony*) 1963 – is certainly full, with more ample textures than we would expect today.

Symphonies Nos. 88 in G; 104 in D (London).
*** CRD CRD 3370; *CRDC 4070* [id.]. Bournemouth Sinf., Ronald Thomas.

Although the orchestra is smaller than the Concertgebouw or LPO, the playing has great freshness and vitality; indeed it is the urgency of musical feeling that Ronald Thomas conveys which makes up for the last ounce of finesse.

Symphonies Nos. 92 in G (Oxford); 94 in G (Surprise); 96 in D (Miracle).
(M) *** Sony SBK 46332 [id.]. Cleveland O, Szell.

Symphonies Nos. 93 in D; 94 in G (Surprise); 95 in C min.; 96 in D (Miracle); 97 in C; 98 in B flat (London Symphonies).
(M) *** Sony MY2K 45673 (2) [id.]. Cleveland O, Szell.

With superb polish in the playing and precise phrasing it would be easy for such performances as these to sound superficial, but Haydn's music obviously struck a deep chord in Szell's sensibility and there is humanity underlying the technical perfection. Indeed there are many little musical touches from Szell to show that his perfectionist approach is a dedicated and affectionate one. The recordings have been splendidly remastered and the sound is fuller and firmer than it ever was on LP.

Symphonies Nos. 92 in G (Oxford); 96 in D (Miracle).
☞ ** Ph. Dig. 434 915-2 [id.]. VPO, Previn.

The days when a record company can get away with issuing only two Haydn symphonies on a full-priced CD are surely numbered. This one plays for just over 49 minutes: there would have been plenty of room for a third work. The performances are warm and affectionate, with fine, spacious phrasing in slow movements and sprightly finales, but with the full textures of modern instruments made to sound a bit heavy by the resonant acoustics of the Musikverein.

Symphonies Nos. 92 in G (Oxford); 101 in D (Clock).
☞ (B) ** Hung. White Label HRC 089. Hungarian State O, Ervin Lucas.

Warm, polished performances, with elegantly phrased slow movements and sprightly finales; the sound is pleasing and full, if not especially transparent.

Symphonies Nos. 92 in G (Oxford); 104 in D (London).
(B) *** Pickwick Dig. PCD 916; *CIMPC 916*. E. Sinfonia, Groves.

Sir Charles Groves's performances are robust yet elegant as well; both slow movements are beautifully shaped, with Haydn's characteristic contrasts unfolding spontaneously. In the last movement of the *Oxford*, the dancing violins are a special delight in what is one of the composer's most infectious finales.

Symphonies Nos. 93 in D; 94 in G (Surprise); 95 in C min.
☞ *** HM/BMG Dig. 05472 77275 [id.]. La Petite Bande, Sigiswald Kuijken.

Sigiswald Kuijken has changed record companies and orchestras, but he still provides polished performances that are at once extremely alive and convey enjoyment in the music's drama and genial craftsmanship. The playing is less earthily robust than with Goodman (who has this same triptych – see above), but the virtuosity here in Allegros is both precise and infectious. The *Largo* slow movement of No. 93 may be pressed on rather strongly for some tastes, but not the slow movement of the *Surprise*, and the minuets have a nice lift. The recording gives a slightly more mellow effect than the Hyperion, without losing transparency.

Symphonies Nos. 93–98.
(M) (***) EMI mono CMS7 64389-2 (2) [id.]. RPO, Sir Thomas Beecham.

Symphonies Nos. 99–104.
⊛ (M) *** EMI CMS7 64066-2 (2) [id.]. RPO, Sir Thomas Beecham.

The art of phrasing is one of the prime secrets of great music-making, and no detail in Beecham's performances of the *London Symphonies* goes untended. They have also great warmth, drama too, and perhaps a unique geniality. The sound throughout is full and fresh, with plenty of body, sweet violin-timbre and no edge. The first box are mono recordings; they sound admirably full-bodied and have been transferred amazingly successfully. The performances profess an inner life and vitality that put them in a class of their own.

Symphonies Nos. 93 in D; 94 in G (Surprise); 95 in C min.; 96 in D (Miracle); 97 in C; 98 in B flat; 99 in E flat; 100 in G (Military); 101 in D (Clock); 102 in B flat; 103 in E flat (Drum Roll); 104 in D (London Symphonies).

☞ (B) *** DG 437 201-2 (4). LPO, Jochum.
☞ (M) **(*) Decca Dig. 436 290-2 (6). LPO, Solti.
☞ (M) **(*) Sony S3MK 47553 (3) (*Nos. 93–99* only) [id.]. NYPO, Bernstein.
☞ (M) **(*) Sony SM2K 47557 (2) (*Nos. 100-104* only) [id.]. NYPO, Bernstein.

Symphonies Nos. 93 in D; 99 in E flat.
☞ ⊛ *** Decca Dig. 417 620-2 [id.]. LPO, Solti.

Symphonies Nos. 94 in G (Surprise); 100 in G (Military).
☞ **(*) Decca Dig. 416 617-2 [id.]. LPO, Solti.

Symphonies Nos. 95 in C min.; 104 in D (London).
☞ *** Decca Dig. 417 330-2 [id.]. LPO, Solti.

Symphonies Nos. 97 in C; 98 in B flat.
☞ **(*) Decca Dig. 433 396-2 [id.]. LPO, Solti.

Jochum recorded the twelve *London Symphonies* between October 1971 and February 1973 in Barking Town Hall as part of DG's 75th-birthday symphony project. Linking the recording sessions with four concerts spaced over a year, he secured fine, stylish playing from the LPO, challenging them with often very fast tempi in outer movements. Those fast tempi sometimes prevent the music from having quite the lilt it has with Beecham or the gravitas of Sir Colin Davis; but the athletic exuberance of Jochum in Haydn, his ability to mould slow movements with tenderness that never spills over into unstylish mannerism (and to handle the sets of themes and variations to bring great diversity of atmosphere and mood), makes these wonderfully satisfying readings of Haydn's greatest symphonies. The spacious *Adagio* of No. 99 inspires radiant playing in the reprise, while the beautiful slow movement of No. 97 is serenely poised.

In No. 98 the quotation of '*God save the King*' is made to sound surprisingly refined; conversely, the *Andante* of No. 94 brings a real fortissimo 'surprise', following a pianissimo echo of the main theme; and the *Andante* of the *Clock*, fairly brisk, ticks crisply with delightful humour. The opening of No. 103 brings a thunderous drum-roll, and this performance has much character. In first movements generally lifted rhythms and the resilience of the LPO playing bring grace as well as vitality, and the introduction of secondary themes is managed with great felicity (as in the *Miracle*, which also has a particularly engaging *Andante*). Finales are neat and sparkling: in the closing *Presto* of No. 100 the triplets are miraculously well defined. In the finale of No. 98 Jochum adds a harpsichord to the texture so that Haydn's charming little joke at the end can make its point all the better. Overall, this set will give much refreshment, and the recording is naturally balanced and clear, with its warm reverberation presenting these works on a somewhat bigger scale than with Dorati, yet with rather less weight than Davis brings. Many will feel this to be a perfect compromise.

Solti made his recordings, with the same orchestra, over a decade between 1981 and 1992. He began with the *Miracle* and the *Clock*, and these early performances, although brilliantly played, were rather too taut to convey all Haydn's charm. Again in Nos. 102 and 103, a year later, even though the beauty and refinement of the LPO playing and the fine Decca recording cannot help but give pleasure, the tensions speak of the twentieth rather than the eighteenth century, with even the lovely *Adagio* of No. 102 failing quite to relax.

In the *Surprise* and *Military Symphonies*, which came next and which has been reissued separately as part of the Solti Edition, the conductor stresses the brilliance and fire of the outer movements, which are a bit hard-driven, but there is no lack of *joie de vivre*. The recording, hitherto excellent, here approaches demonstration standard in its fullness and transparency, and this is even more striking in the pairing of Nos. 95 and *104 in C minor*. Here at last Solti finds a perfect balance between energy and repose. The pacing is admirable and the LPO playing is smiling and elegant, yet full of bubbling vitality. No. 95 has a striking sense of cohesion and purpose, and there is no finer version of No. 104. Solti uses a full body of strings and all the resources of modern wind instruments with the greatest possible finesse, yet the spontaneity of the music-making is paramount.

Nos. 93 and 99, which followed, are the pick of the cycle. Sir Georg's relaxed manner is tangible: the atmosphere is sunny and civilized. There is no lack of brilliance – indeed the LPO are consistently on their toes – but the music-making is infectious rather than hard-driven. The string phrasing is as graceful as the woodwind articulation is light and felicitous. The lovely slow movement of No. 93 has both delicacy and gravitas, and that of No. 99 is serenely spacious. The Minuets are shown to have quite different characters, and both finales sparkle in the happiest manner.

The last disc celebrated Solti's eightieth birthday and contains a splendid account of No. 98, one of Haydn's very greatest symphonies. The *Adagio* slow movement produces a solemnly gracious rendering of '*God save the King*', and both here and in the vigorous Minuet the LPO are on top form. The jokey finale is delightfully handled. No. 97 is equally spirited, but here there is hint of the earlier problem: too much tautness in the first two movements, although the LPO are very responsive and their playing is always elegantly polished. The Minuet and finale, however, are buoyant and infectious, and this is still very enjoyable music-making given beautifully balanced sound. The complete set, however, is uneconomically spread over six mid-priced discs; Solti fans would surely do better to invest in the pair of full-priced issues containing Nos. 93, 95, 99 and 104.

Bernstein offers large-scale performances of Nos. 93 to 99, recorded between 1970 and 1975, either in the Avery Fisher Hall or in a New York studio. The sound is quite full, although there is a degree of fierceness on the violins. The performances show Bernstein's warmth and the spirited NYPO response to the conductor's often grand manner. But while there are many fine individual moments, like the *Andante* of No. 96 or the *vivace* finale of No. 99, often the phrasing is rather heavily expressive, lacking the lightness and grace of Jochum, and this especially applies to the Minuets. The last five symphonies are among the most successful, particularly the *Drum Roll*, with slow movements always individual. The *Andante* of *The Clock* is particularly engaging, and the *Allegretto* of the *Military* brings spectacular percussion – no holds barred. No. 104 was the earliest to be recorded (in 1958) and sounds thinner than the others. Whatever one's reservations, this music-making is full of personality and is always committed.

Symphonies Nos. 94 in G (Surprise); 96 in D (Miracle).
*** O-L Dig. 414 330-2 [id.]. AAM, Hogwood.

The playing here is superb: polished, feeling, and full of imaginative detail. The account of No. 94 is particularly dramatic and in the *Andante* there is not just the one 'surprise' (and that pretty impressive) but two more *forte* chords to follow at the beginning of each subsequent phrase – a most telling device. The presence of Hogwood's fortepiano can also be subtly felt here, and later the wind solos are full of character. With superb recording, full yet transparent, this is an issue to make converts to the creed of authenticity.

Symphonies Nos. 94 in G (Surprise); 96 in D (Miracle); 100 in G (Military).
(M) *** Decca 417 718-2 [id.]. Philh. Hungarica, Dorati.

These three symphonies, collected from Dorati's historic complete Haydn cycle, make a delightful group. The only controversial speed comes in the *Andante* of the *Surprise*, much faster than usual, but the freshness of the joke is the more sharply presented.

Symphonies Nos. (i) 94 in G (Surprise); (ii) 96 in D (Miracle); (i) 104 in D (London).
☞ (M) **(*) EMI CDM5 65178-2 [id.]. (i) Pittsburgh SO; (ii) LSO; Previn.

In coupling what are arguably Haydn's two most popular symphonies with the *Miracle*, Previn offers an attractive triptych for those favouring Haydn on a larger scale. The performances of Nos. 94 and 104 are lively and very well played and recorded. The only reservations concern the slow movements, which sound just a little perfunctory and lacking in poise. No. 96, however, recorded two years earlier with the LSO, shows Previn at his finest, with the pointing and attention to detail matched by the genial atmosphere. Indeed there is a Beechamesque touch to this music-making. The concertante element is a delight and the finale has real wit. The late-1970s recordings have all been very successfully remastered.

Symphonies Nos. 94 in G (Surprise); 98 in B flat; 101 in D (Clock); 104 in D (London).
☞ (B) *** Erato/Warner Dig. 4509 91933-2 [id.]. SCO, Raymond Leppard.

Three favourite Haydn symphonies are offered here at bargain price in an Erato Bonsai Duo reissue, together with the surprisingly rare *No. 98 in B flat*, an unquestioned masterpiece. This attractive pair of discs offers eminently sane, likeable performances from Raymond Leppard and the Scottish Chamber Orchestra. These artists convey a pleasure in what they are doing, and that is more than half the battle. They bring not only geniality and high spirits to these symphonies but also grace and considerable poetic feeling. The recording is agreeably natural and as fresh and warm as the performances themselves. A very useful chamber-sized alternative to the larger orchestras favoured in this repertoire on other labels.

Symphonies Nos. 94 in G (Surprise); 101 in D (Clock).
(M) *** DG 423 883-2 [id.]. LPO, Jochum.

Jochum's are marvellously fresh, crisp accounts of both symphonies, elegantly played and always judiciously paced. The sound remains first class, with added clarity but without loss of bloom, the bass cleaner and only slightly drier.

Symphonies Nos. 94 in G (Surprise); 104 in D (London).
(M) *** Ph. Dig./Analogue 434 153-2 [id.]. Concg. O, Sir Colin Davis.

Davis's *Surprise* was recorded in 1981 and is digital; No. 104 dates from four years earlier and is analogue, but the digital transfer is of high quality. Both performances have breadth and dignity, yet are full of sparkle and character.

Symphonies Nos. 100 in G (Military); 104 in D (London).
*** O-L Dig. 411 833-2 [id.]. AAM, Hogwood.

Those looking for performances on period instruments will find Hogwood's accounts are uncommonly good ones. The change in the balance in the orchestral texture is often quite striking, particularly where the bassoon cuts through the lower strings. The 'Turkish' percussion instruments in the *Military symphony* are most effectively placed. The recording has clarity and presence.

Symphonies Nos. 103 in E flat (Drum Roll); 104 in D (London).
☞ ** EMI Dig. CDC5 55002-2 [id.]. L. Classical Players, Norrington.

High drama is the keynote to Norrington's Haydn; there is little here of the composer's geniality. The opening *Drumroll* of No. 103 is predictably arresting, and the following Allegro is lean-spirited and supercharged; the finale is similarly unbridled. All well and good, but the fast slow movements in both symphonies, high in tension, make little contrast. There is no doubt about the vitality and surface excitement here, but Haydn needs more. The Abbey Road recording seems well judged, with both fullness and presence.

CHAMBER MUSIC

Baryton trios Nos. 71 in A; 96 in B min.; 113 in D; 126 in C.
*** Gaudeamus CDGAU 109 [id.]. John Hsu, Miller, Arico.

Baryton trios Nos. 87 in A min.; 97 in D (Fatto per la felicissima nascita de S:ai:S Principe Estorhazi); 101 in C; 111 in G.
*** Gaudeamus CDGAU 104 [id.]. John Hsu, Miller, Arico.

As John Hsu puts it on the sleeve, 'the baryton is a kind of viola da gamba with a broadened neck, behind which is a harp ... the metal harp-strings are exposed within the open-box-like back of the neck so that they may be plucked by the thumb of the left hand'. These are most beguiling performances which have subtlety and finesse. Natural and well-balanced recorded sound. The second collection is no less desirable than the first.

Duo sonatas for violin and viola Nos. 1–6.
(B) *** Hung. White Label HRC 071 [id.]. Dénes Kovács, Géza Németh.

Haydn's diversity of invention seems inexhaustible. The performances here are expert and spontaneous – the players are obviously enjoying the music, and so do we.

Flute trios for 2 flutes and cello (bassoon) Nos. 1–4 (London), Hob IV/1–4; Duo for 2 flutes (arr. of String quartet in D, Op. 76/5); Echo for 2 flutes (arr. of Divertimento for 2 string trios in E flat).
☞ **(*) Sony Dig. SK 48061 [id.]. Rampal, Schulz, Audin.

Haydn wrote his four *London Trios* in 1794. They are slight but elegant pieces of some charm, but not to be taken all at one sitting. The use of optional bassoon instead of cello makes the sound blander but more piquant. The arrangement of the *String quartet*, Op. 76/5, for two flutes was the work of a London musician, Samuel Arnold. This is essentially for collectors with a very sweet musical tooth indeed, although undoubtedly the *Presto* finale heard by itself is captivating. Fine performances and excellent recording.

Piano trios (complete).
⊛ (M) *** Ph. 432 061-2 (9). Beaux Arts Trio.

It is not often possible to hail one set of records as a 'classic' in quite the way that Schnabel's Beethoven sonatas can be so described. Yet this set can be described in those terms, for the playing of the Beaux Arts Trio is of the very highest musical distinction. The contribution of the pianist, Menahem Pressler, is little short of inspired, and the recorded sound on CD is astonishingly lifelike. The CD transfer has enhanced detail without losing the warmth of ambience or sense of intimacy.

Piano trios, Hob XV, Nos. 24–27.
(M) *** Ph. 422 831-2. Beaux Arts Trio.

These are all splendid works. No. 25 with its *Gypsy rondos* is the most famous, but each has a character of its own, showing the mature Haydn working at full stretch. The playing here is peerless and the recording truthful and refined.

Piano trios Nos. 42 in E flat, Hob XV/30; 43 in C, Hob XV/27; 44 in E, Hob XV/28; 45 in E flat, Hob XV/29.
☞ ⊛ *** Sony Dig. SK 53120 [id.]. Vera Beths, Anner Bylsma, Robert Levin.

Outstanding performances in every way. This Sony group plays with immense flair and spirit and conveys the exhilaration of the finale of the *C major Trio* (No. 43, Hob. XV/27) superbly well and the depth and poetry of the middle movements. Infectious in its high spirits and delight in music-making. And how well they are recorded! It is good to have modern digital alternatives to the justly famous Beaux Arts versions. Strongly recommended.

String quartets: in E flat, Op. 1/0; Nos. 43 in D min., Op. 42; 83 in B flat, Op. 103.
**(*) Mer. ECD 88117; *CDE 77117* [id.]. English Qt.

These fine players rise to all the challenges posed by this music, and the recorded sound is eminently truthful. There would have been room for another *Quartet* on this disc, which offers rather short measure at 43 minutes.

String quartets Nos. 1 in B flat; 2 in E flat; 3 in D; 4 in G, Op. 1/1–4.
☞ (BB) **(*) Naxos Dig. 8.550398 [id.]. Kodály Qt.

String quartets Nos. 5 in E flat; 6 in C, Op. 1/5–6; 7 in A; 8 in E, Op. 2/1–2.
☞ (BB) **(*) Naxos Dig. 8.550399 [id.]. Kodály Qt.

Haydn is credited with 'inventing' the string quartet, but he claimed that he had come across the form by accident. The Op. 1 and Op. 2 quartets are in essence five-movement divertimenti scored for four string players. The first four were published in Paris in 1764, together with two other works, under the collective title, 'Six Simphonies ou Qutuors dialogués'. These earliest works have not quite the unquenchable flow of original ideas that the early symphonies have but, in such fresh performances as these, they make easy and enjoyable listening even if, with the performances generous in observing repeats, some movements outstay their welcome. The Kodály players rightly play adagios as adagios, and there are two striking early examples here, that of Op. 1/2, which has surprise pizzicato interludes, and the opening slow movement of Op. 1/3, which sounds remarkably mature. There are other notable individual movements, the winning Scherzo third movement of the same work, the jolly, dance-like opening Presto of Op. 1/4, and the extended finale of the same quartet. The first movement of Op. 1/5 also sounds remarkably alert and fresh and, after a similarly buoyant opening, the slow movement of Op. 1/6 offers a charming violin melody over pizzicato accompaniment. The first quartet of Op. 2 brings another amiable, flowing *Adagio*, framed by two Minuets, each with agreeable Trios, and Op. 2/2 brings another forward-looking *Adagio*, where the first violin is given free rein. Apart from Op. 4/4, all the finales are briefly energetic; the *Presto* that ends the last work on the disc is rather less predictable. The resonant ambience of the Unitarian Church in Budapest seems not unsuitable for works which lie midway between divertimenti and quartets, and the focus seems brighter and sharper on the second CD, recorded in June 1991, two months after the first.

String quartets Nos. 1 in B flat, Op. 1/1; 67 in D, Op. 64/5 (Lark); 74 in G min., Op. 74/3 (Rider).
*** DG Dig. 423 622-2 [id.]. Hagen Qt.

The Hagen are supple, cultured and at times perhaps a little overcivilized, but in these three Haydn quartets they play flawlessly and are wonderfully alert and intelligent.

String quartet No. 3 in D, Op. 1/3.

(M) ** Decca 433 691-2 [id.]. Weller Qt – *Quartets Nos. 37–39.* ***

The Weller Quartet's performance is accurate and musical, but it really springs to life only in the vivacious Scherzo, which is admittedly by far the best movement.

String quartets Nos. 9 in F; 10 in B flat, Op. 2/4 & 6; 35 in D min., Op. 42.

☞ (BB) **(*) Naxos Dig. 8.550732 [id.]. Kodály Qt.

The Kodály Quartet here move to the Unitarian Church, Budapest, which provides a warm, flattering tonal blend of much aural beauty, but a texture that is a little too ample for early Haydn, while the fairly close microphones reduce the dynamic range. However, their friendly style and elegant finish suit early Haydn. (Both Op. 2 quartets are simple five-movement works, each with a pair of minuets.) These performers find exactly the right degree of expressiveness for the *Adagio* of Op. 2/4 and are equally at home in the engaging *Andante ed innocentemente* which opens the first movement of Op. 42, a splendid work, written a quarter of a century later.

String quartets Nos. 17 in F (Serenade), Op. 3/5; 38 in E flat (Joke), Op. 33/2; 76 in D min. (Fifths), Op. 76/2.

(M) *** Decca 425 422-2; 425 422-4. Janáček Qt.

☞ (BB) **(*) Discover Dig. DIDCD 920172 [id.]. Sharon Qt.

These Decca performances are strong and dedicated. Whether Haydn or Hoffstetter wrote that delicious tune which forms the slow movement of the *Serenade quartet* seems irrelevant; it is an attractive little work and makes a good foil for the really splendid music of its companions.

The Sharon Quartet are an excellent group and they give warm and spirited accounts of these three favourite quartets. They are recorded in the resonant acoustics of St John's Church in Cologne and, like some of the recordings made for Naxos by the Kodály Quartet, the resonance expands the texture, although not seriously enough to prevent enjoyment, for they make a bright, clean sound. They find charm in the famous '*Serenade*' of Op. 3 and are equally good in the *Variations* which form the slow movement of the *Fifths*; at the same time, they find the right approach to the '*Joke*' in the finale of Op. 33/2. This record is well worth its very modest cost.

String quartets Nos. 17 in F (Serenade), Op. 3/5; 63 in D (Lark), Op. 64/5; 76 in D min. (Fifths), Op. 76/2.

(M) *** Ph. 426 097-2. Italian Qt.

First-class playing here; although the first movement of the *Lark* is a bit measured in feeling, the *Serenade quartet* is made to sound inspired, its famous slow movement played with exquisite gentleness. The *D minor Quartet* is admirably poised and classical in feeling.

String quartets Nos. 17 in D (Serenade), Op. 3/5 (now attrib. Hoffstetter); 76 in D min. (Fifths); 77 in C (Emperor), Op. 76/2–3.

☞ (M) ** Denon Dig. DC 8122 [id.]. Berlin Philh. Qt.

These performances are by the Philharmonia Quartet of Berlin whose first violin is leader of the Radio Orchestra, while two of his colleagues come from the Philharmonic. Their playing communicates a slightly bland geniality, and they are at their best in the famous *Serenade* quartet now thought to be composed by Hoffstetter. The slow movement of the *Emperor* is also presented with warmth, and detail is well observed. However, overall, although they play well enough, neither in vitality nor in musical imagination can they be said to match the finest accounts of these works currently available. The recording is of good quality and is naturally balanced.

String quartets Nos. 19 in C; 21 in G; 22 in D min., Op. 9/1, 3 & 4.

☞ (BB) *** Naxos Dig. 8.550786 [id.]. Kodály Qt.

String quartets Nos. 20 in E flat; 23 in B flat; 24 in A, Op. 9/2, 5 & 6.

☞ (BB) *** Naxos Dig. 8.550787 [id.]. Kodály Qt.

Though few of Haydn's early quartets are consistently inspired from beginning to end, all six offered here contain more than their share of moments of magic, and so committed is the playing that Haydn never fails to hold the listener's attention. The Kodály Quartet are in excellent form throughout. Their simple eloquence in all three slow movements on the first disc serves Haydn well: the *Largo* of Op. 9/3 is ideally paced and beautifully poised. The players then go on to give a captivating account of the finale. Indeed, all the finales here are superb, showing Haydn at full stretch. On the second disc, *No. 23 in B flat*, Op. 9/5, unusually opens with a substantial *Poco adagio* which turns out to be a theme with four variations. The last of the set in A major opens with a very attractive *Presto* in 6/8, which is delightfully buoyant here. It too has a beautiful *Adagio*, dominated by a favourite Haydn triplet rhythm and giving much scope to the solo violin, who soars above the texture in a long cantilena and is even given space for a brief cadenza just before the movement ends. The busy finale then is remarkably succinct, 53 bars and 1½ minutes in length. Fortunately the Naxos recording team (in December 1992 and January 1993) have mastered the acoustics of the Unitarian Church in Budapest. The microphones are in the right place, the sound is not inflated: in fact the balance brings a vividly realistic impression. Those collecting this series will not be disappointed with this excellent pair of inexpensive CDs.

String quartets Nos. 31 in E flat; 32 in C; 33 in G min.; 34 in D; 35 in F min.; 36 in A, Op. 20/1–6.
☞ ⊛ *** Astrée Dig. E 8784 (2) [id.]. Mosaïques Qt.
☞ ** Orfeo Dig C 313 101A (*Nos. 31–33*); C 313 201A (*Nos. 34–36*) [id.]. Kocian Qt.
☞ ** Medici MQCD 5002 (2) [id.]. Medici Qt.

String quartets Nos. 31 in E flat; 32 in C; 33 in G min., Op. 20/1–3.
☞ (BB) ** Naxos Dig. 8.550701 [id.]. Kodály Qt.

String quartets Nos. 34 in D; 35 in F min.; 36 in A (Sun quartets), Op. 20/4–6.
☞ (BB) ** Naxos Dig. 8.550702 [id.]. Kodály Qt.

The Mosaïques Quartet (two men and two women) use original instruments with a difference. The leader, Erich Höbarth, plays a Guarnerius, made in Cremona in 1683; the second violin, Andrea Bischof, has an eighteenth-century French instrument; and the violist, Anita Mitterer, plays a modern copy of an Amati; the cellist, Christophe Coin, uses a Testore made in Milan in 1758. They create individual timbres which are pleasing to the ear without any overt opulence, textures which have body and transparency, are perfectly matched and never edgy. There is no squeezed phrasing, and the use of vibrato is as subtle as the control of colour and dynamic. Intonation and ensemble are remarkably exact. The effect, not as genially friendly or casual as the Kodály series on Naxos, is often breathtaking in its rapt concentration. Such is the calibre of this music-making and the strength of insight of these players that the character of these fine, relatively early works is communicated with seemingly total spontaneity. The fresh simplicity of the opening of Op. 20/1 is deceptive, for the slow movement (marked *Affettuoso e sostenuto*) has a remarkable hushed inwardness of intimate feeling. The second movement of Op. 20/2, marked *Capriccio/Adagio*, brings an unforgettable dark cello-line from Christophe Coin. After another remarkable *Adagio e affettuoso* in Op. 20/4, the extrovert *Minuet alla Zingarese* is followed by a finale that is as light as thistledown, while a similarly deft articulation of the brilliant *scherzando* first movement of Op. 20/6 is followed by the utmost delicacy in the *Cantabile Adagio* which follows. This is playing of rare distinction which is immensely revealing and rewarding, helped by state-of-the-art recording of complete realism and presence within an acoustic that provides the necessary intimacy of ambience.

The Naxos Kodály series continues to bring polished, sympathetic playing of considerable warmth. Allegros are lively, but the acoustics of the Unitarian Church, Budapest, though providing beautifully rich string-textures, here make the effect almost orchestral and bring an element of blandness to the fine *Adagio* slow movements; throughout, the dynamic range of the playing is reduced by the microphone positioning. The *Adagio* of Op. 20/2 brings some fine playing, and the theme and variations of the *Poco adagio e effettuoso* of the *D major Quartet*, Op. 20/4, are attractively characterized but badly need a wider dynamic contrast. This is even more striking in the *Fuga a quattro soggetti* which forms the finale of Op. 20/2.

The Kocian Quartet give eminently enjoyable performances, fresh and polished, faithful to the spirit of Haydn. But they are let down by another ecclesiastical recording site, the Kirche der Karlshöhe, Ludwigsburg, where close microphones throw everything forward and narrow the dynamic range unacceptably. The sound is not as inflated here as in some of the Naxos recordings made in the Unitarian Church, Budapest, but at full price these recordings cannot compare with the performances on original instruments by the Mosaïques Quartet.

The Medici performances have plenty of life but are missing the last veneer of polish. These players are highly musical and responsive (the cellist, Anthony Lewis, makes an appealing contribution), but one feels at times that they needed to have lived with the music a little longer before making their recordings. Undoubtedly the second disc containing the last three works brings some fine moments, especially in the slow movements of the *F minor* and *A major Quartets*, but the recording, made in East Woodhay Parish Church, brings the microphones a fraction too close. There is a degree of edginess on the first violin, who dominates the aural picture; otherwise the sound is nicely blended and clear.

String quartets Nos. 32 in C, Op. 20/2; 44 in B flat, Op. 50/1; 76 in D min. (Fifths), Op. 76/2.
*** ASV Dig. CDDCA 622 [id.]. Lindsay Qt.

These are public performances. There is splendid character in the performances and plenty of musical imagination. These readings have a spontaneity which is refreshing. The recordings are eminently truthful and audience noise is minimal.

String quartets Nos. 34 in D, Op. 20/4; 47 in C sharp min., Op. 50/4; 77 in C (Emperor), Op. 76/3.
*** ASV Dig. CDDCA 731 [id.]. Lindsay Qt.

The Lindsay performances were again recorded at public performances, on this occasion in London's Wigmore Hall. The advantages this brings are twofold: higher spontaneity and a greater propensity to take risks. In all three performances the gains outweigh any loss, though the balance tends to cause some coarse-sounding tone in fortissimo passages.

String quartets Nos. 37 in B min.; 38 in E flat (Joke); 39 in C (Bird), Op. 33/1–3.
☞ *** Kingdom KCLCD 2014 [id.]. Bingham Qt.
(M) *** Decca 433 691-2 [id.]. Weller Qt – *Quartet No. 3.* **

String quartets Nos. 40 in B flat; 41 in G; 42 in D (How do you do), Op. 33/4–6.
☞ *** Kingdom KCLCD 2015 [id.]. Bingham Qt.
(M) *** Decca 433 692-2 [id.]. Weller Qt – *Quartet No. 83.* **

Although Haydn had written some fine quartets before these were published in 1782, this Op. 33 set proved a watermark. Here he finally established himself as complete master of a new medium with such skill, musical fecundity and wit that he never surpassed them in terms of cultivated musical pleasure, even if later works, Op. 76 for instance, embrace a somewhat wider range of mood and feeling. In short, and especially when they are played as well as they are here, this is desert island material. It is not for nothing that they have nicknames. The wit of the *Joke* finale (well appreciated here in a sparkling performance of real bravura) is matched by the charming opening of *The Bird*, who on this occasion immediately soars aloft. But this music offers far more than good-humoured pictorialism. First movements are full of structural imagination and they are teeming with ideas. Haydn is ever exploring, as indeed in the first movement of No. 3, while its *Largo* has the simple eloquence of great music, if it is not quite as intense as the *Largo sostenuto* of No. 2. How beautifully these are both paced here, as are all the slow movements. The *Largo cantabile* of No. 5 floats along delightfully and, after its charming Minuet with its *Laendler* trio, the 6/8 finale (a set of rustic variations) is enchanting.

The Bingham Quartet have been in existence a decade or so. The players met at the Royal Academy of Music and received initial training under Sidney Griller (an aptly distinguished name from the world of British chamber music). It has borne fruit, for their tonal matching and ensemble are most impressive, with the leader, Stephen Bingham, a remarkably stylish player who really understands how to shape a Haydn phrase. Above all the Binghams convey their pleasure in the music, and every performance here sounds fresh. The recording was made at the Conway Hall, London, in 1990. The balance is a shade close, but the instruments are naturally focused, individually and as a group, the sound rather less robust and mellow than with the Budapest Kodály recordings, although the effect is certainly real. Even if the range of dynamic is a little affected, the playing itself is full of light and shade so that if the volume level is carefully set one soon forgets this reservation in the sheer pleasure this music affords.

The Weller Quartet offer very polished and lively playing and they are beautifully recorded. They also offer the bonus of two extra works. If the performances are not as penetrating as those of the young Bingham group, they are sunny and civilized and always enjoyable. In all three performances tempi are generally well considered, even if the finale of the *Joke* is perhaps too fast; on the other hand the last movement of Op. 33/4 is beautifully judged.

String quartets Nos. 50–56 (The Seven Last Words of our Saviour on the Cross), Op. 51.
☞ ⊛ *** ASV Dig. CDDCA 853 [id.]. Lindsay Quartet.
*** Olympia Dig. OCD 171 [id.]. Shostakovich Qt.

String quartets Nos. 50–56 (The Seven Last Words of our Saviour on the Cross), Op. 51; 83 in B flat, Op. 103.
(BB) *** Naxos Dig. 8.550346 [id.]. Kodály Qt.

No work for string quartet, not even late Beethoven, presents more taxing interpretative problems than Haydn's *Seven Last Words of our Saviour on the Cross*. This sequence of intense slow movements, an introduction followed by seven so-called sonatas, each devoted to one of Christ's words, is unparalleled in the repertory. Each one of those slow movements presents problems enough, but the need to give variety to the long sequence multiplies them enormously. The recording by the Lindsay Quartet, while offering all the devotional gravity that Haydn demands, brings not just an illuminating variety but also a sense of drama. As in the late Beethoven quartets, the Lindsays have gained from playing the *Seven Last Words* many times in concert, always preferring to perform it, as Haydn wanted, with a brief spoken address between movements explaining the title of each. The CD booklet provides the text of just such a commentary by Dr John Taylor, formerly Bishop of Winchester, and the performance makes no compromise for, unlike others, the Lindsays observe the first-half repeats in each movement, extending the work to a full 70 minutes, instead of under an hour. Their range of expression, in dynamic, tempo and phrasing, is extremely wide, and they intensify the fundamental darkness of Haydn's minor-key inspirations with magical contrasts into the major mode. The opening of the fifth *Sonata, Sitio, I thirst*, is breathtaking when the plucked pizzicati of second violin and viola are magically gentle, suggesting the flowing of water such as the Saviour craves. After the long sequence of slow movements, the Lindsays' account of the final, brief Presto, *Il terremoto*, then conveys the full, elemental force of the earthquake. It is thrilling with so elusive a work to have so complete an answer in a single recording, with sound both well defined and glowingly beautiful, set against an apt church acoustic.

The Kodály Quartet give a memorable performance, strongly characterized and beautifully played, with subtle contrasts of expressive tension between the seven inner slow movements. They also offer an appropriate bonus in Haydn's last, unfinished, two-movement *Quartet*. The recording is first rate, vividly present yet naturally balanced, like the other issues in this attractive Naxos series.

The Shostakovich Quartet also gives an eloquent and thoughtful account of Haydn's score. There is no overstatement and no point-making, yet the playing is tremendously felt – and they are a quartet who produce a beautifully integrated and cultured sound.

String quartets Nos. 50–56 (The Seven Last Words of Christ); 63–68, Op. 64 1–6 (Tost quartets).
(M) **(*) DG 431 145-2 (3). Amadeus Qt.

It is perhaps a pity that the Amadeus version of *The Seven Last Words of Christ* is linked on CD with Op. 64, for the immaculate Amadeus style, though not lacking in drama, does tend to smooth over the darker side of Haydn. The last six of the twelve *Tost quartets* are another matter. Here the superb ensemble and cultivated playing are always easy on the ear when the recording is so well balanced and natural. Indeed, overall these performances give much pleasure.

String quartets Nos. 57 in G; 58 in C; 59 in E, Op. 54/1–3.
(BB) *** Naxos Dig. 8.550395; 4550395 [id.]. Kodály Qt.
*** ASV Dig. CDDCA 582 [id.]. Lindsay Qt.
☞ (M) *** Virgin/EMI Dig. CUV5 61127-2 [id.]. Endellion Qt.

The present works show Haydn at his most inventive. The Kodály players enter animatedly into the spirit of the music; the leader, Attila Falvay, shows himself fully equal to Haydn's bravura embellishments in the demanding first violin writing. The Naxos sound is fresh and truthful.

The playing of the Lindsay Quartet is splendidly poised and vital, and the recording is very fine indeed.

The Endellion Quartet on Virgin are bright-eyed, fresh and vital. The overall sound is beautifully integrated. Yet the Lindsays' insights go deeper, even if at times they have marginally less surface polish.

String quartets Nos. 57 in G; 58 in C; 59 in E, Op. 54/1–3; 60 in A; 61 in F min. (Razor); 62 in B flat, Op. 55/1–3.
☞ (M) **(*) DG 437 134-2 (2) [id.]. Amadeus Qt.

These are the first six of the twelve quartets dedicated to a rich, self-made patron, Johann Tost, who was also a violinist, and they include a number of masterpieces. Op. 55/2 acquired its nickname, *The Razor*, from a curious story. 'My best quartet for a decent razor,' Haydn said one day, and an enterprising publisher successfully took up the challenge. Though the Amadeus Quartet does not always play with the fullest intensity in some of the great slow movements, the ensemble is superb and the results are always easy on the ear. The CD transfers of recordings made in Munich in 1971/2 are fresh and clean.

String quartets Nos. 60 in A; 61 in F min. (Razor); 62 in B flat, Op. 55/1–3 (Tost Quartets).
(BB) **(*) Naxos Dig. 8.550397. Kodály Qt.

Opus 55 brings playing which is undoubtedly spirited and generally polished, but the music-making at times seems plainer than usual in the Naxos series. The recording is bright and clear, with a realistic presence.

String quartets Nos. 63 in C; 64 in B min.; 65 in B flat, Op. 64/1–3.
☞ (BB) *** Naxos Dig. 8.550673 [id.]. Kodály Qt.

String quartets Nos. 66 in G; 67 in D (Lark); 68 in E flat, Op. 64/4–6.
☞ (BB) *** Naxos Dig. 8.550674 [id.]. Kodály Qt.

The Kodály players open Op. 64/1 with a smile: this is warm, somewhat robust playing but with plenty of finesse. These performances are all enjoyable, but the set seems to get better and better as it progresses. Op. 64/1–3 were recorded 25–29 April 1992; the last to be done, the B flat major, is remarkably successful, with a vigorous opening *Vivace assai* and a rapt *Adagio*. The other three works were taped 1–3 May, and clearly the group had found its top form. The *Adagio cantabile e sostenuto* of No. 4 finds them at their most concentrated: the *Lark* has never soared aloft more spontaneously and the Minuet and finale of No. 6 close the set in a winningly spirited fashion. The warm acoustics of the Budapest Unitarian Church provide a mellow and expansive sound-image, but not an orchestral one, and detail remains clear. A most enjoyable set.

String quartets Nos. 69 in B flat; 70 in D; 71 in E flat, Op. 71/1–3 (Apponyi).
☞ **(*) Chan. Dig. CHAN 9416 [id.]. Chilingirian Qt.

The Chilingirians' opening of the first of the *Apponyi Quartets* (so named because their 'onlie begetter' was Count Antal Apponyi) is very positive. This is spick-and-span playing, highly musical and full of character. Slow movements are well shaped and expressive and there are moments of wit, notably in the Minuet and Trio of No. 3. The recording is truthful. Yet this playing, although by no means plain, lacks something of the sunny quality the Kodály Quartet brings to this music.

String quartets Nos. 69 in B flat; 70 in D; 71 in E flat, Op. 71/1–3; 72 in C; 73 in F; 74 in G min. (Reiter), Op. 74/1–3 (Apponyi quartets).
(BB) *** Naxos Dig. 8.550394 (*Nos. 69–71*); 8.550396 (*Nos. 72–74*) [id.]. Kodály Qt.

The *Apponyi quartets* are among the composer's finest. The Naxos recordings by the Kodály Quartet are outstanding in every way and would be highly recommendable even without their considerable price advantage. The digital recording has vivid presence and just the right amount of ambience: the effect is entirely natural.

String quartets Nos. 71 in E flat, Op. 71/3; 72 in C, Op. 74/1.
*** Hyp. CDA 66098 [id.]. Salomon Qt.

String quartets Nos. 73 in F; 74 in G min., Op. 74/2–3.
*** Hyp. CDA 66124 [id.]. Salomon Qt.

The appropriately named Salomon Quartet use period instruments. They are vibrato-less but vibrant; the sonorities, far from being nasal and unpleasing, are clean and transparent. There is imagination and vitality here, and the Hyperion recording is splendidly truthful.

String quartets Nos. 69 in B flat; 70 in D; 71 in E flat, Op. 71/1–3; 72 in C; 73 in F; 74 in G min. (Reiter), Op. 74/1–3; Op. 77/1–2; in D min., Op. 103.
(M) *** DG 429 189-2 (3). Amadeus Qt.

This excellent set shows the Amadeus on their finest form; there is a sense of spontaneity as well as genuine breadth to these readings. The recordings have a warm acoustic and plenty of presence.

String quartets Nos. 72 in C; 73 in F; 74 in G min., Op. 74/1–3.
*** Virgin/EMI Dig. VC7 91097-2; VC 791097-4 [id.]. Endellion Qt.

The Endellion Quartet are also proving sound guides to this rewarding repertoire; this record can be recommended alongside their comparably well-played and -recorded set of Op. 54.

String quartets Nos. 75 in G; 76 in D min. (Fifths); 77 in C (Emperor); 78 in B flat (Sunrise); 79 in D; 80 in E flat, Op. 76/1–6.
⊛ (BB) *** Naxos Dig. 8.550314; 4550314 (*Nos. 75–77*); 8.550315; 4550315 (*Nos. 78–80*). Kodály Qt.
*** Hung. HCD 12812/3-2 [id.]. Tátrai Qt.
☞ (B) **(*) Sony SB2K 53522 (2). Tokyo Qt.

String quartets Nos. 76 in D min. (Fifths); 77 in C (Emperor); 78 in B flat (Sunrise), Op. 76/2–4.
⊛ (BB) *** Naxos Dig. 8.550129; 4550129 [id.]. Kodály Qt.

Haydn's six *Erdödy quartets*, Op. 76, contain some of his very greatest music, and these performances by the Kodály Quartet are fully worthy of the composer's inexhaustible invention. Their playing brings a joyful pleasure in Haydn's inspiration and there is not the slightest suspicion of over-rehearsal or of routine: every bar of the music springs to life spontaneously, and these musicians' insights bring an ideal combination of authority and warmth, emotional balance and structural awareness.

The Tátrai's performances are unforced and natural, as intimate as if they were playing for pleasure, and as authoritative as one could hope for. The splendours of this set are as inexhaustible as those of the Beaux Arts set of the *Trios*.

The Tokyo Quartet offer superb playing and an immaculate tonal blend, and they are unfailingly intelligent. Yet it is a pity that they do not relax a little more and allow the music to unfold at greater leisure, as do the Kodály players, for they do not convery the humanity and charm that distinguish the Naxos set. The recording is faithful, but they are not as well served by the engineers as they were by DG for their prize-winning Bartók cycle; the sound, though fresh, is a little lacking in bloom at upper dynamic levels.

String quartets Nos. 76 in D min. (Fifths); 77 in C (Emperor); 78 in B flat (Sunrise), Op. 76/2–4.
☞ (M) *** Teldec/Warner Dig. 9031 77602-2 [id.]. Eder Qt.

These are elegant performances that are unlikely to disappoint even the most demanding listener, save perhaps in the finale of the *Emperor*, which is taken a little too quickly. But this is unfailingly thoughtful quartet-playing whose internal balance and tonal blend are practically flawless.

String quartet No. 77 in C (Emperor), Op. 76/3.
(M) *** Teldec/Warner 2292 42440-2 [id.]. Alban Berg Qt – MOZART: *Quartet No. 17.* ***

This performance of Haydn's *Emperor quartet*, dating from 1975, has playing of striking resilience and sparkle. The famous slow movement has seldom been put on record with such warmth and eloquence.

String quartets Nos. 81 in G; 82 in F, Op. 77/1–2; 83 in D min., Op. 103.
☞ *** Astrée Dig. E 8799 [id.]. Mosaïques Qt.
*** Decca Dig. 430 199-2; *430 199-4* [id.]. Takács Qt.
*** Hyp. Dig. CDA 66348 [id.]. Salomon Qt.
☞ (B) ** HM Dig. HMA 1903301 [id.]. Festetics Qt.
☞ ** Nimbus Dig. NI 5312 [id.]. Franz Schubert Qt.

Using original instruments to totally convincing effect, the Mosaïques Quartet give outstanding performances of Haydn's last three quartets. They play with much subtlety of colour and dynamic and bring total concentration to every bar of the music. The crisp, bouncing rhythm of the first movement of Op. 77/1 is engagingly arresting, and the *Adagio* is ideally paced and extremely eloquent; the *presto* Minuet of Op. 77/2 is bracingly crisp in articulation, followed by a rapt *sotto voce* introduction for the following *Andante*. The *E flat Quartet*, Haydn's last, is beautifully judged. The recording is absolutely real: the sound is transparent as well as immediate, within an ideally chosen acoustic. Moreover there is never a hint of acerbity of timbre from any of the four players, nor of the unattractive squeezing of lyrical lines which has spoiled so many authentic performances. This is among the finest of all Haydn quartet records.

The Takács Quartet play with warmth, expressive refinement and vitality. The sound is clean and well focused, with just the right amount of resonance.

The Salomon, recorded in a less ample acoustic, produce an altogether leaner sound but one that is thoroughly responsive to every shift in Haydn's thought. They seem to have great inner vitality and feeling.

Although the opening of Op. 77/1 has a pleasing rhythmic character, there is a coolness about the playing of the Festetics Quartet that lends itself less well to Haydn's expressive slow movement. They are at their best in the last quartet; and the transparency of texture from the use of original instruments brings some refreshing textures elsewhere, but in the last resort the effect is too austere.

The Franz Schubert Quartet are generally vital, but they are closely recorded and that gives a slight edge to the leader's tone; the attack on the *Presto* Minuet of Op. 77/1 sounds positively gritty. There is some enjoyable playing here, but this is not in any way distinctive.

String quartet No. 83 in B flat, Op. 103.
(M) ** Decca 433 692-2 [id.]. Weller Qt – *Quartets Nos. 40–42.* ***

The Weller give an eminently smooth and polished account of the incomplete two-movement quartet of Haydn's old age.

KEYBOARD MUSIC

Andante with variations in F min., Hob XVII/6; Fantasia in C, Hob XVII/4; Piano sonata No. 53 in E min., Hob XVI/34.
☞ (M) **(*) Decca 433 901-2 [id.]. Wilhelm Backhaus – BACH: *English & French suites* etc. **

Backhaus's positive, classical manner is perhaps more naturally suited to Haydn than to Mozart and, while his style can at times seem almost unrelenting in its directness, generally the spontaneous imagination behind this playing bubbles out and silences any reservations on minor stylistic points.

Andante with variations in F min., Hob XVII/6; Piano sonatas Nos. 33 in C min., Hob XVI/20; 48 in C, Hob XVI/35; 59 in E flat, Hob XVI/49.
☞ ** Athene Dig. ATHCD 2 [id.]. Joanna Leach (fortepiano).

Joanna Leach is certainly a musical player, and her sensibility in this repertoire is in no doubt. But for some ears she puts herself at a disadvantage by using four different square pianos dating from the composer's lifetime, so that in the end one tends to listen as much to the instruments as to the music. They vary a great deal in effectiveness, but the result of the rather bare sonorities is to make the music's accompanimental figures unduly noticeable. The 1789 Broadwood on which she plays the *C major Sonata* is an effective instrument, but the *E flat* work is played on a very twangy Astor (*c.* 1800). Best by far is the Longman and Broderip (1787) on which we hear the *C minor Sonata* sounding fresh and appealing.

Piano sonatas Nos. 11 in B flat, Hob XVI/2; 31 in A flat, Hob XVI/46; 39 in D min., Hob XVI/24; 47 in B min., Hob XVI/32.
☞ *** Decca Dig. 436 455-2 [id.]. Sviatoslav Richter.

Although there is no question as to the distinction of Richter's two Haydn recitals recorded on tour, the earlier (1986) collection shows him in the more austere mood. His crisp, classical style, with sparing use of the pedal and strong rhythmic feeling is immediately noticeable at the opening of the *B minor* work, bringing a feeling almost of a *moto perpetuo*, although the variations of colour and dynamic prevent any hint of monotony. The *Andante* is cool and gentle and the finale brings toccata-like brilliance of execution. So it is with the others here, though the *Adagios* of both the *D minor* and (especially) the *A flat major* are gentle and touching, while the two closing movements of the early *B flat Sonata* have an engaging simplicity. Clear, realistic sound and not too much applause.

Piano sonatas Nos. 30 in D, Hob XVI/19; 13 in A flat, Hob XVI/46.
☞ (**) DG Dig. 435 618-2 [id.]. Ivo Pogorelich.

In terms of pianistic finesse, few will find anything to quarrel with in Pogorelich's Haydn disc. It is very beautiful, if highly self-conscious, piano playing and, as such, will commend itself to all his admirers. But if you care about Haydn sonatas first and foremost, it will be better to give this disc a miss. These two sonatas are beautified, dragged out to 52 minutes and are drenched with generous dousings of perfume on the way.

Piano sonatas Nos. 32 in G min., Hob XIV/44; 33 in C min., Hob XVI/20; 56 in D, Hob XVI/42; Variations in F, Hob XVII/6.
(M) *** Collins Dig. 3017-2 [id.]. Andrew Wilde.

These performances have a simplicity and directness of approach which is very winning. The playing is unidiosyncratic but does not lack character. It has purpose and a sense of classical proportion and is fresh in its use of colour. Moreover the recording is wholly natural and real.

Piano sonatas Nos. 32 in G min., Hob XVI/44; 54 in G, Hob XVI/40; 55 in B flat, Hob XVI/41; 58 in C, Hob XVI/48; 62 in E flat, Hob XVI/52.
☞ *** Decca Dig. 436 454-2 [id.]. Sviatoslav Richter.

Richter's second Decca Haydn CD, made in Mantua in 1987, is undoubtedly the more attractive of the two, the playing no less direct but with less of a sense of classical austerity. The opening of the *G minor Sonata* is very winning indeed, and his softness of approach is carried over to the following *G major* work, where Richter catches perfectly the mood of the first movement, *Allegretto e innocente*, with a scintillating *Presto* to follow. Both the *C major* (Hob XVI/48) and the well-known *E flat major* (Hob XVI/52) are among Haydn's finest works for the piano – and that means very fine indeed. Richter's playing is fully worthy of this marvellous music, and the account of the witty finale of the *E flat major* with its characteristic pauses and fresh beginnings is both genial and technically breathtaking. Again the sound is vivid and immediate.

Piano sonatas Nos. 33 in C min., Hob XVI/20; 38 in F, Hob XVI/23; 58 in C, Hob XVI/48; 60 in C, Hob XVI/50.
*** Sony Dig. MK 44918 [id.]. Emanuel Ax.

Ax is a fine stylist and his playing is full of colour, without being quite so personal. He brings sparkle, refined musicianship and fluent fingers to these pieces and he is well enough recorded.

Piano sonatas Nos. 33 in C min., Hob XVI/20; 47 in B min., Hob XVI/32; 53 in E min., Hob XVI/34; 50 in D, Hob XVI/37; 54 in G, Hob XVI/40; 56 in D, Hob XVI/42; 58 in C; 59 in E flat; 60 in C; 61 in D; 62 in E flat, Hob XVI/48–52; Adagio in F, Hob XVII/9; Andante with variations in F min., Hob XVII/6; Fantasia in C, Hob XVII/4.
*** Ph. 416 643-2 (4). Alfred Brendel.

This collection offers some of the best Haydn playing on record – and some of the best Brendel, too. The eleven sonatas, together with the *F minor Variations* and the *C major Fantasia*, have been recorded over a number of years and are splendidly characterized and superbly recorded. The first is analogue, the remainder digital.

Piano sonatas Nos. 33 in C min., Hob XVI/20; 58 in C, Hob XVI/48; 60 in C, Hob XVI/50.
*** Denon Dig. C37 7801 [id.]. András Schiff.

Schiff plays with an extraordinary refinement and delicacy; he is resourceful and highly imaginative in his use of tone-colour; his phrasing and articulation are a constant source of pleasure. Superb in every way and beautifully recorded, too.

Piano sonatas: 33 in C min., Hob XVI/20; 60 in C, Hob XVI/50; 62 in E flat, Hob XVI/52; Andante & Variations in F min., Hob XVII/6.
*** Virgin/EMI Dig. VC7 59258-2 [id.]. Mikhail Pletnev.

Pletnev's reading of the *Sonatas* is full of personality and character. The *C major* is given with great elegance and wit, and the great *E flat Sonata* is magisterial. This playing has a masterly authority, and Pletnev is very well recorded.

Piano sonatas Nos. 38 in F, Hob XVI/23; 51 in E flat, Hob XVI/38; 52 in G, Hob XVI/39.
*** Mer. CDE 84155; *KE 77155* [id.]. Julia Cload.

Julia Cload's cool, direct style is heard at its best in her second group of sonatas. The piano image is bright and clear, with just a touch of hardness on *fortes*.

Piano sonatas Nos. 42 in G, Hob XVI/27; 43 in E flat, Hob XVI/28; 44 in F, Hob XVI/29; 45 in A, Hob XVI/30; 46 in E, Hob XVI/31; 47 in B min., Hob XVI/32.
☞ (BB) *** Naxos Dig. 8.550845 [id.]. Jenö Jandó (piano).

After the success of his set of Beethoven piano sonatas, Jenö Jandó was in a good position to approach Naxos to let him record the complete piano works of Haydn, a project for which he had spent much time in preparation. The six sonatas offered here (in what is Volume II of the ongoing series) were written between 1774 and 1776 and were later grouped together and published by Hummel as Haydn's Op. 14. Although they are all comparatively straightforward three-movement classical sonatas, such a comment is deceptive for Haydn consistently has something individual to contribute. *No. 44 in F*, supposedly influenced by C. P. E. Bach, has a somewhat quirky first movement and a characteristically imaginative final Minuet which goes unexpectedly into the minor and has much of the format of a theme and variations. *No. 45 in A* opens refreshingly like a spring morning, even with evocations of a hunt, then, near the end of the first movement, Haydn unexpectedly moves into a brief and rather touching *Adagio*. The Minuet which follows is another (almost Mozartian) set of variations. No. 46 shows the composer at his most resourceful: it opens elegantly, but the theme is treated intricately. Jandó catches its mood perfectly, as he does in the engagingly simple *Allegretto* which follows and the delightful variants of the finale. This last work of the set in B minor opens with perhaps the most striking idea of all and, after the gracious central Minuet, ends in a flurry of precocious virtuosity, with Jandó clearly in his element. He shows himself a complete master of this repertoire, and the recording, crisp and clean but not too dry, is first class.

Piano sonatas Nos. 50 in D, Hob XVI/37; 54 in G, Hob XVI/40; 55 in B flat, Hob XVI/41; Adagio in F, Hob XVII/9.
*** Mer. ECD 84083; *KE 77083* [id.]. Julia Cload.

Julia Cload's playing is fresh, characterful and intelligent, and will give considerable pleasure. She has the advantage of very truthful recorded sound.

Piano sonatas Nos. 53 in E min., Hob XVI/34; 54 in G, Hob XVI/40; 55 in B flat, Hob XVI/41; 56 in D, Hob XVI/42; 58 in C, Hob XVI/48; Variations in F min. (Sonata, un piccolo divertimento), Hob XVII/6.

☞ (BB) *** Naxos Dig. 8.550845 [id.]. Jenö Jandó (piano).

These are distinctly appealing performances of the three *Sonatas*, Hob XVI/40–42, written in 1783/4 and dedicated to Princess Marie Esterházy, who had married the grandson of Haydn's princely patron. They are each in two movements, and in the case of the *G major* the first is marked *Allegretto e innocente*, an obvious tribute to feminine charm. But all three are fine works and not as simple as they at first appear. Jandó also gives a splendid account of the more ambitious three-movement *Sonata in E minor*, Hob XVI/34, with a particularly strong and brilliant opening movement and a hardly less fine central *Adagio*, of which the pianist has the full measure. The flowing account of the *F minor Variations* (with two themes, in F minor and F major respectively) is assured and its expressive qualities nicely calculated. Jandó is a true Haydn player and this (Volume III of his projected series) is in every way recommendable, particularly as the recording is so vivid and clean: just right for the repertoire.

Piano sonatas Nos. 56 in D, Hob XVI/42; 58 in C; 59 in E flat; 60 in C; 61 in D; 62 in E flat, Hob XVI/48–52.

☞ (M) *(**) Sony Dig. SM2K 52623 [id.]. Glenn Gould.

A problematic issue. You are in a good seat at a recital, settling down to enjoy the opening phrases of the Haydn *D major sonata* played with character and some elegance. Suddenly you are disturbed by what appears to be some neighbours muttering – and quite loudly at that – and someone else humming or moaning. You would take steps to silence them, but here the disruption comes from the pianist himself – and is no less insupportable. Gould's clean, classical style in Haydn is often refreshing, but after a while the squeaky-clean articulation, although quite remarkably crisp, becomes a little wearing and the ear craves a less staccato, less percussive approach to allegros. This is not a fortepiano imitation but a pianoforte played with the most sparing sonority. Gould undoubtedly makes a sensitively expressive response to slow movements, but an air of eccentricity remains in the overall shaping of phrases. The digital recording is clear, to match the playing. All the same, listeners who are put off by these drawbacks will lose some very good playing and what is in many ways a unique approach to this repertoire. If you persevere, there are artistic rewards.

Piano sonatas Nos. 58 in C; 59 in E flat; 60 in C; 61 in D; 62 in E flat, Hob XVI/48–52.
*** BMG/RCA Dig. RD 77160 [77160-2-RC]. Andreas Staier (fortepiano).

Andreas Staier plays a recent copy by Christopher Clarke of a fortepiano from around 1790 by the Viennese maker, Anton Walter, and proves a highly sensitive and imaginative interpreter. He brings a surprisingly wide dynamic range as well as a diversity of keyboard colour to these pieces and holds the listener throughout. He is very well recorded indeed.

Piano sonatas Nos. 58 in C, Hob XVI/48; 62 in E flat, Hob XVI/52.
☞ (M) **(*) Decca 433 900-2 [id.]. Wilhelm Backhaus – MOZART: *Sonatas.* **(*)

There is some of Haydn's greatest keyboard music here – the *C major* and *E flat Sonatas* are especially fine – and its greatness is not minimized by Backhaus, even though his clean articulation with its light pedalling misses the composer's genial side. The 1957 piano recording is very truthful.

Piano sonatas Nos. 59 in E flat; 60 in C; 61 in D; 62 in E flat, Hob XVI/49–52.
☞ (BB) *** Naxos Dig. 8.550657 [id.]. Jenö Jandó.

In beginning his integral Haydn series, Jenö Jandó here shows himself as strong and sympathetic as in Beethoven. Although the performances are straighter, Nos. 60 and 62 compare remarkably favourably with Pletnev's masterly accounts. Without allowing himself stylistic idiosyncrasies, Jandó shows himself a thoughtfully imaginative player as well as a bold one, and the finale of the great *E flat Sonata* has splendid, unforced bravura. The recording, made in the Unitarian Church, Budapest, provides an attractive ambience without an excess of ecclesiastical resonance.

VOCAL MUSIC

The Creation (complete; in English).
*** EMI Dig. CDS7 54159-2 [Ang. CDCB 54159]; *EX 754159-4* (2). Augér, Langridge, David Thomas, CBSO & Ch., Simon Rattle.
*** Decca Dig. 430 397-2 (2) [id.]. Kirkby, Rolfe Johnson, George, New College, Oxford, Ch., AAM Ch. & O, Hogwood.

The English version may have its oddities – like the 'flexible tiger' leaping – but it is above all colourful, and Rattle brings out that illustrative colour with exceptional vividness: birdsong, lion-roars and the like. He has plainly learnt from period performance, not only concerning speeds – often surprisingly brisk, as in the great soprano aria, *With verdure clad* – but as regards style too. The male soloists sound none too sweet as recorded, but they characterize positively; and there is no finer account of the soprano's music than that of Arleen Augér. The weight of the Birmingham chorus is impressive, achieved without loss of clarity or detail in a full, well-balanced recording.

Hogwood defies what has become the custom in period performance and opts for large forces. The result, for all its weight, retains fine clarity of detail and an attractive freshness. The choir of New College, Oxford, with its trebles adds to the brightness of choral sound, and the trio of soloists is admirably consistent – Emma Kirkby brightly distinctive, and Anthony Rolfe Johnson sweet-toned. Hogwood may lack some of the flair and imagination of Rattle, but it would be hard to find a period performance to match this. The sound has fine presence and immediacy.

The Creation (Die Schöpfung; in German).
(M) *** DG 435 077-2 (2). Janowitz, Ludwig, Wunderlich, Krenn, Fischer-Dieskau, Berry, V. Singverein, BPO, Karajan.
*** DG Dig. 419 765-2 (2) [id.]. Blegen, Popp, Moser, Ollmann, Moll, Bav. R. Ch. & SO, Bernstein.
☞ (B) (**(*)) DG Double mono 437 380-2 (2) [id.]. Irmgard Seefried, Richard Holm, Kim Borg, St Hedwig's Cathedral Choir, BPO, Markevitch.
☞ (B) ** Erato/Warner Dig. Duo 4509 95306-2 (2) [id.]. Marshall, Branisteanu, Tappy, Rydl, Huttenlocher, SRO Ch. & Lausanne Pro Arte Ch., Jordan.

(i) *The Creation;* (ii) *Mass No. 7 in B flat (Little organ mass): Missa brevis Sancti Johannis de Deo.*
(M) *** Decca 425 968 (2). (i; ii) Ameling; (i) Krenn, Krause, Spoorenberg, Fairhurst; (ii) P. Planyavsky (organ); (i; ii) V. State Op. Ch., VPO, Münchinger.

(i) *The Creation (Die Schöpfung):* complete (in German); (ii) *Salve regina.*
☞ (B) *** Double Decca 443 027-2 (2) [id.]. (i) Lucia Popp, Werner Hollweg, Kurt Moll, Helena Döse, Benjamin Luxon, Brighton Festival Ch., RPO, Dorati; (ii) Arleen Augér, Alfreda Hodgson, Anthony Rolfe Johnson, Gwynne Howell, L. Chamber Ch., Argo CO, László Heltay.

Among versions of *The Creation* sung in German, Karajan's 1969 set remains unsurpassed and, at mid-price, is a clear first choice despite two small cuts (in Nos. 30 and 32). The combination of the Berlin Philharmonic at its most intense and the great Viennese choir makes for a performance that is not only polished but warm and dramatically strong too. The soloists are an extraordinarily fine team, more consistent in quality than those on almost any rival version.

Dorati, as one would expect, directs a lively and well-sprung account. The very opening is magnetic and its imaginative touches and joyfulness of spirit more than compensate for any minor lapses in crispness of ensemble. The soloists are a splendid team: Lucia Popp's *Nun beut die Flur* ('With verdure clad') certainly does not disappoint; Werner Hollweg is an equally sympathetic Uriel and Kurt Moll is splendidly dramatic as Raphael. The chorus is as gutsy as you like in *Die Himmel erzählen*, with the soloists nicely balanced. While Karajan is not superseded, Dorati's enjoyably spontaneous 1976 account is certainly well worth considering, especially as it is offered for the cost of a single premium-priced CD. The set opens gloriously with Heltay's lovely 1979 recording of the *Salve regina*, an early work dating from 1771, comparable in its depth of feeling with his finest vocal music. Although solo voices alone were originally intended here, it is presented using four splendid soloists in alternation with a full chorus. The recording is most realistic and the CD transfer of *The Creation* is strikingly vivid and immediate.

Bernstein's DG version, recorded at a live performance in Munich, uses a relatively large chorus, encouraging him to adopt rather slow speeds at times. What matters is the joy conveyed in the story-telling, with the finely disciplined chorus and orchestra producing incandescent tone, blazing away in the big set-numbers, and the performance is compulsive from the very opening bars. Five soloists are used instead of three, with the parts of Adam and Eve sung by nicely contrasted singers, confirming this as an unusually persuasive version, well recorded in atmospheric sound.

Münchinger provides another excellent, mid-price *Creation*. It is a fine performance that stands up well, even in comparison with Karajan's set, and the Decca recording is much better balanced. Münchinger has rarely conducted with such electric tension on record and although his direct style is somewhat square, his soloists make a satisfying team. The set also includes Haydn's *Little organ mass*, so called because the solo organ is used to add colour to the soprano's *Benedictus*, a most delightful setting. Ameling here matches her appealing contribution to the main work and the choral singing is pleasingly crisp. The sound is first class, the remastering highly successful.

Markevitch's recording was made at the very end of the mono LP era and was first published in 1958. It shows the extraordinary expertise of the DG engineers at that time, for only the somewhat thin orchestral violins really betray the age of the recording. The soloists are naturally caught and the chorus is brilliantly and cleanly recorded. Markevitch is nothing if not dramatic. The opening *Prelude* is full of electric tension and the choruses have great energy and bite. All three soloists are excellent: Richard Holm sings with heady tone and Irmgard Seefried's 'With verdure clad' shows her in splendid lyrical form. And no one will be disappointed with the vigour of 'The heavens are telling'. Altogether a compelling account, but Haydn's oratorio is singularly lucky on record and, with so many fine stereo versions available, this cannot be a major recommendation.

The glory of Jordan's version, recorded with the combined Swiss Radio and Lausanne choirs, is the glorious singing of Margaret Marshall in the first two parts, with *Nun beut die Flur* ('With verdure clad') sounding radiant at a very slow speed. There is much else to commend; though Kurt Rydl is a gruff bass soloist, the tenor Eric Tappy sings freshly, and the choir is well disciplined. But, in spite of digital recording, the chorus words are unclear and the effect is less biting and vital than with Dorati. The Decca set comes at much the same price and includes documentation, whereas the Erato Bonsai Duo reissue merely gives details of the performers and cues the individual numbers.

(i) *The Creation;* (ii) *Mass No. 14 in B flat (Harmoniemesse), Hob XXII/14.*
☞ (M) ** Sony SM2K 47560 (2). (i) Raskin, Young, Reardon, Camerata Singers: (ii) Blegen, Von Stade, Riegel, Estes, Westminster Ch.; NYPO, Bernstein.

Bernstein's first recording of *The Creation* was made in the Avery Fisher Hall in 1966. It is a fine, spontaneous account with bouncy choruses and an excellent team of soloists. The sound is not ideally refined in the upper range but it is reasonably spacious, and the warmth and vigour of the performance carry the day. The *Harmoniemesse* was done in the Manhattan Center in 1973 and the recording is obviously more modern and rather more spacious, though closely balanced. The performance has characteristic energy and pace, and the *Agnus Dei* brings fine blending from the soloists, who are also individually impressive. The brass-led *Dona nobis pacem* ends the work in a blaze of splendour. Good value, though Bernstein's digital DG set of *The Creation* is preferable on almost all counts, including recording quality (DG 419 765-2).

Masses

Masses Nos. 1a in G (Rorate coeli desuper), Hob XXII/3; (i) 5 in E flat (Grosse Orgelmesse): Missa in honorem Beatissimae Virginis Mariae, Hob XXII/4; (ii) 6 in G (Missa Sancti Nicolai), Hob XXII/6.
*** O-L 421 478-2 [id.]. Christ Church Cathedral, Oxford, Ch., AAM, Preston, with (i) Nelson, Watkinson, Hill, D. Thomas; (ii) Nelson, Minty, Covey-Crump, D. Thomas.

In the early *E flat Mass* Haydn followed the rococo conventions of his time, generally adopting a style featuring Italianate melody which to modern ears inevitably sounds operatic. The *Missa Sancti Nicolai* has a comparable freshness of inspiration. The performance is first rate in every way, even finer than that of the earlier Mass, beautifully sung, with spontaneity in every bar and a highly characterized accompaniment. The little *Missa rorate coeli desuper* was written by Haydn when he was still a choirboy in Vienna, and it may well be his earliest surviving work. Excellent recording ensures that this CD receives a warm welcome.

Mass No. 2 in F (Missa brevis), Hob XXII/1.
*** O-L 421 654-2 [id.]. Kirkby, Nelson, Ch. of Christ Church Cathedral, Oxford, AAM, Preston –
HANDEL: *Anthem for Foundling Hospital* etc. ***

Haydn's early *Missa brevis* is engagingly unpretentious; some of its sections last for under two minutes and none takes more than three and a half. The two soprano soloists here match their voices admirably and the effect is delightful.

Masses No. 2a (1768): Sunt bona mixta malis (fragment), Hob XXII/2; 7 in B flat (Little organ mass): Missa brevis Sancti Joannis de Deo, Hob XXII/7; Ave Regina, Hob XXIIIb/3; Offertorium: Non nobis, Domine, Hob XXIIIa/1; Responsorium ad absolutionem: Libera me, Hob XXIIb/1; 4 Responsoria de Venerabili, Hob XXIIIc/4 a–d; Salve Regina, Hob XXIIIb/1.
☞ ⊛ *** Sony Dig. SK 53368 [id.]. Marie-Claude Vallin, Ann Monoyios, Tölz Boys' Ch., L'Archibudelli, Tafelmusik, Bruno Weill.

The Mass fragment, *Sunt bona mixta malis* (consisting of a *Kyrie* and part of the *Gloria* of an incomplete mass in D minor), was recently discovered in the attic of a country house in Northern

Ireland, where it had been left more than a century ago by the publisher, Vincent Novello. The autograph is clearly dated 1768 (the remarkable year of *Symphony No. 49, La Passione*) and establishes that at that time Haydn was composing vocal music in an austere, antique, contrapuntal style, looking back towards Palestrina. The four *Responsoria de Venerabili* also date from 1768. Written for the Corpus Christi celebration, they are more extrovert in feeling, but the second is again in the older style. Other works on this record – the *Responsorium ad absolutionem, Libera me,* and the *Offertorium, Non nobis, Domine* – reflect this same grave contrapuntal idiom and have had to be re-dated in consequence. For the listener this record provides yet another facet of Haydn's ever-questing genius. The collection is completed with a later Mass and two fine early works from the 1750s, the *Ave Regina,* in which Marie-Claude Vallin sings with the purity of a boy treble, and the poignant *Salve Regina in E.* This was written at the time when Haydn was heartbroken as his first great love, Therese Keller, took the veil. Here the soprano solo is superbly and touchingly sung by Ann Monoyios. It is undoubtedly a profoundly felt work, certainly the finest of Haydn's youthful period. The *Missa brevis: Sancti Joannis de Deo* features a solo organ which delightfully accompanies the boy treble soloist in the *Benedictus* (sung here by a member of the Tölz Boys' Choir). This fascinating record cannot be recommended too highly. The performances are admirably stylish and very fresh and alive. The authentic style brings appropriate intensity, natural spontaneity and absolutely no feeling of scholarly rectitude, while the transparently clear yet richly ambient recording could not be bettered. The enthusiastic notes are by the great Haydn Scholar, H. C. Robbins Landon, who appears to have cast a fatherly eye over the project. More of Haydn's Masses are to follow and we look forward to them with keen anticipation.

Mass No. 3 (Missa Cellensis): Missa Sanctae Caeciliae, Hob XXII/5.
*** O-L Dig. 417 125-2 [id.]. Nelson, Cable, Hill, Thomas, Ch. of Christ Church Cathedral, AAM, Preston.

The *Missa Cellensis* is Haydn's longest setting of the liturgy. Preston directs an excellent performance with fine contributions from choir and soloists, set against a warmly reverberant acoustic.

Masses Nos. (i) *7 in B flat (Little organ mass): Missa brevis Sancti Joannis de Deo, Hob XXII/7;* (ii) *8 in C (Mariazellermesse): Missa Cellensis, Hob XXII/8;* (iii) *Organ concerto No. 1 in C, Hob XVIII/1.*
(M) *** Decca 430 160-2 [id.]. (i) J. Smith; Scott; (ii) J. Smith, Watts, Tear, Luxon; (i; ii) St John's College, Cambridge, Ch., Guest; (i–iii) ASMF; (iii) Preston, Marriner.

With excellent singing and fine orchestral playing, this is a very desirable issue in the splendid Guest series. The CD transfers are admirably fresh and well focused, and for a bonus we are given Simon Preston's persuasive account of an early organ concerto. Preston's vivid registration and Marriner's spirited accompaniment ensure the listener's pleasure.

Mass No. 9 in B flat (Heiligmesse): Missa Sancti Bernardi von Offida, Hob XXII/10.
(M) *** Decca 430 158-2 [id.]. Cantelo, Minty, Partridge, Keyte, St John's College, Cambridge, Ch., ASMF, Guest – MOZART: *Litaniae de venerabili.* ***

Of all Haydn's Masses the *Heiligmesse* is one of the most human and direct in its appeal. Its combination of symphonic means and simple vocal style underlines its effectiveness. Like the other records in this series, this is a splendid performance, and the vintage Argo sound has been transferred very successfully to CD.

Mass No. 10 in C (Paukenmesse): Missa in tempore belli, Hob XXII/9.
(M) *** Decca 430 157-2 [id.]. Cantelo, Watts, Tear, McDaniel, St John's College, Cambridge, Ch., ASMF, Guest – MOZART: *Vesperae sollennes.* ***

Guest provides a clean, brightly recorded account with good soloists. The Argo performance sounds very fresh in its remastered format.

Masses Nos. (i) *10 in C (Paukenmesse): Missa in tempore belli, Hob. XXII/9;* (ii) *11 in D min. (Nelson): Missa in angustiis.*
☞ (M) ** Sony SM2K 47563 (2). Killebrew, (i) Wells, Devlin, Titus, Norman Scribner Ch., O; (ii) Blegen, Riegel, Estes, Westminster Ch., NYPO; Bernstein – *Symphony No. 88 in G.* **(*)

Bernstein recorded the *Paukenmesse* in Washington National Cathedral in 1973 in connection with a peace demonstration. The result has great emotional intensity, and within the acoustics of the cathedral the choir produces gloriously rich sounds. Stylistically the performance is more questionable, but it certainly has a sense of occasion, and the remastered recording – originally produced for quadrophony – is fuller than usual from this source. The account of the *Nelson Mass,* recorded in the

Manhatten Center three years later, has comparable intensity and a striking choral vitality and bite. The soloists are good, and this, too, has the spontaneity of a live occasion. A fine performance of the *Symphony No. 88* is thrown in for good measure – see above.

Mass No. 11 in D min. (Nelson): Missa in angustiis.
(M) *** Decca 421 146-2. Stahlman, Watts, Wilfred Brown, Krause, King's College, Cambridge, Ch., LSO, Willcocks – VIVALDI: *Gloria.* ***
☞ (M) **(*) Decca Dig. 436 470-2 [id.]. Bonney, Howells, Rolfe Johnson, Roberts, L. Symphony Ch., City of L. Sinfonia, Hickox – MOZART: *Coronation mass.* **(*)

Mass No. 11 in D min. (Nelson); Te Deum in C, Hob XXIIIc/2.
*** DG Dig. 423 097-2 [id.]. Lott, C. Watkinson, Maldwyn Davies, Wilson-Johnson, Ch. & E. Concert, Pinnock.

The *Nelson Mass* (*Missa in angustiis*: 'Mass in times of fear') brings a superb choral offering from Trevor Pinnock and the English Concert. With incandescent singing from the chorus and fine matching from excellent soloists, Pinnock brings home the high drama of Haydn's autumnal inspiration. Similarly, the *Te Deum* leaps forward from the eighteenth century all the more excitingly in an authentic performance such as this. Excellent, full-blooded sound, with good definition.

The CD of the famous Willcocks account is admirably full-bodied and vivid; those not wanting to stretch to Pinnock's full-priced digital CD will find this a satisfactory alternative with its very generous Vivaldi coupling.

Hickox conducts a lively, well-sung reading of the most celebrated of Haydn's late Masses, most impressive in the vigorous, outward-going music which – with Haydn – makes up the greater part of the service. What is disappointing is the recessed sound of the choir, with inner parts less well defined than they should be. The soloists are good but, as recorded, Barbara Bonney's soprano has a thinness along with the purity. Enjoyable as this is, it falls short of the superb Argo version of 20 years earlier from Sir David Willcocks and the King's College Choir, which is preferable even in its better-focused, more atmospheric sound. However, Hickox's performance remains very enjoyable and is grippingly spontaneous. Those wanting a mid-priced digital version of Haydn's masterpiece will find Cleobury's coupled account of Mozart's *Coronation Mass* of comparable calibre.

Mass No. 12 in B flat (Theresienmesse), Hob XXII/12.
(M) *** Decca 430 159-2 [id.]. Spoorenberg, Greevy, Mitchinson, Krause, St John's College, Cambridge, Ch., Guest – M. HAYDN: *Ave Regina;* MOZART: *Ave verum corpus.* ***
(M) *** Sony Dig. SM2K 47522 (2). Popp, Elias, Tear, Hudson, London Symphony Ch., LSO, Bernstein – BEETHOVEN: *Choral fantasia* etc. ***

The *Theresa Mass* may be less famous than the *Nelson Mass* but its inspiration is hardly less memorable. George Guest injects tremendous vigour into the music and the St John's Choir, in splendid form, makes the very most of this fine work. Good solo singing and brilliant, vivid, 1965 recording.

Bernstein's grand manner goes with playing and singing of infectious bounce and resilience, typical of this conductor. The soloists are first rate, and this can be warmly recommended as an enjoyably spontaneous large-scale alternative to Guest's fine version on Decca.

Mass No. 13 in B flat (Schöpfungsmesse), Hob XXII/13.
(M) *** Decca 430 161-2 [id.]. Cantelo, Watts, Tear, Forbes Robinson, St John's College, Cambridge, Ch., ASMF, Guest – MOZART: *Mass No. 12 (Spaur).* ***

Guest again draws an outstanding performance from his own St John's College Choir and an excellent band of professionals, a fresh and direct reading to match the others of his highly successful Argo series.

Mass No. 14 in B flat (Harmoniemesse), Hob XXII/14.
(M) *** Decca 430 162-2 [id.]. Spoorenberg, Watts, Young, Rouleau, St John's College, Cambridge, Ch., Guest – MOZART: *Vesperae de Dominica.* ***

Haydn was over seventy when he started writing this Mass, but his freshness and originality are as striking as in any of the earlier works. The fine performance caps the others in this outstanding series. The quartet of soloists is strong, with Helen Watts in particular singing magnificently. The brilliant and well-balanced 1966 recording has been transferred splendidly to CD, which now offers a substantial bonus in the Mozart *Vespers*, recorded at St John's over a decade later.

Il ritorno di Tobia (oratorio).

☞ (M) *** Decca 440 038-2 (3) [id.]. Hendricks, Zoghby, Della Jones, Langridge, Luxon, Brighton Festival Ch., RPO, Dorati.

Haydn's first commission from Vienna, written while he was still at Esterháza, is by modern standards a great whale of a piece, full of marvellous material but absurdly long for concert conditions. Based on a subject from the Apocrypha, the story of Tobias and the Angel, it has a libretto which undermines dramatic interest; but on record this objection largely disappears and Haydn's inspiration can at last be appreciated once more. This is the equivalent in oratorio terms of *opera seria*, and though the arias are very long they generally avoid *da capo* form. Most invigorating are the coloratura arias for the Archangel Gabriel (here the dazzling Barbara Hendricks) and the arias for the other soprano, Sara (the radiant Linda Zoghby), which include a lovely meditation, accompanied unexpectedly by antiphonies between oboes and cors anglais in pairs. The other soloists do not quite match the sopranos, but the Brighton Festival Chorus is lively and fresh-toned; except in the rather heavy recitatives, Dorati springs the rhythms beautifully, with the five magnificent choruses acting as cornerstones for the whole expansive structure. The (1979) Kingsway Hall recording is both brilliant and atmospheric. A first-class achievement, with full libretto and back-up notes by H. C. Robbins Landon.

The Seasons (complete; in English).

☞ (M) *** Ph. 434 169-2 (2) [id.]. Harper, Ryland Davies, Shirley-Quirk, BBC Ch. & SO, Sir Colin Davis.

Like Boehm on DG (see below), Sir Colin Davis directs a tinglingly fresh performance of Haydn's mellow last oratorio. In this work – based with flamboyant freedom on a German translation of James Thomson's poem in English – there is more than usual reason for using a translation, and the excellent soloists and chorus get most of the words across to the listener. Indeed the fine (1968) recording does not sound in the least dated – it is full and clear, with a most pleasing bloom. Those who have a preference for an English text will not find this in any way musically inferior to the recommended German-language recordings.

The Seasons (in German).

*** DG Dig. 431 818-2 (2). Bonney, Rolfe Johnson, Schmidt, Monteverdi Ch., E. Bar. Soloists, Gardiner.

☞ (B) *** Ph. Dig. 438 715-2 (2) [id.]. Edith Mathis, Siegfried Jerusalem, Dietrich Fischer-Dieskau, Ch. & ASMF, Marriner.

(M) *** DG 423 922-2 (2) [id.]. Janowitz, Schreier, Talvela, VSO, Boehm.

As in so many of his choral recordings, Gardiner brushes away any cobwebs from the music in Haydn's last oratorio. Gardiner here more than ever rejects the idea prevalent among period performers that slow, measured speeds should be avoided, and almost always gets the best of both worlds in intensity of communication, whatever the purists may say. Even more than usual, this studio performance conveys the electricity of a live event. The silver-toned Barbara Bonney and Anthony Rolfe Johnson at his most sensitive are outstanding soloists, and though the baritone, Andreas Schmidt, is less sweet on the ear, he winningly captures the bluff jollity of the role of Simon.

Sir Neville Marriner followed up the success of his resilient recording of *The Creation* with this superbly joyful performance of Haydn's last oratorio, effervescent with the optimism of old age. Edith Mathis and Dietrich Fischer-Dieskau are as stylish and characterful as one would expect, pointing the words as narrative. The tenor too is magnificent: Siegfried Jerusalem is both heroic of timbre and yet delicate enough for Haydn's most elegant and genial passages. The chorus and orchestra, of authentic size, add to the freshness. The recording, made in St John's, Smith Square, is warmly reverberant without losing detail. The CD virtually transforms the sound, with added definition for both chorus and soloists, with cues for every individual item, and a total playing time of nearly two hours and a quarter. Highly recommended – a remarkable bargain by any standards.

Boehm's performance enters totally into the spirit of the music. The soloists are excellent and characterize the music fully; the chorus sing enthusiastically and are well recorded. But it is Boehm's set. He secures fine orchestral playing throughout, an excellent overall musical balance and real spontaneity in music that needs this above all else.

Stabat Mater.

(M) *** Decca 433 172-2 [id.]. Augér, Hodgson, Rolfe Johnson, Howell, L. Chamber Ch., Argo CO, Laszlo Heltay.

Haydn's *Stabat Mater* is scandalously neglected and it is good that Heltay's reading conveys its essential greatness, helped by excellent soloists and vividly atmospheric recording.

Te Deum in C, Hob XXIIIc/2.
(M) **(*) BMG/RCA GD 86535 [6535-2-RG]. V. Boys' Ch., Ch. Viennensis, VCO, Gillesberger –
   MOZART: *Requiem mass; Ave verum.* **(*)

A fine, vigorous account of the *Te Deum* by these Viennese forces, very vividly recorded, coupled to a
not inconsiderable account of Mozart's *Requiem.* At mid-price it is excellent value.

OPERA

L'anima del Filosofo (Orfeo ed Euridice).
** BMG/RCA Dig. RD 77229 [77229-2] (2). Prégardien, Schmiege, McFadden, Schwarz, Schneider,
   Netherlands Chamber Ch., La Stagione, Frankfurt, Michael Schneider.

Though the subject of the Orpheus story failed signally to draw from Haydn the sort of tragic music
that it requires, there are many delightful numbers even if few are really ambitious solos. This first
CD recording is generally well sung, with the clean-toned tenor, Christoph Prégardien, as Orfeo, the
warm, expressive Marilyn Schmiege as Eurydice and the baritone Gotthold Schwarz a resonant
Creonte. Unfortunately, Michael Schneider and La Stagione Frankfurt, lively in the brisk numbers,
too often make heavy weather of the broader, more spacious passages.

Armida (complete).
☞ *** Ph. 432 438-2 (2) [id.]. Norman, Ahnsjö, Norma Burrowes, Ramey, Leggate, Rolfe Johnson,
   Lausanne CO, Dorati.

Armida, considered in Haydn's time to be his finest opera, was the last he produced at Esterháza and
the one most frequently performed there. It is a piece in which very little happens. Rinaldo, a
crusader seduced away from crusading by the sorceress Armida, who is heavily disguised as a goody,
takes three Acts to decide to cut down the myrtle tree which will undermine Armida's wicked power.
There is a sub-plot: on the way to try to rescue Rinaldo, Clotarco, one of Rinaldo's knights, meets
Zelmira, daughter of the Sultan of Egypt, who has been sent by Armida to seduce him too; but at the
sight of him she experiences love at first sight and promptly leads him to safety. More than most
works in this form, *Armida* presents a psychological drama, with the myrtle tree the most obvious of
symbols. On CD it makes a fair entertainment, with splendid singing from Jessye Norman, even if
she scarcely sounds malevolent. Claes Ahnsjö as the indecisive Rinaldo does better than most tenors
in coping with the enormous range. Indeed the whole team of soloists is one of the most consistent in
Dorati's Haydn opera series, with Norma Burrowes particularly sweet as Zelmira. As well as some
advanced passages, *Armida* also has the advantage that there is little *secco* recitative. The 1978
recording quality is outstanding and the transfer on to a pair of CDs is characteristic of the high
standard of this pioneering Philips series, with the one break quite conveniently placed in the middle
of the second of the three Acts.

La fedeltà premiata (complete).
☞ *** Ph. 432 430-2 (3) [id.]. Valentini Terrani, Landy, Von Stade, Titus, Cotrubas, Alva, Mazzieri,
   Lövaas, SRO Ch., Lausanne CO, Dorati.

The operatic mastery of Mozart has always dogged the reputation of Haydn in this field, but *La
fedeltà premiata* shows its composer on his finest form. It may have a preposterous plot, but this
sparkling performance suggests that in all the complications of who is in love with whom, Haydn was
sending up classical conventions with tongue firmly in cheek, almost like eighteenth-century G&S.
That at least would tie in with the concept of court entertainment at Esterháza, designed for
particular singers and players performing before a select and familiar group of patrons. We can only
guess what private jokes were involved but, above all in the extended finales to the first and second
Acts, one finds Haydn as opera composer setting a dramatic and musical pattern not so far different
from Mozart.

   This was the first of Dorati's series of Haydn opera recordings for Philips, launched with
characteristic effervescence, helped by an excellent Haydn-sized orchestra and a first-rate cast. The
proud Aramanta is superbly taken by Frederica von Stade, while Haydn's unconventional allocation
of voices brings a fine baritone, Alan Titus, to match her as the extravagant Count Perrucchetto. But
the sweetest and most tender singing comes from Ileana Cotrubas as the fickle nymph, Nerina. The
recording is intimate but with plenty of atmosphere. It is well transferred to CD, but at times one
feels the cueing could be more generous.

(i) *L'incontro improviso* (complete). Arias for: (ii) *Acide e Galatea.* (iii) SARTI: *I finti eredi.* (iv)

TRAETTA: *Ifigenia in Tauride*. (ii–iv) Terzetto from: PASTICCIO: *La Circe, ossia L'isola incantata*.
☞ *** Ph. 432 416-2 (3) [id.]. (i; iv) Ahnsjö; (i) Zoghby, Trimarchi, Luxon, M. Marshall, Della
Jones, Prescott; (ii) Devlin; (iii) Baldin; Lausanne CO, Dorati.

In eighteenth-century Vienna the abduction opera involving Moorish enslavement and torture
became quite a cult – a strangely masochistic taste when Turkish invasions were not that distant. The
greatest instance is Mozart's *Entführung*, but this example of the genre from Haydn, a light
entertainment for Prince Esterházy's private theatre, is worthy of comparison, with its very similar
story. In 47 generally brief numbers, but with finales of almost Mozartian complexity, the opera may
lack depth of characterization (Haydn was using a libretto also set by Gluck), but the result is
musically delightful. The most heavenly number of all is a trio for the three sopranos in Act I, *Mi
sembra un sogno*, which, with its high-flown legato phrases, keeps reminding one of *Soave sia il vento*
in *Così fan tutte*. The tenor's trumpeting arias are beautifully crisp and the vigorous canzonettas for
the two *buffo* basses include a nonsense song or two. Benjamin Luxon and Domenico Trimarchi are
delectable in those roles. Claes Ahnsjö is at his finest, resorting understandably to falsetto for one
impossible top E flat; the role of the heroine is superbly taken by Linda Zoghby, and she is well
supported by Margaret Marshall and Della Jones.

The *secco* recitatives are rather heavy, as ever contradicting Dorati's well-sprung style in Haydn.
The recording conveys a most convincing theatre atmosphere, well transferred to CD, though voices
are not always as cleanly focused as in some of this fine series. An indispensable set, just the same.
The layout places each of the three Acts on a single CD and makes room on the third for two arias
which Haydn devised for other men's operas, plus one for his own *Acide e Galatea*. The selection ends
with an amazing eating and drinking trio.

L'infedeltà delusa (complete).
☞ *** Ph. 432 413-2 (2) [id.]. Mathis, Hendricks, Baldin, Ahnsjö, Devlin, Lausanne CO, Dorati.
☞ (M) **(*) HM/BMG 05472 77316-2 (2) [id.]. Argenta, Lootens, Prégardien, M. Schäfer, Varcoe,
La Petite Bande, Sigiswald Kuijken.

More than Haydn's other operas, *L'infedeltà delusa*, a rustic comedy, makes one wonder whether
Mozart and Da Ponte had access to it before they created their three supreme operatic masterpieces.
Vespina is first cousin to Despina in *Così fan tutte*, and there is a splendid Mozartian anticipation
when in the finale of Act I she slaps Nencio's face - it might almost be Susanna in *Figaro*. As there,
the effect is totally refreshing, with sudden realism in the midst of formality, and some of the scenes
are also very complex for their period. Musically, the surprises come less in the melodic writing –
which, in one jolly number after another, is relatively conventional – than in ear-catching twists and
striking instrumental effects. Haydn was proud of the Esterházy horns, for example, and they have
some marvellous whooping to do. This was the last of the admirable Philips series of Haydn
operas recorded with Antal Dorati and the Lausanne Chamber Orchestra, providing an important
nucleus of the works written for performance at Esterháza.

L'infedeltà delusa may not be dramatically the most imaginative of stage works, but by the
standards of the time it is a compact piece, punctuated by some sharply noteworthy ideas. The opera
brings many memorable numbers, such as a laughing song for Nencio (on Philips the admirable Claes
Ahnsjö) and a song of ailments for the spirited and resourceful heroine, Vespina (Edith Mathis, lively
and fresh). Dorati draws vigorous, resilient performances from everyone (not least from the delightful
Barbara Hendricks). The Philips recording is splendidly full-blooded and neatly transferred on to a
pair of CDs, with one Act complete on each.

The plot of the opera is unusual for the time in giving the role of the heavy father to the tenor
(well taken on RCA by Christoph Prégardien), reflecting the fact that it was expressly designed for
Karl Friberth, literary adviser to Prince Esterházy as well as a singer. This alternative version on
period instruments nicely captures the flavour of a semi-domestic performance in the prince's country
palace. Both the RCA sopranos, Nancy Argenta and Lena Lootens, are agile and precise, if a little
edgy. Both tenors, Markus Schäfer as well as Prégardien, are stressed by the range demanded but,
like the bass, Stephen Varcoe, they have clean voices, apt for Haydn on a small scale. The scale of the
whole work, much shorter than was common in the late eighteenth century, makes it the more apt for
revival today. *L'infedeltà delusa* may be no *Così fan tutte* but this too is a most enjoyable set, worth
considering at mid-price, even if the Dorati version is a pretty clear first choice.

L'isola disabitata (complete).
☞ *** Ph. 432 427-2 (2) [id.]. Lerer, Zoghby, Alva, Bruson, Lausanne CO, Dorati.

By eighteenth-century standards *L'isola disabitata* ('The uninhabited island') is an extremely compact
opera. Costanza, her husband, Gernando, and her sister, Silvia, are shipwrecked on an island;

Gernando has been kidnapped by pirates and the two ladies are left behind, sure that they have been abandoned. Thirteen years later Gernando returns with his friend, Enrico. Silvia, in hiding, spots them but does not recognize them. Fortunately
Enrico and Silvia then also fall in love (at first sight) and after some confusion and explanations - which are at first resisted by Costanza - everything ends happily. General rejoicing.

Were it not for the preponderance of accompanied recitative over set numbers, this would be an ideal Haydn opera to recommend to the modern listener. As it is, many passages reflect the *Sturm und Drang* manner of middle-period Haydn – and this is hinted at immediately in the overture – often urgently dramatic, with tremolos freely used. But in Act I it is only after twenty minutes that the first aria appears, a delightful piece for the heroine with a hint of *Che farò* in Gluck's *Orfeo*. Vocally, it is the second soprano here, Linda Zoghby, who takes first honours, though the baritone, Renato Bruson, is splendid too. The piece ends with a fine quartet of reconciliation, only the eighth number in the whole piece. The direction of recitatives is unfortunately not Dorati's strong point – here, as elsewhere in the series, rather too heavy – but with excellent recording, very vividly transferred to CD, and with just the right degree of ambience, this makes a fascinating issue. The two Acts are given a CD apiece.

(i) *Il mondo della luna* (complete). (ii) Arias for: Cantata: *Miseri noi, misera patria*; Petrarch's sonnet from *Il Canzoniere: Solo e pensoso.* BIANCHI: *Alessandro nell'Indie.* CIMAROSA: *I due supposti conti.* GAZZANIGA: *L'isola di Alcina.* GUGLIELMI: *La Quakera spiritosa.* PAISIELLO: *La Frascatana.* PASTICCIO: *La Circe, ossia l'Isola incantana.*
☞ *** Ph. 432 420-2 (3) [id.]. (i) (i) Trimarchi, Alva, Von Stade, Augér, Mathis, Valentini Terrani, Rolfe Johnson, Lausanne CO, Dorati ; (ii) Edith Mathis, Lausanne CO, Jordan.

Il mondo della luna ('The world on the moon') is better known (by name at least) than the other Haydn operas that the Philips series has disinterred. Written for an Esterházy marriage, it uses the plot of a naïve but engaging Goldoni comedy. A bogus astronomer, Ecclitico (played by Luigi Alva) hoodwinks the inevitable rich old man, Buonafede (Domenico Trimarchi, sparkling and stylish in comic vocal acting), into believing he has been transported to the moon. All this is in aid of getting the rich man's lovelorn daughter, Clarice, the hero of her choice. Two other couples come into the plot, Ernesto who is in love with Flaminia, Buonafede's other daughter, while Cecco, Ernesto's valet, fancies Lisetta, Buonafede's serving maid. Ecclitico dresses up his garden into a fantastic moonscape and Buonafede wakes up from a drugged sleep and is very impressed by everything he sees, including a dance divertissement in which he is brought lavish garments to wear; he reluctantly agrees to the proposed matches. Back on Earth the nuptials are confirmed under a degree of duress, but in the end, needless to say, there is general rejoicing. Although the plot is simple by the standards of the time, it takes an age in the resolving. Much of the most charming music comes in the brief instrumental interludes, and most of the arias are correspondingly short. That leaves much space on the discs devoted to *secco* recitative and, as on his other Haydn opera issues, Dorati proves a surprisingly sluggish harpsichord player. Nevertheless, with splendid contributions from the three principal women singers, this is another Haydn set which richly deserves investigation by anyone devoted to opera of the period. The eight substitution arias (including *Solo e pensoso*, the lovely setting of Petrarch's twenty-eighth sonnet – the last Italian aria Haydn wrote) are simply and stylishly sung by Edith Mathis. The 1977 recording is first class throughout, as is the CD transfer; and the layout, with one Act allotted to each of the three CDs, leaves room for the eight substitution arias (recorded three years later) on the last disc.

Orlando paladino (complete).
☞ *** Ph. 432 434-2 (3) [id.]. Augér, Ameling, Killebrew, Shirley, Ahnsjö, Luxon, Trimarchi, Mazzieri, Carelli, Lausanne CO, Dorati.

One might infer from this delightful send-up of a classical story in opera that Haydn in his pieces for Esterháza was producing sophisticated charades for a very closed society. Though long for its subject-matter, this is among the most delightful of all, turning the legend of Roland and his exploits as a medieval champion into something not very distant from farce. Roland's madness (*Orlando furioso*) becomes the amiable dottiness of a Disney giant with a club. Finally, with the assistance of Charon, the famous ferryman, Alcina lifts Orlando's madness with water from the river Lethe and all ends happily.

There are plenty of touches of parody in the music: the bass arias of the King of Barbary suggest mock Handel and Charon's aria (after Orlando is whisked down to the Underworld) brings a charming exaggeration of Gluck's manner. Above all the Leperello-like servant figure, Pasquale, is given a series of numbers which match and even outshine Mozart, including a hilarious duet when, bowled over by love, he can only utter monosyllables – cue for marvellous *buffo* singing from Domenico Trimarchi. The overall team is strong, with Arleen Augér as the heroine outstandingly sweet and pure. George Shirley as Orlando snarls too much in recitative, but it is an aptly heroic performance; and Elly Ameling and Gwendoline Killebrew in subsidiary roles are both excellent. The recitatives here, though long, are rather less heavily done than in some other Dorati sets, and the 1976 recording is first rate and splendidly transferred to three CDs, one for each Act.

La vera costanza (complete).
☞ *** Ph. 432 424-2 (2) [id.]. Norman, Donath, Ahnsjö, Ganzarolli, Trimarchi, Lövaas, Rolfe Johnson, Lausanne CO, Dorati.

Written, like most of Haydn's operas, for private performance at Esterháza, *La vera costanza* keeps an elegantly urbane tone of voice, illustrating what is on the face of it a preposterous story of a shipwreck and a secret marriage. Like Mozart's *Marriage of Figaro*, the piece has serious undertones, if only because it is the proletarian characters who consistently inspire sympathy while the aristocrats come in for something not far short of ridicule. The individual numbers may be shorter-winded than in Mozart, but Haydn's sharpness of invention never lets one down, and the big finales to each of the first two Acts are fizzingly impressive, pointing clearly forward to *Figaro*. Overall, the opera is nicely compact. In every way bar one this is a delectable performance. The conducting of Dorati sparkles, Jessye Norman is superb as the virtuous fisher-girl, Rosina, while the others make up an excellent team, well cast in often difficult roles designed for the special talents of individual singers at Esterháza. The snag is the continuo playing of Dorati himself, heavy and clangorous, holding up the lively singing of the *secco* recitatives. Apart from some discrepancy of balance between the voices and a touch of dryness in the acoustic, the recorded sound is excellent. The CD transfer is first rate, too, and the opera fits snugly on a pair of CDs.

Haydn, Michael (1737–1806)

Concertino for horn and orchestra in D.
(M) *** Teldec/Warner Dig. 9031 74790-2 [id.]. Dale Clevenger, Liszt CO, Rolla – J. HAYDN: *Concertos*. ***

Michael Haydn's *Concertino* is played with fine style by Dale Clevenger, whose articulation is a joy in itself. Rolla and his orchestra clearly enjoy themselves and the recording, like the coupled concertos by Josef Haydn, is very realistic indeed.

(i) *Horn concerto in D;* (ii) *Duo concertante for organ, viola and orchestra, P.55; 6 Minuets, P.70;* (iii) *Divertimento in G.*
☞ (M) *** Decca 436 222-2 [id.]. (i) Barry Tuckwell; (ii) Simon Preston, Stephen Shingles, ASMF, Marriner; (iii Vienna Octet (members).

A robust performance of a lesser horn concerto (not a patch on those by Mozart, but with a vigorous, bravura central allegro). The *Duo concertante*, however, brings an unusual and attractive combination that is more effective in terms of colour than one might have expected. The work's outer movements are well made and spirited, but it is the gracious and elegant *Adagio* that makes the strongest impression. It has a most imaginative middle section, where the organ is delicately florid and the viola sustains the melodic interest. The performance in the main is excellent and the Kingsway Hall recording from the mid- to late 1960s solves the balance problems skilfully. The *Minuets* are placed between the two concertos and are beautifully played: they are almost worthy of Josef! The *Divertimento* is agreeable if less memorable, and here the CD transfer, hitherto smooth and realistic, becomes slightly less well focused, and the ear is aware that the recording is earlier (1962).

Violin concerto in B flat.
(M) **(*) Teldec/Warner Dig. 9031 74784-2 [id.]. Zehetmair, Liszt CO – J. HAYDN: *Concerto* ***; SIBELIUS: *Concerto*. **

A *Violin concerto* from Michael Haydn (written in 1760) makes an enterprising coupling for the better-known work by his brother, Josef. The finale is the weakest part, though not lacking in spirit. The performance with Thomas Zehetmair combining roles of soloist and conductor is strongly characterized and very well recorded.

Symphonies Nos. 19 in C, P.10; 21 in C, P.12; 23 in D, P.43; 26 in G, P.16; 29 in C, P.19; 37 in B flat, P.28; 39 in F, P.30; 41 in F, P.32.
(B) **(*) VoxBox 1155012 (2) [CDX 5020]. Bournemouth Sinf., Harold Fabermann.

It is good that Harold Fabermann is exploring the symphonies of Michael Haydn, even if the resonant recording often makes tuttis sound opaque and not too cleanly focused. The composer's inspiration is uneven but the slow movements are always pleasing, and many of the symphonies are notable for their helter-skelter finales which have great energy. The performances are well made and sympathetic, suitably athletic in the allegros; but they lack the final degree of flexibility and imagination in the expressive writing. The documentation with the set is admirable; the Perger numbers, incidentally, realign the symphonies in order of composition.

Symphony in C, P.12.
(M) *** Teldec/Warner Dig. 9031 74788-2 [id.]. Liszt CO, János Rolla – ROSSINI: *String sonatas.* ***

This *Symphony in C major* contains a strikingly beautiful inspiration, the central elegiac *Andante in A minor* for strings with solo oboe. It is very well played throughout and is freshly recorded.

Symphonies: in C, P.12; in F, P.32; in D, P.43; in E, P.44.
☞ ** Olympia Dig OCD 435 [id.]. Oradea PO, Romeo Rimbu.

As we know from their Pichel collection (see below) the Oradea Philharmonic are not the world's most polished ensemble, but here they play with lots of spirit in music with which they seem more acclimatized. The conductor is certainly a persuasive advocate of these symphonies of Michael Haydn, another composer who had Oradean associations – although it was called Grosswardein in the eighteenth century. Each is an impressive work, showing the composer with almost as strong a symphonic personality as Joseph. They are well recorded, and this CD is well worth exploring.

Divertimenti: in C, P. 98; in C, P. 115.
*** Denon Dig. C37 7119 [id.]. Holliger, Salvatore Qt – J. C. BACH: *Oboe quartet;* MOZART: *Adagio.* ***

Both these *Divertimenti* contain captivating and original inspirations. The longer of the two, P. 98, has a fizzing first movement and a joyful *Presto* finale, while P. 115 brings unexpected timbres. Well coupled and vividly recorded.

String quintets: in B flat, P.105; in C, P.108; in G, P.109.
☞ **(*) Sony Dig. SK 53897 [id.]. L'Archibudelli.

It is good to have modern recordings of Michael Haydn's *String quintets.* P.108/9 date from 1773, and Mozart knew and admired them. The *C major* with its engaging *Andante cantabile* slow movement was very popular in its day (and was attributed to Michael's brother Joseph by one publisher). P.105 is more of a cassation or serenade and has seven movements, including an attractive fourth-movement set of variations and a *marcia* finale. All the works are inventive. Here they are played freshly, elegantly and authentically, without edginess, and the only drawback for some ears may be the modest squeezing of phrases in slow movements plus some rather strong accents in minuets. The recording is fresh with firmly focused yet transparent textures.

Ave Regina.
(M) *** Ph. 430 159-2; *430 159-4* [id.]. St John's College, Cambridge, Ch., Guest – J.HAYDN: *Theresienmesse;* MOZART: *Ave verum corpus.* ***

This lovely antiphon, scored for eight-part double choir, looks back to Palestrina and the Venetian school of the Gabrielis and the young Monteverdi. It is beautifully sung and recorded.

Headington, Christopher (born 1930)

Violin concerto.
⊛ *** ASV CDDCA 780 [id.]. Xue Wei, LPO, Glover – R. STRAUSS: *Violin concerto.* ***

The Headington *Violin concerto* is a warmly lyrical, unashamedly tonal work in which a fiery central Scherzo is framed by two longer, more reflective movements, both with a vein of melancholy which echoes the comparable movements in the violin concertos of Walton and Prokofiev. The finale is a spacious set of variations in which the last and longest acts as a movingly meditative summary. Xue Wei plays with a passionate commitment to match that in his Brahms and Tchaikovsky recordings, with Jane Glover and the London Philharmonic providing warmly sympathetic accompaniments. Excellent sound. Those looking for twentieth-century music that is accessible and rewards familiarity need not hesitate.

Heath, Dave (born 1956)

The Frontier.

☞ (M) *** Virgin/EMI CUV5 61121-2 [id.]. LCO, Warren-Green – ADAMS: *Shaker loops* *** ⊛;
GLASS: *Company* etc. ***; REICH: *8 Lines.* ***

Most minimalist composers are American and, although Dave Heath was born in Manchester, the
influences on his music are transatlantic. In *The Frontier* the incisive rhythmic astringency is tempered
by an attractive, winding lyrical theme which finally asserts itself just before the spiky close. The work
was written for members of the LCO, and their performance, full of vitality and feeling, is admirably
recorded.

Hebden, John (18th century)

6 Concertos for strings (ed. Wood).
**(*) Chan. Dig. CHAN 8339 [id.]. Cantilena, Shepherd.

Little is known about John Hebden except that he was a Yorkshire composer who also played the
cello and bassoon. These concertos are his only known works, apart from some flute sonatas.
Although they are slightly uneven, at best the invention is impressive. The concertos usually feature
two solo violins and are well constructed to offer plenty of contrast. The performances here are
accomplished, without the last degree of polish but full of vitality. The recording is clear and well
balanced, and given good presence.

Heinichen, Johann David (1683–1729)

*Dresden concerti: in C, S 211; in G, S 213; in G (Darmstadt), S 214; in G (Venezia), S 214; in G, S
215; in F, S 217; in F, S 226, in F, S 231; in F, S 232; in F, S 233; in F, S 234; in F, S 235; Concerto
movement in C min., S 240; Serenata di Moritzburg in F, S 204; Sonata in A, S 208.*
☞ *** DG Dig. 437 549-2 (2) [id.]. Col. Mus. Ant., Reinhard Goebel.

*Dresden concerti: in F, S 231; 233/5; in G, S 213; Concerto movement in C min., S 240; Sonata in A, S
208.*
☞ *** DG Dig. 437 849-2 [id.]. Col. Mus. Ant., Reinhard Goebel.

Winner of the *Gramophone* non-vocal Baroque award, this fascinating set represents the current high-
water mark of the achievement of Goebel's Cologne Musica Antiqua in the recording studio. Johann
David Heinichen, a contemporary of Bach, was a Dresden court musician and the concertos here
were intended for the (obviously excellent) Dresden court orchestra. Their personnel must have
included some very good horn players, for the horn parts in the F major concertos are hair-raisingly
spectacular, and the sprightly flute solos and delicate oboe parts suggest fine woodwind as well as
alert string players. It is the orchestral colour that makes these concertos so appealing rather than
their invention, which is more predictable, although often very charming (witness the grace of the
oboe theme in the *Larghetto* of the *G major Concerto*, Seibel 213). The siciliano for a pair of flutes
which forms the *Andante* of the F major work, Seibel 235, is hardly less engaging. Goebel's Cologne
forces have not always been strong on charm in previous recordings, but they obviously relish the
delicacy of Heinichen's wind scoring and his neat and busily vital allegros. Heinichen was no Zelenka;
however, though his writing is often fairly predictable, these spirited performances bring it fully to
life, and the players convey their enthusiasm in placing a striking series of newly rediscovered works
before the public. The recording is freshly vivid, clean and realistic. Goebel's notes are scholarly if not
especially detailed in relation to individual concertos. One would be tempted to recommend the
single-disc selection, but DG have cunningly not included therein the lollipop of the set. This is the
Pastorell second movement of the *C major Concerto*, Seibel 211, with its piquant drone (track 5 of the
second CD); the effect for all the world sounds like an unusually refined set of bagpipes. It is
immediately followed by a peaceful *Adagio* for flute and strings and a sparkling finale.

Henze, Hans Werner (born 1926)

Symphonies Nos. (i) *1–5;* (ii) *6.*
(M) *** DG 429 854-2 (2) [id.]. (i) BPO, (ii) LSO, composer.

The Henze *Symphonies* are remarkable pieces which inhabit a strongly distinctive sound-world. The *First* with its cool, Stravinskian slow movement is a remarkable achievement, and there is a dance-like feel to the *Third*. It is rich in fantasy. The *Fourth* is among the most concentrated and atmospheric of his works; there is at times an overwhelming sense of melancholy. The *Fifth* is strongly post-expressionist. The *Sixth Symphony* was composed while Henze was living in Havana. The performances are excellent and the recorded sound amazingly vivid. An important and indispensable set, recommended with enthusiasm.

Symphony No. 7; Barcarola.
☞ *** EMI Dig. CDC7 54762-2 [id.]. CBSO, Rattle.

Rattle conducts his Birmingham orchestra in one of the most powerful recordings of Henze's music. The *Seventh Symphony* is not only the longest he has written, it is also the weightiest and most traditionally symphonic, Beethoven-like in four substantial movements. As Henze says himself, it is his 'German symphony', written for the Berlin Philharmonic in 1983/4. With a lyrical slow movement and a violent Scherzo (inspired by the madness of the poet, Holderlin), it closes movingly with a chill, disturbing 'setting' of a Holderlin poem for orchestra alone, without voice. Rather belying its title, the *Barcarola* presents a similarly weighty and massive structure, an elegiac piece of over 20 minutes, written in memory of Paul Dessau and inspired by the myth of the ferryman, Charon, crossing the Styx. The dramatic bite of both performances, recorded live in Symphony Hall, Birmingham, makes them instantly compelling, encouraging the sort of repetition that the complex arguments demand. Full, colourful recording to bring out the richness of Henze's orchestral writing.

OPERA

Die Bassariden (The Bassarids).
*** Koch Schwann 314 006-2 (2) [id.]. Tear, Schmidt, Armstrong, Riegel, Lindsley, Wenkel, Burt, Murray, Berlin RIAS Chamber Ch. & RSO, Albrecht.

Henze's *The Bassarids*, based on the *Bacchae* of Euripides, presents a contrast of rival philosophies between the Dionysiac and the Apollonian, the sensual and the intellectual. With its meaty musical argument and consciously symphonic shape, it is an opera that has cried out for a complete recording, and this fine account from Berlin fills the bill well, amply confirming the work's power. The cast is first rate, including Kenneth Riegel, Andreas Schmidt, Robert Tear and Karen Armstrong, and the choral writing adds greatly to the impact, splendidly realized here by the RIAS Choir.

Der junge Lord ('The Young Lord'; complete).
☞ (M) *** DG 455 248-2 (2) [id.]. Mathis, Grobe, McDaniel, Driscoll, Johnson, German Op., Berlin, Christoph von Dohnányi.

As a reaction against his earlier, generally very serious operas, Henze in 1965 completed this piece designed as an *opera buffa*. This is Henze at his most amiable, and it results for much of the time in his Stravinskian side dominating, though he also allows himself a warmer vein of lyricism than usual. The plot in its comedy is consciously cynical, involving a snobbish community duped by a titled Englishman. He introduces an alleged English lord who finally turns out to be an ape. There is an underlying seriousness to the piece, and in this excellent performance, recorded with the composer's approval, the full range of moods and emotions is conveyed. Very good (1967) sound; in this mid-price reissue a full libretto and translation are provided.

Hérold, Ferdinand (1791–1833)

La Fille mal gardée (ballet, arr. Lanchbery): complete.
(M) *** Decca Dig. *430 849-2* (2) [id.]. ROHCG O, Lanchbery – LECOCQ: *Mam'zelle Angot.* ***

Lanchbery himself concocted the score for this fizzingly comic and totally delightful ballet, drawing primarily on Hérold's music, but interpolating the famous comic *Clog dance* from Hertel's alternative score, which must be one of the most famous of all ballet numbers outside Tchaikovsky. There is much else of comparable delight. Here, with sound of spectacular Decca digital fidelity, Lanchbery conducts a highly seductive account of the complete ballet with an orchestra long familiar with playing it in the theatre, now reissued coupled with Gordon Jacob's equally delicious confection, based on the music of Lecocq.

La Fille mal gardée: extended excerpts.
☞ ⊛ (M) *** Decca 430 196-2 [id.]. ROHCG O, Lanchbery.
*** EMI Dig. CDC7 49403-2. RLPO, Wordsworth.

La Fille mal gardée ('The badly guarded daughter') dates originally from 1789, when it received a hasty première just before the French Revolution. Since then the ballet has had a long and chequered history. The tale is a simple one of thwarted rustic love which comes right in the end, and the original score was made up from folk melodies and 'pop' songs of the time. Since 1789 it has been revised and re-written by Hérold (1828), Hertel (1864) and Feldt (1937). The present version, commissioned by Fredrick Ashton for the Royal Ballet revival, was prepared and scored exceedingly skilfully by John Lanchbery, who drew mainly on Hérold's version. However, Lanchbery also interpolates a single Hertel number, a gorgeously vulgar *Clog dance* for Simone (who, as a character in drag, is one of the ancestors of our pantomime dame).

Hérold's score also included tunes from Rossini's *Barber of Seville* and *Cenerentola*, together with a Donizetti selection (mainly from *L'elisir d'amore*). That the music is therefore a complete hotch-potch does not prevent it from being marvellously entertaining. This is one of those ballets that one can listen to all through without being bored for a minute. The writing is direct in its popular appeal but, being French, is also witty. The performance here is wonderfully persuasive and brilliantly played, displaying both affection and sparkle in ample quantity. The Kingsway Hall recording quality (produced by Ray Minshull and engineered by Arthur Lillie) is of vintage Decca excellence. One cannot believe that it dates from 1962, for the combination of ambient bloom and the most realistic detail still places it in the demonstration bracket. Lanchbery later recorded the complete ballet digitally for Decca, and that is also an outstanding set but it involves two CDs (and includes Lecocq's *Mam'zelle Angot* ballet music as a fill-up).

Barry Wordsworth's scintillating account of a generous extended selection from the ballet on CD includes all the important sequences. With playing from the Royal Liverpool Philharmonic Orchestra that combines refinement and delicacy with wit and humour, this also is very highly recommendable.

Herrmann, Bernard (1911–75)

(i) *The Devil and Daniel Webster:* suite; (ii) *Obsession* (abridged score); (i) *Welles raises Kane:* suite.
☞ (M) *** Unicorn UKCD 2065 [id.]. (i) LPO; (ii) Nat. SO; composer.

The Devil and Daniel Webster suite is not first-grade Herrmann: the musical material is not always distinguished enough and one or two of the movements outlast their welcome. *Welles raises Kane* is another matter. Beecham himself gave one of its first performances in New York during the war. The music is drawn from both Orson Welles's *Citizen Kane* and *The Magnificent Ambersons*, but the music itself (unlike the atmosphere of those films) is snappily and evocatively extrovert, showing a brilliant flair for orchestral colour. It is superbly played. For the reissue Unicorn have added a brilliant Decca recording of an abridged version of the music Herrmann wrote for *Obsession* (some 39 minutes overall). His collaborations with Hitchcock formed the apex of Herrmann's Hollywood career, and this highly atmospheric score contributed greatly to the success of the movie. Christopher Palmer tells us in the notes accompanying this CD that the composer was curiously obsessed with the story and its two principal characters. It offers some of his most spectacular and evocative writing, including choral effects.

Film scores: *Beneath the Twelve-mile Reef;* (i) *Citizen Kane: suite; Hangover Square:* (ii) *Concerto macabre. On Dangerous Ground: Death hunt. White Witch Doctor: suite.*
(M) *** BMG/RCA GD 80707 [0707-2-RG]. Nat. PO, Gerhardt, (i) with Te Kanawa, (ii) Achucarro.

Bernard Herrmann's remarkable 1940 score for *Citizen Kane* is well able to stand up on its own and includes a fascinating pastiche aria from a fictitious opera, *Salammbo*, eloquently sung here by Kiri Te Kanawa. The collection opens with an exhilarating example of the composer's ferocious chase music, the *Death hunt* from *On Dangerous Ground*, led by eight roistering horns with the orchestral brass augmented. *Beneath the Twelve-mile Reef* displays Herrmann's soaring melodic gift and his orchestral flair. The Busoni/Liszt-derived *Concerto macabre* is brilliantly played by Joaquin Achucarro. Charles Gerhardt and his splendid orchestra obviously relish the hyperbole and the recording is spectacular.

Symphony; (i) *The Fantasticks* (song-cycle).
☞ (M) *** Unicorn UKCD 2063 [id.]. (London) National PO, composer, (i) with Michael Rippon; Meriel Dickinson; John Amis; Gillian Humphreys; Thames Chamber Ch.

As his superbly professional film music made plain, Bernard Herrmann was a generously eclectic composer and in his ambitious symphony, written in 1941, one can spot the borrowings from Walton, Vaughan Williams and Stravinsky, not to mention Berlioz and Verdi. Underlying everything in this generally enjoyable work, however, the argument reflects the approach of a dedicated Sibelian and, though the pretensions may not always be supported by equivalent matter, it is good to hear Herrmann extending himself and giving what is in effect a musical self-portrait. Admirable perform-ance and very good recording, made in 1974, not long before the composer's untimely death. The coupled song-cycle – virtually a cantata – set to words by the Elizabethan poet Nicolas Breton, has more of the composer's own personality and is obviously deeply felt music. *The Fantasticks* is the title of Breton's last published group of prose poems. Its theme is the changing seasons: January 'a time of little comfort', February 'sharp and piercing and the winds blow cold', while 'the air is sharp' in March, yet 'the tree begins to bud and the grass to peep abroad'. Finally in May comes the promise of summer ('Heigh ho Heigh nonny nonny', with the chorus relishing the sensuous blossoming – 'the sweetness of the air refreshed every spirit'). With its nicely spiced word-imagery, the music communi-cates readily, and it is perhaps April that brings the most seductive setting of all (written for soprano with exquisite violin obbligato), and here it is a pity that Gillian Humphreys, who is very sympathetic, has such a close vibrato. Otherwise the soloists are excellent and the orchestral playing quite lovely. Most rewarding when the sound is so atmospheric.

(i) *Moby Dick* (cantata); (ii) *For the fallen.*
☞ (M) *** Unicorn UKCD 2061 [id.]. (i) John Amis, Robert Bowman, Kelly, Rippon, Aeolian Singers, LPO; (ii) Nat. PO; composer.

Herrmann's *Moby Dick* is written in an immediately approachable idiom and it deserves the attention of choral societies, for it makes a maximum impact at first hearing. The present, extremely dramatic and spontaneous performance should recommend it to any listener who can enjoy a setting of the English language by a composer who shows a real feeling for words. The soloists, notably John Amis as Ishmael and David Kelly as Ahab, are first rate, and the chorus and orchestra convey their enthusiasm and excitement in such effective and rewarding music. The recording is also outstanding, and so is the CD transfer. *For the fallen* is a short elegiac obituary for the dead of the Second World War. Its pastoral feeling and understatement are gently haunting. It is beautifully played and recorded.

Wuthering Heights (opera): complete.
(M) *** Unicorn UKCD 2050/52 [id.]. Bainbridge, Kelly, Bell, Beaton, Kitchiner, Rippon, Ward, Bowden, Elizabethan Singers, Pro Arte O, composer.

Bernard Herrmann, best known for his film scores and as conductor, spent many years working on his operatic adaption of Emily Brontë's novel, and the result is confident and professional. Though the writing is purely illustrative rather than musically original, this performance, strongly conducted by the composer, makes for a colourful telling of the story. The solo singing is consistently good and the recording beautifully clear.

Hertel, Johann (1727–89)

Trumpet concerto in D.
*** Ph. Dig. 420 203-2; *420 203-4* [id.]. Hardenberger, ASMF, Marriner – HAYDN *** ⑱; HUMMEL *** ⑱; STAMITZ: *Concertos.* ***

Johann Hertel's *Trumpet concerto* is typical of many works of the same kind written in the Baroque era. Håkan Hardenberger clearly relishes every bar and plays with great flair.

Hildegard of Bingen (1098–1179)

Ordo virtutum (The Play of the Virtues).
(M) *** HM/BMG Dig. GD 77051 (2) [77051-2-RG]. Köper, Mockridge, Thornton, Laurens, Feldman, Monahan, Lister, Trevor, Sanford, Smith, Sequentia.

The more one learns about Abbess Hildegard of Bingen, the more astonishing her achievement appears. She was not just a leading poet and composer of the twelfth century, she was a major political figure who not only founded her own Abbey but corresponded with popes and emperors. *Ordo virtutum* is a mystery play, and this 90-minute piece includes strikingly dramatic passages, with the Devil himself intervening. This recording, made in collaboration with West German Radio of Cologne, is outstandingly fine.

Hymns and sequences: *Ave generosa; Columba aspexit; O Ecclesia; O Euchari; O Jerusalem; O ignis spiritus; O presul vere civitatis; O viridissima virga.*
*** Hyp. CDA 66039; *KA 66039* [id.]. Gothic Voices, Muskett, White, Page.

This record draws on the Abbess Hildegard of Bingen's collection of music and poetry, the *Symphonia armonie celestium revelationum* – 'the symphony of the harmony of celestial revelations'. These hymns and sequences, most expertly performed and recorded, have excited much acclaim – and rightly so. A lovely CD.

Hindemith, Paul (1895–1963)

Concert music for brass and strings, Op. 50; Viola concerto (Schwanendreher); Nobilissima visione.
☞ *** Decca Dig. 433 809-2 [id.]. San Francisco SO, Herbert Blomstedt.

Blomstedt's Hindemith triptych may help to defuse the idea that this is a grittily uningratiating composer. The three substantial works on the disc include his most sensuously beautiful score, *Nobilissima visione*, taken from a ballet about St Francis. Inspired by the frescos of Giotto in Florence, it ends with a noble *Passacaglia*. The *Concert music* is characteristic of Hindemith's early music, with its chunky tonal contrasts and emphatic rhythms set against a brief lyrical interlude. *Schwanendreher* is a concerto for viola (Hindemith's own instrument), based on German folk-themes, ending with a jolly set of variations. As in their previous Hindemith coupling of *Mathis der Mahler*, *Trauermusik* and the *Metamorphosis on themes of Weber*, Blomstedt and the orchestra bring out the warmth as well as the rugged power.

(i) *Concert music for brass and strings; Mathis der Maler* (symphony); (ii) *Viola concerto (Der Schwanendreher).*
(M) **(*) DG 423 241-2 [id.]. (i) Boston SO, Steinberg; (ii) Benyamini, O de Paris, Barenboim.

William Steinberg's accounts of *Mathis* and the *Concert music* are first class, even if the balance is a little recessed. Hindemith was a fine violist and *Der Schwanendreher* is based on folksongs and the unusual title (*The Swan-Turner*) is of the tune he uses in the finale. Benyamini and the Orchestre de Paris under Barenboim give a very full-bodied account of it.

Concert music for brass and strings, Op. 50; Nobilissima visione; (i) *Viola concerto (Der Schwanendreher).*
☞ ** Decca Dig. 433 809-2 [id.]. (i) Walther; San Francisco SO, Blomstedt.

Herbert Blomstedt's CD of the *Mathis der Maler* coupled with the *Trauermusik* and the *Symphonic metamorphoses on themes of Weber* is one of the mainstays of the modern Hindemith discography. The present disc is less successful: the performances have breadth and dignity in the best Blomstedt manner, but the sound is rather less persuasive. The opening of the *Konzertmusik* would sound less lumbering and ungainly had the engineers adopted a slightly more backward balance; and the wind in *Der Schwanendreher* certainly need more space round them. Geraldine Walther is a brilliant and thoughtful soloist, and Blomstedt gives a thoroughly felt account of the *Nobilissima visione* suite.

Concert music for brass and strings, Op. 50; Symphonic metamorphoses on themes of Weber; Symphony in E flat.
☞ (M) ** Sony SMK 47566 [id.]. NYPO, Bernstein.

The *Concert music* and the *Symphonic metamorphoses* are much recorded and, although Bernstein's performances are vital and brilliantly played, the rather coarse (1961) recording of the former is not an asset to the music's presentation. The 1968 quality in the *Symphonic metamorphoses* is fuller; if not particularly refined it is acceptable, as is the sound in the *Symphony*, recorded a year earlier, also in the unflattering Avery Fisher Hall. Bernstein's performance teems with energy in the first movement of this eloquent and surprisingly little-heard piece. Those seeking a modern version will turn to Yan Pascal Tortelier on Chandos (CHAN 9060), but Bernstein's account is very charismatic and triumphs over the shallow sound.

Cello concerto; (i) *Clarinet concerto.*

*** Etcetera KTC 1006 [id.]. Tibor de Machula; (i) George Pieterson; Concg. O, Kondrashin.

The *Cello concerto* is exhilarating and inventive, and Tibor de Machula proves an excellent protagonist. The *Clarinet concerto* is lyrical and eventful. The recordings (made in the Concertgebouw, Amsterdam) are public performances and emanate from the Hilversum Radio archives.

(i) *Cello concerto;* (ii) *The Four Temperaments* (Theme and variations for piano and strings).

☞ *** Chan. Dig. CHAN 9124 [id.]. (i) Raphael Wallfisch; (ii) Howard Shelley; BBC PO, Tortelier.

Both the *Cello concerto* and *The Four Temperaments* come from 1940, the year in which Hindemith settled in the United States. The concerto is very different in character from its predecessor from the *Kammermusik* collection, and was written for Piatigorsky and the Boston Symphony, who premièred it in 1941. It is vintage Hindemith and well worth adding to your collection, though it is not as inspired as *The Four Temperaments.* This began life as a score for Massine, written to illustrate various paintings by Brueghel. The idea came to nothing, but the score on which he had embarked found its way into a ballet by Balanchine. This is based on the Ancient Greek idea that the health of the body depends on the proper balance of the four humours: the melancholic, the sanguine, the phlegmatic and the choleric. Hindemith's four variations are ingenious and subtle and are splendidly realized by Howard Shelley and the BBC Philharmonic under Yan Pascal Tortelier. Raphael Wallfisch is the eloquent soloist in the *Cello concerto.* The Chandos recording is very good indeed. These recordings set new standards in both works.

Kammermusik Nos. 1 for 12 instruments, Op. 24/1; (i) *2 (Piano concerto), Op. 36/1;* (ii) *3 (Cello concerto), Op. 36/2;* (iii) *4 (Violin concerto), Op. 36/3;* (iv) *5 (Viola concerto), Op. 36/4;* (v) *6 (Viola d'amore concerto), Op. 46/1;* (vi) *7 (Organ concerto), Op. 46/2; Kleine Kammermusik for wind quintet, Op. 24/2.*

☞ *** Decca Dig. 433 816-2 (2). (i) Brautigam; (ii) Harrell; (iii) Kulka; (iv) Kaskkashian; (v) Blume; (vi) van Doeselaar; Concg. O, Chailly.

The seven pieces Hindemith called *Kammermusik* were written, as their opus numbers indicate, in three batches. They all come from the 1920s: No. 1 (for twelve instruments, including accordion) from 1921; the next, the concertos for piano, cello and violin, from 1924–5; and the concertos for Hindemith's own instrument, the viola, for the viola d'amore, which he also played, and for the organ all come from 1927. The miniature *Concerto for Cello and ten instruments* is probably the most often heard and was composed for his brother, Rudolf. The *Violin concerto* was composed for Licco Amar, the leader of the Amar Quartet, of which Hindemith himself was violist. Described as a kind of twentieth-century equivalent of the *Brandenburg concertos,* they show Hindemith at his most fertile and inventive and are mandatory listening. Those who think of Hindemith in terms of some of the more academic neo-Baroque works of his later years (such as the *Octet* or the *Sixth String quartet*) will find these all highly refreshing and imaginative. The set also includes the delightful little *Wind quintet (Kleine Kammermusik),* one of his most frequently performed pieces. This set supersedes its predecessors in every way, not least in the exemplary quality of the Decca recording. The playing of the distinguished soloists and the members of the Concertgebouw is beyond praise.

(i; ii) *Kammermusik No. 3 (Cello concerto), Op. 36/2;* (i) *Sonata for solo cello, Op. 25;* (iii) *Kleine Kammermusik, Op. 24/2.*

☞ **(*) Nuova Era Dig. 7075 [id.]. (i) Luco Signorini; (ii) Solisti dell' Academia Musicale Napoletana, Franco Trinca; (iii) Quintetto Scarlatti.

No quarrels with any of these performances; the *Kleine Kammermusik* is given with wit and spirit by the Quintetto Scarlatti, and Luco Signorini and his Neapolitan musicians give a very musicianly and characterful account of the *Cello concerto* that can hold its own alongside the splendid Concertgebouw account from Lynn Harrell, and that is no mean praise! The sound is well balanced, clear and warm throughout. Signorini is a virtuoso of the old order for whom everything is subservient to purely musical considerations, and he makes out a much better case for the rather arid *Sonata for solo cello* than many of his predecessors on disc (including Kurt Reher on a transparent vinyl 78-r.p.m. disc which R.L. still has). However, the playing time is only 43 minutes and, good though it is, it cannot rate an outright recommendation when such a competitive alternative as the Chailly complete set of *Kammermusik* is on the market.

(i; iii) *Clarinet concerto*. (ii; iii) *Horn concerto*. (iii) *Concert music for brass and strings, Op. 50; Nobilissima visione: suite; Symphonia serena*. (iv–v) *Scherzo for viola and cello*. (iv) *Sonata for solo viola, Op. 25/1*. (iv–vi) *String trio No. 2*.

☞ (M) *** EMI mono/stereo CDC5 55032-2 (i) Louis Cahuzac; (ii) Dennis Brain; (iii) Philh. O, cond. composer; (iv) composer (viola); (v) Emanuel Feuermann; (vi) Szymon Goldberg.

At last EMI have restored virtually all the records Hindemith made with the Philharmonia Orchestra in 1956, which originally ran to three Columbia blue-label LPs. (The only omission is the *Symphony in B flat for concert band*, which appeared on a single CD in 1990.) Particularly welcome is the *Clarinet concerto*, written for Benny Goodman in 1947 and played here by the French virtuoso, Louis Cahuzac, whose pioneering account of the Nielsen concerto is also back in currency. A good track to sample is the second movement, which is full of high spirits and wit and which sounds amazingly present and vivid. Dennis Brain's classic account of the *Horn concerto* and the 1956 version of the *Nobilissima visione* suite are both well known, but the *Symphonia serena* has not been reissued in the UK since the 1950s and is a splendid affair, a useful supplement to Yan Pascal Tortelier's newly recorded version with the BBC Philharmonic. Of particular interest to Hindemithians will be the pre-war collectors' items featuring Hindemith's viola playing: the 1934 Abbey Road recordings of the *Sonata for solo viola* and the *String trio No. 2* with Szymon Goldberg and Emanuel Feuermann, along with the *Scherzo for viola and cello*, written between 5 a.m. and 8 a.m. on the day of the recording to fill up the sixth side of the *Trio*! The *Clarinet concerto* makes its first appearance in stereo and, as we have suggested, sounds astonishingly good – but then so do all the Philharmonia recordings. Each of the two discs lasts nearly 80 minutes and offers exceptional value. Recommended to all who like Hindemith, as well as those who think they don't!

Viola concerto (Der Schwanendreher).
☞ *** EMI Dig. CDC7 54101-2 [id.]. Tabea Zimmermann, Bav. RSO, David Shallon – BARTOK: *Viola concerto*. ***

Record companies are not their own best friends. To encumber such an excellent performance of Hindemith's *Der Schwanendreher* with such meagre playing-time and so reduce its attractiveness to the public is unfair to both the collector, the artists and the engineers. Everything about this performance is excellent – indeed it is arguably the best now before the public – and is certainly better recorded than the rather cool sound Decca get for Geraldine Walther and Blomstedt in San Francisco. If you are prepared to pay full price for such short measure, you will be well rewarded in terms of both artistic and technical quality.

Violin concerto.
☞ (M) **(*) Sony SMK 47599-2. Isaac Stern, NYPO, Bernstein – NIELSEN: *Clarinet concerto* etc. **(*)

While the composer's own recording with David Oistrakh has a unique authority, this alternative account is also very fine indeed. Stern plays with eloquence and Bernstein's accompaniment is sympatehtic. In places it scores over the composer's own (towards the very end of the slow movement, for example) but the recording is less vividly detailed than the Decca. A curious coupling, however.

(i) *Violin concerto;* (ii) *Mathis der Maler (Symphony);* (iii) *Symphonic metamorphoses on themes of Weber*.
🏵 (M) *** Decca 433 081-2 [id.]. (i) David Oistrakh, LSO, composer; (ii) SRO, Kletzki; (iii) LSO, Abbado.

Oistrakh's performance of the Hindemith *Violin concerto* is a revelation. The composer, clearly inspired by the marvellous contribution of his soloist, provides an overwhelmingly passionate accompaniment and the 1962 recording still sounds extraordinarily vivid and spacious. The Rosette is for the concerto but the couplings are well chosen, both also offering vintage late 1960s Decca sound. Abbado's *Symphonic metamorphoses on themes of Weber* is second to none. Kletzki's account of *Mathis der Maler* is also impressive, very well prepared and with a similar attention to detail. He, too has the advantage of finely balanced and truthful recording, and the Suisse Romande Orchestra still plays very well for him. With 77 minutes of music offered, this is an indispensable disc for all Hindemithians, even if some duplication is involved.

(i) *The Four Temperaments; Nobilissima visione*.
**(*) Delos Dig. D/CD 1006 [id.]. (i) Carole Rosenberger; RPO, James de Preist.

The Four Temperaments, a set of variations, is one of Hindemith's finest and most immediate works.

Carole Rosenberger gives a formidable reading of this inventive and resourceful score. James de Preist also secures responsive playing from the RPO strings and gives a sober, well-shaped account of the *Nobilissima visione* suite, doing justice to its grave nobility.

Mathis der Maler (symphony).
☞ (*) Teldec/Warner mono 9031 76440-2 [id.]. BPO, composer – STRAVINSKY: *Jeu de cartes*. (*)

(i) *Mathis de Maler* (symphony); (ii) *String quartet No. 2, Op. 22;* (iii) *String trio No. 2.*
☞ (**) Koch Schwann mono 3-1134-2 [id.]. (i) BPO, Hindemith; (ii) Amar Qt; (iii) Goldberg, Hindemith, Feuermann.

Hindemith made two records of the *Mathis symphony*, both with the Berlin Philharmonic, one in 1934 and the second in 1955. This is the pioneering account, made only a year after Hitler's advent to power and at the height of the controversy that enveloped the opera right from its inception. The present performance was much admired in its day, and the 78s were eminently satisfactory. Writing of its post-war LP transfer, the authors of *The Record Guide* were critical of its tonal deficiencies, and the Teldec transfer does not do justice to the Berlin strings. Moreover it offers short measure in the form of Stravinsky's *Jeu de cartes* at well under 50 minutes. The Koch transfer is better, and the coupling is valuable in that it offers the *Second String quartet*, recorded in 1927 by the Amar Quartet in which Hindemith was the violist and his brother, Rudolph, the cellist. The copy used for the transfer is not without blemish – and nor is the playing. The transfer of the *String trio* is not as good as in the EMI set, but the disc makes a useful supplement to it.

Mathis der Maler (symphony); *Concert music, Op. 50; Symphonic metamorphoses on themes by Weber.*
*** DG Dig. 429 404-2 [id.]. Israel PO, Bernstein.

Mathis der Maler (symphony); *Symphonic metamorphoses on themes of Carl Maria von Weber; Trauermusik.*
*** Decca Dig. 421 523-2 [id.]. San Francisco SO, Blomstedt.

Blomstedt has a strong feeling for *Mathis der Maler* and presents a finely groomed and powerfully shaped performance, with lucid and transparent textures. The famous *Trauermusik* has an affecting quiet eloquence and dedication: the solo viola, Geraldine Walther, is exceptionally sensitive. Blomstedt's reading of the *Symphonic metamorphoses on themes of Carl Maria von Weber* is appropriately light in touch; and the recording is exemplary in the naturalness of its balance.

High-voltage Hindemith from Bernstein and the Israel Philharmonic; it was recorded live in the Robert Mann Auditorium in Tel Aviv whose dry acoustic is a handicap. In both the *Concert music for brass and strings* and the *Weber metamorphoses* the playing is exhilarating, and the *Mathis der Maler* performance is thrilling.

Sinfonia serena; Symphony (Die Harmonie der Welt).
☞ ⊛ *** Chan. Dig. CHAN 9217 (id.]. BBC PO, Yan Pascal Tortelier.

Two major works from the post-war years coupled together on an exemplary Chandos recording. The *Sinfonia serena* (1946) is a rarity: Hindemith himself recorded it with the Philharmonia Orchestra in the 1950s, but since then it has languished in obscurity. It is a brilliant and inventive score, full of humour and melody. Were audiences more inquiring, this piece would figure prominently on concert programmes. The scoring is inventive and imaginative, the textures varied and full of genial touches (one passage in the first movement has an accompaniment of wooden blocks, pizzicato strings and bass drum over which there is a delightful idea for cor anglais followed by piccolo). There is plenty of wit in the Scherzo, which paraphrases a Beethoven march from 1809. The *Symphony, Die Harmonie der Welt* (1951), is another powerful and consistently underrated score: Hindemith recorded it himself for DG not long after its composition, and Mravinsky's 1960s account was briefly available, but otherwise it too has suffered neglect. Like *Mathis der Maler*, it is related to an opera, in this case based on the life of the seventeenth-century astronomer, philosopher and musician, Johannes Kepler. The latter's attempts to relate the mathematical proportions in the structure of musical sounds to proportions in the orbits of the planets and his consequent excommunication from the Lutheran Church engaged Hindemith's sympathies. These well-prepared and finely shaped performances are given state-of-the-art recording quality. An outstanding issue.

Symphonic metamorphoses on themes by Weber.
*** Ph. Dig. 422 347-2 [id.]. Bav. RSO, C. Davis – REGER: *Mozart variations*. *** ⊛
☞ (M) **(*) EMI CDM5 65175-2 [id.]. Phd. O, Ormandy – BARTOK: *Miraculous Mandarin* etc.
   **(*)

Sir Colin Davis's account of the *Symphonic metamorphoses* is first class, though not perhaps as gutsy as Bernstein (DG). However, the reading has plenty of character and enormous finesse and is given state-of-the art Philips recording. Recommended with enthusiasm.

The Philadelphia Orchestra play with splendid panache and brilliance, the humour of the second movement perhaps realized less effectively in their hands than with, say, Blomstedt. In every other respect this is first class, and the recording is full-bodied and does justice to the Philadelphia sound.

Symphony in E flat; Overture Neues vom Tage; Nobilissima visione.
*** Chan. Dig. CHAN 9060 [id.]. BBC PO, Tortelier.

The *Symphony in E flat* is an inventive and resourceful score and is well worth investigating. Yan Pascal Tortelier gets excellent results from the BBC Philharmonic. Good, musicianly performances of *Nobilissima visione* and the much earlier *Neues vom Tage* Overture complete an admirable addition to the Hindemith discography.

Trauermusik (for viola and string orchestra).
☞ (M) *** EMI CDM5 65079-2 [id.]. ECO, Daniel Barenboim – BARTOK: *Divertimento for strings*;
     SCHOENBERG: *Verklaerte Nacht ***.

This piece of *Gebrauchsmusik* ('utility music') was written in 24 hours in January 1936 when the composer was informed of the death of King George V. Its gentle, elegiac quality was highly suitable for the occasion, and the piece – in four sections – is not too long and is enjoyable for its simple, restrained eloquence. It is excellently performed and recorded here, and the couplings are equally successful in a quite different way.

(i) *Alto saxophone sonata;* (ii) *Bass tuba sonata;* (iii) *Bassoon sonata;* (iv) *Morgenmusik;* (v) *Trio;* (vi) *Trombone sonata;* (vii) *Trumpet sonata.*
☞ ** BIS CD159 [id.]. (i) Savijoki, Siirala; (ii) Lind, Harlos; (iii) Sonstevold, Knardahl; (iv) Malmö
     Brass Ens.; (v) Pehrsson, Jonsson, Mjönes; (vi) Lindberg, Pöntinen; (vii) Tarr, Westenholz.

(i) *Alto horn sonata in E flat;* (ii) *Bass tuba sonata;* (i) *Horn sonata;* (iii) *Trombone sonata;* (iv) *Trumpet sonata.*
☞ (M) ** Sony SM2K 52671 (2) [id.]. (i) Mason Jones; (ii) Abe Torchinsky; (iii) Henry Charles
     Smith; (iv) Gilbert Johnson; Glenn Gould.

The *Alto saxophone sonata* and the *Alto horn sonata* are one and the same work. The BIS recordings were made at various times during the mid-1970s and early 1980s and, with the exception of the *Trombone sonata*, are analogue. They are for the most part rather closely balanced though not disturbingly so. The Sony recordings are all from 1976 but unfortunately do not offer the *Recorder trio*, expertly played on the BIS by Claes Pehrsson, Anders-Per Jonsson and Anders Mjönes, or the exhilarating *Morgenmusik* for brass – not to mention the inventive *Bassoon sonata*. On the other hand, Sony's mid-price two-CD set gives you the *Alto horn sonata* with Mason Jones. Glenn Gould has great feeling for Hindemith and plays with strong personality and commitment throughout, even though the tiresome vocalise is a strain. Despite the eminence of his soloists and the somewhat forward quality of the BIS balance, the latter is probably the safer recommendation.

Octet (for wind and strings).
(M) ** Sony SMK 46250 [id.]. Members of the Marlboro Festival – BARBER: *Summer music **(*)*;
     NIELSEN: *Woodwind quintet. **
☞ * Teldec/Warner Dig. 9031 73400-2 [id.]. Berliner Solisten with Elena Bashkirova – PROKOFIEV:
     Overture on Hebrew themes etc. *

Those unsympathetic to the composer will find Hindemith at his ugliest and most manufactured in the *Octet* (1957–8). However, the artists recorded on Sony play it more persuasively than most predecessors on disc. The close balance that Teldec provide for the excellent Berliner Solisten does not enhance its beauty.

(i) *Viola sonatas* (for viola and piano) *Op. 11/4; Op. 25/4;* (Unaccompanied) *Viola sonatas: Op. 11/5; Op. 25/1; Op. 31/4.*
*** ECM Dig. 833 309-2 (2) [id.]. Kim Kashkashian, (i) Robert Levin.

The solo *Sonatas* are played with superb panache and flair – and, even more importantly, with remarkable variety of colour – by Kim Kashkashian, who has an enormous dynamic range. The performances of the sonatas with piano are hardly less imaginative and the recording is good.

PIANO MUSIC

Berceuse; In einer Nacht, Op. 15; Kleines Klavierstück; Lied; 1922 Suite, Op. 26; Tanzstücke, Op. 19.
**(*) Marco Polo Dig. 8.223335 [id.]. Hans Petermandl.

Exercise in three pieces, Op. 31/I; Klaviermusik, Op. 37; Series of little pieces, Op. 37/II; Sonata, Op. 17; Two little piano pieces.
** Marco Polo Dig. 8.223336 [id.]. Hans Petermandl.

Ludus Tonalis; Kleine Klaviermusik, Op. 45/4.
** Marco Polo Dig. 8.223338 [id.]. Hans Petermandl.

Piano sonatas Nos. 1–3; Variations.
** Marco Polo Dig. 8.223337 [id.]. Hans Petermandl.

Hans Petermandl is an expert guide in this repertoire and presents it with real sympathy for, and understanding of, the idiom; his performances are very persuasive. The textures in Hindemith's piano music are often unbeautiful and less than transparent and, although neither the piano nor the acoustic of the Concert Hall of Slovak Radio is outstanding, the sound is perfectly acceptable.

Organ sonatas Nos. 1–3.
☞ *** Chan. Dig. CHAN 9097 [id.]. Piet Kee – REGER: *Four organ pieces.* ***

The *Sonatas* of Hindemith are one of the mainstays of the twentieth-century organ repertoire, and the appearance of this new CD restores them to their rightful place in the catalogue. (Neither Simon Preston (Argo) nor Peter Hurford (Decca) is currently in circulation.) Piet Kee plays on the Müller organ of St Bavo in Haarlem, an instrument more suited to Hindemith than the somewhat spacious acoustic in which it is recorded. This small point apart, Kee plays with his customary distinction and character. All three sonatas are rewarding, and no one investing in this disc is likely to be disappointed on either artistic or technical grounds.

When lilacs last in the dooryard bloom'd (Requiem).
*** Telarc Dig. CD 80132 [id.]. DeGaetani, Stone, Atlanta Ch. & SO, Robert Shaw.
(M) **(*) Sony/CBS MPK 45881. Louise Parker, George London, NY Schola Cantorum, NYPO, composer.

Robert Shaw commissioned Hindemith to compose this 'Requiem for those we loved' at the end of the 1939–45 war. It is one of the composer's most deeply felt works and one of his best. Shaw gives a performance of great intensity and variety of colour and nuance. Both his soloists are excellent, and there is both weight and subtlety in the orchestral contribution. Splendid recording.

On Sony, Hindemith himself is at the helm, so the performance carries a special authority. The music has surpassing beauty and eloquence. Louise Parker and George London are committed soloists and the recording has a full and realistic acoustic.

(i) Cardillac (opera) complete; (ii) Mathis der Maler: excerpts.
(M) *** DG 431 741-2 (2) [id.]. Fischer-Dieskau, Grobe, (i) Kirschstein, Kohn, Cologne R. Ch. & SO, Keilberth; (ii) Lorengar, Berlin RSO, Ludwig.

Taken from a radio performance, this reissue of *Cardillac* shows Hindemith at his most vigorous. Fischer-Dieskau as the goldsmith has a part which tests even his artistry, and though the other soloists are variable in quality the conducting of Keilberth holds the music together strongly. As a generous and ideal coupling, the second disc contains an hour of excerpts from Hindemith's even more celebrated opera, *Mathis der Maler*, again with Fischer-Dieskau taking the lead, and with Donald Grobe in a supporting role. Regina is beautifully sung by Pilar Lorengar. The 1960s recordings of both operas are excellently transferred, with voices full and fresh. No texts are given, but instead there are detailed summaries of the plots, with copious quotations.

Holloway, Robin (born 1943)

Second Concerto for orchestra, Op. 40.
☞ *** NMC Dig. D015M [id.]. BBC SO, Oliver Knussen.

Another valuable issue among those CD 'singles' marketed at a special price and devoted to new music. Holloway's *Second Concerto* made a powerful impression when it was first performed in 1979. The composer tells us that the background inspiration was a visit in 1977–8 to North Africa with its strong contrasts of colour and texture, opulence and austerity, brilliant light and dense shadow. It is a richly imaginative score and shows a sensitivity of high quality, as well as a considerable mastery of instrumental resource. The *Concerto* is a work of substance that is well worth getting to know and is well served by the BBC Symphony Orchestra and Oliver Knussen. The engineers produce a better sound from the Maida Vale Studios than we have heard on any other occasion.

(i) *Romanza for violin and small orchestra, Op. 31;* (ii) *Sea-surface full of clouds, Op. 28.*

☞ *** Chan. Dig. CHAN 9228 [id.]. (i) Gruenberg; (ii) Walmsley-Clark, Cable, Hill, Brett, Hickox Singers; City of L. Sinfonia, Richard Hickox.

Robin Holloway is one of the most imaginative of contemporary composers, and the two works recorded here show his sensitivity to colour and marvellous feeling for the orchestra. The *Sea-surface full of clouds* begins luminously, rather like Szymanowski, and has an at times magical atmosphere. There is an affecting and consuming melancholy about the *Romanza* for violin and orchestra. A composer of a refined intelligence and real sensibility.

Holmboe, Vagn (born 1909)

(i) *Cello concerto, Op. 120;* (ii) *Brass quintet, Op. 79;* (iii) *Triade, Op. 123;* (iv) *Benedic Domino, Op. 59.*

☞ *** BIS Analogue/Dig. CD-78 [id.]. (i) Bløndahl Bengtsson, Danish RSO, Ferencsik; (ii) Swedish Brass Quintet; (iii) Edward Tarr, Elisabeth Westenholz; (iv) Camerata Ch., Per Enevold.

An admirable introduction to the work of the doyen of Danish composers. Vagn Holmboe's magificent *Cello concerto*, along with the Dutilleux *Concerto*, is one of the finest examples of the genre to have appeared in recent years; it is the most substantial piece on the present CD. In Holmboe's music it is the subtle shaping of thematic ideas and their organic transformation that constitute the basis of his musical processes. The textures are transparent and luminous, and the music inhabits a distinctive world of its own. The ideas heard at the outset provide the basis for almost all the subsequent developments; there is a gentle figure on the strings, muted and pianissimo, restless and questioning, that occurs at about two minutes in, which is quite haunting. An excellent performance of an eloquent work. The choral piece, *Benedic Domino*, is one of a cycle of motets comprising the *Liber canticorum*, composed in the 1950s, that have an austere beauty and elevation of feeling that is rare in contemporary music. The *Brass quintet* (1961) is an effective and stirring piece, written for the New York Brass Quintet; and the *Triade* for trombone and organ comes from the 1970s, as does the *Cello concerto*, and is hardly less striking. Only the *Quintet* is a digital recording but its companions here are also strikingly good as sound.

Symphonies Nos. (i) *4 (Sinfonia sacra), Op. 29. 5, Op. 35.*

☞ **(*) BIS Dig. CD 572 [id.]. (i) Jutland Op. Ch.; Aarhus SO, Owain Arwell Hughes.

The *Fifth Symphony* makes a good entry point into Holmboe's world. Its opening movement has an extraordinary vitality and a marvellous sense of line. In outlook it is strongly tonal and neo-classical: the Stravinsky of the *Symphony in C* briefly comes to mind, but Holmboe is very much his own man and a distinctive musical landscape is immediately established. There is a strong sense of organic continuity; new ideas appear exactly where you feel they should and there is a communicative urgency about the score that makes it all the more puzzling to think that it has taken almost half a century to reach the gramophone. The only word to describe its outer movements is exhilarating. The slow movement has a modal character, but an anguished outburst in the middle serves as a reminder that this is a wartime work, composed in 1944 during the dark days of the Nazi occupation. The *Fourth (Sinfonia sacra),* written in 1941 and revised in 1945, is a six-movement choral piece dedicated to the memory of his brother who perished in a Nazi concentration camp. It encompasses a bracing vigour and underlying optimism alongside moments of sustained grief. Very good performances, though the strings are a little under-strength and the acoustic is on the dry side. But don't let this put you off this inspiriting music.

Symphonies Nos. 6, Op. 43; 7, Op. 50.

☞ **(*) BIS Dig. CD 573. Aarhus SO, Owain Arwell Hughes.

Holmboe's *Sixth Symphony* is a much darker piece than its predecessor. Its opening fourths bear a superficial kinship with Bartók (he, too, spent a good deal of time in the Balkans studying folk music in the 1930s), but any resemblance soon fades. This is a distinctively Nordic world and the brooding, slow-moving fourths of the long introduction prompt astronomical analogies: one seems to be surveying some forces in outer space; and there is writing of great luminosity too. Some of the climaxes in the quicker sections are a bit overscored, but as a whole this is a very powerfully argued and eloquent work. The one-movement *Seventh Symphony* is a highly concentrated score, individual in both form and content, which encompasses great variety of pace and mood. The three intermedia which punctuate it are wonderfully luminous. Owain Arwell Hughes, who stepped into the breach at a few days' notice to make this record, acquits himself very well. Frandsen's 1975 recording had the benefit of weightier and more opulent string-tone and a richer, warmer acoustic, but this is music that speaks with so strong and distinctive a voice that it is self-recommending. There are few if any Nordic symphonies post-Nielsen and -Sibelius of this quality.

String quartets Nos. 1, Op. 46; 3, Op. 48; 4, Op. 63.
☞ *** Marco Polo Dacapo Dig. CDDC 9203 [id.]. Kontra Qt.

The quartet medium has fascinated Holmboe all his life; he composed his first in 1926 when he was seventeen and followed it with nine more before feeling confident about publishing his first numbered quartet, Op. 46, in 1949. As a result the influences of Bartók and Hindemith are completely absorbed and a distinctive voice emerges. These quartets have a certain reserve: nothing is overstated, everything is quietly but cogently argued and, once one has broken through its reticence, its rewards are rich. This issue is the first in a complete survey from the Kontra Quartet, and if all the performances are as committed as this it will be a landmark in the catalogue. A previous cycle by the Copenhagen Quartet never reached completion. This is easily the finest post-war quartet cycle in Scandinavia, and those who respond to the quartets of Shostakovich or Robert Simpson should lose no time in investigating them.

Holst, Gustav (1874–1934)

(i) *Beni Mora (oriental suite), Op. 29/1; A Fugal overture, Op. 40/1; Hammersmith – A Prelude and scherzo for orchestra, Op. 52;* (ii) *Japanese suite;* (i) *Scherzo (1933/4); A Somerset rhapsody, Op. 21.*
*** Lyrita SRCD 222 [id.]. (i) LPO; (ii) LSO; Boult.

Beni Mora (written after a holiday in Algeria) is an attractive, exotic piece that shows Holst's flair for orchestration vividly. Boult clearly revels in its sinuosity. *The Japanese suite* is not very Japanese, although it has much charm, particularly the piquant *Marionette dance* and the innocuous *Dance under the cherry tree*. The most ambitious work here is *Hammersmith*, far more than a conventional tone picture, intensely poetic. Although conceived for military band, it was orchestrated a year later (1931). The *Scherzo*, from a projected symphony that was never completed, is strong, confident music. The *Somerset rhapsody* is unpretentious but very enjoyable, and the brief, spiky *Fugal overture* is given plenty of lift and bite to open the concert invigoratingly. As with other records in this Lyrita series the first class analogue recording has been splendidly transferred to CD.

Brook Green suite for strings; Capriccio for orchestra; (i) *Double violin concerto, Op. 49;* (ii) *Fugal concerto for flute, oboe and strings, Op. 40/2. The Golden Goose* (ballet music, arr. Imogen Holst), *Op. 45/1;* (iii) *Lyric movement for viola and small orchestra. A Moorside suite: Nocturne* (arr. for strings); *2 Songs without words, Op. 22.*
☞ **(*) Lyrita SRCD 223 [id.]. ECO, Imogen Holst, with (i) Emanuel Hurwitz, Kenneth Sillito; (ii) William Bennett, Peter Graeme; (iii) Cecil Aronowitz.

Although not all of this is top-quality Holst, the programme is generous (75 minutes) and there are some interesting rarities here. The *Capriccio* was originally written on an American commission for 'jazz band', but was never performed because it lacked the essential folk-theme. Rescued by the composer's daughter, who arranged it for more conventional orchestra (if with some unexpected brass and percussion), it proves an exuberant piece, with some passages not at all capriccio-like. *The Golden Goose* was written as a choral work for St Paul's Girls' School; these orchestral snippets were put together by Imogen Holst and, if comparatively slight, reflect the sharpness of an imagination which was often inspired by the needs of an occasion. The *Double concerto*, with its bi-tonality and cross-rhythms, is grittier and with much less obvious melodic appeal, but it remains an interesting example of the late Holst. The first two movements of the *Fugal concerto* are much more appealing with their cool interplay of wind colour, particularly when the soloists are so distinguished. The *Lyric movement for viola and small orchestra* is certainly persuasive in the hands of Cecil Aronowitz and is one of the most beautiful of Holst's later pieces. The slow movement from the *Moorside suite* – originally written for brass band – is heard here in the composer's own arrangement for strings; and the concert is completed with the comparatively familiar *Brook Green suite* and two *Songs without words*, early works that are tuneful and colourful. All the performances are sympathetically authentic and the recording is well up to Lyrita's usual high standard.

Brook Green suite for string orchestra; (i) *A Fugal concerto, Op. 40/2;* (ii) *Lyric movement for viola and small orchestra; St Paul's suite for string orchestra, Op. 29/2. Arrangements of Morris dance tunes: Bean setting; Constant Billy; Country gardens; How d'ye do; Laudanum bunches; Rigs o'Marlow; Shepherd's hey.*

*** Koch Dig. 3-7058-2 [id.]. New Zealand CO, Nicholas Braithwaite; with (i) Alexa Still, Stephen Popperwell; (ii) Vyvyan Yendoll.

The Fugal concerto features concertante solos for flute and oboe and is a beautifully crafted triptych of miniatures; the rather more ambitious *Lyric movement* is hardly less appealing and is warmly played here by Vyvyan Yendoll, who has a fine, rich timbre. The New Zealand Chamber Orchestra respond sensitively and persuasively to Nicholas Braithwaite who is thoroughly at home in this repertoire. The textures of the *Brook Green suite* are pleasingly light and airy and in the *St Paul's suite* the gutsy opening *Jig* makes a complete contrast with the pianissimo delicacy of the *Ostinati*. The set of country dances is agreeably spontaneous. The recording is in the demonstration bracket.

Brook Green suite; (i) *Double violin concerto, Op. 49;* (ii) *Fugal concerto for flute, oboe and strings, Op. 40/2;* (iii) *Lyric movement for viola and small orchestra; 2 Songs without words, Op. 22; St Paul's suite, Op. 29/2.*

☞ *** Chan. Dig. CHAN 9270 [id.]. (i) Ward, Watkinson; (ii) Dobing, Hooker; (iii) Tees; City of L. Sinf., Hickox.

In every respect this latest Holst anthology from Chandos will be hard to beat. Hickox's collection brings together a delightful group of Holst's shorter pieces, including both of the suites he wrote for St Paul's Girls' School, not just the *St Paul's suite* but also the *Brook Green suite*. The most striking piece of all, a fine example of Holst's later, sparer style, is the *Double concerto* for two violins and small orchestra, very taut and intense. The delicacy of the solo playing in the central *Lament* of this fine work is matched by the ethereal pianissimo from Stephen Tees at the opening of the *Lyric movement* for viola and small orchestra, one of Holst's very last works, written for Lionel Tertis in 1933. Tees is satisfyingly rich-toned and, if not absolutely flawless on intonation, clear parallels with Vaughan Williams's viola writing are readily drawn. The woodwind playing is delightful here too, as is the gentle clarinet solo which opens the *Country song*, the first of Holst's two *Songs without words*; the second, appropriately, is more robust. The *Brook Green suite* is wonderfully fresh and there is a comparable lightness of touch at the opening of the delightful *Fugal concerto*, a nice example of early neo-classicism, which does not sound in the least pedagogic. The *St Paul's suite* combines infectious vigour in the outer movements with wistful delicacy in the *Ostinato* and an intensely felt *Intermezzo*. What matters throughout this programme is the surging warmth that Richard Hickox draws from his modest forces. The recording is superb – very real indeed.

Hammersmith: Prelude and scherzo, Op. 52.

(M) *** Mercury 432 009-2 [id.]. Eastman Wind Ens., Fennell – BENNETT: *Symphonic songs* ***; JACOB: *William Byrd suite* ***; WALTON: *Crown Imperial.* *** ⊛

Holst's highly original and characteristically individual piece is scored for 25 individual wind instruments (there is no doubling of parts in this recording). Fennell's pioneering stereo recording is superbly played by these expert students from the Eastman School, and the effect is totally spontaneous. The recording remains demonstration-worthy, though it dates from 1958!

Invocation for cello and orchestra, Op. 19/2.

*** BMG/RCA RD 70800. Lloyd Webber, Philh. O, Handley – DELIUS: *Concerto;* VAUGHAN WILLIAMS: *Folksongs fantasia.* ***

Holst's *Invocation for cello and orchestra* is a highly attractive and lyrical piece, well worth reviving. Both the performance and recording are of admirable quality. Recommended.

Military band suites Nos. 1 in E flat; 2 in F.

⊛ *** Telarc Dig. CD 80038 [id.]. Cleveland Symphonic Winds, Fennell – HANDEL: *Royal Fireworks music.* ***

☞ (M) *** EMI Dig. CDM5 65122-2 [id.]. Central Band of the RAF, Wing Commander Eric Banks – GRAINGER: *Lincolnshire posy* etc.; VAUGHAN WILLIAMS: *English folk songs suite.* ***

Holst's two *Military band suites* contain some magnificent music. Frederick Fennell's new versions have more gravitas though no less *joie de vivre* than his old Mercury set. They are magnificent, and the recording is truly superb – digital technique used in a quite overwhelmingly exciting way. The *Chaconne* of the *First Suite* makes a quite marvellous effect here. The playing of the Cleveland wind group is of the highest quality.

The new EMI/RAF version of the suites is extraordinarily successful. It has a great sense of style and conveys a marvellous projection of high spirits. The highly original *Song of the blacksmith* in the *Second suite* is particularly sharply characterized and throughout the band is in splendid form: the only blot is the dead-sounding bass drum at the end of the great *Chaconne* of the *First suite*. Wing Commander Banks could, with advantage, have taken this movement (or at least its closing section) a fraction more slowly, and perhaps next time he is recording for EMI he can persuade the producer, Brian Culverhouse, to borrow an orchestral bass drum and re-record just this movement again. The Vaughan Williams and Grainger couplings are just as distinguished; the recording throughout, made in Watford Town Hall, is in the demonstration bracket: it has crisp, clean transients and fine amplitude.

Military band suites Nos. 1–2. Hammersmith: Prelude and scherzo, Op. 52.
(BB) *** ASV CDQS 6021; *ZCQS 6021.* L. Wind O, Denis Wick – VAUGHAN WILLIAMS: *English folksong suite* etc. ***

The London performances have great spontaneity, even if they are essentially lightweight, especially when compared with the Fennell versions. The sound is first class.

The Perfect fool: ballet suite.
*** Collins Dig. 1124-2 [id.]. Philh. O, Barry Wordsworth – VAUGHAN WILLIAMS: *Job.* ***

Wordsworth conducts a colourful, warmly idiomatic performance of these popular ballet movements, vividly recorded.

The Planets (suite), *Op. 32.*
☞ *** Denon Dig. CO 75076 [id.]. King's College Ch., RPO, James Judd.
*** Decca Dig. 417 553-2; *417 553-4* [id.]. Montreal Ch. & SO, Dutoit.
*** Collins Dig. 1036-2 [id.]. LPO & Ch., Hilary Davan Wetton.
☞ (M) *** EMI CDM7 64748-2 [id.]. LPO, Boult (with G. Mitchell Ch.) – ELGAR: *Enigma variations.* ***
☞ *** DG Gold Dig. 439 011-2 [id.]. Berlin Ch., BPO, Karajan.
☞ (BB) *** DG 439 446-2 [id.]. Boston SO, Steinberg – ELGAR: *Enigma variations.* ***
☞ (M) *(**) Sony SMK 47567 [id.]. NYPO, Bernstein (with ELGAR: *Pomp and circumstance march No. 1* **(*)) – BARBER: *Adagio.* **(*)
☞ (M) ** EMI Dig. CDM7 64300-2 [id.]. Toronto SO & Ch., Andrew Davis – BRITTEN: *Young person's guide.* **

(i) *The Planets;* (ii) *Egdon Heath, Op. 47;* (iii) *The Perfect Fool* (suite); *Op. 39.*
☞ (M) *** Decca 440 318-2 [id.]. LPO, cond. (i) Solti, with LPO Ch.; (ii; iii) Boult.
☞ (B) *** EMI CDU5 65041-2 [id.]; *EU 565041-4.* (i) LPO Ch., LPO, Boult; (ii) LSO, Previn; (iii) RPO, Sargent.

(i) *The Planets;* (ii) *The Perfect Fool* (suite).
(B) *** Decca 433 620-2; *433 620-4* [id.]. (i) LAPO, Mehta; (ii) LPO, Boult.
(BB) **(*) Virgin/EMI Dig. VJ7 91457-2; *VJ7 91457-4* [id.]. RLPO, Mackerras.

(i) *The Planets;* (i) *St Paul's suite, Op. 29/2.*
☞ (BB) *** Tring Dig. TRP 007. RPO, Vernon Handley, (i) with Ladies of Ambrosian Ch.

An outstanding new version of *The Planets*, traditional in the best sense, yet full of imaginative detail. The RPO play marvellously under James Judd, while the Denon recording, very much in the demonstration class, is very spectacular, with a wide dynamic range – but not too wide for comfort. The glowing Walthamstow acoustics bring out Holst's many characteristically original touches of colour, and his special effects are superbly realized, not least the sonorously understated pedal towards the close of *Saturn*, and the contrasts between the subtle pianissimo combination of harp and strings and the fat brass chords at the end of a genially spirited *Uranus*. *Mars*, taken fast and pungently laced with percussion, is both ferocious and sinisterly evil, and the peaceful *Venus*, translucently beautiful (lovely horn and flute playing), is rich textured yet not voluptuous. *Mercury* sparkles and fizzes across the heavens with exquisitely light woodwind articulation and a delicious pianissimo coda. *Jupiter* blazes boisterously: here Judd unerringly builds the famous central melody to a gloriously expansive climax; then a tremendous splash from the percussion heralds the ebullient reprise. *Saturn* has a desperate melancholy: the string and brass bring a resigned desolation, and the gentle anguish of the clearly defined bass-line is very poignant. After the gleeful impetus of *Uranus*, *Neptune* makes a haunting conclusion, the King's College Choir entering gently but rapturously and fading into silence at the end. The feeling of mysticism is enhanced if the listener reduces the volume level slightly for this last piece – but this is not to criticize the balance, which is wholly natural, or the beauty and vividness of the overall sound-picture, for which Hiroshi Goto, the Denon producer, must receive the fullest credit.

Charles Dutoit's natural feeling for mood, rhythm and colour, so effectively used in his records of Ravel, here results in an outstandingly successful version, both rich and brilliant, and recorded with an opulence to outshine almost all rivals. It is remarkable that, whether in the relentless build-up of *Mars*, the lyricism of *Venus*, the rich exuberance of *Jupiter* or in much else, Dutoit and his Canadian players sound so idiomatic. The final account of *Saturn* is chillingly atmospheric.

Hilary Davan Wetton's set of *Planets* has a superb digital recording which creates a gripping sense of spectacle in *Mars*, given with a biting attack and forceful rhythms. After a delicately translucent *Venus*, combining serenity with restrained ardour, the delicacy of *Mercury* lacks the sharpest definition. But the resonance adds to the impact of *Jupiter* with its ebullient horns, although here the big tune could be more expansive. With potent, measured melancholy, *Saturn* moves to a forceful climax, dominated by the timpani; then *Uranus*, with its ringing brass chords and rollicking horns, makes a dramatic contrast, while *Neptune*'s ethereal chorus returns us to a silent infinity.

Those wanting a super-bargain digital set surely will not better the new Tring/RPO issue. Sumptuously recorded in St Augustine's Church, Kilburn, Vernon Handley's performance brings a traditional reading of considerable power, very well played by the RPO, who are obviously enjoying themselves. After a sinister opening, Handley builds the climax of *Mars* impressively and the well-separated closing chords have malignant impact. The noble tune of *Jupiter* develops a similar build-up of intensity, well maintained in the spirited reprise of the opening section which has a rumbustious coda. *Saturn*, too, brings a well-graduated, melancholy climax, and the choral diminuendo to silence in *Neptune* is beautifully managed by the Ambrosians. *Venus* is warm and beautiful rather than sensuous or withdrawn, and the resonance provides a lustrous *Mercury*, undoubtedly chimerical if less sharply etched than in some versions. But the sound overall is attractively rich, giving glowing orchestral colour, the horns expansively opulent. What makes this bargain disc especially worth considering is the bracingly fresh account of the *St Paul's suite*, offered as a bonus, with the arrival of *Greensleeves* near the end of the *Dargason* finale particularly deftly managed. The recording of the string body is also very realistic. For some reason Tring have decided to omit both overall timings and those of individual movements.

The Decca recording for Solti's Chicago version is extremely brilliant, with *Mars* given a vivid cutting edge at the fastest possible tempo. Solti's directness in *Jupiter* (with the trumpets coming through splendidly) is certainly riveting, the big tune red-blooded and with plenty of character. In *Saturn* the spareness of texture is finely sustained and the tempo is slow, the detail precise; while in *Neptune* the coolness is even more striking when the pianissimos are achieved with such a high degree of tension. The CD gives the orchestra great presence, and the addition of Boult's classic versions of *Egdon Heath* and *The Perfect Fool* ballet music makes this reissue very competitive and marginally preferable to the EMI alternative of the same three works.

It was Sir Adrian Boult who, well over 70 years ago, first 'made *The Planets* shine', as the composer put it, and in his ninetieth year he recorded it for the last time. It is a performance at once intense and beautifully played, spacious and dramatic, rapt and pointed. The great melody of *Jupiter* is calculatedly less resonant and more flowing than previously but is still affecting, and *Uranus* as well as *Jupiter* has its measure of jollity. The spacious slow movements are finely poised and the recording still stands up well, with added presence and definition, but in its latest remastering it is not quite as brilliant and full or as firmly focused as the competing Solti version. Previn's *Egdon Heath*, darkly intense, is very well transferred, while Sargent's account of the rip-roaring ballet music from *The Perfect Fool* will disappoint nobody and the early recording is extremely vivid – the opening trombones leap out from the speakers. Boult's performance is also available coupled with Elgar's *Enigma variations*.

Mehta's set of *Planets* set a new standard for sonic splendour when it was first issued in 1971. The new ADD transfer still provides outstanding sound, but there is a touch more edge on the strings and the quality has lost just a little of its richness and amplitude; though definition is sharper, the background hiss is fractionally more noticeable. Even so, this is a superb disc and a clear first bargain choice. As on the Solti *Planets*, Boult's splendid account of the ballet suite from *The Perfect Fool* has now been added. This was recorded a decade earlier, but the vintage Decca sound remains spectacular, with the LPO brass hardly less resplendent than their colleagues in Los Angeles.

On this new Classikon super-bargain reissue, recorded in 1971, Steinberg's Boston set of *Planets* was another outstanding version from a vintage analogue period. It remains one of the most exciting and involving versions and now sounds brighter and sharper in outline, though with some loss of opulence. *Mars* in particular is intensely exciting. At his fast tempo, Steinberg may get to his fortissimos a little early, but rarely has the piece sounded so menacing on record. The testing point for most will no doubt be *Jupiter*, and here Steinberg the excellent Elgarian comes to the fore, giving a wonderful *nobilmente* swagger.

Karajan's early (1981) digital recording has been remastered spectacularly, using Original-image-bit processing, in DG's Karajan Gold series, and the improvement in sound-quality is marked. It is spectacularly wide-ranging, while the marvellously sustained pianissimo playing of the Berlin Philharmonic – as in *Venus* and the closing pages of *Saturn* – is very telling indeed. *Mars* has great impact, and the sound, fuller and firmer in the bass, gives the performance throughout a gripping immediacy and presence. *Jupiter*, at its climax, still seems a bit fierce: ideally it needs a riper body of tone, although the syncopated opening erupts with joy, the unison horns are superbly robust, and the big melody has a natural flow and nobility. *Venus* brings sensuous string-phrasing, *Mercury* and *Uranus* have beautiful springing in the triplet rhythms, and the climax of that last movement brings an amazing glissando on the organ. In short this is a thrilling performance and highly recommendable, but it remains at full price and without a coupling.

Mackerras's usual zestful approach communicates readily and the Liverpool orchestra bring a lively response, but the over-reverberant recording tends to cloud the otherwise pungently vigorous *Mars*, and both *Venus* and *Saturn* seem a little straightforward and marginally undercharacterized, while again in the powerful climax of *Uranus* there is some blurring from the resonance. *The Perfect Fool*, with its vivid colouring and irregular rhythms, has much in common with *The Planets* and makes a fine coupling, especially when played with such flair.

Bernstein's 1971 version demonstrates the problems of recording in the Avery Fisher Hall: the close microphones bring a characteristically over-brilliant transatlantic balance, unflattering to the fortissimo violins, although adding edge to *Mars* and impact to *Uranus*. The performance is charismatic, with moments of striking individuality, not least in *Venus* which is touchingly restrained. The choral singing in *Neptune*, too, is most refined and the closing diminuendo very beautiful. *Jupiter* brings a boldly stoical treatment of the big central tune, comparable with the slow, dignified account of Elgar's famous melody in the *Pomp and circumstance march* which acts as a vivid encore.

Andrew Davis recorded *The Planets* with the Toronto orchestra as the first of a series for EMI, taking the players to a new and more helpful venue outside the city. Alas for good intentions, the results do not quite match those achieved in very similar circumstances by the Toronto orchestra's direct rival in Montreal. Though full and firm, the sound is not as open or as atmospheric as that on the finest versions (as, for example, Dutoit's Decca) and Davis's taut control of the music, with fast speeds in *Mars* and *Saturn* diminishing the relentlessness of the argument, makes the result sound just a little inhibited. It is a good, beefy account – but in so strong a field there are many finer versions.

Air and variations; 3 Pieces for oboe & string quartet, Op. 2.
*** Chan. Dig. CHAN 8392; *ABTD 1114* [id.]. Francis, English Qt – BAX: *Quintet;* MOERAN: *Fantasy quartet;* JACOB: *Quartet.* ***

The three pieces here are engagingly folksy, consisting of a sprightly little *March*, a gentle *Minuet* with a good tune, and a *Scherzo*. Performances are first class, and so is the recording.

VOCAL MUSIC

Choral hymns from the Rig Veda (Groups 1–4), *H. 97–100; 2 Eastern pictures for women's voices and harp, H. 112; Hymn to Dionysus, Op. 31/2.*
**(*) Unicorn Dig. DKPCD 9046; *DKPC 9046* [id.]. Royal College of Music Chamber Ch., RPO, Willcocks; Ellis.

The *Choral hymns from the Rig Veda* show Holst writing with deep understanding for voices, devising textures, refined, very distinctively his, to match atmospherically exotic texts. Though performances are not always ideally polished, the warmth and thrust of the music are beautifully caught. The *Hymn to Dionysus*, setting words from the *Bacchae* of Euripides in Gilbert Murray's translation, a rarity anticipating Holst's *Choral symphony*, makes a welcome and substantial fill-up, along with the two little *Eastern pictures*. Beautifully clean and atmospheric recording.

Choral hymns from the Rig Veda (Group 3), *H. 99, Op. 26/3.*
*** Hyp. CDA 66175 [id.]. Holst Singers & O; Davan Wetton; T. Owen – BLISS: *Lie strewn the white flocks;* BRITTEN: *Gloriana: Choral dances.* ***

The third group of *Choral hymns from the Rig Veda*, like the whole series, reveals Holst in his Sanskritic period at his most distinctively inspired. In this responsive performance, it makes an excellent coupling for the attractive Bliss and Britten items, atmospherically recorded.

The Cloud messenger, Op. 30; The Hymn of Jesus, Op. 37.
*** Chan. Dig. CHAN 8901; *ABTD 1510* [id.]. Della Jones, London Symphony Ch. & LSO,
  Richard Hickox.

Hickox's account of Holst's choral masterpiece, *The Hymn of Jesus*, dramatic and highly atmospheric,
easily outshines even Sir Adrian Boult's vintage version for Decca. Not only does modern digital
sound make an enormous difference in a work where the choral sounds are terraced so tellingly, but
Hickox secures tauter and crisper ensemble, as well as treating the sections based on plainchant with
an aptly expressive freedom. The long-neglected choral piece, *The Cloud messenger*, may lack the
concentration of *The Hymn of Jesus* but it brings similarly incandescent choral writing. Warmly and
positively realized by Hickox and his powerful forces, with Della Jones a fine soloist, it makes a
major discovery, whatever its incidental shortcomings. Rich and ample Chandos recording adds to
the involvement.

Dirge and Hymeneal, H. 124; 2 Motets, H. 159/60; 5 Part-songs, H. 61.
*** Conifer Dig. CDCF 142 [id.]. CBSO Ch., Halsey, R. Markham (piano) – ELGAR: *Scenes from
  the Bavarian Highlands.* ***

It is fascinating to find among these Holst part-songs the original musical idea that he used later in
the *Saturn* movement of *The Planets* suite, with the piano accompaniment pivoting back and forth.
That is from the *Dirge and Hymeneal*. The other items – all unaccompanied – bring writing just as
hauntingly lovely and original. Beautiful, refined performances, atmospherically recorded.

*The Evening watch, H.159; 6 Choruses, H.186; Nunc dimittis, H.127; 7 Partsongs, H.162; 2 Psalms,
H.117.*
*** Hyp. Dig. CDA 66329 [id.]. Holst Singers & O, Hilary Davan Wetton.

Having given us a splendid set of *Planets*, Hilary Davan Wetton now turns to the often more austere
but no less inspired choral music. *The Evening watch* creates a rapt, sustained pianissimo until the
very closing bars, when the sudden expansion is quite thrilling. The *Six Choruses* for male voices
show the composer at his most imaginative, while the comparable *Partsongs* for women often
produce a ravishingly dreamy, mystical beauty. The final song, *Assemble all ye maidens*, is a narrative
ballad about a lost love, and its closing section is infinitely touching. The performances are gloriously
and sensitively sung and unerringly paced.

OPERA

(i) *Savitri* (complete); (ii) *Dream city* (song cycle, orch. Matthews).
**(*) Hyp. Dig. CDA 66099 [id.]. (i) Langridge, Varcoe, Palmer, Hickox Singers; (ii) Kwella; City of
  L. Sinfonia, Hickox.

Felicity Palmer is more earthy, more vulnerable as Savitri than Janet Baker was in the earlier Argo
recording, her grainy mezzo well caught. Philip Langridge and Stephen Varcoe both sing sensitively
with fresh, clear tone, though their timbres are rather similar. Hickox is a thoughtful conductor both
in the opera and in the orchestral song-cycle arranged by Colin Matthews from Holst's settings of
Humbert Wolfe poems. Patrizia Kwella's soprano at times catches the microphone rather shrilly.

Holst, Imogen (1907–84)

String quartet No. 1.
*** Conifer Dig. CDCF 196. Brindisi Qt – BRIDGE: *3 Idylls;* BRITTEN: *String quartet No. 2.* ***

Imogen Holst's two-movement *Quartet* is a shortish work; although not strongly personal, it is full of
interest. Both performance and recording are of high quality.

Holt, Simon (born 1958)

. . . era madrugada . . .; Shadow realm; Sparrow night; (i) Canciones.
☞ *** NMC Dig. D008 [id.]. (i) Fiona Kimm; Nash Ens., Lionel Friend.

Among British composers of the younger generation there is none more thoughtful and concentrated
than Simon Holt, and, thanks to NMC, it is good to have at last a complete disc of his music.
Regularly he has found inspiration in Spanish sources, particularly Lorca, and two of the four pieces
are fine examples – *. . . era madrugada*, a sinister evocation of a Lorca poem about a man found

murdered in the hour just before dawn (*madrugada*). Like the other three pieces, it was written for the Nash Ensemble, who here under Lionel Friend respond superbly to Holt's virtuoso demands in writing that is often thorny in its textures – with Birtwistle an influence in the wind-writing – but totally clear in its purpose. Fiona Kimm is the formidable mezzo soloist in three Spanish settings, *Canciones*; but rather more approachable are the two highly atmospheric instrumental works, *Shadow realm* and *Sparrow night*, which round the disc off. These two also bring sinister nightmare overtones. From its eerie opening onwards, *Sparrow night* particularly shows Holt's acute aural imagination: music both atmospheric and sharp in focus. The superb recording is engineered by Holt's fellow-composer, Colin Matthews.

Holten, Bo (born 1948)

(i) *Clarinet concerto* (1987); (ii) *Sinfonia concertante for cello and orchestra* (1985–6).
☞ *** Chan. Dig. CHAN 9272 [id.] (i) Jens Schou; (ii) Morten Zeuten; Danish National RSO; (i) Jorma Panula; (ii) Hans Graf.

Bo Holten is a highly talented Danish composer now in his mid-forties and best known in the UK for his work as a choral conductor with the BBC Singers. The *Clarinet concerto* is certainly appealing. The *Sinfonia concertante* comes from a broadcast of 1987 and is long on complexity (36 minutes 6 seconds) and short on substance, but there are sufficient moments of poetic vision to encourage one to return to it. It is played with great zest and conviction by Morten Zeuten (cellist of the Kontra Quartet), and the recording has exemplary presence and clarity.

Honegger, Arthur (1892–1955)

Le chant de Nigamon; Monopartita; Napoleon (film incidental music); *Les hombres. Phaedre: Prelude. Prélude, fugue and postlude; The Tempest: Prelude.*
☞ **(*) Erato/Warner Dig. 2292 45862-2 [id.]. Monte Carlo PO, Constant.

Honegger wrote prolifically for the theatre and cinema, and much of the music he later extracted or refashioned for concert use is highly impressive. Despite its lack of intensity, a warm welcome must be given to this issue, for it fills in some important gaps in the Honegger discography – in particular the music for *Phaedre*, which is highly imaginative and atmospheric. The earliest work recorded here is *Le chant de Nigamon* (1917), a tone-poem concerning the fate of an American Indian chief who is burnt at the stake; and it is both graphic and powerful. The *Monopartita* is Honegger's last orchestral piece, coming from the same period as the *Fifth Symphony*. Again the invention is of the highest quality. Decent performances and acceptable, though not first-class, recorded sound.

(i) *Concerto da camera;* (ii) *Antigone;* (iii) *Petite suite.*
☞ *** Ph. Dig. 434 105-2 [id.]. Heinz Holliger, with (i) Nicolet, ASMF, Marriner; (ii) Ursula Holliger; (iii) Nicolet, Constable – MARTIN: *Trois danses* etc.; MARTINU: *Oboe concerto.* ***

A valuable release from Heinz and Ursula Holliger who are joined by Aurèle Nicolet in the *Concerto da camera*, a captivating score in Honegger's pastoral mode from the immediate post-war years and contemporaneous with the *Fourth Symphony* (*Deliciae Basilienses*). A splendid performance and recording of the concerto and the two smaller pieces add to the attractions of this civilized programme.

Cello concerto.
**(*) Ph. Dig. 432 084-2 [id.]. Julian Lloyd Webber, ECO, Yan Pascal Tortelier – FAURE: *Elégie* **; D'INDY: *Lied* **(*); SAINT-SAENS: *Concerto* etc. **(*)

Honegger's pastoral *Concerto* is a work of immense appeal. Lloyd Webber plays with refined musicianship and conveys the charm and character of this piece very effectively. He is well supported by Yan Pascal Tortelier, and the Philips recording is eminently natural and well balanced.

(i) *Cello concerto;* (ii) *Pastorale d'été.*
☞ (M) (***) EMI mono CDC5 55036-2 (i) Maurice Maréchal, Paris Conservatoire O; (ii) SO; composer – POULENC: *Aubade* etc. (***)

Honegger recorded a number of his own works, including the *Symphonie liturgique*. His 1930 account of the enchanting and atmospheric *Pastorale d'été* is coupled here with a wartime account of the *Cello concerto* by its dedicatee, Maurice Maréchal, made in 1943 and sounding remarkably fresh for its period. It is not a long piece, but what it lacks in length it makes up for in eloquence, character and elegance. A valuable addition to the 'Composer in Person' series.

Horace victorieux; Mermoz: La traversée des Andes; Le vol sur l'Atlantique; Pacific 231; Rugby; Pastoral d'été; La tempête: Prélude.
☞ *** DG Dig. 435 438-2 [id.]. Toulouse Capitole O, Plasson.

Michel Plasson and his fine Toulouse orchestra give excellent performances of these Honegger pieces. *Horace victorieux* comes from 1920–21 and was intended as a *symphonie mimée*, though it was not staged until 1927, long after it had established itself in the concert hall under Ansermet. It is a noisy score but full of imaginative touches, as are the two scenes recorded here for the film *Mermoz*. We are also offered a beautifully languorous account of *Pastoral d'été*, among the best committed to disc, and Plasson's accounts of *Pacific 231* and *Rugby* are full of high spirits. His version of the *Prélude*, composed for a production of Shakespeare's *Tempest* in the late 1920s, is as fierce and violent as the composer's own pioneering Parlophone 78-r.p.m. disc. DG provide a realistic and natural sound-picture with plenty of detail. Strongly recommended.

Nocturne; Pastorale d'été; (i) La Danse des morts.
☞ ** Calliope CAL 9855 [id.]. (i) Davy, Collart, Piquemal, Lassus Vocal Ens.; Jeune SO de Douai, Vachey.

Recordings of Honegger's *La Danse des morts* have been thin on the ground, though the pioneering version with Jean-Louis Barrault as the *récitant* and a cast including Charles Panzera under Charles Munch must have cast a long and intimidating shadow. Written in the wake of *Jeanne d'Arc au bûcher* during the months leading up to the Second World War, also to words of Claudel, *La Danse des morts* is a powerful and imaginative score, concentrated in atmosphere and marked by much depth of feeling. This analogue (1981) performance, performed by the Jeune Orchestre Symphonique de Douai, is first class in terms of youthful commitment and enthusiasm, and the recorded sound is very present. The Ensemble Vocale de Roland de Lassus is not always in tune, and the intonation of the soprano is also vulnerable, although both the baritone and spoken parts are very well done. However, this is such a marvellous score that in the absence of any alternative it must carry a recommendation. The disc offers another rarity in the *Nocturne for Orchestra* of 1936, not the equal of the *Pastoral d'été* in inspiration but, as always with Honegger, full of character and harmonic interest. The Douai Youth Orchestra are not quite up to the exposed divided string-writing with which it opens (and which returns in the closing section) and their expertise is strained elsewhere, but they play with real dedication. They do not, alas, possess all the tonal finesse required in the *Pastoral d'été*.

Pacific 231.
☞ **(*) Ph. Dig. 432 993-2 [id.]. O de Paris, Semyon Bychkov – MILHAUD: *Le bœuf sur le toit*; POULENC: *Les biches*. **(*)

Semyon Bychkov gives us a good ride on his train, though there are one or two oddities of balance (bassoons are very forward at one point), puzzling in so splendidly engineered an issue. It comes with goodish accounts of *Les biches* and *Le bœuf sur le toit*.

Symphonies Nos. 1; 2 for strings with trumpet obbligato; 3 (Symphonie liturgique); 4 (Deliciae Basilienses); 5 (Di tre re); Mouvement symphonique No. 3; Pacific 231; The Tempest: Prelude.
☞ (M) *** Sup. 11 1566-2 (2). Czech PO, Baudo.

These performances come from the 1960s, but they are more than merely serviceable. The sound comes up very well indeed and the playing of the Czech Philharmonic for Baudo is totally committed. The performance of the *Fifth Symphony* has never been surpassed (except possibly by the pioneering Munch recording) and has amazing presence and detail for its period. This collection is much to be preferred to the Plasson set on EMI.

Symphony No. 1; Pastorale d'été; 3 Symphonic movements: Pacific 231; Rugby; No. 3.
*** Erato/Warner Dig. 2292 45242-2 [id.]. Bav. RSO, Dutoit.

Honegger's *First Symphony* is a highly stimulating and rewarding piece. Charles Dutoit gets an excellent response from the Bavarian Radio Symphony Orchestra, who produce a splendidly cultured sound and particularly beautiful phrasing in the slow movement. Dutoit also gives an atmospheric and sympathetic account of the *Pastorale d'été* and in addition offers the *Three Symphonic movements*, of which *Pacific 231* with its robust and vigorous portrait of a railway engine is by far the best known.

Symphony No. 2 for strings and trumpet.
☞ *** Delos Dig. DE 3121 [id.]. Seattle SO, Gerard Schwarz – R. STRAUSS: *Metamorphosen;*
  WEBERN, arr. Schwarz: *Langsamer satz*. ***

Gerard Schwarz follows up his splendid recordings of modern American works, including William Schuman's *Symphony for strings*, with two more wartime works for this medium, Honegger's *Second Symphony* and Strauss's *Metamorphosen*. In terms of recording quality, his account can hold its own alongside the very best, and the playing of the Seattle strings is splendidly responsive. He is just a bit too slow at the very beginning (conductors like Karajan and Munch manage to convey a sense of movement as well as darkness and introspection) and the same reservation could be made against the slow movement, but there is plenty of atmosphere. Although it does not displace the Jansons or Karajan accounts or other recommendations, this performance is very fine indeed and will give much pleasure.

Symphonies Nos. 2 & 3 (Symphonie liturgique).
⊛ (M) *** DG 423 242-2 [id.]. BPO, Karajan.

Symphonies Nos. 2 for strings and trumpet obbligato; 3 (Liturgique); Pacific 231.
☞ ⊛ *** EMI Dig. CDC5 55122-2 [id.]. Oslo PO, Jansons.

Jansons's account of these two symphonies is the first successful challenge to the classic Karajan record from the 1970s. It is arguably the Oslo orchestra's best record to date. The playing has a virtuosity and tonal sophistication that are almost the equal of the Berliners' sumptuous string-tone in the *Symphony for strings*, and superb concentration and control. The recording is magnificently rich and present, detail is splendidly focused. The *Symphonie liturgique* is thrilling in their hands, and there is an excellent account of *Pacific 231* as well. This can now serve as a key recommendation in the Honegger discography and, though it does not displace the Karajan, one never knows how long that will remain in circulation.

  Karajan's CD includes arguably the finest versions of any Honegger works ever put on record. In No. 2 the Berlin strings have extraordinary sensitivity and expressive power, and Karajan conveys the sombre wartime atmosphere to perfection. At the same time, there is astonishing refinement of texture in the *Liturgique*, whose slow movement has never sounded more magical. The recording was always one of DG's best, and this transfer brings to life more detail and greater body and range. A great record, completely in a class of its own.

Symphonies Nos. 2 for strings with trumpet obbligato; 4 (Deliciae Basilienses); Pastorale d'été;
Prélude, arioso et fughette sur le nom de Bach (for strings).
*** Virgin/EMI Dig. VC7 59064-2 [id.]. Lausanne CO, Jesús López-Cobos.

In the *Fourth Symphony* (*Deliciae Basilienses*) Jesús López-Cobos and the Lausanne orchestra correspond in scale to the forces used in the first performance by Paul Sacher and his Basle Chamber Orchestra who commissioned it. Both symphonies are given with great sensitivity and atmosphere; and so, too, are the *Pastorale d'été*, a most poetic account, and the *Prélude, arioso et fughette sur le nom de Bach*, a 1936 transcription of a piano piece written four years earlier. Excellent performances which, while they do not displace Karajan in the *Second Symphony* or Munch in the *Fourth*, can be recommended alongside them – no mean compliment! They are superbly recorded.

Symphonies Nos. 2 for strings; 5 (Di tre re).
(M) (***) BMG/RCA mono/stereo GD 60685 [60685-2-RG]. Boston SO, Charles Munch –
  MILHAUD: *La création du monde* etc. ***

Charles Munch made the first recordings of both *Symphonies*; in fact this transfer of the *Fifth* is one of them. The *Second*, made in 1953, is a bit harder-driven than his later version with the Orchestre de Paris. The performance of the *Fifth* is full of character though the sound is a bit dry. The witty and enigmatic middle movement has never been surpassed on record. Some (but relatively little) allowance needs to be made for the actual sound-quality of the 1952 mono recording.

Symphony No. 3 (Symphonie liturgique).
☞ *(*) Capriccio Dig. 10428 [id.]. Stuttgart R. SO, Marriner – BRITTEN: *Sinfonia da requiem*. **

The *Symphonie liturgique* is decently played and recorded except in the finale, which is distinctly lacking in power and vitality. The Stuttgart Radio strings are wanting in weight and opulence. But there is nothing particularly special about Marriner's reading and, given both the quality and quantity of rival versions (and particularly Karajan's classic reading), this hybrid issue is uncompetitive; but even were it all-Honegger or all-Britten, this verdict would, alas, still hold.

Symphonies Nos. 3 (Symphonie liturgique); 5 (Di tre re); Chant du joie; Pacific 231; Pastoral d'été.
(M) *** Sup. 11 0667-2. Czech PO, Serge Baudo.

Symphonies Nos. 3; 5; Pacific 231.
☞ *** Chan. Dig. CHAN 9176 [id.]. Danish Nat. R. O, Järvi.

Honegger's *Symphonie liturgique*, composed at the conclusion of the Second World War, is one of his greatest achievements, just as *Pacific 231* is one of his most onomatopoeic. The latter has thundered along the tracks to more striking effect than it does here (Honegger himself steered it more briskly into the station in the days of steam), but the two symphonies are splendidly played and recorded. The *Symphonie liturgique* has stiff competition to meet in the classic Karajan account from the 1970s (one of the greatest orchestral records he made with the Berlin Philharmonic), but Neeme Järvi and the Danish orchestra serve it very well indeed, and the digital Chandos recording is even more detailed and present, and certainly fuller, than the DG version. Järvi's version of the *Fifth Symphony* is also masterly, even if it does not match the hell-for-leather abandon of Baudo's Supraphon set. But that is now over 30 years old and, though it still sounds pretty amazing, this is undeniably superior.

Serge Baudo's 1960s recording of the *Fifth* still remains among the very best versions of the work, superior in sonic terms to the Munch and infinitely more vital than the Dutoit. The *Liturgique* is not quite in the Karajan class but it is very good indeed as are the remaining pieces on offer. Given the modest price of this disc plus the generous playing time, this deserves a very strong recommendation.

Symphony No. 4 (Deliciae Basilienses).
(M) *** Erato/Warner 2292 45689-2 [id.]. French Nat. RSO, Munch – DUTILLEUX: *Métaboles.* ***

Munch's 1967 account of the delightful *Fourth Symphony* remains by far the most characterful on disc – it is to be preferred to any of the full-price rivals and has the right blend of energy and atmosphere. The recording is also eminently acceptable. An additional attraction is the interesting coupling. Strongly recommended.

Le cahier Romand; 2 Esquisses; Hommage à Albert Roussel; 3 Pièces (2 sets); 7 Pièces brèves;
Prélude, arioso et fughette sur le nom de Bach; Sarabande; Souvenir de Chopin; Toccata et variation.
☞ *(*) Koch/Schwann Dig. 3-1220-2 [id.]. Annette Middelbeek.

Honegger's piano music is a small but far from unrewarding area of his output which has received relatively little attention on CD. (Its neglect may be understandable up to a point as it offers few opportunities for overt pianistic display of the kind favoured by Bartók or Prokofiev.) The last complete survey by Jürg von Vintschger appeared over 20 years ago on a Vox-Turnabout LP. Despite her clearer digital sound, the Dutch pianist Annette Middelbeek proves a good deal less persuasive; her command of keyboard colour is limited and she seems unresponsive and unsubtle in her handling of tone. She is obviously an intelligent player, but the sound is just a little too monochrome to advance the cause of this repertoire.

Les aventures du Roi Pausole.
☞ **(*) MGM Musiques Suisses Dig. CD 6114 (2) [id.]. Bacquier, Sénéchal, Barbaux, Yakar, Basle Madrigalists, Swiss Youth PO, Maro Venzàgo.

One doesn't associate Honegger with light operetta, but this is exactly what *Les aventures du Roi Pausole* is. Moreover it was very successful in its day, notching up 400 performances in Paris and as many in the rest of France. It was composed in 1929–30, at the same time as the *Cello concerto* and the *First Symphony*, and is an almost unqualified delight. The libretto by Albert Willemetz, based on a book by Pierre Louÿs (who had intended it for Debussy), has both wit and pace, and the score itself sparkles. The models are Mozart, Chabrier, Messager and Offenbach, and the invention is often piquant and, at its best, memorable. The singing is lively and characterful, though Christine Barbaux's Aline is not flattered by the microphones. The orchestral playing is spirited rather than elegant; but the recording is not distinguished and suffers from inconsistencies of level. At times you have to turn up the dialogue, after which the next musical number is too loud. Hence, some reservations about the third star – but the score is good fun. There are some 45 minutes of spoken dialogue and 75 of music; the set includes a libretto in French and a summary in other languages.

Jeanne d'Arc au bûcher.
⊛ *** DG Dig. 429 412-2 [id.]. Keller, Wilson, Escourrou, Lanzi, Pollet, Command, Stutzman, Aler, Courtis, R. France Ch., Fr. Nat. O, Seiji Ozawa.

Honegger's 1935 setting of the Claudel poem is one of his most powerful and imaginative works, full of variety of invention, colour and textures. It is admirably served by these forces, and in particular by the Joan of Marthe Keller. The singers, too, are all excellent and the Choir and the six soloists of the Maîtrise of Radio France are as top-drawer as the orchestra. The DG engineers cope excellently with the large forces and the acoustic of the Basilique de Saint-Denis.

Judith.
☞ **(*) Van. 89054 71 [id.]. Devrath, Christiansen, Madeleine Milhaud (nar.), Salt Lake Symphonic Ch., Utah SO, Abravanel.

Judith dates from 1925, four years after *Le roi David*, and is set to a libretto by the Swiss poet, René Morax, to whom Honegger had turned for his more celebrated oratorio. He calls it 'a Biblical Music Drama' and its form, like that of its predecessor, is a dramatic vocal–orchestral concert work with interspersed narration. This was premièred at the Théâtre du Jurat in Mézières, Switzerland, in 1925. He was subsequently persuaded to turn it into an opera, replacing narration with sung recitative, in which form it was first performed the following year in Monte Carlo. Abravanel uses the first version of the score. The plot tells how the Assyrians, having laid siege to Bethulie, have cut off their water supply; if the Lord does not replenish the water in the coming five days, they will surrender. Judith and her servant go into the wilderness and cross into Holophernes' camp where they are well received. She ingratiates herself into his favour; during the festivities on the eve of their planned attack, Holophernes is overcome by wine and dismisses his servants and takes Judith, at which point she slays him. On her return with his severed head in her hand, she urges the Israelites to battle and victory. In some respects it scores over *Le roi David* in musical concentration, variety of pace and range of musical devices; some passages are marvellously imaginative and atmospheric (the Choral Invocation to protect Judith on her voyage through the valley of fear to cross into the Assyrian lines is quite chilling). The performance dates from 1964 and is totally committed; the only let-down is in some of the choral singing, which could be stronger. The work is short (just under 45 minutes) and it would have added to the competitiveness of the issue to provide a fill-up. But if it is short on quantity, it is long on musical and dramatic interest.

Le Roi David (complete).
(M) *** Erato/Warner 2292 45800-2 [id.]. Eda Pierre, Collard, Tappy, Petel, Valere, De Dailly, Philippe Caillard Ch., Ens. Instrumental, Dutoit.
(M) *** Van. 08.4038.71 [OVC 4038]. Davrath, Sorensen, Preston, Singher, Madeleine Milhaud, Utah University Ch., Utah SO, Abravanel.

Charles Dutoit's *Le Roi David* uses the original instrumental forces and not the full orchestra favoured by most of his rivals. The recording comes from 1970, not that anyone coming to it afresh would guess that. It is a compelling performance of strong dramatic coherence.

The Vanguard version was made in 1961. It is remarkably vivid, well detailed and present, and the playing of the Utah Symphony under Maurice Abravanel is very fine. The recording also stands up well. Netania Davrath is excellent too, and so is Madeleine Milhaud, the composer's wife, as the Witch of Endor. Thoroughly recommendable.

Hovhaness, Alan (born 1911)

Symphony No. 2 (Mysterious mountain), Op. 32; And God created great whales; Alleluia and fugue; Celestial fantasy; Prayer of St Gregory; Prelude and quadruple fugue.
☞ *** Delos Dig. DE 3157 [id.]. Seattle SO, Gerard Schwarz.

This music is spacious, amiably melodic and easy to come to terms with. The *Symphony No. 2* begins with pastoral, modal writing, leading to a central fugal climax and returning to rich, expressive serenity. The *Prayer of St Gregory* is essentially a chorale and is rather appealing in its innocence. But the most sensational piece here is *And God created great whales*, which reaches a huge climax and interpolates tapes of the actual song of the humpbacked whale. The effect is really very grandiose indeed, and everybody here rises to the occasion, including both the whales and the recording engineers.

Symphonies Nos. 22 (City of light), Op. 236; 50 (Mount St Helens), Op. 360.
☞ *** Delos Dig. DE 3137 [id.]. Seattle SO, composer.

If you enjoyed the spectacle of Symphony No. 2, you'll really respond to the extravagant *Mount St Helens Symphony* with its haunting *Spirit Lake* central movement and awe-inspiring *Volcano* eruption for a finale, where some of the orchestral effects are quite grotesquely shattering. *City of Light* is more conventional, but agreeable enough. Performances and recording are first class, but this is not a record for a flat with thin walls.

Howells, Herbert (1892–1983)

PIANO MUSIC

The Chosen tune; Cobbler's hornpipe; Gadabout; Lambert's clavichord: Lambert's fireside (Hughes' ballet; De la Mare's pavanne; Sir Hugh's galliard); Musica sine nomine; 3 Pieces, Op. 14; Sarum sketches; Slow dance (Double the Cape); Snapshots, Op. 30; Sonatina.
☞ *** Chan. Dig. CHAN 9273 [id.]. Margaret Fingerhut.

Howells's output for piano is not perhaps among his most important music but, as this survey shows, he has a good feeling for keyboard sonorities and the invention among these works is remarkably high. The high-spirited writing, as in *Gadabout* (1928) and *Jackanapes* (the third of the *Three Pieces*, Op. 14), has a Grainger-like rhythmic exuberance, while Howells can also be touchingly solemn, as in the dark processional which is the last item of Op. 14 or in the second of the *Sarum sketches*: *The Drudge talks to himself*. His sense of the picturesque is shown at its most appealing in the *Three Snapshots*, with *The Street dance* winningly piquant, *The Polar bear* growlingly lugubrious and *Wee Willie Winkee* tripping along, as light as thistledown. The *Sarum sketches* (1917) are reminiscences of Howells's sojourn as assistant to the Musical Director of Salisbury Cathedral, where one of the choristers, John Steward, diffidently shy, prompted some charming personal vignettes. The *Sonatina* is late, written when the composer was nearly eighty. It is astonishingly fresh, one of his very best works, spikily high-spirited and with a thoughtfully tender slow movement marked *serioso ma teneramente*, with something of Ravel in its thinking. Margaret Fingerhut captures its slightly reticent atmosphere perfectly, as she does the mood of the *Musica sine nomine*, a nostalgically beautiful tribute to John Ireland on his eightieth birthday in 1959. This is probably the first performance of a piece, previously unpublished. Throughout this highly stimulating and enjoyable programme this fine pianist readily catches the composer's moods, light or grave, and she is most realistically recorded. However, in the excerpts from *Lambert's Clavichord*, while *De la Mare's pavane* sounds effective on the piano, *Hughes' ballet* and *Sir Hugh's galliard* cry out to be heard on a harpsichord.

Howells' clavichord (20 pieces for clavichord or piano): *Books I–II; Lambert's clavichord* (12 pieces for clavichord), *Op. 21.*
☞ ** Hyp. Dig. CDA 66689 [id.]. John McCabe (piano).

Howells felt an affinity with the Tudor period of English music and he dedicated his first set of Elizabethan keyboard pieces, written in 1927, to a clavichord- and harpsichord-maker in Bath, Herbert Lambert. The second set, inspired by an instrument constructed by Thomas Goff of Chelsea, came much later (1941). Each of the pieces is short and precise, averaging a duration of two minutes. Just like those Elizabethan works of Byrd, Dowland and others, they have agreeably inconseqential titles like *Samuel's air*, *H.H. his Fancy*, *Sir Richard's Toye* and, later, *Goff's fireside*. What is extraordinary is John McCabe's decision to record all of them on the piano. Certainly, as John McCabe suggests, 'the bittersweet harmonies can benefit from the greater tonal range of the modern instrument', but despite his judicious use of the sustaining pedal many of these miniatures could be even more effective on the clavichord or harpsichord. They are very well played and well recorded, but this collection has a question mark hanging over it: 'How would they have sounded if. . .?'

VOCAL MUSIC

3 Children's songs (Eight o'clock, the postman's knock; The days are clear; Mother, shake the cherry-tree); 3 Folksongs (I will give my love an apple; The brisk young widow; Cendrillon); 4 French chansons, Op. 29; A Garland for de la Mare (group of 11 unpublished songs); *In green ways* (song-cycle), *Op. 43; Peacock Pie* (song-cycle), *Op. 33; 2 South African settings (Loneliness; Spirit of freedom); 4 Songs, Op. 22 (There was a maiden; Madrigal; The widow bird; Girl's song).* Miscellaneous songs: *An old man's lullaby; Come sing and dance; Flood; Gavotte; Goddess of the Night; Here she lies; King David; The little boy lost; Lost love; Mally O!; The Mugger's song; O garlands, hanging by the doors; O my deir hert; Old Meg; Old skinflint; The restful branches.*
☞ *** Chan. Dig. CHAN 9185/6 (2) [id.]. Lynne Dawson; Catherine Pierard; John Mark Ainsley; Benjamin Luxon; Julius Drake.

This two-disc collection covers virtually all of Howells's completed songs, most of them previously unrecorded and many still unpublished. One of the driving forces behind the project is the pianist Julius Drake, who plays the accompaniments with a consistent rhythmic spring and a sense of fantasy. Two of the finest songs are among the best known, *King David* and *Come sing and dance*, and such a group of miniatures as *Peacock Pie*, settings of Walter de la Mare written early in Howells's career, have a characteristic point and charm. Yet this collection, which has benefited from the scholarly work of Christopher Palmer both on the texts and on the notes for these discs, puts such published songs into quite a new context. Howells had a special sympathy for de la Mare as both person and poet. Far more searching are the 11 much longer settings of de la Mare poems. In this 40-minute sequence, *Garland for de la Mare*, Howells shows what close sympathy he had not just for the child-like, nursery-style poems of *Peacock Pie* but for those which in a subtle way capture a childish sense of mystery and new discovery, so typical of the poet. As Palmer explains, this song-cycle was 'a life-time's work, on and off, essentially completed but never definitively prepared for publication'. Among the other fascinating examples are two South African settings to words by the Afrikaans poet, Jan Celliers, including one very topical at the time the discs appeared in May 1994, *Spirit of freedom*. Christopher Palmer deduces that they must have been written when in 1921 Howells went to South Africa to judge Associated Board examinations. The sopranos, Catherine Pierard and Lynne Dawson, both have aptly fresh, English-sounding voices, with John Mark Ainsley as the thoughtful tenor and Benjamin Luxon the characterful baritone, a fine team, even though the recording brings out some unevenness in the vocal production of both Ainsley and Luxon.

Chichester service: Magnificat; Nunc dimittis. A Hymn for Saint Cecilia; Like as the hart desireth the waterbrooks; My eyes for beauty pine; O salutaris Hostia; Salve Regina.
☞ **(*) ASV Dig. CDDCA 851 [id.]. David Went, Ch. of The Queen's College, Oxford, Matthew Owens – LEIGHTON: *Crucifixus pro nobis* etc. ***

Whereas some of his orchestral and chamber music has a certain pallor, Howells is at his best in his choral work and the pieces gathered here are all worth having. Neither in terms of ensemble nor intonation is The Queen's College, Oxford, choir in the first league, but the performances are committed and give pleasure, and they are well recorded. The disc has the advantage of coupling rarely heard music of quality by Kenneth Leighton.

Collegium regale: canticles; Behold, O God our defender; Like as the hart; St Paul's service: Canticles. Take him to earth for cherishing. (Organ): *Psalm prelude: De profundis; Master Tallis's testament.*
*** Hyp. Dig. CDA 66260 [id.]. St Paul's Cathedral Ch., Scott; Christopher Dearnley.

All the music here is of high quality and the recording gives it resonance, in both senses of the word, with the St Paul's acoustic well captured by the engineers. A fine representation of a composer who wrote in the mainstream of English church and cathedral music but who had a distinct voice of his own.

Collegium regale: Te Deum and jubilate; Office of Holy Communion; Magnificat and Nunc dimittis. Preces & Responses I & II; Psalms 121 & 122; Take him, earth for cherishing. Rhapsody for organ, Op. 17/3.
⊛ *** Decca Dig. 430 205-2 [id.]. Williams, Moore, King's College, Cambridge, Ch., Cleobury.

Here is an unmatchable collection of the settings inspired by the greatest of our collegiate choirs, King's College, Cambridge, presented in performances of heartwarming intensity in that great choir's 1989 incarnation. The boy trebles in particular are among the brightest and fullest ever to have been recorded with this choir. The disc sensitively presents the sequence in what amounts to liturgical order, with the service settings aptly interspersed with responses, psalm-chants, anthems with organ introits and voluntaries all by Howells. Even those not normally attracted by Anglican church music should hear this.

Hymnus Paradisi, An English Mass.
*** Hyp. Dig. CDA 66488 [id.]. Kennard, Ainsley, RLPO Ch., RLPO, Handley.

Hymnus Paradisi is a heartfelt expression of grief over the death of the composer's son at the age of nine; Handley conveys a mystery, a tenderness rather missing from the previous recording, made by Sir David Willcocks for EMI, strong as that is. Handley's soloists bring a moving compassion, as in the haunting setting of the 23rd Psalm which makes up the third movement. The Hyperion digital recording is warm, full and atmospheric. *An English Mass* is simpler yet also hauntingly beautiful.

(Organ) *Psalm prelude, Set 1/1; Paen; Prelude: Sine nomine.* (Vocal): *Behold, O God our defender; Here is the door; Missa Aedi Christi: Kyrie; Credo; Sanctus; Benedictus; Agnus Dei; Gloria. Sing lullaby; A spotless rose; Where wast thou?.*
*** CRD Dig. CRD 3455; *CRDC 4155* [id.]. New College, Oxford, Ch., Edward Higginbottom (organ).

A further collection of the music of Herbert Howells, splendidly sung by Edward Higginbottom's fine choir, while he provides the organ interludes in addition. Among the shorter pieces, the carol-anthem,

Sing lullaby, is especially delightful, and the programme ends with the motet, *Where wast thou?*, essentially affirmative, in spite of the question posed at the opening. Beautifully spacious sound makes this a highly rewarding collection.

Requiem. Motets: *The House of the Mind; A Sequence for St Michael.*
*** Chan. Dig. CHAN 9019 [id.]. Finzi Singers, Spicer – VAUGHAN WILLIAMS: *Lord thou hast been our refuge* etc. ***

Howells' *Requiem* is the work which prepared the way for *Hymnus Paradisi*, providing some of the material for it. For unaccompanied chorus, it presents a gentler, compact view of what in the big cantata becomes powerfully expansive. The Finzi singers, 18-strong, give a fresh and atmospheric, beautifully moulded performance, well coupled with two substantial motets with organ by Howells as well as choral pieces by Vaughan Williams.

Humfrey, Pelham (1647–74)

Verse anthems: *By the waters of Babylon; Have mercy on me, O God; Hear, O Heav'ns; Hear my prayer, O God; Hear my crying, O God; Lift up your heads; Like as the hart; O give thanks unto the Lord; O Lord my God.*
☞ *** HM Dig. HMU 907053 [id.]. Donna Deam, Drew Minter, Rogers Covey-Crump, John Potter, David Thomas, Clare College, Cambridge, Ch., Romanesca, Nicholas McGegan.

Verse anthem: *O Lord my God.*
☞ (M) *** Erato/Warner 2292 45987-2 [id.]. Charles Brett, Martyn Hill, David Thomas, Monteverdi Ch., E. Bar. Sol., Gardiner – Concert: *'Music of the Chapels Royal'.* ***

Here yet another name from the past emerges as a remarkably strong musical personality. Pelham Humfrey (or Humphrey) began his career about 1660 as a chorister at the Chapel Royal and made such an impression that he was sent abroad at the expense of the royal purse of Charles II to study in France and Italy. After more than one visit he returned as a Gentleman of the Chapel Royal, and when the incumbent died in 1672 he took over as Master of the choristers. He married and his short life ended at the age of 27. He brought back from Italy (and from Lully in France) a thorough absorption of the operatic style, and his verse anthems are remarkably dramatic and powerfully expressive, using soloists almost like operatic characters. *By the waters of Babylon* and, especially, *O Lord my God* are very striking indeed. Nicholas McGegan's fine performances reflect this histrionic dimension, helped by his soloists who at times approach stylistic boundaries in their performance of what is essentially devotional music, even if intensely felt. Nevertheless no one could say that these authentic performances are in any way dampened down by scholarly rectitude. With a highly sensitive instrumental contribution from the excellent Romanesca, this collection (about half of Humfrey's surviving output) is very freshly recorded and is strongly recommended to the adventurous collector.

Those seeking just a single example of Humfrey's unique combination of operatic drama and pathos should sample John Eliot Gardiner's telling account of one of the very finest of these verse anthems, *O Lord my God!*, in which the very moving supplication has faint echoes of Purcell's Dido's lament and the declamation, 'For many dogs are come about me, and the counsel of the wicked lay'th siege against me,' is very dramatic indeed. This is part of a well-chosen anthology of anthems and motets associated with the Chapels Royal, including fine examples by Matthew Locke and John Blow, as well as Purcell.

Hummel, Johann (1778–1837)

Bassoon concerto in F.
*** Denon Dig. CO 79281 [id.]. Werba, V. String Soloists, Honeck – MOZART; WEBER: *Concertos.* ***

A good modern recording of Hummel's engaging *Bassoon concerto* was needed and Michael Werba is a personable and characterful soloist. He is well accompanied and recorded and the couplings are attractive.

Piano concertos: in A min., Op. 85; B min., Op. 89.
*** Chan. Dig. CHAN 8505; *ABTD 1217* [id.]. Stephen Hough, ECO, Bryden Thomson.
☞ (BB) *** Discover Dig. DICD 920117 [id.]. Dana Protopopescu, Slovak R. New PO, Rahbari.

The *A minor* is Hummel's most often-heard piano concerto, never better played, however, than by Stephen Hough on this Chandos disc. The coda is quite stunning; it is not only his dazzling virtuosity that carries all before it but also the delicacy and refinement of colour he produces. The *B minor*, Op. 89, is more of a rarity, and is given with the same blend of virtuosity and poetic feeling which Hough brings to its companion. He is given expert support by Bryden Thomson and the ECO – and the recording is first class.

At bargain price Discover offers an outstanding alternative coupling. Well accompanied by the Slovak Radio New Philharmonic, Dana Protopopescu, always sounding fresh and spontaneous, plays with lightness, point and poetry. On her smaller scale, she even rivals Stephen Hough in his prize-winning recording of the same two concertos for Chandos at full price, though Hough is more impulsive.

Trumpet concerto in E.
⑧ *** Ph. Dig. 420 203-2; *420 203-4* [id.]. Hardenberger, ASMF, Marriner – HAYDN *** ⑧; HERTEL
***; STAMITZ: *Concertos.* ***

Trumpet concerto in E flat.
*** Sony CD 37846 [id.]. Marsalis, Nat. PO, Leppard – HAYDN: *Concerto* *** (with L. MOZART:
Concerto ***).

(i) *Trumpet concerto in E;* (ii) *Introduction, theme and variations for 2 trumpets, Op. 102.*
(M) *** Erato/Warner 2292 45061-2 [id.]. Maurice André; (i) LOP, Mari; (ii) with Raymond André,
Paillard CO, Paillard – MOLTER: *Concertos.* **(*)

Hummel's *Trumpet concerto* is usually heard in the familiar brass key of E flat, but the brilliant Swedish trumpeter, Håkan Hardenberger, uses the key of E, which makes it sound brighter and bolder than usual. Neither he nor Marriner miss the genial lilt inherent in the dotted theme of the first movement, the slow-movement cantilena soars beautifully over its jogging pizzicato accompaniment, and the finale captivates the ear with its high spirits and easy bravura. This is the finest version of the piece in the catalogue, for Marriner's accompaniment is polished and sympathetic.

Like Hardenberger, Maurice André plays Hummel's concerto in the bright key of E, and he has the advantage of a splendid accompaniment directed by Jean-Baptiste Mari. They capture the work's *galant* style admirably and the finale is infectious. Good sound too, and the I*ntroduction, theme and variations* is presented with flair.

Marsalis gives a fine account of Hummel's *Concerto*, but does not quite catch its full *galant* charm. In matters of bravura, however, he cannot be faulted; he relishes the sparkling finale.

Introduction, theme and variations in F min./maj., Op. 102.
*** Capriccio Dig. 10 308 [id.]. Lajos Lencsés, Stuttgart RSO, Marriner – HAYDN; MARTINU:
Concertos. ***

Lajos Lencsés – the principal oboe of the Stuttgart orchestra – plays with both poise and an obvious relish for Hummel's engaging invention. He is very well recorded.

Piano quintet in E flat, Op. 87; Piano septet in D min., Op. 74.
(M) *** Decca 430 297-2 [id.]. Melos Ens. – WEBER: *Clarinet quintet.* ***

These two highly engaging works show the composer at his melodically most fecund and his musical craftsmanship at its most apt – just try the opening movement of the *Septet* to sample the composer's felicity.

Septet in D min., Op. 74.
*** CRD CRD 3344; *CRDC 4044* [id.]. Nash Ens. – BERWALD: *Septet.* ***

Hummel's *Septet* is an enchanting and inventive work with a virtuoso piano part, expertly dispatched here by Clifford Benson. A fine performance and excellent recording make this a highly desirable issue, particularly in view of the enterprising coupling.

String quartets: in C; in G; in E flat, Op. 30/1–3.
*** Hyp. Dig. CDA 66568 [id.]. Delmé Qt.

Hummel wrote his three *String quartets* – his only contribution to the form – in 1803/4. Hummel's works are closer to Haydn than Beethoven, though the first of the set in C major with its impressive opening *Adagio e mesto* in the minor key, fine *Adagio*, and brisk, scherzo-like Minuet, with its forward-looking structure, obviously lean towards the influence of the later composer, while the audacious quotation of *Comfort ye* from Handel's *Messiah* in the preceding *Andante*, brings yet another example of Hummelian sleight of hand. In short these are fascinating works, highly inventive, and crafted with the composer's usual fluent charm. They are splendidly played by the Delmé group, who provide plenty of vitality and warmth. The Hyperion recording is fresh and believable.

Violin sonatas: in E flat, Op. 5/3; in D, Op. 50; Nocturne, Op. 99.
*** Amon Ra CD-SAR 12 [id.]. Ralph Holmes, Richard Burnett.

Ralph Holmes's violin timbre is bright and the Graf fortepiano under the fingers of Richard Burnett has plenty of colour and does not sound clattery. Burnett has a chance to catch the ear in the finale of the *D major Sonata* when he uses the quaintly rasping cembalo device (without letting it outstay its welcome). The *Nocturne* is an extended piece (nearly 16 minutes) in variation form. A thoroughly worthwhile issue, 'authentic' in the most convincing way, which shows this engaging composer at his most assured and inventive.

Mass in B flat, Op. 77; Tantum ergo (after Gluck).
*** Koch Dig. 3-7117-2 [id.]. Westminster Oratorio Ch., New Brunswick CO, John Floreen.

Hummel wrote his *Mass in B flat* while working for the Esterházys. It is an unpretentious work of great charm and a real discovery. The Westminster Choir (from the College of that name in Princeton, New Jersey) give exactly the right kind of modest performance, emphasizing the work's warm lyricism; the conductor, while not lacking vigour, is careful not to be too forceful at climaxes. The orchestral accompaniment is nicely in scale, and the recording, though not crystal clear, has the most agreeable ambience.

Humperdinck, Engelbert (1854–1921)

The Canteen Woman (Die Marketenderin): Prelude. The Merchant of Venice: Love scene. Moorish rhapsody: Tarifa (Elegy of summer); Tangier (A night in a moorish coffe-house); Tetuan (A night in the desert). The Sleeping Beauty: suite.
**(*) Marco Polo Dig. 8.223369 [id.]. Slovak RSO (Bratislava), Martin Fischer-Dieskau.

The Love scene from *The Merchant of Venice* ('On such a night') is beautiful but rather over-extended, and all three sections of the *Moorish rhapsody* are much too long (the composite piece lasts some 32 minutes). The opening of the *Summer elegy* begins with raptly ethereal writing for the violins, but the jolly Moorish coffee-house sequence sounds as if the restaurant has been leased from the owner of a Bavarian bier-keller. The Slovak performances under Martin Fischer-Dieskau (the famous Lieder singer's grandson) are not ideally polished but have freshness and vitality, while the Marco Polo recording is open and reasonably full.

Hänsel und Gretel (complete).
*** EMI Dig. CDS7 54022-2 (2) [Ang. CDCB 54022]; *EX 754022-2.* Von Otter, Bonney, Lipovšek, Schwarz, Schmidt, Hendricks, Lind, Tölz Boys' Ch, Bav. RSO, Tate.
(M) *** EMI CMS7 69293-2 (2) [Ang. CDMB 69293]. Schwarzkopf, Grümmer, Metternich, Ilsovay, Schürhoff, Felbermayer, Children's Ch., Philh. O, Karajan.

Tate brings a Brucknerian glow to the *Overture*, and then launches into a reading of exceptional warmth and sympathy at speeds generally faster than those in rival versions. He relates the opera to the Wagner of Act II of *Die Meistersinger*, rather than to anything weightier. The Witch of Marjana Lipovšek is firm and fierce, using the widest range of expression and tone. The chill that Lipovšek conveys down to a mere whisper makes one regret, more than usual, that the part is not longer. All the casting matches that in finesse, with no weak link. Barbara Bonney as Gretel and Anne Sofie von Otter as Hänsel are no less fine than the exceptionally strong duos on the rival sets. There is only a slight question mark over the use of the Tölz Boys' Choir for the gingerbread children at the end. Inevitably they sound what they are, a beautifully matched team of trebles, and curiously the heart-tug is not quite so intense as with the more childish-sounding voices in the rival choirs. That is a minimal reservation, however, when the breadth and warmth of the recording add to the compulsion of the performance.

Karajan's classic 1950s set of Humperdinck's children's opera, with Schwarzkopf and Grümmer peerless in the name-parts, is enchanting; this was an instance where everything in the recording went right. The original mono LP set was already extremely atmospheric. In most respects the sound has as much clarity and warmth as rival recordings made in the 1970s. There is much to delight here; the smaller parts are beautifully done and Else Schürhoff's Witch is memorable. The snag is that the digital remastering has brought a curious orchestral bass emphasis, noticeable in the overture and elsewhere, but notably in the *Witch's ride*. (Karajan's set is currently withdrawn as we go to press.)

Humphrey, Pelham – see Humfrey, Pelham

Hvoslef, Ketil (born 1937)

(i) *Antigone (1982);* (ii) *Violin concerto.*

☞ *** Aurora Dig. ACD4969 [id.]. (ii) Trond Saeverud; Bergen PO, cond. (i) Eggen; (ii) Kitaienko.

Ketil Hvoslef is the son of Harald Saeverud and one of the brightest and most individual figures in the Norwegian musical firmament. He has the same craggy, salty quality as his father, the same rugged independence of personality and creative resource. This CD offers *Antigone*, which comes from the early 1980s, and the *Violin concerto*, composed almost ten years later, in which the soloist is his son, Trond.

Ibert, Jacques (1890–1962)

Bacchanale; Bostoniana; (i) *Flute concerto. Escales (Ports of call); Hommage à Mozart; Louisville concerto; Paris (suite).*

☞ *** Decca Dig. 440 332-2 [id.]. (i) Timothy Hutchins; Montreal SO, Charles Dutoit.

A self-recommending collection for those who rightly respond to Decca's Montreal sound, have already discovered Ibert's *Divertissement* and want to explore his orchestral music further. Dutoit knows exactly where he is going in this repertoire: *Escales* has all the required sensuous, Mediterranean feeling and colour, and Timothy Hutchins is an estimable soloist in the *Flute concerto*. If the unknown music is not quite so indelible as these three best-known works it is still most enjoyable when played with such idiomatic flair. *Bostoniana* is in fact the only finished movement of the composer's second symphony, written for the Boston Symphony; the *Louisville concerto* was commissioned by yet another American ensemble and the Ibertian tribute to Mozart came in time for the bicentennial celebrations of Mozart's birth. Needless to say, the recording with rich, clear textures is yet another example of Decca expertise in St Eustache, Montreal.

La Ballade de la Geôle de Reading; Féerique; 3 Pièces de Ballet (Les Rencontres); (i) *Chant de Folie; Suite Elisabéthaine.*

☞ **(*) Marco Polo Dig. 8.223508 [id.]. (i) Slovak Ph. Ch.; Slovak RSO (Bratislava), Adriano.

Four of these pieces come from the early 1920s, the *Suite Elisabéthaine* from 1942. The latter is a nine-movement suite taken from the incidental music Ibert composed for Shakespeare's *A Midsummer Night's Dream*. It is largely pastiche and four of the movements draw on Blow, Purcell, Bull and Gibbons. More characteristic is *La Ballade de la Geôle de Reading*, composed in 1921, Ibert's first orchestral score, an exercise in neo-impressionism and, as one would expect from a pupil of Fauré and André Gedalge – who taught both Milhaud and Honegger – highly accomplished. The writing in the companion pieces is polished, albeit at times overscored, but the thematic substance is neither memorable nor distinctive. The *Chant de Folie* is an effective four-minute choral and orchestral piece inspired by the composer's experiences in the First World War and at one time championed by Koussevitzky. Its brevity has doubtless inhibited modern performances. Good performances and eminently serviceable recording.

(i) *Concertino da camera. Divertissement.*

☞ * Koch Int. Dig. 37094-2 [id.]. (i) Michael Whitcombe; San Diego CO, Donald Barra –
POULENC: *Sinfonietta.* *

The San Diego orchestra under Donald Barra need to bring an altogether lighter touch to the *Divertissement*, but the disc is of some value in offering the *Concertino da camera* for saxophone with Michael Whitcombe the excellent soloist. He receives less-responsive orchestral support than he deserves.

Divertissement.
*** Chan. Dig. CHAN 9023 [id.]. Ulster O, Yan Pascal Tortelier – MILHAUD: *Le Boeuf; Création;*
POULENC: *Les Biches.* ***
☞ (M) *** BMG/RCA 09026 61429-2 [id.]. Boston Pops O, Arthur Fiedler – OFFENBACH: *Collection.*
**

Yan Pascal Tortelier provides at last a splendid, modern, digital version of Ibert's *Divertissement.*
There is much delicacy of detail, and the coupled suite from Poulenc's *Les Biches* is equally
delectable. Marvellous, top-drawer Chandos sound.

Fiedler's racy account of Ibert's *Divertissement* is as sparkling as you could wish, with genuine
Gallic insouciance. The *Valse*, *Parade* and exuberant *Finale* have tremendous élan. The recording too
is splendidly lively and atmospheric, and this can be recommended alongside Fiedler's equally
dazzling account of *Gaîté parisienne.* It is a pity that the Offenbach collection which acts as coupling
for the *Divertissement* is recorded less successfully.

Escales (Ports of call).
☞ (M) *** BMG/RCA 09026 61500-2 [id.]. Boston SO, Munch – DEBUSSY: *La Mer* **(*); SAINT-
SAENS: *Symphony No. 3.* *** ⊛
(M) **(*) Mercury 432 003-2 [id.]. Detroit SO, Paray – RAVEL: *Alborada* etc. ***

Ibert favours three-piece suites; the three places described in *Escales* are *Palermo, Tunis-Nefta* and
Valencia. Short though it is, this is a first-rate work. The opening of *Palermo* offers some ravishing
textures from the Boston violins (French impressionism at its most seductive); the second evocation
has a piquantly oriental favour and the finale, *Valencia*, has gay dance rhythms. Munch's performances are splendid and the 1956 recording, if balanced rather closely, has brilliance and transparency;
although it does not sound as rich and sumptuous as the outstanding Saint-Saëns symphony with
which it is coupled, the effect is slightly preferable to Paray's fine Mercury version.

Paray's recording catches the Mediterranean exoticism of *Escales* admirably, and the 1962
Mercury recording has plenty of atmosphere as well as glittering detail. The Ravel couplings are very
impressive too.

Escales; Ouverture de fête; Tropisms pour des amours imaginaires.
(M) *** EMI CDM7 64276-2 [id.]. Fr. Nat. R. O, Jean Martinon.

The well-known *Escales* have genuine atmosphere in Martinon's exemplary performance, and the
1974 recording is spacious, at times sensuously so, and pleasingly natural. The strings here have more
allure than in Paray's Mercury version. *Tropisms* has moments of real imagination and is a piece of
greater substance than the *Ouverture de fête* which, though it has a striking principal theme, is rather
inflated. All three performances are expert and the CD transfer is most impressive.

Symphonie concertante (for oboe and string orchestra).
(M) *** BMG/RCA GD 87989 [7989-2-RG]. John de Lancie, LSO, Previn – FRANCAIX: *L'horloge
de flore* *** ⊛; R. STRAUSS: *Oboe concerto.* ***

Ibert's *Symphonie concertante* has vitality and impulse and demands great virtuosity from the
orchestra, and the extended *Adagio* has a wan, expressive poignancy. John de Lancie is a first-class
soloist. André Previn directs with much conviction and spirit. The sound is very good – its slight lack
of opulence suits the music.

d'India, Sigismondo (c. 1582–c. 1630)

Duets, Laments and Madrigals: *Amico, hai vinto; Ancidetemi pur, dogliosi affanti; Che nudrisce tua
speme; Giunto a la tomba; Langue al vostro languir; Occhi della mia vita; O leggiadr' occhi; Quella
vermiglia rosa; Son gli accenti che ascolto; Torna il sereno Zefiro.*
(B) **(*) HM HMA 901011 [id.]. Concerto Vocale – CESTI: *Cantatas.* **(*)

Sigismondo d'India was among the vanguard of the new movement founded by Monteverdi at the
beginning of the seventeenth century, and his laments show him to be a considerable master of
expressive resource. The performances are authoritative, though there are moments of slightly self-
conscious rubato that hold up the flow. The recording is fully acceptable and the coupling is also of
considerable interest; this is worth exploring.

Amico hai vinto; Diana (Questo dardo, quest' arco); Misera me (Lamento d'Olympia); Piangono al pianger mio; Sfere fermate; Torna il sereno zefiro.
*** Hyp. CDA 66106 [id.]. Emma Kirkby, Anthony Rooley (chitarone) – MONTEVERDI: *Lamento d'Olympia* etc. ***

Sigismondo d'India's setting of the *Lamento d'Olympia* makes a striking contrast to Monteverdi's and is hardly less fine. This is an affecting and beautiful piece and so are its companions, particularly when they are sung as superbly and accompanied as sensitively as they are here. A very worthwhile CD début.

d'Indy, Vincent (1851–1931)

Jour d'été à la montagne, Op. 61; Tableaux de voyage, Op. 36.
☞ (M) **(*) EMI CDM7 64364-2 [id.]. Loire PO, Pierre Dervaux.

Jour d'été à la montagne, a comparatively substantial piece, was composed just after Debussy's *La Mer* and was inspired by the beauties of the Vivarais region of central France where d'Indy was born. He was a devoted Wagnerian, but that influence is more completely assimilated in this triptych than in other works such as *Fervaal* or the early tone-poem, *La forêt enchantée. Tableaux de voyage* is a delightful suite, written originally for piano. This is a most enjoyable coupling that reveals d'Indy as a far richer and more rewarding composer than most people give him credit for, and the performances are in no sense second-rate, even though the Orchestre Philharmonique des Pays de Loire is scarcely of international standing. The recording is very good and well transferred to CD, but the measure is short (47 minutes): the original LP included also *La forêt enchantée.*

Lied, Op. 19.
**(*) Ph. Dig. 432 084-2 [id.]. Julian Lloyd Webber, ECO, Yan Pascal Tortelier – FAURE: *Elégie* **; HONEGGER: *Concerto* **(*); SAINT-SAENS: *Concerto* etc. **(*)

Vincent d'Indy's *Lied for cello and orchestra* has something of the nobility that always distinguished this composer, and it comes with an interesting coupling in the shape of the Honegger *Concerto.*

Symphonie sur un chant montagnard français (Symphonie cévenole).
*** Decca Dig. 430 278-2 [id.]. Jean-Yves Thibaudet, Montreal SO, Dutoit – FRANCK: *Symphony.* ***

(M) **(*) BMG/RCA GD 86805 [6805-2-RG]. Nicole Henriot-Schweitzer, Boston SO, Munch – FRANCK: *Symphony.* **(*) ⊛
☞ *(*) Pickwick Dig. MCD 71 [id.]. Valerie Traficante, RPO, Serebrier – FAURE: *Ballade for piano and orchestra;* SAINT-SAENS: *Piano concerto No. 2.* *(*)

Jean-Yves Thibaudet's Decca account is sensitively played and outstandingly well recorded.

Nicole Henriot-Schweitzer plays the piano part most sympathetically and Munch presents a fresh and crisp performance. The early (1958) stereo recording comes up well.

A good performance from Valerie Traficante on Pickwick, but the resonant recording sounds a bit overblown: the first climax is almost explosive in its opulence.

(i) *Symphonie sur un chant montagnard français;* (ii) *Symphony No. 2 in B flat, Op. 57.*
(M) *** EMI CDM7 63952-2. (i) Ciccolini, O de Paris, Baudo; (ii) Toulouse Capitole O, Plasson.

Aldo Ciccolini gives a good account of himself in the demanding solo part of the *Symphonie*, and the Orchestre de Paris under Serge Baudo give sympathetic support. The recording is pleasing and with a convincing piano image. In the *Second Symphony* Michel Plasson proves a sympathetic and committed advocate, and his orchestra responds with enthusiasm and sensitivity to his direction. The recording too is spacious, full and well focused.

String quartets Nos. 1 in D, Op. 35; 2 in E, Op. 45.
**(*) Marco Polo Dig. 8.223140 [id.]. Kodály Qt.

The *First Quartet* is a large-scale piece and beautifully crafted. The *Second* (1897) is hardly less ambitious and shows something of his admiration for late Beethoven. Neither work has the eloquence or poetry of Fauré's chamber music; it must also be said that greater variety of texture would be welcome. The excellent Kodály Quartet are recorded in the Italian Institute in Budapest, where the rather close balance tends to iron out dynamic extremes.

Ippolitov-Ivanov, Mikhail (1859–1935)

Caucasian sketches (suite), *Op. 10.*
*** ASV Dig. CDDCA 773; *ZCDCA 773*. Armenian PO, Tjeknavorian – KHACHATURIAN:
  Gayaneh etc. **(*)

Ippolitov-Ivanov's fames rests on a single movement, the *Procession of the Sardar*, the hit number from the *Caucasian sketches*, which is played by the Armenians with great brio. The other items rely mainly on picaresque oriental atmosphere for their appeal, which Tjeknavorian also captures evocatively in this brightly lit recording.

Ireland, John (1879–1962)

Piano concerto in E flat.
*** Conifer Dig. CDCF 175; *MCFC 175* [id.]. Kathryn Stott, RPO, Handley – BRIDGE: *Phantasm;*
  WALTON: *Sinfonia concertante.* ***
*** Unicorn Dig. DKPCD 9056; *DKPC 9056* [id.]. Tozer, Melbourne SO, Measham – RUBBRA:
  Violin concerto. ***

Piano concerto in E flat; Legend for piano and orchestra; Mai-Dun (symphonic rhapsody).
*** Chan. Dig. CHAN 8461; *ABTD 1174* [id.]. Parkin, LPO, Thomson.
☞ (M) (***) Dutton Laboratories mono CDAX 8001 [id.]. Eileen Joyce, Hallé O, Leslie Heward –
  MOERAN: *Symphony.* *** ⊛

(i) *Piano concerto in E flat;* (ii; iv) *A London overture;* (iii; iv) *Mai-Dunn* (symphonic rhapsody); (v)
Comedy overture; (vi) *Greater love hath no man;* (vii) *The Sally Gardens;* (viii) *Sea fever.*
☞ (M) (***) EMI mono CDM7 64716-2. (i) Colin Horsley, RPO, Basil Cameron; (ii) LSO; (iii)
  Hallé O; (iv) Barbirolli; (v) GUS, Kettering, Band, Geoffrey Brand; (vi) Chichester Cathedral
  Ch., John Birch; (vii) Dame Janet Baker, Gerald Moore; (viii) Robert Lloyd, Nina Walker.

Kathryn Stott gives the most sympathetic reading of Ireland's *Piano concerto* on record since the original interpreter on disc, Eileen Joyce. Spaciously expressive in the lyrical passages and crisply alert in the jazzy finale, Stott plays with a sense of spontaneity, using freely idiomatic rubato. Generously and aptly coupled with the much more neglected Walton and Bridge works, and very well recorded, this version makes an easy first choice for the work.

  Eric Parkin gives a splendidly refreshing and sparkling performance and benefits from excellent support from Bryden Thomson and the LPO. They are no less impressive in *Mai-Dun* and the beautiful *Legend for piano and orchestra*.

  Geoffrey Tozer also gives a characterful account of Ireland's lyrical and often whimsical *Concerto*. Tozer conveys the poetic feel of the slow movement and, though he takes a rather measured tempo in the finale, the music loses none of its freshness. The recording is a little studio-bound, but too much should not be made of this. Doubtless the coupling will decide matters for most collectors.

  When Leslie Heward died in 1943 at the age of 45, he was due to become conductor of the Hallé. His mastery is splendidly illustrated in two of his last recordings, the *Symphony in G minor* of E. J. Moeran and John Ireland's *Piano concerto* with Eileen Joyce giving an inspired performance, both sparkling and deeply expressive. These were the first ever recordings of two works which stand among the very finest British music of the inter-war period, pioneer recordings of performances which have a warmth and intensity never quite matched since. Eileen Joyce's recording of this delightful concerto readily demonstrates the flamboyant romanticism for which she was famous and even a moment or two of fantasy, plus the freshness of discovery. Leslie Heward accompanies with flair, and the orchestral playing is impressive. This highly spontaneous performance is special and Walter Legge's recording, made in the Houldsworth Hall, Manchester, in 1942, was very naturally balanced. The superb transfers of the original 78s show the work of Dutton Laboratories at its finest, offering sound that in its body and sense of presence sets new standards in re-creating what it felt like listening to the original 78s, with the one snag that, as the original shellac pressings were the source, there is noticeable wow on the piano tone, especially striking in the central *Lento*. One adjusts, but it is a pity this could not have been avoided, when the piano timbre itself is so full and realistic. No complaints about the orchestra: the strings are full and warm.

  However, many listeners will prefer the later, stereo recording by Colin Horsley with Basil Cameron which retains that initial freshness and has excellent sound, except for a degree of thinness on the high violins. In this performance the slow movement is more leisured but has a serene poise and beauty which are ravishingly memorable. In the finale Eileen Joyce has marginally greater dash, but Colin Horsley still offers plenty of sparkle and Basil Cameron proves a fine partner. The rest of the programme includes the *London overture* (its main theme rhythmically conjuring up the bus conductor's call, 'Piccadily') and also the brass band piece on which it was based. *Mai-Dun* receives persuasive advocacy from Barbirolli, but this is not Ireland at his finest. The composer's two most famous songs are also very welcome.

A Downland suite; Elegiac meditation; The Holy Boy.
*** Chan. Dig. CHAN 8390; *ABTD 1112* [id.]. ECO, David Garforth – BRIDGE: *Suite for strings.*
***

A Downland suite was originally written for brass band, and in 1941 Ireland began to make a version for strings, completely reconceiving it. However, his reworking was interrupted and the present version was finished and put into shape by Geoffrey Bush, who also transcribed the *Elegiac meditation.* David Garforth and the ECO play with total conviction and seem wholly attuned to Ireland's sensibility. The recording is first class, clear and naturally balanced.

Epic march; The Overlanders (film incidental music): *suite* (arr. Mackerras).
☞ (M) *** Unicorn UKCD 2062 [id.]. W. Australian SO, David Measham – VAUGHAN WILLIAMS:
   On Wenlock Edge. ***

The Overlanders is not the best of Ireland, but it contains some good ideas (the Scherzo, *The Brumbles*, is particularly effective) and it is persuasively presented here. The *Epic march* is jolly and rhythmically folksy, then presents an almost elegiac grand tune, for which Measham slows in respect but presents grandly at the end. This is all recommendable enough, for the CD transfers are first rate and the Vaughan Williams coupling is most appealing.

The Forgotten rite (Prelude); (i) *These things shall be*; (ii) (Piano) *April.*
(M) (***) EMI CDH7 63910-2. Hallé O, Barbirolli; (i) with Parry Jones, Hallé Ch.; (ii) composer –
   BAX: *Symphony No. 3.* (***)

Barbirolli's account of *The Forgotten rite* has something quite special: there is a quiet, inward-looking quality that has eluded subsequent performers. The 1949 sound may not have the freshness and bloom we expect from modern recording but the performance has both. *These things shall be* is a rather conventional piece, though this stirring account does its best to show it in a positive light. There is a welcome bonus in Ireland himself playing *April.*

A London overture.
☞ (M) **(*) EMI CDM5 65109-2 [id.]. LSO, Barbirolli – VAUGHAN WILLIAMS: *London symphony.*
   **(*)

One of Ireland's most immediately attractive works, and Barbirolli's performance of it is a great success, as is the remastering of an outstanding recording: the effect is tangible and real in its crisply vivid focus. The main theme (rhythmically conjuring up the bus conductor's call of 'Piccadilly!') is made obstinately memorable, and the ripe romanticism of the middle section is warmly expansive in Barbirolli's hands. The freshness of the sound makes the performance sound newly minted.

A London overture; Epic march; (i) *The Holy Boy; Greater love hath no man; These things shall be; Vexilla regis.*
*** Chan. Dig. CHAN 8879; *ABTD 1492* [id.]. (i) Bryn Terfel, London Symphony Ch., LSO,
   Richard Hickox.

This CD forms as good an introduction as any to John Ireland's music. Richard Hickox is a sympathetic interpreter of the composer and obtains sensitive results (and good singing) in *The Holy Boy* and *These things shall be.* The disc is of particular interest in that it brings a rarity, *Vexilla Regis* for chorus, brass and organ. First-class recorded sound.

Phantasie (trio) in A min.
*** Gamut Dig. GAM CD 518 [id.]. Hartley Trio – BRIDGE; CLARKE: *Trios.* ***

Built on striking material, energetically argued, the Ireland *Phantasie* is well played and recorded, and it makes an excellent fill-up for the similar Bridge *Phantasie* and the splendid *Piano trio* of Rebecca Clarke.

PIANO MUSIC

The Almond tree; Decorations; Merry Andrew; Preludes: (The undertone; Obsession; The Holy Boy; Fire of spring); Rhapsody; Sonata in E min.; Summer evening; The Towing-path.
*** Chan. Dig. CHAN 9056 [id.]. Eric Parkin.

Amberley Wild Woods; Ballad; The darkened valley; Equinox; For remembrance; Greenways; In those days; Leaves from a child's sketchbook; London pieces; 2 Pieces; Prelude in E flat; Sonatina.
☞ *** Chan. Dig. CHAN 9140 [id.]. Eric Parkin.

Ballade of London nights; Columbine; Month's mind; On a birthday morning; 3 Pastels; 2 Pieces (February's child; Aubade); 2 Pieces (April; Bergomask); Sarnia; A Sea idyll; Soliloquy; Spring will not wait.
☞ *** Chan. Dig. CHAN 9250 [id.]. Eric Parkin.

Eric Parkin has now completed another survey on Chandos. It goes without saying that he is completely inside Ireland's idiom and he brings both dedication and sympathy to this repertoire. Moreover the sound is clean, well-rounded and pleasing.

Isaac, Heinrich (c. 1450–1517)

Missa de Apostolis. Motets: *Optime pastor; Tota pulchra es; Regina caeli laetare; Resurrexi et adhuc tecum sum; Virgo prudentissima.*
*** Gimell Dig. CDGIM 023; *1585T23* [id.]. Tallis Scholars, Peter Phillips.

The German contemporary of Josquin des Pres, Heinrich Isaac has not until recently been widely appreciated. The Mass setting is glorious, culminating in an ethereal version of *Agnus Dei*, flawlessly sung by the Tallis Scholars. Among the many striking passages is the opening of the six-part setting of *Virgo prudentissima* for two upper voices only, with women's rather than boys' voices all the more appropriate with such a text. Ideally balanced recording.

Ives, Charles (1874–1954)

Calcium light night; Country band march; Largo cantabile: Hymn; 3 Places in New England; Postlude in F; 4 Ragtime dances; Set for theatre orchestra; Yale–Princeton football game.
*** Koch Dig. 37025-2; *37025-4* [id.]. O New England, Sinclair.

This selection of shorter Ives pieces makes an ideal introduction for anyone wanting just to sample the work of this wild, often maddening, but always intriguing composer. Excellent performances and recording.

Central Park in the dark; New England Holidays symphony; The unanswered question (original and revised versions).
*** Sony Dig. MK 42381 [id.]. Chicago Symphony Ch. & O, Tilson Thomas.

The *New England Holidays symphony* comprises four fine Ives pieces normally heard separately. The performance from Michael Tilson Thomas and his Chicago forces is in every way superb, while the wide-ranging CBS recording provides admirable atmosphere. This is now among the most impressive Ives records in the catalogue.

Symphony No. 1 in D min.
*** Chan. Dig. CHAN 9053; *ABTD 1589* [id.]. Detroit SO, Järvi – BARBER: *Essays 1–3.* ***

There is a certain freshness about the melodic invention of the *First Symphony* that is appealing; the idiom is polite and generally conservative with Dvořák as perhaps the strongest influence, but there are already glimpses of iconoclasm in the modulatory shifts. Neeme Järvi gives a very persuasive account of it and there is a fresh and unforced virtuosity from the Detroit orchestra. Excellent, very natural recorded sound, excellently balanced.

Symphonies Nos. 1; 4.
**(*) Sony Dig. SK 44939 [id.]. Chicago SO, Michael Tilson Thomas.

Tilson Thomas's strong and brilliant Chicago performances make a generous and apt coupling, the more valuable for providing first recordings of the revised editions of the composer's tangled scores, with bright, well-detailed sound and superb playing.

Symphony No. 2; Central Park in the dark; The gong on the hook and ladder; Hallowe'en; Hymn for strings; Tone roads No. 1; The unanswered question.
*** DG Dig. 429 220-2 [id.]. NYPO, Bernstein.

Bernstein's disc brings one of the richest offerings of Ives yet put on record, offering the *Symphony No. 2* plus six shorter orchestral pieces. They include two of his very finest, *Central Park in the dark* and *The unanswered question*, both characteristically quirky but deeply poetic too. The extra tensions and expressiveness of live performance here heighten the impact of each of the works. The difficult acoustic of Avery Fisher Hall in New York has rarely sounded more sympathetic on record.

Symphonies Nos. 2; 3 (The Camp meeting).
**(*) Sony Dig. SK 46440 [id.]. Concg. O, Michael Tilson Thomas.

Tilson Thomas's performances may not have the fervour of a Bernstein in this music – perhaps reflecting the fact that this is not an American orchestra – but they are strong and direct, and in No. 3 the revised edition is used on record for the first time.

Symphonies Nos. 2; 3 (The Camp Meeting); (i) Central Park in the dark.
☞ (M) **(*) Sony SMK 47568 [id.]. NYPO, Bernstein; (i) with Seiji Ozawa; Maurice Peress.

Bernstein has re-recorded this music more recently for DG, but these earlier recordings from the 1960s have characteristic conviction and intensity and there is nothing wrong with the remastered sound which is full and atmospheric, if closely balanced. But the dynamics of the playing convey the fullest range of emotion. The *Symphony No. 2* has many characteristically Ivesian touches and contains references to Bach, Beethoven, Brahms and Wagner. The *Third* is (for Ives) rather mild and unambitious, being adapted from quartet movements and organ voluntaries written earlier. But *Central Park in the dark* is another matter, wildly individual in its evocation. The playing of the New York Philharmonic, whether under Bernstein or his younger assistants, is of high quality.

Symphony No. 3 (The Camp meeting).
*** Argo 417 818-2 [id.]. ASMF, Marriner – BARBER: *Adagio;* COPLAND: *Quiet City;* COWELL: *Hymn;* CRESTON: *Rumor.* ***
*** Pro Arte Dig. CDD 140 [id.]. St Paul CO, Russell Davies – COPLAND: *Appalachian spring* etc. ***

Symphony No. 3 (The Camp meeting); (i) Orchestral set No. 2.
*** Sony Dig. MK 37823 [id.]. Concg. O, Tilson Thomas; (i) with Concg. Ch.

Tilson Thomas's version of Ives's most approachable symphony is the first to use the new critical edition, prepared with reference to newly available Ives manuscripts. The *Second Orchestral set*, with its three substantial atmosphere pieces, brings performances of a comparable sharpness. First-rate recording to match the fine performances.

Russell Davies does not use the new edition of Ives's score; nevertheless, he gives a fine account of this gentlest of Ives's symphonies, with its overtones of hymn singing and revivalist meetings, and the beauty of the piece still comes over strongly.

Marriner's account is first rate in every way. It does not have the advantage of a digital master, but the 1976 analogue recording has slightly sharper detail in this remastered format.

Symphony No. 3; Three places in New England.
(M) *** Mercury 432 755-2 [id.]. Eastman-Rochester O, Howard Hanson – SCHUMAN: *New England triptych* ***; MENNIN: *Symphony No. 5.* **(*)

Ives's quixotic genius is at its most individual in the *Three places in New England*. Both works are most understandingly presented here under Howard Hanson, who is equally at home in the folksy imagery of the *Third Symphony*. The acoustics of the Eastman Theatre are less than ideally expansive, but the 1957 recording is remarkably full-bodied and vivid.

(i) *Symphony No. 4; Robert Browning Overture;* (ii) Songs: *An Election, Lincoln the great commoner; Majority, They are There!*
(M) *** Sony MPK 46726 [id.]. (i) NY Schola Cantorum; (ii) Gregg Smith Singers; American SO, Stokowski.

The (originally 1965) recording of the *Fourth Symphony*, made at the same period as the belated première of the work, brings a stunning performance, with sound that is still amazingly full and vivid. Stokowski also brings out the often aggressive vigour of the *Robert Browning Overture*. The choral songs with orchestra provide an attractive makeweight.

Variations on America.
☞ ** Teldec/Warner Dig. 9031 74007-2 [id.]. NYPO, Masur – BRAHMS: *Variations on a theme of Haydn;* REGER: *Variations and fugue on a theme of Mozart.* **

Ives' *Variations on America* are the bonus in this all-variations programme, and readers wanting the disc are more likely to be attracted to the not inconsiderable virtues of the Reger or the Brahms rather than to this set whose slender attractions are hardly likely to sway the collector one way or the other. It is given a musicianly and well-groomed performance without any exaggeration, but ideally calls for more flamboyance.

Piano trio (1904).
*** Teldec/Warner Dig. 2292 44924-2 [id.]. Trio Fontenay – BRAHMS: *Piano trio No. 1.* ***

The Ives *Trio* is an amazing piece for 1904 and it is excellently played by the Trio Fontenay. They are given eminently clear but not overbright recording.

String quartets Nos. 1–2.
☞ *** DG Dig. 435 864-2 [id.]. Emerson Qt – BARBER: *Quartet.* **(*)

The Ives *String quartets* have been neglected in recent years, and this new version by the Emerson Quartet is the most commanding to have appeared since the Juilliard Quartet's LP version from the 1970s. The *First* (1896) comes from the composer's early twenties and makes liberal use of hymn-tunes in the first movement fugue. The *Second* (1913) is made of sterner stuff and its high norm of dissonance prompts one's thoughts to turn to the Bartók of the *Third* and *Fourth quartets.* Whether or not you find the work consistently satisfying, it is undeniably an extraordinary musical document and is well worth study. The Emerson Quartet give it a performance of stunning efficiency and brilliance. Ensemble is impeccable, the tone carefully nourished and honed, with every detail of dynamic meticulously calculated and in place. All the same, the musical argument unfolds more naturally and effortlessly with the Juilliards and, for that reason, were it to reappear in the lifetime of this volume it would probably take precedence over the Emerson in spite of the full-blooded and very present quality of the DG recording.

Songs: *An old flame; At the river; Charlie Rutlage; The children's hour; The circus band; He is there!; In the alley; A night song; Romanzo di Central Park; Slow march.*
*** Argo Dig. 433 027-2 [id.]. Samuel Ramey, Warren Jones – COPLAND: *Old American songs.* ***

With some characteristically vigorous songs as well as many that might almost be Edwardian ballads (spiced Ives-style), this group of ten songs is superbly done. Ramey deftly avoids the obvious pitfalls in writing which is only parodistic in part, whether in the overtly sentimental fragments or the rousing songs like *The circus band* and the patriotic First World War song, *He is there!.* It makes an illuminating contrast having Ives's much more idiosyncratic setting of *At the river* as well as Copland's on the disc. Warren Jones's accompaniments are highly sympathetic. Excellent recording. A coupling not to be missed.

Songs: *Autumn; Berceuse; The cage; Charlie Rutlage; Down East; Dreams; Evening; The greatest man; The Housatonic at Stockbridge; Immortality; Like a sick eagle; Maple leaves; Memories: 1, 2, 3; On the counter; Romanzo di Central Park; The see'r; Serenity; The side-show; Slow march; Slugging a vampire; Songs my mother taught me; Spring song; The things our fathers loved; Tom sails away; Two little flowers.*
*** Etcetera Dig. KTC 1020 [id.]. Roberta Alexander, Tan Crone.

Roberta Alexander presents her excellent and illuminating choice of Ives songs in chronological order, starting with one written when Ives was only fourteen, *Slow march*, already predicting developments ahead. Sweet, nostalgic songs predominate, but the singer punctuates them with leaner, sharper inspirations. Her manner is not always quite tough enough in those, but this is characterful singing from an exceptionally rich and attractive voice. Tan Crone is the understanding accompanist, and the recording is first rate.

Jacob, Gordon (1895–1987)

Mini-concerto for clarinet and string orchestra.
*** Hyp. CDA 66031 [id.]. Thea King, NW CO of Seattle, Alun Francis – COOKE; RAWSTHORNE: *Concertos.* ***

Gordon Jacob in his eighties responded to an earlier recording of his music by Thea King by writing this miniature concerto for her, totally charming in its compactness, with not a note too many. Thea King is the most persuasive of dedicatees, splendidly accompanied by the orchestra from Seattle and treated to first-rate 1982 analogue sound, splendidly transferred.

William Byrd suite.
(M) *** Mercury 432 009-2 [id.]. Eastman Wind Ens., Fennell – BENNETT: *Symphonic songs* ***; HOLST: *Hammersmith* ***; WALTON: *Crown Imperial.* *** ⊛

Gordon Jacob's arrangement of the music of Byrd is audaciously anachronistic, but it is very entertaining when played with such flair. The recording is up to the usual high Mercury standard in this repertoire.

Divertimento for harmonica and string quartet.
*** Chan. Dig. CHAN 8802; *CBTD 026* [id.]. Tommy Reilly, Hindar Qt – MOODY: *Quintet; Suite.* ***

Gordon Jacob's set of eight sharply characterized miniatures shows the composer at his most engagingly imaginative and the performances are deliciously piquant in colour and feeling. The recording could hardly be more successful.

Oboe quartet.
*** Chan. Dig. CHAN 8392; *ABTD 1114* [id.]. Francis, English Qt – BAX: *Quintet;* HOLST: *Air and variations* etc.; MOERAN: *Fantasy quartet.* ***

Gordon Jacob's *Oboe quartet* is well crafted and entertaining, particularly the vivacious final Rondo. The performance could hardly be bettered, and the recording is excellent too.

Janáček, Leoš (1854–1928)

Adagio for orchestra; Ballad of Blaník; Cossack dance; (i) *Danube Symphony. The Fiddler's child* (ballad); *Idyll for strings; Jealousy overture; Lachian dances;* (ii) *The Pilgrimage of the soul (Violin concerto);* (iii) *Schluck und Jau* (incidental music): excerpts: *Andante & Allegretto. Serbian Kolo. Sinfonietta; Suite, Op. 3; Suite for strings; Taras Bulba* (rhapsody).
☞ *** Sup. Dig. 11 1834-2 (3) [id.]. Brno State PO, František Jílek, with (i) Karolína Dvořáková; (ii) Ivan Zenatý; (i; iii) Jiří Beneš.

(i) *Danube Symphony. Sinfonietta;* (ii) *The Pilgrimage of the soul (Violin concerto);* (iii) *Schluck und Jau.*
☞ *** Sup. Dig. 11 1422-2 [id.]. Brno State PO, František Jílek, with (i) Karolina Dvořáková; (ii) Ivan Zenatý; (i; iii) Jiří Beneš.

The most important and in a way interesting of the three discs in this valuable Janáček discography is available separately. Yet with its two companions as a package, the three CDs provide an idiomatic basis for any Janáček collection on CD. The performance of the *Sinfonietta* can hold its own with the best in terms of atmosphere and authority, though the recording is admittedly not in the demonstration bracket. The remaining works on the separate disc are reconstructions. The *Danube Symphony* is a four-movement work, conceived in 1923 at the time Janáček was exhilarated with a production of *Katya Kabanová*, but the score was in an advanced state and was completed by Osvald Chlubna. This new version, prepared by the scholars Leoš Faltus and Miloš Stědrů, contains only Janáček's text. There is some invention of great imagination here, as, indeed, there is in the *Violin concerto (The Pilgrimage of the soul).* Ivan Zenatý is an aristocrat of the violin and his performance is no less poignant than the Teldec alternative by Thomas Zehetmair. The incidental music to Gerhart Hauptman's play, *Schluck und Jau,* was planned for a production at Heidelberg in 1928, but Janáček died before completing it. The score was reconstructed in the 1970s by Jarmil Burghauser and is a two-movement piece about as long as the *Violin concerto* and likewise full of characteristic ideas. Of the other two discs, the first offering the *Lachian dances,* the early *Suite for strings* and its seven-movement companion, the *Idyll,* is well filled (71 minutes 32 seconds), and the other disc brings such valuable scores as *Blaník, The Fiddler's Child* and *Taras Bulba* (73 minutes 7 seconds). Good, idiomatic performances and very good, though not demonstration-quality recordings. The Brno studios are less reverberant than the House of the Artists in Prague, and the results here are much more than just agreeable.

(i; ii) *Capriccio for piano and wind;* (iii; i) *A Fairy tale; Presto;* (i) *In the mists; Sonata 1.X.1905.*
☞ *** Decca Dig. 440 312-2 [id.]. (i) András Schiff; (ii) Musiktage Mondsee Ens.; (iii) Boris Pergamenschikow.

(i; ii) *Concertino for piano and chamber ensemble;* (i; iii) *Violin sonata;* (i) *On an overgrown path.*
☞ *** Decca Dig. 440 313-2 [id.]. (i) András Schiff; (ii) Musiktage Mondsee Ens.; (iii) Yuuko Shiokawa.

Two CDs comprising recordings made at the Mondsee Festival near Salzburg, whose artistic director is the pianist, András Schiff, who features in all the pieces on both discs. The instrumental ensemble draws on some distinguished players and such familiar soloists as, for example, the bassoonist Klaus Thunemann and the flautist, Wolfgang Schultz. Generally speaking the performances are highly satisfying, even though there have been more sharply focused accounts of both the *Capriccio* and the *Concertino* from native Czech ensembles or from Firkušný and colleagues. Not that these artists are in the least bland, but they are less acerbic than some earlier accounts and produce less astringent sonorities. The same goes for Schiff's solo contributions: there are more strongly characterized accounts of the *Sonata* and *In the mists* (from Andsnes) or of *On an overgrown path* from Firkušný. Boris Pergamenschikow plays the *Fairy Tale* and the *Presto* which was possibly intended for it with strong personality. There is no reason to withhold a three-star rating for these well-defined recordings or thoughtful performances, but none are quite first choices.

Capriccio for piano left-hand and wind; Concertino for piano and seven instruments.
*** BMG/RCA Dig. RD 60781 [60781-2]. Rudolf Firkušný, Czech PO, Václav Neumann –
DVORAK: *Piano concerto in G min.* ***

Firkušný himself is now older than Janáček was when he wrote these remarkable pieces, but he conveys a youthful fire which seems to burn almost as brightly as the earlier recordings he made in the 1950s and 1970s. A thoroughly worthwhile coupling with Dvořák.

(i) *Concertino for piano and seven instruments;* (ii) *Sinfonietta; Taras Bulba.*
☞ ⊛ *** (B) *** DG 439 437-2 [id.]. (i) Rudolf Firkušný (Bav. RSO members); Bav. RSO; Kubelik.

A quite outstanding bargain triptych that would make a worthwhile addition to any collection, large or small. Kubelik has a special feeling for this repertoire and partners Rudolf Firkušný in a thoroughly idiomatic account of the *Concertino,* with the dialogue between keyboard and sparsely scored accompaniment both plangent and witty. *Taras Bulba* with its unpleasant scenario of death and torture is powerfully evoked, with a discerning balance between passion and subtlety. The organ part is integrated into the texture most delicately in the first section, yet adds grandiloquence to the work's triumphant apotheosis, with its vision of a triumphant Cossack future. Virtuoso playing from the Bavarian orchestra throughout, with much excitement generated in the last two sections. The orchestra is hardly less impressive in the *Sinfonietta* (and particularly so in the central movements), while at the opening and close of the work the spacious acoustic of the Munich Herculessaal is especially suited to the massed brass effects. The vintage (1970) recording has been superbly remastered and sounds amazingly fresh.

Violin concerto (Pilgrimage of the soul) – reconstructed Faltus & Stědrů.
☞ *** Teldec/Warner Dig. 2292-46449-2 [id.]. Zehetmair, Philh. O, Holliger – BERG: *Violin concerto;*
HARTMANN: *Concerto funèbre.* ***

In his last year Janáček worked on his opera, *From the House of the Dead,* based on Dostoevsky, the autograph score of which contains sketches for a violin concerto he had planned to call *Pilgrimage of the soul.* He used some of its ideas in the overture to the opera, but the concerto remained in fragmentary form. On his death, his pupil, Břetislav Bakala, who had seen the opera through the press, prepared a performing version of the piece. The present version, the work of Leoš Faltus and Miloš Stědrů, revived interest in the piece when it was premièred in 1988, and there are two rival accounts currently on the market (from Josef Suk on Supraphon and Christian Tetzlef on Virgin). This is highly original music, albeit with some top-heavy orchestral writing, searing in its intensity – particularly as played here by Thomas Zehetmair and the Philharmonia under Heinz Holliger. Excellent recorded sound.

The Fiddler's child (ballad for orchestra); *Jealousy: overture; Taras Bulba; The Cunning little vixen* (suite).
☞ *** Chan. Dig. CHAN 9080 [id.]. Czech PO, Bělohlávek.

Bělohlávek is perhaps less at home in *Taras Bulba* than in the nature mysticism of the suite from *Cunning little vixen* or the pathos of *The Fiddler's child.* There are more dramatic and fiery accounts of *Taras*, but the beauty of the orchestral playing and the opulence and detail of the recording still just earn it a three-star rating.

Sinfonietta.
*** EMI Dig. CDC7 47504-2 [id.]. Philh. O, Rattle – *Glagolitic Mass.* ***
☞ (M) *** DG 437 254-2 [id.]. Bav. RSO, Kubelik – SMETANA: *Symphonic poems.* ***
(M) *** Decca 425 624-2 [id.]. LSO, Abbado – *Glagolitic Mass.* ***
☞ (M) **(*) Telarc CD 82010 [id.]. LAPO, André Previn – BARTOK: *Concerto for orchestra.* **(*)

Sinfonietta; Lachian dances; Taras Bulba.
(BB) *** Naxos Dig. 8.550411 [id.]. Slovak RSO (Bratislava), Ondrej Lenárd.

Sinfonietta; Taras Bulba.
(M) *** Decca Dig. 430 727-2 [id.]. VPO, Mackerras – SHOSTAKOVICH: *Age of gold.* ***

Mackerras's coupling comes as a superb supplement to his Janáček opera recordings with the Vienna Philharmonic. The massed brass of the *Sinfonietta* has tremendous bite and brilliance as well as characteristic Viennese ripeness, thanks to a spectacular digital recording. *Taras Bulba* too is given more weight and body than is usual, the often savage dance rhythms presented with great energy.

Rattle gets an altogether first-class response from the orchestra and truthful recorded sound from the EMI engineers; many collectors may find the EMI sound more pleasing. The Decca has greater clarity and presence in its favour, as well as Mackerras's authority in this repertoire. However, Rattle's coupling with the *Glagolitic Mass* is very attractive indeed.

Abbado gives a splendid account of the *Sinfonietta* and evokes a highly sympathetic response from the LSO. His acute sensitivity to dynamic nuances and his care for detail are felt in every bar. The recording balance, too, allows the subtlest of colours to register while still having plenty of impact.

Jiři Bělohlávek's exultant and imaginative account of the *Sinfonietta* is one of the best currently on offer and is coupled with an outstanding version of Martinů's *Sixth Symphony*; the recording, made in the Smetana Hall, Prague, is impressive.

On Naxos we have the normal LP coupling of the *Sinfonietta* and *Taras Bulba*, but with the *Lachian dances* thrown in for good measure, all played by musicians steeped in the Janáček tradition – and all at a very modest cost. These are excellent performances and well worth the money involved; the recording, made in a fairly resonant studio, is natural and free from any artificially spotlit balance.

The Bavarian orchestra is in virtuoso form and there is some fine playing here and much vitality. The recording was made in the Hercules Hall in Munich which is very suited to Janáček's plangent brass sonorities. Kubelik's performance makes an enjoyably vibrant coupling for the Smetana symphonic poems, but this performance is also included in an even more attractive bargain collection – see above.

The amiability of Janáček's colourful and brassy work is what dominates Previn's performance rather than any more dramatic qualities. It matches his relaxed view of the Bartók *Concerto for orchestra*, which comes as a unique coupling. The Los Angeles Philharmonic has never been recorded with a warmer and more realistic bloom than here by Jack Renner of Telarc in Royce Hall, UCLA. However, those looking for more bite and brilliance in this work will probably be happier with either the splendidly vital Mackerras recording, coupled with *Taras Bulba*, or the Rattle version.

Taras Bulba (rhapsody).
*** Decca Dig. 430 204-2 [id.]. Cleveland O, Dohnányi – DVORAK: *Symphony No. 6.* ***

Opulently recorded in Decca's finest Cleveland style, like the Dvořák symphony with which it is coupled, Dohnányi's version of *Taras Bulba* provides a generous makeweight on a fine disc.

String quartet No. 1 (Kreutzer sonata).
☞ *** BMG/RCA Dig. 09026 61816-2 [id.]. Vogler Qt – DEBUSSY; SHOSTAKOVICH: *Quartets.* ***

Hybrid CDs or those coupling more than one composer endanger themselves for the simple reason that those who want the Debussy *Quartet* do not necessarily need Shostakovich No. 11 if they have a complete cycle, or alternatively a Janáček *First* if they want (or have) both. However, to miss this performance by the Vogler Quartet would be a pity. Taken on its own merits, it is very impressive: intelligent and alive, and well recorded too.

String quartets Nos. 1 (Kreutzer); 2 (Intimate letters).
(M) *** Decca 430 295-2 [id.]. Gabrieli Qt – SMETANA: *Quartet No. 1.* ***
*** ASV Dig. CDDCA 749 [id.]. Lindsay Qt (with DVORAK: *Cypresses* ***).
☞ **(*)* HM Dig. HMC 901380; *HMC 401380* [id.]. Melos Qt.
☞ *(*) Nimbus Dig. NI 5113 [id.]. Medici Qt.

(i) *String quartets Nos. 1–2;* (ii) *Mladi: suite for wind sextet.*
☞ **(*) Koch/Panton 11203-2 [id.]. (i) Vlach Qt; (ii) Foerster Wind Quintet, Josef Horák.

(i) *String quartets Nos. 1–2;* (ii; iii) *Pohádka (A Tale)* for cello & piano; (iv; iii) *Violin sonata.*
☞ ** EMI Dig. CDC7 54787-2 [id.]. (i) Britten Qt; (ii) Andrew Schulman; (iii) Ian Brown; (iv) Peter Maning.

(i) *String quartets Nos. 1–2;* (ii) *On an overgrown path: suite No. 1.*
*** Calliope Dig. CAL 9699 [id.]. (i) Talich Qt; (ii) Radoslav Kvapil.

The Gabrieli Quartet have the measure of this strikingly original music and give a highly idiomatic and strongly felt account of these masterpieces. They have the advantage of a well-focused and truthfully balanced recording.

Otherwise pride of place must go to the Talich Quartet on Calliope, not because their recording is the best – it is by no means as vivid as the Decca – but because of their extraordinary qualities of insight. They play the *Intimate letters* as if its utterances came from a world so private that it must be approached with great care. The disc's value is much enhanced by a fill-up in the form of the *First suite, On an overgrown path.* Radoslav Kvapil is thoroughly inside this repertoire.

The Lindsays on ASV are eminently competitive and have the right blend of sensitivity and intensity. Theirs must certainly rank very highly among current recommendations. It is played with the same concentration and sensitivity they bring to all they do, and recorded with great naturalness.

The most recent contender of note is EMI's Britten Quartet, who also offer a generous bonus in the form of *Pohádka* and the *Violin sonata.* They play with stunning accuracy and vehemence and are splendidly recorded; at the same time, as a comparison with such rivals as the Lindsay (ASV) and the Talich (Calliope) reveal, there is something missing, and the listener remains untouched.

These days the two Janáček *Quartets* alone do not really represent the good value for money they represented in the days of LP. The Melos Quartet offer nothing in addition to the two *Quartets,* but theirs are performances of considerable character and fire and, though the playing-time is ungenerous and the recording a bit fierce, they are worth consideration.

All the same, the Koch/Panton coupling with the Vlach Quartet, recorded in 1969, and a 1970 version of *Mladi* should not automatically be dismissed on grounds of age. The performances are very idiomatic and appealing, the recording far from inferior; and this record will give pleasure.

The Nimbus/Medici CD plays for 43 minutes 20 seconds and even with a highly competitive price-tag this would be poor value. The playing and recording are perfectly acceptable and recommendable but fall short of distinction.

Violin sonata.
*** Virgin/EMI Dig. VC5 45002-2 [id.]. Dmitry Sitkovetsky, Pavel Gililov – DEBUSSY: *Sonata* **; R. STRAUSS: *Sonata.* ***
(*) DG Dig. 427 351-2 [id.]. Gidon Kremer, Martha Argerich – BARTOK: *Sonata No. 1;* MESSIAEN: *Theme and variations.* *

The Janáček *Sonata* is a powerfully impassioned and original work. Dmitry Sitkovetsky and Pavel Gililov seem completely attuned to its thoughtful, impulsive, improvisatory idiom, and the engineers produce a natural, well-balanced sound.

It is also played with great imaginative intensity and power by Gidon Kremer and Martha Argerich, though it is less selfless here than with Sitkovetsky on Virgin: there is some expressive exaggeration. Excellent DG recording.

Along an overgrown path: Suite No. 1; In the mists; Piano sonata (I.X.1905).
*** Virgin/EMI Dig. VC7 59639-2 [id.]. Leif Ove Andsnes.

Leif Ove Andsnes gives us a very well-thought-out and imaginatively realized recital, including a highly sensitive account of *In the mists,* which is second to none in conveying the pervasive melancholy and evocative atmosphere of these pieces. This is every bit as telling as Mikhail Rudy's EMI account, and beautifully recorded.

Piano sonata (1.X.1905); In the mists; 3 Moravian dances; On an overgrown path: Books 1 & 2; A recollection.
*** EMI Dig. CDC7 54094-2 [id.]. Mikhail Rudy.

Piano sonata (1.X.1905); In the mists; On the overgrown path, Book 2; A recollection; Theme & variations.
(M) *** DG 429 857-2 [id.]. Rudolf Firkušný.

Rudolf Firkušný recorded these pieces for DG in the early 1970s and he produces seamless legato lines, hammerless tone and rapt atmosphere. Given its competitive price, many collectors will opt for this anthology, which still sounds very good and also includes the *Zdenka Theme and variations*.

Mikhail Rudy proves a perceptive and sympathetic guide in this music. His is a fine account of the *Sonata*, and he succeeds in penetrating the world of the *Overgrown path* miniatures to perfection. He conveys their acute sense of melancholy and their improvisatory character with distinction, and the recorded sound is very natural.

VOCAL MUSIC

Glagolitic Mass.
*** EMI Dig. CDC7 47504-2 [id.]. Palmer, Gunson, Mitchinson, King, CBSO & Ch., Rattle – *Sinfonietta.* ***
(M) *** Decca 425 624-2 [id.]. Kubiak, Collins, Tear, Schone, Brighton Festival Ch., RPO, Kempe – *Sinfonietta.* ***
☞ (M) **(*) Sony SMK 47569 [id.]. Pilarczyk, Gedda, Gaynes, Westminster Ch., NYPO, Bernstein – POULENC: *Gloria.* ***
☞ (B) ** DG Double 437 937-2 (2) [id.]. Lear, Haefliger, Rössel-Majdan, Crass, Bav. R. Ch. & O, Kubelik – DVORAK: *Stabat Mater.* ***

Written when Janáček was over seventy, this is one of his most important and most exciting works, full of those strikingly fresh uses of sound that make his music so distinctive. The text is taken from native Croatian variations of the Latin text, but its vitality bespeaks a folk inspiration. Rattle's performance, aptly paired with the *Sinfonietta*, is strong and vividly dramatic, with the Birmingham performers lending themselves to Slavonic passion. The recording is first class.

The Decca recording is an extremely good one. Kempe's reading is broad but has plenty of vitality, and the Brighton chorus sings vigorously. The playing of the Royal Philharmonic is wonderfully committed and vivid, and there is first-rate solo singing, with Teresa Kubiak particularly impressive.

Though Bernstein's reading of the *Glagolitic Mass* is not entirely idiomatic, it is a fine red-blooded performance and one which has the merit of distinguished soloists who add much to the performance. The vivid (1963) recording is one of the best of those Bernstein made in the Avery Fisher Hall.

Kubelik's DG version is fresh and well sung and fully acceptable if you want the Dvořák coupling, but at almost every point the versions by Rattle and Kempe are preferable.

OPERA

The Cunning Little Vixen (complete); Cunning little vixen (suite, arr. Talich).
*** Decca Dig. 417 129-2 (2) [id.]. Popp, Randová, Jedlická, V. State Op. Ch., Bratislava Children's Ch., VPO, Mackerras.

Mackerras's thrusting, red-blooded reading is spectacularly supported by a digital recording of outstanding, demonstration quality. The inspired choice of Lucia Popp as the vixen provides charm in exactly the right measure: sparkling and coquettish, spiteful as well as passionate. The supporting cast is first rate, too. Talich's splendidly arranged orchestral suite is offered as a bonus in a fine new recording.

(i) *The Cunning Little Vixen (sung in English); (ii) Taras Bulba.*
*** EMI CDS7 54212-2 (2) [id.]. (i) Watson, Tear, Allen, ROHCG Ch. & O; (ii) Philh. O; Simon Rattle.

For anyone who wants the work in English, Simon Rattle's recording provides an ideal answer, with Rattle's warmly expressive approach to the score giving strong support to the singers, who equally have gained in expressiveness from singing their roles on stage in the theatre. The cast is outstanding, with Lillian Watson delightfully bright and fresh as the Vixen and Thomas Allen firm and full-toned as the Forester. If Mackerras's Janáček style is more angular and abrasive, bringing out the jagged, spiky rhythms and unexpected orchestral colours, Rattle's is more moulded, more immediately persuasive, if less obviously idiomatic.

(i) *From the house of the dead;* (iii) *Mládí* (for wind sextet); (ii; iii) *Říkadla* (for Chamber Ch. & 10 instruments).
*** Decca Dig. 430 375-2 (2) [id.]. (i) Jedlička, Zahradníček, Zídek, Zítek, V. State Op. Ch., VPO, Mackerras; (ii) L. Sinf. Ch.; (iii) L. Sinf., Atherton.

With one exception, the cast here is superb, with a range of important Czech singers giving sharply characterized vignettes. The exception is the raw Slavonic singing of the one woman in the cast, Jaroslav Janska as the boy, Aljeja, but even that fails to undermine the intensity of the innocent relationship with the central figure, which provides an emotional anchor for the whole piece. The chamber-music items added for this reissue are both first rate.

Jenůfa (complete).
⊛ *** Decca Dig. 414 483-2 (2) [id.]. Söderström, Ochman, Dvorský, Randová, Popp, V. State Op. Ch., VPO, Mackerras.

This is the warmest and most lyrical of Janáček's operas, and it inspires a performance from Mackerras and his team which is deeply sympathetic, strongly dramatic and superbly recorded. Elisabeth Söderström creates a touching portrait of the girl caught in a family tragedy. The two rival tenors, Peter Dvorský and Wieslav Ochman as the half-brothers Steva and Laca, are both superb; but dominating the whole drama is the Kostelnitchka of Eva Randová. Some may resist the idea that she should be made so sympathetic but, particularly on record, the drama is made stronger and more involving.

Káta Kabanová (complete).
☞ **(*) Sup. 10 8016-2 612 (2) [id.]. Tikalová, Blachut, Komancová, Vích, Mixová, Kroupa, Prague Nat. Theatre Ch. & O, Jaroslav Krombholc.

(i) *Káta Kabanová* (complete); (ii) *Capriccio for piano and 7 instruments; Concertino for piano and 6 instruments*.
☞ *** Decca 421 852-2 (2) [id.]. (i) Söderström, Dvorský, Kniplová, Krejčik, Márová, V. State Op. Ch., VPO, Mackerras; (ii) Paul Crossley, L. Sinf., Atherton.

Káta Kabanová is based on Ostrovsky's play, *The Storm*, which has inspired other operas as well as Tchaikovsky's overture and was Janáček's first stage work after the First World War. It is worth adding that this Decca recording was the first of a Janáček opera ever made outside Czechoslovakia. Elisabeth Söderström dominates the cast as the tragic heroine and gives a performance of great insight and sensitivity; she touches the listener deeply and is supported by Mackerras with imaginative grip and flair. He draws playing of great eloquence from the Vienna Philharmonic Orchestra. The plot (very briefly) centres on Kátya, a person of unusual goodness whose marriage is loveless, and her husband, who is dominated by his mother. Her infatuation with Boris (Peter Dvorský), her subsequent confession of adultery and her ultimate suicide are pictured with music of the most powerful and atmospheric kind. The other soloists are all Czech and their characterizations are brilliantly authentic. But it is the superb orchestral playing and the inspired performance of Söderström that make this set so memorable. The recording has a truthfulness and realism that do full justice to Janáček's marvellous score, vividly transferred to CD, with a double bonus added in the shape of the two concertante keyboard works, in which Paul Crossley is the impressive soloist. These are performances that can be put alongside those of Firkušný – and no praise can be higher.

The alternative Czech recording, made in 1959, also has the distinction of being one of the first complete recordings of a Janáček opera made by Supraphon, and the early stereo is remarkably full and atmospheric. The performance has the loving authenticity one expects from this source. Something of the original sharpness of sound is lost – in part because of the recording, in part because Vaclav Talich's reorchestration is used. The cast is strong, with a superb performance from the tenor Blachut at the peak of his career. However, Drahomíra Tikalová in the name-role cannot match Söderström in intensity of expression and feeling.

(i) *The Makropulos affair (Věc Makropulos)*: complete; (ii) *Lachian dances*.
*** Decca 430 372-2 (2) [id.]. (i) Söderström, Dvorský, Blachut, V. State Op. Ch., VPO, Mackerras; (ii) LPO, Huybrechts.

Mackerras and his superb team provide a thrilling new perspective on this opera, with its weird heroine preserved by magic elixir well past her 300th birthday. Elisabeth Söderström is not simply malevolent: irritable and impatient rather, no longer an obsessive monster. Framed by richly colourful singing and playing, Söderström amply justifies that view, and Peter Dvorský is superbly fresh and ardent as Gregor. The recording, like others in the series, is of the highest Decca analogue quality. The performance of the *Lachian dances* is highly idiomatic and makes a good bonus.

Osud (complete).

*** EMI Dig. CDC7 49993-2 [Ang. CDC 49993]. Langridge, Field, Harries, Bronder, Kale, Welsh National Op. Ch. & O, Mackerras.

Janáček's – most unjustly neglected – opera, richly lyrical, more sustained and less fragmented than his later operas, is not just a valuable rarity but makes an ideal introduction to the composer. Philip Langridge is superb in the central role of the composer, Zivny, well supported by Helen Field as Mila, the married woman he loves, and by Kathryn Harries as her mother – a far finer cast than was presented on a short-lived Supraphon set. This performance uses Rodney Blumer's excellent English translation, adding to the immediate impact. Sir Charles Mackerras matches his earlier achievement in the prize-winning series of Janáček opera recordings for Decca, capturing the full gutsiness, passion and impetus of the composer's inspiration. The warmly atmospheric EMI recording, made in Brangwyn Hall, Swansea, brings out the unusual opulence of the Janáček sound, yet it allows words to come over with fine clarity.

Joachim, Joseph (1831–1907)

(i) *Violin concerto in the Hungarian manner, Op. 11. Overtures: Hamlet, Op. 4; Henry IV, Op. 7.*

(M) *** Pickwick Dig. MCD 27; *M CC 27*. (i) Elmer Oliveira; LPO, Leon Bottstein.

Joseph Joachim's fame rests as a legendary performer and the dedicatee of the Brahms *Violin concerto*, rather than as a composer. Nevertheless his concerto is one of the most demanding works written for the instrument in the nineteenth century. Conservative in outlook and indebted to Mendelssohn and Beethoven, it is a very considerable achievement – as, for that matter, is the playing of Elmer Oliveira in this truthful, present and well-balanced recording. The conductor Leon Bottstein also gives committed accounts of the splendid *Henry IV* and *Hamlet Overtures*. An enterprising and rewarding release.

Johnson, Robert (c. 1582–1633)

Lute and Theatre music: *Almans I–III; Corant; Fantasia; Galliard; Pavan;* Ayres: *Adieu, fond love; Arm, arm!; As I walked forth; Away delights; Care-charming sleep; Charon, oh Charon; Come away, Hecate; Come away, thou lady gay; Come, heavy sleep; Come hither, you that love; Full fathom five; Hark! hark! the lark!; Have you seen the white lily grow?; O let us howl; Tell me dearest; 'Tis late and cold; Where the bee sucks; Woods, rocks and mountains.*

☞ ❀ *** Virgin/EMI Dig. VC7 59321-2 [id.]. Emma Kirkby, David Thomas, Anthony Rooley.

It is good to have a CD devoted to the youngest of the English writers of lute-songs. Robert Johnson was born two decades after Dowland and Campion, and he had the most individual musical personality. His feeling for expressive Elizabethan melancholy was profound, if not as overwhelmingly introverted as Dowland's, and his muse could display humour and drama with equal facility. In this most engaging recital, Emma Kirkby sings with characteristic freshness and charm in Shakespearean numbers like *Hark! hark! the lark!*, *Where the bee sucks* and *Away delights* from Beaumont and Fletcher's *The Captain*, and she is utterly ravishing in the poignant *Come, heavy sleep*, and the following, equally beautiful *Care-charming sleep*. David Thomas is hardly less expressive in Ariel's *Full fathom five* from *The Tempest* with its gently tolling bell and *Have you seen the white lily grow?* (Ben Jonson). Like Kirkby, his decoration is felicitous, often florid but never fussy. After the drama of the male solo songs, *Arm, arm* (recalling a famous battle, written for Beaumont and Fletcher's *Mad Lover*) and the grotesquely malignant *O let us howl* (provided for Webster's *Duchess of Malfi*), Thomas is joined by Emma Kirkby in the dialogue interchange of *Come away, Hecate* (from Middleton's *The Witch*) complete with vociferous growls which suggest that the angst is not to be taken too seriously. Anthony Rooley then calms the atmosphere with delicately played lute solos, which demonstrate the composer's ready versatility. Two more duets end the programme, *Come away thou lady gay*, with a garrulous cackling response from Kirkby, and *Tell me dearest*, in which she is altogether more demure. The recording is absolutely natural, the presence of the singers enhanced by the pleasing acoustic, and the lute is never made to seem larger than life. This is a programme that can be listened to straight through with much pleasure, admirably simulating a live recital.

Jolivet, André (1905–74)

(i) *Concertino for trumpet, piano and strings; Trumpet concerto.*
*** Sony Dig. MK 42096 [id.]. Wynton Marsalis, (i) Craig Shepherd, Philh. O, Salonen – TOMASI: *Concerto.* ***

As crossover music goes, this is rather successful, with the brilliant musicianship, dizzy bravura and natural idiomatic feeling of Wynton Marsalis tailor-made for this repertoire. There is not a great deal for Craig Shepherd to do in the duet concertino, but he does it well enough. The recording is not especially clear, though some ears will detect background hum at times. The CD offers poor value at only 35 minutes.

Chant de Linos.
*** Koch Dig. 3-7016 [id.]. Atlantic Sinf. – JONGEN: *Concert;* DEBUSSY: *Sonata.* ***

The *Chant de Linos* was originally composed for flute and piano, but Jolivet subsequently made this highly effective transcription for flute, violin, viola, cello and harp. It is played with exemplary taste and effortless virtuosity by Bradley Garner and his colleagues of the Atlantic Sinfonietta and is most beautifully recorded.

Jongen, Joseph (1873–1953)

(i) *Allegro appassionato for viola and orchestra, Op. 79; Suite for viola and orchestra, Op. 48.* (ii) *Symphonie concertante for organ and orchestra, Op. 81.*
☞ **(*) Koch Schwann Dig. CD 315 012 [id.) (i) Therèse-Marie Gilissen, RTBF SO, Brian Priestman; (ii) Hubert Schoonbroodt, Liège SO, René Defossez.

Symphonie concertante for organ and orchestra, Op. 81.
*** Telarc Dig. CD 80096 [id.]. Michael Murray, San Francisco SO, De Waart – FRANCK: *Fantaisie* etc. ***
☞ (M) ** EMI CDM5 65075-2 [id.]. Virgil Fox, Fr. Nat. Theatre Op. O, Prêtre – DE GREEF: *Piano concerto.* **

Anyone who likes the Saint-Saëns *Third Symphony* should enjoy the Jongen *Symphonie concertante.* Even if the music is on a lower level of inspiration, the passionate *Lento misterioso* and hugely spectacular closing *Toccata* make a favourable impression at first hearing and wear surprisingly well afterwards. Michael Murray has all the necessary technique to carry off Jongen's hyperbole with the required panache. He receives excellent support from Edo de Waart and the San Francisco Symphony Orchestra. The huge Ruffatti organ seems custom-built for the occasion and Telarc's engineers capture all the spectacular effects with their usual aplomb. A demonstration disc indeed.

Joseph Jongen has a more individual profile than his countryman, Arthur de Greef, with whom he shares the EMI issue. In spite of his academic duties (he was professor of fugue at the Brussels conservatoire whose director he became), he was a prolific composer with over 400 works to his credit. The *Sinfonia concertante* begins fugally, but there is a lot of Franck, d'Indy and Ravel in its writing. Jongen himself was the soloist in its first performance in 1924 and would presumably find the Schoonbroodt–Defossez recording more congenial than the brash and brassy Virgil Fox account recorded at Les Invalides in the 1960s.

The Koch Schwann version comes from 1975 and is less aggressively recorded than the Koch version, although needing greater transparency. It has the advantage of being coupled with the *Suite for viola and orchestra,* Op. 48, whose first movement almost calls to mind the elegiac tone of Lekeu's *Adagio* for quartet and strings. Neither version is top-drawer, and the spectacular Telarc version by Michael Murray remains an easy first choice.

Concert à cinq.
*** Koch Dig. 3-7016-2 [id.]. Atlantic Sinf. – DEBUSSY: *Sonata;* JOLIVET: *Chant de Linos.* ***

The three-movement *Concert à cinq* for flute, harp and string trio is a civilized piece very much in the post-impressionist style. It remains more pleasing than memorable, though these players do their utmost for it.

Joplin, Scott (1868–1917)

Rags: *Bethena (concert waltz); Cascades rag; Country club (ragtime two-step); Elite syncopations; The Entertainer; Euphonic sounds (A syncopated novelty); Fig leaf rag; Gladiolus rag; Magnetic rag (syncopations classiques); Maple leaf rag; Paragon rag; Pine apple rag; Ragtime dance; Scott Joplin's new rag; Solace (Mexican serenade); Stoptime rag; Weeping willow (ragtime two-step).*
(M) *** Nonesuch Elektra/Warner 7559 79159-2. Joshua Rifkin (piano).

Joshua Rifkin is the pianist whose name has been indelibly associated with the Scott Joplin revival, originally stimulated by the soundtrack music of the very successful film, *The Sting*. His relaxed, cool rhythmic style is at times more subtle than Dick Hyman's more extrovert approach and, although the piano timbre is full, there is a touch of monochrome in the tone-colour.

Rags: *A Breeze from Alabama; The Cascades; The Chrysanthemum; Easy winners; Elite syncopations; The Entertainer; Maple leaf rag; Original rags; Palm leaf rag; Peacherine rag; Something doing; The Strenuous life; Sunflower slow drag; Swipesy; The Sycamore.*
(M) *** BMG/RCA GD 87993 [7993-2-RG]. Dick Hyman.

Dick Hyman's playing is first rate. His rhythmic spring, clean touch and sensibility in matters of light and shade – without ever trying to present this as concert music – mean that pieces which can easily appear stereotyped remain fresh and spontaneous-sounding throughout. The recording has fine presence; the piano image seems just right.

Treemonisha (opera: arr. and orch. Schuller): complete.
(M) **(*) DG 435 709-2 (2) [id.]. Balthrop, Allen, Rayam, White, Houston Grand Op. Ch. and O, Schuller.

The deliciously ingenuous score will not appeal to all tastes, with its mixture of choral rags, barber's shop quartets, bits of diluted Gilbert and Sullivan, Lehár and Gershwin, and much that is outrageously corny, but – to some ears – irresistibly so. The work has the ethos of the musical rather than of the opera house. But (with the exception of some unlovable singing from Betty Allen as Monisha) the performance and recording are first class and many will find themselves warming to the spontaneity of Joplin's invention.

Josquin des Prés (c. 1450–1521)

Motets: *Ave Maria, gratia plena; Ave, nobilissima creatura; Miserere mei, Deus; O bone et dulcissime Jesu; Salve regina; Stabat mater dolorosa; Usquequo, Domine, oblivisceris me.*
*** HM Dig. HMC 901243; *HMC 401243* [id.]. Chapelle Royale Ch., Herreweghe.

The Chapelle Royale comprises some nineteen singers, but they still produce a clean, well-focused sound and benefit from excellent recording. Their account of the expressive *Stabat mater* sounds thicker-textured than the New College forces under Edward Higginbottom, but there is a refreshing sense of commitment and strong feeling.

Antiphons, Motets and Sequences: *Inviolata; Praeter rerum serium; Salve regina; Stabat mater dolorosa; Veni, sancte spiritus; Virgo prudentissima; Virgo salutiferi.*
*** Mer. ECD 84093; *KE 77093* [id.]. New College, Oxford, Ch., Higginbottom.

The Meridian anthology collects some of Josquin's most masterly and eloquent motets in performances of predictable excellence by Edward Higginbottom and the Choir of New College, Oxford. An admirable introduction to Josquin, and an essential acquisition for those who care about this master.

Missa: Faisant regretz; Missa di dadi.
*** O-L Dig. 411 937-2 [id.]. Medieval Ens. of London, Peter and Timothy Davies.

The two Josquin Masses recorded here are both ingenious works and, more to the point, very beautiful, particularly when sung with such dedication and feeling as here. Nine singers are used for this recording, the number that would have been available in an average-size choir of one of the smaller religious establishments before the 1480s, the last decade when these Masses could have been composed. The Medieval Ensemble of London sing superbly; they not only blend perfectly but are blessed with perfect intonation. This deserves the strongest recommendation to all with an interest in this period.

Missa: L'homme armé super voces musicales.
*** DG 415 293-2 [id.]. Pro Cantione Antiqua, Bruno Turner – OCKEGHEM: *Missa pro defunctis.* ***

This Mass on the *L'homme armé* theme is both one of the most celebrated of all Mass settings based on this secular melody and at the same time one of Josquin's most masterly and admired works. Jeremy Noble's edition is used in the present (1977) performance, which must be numbered among the very finest accounts not only of a Josquin but of any Renaissance Mass to have appeared on record. On CD, the transparency of each strand in the vocal texture is wonderfully clear and the singers are astonishingly present.

Missa Pange lingua; Missa La sol fa re mi.
*** Gimell Dig. CDGIM 009; *1585T-09* [id.]. Tallis Scholars, Peter Phillips.

The Gimell recording of the *Missa Pange lingua* has collected superlatives on all counts and was voted record of the year in the *Gramophone* magazine's 1987 awards. The tone the Tallis Scholars produce is perfectly blended, each line being firmly defined and yet beautifully integrated into the whole sound-picture. Their recording, made in the Chapel of Merton College, Oxford, is first class, the best of the *Missa Pange lingua* and the first of the ingenious *Missa La sol fa re mi*. Not to be missed.

Kabalevsky, Dmitri (1904–87)

Cello concertos Nos. 1 in G min., Op. 49; 2 in C min., Op. 77; (ii) *Improvisato, Op. 21/1; Rondo, Op. 69* (both for violin & piano).
☞ *** Olympia Dig. OCD 292 [id.]. (i) Marina Tarasova, SO of Russia, Veronika Dudarova; (ii) Natalia Likopoi, Ludmila Kuritskaya.

Marina Tarasova made a great impression in the mid-1980s when she appeared at a forum for young artists in Hungary. She had a vibrant intensity, enormous tonal eloquence and a dazzling technique, much of which registers in these performances of the two *Cello concertos*, and this is surely an ideal coupling. She does not bring as much elegance or character to the endearing *First Concerto* (composed in the immediate wake of the 1948 Zhdanov affair) as do Yo-Yo Ma and Ormandy on CBS, though the poignant ending of the middle movement comes off beautifully. Nor does her account of the sombre *Second Concerto in C minor* banish memories of Wallfisch. Still she is very good indeed and no one investing in these performances is likely to be disappointed. Viktoria Dudarova gets decent playing from the orchestra and the recording is very good, full and clear. The two violin-and-piano pieces are very well played indeed but are of no great consequence.

Cello concerto No. 1 in G min.
*** Sony Dig. MK 37840 [id.]. Yo-Yo Ma, Phd. O, Ormandy – SHOSTAKOVICH: *Cello concerto No. 1.* ***

The excellence of Ma's performance is matched by a fine recording which adds considerably to the refinement and presence of the sound, and its vividness is such as to seem to add stature to the music itself.

Cello concerto No. 2, Op. 77.
*** Chan. Dig. CHAN 8579; *ABTD 1273* [id.]. Wallfisch, LPO, Thomson – GLAZUNOV: *Chant du ménestrel;* KHACHATURIAN: *Concerto.* ***

The *Second Cello concerto* is played eloquently – and with the greatest virtuosity – by Raphael Wallfisch, who is well supported by Bryden Thomson and the LPO. Excellent recording too.

Violin concerto in C, Op. 48.
*** Chan. Dig. CHAN 8918; *ABTD 1519* [id.]. Lydia Mordkovitch, SNO, Järvi - KHACHATURIAN: *Violin concerto.* ***
(**) Chant du Monde mono LDC 278883 [id.]. David Oistrakh, USSR Nat. O, composer – KHACHATURIAN: *Violin concerto.* *** ⊛

Kabalevsky's *Violin concerto* is most persuasively presented by these artists. Throughout, Lydia Mordkovitch plays with great flair and aplomb and is given first-class Chandos recording.

David Oistrakh's 1955 mono recording is in most ways definitive, with the composer helping to make the delightfully atmospheric slow movement quite memorable. Oistrakh's clean articulation and sparkle in the finale are also outstanding – and it is a pity that so much allowance has to be made for the sound, which is papery, with a shrill solo image and whistly orchestral strings.

Symphony No. 2, Op. 19.

☞ (M) **(*) Unicorn UKCD 2066 [id.]. New Philh. O, David Measham – MIASKOVSKY: *Symphony No. 21* ***; SHOSTAKOVICH: *Hamlet.* **(*)

Kabalevsky's *Second Symphony* enjoyed some popularity in the 1940s and is high-spirited, well crafted and far from unappealing. It has not the substance or depth of Miaskovsky, with which it is coupled, but is nevertheless worth having as an example of the 'official' Soviet symphony. David Measham secures excellent results from the New Philharmonia, and though the sound is not absolutely top-drawer it is well focused and spacious.

(i) *Symphony No. 4 in C min., Op. 54;* (ii) *Requiem, Op. 72.*

☞ *(*) Olympia OCD 290 (2) [id.]. (i) Leningrad PO; (ii) Valentina Levko, Vladimir Valaitis,
  Moscow Artistic Educational Institute Ch., Moscow SO; Kabalevsky.

For years Kabalevsky's reputation in the West rested on his *Third Piano sonata*, the *Second Symphony*, also in C minor, and the *Overture, Colas Breugnon.* Both of the works recorded here are post-Stalin; the symphony was composed in 1955, two years after Shostakovich's *Tenth* and some two decades after his own *Second*, and the *Requiem* is from the early 1960s. Both recordings are analogue and were briefly available on LP on both sides of the Atlantic. The *Fourth Symphony* is the earlier of the two, made in 1956, and rather sounding its age – it never seemed particularly spectacular even at the time – and the *Requiem* comes from 1964. The *Fourth* is a rather conventional work which goes through the correct motions of sonata procedure, but the ideas are only intermittently engaging; indeed, many border on the commonplace. Kabalevsky conducts with great abandon and the Leningrad orchestra respond with some enthusiasm to his direction. The *Requiem* is a more rewarding piece, even if much of it is hard work. But the longueurs are offset by some moving passages and a genuine, unforced dignity that grips the listener. The performers are committed and the singing of high standard. It is good to have these performances restored to circulation for, even if they do not reveal a great musical personality at work, the fact remains that Kabalevsky's music is not negligible either. The sound in the *Requiem* is very good indeed for the period – and the place.

Piano sonata No. 3, Op. 46.

☞ (M) (***) BMG/RCA mono GD 60377 [id.]. Vladimir Horowitz – BARBER; PROKOFIEV: *Sonatas* etc. (***)

Horowitz cannot give Kabalevsky's music the calibre of the Barber or Prokofiev sonatas with which it is coupled, and the 1947 recording is a bit subfusc. But the power of the playing certainly comes through, especially in the brilliant finale.

Colas Breugnon (complete).

☞ *** Olympia OCD 291 A/B (2) [id.]. Boldin, Isakova, Kayevchenko, Maksimenko, Duradev,
  Gutorovich, Mishchevsky, Stanislavsky & Nemirovich-Danchenko Moscow Music Theatre Ch. &
  O, Zhemchuzhin.

Few pieces this century can match in high spirits the overture which the Russian, Dmitri Kabalevsky, wrote for his opera, *Colas Breugnon.* It has an effervescence comparable to that of Bernstein's *Candide* or Walton's *Scapino.* Yet the opera which it introduces has remained virtually unknown in the West, except for a promising suite of genre pieces. This complete recording, made in Russia in the 1970s, confirms that the overture is not just a flash in the pan but part of an exceptionally winning piece, rhythmically inventive and full of good tunes, many of them drawn from French folksong. There is a patter-song for the hero in Act I directly based on one of the jaunty themes of the overture. The opera, based on a novel by Romain Rolland, tells of Breugnon's fight as man and artist with the tyrannical duke who rules the town, as well as with his officials. You can see why the novel was so popular in the Soviet Union in the 1930s, and why the young Kabalevsky responded to it. Latterly the irony emerged ever more clearly in Russia that the attack is at least as much on bureaucracy as on the aristocracy. The snag is that between Acts I and II in the three-Act layout there is a story-gap of 40 years. Enough of the same characters are still around to maintain continuity, but youthful effervescence is less apt for the aged characters in Acts II and III. Nevertheless the Russian performance and recording, made by members of the Moscow Music Theatre, is most convincing, with a cast superbly led by the baritone, Leonid Boldin, in the title-role. The other male singers are first rate too, with splendidly alert singing from the chorus (which, in good proletarian fashion, plays a key part in the opera). The women soloists are raw-toned in a very Russian way, and the whole performance under Georgy Zhemchuzhin reflects the confidence of experience on stage. The 1973 recording, rather dry but with fine presence, catches the voices splendidly, though the orchestra is backwardly placed. But reservations may be put to one side; this is a thoroughly worthwhile set.

Kalinnikov, Vasily (1866–1901)

Intermezzos Nos. 1 in F sharp min.; 2 in G.
*** Chan. Dig. CHAN 8614; *ABTD 1303* [id.]. SNO, Järvi – RACHMANINOV: *Symphony No. 3.* ***

These two colourful *Intermezzos* with a flavour of Borodin are charming.

Symphony No. 1 in G min.
*** Chan. Dig. CHAN 8611; *ABTD 1299* [id.]. SNO, Järvi – GLAZUNOV: *The Sea; Spring.* ***

Kalinnikov's *First Symphony* contains something akin to the flow and natural lyricism of Borodin, and the second movement has something of the atmosphere and character of early Rachmaninov or his almost exact contemporary, Glazunov. Neeme Järvi and the Scottish National Orchestra seem fired with enthusiasm for this appealing work, and the engineers serve them admirably. Strongly recommended.

Symphonies Nos. 1 in G min.; 2 in A.
☞ *(*) Olympia Dig. OCD 511 [id.]. SO of Russia, Veronika Dudarova.

Veronika Dudarova and the Symphony Orchestra of Russia enjoy the advantage of offering these two attractive symphonies on the one CD – on the face of it good value at 77 minutes 37 seconds. Neeme Järvi's Chandos accounts run to two separate discs, although they come with interesting and attractive fill-ups. However, neither artistically nor in terms of recording quality is this a match for the competition. The playing is routine and wanting in subtlety, and the sound does not have the bloom and depth of the Järvi set. The two Chandos CDs are really worth the extra outlay.

Symphony No. 2 in A; The Cedar and the palm; Overture: Tsar Boris.
*** Chan. Dig. CHAN 8805; *ABTD 1433* [id.]. SNO, Järvi.

The *Second Symphony*, though not quite as appealing as No. 1, is played by the Scottish orchestra under Neeme Järvi with enthusiasm and commitment, and the Chandos recording is in the demonstration class. Both the *Overture* and *The Cedar and the palm* are worth having on disc.

Kern, Jerome (1885–1945)

Showboat (complete recording of original score).
⊛ *** EMI Dig. CD-RIVER 1 (3) [Ang. A23 49108]. Von Stade, Hadley, Hubbard, O'Hara, Garrison, Burns, Stratas, Amb. Ch., L. Sinf., John McGlinn.

In faithfully following the original score, this superb set at last does justice to a musical of the 1920s which is both a landmark in the history of Broadway and musically a work of strength and imagination hardly less significant than Gershwin's *Porgy and Bess* of a decade later. The original, extended versions of important scenes are included, as well as various numbers written for later productions. As the heroine, Magnolia, Frederica von Stade gives a meltingly beautiful performance, totally in style, bringing out the beauty and imagination of Kern's melodies, regularly heightened by wide intervals to make those of most of his Broadway rivals seem flat. The London Sinfonietta play with tremendous zest and feeling for the idiom; the Ambrosian Chorus sings with joyful brightness and some impeccable American accents. Opposite von Stade, Jerry Hadley makes a winning Ravenal, and Teresa Stratas is charming as Julie, giving a heartfelt performance of the haunting number, *Bill* (words by P. G. Wodehouse). Above all, the magnificent black bass, Bruce Hubbard, sings *Ol' man river* and its many reprises with a firm resonance to have you recalling the wonderful example of Paul Robeson, but for once without hankering after the past. Beautifully recorded to bring out the piece's dramatic as well as its musical qualities, this is a heart-warming issue.

Ketèlbey, Albert (1875–1959)

The Adventurers: overture; Bells across the meadow; Caprice pianistique; Chal Romano; The Clock and the Dresden figures; Cockney suite, excerpts: Bank holiday; At the Palais de Danse. In a Monastery garden; In the moonlight; In a Persian market; The Phantom melody; Suite romantique; Wedgewood blue.
☞ ** Marco Polo Dig. 8.223442 [id.]. Slovak Philharmonic Male Ch., Slovak RSO (Bratislava), Adrian Leaper.

The Marco Polo collection has the advantage of modern digital recording and a warm concert-hall acoustic, and the effect is very flattering to *In a Monastery garden*. Adrian Leaper's performance is romantically spacious and includes the chorus. If elsewhere his characterization is not always as apt as Lanchbery's, this is still an agreeable programme. It offers several novelties and, though some of these items (for instance *The Adventurers overture*) are not vintage Ketèlbey, there is nothing wrong with the lively Slovak account of the closing *In a Persian market*, again featuring the chorus.

Bells across the meadow; Chal Romano (Gypsy lad); The Clock and the Dresden figures; In a Chinese temple garden; In a monastery garden; In a Persian market; In the moonlight; In the mystic land of Egypt; Sanctuary of the heart.

☞ (B) *** CfP CD-CFP 4637; *TC-CFP 4637* [id.]. Vernon Midgley, Jean Temperley, Leslie Pearson (piano), Amb. S., Philh. O, Lanchbery – LUIGINI: *Ballet Egyptien.* ***

A splendid collection in every way. John Lanchbery uses every possible resource to ensure that, when the composer demands spectacle, he gets it. *In the mystic land of Egypt*, for instance, uses soloist and chorus in canon in the principal tune (and very fetchingly too). In the *Monastery garden* the distant monks are realistically distant, in *Sanctuary of the heart* there is no mistaking that the heart is worn firmly on the sleeve. The orchestral playing throughout is not only polished but warm-hearted – the middle section of *Bells across the meadow*, which has a delightful melodic contour, is played most tenderly and loses any hint of vulgarity. Yet when vulgarity is called for, it is not shirked – only it's a stylish kind of vulgarity! The recording is excellent, full and brilliant, and it has transferred to CD with striking presence and very little loss of ambient warmth. The CD has a splendid autobiographical note about the composer by Peter Gammond. The Luigini coupling (and the price) make this selection most desirable.

Khachaturian, Aram (1903–78)

Cello concerto.
*** Chan. Dig. CHAN 8579; *ABTD 1273* [id.]. Wallfisch, LPO, Thomson – GLAZUNOV: *Chant du ménestrel;* KABALEVSKY: *Cello concerto No.2.* ***
☞ (M) ** Ph. 434 166-2 [id.]. Walevska, Monte Carlo Opera O, Inbal – PROKOFIEV: *Cello concerto.* **

Khachaturian's *Cello concerto* of 1946 has some sinuous Armenian local colour for its lyrical ideas, but none of the thematic memorability of the concertos for violin and piano and the *Gayaneh ballet* score, on which Khachaturian's reputation must continue to rest. Raphael Wallfisch plays with total commitment and has the benefit of excellent and sympathetic support. The recording is of the usual high standard we have come to expect from Chandos.

Christine Walevska gives a committed account of the work and she is well accompanied by Inbal, but the Philips sound is not especially vivid. This CD is issued as a limited edition.

Flute concerto (arr. Rampal/Galway); *Gayaneh: Sabre dance. Masquerade: Waltz. Spartacus: Adagio of Spartacus and Phrygia.*
*** BMG/RCA Dig. RD 87010; *RK 87010.* Galway, RPO, Myung-Whun Chung.

Khachaturian's *Flute concerto* is a transcription of the *Violin concerto*; Galway has prepared his own edition of the solo part. Needless to say, the solo playing is peerless; if in the finale even Galway cannot match the effect Oistrakh makes with his violin, the ready bravura is sparklingly infectious. As encores, he offers three of Khachaturian's most famous melodies.

Piano concerto in D flat.
(***) Olympia mono OCD 236 [id.]. Moura Lympany, LPO, Fistoulari – SAINT-SAENS: *Piano concerto No. 2.* (**(*))

The 1952 Lympany/Fistoulari account has a dash, sparkle and bravura which have never been matched on record since: even the Flexatone warbling in the *Andante* is made to seem convincing, and Khachaturian's melancholy Armenian melodies are given their full character. The recording, first rate in its day, now sounds curiously cavernous, though perfectly acceptable; the sheer élan of the performance soon makes one forget the aural deficiencies.

(i) *Piano concerto in D flat; Gayaneh (ballet) suite; Masquerade: suite.*
**(*) Chan. Dig. CHAN 8542; *ABTD 1250* [id.]. (i) Orbelian, SNO, Järvi.

The Chandos recording is splendid technically, well up to the standards of the house. Constantin Orbelian, an Armenian by birth, plays brilliantly and Järvi achieves much attractive lyrical detail. Overall it is a spacious account, and though the finale has plenty of gusto, the music-making seems just a shade too easygoing in the first movement. The couplings, sumptuously played, are both generous and appealing.

Violin concerto in D min.

✦ *** Chant du Monde LDC 278883 [Mobile Fidelity MFCD 899 with SIBELIUS: *Concerto*]. David Oistrakh, USSR RSO, composer – KABALEVSKY: *Violin concerto.* (**)

*** Chan. Dig. CHAN 8918; *ABTD 1519* [id.]. Lydia Mordkovitch, SNO, Järvi - KABALEVSKY: *Violin concerto.* ***

☞ (M) ** Mercury 434 318-2 [id.]. Szeryng, LSO, Dorati – BRAHMS: *Violin concerto.* *(*)

David Oistrakh, for whom the *Concerto* was written, is peerless in its performance, not only in projecting its very Russian bravura, but also in his melting phrasing and timbre in the sinuous secondary theme of the first movement. Indeed this quite marvellous performance is unlikely ever to be surpassed. The composer creates a rapt degree of tension in the slow movement and affectionately caresses the Armenian colour and detail in the very atmospheric orchestral accompaniment. The finale has an irresistible exhilaration. The (1970) Russian recording is warm and very well balanced, especially in its relationship of soloist with orchestra. The *Concerto* is coupled differently in the USA.

Among more recent performances of this attractively inventive concerto, Lydia Mordkovitch is probably the most competitive. She plays with real abandon and fire, and Chandos balance her and the orchestra in a thoroughly realistic perspective. This new version has far superior sound to Oistrakh on Chant du Monde.

Although more successful than the coupled Brahms concerto, Szeryng's 1964 recording of the Khachaturian does not measure up to the finest versions of the past, notably those of Leonid Kogan and David Oistrakh and, more recently, Perlman. It is a lightweight account, at its most convincing in the folksy lyricism of the *Andante* and in the sparkle of the finale, where the soloist is on top technical form. The recording is good but does not flatter the solo violin timbre.

(i) *Violin concerto in D min.; Gayaneh* (extended suite); *Masquerade suite.*

☞ (***) EMI mono CDC5 55035-2 [id.]. (i) David Oistrakh; Philh. O, composer.

David Oistrakh's EMI mono recording of the *Violin concerto* was made in the Kingsway Hall in 1954. He had recorded it before on a Russian film soundtrack, and that vivid account – distorted by wow and flutter – was once available from Decca. But the EMI version had the advantage of first-class recording, and such is the freshness and power of the performance that one adjusts almost immediately to the absence of stereo, for the sound is well balanced and spacious. The slow movement and dancing finale are particularly memorable and, throughout, Oistrakh's reading combines warmth and Slavic intensity with easy brilliance. The couplings on EMI are more obviously attractive than the alternative Russian stereo CD, and again no apologies have to be made for the bright EMI recording with its attractive ambience. The *Masquerade suite* and the eight best numbers from *Gayaneh* bring a refreshing sense of newness and discovery: the lyrical music is full of atmosphere, finding delicacy as well as warmth, while the famous *Sabre dance* bursts at the seams with energy.

Gayaneh (ballet): extended suite.

☞ (M) **(*) Mercury 434 323-2 [id.]. LSO, Dorati – SHOSTAKOVICH: *Symphony No. 5.* **(*)

Dorati understands this music as well as anyone, and his *Sabre dance* has plenty of energy; and the other dances admirably celebrate Khachaturian's local colour. The 1960 Mercury recording is brilliant, with a tendency to fierceness in the strings, which suits the music well enough. There are eight items here; Dorati omits *Gayaneh's Adagio*.

Gayaneh (ballet): suite; *Masquerade: suite; Spartacus* (ballet): *suite.*

(*) ASV Dig. CDDCA 773; *ZCDCA 773.* Armenian PO, Tjeknavorian – IPPOLITOV-IVANOV: *Caucasian sketches.* *

Gayaneh: suite; Spartacus: suite.

(M) **(*) Decca 417 737-2 [id.]. VPO, composer – PROKOFIEV: *Romeo and Juliet.* ***

The composer's own first selection on Decca was recorded in 1962 and offers five items from *Gayaneh* and four from *Spartacus*. Khachaturian achieves a brilliant response from the VPO and everything is most vivid, notably the famous *Adagio* from *Spartacus*, which is both expansive and passionate. It is a pity that the Decca remastering process has brought everything into such strong focus; the massed violins now have an added edge and boldness of attack, at the expense of their richness of timbre.

The Armenians clearly relish the explosive energy of this music. The *Masquerade suite* relies rather more on charm for its appeal, but Tjeknavorian and his players bring a determined gusto, even to the

Waltz and certainly to the ebullient closing *Galop*. Then the vibrant Spartacus and his ardent lover Phrygia come on stage with a great flair of passion in a melody that is justly famous. One wishes the recording were more sumptuous here, but for the most part its burnished primary colours suit the dynamic orchestral style.

Gayaneh (ballet): highlights; *Spartacus* (ballet): highlights.
☞ (B) *** CfP CD-CFP 4634; *TC-CFP 4634*. LSO, composer (with GLAZUNOV: *The Seasons: Autumn:* Philh. O, Svetlanov ***).

The composer's 1977 pairing for EMI of selections from his two famous ballets offers one more item from *Gayaneh* than on his earlier (1962) Decca coupling. The EMI sound, obviously more modern than the Decca, is a shade reverberant for the more vigorous numbers, but the present remastering presents a firmer focus than on LP. The effect is realistically spectacular with full, rich strings so that the famous *Adagio of Spartacus and Phrygia* expands opulently as well as ardently. The LSO play excitingly throughout. There is a gorgeous response from the violins in the extra item, called *Invention*, from *Gayaneh*. The inclusion of *Autumn*, the most memorable section of Glazunov's *Seasons* – its vigorously thrusting string theme stirringly conducted by Svetlanov – increases the appeal of this CD. At bargain price it is now a best buy for those wanting a suite from the two Khachaturian ballets.

Spartacus (ballet): *suites Nos. 1–3*.
*** Chan. Dig. CHAN 8927; *ABTD 1529* [id.]. SNO, Neeme Järvi.

The ripe lushness of Khachaturian's scoring in *Spartacus* narrowly skirts vulgarity. Järvi and the SNO clearly enjoy the music's tunefulness and primitive vigour, while the warmly resonant acoustics of Glasgow's Henry Wood Hall bring properly sumptuous orchestral textures, smoothing over the moments of crudeness without losing the Armenian colouristic vividness.

Symphonies Nos. 1 in E min.; 3 in C (Symphonic poem).
☞ *** ASV Dig. CDDCA 858 [id.]. Armenian PO, Loris Tjeknavorian.

Symphony No. 1 in E min.; (i) *Masquerade suite*.
☞ ** Russian Disc RDCD11005 [id.]. Moscow R. SO, Alexander Gauk; (i) composer.

The *First Symphony* was Khachaturian's exercise on graduating from Miaskovsky's class in 1934. It is a long piece of some 40 minutes and has been out of circulation for many years. It is far from negligible and in some ways is superior to some of his later work – certainly to the bombastic *Third* (1947) with its 15 trumpets and organ (written to mark the 30th anniversary of the October Revolution). Now there are two recordings: a modern account from Armenia under Tjeknavorian which enjoys the advantage of good digital recording, and an older one from the redoubtable Alexander Gauk, made in the late 1950s. While the Russian Disc transfer is a great improvement on the original Melodiya LP, its sonic limitations may deter some enthusiasts. It does, however, have the advantage of the composer's performance of the *Masquerade* suite, recorded in stereo. Gauk keeps a stronger grip on proceedings than Tjeknavorian, but the better technical quality will doubtless be more widely preferred. The Armenian orchestra play well for Tjeknavorian, and his is probably the safer recommendation.

Symphony No. 2 in E min. (The Bell); Battle of Stalingrad (suite).
☞ **(*) ASV Dig. CDDCA 859 [id.]. Armenian PO, Loris Tjeknavorian.

Symphony No. 2 (original version); *Gayaneh: suite* (excerpts).
☞ (M) *** Decca 425 619-2 [id.]. VPO, composer.
☞ *** Chan. Dig. CHAN 8945 [id.]. Royal Scottish O, Järvi.

The *Second Symphony* comes from 1943 but the composer subsequently made a number of revisions, the last in 1969, which Tjeknavorian has recorded. It acquired its nickname, '*The Bell*', because of a motive heard on tubular bells, and in the slow movement makes fascinating use of the *Dies irae*. Neeme Järvi and his Scottish forces give a very fine account of themselves and they enjoy the benefit of a superb recording. Like the composer's own account with the Vienna Philharmonic, it runs to some 51 minutes, while Tjeknavorian's final revision prunes the score down to 42 minutes 45 seconds. The suite from *The Battle of Stalingrad* is taken from a score composed for a patriotic film and is empty and inflated. Khachaturian's own recording remains a first recommendation and still sounds excellent. The performance gives the music passionate advocacy and the recording is superbly spectacular (although the CD remastering doesn't help its garish qualities).

The Valencian Widow (incidental music): *suite; Gayaneh* (ballet): *suite No. 2.*
☞ *** ASV Dig. CDDCA 884 [id.]. Armenian PO, Loris Tjeknavorian (with TJEKNAVORIAN:
Danses fantastiques **(*)).

Khachaturian's early suite from his incidental music to the Spanish comedy, *The Valencian Widow* (1940), is probably his first major score and, brimming over with striking tunes as it is, one is surprised that it has not been discovered by the gramophone before this. With its characteristically sinuous melodic invention, its flavour is more Armenian than Spanish, though Carmen does make a momentary appearance at the beginning of the *Intermezzo*, and the briefly flashing dance-sequence which appears later in the same piece is also authentic in feeling. But on the whole this is the Khachaturian of *Gayaneh*, so the coupling of seven lesser-known but indelible excerpts from that fine ballet score – undoubtedly the composer's masterpiece – is very appropriate. Tjeknavorian and his orchestra play this music with great spirit and relish its Armenian flavours; they are equally at home in Tjeknavorian's own suite of *Danses fantastiques*, full of energy and colour if essentially sub-Khachaturian. Its opening *Danse rhythmique* is a bit like the *Sabre dance* without the tune. Splendidly vivid, yet spacious sound.

PIANO MUSIC

10 Children's pieces; 2 Pieces; Poem; Sonata; Sonatina; Toccata; Waltz (from *Masquerade*).
☞ **(*) Olympia Dig. OCD 423 [id.]. Murray McLachlan.

Apart from the *Toccata* (1932), which is a frequent encore, Khachaturian's piano music rarely features in piano recitals. At 80 minutes, this CD offers all of it with the exception of the *Scenes from childhood* and the *Recitative and fugues*. The early pieces, *Poem* (1927) and the *Valse-Caprice* and *Dance* (1926), are much like the *Toccata*, pretty empty, but the later pieces including the *Sonatina* (1959), the *Ten Children's pieces* (1964) and the *Sonata* (1961) are worth a hearing, even though they are limited in range and rely on a small vocabulary of musical devices. The slow movement of the *Sonatina* is rather touching, as are some of the *Ten Children's pieces*, like *An evening tale*. Murray McLachlan, who as usual provides informative and intelligent notes, is a persuasive guide, though not even he can persuade one that this is remotely comparable as piano music to that of Shostakovich or Miaskovsky, let alone Prokofiev. His recording, made at All Saints' Church, Petersham, is eminently serviceable though there are times when the attentions of a tuner would not have come amiss (particularly in the garrulous first movement of the *Sonata*).

Klami, Uuno (1900–61)

Kalevala suite, Op. 23; Karelian rhapsody, Op. 15; Sea pictures.
☞ **(*) Chan. Dig. CHAN 9268 [id.]. Iceland SO, Sakari.

Uuno Klami is relatively little known and rarely if ever features in concert programmes outside his native Finland. After studying in Helsinki he went to Paris, where he fell under the spell of Florent Schmitt and Ravel to whom he showed his compositions. The *Kalevala suite*, written between 1929 and 1933 and revised during the war, is his best-known work but, like the other two pieces on this disc, both written in the late 1920s/early 1930s, it is highly derivative. Ravel and Schmitt mingle with Falla, Sibelius and early Stravinsky; while there are some imaginative and inspired passages (such as the opening of the *Terheniemi* or Scherzo), there is some pretty empty stuff as well. The performances under Petri Sakari are very good indeed. Playback level needs to be high if the recording is to be heard to anywhere near best advantage; there is good perspective and a wide dynamic range. On high-grade equipment it yields good results but it does not reproduce so well on more modest machines. Colourful scores, though essentially too derivative to make much headway in the wider world.

Knipper, Lev (1898–1974)

(i) *Concert poem for cello and orchestra; Sinfonietta for strings.*
** Olympia OCD 163 [id.]. (i) Shakhovskaya; Moscow Conservatoire CO, Teryan – MIASKOVSKY:
Symphony No. 7. **

This *Sinfonietta* is well-fashioned but rather anonymous music, albeit with some moments of beauty. The *Concert poem* opens strikingly and is played magnificently, but is not strongly individual either.

Knussen, Oliver (born 1952)

(i) *Songs without voices, Op. 26;* (ii) *Sonya's lullaby, Op. 16; Variations, Op. 24;* (iii; i) *Hums and songs of Winnie-the-Pooh, Op. 6;* (iii) *4 Late poems and and epigram of Rainer Maria Rilke, Op. 23;* (iv; i) *Océan de terre, Op. 10;* (iv; ii) *Whitman settings, Op. 25.*

☞ *** Virgin/EMI Dig. VC7 59308-2 [id.]. (i) Chamber Music Soc. of Lincoln Center, composer; (ii) Peter Serkin; (iii) Lisa Saffer; (iv) Lucy Shelton.

Some of Oliver Knussen's shorter works, all sharply characterful, here receive superb performances from American musicians, biting and committed, making light of the complexities of argument and texture. Serkin, for whom the solo piano works were written, plays incisively, both warmly responsive and muscular, not just in those works but also as accompanist to Lucy Shelton in the angular Whitman settings. The *Pooh songs*, with Lisa Saffer another bright, clear soprano, reflect Knussen's fascination with children's literature; but they are certainly not music for children, reflecting simply a mood of playfulness. The most complex work is the earliest, *Océan de terre*, but even that is clarified in such a performance as this. Good, well-focused sound.

Symphony No. 3.
*** RPO Dig. CDRPO 8023 [id.]. RPO, Ashkenazy – BRITTEN: *Serenade;* WALTON: *Symphony No. 2.* ***

This performance of Knussen's powerfully concentrated symphony was recorded live. Next to the Philharmonia players in Tilson Thomas's studio recording for Unicorn Kanchana, the RPO sounds liberated, bringing out the mystery of the opening far more intensely and regularly revealing the emotional thrust of Knussen's beautiful and complex writing. This closely argued one-movement symphony, lasting in this performance 16½ minutes, is the work which most clearly reveals his weight as a composer.

Where the Wild Things are (complete).
*** Unicorn Dig. DKPCD 9044; *DKPC 9044* [id.]. Rosemary Hardy, Mary King, Herrington, Richardson, Rhys-Williams, Gallacher, L. Sinf., composer.

Oliver Knussen has devised a one-act opera that beautifully matches the grotesque fantasy of Maurice Sendak's children's book of the same name. The record presents the piece with all the bite and energy of a live performance. The final rumpus music here feels like the culmination intended. Rosemary Hardy makes a superb Max; Mary King sings warmly in the small part of the Mother. The brilliant recording vividly conveys a sense of presence and space.

Kodály, Zoltán (1882–1967)

Concerto for orchestra; Dances of Galánta; Dances of Marosszék; Háry János: suite; Symphony in C; Summer evening; Theatre overture; Variations on a Hungarian folksong (The Peacock).
☞ (B) *** Double Decca 443 006-2 (2) [id.]. Philh. Hungarica, Antal Dorati.

In 1973 when Dorati and the Philharmonia Hungarica finished their monumental task of recording Haydn's symphonies complete, they turned to the music of their compatriot, Kodály. Though, of course, the string section is augmented, there is the same sense of commitment here as in the Haydn. This is all to the good in music which, though it is always beautifully written and often colourful, is not always as cogent as it might be. Only the *Ballet music*, the *Hungarian rondo* and *Minuetto serio* are left out of this bargain Double Decca compilation, but it must be admitted that the single CD listed below contains the four finest works. The more ambitious pieces like the *Concerto for orchestra* and the three-movement *Symphony in C* are certainly enjoyable, but they lack the sharpness of inspiration that pervades the music of Kodály's friend Bartók. The *Symphony* comes from the composer's last years and is by general consent one of his least imposing works: it lacks real concentration and cohesion. Even so, in Dorati's hands the passionate *Andante* is strong in gypsy feeling and the jolly, folk-dance finale, if repetitive, is colourful and full of vitality. *Summer evening*, too, is warmly evocative, but in the *Theatre overture*, brightly and effectively scored, the invention is thin. The sound remains of vintage quality and the CD transfers are first rate.

Dances of Galánta.
*** Ph. 416 378-2 [id.]. Concg. O, Zinman – BARTOK: *Concerto for 2 Pianos, percussion & celesta.* ***

David Zinman offers an attractively vivid performance of the *Dances of Galánta*. Although this is not a very generous coupling for the Bartók *Concerto*, the recording is very much in the demonstration class.

(i) *Dances of Galánta; Dances of Marosszék;* (ii) *Háry János: suite.*
(M) *** Mercury 432 005-2 [id.]. (i) Philharmonia Hungarica; (ii) Minneapolis SO, Dorati – BARTOK: *Hungarian sketches* etc. ***

Dances of Galánta; Dances of Marosszék; Háry János suite; Variations on a Hungarian folksong (The Peacock).
(M) *** Decca 425 034-2; *425 034-4* [id.]. Philharmonia Hungarica, Dorati.

Dances of Galánta; Háry János: suite.
*** Delos Dig. DE 3083 [id.]. Seattle SO, Garard Schwarz – BARTOK: *Miraculous Mandarin.* **(*)

From sneeze to finale, the Minneapolis orchestral playing in the *Háry János suite* is crisp and vigorous; given the excellent 1956 Mercury stereo, Dorati went on to record the other two sets of dances with the Philharmonia Hungarica in 1958. The playing of the woodwind soloists in the slow dances is intoxicatingly seductive, and the power and punch of the climaxes come over with real Mercury fidelity. An outstanding disc, since the Bartók couplings are equally successful.

The Philharmonia Hungarica performances of the *Galánta dances* and the familiar *Háry János suite* are also first class, and the *Peacock variations* – luxuriantly extended, highly enjoyable and deserving of greater popularity – are equally fine. While the older, Mercury performances have a very special electricity of their own, the 1973 Decca recording is more modern and is of vintage quality.

The Seattle Symphony Orchestra play Kodály's music with great vividness and warmth. The *Háry János suite* is more spaciously romantic in feeling than some versions – helped by the rich acoustics of Seattle Opera House – and there is less surface glitter. But *The Battle and defeat of Napoleon* and the *Entrance of the Emperor and his Court* have all the necessary mock-drama and spectacle, and it is good to hear the cimbalom again balanced so effectively within the orchestra. The *Galánta dances* have splendid dash. The recording is outstandingly real.

Háry János suite.
(BB) *** Naxos Dig. 8.550142; *4550142* [id.]. Hungarian State O, Mátyás Antal (with Concert: *'Hungarian festival'* ***).

The Hungarian performance of the *Háry János suite* is wonderfully vivid, with the cimbalom – perfectly balanced within the orchestra – particularly telling. The grotesque elements of *The Battle and defeat of Napoleon* are pungently and wittily characterized and the *Entrance of the Emperor and his Court* also has an ironical sense of spectacle. The brilliant digital sound adds to the vitality and projection of the music-making, yet the lyrical music is played most tenderly.

(Unaccompanied) *Cello sonata, Op. 8;* (i) *Duo for violin and cello.*
*** Delos D/CD 1015 [id.]. Janos Starker, (i) Josef Gingold.

When, not long before the composer's death, Kodály heard Starker playing this *Cello sonata*, he apparently said: 'If you correct the ritard in the third movement, it will be the Bible performance.' The recording is made in a smaller studio than is perhaps ideal; the *Duo*, impressively played by Starker and Josef Gingold, is made in a slightly more open acoustic. There is a small makeweight in the form of Starker's own arrangement of the Bottermund *Paganini variations.*

String quartet No. 2, Op. 10.
*** DG Dig. 419 601-2 [id.]. Hagen Qt – DVORAK: *String quartet No. 12* etc. ***

The Hagen give a marvellously committed and beautifully controlled performance of the *Second* – indeed as quartet playing it would be difficult to surpass. In range of dynamic response and sheer beauty of sound, this is thrilling playing and welcome advocacy of a neglected but masterly piece. The recording is well balanced and admirably present.

Budavári Te Deum; Missa brevis.
*** Hung. HCD 11397-2 [id.]. Andor, Ekert, Makkay, Mohácsi, Szirmay, Réti, Gregor, Hungarian R. & TV Ch., Budapest SO, Ferencsik.

The *Budavári Te Deum* is predictably nationalist in feeling. The *Missa brevis* is also one of Kodály's strongest works, almost comparable in stature to the *Psalmus Hungaricus.* The singing is accurate and sensitive, and the playing of the Budapest orchestra under Ferencsik absolutely first class.

Háry János (musical numbers only).
**(*) Hung. HCD 12837/8-2 [id.]. Sólyom-Nagy, Takács, Sudlik, Póka, Mésozöly, Gregor, Palcsó, Hungarian R. & TV Children's Ch., Hungarian State Op. Ch. and O, Ferencsik.

For the CD transfer the dialogue has been cut out, which means there is no dramatic continuity but, when Kodály's score is so colourful, the piece becomes a rich chocolate-box of delights. Ferencsik's performance with Hungarian singers and players is committedly idiomatic, with strong singing, not always ideally well characterized but very stylish, from some of the most distinguished principals of the Budapest Opera.

(i) *Hymn of Zrinyi;* (ii) *Psalmus Hungaricus.*
(M) *** Decca 421 810-2 (2). (i) Luxon, Brighton Festival Ch., Heltay; (ii) Kozma, Brighton Festival
   Ch., Wandsworth School Boys' Ch., LSO, Kertész – DVORAK: *Requiem.* ***

Psalmus Hungaricus is Kodály's most vital choral work, and this Decca version comes as close to an ideal performance as one is likely to get. The results are electrifying, and the recording is outstandingly brilliant too. The light tenor tone of Lajos Kozma is not ideal for the solo part, but again the authentic Hungarian touch helps. The *Hymn of Zrinyi,* for unaccompanied chorus and baritone solo, celebrates a Magyar hero, and Heltay is persuasive. With first-class remastered sound, this generous coupling with Dvořák is strongly recommended.

(i; ii; v) *Missa brevis;* (ii; v) *Pange lingua;* (iii) *Psalmus Hungaricus;* (iv; v) *Psalm 114.*
⊛ (M) *** Decca 433 080-2 [id.]. Brighton Festival Ch. with (i) Gale, Le Sage, Francis, Hodgson,
   Caley, Rippon; (ii) Bowers-Broadbent (organ); (iii) Kozma, Wandsworth School Boys' Ch.,
   LSO, Kertész; (iv) Weir (organ); (v) cond. Heltay.

László Heltay directs all the music except the *Psalmus Hungaricus,* which is splendidly vibrant in the hands of István Kertész and there is no doubt that Heltay's meticulous training contributed to the fluency of that outstanding performance, idiomatically presented in Hungarian. The *Missa brevis* is literally a short setting of the Mass, not one which omits the *Credo.* The *Pange lingua* is a more searching piece, sung here with glorious tone and great intensity. The short setting of *Psalm 114,* from the Geneva Psalter, is also very moving and shows Kodály's relatively gentle art at its most persuasive, and here Gillian Weir makes an impressive contribution. A highly rewarding 70-minute collection, given vintage Decca sound from the mid- to late 1970s.

Koechlin, Charles (1867–1961)

(i) *Ballade for piano and orchestra, Op. 50. 7 Stars Symphony (suite), Op. 13.*
☞ (M) *** EMI Dig. CDM7 64369-2 [id.]. (i) Bruno Rigutto; Monte Carlo PO, Myrat.

The 'stars' of the *Symphony* are terrestrial rather than galactic: Fairbanks and Marlene Dietrich, not Betelgeuse and Sirius. Koechlin is an interesting figure whose output ran to more than 350 works. In some quarters he has been spoken of as a French Charles Ives, though so glib a comparison does not do justice to his individuality of mind. There is never any want of finesse and his imagination is richly stocked, yet there is a sense in which his works contain the raw material of a work of art rather than achieving artistic fulfilment. The *Seven Stars Symphony* is not, strictly speaking, a symphony, rather a series of sketches evoking the great personalities of the cinema in the 1920s and '30s, and it is coupled here with an earlier work written for the pianist Henriette Fauré. Koechlin's music lacks the concentration and distinction of Magnard or the perfection of Roussel and, ultimately, offers less than real nourishment, yet he is a stimulating figure and, given the keen advocacy of these artists and the excellence of the CD sound, this enterprising reissue well rewards investigation.

Les Bandar-log (symphonic poem), *Op. 176.*
(M) *** EMI CDM7 63948-2 [id.]. BBC SO, Dorati – BOULEZ: *Le soleil des eaux;* MESSIAEN:
   Chronochromie etc. ***

Les Bandar-log is a symphonic poem based on the Kipling story, but used to satirize the vagaries of twentieth-century composers with fluent mastery, and the score is aurally fascinating, especially in a performance as finely played and dedicated as this and with a 1964 recording which in its CD transfer approaches the demonstration class.

Les heures persanes, Op. 65.
☞ *** Marco Polo Dig. 8.223504 [id.]. Reinland-Pfalz PO, Segerstam.

Koechlin's powers as an orchestrator are evident in such works as Debussy's *Khamma* and Fauré's *Pelléas et Mélisande.* Small wonder that he was a much-sought-after teacher whose pupils included Poulenc, Taillefaire and Sauguet. These 16 exotic mood-pictures *d'après Vers Isphahan de Pierre Loti* were originally composed for the piano in 1913 and were scored after the First World War in 1921. They evoke a journey recorded by Pierre Loti in 1900. 'He who wants to come with me to see at

Isfahan the season of roses should travel slowly by my side, in stages, as in the Middle Ages' (to quote Loti's preface), and the cynic might be tempted to say that we do. The work is generally slow-moving and one would expect it to pall during the course of 68 minutes 56 seconds. But this music has tremendous atmosphere and exotic colours, and the very titles of the movements (*Les collines au coucher de soleil, A l'ombre près de la fontaine marbre*, for example) conjure up some idea of its character. In the hands of Leif Segerstam and the Reinland-Pfalz Orchestra this music casts a powerful spell. It is also beautifully recorded.

The Jungle Book (Le livre de la Jungle).
☞ *** Marco Polo Dig. 8.223484 [id.]. Reinland-Pfalz PO, Segerstam.

The Jungle Book (Le livre de la Jungle); (i) 3 songs (Seal Lullaby, Night-Song in the Jungle; Song of Kala Nag) for soloists, chorus and orchestra, Op. 18.
☞ (M) *** BMG/RCA Dig. 09026 61955-2 (2) [id.]. Berlin RSO, Zinman, (i) with Vermillion, Botha, Lukas & Ch.

Koechlin's lifelong fascination for Kipling's *Jungle Book* is reflected in this extraordinary four-movement tone-poem whose composition extended over several decades. The first ideas for it came to the composer in 1899, while in his early thirties. *La loi de la jungle*, Op. 175, was eventually finished in 1934. *Les bandar-log*, Op. 176, depicting Kipling's monkeys, comes from 1939–40; *La méditation de Purun Baghat*, Op. 159, from 1936 and *La course de printemps*, Op. 95, the longest of them all, occupied Koechlin for more than a decade and a half between 1911 and 1927. *La course de printemps*, Op. 95, is extraordinarily imaginative and pregnant with atmosphere: you can feel the heat and humidity of the rainforest and sense the presence of strange and menacing creatures. Powerful though it is, Koechlin does not quite sustain its length (over half an hour) but it remains quite hypnotic. Evocative though these scores are, it must be admitted that they are uneven: *La loi de la jungle* is the most static and the least interesting. Leif Segerstam is excellent in this repertoire and with his refined ear for texture distils a heady atmosphere. His reading of *Les bandar-log* may not be superior to Dorati's pioneering EMI version with the BBC Symphony Orchestra (see above) but it more than holds its own and, like its companions, is beautifully recorded. Anyone with a feeling for the exotic will respond to this original and fascinating music.

David Zinman and the Berlin Radio Symphony Orchestra on RCA include three Op. 18 songs (*Seal lullaby, Night-song in the jungle* and *Song of Kala Nag*) for soloists, chorus and orchestra, dating from the turn of the century and comprising an additional 17 minutes 32 seconds and necessitating an additional disc, albeit accommodated economically on a two-for-the-price-of-one Duo set, as in the Double Decca and Philips Duo series. Generally speaking, Zinman's performance is almost as atmospheric, though the texture is more brightly lit and clearly defined. Either can be safely recommended with three stars, but, if your shop stocks both, Segerstam has the stronger atmosphere and would be a first recommendation.

Kohaut, Carl (Joseph) (1736–93)

Lute concerto in F.
☞ (M) **(*) BMG/RCA 09026 61588-2. Julian Bream, Monteverdi O, Gardiner – HANDEL; VIVALDI: *Concertos*. **(*)

Kohaut, a Bohemian composer, was himself a lutenist and this is a well-made little work, *galant* in style and with an attractively simple *arioso* forming the slow movement. The performance is excellent and the recording good, except for the larger-than-life solo instrument caused by the forward balance.

Kokkonen, Joonas (born 1921)

(i) *Cello concerto; Symphonic sketches; Symphony No. 4.*
*** BIS Dig. CD 468 [id.]. (i) Torleif Thedéen, Lahti SO, Osmo Vänskä.

The *Fourth Symphony* is the strongest work here: its ideas are symphonic, its structure organic and its atmosphere powerful. The *Cello concerto* is a lyrical piece, very accessible. The Swedish cellist, Torleif Thedéen, gives a performance of great restraint, mastery and sensitivity. Good orchestral playing and recording.

(i) *Cello concerto;* (ii) *Symphony No. 3;* (iii) *Cello sonata.*

(M) *** Finlandia FACD 027 [id.]. (i; iii) Noras; (i) Helsinki PO, Freeman; (ii) Finnish RSO, Berglund; (iii) Heinonen.

There is precious little to choose between Arto Noras's version of the *Cello concerto* and that of the young Swedish cellist, Torleif Thedéen; both play with aristocratic finesse and convey the composer's intentions with admirable fidelity; both were recorded in close collaboration with the composer, though Thedéen on BIS has the advantage of digital recording. Paavo Berglund's excellent recording of the *Third Symphony* was made in the early 1970s and briefly appeared on Decca in the UK. This Finlandia record has the advantage of economy.

(i) *Sinfonia da camera; Il paesaggio* ; (ii) '. . . *durch einen Spiegel . . .'* (iii) *Wind quintet.*

*** BIS Dig. CD 528 [id.]. (i; ii) Lahti SO; (i) Vänskä; (iii) Söderblom; (ii) with Tiensuu; (iii) Lahti Sinf. Wind Quintet.

Those coming new to Kokkonen's musical idiom, should try the pretentiously titled but resourceful and imaginative '. . . *durch einen Spiegel . . .*', subtitled *Metamorphosis* for twelve strings and harpsichord. There are some rewardingly individual sonorities. *Il paesaggio* is an evocative landscape study, and the earlier *Wind quintet* is a lively piece. The early *Sinfonia da camera* is grey general-purpose modern music deriving from Bartókian–Hindemithian roots. Very good performances and splendid recording.

Symphony No. 1; Music for string orchestra; (i) *The Hades of the birds* (song-cycle).

*** BIS Dig. CD 485 [id.]. Lahti SO, Söderblom; (i) Monica Groop.

The *Music for string orchestra* is a rather powerful piece lasting almost half-an-hour, well wrought and its invention finely sustained if slightly anonymous. The colourings are dark. *The Hades of the birds* is a short song-cycle, which shows Monica Groop's talents to strong effect, but it is the *First Symphony* which is the strongest piece on the disc. It is serious in purpose and as far as the orchestra is concerned shows considerable mastery of colour.

Symphony No. 2; Inauguratio; Erekhtheion (cantata); *The Last temptations* (opera): *Interludes.*

**(*) BIS Dig. CD 498 [id.]. Vihavainen, Grönroos, Akateeminen Laulu Ch., Lahti SO, Vänskä.

The *Second Symphony* is a work of some eloquence and its invention has a certain freshness and quality, even if it remains ultimately unmemorable. The interludes from his opera, *The Last temptations*, make a strong impression. Not an essential purchase for admirers of this composer.

Symphony No. 3; (i) *Opus sonorum;* (ii) *Requiem.*

*** BIS Dig. CD 508 [id.]. Lahti SO, Söderblom; (i) with Ilkka Sivonen; (ii) Iskoski, Grönroos, Savonlinna Op. Festival Ch.

Söderblom's account of the *Third Symphony* has detail and atmosphere, and the same must be said of the *Requiem*. In the *Opus sonorum*, written in reaction to the sight of the vast battery of percussion so common in the 1960s, Kokkonen assigns all the percussion part to a piano, played with great delicacy here.

(i) *Piano quintet; String quartets Nos. 1–3.*

*** BIS Dig. CD 458 [id.]. (i) Valsta; Sibelius Ac. Qt.

The *Quintet* is a slight but not unpleasing work; the *First Quartet*, which sounds like any chamber work of the period, has seriousness. Like its companions it is very well played, but even such eloquent advocacy cannot disguise a certain facelessness. But three stars for the performers and the engineers.

The Last Temptations (opera): complete.

**(*) Finlandia FACD 104 (2) [id.]. Auvinen, Ruohonen, Lehtinen, Talvela, Savonlinna Op. Festival Ch. & O, Söderblom.

The Last Temptations tells of a revivalist leader, Paavo Ruotsalainen, from the Finnish province of Savo and of his inner struggle to discover Christ. The opera is dominated by the personality of Martti Talvela, and its invention for the most part has a dignity and power that are symphonic in scale. All four roles are well sung, and the performance under Ulf Söderblom is very well recorded indeed.

Koppel, Herman D. (born 1908)

Cello concerto, Op. 56.
*** BIS CD 80 [id.]. Erling Blondal Bengtsson, Danish Nat. RSO, Schmidt – NORHOLM: *Violin concerto.* ***

Herman D. Koppel's idiom stems from Stravinsky and Bartók, but the opening of his *Cello concerto* has something of the luminous quality of Tippett's *Midsummer Marriage.* Very good recording of an inventive and original piece that deserves to enter the wider international repertoire. It is more satisfying than either the Kokkonen or Sallinen concertos.

Korngold, Erich (1897–1957)

Violin concerto in D, Op. 35.
☞ *** EMI CDC7 47846-2 [id.]. Perlman, Pittsburgh SO, Previn – GOLDMARK: *Concerto.* ***

The *Violin concerto* draws its material largely from Korngold's film scores. It was written for Huberman but was a favourite of Heifetz's. He gave the first performance, and one would have thought that his recording would remain forever the supreme interpretation. It has to be played as if it is a masterpiece and with consummate virtuosity, if it is to carry conviction. Perlman, dashing and romantic, with more of a sense of fun than the older maestro, gives just such a superlative account and, though he is placed too close to the microphone, the recording overall is vivid, with Previn and the Pittsburgh orchestra warmly committed in their accompaniment. Although it is pure kitsch, there is something endearing about this piece and it deserves a place in the catalogue, if only to remind us of the calibre of this famous Hollywood musician. It is also marvellous violin music. The remastered sound has gained in presence but lost a little amplitude and warmth. This appropriately coupled disc now returns to the EMI catalogue at full price and can be recommended.

Film scores: The Adventures of Robin Hood (suite); *Captain Blood: Ship in the Night;* (i) *The Sea Hawk* (suite).
(M) *** BMG/RCA GD 80912; *GK 80912* [0912-2-RG; *0912-4-RG*]. Nat. PO, Charles Gerhardt; (i) with Amb. S. – STEINER: *Film scores.* ***

Curiously, although this collection, centring on the swashbuckling movies of Errol Flynn, is entitled *'Captain Blood'*, only a fragment – if a potent one – is included from Korngold's music for this film. Juxtaposed with the more flamboyant Steiner scores for other Flynn vehicles, this makes for one of the very best of these Hollywood anthologies. As in the rest of the series, the dedication of Charles Gerhardt and the superb playing of the National Philharmonic Orchestra, coupled with sumptuous RCA recording, means that these performances communicate strongly.

Film scores: excerpts from: Another Dawn; Anthony Adverse; Deception: (i) *Cello concerto in C, Op. 37. Of Human Bondage; The Prince and the Pauper; The Private Lives of Elizabeth and Essex; The Sea Wolf.*
(M) *** BMG/RCA GD 80185; *GK 80185* [0185-2-RG; *0185-4-RG*]. Nat. PO, Gerhardt, (i) with Gabarro.

Korngold drew on the attractive, lightweight score for *The Prince and the Pauper* as a basis for the variations in the last movement of the *Violin concerto*, while *Night scene* from *Another Dawn* – very effective in its own right – was to provide the principal theme of the first movement. For *Deception* he invented a miniature cello concerto, which is heard here in its expanded complete format. The performances by Gerhardt and the National Philharmonic are as persuasive as ever, with brilliant, spacious recording to match.

Film scores: excerpts from: Anthony Adverse; Between Two Worlds; (i) *The Constant Nymph; Deception; Devotion; Escape Me Never; King's Row; Of Human Bondage; The Sea Hawk* (suite); *The Sea Wolf* (suite).
(M) *** BMG/RCA GD 87890 [7890-2-RG]. Nat. PO, Gerhardt; (i) with Procter, Amb. S.

This was the first of the Korngold film collections to be reissued on CD and it makes a good summation of the scope of his achievement, and the remastered recording, with its panoply of brass and strings, is attractively full and spacious.

Symphony in F sharp, Op. 40; (i) *Abschiedslieder, Op. 14.*
☞ *** Chan. Dig. CHAN 9171 [id.]. (i) Linda Finnie; BBC PO, Downes.

Writing a year or so before the First World War, Sibelius spoke of Korngold with admiration as 'a young eagle' and, though the obvious hopes that were centred on the adolescent composer were not fully realized, this remarkable symphony shows just how prodigious his gifts were. To reverse the oft-quoted jibe, there is certainly far more gold than corn here; indeed the *Symphony*, composed in America during the years 1947–52, is a work of real imaginative power. It is scored for large forces –a big percussion section including piano, celeste, marimba, etc., and the orchestra is used with resource and flair. A big, 50-minute work, its opening almost calls to mind Prokofiev's textures, though there is also a fair amount of Mahler. It is now over 20 years since Rudolf Kempe made his pioneering LP in 1971, and the present performance is every bit as impressive, the Chandos recording particularly wide-ranging and lifelike. The BBC Philharmonic play with enthusiasm and sensitivity for Edward Downes. The *Abschiedslieder* are much earlier and were completed in 1920; there is a great deal of Strauss, Mahler and Zemlinsky here. Linda Finnie is a persuasive soloist, and the balance is eminently well judged.

String sextet, Op.10.
*** Hyp. Dig. CDA 66425 [id.]. Raphael Ens. – SCHOENBERG: *Verklaerte Nacht*. ***

The Korngold *Sextet* is an amazing achievement for a seventeen-year-old. Not only is it crafted with musicianly assurance and maturity it is also inventive and characterful. The Raphael Ensemble play it with great commitment and the Hyperion recording is altogether first class.

3 Lieder, Op. 18. Lieder: *Alt-spanisch; Gefasster Abschied; Glückwunsch; Liebesbriefchen; Sonett für Wien; Sterbelied.*
☞ *** DG Dig. 437 515-2 [id.]. Anne Sofie von Otter, Bengt Forsberg – BERG: *7 Early songs;* STRAUSS: *Lieder*. ***

Anne Sofie von Otter and Bengt Forsberg follow up the success of their prize-winning disc of Grieg songs with inspired playing and singing, not just in Berg and Strauss, relatively well known, but in these rare and immediately attractive songs by Erich Korngold. Though a few date from his early, precocious years in Vienna, including some of the most sensuously beautiful, such a charming miniature as *Alt-spanisch* is taken from the film music he wrote in 1940 for the swashbuckling Hollywood film, *The Sea Hawk*. Singer and pianist draw out the intensity of emotion to the full without exaggeration or sentimentality. A fascinating programme.

OPERA

Die tote Stadt (complete).
(M) *** BMG/RCA GD 87767 (2) [7767-2-RG]. Neblett, Kollo, Luxon, Prey, Bav. R. Ch., Tölz Ch., Munich R. O, Leinsdorf.

At the age of twenty-three Korngold had his opera, *Die tote Stadt*, presented in simultaneous world premières in Hamburg and Cologne! The score includes many echoes of Puccini and Richard Strauss, but its youthful exuberance carries the day. Here René Kollo is powerful, if occasionally coarse of tone, Carol Neblett sings sweetly in the equivocal roles of the wife's apparition and the newcomer, and Hermann Prey, Benjamin Luxon and Rose Wagemann make up an impressive cast. Leinsdorf is at his finest.

Violanta (complete).
**(*) Sony CD 79229 [MK 35909]. Marton, Berry, Jerusalem, Stoklassa, Laubenthal, Hess, Bav. R. Ch., Munich R. O, Janowski.

Korngold was perhaps the most remarkable composer-prodigy of this century; he wrote this opera at the age of seventeen. Though luscious of texture and immensely assured, the writing lets one down by an absence of really memorable melody but, with a fine, red-blooded performance and with Siegfried Jerusalem a youthfully fresh hero, it makes a fascinating addition to the recorded repertory. Eva Marton, not always beautiful of tone, combines power and accuracy in the key role of the heroine. The recording is quite full if not especially refined.

Das Wunder der Heliane (complete).
☞ *** Decca Dig. 436 636-2 (3) [id.]. Tomowa-Sintow, Welker, De Haan, Runkel, Pape, Gedda, Berlin R. Ch. & RSO, Mauceri.

Like the Decca set of Krenek's *Jonny spielt auf*, this Korngold opera, also first performed in Vienna in 1927, comes in a series devoted to works banned by the Nazis, '*Entartete Musik*', so-called decadent music. Far more exotic, *Das Wunder der Heliane* was the opera which was initially presented in direct confrontation with the Krenek. Korngold's father, Julius, as the leading Viennese critic, vilified the Krenek piece so bitterly (ironically bringing in the Nazis as allies) that there was a backlash, and this symbolic fairytale opera with opulent orchestration to out-Strauss Strauss was quickly withdrawn. The narrative itself is full of overt eroticism.

Though the plot, with its tyrannical ruler, his wife and a mysterious stranger, is unconvincing, Decca's magnificent recording amply confirms the view that this is Korngold's masterpiece, musically even richer than his better-known opera, *Die tote Stadt*. The opening prelude, with its exotic harmonies and heavenly choir, will seduce anyone with a sweet tooth, and though in three Acts of nearly an hour each it is overlong, Korngold – who had just emerged from his years as a child prodigy to rival Mozart – sustains the story with a ravishing score. Puccini as well as Strauss is often very close, with one passage in the big Act I love-duet bringing languorous echoes of the end of *Fanciulla del West*. Korngold's lavish Hollywood scores of the 1930s are thin by comparison. John Mauceri draws glorious sounds from the Berlin Radio Symphony Orchestra, and the cast is headed by three outstanding singers, the soprano Anna Tomowa-Sintow at her richest, an impressive American Heldentenor, John David de Haan, as the Stranger and Hartmut Welker as the Ruler.

Kozeluch, Leopold (1747–1818)

Clarinet concerto No. 2 in E flat.
☞ *** ASV Dig. CDDCA 763; *ZCDCA 763* [id.]. Emma Johnson, RPO, Herbig – CRUSELL; KROMMER: *Concertos.* ***

The Bohemian composer, Leopold Kozeluch, was the cousin of the slightly better-known Jan (Johann), and his concerto is a highly agreeable work, especially when performed so magnetically by Emma Johnson. There is plenty of Johnsonian magic here to light up even the most conventional passage-work, and the 'naturally flowing melodies' (the soloist's own description), and she is well accompanied and admirably recorded, with the slow movement made to sound recessed and delicate.

Kramář, František – see Krommer, Franz

Kreisler, Fritz (1875–1962)

Allegretto in the style of Boccherini; Allegretto in the style of Porpora; Caprice viennoise; Cavatina; La Chasse in the style of Cartier; La Gitana; Grave in the style of W. F. Bach; Gypsy caprice; Liebesfreud; Liebesleid; Praeludium and allegro in the style of Pugnani; Recitative and scherzo; Schön Rosmarin; Shepherd's madrigal; Sicilienne et rigaudon in the style of Francoeur; Toy soldiers' march; Viennese rhapsodic fantasia; arr. of Austrian National Hymn.
(BB) **(*) ASV CDQS 6039. Oscar Shumsky, Milton Kaye.

Oscar Shumsky's combination of technical mastery and musical flair is ideal for this music; and it is a pity that the rather dry recording and forward balance – well in front of the piano – makes the violin sound almost too close.

Caprice viennoise; Chanson Louis XIII & Pavane in the style of Couperin; La Gitana; Liebeslied; Liebesfreud; Polinchinelle; La Précieuse in the style of Couperin; Rondino on a theme by Beethoven; Scherzo alla Dittersdorf; Tambourin chinois; Schön Rosmarin. Arrangements: BACH: *Partita No. 3 in E, BWV 1006: Gavotte.* BRANDL: *The old refrain.* DVORAK: *Humoresque.* FALLA: *La vida breve: Danza española.* GLAZUNOV: *Sérénade espagnole.* HEUBERGER: *Midnight bells (Im chambre séparée).* POLDINI: *Poupée valsante.* RIMSKY-KORSAKOV: *Sadko: Chanson hindoue.* SCHUBERT: *Rosamunde: Ballet music No. 2.* SCOTT: *Lotus Land.* TCHAIKOVSKY: *Andante cantabile from Op. 11.* WEBER: *Violin sonata No. 1 in F, Op. 10: Larghetto.* TRAD.: *Londonderry air.*
☞ (M) (***) EMI mono CDH7 64701-2 [id.]. Fritz Kreisler, Franz Rupp or Michael Rachelsein; or (in *Scherzo*) Kreisler String Qt.

Impeccable and characterful performances by Fritz Kreisler of his own lollipops, including those 'in the style of' pieces with which – until he owned up – he fooled his audiences into believing they were actually written by the composers in question. Most of the recordings were made with Franz Rupp in 1936 or 1938, and the transfers offer a convincingly realistic if studio-ish balance and are of excellent technical quality; a few (the *Polinchinelle*, the pieces in the style of Couperin, the Schubert *Rosamunde ballet music*, the Glazunov and Weber arrangements, *The old refrain* (especially) and an indulgent performance of Heuberger's *Im chambre séparée*) date from 1930 and here the piano balance is poor, the piano badly defined. However, these were recorded before Kreisler's accident and the violin timbre is noticeably more opulent. A valuable document.

Caprice viennoise, Op. 2; La Gitana; Liebesfreud; Liebesleid; Polichinelle; La Précieuse; Recitativo and scherzo caprice, Op. 6; Rondo on a theme of Beethoven; Syncopation; Tambourin chinois; Zigeuner (Capriccio). Arrangements: ALBENIZ: *Tango, Op. 165/2.* WEBER: *Larghetto.* WIENIAWSKI: *Caprice in E flat.* DVORAK: *Slavonic dance No. 10 in E min.* GLAZUNOV: *Sérénade espagnole.* GRANADOS: *Danse espagnole.*
(M) *** DG 423 876-2; *423 876-4* [id.]. Shlomo Mintz, Clifford Benson.

Shlomo Mintz plays with a disarmingly easy style and absolute technical command, to bring out the music's warmth as well as its sparkle. A very attractive programme, given first-class recording and splendid presence without added edge on CD.

Krenek, Ernst (1900–1991)

Jonny spielt auf (complete).
☞ **(*) Decca Dig. 436 631-2 (2) [id.]. Kruse, Marc, St Hill, Kraus, Posselt, Leipzig Op. Ch., Leipzig GO, Zarogsek.

Read any musical history of the 1920s written at the time, and Ernst Krenek's opera, *Jonny spielt auf* ('Jonny plays on'), will have a prominent place. It was acclaimed as the first jazz opera, even though the composer always resisted that description. In Berlin in 1927 it scored a phenomenal success, reviled by the critics but loved by the public, and within the year there had been 50 productions through Europe. Yet it all proved a flash in the pan. Paris was unimpressed, and back in Germany it was quickly banned by the Nazi regime, which condemned it as '*Entartete Musik*', decadent music. Krenek (not a Jew) found refuge in America, and in New York the piece was a flop. It did not help that as late as 1938 the singer taking the role of Jonny had to be a 'blacked-up' white man. However, Jonny does not make his entry until the third scene.

Hearing the opera now in a fine recording, based on a 1990 Leipzig production – made just before the composer died at the age of ninety – it stands as more than a historical curiosity. Contradicting its reputation, it is a lyrical post-romantic piece. It is primarily about a frustrated musician, Max, in which the story of Jonny stealing a violin is merely a sub-plot; and the jazzy passages – blues, tango and so on – are superimposed, like cherries on a cake. One's first disappointment is that it hardly matches the Kurt Weill operas. The idiom is far milder, with syncopations used more gently in the jazzy passages and with the instrumentation less abrasive. The cavortings of Jonny, complete with Keystone Cops-style chases, were what originally attracted attention, and in the recording – helped by spectacular sound effects – they come over with colour and energy; but Max (symbolically addicted to exploring glaciers) with his process of self-discovery, touchingly treated, provides a far more important element. Though the Leipzig Gewandhaus Orchestra under Lothar Zagrosek does not always sound at home in the jazzy sequences, the recording provides the most convincing evidence yet that the piece deserves reappraisal. Heinz Kruse as Max sustains his long monologues impressively, and Krister St Hill as Jonny also sings well, even if the microphone catches an unevenness in their voices. It is Alessandra Marc as the heroine, Anita, who emerges as the main star, relishing lush Krenek melodies that yet never quite stick in the mind.

Kreutzer, Joseph (c. 1820)

Grand Trio.
*** Mer. Dig. CDE 84199; *KE 77199* [id.]. Conway, Silverthorne, Garcia – BEETHOVEN: *Serenade;* MOLINO: *Trio.* ***

Joseph Kreutzer, thought to be the brother of Rodolphe Kreutzer, dedicatee of Beethoven's *A major Violin sonata*, wrote many works for the guitar, of which this is a delightful example. The guitar, given at least equal prominence with the other instruments, brings an unusual tang to the textures of this charming piece, ending with a rousing *Alla Polacca*. A nicely pointed performance, very well recorded in warm, faithful sound.

Krommer, Franz (1759–1831)

Clarinet concerto in E flat, Op. 36.
☞ *** ASV Dig. CDDCA 763; *ZCDCA 763* [id.]. Emma Johnson, RPO, Herbig – CRUSELL: *Concerto No. 1;* KOZELUCH: *Concerto No. 2.* ***

Emma Johnson is at her most winning in this attractive concerto which is made to sound completely spontaneous in her hands, particularly the engaging finale, lolloping along with its skipping main theme. The *Adagio* is darker in feeling, its mood equally well caught. Excellent accompaniments and warm, refined rercording make this a most engaging triptych.

Symphonies Nos. 2 in D, Op. 40; 4 in C min., Op. 102.
☞ *** Chan. Dig. CHAN 9275 [id.]. LMP, Bamert.

A delightful addition to the representation of Krommer (born František Kramář) in the catalogue. Collectors who acquired the *Harmonien*, played by the Netherlands Wind Ensemble, or the *Octets* (now deleted), which the Sabine Meyer wind ensemble recorded for EMI (see our last volume), will know how infectiously high-spirited this composer is; and they will not be disappointed by the two symphonies played here by the London Mozart Players under Matthias Bamert. They present a different picture of him: the *D major Symphony* (1803) opens in something of the manner of *Don Giovanni*, while much else conveys a distinctly Beethovenian visage. The *C minor*, Op. 102, composed towards the end of the second decade of the nineteenth century, already has a whiff of the changing sensibility that we find in Schubert and Weber. Very interesting and refreshing music, played with evident enthusiasm and well recorded.

Kuhlau, Friedrich (1786–1832)

(i) *Concertino for two horns, Op. 45;* (ii) *Piano concerto in C, Op. 7; Overture Elverhøj (The elves' hill), Op. 100.*
*** Unicorn Dig. DKPCD 9110; *DKPC 9110* [id.]. (i) Ib Lansky-Otto, Frøydis Ree Wekre; (ii) Michael Ponti; Odense SO, Othmar Maga.

The overture *Elverhøj* or *The elves' hill* is probably Kuhlau's best-known work and is certainly the finest piece on this disc. The *Piano concerto in C*, Op. 7, is modelled on Beethoven's concerto in the same key. The *Concertino for two horns* (1821) is full of initially engaging, but eventually unmemorable, ideas. Very good performances from all concerned, and satisfactory recording.

Elverhøj (The elves' hill), Op. 100.
** Dacapo Dig. DCCD 8902 [id.]. Gobel, Plesner, Johansen, Danish R. Ch. & SO, John Frandsen.

Kuhlau's incidental music to J. L. Heiberg's play, *Elverhøj*, is endearingly fresh. Not so the recording however; this sounds really rather dryish, as if recorded in a fully packed concert hall. The music has great charm and the performance too under John Frandsen is very sympathetic.

(i) *Elverhoj (The elves' hill): suite;* (ii) *Overtures: Lulu; The Robber's hill; The Three brothers from Damascus; William Shakespeare.*
☞ **(*) Unicorn Dig. DKPCD 9132 [id.]. Odense SO, cond. (i) Maga; (ii) Serov.

A useful companion issue to the Odense orchestra's recordings of Kuhlau's *C major Piano concerto* and the *Concertino for two horns* (see above). No great claims can be made for this repertoire but it has a certain freshness and grace that compensate for the absence of any great individuality. Only the Overture to *Elverhøj* is duplicated. *Røverborgen* ('The robbers' hill'), Kuhlau's first singspiel (or rather *syngespil*), scored a great success in 1814 and its short overture (it lasts only 4½ minutes) is engaging, as are its three companions from the 1820s. There are plenty of reminders of Weber, Spohr and other contemporaries, and few of the ideas resonate long in the memory (some, it must be admitted, not at all!). In the *Elverhøj* music, Othmar Maga gets pleasing results as, for that matter, does his younger Russian colleague in the overtures. Not mandatory listening, but pleasing all the same. Decent, if rather bright-and-breezy recording, with not quite enough air round it.

Lulu (opera): complete.
*** Kontrapunkt/HM 32009/11 [id.]. Saarman, Frellesvig, Kiberg, Cold, Danish R. Ch. & SO, Schönwandt.

This *Lulu* comes from 1824 and is surely too long: the spoken passages are omitted here – but, even so, the music takes three hours. The opening of Act II has overtones of the Wolf's Glen scene in *Der Freischutz* and the dance of the black elves in the moonlight is pure Mendelssohn – and has much charm. The invention is generally fresh and engaging, though no one would claim that it has great depth. The largely Danish cast cope very capably with the not inconsiderable demands of Kuhlau's vocal writing, the Danish Radio recording is eminently truthful and vivid, and Michael Schönwandt draws excellent results from the Danish Radio Chorus and Orchestra.

Lachner, Franz (1803–90)

Septet in E flat.
*** Marco Polo Dig. 8.223282 [id.]. Ens. Villa Musica – FUCHS: *Clarinet quintet.* ***

Franz Lachner was a friend of Schubert, and his *Septet* dates from 1824, the same year as the Schubert *Octet*. The *Septet* is not great music but has an easy-going charm that is really quite winning, and it is nicely played and well recorded by this Mainz-based group.

Lajtha, László (1892–1963)

3 Berceuses; Contes, Op. 2; Des Ecrits d'un musicien, Op. 1; 6 Piano pieces; Prélude.
☞ ** Marco Polo Dig. 8.223473 [id.]. Klára Körmendi.

Although two of László Lajtha's symphonies and some of his other orchestral music have been recorded, his piano music has not been readily available except, perhaps, in Hungary. No doubt the centenary of his birth – in the same year as Honegger and Milhaud – prompted the release of this issue. Lajtha was a highly accomplished pianist (he was a Stavenhagen student in the first decade of the century). Most of these pieces date from the earlier part of his career (1913–18) and show a responsiveness to the modern music of the period, Bartók and Debussy, and there is also an awareness of Schoenberg. The *Six Piano Pieces* of 1930 are obviously Bartókian and the *Three Berceuses* (1955–7) have a certain charm. A fastidious craftsman and a composer of culture, the piano music is a little too anonymous to make strong claims on the repertoire, though Klára Körmendi plays with evident conviction. The recording is clean and decent without being in any way distinguished; and there seems to be a different balance between the *Toccata* of Op. 14 and the *Berceuses*.

Lalo, Eduard (1823–92)

Cello concerto No. 1 in D min., Op. 33.
☞ *** ASV Dig. CDDCA 867 [id.]. Sophie Rolland, BBC PO, Gilbert Varga – MASSENET: *Fantaisie;* SAINT-SAENS: *Cello concerto No. 1.* ***
*** DG Dig. 427 323-2 [id.]. Matt Haimovitz, Chicago SO, Levine – SAINT-SAENS: *Concerto No. 1;* BRUCH: *Kol Nidrei.* ***
(B) *** DG 431 166-2. Heinrich Schiff, New Philh. O, Mackerras – FAURE: *Elégie;* SAINT-SAENS: *Cello concerto No. 1.* ***
(M) **(*) Mercury 432 010-2 [id.]. Janos Starker, LSO, Skrowaczewski – SAINT-SAENS; SCHUMANN: *Concertos.* ***
☞ (M) **(*) Sony SBK 48278 [id.]. Leonard Rose, Phd. O, Ormandy – BLOCH: *Schelomo;* FAURÉ: *Elégie;* TCHAIKOVSKY: *Rococo variations.* ***

The young Canadian cellist, Sophie Rolland, has been hailed in flattering terms by both Charles Dutoit and William Pleeth, with whom she studied, and her account of the endearing Lalo *Cello concerto in D minor* reveals her as a formidable talent. She plays with effortless eloquence and is given responsive support from the BBC Philharmonic under Gilbert Varga (the son of the violinist, Tibor), though he is a little brusque in the *Intermezzo*. An enjoyable and convincing performance, probably the finest to appear since Yo-Yo Ma's Sony account (which is currently withdrawn). The excellence of the BBC/ASV recording makes for a strong recommendation.

An outstandingly impressive début from the young cellist, Matt Haimovitz; the performance throughout combines vitality with expressive feeling in the most spontaneous manner. The recording is very well balanced indeed and highly realistic.

This was Heinrich Schiff's début recording in 1977, made when he was still very young. His account of the Lalo *Concerto* is fresh and enthusiastic and very well recorded for its period. With its excellent coupling it makes a real bargain.

Janos Starker's 1962 recording with the LSO under Stanislaw Skrowaczewski sounds remarkably good for its age. Though the tutti chords are brutal and clipped, Starker plays splendidly, and the famous Mercury recording technique lays out the orchestral texture quite beautifully and with remarkable transparency.

Leonard Rose gives a strong, spontaneous account of this sometimes intractable concerto, bringing out its melodic character as well as its vitality of invention. Ormandy's accompaniment is wonderfully supportive and it is a pity that the orchestral sound has a hint of edginess in the violins and is a bit two-dimensional. However, one can adjust use the controls and the ear adjusts when the music-making is so compelling, as it is throughout this fine anthology.

(i) *Cello concerto in D min.;* (ii) *Symphonie espagnole, Op. 21.*

☞ (M) *** Decca Dig. 436 483-2 [id.]. (i) Lynn Harrell, Berlin RSO, Chailly; (ii) Kyung Wha Chung, Montreal SO, Dutoit – SAINT-SAENS: *Violin concerto No. 1.* ***

☞ (B) *(**) Erato/Warner 2292 45949-2 [id.]. (i) Pierre Amoyal, Monte-Carlo Opéra O, Paray; (ii) Frédéric Lodéon.

Lynn Harrell's Decca account was recorded within the attractive acoustic of the Jesus-Christus-Kirche, Berlin (the venue of many of Furtwängler's successful mono LPs of the 1950s). The orchestra is given vivid colour and presence. Chailly's accompaniment is attractively bold, more assertive than usual. Lynn Harrell's performance is an extremely fine one, perhaps less subtle but no less ardent than Sophie Rolland's and certainly no less convincing. While the playing remains refined in polish and detail, there is a yearning intensity in the *Intermezzo*, while the outer movements combine spontaneity and vigour. The cello image is very tangible on CD (though, like Yo-Yo Ma's, it is modest in scale) and, while the orchestra creates a dramatic contrast, the balance remains totally believable. Harrell's CD now comes at mid-price and the coupling, with not only Kyung Wha Chung's *Symphonie espagnole* but also Saint-Saëns's lesser-known but very attractive *First violin concerto*, makes this reissue very attractive, particularly as the digital sound is first class throughout.

Chung's is an athletic, incisive account, at its most individual in the captivatingly lightweight finale, with an element almost of fantasy. For some ears, the lack of sumptuousness of style as well as of timbre may be a drawback; Miss Chung does not have quite the panache of Perlman. But Charles Dutoit's accompaniment is first class and the orchestral characterization is strong throughout.

Here on Erato is a case where a marvellous solo performance triumphs over indifferent orchestral recording which, in the *Symphonie espagnole*, is boomy in the bass, though the treble is free enough and the solo violin truthfully caught. Amoyal's account of the solo role is glorious, his playing consistently seductive (and totally free from schmaltz), as well as warm and polished. The infectious finale is like quicksilver and the *Andante* (with rich orchestral brass) has unexpected nobility. Moreover Lodéon's performance of the *Cello concerto* is recommendable in every way – the *Intermezzo* is ravishingly done and the finale spontaneously volatile – with the Philharmonia under Dutoit providing excellent backing. Here the recording, though not brilliant, is much better balanced and it gives the soloist a rich, firmly focused timbre that is most appealing.

Namouna (ballet): extended excerpts: *(suites Nos. 1–2 & Allegro vivace; Tambourin; La Gitane; Bacchanale).*

☞ **(*) Audivis Valois Dig. V 4677 [id.]. Monte-Carlo PO, David Robertson.

Namouna (ballet): *suites Nos. 1–2; Valse de la cigarette.*

☞ **(*) ASV Dig. CDDCA 878 [id.]. RPO, Yondani Butt (with GOUNOD: *Mors et Vita: Judex*).

Pierre Boulez has commented that 'symphonic music in France has often evolved more inventively thanks to the great ballets – starting with *Namouna* – rather than to the symphonies with their more formalist principles of composition'. There is no complete version available of Lalo's ballet, which dates from 1882 and which Debussy admired, but David Robertson has added four more items to the content of Lalo's two suites, plus the charmingly Gallic *Valse de la cigarette* (which the composer extracted as a separate number). He has also re-established the music in ballet-order, whereas in the suites Lalo reassembled the items for concert performance. There is much engaging music here, especially the Beechamesque lollipop, *La Sieste*. Robertson secures sensitive, polished playing from his Monte Carlo orchestra, who resound with warmth, and the recording, if not quite top-drawer, has plenty of colour and ambience.

Yondani Butt achieves performances of the suites and the *Valse de la cigarette* which have comparable colour and finesse, and the RPO play extremely well. Even so, they don't necessarily upstage their French competitors and they offer less music. Where they gain is in the *Prélude*, which is an unashamed crib from Wagner's *Das Rheingold*. Clearly the British players relish the connection and make the most of the rumbustious climax (aided by Brian Culverhouse's vibrantly expansive recording), where the French orchestra tries not to wallow in Wagnerian amplitude. The ASV disc offers a big *religieuse* Gounod tune as an encore, but more of *Namouna* would have been preferable.

Symphonie espagnole (for violin and orchestra), *Op. 21.*

(M) *** DG Dig. 429 977-2 [id.]. Perlman, O de Paris, Barenboim – SAINT-SAENS: *Concerto No. 3.* ***

*** DG Dig. 427 676-2 [id.]. Mintz, Israel PO, Mehta – SAINT-SAENS: *Introduction & Rondo capriccioso;* VIEUXTEMPS: *Concerto No. 5.* ***

☞ (M) **(*) Sony SBK 48274 [id.]. Zukerman, LAPO, Mehta – VIEUXTEMPS: *Concerto No. 5.* **(*)
**(*) BMG/RCA Dig. RD 60942 [09026 60942-2]. Anne Akiko Meyers, RPO, Lópes-Cobos –
  BRUCH: *Scottish fantasia.* ***

☞ (BB) ** Naxos Dig. 8.550494 [id.]. Marat Bisengaliev, Polish Nat. RSO, Wildner (with: SARASATE:
  Zigeunerweisen ***; SAINT-SAENS: *Havanaise;* RAVEL: *Tzigane* **(*)).

Lalo's brilliant five-movement distillation of Spanish sunshine is well served by DG. Barenboim
combines rhythmic buoyancy with expressive flair and the richness and colour of Perlman's tone are
never more telling than in the slow movement, which opens tenderly but develops a compelling
expressive ripeness. The brilliance of the scherzo is matched by the dancing sparkle of the finale. The
recording is extremely lively but fairly dry.

Mintz, too, plays with much panache; he is highly seductive in the lilting secondary theme of the
first movement, and he brings a comparable touch of restrained voluptuousness to the habanera
rhythms of the *Intermezzo*, while the Scherzo is light as thistledown. Mehta opens a bit heavily but
provides a satisfactory accompaniment, while the recording, made live in the Israel Mann Auditorium,
is acceptable, full, if not ideally transparent.

Kyung Wha Chung has the advantage of a first-class Decca digital recording, fuller than the DG
alternative, and with a highly effective, natural balance. Hers is an athletic, incisive account, at its
most individual in the captivatingly lightweight finale, with an element almost of fantasy.

Zukerman's performance is outstandingly successful. He plays with great dash and fire yet brings
a balancing warmth. The rhythmic zest of the Scherzo, with its subtle control of dynamic shading, is
contrasted with a richly expressive *Andantino*, to be followed by a dazzling display of fireworks in the
finale. Mehta accompanies with sympathetic gusto, and the reverberant, larger-than-life recording
suits the style of the music-making, the soloist balanced very forwardly indeed. Zukerman's couplings
are more generous than Perlman's, but the effect of the DG recording is to give Perlman's account
slightly more romantic finesse.

Anne Akiko Meyers' account offers a genuine alternative view. Her approach to the first
movement's secondary theme has a beguilingly light touch, the seductive Spanish lilt pastel-shaded,
and her sense of fantasy brings a similar airy lightness to the Scherzo. She introduces the lovely
melody of the *Andante* with magically hushed intensity. The finale brings appealing sparkle and
delicacy of articulation. López-Cobos does not quite match his young soloist in concentration.
However, he has the advantage of really first-class recording, achieving a natural balance with the
soloist.

Lalo's tuttis are rather thickly scored, with frequent orchestral unisons, and the effect on Naxos
produces rather ample textures. The resonance of the Concert Hall of the Polish Radio in Katowice
suits Lalo less well than it does Paganini (see below). The soloist here, Marat Bisengaliev, was born in
Kazakhstan but studied in Moscow. He is an accomplished player with a rich tone and secure
technique, and his Slavonic temperament means that Lalo's Spanish ideas are presented with sultry
flair. Jonathan Wildner is a musical accompanist; he is lively enough in the first movement and
manages to make Lalo's quiet woodwind detail register in spite of the resonance. But he takes the
Andante rather steadily, and the finale again could have used more sheer sparkle from the orchestra.
There is nothing wrong with the solo playing. The three encores are very successful. *Zigeunerweisen*,
the highlight, has glowing gypsy panache and the luscious lyrical tune sounds properly beguiling,
Saint-Saëns's *Havanaise* is stylishly sympathetic, and Ravel's *Tzigane* has real temperament and fire.
The recording acoustic suits these pieces much better than the Lalo.

Symphony in G min.
(M) **(*) CDM7 63396-2 [id.]. O Nat. de l'ORTF, Sir Thomas Beecham – FRANCK: *Symphony*.
  **(*)

The *Symphony*'s second-movement Scherzo with its delectable flute-writing inspires Beecham to a
delectably pointed performance; but he has to work harder with the rest, when the material is thinner,
and the argument in the first movement lacks tautness. The EMI recording has good body and
presence, but the transfer adds an edge on top.

Le roi d'Ys (complete).
*** Erato/Warner Dig. 2292 45015-2 (2) [id.]. Courtis, Ziegler, Hendricks, Villa, Fr. R. Ch. & PO,
  Jordan.

The American mezzo-soprano, Delores Ziegler, is very convincingly cast. Her dramatic, unfruity
voice is perfectly contrasted against the ravishing Rozenn of Barbara Hendricks. Eduardo Villa as the
hero, Mylio, may not be delicate enough in the famous *Aubade*, but his heady tenor has no trouble
with the high tessitura. Jean-Philippe Courtis as the King, in this improbable Breton legend of

medieval chivalry, and Marcel Vanaud as the villain, Karnac, have dark, weighty voices, marred at times by flutter.

Lambert, Constant (1905–51)

Aubade héroïque; (i) *The Rio Grande; Summer's last will and testament.*
⊛ *** Hyp. Dig. CDA 66565 [id.]. Sally Burgess, Jack Gibbons, William Shimell, Ch. of Opera North and Leeds Festival, (i) with Jack Gibbons; English N. Philh., Lloyd-Jones.

The Rio Grande, Lambert's jazz-based choral concerto setting a poem by Sacheverell Sitwell, is one of the most colourful and atmospheric works from the 1920s. David Lloyd-Jones directs a scintillating performance that directly reflects the original recording, conducted by the young composer in 1930 with Sir Hamilton Harty as piano soloist. With Sally Burgess a warmly expressive soloist, sharply dramatic choral singing, and Jack Gibbons the brilliant, keenly responsive pianist, Lloyd-Jones gives a totally idiomatic account of music that requires crisp attack combined with a jazzy freedom of rhythm. The *Aubade héroïque* is an evocative tone-poem inspired by Lambert's memory of a beautiful morning in Holland in 1940 when, with the Nazi invasion, it was far from certain whether he and his colleagues would be able to get back to England. Inspired by the death of his friend (and alcoholic evil influence) Peter Warlock/Philip Heseltine, *Summer's last will and testament* is a big, 50-minute choral work setting lyrics by the Elizabethan, Thomas Nashe, on the unpromising subject of the threat of plague. Lloyd-Jones and his outstanding team, mainly from Opera North, bring out the vitality and colour of the writing, with each of the nine substantial sections based on Elizabethan dance-rhythms. The recording in all three works is full, vivid and atmospheric.

(i) *Piano concerto; Horoscope* (ballet): *suite;* (i; ii) *The Rio Grande.*
**(*) Argo Dig. 436 118-2 [id.]. (i) Kathryn Stott; (ii) Della Jones, BBC Singers; BBC Concert O, Wordsworth.

With bright, forward recording this Argo account of *The Rio Grande* is rather more aggressive than the Hyperion one and is a degree more literal, less idiomatic in its interpretation of jazzy syncopations, but the power and colour of the writing come across with fine bite and clarity. In the ballet suite from *Horoscope* there is one more movement than Lambert ever recorded, the *Palindromic prelude*, less striking than the other movements but still beautifully written. Here again Wordsworth and the BBC Concert Orchestra are a degree more literal than Lambert himself was in jazz-rhythms. Kathryn Stott with members of the orchestra gives splendid point to the angular *Concerto* for piano and nine players, where the emotional element is much more severely repressed than in the other works on the disc.

Horoscope (ballet): *suite.*
⊛ *** Hyp. CDA 66436 [id.]. E. N. Philh. O, Lloyd-Jones – BLISS: *Checkmate;* WALTON: *Façade.*
***

The music for *Horoscope* is sheer delight, and it seems incredible that the only previous complete recording of the suite was made in the mid-1950s by Irving for Decca. David Lloyd-Jones is equally sympathetic to its specifically English atmosphere. He wittily points the catchy rhythmic figure which comes both in the *Dance for the followers of Leo* and, later, in the *Bacchanale*, while the third-movement *Valse for the Gemini* has a delectable insouciant charm. Excellent playing and first-class sound, perhaps a shade resonant for the ballet pit, but bringing plenty of bloom.

Lambert, Michel (c. 1610–96)

Airs de cour: Admirons notre jeune et charmante Déesse; Ah! qui voudra desormais s'engager; C'en est fait, belle Iris; D'un feu secret je me sens consumer; Il faut mourir plutost que le changer; Iris n'est plus, mon Iris m'est ravie; Je suis aymé de celle que j'adore; Ma bergere est tendre et fidelle; Ombre de mon amant; Par mes chants tristes et touchants; Pour vos beaux yeux, Iris; Le repos, l'ombre, le silence; Tout l'univers obéit à l'amour; Trouver sur l'herbette.
(B) *** HM HMA 901123 [id.]. Les Arts Florissants, William Christie.

Grove speaks of Michel Lambert's airs as models of elegance and grace, in which careful attention was paid to direct declamation. The 300 or so that survive show his artistry in characterization and dialogue to have been of the highest order. They are beautifully performed and expertly recorded by members of Les Arts Florissants and William Christie and are altogether delightful. Unlike some bargain issues, there is excellent documentation with the original texts and translation.

Lanchbery, John (born 1923)

Tales of Beatrix Potter (ballet arranged from popular tunes of the Victorian era).
☞ **(*) EMI CDC7 54537-2 [id.]. ROHCG O, Lanchbery.

Here is a companion score for John Lanchbery's clever adaptation of Hérold's *La Fille mal gardée*. In this instance he chose tunes from the period of the Beatrix Potter stories (including some of Sullivan) and they are all so skilfully linked that one would think the score 'through-composed'. The material is not quite as distinguished melodically as the compilation of ideas (not all by Hérold) in that earlier arrangement, but the colourful and witty orchestration is a source of delight. The 1971 Abbey Road recording was out of EMI's top drawer at the time, and the CD remastering is highly successful. But why is this reissued at full price?

Landowski, Marcel (born 1915)

Symphonies Nos. 1 (Jean de la peur); 3 (Des espaces); 4.
☞ *** Erato/Warner Dig. 2292 45018-2 [id.]. Fr. Nat. O, Prêtre.

Marcel Landowski is little more than a name outside France, where he is much respected – and rightly so, if these symphonies are anything to go by. He is firmly rooted in the tradition of Honegger and Roussel, and though he is perhaps not as resourceful as, say, Dutilleux, his handling of complex orchestral textures and orchestral colours is highly imaginative. The three symphonies recorded here cover a considerable period: the *First* comes from the immediate post-war years, while the *Fourth* was a French Radio commission from the 1980s. The overwhelming inspiration is undoubtedly Honegger, but the musical invention is well sustained, and interest never flags. A most worthwhile issue, with good performances and recordings too.

Langgaard, Rued (1893–1952)

Symphony No. 1 (Klippepastoraler); Fra Dybet.
☞ *** Chan. Dig. CHAN 9249 [id.]. Danish Nat. RSO & Ch., Segerstam.

Rued Langgaard began this symphony when he was fourteen; he was only eighteen when he finished revising it. Bendt Vinholt Nielsen makes out a sympathetic case for the work in his authoritative, 580-page study of the composer and in his excellent notes; so, too, do the Danish Radio forces under Leif Segerstam. Langgaard was a figure of undoubted but flawed talent (and his *Sfærernes Musik* shows a composer who possessed flashes of real vision), but as this banal, five-movement overblown sprawl slowly unwinds its 67 minutes, one realizes that the composer subjected this particular piece to no real critical scrutiny. Not to put too fine a point upon it, he was essentially a windbag. There are some imaginative moments in the finale. *Fra Dybet* ('From the Deep') comes from the other end of his career and was completed not long before his death: it opens rather bombastically but soon lapses into sentimentality at the entrance of the choir. Good recording.

Symphonies Nos. 4 (Løfvald: The falling of the leaf); 5 (Steppelands); 6 (Himmelrivende: The storming of the heavens).
☞ *** Chan. Dig. CHAN 9064 [id.]. Danish Nat. RSO, Neeme Järvi.

The revival of Rued Langgaard's remarkable *Sfærernes Musik* ('Music of the spheres') during the 1968 Nordic Music Days in Stockholm stimulated something of an upturn in the fortunes of this neglected Danish composer. His *Fourth Symphony* (1916, revised 1920), subtitled *The falling of the leaf* or, rather less romantically, *Defoliation*, had several performances but retained little more than a foothold on the repertoire. The *Sixth (Himmelrivende* – variously translated as *The storming of the heavens* or, on this CD, as *Heavens asunder)* is another work which hovers on the periphery of the catalogue. Both were recorded in the 1970s. In fact this Chandos collaboration with Danish Radio makes a useful introduction to this far from uninteresting composer, for these works have passages that almost persuade one as to the justice of the claims made by his admirers – almost, but not quite. The parallels so often made with Charles Ives and Havergal Brian seem difficult to sustain: what is lacking in Langgaard is any real sense of organic growth and ultimately, it must be said, a distinctive and original personality. However, Neeme Järvi makes out a strong case for this music and the Danish Radio Orchestra play with conviction and sympathy. They are given excellent recorded sound.

Symphonies Nos. 10 (Yon Dwelling of Thunder); 11 (Ixion); 12 (Helsingeborg); Sfinx (tone-poem).
☞ ** Danacord Dig. DACOCD 408 [id.]. Artur Rubinstein PO, Ilya Stupel.

The *Eleventh* and *Twelfth Symphonies* are shorter than they seem; in fact the *Eleventh* lasts less than six minutes but its main theme is of awesome vapidity. It could easily pass muster in some Hollywood feature about a misunderstood and neglected composer. The language is openly neo-romantic, which would not in itself matter were the musical invention tinged with a flicker of real distinction. The Artur Rubinstein Philharmonic Orchestra turns in serviceable performances and are decently enough recorded, but do not dispel the impression that this is music of shadows rather than substance.

Symphonies Nos. 13 (Faithlessness); 16 (The Deluge of Sun); Anti-Christ (opera): *Prelude.*
☞ ** Danacord Dig. DACOCD 410. Artur Rubinstein PO, Ilya Stupel.

The *Sixteenth Symphony* (1951) betrays more of Langgaard's weaknesses than his strengths. Its first movement opens rather like Strauss, then comes to an abrupt stop, before launching into a short, Schumannesque Scherzo of about 1½ minutes in the same key, and thence into a *Dance of chastisement.* The *Elegy* which follows also has touches of Schumann and there is a short and unconvincing finale. The *Thirteenth* (*Undertro*, 'Faithlessness') was apparently rejected when it was submitted to the Danish Radio, and one can well understand why. In it the composer returns to material he had first used in his *Seventh Symphony*, which he had in turn borrowed from his countryman, Axel Gade. What it lacks in substance it makes up for in bombast. Probably the best thing here is the *Prelude* to the opera, *Anti-Christ*, a much earlier piece dating from the 1920s. The performances and recordings are respectable rather than distinguished.

Langlais, Jean (born 1907)

(i) *Messe solennelle;* (i; ii; iii) *Missa Salve regina;* (Organ): (i) *Paraphrases grégoriennes, Op. 5: Te Deum. Poèmes évangéliques, Op. 2: La Nativité. Triptyque grégorien: Rosa mystica.*
*** Hyp. Dig. CDA 66270 [id.]. Westminster Cathedral Ch., David Hill, (i) with J. O'Donnell; (ii) A. Lumsden; (iii) ECO Brass Ens.

Jean Langlais' organ music owes much to Dupré's example, and the two Masses are archaic in feeling, strongly influenced by plainchant and organum, yet with a plangent individuality that clearly places the music in the twentieth century. The style is wholly accessible and the music enjoys fervent advocacy from these artists, who are accorded sound-quality of the high standard one expects from this label.

Larsson, Lars-Erik (1908–86)

(i) *Violin concerto, Op. 42.* (ii) *Förklädd Gud (A god in disguise), Op. 24; Pastoral suite, Op. 19.*
☞ ** Sony Dig. SK 64140 [id.]. (i) Arve Tellefsen, Swedish RSO, Esa-Pekka Salonen; (ii) Hillevi Martinpelto, Håkan Hagegård, Erland Josephson, Swedish R. Ch. & O, Salonen.

A good introduction to this delightful Swedish composer. Like the well-known *Pastoral Suite*, *Förklädd Gud* ('A god in disguise') comes from his time in the Swedish Radio in the days when radio stations had cultural ambitions and employed poets and composers on their staffs. *A god in disguise* has charm and is full of naïve and folk-like but captivating ideas, and it is well done by both the two soloists and the distinguished narrator. Salonen does not let the music speak for itself as Stig Westerberg and Sten Frykberg did on earlier recordings, but his direction is smart and crisp. The recording, made in Stockholm's Berwald Hall, is not state-of-the-art, being very two-dimensional (there is no back-to-front perspective), and there is not enough air round the musicians. Frykberg's BIS recording, coupled with the *Third Symphony*, is much better, and Håkan Hagegård's voice was fresher and more youthful then. Larsson's *Violin concerto* is one of his best works, very much in the manner of Walton and Prokofiev, lyrical and atmospheric with a quiet Nordic melancholy all its own. A beautiful piece, very well played by Arve Tellefsen and the Swedish Radio Orchestra, but the recording is again decent and acceptable but no more.

Symphonies Nos. 1 in D, Op. 2; 2, Op. 17.
**(*) BIS Dig. CD 426 [id.]. Helsingborg SO, Hans-Peter Frank.

The *First Symphony* is derivative but a work of obvious promise, fluent and well put together. There are obvious echoes of the Russian post-nationalists as well as Nielsen and Sibelius. Much the same could be said of the more mature *Second Symphony* (1936–7), which is genial and unpretentious. Good performances and recording, but the music itself is not Larsson at his strongest.

Symphony No. 3 in C min., Op. 34; (i) *Förklädd Gud (A God in disguise), Op. 24.*
** BIS CD 96 [id.]. (i) Nordin, Hagegård, Jonsson, Helsingborg Concert Ch.; Helsingborg SO, Frykberg.

A God in disguise was a production for Swedish Radio. The choral suite for two soloists and narrator that Larsson fashioned from it has great freshness and charm. This 1978 performance has some fine singing from Håkan Hagegård, and the Helsingborg chorus and orchestra give a serviceable account of the score. It is as diatonic as *A God in disguise* and, though not completely successful, is strong enough to deserve rescue.

Lassus, Orlandus (c. 1532–94)

Madrigals: *Al dolce suon'; Ben convenne; Bestia curvafia pulices; Ove d'alta montagna; Praesidium sara; Spent'è d'amor.* Motets: *Beati pauperes/Beati pacifici; Da pacem, Domine; Domine, quando veneris; Gloria patri et filio.* Chansons: *Lucescit jam o socii; Voir est beaucoup.*
☞ (M) ** Teldec/Warner Dig. 4509 93685-2 [id.]. Alsfelder Vocal Ens., Helbich.

Expertly directed performances with good intonation and tonal blend. Wolfgang Helbich does not vary the forces here, however; everything is done with full chorus, whereas many of the items would have benefited from greater variety of vocal texture. Thus, in spite of beautiful recording, the overall impact of this reissue is less than the sum of its parts.

(i) Motets: *Ave Regina caelorum; O mors, quam amara est; Salve Regina; Penitential Psalms: I, Domine, ne in furore tuo;* (ii) *III, Domine, ne in furore tuo;* (i) *Miserere mei Deus;* (iii) *Missa super Bell' Amfitrit'altera;* Motets: *Domine convertere; In convertendo; In monte Oliveti; Lauda Sion Salvatorem; Tristis est anima mea.*
☞ (M) **(*) DG 439 958-2 (2) [id.]. (i) Pro Cantione Antiqua, Hamburger Bläserkreis, Bruno Turner; (ii) Regensburger Domchor, Instrumental Ens., Hans Schrewmsl Aachener Domsingknaben, Krebs, Rotzsch, Hudemann, Ens. Rudolf Pohl.

This handsomely produced two-CD set does not offer new material but it is well worth considering nevertheless. The *Missa super Bell' Amfitrit'altera* and the Motets on the first CD were recorded in 1968, the third *Penitential Psalm* in 1958; the remaining two and the motets *Ave Regina caelorum, O mors quam amara est* and the *Salve Regina* in 1974. The *Mass* differs from the slightly later version by Simon Preston and the Choir of Christ Church, Oxford, now on Decca Ovation (see below) in employing instrumental support, and the results are more opaque. (The Oxford performance has a sweeter tone, wider expressive range and greater transparency.) The same reservation may be levelled against the 1974 recordings with the Pro Cantione Antiqua and the Hamburger Bläserkreis and Bruno Turner. They are eloquent performances, beautifully sung (the singers include James Bowman, Paul Esswood and Ian Partridge), and accompanied by cornett, trombones etc. (see below).

Motets: *Ave Regina caelorum; O mors, quam amara est; Salve Regina. First Penitential Psalm: Domine, ne in furore tuo.*
☞ (M) **(*) DG 437 072-2. Pro Cantione Antiqua, Hamburg Wind Ens., Bruno Turner –
PALESTRINA: *Missa Aeterna Christi munera* etc. **

We are offered here one of the *Penitential Psalms* plus three motets in expert performances by the London Pro Cantione Antiqua under Bruno Turner. This is very beautiful music and there is plenty of historical evidence to support the view that the Psalms were accompanied, though whether the instruments chosen here would be used together is conjectural. The blend between the expressive vocal style favoured by Turner and his distinguished group (which includes James Bowman, Paul Esswood, Ian Partridge and others) and the more restrained instrumental style may not convince all listeners, but it makes for noble, eloquent music-making. The CD transfers of 1974 recordings offer sound of remarkable refinement and realism – even better than in the set above.

De profundis clamavi; Exaltabo te, Domine; Missa octavi toni; Missa qual donna.
*** Nimbus Dig. NI 5150 [id.]. Christ Church Cathedral Ch., Oxford, Stephen Darlington.

Given the stimulus of the quatercentenary of his death in 1994, we can expect a spate of new Lassus recordings and reissues. His output is enormous, as are his versatility and range – there are no fewer than 530 motets alone and some 2,000 works in almost every genre, in Latin, Italian, French and German.

The *Missa qual donna* is a late work, expressive and mellifluous, and very well sung by the choir of Christ Church Cathedral, Oxford. As a pendant, the disc also includes Cipriano de Rore's Petrarch setting, *Qual donna a gloriosa fama*, which the Mass takes as its inspiration. The contrast between this and the *Missa octavi toni*, also known as the *Missa Jäger* (*Hunting Mass*), could hardly be more striking. The motet, *De profundis clamavi*, one of the great penitential Psalms, is almost the most eloquent and expressive of the pieces here. At times one could wish for more ardent tone from the trebles; but unquestionably these are fine performances, and the recording is very good indeed.

La Lagrime di San Pietro a 7.
☞ *** HM Dig. HMC 901483 [id.]. Kiehr, Koslowsky, Berridge, Türk, Lamy, Koay, Peacock, Ens.
   Voc. Européen, Herreweghe.
☞ (M) *** O-L 443 197-2 [id.]. Emma Kirkby, Nigel Rogers, Consort of Musicke, Rooley.

The *Lagrime di San Pietro* is one of Lassus's most perfect works and his last musical utterance; within three weeks of its completion he was dead. It is a cycle of 20 spiritual madrigals to texts by the poet, Luigi Tonsillo (1510–68), whose 42 *ottave rime* on the grief and repentance of St Peter after his denial of Christ were held in great esteem at the time. The cycle is full of symbolism – seven being the number associated with suffering; the writing is in seven parts, and there are 21 pieces in all (a multiple of seven), the last of which is a Latin motet on the theme of suffering. It is a work of great expressive purity and is performed by Herreweghe's forces with dedication and perfection in the matter of intonation. Excellent recording.

Like much Renaissance music, *La Lagrime di San Pietro* ('The Tears of St Peter') can be performed by a vocal consort or a choir, with or without instruments. The work is rich in variety of expressive means: Howard Mayer Brown calls it a work 'of almost baroque religious fervour', and much of its eloquence is communicated by these performers. The performance is here given one voice to a part and its impact might have been heightened had the artists permitted themselves an even wider tone-colour. The absence of vibrato produces a whiteness of tone that eventually tires the ear, even though there is every sensitivity to the words and great clarity of texture. Instruments are used in the closing motet, but otherwise much is made of the madrigalian character of this work. There are of course many legitimate approaches to this music and this admirably recorded and well-annotated CD will surely give much satisfaction, despite the noted reservations.

9 Lamentationes Hieremiae.
*** HM Dig. HMC 901299 [id.]. Paris Chapelle Royale Ens., Herreweghe.

9 Lamentationes Hieremiae. Aurora lucis rutilat; Christus resurgens; Magnificat Aurora lucis rutilat; Missa Pro defunctis; Regina coeli; Surgens Jesu.
*** Hyp. Dig. CDA 66321/2 [id.]. Pro Cantione Antiqua, Bruno Turner.

The Harmonia Mundi set of the *Lamentations* enjoys one obvious advantage over its rival on Hyperion in that the nine *Lamentations* are all accommodated on the one disc, while Bruno Turner's 1981 digital recording spills over on to two. However, in addition to the *Lamentations* for Maundy Thursday, Good Friday and Holy Saturday, the Hyperion recording offers music for Easter Sunday including the glorious *Aurora lucis rutilat* for two five-part choirs and the *Magnificat* based on the motet. The performances by the Pro Cantione Antiqua under Bruno Turner are very persuasive, expressive and vital. The recording too is spacious and warm. So, for that matter, is the Harmonia Mundi recording for the Chapelle Royale and Philippe Herreweghe, whose performances are wholly admirable.

Missa Osculetur me; Motets: *Alma Redemptoris Mater; Ave regina caelorum; Hodie completi sunt; Osculetur me; Regina caeli; Salve Regina; Timor et tremor.*
*** Gimell Dig. CDGIM 018; 1585T-18 [id.]. Tallis Scholars, Peter Phillips.

Lassus learned the technique of double-choir antiphonal music in Italy. The Mass is preceded by the motet, *Osculetur me* (*Let him kiss me with the kisses of his lips*), which provides much of its motivic substance and is glorious in its sonorities and expressive eloquence. The singing of the Tallis Scholars under Peter Phillips is as impressive as it was on their earlier records, and the recording is beautifully present.

Missa super Bell' Amfitrit'altera; Psalmus penitentialis VII (Psalm 143); Motets: *Alma redemptoris Mater; Omnes de Saba venient; Salve regina, mater misericordiae; Tui sunt coeli.*
✿ (M) *** Decca 433 679-2 [id.]. Christ Church Cathedral, Oxford, Ch., Simon Preston.

The *Mass* is Venetian in style, scored for double choir, each comprising SATB. The seventh *Penitential Psalm* uses a five-part choir with divided tenors, and at *Sicut erat* expands to a six-part choir with divided trebles. The trebles here are firm in line, strong in tone. Indeed, throughout, the singers produce marvellously blended tone-quality and Simon Preston secures magical results. As if this were not enough, the choir conclude with the four eight-part motets, amazingly rich in texture, including a Christmas motet, *Tui sunt coeli.* The acoustic is warm and atmospheric (the recordings were made in Merton College Chapel, Oxford, in 1974/5) and these performances have an admirable vitality and plenty of expressive range. The CD transfer further enhances the sound and the effect is uncannily real and vivid.

Prophetiae Sibyllarum. Settings of Petrarch, Ronsard and du Bellay: Chansons: *Amour donne-moy pays; Bon jour mon coeur; Comme un qui prend; J'ay de vou voir; J'espère et crains; La nuict froide et sombre; O foible esprit; Ronds-moi mon cœur; La terre les eaux va Beuvant; La vita fugge.* Madrigals: *Crudele acerba; I vo piangendo; Mia benigna fortun'e; Soleasi nel mio cor; Standomi un giorno.*
☞ *** HM/BMG Dig. 05472 77304-2 [id.]. Cantus Cölln, Konrad Junghänel.

The *Prophetiae Sibyllarum* ('Sibylline Prophecies') almost certainly comes from Lassus's Italian period before 1555, when he was in his early twenties. It sets a cycle of humanistic Latin verse based on Neapolitan legends that tell how the caves at Cumae were the home of the Sibyls who foretold the coming of God. These settings were much influenced by the highly chromatic style of Vicentino, which hardly surfaces so strongly elsewhere in Lassus's music. Jerome Roche in his 1982 monograph writes of it as 'mysterious, brooding music, but never unsettling emotionally in the manner of Gesualdo'. In addition, we have the madrigal-cycle, *Standomi un giorno,* and five other Petrarch settings, as well as settings by two of *La Pléiade,* Pierre de Ronsard and Joachim du Bellay. It is difficult to imagine these better performed than they are here by the Cantus Cölln and Konrad Junghänel, and they are excellently recorded too.

St Matthew Passion; Exsultet; Visitatio.
☞ **(*) HM Dig. HMU 907076 [id.]. Paul Elliot, Theatre of Voices, Paul Hillier.

Lassus set each of the four Passion narratives, but only the *St Matthew Passion* was published in his lifetime (in Munich, in 1575). It must have enjoyed some acclaim since it was reprinted in Paris. Lassus's setting is interspersed with the chant version of the Passions in use at the St Franciscan monastery in Munich; in this manuscript the chant sections that represent the various speaking characters correspond very closely to the cantus firmus. This is Lassus at his most austere and devotional, with more chant than polyphony; it is not the best entry-point into his music for those unfamiliar with its opulence. The *Visitatio (Easter Dialogue),* which uses the edition by John Stevens, and the *Exsultet* from the Paschal Vigil, are purely chant. In the *Passion* Paul Elliot sings the part of the Evangelist, Paul Hillier that of Christ. The recording, made in California where Hillier now teaches, is exemplary.

Lawes, Henry (1596–1662)

Songs: *Amintor's welladay; The angler's song; Come sad turtle; Fairwell despairing hopes; Hark, shepherd swains; I laid me down; I prithee send me back my heart; The Lark; My soul the great God's praises sings; O King of heaven and hell; Sing, fair Clorinda; Sitting by the streams; Slide soft you silver floods; Sweet stay awhile; Tavola; Thee and thy wondrous deeds; This mossy bank.*
☞ *** Hyp. CDA 66315 [id.]. Emma Kirkby, Consort of Musicke, Anthony Rooley.

'Songs of an English cavalier': *Anakreontos; As on a day Clorinda fair was bathing; A beautiful mistress; The celestial mistress; Come, lovely Phyllis; Cupid scorned; A despairing lover; A divine mistress; An echo; The excellency of wine; Fie, away, fie! what mean you by this?; Go, lovely rose; Inconstancy in woman; I rise and grieve; Lágrimas que no pudieron; Like to the damask rose; Loath to depart; Murdering beauty; Nightpiece to Julia; No reprieve; Tavola; To Amarantha that she would dishevel her hair; To Amoret; To Anthea; To his mistress on his going to travel; To Lucasta, going beyond the seas; Why should only man be tied?; You are fair and lovely.*
☞ *** Virgin/EMI Dig. VC5 45004-2 [id.]. Nigel Rogers, Paul O'Dette, Francis Kelly.

The music of Henry Lawes is less familiar today than that of his brother Thomas (who was killed during the Civil War, at the Siege of Chester). Henry, too, was affected by the war, but not so disastrously, and at the Restoration he reassumed his position at court. He composed over 400 songs, most during the pre-war period when he was very prolific. John Milton wrote a genial Ode to his Aires beginning, 'Harry whose tuneful and well measur'd song first taught our English musick how to span . . . that with smooth aire could humour best our tongue', and the Lawes songs were enormously popular in their time. Today their direct, declamatory style seems comparatively unsubtle, alongside Purcell. Often the effect is like a folksong. *Why should only man be tied to a foolish female thing?* shows a twinkle of humour, while the praise of *The Celestial mistress* and *Come, lovely Phyllis* certainly have charm. The melancholy is tangible, but not overtly expressive, in songs like *No reprieve* and *I rise and grieve*, and the rather lovely *Làgrimas que no pudieron*. The sparkling *Nightpiece to Julia* is delightfully frothy with its allusions to shooting stars and will-o'-the-wisp, and the brief but effective *Tavola* (common to both recitals here) is like an arietta from an Italian opera. In the Virgin Veritas collection Nigel Rogers brings a forthright manner to his presentation. Perhaps the accompaniments are a shade too discreet but this is a lively, spontaneous recital, though not to be taken at a single sitting. The recording has fine presence.

The earlier, Hyperion collection, though less generous in content, is somewhat wider in its range: the title-number (*Sitting by the streams*) is a verse anthem. There are plenty of secular songs too, notably the engaging *Angler's song*. There is little duplication between the two CDs and, while the Virgin recital is probably a first choice, admirers of Emma Kirkby – here in radiant voice – and Rooley's immaculately stylish Consort of Musicke will find much to enjoy on Hyperion.

Leclair, Jean-Marie (1697–1764)

Violin concertos: Op. 7/2 in D; 7/5 in A min.; Op. 10/1 in B flat; 10/5 in E min.
☞ *** Chan. Dig. CHAN 0551 [id.]. Simon Standage, Coll. Mus. 90.

The twelve concertos of Opp. 7 and 10 make up Leclair's complete orchestral output. Op. 7 was composed in 1737 and Op. 10 in 1743–4; generally speaking, they are underrated and their merits are considerable. Although one cannot include among them a strongly individual lyrical power, the opening *Adagio* of Op. 7/2 demonstrates an espressivo of some gravity and the *Largo* of Op. 7/5 is distinctly appealing. The works are all fresh and well constructed and often highly expressive, even when the ideas are not in themselves memorable. Chandos plan to record both complete sets and the first CD speaks well for the project. Simon Standage is a stylish soloist of impeccable technique and the Collegium Musicum 90 (4.4.2.2.1) provide authentic, spirited accompaniments. The recording was made in St Jude's in north-west London, and textures are transparent and have good sonority.

Violin concertos: in C & A min., Op. 7/3 & 5; in G min., Op. 10/6.
☞ (M) *** Teldec/Warner 4509 92180-2 [id.]. Jaap Schröder, Concerto Amsterdam (with NAUDOT: *Recorder concerto in G, Op. 17/5:* Brüggen, VCM, Harnoncourt **).

Distinguished playing from Jaap Schröder and his colleagues, who make outstanding advocates of these concertos. Leclair is a stronger composer than he is often given credit for. The *G minor Concerto*, Op. 10/6, is a work of real sensibility and imagination, and one only has to sample the slow movements of both the other concertos to discover that Leclair's melodic lines are individual and pleasing. The performances are on period instruments or copies and can be recommended to *aficionados*, as the 1978 analogue sound is both flattering and vivid. The *Recorder concerto* by Jacques-Christophe Naudot (c. 1690–1762) which is provided as a bonus is less individual but very well played. However, here the sound of the supporting group is thin and less well focused.

Lecocq, Alexandre (1832–1918)

Mam'zelle Angot (ballet, arr. Gordon Jacob).
(M) *** Decca 430 849-2 (2) [id.]. Nat. PO, Bonynge – HEROLD: *La Fille mal gardée.* ***

Mam'zelle Angot is a gay, vivacious score with plenty of engaging tunes, prettily orchestrated in the modern French style. Bonynge offers the first recording of the complete score, and its 39 minutes are consistently entertaining when the orchestral playing has such polish and wit. The Kingsway Hall recording is closely observed: the CD brings sharp detail and tangibility, especially at lower dynamic levels.

Lehár, Franz (1870–1948)

The Merry Widow (Die lustige Witwe; complete, in German).
🏵 *** EMI CDS7 47178-8 (2) [Ang. CDCB 47177]. Schwarzkopf, Gedda, Waechter, Steffek,
Knapp, Equiluz, Philh. Ch. and O, Matačić.
(M) (***) EMI mono CDH7 69520-2 [id.]. Schwarzkopf, Gedda, Kunz, Loose, Kraus, Philh. Ch. &
O, Ackermann.
☞ ** EMI Dig. CDS5 55152-2 (2). Lott, Hampson, Szmytka, Aler, Dirk Bogarde (nar.),
Glyndebourne Ch., LPO, Welser-Möst.

Matačić provides a magical set, guaranteed to send shivers of delight through any listener with its
vivid sense of atmosphere and superb musicianship. It is one of Walter Legge's masterpieces as a
recording manager, creating a sense of theatre that is almost without rival in gramophone literature.
The CD opens up the sound yet retains the full bloom, and the theatrical presence and atmosphere
are something to marvel at.

It was the mono set, of the early 1950s, which established a new pattern in recording operetta. Ten
years later in stereo Schwarzkopf was to record the role again, if anything with even greater point and
perception, but here she has extra youthful vivacity, and the *Viljalied* – ecstatically drawn out – is
unique. Some may be troubled that Kunz as Danilo sounds older than the Baron, but it is still a
superbly characterful cast, and the transfer to a single CD is bright and clear.

This live Welser-Möst recording was made at the Royal Festival Hall in July 1993, when the
Glyndebourne company was temporarily without a home, while the new theatre was being rebuilt in
Sussex. Much will depend on the listener's response to Dirk Bogarde's narration which punctuates
the separate numbers: it aims to be a witty text, written by Tom Stoppard, which Bogarde delivers
with an arch knowingness. The music-making is disappointing too, for though Welser-Möst has a fair
idea of the idiom, his slowish speeds often diminish the sparkle, as in the *March septet* in Act II,
celebrating women. Thomas Hampson makes a handsome, swaggering Danilo, but not even he is
vocally at his sweetest and, when the other three principals all sing with more uneven production than
usual, one suspects the recording is partly to blame. Even John Aler, normally sweet-toned, is gritty
as Camille, and Elzbieta Szmytka makes a strained and wobbly Valencienne, so that their duets –
among the most delightful of all the numbers in the piece – lose their charm. Felicity Lott has plenty
of charm and dignity as the Widow herself, but her voice too is given an unpleasant edge at times, not
nearly as sweet as it can be. As well as the dialogue, the applause is also intrusive.

The Merry Widow (English version by Bonynge): highlights.
(M) **(*) Decca 421 884-2; *421 884-4* [id.]. Sutherland, Krenn, Resnik, Masterson, Ewer, Brecknock,
Fryatt, Egerton, Amb. S., Nat. PO, Bonynge.

Although not everyone will take to Sutherland's Widow, this is generally an attractive English
version. The chorus sings with great zest and the ensembles are infectious. The Parisian atmosphere
may seem a trifle overdone, but enjoyably so. Earlier, Sutherland's *Vilja* loses out on charm because
of her wide vibrato, but the *Waltz duet* with Krenn is engaging.

Der Zarewitsch (complete).
*** Eurodisc 610 137 (2). Kollo, Popp, Rebroff, Orth, Hobarth, Bav. R. Ch., Munich R. O,
Wallberg.

René Kollo may not have the finesse of a Tauber, but he sings with a freshness and absence of
mannerism that bring out the melodic beauty. Lucia Popp as the heroine, Sonya, sings ravishingly,
and there is no weak link in the cast elsewhere, and the exhilaration of the entertainment comes over
all the more refreshingly in the excellent CD transfer. No text is given, only notes in German.

Leighton, Kenneth (1929–88)

(i) *Cello concerto;* (ii) *Symphony No. 3 (Laudes Musicae).*
*** Chan. Dig. CHAN 8741; *ABTD 1380* [id.]. (i) Wallfisch; (ii) Mackie; SNO, Bryden Thomson.

The symphony is in part a song-cycle, and its glowing, radiant colours and refined textures are
immediately winning. Raphael Wallfisch plays the *Concerto* as if his life depended on it, and the
Symphony draws every bit as much dedication from its performers. The recording is very immediate,
and has stunning clarity and definition.

Veris gratia (for cello, oboe and strings), *Op. 9.*
*** Chan. Dig. CHAN 8471; *ABTD 1182* [id.]. Wallfisch, Caird, RLPO, Handley – FINZI: *Cello concerto.* ***

Finzi is the dedicatee of Kenneth Leighton's *Veris gratia*, and so it makes an appropriate coupling for his *Cello concerto*, more particularly as its English pastoral style nods in his direction. The performance is highly sympathetic, George Caird the excellent oboist, and the naturally balanced recording is first class.

Conflicts, Op. 51; Fantasia contrappuntistica, Op. 24; Household pets, Op. 86; Sonatina No. 1; 5 Studies, Op. 22.
**(*) Abacus Dig. ABA 402-2 [id.]. Eric Parkin.

Kenneth Leighton was one of the most musical of pianists and wrote beautifully for the instrument. The *Household pets* is a sensitive piece, refined in craftsmanship, and the *Fantasia contrappuntistica* is comparably powerful. Eric Parkin plays it with total sympathy, and the recording is eminently serviceable.

Crucifixus pro nobis; Give me the wings of faith; O sacrum convivium; The second service: Magnificat; Nunc dimittus. Solus ad victimam.
☞ *** ASV Dig. CDDCA 851 [id.]. David Went, Ch. of The Queen's College, Oxford, Matthew Owens – HOWELLS: *Chichester service* etc. **(*)

Kenneth Leighton studied with Bernard Rose in Oxford and later with Petrassi, and he is an eclectic yet individual figure. As a chorister in his youth, he wrote with an inborn sympathy for the voice and a natural feeling for line. These are beautiful pieces with an occasional reminder of Britten, and they are well sung, too, by the Choir of The Queen's College, Oxford, at which Leighton was a student.

Lekeu, Guillaume (1870–94)

(i) *Piano quartet* (2nd movt ed. d'Indy); (ii) *Cello sonata in F.*
☞ *** Koch Schwann Dig. 310 185 [id.] (i–ii) Blumenthal, (i) Adamopoulos, Desjardins, (i–ii) Zanlonghi.

Although he is best known by his moving *Adagio for strings*, which is as deeply felt as Barber's and ought to be as well known, and the *Violin sonata*, Lekeu's output is rich in quality and (given that he only lived to be 23 and had been a late starter) extensive. The *Cello sonata* was written when he was a mere eighteen and is a powerful, big-boned piece whose first movement alone takes well over 20 minutes (the whole work lasts just under 50). The *Piano quartet*, composed at the instigation of Ysaÿe, was left incomplete when Lekeu succumbed to typhus; it was finished by d'Indy, who was a supportive figure after the death of Franck. The style is heavily indebted to these masters, but there is a dignity and melancholy at the heart of Lekeu's music which is moving. Excellent performances and vividly present recording.

Piano trio in C min.
☞ **(*) Koch Schwann Dig. 310 060 [id.] Blumenthal, Adamopoulos, Zanlonghi.

The *Piano trio* is a long and ambitious work, lasting almost an hour; it was written in 1890, the year in which César Franck's death brought to an end the composer's studies with him. It is an astonishing achievement for a twenty-year-old, secure in its grasp of form and full of expressive intensity. The main influence, apart from that of his master, is Wagner, whose music Lekeu had encountered the previous year. Lekeu is a thoughtful composer and, though the slow movement perhaps outstays its welcome (it lasts 19 minutes), there are relatively few *longueurs*. The performance is dedicated, and the only reservation is the quality of the piano-tone which is thick at the bottom end of the register; the acoustic is a bit over-reverberant. Despite some academic touches, this is music of quality.

Lemba, Artur (1885–1960)

Symphony in C sharp min.
*** Chan. Dig. CHAN 8656; *ABTD 1342* [id.]. SNO, Järvi (with Concert: *'Music from Estonia':* Vol. 2***).

Lemba's *Symphony in C sharp minor* was the first symphony ever to be written by an Estonian. It sounds as if he studied in St Petersburg: at times one is reminded fleetingly of Glazunov, at others of Dvořák (the scherzo) – and even of Bruckner (at the opening of the finale) and of Elgar. This is by far the most important item in an enterprising collection of Estonian music.

Leoncavallo, Ruggiero (1858–1919)

I Pagliacci (complete).
*** DG 419 257-2 (3) [id.]. Carlyle, Bergonzi, Benelli, Taddei, Panerai, La Scala, Milan, Ch. & O,
   Karajan – MASCAGNI: *Cavalleria rusticana.* ***
(M) *** BMG/RCA GD 60865 (2) [60865-2]. Caballé, Domingo, Milnes, John Alldis Ch., LSO,
   Santi – PUCCINI: *Il Tabarro.* **(*)
(***) EMI mono CDS7 47981-8 (3) [Ang. CDCC 47981]. Callas, Di Stefano, Gobbi, La Scala,
   Milan, Ch. & O, Serafin – MASCAGNI: *Cavalleria rusticana.* (***)
☞ (B) **(*) Naxos Dig. 8.660021 [id.]. Gauci, Martinucci, Tumagian, Dvorsky, Skovhus, Slovak
   Philh. Ch., Czech RSO, Rahbari.
☞ (M) (**(*)) Nimbus mono NI 7843/4 [id.]. Gigli, Pacetti, Basiola, Nessi, Paci, La Scala Ch. & O,
   Ghione – MASCAGNI: *Cavalleria rusticana.*
☞ * Ph. Dig. 434 131-2 [id.]. Pavarotti, Dessì, Pons, Gavazzi, Coni, Westminster Symphonic Ch.,
   Phd. Boys Ch., Phd. O, Muti.

Karajan does nothing less than refine Leoncavallo's melodrama, with long-breathed, expansive tempi and the minimum exaggeration. Karajan's choice of soloists was clearly aimed to help that – but the passions are still there; and rarely if ever on record has the La Scala Orchestra played with such beautiful feeling for tone-colour. Bergonzi is among the most sensitive of Italian tenors of heroic quality, and it is good to have Joan Carlyle as Nedda, touching if often rather cool. Taddei is magnificently strong, and Benelli and Panerai could hardly be bettered in the roles of Beppe and Silvio. As a filler, DG provides a splendid set of performances of operatic intermezzi.

For those who do not want that obvious coupling, the RCA set is a first-rate recommendation, with fine singing from all three principals, vivid playing and recording, and one or two extra passages not normally included – as in the Nedda–Silvio duet. Milnes is superb in the Prologue.

It is thrilling to hear *Pagliacci* starting with the Prologue sung so vividly by Tito Gobbi. Di Stefano, too, is at his finest, but the performance inevitably centres on Callas and there are many points at which she finds extra intensity, extra meaning. Serafin's direction is strong and direct. The mono recording is dry, with voices placed well forward but with choral detail blurred, and this set is overpriced.

Alexander Rahbari conducts his Slovak forces in a vigorous, red-blooded reading which with first-rate solo singing makes an excellent bargain recommendation, very well recorded, if with the chorus a little distant. Miriam Gauci is a warmly vibrant Nedda, with plenty of temperament, and Eduard Tumagian is an outstanding Tonio, not only firm and dark of tone but phrasing imaginatively. As Canio, Nicola Martinucci has an agreeable tenor that he uses with more finesse and a better line than many more celebrated rivals, even though his histrionics at the beginning and end of *Vesti la giubba* are unconvincing.

The Nimbus transfer of the classic 1934 recording with Gigli focuses the voices effectively enough, giving them a mellow bloom – though the orchestra, often rather recessed, is relatively muffled. Gigli is very much the centre of attention, with Iva Pacetti as Nedda clear and powerful rather than characterful.

The Philips set with Riccardo Muti conducting the Philadelphia Orchestra and a cast headed by Luciano Pavarotti is spliced together from live concert performances in the unhelpful acoustic of the Music Academy in Philadelphia, with sound that is muddy in the bass and harsh at the top. The tenor's tone is glorious but unremittingly loud, with effortful grunts at the end of each phrase. He sings better in his earlier, Decca set, and Muti is less effortful too in his earlier, EMI recording, timing the dramatic conclusion more effectively. What then puts this version out of court is the Nedda of Daniella Dessì, recalling the classic phrase of Philip Hope-Wallace describing sopranos who, when Nedda is communing with the birds, 'sound like a jungle locomotive scaring the macaws'. Dessì is one such, disturbing the vocal line with squally, unsteady notes and sounding much too hefty for the delicate passages. Juan Pons sings with strong, forthright tone as Tonio (and in the Prologue) but, like Paolo Coni as Silvio, is dramatically unconvincing.

Liadov, Anatol (1855–1914)

About olden times, Op. 21b; Baba-Yaga, Op. 56; The enchanted lake, Op. 62; 3 Fanfares; Kikimora,
Op. 63; The musical snuff-box, Op. 32; Polonaises, Opp. 49 & 55; 8 Russian folksongs, Op. 58.
**(*) ASV Dig. CDDCA 657 [id.]. Mexico City SO, Bátiz.

Three stars for the ASV recording by Brian Culverhouse – but the performances under Enrique Bátiz
fall just short of that rating: the magical world of the finest of these scores could perhaps be conveyed
with a more subtle atmosphere.

(i) *Baba Yaga, Op. 56; The enchanted lake, Op. 62; Kikimora, Op. 63;* (ii) *8 Russian folksongs.*
(BB) **(*) Naxos Dig. 8.550328 [id.]. Slovak PO, (i) Gunzenhauser; (ii) Kenneth Jean – Concert:
    'Russian Fireworks'.

It is good to have inexpensive recordings of these key Liadov works, particularly the *Russian
folksongs*, eight orchestral vignettes of great charm, displaying a winning sense of orchestral colour.
The performances are persuasive, and the digital recording is vivid and well balanced.

Ligeti, György (born 1923)

(i) *Cello concerto; Chamber concerto;* (ii) *Piano concerto.*
☞ *** Sony Dig. SK 58945 [id.]. (i) Miklós Perényi; (ii) Ueli Wiget; Modern Ens., Peter Eötvös.

These three concertos span two decades of Ligeti's output. The *Cello concerto* (1966) and the
Chamber concerto, for 13 instruments, (1970) are vivid in colour, complex in detail and undoubtedly
full of energy. To some ears their content may not match their undoubted prolixity of surface
comment. The *Piano concerto*, completed in 1988, has five movements, the last two having been
composed separately twelve months after the first three. The most striking movement is the second;
perhaps the others, exuberant as they are, outlast their welcome. Dedicated Ligetians (are there
many, we wonder) will welcome these obviously skilled and committed performances, well recorded,
with Wiget a striking advocate of the demanding solo role in the concertante work for piano.

Chamber concerto.
☞ (B) *** DG Dig. 439 452-3 [id.]. Ens. InterContemporain, Boulez – LUTOSLAWSKI: *Chain 3* etc.;
    SCHNITTKE: *Concerto grosso No. 1.* ***

This bargain DG CD presents a performance of the *Chamber concerto* that is a useful supplement to
that offered below, and admirers of this composer's cloudy sound-textures can safely investigate. In
this work the specific notes matter less than the washes of colour. Excellent performance and
recording.

(i) *Chamber concerto for 13 instrumentalists;* (ii) *Double concerto for flute, oboe and orchestra;*
Melodien for orchestra; (iii) *10 Pieces for wind quintet.*
(M) *** Decca 425 623-2. (i) L. Sinf., Atherton; (ii) with Nicolet, Holliger; (iii) Vienna Wind Soloists.

The *Double concerto* makes great play with micro-intervals, not exactly quarter-tones but deviations.
The distinguished soloists and the London Sinfonietta give accomplished accounts of these complex
scores and the Vienna performances of the wind pieces are hardly less stimulating.

Bagatelles.
*** Crystal CD 750 [id.]. Westwood Wind Quintet – CARLSSON: *Nightwings;* MATHIAS: *Quintet;*
    BARBER: *Summer music.* ***

Ligeti's folk-inspired *Bagatelles* are highly inventive and very attractive; and they are played with
dazzling flair and unanimity of ensemble by this American group.

Liszt, Franz (1811–86)

Piano concertos Nos. 1–2; Fantasia on Hungarian folksongs; Fantasia on themes from Beethoven's
'Ruins of Athens'; Grande fantaisie symphonique on themes from Berlioz's 'Lélio'; Malédiction;
Polonaise brillante on Weber's Polonaise brillante in E (L'Hilarité); Totentanz (paraphrase on the
Dies Irae); SCHUBERT/LISZT: *Wanderer fantasia.*
(B) *** EMI CZS7 67214-2 (2) [id.]. Michel Béroff, Leipzig GO, Kurt Masur.

Béroff's account of the two concertos can hold its own with the best of the competition: here there is
nothing routine or slapdash, but instead excitement, warmth and spontaneity, along with his

remarkable technical prowess. The Leipzig recording, too, sounds first rate in its remastered form and the distinguished orchestral playing under Masur is given plenty of body and weight. This is especially satisfying in the Schubert *Wanderer* arrangement, while the opening of the Beethoven and Berlioz *Fantasias* are full of atmosphere. The piano timbre has plenty of body and colour as well as sparkle. This is an exhilarating and rewarding set which can be given the strongest recommendation on all counts.

Piano concertos Nos. 1–2.
(M) *** Ph. 434 163-2 [id.]. Sviatoslav Richter, LSO, Kondrashin (with BEETHOVEN: *Cello sonata No. 2, Op. 5/2* with Rostropovich and Richter ***).

Piano concertos Nos. 1–2; Totentanz.
⊛ *** DG Dig. 423 571-2 [id.]. Zimerman, Boston SO, Ozawa.
(M) *** Ph. 426 637-2. Alfred Brendel, LPO, Haitink.

Piano concertos Nos. (i) *1 in E flat;* (ii) *2 in A. Années de pèlerinage: Sonetto 104 del Petrarca. Hungarian rhapsody No. 6; Valse oubliée.*
(M) *** Mercury 432 002-2 [id.]. Byron Janis, (i) Moscow PO, Kondrashin; (ii) Moscow RSO, Rozhdestvensky (also with SCHUMANN: *Romance in F sharp; Novellette in F.* FALLA: *Miller's dance.* GUION: *The harmonica player ***).

Krystian Zimerman's record of the two *Concertos* and the *Totentanz* is altogether thrilling, and he has the advantage of excellent support from the Boston orchestra under Ozawa. It has poise and classicism and, as one listens, one feels this music could not be played in any other way – surely the mark of a great performance! This record is outstanding in every way, and it now makes a first choice for this repertoire.

Sviatoslav Richter's 1961 recordings are very distinguished indeed, and the remastering makes the very most of the recording, originally engineered by the Mercury team. Richter's playing is unforgettable and so is his rapport with Kondrashin and the LSO, whose playing throughout is of the very highest order. Rostropovich then joins Richter in Beethoven's *G minor Cello sonata*, a most satisfying encore, given a recording full of presence.

Around the time they were recording Richter's Liszt *Concertos* for Philips in London (1962), the Mercury engineers paid a visit to Moscow to record Byron Janis in the same repertoire, and his is a comparably distinguished coupling. Janis's glittering articulation is matched by his sense of poetry and drama, and there is plenty of dash in these very compelling performances, which are afforded characteristically brilliant Mercury sound, although the piano is too close. The encores which follow the two *Concertos* are also very enjoyable.

Brendel's Philips recordings from the early 1970s hold their place at or near the top of the list. There is a valuable extra work offered here and the recording is of Philips's best. The performances are as poetic as they are brilliant, and those who doubt the musical substance of No. 2 will find their reservations melt away.

Piano concertos Nos. 1–2; Hungarian fantasia for piano and orchestra.
☞ (M) ** Erato/Warner 4509 92406-2 [id.]. Duchable, LPO, Conlon.

Duchable's performances are flamboyantly extrovert, and the bold, forwardly balanced piano helps to underline that effect. The orchestra makes a strong impression, however, and Conlon matches his soloist with firm and vigorous accompaniments. On CD the *Second Concerto* comes first and is made to sound more melodramatic than usual. In both works, while the lyrical episodes do not lack expressive feeling, they are without the melting spontaneity of the famous Richter versions. The dash and brilliance of the playing best suit the *Hungarian fantasia*. Certainly on CD the sound has plenty of presence.

Piano concerto No. 1 in E flat.
☞ *** Chesky CD 93 [id.]. Earl Wild, RPO, Sargent – CHOPIN: *Concerto No. 1 **(*); FAURE: Ballade for piano and orchestra. ***

Earl Wild is in his element and gives a glittering and powerful account of Liszt's famous warhorse, yet one that does not lack either delicacy or warmth. The famous triangle Scherzo is crystalline in its clarity and the full-blooded recording matches the extravagance of Liszt's exciting finale.

(i; ii) *Piano concerto No. 1 in E flat;* (i) *Sonata in B min.; Hungarian rhapsody No. 6;* (iii) *Années de pèlerinage: Vallée d'Obermann; Les jeux d'eau à la Villa d'Este.*

☞ (B) ** DG 439 409-2 [id.]. (i) Martha Argerich; (ii) LSO, Abbado; (iii) Lazar Berman.

For some reason Martha Argerich (in 1968) recorded only Liszt's *First concerto* and not the *Second.* However, in the *E flat Concerto* there is an excellent partnership between the pianist and Abbado, and this is a performance of flair and high voltage which does not ever become vulgar. It is very well recorded. Argerich recorded the *Sonata* three years later, and her account has tremendous assurance and vigour. There is no lack of spontaneity, but the work's lyrical feeling and indeed its breadth are sacrificed to some extent to the insistent forward pulse of the playing. The *Rhapsody* gives no cause for complaint and the recording is clear (if not especially rich), but Lazar Berman's performances of the two excerpts from the *Années de pèlerinage* which complete the CD show how Liszt playing can be controlled as well as seemingly impulsive and poetic.

Piano concerto No. 2 in A.
*** Virgin/EMI Dig. VC7 59613-2 [id.]. Leif Ove Andsnes, Bergen PO, Dmitri Kitaenko – GRIEG:
    Piano concerto etc. ***

Leif Ove Andsnes is a real musician who plays with great tenderness and poetic feeling as well as bravura. Marvellous sound, too, with a piano in perfect condition (not always the case on records) and an excellent balance.

Dante Symphony.
*** Hung. HCD 11918-2 [id.]. Kincses, Hungarian R. & TV Ch., Budapest SO, Lehel.

Lehel's account is better than most previous versions. Veronika Kincses is a fine singer, and Lehel gives a strongly characterized performance with well-focused singing and fiery, intense orchestral playing. The Hungaroton recording has plenty of detail and presence. But this version is now virtually eclipsed by the new Barenboim/Teldec CD.

(i) *Dante Symphony;* (ii) *Années de pèlerinage, Book 2: Après un lecture du Dante (Fantasia quasi sonata).*
☞ *** Teldec/Warner Dig. 9031 77340 [id.]. (i) Women's voices of Berlin R. Ch., BPO, Daniel
    Barenboim; (ii) Barenboim (piano).

Liszt's *Dante Symphony* divides naturally into two very expansive, equally balanced halves – *Inferno* and *Purgatorio* – each lasting about 21 minutes, with a relatively short choral *Magnificat* as a finale. (There is a flamboyant alternative closing section, but Barenboim was wise to take Wagner's advice and settle instead for Liszt's romantic vision of Paradise.) The work opens diabolically, with the rasping trombones evoking the gates of Hell, followed by a sustained frenzy of writing for strings and brass; later in a romantic interlude we meet Francesca da Rimini in all her grief. Interestingly, she is introduced by a bass clarinet in a not dissimilar way to her entrance on the clarinet in Tchaikovsky's symphonic poem. Other woodwind, including flutes and cor anglais, complete her portrait before the neurotically restless strings tell her story. A blinding flash of harps introduces the malignant Scherzo, and the movement reaches a tremendous climax; with the return of the malevolent trombone theme from the opening we are left with a desperate feeling that all is hopeless. The second movement is calming – some might say becalmed in its spacious paragraphs. While it has its more modest climax, it is mostly reflective, although increasingly confident, preparing the way for the entry into Paradise. Finally the heavenly chorus enters and lusciously proclaims salvation. Barenboim really has the measure of this somewhat rambling work and controls its rhapsodic structure admirably, holding the tension throughout the first movement and creating enormous visceral excitement at the close. He is helped by marvellous playing from the BPO, who really sound as if they believe in it all, and the radiant choral effects are superbly brought off. The resonant acoustic of Berlin's Schaulspielhaus lets everything expand with Wagnerian amplitude and the result is very impressive indeed. As an encore, Barenboim leaves the rostrum for the piano and offers the *Dante Sonata*, which has the same literary basis but offers a quite different musical treatment. The performance is flamboyantly arresting, but the piano recording is curiously shallow.

*2 Episodes from Lenau's Faust: Der nächtliche Zug; Mephisto waltz No. 1 (Der Tanz in der
Dorfschenke). 2 Legends; Les Préludes* (symphonic poem).
(M) **(*) Erato/Warner Dig. 2292 45256-2 [id.]. Rotterdam PO, James Conlon.

Conlon secures responsive playing from the Rotterdam orchestra, and the engineering is excellent without being in any way spectacular.

(i) *Fantasia on Hungarian folk tunes; Hungarian rhapsodies Nos. 2 & 5.*
(B) *** DG 429 156-2 [id.]. (i) Shura Cherkassky; BPO, Karajan (with BRAHMS: *Hungarian dances Nos. 17–20* ***).

(i) *Fantasia on Hungarian folk tunes. Hungarian rhapsodies Nos. 2 & 5; Mephisto waltz No. 2.*
(M) *** DG 419 862-2 [id.]. (i) Cherkassky; BPO, Karajan.

Shura Cherkassky's glittering 1961 recording of the *Hungarian fantasia* is an affectionate performance with some engaging touches from the orchestra, though the pianist is dominant and his playing is superbly assured. The rest of the programme is comparably charismatic.

(i) *Fantasia on Hungarian folk tunes. Hungarian rhapsodies; Symphonic poems: Mazeppa; Les Préludes; Tasso, lamento e trionfo. Mephisto waltz No. 2.*
**(*) DG 415 967-2 (2). (i) Shura Cherkassky; BPO, Karajan.

The cellos and basses sound marvellous in the *Fifth Rhapsody* and *Tasso*, and even the brashness of *Les Préludes* is a little tempered. *Mazeppa* is a great performance, superbly thrilling and atmospheric. A superb achievement, showing Karajan and his Berlin orchestra at their finest. However, this set now seems overpriced.

A Faust symphony.
(M) *** DG 431 470-2; *431 470-4.* Kenneth Riegel, Tanglewood Festival Ch., Boston SO, Bernstein.
(M) *** EMI CDM7 63371-2 [id.]. Alexander Young, Beecham Ch. Soc., RPO, Beecham.
☞ **(*) Denon Dig. CO 75634 [id.]. Jianyi Zhang, Berlin R. Ch., RSO, Inbal.
☞ (B) **(*) Pickwick Dig. PCD 1071; *PK 515* [id.]. Antonio Necolescu, Hung. R. Ch., Budapest & State SO, Francesco D'Avalos.
☞ (M) ** Sony SMK 47570 [id.]. Charles Bressler, Choral Art Soc., NYPO, Bernstein.
☞ ** Decca Dig. 436 359-2. Blochwitz, Groot Omroepkoor NOB, Concg. O, Chailly.

Bernstein on DG seems to possess the ideal temperament for holding together grippingly the melodrama of the first movement, while the lovely *Gretchen* centrepiece is played most beautifully. Kenneth Riegel is an impressive tenor soloist in the finale, there is an excellent, well-balanced choral contribution, and the Boston Symphony Orchestra produce playing which is both exciting and atmospheric.

Sir Thomas Beecham's classic 1959 recording, well transferred to CD, shows this instinctive Lisztian at his most illuminatingly persuasive. His control of speed is masterly, spacious and eloquent in the first two movements without dragging, brilliant and urgent in the finale without any hint of breathlessness. Though in the transfer string-tone is limited in body, balances are very convincing.

The two newest digital recordings have individual merits but neither displaces current recommendations, though the Pickwick CD makes a very acceptable bargain version. D'Avalos's performance has much vitality and makes up in gutsy spontaneity for any lack of finesse, while the Hungarian orchestral playing is really very good. His tenor soloist, Antonio Necolescu, has a rather wide vibrato, and that offers minor problems in the work's passionate apotheosis, but the Hungarian choir sings with plenty of bite and D'Avalos's reading of the last movement (*Mephistofeles*) has more pungency than Inbal's version. The Pickwick recording is vivid, but has fullness too.

Where Inbal scores is in his added gravitas and his sense of architecture. Helped by the resonant acoustic, the Berlin Radio Orchestra provides warmly full-bodied textures and the element of vulgarity in Liszt's inspiration is minimized, if some of the music's gusto is simultaneously lost. Gretchen's portrayal in the central movement is poetically refined and *Mephistofeles* is a strong rather than a grotesquely Satanic portrait. But Inbal comes into his own in the closing pages when, with his splendidly ardent soloist and fine chorus, he creates a hugely expansive final climax, anticipating Wagner in its richness of amplitude and drama.

Bernstein's first recording of the *Faust Symphony* was made in the Manhattan Center in 1960, not very long after Beecham made his pioneering stereo version. Bernstein does not match the sort of magic that was uniquely Beecham's, but there is a great deal to be said for a really high-powered approach to a high-romantic work that is basically extrovert. It goes without saying that the New York orchestra plays superbly, and Bernstein brings all his charismatic qualities to the performance. The recording too is very good for its time.

Decca produce an impressive clarity for Riccardo Chailly, and his performers are in every way impressive. All the same, the performance as a whole is not strongly characterized or involving and, while everything is laid out with impeccable respect for detail, the sum of the parts is less than the whole. By the side of Beecham and Bernstein, this seems, for all its technical merits, short on personality. Bernstein probably remains the best buy. He is at mid-price and this is one of his most compelling DG records, admirably recorded in Boston.

Hungarian rhapsodies Nos. 1–6.
(M) **(*) Mercury 432 015-2 [id.]. LSO, Dorati – ENESCU: *Roumanian rhapsody No. 1.* ***

Hungarian rhapsodies Nos. 1–6; Hungarian battle march; Rákóczy march.
☞ (M) **(*) EMI CDM7 64627-2. Philh. Hungarica or LPO, Boskovsky.

Dorati's is undoubtedly the finest set of orchestral *Hungarian rhapsodies*. He brings out the gypsy flavour and, with lively playing from the LSO, there is both polish and sparkle. The Mercury recording is characteristically vivid.

Boskovsky does not fully catch the mercurial element, the sudden changes of mood which is the gypsy heritage of these pieces, but the Philharmonia Hungarica (who play in Nos. 1, 4 and 6 – *Carnival in Pest*) are obviously at home; and the LPO clearly enjoy the famous No. 2, while the *Third* with its effective use of the cimbalom, has plenty of colour. The *Rákóczy march* (No. 15 for piano) is done spiritedly by the Hungarian group, but the little-known *Hungarian battle march* does not emerge here as a lost masterpiece. The freshly remastered recordings (from 1977/8) sound well and, though Dorati on Mercury takes pride of place in this repertoire, this EMI disc certainly gives pleasure.

Hungarian rhapsodies Nos. 1 in F min.; 4 in D min.; Les Préludes.
☞ (M) **(*) Sony SMK 47572 [id.]. NYPO, Bernstein – ENESCU: *Roumanian Rhapsody No. 1* (with BRAHMS: *Hungarian dances Nos. 5–6* **(*)).

Notable for the vivid coupled performance of the Enescu *Rhapsody*, this collection shows characteristic Bernstein brilliance, with first-rate orchestral playing throughout. The sound is a bit glossy in the violins, but has weight too, especially for the heavy brass in the final peroration of *Les Préludes*, which is wonderfully pontifical. Indeed Bernstein is very much at home in this melodramatic piece, not missing its noble lyricism alongside its excitement. The two Brahms *Hungarian dances* are played with plenty of dash.

SYMPHONIC POEMS

Ce qu'on entend sur la montagne; Festklänge; Mazeppa; Orpheus; Les Préludes; Prometheus; Tasso, lamento e trionfo.
☞ (B) **(*) Ph. Duo 438 751-2 (2) [id.]. LPO, Bernard Haitink.

Hamlet; Héroïde funèbre; Hungaria; Hunnenschlacht; Die Ideale; Mephisto waltz No. 1; Von der Wiege bis zum Grabe.
☞ (B) **(*) Ph. Duo 438 754-2 (2) [id.]. LPO, Bernard Haitink.

Apart from *Les Préludes*, the splendid *Mazeppa* and, to a lesser extent, *Tasso*, Liszt's symphonic poems enjoy a fairly limited popularity, though Sir Thomas Beecham was very fond of *Orpheus* and his endearing gentleness in this work makes it seem genuinely inspired. Though they undeniably contain their longueurs, these pioneering works display a wider range of imagination than most listeners will realize. The relatively popular pieces have by no means the monopoly of Liszt's inspiration; some of his earlier efforts, such as *Ce qu'on entend sur la montagne* (a full half-hour long) and *Festklänge*, suffer not only from formal weakness but also from a lack of interesting melodic invention, and many of their pages are let down by rhetorical bursts and by the repetition of melodramatic flourishes. But the final work, *From the cradle to the grave*, has a visionary quality which shows Liszt thinking far ahead of his time. Understandably the wider musical public have chosen *Les Préludes* in preference to all the rest; with its ready tunefulness and strong contrasts between drama and pastoral lyricism it triumphs over an inherent tendency to bombast. But elsewhere, in *Hamlet*, for instance, there is a lot to admire; the *Héroïde funèbre* is nobly conceived, and Haitink's restrained yet powerful performance does it full justice. *Prometheus* is also successful and *Hungaria* has an agreeable gypsy violin sequence to offset its patriotic fervour and brass chorales. *Hamlet* brings great dramatic intensity and plenty of atmosphere; *Festklänge* mixes polonaise dance-rhythms with more romantic sections. *Die Ideale* is based on Schiller's poem and has a pleasing rhapsodical feeling imbued with melancholy until the self-assurance of its closing pages. It is not an easy work to bring off, and Haitink's direct, dedicated manner does not always catch its changing moods. The performance of *Festklänge* is more successful but, like *Hunnenschlacht* ('The battle of the Huns'), it lacks extrovert bravura, although no one could complain about the impressive organ effects at the close of the latter piece. *Les Préludes* and *Mazeppa* (which sounds marvellous in Karajan's hands), though structurally well conceived, lack that strain of histrionic vulgarity which makes them more ear-catching, and in the familiar *Mephisto waltz* there is a hint of reserve not entirely in the spirit of a Bacchanalian dance. Nevertheless the orchestral playing is first rate throughout these four discs and the recording has never sounded better – far more vivid than on the original LPs. Liszt invented the symphonic poem; here is an inexpensive and, for the most part, rewarding way to sample his achievement overall. There is good documentation.

Hunnenschlacht (symphonic poem).
** Telarc Dig. CD 80079 [id.]. Cincinnati SO, Kunzel – BEETHOVEN: *Wellington's victory*. **

A direct, unsubtle performance of a rarely recorded piece. The Telarc sound, however, is highly spectacular. Those wanting the *'Battle' symphony* of Beethoven won't be disappointed with this, although the CD is rather short measure.

Symphonic poems: *Mazeppa; Orpheus; Les Préludes; Tasso, lamento e trionfo. Mephisto waltz No. 2.*
☞ (M) ** EMI CDM7 64850-2 [id.]. Leipzig GO, Kurt Masur.

The five works gathered here (the less often heard *Mephisto waltz No. 2* has been added for the present reissue) play for just over 72 minutes and, although the digital remastering has robbed the sound of some of its rich sonority in the lower strings, the brightness of the new sound-balance has a different kind of appeal. Masur is not altogether at home in the melodrama of *Les Préludes* and *Mazeppa* – although the latter is excitingly done, if without the panache of Karajan. He breezes through *Orpheus* at record speed and misses the endearing gentleness that Beecham brought to it in the early 1960s. Nevertheless these performances are all strongly characterized and extremely well played.

Mazeppa; Les Préludes; Prometheus; Tasso, lamento e trionfo (symphonic poems).
(BB) *** Naxos Dig. 8.550487 [id.]. Polish Nat. RSO (Katowice), Michael Halász.

Michael Halász has the full measure of this repertoire and this is one of the most successful collections of Liszt's symphonic poems to have emerged in recent years. He draws some remarkably fine playing from the Katowice Radio Orchestra. The brass playing is very impressive throughout, especially the trombones and tuba, who have the epic main theme of *Mazeppa*, but its grandiloquence is no less powerful in *Les Préludes*, weighty and never brash. The recording is spacious, with full natural string textures, but it is the resounding brass one remembers most .

Les Préludes (symphonic poem); *Hungarian rhapsody No. 2 in C sharp min.*
(B) *** EMI CDZ7 62860-2. Philh. O, Karajan – MUSSORGSKY: *Pictures*. ***

Karajan's 1958 *Les Préludes* found much favour in its day, as well it should. It still sounds thrilling now, and demonstrates the fine musical judgement of the original balance engineers.

Totentanz (for piano and orchestra).
☞ (M) *** BMG/RCA 09026 61250-2 [id.]. Byron Janis, Chicago SO, Reiner – Concert: *'The Reiner sound'*. ***

Recorded in 1959, this is still one of the most exciting accounts of Liszt's *Dance of death* in the catalogue. It opens in thrillingly dramatic fashion, but the scherzando element later is no less successful. A powerful partnership between Janis and Reiner ensures that the tension is well held throughout, and the Chicago ambience makes its own evocative contribution. Though the close balance is not as natural as some of the earlier Chicago recordings, the sound here is fuller and more realistic than on the original LP.

PIANO MUSIC

Complete piano music, Vol. 1: *Albumblatt in waltz form; Bagatelle without tonality; Caprice-valses Nos. 1 & 2; Ländler in A flat; Mephisto waltzes Nos. 1–3; Valse impromptu; 4 Valses oubliées.*
*** Hyp. Dig. CDA 66201 [id.]. Leslie Howard.

Complete piano music, Vol. 2: *Ballades Nos. 1–2; Berceuse; Impromptu (Nocturne); Klavierstück in A flat; 2 Légendes; 2 Polonaises.*
**(*) Hyp. Dig. 66301. Leslie Howard.

Complete piano music, Vol. 3: *Fantasia and fugue on B-A-C-H; 3 Funeral odes: Les morts; La notte; Le triomphe funèbre du Tasse; Grosses Konzertsolo; Prelude on Weinen, Klagen, Sorgen, Sagen; Variations on a theme of Bach.*
** Hyp. Dig. CDA 66302 [id.]. Leslie Howard.

Complete piano music, Vol. 4: *Adagio in C; Etudes d'éxécution transcendante; Elégie sur des motifs de Prince Louis Ferdinand de Prusse; Mariotte.*

** Hyp. Dig. CDA 66357 [id.]. Leslie Howard.

Complete piano music, Vol. 5: Concert paraphrases: BERLIOZ: *L'Idée fixe; Overtures: Les Francs-Juges; Le Roi Lear; Marche des pèlerins; Valse des Sylphes.* CHOPIN: *6 Chants polonais.* SAINT-SAENS: *Danse macabre.*
*** Hyp. Dig. CDA 66346 [id.]. Leslie Howard.

Complete piano music, Vol. 6: Concert paraphrases: AUBER: *3 Pieces on themes from La muette de Portici.* BELLINI: *Réminiscences de Norma.* BERLIOZ: *Benvenuto Cellini: Bénédiction et serment.* DONIZETTI: *Réminiscences de Lucia di Lammermoor; Marche funèbre et Cavatina (Lucia).* ERNST (Duke of Saxe-Coburg-Gotha): *Tony: Hunting chorus.* GLINKA: *Russlan and Ludmilla: Tscherkessenmarsch.* GOUNOD: *Waltz from Faust.* HANDEL: *Almira: Sarabande and Chaconne.* MEYERBEER: *Illustrations de L'Africaine.* MOZART: *Réminiscences de Don Juan.* VERDI: *Aida: Danza sacra & Duetto finale.* TCHAIKOVSKY: *Eugene Onegin: Polonaise.* WAGNER: *Tristan: Isoldes Liebestod.* WEBER: *Der Freischütz: Overture.*
*** Hyp. Dig. CDA 66371/2 [id.]. Leslie Howard.

Complete piano music, Vol. 7: Chorales: *Crux ave benedicta; Jesu Christe; Meine Seele; Nun danket alle Gott; Nun ruhen all Wälder; O haupt; O Lamm Gottes; O Traurigkeit; Vexilla Regis; Was Gott tut; Wer nur den Lieben; Via Crucis; Weihachtsbaum; Weihnachtslied.*
** Hyp. Dig. CDA 66388 [id.]. Leslie Howard.

Complete piano music, Vol. 8: *Alleluia and Ave Maria; Ave Marias 1–4; Ave Maria de Arcadelt; Ave Maris stella; Harmonies poétiques et religieuses* (complete); *Hungarian Coronation Mass; Hymnes; Hymne du Pape; In festo transfigurations; Invocation; O Roma nobilis; Sancta Dorothea; Slavimo slavno slaveni!; Stabat mater; Urbi et orbi; Vexilla regis prodeunt; Zum Haus des Herrn.*
** Hyp. Dig. CDA 66421/2 [id.]. Leslie Howard.

Complete piano music, Vol. 9: *6 Consolations; 2 Elégies; Gretchen* (from *Faust Symphony*); *Sonata in B min.; Totentanz.*
** Hyp. Dig. CDA 66429 [id.]. Leslie Howard (piano).

Complete piano music, Vol. 10: Concert paraphrases: BELLINI: *Hexaméron (Grand bravura variations on the March from I Puritani).* BERLIOZ: *Symphonie fantastique. Un portrait en musique de la Marquise de Blocqueville.*
**(*) Hyp. Dig. CDA 66433 [id.]. Leslie Howard.

Complete piano music, Vol. 11: *Abschied (Russisches Volkslied); Am Grabe Richard Wagners; Carrousel de Madame P-N; Dem Andenken Petöfis; Epithalium; Klavierstück in F sharp; En Rêve; 5 Klavierstücke; Mosonyis Grabgeleit; Recueillement; Resignazione; Romance oubliée; RW (Venezia); Schlaflos! Frage und Antwort; Sospiri; Toccata; Slyepoi (Der blinde Sänger); Die Trauergondel (La lugubre gondola); Trauervorspiel und Trauermarsch; Trübe Wolken (Nuages gris); Ungams Gott; Ungarisches Königslied; Unstern: Sinistre; Wiegenlied (Chant de berceau).*
**(*) Hyp. Dig. CDA 66445 [id.]. Leslie Howard.

Complete piano music, Vol. 12: *Années de Pèlerinages, 3rd Year (Italy); 5 Hungarian folksongs; Historical Hungarian portraits.*
** Hyp. Dig. CDA 66448 [id.]. Leslie Howard.

Complete piano music, Vol. 13: Concert paraphrases: ALLEGRI/MOZART: *A La Chapelle Sistine: Miserere d'Allegri et Ave verum corpus de Mozart.* BACH: *Fantasia and fugue in G min.; 6 Preludes and fugues for organ.*
** Hyp. Dig. CDA 66438 [id.]. Leslie Howard.

Complete piano music, Vol. 14: *Christus; Polonaises de St Stanislas; Salve Polonia; St Elizabeth.*
**(*) Hyp. Dig. CDA 66466 [id.]. Leslie Howard.

Complete piano music, Vol. 15: Concert paraphrases of Lieder: BEETHOVEN: *Adelaïde; An die ferne Geliebte; 6 Gellert Lieder; 6 Lieder von Goethe; An die ferne Geliebte.* DESSAUER: *3 Lieder.* FRANZ: *Er ist gekommenin Sturm und Regen; 12 Lieder.* MENDELSSOHN: *7 Lieder* including *Auf Flügeln des Gesanges.* CLARA & ROBERT SCHUMANN: *10 Lieder* including *Frülingsnacht; Widmung.*
**(*) Hyp. Dig. CDA 66481/2 [id.]. Leslie Howard.

Complete solo piano music, Vol. 16: Piano transcriptions: DAVID: *Bunte Reihe* (24 character pieces for violin and piano), *Op. 30.*
*** Hyp. Dig. CDA 66506 [id.]. Leslie Howard.

Complete piano music, Vol. 17: Concert paraphrases: DONIZETTI: *Spirito gentil* from *La Favorita; Marche funèbre* from *Don Sebastien*. GOUNOD: *Les Sabéennes (Berceuse)* from *La Reine de Saba*. GRETRY: *Die Rose (Romance)* from *Zémire et Azor*. MEYERBEER: *3 Illustrations du Prophète; Fantasia and fugue* on *Ad nos, ad salutarem undam* on a theme from *Le Prophète*. MOSONYI: *Fantasy on Szép Ilonka* (Mosonyi). WAGNER: *Spinning song and Ballade* from *Der fliegende Holländer; Pilgrims' chorus and O du, mein holder Abendstern* from *Tannhäuser; Valhalla* from *The Ring; Feierlicher Marsch zum heiligen Grail* from *Parsifal*.
**(*) Hyp. Dig. CDA 66571/2 [id.]. Leslie Howard.

Complete piano music, Vol. 18: Concert paraphrases: BEETHOVEN: *Capriccio alla turca; Fantasy* from *Ruins of Athens*. LASSEN: *Symphonisches Zwischenspiel zu Calderons Schauspiel über allen Zauber Liebe*. MENDELSSOHN: *Wedding march and dance of the elves* from *A Midsummer night's dream*. WEBER: *Einsam bin ich, nicht alleine from La Preciosa*. HEBBEL: *Nibelungen*.
**(*) Hyp. Dig. CDA 66575 [id.]. Leslie Howard.

Leslie Howard's ambitious project to record the complete music of Liszt proceeds apace and at least two of these issues have already collected a Grand Prix du Disque in Budapest (Volumes 5 and 6). The performances are very capable and musicianly, and there are moments of poetic feeling, but for the most part his playing rarely touches distinction. The kind of concentration one finds in great Liszt pianists such as Arrau, Kempff and Richter (and there are many younger artists whose names also spring to mind) rarely surfaces. Howard's technical equipment is formidable but poetic imagination and the ability to grip the listener are here less developed. The very first recital, which collected all of Liszt's original piano pieces that might be described as waltzes, promised well, including a fourth *Valse oubliée* that the pianist himself notionally completed from material long buried, and it is no accident that the prize-winning discs are orchestral or operatic paraphrases, which – alongside the Lieder transcriptions – Howard does impressively. However, his rushed account of the *Sonata* does not really stand up against the current competition. One of the most interesting issues is Volume 16, the *Bunte Reihe* of Ferdinand David (1810–70), a contemporary of Mendelssohn. These are transcriptions of music for violin and piano in which the violin seems hardly to be missed at all. Leslie Howard plays them beautifully. Certainly the coverage so far is remarkable and, if this playing rarely takes the breath away either by its virtuosity or poetic insights, it is unfailingly intelligent and the recordings are first class.

Complete piano music, Vol. 19: *Die Lorelei; 3 Liebesträume; Songs for solo piano, Books 1–2*.
☞ *** Hyp. Dig. CDA 66593 [id.]. Leslie Howard.

Complete piano music, Vol. 20: *Album d'un voyageur: Années de pèlerinage*, 1st, 2nd & 3rd years (first versions); *Chanson du Béarn; Fantaisie romantique sur deux mélodies suisses; Faribolo pastour*.
☞ *** Hyp. Dig. CDA 66601/2 [id.]. Leslie Howard.

Complete piano music, Vol. 21: ROSSINI: *Soirées musicales; Grande fantaisie on motifs from Soirées musicales; 2nd Fantaisie on motifs from Soirées musicales*. DONIZETTI: *Nuits d'été à Pausilippe*. MERCADANTE: *Soirées italiennes. 3 Sonetti di Petrarca* (1st version); *Venezia e Napoli* (1st set).
☞ *** Hyp. Dig. CDA 66661/2 [id.]. Leslie Howard.
Complete piano music, Vol. 22: Concert paraphrases of Beethoven Symphonies: *Symphonies Nos. 1–9*.
☞ ** Hyp. Dig. CDA 66671/5 [id.]. Leslie Howard.

Complete piano music, Vol. 23: BERLIOZ: (i) *Harold in Italy*. LISZT: (i) *Romance oubliée*. GOUNOD: *Hymne à Sainte Cécile*. MEYERBEER: *Le moine; Festmarsch*.
☞ **(*) Hyp. Dig. CDA 66683 [id.]. Leslie Howard, (i) with Paul Coletti.

Complete piano music, Vol. 24: Concert paraphrases: BEETHOVEN: *Septet, Op. 20*. MOZART: *Requiem mass, K.626: Confutatis; Lacrimosa. Ave verum corpus, K.618*. VERDI: *Requiem mass: Agnus dei*. ROSSINI: *Cujus animam: Air du Stabat Mater; 3 Chœurs religieux: La Charité*. GOLDSCHMIDT: *7 Tödsunden: Liebesszene und Fortunas Kugel*. MENDELSSOHN: *Wasserfahrt und der Jäger Abschied*. WEBER: *Schlummerlied mit Arabesken; Leyer und Schwert-Heroïde*. HUMMEL: *Septet No. 1 in D min*.
☞ ** Hyp. Dig. CDA 66761/2 [id.]. Leslie Howard.

Complete piano music, Vol. 25: *San Francesco: Prelude: The canticle of the sun; Canticle of the sun of St Francis of Assisi. Ave maris stella; Gebet; Ich liebe dich; Il m'aimait tant; O pourquoi donc; Ora pro nobis; O sacrum convivium* (2 versions); *Rezignazione – Ergebung; Salve regina; Von der Wiege bis zum Grabe; Die Zelle in Nonnenwerth*.
☞ **(*) Hyp. Dig. CDA 66694 [id.]. Leslie Howard.

Complete piano music, Vol. 26: *Allegro di bravura; Apparitions; Berceuse; 12 Etudes; Feuilles d'album; Galop de bal; Hungarian recruiting dances; Impromptu brillant on themes of Rossini and Spontini; Klavierstücke (aus der Bonn Beethoven-Kantatej); 2 Klavierstücke; Marche hongroise; Notturno No. 2; Rondo di bravura; Scherzo in G min.; Variation on a waltz of Diabelli; Variations on a theme of Rossini; 5 Variations on a theme from Méhul's Joseph; Waltz in A; Waltz in E flat.*
☞ **(*) Hyp. Dig. CDA 66771/2 [id.]. Leslie Howard.

Complete piano music, Vol. 27: *Canzone napolitana* (2 versions); *La cloche sonne; Gleanings from Woronince; God save the Queen; Hungarian national folk tunes (Ungarische Nationalmelodien); Hussite song; La Marseillaise; Rákóczi march; Szózat and Hungarian hymn; Vive Henri IV.*
☞ *** Hyp. Dig. CDA 66787 [id.]. Leslie Howard.

Complete piano music, Vol. 28: *Bulow-Marsch; Heroischer Marsch im Ungarischer Geschwindmarsch; Csárdás; Csárdás macabre; Csárdás obstiné; Festmarsch zur Goethejubiläumsfeier; Festpolonaise; Festvorspiel; Galop in A min.; Grand galop chromatique; Huldigungsmarsch; Kunstierfestzug zur Schillerfeier; Marche héroïque; Mazurka brillante; Mephisto polka; Petite valse; Rákóczy Marsch; Vorn Fels zurn Meer; La favorite; Scherzo and march; Siegesmarsch; Ungarischer Marsch zur Krönungsfeier in Ofen-Pest; Ungarischer Stürmmarsch; Zweite Festmarsch.*
☞ **(*) Hyp. Dig. CDA 66811/2 [id.]. Leslie Howard.

Ten more volumes of Leslie Howard's distinguished continuing Liszt series, and a great deal of repertoire otherwise unavailable. The two Liszt *Songbooks* offer 12 early Lieder in engagingly simple transcriptions. Leslie Howard plays them beautifully, as he does the three *Liebesträume*, of which only the third is really familiar. Volume 20 centres on what Leslie Howard prefers to call *Album d'un Voyager*, the early edition of what we know as the *Années de pèlerinage* (which the composer tried, unsuccessfully, to suppress). Book I includes a flamboyant extra item, *Lyon*, inspired by a workers' uprising, and only two of the pieces in Book II, *Fleurs mélodiques des Alpes*, were retained in the final set of *Années de pèlerinage*. Apart from the *Paraphrases* in Book III, this collection also includes an unknown major improvisatory work of the same period and inspiration, the 18-minute-long *Fantaisie romantique sur deux mélodies suisses*, with plenty of opportunities for bravura in the latter part. A fascinating collection, very well played indeed. Volume 21 is lightweight, opening with the Rossini *Soirées musicales*, which we know from the much later Britten orchestrations, and *Soirées italiennes*, based on rather less interesting music by Mercadante. For the second disc Howard returns to the initial versions of the *Années de pèlerinage*, including the *Petrarch Sonnets* and *Venezia e Napoli*. The second CD ends with a pair of *Grand fantasias* on themes from the *Soirées* which began the recital.

Volume 22 brings us to Liszt's paraphrases of the nine Beethoven symphonies. Leslie Howard's 'interpretations' are sound throughout; he makes more of some movements than others (the first movement of the *Eroica* could be more compelling) and the resonance of the recording is not ideal for revealing detail. The *Ninth* works impressively, if not as earth-shaking as Katsaris's version on Teldec. Overall, this is surprisingly enjoyable to listen to; without the orchestral colour, one notices the more what is happening in the internal arguments of these inexhaustible works.

Volume 23 is an effective transcription of Berlioz's *Harold in Italy* for viola and piano, and Howard takes the opportunity to include Liszt's own *Romance oubliée* for the same combination. Here Paul Coletti joins the pianist, and the performances are well played and spontaneous, if not earth-shaking. The transcriptions of the Beethoven and Hummel *Septets*, however, do not really work at all. This music either needs the instrumental colour or a much more witty approach (and the resonant recording is not helpful). However, there are some other paraphrases here that are much more effective, notably the excerpts from Goldschmidt's *Die sieben Todsünden* and two transcribed Mendelssohn choruses. Incidentally, it was the Liszt arrangement of Mozart's *Ave verum corpus* that Tchaikovsky orchestrated for a movement in his *Mozartiana suite*.

The *Cantico del Sol di San Francesco d'Assisi* is pleasantly based on *In dulci jubilo*. Then comes the chrysalis of the symphonic poem, *From the cradle to the grave*, which was greatly expanded in its orchestral form (not entirely to advantage!). Next, a series of shorter pieces, some quite bare and simple, but none the less effective for that, and the programme ends with more song transcriptions. Volume 26 is almost entirely devoted to works written when Liszt was a teenager, and the *Variations* show his mettle. Volume 27 offers patriotic songs and airs in a much more interesting and varied programme than it looks at first glance. *God save the Queen* was written for a British tour in 1840/41 and the tune is immediately interestingly varied in the opening bars. *La Marseillaise* starts off straightforwardly and the variants come later, but the tune reasserts itself strongly. The *Ungarische Nationalmelodien* is in effect a sketch for the *Sixth Hungarian rhapsody*. But there are plenty of enticing ideas here, notably the three-part suite, *Glanes de Woronince*, and the delightful French folksong arrangements, *Vive Henry IV* and *La cloche sonne*. Howard is at his most imaginative. Volume 28 is essentially a collection of marches and lively extrovert pieces, but they are very well presented.

Années de pèlerinage (complete): *Book 1, 1st Year: Switzerland; Book 2, 2nd Year: Italy; Supplément: Venezia e Napoli; Book 3, 3rd Year: Italy.*
☞ (B) *** DG 437 206-2 (3). Lazar Berman.

The *Années de pèlerinage* contain some of Liszt's very finest inspiration, and Lazar Berman's 1977 complete recording is fully worthy of it. Berman's technique is fabulous, more than equal to the demands made by these 26 pieces. The playing is enormously authoritative and quite free of empty display and virtuoso flamboyance, even though its brilliance is never in question. Indeed Berman brings searching qualities to this music: much of the time he is thoughtful and inward-looking in pieces like *Angelus* and *Sunt lachrymae rerum*. The imaginative colour and flair he displays in *Les cloches de Genève* and the simple freshness of *Eglogue* are matched by the felicity of the watery evocations, *Au lac de Wallenstadt* and *Les jeux d'eaux à la Villa d'Este*, while the power of the *Dante sonata* is equalled by the coruscating glitter of his articulation of the *Tarantella* from the *Supplément, Venezia e Napoli*. The recording, made in the Munich Alter Herkulessaal, is excellent. It is firmly and faithfully transferred to CD and does full justice to Berman's range of colour and dynamics. Moreover this box is remarkably inexpensive.

Années de pèlerinage: 1st Year (Switzerland); 2nd (with supplement) & 3rd Years (Italy): complete. *Hungarian rhapsodies Nos. 1–19* (complete).
☞ (M) **(*) EMI CMS7 64882-2 (4) [id.]. Georges Cziffra.

Cziffra's accounts of the complete *Années de pèlerinage* show the same prodigious virtuosity and keyboard command that make his set of *Hungarian rhapsodies* unforgettable. His account of the *Dante sonata* is enormously dramatic and produces the same fabulous digital dexterity that makes the *Tarantella* from the Italian Supplement, *Venezia e Napoli*, so breathtaking. In the more poetic pieces from Book 1, *Au lac de Wallenstadt* and *Au bord d'une source*, he finds more restrained romantic feeling, and in the Third Year *Les jeux d'eau à la Villa d'Este* brings some most delicate articulation. But at times the music's passion takes him over the top (as with *Aux cyprès de la Villa d'Este*) and he is not helped by a degree of hardness on piano timbre that is already somewhat dry. Remarkable pianism just the same.

Années de pèlerinage, 1st Year (Switzerland).
*** Decca Dig. 410 160-2 [id.]. Jorge Bolet.

This recording of the Swiss pieces from the *Années de pèlerinage* represents Bolet at his very peak, with playing of magical delicacy as well as formidable power. The piano sound is outstandingly fine.

Années de pèlerinage, 2nd Year (Italy) (complete).
*** Decca Dig. 410 161-2 [id.]. Jorge Bolet.

The pianistic colourings in this fine instalment in Bolet's Liszt series are magically caught here, whether in the brilliant sunlight of *Sposalizio* or the visionary gloom of *Il penseroso*. The *Dante sonata* brings a darkly intense performance, fresh and original and deeply satisfying.

Années de pèlerinage, 3rd Year (Italy) (complete).
*** Ph. Dig. 420 174-2 [id.]. Zoltán Kocsis.

Zoltán Kocsis gives the most compelling account of these sombre and imaginative pieces; apart from beautiful pianism, he also can convey the dark power of the music without recourse to percussive tone. He is splendidly recorded by the Philips engineers.

Années de pèlerinage, Book 2; Supplement: Venezia e Napoli (Gondoliera; Canzone; Tarantella); 3rd Year: Les jeux d'eau à la Villa d'Este; Ballade No. 2 in B min.; Harmonies poétiques et religieuses: Bénédiction de Dieu dans la solitude.
*** Decca Dig. 411 803-2 [id.]. Jorge Bolet.

A dazzling pendant to Liszt's Italian *Années de pèlerinage*, and the recital includes two of Liszt's weightiest conceptions, the *Bénédiction* and the *Ballade*, both spaciously conceived and far too little known. Vivid and full piano recording.

Années de pèlerinage: 1st Year: Au bord d'une source; Au lac de Wallenstadt; 3rd Year: Les jeux d'eau à la Villa d'Este. Bénédiction de Dieu dans le solitude; Liebestraum No. 3; Mephisto Waltz No. 1; Hungarian rhapsody No. 12; Variations on B-A-C-H.
ⓑ (BB) *** Virgin/EMI VJ7 59646-2; *VJ 759646-4* [id.]. Kun Woo Paik.

Kun Woo Paik is an outstanding Lisztian and this 78-minute recital, very realistically recorded and offered in the lowest price range, is in every way recommendable. This is playing of a high order. The famous *Liebestraum* is presented more gently than usual and the wide range of mood of the *Bénédiction* is controlled very spontaneously; it is only in the climax of the *BACH variations* that perhaps a touch more restraint would have been effective. A most exciting issue and a very real bargain.

Années de pèlerinage, 1st Year: Au bord d'une source; 2nd Year: Sonetto 104 del Petrarca; 3rd Year: Les jeux d'eau à la Villa d'Este; Supplement: Tarantella. Concert paraphrases of Schubert Lieder: *Auf dem Wasser zu singen; Die Forelle.* Concert studies: *Gnomenreigen; Un sospiro. Liebestraum No. 3.* (i) SCHUBERT/LISZT: *Wanderer fantasia* (arr. for piano and orchestra).
(B) *** Decca Dig. 425 689-2 [id.]. Jorge Bolet; (i) with LPO, Solti.

Intended by Decca as a bargain sampler for Bolet's distinguished Liszt series, this makes a unique recital in its own right. The recording is very real and present.

Années de pèlerinage, 1st Year: Au bord d'un source. 2nd Year: Sonetto del Petrarca No. 104. 2 Concert studies: Waldesrauschen; Gnomenreigen. Mephisto waltz No. 1; Rhapsodie espagnole.
*** Sony Dig. SK 47180 [id.]. Murray Perahia – FRANCK: *Prélude, choral et fugue.* ***

Murray Perahia's Liszt shows all the keyboard distinction and poetic insight we associate with him. This is memorable and very distinguished Liszt playing, and the Sony engineers do full justice to him.

Années de pèlerinage, 1st Year: Vallée d'Obermann; 2nd Year: Après une lecture du Dante (Dante sonata); Sonetto 104 del Petrarca; 3rd Year: Les jeux d'eau à la Villa d'Este. Ballade No. 2 in B min.; 6 Chants polonais de Chopin; Concert paraphrases on operas by Verdi; 2 Concert studies: Waldesrauschen; Gnomenreigen. 3 Etudes de concert; 12 Etudes d'exécution transcendante; Funérailles; Harmonies poétiques et religieuses: Bénédiction de Dieu dans la solitude; Sonata in B min.; Valse oubliée No. 1 in F sharp.
(M) *** Ph. Dig. 432 305-2 (5) [id.]. Claudio Arrau.

Claudio Arrau's Liszt performances combine an aristocratic finesse with just the proper amount of virtuoso abandon. His rubato is never excessive and always idiomatic. The performances are always completely within the sensibility of the period, yet are completely of our time as well. The excellent Philips recordings do justice to his thoroughly individual sound-world.

Années de pèlerinage, 2nd year: 3 Sonetti di Petrarca (Nos. 47, 104 & 123). Concert paraphrase on the *Quartet* from Verdi's *Rigoletto; Consolations Nos. 1–5; Liebesträume Nos. 1–3.*
(M) *** DG 435 591-2 [id.]. Daniel Barenboim.

Daniel Barenboim proves an ideal advocate for the *Consolations* and *Liebestraume*, and he is highly poetic in the *Petrarch sonnets*. His playing has an unaffected simplicity that is impressive and throughout there is a welcome understatement and naturalness, until he arrives at the *Rigoletto paraphrase* which is played with plenty of flair and glitter. The quality of the recorded sound is excellent.

Concert paraphrases of Schubert Lieder: *Auf den Wasser zu singen; Aufenthalt; Erlkönig; Die Forelle; Horch, horch die Lerch; Lebe wohl!; Der Lindenbaum; Lob der Tränen; Der Müller und der Bach; Die Post; Das Wandern; Wohin.*
*** Decca Dig. 414 575-2 [id.]. Jorge Bolet.

Superb virtuosity from Bolet. He is not just a wizard but a feeling musician, though here he sometimes misses a feeling of fun. First-rate recording.

Concert paraphrase of Verdi's *Rigoletto; Etudes d'exécution transcendante d'après Paganini: La Campanella. Harmonies poétiques et religieuses: Funérailles. Hungarian rhapsody No. 12; Liebestraum No. 3. Mephisto waltz No. 1.*
*** Decca Dig. 410 257-2 [id.]. Jorge Bolet.

Bolet's playing is magnetic, not just because of virtuosity thrown off with ease, but because of an element of joy conveyed, even in the demonic vigour of the *Mephisto waltz No. 1.* The relentless thrust of *Funérailles* is beautifully contrasted against the honeyed warmth of the famous *Liebestraum No. 3* and the sparkle of *La Campanella.* First-rate recording.

3 Concert studies; 2 Concert studies; 6 Consolations; Réminiscences de Don Juan (Mozart).
*** Decca 417 523-2 [id.]. Jorge Bolet.

In the *Concert studies* the combination of virtuoso precision and seeming spontaneity is most compelling in the splendid account of the *Don Juan* paraphrase. The *Consolations* show Bolet at his most romantically imaginative: he plays them beautifully.

Etudes d'exécution transcendante (complete).
**(*) Ph. 416 458-2 [id.]. Claudio Arrau.
**(*) Decca Dig. 414 601-2 [id.]. Jorge Bolet.

Arrau always plays with great panache and musical insight which more than compensate for the occasional smudginess of the recorded sound.

Bolet is a little disappointing, lacking a little in demonry; but as a searching interpreter of the composer and his musical argument he has few rivals.

Hungarian rhapsodies Nos. 1–19.
(M) *** DG 423 925-2 (2) [id.]. Roberto Szidon.
☞ (B) ** Ph. Duo 438 371-2 (2) [id.]. Michele Campanella.

Roberto Szidon's set of the *Hungarian rhapsodies* is highly recommendable. There is plenty of fire and flair here, and much that will dazzle the listener! The recording, too, sounds excellent.

Michele Campanella's bargain survey of the Liszt *Hungarian rhapsodies* has no want of technical command or finesse, and there are moments when the bravura provides excitement, as in the closing pages of the famous *No. 2 in C sharp minor*. But for the most part these performances lack the flair and spontaneity of Roberto Szidon's set, where the playing is not only more gripping but also much more imaginatively illuminating. The Philips set is provided with adequate documentation and has characteristically fine recording.

Hungarian rhapsodies Nos. 1–15; Rhapsodie espagnole.
☞ (B) *** EMI CZS7 67888-2 (2) [id.]. György Cziffra.

Cziffra's performances are dazzling. They are full of those excitingly chimerical spurts of energy and languorous rubato that immediately evoke the unreasonably fierce passions of gypsy music. Yet the control is absolute (try the delectably free opening of *No. 12 in C sharp minor*, or the *D minor* (No. 7). There is plenty of power in reserve and poetry too (the introduction to *No. 5 in E minor* is made to seem very like Chopin). For sheer glitter, sample *No. 10 in E major*. The high degree of temperament in the playing, with hardly two consecutive phrases at an even tempo, makes even Szidon (who has the full measure of the music) seem almost staid. Cziffra with coruscating brilliance sets every bar of the music on fire. Some might find him too impulsive for comfort (and they should turn to the DG alternative), but this is surely the way Liszt would have played them: the *Rákóczy march* (No. 15) is a *tour de force*. The recording, made in the Salle Wagram, Paris, in 1957/8 (or, in the case of Nos. 2, 6, 12 and 15, in the Hungaraton Budapest Studio a year earlier), is a little dry and close but otherwise truthful, and it does not lack sonority.

Hungarian rhapsodies Nos. 2–3, 8, 13, 15 (Rákóczy march); 17; Csárdás obstinée.
(M) *** Van. 08.4024.71 [OVC 4024]. Alfred Brendel.

Although the Vanguard recording is not a recent one, it sounds very good in this excellent CD transfer, and the playing is very distinguished indeed. There are few more charismatic or spontaneous accounts of the *Hungarian rhapsodies* available, and there is no doubt about the brilliance of the playing nor the quality of musical thinking that informs it.

Impromptu (Nocturne); Mephisto waltz No. 1.
☞ (M) *** Decca 425 046-2 [id.]. Vladimir Ashkenazy – PROKOFIEV: *Sonatas Nos. 7–8.* ***

Liszt wrote his short *Impromptu* for Olga Meyendorff, a baroness-pianist whom he admired. It combines romanticism with brilliance of display, as does the more famous *Mephisto waltz*. Ashkenazy is dazzling in both – the waltz sounds uncommonly fresh. The recording is rather brightly lit (not inappropriately so) but otherwise truthful.

Piano sonata in B min.
☞ (M) *** BMG/RCA 09026 61614-2 [id.]. Emil Gilels – SCHUBERT: *Sonata No. 17.*

Piano sonata; Années de pèlerinage, 2nd Year: Il Penseroso; 3rd Year: Les jeux d'eau à la Villa d'Este. Hungarian rhapsody No. 15 (Rákóczy march); Mephisto waltz No. 1.
⊛ *** Olympia Dig. OCD 172 [id.]. Mikhail Pletnev.

Piano sonata; Années de pèlerinage, 2nd Year: Après une lecture du Dante (Dante sonata). Mephisto waltz No. 1.
*** Denon Dig. C37 7547 [id.]. Dezsö Ránki.

Piano sonata; 3 Concert studies.
*** Chan. Dig. CHAN 8548; *ABTD 1223* [id.]. Louis Lortie.

Piano sonata; Grand galop chromatique; Liebesträume Nos. 1–3; Valse impromptu.
*** Decca Dig. 410 115-2. Jorge Bolet.

Piano sonata; Hungarian rhapsody No. 6.
☞ (M) ** DG 437 252-2 [id.]. Martha Argerich – BRAHMS: *Rhapsodies* **(*); SCHUMANN: *Sonata No. 2.* *(*)

Piano sonata; 2 Legends; Scherzo and March.
☞ *** Hyp. Dig. CDA 66616 [id.]. Nikolai Demidenko.

Mikhail Pletnev has a commanding musical authority, a highly distinctive timbre and an amazing dynamic range and variety of colour. His technique is transcendental, and there is a refinement and poetry that are hardly less remarkable. He dispatches the *Sonata* with an awesome brilliance and sense of drama, and his *Mephisto Waltz* is altogether thrilling. While the recording does not do full justice to his highly personal sound-world, it is eminently satisfactory. A most exciting disc.

Gilels's version of the Liszt *Sonata* is masterly. It has something in common with Curzon's stunning account (at present awaiting restoration to the catalogue) and can be spoken of alongside Pletnev. It is as penetrating in its way as Horowitz's famous pre-war record was virtuosic, and the playing here is equally astonishing technically. The 1964 recording leaves little cause for complaint on CD. It is vividly transferred and is not without body.

Nikolai Demidenko's account of the *Sonata* has won golden opinions, and rightly so. His is a keenly dramatic and powerfully projected account that has the listener on the edge of his or her seat. It must be numbered among the finest performances that this young Russian pianist has given us and is free from the slight mannerisms and the disruptive rubati that sometimes mar his recitals. The excitement and virtuosity are second to none and almost call to mind Horowitz, and his playing can be measured against that of Brendel and Pletnev. He has the advantage of exceptionally vivid recorded sound, and the remainder of the recital goes equally well.

Louis Lortie gives almost as commanding a performance of the Liszt *Sonata* as any in the catalogue; its virtuosity can be taken for granted and, though he does not have the extraordinary intensity and feeling for drama of Pletnev, he has a keen awareness of its structure and a Chopinesque finesse that win one over. The Chandos recording, though a shade too reverberant, is altogether natural.

The power, imagination and concentration of Bolet are excellently brought out in his fine account of the *Sonata*. With the famous *Liebestraum* (as well as its two companions) also most beautifully done, not to mention the amazing *Grand galop*, this is one of the most widely appealing of Bolet's outstanding Liszt series. Excellent recording.

Dezsö Ránki's account of the *Sonata* is very impressive indeed and can hold its own with almost any of its rivals. The *Mephisto waltz* and the *Dante sonata* are hardly less powerful in the hands of the young Hungarian master, the latter with real fire and a masterly control of dramatic pace. The Denon recording is absolutely first class.

Martha Argerich's 1971 account of the Liszt *Sonata* has tremendous assurance and vigour. Indeed the bravura is breathtaking. There is no lack of spontaneity, but both the work's lyrical feeling and its breadth are to some extent sacrificed to the insistent forward impulse of the playing. The *Hungarian rhapsody* has plenty of temperament. The recording, however, is clear rather than richly resonant.

ORGAN MUSIC

Ave Maria; Prelude and fugue on B-A-C-H; Symphonic poems: Orpheus (arr. Jean Guillou); Prometheus (arr. Schaab/Liszt).
*** Argo Dig. 430 244-2 [id.]. Thomas Trotter (Klais organ of Ingolstadt Minster) – REUBKE: *Sonata on Psalm 94.* ***

Evocation à la Chapelle Sixtine; Fantasia and fugue on 'Ad nos, ad salutarem undam'; Orpheus (symphonic poem; arr. Jean Guillou); *Variations on a theme by Bach: 'Weinen, Klagen, Sorgen, Zagen'.*
*** Collins Dig. 1249-2 [id.]. Jane Parker-Smith (Klais organ of Ingolstadt Minster).

Fantasia and fugue on 'Ad nos, ad salutarem undam'; Prelude and fugue on B-A-C-H; Variations on 'Weinen, Klagen, Sorgen, Zagen'.
☞ (BB) *** ASV CDQS 6127 [id.]. Jennifer Bate (Royal Albert Hall organ) – SCHUMANN: *4 Sketches.* ***

The Argo and Collins records are complementary not only in terms of repertoire but, because both artists have coincidentally chosen the same organ at Ingolstadt. It is obviously very suitable for this music, with its long reverberation period providing a highly spectacular effect. The only work common to both CDs is the arrangement of the symphonic poem, *Orpheus.* Comparing them is to discover the principal differences between the two sets of performances. Thomas Trotter is direct, with a firm forward impulse, Jane Parker-Smith is altogether more imaginative. She has a remarkable sense of fantasy, and the atmospheric writing at the beginning of the piece glows with a haunting aura. The sound of the two recordings is subtly different, with a slightly firmer focus on the Collins CD. There is no doubt that Parker-Smith's performances are inspirational. Thomas Trotter's playing is positive and firm, and his account of the *Prelude and fugue on B-A-C-H* is strongly controlled and very powerful, in contrast to the gently serene *Ave Maria*, which is most delicately registered.

Jennifer Bate, too, gives superb performances of the three major Liszt warhorses. The clarity and incisiveness of her playing go with a fine sense of line and structure, and there is plenty of exuberance in the *'Ad nos' Fantasia and fugue.* Even making no allowance for the Royal Albert Hall's acoustic problems, the analogue recording captures an admirable combination of definition and atmosphere, well conveyed on CD. This makes a fine super-bargain alternative to the competing digital versions, which are only marginally more sharply defined.

VOCAL MUSIC

Lieder: *Blume und Duft; Der du von dem Himmel bist; Du bist wie eine Blume; Die drei Zigeuner; Einst; Es war ein König in Thule; Freudvoll und leidvoll; Hohe Liebe; Ich möchte hingehn; Ihr Auge; Im Rhein, im schönen Strome; Mignons Lied (Kennst du das Land); O lieb' so lang du dieben kannst; Uber allen Gipfeln ist Ruh; Und wir dachten der Toten; Was Liebe sei; Wieder möcht' ich dir begegnen.*
☞ *** Decca Dig. 430 512-2 [id.]. Brigitte Fassbaender, Jean-Yves Thibaudet.

The sensitive poetry of Thibaudet's playing goes with powerful singing from Fassbaender in superb, characterful voice, with each highly individual artist challenging the other in imagination. There are few collections of Liszt songs to match this generous one in either range or intensity. Outstanding in every way, with excellent, helpful sound.

Lieder: *Blume und Duft; Der drei Zigeuner; Der du von dem Himmel bist (2 settings); Ein Fichtenbaum steht einsam; Es muss ein Wunderbares sein; Es rauschen die Winde; Der Hirt; Ihr Auge; Ihr Glocken von Marling; Freudvoll und leidvoll; Die Loreley; O komm im Traum; Des Tages laute Stimmen schweigen; Uber allen Gipfeln ist Ruh; Vergiftet sind meine Lieder.*
*** Capriccio Dig. 10 294 [id.]. Mitsuko Shirai, Hartmut Höll.

There are only one or two collections of Liszt songs as searchingly persuasive as this, and none more beautiful. Provocatively the record starts with Shirai at her most vehement in *Vergiftet sind meine Lieder* (My songs are poised), written when Liszt's long relationship with the Countess d'Agoult was breaking up. Regrettably, no English translations are provided with the text, only a commentary.

Lieder: *Comment, disaient-ils; Die drei Zigeuner; Ein Fichtenbaum steht einsam; Enfant, si j'étais roi; Es muss ein Wunderbares sein; Oh, quand je dors; S'il est un charmant gazon; Uber allen Gipfeln ist Ruh; Vergiftet sind meine Lieder.*
*** DG Dig. 419 238-2 [id.]. Brigitte Fassbaender, Irwin Gage – R. STRAUSS: *Lieder.* ***

This is singing which, in its control of detail, both in word and in note, as well as in its beauty and range of expression, is totally commanding. Fassbaender proves just as much at home in the four Victor Hugo settings in French as in the German songs. Sensitive accompaniment, well-placed recording.

Lieder: *Comment, disaient-ils; Es muss ein Wunderbares sein; Es rauschen die Winde; Go not happy day; Ihr Auge; Im Rhein, im schönen Strome; Oh, quand je dors; La tombe et la rose; Die Vätergruft; Vergiftet sind meiner Lieder; Wanderers Nachtlied.*

☞ ⊛ *** EMI Dig. CDC5 55047-2 [id.]. Thomas Hampson, Geoffrey Parsons – BERLIOZ; WAGNER: *Lieder.* *** ⊛

On his disc of romantic songs, Thomas Hampson ranges wide in his selection of 11 by Liszt, ending magically with one of the best-known, his setting in French of Victor Hugo, *Oh, quand je dors*. Characteristic, in that he finds a wider range of expressiveness and dynamic than almost any of his rivals, building from the drawing-room charm of the opening to a tremendous climax. He is helped by Parsons' accompaniment and the fine, warm recording. Other fascinating songs include Liszt's setting of Tennyson in English, *Go not happy day*, with the words oddly stressed. There is also a still, hushed and intense setting of Goethe's *Wanderers Nachtlied*, best known from Schubert. Magnetic, rich-voiced performances.

Hungarian Coronation Mass.
*** Hung. HCD 12148-2 [id.]. Kincses, Takács, Gulyás, Polgár, Hungarian R. & TV Ch., Budapest SO, Lehel.

Sung here with dedication by excellent Hungarian forces under György Lehel, the plain homophonic textures of the Mass – with the soloists generally used together as a quartet – make a strong impact, and the reverberant recording allows plenty of detail to be heard against an apt church acoustic.

The Legend of St Elisabeth.
*** Hung. Dig. HCD 12694/6-2 [id.]. Marton, Kováts, Farkas, Solyom-Nagy, Gregor, Gáti, Budapest Ch., Hungarian Army Male Ch., Children's Ch., Hungarian State O, Joó.

Though uneven in inspiration, Liszt's oratorio on *The Legend of St Elisabeth* contains some of his finest religious music in its span of six tableaux. Arpad Joó drives the work hard, but never to undermine the expressiveness of chorus and soloists, with Eva Marton as Elisabeth more firmly controlled than she has sometimes been in opera, and with no weak link in the rest of the team of principals.

Missa choralis.
(M) *** Decca 430 364-2 [id.]. Atkinson, Tinkler, Royall, Kendall, Suart, St John's College, Cambridge, Ch., Guest; Cleobury (organ) – DVORAK: *Mass in D.* ***

Missa choralis; Via crucis.
⊛ (M) *** Erato/Warner 2292 45350-2 [id.]. Donna Brown, Tantcheff, Alary, Oudor, Piquemal, Audita Nova de Paris Vocal Ens., Jean Sourisse; Marie-Claire Alain.
☞ (M) ** Saga EC 3399-2 [id.]. BBC N. Singers, Gordon Thorne; Francis Jackson.

This Erato performance is superbly sung and recorded, and the performance has a pulsing Latin ardour that is unforgettable in its spontaneous surges of feeling. It is ideally coupled to the other great ecclesiastical choral work of Liszt's final period, *Via crucis*, a provision of music for the Stations of the Cross, which he wrote between 1876 and 1878. This is even more original and certainly more daring in its spare treatment of the Crucifixion story. The organ intervenes with brief interludes to suggest some of the events, with the chorus continuing the tragic ongoing narrative. Liszt's forward-looking setting is most movingly realized here, by chorus, soloists who are excellent throughout both works, and not least, Marie-Claire Alain's restrained yet moving organ contribution. The acoustics of Saint-Antoine, Paris, seem quite ideal for this music. Very highly recommended.

On Decca Guest provides an inspired and beautifully sung version of just the *Missa choralis*, with well-blended tone. It has the benefit of spacious and richly detailed (originally Argo) recording.

It was Saga (now, alas, a mid-price rather than a bargain label) who pioneered the coupling of Liszt's *Missa choralis* and *Via crucis*, and the performances – especially of the latter – are committed and effective, with Francis Jackson's powerful organ-playing very impressively dramatic. The vocal style, however, is less free and uninhibitedly passionate than that of the French choir on Erato, and the Saga recording is comparatively studio-ish, with the organ very forward.

Missa solemnis.
**(*) Hung. HCD 11861-2 [id.]. Kincses, Takács, Korondy, Gregor, Hungarian R. & TV Ch., Budapest SO, Ferencsik.

This ambitious setting of the Mass is one of Liszt's finest choral inspirations. Ferencsik's recording, made in the mid-1970s, brings a spacious, powerful performance, well played and sung, with four of

Hungary's most distinguished singers as soloists. The analogue recording is not ideal but this is a noble account of a masterly choral work.

OPERA

Don Sanche (complete).
**(*) Hung. Dig. HCD 12744/5-2 [id.]. Garino, Hamari, Gáti, Farkas, Hungarian R. & TV Ch., Hungarian State Op. O, Tamás Pál.

Don Sanche or the Castle of Love was the teenage composer's first essay at a stage work. The only really Lisztian quality is the way he lights on instruments relatively exotic at the time, loading piccolos and trombones on to writing which suggests Weber or Rossini with dashes of Haydn, Schubert or even an occasional watered-down echo of Beethoven's *Fidelio*. The pity is that, after a promising start, the 90-minute one-acter tails off. Tamás Pál conducts a lively performance, with some stylish singing from the lyric tenor, Gerard Garino, in the name-part. Other principals are variable, including Julia Hamari as the hard-hearted heroine; but as long as you keep firmly in mind that this is the work of a thirteen-year-old, it will give much pleasure. The sound is bright and close.

Litolff, Henri (1818–91)

Concerto symphonique No. 4: Scherzo.
*** Ph. Dig. 411 123-2 [id.]. Misha Dichter, Philh. O, Marriner (with Concert of concertante music***).

Misha Dichter gives a scintillating account of Litolff's delicious *Scherzo*, played at a sparklingly brisk tempo. Marriner accompanies sympathetically and the recording is excellent.

Lloyd, George (born 1913)

Piano concerto No. 3.
**(*) Albany Dig. TROY 019-2; *TROY 019-4* [id.]. Kathryn Stott, BBC PO, composer.

The *Third Piano concerto* is very eclectic in style, with flavours of Prokofiev (with diluted abrasiveness) and even of Khachaturian – minus vulgarity – in outer movements which have a toccata-like brilliance and momentum. Kathryn Stott plays with a pleasing, mercurial lightness and makes the most of the music's lyrical feeling. But the slow movement is too long (19½ minutes) and its passionate climax uses material which does not show Lloyd at his best. On the other hand, the wistful tune at the centre of the finale is rather appealing. The composer achieves a fine partnership with his soloist and the performance has undoubted spontaneity.

(i) *Piano concerto No. 4; The lily-leaf and the grasshopper; The transformation of that Naked Ape.*
*** Albany AR 004 [id.]. Kathryn Stott; (i) LSO, composer.

The *Fourth Piano concerto* is a romantic, light-hearted piece with a memorable 'long singing tune' (the composer's words), somewhat Rachmaninovian in its spacious lyricism contrasting with a 'jerky' rhythmic idea. The performance by Kathryn Stott and the LSO under the composer is ardently spontaneous from the first bar to the last. The solo pieces are eclectic but still somehow Lloydian. The recording is first rate.

Symphonies Nos. 1 in A; 12.
*** Albany Dig. TROY 032-2; *TROY 032-4* [id.]. Albany SO, composer.

The pairing of George Lloyd's first and last symphonies is particularly appropriate, as both share a theme-and-variations format. The *First*, written in 1932 but recently revised, is relatively lightweight. The mature *Twelfth* uses the same basic layout but ends calmly with a ravishingly sustained pianissimo, semi-Mahlerian in intensity, that is among the composer's most beautiful inspirations. At the beginning of the work, the listener is soon aware of the noble lyrical theme which is the very heart of the *Symphony*. The Albany Symphony Orchestra gave the work its première and they play it with enormous conviction and eloquence. The concentration of the music-making throughout is that of a live performance, helped by the superb acoustics of the Troy Savings Bank Music Hall, which produces sound of demonstration quality. This record therefore makes an admirable starting point for anyone wishing to begin an exploration of the music of a composer who communicates readily.

Symphonies Nos. 2 and 9.
*** Conifer Dig. TROY 055 [id.]. BBC PO, composer.

Lloyd's *Second Symphony* is a lightweight, extrovert piece, conventional in form and construction, though in the finale the composer flirts briefly with polytonality, an experiment he did not repeat. The *Ninth* (1969) is similarly easygoing; the *Largo* is rather fine, but its expressive weight is in scale, and the finale, 'a merry-go-round that keeps going round and round', has an appropriately energetic brilliance. Throughout both works the invention is attractive, and in these definitive performances, extremely well recorded, the composer's advocacy is very persuasive.

Symphony No. 3 in F; Charade (suite).
☞ *** TROY Dig. TROY 90 [id.]. BBC PO, composer.

The *Third Symphony* dates from the composer's nineteenth year, and after some consideration he decided to leave it unrevised. On the whole it works well, its idiom undemanding but agreeable. Although it is described as a one-movement piece, it clearly subdivides into three sections. There are attractive lyrical ideas throughout, but it is the central *Lento* which has *the* tune, a winding, nostalgic theme that persists in the memory. It is atmospherically prepared and eventually blossoms sumptuously. Given sufficient exposure, it could surely become a hit. The finale, introduced with a dramatically regal fanfare, is vigorously light-hearted. *Charade* dates from the 1960s and attempts to portray the London scene of the time, from aggressive *Student power* and *LSD* to *Flying saucers* and *Pop song* (the most memorable number – swinging along, but not a bit like 'pop' music of the time). The ironic final movement, *Party politics*, is amiable rather than wittily abrasive. The composer is good at bringing his music vividly to life, and he is very well recorded indeed.

Symphony No. 4.
*** Albany AR 002; *AR 002C* [id.]. Albany SO, composer.

George Lloyd's *Fourth Symphony* was composed during his convalescence after being badly shell-shocked while serving in the Arctic convoys of 1941/2. The first movement is directly related to this period of his life, and the listener may be surprised at the relative absence of sharp dissonance. After a brilliant scherzo, the infectious finale is amiable, offering a series of quick, 'march-like tunes', which the composer explains by suggesting that 'when the funeral is over the band plays quick cheerful tunes to go home'. Under Lloyd's direction, the Albany Symphony Orchestra play with great commitment and a natural, spontaneous feeling. The recording is superb.

Symphony No. 5 in B flat.
*** Albany Dig. TROY 022-2; *TROY 022-4* [id.]. BBC PO, composer.

The *Fifth Symphony* is a large canvas, with five strong and contrasted movements, adding up to nearly an hour of music. It was written during a happy period spent living simply on the shore of Lac Neuchâtel, during the very hot summer of 1947. In the finale the composer tells us: 'everything is brought in to make as exhilarating a sound as possible – strong rhythms, vigorous counterpoints, energetic brass and percussion'. The symphony is played with much commitment by the BBC Philharmonic under the composer, who creates a feeling of spontaneously live music-making throughout. The recording is first class.

(i) *Symphonies Nos. 6;* (ii) *10 (November journeys);* (i) *Overture: John Socman.*
**(*) Albany Dig. TROY 15-2; *TROY 15-4* [id.]. (i) BBC PO; (ii) BBC PO Brass, composer.

The bitter-sweet lyricism of the first movement of *November journeys* is most attractive, but the linear writing is more complex than usual in a work for brass. In the finale a glowing *cantando* melody warms the spirit, to contrast with the basic *Energico*. The *Calma* slow movement is quite haunting, no doubt reflecting the composer's series of visits to English cathedrals, the reason for the subtitle. The *Sixth Symphony* is amiable and lightweight; it is more like a suite than a symphony. Lloyd's performances are attractively spontaneous and well played, and the equally agreeable *John Socman* overture also comes off well, although it is rather inconsequential.

Symphony No. 7.
*** Conifer Dig. TROY 057 [id.]. BBC PO, composer.

The *Seventh Symphony* is a programme symphony, using the ancient Greek legend of Proserpine. The slow movement is particularly fine, an extended soliloquy of considerable expressive power. The last and longest movement is concerned with 'the desperate side of our lives – "Dead dreams that the snows have shaken, Wild leaves that the winds have taken",' yet, as is characteristic with Lloyd, the darkness is muted; nevertheless the resolution at the end is curiously satisfying. Again he proves an admirable exponent of his own music. The recording is splendid.

Symphony No. 11.
*** Conifer Dig. TROY 060 [id.]. Albany SO, composer.

The urgently dynamic first movement of the *Eleventh* is described by the composer as being 'all fire and violence', but any anger in the music quickly evaporates, and it conveys rather a mood of exuberance, with very full orchestral forces unleashed. With the orchestra for which the work was commissioned, Lloyd conducts a powerful performance, very well played. The recording, made in the Music Hall of Troy Savings Bank near Albany, is spectacularly sumptuous and wide-ranging.

PIANO MUSIC

An African shrine; The aggressive fishes; Intercom baby; The road through Samarkand; St Anthony and the bogside beggar.
**(*) Albany Dig. AR 003; *C-A R 003* [id.]. Martin Roscoe.

The most ambitious piece here is *An African shrine*, in which the composer's scenario is linked (not very dissonantly) to African violence and revolution. *The road through Samarkand* (1972) has travellers from the younger generation leaving for the East; while *The aggressive fishes* are tropical and violently moody, changing from serenity to anger at the flick of a fin. The two most striking pieces are the picaresque tale of the *Bogside beggar* and the charming lullaby written for a baby whose mother is in another room listening with the aid of modern technology. Martin Roscoe's performances are thoroughly committed and spontaneous, and the recording is first class.

VOCAL MUSIC

A Symphonic Mass.
☞ ⊛ *** Albany Dig. TROY 100 [id.]. Brighton Festival Ch., Bournemouth SO, composer.

George Lloyd's *Symphonic Mass* is the composer's masterpiece. It was commissioned for the 1993 Brighton Festival, was first performed in May and recorded a month later by the same forces that gave it its première. Lloyd tells us that, although he is a believer, he attends no church; he therefore had some difficulties with setting the Latin text of the Mass. But he managed to 'square them' with his own beliefs, and his title is intended to denote that the work is non-liturgical. Written for chorus and orchestra (but no soloists) on the largest scale, the piece covers the widest range of feeling, doubt as well as faith, violence as well as peaceful conviction and, finally, repose which is the essence of the quietly intense closing *Agnus Dei*.

The work is linked by a recurring main theme, a real tune which soon lodges insistently in the listener's memory, even though it is modified at each reappearance. It first appears as a quiet setting of the words *Christe eleison*, nearly four minutes into the *Kyrie* which dazzles by its choral energy and returns again, richly intoned, first for the *Miserere nobis* of the exultant *Gloria*, then again for the choir's confident main statement of the *Credo*, now reinforced by the brass. The climax of the whole work is the combined *Sanctus* and *Benedictus*, with the latter framed centrally. To the words *Dominus Deus* the great melody finds its apotheosis in a passage marked *largamente con fevore*. Then the *Sanctus* reasserts itself dramatically and, after a cry of despair from the violins, the movement reaches its overwhelmingly powerful and dissonant dénouement. Peace is then restored in the *Agnus Dei*, where the composer tells us the words *Dona nobis pacem* became almost unbearably poignant for him.

The performance is magnificent. The choir had obviously become completely at home in the music during the preparation for the work's première, and the recorded account is every bit as powerful in its fervour and conviction and, if anything, seemingly even more spontaneous. The recording is fully worthy, spaciously balanced within the generous acoustic of the Guildhall, Southampton, and overwhelmingly realistic, even in the huge climax of the *Sanctus* with its shattering percussion.

The Vigil of Venus (Pervigilium Veneris).
*** Argo Dig. 430 329-2 [id.]. Carolyn James, Thomas Booth, Welsh Nat. Op. Ch. & O, composer.

Following up the success of his recordings of his symphonies, George Lloyd here directs Welsh National Opera forces in this ambitious oratorio. Here, as in the symphonies, he thumbs his nose at fashion in a score which both pulses with energy and cocoons the ear in opulent sounds. Delian ecstasy is contrasted against the occasional echo of Carl Orff, an attractive mixture, even if – for all the incidental beauties – there is dangerously little variety of mood in the nine substantial sections. The composer was not entirely happy with what he was able to achieve in that first recording; even so, his performance certainly does not lack intensity and the recording is excellent, given the inherent problems of the recording venue in Swansea.

Lloyd Webber, Andrew (born 1948)

Requiem.
*** EMI Dig. CDC7 47146-2 [id.]. Brightman, Domingo, Miles-Kingston, Drew, Winchester
   Cathedral Ch., ECO, Maazel; J. Lancelot (organ).

This *Requiem* may be derivative at many points, with echoes of Carl Orff – not to mention the
Requiems of both Verdi and Fauré – but, with Maazel conducting a performance of characteristic
intensity, it certainly has a life of its own. Radiant sounds from the Winchester Cathedral Choir, not
least the principal treble, Paul Miles-Kingston. Above all, this is music to which one returns with
increasing appreciation and pleasure. The CD gives presence and clarity to the excellent sound.

Lloyd Webber, William (1914–82)

(i) *Missa Sanctae Mariae Magdalenae;* (ii) Arias: *The Divine compassion: Thou art the King. The
Saviour: The King of Love. 5 Songs.* (iii; iv) *In the half light (soliloquy); Air varié* (after Franck); (iv)
6 Piano pieces.
*** ASV Dig. CDDCA 584 [id.]. (i) Richard Hickox Singers, Hickox; I. Watson (organ); (ii) J.
   Graham Hall; P. Ledger; (iii) Julian Lloyd Webber; (iv) John Lill.

William Lloyd Webber was a distinguished academic who, in a few beautifully crafted works, laid
bare his heart in pure romanticism. In his varied collection, the *Missa Sanctae Mariae Magdalenae* is
both the last and the most ambitious of his works, strong and characterful. John Lill is a persuasive
advocate of the *Six Piano pieces*, varied in mood and sometimes quirky, and accompanies Julian
Lloyd Webber in the two cello pieces, written – as though with foresight of his son's career – just as
his second son was born. Graham Hall, accompanied by Philip Ledger, completes the recital with
beautiful performances of a group of songs and arias. Recording, made in a north London church, is
warm and undistracting.

Locatelli, Pietro (1695–1764)

L'Art del violino (12 violin concertos), *Op. 3.*
☞ *** Hyp. Dig. CDA 66721/3 [id.]. Elizabeth Wallfisch, Raglan Bar. Players, Nicholas Kraemer.

Pietro Locatelli, an almost exact contemporary of Handel and Vivaldi, was born in northern Italy.
He was a pupil of Corelli and he travelled much as a virtuoso violinist until, around 1729, he finally
settled in Amsterdam, where he spent the rest of his life. It was here in 1733 that he wrote the present
set of concertos, in some ways anticipating Paganini by more than half a century. Each concerto is
fitted out in both outer movements with an extended *Capriccio*, obviously of enormous technical
difficulty to players of the time, with fast, complicated, sometimes stratospheric upper tessitura. Trills
and double-stopping abound, so that each time the ripieno returns one feels almost a sense of relief
that the soloist has reached home base, having tackled all the hurdles with such aplomb. Certainly
that is the case with Elizabeth Wallfisch, who not only throws off the fireworks with ease but also
produces an appealingly gleaming lyrical line. Although Locatelli has not as strong a melodic
personality as his famous contemporaries, the invention here has rhythmic vitality (which at times
mirrors Vivaldi) and, in the Largo slow movements, a series of flowing ideas that have an inherent
Handelian grace. (This latter aspect of the music came out more fully on the older-fashioned if less
polished Vox recording with Susanne Lautenbacher and the Munich Chamber Orchestra under
Kehr.) With excellent, vital and stylish support from Kraemer and his Raglan Baroque Players, this
may be counted a stimulating authentic re-creation of a set of concertos which had a profound
influence on the violin technique of the time. The very well-balanced recording (the soloist real and
vivid) is admirably clear yet has plenty of ambience. If you are doubtful about the interest of this
music, try to sample the last (twelfth) concerto, appropriately subtitled *Il Laberinto Armonico, facilis
aditus, difficilis exitus.*

12 Flute sonatas, Op. 2.
☞ *** O-L 436 191-2 (2). Stephen Preston (with McGegan in *No. 12*), Pleeth, Hogwood.

Apart from the concertos, the 12 *Flute sonatas* are perhaps the most important collection among
Locatelli's works. Published in 1732, they take a traditional line in their use of binary form, but the
amiable freshness of the writing is most persuasive in fine, authentic performances like these. No. 12
here is offered in its optional rendering as a double canon, with Nicholas McGegan taking the second

flute part. In effect the work is heard with a following echo, although the harpsichord continuo is shadowed by the cello, so the continuo echo is barer than the first statement. The results are aurally fascinating. The recording is most realistic.

Locke, Matthew (c. 1621–77)

(i) *The Tempest* (incidental music written in collaboration with Pelham Humphrey, Pietro Reggio, John Bannister, James Hart); (ii) *Music for His Majesty's sackbuts and cornetts*.

☞ *** O-L 433 191-2 [id.]. (i) Nelson, Hill, Thomas, AAM, Christopher Hogwood; (ii) Michael Laird Cornett and Sackbut Ens. – PURCELL: *Abdelazar*. ***

This admirable recording was first issued in 1977, the tercentenary of Matthew Locke's death, and it is a worthy tribute. *The Tempest* music was the work for which he was renowned in his lifetime and for a century afterwards. The performance could not be bettered, and the balance of the recording is judged with taste and discretion. The CD transfer is immaculate: every detail is firmly in focus and every singer and instrument is life-size and lifelike. The performance of the *Music for His Majesty's sackbuts and cornetts* is no less impressive, even if as music this is more conventional. But *The Tempest* is a very fine score indeed.

Loeffler, Charles (1861–1935)

A Pagan poem, Op. 14.

☞ (M) **(*) EMI CDM5 65074-2 [id.]. SO, Stokowski with Robert Hunter, William Kosinski – GLIÈRE: *Symphony No. 3.* **(*)

Loeffler was born in Alsace (then still part of France) and moved to America in 1887. He spent the bulk of his life in Boston. Franck, Wagner and *fin-de-siècle* romanticism are the predominant influences here. He does not possess as strongly individual a personality as, say, his younger American contemporary, Griffes. His highly eclectic but richly coloured *Pagan poem* is his only claim to fame; it is based on Vergil's *Eighth Eclogue* and tells of a young girl, Thessaly, who tries, with the aid of sorcery, to win back the lover who has left her. The ambitious scoring includes obbligato piano and a cor anglais solo, but it is the brass that carry the day at the triumphant conclusion. Its hyperbole is well understood by Stokowski, who gives a sumptuously exciting performance in the tradition of Hollywood film music, with virtuoso playing throughout, yet with the gentler passages poetically caught using the widest palette of colour. An ideal coupling for Glière with the early (1957) stereo providing plenty of opulent spectacle.

Lourié, Arthur (1892–1966)

Concerto da camera; (i) *A little chamber music;* (ii) *Little Gidding.*

☞ *** DG Dig. 437 788-2 [id.]. Gidon Kremer, (i) Thomas Klug; (ii) Kenneth Riegel, Deutsche Kammerphilharmonie.

Arthur Lourié was one of the pioneers of modernism in the early years of the Soviet Union; a futurist and a proto-serialist in the days of Lunacharsky, one of whose cultural commissars he briefly became. But, presciently, in 1923 he did not return from a trip to the West; and he settled in Paris, where he became drawn into Stravinsky's orbit, acting for him as an assistant, before their eventual estrangement. In the course of time he became disenchanted with modernism and in 1941 settled in the United States. *A little chamber music* comes from the 1920s and in its obvious neo-classicism betrays a certain closeness to Stravinsky's aesthetic, as well as a touch of Shostakovich's sardonic humour. The *Concerto da camera* was written in America and is a six-movement work in a quasi-baroque style. The melodic ideas all tend to be short-breathed but characterful. Lourié's setting of T. S. Eliot's *Little Gidding*, the first of the *Four Quartets*, shows great affinity with Eliot's world and is arguably the most imaginative thing on the disc. Kremer and the Deutsche Philharmonie play with a sense of real discovery and commitment, and Kenneth Riegel is at his usual best. Interesting repertoire rather than great music, but very rewarding all the same, and well worth acquiring, particularly in so fine a recording.

Lovenskiold, Herman (1815–70)

La Sylphide (ballet) complete.
(M) *** Chan. Dig. CHAN 6546; *MBTD 6546* [id.]. Royal Danish O, David Garforth.

La Sylphide (1834) predates Adam's *Giselle* by seven years. It is less distinctive than Adam's score, but it is full of grace and the invention has genuine romantic vitality – indeed the horn writing in the finale anticipates Delibes. The wholly sympathetic playing is warm, elegant, lively and felicitous in its detailed delicacy, yet robust when necessary and always spontaneous. A most enjoyable disc, superbly recorded.

Ludford, Nicholas (1485–1557)

Missa: Christi Virgo Dilectissima; Motet Domine Ihesu Christe.
☞ *** Gaudeamus/ASV Dig. CDGAU 133 [id.]. The Cardinall's Musick, Andrew Carwood.

Missa: Videte miraculum; Motet: *Ave cuius conceptio.*
☞ *** Gaudeamus/ASV Dig. CDGAU 131 [id.]. The Cardinall's Musick, Andrew Carwood.

Nicholas Ludford is one of the least familiar of the Tudor masters; he never enjoyed the fame of his older contemporary, Fayrfax, or the much younger Tallis. Ludford was in the employ of St Stephen's Chapel, Westminster (which was destroyed by fire in 1834, three centuries after his death), and he has remained outside the repertoire of most cathedral choirs, little more than a name to those with an interest in early music. According to Dr John Bergsagel's *Grove* article, Ludford composed 11 complete Masses and three incomplete, thus making him 'the most prolific of English composers of masses'. This CD is the first in a projected series to bring his work to modern audiences, and one for which we should feel gratitude; this is music of great beauty, whose expressive eloquence and floating lines quite carry the listener away. Andrew Carwood proves an excellent advocate of this composer, and the sound is also spacious and well balanced.

Luigini, Alexandre (1850–1906)

Ballet Egyptien, Op. 12 (suite).
☞ (B) *** CfP CD-CFP 4637; *TC-CFP 4637*. RPO, Fistoulari – KETELBEY: *Collection.* ***

Because of its bandstand popularity, Luigini's amiable and tuneful *Ballet Egyptien* has never been taken very seriously and there is some sparkling doggerel by Richard Murdoch which snappily fits bizarre words about 'Dame Ella Wheeler Wilcox' neatly to the famous opening rhythm. However, the four-movement suite is highly engaging (both the two central sections have good tunes), especially when played as affectionately and stylishly as here under that master conductor of ballet, Anatole Fistoulari. The 1958 recording has come up remarkably freshly, and this makes an excellent bonus for an outstanding Ketèlbey concert.

Lully, Jean-Baptiste (1632–87)

Atys (opera): complete.
*** HM Dig. HMC 901257/9; *HMC 701257/9* (3). Guy de Mey, Mellon, Laurens, Gardeil,
    Semellaz, Rime, Les Arts Florissants Ch. & O, Christie.

Christie and his excellent team give life and dramatic speed consistently to the performance of *Atys*, and there are many memorable numbers, not least those in the sleep interlude of Act III. Outstanding in the cast are the high tenor, Guy de Mey, in the name-part and Agnès Mellon as the nymph, Sangaride, with whom he falls in love.

Le bourgeois gentilhomme (comédie-ballet; complete).
(M) *** HM/BMG GD 77059 (2) [77059-2-RG]. Nimsgern, Jungmann, Schortemeier, René Jacobs,
    Tölz Ch., La Petite Bande, Leonhardt – CAMPRA: *L'Europe galante.* ***

Lully's score is unmemorable and harmonies are neither original nor interesting; but the performance puts Lully's music into the correct stage perspective and, with such sprightly and spirited performers as well as good 1973 recording, this can hardly fail to give pleasure. The orchestral contribution under the direction of Gustav Leonhardt is distinguished by a splendid sense of the French style.

Lumbye, Hans Christian (1810–74)

*Amager polka; Amelie waltz; Champagne galop; Columbine polka mazurka; Copenhagen Steam
Railway galop; Dream pictures fantasia; The Guard of Amager* (ballet): *Final galop. Helga polka
mazurka; Hesperus waltz; Lily polka (dedicated to the ladies); Queen Louise's waltz; Napoli* (ballet):
Final galop. Salute to August Bournonville; Salute to our friends; Sandman galop fantastique.
⊛ *** Unicorn Dig. DKPCD 9089; *DKPC 9089* [id.]. Odense SO, Peter Guth.

This superb Unicorn collection offers 75 minutes of the composer's best music, with wonderfully
spontaneous performances demonstrating above all its elegance and gentle grace. It opens with a
vigorous *Salute to August Bournonville* and closes with a *Champagne galop* to rival Johann junior's
polka; and here the hitherto silent audience joins in with enthusiastic, if undisciplined hand-claps, to
recall the *Radetzky march* of Johann senior. In between comes much to enchant, not least the
delightful *Amelie waltz* and the haunting *Dream pictures fantasia* with its diaphanous opening textures
and lilting main theme. Another charmer is the *Sandman galop fantastique*, a vivacious pot-pourri
which never wears out its welcome by becoming too vociferous, while *Queen Louise's waltz* has an
appropriate melodic poise. But Lumbye's masterpiece is the unforgettable *Copenhagen Steam Railway
galop*. This whimsical yet vivid portrait of a local Puffing Billy begins with the gathering of
passengers at the station – obviously dressed for the occasion in a more elegant age than ours. The
little engine then wheezingly starts up and proceeds on its journey, finally drawing to a dignified halt
against interpolated cries from the station staff. Because of the style and refinement of its imagery, it
is much the most endearing of musical railway evocations, and the high-spirited lyricism of the little
train racing through the countryside, its whistle peeping, is enchanting. This is a superbly entertaining
disc, showing the Odense Symphony Orchestra and its conductor, Peter Guth, as naturally suited to
this repertoire as are the VPO under Boskovsky in the music of the Strauss family. The recording has
a warm and sympathetic ambience and gives a lovely bloom to the whole programme.

Amelie waltz; Britta polka; Champagne galop; Columbine polka mazurka; Concert polka (for 2 violins
and orchestra); *Copenhagen Steam Railway galop; Dream pictures* (fantasy); *The Lady of St Petersburg*
(polka); *The Guards of Amager: Final galop. My salute to St Petersburg* (march); *Napoli* (ballet):
*Final galop. Polonaise with cornet solo; Queen Louise's waltz; Salute to August Bournonville; St
Petersburg champagne galop.*
☞ *** Chan. Dig. CHAN 9209 [id.]. Danish Nat. RSO, Rozhdestvensky.

No record collection is complete without a Lumbye anthology. The Danish contemporary of Johann
Strauss wrote a great deal of dance music which in its tuneful vitality is fully worthy of that master;
his enchanting *Copenhagen Steam Railway galop* remains the most vivid and entertaining musical
train evocation ever conceived. This new Chandos disc opens with an arresting fanfare and sets off
into the *Champagne galop* with much brio. Throughout his programme, Rozhdestvensky's approach
is altogether more extrovert than Guth's on Unicorn, and the Royal Danish Orchestra, without loss
of finesse, play almost everything here with great gusto. The Copenhagen Steam Railway engine
becomes a mainline express and reaches an exhilarating momentum before slamming on its brakes, to
be vociferously welcomed by the Danish porters as it arrives at its destination. One cannot but
respond to the energy and vivacity of the playing here, while the lovely *Dream pictures* creates a total
contrast and is most poetically done. Incidentally, the lively *Britta polka* (unwittingly?) quotes
Sullivan's *A magnet hung in a hardware shop* (from *Patience*). This is one of five items not duplicated
on the Unicorn disc, but collectors who already have this will surely want the new Chandos collection
as a supplement, if only to experience the exuberance of Rozhdestvensky's response to some
splendidly entertaining music. The recording is spectacularly resonant and adds to the impact.

*Britta polka; Canon galop; Cecilie waltz; Dancing tune from Kroll Waltz; Indian war dance; King
Christian IX March of honour; King George I March of honour; Manoeuvre galop; Memories from
Vienna waltz; Nordic brotherhood; Pegasus galop; Sommernight at Møns Cliff galop; Sophie waltz;
Velocipedes galop; Victoria quadrille; Welcome mazurka; Les Zouaves galop.*
☞ *** Unicorn Dig. DKPCD 9143; *DKPC 9143.* Odense SO, Peter Guth.

A further, essentially energetic selection of sparkling Lumbye repertoire, splendidly played with much
spirit by the excellent Odense orchestra under Guth. The *Velocipedes galop* makes an engaging and
vivacious opener, and the *Canon galop* which closes the concert has properly spectacular effects, plus
a final bang to make the listener jump. The *Memories from Vienna waltz* has a particularly winning
lilt, but there is nothing here that quite matches the *Copenhagen Steam Railway galop*.

Lutoslawski, Witold (1916–94)

Chain II; Partita.
*** DG Dig. 423 696-2 [id.]. Mutter, BBC SO, composer – STRAVINSKY: *Violin concerto.* ***

Chain II, a *Dialogue for violin and orchestra*, follows up the technique of *Chain I*, contrasting fully written sections with *ad libitum* movements, where chance plays its part within fixed parameters. The *Partita* is a development of a piece for violin and piano which Lutoslawski originally wrote for Pinchas Zukerman, with the first, third and fifth movements written for violin and orchestra. With Mutter and the composer the most persuasive advocates, both pieces establish themselves as among the finest examples of Lutoslawski's latterday work, provocative and ear-catching in their fantasy. First-rate sound.

Chain 3; Novelette.
☞ (B) *** DG Dig. 439 452-3 [id.]. BBC SO, composer – LIGETI: *Chamber concerto;* SCHNITTKE: *Concerto grosso No. 1.* ***

On this Classikon reissue of material which first appeared at full price only in 1992, DG are obviously treading water, wondering if they can sell this kind of *avant-garde* music in a wider marketplace at budget price. *Novelette* (1979) is an attractive, Scherzo-like piece, full of incandescent energy, while *Chain 3* makes a more sustained contrast with its ear-catching orchestral colours. Both are well played under the composer, and the digital sound has plenty of ambience.

Concerto for orchestra.
*** Decca Dig. 425 694-2. Cleveland O, Dohnányi – BARTOK: *Concerto for orchestra.* **(*)
☞ **(*) BMG/RCA Dig. 09026 61520-2 (2) [id.]. Fr. R. PO, Janowski – MESSIAEN: *Turangalîla Symphony* etc. **(*)

Lutoslawski's brilliant showpiece is played on Decca with a thrust and precision to bring out the full colour and energy of the work. Dohnányi's dedicated performance is recorded with a fullness and brilliance outstanding even by Decca standards.

Janowski is a sympathetic interpreter of this most popular of Lutoslawski's orchestral works, but it comes unnecessarily coupled with two Messiaen works in a two-disc set.

Cello concerto.
☞ *** EMI CDC7 49304-2 [id.]. Rostropovich, O de Paris, composer – DUTILLEUX: *Cello concerto.* ***

The *Cello concerto* was written in response to a commission by Rostropovich, whose 1975 recording is now reissued at full price, retaining the original catalogue number and still sounding extremely vivid. As in some other Lutoslawski pieces, there are aleatory elements in the score, though these are carefully controlled. The sonorities are fascinating and heard to good advantage on the EMI CD. The soloist is rather forward, but in every other respect the recording is extremely realistic. Rostropovich is in his element and gives a superb account of the solo role, and the composer's direction of the accompaniment is grippingly authoritative.

(i) Piano concerto. Chain 3; Novelette.
☞ *** DG Dig. 431 664-2 [id.]. (i) Krystian Zimerman; BBC SO, composer.

The *Piano concerto* (1987) was commissioned for the Salzburg Festival where the dedicatee, Krystian Zimerman, and the composer gave its first performance in 1988. The piece is full of imaginative ideas and opens with some shimmering, sensitively laid-out textures. It is sympathetically written for the piano, Lutoslawski's own instrument (although he has composed rather little for it) and is marvellously played by Zimerman and the BBC Symphony Orchestra under the composer. It is beautiful to listen to, but for all its diversity of aural incident and activity one is left wondering whether there is much of enduring substance. The two remaining works were written for American orchestras; *Novelette* in 1978–9 for Rostropovich and the Washington orchestra, and *Chain 3* in 1986 for San Francisco. Absolutely first-rate recording.

Dance preludes (for clarinet and orchestra).
*** Hyp. Dig. CDA 66215 [id.]. Thea King, ECO, Litton – BLAKE: *Clarinet concerto;* SEIBER: *Concertino.* ***
*** Chan. Dig. CHAN 8618; *ABTD 1307* [id.]. Janet Hilton, SNO, Bamert – COPLAND; NIELSEN: *Concertos.* ***

Lutoslawski's five folk-based vignettes are a delight in the hands of Thea King and Andrew Litton, who give sharply characterized performances, thrown into bold relief by the bright, clear recording.

Janet Hilton also emphasizes their contrasts with her expressive lyricism and crisp articulation in the lively numbers. Excellent recording.

Paganini variations for piano and orchestra.
☞ *** Decca Dig. 436 239-2 [id.]. Jablonski, RPO, Ashkenazy – RACHMANINOV: *Rhapsody on a theme of Paganini* **(*); SHOSTAKOVICH: *Piano concerto No. 1.* ***

The *Paganini variations* for two pianos is one of Lutoslawski's earliest works and dates from 1941. The young Swedish pianist, Peter Jablonski, plays it in its much later orchestral transcription with evident pleasure and delight.

Symphonies Nos. 1–2; Symphonic variations.
☞ (M) *** EMI CDM5 65076-2 [id.]. Polish R. Nat. SO, composer.

The wholly beguiling *Symphonic variations*, with its Szymanowskian palette and luminosity, is an early work (1938); the symphonies date from 1947 and 1966/8, respectively. The latter consolidates the new language the composer formed after his change of style in the mid-1950s; the *First* is written against a musical background influenced by Hindemith, Bartók and Prokofiev and perhaps by Stravinsky too. But the work has its own individuality and is well worth hearing. The composer is an eloquent advocate, and the 1976/7 recordings are spacious and full-bodied with bright detail.

Symphony No. 3; (i) Les espaces du sommeil.
*** Sony Dig. M2K 42271 (2) [id.]. (i) Shirley-Quirk; LAPO, Salonen – MESSIAEN: *Turangalîla symphony.* **(*)

Even next to Lutoslawski's own interpretation, Salonen's brings an extra revelation. This is a deeply committed, even passionate account of a work which may be rigorous in its argument but which is essentially dramatic in one massive, continuous span. In *Les espaces du sommeil* Salonen also presents a different slant from the composer himself, making it – with the help of John Shirley-Quirk as an understanding soloist – much more evocative and sensuous in full and well-balanced sound.

String quartet.
*** Olympia OCD 328 [id.]. Varsovia Qt – SZYMANOWSKI: *Quartets;* PENDERECKI: *Quartet No. 2.* ***

Lutoslawski tells us that in his *String quartet* he uses 'chance elements to enrich the rhythmic and expressive character of the music without in any way limiting the authority of the composer over the final shape of the piece'. Whatever its merits, it has a highly developed and refined feeling for sonority and balance and, generally speaking, succeeds in holding the listener.

Lyapunov, Sergei (1859–1924)

Hashish, Op. 53; Polonaise, Op. 16; Solemn overture on Russian themes, Op. 7; Zelazowa Wola, Op. 37.
** Olympia OCD 129 [id.]. USSR Ac. SO, Svetlanov – BALAKIREV: *Islamey.* **

The *Solemn overture on Russian themes* is much influenced by Balakirev's examples in this genre, and the spirited *Polonaise* is very much in the processional style of Glinka and Tchaikovsky. The tone-poem, *Zelazowa Wola* (Chopin's birthplace), is a tribute to Chopin. The intriguingly entitled *Hashish* takes its cue from Balakirev's *Tamara* and is colourful stuff. If you respond to Balakirev, you should investigate this attractive music. Svetlanov is in his element in this kind of repertoire and the playing is very good. The recording, though not top-drawer, is perfectly acceptable.

MacCunn, Hamish (1868–1916)

The Land of the mountain and the flood (concert overture).
☞ (B) *** CfP CD-CFP 4635; *TC-CFP 4635.* RSNO, Gibson – GERMAN: *Welsh rhapsody;* HARTY: *With the wild geese;* SMYTH: *Wreckers overture.* ***

MacCunn's descriptive overture is no masterpiece, but it has a memorable tune, is attractively atmospheric and is constructed effectively. Sir Alexander Gibson's performance is quite outstanding in its combination of warmth, colour and drama, and the recording is excellent. So is the CD transfer, and this enterprising collection is a real bargain.

MacDowell, Edward (1861–1908)

Piano concertos Nos. 1 in A min., Op. 15; 2 in D min., Op. 23.
⊛ *** Olympia Dig. OCD 353 [id.]. Donna Amato, LPO, Paul Freeman.

Of MacDowell's two *Piano concertos* the *First* is marginally the lesser of the two: the melodic content, though very pleasing, is slightly less memorable than in the *Second*. This is a delightful piece, fresh and tuneful, redolent of Mendelssohn and Saint-Saëns. Donna Amato's scintillating performance is entirely winning, and she is equally persuasive in the *A minor*. This music needs polish and elegance as well as fire, and Paul Freeman's accompaniments supply all three. The recording, made in All Saints', Tooting, has an agreeable ambient warmth. A highly rewarding coupling in all respects.

Piano concerto No. 2 in D min., Op. 23.
☞ *** Chesky CD 76 [id.]. Earl Wild, RCA Victor SO, Freccia – RACHMANINOV: *Piano concerto No. 3.* ***

Earl Wild never played more brilliantly or more appealingly on record than in these coupled recordings of MacDowell and Rachmaninov, engineered by Decca in the mid-1960s. The performance of the finer of the two MacDowell concertos is technically dazzling – both the delicious Scherzo and the finale erupt with scintillating pianistic bravura – and so assured and sympathetic is Wild's style that the concerto is almost made to sound a masterpiece. Massimo Freccia and the so-called RCA Victor Symphony Orchestra (probably including members of the RPO) provide excellent support, and Wild is much better balanced and recorded than his competitor on RCA, Van Cliburn.

(i) *Piano concerto No. 2 in D min., Op. 23. Woodland sketches: To a wild rose, Op. 51/1.*
(M) **(*) BMG/RCA GD 60420 [60420-2-RG]. Van Cliburn, (i) Chicago SO, Hendl – SCHUMANN: *Concerto.* **(*)

Van Cliburn is not helped by a recording balance which consistently makes him sound rather too loud; but the performance otherwise has the advantage of warm Chicago acoustics, and Walter Hendl's vigorous and sympathetic support, with its fire and spontaneity, triumph over the technical problems. The Scherzo is superb. MacDowell's most famous solo piano piece makes a pleasing encore, though the performance is a trifle cool.

PIANO MUSIC

Fireside tales, Op. 61; New England idyls, Op. 62; Sea pieces, Op. 55; Woodland sketches, Op. 51.
☞ **(*) Marco Polo Dig. 8.223631 [id.]. James Baragallo.

MacDowell's most famous piano piece opens this recital: *To a wild rose* (named by his wife) is the first of the ten *Woodland sketches*. They are all pleasant if not distinctive vignettes, most lasting a little over a minute. The second piece, *Will-o'-the Wisp*, has a fragile charm and *At an old trysting place* and *By a deserted farm* a simple nostalgia. The other three suites are very similar. The *Sea pieces* are without any striking oceanic evocation: the thoughtful suggestion of the composer's response to *Starlight* is perhaps most memorable. Of the *Fireside tales*, the opening *An old love story* immediately sets the cosy atmosphere, and *From a German forest* brings another simple evocation that is engaging in its simplicity. This is certainly not a CD to listen to all at once but to be dipped into; one can appreciate that James Baragallo is a thoroughly sympathetic exponent, and he is well recorded too.

MacMillan, James (born 1959)

(i). . . *as others see us; 3 Dawn rituals; Untold;* (ii) *Veni, veni, Emmanuel (concerto for percussion and orchestra);* (iii) *After the Tryst (miniature fantasy for violin and piano).*
☞ ⊛ *** BMG/RCA Catalyst Dig. 09026 61916-2 [id.]. (i) Scottish CO (members), composer; (ii) Evelyn Glennie, SCO, Saraste; (iii) Ruth Crouch, composer.

As in 1990 with *The Confession of Isobel Gowdie* – see below – so in the 1992 Proms James MacMillan had wild success with the percussion concerto, *Veni, veni, Emmanuel,* written for Evelyn Glennie, the major work recorded here. This also instantly reveals the composer's rare gift of communicating with electric intensity to a wide audience, rare in new music today. His dedication, strongly motivated by his devout Catholicism and his equally passionate left-wing stance, invariably colours what he writes, making us share not his precise beliefs but the spiritual intensity that goes with them. That provides a link with Gorecki's *Third Symphony* and Tavener's *The Protecting Veil* with a physical, even sensual impact in the music alongside the spiritual.

The difference with MacMillan is that he cannot be accused of dabbling in minimalism. In *Veni,*

veni, Emmanuel he has written a concerto for percussion that in its energy as well as its colour consistently reflects both the virtuosity and the charismatic personality of Evelyn Glennie. Taking the Advent plainsong of the title as his basis, he reflects in his continuous 26-minute sequence the theological implications behind the period between Advent and Easter. The five contrasted sections are in a sort of arch form, with the longest and slowest section in the middle. That section, *Gaude, Gaude,* expresses not direct joy as the Latin words might suggest but a meditative calm, using the four relevant chords from the plainsong's refrain as a hushed ostinato, with the soloist on the marimba playing an elaborate but gentle, poetic cadenza. The main sections on either side are related dances based on hocketing repeated notes and full of jazzy syncopations, with powerful sections for Advent and Easter respectively framing the whole. The plainsong emerges clearly and dramatically as a full chorale at the climax of the second dance-section, a telling moment. Finally comes a dramatic coup when, with the musicians in the orchestra playing little jingling bells, the soloist progresses up to the big chimes set on a platform above the rest of the orchestra. The very close of the work brings a crescendo of chimes intended to reflect the joy of Easter in the Catholic service and the celebration of the Resurrection. In this superb recording the orchestra as well as Evelyn Glennie play with both brilliance and total commitment, if not with quite the extra thrill that at the end is experienced in live performances. This is a magnificent representation of one of the most striking and powerful works written by any British composer of the younger generation. In the fill-up works – brief pieces marked by the same dramatic intensity – MacMillan himself as conductor inspires strong, positive performances from various groups of SCO players. With first-rate, atmospheric sound – *Veni, veni, Emmanuel* recorded in Usher Hall, Edinburgh, the rest in City Hall, Glasgow – this is an outstanding first issue on BMG's Catalyst label.

The Confession of Isobel Gowdie; Tryst
*** Koch/Schwann Dig. 3-1050-2 [id.]. BBC Scottish SO, Maksymiuk.

James MacMillan from Glasgow is the most exciting young British composer to have emerged in the 1990s. Inspired by the horrific execution in 1662 of Isobel Gowdie, tortured into confessing herself a witch, MacMillan has used the story as a metaphor for twentieth-century witch-hunting, including what he sees as resurgent fascism today. The result is rather like Vaughan Williams's *Tallis fantasia* updated and then invaded by Stravinsky's *Rite of spring*. The other piece on the disc, *Tryst* – marginally longer at 28 minutes – has similar qualities. In juxtaposition it emerges as the obverse of *Isobel Gowdie*, similarly a massive single movement in arch form. This time the music works from violence at the beginning and end to a long slow meditation in the middle, again with echoes of ecclesiastical chant a basic element. Maksymiuk proves a dedicated interpreter.

Maconchy, Elizabeth (born 1907)

Concertinos Nos. 1 (1945); 2 (1984).
☞ *** Hyp. Dig. CDA 66634 [id.]. Thea King, ECO, Wordsworth – ARNOLD: *Clarinet concertos* etc.; BRITTEN: *Clarinet concerto movement.* ***

The two Maconchy *Concertinos*, each in three movements and under ten minutes long, have a characteristic terseness, sharp and intense, that runs no risk whatever of seeming short-winded. One keeps wishing that other composers could be as crisp in their material and argument. Not only Thea King but the ECO (the orchestra in which she has been a distinguished principal for many years) under Barry Wordsworth bring out the warmth as well as the rhythmic drive, as in the other attractive works on the disc.

Five sketches.
☞ *** Gamut Dig. GAMCD 537 [id.]. Philip Dukes – CLARKE: *Sonata;* SHOSTAKOVICH: *Sonata.* ***

Maconchy's *Five sketches* for unaccompanied viola are improvisational in feeling, primarily exploring the instrument's range and colour. They are very well played and recorded.

String quartets Nos. 1–4.
*** Unicorn Dig. DKPCD 9080; *DKPC 9080* [id.]. Hanson Qt.

String quartets Nos. 5–8.
*** Unicorn Dig. DKPCD 9081; *DKPC 9081* [id.]. Bingham Qt.

Elizabeth Maconchy has excited the admiration of musicians far and wide. The four quartets recorded by the Hanson Quartet encompass the period 1932–43; while the second disc spans the years

1948–67, and the Bingham Quartet seem equally at home in this rewarding repertoire. All these works testify to the quality of Maconchy's mind and her inventive powers. She speaks of the quartet as 'an impassioned argument', and there is no lack of either in these finely wrought and compelling pieces. Even if there is not the distinctive personality of a Bartók or a Britten, her music is always rewarding. Though the playing may occasionally be wanting in tonal finesse, both groups play with total commitment and are well recorded.

Maderna, Bruno (1920–73)

Aura; Biogramma; Quadrivium.
*** DG 423 246-2 [id.]. N. German RSO, Sinopoli.

This record usefully brings together three of Bruno Maderna's key works, *Quadrivium*, for four orchestral groups, each with percussion, is a work designed 'to entertain and to interest, not to shock the bourgeoisie'. In 1972 came *Aura* and *Biogramma*. Excellent recording for dedicated performances.

Madetoja, Leevi (1887–1947)

Symphonies Nos. 1 in F, Op. 29; 2 in E flat, Op. 35.
☞ *** Chan. Dig. CHAN 9115 [id.]. Iceland SO, Petri Sakari.

Sibelius had only three pupils: Leevi Madetoja, Toivo Kuula and Bengt de Törne. Madetoja was the most important, and his three symphonies and the opera, *Pohjalaisia*, are well worth investigating. The *First Symphony* comes from 1914–15, at a time when his relations with Sibelius were briefly strained; no doubt the younger man was anxious to assert an independent identity and outlook. Apart from Sibelius himself, the work is indebted to various contemporaries; there is a dash of Straussand of the Russian post-nationalists, a touch of Reger and, above all, of the French. Madetoja had hoped to study with Vincent d'Indy and lived in France for some time. The *Second Symphony* is an almost exact contemporary of Sibelius's *Fifth* and is expertly fashioned and appealing. The slow movement is very Sibelian, but all the same there are distinctive accents too. Petri Sakari is a first-rate exponent of these pieces and he secures an excellent response from his Icelandic players. The Chandos recording is very naturally balanced and difficult to flaw.

Symphony No. 3 in A, Op. 55; Huvinäytelmäalkusoitto (Comedy overture), *Op. 53; Okon Fuoko: suite No. 1, Op. 58; Pohjalainen sara (The Ostrobothnians): suite, Op. 52.*
*** Chan. Dig. CHAN 9036 [id.]. Iceland SO, Petri Sakari.

Leevi Madetoja belongs to the first generation of Finnish composers after Sibelius. This new version of the *Third Symphony* is both Finnish, in its modality and melancholy, and Gallic, in its clarity of line and elegant orchestration. Its only failing, perhaps, is in its finale where invention flags a little but otherwise it is a first-rate score which ought to enjoy wide appeal. So, too, should the couplings, the delightfully high-spirited and attractive *Comedy Overture* and the imaginative suites. The Iceland orchestra give dedicated and persuasive accounts of both scores.

The Ostrobothnians (Pohjalaisa) (opera in 3 Acts).
☞ *** Finlandia 511002 (2). Hynninen, Erkkila, Lokka, Finnish Nat. Op. Ch. & O, Panula.

Madetoja's opera was first produced in Helsinki in 1924 and is an adaptation by the composer himself of a play by Artturi Järviluoma. The setting is the western Finnish plains of Ostrobothnia (which Madetoja knew well) and its central theme is the Bothnian farmer's love of personal liberty and his abhorrence of all authoritarian restraints. The nationalist tone of the original play was prompted by the growing Russification of Finland in the period leading up to and including the First World War. In the nineteenth century the peasantry had been prepared to co-operate with a centrally appointed governor or sheriff, but the brutal authority into which it had turned inspires strong hostility. Against the background of these tensions is set a simple love story. Antti, one of the farmers, is imprisoned after a stabbing incident; the first Act centres on his relationship with Maija, and the increased tension between her brother (Jussi) and the sheriff. In the second, Antti escapes during an attack by the sheriff's thugs, whose leader is soundly beaten by Jussi. In the last Act a chance remark leads the sheriff mistakenly to believe that Jussi was implicated in the escape, and the opera ends with Jussi's death at the sheriff's hands. The opera is also interspersed with humorous elements that lighten the mood and lend the work variety. Unlike Merikanto's *Juha*, composed at much the same time, Madetoja's language is not ahead of its time: it springs from much the same soil as most Scandinavian post-nationalists. However, the score makes often imaginative use of folk material, and Madetoja's sense of theatre and lyrical gift are in good evidence. Although it is unlikely to find a place on the international opera circuit, *Pohjalaisa* is a good work that well rewards attention, and this 1975 performance has the benefit of excellent teamwork from the soloists, and keen and responsive playing from the orchestra. The analogue recording is very good indeed.

Mahler, Gustav (1860–1911)

Symphonies Nos. 1–9.

(B) *** Decca Dig./Analogue 430 804-2 (10). Buchanan, Zakai, Chicago Ch. (in No. 2); Dernesch, Ellyn Children's Ch., Chicago Ch. (in No. 3); Te Kanawa (in No. 4); Harper, Popp, Augér, Minton, Watts, Kollo, Shirley-Quirk, Talvela, V. Boys' Ch., V. State Op. Ch. & Singverein (in No. 8); Chicago SO, Solti.

Symphonies Nos. 1–9; 10 (Adagio).

☞ (B) **(*) Ph. 442 050-2 (10). Concg. O, Haitink (with Ameling, Heynis & Netherlands R. Ch. in No. 2; Forrester, Netherlands R. Ch. & St Willibrord Boys' Ch. in No. 3; Ameling in No. 4; Cotrubas, Harper, Van Bork, Finnila, Dieleman, Cochran, Prey, Sotin, Amsterdam Choirs in No. 8).

Symphonies Nos. 1–10.

(M) **(*) DG 435 162-2 (13) [id.]. Hendricks, Ludwig, Wittek, M. Price, Blegen, Zeumer, Baltsa, Schmidt, Reigel, Prey, Van Dam, Brooklyn Boys' Ch., Westminster Ch., N Y Choral Artists, V. Boys' Ch., V. Singverein, V. State Op. Ch., Concg. O, NYPO, or VPO, Bernstein.

Solti's achievement in Mahler has been consistent and impressive, and this reissue is a formidable bargain that will be hard to beat. Nos. 1–4 and 9 are digital recordings, Nos. 5–8 are digitally remastered analogue. Solti draws stunning playing from the Chicago Symphony Orchestra, often pressed to great virtuosity, which adds to the electricity of the music-making; if his rather extrovert approach to Mahler means that deeper emotions are sometimes understated, there is no lack of involvement; and his fiery energy and commitment often carry shock-waves in their trail. All in all, an impressive achievement.

It is a measure of Bernstein's greatness as a Mahler interpreter and the electricity he consistently conveys in these edited live recordings that, despite obvious shortcomings, they so readily add up to more than the sum of their parts. The wilfulness of some of the readings, the heaviness of underlining, the exaggeratedly slow speeds, notably in Nos. 3 and 9, even seem to enrich the total experience. This is a personal statement by one great musician on another, and represents a monumental achievement.

Haitink's set of Mahler *Symphonies* comes at bargain price and offers characteristically refined and well-balanced Philips recording. The performances bring consistently fine playing from the Concertgebouw Orchestra, but Haitink is not by nature an extrovert Mahlerian. While he is always sensitive and thoughtful – and this works well enough in Nos. 1 (his earlier recording is included) and 4 (with Elly Ameling a freshly appealing soloist) and they have an attractive simplicity of approach – Nos. 2 and 8 lack the necessary sense of occasion, and No. 8 also needs greater overall grip and a more expansive recording. No. 5 is fresh and direct (the *Adagietto* a little cool) but No. 6 has more refinement than fire. The finest of the set are the deeply satisfying accounts of No. 3 (with fine contributions from both Maureen Forrester and the choristers) and the finely wrought and intensely convincing performance of No. 7. However, the series is capped by an outstanding performance of No. 9. Here Haitink is at his most inspirational and the last movement has a unique concentration, with its slow tempo maintained to create the greatest intensity of feeling. As usual from Philips, the original recordings are consistently enhanced by the CD transfers, and only No. 8 is technically disappointing.

Symphonies Nos. 1–4.

☞ (M) **(*) EMI CMS7 64471-2 (4). Mathis, Soffel (in *No. 2*); LPO Ch. (in *Nos. 2 & 3*); Wenkel, Southend Boys' Ch. (*in No. 3*); Lucia Popp (*in No. 4*), LPO, Klaus Tennstedt.

Tennstedt's complete Mahler cycle is offered, spread over three separate mid-priced boxes, and will be a perfect antidote for those who find Solti's view of Mahler over-intense to the point of neurosis and the Chicago sound too massively voluptuous and brightly lit. No. 1 – the first to be recorded, in Abbey Road in 1977 – sets the style of Tennstedt's approach, with textures fresh and neat, the opening evocation of spring comparatively gentle and the style of phrasing less moulded than we have come to expect. The precision and directness, however, do not preclude coaxing use of rubato in the slow movement, while the big string melody in the finale (which comes after a powerfully dramatic opening) is both spacious and passionate at its climax. The analogue recording is first class, warm and vividly coloured and transferred admirably. In the *Resurrection Symphony*, however, most Mahlerians will prefer a more tinglingly dramatic performance than this, though Tennstedt's account is consistently dedicated, and especially so in the finale, conveying Mahlerian certainties in the light of day, underplaying neurotic tensions. The digital recording is excellent. No. 3, with its arrestingly powerful introduction, is one of the finest of the cycle. Tennstedt gives an eloquent reading, spaciousness underlined, with measured tempi. With Ortrud Wenkel a fine soloist and the Southend Boys adding lusty freshness to the bell music in the fifth movement, this performance with its movingly noble finale is very impressive, again splendidly recorded, digitally. No. 4 is hardly less successful. Again the reading conveys spaciousness and strength, yet Tennstedt's agreeably light touch in the outer movements brings an innocence entirely in keeping with this most endearing of the Mahler symphonies. He makes the argument seamless in his easy transitions of speed, yet here he never deliberately adopts a coaxing, overtly charming manner, and in that he is followed most beautifully by Lucia Popp, the pure-toned soloist in the finale. The peak of the work as Tennstedt presents it lies in the long slow movement, here taken very slowly and intensely. The 1982 digital recording, made in the Kingsway Hall, is among EMI's finest, full and well balanced.

(i) *Symphony No. 1 in D* (1896 version); (ii) *Blumine*.
(M) **(*) Collins Dig. 3005-2 [id.]. (i) LSO; (ii) Philh. O; Jacek Kaspszyk.
(B) **(*) Hung. White Label HRC 077 [id.]. Hungarian State O, Iván Fischer.

Kaspszyk has the advantage of excellent, modern, digital recording with a wide dynamic range and a spacious acoustic. The LSO plays with commitment and drama and responds persuasively to the conductor's rather wayward reading, leading to a tense and exciting finale.

The bargain version on Hungaroton White Label also includes the original second movement, *Blumine*, placing it where the composer intended. Fischer's reading of the symphony is spaciously conceived, with relaxed tempi throughout, but the Hungarian State Orchestra sustain his conception with very fine playing, especially from the strings in the last movement.

Symphony No. 1 in D (Titan).
☞ *** DG Dig. 427 303-2; *427 303-4* [id.]. Concg. O, Bernstein.
(M) *** Decca 417 701-2 [id.]. LSO, Solti.
*** DG Dig. 429 228-2 [id.]. Philh. O, Sinopoli.
(M) *** Unicorn UKCD 2012. LSO, Horenstein.

Symphony No. 1 in D min.; (i) *Lieder eines fahrenden Gesellen*.
☞ (B) **(*) DG 439 446-2 [id.]. Bav. RSO, Kubelik, (i) with Dietrich Fischer-Dieskau.

Bernstein and the Concertgebouw Orchestra, recorded live, give a wonderfully alert and imaginative performance of Mahler's *First*. This is among Bernstein's finest Mahler issues, very well recorded, even making no allowance for the extra problems encountered at live concerts.

The London Symphony Orchestra under Solti play Mahler's *First* like no other orchestra. They catch the magical opening with a singular evocative quality, at least partly related to the peculiarly characteristic blend of wind timbres, and throughout there is wonderfully warm string-tone. The remastering for CD has improved definition without losing the recording's bloom.

Sinopoli's, too, is a warmly satisfying reading, passionately committed, with refined playing from the Philharmonia. The sound is rich and refined to match.

Horenstein's version has a freshness and concentration which put it in a special category among the many rival accounts. Fine recording from the end of the 1960s, though the timpani is balanced rather too close.

On DG Classikon, Kubelik gives an intensely poetic reading. He is here at his finest in Mahler and though, as in later symphonies, he is sometimes tempted to choose a tempo on the fast side, the result could hardly be more glowing. The rubato in the slow funeral march is most subtly handled. In its bargain CD reissue the quality is a little dry in the bass and the violins have lost some of their warmth, but there is no lack of body. In the *Lieder eines fahrenden Gesellen* the sound is fuller, with more atmospheric bloom. No one quite rivals Fischer-Dieskau in these songs, and this is a very considerable bonus, especially at bargain price.

Symphonies Nos. (i) *1*; (ii) *2 (Resurrection)*.
(B) *** Sony M2YK 45674. (i) Columbia SO; (ii) Cundari, Forrester, Westminster College Ch.,
    NYPO; Bruno Walter.
(M) **(*) Decca 425 005-2 (2) [id.]. (ii) Harper, Watts, London Symphony Ch.; LSO, Solti.

☞ (M) ** Sony SM2K 47573 [id.]. (i) NYPO; (ii) J. Baker, S. Armstrong, Edinburgh Festival Ch.,
LSO; Bernstein.

Bruno Walter's recordings of Mahler's *Symphonies Nos. 1* and *2* are now economically coupled
together. The recording of No. 1 sounds splendid in this new format and Walter is at his most
charismatic here, while the *Resurrection Symphony* is among the gramophone's indispensable classics.
In the first movement there is a restraint and in the second a gracefulness which provide a strong
contrast with a conductor like Solti. In remastering for CD, the glowing sound brings an evocative
haze to the score's more atmospheric moments, with the closing section thrillingly expansive.

Solti's 1964 LSO account of No. 2 remains a demonstration of the outstanding results Decca
were securing with analogue techniques at that time, although on CD the brilliance of the fortissimos
may not suit all ears. Helen Watts is wonderfully expressive, while the chorus has a rapt intensity that
is the more telling when the recording perspectives are so clearly delineated.

Bernstein's earlier (1966) account of the *First Symphony* is an excellent, red-blooded version but,
when competition is so intense in this work, it falls below a top recommendation because of the close-
up (originally CBS) sound. Similarly the *Resurrection Symphony*, recorded in Ely Cathedral in
September 1973 and concluded in George Watson's College, Edinburgh, a few months later, is far too
badly balanced for the discs to have a general recommendation. The performance is idiosyncratic but
deeply felt and has superb contributions from the two soloists, not to mention the chorus and the
orchestra. Although the CD transfers make the best of the original sound, the later, DG versions of
both symphonies are clearly superior. Both were recorded live. No. 1, with the Concertgebouw
Orchestra, is a top recommendation, one of Bernstein's very finest records. No. 2, made in the Avery
Fisher Hall, is remarkably successful technically as well as musically, if somewhat more self-indulgent
than before (DG 423 395-2).

Symphonies Nos. (i) *1 in D;* (ii) *3 in D min.*
☞ (B) ** Double Decca 443 030-2 (2) [id.]. (i) Israel PO; (ii) Maureen Forrester, LAPO Ch., LAPO;
Mehta.

Mehta in his years in Los Angeles rarely recorded a performance so authentically Viennese as this
1978 Decca account of Mahler's *Third*. The crisp spring of the first movement leads to a fruitily
Viennese view of the second and a carefree account of the third in which *Wunderhorn* overtones come
out vigorously. The singing is excellent and the sharpness of focus of the reading as a whole is
impressive, underlined by brilliant (if rather too close) recording. This means that, while the score's
gentler moments come over affectionately, the spectacularly vivid sound underlines a feeling of
aggressiveness which detracts from the warmer side of the reading. The other snag is that on this
Double Decca reissue the *Third* comes in harness with a much less attractive version of the *First*,
recorded with the Israel Philharmonic four years earlier, in which the hard-driving, frenetic quality of
the outer movements is unattractive and the warmth of the slow movement offers insufficient
compensation. The recording is very brilliant to match.

Symphonies Nos. (i) *1 in D (Titan);* (ii) *10: Adagio* (arr. Krenet, ed. Jokl).
☞ (B) **(*) Sony Dig./Analogue SBK 53259 [id.]. (i) NYPO, Mehta; (ii) Cleveland O, Szell.

Mehta's Sony/CBS digital version of the *First Symphony*, successfully recorded in the Avery Fisher
Hall in 1980, is far preferable to his Israeli Decca CD. It has no less urgency and drama, but here
Mehta's Viennese training comes out in the lilt of the Ländler second movement while his freely
expressive rubato in the third, after the dark opening, is very appealing. While the strings lack a
genuine pianissimo in the slow introduction, detail is attractively colourful and the reading overall
has undoubted spontaneity. Many will also welcome the reissue of Szell's 1958 recording of the
Adagio from the *Tenth Symphony* in Jokl's edition. Although today we are used to hearing the whole
work in Deryck Cooke's completion, the *Adagio* is a magnificent piece in its own right, the equal in
its nobility and architecture of the comparable movement in the *Ninth*. These qualities are fully
realized here, and the Cleveland orchestral playing is stylish as well as eloquent. The sound, too, is
very good.

Symphony No. 2 in C min. (Resurrection).
⊛ *** EMI CDS7 47962-8 (2) [Ang. CDCB 47962]. Augér, J. Baker, CBSO Ch., CBSO, Rattle.
☞ *** Ph. Dig 438 935-2 (2) [id.]. McNair, Van Nes, Ernst-Senff Ch., BPO, Haitink.
☞ (M) *** Chan. CHAN 6595/6 [id.]. Lott, Hamari, Latvian State Ac. Ch., Oslo Philharmonic Ch.,
Oslo PO, Jansons.
☞ (B) *** Double Decca 440 615-2 (2) [id.]. Ileana Cotrubas, Christa Ludwig, V. State Op. Ch.,
Mehta – SCHMIDT: *Symphony No. 4.* ***

(M) *** EMI CDM7 69662-2 [id.]. Schwarzkopf, Rössl-Majdan, Philh. Ch. & O, Klemperer.

☞ *** DG 439 953-2 (2) [id.]. Studer, Meyer, Arnold Schoenberg Ch., VPO, Abbado.

(B) **(*) Pickwick Dig. DPCD 910; *CIMPC 910* (2) [MCA MCAD 11011]. Valente, Forrester,
London Symphony Ch., LSO, Kaplan.

Simon Rattle's reading of Mahler's *Second* is among the very finest records he has yet made, superlative in the breadth and vividness of its sound and with a spacious reading which in its natural intensity unerringly sustains generally slow, steady speeds to underline the epic grandeur of Mahler's vision. The playing of the CBSO is inspired. The choral singing, beautifully balanced, is incandescent, while the heart-felt singing of the soloists, Arleen Augér and Dame Janet Baker, is equally distinguished and characterful.

Bernard Haitink's 1993 version with the Berlin Philharmonic also brings one of his very finest Mahler recordings, weighty and bitingly powerful. The sound of the Berlin Philharmonic in the Philharmonie is caught with a vividness and sense of presence rarely matched. Above all Haitink conveys the tensions of a live occasion, even though this was a studio performance, leading up to a glorious apotheosis in the Judgment Day finale. The soloists are outstanding, and the chorus immaculately expands from rapt, hushed singing to incandescent splendour. Outstanding in every way, this can be placed alongside Rattle's superb CBSO set.

The crisp attack at the start of the opening funeral march sets the pattern for an exceptionally refined and alert reading of the *Resurrection Symphony* from Jansons and his Oslo orchestra. Transparent textures are beautifully caught by the glowing recording – one of the last big projects of the outstanding recording producer and engineer, Jimmy Burnett. During the first four movements, this may seem a lightweight reading, but the extra resilience and point of rhythm bring out the dance element in Mahler's *Knaben Wunderhorn* inspirations rather than ruggedness or rusticity. That Jansons intends this is confirmed when, at the finale, the whole performance erupts in an overwhelming outburst for the vision of Resurrection. That transformation is intensified by the breathtakingly rapt and intense account of the song, *Urlicht*, which precedes it. At a very measured speed, with Julia Hamari the warmly dedicated soloist, Jansons secures the gentlest of pianissimos. The chorale for pianissimo trumpets at the start is far more hushed than usual, magically distanced. In the finale, power goes with precision and meticulous observance of markings, when even Mahler's surprising diminuendo on the final choral cadence is observed. With the Oslo Choir joined by singers from Jansons's native Latvia, the choral singing is heartfelt, to crown a version which finds a special place even among the many distinguished readings on a long list.

Zubin Mehta sounds a different conductor, not at all like his NYPO self, when he is drawing as sympathetic a Mahler performance as this from the Vienna Philharmonic. The refinement of the playing, recorded with vivid clarity and warmth, puts this among the finest versions of the symphony. At the very start Mehta's fast tempo brings resilience, not aggressiveness, and the *espressivo* lyricism is equally persuasive. The second movement has *grazioso* delicacy and, though the third movement begins with the sharpest possible timpani strokes, there is no hint of brutality, and the *Wunderhorn* rhythms have a delightful lilt. After that comes *Urlicht*, pianissimo in D flat after the Scherzo's final cadence in C minor, and Christa Ludwig is in superb form. The enormous span of the finale brings clarity as well as magnificence, with fine placing of soloists and chorus and glorious atmosphere in such moments as the evocation of birdsong over distant horns, as heavenly a moment as Mahler ever conceived. The CD transfer has brightened the analogue sound somewhat, but there is still plenty of ambient warmth.

Klemperer's performance – one of his most compelling on record – comes on a single CD, and the remastered sound is impressively full and clear, with the fullest sense of spectacle in the closing pages. The first movement, taken at a fairly fast tempo, is intense and earth-shaking, and though in the last movement some of Klemperer's speeds are designedly slow, he conveys supremely well the mood of transcendent heavenly happiness in the culminating passage, with chorus and soloists themselves singing like angels.

Abbado's recording with the Vienna Philharmonic was made live in 1992 in the Musikverein, offering a predictably fine, beautifully paced performance, but one that rather suffers, compared both with his Berlin version of the *Fifth*, recorded live six months later, and with Haitink's Berlin account of the *Second*, issued simultaneously. The Vienna Philharmonic's ensemble is less refined than that of the Berliners, even in the strings, and the sound is less immediate and involving. Tensions are not helped when the audience is so noisy. Yet with powerful soloists and a superb choir, it is still a strong reading.

Under Gilbert Kaplan the LSO plays with a biting precision and power to shame many an effort on record under a world-renowned conductor. Added to that, the sound is exceptionally brilliant and full, bringing home the impact of the big dramatic moments, which are what stand out in the performance. Valente and Forrester, as well as the fine chorus, sing with a will, crowning a performance that is never less than enjoyable, thanks above all to the playing and to superb sound.

Symphony No. 3 in D min.
*** Ph. Dig. 432 162-2 (2) [id.]. Jard van Nes, Tölz Boys' Ch., Ernst-Senff Ch., BPO, Haitink.
*** DG Dig. 410 715-2 (2) [id.]. J. Norman, V. State Op. Ch., V. Boys' Ch., VPO, Abbado.
(M) *** Unicorn UKCD 2006/7 [id.]. Procter, Wandsworth School Boys' Ch., Amb. S., LSO, Horenstein.

(i) *Symphony No. 3 in D min.;* (ii) *Kindertotenlieder; Des Knaben Wunderhorn: Das irdische Leben. 3 Ruckert Lieder: Ich atmet' einem linden Duft; Ich bin der Welt abhanden gekommen; Um Mitternacht.*
☞ (M) *** Sony SM2K 47576 (2) [id.]. (i) Martha Lipton, Schola Cantorum Ch., Boys' Ch. of Church of Transfiguration; (ii) Jennie Tourel; NYPO, Bernstein.

Symphony No. 3; 5 Rückert Lieder.
*** Sony M2K 44553 (2) [id.]. Janet Baker, London Symphony Ch., LSO, Tilson Thomas.

Michael Tilson Thomas inspires the orchestra to play with bite and panache in the bold, dramatic passages and to bring out the sparkle and freshness of the *Knaben Wunderhorn* ideas; but what crowns the performance is the raptness of his reading of the noble, hymn-like finale, hushed and intense, beautifully sustained. There is a formidable bonus in Dame Janet Baker's searching performances of the five *Rückert Lieder*. Excellent CBS sound, both warm and brilliant.

With the Berlin Philharmonic producing glorious sounds, recorded with richness and immediacy, Haitink conducts a powerful, spacious reading. It culminates in a glowing, concentrated account of the slow finale, which gives the whole work a visionary strength often lacking. The mystery of *Urlicht* is then beautifully caught by the mezzo soloist Jard van Nes.

With sound of spectacular range, Abbado's performance is sharply defined and deeply dedicated. The range of expression, the often wild mixture of elements in this work, is conveyed with extraordinary intensity, not least in the fine contributions of Jessye Norman and the two choirs. The recording has great presence and detail on CD.

Horenstein is at his most intensely committed. The manner is still very consistent in its simple dedication to the authority of the score and its rejection of romantic indulgence; but with an extra intensity the result has the sort of frisson-creating quality one knew from live Horenstein performances and the recording quality is both full and brilliant. Fine vocal contributions from Norma Procter, the Ambrosian Singers and the Wandsworth School Boys' Choir.

Bernstein's 1961 account of Mahler's *Third Symphony* – one of the first to be recorded in his earlier Mahler cycle for CBS – remains one of his most satisfying records. The reading, strong and passionate, has few of the stylistic exaggerations that sometimes overlay his interpretations. (His later version for DG, available only within the complete cycle – 435 162-2 – has some exaggeratedly slow speeds, though he certainly carries them by the sheer concentration of the performance.) Here his style in the slow movement is more heavily expressive than Horenstein's, the other mid-priced contender, but many will respond to his extrovert involvement. The remastered recording, made in New York's Manhattan Center, the venue of so many of the best of his early records, has added spaciousness and body in this very successful remastering for CD; it is rather less refined than the Unicorn sound but is better balanced. The vocal contributions from Martha Lipton and the two choirs contribute to the success of this venture and the generous Lieder coupling is well worth having. It was made the previous year in the St George Hotel, Brooklyn, which provides a sympathetic acoustic, and Jennie Tourel is in excellent voice. There are no couplings with the Horenstein set.

Symphony No. 4 in G.
☞ *** Sony Dig. SK 39072 [id.]. Kathleen Battle, VPO, Maazel.
(M) *** EMI Dig. CD-EMX 2139; *TC-EMX 2139.* Felicity Lott, LPO, Welser-Möst.
(M) *** DG 419 863-2 [id.]. Edith Mathis, BPO, Karajan.
☞ (M) *** EMI CDM5 65179-2 [id.]. Elly Ameling, Pittsburgh SO, Previn (with SCHUBERT: Lieder: *An die Musik;* (i) *Der Hirt auf dem Felsen; Ständchen* – Ameling, Irwin Gage or Joerg Demus; (i) with George Pieterson ***).
*** Denon Dig. C37 7952 [id.]. Helen Donath, Frankfurt RSO, Inbal.
*** Ph. Dig. 412 119-2 [id.]. Roberta Alexander, Concg. O, Haitink.
☞ (M) *(*) Sony SMK 47579 [id.]. Reri Grist, NYPO, Bernstein.

(i) *Symphony No. 4 in G;* (ii) *Lieder eines fahrenden Gesellen.*

⊛ (M) *** Sony SBK 46535 [id.]; *40-46535.* (i) Judith Raskin, Cleveland O, Szell; (ii) Frederica von
Stade, LPO, Andrew Davis.

Maazel's 1983 VPO recording now returns to the catalogue – the most completely successful issue in
his cycle, to make a strong current recommendation. The superbly refined and warmly atmospheric
recording enhances a performance that – unlike other Mahler from this conductor – reflects the
Viennese qualities of the work while still conveying structural strength, above all in the beautiful,
wide-ranging slow movement, played with great inner intensity. Kathleen Battle with her radiant
soprano brings aptly child-like overtones to the *Wunderhorn* solo in the finale, until the final stanza is
given with rapt intimacy to match Maazel's whole reading.

George Szell's 1966 record of Mahler's *Fourth* represented his partnership with the Cleveland
Orchestra at its highest peak and the digital remastering for CD brings out the very best of the
original recording. The performance remains uniquely satisfying: the music blossoms, partly because
of the marvellous attention to detail (and the immaculate ensemble), but more positively because of
the committed and radiantly luminous orchestral response to the music itself. In the finale Szell found
the ideal soprano to match his conception. An outstanding choice, generously coupled. In contrast
with most other recorded performances, Frederica von Stade insinuates a hint of youthful ardour into
her highly enjoyable account of the *Wayfaring Lad* cycle.

Welser-Möst's outer movements are fresh and beautifully shaped, with Felicity Lott a youthful-
sounding soloist, and the Laendler second movement clean-cut and crisp. It is the third movement
Adagio that crowns the performance, hushed and intense from the start, with the emotional outbursts
strongly controlled. At mid-price with excellent modern digital sound, spacious like the performance,
it makes an outstanding mid-priced recommendation, a fine alternative to Szell.

Karajan's refined and poised, yet undoubtedly affectionate account remains among the finest
versions of this lovely symphony, and Edith Mathis's sensitively composed contribution to the finale
matches the conductor's meditative feeling. With glowing sound, this makes an outstanding mid-
priced recommendation alongside Szell's renowned Cleveland CD.

Previn recorded this symphony in 1978, immediately before taking the Pittsburgh Orchestra on a
European tour, where they proved – as on this record – what an outstanding band they have become.
Previn starts the first movement more slowly than usual, underlining the marked speed-changes very
clearly, and the second movement is unusually light and gentle. But it is the spaciousness of the slow
movement, at a very measured pace, that provides total fulfilment, followed by a light and playful
account of the finale, with Ameling both sweet-toned and characterful. The recording, made in Heinz
Hall, Pittsburgh, has fine depth and range. It was a happy idea then to give Elly Ameling three
Schubert songs as encores. She sings *An die Musik* and *Ständchen* quite simply and is even more
eloquent in *Der Hirt auf dem Felsen* ('The shepherd on the rock'). Here the contribution of the
clarinettist, George Pieterson, is sensitive, if without any special magic.

There is a pastoral element in Inbal's approach all through, reflecting the *Wunderhorn* basis, and
even the spacious slow movement is easily songful rather than ethereal. Helen Donath brings boyish,
Hansel-like timbre to her solo in the finale.

Haitink's reading, too, has a fresh innocence that is most winning. Thus the lovely *Adagio*, rather
than conveying the deepest meditation, presents an ecstatic, songful musing in the long paragraphs of
the main theme, and Roberta Alexander makes a perceptive choice of soloist.

Bernstein's version, dating from 1960, brings a rather erratic reading, less controlled than his
finest Mahler performances and, although well transferred, not really competitive in quality of sound.
His later, DG, digital version (423 607-2) with the Concertgebouw Orchestra makes the earlier
performance sound heavy-handed by comparison, although not everyone will respond to his use of a
boy treble in the finale. In that respect Reri Grist's contribution is less controversial.

Symphony No. 5 in C sharp min.

☞ *** DG Dig. 437 789-2 [id.]. BPO, Abbado.

(M) *** EMI Dig. CD-EMX 2164; *TC-EMX 2164.* RLPO, Mackerras.

☞ ⊛ (M) *** EMI CDM7 64749-2 [id.]. New Philh. O, Barbirolli.

☞ (B) *** DG 439 429-2 [id.]. BPO, Karajan.

(M) *** DG Dig. 431 037-2. VPO, Bernstein.

*** EMI Dig. CDC7 49888-2 [id.]. LPO, Tennstedt.

*** DG Dig. 415 476-2 [id.]. Philh. O, Sinopoli.

*** Decca Dig. 425 438-2 [id.]. Cleveland O, Dohnányi.

*** Denon Dig. CO 1088 [id.]. Frankfurt RSO, Inbal.

☞ (M) ** Sony SMK 47580 [id.]. NYPO, Bernstein.

☞ (B) ** Pickwick PCD 1033 [id.]. Symphonica of L., Wyn Morris.
☞ (B) ** Belart 450 135-2. LAPO, Zubin Mehta.

Abbado's is an outstanding new version, recorded live in the Philharmonie, Berlin, with the dramatic tensions of a concert performance vividly captured. Abbado's view is clean-cut and taut, bringing out the high contrasts between movements, pointing rhythms not just precisely but with often-Viennese seductiveness. The great *Adagietto* is raptly done, wistful rather than openly romantic at a flowing tempo, and the *Wunderhorn* finale is at once refined and exuberant. With excellent sound, there are few versions to match this, presenting Abbado at his peak.

Mackerras in his well-paced reading sees the work as a whole, building each movement with total concentration. There is a thrilling culmination on the great brass chorale at the end, with polish allied to purposefulness. Barbirolli in his classic reading may find more of a tear-laden quality in the great *Adagietto*; but Mackerras, with fewer controversial points of interpretation and superb modern sound, makes an excellent first choice.

Barbirolli's famous 1969 version now reappears with a new catalogue number. On any count it is one of the greatest, most warmly affecting performances ever committed to disc, expansive, yet concentrated in feeling: the *Adagietto* is very moving. The recording was made in Watford Town Hall and has been remastered most successfully. A classic version, and still a fine bargain.

Karajan's 1973 recording (previously issued on two full-price CDs in harness with *Kindertoten-lieder*) now becomes instantly competitive on a single disc at bargain price. Karajan's characteristic emphasis on polish and refinement goes with sharpness of focus. His is at once one of the most beautiful and one of the most intense versions available, starting with an account of the first movement which brings more biting funeral-march rhythms than any rival. Radiant playing from the Berlin Philharmonic and full, atmospheric recording, made in the Berlin Jesus-Christus-Kirche. However, the CD transfer is very brightly lit and some softening of the brilliance on top is needed for complete comfort.

Bernstein's is also an expansive version, characteristic of his latterday Mahler style. The whole performance (recorded at live concerts) has his personal stamp on it, at times idiosyncratic but luminous and magnetically compelling, one of the best in his DG Mahler series.

Tennstedt's later, digital recording of the *Fifth* was also made live, at the Festival Hall. The emotional tension of the occasion is vividly captured. As a Mahler interpretation, it is at once more daring and more idiosyncratic than Tennstedt's earlier, studio recording, but the tension is far keener. The experience hits one at full force.

Sinopoli's version draws the sharpest distinction between the dark tragedy of the first two movements and the relaxed *Wunderhorn* feeling of the rest. Sinopoli seems intent on not overloading the big melodies with excessive emotion. This comes out the more clearly in the central movements, where relaxation is the keynote, often with a pastoral atmosphere. The celebrated *Adagietto* brings a tenderly wistful reading, songful and basically happy, not tragic. Warmly atmospheric recording, not lacking brilliance, but not always ideally clear on detail.

Dohnányi conducts the Cleveland Orchestra in an exceptionally high-powered reading, superbly played and recorded, which can still relax totally in expressive warmth. Though the hushed *Adagietto* keeps a degree of reserve, the songful freshness and purity are very sympathetic, before the thrustful and dramatic finale, dramatically done.

Inbal brings out the *Wunderhorn* element in the *Fifth* very convincingly. He may not be as exciting as some rivals, but, with superb playing and beautifully balanced sound, full and atmospheric, it is an exceptionally sympathetic reading. The second and third movements, unusually relaxed, lead to an account of the *Adagietto* that is warmly songful yet hushed and sweet, while the finale conveys the happiness of pastoral ideas leading logically to a joyful, triumphant close.

The *Adagietto* is the highlight of Bernstein's earlier performances, reissued on Sony. It brings a heady beauty so delicate that one holds one's breath. Elsewhere Bernstein's care for detail means that he never seems quite to plumb the depths of Mahler's inspiration. The first movement, for example, seems too careful, for all the virtuosity of the playing. The recording, too, made in the Avery Fisher Hall in 1963, is not entirely flattering. Fortunately he re-recorded the work digitally with the VPO for DG and this record – also at mid-price – is one of the very finest of his last series of records and includes an equally elegiac account of the *Adagietto* – the music he conducted at the funeral of President Kennedy.

Wyn Morris starts with a strikingly commanding account of the *Funeral march*, but then the second movement is more cautious with the ensemble less crisp than elsewhere. In the third movement Morris captures the Viennese lilt very winningly; he takes the *Adagietto* at a flowing tempo and the finale in a broad, expansive sweep, not quite as sharply focused as it might be. In many ways it is a sympathetic reading, but not consistent in its success. The recording is both atmospheric and brightly lit, not absolutely refined in its definition at climaxes.

Brilliant as the 1977 recording is of Mehta's Los Angeles version, and the playing too, yet it misses the natural warmth of expression that the same conductor found in his reading of No. 2 with the Vienna Philharmonic (see above). Most impressive is the virtuoso Scherzo, but in their different ways the opening Funeral march and the beautiful *Adagietto* both lack the inner quality which is essential if the faster movements are to be aptly framed. The animation of the finale is exaggerated by Mehta's very fast tempo, missing the *Wunderhorn* overtones of this most optimistic of Mahler's conclusions.

Symphonies Nos. 5; 9; 10 (Adagio).
☞ (M) *** EMI CMS7 64481-2 (3). LPO, Klaus Tennstedt.

Rather like Barbirolli, Tennstedt takes a ripe and measured view of the *Fifth* and, though his account of the lovely *Adagietto* lacks the full tenderness of Barbirolli's (starting with a slightly intrusive balance for the harp), this is an outstanding performance, on the one hand thoughtful, on the other warm and expressive. The *Ninth* brings another performance of warmth and distinction, characteristically underlining nobility rather than any neurotic tension, so that the outer movements, spaciously drawn, have architectural grandeur. The second movement is gently done, and the third, crisp and alert, lacks just a little in adrenalin. The playing is excellent both here and in the *Adagio* of the *Tenth*, and the CD transfers are exemplary. These 1978/9 analogue recordings were made at Abbey Road and the effect is full and spacious. A highly recommendable set.

Symphony No. 6 in A min.
*** DG 415 099-2 (2) [id.]. BPO, Karajan – 5 Rückert Lieder. **(*)
(M) *** Sony SBK 47654 [id.]. Cleveland O, Szell.
*** Ph. Dig. 426 257-2 [id.]. BPO, Haitink – Lieder eines fahrenden Gesellen. ***
(M) *** Unicorn UKCD 2024/5. Stockholm PO, Jascha Horenstein.
☞ (M) **(*) Decca 425 040-2 [id.]. Chicago SO, Solti.
☞ **(*) EMI Dig. CDS7 54047-2 [Ang. CDCB 54047]. CBSO, Simon Rattle.

With superlative playing from the Berlin Philharmonic, Karajan's reading of the *Sixth* is a revelation, above all in the slow movement, which emerges as one of the greatest of Mahler's slow movements, and the whole balance of the symphony is altered. Though the outer movements firmly stamp this as the darkest of the Mahler symphonies, in Karajan's reading their sharp focus makes them both compelling and refreshing. The superb DG recording, with its wide dynamics, adds enormously to the impact. Christa Ludwig's set of the *Five Rückert Songs* has been added as a bonus.

Szell's powerful outer movements are masterfully shaped and unerringly paced, with the second-movement scherzo beautifully sprung to bring out the grotesquerie. The *Andante moderato* then brings a uniquely delicate and moving account, hauntingly wistful, tender without a hint of sentimentality. The CD transfer gives a fuller, more atmospheric impression of what the orchestra sounded like in Severance Hall, Cleveland, than most of the studio recordings of the time. At budget price, squeezed on to a single disc, this is buried treasure and a fine counterpart to Szell's classic reading of Mahler's *Fourth*.

Haitink conducts a noble reading of this difficult symphony, underplaying the neurosis behind the inspiration, but, in his clean-cut concentration and avoidance of exaggeration, making the result the more moving in its degree of reticence, yet intensely committed. Jessye Norman's rich-toned account of *Lieder eines fahrenden Gesellen* makes a powerful bonus. Excellent sound, both full-blooded and refined.

In the first movement, Horenstein finds extra weight by taking a more measured tempo than most conductors. It is a sober reading that holds together with wonderful concentration, yet the slow movement brings the most persuasive rubato. The finale brings another broad, noble reading. Yet some will feel that 33 minutes is short measure for the second CD.

Solti draws stunning playing from the Chicago orchestra. The sessions were in March and April 1970, and this was the first recording he made with them after he took up his post as principal conductor; as he himself said, it represented a love-affair at first sight. The electric excitement of the playing confirms this, with brilliant, immediate but atmospheric sound. Solti's rather extrovert approach is here at its most impressive. His fast tempi may mean that he misses some of the deeper emotions, and the added brightness of the CD transfer perhaps emphasizes this, but it is still a very convincing and involving performance.

At spacious speeds Rattle directs a thoughtful, finely detailed reading of what has become a favourite symphony for him. The performance yet lacks the electric tension which usually marks his work with this orchestra, with ensemble less crisp. One admires without being involved in the way Mahler demands, even in Rattle's tender and hushed account of the slow movement, which he places second in the scheme instead of third, following Mahler's last thoughts on the work rather than what is published. It was thoughtless of EMI, therefore, to divide the two-disc set between slow movement and Scherzo, thus preventing the listener from programming whichever order he or she prefers, as can be done on rival sets. The sound is full and warm, but in its diffuseness it undermines tension further compared with the finest versions.

Symphonies Nos. 6, 7 & 8.

⊛ (M) *** EMI Dig. CMS7 64476-2 (4) [id.]. LPO, Klaus Tennstedt (with, in *No. 8*, Connell, Wiens, Lott, Schmidt, Denize, Versalle, Hynninen, Sotin, Tiffin School Boys' Ch., LPO Ch.).

There seems no reason to withhold the Rosette we awarded to Tennstedt's magnificent account of the *Eighth* in its original full-priced issue (CDS7 47625-8) from this mid-priced boxed set which includes also Nos. 6 and 7. While the *Eighth* marks a superb culmination the finest of his whole cycle, and is magnificently recorded, Nos. 6 and 7 are also a very considerable achievement, and this four-CD digital box is a real bargain. Tennstedt's reading of the *Sixth* is characteristically strong, finding more warmth than usual, even in this dark symphony. So the third-movement *Andante* is warmly beautiful, open and song-like, almost Schubertian in its sweetness, though there is never any question of Tennstedt taking a sentimental view of Mahler. His expressiveness tends towards conveying joy rather than Mahlerian neurosis, and for some that may make this too comfortable a reading. Karajan has more power and bite; his scale is bigger and bolder and the Berlin playing is more brilliant. Yet the EMI digital recording brings extra range and impact in the famous hammer-blows of fate in the finale and the result overall is most satisfying. The *Seventh* is even finer. Tennstedt is predictably spacious, and the first movement's architectural span is given the kind of expansive structural unity that one associates with Klemperer; but the concentration of the LPO playing under Tennstedt brings much greater success here than Klemperer found in his disappointing New Philharmonia version. In the central movements Tennstedt is not as imaginative as Solti, who is more mercurial in the second *Nachtmusik*, but the former is again at his most impressive in the finale, showing his directness and strength, and with vigorous support from the LSO players, who are on top form throughout the symphony. The digital recording is full, yet beautifully clear in detail. As for the *Eighth*, Tennstedt's broader, grander view makes at least as powerful an impact as Solti's Decca set; even though the playing does not always have the searing intensity of the Chicago orchestra, the singing of the LPO Choir combined with the Tiffin School Boys' Choir is unforgettable, with concentrated pianissimos matched by the expansive climaxes, where the opulent sound of the Westminster Cathedral organ adds to the feeling of weight and power.

Symphonies Nos. (i) 6 in A min.; (i) 8 in E flat (Symphony of 1000).

☞ (M) *(**) Sony SM3K 47581 [id.]. (i) NYPO; (ii) Spoorenberg, Gwyneth Jones, Annear, Reynolds, Procter, Mitchinson, Ruzdjak, McIntyre, Leeds Festival Ch., London Symphony Ch., Orpington Junior Singers, Highgate School Boys' Ch., Finchley Children's Music Group, LSO; Bernstein.

Bernstein's first CBS recording of the *Sixth* was made in the Avery Fisher Hall in 1967. Like the *Third*, it stood out from the others in the set, but the bright, close-up sound remains a drawback. Like the later, digital version with the VPO, one can argue that his tempi are inclined to be too fast (particularly in the first movement, which no longer sounds like a funeral march) but the searing intensity of the performance – like a live concert – comes over readily. The later version brings more refinement of expression, but not more concentration, and involves two full-priced CDs (DG 427 697-2). The New York recording is reissued on three mid-priced CDs but includes also the *Eighth Symphony*, recorded at Walthamstow in 1966 in the days immediately following a hazard-ridden performance at the Royal Albert Hall, in which emergency measures had to be taken to reinforce the choral strength. You would hardly know this from the records, though the hazards still left their mark. One of them was entirely to the good, the last-minute inclusion of John Mitchinson among the soloists, following his predecessor's indisposition. The Orpington Junior Singers too did valiant work in taking on more than their share of the children's choir music. In the final recorded account, the Leeds Festival Chorus is strongly stiffened by professional choristers, and the result is splendidly incisive. The unfortunate point, undermining much of the superb achievement in the performance, is the closeness of sound and the resultant lack of atmosphere in the recording quality.

Symphony No. 7 in E min.
*** DG Dig. 419 211-2 (2) [id.]. NYPO, Bernstein.
☞ (M) *** Decca 425 041-2 [id.]. Chicago SO, Solti.
*** Denon Dig. CO 1553/4 [id.]. Frankfurt RSO, Inbal.
☞ **(*) EMI Dig. CDC7 54344-2 [id.]. CBSO, Rattle.

Leonard Bernstein's *Seventh* for DG was recorded from live performances. It is a riveting performance from first to last, ending with a searingly exciting account of the finale which triumphantly flouts the idea of this as a weak conclusion. It is a performance to send you off cheering – a splendid example of Bernstein's flair in Mahler. The recording is a little harsh at times, next to the finest modern digital sound.

In interpretation, this is as successful as Solti's fine account of the *Sixth Symphony*, extrovert in display but full of dark implications. The tempi tend to be challengingly fast – at the very opening, for example, and in the Scherzo (where Solti is mercurial) and in the finale (where his energy carries shock-waves in its trail). The second *Nachtmusik* is enchantingly seductive, and throughout the orchestra plays superlatively. This is one of Solti's finest Mahler records and the recording is brilliant and full – the CD transfer increases the brightness.

Inbal's account of the *Seventh* is one of the high points of his Mahler series, masterfully paced, relaxed and lyrical where appropriate, but incorporating all the biting tensions that are missing in his version of the *Sixth*, the other dark, middle symphony. The recording is outstandingly fine in its vivid, natural balances.

Rattle, as ever, proves a sensitive and persuasive Mahlerian, in this most equivocal Mahler symphony. He made this recording live in The Maltings at Snape, disappointed with an earlier, studio version, which he did not want to have issued. Sadly, live or not, this performance does not have the biting tension and thrust that makes Rattle's recording of the *Second Symphony* so compelling, and the sound is not as full. The first movement suffers most, and the finale is the most successful. But as a single-disc version of the symphony – when most other versions take two CDs – this is still well worth considering.

Symphonies Nos. 7; 9; 10 (Adagio).
☞ (M) **(*) Sony SM3K 47585 (3) [id.]. NYPO, Bernstein.

In 1965 Bernstein drew a performance of the *Seventh* of characteristic intensity and beauty from the New York Philharmonic; his love of the music is evident in every bar. The playing is fabulous, yet there are also reservations. His warmth of phrasing in the second subject makes Bernstein's pointing sound self-conscious and tense, and in the *Night music* of the second and fourth movements, where the New York orchestra produces playing of heavenly refinement, the same feeling is present. Even in the finale, where Bernstein's thrusting dynamism holds the disparate structure together, there is the feeling that he is unable to relax into simplicity. The recording, made in the Avery Fisher Hall, is vivid and forward, not as full-bodied or refined as the later, DG version, which on two full-priced discs costs far more but is worth the extra outlay. The New York *Ninth* – a lucky symphony on records – is undoubtedly a great performance. Here Bernstein's sense of urgency has its maximum impact, though in the finale he does not quite achieve the visionary intensity of his later recording for DG with the Berlin Philharmonic. In the *Adagio* from the *Tenth*, recorded a decade after the others in 1975, Bernstein uses the old, fallible edition, but again the passionate commitment of his performance is hard to resist, with contrasts underlined between the sharpness of the *Andante* passages and the free expressiveness of the main *Adagio*. The recording is characteristically close but quite full, and for Bernstein admirers with limited budgets this box is certainly good value.

Symphony No. 8 (Symphony of 1000).
⊛ *** EMI Dig. CDS7 47625-8 (2) [Ang. CDCB 47625]. Connell, Wiens, Lott, Schmidt, Denize,
    Versalle, Hynninen, Sotin, Tiffin School Boys' Ch., LPO Ch., LPO, Tennstedt.
*** Decca 414 493-2 (2) [id.]. Harper, Popp, Augér, Minton, Watts, Kollo, Shirley-Quirk, Talvela,
    V. Boys' Ch., V. State Op. Ch. & Singverein, Chicago SO, Solti.

(i) *Symphony No. 8 (Symphony of 1000). Symphony No. 10: Adagio.*
**(*) DG 435 102-2 (2) [id.]. VPO, Bernstein, (i) with Price, Blegen, Zeumer, Schmidt, Baltsa,
    Riegel, Prey, Van Dam, V. Op. Ch., V. Boys' Ch.

Tennstedt's magnificent account of the *Eighth* makes a superb culmination. Though it does not always have the searing intensity that marks Solti's overwhelming Decca version, Tennstedt's broader, grander view makes at least as powerful an impact, and with the extra range and richness of the modern EMI recording, coping superbly with even the heaviest textures, for most listeners it will be even more satisfying. It is the urgency and dynamism of Solti which make his reading irresistible, ending in an earth-shattering account of the closing hymn. Tennstedt, both there and elsewhere, finds more light and shade. His soloists, though a strong, characterful team, are not as consistent as Solti's. The great glory of the EMI set is the singing of the London Philharmonic Choir, assisted by Tiffin School Boys' Choir. The chorus may be rather smaller than in live performance, but diction and clarity are aided, with no loss of power.

Bernstein's DG version of the *Eighth* is more compelling and better recorded (in 1975) than his earlier, CBS/Sony recording; but at full price it is hardly a primary recommendation, even though the sound is quite full and atmospheric.

Symphony No. 9 in D min.
*** DG Dig. 410 726-2 (2) [id.]. BPO, Karajan.
(M) *** EMI CDM7 63115-2 [id.]. BPO, Barbirolli.
*** DG 435 378-2 [id.]. BPO, Leonard Bernstein.
(M) *** EMI CMS7 63277-2 (2) [Ang. CDMB 63277]. New Philh. O, Klemperer – WAGNER: *Siegfried idyll.* **(*)
(M) (**(*)) EMI mono CDH7 63029-2. VPO, Bruno Walter.
☞ (B) ** DG Double 437 467-2 (2) [id.]. Chicago SO, Giulini.

Symphony No. 9; Symphony No. 10: Adagio.
*** Nuova Era Dig. 6906/7 (2). Mahler-Jugend O, or European Community Youth O, James Judd.
*** Denon Dig. CO 1566/7 [id.]. Frankfurt RSO, Inbal.

The combination of richness and concentration in the outer movements of Karajan's version of Mahler's *Ninth* makes for a reading of the deepest intensity. In the middle movements, point and humour are found, as well as refinement and polish, with a new dimension of glowing optimism in the finale, rejecting any Mahlerian death-wish. A supreme achievement. Despite the problems of live recording, the sound is bright and full, if somewhat close.

Judd conducts the brilliant young players of the Mahler-Jugend Orchestra in a deeply moving account of the *Ninth*, recorded live in Bratislava in April 1990. With recording of spectacular range and vividness, this makes one of the most appealing of all versions. The searing emotional commitment of the players comes out consistently, and no allowance whatever need be made on technical grounds for their youth. The performance of the *Adagio* from *No. 10* is not quite so distinguished, though warmly satisfying; it was recorded in August 1987 by the rival band from EEC countries, the European Community Youth Orchestra.

Barbirolli greatly impressed the Berliners with his Mahler performances live, and this recording reflects the players' warmth of response. He opted to record the slow and intense finale before the rest, and the beauty of the playing makes it a fitting culmination. The other movements are strong and alert too, and the sound remains full and atmospheric, though now more clearly defined. An unquestionable bargain.

Bernstein's version of Mahler's *Ninth*, made live in 1979, was the solitary occasion when he was permitted to conduct Karajan's own orchestra, and the response is electric, with playing not only radiant and refined but also deeply expressive in direct response to the conductor. Highly spontaneous, with measured speeds superbly sustained in a tautly concentrated reading. Bernstein conveys a comparably hushed inner quality.

Klemperer's performance was recorded in 1967 after a serious illness. His refusal to languish pays tribute to his spiritual defiance, and the physical power is underlined when the sound is full-bodied and firmly focused. The sublimity of the finale comes out the more intensely, with overt expressiveness held in check and deep emotion implied rather than made explicit.

Inbal's reading may not have the epic power or the sweeping breadth of Karajan, but his simple dedication brings a performance just as concentrated in its way, simulating the varying tensions of a live performance and leading to a wonderfully hushed culmination, not tragic as with Karajan, but in its rapt ecstasy looking forward to the close, on murmurs of 'Ewig', of *Das Lied von der Erde*. As a logical fill-up, the *Adagio* from the *Tenth Symphony* brings a similarly natural and warm reading. The sound in both works is excellent in its natural balance, a fine example of the Denon engineers' work.

Bruno Walter's 1938 version with the Vienna Philharmonic was the first recording of this symphony ever issued. The opening is not promising, with coughing very obtrusive; but then, with the atmosphere of the Musikvereinsaal caught more vividly than in most modern recordings, the magnetism of Walter becomes irresistible in music which he was the first ever to perform. Ensemble is often scrappy in the first movement, but intensity is unaffected; and, even at its flowing speed, the finale brings warmth and repose with no feeling of haste.

Giulini's version lacks the very quality one expects of him, dedication. He sets tempi that are a shade too measured for a sense of impetus to assert itself. The orchestral playing is of the highest quality, and the recording (from the late 1970s) is excellent, although the sound itself does not help in conveying hushed concentration. At two discs for the price of one, this would still seem good value, but the total playing time is only 88 minutes.

Symphony No. 10 in F sharp (Unfinished) (revised performing edition by Deryck Cooke).
*** EMI Dig. CDC7 54406-2 [id.]. Bournemouth SO, Rattle.

With digital recording of outstanding quality, Simon Rattle's vivid and compelling reading of the Cooke performing edition has one convinced more than ever that a remarkable revelation of Mahler's intentions was achieved in this painstaking reconstruction. The Bournemouth orchestra plays with dedication, marred only by the occasional lack of fullness in the strings.

Piano quartet movement.
*** Virgin/EMI Dig. VC7 90739-2 [id.]. Domus – BRAHMS: *Piano quartet No. 2.* ***

Mahler's *Piano quartet movement* comes from his student days. Ideas unfold at the right pace and in a way that shows the composer to have mastered the received tradition. Domus play with sensitivity and dedication and, though the acoustic is undeniably reverberant, the sound is far from unpleasing. Alas, this CD is currently withdrawn.

LIEDER AND SONG-CYCLES

7 frühe Lieder (with piano); *11 frühe Lieder* (arr. Berio); *Lieder eines fahrenden Gesellen.*
☞ *** Teldec/Warner Dig. 9031 74002-2. Thomas Hampson, David Lutz or Philh. O, Berio.

Thomas Hampson is in magnificent voice for his unusual collection of Mahler songs. He does the first seven of the early songs and the *Wayfaring Lad* songs with piano accompaniment by David Lutz. He then turns to the remaining early songs in the distinctive orchestral arrangements made by Luciano Berio. Though Berio follows Mahlerian practice in many of his orchestral colourings, notably in the woodwind, his instrumentation overall is far thicker and weightier, making it harder for the voice. Though these arrangements are far less 'authentic' than those made of a group of the same songs by Colin and David Matthews (available on Unicorn Kanchana), they have their fascination when sung as warmly and sensitively as by Thomas Hampson. First-rate sound.

7 early Lieder: Ablosung im Sommer; Fruhlingsmorgen; Hans und Grete; Nicht Wiedersehen!; Selbstgefühl; Starke Einbildungskraft; Zu Strassburg Auf der Schanz' (orch. D. and C. Matthews).
☞ *** Unicorn Dig. DKPCD 9120 [id.]. Jill Gomez, Bournemouth Sinf., Carewe – MATTHEWS: *Cantiga, Introit; September music.* ***

Some years before they took on the task of helping Deryck Cooke with the performing edition of Mahler's *Tenth Symphony*, David and Colin Matthews made this orchestration of Mahler's so-called 'Youth' songs. As is shown in this sensitive performance from Jill Gomez and the Bournemouth Sinfonietta under John Carewe, their feeling for the Mahler sound is unerring, making these a most rewarding addition to the tally of regular Mahler song-cycles with orchestra. It proves a very apt coupling for the warmly sympathetic works of David Matthews on the disc, notably the dramatic scena, *Cantiga*, powerful and immediately attractive.

Kindertotenlieder.
☞ (M) (**) Decca mono 425 995-2 [id.]. Kathleen Ferrier, Concg. O, Klemperer – BRAHMS: *Liebeslieder Waltzes.* (***)
Kindertotenlieder; Des Knaben Wunderhorn: 3 songs; Leider eines fahrenden Gesellen; 4 Rückert Lieder.
☞ **(*) Decca Dig. 425 790-2 [id.]. Brigitte Fassbaender, Deutsches SO, Berlin, Chailly.

(i) *Kindertotenlieder;* (ii) *Lieder eines fahrenden Gesellen.*
☞ (M) *(*) Decca 436 200-2 [id.]. Marilyn Horne; (i) RPO, Henry Lewis; (ii) LAPO, Mehta – WAGNER: *Wesendonck Lieder.* *(*)

(i) *Kindertotenlieder; Lieder eines fahrenden Gesellen;* (ii) *5 Rückert Lieder.*
*** EMI CDC7 47793-2 [id.]. Dame Janet Baker, (i) Hallé O; (ii) New Philh. O, Barbirolli.

Dame Janet Baker's collaboration with Barbirolli represents the affectionate approach to Mahler at its warmest, intensely beautiful, full of breathtaking moments. The spontaneous feeling of soloist and conductor for this music comes over as in a live performance and brings out the tenderness to a unique degree. An indispensable CD.

Fassbaender gives fearless, vividly characterized performances of Mahler's three shorter orchestral song-cycles, adding for good measure three songs from *Des Knaben Wunderhorn*, including *Urlicht*, usually heard as part of the *Symphony No. 2*. In that last, her voice is not quite as even as usual, and the orchestra in *Kindertotenlieder* is slacker than elsewhere; but otherwise this is an issue to recommend to anyone who fancies these songs with a woman's voice, though Dame Janet Baker's vintage performances with Barbirolli are more beautiful, with gentleness part of the mixture.

The Ferrier version with Klemperer is a live recording taken from a broadcast in July 1951, some two years after her EMI recording with Bruno Walter. Though the voice is caught vividly and the richness of her interpretation has, if anything, intensified, the surface-hiss is daunting. Unusually coupled with the Brahms in which Ferrier's role is only incidental.

In the *Kindertotenlieder* Marilyn Horne's voice has a statuesque quality that does not suit Mahler's intensely personal inspiration. There is much to admire and the voice itself is beautiful, but tenderness is missing. In the *Lieder eines fahrenden Gesellen* the vocal production is uneven; this is exaggerated by the close recording, and that balance undermines the refinement in the orchestral accompaniment. The CD transfer is firm, full and clear.

(i) *Kindertotenlieder;* (ii) *Lieder eines fahrenden Gesellen;* (i) *4 Rückert Lieder (Um Mitternacht; Ich atmet' einen linden Duft; Blicke mir nicht in die Lieder; Ich bin der Welt).*
*** DG 415 191-2 [id.]. Dietrich Fischer-Dieskau, (i) BPO, Boehm; (ii) Bav. RSO, Kubelik.

Only four of the *Rückert Lieder* are included (*Liebst du um Schönheit* being essentially a woman's song), but otherwise this conveniently gathers Mahler's shorter and most popular orchestral cycles in performances that bring out the fullest range of expression in Fischer-Dieskau at a period when his voice was at its peak.

Das klagende Lied: complete *(Part 1, Waldmärchen; Part 2: Der Spielmann; Part 3, Hochzeitsstücke).*
*** EMI Dig. CDC 747089-2 [id.]. Döse, Hodgson, Tear, Rea, CBSO and Ch., Rattle.
*** Decca Dig. 425 719-2 [id.]. Susan Dunn, Markus Baur, Fassbaender, Hollweg, Schmidt, Düsseldorf State Musikverein, Berlin RSO, Chailly.
(M) **(*) Sony SK 45841 [id.]. Hoffman, Söderström, Haefliger, Nienstedt, Lear, Burrows, LSO, Boulez.

Rattle brings out the astonishing originality but adds urgency, colour and warmth, not to mention deeper and more meditative qualities. So the final section, *Wedding Piece*, after starting with superb swagger in the celebration music, is gripping in the minstrel's sinister narration and ends in the darkest concentration on a mezzo-soprano solo, beautifully sung by Alfreda Hodgson. The ensemble of the CBSO has a little roughness, but the bite and commitment could not be more convincing.

The strength of the Chailly version lies with the splendid singing of the Düsseldorf Choir and the demonstration-worthy Decca recording, full of presence. While not quite upstaging Simon Rattle in revealing the music's marvellously imaginative detail, Chailly pulls one special trick out of the hat in *Waldmärchen* by using a boy alto (Markus Baur) to represent the voice from the grave, a tellingly sepulchral effect, and again after the off-stage band sequence.

Boulez is a distinctive Mahlerian. His clear ear concentrates on precision of texture, but the atmospheric ambience adds warmth despite the forward balance, which also ensures very little difference in sound between the two recordings. Certainly the chill at the heart of this gruesome story of the days of chivalry and knights in armour is the more sharply conveyed. *Waldmärchen* is less effective than the rest. Good singing from the chorus, less good from the soloists.

(i) *Das klagende Lied* (published version); (ii) *Lieder und Gesänge aus der Jugendzeit.*
☞ (B) **(*) Pickwick PCD 1053 [id.]. (i) Anna Reynolds, Teresa Zylis-Gara, Andor Kaposy, Amb. S., New Philh. O, Wyn Morris; (ii) Reynolds, Geoffrey Parsons.

The reissue of Wyn Morris's 1967 Delysé recording, carefully remastered at bargain price on Pickwick, is most welcome. These are committed, idiomatic performances with fine solo singing, and the recording is as atmospheric as ever, with the off-stage band at the wedding celebrations vividly caught and the sound generally full and atmospheric. Anna Reynolds is the excellent mezzo soloist and it is she who provides the coupling. Though in the *Jugendzeit Lieder* she does not characterize each song as sharply as some more famous Lieder singers, they emerge tastefully in an entirely fresh and musical way. Geoffrey Parsons is the sensitive accompanist, though the recording of the piano is less vivid than that of the voice. The snag of this reissue is that the two regularly published sections of *Das klagende Lied* (39 minutes) are given without any internal dividing bands.

Des Knaben Wunderhorn.
*** EMI CDC7 47277-2. Schwarzkopf, Fischer-Dieskau, LSO, Szell.
☞ (M) **(*) Sony SMK 47590-2 [id.]. Christa Ludwig, Walter Berry, NYPO, Bernstein.

Szell's warmth and tenderness, coupled with the most refined control of pianissimo in the orchestra matches the tonal subtleties of his two incomparable soloists. Wit and dramatic point as well as delicacy mark these widely contrasted songs, and the device of using two voices in some of them is apt and effective.

It is arguable that orchestral Lieder need a more robust approach than comparable Lieder with piano, and there is a strong case to be made for Bernstein's rich, robust account of these endlessly fascinating songs. Full-blooded sound from 1969.

(i) *Des Knaben Wunderhorn;* (ii) *Lieder eines fahrenden Gesellen.*
☞ (B) **(*) Pickwick PCD 1035 [id.]. (i) Dame Janet Baker, Sir Geraint Evans, LPO; (ii) Roland
   Hermann, Symphonica of L.; (i; ii) Wyn Morris.

Des Knaben Wunderhorn; Lieder eines fahrenden Gesellen; 11 Lieder Aus der Jugendzeit; 4 Rückert Lieder.
(M) **(*) Sony SM2K 47170 (2) [id.]. Christa Ludwig, Walter Berry, Dietrich Fischer-Dieskau,
   Leonard Bernstein (piano).

Dame Janet and Sir Geraint recorded Mahler's cycle in 1966 for Delysé, long before they both received the royal accolade. This was also Wyn Morris's first major essay in the recording studio; though he secures crisp playing from the LPO, the orchestral phrasing could ideally show more affection and be less metrical in charming songs that need some coaxing. Dame Janet in particular turns her phrases with characteristic imagination, and her flexibility is not always matched by the orchestra. Baker could hardly be more ideally cast, but Sir Geraint is more variable. He points the humour of the song about the cuckoo and the donkey with typical charm, but sometimes the voice does not sound perfectly focused. That may be attributed partly to the recording which, although vivid and warmly atmospheric, is not always cleanly focused, as at the very opening with its resonance in the bass. However, it is good to have this recording available again at bargain price. Roland Hermann's performance of the *Lieder eines fahrenden Gesellen* is fresh, committed and intelligent, though his baritone is not always flattered by the otherwise atmospheric stereo. At times expressiveness is underlined too heavily, but better this than a lack of warmth, and there is plenty of drama. The orchestra is well caught, full and spacious. Where the *Wunderhorn* songs with Christa Ludwig and Walter Berry keep constantly in touch with the folk-inspiration behind them, the other groups with Fischer-Dieskau bring an even subtler and more sophisticated partnership between pianist and singer. It is true that, even in the *Wunderhorn* songs, Bernstein allows himself the most extreme rubato and tenuto on occasion, and with the Fischer-Dieskau performances both singer and pianist adopt a far more extreme expressive style all through.

Des Knaben Wunderhorn (excerpts): *Verlor'ne Müh; Rheinlegendchen; Wo die schönen Trompeten blasen; Lob des hohen Verstandes; Aus! Aus!. Lieder: Erinnerung; Frühlingsmorgen; Ich ging mit Lust durch einen grünen Wald; Phantasie aus Don Juan; Serenade aus Don Juan.*
*** DG Dig. 423 666-2 [id.]. Anne Sofie von Otter, Rolf Gothoni – WOLF: *Lieder.* ***

The Mahler half of Anne Sofie von Otter's brilliant recital is just as assured and strongly characterized as the formidable group of Wolf songs. Rolf Gothoni's sparkling and pointed playing makes this a genuinely imaginative partnership, bringing out the gravity as well as the humour of the writing. Excellent, well-balanced recording.

Lieder eines fahrenden Gesellen.
*** Ph. Dig. 426 257-2 [id.]. Jessye Norman, BPO, Haitink – Symphony No. 6. ***

Jessye Norman is a joy to the ear, with Haitink, in his accompaniment for the jaunty second song, providing the necessary lightness. The stormy darkness of the third song fits the soloist more naturally, always a magnetic singer. It makes a valuable extra for Haitink's deeply satisfying version of the *Sixth Symphony.*

Lieder eines fahrenden Gesellen; Lieder und Gesänge (aus der Jugendzeit); Im Lenz; Winterlied.
⊛ *** Hyp. CDA 66100 [id.]. Dame Janet Baker, Geoffrey Parsons.

Dame Janet presents a superb collection of Mahler's early songs with piano, including two written in 1880 and never recorded before, *Im Lenz* and *Winterlied*; also the piano version of the *Wayfaring Lad* songs in a text prepared by Colin Matthews from Mahler's final thoughts, as contained in the orchestral version. The performances are radiant and deeply understanding from both singer and pianist, well caught in atmospheric recording. A heart-warming record.

Das Lied von der Erde.
⊛ (M) *** Ph. 432 279-2 [id.]. Dame Janet Baker, James King, Concg. O, Haitink.
(M) *** DG 419 058-2 [id.]. Ludwig, Kollo, BPO, Karajan.
*** DG Dig. 413 459-2 [id.]. Fassbaender, Araiza, BPO, Giulini.
☞ ** Decca Dig. 440 314-2 [id.]. Marjana Lipovšek, Thomas Moser, Concg. O, Solti.
(**) Decca mono 414 194-2. Ferrier, Patzak, VPO, Walter.
☞ (M) *(*) Sony SMK 47589-2 [id.]. Christa Ludwig, René Kollo, Israel PO, Bernstein.

The combination of this most deeply committed of Mahler singers with Haitink, the most thoughtfully dedicated of Mahler conductors, produces radiantly beautiful and moving results, helped by refined and atmospheric recording. The concentration over the long final *Abschied* has never been surpassed on record. James King cannot match his solo partner, often failing to create fantasy, but his singing is intelligent and sympathetic.

Karajan presents *Das Lied* as the most seductive sequence of atmospheric songs, combining characteristic refinement and polish with a deep sense of melancholy. He is helped enormously by the soloists, both of whom have recorded this work several times, but never more richly than here. The sound on CD is admirably vivid and does not lack a basic warmth.

Giulini conducts a characteristically restrained reading. With Araiza a heady-toned tenor rather than a powerful one, the line *Dunkel ist das Leben* in the first song becomes unusually tender and gentle, with rapture and wistfulness keynote emotions. In the second song, Fassbaender gives lightness and poignancy rather than dark tragedy to the line *Mein Herz ist müde*; and even the final *Abschied* is rapt rather than tragic, following the text of the poem; and the playing of the Berlin Philharmonic could hardly be more beautiful.

As in his earlier recording, made in Chicago 20 years earlier, Solti in his Concertgebouw version of 1992 takes a clean-cut, dry-eyed view of Mahler's great symphony/song-cycle. Beautifully played in a detached way, the performance lacks mystery even in the long final song, *Abschied*, with Marjana Lipovšek characterful but not as pure-toned as she can be. Thomas Moser too is a disappointing soloist, powerful but often rough in tone and occasionally strained. Good, atmospheric sound.

It is a joy to have the voice of Kathleen Ferrier so vividly caught on CD – not to mention that of the characterful Patzak – in Bruno Walter's classic Vienna recording for Decca. The sad thing is that the violin tone in high loud passages has acquired a very unattractive edge, not at all like the Vienna violins, and this makes for uncomfortable listening.

Bernstein, Ludwig and Kollo had all earlier appeared in other versions of *Das Lied*, but the conjunction of the three in Israel in 1972 did not produce extra illumination, rather the reverse. This recording, idiosyncratically balanced and put together from a series of live performances, hardly rivals the best available.

(i) *Das Lied von der Erde;* (ii) *5 Rückert Lieder.*
☞ (B) *(*) Sony SBK 53518 [id.]. (i) Lili Chookasian, Richard Lewis, Phd. O, Ormandy; (ii) Frederica von Stade, LPO, Andrew Davis.

This CBS/Sony version of *Das Lied* from the late 1960s is disappointing. Chookasian has a marvellously rich tone but she does not begin to bring the full meaning of the words out, while Richard Lewis is not in his best voice, with disagreeably gritty tone, though the close-up recording does him less than justice. Von Stade too, normally so assured and stylish, has moments of ungainliness in the taxing *Rückert Lieder*, although the compensating factor is the hint of youthful ardour which contrasts with most other recorded performances. Again the close recording-balance robs the music-making (here in the orchestral accompaniment) of a degree of refinement.

5 Rückert Lieder.
(*) DG 415 099-2 (2) [id.]. Christa Ludwig, BPO, Karajan – *Symphony No. 6.* *

Christa Ludwig's *Rückert Lieder* are fine, positive performances, but it is the distinction and refinement of the orchestral playing and conducting that make this reissue valuable.

Rückert Lieder: Ich atmet' einen Linden Duft; Ich bin der Welt; Um Mitternacht.
(***) Decca 421 299-2. Kathleen Ferrier, VPO, Bruno Walter – BRAHMS: *Alto rhapsody* etc. (***)

Ferrier's recording of three of Mahler's *Rückert Lieder*, heartfelt and monumental, are not as delicately expressive as many since, but magnetically intense. While the extra clarity of CD is not kind to the orchestral strings, the voice emerges realistically with good presence.

Malipiero, Gianfrancesco (1882–1973)

Symphonies No. 3 (delle campane); No. 4 (In memoriam); Sinfonia del mare.
☞ *(*) Marco Polo Dig. 8.223602 [id.]. Moscow SO, de Almeida.

The Malipiero *Symphonies* are worth exploring and deserve more convincing advocacy. It sounds as if Antonio de Almeida had all too little time for rehearsal; the performances are well prepared but the players do not sound as if they have lived with the music or really believe in it. Decent recording and playing, but not quite persuasive enough for those who have yet to see the light.

String quartets Nos. 1–8.
*** ASV Dig. CDDCD 457 (2) [id.]. Orpheus Qt.

Malipiero's eight *String quartets* are all modest in length: the longest being the *First* (*Rispetti e strambotti*) (1920), which runs to twenty minutes, while the *Eighth* (1963–4), written when the composer was in his early eighties, takes only twelve. None fall below a certain level of distinction, all are beautifully crafted and there is much freshness and fertility of invention. They are all played with expertise and conviction by the Orpheus Quartet, and very well recorded indeed.

Manzoni, Giacomo (born 1932)

Masse: Omaggio a Edgard Varèse.
*** DG Dig. 423 307-2 [id.]. Pollini, BPO, Sinopoli – SCHOENBERG: *Chamber symphony No. 1.* ***

Masse has nothing to do with church liturgy but refers to measures or quantities, and follows up a science-based mode of thought which proves surprisingly dramatic and colourful. Only the piano solo has much in the way of melodic interest, and Pollini exploits it all he can, not least in the elaborate cadenza-like passages. Sinopoli too reveals the feeling for texture and dynamic which so often makes his conducting so memorable.

Marais, Marin (1656–1728)

L'Arabesque; Le Badinage; Le Labyrinthe; Prélude in G; La Rêveuse; Sonnerie de Sainte Geneviève du Mont de Paris; Suite in G; Tombeau pour Monsieur de Sainte-Colombe.
☞ (BB) *** Naxos Dig. 8.550750 [id.]. Spectre de la Rose – SAINTE-COLOMBE: *Le Retour* etc. ***

Naxos have stepped in enterprisingly and chosen a programme that is not only most attractive in its own right, but which also includes the key items used in the fascinating conjectural film about the relationship between Marin Marais and his reclusive mentor, Sainte-Columbe (*Tous les matins du monde*). Spectre de la Rose consists of a first-rate group of young players using original instruments (not that a viola da gamba could be anything else), led by Alison Crum, who plays in a dignified but austere style which at first seems cool but which is very effective in this repertoire. *Le Badinage* is perhaps a little stiff and unsmiling, but the key item, Marais' eloquent lament for his teacher, *Tombeau pour Monsieur de Sainte-Colombe*, is restrained and touching. Good, bright, forward recording, vividly declaiming the plangent viola da gamba timbre. But be careful not to play this record at too high a volume setting.

La Gamme en forme de petit opéra; Sonata à la marésienne.
(B) *** HM HMA 901105; *HMA 431105* [id.]. L. Baroque.

La Gamme is a string of short character-pieces for violin, viola de gamba and harpsichord that takes its inspiration from the ascending and descending figures of the scale. Although it is *en forme de petit opéra*, its layout is totally instrumental and the varied pieces and dramatic shifts of character doubtless inspire the title. The *Sonata à la marésienne* also has variety and character. The London Baroque is an excellent group, and they are well recorded too.

6 Recorder suites (in B flat; C; E min.; F; 1–2 in G min.).
☞ (M) **(*) Teldec/Warner 9031 77617-2 (2) [id.]. Quadro Hotteterre.

With the advent of the recent French biographical film, Marin Marais is likely to emerge from relative obscurity into the realm of public consciousness. He is a sophisticated and subtle composer whose music deserves more than just specialist attention. He was a great master of the gamba, in which his innate melancholy found a natural outlet. These recorder suites date from 1692, when Marais was a famous musician and public figure, but was not yet known as a composer. They form a collection of *Pièces en trio pour le flute, violon et dessus de viole avec b.c.* (basso continuo) and are

played throughout by two recorders, cello and harpsichord. The performances are of the highest
sensitivity and virtuosity. The music is often doleful in its expressive feeling, but it would be idle to
pretend that it always sustains attention. Unlike some of Marais's gamba writing, these suites are of
limited interest and belong among that repertoire which is more rewarding to play than to hear.
Aficionados can be assured of the excellence of both performance and recording, although the close
balance limits the dynamic range.

Suites for viols: in D min.; in G; Tombeau de Mr Meliton.
*** HM/BMG Dig. RD 77146 [77146-2-RC]. Kenneth Slowik, Jaap ter Linden, Konrad Junghänel.

The viol music of Marin Marais is, like certain white wines, an acquired taste; however, once
acquired, it is quite addictive. The present artists, Kenneth Slowik and Jaap ter Linden, alternate
between bass viol and gamba in the two suites, with Konrad Junghänel on theorbo, and they give
vibrant, spirited performances that are most persuasive. The recording needs to be played at a lower
than usual level-setting if a realistic result is required.

Marcello, Alessandro (1669–1747)

6 Oboe concertos (La Cetra).
(M) *** DG 427 137-2 [id.]. Heinz Holliger, Louise Pellerin, Camerata Bern, Füri.

The six concertos of *La Cetra* reveal a pleasing mixture of originality and convention; often one is
surprised by a genuinely alive and refreshing individuality. These performances are vital and keen,
full of style and character, and the recording is faithful and well projected.

Oboe concerto in D min.
☞(BB) **(*) Naxos Dig. 8.550556 [id.]. József Kiss, Ferenc Erkel CO – C. P. E. BACH: *Concertos.*
   **(*)
☞(BB) *(*) Virgin/EMI Dig. VJ7 59686-2 [id.]. Ray Still, Ac. of L., Stamp – BACH: *Oboe d'amore
   concerto* etc.; R. STRAUSS: *Oboe concerto.* *(*)

This enjoyable concerto, once attributed (in a different key) to Benedetto Marcello, is given a good
performance here by József Kiss and is very well recorded. One might have preferred more dynamic
contrast from the soloist, but his timbre is right for baroque music and he plays with plenty of spirit.
This disc is well worth its modest cost for the C. P. E. Bach couplings.
    A stylish if slightly cool performance on Virgin, generously coupled and well recorded. But this is
in no way a distinctive issue.

Marenzio, Luca (1553–99)

*Madrigals: Come inanti de l'alba; Crudele acerba; Del cibo onde il signor; Giunto a la tomba; Rimanti
inpace; Sola angioletta* (sestina); *Strider faceva; Tirsi morir volea; Venuta era; Vezzosi augelli.*
(B) *** HMA 901065 [id.]. Concerto Vocale, René Jacobs.

Luca Marenzio enjoyed an enormous reputation during his lifetime, particularly in England, and this
record gives an altogether admirable picture of his breadth and range. There are poignant and
expressive pieces such as *Crudele, acerba*, from the last year of his life, which is harmonically daring,
and lighter pastoral madrigals such as *Strider faceva* and the more ambitious sestina, *Sola angioletta*,
which this excellent group of singers, occasionally supported by theorbo and lute, project to striking
effect. Fine singing and recording and a modest price serve to make this a most desirable issue.

Marsh, John (1752–1828)

Symphonies Nos. 1 in B flat (ed. Robins); *3 in D; 4 in F; 6 in D; A Conversation Symphony for 2
Orchestras* (all ed. Graham-Jones).
** Olympia Dig. OCD 400 [id.]. Chichester Concert, Ian Graham-Jones.

John Marsh was essentially a musical amateur (in the best sense). In his way he was innovative:
because of the continuing influence of Handel the symphony format was not fashionable in England
at that time. For the most part they each consist of three short movements and, while the tunes
sometimes have a whiff of Handel, there is a strong element of the English village green. The
Conversation Symphony does not divide into two separate ensembles but makes contrasts between

higher and lower instrumental groupings. Five of his works are presented here with enthusiasm by an aptly sized authentic Baroque group; they play well and are quite effectively recorded.

Martin, Frank (1890–1974)

(i) *Ballade for flute, piano and strings. Concerto for seven wind instruments, timpani, percussion and strings; Petite symphonie concertante.*
☞ *(*) Koch Schwann Dig. 3-1083-2 [id.]. (i) Elizabeth Brown; Philh. Virtuosi, Richard Kapp.

This New York group gives expert performances of all three pieces, though neither the acoustic nor the engineering shows them in as flattering a light as their rivals on DG and Erato. Moreover the short playing time (48 minutes 49 seconds – not 66 minutes 48 seconds, as inadvertently shown on the label) hardly enhances the Koch issue's competitiveness. The playing is vital and sensitive but the good is the enemy of the better, and this *Concerto for seven wind instruments* is no match for the superb DG disc from the Chamber Orchestra of Europe under Thierry Fischer, nor is the *Petite symphonie concertante* superior to existing recommendations. There is not enough air round the individual instruments and the strings are a little wanting in bloom.

(i) *Ballade for piano and orchestra;* (ii) *Ballade for trombone and orchestra;* (iii) *Concerto for harpsichord and small orchestra.*
**(*) Jecklin-Disco JD 529-2. (i) Sebastian Benda; (ii) Armin Rosin; (iii) Christiane Jaccottet; Lausanne CO, composer.

The *Harpsichord concerto* is a highly imaginative and inventive piece, arguably the most successful example of the genre since the Falla *Concerto*. The orchestral texture has a pale, transparent delicacy that is quite haunting, and the atmosphere is powerful – as, indeed, it is in the fine *Ballade*. Christiane Jaccottet is a committed advocate and her performance has the authority of the composer's direction.

(i) *Cello concerto. The Four elements.*
(M) *** Preludio PRL 2147 [id.]. (i) Jean Decroos, Concg. O, Haitink.

Jean Decroos, from the first desk of the Concertgebouw, gives an impressive account of the *Cello concerto* and Haitink secures excellent playing from the Concertgebouw Orchestra. *The Four elements* is another Martin rarity, rich in invention and imaginative resource: its neglect is little short of scandalous. Both performances were recorded at public concerts in 1965 and 1970 respectively, but audience noise is minimal and the quality first rate.

(i) *Piano concerto No. 2;* (ii) *Violin concerto.*
** Jecklin Disco JD 632-2 [id.]. (i) Badura-Skoda; (ii) Schneiderhan; Luxembourg RSO, composer.

The *Violin concerto* is a score of great subtlety and beauty. Don't be put off by the less than lustrous sound, for this is a masterpiece and has the benefit of having Martin himself at the helm. The *Second Piano concerto* is not as lyrical as the *Violin concerto* but is still worth investigation for its thoughtful slow movement.

Concerto for seven wind instruments, percussion and strings; (i) *Erasmi monumentum* (for organ and orchestra); *Etudes for strings.*
☞ *** Chan. Dig. CHAN 9283 [id.]. (i) Leslie Pearson; LPO, Matthias Bamert.

The main interest of the Chandos issue is *Erasmi monumentum*, for organ and orchestra, written in the late 1960s at the behest of the Rotterdam Arts Foundation. This is its first recording as far as the UK is concerned. It is a substantial piece of some 25 minutes. The first movement, *Homo pro se* ('The independent man'), alludes to the name given to Erasmus by his contemporaries; the second is *Stulticiae Laus* ('In praise of folly'), and the third is *Querela Pacis* ('A plea for peace'). The outer movements are pensive and atmospheric; the middle movement is less convincing. Matthias Bamert's account of the *Concerto for seven wind instruments* is very assured, more relaxed and less keenly animated than either the highly imaginative Thierry Fischer on DG or Armin Jordan on Erato, but thoroughly persuasive all the same. He makes rather heavy weather of the *Etudes*, which are not as strongly characterized as Fischer's; neither the concerto nor the *Etudes* displaces the DG, which fully deserves its Rosette.

Concerto for 7 wind instruments, percussion and strings; Etudes; (i) *Polyptique for violin and two string orchestras.*
⊛ *** DG Dig. 435 383-2 [id.]. (i) Marieke Blankestijn; COE, Thierry Fischer.

This is a remarkable record and quite in a class of its own. The *Polyptique* is a work of serene profundity, inspired by a polyptych, a set of very small panels depicting scenes from the Passion which Martin saw in Siena. It is a work of great power and is played with rapt concentration and dedication by Marieke Blankestijn and the European Chamber Orchestra under Thierry Fischer. In the *Concerto for seven wind instruments, percussion and strings* there is a lightness of accent and refinement of tone and dynamics that are quite exceptional, and the *Etudes pour cordes* similarly outclasses its predecessors. The tone is pure and there is the widest possible range of timbre, colour and dynamics without ever the slightest hint of self-consciousness. Music of great quality, playing of great artistry, and recording to match.

Concerto for 7 wind instruments, timpani, percussion and strings; Etudes for strings; (i) *Petite symphonie concertante for harp, harpsichord, piano and double string orchestra.*
(M) (***) Decca mono 430 003-2. (i) Jamet, Vauchet-Clerc, Rossiaud, SRO, Ansermet.

Concerto for 7 wind instruments, timpani, percussion and strings; (i) *Petite symphonie concertante for harp, harpsichord, piano and double string orchestra;* (ii) *6 Monologues from Everyman.*
*** Erato Dig. 2292 45694-2. (i) Guibentif, Jaccottet, Ruttimann; (ii) Gilles Cachemaille; OSR, Armin Jordan.

This well-recorded Erato disc serves as an admirable introduction to Martin's music, and newcomers to this composer should almost certainly start here, for the *Petite symphonie concertante* makes an ideal entry point into Martin's world. Armin Jordan's account of the *Concerto for seven wind instruments* is very good indeed, and his recording of the *Petite symphonie concertante* must now be a first recommendation; it is excellently played and recorded. Gilles Cachemaille proves an impressive and thoughtful exponent of the powerful *Everyman* monologues.

The Decca mono CD contains the pioneering record of the *Petite symphonie concertante*. This authoritative performance has a concentration and an atmosphere that have rarely been matched since. The 1951 recording does not sound as spectacular as it seemed at the time, and the string-tone shows its age. No apologies need be made for the remarkably vivid recording of the *Etudes for strings* and the masterly *Concerto for 7 wind instruments*.

(i) *3 Danses;* (ii) *Pièce breve;* (iii) *Petite complainte.*
☞ *** Ph. Dig. 434 105-2 [id.]. Heinz Holliger, with (i) Ursula Holliger, ASMF, Marriner; (ii) Ursula Holliger, Nicolet; (iii) Constable – HONEGGER: *Concerto da camera*, etc.; MARTINU: *Oboe concerto.* ***

The *Trois danses* were composed for Heinz and Ursula Holliger, man and wife, oboe and harp, respectively, together with string quintet and orchestra. It is a work of great refinement and imaginative resource and this is its first recording. It is unlikely to be bettered either artistically or technically.

Piano quintet; String quintet (Pavane couleur de temps); String trio; Trio sur des mélodies populaires irlandaises.
*** Jecklin-Disco JD 646-2 [id.]. Zurich Ch. Ens.

The *Piano quintet* has an eloquence and an elegiac dignity that are impressive; the short string quintet, subtitled *Pavane couleur de temps* (the title is taken from a fairy story in which a young girl wishes for 'a dress the colour of time'), is a beautiful piece. The *Piano trio on Irish popular themes* is full of imagination and rhythmic life. The *String trio* is a tougher nut to crack; its harmonies are more astringent and its form more concentrated. To summarize: altogether a most satisfying disc, offering very good performances and recordings.

Trio sur des mélodies populaires irlandaises.
☞ * Victoria Dig. VCD19079 [id.]. Nilsson, Kvalbein, Bratlie – GRIEG: *Andante con moto* *(*); TCHAIKOVSKY: *Trio.* *

The Oslo Trio is an accomplished ensemble who play Martin's *Trio sur des mélodies populaires irlandaises* with personality and intelligence. Indeed the performance holds its own in almost all respects, but unfortunately the recording lets it down: it is too closely balanced to warrant the strong recommendation to which the performance is entitled.

PIANO MUSIC

8 Préludes; Clair de lune; Etude rhythmique, Etude de concert; Esquisse; Fantaisie sur les rhythmes flamenco; Guitare.
☞ (*) Koch Schwann Dig. CD-312212 [id.]. Christiane Mathé.

Martin's piano music – and in particular the *Eight Préludes* written for Lipatti – deserves better advocacy than it receives here. This pianist shows little subtlety or finesse and the recording, made in collaboration with Bavarian Radio, is not of the best. At full price and only 48 minutes, this is indifferent in all respects.

Der Cornet.
*** Orfeo Dig. S 164881A [id.]. Marjana Lipovšek, Austrian RSO, Zagrosek.

Rilke's celebrated collection of poems, *Die Weise von Liebe und Tod des Cornets Christoph Rilke*, tells of a youthful ensign who in 1660 fell under 'the sabres of the Turks into an ocean of flowers'. The shadowy, half-real atmosphere often reminds one of *Pelléas*; and Martin's responsiveness to the rhythm and music of the words is thoroughly Debussian (German was not his native tongue). The performance by the contralto, Marjana Lipovšek, is a *tour de force*, and the orchestral playing under Lothar Zagrosek is highly sympathetic. The recording is very faithful, and the performance puts one completely under the spell of this strongly atmospheric work.

(i) *Golgotha;* (ii) *Mass for unaccompanied double choir.*
*** Erato/Warner Analogue/Dig. 2292 45779-2 (2) [id.]. (i) Staempfli, De Montmollin, Tappy, Mollet, Huttenlocher, Faller Ch. & SO, Robert Faller; (ii) Choeur de Chambre du Midi, Denis Martin.

The *Mass for unaccompanied double choir* is an early and not entirely characteristic work whose beauties are gaining wider recognition. *Golgotha* is one of Martin's major works, of greater emotional power than *Le vin herbé*, and arguably the greatest Passion since Bach but, in contradistinction to Bach, the narrative passes freely between the various soloists and the body of the choir. The eloquence, power and dignity of this music are well conveyed by the conviction of the performance. The *Mass* is a digital recording, and the singing of the Choeur de Chambre du Midi under Denis Martin is very good indeed.

Mass for double choir.
*** Koch Bayer Dig. BR 100084 [id.]. Frankfurt Vocal Ens., Ralf Otto – REGER: *Geistliche Gesänge.* ***

(*) Nimbus Dig. NI 5197 [id.]. Christ Church Cathedral Ch., Oxford, Stephen Darlington – POULENC: *Mass in G* etc. *

Ralf Otto's fine Frankfurt choir have a great understanding of and feeling for this work, and convey its poignancy and depth. Their performance is quite a powerful and moving experience, and they produce a refined and expressive tonal blend as well as a wide dynamic range, which are well captured by the engineers.

The Choir of Christ Church Cathedral, Oxford, under Stephen Darlington also give a good account of themselves: their tone is clean and beautifully balanced. The boys' voices are moving in a different way from that of the Frankfurt choir, but the English performance does not add up to quite as impressive or richly imaginative a musical experience. The Nimbus disc is eminently well recorded.

6 Monologues from Everyman; The Tempest: 3 excerpts.
🏵 (M) *** DG 429 858-2 [id.]. Fischer-Dieskau, BPO, composer – EGK: *The temptation of St Anthony.* ***

The *Everyman Monologues* is a masterpiece – one of the great song-cycles of the twentieth century – on the theme of a rich man dying. The music is of extraordinary vision and imaginative power, and this classic performance from Fischer-Dieskau and the composer sounds as vivid and fresh as ever. The three excerpts from *The Tempest* make one long to hear the rest of the opera. The orchestral *Prelude* casts a strong and powerful spell and the two arias, from Act III (*My Ariel! Hast thou, which art but air*) and the Epilogue (*Now my charms are all o'erthrown*), are hardly less magical.

Requiem.
*** Jecklin Disco JD 631-2 [id.]. Speiser, Bollen, Tappy, Lagger, Lausanne Women's Ch., Union Ch., SRO, composer.

This is arguably the most beautiful *Requiem* to have been written since Fauré's and, were the public to have ready access to it, would be as popular. The recording, made at a public performance that the (then 83-year-old) composer conducted in Lausanne Cathedral, is very special. The analogue recording is not in the demonstration class, but this music and performance must have three stars.

Le vin herbé (oratorio).
*(**) Jecklin Disco JD 581/2-2 [id.]. Retchitzka, Tuscher, Comte, Morath, De Montmollin, Diakoff, De Nyzankowskyi, Tappy, Jonelli, Rehfuss, Vessières, Olsen, composer, Winterthur O (members), Desarzens.

Martin's oratorio on the Tristan legend is laid out for a madrigal choir of twelve singers, who also assume solo roles, and a handful of instrumentalists, including the piano, played here by the septuagenarian composer himself. It is powerful and hypnotic, and there is some fine singing here from Tuscher, Tappy and Rehfuss. The instrumental playing, though not impeccable, is dedicated (and the same must be said for the choral singing). The 1960s sound is much improved in the CD format.

Martinů, Bohuslav (1890–1959)

La Bagarre; Half-time; Intermezzo; The Rock; Thunderbolt.
*** Sup. SUP 001669 [id.]. Brno State O, Vronsky.

La Bagarre and *Half-time* are early evocations, the latter a Honeggerian depiction of a roisterous half-time at a football match that musically doesn't amount to a great deal. The three later works are much more interesting – *Intermezzo* is linked to the *Fourth Symphony* – and the collection as a whole will be of great interest to Martinů addicts, if perhaps not essential for other collectors. All the performances are alive and full of character, and the recording is vividly immediate.

(i) *Concertino in C min. for cello, wind instruments and piano;* (ii) *Harpsichord concerto;* (iii) *Oboe concerto.*
☞ *** Sup. Dig. 11 0107-2 031 [id.]. (i) Alexandr Večtomov, Vladimir Topinka, members of Czech PO; (ii) Zuzana Růžičková, Václav Rehák; (iii) Jiří Krejči; (ii; iii) Czech Philharmonic Chamber O; (i, iii) Petr Skvor; (ii) Václav Neumann.

Zuzana Růžičková has made a number of recordings of the *Harpsichord concerto* but this is her most successful. The sound is agreeably spacious, though the balance is synthetic and the piano has equal prominence with the solo harpsichord. However, the playing is spirited and sympathetic; and the *Oboe concerto* is heard to excellent advantage too, with very good playing and a well-laid-out sound-picture. The early *Concertino for cello with piano, wind and percussion* does not make as strong an impression as in Navarra's LP or Večtomov's earlier record from the mid-1970s, but it is more than acceptably played and recorded.

(i) *Concerto for double string orchestra, piano and timpani;* (ii) *Concerto for string quartet and orchestra;* (iii) *Sinfonia concertante for oboe, bassoon, violin, cello and orchestra.*
*** Virgin/EMI Dig. VC7 59575-2 [id.]. (i) Alley, Fullbrook; (ii) Endellion Qt; (iii) Daniel, Reay, Watkinson, Orton; City of L. Sinfonia, Hickox.

The *Double concerto* has splendid vitality in Hickox's hands and he has obvious sympathy for this repertoire. The *Sinfonia concertante* is more rewarding than the neo-Baroque *Concerto for string quartet and orchestra*, which is very manufactured. However, this is a useful addition to the growing Martinů discography, and Richard Hickox is an enthusiastic and expert guide in this terrain.

Concerto for double string orchestra, piano and timpani; 3 Frescoes of Piero della Francesca. (i) *Rhapsody-concerto for viola and orchestra.*
*(**) BIS Dig. CD 501 [id.]. (i) Nobuko Imai; Malmö SO, James DePreist.

Nobuko Imai's performance of the *Rhapsody-concerto* is quite special. It has the feel of live music-making, as if the musicians were all swept along by the current this all generates. She is excellently supported by the Malmö orchestra, who play very well indeed throughout. The *Double concerto* receives a dignified reading, but the acoustic unfortunately lets things down: it is far too reverberant; nor is the balance ideal in the *Frescoes*, where wind and brass come dangerously close to swamping the strings.

Concerto for double string orchestra, piano and timpani; (i) *Sinfonietta giocosa for piano and orchestra;* (ii) *Rhapsody-concerto for viola and orchestra.*
**(*) Conifer Dig. CDCF 210. Brno State PO, Mackerras; (i) Dennis Hennig, Australian CO, Mackerras; (ii) Rivka Golani, Berne SO, Peter Maag.

Rivka Golani's unaffected account of the *Rhapsody-concerto*, all the more eloquent for being understated, is here added to the *Double concerto* reviewed below, and the delightful *Sinfonietta giocosa*, both previously coupled with music by different composers. The wartime but apparently carefree *Sinfonietta giocosa* gets a delightfully fresh performance and an acceptable recording, though the balance is a bit synthetic with little back-to-front depth.

Concerto for double string orchestra, piano and tympani; Spaliček – ballet suites.
*** Conifer Dig. CDCF 202; *MCFC 202* [id.]. Brno State PO, Mackerras.

The ballet *Spaliček* is an engaging score, based on traditional Czech fairytale tunes and nursery rhymes. The music is delightful and some of the numbers, particularly the *Dance of the Ladies of Honour*, captivating. If you enjoy the Dvořák of the *Slavonic dances*, you will respond to this fresh and open-hearted music. Mackerras also includes the powerful *Concerto for double string orchestra, piano and tympani*, again well played and recorded, though the pianist produces some less-than-elegant tone at climaxes. Eminently recommendable though in the *Double concerto*, Bělohlávek perhaps gives the more concentrated reading.

Concerto for double string orchestra, piano and tympani; Symphony No. 1.
*** Chan. Dig. CHAN 8950; *ABTD 1544* [id.]. Czech PO, Jiří Bělohlávek.

Jiří Bělohlávek's dedicated and imaginative account of the *First Symphony* is very good indeed. Bělohlávek is totally inside this music, and the recording, made in the agreeably resonant Spanish Hall of Prague Castle, is very natural. The *Double concerto* is one of the most powerful works of the present century, and its intensity is well conveyed in this vital, deeply felt performance. Strongly recommended for both works.

(i) *Harpsichord concerto;* (ii; iii) *Piano concertos Nos. 4 (Incantations);* (ii; iv) *5 (Fantasia concertante).*
☞ (**) Campion mono RRCD 1321 [id.]. (i) Růžičková, Slovak R. CO, Košler; (ii) Havlikova, Slovak RSO; (iii) Lenárd; (iv) Koutnik.

Three Martinů rarities taken from the archives of Slovak Radio. The *Harpsichord concerto* comes from 1936 and, like Poulenc's *Concert champêtre* and Falla's *Concerto*, was written for Wanda Landowska. It is a likeable and diverting piece with good ideas and, though not top-drawer Martinů, is eminently enjoyable. Růžičková recorded it for Supraphon (coupling it with the Poulenc) way back in the late 1960s and she gives a good account of it here. The recording is well balanced though it is a radio, not a natural concert-hall, perspective (the orchestral piano and the wind loom as large as the soloist) but the overall sound is warm and clean. The other two concertos come from the 1950s, *Incantations* from the turn of 1955–6 and the *Fifth (Fantasia concertante)* from the last months of the composer's life. *Incantations* is a highly imaginative piece, one of the best works of Martinů's last years, full of exotic effects of colour and texture. This recording, however, does it scant justice; the orchestra is well enough reproduced but the piano, which is not in good shape, sounds dull and blanketed and is not cleanly focused. The *Fifth* sounds much better, the instrument is in better condition, decently balanced, and both soloist and orchestra play well. Neither performance is quite as finished as one would find in a commercial recording.

Oboe concerto.
☞ *** Ph. Dig. 434 105-2 [id.]. Holliger, ASMF, Marriner – HONEGGER: *Concerto da camera* etc.
***; MARTIN: *3 danses* etc. ***
*** Nimbus Dig. NI 5330 [id.]. John Anderson, Philh. O, Simon Wright – FRANCAIX: *L'horloge de flore;* R. STRAUSS: *Concerto.* ***
*** Capriccio Dig. 10 308 [id.]. Lajos Lencsés, Stuttgart RSO, Marriner – HAYDN: *Concerto;* HUMMEL: *Intro., theme & variations.* ***

An excellent account of Martinů's lightweight but attractive *Oboe concerto* makes a splendid makeweight to the Frank Martin and Honegger couplings. Holliger plays the original cadenzas to the concerto. All in all a first-rate issue, offering some eminently civilized music in a state-of-the-art recording of striking clarity and definition. Strongly recommended.

Not surprisingly, Martinů's *Concerto* is full of individual touches. The newest Nimbus account, by John Anderson, principal of the Philharmonia, is outstanding in every way, with the *Andante* quite ravishing when the soloist's timbre is so rich. The recording is first class and the couplings particularly attractive.

Lajos Lencsés plays with a rather more plangent timbre, and the *Poco andante* – with its two piano-accompanied improvisatory interludes – is memorable in its bitter-sweet lyricism. Marriner accompanies sympathetically and the recording is first rate.

Piano concertos Nos. 1–3; 4 (Incantations) (1956); 5 in B flat (Fantasia concertante); Piano concertino.
☞ *(*) Sup. Dig. 11 1313-2 032 (2) [id.]. Emil Leichner, Czech PO, Jiří Bělohlálek.

Although the five piano concertos are obviously of far less importance in Martinů's output than the symphonies, the best of them are well worth hearing. The weakest is the *First*, written during his Paris years and whose neo-classical pastiche wears thin, particularly in the slow movement. The *Fourth* (*Incantations*) is a highly imaginative work full of splendid sonorities, and there is much to admire in the *Fifth* (*Fantasia concertante*) but, for the most part, the concertos do not show the composer at his most inspired. None is as exhilarating or as inventive as the *Sinfonietta giocosa* for piano and orchestra. These performances were all recorded between 1986 and 1989 and, although Emil Leichner is a capable artist, his piano sounds curiously tubby in all five concertos and wanting in real timbre, though it is clean at the very top. Jiří Bělohlávek gives excellent support, but the recording is reverberant and mushy; detail is not clearly defined in fully scored passages.

Merry Christmas 1942; La revue de cuisine; 3 ricercari; Sinfonietta La Jolla; Toccata e due canzoni.
☞ *** Decca Dig. 433 660-2 [id.]. St Paul CO, Hogwood.

Martinů is hardly the repertoire one associates with Christopher Hogwood, but his accounts of these scores show his musicianship responding with flair to the challenges posed by the Czech master. Hogwood's version of these (relatively familiar) pieces has one inestimable advantage over its rivals in the superiority of the Decca recording, which is beautifully clean, clear and present. Although the *Sinfonietta la Jolla* and the *Toccata e due canzoni* have previously been well represented on LP, these new performances supersede them, even if the St Paul upper strings could do with more bloom and sonority. (They are not really a match for the strings of the Orpheus or the Franz Liszt Chamber Orchestras.) The disc is supplemented by *La revue de cuisine*, perhaps the best-known work of the composer's 1920s Parisian years, with its high spirits and fetching Charleston. Although here there is a strong rival in the Dartington Ensemble on Hyperion, given the presence of excellent performances of the *Tre ricicare* and a bonne-bouche in the form of a Christmas trifle not even listed in Harry Halbreich's catalogue, this Decca collection can be cordially recommended. *Merry Christmas 1942* was originally for piano and written as a thankyou to the composer's American hosts; here it is transcribed for wind quintet. The excellent notes show Hogwood can write as persuasively about Martinů as he does about the Trio Sonata.

Spalíček (ballet; complete); Dandelion (Romance); 5 Duets on Moravian folksongs.
☞ *** Sup. Dig. 11 0752-2 (2). Soloists, Kantilena Children's Ch., Kühn Mixed Ch., Brno State PO, František Jílek.

The original of Martinů's engaging ballet, *Spalíček*, dates from 1931–2 and must in some sense have been a reaction against the sophistication of life in Paris. This is the first recording of the complete score and it makes an even more positive impression than the more conventionally scored suites (see above). On the autograph Martinů speaks of it as 'a ballet of popular plays, customs and fairy-tales – ballet-revue', and the score draws on folklore and children's songs to striking effect. To some extent the work reflects Martiů's homesickness, but its cultivation of a naïve-sounding, expressive simplicity and the use of children's stories is so unaffected and natural as to disarm criticism completely. The dances familiar from the suites are interspersed with vocal episodes, both solo and choral, and there is inevitably far greater variety of texture and pace than is evident from the suites. Its three Acts last some 97 minutes and, although there are some longueurs, they are very few. For the most part this music is quite captivating, particularly given the charm of this performance. Two shorter works complete the set: *Dandelion Romance* for mixed chorus and soprano, and *Five Duets on Moravion folksong texts* for female voices, violin and piano, both of which come from his last years. All in all, a delightful addition to the Martinů discography.

Symphonies Nos. 1–6 (Fantaisies symphoniques).
(m) *** Sup. 11 0382-2 (3) [id.]. Czech PO, Václav Neumann.

Symphonies Nos. 1–4.
*** BIS Dig. CD 362-3 [id.]. Bamberg SO, Järvi.

Martinů always draws a highly individual sound from his orchestra and secures great clarity, even when the score abounds in octave doublings. He often thickens his textures in this way, yet, when played with the delicacy these artists produce, they sound beautifully transparent. On hearing the *First*, Virgil Thomson wrote, 'the shining sounds of it sing as well as shine', and there is no doubt this music is luminous and life-loving. The BIS recording is in the demonstration class yet sounds completely natural, and the performances under Neeme Järvi are totally persuasive and have a spontaneous feel for the music's pulse.

Neumann's set was recorded in the Dvořák Hall of the House of Artists, Prague, between January 1976 (No. 6) and 1978 (No. 5). The transfers to CD are excellently done: the sound is full, spacious and bright; it has greater presence and better definition than the original LPs, yet with no edginess in the strings. Václav Neumann's performances have an impressive spaciousness and, though there could be more urgency and fire in places, the readings have life, colour and impetus, and are thoroughly compelling when the Czech orchestra play so vividly.

Symphonies Nos. 1; 3; 5.
*** Multisonic 31 0023-2 (2). Czech PO, Ančerl.

This is the real thing. Whether or not you have modern versions of these Martinů symphonies, you should obtain these powerful, luminous performances; they come from Czech Radio recordings made in 1963, 1966 and 1962 respectively. They are such superb and convincing readings that readers should not hesitate. The music glows in Ančerl's hands and acquires a radiance that quite belies its date.

Symphony No. 4; Memorial to Lidice; (i) Field Mass.
☞ *** Chan. Dig. CHAN 9138 [id.]. (i) Ivan Kusjner, Czech Ph. Ch.; Czech PO, Jiří Bělohlávek.

The Chandos Martinů cycle from the Czech Philharmonic under Jiří Bělohlávek goes from strength to strength. Their account of the *Sixth*, coupled with the Janáček *Sinfonietta* and Suk's adorable *Scherzo fantastique* (see below), was impressive enough, and the *First Symphony* (coupled with a powerfully dark account of the *Concerto for double string orchestra, piano and timpani*) was warmly greeted in our 1992 edition (see above). This newcomer is if anything even finer; rhythms are crisp and buoyant, accents light, and there is an inexorable sense of momentum. The Chandos recording is spacious and transparent and, though not perhaps as finely detailed as in a demonstration Decca recording, very realistic and full-bodied all the same. Despite its wartime provenance the *Fourth Symphony* is one of the composer's sunniest works; the infectious high spirits of the Scherzo and the luminous, glowing textures of the slow movement and its harmonic resource (at one point there is a reminder of Roussel with whom he studied) are irresistible. There is a radiance about this work that is quite special, and Bělohlávek's account of it is quite the best that has appeared in recent years. It is better played than the Järvi, though perhaps the latter scores in the eloquence of the slow movement. The *Memorial to Lidice*, composed in response to a Nazi massacre, is a powerful and haunting piece, and so is the *Field Mass*, which receives its best performance until now – by far. The soloist is excellent and the choral singing has an appropriate ardour. Thoroughly convincing performances and an indispensable item in any Martinů discography.

Symphony No. 5; Memorial to Lidice; Les Fresques de Piero della Francesca; The Parables.
☞ ** Sup. mono/stereo 111931-2 001 [id.]. Czech PO, Ančerl.

Most of these are pioneering recordings (only Kubelik's recording of the *Three Frescoes* precedes Ančerl). The *Fifth Symphony* comes from 1955 and the *Memorial to Lidice* from 1957, and they do not wear their years as lightly as some Western recordings of the period. The sound is constricted in range, though the quality and conviction of the performances are such that sonic limitations are almost (but never completely) forgotten. The *Three Frescoes* and *The Parables* are stereo, made in 1959 and 1961 respectively. The *Three Frescoes* are given a marvellously glowing performance and, though it has still not been possible to remove the slight glassiness and shrillness in the string-tone above the stave, there is rather more detail than in the LP. *The Parables*, never released in stereo in the UK, sound better and the performances have much authority and convey that luminous quality that make the Martinů sound-world so special.

Symphonies Nos. 5; 6 (Fantaisies symphoniques).
*** BIS Dig. CD 402 [id.]. Bamberg SO, Järvi.

The *Fifth* is a glorious piece and Järvi brings to it that mixture of disciplined enthusiasm and zest for life that distinguishes all his work. Wonderfully transparent, yet full-bodied sound, in the best BIS manner.

Symphony No. 6 (Fantaisies symphoniques).
*** Chan. Dig. CHAN 8897; *ABTD 1508* [id.]. Czech PO, Bělohlávek – JANACEK: *Sinfonietta;* SUK: *Scherzo.* ***

This Chandos reading has the inestimable benefit of the Czech Philharmonic. Moreover the interpretation has great dramatic strength and is fully characterized; undoubtedly these players believe in every note. It is an outstanding performance that does full justice to the composer's extraordinarily imaginative vision and is very well recorded.

CHAMBER MUSIC

Cello sonatas Nos. 1–3.
*** Hyp. Dig. CDA 66296 [id.]. Steven Isserlis, Peter Evans.

Steven Isserlis and Peter Evans have done well to collect all three Martinů *Cello sonatas* on one disc. Very good playing and very acceptable recording.

Duo for violin and cello.
(M) *** BMG/RCA GD 87871 [7871-2-RG]. Heifetz, Piatigorsky – DEBUSSY: *Sonata* etc. (**);
   RESPIGHI: *Sonata* (***); RAVEL: *Trio* etc. (**)

A short but powerful piece, this *Duo* was recorded in 1964 and, though the acoustic is a bit dryish, the playing is fabulous.

Flute sonata.
*** BMG/RCA Dig. RD 87802 [7802-2-RC]. James Galway, Phillip Moll – DVORAK: *Sonatina;*
   FELD: *Sonata.* ***

With the outer movements generally jolly and extrovert, bringing distinctive Martinů touches, the main weight of the *Flute sonata* comes in the central *Adagio.* Galway is characteristically individual but without mannerism in his performance, and is most sympathetically accompanied by Moll. Relatively dry recording, with a fine sense of presence.

4 Madrigals for oboe, clarinet and bassoon; 3 Madrigals for violin and viola; Madrigal sonata for piano, flute and violin; 5 Madrigal stanzas for violin and piano.
*** Hyp. Dig. CDA 66133 [id.]. Dartington Ens.

These delightful pieces exhibit all the intelligence and fertility of invention we associate with Martinů's music. The playing of the Dartington Ensemble is accomplished and expert, and the recording, though resonant, is faithful.

Nonet; Trio in F for flute, cello and piano; La Revue de cuisine.
*** Hyp. CDA 66084 [id.]. Dartington Ens.

A delightful record. Only one of these pieces is otherwise available on CD and all of them receive first-class performances and superb recording. The sound has space, warmth, perspective and definition. An indispensable issue for lovers of Martinů's music.

Piano quintet No. 2.
☞ *** ASV Dig. CDDCA 889 [id.]. Peter Frankl, Lindsay Qt – DVORAK: *Piano quintet.* ***

Martinů's *Second Piano quintet* was written in 1944, soon after the composer's arrival in the United States. It is a remarkably successful piece, characteristically original in its content and rhythmic style. The Lindsays with Peter Frankl have its full measure and – as in the coupled Dvořák *Quintet* – after the impulsive opening movement it is the central movements which bring playing of striking insight and subtlety, with rapt concentration at the opening of the finale. The recording is lively and present, with the piano well integrated, although there is just a touch of thinness on the strings. An outstanding coupling.

Sonata for 2 violins and piano.
**(*) Hyp. Dig. CDA 66473 [id.]. Ososowicz, Kovacic, Tomes – MILHAUD: *Violin duo* etc. **(*);
   PROKOFIEV: *Violin sonata.* ***

Martinů's *Sonata for two violins and piano* finds him full of invention and vitality. Krsyia Osostowicz, Ernst Kovacic and Susan Tomes play it with all the finesse and sensitivity you could want and are excellently recorded. The disc would be even more recommendable if it had a longer playing time than 46 minutes.

Violin sonatas Nos. 2–3; 5 Madrigal sonatas.
** Sup. Dig. 11 0099-2 [id.]. Josef Suk, Josef Hála.

The *Second Violin sonata* is a short and attractive work, while the bigger-boned *Third* speaks much the same language as the symphonies. Josef Suk and Josef Hála give excellent acounts of all three pieces, though the 1987 recording is less than appealingly balanced. The sound is rather synthetic and too close.

Etudes and Polkas; Fantasy and Toccata; Moderato (Julietta Act II), arr. Firkušný; *Les Ritournelles; Piano sonata No. 1.*
**(*) BMG/RCA Dig. RD 87987 [7987-2-RC]. Rudolf Firkušný.

Firkušný was long associated with Martinů and gave the first performances of most of these pieces. The *Fantasy and Toccata* was written for him in the dark days of 1940. No doubt had he recorded it when he was younger (he is in his late seventies), the rhythmic contours would be more sharply etched and would have more bite, but it could not be more delicate in its keyboard colouring, more authoritative or refined. The recording is not made in a large enough acoustic but is otherwise truthful.

The Epic of Gilgamesh (oratorio).
⊛ *** Marco Polo Dig. 8.223316 [id.]. Depoltová, Margita, Kusnjer, Vele, Karpílšek, Slovak Ph. Ch. & O, Zdeněk Košler.

The Epic of Gilgamesh comes from Martinů's last years and is arguably his masterpiece. It evokes a remote and distant world, full of colour and mystery. Gilgamesh is the oldest poem known to mankind: it predates the Homeric epics by 1,500 years, which places it at 7000 BC or earlier. The work abounds with invention of the highest quality and of consistently sustained inspiration. The performance is committed and sympathetic and the recording very natural in its balance.

(i) *Hymn to St James;* (ii) *Mount of three lights;* (iii) *The Prophecy of Isaiah.*
☞ ** Sup. Dig. 11 0751-2 (2). (i) Doležal, Novák, Haničinec; (i; ii) Kuhn Mixed Ch., Prague SO, Pavel Kühn; (ii; iii) Romanová, Drobková; (iii) Kozderka, Pěruška, Haničinec, Boguna, Kiezlich, Prague R. Ch., Hora.

This disc gathers three cantatas Martinů composed towards the end of his life. The *Hymn to St James* and the *Mount of three lights* were both composed during 1954, when he was living in Nice, while *The Prophecy of Isaiah* was his very last work. The *Mount of three lights* is a rarity and new to the catalogue in this country. It is based on a bizarre mixture of Czech folksong, bits of H. V. Morton's book, *In the Steps of the Master,* and *The Gospel according to St Matthew!* Though it is not quite as concentrated or haunting as *The Epic of Gilgamesh* or *The Prophecy of Isaiah,* it is powerful stuff and well worth the attention of all admirers of the composer. It is for the unusual combination of narrator, tenor, bass, chorus and organ, and is very well performed by these forces, save perhaps for the bass, Richard Novák, whose wobble may prove too much for some listeners. The *Hymn of St James* has moments of a disarming simplicity of utterance; generally speaking, though, it is not top-drawer Martinů. However, *The Prophecy of Isaiah* is; scored for soprano, contralto, bass, male chorus, trumpet, viola, timpani and piano, it is a work of great substance and depth. Its austere sound-world and seriousness resonate in the mind, though the performance is less impressive than the old LP under Karel Ančerl, which deserves reissue; and readers should be cautioned that the bass has a terribly wide vibrato. The disc comes in an uneconomical two-CD format, though it lasts less than an hour.

OPERA

Ariane.
☞ ** Sup. Dig. 10 4395-2. Lindsley, Phillips, Doležal, Novák, Czech PO, Vaclav Neumann.

Ariane is a slight work to which Martinů turned as a relaxation from *The Greek Passion.* It is based on the play, *Le voyage de Thésée,* by Georges Neveux. Apparently the demanding role of Ariane was inspired by Callas; it is all quite engaging and high-spirited without being Martinů at his very best. Written in the course of a month, it is a short piece, no longer than 43 minutes, though it is housed in a two-CD format so as to accommodate a multi-lingual booklet and libretto. The singers (and in particular Celina Lindsley) are very good indeed: only Richard Novák's wide vibrato is problematic. Decent rather than outstanding recording quality.

The Greek Passion (sung in English).
*** Sup. Dig. 10 3611/2 [id.]. Mitchinson, Field, Tomlinson, Joll, Moses, Davies, Cullis, Savory, Kuhn Children's Ch., Czech PO Ch., Brno State PO, Mackerras.

Written with much mental pain in the years just before Martinů died in 1959, this opera was the work he regarded as his musical testament. It tells in an innocent, direct way of a village where a Passion play is to be presented; the individuals – tragically, as it proves – take on qualities of the New Testament figures they represent. This extraordinarily vivid recording – almost stereoscopic in its clear projection of the participants – was made by a cast which had been giving stage performances for the Welsh National Opera in what in effect is the original language of Martinů's libretto, English. The combination of British soloists with excellent Czech choirs and players is entirely fruitful. Mackerras makes an ideal advocate, and the recording is both brilliant and atmospheric. With the words so clear, the absence of an English libretto is not a serious omission, but the lack of any separate cues within the four Acts is a great annoyance.

Julietta (complete).
☞ *** Sup. 10 8176-2 (3) [id.]. Tauberová, Zídek, Zlesák, Otava, Bednář, Mixová, Jedenáctík, Procházková, Hanzalíková, Soukupová, Jindrák, Veverka, Svehla, Zlesák, Lemariová, Berman, Prague Nat. Theatre Ch. & O, Jaroslav Krombholc.

Described by the composer as a Dreambook, *Julietta* was given first in Prague in March 1938, the year which brought the Munich Agreement and the dismemberment of Czechoslovakia at the hands of Hitler, itself a surreal period for the Czech nation. This vintage Supraphon recording, made in 1964, captures that surreal quality vividly. You would never guess the date of the recording, for the ear is mesmerized from the very start, when the howling of a high bassoon introduces the astonishingly original prelude. The voices as well as the orchestra are then presented with a bright immediacy which reinforces the power and incisiveness of Krombholc's performance. The sharpness of focus adds to the atmospheric intensity, as when in the first Act The Man in the Window plays his accordion. Ivo Zídek gives a vivid portrait of the central character, Michel, perplexed by his dream-like search, and there is no weak link in the rest of the cast. The snag is that the set stretches extravagantly to three discs, when the opera could have been fitted on to two, though that layout brings the advantage of having each Act complete on a single disc. Informative notes and libretto come with multiple translations.

Martucci, Giuseppe (1856–1909)

(i) *Piano concerto No. 1 in D min.;* (ii) *La canzone dei Ricordi.*
** ASV Dig. CDDCA 690 [id.]. (i) Caramiello; (ii) Yakar; Philh. O, D'Avalos.

The *First Piano concerto* (with Francesco Caramiello a capable soloist) is inevitably derivative, and it is the song-cycle that is the chief attraction here: Rachel Yakar sings beautifully and is particularly affecting in the Duparc-like *Cantavál ruscello la gaia canzone*. The recording is generally faithful.

(i) *Piano concerto No. 2 in B flat min., Op. 66. Canzonetta, Op. 55/1; Giga, Op. 61/3; Minuetto, Op. 57/2; Momento musicale, Op. 57/3; Serenata, Op. 57/1; Tempo di gavotta, Op. 55/2.*
** ASV Dig. CDDCA 691 [id.]. Francesco Caramiello; (i) Philh. O, D'Avalos.

The *Second Piano concerto* is a big, 40-minute piece in a Brahmsian mould but is nevertheless full of individual touches. Caramiello copes very successfully with its very considerable demands, and the results all round are eminently acceptable. The fill-ups derive mainly from piano pieces and are wholly delightful. The recording is good.

Giga, Op. 61/3; Notturno, Op. 70/1; Novelletta, Op. 82.
☞ *** Sony Dig. SK 53280 [id.]. La Scala PO, Muti – BUSONI: *Turandot suite;* CASELLA: *Paganiniana.* ***

The three Martucci pieces are played with infinitely greater sensitivity and finesse than in the ASV survey of Martucci's symphonies and concertos by D'Avalos. They were all composed at about the turn of the century and have the gentleness and elegiac quality of Fauré and Elgar with a touch of Wagner (Martucci conducted the Italian première of *Tristan*). This is altogether a most valuable issue and can be strongly recommended.

Symphony No. 1 in D min., Op. 75; Notturno, Op. 70/1; Novelletta, Op. 82; Tarantella, Op. 44.
** ASV Dig. CDDCA 675 [id.]. Philh. O, D'Avalos.

The *First Symphony* is greatly indebted to Brahms, but elsewhere there is a vein of lyricism that is more distinctive. The *Notturno* has the nobility and eloquence of Elgar or Fauré and deserves to be much better known. The performances by the Philharmonia under Francesco D'Avalos are serviceable rather than distinguished, but the recording is very truthful and well balanced.

Symphony No. 2 in F, Op. 81; Andante in B flat, Op. 69; Colore orientale Op. 44/3.
** ASV Dig. CDDCA 689 [id.]. Philh. O, D'Avalos.

The *Second Symphony* is a relatively late work. Though the performance falls short of distinction, it leaves the listener in no doubt as to Martucci's quality as a composer and the nobility of much of his invention. The *Colore orientale* is an arrangement of a piano piece; the beautiful *Andante*, a work of depth, has a Fauréan dignity. The recording is a bit too closely balanced.

Le canzone dei ricordi; Notturno, Op. 70/1.
*** Hyp. Dig. CDA 66290 [id.]. Carol Madalin, ECO, Bonavera – RESPIGHI: *Il tramonto*. ***

Le canzone dei ricordi is a most beautiful song-cycle, and its gentle atmosphere and warm lyricism are most seductive. At times Carol Madalin has a rather rapid vibrato, but she sings the work most sympathetically and with great eloquence. The *Notturno* is beautifully played. Recommended with all possible enthusiasm.

Mascagni, Pietro (1863–1945)

Cavalleria rusticana (complete).
*** BMG/RCA RD 83091. Scotto, Domingo, Elvira, Isola Jones, Amb. Op. Ch., Nat. PO, Levine.
*** DG 419 257-2 (3) [id.]. Cossotto, Bergonzi, Guelfi, Ch. & O of La Scala, Milan, Karajan –
   LEONCAVALLO: *I Pagliacci* *** (also with collection of Operatic intermezzi ***).
(***) EMI mono CDS7 47981-8 (3) [Ang. CDCC 47981]. Callas, Di Stefano, Panerai, Ch. & O of
   La Scala, Milan, Serafin – LEONCAVALLO: *I Pagliacci*. (***)
(M) **(*) Decca 425 985-2 [id.]. Tebaldi, Bjoerling, Bastianini, Maggio Musicale Fiorentino Ch. & O,
   Erede.
(M) (***) BMG/RCA mono GD 86510 [RCA 6510-2-RG]. Milanov, Bjoerling, Merrill, Robert
   Shaw Chorale, RCA O, Cellini.
☞ (B) **(*) Naxos Dig. 8.660022 [id.]. Evstatieva, Aragall, Tumagian, Di Mauro, Michalková,
   Slovak Philh. Ch., Czech RSO, Rahbari – LEONCAVALLO: *I Pagliacci*. **(*)
☞ (M) (**) Nimbus mono NI 7843/4 [id.]. Gigli, Bruna Rasa, Marcucci, Bechi, Simionato, La Scala
   Ch. & O, composer – LEONCAVALLO: *I Pagliacci*. (**(*))

On balance, in performance the RCA issue stands as the best current recommendation, with Domingo giving a heroic account of the role of Turiddù, full of defiance. Scotto is strongly characterful too, and James Levine directs with a splendid sense of pacing, by no means faster than his rivals (except the leisurely Karajan) and drawing red-blooded playing from the National Philharmonic. The recording is very good, strikingly present in its CD format.

Karajan pays Mascagni the tribute of taking his markings literally, so that well-worn melodies come out with new purity and freshness, and the singers have been chosen to match that. Cossotto quite as much as Bergonzi keeps a pure, firm line that is all too rare in this much-abused music. Not that there is any lack of dramatic bite. The CD transfer cannot rectify the balance, but voices are generally more sharply defined, while the spacious opulence is retained.

Dating from the mid-1950s, Callas's performance as Santuzza reveals the diva in her finest form, with edginess and unevenness of production at a minimum and with vocal colouring at its most characterful. The singing of the other principals is hardly less dramatic and Panerai is in firm, well-projected voice.

The early (1957) Decca recording with Tebaldi offers a forthright, lusty account of Mascagni's piece of blood and thunder and has the distinction of three excellent soloists. Tebaldi is most moving in *Voi lo sapete*, and the firm richness of Bastianini's baritone is beautifully caught. As always, Bjoerling shows himself the most intelligent of tenors, and it is only the chorus that gives serious cause for disappointment; they are very undisciplined. The CD sound is strikingly bright and lively.

Admirers of Milanov will not want to miss her beautiful singing of *Voi lo sapete*, and in the duet Merrill's dark, firm timbre is thrilling. Bjoerling brings a good measure of musical and tonal subtlety to the role of Turiddù, normally belted out, while Cellini's conducting minimizes the vulgarity of the piece.

As in his parallel recording of *Pag.*, Alexander Rahbari conducts a red-blooded reading of *Cav.*, making it a first-rate super-bargain choice. Stefka Evstatieva is a warmly vibrant Santuzza, well controlled, no Slavonic wobbler, and Giacomo Aragall as Turiddù, not quite as fresh-sounding as he once was, yet gives a strong, characterful performance, with Eduard Tumagian excellent as Alfio, firm and dark. Well-focused digital recording. This set is a real bargain.

EMI's vintage (1940) version of *Cav.*, conducted by the composer with Gigli as Turiddù, came out on CD in an ungenerous two-disc package from EMI, and we await its reissue. It is good to have it again available on CD from Nimbus, along with the curious little speech of introduction that Mascagni himself recorded. Yet the composer's sluggish speeds mean that this opera has to start awkwardly at the end of the *Pag*. disc. Nimbus's transfer captures the voices well, giving them a mellow bloom, though the focus is not nearly as sharp as on the old EMI transfer, and the orchestral sound becomes muzzy.

Iris (complete).
*** Sony Dig. M2K 45526 (2) [id.]. Domingo, Tokody, Pons, Giaiotti, Bav. R. Ch., Munich R. O, Patanè.

Musically, *Iris* brings a mixture of typical Mascagnian sweetness and a vein of nobility often echoing Wagner. With a strong line-up of soloists including Domingo, and with Giuseppe Patanè a persuasive conductor, this recording makes as good a case for a flawed piece as one is ever likely to get. Domingo's warm, intelligent singing helps to conceal the cardboard thinness of a hero who expresses himself in generalized ardour. The Hungarian soprano, Ilona Tokody, brings out the tenderness of the heroine, singing beautifully except when under pressure. Juan Pons, sounding almost like a baritone Domingo, is firm and well projected as Kyoto, owner of a geisha-house, and Bonaldo Giaiotti brings an authentically dark Italian bass to the role of Iris's father. Full, atmospheric recording.

Lodoletta (complete).
*** Hung. Dig. HCD 31307/8 [id.]. Maria Spacagna, Kelen, Szilágyi, Polgár, Kálmándi, Hungarian State Op. Children's Ch., Hungarian R. & TV Ch. & State O, Charles Rosekrans.

In vivid sound and with some excellent singing, this valuable first recording from Hungaroton makes a persuasive case for Mascagni's unashamed mixture of charm and sentimentality. As the little Dutch girl, Lodoletta, Maria Spacagna sings most sensitively, even if the voice is too warm and full to suggest extreme youth. As the dissolute painter who unwittingly drives her to her death Péter Kelen proves a stylish and heady-toned lyric tenor. The American, Charles Rosekrans, makes a very sympathetic conductor, in charge of a strong cast from the Hungarian State Opera.

Mason, Benedict (born 1954)

Lighthouses of England and Wales.
**(*) Collins Dig. Single 2004-2 [id.]. BBC SO, Zagrosek.

Mason's piece is based on the distinctively rhythmic light signals of dozens of specific lighthouses (plus a fog-signal or two). It then develops into an evocative seascape, in its way a descendant of Debussy's *La mer*. Lothar Zagrosek directs a finely concentrated performance, and the recorded sound is outstanding.

Massenet, Jules (1842–1912)

Le Carillon (ballet): complete.
(M) *** Decca 425 472-2 (2). Nat. PO, Richard Bonynge – DELIBES: *Coppélia*. ***

Le Carillon was written in the same year as *Werther*. The villains of the story who try to destroy the bells of the title are punished by being miraculously transformed into bronze jaquemarts, fated to continue striking them for ever! The music of this one-act ballet makes a delightful offering – not always as lightweight as one would expect. With his keen rhythmic sense and feeling for colour, Bonynge is outstanding in this repertory, and the 1984 Decca recording is strikingly brilliant and colourful. A fine bonus (37 minutes) for a highly desirable version of Delibes' *Coppélia*.

Le Cid: ballet suite.
(M) *** Decca 425 475-2 (2). Nat. PO, Richard Bonynge – DELIBES: *Sylvia*. ***

Bonynge's version of the ballet music from *Le Cid* is the finest yet, with the most seductive orchestral playing, superbly recorded.

Cigale (ballet): complete.
(M) *** Decca 425 413-2 (3). Enid Hartle, Nat. PO, Bonynge – TCHAIKOVSKY: *Swan Lake*. **(*)

Cigale recounts the La Fontaine fable about the grasshopper and the ant. The melodic invention does not match Massenet's finest, but the score is charming and colourful; it is played and sung brightly and atmospherically and is brilliantly recorded.

(i) *Piano concerto in E flat. Papillons noirs, Papillons blancs; Devant la Madone; 10 Pièces de genre, Op. 10; Eau dormante; Eau courante; Musique pour 'bercer les petits enfants'; Toccata; Valse folle; Valse triste.*
(M) ** EMI CDM7 64277-2 [id.]. Aldo Ciccolini, (i) Monte Carlo Nat. Op. O, Cambreling.

Massenet's *Piano concerto in E flat* has perhaps the manners of the Saint-Saëns but none of the flair, and though some of the genre pieces and certainly the two impromptus, *Eau dormante* and *Eau courante*, have a certain charm, this has greater curiosity than musical value. Aldo Ciccolini plays with conviction and is well supported in the concerto by Sylvain Cambreling and the Monte Carlo Opera Orchestra. The sound is a bit shallow, and the piano pieces are recorded rather closely in the Salle Wagram.

Don Quichotte: 2 Interludes; Scènes alsaciennes; Scènes pittoresques.
☞ (M) ** Erato/Warner 2292 45859-2 [id.]. Monte Carlo Op. O, Gardiner.

Scènes de féerie; Scènes dramatiques; La Vierge: The last sleep of the Virgin.
☞ (M) ** Erato/Warner 2292 45858-2 [id.]. Monte Carlo Op. O, Gardiner.

This pair of CDs, recorded in 1978, gathers together four of Massenet's seven orchestral suites, plus a few encores, including one of Sir Thomas Beecham's favourites, *The last sleep of the Virgin*. In fact this is all music which would respond to the Beecham touch. John Eliot Gardiner secures quite impressively characterized performances. The strings play sensitively in *Le sommeil de Desdémone*, the central movement of the *Scènes dramatiques* (which all have Shakespearean connotations) while the violins are also impressive in the *Apparition*, the most memorable movement of *Scènes de féerie*. The *Scènes pittoresques* are bright and fresh, the horns tolling in the *Angelus* with resonant impact. The *Scènes alsaciennes* also come off colourfully. The Monte Carlo orchestra play well enough, and the full recording – just a little studio-ish in acoustic – disguises any deficiencies, for the wind solos are well taken. But the reissue on two discs, playing for 45 and 41 minutes respectively, is ungenerous, even at mid-price. The four suites could easily have been fitted on to a single CD.

Fantaisie.
☞ *** ASV Dig. CDDCA 867 [id.]. Sophie Rolland, BBC PO, Gilbert Varga – LALO: *Cello concerto;* SAINT-SAENS: *Cello concerto No. 1.* ***

Massenet composed his three-movement *Fantaisie for cello and orchestra* in 1897 while on holiday in Aix-les-Bains. It is something of a rarity both in the concert hall and on record. Music for the sweet-toothed (and none the worse for that), though its ideas are not anywhere near as memorable as those of its two companions on this disc, and the work as a whole overstays its welcome. The Canadian cellist, Sophie Rolland, and the BBC forces under Gilbert Varga play it with total commitment and fervour as if they believe every note. Excellent recording.

Manon (ballet) complete (arr. Lucas).
*** Decca Dig. 414 585-2 (2) [id.]. ROHCG O, Bonynge.

This confection of Massenet lollipops – with the famous *Elégie* returning as an idée fixe – is the work of Leighton Lucas; with characteristically lively and colourful playing from the Covent Garden Orchestra under Richard Bonynge, it makes a delightful issue, the more attractive when the Decca engineers deliver sound of spectacular quality.

Orchestral suite No. 1, Op. 13; Cendrillon (opera): *suite. Esclarmonde* (opera): *suite.*
** Marco Polo Dig. 8.223354 [id.]. Hong Kong PO, Kenneth Jean.

The delicate atmosphere of *L'île magique* and *Hymenée* from *Esclarmonde*, and the charming *Nocturne* from the *Suite*, Op. 13, is matched by the vigour of the finales from both, the *Marche et Strette* of Op. 13 and *La Chasse*, with its hunting horns in the operatic suite. The charming *Cendrillon* vignettes also have plenty of sparkle. The playing does not find the degree of Beechamesque finesse that makes for totally memorable results in such repertoire, but this remains an enjoyable collection.

Mélodies: *Berceuse; Elégie; Les mains; La mort de la cigale.*
☞ **(*) EMI Dig. CDC7 54818-2 [id.]. José van Dam, Jean-Philippe Collard – GOUNOD; SAINT-SAENS: *Songs.*

As in Gounod and Saint-Saëns, José van Dam's firm, dark tone brings out the beauty of these five Massenet songs, with the celebrated *Elégie* enhanced by the cello solo of Guy Rogé. Except in *Les mains*, Collard is heavier-handed here than in his solo playing. Altogether an unusual and enjoyable recital.

OPERA

Cendrillon (complete).
**(*) Sony CD 79323 (2) [M2K 35194]. Von Stade, Gedda, Berbié, Welting, Bastin, Amb. Op. Ch.,
   Philh. O, Rudel.

Julius Rudel directs a winning performance of Massenet's Cinderella opera. The Fairy Godmother is
the bright-toned Ruth Welting and Cendrillon a soprano. Von Stade gives a characteristically strong
and imaginative performance, untroubled by what for her is high tessitura. The pity is that the role of
the prince, originally also written for soprano, is here taken by a tenor, Gedda, whose voice is no
longer fresh-toned. Jules Bastin sings most stylishly as Pandolfe, and the others make a well-chosen
team. The recording is vivid, but spacious too. Worth exploring, even at full price.

Chérubin (complete)
☞ ⊛ *** RCA/BMG Dig. 09026 60593-2 (2) [60593-2]. Von Stade, Ramey, Anderson, Upshaw,
   Bav. State Op. Ch., Munich RSO, Steinberg.

What Massenet did in this delightful *comédie chantée* of 1903 (he was sixty at the time) was to follow
up what happened to Cherubino after the *Marriage of Figaro*. There is none of the social comment of
Beaumarchais, or of da Ponte or Mozart, just a frothy entertainment, one brimming with ear-tickling
ideas, from the dazzlingly witty overture onwards. The inconsequential plot involves Cherubino
having a fling with a celebrated dancer, favourite of the king, only to return at the end to the simple
girl who adores him. What matters is that the characterization, though plain, is convincing, with each
of the main figures sharply contrasted, both dramatically and musically. So Cherubino, as in Mozart,
is taken by a high mezzo; L'Ensoleillad, the dancer, by a dramatic soprano; and the ingénue, Nina, by
a soubrettish soprano. The only other main character is Cherubino's tutor, the Philosopher. In this
superb RCA recording the cast is both starry and ideal, with June Anderson powerful and
flamboyant as the dancer, Dawn Upshaw sweet and pure as Nina and Samuel Ramey warm and firm
as the Philosopher. Yet finest of all is Frederica von Stade in the title-role. Cherubino is a perky
figure, much more self-confident and pushy than in Mozart, master of his own household, though
still full of youthful high spirits. The delight is to find one tiny gem of an aria after another, with
Massenet at this late stage in his career able to establish a mood and make a dramatic point even in a
solo of just a minute or so. What seals this as an exhilarating experience is the conducting of Pinchas
Steinberg with the Munich Radio Symphony Orchestra, strong and thrustful yet responsive to the
dramatic subtleties, plainly a conductor who should be used more often in recordings. The sound is
fresh and atmospheric, bringing out the sparkle and fantasy of the piece.

Le Cid (complete).
** Sony CD 79300 (2) [M2K 34211]. Bumbry, Domingo, Bergquist, Plishka, Gardner, Camp
   Chorale, NY Op. O, Queler.

The CBS recording is taken from a live performance in New York and suffers from boxy recording
quality. Only with the entrance of Domingo in the second scene does the occasion really get going,
and the French accents are often comically bad. Domingo, not always as stylish as he might be, is in
heroic voice and Grace Bumbry as the proud heroine responds splendidly. The popular ballet music is
given a sparkling performance. But this should have been reissued at mid-price.

Cléopâtre (complete).
☞ **(*) Koch/Schwann Dig. 3 1032-2 (2) Harries, Streiff, Olmeda, Henry, Maurette, Hacquard,
   Festival Ch., Nouvel O de Saint-Étienne, Fournillier.

Cléopâtre was the very last of Massenet's operas, written in 1912, the year he died. Reacting against
a Shakespeare adaptation that had just proved a failure, he and his librettist deliberately made the
plot and characterization simple and direct to suit operatic needs. With exotic choruses, fanfares,
dances and marches, it makes one regret that Massenet – unlike Erich Korngold – did not live to
become a Hollywood composer: *Cléopâtre* has much of the easy opulence of a film spectacular. It is
sad that it has never been appreciated as a major addition to the Massenet canon but had to wait
until 1914, two years after the composer's death, for its première – and then it was given in a garbled
form, with the role of Cléopâtre modified to suit a soprano. Yet with its echoes of Verdi's *Aida*, as
well as of Wagner, it could yet prove viable on stage.

   This première recording was taken from a live performance at the Massenet Festival in Saint-
Etienne in 1990, with Patrick Fournillier conducting. The cast has no serious weakness, and the two
principal roles are splendidly taken, with Didier Henry firm and responsive as Mark Antony and with
Kathryn Harries demonstrating what a rich role for a singing actress this Cléopâtre is, a woman who

consciously breaks men's hearts, toying with them. Miss Harries with her rich mezzo should be used more on record, when her expressive intensity here in her big solos is magnetic. That is particularly so in the concluding scenes. Antony's death-throes bring first an extended love-duet leading to what becomes a Massenet equivalent of Isolde's *Liebestod*. The excellent notes in the well-produced booklet and libretto even suggest that Massenet, anticipating his own death, was composing an equivalent to Mahler's *Tenth Symphony*, written at exactly the same time. The Koch live recording is not helped by the dryness of the orchestral sound, though only the brass is seriously affected, and the voices are vividly caught.

Don Quichotte (complete).

☞ *** EMI Dig. CDS7 54767-2 (2) [id.]. Van Dam, Fondary, Berganza, Toulouse Capitole Ch. & O, Plasson.

(i) *Don Quixote;* (ii) *Scènes alsaciennes.*

☞ (M) *** Decca 430 636-2 (2) [id.]. (i) Ghiaurov, Bacquier, Crespin, SRO Ch. & O, Kord; (ii) Nat. PO, Bonynge.

Massenet's operatic adaptation of Cervantes' classic novel gave him his last big success. There is genuine nobility as well as comedy in the portrait of the knight, and that is well caught here by Ghiaurov, who refuses to exaggerate the characterization. Bacquier makes a delightful Sancho Panza, but it is Régine Crespin as a comically mature Dulcinée, who provides the most characterful singing, flawed vocally but commandingly positive. Kazimierz Kord directs the Suisse Romande Orchestra in a performance that is zestful and electrifying, and the recording is outstandingly clear and atmospheric.

Michel Plasson conducts a sumptuous account of Massenet's charming Cervantes-based opera, with José van Dam singing gloriously as the Don, producing consistently firm and velvety tone. Alain Fondary as Sancho Panza is equally strong and firm vocally, shadowing and matching his master instead of contrasting, never indulging in exaggeratedly comic effects. Teresa Berganza as Dulcinée adds to the sensuousness of the performance, with the Toulouse acoustic bringing out the richness and beauty of Massenet's orchestral writing. No one will be disappointed, but the 1977 Decca set still has clear advantages. With Ghiaurov and Bacquier, the two central roles are more aptly characterized as well as more clearly contrasted, and Régine Crespin too is a formidably characterful Dulcinée. The Decca analogue sound is more clearly focused than the EMI digital, with the chorus full and immediate and with stage effects creating a vivid atmosphere. At mid-price the Decca set also comes with an attractive fill-up, the *Scènes alsaciennes*, brightly and colourfully presented by Bonynge and the National Philharmonic Orchestra.

Esclarmonde (complete).

(M) *** Decca 425 651-2 (3) [id.]. Sutherland, Aragall, Tourangeau, Davies, Grant, Alldis Ch., Nat. PO, Bonynge.

Joan Sutherland is the obvious diva to encompass the demands of great range, great power and brilliant coloratura of the central role of *Esclarmonde*, and her performance is in its way as powerful as it is in Puccini's last opera. Aragall proves an excellent tenor, sweet of tone and intelligent, and the other parts are well taken too. Richard Bonynge draws passionate singing and playing from chorus and orchestra, and the recording has both atmosphere and spectacle to match the story, based on a medieval romance involving song-contests and necromancy.

Le Roi de Lahore (complete).

☞ ⊛ (M) *** Decca Dig. 433 851-2 (2) [id.]. Sutherland, Lima, Milnes, Ghiaurov, Morris, Tourangeau, L. Voices, Nat. PO, Bonynge.

With a libretto that sets high melodrama against an exotic background, *Le Roi de Lahore* was Massenet's first opera for the big stage of L'Opéra in Paris and marked a turning point in his career, even introducing the supernatural, with one Act set in the Paradise of Indra. The characters may be stock figures out of a mystic fairytale, but in the vigour of his treatment Massenet makes the result red-blooded in an Italianate way. This vivid performance under Bonynge includes passages added for Italy, notably a superb set-piece aria which challenges Sutherland to some of her finest singing. Massenet's idea of the exotic extends to a saxophone waltz (here made deliciously Parisian), but generally the score reflects the eager robustness of a young composer stretching his wings for the first time. Sutherland may not be a natural for the role of the innocent young priestess, but she makes it a magnificent vehicle with its lyric, dramatic and coloratura demands. Luis Lima as the King is somewhat strained by the high tessitura, but his is a ringing tenor, clean of attack. Sherrill Milnes as the heroine's wicked uncle sounds even more Italianate, rolling his 'r's ferociously; but high melodrama is apt, and with digital recording of demonstration splendour and fine perspective this shameless example of operatic hokum could not be presented more persuasively on CD.

Werther (complete).

*** Ph. 416 654-2 (2) [id.]. Carreras, Von Stade, Allen, Buchanan, Lloyd, Children's Ch., ROHCG O, C. Davis.

(M) **(*) EMI CMS7 63973-2 (2) [Ang. CDMB 63973]. Gedda, De los Angeles, Mesplé, Soyer, Voix d'Enfants de la Maîtrise de l'ORTF, O de Paris, Prêtre.

Sir Colin Davis has rarely directed a more sensitive or more warmly expressive performance on record than his account of *Werther*, based on a stage production at Covent Garden. Frederica von Stade makes an enchanting Charlotte, outshining all current rivals on record. Carreras uses a naturally beautiful voice freshly and sensitively. Thomas Allen as Charlotte's husband Albert and Isobel Buchanan as Sophie, her sister, are excellent, too. The CD transfer on to a pair of discs has been highly successful, with a single serious reservation: the break between the two CDs is badly placed in the middle of a key scene between Werther and Charlotte, just before *Ah! qu'il est loin ce jour!*

Victoria de los Angeles's golden tones, which convey pathos so beautifully, are ideally suited to Massenet's gentle melodies and, though she is recorded too closely (closer than the other soloists), she makes an intensely appealing heroine. Gedda makes an intelligent romantic hero, though Prêtre's direction could be subtler.

Mathias, William (1934–92)

Lux aeterna, Op. 88.

*** Chan. Dig. CHAN 8695 [id.]. Felicity Lott, Cable, Penelope Walker, Bach Ch., St George's Chapel Ch., Windsor, LSO, Willcocks; J. Scott (organ).

Just as Britten in the *War Requiem* contrasted different planes of expression with Latin liturgy set against Wilfred Owen poems, so Mathias contrasts the full choir singing Latin against the boys' choir singing carol-like Marian anthems, and in turn against the three soloists, who sing three arias and a trio to the mystical poems of St John of the Cross. Overall, the confidence of the writing makes the work far more than derivative, an approachable and colourful piece, full of memorable ideas, especially in this excellent performance, beautifully sung and played and atmospherically balanced.

Wind quintet.

*** Crystal CD 750 [id.]. Westwood Wind Quintet – CARLSSON: *Nightwings;* LIGETI: *Bagatelles;* BARBER: *Summer music.* ***

Of the five movements of this spirited *Quintet* the Scherzo is particularly felicitous and there is a rather beautiful *Elegy.* The playing of the Westwood Wind Quintet is highly expert and committed, and the recording is very good indeed.

Matthews, Colin (born 1946)

(i) *Cello concerto;* (ii) *Sonata No. 5 (Landscape), Op. 17.*

☞ (M) *** Unicorn Dig. UKCD 2058 [id.]. (i) Alexander Baillie, L. Sinf.; (ii) Berlin RSO, John Carewe.

Colin Matthews' *Sonata No. 5*, subtitled *Landscape*, is one of the most powerful and ambitious orchestral works to have been written by a British composer of the younger generation, in effect a large-scale symphony in a single movement, richly and evocatively scored. In its concentration over a broad span it rises well above mere atmospheric associations of dark into light (the composer's broad theme), presenting a natural logic which the ear can appreciate even before the brain can analyse it. This is a formidable achievement and, though the Berlin live performance conducted by John Carewe is not as strong or committed as that which the BBC broadcast earlier, this is a splendid celebration of a fast-growing talent. The *Cello concerto* too is an impressive piece, again confidently argued on a broad scale. It is a pity that, with this of all instruments, Matthews does not allow himself a warmer lyricism; but with Alexander Baillie brilliantly bringing out the power of the declamatory writing and intensifying the underlying darkness of the piece, this too emerges as a fine, ambitious work, warm in its emotions. On this CD it is as well recorded as it is dedicatedly played. The sound has plenty of atmosphere and yet good definition.

Matthews, David (born 1942)

Symphony No. 4, Op. 52.
☞ **(*) Collins Single Dig. 2008-2 [id.]. East of England O, Malcolm Nabarro.

One of Collins's exemplary series devoted to contemporary British music and generally offering only one work at a special price. David Matthews is a gifted and imaginative composer with a good musical mind, whose work deserves wider exposure. There is a lot of Britten, Stravinsky and Tippett (on whose music he has written a book) in his musical thinking, but all the same he is his own man. His *Fourth Symphony* takes 27 minutes 17 seconds and is well worth hearing. The orchestral playing is spirited, though the strings are not world class; but the recording is very vivid and well detailed.

Cantiga (Dramatic scena for soprano and orchestra), *Op. 45, Introit Op. 28; September music, Op. 24.*
☞ *** Unicorn Dig. DKPCD 9120 [id.]. Jill Gomez, Bournemouth Sinf., Carewe – MAHLER: *7 early Lieder.* ***

With his younger brother, Colin, David Matthews played an important part both in helping Deryck Cooke with the performing edition of Mahler's *Tenth Symphony* and together, as assistants to Benjamin Britten during his long final illness, David and Colin played a key part in ensuring that Britten's last, painfully created works were completed. Until now David Matthews has tended to attract less attention than Colin as a composer, so it is welcome to have a major recording of David Matthews' music, perfectly designed to bring out his positive and immediately appealing qualities, confirming him as one of the most gifted composers of his generation. In the Matthews family, lightning has clearly struck twice!

The major work on this Unicorn-Kanchana CD is *Cantiga*, a 25-minute dramatic scena which in a warmly lyrical idiom with luscious textures tells the haunting story, set in medieval Portugal, of Dom Pedro and his mistress, Dona Inez de Castro. The king, Dom Pedro's father, had Dona Inez savagely murdered, yet when Pedro succeeded to the throne he had the embalmed body of his beloved treated to a coronation, as if she were a living queen. The four linked narrative poems by Maggie Hemingway represent a commentary by Dona Inez from beyond the grave, involving strong dramatic contrasts, vividly presented here by the singer for whom *Cantiga* was written, Jill Gomez, most sympathetically accompanied by the Bournemouth Sinfonietta under John Carewe. So the sensuousness of the first two songs gives way to the violence of the third, involving the murder of Dona Inez, and leads to the sweet-sour mood of the final number, with bitterness sharpening the stately coronation ceremonial. *Cantiga*, powerful and immediately attractive, is well coupled here with two shorter orchestral pieces by Matthews, *September music* – full of glowing colours from the opening horn solo onwards – and another ceremonial piece, *Introit*, with sustained string-writing and elaborate solos aiming to echo Gothic architecture. What crowns the disc is the final work, the orchestration of Mahler's *Seven Early Lieder* made at the beginning of their careers by David and Colin Matthews together. In anticipation of their work for Deryck Cooke, their feeling for the Mahler sound is unerring, making these a most rewarding addition to the tally of regular Mahler song-cycles.

Matthus, Siegfried (born 1936)

Nachtlieder, for baritone, string quartet and harp.
☞ *(*) EMI Dig. CDC7 54520-2 [id.]. Fischer-Dieskau, Graf, Cherubini Qt – SCHOECK: *Notturno.* *(*)

Siegfried Matthus is one of the leading composers of the former DDR who enjoyed little exposure on the other side of the Wall. His *Nachtlieder*, dedicated to Fischer-Dieskau, sets for baritone, string quartet and harp various texts on the theme of Night from Herder's *Alte ägyptische Philosophie* through to Heine and Morgenstern. It is a most imaginative and atmospheric work (not wholly uninfluenced by Schoeck as well as by the example of Ravel's *Mallarmé* settings). It is very well played here and deserves the attention of all connoisseurs of song; but Fischer-Dieskau was in his mid-sixties when he made this recording, and it finds the voice wanting in timbre and bloom. To be brutal, the voice has almost gone, though one can admire the intelligence, finesse and taste with which what little that is left is used.

Maunder, John (1858–1920)

Olivet to Calvary (cantata).
☞ (B) **(*) CfP CD-CFP 4619. John Mitchinson, Frederick Harvey, Guildford Cathedral Ch.,
Barry Rose; P. Morse (organ).

It is easy to be patronizing about music like this. For many tastes its melodic and harmonic flavour
will seem too highly coloured and sugary for the subject but, provided one accepts the conventions of
style in which it is composed, the music is effective and often moving. The performance has an
attractive simplicity and genuine eloquence. Just occasionally the soloists overdo the drama in their
enunciation, but for the most part they are sensitive to the text and the obvious dedication of the
music. Frederick Harvey is particularly moving at the actual moment of Christ's death; in a passage
that, insensitively handled, could be positively embarrassing, he creates a magical, hushed intensity.
The choir sing beautifully, and in the gentler, lyrical writing (the semi-chorus *O Thou whose sweet
compassion*, for example) sentimentality is skilfully avoided. The 1964 recording is first class in every
way, and it has been admirably transferred to CD.

Maw, Nicholas (born 1935)

Odyssey.
*** EMI Dig. CDS7 54277-2 (2) [Ang. CDCB 54277]. CBSO, Simon Rattle.

Spanning an hour and 40 minutes, Nicholas Maw's *Odyssey* has been counted the biggest continuous
orchestral piece ever written. As in Mahler, if not so readily, one comes to recognize musical
landmarks in the six substantial movements. The slow movement alone lasts over half an hour, while
the allegros bring a genuine sense of speed, thrusting and energetic. It was at Rattle's insistence that
this superb recording was made at live concerts. The result is astonishingly fine, with the engineers
totally disguising the problems of recording in Birmingham Town Hall.

Maxwell Davies, Peter (born 1934)

Ave maris stella; Image, reflection, shadow; (i) *Runes from a holy island.*
(M) *** Unicorn UKCD 2038; *UKC 2038*. Fires of London, (i) cond. composer.

This is a CD compilation of key Maxwell Davies works. *Ave maris stella*, essentially elegiac, finds the
composer at his most severe and demanding. The second piece, *Image, reflection, shadow*, is a kind of
sequel. *Runes*, conducted by the composer, is much shorter yet just as intense in its rapt slowness.
Ideal performances, well recorded, from the group for which all this music was written.

The Boyfriend; The Devils (film-scores): suites. (i) *Seven in nomine.*
*** Collins Dig. 1095-2 [id.]. (i) Mary Thomas; Aquarius, Nicholas Cleobury.

In 1971 Maxwell Davies did the sharply imagined scores for two Ken Russell films. Maxwell Davies's
distorting lens works surprisingly well in both. Nicholas Cleobury draws alert playing from Aquarius,
though in *The Boyfriend* the distant recording takes away some of the necessary bite. From the same
crisply economical period *Seven in nomine* is a series of rather severe reworkings of the *In nomine*
theme of John Taverner, which somewhat obsessed Maxwell Davies while writing his opera on that
Tudor composer.

Caroline Mathilde – concert suite
*** Collins Dig. Single 2002-2. BBC PO, composer.

The composer conducts the BBC Philharmonic in these vivid performances, brilliantly recorded. A
valuable addition to Collins's 20th-Century Plus series of CD singles.

(i) *Trumpet concerto;* (ii) *Symphony No. 4.*
*** Collins Dig. 1181-2 [id.]. (i) John Wallace, SNO; (ii) SCO; composer.

Inspired by the dazzling and poetic playing of the Philharmonia principal, John Wallace, the soloist
on the record, the *Trumpet concerto*, written in 1988, is one of the most rewarding of Maxwell
Davies's later works. Another source of inspiration has been St Francis, and the slow movement links
with the saint's sermon to the birds, deeply meditative; the final coda in its Messiaenic jangling
represents sublime glorification when St Francis receives the stigmata. The *Fourth Symphony* of 1984
brings similarly striking landmarks. Though it uses chamber forces, this four-movement work is
texturally the thorniest of the composer's symphonies, not an easy piece but one with a powerful

physical impact. The playing both of the SNO in the concerto and of the SCO in the symphony is strongly committed, with excellent recorded sound.

Violin concerto.
☞ (M) *** Sony Dig. SMK 58928 [id.]. Isaac Stern, RPO, Previn – BRITTEN: *Cello symphony.* ***

Maxwell Davies wrote his *Violin concerto* specifically with Isaac Stern in mind, and there are parallels here with the Walton *Violin concerto* of over 40 years earlier. The composer was inspired to draw on a more warmly lyrical side that he has rarely displayed. Yet for all its beauties, this is a work which has a tendency to middle-aged spread, not nearly as taut in expression as the Walton or, for that matter, Britten's *Cello symphony*, with which it is coupled. Stern seems less involved here than in that other work, though this coupling makes a strong, meaty issue for anyone wanting to investigate the recent development of these characterful composers.

Renaissance and Baroque realisations: (PURCELL: *Fantasia & 2 pavans; Fantasia upon one note.* BACH: *Well-tempered Clavier: Preludes & fugues in C sharp major and min.* (i) GESUALDO: *Tenebrae super Gesualdo.* DUNSTABLE: *Veni sancte – Veni creator spiritus.* KINLOCH: *His fantaisie. 3 Early Scottish motets*).
(M) *** Unicorn UKCD 2044 [id.]. Fires of London, (i) with Mary Thomas; composer.

These pieces mainly represent the composer in the 1960s abrasively distorting into foxtrot and other dance rhythms pieces by Purcell, Bach, Dunstable and others. It is like painting a moustache on the Mona Lisa, only more fun.

Sinfonia; Sinfonia concertante.
(M) *** Unicorn Dig. UKCD 2026; *UKC 2026* [id.]. SCO, composer.

In his *Sinfonia* of 1962 Peter Maxwell Davies took as his inspirational starting point Monteverdi's *Vespers* of 1610, and the dedication in this music, beautifully played by the Scottish Chamber Orchestra under the composer, is plain from first to last. The *Sinfonia concertante* is a much more extrovert piece for strings plus solo wind quintet and timpani. In idiom this is hardly at all neo-classical and, more than usual, the composer evokes romantic images, as in the lovely close of the first movement. Virtuoso playing from the Scottish principals, not least the horn. Well-balanced recording.

Sinfonia accademica; (i) *Into the labyrinth.*
(M) *** Unicorn UKCD 2022. (i) Neil Mackie; SCO, composer.

Into the labyrinth, in five movements, might be regarded more as a song-symphony than as a cantata, a prose-poem inspired by the physical impact of Orkney. The fine Scottish tenor, Neil Mackie, gives a superb performance, confirming this as one of Maxwell Davies's most beautiful and moving inspirations. The *Sinfonia accademica* provides a strong and attractive contrast, and again evokes the atmosphere of Orkney. Strong, intense performances under the composer, helped by first-rate recording.

Symphony No. 2.
☞ *** Collins Dig. 1403-2 [id.]. BBC PO, composer.

With its four movements lasting nearly an hour, the *Symphony No. 2* on its appearance in 1980 confirmed the new pattern of Maxwell Davies's creative drive earlier set by the *First Symphony*, similarly weighty in its form and arguments. Written for the centenary of the Boston Symphony Orchestra, the *Second* represents the composer's search for a latter-day equivalent, personal to him, of the traditional conflicts of symphonic form. He sets out his aims lucidly in the notes. Though the textures are complex, he hopes in the four conventionally balanced movements to make the musical logic speak for itself. Like Sibelius, he has also taken inspiration directly from nature, the seascape near his Orkney home which has been an important force in many of his later works. The outer, most obviously symphonic, movements are the ones that benefit most from repetition on disc, but the whole work, with its reposeful slow movement and shadowy Scherzo, makes an immediate impact, though under the composer the playing of the BBC Philharmonic is not as taut as it might be. Excellent sound.

OPERA

The Martyrdom of St Magnus.
*** Unicorn Dig. DKPCD 9100 [id.]. Dives, Gillett, Thomson, Morris, Kelvin Thomas, Scottish Chamber Op. Ens., Michael Rafferty.

With Gregorian chant providing an underlying basis of argument, Davies has here simplified his regular idiom. The musical argument of each of the nine compact scenes is summarized in the interludes which follow. The story is baldly but movingly presented, with St Magnus translated to the present century as a concentration camp victim, finally killed by his captors. Outstanding among the soloists is the tenor, Christopher Gillett, taking among other roles that of the Prisoner (or saint).

Mayerl, Billy (1902–59)

Aquarium suite; Autumn crocus; Bats in the belfry; Four Aces suite: Ace of Clubs; Ace of Spades. 3 Dances in syncopation, Op. 73; Green tulips; Hollyhock; Hop-o'-my-thumb; Jill all alone; Mistletoe; Parade of the sandwich-board men; Sweet William; White heather.
**(*) Chan. Dig. CHAN 8848; *LBTD 028* [id.]. Eric Parkin.

Billy Mayerl left an indelible legacy of light pieces of high quality, with writing that is often much more complex and sophisticated than the rags of Joplin and his contemporaries. Mayerl's most famous lyrical numbers, such as *Marigold* and *Autumn crocus*, combine 'a blend of elegance, wistfulness, nonchalance and high spirits – qualities which stamped his whole output'. The best of his pieces sound surprisingly undated. Eric Parkin obviously enjoys this repertoire and plays the music with much sympathy and vivacious rhythmic freedom, even if his shoulders are not quite as loose as those of Susan Tomes, whose Virgin collection has been withdrawn. His programme is well chosen to suit his own approach to Mayerl's repertoire, and this Chandos record is certainly very enjoyable as he is very well treated by the recording engineers.

Medtner, Nikolai (1880–1951)

(i) *Piano concertos Nos. 1 in C min., Op. 33; 2 in C min., Op. 50; 3 in E min. (Ballade), Op. 60.* (Piano) *Sonata-Ballade in F sharp, Op. 27.*
*** Chan. Dig. CHAN 9040 (2) [id.]. Geoffrey Tozer; (i) LPO, Järvi.

Piano concerto No. 1 in C min., Op. 33.
☞ **(*) Russian Disc MK 417087 [id.]. Igor Zhukov, USSR R. & TV Large SO, Alexander Dmitriev – BALAKIREV; RIMSKY-KORSAKOV: *Piano concertos.* **(*)

(i) *Piano concerto No. 1 in C min., Op. 33; Sonata-Ballade in F sharp, Op. 27.*
*** Chan. Dig. CHAN 9038 [id.]. Tozer, (i) LPO, Järvi.

Piano concertos Nos. 2 in C min., Op. 50; 3 in E min., Op. 60.
*** Hyp. Dig. CDA 66580 [id.]. Nikolai Demidenko, BBC Scottish SO, Jerzy Maksymiuk.
*** Chan. Dig. CHAN 9039 [id.]. Tozer, LPO, Järvi.

After some years of neglect, the recording industry is taking more interest in Medtner, this Russian aristocrat of the piano who spent his last years in London. Chandos offer the three concertos together as a package or separately. Their soloist is the Australian Geoffrey Tozer, who also plays the *Sonata-Ballade, Op. 27*, for good measure. In the *Second* and *Third* concertos they come into direct competition with Hyperion with Nikolai Demidenko as soloist. Tozer has obvious feeling for this composer, and his playing has no lack of warmth and virtuosity. He has the advantage over his rival of a richer, more transparent recording and a more sympathetic and responsive accompanist in Järvi and the London Philharmonic. Demidenko, on the other hand, has the greater fire and dramatic flair, and his performance with the BBC Scottish Orchestra under Jerzy Maksymiuk has one very much on the edge of one's chair. He is by no means as well recorded as Tozer, the sound of the piano is shallow, and the orchestra lacks real transparency and is a bit two-dimensional in terms of front-to-back perspective. All the same, many will feel that this is a small price for playing of such thrilling quality.

The *First Piano concerto* comes on this Russian CD in a virtuosic account from Igor Zhukov, made in the 1960s. It forms part of an interesting collection of one-movement concertos (the first of Balakirev and the only one of Rimsky-Korsakov), decently enough recorded but with some less-than-elegant orchestral support.

Piano concertos Nos. 2 in C min., Op. 50; 3 in E min., Op. 60 (Ballade); Arabesque in A min., Op. 7/ 2; Tale in F min., Op. 26/3.

☞ (***) Testament mono SBT 1027 [id.]. Composer, Philh. O, Dobrowen.

At last we have two of the celebrated set of Medtner concerto recordings which the Maharajah of Mysore funded in the late 1940s. Medtner was then in his sixties but his playing is still pretty magisterial. These concertos could really have been written in the 1880s in the days of Anton Rubinstein, and despite their date are firmly in the romantic tradition. Hailed in his youth as the Russian Brahms, Medtner set his face against 'modernist' trends in music. When critics complained after the first performance of Rachmaninov's *Third Symphony* that his music was too old-fashioned ('a castle without royalty. Rachmaninov still gives lavish parties in the old style but none of the guests turn up', was Richard Capell's memorable phrase), Medtner spent a sleepless night worrying that his writing was too modernistic! These two concertos and the early miniatures that make up the disc still possess an aristocratic allure and a musical finesse that it is difficult to resist. The performances were never reissued in the UK in the days of LP, and their reappearance at long last is as welcome as it is overdue. Good transfers.

Violin sonatas Nos. 1 in B min., Op. 21; 2 in G, Op. 44; 3 in E min., Op. 57 (Epica); Canzonas and Dances, Op. 43; 3 Nocturnes, Op. 16.

☞ **(*) Russian Disc MK Dig. 417109(2) [id.]. Alexander Shirinsky, Dmitri Galynin.

These two CDs comprise Medtner's complete output for violin and piano – indeed his entire chamber music save for the *Piano quintet*. The *Second* and *Third Sonatas* are both big-boned works, lasting almost 50 minutes apiece, and despite their apparent air of rhapsody are held together closely. The latter was once recorded by Oistrakh. They are not easy listening and call for keen concentration; more approachable is the much shorter *First Sonata* which has genuine charm. The *Nocturnes* and their lyrical companions on this disc should be repertoire pieces. The performances are good and the recorded balance decently judged and sonically acceptable but not top-drawer.

PIANO MUSIC

(Piano, four hands) (i) *Russian round dance, Op. 58/1;* (Piano) *Forgotten melody: Danza festivo, Op. 38/3; 2 Tales, Op. 20; 3 Tales, Op. 51/1–3.* Songs: (ii) *Down in the garden;* (iii) *The Muse; The Rose;* (ii) *The Ravens; Serenade; To a dreamer; The wagon of life;* (iii) *When roses fade;* (ii) *The willow; Winter evening.* (iii) Goethe *Lieder; Aus Lila; Einsamkeit; Elfenliedchen; Glückliche Fahrt; Selbstbetrug; Im Vorübergehn; 3 Lieder, Op. 46: Praeludium; Die Quelle; Winternacht.*

☞ (***) EMI mono EMI CDC7 54839-2 [id.]. Composer, with (i) Moiseiwitsch; (ii) Oda Slobodskaya; (iii) Elisabeth Schwarzkopf.

Apart from the pieces from Opp. 20, 51 and 58, which were recorded in 1936, these recordings all date from 1946–7 and 1950. They add a further dimension to the picture of the composer's music-making that we have from the concertos. Both Slobodskaya and Schwarzkopf give finely characterized accounts of these songs, all too few of which have been recorded since. There is nearly 80 minutes of Medtner playing either as solo pianist, as accompanist or, with his friend Benno Moiseiwitsch, as duo-pianist, and no one with an interest in Russian music should be without them.

Russian round dance; Knight errant, Op. 58/1–2.

☞ *** Hyp. Dig. CDA 66654 [id.]. Nikolai Demidenko, Dmitri Alexeev – RACHMANINOV: *Suite* etc. ***

The Russian round-dance or *khorovod* was written in 1946 and Medtner and Moiseiwitsch recorded it the same year for EMI. Here it is given with great lightness of touch, though this partnership lose beauty of tone-production above fortissimo.

Canzona matinata, Op. 39/4; Canzona serenata, Op. 38/6; Dithyrambe, Op. 10/2; Fairy tale, Op. 20/1; Sonata elegia in D min., Op. 11/2; Sonata reminiscenza in A min., Op. 38/1; Sonata tragica in C min., Op. 39/5; Theme and variations in C sharp min., Op. 55.

☞ ** Hyp. Dig. CDA 66636 [id.]. Nikolai Demidenko.

Demidenko's Medtner recital has collected rave reviews and there is no question that he brings many poetic insights to some of these pieces and great pianistic finesse. But his accomplishments are all too often in the service of interpreter rather than composer. No one who has heard Medtner's own playing, which is simple, direct and totally free of any affectation, or who recalls Gilels's account of the *Sonata reminiscenza* will find Demidenko's perfumed account entirely acceptable. Gilels went directly to the heart of this piece and his selfless 1969 account should be restored to circulation within the lifetime of this book. By its side Demidenko sounds posturing and self-regarding. As a guide to Medtner, the less glamorous Hamish Milne (CRD) remains the truer interpreter. Demidenko's formidable pianism is not in question but some of his artistic judgements are less sound, and the quality of the Hyperion recording has also been overpraised. It is good without being distinguished and there is a lack of transparency, particularly in the middle range.

Dancing fairy tale, Op. 48/1; Fairy tale (1915); Fairy tales in D min., Op. 51/1; in E min., Op. 34/2; in F min., Op. 26/3; in G sharp min., Op. 31/3. Funeral march, Op. 31/2; The Organ grinder, Op. 54/3; Russian fairy tale, Op. 42/1; Sonata in G min., Op. 22; Sonata reminiscenza in A min., Op. 38/1.
☞ *** Chan. Dig. CHAN 9050 [id.]. Geoffrey Tozer.

The more romantically named Demidenko has put the less romantic Tozer in the shade in some (but not all) sections of the press. But although Demidenko's pianistic wizardry is unassailable, Tozer is often to be preferred on interpretative grounds. He takes much less time over the *Sonata reminiscenza*, for example, but creates the illusion of unhurried calm. His playing has the classic virtues of being truthful to the letter (and the spirit) of the score and he allows the music to speak for itself without recourse to ostentation or flamboyance. The lifelike recording enhances the claims of this issue and bodes well for the enterprise (a complete survey of the keyboard music) as a whole.

Dithyramb, Op. 10/2; Elegy, Op. 59/2; Skazki (Fairy tales): No. 1 (1915); in E min., Op. 14/2; in G, Op. 9/3; in D min. (Ophelia's song); in C sharp min., Op. 35/4. Forgotten melodies, 2nd Cycle, No. 1: Meditation. Primavera, Op. 39/3; 3 Hymns in praise of toil, Op. 49; Piano sonata in E min. (The Night Wind), Op. 25/2; Sonata Triad, Op. 11/1–3.
*** CRD CRD 3338/9 [id.]. Hamish Milne.

Improvisation No. 2 (in variation form), Op. 47; Piano sonata in F min., Op. 5.
*** CRD Dig. CRD 3461 [id.]. Hamish Milne.

3 Novelles, Op. 17; Romantic sketches for the young, Op. 54; Piano sonatas in G min., Op. 22; A min., Op. 30; 2 Skazki, Op. 8.
*** CRD Dig. CRD 3460 [id.]. Hamish Milne.

Medtner's art is subtle and elusive. He shows an aristocratic disdain for the obvious, a feeling for balance and proportion, and a quiet harmonic refinement that offer consistent rewards. The *G minor Sonata* (1911), which Moiseiwitsch and Gilels recorded, makes a good starting point to discovering Medtner, and there is no better guide than this splendid pianist. There is hardly a weak piece here, and Milne is a poetic advocate whose technical prowess is matched by first-rate artistry. The recording too is very truthful and vivid.

Méhul, Etienne-Nicolas (1763–1817)

Symphonies Nos. 1–4; Overtures: La chasse de jeune Henri; Le trésor supposé.
*** Nimbus Dig. NI 5184/5 [id.]. Gulbenkian Foundation O, Swierczewski.

Méhul was a contemporary of Cherubini and flourished during the years of Napoleon. He was enormously prolific and wrote no fewer than 25 operas in the period 1790–1810. The four symphonies recorded here come from 1808–10 (Nos. 3 & 4 have been discovered only in recent years by David Charlton, who has edited them) and are well worth investigating. The invention is felicitous and engaging, and in *No. 4 in E major* Méhul brings back a motif of the *Adagio* in the finale, a unifying gesture well ahead of its time. The performances are eminently satisfactory even if the strings sound a shade undernourished.

Piano sonatas Nos. 1 in D; 2 in C min.; 3 in A, Op. 1/1–3; 4 in D; 5 in A min.; 6 in C, Op. 2/1–3.
☞ ⑧ (B) *** Discover Dig. DICD 920152 [id.]. Brigitte Haudebourg (fortepiano).

This is a fascinating rarity, well worth investigating on the new bargain label, Discover. Beethoven admired Etienne-Nicolas Méhul, one of the musical standard-bearers of the French Revolution, who wrote these six keyboard sonatas very early in his career. He is credited with having an influence on the German master and, on the evidence of this CD, that claim is well founded. Beethoven's first three major numbered *Sonatas* (Op. 2) were written in 1795. Méhul's first three *Piano sonatas* date from 1783 (Op. 1) and are for the most part charming miniatures, but the remaining three, dating from 1788, are on a broader scale, and bring fascinating anticipations of Beethoven. There is a D major work (Op. 2/1) that Beethoven must have known when writing his own D major, Opus 10, No. 3, so similar is the opening theme. Méhul's earlier *C minor Sonata*, Op. 1/2, has a strong profile and in its less sophisticated way anticipates the kind of drama that Beethoven was to bring to the keyboard. Méhul's opening movement, marked *fièrement*, almost immediately brings a passage that gives a whiff of the German master. Of course there is much keyboard writing here that is comparatively primitive, but nearly all of it is appealing and melodic: the *Andante* of No. 4 (Op. 2/1) is a set of variations on a tune which sounds very like 'Ten green bottles hanging on the wall'. The opening movements of Nos. 5 and 6 (Op. 2/2 and /3) are far from conventional – the latter beginning very grandly, with another attractive slow movement to follow. Brigitte Haudebourg gives sparkling performances, with much conviction and flair, on a fortepiano – a modern copy of a Dulcken from The Hague. It is a fine instrument with a resonant yet attractively gentle tone which suits the music exactly. Well worth exploring. A Rosette for successful enterprise.

Melartin, Erkki (1875–1937)

Symphonies Nos. 5, Op. 90 (Sinfonia brevis); 6, Op. 100.
☞ ** Ondine Dig. ODE 799-2 [id.]. Tampere PO, Leonid Grin.

Erkki Melartin's dates coincide exactly with those of Ravel and he, too, has a good feel for orchestral colour though he was less responsive to French influence than his fellow-countrymen, Madetoja and Klami. He followed Sibelius's footsteps in studying first with Martin Wegelius and then with Robert Fuchs, and he was active as teacher and conductor. He was widely travelled for his period, visiting India, Egypt and North Africa and conducting in St Petersburg, Riga and Berlin. (He can claim the distinction of conducting in 1908 the first performance of a Mahler work in any of the Nordic countries.) There is an *art nouveau* feel to his music (Glière, Scriabin and Mahler) and, though some of his ideas are empty and overblown, his was obviously a considerable talent. The *Fifth* (1915) has an extremely attractive *Intermezzo* and the melodramatic *Sixth* (1924) is also worth investigating. One can see why these symphonies have not made their way into the repertoire (though there are worse that have), but they are the product of an intelligent mind. Well-conducted performances and goodish recording.

Mendelssohn, Fanny (1805–47)

Piano trio in D, Op. 11.
*** Hyp. Dig. CDA 66331 [id.]. Dartington Piano Trio – Clara SCHUMANN: *Trio in G min.* ***

Like Clara Schumann's *G minor Trio* with which it is coupled, the *Piano trio* has impeccable craftsmanship and great facility. Its ideas are pleasing, though not strongly individual. The Dartington Piano Trio play most persuasively and give much pleasure. Excellent recording.

3 Pieces for piano, 4 hands.
☞ *** Sony Dig. SK 48494 [id.]. Tal & Groethuysen – Felix MENDELSSOHN: *Andante and allegro*
    etc. ***

Yaara Tal and Andreas Groethuysen are a wonderful duo and have the capacity to transform dust into gold – not that Fanny Mendelssohn's *Pieces* are inferior. They have charm, and seem even more charming than they are in this duo's hands.

Mendelssohn, Felix (1809–47)

(i) *Piano concerto in A min.* (for piano and strings); (ii) *Piano concertos Nos. 1–2; Capriccio brillant, Op. 22.*
(M) *** Teldec/Warner Dig. 9031 75860-2; *9031 78560-4* [id.]. Cyprien Katsaris; (i) Franz Liszt CO, Rolla; (ii) Leipzig GO, Masur.

It was a happy idea to pair the early *A minor Piano concerto* with the two mature works in this form. The former is an extended piece, lasting over half an hour, far longer than the two numbered concertos, an amazing work for a thirteen-year-old, endlessly inventive. It is impossible not to respond to Katsaris's vitality, even if at times there is a feeling of his rushing his fences. He plays with enormous vigour in the outer movements and receives strong support from Masur. There is nothing heavy, yet the music is given more substance than usual, while the central slow movements bring a relaxed lyrical *espressivo* which provides admirable contrast. The full, well-balanced recording has attractive ambience and sparkle.

(i) *Piano concerto in A min.* (for piano and strings); (i; ii) *Double piano concerto in E. String symphony No. 12 in G min.*

☞ (M) *** Decca 433 729-2 [id.]. (i) John Ogdon; (ii) Brenda Lucas; ASMF, Marriner.

Here is a highly attractive (and generous: 74 minutes) compilation from Mendelssohn's precocious teenage years. The remarkably ambitious and successful *A minor Concerto* was written when he was thirteen and the *Double Concerto* and *String Symphony* (in which the flowing tranquillity of the *Andante* is most appealing) come from approximately two years later. The delightful concertante rarities both have engaging ideas and are played with great verve and spirit by John Ogdon and his wife. The orchestral playing is equally lively and fresh throughout the disc, and the vivid (originally Argo) Kingsway Hall recording from the late 1960s has hardly dated.

Piano concertos Nos. 1 in G min., Op. 25; 2 in D min., Op. 40; Capriccio brillant in B min., Op. 22.

☞ ⊛ *** Chan. Dig. CHAN 9215 [id.]. Howard Shelley, LMP.

☞ *(*) (M) Pickwick PCD953 *CIMPC953* [id.]. Anton Kuerti, LPO, Paul Freeman.

Piano concertos Nos. 1–2; Capriccio brillant, Op. 22; Rondo brillant in E flat, Op. 29.

☞ (BB) *** Naxos Dig. 8.550691-2 [id.]. Benjamin Frith, Slovak State PO (Košice), Robert Stanovsky.

After his successful series of Mozart concertos which, along with the Schiff–Végh cycle, is the first that can be named in the same breath as Murray Perahia's, Howard Shelley has ventured into another area of the catalogue dominated by the great American pianist – and again with no less distinction. Indeed this is marvellous playing in every respect: fresh, sparkling and dashing in the fast movements, poetic and touching in the slower ones. The London Mozart Players are a group of exactly the right size for these works and they point rhythms nicely and provide the necessary lift. Shelley is particularly good in the finales and certainly conveys the scherzando quality in the closing *Presto* of No. 2. He despatches the *Capriccio brillant* with similar aplomb, and the recording-balance is admirably judged, with rich, truthful recorded sound. For many collectors this will be a first choice. In any event it is recommended with enthusiasm and deserves to be placed alongside the Perahia, which is no mean honour!

But Howard Frith on Naxos is a hardly less personable and nimble soloist: he is sensitively touching in the slow movements and makes much of the fine *Adagio* of No. 2. The Slovak orchestra accompany with vigour and enthusiasm, and if the effect is at times less sharply rhythmic this is partly the effect of a somewhat more reverberant acoustic. The piano balance here is bolder, more forward, although the orchestra certainly makes a strong impression. What gives the Naxos disc an extra edge (apart from its price) is the inclusion of the *Rondo brillant*, which Frith despatches with admirable vigour and sparkle. This disc is enjoyable in every way and is undoubtedly very good value indeed.

Despite a competitive price-tag and decent recording, Anton Kuerti is not in the same bracket. He rattles off the brilliant movements with great dexterity and there is much that gives satisfaction. But this is not in any way an outstanding performance, and the LPO sound pretty uninvolved.

(i) *Piano concertos Nos. 1–2. Prelude and fugue, Op. 35/1; Rondo capriccioso, Op. 14; Variations sérieuses, Op. 54.*

*** Sony MK 42401 [id.]. Murray Perahia; (i) ASMF, Marriner.

Perahia's playing catches the Mendelssohnian spirit with admirable perception. There is sensibility and sparkle, the slow movements are shaped most beautifully and the partnership with Marriner is very successful, for the Academy give a most sensitive backing. The recording could be more transparent but it does not lack body, and the piano timbre is fully acceptable.

(i) *Piano concerto No. 1 in G min., Op. 25;* (ii) *Violin concerto in E min., Op. 64. Symphony No. 4 in A (Italian).*

**(*) Nimbus Dig. NI 5158 [id.]. (i) Kite; (ii) Hudson; Hanover Band, Goodman.

The *G minor Concerto* works surprisingly well on a fortepiano, but the *Violin concerto* is rather less successful when the relative closeness of the solo violin – played by the leader of the Hanover Band, Benjamin Hudson – exaggerates the cutting edge of the instrument, with little or no vibrato used, and each portamento, however authentic, is obtrusive. Yet, with well-chosen speeds – a really flowing *Andante* in the second movement – there is still much to enjoy. If anything, Goodman's performance of the *Italian Symphony*, with string ensemble surprisingly large, is even more sympathetic than Sir Charles Mackerras's earlier period recording for Virgin Classics, when here both speeds and manner are more relaxed, notably in the first two movements.

Double piano concertos: in A flat; in E.
*** Hyp. Dig. CDA 66567 [id.]. Coombs, Munro, BBC Scottish SO, Maksymiuk.

Mendelssohn's *Double concerto in A flat* is the most ambitious of all his concertante works, and the work in E brings an expansive first movement too; they provide formidable evidence of the teenage composer's fluency and technical finesse. Stephen Coombs and Ian Munro prove ideal advocates, playing with delectable point and imagination, finding a wit and poetry in the writing that might easily lie hidden, with even the incidental passagework magnetizing the ear. The recording of the pianos is on the shallow side, and the string-tone is thin too, but that is not inappropriate for the music.

Double piano concerto in E.
☞ **(*) Ph. Dig. 432 095-2 [id.]. Katia and Marielle Labèque, Philh. O, Bychkov – BRUCH: *Double concerto.* **(*)

The fourteen-year-old Mendelssohn's ambitious *E major Double concerto* was written for its young composer to play with his sister Fanny and was first performed by them on her birthday in November 1824. It is not an early masterpiece but is well crafted (if a bit long) and enjoyable. The Labèques play it with enthusiasm and flair, and Bychkov accompanies manfully. But, partly because of the resonant acoustic, the effect is rather inflated and the ear looks for more transparency and lightness of texture in such an amiable piece.

Violin concertos: in D min. (for violin & strings); in E min., Op. 64.
*** Ph. Dig. 432 077-2; *432 077-4* [id.]. Viktoria Mullova, ASMF, Marriner.

Mendelssohn's early *D minor Violin concerto* was completed when he was thirteen. As a structure it is amazingly accomplished; but only the finale, with its dancing main theme, is really memorable. Purity is the keynote of Mullova's fresh and enjoyable readings of both concertos, the early *D minor* as well as the great *E minor* which is tenderly expressive rather than flamboyant in the expression of emotion, yet with concentration keenly maintained. So the central *Andante* is sweet and songful and the finale, light and fanciful, conveys pure fun in its fireworks. The early work follows a similar pattern, with youthful emotions given full rein and with the finale turned into a headily brilliant Csardas. The Philips recording is admirably natural and beautifully balanced.

Violin concerto in E min., Op. 64.
(M) *** Sony Dig. MDK 44902; *40-44902* [id.]. Cho-Liang Lin, Philh. O, Tilson Thomas – BRUCH: *Concerto No. 1* *** (with encores by SARASATE and KREISLER ***).
☞ (M) Decca *** Dig. 430 752-2; *430 752-4* [id.]. Kyung Wha Chung, Montreal SO, Dutoit – BEETHOVEN: *Concerto.* **
(BB) *** Naxos Dig. 8.550153 [id.]. Nishizaki, Slovak PO, Jean – TCHAIKOVSKY: *Concerto.* ***
☞ *** BMG/RCA Dig. 09026 61700-2. Anne Akiko Meyers, Philh. O, Andrew Litton (with DVORAK: *Romance, Op. 11;* MASSENET: *Thaïs: Méditation* ***) – VAUGHAN WILLIAMS: *Lark ascending.* ***
*** EMI Dig. CDC7 49663-2 [id.]. Nigel Kennedy, ECO, Tate – BRUCH: *Concerto No. 1;* SCHUBERT: *Rondo.* ***
*** ASV CDDCA 748 [id.]. Xue-Wei, LPO, Ivor Bolton – BRAHMS: *Violin concerto.* ***
(B) *** Pickwick Dig. PCD 829; *CIMPC 829* [id.]. Jaime Laredo, SCO – BRUCH: *Concerto No. 1.* ***
(M) *** EMI CDM7 69003-2 [id.]; *EG 769003-4.* Menuhin, Philh. O, Kurtz – BRUCH: *Concerto No. 1.* ***
(M) *** DG 419 067-2 [id.]. Milstein, VPO, Abbado – TCHAIKOVSKY: *Concerto.* ***
**(*) BMG/RCA RD 85933 [RCA 5933-2-RC]. Heifetz, Boston SO, Munch – TCHAIKOVSKY: *Concerto* etc. **(*)
☞ (***) Testament mono SBT 1037 [id.]. Martzy, Philh. O, Kletzki – BRAHMS: *Concerto.* (***)
(M) (***) EMI mono CDH7 69799-2 [id.]. Yehudi Menuhin, BPO, Furtwängler – BEETHOVEN: *Concerto.* (***)
☞ (BB) **(*) Discover Dig. DICD 920122 [id.]. Evgeny Bushkov, Slovak New PO, Rahbari – TCHAIKOVSKY: *Concerto.* **
☞ (M) ** EMI Dig. CD-EMX 2217 [id.]. Monica Huggett, O of Age of Enlightenment, Mackerras – BEETHOVEN: *Concerto.* **
☞ (M) (***) EMI mono CDH7 64562-2 [id.]. Szigeti, LPO, Beecham – MOZART: *Violin concerto No. 4;* PROKOFIEV: *Violin concerto No. 1.* (***)
☞ (**) Pearl mono GEMM CD 9377 [id.]. Szigeti, LPO, Beecham – MOZART: *Violin concerto No. 4;* PROKOFIEV: *Violin concerto No. 1.* (**)

☞ (**) Pearl mono GEMM CDS 9996 [id.]. Kreisler, Berlin State Op. O, Leo Blech – BACH: *Double violin concerto;* BEETHOVEN; BRAHMS; MOZART: *Violin concertos.* (**)

Cho-Liang Lin's vibrantly lyrical account now reappears with the Bruch *G minor* (plus some attractive encores) to make an unbeatable mid-priced coupling. These are both immensely rewarding and poetic performances, given excellent, modern, digital sound, and Michael Tilson Thomas proves a highly sympathetic partner in the Mendelssohn *Concerto.*

Chung favours speeds faster than usual in all three movements, and the result is sparkling and happy, with the lovely slow movement fresh and songful, not at all sentimental. With warmly sympathetic accompaniment from Dutoit and the Montreal orchestra, amply recorded, the result is one of Chung's happiest records. Alas, the Beethoven coupling is altogether less recommendable.

Takako Nishizaki gives an inspired reading of the *Concerto,* warm, spontaneous and full of temperament. The central *Andante* is on the slow side, but well shaped, not sentimental, while the outer movements are exhilarating, with excellent playing from the Slovak Philharmonic. Though the forwardly placed violin sounds over-bright, the recording is full and warm. A splendid coupling at super-bargain price.

The sweet, gentle opening of the Mendelssohn *Concerto* as presented by Anne Akiko Meyers immediately sets the pattern not only for that central work but for the whole unusual collection on this disc. As her previous discs for RCA have demonstrated, this violinist, born in California in 1970, is a thoughtful rather than a flamboyant virtuoso, and the four items suit her exceptionally well. There is no feeling that the shorter pieces are in any way mere fillers, so rapt is her playing. This is a small-scale reading of the Mendelssohn, but in context that hardly matters. From the limited range of dynamic here, as well as the total absence of forcing, one gathers that Miss Meyers' tone is not large, but she compensates in sweetness and poetry. At a flowing speed her sweetly lyrical account of the *Andante* completely avoids sentimentality. The Dvořák then emerges as far more than just a salon piece with a Slavonic flavour. The Massenet too, which can seem all too sweet, is played with natural gravity. Though there are many other versions of the Mendelssohn with obviously higher priorities, this one, offering an unusual sequence of other items, all played with compelling dedication and poetry and recorded in vivid sound, clearly has its place.

Kennedy establishes a positive, masculine view of the work from the very start, but fantasy here goes with firm control. The slow movement brings a simple, songful view of the haunting melody, and the finale sparkles winningly, with no feeling of rush. With a bonus in the rare Schubert *Rondo* and clear, warm recording, it makes an excellent recommendation.

Xue-Wei's version, clean and fresh if a little reticent emotionally, makes a generous and attractive coupling for his equally recommendable version of the Brahms. There are more strongly characterized readings than this but, with its pastel-shaded lyricism, this is undoubtedly satisfying, helped by first-rate recording.

Laredo's version on a bargain-price CD brings an attractively direct reading, fresh and alert but avoiding mannerism, marked by consistently sweet and true tone from the soloist. The orchestral ensemble is amazingly good when you remember that the soloist himself is directing. The recording is vivid and clean.

The restrained nobility of Menuhin's phrasing of the famous principal melody of the slow movement has long been a hallmark of his reading with Efrem Kurtz, who provides polished and sympathetic support. The sound of the CD transfer is bright, with the soloist dominating but the orchestral texture well detailed.

Milstein's DG version comes from the early 1970s. His is a highly distinguished performance, very well accompanied. His account of the slow movement is more patrician than Menuhin's, and his slight reserve is projected by DG sound which is bright, clean and clear in its CD remastering.

As one might expect, Heifetz gives a fabulous performance. His speeds are consistently fast, yet in the slow movement his flexible phrasing sounds so inevitable and easy that it is hard not to be convinced. The finale is a tour de force, light and sparkling, with every note in place. The recording has been digitally remastered with success and the sound is smoother than before.

Johanna Martzy gives an exceptionally beautiful account of this lovely concerto, and it is sad that, coming at the very end of the mono era, it has been out of currency for so long, until Testament issued this superb transfer, ideally coupled with an equally inspired account of the Brahms. It is not just the perfect sweetness and purity of Martzy's tone that is so impressive, coupled with flawless intonation, but also her natural imagination in phrasing. So her freely flexible rubato always sounds spontaneous, and the hushed tenderness of her pianissimo playing is breathtaking, as in the link into the second subject of the first movement and in the central *Andante.* The performance is also remarkable for the quicksilver energy of the finale and, with the soloist well forward, the mono sound is full and clear.

Menuhin's unique gift for lyrical sweetness has never been presented on record more seductively than in his classic, earlier version of the Mendelssohn *Concerto* with Furtwängler. The digital transfer is not ideally clear, yet one hardly registers that this is a mono recording from the early 1950s.

The latest bargain-basement digital recording from Discover introduces a brilliant young Russian soloist, Evgeny Bushkov, a pupil of Leonid Kogan. His small, sweet, silvery timbre suits the Mendelssohn concerto admirably, and he prepares and plays the secondary theme of the opening movement with appealing tenderness. The *Andante*, too, has a matching simplicity and the finale no lack of bravura and fire. He is well accompanied, and the recording, made in the Concert Hall of Slovak Radio, Bratislava, is full and well balanced. Not a first choice, however, for the coupled Tchaikovsky *Concerto* sounds less spontaneous.

Monica Huggett's 'authentic' version is a disappointment. Without a memorably lyrical slow movement, any recording of this concerto is a non-starter.

It is good to have Szigeti's wonderfully intense performance of the Mendelssohn *Violin concerto* back in circulation, together with the other classic records he did in the 1930s with Sir Thomas Beecham. The EMI transfer is the one to have. The Pearl is nowhere near so smooth; the top is slightly acidulated and is difficult to tame, and detail in the middle range is far more in focus, smoother and fuller-bodied in the EMI transfer.

Kreisler's 1926 version of the concerto was its very first complete recording. It is beautifully played, but the performance is ill-served by the Pearl transfer, with heavy background and a badly managed join between the first and second movements.

(i) *Violin concerto in E min., Op. 64. Symphony No. 4 in A (Italian), Op. 90; From Athalie, War march of the priests, Op. 74; Overture: The Hebrides (Fingal's Cave), Op. 26.*
☞ (M) **(*) Sony SMK 47592-2. (i) Pinchas Zukerman; NYPO, Bernstein.

Zukerman gives a sweet-toned but never cloying account of the *Violin concerto*. His playing is impeccable from the technical point of view, and the support he receives from Bernstein is thoroughly sympathetic. An extremely fine performance and one which would be a match for any – were it not for the recording, which is balanced unnaturally with the violin well forward and the orchestra recessed. There are rushed tempi and some distracting mannerisms in the *Italian Symphony*, though the recording has been greatly improved on the original LP pressings.

Overtures: *Athalia, Op. 74; Calm sea and prosperous voyage, Op. 27; The Hebrides (Fingal's Cave), Op. 26; The Marriage of Camacho, Op. 10; A Midsummer Night's Dream, Op. 21; Ruy Blas, Op. 95.*
⊛ *** BMG/RCA Dig. RD 87905 [7905-2-RC]. Bamberg SO, Flor.

This is the most desirable collection of Mendelssohn overtures the catalogue has ever offered; the evocatively atmospheric opening of *Calm sea and prosperous voyage*, followed by an allegro of great vitality, is a demonstrable example of the spontaneous imagination of these performances, and there is no finer version of *Fingal's Cave*, with its lyrical secondary theme phrased with memorable warmth. *The Marriage of Camacho*, with its brass opening, reminds us somewhat of *Ruy Blas*, and also a little of Weber: it is a most attractive piece with some engaging writing for woodwind. *Athalia* is very enjoyable too, especially when played with such freshness and polish. The recording, made in the Dominikanerbau, Bamberg, has splendid warmth and bloom and a most attractive hall ambience.

Symphonies for string orchestra Nos. 1 in C; 2 in D; 3 in E min.; 4 in C min.; 5 in B flat; 6 in E flat.
*** Nimbus Dig. NI 5141 [id.]. E. String O, William Boughton.

Symphonies for string orchestra Nos. 7 in D min.; 8 in D; 10 in B min.
*** Nimbus Dig. NI 5142 [id.]. E. String O, William Boughton.

Symphonies for string orchestra Nos. 9 in C; 11 in F; 12 in G min.
*** Nimbus Dig. NI 5143 [id.]. E. String O, William Boughton.

Mendelssohn's twelve *String symphonies*, written for family performance by one of the most brilliant boy-geniuses in the history of music, contain delectable inspirations by the dozen. William Boughton conducts the English String Orchestra in winningly energetic readings of these delightful works, not as polished in ensemble as some rivals, but with warmly atmospheric recording helping to make them very persuasive.

Symphonies for strings Nos. 2 in D; 3 in E min.; 9 in C; 10 in B min.
☞ *** BIS Dig. CD 643 [id.]. Amsterdam New Sinf., Lev Markiz.

The recordings by the Amsterdam New Sinfonietta are the first instalment of a new, complete survey. They are very well if resonantly recorded, but the playing, both vital and expressive, is of high quality and the sound is clearly textured as well as full. Recommendable, alongside the current alternatives, and on grounds of recording a possible first choice.

Symphonies for string orchestra, Nos. 9 in C min.; 10 in B min.; 12 in G min.
*** Hyp. CDA 66196 [id.]. L. Festival O, Ross Pople.

Ross Pople achieves performances that are as polished and spirited as they are lyrically responsive. No. 9 has a particularly gracious slow movement following the drama of its opening, but No. 12 with its clear debt to Bach is also most impressive. Excellent sound.

Symphonies Nos. 1–5.
(M) *** DG 429 664-2 (3). Mathis, Rebman, Hollweg, German Op. Ch., BPO, Karajan.

Symphonies Nos. 1–5; Overtures: Fair Melusina, Op. 32; The Hebrides (Fingal's Cave), Op. 26; A Midsummer Night's Dream, Op. 21; Octet, Op. 20: Scherzo.
*** DG Dig. 415 353-2 (4) [id.]. LSO, Abbado (with Connell, Mattila, Blochwitz and London Symphony Ch. in Symphony No. 2).

Abbado's is a set to brush cobwebs off an attractive symphonic corner; in the lesser-known symphonies it is his gift to have you forgetting any weaknesses of structure or thematic invention in the brightness and directness of his manner. So the youthful *First* has plenty of C minor bite. The toughness of the piece makes one marvel that Mendelssohn ever substituted the scherzo from the *Octet* for the third movement (as he did in London), but helpfully Abbado includes that extra scherzo, so that on CD, with a programming device, you can readily make the substitution yourself. Good, bright recording, though not ideally transparent.

Karajan's distinguished set of the Mendelssohn *Symphonies* was recorded in 1971/2 in the Berlin Jesus Christus Kirche. The early C minor work sounds particularly fresh, and the *Hymn of praise* brings the fullest sound of all; the very fine choral singing is vividly caught. The soloists make a good team, rather than showing any memorable individuality; but overall Karajan's performance is most satisfying. The *Scottish Symphony* is a particularly remarkable account and the *Italian* shows the Berlin Philharmonic in sparkling form: the only drawback is Karajan's characteristic omission of both first-movement exposition repeats. There are some reservations to be made about the *Reformation Symphony*, but the sound has been effectively clarified without too much loss of weight.

Symphonies Nos. 1 in C min., Op. 11; 5 in D (Reformation), Op. 107.
**(*) Teldec/Warner Dig. 2292 44933-2 [id.]. Leipzig GO, Kurt Masur.
☞ **(*) Unicorn Dig. DKPCD 9117; *DKPC 9117* [id.]. Milton Keynes CO, Hilary Davan Wetton.

Symphonies Nos. 1; 5; Hebrides overture (Fingal's cave), Op. 26.
☞ *** Chan. Dig. CHAN 9099 [id.]. Philh. O, Weller.

Weller plays the *First Symphony* as if it were a mature work, not the inspiration of a fifteen-year-old, making the strongest contrast between the fast outer movements and the *Andante* which is spaciously moulded. In the *Reformation Symphony* and in *Fingal's Cave* there is an emotional thrust that is very involving, leading to a joyfully exultant conclusion in the finale. With Weller there are even Wagnerian associations, especially in his rapt treatment of the *Dresden Amen* at the close of the introduction. Again, in the slow movement of No. 5 he is exceptionally spacious – but convincingly so because of the degree of concentration. The Chandos recording is richly full-bodied, though not sharply defined.

Masur's mastery in Mendelssohn is due in good measure to his ability to adopt a relatively fast speed and make it sound easy and relaxed, not hurried and breathless. As recorded, the Leipzig sound is on the heavy side for No. 1, with some clouding of tuttis, but when separate discs of No. 1 are rare, this is a welcome issue, part of Masur's latest Mendelssohn cycle.

Davan Wetton presents both symphonies, crisply, elegantly and with keen sympathy on a chamber scale, with the first movement of No. 1, at a restrained speed with light textures given Mozartian elegance. The *Reformation Symphony* too works surprisingly well on this limited scale. Despite the transparent textures, these are warmly expressive performances, though dramatic tension tends to be a degree lower than with such a rival in this coupling as Weller and Masur. The Milton Keynes Chamber Orchestra, fully professional, plays with point and polish.

Symphony No. 2 in B flat (Hymn of praise), Op. 52.
☞ *** Opus 111 OPS 30-98. Soile Isokoski, Mechthild Bach, Frieder Lang, Chorus Musicus Köln, Das neue Orchester, Christoph Spering.
(M) *** DG 431 471-2. Mathis, Rebmann, Hollweg, German Op. Ch., BPO, Karajan.
*** DG Dig. 423 143-2 [id.]. Connell, Mattila, Blochwitz, London Symphony Ch., LSO, Abbado.

It is timely that Spering, following up the success of Herreweghe's Harmonia Mundi version of *Elijah*, here presents a performance of the *Hymn of Praise* in period style. When the composer's preference for fast speeds is well documented and has been followed up so convincingly by his latter-day successor at the Leipzig Gewandhaus, Kurt Masur, it is perhaps surprising that Spering is far more relaxed in his choice of tempos, but in no way does he let the music drag or become sentimental. With clean, crisp textures this is a most refreshing performance, full of incidental beauties, of a work that for several generations was regarded as too sweet on the one hand, over-inflated on the other. Spering's clean directness and his obvious affection for the music reverse that jaundiced judgement. For example, the once-celebrated duet for the two soprano soloists, *Ich harrete des Herrn* ('I waited for the Lord'), is intensely beautiful in its simplicity, with Soile Isokoski (also in Herreweghe's *Elijah*) and Mechthild Bach both angelically sweet yet nicely contrasted. The tenor soloist, Frieder Lang, is also exceptionally sweet-toned, though his projection is keen enough to make the *Huter, ist die Nacht bald hin?* ('Watchman, what of the night?') episode very intense and dramatic. Though not always clear in inner definition, the freshness of the choral singing matches that of the whole performance.

We have already praised the 1972 Karajan recording of the *Hymn of praise* within the context of his complete set of Mendelssohn symphonies above. In some ways Abbado's full-price digital version is even finer, if not more clearly recorded, brushing aside all sentimentality, both fresh and sympathetic and, though the recording is not ideally clear on inner detail, the brightness reinforces the conductor's view. The chorus, well focused, is particularly impressive, and the sweet-toned tenor, Hans-Peter Blochwitz, is outstanding among the soloists.

Symphony No. 3 in A min. (Scottish), Op. 56; Overtures; Calm sea and a prosperous voyage; The Hebrides (Fingal's Cave); Ruy Blas.
(BB) **(*) Naxos Dig. 8.550222; 4.550222 [id.]. Slovak PO, Oliver Dohnányi.

Oliver Dohnányi conducts a joyful account of the *Scottish Symphony* on Naxos, given the more impact by forward recording. Mendelssohn's lilting rhythms in all the fast movements are delightfully bouncy, and though the slow movement brings few hushed pianissimos, its full warmth is brought out without sentimentality. The three overtures, also very well done, not least the under-appreciated *Ruy Blas*, make an excellent coupling.

Symphonies Nos. 3 in A min. (Scottish); 4 in A (Italian), Op. 90.
☞ *** Decca Dig. 433 811-2 [id.]. San Francisco SO, Herbert Blomstedt.
(M) *** DG Dig. 427 810-2 [id.]. LSO, Abbado.
(BB) *** ASV CDQS 6004. O of St John's, Lubbock.
☞ (M) *** Teldec/Warner Dig. 4509 92148 [id.]. Leipzig GO, Kurt Masur.
☞ *** Teldec/Warner Dig. 9031 72308-2 [id.]. COE, Harnoncourt.
*** EMI CDC7 54000-2 [id.]. L. Classical Players, Norrington.
(M) *** Decca 425 011-2; 425 011-4 [id.]. LSO, Abbado.
☞ **(*) Chan. Dig. CHAN 9032 [id.]. Philh. O, Weller.
☞ ** DG Dig. 427 670-2 [id.]. BPO, Levine.
☞ ** EMI Dig. CDC7 54263-2 [id.]. LPO, Welser-Möst.
☞ (M) ** Ph. 438 304-2 [id.]. LPO, Bychkov.

Of all the many discs coupling Mendelssohn's two most popular symphonies, the *Scottish* and the *Italian*, there is none finer than Blomstedt's. Not only does he choose ideal speeds – not too brisk in the exhilarating first movement of the *Italian* or sentimentally drawn out in slow movements – he conveys a feeling of spontaneity throughout, springing rhythms infectiously. The sound is outstandingly fine, outshining any direct rival.

Abbado's fine digital recordings of the *Scottish* and *Italian Symphonies*, coupled together from his complete set, make a splendid mid-price bargain. The recording is admirably fresh and bright – atmospheric, too – and the ambience, if not absolutely sharply defined, is very attractive. Both first-movement exposition repeats are included.

Lubbock's coupling of the *Scottish* and *Italian Symphonies* makes an outstanding super-bargain issue, offering performances of delightful lightness and point, warmly and cleanly recorded. The string section may be of chamber size but, amplified by a warm acoustic, the result sparkles, with rhythms exhilaratingly lifted. The slow movements are both on the slow side but flow easily with no suspicion of sentimentality, while the *Saltarello* finale of No. 4, with the flute part delectably pointed, comes close to Mendelssohnian fairy music.

Masur observes exposition repeats in both symphonies, and his choice of speeds brings out the freshness of inspiration judiciously, avoiding any suspicion of sentimentality in slow movements which are taken at flowing tempi. Conversely, the allegros are never hectic to the point of breathlessness. The one snag is that the reverberant Leipzig recording tends to obscure detail in tuttis; the Scherzo of the *Scottish*, for example, becomes a blur, losing some of its point and charm. Otherwise, the sound of the orchestra has all the characteristic Leipzig bloom and beauty. Indeed the orchestral sound is glorious and the cultured playing always a joy to listen to, while at the climax of the first movement, by bringing out the timpani strongly, Masur finds a storm sequence almost to match *Fingal's Cave*. This disc is not a first choice, but as an alternative coupling it can be strongly recommended, for the effect has a natural concert-hall feel and the performances are very satisfying.

As in Beethoven and Schubert, Nikolaus Harnoncourt's happy relationship with the Chamber Orchestra of Europe brings performances which on modern instruments might be counted 'historically aware', with shortened phrasing, limited string vibrato, rasping horns and clean-cut timpani. The cleanness of texture is enhanced by Harnoncourt's generally relaxed speeds, which allow Mendelssohnian rhythms to have an infectious spring. Natural, well-balanced sound.

As in his Schumann, Norrington opts for unexaggerated speeds in the outer movements, relatively brisk ones for the middle movements. The results are similarly exhilarating, particularly in the clipped and bouncy account of the first movement of the *Italian*. The *Scottish Symphony* is far lighter than usual, with no hint of excessive sweetness. The scherzo has rarely sounded happier, and the finale closes in a fast gallop for the 6/8 coda with the horns whooping gloriously. Good, warm recording, only occasionally masking detail in tuttis.

Abbado's outstanding Decca *Scottish Symphony* is beautifully played and the LSO responds to his direction with the greatest delicacy of feeling, while the *Italian Symphony* has a comparable lightness of touch, matched with lyrical warmth. The vintage 1968 Kingsway Hall recording is in some ways preferable to the DG sound; however, the absence of the first-movement exposition repeat in the *Scottish Symphony* (though not in the *Italian*) is a drawback.

Walter Weller conducts the Philharmonia in refreshingly spontaneous-sounding performances full of vitality. The sense of live performances caught on the wing compensates for the occasional lack of crispness in the ensemble. The reverberant Chandos recording, warmly atmospheric, at times obscures inner detail in orchestral tuttis, but these are warm, amiable readings which build excitingly to climaxes as in live performance. The only speeds that might be counted controversial are those for the slow movements in both symphonies, as well as for the introduction to the *Scottish*. More expansive than usual, Weller sustains them well, avoiding sentimentality.

Levine and the Berlin Philharmonic give performances that are both powerful and refined, with characteristically polished playing bringing fine detail of expression and texture. Though they are rather short on Mendelssohnian magic, the close-up recording adds to their power. Even so, the sound lacks something in presence, failing to give the violins much bloom. Exposition repeats are observed in both symphonies.

Welser-Möst's are light, consciously controlled readings, very well paced, fresh and unsentimental. He brings out the refinement of the playing of the LPO, of which he had recently become music director, helped by slightly distant recording. The strings lead the ensemble in refinement, with the splendid LPO horns cutting through the texture well, though the big horn whoops in the coda of the *Scottish* are disappointingly thin and uninvolving. Elsewhere, too, Welser-Möst's concern for refinement means that in places the performances fail to lift in the way they would in a concert hall. He observes the exposition repeat in the first movement of the *Italian*, but not in the *Scottish*.

Bychkov also observes the exposition repeat in the first movement of the *Italian* but not in the *Scottish*. He gets good playing from the LPO but his reading is not free from point-making: fast tempi tend to be hectic and slow movements too measured and laboured. There are good things all the same, and the recording is admirably truthful: nevertheless this is not a first recommendation.

Symphonies Nos. 3 in A min. (Scottish); 4 in A (Italian); Octet, Op. 30: Scherzo.
☞ **(*) ASV Dig. CDDCA 700 [id.]. SCO, Serebrier.

Serebrier offers a chamber-sized version in bright, close-up sound, which has plenty of power, with relatively more weight given to the wind. Some minor imperfections of ensemble are exposed but, with speeds generally thrustful and urgent, these are positive, enjoyable readings. In the horn passage of the third-movement Trio of the *Italian*, Serebrier compensates for any lack of magic in rustic directness. He observes the exposition repeat in the *Italian*, but not in the *Scottish*, though he provides a makeweight in the *Scherzo* from the *Octet* in the composer's orchestral arrangement.

Symphony No. 4 in A (Italian), Op. 90.
(M) *** EMI Dig. CDD7 64085-2 [id.]. BPO, Tennstedt – SCHUBERT: *Symphony No. 9.* ***
(B) *** DG 429 158-2. BPO, Karajan – SCHUMANN: *Symphony No. 1.* ***

Tennstedt's account of the *Italian* is vividly articulated and obviously felt. The quality of the

Berliners' playing is superb, with the *Saltarello* finale exhilarating in its witty, polished bravura and the woodwind achieving the lightest possible touch. The central movements are elegant and relaxed, with the *Andante* warmly flowing and gentle horns in the Trio of the Minuet. The digital sound has admirable body and clarity to recommend it and this is certainly a version to be considered if the splendid Schubert coupling is wanted.

Karajan's performance of the *Italian* is superbly polished and well paced. The reading is straighter than usual, notably in the third movement, though the effect of Karajan's slower pace is warm, never bland. The recording is very brightly lit in its remastered transfer and has lost some of its depth. The coupling with Schumann comes at bargain price.

Symphony No. 4 (Italian); Overtures: Fair Melusina, Op. 32; The Hebrides (Fingal's Cave), Op. 26; Son and stranger (Die Heimkehr aus der Fremde), Op. 89.

(B) *** Pickwick Dig. PCD 824; *CIMPC 824* [id.]. Berne SO, Peter Maag.

Peter Maag, making a welcome return to the recording studio with his Berne orchestra, here offers a winningly relaxed performance of the *Italian Symphony* (including exposition repeat), plus an attractive group of overtures, which once more confirms him as a supreme Mendelssohnian, particularly *Son and stranger*, which in Maag's hands conveys radiant happiness. At bargain price, with full and brilliant recording, it is first rate.

(i) *Symphony No. 4 in A (Italian), Op. 90; Overture Fingal's Cave;* (ii) *A Midsummer Night's Dream: Overture, Op. 21; Scherzo; Nocturne; Wedding march, Op. 61.*

☞ (B) *** DG 439 411-2 [id.]. (i) Israel PO, Bernstein; (ii) Bav. RSO, Kubelik.

Bernstein's performance of the *Italian Symphony* (exposition repeat included) is sparkling and persuasive. The 1978 recording was made at a public concert and, though speeds are often challengingly fast in outer movements, they never fail to convey the exhilaration of the occasion. *Fingal's Cave* is also a live recording, made a year later, and while it has plenty of romantic warmth and Bernstein is slightly more indulgent, it too sounds spontaneously alive. In the items from *A Midsummer Night's Dream* the Bavarian orchestra are on top form, especially in the *Overture* which is beautifully played. The *Scherzo*, too, has the lightest touch from the woodwind, the *Nocturne* brings a fine horn solo and the *Wedding march* is suitably vigorous. The 1964 recording, made in the Herkules-Saal, Munich, still sounds excellent, and this bargain Classikon CD would grace any collection.

(i) *Symphony No. 4 (Italian);* (ii) *A Midsummer Night's Dream: Overture, Op. 21; Incidental music, Op. 61: Fairy march; Wedding march; Intermezzo; Nocturne; Dance of the Clowns; Scherzo.*

(BB) *** LaserLight Dig. 15 526 [id.]. (i) Philh. O, János Sándor; (ii) Budapest PO, Kovacs.

A first-class coupling in the super-bargain range from LaserLight. Sándor gives a fresh and exhilarating account of the *Italian Symphony*, with particularly elegant Philharmonia playing, and the digital sound is excellent. The performance of a generous selection from the *Midsummer Night's Dream incidental music* also shows the Budapest orchestra on top form: this is most beguiling and is recorded in a pleasingly warm acoustic which does not cloud detail.

(i) *Symphonies Nos. 4 in A (Italian), Op. 90; 5 in D min. (Reformation);* (ii) *A Midsummer Night's Dream overture.*

☞ (B) *** Erato/Warner 2292 45932-2 [id.]. (i) ECO; (ii) LPO; Leppard.

Couplings of the *Italian* and *Reformation Symphonies* are surprisingly rare and this one, in the bargain range, is hard to beat, particularly as a sensitive account of the *Midsummer Night's Dream overture* is thrown in for good measure. Raymond Leppard directs joyful performances of both symphonies. Consistently he shows how infectiously he can lift rhythms, so that the first movement of the *Italian* (exposition repeat included) has exhilaration with no feeling of rush. The relatively small string section of the ECO may sound a little thin in the first and third movements, but the *Saltarello* finale brings superbly clean articulation of triplets. In the *Reformation* – one of the best performances in the catalogue – the scale of the reading, coupled with Leppard's rhythmic flair, helps to lighten a work that can sometimes seem too heavy for its material. The *Allegro con fuoco* of the opening movement gets its fire not from high speed but from crisp precision; the Scherzo too is beautifully lilting, and the *Allegro maestoso* of the finale firmly replaces pomposity with joy. The recording is full and pleasing.

CHAMBER AND INSTRUMENTAL MUSIC

Cello sonatas Nos. 1 in B flat, Op. 45; 2 in D, Op. 58; Assai tranquillo; Song without words, Op. 109;
Variations concertantes, Op. 17.
*** Hyp. Dig. CDA 66478 [id.]. Richard Lester, Susan Tomes.

There are few cello sonatas so exhilarating as the second of the two written by Mendelssohn. Susan Tomes, the inspired pianist of the group, Domus, and her cellist colleague, Richard Lester, give a performance full of flair on this ideally compiled disc of Mendelssohn's collected works for cello and piano, brimming with charming ideas. As well as the works with opus number they include a delightful fragment, *Assai tranquillo*, never previously recorded.

Cello sonatas Nos. 1 in B flat, Op. 45; 2 in D, Op. 58; Songs without words, Op. 19/1; Op. 109;
Variations concertantes, Op. 17.
☞ *** Decca Dig. 430 198-2 [id.]. Lynn Harrell, Bruno Canino.
☞ (BB) ** Naxos Dig. 8.550655 [id.]. Maria Kliegel, Kristin Merscher.

Big names are in themselves no guarantee of great music-making, but Lynn Harrell and Bruno Canino do offer something of special quality that justifies a full-price tag. Their playing has an ardour and expressive vitality that are totally compelling. Both *Sonatas* and the *Variations concertantes* are played with a conviction that is completely persuasive, and the recording serves them well.

Maria Kliegel and Kristin Merscher play in a lively and spirited fashion and are very decently recorded; at a third of the price of its competitors, this Naxos CD has a lot going for it. However, the performances are nowhere near as strong in personality or as compelling as the rival versions. Their partnership does not seem anywhere near as strong either.

Octet in E flat, Op. 20.
*** Hyp. Dig. CDA 66356 [id.]. Divertimenti – BARGIEL: *Octet.* ***
(B) **(*) Decca 421 637-2. ASMF – BOCCHERINI: *Cello quintet.* **(*)
☞ ** Sony Dig. SK 48307 [id.]. L'Archibudelli, Smithsonian Chamber Players – GADE: *Octet in F.*
**
☞ *(*) Nimbus Dig. NI 5140 [id.]. Alberni & Medici Qts – SHOSTAKOVICH: *2 pieces* etc. *(*)

Divertimenti give a very natural and unforced account of the celebrated *Octet* which, though it may not be the most distinguished in the catalogue, still gives great pleasure. Excellent recorded sound.

The 1968 (originally Argo) performance by the ASMF is fresh and buoyant, and the recording wears its years fairly lightly. It offered fine judgement in matters of clarity and sonority, and the digital remastering has not lost the original ambient bloom, although the violin timbre now has noticeable thinness. A good bargain version.

In their performance of the *Octet*, L'Archibudelli and the Smithsonian Chamber Players give a spirited but hurried and not always cleanly articulated account of Mendelssohn's ravishing score. They offer an interesting rarity in the form of Gade's essay in the same genre, clearly modelled on the Mendelssohn, and are well recorded; but this is not enough to put this in a commanding position in the *Octet* lists!

Nor do the Medici and Alberni Quartets offer more than a serviceable account, which they couple with some Shostakovich rarities. Goodish recording too. However, at 47 minutes 44 seconds this is not really competitive, given the quality and range of the opposition.

Octet in E flat, Op. 20; Symphonies for string orchestra Nos. 6 in E flat; 10 in B min.
*** Denon Dig. CO 73185 [id.]. I Solisti Italiani.

I Solisti Italiani are none other than the old Virtuosi di Roma, and they play with all the finesse and grace you would expect from them. The *Octet* is delightful and could be a first choice, were the acoustic not quite so resonant. The two early *Symphonies* are given with not only elegance but also a conviction that is very persuasive indeed.

Octet in E flat, Op. 20; String quintet No. 1 in A, Op. 18.
*** EMI Dig. CDC7 49958-2. Hausmusik.

Using period instruments, the British-based group, Hausmusik, gives a most refreshing performance of the *Octet* and couples it with another miraculous masterpiece of Mendelssohn's boyhood. The period performance gives extra weight to the lower lines compared with the violins, with the extra clarity intensifying the joyfulness of the inspiration. Most revealing of all is the way that the last two movements of the *Octet*, the feather-light *Scherzo* and the dashing finale, with their similar figuration, are presented in contrast, the one slower and more delicately pointed than usual, the other more exhilarating at high speed.

Octet in E flat, Op. 20; String quintet No. 2 in B flat, Op. 87.
*** Ph. 420 400-2 [id.]. ASMF Chamber Ens.

This Philips successor comes from just over a decade after the Academy's earlier record of Mendelssohn's *Octet* and the playing has greater sparkle and polish. The recorded sound is also superior and sounds extremely well in its CD format. The *Second Quintet* is an underrated piece and it too receives an elegant and poetic performance that will give much satisfaction.

Piano quartets Nos. 1 in C min.; 2 in F min.; 3 in B min., Op. 1–3.
*** Virgin/EMI Dig. VC7 59628-2 [id.]. Domus.

Piano quartet No. 1 in C min., Op. 1; Piano sextet in D, Op. 110.
☞ (BB) **(*) Naxos Dig. 8.550966 [id.]. Bartholdy Piano Qt (augmented).

Piano quartets Nos. 2 in F min., Op. 2; 3 in B min., Op. 3.
☞ (BB) **(*) Naxos Dig. 8.550967 [id.]. Bartholdy Piano Qt.

The *Piano quartet No. 1 in C minor* was the composer's first published composition and was succeeded the following year by another, dedicated to '*Monsieur le Professeur Zelter par son élève Felix Mendelssohn-Bartholdy*', equally fluent and accomplished. However, none of the ideas of this *F minor* work are as remarkable as those of its successor in *B minor* of 1825. All three pieces have charm, vitality and musicianship, particularly in the hands of this ensemble, who play with the taste and discernment we have come to expect from them. Excellent recording.

The Bartholdy Quartet have an excellent pianist in Pier Narciso Masi, and his mercurial style is just right for these early works. The string players are always fluent and show a light-hearted vivacity in Mendelelssohn's scherzos (especially in the very winning *Allegro molto* of No. 3) and finales, and they play the simple slow movements gracefully. The *Piano sextet* also comes from the composer's youth and, like the other works, it has an engaging immediacy. The recording was made in the fairly resonant Clara Wieck Auditorium in Heidelberg, which means that the microphones are fairly close to the strings and the balance is slightly contrived. Nevertheless the sound is good and the piano well caught. While Domus remain a clear first choice, this Naxos set is worth considering.

Piano trios Nos. 1 in D min., Op. 49; 2 in C min., Op. 66.
**(*) Chan. Dig. CHAN 8404; ABTD 1141 [id.]. Borodin Trio.
**(*) Teldec/Warner Dig. 2292 44947-2. Trio Fontenay.

The Borodin Trio are recorded in a very resonant acoustic and are rather forwardly balanced. They give superbly committed but somewhat overpointed readings. All the same, there is much musical pleasure to be found here.

The Trio Fontenay are rather brightly recorded and they play with passionate commitment and great virility. Undoubtedly powerful and keenly alive though both performances are, they do not communicate much charm.

String quartets: in E flat; Nos. 1 in E flat, Op. 12; 2 in A min., Op. 13; 3–5, Op. 44/1–3; 6 in F min., Op. 80; 4 Pieces, Op. 81.
☞ *** Hyp. Dig. CDS 44051/3 [id.]. Coull Qt.

Mendelssohn's string quartets are increasingly well served on CD and there is a good choice of individual couplings. But for those wanting a complete set, the Coull survey is eminently satisfactory, the playing alive and spontaneous. Even if the group may not have the unanimity or finesse of the old Melos recordings on DG, these Coull accounts are better-paced and musically more penetrating. Moreover they bring the advantage of both freshness and completeness (including the early (1823) *Quartet*, written a year before the *First C minor Symphony*). The quietly intense playing in the slow movements of the later works – and indeed in Op. 13 – and the charming, graceful *Intermezzo* of this same quartet show the group's affinity with this repertoire, while the *Canzonetta* of Op. 12 introduces Mendelssohn's fairies, tripping in gracefully. The Scherzo of Op. 44/3 is another highlight, and the opening of Op. 44/2 is particularly warm and well paced. The recording is realistic and well balanced.

String quartets Nos. 1 in E flat, Op. 12; 2 in A min., Op. 13; 3–5, Op. 44/1–3; 6 in F min., Op. 30.
☞ *** EMI CDS7 54514-2 (3) [id.]. Cherubini Qt.

The young Mendelssohn in Berlin in his teens was able to study the scores of late Beethoven quartets even before he had a chance to hear the music performed. His own youthful quartets reflect that influence from what at the time was the most avant-garde music imaginable. The results are fascinating, and a new set of the six regular Mendelssohn *Quartets* is most welcome from the young members of the Cherubini Quartet who consistently play with warmth as well as intensity. Here with a light touch they bring out the mercurial charm of Mendelssohn as well as his vigour and high spirits. The pity is that, unlike the set from the Coull Quartet, this one does not include two works from opposite ends of Mendelssohn's career that provide an extra insight into his development: the early *E flat Quartet* (without opus number), written when he was only fourteen, and the collection of four movements, Op. 81, that in shape and sequence group themselves satisfyingly together. One only wishes that the Cherubinis, consistently imaginative, had been persuaded to do the extra items as well.

String quartet No. 1 in E flat, Op. 12.
*** Ph. 420 396-2 [id.]. Orlando Qt – DVORAK: *String quartet No. 12.* ***

The Orlando performance of Mendelssohn's *E flat Quartet* is one of the very best ever put on record. It is played with lightness of touch, delicacy of feeling and excellent ensemble. The CD transfer has added a touch of glare on the first violin. However, it responds to the controls and we see no reason to withhold a strong recommendation.

String quartets Nos. 1 in E flat, Op. 12; 2 in A, Op. 13.
*** Hyp. Dig. CDA 66397 [id.]. Coull Qt (with *2 Pieces, Op. 81* ***).

The Coull Quartet on Hyperion give fresh and unaffected accounts of both *Quartets* and have the benefit of very good recorded sound. Tempi are well judged and everything flows naturally. The Coull offer the additional inducement of two of the *Four pieces*, Op. 81, which were published after Mendelssohn's death.

String quartet No. 2 in A min., Op. 14.
☞ *(*) Nimbus Dig. NI 5156 [id.]. John Bingham, Medici Qt – SHOSTAKOVICH: *Piano quintet.* *(*)

The Medici give a straightforward account of the *A minor Quartet* and are decently recorded. All the same, this is not special enough to represent a challenge to current alternatives and is encumbered with a poorly balanced recording of the Shostakovich *Piano quintet*.

String quartets Nos. 3 in D, Op. 44/1; 4 in E min., Op. 44/2.
☞ *** Decca Dig. 440 369-2 [id.]. Ysaÿe Qt.

The Ysaÿe Quartet play without the slightly overdriven quality in the Melos set that worried some collectors, still available in a mid-price complete DG set (415 883-2). They observe the exposition repeats in the first movements and their approach is agreeably civilized and urbane as befits this endearing music. Perhaps the Scherzos could be keener and more pointed, but this is still very enjoyable music-making. The recording has warmth and good definition.

String quintets Nos. 1 in A, Op. 18; 2 in B flat, Op. 87.
(M) *** Sony/CBS CD 45883. Laredo, Kavafian, Ohyama, Kashkashian, Robinson.

Laredo and his ensemble achieve good matching of timbre, and they give lively accounts of both these neglected works, lacking neither warmth nor finesse. The 1978 recording has responded well to remastering, and has body and presence.

Violin sonata in F min., Op. 4.
☞ (M) *** O-L 443 196-2 [id.]. Jaap Schröder, Christopher Hogwood (fortepiano) – SCHUBERT:
    Violin sonatinas. ***

As the early opus number indicates, this Mendelssohn *Violin sonata* is an early piece. It is not the most memorable of his early works, though it has many endearing moments, and it is here presented most persuasively on period instruments. Jaap Schröder plays a Stradivarius of 1709 and Christopher Hogwood a fortepiano of the mid-1820s. Alive and natural recording.

Violin sonatas: in F min., Op. 4; in F (1838).
*** DG Dig. 419 244-2 [id.]. Shlomo Mintz, Paul Ostrovsky.

Mendelssohn was only fourteen when he composed the *F minor Sonata*, but the 1838 *Sonata* comes from Mendelssohn's productive Leipzig period. The performances are beyond reproach; the playing of both artists is a model of sensitivity and intelligence, and the recording is absolutely first class. Strongly recommended.

PIANO MUSIC

*Andante and allegro brilliant in A, Op. 92; Andante and variations in B flat, Op. 83a; Piano trio No. 2
in C min., Op. 66.*
☞ *** Sony Dig. SK 48494 [id.]. Tal & Groethuysen – Fanny MENDELSSOHN: *3 Pieces for piano, 4
hands.* ***

Playing of exceptional quality from this remarkable duo. Everything, including the transcription of
the *C minor Piano trio*, sparkles, and the recording does them full justice.

*Andante and rondo capriccioso in E min., Op. 14; Prelude and fugue in E minor/major, Op. 35/1;
Sonata in E, Op. 6; Variations sérieuses in D min., Op. 53.*
*** Sony Dig. MK 37838 [id.]. Murray Perahia.

Perahia is perfectly attuned to Mendelssohn's sensibility and it would be difficult to imagine these
performances being surpassed. The quality of the CBS recording is very good indeed.

Etude in F min.; Preludes & 3 Etudes, Op. 104; 6 Preludes & fugues, Op. 35; Prelude & fugue in E min.
**(*) Nimbus NI 5071 [id.]. Martin Jones.

*Fantasy in F sharp min., Op. 28; 3 Fantaisies et caprices, Op. 16; Fantasy on 'The last rose of summer',
Op. 15; Variations: in E flat, Op. 82; in B flat, Op. 83; Variations sérieuses in D min., Op. 53.*
**(*) Nimbus NI 5072 [id.]. Martin Jones.

Sonatas: in E, Op. 6; in G min., Op. 105; in B flat, Op. 106; Kinderstücke, Op. 72.
**(*) Nimbus NI 5070 [id.]. Martin Jones.

In his collection of Mendelssohn piano music, Martin Jones provides a fascinating slant on the
composer, particularly his youthful inspirations. In many ways the disc of sonatas is the most
interesting of all, reflecting Mendelssohn's devotion to Beethoven and his sonatas. The *Preludes and
fugues* inevitably reflect his even deeper devotion to Bach, then still under-appreciated. The sets of
variations on the third disc were mostly written later in his career, examples of his high skill and love
of the keyboard, rather than works of genius. Martin Jones is an excellent advocate, playing
dedicatedly and persuasively, not always immaculately but without mannerism. The recordings, made
in the 1970s, come up very well in the CD transfers, with the atmosphere of a small hall realistically
conveyed.

*Rondo capriccioso, Op. 14; Songs without words: in G; in A (Spring song), Op. 62/1 & 6; in C
(Spinning song), Op. 67/4.*
☞ (M) *** Decca 433 902-2 [id.]. Wilhelm Backhaus – SCHUBERT: *Impromptus* etc. **(*)

Perhaps surprisingly, Backhaus is at his most persuasive in this well-planned and expertly played
miniature Mendelssohn programme. The 1955 recording, too, is remarkably good.

Scherzo from A Midsummer Night's Dream, Op. 61 (trans. Rachmaninov).
*** Hyp. CDA 66009 [id.]. Howard Shelley – RACHMANINOV: *Variations* etc. ***

Howard Shelley, with fabulously clear articulation and delectably sprung rhythms, gives a performance of which Rachmaninov himself would not have been ashamed.

Songs without words, Books 1–8 (complete).
**(*) Hyp. Dig. CDA 66221/2 [id.]. Lívia Rév.

*Songs without words, Books 1–8 (complete); Albumblatt, Op. 117; Gondellied; Kinderstücke, Op. 72; 2
Klavierstücke.*
☞ (B) *** DG Double 437 470-2 (2) [id.]. Daniel Barenboim.

*Songs without words (complete); Andante and variations in E flat, Op. 82; Andante cantabile e presto
agitato in B; Variations in B flat, Op. 83.*
☞ (B) *** Ph. Duo 438 709-2 (2) [id.]. Ilse von Alpenheim.

This 1974 set of Mendelssohn's complete *Songs without words*, which Barenboim plays with such
affectionate finesse, has dominated the catalogue for nearly two decades. For this reissue, the six
Kinderstücke (sometimes known as 'Christmas pieces') have been added, plus other music, so that the
second of the two CDs plays for 73 minutes. The sound is first class. At Double DG price (two CDs
for the price of one) this sweeps the board in this repertoire, although it is a pity that there is no back-
up documentation except for a list of titles.

Ilse von Alpenheim's set of *Songs without words* may not have quite the distinctive character of
Barenboim, but she plays this music with an appealing spontaneous simplicity. Her sensibility is at

times a little solemn, and just occasionally in the faster pieces she has a slight tendency to rush her fences. But these are performances which show individuality without self-conscious idiosyncrasy: the famous *Spring song*, for instance, brings an attractively light chimerical touch, and elsewhere there are many agreeable moments of poetic tranquillity. Of the encores, the *Andante and variations in E flat* is particularly appealing in this respect. The (1980) recording of the piano is first class, well up to Philips's usual high standard. Not a first choice, perhaps, but an undoubted bargain.

Lívia Rév is a thoughtful, sensitive and aristocratic artist. Her survey of the *Songs without words* has charm and warmth, and she includes a hitherto unpublished piece. The set is handsomely presented and the recording is warm and pleasing; it is, however, somewhat bottom-heavy. Yet the slightly diffuse effect suits the style of the playing.

Songs without words, Op. 19/1–2 & 5; Op. 30/4–5; 6 (Venetian gondola song); Op. 38/2–3; 5 & 6; Op. 53/1–3; Op. 67/6; Op. 62/1; Op. 102/1.
☞ (BB) ** Discover Dig. DICD 920155 [id.]. Sergei Babayan (with LISZT/SCHUBERT: *Lieder concert paraphrases* *).

It is curious to offer a selection from Mendelssohn's *Songs without words* that misses out both the *Spring song* and *Spinning song*, but those looking for a disc of the less familiar examples from the series will be pleased enough. Sergei Babayan plays his programme agreeably enough and seems to relish the agitato numbers, in which he is thoroughly involved. He is very well recorded. He is less successful in the four Liszt *Concert paraphrases* of Schubert Lieder (why include these instead of more Mendelssohn?), where the flow of the melodic line is broken with excessive rubato, while *Erlkönig* is made to sound very melodramatic.

VOCAL MUSIC

Lieder: *Allnächtlich im Traume; Altdeutsches Liede; And'res Maienlied; An die Entfernte; Auf der Wanderschaft; Auf Flügeln des Gesanges ('On wings of song'); Bei deder Wiege; Der Blumenkranz; Da lieg' ich unter den Bäumen; Entelied; Erster Verlust; Das erste Veilchen; Es lauschte das Lamb; Frühlingslied* (3 versions: Lenau, Lichtenstein and Klingemann settings); *Grüss; Hirtenlied; Jagdlied; Minnelied* (Deutsches Volkslied); *Minnelied* (Tieck); *Der Mond; Morgengruss; Nachtlied; Neue Liebe; O Jugend; Pagenlied; Reiselied* (2 versions: Heine and Ebert); *Scheindend; Schiflied; Schlafloser Augen Leuchte; Tröstung; Venetianisches Gondellied; Volkslied (Feuchtersleben); Das Waldschloss; Wanderlied; Warnung vor dem Rhein; Wenn sich zwei Herzen scheiden; Winterlied.*
☞ (M) **(*) EMI CMS7 64827-2 (2) Fischer-Dieskau, Sawallisch.

Though Mendelssohn generally reserved his finest song-like inspirations for the *Songs without words*, the lyrical directness of these settings of Heine, Eichendorff, Lenau and others assures him of a niche of his own among contemporary composers of Lieder. Fischer-Dieskau conveys the joy of fresh discovery but in some of the well-known songs – *Grüss* or *On wings of song* – he tends to overlay his singing with heavy expressiveness. Lightness should be the keynote, and that happily is wonderfully represented in the superb accompaniments of Sawallisch. Excellent, natural recording.

Elijah (oratorio), *Op. 70.*
*** Chan. Dig. CHAN 8774/5; *DBTD 2016* [id.]. White, Plowright, Finnie, A. Davies, London Symphony Ch., LSO, Hickox.
☞ **(*) Teldec/Warner Dig. 9031 73131-2 (2) [id.]. Alastair Miles, Helen Donath, Jard van Nes, Donald George, Leipzig MDR Ch., Israel PO, Masur.
☞ **(*) Ph. Dig. 432 984-2 (2) [id.]. Kenny, Dawson, Von Otter, Rigby, Rolfe Johnson, Begley, Allen, Connell, Hopkins, ASMF Ch., ASMF, Marriner.
☞ **(*) HM Dig. HMC 901463/4. Petteri Salomaa, Soile Isokoski, Monica Groop, John Mark Ainsley, Delphine Collot, La Chapelle Royale, Coll. Voc., O des Champs-Elysées, Herreweghe.

Richard Hickox with his London Symphony Chorus and the LSO secures a performance that both pays tribute to the English choral tradition in this work and presents it dramatically as a kind of religious opera. Hickox shows what fresh inspiration it contains, what a wealth of memorable ideas. The choice of soloists reflects that approach. Willard White may not be ideally steady in his delivery, sometimes attacking notes from below, but he sings consistently with fervour, from his dramatic introduction to the overture onwards. Rosalind Plowright and Arthur Davies combine purity of tone with operatic expressiveness, and Linda Finnie, while not matching the example of Dame Janet Baker in the classic EMI recording, sings with comparable dedication and directness in the solo, *O rest in the Lord*. The chorus fearlessly underlines the high contrasts of dynamic demanded in the score. The Chandos recording, full and immediate yet atmospheric too, enhances the drama.

Masur as a Mendelssohnian consistently eliminates any hint of sentimentality, but in *Elijah* his determination to use a new broom involves many fast speeds that fail to let this dramatic music blossom, not least in the exuberant final chorus. Yet anyone wanting a fine, modern, digital recording using the German text, crisply and urgently done, should not be too disappointed, particularly when Alastair Miles sings so freshly and intelligently in the title-role.

Marriner in his line-up of soloists may look unmatchable, and there is much fine singing; but with the mellifluous Elijah of Thomas Allen balanced rather backwardly in the live recording, less dominant than he should be, the result is refined rather than dramatically powerful. The Old Testament subject benefits from more rugged treatment, not just in that, but generally. Marriner and his splendid forces are in danger of sounding too well-mannered and, though Hickox's Chandos version has some rough edges, it conveys more tellingly the strength of the work as embodied in the English choral tradition. Marriner gives the quartets and double-quartets to the soloists, whereas Hickox, following the English tradition, has the chorus singing them.

Herreweghe's reading, using period forces, recorded live in Metz in February 1993, is predictably clean, fresh and light-textured. With a German text, this is as far removed from the English choral tradition as could be, and probably far removed too from the first performance in Birmingham in 1846. Yet in its way it is quite compelling, thanks to the bright, clear choral singing. Petteri Salomaa is a lightweight Elijah, occasionally fluttery in timbre, and Soile Isokoski is less sweet-toned than in the Opus 111 recording of the *Hymn of Praise*, but John Mark Ainsley and Monica Groop are both excellent. Clear, atmospheric recording.

Infelice; Psalm 42 (As the hart pants), Op. 42.
*** Virgin/EMI Dig. VC7 59589-2 [id.]. J. Baker, London Symphony Ch., City of L. Sinf., Hickox – BRAHMS: *Alto rhapsody* etc. ***

The scena, *Infelice* – a piece which harks back to an earlier tradition – and the Psalm-setting both have the solos prescribed for soprano, but they suit Dame Janet well. The voice is in superb condition, with the weight of expressiveness as compelling as ever.

A Midsummer Night's Dream: Overture, Op. 21; Incidental music, Op. 61 (complete).
*** EMI CDC7 47163-2 [id.]. Watson, Wallis, Finchley Children's Music Group, LSO, Previn.
*** BMG/RCA Dig. RD 87764 [7764-2-RC]. Popp, Lipovšek, Bamberg Ch. & SO, Flor.
(B) *** CfP Dig. CD-CFP 4593; *TC-CFP 4593*. Wiens, Walker, LPO Ch. & O, Litton.
(M) *** DG 415 840-2 [id.]. Mathis, Boese, Bav. R. Ch. & SO, Kubelik – WEBER: *Overtures: Oberon; Der Freischütz.* ***
(M) (***) BMG/RCA mono GD 60314. Eustis, Kirk, University of Pennsylvania Women's Glee Club, Phd. O., Toscanini – BERLIOZ: *Romeo and Juliet: Queen Mab scherzo.* (**)

On EMI, Previn offers a wonderfully refreshing account of the complete score; the veiled pianissimo of the violins at the beginning of the Overture and the delicious woodwind detail in the Scherzo certainly bring Mendelssohn's fairies into the orchestra. Even the little melodramas which come between the main items sound spontaneous here, and the contribution of the soloists and chorus is first class. The *Nocturne* (taken slowly) is serenely romantic and the *Wedding march* resplendent. The recording is naturally balanced and has much refinement of detail.

Claus Peter Flor's account omits the little melodramas, which is a pity; but for those who require the major items only, this beautiful RCA CD could well be a first choice. Recorded in the warmly resonant acoustics of the Dominikanerbau, Bamberg, the orchestra is given glowingly radiant textures; but Flor's stylish yet relaxed control brings the kind of intimacy one expects from a chamber group. Lucia Popp's vocal contribution is delightful, especially when she blends her voice so naturally with that of Marjana Lipovšek in *You spotted snakes*.

Andrew Litton also includes the melodramas and, like Previn, he uses them most effectively as links, making them seem an essential part of the structure. He too has very good soloists; in the *Overture* and *Scherzo* he displays an engagingly light touch, securing very fine wind and string playing from the LPO. The wide dynamic range of the recording brings an element of drama to offset the fairy music. Both the *Nocturne*, with a fine horn solo, and the temperamental *Intermezzo* are good examples of the spontaneity of feeling that permeates this performance throughout and makes this disc a bargain.

Although Kubelik omits the melodramas, this makes room for an appropriate coupling of the two finest Weber overtures (both also associated with magic) with *Oberon* drawing an obvious parallel with Mendelssohn. They are marvellously played and the sound and 1965 recording are strikingly fresh.

Toscanini's Philadelphia recording offers the seven most popular numbers from the *Midsummer*

Night's Dream music, including the song with chorus, *You spotted snakes*, and the final melodrama. In sparkling performances it offers a fine example of his more relaxed manners in his one Philadelphia season.

A Midsummer Night's Dream: Overture, Op. 21 (incidental music): suite.
☞ (M) *** Sony SBK 48264 [id.]. Cleveland O, Szell – BIZET: *Symphony;* SMETANA: *Vltava.* ***

Seldom can Mendelssohn's score have been played so brilliantly on record as under Szell. The orchestral ensemble is superb, the fairies dance with gossamer lightness in the violins, yet the tension is high so that the listener is gripped from the first bar to the last of the *Overture*. Its basic tempo and that of the *Intermezzo* are fast, but the playing is so well disciplined that there is never a feeling of hurry. The *Scherzo* is infectious and in the *Nocturne* the solo horn is cool but very sensitive. This may not be everyone's idea of Mendelssohn but of its kind it is first class, and the 1967 recording sounds smoother and fuller than on the old LP.

A Midsummer Night's Dream: Overture, Op. 21 (incidental music): excerpts; *Overtures: Fingal's Cave (The Hebrides), Op. 26; Die Schöne Melusine, Op. 32.*
☞ ** Erato/Warner Dig. 4509 91734-2 [id.]. SRO, Jordan.

No one could fail to enjoy these Suisse Romande performances under Jordan who secures playing of much more finesse and elegance from his orchestra than was possible only a few years back. The overtures are also very well done, warmly atmospheric rather than arresting. The recording, too, is very good. But this collection at 52 minutes is ungenerous, and there are better ways of acquiring this repertoire.

3 Psalms, Op. 78.
**(*) Nimbus Dig. NI 5171 [id.]. Oslo Cathedral Ch., Terje Kvam – GRIEG: *4 Psalms.* **(*)

All three *Psalms* have considerable beauty and dignity, especially the first, a setting of Psalm 11 with its ingenious four-part canon. Good performances by the Oslo Cathedral Choir, and eminently serviceable recording. However, at under 45 minutes, the CD offers short measure.

Psalms Nos. 98: Singet dem Herrn ien neues Lied; 114: Da Israel aus Aegypten Zog; (i) *Lass', O Herr, mich Hülfe finden, Op. 96;* (ii) *Lauda Sion, Op. 73.*
☞ *** Erato/Warner Dig. 4509 94359-2 [id.]. (i) Stutzmann; (ii) Brunner, Ihara, Ramirez, Huttenlocher, Gulbenkian Foundation Ch. & O, Lisbon, Corboz.

These two Psalm settings inspire Mendelssohn to some of his most effectively Bach-like writing. The text of Psalm 98 inspired Bach too and, though austerity periodically turns into sweetness, both pieces are welcome in performances as fresh and alert as these. *Lauda Sion* is less varied in its expression, a persistent hymn of praise, but *Lass', O Herr* ('Let me find your help, O Lord'), a paraphrase of Psalm 13, is set in four contrasted sections featuring contralto and chorus and ending with a Fugue. Excellent performances and fine recording.

St Paul, Op. 36.
**(*) Ph. 420 212-2 (2). Janowitz, Lang, Blochwitz, Stier, Polster, Adam, Leipzig R. Ch. & GO, Masur.

Masur, always a persuasive interpreter of Mendelssohn, here directs a performance which, without inflating the piece or making it sanctimonious, conveys its natural gravity. Theo Adam is not always steady, but otherwise the team of soloists is exceptionally strong, and the chorus adds to the incandescence, although placed rather backwardly. The Leipzig recording is warm and atmospheric.

Mennin, Peter (1923–83)

Symphony No. 5.
(M) **(*) Mercury 432 755-2 [id.]. Eastman-Rochester O, Howard Hanson – IVES: *Symphony No. 3* etc.; SCHUMAN: *New England triptych.* ***

Peter Mennin is not as individual a musical personality as William Schuman, let alone Charles Ives; but the *Canto* central movement of his *Fifth Symphony* has a piercing melancholy which is slightly reminiscent of the Barber *Adagio for strings*. The outer movements develop plenty of polyphonic energy, but the toccata-like linear writing lacks real memorability. Hanson's performance is persuasive and vital, and the 1962 Mercury sound makes the very most of the relatively unexpansive acoustics of the Eastman Theatre.

Menotti, Gian-Carlo (born 1911)

Piano concerto in F.
(M) **(*) Van. 08.4029.71 [OVC 4071]. Earl Wild, Symphony of the Air, Jorge Mester – COPLAND: *Concerto.* ***

Menotti's *Piano concerto*, like most of his music, is easy and fluent, never hard on the ear. Its eclectic style brings a pungent whiff of Shostakovich at the opening, and there are hints of Khachaturian elsewhere. Even if it is unlikely to bear repeated listening, the charisma and bravura of Earl Wild's playing make the music sound more substantial than it is.

Amahl and the Night Visitors (opera): complete.
*** That's Entertainment CDTER 1124. Lorna Haywood, John Dobson, Curtis Watson, Christopher Painter, James Rainbird, ROHCG Ch. & O, David Syrus.

Recorded under the supervision of the composer himself, this is a fresh and highly dramatic performance, very well sung and marked by atmospheric digital sound of striking realism. Central to the success of the performance is the astonishingly assured and sensitively musical singing of the boy treble, James Rainbird, as Amahl, while Lorna Haywood sings warmly and strongly as the Mother, with a strong trio of Kings.

Amahl and the night visitors: Introduction; March; Shepherd's dance. Sebastian (ballet): suite.
*** Koch Dig. 3-7005-2 [id.]. New Zealand SO, Schenck – BARBER: *Souvenirs.* ***

This seven-movement suite from *Sebastian* is beautifully crafted and expertly scored music whose attractions are strong, as are the three movements from *Amahl and the night visitors*. The players under Andrew Schenck, who sound as if they are enjoying themselves, are well recorded.

Mercadante, Saverio (1795–1870)

Clarinet concerto in B flat.
*** Claves CD 50-813 [id.]. Friedli, SW German CO, Angerer – MOLTER; PLEYEL: *Concertos.* ***

Mercadante's *Concerto* consists of an *Allegro maestoso* and a galant *Andante with variations*. The music is agreeably fluent and very well played by the soloist.

Flute concertos: in D; E; E min.
☞ *** BMG/RCA Dig. 09026 61447-2 [id.]. James Galway, Sol. Ven., Scimone.

These three *Flute concertos* show Mercadante to be an excellent craftsman with a nice turn for lyrical melody in the slow movements with their simple, song-like cantilenas. Both the *Andante alla siciliana* of the *D major Concerto* and the *Largo* of the *E minor* are appealing, especially with Galway as soloist, while the *Rondo Russo* or *Polacca* finales are inventively spirited. Scimone makes the most of the often exuberantly florid tuttis of the opening movements, and elsewhere he accompanies Galway's silvery melodic line, sparkling and delicate by turns, with style and polish. The sound is excellent.

Merikanto, Aarre (1893–1958)

(i) *Violin concertos Nos. 2; 4;* (ii) *10 Pieces;* (iii) *Genesis.*
*** Finlandia Dig. FACD 387 [id.]. (i) Saatikettu, Helsinki PO, James De Priest; (ii) Avanti CO, Angervo; (iii) Mattila, Savonlinna Op. Festival Ch., Lahti SO, Söderblom.

Merikanto's *Second Violin concerto* is quite a find, a most imaginative work which will appeal to anyone who likes the exoticism of Szymanowski and the nature mysticism of Janáček. The expressionist *Ten Pieces* and in particular the first, the *Largo misterioso*, cast a strong spell. The *Fourth Violin concerto* – he burned the *Third* – has a folksy Prokofiev-like character but has no lack of astringency. Merikanto's works emanate from an altogether distinctive sound-world. Very good performances and recording. Strongly recommended.

(i) *Fantasy for orchestra; Largo misterioso;* (ii) *Notturno;* (i) *Pan; Symphonic study.*
*** Finlandia Dig. FACD 349 [id.]. Finnish RSO, (i) Segerstam; (ii) Saraste.

The *Fantasy for orchestra* is a work of an extraordinarily rich imagination. Both the *Fantasy* and the tone-poem, *Pan*, are sensitively conducted by Leif Segerstam, who successfully conveys their haunting, other-worldly atmosphere. The *Notturno* and *Largo misterioso* are also beautiful pieces that immediately cast a strong spell.

Juha (opera) complete.

**(*) Finlandia FACD 105 (2) [id.]. Lehtinen, Kostia, Krumm, Kuusoja, Finnish Nat. Op. Ch. and O, Ulf Söderblom.

The musical language of *Juha* reflects the composer's international sympathies and yet the music is far more than merely eclectic. It is atmospheric and highly expert in scoring and, in its way, bears a quite distinctive stamp. The singing on the whole is more than respectable, and Matti Lehtinen in the title-role is outstanding. The opera is not long – under two hours – and is very well worth investigating.

Messager, André (1853–1929)

Le deux pigeons (ballet) complete.

☞ *** Decca Dig. 433 700-2 [id.]. Welsh Nat. Op. O, Richard Bonynge.

Messager's charming gypsy ballet was premièred at the Paris Opéra in 1886 on the same bill as Donizetti's *La Favorita*. But it swiftly established its independence, to remain in the repertory and be revived (with new choreography by Frederick Ashton) by the Sadler's Wells Royal Ballet in 1961. We are familiar with the suite, but this is the first complete recording. The music is slight but cleverly scored, after the manner of Delibes; agreeably tuneful, it does not wear out its welcome. Bonynge secures playing from the Wesh Opera Orchestra that is consistently graceful and sparkling. He does not reveal a missing masterpiece but entertains the listener pleasingly for just over an hour. The recording, made in the slightly intractable Brangwyn Hall, Swansea, is vivid and naturally balanced, if not quite out of Decca's very top drawer.

Fortunio (complete).

☞ ✧ (M) *** Erato/Warner Dig. 2292 45983-2 (2) [id.]. Dran, Alliot-Lugaz, Cachemaille, Dudziak, Tremplant, Rocca, Ch. & O de l'Opéra de Lyon, Gardiner.

Dating from 1907, *Fortunio*, based on a play by Alfred de Musset, has all the effervescence and heady lyricism of an operetta combined with the strength and subtlety of a full opera. The tuneful score has ravishing solos for the lovelorn hero – with the heady-toned Thierry Dran very well cast – which are beautifully woven into the through-composed structure in four compact Acts.

Its story of the triumph of youthful love, and the outwitting of the older generation – husband and paramour alike – by a personable and essentially innocent hero, was bound to appeal to the Parisian public. Gardiner is in his element, and the Lyon Opéra cast includes such outstanding singers as Colette Alliot-Lugaz, rich-toned and characterful as the vivaciously provocative heroine, Jacqueline, and Thierry Dran as Fortunio, with Pierre Cachemaille as the handsome Captain Clavaroche, rival suitor for the heroine's attentions. On two mid-priced discs in Erato's Libretto series, it makes an ideal rarity to recommend not just to opera-lovers but also to those normally limiting themselves to operetta.

Messiaen, Olivier (1908–92)

L'Ascension (4 méditations symphoniques).

☞ *** DG Dig. 435 854-2 [id.]. Bastille Opéra O, Myung-Whun Chung – SAINT-SAENS: *Symphony No. 3*. **

Myung-Whun Chung creates just the right degree of intensity in his fine performance of one of Messiaen's most directly involving orchestral works. The *Majesté* of the first movement is balanced by the evocative and sensuous mysticism of the last, and the *Alléluias sereins* and *sur la trompette* of the central sections are radiantly and freshly played. Outstanding recording too – it is a pity that the coupling is disappointing.

Des canyons aux étoiles; Couleurs de la cité céleste; Oiseaux exotiques.

*** Sony Dig. MK 44762 [id.]. Paul Crossley, L. Sinf., Salonen.

The power of the writing in Messiaen's vast symphonic cycle, *Des canyons aux étoiles*, comes out vividly in Esa-Pekka Salonen's CBS version, with Paul Crossley as soloist both incisive and deeply sympathetic. Salonen's performance is not obviously devotional in the first five movements; but then, after Michael Thompson's virtuoso horn solo, in the sixth movement Salonen and his players increasingly find a sharper focus, with the playing of the London Sinfonietta ever more confident and idiomatic. *Oiseaux exotiques* find Crossley in inspired form as soloist, and with *Couleurs de la cité céleste* made tough rather than evocative. The recording is sharply focused, but has good presence and atmosphere.

(i) *Chronochromie;* (ii) *Et exspecto resurrectionem mortuorum.*
(M) *** EMI CDM7 63948-2 [id.]. (i) BBC SO, Dorati; (ii) O de Paris & Ens. de Percussion, Baudo
– BOULEZ: *Le soleil des eaux;* KOECHLIN: *Les Bandar-log.* ***

Messiaen's *Chronochromie* characteristically has its inspiration in nature, the composer's long-established preoccupation with birdsong, and the culminating *Epode*, readily understandable as a climactic representation of the birds' dawn chorus. This fine performance and immensely vivid recording are worthy of the music, and for the reissue EMI have added Serge Baudo's excellent 1968 recording of *Et exspecto resurrectionem mortuorum*. Baudo conducted its first performances in Paris and Chartres.

(i) *Hymne au Saint-sacrement; Les offrandes oubliées;* (ii) *Visions de l'amen.*
☞ (M) **(*) Erato/Warner 4509 91707-2 [id.]. (i) O de l'ORTF, Marius Constant; (ii) Katia and
Marielle Labèque.

Constant gives atmospheric yet passionate accounts of these two early works, catching also their rich vein of mysticism. The recordings, from the beginning of the 1970s, have a pleasingly warm ambience and do not sound too dated. The Labèque duo play the *Visions de l'amen* brilliantly, their performance bolder in profile and less withdrawn in atmosphere than rival versions, but compelling nevertheless.

Turangalîla Symphony.
☞ *** Decca Dig. 436 626-2 [id.]. Jean-Yves Thibaudet, Takashi Harada, Concg. O, Chailly.
☞ *** DG Dig. 431 781-2 [id.]. Yvonne & Jeanne Loriod, Bastille O, Chung.

(i) *Turangalîla Symphony. Un sourire.*
☞ ** BMG/RCA Dig. 09026 61520-2 (2) [id.]. (i) Roger Muraro, Valerie Hartmann-Claverie; Fr. R.
PO, Janowski – LUTOSLAWSKI: *Concerto for orchestra.* **(*)

(i) *Turangalîla symphony;* (ii) *Quartet for the end of time.*
*** EMI Dig. CDS7 47463-8 [id.] (2). (i) Donohoe, Murail, CBSO, Rattle; (ii) Gawriloff, Deinzer,
Palm, Kontarsky.

Among the new generation of one-disc versions of *Turangalîla*, Chailly's powerful, dramatic reading with the Concertgebouw makes an outstanding first choice. The richness of the sound goes with beautiful balance, fine clarity and a keen sense of presence, heightening the impact of Chailly's clean-cut, brilliant interpretation. Chailly's sharpness at a fast tempo in the catchy fifth movement, *Joie du sang des étoiles*, conveys its joy with a jazzy lilt, and the following *Jardin du sommeil d'amour* conveys sensuousness rather than spiritual intensity, taken at a flowing tempo. In the seventh movement, *Turangalîla II*, the wit and point of Thibaudet's playing heighten the sharpness of focus and, though some will prefer a warmer reading, no one will fail to appreciate the concentration and intensity of Chailly's performance. The Decca recording is in the demonstration class.

Chung's reading with the Bastille Orchestra was recorded in 1990 in the composer's presence, not long before he died. Messiaen's endorsement is confirmed when the soloists are his wife and his sister-in-law, at times less precise than rivals, but bringing a unique, expressive intensity. Their contributions, particularly the pointed piano-playing of Yvonne Loriod, heighten the natural warmth of Chung's reading, less high-powered and at times less precise than Chailly's rival one-disc version, and less cleanly recorded, but very persuasive.

Simon Rattle conducts a winning performance of *Turangalîla*, not only brilliant and dramatic but warmly atmospheric and convincing. It is not just that his rendering of the love music is ripely sensuous: in his rhythmic control of the fast dramatic movements he is equally understanding. The recording is warm and richly co-ordinated while losing nothing in detail. Peter Donohoe and Tristan Murail play with comparable warmth and flair. Led by Aloys Kontarsky, the performance of the *Quartet for the end of time* provides a contrasted approach to Messiaen from Rattle's, when atmospheric warmth is only an incidental.

When Janowski's version of *Turangalîla* is fitted complete on to a single disc, it seems an odd idea to shackle it to another CD, containing two works which together last only 37 minutes. In any case, Janowski's reading, though perceptive and idiomatic, has neither the power of Chailly's nor the warmth of Chung's. *Sourire*, here given a début recording, was the brief work (7½ minutes) which Messiaen wrote for the Mozart bicentenary, a simple alternation of a song-like theme and bird-song, ideas very typical of the composer. The Lutoslawski is very well done but is hardly a consistent coupling.

Quatuor pour la fin du temps.
*** Delos Dig. D/CD 3043 [id.]. Chamber Music Northwest – BARTOK: *Contrasts.* ***
(M) *** Ph. 422 834-2. Beths, Pieterson, Bylsma, De Leeuw.

(i) *Quatuor pour la fin du temps (Quartet for the end of time); (ii) Le merle noir.*
(M) *** EMI CDM7 63947-2 [id.]. (i) Gruenberg, De Peyer, Pleeth, Béroff; (ii) Zöller, Kontarsky.

Messiaen's visionary and often inspired piece was composed during his days in a Silesian prison camp. Among his fellow-prisoners were a violinist, a clarinettist and a cellist who, with the composer at the piano, made its creation possible. The 1968 EMI account, led by Erich Gruenberg and with Gervase de Peyer the inspirational clarinettist, is in the very highest class, the players meeting every demand the composer makes upon them, and the fine, clear Abbey Road recording gives the group striking presence while affording proper background ambience. The bonus, *Le merle noir*, exploits the composer's love of birdsong even more overtly and is splendidly played and recorded here.

We already know the calibre of David Shifrin's playing from his recording of Copland's *Clarinet concerto*. Here, like his colleagues, he fully captures the work's sensuous mysticism, while the solos of Warren Lash (cello) and Williams Doppmann have a wistful, improvisatory quality: both *Louange à l'éternité de Jésus* and the closing *Louange à l'immortalité de Jésus* are played very beautifully. The Delos recording is naturally balanced and very realistic, while the ambience is suitably evocative.

The Dutch team on Philips are also given the benefit of very good recording which has transferred well to CD; moreover their account has the merit of outstanding team-work and Reinbert de Leeuw has a keen sense of atmosphere, though he does not dominate the proceedings. There is also some superbly eloquent playing from George Pieterson and Anner Bylsma.

(i) *Quatuor pour la fin du temps; (ii) Cinq rechants* (for 12 voices).
☞ (M) *** Erato/Warner 4509 91708 [id.]. Fernandez, Deplus, Neilz, Petit; (ii) Solistes des Chœurs de l'ORTF, Marcel Couraud.

The French Ensemble on Erato give a strong, powerfully integrated performance, well held together by the pianist, Marie-Madeleine Petit. Among her colleagues, Jacques Neilz, the cellist, is raptly inspirational in the fifth movement (*Louange à l'Eternité de Jésus*) and is all but matched by the playing of his violinist colleague, Huguette Fernandez; the clarinettist, Guy Deplus, does not quite manage to achieve an opening crescendo out of nothingness but still makes a sensitive contribution. The recording is very good, clear and well balanced. The coupling is the extraordinary vocal work, *Cinq rechants*, written for a choir of twelve soloists. The composer's inspiration of human passion brings both lyrical intensity and extraordinary irregular rhythmic effects (some of which have an Indian source) and the various bursts and cascades of vocal tone give the work a stimulatingly original vitality. The performance is remarkably assured and full of ardent spontaneity, and the group are vividly recorded. Excellent notes are provided by the composer.

Theme and variations.
*** DG Dig. 427 351-2 [id.]. Gidon Kremer, Martha Argerich – BARTOK: *Sonata No. 1* ***; JANACEK: *Sonata.* **(*)

Messiaen's *Theme and variations* is an early work and the music's fervour is well captured here.

PIANO MUSIC

Cantéyodjaya; Fantaisie burlesque; 4 études de rythme; Rondeau.
*** Unicorn Dig. DKPCD 9051 [id.]. Peter Hill.

Peter Hill, playing a Bösendorfer, is a sympathetic guide in this repertoire; he has a good feeling for atmosphere and makes out an excellent case for all these pieces, save perhaps for the somewhat repetitive *Fantaisie burlesque* of 1932, which outstays its welcome. The recording is unobtrusively natural.

Catalogue d'oiseaux (complete); *La fauvette des jardins.*
☞ **(*) DG Dig. 439 214-2 (3) [id.]. Anatol Ugorski.

It is good to have such a bold, powerful, obviously deeply felt and essentially Slavonic approach to Messiaen's multi-faceted evocations of birdsong heard against graphically depicted landscapes, often rough-hewn, with all the extravagance of nature. It is impossible not to respond to such vivid pictorialism, even if Ugorski's response is essentially extrovert and at times almost melodramatic in its dynamism and sense of contrast. This would make a spectacular impression at a live performance, but under domestic circumstances the greater intimacy and the less flamboyant, more subtle approach of Peter Hill on Unicorn is the more satisfying. And the DG recording is very immediate, not necessarily an advantage when the playing creates its own presence.

Catalogue d'oiseaux, Books 1–3.
*** Unicorn Dig. DKPCD 9062; *DKPC 9062* [id.]. Peter Hill.

Catalogue d'oiseaux, Books 4–6: L'alouette calandrelle; La bouscarle; La merle de roche; La rousserolle effarvatte.
*** Unicorn Dig. DKPCD 9075; *DKPC 9075* [id.]. Peter Hill.

These scores derive their inspiration from Messiaen's beloved birdsong. Little of the piano writing is conventional and the music is vivid and colourful to match the plumage of the creatures which Messiaen depicts so strikingly. Peter Hill prepared this music in Paris with the composer himself and thus has his imprimatur. He evokes the wildlife pictured in this extraordinary music to splendid effect, and is recorded with the utmost clarity and definition.

Catalogue d'oiseaux, Book 7; Supplement: La fauvette des jardins.
*** Unicorn Dig. DKPCD 9090; *DKPC 9090* [id.]. Peter Hill.

In addition to the last book of the *Catalogue d'oiseaux* we have here *La fauvette des jardins*, which the sleeve annotator describes as the perfect parergon to the cycle. The composer himself has spoken with great warmth of this artist and, given what we hear on this disc, he has every reason to.

Préludes (complete); *Vingt regards sur l'enfant Jésus.*
(B) **(*) EMI CMS7 69161-2 (2) [id.]. Michel Béroff.

The *Préludes* are early works but, like *Vingt regards*, show Béroff at his most inspired, generating the illusion of spontaneous creation. Clean, well-focused sound – but, even though the venue was the Salle Wagram, the close balance brings a lack of rich sonority.

Vingt regards sur l'enfant Jésus.
☞ (M) *** Erato/Warner 4509 91705-2 (2) [id.]. Yvonne Loriod.
☞ (BB) *** Naxos Dig. 8.550829/30 [id.]. Håkon Austbø.

Vingt regards sur l'enfant Jésus; 4 Etudes de rythme; Petites esquisses d'oiseaux; 8 Préludes.
☞ (M) *** Erato/Warner 4509 96222-2 (3) [id.]. Yvonne Loriod.

The 1973 recording by Yvonne Loriod – the composer's second wife – of *Vingt regards* has long been considered very special in its understanding and feeling for the composer's mystical sound-world. The piano recording is full but is otherwise acceptable rather than outstanding – yet the magnetism of the playing overcomes the lack of the sharpest focus. This comes either separately (on two mid-priced CDs) or on three (together with other key repertoire, played with equal distinction).

Håkon Austbø as one-time prize-winner of the Olivier Messiaen Competition for Contemporary Music in Royan – he also studied at the Paris Conservatoire – has excellent credentials for performing this repertoire, and his is an individual view, with a wider range of tempi and dynamic than Loriod. His account of the opening *Regard du Père* and the later *Regard du Fils sur le Fils* is paced much more slowly, but his playing has great concentration and evocative feeling so that he readily carries the slower tempo, and in *Par lui tout a été fait* articulation is bolder, giving the music a stronger profile, helped by the clearer, Naxos digital focus. This is undoubtedly a performance that grips the listener and can be strongly recommended as an alternative view.

Visions de l'Amen.
*** EMI CDC7 54050-2 [id.]. Alexandre Rabinovitch, Martha Argerich.
*** New Albion Dig. NA 045 CD [id.]. Double Edge (Edmund Niemann & Nurit Tilles).

Messiaen's *Visions de l'Amen* for two pianos is a long, eloquent work in seven sections with a powerful sense of mystery, and is played with uncommon conviction by the Russian pianist-composer, Alexandre Rabinovitch, with Martha Argerich at the second piano.

The performance from Edmund Niemann and Nurit Tilles is hardly less arrestingly spontaneous. They capture the work's colour and atmosphere powerfully and evocatively – it is Messiaen at his most compelling – and some may prefer the sound of the New Albion recording. The two pianists are set back in a fairly reverberant but not blurring acoustic, which enhances the work's plangent palette.

ORGAN MUSIC

Complete works for organ: *Apparition de l'Eglise éternelle; L'Ascension* [4 *Méditations*]*; Le banquet céleste; Le corps glorieux* [7 *Visions de la vie des ressuscités*]*; Diptyque* [*Essai sur la vie terrestre et l'éternité religieuse*]*; Livre d'Orgue* [*Reprises par interversion; Première pièce en trio; Les mains de*

l'abîme; Chants oiseaux; Deuxième pièce en trio; Les yeux dans les roues; Soixante-quatre durées].
Messe de la Pentecôte; La Nativité du Seigneur [*9 Méditations*].
(M) *** EMI mono CZS7 67400-2 (4) [id.]. Composer (Cavaillé-Coll organ de L'Eglise de la Sainte-Trinité, Paris).

In an intensive series of sessions which began at the end of May and continued through June and July 1956, Olivier Messiaen returned to the organ in Sainte-Trinité, with which all his music is associated, and recorded everything he had written and published before that date. These performances not only carry the imprint of the composer's authority, but also the inspiration of the occasion. It is remarkable that the concentration of the playing comes over from the very opening bars of each movement, to grip the listener in its spell; and this applies especially to the more elusive works which create a pervasive atmosphere of spiritual mysticism. The large-scale works have a concentration and compelling atmosphere that are unforgettable. No apologies at all need be made for the range, breadth and faithfulness of the recording, although some must be made for the organ itself, which is not always perfectly tuned. There is minor background hiss, which is not troublesome, and technically the CD transfers are a remarkable achievement.

Livre du Saint Sacrement.
*** Unicorn Dig. DKPCD 9067/8; *DKPC 9067/8* [id.]. Jennifer Bate (organ of Sainte-Trinité, Paris).

What a sound! This is a quite spectacular recording and carries the composer's imprimatur. Jennifer Bate makes an impressive and compelling case for these hypnotic pieces, and the recording is in the demonstration bracket.

(i) *Méditations sur le mystère de la Sainte Trinité;* (ii) *3 Petites Liturgies de la Presence Divine.*
☞ (M) *** Erato/Warner 4509 92007-2 [id.]. (i) composer (Cavaillé-Coll organ, L'Eglise de la Sainte-Trinité, Paris); (ii) Yvonne & Jeanne Loriod, ORTF Ch. & CO, Couraud.

The composer's own performance of the *Méditations* is uniquely powerful, and the Sainte-Trinité organ is very well recorded. The balance in the mystically exotic choral work with its piano obbligato, and onde martenot, has the instruments placed rather forwardly but the chorus is well in the picture, and the effect is to embroider and comment on the choral texture very colourfully. The performance is vital and spontaneous; the sensuousness of the more luscious choral sections and the spectacular oriental percussion in Part II come over splendidly. The *Trois Petites Liturgies* has an immediate appeal, and this would be a good starting-point for newcomers to this composer's music. The recording is not always absolutely refined but it has great immediacy and impact.

La Nativité du Seigneur [*9 meditations*].
(M) *** Decca 425 616-2 (2) [id.]. Simon Preston (organ of Westminster Abbey) – *La Transfiguration*.
***

La Nativité du Seigneur [*9 meditations*]; *Le banquet céleste.*
⊛ *** Unicorn Dig. DKPCD 9005; *DKPC 9005* [id.]. Jennifer Bate (organ of Beauvais Cathedral).

'*C'est vraiment parfait!*' said Messiaen after hearing Jennifer Bate's Unicorn recording of *La Nativité du Seigneur*, one of his most extended, most moving and most variedly beautiful works. For the CD issue, *Le banquet céleste* also provides an intense comment on the religious experience which has inspired all of the composer's organ music. The recording of the Beauvais Cathedral organ is of demonstration quality.

Simon Preston is a convinced advocate of this score and conveys its hypnotic power most successfully. The Westminster Abbey organ produces the right kind of veiled colours to evoke the work's mysticism. This performance is by no means second best and makes a very generous bonus for *La Transfiguration*.

VOCAL MUSIC

Chants de terre et de ciel; Harawi [*Chants d'amour et de mort*]. *3 Mélodies* [*Pourquoi; Le sourire; La fiancée*]; *Poèmes pour Mi*
(M) *** EMI CMS7 64092-2 (2). Michèle Command, Marie-Madeleine Petit.

Michèle Command is here most characterful and firmly focused, with her accompanist just as warmly idiomatic. The three early songs of 1930 lead naturally to the two cycles from the late 1930s, more complex in their melodic lines. It is then that the ambitious Harawi cycle of 1945 reveals the full scope of the mature Messiaen's style, with its echoes of birdsong. This hour-long cycle belongs to what the composer regarded as his 'Tristan and Isolde' trilogy, along with the *Turangalîla Symphony* and the choral cycle, *Cinq Rechants*. Clear, undistracting sound.

La Transfiguration de Notre Seigneur Jésus-Christ.
(M) *** Decca 425 616-2 (2) [id.]. Sylvester, Aquino, Westminster Symphonic Ch., Loriod,
   Instrumental Soloists, Washington Nat. SO, Dorati – *La Nativité du Seigneur*. ***

This massive work of fourteen movements, divided into two parallel septenaries, sums up the whole achievement of Messiaen. Dorati holds the unwieldy structures together magnificently, and the brilliance and immediacy of the recording are most impressive.

Meyerbeer, Giacomo (1791–1864)

Les Patineurs (ballet suite, arr. & orch. Lambert).
(M) *** Decca 425 468-2 (3). Nat. PO, Richard Bonynge – TCHAIKOVSKY: *Sleeping Beauty*. **(*)

Les Patineurs was arranged by Constant Lambert using excerpts from two of Meyerbeer's operas, *Le Prophète* and *L'Etoile du Nord*. Bonynge's approach is warm and comparatively easy-going but, with such polished orchestral playing, this version is extremely beguiling. The sound too is first rate.

Il Crociato in Egitto (complete).
*** Opera Rara OR 10 (4). Kenny, Montague, Della Jones, Ford, Kitchen, Benelli, Platt, Geoffrey
   Mitchell Ch., RPO, David Parry.

This was the sixth and last opera which the German-born Meyerbeer wrote for Italy. The musical invention may not often be very distinctive, but the writing is consistently lively, notably in the ensembles. With one exception – Ian Platt, ill-focused in the role of the Sultan – the cast is a strong one, with Dianna Montague outstanding in the castrato role of the Crusader-Knight, Armando. Della Jones, too, in the mezzo role of Felicia, whom Armando has abandoned in favour of Palmide, the Sultan's daughter, sings superbly with agile coloratura and a rich chest register. Yvonne Kenny is brilliant as Palmide. Bruce Ford, with his firm, heroic tone, and Ugo Benelli are very well contrasted in the two tenor roles. Though the chorus is small, the recording is clear and fresh.

Les Huguenots (complete).
(M) *** Decca 430 549-2 (4) [id.]. Sutherland, Vrenios, Bacquier, Arroyo, Tourangeau, Ghiuselev,
   New Philh. O, Bonynge.

Sutherland is predictably impressive, though once or twice there are signs of a 'beat' in the voice, previously unheard on Sutherland records. The rest of the cast is uneven, and in an unusually episodic opera, with passages that are musically less than inspired, that brings disappointments. Gabriel Bacquier and Nicola Ghiuselev are fine in their roles and, though Martina Arroyo is below her best as Valentine, the star quality is unmistakable. The tenor, Anastasios Vrenios, copes with the extraordinarily high tessitura and florid diversions. Vrenios sings the notes, which is more than almost any rival could. Fine recording to match this ambitious project, well worth investigating by lovers of French opera. The work sounds newly minted on CD.

Le Prophète (complete).
**(*) Sony M3K 79400 (3) [id.]. Horne, Scotto, McCracken, Hines, Dupony, Bastin, Boys' Ch. of
   Haberdasher's Aske's School, Amb. Op. Ch., RPO, Henry Lewis.

This recording anticipated the 1977 production at the New York Met. with the same conductor and principal soloists. None of the soloists is quite at peak form, though they all sing more than competently. Nevertheless, with vigorous direction by Henry Lewis – rather brutal in the Coronation scene – there is much to enjoy. The recording is vividly transferred to CD but would have benefited from a more atmospheric acoustic.

Miaskovsky, Nikolay (1881–1950)

Cello concerto.
*** Ph. Dig. 434 106-2 [id.]. Julian Lloyd Webber, LSO, Maxim Shostakovich (with SHOSTAKOVICH:
   The *Limpid Stream: Adagio*) – TCHAIKOVSKY: *Rococo variations*. ***

Miaskovsky's *Cello concerto* is a work of great beauty and its neglect is baffling. It radiates an all-pervasive nostalgia, a longing for a world lost beyond recall. In its predominantly elegiac tone and its gentle resigned melancholy, it recalls the Elgar concerto. All credit to Julian Lloyd Webber for championing this piece and doing so with eloquence, and to Philips for recording it. Highly recommended.

(i) *Violin concerto, Op. 44;* (ii) *Symphony No. 22 in B min., Op. 54.*
**(*) Olympia OCD 134 [id.]. Grigori Feigin, USSR RSO, Dmitriev; (ii) USSR SO, Svetlanov.

The *Violin concerto* has a distinctive personality and a rich vein of lyricism. The ideas flow generously and the architecture is well held together. Grigori Feigin is the excellent soloist and plays with the right amount of warmth and virtuosity. The *Symphony* is a more powerful and ambitious piece and far more substantial than its immediate neighbours. Neither recording is new; both were made in 1974.

(i) *Lyric concertino for flute, clarinet, horn, bassoon, harp and string orchestra, Op. 32/3; Salutatory overture in C, Op. 48; Serenade for chamber orchestra in E flat, Op. 32/1; Sinfonietta for string orchestra in B min., Op. 32/2.*
☞ *** Olympia Dig. OCD 528 [id.]. Moscow New Op. O, Samoilov.

While he was working on his *Tenth Symphony*, Miaskovsky conceived the idea of three suites 'in song and dance idioms', though ultimately the dance element failed to achieve full expression. In fact the three pieces comprising Op. 32 were the only orchestral pieces he wrote between 1927 and 1931. The *Serenade* has great charm and strong lyrical appeal; the *Lyric concertino*, and particularly its slow movement, has considerable harmonic subtlety. The performance under Yevgeny Samoilov is much finer than the earlier account by Vladimir Verbitzky, and he gives a sensitive reading of the *Sinfonietta for strings*. These are endearing pieces; not so the *Salutatory Overture*, written for Stalin's 60th birthday, which is worth giving a miss. Very good recording.

(i) *Lyric concertino in G, Op. 32/3;* (ii) *Symphony No. 3 in A min., Op. 15.*
** Olympia OCD 177 [id.]. USSR SO; (i) Verbitzky, (ii) Svetlanov.

The *Third Symphony* is an epic, ambitious work, a dark and powerful piece, and Svetlanov is a persuasive advocate. The *Lyric concertino* is less satisfactorily recorded. The playing is a little less polished, too – which is a pity, as there are imaginative and original touches in the slow movement which show that Miaskovsky knew his French music.

(i) *Sinfonietta No. 2 in A min. for strings, Op. 68;* (ii) *Symphony No. 27 in C min., Op. 85.*
** Olympia OCD 168 [id.]. USSR Ac. SO; (i) Verbitzky, (ii) Svetlanov.

The *Symphony* is an endearingly old-fashioned work, and is very much better played and recorded than the *Sinfonietta*, written in a similar idiom. The recording, which dates from 1980, was made in a warm acoustic; the sound image is in excellent perspective, even if the balance will be too recessed for some tastes.

Symphonies Nos. (i) *1 in C min., Op. 3;* (ii) *19 in E flat for wind band, Op. 46.*
☞ **(*) Russian Disc RDCD 11 007 [id.]. (i) USSR Ministry of Culture SO, Gennady
  Rozhdestvensky; (ii) Russian State Brass O, Nikolai Sergeyev.

Miaskovsky's *First Symphony* comes from 1908, two years after he had resigned from the army to study composition at St Petersburg with Liadov and Rimsky-Korsakov; he had previously studied with Glière. This is a student work, very much in the received tradition, observing all the conventions one would expect to find in a symphonist of the post-nationalist Russian school. The composer's contrapuntal facility almost suggests Taneyev. The work is generously proportioned (it runs to 42 minutes) and although its melodic substance offers the occasional glimpse of the Miaskovsky to come the musical personality is not as yet fully formed. All the same, if the thematic ideas may not be highly individual, they betray (as so often with this composer) an endearing generosity of feeling, and there is a strongly Russian atmosphere throughout. It is obvious from the very start of the work that Miaskovsky was a composer who could think on a big scale. The *Nineteenth Symphony in B flat* for military band was written in 1939 for the 21st anniversary of the Red Army and is a slighter piece, worth hearing for its inner movements, a wistful *Moderato* and a well-written *Andante*. The *First Symphony* is well played by the Ministry of Culture Orchestra under Gennady Rozhdestvensky, though the brass sound a bit raw, as indeed do the upper strings. Climaxes, too, could be more transparent. The *Nineteenth* is played with great brio and genuine affection. The less-than-three-star recording-quality should not deter collectors from investigating this work.

Symphonies Nos. 5 in D, Op. 18; 9 in E min., Op. 28.
☞ *** Marco Polo Dig. 8.223499 [id.]. BBC PO, Downes.

The *Fifth Symphony* is a sunny, pastoral score dating from 1918, very much in the tradition of Glazunov and Glière. Downes's recording with the BBC Philharmonic, recorded in an admittedly over-resonant venue in Derby, is to be preferred both artistically and sonically to its earlier rival by the USSR Symphony Orchestra under Ivanov (coupled with No. 11 on Olympia). Nicolai Malko conducted its Moscow première in 1920 and it is to him that the *Ninth Symphony* of 1926–7 is dedicated. That symphony is not otherwise recorded and is somewhat better served than No. 5 so far as the sound is concerned. It is vintage Miaskovsky, more cogently argued and more interesting in thematic substance than the *Eighth*. Very good performances and good enough recording to make three stars.

Symphonies Nos. (i) *5 in D, Op. 18;* (ii) *11 in B flat, Op. 34.*
**(*) Olympia OCD 133 [id.]. (i) USSR SO, Ivanov; (ii) Moscow SO, Dudarova.

Miaskovsky himself called the *Fifth* his 'quiet' symphony; it is also pastoral in feeling and more introspective than Glazunov. The *Eleventh* is also conservative in idiom, yet the language is unpredictable; its distinctive melodic style is particularly evident in the finale. The recording, if not outstanding, is eminently serviceable.

Symphony No. 6 in E flat min. (Revolutionary), Op. 23.
☞ ** Olympia Dig. OCD 510. Anima Moscow Chamber Ch., Russian SO, Veronika Dudarova.
☞ * Marco Polo Dig. 8.223301. Bratislava Nat. Op. Ch. & RSO, Robert Stankovsky.

The *Sixth* is Miaskovsky's most ambitious symphony and it enjoyed considerable success in the 1920s. It is a 70-minute work of considerable power which, after long neglect, appears in two new recordings. Neither is ideal, but either is better than nothing. The ravages and privation of the First World War and then the October Revolution, as well as private tragedies, served to make this a symphony of both tragic dimensions and dramatic vigour. There are echoes of his master, Glière, and of Scriabin, and in the trio of the Scherzo Miaskovsky strikes that note of nostalgia and lost innocence he was to make so much his own in the *Cello concerto* (and at times in the *Violin concerto* too). It is a highly individual and often masterly score, let down perhaps by its somewhat inflated choral finale, which employs folk and revolutionary songs which earned the symphony its name, *The Revolutionary*.
    Of the two versions now offered, the Olympia under Veronika Dudarova is more inside the idiom. If the strings are lacking in weight (they are distinctly vinegary above the stave in the first movement and less than opulent elsewhere) and the brass sound a bit raw, the essential character of the work is conveyed well enough. The recording is not top-drawer but is more than acceptable and is to be preferred to the rather congested sound Marco Polo offers to Robert Stankovsky. Longer rehearsal time would undoubtedly have benefited the Bratislava performance, which is really rather ordinary and uncommitted.

Symphony No. 7 in B min., Op. 24.
** Olympia OCD 163 [id.]. USSR RSO, Ginsburg – KNIPPER: *Concert poem* etc. **

The *Seventh Symphony* (1922) is one of Miaskovky's finest symphonies, a much shorter work than its vast predecessor. The pastoral writing in the *Andante* movement has great beauty, and the performance under Leo Ginsburg is very persuasive. The sound is very agreeable and better balanced than the Knipper with which it is coupled.

Symphony No. 8 in A, Op. 26.
** Marco Polo Dig. 8.223297 [id.]. Slovak RSO (Bratislava), Robert Stankovsky.

Although the *Eighth* is not one of Miaskovsky's finest symphonies, it is still worth investigating. There are some characteristic ideas, and initially unfavourable impressions are soon dispelled as one comes closer to it. Neither the performance nor the recording is distinctive, but both are thoroughly acceptable; there is a lack of subtlety here, but not of vitality and commitment.

Symphony No. 12 in G min., Op. 35; Silence (symphonic poem after Poe), *Op. 9.*
**(*) Marco Polo Dig. 8.223302 [id.]. Slovak RSO (Bratislava), Robert Stankovsky.

The *Twelfth Symphony* comes from 1932; it is endearingly old-fashioned and has strong appeal. Although some of the big rhetorical gestures of the *Sixth Symphony* are to be found in the second movement, there are also some pre-echoes of things to come in the later symphonies. It is highly enjoyable, particularly when it is as well played as it is here by the Bratislava Radio Orchestra under their gifted young conductor, Robert Stankovsky. The tone-poem *Silence* draws for its inspiration on Edgar Allan Poe's *The Raven* and has a strongly atmospheric quality with a distinctly *fin-de-siècle* air: if you enjoy Rachmaninov's *Isle of the dead*, you should investigate it. The orchestra play with enthusiasm and they are decently recorded.

Symphony No. 21, Op. 51.
☞ (M) *** Unicorn UKCD 2066 [id.]. New Philh., David Measham – KABALEVSKY: *Symphony No. 2;* SHOSTAKOVICH: *Hamlet.* **(*)

The *Twenty-first* is arguably Miaskovsky's finest symphony. David Measham has the measure of the composer's special blend of melancholy and nostalgia, and in both the contemplative opening and the poetic closing pages he does this score full justice. Though it is conservative in idiom, the work stands the test of time remarkably well, and Miaskovsky's elegiac musings ring far truer than many more overtly 'modern' scores of the early 1940s. The sound is fully acceptable: the timbre of the various instruments reproduces faithfully and, although the recording is not top-drawer, it is spacious and clear.

String quartets Nos. 3 in D min., Op. 33/3; 10 in F, Op. 67/1; 13 in A min., Op. 86.
**(*) Olympia OCD 148 [id.]. Leningrad Taneiev Qt.

The *Thirteenth Quartet* is Miaskovsky's last work, one of fastidious craftsmanship and refined musicianship. It is a beautifully wrought score, in which ideas of great lyrical fervour flow abundantly. The Leningrad Taneiev Quartet, a first-class ensemble, play with dedication in all three works and the recordings, though not of the very highest quality, are very acceptable indeed.

PIANO MUSIC

Piano sonatas Nos. 1 in D min., Op. 6; 2 in F sharp min., Op. 13; 3 in C min., Op. 19; 6 in A flat, Op. 64/2.
**(*) Olympia Dig. OCD 214 [id.]. Murray McLachlan.

In its way, the *First Sonata* is an oddity; its opening, like that of the Balakirev *B flat minor Sonata* written two years earlier, is fugal, but much of the second movement is more akin to the early Scriabin sonatas. So, too, is the *Second,* though Taneyev, Glazunov and Medtner also spring to mind. The pianist, Murray McLachlan, possesses a very considerable talent. An enterprising issue in every way, and well recorded.

Piano sonatas Nos. 4 in C min., Op. 27; 5 in B, Op. 64/1; Sonatine in E min., Op. 57; Prelude, Op. 58.
*** Olympia Dig. OCD 217 [id.]. Murray McLachlan.

The middle movement of the *Sonatine,* marked *Narrante e lugubre,* is dark and pessimistic, and quite haunting. McLachlan speaks of the 'enormous tactile pleasure' it gives to the performer, and his playing is both authoritative and persuasive. Perhaps this is the record to try first, since both *Sonatas,* not just the more 'radical' *Fourth,* are of interest and substance. Good recording.

Piano sonatas Nos. 6 in A flat, Op. 62/2; 7 in C, Op. 82; 8 in D min., Op. 83; 9 in F, Op. 84.
**(*) Marco Polo Dig. 8.223178 [id.]. Endre Hegedüs.

Piano sonatas Nos. 7 in C, Op. 82; 8 in D min., Op. 83; 9 in F, Op. 84; Reminiscences, Op. 29; Rondo-Sonata in B flat min., Op. 58; String quartet No. 5: Scherzo (trans. Aliawdina): *Yellowed Leaves, Op. 31.*
**(*) Olympia Dig. OCD 252 [id.]. Murray McLachlan.

The sonatas on the Olympia disc are all from 1949. The music is of the utmost simplicity but has an endearing warmth. As in the earlier discs, McLachlan provides scholarly and intelligent notes. The recording is good though the acoustic ambience is perhaps not absolutely ideal.

The Marco Polo disc brings the last four sonatas. The young Hungarian pianist, Endre Hegedüs, is often the more imaginative interpreter: he colours the second theme of the *Barcarolle* section of the *Eighth Sonata* with greater tenderness and subtlety than Murray McLachlan on Olympia, though the latter has great freshness. The sound is a little wanting in bloom. On balance, then, honours are fairly even between these two artists.

Milán, Luis de (c. 1500–c. 1561)

El Maestro: Fantasias Nos. 7, 8, 9 & 16; Pavanas Nos. 1, 4, 5 & 6; Tento No. 1.
☞ (M) *** BMG/RCA 09026 61606-2. Julian Bream (lute) (with MUDARRA: *Fantasia*) – NARVAEZ: *Collection.* ***

This music was originally written for the vihuela, a hybrid instrument popular in sixteenth-century Spain, looking like a guitar but tuned like a lute. It was Milán who produced the first published book of this music in 1535, calling it *El Maestro* and including also instruction. Julian Bream seeks and achieves nobility of feeling in this repertoire and often chooses slow, dignified tempi. It all sounds splendid here on a proper lute, especially when so beautifully recorded.

Milhaud, Darius (1892–1974)

L'Apothéose de Molière, Op. 286; Le bœuf sur le toit, Op. 58; (i) Le carnaval d'Aix, Op. 83b. Le carnaval de Londres, Op. 172.

☞ *** Hyp. Dig. CDA 66594 [id.]. (i) Jack Gibbons; New L. O, Ronald Corp.

The best thing in the well-filled Hyperion disc is *Le carnaval d'Aix*, which originally served as the music to Milhaud's ballet, *Salade*. It is a work full of carefree high spirits and is bathed in Mediterranean sun with the occasional poignant moment of nostalgia – a delight from start to finish, and very expertly played by Jack Gibbons and the New London Orchestra under Ronald Corp. They also convey the Satie-like circus-music character of *Le bœuf sur le toit* to excellent effect. What delightful music this is, and so expertly fashioned by this lovable composer. The Molière pastiche and the arrangement of melodies from *The Beggar's Opera* are not top-drawer Milhaud, but they are still worth having. Very good recording from the Hyperion team.

Ballade, Op. 61; Le carnaval d'Aix; Piano concertos Nos. 1 & 4; 5 Etudes, Op. 63.

☞ *** Erato/Warner Dig. 2292 45992-2 [id.]. Claude Heffler, O Nat. de France, David Robertson.

Not many years ago Milhaud's delightful *Le carnaval d'Aix* for piano and orchestra was unrepresented on CD. Now there are several versions to hand, among which Claude Heffler's account with the Orchestre National must rank high in terms of easy-going charm and Mediterranean-like atmosphere, an altogether delightful performance. All the pieces on this disc, incidentally, are for piano and orchestra. The *Ballade*, Op. 61, and the *Cinq Etudes*, Op. 63, are both early works, coming from 1920. The *Ballade* was composed for Roussel, and Milhaud made his piano début at its première in New York: its languorous opening seems to hark back to his days in Brazil. The first of the *Cinq Etudes* shows Milhaud in window-breaking, polytonal mode, as does the third, *Fugues*, while the fourth, *Sombre*, also has a high norm of dissonance; on the other hand, the second, *Doucement*, has a beguiling charm. The *First Piano concerto*, Op. 127, No. 1, (1934) was written for Marguerite Long and is a relaxed, charming work not dissimilar to, though more complex in texture than, Jean Françaix's well-known *Concertino*. The *Fourth Piano concerto*, Op. 295 (1949), written for the virtuoso, Sadel Zkolowsky, is an inventive piece of some substance with a particularly imaginative, dream-like slow movement. Of the new CDs to have appeared in the wake of the Milhaud centenary this is among the very best, and it is beautifully and naturally recorded.

Le Bœuf sur le toit.

☞ (M) *** Mercury 434 335-2 [id.]. LSO, Dorati – AURIC: *Overture;* FETLER: *Contrasts;* FRANCAIX: *Piano concertino;* SATIE: *Parade.* ***

☞ **(*) Ph. Dig. 432 993-2 [id.]. Ch & O de Paris, Bychkov – HONEGGER: *Pacific 231;* POULENC: *Les biches.* **(*)

Dorati's reading, effervescent and light-hearted, catches the idiom splendidly and the music's lilt is infectiously conveyed. The LSO are obviously enjoying themselves and their playing, subtle as well as vivid, catches the audacious mood of a piece which is a trifle long for its content but which still entertains. The (1965) Mercury recording is perfectly judged, giving the music both transparency, vibrant colour and its proper edge.

   A highly proficient account of *Le bœuf sur le toit* from the Orchestre de Paris, which plays with appropriate brilliance under Bychkov. But the performance does not have the abandon and *joie de vivre* which distinguish the Dorati LSO account which is now happily restored to circulation and which still sounds pretty amazing.

(i) *Le bœuf sur le toit, Op. 58a;* (ii) *Le carnaval d'Aix, Op. 83b;* (iii) *Chamber symphony for winds No. 5, Op. 75;* (iv) *Flute sonatina, Op. 76;* (v) *Violin sonata No. 2, Op. 40.*

☞ ** Praga stereo/mono PR 250 007 [id.]. (ii) Hála; (iv) Jelínek, Leichner; (v) Gertler, Holeček; (iii) Prague Wind Band; (i) Czech PO; (i; iii) Pešek; (ii) Prague SO, Rohan.

These Czech performances are of varying quality: *Le bœuf sur le toit* is the most recent, from 1989, and finds the Czech Philharmonic under Libor Pešek in excellent form – though by comparison with, say, Dorati, they are wanting in abandon and zest. *Le carnaval d'Aix* with Josef Hála and the Prague Symphony under Jindřich Rohan is also a little strait-laced. Older collectors will recall André Gertler's 1957 mono recording of the *Second Violin sonata* with Josef Holeček, which rather shows its age. The little *Chamber symphony No. 5 for winds*, also mono, comes from the 1960s and is well played but could do with a bit more charm. None of these versions would be a first choice and all are otherwise available on CD, but those who want this particular compilation will still derive some pleasure from it.

Le bœuf sur le toit, Op. 58; (i) *Harp concerto, Op. 323. La création du monde, Op. 81.*
☞ *** Erato/Warner Dig. 2292 45820 [id.]. (i) Frédérique Cambreling; Lyon Op. O, Kent Nagano.

This Erato CD, made in collaboration with French Radio, brings together Milhaud's most celebrated ballets from the immediate post-war years (1919–23), *La création du monde* and *Le bœuf sur le toit*, with one of the numerous concertos he wrote in the 1950s. Kent Nagano and the Orchestra of the Opéra de Lyon give a splendid account of themselves in both the ballets. In *La création* the playing is full of character (the jazz fugue comes off marvellously) and the opening has splendid atmosphere; and much the same may be said of Nagano's exhilarating account of the Cocteau-inspired *Le bœuf sur le toit*. These scores have been recorded by the likes of Munch (RCA) and Bernstein (EMI), but this Erato disc need not fear comparisons: the playing is first rate and so, too, is the digital recording. The 1953 *Harp concerto* was written in America for Nicanor Zabaleta. It is not top-drawer Milhaud; there is more activity than substance for much of the time, but the slow movement has many beautiful things and Cambreling makes out a very good case for the high-spirited finale. Recommendable – eminently so in the case of the ballets.

Le bœuf sur le toit, Op. 58; La création du monde, Op. 81.
*** Chan. Dig. CHAN 9023 [id.]. Ulster O, Yan Pascal Tortelier – IBERT: *Divertissement*; POULENC: *Les Biches*. ***

A most engaging account of *Le bœuf sur le toit* from Tortelier and his Ulster players, full of colourful detail, admirably flexible, and infectiously rhythmic. Perhaps *La Création du monde* is without the degree of plangent jazzy emphasis of a French performance, but its gentle, desperate melancholy is well caught, and the playing has plenty of colour and does not lack rhythmic subtlety. The Chandos recording, although resonant, is splendid in every other respect, and so are the couplings.

(i) *Le bœuf sur le toit;* (ii) *La création du monde;* (iii) *Saudades do Brasil; Suite provençale;* (iv) *Scaramouche* (for 2 pianos).
☞ (***) EMI mono/stereo CDC7 54604-2 [id.]. (i) Champs-Elysées Theatre O; (ii) Ens. of 19 soloists; (iii) Concert Arts O, composer; (iv) Marcel Meyer, composer.

These recordings encompass both the pre- and post-war eras. Among the earliest are *La création du monde*, made with its chamber forces in 1932, and *Scaramouche*, which Milhaud recorded with Marcelle Meyer in 1938. (Both were included on an excellent Pearl CD, together with some highly desirable Honegger conducted by the composer, but the present transfers are undoubtedly superior.) Milhaud's own account of *La création du monde* has a certain want of abandon but is otherwise well played, and this *Scaramouche* has an altogether special charm. Older collectors will recall the Capitol mono LP coupling of the captivating *Suite provençale* and the carefree and catchy *Saudades do Brasil*, which now appears for the first time in stereo sounding very sprightly indeed. The Hollywood players who comprised the 'Concert Arts' orchestra respond to the composer with evident delight, and they make this a most desirable issue. In addition there is *Le Bœuf sur le toit* that Milhaud made with a Champs-Elysées orchestra in 1958 which will be new to most collectors and which makes a welcome makeweight to an altogether delightful (and, for lovers of this composer, indispensable) issue. However, it was curmudgeonly of EMI to put the disc in the full-price range.

La création du monde.
*** Virgin/EMI Dig. VJ5 61104-2 [id.]. Lausanne CO, Zedda – DEBUSSY: *Danse; Sarabande;* PROKOFIEV: *Sinfonietta*. ***

La création du monde; Suite provençale.
(M) *** BMG/RCA GD 60685 [60685-2-RG]. Boston SO, Charles Munch – HONEGGER: *Symphonies Nos. 2 & 5.* (***)

Both Munch performances come from the early 1960s and are full of all the style and spirit you would expect from this combination. Munch's account of *La création du monde* has great virtuosity and panache, though the Boston recording always sounded a bit too reverberant, and still does. The *Suite provençale*, based on tunes by another Provençal composer, André Campra, is one of Milhaud's most captivating pieces. A thoroughly enjoyable disc.

Milhaud's ballet, with its mixture of yearning melancholy and jazzy high spirits, comes off splendidly in Alberto Zedda's highly spontaneous account, its witty syncopations and brassy exuberance bringing an unbridled effervescence to offset the restrained blues feeling of the main lyrical theme. The performance doesn't miss the Gershwin affinities, and the very vivid recording makes a bold dynamic contrast between the work's tender and abrasive moments. An excellent bargain.

Suite française.
(M) *** CDWHL 2067. L. Wind O, Wick – GRAINGER: *Irish tune from County Derry* etc.; POULENC: *Suite française.*

Milhaud's *Suite française* for wind is an enchanting piece, full of Mediterranean colour and vitality. It would be difficult to imagine a more idiomatic or spirited performance than this one, which has excellent blend and balance. Vivid recording.

Suite provençale.
☞ ** Chan. Dig. CHAN 9072 [id.]. Detroit SO, Järvi – DEBUSSY: *La Mer;* ROUSSEL: *Sinfonietta* etc. **

The *Suite provençale* is well enough played by Järvi's Detroit forces and is well recorded, too, but this captivating score needs greater lightness of touch if it is to charm the listener as it should. Not a first choice, and it must be conceded that neither the Roussel symphony nor *La Mer* are front-runners, though both have strong merits.

Symphonies for chamber orchestra Nos. 1 (Le Printemps); 2 (Pastoral); 3 (Serenade); 5 (Dixtour d'instruments).
☞ ** Koch Dig. 3-7067-2 [id.]. Sinfonia O of Chicago, Barry Faldner – DEBUSSY: *Symphony in B min.;* GOUNOD: *Petite symphonie for winds.*

Barry Faldner and his Chicago Sinfonia, drawn from principals and other winds of the Chicago Symphony, give expert accounts of four of the little symphonies Milhaud composed in the 1920s. It would have made better sense (as well as rendering them more competitive) to have recorded all six rather than offering Faldner's orchestral transcription of Debussy's 10-minute symphony, a piece of little significance and not very characteristic of the composer. The performances of the Milhaud are very alert, characterful and polished – and very well recorded indeed. They give much pleasure.

Symphonies Nos. 1 (1939); 2 (1944); Suite provençale.
⊛ *** DG Dig. 435 437-2 [id.]. Toulouse Capitole O, Michel Plasson.

The *Second Symphony* is richly imaginative, melodically inventive and rewarding. Sample the fourth movement, *Avec sérénité,* and you will see just how sunny, relaxed and easy-going this music is; try also the slow movement of the *First* for its powerful, nocturnal atmosphere. The Orchestre du Capitole de Toulouse and Michel Plasson play these melodious scores with total commitment and convey their pleasure in rediscovering this music. The recording is very natural with a refined tone and well-balanced perspective. The delightful *Suite provençale* is as good as a holiday in the south of France – and cheaper!

Symphonies Nos. 4, Op. 281; 8 (Rhodanienne), Op. 362.
☞ (M) *** Erato/Warner 2292 45841-2 [id.]. O Philh. RTF, cond. composer.

The sheer size of Milhaud's output has an intimidating effect on the collector. Wherever does one start in so vast an output? Yet the appearance during the Milhaud centenary year of the rosetted DG coupling of the *First* and *Second Symphonies* from Michel Plasson and the Toulouse Capitole Orchestra will have alerted many collectors that there is more to Milhaud than *La création du monde* and *Le Bœuf sur le toit* and that the larger symphonies are of some quality and substance. The *Fourth Symphony* was commissioned by the French Radio in commemoration of the centenary of the 1848 Revolution, and its four movements offer a vivid portrayal of those events. It is scored for unusually large forces, including two saxophones and a vast array of percussion, all heard to good effect in the first movement, which depicts the uprising with massive polytonal and dissonant clashes; the second laments the fallen, the third describes liberty rediscovered and the finale is almost festive. The *Eighth Symphony,* Op. 362, written in the late 1950s for a new concert hall at the University of California in Berkeley, is subtitled *Rhodanienne* and evokes the course of the river Rhône from its beginnings in the Alps down to the Camargue. Rich in instrumental resource, it is full of imaginative colours and textures, and the playing of the Orchestre Philharmonique de l'ORTF for Milhaud himself is absolutely first rate. Both performances date from 1968, when they were briefly available on an Erato LP; the sound is much cleaned-up for this CD, which commands an unqualified recommendation.

(i) *Symphony No. 8 (Rhodanienne), Op. 362;* (i; ii) *Scaramouche for saxophone, Op. 165c;* (iii) *La Cheminée du Roi René, Op. 205;* (iv) *Organ preludes, Op. 231b/3, 7–8;* (v) *Cantique du Rhône, Op. 155.*

☞ ** Praga PR 250 013 [id.]. (i) Czech PO, Neumann, (ii) with Neidenbach-Rahbari; (iii) Mihule, Vaček, Hůlka, Uher, Svárovsky; (iv) Tvrzský; (v) Czech R. Mixed Ch., Kühn.

The 1966 performance of the *Eighth Symphony* (*Rhodanienne*) is not superior to the composer's own on Erato, but the disc is well worth acquiring even if it involves duplication. (The *Cantique du Rhône* for *a cappella* choir, a setting of words by Claudel in praise of the Rhône, composed in Aix in 1936, is a beautiful piece, well sung here by the Pavel Kühn Choir and, like *Scaramouche*, recorded in 1987.) After the success of the two-piano version of *Scaramouche* in 1937, Milhaud made two transcriptions, one for saxophone and orchestra and the other for clarinet (for Benny Goodman). The saxophone version is played with plenty of character and a certain artful charm by Sohre Neidenbach-Rahbari and the Czech Philharmonic and was recorded at a live performance. *La Cheminée du Roi René* for wind quintet, originating from the film music to *Cavalcade d'amour*, has an abundant charm, much of which is conveyed in this 1979 studio performance.

(i; ii) *Symphony No. 10, Op. 382;* (i; iii) *Concertino d'hiver for trombone and strings, Op. 327;* (iv) *Music for Prague, Op. 415;* (i; v) *Hommage à Comenius, Op. 421.*

☞ ** Praga PR 250 012 [id.]. (i) Prague R.O; (ii) Košler; (iii) Pulec, cond. Krombholc; (iv) Czech PO, composer; (v) Zikmundová, Jindrák, Hrnčíř.

Another disc commemorating Milhaud's association with Prague on the occasion of the centenary of his birth. The *Concertino d'hiver* (1953) comes from the set of 'Four Seasons' that he composed over a period of two decades and subsequently linked together. Not as inventive as the pre-war *Concertino de printemps*, it is given a very good performance by Zdenek Pulec and the Prague Radio Orchestra under Jaroslav Krombholc (1976). The quality of sound in the 1970 performance of the *Tenth Symphony* with Zdenek Košler conducting is sonically superior to Milhaud's own account on Koch. *Musique pour Prague* was commissioned for the Prague Spring Festival in 1966, and this performance under Milhaud's own baton sounds a little better than the Koch rival. The textures are occasionally thick and hyperactive, but on the whole it is more rewarding than the symphony itself. Also associated with Prague is the cantata for soprano and baritone Milhaud composed in honour of the Czech philosopher and bishop Comenius (1592–1670), a pioneer of universal education, which is new to the catalogue. This, like the symphony, is a studio performance from 1970, though the soprano, Eva Zikmundová, has a characteristic Slavonic vibrato.

CHAMBER MUSIC

Duo for 2 violins, Op. 243; (i) *Sonata for 2 violins and piano, Op. 15.*
(*) Hyp. Dig. CDA 66473 [id.]. Ososowicz, Kovacic, (i) Tomes – MARTINU: *Violin sonata* **(*); PROKOFIEV: *Violin sonata.* *

The *Sonata for two violins and piano* of 1914 is beautifully crafted and has a charming slow movement but is very slight. Not as slight, though, as the *Duo*, the first two movements of which were composed at a dinner party; the finale was written the following morning. Musically it is all rather like having *canapés* and *petits fours* and missing out the meal! Elegant performances from Krysia Ososowicz and Ernst Kovacic – and in the *Sonata* Susan Tomes.

Music for wind: *La Cheminée du Roi René, Op. 105; Divertissement en trois parties, Op. 399b; Pastorale, Op. 47; 2 Sketches, Op. 227b; Suite d'après Corrette, Op. 161b.*
(M) **(*) Chan. CHAN 6536; *MBTD 6536* [id.]. Athena Ens., McNichol.

Though none of this is first-class Milhaud, it is still full of pleasing and attractive ideas, and the general air of easy-going, life-loving enjoyment is well conveyed by the alert playing of the Athena Ensemble. One's only quarrel with this issue is the somewhat close balance. However, this can be remedied a little by a lower-level setting; even if the overall playing time is not very generous, this is an excellent entertainment.

Sonatina for clarinet and piano; Sonatina for flute and piano; Sonata for flute, oboe, clarinet and piano; Sonatina for oboe and piano.
*** Orfeo Dig. CO 60831A [id.]. Brunner, Nicolet, Holliger, Maisenberg.

The *Sonata* is an ingenious and delightful piece, most expertly played here. The later *Sonatinas* have no less charm and polish, and are beautifully played and very naturally recorded. A strong recommendation for a very attractive concert.

(i) *Oboe sonatina, Op. 337;* (ii) *Suite après Corette, Op. 161b;* (iii) *Violin sonata No. 1, Op. 240;* (iv) *4 Visages, Op. 238;* (v) *Organ pastorale, Op. 229;* (vi) *3 Chansons de Négresse, Op. 148b;* (vii) *2 Poems by Blaise Cendrars, Op. 113.*

☞ *** Praga PR 250 008 [id.].(i) Adamus, Bogunia; (ii) Hedba, Nechvatal, Zedník; (iii) Spelina, Friesl; (iv) Christ, Klánský; (v) Grubich; (vi) Fassbaender, Gage; (vii) Smíšený, Kühn Mixed Ch., Kühn.

Another compilation from Prague to honour the Milhaud centenary. All are live performances, made in Prague between 1981 and 1990, and are of decent to excellent quality. The two choral settings of poems by Blaise Cendrars, which open the CD, are of striking quality and are very well sung by Pavel Kühn's choir. The *Trois Chansons de Négresse* hark back to Milhaud's years in Rio, where he served as secretary to Paul Claudel at the French Embassy, and are sung with great character and charm by Brigitte Fassbaender. The *Pastorale, Op. 229,* for organ is a rather lovely and meditative piece. Wolfram Christ is the excellent soloist in the *Sonata No. 1,* based on eighteenth-century French tunes, and the *Quatre Visages* for viola and piano, the latter a portrait of four ladies from California, Wisconsin, Brussels and Paris. Like Jean Françaix's *Cinq Portraits de jeunes filles* for piano, it has character and a winning charm – as, for that matter, have most of the other pieces. The *Suite d'après Corette* for oboe, clarinet and bassoon is elegantly played and sounds more persuasive here than in some French performances we have heard. A welcome issue and a valuable addition to the Milhaud discography.

String quartets Nos. 1, Op. 5; 7 in B flat, Op. 87; 10, Op. 218; 16, Op. 303.
*** Cybella Dig. CY 804 [id.]. Aquitaine National Qt.

The *First Quartet* is a beautifully relaxed, sunny work, rather Debussian in feel. The *Seventh* speaks Milhaud's familiar, distinctive language; its four short movements are delightful, full of melody and colour. The *Tenth* is attractive too, while the *Sixteenth* was a wedding anniversary present for the composer's wife: its first movement has great tenderness and warmth. The Aquitaine Quartet has excellent ensemble, intonation is good and their playing is polished. The recording has a wide dynamic range and a spacious tonal spectrum.

String quartets Nos. 5, Op. 64; 8, Op. 121; 11, Op. 232; 13, Op. 268.
*** Cybella Dig. CY 805 [id.]. Aquitaine National Qt.

The *Fifth Quartet* is not one of Milhaud's most inspired; the *Eighth*, on the other hand, has much to commend it, including a poignant slow movement. No. 11 has a splendid pastoral third movement and a lively jazzy finale; No. 13 has overtones of Mexico in its finale and a beguiling and charming *Barcarolle*. Both performance and recording are very good.

Minkus, Léon (1826–1917)

La Bayadère (complete; arr. Lanchbery)
☞ *** Decca Dig. 436 917-2 (2) [id.]. ECO, Richard Bonynge.

John Lanchbery has a good track record, and the fact that he has had a hand in this new complete set of *La Bayadère* augurs well. The ballet itself was a key work in the repertoire of Petipa's Russian Ballet in St Petersburg before Tchaikovsky began to dominate the scene, and the piece still has stage life in it, having been revived fairly recently in New York and London. Lanchbery has provided the present score, and though officially he is responsible for the orchestration, who knows, perhaps he had a hand in its content, as in his vintage arrangement of Hérold's *La fille mal gardée*. Whatever the case, the result is highly engaging. Unlike Adam's rather disappointing *Le Corsaire* (also recorded by the same forces), this work is full of attractive melody and sparkling orchestral effects. If you like late-nineteenth-century ballet music, then here is nearly two hours of it, played with much vivacity, elegance and drama, and given Decca's top-drawer sound.

La Source (ballet): Act I; Act III, scene ii.
*** Decca Dig. 421 431-2 (2) [id.]. ROHCG O, Bonynge – DELIBES: *La Source* (Act II; Act III, scene i); DRIGO: *Flûte magique.* ***

Composed in partnership with Delibes, it is the contribution of Minkus that sets the style and atmosphere of *La Source*, very much inherited from Adam; the writing has distinct charm and its picaresque evocation suits the slight narrative line. The score is beautifully played and Bonynge's affection is obvious; there is both grace and sparkle here. First-class Decca sound, too.

Moeran, Ernest J. (1894–1950)

(i) *Cello concerto. Sinfonietta.*
*** Chan. Dig. CHAN 8456; *ABTD 1167* [id.]. (i) Raphael Wallfisch; Bournemouth Sinf., Del Mar.

Raphael Wallfisch brings an eloquence of tone and a masterly technical address to the *Cello concerto* and he receives responsive orchestral support from Norman Del Mar and the Bournemouth players. The well-crafted *Sinfonietta* is among Moeran's most successful pieces: its invention is delightfully fresh, and there is that earthy, unpretentious musicality that makes Moeran so appealing a composer. The recording is a little on the reverberant side but well balanced and present.

(i) *Violin concerto. 2 Pieces for small orchestra: Lonely waters; Whythorne's shadow.*
*** Chan. Dig. CHAN 8807; *ABTD 1435* [id.]. (i) Lydia Mordkovitch; Ulster O, Vernon Handley.

The *Violin concerto* is strongly lyrical in feeling. The first movement is ruminative and rhapsodic, its inspiration drawn from Moeran's love of the west coast of Ireland; the middle movement makes use of folk music; while the finale, a ruminative elegy of great beauty, is the most haunting of the three. Lydia Mordkovitch plays with great natural feeling for this music and, quite apart from his sensitive support in the *Concerto*, Vernon Handley gives an outstanding (and affecting) account of *Lonely waters*. Superb recording.

2 Pieces for small orchestra: (i) *Lonely waters; Whythorne's shadow.*
☞ (M) *** EMI Dig. CDM7 64200-2 [id.]. (i) Ann Murray; ECO, Tate – BAX: *3 Pieces* ***;
  BRIDGE: *There is a willow;* BUTTERWORTH: *Banks of green willow* etc. **(*)

The two Moeran pieces in Tate's English recital present a complete contrast with each other, the first atmospheric and impressionistic, the second reflecting the composer's interest in the Elizabethan madrigal. They are given finely judged, refined performances, warmly recorded.

Serenade in G (complete original score); (i) *Nocturne.*
*** Chan. Dig. CHAN 8808; *ABTD 1436* [id.]. Ulster O, Vernon Handley – WARLOCK: *Capriol suite* etc. ***

The *Serenade in G* is a welcome addition to the catalogue, a work which has a good deal in common with Warlock's *Capriol suite* in its orchestral dress. Both use dance forms from a previous age and transform them with new colours and harmonic touches. Handley and the Ulster Orchestra present it with striking freshness and warmth in its original version. Handley also offers the lovely *Nocturne*, a setting of a poem by Robert Nichols for baritone solo and eight-part chorus, which was much admired by Britten. It is given a wholly sympathetic performance and recording here, and the resonant acoustics of the Ulster Hall, Belfast, provide a warmly atmospheric ambient glow.

Serenade in G; Sinfonietta.
☞ (M) **(*) EMI Dig. CDM7 64721-2 [id.]. N. Sinfonia, Hickox – FINZI: *The Fall of the leaf* etc.
  ***

The Hickox performance of the *Serenade* is very pleasing, if lacking as strong a profile as Handley's account; moreover, by playing just the published score, it omits the two rediscovered movements. However, the coupling of a fine account of the *Sinfonietta*, one of Moeran's very best works, almost rights the balance. The recording, made in All Saints', Newcastle-upon-Tyne, is agreeably flattering but brings a less well-defined bass than on the Chandos disc. Even so, with its attractive Finzi couplings, this is still worth considering.

Symphony in G min.
☞ ⊛ *** Dutton Laboratories CDAX 8001 [id.]. Hallé O, Leslie Heward – IRELAND: *Piano concerto.*
  (***)

There is always something special about first recordings, but this is remarkable in more than one respect. First, it is a wonderful performance of a great British symphony which, in its natural spontaneity – combining creative freedom with complete faithfulness to the score – has never been surpassed. Secondly, it celebrates a great British conductor, working at white-hot intensity, who died (so prematurely) just over a year after the original 78s appeared. Thirdly, it was the first recording of British music sponsored by the British Council, which went on to provide us with many more cherishable records. Walter Legge produced the sessions in Manchester's Houldsworth Hall, and his mono sound-balance was completely natural, using the slightly dry hall acoustics to maximum advantage. Finally, no praise can be too great for Michael Dutton's CD transfer, made direct from the 78-r.p.m. shellac pressings, using the Cedar system to suppress the surface noise, yet providing sound for which no apologies whatsoever need to be made, with no edginess to ruin the strings: the violins sound particularly fresh. The sense of orchestral presence and the truthfulness of the overall sound-picture are uncanny: this is far ahead of most transfers of mono LPs, let alone 78s. The composer was present at the sessions and gave his imprimatur, afterwards saying, 'The symphony has had such a performance as it never had before.' This CD is fully worthy of it. The Ireland coupling is hardly less indispensable.

Symphony in G min.; Overture for a masque.
*** Chan. Dig. CHAN 8577; *ABTD 1272* [id.]. Ulster O, Vernon Handley.

Moeran's superb *Symphony in G minor* is in the best English tradition of symphonic writing and worthy to rank with the symphonies of Vaughan Williams and Walton. But for all the echoes of these composers (and Holst and Butterworth, too) it has a strong individual voice. Vernon Handley gives a bitingly powerful performance, helped by superb playing from the Ulster Orchestra, totally committed from first to last. The *Overture for a masque*, a brash, brassy piece in its fanfare opening and Waltonian cross-rhythms, makes an attractive and generous fill-up. The recording is superb.

Fantasy quartet for oboe and strings.
*** Chan. Dig. CHAN 8392; *ABTD 1114* [id.]. Francis, English Qt – BAX: *Quintet;* HOLST: *Air and variations* etc.; JACOB: *Quartet.* ***

Moeran's folk-influenced *Fantasy quartet*, an attractively rhapsodic single-movement work, is played admirably here, and the recording is excellent, well balanced too.

(i) *String quartet in A min.;* (ii) *Violin sonata in E min.*
*** Chan. Dig. CHAN 8465; *ABTD 1168* [id.]. (i) Melbourne Qt; (ii) Donald Scotts, John Talbot.

There is a strong folksong element in the *Quartet*, and some French influence too; these pieces are stronger than they have been given credit for. Good performances and recording.

Molino, Francesco (1775–1847)

Trio, Op. 45.
*** Mer. Dig. CDE 84199; *KE 77199* [id.]. Conway, Silverthorne, Garcia – BEETHOVEN: *Serenade;* JOSEPH KREUTZER: *Grand Trio.* ***

Italian-born, Molino first settled in Spain, before going on to London and Paris, where he built a reputation as a violinist and guitarist. Undemanding music to complete a charming disc for a rare combination. First-rate playing and recording.

Molter, Johann (1696–1765)

Clarinet concerto in D.
*** Claves CD 50-813 [id.]. Friedli, SW German CO, Angerer – MERCADANTE; PLEYEL: *Concertos.* ***

Molter's *Concerto* is for D clarinet and its high tessitura means that, when heard on a modern version of the instrument for which it was written, the timbre sounds uncannily like a soft-grained trumpet – and very effective, too, especially when the playing is both expert and sympathetic. Here the accompaniment is good rather than outstanding. Nevertheless, this remains a most enjoyable collection, for the coupled works are equally interesting.

Trumpet concertos Nos. 1–3 in D, MWV IV/12–14; (i) *Double trumpet concertos in D, MWV IV/7, 8, 10–11.*
☞ *** BMG/RCA Dig. 09026 61200-2. Guy Touvron; (i) Guy Messler; Württemberg CO, Heilbronn, Joerg Faerber.

Johann Molter was born in Tiefenort, a violinist and a court musician who became Kapellmeister at Karlsruhe. During his career he made two separate tours of Italy, bringing back influences from Vivaldi and Albinoni and, later, from Pergolesi and Sammartini; so his style ranges from the baroque to the *galant*. He was a composer of accomplishment and, although most of his vocal music is lost, he is well remembered for his concertos, especially those for the trumpet, for which he wrote with innate skill, even though he was not a brass player himself. His melodic lines lie high in the clarino range, and the brilliantly felicitous bravura writing makes the utmost demands on his soloists. In all four double concertos here, both trumpeters are thoughtfully left resting in the engaging *Andante* slow movements, which are usually for strings alone. MWV IV/10 is an exception, bringing a divertimento-like interlude, scored for woodwind alone. In the solo concertos, although outer movements are hardly less brilliant, and rewardingly so, the trumpeter also has a central slow melody in the highest tessitura. The performances here are persuasively accomplished and, while the concertos are all very similar, each has its own individual inventiveness; taken singly, they are easy to enjoy. Joerg Faerber and his excellent Württemberg players provide alert and spirited accompaniments and are particularly sympathetic in the serene *Andantes*. The two Guys match timbres and phrasing as one in the duo works. The recording is most realistic: it has an exemplary balance and a warm, pleasingly spacious acoustic, yet is not too resonant.

Trumpet concertos in D (M S 331 & 333); (i) *Double trumpet concerto in D (M S 330).*
(M) **(*) Erato/Warner 2292 45061-2 [id.]. Maurice André; (i) with Raymond André; Paillard CO, Paillard – HUMMEL: *Concerto.* ***

The *Double concerto* here is rather more striking than the solo concertos, but all three works here are very well played and accompanied.

Mompou, Federico (1893–1987)

Escenas infantiles (orch. Tansman); *Suburbis* (orch. Rosenthal); (i) *Combat del Sueño;* (ii) *Los Improperios.*
☞ *** HM Dig. HMC 901482 [id.]. O of Cambra Theatre, Lliure, Josep Pons, with (i; ii) Virginia Parramon; (ii) Jerzy Artysz, Valencia Ch.

We are already familiar with Mompou's highly engaging piano music; the present disc suggests that this Barcelona-born composer who divided his musical career between Paris and the city of his birth is a more substantial figure than hitherto suspected. Admittedly the two orchestral works were scored by other hands, but the writing itself has much charm and the pastel-shaded colouring is inherent in the music itself. Not surprisingly, the flavour and impressionistic influences are both Spanish and French, with whiffs of Ravel and the Debussy of *Ibéria* in these haunting evocations of the innocent world of children playing and scenes of Barcelona (including portraits of two gypsies, a little blind girl and a barrel-organ grinder). The oratorio, *Los Improperios*, is much more ambitious and – although there are reminders of Poulenc and even of Delius – the music has an individual voice, both orchestrally and in its serene, gleaming choral writing. *Combat del Sueño* is a triptych of ardent yet poignant love songs – somewhat like Ravel's *Shéhérazade* – combining memorable melodic lines with spare and delicate orchestration. They are seductively sung here by Virginia Parramon. Jerzy Artysz joins her in the oratorio, and the excellent choral and orchestral contributions under the persuasive Josep Pons, plus warm yet vividly atmospheric recording, ensure a strong recommendation for this very rewarding collection. Mompou may be eclectic, but he is also very personable.

Suite compostellana (for guitar).
☞ (M) *** BMG/RCA Dig. 09026 61596-2 [id.]. Julian Bream – RECITAL: *'Twentieth-century guitar'.* ***

Mompou's *Suite compostellana* is his only work for guitar – and very fine it is, beautifully written for the instrument and with a prevailing mood of wistful melancholy. Its opening *Preludio* has an obvious reminder of Albéniz's famous *Asturias*, but Mompou's sound-world is altogether more intimate and any flamenco associations are muted. The second movement, *Coro*, has a Satiesque flavour, the third, *Cuna*, is a gently rocking cradle song. After the interplay of two different moods in *Recitativo*, we reach a charming *Canción*, almost a folk tune, and the piece ends with an infectious, lightly sparkling *Muñeira*, a gypsy dance from Galicia, but heard in a cultivated metamorphosis. Bream's performance is wonderfully sympathetic and spontaneous and the digital recording is first class.

7 Cançons y dansas; Impresiones intimas; Música callada IV; Preludio VII a Alicia de Larrocha.
⊛ (M) *** Decca 433 929-2 (2) [id.]. Alicia de Larrocha – Recital: *'Musica española'.* ***

This is gentle, reflective music which brings peace to the listener. Its quiet ruminative quality finds an eloquent exponent in Alicia de Larrocha, to whom Mompou dedicated one of his preludes. The *Impresiones intimas* date from 1911–14 and is his first work of note. Like Falla and Turina, Mompou was drawn to Paris, and these pieces have absorbed something of the delicacy of Debussy in their poetic feeling, fine detail and well-calculated proportions. Alicia de Larrocha plays these poetic miniatures *con amore*, and the Decca recording is quite superb. This is reissued as part of a generous and stimulating recital of piano music by Mompou's Spanish contemporaries.

8 Canciones y danzas; Escenas de niños; Fiestas lejanas; Paisajes; Pessebres; Suburbis.
☞ (M) *** EMI CDM7 64470-2 [id.]. Gonzalo Soriano or Carmen Bravo.

This EMI collection, which comes from the Spanish Hispavox catalogue, is valuable in duplicating only the *Canciones y danzas* included on Alicia de Larrocha's two-disc Decca recital of 'Musica española'. Gonzalo Soriano plays these reflective miniatures simply and with the right degree of restrained eloquence. Mompou is the very antithesis of a gaudy impressionist; his musical pictures are restrained and delicately delineated. Carmen Bravo also finds poetry in the rest of the programme and is charmingly perceptive in his portrayal – in *Suburbis* – of *L'home de l'aristo* (the *aristo* was a cross between a hand-held miniature barrel-organ and a hurdy-gurdy). The *Escenas de niños* are gentle children's pictures, while the *Fiestas lejanas* are a series of brief vignettes, echoes and memories of past festivities. The two closing *Paisajes* with evocations of fountain, bell and lake are delightful, and the playing here catches well their delicately picaresque understatement. A rewarding and generous recital, given remarkably good recording, even though it dates from the early days of stereo. (Alas, it has been withdrawn as we go to press.)

Jeunes filles au jardin; El carrer, el guitarrista i el vell cavall; Canción y danza Nos. 5, 6 & 8; La fuente y la compaña.
☞ (M) (***) EMI mono CDC7 54836-2 [id.]. (i) Composer – FALLA: *Harpsichord concerto etc.*;
    GRANADOS: *Danzas españolas etc.*; NIN: *Cantos populares españolas.* (***)

One of the most valuable of the marvellously documented and beautifully restored 'Composers in Person' CDs that EMI have recently published. Federico Mompou was the most long-lived of the Spanish composers recorded on this disc. (When R.L. was in Barcelona, some years before the composer's death, he was told that Mompou claimed never to have gone to bed before 3 o'clock in the morning during the whole of his life!) He remains the most intimate and the most intensely private of Spanish composers. He recorded these six pieces while in London in 1950, though unaccountably they were never published until now. They are slight but beautiful and enhance what is a highly interesting disc.

Mondonville, Jean-Joseph Cassanea de (1711–72)

Titon et L'Aurore (complete).
*** Erato/Warner Dig. 2292 45715-2 (2) [id.]. Fouchécourt, Napoli, Huttenlocher, Smith, Monnoyios, Les Musiciens du Louvre, Minkowski.

Described as a 'heroic-pastoral', *Titon et L'Aurore* fluently pours forth a sequence of crisp ideas in each of the three acts of this formal classical tale of the mortal Titon who has the temerity to fall in love with Aurora, goddess of the dawn. Some of the instrumental effects are most vivid and the work is full of charming ideas, presented with freshness and vigour. Marc Minkowski proves an ideal interpreter, directing a performance of the highest voltage, which yet allows the singers a full range of expressiveness. Jean-Paul Fouchécourt proves an outstanding example of the French *haute-contre*, sustaining stratospheric lines with elegance and no strain. Catherine Napoli is bright and clear, if shallow at times as Aurore, while Anne Monnoyios sings with ideal sweetness as L'Amour.

Monteverdi, Claudio (1567–1643)

Ab aeterno ordinata sum; Confitebor tibi, Domine (3 settings); Deus tuorum militum sors et corona; Iste confessor Domini sacratus; Laudate Dominum, O omnes gentes; La Maddalena: Prologue: Su le penne de venti. Nisi Dominus aedificaverit domum.
⊕ *** Hyp. Dig. CDA 66021; *KA 66021* [id.]. Kirkby, Partridge, Thomas, Parley of Instruments.

There are few records of Monteverdi's solo vocal music as persuasive as this. The three totally contrasted settings of *Confitebor tibi* (Psalm 110) reveal an extraordinary range of expression, each one drawing out different aspects of word-meaning. Even the brief trio, *Deus tuorum militum*, has a haunting memorability – it could become to Monteverdi what *Jesu, joy of man's desiring* is to Bach – and the performances are outstanding, with the edge on Emma Kirkby's voice attractively presented in an aptly reverberant acoustic. The accompaniment makes a persuasive case for authentic performance on original instruments. The CD sounds superb.

Madrigals, Book 4 (complete).
*** O-L Dig. 414 148-2 [id.]. Cons. of Musicke, Anthony Rooley.

Under Anthony Rooley the fine, well-integrated singers of the Consort of Musicke give masterly performances of this dazzling collection of madrigals. The flexibility and control of dramatic contrast, conveying consistent commitment, make this one of this group's finest records, helped by atmospheric but aptly intimate recording.

Madrigals, Book 6 (complete).
*** Virgin/EMI Dig. VC7 59605-2 [id.]. Consort of Musicke, Anthony Rooley.

Il sesto libro de madrigali (1614) includes the five-part transcription of the *Lamento d'Arianna* and *Zefiro torno*, and also pieces from Monteverdi's years at Mantua. The Consort of Musicke maintain the high standards of taste and artistry with which we associate them. Excellent recording.

Madrigals from Books 7 and 8: *Amor che deggio far; Altri canti di Marte; Chiome d'oro; Gira il nemico insidioso; Hor ch'el ciel e la terra; Non havea Febo ancora – Lamento della ninfa; Perchè t'en fuggi o Fillide; Tirsi e Clori (ballo concertato for 5 voices and instruments).*
(B) *** HM HMA 901068; *HMA 431068* [id.]. Les Arts Florissants, Christie.

The singing of this famous group is full of colour and feeling and, even if intonation is not absolutely flawless throughout, it is mostly excellent. Much to be preferred to the bloodless white tone favoured by some early-music groups. Good recording. A bargain.

Madrigals, Book 8: *Madrigali guerrieri et amorosi (Madrigals of love and war).*
⊛ (M) *** Ph. 422 503-2 (2) [id.]. Armstrong, Bostock, Fuller, Harper, Howells, Watson, Hodgson, Collins, Alva, Davies, Oliver, Tear, Wakefield, Dean, Grant, Glyndebourne Ch. (members), ECO, Leppard.

This set provided a richly enjoyable start to a magnificent project of the early 1970s, nothing less than the complete recording by Leppard and his varied forces of Monteverdi's enormous total output of madrigals. With his star-studded cast Leppard ensures that there is nothing earnest or pedestrian about the results. Some – used to more acerbic textures – may complain at the warmth and richness, not only of the opening *Sinfonia* but also of the pair of magnificent six-part choruses which open each set (both *guerrieri* and *amorosi*), but here as elsewhere Leppard is demonstrating the enormous variety of expression of the composer's three described musical styles, *concitato*, *temperato* and *molle*, and the string accompaniments on modern instruments sound very much in place. First-class, atmospheric recording and CD transfers of the very highest Philips quality.

Madrigals, Book 8: Madrigali amorosi.
*** Virgin/EMI Dig. VC7 59621-2 [id.]. Consort of Musicke, Anthony Rooley.

Monteverdi published his *Eighth Book* in 1638 after a long gap in his madrigal output. One of the very greatest of the songs is *Lamento della ninfa* (which Nadia Boulanger so memorably recorded) in what Monteverdi called the *stile rappresentativo* or theatre style, and that is affectingly done here.

Madrigals: *Addio Florida bella; Ahi com'a un vago sol; E così a poco a poco torno farfalla; Era l'anima mia; Luci serene e chiare; Mentre vaga Angioletta ogn'anima; Ninfa che scalza il piede; O mio bene, a mia vita; O Mirtillo, Mirtill'anima mia; Se pur destina; Taci, Armelin deh taci; T'amo mia vita; Troppo ben può questo tiranno amore.*
(B) *** HM HMA 901084; *HMA 431084* [id.]. Concerto Vocale.

A highly attractive collection of generally neglected items, briskly and stylishly performed. The most celebrated of the singers is the male alto, René Jacobs, a fine director as well as soloist. With continuo accompaniment, the contrasting of vocal timbres is achieved superbly. Excellent recording and very good value.

Madrigals: *A Dio, Florinda bella; Altri canti d'amour; Amor che deggio far; Hor che'l ciel e la terra; Presso un fiume tranquillo; Questi vaghi concenti; Quio rise, O Tirsi.*
☞ (M) ** Teldec/Warner 4509 93268-2 [id.]. Jacobeit, Förster-Dürlich, Van t'Hoff, Runge, Villisech, Hamburg Monteverdi Ch., Leonhardt Consort.

Highly regarded when first issued, this 1963 recording now brings some problems in its CD transfer, caused by the generous acoustics of the Christ-König-Kirche, Hamburg. The choral focus is somewhat blurred and the resonance also affects the accompanying group. However, many of these items are dialogue madrigals with the interplay of excellent soloists (*A Dio, Florida bella* is a delightful example), and in *Hor che'l ciel e la terra* the solemn choral section is undoubtedly enhanced by the reverberations. The Hamburg Monteverdi Choir is a splendid ensemble and throughout these performances are as stylish as they are sensible. But the measure is short: 43½ minutes.

Madrigals: *Altri canti di Marte; Ardo avvampo; Hor che'l ciel e la terra; Ballo: Movete al mio bel suon; O ciecchi, ciecchi; Questi vaghi concenti.* (i) *Sestina: Lagrime d'amante al sepolcro dell'amata.*
(M) *** Decca 433 174-2 [id.]. Palmer, Holt, Bowen, Evans, Elwes, Thomas, Heinrich Schütz Ch., Norrington; (i) Schütz Cons.

These fine madrigals are given crisp, well-drilled performances by Norrington, not as relaxedly expressive as Leppard's outstanding Philips set, but most refreshing. The ample acoustic of St John's, Smith Square, adds agreeable atmosphere. The eloquent and moving *Sestina* is one of Monteverdi's most unusual and original extended settings.

Madrigali erotici: Chiome d'oro; Come dolci hoggi l'auretta; Con che saovita; Mentre vaga Angioletta; Ogni amante e guerrier; Ohimè, dov'è il mio ben?; Parlo misero, o taccio; S'el vostro cor, Madonna; Tempro la cetra; Vorrei baciarti o Filli.
*** O-L Dig. 421 480-2 [id.]. Emma Kirkby, Nelson, Holden, Elliot, King, Thomas, Cons. of Musicke, Rooley.

Most of the madrigals on this CD come from the Seventh Book of 1619, very much a watershed in Monteverdi's output. In many instances they are for virtuoso singers and make a break with the past in that they call for instrumental accompaniment. The recording is excellently balanced. Strongly recommended.

Madrigals (Duets and solos): *Chiome d'oro, bel thesoro; Il son pur vezzosetta pastorella; Non è di gentil core; O come sei gentile, caro augellino; Ohimè dov'è il mio ben?; Se pur destina e vole il cielo, partenza amorosa.* Sacred music: *Cantate Domino; Exulta, filia Sion; Iste confessoe II; Laudate Dominum in sanctis eius; O bone Jesu, o piissime Jesu; Sancta Maria, succurre miseris; Venite, siccientes ad aquas Domini.* (Opera) *Il Ritorno d'Ulise in patria: Di misera regina (Penelope's lament).*
☞ (B) *** Pickwick PCD 881 [id.]. Emma Kirkby, Evelyn Tubb, Consort of Musicke, Rooley.

We are indebted to a reader for drawing our attention to this Pickwick CD, issued in 1988, which has hitherto escaped our notice. Those who have enjoyed the Hyperion disc listed above, also featuring the delightful artistry of Emma Kirkby, will surely revel in this bargain collection, mostly of duets in which she is joined by Evelyn Tubb. The two voices are admirably matched and both artists ornament their lines attractively and without overdoing it. Evelyn Tubb is given a solo opportunity in Penelope's lament from *Il ritorno d'Ulise*, which she sings dramatically and touchingly. Anthony Rooley's simple accompaniments with members of the Consort of Musicke are also imaginatively stylish. It is a pity that the documentation is inadequate; otherwise this collection is a genuine bargain.

Lamento d'Olympia; Maladetto sia l'aspetto; Ohimè ch'io cado; Quel sdengosetto; Voglio di vita uscia.
*** Hyp. CDA 66106 [id.]. Emma Kirkby, Anthony Rooley (chitarone) – D'INDIA: *Lamento d'Olympia* etc. ***

A well-planned recital from Hyperion contrasts the two settings of *Lamento d'Olympia* by Monteverdi and his younger contemporary, Sigismondo d'India. The performances by Emma Kirkby, sensitively supported by Anthony Rooley, could hardly be surpassed; her admirers can be assured that this ranks among her best records.

Motets and madrigals: *Adoramus te; Cantate Domino; Domine, ne in furore tuo; Era l'anima mia; Ohimè se tanto amate; Zefiro torna.*
☞ (M) ** Decca 440 032-2 [id.]. Monteverdi Ch., John Eliot Gardiner – GESUALDO: *Motets.* **

These performances are marked by excellent singing, with firm tone and intonation, but there is an element of interpretative exaggeration that looks forward to Eliot's later 'authentic' style and is not always wholly convincing here. Dynamics and tempi are rather extreme but there is no lack of life and vitality, and the really excellent recording – firm and clearly focused – will undoubtedly tempt many collectors.

Motets: *Ego flos campi; Ego sum pastor bonus; Exulta, filia Sion; Fuge, fuge anima mea, mundum; Iusti tulerunt spolia; Lapidabant Stephanum; Lauda, Jerusalem; Laudate Dominum; Nigra sum; O bone Jesu, illumina oculos meos; O bone Jesu, O piissime Jesu; O quam pulchra es; Pulchra es; Salve regina; Spuntava al dì; Sugens Jesus, Dominus noster; Surge propera, amica mea; Veni in hortum meum* (with PICCININI: *Toccata X*).
*** Virgin/EMI Dig. VC7 59602-2 [id.]. Brigitte Lesne, Gérard Lesne, Josep Benet, Josep Cabré, Il Seminario Musicale, Tragicomedia.

The music on this disc encompasses all periods of Monteverdi's career; the earliest comes from his first published collection, the *Sacrae Canticulicae* (1582) composed when he was only fifteen. Other pieces, such as the *Salve Regina*, come from the *Selva Morale* (1640), while *Pulchra es* and *Nigra sum* are performed on instruments alone. The solo motet *O quam pulchra es* is preceded by a *Toccata* by Alessandro Piccinini about which the excellent notes are silent. The performances here are expert and totally committed. Excellent recording.

Mass of thanksgiving (Venice 1631).
*** EMI Dig. CDS7 49876-2 (2) [Ang. CDCB 49876]. Taverner Consort, Ch. & Players, Parrott.

Parrott here presents a reconstruction of the *Mass of thanksgiving* as performed in Venice on 21 November 1631. What he and his team have sought to assemble is a likely sequence of music for the liturgy, surrounding it with introits, toccatas, sonatas and recessionals, as well as linking chant. At the heart of the celebration lies Monteverdi's magnificent seven-part *Gloria* from his great collection, *Selva morale e spirituale*. The *Kyrie*, sections of the *Credo* (including an amazing chromatic *Crucifixus*), the *Offertory*, *Sanctus*, *Agnus Dei* and a final *Salve regina* also come from that great collection. Other contemporaries of Monteverdi contributing incidental items include Giovanni Rovetta, Girolami Fantini, Giuseppe Scarani and Francesco Usper, to make a very grand whole. The recording is warmly atmospheric. The performance is superb; the only reservation to make is that with only a little less linking material it would have been possible to fit the whole on to a single CD.

Missa de cappella a 4; Missa de cappella a 6 (In illo tempore); Motets: *Cantate domino a 6; Domine ne in furore a 6.*
*** Hyp. Dig. CDA 66214 [id]. The Sixteen, Christophers; M. Phillips.

Harry Christophers draws superb singing from his brilliant choir, highly polished in ensemble but dramatic and deeply expressive too, suitably adapted for the different character of each Mass-setting, when the four-part Mass involves stricter, more consistent contrapuntal writing and the six-part, in what was then an advanced way, uses homophonic writing to underline key passages. Vivid, atmospheric recording.

Vespro della Beata Vergine (Vespers).
⊛ *** DG Dig. 429 565-2; *429 565-4* (2) [id.]. Monoyios, Pennicchi, Chance, Tucker, Robson, Naglia, Terfel, Miles, H. M. Sackbutts & Cornetts, Monteverdi Ch., London Oratory Ch., E. Bar. Soloists, Gardiner.
*** Hyp. Dig. CDA 66311/2; *KA 66311/2* [id.]. The Sixteen, Harry Christophers.
*** EMI Dig. CDS7 47078-8 [Ang. CDCB 47077] (2). Kirkby, Nigel Rogers, David Thomas, Taverner Ch., Cons. & Players, Canto Gregoriano, Parrott.
☞ (M) **(*) Teldec/Warner Dig. 4509 92629-2 (2) [id.]. Marshall, Palmer, Langridge, Equiluz, Hampson, Korn, Tölz Boys' Ch., V. Hofburg Ch. Choral Scholars, Schoenberg Ch., VCM, Harnoncourt.
☞ (M) **(*) Teldec/Warner 4509 92175-2 (2) [id.]. Hansmann, Jacobeit, Rogers, Van t'Hoff, Van Egmond, Villisech, V. Boys' Ch. soloists, Hamburg Monteverdi Ch., Plainsong Schola of Munich Capella Antiqua, VCM, Jürgen Jürgens.

Gardiner's second recording of the *Vespers* vividly captures the spatial effects that a performance in the Basilica of St Mark's, Venice, made possible. Gardiner made his earlier recording for Decca in 1974 using modern instruments, but since then the art of period performance has developed out of all recognition. Here, with the English Baroque Soloists and a team of soloists less starry but more aptly scaled than in 1974, all of them firm and clear, he directs a performance even more compellingly dramatic. It would be hard to better such young soloists as the counter-tenor Michael Chance, the tenor Mark Tucker and the bass Bryn Terfel. Unashamedly Gardiner refuses to miniaturize this most magnificent of early choral works. Without inflating the instrumental accompaniment – using six string-players only, plus elaborate continuo and six brass from His Majesties Sackbutts and Cornetts – he combines clarity and urgency with grandeur. Gardiner's version more than any other conveys the physical thrill which above all has established this long-neglected work as music for today, bringing it into the central repertory alongside the choral masterpieces of later centuries. Gardiner (as before) does not include plainchant antiphons, and so has room on the two discs for the superb alternative setting of the *Magnificat*, in six voices instead of seven, in another dedicated performance.

The Sixteen's version of Monteverdi's 1610 *Vespers* on Hyperion, beautifully scaled, presents a liturgical performance of what the scholar, Graham Dixon, suggests as Monteverdi's original conception. As it is, with a liturgical approach, the performance includes not only relevant Gregorian chant but antiphon substitutes, including a magnificent motet of Palestrina, obviously relevant,

Gaude Barbara. The scale of the performance is very satisfying, with The Sixteen augmented to 22 singers (7.4.6.5) and with members of the group taking the eight solo roles.

Though Andrew Parrott uses minimal forces, with generally one instrument and one voice per part, so putting the work on a chamber scale in a small church setting, its grandeur comes out superbly through its very intensity. Brilliant singing here by the virtuoso soloists, above all by Nigel Rogers, whose distinctive timbre may not suit every ear but who has an airy precision and flexibility to give expressive meaning to even the most taxing passages. Fine contributions too from Parrott's chosen groups of players and singers, and warm, atmospheric recording.

Harnoncourt's admirers may well be attracted to his 1986 recording, particularly now that it is reissued at mid-price. It was recorded live and gives a keen sense of occasion, with the grandeur of the piece linked to a consciously authentic approach. There is a ruggedness in the interpretation, entirely apt, which is lightened by the characterful refinement of the solo singing from an exceptionally strong team of soloists, not to mention the fine singing from all three choirs. Ample, atmospheric recording.

Recorded in Vienna in 1966/67 the Jürgens set is scholarly yet not without warmth. The liturgical sequence is respectful, and authentic instruments are used. The continuo tends to be somewhat lightweight, but there is a sure sense of style. The opening chorus is vivid with the colour of renaissance trumpets and recorders, but the CD transfer cannot disguise a lack of sharpness of focus here and in the more complex analogue choral textures. Some might feel that Jürgens's approach, though not lacking momentum or motivation, could be less smooth, more dramatic; yet in the music's quieter, more expressive pages (and especially for the soloists) the well-judged aural perspective of the Teldec analogue recording gives atmosphere and a proper feeling of space and beauty. At mid-price this is fair value, for the soloists are all fine artists and the choral singing is committed and polished. Documentation is excellent.

Vespri di S. Giovanni Battista.
*** Ph. Dig. 422 074-2 [id.]. Netherlands Chamber Ch., Ch. Viennensis, Amsterdam Monteverdi Ens., Gustav Leonhardt.

This is a conjectural reconstruction of an actual performance directed by the composer. Apart from Monteverdi's settings of *Dixit Dominus, Confitebor tibi, Laudate pueri* and *Magnificat*, there are toccatas by Giovanni Gabrieli, a motet by Alessandro Grandi (*c.* 1575–1630), and two sonatas by Dario Castello (whose dates are uncertain). The recording, made in Utrecht in an ideal acoustic, is a model of its kind.

OPERA AND OPERA-BALLET

(i) *Il ballo delle ingrate;* (ii) *Lamento d'Arianna.*
☞ (M) **(*) Van. 08.2030.71 [id.]. (i) Alfred Deller, McLoughlin, Ward, Cantelo, Amb. S., L. Chamber Players, Denis Stevens; (ii) Shepppard, Le Sage, Worthley, Todd, Deller, Bevan, Deller Consort, Deller.

Denis Stevens's pioneering stereo version of Monteverdi's *Il ballo delle ingrate* dates from 1956 and has an impressive cast, well backed up by the Ambrosian Singers and London Chamber Players. Although the orchestral sound seems rather ample to ears used to original instruments, this account rings true and there is much that is authentic, not least the decoration of the vocal line, especially by Deller himself who is most moving as Venus. Eileen McLoughlin makes a delightful Amor, and David Ward is suitably stentorian as Pluto. Readers will remember that Monteverdi wrote his early opera-ballet for performance at the wedding celebrations of Duke Francesco Gonzaga of Mantua. The Duke was to marry the young Infanta Margherita of Savoy, and the message of the opera is that she should be passionately generous in the arms of her husband-to-be. In *Il ballo* the ungrateful ladies have been confined to Hades for refusing their lovers' advances and at the end of the opera they sing a touching chorus of penitence for their unfortunate lack of ardour, followed by a plea from their leader (the sweet-voiced April Cantelo) that the noble ladies of the court should learn from their experience! It is all emotively communicated here and the recording is vivid, if rather close. In addition Deller directs a performance of the famous *Lamento d'Arianna*, sung by a vocal sextet comprising Honor Sheppard, Sally le Sage, Max Worthley, Philip Todd, Maurice Bevan and Deller himself. Here the individual voices, while having plenty of character, do not always match ideally in consort. Nevertheless a thoroughly worthwhile reissue.

Il ballo delle ingrate; Sestina: Lagrime d'amante al sepolcro dell'amata.
**(*) HM Dig. HMC 901108; *HMC 401108* [id.]. Les Arts Florissants, Christie.

William Christie directs refreshingly dramatic accounts of both *Il ballo delle ingrate* and the *Sestina.*

His singers have been chosen for character and bite rather than for beauty of tone, and the final lament of *Il ballo* is spoilt by exaggerated plaintiveness, but (particularly in the *Sestina*) the boldness of Christie's interpretation makes for very compelling performances, beautifully recorded. The note on the CD version irritatingly omits details of the soloists.

(i) *Il combattimento di Tancredi e Clorinda. Lamento della Ninfa; Mentre vaga Angioletta; Ogni amante e guerrier.*

☞ (M) *** Teldec/Warner Dig. 4509 92181-2 [id.]. (i) Equiluz, Schmidt, Hollweg, Murray, Langridge, Hartman, Perry, Palmer, Mühle, Franzden; VCM, Harnoncourt.

Harnoncourt directs sharply characterized readings of substantial items from Monteverdi's eighth Book of Madrigals plus two *Canti amorosi.* The substantial scena telling of the conflict of Tancredi and Clorinda is made sharply dramatic in a bald way. *Ogni amante e guerrier*, almost as extended, is treated with similar abrasiveness, made attractively fresh but lacking subtlety. The two *Canti amorosi* are treated quite differently, in a much warmer style, with the four sopranos of *Mentre vaga Angioletta* producing sensuous sounds. *Lamento della Ninfa*, perhaps the most celebrated of all Monteverdi's madrigals, brings a luscious performance with the solo voice (Ann Murray) set evocatively at a slight distance behind the two tenors and a bass. On CD the recording is extremely vivid, with voices and instruments firmly and realistically placed. The documentation is first class in every way, with full translations and the composer's own fascinatingly detailed instructions as to how *Il Combattimento* should be staged.

L'Incoronazione di Poppea.

*** Virgin/EMI Dig. VCT7 59606-2 (3) [id.]. Arleen Augér, Della Jones, Linda Hirst, James Bowman, City of L. Bar. Sinfonia, Hickox.

☞ (M) **(*) Teldec/Warner 2292 42547-2 (4) [id.]. Donath, Söderström, Berberian, Esswood, VCM, Harnoncourt.

The tender expressiveness of Arleen Augér in the title-role of Monteverdi's elusive masterpiece goes with a very spare accompaniment of continuo instruments, contrasting not just with the opulent score presented at Glyndebourne by Raymond Leppard, but with the previous period performance on record, that of Nikolaus Harnoncourt and the Concentus Musicus of Vienna, who has a far wider, more abrasive range of instrumental sound. Hickox overcomes the problems of that self-imposed limitation by choosing the widest possible range of speeds. The purity of Augér's soprano may make Poppea less of a scheming seducer than she should be, but it is Monteverdi's music for the heroine which makes her so sympathetic. Taking the castrato role of Nero, Della Jones sings very convincingly with full, rather boyish tone, while Gregory Reinhart is magnificent in the bass role of Seneca. James Bowman is a fine Ottone, with smaller parts taken by such excellent young singers as Catherine Denley, John Graham-Hall, Mark Tucker and Janice Watson. This set has been withdrawn as we go to press, but we feel sure it will be restored during the lifetime of this book.

Nikolaus Harnoncourt's well-paced and dramatic version makes a welcome reappearance at mid-price in Teldec's Harnoncourt series. First issued in 1974, it offers a starry cast, with Elisabeth Söderström as Nero (imaginative but not always ideally steady), Helen Donath pure-toned as Poppea and Cathy Berberian as the most characterful and moving Ottavia on disc. Others include Paul Esswood and Philip Langridge, and Harnoncourt's bold and brassy instrumentation adds to the bite. The snag is that, unnecessarily, the set stretches to four discs instead of three, which cancels out the price advantage over the excellent rival set from Richard Hickox.

Orfeo (opera): complete.

☞ *** O-L Dig. 433 545-2 (2) [id.]. Ainsley, Gooding, Bott, Bonner, George, Grant, New L. Cons., Pickett.

*** DG Dig. 419 250-2 (2) [id.]. Rolfe Johnson, Baird, Lynne Dawson, Von Otter, Argenta, Robson, Monteverdi Ch., E. Bar. Soloists, Gardiner.

☞ (M) *** EMI Dig. CMS7 64947-2 (2). Rogers, Kwella, Kirkby, J. Smith, Chiaroscuro, L. Bar. Ens., L. Cornett & Sackbut Ens., Charles Medlam.

☞ (M) ** Teldec/Warner 2292 42494-2 (2). Kozma, Hansmann, Berberian, Katanosaka, Villisech, Van Egmond, Munich Cappela Antiqua, VCM, Harnoncourt.

Philip Pickett and the New London Consort triumphantly establish how vibrantly alive this music of 1607 can be. Thoughtful and scholarly as he is, Pickett has not tried to treat *Orfeo* with kid gloves but has aimed above all to bring out its freshness. Compared with John Eliot Gardiner, whose DG Archiv recording combines precision and alertness in presenting the drama, Pickett is rougher, not caring quite so much about pinpoint ensemble, preferring less extreme speeds and characteristically relying more on dramatic contrasts in instrumentation. So, in the dark *Sinfonia* with its weird chromatic writing which at the opening of Act III represents Orfeo's arrival in the underworld, Pickett cuts out strings and uses brass instruments alone. He has the cornetts, sackbutts and a rasping regal organ playing at a lower pitch than usual, deducing that transposition from Monteverdi's use of high clefs. The result is all the more darkly menacing. While planning his recording, Pickett visited the Gonzaga Palace in Mantua, scene of the first performances of *Orfeo*, trying to establish in which room precisely the event took place. That has dictated both the scale and the acoustic chosen for the recording, drier than Gardiner's DG, with the performers placed more immediately. As Orfeo, John Mark Ainsley may have a less velvety tenor than Anthony Rolfe Johnson on the Gardiner set, but his voice is more crisply flexible in the elaborate decorations of *Possente spirto*, Orfeo's plea to Charon. Outstanding among the others, establishing the characterful style of the solo singing from the start, is Catherine Bott, who was also the vocal star of Pickett's exciting set, *The Pilgrimage to Santiago*. In *Orfeo* she not only sings the elaborate role given to La Musica in the Prologue, sensuously beautiful and seductive in her coloration, but also the part of Proserpina and the key role of the Messenger, who graphically describes the death of Euridice. Excellent among the others are Julia Gooding as Euridice, the counter-tenor Christopher Robson as Hope and Tessa Bonner as the Nymph.

John Eliot Gardiner very effectively balances the often-conflicting demands of authentic perform- ance – when this pioneering opera was originally presented intimately – and the obvious grandeur of the concept. So the 21-strong Monteverdi Choir conveys, on the one hand, high tragedy to the full, yet sings the lighter commentary from nymphs and shepherds with astonishing crispness, often at top speed. However, Gardiner is strong on pacing. He gives full and moving expansion to such key passages as the messenger's report of Euridice's death, sung with agonizing intensity by Anne Sophie von Otter. Lynne Dawson is also outstanding as the allegorical figure of Music in the *Prologue*, while Anthony Rolfe Johnson shows his formidable versatility in the title-role. This is a set to take you through the story with new involvement. Though editing is not always immaculate, the recording on CD is vivid and full of presence.

Nigel Rogers – who recorded the role of Orfeo ten years earlier for DG Archiv – in the EMI version has the double function of singing the main part and acting as co-director. In the earlier recording under Kurt Jürgens, ample reverberation tended to inflate the performance but, this time in a drier acoustic, Rogers has modified his extraordinarily elaborate ornamentation in the hero's brilliant pleading aria before Charon and makes the result all the freer and more wide-ranging in expression, with his distinctive fluttering timbre adding character. With the central singer directing the others, the concentration of the whole performance is all the greater, telling the story simply and graphically. The sound of thunder that fatefully makes Orpheus turn around as he leads Euridice back to earth is all the more dramatic for being drily percussive; and Euridice's plaint, beautifully sung by Patrizia Kwella, is the more affecting for being accompanied very simply on the lute. The other soloists make a good team, though Jennifer Smith as Proserpina, recorded close, is made to sound breathy. The brightness of the cornetti is a special delight, when otherwise the instrumentation used – largely left optional in the score – is modest. Excellent, immediate recording, making for a fine mid-priced alternative to Gardiner.

In Harnoncourt's version, the ritornello of the Prologue might almost be by Stravinsky, so sharply do the sounds cut. He is an altogether more severe Monteverdian than John Eliot Gardiner. In compensation, the simple and straightforward dedication of this performance is most affecting, and the solo singing, if not generally very characterful, is clean and stylish. One exception to the general rule on characterfulness comes in the singing of Cathy Berberian as the Messenger. She is strikingly successful and, though slightly differing in style from the others, she sings as part of the team. Excellent, restrained recording, as usual in Harnoncourt's remastered Telefunken CD series, projecting the performance even more vividly than on LP. The extra clarity and sharpness of focus – even in large-scale ensembles – add to the abrasiveness from the opening *Toccata* onwards, and the 1968 recording certainly sounds immediate, with voices very realistic.

Il ritorno d'Ulisse in patria (complete).
☞ *** HM Dig. HMU 90 1427/9 [id.]. Prégardien, Fink, Högeman, Hunt, Visse, Tucker, D. Thomas, Concerto Vocale, René Jacobs.
☞ (M) **(*) Teldec/Warner 2292 42496-2 (3) [id.]. Eliasson, Lerer, Hansen, Baker-Genovesi, Hansmann, Equiluz, Esswood, Wyatt, Walters, Van Egmond, Mühle, Junge Kantorei, VCM, Harnoncourt.

The second of Monteverdi's three surviving operas, *Il ritorno d'Ulisse in patria*, neglected for so long in the CD catalogue, is here treated to a most enjoyable version by René Jacobs with the same cast as in the Montpellier Festival. Following up Jacobs's earlier set of Monteverdi's *L'Incoronazione di*

Poppea, also from Montpellier, it offers a scholarly performance that is not afraid of being warmly expressive. This is not just a far longer opera than *Orfeo*, it contains much more of what one might describe as madrigal material – relatively brief solos and ensembles that form landmarks amid Monteverdi's free-running recitative.

Jacobs as a singer himself is most understanding of the need to give his soloists free rein, and they make a first-rate team, with the clear-toned German tenor Christoph Prégardien splendid as Ulisse, firm and heroic but light enough to cope with the elaborate ornamentation. Bernarda Fink with her rich, firm mezzo gives full weight to Penelope's agony, and it is encouraging to find such excellent British singers as the tenors Martyn Hill and Mark Tucker and the baritone David Thomas taking character roles. The French counter-tenor Dominique Visse is also excellent, both as Human Frailty in the Prologue and as one of Penelope's suitors, with Guy de Mey in the comic role of the glutton, Iro. The five Acts fit neatly on the three CDs of around an hour each, with no internal breaks within Acts. Jacobs explains that with the surviving manuscripts raising dozens of textual questions, he decided to return to the original five-Act division of the text which, as he suggests, is better-balanced. He also inserts music by Rossi and Caccini for the choruses included in the text but missing from the score, all adding to the impact of the whole piece.

Harnoncourt's 1971 recording of *Il ritorno d'Ulisse* brings a sympathetic performance, generally not quite as brisk as Jacobs in his recording from the Montpellier Festival, and rather more square in rhythm, but bringing a keener sense of repose, important in Monteverdi. The solo singing is not as characterful as that on the Jacobs set, nor as Harnoncourt's *Poppea*, though Norma Lerer makes a touching Penelope, with Sven Olaf Eliasson a stylish Ulisse, not ideally pure of timbre.

Moody, James (born 1907)

(i) *Quintet for harmonica and string quartet;* (ii) *Suite dans le style français.*
*** Chan. Dig. CHAN 8802; *ABTD 1202* [id.]. Tommy Reilly; (i) Hindar Qt; (ii) Skaila Kanga –
JACOB: *Divertimento.* ***

James Moody's *Suite in the French style* may be pastiche but its impressionism is highly beguiling. The *Quintet* is more ambitious, less charming perhaps, but likely to prove even more rewarding on investigation, especially the very diverse theme and variations of the finale, the longest movement. The performance and recording are hardly likely to be bettered.

Morley, Thomas (1557/8–1602)

Ayres and Madrigals: *Absence, hear thou my protestation; Arise, awake; Besides a fountain; Deep lamenting; Fire and lightning; Hard by a crystal fountain; Hark! Alleluia; In every place; Mistress mine; No, no, no, Nigella; O grief ev'n on the bud; Phyllis I fain would die now; Singing alone; Sleep slumb'ring eyes; Stay heart, run not so fast; With my love.*
☞ *** O-L Dig. 436 862-2 [id.]. Consort of Musicke, Anthony Rooley.

Morley is generally thought of as a lesser figure than his contemporaries, even though he was the pioneering English madrigalist. This CD should do something to modify the picture of him for, although the lighter *canzonetti* and *balletti* based on Italian models (and in particular Gastoldi) are in evidence, there are more searching and thoughtful pieces. *Deep lamenting, grief betraying* is one such piece, and there are others which make one feel that the range of Morley's musical personality has not been adequately reflected heretofore. This is an interesting and attractive recital and has the benefit of well-projected performances and good recorded sound.

Moszkowski, Moritz (1854–1925)

Air de ballet, Op. 36/5; Albumblatt, Op. 2; Au Crépuscule, Op. 68/3; Barcarolle from *Offenbach's Tales of Hoffmann; Chanson bohème* from *Bizet's Carmen; Danse Russe; En Automne, Op. 36/4; Expansion, Op. 36/3; La Jongleuse, Op. 52/4; Minuetto, Op. 68/2; Nocturne, Op. 68/1; Poème de Mai; Près de berceau; Rêverie, Op. 36/2; Serenata, Op. 15/1; Tarantella, Op. 27/2; Valse Mignonne.*
☞ **(*) Collins Dig. 1412-2. Seta Tanyel.

The composer/pianist Moszkowski once came to London to conduct his *Spanish dances* at a Henry Wood Promenade Concert. Famous in their day, they are all but forgotten now, and his piano music seems faded too. Pieces like *Au Crépuscule* have a certain sub-Lisztian charm, and *La Jongleuse* is an engaging *moto perpetuo*, while *Près de berceau* is the epitome of a salon piece. Seta Tanyel characterizes the music well enough, but she is hard put to sustain interest through a 69-minute recital of genre pieces that are heard most effectively as encores at the end of a more substantial programme. The *Air de ballet* is an ideal example with its brilliant filigree at the close which sparkles readily in her hands. Good recording.

Mourant, Walter (born 1910)

The Pied Piper.
*** ASV Dig. CDDCA 568 [id.]. MacDonald, N. Sinfonia, Bedford – COPLAND; FINZI: *Concertos.*
***

Walter Mourant's *Pied Piper* is a catchy, unpretentious little piece for clarinet, strings and celeste, which in a gently syncopated style effectively contrasts 3/4 and 6/8 rhythms. It makes an attractive filler after the Copland *Concerto.*

Mozart, Leopold (1719–87)

Cassation in G: Toy symphony (attrib. Haydn). (i) *Trumpet concerto in D.*
*** Erato/Warner Dig. 2292 45199-2. (i) Touvron; Paillard CO, Paillard – W. A. MOZART: *Musical Joke.* ***

One could hardly imagine this *Cassation* being done with more commitment from the effects department directed by Paillard, while the music itself is elegantly played. After this, the more restrained approach to the excellent two-movement *Trumpet concerto* seems exactly right. The recording has plenty of presence and realism.

Trumpet concerto in D.
☞ (M) *(*) Teldec/Warner 9031 77603-2 [id.]. Immer, VCM, Harnoncourt – W. A. MOZART: *Bassoon concerto* etc. *(*)

Leopold Mozart's *Trumpet concerto* is a pretty florid piece, and Friedemann Immer does not make a very good case for playing it on an 'authentic'-keyed trumpet, which at times produces an unattractively strangulated tone. He is brightly accompanied. Strictly for authenticists only.

Mozart, Wolfgang Amadeus (1756–91)

Adagio in E, K.261; Rondo in C, K.373 (both for violin & orchestra).
(B) *** Ph. 426 977-2. Grumiaux, New Philh. O, Leppard – HAYDN: *Violin concertos;* SCHUBERT: *Rondo.* ***

These two Mozart movements are far from slight: the *Adagio* is really lovely on Arthur Grumiaux's bow and the *Rondo* sparkles. Excellent, stylish accompaniments and very good sound. This makes a strong contribution to a splendid bargain anthology.

Adagio and fugue in C minor: see also below, in VOCAL MUSIC, under Complete Mozart Edition, Volume 22.

Complete Mozart Edition, Volume 3: *Cassations Nos. 1 in G, K.63; 2 in B flat, K.99; Divertimento No. 2 in D, K.131; Galimathias musicum, K.32; Serenades Nos. 1 in D, K.100* (with *March in D, K.62); 3 in D, K.185* (with *March in D, K.189); 4 in D (Colloredo), K.203* (with *March in D, K.237); 5 in D, K.204* (with *March in D, K.215); 6 in D (Serenata notturna), K.239; 7 in D (Haffner), K.250* (with *March in D, K.249); 8 in D (Notturno for 4 orchestras), K.286; 9 in D (Posthorn), K.320* (with *Marches in D, K.335/1–2); 13 in G (Eine kleine Nachtmusik), K.525.*
(M) *** Ph. Dig. 422 503-2 (7) [id.]. ASMF, Sir Neville Marriner.

Marriner and his Academy are at their very finest here and make a very persuasive case for giving these works on modern instruments. The playing has much finesse, yet its cultivated polish never brings a hint of blandness or lethargy; it is smiling, yet full of energy and sparkle. In the concertante violin roles Iona Brown is surely an ideal soloist, her playing full of grace. Throughout this set the digital recording brings an almost ideal combination of bloom and vividness.

Cassations Nos. 1 in G, K.63; 2 in B flat, K.99; Adagio and fugue in C min., K.546.
*** Capriccio Dig. 10 192 [id.]. Salzburg Camerata, Végh.

These excellent performances of the early *Cassations*, so full of attractive invention, can be strongly recommended. The playing combines vitality with finesse and, to make a proper contrast, the Camerata find plenty of drama in the *Adagio and fugue*. Very good recording.

CONCERTOS

Complete Mozart Edition, Volume 9: (i) *Bassoon concerto;* (ii) *Clarinet concerto;* (iii) *Flute concertos Nos. 1–2; Andante in C for flute & orchestra;* (iii; iv) *Flute and harp concerto;* (v) *Horn concertos Nos. 1–4; Concert rondo in E flat for horn and orchestra;* (vi) *Oboe concerto. Sinfonia concertante in E flat, K.297b; Sinfonia concertante in E flat, K.297b* (reconstructed R. Levin).
(M) **(*) Ph. Dig. 422 509-2 (5) [id.]. (i) Thunemann; (ii) Leister; (iii) Grafenauer; (iv) Graf; (v) Damm; (vi) Holliger; ASMF, Marriner (except (vi) Holliger).

The principal wind concertos here are recent digital versions. They are all well played and recorded. However, there is a slightly impersonal air about the accounts of the *Bassoon* and *Clarinet concertos*, well played though they are; and there are more individual sets of the works for horn. The *Sinfonia concertante* is offered both in the version we usually hear (recorded in 1972, with the performance attractively songful and elegant) and in a more modern recording of a conjectural reconstruction by Robert Levin, based on the material in the four wind parts.

Bassoon concerto in B flat.
*** Denon Dig. CO 79281 [id.]. Werba, V. String Soloists, Honeck – HUMMEL; WEBER: *Concertos.* ***

☞ *** Caprice Dig. CAP 21411. Knut Sönstevold, Swedish RSO, Comissiona – PETTERSSON: *Symphony No. 7.* ***

Though not quite as individual as some versions, Michael Werba's account does not lack character or geniality and he is well accompanied and recorded. He features the cadenzas by Eusebius Mandycze-wski to good effect. If the couplings are suitable, this is recommendable.

Knut Sönstevold's performance of Mozart's concerto with the Swedish Radio Orchestra under Sergiu Comissiona comes as a fill-up to the Pettersson *Seventh Symphony* and sits uncomfortably in this coupling. It is good enough to compete in an already crowded market, but Mozartians are likely to turn elsewhere in search of a more logical coupling. A good, big-band performance, which does give pleasure, and very well recorded.

(i) *Bassoon concerto in B flat, K.191;* (ii) *Clarinet concerto in A, K.622;* (iii) *Flute concerto No.1 in G, K.313; Andante in C, K.315;* (iii; iv) *Flute and harp concerto in C, K.299;* (v) *Horn concertos Nos. 1–4;* (vi) *Oboe concerto in C, K.314; Sinfonia concertante in E flat, K.197b.*
(M) *** DG Dig. 431 665-2 (3). (i) Morelli; (ii) Neidlich; (iii) Palma; (iv) Allen; (v) Jolley or Purvis; (vi) Wolfgang; Orpheus CO.

Randall Wolfgang's plaintive, slightly reedy timbre is especially telling in the *Adagio* of the *Oboe concerto* and he plays the finale with the lightest possible touch, as does Susan Palma the charming Minuet which closes the *Flute concerto*. The *Sinfonia concertante* for wind is pleasingly fresh. All the works are given excellent modern recordings and this is a very persuasive collection, probably a 'best buy' for those wanting all the music in a digital format.

(i) *Bassoon concerto in B flat, K.191;* (ii) *Clarinet concerto in A, K.622;* (iii) *Flute concerto No. 1 in G, K.313; Andante in C, K.315;* (iv) *Flute and harp concerto in C, K.299;* (v) *Oboe concerto in C, K.314.*
☞ (B) *** Erato/Warner Duo 4509 95361-2 (2) [id.]. (i) Paul Hogne, Bamberg SO, Guschlbauer; (ii) Jacques Lancelot, Paillard CO, Paillard; (iii) Jean-Pierre Rampal, VSO, Guschlbauer; (iv) Rampal, Lily Laskine, Paillard CO, Paillard; (v) Pierre Pierlot, ECO, Rampal.

This Erato Bonsai Duo set attractively combines the two recommendable bargain CDs listed and discussed individually below.

(i) *Bassoon concerto;* (ii) *Clarinet concerto;* (iii) *Oboe concerto, K.314.*
☞ (B) *** Erato/Warner 2292 45937-2 [id.].(i) Paul Hogne, Bamberg SO, Guschlbauer; (ii) Jacques Lancelot, Paillard CO, Paillard; (iii) Pierre Pierlot, ECO, Rampal.
(BB) **(*) Naxos Dig. 8.550345 [id.]. (i) Turnovský; (ii) Ottensamer; (iii) Gabriel, V. Mozart Academy, Wildner.
☞ (M) ** EMI CDM7 64385-2 [id.]. (i) Günter Piesk; (ii) Karl Leister; (iii) Lothar Koch; BPO, Karajan.

Three first-class French soloists here provide a bargain triptych of highly enjoyable Mozartian performances, distinctly Gallic in style in their elegance and sense of wit, with Pierlot's small, sweet oboe timbre matched by Paul Hogne's woody French bassoon. Lancelot's slow movement for the *Clarinet concerto* is gloriously expressive and, with lively accompaniments, all three performances sound remarkably fresh, each with a character of its own. The recordings (from 1963, 1969 and 1979) are well matched – the sound is always very good and musically balanced.

In the *Oboe concerto* the soloist on Naxos, Martin Gabriel, is excellent. The clarinettist, Ernst Ottensamer, is also a sensitive player, his slow movement is full of feeling; and there is an accomplished performance of the *Bassoon concerto* from Stepan Turnovský, who has the measure of the work's character and wit. Recommendable, particularly at the price.

The three performances on this EMI reissue come from a series of recordings of Mozart's concertante wind works that Karajan made in 1971. Günter Piesk gives a predictably fine account of the *Bassoon concerto*, but the *Clarinet concerto* is a little bland and, while Koch is also an estimable soloist in the work for oboe, the richly homogeneous orchestral accompaniments without much analytical detail, although pleasingly warm and elegantly phrased, tend to rob the music of vitality. No complaints about the CD transfers.

(i) *Bassoon concerto in B flat, K.191;* (ii) *Clarinet concerto in A, K.622;* (iii) *Violin concerto No. 3 in G, K.216.*

(M) **(*) EMI stereo/mono CDM7 63408-2 [id.]; *EG 763408-4.* (i) Brooke; (ii) Brymer; (iii) De Vito; RPO, Beecham.

Beecham's romantically expansive reading of the Mozart *Clarinet concerto* with Jack Brymer the glowing soloist is a 1958 classic recording, totally individual in every phrase, with conductor and soloist inspiring each other. The account of the *Bassoon concerto* has equal magic, thanks to the comparable partnership between Beecham and Gwydion Brooke. But the surprise here is the equally inspired and highly personal 1949 mono account of the *G major Violin concerto*, with Gioconda de Vito as soloist. She too conveys magic comparable to Beecham's own, with the slow movement again luxuriantly expansive.

(i) *Bassoon concerto in B flat, K.191; Notturno for 4 orchestras, K.286; Serenade No. 6 (Serenata notturna), K.239.*

☞ (M) *(*) Teldec/Warner 9031 77603-2 [id.]. (i) Milan Turkovič; VCM, Harnoncourt – L. MOZART: *Trumpet concerto.* *(*)

By far the most attractive music-making here is from Milan Turkovič, who plays Mozart's *Bassoon concerto* convincingly and with considerable character on a Viennese Tauber seven-key bassoon, which may be primitive but which can be made to sound colourfully attractive. However, in the *Serenata notturna*, which opens the concert, Harnoncourt creates explosive fortissimos with his drums, together with plentiful accents. The *Notturno* is made to sound ungratefully harsh and utterly fails to create the atmosphere of an evening serenade, and the antiphonal horn effects seem crude. Vivid recording.

Clarinet concerto in A, K.622.

☞ (M) *** Decca 433 727-2 [id.]. Gervase de Peyer, LSO, Maag – SPOHR; WEBER: *Concertos.* ***

☞ *** Denon Dig. CO 75289 [id.]. Paul Meyer, ECO, Zinman – BUSONI: *Adagio* ***; COPLAND: *Concerto.* **(*)

Gervase de Peyer made his recording in the Kingsway Hall in 1959, and the famous Kingsway ambience disguises its age, although the violins are not quite as full as we would expect today. The performance is as fine as any available. De Peyer's timbre is succulent, his control of colour subtle, and the playing is fluent and lively, with masterly phrasing in the slow movement and a vivacious finale. The couplings, too, are thoroughly worth while.

An enjoyably bracing performance from Paul Meyer and David Zinman, cool and elegant and given refined, truthful recording of Denon's best quality. This is not to say that the playing lacks warmth, but the heart is not worn on the sleeve and the lovely slow movement is refreshing and touching, without having sensuous overtones. The finale is delightfully spirited. Excellent recording, too.

Clarinet concerto; Flute concerto No. 1, K.313; Andante for flute & orchestra, K.315; Flute & harp concerto; Oboe concerto; Horn concertos Nos. 1–4; Rondo for horn & orchestra, K.371.

(B) *** Ph. 426 148-2 (3). Brymer, Claude Monteux, Ellis, Black, Civil, ASMF, Marriner.

Jack Brymer's recording of the *Clarinet concerto* is the third he has made; in some ways it is his best, for he plays with deepened insight and feeling. The *Flute* and *Oboe concertos* are hardly less recommendable and the *Flute and harp concerto* is delightful, even if the instruments are made to seem jumbo-sized! Alan Civil's third recording of the *Horn concertos* was made in 1973, and the performances are highly enjoyable, with Sir Neville Marriner's polished and lively accompaniments giving pleasure in themselves.

(i) *Clarinet concerto;* (ii) *Flute and harp concerto in C, K.299.*
*** ASV Dig. CDDCA 532 [id.]. (i) Emma Johnson; (ii) Bennett, Ellis; ECO, Leppard.
(B) *** Pickwick Dig. PCD 852; *CIMPC 852* [id.]. (i) Campbell; (ii) Davies, Masters; City of L.
   Sinfonia, Hickox.

Emma Johnson's account of the *Clarinet concerto* has a sense of spontaneity, of natural magnetism which traps the ear from first to last. There may be some rawness of tone in places, but that only adds to the range of expression, which breathes the air of a live performance. Leppard and the ECO are in bouncing form, as they are too for the *Flute and harp concerto*, though here the two excellent soloists are somewhat on their best behaviour, until the last part of the finale sends Mozart bubbling up to heaven. First-rate recording.

David Campbell's agile and pointed performance of the clarinet work brings fastish speeds and a fresh, unmannered style in all three movements. His tonal shading is very beautiful. The earlier flute and harp work is just as freshly and sympathetically done, with a direct, unmannered style sounding entirely spontaneous.

(i) *Clarinet concerto in A;* (ii) *Oboe concerto in C, K.314;* (i; ii; iii) *Sinfonia concertante, K.297b.*
*** ASV Dig. CDCDO 814 [id.]. (i) Richard Hosford; (ii) Douglas Boyd; (iii) O'Neill, Williams;
   COE, Schneider.

It would be hard to imagine a performance of the *Oboe concerto* that conveys more fun in the outer movements, infectiously pointed and phrased, both by the ever-imaginative Douglas Boyd and by his colleagues. The wind soloists in this live recording of the *Sinfonia concertante* are four COE artists who each know when to take centre stage and when to hold back in turn. The variations of the finale are pure delight. Richard Hosford in his reading of the *Clarinet concerto* uses a basset clarinet with its extended lower range, allowing Mozart's original intentions to be realized. At slowish speeds he leans towards the lyrical rather than the dramatic, even in the first movement, and ends with a delightfully bouncy account of the finale. Full, atmospheric recording.

(i) *Clarinet concerto;* (ii) *Clarinet quintet in A, K.581.*
*** Hyp. Dig. CDA 66199; *KA 66199* [id.]. Thea King, (i) ECO, Tate; (ii) Gabrieli Qt.

Thea King's coupling brings together winning performances of Mozart's two great clarinet master-pieces. She steers an ideal course between classical stylishness and expressive warmth, with the slow movement becoming the emotional heart of the piece. The Gabrieli Quartet is equally responsive in its finely tuned playing. For the *Clarinet concerto* Thea King uses an authentically reconstructed basset clarinet such as Mozart wanted. With Jeffrey Tate an inspired Mozartian, the performance – like that of the *Quintet* – is both stylish and expressive, with the finale given a captivating bucolic lilt. Excellent recording.

(i) *Flute concertos Nos. 1–2; Andante in C, K.315;* (ii) *Flute and harp concerto, K.299;* (iii) *Sinfonia concertante for flute, oboe, horn & bassoon, K.297b* (reconstructed R. Levin); (iv) *4 Flute quartets, K.285, K.285a, K.285b; K.298.*
☞ (B) **(*) Ph. Duo 442 299-2 [id.]. (i) Aurèle Nicolet, Cong. O, Zinman; (ii) Hubert Barwahser,
   Osian Ellis, LSO, C. Davis; (iii) Nicolet, Holliger, Baumann, Thunemann, ASMF, Marriner; (iv)
   William Bennett, Grumiaux Trio.

The Philips Duo set is perhaps less attractive than it first looks as it is filled out with a reconstruction of the wind *Sinfonia concertante* in which the oboe and clarinet parts are replaced by flute and oboe respectively, an interesting conjectural experiment rather than an essential part of a Mozart collection. Aurèle Nicolet's performances of the *Flute concertos* and *Andante for flute and orchestra* are very positive, with the flute balanced well forward and dominating the proceedings, though David Zinman's accompaniments are alert and strong. Both finales are particularly attractive, briskly paced, and the solo playing throughout is expert and elegantly phrased. Barwahser, (the first flute of the Concertgebouw at the time) and Ellis give a sparkling account of the *Flute and harp concerto* and Sir Colin Davis accompanies them with the greatest sprightliness and sympathy. If these are not a top choice in this repertoire, the William Bennett accounts of the four *Flute quartets* with the Grumiaux Trio certainly are. They are, to put it in a nutshell, exquisitely played and very well recorded, in every way finer than most other versions which have appeared and disappeared over the years. The recordings throughout are smoothly remastered and sound fine.

Flute concertos Nos. (i) *1 in G, K.313;* (ii) *2 in D, K.314.*
(B) *** Pickwick Dig. PCD 871; *CIMPC 871.* Judith Hall, Philh. O, Peter Thomas.
(B) *** Pickwick PCD 807; *CIMPC 807.* Galway, New Irish Chamber Ens., Prieur.

Flute concertos Nos. 1 in G, K.313; 2 in D, K.314; Andante in C, K.315.
(BB) **(*) Naxos Dig. 8.550074; *4550074* [id.]. Herbert Weissberg, Capella Istropolitana, Sieghart.

Judith Hall produces a radiantly full timbre. Moreover she is a first-class Mozartian, as she demonstrates in her cadenzas as well as in the line of the slow movements, phrased with a simple eloquence that is disarming. There is plenty of vitality in the allegros, and Peter Thomas provides polished, infectious accompaniments to match the solo playing. The balance is most realistic and the sound overall is in the demonstration bracket.

   Galway's Pickwick alternative is a bargain. The accompaniments, ably directed by André Prieur, are reasonably polished and stylish, and the recording (although it gives a rather small sound to the violins) is excellent, clear and with good balance and perspective. It might be argued that Galway's vibrato is not entirely suited to these eighteenth-century works and that his cadenzas, too, are slightly anachronistic. But the star quality of his playing disarms criticism.

   The Naxos record by Herbert Weissberg and the Capella Istropolitana under Martin Sieghart can hold its head quite high alongside the competition. Weissberg does not have the outsize personality of some of his rivals but he is a cultured player, and the quality of the recording is excellent. In short, good value for money and very pleasant sound.

(i) *Flute concerto No. 1 in G, K.313; Andante in C, K.315;* (ii) *Flute and harp concerto in C, K.299.*
(M) *** BMG/RCA GD 86723; *GK 86723* [6723-2-RG]. James Galway; (i) Lucerne Festival O,
   Baumgartner; (ii) with Marisa Robles, LSO, Mata.
☞ (B) *** Erato/Warner 2292 45936-2 [id.]. Rampal, (i) VSO, Guschlbauer; (ii) Lily Laskine,
   Paillard CO, Paillard.

James Galway's silvery timbre seems as unlike an original instrument as could possibly be imagined. Galway is well supported by the Lucerne orchestra, rather reverberantly recorded, with the solo flute placed well forward. The coupled *Flute and harp concerto* has seldom sounded more lively than it does here, with an engaging element of fantasy in the music-making, a radiant slow movement and a very spirited finale. Marisa Robles makes a characterful match for Galway and they are well accompanied.

   Rampal and Lily Laskine also create a genuine symbiosis in the *Flute and harp concerto:* their interplay has great charm and delicacy, and the slow movement is a delight. The solo concerto and *Andante* find Rampal in equally good form and he is well accompanied in both instances. With well-transferred recordings from the mid-1960s, this CD is well worth its modest price.

Flute concertos Nos. 1–2, K.313/4; (i) *Flute and harp concerto in C, K.299.*
☞ (M) *** Decca 440 080-2 [id.]. (i) William Bennett, ECO, Malcolm; (ii) Werner Tripp, Hubert
   Jellinek, VPO, Münchinger.
☞ (B) *** Virgin/EMI Dig. VJ5 61108-2 [id.]. Samuel Coles, (i) with Naoko Yoshino; ECO, Sir
   Yehudi Menuhin.

William Bennett gives a beautiful account of the concertos, among the finest in the catalogue. Every phrase is shaped with both taste and affection, and the playing of the ECO under George Malcolm is fresh and vital. The (1978) Kingsway Hall recording is clean and well detailed and has just the right degree of resonance to add bloom to the sound. The earlier (1962) Vienna recording of the *Flute and harp concerto* has also stood the test of time, and again the recording is smooth, full, nicely reverberant and with good detail. The balance between the soloists is finely calculated and the performance is admirable. Refinement and beauty of tone and phrase are a hallmark throughout, and Münchinger provides most sensitive accompaniments. A first-rate (75 minutes) compilation.

   Both the solo *Flute concertos* are stylishly and pleasingly played by Samuel Coles, and when he is joined by Naoko Yoshino in the delectable *Flute and harp concerto* the interplay is fluently appealing. Menuhin directs the orchestra very precisely in the opening movement of this work; his is a firmly accented, classical view of Mozart, but the *Andantino* is warm and flexible and the finale gay and sprightly. The result is distinctly enjoyable. No complaints about the sound either, and there is no doubting the character of these performances. An excellent bargain.

(i) *Flute and harp concerto;* (ii) arr. of *Violin sonatas Nos. 17 in C, K.296; 24 in F, K.376* (for flute and piano).
☞ ** BMG/RCA Dig. 09026 61789-2 [id.]. James Galway, (i) Marisa Robles, LSO, Tilson Thomas; (ii) with Phillip Moll.

Apart from the excellence of the modern, digital recording, there seems no reason to prefer James Galway's newest recording of the *Flute and harp concerto* to his earlier version with the same partner, Marisa Robles (GD 86723). That was more appropriately coupled, whereas the transcription of some *Violin sonatas* seems a less valuable exercise when there is ample flute repertoire available. In any case, when the second subject of the first movement of the concerto appears, Galway produces a mannered slowing of tempo which could become irritating on repetition.

(i) *Flute and harp concerto in C, K.299; Sinfonia concertante in E flat, K.297b.*
(BB) *** Naxos Dig. 8.550159; *4550159* [id.]. (i) Jiri Válek, Hana Müllerová; Capella Istropolitana, Richard Edlinger.

Richard Edlinger's account of the *Flute and harp concerto* is thoroughly fresh and stylish, and the two soloists are excellent. Although the *Sinfonia concertante in E flat*, K.297b, is not quite so successful, it is still very impressive, and it gives much pleasure. Both performances are very decently recorded; in the lowest price-range they are a real bargain.

Horn concertos Nos. 1 in D, K.412; 2–4 in E flat, K.417, 447 & 495.
(M) *** Decca 417 767-2. Barry Tuckwell, LSO, Maag – HAYDN: *Concerto No. 1.* ***
(B) *** CfP Dig. CD-CFP 4589. Claire Briggs, RLPO, Stephen Kovacevich – HAYDN: *Trumpet concerto.* ***
(M) *** Teldec/Warner 2292 42757-2 [id.]. Hermann Baumann (hand-horn), VCM, Harnoncourt.

Horn concertos Nos. 1 in D, K.412 (with alternative versions of Rondo); *2–4 in E flat, K.417, K.447 & K.495; Allegro, K.370b & Concert rondo in E flat* (ed. Tuckwell); *Fragment in E, K.494a.*
*** Collins Dig. 1153-2; *1153-4* [id.]. Barry Tuckwell, Philh. O.

Horn concertos Nos. 1–4; Concert rondo in E flat, K.371 (ed. Civil or E. Smith).
☞ *** Sony Dig. SK 53369 [id.]. Ab Koster, Tafelmusik, Bruno Weil.
☞ *** Chan. Dig. CHAN 9150 [id.]. Frank Lloyd, N. Sinfonia, Richard Hickox.
☞ (BB) *** Naxos Dig. 8.550148; *4.550148* [id.]. Miloš Stevove, Capella Istropolitana, Josef Kopelman.
(M) *** EMI CD-EMX 2004. Alan Civil, RPO, Kempe.

Horn concertos Nos. 1–4; Concert rondo in E flat, K.371 (arr. Tuckwell).
☞ (M) *** EMI Dig. CDM7 64851-2 [id.]. Radovan Vlatković, ECO, Tate – R. STRAUSS: *Horn concerto No. 1.* ***

Horn concertos Nos. 1–4; Concert rondo, K.371 (ed. Tuckwell); *Fragment, K.494a.*
*** Virgin/EMI Dig. VC7 59558-2 [id.]. Timothy Brown (hand horn), O of Age of Enlightenment, Kuijken.
(M) *** EMI CDM7 69569-2. Barry Tuckwell, ASMF, Marriner.

For three decades Barry Tuckwell, following on after Dennis Brain (see below), has offered a yardstick by which other versions have been judged; his Collins CD, his fourth recording of the Mozart *Horn concertos*, remains a first choice for those wanting these works in a modern-instrument performance with first-class, digital sound. They are fresh, without a suspicion of routine, and are played with rounded tone and consistently imaginative phrasing. Moreover the Collins collection is unusually complete. Besides the *Fragment*, K.494a, Tuckwell includes both the familiar *Concert Rondo*, K.371, plus an *Allegro* first movement which Mozart wrote to go with it. Tuckwell also includes his own alternative *Rondo* finale of the *Concerto in D*, K.412, which is called No. 1 but which was the last to be written. This is based directly on Mozart's autograph, and the two alternative finales are placed side by side on this 71-minute CD.

We must also give the most cordial welcome to a splendid new authentic set from Tafelmusik, which makes a very tempting alternative. Ab Koster is a very personable soloist and he plays on an Austrian hand-horn, built by Ignaz Lorenz of Linz. His plump timbre is very different from Tuckwell's – obviously very like the sound Mozart would have recognized, with stopped notes neatly incorporated into the melodic line. Surprisingly for 'authentic' performances, tempi are relaxed, and this means that the melodic lines are allowed to breathe in the most attractive way while allegros are as spirited as one would wish. But the phrasing in slow movements is particularly warm and appealing, and the fresh, transparent textures of the accompanying Tafelmusik group (a sizeable band: 9.8.4.3.2, plus wind) are equally refreshing. Splendid recording, but this CD includes only the four *Concertos* plus the *Rondo*, K.371.

The other performance on original instruments is hardly less enjoyable. Timothy Brown also uses an open hand-horn without valves, and it might be useful here to say something about this technique. Notes in the instrument's harmonic sequence which are not naturally in tune, are 'lipped' into pitch with admirable skill and precision. Other notes which are not available in the harmonic sequence are produced by 'stopping' the bell of the horn with the hand, which simultaneously alters both pitch and timbre. Brown uses stopped notes with especially smart effect in the Rondos, and more sparingly and more subtly in the lyrical music. His control of the upper range of the instrument is remarkably free and even, yet the ear is often subtly aware that certain notes are being contrived. Far from being a drawback, this tends to increase the range of colour. Brown's lyrical line is very persuasive indeed, and he handles the chromatics in slow movements very beautifully. In short these performances sound delightfully fresh, and give constant pleasure. Timothy Brown includes the additional *Rondo* and also the *Fragment*, which (like Tuckwell) he leaves in mid-air, at the point at which the composer abandoned his manuscript.

Choice between Brown and Koster will be subjective; Koster makes no concessions to 'modern' horn sound; Brown, although he plays a narrow-bore open horn, articulates and creates a tone nearer the effect possible with a modern instrument. Kuijken's accompaniments, while light, bright and transparent, are also pleasingly smooth and cultivated. With first-rate recording this is also highly recommendable.

Like Timothy Brown, Hermann Baumann successfully uses the original hand-horn, without valves, for which the concertos were written, and the result is not achieved at the expense of musical literacy or expressive content. Baumann lets the listener hear the stopped effect only when he decides that the tonal change can be put to good artistic effect. In his cadenzas he also uses horn chords (where several notes are produced simultaneously by resonating the instrument's harmonics), but as a complement to the music rather than as a gimmick. While the horn is given added presence and tangibility in the digital remastering, the brightness of the strings has brought some roughness of focus, since the original recording was mellow and reverberant.

Among the more recent versions is a fine set by Frank Lloyd, an outstanding soloist of the new generation. He plays these works with great character and poetic warmth; his phrasing is supple and his tone full, though never suave. Like Tuckwell, he uses a modern German double horn with great skill and sensitivity. Hickox provides admirable accompaniments, and the Chandos recording is well up to the high standards of the house.

Those looking for a super-bargain version will surely not be disappointed with the Naxos disc. Miloš Stevove is principal horn with the Slovak Philharmonic Orchestra, and with his Bohemian background he is naturally at home in this genial music. He uses the slightest trace of vibrato but it is never obtrusive, and one has only to listen to the *Larghetto* of K.447 or the *Andante cantabile* of K.495 to discover his naturally warm feeling for a Mozartian phrase. Allegros are lively and the Rondos have agreeable lift. In short, with excellent, stylish accompaniments from the Capella Istropolitana this is enjoyably spontaneous. The recording is very good too; though not quite as beautiful as the Chandos, it has a compensating freshness.

Radovan Vlatković was born in Zagreb and is principal horn of the Berlin Radio Symphony Orchestra. His tone is very full, with the lower harmonics telling more resonantly than is characteristic of a British soloist; there is also at times the slightest hint of vibrato, but it is applied with great discretion and used mostly in the cadenzas. His performances are full of imaginative touches and he has the perfect partner in Jeffrey Tate, who produces sparkling accompaniments. The strings dance in the allegros and provide gracious elegance in the lyrical music. The *Romanza* of K.447 is more deliberate than usual, but the soloist's flexibility prevents any heaviness, while the Rondos have the lightest rhythmic bounce throughout; the opening movement of No. 1, too, is particularly characterful. All in all, another outstanding set, most winningly different from the playing of the British generation. Moreover Vlatković includes both the *Concert rondo*, K.371, and, very appropriately, a quite outstanding account of the *First Horn concerto* of Richard Strauss which, although more romantic, has so much in common with the spirit of the Mozart concertos.

Tuckwell's first (1960) stereo recording of the *Horn concertos* re-emerges freshly on Decca's mid-price label, now shorn of the *Fragment*, K.494a, but offering instead Haydn's best concerto to make it more competitive. Peter Maag's accompaniments are admirably crisp and nicely scaled, giving his soloist buoyant support, and the vintage recording still sounds astonishingly well. However, EMI have also effectively remastered Tuckwell's second set with Marriner, and the 1972 recording sounds fuller, with slightly more body to the violins. This CD has the advantage of including not only the *Concert rondo* but also the *Fragment in E*.

Alan Civil recorded the concertos three times, but the earliest set, with Kempe, is the freshest and most rewarding. His sensitivity is present in every bar and Kempe accompanies benignly and with great affection. The warm 1967 recording has been cleanly remastered, although the RPO violins sound somewhat thin above the stave.

For those seeking a bargain digital set, Claire Briggs, principal horn of the City of Birmingham orchestra, here gives brilliant performances of all four *Concertos*, with the celebrated finale of No. 4 taken exceptionally fast. Even that is superbly articulated without any feeling of breathlessness, though it lacks some of the fun that others have brought.

(i) *Horn concertos Nos. 1–4;* (ii) *Piano and wind quintet in E flat, K.452.*
☞ (***) EMI mono CDC5 55087-2 [id.]. Dennis Brain; (i) Philh. O, Karajan; (ii) Colin Horsley & members of Dennis Brain Wind Ens.

As we go to press, EMI have reissued Dennis Brain's famous (1954) mono record of the concertos with Karajan. EMI assure us that the remastering has been done with the latest Abbey Road technology, with great orchestral body and warmth resulting. Brain's horn timbre was unique. As for the playing, Brain's glorious tone and phrasing – every note is alive – is life-enhancing in its warmth; the *espressivo* of the slow movements is matched by the joy of the Rondos, spirited, buoyant, infectious and smiling. Karajan's accompaniments, too, are a model of Mozartian good manners and the Philharmonia at their peak play wittily and elegantly. Brain's distinguished earlier recording of the *Piano and wind quintet* has been added, with Colin Horsley making a fine contribution on the piano. However, the CD has now reverted to full price.

Horn concertos Nos. (i; iii) *2 in E flat, K.417;* (ii; iv) *3 in E flat, K.417;* (i; ii; v) *Divertimento No. 17 in D, K.334.*
☞ (M) (***) EMI mono CDH7 64198-2 [id.]. (i) Dennis Brain; (ii) Aubrey Brain; (iii) Philh. O, Susskind; (iv) BBC SO, Boult; (v) Léner Qt.

It was a happy idea of EMI to make this compilation of the recordings of the two great Brains, *père et fils*, opening with the unique 1939 recording of father and son together in the *Divertimento*, K.334, with members of the Léner Quartet. The horn parts are not particularly demanding, but Dennis was only seventeen at the time and had been playing for only two years. He recorded the *Second Concerto* in 1946 with a French horn (a Raoux-Millereau) although, interestingly, using a B flat crook – which follows modern practice with the wider-bore German double horn used in orchestras today. However, the sharper focus of articulation possible with the narrow-bore French instrument gives special point to the infectious finale. The performance is strikingly fresh and the listener will soon be aware that the work was a favourite with its illustrious young soloist. Father, Aubrey, made his recording of No. 3 while principal of the BBC Symphony Orchestra in 1940, and his firm line and easy flexibility anticipate a style which his son was to make famous. Excellent transfers bring very satisfactory sound.

Oboe concerto in C, K.314.
*** ASV Dig. CDCOE 808 [id.]. Douglas Boyd, COE, Berglund – R. STRAUSS: *Oboe concerto.* ***

Douglas Boyd is never afraid to point the phrasing individually, spontaneously and without mannerism. Others may be purer in their classicism, but this is a very apt reading next to Strauss. Recorded in Henry Wood Hall, the sound is full and vivid.

Piano concertos

Complete Mozart Edition, Volume 7: (i) *Piano concertos, K.107/1–3;* (ii) *Nos. 1–4;* (iii) *5, 6, 8, 9, 11–27; Concert rondos 1–2;* (iii; iv) *Double piano concertos, K.242 & K.365;* (v) *Triple concerto in F, K.242.*
(M) **(*) Ph. Analogue/Dig. 422 507-2 (12) [id.]. (i) Ton Koopman, Amsterdam Bar. O; (ii) Haebler, Vienna Capella Academica, Melkus; (iii) Brendel, ASMF, Marriner; (iv) Imogen Cooper; (v) Katia and Marielle Labèque, Bychkov, BPO, Bychkov.

Piano concertos Nos. 1–6; 8–9; 11–27; Rondo in D, K.382.
(M) *** EMI CZS7 62825-2 (10). Daniel Barenboim, ECO.

Piano concertos Nos. 1–6; 8–9; 11–27; Rondos Nos. 1–2, K.382 & 386.
(M) *** Sony Analogue/Dig. SK12K 46441 (12). Murray Perahia, ECO.

By omitting the four early concertos after J. C. Bach, Sony have been able to reissue the Perahia set on twelve mid-priced CDs. The cycle is a remarkable achievement; in terms of poetic insight and musical spontaneity, the performances are in a class of their own. There is a wonderful singing line and at the same time a sensuousness that is always tempered by spirituality. There is one slight snag: about half the recordings are digital and of excellent quality, but the remastering of the earlier, analogue recordings, especially those made in 1976/7, has not enhanced the violin timbre. Nos. 5, 12, 21, 22, 24 and 27 are acceptable, although there is a loss of bloom; but Nos. 8, 11 and especially 20 have varying amounts of edginess or shrillness, while Nos. 9, 13 and 14 have a lesser degree of thinness – which admirers of the authentic school may welcome. Others will prefer the rounder, more natural sound of the digital recordings.

The sense of spontaneity in Barenboim's performances of the Mozart concertos, his message that this is music hot off the inspiration line, is hard to resist, even though it occasionally leads to over-exuberance and idiosyncrasies. These are as nearly live performances as one could hope for on record, and the playing of the English Chamber Orchestra is splendidly geared to the approach of an artist with whom the players have worked regularly. They are recorded with fullness, and the sound is generally freshened very successfully in the remastering.

The Philips Mozart Edition *Piano concertos* box is based on Brendel's set with the ASMF under Marriner. Throughout, his thoughts are never less than penetrating. The transfers are consistently of the very highest quality, as is the playing of the Academy of St Martin-in-the-Fields under Sir Neville Marriner. To make the set complete, Ingrid Haebler gives eminently stylish accounts of the first four *Concertos* on the fortepiano, accompanied by Melkus and his excellent Vienna Capella Academica; the sound is admirably fresh. However, on disc two the ear gets rather a shock when Ton Koopman presents the three works after J. C. Bach. Convincing though these performances are, it seems a strange idea to offer an authentic approach to these three concertos alone, particularly as at the end of the disc we return to a delightfully cultured performance on modern instruments of the alternative version for three pianos of the so-called *Lodron Concerto*, K.242, provided by the Labèque duo.

Piano concertos Nos. 1 in F, K.37; 2 in B flat, K.39; 3 in D, K.40; 4 in G, K.41.
*** Sony Dig. MK 39225 [id.]. Murray Perahia, ECO.
☞ (BB) ** Naxos Dig. 8.550212. Jenö Jandó, Concentus Hungaricus, Idikó Helgi.

The first four concertos which occupy Perahia's present issue date from the spring or summer of 1767, when Mozart was eleven. Of course, they are not the equal of any of his more mature concertos; however, played with such grace and affection as here, they make delightful listening.

These early concertos are also given crisp, direct performances by Jandó, well accompanied. But the resonance of the Italian Institute in Budapest does not provide as sharp a focus as with the best of his other recordings of this repertoire.

Piano concertos Nos. 5 in D, K.175; 6 in B flat, K.238; 8 in C (Lützow); 9 in E flat (Jeunehomme); 11 in F, K.413; 12 in A, K.414; 13 in C, K.415; 14 in E flat, K.449; 15 in B flat, K.450; 16 in D, K.451; 17 in G, K.453; 18 in B flat, K.456; 19 in F, K.459; 20 in D min., K.466; 21 in C, K.467; 22 in E flat, K.482; 23 in A, K.488; 24 in C min., K.491; 25 in C, K.503; 26 in D (Coronation), K.537; 27 in B flat, K.595. Rondo in D, K.382.
☞ **(*) Ph. Dig. 438 207-2 (9) [id.]. Mitsuko Uchida, ECO, Jeffrey Tate.

Mitsuko Uchida, following up her stylish and sensitive accounts of the *Piano sonatas*, began a cycle of the concertos in 1985 with Nos. 20 and 21, which set the style for the series (recorded over a period of nearly five years) with playing of considerable beauty and performances guaranteed never to offend and most likely to delight. But on the highest level their degree of reticence – despite the superb orchestral work of the ECO under Tate – makes them often less memorable than the very finest versions. However, as it happens, the second of her series showed the partnership at its most illuminating. Their coupling of the late *E flat*, K.482, with its immediate successor, the beautiful *A major*, was a striking success – see below. The earlier concertos are neatly and elegantly done, although at times one would welcome more extrovert sparkle: the first movement of the *A major*, K.414 (No. 12), swings along nicely in the orchestra, but at the piano entry Uchida's tone-production is rather too recessive to bring out the full sparkle to contrast with the following raptly gentle *Andante*. There is some lovely playing in K.415 (No. 13), although her cultured reading of the slow movement offers more than a glimpse of Dresden china. She is unfailingly elegant in K.449, although again its slow movement (like that of K.595) is a little over-civilized; some will find a faint hint of preciosity here and particularly in the finale, which needs more abandon and character. The couplings of Nos. 16 and 17 (K.451 and K.453) and 18 and 19 (K.456 and K.459) are both successful, with plenty of flowing lyrical momentum in outer movements, slow movements attractively thoughtful and sympathetic, finales agreeably lighthearted. There is some fine orchestral playing, especially from the woodwind. Uchida is eminently alive and imaginative in her coupling of Nos. 24 and 25, although again the slow movement of K.503 may strike some listeners as a bit too measured. At times one would welcome a greater robustness of spirit, a lively inner current, and this applies particularly to the last two concertos, K.537 and K.595. Throughout, Jeffrey Tate draws splendid playing from the ECO, and these artists have the benefit of exceptionally good recorded sound; although the perspective favours the piano, the timbre of the solo instrument is beautifully captured. (Incidentally, the first of the two boxes is hinged both ways and the CDs are not easy to manipulate.)

Piano concertos Nos. 5, 6, 8, 9, 11–27; (i) *Double piano concerto, K.365;* (i; ii) *Triple piano concerto, K.242. Concert Rondos 1–2.*
(M) *** DG Dig. 431 211-2 (9) [id.]. Malcolm Bilson (fortepiano), E. Bar. Soloists, Gardiner, (i) with Robert Levin; (ii) Melvyn Tan.

Malcolm Bilson's complete set of the Mozart *Piano concertos* appears on nine mid-price CDs. Bilson is an artist of excellent musical judgement and good taste, and his survey is the only one at present available on the fortepiano, though we gather that one is under way from Melvyn Tan, who features here in the *Triple concerto*. For the most part, there is little to quarrel with here and much to enjoy.

Piano concertos Nos. 5 in D, K.175; 25 in C, K.503.
*** Sony Dig. MK 37267 [id.]. Murray Perahia, ECO.

Murray Perahia has the measure of the strength and scale of the *C major*, K.503, as well as displaying tenderness and poetry; while the early *D major*, K.175, has an innocence and freshness that are completely persuasive. The recording is good, but the upper strings are a little fierce and not too cleanly focused.

Piano concertos Nos. 6 in B flat, K.238; 8 in C, K.246; 19 in F, K.459.
(BB) *** Naxos Dig. 8.550208; *4550208* [id.]. Jenö Jandó, Concentus Hungaricus, Mátyás Antal.

No. 19 in F is a delightful concerto and it receives a most attractive performance, aptly paced, with fine woodwind playing, the finale crisply sparkling. No. 6 is hardly less successful; if No. 8 seems plainer, it is still admirably fresh. With excellently balanced recording this is a genuine bargain.

Piano concertos Nos. 6 in B flat, K.238; 13 in C, K.415.
*** Sony MK 39223 [id.]. Murray Perahia, ECO.

Perahia brings a marvellous freshness and delicacy to the *B flat Concerto*, K.238, but it is in the *C major*, with its sense of character and subtle artistry, that he is at his most sparkling and genial. Even if the acoustic ambience is less than ideally spacious, the CBS sound is still good.

Piano concertos Nos. 8 in C, K.246; 11 in F, K.413; Rondo in A, K.386.
☞ *** Decca Dig. 433 042-2 [id.]. Schiff, Camerata Ac. des Mozarteums Salzburg, Végh.

András Schiff's Mozart cycle goes from strength to strength. These are lovely performances, much enhanced by the quality of the accompaniment under Sándor Végh. Schiff offers playing of consummate artistry and excellent taste, and Végh and his Salzburg orchestra are unfailingly supportive. Along with the new Shelley cycle on Chandos, this is the best Mozart cycle since Perahia.

(i) *Piano concertos Nos. 9 in E flat, K.271; 14 in E flat, K.449. Fantasia in C min., K.396.*
(M) *** Van. 8.4015.71 [OVC 4015]. Alfred Brendel; (i) I Solisti di Zagreb, Janigro.

Brendel's 1968 performance of No. 9 is quite outstanding, elegant and beautifully precise. The classical-sized orchestra is just right and the neat, stylish string-playing matches the soloist. The performance of K.449 is also first rate, with a memorably vivacious finale. Altogether this is an outstanding reissue with natural sound which hardly shows its age in the clean remastering.

Piano concertos Nos. 9 in E flat, K.271; 17 in G, K.453.
☞ *** Chan. Dig. CHAN 9068 [id.]. Howard Shelley, LMP.
☞ **(*) Teldec/Warner Dig. 9031 73128-2 [id.]. Daniel Barenboim, BPO.

Howard Shelley is the latest to embrace the challenge of directing Mozart concertos from the keyboard, a practice favoured by artists from Edwin Fischer through to Murray Perahia. Shelley's playing is a delight and is possessed of a refreshing naturalness which should win many friends. There is spontaneity and elegance, a strong vein of poetic feeling and extrovert high spirits. His *G major concerto* belongs in the most exalted company and can withstand comparison with almost any rival. But both performances are touched by distinction, and they are beautifully recorded too.

Barenboim in the same coupling is free from affectation and self-indulgence. His playing is in exemplary taste without any trace of the tendency to beautify and italicize this or that phrase which one recalls from some of his old ECO cycle, good though that was in so many other respects. The orchestral sonority may be a little overnourished for those accustomed to period-instrument groups, but this will not worry most collectors. The engineers serve both pianist and orchestra well; these are satisfying accounts which will not disappoint.

Piano concertos Nos. 9 in E flat (Jeunehomme), K.271; 20 in D min., K.466; 21 in C, K.467; 23 in A, K.488; 27 in B flat, K.595.
☞ (B) **(*) EMI CZS7 67878-2 (2) [id.]. Daniel Barenboim, ECO.

The youthful *Jeunehomme concerto*, K.271, sets the style of these highly enjoyable performances, full of spirit and demonstrating masterly pianism, with an alert and musical direction of the orchestra. It also demonstrates Barenboim's willingness at times to display too great an awareness of refinements of tone and dynamics that are, strictly speaking, anachronistic. In K.271 the most serious reservation concerns the minuet at the centre of the final rondo which is far too measured. Barenboim's performances of *No. 20 in D minor* and No. 23, K.488, have all the sparkle and sensitivity one could ask for. The orchestral accompaniment is admirably alive, and one's only serious reservation concerns the somewhat fast tempo he adopts in the finale of K.466. The account of No. 23 is enchanting. There are moments when his delicacy of fingerwork comes close to preciosity, but it never quite goes over the edge. (The only snag is that this concerto is split between the two CDs.) There need be no reservations about the performance of No. 21 either; it is accomplished in every way. His version of K.595 is, however, more controversial. He again indulges in great refinement of touch and his reading of the slow movement is overtly romantic. The recordings (from the late 1960s) are fresh and naturally balanced; they are admirably transferred to CD.

Piano concertos Nos. 9 in E flat (Jeunehomme), K.271; 23 in A, K.288; Concert rondo in A, K.386.
☞ (B) **(*) Erato/Warner 2292 45935-2 [id.]. Maria-João Pires, Gulbenkian Foundation CO of Lisbon, Guschlbauer.

(i) *Piano concertos Nos. 20 in D min., K.466;* (ii) *21 in C, K.467. Rondo in A min., K.511.*
☞ (B) ** Erato/Warner 2292 45933-2 [id.]. Pires; (i) Lausanne CO, Jordan; (ii) Gulbenkian Foundation CO of Lisbon, Guschlbauer.

(i) *Piano concertos Nos. 26 in D min. (Coronation), K.537;* (ii) *27 in B flat, K.595;* (i) *Concert rondo in D, K.382.*
☞ (B) **(*) Erato/Warner 2292 45934-2 [id.]. Pires; (i) Gulbenkian Foundation CO of Lisbon, Guschlbauer; (ii) Lausanne CO, Jordan.

Erato are reissuing on the bargain Bonsai label some of Maria-João Pires's recordings from the mid- to late 1970s. She plays here with evident spirit and taste as well as immaculate fingerwork. Her playing reminds one a little of Ingrid Haebler's early Vox accounts (before her Mozart acquired some of the gentility and rectitude that have sometimes eroded the freshness of her playing, much though one admires it in many respects). Miss Pires is at her best in the *Jeunehomme*, K.271 (she is especially sensitive in the middle section of the closing Rondo). The coupling of K.466 and K.467 has less individuality, though neither performance is without atmosphere. Greater dash and fire in outer movements would have been welcome, but Miss Pires offers many insights and she is impressive in the *Coronation concerto*. Guschlbauer gives her most musical support; so too does Armin Jordan, although he is inclined to display a less striking profile. Smooth transfers of well-balanced analogue sound. Good value, but in the last resort not distinctive.

Piano concertos Nos. 9 in E flat, K.271; 21 in C, K.467.
*** Sony MK 34562 [id.]. Murray Perahia, ECO.

Perahia's reading of K.271 is wonderfully refreshing and delicate, with diamond-bright articulation, urgently youthful in its resilience. The famous *C major Concerto* is given a more variable, though still highly imaginative performance. Faithful, well-balanced recording.

Piano concertos Nos. 11 in F, K.413; 12 in A, K.414; 14 in E flat, K.449.
*** Sony MK 42243 [id.]. Murray Perahia, ECO.

These performances remain in a class of their own. When it first appeared, we thought the *F major*, K.413, the most impressive of Perahia's Mozart concerto records so far, its slow movement wonderfully inward; and the *E flat Concerto*, K.449, is comparably distinguished.

Piano concertos Nos. 12 in A, K.414; 14 in E flat, K.449; 21 in C, K.467.
(BB) *** Naxos Dig. 8.550202; *4550202* [id.]. Jenö Jandó, Concentus Hungaricus, András Ligeti.

In Jandó's hands the first movement of K.449 sounds properly forward-looking; the brightly vivacious K.414 also sounds very fresh here, and its *Andante* is beautifully shaped. The excellent orchestral response distinguishes the first movement of K.467: both grace and weight are here, and some fine wind playing. An added interest in this work is provided by Jandó's use of cadenzas provided by Robert Casadesus. Jandó is at his most spontaneous throughout these performances and this is altogether an excellent disc, well recorded.

Piano concertos Nos. 12 in A, K.141; 19 in F, K.459.
☞ (M) *** Chan. Dig. CHAN 9256 [id.]. Howard Shelley, LMP.

Another fine disc in Howard Shelley's musically rewarding and beautifully recorded series. Admirers of this artist need not hesitate in investing here, with the music's expressive range fully encompassed without mannerism, slow movements eloquently shaped and outer movements aptly paced and alive with vitality.

Piano concertos Nos. 12 in A, K.414; 20 in D min., K.466; Rondo in D, K.382.
☞ *** BMG/RCA Dig. 09026 60400 [id.]. Kissin, Moscow Virtuosi, Spivakov.

It is now more than a decade since the twelve-year-old Yevgeni Kissin made his Moscow début and then went on to record the two Chopin *Concertos* before he was thirteen. While the brilliant technique that dazzled us then and in the remarkable Tokyo (Sony) and Carnegie Hall (RCA) recitals is not necessarily a guarantee that he will prove a natural Mozartian, such he proves to be. The *D major Rondo*, K.382, has an elegance and delicacy worthy of the greatest Mozart players of the day. The *A major Concerto* shows the same immaculate technical finesse and musical judgement (save, perhaps, in the slow movement, which some could find a little oversweet). There are perhaps greater depths in the *D minor Concerto* than he finds but, even so, the playing is musical through and through and gives unfailing pleasure. The recorded sound is very good and the disc as a whole deserves the attention of any Mozartian.

Piano concertos Nos. 14 in E flat, K.449; 15 in E flat, K.450; 16 in D, K.451.
(M) *** EMI CDM7 69124-2 [id.]. Barenboim, ECO.

Barenboim's playing is spontaneous and smiling, while the orchestra respond with genuine vitality and sparkle. K.451 is particularly enjoyable, with a brisk, jaunty account of the first movement, a flowing, expressive slow movement and an exuberant finale. Good recording.

Piano concertos Nos. 14 in E flat, K.449; 27 in B flat, K.595.
☞ (M) *** Chan. Dig. CHAN 9137 [id.]. Howard Shelley, LMP.

Admirable performances, stylish and with a fine Mozartian sensibility. This is altogether most refreshing, and the recording is very good indeed.

Piano concertos Nos. 15 in B flat, K.450; 16 in D, K.451.
*** Sony Dig. MK 37824 [id.]. Murray Perahia, ECO.

Perahia's are superbly imaginative readings, full of seemingly spontaneous touches and turns of phrase very personal to him, which yet never sound mannered. His version of the *B flat Concerto* has sparkle, grace and intelligence; both these performances are very special indeed. The recording is absolutely first rate.

Piano concertos Nos. 16 in D, K.451; 25 in C, K.503; Rondo in A, K.386.
(BB) *** Naxos Dig. 8.550207; 4550207 [id.]. Jenö Jandó, Concentus Hungaricus, Mátyás Antal.

Jenö Jandó gives a very spirited and intelligent account of the relatively neglected *D major Concerto*, K.451, in which he receives sensitive and attentive support from the excellent Concentus Hungaricus under Mátyás Antal. The performance has warmth. The players sound as if they are enjoying themselves and, although there are greater performances of the *C major Concerto*, K.503, on record, they are not at this extraordinarily competitive price.

Piano concertos Nos. 17 in G, K.453; 18 in B flat, K.456.
*** Sony MK 36686 [id.]. Murray Perahia, ECO.
(BB) *** Naxos Dig. 8.550205; 4550205 [id.]. Jenö Jandó, Concentus Hungaricus, Mátyás Antal.

The *G major Concerto* is one of the most magical of the Perahia cycle and is on no account to be missed. The *B flat*, too, has the sparkle, grace and finesse that one expects from him. Even if you have other versions, you should still add this to your collection, for its insights are quite special.

This is also one of the finest in Jandó's excellent super-bargain series. Tempi are admirably judged and both slow movements are most sensitively played. The variations which form the *Andante* of K.456 are particularly appealing in their perceptive use of light and shade, while the very lively *Allegro vivace* finale of the same work is infectiously spirited. Jandó uses Mozart's original cadenzas for the first two movements of K.453 and the composer's alternative cadenzas for K.546. Excellent sound.

Piano concertos Nos. 17 in G, K.453; 21 in C, K.467.
*** Decca 411 947-2 [id.]. Vladimir Ashkenazy, Philh. O.
☞ **(*) Collins Dig. 1066-2 [id.]. Vásáry, Philh. O.

Ashkenazy's performances combine a refreshing spontaneity with an overall sense of proportion and balance. There is a fine sense of movement, and yet nothing is hurried; detail is finely characterized, but nothing is fussy. Moreover the recording is clear and lucid, with the balance between soloist and orchestra finely judged.

Very musicianly performances, directed from the keyboard by Tamás Vásáry, well shaped and expertly recorded. Rival accounts of the *G major*, K.453, by Perahia and Shelley among others have a stronger sense of characterization, and Vásáry is not to be preferred to either. Nor, for that matter, does his *C major*, K.467, represent much of a challenge to the strongest versions (Kovacevich, Perahia, Casadesus and others) in terms of sheer personality and presence.

Piano concertos Nos. (i) *17 in G, K.453;* (ii) *23 in A, K.488.*
☞ (M) *(*) BMG/RCA Stereo/mono 09026 61859-2 [id.]. Rubinstein, (i) RCA Victor SO,
    Wallenstein; (ii) St Louis SO, Golschmann.

Rubinstein's 1961 account of the *G major Concerto* is not one of the most spontaneous of his recordings. Wallenstein opens vigorously, and everything is musically shaped, but it is only in the finale that the music really sparkles. The *A major*, a mono recording from 1949, is not memorable either. Others have found more magic in the lovely *Andante*, and once again it is the spirited finale that remains in the memory. Acceptable sound.

(i) *Piano concerto No. 17 in G, K.453;* (ii) *Piano and wind quintet in E flat, K.452.*
☞ ** Ph. Dig. 422 592-2 [id.]. Uchida; (i) ECO, Tate; (ii) Neil Black, Thea King, Frank Lloyd,
    Robin O'Neill.

Instead of two concertos, Mitsuko Uchida offers the less usual but no less logical coupling of the *G major Concerto* with the *E flat Quintet* for piano and wind, which immediately preceded it. The *G major Concerto* does not offer serious competition to such artists as Murray Perahia (Sony) or Howard Shelley (Chandos). Uchida is her usual polished, elegant self but is not content to let this music proceed without interposing little touches of beautification which sweeten and thus diminish its purity. The slow movement is particularly mannered. The *E flat Quintet* is less so and unfolds more naturally. There is a pleasing interplay among the distinguished musicians and they offer much that is refreshing and vital. All the same, rival versions with Perahia (Sony) and Brendel (Philips) are not superseded. The acoustic of The Maltings, Snape, offers a rather warm glow; the concerto was recorded in a different venue (St John's, Smith Square) which Philips have used for the remainder of the cycle.

*Piano concertos Nos. 19, K.459; 20, K.466; 21, K.467; 23, K.488; 24, K.491; Concert rondos Nos. 1–2,
K.382 & 386.*   442-571-2
☞ ⊛ (B) *** Ph. Duo 442 269-2 [id.]. Alfred Brendel, ASMF, Marriner.

This must be the Mozartian bargain of all time, five piano concertos and two concert rondos – all for the cost of one premium-price CD. A Rosette then for generosity, to say nothing of the distinction of the performances. Indeed, throughout, the playing exhibits a sensibility that is at one with the composer's world. With Brendel, the first movement of K.459 is presented at a slightly quicker tempo than usual, but the performance sparkles all the way through and the playing of the ASMF could hardly be improved on. The slow movement is quite magical and the finale again has great zest and brilliance. The two minor-key concertos (*20 in D minor, 24 in C minor*) are also superbly played and recorded, though perhaps they miss the last ounce of tragic intensity. There are minor qualms about K.467. Brendel's outer movements are brisk, but tempo itself is not a problem. Each detail of a phrase is meticulously articulated, every staccato and slur carefully observed. The finale sounds over-rehearsed, and some of the joy and high spirits are sacrificed in the sense of momentum. Yet there remains much to delight. There are no reservations whatsoever about Brendel's account of K. 488, which is among the best in the catalogue. It is more spontaneous in feeling than Curzon's (masterly though that is) and in better taste than Barenboim's, and it is impeccably played. The decoration of the solo part in the slow movement is never obtrusive, always in style. The two *Concert rondos* – the first (K.382) is the Viennese alternative to the *Salzburg concerto* (K.175) – are no less elegantly performed, and throughout the set the Philips sound-balance is impeccable.

Piano concertos Nos. 19 in F, K.459; 23 in A, K.488.
⊛ *** Sony Dig. MK 39064 [id.]. Murray Perahia, ECO.

Murray Perahia gives highly characterful accounts of both *Concertos* and a gently witty yet vital reading of the *F Major*, K.459. As always with this artist, there is a splendidly classical feeling allied to a keenly poetic sensibility. His account of K.488 has enormous delicacy and inner vitality, yet a serenity that puts it in a class of its own.

Piano concertos Nos. 19 in F, K.459; 27 in B flat, K.595.
*** Decca Dig. 421 259-2 [id.]. András Schiff, Salzburg Mozarteum Camerata Academica, Végh.

This is agreeably relaxed, leisurely music-making though not in the least lacking in intensity or weight (Sandor Végh is very much the hero of the occasion). Occasionally András Schiff dots his 'i's and crosses his 't's a little too precisely, but his playing for the most part is so musicianly and perceptive that this does not seem important. These two readings can be warmly recommended – with the proviso that the resonant acoustic may trouble some listeners.

Piano concertos Nos. 20 in D min., K.466; 21 in C, K.467.
⊛ *** DG Dig. 419 609-2 [id.]. Malcolm Bilson (fortepiano), E. Bar. Soloists, Gardiner.
*** Decca Dig. 430 510-2 [id.]. Schiff, Salzburg Mozarteum Camerata Academica, Végh.
(M) *** BMG/RCA GD 87967 [7967-2-RG]. Rubinstein, RCA Victor SO, Wallenstein (with
HAYDN: *Andante & variations in F min.* ***).

These are vital, electric performances by Bilson and the English Baroque Soloists, expressive within their own lights, neither rigid nor too taut in the way of some period Mozart, nor inappropriately romantic. This is a disc to recommend even to those who would not normally consider period performances of Mozart concertos, fully and vividly recorded with excellent balance between soloist and orchestra – better than you would readily get in the concert hall.

András Schiff's Mozart cycle with the Salzburg Mozarteum Camerata Academica under Sándor Végh is proving one of the more satisfying of recent years – and arguably the finest since Murray Perahia's cycle of the late 1970s. There is plenty of dramatic fire in the *D minor*, K.466, which is marvellously controlled and the *C major*, K.467, comes up sounding beautifully fresh too.

Rubinstein has seldom been caught so sympathetically by the microphones, and the remastered 1961 recording has the orchestral sound admirably freshened. In each concerto the slow movement is the kernel of the interpretation. Rubinstein's playing is melting. Altogether Wallenstein is an excellent accompanist, for finales have plenty of sparkle. The Haydn *Andante and variations*, a substantial bonus recorded a year earlier, again demonstrates Rubinstein's aristocratic feeling for a classical melodic line: it is played most beautifully.

(i) *Piano concertos Nos. 20 in D min., K.466; 21 in C, K.467; 23 in A, K.488; 27 in B flat, K.595.*
Piano sonata No. 17 in D, K.576; Rondo in A min., K.511.
☞ ⊛ (B) *** Double Decca Analogue/Dig. 436 383-2 (2). Vladimir Ashkenazy, Philh. O.

This set – with two CDs offered for the price of one – deserves to be successful and is highly recommendable on all counts. With the three favourite Mozart piano concertos included, plus a splendid *Sonata* and a charming *Rondo*, this is real bounty. Ashkenazy's performance of the famous *C major Concerto* combines a refreshing spontaneity with an overall sense of proportion and balance. His *A major*, too, is beautifully judged, alive and fresh, yet warm – one of the most satisfying accounts yet recorded, even finer than Brendel's. No quarrels either with the *B flat*, which is as finely characterized as one would expect. The recording focuses closely on the piano, yet no orchestral detail is masked and the overall impression is very bright and lifelike. These latter two recordings are digital; the *C major* and *No. 20 in D minor* are analogue, but the sound is just as clean and well-focused. The *Sonata* and *Rondo* were recorded earlier (in 1967); the playing is equally fine and the sound first class. This makes an equally desirable alternative to Brendel's Duo set, above.

Piano concertos Nos. 20 in D min., K.466; 23 in A, K.488.
*** EMI Dig. CDC7 54366-2 [id.]. Melvyn Tan, L. Classical Players, Norrington.
☞ (M) *** Chan. Dig. CHAN 8992 [id.]. Howard Shelley, LMP.

Melvyn Tan radiates infectious delight in what he is doing, and the playing has both imagination and poise. Although the fortepiano may be less able than a modern concert grand to convey the dark *Don Giovanni* colourings of the *D minor Concerto*, K.466, these readings have an impressive flair, and the London Classical Players under Norrington are generally supportive. The EMI recording does justice to their artistry.

Those wanting this coupling with modern instruments will find Howard Shelley's performances no less rewarding. Characterization is strong, yet the slow movement of K.488 is very beautiful and touching. Splendid Chandos recording.

Piano concertos Nos. (i) *20 in D min., K.466;* (ii) *27 in B flat, K.595.*
*** Sony MK 42241 [id.]. Murray Perahia, ECO.

Perahia produces wonderfully soft colourings and a luminous texture in the *B flat Concerto*, yet at the same time he avoids underlining too strongly the valedictory sense that inevitably haunts this magical score. In the *D minor Concerto* none of the darker, disturbing undercurrents go uncharted, but at the same time we remain within the sensibility of the period. An indispensable issue, well recorded.

Piano concerto No. 20 in D min., K.466; (i) *Double piano concerto in E flat, K.365.*
☞ (M) ** EMI CDM5 65180-2 [id.]. André Previn; (i) Radu Lupu; LSO.

André Previn is the soloist in the *D minor Concerto* and, with the best will in the world, this reading of the solo part cannot be said to match those of Perahia, Ashkenazy, Brendel or Barenboim. Needless to say everything is musical enough, but the performance as a whole lacks real personality. It is fluent, intelligent and far from unenjoyable, yet ultimately bland; and the *Double concerto* does not possess the sparkle and distinction of Gilels and his daughter on DG. In a cruelly competitive world this issue, for all its merits, including a well-detailed and admirably balanced recording, does not stand out.

Piano concertos Nos. (i) *21 in C, K.467;* (ii) *22 in E flat, K.482; 23 in A, K.488;* (i) *24 in C min., K.491;* (ii) *26 in D (Coronation), K.537; 27 in B, K.595;* (iii) *Double piano concerto in E flat, K.365.*
⊛ (M) **(*) Sony SM3K 46519 (3) [id.]. Robert Casadesus, with (i) Cleveland O, Szell; (ii) Columbia SO, Szell; (iii) Gaby Casadesus, Phd. O, Ormandy.

A very distinguished set, effectively transferred to CD. Casadesus's Mozart may at first seem understated, but the imagination behind his readings is apparent in every phrase and the accompaniment could hardly be more stylish. The balance is better than we had remembered it. Although the orchestra tends to dwarf the soloist in tuttis, the placing of the piano is very pleasing, and the subtleties of the solo playing are naturally caught. Mozart's last piano concertos inspire two extremely memorable performances, each of them underlining the dramatic contrast of soloist and orchestra, almost as a meeting of heroine and hero. The *Double concerto* is essentially a genial work, and this is the one quality completely missing from Casadesus's performance, which has a matching dry recording. All the solo concertos, however, were recorded in Severance Hall, Cleveland, between 1959 and 1962 (except for No. 23, which dates from 1969) and the hall ambience provides an attractive fullness to the overall sound.

Piano concertos Nos. 21 in C, K.467; 24 in C min., K.491.
(B) *** Pickwick Dig. PCD 832; *CIMPC 832* [id.]. Howard Shelley, City of L. Sinfonia.

Howard Shelley gives delightfully fresh and characterful readings of both the popular *C major* and the great *C minor* concertos, bringing out their strength and purposefulness as well as their poetry, never overblown or sentimental. His Pickwick disc makes an outstanding digital bargain, with accompaniment very well played and recorded.

Piano concertos Nos. 21 in C, K.467; 25 in C, K.503.
⊛ (B) *** Ph. 426 077-2. Kovacevich, LSO, C. Davis.

The partnership of Kovacevich and Davis almost invariably produces inspired music-making. Their balancing of strength and charm, drama and tenderness, make for performances which retain their sense of spontaneity but which plainly result from deep thought, and the weight of both these great C major works is formidably conveyed. The 1972 recording is well balanced and refined.

Piano concertos Nos. 21 in C, K.467; 27 in B flat, K.595.
*** Sony Dig. SK 46485 [id.]. Murray Perahia, COE.
☞ **(*) Pickwick MCD 74; *MCC 74* [id.]. Fou Ts'ong, Sinfonia Varsovia.

Murray Perahia gives performances of characteristic understanding and finesse with the Chamber Orchestra of Europe. There are new and different insights into both works though neither reading necessarily displaces his earlier accounts with the ECO, which may have a slight edge on the newcomer in terms of freshness and spontaneity.

Fou Ts'ong and the Sinfonia Varsovia give us very musical playing and have the advantage of exemplary recording, well balanced and in a warm, beautifully spacious acoustic. There is much to admire, though the occasional mannerism must be noted. In the first movement of the *C major Concerto* the last orchestral chord before the cadenza drops in level while the piano leaps forward.

The *B flat Concerto* is also beautifully played, though there are times in both works when one feels that the vital sense of flow is not quite vital enough. All the same there is a great deal to enjoy here and, were it at a proper mid- or bargain-price level, it would be competitive. However, for all his undoubted distinction, Fou Ts'ong does not have the commanding keyboard personality or stature of Perahia or the Schiff–Végh partnership. The pianist-conductor's humming is occasionally audible and, though less obtrusive than Glenn Gould in this respect, is unwelcome.

Piano concertos Nos. 22 in E flat, K.482; 23 in A, K.488.
*** Ph. Dig. 420 187-2 [id.]. Mitsuko Uchida, ECO, Tate.

In balance, fidelity and sense of presence, few recordings of Mozart piano concertos can match Uchida's fine coupling of the late *E flat*, K.482, with its immediate successor, the beautiful *A major*, and Uchida's thoughtful manner, at times a little understated, is ideally set against outstanding playing from the ECO with its excellent wind soloists.

Piano concertos Nos. 22 in E flat, K.482; 24 in C min., K.491.
*** Sony MK 42242 [id.]. Murray Perahia, ECO.
☞ **(*) Pickwick Dig. MCD 79; *MCC 79* [id.]. Fou Ts'ong, Sinfonia Varsovia.

Not only is Perahia's contribution inspired in the great *E flat Concerto*, but the wind players of the ECO are at their most eloquent in the slow movement. Moreover the *C minor Concerto* emerges here as a truly Mozartian tragedy, rather than as foreshadowing Beethoven, which some artists give us. Both recordings are improved in focus and definition in the CD transfer.

Like his coupling of Nos. 21 and 27, Fou Ts'ong gives accomplished, highly musical accounts of these two concertos, the playing lacking in neither style nor vividness. On the whole, K.482 is more memorable than K.491, with expressive and bracing playing in good balance, but there are more deeply searching readings of the *C minor*, and one again wishes that Pickwick had issued this record in their bargain range when it would have been far more competitive.

Piano concertos Nos. 23 in A, K.488; 24 in C min., K.491.
(M) *** DG 423 885-2 [id.]. Kempff, Bamberg SO, Leitner.
(B) *** Decca 430 497-2. Cîifford Curzon, LSO, Kertész (with SCHUBERT: *Impromptus: in G flat & A flat, D.899/3 & 4* ***).
☞ **(*) Virgin/EMI Dig. VC7 59280-2 [id.]. Mikhail Pletnev, Deutsche Kammerphilharmonie.
☞ * BMG/RCA Dig. 09026 60989-2 [id.]. Alicia de Larrocha, ECO, Sir Colin Davis.

(i) *Piano concertos Nos. 23 in A, K.488;* (ii) *24 in C min., K.491; Rondo in A, K.511.*
(M) *** BMG/RCA GD 87968 [7968-2-RG]. Rubinstein, RCA Victor SO, (i) Alfred Wallenstein; (ii) Josef Krips.

Rubinstein brings characteristic finesse and beauty of phrasing to his coupling; K.488 is especially beautiful. In K.49l the crystal-clear articulation is allied to the aristocratic feeling characteristic of vintage Rubinstein: the slow movement is memorable in its poise. Krips's accompaniment acts as a foil to the tragic tone of this great and wonderfully balanced work. The recordings, from 1958 and 1961 respectively, sound fresh, and the *Rondo*, recorded in 1959, is equally distinguished.

Kempff's outstanding performances of these concertos are uniquely poetic and inspired, and Leitner's accompaniments are comparably distinguished. The 1960 recording still sounds well, and this is strongly recommended at mid-price.

Curzon's account of these two concertos is immaculate; no connoisseur of the piano will fail to derive pleasure and refreshment from them. Curzon has the advantage of sensitive support both from Kertész and from the Decca engineers, and the remastering has added life and vividness to the music-making. Two of the Schubert Op. 90 *Impromptus*, making an attractive fill-up, add to the appeal of this reissue.

Pletnev and the Deutsche Kammerphilharmonie have obviously established a close rapport and there is great personality here – whether you like everything about it or not. In Pletnev's hands the slow movement of the *A major Concerto* is among the most beautiful on record, the finale the most rushed – many may find it unacceptable. In the *C minor Concerto* he is intensely dramatic, Beethovenian in feeling and powerful in conception: his own first-movement cadenza looks even more forward into the nineteenth century. There is nothing bland here: commanding playing from all concerned, but not to all tastes.

Alicia de Larrocha is a fine Mozartian as, of course, is Sir Colin Davis, but neither seems wholly at ease on this occasion. Nothing sparkles: Larrocha's playing, so often touched by distinction, borders on the routine, and not even Sir Colin's vital opening of the *C minor Concerto* evokes much of a response. The actual sound of the RCA recording is very lifelike and well balanced, but artistically this is not the success that one might have hoped for.

Piano concertos Nos. 23 in A, K.488; 26 (Coronation), K.537.
☞ (M) **(*) Teldec/Warner Dig. 4509 92150-2 [id.]. Friedrich Gulda, Concg. O, Harnoncourt.

Friedrich Gulda discreetly participates in the orchestral *ritornelli*. The playing of the Concertgebouw Orchestra is careful in handling both balance and nuances, and Nikolaus Harnoncourt is particularly successful in conducting the *Coronation concerto*. Gulda gives an admirably unaffected and intelligent account of the *A major*, which is enjoyable – as, for that matter, is his reading of the *Coronation* – but it does not constitute a challenge to such rivals as Perahia or Brendel or Ashkenazy in K.488.

Piano concertos Nos. 24 in C min., K.491; 25 in C, K.503.
*** EMI Dig. CDC7 54295-2 [id.]. Melvyn Tan (fortepiano), L. Classical Players, Norrington.

Melvyn Tan tries not to see the C minor through Beethovenian eyes, and approaches it both imaginatively and with great freshness. His playing has both poise and grace, and so does that of the London Classical Players too. The fortepiano is less well equipped to penetrate the tragic overtones of the slow movement and here Tan does not help himself by adopting too brisk a tempo. He shapes the finale with subtlety and finesse, and is equally thought-provoking in the *C major Concerto*, K.503. The EMI recording is most naturally and truthfully balanced.

Piano concerto No. 25 in C, K.503.
(M) *** Sony MYK 44832 [MYK 37762]. Leon Fleisher, Cleveland O, Szell – BEETHOVEN: *Piano concerto No. 4.* ***

Fleisher and Szell achieve a memorable partnership in this 1959 recording. The kernel of the performance is the beautiful slow movement, classically serene. The commanding outer movements have great vitality: Fleisher shapes the first movement's second subject most engagingly and is wonderfully nimble in the finale, while Szell's orchestral detail is a constant source of pleasure.

Piano concertos Nos. (i) 26 in D (Coronation), K.537; (ii) 27 in B flat, K.595.
(M) *** DG 429 810-2; 429 810-4 [id.]. (i) Vásáry, BPO; (ii) Gilels, VPO, Boehm.

Tamás Vásáry is a fine Mozartian with exemplary taste and judgement, and his account of the *Coronation concerto* has grandeur as well as vitality. The quality of the 1974 sound is very good in this transfer.

Piano concerto No. 26 in D (Coronation), K.537; Concert rondos, Nos. 1 in D, K.382; 2 in A, K.386.
*** Sony Dig. MK 39224 [id.]. Murray Perahia, ECO.

Perahia succeeds in making K.537 mean more than do most of his rivals. This is a magical performance in which the level of inspiration runs high. The *Concerto* is coupled with superb accounts of the two *Concert rondos*, K.382 and K.386, which for the first time on record incorporate the closing bars newly discovered by Professor Alan Tyson. The recording is naturally balanced within a fairly resonant ambience.

Piano concerto No. 27 in B flat, K.595; (i) Double piano concerto in E flat, K.365.
⊛ (M) *** DG 419 059-2; 419 059-4 [id.]. Emil Gilels, VPO, Boehm, (i) with Elena Gilels.

Gilels's is supremely lyrical playing that evinces all the classical virtues. No detail is allowed to detract from the picture as a whole; the pace is totally unhurried and superbly controlled. All the points are made by means of articulation and tone, and each phrase is marvellously alive, while Boehm and the Vienna Philharmonic provide excellent support. The performance of the marvellous *Double concerto* is no less enjoyable. Its mood is comparatively serious, but this is not to suggest that the music's sunny qualities are not brought out. The quality on CD is first class, refining detail yet not losing ambient warmth.

(i) *Piano concerto No. 27 in B flat, K.595. Piano sonatas Nos. 11 in A, K.331; 14 in C min., K.457.*
☞ (M) **(*) Decca 433 898-2 [id.]. Backhaus, (i) VPO, Karl Boehm.

Backhaus is magisterial and, if he is rhythmically rather uneven and the performance of the concerto does not always flow smoothly, the performance, very well accompanied by Boehm, has great character. The two *Sonatas* are also welcome. The manner is a little unsmiling in its directness, but the classicism is appealing in its total lack of romantic overlay. There is something very compelling about this music-making, for Backhaus's personality projects strongly in every bar. The early (1955) stereo is remarkably truthful.

(i) *Double Piano concerto in E flat, K.365; (i–ii) Triple Piano concerto in F, K.242; Concert rondos: (iii) in D, K.382; (iv) in A, K.386.*

☞ (M) ** Decca 425 044-2 [id.]. Vladimir Ashkenazy, with (i) Barenboim, ECO, cond. Barenboim; (ii) Fou Ts'ong; (iii) Philh. O; (iv) LSO, Kertész.

Barenboim's 1972 partnership with Ashkenazy in the *Double Piano concerto* finds both artists slightly self-conscious, particularly in the slow movement, which is taken very slowly. There is slackness too in the *Triple concerto*, in which they are joined by Fou Ts'ong. Ashkenazy's versions of the two *Concert rondos* have plenty of freshness and sparkle.

(i) *Double piano concerto in E flat, K.365; Triple piano concerto in F (Lodron), K.242* (arr. for 2 pianos); *Fantasia in F min., K.608* (arr. Busoni); *5 Variations in G, K.501.*
*** Sony Dig. SK 44915 [id.]. Murray Perahia, Radu Lupu, (i) ECO.

Murray Perahia and Radu Lupu are in good form in both the *Double concerto*, K.365, and the two-piano arrangement of the *Lodron*. The performances emanate from public concerts at The Maltings, Snape, and have much of the excitement and spontaneity of live music-making. The two pianists are beautifully matched in both pieces, and again in the G major variations, K.501 and Busoni's transcription of the *F minor Fantasy*.

Violin concertos

Violin concertos Nos. 1–7; Adagio, K.261; Rondos Nos. 1–2, K.269 & K.373 (all for violin and orchestra).
(BB) *** BMG/Eurodisc VD 69255 (3) [69255-2-RG]. Josef Suk, Prague Chamber O, Libor Hlaváček.

Josef Suk's recordings date from 1972. He includes Nos. 6 and 7 which are almost certainly spurious (although some authorities suggest that No. 7 is largely the work of Mozart). Suk makes a good case for them and throughout the set his performances are highly distinguished. The solo playing has character, warmth and humanity, and its unaffected manner is especially suited to the first two concertos. Hlaváček does not always make enough of the dynamic contrasts and, throughout, this music-making is dominated by Suk. This is partly a matter of the recording balance. But with any reservations noted, these are delightful performances.

Complete Mozart Edition, Volume 8: (i) *Violin concertos Nos 1–5; 7 in D, K.271; Adagio in E, K.361; Rondo in B flat, K.269; Rondo in C, K.373.* (i; ii) *Concertone, K.190;* (iii; iv) *Double Concerto in D for violin, piano and orchestra, K.315f;* (iii; v; vi) *Sinfonia concertante in A, for violin, viola, cello and orchestra, K.320e.* (iii; v) *Sinfonia concertante in E flat, K.364.*
(M) **(*) Ph. Analogue/Dig. 422 508-2 (4). (i) Szeryng, (ii) with Poulet, Morgan, Jones; New Philh. O, Gibson; (iii) Iona Brown, with (iv) Shelley; (v) Imai; (vi) Orton; ASMF, Marriner.

Philip Wilby has here not only completed the first movement of an early *Sinfonia concertante for violin, viola and cello* (Mozart's only music with concertante cello) but also, through shrewd detective work, has reconstructed a full three-movement *Double concerto* from what Mozart left as 'a magnificent torso', to use Alfred Einstein's description; it is for violin, piano and orchestra. The result here is a delight, a full-scale 25-minute work which ends with an effervescent double-variation finale, alternately in duple and compound time. That is superbly done with Iona Brown and Howard Shelley as soloists; and the other ASMF items are very good too, with Iona Brown joined by Nobuko Imai most characterfully on the viola in the great *Sinfonia concertante*, K.364. What is a shade disappointing is to have Henryk Szeryng's readings of the main violin concertos from the 1960s instead of the Grumiaux set. Szeryng is sympathetic but a trifle reserved and not as refreshing as Grumiaux.

(i) *Violin concertos Nos. 1 in B flat, K.207;* (ii) *2 in D, K.211;* (iii) *3 in C, K.216;* (ii) *4 in D, K.218;* (i) *5 in A (Turkish), K.219;* (ii) *Adagio in C, K.261; Rondo No. 2 in C, K.373; Haffner Serenade, K.250: Rondo* (all for violin & orchestra); (iv) *Sinfonia concertante in E flat, K.364;* (v) *Divertimento in E flat for string trio* (violin, viola & cello), *K.563.*
(M) **(*) Sony SM3K 46523 [id.]. Isaac Stern, with (i) Columbia SO, Szell; (ii) ECO, Schneider; (iii) Cleveland O, Szell; (iv) Zukerman, ECO, Barenboim; (v) Pinchas Zukerman, Leonard Rose.

It goes without saying that Stern's solo playing is always splendid; it is simply that he is not always as sensitive on detail as his rivals, and this especially applies to No. 1 and rather less so to No. 5 where the accompaniment is provided by the Columbia Symphony Orchestra under Szell. The interpretation of No. 3, however, displays Stern's qualities of sparkling stylishness at their most intense in a very satisfying reading, with a beautifully poised and pointed accompaniment from the same conductor but now with the splendid Cleveland Orchestra. In Nos. 2 and 4, Stern has the benefit of rather fuller recording and his playing, as always, is full of personality. The great *Sinfonia concertante* stands among the finest available and is certainly the jewel in this set, presenting as it does two soloists of equally strong musical personality. The trio of famous virtuosi, Stern, Zuckerman and Rose, brings an individually characterized performance of the *Divertimento for string trio* with hushed playing accurately conveyed and the players clearly separated within an atmospheric acoustic, even though the recording is rather close and bright.

Violin concertos Nos. 1–5; Adagio in E, K.261; Rondo in C, K.373; Rondo concertante in B flat, K.269.
☞ (B) *** Double Decca 440 621-2 (2). Mayumi Fujikawa, RPO, Weller.

(i) *Violin concertos Nos. 1–5;* (ii) *Adagio in E, K.261; Rondo in C, K.373;* (i; iii) *Sinfonia concertante in E flat, K.364.*
☞ (B) *** Ph. Duo 438 323-2 (2) [id.]. Arthur Grumiaux, (i) LSO, C. Davis; (ii) New Philh. O, Leppard; (iii) with Arrigo Pellicia.

Grumiaux's accounts of the Mozart *Violin concertos* come from the early 1960s and are among the most beautifully played in the catalogue at any price. The orchestral accompaniments have sparkle and vitality, and Grumiaux's contribution has splendid poise and purity of tone. There are many delights here and the music-making has warmth as well as refinement; the recording sounds remarkably good, with clean, fresh string-tone and well-defined bass. For this remarkably generous reissue on their bargain Duo label, Philips have added the *Adagio*, K.261, and *Rondo*, K.373, recorded later in 1967, and also, to make the package uniquely desirable, a fine performance of the great *Sinfonia concertante*, K.364, with Arrigo Pellicia proving a sensitive partner for Grumiaux, especially in the *Andante*. The new CD transfers are brightly lit but still faithful.

Mayumi Fujikawa made her recording début for Decca with this impressive set of the Mozart *Violin concertos*, recorded in 1979/80. She has the advantage of admirably stylish and sympathetic accompaniments from Walter Weller, who secures consistently warm and polished playing from the RPO. Throughout there is much evidence of the soloist's musicianship and imagination, and every one of these performances comes sparklingly to life. Particularly to be admired is the first *B flat Concerto*, which can easily sound routine, but not here. Her espressivo in slow movements is very appealing, notably in the *G major Concerto*, K.216, but the lovely *Andante* of *No. 4 in D major* is obviously heartfelt and its finale has an attractive, chimerical lightness of touch. No. 5 also reinforces the very positive impression she makes. Of course this set comes into direct competition with Grumiaux, also at bargain price, which must still remain a first choice. Yet the Decca recording is much warmer than the Philips, the violin is caught with complete naturalness and the orchestra is recorded so beautifully that this Double Decca set certainly holds its place.

Violin concertos Nos. 1 in B flat, K.207; 3 in G, K.216; 5 in A (Turkish), K.219.
(M) *** Decca Dig./Analogue 433 170-2 [id.]. Iona Brown, ASMF.

Violin concertos Nos. 2 in D, K.211; 4 in D, K.218; (i) *Sinfonia concertante in E flat, K.364.*
(M) *** Decca Dig./Analogue 433 171-2 [id.]. Iona Brown, (i) Josef Suk; ASMF.

Iona Brown's (originally Argo) set of the Mozart *Violin concertos*, on a pair of mid-priced Decca Serenata discs, has the advantage of including a fine account of the great *Sinfonia concertante*, in which she is joined by Josef Suk. The performances of the solo concertos, too, are first rate. The playing has a freshness and vigour that are winning and the participants convey a sense of pleasure in what they are doing.

Violin concerto No. 1 in B flat, K.207.
☞ (M) *** Ph. 434 167-2 [id.]. David Oistrakh, LOP, Haitink – STRAVINSKY: *Concerto.* ***

David Oistrakh's playing is so persuasive that one is compelled to think of this least-performed of Mozart's violin concertos as quite the equal of the later works in the same group. Haitink's stylish accompaniments temper the tendency to romanticism from the soloist, and the result is very satisfying. The recording sounds much better on CD than on LP, with the orchestral focus firmer. Such masterly fiddling makes up for the short playing time of this reissue (43 minutes, but all highly stimulating). This is a limited edition and is unlikely to be available beyond the lifetime of this book.

Violin concertos Nos. 1 in B flat, K.207; 2 in D, K.211; Rondo No. 1 in B flat, K.269.
*** Denon Dig. C37 7506 [id.]. Jean-Jacques Kantorow, Netherlands CO, Hager.

Violin concertos Nos. 1 in B flat, K.207; 2 in D, K.211; Rondo in B flat, K.269; Andante in F (arr. Saint-Saëns from *Piano concerto No. 21, K.467*).
(BB) **(*) Naxos Dig. 8.550414 [id.]. Takako Nishizaki, Capella Istropolitana, Johannes Wildner.

Kantorow's coupling makes an excellent start to his Mozart series. He is given alert, stylish accompaniments by Leopold Hager and the Netherlands Chamber Orchestra, and the recording is eminently realistic. The *B flat Rondo* makes an excellent bonus. Kantorow plays his own cadenzas – and very good they are.

This was the last disc to be recorded (in 1990) of Takako Nishizaki's fine survey of the violin concertos. The opening movement of K.207 is brisk and fresh, although this is the least individual of Nishizaki's readings. The *Second Concerto*, K.211, has rather more flair, the *Andante* touchingly phrased, and the finale has a winning lightness of touch. The *Rondo* is also an attractively spontaneous performance, and as an encore we are offered Saint-Saëns's arrangement of the famous *'Elvira Madigan'* theme from the *C major Concerto*, K.467.

Violin concertos Nos. 1 in B flat, K.207; 4 in D, K.218; Rondo in B flat, K.269.
*** Sony MK 44503 [id.]. Cho-Liang Lin, ECO, Leppard.

As in his coupling of K.216 and K.219, Lin creates a ready partnership with Leppard and the ECO, and his combination of effervescence and delicacy is matched by the orchestra, with appealing tenderness in both slow movements and plenty of dash in the last movement of K.207. Excellent recording, naturally balanced.

Violin concertos Nos. (i) 2 in D, K.211; (ii) 3 in G, K.216; (i) 5 in A (Turkish), K.219.
☞ (M) **(*) Sony mono/stereo MPK 52526 [id.]. Zino Francescatti, (i) Zurich CO, Edmond de Stoutz; (ii) Columbia SO, Bruno Walter.

Francescatti's 1958 recording of the *Third Concerto* with Bruno Walter is one of his finest records. The playing is at times a little wayward, but Walter accompanies throughout with his usual warmth and insight and falls into line sympathetically with his soloist. The slow movement is beautifully played, albeit with an intensity that barely stops short of romanticism, and the changing moods of the finale are admirably contrasted. In the other two concertos, Francescatti's timbre and style are equally sweet and Edmond de Stoutz provides neat, crisply profiled accompaniments which are straighter than with Walter, but he too follows his soloist flexibly. The mono recordings are made in a resonant acoustic and the sound is surprisingly expansive; indeed there are no complaints about a lack of fullness. There is much competition in this repertoire, but admirers of Francescatti will not be disappointed with this strikingly well-transferred reissue.

Violin concertos Nos. 2 in D, K.211; 4 in D, K.218.
*** EMI Dig. CDC7 47011-2 [id.]. Anne-Sophie Mutter, Philh. O, Muti.

Anne-Sophie Mutter is given very sensitive support from the Philharmonia under Muti. Her playing combines purity and classical feeling, delicacy and incisiveness, and is admirably expressive. The EMI recording is very good; the images are sharply defined, but the balance is convincing.

Violin concertos Nos. 2 in D, K.211; 7 in D, K.271a; Rondo in C, K.373.
*** Sony Dig. SK 44913 [id.]. Cho-Liang Lin, ECO, Leppard.

Lin's coupling of the early *D major concerto* and the doubtfully attributed K.271a follows the pattern of his earlier Mozart recordings in sweet, elegant playing, beautifully supported by Leppard in a traditional but uninflated style. First-rate recording.

(i) Violin concertos Nos. 3 in G, K.216; 4 in D, K.218; (ii) Duo for violin and viola in G, K.423.
☞ (M) **(*) DG Dig. 439 525-2 [id.]. Gidon Kremer; (i) VPO, Harnoncourt; (ii) Kim Kashkashian.

Kremer and Harnoncourt make a characterful partnership in the Mozart violin concertos, although Harnoncourt is nothing if not eccentric. In the *G major*, K.216, the first movement flows at just the right pace, and then in the *Andante* a comma is placed to romanticize the climbing opening phrase of the main theme slightly. But with Kremer playing sweetly throughout, such individual touches may be found very acceptable (including a long cadenza in the first movement of No. 3) when there is plenty of vitality and Harnoncourt's tuttis are always strong. The *Duo* (quite substantial at 17 minutes) makes an interesting bonus, with skilful playing and a good balance between Kremer and Kashkashian. But there is more to this music than these players find.

Violin concertos Nos. 3 in G, K.216; 5 in A (Turkish), K.219.
(BB) *** Naxos Dig. 8.550063 [id.]. Takako Nishizaki, Capella Istropolitana, Stephen Gunzenhauser.

Violin concertos Nos. 3, K.216; 5 (Turkish); Adagio in E, K.261.
*** Sony Dig. MK 42364 [id.]. Cho-Liang Lin, ECO, Leppard.

This is the finest of Nishizaki's three discs of the Mozart violin concertos on Naxos. The readings are individual and possess the most engaging lyrical feeling and the natural response of the soloist to

Mozartian line and phrase. A good balance, the soloist forward, but convincingly so, and the orchestral backcloth in natural perspective. A real bargain.

Lin's persuasive style brings out the tenderness of both slow movements. Lin is full of fancy and imagination, apt for the music of a teenager. Leppard and the ECO are the most responsive of partners, and the recording is first rate.

Violin concerto No. 4 in D, K.218.
☞ (***) EMI mono CDH7 64562-2 [id.]. Szigeti, LPO, Beecham – MENDELSSOHN: *Violin concerto;* PROKOFIEV: *Violin concerto No. 1.* (***)
☞ (**) Pearl mono GEMM CD 9377 [id.]. Szigeti, LPO, Beecham – MENDELSSOHN: *Violin concerto;* PROKOFIEV: *Violin concerto No. 1.* (**)
☞ (**) Pearl mono GEMM CDS 9996 [id.]. Kreisler, LSO, Sir Landon Ronald – BACH: *Double violin concerto;* BEETHOVEN; BRAHMS; MENDELSSOHN; *Violin concertos.* (**)

Szigeti recorded the *D major Concerto* with that consummate Mozartian, Sir Thomas Beecham, a decade after the Kreisler version, and the combination produces music-making of a high order. It comes with a magical account of the Prokofiev *D major Concerto* and a fine Mendelssohn. Of the two transfers of the same coupling now on offer, the EMI is far smoother and more revealing. Pearl's transfer produces rougher and more congested sound and untamed surfaces.

The Kreisler account with Sir Landon Ronald comes from 1924 and his thrilling, glorious tone survives acoustic technique and the inevitable surface noise which Pearl have not fully succeeded in taming. It comes in harness with a host of other remarkable performances.

Violin concerto No. 4 in D, K.218; (i) *Sinfonia concertante in E flat, for violin, viola and orchestra, K.364.*
(BB) **(*) Naxos Dig. 8.550332 [id.]. Takako Nishizaki, (i) Ladislav Kyselak; Capella Istropolitana, Stephen Gunzenhauser.

A fine account of No. 4, with Takako Nishizaki's solo playing well up to the high standard of this series and with Stephen Gunzenhauser's perceptive pacing adding to our pleasure. The *Sinfonia concertante* is very enjoyable too, if perhaps slightly less distinctive. The finale is infectious in its liveliness, its rhythms buoyantly pointed. Again, a good balance and excellent sound.

Violin concertos Nos. 4, K.218; 5 (Turkish), K.219.
*** Nimbus Dig. NI 5009. Oscar Shumsky, SCO, Yan Pascal Tortelier.

Shumsky's performances with the Scottish Chamber Orchestra have the advantage of being totally unaffected, natural and full of character. Yan Pascal Tortelier secures a very alive and thoroughly musical response from the orchestra. The recording is nicely balanced.

Violin concertos Nos. 4 in D, K.218; 5 in A (Turkish), K.219; Adagio in E, K.261; Rondos Nos. 1 in B flat, K.269; 2 in C, K.373.
☞ (M) **(*) EMI CDM7 64868-2 [id.]. David Oistrakh, BPO.

David Oistrakh's performances come from his complete set, recorded in 1970/71. The remastering has lightened the sound and the touch of rhythmic heaviness in the accompaniments from the Berlin Philharmonic is less striking. The slow movement of K.219 is particularly fine, and so too is the finale. The three shorter concertante works also show the soloist at his finest; though the accompaniment for the *Adagio*, K.261, remains richly upholstered, this is played very beautifully. With 77 minutes of music this is excellent value, for the soloist is truthfully caught and the balance is convincing.

Violin concerto No. 5 in A (Turkish), K.219.
(M) *** BMG/RCA GD 87869 [7869-2-RG]. Heifetz with CO – *String quintet, K.516* etc. ***

Marvellously exhilarating Mozart from Heifetz, though his actual entry in the first movement is quite ethereal. He directs the accompanying group himself, the only time he did so on record. The early (1954) stereo is fully acceptable and the performance memorable, with the crystalline clarity of articulation matched by warmth of timbre and aristocratic phrasing.

(i) *Concertone in C, K.190;* (ii) *Sinfonia concertante in E flat, for violin, viola and orchestra, K.364.*
⊛ *** DG 415 486-2 [id.]. Perlman, Zukerman, Israel PO, Mehta.
*** Sony Dig. SK 47693 [id.]. Cho-Liang Lin, Jaime Laredo, ECO, Leppard.
☞ **(*) BMG/RCA Dig. 09026 60467-2 [id.]. Vladimir Spivakov, with (i) Boris Garlitski; (ii) Shlomo Mintz; Moscow Virtuosi.

The DG version of the *Sinfonia concertante* was recorded in Tel Aviv at the Huberman Festival in

December 1982. It is balanced with the soloists a fraction too near the microphones. The performance is in a special class and is an example of 'live' recording at its most magnetic, with the inspiration of the occasion caught on the wing. Zubin Mehta is drawn into the music-making and accompanies most sensitively. The *Concertone* is also splendidly done; the ear notices the improvement in the sound-balance of the studio recording of this work. But the *Sinfonia concertante*, with the audience incredibly quiet, conveys an electricity rarely caught on record.

Cho-Liang Lin's outstanding performance of the *Sinfonia concertante* is also mandatory listening. The playing has great finesse and style, and Lin makes a natural partnership with Laredo. Neil Black (oboe) and Charles Tunnell (cello) add to the distinction of the *Concertone*. The recording is reverberant, which brings a large-scale orchestral image, but it is fuller and smoother than the DG alternative.

Highly accomplished playing from Vladimir Spivakov and Shlomo Mintz on the viola. Mintz is by far the stronger personality of the two and produces a big, rich and creamy sound which is in danger of outbalancing Spivakov's leaner timbre. This does not seriously challenge the recent Lin/Laredo set on Sony, or other first recommendations, but is eminently vital and musicianly, as is the playing of the Moscow Virtuosi both in the *Sinfonia concertante* and in the *Concertone*. Boris Garlitski is Spivakov's excellent partner in the latter, and the oboist Mikhail Evstigoreev is worth special mention for his purity of tone and style. Both performances give pleasure but do not resonate in the memory in the way that classic accounts do. The recordings, made in the Herkulessaal in Munich, are clean and well focused.

Dances and Marches

Contredanses: La Bataille, K.535; Das Donerwetter, K.534; Les filles malicieuses, K.610; Der Sieg vom Helden Koburg, K.587; Il trionfo delle donne, K.607. Gallimathias musicum (quodlibet), K.32; 6 German dances, K.567; 3 German dances, K.605; German dance: Die Leyerer, K.611. March in D, K.335/1. A Musical joke, K.522.
*** DG Dig. 429 783-2 [id.]. Orpheus CO.

A splendid sampler of the wit and finesse, to say nothing of the high quality of entertainment, provided by Mozart's dance music, which kept people on their feet till dawn at masked balls in the 1780s and early 1790s. The playing of the Orpheus group is winningly polished, flexible and smiling, and they bring off the *Musical joke* with considerable flair, both in the gentle fun of the *Adagio cantabile*, which is exquisitely played, and in the outrageous grinding dissonance of the 'wrong notes' at the end. First-class sound, fresh, transparent and vividly immediate.

Complete Mozart Edition, Volume 6: La Chasse, KA.103/K.299d; Contredanses, K.101; K.123; K.267; K.269b; K.462; (Das Donnerwetter) K.534; (La Bataille) K.535; 535a; (Der Sieg vom Helden Koburg) K.587; K.603; (Il trionfo delle donne) K.607; (Non più andrai) K.609; K.610; Gavotte, K.300; German dances, K.509; K.536; K.567; K.571; K.586; K.600; K.602; K.605; Ländler, K.606; Marches, K.214; K.363; K.408; K.461; Minuets, K.61b; K.61g/2; K.61h; K.94, 103, 104, 105; K.122; K.164; K.176; K.315g; K.568; K.585; K.599; K.601; K.604; Minuets with Contredanses, K.463; Overture & 3 Contredanses, K.106.
⊛ (M) *** Ph. 422 506-2 (6). V. Mozart Ens., Willi Boskovsky.

Much of the credit for this remarkable undertaking should go to its expert producer, Erik Smith, who, besides providing highly stylish orchestrations for numbers without Mozart's own scoring, illuminates the music with some of the most informative and economically written notes that ever graced a record. The CD transfers preserve the excellence of the mid-1960s sound. The collector might feel that he or she is faced here with an *embarras de richesses* with more than 120 *Minuets*, nearly 50 *German dances* and some three dozen *Contredanses*, but Mozart's invention is seemingly inexhaustible, and the instrumentation is full of imaginative touches.

2 Contredanses, K.603; Contredanse, K.610; 19 German Dances, K.571/1–6; K.600/1–6; K.602/1–4; K.605/1–3; Marches: in D, K.335/1; in C & D, K.408/1–3; 10 Minuets, K.599/1–6; K.601/1–4.
(M) *** Decca 430 634-2 [id.]. V. Mozart Ens., Willi Boskovsky.

A self-recommending single-disc selection from Boskovsky's admirable survey of Mozart's dance music. The selection, of course, includes the famous *Sleigh ride* (within K.605) which has some superb posthorn playing, and there are other special effects, notably the charming hurdy-gurdy of K.602. The transfers are impeccable.

6 German dances, K.571; Les petits riens: ballet music, K.299b; Serenade No. 13 (Eine kleine Nachtmusik), K.525.
*** Erato/Warner Dig. 2292 45198-2 [id.]. SCO, Leppard.

An excellent collection. The performance of *Les petits riens* is delightful, spirited and polished, and the *German dances* are no less lively and elegant; the famous *Nachtmusik* is nicely proportioned and very well played. The sound is especially believable on CD.

12 German dances, K.586; 6 German dances, K.600; 4 German dances, K.602; 3 German dances, K.605.
(BB) *** Naxos Dig. 8.550412 [id.]. Capella Istropolitana, Johannes Wildner.

Fresh, bright, unmannered performances of some of the dance music Mozart wrote right at the end of his life. The playing is excellent and the recording is bright and full. An excellent super-bargain alternative to the Boskovsky Decca CD.

Complete Mozart Edition, Volume 45: *'Rarities and curiosities': Contredanses in B flat & D* (completed Smith); *The London Sketchbook:* (i) *3 Contredanses in F; 2 Contredanses in G; 6 Divertimenti.* (ii) *Wind divertimenti* arr. from operas: *Don Giovanni* (arr. Triebensee); *Die Entführung aus dem Serail* (arr. Wendt) & (i) *March, K 384.* (i; iii) *Rondo in E flat for horn and orchestra, K 371* (completed Smith); (iv) *Larghetto for piano and wind quintet, K 452a;* (v) *Modulating prelude in F/E min.* (vi) *Tantum ergo in B flat, K 142; in D, K 197;* (vii) *Idomeneo: Scene & rondo.* (viii) *Musical dice game, K.516.*
(M) *** Ph. 422 545-2 (3) [id.]. (i) ASMF, Marriner; (ii) Netherlands Wind Ens.; (iii) Timothy Brown; cond. Sillito; (iv) Uchida, Black, King, Farrell, O'Neil; (v) Erik Smith (harpsichord); (vi) Frimmer, Leipzig R. Ch. & SO, Schreier; (vii) Mentzler, Hendricks, Bav. RSO, C. Davis; (viii) Marriner & Smith.

The first CD includes the innocent little piano pieces from the child Mozart's 'London Notebook'. Erik Smith has orchestrated them and, if the results may not be important, they charm the ear at least as much as Mozart's early symphonies, with many unexpected touches. Marriner and the Academy are ideal performers and the 1971 recording is warm and refined. Then come the arrangements for wind of selections from two key operas, elegantly played by the Netherlands Wind Ensemble. Finally come the rarities and curiosities, the *Rondo for horn and orchestra* with the missing 60 bars (discovered only in 1989) now added, and the other music made good by Erik Smith. There is a curious finale in which Erik Smith and Sir Neville Marriner participate (with spoken comments) in a *Musical dice game* to decide the order of interchangeable phrases in a very simple musical composition. The result, alas, is something of a damp squib.

Divertimenti and Serenades

Complete Mozart Edition, Volume 4: *Divertimenti for strings Nos. 1–3, K.136/8; Divertimenti for small orchestra Nos. 1 in E flat, K.113; 7 in D, K.205* (with *March in D, K.290); 10 in F, K.247* (with *March in F, K.248); 11 in D, K.251; 15 in B flat, K.287; 17 in D, K.334* (with *March in D, K.445); A Musical joke, K.622; Serenade (Eine kleine Nachtmusik), K.525.*
(M) *** Ph. Dig. 422 504-2 (5) [id.]. ASMF CO.

This is one of the most attractive of all the boxes in the Philips Mozart Edition. The music itself is a delight, the performances are stylish, elegant and polished, while the digital recording has admirable warmth and realistic presence and definition.

Divertimenti for strings Nos. 1–2, K.136/7; Serenades Nos. 6 (Serenata notturna), K.239; 13 (Eine kleine Nachtmusik), K.525.
*** Capriccio 10185 [id.]. Salzburg Mozarteum Camerata Academica, Végh.

Delightfully bold, fresh and characterful performances from the Salzburg group, very well recorded. Only in the slow movement of *Eine kleine Nachtmusik*, taken rather slowly, is the playing a shade less refined. Curiously, Végh changes the regular order of movements in K.137, making it a conventional fast-slow-fast piece, though neither the label nor the note recognizes the change.

Complete Mozart Edition, Volume 5: *Divertimentos for wind Nos. 3 in E flat, K.166; 4 in B flat, K.186; 6 in C, K.188; 8 in F, K.213; 9 in B flat K.240; 12 in E flat, K.252; 13 in F, K.253; 14 in B flat, K.270; 16 in E flat, K.289; in E flat, K. Anh. 226; in B flat, K. Anh. 227; Divertimentos for 3 basset horns, K.439b/1–5; Duos for 2 horns, K.487/1–12; Serenades for wind No. 10 in B flat, K.361; 11 in E flat, K.375; 12 in C min., K.388; Adagios: in F; B flat, K.410–11.*
(M) *** Ph. Analogue/Dig. 422 505-2 (6) [id.]. Holliger Wind Ens. (or members of); Netherlands Wind Ens., De Waart (or members of); ASMF, Marriner or Laird.

Mozart's wind music, whether in the ambitious *Serenades* or the simpler *Divertimenti*, brings a naturally felicitous blending of timbre and colour unmatched by any other composer. It seems that even when writing for the simplest combination of wind instruments, Mozart is incapable of being dull. The playing of the more ambitious works is admirably polished and fresh, and it is interesting to note that Holliger's group provides a stylishly light touch and texture with the principal oboe dominating, while the blending of the Netherlanders is somewhat more homogeneous, though the effect is still very pleasing.

Divertimenti Nos. 7 in D, K.205; 17 in D, K.334; March in D, K.290.
(B) *** Hung. White Label HRC 080 [id.]. Liszt CO, Rolla or Sándor.

An outstanding bargain coupling of two of Mozart's finest *Divertimenti*, in stylish chamber orchestra versions, elegantly played and truthfully recorded in a most pleasing acoustic. K.334 is perhaps the most familiar of all Mozart's large-scale works in this form, and its famous Minuet has more natural rhythmic pulse here than in the Decca version by members of the Vienna Octet, now withdrawn.

Divertimenti Nos. 10 in F, K.247; 11 in D, K.331.
**(*) Capriccio 10 203 [id.]. Salzburg Mozarteum Camerata Academica, Végh.

The playing, as in Végh's previous issues, has striking freshness and vitality; these are chamber orchestral performances on modern instruments, but the scale is admirable and the resonance adds a feeling of breadth. Although slow movements tend to be on the slow side, while not lacking grace, allegros sparkle and have dash without ever seeming hurried, even if ensemble isn't always absolutely immaculate.

Divertimento No. 11 in D, K.251; Serenade No. 9 in D (Posthorn), K.320; 2 Marches in D, K.335/1–2.
☞ **(*) Sony Dig. SK 53277 [id.]. BPO, Claudio Abbado.

Abbado uses a modest chamber group from the orchestra for the *Divertimento* and larger forces for the *Posthorn Serenade*. The playing is lively and cultivated, with plenty of rhythmic character and much finesse from the strings and a charming delicacy from the woodwind in the *concertante* movement of the *Serenade*. In the first Trio of the second Minuet of the latter work, Andrea Blau plays what sounds very like a treble recorder, a curious but effective change of colour. This is an enjoyable concert, very well recorded (the serenade at a live performance), but a smaller scale can be even more effective in this repertoire.

Divertimento No. 17; Divertimento for strings No. 1, K.136.
*** Denon Dig C37 7080 [id.]. Augmented Berlin Philh. Qt.

Divertimento No. 17; Notturno (Serenade) in D, K.286; Serenade No. 13 in G (Eine kleine Nachtmusik), K.525.
(M) *** Decca 430 496-2. ASMF, Marriner.

Mozart's innocently tricky *Notturno for four orchestras*, with its spatial interplay, is here played with superb style and is very well recorded. The *Divertimento*, equally, finds the Academy of St Martin's at its peak, relishing the technical problems of co-ordinating music which is often performed by solo strings and playing with great finesse.

On Denon, a hardly less successful account from the augmented Berlin Philharmonia Quartet. The music-making is polished, spirited and full of warmth. The *String divertimento* is equally attractive but makes a less substantial encore than the ASMF programme. The digital recording is fresh and believable.

Galimathias musicum (Quodlibet), K.32; Wind divertimenti (arr. from operas by Johann Wendt): *Die Entführung aus dem Serail; Le nozze di Figaro.*
(BB) *** HM/BMG VD 77576 [id.]. Coll. Aur.

It is good to have a fine, inexpensive version of Mozart's engaging *Quodlibet* (written at the tender age of ten), coupled with the entertaining Wendt wind arrangements, which select the best tunes from two favourite operas. *Le nozze di Figaro* overture sounds very personable here, but the *Overture* for *Die Entführung* is cut back to 1½ minutes. The account of the *Galimathias musicum* is pleasingly sprightly. The variety of the scoring in this series of seventeen vignettes is amazing: there is some fine writing for solo oboe and horns, an engaging harpsichord solo, plus a remarkable fugato finale. Good, natural sound.

Complete Mozart Edition, Volume 25: (i) *Idomeneo* (ballet music), *K.367;* (ii) *Les petits riens* (ballet), *K.299b; Music for a pantomime (Pantalon und Colombine), K.446* (completed and orch. Beyer); *Sketches for a ballet intermezzo, K.299c* (completed and orch. Erik Smith); (iii) *Thamos, King of Egypt* (incidental music), *K.345.*

(M) *** Ph. 422 525-2 (2) [id.]. (i) Netherlands CO, David Zinman; (ii) ASMF, Marriner; (iii) Eickstädt, Pohl, Büchner, Polster, Adam, Berlin R. Ch. & State O, Klee.

This volume collects together Mozart's theatre music and makes a particularly enticing package. Zinman and his Netherlanders give a neatly turned account of the ballet from *Idomeneo*, musical and spirited. Marriner takes over with modern digital sound for *Les petits riens* and the two novelties, and the ASMF playing has characteristic elegance and finesse. The *Sketches for a ballet intermezzo* survive only in a single-line autograph, but Erik Smith's completion and scoring provide a series of eight charming vignettes, most with descriptive titles, ending with a piquant *Tambourin.* The music for *Pantalon and Columbine* (more mime than ballet) survives in the form of a first violin part, and Franz Beyer has skilfully orchestrated it for wind and strings, using the first movement of the *Symphony*, K.84, as the overture and the last movement of *Symphony*, K.120, as the finale. Beautifully played as it is here, full of grace and colour, this is a real find and the digital recording is first rate. *Thamos, King of Egypt* is marvellous music which it is good to have on record, particularly in such persuasive hands as these. The choral singing is impressive and the orchestral playing is excellent.

Masonic funeral music: see also below, in VOCAL MUSIC, under Complete Mozart Edition, Volume 22

A Musical joke, K.522.
*** Erato/Warner Dig. 2292 45199-2 [id.]. Paillard CO, Paillard – L. MOZART: *Cassation* etc. ***

(i) *A Musical Joke, K.522;* (ii) *Notturno for 4 orchestras, K.286; Serenades Nos. 6 (Serenata notturna), K.239;* (iii) *13 in G (Eine kleine Nachtmusik), K.525.*
(M) *** Decca 430 259-2; *430 259-4.* V. Mozart Ens., Boskovsky.

Boskovsky's recordings were made in the Sofiensaal in 1968–9 and 1978 (K.239 and K.286); in remastered form they all sound wonderfully fresh and realistic. We have often praised this version of *Eine kleine Nachtmusik* for its grace and spontaneity – one has the impression that one is hearing the piece for the first time – and the same comment could be applied to the string playing in the *Musical joke* (especially the delectable Minuet and the neat, zestful finale which ends with spectacular dissonance). The *Notturno for four orchestras* is a less inspired piece, but its spatial echoes are ingeniously contrived and their perspective admirably conveyed by the recording.

Happily paired with a high-spirited version of Leopold Mozart's *Toy symphony*, Paillard's account of Mozart's fun piece makes the most of its outrageous jokes, with the horns in the opening movement boldly going wrong and the final discordant clash sounding positively cataclysmic; yet it takes into account the musical values, too.

Notturno for four orchestras, K.286; Serenade No. 6 (Serenata notturna), K.239; Serenade No. 13 (Eine kleine Nachtmusik), K.525.
*** O-L Dig. 411 720-2 [id.]. AAM, Hogwood.

In *Eine kleine Nachtmusik* Christopher Hogwood uses an additional minuet that Mozart composed in collaboration with his English pupil, Thomas Attwood. All the repeats in every movement save one are observed – which is perhaps too much of a good thing. The performance is given one instrument to a part and is sprightly and alive. The *Serenata notturna* and the *Notturno for four orchestras* are for larger forces and are given with considerable panache. Technically, this is first class.

Overtures: *Apollo et Hyacinthus; Bastien und Bastienne; La clemenza di Tito; Così fan tutte; Don Giovanni; Die Entführung aus dem Serail; La finta giardiniera; Idomeneo; Lucio Silla; Mitridate, rè di Ponto; Le nozze di Figaro; Il rè pastore; Der Schauspieldirektor; Die Zauberflöte.*
(BB) *** Naxos Dig. 8.550185; *4550185* [id.]. Capella Istropolitana, Barry Wordsworth.

Wordsworth follows up his excellent series of Mozart symphonies for Naxos with this generous collection of overtures, no fewer than 14 of them, arranged in chronological order and given vigorous, stylish performances. In Italian overture form, *Mitridate* and *Lucio Silla*, like miniature symphonies, have separate tracks for each of their three contrasted sections. Very well recorded, the disc is highly recommendable at super-bargain price.

Les Petits Riens: Overture and ballet music.
☞ (M) *** Decca 436 782-2 [id.]. V Mozart Ens., Boskovsky – BEETHOVEN: *Contretänze* etc. **(*)

This beautifully elegant and polished performance of some of Mozart's most delightful ballet music was originally part of Boskovsky's complete survey of the dance music, made for Decca in the late 1960s. With first-rate vintage sound, the effect is enchanting.

Serenades Nos. 3 in D, K.185; 4 in D (Colloredo), K.203.
(BB) *** Naxos Dig. 8.550413; 4550413 [id.]. Salzburg CO, Harald Nerat.

Well-played, nicely phrased and musical accounts on Naxos, recorded in a warm, reverberant acoustic, but one in which detail clearly registers. The Salzburg Chamber Orchestra has real vitality, and most readers will find these accounts musically satisfying and very enjoyable.

Serenades Nos. 3 in D, K.185; 9 in D (Posthorn), K.320.
☞ (M) *** Decca 440 036-2 [id.]. V. Mozart Ens., Willi Boskovsky.

Boskovsky's performance of the *Posthorn Serenade* is renowned for its natural musicality and sense of sparkle, and the earlier work is similarly stylish. The CD transfer is a shade dry in the matter of string timbre, but there is bloom on the wind, detail is clean and the posthorn's modest contribution is tangible in its presence.

Serenades Nos. 6 in D (Serenata notturna), K.239; 7 in D (Haffner), K.250.
*** Telarc Dig. CD 80161 [id.]. Prague CO, Mackerras.

In Mackerras's coupling the playing is lively and brilliant, helped by warm recorded sound, vivid in its sense of presence, except that the reverberant acoustic clouds the tuttis a little. The violin soloist, Oldrich Viček, is very much one of the team under the conductor rather than a virtuoso establishing his individual line. By omitting repeats in the *Haffner*, Mackerras leaves room for the other delightful *Serenade*, just as haunting, with the terracing between the solo string quartet (in close focus) and the full string band aptly underlined.

Serenades Nos. 6 in D (Serenata notturna), K.239; 9 in D (Posthorn), K.320.
*** Novalis Dig. 150 013-2 [id.]. Bav. RSO, C. Davis.

Davis secures consistently spirited and responsive playing from the Bavarian Radio Orchestra. With apt tempi and a fine sense of spontaneity throughout, this is very refreshing. The *Serenata notturna* is also well done, if without quite the sparkle of K.320 – here the backwardly balanced drums sound a shade too resonant.

Serenades Nos. 6 in D (Serenata notturna), K.239; 13 in G (Eine kleine Nachtmusik), K.525.
(B) *** Pickwick Dig. PCD 861; *CIMPC 861* [id.]. Serenata of London – ELGAR: *Serenade;* GRIEG: *Holberg suite.* ***

The performance of the *Night music* by the Serenata of London is as fine as any available. There is not a suspicion of routine here; indeed the players, for all the excellence of their ensemble, give the impression of coming to the piece for the first time. The *Serenata notturna* is perhaps not quite so inspired a work, but these excellent players make a good case for it and are agreeably sprightly whenever given the opportunity. The recording has striking naturalness and realism; this is an outstanding CD bargain.

Serenades Nos. 6 in D (Serenata notturna), K.239; 13 (Eine kleine Nachtmusik), K.525; Serenade for wind No. 12 in C min., K.388.
☞ (M) **(*) DG Dig. 439 524-2 [id.]. Orpheus CO.

The *Serenata notturna*, which can easily sound bland, has a fine sparkle here. The famous *Night music*, however, is rather lacking in charm with a very brisk opening movement, alert enough and very polished, but somewhat unbending. The *Wind serenade* restores the balance of excellence, alert and sympathetic and full of character. The digital recording is first class throughout.

Serenade No. 7 in D (Haffner), K.250; March in D, K.249.
*** Ph. Dig. 416 154-2 [id.]. I. Brown, ASMF, Marriner.

A spacious, yet warm and polished account of the *Haffner serenade* from Marriner and his Academy players, with Iona Brown making a superb contribution in the concertante violin role. There is sparkle here as well as expressive grace.

Serenade No. 9 in D (Posthorn), K.320; 2 Marches in D, K.335/1–2.
☞ (M) ** Teldec/Warner Dig. 4509 92149-2 [id.]. Dresden State O, Harnoncourt.

Serenade No. 9 in D (Posthorn), K.320; A Musical joke, K.522.
(BB) *** HM/BMG VD 77544 [77544-2-RV]. Coll. Aur., Franzjosef Maier.

The Collegium Aureum period-instrument version of the *Posthorn Serenade* is sensitive and vital and never sounds pedantic. Indeed the woodwind sounds in the first-movement *Allegro con spirito* are full of character and quite delightful in the concertante, *Andante grazioso*. The remastered recording (from 1976), made in the spacious acoustics of Schloss Kirchheim, gives the players a striking presence. The *Musical joke* (recorded in 1979) is effectively presented on a chamber sextet. The use of one instrument to each part is especially telling in the vivacious finale.

The Dresden State Orchestra, not surprisingly, play well for Harnoncourt and produce a certain overt charm, but the ample Dresden acoustic helps to inflate the performances, which are quite unlike those we are used to from this conductor. Boskovsky is altogether fresher and offers a much more substantial coupling (see above).

Serenades Nos. 9 in D (Posthorn); 13 (Eine kleine Nachtmusik), K.525.
**(*) Telarc CD 10108 [id.]. Prague CO, Mackerras.

(i) *Serenades Nos. 9 in D (Posthorn), K.320; 13 in G (Eine kleine Nachtmusik), K.525;* (ii) *6 German dances, K.509; Minuet in C, K.409.*
☞ (M) **(*) Sony SBK 48266 [id.]. (i) Cleveland O, George Szell; (ii) LSO, Leinsdorf.

The Prague strings have great warmth and Mackerras gets vital results from his Czech forces. Rhythms are lightly sprung and the phrasing is natural in every way. The Telarc acoustic is warm and spacious with a wide dynamic range (some might feel it is too wide for this music), and most ears will find the effect agreeable.

Marvellously vivacious playing from the Clevelanders in the *Posthorn Serenade*, especially in the exhilarating *presto* finale, yet there is no lack of tenderness in the *concertante* third movement marked *Andante grazioso*. *Eine kleine Nachtmusik* is similarly polished and vital, and in both works the Severance Hall acoustic provides a full ambience, but it is a pity that the close balance means a reduced dynamic range. Even so, this is music-making of great character. Leinsdorf's *German dances* make a lively bonus, if not as distinctive as the Szell performances.

Serenade No. 10 in B flat for 13 wind instruments, K.361.
*** ASV Dig. CDCOE 804 [id.]. COE Wind Soloists, Schneider.
*** Ph. Dig. 412 726-2 [id.]. ASMF, Marriner.
**(*) Accent ACC 68642D [id.]. Octophorus, Kuijken.
(B) **(*) Hung. White Label HRC 076 [id.]. Hungarian State Op. Wind Ens., Ervin Lukacs.

Serenade No. 10 in B flat for 13 wind instruments, K.361; Divertimento in F (for 2 oboes, 2 horns & 2 bassoons), K.213.
☞ (M) **(*) Chan. Dig. CHAN 6575. SNO Wind Ens., Paavo Järvi.

The brilliant young soloists of the Chamber Orchestra of Europe, inspired by the conducting of Alexander Schneider, give an unusually positive, characterful reading. Right at the start, the flourishes from the first clarinet are far more effective when played as here, not literally, but with Schneider leading them on to the first forte chord from the full ensemble. From then on the individual artistry of the players is most winning. The sound is exceptionally vivid and faithful.

The Marriner version fits very stylishly in the Academy's series of Mozart wind works, characteristically refined in its ensemble, with matching of timbres and contrasts beautifully judged, both lively and graceful with rhythms well sprung and speeds well chosen, yet with nothing mannered about the result. Full, warm recording that yet allows good detail.

On period instruments Barthold Kuijken directs his talented team in an authentic performance where the distinctive character of eighteenth-century instruments brings a sparer, lighter texture, as it should. Speeds tend to be on the cautious side but the liveliness of the playing makes up for that. The recording adds to the clarity.

Of the bargain versions of Mozart's large-scale wind serenade the Hungaroton is the other one to go for. The blending of the wind players from the Hungarian State Opera is impressive and their performance has an attractively robust character with buoyant allegros, and plenty of flexibility in slow movements. The sound is vivid within an attractive ambience.

The SNO Wind Ensemble's version under Paavo Järvi (son of a famous father) is enjoyably spontaneous-sounding, though ensemble is not quite as polished as in the finest versions. Speeds are well chosen, and the recording is warm, though the detail is sometimes masked by the lively acoustic. The little *Divertimento* makes an attractive bonus. Not a first choice but, at mid-price and with digital recording, worth considering.

Serenades Nos. 10 in B flat; 12 in C min., K.388.
☞ (B) *** HM Dig. HMA 1903051 [id.]. Budapest Wind Ens., Zoltán Kocsis.

A particularly winning bargain coupling from Harmonia Mundi, beautifully recorded and directed with fine spirit by Zoltán Kocsis. The Budapest wind players blend beautifully in slow movements and phrase with pleasingly simple, expressive warmth; allegros are infectiously buoyant, especially the Rondo finale of the so-called *Grand Partita in B flat*, which also has a satisfyingly full sonority. Both works contain a notable set of variations: in K.361 it is the penultimate movement, in K.388 the finale, and the colour and diversity of the playing make a high point in each work. Kocsis himself composes a brief oboe cadenza for the latter and a clarinet cadenza for the lovely *Romance* in K.361.

Serenades for wind Nos. 11 in E flat, K.375; 12 in C min., K.388.
*** ASV Dig. CDCOE 802 [id.]. COE, Schneider.

With Schneider as a wise and experienced guide, the COE Wind give performances which combine brilliance and warmth with a feeling of spontaneity. K.375 in particular is a delight, as genial as it is characterful, conveying the joy of the inspiration. K.388 might have been more menacing at the C minor opening, but the result is most persuasive, with excellent digital sound set against a warm but not confusing acoustic.

Serenade No. 13 in G (Eine kleine Nachtmusik), K.525.
*** Ph. Dig. 410 606-2 [id.]. I Musici (with concert of Baroque music***).

I Musici play the music with rare freshness, giving the listener the impression of hearing the work for the first time. The playing is consistently alert and sparkling, with the *Romanze* particularly engaging. The recording is beautifully balanced.

Sinfonia concertante for violin, viola and orchestra in E flat, K.364.
☞ (M) ** EMI CDM7 64632-2 [id.]. David & Igor Oistrakh, BPO, D. Oistrakh – BRAHMS: *Violin concerto.* **(*)

Although the solo playing is rich-timbred and beautifully matched, the orchestral accompaniment polished and the recording full and pleasing, there is a curiously literal approach to the music-making here, and the imaginative spark which can bring this glorious work fully to life is missing.

Complete Mozart Edition, Volume 21: (i) *Sonatas for organ and orchestra (Epistle sonatas) Nos. 1–17* (complete). *Adagio & allegro in F min., K.594; Andante in F, K.616; Fantasia in F min., K.608.*
(M) **(*) Ph. 422 521-2 (2). Daniel Barenboim (organs at Stift Wilhering, Linz, Austria; Schlosspfarrkirche, Obermarchtal, Germany – K.594; K.608); (i) German Bach Soloists, Helmut Winschermann.

The *Epistle sonatas* derive their name from the fact that they were intended to be heard between the Epistle and Gospel in the Mass. Admittedly they are not great music or even first-class Mozart; however, played with relish they make a strong impression. The final *Sonata*, K.263, becomes a fully fledged concerto. The set is completed with the other works by Mozart which are usually heard on the organ, and here Barenboim's registration is particularly appealing.

Sonatas Nos. 1–17 (Epistle sonatas) for organ and chamber orchestra.
☞ (BB) **(*) Naxos Dig. 8.550512 [id.]. János Sebestyén, Budapest Ferenc Erkel CO.

While it is understood that, apart from No. 16 in C, K.329, which has a specific solo part, the organ is not intended as a solo instrument in these *Chiesa sonatas*, it seems perverse to balance the instrument so that it blends in completely with the orchestral texture, as the Naxos engineers have done. Otherwise these alert, polished and nicely scaled performances could hardly be improved on and, apart from the controversial matter of the relationship of the organ to the orchestra, the recording is first class.

SYMPHONIES

Symphonies Nos. 1–47 (including alternative versions); in C, K.35; in D, K.38; in F, K.42a; in B flat, K.45b; in D, K.46a (K.51); in D, K.62a (K.100); in B flat, K.74g (K.216); in F, K.75; in G, K.75b (K.110); in D, K.111a; in D, K.203, 204 & 196 (121); in G, K.425a (K.444); in A min. (Odense); in G (New Lambacher).

(M) **(*) O-L Analogue/Dig. 430 639-2 (19) [id.]. AAM, Schröder, Hogwood.

With Jaap Schröder leading the admirably proportioned string group (9.8.4.3.2) and Christopher Hogwood at the keyboard, this is a remarkably successful joint enterprise. The playing has great style, warmth and polish and, if intonation is not always absolutely refined, that seemed only to be expected with old instruments. The survey is complete enough to include No. 37 – in fact the work of Michael Haydn but with a slow introduction by Mozart. The *Lambacher* and *Odense Symphonies* are also here, plus alternative versions, with different scoring, of No. 40; while the *Paris Symphony* is given two complete performances with alternative slow movements. These recordings are also available in seven separate boxes of two or (mainly) three CDs, but they are still offered at premium price.

Symphonies Nos. 1 in E in E flat, K.16; in F, K.19a; 4 in D, K.19; 5 in B flat, K.22; in G, K.45a; 6 in F, K.43; 7 in D, K.45; 8 in D, K.48; 9 in C, K.73; in F, K.76; in B flat, K.45b; in D, K.81; in D, K.97; in D, K.95; 11 in D, K.84; in B flat, K. Anh. 214; in F, K.75; in C, K.96; 10 in G, K.74; 12 in G, K.110; 13 in F, K.112; 14 in A, K.114; 15 in G, K.124.
☞ *** DG Dig. 437 792-2 (4) [id.]. E. Concert, Pinnock.

This is repertoire that Hogwood pioneered on original instruments in a most arresting way. But Pinnock's Mozartian enterprise has the advantage of some years' experience of authentic performance, and certain exaggerated elements have been absorbed into a smoother but not less vital playing style. Moreover players have accommodated themselves to 'authentic' manners, and intonation has improved very considerably. So in these new performances we have greater polish, smoother and less edgy violins, and even a hint of vibrato. Slow movements have more lyrical feeling. These four discs explore early Mozartian symphonic territory and show the remarkable advance from the childhood works, which are often rather engaging, to those symphonies written at the beginning of the 1770s when a recognizable Mozartian personality was formed. A clear first choice for authenticists.

Complete Mozart Edition, Volume 1: *Symphonies Nos. 1 in E in E flat, K.16; 4 in D, K.19; in F, K.19a; 5 in B flat, K.22; 6 in F, K.43; 7 in D, K.45; in G (Neue Lambacher), G.16; in G (Alte Lambacher), K.45a; in B flat, K.45b; 8 in D, K.48; 9 in C, K.73; 10 in G, K.74; in F, K.75; in F, K.76; in D, K.81; 11 in D, K.84; in D, K.95; in C, K.96; in D, K.97; 12 in G, K.110; 13 in F, K.112; 14 in A, K.114; 15 in G, K.124; 16 in C, K.128; 17 in G, K.129; 18 in F, K.130; 19 in E flat, K.132* (with alternative slow movement); *20 in D, K.133; in D, K.161 & 163; in D, K.111 & 120; in D, K.196 & 121; in C, K.208 & 102. Minuet in A, K.61g/1.*
(M) *** Ph. 422 501-2 (6) [id.]. ASMF, Marriner.

The reissue, in the Philips Complete Mozart Edition, of Marriner's recordings of the early symphonies confirms the Mozartian vitality of the performances and their sense of style and spontaneity. There are some important additions, notably the *Symphony in F*, K.19a, written when the composer was nine. Also now included are alternative Minuets for the Salzburg *Symphony No. 14 in A*, K.114. The layout remains on six compact discs and the ear is again struck by the naturalness and warm vividness of the transfers. Except perhaps for those who insist on original instruments, the finesse and warmth of the playing here is a constant joy.

Complete Mozart Edition, Volume 2: *Symphonies Nos. 21–36; 37: Adagio maestoso in G, K.44* (Introduction to a symphony by M. Haydn); *38–41; Minuet for a Symphony in C, K.409.*
(M) **(*) Ph. 422 502-2 (6) [id.]. ASMF, Marriner.

*compare p. 747

As with the early works, the later symphonies in the Marriner performances, as reissued in the Philips Mozart Edition, are conveniently laid out on six mid-priced CDs, offered in numerical sequence, without a single symphony having to be divided between discs. However, the over-resonant bass remains in the recording of No. 40 and the *Haffner* (both of which date from 1970, nearly a decade before the rest of the cycle was recorded). Otherwise the transfers are of Philips's best quality, and the performances generally give every satisfaction, even if their style does not show an awareness of the discoveries made – in terms of texture and balance – by the authentic school.

Symphonies Nos. 1 in E flat, K.16; in A min. (Odense), K.16a; 4 in D, K.19; in F, K.19a.
(M) **(*) Unicorn Dig. UKCD 2018. Odense SO, Vetö.

It was in Odense that the lost symphony, K.16a, was discovered by the archivist, Gunnar Thygesen. Alas for everyone's hopes, it seems very unlikely, from stylistic evidence and even the key, A minor, that it is genuine Mozart. It remains a charming work in the *Sturm und Drang* manner, and is well coupled here with an apt group of other early Mozart symphonies, done with warmer tone than those in the Hogwood complete set. First-rate recording.

Symphonies Nos. 1, K.16; 4, K.19, in F, K.19a; 5 in K.22; in G, K.45a; 6–36; 38–41.
☞ (M) *** Telarc Dig. CD 80300 (10) [id.]. Prague CO, Mackerras.
☞ **(*) DG Dig. 435 360-2 (11) [id.]. VPO, Levine.

Mackerras's is an outstanding series, with electrifying performances of the early as well as the later symphonies. Even in the trivial boyhood works there is not a suspicion of routine, with the playing full of dramatic contrasts in rhythm, texture or dynamic. Mackerras has a keen feeling for Mozart style, not least in the slow movements and minuets, which he regularly takes faster than usual. His flowing andantes are consistently stylish too, with performances on modern instruments regularly related to period practice. An outstanding instance comes in the G minor *Andante* of *No. 5 in B flat*, K.22, where Mackerras, fastish and light, makes others seem heavy-handed in this anticipation of romanticism, underlining the harmonic surprises clearly and elegantly. Consistently Mackerras finds light and shade in Mozart's inspirations, both early and late, though some may feel that, with warm reverberation characteristic of this Prague orchestra's recording venue, the scale is too large, particularly in the early symphonies. Harpsichord continuo, where used, is usually well balanced.

Levine directs the Vienna Philharmonic in lively accounts of all the symphonies, both early and late, regularly giving the feeling of new discovery. The players themselves voted to have Levine conducting them in this long series, and plainly they responded keenly. Not surprisingly, in comparison with other modern rivals like Mackerras, the playing seems smooth, with rhythms not always sprung infectiously. In slow movements on occasion the results sound heavy-handed. The set takes an extra disc compared with the Mackerras, but Levine is more generous over repeats, observing them even in the *da capos* of minuets, as Hogwood does in his period-performance set. The DG recording for Levine is aptly scaled, even intimate, but the textures are often relatively opaque. Where used, harpsichord continuo is well balanced.

√ *Symphonies Nos. 13 in F, K.112; 14 in A, K.114; 15 in G, K.124; 16 in C, K.128; 23 in D, K.181; 24 in B flat, K.182.*
☞ (M) *** Decca 436 223-2 [id.]. ASMF, Marriner.

Brisk, fresh, yet gracefully sympathetic performances of four early symphonies, plus two slightly later ones. Nos. 13–16 come from the period after Mozart's initial essays, when he was beginning to imitate rather than to express his own untrammelled if immature genius. However, A major was always a good key for him and No. 14 (with striking horn parts) is made to sound particularly inviting here. No. 16 has a most engaging *Andante*, full of rhythmic character, nicely pointed by the ASMF, and none of this music is without interest. Nos. 23 and 24 belong to the last symphonies that Mozart wrote before the sequence of really great works starts (with Nos. 25 and 29) but they have plenty of spirited invention and No. 23 introduces a charming siciliano oboe solo in its *Andantino grazioso*. This is beautifully played, and both performances are effervescent and finely detailed in their lightness and understanding. Any interpretative freedoms are a positive addition to enjoyment and, with an aptly sized group, splendidly recorded in the late 1960s, the bright CD transfers make a very good case for using modern instruments in these works.

Symphonies Nos. 14 in A, K.114; 15 in G, K.124; 16 in C, K.128; 17 in G, K.129; 18 in F, K.130.
☞ *** Telarc Dig. CD 80242 [id.]. Prague CO, Mackerras.

If you want modern instruments used in performing these sprightly early symphonies, then Mackerras fits the bill rather well. *No. 14 in A* is a particularly fine work (as indeed are all Mozart's A major symphonies) and, like the others here, it receives an invigorating account with brisk Allegros and a strong, one-in-a-bar tempo for the Minuet (this suits the Minuet of *No. 18 in F* even better as it is very folksy). Slow movements, however, are very direct and are pressed onwards, slightly unbending; here some might find Mackerras's approach too austere. The bright recording is resonant, which prevents absolute clarity, but the clean lines of the playing ensure plenty of stimulating impact.

Symphonies No. 19 in E flat, K.132; 20 in D, K.133; 21 in A, K.134; 22 in C, K.162; 23 in D, K.162b.
*** Telarc Dig. CD 80217 [id.]. Prague CO, Mackerras.

Mackerras, having had great success with his Telarc recordings of the later symphonies, is equally lively in these early works from Mozart's Salzburg period. The surprising thing is how fast his speeds tend to be. In one instance the contrast is astonishing, when at a very brisk *Andantino grazioso* Mackerras turns the slow middle movement of No. 23 into a lilting Laendler, quite different from other performances. The recording is reverberant, as in the later symphonies, giving relatively weighty textures; with such light scoring, however, there is ample clarity, with braying horns riding beautifully over the rest.

Symphonies Nos. 21 in A, K.134; 23 in D, K.181; 24 in B flat, K.182; 27 in G, K.199.
*** Erato/Warner Dig. 2292 45544-2 [id.]. Amsterdam Bar. O, Koopman.

Koopman's readings of these delightful early symphonies are much less severe than most on period instruments, and are sparklingly recorded. Helped by the sound-quality, Koopman consistently catches the fun of early Mozart, as in the delectable finale of No. 21. He also brings out the lightness and elegance of slow movements.

Symphonies Nos. 24 in B flat, K.173; 26 in E flat, K.161a; 27 in G, K.161b; 30 in D, K.202.
*** Telarc Dig. CD 80186 [id.]. Prague CO, Mackerras.

With discreet use of harpsichord continuo, Mackerras's readings are consistently stylish in their refreshing Mozart manners. Where in later symphonies Mackerras chooses more relaxed speeds, here he tends to be more urgent, as in the finale of No. 26 or the *Andantino grazioso* slow movement of No. 27, where he avoids the questionable use of muted strings. The reverberation of the recording gives the impression of a fairly substantial orchestra, without loss of detail, and anyone fancying this particular group of early Mozart symphonies need not hesitate.

Symphonies Nos. 25 in G min., K.183; 26 in E flat, K.184; 27 in G, K.199; 29 in A, K.201; 32 in G, K.318.
(M) *** Decca 430 268-2; *430 268-4.* ASMF, Marriner.

With an aptly sized group, very well balanced by the engineers, Marriner secures effervescent performances of the earlier symphonies, especially the little *G minor*, the first of the sequence of really great works. The scale of No. 29 is broad and forward-looking, yet the continuing alertness is matched by lightness of touch, while the imaginative detail of any interpretative freedoms adds positively to the enjoyment.

Symphonies Nos. 25 in G min., K.183; 26 in E flat, K.184; 28 in C, K.200.
(M) ** Teldec/Warner Dig. 4509 91189-2 [id.]. Concg. O, Harnoncourt.

Symphonies Nos. 29 in A, K.201; 30 in D, K.202; 31 in D (Paris).
(M) **(*) Teldec/Warner Dig. 4509 91187-2 [id.]. Concg. O, Harnoncourt.

Symphonies Nos. 32 in G, K.218; 33 in B flat, K.319; 34 in C, K.338.
(M) **(*) Teldec/Warner Dig. 4509 91190-2 [id.]. Concg. O, Harnoncourt.

Harnoncourt's Mozart, for all its merits, is nothing if not eccentric. He secures consistently fine playing from the Royal Concertgebouw Orchestra, but the results are variably successful. Speeds are often extreme. The contrasts in No. 25 are effective, but explosive tuttis bring a somewhat unsettled mood to the earlier symphonies, notably in the *molto presto* first movement of No. 26 and the *Allegro spirito* of No. 28, both markings taken very literally. Minuets also tend to be fast, and the pacing of the slow movement of No. 29 has little feeling of serenity or repose. The *Paris* is given with its alternative slow movement, the second added as a pendant at the end, and is among the most successful performances with beautiful, cleanly articulated playing.

The most successful of the three discs contains a very vital account of the Italian overture structure of *No. 32 in G* (the *Andante's* expressiveness well judged in relation to the vigorously eruptive outer movements), plus Nos. 33 and 34. In No. 33 Harnoncourt overdoes his slowness in the *Andante* but adds to the breadth of the finale by giving the repeats of both halves. It thus becomes the longest movement, but the lively playing ensures that it does not wear out its welcome. No. 34 goes well, too, refreshing and directly dramatic, with tempi unforced. Charm is missing until the finale, which fizzes along, neatly articulated.

The recorded sound is not consistent with the natural acoustics of the Concertgebouw, resonant, yet very bright, with a tendency to fierceness on the brass (which are almost made to sound 'authentic') and strings alike. Altogether stimulating, but not for all tastes.

Symphonies Nos. 25 in G min., K.183; 28 in C, K.200; 29 in A, K.201.
*** Telarc Dig. CD 80165 [id.]. Prague CO, Mackerras.

If you want performances on modern (as opposed to period) instruments, these are at least as fine as any, fresh and light, with transparent textures set against a warm acoustic and with rhythms consistently resilient. Mackerras's speeds are always carefully judged to allow elegant pointing but without mannerism, and the only snag is that second-half repeats are omitted in slow movements, and in the finale too of No. 29.

Symphonies Nos. 25 in G min., K.183; 32 in G, K.318; 41 in C (Jupiter), K.551.
(BB) *** Naxos Dig. 8.550113; *4550113* [id.]. Capella Istropolitana, Barry Wordsworth.

Symphonies Nos. 27 in G, K.199/161b; 33 in B flat, K.319; 36 in C (Linz), K.425.
(BB) *** Naxos Dig. 8.550264; *4550264* [id.]. Capella Istropolitana, Barry Wordsworth.

Symphonies Nos. 28 in C, K.200; 31 in D (Paris), K.297; 40 in G min., K.550.
(BB) *** Naxos Dig. 8.550164; *4550164* [id.]. Capella Istropolitana, Barry Wordsworth.

Symphonies Nos. 29 in A, K.201; 30 in D, K.202; 38 in D (Prague), K.504.
(BB) *** Naxos Dig. 8.550119; *4550119* [id.]. Capella Istropolitana, Barry Wordsworth.

Symphonies Nos. 34 in C, K.338; 35 in D (Haffner), K.385; 39 in E flat, K.543.
(BB) *** Naxos Dig. 8.550186; *4550186* [id.]. Capella Istropolitana, Barry Wordsworth.

Symphonies Nos. 40 in G min., K.550; 41 in C (Jupiter), K.551.
(BB) *** Naxos Dig. 8.550299 [id.]. Capella Istropolitana, Barry Wordsworth.

Barry Wordsworth's series of 15 symphonies on the Naxos super-bargain-priced label brings consistently refreshing and enjoyable performances. The Capella Istropolitana consists of leading members of the Slovak Philharmonic Orchestra of Bratislava; though their string-tone is thinnish, it is very much in scale with the clarity of a period performance but tonally far sweeter. The recording is outstandingly good, with a far keener sense of presence than in most rival versions and with less reverberation to obscure detail in tuttis. Wordsworth observes exposition repeats in first movements, but in the finales only in such symphonies as Nos. 38 and 41, where the movement particularly needs extra scale. In slow movements, as is usual, he omits repeats. He often adopts speeds that are marginally slower than we expect nowadays in chamber-scale performances; but, with exceptionally clean articulation and infectiously sprung rhythms, the results never drag, even if No. 29 is made to sound more sober than usual. In every way these are worthy rivals to the best full-priced versions, and they can be recommended with few if any reservations. Anyone wanting to sample might try the coupling of Nos. 34, 35 and 39 – with the hard-stick timpani sound at the start of No. 39 very dramatic. The *Linz* too is outstanding. For some, the option of having the last two symphonies coupled together will be useful.

Symphonies Nos. 25–36 (Linz); 38 (Prague); 39–40; 41 (Jupiter).
☞ (M) *** EMI Dig. CMS7 63857-2 (6) [Ang. CDC 63857]. ECO, Jeffrey Tate.

Tate is generally smoother in style than Mackerras, but the characterization is marked, with fine detail and clean articulation freshening the result. In all these works he provides a winning combination of affectionate manners, freshness and elegance. Like Mackerras in his brighter, more thrustful account of the *Paris*, Tate provides the alternative *Andante* slow movement, an interesting curiosity, and on CD you can readily programme whichever you prefer. Tate's account of the *Jupiter* has an apt scale which yet allows the grandeur of the work to come out. On the one hand it has the clarity of a chamber orchestra performance, but on the other, with trumpets and drums, its weight of expression never underplays the scale of the argument which originally prompted the unauthorized nickname. In both Nos. 40 and 41 exposition repeats are observed in outer movements, particularly important in the *Jupiter* finale. Tate's keen imagination on detail, as well as over a broad span, consistently conveys the electricity of a live performance. The recording is well detailed, yet has pleasant reverberation, giving the necessary breadth. A fine set overall.

Symphonies Nos 26 in E flat, K.184; 27 in G, K.199; 28 in C, K.200; 30 in D, K.202; 32 in G, K.318.
*** ASV Dig. CDDCA 762 [id.]. LMP, Jane Glover.

Glover's generous coupling of five early symphonies brings typically fresh and direct readings, marked by sharp attack and resilient rhythms, at speeds on the fast side. With tuttis a little weightier than with most rivals, these are brightly enjoyable performances.

Symphonies Nos. 28 in C, K.200; 29 in A, K.201; 30 in D, K.202; 40 in G min., K.550; 41 in C (Jupiter), K.551.
☞ (B) **(*) EMI Dig. CZS7 67564-2 [id.]. ASMF, Marriner.

In his continuing series for EMI, Marriner secures warm and gracious playing from the Academy in the three early symphonies. The spacious acoustic of EMI's No. 1 Studio at Abbey Road adds an agreeable fullness and colour to the orchestral sound, which makes very pleasurable listening; but, with articulation that brings neat rather than sharp rhythmic incisiveness, the effect is somewhat more bland than with Marriner's earlier, Argo (Decca) recordings. Slow movements are very persuasive, in both their delicacy of touch and elegant contours, and the first movement of No. 28 is admirably spirited, with the genial nature of the finale also giving much pleasure. In No. 29 Marriner observes more repeats than before and the performance has an affectionate breadth, with plenty of energy reserved for the last movement. The *Molto allegro* which opens No. 30 has energy without forcefulness, and again the dancing finale brings the most sophisticated lightness of touch. Marriner is at his very best in No. 40, a work he always did very sympathetically. In the last two movements he is strikingly dramatic, with crisper articulation and faster speeds than in his earlier recording for Philips, and this time in the slow movement he observes the first-half repeat. The *Jupiter* is also very well done, but the effect is less charismatic – though, as in the others in this digital series, the recording is first rate.

Symphonies Nos. 28 in C, K.200; 29 in A, K.201; 35 in D (Haffner).
*** Sony Dig. SK 48063 [id.]. BPO, Claudio Abbado.

Though Abbado's Berlin sound is weighty, the results are not just big-scaled but elegant too, with horns whooping out brightly. Abbado is never mannered and his phrasing and pointing of rhythm are delicately affectionate, conveying an element of fun and with speeds never allowed to drag. Slow movements are kept flowing, and finales are hectically fast, but played with such verve and diamond-bright articulation that there is no feeling of breathlessness. The Sony engineers have coped splendidly with the acoustic problems of the Philharmonie to give a full and forward sound, with good presence.

Symphonies Nos. 29–36; 38–41; Divertimento No. 7 in D, K.205; 2 Marches, K.335.
(M) **(*) EMI CZS7 67301-2 (4). ECO, Barenboim.

Barenboim's recordings were made at Abbey Road over a five-year span, between 1966 and 1971. The use of an authentic-sized orchestra of modern instruments ensures that the balance between sections is accurate, although the sound caught by the EMI engineers is forward and full-bodied, with a resonant bass. With fine rhythmic pointing and consistently imaginative phrasing, these performances certainly have a place in the catalogue. Nos. 29 and 34 are particularly successful, and the *Paris* (No. 31) is also given an outstanding performance, the contrasts of mood in the first movement underlined and the finale taken at a hectic tempo that would have sounded breathless with players any less brilliant than the ECO. The box also includes the *D major Serenade*, K.205, which responds well to Barenboim's affectionate treatment, while the two *Marches* are attractively jaunty and colourful.

Symphonies Nos. 29 in A, K.201; 32 in G, K.318; 33 in B flat, K.319; 35 (Haffner), 36 (Linz); 38 (Prague); 39 in E flat, K.543; 40 in G min., K.550; 41 (Jupiter).
(M) *** DG 429 668-2 (3) [id.]. BPO, Karajan.

With Nos. 29, 32 and 33 added to the original LP box, these are beautifully played and vitally alert readings; and the recordings, made between 1966 and 1979, are well balanced and given full, lively transfers to CD. There are details about which some may have reservations, and the opening of the *G minor*, which is a shade faster than in Karajan's earlier, Vienna performance for Decca, many not be quite dark enough for some tastes. But the *Jupiter*, although short on repeats, has weight and power as well as surface elegance.

Symphonies Nos. 29 in A, K.201; 33 in B flat, K.319.
*** Ph. Dig. 412 736-2 [id.]. E. Bar. Soloists, Gardiner.

Although the opening is deceptively gentle, the first movement of John Eliot Gardiner's *A major Symphony* soon develops an athletic strength. Delicacy returns in the *Andante*, nicely proportioned and beautifully played. The account of *No. 33 in B flat* is outstandingly successful and overall this is authenticity with a winning countenance and without the abrasiveness of the Academy of Ancient Music in this repertoire. The recording is fresh and immediate and very well balanced.

Symphonies Nos. 29 in A, K.201; 39 in E flat, K.543; 40 in G min., K.550; 41 (Jupiter), K.551.
☞ (B) *(*) DG Double 437 386-2 (2) [id.]. VSO, Ferenc Fricsay.

Fricsay, normally a reliable Mozart interpreter, is on uneven form here. The tempi of the first two movements of No. 29 are a shade too slow for the comfort of the phrase (especially when the violins as recorded are a trifle shrill) and, although the finale possesses adequate spirit, one feels that recovery is then too late. He then overloads both the *G minor* and the *E flat Symphonies* with nineteenth-century phrasing, tempi and forces. The music-making is undoubtedly alive but the purity of Mozart's lines is at times obscured and the spirit of the music affected. However, the *Jupiter* clearly suits the conductor's temperament more readily. He puts tremendous energy and concentration into this performance, and the first movement has all the breadth and dignity it needs and the finale ample brilliance. In the slow movement there is much to admire in the wind playing, but the strings have less allure. It must be faced that the Vienna Symphony Orchestra is not as good an orchestra as the Philharmonic, and a less-than-ideal recording does not help matters. Even at Double DG price, this is hardly a bargain, especially remembering that the overall playing time is only 109 minutes.

Symphonies Nos. 29 in A, K.201; 40 in G min., K.550; 41 (Jupiter), K.551.
☞ (M) ** EMI CDM7 64327-2 [id.]. BPO, Karajan.

Karajan's EMI recordings are separated by a decade. No. 29 – by far the most impressive – was made in the Grünewaldkirche in 1960. It is a warm, polished performance, realized with much finesse, and it has plenty of life. The recording, balanced by Walter Legge, is also remarkably good. Nos. 40 and 41 were made in the Jesus-Christus Kirche in 1970; the sound is thicker, the effect more resonant and less sharply focused, though the CD transfers are well done. The playing of the orchestra remains a joy in itself and the interpretations are purposeful and considered, but Karajan's earlier performances with the VPO for Decca sound fresher and were made not long after the EMI version of K.201 (433 607-2). However, this latter disc, though in the bargain range, includes only K.550 and K.551.

Symphonies Nos. 31 in D (Paris), K.207; 33 in B flat, K.319; 34 in C, K.338.
**(*) Telarc Dig. CD 80190 [id.]. Prague CO, Mackerras.

Mackerras and the Prague Chamber Orchestra give characteristically stylish and refined performances, clean of attack and generally marked by brisk speeds. As in their accounts of the later symphonies, all repeats are observed – even those in the *da capos* of minuets – and the only snag is that the reverberant Prague acoustic, more than in others of the Telarc series, clouds tuttis: the Presto finale of the *Paris* brings phenomenal articulation of quavers at the start, which then in tuttis disappear in a mush.

(i) *Symphonies Nos. 31 in D (Paris), K.297; 36 in C (Linz), K.425;* (ii) *Overture: Le nozze di Figaro.*
(BB) *** ASV CDQS 6033. (i) LSO; (ii) RPO, Bátiz.

After a sprightly account of the *Figaro overture* from the RPO, the LSO under Bátiz provide two spirited and polished accounts of favourite named symphonies. Tempi in outer movements are brisk, but the *Presto* finale of the *Linz* (for instance) produces some sparkling playing from the strings; and in both slow movements the phrasing is warm and gracious. With excellent digital recording, this makes an enjoyable super-bargain pairing.

Symphonies Nos. 31 in D (Paris), K.297; 36 in C (Linz), K.425; 38 in D (Prague), K.504.
*** ASV Dig. CDDCA 647 [id.]. LMP, Jane Glover.

Jane Glover and the London Mozart Players offer a particularly attractive and generous coupling in the three Mozart symphonies associated with cities. Happily, exposition repeats are observed in the outer movements. The performances are all fresh and vital in traditional chamber style, with little influence from period performance. Tuttis are not always ideally clear on inner detail; but the result is nicely in scale, not too weighty, with the delicacy beautifully light and airy.

Symphonies Nos. 31 in D (Paris), K.297; 36 in C (Linz), K.425; 38 in D (Prague), K.504.
☞ (B) ** Erato/Warner 2292 45938-2 [id.]. Bamberg SO, Guschlbauer.

(i) *Symphonies Nos. 39 in E flat, K.543; 40 in G min., K.550;* (ii) *Serenade No. 13 (Eine kleine Nachtmusik).*
☞ (B) ** Erato/Warner 2292 45939-2 [id.]. (i) Bamberg SO; (ii) Bournemouth Sinf.; Guschlbauer.

Guschlbauer is a brisk, alert Mozartian and his well-drilled orchestra play with considerable brilliance, especially in the *Paris* and *Prague Symphonies*. All the performances are enjoyable, but the *Prague* and *No. 39 in E flat* stand out. The recordings have plenty of brightness and immediacy, and the two discs are fair value at bargain price, if not distinctive.

Symphonies Nos. 32 in G, K.318; 33 in B flat, K.319; 35 in D (Haffner), K.385; 36 in C (Linz), K.425.
(M) *** DG 435 070-2 [id.]. BPO, Karajan.

Here is Karajan's big-band Mozart at its finest. Although there may be slight reservations about the Minuet and Trio of the *Linz*, which is rather slow (and the other minuets are also somewhat stately), overall there is plenty of life here and slow movements show the BPO at their most graciously expressive. The remastered sound is clear and lively, full but not over-weighted.

Symphonies Nos. 32 in G, K.318; 35 in D (Haffner), K.385; 36 in C (Linz), K.425.
☞ (BB) *** Virgin/EMI Dig. VJ7 59679-2 [id.]. SCO, Saraste.

More than most other versions on modern instruments, Saraste's accounts reflect the new lessons of period performance. These are more detached, less sostenuto performances than those of, for example, Jeffrey Tate and the ECO in these works and, with all repeats observed, make an excellent alternative. The recording, helpfully reverberant, yet gives lightness and transparency to textures, conveying an apt chamber scale.

Symphonies Nos. 32 in G, K.318; 35 in D (Haffner), K.385; 39 in E flat, K.543.
*** Telarc Dig. CD 80203 [id.]. Prague CO, Mackerras.
(BB) *** ASV CDQS 6071. ECO, Mackerras.

On Telarc, Mackerras is fresh rather than elegant, yet with rhythms so crisply sprung that there is no sense of rush. His whirling one-in-a-bar treatment of Minuets may disconcert traditionalists, but brings exhilarating results. The third movements of both the *Haffner* and No. 39 become scherzos, not just faster but fiercer than regular minuets, and generally his account of No. 39 is as commanding as his outstanding versions of the last two symphonies. The clanging attack of harpsichord continuo is sometimes disconcerting, but this music-making is very refreshing.

Mackerras's ASV version was recorded digitally, in 1985, before he moved on to make his integral set for Telarc. Mackerras here anticipates the urgent style of the later recordings, especially in the Minuets and, with generally brisk speeds, the ASV readings are attractively fresh and full of momentum. Mackerras rarely seeks to charm, but unfussily presents each movement with undistractingly direct manners. The strong character of the music-making is in no doubt, and the sound is appealingly bright and vivid; at super-bargain price this undoubtedly remains competitive.

Symphonies Nos. 34 in C, K.388; 35 in D (Haffner), K.385; 39 in E flat, K.543.
*** ASV Dig. CDDCA 615 [id.]. LMP, Jane Glover.

Tackling three major works, Jane Glover provides freshly imaginative performances that can compete with any in the catalogue, given the most vividly realistic recorded sound; Nos. 34 and 39 are especially striking. This collection can be recommended with enthusiasm.

(i) *Symphonies Nos. 35 (Haffner); 36 (Linz);* (ii) *Divertimento No. 1 in D for strings, K.136; Serenade No. 6 (Serenata notturna).*
☞ *** Virgin/EMI Dig. VC7 59302-2 [id.]. (i) Sinfonia Varsovia; (ii) Lausanne CO, Sir Yehudi Menuhin.

As in Menuhin's winning version of the last four Mozart symphonies, Mozart is again presented with a smile on his face. Though modern instruments are used, the scale is intimate with textures beautifully clear. The Sinfonia Varsovia, comprising players drawn from a range of Polish orchestras, responds warmly to Menuhin as the group's chosen President. There is elegance and charm as well as energy in outer movements, and in the slow movements Menuhin moulds the phrasing with Beechamesque magic, yet never adopts excessively slow speeds or over-romantic manners. The *Serenata notturna* and the *Divertimento* (first of the so-called 'Salzburg Symphonies') make a generous coupling, both of them favourites among Mozart's shorter works. Performances are similarly fresh and elegant, though, as recorded, the strings of the Lausanne Chamber Orchestra are a degree less sweet, and the acoustic is bigger and more reverberant.

Symphonies Nos. 35 (Haffner); 36 (Linz); 38 (Prague); 39 in E flat; 40 in G min.; 41 (Jupiter).
(B) *** Sony M2YK 45676 (2). Columbia SO, Bruno Walter.

Walter's set of Mozart's last and greatest symphonies comes from the beginning of the 1960s, his final recording period. The sound remains wonderfully fresh and full. The performances are crisp and classical, while still possessing humanity and warmth. Slow movements are outstanding for their breadth and the natural flow of the phrasing. Melodic lines are moulded nobly and pacing always seems inevitable. Finales are sparkling and brilliant, but never forced. The *G minor Symphony* is given a treasurable performance; in the *Jupiter*, if neither the first-movement exposition nor the finale carries repeats, Walter structures his interpretation accordingly, and the reading wears an Olympian mantle.

'The birth of a performance': (recorded rehearsals of *Symphony No. 36*). *Symphonies Nos. 35 (Haffner); 36 (Linz); 38 (Prague); 39 in E flat; 40 in G min.; 41 (Jupiter).*
(M) *** Sony stereo/mono SM3K 46511 (3) [id.]. Columbia SO, Bruno Walter.

This set includes Walter's earlier version of the *Linz*, recorded in mono in New York City in 1955.

Also included are the famous rehearsals of the *Linz Symphony*, called 'The birth of a performance', occupying the first disc. The second disc comprises Walter's mono performance of the *Linz* together with the stereo *Prague* and No. 40, while the third disc contains performances of the *Haffner*, No. 39 and the *Jupiter* symphonies.

Symphonies Nos. 35 in D (Haffner); 36 in C (Linz), K.425.
☞ (M) ** Teldec/Warner Dig. 9031-77595-2 [id.]. Concg. O, Harnoncourt.

With bright, clear, digital recording – quite different from the sound which Philips engineers get from this orchestra and with a dryness in tuttis which borders on harshness – the Harnoncourt coupling provides directly dramatic performances of these two symphonies. Tempi are unforced and the strongly rhythmic accenting brings vitality, but there is a total absence of charm, even in the *Haffner*. Like the *Prague*, below, the *Linz* is given with all repeats and plays for over 39 minutes, the longest account on record.

(i) *Symphonies Nos. 35 in D (Haffner), K.385; 36 in C (Linz);* (ii) *Rondo for violin and orchestra in B flat, K.269.*
(M) *** Sony Dig. MDK 44647 [id.]. (i) Bav. RSO, Kubelik; (ii) Zukerman, St Paul CO.

First-class performances from Kubelik and the Bavarian Radio orchestra, well paced and alive in every bar. The *Haffner* is particularly strong, and Kubelik's spacious presentation of the *Linz* is also satisfying. Both slow movements are beautifully played. At the end, Zukerman provides a sparkling encore. The CBS recording is admirable, full, yet clear and well balanced.

Symphonies Nos. 35 in D (Haffner), K.385; 40 in G min., K.550; 41 in C (Jupiter), K.551.
(M) *** Sony SBK 46333 [id.]. Cleveland O, Szell.

As in his companion triptych of late Haydn symphonies, Szell and his Clevelanders are shown at their finest here. The sparkling account of the *Haffner* is exhilarating, and the performances of the last two symphonies are equally polished and strong. Yet there is a tranquil feeling to both *Andantes* that shows Szell as a Mozartian of striking sensibility and finesse. He is at his finest in the *Jupiter*, which has great vigour in the outer movements and a proper weight to balance the rhythmic incisiveness; in spite of the lack of repeats, the work's scale is not diminished. Here the sound is remarkable considering the early date (late 1950s), and the remastering throughout is impressively full-bodied and clean.

Symphonies Nos. 36 in C (Linz); 38 in D (Prague); 39 in E flat, K.543; 40 in G min., K.550; 41 in C (Jupiter).
☞ (B) *** Ph. Duo 438 332-2 (2) [id.]. ASMF, Marriner.

This is an inexpensive way of acquiring first-class performances of Mozart's last five symphonies. The recordings are of high quality, all being made in 1978 or 1980, except for No. 40, which dates from a decade earlier (1970). Here the bass is a shade over-resonant, but the present transfer has made it seem firmer than previously. In terms of finesse and elegance of phrasing, the orchestral playing is of very high quality and Marriner's readings are satisfyingly paced, full of vitality and warmth. There is not a whiff of original-instrument style here, but those who enjoy the sound of Mozart in a modern orchestra of a reasonable size should be well satisfied.

Symphonies Nos. 37 in G, K.444: Introduction (completed by M. Haydn); *40 in G min., K.550; 41 in C (Jupiter), K.551.*
*** ASV Dig. CDDCA 761 [id.]. LMP, Jane Glover.

This is an excellent example of Jane Glover's work with the LMP. Anyone who fancies this generous coupling need hardly hesitate, particularly when in the two last Mozart symphonies Glover does not skimp on repeats, as she might have done. She omits them – as most versions do – in the slow movements, but includes exposition repeats in the finales as well as in first movements, particularly important in the *Jupiter*, with its grandly sublime counterpoint. There Glover's speed is exceptionally fast, with ensemble not quite so refined or crisp as in some rival versions, but still making for a strong and enjoyable reading.

Symphonies Nos. 38 (Prague); 39 in E flat, K.543; 40 in G min., K.550; 41 (Jupiter).
☞ (B) * Erato/Warner Duo Dig. 4509 95356-2 (2) [id.]. Ens. O de Paris, Armin Jordan.

Armin Jordan with his Parisian chamber-group, founded in 1978 as a 'Mannheim-style permanent ensemble', brings intelligent readings which never commit any major sin but which lack the tension of live music-making. They are run-throughs rather than real performances; slow movements sound routine, and the *Jupiter* in particular lacks any sense of stature.

Symphonies Nos. 38 in D (Prague), K.504; 39 in E flat, K.543.
*** Virgin/EMI Dig. VC7 59561-2 [id.]. Sinfonia Varsovia, Sir Yehudi Menuhin.
(M) *** Sony Dig. MDK 44648 [id.]. Bav. RSO, Rafael Kubelik.
☞ **(*) Ph. Dig. 426 283-2 [id.]. E. Bar. Soloists, Gardiner.
☞ (M) ** Teldec/Warner Dig. 9031 77596-2 [id.]. Concg. O, Harnoncourt.

Menuhin's Mozart with this hand-picked orchestra – of which he is the Principal Conductor – has a clear place for those who, resisting period instruments, yet want many of the benefits of an authentic approach without sacrificing sweetness of string sound. It may be surprising to some that Menuhin is such a complete classicist here, with speeds on the fast side. Yet he does not sound at all rushed. He treats the third-movement trio of No. 39 as a brisk Laendler, almost hurdy-gurdy-like, refusing – after consultation with the autograph – to allow a rallentando at the end. Otherwise the only other oddity is his omission of the exposition repeat in the first movement when as a rule he is generous with repeats. The fresh, immediate sound highlights the refined purity of the string-playing.

Kubelik has the advantage of first-class, modern, digital recording. The playing has verve and is highly responsive. No. 39 is especially invigorating in its racy finale but has plenty of strength too.

For many listeners, Gardiner represents a happy medium in period performance. He is able to relax while at the same time preserving sparkle and plenty of rhythmic character. Here he is cooler than usual, and slow movements seem marginally less penetrating. Even so, there is an inherent vitality that it is difficult to resist, and the playing is wonderfully polished, far smoother and indeed with a more human profile than Hogwood shows.

Harnoncourt's strongly dramatic account of the *Prague Symphony* is generally very successful. With all repeats included, it runs for 37 minutes and was originally allotted a full-price disc to itself! Harnoncourt secures superb playing from the Royal Concertgebouw Orchestra, and the lack of charm is less noticeable in the *Prague* than it is in No. 39, which could use more geniality. But the finale (which, with repeats, plays for 7 minutes 53 seconds) is fizzingly brilliant. Bright, clear sound.

Symphonies Nos. 39 in E flat, K.543; 41 in C (Jupiter), K.551.
(BB) *** Virgin/EMI Dig. VJ7 91461-2; *VJ7 91461-4* [id.]. SCO, Saraste.

Jukka-Pekka Saraste's bargain issue on the Virgin Virgo label offers two of the finest performances of these late symphonies available on any disc: fresh, light and resilient in allegros, elegant in the slow movements and with clean, transparent recording. Wordsworth with the Capella Istropolitana may have more weight in these works, but Saraste has extra polish and refinement, with generally brisker speeds, notably in slow movements and minuets.

Symphony No. 40 in G min., K.550.
(B) **(*) Pickwick Dig. PCD 820; *CIMPC 820* [id.]. O of St John's, Smith Square, Lubbock –
   HAYDN: *Symphony No. 44.* ***
(M) (**) BMG/RCA mono GD 60271 [60271-2-RG]. NBC SO, Toscanini – BEETHOVEN: *Symphony No. 3.* (***)

Lubbock's is a pleasingly relaxed account of Mozart's *G minor Symphony*, well played – the Minuet particularly deft – and nicely proportioned. The last ounce of character is missing from the slow movement, but the orchestra is responsive throughout, and the recording is in the demonstration class.

Dating from March 1950, Toscanini's version was recorded in the notoriously dry Studio 8-H in Radio City, New York; though the sound is uncomfortable, the high voltage of the interpretation makes considerable amends, with expressive warmth tempering the conductor's characteristic urgency. The slow movement is elegantly done, and even though the finale brings a measure of fierceness, Toscanini eases lovingly into the second subject.

Symphonies Nos. 40 in G min., K.550; 41 in C (Jupiter), K.551.
☞ (M) *** Virgin/EMI Dig. CUV5 61133-2 [id.]. Sinfonia Varsovia, Sir Yehudi Menuhin.
☞ *** Ph. Dig. 426 315-2 [id.]. E. Bar. Soloists, Gardiner.
*** Telarc Dig. CD 80139 [id.]. Prague CO, Mackerras.
(B) *** CfP CD-CFP 4253; *TC-CFP 40243.* LPO, Mackerras.
☞ (M) **(*) O-L Dig. 443 180-2 [id.]. AAM, Schröder (leader), Hogwood (continuo).
☞ (M) *(*) BMG/RCA Dig. 09026 61397-2 [id.]. Chicago SO, James Levine.

Symphonies Nos. 40–41; Overture: The Marriage of Figaro.
☞ (B) *** RPO TRP 004 [id.]. RPO, Glover.

Recorded in exceptionally vivid, immediate sound, Menuhin's versions of both symphonies with the

Sinfonia Varsovia find a distinctive place in an overcrowded field, with playing of precision, clarity and bite which is consistently refreshing, giving a feeling of live music-making. Menuhin reveals himself again as very much a classicist, preferring speeds on the fast side, rarely indulging in romantic tricks. He is generous with repeats – observing exposition repeats in both first movement and finale of the *Jupiter*, for example. With such vivid sound, this is the best current recommendation for this favourite pairing.

Gardiner's coupling is also very impressive indeed and, for those wanting period instruments, this is a clear first choice. These are both large-scale conceptions with the strings fuller and with less edge than usual, and there are no eccentric tempi. Allegros are strongly motivated and slow movements spacious, that of the *Jupiter* strikingly so, and played with great eloquence. The finale has great vitality and purpose yet certainly does not lack weight. The second repeat is not taken here, which is a pity; but these remain powerful and stimulating readings, very well played and recorded.

On Telarc, with generally fast speeds, so brisk that he is able to observe every single repeat, Mackerras takes a fresh, direct view which, with superb playing from the Prague Chamber Orchestra, is also characterful. The speeds that might initially seem excessively fast are those for the Minuets, which – with fair scholarly authority – become crisp country dances, almost Scherzos. On the question of repeats, the doubling in length of the slow movement of No. 40 makes it almost twice as long as the first movement, a dangerous proportion – though it is pure gain having both halves repeated in the magnificent finale of the *Jupiter*.

On Classics for Pleasure, Mackerras directs excellent, clean-cut performances which can stand comparison with any at whatever price. He observes exposition repeats in the outer movements of the *G minor* but not the *Jupiter*, which is a pity for so majestic a work.

At super-bargain price in the Royal Philharmonic Collection, Jane Glover conducts fresh, urgent performances, stylishly moulded, which include exposition repeats that generally outshine her own earlier, smaller-scale readings with the London Mozart Players on ASV. With rhythms crisply sprung in fast movements and with slow movements warmly lyrical and relaxed without becoming over-romantic, these performances, brightly recorded, stand comparison with almost any version, and the *Figaro overture* provides a welcome makeweight, though on ASV the *Symphony No. 37* (mainly by Michael Haydn) was even more generous.

The separate issue of Nos. 40 and 41 from Hogwood's collected edition makes an alternative recommendation for those wanting period performances: brisk and light, but still conveying the drama of No. 40 and the majesty of the *Jupiter*.

Levine's Chicago performances cannot be recommended with any enthusiasm. The *G minor* is matter-of-fact and wanting in real warmth; while the *Jupiter* is more than routine, it is less than distinguished, given the reputation of the orchestra and the musicianship and insight of this conductor. The recording, made in the Medinah Temple, Chicago, has no want of clarity and presence, but its claims cannot be pressed over rival performances.

CHAMBER MUSIC

Complete Mozart Edition, Volume 14: (i) *Adagio in C for glass harmonica, K.356;* (i; ii) *Adagio in C min. & Rondo in C for glass harmonica, flute, oboe, viola & cello;* (iii) *Clarinet trio in E flat (Kegelstatt), K.498;* (iv; v) *Piano quartets Nos. 1–2;* (iv) *Piano trios Nos. 1–6; Piano trio in D min., K.442;* (vi) *Piano and wind quintet in E flat, K.452.*
(M) *** Ph. Dig./Analogue 422 514-2 (5) [id.]. (i) Bruno Hoffmann; (ii) with Nicolet, Holliger, Schouten, Decroos; (iii) Brymer, Kovacevich, Ireland; (iv) Beaux Arts Trio, (v) with Giuranna; (vi) Brendel, Holliger, Brunner, Baumann, Thunemann.

This compilation of Mozart's chamber music with piano has no weak link. The last three discs contain the complete set of the Mozart *Piano trios* recorded by the Beaux Arts Trio in 1987, a first-rate cycle which includes not only the six completed trios but also the composite work, put together by Mozart's friend, the priest Maximilian Stadler, and listed by Köchel as K.442. The Beaux Arts' teamwork – with the pianist Menahem Pressler leading the way – brings consistently fresh and winning performances, as it also does in the two great *Piano quartets* where, in recordings made in 1983, they are joined by the viola-player, Bruno Giuranna. The *Piano and wind quintet*, K.452, recorded in 1986, subtly contrasts the artistry of Alfred Brendel at the piano with that of the oboist, Heinz Holliger, leading a distinguished team of wind-players. The only non-digital recordings are those of the *Kegelstatt trio*, characterfully done by Stephen Bishop-Kovacevich with the clarinettist Jack Brymer and the viola-player Patrick Ireland, and of the two shorter works involving glass harmonica. Those last are conveniently included here as an extra, both with Bruno Hoffmann playing that rare instrument, so titillating to the ear if heard in fairly brief spans.

Adagio in C for cor anglais, 2 violins & cello, K.580a.
*** Denon Dig. C37 7119 [id.]. Holliger, Salvatore Qt – M. HAYDN: *Divertimenti;* J. C. BACH: *Oboe quartet.* ***

Though the shortest of the four works on Holliger's charming disc, this Mozart fragment is in a world apart, deeply expressive. Excellent performances and recording.

Canons for strings; Canons for woodwind: see below, under VOCAL MUSIC: Complete Mozart Edition, Volume 23

Complete Mozart Edition, Volume 10: (i; vi) *Clarinet quintet;* (ii) *Flute quartets Nos. 1–4;* (iii; vi) *Horn quintet;* (iv; vi) *Oboe quartet;* (v) *Sonata for bassoon and cello, K.292.* (vi) Fragments: *Allegro in F, K.App. 90/580b for clarinet, basset horn, & string trio; Allegro in B flat. K.App. 91/K.516c for a clarinet quintet; Allegro in F, K.288 for a divertimento for 2 horns & strings; String quartet movements: Allegro in B flat, K.App. 72/464a; Allegro in B flat, K.App. 80/514a; Minuet in B flat, K.68/589a; Minuet in F, K.168a; Movement in A, K.App. 72/464a. String quintet No. 1 in B flat, K.174: 2 Original movements: Trio & Finale. Allegro in A min., K.App. 79 for a string quintet. Allegro in G, K.App. 66/562e for a string trio* (completed, where necessary, by Erik Smith).
(M) *** Ph. Analogue/Dig. 422 510-2 (3) [id.]. (i) Pay; (ii) Bennett, Grumiaux Trio; (iii) Brown; (iv) Black; (v) Thunemann; Orton; (vi) ASMF Chamber Ens.

These are highly praised performances of the major chamber works featuring modern wind instruments (Antony Pay uses a normal clarinet). The rest of the items are by no means inconsequential offcuts but provide music of high quality, notably the *String quartet movement,* K.514a. The *Minuet in B flat,* K.589a, in the rhythm of a polonaise and possibly the first draft for the finale of the *Hunt quartet,* is a real charmer which, had it received more exposure, might well have become a Mozartian lollipop like the famous and not dissimilar Minuet in the *D major Divertimento,* K.334. The two pieces with solo clarinet are also very winning. The performances here are all polished and spontaneous and beautifully recorded.

(i) *Clarinet quartet in E flat, K.347a; Clarinet quintet in A, K.581;* (ii) *Quintet for clarinet, basset horn and string trio.*
☞ (BB) ** Naxos Dig. 8.550390 [id.]. József Balogh; (i) Béla Kovács; Danubius Qt (members).

(i) *Clarinet quartets: in B flat, K.317d; in F, K.496;* (ii) *Clarinet trio (Kegelstatt) for clarinet, viola and piano, K.498.*
☞ (BB) **(*) Naxos Dig. 8.550439 [id.]. József Balogh; (i) Daniubius Qt (members); (ii) Jenö Jandó, György Konrád.

Mozart's *Clarinet quartets* are arrangements, with the first two based on violin sonatas (K.378 and K.380) while the third is a version of the piano trio, K.496. They were published posthumously in 1799 and it seems unlikely that Mozart made the arrangements himself. Never mind, they are most enjoyable in this form and suit the clarinet very well, especially the lovely *Andante con moto* of K.347f and the melting *Andantino sostenuto e cantabile* of K.317d, while the perky finale (*Allegro non tanto*) of K.496 is sheer delight. They are most persuasively presented here, and very well recorded. Unfortunately József Balogh, who plays so sympathetically in the *Quartets,* is less memorable in the *Quintet,* where he paces the famous *Larghetto* a shade too fast. However, he makes up a good team with Jandó and Konrád for the fine *Kegelstatt trio.* Here the performance is relaxed but enjoyable (it could have used a shade more momentum in the first movement).

(i) *Clarinet quintet in A, K.581; Divertimento No. 1 for strings in D, K.136* (quartet version).
☞ (M) *** Saga EC 3387-2. (i) Thea King; Aeolian Qt.

Clarinet quintet in A, K.581; Clarinet quintet fragment in B flat, K.516c; (i) *Quintet fragment in F for clarinet in C, basset-horn and string trio, K.580b* (both completed by Duncan Druce).
*** Amon Ra/Saydisc CD-SAR 17 [id.]. Alan Hacker, Salomon Qt, (i) with Lesley Schatzberger.

Leading the CD versions of the *Clarinet quintet* (alongside Thea King's outstanding coupling with the *Clarinet concerto* on Hyperion – see above) is a superb recording by Alan Hacker with the Salomon Quartet, using original instruments. Hacker's gentle sound on his period instrument is displayed at its most ravishing in the *Larghetto.* He is matched by the strings, and especially by the leader, Simon Standage, who blends his tone luminously with the clarinet. Tempi are wonderfully apt throughout the performance, the rhythms of the finale are infectiously pointed, the music's sense of joy fully projected. The recording balance is near perfect. Hacker includes a fragment from an earlier projected *Quintet* and a similar sketch for a work featuring C clarinet and basset-horn with string trio. Both are skilfully completed by Duncan Druce.

This Saga recording helped to establish Thea King's reputation as both a first-rate soloist and a fine Mozartian. With great refinement in matters of tonal shading, and consistently beautiful phrasing, this remains among the most attractive versions of the *Quintet*. There is, it is true, a touch of coolness in the first two movements but the music still glows. Miss King's articulation in the third-movement solos and in the delightfully pointed finale is a joy. The closing pages of the work are especially beautiful. This is all helped by excellent support from the Aeolian Quartet and a most realistically balanced recording from Saga. The ungenerous filler is bright and breezy, with very fast tempi for the outer movements and a graceful, if matter-of-fact account of the *Andante*.

(i) *Clarinet quintet in A, K.581;* (ii) *Flute quartets Nos. 1–4, K.285; 285a; 285b; 298;* (iii) *Horn quintet in E flat, K.407;* (iv) *Oboe quartet in F, K.370.*
☞ (M) *** DG 437 137-2 (2). (i) De Peyer; (ii) Blau; (iii) Seifert; (iv) Koch; Amadeus Qt.

The Amadeus set can receive a strong recommendation. Gervase de Peyer gives a warm, smiling account of the *Clarinet quintet* with a sunny opening movement, a gently expressive *Larghetto* and a delightfully genial finale. Andreas Blau is hardly less appealing in the *Flute quartets*. He is a splendid artist and the Amadeus accompany him with subtlety and distinction. The enchanting slow movement of the *D major Quartet*, where the flute cantilena is floated over a pizzicato accompaniment, is very beautifully done. Moreover the balance is exceptionally well managed, the flute very well integrated with the strings, yet allowed to dominate naturally. In the *Oboe quartet* Koch provides creamy tone and stylish phrasing, the Amadeus accompany with much sensibility and the recording is refined to match. Gerd Seifert is an accomplished horn player and is sensitive in matters of phrasing and dynamics. It is not a high-spirited account, but a very pleasing one nevertheless, and the closing *Rondo* goes well enough. The recordings, made over a period between 1969 and 1977, have all transferred admirably to CD.

(i) *Clarinet quintet in A, K.581;* (ii) *Horn quintet in E flat, K.407;* (iii) *Oboe quartet in F, K.370.*
(M) *** Ph. 422 833-2; *422 833-4.* (i) Antony Pay; (ii) Timothy Brown; (iii) Neil Black; ASMF Chamber Ens.

It is a delightful idea to have the *Clarinet quintet*, *Oboe quartet* and *Horn quintet* on a single CD. Here, Antony Pay's earlier account of the *Clarinet quintet*, played on a modern instrument, with the Academy of St Martin-in-the-Fields players must be numbered among the strongest now on the market for those not insisting on an authentic basset clarinet. Neil Black's playing in the *Oboe quartet* is distinguished, and again the whole performance radiates pleasure, while the *Horn quintet* comes in a well-projected and lively account with Timothy Brown. The recording, originally issued in 1981, is of Philips's best.

(i) *Clarinet quintet;* (ii) *Oboe quartet in F, K.370.*
(B) *** CfP CD-CFP 4377; *TC-CFP 4377.* (i) Andrew Marriner; (ii) Gordon Hunt, Chilingirian Qt.
(B) *** Pickwick Dig. PCD 810; *CIMPC 810* [id.]. (i) Puddy; (ii) Boyd, Gabrieli Qt.

On the bargain-priced CfP version, recorded in 1981, the young Andrew Marriner's persuasive account occupies the front rank, quite irrespective of price. Marriner's playing in the *Quintet* is wonderfully flexible; it reaches its apex in the radiantly beautiful reading of the slow movement, although the finale is also engagingly characterized. The *Oboe quartet* is delectable too, with Gordon Hunt a highly musical and technically accomplished soloist. The CfP issue was recorded in the Wigmore Hall and the sound-balance is most believable.

The alternative bargain-priced Pickwick CD brings a reading of the *Clarinet quintet* which is clean and well paced and, if lacking the last degree of delicacy in the slow movement, is never less than stylish. The young oboist, Douglas Boyd, then gives an outstanding performance in the shorter, less demanding work, with the lilting finale delectably full of fun. The digital recording is vividly immediate and full of presence, with even the keys of the wind instruments often audible.

(i) *Clarinet quintet in A, K.581; String quartet No. 20 in D (Hoffmeister), K.499.*
☞ (M) **(*) Whitehall Associates Dig. MQCD 6001 [id.]. (i) Jack Brymer; Medici Qt.

The Medici String Quartet have set up their own label. Jack Brymer joins them for their first Mozart CD and has a benign influence in a fine, mellifluous performance of the *Clarinet quintet*. He plays the *Adagio* as a sustained half-tone and conjures from the strings comparably soft playing. Perhaps a little more dynamic variety would have been an advantage, but the concentration is sustained right through. The finale is delightful; there is an attractive improvisational feeling in the lyrical variation before the main theme makes its joyful return. The recording is truthful, but the close balance is more noticeable in the coupled *Hoffmeister quartet*, which is a lively, well-integrated performance, if without the individuality of the *Quintet*. However, at mid-price this coupling is certainly worth considering.

(i) *Clarinet quintet in A, K.581;* (ii) *String quintets Nos. 1 in B flat, K.174; 2 in C min., K.406.*
☞ *** Calliope Dig. CAL 9232 [id.]. Talich Qt, with (i) Bohuslav Zahradnik; (ii) Karel Rehak.

The Talich performances here are of the highest quality: just sample the delicacy of the playing in the lovely *Adagio* of K.174 or the energy of the simple yet spirited finale. The *C minor Quintet* is of course the composer's transcription of the *Serenade for wind*, K.388, and the players make the very most of the splendid variations which form the finale. The *Clarinet quintet* is exquisitely done. Bohuslav Zahradnik's contribution has much delicacy of feeling and colour; he is highly seductive in the slow movement, and even in the finale the effect is gentle in the most appealing way without any loss of vitality. The recording balance is exemplary in all three works and the acoustic admirably chosen. A rewarding triptych in every way – and a playing time of 80 minutes 17 seconds!

Complete Mozart Edition, Volume 13: (i) *Divertimento in E flat for string trio, K.563;* (ii) *Duos for violin and viola Nos. 1–2, K.423/4;* (i) *6 Preludes and fugues for string trio, K.404a;* (iii) *Sonata (String trio) in B flat, K.266.*
(M) *** Ph. 422 513-2 (2) [id.]. (i) Grumiaux, Janzer, Szabo; (ii) Grumiaux, Pelliccia; (iii) ASMF Chamber Ens.

Grumiaux's 1967 recorded performance of the *Divertimento in E flat* remains unsurpassed; he is here joined by two players with a similarly refined and classical style. The recording has been remastered again: the balance still favours Grumiaux but he also dominates the performance artistically (as he does also in the *Duos*) and the result is now fully acceptable. In the *Duos*, which are ravishingly played, the balance is excellent, and Arrigo Pelliccia proves a natural partner in these inspired and rewarding works. The *Sonata for string trio* is well played by the ASMF Chamber Ensemble and it has a modern, digital recording. Of the six *Preludes and fugues*, the first three derive from Bach's *Well-tempered clavier*, the fourth combines an *Adagio* from the *Organ sonata*, BWV 527, with *Contrapunctus 8* from the *Art of fugue*, the fifth is a transcription of two movements from the *Organ sonata*, BWV 526, and the sixth uses music of W. F. Bach. The performances here are sympathetic and direct, the recorded sound bold, clear and bright.

Divertimento in E flat for string trio, K.563.
*** Sony Dig. MK 39561 [id.]. Kremer, Kashkashian, Ma.

Gidon Kremer, Kim Kashkashian and Yo-Yo Ma turn in an elegant and sweet-toned account on CBS and are excellently recorded. Indeed, the sound is fresh and beautifully realistic. There are many perceptive insights, particularly in the *Adagio* movement which is beautifully done.

Divertimento in E flat for string trio, K.563; Duos for violin and viola, Nos. 1–2, K.423/4.
(B) **(*) Hung. White Label HRC 072 [id.]. Dénes Kovács, Géza Németh, Ede Banda.

If not quite a match in subtlety for the Grumiaux version, the account of this masterly *Divertimento* by the three Hungarian players is freshly enjoyable, the playing vital, spontaneous and agreeably without mannered idiosyncrasy, both in the *Trio* and in the highly rewarding pair of *Duos* which make the substantial coupling. The Hungaroton recording is forward but better balanced than the Philips version.

Flute quartets Nos. 1 in D, K.285; 2 in G, K.285a; 3 in C, K.285b; 4 in A, K.298.
(M) *** Van. 08.4001.71 [OVC 4001]. Paula Robinson, Tokyo Qt (members).
*** Accent ACC 48225D. Bernhard and Sigiswald Kuijken, Van Dael, Wieland Kuijken.
*** Sony Dig. MK 42320 [id.]. Rampal, Stern, Accardo, Rostropovich.
☞ (BB) ** ASV CDQS 6099. Richard Adeney, Melos Ens. (members).

Mozart professed an aversion for the flute (partly because at the time its intonation was suspect and its timbre could be watery), yet he wrote some delightful music for it, none more so than these delicious, lightweight quartets. The Vanguard recording of the *Flute quartets* (presumably from the 1960s – no date is given) is most winning. Paula Robinson displays a captivating lightness of touch and her silvery timbre seems eminently suited to Mozart. Needless to say, the Tokyo Quartet provide polished accompaniments which combine warmth with much finesse, and the recording is most naturally balanced.

Readers normally unresponsive to period instruments should hear these performances by Bernhard Kuijken, for they have both charm and vitality; they radiate pleasure and bring one close to this music. This record is rather special and cannot be recommended too strongly. The playing is exquisite and the engineering superb.

It would be hard to dream up a more starry quartet of players than that assembled on the CBS disc. But the recording was made in a relatively dry studio, and the acoustic emphasizes the dominance of Rampal's flute in the ensemble, with the three superstar string-players given little chance to shine distinctively except in the finale of K.285. A delectable record none the less.

The performances by Richard Adeney with distinguished members of the Melos Ensemble (Hugh Maguire, Cecil Aronowitz, Terence Weill) date from 1978 and were produced by John Boyden for the now-defunct Enigma label. The balance treats the flute very much in a solo capacity and is vividly close, although the characterful playing of Adeney's colleagues is not masked. The effect is undoubtedly lively and spontaneous but has not the imaginative insight or persuasive charm of the best versions. However, this excellently transferred CD is in the lowest price-range and represents good value.

Flute quartets Nos. 1–4; Oboe quartet (arr. for flute, Galway), K.370.
☞ **(*) BMG/RCA Dig. 09026 60442-2 [id.]. James Galway, Tokyo Qt.

James Galway is an impeccable soloist and the Tokyo Quartet provide admirable support. The recording too is fresh and well balanced and, if Galway dominates, that is partly the result of Mozart's writing and the use of a modern instrument. Some may feel that in slow movements his sweet, silvery timbre and individual vibrato are too much of a good thing, and this is particularly noticeable in the famous cantilena of the *G major* work. But this is perhaps carping – if Galway brings this music to the attention of a wider public, well and good. The transcription of the *Oboe quartet* is more questionable, although it must be admitted that here the *Adagio* sounds refreshingly different on the flute, and the performance cannot be faulted.

(ii) *Horn quintet in E flat, K.407;* (ii) *Oboe quartet in F, K.370; A Musical Joke, K.522.*
☞ (BB) **(*) Naxos Dig. 8.550437 [id.]. (i) József Kiss; (ii) Jenö Keveházi; Kodály Qt.

Highly musical if not especially individual performances of the *Horn quintet* and *Oboe quartet*; in the latter the oboe is balanced forwardly and seems a bit larger than life; but no matter, the recordings have a pleasingly resonant bloom. The *Musical Joke* really comes off well: the horn players have a great time with their wrong notes.

Piano quartets Nos. 1 in G min., K.478; 2 in E flat, K.493 (see also above, under Complete Mozart Edition, Volume 14).
*** Ph. Dig. 410 391-2 [id.]. Beaux Arts Trio with Giuranna.
(B) *** Hung. White Label HRC 170 [id.]. Gyula Kiss, Tátrai Trio.
*** DG Dig. 423 404-2 [id.]. Bilson (fortepiano), Wilcock, Schlapp, Mason.

The Beaux Arts group provide splendidly alive and vitally sensitive accounts that exhilarate the listener, just as does the Curzon–Amadeus set (see below), and they have the advantage of first-class digital recording. The Beaux Arts play them not only *con amore* but with the freshness of a new discovery, and the sound (particularly that of the piano) is exceptionally lifelike.

Gyula Kiss, the pianist, is a fine and characterful Mozartian, and he dominates performances which are convincingly paced and alive, with the Tátrai string group making an excellent partnership. Natural sound with good presence yet no edginess on the strings.

The balance between the three stringed instruments and the keyboard is immediately altered when heard on period instruments. The playing of Malcolm Bilson and his colleagues is excellent and has both sparkle and grace. The recording is outstandingly natural and lifelike.

(i) *Piano quartets Nos. 1–2;* (i) *Horn quintet in E flat, K.407.*
⊛ (M) *** Decca mono 425 960-2 [id.]. (i) Clifford Curzon, Amadeus Qt; (ii) Dennis Brain, Griller Qt.

All versions of the Mozart *Piano quartets* rest in the shadow of the recordings by Clifford Curzon and members of the Amadeus Quartet. No apologies need be made for the 1952 mono recorded sound. The performances have a unique sparkle, slow movements are elysian. One's only criticism is that the *Andante* of K.478 opens at a much lower dynamic level than the first movement, and some adjustment of the controls needs to be made. The *Horn quintet* coupling was recorded in 1944 and the transfer to CD is even more miraculous. The slight surface rustle of the 78-r.p.m. source is in no way distracting and Dennis Brain's performance combines warmth and elegance with a spirited spontaneity, and the subtleties of the horn contribution are a continuous delight. A wonderful disc that should be in every Mozartian's library.

Piano trios – see also above, under Complete Mozart Edition, Volume 14.
Piano trios Nos. 1–6; Piano trio in D min., K.442.

*** Ph. Dig. 422 079-2 (3). Beaux Arts Trio.

Piano trios Nos. 1–6.
*** Chan. Dig. CHAN 8536/7; *DBTD 2008* (2). Borodin Trio.

Apart from including an extra work, the Beaux Arts are more generous with repeats, which accounts for the extra disc. Their performances are eminently fresh and are no less delightful and winning. There is a somewhat lighter touch here compared with the Chandos alternative, thanks in no small degree to the subtle musicianship of Menahem Pressler. The Philips recording is strikingly realistic and present.

The Borodin Trio are slightly weightier in their approach and their tempi are generally more measured than the Beaux Arts', very strikingly so in the *Allegretto* of the *G major*. All the same, there is, as usual with this group, much sensitive playing and every evidence of distinguished musicianship. The balance in the Philips set tends to favour the piano a little; the Chandos, recorded at The Maltings, Snape, perhaps produces the more integrated sound.

Piano and wind quintet in E flat, K.452.
*** Sony Dig. MK 42099 [id.]. Perahia, members of ECO – BEETHOVEN: *Quintet.* ***
(M) *** Decca 421 151-2. Ashkenazy, L. Wind Soloists – BEETHOVEN: *Quintet.* ***
☞ (B) * HM Dig. HMA 1903020 [id.]. Zoltán Kocsis, Budapest Wind Ens. – BEETHOVEN: *Piano and wind quintet* etc. *(*)

An outstanding account of Mozart's delectable *Piano and wind quintet* on CBS, with Perahia's playing wonderfully refreshing in the *Andante* and a superb response from the four wind soloists, notably Neil Black's oboe contribution. Clearly all the players are enjoying this rewarding music, and they are well balanced, with the piano against the warm but never blurring acoustics of The Maltings at Snape.

Ashkenazy's performance in Mozart's engaging *Quintet* is also outstandingly successful, polished and urbane, yet marvellously spirited. His wind soloists are a distinguished team and their playing comes fully up to expectations. The balance and sound-quality are of the highest order and the CD sounds very natural, although the balance is forward. A first-class mid-priced alternative to the full-price versions led by Perahia and Lupu.

The Budapest account on Harmonia Mundi is a non-starter. Kocsis dominates and sets too fast a pace for comfort in the opening movement, and even he sounds rushed. The engaging character of one of Mozart's most winning chamber works all but evaporates.

Complete Mozart Edition, Volume 12: *String quartets Nos. 1–23.*
(M) *** Ph. 422 512-2 (8) [id.]. Italian Qt.

The earliest recordings by the Italians now begin to show their age (notably the six *Haydn Quartets*, which date from 1966): the violin timbre is thinner than we would expect in more modern versions. But the quality is generally very satisfactory, for the Philips sound-balance is admirably judged. As a set, the performances have seen off all challengers for two decades or more; one is unlikely to assemble a more consistently satisfying overview of these works, or one so beautifully played. They hold a very special place in the Mozartian discography.

String quartets Nos. 1 in G, K.80; 2 in D, K.155; 3 in G, K.156; 4 in C, K.157; 5 in F, K.158; 6 in B flat, K.159; 7 in E flat, K.160; 8 in F, K.168; 9 in A, K.169; 10 in C, K.170; 11 in E flat, K.171; 12 in B flat, K.172; 13 in D min., K.173; Divertimenti: in D, K.136; in B flat, K.137; in F, K.138.
*** DG Dig. 431 645-2 (3) [id.]. Hagen Qt.

This set of three CDs presents all of Mozart's music for string quartet up to the age of seventeen and it is played with much charm and polish. Unlike the Quartetto Italiano, the Hagens include the *Divertimenti*, K.136–8. In this present set they strike an excellent balance between naturalness of utterance and sophistication of tone, and the DG recording is in the very first flight.

String quartet No. 1 in G, K.80.
☞ (BB) *** Discover Dig. DICD 920171 [id.]. Sharon Qt – BEETHOVEN: *Harp quartet;* RAVEL: *Quartet in F.* **(*)

The Sharon Quartet give an excellent account of Mozart's *First* divertimento-like *Quartet*, which he wrote in Italy at the age of fifteen. The playing has life and finesse and, although the recording (made in a Cologne Church) is reverberant, detail is clear; indeed the acoustic rather suits the music.

String quartets Nos. 1 in G, K.80; 2 in D, K.155; 4 in C, K.157.
(BB) ** Naxos Dig. 8.550541 [id.]. Eder Qt.

String quartets Nos. 3 in G, K.156; 5 in F, K.158; 6 in B flat, K.159; 17 in B flat (Hunt), K.458.
(B) ** Naxos Dig. 8.550542 [id.]. Eder Qt.

This new, super-bargain Naxos series of the Mozart *Quartets* has much in its favour. The playing of the Eder Quartet is polished and responsive. Their phrasing is warm and elegant; their ensemble is impressive; allegros are vital and they certainly bring the music to life. The snag is the venue, the Sashalom Reformed Church in Budapest, which affords the group the most beautiful sound; but the effect overall is almost orchestral and loses virtually all the intimacy of the medium.

String quartets Nos. 6 in B flat, K.160; 8 in F, K.168; 9 in A, K.169; 22 in B flat (Prussian No. 2), K.589.
☞ (BB) **(*) Naxos Dig. 8.550544 [id.]. Eder Qt.

This is the finest issue so far in the Naxos Eder series. The three early quartets in their first-movement allegros keep reminding us of the Salzburg *Divertimenti* (K.136–8), yet they are already becoming fully fledged string quartets, with K.168 and K.169 each in four movements. Indeed the slow movement of the F major is very touching, and it is beautifully played here. The *Second Prussian Quartet* is also elegantly done, though once again the resonant acoustic of the Unitarian Church in Budapest gives an almost orchestral expansion of tone and takes some of the edge off the playing. The sound itself is beautiful, and with a careful setting of the volume control this is enjoyable.

String quartets Nos. 8 in F, K.168; 9 in A, K.169; 10 in C, K.170; 11 in E flat, K.171; 12 in E flat, K.172.
☞ *** Calliope Dig. CAL 9247 [id.]. Talich Qt.

Mozart composed these six quartets in Vienna in the late summer and early autumn of 1773. They are remarkably mature works, laid out in four movements in the manner of Haydn, even using a fugal format, as in the succinct finale of K.168. One has only to listen to the *Andante* of this work (introducing the mute) or the nostalgic lyricism of the *Adagio* in K.170 to realize that these quartets marked a step forward for the composer, and this is confirmed in the engaging gravitas of the *Variations* which form the first movement of the same work. K.171 then opens with an *Adagio* of real depth, which is recapitulated at the movement's close, while its *Andante* (again using mutes) brings a quiet nocturnal atmosphere. In K.172 the slow movement has a distinct, operatic sensibility and a reminder of the outline of one of the composer's most famous arias, while its finale finds the composer at his most vital and spirited. The Talich players are the soul of finesse and bring the intimacy of familiarity. They play with expressive simplicity, while bringing vitality to allegros and conveying a consistent feeling of spontaneous liveliness throughout. They are naturally if forwardly balanced, and beautifully recorded. There are few records of Mozart's earlier quartets to match this collection.

String quartets Nos. 14 in G, K.387; 15 in D min., K.421; 16 in E flat, K.428; 17 in B flat (Hunt), K458; 18 in A, K.464; 19 in C (Dissonance), K.465 (Haydn Quartets).
⊛ *** CRD CRD 3362; *CRD C 4062* (*Nos. 14–15*); 3363; *4063* (*Nos. 16–17*); 3364; *4064* (*Nos. 18–19*) [id.]. Chilingirian Qt.
*** Hyp. Dig. CDS 44001/3 [id.]. Salomon Qt.

String quartets Nos. 14 in G, K.387; 15 in D min., K.421.
☞ (M) **(*) Whitehall Associates Dig. MQCD 6004 [id.]. Medici Qt.

String quartets Nos. 16 in E flat, K.428; 19 in C (Dissonance), K.465.
☞ (M) **(*) Whitehall Associates Dig. MQCD 6002 [id.]. Medici Qt.

String quartets Nos. 17 in B flat (Hunt), K.458; 18 in A, K.464.
☞ (M) **(*) Whitehall Associates Dig. MQCD 6003 [id.]. Medici Qt.

The set of six quartets dedicated to Haydn contains a high proportion of Mozart's finest works in the genre. The Chilingirian Quartet plays with unforced freshness and vitality, avoiding expressive mannerism but always conveying the impression of spontaneity, helped by the warm and vivid recording. Unlike most quartets, they never sound superficial in the elegant but profound slow movements. The three CDs are packaged separately and offer demonstration quality.

The playing of the Salomon Quartet is highly accomplished and has a real sense of style; they do not eschew vibrato, though their use of it is not liberal, and there is admirable clarity of texture and vitality of articulation. There is no want of subtlety and imagination in the slow movements. The recordings are admirably truthful and lifelike, and those who seek 'authenticity' in Mozart's chamber music will not be disappointed.

The Medici provide a polished, well-integrated set of 'Haydn' quartets, fresh and alert, if without always the touch of extra individuality that appears in their account of the *Clarinet quintet*. The studio recordings are rather closely balanced (although they are not airless) and the leader is obviously near the microphone, which adds a degree of digital brightness to his timbre and increases his dominance. The most enjoyable of the three couplings is that of K.387 – where the Haydnesque influence on the *Andante* and Minuet and the humour of the polyphony of the finale are well appreciated – and K.421 (with a finely judged slow movement and a light touch for the siciliano variations which close the work). These records are competitively priced and certainly give pleasure.

String quartets Nos. 14 in G, K.387; 15 in D min., K.421; 3 in G, K.156.
☞ *** Calliope CAL 9241 [id.]. Talich Qt.

String quartets Nos. 16 in E flat, K.428; 17 in B flat (Hunt), K.458.
☞ *** Calliope CAL 9242 [id.]. Talich Qt (with HAYDN: *String quartet No. 74 in G min., Op. 74/3.*
**(*))

(i) *String quartets Nos. 18 in A, K.464; 19 in C, K.465;* (ii) *Violin sonata No. 18 in G, K.301.*
☞ *** Calliope CAL 9243 [id.]. (i) Talich Qt; (ii) Peter Messiereur, Stanislav Bogunia.

These performances by the Talich Quartet are immaculate in ensemble and the performances have a special kind of shared intimacy which is yet immediately communicative. There is complete understanding of what Mozart is trying to say and a warmth and elegance of phrasing which is totally appealing. The Minuets are delightfully done, the Trio of K.421 is exquisite, and the 6/8 finale of that remarkable work begins with simple charm then becomes more searching in the variations, which surely anticipate Beethoven. The *Hunt* opens swingingly yet is agreeably relaxed and its slow movement has a natural gravity. The analogue recordings are beautiful, very smooth on top, the balance slightly middle- and bass-orientated, more noticeably so on CAL 9242. After the finale of K.421 and a pause of about twelve seconds, the Haydn Op. 74/3 begins with the level disconcertingly higher and the transfer much brighter. This too is a very fine performance – but be prepared! Perhaps the *Dissonance* could have a stronger profile but it, too, is beautifully played and recorded.

String quartets Nos. 15 in D min., K.421; 17 in B flat (Hunt), K.458.
*** Denon C37 7003 [id.]. Smetana Qt.

The Smetana find just the right tempo for the first movement of the *D minor*, unhurried but forward-moving. *The Hunt*, which is placed first on the disc, is given a spirited performance and is rather more polished than most of its CD rivals; it is a pleasure to report with enthusiasm on these well-paced accounts.

String quartets Nos. 16 in E flat, K.428; 18 in A, K.464.
(M) ** Naxos Dig. 8.550540 [id.]. Eder Qt.

Like the earlier issue in this super-bargain Naxos series, the playing of the Eder Quartet can hardly be faulted, but the resonant recording, made in a Budapest church, gives almost a string orchestral illusion at times and robs the music-making of intimacy.

String quartet No. 17 in B flat (Hunt), K.458.
(M) *** Teldec/Warner 2292 42440-2 [id.]. Alban Berg Qt – HAYDN: *Quartet No. 77.* ***

String quartets Nos. 17 in B flat (Hunt), K.458; 19 in C (Dissonance), K.465.
⊛ *** Teldec/Warner 2292 43037-2 [id.]. Alban Berg Qt.

The Alban Berg version of the *Hunt quartet* dates from 1979 and is still possibly the finest account on the market. It is also available coupled with Haydn, and has great polish and freshness and well withstands all the competition that has come since. The *Dissonance* is of similar vintage. It, too, is first class, with a wonderfully expressive account of the slow movement; there is a sense of total dedication about these wholly excellent performances, which are recommended with enthusiasm. No reservations about the transfers.

String quartet No. 19 in C *(Dissonance), K.465; Divertimenti: in D, K.136; in B flat, K.137; in F, K.138.*
☞ (BB) ** Naxos Dig. 8.550543 [id.]. Eder Qt.

The playing here is enjoyably warm and polished. The *Dissonance* opens with the Eder group creating considerable atmosphere, then the Allegro sets off rather determinedly. The fairly close balance in the resonant Budapest Unitarian Church prevents a real pianissimo, but the effect is real if inflated. The three *Divertimenti* (which we also often hear in chamber-orchestra presentation) are better suited by the acoustic and are given sympathetic, lively performances, if lacking the last ounce of sparkle.

String quartets Nos. 20 in D (Hoffmeister), K.499; 21 in D, K.575; 22 in B flat, K.589; 23 in F, K.590 (Prussian Quartets Nos. 1–3).
*** CRD CRD 3427/8; *CRDC 4127/8* [id.]. Chilingirian Qt.

The Chilingirian Quartet give very natural, unforced, well-played and sweet-toned accounts of the last four *Quartets*. They are very well recorded too, with cleanly focused lines and a warm, pleasing ambience; indeed in this respect these two discs are second to none.

(i) *String quartets Nos. 20 in D, K.499; 21 in D, K.575;* (ii) *Violin sonata No. 17 in C, K.296.*
☞ *** Calliope CAL 9244 [id.]. (i) Talich Qt; (ii) Peter Messiereur, Stanislav Bogunia.

The Talich coupling of K.499 and K.575 is digital and the recording brighter and more present than in the *Haydn Quartets*. The playing has comparable sensibility and plenty of vitality.

String quartets Nos. 21 in D, K.575; 22 in B flat, K.589.
☞ *** Nimbus Dig. NI 5351 [id.]. Franz Schubert Qt.

An enjoyable and well-recorded issue. The Franz Schubert Quartet play with refreshing lack of affectation and great sweetness of tone. They are to a certain extent devotees of beauty: there are no rough edges and contours are consistently smooth. There is perhaps more sweetness than depth in the slow movements; but at the same time it must be said that there is nothing narcissistic about the playing, and the listener is held from start to finish. They are very well recorded too. At 51 minutes 46 seconds there would be room for another quartet, but, as a glance above and below will confirm, this is a criticism that can be widely levelled.

Complete Mozart Edition, Volume 11: *String quintets Nos. 1–6.*
(M) *** Ph. 422 511-2 (3). Grumiaux Trio, with Gerecz, Lesueur.

(i) *String quintets Nos. 1–6;* (ii) *Clarinet quintet in A, K.581.*
(M) *** Sony M3YK 45827 (3). (i) Juilliard Qt with John Graham; (ii) Harold Wright, Marlboro
    Ens. (Alexander Schneider, Isidore Cohen, Samuel Rhodes, Leslie Parnas).

The Grumiaux ensemble's survey of the *String quintets* offers immensely civilized and admirably conceived readings. Throughout the set the vitality and sensitivity of this team are striking, and in general this eclipses all other recent accounts. The remastering of the 1973 recordings for CD is very successful indeed.

While the Grumiaux box remains a first choice, the Juilliard set on the Sony makes a very good alternative. The performances are finely shaped and very alive, and even those who do not always warm to this ensemble will find them both alive and responsive here. There is depth in slow movements and plenty of spirit elsewhere. The first movement of the *D major*, K.593, for example, is a delight. The recordings, which emanate from the late 1970s, have come up very well and the set has the additional inducement of offering a very musical account of the *Clarinet quintet* from 1970.

String quintets Nos. 3 in C, K.515; 4 in G min., K.516.
☞ ** RCA Dig. 09026 60940-2 [id.]. Tokyo Qt, Pinchas Zukerman.

Wonderfully accomplished performances from the Tokyo Quartet and Zukerman, but music-making which is rather less satisfying as Mozart playing. In terms of unanimity of ensemble, technical finesse and tonal blend, the Tokyo is one of the finest quartets now before the public and their accounts of both these great works is marked by impeccable technical address. But feeling resides on the surface and there is too little sense of spontaneity or the depth and poignancy this great music must have. Compare the humanity and naturalness of the old Pro Arte set or, turning to more recent times, the Grumiaux on Philips, and one is in a different world.

(i) *String quintet No. 4 in G min., K.516;* (i) *Violin sonata No. 26 in B flat, K.378.*
(M) *** BMG/RCA GD 87869 [7869-2-RG]. Heifetz, with (i) Baker, Primrose, Majewski,
    Piatigorsky; (ii) Brooks Smith – *Violin concerto No. 5.* ***

The illustrious ensemble adopts a very fast pace for the first movement of the *G minor Quintet*, and some might feel that its urgency is over-pressed; yet so fine is the playing that, after a minute or two, one adjusts as at a live performance. There are wonderful moments in the rest of the work, not least the viola playing of William Primrose. The acoustic is a little dry, but the sound itself is full and warmly blended, with good detail. The *Violin sonata* was recorded two years later and shows splendid rapport between the great violinist and his partner, Brooks Smith.

Complete Mozart Edition, Volume 15: *Violin sonatas Nos. 1–34; Sonatinas in C & F, K.46d & 46e; Sonatina in F (for beginners), K.547; Sonata in C, K.403* (completed Stadler); *Adagio in C min., K.396; Allegro in B flat, K.372; Andante & allegretto in C, K.404; Andante in A & Fugue in A min., K.402* (completed Stadler); *12 Variations on 'La bergère Célimène', K.359; 6 Variations on 'Hélas, j'ai perdu mon amant', K.360.*

(M) **(*) Ph. Analogue/Dig. 422 515-2 (7). Gérard Poulet, Blandine Verlet; Arthur Grumiaux, Walter Klien; Isabelle van Keulen, Ronald Brautigan.

The early sonatas, from K.6 through to K.31, were recorded in the mid-1970s by Gérard Poulet with Blandine Verlet on harpsichord. The various fragments, sonatinas, sonatas (K.46d, K.46e, K.403 and K.547) and variations were recorded in 1990 by Isabelle van Keulen and Ronald Brautigan. For the remaining four CDs, Philips have turned to the set by Arthur Grumiaux and Walter Klien, recorded digitally in the early 1980s. There is a great deal of sparkle and some refined musicianship in these performances, and pleasure remains undisturbed by the balance which, in the 1981 recordings, favours the violin. The later recordings, from 1982 and 1983, are much better in this respect.

Violin sonatas Nos. 1–16, K.6–15 & 26–31.
☞ (B) *** Ph. Duo 438 803-2 [id.]. Gérard Poulet, Blandine Verlet.

These early *Violin sonatas* include the young Mozart's first works to appear in print. K.6–9 were composed during the composer's five-month-long Paris visit of 1763–4, and K.10–15 followed on in 1765 when the Mozarts resided in Chelsea, London, for over a year; K.26–31 appeared a few weeks later when the family moved on to The Hague. It seems impossible to determine how much there is of Mozart's father, Leopold, in their composition; certainly he masterminded the project (and the music of J. C. Bach was also a probable influence), but the precociously sprightly invention is consistently ear-catching and, even if the keyboard dominates the musical argument, the violinist is always making attractive comments. The performances here are most persuasive in their vitality and freshness, and they are very well balanced and recorded (in 1975). This set derives from Volume 15 of Philips's Complete Mozart Edition and is well worth having as a separate issue. There is much to delight and fascinate the ear, although these are records to dip into rather than to play all through!

Violin sonatas Nos. 26 in B flat, K.378; 28 in E flat, K.380; 32 in B flat, K.454; Violin sonatina in F, K.457.
*** Olympia OCD 125 [id.]. Igor Oistrakh, Natalia Zertsalova.

Igor Oistrakh has not as assertive a personality as his father, and he makes a very real partnership here with Zertsalova, who is an excellent Mozartian. These are all splendid works and they are played with fine classical feeling and impetus; the Rondo finale of K.380 is a demonstrable example of the sparkle of this music-making. The recording, too, is truthful.

Violin sonatas Nos. 33 in E flat, K.481; 34 in A, K.526; Violin sonatina in F, K.547.
(M) *** Decca 425 420-2. Szymon Goldberg, Radu Lupu.

Goldberg's playing has great depth, though at times his age perhaps begins to show (a slight lack of bloom on his tone); but this does not inhibit the strength of the recommendation, for Lupu is marvellously sensitive. The CD transfer is first class, and this is one of the most rewarding single discs of these *Sonatas*.

PIANO MUSIC

Piano duet

Complete Mozart Edition, Volume 16: (i) *Andante with 5 variations, K.501; Fugue in C min., K.426; Sonatas for piano duet in C, K.19d; D, K.381; G, K.357; B flat, K.358; F, K.497; C, K.521; Sonata in D for two pianos, K.448;* (ii) *Larghetto and Allegro in E flat* (reconstructed Badura-Skoda).
(M) ** Ph. 422 516-2 (2) [id.]. (i) Ingrid Haebler, Ludwig Hoffman; (ii) Jörg Demus, Paul Badura-Skoda.

This two-CD set includes all the music Mozart composed for piano duet or two pianos, in elegant (if at times a little too dainty) performances by Ingrid Haebler and Ludwig Hoffman in recordings dating from the mid-1970s. Also included is a Mozart fragment, the *Larghetto and Allegro in E flat*, probably written in 1782–3 and completed by Paul Badura-Skoda, who recorded it in 1971 for the Amadeo label with Jörg Demus. Despite the occasional distant clink of Dresden china, all these performances give pleasure and are very decently recorded.

Andante with 5 variations, K.501; Sonata in D for 2 pianos, K.448.
☞ *** Chan. Dig. CHAN 9162 [id.]. Louis Lortie, Hélène Mercier (with SCHUBERT: *Fantasia in F min.* ***).

The Louis Lortie–Hélène Mercier partnership was quite special in Ravel and proves no less successful here. In fact theirs is one of the most sensitive accounts of the *D major Sonata,* K.448, currently available on disc, and their account of the *Andante and variations* can be put without embarrassment alongside the classic (currently deleted) Argerich/Bishop or Lupu/Perahia versions. The Schubert coupling is also recommendable. Very good recording.

Sonata in D, K.448.
*** Sony MK 39511 [id.]. Murray Perahia, Radu Lupu – SCHUBERT: *Fantasia in D min.* ***

With Perahia taking the primo part, his brightness and individual way of illuminating even the simplest passage-work dominate the performance, producing magical results and challenging the more inward Lupu into comparably inspired playing. Pleasantly ambient recording made at The Maltings, Snape, and beautifully caught on CD.

Sonatas in F, K.497; in B flat, K.358; Adagio and allegro in F min., K.594.
☞ *(*) Ara. Dig. Z 6635 [id.]. Artur Balsam & Gena Raps.

With Artur Balsam leading the duo, it is not surprising that the Arabesque performances are musically satisfactory. However, here the rather resonant piano emphasizes the middle and lower range; one needs clearer, brighter textures for this repertoire. Also the playing time is ungenerous: 45 minutes 34 seconds.

Sonatas: in F, K.497; in C, K.521; Andante and 5 variations in G, K.501. Pieces for mechanical organ: Adagio and allegro in F min., K.594; Adagio and allegro in F min., K.608.
☞ * Decca Dig. 440 474-2 [id.]. George Malcolm & András Schiff (fortepiano).

Malcolm and Schiff use a fortepiano in the Salzburg Mozarteum traditionally reputed to have once belonged to the composer. It is closely recorded and the result is, to say the least, clattery. The playing is strong, the effect percussive and the results are entirely lacking in charm and soon tire the ear.

Sonatas: in F, K.497; in C, K.521; Pieces for mechanical organ: Adagio and allegro in F min., K.594; Adagio and allegro in F min., K.608.
☞ ⊛ *** Ottavio Dig. OTR C129242. Imogen Cooper and Anne Queffélec.

The partnership of Imogen Cooper and Anne Queffélec is highly suited to this repertoire, recalling the earlier association of Brendel and Klien on Vox in its spontaneity and musicianship. Yet they have the advantage of first-class modern recording, with the acoustic and degree of resonance nicely judged; indeed the piano image is all but ideal. Above all, these performances convey a sense of joy in the music. The *Sonatas* – both highly inspired – are framed by the two works for mechanical clock, which here sound both thoughtful and unusually commanding: the opening *Adagio* of K.594 is wonderfully serene. The first movement of the *C major Sonata* sets off with great spirit, yet detail is always imaginatively observed; the *Andante* which follows is delightfully poised, and the finale has the lightest touch. The slow movement of K.497 reminds the listener immediately of the horn concertos, a lovely, flowing melody, so persuasively presented, while the finale has a most engaging lilt. Altogether this is playing of great distinction. Everything is marvellously fresh and there is never the least suspicion of Dresden china. Very strongly recommended.

Solo piano music

Piano sonatas Nos. 1–10.
☞ ⊛ (B) *** VoxBox 11 58422 (2) [CDX 5026]. Walter Klien.

Piano sonatas Nos. 11–18; Fantasy in C min., K.475.
☞ ⊛ (B) *** VoxBox 11 59222 (2) [CDX 5046]. Walter Klien.

Piano sonatas Nos. 1–18; Fantasia in C min., K.475.
⊛ (M) *** Ph. Dig. 422 517-2 (5) [id.]. Mitsuko Uchida.

Piano sonatas Nos. 1–18; Sonatas in C, K.46d; in F, K.46e.
☞ (B) *** DG 419 445-2 (5) [id.]. Christoph Eschenbach.

On Philips, Mitsuko Uchida's collection, with beautiful and naturally balanced digital recording made in the Henry Wood Hall, London, has now been reissued on 5 mid-priced CDs by omitting the shorter pieces, except for the *C minor Fantasia*. Miss Uchida's set of the Mozart *Sonatas* brings playing of consistently fine sense and sound musicianship. There is every indication that this will come to be regarded as a classic series to set alongside those of Gieseking and Walter Klien. Every phrase is beautifully placed, every detail registers, and the early *Sonatas* are as revealing as the late ones. The piano recording is completely realistic, slightly distanced in a believable ambience.

Klien is an outstanding Mozartian; his playing has consistent freshness and is in exemplary taste. It gives enormous pleasure and is at times slightly more robust in its vitality than the playing of Mitsuko Uchida. There is nothing remotely self-conscious about it; the phrasing is unfailingly musical and every detail is beautifully placed without there being the slightest suggestion of preciosity. The balance is rather forward but the tone is rounded and full. The set has been successfully accommodated on four bargain-priced discs.

Christoph Eschenbach made his recordings over 3½ years between 1967 and 1970, and the sound is of admirable quality, the piano well focused and clear with just the right degree of sonority for his repertoire. He gives consistently well-turned, cool and elegant performances without affectation or mannerism. Those looking for an unidiosyncratic, direct approach to Mozart, entirely free from any suggestion of Dresden china, should find this poised, immaculate pianism to their taste. The famous *Andante grazioso* variations which form the first movement of the *Sonata in A*, K.331, are entirely characteristic, played very simply and directly. Other pianists are gentler, more romantic, but Eschenbach's taste cannot be faulted and the clean precision of the *Rondo Alla Turca* finale is very impressive.

Piano sonatas Nos. 1–18; Fantasias: in D min., K.397; C min., K.475.
☞ *** DG Dig. 431 760-2 (6). Maria João Pires.

Piano sonatas Nos. 1 in C, K.279; 2 in F, K.280; 9 in D, K.311; 18 in D, K.576.
☞ *** DG Dig. 435 882-2 [id.]. Maria João Pires.

Piano sonatas Nos. 3 in B flat, K.281; 4 in E flat, K.282; Sonata in F: andante and allegro, K.533; Rondo, K.494.
☞ *** DG Dig. 437 546-2 [id.]. Maria João Pires.

Piano sonatas Nos. 5 in G, K.283; 6 in D, K.284; 10 in C, K.330.
☞ *** DG Dig. 437 791-2 [id.]. Maria João Pires.

Piano sonatas Nos. 7 in C, K.309; 12 in F, K.332; 16 in B flat, K.570.
☞ *** DG Dig. 439 769-2 [id.]. Maria João Pires.

Piano sonatas Nos. 8 in A min., K.310; 13 in B flat, K.333; 15 in C, K.545.
☞ *** DG Dig. 427 768-2 [id.]. Maria João Pires.

Piano sonatas Nos. 11 in A, K.331; 14 in C min., K.457; Fantasias: in C min., K.475; in D min., K.397.
☞ *** DG Dig. 429 739-2 [id.]. Maria João Pires.

Maria João Pires is a stylist and a fine Mozartian, as those who have heard any of her cycle on Denon will know. But this splendid new DG set marks a step forward over her earlier interpretations. Pires is always refined yet never wanting in classical feeling, and she has a vital imagination. In these new readings there is even more life: she strikes an ideal balance between poise and expressive sensibility, conveying a sense of spontaneity in everything she does. Moreover, the DG recording is fuller, with greater depth than the Denon set, and the slight dryness to the timbre suits the interpretations, which are expressively fluid and calm without a trace of self-consciousness. Her thoughtful, poetic feeling is heard at its very finest in the *Adagio* of the *F major Sonata*, K.332, and the slow movement of K.570 has a comparable grace and quiet dignity. The *Andante un poco Adagio* of the early *Sonata*, K.309 (an unusually structured movement), is hardly less successful, so this makes DG 439 769-2 (which includes these three works) a positive point of entry into her cycle. With allegros always alert and vital yet never too predictable in their expressive contrasts, this is playing to stimulate the listener consistently – even the hackneyed *C major Sonata*, K.545, sounds freshly minted. While Uchida's much-praised versions are full of personal intimacy, Pires's more direct style with its tranquil eloquence is no less satisfying.

Piano sonatas Nos. 2 in F, K.280; 4 in E flat, K.282; 14 in C min., K.457; Fantasia in C min., K.475.
☞ (BB) ** Discover Dig. DICD 920144 [id.]. Aldo Ciccolini.

Piano sonatas Nos. 3 in B flat, K.281; 12 in F, K.332; 13 in B flat, K.333.
☞ (BB) ** Discover Dig. DICD 920148 [id.]. Aldo Ciccolini.

Piano sonatas Nos. 7 in C, K.309; 10 in C, K.330; 15 in C, K.545.
☞ (BB) ** Discover Dig. DIDC 920145 [id.]. Aldo Ciccolini.

Aldo Ciccolini's new digital survey of the Mozart *Sonatas* is strikingly well recorded: the presence of the piano is very tangible. However, the forwardness emphasizes the playing style, which is very strong, even percussive, in its directness of articulation. That is not to suggest a lack of sensibility, only that (for some ears) the effect may seem too forceful for this repertoire. *Andante* movements are nicely paced, and allegros are certainly spirited. On the disc containing the three *C major Sonatas*, Ciccolini lightens his touch for the famous first movement of K.545, and this is a very appealing performance; but the *Allegro con spirito* opening of K.309 brings a very wide dynamic range and a forceful sonority more appropriate for Beethoven. When Ciccolini relaxes and plays lightly, he can readily charm the ear, but the fortissimos are very strongly accented indeed.

Piano sonatas Nos. 4 in E flat, K.282; 5 in G, K.283; 10 in C, K.330; 12 in F, K.332.
☞ (M) **(*) Decca 433 900-2 [id.]. Wilhelm Backhaus – HAYDN: *Sonatas.* **(*)

Backhaus was always magisterial and here his playing, strongly classical in style, commands the listener's interest throughout, managing to do so without any attempt at surface charm. The rhythmic control is not always exact, but this slight fluctuation gives the melodic flow a certain rugged individuality. The whole effect is far removed from the scented periwig style of Mozart pianism, and if the sonatas are taken one at a time the spontaneous quality of the playing is enjoyable for its sheer strength of personality. However, listening to the recital as a whole, one is conscious that rather more lightening of the texture is needed in slow movements. The recording, from the 1960s, is faithful and clear.

Piano sonatas Nos. 8 in A min., K.310; 11 in A, K.331; 14 in C min., K.457; Fantasy in C min., K.475.
☞ (B) ** Virgin/EMI Dig. VJ5 61101-2 [id.]. Jean-Bernard Pommier (piano).

This is thoughtfully musical playing, but Pommier does not project a strongly individual profile. He is at his best in the improvisatory style of the *Fantasy in C minor* which is very effective, but in the variations which form the opening *Andante* of the favourite *A major Sonata*, K.331, the clear, clean articulation of the melody fails to find its simple, *grazioso* character, and the effect becomes too formal. The recording is most lifelike.

Piano sonatas No. 8 in A min., K.310; 11 in A, K.331; 15 in F, K.533.
☞ ⊛ *** Sony Dig. SK 48233 [id.]. Murray Perahia.

Murray Perahia celebrates his return to the recording studios with this recital, which is easily the finest Mozart sonata record for some years. Such is his artistry that one is never consciously aware of it. Again we have the old story of the search for truth producing beauty almost as a by-product. Nothing is beautified, nor does he shrink from conveying that hint of pain that fleetingly disturbs the symmetry of the slow movements. The Sony engineers provide excellent sound. Here is one of the records that will be reissued in 2010 or thereabouts as a 'Great Recording of the Last Century'.

Piano sonata No. 11 in A, K.331; 9 Variations in D on a Minuet by Dupont, K.373.
☞ (M) *** Ph. 438 306-2 [id.]. Alfred Brendel – BEETHOVEN: *Sonata No. 12* etc. ***

Very distinguished playing indeed. One is tempted to suggest that the reader adds this CD to his or her collection even at the cost of duplication, so thoughtful and illuminating are Brendel's insights. K.331 is a joy, and beautifully recorded too (in 1975), and the Beethoven coupling is equally recommendable.

Piano sonatas Nos. 12 in F, K.332; 13 in B flat, K.333; 14 in C min., K.457; Fantasy in C min.
*** Sony Dig. SK 46748 [id.]. Andreas Haefliger.

The Swiss-born, Juilliard-trained Andreas Haefliger is still in his twenties and shows himself to be an impressive Mozartian. These are finely poised and well-integrated performances without any touch of Dresden china but with plenty of sensitivity. The Sony recording is very clean and firm. Eminently recommendable.

Piano sonatas Nos. 14 in C min., K.457; 15 in C, K.545; 17 in D, K.576; Adagio in B min., K.540; Fantasias: in C min., K.475; D min., K.397; Sonata in F (Allegro and Andante in F), K.533; Rondo, K.494; Rondo in A min., K.511; 10 Variations in G, K.455.
☞ ** Ph. Dig. 432 989-2 [id.]. Mitsuko Uchida.

These recordings were made in Osaka and Tokyo on a Japanese concert tour in 1991 and – apart from the intrusive applause, which is unnecessarily loud – are technically of the highest quality. But while they obviously bring the spontaneous interplay between pianist and audience, they also, alas,

demonstrate Uchida's willingness to posture and move away from her natural Mozartian sensibility
into a more romantic style of playing. The *Adagio in B minor* is very free, but not as much so as the
Fantasia in D minor, which opens with a crescendo and diminuendo and then becomes very wayward
indeed. The nostalgic manner of the *A minor Rondo* also seems too self-aware, and even the *Andante*
of the crisply classical *Sonata in C* has an unnecessary degree of rubato. The famous *Variations*
(Tchaikovsky's choice for his *Mozartiana suite*) have plenty of vigour and colour but, as in the
Fantasia, the dynamic range is surely too wide to encompass a truly Mozartian ethos. Readers should
turn back to Uchida's earlier and admirable complete set of the *Sonatas* (Philips 422 517-2) which,
with the *D minor Fantasia*, is offered on five CDs at mid-price and to which we give a Rosette.

Complete Mozart Edition, Volume 18: *8 Variations in G, K.24; 7 Variations in D, K.25; 12 Variations
in C, K.179; 6 Variations in G, K.180; 9 Variations in C, K.264; 12 Variations in C, K.265; 8
Variations in F, K.352; 12 Variations in E flat, K.353; 12 Variations in E flat, K.354; 6 Variations in
F, K.398; 10 Variations in G, K.455; 12 Variations in B flat, K.500; 9 Variations in D, K.573; 8
Variations in F, K.613; Adagio in B min., K.540; Eine kleine Gigue in G, K.574; Fantasia in D min.,
K.397; Minuet in D, K.355; Rondos: in D, K.485; in A min., K.511; 21 Pieces for keyboard, K.1, K.1a–
1d;1f; K.2–5; K.5a; K.33b; K.94; K.312; K.394–5; K.399–401; K.408/1; K.453a; K.460.*
(M) ** Ph. Analogue/Dig. 422 518-2 (5) [id.]. Ingrid Haebler or Mitsuko Uchida (both piano), Ton
   Koopman (harpsichord).

Although the gentle clink of Dresden china can occasionally be heard, Ingrid Haebler is an intelligent
and perceptive artist who characterizes these variations with some subtlety. The quality of the sound
is very good indeed: there is both warmth and presence. Mitsuko Uchida gives us various short
pieces, such as the *A minor Rondo*, K.511, and the *B minor Adagio*, K.540, which she plays beautifully
– though at less than 40 minutes her disc offers rather short measure. However, Haebler and
Koopman make up for that, the latter offering 21 short pieces, including some juvenilia, which he
dispatches with some degree of brusqueness. He is very brightly recorded.

VOCAL MUSIC

Complete Mozart Edition, Volume 22: (i) *Adagio and fugue in C min., K.546; Maurerische
Trauermusik, K.477.* (ii) *La Betulia liberata* (oratorio), *K.118.* (iii) *Davidde penitente* (cantata), *K.469.*
(iv) *Grabmusik (Funeral music), K.42.* (v; i) Masonic music: *Dir, Seele des Weltalls, K.429; Ihr unsre
neuen Leiter, K.484; Die ihr unermesslichen Weltalls Schöpfer, ehrt, K.619; Lasst uns mit
geschlung'gnen Händen, K.623; Laut verkünde unsre Freude, K.623; Lied zur Gesellenreise, K.468;
Lobgesang auf die feierliche Johannisloge, K.148; Die Maurerfreude, K.471; Zerfliesset heut, geliebte
Brüder, K.483.* (vi) *Passionslied: Kommet her, ihr frechen Sünder, K.146.* (vii) *Die Schuldigkeit des
ersten Gebots* (Singspiel), K.35.
(M) **(*) Ph. Analogue/Dig. 422 522-2 (6) [id.]. (i) Dresden State O, Schreier; (ii) Schreier, Cotrubas,
   Berry, Fuchs, Zimmermann, Salzburg Chamber Ch. & Mozarteum O, Hagen; (iii) M. Marshall,
   Vermillion, Blochwitz; (iv) Murray, Varcoe; (v) Schreier, Blochwitz, Schmidt, Leipzig R. Ch.; (vi)
   Murray; (vii) M. Marshall, Murray, Nielsen, Blochwitz, Baldin; (iii; iv; vi; vii) Stuttgart RSO,
   Marriner.

The two big oratorios are both early works, *La Betulia liberata* and (even earlier, dating from his
twelfth year) *Die Schuldigkeit des ersten Gebots* ('The Duty of the First Commandment'). *Davidde
penitente* is the cantata largely derived from the torso of the *C minor Mass*, while the sixth disc, in
many ways the most inspired of all, contains the Masonic music, vividly done in Dresden under the
direction of Peter Schreier. For convenience that disc also includes the purely instrumental Masonic
music, the *Mauerische Trauermusik* and the *Adagio and fugue in C minor*. Directed by Leopold Hager,
La Betulia liberata is a plain, well-sung performance that does not quite disguise the piece's excessive
length. Sir Neville Marriner is the conductor both of *Die Schuldigkeit* and of *Davidde penitente*, giving
sparkle to the early oratorio and vigour to the cantata, a fine piece. Full texts are given, and
informative notes on individual works.

Complete Mozart Edition, Volume 20: (i) *Alma Dei creatoris, K.277;* (ii) *Ave verum corpus, K.618;* (i)
Benedictus sit Deus Pater, K.117; Cibavit eos ex adipe frumenti, K.44; (iii) *Dixit et Magnificat, K.193;*
(i) *Ergo interest, an quis, K.143;* (ii) *Exsultate jubilate, K.165;* (i) *God is our refuge* (motet), *K.20; Inter
natos Mulierum, K.72;* (iii) *Litaniae de BMV (Lauretanae), K.109 & K.195;* (i) *Kyries, K.33; K.90–
91; K.322–3;* (ii) *Kyrie, K.341;* (iii) *Litaniae de venerabili altaris sacramento, K.125 & K.243;* (i)
*Miserere mei, Deus, K.85; Misercordias Domini, K.222; Quaerite primum regnum Dei, K.86; Regina
coeli, laetare, K.108; K.127; K.276; Sancta Maria, mater Dei, K.273; Scande coeli limina, K.34; Sub*

tuum praesidium, K.198; Te Deum laudamus, K.141; Veni, Sancte Spiritus, K.47; Venite, populi, venite, K.260; (ii) *Vesperae solennes de confessore, K.339;* (iii) *Vesperae solennes de Domenica, K.321.*

(M) *** Ph. 422 520-2 (5) [id.]. (i) Nawe, Reinhardt-Kiss, Schellenberger-Ernst, Selbig, Burmeister, Lang, Büchner, Eschrig, Ribbe, Pape, Polster; (ii) Te Kanawa, Bainbridge, Ryland Davies, Howell, London Symphony Ch. & LSO, Sir Colin Davis; (iii) Frank-Reinecke, Shirai, Burmeister, Riess, Büchner, Polster, (i; iii) Leipzig R. Ch. & SO, Kegel.

It is fascinating to find that the boy Mozart's very first religious piece is an unaccompanied motet, written in London to an English text, *God is our refuge* – which here the Leipzig singers very forgivably pronounce 'reefuge'. Herbert Kegel with the Dresden Staatskapelle and his Leipzig Radio Choir are responsible for the great majority of the pieces here, fresh and alert if on occasion rhythmically too rigid. The big exception is the great setting of the *Solemn vespers,* K.339, for which Sir Colin Davis's 1971 version has understandably been preferred, when the young Kiri Te Kanawa sings the heavenly soprano setting of *Laudate Dominum* so ravishingly. She is also the soloist in the early cantata *Exsultate jubilate* with its brilliant *Alleluia.* Those 1971 recordings, made in London, are bass-heavy, but the rest brings very fresh and clean recording, with the choir generally more forwardly placed than in the recordings of Mozart's Masses, made by the same forces.

Complete Mozart Edition, Volume 23: (i) *2 Canons for strings; 14 Canons for woodwind; 10 Interval canons for woodwind;* (ii) *6 Canons for female voices; 3 Canons for mixed voices; 13 Canons for male voices; 4 puzzle canons for mixed voices.* (iii) *53 Concert arias. Aria* (with ornamentation by Mozart) for: J. C. BACH: *Adriano in Siria.* (iv) *8 Vocal Duets, Trios and Quartets.* (v) Alternative arias and duets for: *Così fan tutte; Don Giovanni; Die Entführung aus dem Serail; La finta semplice; Idomeneo; Lucio Silla; Mitridate; Le nozze di Figaro.*

(M) *** Ph. 422 523-2 (8) [id.]. (i) Bav. RSO (members); (ii) Ch. Viennensis, Mancusi or Harrer; (iii) Moser, Schwarz, Popp, Mathis, Gruberová, Sukis, Araiza, Ahnsjö, Lloyd, Berry, Kaufmann, Blochwitz, Lind, Burrows, Eda-Pierre; (iv) Blochwitz, Schariner, Pape, Kaufman, Lind, Jansen, Schreier; (v) Blochwitz, Szmytka, Wiens, Gudbjörnson, Vermillion, Schreier, Mathis, Burrows, Tear, Terfel, Kaufmann, Lind, Scharinger.

Taking three more records than the Decca collection of concert arias (see below), the Philips set offers substantial extras, not just a collection of a dozen or so ensembles and a whole disc of 35 canons (some of them instrumental) but some fascinating alternative versions and substitute arias for different Mozart operas, from *La finta semplice* and *Mitridate* through to the three Da Ponte masterpieces. It is fascinating to have Bryn Terfel, for example, as Figaro in a varied recitative and slightly extended version of the Act I aria, *Non piu' andrai.* Eva Lind is vocally a less happy choice for the items involving Susanna and Zerlina, and generally the sopranos chosen for this collection, stylish Mozartians as they are, have less sumptuous voices than those on the Decca set.

Complete Mozart Edition, Volume 24: (i) Lieder: *Abendempfindung; Als Luise die Briefe ihres ungetreuen Liebhabers; Die Alte; An Chloe; An die Freude; An die Freundschaft; Die betrogene Welt; Dans un bois solitaire; Geheime Liebe; Der Frühling; Gessellenreise; Die grossmütige Gelassenheit; Ich würd' auf meinem Pfad; Das Kinderspiel; 2 Kirchenlieder (O Gottes Lamm; Als aus Agypten); Des kleinen Friedrichs Geburtstag; Die kleine Spinnerin; Komm, liebe Zither, komm; Lied der Freiheit; Das Lied der Trennung; Un moto di gioia; Oiseaux, si tous les ans; Ridente la calma; Sehnsucht nach dem Frühling; Sei du mein Trost; Das Traumbild; Das Veilchen; Verdankt sei es dem Glanz der Grossen; Die Verschweigung; Warnung; Wie unglücklich bin ich nit; Der Zauberer; Die Zufriedenheit (2): (Was frag' ich viel nach Geld und Gut; Wie sanft, wie ruhig fühl' ich hier); Die Zufriedenheit im niedrigen Stande.* (ii) *6 Notturni for voices and woodwind, K.346; K.436/9 & K.549.*

(M) *** Ph. 422 524-2 (2) [id.]. Elly Ameling, (i) with Dalton Baldwin (piano or organ) or Benny Ludemann (mandolin); (ii) with Elisabeth Cooymans, Peter van der Bilt, Netherlands Wind Ens. (members).

Elly Ameling is the ideal soprano for such fresh and generally innocent inspirations, with her voice at its purest and sweetest when she made the recordings in 1977. In the 1973 recordings of the *Notturni* (setting Italian texts by Metastasio) she is well matched by her soprano and baritone partners, though these are mostly plainer, less distinctive miniatures. Included are two hymns with organ and two tiny songs with mandolin, while aptly the very last of the series, K.598, is one of the lightest of all, *Children's games,* sparklingly done. The recordings come up with fine freshness and presence.

Lieder: *Abendempfindung; Als Luise die Briefe; An die Einsamkeit; An die Freundschaft; An die Hoffnung; Dans un bois solitaire; Eine kleine deutsche Kantate; Gesellenreise; Die grossmütige Gelassenheit; Die kleine Spinnerin; Das Lied der Trennung; Oiseaux, si tous les ans; Ridente la calma;*

Sehnsucht nach dem Frühlinge; Das Veilchen; Der Zauberer; Die Zufriedenheit.
(M) **(*) Saga SCD 9037 [id.]. Jill Gomez, John Constable.

Recorded early in Jill Gomez's career, this collection of Mozart songs offers much fresh and charming singing, with the girlish simplicity of some of the songs delightfully brought out, and with fine shading of tone-colour. For all her beauty of tone, the singer is taxed by some of the more demanding songs like *Abendempfindung*, not always helped by John Constable's accompaniments, less imaginative than usual.

Concert arias: *Ah! lo previdi . . . Ah t'invola, K.272; Bella mia fiamma . . . Resta oh cara, K.528; Chi sa, K.582; Nehmt meinen Dank, ihr holden Gönner, K.383; Non più, tutto ascolta . . . Non temer, amato bene, K.490; Oh temerario Arbace! . . . Per quel paterno amplesso, K.79/K.73d; Vado, ma dove?, K.583.* Opera arias: (ii) *Le nozze di Figaro: Porgi amor; E Susanna non vien! . . . Dove sono.* (iii) *Der Schauspieldirektor: Bester Jüngling!*
☞ *** Decca 440 401-2 [id.]. Kiri Te Kanawa: (i) V. CO, György Fischer; (ii) LPO, Solti; (iii) VPO, Pritchard.

Kiri Te Kanawa's Decca set of Mozart's concert arias for soprano, recorded in 1982, makes a beautiful and often brilliant recital. Items range from one of the very earliest arias, *Oh temerario Arbace*, already memorably lyrical, to the late *Vado, ma dove*, here sung for its beauty rather than for its drama. Atmospheric, wide-ranging recording, which has transferred well to CD. The arias from *Figaro* and *Schauspieldirektor* come from the complete Decca sets and show the singer at her finest.

Concert arias: *Alma grande e nobil core, K.578; Ch'io mi scordi di te?, K.505; Nehmt meinen Dank, K.383; Vado, ma dove?, K.583.* Lieder: *Abendempfindung; Als Luise die Briefe; Die Alte; An Chloë; Dans un bois solitaire; Im Frühlingsanfang; Das Kinderspiel; Die kleine Spinnerin; Das Lied der Trennung; Oiseaux, si tous les ans; Ridente la calma; Sehnsucht nach dem Frühling; Das Trumbild; Das Veilchen; Der Zauberer; Die Zuhfriedenheit.*
(M) *** EMI mono/stereo CDH7 63702-2 [id.]. Schwarzkopf, Gieseking; Brendel; LSO, Szell.

Schwarzkopf's classic series of the Mozart songs with Gieseking makes a splendid reissue at mid-price; it includes the most famous one, *Das Veilchen*. As a generous coupling, the disc also includes Schwarzkopf's much later recordings, with Szell conducting four concert arias – including the most taxing of all, *Ch'io mi scordi di te?*, with Brendel playing the piano obbligato. Though the voice is not quite so fresh in the concert arias, the artistry and imagination are supreme, and stereo recording helps to add bloom.

Concert arias: *A questo seno . . . Or che il cielo, K.374; Basta, vincesti . . . An non lasciarmi, K.486a; Voi avete un cor fedele, K.217. Exsultate, jubilate* (motet), *K.165. Litaniae de venerabili altaris sacramento, K.243: Dulcissimum convivium. Vesperae de Dominica, K.321: Laudate dominum.*
(B) *** Ph. 426 072-2. Elly Ameling, ECO, Leppard.

Elly Ameling's singing, besides being technically very secure, has a simple radiance in the phrasing which is very beautiful. She is equally happy in the concert arias, sung with delightful flexibility of phrase, and in the ecclesiastical music, where the style has a serene simplicity, while *Exsultate, jubilate* has an infectious sense of joy.

Concert arias: *Bella mia fiamma . . . Resta, o cara!, K.528; Ch'io mi scordi di te, K.505.* Arias: *Don Giovanni: Or sai chi l'onore; Crudele! Ah, no, mio bene; Non mi dir. Idomeneo: Se il padre perdei; O smania! . . . D'Oreste e d'Ajace. Le nozze di Figaro: Porgi, amor; Deh vieni non tardar; E Susanna non vien! . . . Dove sono. Il rè pastore: L'amerò, sarò costante. Die Zauberflöte: Ach, ich fühl's.*
☞ (M) *** BMG/RCA 09026 61357-2 [id.]. Leontyne Price, New Philh. O, Adler or Santi; RCA Italiana Op. O, Molinari-Pradelli; LSO, Downes.

This record is an adjunct to Leontyne Price's four-disc 'Prima donna' collection (see Recitals, below) and the items here make an equally outstanding representation of her art. One does not think of her primarily as a Mozartian, yet the very opening concert aria, *Ch'io mi scordi*, shows the extra dimension of drama in her vocal personality, never at the expense of the vocal line. She is thrilling as Electra, snorting fire in *O smania! O Furie! (Idomeneo)*, and *Or sai chi l'onore (Don Giovanni)* is scarcely less vehement. The glorious legato line is heard at its most ravishing in the major *Figaro* arias, whether as Susanna (*Deh vieni*) or the Countess (*Dove sono*), and the excerpt from *Il rè pastore*, *L'amerò, sarò costante*, with its weaving violin obbligato, is radiant. Nearly all these recordings were made in the late 1960s, when the voice was at its freshest. Accompaniments are highly sympathetic and the vocal quality is most natural and vivid, and with lovely orchestral sound.

Concert arias: (i) *Ch'io mi scordi di te ... Non temer, K.505;* (ii) *Misero me! ... Misero pergoletto, K.77; Ombra felice! ... Io ti lascio, K.255.* Arias: (iii) *La clemenza di Tito: Parto, parto;* (iv) *Deh per questo istante solo.* (iii) *Così fan tutte: Temerari! ... Come scoglio; E Amore un ladroncello; Ei parte ... Per pietà;* (v) *Ah! Scostati! ... Smanie implacabili.* (iii) *Le nozze di Figaro: Non so più; Voi che sapete;* (ii) (Replacement aria): *Giunse alfin il momento ... Al desio di chi t'adora.*

☞ (M) *** Decca 421 899-2 [id.]. Teresa Berganza, with (i) Geoffrey Parsons; (ii) VSO, György Fischer; (iii) LSO, Pritchard; (iv) V. State Op. O, Kertész; (iv) LPO, Solti.

The greater part of this CD represents Berganza's Mozart début recital, which received universal praise when it first appeared in 1962. It was obvious that a new recording star had arrived, and at the time we praised her technical virtuosity and noted her tone-colour to be unfailingly beautiful and the sense of style immaculate. We also noted that the last degree of dramatic urgency was missing but that this was only the smallest drawback when separate arias are involved. Now the collection has been made more up to date by the inclusion of an excerpt from her complete set, *La Clemenza di Tito* of 1967, and *Smanie implacabili* from the 1973 *Così fan tutte* with Solti. To complete the picture, two more concert arias and a replacement aria which Mozart composed in 1789 for a revival of *Figaro* are added, recorded in 1981 as part of Decca's compilation of concert and insertion arias, featuring different artists. Here one notices the extra vocal maturity, but throughout it is the consistency that is so striking, the rich voice controlled with the sort of vocal perfection one associates with her compatriot, Victoria de los Angeles, which means that she can be equally convincing as Cherubino and Susanna in *Figaro*, and Fiordiligi and Dorabella in *Così*. Bright, vivid transfers throughout.

Ave verum corpus, K.618.

(M) *** Decca 430 159-2 [id.]. St John's College, Cambridge, Ch., Guest – J. HAYDN: *Theresienmesse;* M. HAYDN: *Ave regina.* ***

This simple and eloquent account of Mozart's choral lollipop is beautifully recorded and, it is to be hoped, may introduce some collectors to the inspired late Haydn Mass with which it is coupled.

Ave verum corpus, K.618; Exsultate, jubilate, K.165; Kyrie in D minor, K.341; Vesperae solennes de confessore in C, K.339.

**(*) Ph. 412 873-2 [id.]. Te Kanawa, Bainbridge, Ryland Davies, Howell, London Symphony Ch., LSO, C. Davis.

This disc could hardly present a more delightful collection of Mozart choral music, ranging from the early soprano cantata, *Exsultate, jubilate*, with its famous setting of *Alleluia*, to the equally popular *Ave verum*. Kiri Te Kanawa is the brilliant soloist in the cantata, and her radiant account of the lovely *Laudate Dominum* is one of the highspots of the *Solemn vespers*, here given a fine, responsive performance. The 1971 recording has been remastered effectively, although the choral sound is not ideally focused.

(i–ii) *Ave verum corpus, K.618;* (iii–iv) *Exsultate, jubilate, K.165; Masses Nos.* (i–iii; v) *10 in C (Missa brevis): Spatzenmesse, K.220;* (ii–iii; vi) *16 in C (Coronation), K.317.*

(M) *** DG 419 060-2. (i) Regensburg Cathedral Ch.; (ii) Bav. RSO, Kubelik; (iii) Edith Mathis; (iv) Dresden State O, Klee; (v) Troyanos, Laubenthal, Engen; (vi) Procter, Grobe, Shirley-Quirk, Bav. R. Ch.

Kubelik draws a fine, vivid performance of the *Coronation Mass* from his Bavarian forces and is no less impressive in the earlier *Missa brevis*, with excellent soloists in both works. Then Edith Mathis gives a first-class account of the *Exsultate, jubilate* as an encore. The concert ends with Bernard Klee directing a serenely gentle account of the *Ave verum corpus* (recorded in 1979).

(i) *Ave verum corpus, K.618;* (ii) *Exsultate jubilate, K.65;* (i–iii) *Masses Nos. 10 in C (Spatzenmesse; 'Sparrow Mass');* (iv) *16 in C (Coronation), K.317;* (i) *Offertorium de tempore (Misericordias Domine), K.222;* (iv) *Vesperae de Dominica, K.321;* (i–iii) *Vesperae solennes de confessor, K.339.*

☞ (B) **(*) Erato/Warner Duo 4509 95362-2 (2) [id.]. (i) Philippe Caillard Chorale; (ii) Rotraud Hansmann; (iii) Annie Bartelloni, Michel Sénéchal, Roger Soyer; V. Bar. Ens.; (iv) Patricia Wise, Monika Bürgener, Michael Cousins, Heinz Ecker, Lisbon Gulbenkian Foundation Ch. & O; all cond. Guschlbauer.

A splendid Erato Bonsai Duo collection of Mozart church music that is much more than the sum of its parts. Throughout, Theodor Guschlbauer knows just where he is going and his pacing always feels right. The choral contributions, whether of the Lisbon Chorus or the smaller, Philippe Caillard group, have both discipline and commitment: these singers really rise to the occasion. The performance of the *Spatzenmesse* is particularly attractive. It is full of high spirits and is a remarkably concise piece (the *Kyrie* lasts only 1 minute 44 seconds and the *Sanctus* is a burst of joy merely 57 seconds long). The *Benedictus* provides a fine ensemble for the solo team. Before that, we have heard the excellent soprano soloist, Rotraud Hansmann, showing her mettle in the *Exsultate jubilate*, where the famous *Alleluia* sparkles, and she is no less impressive in the more demanding and equally well-known *Laudate Dominum* of the *Solemn Vespers*, which she sings with serene radiance. In the *Laudate Dominum* of the *Vesperae de Dominica*, Patricia Wise is not her match. This is a more florid piece, much more difficult technically; it is well enough managed, but one feels that the singer is under pressure. But she leads the solo team confidently in the *Benedictus* of the *Coronation Mass*, another very lively performance, and seems altogether more at ease in the final *Agnus Dei*, where she is joined at the end by her colleagues; then the chorus closes the work vigorously in a glorious culmination, very operatic in feeling. These reservations are of minor account: all this music is greatly enjoyable, and the analogue recordings, all from the late 1960s (except K.317 and K.321, which are a decade later), are of good quality and excellently transferred. This is well worth exploring – but be warned: no documentation is provided about the music except for the cued list of tracks.

Exsultate, jubilate, K.165 (Salzburg version); Motets: *Ergo interest, K.143; Regina coeli* (2 settings), *K.108, K.127.*
*** O-L Dig. 411 832-2 [id.]. Emma Kirkby, Westminster Cathedral Boys' Ch., AAM Ch. and O, Hogwood.

The boyish, bell-like tones of Emma Kirkby are perfectly suited to the most famous of Mozart's early cantatas, *Exsultate, jubilate*, culminating in a dazzling account of *Alleluia*. With accompaniment on period instruments, that is aptly coupled with far rarer but equally fascinating examples of Mozart's early genius, superbly recorded.

(i) *Exsultate jubilate, K.165;* (ii) *Litaniae Lauretanae in D, K.195; Mass No. 16 (Coronation), K.317;* (iii) *Requiem mass (No. 19) in D min., K.626.*
☞ (B) **(*) Double Decca 443 009-2 (2) [id.]. (i) Erna Spoorenberg; (ii; iii) Cotrubas, Watts, Tear, Shirley-Quirk; (ii) Oxford Schola Cantorum; (iii) ASMF Ch; (i–iii), ASMF, Marriner.

It is good to have Marriner's 1971 (Argo) recordings of two of Mozart's most appealing early choral works, the *Litaniae Lauretanae* and the *Coronation Mass*, back in the catalogue on this Double Decca set. The solo work is particularly good (notably Ileana Cotrubas in the two lovely *Agnus Dei* versions) and the Academy Choir is on its best form. Erna Spoorenberg's impressive *Exsultate jubilate* was recorded earlier (1966). However, Marriner generates less electricity than usual in the coupled (1977) *Requiem Mass*. It is interesting to have a version which uses the Beyer Edition and a text which aims at removing the faults of Süssmeyer's completion, amending points in the harmony and instrumentation; but few will register any significant differences except in such points as the extension of the *Osanna*. Solo singing is good, and some of the choruses (the *Dies irae*, for instance) are vibrant, but at other times they are less alert and the tension slackens. The sound is excellent, well balanced and vivid.

(i) *Exsultate jubilate, K.165;* (i; ii) *Vesperae solemnes de confessore, K.339: Laudate Dominum;* (iii) *Requiem mass (No. 19) in D min., K.626.*
☞ (B) *(*) DG Classikon 439 412-2 [id.]. (i) Maria Stader; (ii) Berlin RIAS Chamber Ch.; (i;ii) Berlin RSO, Fricsay; (iii) Lipp, Rössel-Majdan, Dermota, Berry, V. Singverein, BPO, Karajan.

Maria Stader's performances are accomplished, but Karajan's earlier (1962) reading of the *Requiem* took a suave view of the work. The chief objection to this version is that detail tends to be sacrificed in favour of warmth and atmosphere. The solo quartet are wonderfully blended, a rare occurrence in this work above all, and, although the chorus lacks firmness of line, they are helped out by the spirited playing of the Berlin Philharmonic. However, the sound is nothing special, and both Karajan's digital version and the 1976 analogue recording are greatly preferable.

Litaniae de venerabili altaris sacramento, K.243.
(M) *** Decca 430 158-2 [id.]. Marshall, Cable, Evans, Roberts, St John's College, Cambridge, Ch., Wren O, Guest – HAYDN: *Heiligmesse.* ***

Mozart made four settings of the Litany, of which this is the last, written in 1776. It is ambitiously scored for an orchestra of double wind, two horns and three trombones – used to add sonorous gravity to many of the choral passages and to bring point and drama to the choral fugue, *Pignus futurae gloriae*; in the beautiful *Dulcissimum convivium* the solo soprano is accompanied with flutes added to the orchestra in place of the oboes. It is Mozart at his most imaginative and vital; the artists here rise to the occasion and give a highly responsive performance, with Margaret Marshall outstanding among the soloists. Excellent 1980 sound.

Masonic music (see also above, in Complete Mozart Edition, Volume 22)

Masonic music: *Masonic funeral music (Maurerische Trauermusik), K.477; Die ihr des unermesslichen Weltals Schöpfer ehrt* (cantata), *K.619; Die ihr einen neuen Grade, K.468; Dir, Seele des Weltalls* (cantata), *K.429; Ihr unsre neuen Leiter* (song), *K.484; Lasst uns mit geschlungnen Händen, K.623a; Laut verkünde unsre Freude, K.623; O heiliges Band* (song), *K.148; Sehen, wie dem starren Forscherange, K.471; Zerfliesset heut', geliebte Brüder, K.483.*

(M) *** Decca 425 722-2. Werner Krenn, Tom Krause, Edinburgh Festival Ch., LSO, Kertész.

This Decca reissue contains the more important of Mozart's masonic music in first-class performances, admirably recorded. Most striking of all is Kertész's strongly dramatic account of the *Masonic funeral music*; the two lively songs for chorus, *Zerfliesset heut'* and *Ihr unsre neuen Leiter*, are sung with warm humanity and are also memorable. Indeed the choral contribution is most distinguished throughout, and Werner Krenn's light tenor is most appealing in the other items which he usually dominates.

Complete Mozart Edition, Volume 19: *Masses Nos. 1 in G (Missa brevis), K.49; 2 in D min. (Missa brevis), K.65; 3 in C ('Dominicus'), K.66; 4 in C min. (Waisenhaus), K.139; 5 in G (Pastoral), K.140; 6 in F (Missa brevis), K.192; 7 in C (Missa in honorem Ssmae Trinitatis), K.167; 9 in D (Missa brevis), K.194; 10 in C (Spatzenmesse; 'Sparrow Mass'), K.220; 11 in C ('Credo'), K.257; 12 in C (Spaur-Messe), K.258; 13 in C ('Organ solo'), K.259; 14 in C (Missa longa), K.262; 15 in B flat (Missa brevis), K.275; 16 in C ('Coronation'), K.317; 17 in C (Missa solemnis), K.337; 18 in C min. (Great), K.427; 19 in D min. (Requiem), K.626.*

(M) **(*) Ph. Analogue/Dig. 422 519-2 (9) [id.]. Mathis, Donath, M. Price, McNair, Montague, Shirai, Casapietra, Trudeliese Schmidt, Lang, Schiml, Markert, Burmeister, Knight, Schreier, Araiza, Heilmann, Baldin, Ryland Davies, Rolfe Johnson, Ude, Jelosits, Adam, Polster, Andreas Schmidt, Hauptmann, Rootering, Grant, Eder; Leipzig R. Ch.; Monteverdi Ch.; V. Boys' Ch.; John Alldis Ch.; Ch. Viennensis; Leipzig RSO; E. Bar. Soloists; Dresden State O; LSO; VSO; Dresden PO; Kegel; C. Davis; Gardiner; Schreier; Harrer.

Only the *C minor Mass* has period performers. John Eliot Gardiner's inspired reading, with superb soloists as well as his Monteverdi Choir and English Baroque Soloists, has rightly been chosen, and the *Requiem* comes in another outstanding modern version, with the Dresden Staatskapelle and Leipzig Radio Choir conducted by Peter Schreier, as imaginative a conductor as he is a tenor. That same choir and orchestra under the choir's regular conductor, Herbert Kegel, is responsible for the great bulk of the rest of the Masses. With the chorus tending to be placed a little backwardly, it does not always sound its freshest, but performances – with consistently clean-toned soloists, including latterly Mitsuko Shirai – are bright and well sprung. Sir Colin Davis and the LSO in the earliest recording here, dating from 1971, take a weightier view than any in the *Credo Mass*, K.257, with sound bass-heavy, but again his vigour and freshness are very compelling. Two favourite Masses, the *Coronation Mass* and the *Spatzenmesse* (Sparrow Mass), come in performances conducted by Uwe Christian Harrer with the Vienna Symphony Orchestra and the Vienna Boys' Choir; boys also distinctively take the soprano and alto solos. Though Harrer's speeds tend to be slow, the rhythmic buoyancy is most compelling, with choral sound full and forward.

Mass No. 4 in C min. (Weisenhausmesse), K.139.
(M) *** DG 427 255-2. Janowitz, Von Stade, Moll, Ochman, V. State Op. Ch., VPO, Abbado.

By any standards this is a remarkably sustained example of the thirteen-year-old composer's powers, with bustling allegros in the *Kyrie*, *Gloria* and *Credo*, as well as at the end of the *Agnus Dei*, while the *Gloria* and *Credo* end with full-scale fugues. This far from negligible piece sounds at its very best in Abbado's persuasive hands.

Mass No. 12 in C (Spaur), K.258.
(M) *** Decca 430 161-2 [id.]. Palmer, Cable, Langridge, Roberts, St John's College, Cambridge, Ch., Wren O, Guest – HAYDN: *Schöpfungsmesse.* ***

The *Spaur Mass* is not among Mozart's most inspired, but its directness is appealing and the *Benedictus* offers a fine Mozartian interplay of chorus and soloists. In a vigorous performance like this, it is most enjoyable.

Mass No. 16 in C (Coronation), K.317.
☞ (M) **(*) Decca Dig. 436 470-2 [id.]. Margaret Marshall, Murray, Covey-Crump, Wilson-Johnson, King's College Ch., ECO, Cleobury – HAYDN: *Nelson Mass.* **(*)

Though in terms of its rhythms Cleobury's performance is not as lively as the finest versions of
King's College Ch., ECO, Cleobury – HAYDN: *Nelson Mass.* **(*)
Though in terms of its rhythms Cleobury's performance is not as lively as the finest versions of
K.317, this performance can be recommended warmly, with its excellent soloists and fresh choral
singing all beautifully recorded. It is generously coupled to an even more vibrant account of Haydn's
Nelson Mass.

(i) *Mass No. 16 in C (Coronation), K.317;* (ii; iii) *Missa brevis in C (Spatzenmesse), K.220;* (iii) *Ave
verum corpus;* (iv) *Exsultate, jubilate, K.165; Vesperae solennes de Confessore, K.339: Laudate
Dominum.*
(M) **(*) DG 429 820-2 [id.]. (i) Tomowa-Sintow, Baltsa, Krenn, Van Dam, V. Singverein, BPO,
Karajan; (ii) Mathis, Troyanos, Laubenthal, Engen; (iii) Regensberger Cathedral Ch., Bav. RSO,
Kubelik; (iv) Mathis, Dresden Ch. & State O, Klee.

Karajan's 1976 recording of the *Coronation Mass* is a dramatic reading, lacking something in
rhythmic resilience perhaps; but, with excellent solo singing as well as an incisive contribution from
the chorus, there is no lack of strength and the score's lyrical elements are sensitively managed.
Kubelik draws a fine, lively account of the earlier *Missa brevis*, and again the solo singing is of high
quality. Bernard Klee contributes a serene performance of the lovely *Ave verum corpus*, and Edith
Mathis offers a first-class account of the *Exsultate, jubilate* and a slightly less appealing *Laudate
Dominum* (recorded in 1979, six years after the motet). The remastering is vivid.

Masses Nos. (i; ii) *16 in C (Coronation), K.317;* (i; iii) *18 in C min. (Great), K.427;* (i; iv) *Requiem
Mass, K.526.*
☞ (B) **(*) Ph. Duo 438 800-2 (2) [id.]. (i) Helen Donath, Ryland Davies; (ii) Gillian Knight,
Stafford Dean; John Alldis Ch., LSO; (iii) Heather Harper, Stafford Dean, L. Symphony Ch.,
LSO; (iv) Yvonne Minton, Gerd Nienstedt, Alldis Ch., BBC SO; Sir Colin Davis.

These very successful CD transfers demonstrate the best features of the original recordings, which
date from between 1967 and 1971. Sir Colin Davis's vital account of the *Coronation Mass* is given
with a strong team of soloists; and in the so-called *'Great' Mass in C minor* the use of the Robbins
Landon edition – which rejects the accretions formerly used to turn this incomplete torso of a work
into a full setting of the liturgy – prompts him to a strong and intense performance which brings out
the darkness behind Mozart's use of the C minor key. Again he is helped by fine soprano singing
from Helen Donath, and from Heather Harper too. The *Requiem*, with a smaller choir, is more
intimate and the soloists are more variable, yet with his natural sense of style Davis finds much
beauty of detail. While the scale is authentic and the BBC orchestra is in good form, this reading,
enjoyable as it is, does not provide the sort of bite with which a performance on this scale should
compensate for sheer massiveness of tone.

Mass No. 18 in C min. (Great), K.427.
☞ *** DG Gold Dig. 439 012-2 [id.]. Hendricks, Perry, Schreier, Luxon, V. Singverein, BPO,
Karajan.
*** Ph. Dig. 420 210-2 [id.]. McNair, Montague, Rolfe Johnson, Hauptmann, Monteverdi Ch., E.
Bar. Soloists, Gardiner.
*** Decca Dig. 425 528-2. Augér, Dawson, Ainsley, D. Thomas, Winchester Cathedral Ch. &
Winchester College Quiristers, AAM, Hogwood.

In his (1982) digital recording of the *C minor Mass* Karajan gives Handelian splendour to this
greatest of Mozart's choral works and, though the scale is large, the beauty and intensity are hard to
resist. Solo singing is first rate, particularly that of Barbara Hendricks, the dreamy beauty of her
voice ravishingly caught. Woodwind is rather backward, yet the sound is both rich and vivid –
though, as the opening shows, the internal balance is not always completely consistent. Nevertheless
this digitally remastered CD in the Karajan Gold series sounds more vivid than ever, and the chorus
is tangibly present.

John Eliot Gardiner, using period instruments, gives an outstandingly fresh performance of high
dramatic contrasts, marked by excellent solo singing – both the sopranos pure and bright-toned and
Anthony Rolfe Johnson in outstandingly sweet voice. With the recording giving an ample scale
without inflation, this can be warmly recommended.

Hogwood's version can be considered alongside the fine Gardiner account, even though his
control of rhythm is less resilient and often squarer. The soloists if anything are even finer, and many
Mozartians will prefer having boy trebles in the chorus and German pronunciation of Latin.
Hogwood also opts for an edition by Richard Maunder which, among other things, adds appropriate
instruments to the incomplete orchestrations of the *Credo* and *Et incarnatus est.* This is particularly
impressive in the *Credo*, where trumpets and timpani bring an aptly festive flavour, adding to the

panache of the opening. The sound has a vivid sense of presence, with treble tone cutting through very freshly.

Masses Nos. (i) *18 in C min. (Great), K.427;* (ii) *19 in D min. (Requiem), K.626.*
☞ (B) (**(*)) DG Double stereo/mono 437 389-2 (2) [id.]. (i) Stader, Töpper, Haefliger, Sardi, St Hedwig's Cathedral Ch., Berlin RSO, Fricsay; (ii) Seefried, Pitzinger, Holm, Borg, V. State Op. Ch., VPO, Jochum.

Fricsay's powerful 1960 recording of the *C minor Mass* brings often bitingly dramatic choral singing. The performance is not without its eccentricities (the accelerando at the close of the *Osanna*, for instance) but the conductor's volatile approach adds to the feeling of freshness. Maria Stader distinguishes herself in the *Laudamus te* and concludes the *Credo* most beautifully. Hertha Töpper, however, is less satisfactory and in the *Domine Deus* she tends to mar the duet she shares with Stader by conveying a lack of comfort in certain high passages where a similar phrase passes from one singer to the other. But even with such blemishes, this music-making communicates very directly, and the focus is remarkably clear on CD, with plenty of depth to back up the bright upper range. The coupling, Jochum's 1956 mono recording of the *Requiem Mass*, is a characteristically inspirational account with powerfully committed choral singing (witness the fervour of the *Dies irae* and *Sanctus*), capped by the splendid closing *Lux aeterna*. There are good soloists who work well together as a team and Kim Borg is particularly strong. No apologies need be made for the mono sound, which is forward, vivid and well focused.

Requiem Mass (No. 19) in D min., K.626.
(BB) *** Virgin/EMI Dig. VJ7 59648-2; *VJ 759648-4* [id.]. Yvonne Kenny, Alfreda Hodgson, Arthur Davies, Gwynne Howell, N. Sinfonia Ch., London Symphony Ch., N. Sinfonia, Richard Hickox.
(M) *** DG Dig. 431 288-2. Tomowa-Sintow, Müller Molinari, Cole, Burchuladze, V. Singverein, VPO, Karajan.
*** Ph. Dig. 411 420-2 [id.]. Margaret Price, Schmidt, Araiza, Adam, Leipzig R. Ch., Dresden State O, Schreier.

Requiem Mass, K.626; Ave verum corpus, K.618.
(M) **(*) BMG/RCA GD 86535 [RCA 6535-2-RG]. Equiluz, Eder, Vienna Boys' Ch., V. State Op. Ch. & O, Gillesberger; or VSO, Froschauer – HAYDN: *Te Deum.* **(*)

Requiem Mass, K.626; Kyrie in D min., K.341.
*** Ph. Dig. 420 197-2 [id.]. Bonney, Von Otter, Blochwitz, White, Monteverdi Ch., E. Bar. Soloists, Gardiner.

John Eliot Gardiner with characteristic panache gives one of the most powerful performances ever, for while the lighter sound of the period orchestra makes for greater transparency, the weight and bite are formidable. The soloists are an outstanding quartet, well matched but characterfully contrasted too, and the choral singing is as bright and luminous as one expects of Gardiner's Monteverdi Choir. The superb *Kyrie in D minor* makes a very welcome and generous fill-up, to seal a firm recommendation.

At super-bargain price, Richard Hickox's excellent version of the *Requiem Mass* on the Virgin Virgo label matches any in the catalogue. With generally brisk speeds and light, resilient rhythms, it combines gravity with authentically clean, transparent textures in which the dark colourings of the orchestration, as with the basset horns, come out vividly. All four soloists are outstandingly fine, and the choral singing is fresh and incisive, with crisp attack. The voices, solo and choral, are placed rather backwardly; otherwise the recording is excellent.

Karajan's 1987 digital version of the *Requiem* is a large-scale reading, but one that is white-hot with intensity and energy. The power and bite of the rhythm are consistently exciting. The solo quartet is first rate, though Helga Müller Molinari is on the fruity side for Mozart. Vinson Cole, stretched at times, yet sings very beautifully, and so does Paata Burchuladze with his tangily distinctive Slavonic bass tone. The close balance adds to the excitement.

Peter Schreier's is a forthright reading of Mozart's valedictory choral work, bringing strong dramatic contrasts and marked by superb choral singing and a consistently elegant and finely balanced accompaniment. The singing of Margaret Price in the soprano part is almost finer than any other yet heard on record, and the others make a first-rate team, if individually more variable. Only in the *Kyrie* and the final *Cum sanctis tuis* does the German habit of using the intrusive aitch annoy. Altogether this is most satisfying.

The surprise version is Gillesberger's. Using treble and alto soloists from the Vienna Boys' Choir, who sing with confidence and no little eloquence, this performance also has the advantage of a dedicated contribution from Kurt Equiluz. Gillesberger's pacing is well judged and the effect is as fresh as it is strong and direct. The 1982 recording is excellent, vivid yet full, and the result is powerful but not too heavy. Mozart's *Ave verum* is also very well sung.

Requiem mass (No. 19) in D min. (ed. Maunder).
**(*) O-L Dig. 411 712-2 [id.]. Emma Kirkby, Watkinson, Rolfe Johnson, David Thomas,
     Westminster Cathedral Boys' Ch., AAM Ch. and O, Hogwood.

Hogwood's version cannot be compared with any other, using as it does the edition of Richard Maunder, which aims to eliminate Süssmayr's contribution to the version of Mozart's unfinished masterpiece that has held sway for two centuries. So the *Lacrimosa* is completely different, after the opening eight bars, and concludes with an elaborate *Amen*, for which Mozart's own sketches were recently discovered. This textual clean-out goes with authentic performance of Hogwood's customary abrasiveness, very fresh and lively to underline the impact of novelty.

Vesperae de dominica, K.321.
(M) *** Decca 430 162-2 [id.]. Marshall, Cable, Evans, Roberts, St John's College, Cambridge, Ch.,
     Wren O, Guest – HAYDN: *Harmoniemesse*. ***

Aptly coupled with Haydn's *Harmoniemesse*, Mozart's vibrant *Vesperae de dominica* opens with a series of brilliant choral settings (with contrasting solo quartet), accompanied by trumpets and strings. Margaret Marshall is appropriately agile in the lively soprano solo of the *Laudate Dominum*, and the work closes with an ambitious *Magnificat* in which all the participants are joined satisfyingly together. The St John's performance is full of vigour and the 1980 recording is full and vivid.

Vesperae solennes de confessore, K.339.
(M) *** Decca 430 157-2 [id.]. Palmer, Cable, Langridge, Roberts, St John's College, Cambridge,
     Ch., Wren O, Guest – HAYDN: *Paukenmesse*. ***

Although Guest's version of Mozart's masterpiece does not always match the full-price recording by Sir Colin Davis for Philips (see above under *Ave verum corpus*) – with Felicity Palmer a less poised soloist than Kiri Te Kanawa – the Decca account has the advantage of authenticity in the use of boys in the chorus. Moreover the CD transfer of the 1979 Argo recording is preferable to the less well-defined Philips sound.

OPERA

Complete Mozart Edition, Volume 26: *Apollo et Hyacinthus* (complete).
(M) *** Ph. 422 526-2 (2) [id.]. Augér, Mathis, Wulkopf, Schwarz, Rolfe Johnson, Salzburg Chamber
     Ch. & Mozarteum O, Hager.

The opera was written when Mozart was eleven, with all but two of the parts taken by schoolchildren. The style of the writing and vocalization is rather simpler than in other dramatic works of the boy Mozart, but the inspiration is still remarkable, astonishingly mature. The orchestration is assured and full of imaginative touches. The performance here is stylish and very well sung. Excellent, clear and well-balanced recording, admirably transferred to CD.

Complete Mozart Edition, Volume 30: *Ascanio in Alba* (complete).
(M) **(*) Ph. 422 530-2 (3) [id.]. Sukis, Baltsa, Mathis, Augér, Schreier, Salzburg Chamber Ch.,
     Salzburg Mozarteum O, Hager.

Written when he was fifteen, *Ascanio in Alba* came between the boy composer's two other Milan commissions, *Mitridate* and *Lucio Silla*. Hager makes an excellent start with an exceptionally lively account of the delightful overture, but then the choruses seem relatively square, thanks to the pedestrian, if generally efficient singing of the Salzburg choir. Hager's speeds are sometimes on the slow side, but the singing is excellent, with no weak link in the characterful cast, though not everyone will like the distinctive vibrato of Lilian Sukis as Venus. The 1976 analogue recording is full and vivid.

Bastien und Bastienne (complete). Concert arias: *Mentre ti lascio, o figlia, K.513; Misero ! o sogno . . . Aura, che intorno spiri, K.431. Le nozze di Figaro: Giunse alfin il momento . . . Deh vieni; Un moto di gioia.*
*** Sony Dig. SK 45855 [id.]. Gruberová, Cole, Polgar, Liszt CO, Leppard.

Complete Mozart Edition, Volume 27: *Bastien und Bastienne* (complete); Lieder: *Komm, liebe Zither, komm; Die Zufriedenheit.*

(M) *** Ph. Dig. 422 527-2 [id.]. Dominik Orieschnig, Georg Nigl, David Busch, V. Boys' Ch., VSO, Harrer.

Leppard conducts a near-ideal performance of the eleven-year-old Mozart's charming little one-Acter, very well recorded. Edita Gruberová is delectably fresh and vivacious as the heroine, Vinson Cole is a sensitive and clean-voiced Bastien and Laszlo Polgar is full of fun in the buffo role of Colas. The Liszt Chamber Orchestra of Budapest plays with dazzling precision. As a generous fill-up, the three soloists sing Mozart arias, including the big scena for tenor, *Misero! o sogno*, and a replacement aria for Susanna, especially written for the 1789 production of *Le nozze di Figaro*: *Un moto di gioia*.

On Philips, the opera is performed by boy trebles instead of the soprano, tenor and bass originally intended. Members of the Vienna Boys' Choir give a refreshingly direct performance under Uwe Christian Harrer, missing little of the piece's charm. The two songs with mandolin accompaniment, also sung by one of the trebles, make an attractive fill-up. First-rate 1986 digital sound.

Complete Mozart Edition, Volume 44: *La clemenza di Tito* (complete).

(M) *** Ph. 422 544-2 (2) [id.]. Dame Janet Baker, Minton, Burrows, Von Stade, Popp, Lloyd, ROHCG Ch. & O, Sir Colin Davis.

La clemenza di Tito (complete).

*** DG Dig. 431 806-2 (2). Rolfe Johnson, Von Otter, McNair, Varady, Robbin, Hauptmann, Monteverdi Ch., E. Bar. Soloists, Gardiner.

☞ *** Teldec/Warner Dig. 4509 90857-2 (2) [id.]. Langridge, Popp, Ziesack, Murray, Ziegler, Polgár, Zurich Op. Ch. & O, Harnoncourt.

(M) *** DG 429 878-2 (2) [id.]. Berganza, Varady, Mathis, Schreier, Schiml, Adam, Leipzig R. Ch., Dresden State O, Boehm.

Sir Colin Davis's superb set is among the finest of his many Mozart recordings. Not only is the singing of Dame Janet Baker in the key role of Vitellia formidably brilliant; she actually makes one believe in the emotional development of an impossible character, one who progresses from villainy to virtue with the scantiest preparation. The two other mezzo-sopranos, Minton as Sesto and Von Stade in the small role of Annio, are superb too, while Stuart Burrows has rarely if ever sung so stylishly on a recording as here. Davis's swaggering manner transforms what used to be dismissed as a dry *opera seria*. Excellent recording.

Again, with his vitality and bite, Gardiner turns the piece into a genuinely involving drama. Though the team of soloists is not quite as consistent as on Sir Colin Davis's 1977 recording, Anthony Rolfe Johnson is outstanding in the title-role, matching the vivid characterization of both Anne Sofie von Otter as Sesto and Julia Varady as Vitellia. Sylvia McNair is an enchanting, pure-toned Servilia and Catherine Robbin a well-matched Annio, though the microphone catches an unevenness in the voice, as it does with Cornelius Hauptmann in the incidental role of Publio. More seriously, DG's vivid, immediate recording picks up a distracting amount of banging and bumping on stage in the Süssmayr recitatives.

Nikolaus Harnoncourt in his commentary for his set of *Clemenza* underlines the way that within the Mozart canon it points forward to a new simplicity, foreshadowing nineteenth-century developments. He conducts the piece to bring that out, adopting a far more romantic manner than Gardiner on his fine DG Archiv set. He is so expansively romantic that, in Act II alone, he takes almost 10 minutes longer. In keeping with this approach, Harnoncourt uses modern, not period instruments, as in his previous Mozart opera recordings based on Zurich productions. The trumpets and timpani in the *March* are fearsomely dramatic. Even so, he has not forgotten his early devotion to period performance, making this a very viable account for anyone wanting a half-way approach. Though recorded in association with Zurich Opera, this is a studio, not a live, recording like Gardiner's. It gains from not having stage noises in recitative, even if the less reverberant acoustic for Gardiner is more apt for the music. Ann Murray is at her finest as Sesto, if not quite as firm or dominant as von Otter for Gardiner. Philip Langridge is a splendid Tito, and it is good to have Lucia Popp so affecting in her very last recording. Ruth Ziesak and Delores Ziegler complete a strong team which will not disappoint anyone, even if it cannot quite compare with Gardiner's, singer for singer.

Boehm gave the work warmth and charm, presenting the piece more genially than we have grown used to. The atmospheric recording helps in that, and the cast is first rate, with no weak link, matching at every point that of Sir Colin Davis on his full-price Philips set. Yet, ultimately, even Julia Varady for Boehm can hardly rival Dame Janet Baker for Davis, crisper and lighter in her coloratura. Davis's incisiveness, too, has points of advantage; but, to summarize, any Mozartian can safely leave the preference to his feelings about the two conductors, the one more genial and glowing, the other more urgently dramatic.

Complete Mozart Edition, Volume 42: *Così fan tutte* (complete).
(M) *** Ph. 422 542-2 (3) [id.]. Caballé, Dame Janet Baker, Cotrubas, Gedda, Ganzarolli, Van Allan, ROHCG Ch. & O, Sir Colin Davis.

Così fan tutte (complete).
❀ (M) *** EMI CMS7 69330-2 (3) [Ang. CDMC 69330]. Schwarzkopf, Ludwig, Steffek, Kraus, Taddei, Berry, Philh. Ch. & O, Boehm.
*** Ph. Dig. 422 381-2 (3) [id.]. Mattila, Von Otter, Szmytka, Araiza, Allen, Van Dam, Amb. Op. Ch., ASMF, Marriner.
❀ (M) (***) EMI mono CHS7 69635-2 (3) [Ang. CDHC 69635]. Schwarzkopf, Otto, Merriman, Simoneau, Panerai, Bruscantini, Philh. Ch. & O, Karajan.
☞ *** EMI Dig. CDS7 47727-8 (3) [Ang. CDCC 47727]. Vaness, Ziegler, Watson, Aler, Duesing, Desderi, Glyndebourne Ch., LPO, Haitink.
(M) *** Erato/Warner 2292 45683-2 (3) [id.]. Te Kanawa, Stratas, Von Stade, Rendall, Huttenlocher, Bastin, Rhine Op. Ch., Strasbourg PO, Lombard.
**(*) O-L Dig. 414 316-2 (3) [id.]. Yakar, Resick, Nafé, Winberg, Krause, Feller, Drottningholm Court Theatre Ch. & O, Ostman.
(M) (***) EMI mono CHS7 63864-2 (2) [Ang. CDHB 63864]. Souez, Helletsgruber, Nash, Domgraf-Fassbaender, Brownlee, Eisinger, Glyndebourne Festival Ch. & O, Fritz Busch.
☞ (M) (**(*)) Ph. mono 438 678-2 (3) [id.]. Stich-Randall, Malaniuk, Sciutti, Kmentt, Berry, Ernster, V. State Op. Ch., VSO, Rudolf Moralt.
☞ ** Telarc Dig. CD 80360 (3) [id.]. Lott, McLaughlin, Focile, Hadley, Corbelli, Cachemaille, Edinburgh Festival Ch., SCO, Mackerras.

First choice remains with Boehm's classic set, reissued on three mid-priced CDs, with its glorious solo singing, headed by the incomparable Fiordiligi of Schwarzkopf and the equally moving Dorabella of Christa Ludwig, a superb memento of Walter Legge's recording genius. It still bears comparison with any other recordings, made before or since.

Marriner directs a fresh and resilient performance, beautifully paced, often with speeds on the fast side, and with the crystalline recorded sound adding to the sparkle. Though the women principals make a strong team, the men are even finer: Francisco Araiza as Ferrando, Thomas Allen as Guglielmo and José van Dam as Alfonso all outstanding so that, though the reading is lighter in weight than those of Boehm, Karajan, Haitink or Davis, it has more fun in it, bringing out the laughter in the score.

Commanding as Schwarzkopf is as Fiordiligi in the 1962 Boehm set, the extra ease and freshness of her singing in the earlier (1954) version under Karajan makes it even more compelling. Nan Merriman is a distinctive and characterful Dorabella, and the role of Ferrando has never been sung more mellifluously on record than by Leopold Simoneau. The young Rolando Panerai is an ideal Guglielmo, and Lisa Otto a pert Despina; while Sesto Bruscantini in his prime brings to the role of Don Alfonso the wisdom and artistry which made him so compelling at Glyndebourne. Karajan has never sparkled more naturally in Mozart than here, for the high polish has nothing self-conscious about it. Though the mono recording is not as clear as some others of this period, the subtleties of the music-making are very well caught.

Like his recordings of the other two Lorenzo da Ponte Italian operas, Bernard Haitink's *Così* has been remastered to celebrate the reopening of the new Glyndebourne Opera House in May 1994. With speeds often more measured than usual, Haitink's EMI version still conveys the sparkle of live performances at Glyndebourne. The excellent teamwork, consistently conveying humour, makes up for a cast-list rather less starry than that on some rival versions. This is above all a sunny performance, sailing happily over any serious shoals beneath Da Ponte's comedy. Claudio Desderi as Alfonso helps to establish that Glyndebourne atmosphere, with recitatives superbly timed and coloured. If Carol Vaness and Delores Ziegler are rather too alike in timbre to be distinguished easily, the relationship becomes all the more sisterly when, quite apart from the similarity, they respond so beautifully to each other. John Aler makes a headily unstrained Ferrando, beautifully free in the upper register; and Lilian Watson and Dale Duesing make up a strong team. The digital recording gives fine bloom and an impressive dynamic range to voices and orchestra alike.

The energy and sparkle of Sir Colin Davis are set against inspired and characterful singing from the three women soloists, with Montserrat Caballé and Janet Baker proving a winning partnership, each challenging and abetting the other all the time. Cotrubas equally is a vivid Despina, never merely arch. Though Gedda has moments of rough tone and Ganzarolli falls short in one of his prominent arias, they are both spirited, while Richard van Allan sings with flair and imagination. Sparkling recitative, and recording which has you riveted by the play of the action.

On Erato, Kiri Te Kanawa's voice sounds radiant, rich and creamy of tone; she is commanding in *Come scoglio*, and tenderly affecting in *Per pietà*, which is more moving here than with Levine. Lombard is a sympathetic accompanist, if not always the most perceptive of Mozartians; some of his tempi are on the slow side, but his sextet of young singers make up a team that rivals almost any other, giving firm, appealing performances. With warm recording of high quality, this is most enjoyable and could be a first choice for any who follow the singers in question.

Except that soloists of international standing have been introduced – an aptly fresh-voiced team, stylishly Mozartian – this Oiseau-Lyre recording aims to reproduce one of the most successful of Arnold Ostman's authentic productions at Drottningholm. The point to marvel at initially is the hectic speed of almost every number, yet Ostman refreshingly establishes a valid new view. Few Mozartians would want to hear *Così fan tutte* like this all the time but, with no weak link in the cast and with the drama vividly presented, it can be recommended to all who are prepared to listen afresh.

The legendary Glyndebourne performance, the first ever recording of *Così fan tutte*, is the finest of the three pioneering sets recorded on 78s in the mid-1930s with the newly founded Glyndebourne company. The sound in the CD transfer, though limited, is amazingly vivid, with voices very well focused and with a keener sense of presence than on many recordings of the 1990s. Busch at the time was a progressive Mozartian, preferring athletic treatment, and nowadays even the use of a piano for the recitatives instead of a harpsichord seems less outlandish with the emergence of the fortepiano. John Brownlee as Don Alfonso is very much the English aristocrat, with 'fruffly-fruffly' English vowels instead of Italianate ones, but he is a fine, stylish singer. Ina Souez and Luise Helletsgruber are technically superb; and Heddle Nash and Willi Domgraf-Fassbaender as their lovers are at once stylish and characterful, with Irene Eisinger as a delightfully soubrettish Despina. Cuts are made in the recitatives according to the custom of the time and, more seriously, four numbers disappear – including, amazingly, Ferrando's *Tradito, schernito* and Dorabella's *E amore un ladroncello*. The bonus is that, with those cuts, the opera fits on to only two mid-price CDs.

We discussed the 1956 Moralt mono set of *Così* (together with his *Don Giovanni*) in our first *Penguin Guide to Bargain Records*, a 500-page book published in 1966 at 25/- (£1.25), well before the *Penguin Stereo Guides* first appeared. The three LPs together then cost around £3.15, and at the time we commented that 'at bargain price this is a winner!'. To have remained competitive, the present set should surely have been reissued on CD at bargain price. Moralt in all honesty cannot really compare with Karajan, Marriner or Karl Boehm as an interpreter of Mozart. There is not quite the same sense of style and polish, but that is a comparison on the highest level, and not every Mozart opera recording is conducted as well as this. Among the soloists it is the Despina of Graziella Sciutti who shines out – a glorious performance. Teresa Stich-Randall sings exquisitely too. In the opera house her voice might not be quite big enough for *Come scoglio*, but the precision and clarity here are splendid. Kmentt has a somewhat strained and Germanic tone but he sings intelligently; Walter Berry, as always, is a very reliable Guglielmo and the men's voices match well together in the many trios in which this opera abounds. Two numbers sometimes cut are included here – a duettino from Act I, *Al fato dan legge* and Ferrando's Act II aria, *Ah! Lo veggio quell'anima bellsa*. Minor cuts are made in the long recitatives. The mono sound is full and quite atmospheric; the ear adjusts immediately and the opera moves forward with enjoyable liveliness, with the voices vividly caught. Libretto and translation are included in what is to be a limited edition.

Sir Charles Mackerras follows up his strong, dramatic account of *Zauberflöte* with an equally sympathetic version of *Così fan tutte*. Mackerras here again aims to present a performance on modern instruments which echoes the practices and manner of a period performance, in principle an excellent course. Mackerras is not just a scholarly Mozartian – insisting on appoggiaturas, for example – but a vigorous one, skilled at heightening dramatic moments, making ensembles brisk and exciting. Unfortunately, as in the previous recording, the sound is too reverberant, which is even less apt for this frothy comedy. It inflates the scale of the performance, with recitative sounding as though delivered in a church. It blunts the crispness and undermines the clarity of ensembles. The cast is strong but, whether or not affected by the acoustic and the recording, Mozart manners are on the rough side. Felicity Lott sings a powerful *Come scoglio*, with wonderfully precise triplets, but the voice is not at its purest, with a hint of flutter. It is much the same with Jerry Hadley as Ferrando, who is heavy rather than elegant, with a hint of strain in his aria, *Un aura amorosa*. A flawed set, but enjoyable if you can adjust to the acoustic.

Così fan tutte (excerpts).

☞ (***) Testament mono SBT 1040 [id.]. Jurinac, Thebom, Lewis, Kunz, Borriello, Glyndebourne
Festival O, Fritz Busch; Alda Noni, Philh. O, Susskind.

The superb Testament transfer of excerpts from *Così fan tutte* in the 1950 Glyndebourne production
gives a vivid idea of the way that even in the first year when the re-established Glyndebourne Festival
was recovering its pre-war format, standards were never higher. Sadly, only excerpts were recorded,
but the 73 minutes of items include substantial sections of the first three scenes, as well as other arias
and ensembles. Fritz Busch in his penultimate season was as incisive as before the war, directing
performances at once superbly disciplined yet easy and amiable. Sena Jurinac as Fiordiligi, clear and
vibrant, provides the central glory, with both her two big arias included, as well as six of her ensemble
numbers, and three substantial rehearsal 'takes'. Blanche Thebom too, as Dorabella, sings with
clarity and freshness, and the others make a splendid team. Alda Noni, the Despina, was not
recorded at the Glyndebourne sessions but later, at Abbey Road, with Susskind and the Philharmonia.
The recording brings out a flutter in her voice, less steady than the others. As in pre-war days, a
piano is used instead of harpsichord for recitatives.

Così fan tutte: highlights.
(M) **(*) DG Dig. 431 290-2 [id.]. Te Kanawa, Murray, McLaughlin, Blochwitz, Hampson,
Furlanetto, Concert Group of V. State Op., VPO, Levine.

☞ **(*) Teldec/Warner Dig. 9031 76455-2 [id.]. Margiono, Ziegler, Steiger, Van der Walt,
Cachemaille, Hampson, Netherlands Op. Ch., Concg. O, Harnoncourt.

A generous selection (75 minutes) from Levine's brisk, rather unsmiling full-price *Così*, especially
useful for sampling Dame Kiri's Fiordiligi, one of her finest Mozartian performances on record, and
Thomas Hampson's characterfully rich portrayal of Guglielmo.

Many may enjoy the highlights from Harnoncourt's characterful but somewhat eccentric version,
rather than the complete set. The selection includes the controversially fast *O soave si il vento*,
Fiordiligi's *Come scoglio* and *Per Pietà* within a generally comprehensive and well-selected 74-minute
sampler. However, this would have been even more enticing at mid-price.

Complete Mozart Edition, Volume 41: *Don Giovanni* (complete).
(M) *** Ph. 422 541-2 (3) [id.]. Wixell, Arroyo, Te Kanawa, Freni, Burrows, Ganzarolli, ROHCG
Ch. & O, Sir Colin Davis.

Don Giovanni (complete).
*** EMI CDS7 47260-8 (3) [Ang. CDCC 47260]. Waechter, Schwarzkopf, Sutherland, Alva, Frick,
Sciutti, Taddei, Philh. Ch. & O, Giulini.
(M) *** Decca 411 626-2 (3). Siepi, Danco, Della Casa, Corena, Dermota, V. State Op. Ch., VPO,
Krips.
*** DG Dig. 419 179-2 (3) [id.]. Ramey, Tomowa-Sintow, Baltsa, Battle, Winbergh, Furlanetto,
Malta, Burchuladze, German Op. Ch., Berlin, BPO, Karajan.
☞ *** EMI Dig. CDS7 47037-2 (3) [Ang. CDCC 47036]. Allen, Vaness, Ewing, Gale, Lewis, Van
Allan, Rawnsley, Kavrakos, Glyndebourne Ch., LPO, Haitink.
(M) (***) EMI mono CHS7 63860-2 (3) [Ang. CDHB 63860]. Siepi, Schwarzkopf, Berger, Grümmer,
Dermota, Edelmann, Berry, Ernster, V. State Op. Ch., VPO, Furtwängler.
**(*) O-L Dig. 425 943-2 (3) [id.]. Hagegård, Cachemaille, Augér, Della Jones, Van der Meel,
Bonney, Terfel, Sigmundsson, Drottningholm Court Theatre Ch. & O, Ostman.
(M) (***) EMI mono CHS7 61030-2 (3) [Ang. CDHB 61030]. Brownlee, Souez, Von Pataky,
Helletsgruber, Baccaloni, Henderson, Mildmay, Glyndebourne Fest. Ch. & O, Fritz Busch.
☞ (M) **(*) DG 437 341-2 (3) [id.]. Fischer-Dieskau, Jurinac, Stader, Seefried, Haefliger, Kohn,
Sardi, Kreppel, Berlin RIAS Chamber Ch. & R.O, Fricsay.
☞ (M) (**) Ph. mono 438 674-2 (3) [id.]. London, Zadek, Jurinac, Sciutti, Simoneau, Berry,
Waechter, Weber, V. Chamber Ch., VSO, Rudolf Moralt.
☞ ** EMI Dig. CDS7 54859-2 (3) [Ang. CDCB 54859]. Schmidt, Halgrimson, Dawson, Ainsley,
Yurisch, Argenta, Finley, Miles, Schütz Ch., LCP, Norrington.
☞ ** Chan. Dig. CHAN 8920/2 [id.]. Bruson, Ghazarian, Ottenthal, Pace, Ghiuselev, Sabbatini,
Cologne R. Ch. & SO, Järvi.
☞ (M) (**) EMI mono CMS7 643772 (3). Campo, Stich-Randall, Danco, Moffo, Cortis, Gedda,
Aix-en-Provence Festival Ch., Paris Conservatoire O, Rosbaud.
☞ *(*) Erato/Warner Dig. 2292 45588-2 (3) [id.]. Furlanetto, Cuberli, Meier, Tomlinson, Heilmann,
Pertusi, Salminen, Rodgers, Berlin RIAS Chamber Ch., BPO, Barenboim.

☞ * Koch Schwann Dig. 314 088 (2) [id.]. Dohmen, Pedaci, Galgani, Turco, Berti, Lucarini, Cauli, Silvestrelli, Bellini Lyric Ch., Marchigiano Philh. O, Kuhn.

The classic Giulini EMI set, lovingly remastered to bring out even more vividly the excellence of Walter Legge's original sound-balance, sets the standard by which all other recordings have come to be judged. Elisabeth Schwarzkopf, as Elvira, emerges as a dominant figure to give a distinctive but totally apt slant to this endlessly invigorating drama. The young Sutherland may be relatively reticent as Anna but, with such technical ease and consistent beauty of tone, she makes a superb foil. Taddei is a delightful Leporello, and each member of the cast – including the young Cappuccilli as Masetto – combines fine singing with keen dramatic sense.

Sir Colin Davis has the advantage of a singing cast that has fewer shortcomings than almost any other on disc and much positive strength. Martina Arroyo controls her massive dramatic voice more completely than one would think possible, and she is strongly and imaginatively contrasted with the sweetly expressive Elvira of Kiri Te Kanawa and the sparkling Zerlina of Mirella Freni. As in the Davis *Figaro*, Ingvar Wixell and Wladimiro Ganzarolli make a formidable master/servant team with excellent vocal acting, while Stuart Burrows sings gloriously as Don Ottavio, and Richard Van Allan is a characterful Masetto. Davis draws a fresh and immediate performance from his team, riveting from beginning to end, and the recording is now better defined and more vivid than before.

Krips's recording of this most challenging opera has kept its place as a mid-priced version that is consistently satisfying, with a cast of all-round quality headed by the dark-toned Don of Cesare Siepi. The women are not ideal, but they form an excellent team, never overfaced by the music, generally characterful, and with timbres well contrasted. To balance Siepi's darkness, the Leporello of Corena is even more saturnine, and their dramatic teamwork is brought to a superb climax in the final scene – quite the finest and most spine-tingling performance of that scene ever recorded. The 1955 recording – genuine stereo – still sounds remarkably well.

Even if ensemble is less than perfect at times in the Karajan set and the final scene of Giovanni's descent to Hell goes off the boil a little, the end result has fitting intensity and power. Though Karajan was plainly thinking of a big auditorium in his pacing of recitatives, having Jeffrey Tate as continuo player helps to keep them moving and to bring out word-meaning. The starry line-up of soloists is a distinctive one. Samuel Ramey is a noble rather than a menacing Giovanni, consistently clear and firm.

Haitink's set superbly captures the flavour of Sir Peter Hall's memorable production at Glyndebourne, not least in the inspired teamwork. The only major change from the production on stage is that Maria Ewing comes in as Elvira, vibrant and characterful, not ideally pure-toned but contrasting characterfully with the powerful Donna Anna of Carol Vaness and the innocent-sounding Zerlina of Elizabeth Gale. Keith Lewis is a sweet-toned Ottavio, but it is Thomas Allen as Giovanni who – apart from Haitink – dominates the set, a swaggering Don full of charm and with a touch of nobility when, defiant to the end, he is dragged down to hell – a spine-chilling moment as recorded here. Rarely has the Champagne aria been so beautifully sung, with each note articulated – and that also reflects Haitink's flawless control of pacing, not always conventional but always thoughtful and convincing. Excellent playing from the LPO – well practised in the Glyndebourne pit – and warm, full recording, far more agreeable than the dry sound in the old auditorium at Glyndebourne.

The historic Furtwängler performance was recorded live by Austrian Radio at the 1954 Salzburg Festival, barely three months before the conductor's death. Though speeds are often slow by today's standards, his springing of rhythm never lets them sag. Even the very slow speed for Leporello's catalogue aria is made to seem charmingly individual. With the exception of a wobbly Commendatore, this is a classic Salzburg cast, with Cesare Siepi a fine, incisive Don, dark in tone, Elisabeth Schwarzkopf a dominant Elvira, Elisabeth Grümmer a vulnerable Anna, Anton Dermota a heady-toned Ottavio and Otto Edelmann a clear and direct Leporello. Stage noises often suggest herds of stampeding animals, but both voices and orchestra are satisfyingly full-bodied in the CD transfer, and the sense of presence is astonishing.

Ostman follows up his earlier recordings of *Così fan tutte* and *Le nozze di Figaro* with this period performance of *Don Giovanni*. This time, with a far darker score, he has modified his stance. Though speeds are still often fast, this time they rarely seem breathless. Håkan Hagegård as Giovanni could be sweeter-toned, but his lightness and spontaneity, particularly in exchanges with the vividly alive Leporello of Gilles Cachemaille, are most winning, with recitative often barely vocalized. Arleen Augér is a radiant Donna Anna, while Della Jones is a full-toned Elvira and Bryn Terfel a resonant Masetto. Understandably, the original Prague text is used. Such essential additions as Ottavio's *Dalla sua pace* (beautifully sung by Nico van der Meel) and Elvira's *Mi tradi* are given in an appendix on the third disc.

The early Glyndebourne set shows Fritz Busch an inspired Mozartian, pointing the music with a freshness and absence of nineteenth-century heaviness rare at the time. A piano is used for the *secco* recitatives; but the interplay of characters in those exchanges has never been caught more infectiously on disc. John Brownlee as Giovanni may have a rather British-stiff-upper-lip Italian accent but his is a noble performance, beautifully sung, and he is brilliantly set against the lively, idiomatically Italian Leporello of Salvatore Baccaloni. Audrey Mildmay as Zerlina makes a delightful foil for the excellent, if otherwise little-known Ina Souez and Luise Helletsgruber. Koloman von Pataky uses his light, heady tenor well as Ottavio, and David Franklin and Roy Henderson are first rate as the Commendatore and Masetto respectively. Keith Hardwick's digital transfers are astonishingly vivid, with very little background noise.

As he has shown in his recording of *Die Zauberflöte*, Fricsay is a forceful, dramatic Mozart conductor. This might suggest that *Don Giovanni* is exactly the Mozart opera best suited to his talents. In fact, though there is fine crispness throughout and the ensembles are superb, the absence of charm is serious. This is mainly felt in some ridiculously fast speeds. Zerlina, Masetto and their rustic friends are hustled unmercifully along in 6/8, and poor Zerlina has an even worse time when it comes to her aria, *Batti batti*. Seefried being the superb artist she is, her charm comes through, but how much more charming it would have been if she had been allowed more time to breathe. The cast is generally strong, but unfortunately there is a serious blot in the Donna Elvira of Maria Stader; she is made to sound shrill and some of her attempts to get round the trickier florid passages leave a good deal to be desired. Yet most of the singing is very stylish. Haefliger shows himself as one of the finest Mozart tenors of the time, Karl Kohn is a fine, incisive Leporello, Ivan Sardi an exceptionally rich-voiced Masetto, and Seefried a truly enchanting Zerlina. As so often on records, Sena Jurinac is not quite as thrilling here as one remembers her in the flesh. The timbre of the voice is harder, but what wonderful singing this is nevertheless. Fischer-Dieskau is a particularly interesting choice of Don; his characterization proves powerful and forwardly projected: there is no suspicion of his singing being mannered, even if at the beginning of *Là ci darem* his tone is not as pure as it normally is. Yet with all these plus points, the set does not quite add up to the sum of its parts, even though there is much to enjoy. The 1958 recording was made in the Berlin Jesus-Christus Kirche, so the stereo is remarkably atmospheric, although Zerlina's scream at the end of Act I is decidedly disappointing (not Seefried's fault either) and that because it is too loud rather than too soft.

At the time it was issued (1955), Moralt's Vienna set compared favourably with much of the full-priced competition, but today it is something of an also-ran, with London on the coarse side in the principal role. The compensation is that Jurinac is really on top form as Donna Elvira, while Sciutti makes a charming Zerlina. On CD the recording of the voices is vivid, but there is a touch of edginess on top and the backwardly balanced orchestra tends to lessen the overall dramatic account somewhat. Overall, this is less appealing than the companion set of *Così fan tutte*. Like that, this is a limited edition and includes a full translation.

Roger Norrington's EMI version not only provides a period performance which on the orchestral side outshines the Ostman Drottningholm set on Oiseau-Lyre but which ingeniously offers the alternative of playing the original Prague version or Mozart's revision for Vienna. This it does by having long sections on separate tracks, instead of tracking each individual number. The snag is that if you want to find a particular aria, it is far less convenient, and many numbers are duplicated when there are alternative sections for Prague or Vienna. Sadly, the singing cast cannot match that in the Ostman set. Though Lynne Dawson as Elvira, John Mark Ainsley as Ottavio, Gregory Yurisch as Leporello and Alastair Miles as the Commendatore all sing impressively, they hardly outshine their Drottningholm opposite numbers, and most of the others fall seriously short, including Andreas Schmidt as an ill-focused Don and Amanda Halgrimson as a shrill Donna Anna. Good, well-balanced sound.

Järvi's Cologne version for Chandos has many points in its favour, with a powerfully dramatic Donna Anna in Sona Ghazarian and a remarkable Elvira, true, clean-cut and agile, in the young German, Gertrud Ottenthal, who developed her Mozart roles in Berlin and Vienna. Nicolai Ghiuselev is a powerful, if unsteady, Leporello, while others like the tenor, Giuseppe Sabbatini, as Ottavio have full, firm voices, but are coarse Mozartians. Renato Bruson as the Don too has a magnificent voice but too often uses it roughly; maybe Järvi is partly to blame, a strong, thrustful conductor but not really an elegant Mozartian. The Chandos sound catches the voices well, but with a heavy bass the orchestral sound is less clean.

Rosbaud's recording, based on the 1957 production at the Aix-en-Provence Festival, was recorded in the studio but surprisingly in mono only. Orchestral sound is clear but limited, while the voices are well caught, though the chorus is very backward. The set can be recommended to those who want to know more about fine singers who should have recorded more, notably Teresa Stich-Randall, best known as the Sophie in Karajan's 1956 *Rosenkavalier*, who here is a superb Donna Anna. Suzanne Danco, a favourite French singer, is more firmly caught here than in her Decca recordings, making a positive Elvira, while Anna Moffo is an enchanting Zerlina. The young Nicolai Gedda as Ottavio produces his most golden tone, but the other men are disappointing. Antonio Campo is a lyrical Don who projects well but is not always steady, while Marcello Cortis is a dry-toned Leporello.

Though Barenboim's Berlin version has a distinguished line-up of soloists, most of them are vocally below form, notably Lella Cuberli, too often shrill and ungainly as Donna Anna. Even Joan Rodgers as Zerlina sounds less firm and pure than usual, while John Tomlinson's fine bass is not always ideally steady either, though he characterizes well as Leporello. Ferruccio Furlanetto, expressive as he is, makes an old-sounding Don, and surprisingly the most successful of the soloists is Waltraud Meier as Elvira, not usually counted a Mozartian. Added to that, Barenboim regularly opts for slow speeds, which are allowed to drag.

Gustav Kuhn's version for Koch-Schwann was recorded live at the Macerata Festival in 1991, and the dry acoustic goes with a presentation on a small scale. Albert Dohmen makes a rough, ill-focused Don, and most of the others in the otherwise Italian cast are disappointing, with Francesca Pedaci a painfully shrill and fluttery Anna.

Don Giovanni: highlights.
(M) *** EMI CDM7 63078-2 (from above recording with Sutherland, Schwarzkopf, Waechter; cond. Giulini).

Not surprisingly, the Giulini EMI selection concentrates on Sutherland as Donna Anna and Schwarzkopf as Donna Elvira, so that the Don and Leporello get rather short measure, but Sciutti's charming Zerlina is also given fair due.

Die Entführung aus dem Serail (complete).
☞ *** DG Dig. 435 857-2 (2) [id.]. Orgonasova, Sieden, Olsen, Peper, Hauptman, Mineti, Monteverdi Ch., E. Bar. Soloists, Gardiner.
(M) *** DG 429 868-2 (2) [id.]. Augér, Grist, Schreier, Neukirch, Moll, Leipzig R. Ch., Dresden State O, Boehm.
*** Teldec/Warner Dig. 2292 42643-2 (3) [id.]. Kenny, Watson, Schreier, Gamlich, Salminen, Zurich Op. Ch. & Mozart O, Harnoncourt.

Unlike *Idomeneo* and *La clemenza di Tito* (the first two in Gardiner's series of Mozart opera recordings with the English Baroque Soloists) *Entführung* was not recorded live but in the studio immediately after a concert performance. With a comedy like this, studded with spoken dialogue, that was a wise decision. The direct comparison in a period performance of the opera is with Christopher Hogwood and the Academy of Ancient Music and, like him, Gardiner includes some minor additions to the text, sanctioned by recent scholarship. The overture immediately establishes the extra zest of the Gardiner performance, with wider dynamic contrasts, more body in the sound, and with more spring in the rhythm and a keener sense of fun. Though Gardiner's speeds are often fast they never sound breathless, thanks to his rhythmic flair, making the music lift and allowing time for imaginative phrasing. So Konstanze's great heroic aria, *Martern aller Arten*, has tremendous swagger; thanks also to glorious singing from Luba Orgonasova, at once rich, pure and agile, the close is triumphant. Curiously, Gardiner exaggerates the *ad lib.* markings in the first half of that climactic aria. Orgonasova sounds far richer than Lynne Dawson, the outstanding Konstanze for Hogwood; and in the other great aria, *Traurigkeit*, she is warmer too, less withdrawn. As Belmonte, Stanford Olsen for Gardiner is firmer and more agile than the fluttery Uwe Heilmann for Hogwood, and though Cornelius Hauptmann, Gardiner's Osmin, lacks a really dark bass, he too is firmer and more characterful than the unsteady Günther von Kannen for Hogwood. Add to that a recording which gives a clearer idea of staging, and you have a version of *Entführung* to be recommended as first choice even for those who would not normally go for a period performance.

Boehm's is a delectable performance, superbly cast and warmly recorded. Arleen Augér proves the most accomplished singer on record in the role of Constanze, girlish and fresh, yet rich, tender and dramatic by turns, with brilliant, almost flawless coloratura. The others are also outstandingly good, notably Kurt Moll whose powerful, finely focused bass makes him a superb Osmin, one who relishes the comedy too. The warm recording is beautifully transferred, to make this after Gardiner easily the most sympathetic version of the opera on CD, with the added attraction of being at mid-price.

Harnoncourt's version establishes its uniqueness at the very start of the overture, tougher and more abrasive than any previous recording, with more primitive percussion effects than we are used to in his Turkish music. It is not a comfortable sound, compounded by Harnoncourt's often fast allegros, racing singers and players off their feet. Slow passages are often warmly expressive, but the stylishness of the soloists prevents them from seeming excessively romantic. The men are excellent: Peter Schreier singing charmingly, Wilfried Gamlich both bright and sweet of tone, Matti Salminen outstandingly characterful as an Osmin who, as well as singing with firm dark tone, points the words with fine menace. Yvonne Kenny as Constanze and Lilian Watson as Blonde sound on the shrill side, partly a question of microphones.

Complete Mozart Edition, Volume 33: *La finta giardiniera* (complete).
(M) *** Ph. 422 533-2 (3) [id.]. Conwell, Sukis, Di Cesare, Thomas Moser, Fassbaender, Ihloff, McDaniel, Salzburg Mozarteum O, Hager.

Leopold Hager has a strong vocal team, with three impressive newcomers taking the women's roles – Jutta-Renate Ihloff, Julia Conwell (in the central role of Sandrina, the marquise who disguises herself as a garden-girl) and Lilian Sukis (the arrogant niece). Brigitte Fassbaender sings the castrato role of Ramiro, and the others are comparably stylish. It is a charming – if lengthy – comedy, which here, with crisply performed recitatives, is presented with vigour, charm and persuasiveness. The recording, made with the help of Austrian Radio, is excellent.

Complete Mozart Edition, Volume 28: *La finta semplice* (complete).
(M) *** Ph. Dig. 422 528-2 (2) [id.]. Hendricks, Lorenz, Johnson, Murray, Lind, Blochwitz, Schmidt, C. P. E. Bach CO, Schreier.

Schreier's version replaces the earlier, Orfeo full-priced set from Leopold Hager, particularly when it comes at mid-price on two discs instead of three. The digital recording is wonderfully clear, with a fine sense of presence, capturing the fun of the comedy. Ann Murray has never sung more seductively in Mozart than here as Giacinta, and the characterful Barbara Hendricks is a delight in the central role of Rosina.

Idomeneo (complete).
⊛ *** DG Dig. 431 674-2 (3) [id.]. Rolfe Johnson, Von Otter, McNair, Martinpelto, Robson, Hauptmann, Monteverdi Choir, E. Bar. Soloists, Gardiner.
(M) *** DG 429 864-2 (3) [id.]. Ochman, Mathis, Schreier, Varady, Winkler, Leipzig R. Ch., Dresden State O, Boehm.
*** Decca Dig. 411 805-2 (3) [id.]. Pavarotti, Baltsa, Popp, Gruberová, Nucci, V. State Op. Ch., VPO, Pritchard.
☞ (M) ** Ph. 422 537-2 (3) [id.]. Francisco Araiza, Susanne Mentzer, Barbara Hendricks, Roberta Alexander, Uwe Heilmann, Werner Hollweg, Harry Peeters, Bav. R. Ch. & RSO, Sir Colin Davis.

With its exhilarating vigour and fine singing, Gardiner's revelatory recording, taken from live performances, will please many more than period-performance devotees. Gardiner's aim has been to include all the material Mozart wrote for the original 1781 production, whether it was finally used or not, and he recommends the use of the CD programming device for listeners to select the version they prefer, with supplementary numbers put at the end of each disc. Gardiner's Mozartian style is well sprung and subtly moulded rather than severe, and his choice of singers puts a premium on clarity and beauty of production rather than weight. Even Hillevi Martinpelto, the young soprano chosen to sing the dramatic role of Elettra, keeps a pure line in her final fury scene, avoiding explosiveness – a passage given in alternative versions. The other principals sing beautifully too, notably Anne Sofie von Otter as Idamante and Sylvia McNair as Ilia, while Anthony Rolfe Johnson, a tenor on the light side for the role of Idomeneo in a traditional performance, is well suited here, with words finely projected. The electrifying singing of the Monteverdi Choir adds to the dramatic bite, and the sound is excellent, remarkably fine for a live performance in a difficult venue.

Boehm's conducting is a delight, often spacious but never heavy in the wrong way, with lightened textures and sprung rhythms which have one relishing Mozartian felicities as never before. As Idomeneo, Wieslaw Ochman, with tenor tone often too tight, is a comparatively dull dog, but the other principals are generally excellent. Peter Schreier as Idamante also might have sounded more consistently sweet, but the imagination is irresistible. Edith Mathis is at her most beguiling as Ilia, but it is Julia Varady as Elettra who gives the most compelling performance of all, sharply incisive in her dramatic outbursts, but at the same time precise and pure-toned, a Mozartian stylist through and through.

In the Decca version, spaciously conducted by Sir John Pritchard, Pavarotti is the only tenor among the principal soloists. Not only is the role of Idamante given to a mezzo instead of a tenor – preferable, with what was originally a castrato role – but that of the High Priest, Arbace, with his two arias is taken by a baritone, Leo Nucci. The wonder is that though Pavarotti reveals imagination in every phrase, using a wide range of tone colours, the result remains well within the parameters of Mozartian style. Casting Baltsa as Idamante makes for characterful results, tougher and less fruity than her direct rivals. Lucia Popp as Ilia tends to underline expression too much, but it is a charming, girlish portrait. Gruberová makes a thrilling Elettra, totally in command of the divisions, as few sopranos are; owing to bright Decca sound, the projection of her voice is a little edgy at times.

To have a major new opera-set like this, issued from the start on a mid-priced label, is generous, but Sir Colin Davis's second version of Mozart's great *opera seria* was designed as part of the Philips Complete Mozart Edition and is priced accordingly. It comes with the fine qualities of presentation associated with the series; the text aims at completeness, with an appendix on the third disc containing major numbers like Arbace's two arias, omitted in the main text, as well as the ballet music designed to be performed after the drama is over. It also has the advantage over Davis's previous recording that the role of Idamante is given to a mezzo instead of a tenor, following Mozart's original Munich text. Such a number as the great Quartet of Act III benefits much by that – but unfortunately, as in Davis's previous version, there are flaws in the casting; his reading has also grown smoother and less incisive, less fresh than before, if now at times grander.

Francisco Araiza's efforts to produce the heroic tone needed often sound strained, and he is not clean enough in his attack; while Barbara Hendricks as Ilia adopts an even less apt Mozartian style, with too much sliding and under-the-note attack, missing the purity needed for this character. Uwe Heilmann as Arbace is also disappointing, and it is as well that his arias are left to the appendix. Others in the cast are far finer, but the total result is less than completely satisfactory, particularly arriving so soon after John Eliot Gardiner's brilliant and dramatic full-priced version for DG Archiv using period instruments. The Philips recording is full and warm, but the Gardiner set is well worth its extra cost.

Complete Mozart Edition, Volume 32: *Lucio Silla* (complete).
(M) *** Ph. 422 532-2 (3) [id.]. Schreier, Augér, Varady, Mathis, Donath, Krenn, Salzburg R. Ch. & Mozarteum Ch. & O, Hager.

Lucio Silla (slightly abridged).
*** Teldec/Warner Dig. 2292 44928-2 (2). Schreier, Gruberová, Bartoli, Kenny, Upshaw, Schoenberg Ch., VCM, Harnoncourt.

The sixteen-year-old Mozart wrote his fifth opera, on the subject of the Roman dictator Sulla (Silla), in double quick time. There are many pre-echoes of later Mozart operas, not just of the great *opera seria*, *Idomeneo*, but of *Entführung* and even of *Don Giovanni*. On Philips the castrato roles are splendidly taken by Julia Varady and Edith Mathis, and the whole team could hardly be bettered. The direction of Hager is fresh and lively, and the only snag is the length of the *secco* recitatives. However, with CD one can use these judiciously.

What Harnoncourt has done is to record a text which fits on to two generously filled CDs, not just trimming down the recitatives but omitting no fewer than four arias, all of them valuable. Yet his sparkling direction of an outstanding, characterful team of soloists brings an exhilarating demonstration of the boy Mozart's genius, with such marvels as the extended finale to Act I left intact. As in the earlier set, Schreier is masterly in the title-role, still fresh in tone, while Dawn Upshaw is warm and sweet as Celia, and Cecilia Bartoli is full and rich as Cecilio. The singing of Edita Gruberová as Giunia and Yvonne Kenny as Cinna is not quite so immaculate, but still confident and stylish. The Concentus Musicus of Vienna has rarely given so bright and lightly sprung a performance on record. Excellent digital sound.

Complete Mozart Edition, Volume 29: *Mitridate, rè di Ponto* (complete).
(M) **(*) Ph. 422 529-2 (3) [id.]. Augér, Hollweg, Gruberová, Baltsa, Cotrubas, Salzburg Mozarteum O, Hager.

Hager's fresh and generally lively performance (the rather heavy recitatives excepted) brings splendid illumination to the long-hidden area of the boy Mozart's achievement. Two of the most striking arias (including an urgent G minor piece for the heroine, Aspasia, with Arleen Augér the ravishing soprano) exploit minor keys most effectively. Ileana Cotrubas is outstanding as Ismene, and the soloists of the Salzburg orchestra cope well with the often important obbligato parts. The CD transfer is vivid and forward and a little lacking in atmosphere.

Complete Mozart Edition, Volume 40: *Le nozze di Figaro* (complete).
(M) *** Ph. 422 540-2 (3) [id.]. Freni, Norman, Minton, Ganzarolli, Wixell, Grant, Tear, BBC Ch. &
SO, Sir Colin Davis.

Le nozze di Figaro (complete). .
*** Decca Dig. 410 150-2 (3). Te Kanawa, Popp, Von Stade, Ramey, Allen, Moll, LPO & Ch., Solti.
🏵 (B) *** CfP CD-CFPD 4724; *TC-CFPD 4724* (2). Sciutti, Jurinac, Stevens, Bruscantini, Calabrese,
Cuénod, Wallace, Sinclair, Glyndebourne Ch. & Festival O, Gui.
(M) *** EMI CMS7 63266-2 (2) [Ang. CDMB 63266]. Schwarzkopf, Moffo, Cossotto, Taddei,
Waechter, Vinco, Philh. Ch. & O, Giulini.
(M) **(*) Decca 417 315-2 (3) [id.]. Gueden, Danco, Della Casa, Dickie, Poell, Corena, Siepi, V.
State Op. Ch., VPO, Erich Kleiber.
(M) *** DG 429 869-2 (3) [id.]. Janowitz, Mathis, Troyanos, Fischer-Dieskau, Prey, Lagger, German
Op. Ch. & O, Boehm.
☞ **(*) EMI Dig. CDS7 49753-2 (3) [Ang. CDCC 49753]. Desderi, Rolandi, Stilwell, Lott, Esham,
Glyndebourne Ch., LPO, Haitink.
(M) (**(*)) EMI mono CMS7 69639-2 (2) [Ang. CDMB 69639]. Schwarzkopf, Seefried, Jurinac,
Kunz, Majkut, London, V. State Op. Ch., VPO, Karajan.
☞ (M) ** Ph. mono 438 670-2 (3) [id.]. Berry, Streich, Schoeffler, Jurinac, Ludwig, Majkut, V. State
Op. Ch., VSO, Karl Boehm.

Solti opts for a fair proportion of extreme speeds, slow as well as fast, but they rarely if ever intrude
on the quintessential happiness of the entertainment. Samuel Ramey, a firm-toned baritone, makes a
virile Figaro, superbly matched to the most enchanting of Susannas today, Lucia Popp, who gives a
sparkling and radiant performance. Thomas Allen's Count is magnificent too, tough in tone and
characterization but always beautiful on the ear. Kurt Moll as Dr Bartolo sings an unforgettable *La
vendetta* with triplets very fast and agile 'on the breath', while Robert Tear far outshines his own
achievement as the Basilio of Sir Colin Davis's amiable recording. Frederica von Stade is a most
attractive Cherubino, even if *Voi che sapete* is too slow; but crowning all is the Countess of Kiri Te
Kanawa, challenged by Solti's spacious tempi in the two big arias, but producing ravishing tone,
flawless phrasing and elegant ornamentation throughout. With superb, vivid recording this now
makes a clear first choice for a much-recorded opera. However, in view of the strong competition,
Decca should find a way of reducing its price.

The most effervescent performance of *Figaro* on disc, brilliantly produced in early but well-
separated stereo, the 1955 Glyndebourne recording makes a bargain without equal on only two CDs
from CfP. The transfer on CD brings sound warmer, more naturally vivid and with more body than
on many modern recordings. Just as Sesto Bruscantini is the archetypal Glyndebourne Figaro, Sena
Jurinac is the perfect Countess, with Graziella Sciutti a delectable Susanna and Risë Stevens a well-
contrasted Cherubino, vivacious in their scenes together. Franco Calabrese as the Count is firm and
virile, if occasionally stressed on top; and the three character roles have never been cast more vividly,
with Ian Wallace as Bartolo, Monica Sinclair as Marcellina and the incomparable Hugues Cuénod as
Basilio. The only regret is that Cuénod's brilliant performance of Basilio's aria in Act IV has had to
be omitted (as it so often is on stage) to keep the two discs each within the 80-minute limit. There is
no libretto; instead a detailed synopsis is provided, with cueing points conveniently indicated. But this
set costs little more than a third the price of the Decca/Solti version.

Like his set of *Don Giovanni* – also recorded in 1959 – the Giulini version is a classic, with a cast
assembled by Walter Legge that has rarely been matched, let alone surpassed. Taddei with his dark
bass-baritone makes a provocative Figaro; opposite him, Anna Moffo is at her freshest and sweetest
as Susanna. Schwarzkopf as ever is the noblest of Countesses, and it is good to hear the young
Fiorenza Cossotto as a full-toned Cherubino. Eberhard Waechter is a strong and stylish Count. On
only two mid-priced discs it makes a superb bargain, though – as in the other EMI two-disc version,
the Gui on CfP – Marcellina's and Basilio's arias are omitted from Act IV. It comes in a slip-case,
complete with full libretto and translation, bringing an advantage over the CfP set.

The pacing of Sir Colin Davis has a sparkle in recitative that directly reflects experience in the
opera house, and his tempi generally are beautifully chosen to make their dramatic points. Vocally
the cast is exceptionally consistent. Mirella Freni (Susanna) is perhaps the least satisfying, yet there is
no lack of character and charm. It is good to have so ravishingly beautiful a voice as Jessye Norman's
for the Countess. The Figaro of Wladimiro Ganzarolli and the Count of Ingvar Wixell project with
exceptional clarity and vigour, and there is fine singing too from Yvonne Minton as Cherubino,
Clifford Grant as Bartolo and Robert Tear as Basilio. The 1971 recording has more reverberation
than usual, but the effect is commendably atmospheric and on CD the voices have plenty of presence.

Kleiber's famous set was one of Decca's Mozart bicentenary recordings of the mid-1950s. It remains an attractively strong performance with much fine singing. Few if any sets since have matched its constant stylishness. Gueden's Susanna might be criticized but her golden tones are certainly characterful and her voice blends with Della Casa's enchantingly. Danco and Della Casa are both at their finest. A dark-toned Figaro in Siepi brings added contrast and, if the pace of the recitatives is rather slow, this is not inconsistent within the context of Kleiber's overall approach. It is a pity that the Decca remastering, in brightening the sound, has brought a hint of edginess to the voices, though the basic atmosphere remains. Also, the layout brings a less than felicitous break in Act II. In this respect the cassettes were superior – and they had smoother sound, too.

Boehm's version of *Figaro* is also among the most consistently assured performances available. The women all sing most beautifully, with Janowitz's Countess, Mathis's Susanna and Troyanos's Cherubino all ravishing the ear in contrasted ways. Prey is an intelligent if not very jolly-sounding Figaro, and Fischer-Dieskau gives his dark, sharply defined reading of the Count's role. All told, a great success, with fine playing and recording, enhanced on CD.

As in his other Glyndebourne recordings, Haitink's approach to Mozart is relaxed and mellow, helped by beautifully balanced orchestral sound. Where in *Così* the results were sunny, here in *Figaro* there is at times a lack of sparkle. There is much fine singing and excellent ensemble, and the set is well worth hearing, in particular for Claudio Desderi's idiomatically pointed and characterful Figaro, a vintage Glyndebourne performance. Yet next to the finest versions – as, for example, Solti's – this falls short in the line-up of soloists. That even applies to Felicity Lott as the Countess. Though she sings *Dove sono* with melting simplicity, the voice is not caught as well as it can be, and she does not match such a rival as Kiri Te Kanawa. Gianna Rolandi as Susanna and Faith Esham as Cherubino are both stylish without being specially characterful, and the microphone gives an edge to their voices.

Recorded in 1950, Karajan's first recording of *Figaro* offers one of the most distinguished casts ever assembled; but, curiously at that period, they decided to record the opera without the secco recitatives. That is a most regrettable omission when all these singers are not just vocally immaculate but vividly characterful – as for example Sena Jurinac, later the greatest of Glyndebourne Countesses, here a vivacious Cherubino. The firmness of focus in Erich Kunz's singing of Figaro goes with a delightful twinkle in the word-pointing, and Irmgard Seefried makes a bewitching Susanna. Schwarzkopf's noble portrait of the Countess – not always helped by a slight backward balance in the placing of the microphone for her – culminates in the most poignant account of her second aria, *Dove sono*. The sound, though obviously limited, presents the voices very vividly.

Karl Boehm's early (1956) *Figaro* is strongly cast. Walter Berry sounds a bit gruff as Figaro, but the partnership with the delightfully fresh-voiced Rita Streich works well and the strength of Berry's voice is very effective in *Non più andrai*, bringing out the drama rather than the humour of the situation. Sena Jurinac's line does not always seem absolutely certain as the Countess, but it is a moving performance, and Christa Ludwig is an appealing Cherubino. Although there are some other vocal blemishes in some of the big numbers (often taken slowly), with Karl Boehm rattling the recitatives through, the whole thing comes to life and there is much vitality in the presentation overall. The recording is still very acceptable, but on three mid-priced discs this seems rather expensive. There is a full libretto translation. The reissue is a limited edition.

Le nozze di Figaro: highlights.
☞ (B) *** DG 439 449-2 (from above set, with Janowitz, Mathis, Prey, Fischer-Dieskau; cond. Boehm).
☞ ** DG Dig. 435 488-2 [id.]. Furlanetto, Upshaw, Hampson, Te Kanawa, Von Otter, NY Met. Op. Ch. & O, Levine.

Boehm's selection includes many of the key numbers, but with a little over an hour of music it is less than generous and inadequately documented; but the singing is first class and the sound vivid.

Levine's highlights disc gives one a chance to sample Anne Sofie von Otter's Cherubino (with *Non so più* and *Voi che sapete* included), and Ferruccio Furlanetto's striking Figaro, but Dame Kiri's Countess projects more effectively with Solti on Decca. The 67-minute selection is well balanced, including the *Overture* and finale.

Complete Mozart Edition, Volume 39: *L'Oca del Cairo* (complete).
(M) *** Ph. Dig. 422 539-2 [id.]. Nielsen, Wiens, Coburn, Schreier, Johnson, Fischer-Dieskau, Scharinger, Berlin R. Ch. (members), C. P. E. Bach CO, Schreier – *Lo sposo deluso*. ***

We owe it to the Mozart scholar and Philips recording producer, Erik Smith, that these two sets of Mozartian fragments, *L'Oca del Cairo* and *Lo sposo deluso*, have been prepared for performance and recorded. *L'Oca del Cairo* ('The Cairo goose'), containing roughly twice as much music as *Lo sposo deluso*, involves six substantial numbers, most of them ensembles, including an amazing finale to the projected Act I, with contrasted sections following briskly one after the other. It is very well conducted by Peter Schreier, who also takes part as one of the soloists. Dietrich Fischer-Dieskau takes the *buffo* old-man role of Don Pippo, and Anton Scharinger is brilliant in the patter aria in tarantella rhythm for the major-domo, Chichibio, bringing a foretaste of Donizetti. Fresh, bright digital recording.

Complete Mozart Edition, Volume 35: *Il rè pastore* (complete).
(M) **(*) Ph. Dig. 422 535-2 (2) [id.]. Blasi, McNair, Vermilion, Hadley, Ahnsjö, ASMF, Marriner.

Il rè pastore, the last of Mozart's early operas, is best known for the glorious aria, *L'amero*, one of the loveliest he ever wrote for soprano. The whole entertainment is among the most charming of his early music, a gentle piece which works well on record. This version by Marriner and the Academy, with a first-rate cast and with plenty of light and shade, and superbly played, does not efface memories of the 1979 DG version conducted by Leopold Hager, which offered even purer singing. Here Angela Maria Blasi, despite a beautiful voice, attacks notes from below, even in *L'amero*. Excellent sound.

Complete Mozart Edition, Volume 36: *Der Schauspieldirektor* (complete).
(M) **(*) Ph. 422 536-2 (2) [id.]. Welting, Cotrubas, Grant, Rolfe Johnson, LSO, Sir Colin Davis – *Zaïde*. ***

Der Schauspieldirektor (*The Impresario*): complete.
(M) *** DG 429 877-2 (3) [id.]. Grist, Augér, Schreier, Moll, Dresden State O, Boehm – *Die Zauberflöte*. **(*)

The DG performance of *Der Schauspieldirektor* is without dialogue, so that it is short enough to make a fill-up for Boehm's *Zauberflöte*. Reri Grist's bravura as Madame Herz is impressive, and Arleen Augér is pleasingly fresh and stylish here. The tenor and bass make only minor contributions, but Boehm's guiding hand keeps the music alive from the first bar to the last.

There is no contest whatsoever between the two rival prima donnas presented in the Philips recording. *Ich bin die erste Sängerin* ('I am the leading prima donna'), they yell at each other; but here Ileana Cotrubas is in a world apart from the thin-sounding and shallow Ruth Welting. Davis directs with fire and electricity a performance which is otherwise (despite the lack of spoken dialogue) most refreshing and beautifully recorded (in 1975) in a sympathetic acoustic.

Complete Mozart Edition, Volume 31: *Il sogno di Scipione* (complete).
(M) *** Ph. 422 531-2 (2) [id.]. Popp, Gruberová, Mathis, Schreier, Ahnsjö, Thomas Moser, Salzburg Chamber Ch. & Mozarteum O, Hager.

Il sogno di Scipione presents an allegorical plot with Scipio set to choose between Fortune and Constancy. Given the choice of present-day singers, this cast could hardly be finer, with Edita Gruberová, Lucia Popp and Edith Mathis superbly contrasted in the women's roles (the latter taking part in the epilogue merely), and Peter Schreier is joined by two of his most accomplished younger colleagues. Hager sometimes does not press the music on as he might, but his direction is always alive. With fine recording, vividly and atmospherically transferred to CD, the set is not likely to be surpassed in the immediate future.

Complete Mozart Edition, Volume 39: *Lo sposo deluso*.
(M) *** Ph. 422 539-2 [id.]. Palmer, Cotrubas, Rolfe Johnson, Tear, Grant, LSO, Sir Colin Davis – *L'Oca del Cairo*. ***

The music presented here from *Lo sposo deluso* is the surviving music from an unfinished opera written in the years before *Figaro*, and it contains much that is memorable. The *Overture*, with its trumpet calls, its lovely slow middle section and recapitulation with voices, is a charmer, while the two arias, reconstructed by the recording producer and scholar, Erik Smith, are also delightful: the one a trial run for Fiordiligi's *Come scoglio* in *Così*, the other (sung by Robert Tear) giving a foretaste of Papageno's music in *The Magic Flute*.

Complete Mozart Edition, Volume 36: *Zaïde*.
(M) *** Ph. 422 536-2 (2) [id.]. Mathis, Schreier, Wixell, Hollweg, Süss, Berlin State O, Klee – *Der Schauspieldirektor*. **(*)

Zaïde, written between 1779 and 1780 and never quite completed, was a trial run for *Entführung*. Much of the music is superb, and melodramas at the beginning of each Act are strikingly effective and original, with the speaking voice of the tenor in the first heard over darkly dramatic writing in D minor. Zaïde's arias in both Acts are magnificent: the radiantly lyrical *Ruhe sanft* is hauntingly memorable, and the dramatic *Tiger aria* is like Constanze's *Martern aller Arten* but briefer and more passionate. Bernhard Klee directs a crisp and lively performance, with excellent contributions from singers and orchestra alike – a first-rate team, as consistently stylish as one could want.

Die Zauberflöte (complete).

*** Ph. Dig. 426 276-2 (2) [id.]. Te Kanawa, Studer, Lind, Araiza, Bär, Ramey, Van Dam, Amb. Op. Ch., ASMF, Marriner.

⊛ (M) (***) DG mono 435 742-2 (2). Stader, Streich, Fischer-Dieskau, Greindl, Haefliger, Berlin RIAS Ch. & SO, Fricsay.

(M) *** EMI CMS7 69971-2 (2) [Ang. CDMB 69971]. Janowitz, Putz, Popp, Gedda, Berry, Frick; Schwarzkopf, Ludwig, Hoffgen (3 Ladies), Philh. Ch. & O, Klemperer.

(M) *** EMI mono CHS7 69631-2 (2) [Ang. CDHB 69631]. Seefried, Lipp, Loose, Dermota, Kunz, Weber, V. State Op. Ch., VPO, Karajan.

*** EMI Dig. CDS7 47951-8 (3) [Ang. CDCC 47951]. Popp, Gruberová, Lindner, Jerusalem, Brendel, Bracht, Zednik, Bav. R. Ch. & SO, Haitink.

*** Telarc Dig. CD-80302 (2). Hadley, Hendricks, Allen, Anderson, Lloyd, SCO & Ch., Mackerras.

☞ (B) *** Naxos Dig. 8 660030/31 (2) [id.]. Norberg-Schulz, Kwon, Lippert, Leitner, Tichy, Rydl, Hungarian Festival Ch., Failoni O, Budapest, Halász.

☞ **(*) O-L Dig. 440 085-2 (2) [id.]. Bonney, Sumi Jo, Streit, Cachemaille, Sigmundsson, Drottningholm Court Theatre Ch. & O, Ostman.

(M) **(*) DG 429 877-2 (3) [id.]. Lear, Peters, Otto, Wunderlich, Fischer-Dieskau, Hotter, Crass, Berlin RIAS Chamber Ch., BPO, Boehm – *Der Schauspieldirektor*. ***

(M) (**(*)) Pearl mono GEMMCDS 9371 (2). Lemnitz, Roswaenge, Berger, Hüsch, Strienz, Ch. & BPO, Beecham.

Marriner directs a pointed and elegant reading of *Zauberflöte*, bringing out the fun of the piece. It lacks weight only in the overture and finale, and the cast is the finest in any modern recording. Dame Kiri lightens her voice delightfully, while Olaf Bär, vividly characterful, brings the Lieder-singer's art to the role of Papageno. Araiza's voice has coarsened since he recorded the role of Tamino for Karajan, but this performance is subtler and conveys more feeling. Cheryl Studer's performance as Queen of the Night is easily the finest among modern recordings; and Samuel Ramey gives a generous and wise portrait of Sarastro. This is now the finest digital version, superbly recorded, with the added advantage that it comes on only two discs instead of the three used for most other recent recordings.

From the early LP era Fricsay's is an outstandingly fresh and alert *Die Zauberflöte*, marked by generally clear, pure singing and well-sprung orchestral playing at generally rather fast speeds. In some ways Fricsay anticipates the Mozart tastes of a later generation, even if his approach to ornamentation is hardly in authentic-period style. Maria Stader and Dietrich Fischer-Dieskau phrase most beautifully, but the most spectacular singing comes from Rita Streich as a dazzling Queen of the Night – the finest on record – and the relatively close balance of the voice gives it the necessary power such as Streich generally failed to convey in the opera house. It is this unique contribution which nudges us towards a Rosette; but Ernst Haefliger, too, is at his most honeyed in tone as Tamino, and only the rather gritty Sarastro of Josef Greindl falls short – and even he sings with a satisfyingly dark resonance. This was the first version to spice the musical numbers with brief sprinklings of dialogue, just enough to prevent the work from sounding like an oratorio. Even including that, DG has managed to put each of the Acts complete on a single disc. The transfer of the original 1954 mono recording (made in the Berlin Jesus-Christus-Kirche) is remarkably full-bodied, with a pleasant ambience and sense of presence.

Klemperer's conducting of *The Magic Flute* is one of his finest achievements on record; indeed he is inspired, making the dramatic music sound more like Beethoven in its breadth and strength. But he does not miss the humour and point of the Papageno passages, and he gets the best of both worlds to a surprising degree. The cast is outstanding – look at the distinction of the Three Ladies alone – but curiously it is that generally most reliable of all the singers, Gottlob Frick as Sarastro, who comes nearest to letting the side down. Lucia Popp is in excellent form, and Gundula Janowitz sings Pamina's part with a creamy beauty that is just breathtaking. Nicolai Gedda too is a firm-voiced Papageno. The transfer to a pair of CDs, made possible by the absence of dialogue, is managed expertly.

Apart from the Fricsay set with Rita Streich which includes some spoken dialogue, there has never been a more seductive recording of *Zauberflöte* than Karajan's mono version of 1950. The

Vienna State Opera cast here has not since been matched on record: Irmgard Seefried and Anton Dermota both sing with radiant beauty and great character, Wilma Lipp is a dazzling Queen of the Night, Erich Kunz as Papageno sings with an infectious smile in the voice, and Ludwig Weber is a commanding Sarastro. There is no spoken dialogue; but on two mid-priced CDs instead of three LPs, it is a Mozart treat not to be missed, with mono sound still amazingly vivid and full of presence.

Haitink directs a rich and spacious account of *Zauberflöte*, superbly recorded in spectacularly wide-ranging digital sound. The dialogue – not too much of it, nicely produced and with sound effects adding to the vividness – frames a presentation that has been carefully thought through. Popp makes the most tenderly affecting of Paminas and Gruberová has never sounded more spontaneous in her brilliance than here as Queen of the Night: she is both agile and powerful. Jerusalem makes an outstanding Tamino, both heroic and sweetly Mozartian; and though neither Wolfgang Brendel as Papageno nor Bracht as Sarastro is as characterful as their finest rivals, their personalities project strongly and the youthful freshness of their singing is most attractive. The Bavarian chorus too is splendid.

Though the recording puts a halo of reverberation round the sound, Mackerras and the Scottish Chamber Orchestra find an ideal scale for the work. His speeds are often faster than usual, not least in Pamina's great aria of lament, *Ach, ich fühl's*, but they always flow persuasively. This is the version among recent ones which best conveys the fun of the piece, as well as its power. Jerry Hadley makes a delightfully boyish Tamino, with Thomas Allen the most characterful Papageno, singing beautifully. Robert Lloyd is a noble Sarastro, and though June Anderson is a rather strenuous Queen of the Night, it is thrilling to have a big, dramatic voice so dazzlingly agile. Barbara Hendricks is a questionable choice as Pamina, not clean enough of attack, but the tonal quality is golden. Among modern recordings this is a set to put beside Haitink's very enjoyable EMI version, despite the reverberant sound.

Though Kurt Rydl is the only established recording artist among the soloists, the Naxos set offers a very satisfying performance, well conducted and well recorded, with some very stylish solo singing. At budget price with a fair measure of German dialogue included (but on separate tracks to allow it to be programmed out if preferred), this makes a first-rate recommendation, competitive with some of the classic sets. As Tamino, Herbert Lippert is a good, clean-cut Germanic tenor, hardly ever strained, with fine legato in *Dies Bildnis*. The young Norwegian, Elisabeth Norberg-Schulz, is a bright, girlish Pamina, who sustains a slow speed for *Ach, ich fühl's* very effectively, tenderly making it an emotional high point. Rydl is a powerful Sarastro, if not always perfectly steady, and Tichy is a delightful Papageno, defying Halász's uncharacteristically stodgy tempo for his first aria, and from there consistently conveying characterful humour without vocal exaggeration. Perhaps the most exciting newcomer is Hellen Kwon, an outstanding Queen of the Night, using full, firm tone with bright attack in her two big arias. The recording is clear and well balanced, with the Queen's thunder vividly caught.

In contrast with his earlier Drottningholm recordings of Mozart operas, often rushed and brittle, Ostman in his Oiseau-Lyre series offers a far more sympathetic set of *Zauberflöte*. It may lack weight but it rarely sounds rushed, for consistently Ostman gives a spring to the rhythms. That was something which disappointingly is missing from Roger Norrington on EMI, the rival recording using period forces. Ostman's cast too is markedly preferable to Norrington's, with no weak link. Barbara Bonney is a charming Pamina, with Kurt Streit a free-toned Tamino and with Gilles Cachemaille as Papageno both finely focused and full of fun. Sumi Jo is a bright, clear Queen of the Night and, though the Sarastro of Kristian Sigmundsson is lightweight, that matches the overall approach.

One of the glories of Boehm's DG set is the singing of Fritz Wunderlich as Tamino, a wonderful memorial to a singer much missed. Fischer-Dieskau, with characteristic word-pointing, makes a sparkling Papageno on record and Franz Crass is a satisfyingly straightforward Sarastro. The team of women is well below this standard – Lear taxed cruelly in *Ach, ich fühl's*, Peters shrill in the upper register (although the effect is exciting), and the Three Ladies do not blend well – but Boehm's direction is superb, light and lyrical, but weighty where necessary to make a glowing, compelling experience. Fine recording, enhanced in the CD set, which has also found room for Boehm's admirable account of *Der Schauspieldirektor*, a very considerable bonus to this mid-priced reissue.

Recorded in Berlin between November 1937 and March 1939, Beecham's recording of *Zauberflöte* was also the first opera set produced by Walter Legge. It brings a classic performance. Beecham was at his peak, pacing each number superbly, and the vocal delights are many, not least from Tiana Lemnitz as a radiant Pamina, Erna Berger as a dazzling Queen of the Night, and Gerhard Hüsch as a delicately comic Papageno, bringing the detailed art of the Lieder-singer to the role. Of the three currently available transfers of this Beecham recording to CD, the Pearl is the one which captures the original 78 recording most naturally, with the keenest sense of presence for the voices, even if it leaves it with plentiful surface hiss. The disappointment of the EMI alternative is the dryness of the sound, with a limited top, little sense of presence and no bloom on the voices. The Nimbus attempt finds that company's re-recording process, using an acoustic gramophone, less effective than it can be. The orchestral sound is made thin, almost disembodied, and though the voices have bloom on them, they often jangle.

Die Zauberflöte: highlights.

☞ *** Ph. Dig. 438 495-2 [id.] (from above recording, with Te Kanawa, Studer, Araiza, Bär, Ramey; cond. Marriner).

(M) *** EMI CDM7 63451-2; *EG 763451-4* (from above recording, cond. Klemperer).

☞ (M) (***) EMI mono CD-EMX 2220; *TC-EMX 2220* [id.] (from above recording with Seefried, Lipp; cond. Karajan).

☞ ** Decca Dig. 433 667-2 [id.]. Ziesak, Heilmann, Jo, Leitner, M. Kraus, Moll, V. State Op. Ch., VPO, Solti.

☞ (M) ** Decca Dig. 433 441-2 [id.]. Lorengar, Deutekom, Burrows, Talvela, Prey, Stolze, V. State Op. Ch., VPO, Solti.

First choice goes to Marriner with his outstanding cast and first-class, modern, digital recording. The selection includes the *Overture* and plays for 69 minutes. Otherwise, those looking for a first-rate set of highlights from *Die Zauberflöte* will find the mid-priced Klemperer disc hard to beat. It makes a good sampler of a performance which, while ambitious in scale, manages to find sparkle and humour too. A synopsis details each individual excerpt, and in this case the inclusion of the *Overture* is especially welcome. The remastered sound has plenty of presence, but atmosphere and warmth too.

The Karajan Vienna State Opera selection on Eminence will be a good way for many to sample a highly enticing mono set with a superb cast, all on the top of their form. The selection lasts 68 minutes, but seven of these are taken up by the Overture, a less than sensible idea, even if it is superbly played. It is disgraceful, though, that the front of this CD – aimed at a popular market – does not make it absolutely clear that the sound is mono.

The selection from Solti's recent digital set offers only 58 minutes of music and is a premium-price CD. The disc is notable mainly for Sumi Jo's two arias as Queen of the Night and for the items featuring Ruth Ziesak (Pamina) and Kurt Moll (Sarastro). The disc was issued as part of Solti's birthday celebrations and includes a thick illustrated booklet detailing his career.

This 63-minute highlights disc is perhaps the best way to sample Solti's earlier (1969) Vienna set of *Die Zauberflöte*, though, outside the context of the complete performance, the flaws are the more striking, particularly the absence of Mozartian charm. The sense of drama may be consistently vital and Stuart Burrows is outstanding as Tamino, with stylish and rich-toned singing, and Martti Talvela a superbly strong Sarastro, but some will be worried by Pilar Lorengar's obtrusive vibrato, while Cristina Deutekom's impressively accurate coloratura as Queen of the Night is marred by a curious warbling timbre. Bright, vivid but not especially ingratiating sound to match Solti's toughness of manner.

Arias: *La clemenza di Tito: S'altro che lagrime. Così fan tutte: Ei parte . . . Sen . . . Per pietà. La finta giardiniera: Crudeli fermate . . . Ah dal pianto. Idomeneo: Se il padre perdei. Lucio Silla: Pupille amate. Il rè pastore: L'amerò, sarò costante. Zaïde: Ruhe sanft, mein holdes Leben. Die Zauberflöte: Ach ich fühl's es ist verschwunden.*
*** Ph. Dig. 411 148-2 [id.]. Kiri Te Kanawa, LSO, C. Davis.

Kiri Te Kanawa's is one of the loveliest collections of Mozart arias on record, with the voice at its most ravishing and pure. One might object that Dame Kiri concentrates on soulful arias, ignoring more vigorous ones; but with stylish accompaniment and clear, atmospheric recording, beauty dominates all.

Arias: *Don Giovanni; Die Entführung aus dem Serail; Idomeneo; Le nozze di Figaro; Die Zauberflöte.*
(M) (***) EMI mono CDH7 63708-2. Elisabeth Schwarzkopf (with various orchestras & conductors, including John Pritchard).

Just how fine a Mozartian Schwarzkopf already was early in her career comes out in these 12 items, recorded between 1946 and 1952. The earliest are Konstanze's two arias from *Entführung*, and one of the curiosities is a lovely account of Pamina's *Ach ich fühl's*, recorded in English in 1948. The majority, including those from *Figaro* – Susanna's and Cherubino's arias as well as the Countess's – are taken from a long-unavailable recital disc conducted by John Pritchard. Excellent transfers.

ANTHOLOGIES

'The Complete Mozart Edition': highlights. Excerpts from: *Horn concerto No. 4, K.495; Piano concerto No. 5 in D, K.175; Serenade No. 12 in C min., K.388; Symphony No. 29, K.201; Flute quartet No. 1 in D, K.285; Piano trio No. 4 in E, K.542; Allegretto in B flat for string quartet, K.App.68* (completed by Erik Smith); *String quartet No. 22 in B flat, K.589; Violin sonata No. 25 in F, K.377; Piano sonata No. 8 in A min., K.310; Exsultate Jubilate, K.165. Die kleine Spinnerin.* Excerpts from: *Requiem Mass, K.626; La clemenza di Tito; Così fan tutte; Don Giovanni; Die Entführung aus dem Serail; Le nozze di Figaro; Die Zauberflöte.*

(M) *** Ph. Dig./Analogue 426 735-2 [id.]. Various artists.

Issued as a sampler for Philips's Complete Mozart Edition and designed to tempt purchasers to explore further, this is a thoroughly worthwhile anthology in its own right. The major novelty, previously unrecorded, is the *Allegretto for string quartet* in polonaise rhythm, of which Mozart completed only the first eight bars but then continued with 68 bars for the first violin alone. Smith reconstructed this himself, and very worthwhile it proves. The rest of the programme fits together uncannily well and includes artists of the calibre of the Beaux Arts Trio, Brendel, Grumiaux, Marriner and Uchida, plus many famous vocal soloists, making a fine and certainly a tempting entertainment: some 76 minutes of marvellous music. To make this issue even more of a bargain, the accompanying 204-page booklet offers an excellent potted biography, directly related to Mozart's output, with much about the social background against which his works were composed. Of course it also includes details of the 180 CDs which comprise the 45 volumes of the Edition, and it provides pictures and information about the principal performing artists. Finally, the Index gives a complete Köchel listing of Mozart's works, together with the volume number in which each appears.

'Fifty Years of Mozart singing on record': (i) *Concert arias;* Excerpts from: (ii) *Mass in C min., K.427;* (iii) *La clemenza di Tito;* (iv) *Così fan tutte;* (v) *Don Giovanni;* (vi) *Die Entführung aus dem Serail;* (vii) *La finta giardiniera;* (viii) *Idomeneo;* (ix) *Le nozze di Figaro;* (x) *Il rè pastore;* (xi) *Zaïde;* (xii) *Die Zauberflöte.*

(M) (***) EMI mono CMS7 63350-2 (4) [id.]. (i) Rethberg, Ginster, Francillo-Kaufmann; (ii) Berger; (iii) Kirkby-Lunn; (iv) V. Schwarz, Noni, Grümmer, Hahn, Kiurina, Hüsch, Souez, H. Nash; (v) Vanni-Marcoux, Scotti, Farrar, Battistini, Corsi, Leider, Roswaenge, D'Andrade, Pinza, Patti, Maurel, Renaud, Pernet, McCormack, Gadski, Kemp, Callas; (vi) Slezak, L. Weber, Tauber, Lehmann, Nemeth, Perras, Ivogün, Von Pataky, Hesch; (vii) Dux; (viii) Jurinac, Jadlowker; (ix) Stabile, Helletsgruber, Santley, Gobbi, Lemnitz, Feraldy, Schumann, Seinemeyer, Vallin, Rautawaara, Mildmay, Jokl, Ritter-Ciampi; (x) Gerhart; (xi) Seefried; (xii) Fugère; Wittrisch; Schiøtz, Gedda, Kurz, Erb, Kipnis, Galvany, Hempel, Sibiriakov, Frick, Destinn, Norena, Schöne, Kunz.

This is an astonishing treasury of singing, recorded over the first half of the twentieth century. It begins with Mariano Stabile's resonant 1928 account of Figaro's *Se vuol ballare*, snail-like by today's standards, while Sir Charles Santley in *Non piu andrai* a few tracks later is both old-sounding and slow. The stylistic balance is then corrected in Tito Gobbi's magnificently characterful 1950 recording of that same aria. Astonishment lies less in early stylistic enormities than in the wonderful and consistent purity of vocal production, with wobbles – so prevalent today – virtually non-existent. That is partly the result of the shrewd and obviously loving choice of items, which includes not only celebrated marvels like John McCormack's 1916 account of Don Ottavio's *Il mio tesoro* (breaking all records for breath control, and stylistically surprising for including an appoggiatura), but many rarities. The short-lived Meta Seinemeyer, glorious in the Countess's first aria, Germaine Feraldy, virtually unknown, a charming Cherubino, Johanna Gadski formidably incisive in Donna Anna's *Mi tradi*, Frieda Hempel incomparable in the Queen of the Night's second aria – all these and many dozens of others make for compulsive listening, with transfers generally excellent. There are far more women singers represented than men, and a high proportion of early recordings are done in languages other than the original; but no lover of fine singing should miss this feast. The arias are gathered together under each opera, with items from non-operatic sources grouped at the end of each disc. Helpfully, duplicate versions of the same aria are put together irrespective of date of recording, and highly informative notes are provided on all the singers.

Muffat, Georg (1653–1704)

Concerto No. 1 in D min. (Bonna nova); Indissolubilis Amicitia (ballet): suite.
☞ (M) *** DG 437 081-2. VCM, Harnoncourt – BIBER: *Battalia a 10; Sonatas.* ***

These two attractive works show that the versatile Austrian Court composer, Georg Muffat, who enjoyed the patronage of both Leopold I and the Archbishop of Salzburg – who paid for his Italian visit – could write ballet music after the style of Lully (even including pistol-shots in the fourth movement, *Les Gendarmes*) and a fine orchestral concerto with well-absorbed Italian influences. Both works also have a strong German flavour; in the jolly and inventive *Bonna Nova concerto*, with its impressively noble opening *Grave*, the wind scoring later reminds us of Telemann. This repertoire is well worth having on disc. It is presented with the utmost character and strong rhythmic feeling by Harnoncourt, and his Vienna Concentus Musicus are on top form and are vividly recorded.

Armonico tributo cioè sonata da camera: Nos. 2 in G min.; 5 in G.
☞ **(*) HM/BMG Dig. 05472 77303-2 [id.]. Freiburg Bar. Cons. – BIBER: *Sonatae tam Aris.* **(*)

Muffat's sonatas (1682) are almost exactly contemporary with the Biber sonatas with which they are coupled but they are much more conventional works. Yet they attractively provide a touch of gravitas between the chimerical Biber pieces. They are played authentically and with spirit, and are well recorded. But with a playing time of 59 minutes there would have been room here for yet another work by each composer.

Mundy, William (c. 1529–c. 1591)

Vox Patris caelestis.
*** Gimell CDGIM 339 [id.]. Tallis Scholars, Phillips – ALLEGRI: *Miserere;* PALESTRINA: *Missa Papae Marcelli.* ***

Mundy's *Vox Patris caelestis* was written during the short reign of Queen Mary (1553–8). The work is structured in nine sections in groups of three, the last of each group being climactic and featuring the whole choir, with solo embroidery. Yet the music flows continuously, like a great river, and the complex vocal writing creates the most spectacular effects, with the trebles soaring up and shining out over the underlying cantilena. The Tallis Scholars give an account which balances linear clarity with considerable power. The recording is first class and the digital remastering for CD improves the focus further.

Mussorgsky, Modest (1839–81)

The Capture of Kars (Triumphal march); St John's night on the bare mountain (original score); *Scherzo in B flat. Khovanshchina: Prelude to Act I;* (i) *Introduction to Act IV. The Destruction of Sennacherib.* (i; ii) *Joshua.* (i) *Oedipus in Athens: Temple chorus. Salammbô: Priestesses' chorus* (operatic excerpts all orch. Rimsky-Korsakov).
☞ ⊛ *** BMG/RCA 09026 61354-2 [id.]. (i) London Symphony Ch.; (ii) Zehava Gal; LSO, Abbado.

To commemorate the centenary of Mussorgsky's death, in 1981 Abbado and the LSO came up with this very attractive and revealing anthology of shorter pieces. The *Khovanshchina Prelude*, very beautifully played indeed, is well enough known, but it is good to have so vital and pungent an account of the original version of *Night on the bare mountain*, different in all but its basic material from the Rimsky-Korsakov arrangement. Rimsky was right to prune it: at 12 minutes, without the slow end-piece, it is a shade over-long, but Mussorgsky's scoring is so original and imaginative that the ear is readily held. Best of all are the four choral pieces; even when they are early and untypical (*Oedipus in Athens*, for example), they are immediately attractive and very Russian in feeling, and they include such evocative pieces as the *Chorus of Priestesses* (intoning over a pedal bass) from a projected opera on Flaubert's novel. The recording is first rate and the CD transfer enhances the original considerably, giving the chorus greater presence without loss of atmosphere or perspective. This is one of the most attractive Mussorgsky records in the catalogue and is not to be missed: the performers are on their toes throughout.

Night on the bare mountain (orch. Rimsky-Korsakov).
(M) *** Mercury 432 004-2 [id.]. LSO, Dorati – PROKOFIEV: *Romeo and Juliet suites.* ***
☞ (M) ** Ph. Dig. 434 731-2; *434 731-4* [id.]. Concg. O, C. Davis – STRAVINSKY: *Firebird.* ***

Dorati's fine 1960 account of *Night on the bare mountain* comes as an encore for Skrowaczewski's outstanding Prokofiev, and it is interesting at the end of *Romeo and Juliet* to note the subtle shift of acoustic from the Minneapolis auditorium to Wembley Town Hall.

Davis's performance sounds like a run-through and, though some may like the total absence of vulgarity, with speeds often on the slow side, at times the music sounds disappointingly tame. This was an early digital recording (1979) and, though the heavy brass makes an impressive impact, the recording otherwise lacks a convincing balance and there is less weight in the strings.

Night on the bare mountain (original version); *Khovanshchina: Prelude* (orch. Rimsky-Korsakov); *Pictures at an exhibition* (orch. Ravel).
*** Collins EC 1004-2 [id.]. LSO, Kaspryzk.

The LSO performance of the *Pictures* directed by Jacek Kaspryzk is superbly recorded in London's Henry Wood Hall, rivalling the famous Telarc version in its weight and brilliance and its ripe treatment of the orchestral brass: the sound is rather less sumptuous in the spectacular closing *Great Gate of Kiev* but is more sharply focused. The performance, led onwards convincingly by the various Promenades, is strongly characterized, with the nostalgia inherent in *The old castle* carried on to the portrait of the ox-wagon, which yet does not lose its juggernaut power. There is much orchestral virtuosity, exhilarating in *The Tuileries* and in the bustle of the *Limoges market place*, and the brass has subtlety as well as bite in *The hut on fowl's legs*, yet produces a powerful sonority for the *Catacombs* sequence. The spacious closing apotheosis has plenty of weight and power. Rimsky-Korsakov's glowing scoring of the beautiful *Khovanshchina Prelude* is also made radiant by fine orchestral playing, though perhaps ideally Kaspryzk could have moved the music on a little more firmly. He finds plenty of gusto, however, in the bizarre wildness of Mussorgsky's original draft for *Night on the bare mountain* (without the serene closing section).

Night on the bare mountain (original version); *Pictures at an exhibition* (orch. Ravel).
☞ (M) ** Teldec/Warner Dig. 9031 77600-2 [id.]. Cleveland O, Christoph von Dohnányi.

Dohnányi's coupling of the *Pictures* with *Night on the bare mountain* fails to match the electrifying impact of the famous earlier Telarc record of these same two works (CD 80042). Well, not quite the same, since Dohnányi chooses Mussorgsky's original score of the latter piece rather than the Rimsky-Korsakov arrangement. His somewhat cultivated approach tends to smooth over the music's crudities; Kaspryzk makes a much better case for this work. Although the Cleveland acoustics add considerably to the sound of the new record and there is some very fine orchestral playing in the various *Pictures* (the *Unhatched chicks* and *The Tuileries* both offer superb, restrained instrumental virtuosity), the more dramatic and grotesque elements of the score are less effectively characterized.

(i) *Night on the bare mountain* (arr. Rimsky-Korsakov); (ii) *Pictures at an exhibition* (orch. Ravel).
*** DG Dig. 429 785-2; *429 785-4* [id.]. NYPO, Sinopoli – RAVEL: *Valses nobles et sentimentales.* **(*)
*** Telarc Dig. CD 80042 [id.]. Cleveland O, Maazel.
☞ (M) *** BMG/RCA [id.]. 09026 61958-2 [id.]. Chicago SO, Reiner – *Concert of Russian showpieces.* ***
(BB) **(*) Naxos 8.550051 [id.]. Slovak PO, Nazareth – BORODIN: *In the Steppes of Central Asia* etc. **(*)

Sinopoli's electrifying New York recording of Mussorgsky's *Pictures at an exhibition* not only heads the list of modern digital versions but also it again displays the New York Philharmonic as one of the world's great orchestras, performing with an epic virtuosity and panache that recall the Bernstein era of the 1960s. The playing of violins and woodwind alike is full of sophisticated touches, so well demonstrated by their colourful, brilliant articulation in *Tuileries Gardens* and *Limoges*, the wittily piquant portrayal of the *Unhatched chicks*, and the firm, resonant line of the lower strings in *Samuel Goldenberg and Schmuyle*. But it is the brass that one rememembers most, from the richly sonorous opening *Promenade*, through the ferocious bite and subtle grotesquerie of *Gnomus*, the bleating trumpet of *Schmuyle*, the stabbing sforzandos at the opening of *Catacombs*, to the malignantly forceful rhythms of *The hut on fowl's legs*, with the playing of the trombones and tuba often assuming an unusual yet obviously calculated dominance of the texture. The finale combines power with dignified splendour, and the bells toll out from their tower to emphasize the Byzantine character of Hartmann's picture of the *Kiev Gate*. *A Night on the bare mountain* is comparably vibrant, with the Rimskian fanfares particularly vivid and the closing pages full of Russian nostalgia. The splendid digital recording, made in New York's Manhattan Center, has breadth and weight, and its fullness comes with a believable overall perspective and excellent internal definition.

The quality of the Telarc Cleveland recording is apparent at the very opening of *Night on the bare mountain* in the richly sonorous presentation of the deep brass and the sparkling yet unexaggerated percussion. With the Cleveland Orchestra on top form, the *Pictures* are strongly characterized; this may not be the subtlest reading available, but each of Mussorgsky's cameos comes vividly to life. After a vibrantly rhythmic *Baba-Yaga*, strong in fantastic menace, the closing *Great Gate of Kiev* is overwhelmingly spacious in conception and quite riveting as sheer sound, with the richness and amplitude of the brass which make the work's final climax unforgettable. Unfortunately the *Pictures* are not cued separately.

Reiner's RCA *Pictures* (recorded in 1957) is another demonstration of vintage stereo using simple microphone techniques to achieve a natural concert-hall balance. The recording was originally issued in the UK in 1959, a few months after Karajan's Philharmonia account (see below). The RCA sound-balance is fuller and more atmospheric than the EMI recording, if less sharply focused. But Reiner's approach is evocative to match – the sombre picture of *The old castle*, the lumbering *Ox-wagon*, the unctuous picture of *Samuel Goldenberg* (powerfully drawn in the strings) and the superb brass playing in the *Catacombs* sequence are all memorable. The final climax of *The Great Gate of Kiev* is massively effective, if not quite matching the Cleveland Telarc version in sheer spectacle. The Chicago brass is again very telling in *Night on a bare mountain*, made two years later, a performance just as strongly characterized. The current CD transfers are very impressive indeed.

The super-bargain Naxos coupling is vividly played and recorded and is well worth its modest price. *A night on the bare mountain* is played flexibly, yet does not lack excitement. The *Pictures*, too, have plenty of character. The climax of *Bydlo* is dramatically enhanced by a fortissimo contribution from the timpanist, and the detail throughout is well observed, from the bleating Schmuyle to the chirping chicks. *Tuileries* and *Limoges* bring lightly etched orchestral bravura, while the closing picture of the Kiev Gate has architectural grandeur and a sense of majesty. Enjoyable, if lacking the last touch of individuality.

(i) *Night on the bare mountain* (arr. Rimsky-Korsakov); *Pictures at an exhibition* (arr. Funtek). (ii) *Songs and dances of death* (arr. Aho).
*** BIS Dig. CD 325 [id.]. (i) Finnish RSO, (i) Leif Segerstam; (ii) Järvi, with Talvela.

This fascinating CD offers an orchestration by Leo Funtek, made in the same year as Ravel's (1922); it is especially fascinating for the way the different uses of colour change the character of some of Victor Hartman's paintings: the use of a cor anglais in *The old castle*, for instance, or the soft-grained wind scoring which makes the portrait of *Samuel Goldenberg and Schmuyle* more sympathetic, if also blander. The performances by the Finnish Radio Orchestra under Leif Segerstam both of this and of the familiar Rimsky *Night on the bare mountain* are spontaneously presented and very well recorded. The extra item is no less valuable: an intense, darkly Russian account of the *Songs and dances of death* from Martti Talvela with the orchestral accompaniment plangently scored by Kalevi Aho.

Pictures at an exhibition (orch. Ravel).
☞ *** DG Gold Dig. 439 013-2 [id.]. BPO, Karajan – RAVEL: *Boléro* etc. ***
*** Sony Dig. SK 45935 [id.]. BPO, Giulini – STRAVINSKY: *Firebird suite.* **(*)
*** DG Dig. 423 901-2 [id.]. LSO, Abbado – STRAVINSKY: *Petrushka.* ***
(M) *** DG 415 844-2 [id.]. Chicago SO, Giulini – RAVEL: *Ma mère l'Oye; Rapsodie espagnole.* ***
(M) *** EMI Dig. CDM7 64516-2 [id.]. Phd. O, Muti – STRAVINSKY: *Rite of spring.* ***
(B) *** EMI CDZ7 62860-2 [id.]. Philh. O, Karajan – LISZT: *Hungarian rhapsody No. 2* etc. ***
(M) *** Decca Dig. 417 754-2 [id.]. Chicago SO, Solti – BARTOK: *Concerto for orchestra.* ***
☞ (M) (***) BMG/RCA mono 09026 61392-2 [id.]. Boston SO, Koussevitzky (with DEBUSSY: *Saraband*) – RAVEL: *Boléro, Daphnis et Chloé* etc. (***)
☞ (B) **(*) Belart 450 081-2. New Philh. O, Lorin Maazel – PROKOFIEV: *Piano concerto No. 3.* **(*)
(M) (**) BMG/RCA mono GD 60287 [60287-2-RG]. NBC SO, Toscanini – ELGAR: *Enigma variations.* (***)

Pictures at an exhibition (orch. Ravel); *Khovanshchina: Prelude; Persian dance; Prince Golitsin's departure into exile* (orch. Shostakovich).
☞ (B) **(*) Erato/Warner Dig. 4509 92870-2 [id.]. Rotterdam PO, James Conlon.

Karajan's 1986 recording is one of the most impressive of DG's digital recordings remastered by their Original-image-bit processing. The tangibility of the sound is remarkable, with the opening brass *Promenade* and the massed strings in *Samuel Goldenberg and Schmuyle* notable in their naturalness of sonority. The power of *Bydlo* is as impressive as the tension in the pianissimo tremolando strings in *Cum mortuis in lingua mortua*. With superb Berlin Philharmonic playing and the weight of the climaxes contrasting with the wit of *Tuileries* and the exhilaration of *The market at Limoges*, this is certainly now among the top recommendations. Even the spacious finale, where Karajan fails to detach the massive chords – if not quite as electrifying as his earlier, analogue version – is given greater impact by the added weight and makes a fittingly grandiose culmination.

Giulini's newest account of Mussorgsky's *Pictures* can also be counted among the finest recent versions. Recorded in the Jesus Christus Kirche, Berlin, the sound is rich and spacious, the orchestral playing superb. The reading has a pervading sense of nostalgia which haunts the delicate portrayal of *The old castle* and even makes the wheedling interchange between the two Polish Jews more sympathetic than usual. A powerful and weighty *Baba Yaga*, yet with the bizarre element retained in the subtle rhythmic pointing of the middle section, leads naturally to a majestic finale, with the Berlin brass full-bloodedly resplendent, and the tam-tam flashing vividly at the climax.

Abbado takes a straighter, more direct view of Mussorgsky's fanciful series of pictures than usual. He is helped by the translucent and naturally balanced digital recording; indeed, the sound is first class, making great impact at climaxes yet also extremely refined, as in the delicate portrayal of the unhatched chicks. Abbado's speeds tend to be extreme, with both this and *Tuileries* taken very fast and light, while *Bydlo* and *The Great Gate of Kiev* are slow and weighty.

Giulini's 1976 Chicago recording has always been among the front runners. He is generally more relaxed and often more wayward than Karajan, but this is still a splendid performance and the finale generates more tension than Karajan's most recent, digital version, though it is not as overpowering as the earlier, analogue recording.

Muti's reading, given the excellence of its recorded sound, more than holds its own, although the balance is forward and perhaps not all listeners will respond to the brass timbres at the opening. The lower strings in *Samuel Goldenberg and Schmuyle* have extraordinary body and presence, and *Baba-Yaga* has an unsurpassed virtuosity and attack, as well as being of a high standard as a recording. The coupling is no less thrilling. This can be recommended even to those readers who have not always responded to later records from this conductor.

Karajan's Philharmonia recording of Mussorgsky's *Pictures* was made in the Kingsway Hall in 1955–6. There is extraordinary clarity and projection, yet no lack of body and ambience, and it is matched by the brilliantly polished detail of the orchestral playing – the Philharmonia offering breathtaking standards of ensemble and bite. *The Great Gate of Kiev* brings a frisson-creating climax of great breadth and splendour, achieved as much by Karajan's dignified pacing as by the spread of the sound.

Solti's performance is fiercely brilliant rather than atmospheric or evocative. He treats Ravel's orchestration as a virtuoso challenge, and with larger-than-life digital recording it undoubtedly has demonstration qualities, and the transparency of texture, given the forward balance, provides quite startling clarity.

From Koussevitzky comes the Ravel orchestration of *Pictures at an exhibition* conducted by the man who commissioned it and recorded it in 1930. The shallow sound should not deter readers from hearing this, for it is superbly characterized and splendidly played. Moreover it comes with what is arguably the best *Daphnis et Chloé* suite ever made.

Though Maazel's characterization is direct rather than subtle, this (originally Decca Phase 4) recording cannot match his later Cleveland version for Telarc in richness of sonority. Maazel's Belart account from 1972 offers an immensely vivid reading, brilliantly recorded, with only a touch of brashness at the end. Moreover, this bargain CD has an unexpected and attractive coupling.

Conlon uses Ravel's orchestration but makes a few changes in the light of studying Mussorgsky's piano manuscript (to which Ravel had no direct access). The changes are only slightly more than cosmetic, although two extra bars have been added effectively to the coda of the *Ballet of the unhatched chicks* and two – added by Ravel – have been removed from *Baba-Yaga*. But the most striking change is with the vehement performance of *Bydlo* at one unrelenting dynamic level – which may be what Mussorgsky wrote but which in practice works less well than Ravel's opening crescendo. Otherwise this is a strongly characterized, very well-played performance, which could have clearer detail, for the acoustic of Rotterdam's empty De Doelen Concert Hall is very resonant. However, the closing *Great Gate of Kiev* has much breadth and dignity, even if the tam tam strokes at the end are clouded by the reverberation. The couplings are what make this record really distinctive, with excerpts from *Khovanshchina*, orchestrated by Shostakovich, who (unlike Rimsky-Korsakov) leaves Mussorgsky's music untouched. The wonderfully evocative *Prelude* has never sounded more beautiful than here.

Toscanini was no colourist, and his regimented view of the exotic Mussorgsky–Ravel score is at its least sympathetic in the opening statement of the opening *Promenade*, not just rigidly metrical but made the coarser by the cornet-like trumpet tone. Many of the individual movements are done with greater understanding – for example, the *Ballet of the unhatched chicks* – but too often Toscanini's lack of sympathy undermines the character of this rich score. Clean, bright transfer.

Pictures at an exhibition (original piano version).

⊛ *** Virgin/EMI Dig. VC7 59611-2 [id.]. Mikhail Pletnev – TCHAIKOVSKY: *Sleeping Beauty*: excerpts. *** ⊛

☞ ** EMI Dig. CD-EMX 2213; *TC-EMX 2213* [id.]. Piers Lane – BALAKIREV: *Islamey*. ***

☞ ** EMI Dig. CDC7 54548-2 [id.]. Lars Vogt (with KOMAROVA: *Sonata;* TCHAIKOVSKY: *Dumka, Op. 59; The Seasons, Op. 37b: Nos. 6, 10 & 11* **).

Pictures at an exhibition (piano version, ed. Horowitz).

☞ (M) (***) BMG/RCA mono GD 60321. Vladimir Horowitz – TCHAIKOVSKY: *Piano concerto No. 1.* (***) ⊛

Pictures at an exhibition (piano version, ed. Horowitz); *Sunless: On the river* (arr. Horowitz).

(M) (***) BMG/RCA mono GD 60449 [60449-2-RG]. Horowitz – TCHAIKOVSKY: *Piano concerto No. 1.* (***)

Some of the finest artists play Mussorgsky's *Pictures* as you can only imagine them in your mind's ear; others, like Horowitz and Pletnev, play them as you could never imagine them! There are remarkable effects of colour and of pedalling in Pletnev's performance – easily the most commanding to have appeared since Richter and, one is tempted to say, a re-creation rather than a performance. Pletnev does not hesitate to modify the odd letter of the score in order to come closer to its spirit. *The Ballet of the unhatched chicks* has great wit and the *Great Gate of Kiev* is extraordinarily rich in colour. An altogether outstanding issue.

Horowitz's famous 1951 recording, made at a live performance at Carnegie Hall, is as thrilling as it is perceptive. Mussorgsky's darker colours are admirably caught and the lighter, scherzando evocations are dazzlingly articulated. But it is the closing pictures which are especially powerful, the pungent *Baba-Yaga*, and the spectacular *Great Gate of Kiev*, where Horowitz has embroidered the final climax to add to its pianistic resplendency. This has now been reissued as Volume 44 in the Toscanini Edition, admirably paired with his equally devastating account of Tchaikovsky's *First Piano concerto*, recorded at a live concert in 1943. This is an indispensable coupling and, even though the extra Mussorgsky items (*Sunless* and *By the water*) have disappeared, one can forgive this; no admirer of great pianism should be without this record. RCA have also reissued this version of the *Pictures*, plus Horowitz's arrangement of *On the river* from Mussorgsky's song-cycle, *Sunless*, coupled with the 1941 *studio* recording of the Tchaikovsky concerto, a performance which we find less satisfying.

Lars Vogt does not offer a serious challenge to the best though he, too, is served by excellent recorded sound. He is a marvellous player, much (and rightly) admired. All the same, his reading of the *Pictures* is just a little too measured and too judicious, perhaps, to entice the listener to see these pictures in fresh and vivid colours. His couplings do not particularly enhance the competitiveness of the disc, even though his selfless championship of the Russian-born Tatiana Komarova deserves a plaudit; but the Tchaikovsky pieces, *June, October* and *November* plus the *Dumka*, are, as it were, neither here nor there. No one will buy the record just for them and though he plays them with grace there is more elegance than eloquence.

(i) *Pictures at an exhibition* (arr. Leonard for piano and orchestra); *3 Pictures from the Crimea* (orch. Goehr); *Night on the bare mountain* (arr. & orch. Rimsky-Korsakov); *Scherzo in B flat* (orch. Rimsky-Korsakov); *From my tears* (orch. Kindler); *Khovanshchina: Prelude* (orch. Rimsky-Korsakov); *Golitsyn's journey* (orch. Stokowski). *Sorochinsky Fair: Gopak* (orch. Liadov).

☞ *** Cala Dig. CACD 1012; *CAMC 1012.* (i) Tamás Ungár; Philh. O, Geoffrey Simon.

Lawrence Leonard's arrangement of Mussorgsky's *Pictures* for piano and orchestra is remarkably effective and very entertaining. The concertante format works admirably, especially powerful in *Gnomus* and *The hut on fowl's legs*, charmingly depicting the *Unhatched chicks* (a piquant mixture of keyboard and woodwind, spiced with xylophone). There are many added touches of colour and the wind whistles round *The Old Castle*, to the discomfiture of the melancholy troubadour, and sinisterly accompanies the witch as she flies in on her broomstick at the close of the menacing *Baba-Yaga*. The *Tuileries*, where piano and woodwind alternate, is another delightful variation, and *Samuel Goldenberg* is portentously depicted as the heavy brass joins the strings, with the piano bleating Schmuyles' sycophantic response. After leading the way through the *Catacombs*, the piano dominates the spectacular portrayal of *The Great Gate of Kiev* just like the finale of a grand romantic concerto. The other pieces are all well worth having, notably Rimsky's chimerical scoring (following the composer's orchestral sketch) of the *Scherzo in B flat*. The three *Pictures from the Crimea* are darkly nostalgic, and the lively *Gopak*, like the *Khovanshchina* excerpts (Stokowski's arrangement of *Golitsyn's journey* is sombrely characterful), are very welcome. Hans Kindler's scoring of the Tchaikovskian melody, *From my tears*, is also adeptly managed. All Geoffrey Simon's performances have plenty of life, and Tamás Ungár makes an exciting contribution and is fully equal to all the technical demands of the revised piano-part. The recording is warm, full and expansive, but not always sharply defined.

Pictures at an exhibition (arr. Howarth); *St John's Night on the bare mountain* (arr. Alan Wiltshire).
*** Collins Dig. 1227-2; *1227-4* [id.]. The Wallace Collection, John Wallace (with KHACHATURIAN: *Spartacus: Adagio of Spartacus and Phrygia* (arr. John Miller) **).

There is no reason why Mussorgsky's famous piano work should not be transcribed for brass as effectively as for a full symphony orchestra, and the Collins version by the John Wallace Collection brings a modern, digital recording. Combined with the highly dramatic characterization of the playing, the effect is to increase the brilliance and pungency of the more grotesque portrayals; *Gnomus* and *The hut on fowl's legs* are both given considerable malignant force, *Bydlo* approaches menacingly, and the *Catacombs* sequence is even more powerfully sinister than with Philip Jones. The cheeping chicks, too, are more piquantly vociferous than usual, and the *Great Gate of Kiev* has striking power and impact. What makes this record a collector's item is the inclusion of Alan Wiltshire's dazzling brass arrangement of Mussorgsky's own rather crude original version of what we know as *Night on the bare mountain*. Wiltshire and Wallace create weirdly barbarous climaxes and some ear-tickling pianissimo effects with muted brass and xylophone, so that the starkness of Mussorgsky's inspiration comes over compellingly. The famous *Spartacus Adagio*, which is placed between the two Mussorgsky works, has a thrilling climax, but here one misses the string textures, despite the eloquence of the performance.

The Complete Songs.
⊛ (M) (***) EMI mono CHS7 63025-2 (3) [Ang. CHS 63025]. Boris Christoff, Alexandre Labinsky, Gerald Moore, French R. & TV O, Georges Tzipine.

Boris Christoff originally recorded these songs in 1958; they then appeared in a four-LP mono set with a handsome book, generously illustrated with plates and music examples, giving the texts in Russian, French, Italian and English, and with copious notes on each of the 63 songs. Naturally the documentation cannot be so extensive in the CD format – but, on the other hand, one has the infinitely greater ease of access that the new technology offers. The Mussorgsky songs constitute a complete world in themselves, and they cast a strong spell: their range is enormous and their insight into the human condition deep. Christoff was at the height of his vocal powers when he made the set with Alexandre Labinsky, his accompanist in most of the songs; and its return to circulation cannot be too warmly welcomed. This was the first complete survey, and it still remains the only one.

OPERA

Boris Godunov (original version; complete).
☞ *** Sony Dig. S3K 58977 (3) [id.]. Kotcherga, Leiferkus, Lipovšek, Ramey, Nikolsky, Langridge, Slovak Philharmonic Ch., Bratislava, Tölz Boys' Ch., Berlin RSO, Abbado.
☞ **(*) EMI CDS7 54377-2 (3) [id.]. Talvela, Gedda, Mróz, Kinasz, Haugland, Krakow Polish R. Ch., Polish Nat. SO, Semkow.

Claudio Abbado recorded *Boris Godunov* in its original version in conjunction both with live concert performances in Berlin and with the subsequent stage production at the Salzburg Festival. The result has not only the polish and intensity associated with the Berlin Philharmonic at its finest but also a dramatic cohesion hard to achieve in an ordinary studio recording, particularly of this long, episodic opera. In his approach to Mussorgsky, Abbado is more lyrical than most, moulding phrases more affectionately. The result may initially seem to dilute the essential ruggedness of this work but, with speeds which regularly press ahead, the urgency of the composer's inspiration is conveyed as never before on disc, without reducing the epic scale of the work or its ominously dark colouring. Like others who have recorded the original version rather than Rimsky-Korsakov's highly coloured arrangement, Abbado inserts the beautiful scene in front of St Basil's at the start of Act IV, but then omits from the final Kromy Forest scene the episode about the Simpleton losing his kopek, which would otherwise come in twice – as it does in the Semkow (EMI) set. Vocally, the performance centres on the glorious singing of Anatoly Kotcherga as Boris. Rarely has this music been sung with such firmness and beauty as here and, so far from losing out dramatically compared with rivals who resort to *parlando* effects for emphasis, the performance gains in intensity. Kotcherga may not have as weighty a voice as Talvela on EMI, but with Abbado encouraging high contrasts, the darkly meditative depth of the performance is enhanced without loss of power. The other principal basses, Samuel Ramey as the monk, Pimen, and Gleb Nikolsky as Varlaam, are well contrasted, even if Ramey's voice sounds un-Slavonic. The tenor, Sergei Larin, sings with beauty and clarity up to the highest register as the Pretender, not least in the Polish act, while Marjana Lipovšek is a formidably characterful Marina, if not quite as well focused as usual. Having Philip Langridge as Shuisky and Sergei Leiferkus as Rangoni reinforces the starry strength of the team. The sound is spacious, more atmospheric than usual in recordings made in the Philharmonie in Berlin, and allowing high dynamic contrasts, with the choral ensembles – so vital in this work – full and glowing.

Though the EMI version offers (at full price) only an analogue recording of 1977, its warmth and richness go with a forward balance and a high transfer level that many will prefer to digital rivals. The voices have an extra bite, not least the firm, weighty bass of Martti Talvela as Boris or of Aage Haugland, magnificent as Varlaam. Nicolai Gedda is excellent as the Pretender, if not as free on top as Larin in the Abbado set. The other soloists, as well as the chorus, make up a formidable Polish team, with hardly a weak link. Bozena Kinasz as Marina is particularly impressive. Jerzy Semkow may not convey such bite and beauty as Abbado, but in his rugged, measured way he conveys more intensity at moments of high drama than the other Sony rival, Tchakarov, helped by the firm, full sound. If this were reissued at mid-price it would be a strong contender.

Boris Godunov (arr. Rimsky-Korsakov).
*** Decca 411 862-2 (3) [id.]. Ghiaurov, Vishnevskaya, Spiess, Maslennikov, Talvela, V. Boys' Ch., Sofia R. Ch., V. State Op. Ch., VPO, Karajan.

With Ghiaurov in the title-role, Karajan's superbly controlled Decca version, technically outstanding, comes far nearer than previous recordings to conveying the rugged greatness of Mussorgsky's masterpiece. Only the Coronation scene lacks something of the weight and momentum one ideally wants. Vishnevskaya is far less appealing than the lovely non-Slavonic Marina of Evelyn Lear on EMI, but overall this Decca set has much more to offer. However, Abbado's Sony recording of the original version now makes a clear first choice for this opera, and Decca need to reissue the Karajan at mid-price, when it would still be competitive.

Khovanshchina (complete).
*** DG Dig. 429 758-2 (3) [id.]. Lipovšek, Burchuladze, Atlantov, Haugland, Borowska, Kotscherga, Popov, V. State Op. Ch. & O, Abbado.
**(*) Ph. Dig. 437 147-2 (3) [id.]. Minjelkiev, Galusin, Steblianko, Ohotnikov, Borodina, Kirov Theatre Ch. & O, Gergiev.

Abbado's live recording brings the most vivid account of this epic Russian opera yet on disc. He uses the Shostakovich orchestration (with some cuts), darker and harmonically far more faithful than the old Rimsky-Korsakov version. Yet Abbado rejects the triumphant ending of the Shostakovich edition and follows instead the orchestration that Stravinsky did for Diaghilev in 1913 of the original subdued ending as Mussorgsky himself conceived it. When the tragic fate of the Old Believers, immolating themselves for their faith, brings the deepest and most affecting emotions of the whole opera, that close, touching in its tenderness, is far more apt. Lipovšek's glorious singing as Marfa, the Old Believer with whom one most closely identifies, sets the seal on the whole performance. Aage Haugland is a rock-like Ivan Khovansky and, though Burchuladze is no longer as steady of tone as he was, he makes a noble Dosifei. Stage noises sometimes intrude and voices are sometimes set back, but this remains a magnificent achievement.

Gergiev does not disguise the squareness of much of the writing and his performance lacks the flair and brilliance of Abbado. He stays faithful to the Shostakovich version of the score to the very end. There he simply adds a loud version of the *Old Believers' chorale* on unison brass – hardly a subtle solution! The Kirov soloists make a fine team, but on almost all counts Abbado is more persuasive.

Sorochinsky Fair (complete).
*** Olympia OCD 114 A/B (2) [id.]. Matorin, Mishchevsky, Voinarovsky, Klenov, Temichev, Chernikh, Zhakharenko, Stanislavsky Theatre Ch. & O, Esipov – BORODIN: *Petite suite.* ***

Though the most striking passage in the opera, *St John's Night* at the beginning of Act III, is the original choral version of what Rimsky-Korsakov turned into *Night on the bare mountain*, this is not at all a grim piece but a folk-comedy that is full of fun, as charming and attractive as any, its score spiced with characteristically individual Mussorgskian progressions. In this version, the piece ends joyfully with an exhilarating choral version of the famous *Gopak*, here brilliantly sung. The full-ranging Melodiya recording has fine immediacy and presence, with the bass, Vladimir Matorin, outstanding as the village elder, Tcherevik. An English translation of the libretto is included in the booklet.

Narváez, Luys de (1500–c. 1555)

El Delphin de Musica, Book 1: *Fantasia No. 5.* Book 2: *Fantasias Nos. 5–6;* Book 3: *La canción del Emperor.* Book 4: *O gloriosa domina (Seys differencias).* Book 5: *Arde coracón, arde; Ye se asiente el Rey Raminor.* Book 6: *Conde claros; Guárdame las vacas; Tre diferencias por otra parte; Baxa de contrapunto.*
☞ (M) *** BMG/RCA 09026 61606-2. Julian Bream (lute) – MILAN: *Collection.* ***

Luys de Narváez followed Milán's first book of music for vihuela with his *Los seys libros del Delphin des Musica* of 1538 which included songs as well as instrumental pieces. The collection Bream plays here is more diverse than the coupled Milán pieces and he includes some arrangements of the popular songs of the time and some of the earliest-known *differencias* (variations). Bream is in his element in this repertoire and each piece is eloquently felt and strongly characterized; the music's nobility is readily conveyed. The recording is first class.

Nicolai, Carl Otto (1810–49)

The merry wives of Windsor (Die lustigen Weiber von Windsor): complete.
(M) **(*) EMI CMS7 69348-2 (2) [Ang. CDMB 69348]. Frick, Gutstein, Engel, Wunderlich, Lenz, Hoppe, Putz, Litz, Mathis, Ch. & O of Bav. State Op., Heger.

The great glory of this fine EMI set is the darkly menacing Falstaff of Gottlob Frick in magnificent voice, even if he sounds baleful rather than comic. It is good too to have the young Fritz Wunderlich as Fenton opposite the Anna Reich of Edith Mathis. Though the others hardly match this standard – Ruth-Margret Putz is rather shrill as Frau Fluth – they all give enjoyable performances, helped by the production, which conveys the feeling of artists who have experienced performing the piece on stage. The effectiveness of the comic timing is owed in great measure to the conducting of the veteran, Robert Heger. From the CD transfer one could hardly tell the age of the recording, with the voices particularly well caught. Alas, this enjoyable set is withdrawn as we go to press.

Nielsen, Carl (1865–1931)

Clarinet concerto, Op. 57.
*** Chan. Dig. CHAN 8618; *ABTD 1307* [id.]. Janet Hilton, SNO, Bamert – COPLAND: *Concerto;* LUTOSLAWSKI: *Dance preludes.* ***

Janet Hilton gives a highly sympathetic account of the Nielsen *Concerto,* but it is characteristically soft-centred and mellower in its response to the work's more disturbing emotional undercurrents than Olle Schill's splendid account on BIS – see below. However, those who prefer a record offering other clarinet works will not be disappointed by Janet Hilton's alternative programme. The Chandos recording is first class.

(i) *Clarinet concerto, Op. 57;* (ii) *Flute concerto.*
☞ (M) **(*) Sony 47599-2. (i) Stanley Drucker, (ii) Julius Baker; NYPO, Bernstein – HINDEMITH: *Violin concerto* **(*).

Both soloists are sensitive on the Sony reissue, and the *Clarinet concerto* is very satisfactory, even if Bernstein scrambles through the closing pages and underlines sforzati with gratuitous force. Julius Baker gives a fine account of the *Flute concerto,* although Bernstein again gives a somewhat over-emphatic account of the accompaniment. Above all, these performances have character and the recording is good, even if the balance gives excessive prominence in the *Clarinet concerto* to the side-drum!

(i) *Clarinet concerto, Op. 57;* (ii) *Flute concerto;* (iii) *Violin concerto, Op. 33.*
*** Chan. Dig. CHAN 8894; *ABTD 1505* [id.]. (i) Thomsen; (ii) Christiansen; (iii) Sjøgren; Danish RSO, Schønwandt.

Niels Thomsen's powerfully intense account of the late *Clarinet concerto* is completely gripping.

Michael Schønwandt gives sensitive and imaginative support, both here and in the two companion works. Toke Lund Christiansen is hardly less successful in the *Flute concerto*. Kim Sjøgren and Schønwandt give a penetrating and thoughtful account of the *Violin concerto*; there is real depth here, thanks in no small measure to Schønwandt. The recording is first class.

(i) *Clarinet concerto;* (ii) *Flute concerto. An Imaginary journey to the Faeroe Islands; Saul and David: Prelude.* (iii) *Springtime in Fünen, Op. 42.*

☞ **(*) Sony Dig. SK 53276 [id.]. Swedish RSO, Salonen, with (i) Håkan Rosengren; (ii) Per
   Flemström; (iii) Asa Bäverstam, Kjell Sandve, Per Høyer, Linnéa Ekdale, Andréas Thors,
   Swedish R. Ch. & Boys' Ch.

Generally good performances from Esa-Pekka Salonen and the Swedish Radio Orchestra. Håkan Rosengren has the measure of the *Clarinet concerto*, which he plays with considerable flair, and he receives excellent support from Salonen, not always the most idiomatic interpreter of this repertoire. His version can be recommended alongside but not in preference to Schill (BIS) or Niels Thomsen (Chandos). The *Flute concerto* fares equally well, though in tonal range and sheer character he does not quite match Patrick Gallois on BIS, who comes closer to the heart of this work than anyone since the dedicatee, Holger Gilbert Jespersen, on an early Decca LP. The *Prelude* to *Saul and David* comes off well but the earthy (yet seraphic) innocence and simplicity of *Springtime in Fünen* elude Salonen altogether. The singers do not banish memories of earlier and rival versions either. The concertos, though not first recommendations, deserve three stars but the cantata falls well short of that. Good recording, as one would expect from this source.

(i) *Clarinet concerto, Op. 57;* (ii) *Symphony No. 3 (Sinfonia espansiva). Maskarade overture.*
*** BIS Dig. CD 321 [id.]. (i) Olle Schill; (ii) Pia Raanoja, Knut Skram; Gothenburg SO, Myung-
    Whun Chung.

Olle Schill brings brilliance and insight to what is one of the most disturbing and masterly of all modern concertos. The young Korean conductor secures playing of great fire and enthusiasm from the Gothenburgers in the *Third Symphony* and he has vision and breadth – and at the same time no want of momentum. Two soloists singing a wordless vocalise are called for in the pastoral slow movement, and their contribution is admirable. Myung-Whun Chung also gives a high-spirited and sparkling account of the *Overture* to Nielsen's comic opera, *Maskarade*. The BIS recording is marvellous, even by the high standards of this small company. ᵢ

(i) *Clarinet concerto, Op. 57;* (ii) *Serenata in Vano;* (iii) *Wind quintet, Op. 43.*
☞ (***) Clarinet Classics mono CC 002 [id.]. (i) Cahuzac, Copenhagen Op. O, Frandsen; (ii)
   Oxenvad, Larsson, Sorensen, Jensen, Hegner; (iii) Royal Chapel Wind Quintet.

These are pioneering recordings and an essential part of any Nielsen collection. In 1922, at the time of the *Fifth Symphony*, Nielsen was captivated by the Mozart playing of the wind quintet of the Royal Opera or Theatre Orchestra, Copenhagen, and was immediately inspired to write his *Wind quintet* for them. Indeed it had been his intention to write each of the five players a concerto; he lived to compose only two, one for the flute (1926) and the other for clarinet (1928). The *Clarinet concerto* was to have been recorded by its dedicatee, Aage Oxenvad, who is heard in both the *Quintet* and the *Serenata in Vano*, but death intervened and the eminent French clarinettist Louis Cahuzac filled the breach. These records of the *Quintet* on four 78s with a filler, *Taagen letter* ('The Fog is lifting'), for flute and harp, were the post-war generation's introduction to Nielsen; and this lovely performance is so full of character that in some ways it remains unsurpassed. These transfers are a great improvement on the earlier ones on Danacord LPs and deserve the highest commendation. The original records were close and a little dry in the case of the chamber works, and a bit dry but eminently clean and well detailed in the case of the *Concerto*, which Cahuzac plays with great feeling.

(i) *Flute concerto; Symphony No. 1; Rhapsody overture: An imaginary journey to the Faeroe Islands.*
*** BIS Dig. CD 454 [id.]. (i) Patrick Gallois; Gothenburg SO, Myung-Whun Chung.

The *Flute concerto* is given a marvellous performance by Patrick Gallois, and Myung-Whun Chung and the Gothenburg orchestra have an instinctive feeling for Nielsen. They play with commendable enthusiasm and warmth, and Chung shapes the *Symphony* with great sensitivity to detail and a convincing sense of the whole. The *Rhapsody overture: An imaginary journey to the Faeroe Islands* is not the composer at his strongest, but it has a highly imaginative opening.

Violin concerto, Op. 33.
⊛ *** Sony Dig. MK 44548 [id.]. Cho-Liang Lin, Swedish RSO, Salonen – SIBELIUS: *Violin concerto.* *** ⊛

(i) *Violin concerto, Op. 33. Symphony No. 5, Op. 50.*
*** BIS Dig. CD 370 [id.]. (i) Dong-Suk Kang, Gothenburg SO, Myung-Whun Chung.

Cho-Liang Lin brings as much authority to Nielsen's *Concerto* as he does to the Sibelius and he handles the numerous technical hurdles with breathtaking assurance. His perfect intonation and tonal purity excite admiration, but so should his command of the architecture of this piece; there is a strong sense of line from beginning to end. Salonen is supportive here and gets good playing from the Swedish Radio Symphony Orchestra.

Dong-Suk Kang is more than equal to the technical demands of this concerto and is fully attuned to the Nordic sensibility. He brings tenderness and refinement of feeling to the searching slow movement and great panache and virtuosity to the rest. The *Fifth Symphony* is hardly less successful and is certainly the best-recorded version now available. Myung-Whun Chung has a natural feeling for Nielsen's language and the first movement has real breadth.

En aften paa Giske: Prelude (1889); Bøhmiske-dansk folketone; Helios, Overture, Op. 17; Paraphrase on 'Nearer my God, to thee', for wind band; Rhapsodic overture: An imaginary journey to the Faeroe Islands; Saga-drøm, Op. 39; Symphonic rhapsody (1888).
☞ **(*) Chan. Dig. CHAN 9287 [id.]. Danish Nat. RSO, Rohzdestvensky.

Two new pieces here: the *Prelude* to some incidental music Nielsen composed in 1889 for Andreas Munck's play, *En aften paa Giske* – not particularly characteristic but pleasing none the less, and the *Paraphrase on the Psalm, 'Nearer, my God, to thee', for wind band* from 1912, neither of which has been recorded before. The latter is both noble and individual. Rozhdestvensky gives musicianly, well-prepared and often poetic accounts of the more familiar pieces, though his *Helios, Overture* must be the slowest ever – over 14 minutes! His account of *Saga-drøm* ('The Dream of Gunnar') is also spacious. Very good recording, but in the last analysis these performances are a little deficient in zest. If, as we suspect, Blomstedt's 1975 accounts of this repertoire reappear during the lifetime of this book, they would be a safer choice.

Symphonies Nos. 1 in G min. Op. 7; 2 in B min., Op. 16; (i) 3 (Espansiva), Op. 27. 4 (Inextinguishable), Op. 27; 5, Op. 50; 6 (Sinfonia semplice).
☞ *** Chan. Dig. CHAN 9163/5 [id.]. Royal Scottish O, Thomson.
(M) **(*) Unicorn UKCD 2000/2 [id.]. LSO, Schmidt, (i) with Gomez, Rayner-Cook.

Symphonies Nos. 1 in G min. Op. 7; 2 in B min., Op. 16.
☞ **(*) DG Dig. 439 775-2 [id.]. Gothenburg SO, Neeme Järvi.

Symphonies Nos. (i) 3 (Espansiva), Op. 27; 4 (Inextinguishable), Op. 27.
☞ **(*) DG Dig. 439 776-2 [id.]. Gothenburg SO, Neeme Järvi, (i) with Hynninen.

Symphonies Nos. 5, Op. 50; 6 (Sinfonia semplice).
☞ **(*) DG Dig. 439 777-2 [id.]. Gothenburg SO, Neeme Järvi.

Symphonies Nos. (i) 1 in G min. Op. 7; 2 in B min., Op. 16; (i & ii) 3 (Espansiva), Op. 27; (iii) 4 (Inextinguishable), Op. 27; (i) 5, Op. 50; (iii) 6 (Sinfonia semplice); (i; iv) Clarinet concerto, Op. 57; (i; v) Flute concerto; (i; vi) Violin concerto, Op. 33.
☞ (M) *** BIS Dig. CD 614/616 [id.]. Gothenburg SO, (i) Myung-Whun Chung; (ii) with Raanoja, Skram; (iii) Neeme Järvi; (iv) with Olle Schill; (v) Patrick Gallois; (vi) Dong-Suk Kang.

The merits of the BIS Nielsen cycle (which includes the three concertos) have been well detailed in these pages. Myung-Whun Chung's accounts of the *First* and *Second Symphonies* can hold their own against the very best, and his version of the *Sinfonia espansiva* is one of the very best – and can be recommended alongside Blomstedt (Decca). It has the inestimable advantage of the Gothenburg Hall acoustic and warm, splendidly present recording. The concertos are all excellent – some may even prefer them to the rival collection on Chandos. Dong-Suk Kang's reading of the *Violin concerto* is eloquent in every respect and a worthy alternative to Cho-Liang Lin on Sony; and both Patrick Gallois and Olle Schill are magnificent soloists. The *Fourth* and *Sixth Symphonies* under Neeme Järvi are discussed below, but the package as a whole with four records for the price of three is eminently competitive.

Generally speaking Bryden Thomson's Nielsen symphonies are eminently sound and straightforward, without the extra ounce of finish that we find with the Blomstedt set. If they are not as beautifully recorded as Järvi on DG, they still sound impressive and as performances have the merit of being totally unmannered and unfussy, with generally well-chosen tempi. Thomson's version of the *Sixth* is arguably the best now on the market, and his *Fourth* has great fire. The set can hold its own with most of the first recommendations without displacing any of them – except in the two cases mentioned.

Neeme Järvi's Nielsen cycle is unusual in that two performances (of the *Fourth* and *Sixth Symphonies*) have appeared both in the BIS four-CD compilation that includes the three concertos and also on a separate CD issue. His cycle as a whole has much going for it – absolutely first-class recording with a completely natural balance which enables the strings to sound rich and sonorous in fortissimo passages, delicate and transparent in lightly scored writing; the wind are ideally placed, with no hint of spotlighting yet with every detail registering clearly; and the brass and percussion are equally successfully captured. The Gothenburg orchestra play with great enthusiasm and responsiveness for Järvi, and the celebrated acoustic of the Gothenburg Hall enhances the pleasure their playing gives. At the same time, not all the performances can be wholeheartedly recommended. Järvi does not allow the atmosphere and mystery of the *Fifth Symphony*'s first movement to register fully. He is far too intent to move things on, and the music does need to be a little more spacious; there is splendid playing all the same, particularly in the coda from the excellent Gothenburg clarinettist. In the *First Symphony* he is a shade too brisk in the outer movements though not unacceptably so, and the inner movements are played with real eloquence. The inner movements of the *Second Symphony* have plenty of character, though Järvi does make a little too much of the *allargando* markings in the third, which becomes a little overblown. Again the finale is rather rushed off its feet, particularly at the very end. The *Sinfonia espansiva* is well paced, and the slow movement features some particularly sensitive singing from Hynninen. The finale is let down by some uncharacteristic moments of bombast – Järvi plays the big tune at the right tempo but is unable to resist some disruptive, agogic emphases. There is strong competition in this field and, despite the excellent recorded sound, Blomstedt is the safer all-round buy, though the claims of Bryden Thomson's *Sixth* (Chandos) are also strong.

The performances on Unicorn Kanchana are ablaze with life, warmth and a sense of discovery. The recordings were always a bit rough, but the digital remastering represents an undoubted (though not spectacular) improvement, for the texture still remains coarse in tuttis. In No. 2 and the last three symphonies Ole Schmidt is a sure and penetrating guide and his readings have an authentic ring to them, for he has real feeling for this glorious music. They obviously represent good value.

Symphonies Nos. 1 in G min., Op. 7; 2 in B min., Op. 16 (The 4 Temperaments).
*** Chan. Dig. CHAN 8880 [id.]. Royal Scottish O, Bryden Thomson.

Strong, vigorous accounts of both symphonies from the Royal Scottish Orchestra under Bryden Thomson, with a particularly well-characterized reading of *The Four Temperaments*. The second movement is perhaps a shade too brisk, but in most respects these performances are difficult to flaw.

Symphonies Nos. 1 in G min., Op. 7; 4 (L'Inextinguishible) Op. 29.
☞ *(*) Chan. Dig. CHAN 9260 [id.]. Royal Stockholm PO, Rozhdestvensky.

Excellent playing from the Royal Stockholm Philharmonic and exemplary recording from the Chandos team do not prevent this coupling being a disappointment. Rozhdestvensky produces cultured playing and musically shaped phrasing and shows obvious affection for Nielsen's scores, but something essential is missing: the urgent level of energy and that vital current that carries the listener forward. There are many felicitous details, but tempi are just that little bit too leisurely and expansive.

Symphonies Nos. 1 in G min., Op. 7; 6 (Sinfonia Semplice).
*** Decca Dig. 425 607-2 [id.]. San Francisco SO, Blomstedt.

Blomstedt's record of the *First Symphony* is the best to have appeared for many years. It has vitality and freshness, and there is a good feel for Nielsen's natural lyricism. He inspires the San Francisco orchestra to excellent effect and the lean, well-focused string sound and songful wind playing are lovely. In the *Sixth Symphony* he has no want of intensity, though a broader tempo would have helped generate greater atmosphere in the first movement. Ole Schmidt (Unicorn) is more penetrating here. However, the performance is undeniably impressive and enjoys the advantage of far better recording.

Symphony No. 2 (The Four Temperaments), Op. 16; Aladdin suite, Op. 34.
*** BIS CD 247 [id.]. Gothenburg SO, Myung-Whun Chung.

Symphonies Nos. 2 (The Four Temperaments); (i) 3 (Espansiva), Op. 27.
*** Decca Dig. 430 280-2 [id.]. (i) Kromm, McMillan; San Francisco SO, Blomstedt.

This coupling is possibly the finest of Blomstedt's cycle: he finds just the right tempo for each movement and nowhere is this more crucial than in the finale of the *Espansiva*. The two soloists are good and the orchestra play with all the freshness and enthusiasm one could ask for. The recording, though not quite in the demonstration bracket, is very fine indeed.

Myung-Whun Chung has a real feeling for this repertoire and his account of the *Second Symphony* is also very fine. The Gothenburg Symphony Orchestra proves an enthusiastic and responsive body of players. The recording is impressive, too, and can be recommended with enthusiasm.

Symphonies Nos. 2 (The Four Temperaments), Op. 16; 4 (The Inextinguishable), Op. 29.
☞ (M) ** Sony SMK 47597-2. NYPO, Bernstein.

Symphonies Nos. 3 (Sinfonia espansiva), Op. 27; 5, Op. 50.
☞ (M) **(*) Sony SMK 47598-2. (i) Ruth Guldbaeck, Niels Moller, Royal Danish O; (ii) NYPO, Bernstein.

The *Second Symphony* is one of Nielsen's most attractive works; Bernstein, who had an undoubted feeling for this composer, gives it a fine, powerful reading with plenty of fire in the first movement. But the inner movements are too slow and expressive, detail too heavily underlined to be wholly satisfactory. There is an idiosyncratic agogic change in the coda of the finale. Bernstein's performance of the genial *Espansiva* with the Royal Danish Orchestra has a lot going for it. And yet, for all the excellence of the orchestral playing, this performance misses something of the music's innocence; this is most striking in the slow movement, where Bernstein favours great intensity of string-tone. In the *Fourth*, at times Nielsen's finely drawn lines again quiver with an expressive emphasis that strikes a jarring note. Moreover Bernstein does not hesitate to distort the rhythmic flow of the music to underline an expressive point. But it would be churlish to concentrate on the defects in these performances; they have many merits: liveliness, enthusiasm and admirable orchestral playing. Furthermore Bernstein conveys a genuine love for the music, for all the overstatement in which he occasionally indulges. Bernstein is at his finest in the *Fifth* and gives an immensely powerful reading. The dominating side-drum in the first movement is tellingly played by Elden C. Bailey, and the passion of the string cantilena and the following movement through into the finale are indicative of the spontaneous feeling which pervades the whole symphony. The well-detailed, resonant recording adds to the impact of the performance.

(i) *Symphonies No. 3 (Sinfonia espansvia). 5, Op. 50.*
☞ *** Chan. Dig. CHAN 9067 [id.]. (i) Bott, Roberts; Royal Scottish O, Bryden Thomson.

These performances have the merit of selflessness. At no point does Bryden Thomson interpose himself between the composer and the listener. His chosen tempi in the *Sinfonia espansiva* are just right, particularly in the finale which has posed difficulties for so many interpreters. In the slow movement Catherine Bott and Stephen Roberts are excellent, and the performance has a refreshing directness that is most likeable. The *Fifth Symphony* is equally committed and satisfying. Thomson draws a vibrant response from his players in the second movement and there is much beauty of detail in the first. One is occasionally too aware of the barline in the first movement, which does not always move with that ethereal quality one recalls from the pioneering versions by Erik Tuxen and Thomas Jensen. The recordings are very good indeed, though one feels the need for heavily scored passages to open out a little more. Recommended, albeit not in preference to Blomstedt, who is differently coupled.

Symphonies Nos. 3 (Sinfonia espansiva); 6 (Sinfonia semplice).
*** BMG/RCA Dig. RD 60427 [60427-2-RC]. Royal Danish O, Paavo Berglund.

Paavo Berglund's account of the *Sinfonia espansiva* is the best to appear since Blomstedt's Decca version. The playing of the Royal Danish Orchestra, in which Nielsen once served, is beautifully prepared and full of vitality. His two soloists, though unnamed, are very good and the general architecture of the work is well conveyed. In the more problematic *Sixth Symphony* Berglund proves a perceptive guide. His performance matches Blomstedt's in integrity and insight and is obviously the product of much thought. The RCA engineers produce a recording of splendid body and presence. In any event, Berglund can be strongly recommended alongside (though not necessarily in preference to) Blomstedt.

Symphony No. 4 (Inextinguishable); Pan and Syrinx, Op. 29.
☞ (M) *** EMI CDM7 64737-2 [id.]. CBSO, Rattle – SIBELIUS: *Symphony No. 5.* ***

Simon Rattle's version of the *Inextinguishable* dates from the late 1970s and is very fine indeed, though it is perhaps a shade judicious when put alongside his live broadcast (with the Philharmonia) dating from the same period. All the same, it deserves a strong recommendation, particularly given the fact that it is at mid-price and comes with an altogether outstanding account of *Pan and Syrinx* (the best ever on record) and his classic account of Sibelius's *Fifth Symphony*. Excellent sound.

Symphonies Nos. 4 (Inextinguishable); 5, Op. 50.
*** Decca Dig. 421 524-2 [id.]. San Francisco SO, Blomstedt.

The opening of Blomstedt's *Fourth* has splendid fire: this must sound as if galaxies are forming. Blomstedt conveys Nielsen's image about the soaring string-lines in the slow movement ('like the eagle riding on the wind') most strikingly. The finale is exhilarating, yet held on a firm rein. The *Fifth Symphony*, too, is impressive: it starts perfectly and is almost as icy in atmosphere as those pioneering recordings of the 1950s. The desolate clarinet peroration also comes off most successfully. The recording balance could not be improved upon.

Symphonies Nos. 4 (Inextinguishable), Op. 27; 6 (Sinfonia semplice).
☞ ⊛ *** Chan. Dig. CHAN 9047 [id.]. Royal Scottish O, Bryden Thomson.
☞ **(*) BIS Dig. CD 600 [id.]. Gothenburg SO, Neeme Järvi.

The late Bryden Thomson's coupling of the *Fourth* and *Sixth Symphonies* is by far the most successful of his Nielsen cycle and possibly the finest recording of his career. The *Fourth Symphony* has some of the ardent intensity of Launy Grøndahl's pioneering records, particularly in the anguished string-writing of the slow movement, which calls to mind Nielsen's own image that the melodic line must soar 'like the eagle riding on the wind'. The finale, too, has great sweep and excitement, and though Blomstedt and the San Francisco orchestra on Decca have the greater polish, there is the same directness that has distinguished earlier issues in the cycle but with greater fire. But it is Bryden Thomson's account of the *Sixth Symphony* that crowns the set. This is quite simply the finest version now before the public, and arguably the most penetrating since Thomas Jensen's first recording. Thomson really knew what this writing is all about and was the first to make real sense of the puzzling and problematic *Humoreske* movement. Moreover he strikes just the right tempo for the first movement, a fraction broader than Blomstedt, and gets to the heart of the eloquent *Proposta seria* too: indeed no one brings us closer to the spirit of this music than Thomson, and the recording is very good too. Recommended with enthusiasm.

Neeme Järvi's accounts of the *Fourth* and *Sixth Symphonies* are good performances that are beautifully played and most naturally recorded and can hold their own with most of the competition. In the *Fourth Symphony* (*Inextinguishable*), Blomstedt, Ole Schmidt (save for the recording which now sounds less refined than the latest versions) and Bryden Thomson have greater character; and in the *Sixth*, Järvi's reading does not go quite as deeply as do Thomson and Blomstedt. All the same, this disc has much going for it and readers investing in it should not be disappointed.

Symphony No. 5, Op. 50.
☞ (M) **(*) EMI CDM5 65182 [id.]. Danish Nat. RSO, Kubelik – SIBELIUS: *Luonnotar* etc. **(*)
☞ (M) * Ph. 438 283-2 [id.]. Concg. O, Kondrashin – SHOSTAKOVICH: *Symphony No. 6.* *

Rafael Kubelik's majestic and spacious account of the *Fifth Symphony* must be the slowest on record. It does, however, have great atmosphere, as well as a sense of mystery: he obviously has a great feeling for the score. Not a 'library recommendation', perhaps, but well worth hearing – and a performance of stature. It emanates from a live performance in 1983 in the Concert Hall of Danish Radio. (This CD has been withdrawn as we go to press.)

In spite of impressive orchestral playing from the then un-Royal Concertgebouw, Kirill Kondrashin and the great Dutch orchestra are not quite inside this repertoire in terms of either pacing or feeling. The recording was made at a public performance in the 1970s and is very good, but neither the Nielsen nor the Shostakovich is a real challenge to existing recommendations.

CHAMBER MUSIC

Canto serioso; Fantasias for oboe and piano, Op. 2; The Mother (incidental music), Op. 41; Serenata in vano; Wind quintet, Op. 43.
**(*) Chan. CHAN 8680 [id.]. Athena Ens.

This reissue gathers together Nielsen's output for wind instruments in chamber form, with everything played expertly and sympathetically. The recording is balanced very close; nevertheless much of this repertoire is not otherwise available, and this is a valuable disc.

String quartets Nos. 1 in G min., Op. 13; 2 in F min., Op. 5; 3 in E flat, Op. 14; 4 in F, Op. 44. 5 quartet movements, FS2.
☞ *** Kontrapunkt Dig. 32150-1 [id.]. Danish Qt.

The Nielsen *Quartets* have not been ideally served on CD. The Kontra set on BIS is the better of the two rival versions; the eponymous Carl Nielsen Quartet on a mid-price DG set are very rough-and-ready and the inclusion of a serviceable account of the *Wind quintet* does not tip the scales in their favour. The new set from the Danish Quartet is the best since the Copenhagen Quartet's LPs: these players are sensitive to the shape of the phrase, they produce a wide dynamic range, including really soft pianissimo tone when required. They are not always the last word in polish, but everything they do is musical and leaves one marvelling at the freshness of invention Nielsen commanded, particularly in the *E flat quartet*, Op. 14, and its *F major* companion, Op. 44. Throughout, they judge pace most expertly and play with imagination, which makes one forgive the occasional rough edge and the somewhat dry quality and rather close balance of the recording. This shortcoming should not be overstressed but deserves mention. The set also includes five short movements that Nielsen wrote in his late teens and early twenties, emphatically not great music but of undoubted interest for students of the composer. Recommended.

String quartets Nos. 1 in G min., Op. 13; 2 in F min., Op. 5; 3 in E flat, Op. 14; 4 in F, Op. 44. (i)
String quintet in G (1888); (ii) *Andante lamentoso (At the bier of a young artist)* (1910).
*** BIS Dig. CD 503/4 [id.]. Kontra Qt, (i) Philipp Naegele; (ii) Jan Johansson.

The Nielsen *Quartets* are all from his first period. There is an ardour and temperament to the playing here, which most listeners will find very persuasive. In addition we are given by far the finest account yet recorded of the *G major String quintet*, where the Kontra Quartet are joined by the American violist Philipp Naegele, and the only current account of the *Andante lamentoso (At the bier of a young artist)* in its chamber form. The BIS recordings, made in the Malmö Concert Hall, have plenty of presence and clarity, and are rather forwardly (but not unpleasingly) balanced. Recommended, alongside the Danish Quartet.

String quintet in G (1888), FS5.
☞ *** Chan. Dig. CHAN 9258 [id.]. ASMF Ens. – SVENDSEN: Octet. ***

The *String quintet in G major* is an early piece, written when Nielsen was in his early twenties. Although there is the occasional foretaste of things to come, the work is not really characteristic. It is very well fashioned and owes more to Svendsen, under whose baton the composer was to play, than to his teacher, Gade. It makes both an agreeable and an appropriate companion for Svendsen's early and delightful *Octet*. It receives a three-star performance and recording.

Wind quintet, Op. 43.
*** Sony Dig. CD 45996. Ens. Wien-Berlin – TAFFANEL: *Quintet.* ***
(M) ** Sony SMK 46250 [id.]. Members of the Marlboro Festival – BARBER: *Summer music* **(*);
  HINDEMITH: *Octet.* **

The Ensemble Wien-Berlin gives one of the best accounts of the Nielsen *Wind quintet* to have appeared in years. Their tonal blend and purity of intonation are beyond praise and there are too many felicities of characterization in the variation movement to enumerate. They are also beautifully recorded, and the only reservation must be that, at 50 minutes, this disc gives short measure.

The Marlboro performance of the *Wind quintet* dates from 1971 and is a good one, although the recording balance places the listener just a little too close to the players. There are some perceptive things here, and these players penetrate the spirit of the poignant preamble that opens the *Theme and variations*.

VOCAL MUSIC

(i) *Hymnus amoris, Op. 12;* (ii) *3 Motets, Op. 55; The sleep, Op. 18;* (iii) *Springtime in Fünen, Op. 43.*
*** Chan. Dig. CHAN 8853; *ABTD 1470* [id.]. Soloists; (i) Copenhagen Boys' Ch.; (ii–iii) Danish
  Nat. R. Ch.; (iii) Skt. Annai Gymnasium Children's Ch., Danish Nat. RSO; (i; iii) Segerstam; (ii)
  Parkman.

Hymnus amoris is full of glorious music whose polyphony has a naturalness and freshness that it is difficult to resist, and which is generally well sung. The harsh dissonances of the middle *Nightmare* section of *Søvnen* ('The Sleep') rather shocked Danish musical opinion at the time and still generate a powerful effect. Segerstam gets very good results both here and in the enchanting *Springtime in Fünen*, and the solo singing is good. The three motets actually contain a Palestrina quotation. Generally excellent performances and fine recorded sound.

(i) *Springtime in Fünen. Aladdin suite, Op. 34.*

*** Unicorn Dig. DKPCD 9054; *DKPC 9054* [id.]. (i) Ingo Nielsen, Von Binzer, Klint, Lille Muko University Ch., St Klemens Children's Ch.; Odense SO, Veto.

Springtime in Fünen is one of those enchanting pieces to which everyone responds when they hear it, yet which is hardly ever performed outside Denmark. The engaging *Aladdin* orchestral suite is well played by the Odense orchestra. This disc is a little short on playing time – but no matter, it is well worth its cost and will give many hours of delight.

STAGE WORKS

Aladdin (complete incidental music), *Op. 34.*

☞ *** Chan. Dig. CHAN 9135 [id.]. Ejsing, Paevetalu, Danish R. Chamber Ch. & SO, Rozhdestvensky.

In 1917 the Royal Theatre in Copenhagen commissioned Nielsen to compose incidental music for a lavish production of Adam Oehlenschläger's play, *Aladdin*. (The Royal Theatre performs a dual role in Danish cultural life as a centre not only for classical drama but also for opera, so that Nielsen had large choral and orchestral forces at his disposal.) Up to now the *Aladdin* music has been known only from the 20-minute, seven-movement suite, but the complete score runs to four times its length (no fewer than 275 pages). And so this CD gives us an additional hour of Nielsen that has never been available before. Torben Schousboe, who has prepared the score for this recording, provides an ample discussion of the plot so that it is easy to follow the action as one listens to the 31 pieces. Nielsen conveys the oriental colour and atmosphere with great expertise. The bulk of the processional music and dances comes from Act III, which furnished the majority of the pieces from the suite; indeed, half of the score is purely orchestral. The four oriental dances were conceived almost symphonically with an appropriate contrast of tonality and pace. Some numbers are choral, and there are songs and a short piece for solo flute. Thirteen of the movements are designed to accompany spoken dialogue and, although not all of it is of equal musical interest and substance, most of it is characteristically Nielsenesque, and much of it is delightful. The two soloists, Mette Ejsing and Guido Paevatalu, are very good and the Danish Radio forces respond keenly to Rozhdestvensky's baton. This is not top-drawer Nielsen but, given such a persuasive performance and excellent recording, one is almost lulled into the belief that it is.

OPERA

Maskarade (complete).

**(*) Unicorn DKPCD 9073/4 [id.]. Hansen, Plesner, Landy, Johansen, Serensen, Bastian, Brodersen, Haugland, Danish R. Ch. & SO, Frandsen.

Maskarade is a buoyant, high-spirited score, full of strophic songs and choruses, making considerable use of dance and dance-rhythms, and having the unmistakable lightness of the *buffo* opera. It is excellently proportioned. The performance here is delightful, distinguished by generally good singing and alert orchestral support. The disappointment is the CD transfer which, in trying to clarify textures, has in fact made the focus less clean.

Saul and David (complete).

⊛ *** Chan. Dig. CHAN 8911/12; *DBTD 2026* [id.]. Haugland, Lindroos, Kiberg, Westi, Ch. & Danish Nat. RSO, Järvi.

Nielsen's first opera is here sung in the original language, which is as important with Nielsen as it is with Janáček, and it has the merit of an outstanding Saul in Aage Haugland. The remainder of the cast is very strong and the powerful choral writing is well served by the Danish Radio Chorus. The opera abounds in wonderful and noble music, the ideas are fresh and full of originality. It convinces here in a way that it rarely has before, and the action is borne along on an almost symphonic current that disarms criticism. A marvellous set.

Nin, Joaquín (1879–1949)

Cantos populares españoles Nos. 3, 4, 6, 7, 19 & 20.
☞ (M) (***) EMI mono CDC7 54836-2 [id.]. Ninon Vallin, composer – FALLA: *Harpsichord concerto* etc.; GRANADOS: *Danzas españolas* etc.; MOMPOU: *Piano pieces.* (***)

This is part of another of the marvellously documented and beautifully restored 'Composers in Person' CDs that EMI have recently put on the market. Although Joaquín Nin was born and died in Cuba, he spent the better part of his life in Paris and Berlin, where he was active as a virtuoso pianist and teacher. Less individual than his companions, he was still a highly accomplished and polished composer. His *Cantos populares españoles* are rather similiar in character to the celebrated Falla set. The incomparable Ninon Vallin sings six of them with great simplicity and Nin proves himself a charming accompanist. The recordings, made in Paris in 1929, when Vallin was at the height of her powers, sound remarkably good. They come with highly interesting couplings.

Nono, Luigi (1924–90)

Fragmente; Stille, an Diotima (Silence for Diotima).
☞ (M) ** DG Dig. 437 720-2 [id.]. LaSalle Qt.

If anyone can convert the listener to the music of Luigi Nono, it is the LaSalle Quartet, for whom he wrote this taxing, endlessly pauseful work in two substantial movements of nearly 20 minutes each. The economy-conscious collector might well complain not only of the short overall playing time (38 minutes) but of the high proportion of silence on the disc. But the intensity of the playing will help the uncommitted listener to concentrate on intentionally weighty expression in which late Beethoven was an inspiration – not that one would readily recognize it. Full, immediate recording.

Norby, Erik (born 1936)

The Rainbow snake.
☞ *** BIS CD 79 [id.]. Danish Nat. RO, Frandsen – BENTZON: *Feature on René Descartes;* JORGENSON: *To love music.* **

Erik Norby, now in his late fifties, studied with Per Nørgård, and *The Rainbow snake*, commissioned by the Danish Radio in 1975, is – unusually for our times – purely programmatic. *The Rainbow snake* is an American Indian fable which tells how drought had produced infertility in the land. The snake heard of this and let itself be thrown, coiled up, into the sky where it uncoiled until it touched the earth at both ends. It then arched its back and scraped down the blue ice which had given rise to the drought, thus restoring life to the earth. Every time the sun and rain meet, the snake stretches its luminous body across the heavens. The scoring is highly colourful, the harmonic language impressionist. At times it seems like listening to the Debussyian opening of the second part of *Le sacre du printemps* mixed up with *Daphnis* while sitting in a Turkish bath. All highly atmospheric, with kaleidoscopic changes of harmony against an almost static rhythmic background. It is very well played and recorded.

Nørholm, Ib (born 1931)

Violin concerto, Op. 60.
*** BIS CD 80 [id.]. Leo Hansen, Danish Nat. RSO, Herbert Blomstedt – KOPPEL: *Cello concerto.* ***

Ib Nørholm's *Violin concerto* not only evinces considerable imaginative powers but contains some music of real beauty and is expertly laid out for the orchestra. The Danish Radio recording, while not state of the art, is more than acceptable, and it comes with a rewarding coupling.

Novák, Vitězslav (1870–1949)

(i) Symphonic poems: *About the Eternal longing, Op. 33; In the Tatras, Op. 26;* (ii) *Moravian-Slovak suite, Op. 32.*
☞ (M) **(*) Sup. 11 0682-2 [id.]. (i) Czech PO; (ii) Brno State PO, Karel Sejna.

A valuable reissue from the 1960s. Novák was a pupil of Dvořák and his music has Slavic as well as French and German influences, though he speaks with distinctive accents. *In the Tatras* (1902), an opulent Straussian tone-poem, and *About the Eternal longing* (1903/4) were inspired by unrequited love for a beautiful young pupil, Růžena, who came to him for harmony lessons. But the effect on the composer was joy rather than frustration. The *Slovak suite* is a heavenly score. *Two in love*, its third movement, could well become as widely popular as any piece of music you care to think of. *In the church*, the opening movement, has something in common with Mozart's *Ave verum corpus*, though more obviously romantic, and the closing *At night* is beguilingly atmospheric. All three works here are persuasively played. The recording of the two symphonic poems is atmospheric and clear but a bit pale in the more expansive tuttis; the suite has slightly more body and colour.

Pan (symphonic poem), *Op. 43.*
*** Marco Polo Dig. 8.223325 [id.]. Slovak PO, Zdeněk Bílek.

Novák's five-movement symphonic poem, *Pan*, has some lovely music in it. Novák belonged to the generation of composers (Delius, Mahler, Debussy, Janáček, Sibelius etc.) for whom Nature was still central, and there is a pantheistic sensibility here. The scoring has great delicacy and imaginative resource, and there is a distinctly Gallic feeling to much of it. Lyrical, often inspired (occasionally a bit overlong – particularly the last movement) and rewarding, this score is beautifully played by the Slovak Philharmonic under Zdeněk Bílek, and no less beautifully recorded.

Ockeghem, Johannes (*c.* 1410–97)

Complete secular music: *Au travail suis; L'aultre d'antan l'autrier; Aultre venus estés; Baisiés moy dont fort; Ce n'est pas jeu; Departés vous, male touche; Les desléaux ont la saison; La despourveue et la bannie; D'un aultre amer; D'un aultre la (Rondeau royal); Fors seulement contre ce qu'ay promis; Fors seulement l'attente; Il ne m'en chault plus; Je n'ay dueil que je ne suis morte; Ma bouche rit; Ma maistresse et ma plus grante amye; Malheur me bat; Mort tu es navre; O rosa bella o dolce anima mia; Prenez sur moi vostre exemple; Presque transi; Quant ce viendra; Quant de vous seul; Qu'es mi vida preguntoys; Resjois toy terre de France; Se vostre cuer eslongne; S'elle m'amera; Tant fuz gentement.*
☞ (M) *** O-L Dig. 436 194-2 (2). Medieval Ens. of London, Peter and Timothy Davies.

Ockeghem was not a prolific master; apart from the chansons collected here, there are 11 Masses, a Requiem and a number of motets. This set includes all the chansons attributed to him in fifteenth-century manuscripts, including 22 of whose authenticity there is no doubt. He is generally thought to be the most outstanding composer of chansons after Dufay, and there is no doubting the elegance and refinement of many of the pieces recorded here, nor can there be much about their diversity and range. The performances are intelligent and sensitive, and the use of instrumental support is imaginative. At times the ear tires of the somewhat white timbre of the voices, but there is no denying the accomplishment of these artists or the excellence of the recording. The accompanying essay and texts of the songs are most helpful in going through this rewarding set.

Requiem (Missa pro defunctis).
*** DG 415 293-2 [id.]. Pro Cantione Antiqua, Hamburger Bläserkreis für alte Musik, Turner – JOSQUIN DES PRES: *Missa – L'homme armé.* ***

The DG Archiv version of the *Missa pro defunctis* was originally recorded in Hamburg in 1973. The Pro Cantione Antiqua was unmatched at this period (with such artists as James Bowman and Paul Esswood as their counter-tenors, this is hardly surprising), and Bruno Turner's direction has both scholarly rectitude and musical eloquence to commend it.

Offenbach, Jacques (1819–80)

Cello concerto.
*** BMG/RCA RD 71003. Ofra Harnoy, Cincinnati SO, Kunzel – SAINT-SAENS: *Concerto No. 1;* TCHAIKOVSKY: *Rococo variations.* ***

Offenbach's *Cello concerto* is a delight, with all the effervescence and tunefulness of his operettas. It is played with verve and brio and a full range of colour by Ofra Harnoy and did much to establish her reputation, while the accompaniment from Kunzel and his Cincinnati players is just as lively and sympathetic. Excellent recording throughout.

Gaîté parisienne (ballet, arr. Rosenthal): complete.

☞ ⊛ (M) *** BMG/RCA 09026 61847-2 [id.]. Boston Pops O, Arthur Fiedler – ROSSINI/RESPIGHI: *Boutique fantasque*. ***

Fiedler's *Gaîté parisienne* is irresistible – one of his very finest records. The orchestra are kept exhilaratingly on their toes throughout and are obviously enjoying themselves, not least in the elegantly tuneful waltzes and in the closing *Barcarolle*, which Fiedler prepares beautifully and to which the generous acoustic of Symphony Hall affords a pleasing warmth without in any way blunting or coarsening the brilliance. The percussion, including bass drum in the exuberant *Can-Can*, adds an appropriate condiment and John Pfeiffer's superb new transfer makes the recording sound remarkably fresh and full. Unbelievably it dates from 1954, one of the very first of RCA's 'Living Stereo' records and still one of the finest.

Gaîté parisienne (ballet, arr. Rosenthal): extended excerpts.

☞ (B) *** DG Double 437 404-2 (2) [id.]. BPO, Karajan – CHOPIN: *Les Sylphides* *** ⊛; DELIBES: *Coppélia: suite* ***; GOUNOD: *Faust* etc. **(*); RAVEL: *Boléro* ***; TCHAIKOVSKY: *Sleeping Beauty* (suite). **(*)

Karajan's selection is generous. On the DG disc, only Nos. 3–5, 7 and 19–21 are omitted. The remastering of the 1972 recording is highly successful, although the sound is very brightly lit. However, textures have been lightened to advantage and the effect is to increase the raciness of the music-making, while its polish and sparkle are even more striking. This now comes in a generous compilation of ballet music, all in performances showing characteristic Karajan panache.

Gaîté parisienne (ballet music, arr. Rosenthal): excerpts; *Overture: Orpheus in the Underworld*.

(M) ** Sony SMK 47532 [id.]. NYPO, Bernstein (with SUPPE: *Overture: Beautiful Galathea* ***) – BIZET: Symphony. **(*).

Bernstein's suite includes a good deal of the raciest part of the score and then closes with the *Barcarolle*. The playing is characteristically effervescent, but the rather hard light of the 1969 CBS sound – the recording was made in the Avery Fisher Hall – makes everything seem brittle, and the ear is easily tired, unless a modest volume level is chosen. The Overtures are characteristically boisterous: Bernstein is warmly elegant as well, in Suppé's *Beautiful Galathea*.

(i) *Musette (Air de ballet)*. Overtures: *La Belle Hélène; La Grande-Duchesse de Gérolstein; Orpheus in the Underworld. Les belles Américaines: Waltz* (orch. Robert Russell Bennett). *Contes d'Hoffmann: Intermezzo; Introduction; Minuet; Barcarolle. Geneviève de Brabant: Galop. La Périchole:* Pot-pourri.

☞ (M) ** BMG/RCA 09026 61429-2 [id.]. Boston Pops O, Arthur Fiedler – IBERT: *Divertissement*. ***

For once the CD transfer of this RCA 'Living Stereo' recording from 1956 is disappointing. The Boston resonance intrudes on the music-making and tends to blunt the effect of the playing, so that one has the impression that Fiedler is fielding a second team. But the selection is interesting and generous, and Samuel Mayes is a sympathetic cello soloist in the *'Air de ballet from the 17th Century'*. Curiously, the Ibert *Divertissement* which acts as coupling and which was recorded a month later, is as racy as you could wish, and the recorded sound is comparably lively.

Overtures: *Barbe-Bleue; La Belle Hélène; La Grande-Duchesse de Gérolstein; La fille du tambour-major; Monsieur et Madame Denis; Orpheus in the Underworld; Vert-vert; La vie parisienne.*

☞ *(*) Sony SK 53288 [id.]. VSO, Bruno Weill.

A most disappointing disc. These are well-played but lustreless performances, like champagne gone flat. One remembers nostalgically an early Decca LP of this delightful repertoire by Jean Martinon and the LPO. Those performances had a delectable combination of finesse and sparkle that is entirely missing here.

Overtures: *La Belle Hélène; Bluebeard; La Grande-Duchesse de Gérolstein; Orpheus in the Underworld; Vert-vert. Barcarolle from Contes d'Hoffmann.*

**(*) DG Dig. 400 044-2 [id.]. BPO, Karajan.

Other hands besides Offenbach's helped to shape his overtures. Most are on a pot-pourri basis, but the tunes and scoring are so engagingly witty as to confound criticism. Karajan's performances racily evoke the theatre pit. The Berlin playing is very polished and, with so much to entice the ear, this cannot fail to be entertaining; however, the compact disc emphasizes the dryness of the orchestral sound; the effect is rather clinical, with the strings lacking bloom.

Le Papillon (ballet): complete.
(M) *** Decca 425 450-2 [id.]. LSO, Richard Bonynge – TCHAIKOVSKY: *Nutcracker*. **(*)

Le Papillon is Offenbach's only full-length ballet and it dates from 1860. The quality of invention is high and the music sparkles from beginning to end. In such a sympathic performance, vividly recorded (in 1974) it cannot fail to give pleasure.

Cello duos, Op. 54: Suites Nos. 1–2.
(B) *** HM 901043. Roland Pidoux and Etienne Péclard.

Offenbach was himself a very accomplished cellist, and these two works are tuneful and imaginatively laid out to exploit the tonal possibilities of such a duo. Offenbach's natural wit is especially apparent in the *First Suite in E major*. The performances are excellent and so is the recording.

OPERA

Les brigands (complete).
**(*) EMI Dig. CDS7 49830-2 (2). Raphanel, Alliot-Lugaz, Raffalli, Trempont, Le Roux, Lyon
   Opera Ch. & O, Gardiner.

Les brigands has a Gilbertian plot about brigands and their unlikely association with the court of Mantua, with the carabinieri behaving very like the police in *The Pirates of Penzance*. The tone of the principal soprano, Ghislaine Raphanel, is rather edgily French, but the rest of the team is splendid. Outstanding as ever is the characterful mezzo, Colette Alliot-Lugaz, in another of her breeches roles. Warm, well-balanced recording. (This recording has been deleted as we go to press.)

Les Contes d'Hoffmann (The Tales of Hoffmann): complete.
⊛ *** Decca 417 363-2 (2) [id.]. Sutherland, Domingo, Tourangeau, Bacquier, R. Suisse Romande
   and Lausanne Pro Arte Ch., SRO, Bonynge.
☞ **(*) Ph. 422 374-2 (3) [id.]. Francisco Araiza, Eva Lind, Cheryl Studer, Jessye Norman, Anne
   Sofie von Otter, Samuel Ramey, Dresden Ch. & State O, Tate.

On Decca Joan Sutherland gives a virtuoso performance in four heroine roles, not only as Olympia, Giulietta and Antonia but also as Stella in the *Epilogue*. Bonynge opts for spoken dialogue, and puts the Antonia scene last, as being the more substantial. His direction is unfailingly sympathetic, while Sutherland is impressive in each role, notably as the doll Olympia and in the pathos of the Antonia scene. As Giulietta she hardly sounds like a *femme fatale*, but still produces beautiful singing. Domingo gives one of his finest performances on record, and so does Gabriel Bacquier. It is a memorable set, in every way, much more than the sum of its parts.

Jeffrey Tate in this textually troubled work uses a new edition prepared by Michael Kaye that takes account of the discovery of 350 more manuscript pages in addition to those which expanded the Oeser edition to Wagnerian lengths. One big difference here from the complete Oeser edition, as presented by Cambreling on his deleted EMI set, is that dialogue replaces all the recitatives written by Ernest Guiraud. The Prologue is more extended, showing the transformation of the Muse into Nicklausse, with extra material in the Olympia and Antonia Acts too, such as the striking trio for Hoffmann, Nicklausse and Coppélius. Also, Tate points out that 'the Giulietta act contains music that shows conclusively that Offenbach would have wanted a single voice to embody all of Hoffmann's female infatuations'.

A fascinating illustration of that comes in the jaunty couplets, *L'amour lui dit: la belle*, leading into exchanges and a duet reprise with Hoffmann. It is a jolly little piece, close in style to earlier Offenbach, which in its lightness and use of high coloratura radically alters one's conception of the character of the Venetian *femme fatale*. Needless to say, Cheryl Studer has no problems here over high coloratura, but in context it seems inconsistent with the character as we know it. It is a pity that the logic of the project was not carried through, with a single singer chosen for all the heroines, as in the Bonynge/Sutherland set. As it is, Jessye Norman, the Giulietta of the Cambreling set, has here become the Antonia of the new one. Though she cunningly lightens her voice, making it sound as girlish as she can, and she urges the music on at a brisker speed than usual in the charming duet, *C'est une chanson d'amour*, it is still hard to imagine her as the fragile young girl destined to die. Tate's determination to adopt an authentic text leads him to reject the septet, based on the *Barcarolle* theme, not even including it in an appendix (as Cambreling does). Nor is Dapertutto's *Scintille, diamant* included, drawn originally from another Offenbach work, when the authentic *Tourne, tourne miroir*, is restored at that point.

As a recording, the set's drawback is that it does not feel very theatrical, thanks partly to being recorded in a church but also to the very sparing use of sound effects, with the chorus's contributions sounding rather oratorio-like. The spoken dialogue does not help when, among the principals, only Georges Gautier, in the four grotesque roles, has a French-speaking background, though Jessye Norman's spoken French is a delight. The new set, unlike the Cambreling, uses the sour alternative ending to the Venice Act, with Giulietta accidentally taking poison. Samuel Ramey sings very well in all four villainous roles, with satisfyingly firm, dark tone, even if he finds it hard to sound really sinister, but principal vocal honours go to Anne Sofie von Otter as a superb Muse and Nicklausse, making one relish all the extra music given the character in this version. Eva Lind is bright and clear, if a little edgy and shallow, as Olympia, perfectly doll-like in fact; and Cheryl Studer is technically very strong and confident, even if she does not quite sound in character. Not always helped by the recorded sound, refined and rather lacking in weight, Riccardo Cassinelli, Georges Gautier and Boris Martinovitch give enjoyable but rather undercharacterized performances, and the student leaders in the Prologue sound far too mature. Francisco Araiza makes an agreeable Hoffmann, but he lacks the flair of his finest rivals, and the voice tends to lose its focus under pressure.

Jeffrey Tate secures fine ensemble. He tends to pace on the slow side, but by contrast presses the celebrated *Barcarolle* on faster than usual – a conflation of the vocal and entr'acte versions – with woodwind soloists who in their literal way miss the magic. Even with reservations there is a very strong textual case for this set, and admirers of the opera will surely want to have it alongside the first choice with Sutherland, Domingo and Bacquier.

Les Contes d'Hoffmann: highlights.
(M) *** Decca 421 866-2; *421 866-4* (from above set, cond. Bonynge).

The Decca highlights disc is one of the finest compilations of its kind from any opera. With over an hour of music, it offers a superbly managed distillation of nearly all the finest items and is edited most skilfully.

Orpheus in the Underworld: highlights of English National Opera production (in English).
**(*) That's Entertainment Dig. CDTER 1134. Kale, Watson, Angas, Squires, Bottone, Pope, Belcourt, Styx, Burgess, E. Nat. Op. Ch. & O, Mark Elder.

The sparkling English National Opera production depends a lot for its fun on the racy new adaptation and translation by Snoo Wilson and the ENO producer, David Pountney. Offenbach devotees should be warned: there is little of Parisian elegance in this version and plenty of good knockabout British fun, brilliantly conveyed by the whole company, including Bonaventura Bottone's hilariously camp portrait of a prancing Mercury. Bright, vivid recording to match the performance.

La Périchole (complete).
(M) *** Erato/Warner 2292 45686-2 (2) [id.]. Crespin, Vanzo, Bastin, Lombard, Friedmann, Trigeau, Rhine Op. Ch., Strasbourg PO, Lombard.

Though both Régine Crespin in the title-role and Alain Vanzo as her partner, Piquillo, were past their peak at that time, their vocal control is a model in this music, with character strongly portrayed but without any hint of vulgar underlining. Crespin is fresh and Vanzo produces heady tone in his varied arias, some of them brilliant. Jules Bastin is characterful too in the subsidiary role of Don Andres, Viceroy of Peru. Lombard secures excellent precision of ensemble from his Strasbourg forces, only occasionally pressing too hard. The recorded sound is vivid and immediate, and the libretto provides a detailed synopsis of the action between the texts and translations of numbers.

Robinson Crusoe (sung in English).
☞ *** Opera Rara ORC 7 (3) [id.]. Brecknock, Kenny, Kennedy, Hartle, Hill Smith, Oliver, Browne, Geoffrey Mitchell Ch., RPO, Alun Francis.

It was Opera Rara in 1973 that presented the British première of this *opéra comique*, following it up with several successful revivals. They then gave a concert performance at the Proms in 1980, as a preliminary for this studio recording. More ambitious than Offenbach's operettas, the piece offers a sequence of fresh and tuneful numbers with many striking ensembles. The plot is derived less from Daniel Defoe than from the British pantomime tradition, which in the middle of last century turned regularly to Crusoe as a story. Characterization is strong and amusing, with a secondary couple shadowing Crusoe and his beloved Edwige. The casting is also from strength, with John Brecknock and Yvonne Kenny outstanding as Crusoe and Edwige, while Man Friday, as in the original Paris production, is sung by a mezzo, Sandra Browne. On the three discs are 3¾ hours of music, covering numbers which the composer cut even from the original production. The witty English translation, very freely adapted from the French text, with some changes of plot, is by Don White, and words are admirably clear.

Orff, Carl (1895–1982)

Carmina Burana.

*** Decca Dig. 430 509-2; *430 509-4* [id.]. Dawson, Daniecki, McMillan, San Francisco Boys' & Girls' Choruses, San Francisco Symphony Ch. & SO, Blomstedt.

*** Ph. Dig. 422 363-2 [id.]. Gruberová, Aler, Hampson, Shinyukai Ch., Knaben des Staats & Berlin Cathedral Ch., BPO, Ozawa.

⊛ (M) *** Sony SBK 47668 [id.]. Harsanyi, Petrak, Presnell, Rutgers University Ch., Phd. O, Ormandy.

*** EMI CDC7 47411-2 [id.]. Armstrong, English, Allen, St Clement Danes Grammar School Boys' Ch., London Symphony Ch., LSO, Previn.

(B) *** Pickwick Dig. PCD 855 [id.]. Walmsley-Clark, Graham-Hall, Maxwell, Southend Boys' Ch., London Symphony Ch., LSO, Hickox.

☞ **(*) Teldec/Warner Dig. 9031 74886-2 [id.]. Sumi Jo, Jochen Kowalski, Boje Skovhus, LPO Ch., Southend Boys' Ch., LPO, Mehta.

☞ (M) (***) EMI CDU5 65043-2 [id.]. Popp, Unger, Wolansky, Noble, New Philh. Ch., Wandsworth School Boys' Ch., New Philh. O, Frühbeck de Burgos (with MUSSORGSKY/RIMSKY-KORSAKOV: *Night on a bare mountain;* Bav. State O, Sawallisch **).

Blomstedt's is the finest modern version of Orff's exhilaratingly hedonistic cantata. Throughout the choral singing, men, boys, and girls, all enjoy themselves hugely – as they should, with such stimulating words to sing. They generate great passion and energy and all three soloists are equally outstanding. John Daniecki's use of vocal colouring is entertainingly diverse, while Kevin McMillan is a splendidly unctuous Abbot, and Lynne Dawson portrays the girl in the red tunic with seductive innocence. Blomstedt's reading is full of imaginative touches of light and shade, yet the flow of passionate energy is paramount. He is helped by the remarkable range and sonority of the Decca recording, very much in the demonstration bracket.

Ozawa's digital recording of Orff's justly popular cantata carries all the freshness and spontaneity of his earlier successful Boston version. The *Cours d'amours* sequence is the highlight of his reading, with the soprano, Edita Gruberová, highly seductive; Thomas Hampson's contribution is also impressive. Ozawa's infectious rubato in *Oh, oh, oh, I am bursting out all over*, interchanged between male and female chorus towards the end of the work, is wonderfully bright and zestful, with the contrast of the big *Ave formosissima* climax which follows made to sound spaciously grand. Taken overall, this Philips version readily goes to the top of the list alongside Blomstedt.

Ormandy and his Philadelphians have just the right panache to bring off this wildly exuberant picture of the Middle Ages by the anonymous poets of former days, and there is no more enjoyable analogue version. It has tremendous vigour, warmth and colour and a genial, spontaneous enthusiasm from the Rutgers University choristers, men and boys alike, that is irresistible. The soloists are excellent, but it is the chorus and orchestra who steal the show; the richness and eloquence of the choral tone is a joy in itself. This is quite splendid, one of Ormandy's most inspired recordings and, even if you already have the work in your collection, this exhilarating version will bring additional delights.

Previn's 1975 analogue version, vividly recorded, is even more sharply detailed than Ozawa's. It is strong on humour and rhythmic point. The chorus sings vigorously, the men often using an aptly rough tone; and the resilience of Previn's rhythms, finely sprung, brings out a strain not just of geniality but of real wit. This is a performance which swaggers along and makes you smile. Among the soloists, Thomas Allen's contribution is one of the glories of the music-making, and in their lesser roles the soprano and tenor are equally stylish. The digital remastering is wholly successful: the choral bite is enhanced, yet the recording retains its full amplitude. But this should be reissued at mid-price.

Richard Hickox, on his brilliantly recorded Pickwick CD, like Previn uses the combined London Symphony forces, but adds the Southend Boys' Choir who make sure we know they understand all about sexual abandon – their *Oh, oh, oh, I am bursting out all over* is a joy. Penelope Walmsley-Clark, too, makes a rapturous contribution: her account of the girl in the red dress is equally delectable. The other soloists are good but less individual, and the chorus rises marvellously to climaxes, while the sharp articulation of consonants when the singers hiss out the words of *O Fortuna* in the closing section is a highlight. The documentation provides a vernacular narrative for each band but no translation.

Mehta's newest Teldec version is often enjoyably vigorous, it has good soloists and an excellent choral response, with the Southend boys throatily enjoying their pubescent spree. Sumi Jo is a seductive if rather knowing Girl in the Red Shift who submits willingly, rising nimbly up her ascending scale to a spectacularly floated pianissimo. But Boje Skovhus makes a strongly vibrant rather than a subtle contribution. The recording, made at The Maltings, Snape, is resonantly spectacular, especially in the matter of the orchestral percussion, but the quieter choral passages are a little recessive. In the last resort this is not a first choice, for Mehta's direction is not as imaginative or as spontaneously exuberant as that of his finest competitors.

For some reason the latest CD remastering of the EMI Frühbeck de Burgos recording still produces a curiously artificial treble response, slightly pinched and too insistently bright. This is a great pity for Frühbeck de Burgos gives the kind of performance of *Carmina burana* which is ideal for gramophone listening. Where Ozawa favours a straightforward approach, with plenty of impact in the climaxes, it is in the more lyrical pages that Burgos scores with his much greater imagination and obvious affection. This is not to suggest that the Philharmonia account has any lack of vitality. Indeed the sheer gusto of the singing is the more remarkable when one considers the precision from both singers and orchestra alike. The brass too bring out the rhythmic pungency which is such a dominating feature of the work with splendid life and point. Lucia Popp's soprano solo, *Amor volat*, is really ravishing, and Gerhard Unger, the tenor, brings a Lieder-like sensitivity to his lovely singing of his very florid solo in the tavern scene. The inadequate documentation includes 25 cued titles and no translation. Sawallisch's performance of *Night on a bare mountain* is a more than acceptable bonus, but overall this cannot be recommended.

(i) *Die Kluge;* (ii) *Der Mond.*
(M) *** EMI CMS7 63712-2 (2) [Ang. CDMB 63712]. (i) Cordes, Frick, Schwarzkopf, Wieter, Christ, Kusche; (ii) Christ, Schmitt-Walker, Graml, Kuen, Lagger, Hotter; Philh. Ch. & O, Sawallisch.

Sawallisch's pioneering Orff recordings of the mid-1950s are vivid and immediate on CD, with such effects as the thunderbolt in *Der Mond* impressive still. Elisabeth Schwarzkopf is characterful and dominant as the clever young woman of the title in *Die Kluge*. It is good too to hear such vintage singers as Gottlob Frick and Hans Hotter in unexpected roles. Musically, these may not be at all searching works, but both short operas provide easy, colourful entertainment, with Sawallisch drawing superb playing from the Philharmonia. No texts are provided, but the discs are very generously banded. (This set has currently been withdrawn.)

Oedipus der Tyrann.
☞ **(*) DG 437 290-2. Stolze, Harper, Engen, Varnay, Cramer, Alexander, Kohn, Nöcker, Boysen, Bav. R. Ch. & SO, Kubelik.

In discussing composition with twelve notes, Schoenberg once said that there was 'a great deal of good music to be written in C'. So there is, but this is not it! At least *Carmina burana* has the merit of a certain earthy vitality and some rousing moments. Those who think it thin and repetitive should wait until they hear this! Three hours of declamation on and around middle C may do wonders for your German but it doesn't offer much in the way of musical substance. In spite of the huge forces involved, its sound-world remains austerely monochrome and, as so often with Orff, offers plentiful reminders of Stravinsky's *Les noces*. But there is more music in a page of the latter than there is in any of *Oedipus*'s five Acts. No quarrels with the performances: Astrid Varnay's Jocasta and Gerard Stolze's Oedipus are strongly characterized, and the Bavarian Radio forces under Kubelik are exemplary. The 1966 recording still sounds very impressive.

Pachelbel, Johann (1653–1706)

Canon in D.
☞ (M) *** Virgin/EMI Dig. CUV5 61145-2 [id.]. LCO, Warren-Green – ALBINONI: *Adagio;* VIVALDI: *Four seasons.* ***

A lovely performance of the *Canon* from Christopher Warren-Green and his excellent London Chamber Orchestra, with a delicately graceful opening and a gorgeous climax and with radiant violins. With splendid sound this is as fine as any version in the catalogue. Other enjoyable performances are listed in the Concerts section.

Pacius, Fredrik (1809–91)

Kung Karls Jakt (King Charles's Hunt) (opera): complete.
(M) *** Finlandia Dig. FACD 107. Törnqvist, Lindroos, Krause, Grönroos, Jubilate Ch., Finnish
Nat. Op. O, Söderblom.

Fredrik Pacius became known as 'the father of Finnish music', for he brought the Finnish capital, then a provincial backwater, into contact with the mainstream of European music. His opera *King Charles's Hunt* brings pretty simple musical ideas. Some are pleasant but there is little evidence of much individuality. There is some fine singing from Pirkko Törnqvist as the fisherman's daughter, Leonora, Peter Lindroos as her fiancé, and from Walton Grönroos as the coup leader, Gustaf Gyllenstjerna. The young King is a speaking role. Much care has been lavished on the production and Ulf Söderblom holds things together admirably. No masterpiece is uncovered but it will be of interest to collectors with a specialist interest in the beginnings of opera in the northern countries.

Padilla, Juan Gutierrez de (c. 1590–1664)

Missa: Ego flos campi. Stabat Mater.
(B) *** Pickwick Dig. PCD 970; *CIMPC 970* [id.]. Mixolydian, Piers Schmidt – VICTORIA: *Missa surge propera* etc. ***

Juan Gutierrez de Padilla's Mass, *Ego flos campi*, for double choir is more homophonic than much of his other music. The Mass is nevertheless full of interest, though of course the comparison which the sleeve-writer makes between the two composers on the disc is not to Victoria's disadvantage. Padilla's setting of the *Stabat Mater* lacks the expressive depth of that Renaissance master. Dedicated performances and excellent recording.

Paganini, Niccolò (1782–1840)

Andante amaroso; Balletto campestre (Variations on a comic theme; orch. Tamponi); Larghetto con passione; Moto perpetuo in C, Op. 11; Polacca with variations in A; Sonata for grand viola; Sonata Maria Luisa in E; Sonata Varsavia; Variations on The Carnival of Venice; Variations on a theme from Rossini's Mosè.
☞ (B) *** EMI CZS7 67567-2 (2). Salvatore Accardo, COE, Tamponi.

To supplement his concerto recordings for DG – see below – Salvatore Accardo here explores the by-ways of Paganini's concertante music for violin and orchestra (with one piece for viola), and much of the virtuosity is stunning – sample the *Moto perpetuo*. As can be seen from the listing, Paganini's favourite device was a set of variations on a simple, often ingenuous theme, alternating *galant* lyricism with fiendish bravura. Accardo is equally at home in both; his virtuosity in the *Balletto campestre* and the *Polacca* is breathtaking, although he is no less impressive in the more famous *Carnival of Venice*, or the *Mosè variations* (where for added bite he tunes his G string a minor third higher and uses it throughout!). The orchestral accompaniments are of minimal interest but they are warmly supportive; the flattering ambience of the recording and the good balance ensure that the sounds reaching the listener are pleasingly believable: the CD transfers are admirably faithful. The two discs are offered for the price of one. There are, however, no notes about the music. (This set has been withdrawn as we go to press.)

Violin concertos Nos. 1–6.
☞ (M) *** DG 437 210-2 (3) [id.]. Accardo, LPO, Dutoit.

Violin concertos Nos. 1 in D, Op. 6; 2 in B min. (La Campanella), Op. 7.
*** DG 415 378-2 [id.]. Accardo, LPO, Dutoit.

Violin concertos Nos. 3 in E; 4 in D min.
*** DG 423 370-2 [id.]. Accardo, LPO, Dutoit.

Violin concerto No. 5 in A min.; Maestosa sonata sentimentale; La primavera in A.
*** DG 423 578-2 [id.]. Accardo, LPO, Dutoit.

Violin concerto No. 6 in E min., Op. posth.; Sonata with variations on a theme by Joseph Weigl; Le streghe (Variations on a theme of Süssmayr), Op. 8; Variations of Non più mesta from Rossini's La Cenerentola.
*** DG 423 717-2 [id.]. Accardo, LPO, Dutoit.

Paganini's concertos can too often seem trivial and long-winded; it is a tribute to the virtuosity and artistry of Salvatore Accardo that they reveal so much musical interest in his hands. But – as we have observed before – Accardo's technique is formidable and his intonation marvellously true; these qualities, blended with good taste, make this series of performances distinctive. Apart from No. 5 (which, like No. 6, was orchestrated by Federico Mompellio), these are all genre works written to a formula in which the composer produced a series of contrasting lyrical operatic melodies to offset the fireworks of the outer movements. In No. 5 – thought now to be a product of the composer's later years – a characteristically flamboyant opening introduces a more rhapsodic treatment of the themes than usual, and Mompellio provides very attractive woodwind detail (flute and oboe) to introduce the secondary theme of the first movement. After an expressively serene *Andante*, the finale too is lyrically chimerical. In the other concertos, movements could be interchangeable (the *Rondo galante* finale of No. 4 would fit No. 2 equally well. Having said this, Paganini's invention holds up well throughout these works. Tuttis are stereotyped but have plenty of impulse, the lyrical tunes are all very engaging, and the violinistic display is consistently ear-tickling when presented with such panache. Accardo is beautifully accompanied by Dutoit who always keeps even the most conventional passage-work alive. The recordings were made in Barking Town Hall in 1974/5 and the remastering preserves the hall ambience, yet has a cleaner orchestral bass than the LPs. Accardo is placed forward, but not excessively so, and his timbre is captured with a natural presence and without scratchiness within an overall balance which remains exemplary.

Violin concerto No. 1 in D, Op. 60.
❀ *** EMI CDC7 47101-2 [id.]. Itzhak Perlman, RPO, Foster – SARASATE: *Carmen fantasy.**** ❀
*** Ph. Dig. 422 332-2 [id.]. Mullova, ASMF, Marriner – VIEUXTEMPS: *Concerto No. 5.* ***
*** DG Dig. 429 786-2 [id.]. Gil Shaham, NYPO, Sinopoli – SAINT-SAENS: *Concerto No. 3.* ***
☞ (B) ** Hung. White Label HRC 162 [id.]. Mária Bálint, Budapest SO, Lehel – GOLDMARK: *Violin concerto.* **

Itzhak Perlman demonstrates a fabulously clean and assured technique and, with the help of the EMI engineers, he produces a gleamingly rich tone, free from all scratchiness. Lawrence Foster matches the soloist's warmth with an alive and buoyant orchestral accompaniment. Provided one does not feel strongly about Perlman's traditional cuts, there has been no better record of the *D major Concerto*.

Viktoria Mullova's virtuosity dazzles and holds one enthralled, and she has the advantage of a more modern recording. She copes with all the technical hurdles effortlessly and with great brilliance, and the Academy of St Martin-in-the-Fields under Sir Neville Marriner give sterling support.

Gil Shaham's technical ease in the histrionics of Paganini's stratospheric tessitura, harmonics and all, is breathtaking, and he can phrase an Italianate lyrical melody – and there are some good ones in this *Concerto* – with disarming charm and ravishing timbre. His dancing spiccato in the finale is a joy and, however high he ascends, there is never a hint of scratchiness. Sinopoli's finely graduated and often dramatic accompaniment could hardly be more sympathetic.

A perfectly satisfactory bargain version comes from Mária Bálint, who is well supported by Lehel. The soloist responds to Paganini's lyrical muse persuasively and her bouncing bowing in the finale is most felicitous; indeed she plays with an easy flair. The drawback is the CD remastering, which adds a degree of edge to the violin timbre and makes the high harmonics tingle in the ear. The orchestral sound is spacious.

Violin concertos Nos. 1 in D, Op. 6; 2 in B min. (La Campanella), Op. 7.
*** Denon Dig. CO 77611 [id.]. Kantorow, Auvergne O.
(B) *** DG 429 524-2 [id.]. Shmuel Ashkenasi, VSO, Esser.
☞ (BB) **(*) Naxos Dig. 8.550649 [id.]. Ilya Kaler, Polish Nat. RSO, Gunzenhauser.
☞ ** Erato/Warner Dig. 2292 45788-2 [id.]. Markov, Saar RSO, Viotti.

Kantorow plays superbly and he is very naturally recorded (the microphones in exactly the right place). In both concertos his lyrical line is very appealing indeed and the fireworks are dazzling, especially in the *La Campanella* finale of No. 2. The Denon recording is digital, but the acoustics have a slightly studio-ish feeling.

At bargain price on CD, Ashkenasi's coupling of the two favourite Paganini *Concertos* is also very good value. He surmounts all the many technical difficulties in an easy, confident style and, especially in the infectious *La Campanella* finale of No. 2, shows how completely he is in control. The microphone is close, but his timbre is sweet and the high tessitura and harmonics are always cleanly focused.

The young Russian virtuoso, Ilya Kaler, was born in Moscow in 1963. He was a pupil of Leonid Kogan and is fully equal to Paganini's once devilish technical demands and the phrasing of warm Italianate melody. His bouncing staccato in the sparkling spiccato finales of both concertos is managed adeptly and in every respect his technique is commandingly secure. Stephen Gunzenhauser is a sympathetic accompanist throughout, and the Polish Radio Orchestra play with suppleness and bring a sense of elegance and style to this music. The recordings were made in the Concert Hall of Polish Radio in Katowice, which has a suitably warm acoustic, and the microphones are not too close to the soloist: there is none of the scratchiness in the violin's upper tessitura that can ruin one's pleasure in Paganinian bravura. There is no lack of dazzle in the fireworks, and no damp squibs here. With excellent notes, this is an excellent example of a Naxos super-bargain at its best. Kaler does not possess the charisma of a Perlman but he is an excellent violinist and a fine musician.

Alexander Markov is a brilliant soloist but he is balanced rather near the microphone in a reverberant acoustic, and this brings a slight element of scratchiness to his otherwise able histrionics. There is nothing special about the accompaniments. Viotti sets a fast pace for the first movement of Op. 6, yet by including the Emile Seuret cadenza it still lasts 19 minutes 20 seconds, and these performers have nothing special to offer in this music.

Allegro di concert (Moto perpetuo) in C, Op. 11; Cantabile in D, Op. 17; Centone si sonate: in D; in A, Op. 64/2 & 4; Guitar and violin sonatas: in A; A min.; E min., Op. 3/1, 4 & 6; Grand sonata for violin & guitar in A, Op. posth.; Sonata concertata in A, Op. 61; Sonata a preghiera (arr. Hannibal).
☞ *** DG Dig. 437 837-2; *437 837-4* [id.]. Gil Shaham, Göran Söllscher.

Paganini's expertise as a guitarist is sometimes forgotten, but he played the plucked instrument with considerable skill and wrote much music for it, though usually in subservience to his favourite, the violin. However, while the guitar contribution to the Op. 3 sonatas is designed so that almost any reasonably proficient accompanist would have no trouble at all giving support to the violin line, the *Sonata concertata* is aptly named, giving the guitar a fair share of the limelight, and the *Grand sonata* bristles with bravura for this instrument. Yet the atmosphere of much of this repertoire is comparatively intimate, something these artists readily appreciate, and their playing is immaculate and amiably easy-going. Perhaps at times here the style of performance could with advantage have been more extrovert, but the present hour-long recital will make attractive late-evening entertainment (not taken all at once, of course). The recording has a realistic balance and fine presence.

Violin and guitar: *Cantabile; Centone di sonate No. 1 in A; Sonata in E min., Op. 3/6; Sonata concertata in A.*
*** Sony MK 34508 [id.]. Itzhak Perlman, John Williams – GIULIANI: *Sonata.* ***

Superb playing from Perlman and John Williams, and a good balance; the music-making here gives much pleasure, and this is a generally distinguished disc.

24 Caprices, Op. 1.
(M) *** DG 429 714-2; *429 714-4* [id.]. Salvatore Accardo.
*** EMI CDC7 47171-2 [id.]. Itzhak Perlman.
☞ (M) *** Decca 440 034-2 [id.]. Ruggiero Ricci.
☞ (B) *** Naxos Dig. 8.550717 [id.]. Ilya Kaler.
☞ (M) **(*) Teldec/Warner Dig. 9031 76259-2 [id.]. Thomas Zehetmair.
☞ (M) *(**) EMI CDM7 64560-2 [id.]. Michael Rabin.

Accardo succeeds in making Paganini's most routine phrases sound like the noblest of utterances and he invests these *Caprices* with an eloquence far beyond the sheer display they offer. There are no technical obstacles and, both in breadth of tone and in grandeur of conception, he is peerless. He observes all the repeats and has an excellent CD transfer.

Perlman's playing is also flawless, wonderfully assured and polished, yet not lacking imaginative feeling. Such is the magnetism of his playing that the ear is led on spontaneously from one variation to the next. The transfer to CD of the 1972 recording is extremely natural. But this is at full price.

Ricci's Decca recording dates from 1959 but it is remarkably real, with a vivid presence. Ricci's playing often offers a breathtaking display of bravura and, oddly enough, his very occasional imperfections (usually minor slips of intonation) come at points where they are least expected – in the easier rather than the more difficult parts. The playing has great personality and the quicksilver articulation is often dazzlingly precise, conveying enormous dash, for instance in *No. 5 in A minor*. A most enjoyable and stimulating set, and the violin sounds life-size. However, Perlman and Accardo are even more polished.

Those looking for a bargain will surely not be disappointed with the Russian fiddler, Ilya Kaler, on Naxos. He studied under Kogan and in 1981 won the Grand Prize at the Genoa Paganini competition. His playing is technically very assured, the lyrical bowing vibrant in a Slavic way, and, like Ricci, he projects a strong profile. The 1992 Naxos recording, truthful and real, is very well balanced: the violin is present but the engineers also convey the acoustic of Orum Hall, Valparaiso, Indiana. How attractively this colours the opening of the famous *No. 9 in E major*, which has superb variety of bowing!

Thomas Zehetmair has a somewhat more reticent personality and seems to want to avoid blazing virtuosity for its own sake. His style of articulation in the faster passages at times has an almost throwaway quality, but he soars most agreeably in the lyrical writing and his timbre above the stave is richly caught by the recording. There is much to appreciate and enjoy in these performances, but in the last resort Zehetmair projects less charisma than his competitors.

Michael Rabin was a prodigiously gifted virtuoso whose career was cut short in its prime by a freak accident in 1972 when he was only 36. His playing here is consistently mesmerizing, hardly less astonishing in its fizzing bravura (compare No. 5) than Ricci. The snag is that he was given a closely miked recording (in 1958) in the Capitol studios in New York and, although his technique stands up brilliantly to the immediacy of the aural scrutiny, the effect of the CD transfer is to add a degree of shrillness to the violin timbre above the stave, and at times the upper tessitura is made to sound scratchy.

Paine, John Knowles (1839–1906)

Symphony No. 1 in C min., Op. 23; Overture, As you like it.
*** New World Dig. NW 374-2 [id.]. NYPO, Mehta.

Paine's symphonies were milestones in the history of American music, and it is good that at last Mehta's fine recordings of both of them will allow them to be appreciated more widely. Paine consciously inspires echoes of Beethoven, with little feeling of dilution – though, after his dramatic C minor opening, he tends to relax into sweeter, more Mendelssohnian manners for his second subject and the three other movements. What is striking is the bold assurance, and the overture is also full of charming ideas. Mehta is a persuasive advocate, helped by committed playing and full, well-balanced recording.

Symphony No. 2 in A, Op. 34.
*** New World Dig. NW 350-2 [id.]. NYPO, Mehta.

Written four years after the *First Symphony*, this magnificent work is both more ambitious and more memorable than its predecessor and, far more remarkably, anticipates Mahler. The idiom is notably more chromatic than that of the *First*, and the other movements – introduced by an extended slow introduction – bring an element of fantasy, as in the fragmented rhythms and textures of the Scherzo. Mehta draws a strongly committed performance from the New York Philharmonic, and the sound is first rate.

Paisiello, Giovanni (1740–1816)

Piano concertos Nos. 1 in C; 5 in D; 7 in A; 8 in C.
☞ *** ASV Dig. CDDCA 873 [id.]. Monetti, ECO, Gonley.

Piano concertos Nos. 2 in F; 3 in A; 4 in G min.; 6 in B flat.
☞ **(*) ASV Dig. CDDCA 872 [id.]. Monetti, ECO, Gonley.

It was enterprising of ASV to persuade Mariaclara Monetti to record Paisiello rather than duplicate main-line repertoire for her début recording. She certainly reveals herself to be an artist who can produce a silk purse out of more humble material, for her playing here is both sparkling and elegant. Paisiello obviously was primarily an opera composer, and these concertos, though not wanting grace or fluency, are often very conventional in most other respects. But with a ready facility Paisiello could certainly spin an expressive cantilena. As it happens, the *First Concerto* is one of the finest of the set in this respect, but so is No. 4 on the second disc. Nos. 5, 7 (especially) and 8 all have agreeably melodic slow movements. Paisiello was distinctly better at rondo finales than first movements, and those of both Nos. 1 and 7 stand out for their catchy ideas. There are some good moments elsewhere of course, but this repertoire would be more attractive on a bargain label. No complaints about the recording, and on the whole the first of the two discs is the one to go for.

Il barbiere di Siviglia (opera): complete.

*** Hung. Dig. HCD 12525/6-2 [id.]. Laki, Gulyás, Gregor, Gati, Sólyom-Nagy, Hungarian State O, Adám Fischer.

Paisiello's *Barbiere di Siviglia* for many generations has been remembered only as the forerunner of Rossini's. The musical inspiration may too often be short-winded, but the invention is full of vitality, and that is reflected captivatingly in this Hungarian performance under Adám Fischer. Jószef Gregor is a vividly characterful Bartolo, a role more important here than in Rossini, while István Gati is a strong, robust Figaro. Krisztina Laki is a brilliant Rosina and Dénes Gulyás a clean, stylish Almaviva, relishing his Don Alonso imitation. Full, vivid recording.

Palestrina, Giovanni Pierluigi di (1525–94)

(i) *Good Friday Liturgy: Improperia (Reproaches). Lamentations of Jeremiah: No. 9, Incipit oratorio Jeremiah prophetae:* (iii) original and (ii) revised versions. (i) *Mass and Motet: Dum complerentur; Mass and motet: Tu es Petrus;* (iv) *Missa Papae Marcelli.* Motets: (ii) *Illumina oculos meos; Jubilate Deo; Laudate dominum omnes gentes; Pueri Hebraeorum.*

☞ (M) ** DG Analogue/Dig. 439 961-2 (2). (i) Regensburger Domchor, Hans Schrems; (ii) cond. Theobald Schrems; (iii) Pro Cantione Antiqua, Bruno Turner; (iv) Westminster Abbey Ch., Simon Preston.

An interesting and well-planned Palestrina collection, if not one to laud to the skies, except for the Westminster Abbey performance of the *Missa Papae Marcelli.* The Regensburg Choristers sing wonderfully well in the works of Mozart and Haydn, but they have not quite the same fluency in music of the sixteenth century, where line is of supreme importance and balance a *sine qua non.* The feeling for tension and relief inherent in every true polyphonic line seems to evade these otherwise musical singers. Although the music flows well, the Mass singing is inclined to be square and here, as in the motets, the singers are not always careful to give the music plenty of light and shade. On the whole the solemn *Improperia* for Holy Week with their contrasts between homophony (and simple polyphony) and plainsong more nearly suit the choir's bland style; but even here – although the beauty comes through in the warm acoustic of St Emmergram, Regensburg – there are depths of subtlety in the writing that elude these singers. However, the collection offers a fascinating comparison in presenting two utterly different versions of the ninth *Lamentation of Jeremiah* (sung during Matins on Maundy Thursday, Good Friday and Holy Saturday, services known as Tenebrae because the candles were gradually extinguished, leaving the church in darkness). On the first CD *Incipit oratio Jeremiae prophetae* is heard from the Regensburgers, richly textured, in its shorter, revised version – although it is not absolutely sure that Palestrina himself made the revision. Then on the second disc Bruno Turner and his excellent Pro Cantione Antiqua give the original version containing a longer ending for the section, *Aquam nostram,* with a full repetition of the final phrase 'Lassis non dabatur'. Performance tempi are very similar, but the latter takes over three minutes longer. Moreover Bruno Turner performs the work with a small vocal consort, with no more than two or three voices to each part. The singers are expert (the roster includes names like Paul Esswood, James Griffet, Ian Partridge and David Thomas) and the sound is clear and well blended. Its more limited sonority undoubtedly suits the *Lamentation,* which is beautifully sung. All this music is given good analogue recording from the early 1960s, well transferred, although in St Emmergram, Regensburg, while the effect is warmly atmospheric, the definition of the words is misty. The second of the CDs opens with Simon Preston's digital recording of Palestrina's most famous work, the *Missa Papae Marcelli.* With its apparent simplicity of line and serene beauty which disguises an underlying emotional power, this is not a work which lends itself readily to performers with an Anglican background. The account by the Westminster Abbey choristers, however, transcends any such stylistic limitations. The digital recording is first class. All Saints', Tooting, was used rather than the Abbey, and the acoustics are both intimate and expansive, while detail is beautifully caught – a model of how to manage this repertoire on CD.

Missa Aeterna Christi munera; Motets: *O bonne Jesu; Sicut cervus desiderat; Super flumina Babylonis.*

☞ (M) ** DG 437 072-2. Pro Cantione Antiqua, Bruno Turner – LASSUS: Motets etc. ***

Bruno Turner gives us these Palestrina works with a small consort, no more than two or three voices to a part. The sound is admirably fresh and clear and well blended, but many listeners will feel the need for a warmer acoustic ambience, and the *Mass* cries out for a richer sonority.

Missa: Assumpta est Maria; Missa: Sicut lilium.
*** Gimell Dig. CDGIM 020; *1585T-20* [id.]. Tallis Scholars, Peter Phillips.

After the *Missa Papae Marcelli*, the *Missa: Assumpta est Maria* is one of Palestrina's most sublime works. Its companion on this CD is based on the motet, *Sicut lilium inter spinas* ('Like a lily among thorns'). As is their practice, the Tallis Scholars record the Masses together with the motets on which they are based, and sing with their customary beauty of sound and well-blended tone. They are superbly recorded in the Church of St Peter and St Paul in Salle, Norfolk.

Antiphon: Assumpta est Maria; Missa: Assumpta est Maria. Antiphon, Motet and Missa: Veni sponsa Christi. Magnificat VI toni.
(M) *** Decca 433 678-2 [id.]. St John's College, Cambridge, Ch., Guest.

The older St John's record of *Assumpta est Maria* sounds splendid on CD, if perhaps not so refined in texture as its digital competitor, and the St John's performance is thoroughly persuasive. The Decca couplings are even more generous (70 minutes) than on the Gimell CD and equally attractive. Some may find the presentation a little lacking in Latin fervour: the trebles sound distinctly Anglican. But this is fine singing by any standards, and has great purity of tone and beauty of phrasing.

Hodie Beata Virgo; Litaniae de Beata Virgine Maria in 8 parts; Magnificat in 8 parts (Primi Toni); Senex puerum portabat; Stabat Mater.
(M) *** Decca 421 147-2 [id.]. King's College Ch., Willcocks – ALLEGRI: *Miserere.* ***

The flowing melodic lines and serene beauty which are the unique features of Palestrina's music are apparent throughout this programme, and there is no question about the dedication and accomplishment of the performance. Argo's recording is no less successful, sounding radiantly fresh and clear.

Missa: Benedicta es (with *Plainchant*).
*** Gimell CDGIM 001; *1585T-01* [id.]. Tallis Scholars, Peter Phillips (with JOSQUIN: *Motet: Benedicta es*).

Palestrina's Mass is coupled with the Josquin motet, *Benedicta es*, on which it is based, together with the plainchant sequence on which both drew. It would seem that this Mass was the immediate predecessor of the *Missa Papae Marcelli* and was composed while the music of *Benedictus es* was still at the forefront of the composer's mind. The Tallis Scholars and Peter Phillips sing with impressive conviction and produce an expressive, excellently blended sound.

Missa brevis; Missa: Nasce la gioia mia (with PRIMAVERA: *Madrigal: Nasce la gioia mia*).
*** Gimell Dig. CDGIM 008; *1585T-08* [id.]. Tallis Scholars, Phillips.

The *Missa: Nasce la gioia mia* is a parody Mass, modelled on the madrigal, *Nasce la gioia mia* by Giovan Leonardo Primavera. The Tallis Scholars and Peter Phillips give expressive, finely shaped accounts of both the *Missa brevis* and the *Mass*, which they preface by the madrigal itself. A most rewarding disc: no grumbles about the recording.

Missa: Nigra sum (with motets on *Nigra sum* by LHERITIER; VICTORIA; DE SILVA).
*** Gimell Dig. CDGIM 003; *1585T-03* [id.]. Tallis Scholars, Phillips.

Palestrina's *Missa: Nigra sum* is another parody Mass, based on a motet by Jean Lheritier, and follows its model quite closely; its text comes from the Song of Solomon. On this record, the plainchant and the Lheritier motet precede Palestrina's *Mass*, plus motets by Victoria and Andreas de Silva, a relatively little-known Flemish singer and composer who served in the Papal chapel and later in Mantua. The music is inspiring and the performances exemplary. This is a most beautiful record and the acoustic of Merton College, Oxford, is ideal.

Missa Papae Marcelli.
*** Gimell CDGIM 339; *1585T-39* [id.]. Tallis Scholars, Phillips – ALLEGRI: *Miserere;* MUNDY: *Vox Patris caelestis.* ***

Missa Papae Marcelli; Tu es Petrus (motet).
*** DG 415 517-2 [id.]. Westminster Abbey Ch., Preston (with ANERIO: *Venite ad me omnes;* NANINO: *Haec dies;* GIOVANNELLI: *Jubilate Deo* ***) – ALLEGRI: *Miserere.* **(*)

The account by the Westminster Abbey choristers is a performance of great fervour, married to fine discipline, rich in timbre, eloquent both at climaxes and at moments of serenity. The singing is equally fine in the hardly less distinctive motet, *Tu es Petrus*. Felice Anerio, Giovanni Bernardino Nanino and Ruggiero Giovannelli represent the following generation of composers. Their contributions to this collection are well worth having, particularly Giovannelli's *Jubilate Deo* which makes a splendid closing item. The digital recording is first class.

The Gimell alternative is an analogue recording from 1980. The singing has eloquence, purity of tone, and a simplicity of line which is consistently well controlled.

Missa Papae Marcelli; Alma Redemptoris Mater (antiphon); *Peccantem me quotidie* (motet); *Stabat Mater.*
☞ (BB) **(*) ASV CDQS 6086. L. Pro Cantione Antiqua, Bruno Turner.

A super-bargain recording of Palestrina's most celebrated Mass is not to be ignored. Bruno Turner uses small forces throughout his well-conceived programme (the concert opens with the Mass), and these are most beautiful performances of all four pieces, offering both intelligence and sensitivity in the handling of each line. Partly because of the recording balance, which is rather forward, one can hear the inner parts with uncommon clarity and, although this is not achieved at the expense of the overall sonority, some might feel that the clear and precise acoustic robs the music of some of its mystic atmosphere. This is not the only way of performing and recording Palestrina, but it is none the less impressive, and it makes one listen to the linear detail with fresh ears.

Missa Papae Marcelli; Stabat Mater.
(B) *** Pickwick PCD 863; *IMPCD 863* [id.]. Pro Cantione Antiqua, Mark Brown.

With an all-male choir and no boy trebles, and with one voice per part, the Pro Cantione Antiqua chamber choir yet sings with power and resonance against a warm and helpful church acoustic. The authentic atmosphere is enhanced by the inclusion of relevant plainchants between the sections of the *Mass*. The magnificent eight-part *Stabat Mater* also receives a powerful performance, warm and resonant.

Panufnik, Andrzej (1914–91)

(i) *Arbor Cosmica;* (ii) *Symphony No. 3 (Sinfonia sacra).*
*** Elektra Nonesuch/Warner Dig. 7559 79228-2 [id.]. (i) NY Ch. Symphony; (ii) Concg. O; composer.

The *Sinfonia sacra* is one of Panufnik's most warmly and immediately communicative works, and here receives a magnificent performance from the Concertgebouw under the composer. The first movement, *Three Visions*, is in three distinct sections, a brassy fanfare, a meditation for strings and a longer dashing allegro, which starts with a dramatic timpani cadenza, and works up to a powerful final climax. As the title implies, *Arbor Cosmica* directly reflects a visual concept, this time the branches of a tree. The 12 'evocations' are all generated from a single three-note chord, each with the structure mapped out like a tree. The composer draws dedicated performances both from the Concertgebouw and the New York Chamber Symphony, with the former inevitably sounding richer and fuller.

(i) *Autumn music; Heroic overture;* (i, ii) *Nocturne;* (iii) *Sinfonia rustica;* (i) *Tragic overture.*
(M) *** Unicorn UKCD 2016. (i) LSO, Horenstein; (ii) with Anthony Peebles; (iii) Monte Carlo Op. O, composer.

The *Autumn music* and *Nocturne* may strike some listeners as musically uneventful, but the opening of the *Nocturne* is really very beautiful indeed and there is a refined feeling for texture and a sensitive imagination at work here. The *Sinfonia rustica* is the most individual of the works recorded here and has plenty of character. The performance under the composer is thoroughly committed. The LSO under Horenstein play with conviction and they are very well recorded.

(i) *Bassoon concerto;* (ii) *Violin concerto;* (iii) *Hommage à Chopin.*
*** Conifer Dig. CDFC 182; *MCFC 182* [id.]. (i) Thompson; (ii) Smietana; (iii) K. Jones; L. Musici, Stephenson.

The *Violin concerto* is a strongly atmospheric piece and is well worth a place in the repertory; it is beautifully played here by Krzysztof Smietana. The *Hommage à Chopin* owes its origin to a commission from Unesco. Panufnik composed five vocalises for voice and piano that make use of folk music from Masovia, in 1966 transcribing them for flute and orchestra; they could not have more persuasive advocacy than they do from Karen Jones and the London Musici. The *Bassoon concerto* (1985) is a darker piece, dedicated to the memory of the Polish priest, Jerzy Popieluszko, who was murdered that year; Robert Thompson plays it with great sensitivity. The London Musici under Mark Stephenson play with dedication throughout and, as the recording was made in the presence of the composer, it can be assumed to be authoritative. The Conifer sound, very well balanced at The Maltings, Snape, is first class.

Cello concerto.
☞ *** NMC Dig. Single D 0105 [id.]. Rostropovich, LSO, Hugh Wolff.

The *Cello concerto* of Sir Andrzej Panufnik, his very last work, completed only days before his death in September 1991, is here presented on a CD single from NMC at the very reasonable price of around £5. The inspirer was Rostropovich, who gave the first performance with Hugh Wolff and the LSO at the Barbican in June 1992 and then promptly made this recording. The recording is even more successful at conveying the purposefulness of the writing than that first performance, bringing out the tautness of the palindromic structure, with the two movements, each in arch form, a mirror-image of the other, slow then fast. In all his later works Panufnik preferred to develop his musical ideas by translating geometric shapes and concepts into notes and themes. So here his prime source of inspiration was the almond-shaped figure produced by the intersection of two circles. The result is not a drily schematic work, as one might expect, but a piece that in its warmth reflects the player who inspired it, strong and eventful with a more open lyricism than in many previous Panufnik compositions.

(i) *Piano concerto. Symphony No. 9 (Sinfonia della speranza).*
*** Conifer Dig. CDCF 206 [id.]. (i) Ewa Poblocka; LSO, composer.

In a massive single movement of 41 minutes Panufnik's *Ninth Symphony* brings a formidable example of the composer's fascination with translating geometric concepts into notes. The visual analogy here is with light travelling through a prism, and the accompanying booklet provides a diagram illustrating how the formula works, using a three-note cell refracted in various ways. The shape and colours of the rainbow then provide a related analogy, dictating the framework of the symphony. The result has similarities with a gigantic passacaglia. The close brings a violent crescendo, with massive strings set against powerful percussion. That shattering conclusion may not immediately suggest the message of hope implied by the Italian title, but there is no denying the symphony's strength. Panufnik's *Piano concerto* is not so extended, but carries comparable weight. The opening *Entrata* has a neo-classical flavour in its ostinatos for the solo instrument, leading to a bald, spare central slow movement. The mood is rather like that of some of Bartók's night music. By contrast, the finale is violently rhythmic with jazzy syncopations. Though the piano writing gives the soloist relatively little chance for conventional keyboard display, her playing adds to the power of the composer's purposeful interpretation. The piano tone is a degree too clangy, but otherwise the recording is spacious and full.

(i) *Concerto festivo;* (ii) *Concerto for timpani, percussion and strings; Katyń epitaph; Landscape;* (iii) *Sinfonia sacra (Symphony No. 3).*
(M) *** Unicorn UKCD 2020. (i) LSO, (ii) with Goedicke & Frye; (ii) Monte Carlo Op. O, composer.

This splendidly recorded collection might be a good place for collectors to begin exploring Panufnik's output. The *Concertos* are both readily communicative and the *Katyń epitaph* is powerfully eloquent. The best of this music is deeply felt. The *Sinfonia sacra* serves to demonstrate the spectacular quality of the vividly remastered recording, with its compelling introductory 'colloquy' for four trumpets, followed by a withdrawn section for strings alone. In the finale of the second part of the work, Hymn, the trumpets close the piece resplendently.

(i) *Concerto for timpani, percussion and strings. Harmony* (a poem for chamber orchestra); (ii) *Sinfonia concertante for flute, harp and strings.*
☞ *** Conifer Dig. CDCF 217 [id.]. L. Musici, Mark Stephenson, with (i) Richard Benjafield, Graham Cole; (ii) Karen Jones, Rachel Masters.

The *Concertino* is a highly effective work based on a four-note motif, F-G-B-C; Panufnik creates an imaginative sound-world using both tuned and untuned percussion. The piece projects readily, although perhaps its appeal is enhanced at a live performance when the communication is both aural and visual. The *Sinfonia concertante*, written seven years earlier (1974), is highly atmospheric, often hauntingly so, but somewhat more static. Karen Jones and Rachel Masters make a highly persuasive solo partnership. By far the most impressive work here is *Harmony*, again written for the composer's wife, but as a celebration of their 25th wedding anniversary. Alas, Panufnik died only two years later. Opening with a poignantly ethereal pianissimo on the violins, this distinctive 16-minute piece alternates passages for strings and woodwind; then they finally join together and move to a passionately piercing climax. The performance here has great intensity and, given greater exposure, this piece could become really popular, after the manner of Barber's *Adagio*, though thematically it is more diffuse. Performance and recording throughout are first class.

Symphony No. 8 (Sinfonia votiva).
*** Hyp. Dig. CDA 66050 [id.]. Boston SO, Ozawa – SESSIONS: *Concerto for orchestra.* ***

The *Sinfonia votiva* has a strongly formalistic structure, but its message is primarily emotional. Though Panufnik's melodic writing may as a rule reflect the formalism of his thought rather than tapping a vein of natural lyricism, the result is most impressive, particularly in a performance of such sharp clarity and definition as Ozawa's, very well recorded.

Paray, Paul (1886–1979)

Mass for the 500th anniversary of the death of Joan of Arc.
(M) **(*) Mercury 432 719-2 [id.]. Yeend, Bible, Lloyd, Yi-Kwei-Sze, Rackham Ch., Detroit SO, Paul Paray – SAINT-SAENS: *Symphony No. 3.* ***

Paray's *Mass*, much admired by the composer, Florent Schmitt, could hardly have a more eloquent performance. The soloists are good and the choir are inspired to real fervour by their conductor, who at the close (in a brief recorded speech) expresses his special satisfaction with the singing of the closing, very romantic *Agnus Dei*. Excellent (1957) Mercury stereo, using the Ford Auditorium in Detroit.

Parker, Horatio (1863–1910)

A Northern ballad.
*** New World Dig. NWCD 339 [id.]. Albany SO, Julius Hegyi – CHADWICK: *Symphony No. 2.* ***

Horatio Parker's *Northern ballad* of 1899 was an enormous success in its day and calls both Dvořák and Grieg to mind. It has remained unpublished and unperformed in recent times. Excellent playing and recording. An interesting disc.

Parry, Hubert (1848–1918)

(i) *The Birds: Bridal march;* (ii) *English suite; Lady Radnor's suite* (both for strings); *Overture to an unwritten tragedy; Symphonic variations.*
*** Lyrita SRCD 220 [id.]. (i) LPO; (ii) LSO; Boult.

The *Bridal march* comes from Parry's equivalent to Vaughan Williams's *Wasps*, a suite of incidental music for *The Birds*, also by Aristophanes. Here the rich, *nobilmente* string melody asserts itself strongly over any minor contributions from the woodwind aviary. The two *Suites* of dances for strings have some charming genre music and the *Overture* is very strongly constructed. But best of all is the set of variations, with its echoes of Brahms's *St Anthony* set and its foretastes of *Enigma*: a big work in a small compass. Boult's advocacy is irresistible. and the CD transfer demonstrates the intrinsic excellence of the analogue recordings, with gloriously full string sound.

Lady Radnor's suite.
*** Nimbus Dig. NI 5068 [id.]. E. String O, Boughton – BRIDGE: *Suite;* BUTTERWORTH: *Banks of green willow* etc. ***

Parry's charming set of pastiche dances, now given an extra period charm through their Victorian flavour, makes an attractive item in an excellent and generous English collection, one of Nimbus's bestsellers. Warm, atmospheric recording, with refined playing set against an ample acoustic.

Symphonies Nos. 1–5; Symphonic variations in E min.
☞ *** Chan. Dig. CHAN 9120-22 [id.]. LPO, Matthias Bamert.

The rehabilitation of Parry has been long overdue; Chandos have now done this remarkable British nineteenth-century 'English Renaissance' musician full justice by recording the complete set of the symphonies. Bamert proves a masterly interpreter and takes us convincingly through the symphonic terrain of a highly influential composer about whom Elgar declared, 'He is our leader – no cloud of formality can dim the healthy sympathy and broad influence he exerts upon us. Amidst all the outpourings of modern English music the work of Parry remains supreme.' Bamert's set, discussed in detail below, is offered here complete on three CDs and includes also Parry's best-known orchestral work, the *Symphonic variations*.

Symphony No. 1 in G; Concertstück in G min.
☞ *** Chan. Dig. CHAN 9062; *ABTD 1591* [id.]. LPO, Bamert.

Symphony No. 1 in G; From death to life.
☞ ** Nimbus Dig. NI 5296 [id.]. English SO, Boughton.

Parry began work on his *First Symphony* in December 1880. Only a few weeks previously he had made his acquaintance with Brahms's *First*, and it had an obvious influence on him, not least in the grand main theme of his own finale. Parry's work was ready for an abortive première under Hans Richter in June 1882 but was instead presented in Birmingham in August of that same year, where it was well received. It was played again at the August Manns Crystal Palace Concerts, a year later. After that the symphony was confined to a dusty attic until these recordings were made. The Nimbus CD appeared in 1991 and Bamert's Chandos disc was issued the following year.

Bamert immediately demonstrates his response to the composer's muse in the way the opening *Con fuoco* sails off with a powerful thrust in the first movement. His control of the overall structure with its interrelated thematic material is most convincing, through the eloquent *Andante* and the Scherzo with its double trio, until he brings the finale to an impressively up-beat conclusion. He offers the earlier *Concertstück for orchestra* as coupling, almost equally convincingly performed, even though here the Wagnerian influences remain incompletely absorbed. The spacious Chandos recording seems exactly right for this pre-Elgarian opulence of symphonic thought.

William Boughton starts with the disadvantage of the very reverberant acoustic of the Great Hall of Birmingham University, which brings even greater opulence but a less clean focus and, at times, ill-defined orchestral detail. Boughton's reading displays a less firm grip on Parry's overall symphonic scheme and the resulting performance has altogether less cogency. His coupling, the symphonic poem, *From Death to Life*, is well played but not made to sound really memorable.

Symphony No. 2 in F (Cambridge); Symphonic variations.
☞ *** Chan. Dig. CHAN 8961; *ABTD 1553* [id.]. LPO, Matthias Bamert.

The *Second Symphony* was first performed in Cambridge in 1883 – hence its subtitle – but the composer revised it for its London première, four years later, when Richter redeemed himself by directing it to considerable acclaim. Even so, the work soon became forgotten. It opens confidently (with distinct Mendelssohnian associations) and Brahms's influence reappears in the main lyrical idea of the finale. In between there is a reminder of Dvořák in the Scherzo and of Schumann in the romantic warmth of the *Andante*. But for all its eclecticism and occasional longwindedness, notably in the finale, Parry finds his own voice and the music has a genuinely vital flow. Bamert's advocacy certainly holds the listener's attention and the orchestra responds with obvious relish. The (1897) *Symphonic variations* (27 of them), did retain a foothold in the repertory for a couple of decades, and the work was even heard in America. Admired by Elgar, it is certainly worth having on disc, even if it is nothing like as memorable as *Enigma*. Excellent, full-bodied sound of the best Chandos vintage.

Symphonies Nos. 3 in C (English); 4 in E min.
*** Chan. Dig. CHAN 8896; *ABTD 1507* [id.]. LPO, Matthias Bamert.

No. 3 is the most immediately approachable of the symphonies, with its bold melodies, often like sea-shanties, and its forthright structure. Yet it is No. 4 which proves even more rewarding, a larger-scale and more ambitious work which, amazingly, was never performed at all between the first performance of the revised version in 1910 and the present recording. The bold opening, in its dark E minor, echoes that of Brahms's *First Piano concerto*, leading to an ambitious movement lightened by thematic transformation that can take you in an instant into infectious waltz-time. The elegiac slow movement and jolly and spiky scherzo lead to a broad, noble finale in the major key. Bamert again proves a masterly interpreter, bringing out the warmth and thrust of the writing, akin to that of Elgar but quite distinct. The sound is rich and full to match the outstanding playing.

Symphony No. 5 in B min.; Symphonic variations; Elegy to Johannes Brahms; (i) Blest pair of Sirens.
☞ (M) *** EMI CDM5 65107-2 [id.]. LPO, Boult, (i) with LPO Ch.

Symphony No. 5 in B min.; Elegy for Brahms; From death to life.
*** Chan. Dig. CHAN 8955; *ABTD 1549* [id.]. LPO, Bamert.

The *Fifth* and last of Parry's symphonies, completed in 1912, is in four linked movements, terser in argument than the previous two in the series and often tougher, though still with Brahmsian echoes.

After the minor-key rigours of the first movement, *Stress*, the other three movements are comparably subtitled *Love*, *Play* and *Now*, with the Scherzo bringing echoes of Berlioz and the optimistic finale opening with a Wagnerian horn-call. The *Elegy for Brahms* conveys grief, but its vigour rises above passive mourning into an expression of what might almost be anger. *From death to life* consists of two connected movements, exuberantly melodic, with a theme in the second which echoes Sibelius's *Karelia*. It would be hard to imagine finer, more committed performances or richer sound.

This was the last record made by Sir Adrian Boult, whose recording career was longer than that of any important rival. The *Fifth Symphony*, the last that Parry wrote, is broadly Brahmsian in style but with the four movements linked in a Lisztian cyclic manner; the slow movement is particularly beautiful here. Equally impressive is the *Elegy*, not merely an occasional piece but a full-scale symphonic movement which builds to a powerful climax. The sharply inventive *Symphonic variations* – also recorded by Boult for an earlier, Lyrita disc – fills out the Parry portrait. Recording and performances are exemplary, a fitting coda to Sir Adrian's recording career. To make the CD even more representative, it is good to welcome so enjoyably professional a motet as Parry's *Blest pair of Sirens*. Much of the once-popular music by Parry and his contemporaries is unacceptably inflated, but certainly not this. The performance by the London Philharmonic Choir should be more incisive, but it still conveys much of the right atmosphere. Throughout, the digital remastering has been wholly beneficial. Textures are better defined and the strings sound fresher than originally, while the ambient bloom remains. (This CD appears to have just been withdrawn.)

Nonet in B flat.
*** Hyp. Dig. CDA 66291 [id.]. Capricorn – STANFORD: *Serenade (Nonet)*. ***

Parry's *Nonet* is for flute, oboe, cor anglais and two each of clarinets, bassoons and horns. Although the finale is perhaps a little lightweight, it is a delight from beginning to end. If one did not know what it was, one would think of early Strauss, for it is music of enormous accomplishment and culture as well as freshness. An excellent performance and recording.

(i) *Piano quartet in A flat; Piano trio No. 1 in E min.*
☞ **(*) Mer. Dig. CDE 84248 [id.]. Deakin Piano Trio, (i) with Yuko Inoue.

After the success of the Chandos series of the Parry symphonies, it is good to have his chamber music appearing in a comparable Meridian series. Both these works, dating from 1878 and 1879 respectively, are products of the surge of creativity that followed after Parry's visit to Bayreuth in 1776 to see the *Ring* cycle in its first year. In his actual idiom, Brahms and Schumann, not Wagner, were still the more important influences, with diatonic melody providing clear-cut thematic material, well argued. The *E minor Piano trio*, the first of three that Parry wrote, is both shorter and more direct than the *Piano quartet*, with an urgently passionate first movement, a Mendelssohnian Scherzo, a richly melodic slow movement and a jaunty finale, sparer and more quirky in its arguments than the rest. The *Piano quartet* is more ambitious, with a darkly meditative slow introduction echoing late Beethoven. That leads to a clear-cut and happy main theme, and from then on introspection plays little part in the argument until the very end of the work. Though the performance on the disc is not as polished as one would like, the confidence and technical skill of the 31-year-old composer are never in doubt. Parry's melodic writing is more than distinctive enough to rebut the charge of mere imitation, with such a movement as the dashing tarantella-like Scherzo of the *Piano quartet* very effective indeed. The recording, made in a helpful acoustic at St Olave's School, Orpington, balances the piano rather behind the rest, which is a pity when Catherine Dubois so often takes the lead.

Piano trios Nos. 2 in B min.; 3 in G.
☞ *** Mer. Dig. CDE 84255 [id.]. Deakin Piano Trio.

The two *Piano trios* contained in Volume 2 of the Meridian series date from the following decade. By this time the English element in Parry's invention is more clearly identifiable, with some themes bringing anticipations of Elgar. Equally, the healthy outdoor feel of the triple-time main themes of the finales of both trios has a hint of English folk-music, while the folky element in the third-movement Scherzo of No. 2 is like a cross between Dvořák and Stanford, with Czech and Irish elements attractively intermingled. Both works are richly enjoyable, with the warm, open lyricism of the slow movement of No. 2 particularly attractive. The players of the Deakin Piano Trio seem more happily adjusted to the rigours of recording than in the first volume, with rather better matching and intonation.

Violin sonata in D, Op. 103; Fantasie-sonata in B, Op. 75; 12 short pieces.
*** Hyp. CDA 66157 [id.]. Erich Gruenberg, Roger Vignoles.

The *Fantasie-sonata* provides a fascinating example of cyclic sonata form, earlier than most but also echoing Schumann. The three-movement *Sonata in D* is another compact, meaty piece, the strongest work on the disc. The *Twelve short pieces*, less demanding technically, are delightful miniatures. Gruenberg and Vignoles prove persuasive advocates, and the recording is first rate.

Blest pair of sirens; I was glad (anthems).
*** Chan. Dig. CHAN 8641/2; *DBTD 2014* (2) [id.]. London Symphony Ch. & LSO, Hickox –
    ELGAR: *Dream of Gerontius*. ***

Parry's two finest and most popular anthems make an attractive coupling for Hickox's fine, sympathetic reading of Elgar's *Dream of Gerontius*. The chorus for Parry is rather thinner than in the main work but is very well recorded.

Evening Service in D (Great): Magnificat; Nunc dimittis. Hear my words, ye people; I was glad when they said unto me; Jerusalem; Songs of farewell.
*** Hyp. CDA 66273 [id.]. St George's Chapel, Windsor, Ch., Christopher Robinson; Roger Judd
    (organ).

Everyone knows *Jerusalem*, which highlights this collection resplendently. In the *Songs of farewell* trebles are used and the effect is less robust than in Marlow's version, but undoubtedly very affecting. Perhaps the stirring coronation anthem, *I was glad*, needs the greater weight of an adult choir, but it is still telling here. The excerpts from the *Great Service in D* are well worth having on record, as is the anthem, *Hear my words, ye people*. Excellent recording, the chapel ambience colouring the music without blunting the words.

Songs of farewell.
*** Conifer Dig. CDCF 155 [id.]. Trinity College, Cambridge, Ch., Richard Marlow – STANFORD:
    Magnificat etc. ***

Parry's *Songs of farewell* represent his art at its deepest. Finest and most searching of the set is the Donne setting, *At the round earth's imagined corners*, with its rich harmonies poignantly intense and beautiful. Richard Marlow with his splendid Trinity Choir, using fresh women's voices for the upper lines instead of trebles, directs thoughtful, committed performances, very well recorded, which capture both the beauty and the emotion.

The Soul's ransom (sinfonia sacra); The Lotos eaters.
*** Chan. Dig. CHAN 8990; *ABTD 1572* [id.]. Jones, Wilson-Johnson, LPO and Ch., Bamert.

Using a biblical text *The Soul's ransom*, with its sequence of solos and choruses, forms a broadly symphonic four-movement structure with references back not only to Brahms and the nineteenth century but to much earlier choral composers, notably Schütz. This 45-minute piece is generously coupled with *The Lotos eaters*, a setting for soprano, chorus and orchestra of eight stanzas from Tennyson's choric song of that name, with Della Jones again the characterful soloist. Written in 1892 it strikes a vein of sensuousness rare in the British music of its time, reflecting instead the exoticry of the literary world in the 1890s. Full and atmospheric recording to match the incandescent performances.

Pärt, Arvo (born 1935)

(i) *Arbos* (two performances); (ii) *Pari Intervallo;* (iii) *An den Wassern zu Babel; De Profundis;* (iv; v) *Es sang vor langen Jahren;* (iii) *Summa;* (iii; v; vi) *Stabat Mater.*
*** ECM Dig. 831 959-2 [id.]. (i) Brass Ens., Stuttgart State O, Davies; (ii) Bowers-Broadbent; (iii)
    Hilliard Ens., Hillier; (iv) Bickley; (v) Kremer, Mendelssohn; (vi) Demenga.

All the music recorded here gives a good picture of Pärt's musical make-up with all its strengths and limitations. *Arbos*, which is heard in two different versions, 'seeks to create the image of a tree or family tree'. It does not modulate and has no development, though pitch and tempi are in proportional relationships. Like the *Cantus in memory of Benjamin Britten*, the *Stabat Mater* (1985) for soprano, counter-tenor, tenor and string trio is distinguished by extreme simplicity of utterance and is almost totally static. This music relies for its effect on minimal means and invites one to succumb to a kind of mystical, hypnotic repetition rather than a musical argument. The artists performing here do so with total commitment and are excellently recorded.

(i) *Cantus in memory of Benjamin Britten; Festina lente; Summa;* (i; ii) *Tabula rasa;* (ii) *Fratres; Spiegel im Spiegel.*

☞ (M) *** EMI Dig. CD-EMX 2221; *TC-EMX 2221.* (i) Bournemouth Sinf., Richard Studt; (ii) Tasmin Little, Martin Roscoe.

An admirable and enterprising compilation from EMI Eminence to tempt those who have not yet sampled this composer's highly individual sound-world with its tintinnabulation (ringing bells). *Summa* is another version of the vocal *Creed* and is certainly effective, if not superior in its new costume. In the two chamber works Tasmin Little holds the listener's attention by the intensity of her commitment and the powerful projection of her playing. But most striking of all is the ambitious *Tabula rasa* with strong contrasts between the erupting energy of the opening *Ludus* and the aptly named second-movement *Silentium* which, of course, isn't silent but spins a compulsive atmospheric web. Fine performances and evocative sound, spread within an ecclesiastical acoustic, and first-rate recording combine to give this programme persuasive advocacy, if not to convince the listener that Pärt is one of the greatest composers of our time.

Fratres; Summa (string quartet versions).

☞ *** Virgin/EMI Dig. VC5 45023-2 [id.]. Chilingirian Qt – TAVENER: *Last Sleep of the Virgin* etc.
***

Like the Tavener works with which they are generously coupled on this 74-minute CD, these are both atmospheric works with a liturgical basis, using sparse basic material, which try to convey a sense of eternity. The performances here, obviously felt, make an interesting comparison with the alternative versions discussed above. But it must be admitted that, as music, they are less potent than the Tavener pieces.

Passio Domini Nostrum Jesu Christi secundum Joannem.
*** ECM Dig. 837 109-2 [id.]. Michael George, John Potter, Hilliard Ens., Western Wind Chamber Ch. (Instrumental group), Paul Hillier.

Pärt's *Passion of our Lord Jesus Christ according to St John* was composed in a bleak narrative style that reminds one of a mixture of Stravinsky and Schütz. It repeats the same scraps of ideas over and over again; it takes 70 minutes and never seems to leave the Aeolian mode, and it ought to be intolerable; yet in its way it is a strangely impressive experience, albeit not a wholly musical one. Impeccable recording and a dedicated performance.

Penderecki, Kryszstof (born 1933)

(i) *Anaklasis;* (ii; iii) *Capriccio for violin and orchestra;* (iii) *De natura sonoris I & II; The dream of Jacob; Fonogrammi; Threnody for the victims of Hiroshima;* (iv) *Canticum canticorum Salomonis.*
☞ (M) *** EMI CDM5 65077-2 [id.]. (i) LSO; (ii) Wanda Wilkomirska; (iii) Polish Nat. RSO; (iv) Krakow Philharmonic Ch.; composer.

A splendid anthology and an admirable introduction to Penderecki's music. The longest work is the setting of a text from the *Song of Solomon* for large orchestra and sixteen solo voices. Whether or not the ultimate impression from this glitteringly sonorous music is of sensuality, it represents the familiar brand of individual effect-making, deeply sincere but diffuse of argument. The other, shorter pieces will probably have a more lasting impact. The beautiful and touching *Threnody* for 53 strings (1959–61) is the best-known piece and originally made the composer's name internationally; it is here given a magnificent performance. So is the ambitious *Capriccio* in which Wilkomirska proves a superb soloist. Penderecki's music relies for its appeal on its resourceful use of sonorities, and his sound-world is undoubtedly imaginative, albeit limited. *Anaklasis,* an inventive piece for strings and percussion, and *De natura sonoris* are more obviously brilliant in their use of contrasts, while *The dream of Jacob* of 1974 is as inventive as the rest but sparer and more cogent. Performances are definitive and the recordings, a co-production between EMI and Polish Radio, are very good.

The Awakening of Jacob; (i) *Cello concerto No. 2;* (ii) *Viola concerto. Paradise Lost: Adagietto.*
*** Polski Nagrania PNCD 020 [id.]. (i) Monighetti; (ii) Kamasa; Polish Nat. RSO, Antoni Wit.

The *Cello concerto No. 2* was written for Rostropovich, and this 1984 recording is impressively played by Ivan Monighetti. The *Viola concerto* is rather like skimmed Bartók; it brings masterly playing from Stefan Kamasa and the Polish Radio Orchestra. One cannot escape the suspicion that behind the mask of colour and orchestral trickery there is little real substance. However, these mid-1980s performances have plenty of ardour and commitment and are well recorded.

String quartet No. 2.
* Olympia OCD 328 [id.]. Varsovia Qt – SZYMANOWSKI: *Quartets;* LUTOSLAWSKI: *Quartet.* *****

Penderecki's *First quartet* lasts seven minutes; the *Second* is not much longer and is hardly more substantial. It is full of the gimmicks and clichés of the period. Whatever its merit, it is extremely well played.

St Luke Passion.
**(*) Argo 430 328-2 [id.]. Von Osten, Roberts, Rydl, Warsaw Philharmonic Ch., Polish RSO, composer.

The *St Luke Passion*, with its bold choral effects, including widely spaced choirs uttering crowd noises, was one of the very first avant-garde works to make a breakthrough into a wider public. This first CD version is welcome, but the composer's relatively detached approach exposes a dangerous thinness in the argument, though it remains a powerful and moving piece.

Pepping, Ernst (1901–81)

Passionsbericht des Matthäus.
☞ ** Chan. Dig. CHAN 8854 [id.]. Danish Nat. R. Ch., Parkman.

Ernst Pepping enjoyed some exposure during the 1950s, though his relative conservatism ensured his subsequent neglect in the avant-garde climate that gradually gained ground in post-war Germany. His style derives mainly from Reger, Distler and Hindemith, but he is a composer of quality. The *St Matthew Passion* is a rather extraordinary piece: a motet passion of the kind that flourished in the late Renaissance and early Baroque from Lassus through to Schütz but which was subsequently replaced by the dramatic settings of Bach. An hour and a quarter of *a cappella* singing puts a strain on the singers (and the listeners), but the Danish Radio Choir under Stefan Parkman rise to the challenge and give a generally good account of the piece, though the choral tone is not always cleanly focused. The music has integrity and beauty, and it improves as one comes closer to it, and the Danish Radio recording is good.

Pergolesi, Giovanni (1710–36)

Sinfonia for cello and continuo.
* Decca Dig. 425 614-2 [id.]. Peter Howard, St Paul CO, Hogwood – GALLO: *Trio sonata movements;* STRAVINSKY: *Pulcinella* etc. *****

Though Stravinsky originally thought that all his sources for his ballet, *Pulcinella*, were drawn from Pergolesi, much of the material he used was written by others. Stylishly played here, this charming *Sinfonia for cello* is genuine, providing in its finale the material for the memorable *Vivo* movement, which Stravinsky outrageously scored for trombone and double-bass.

Magnificat.
(M) **(*) Decca 425 724-2; *425 724-4.* Vaughan, J. Baker, Partridge, Keyte, King's College Ch., ASMF, Willcocks – VIVALDI: *Gloria; Magnificat.* **(*)

This Pergolesi *Magnificat* is doubtfully attributed. But the King's College Choir gives a beautiful performance, and the recording matches it in intensity of atmosphere. The CD transfer is expertly managed.

Miserere II in C min.
(M) ***** Decca 430 359-2. Wolf, James, Covey-Crump, Stuart, Magdalen College, Oxford, Ch., Wren O, Bernard Rose – A. and G. GABRIELI: *Motets.* **(*)

Pergolesi's *Miserere* is both ambitious and moving. The singers are all of quality, particularly Richard Stuart, and Bernard Rose secures expressive and persuasive results from the Magdalen College Choir and the Wren Orchestra. The (originally Argo) recording sounds magnificently real and vivid in its CD format.

Stabat Mater.
* DG 415 103-2; *415 103-4* [id.]. Margaret Marshall, Valentini Terrani, LSO, Abbado.

(i; ii) *Stabat Mater;* (ii) *In coelestibus regnis;* (i) *Salve Regina in A.*

*** Hyp. Dig. CDA 66294; *KA 66294* [id.]. (i) Gillian Fisher; (ii) Michael Chance; King's Consort, Robert King.

Abbado's account brings greater intensity and ardour to this piece than any rival, and he secures marvellously alive playing from the LSO – this without diminishing religious sentiment. The DG recording has warmth and good presence and the perspective is thoroughly acceptable. This is now a clear first choice.

The Hyperion recording makes a very good case for authenticity in this work. The combination of soprano and male alto blends well together yet offers considerable variety of colour. Gillian Fisher's *Salve Regina* is quite a considerable piece in four sections, whereas Michael Chance's motet is brief but makes an engaging postlude. Excellent sound.

La serva padrona (opera) complete recording (includes alternative ending and insertion arias).
*** Hung. HCD 12846-2 [id.]. Katalin Farkas, Jószef Gregor, Capella Savaria, Németh.

La serva padrona is ideally suited to disc, and on this Hungaroton issue receives a delightful, sparkling performance with the excellent period-performance group, Capella Savaria. Jószef Gregor sings with splendid buffo stylishness, while Katalin Farkas, as Serpina the maid, brings out the fun of the writing, with the shrewishness of the character kept in check. Bright, clean recording.

Pettersson, Allan (1911–80)

(i) *Viola concerto. Symphony No. 5.*
*** BIS Dig. CD 480 [id.]. (i) Nobuko Imai; Malmö SO, Moshe Atzmon.

Allan Pettersson's *Fifth* is a one-movement work and begins well. However, invention flags and the brooding, expectant atmosphere and powerful ostinatos arouse more promise of development than fulfilment. The *Viola concerto* comes from the last year of Pettersson's life and is pretty amorphous. Both pieces lack the concentration and quality of Tubin or Holmboe. The three stars are for the performers and the recording team.

Symphony No. 7.
☞ *** Caprice Dig. CAP 21411. Swedish RSO, Comissiona – MOZART: *Bassoon concerto.* ***

Allan Pettersson's *Seventh Symphony* established him in the 1960s after a long period of neglect. A Swedish public, nourished on lashings of Blomdahl and a diet of serial and post-serial music, warmed to his tonal, post-Mahlerian language. The *Seventh* is a long, dark work which wears an anguished visage and packs a considerable emotional punch. Its musical substance is less weighty than appears to be the case on first acquaintance, and the ideas seem static and thinly spread; but it has a strong emotional appeal for many music-lovers and its atmosphere is quite powerful. Those who dismiss its composer impatiently as a self-pitying windbag should hear this work, which has an undoubted eloquence. Sergiu Comissiona gives a dedicated and sensitive account of the score that is every bit as fine as Dorati's première recording. The rather bizarre coupling is unlikely to sway the collector one way or the other.

Pfitzner, Hans (1869–1949)

(i) *Duo for violin, cello and orchestra, Op. 43;* (ii) *Symphony in C (An die Freunde), Op. 43;* (iii) Songs: *Abbitte; Die Einsame; Der Gärtner; Hast du von den Fischerkindern das alte Märchen vernommen?; Herbstgefühl; Hussens Kerker; In Danzig; Leuchtende Tage; Michaelskirchplatz; Nachts; Säerspruch; Zum Abschied meiner Tochter.*
(***) Preiser mono 90029. (i) Max Strub, Ludwig Hoelscher, Berlin Staatsoper O; (ii) BPO, composer; (iii) Gerhard Hüsch, composer.

This CD collects recordings made by Hans Pfitzner, both as conductor and as pianist, between 1938 and 1940. The most astonishing performances for the younger generation will be Gerhard Hüsch's remarkable accounts of the songs. What a voice and what diction! The Preiser CD does not run to the full texts of the songs, let alone a translation, but, sung like this, you don't need them. These Lieder inhabit much the same world as those of Brahms and Strauss and have moments of great poignancy. Pfitzner's performances of both the *Duo* and the *Symphony in C* have splendid grip. German recording of this period was much admired at the time and, to judge from the quality of the orchestral sound, rightly so.

Palestrina (opera) complete.
(M) *** DG 427 417-2 (3) [id.]. Gedda, Fischer-Dieskau, Weikl, Ridderbusch, Donath, Fassbaender, Prey, Tölz Boys' Ch., Bav. R. Ch. & SO, Kubelik.

Though Pfitzner's melodic invention hardly matches that of his contemporary, Richard Strauss, his control of structure and drawing of character through music make an unforgettable impact. It is the central Act, a massive and colourful tableau representing the Council of Trent, which lets one witness the crucial discussion on the role of music in the church. The outer Acts – more personal and more immediately compelling – show the dilemma of Palestrina himself and the inspiration which led him to write the *Missa Papae Marcelli*, so resolving the crisis, both personal and public. At every point Pfitzner's response to this situation is illuminating, and this glorious performance with a near-ideal cast, consistent all through, could hardly be bettered in conveying the intensity of an admittedly offbeat inspiration. This CD reissue captures the glow of the Munich recording superbly and, though this is a mid-price set, DG has not skimped on the accompanying booklet.

Philips, Peter (c. 1561–1640)

Motets: *Ave verum corpus; Ave Maria gratia plena; Ecce vicit Leo; Factum est silentium; Gaudent in coelis; Hodie nobis de coelo; O bone Jesu; O crux ave spes unica; O quam suavis.*
**(*) EMI Dig. CDC7 54189-2 [id.]. King's College, Cambridge, Ch., Cleobury – DERING: *Motets.*
**(*)

Both Peter Philips and his younger contemporary, Richard Dering, were Catholics and spent much of their lives on the Continent. This CD contrasts and compares the two composers' beautiful and expressive settings of the same texts. The performances are faithful, but the actual sound is not always perfect in either focus or blend, partly perhaps but not solely due to the recording.

Pichel, Wenzel (1741–1805)

Symphonie concertante in D (Apollo), Op. 6; Symphonies: in D (Mars); in B flat, Op. 1/5; in D, Op. 17.
☞ *(*) Olympia Dig. OCD 434 [id.]. Oradea PO, Romeo Rimbu.

Wenzel Pichel (born Václav Pichl) was a Bohemian composer who spent part of his career in Romania near the home of this orchestra. They play his ingenuous and sometimes unpredictable – if short-breathed – symphonies with more enthusiasm than finesse (although the solo playing in the slow movement of Op. 6 is certainly adequate). This is a new name of some interest, but Pichel needs more polished advocacy and a surer sense of pacing and style from his performers if he is to be revealed as a major minor figure.

Pierné, Gabriel (1863–1937)

Les Cathédrales: Prelude (No. 1); Images, Op. 49; Paysages franciscains, Op. 43; Viennoise (suites de valses et cortège blues), Op. 49 bis.
(M) *** EMI CDM7 63950-2. Loire PO, Pierre Dervaux.

The opening *Prélude* to *Les Cathédrales* is an evocation of the desolation caused by war; while *Images* is full of touches of pastiche – a reference to Dukas's *La Péri* in the opening, an allusion to Debussy's *Gigues*, and so on – and there follows a set of pieces, *Viennoise*, in which Pierné developed two of the numbers in the divertissement as 'valses et cortège blues'. The three picturesque *Paysages franciscains* betray the composer's love of Italy. All of this is rewarding music in the best French tradition, extremely well played, and the recording has plenty of warmth and atmosphere. (But this CD has just been withdrawn.)

Piston, Walter (1894–1976)

(i; ii) *Capriccio for harp and strings;* (ii) *3 New England sketches;* (iii) *Serenata;* (ii) *Symphony No. 4.*
⊛ *** Delos Dig. DE 3106 [id.]. (i) Wunrow; (ii) Seattle SO; (iii) NY CO; Gerard Schwarz.

Piston's *Fourth* is arguably the finest American symphony, as powerful in its forward sweep as the Harris *Third* and better held together than either Barber's *First* or Copland's *Third*. The remaining pieces, not only the *New England sketches* but also the inventive *Capriccio for harp and strings*, are well worth seeking out. The natural recording and Gerard Schwarz's natural and unforced direction make this a most desirable CD. The slow movement of the *Serenata*, equally well played by New York forces, is quite inspired.

The Incredible flutist (ballet; complete); *New England sketches; Symphony No. 6* (1955).
*** BMG/RCA Dig. RD 60798 [60798-2-RC]. St Louis SO, Leonard Slatkin.

Walter Piston's ballet, *The Incredible flutist*, is one of the most refreshing and imaginative of all American scores. Hitherto it has been known as a suite in which the composer selected his more important material, ideas that are instantly memorable. The full score does bring a degree of dilution but a gain in cohesion. The most powerful work on Slatkin's disc is the *Sixth Symphony*, about which Piston wrote rather disarmingly, 'It seemed as though the melodies were being written by the instruments themselves as I just followed along,' and there is an inexorable sense of logic and inevitability. Piston is a cultivated, refined symphonist who does not wear his heart on his sleeve. The playing of the St Louis orchestra under Leonard Slatkin both here and in the *New England sketches* is sensitive and brilliant, and the RCA engineers give them excellent quality.

Symphonies Nos. 5; (i) *7 and 8.*
** Albany AR 011 [id.]. Louisville O, Whitney, (i) Mester.

The *Fifth Symphony* has a sureness of purpose and feeling for organic growth that are the hallmark of the true symphonist. The *Seventh* and *Eighth Symphonies*, though not quite the equal of the finest Piston, are powerful and rewarding works which will speak to those who are more concerned with substance than with surface appeal. The Louisville performances are thoroughly committed and good, without being outstanding. The recordings sound better than they did on LP.

(i) *Piano quintet. Passacaglia; Piano sonata; Toccata.*
**(*) Northeastern/Koch Int. Dig. NR 232-CD [id.]. Leonard Hokanson; (i) Portland Qt.

The *Piano quintet* must be numbered among the finest post-Second World War piano quintets; it is a work of great vitality and integrity. These artists give a more than respectable account of it, and Leonard Hokanson proves no less convincing and responsive in the early *Piano sonata*. The recording is fully acceptable.

String quartets Nos. 1–3.
** Northeastern/Koch Dig. NR 9001-CD [id.]. Portland Qt.

Piston's five *String quartets* are finely crafted pieces, sinewy and Hindemithian at times (the first movement of No. 1), thoughtful and inward-looking at others (the Lento opening of No. 2 and the slow movement of No. 3). His music never wears its heart on its sleeve, but if its emotional gestures are restrained there is no real lack of warmth. The Portland Quartet play well and the recordings are clear, although the acoustic is a little on the small side.

Pizzetti, Ildebrando (1880–1968)

Messa di Requiem. Due composizioni corali: Il giardino di Afrodite; Piena sorgeva la luna. Tre composizioni corali: Cade la sera; Ululate; Recordare, Domine.
*** Chan. Dig. CHAN 8964 [id.]. Danish Nat. R. Chamber Ch., Stefan Parkman.

Pizzetti wrote with exceptional sympathy for voices, and his *Requiem* is a work of striking beauty and purity of utterance. In his note John Waterhouse speaks of it as occupying something of the same position in Italian music as the Vaughan Williams *Mass in G minor* does in English music. This Chandos issue has the merit of offering two other Pizzetti rarities in performances of high quality by the Danish Radio Chamber Choir, and there is no doubt that this is a most rewarding issue, one of the finest choral records of recent years.

Play of Daniel (medieval)

The Play of Daniel (liturgical drama).
☞ (M) *** Decca 433 731-2 [id.]. Pro Cantione Antiqua, Landini Consort, Mark Brown.

The Play of Daniel first became widely known thanks to the re-creation by the American, Noah Greenberg. The manuscript, found at Beauvais, dates from the thirteenth century and Greenberg's dramatic view of this medieval miracle play made an understandably strong impact on record. The

1978 version under Mark Brown is more austere and far more authentic, yet cannot fail to grip the listener. There is a simplicity and restraint in both the performance and the treatment which, with such sensitively felt singing and playing, is most affecting. The (originally Argo) recording is first class. Much convincing use is made of the spacious ecclesiastical perspective. After the opening hymn, *Let all rejoice*, King Belshazzar's procession approaches in the most convincing way, followed by a dramatic cry: *Rex in aeternam vive*; later, the famous episode of the writing on the wall is equally telling. This is definitely not a specialist's record but a vibrantly alive conjectural re-creation which communicates strongly and, with fine, tuneful music, is attractive in the most direct way. Highly recommended, especially to medieval novices.

Pleyel, Ignaz (1757–1831)

Clarinet concerto in C.
*** Claves CD 50-813 [id.]. Friedli, SW German CO, Angerer – MERCADANTE; MOLTER: *Concertos.* ***

Pleyel's *Concerto* is engagingly inventive throughout, with the finale especially attractive. Friedli plays it skilfully and sympathetically and gets good if not outstanding support from Angerer. The overall sound is very pleasing.

Ponce, Manuel (1882–1948)

Folia de España (Theme and variations with fugue).
(M) *** Sony SBK 47669 [id.]. John Williams (guitar) – BARRIOS: *Collection.* ***

Ponce's *Variations on 'Folia de España'* are subtle and haunting, and their surface charm often conceals a vein of richer, darker feeling. The performance is first rate and the sound admirably clean and finely detailed, yet at the same time warm.

Ponchielli, Amilcare (1834–86)

La Gioconda (complete).
*** Decca Dig. 414 349-2 (3) [id.]. Caballé, Baltsa, Pavarotti, Milnes, Hodgson, L. Op. Ch., Nat. PO, Bartoletti.
*** EMI CDS7 49518-2 (3) [Ang. CDCC 49518]. Callas, Cossotto, Ferraro, Vinco, Cappuccilli, Companeez, La Scala, Milan, Ch. & O, Votto.

The colourfully atmospheric melodrama of this opera gives the Decca engineers the chance to produce one of their most vivid opera recordings. Caballé is just a little overstressed in the title-role but produces glorious sounds. Pavarotti has impressive control and heroic tone. Commanding performances too from Milnes as Barnaba, Ghiaurov as Alvise and Baltsa as Laura, firm and intense all three. Bartoletti proves a vigorous and understanding conductor, presenting the blood and thunder with total commitment but finding the right charm in the most famous passage, the *Dance of the hours*.

   Maria Callas gave one of her most vibrant, most compelling, most totally inspired performances on record in the title-role of *La Gioconda*, with flaws very much subdued. The challenge she presented to those around her is reflected in the soloists – Cossotto and Cappuccilli both at the very beginning of distinguished careers – as well as the distinctive tenor Ferraro and the conductor Votto, who has never done anything finer on record. The recording still sounds well, though it dates from 1959.

Porter, Cole (1891–1964)

Ballets: The Snake in the grass (from *Fifty million Frenchmen*); *Within the Quota.* Overtures: *Anything goes; Can-Can; Du Barry was a lady* (with *Gavotte*); *Fifty million Frenchmen; Gay divorce* (with *Night and day*); *Kiss me Kate; Leave it to me; Out of this world; Something for the Boys; You never know.*
*** EMI Dig. CDC7 54300-2 [id.]; *EL* 754300-4. London Sinf., John McGlinn.

A splendid supplement to John McGlinn's series of recordings of American musicals, with 76 minutes of racy vitality and plenty of good tunes. The orchestrations are authentic. The ballet, *Within the*

Quota, has the brittle, jazzy, satirical flavour of its time and could well have been written for the Ballets Russes. The much briefer *Snake in the grass* originally had choreography by Massine. The Overtures were not put together or scored by the composer, but by the professionals of the day. As *Gay divorce* does not include the most famous number from the show, a separate arrangement of *Night and day* has been included, richly scored. The performances here are surely definitive and the bright recording fits the music like a glove.

Song arrangements for orchestra: *Anything goes; Begin the beguine; Blow, Gabriel blow; In the still of the night; It's de-lovely; I've got you under my skin; My heart belongs to Daddy; Night and day; It's all right with me; Ridin' high; So in love; You'd be so nice to come home too* (all orch. Ray Wright).
☞ (M) **(*) Mercury 434 327-2 [id.]. O, Frederick Fennell – GERSHWIN: *Song arrangements.* **(*)

The lyrics are missed more than most with orchestral arrangements of Cole Porter songs and, though Ray Wright's scoring is imaginative and admirably sophisticated, this is essentially a CD to use as a pleasing background for a dinner party, rather than for concentrated listening. Unusually for this label, the recording is multi-miked, so the stereo effects are unashamedly directional. But the sound is silky-smooth as well as being clearly defined and, of its kind, this is very good indeed.

Anything goes (musical).
*** EMI Dig. CDC7 49848-2 [id.]; EL 749848-2. Criswell, Groenendaal, Von Stade, Ambrosian Ch., LSO, McGlinn.

John McGlinn, with a scholarly concern for original sources comparable to that of a baroque specialist, here reconstructs the original (1934) version of Cole Porter's brilliant score, with the plot following the characters on a liner sailing the Atlantic in the 1930s. In the original production Ethel Merman had her first big Broadway success in the unlikely role of Reno, evangelist-turned-nightclub-singer, and here Kim Criswell proves a superb successor. She commandingly establishes her star quality, and she remains the focus of the whole piece, though Frederica von Stade is equally winning as the second heroine, Hope. The well-filled single disc includes as an appendix three extra numbers cut from the 1934 score. Full, satisfyingly beefy sound, bringing out the vigour of playing and singing.

Kiss me Kate (musical).
*** EMI Dig. CDS7 54033-2 (2). Barstow, Hampson, Criswell, Dvorsky, Burns, Evans, Amb. Ch., L. Sinf., John McGlinn.

Having two opera-singers, Josephine Barstow and Thomas Hampson, in the principal roles of the ever-argumentative husband-and-wife team who play Kate and Petruchio in *The Taming of the Shrew* works excellently, both strong and characterful. Kim Criswell is delectable as Lois Lane, brassy but not strident in *Always true to you, darling, in my fashion*. Strong characterization too from George Dvorsky, Damon Evans and Karla Burns, with the London Sinfonietta playing their hearts out. The recording is full and vivid with enough atmosphere to intensify the sense of presence.

Songs: *Begin the Beguine; Bring me back my butterfly; Bull Dog; Don't fence me in; Drink; Easy to love; A fool there was; How's your romance?; I concentrate on you; In the still of the night; It was written in the stars; I've got you under my skin; My cozy little corner in the Ritz; Night and day; Two little babes in the wood; When I had a uniform on; When my baby goes to town; Who said Gay Paree?.*
*** EMI Dig. CDC7 54203-2 [id.]; *EL 754203-4*. Thomas Hampson, Ambrosian Ch., LSO, McGlinn.

Thomas Hampson proves an ideal baritone for this repertory, totally inside the idiom, yet bringing to it a gloriously firm, finely controlled voice. The selection is a delightful one, including not just popular 'standards' but unexpected rarities. Excellent sound.

Let's do it; Miss Otis regrets; My heart belongs to Daddy; The physician; Night and day.
☞ **(*) Unicorn Dig. DKPCD 9138 [id.]. Jill Gomez, Martin Jones, Instrumental Ens. – BRITTEN: *Songs.* ***

Though the accompanist, Martin Jones, is too stiff and deadpan in these five classic Cole Porter songs, Jill Gomez is so warmly expressive a singer that the dry backing serves to add to the poignancy of songs like 'Miss Otis Regrets'. Despite the reservations, a good coupling for the Britten items.

Poulenc, Francis (1899–1963)

(i) *Les animaux modèles;* (ii; iii) *Les biches* (complete ballet); (ii) *Bucolique;* (i; iv) *Concerto champêtre (for harpsichord & orchestra);* (i; v) *Double piano concerto in D min.;* (vi) *2 Marches et un intermède (for chamber orchestra); Les mariés de la Tour Eiffel (La baigneuse de Trouville; Discourse du Général).* (ii) *Matelote provençale; Pastourelle;* (vi) *Sinfonietta; Suite française.*

(B) *** EMI Analogue/Dig. CZS7 62690-2 (2). (i) Paris Conservatoire O; or (ii) Philh. O; (iii) with Amb. S.; (iv) with Van der Wiele, or (v) composer and Février; (vi) O de Paris; all cond. Prêtre.

Les biches comes here in its complete form, with the choral additions that Poulenc made optional when he came to rework the score. The music is a delight, and so too is the group of captivating short pieces, digitally recorded at the same time (1980): *Bucolique, Pastourelle* and *Matelote provençale.* High-spirited, fresh, elegant playing and sumptuous recorded sound enhance the claims of all this music. The *Suite française* is another highlight. It is well played and recorded in a pleasing, open acoustic. Poulenc himself was a pianist of limited accomplishment, but his interpretation (with partner) of his own skittish *Double concerto* is infectiously jolly. In the imitation pastoral concerto for harpsichord, Aimée van de Wiele is a nimble soloist, but here Prêtre's inflexibility as a conductor comes out the more, even though the finale has plenty of high spirits. The *Sinfonietta*, too, could have a lighter touch, but it does not lack personality. *Les animaux modèles* is based on the fables of La Fontaine, with a prelude and a postlude, but here the recording is rather lacking in bloom, and the *Deux Marches* are also a trifle overbright. With nearly 156 minutes' playing time, these CDs are well worth exploring.

Les animaux modèles; Les biches (ballet): *suite; Les mariés de la Tour Eiffel: 2 Marches et un intermède.*
☞ ** Claves Dig. CD 50-9111[id.]. SW German RSO, Baden-Baden, Viotti.

Marcello Viotti gets a more Gallic sound from his Baden-Baden orchestra and more stylish results too in *Les biches* than Bychkov does from the Orchestre de Paris. But neither good playing nor decent recording make for a really strong recommendation, given the brevity of the programme on offer, a mere 48 minutes 39 seconds. Uneconomic, given the fact that this is at full price.

(i) *Aubade (Concerto choréographique);* (ii) *Concert champêtre for harpsichord and orchestra;* (iii) *Organ concerto in G min.;* (i) *Piano concerto in C sharp min.;* (i; iv) *Double piano concerto in D min.*
☞ ⊛ (B) *** Erato/Warner Duo 4509 95303-2 (2) [id.]. Rotterdam PO, James Conlon, with (i) Duchable; (ii) Koopman; (iii) Alain; (iv) Collard.

This Erato Bonsai Duo reissue combines two CDs, each highly recommended by us at premium price. Now issued as two for the price of one, they represent one of the most attractive of all Poulenc issues. The *Aubade* is an exhilarating work of great charm. It dates from the late 1920s and is a send-up of Mozart, Stravinsky etc. The *Piano concerto* has a most beguiling opening theme and evokes the faded charms of Paris in the '30s. The skittish *Double concerto* is infectiously jolly. One could never mistake the tone of voice intended. The performances of two of the solo works by François-René Duchable and the Rotterdam orchestra have a certain panache and flair that are most winning. The *Double concerto* too captures all the wit and charm of the Poulenc score, with the 'mock Mozart' slow movement particularly elegant. The balance is almost perfectly judged. Perhaps in these two solo works Duchable is a shade too prominent, but not sufficiently so to disturb a strong recommendation, for the sound is otherwise full and pleasing. The *Organ concerto*, too, has never come off better on record than in Marie-Claire Alain's performance using the excellent Flenthrop organ in Rotterdam's concert hall, the Doelen. She is fully equal to its many changes of mood and her treatment of the *Allegro giocoso* really catches the music's rhythmic humour. The balance is very well managed and the recording is in the demonstration bracket in this work. The *Concert champêtre* always offers problems of balance as it is scored for a full orchestra, but the exaggerated contrast was clearly intended by the composer. The performance is most perceptive, with a particularly elegant and sparkling finale. James Conlon provides admirable accompaniments throughout a highly recommendable pair of discs.

Aubade (Concerto choréographique); Piano concerto in C sharp min.; (i) *Double piano concerto in D min.*
☞ (M) **(*) EMI CDM7 64714-2 [id.]. Tacchino, (i) Paris Conservatoire O; (ii) Ringeissen, Monte Carlo PO; Prêtre.

On EMI the performance of the *Aubade* is nicely pointed, and the *Concerto* too receives a finely poised and brilliantly executed performance. However, the *Double concerto*, where Gabriel Tacchino is joined by Bernard Ringeissen, is disappointing, with the result brash and hard-driven. It was a great pity that EMI didn't choose the composer's own version of this work with Jacques Février.

Poulenc may have been only an amateur pianist, but his interpretation (with partner) had an agreeable lightness of touch, bringing out all the humour.

Aubade; Sinfonietta.
*** Hyp. Dig. CDA 66347; *KA 66347* [id.]. New London O, Ronald Corp – HAHN: *Le bal de Béatrice d'Este* (ballet suite). ***

The *Sinfonietta* is a fluent and effortless piece, full of resource and imagination, and Ronald Corp and the New London Orchestra do it proud. This performance has a real sense of style and Gallic elegance. Julian Evans is an alert soloist in the *Aubade*: his is a performance of real character and, though less well balanced than the *Sinfonietta*, he can hold his own artistically with the best. The Hahn rarity with which it is coupled enhances the interest and value of this release.

(i) *Aubade for piano and 18 instruments. Improvisations; Mouvements perpétuels; 2 Novelettes; Nocturnes;* (ii) *Trio for oboe, bassoon and piano.*
☞ (***) (M) EMI mono CDC5 55036-2 [id.]. Composer, with (i) Straram CO, Walther Straram; (ii) Roger Lamorlette, Gustave Dhérin – HONEGGER: *Cello concerto* etc. (***)

Most people know Poulenc's own playing from his partnership with Pierre Bernac. While he was not the most elegant or finished of pianists, his playing had plenty of character, nowhere more so than in the 1930 recording of the *Aubade for piano and eighteen instruments* which sounds remarkably fresh, save, perhaps, for the rather papery timbre of the solo instrument. The work is slightly abridged (the second number, *Récitatif: les campagnes de Diane*, is cut by about a minute). The solo pieces generally come off well, though the composer occasionally sounds as if another hour's practice wouldn't have come amiss! Splendid playing from the Walther Straram players (there is a striking period flavour here) and in particular from Roger Lamorlette and Gustave Dhérin, the two wind players in the *Trio*, recorded in 1928. Allowances have to be made for variable quality – but, for all that, this disc is not to be missed.

Les biches (ballet; complete).
☞ **(*) Ph. Dig. 432 993-2 [id.]. Ch. & O de Paris, Semyon Bychkov – HONEGGER: *Pacific 231;* MILHAUD: *Le bœuf sur le toit.* **(*)

Semyon Bychkov and the Orchestre de Paris offer us the complete choral version of *Les biches* – though, to be fair, the chorus are heard in only three movements. Bychkov gives a goodish account of the score, though it is not quite as light or as Parisian as the Prêtre version. At times Bychkov makes slightly heavy weather of one or two of the numbers. Perhaps the beefier recording and the thicker sonority at the bottom end of the range are to blame. The Prêtre is to be preferred (see above).

Les biches (ballet suite).
*** Chan. Dig. CHAN 9023 [id.]. Ulster O, Yan Pascal Tortelier – IBERT: *Divertissement*; MILHAUD: *Le Boeuf; La Création.* ***

Yan Pascal Tortelier and the Ulster Orchestra give an entirely winning account of Poulenc's ballet suite. Here the opening has delightfully keen rhythmic wit, and the playing is equally polished and crisply articulated in the gay *Rag-Mazurka* and infectious *Final*. The lovely *Adagietto* is introduced with tender delicacy, yet reaches a suitably plangent climax. Top-drawer Chandos sound and splendid couplings ensure the overall success of this admirable compilation.

(i) *Concert champêtre; Concerto in G min. for organ, strings and timpani;* (ii) *Gloria.*
(M) *** Decca 425 627-2. (i) Malcolm (harpsichord/organ), ASMF, Iona Brown; (ii) Greenberg, SRO Ch., Lausanne Pro Arte Ch., SRO, López-Cobos.

George Malcolm's excellent version of the *Organ concerto* is attractively paired with the *Concert champêtre*. In the latter work the engineers did not succumb to the temptation to make the harpsichord sound larger than life, and on CD the beautifully focused keyboard image contrasts wittily with the designedly ample orchestral tuttis. Some might feel that in the finale Malcolm rushes things a bit but the music effervesces, and in every other respect this is an exemplary account, with López-Cobos's fine account of the *Gloria* – see below, under its alternative coupling with Saint-Saëns – a splendid bonus.

(i) *Piano concerto in C sharp min.;* (i; ii) *Double piano concerto in D min.;* (iii) *Concerto in G min. for organ, strings and timpani.*
☞ *** Decca Dig. 436 546-2 [id.]. (i) Pascal Rogé; (ii) Silvia Deferne; (iii) Peter Hurford; Philh. O, Dutoit.

Pascal Rogé's credentials as a Poulenc interpreter are well established: his two CDs of solo piano music have been widely and rightly acclaimed both by us and elsewhere, so it will be no surprise that his playing of the *Piano concerto* and (partnered by Silvia Deferne) in the delightful *D minor Concerto for two pianos* is completely attuned to the sensibility and spirit of this still-underrated master. One of Poulenc's most extraordinary qualities is his ability to effect an abrupt change of mood from the highest of spirits to a sudden glimpse of melancholy and desolation. There is much tenderness in his account of the *Piano concerto* as well as the gamin-like *joie de vivre* that are such characteristic ingredients in Poulenc's art. Rogé and Deferne play with subtlety and intelligence. It was a good idea to couple them with the *Organ concerto*, which sounds very convincing in this performance with Peter Hurford. The Philharmonia Orchestra produce a cultivated sound for Dutoit, less characterful and idiomatic, perhaps, than the Paris Conservatoire Orchestra for Prêtre on the recently reissued Tacchino disc from the late 1960s. Good engineering.

Concerto in G min. for organ, strings and timpani.
☞ **(*) Chan. Dig. CHAN 9271 [id.]. Ian Tracey (organ of Liverpool Cathedral), BBC PO, Yan
    Pascal Tortelier – GUILMANT: *Symphony No. 1;* WIDOR: *Symphony No. 5.* ***
☞ (B) (**) Erato/Warner 2292 45943-2 [id.]. Marie-Claire Alain, French Nat. RO, Martinon –
    SAINT-SAENS: *Symphony No. 3* etc. (*(**))

The wide reverberation period of Liverpool Cathedral produces gloriously plushy textures (the orchestra strings are radiantly rich in colour) but little plangent bite, and some may feel that the effect is too overwhelmingly sumptuous for Poulenc's *Concerto*. Yet it is easy to wallow in the gloriously full sounds, and the performance itself, spacious to allow for the resonance, is certainly enjoyable.

Marie-Claire Alain's performance of the *Organ concerto* can be compared with the best. The performance is exhilarating – but, alas, the CD transfer has brightened the original analogue sound unmercifully and the organ is made to sound brash and harsh. The coupling, while better, is still too bright.

Sinfonietta.
☞ * Koch Int. Dig. 37094-2 [id.]. San Diego CO, Donald Barra – IBERT: *Divertissement* etc. *

The San Diego orchestra turns in a decent but a trifle sober account of the *Sinfonietta* which presents no real challenge to the current three-star recommendations. Good but not outstanding recording.

Suite française.
(M) *** ASV CDWHL 2067. L. Wind O, Wick – GRAINGER: *Irish tune from County Derry* etc.;
    MILHAUD: *Suite française.* ***

This engaging suite is based on themes by the sixteenth-century composer, Claude Gervaise. Poulenc scored them for a small ensemble of wind instruments and they come up very freshly in these artists' hands. Excellent recording and couplings. Thoroughly recommended.

CHAMBER MUSIC

Elégie for horn and piano; Sextet for piano, flute, oboe, clarinet, bassoon and horn; Clarinet sonata;
Flute sonata; Trio for piano, oboe and bassoon.
**(*) Decca Dig. 421 581-2 [id., without *Elégie*]. Portal, Gallois, Bourgue, Rogé, Wallez, Cazalet.

The playing of Maurice Bourgue in the *Oboe sonata* is both masterly and touching, and all these artists are on top form. These performances have a wonderful freshness and convey a real sense of delight. Pascal Rogé's pianism throughout is a constant source of pleasure, and the only drawback is the reverberance of the Salle Pleyel. All the same, an enchanting disc.

Sextet for piano & wind; Trio for piano, oboe & bassoon; (i) Le Bal masqué; Le Bestiaire.
*** CRD Dig. CRD 3437; *CRDC 4137* [id.]. (i) Thomas Allen; Nash Ens., Lionel Friend.

Thomas Allen is in excellent voice and gives a splendid account of both *Le Bal masqué* and *Le Bestiaire*. The Nash play both the *Trio* and the *Sextet* with superb zest and character. The wit of this playing and the enormous resource, good humour and charm of Poulenc's music are well served by a recording of exemplary quality and definition. Not to be missed.

Piano duet
Capriccio; Elégie; L'embarquement pour Cythère; Sonata for piano, four hands; Sonata for two pianos.
*** Chan. Dig. CHAN 8519; *ABTD 1229* [id.]. Seta Tanyel, Jeremy Brown.

These two artists have a very close rapport and dispatch this repertoire with both character and sensitivity. The Chandos recording is excellent, very vivid and present.

Solo piano music

Badinage; Bourrée au pavillon d'Auvergne; Feuillets d'album; Française; Humoresque; 6 Impromptus,
Nos. 1–5; 15 Improvisations; 3 Intermezzi; Mélancolie; 3 Mouvements perpétuels; Napoli; 8 Nocturnes;
3 Novelettes; Pastourelle; 3 Pièces; Pièce brève sur le nom d'Albert Roussel; Presto in B flat;
Promenades; Les soirées de Nazelles; Suite in C; Suite française; Thème varié; Valse in C; Valse-
improvisation sur le nom de Bach; Villageoise.
**(*) Sony Dig. M3K 44921 (3). Paul Crossley.

Paul Crossley is a perceptive guide in this repertoire, fleet-fingered and unfailingly intelligent, though
he does not really have the grace and charm of Pascal Rogé. Good recording quality.

Badinage; Les Biches: Adagietto; Intermezzo No. 3 in A flat; 3 Mouvements perpétuels; Napoli; 3
Pièces; Les soirées de Nazelles; Suite in C; Valse-improvisation sur le nom de Bach.
*** Chan. Dig. CHAN 8637; *ABTD 1325* [id.]. Eric Parkin.

Humoresque; 15 Improvisations; Intermezzi Nos. 1 in C; 2 in D flat; Mélancolie; 3 Novelettes; Presto
in B flat; Suite française d'après Claude Gervaise; Thème varié; Villageoises (Petites pièces
enfantines).
*** Chan. Dig. CHAN 8847; *ABTD 1464* [id.]. Eric Parkin.

Eric Parkin is an artist of instinctive taste and a refined musical intelligence who is completely inside
this idiom: he has plenty of spirit and character and abundant sensitivity. Perhaps Rogé has the
greater pianistic finesse plus a gamin-like charm, but Parkin too has charm and, in many of the pieces
where they overlap, there is often little to choose between them. The Chandos recording is rather
more resonant, though not unacceptably so.

Humoresque; Improvisations Nos. 4, 5, 9–11 & 14; 2 Intermezzi; Intermezzo in A flat; Nocturnes;
Presto in B flat; Suite; Thème varié; Villageoises.
*** Decca Dig. 425 862-2; *425 862-4* [id.]. Pascal Rogé.

Pascal Rogé's second Poulenc recital is every bit as captivating as his earlier disc (see below). The
acoustic is somewhat reverberant but not excessively so. Elegant playing, responsive to all the rapidly
changing shifts of tone in Poulenc's music, and strongly recommended.

Improvisations Nos. 1–3; 6–8; 12–13; 15; Mouvements perpétuels; 3 Novelettes; Pastourelle; 3 Pièces;
Les soirées de Nazelles; Valse.
⊛ *** Decca Dig. 417 438-2; *417 438-4* [id.]. Pascal Rogé.

This music is absolutely enchanting, full of delight and wisdom; it has many unexpected touches and
is teeming with character. Rogé is a far more persuasive exponent of it than any previous pianist on
record; his playing is imaginative and inspiriting, and the recording is superb.

VOCAL MUSIC

Mélodies: Allons plus vite; Banalités; Le bestiare; Calligrammes; Chansons galliardes; Dans le jardin
d'Anna; Epitaphe; La Grenouillère; Montparnasse; Le Pont; Priez pour paix.
**(*) Adès 14114-2 & 14115-2 [id.]. Pierre Bernac, composer.

Bernac had enormous charm and great feeling for characterization and, although Poulenc was not the
greatest of pianists, he was a sympathetic accompanist. These recordings were made in Paris in 1959,
when Bernac's vibrato was a little wider than in earlier life but his powers of characterization were
undimmed. What a singer he was! The sound is stereo, and very alive and fresh for its period.

Ave verum corpus; Exsultate Deo; Laudes de Saint-Antoine de Padoue; (i) Litanies à la Vierge Noire;
4 Motets pour le temps de Noël; 4 Motets pour le temps de pénitence; Salve Regina.
☞ (M) *** EMI CDM5 65156-2 [id.]. Groupe Vocale de France, John Alldis; (i) with Marie-Claire
Alain.

An outstanding collection. This is music that ideally needs French voices, and John Alldis has trained
his French group splendidly so that they combine precision and fervour with a natural feeling for the
words. The soaring *Ave verum* is matched by the exhilaration of the *Exsultate Deo* and the originality
of the *Litanies* with its stabbing bursts of organ tone. The *Salve Regina* is very fine too, and the four
Christmas motets have the right extrovert joyfulness and sense of wonder. The recording is made
within an ecclesiastical ambience, yet definition is admirable.

Mélodies: Banalités: Hôtel; Voyage à Paris. Bleuet. C; Calligrammes: Voyage. 4 Chansons pour enfants: Nous voulons une petite soeur. Les chemins de l'amour. Colloque; Hyde Park; Métamorphoses; Miroirs brûlants: Tu vois le feu du soir. Montparnasse; 2 Poèmes de Louis Aragon; 3 Poèmes de Louise Lalanne; Priez pour paix; Tel jour, telle nuit; Toréador.
*** Hyp. Dig. CDA 66147 [id.]. Songmakers' Almanac: Lott, Rolfe Johnson, Murray, Johnson.

Felicity Lott sings the great majority of the songs here, joyful and tender, comic and tragic by turns. The other soloists have one song apiece, done with comparable magnetism, and Richard Jackson joins Felicity Lott (one stanza each) in Poulenc's solitary 'song for two voices', *Colloque.* First-rate recording, though Lott's soprano is not always as sweetly caught as it can be.

Le bestiaire; Chansons gaillardes: La belle jeunesse; Invocation aux Parques. Métamorphoses: C'est ainsi que tu es; Paganini; Reine des mouettes. 2 Poèmes de Guillaume Apollinaire: Dans le jardin d'Anna; Montparnasse. 2 Poèmes de Louis Aragon: 'C'; Fêtes galantes. Tel jour, telle nuit.
☞ (***) EMI mono CDC7 54605-2 [id.]. Pierre Bernac, Francis Poulenc – BRITTEN: *Song cycles.* (***)

It is apt for EMI's 'Composers in Person' series to celebrate two unique partnerships, with Francis Poulenc accompanying Pierre Bernac and Benjamin Britten accompanying Peter Pears. The distinctive voice of each singer was the direct inspiration for most of these songs. That is so, not just with Britten's two sonnet-cycles, but with most of the two-dozen Poulenc songs as well. To hear Bernac performing Poulenc's most moving song, '*C*', as well as his other Aragon setting, the cabaret-inspired *Fêtes galantes*, is to have a new, more intense insight into the two contrasted sides of Poulenc's genius, now dedicated, now flippant. Documentation is good and with complete texts but, like all the other issues in this series, the discs come at full price.

Figure humaine; Laudes de Saint Antoine de Padoue; 4 Motets pour le temps de Noël; 4 Motets pour un temps de pénitence; 4 Petites prières de Saint François d'Assise.
☞ *** Virgin/EMI Dig. VC7 59192-2 [id.]. The Sixteen, Harry Christophers.

A lovely record which assembles the cantata for double choir, *Figure humaine*, with some of the composer's most celebrated *a cappella* motets. These performances can be recommended strongly, both on artistic grounds and for the excellence of the sound.

Gloria.
☞ (M) *** Sony SMK 47569 [id.]. Judith Blegen, Westminster Ch., NYPO, Bernstein – JANACEK: *Glagolitic Mass.* ***
☞ (M) *** Decca 425 077-2 [id.]. Sylvia Greenberg, Wayne Williams, SRO Ch., Lausanne Pro Arte Ch., SRO, López-Cobos – SAINT-SAENS: *Messe.* **(*)

The *Gloria* is one of Poulenc's last compositions and is among his most successful. Bernstein perhaps underlines the Stravinskian springs of its inspiration and produces a vividly etched and clean-textured account which makes excellent sense in every way and is free from excessive sentiment. Judith Blegen is an appealing soloist, and the 1976 recording, made in New York's Manhattan Center, though not the last word in refinement, is clear, well detailed and spacious. With its vibrant Janáček coupling, this is one of the most attractive reissues in the Bernstein Edition.

López-Cobos gives a fine account of the *Gloria*, expansive yet underlining the Stravinskian elements in the score. The recording is first class, full-bodied and with clean definition.

(i; ii) Gloria; Ave verum corpus; Exultate Deo; (ii) Litanies à la Vierge Noire; 4 Motets pour le temps de Noël; 4 Motets pour un temps de pénitence; Salve regina.
*** Coll. COLCD 108; *COLC 108.* (i) Donna Deam, Cambridge Singers, (ii) City of L. Sinfonia, John Rutter.

A generous selection of Poulenc's choral music, much of it of great beauty and simplicity, in very fresh-sounding performances and well-focused sound.

Mass in G; 4 petites prières de Saint François d'Assise; Salve regina.
*** Nimbus Dig. NI 5197 [id.]. Christ Church Cathedral Ch., Oxford, Stephen Darlington – MARTIN: *Mass for double choir.* **(*)

The *Mass in G* is a work of strong appeal and greater dramatic fire than the *Salve Regina* or the more intimate *Quatre petites prières de Saint François d'Assise* for men's voices. The choir of Christ Church Cathedral, Oxford, under Stephen Darlington sing with clean tone and excellent balance, and the Nimbus recording is very good indeed.

(i) Mass in G. Exultate Deo; (ii) Litanies à la Vierge Noire. Salve Regina.

☞ (B) *** Double Decca 436 486-2 (2) [id.]. St John's College, Cambridge, Ch., Guest; (i) with Jonathon Bond; (ii) Stephen Cleobury – FAURE; DURUFLE: *Requiems.* ***

As an extraordinarily generous bonus for the two great *Requiems* of Fauré and Duruflé, this Double Decca set offers the Poulenc *Mass in G minor* together with two motets, *Exultate Deo* and *Salve Regina,* finely wrought pieces in performances of great finish. Then, together with Stephen Cleobury, they give us the cool, gently dissonant *Litanies à la Vierge Noire,* a dialogue between voices and organ in which the voices eventually take dominance. It is beautifully done and the St John's College forces cope with the delicacy and sweetness of Poulenc's chromatic harmony throughout. The (originally Argo) recording is eminently realistic and truthful.

Stabat Mater; Litanies à la vierge noire; Salve Regina.
*** HM Dig. HMC 905149; *HMC 405149* [id.]. Lagrange, Lyon Nat. Ch. and O, Baudo.

In the *Stabat Mater* Serge Baudo certainly makes the most of expressive and dynamic nuances; he shapes the work with fine feeling and gets good singing from the Lyon Chorus. Michèle Lagrange has a good voice and is an eminently expressive soloist. The coupling offers the short *Salve Regina* and the *Litanies à la Vierge Noire,* an earlier and somewhat more severe work.

Dialogue des Carmélites (complete).
☞ *** Virgin/EMI Dig. VCD7 59227-2 (2). Dubosc, Gorr, Yakar, Fournier, Van Dam, Viala, Dupuy, Lyon Opéra O, Kent Nagano.

The opening of Poulenc's *Dialogue des Carmélites* with its very Stravinskian ostinatos for a moment suggests a minimalist opera, written before its time. Yet the relative ease of the idiom, its triviality even, conceals a genuine depth, superbly brought out by Kent Nagano and Lyon Opéra forces in this recording made by Virgin in collaboration with Radio France. It fills an important gap, when the only previous version, recorded soon after the première in 1957, has not been generally available. Much is owed to the dynamic Nagano, who gives an extra momentum and sense of contrast to a work that with its measured speeds and easily lyrical manner can fall into sameness. That the male casting is so strong, with the principal roles taken by José van Dam and the tenor, Jean-Luc Viala, compensates for any lack of variety in having women's voices predominating in an opera about nuns. Catherine Dubosc in the central role of the fear-obsessed, self-doubting Blanche is fresh and appealing, with Brigitte Fournier charming as the frivolous nun, Constance, and the veteran Rita Gorr as the old Prioress and Rachel Yakar as the new Prioress both splendid. The vivid recording, helped by a stage production in Lyon, culminates in a spine-chilling rendering of the final execution scene, with the sound of the guillotine ever more menacing.

Praetorius, Michael (1571–1621)

Dances from Terpsichore (extended suite).
*** Decca Dig. 414 633-2 [id.]. New L. Cons., Philip Pickett.

Dances from Terpsichore (Suite de ballets; Suite de voltes).
☞ (M) **(*) EMI CDM7 67803-2 [id.]. Early Music Cons. of L., Munrow – Concert: *Flemish music.*
**(*)

Terpsichore is a huge collection of some 300 dance tunes used by the French-court dance bands of Henri IV. They were enthusiastically assembled by the German composer, Michael Praetorius, who also harmonized them and arranged them in four to six parts; however, any selection is conjectural in the matter of orchestration. Philip Pickett's instrumentation is sometimes less exuberant than that of David Munrow before him; but many will like the refinement of his approach, with small instrumental groups, lute pieces and even what seems like an early xylophone! There are also some attractively robust brass scorings (sackbuts and trumpets). The use of original instruments is entirely beneficial in this repertoire; the recording is splendid.

One of the great pioneers of the 'authentic' re-creation of early music, David Munrow's main purpose was to bring the music fully to life and at the same time imaginatively to stimulate the ear of the listener. This record, made in 1973, is one of his most successful achievements. The sound is excellent in all respects. Munrow's instrumentation is imaginatively done: the third item, a *Bourrée* played by four racketts (a cross between a shawm and comb-and-paper in sound), is fascinating. The collection has now been intriguingly extended to include vocal and dance music from the early Renaissance Flemish school – see Concerts, below. The one drawback to this reissue is the poor documentation, with titles printed in impossibly small type.

Christmas music: *Polyhymnia caduceatrix et panegyrica Nos. 9–10, 12 & 17. Puericinium Nos. 2, 4 & 5. Musae Sionae VI, No. 53: Es ist ein Ros' entsprungen. Terpsichore: Dances Nos. 1; 283–5; 310.*
*** Hyp. Dig. CDA 66200; *KA 66200* [id.]. Westminster Cathedral Ch., Parley of Instruments, David Hill.

Praetorius was much influenced by the polychoral style of the Gabrielis; these pieces reflect this interest. The music is simple in style and readily accessible, and its performance on this atmospheric Hyperion record is both spirited and sensitive.

Christmas music: *Polyhymnia caduceatrix et panegyrica Nos. 10, Wie schön leuchtet der Morgenstern; 12, Puer natus in Bethlehem; 21, Wachet auf, ruft uns die Stimme; 34, In dulci jubilo.*
*** EMI Dig. CDC7 47633-2 [id.]. Taverner Cons., Ch. & Players, Parrott – SCHUTZ: *Christmas oratorio.* ***

This is the finest collection of Praetorius's vocal music in the current catalogue. The closing setting of *In dulci jubilo*, richly scored for five choirs and with the brass providing thrilling contrast and support for the voices, has great splendour. Before that comes the lovely, if less ambitious *Wie schön leuchtet der Morgenstern*. Both *Wachet auf* and *Puer natus in Bethlehem* are on a comparatively large scale, their combination of block sonorities and florid decorative effects the very essence of Renaissance style. The recording is splendidly balanced, with voices and brass blending and intertwining within an ample acoustic. Alas, this CD is another of EMI's current withdrawals.

Previn, André (born 1929)

'A different kind of blues' (Look at him go; Little face; Who reads reviews?; Night thoughts; A different kind of blues; Chocolate apricot; The five of us; Make up your mind).
☞ (M) **(*) EMI Dig. CDM7 64319-2 [id.]. Perlman, Previn, Manne, Hall, Mitchell.

Perlman, unlike his colleagues here, is no jazz musician, and he had to have the 'improvisations' written out for him; but the challenge of this project with Previn's colourful and appealing pieces dividing sharply between brilliant and sweet, is very clear from first to last. There are (for E. G.) not many better examples of 'middle-of-the-road' records, and the haunting *Chocolate apricot* could become a classic. No information is given on which critic gave rise to *Who reads reviews?*. The 1981 digital recording is vivid and immediate: the artists have great presence, but in the Editor's view this is a record to sample first. It plays for only 37 minutes.

'It's a breeze' (It's a breeze; Rain in my head; Catgut your tongue; It's about time; Bowing and scraping; A tune for Heather; Quiet diddling; The red bar).
☞ (M) **(*) EMI Dig. CDM7 64318-2 [id.]. Perlman, Previn, Manne, Hall, Mitchell.

If you enjoyed the first collection, you may well find the second (recorded in Pittsburgh as a relaxed supplement to more serious sessions) even more persuasive, although, with only 43 minutes of music included, it would have been more generous of EMI to have combined both programmes on a single CD, if necessary omitting a single piece. No prizes are offered by the Editor for the choice. However, a sweet number like *A tune for Heather* is certainly attractive, with a tinge of Walton. As with the first programme, the digital recording presents balances that are closer to pop than to those one would expect in a semi-classical issue, but the sound is very vivid.

Prokofiev, Serge (1891–1953)

Andante for strings, Op. 50 bis; Autumn (symphonic sketch), Op. 8; Lieutenant Kijé: suite, Op. 60; The Stone flower: suite, Op. 118; Wedding suite, Op. 126.
*** Chan. Dig. CHAN 8806; *ABTD 1434* [id.]. SNO, Järvi.

The *Andante* is a transcription for full strings of the slow movement of the *First String quartet*, and its eloquence is more telling in this more expansive format. *Autumn*, on the other hand, is an early piece, much influenced by Rachmaninov, in particular his symphonic poem, *The Isle of the dead*, and is full of imaginative touches. Järvi takes it at a fairly brisk tempo but it remains appropriately atmospheric. The *Wedding suite* is drawn from *The Stone flower* and complements the Op. 118 suite from Prokofiev's last full-length ballet. *The Stone flower* has some engaging lyrical invention, and the music recorded here is still full of appeal. The performances and recording are in the best traditions of the house.

Boris Godunov, Op. 70 bis: Fountain scene; Polonaise. Dreams, Op. 6. Eugene Onegin, Op. 71: Minuet,
Polka, Mazurka. 2 Pushkin waltzes, Op. 120. Romeo and Juliet (ballet): suite No. 2, Op. 64.
*** Chan. Dig. CHAN 8472; *ABTD 1183* [id.]. SNO, Järvi.

Järvi's second suite from *Romeo and Juliet* has sensitivity, abundant atmosphere, a sense of the
theatre, and is refreshingly unmannered. A fuller selection of the music Prokofiev wrote for a
production of *Eugene Onegin* is available – see below – but what is offered here, plus the *Two Pushkin
waltzes*, are rather engaging lighter pieces. The performances are predictably expert, the balance finely
judged and detail is in exactly the right perspective.

Chout (The Buffoon): ballet, Op. 21.
**(*) Olympia Dig. OCD 126 [id.]. USSR MoC SO, Rozhdestvensky.

Chout was the first of Prokofiev's ballets that Diaghilev actually staged, a wonderfully imaginative
score, full of colour and resource. Rozhdestvensky gives a very lively account of the complete score
and gets good playing from his youthful Moscow orchestra. The recording is as vivid as the music;
indeed some may find it a little overbright at the top.

Chout (ballet): suite, Op. 21a; Love for 3 Oranges: suite, Op. 33a; Le pas d'acier: suite, Op. 41a.
*** Chan. Dig. CHAN 8729; *ABTD 1369* [id.]. SNO, Järvi.

Chout (ballet) suite; Romeo and Juliet (ballet), Op. 64: excerpts.
(M) *** Decca 425 027-2 [id.]. LSO, Claudio Abbado.

Abbado's version of the suite from *Chout* with the LSO offers a generous part of the score, including
some of the loosely written connecting material, and he reveals a sensitive ear for balance of texture.
The excerpts from *Romeo and Juliet* include some of the most delightful numbers, which are often
omitted from selections. There is admirable delicacy and a lightness of touch that are most engaging.
The analogue recording, made in the Kingsway Hall in 1966, was a model of its kind.

   Järvi has a natural affinity for this repertoire and gets splendid results from the SNO; and the
recording is pretty spectacular.

Cinderella (ballet; complete), Op. 87.
*** Decca Dig. 410 162-2 (2) [id.]. Cleveland O, Ashkenazy.

Compact disc collectors wanting the complete ballet can safely invest in Ashkenazy without fear of
disappointment. Detail is closely scrutinized by the Decca engineers and Ashkenazy gets excellent
results from the Cleveland Orchestra. On CD, the recording's wonderful definition is enhanced.

Cinderella (ballet): highlights.
(M) *** EMI Dig. CDD7 64289-2 [id.]. LSO, Previn.

This highlights disc is generous (71 minutes) and well laid out to include the most important numbers
from each of the three Acts, including the final resolution of the story and Prokofiev's *Amoroso*
apotheosis, as the Prince and Princess dance together in their enchanted garden. The playing of the
LSO for Previn is extremely alert and beautifully characterized, the wind playing is particularly fine,
and there is a good sense of theatre. With 27 numbers offered, and a synopsis relating the action to
each of the separate cues, this reissue rather sweeps the board. However, it has just been withdrawn!

(i) Cinderella: excerpts; (ii) Romeo and Juliet: excerpts.
(M) *** EMI CD-EMX 2194. (i) RPO, Irving; (ii) Philh. O, Kurtz.

Kurtz's *Romeo and Juliet* comes from the mid-1960s, but Irving's performances are from 1958, yet it
would be difficult to guess the dates of either from the sound here, which is admirable in its definition
and body. Irving secures very fine playing from the RPO, crisply rhythmic and sympathetic. In
Romeo and Juliet Kurtz's performances are slightly lacking in dramatic tension in the longer
movements, but the shorter dances come off superbly. But what beautifully shaped phrasing the
Philharmonia give us and what full timbre.

Cinderella (ballet): suites Nos. 1 & 2, Op. 107–8: excerpts. (i) Peter and the wolf, Op. 67.
*** Chan. Dig. CHAN 8511; *ABTD 1221* [id.]. (i) Lina Prokofiev; SNO, Järvi.

Peter and the wolf is very slow, but the magnetism of Madame Prokofiev (the composer's first wife),
with many memorable lines delivered in her tangily Franco-Russian accent, makes up for that
leisurely manner, with beautiful, persuasive playing from the Scottish National Orchestra. Järvi's
compilation of eight movements from the two *Cinderella suites* has even more persuasive playing,
with the sensuousness of much of the writing brought out. Warmly atmospheric recording, with the
narration realistically balanced.

Cinderella: suite No. 1, Op. 107; Lieutenant Kijé (suite); The Love for 3 Oranges: March; Scherzo;
The Prince and Princess. Romeo and Juliet: Madrigal; Dance of the girls with lilies.
(BB) *** Naxos Dig. 8.550381 [id.]. Slovak State PO, (Košice), Andrew Mogrelia.

The calibre of this excellent Slovak orchestra is well demonstrated here, and its perceptive conductor, Andrew Mogrelia, is at his finest in his gently humorous portrait of *Lieutenant Kijé*, the three 'best bits' from *The Love for Three Oranges* and the charming items from *Romeo and Juliet*. Excellent recording.

Concertino in G min. for cello and orchestra, Op. 132 (completed and orch. Kabalevsky &
Rostropovich); *Sinfonia concertante in E min. for cello and orchestra, Op. 125.*
☞ *** Decca Dig. 436 233-2 [id.]. Lynn Harrell, RPO, Ashkenazy.
☞ (*(**)) Russian Disc mono RDCD 11103 [id.]. Rostropovich, USSR SO, Rozhdestvensky.

Lynn Harrell gives a very impressive account of the *Sinfonia concertante* and sounds as if he is relishing the numerous challenges to his virtuosity that this score poses. His playing of the cadenza of the middle movement (fig. 18 in the score and the ensuing paragraphs) is pretty stunning and Vladimir Ashkenazy gets strongly characterized playing from the RPO, which does full justice to its sardonic humour. A fresh, totally committed and well-prepared performance which blends enthusiasm and spontaneity. The *Concertino*, inspired by his collaboration with Rostropovich in Op. 125, and completed and orchestrated on Prokofiev's death by the then young cellist together with Kabalevsky, is a much slighter piece but is equally well played. Two other plus points: the Decca recording is very truthful and vivid, though it sounds best when played at a highish level setting; and Christopher Palmer's useful notes give a detailed comparison of Op. 125 with its earlier incarnation, the *Cello concerto*, Op. 58. Rostropovich's own performances with the USSR Symphony Orchestra under Rozhdestvensky naturally have a very special authority. They were made at public concerts in 1964 and appear in the UK for the first time. Some allowance must be made for the rather raw sound.

Cello concerto in E min., Op. 58.
☞ (M) ** Ph. 434 166-2 [id.]. Walevska, Monte Carlo Op. O, Inbal – KHACHATURIAN: *Cello concerto.* **

Although it opens strongly, with interesting ideas, Prokofiev's *Cello concerto* (which was later to be reworked into the *Sinfonia concertante*) does not maintain this intensity of inspiration. Even so, making cuts in the closing *Theme and variations* with a view to tightening the structure is not the answer. It is otherwise interesting to hear Prokofiev's first thoughts, and Christine Walevska plays with ardour and is well accompanied. The Philips recording, however, is nothing special, so perhaps it is as well that this is a limited edition.

(i) *Flute concerto* (orch. Palmer); (ii) *Humoresque scherzo, Op. 12 bis; Overture on Hebrew themes,
Op. 34 bis; Sonata for unaccompanied violins, Op. 115; Symphony No. 1 in D (Classical), Op. 25.*
**(*) Conifer Dig. CDCF 173; *MCFC 173* [id.]. (i) Jonathan Snowden; (ii) Alexander, Gatt,
  Mackie, Orford; L. Musici, Mark Stephenson.

The *Flute concerto* is an arrangement of the *Sonata in D major*, expertly scored by Christopher Palmer but is in no sense a concerto, the orchestra's role being confined to that of accompaniment. The *Humoresque scherzo* is in Prokofiev's own transcription for four bassoons, and the *Sonata*, Op. 115, was originally intended to be heard played by violins in unison, and sounds effective in this form. The *Overture on Hebrew themes* is well played and recorded, and so is the *Classical Symphony*, though it is rather on the slow side. Jonathan Snowden gives an excellent account of the arrangement of the *D major Sonata* and the recordings are well balanced, natural and realistic.

Piano concertos Nos. 1–5.
*** Chan. Dig. CHAN 8938; *DBTD 2027* (2) [id.]. Boris Berman (in Nos. 1, 4 & 5); Horacio
  Gutiérrez (in Nos. 2 & 3), Concg. O, Järvi.
(M) **(*) Decca 425 570-2 (2) [id.]. Ashkenazy, LSO, Previn.

Piano concertos Nos. 1 in D flat, Op. 10; 3 in C, Op. 26; 4 in B flat, Op. 53.
(BB) *** Naxos Dig. 8.550566 [id.]. Kun Woo Paik, Polish Nat. RSO (Katowice), Antoni Witt.

Piano concertos Nos. 2 in G min., Op. 16; 5 in G, Op. 55.
(BB) *** Naxos Dig. 8.550565 [id.]. Kun Woo Paik, Polish Nat. RSO (Katowice), Antoni Witt.

(i) *Piano concertos Nos. 1–5;* (ii) *Overture on Hebrew themes. Visions fugitives, Op. 22.*

(B) *** EMI CMS7 62542-2 (2). Michel Béroff; (i) with Leipzig GO, Masur; (ii) with Portal, Parrenin Qt.

The merits of the Berman single discs are discussed below. As a package, their claims are strong, both artistically and in terms of recording quality.

Honours are more evenly divided between Ashkenazy and Béroff than one might expect. Ashkenazy's virtuosity is often challenged by the young Frenchman, and he too plays masterfully; indeed, both sets of performances prove remarkably distinguished on closer acquaintance. However, the remastered Decca recording has a top-heavy balance and the upper strings tend to sound shrill at higher dynamic levels. The EMI CD transfer brings a fairly spiky sound to the violins – one would not guess that this was the Leipzig Gewandhaus Orchestra in the opening tutti of the *First Concerto*, which is bright rather than rich-textured. Nevertheless there is plenty of ambience and the somewhat acerbic sounds are not inappropriate for Prokofiev. Slow movements have plenty of atmosphere. Generous bonuses are offered by the EMI set. Béroff's account of the *Visions fugitives* is particularly distinguished, and the piano recording gives little cause for complaint.

Kun Woo Paik's playing throughout these five concertos has exhilarating bravura. Tempi are dangerously fast at times and occasionally he has the orchestra almost scampering to keep up with him, but they do, and the result is often electrifying. The famous theme and variations central movement of the *Third concerto* is played with great diversity of mood and style and the darkly expressive *Larghetto* of No. 5 is very finely done. The *First concerto*, which comes last on the first CD has great freshness and compares well with almost any version on disc. In short, with vivid recording in the Concert Hall of Polish Radio, which has plenty of ambience, this set is enormously stimulating and a remarkable bargain. It has far better sound than the remastered Decca recording for Ashkenazy.

(i) *Piano concerto No. 1 in D flat. Suggestion diabolique, Op. 4/4.*

(M) *** EMI CDM7 64329-2 [id.]. Gavrilov, (i) LSO, Rattle – BALAKIREV: *Islamey;* TCHAIKOVSKY: *Piano concerto No. 1.* ***

A dazzling account of the *First Piano concerto* from Andrei Gavrilov. This version is second to none for virtuosity and sensitivity. Apart from its brilliance, this performance scores on other fronts too; Simon Rattle provides excellent orchestral support and the EMI engineers offer most vivid recording, while the *Suggestion diabolique* makes a hardly less dazzling encore after the concerto.

(i) *Piano concertos Nos. 1 in D flat, Op. 10; 3 in C, Op. 26. Piano sonata No. 7 in B flat, Op. 83.*

☞ ** ASV Dig. CDDCA 786 [id.]. Mari Kodama, (i) with Philh. O, Kent Nagano.

The *First Piano concerto*, with which Prokofiev astonished the judges and shocked Glazunov, and the *Third in C major* were for long the only two that held a place in the repertoire, and they still remain the most frequently played. ASV's coupling should win great favour since it brings performances of real panache and style, together with a highly competitive account of the *Seventh Sonata*. Mari Kodama is a vital and imaginative player and the performances are wonderfully alert and fresh-eyed; there is splendid rapport between soloist and conductor (not surprisingly since they are husband and wife) and they benefit from first-class recording. A strong recommendation not only for newcomers to Prokofiev but for the experienced collector.

Piano concertos Nos. 1 in D flat, Op. 10; 3 in C, Op. 26; 5 in G, Op. 55.

☞ *** Sony SK 52483 [id.]. Yefim Bronfman, Israel PO, Zubin Mehta.

Yefim Bronfman's Sony recording offers the *Fifth Piano concerto* instead of the *Sonata* (as on ASV), which makes a more logical and (for the collector) competitive choice – and the recording is similarly excellent in quality. Bronfman is hardly less remarkable or sensitive than Mari Kodama; indeed he is a player of subtlety and possesses a formidable technique and a cultured restraint. The Israel orchestra under Mehta gives good, well-phrased and athletic support. Existing recommendations are not displaced, but for those wanting this particular coupling this deserves a three-star recommendation.

Piano concertos Nos. 1 in D flat, Op. 10; 4 in B flat for the left hand, Op. 53; 5 in G, Op. 56.

*** Chan. Dig. CHAN 8791; *ABTD 1424* [id.]. Boris Berman, Concg. O, Järvi.

On Chandos, very fine performances of all three *Concertos*, and the orchestral playing is very distinguished. Boris Berman has established an enviable reputation as interpreter of this composer, and he plays with great panache and (at times) dazzling virtuosity. He holds the music on a taut rein and has the nervous energy and ebullience this music needs. The superb recording quality will sway many collectors in his favour.

Piano concerto No. 1 in D flat; Piano sonata No. 5 in C, Op. 38.
*** ASV Dig. CDDCA 555 [id.]. Osorio, RPO, Bátiz – RAVEL: *Left-hand concerto etc.* ***

Jorge Federico Osorio is a thoroughly perceptive interpreter. He is accompanied well by Bátiz, and readers wanting this coupling need not fear that it is second best; they are excellently recorded. ASV offer an interesting fill-up in the form of the Prokofiev *Fifth Sonata*, which Osorio does in its post-war, revised form.

Piano concertos No. 2 in G min., Op. 16; 3 in C, Op. 26.
*** Chan. Dig. CHAN 8889; *ABTD 1500* [id.]. Horacio Gutiérrez, Concg. O, Neeme Järvi.

Horacio Gutiérrez is keenly responsive to the shifting moods and extreme dynamics of Prokofiev's writing. If you think his fortissimo playing too unrelieved in the first-movement cadenza or elsewhere, it is because the composer marks it so. The Concertgebouw Orchestra under Neeme Järvi play magnificently throughout and, in terms of recording quality alone, this must rank high in the lists.

Piano concerto No. 3 in C, Op. 26.
☞ (M) *** Mercury 434 333-2 [id.]. Byron Janis, Moscow PO, Kondrashin (with PROKOFIEV:
   Toccata; SCHUMANN: *Sonata No. 3;* MENDELSSOHN: *Songs without words, Op. 61/1;* PINTO: *3
   Scenes from childhood* ***) – RACHMANINOV: *Piano concerto No. 3.* ***
☞ (BB) **(*) Belart 450 081-2. Israela Margalit, New Philh. O, Maazel – MUSSORGSKY: *Pictures.*
   **(*)
☞ (M) ** Telarc Dig. CD 82009 [id.]. Jon Kimura Parker, RPO, Previn – TCHAIKOVSKY: *Concerto
   No. 1.* *(*)

Byron Janis's record with Kondrashin has a certain historical éclat in containing the first recordings made in the Soviet Union (in 1962) by non-Russian recording engineers. The result was a triumphant success, artistically and technically. Janis's account of the Prokofiev *Third Concerto* is outstanding in every way, soloist and orchestra plainly challenging each other in a performance full of wit (particularly in the delightfully managed slow-movement variations), drama and warmth. Even though it was made three decades ago, the Mercury recording sounds amazingly clean and faithful. The recital (recorded in Russia the following year – except for the Schumann, which was made in the USA) is comparatively low-key, except perhaps for the captivating *Scenes from childhood* of Octavio Pinto, which combine charm with glittering yet unostentatious bravura.

The performance by Israela Margalit and Maazel is not the most poised available but it has a splendid feeling of spontaneity and enjoyment, and there is no lack of wit in the central theme and variations. The recording balance is somewhat contrived, the resonance of the acoustic competing with the microphone spotlighting, but the end-result is unfailingly vivid and the piano image is tangible. It is not unlikely that those who buy this disc for the Mussorgsky may find themselves turning as readily to the concerto, for the personality and colour of the score emerge strongly here.

Jon Kimura Parker plays the outer movements with considerable vigour, and he and Previn are at their most imaginatively communicative in the slow-movement variations. The Telarc recording is rich and well balanced, and this is enjoyable enough – if in no way distinctive. It obviously has more modern sound than Janis's version on Mercury in the same price-range, but in every other respect that is far more rewarding.

(i) *Piano concerto No. 3 in C. Contes de la vieille grand-mère, Op. 31/2 & 3; Etude, Op. 52; Gavotte
No. 2, Op. 25; Gavotte No. 3, Op. 32; Paysage, Op. 59; Sonatine pastorale, Op. 59; Sonata No. 4, Op.
29: Andante. Suggestions diaboliques, Op. 4/4; Visions fugitives, Op. 22/3, 5, 6, 9–11, 16–18.*
(M) (***) Pearl mono GEMMCD 9470. composer, (i) LSO, Piero Coppola.

An invaluable disc that gives us the only recordings the composer ever made of his own music as a pianist. Prokofiev's playing has the same wit and character as the music itself and, although interpretatively he is straightforward, there is a really strong musical personality in evidence. The recordings, though a bit monochrome and dry, are good for the period.

(i) *Piano concerto No. 3 in C, Op. 26;* (ii; iii) *Violin concerto No. 1 in D, Op. 19;* (iii) *Lieutenant Kijé
(suite), Op. 60.*
☞ (B) *** DG Analogue/Dig. 439 413-2 [id.]. (i) Martha Argerich, BPO; (ii) Shlomo Mintz; (iii)
   Chicago SO; all cond. Abbado.

Martha Argerich's highly individual performance of Prokofiev's *C major Concerto* is justly famous, displaying countless indications of feminine perception and subtlety. Once regarded as tough music, the work here receives a sensuous performance, and Abbado's direction underlines that from the very first with a warmly romantic account of the ethereal opening phrases on the high violins. The recording was made in the Berlin Jesus-Christus-Kirche in 1967 and still sounds excellent, although a little dimming of the treble may be advantageous. The *First Violin concerto* also has a magical opening, and once again Abbado's accompaniment is peerless, while Mintz phrases with imagination and individuality. *Lieutenant Kijé* is hardly less successful and also sounds splendid; Abbado gets both warm and wonderfully clean playing from the Chicago orchestra. This compilation is one of the very finest reissues on DG's bargain Classikon label.

Piano concerto No. 4 in B flat for the left hand, Op. 53.
☞ *** Sony Dig. SK 47188 [id.]. Fleisher, Boston SO, Ozawa – BRITTEN: *Diversions;* RAVEL: *Left-hand concerto.* ***
(M) (***) Sony MPK 46452 [id.]. Rudolph Serkin, Phd. O, Ormandy – REGER: *Piano concerto.* **

Forced to abandon his career at its height as a result of a medical disorder (his right hand was disabled by numbness and cramping caused by what is known as carpal tunnel syndrome), Leon Fleisher has embarked on an ambitious project for Sony to record repertoire for the left hand. The present issue assembles three of the most brilliant and rewarding pieces for the medium. The *Fourth Piano concerto* was commissioned, like the Ravel, for Paul Wittgenstein who lost his right hand during the First World War. He did not like it, however, and the piece remained long neglected (its first UK performance was by Malcolm Binns in 1960). It is a powerful and resourceful piece which Fleisher performs with great sympathy and skill. Although his does not necessarily eclipse earlier versions by Michel Béroff, John Browning and Ashkenazy, it is an interpretation of strong character and comparable stature, and is well accompanied by Ozawa and the Boston orchestra, and is splendidly recorded.

Serkin's recording was made in 1958 and the performance is not likely to be bettered. His mastery helps to disguise some of the work's defects, though even he cannot quite conceal the fact that the vivace finale is far too short to balance the rest properly. The mono recording is excellent.

Piano concerto No. 5 in G, Op. 55.
*** DG 415 119-2 [id.]. Sviatoslav Richter, Warsaw PO, Witold Rowicki – RACHMANINOV: *Piano concerto No. 2.* ***

Richter's 1959 account of the *Fifth Piano concerto* is a classic and it cannot be recommended too strongly to all admirers of Richter, Prokofiev and great piano playing.

Violin concertos Nos. 1 in D, Op. 19; 2 in G min., Op. 63.
*** DG Dig. 410 524-2 [id.]. Mintz, Chicago SO, Abbado.
(M) *** Decca 425 003-2. Kyung Wha Chung, LSO, Previn – STRAVINSKY: *Concerto.* ***

Mintz phrases with imagination and individuality and there is an attractive combination of freshness and lyrical finesse. He has the advantage of Abbado's sensitive and finely judged accompaniments. In short, this partnership casts the strongest spell on the listener and, with recording on CD which is both refined and full, this must receive the strongest advocacy.

Kyung Wha Chung gives performances to emphasize the lyrical quality of these *Concertos*, with playing that is both warm and strong, tender and full of fantasy. Previn's accompaniments are deeply understanding, while the Decca sound has lost only a little of its fullness in the digital remastering, and the soloist is now made very present.

Violin concerto No. 1 in D, Op. 19.
☞ (***) EMI mono CDH7 64562-2 [id.]. Szigeti, LPO, Beecham – MENDELSSOHN: *Violin concerto;* MOZART: *Violin concerto No. 4.* (***)
☞ (**) Pearl mono GEMM CD 9377 [id.]. Szigeti, LPO, Beecham – MENDELSSOHN: *Violin concerto;* MOZART: *Violin concerto No. 4.* (**)
☞ *(*) BMG/RCA Dig. 09026 60990-2 [id.]. Spivakov, RPO, Temirkanov – TCHAIKOVSKY: *Violin concerto.* *(*)

Szigeti's classic (1934) account of Prokofiev's *D major Concerto* with Beecham and the LPO may have been matched but it has hardly been surpassed. It has a virtuosity, a sense of character, an astringency and magic which are quite special. Although the Pearl transfer is serviceable, readers will find the quality rough and edgy at the top end of the spectrum and wanting in warmth and body. The EMI CD transfer is definitely the one to have: much smoother and more refined.

Spivakov's heavily romantic style, excessive in the Tchaikovsky, is much less appropriate in the Prokofiev and, though he adapts to a degree, he does not avoid similar soupiness, missing the necessary refinement in the big melodies. The accompaniment of Temirkanov and the RPO is warmly sympathetic though, thanks to the recording, the orchestra is not well defined.

Violin concerto No. 2 in G min., Op. 63.
*** BMG/RCA RD 87019 [RCD1 7019]. Heifetz, Boston SO, Munch – GLAZUNOV; SIBELIUS: *Concertos.* ***
☞ ** BMG/RCA Dig. 09026 60759-2 Takezawa, Moscow RSO, Fedoseyev – TCHAIKOVSKY: *Violin concerto.* **

In the *arioso*-like slow movement, Heifetz chooses a faster speed than is usual, but there is nothing unresponsive about his playing, for his expressive rubato has an unfailing inevitability. In the spiky finale he is superb, and indeed his playing is glorious throughout. The recording is serviceable merely, though it has been made firmer in the current remastering. But no one is going to be prevented from enjoying this ethereal performance because the technical quality is dated.

Kyoko Takezawa is one of the brightest of the young Japanese instrumentalists now before the public. She belongs to the select band of star violinists who began life as child prodigies before studying with Dorothy DeLay at the Juilliard School. This performance of the *G minor Concerto* was recorded at the Alte Oper in Frankfurt while the Moscow Radio Orchestra was on tour in 1990. It is a very good account without being special enough to displace the top recommendations. There is no doubting Takezawa's accomplishment or beauty of tone and, though Vladimir Fedoseyev is not always the most imaginative of accompanists, there are still many details of colour and phrasing to admire from the Moscow orchestra. Not all the tempo changes in the first movement convince, and the movement does not hold together or have as strong a sense of line as some rivals; the second movement could have greater lightness of touch and the finale could afford to be slightly more sardonic and more strongly characterized. Takezawa is rather (but not too) forwardly balanced, and the recording quality is generally very good. The performance is also available on video, carrying the suffix -3.

Divertimento, Op. 43; The Prodigal Son, Op. 46; Symphonic song, Op. 57; Andante (Piano Sonata No. 4).
*** Chan. Dig. CHAN 8728; *ABTD 1368* [id.]. SNO, Järvi.

The *Divertimento* is a lovely piece: its first movement has an irresistible and haunting second theme. Its long neglect is puzzling since it is highly attractive and ought to be popular. So, for that matter, should *The Prodigal Son*, some of whose material Prokofiev re-used the following year in the *Fourth Symphony*. Another rarity is the *Symphonic song*, a strange, darkly scored piece. The recording is first class – as, indeed, are the performances. An indispensable item in any Prokofiev collection.

The Gambler: 4 Portraits, Op. 49; Semyon Kotko: Symphonic suite, Op. 81 bis.
*** Chan. Dig. CHAN 8803; *ABTD 1431* [id.]. SNO, Järvi.

Prokofiev's *Four Portraits* enshrine the best of the opera and are exhilarating and inventive. *Semyon Kotko*, though not top-drawer Prokofiev, is still thoroughly enjoyable. Järvi gives a thoroughly sympathetic reading in vivid and present sound.

Lieutenant Kijé (incidental music): *suite, Op. 60.*
☞ (M) *** EMI Dig. CD-EMX 2214; *TC-EMX 2214*. LPO, Takuo Yuasa – RIMSKY-KORSAKOV: *Scheherazade.* ***

There are many fine accounts of Prokofiev's *Lieutenant Kijé* currently available, but this ranks among the best, the performance beguiling in its affectionate geniality and sense of nostalgia, yet with the *Troika* strongly rhythmic but without heaviness. The full, warm recording helps in this impression, slightly softer in focus than in the vivid coupling.

(i) *Lieutenant Kijé* (suite); *Love for three oranges:* suite; (ii) *Peter and the wolf;* (iii) *Romeo and Juliet* (ballet): excerpts; (iv) *Scythian suite, Op. 20;* (i) *Symphony No. 1 (Classical).*
☞ (B) ** Ph. Duo 442 278-2 (2) [id.]. (i) LSO, Marriner; (ii) Alec McCowen, Concg. O, Haitink; (iii) Rotterdam PO, Edo de Waart; (iv) LAPO, Previn.

An enjoyable and inexpensive 'basic library' Prokofiev collection, but better versions of all this music are available. Marriner's LSO accounts of the *Lieutenant Kijé* and *Love for three oranges suites* and the *Classical Symphony* are all lively, well played and naturally recorded; but one only has to compare the symphony with his earlier, Decca/Argo version (currently withdrawn) to discover an extra dimension in that performance. In *Peter and the wolf* Alec McCowen uses a new text by Erik Smith which is intelligently prepared to give a fresh look at the story. However, the addition of bird imitations, including the duck quacking 'Let me out!' inside the wolf's stomach at the end, is rather twee and seems designed to appeal to the youngest of listeners. McCowen is recorded closely in a different acoustic from the orchestra, and as the story reaches its climax the vocal reproduction almost becomes strident. Yet taken as a whole the presentation is vivid, and undoubtedly children will enjoy its liveliness. Perhaps the finest performance comes from the Rotterdam Philharmonic, who play (and very well too) 11 well-chosen numbers from Prokofiev's great Shakespearean ballet score. The recording is full and atmospheric. But the most vivid sound of all comes in Previn's *Scythian suite*, which approaches the demonstration bracket. However, the performance does not quite match this degree of drama: for some reason Previn was not on his best form on this occasion.

The Love for 3 oranges: suite.
☞ (B) ** Sony SBK 53621 [id.]. Phd. O, Ormandy – SHOSTAKOVICH: *Symphony No. 5* etc. **(*)

(i) *Love for three oranges* (suite), *Op. 33a; Scythian suite, Op. 20;* (ii) *Symphony No. 5, Op. 100.*
(M) **(*) Mercury 432 753-2 [id.]. (i) LSO; (ii) Minneapolis SO, Antal Dorati.

Dorati's account of Prokofiev's powerful and atmospheric *Scythian suite* was recorded at Watford Town Hall in 1957; the remastering confirms the excellence of the original engineering. The suite from the *Love for three oranges* is similarly striking in its characterization and vivid primary colours, with the resonance not blunting the rhythms. The CD is worth considering for these two performances; but the *Fifth Symphony*, recorded in Minneapolis two years later, is less successful. Dorati's reading is similarly forceful but the effect is hard and often unsympathetic.

Superb orchestral playing of course, but Ormandy's view of the score is larger than life, spectacle seemingly more important than subtlety, which the close recording tends to emphasize. The excitement is undeniable, but the famous *March* seems rather inflated and heavy.

On the Dnieper (ballet), *Op. 51; Le pas d'acier* (ballet), *Op. 41.*
*** Olympia Dig. OCD 103 [id.]. USSR MoC SO, Rozhdestvensky.

Le pas d'acier is full of vitality and – apart from one or two numbers – highly attractive, very much in the *ballet mécanique* style; *On the Dnieper* is a lyrical work not dissimilar to *The Prodigal Son.* Colourful performances and recordings. Lovers of Prokofiev's ballets should not miss this welcome addition to the discography.

Peter and the wolf, Op. 67 (see also above, under Cinderella).
⊛ (M) *** Virgin/EMI Dig. CU5 61137-2 [id.]. Gielgud, Ac. of L., Richard Stamp – SAINT-SAENS: *Carnival.* ***
(BB) *** ASV CDQS 6017. Angela Rippon, RPO, Hughes – SAINT-SAENS: *Carnival.* ***
(M) **(*) EMI Dig. CD-EMX 2165; *TC-EMX 2165.* William Rushton, LPO, Sian Edwards – BRITTEN: *Young person's guide* ***; RAVEL: *Ma Mère l'Oye.* **
☞ **(*) EMI Dig. CDC7 54730-2 [id.]. Phillip Schofield, Toulouse Capitole O, Plasson (with BRITTEN: *Young person's guide to the orchestra* **(*)) – SAINT-SAENS: *Carnival of the animals.* **

(i) *Peter and the wolf;* (ii) *Violin concerto No. 1 in D. Symphony No. 1 in D (Classical).*
☞ **(*) Nimbus NI 5192 [id.]. (i) Christopher Lee; (ii) Hu Kun; E. String O, Sir Yehudi Menuhin.

(i; ii) *Peter and the wolf;* (iii) *Lieutenant Kijé: suite;* (iv) *Love for 3 oranges: suite;* (ii) *Symphony No. 1 in D (Classical).*
⊛ (B) *** Decca 433 612-2 [id.]. (i) Sir Ralph Richardson, (ii) LSO, Sargent; (iii) Paris Conservatoire O, Boult; (iv) LPO, Weller.

Sir John Gielgud's highly individual presentation of Prokofiev's masterly narrative with orchestra brings a worthy successor to our previous favourite version, by Sir Ralph Richardson for Decca; moreover Richard Stamp and the Academy of London have the advantage of a superb, modern, digital recording, warmly atmospheric but with a strikingly wide dynamic range. At the end, Sir John, who has presided over these events with a wonderfully benign involvement, becomes Grandfather himself with his restrained moral questioning of Peter's youthful bravado. Throughout, his obvious relish for the colour as well as the narrative flow of the text has been splendidly matched by the detail and impetus of Richard Stamp's accompaniment.

Sir Ralph Richardson brings a great actor's feeling for words to the narrative; he dwells lovingly on their sound as well as their meaning, and this genial preoccupation with the manner in which the story is told matches Sargent's feeling exactly. Sir Malcolm Sargent's direction of the accompaniment shows his professionalism at its very best. The original coupling, Sargent's amiable, polished account of the *Classical Symphony*, has now been restored. All the tempi, except the finale, are slow but Sir Malcolm's assured elegance carries its own spontaneity. The sound is vivid. Boult's Paris recording of *Lieutenant Kijé* offers more gusto than finesse, but the result is exhilaratingly robust and the very early (1955) stereo comes up remarkably well. Weller's *Love for three oranges* is a first-class performance, given top-drawer 1977 recording. But our Rosette is for *Peter and the wolf.*

Angela Rippon narrates with charm yet is never in the least coy; indeed she is thoroughly involved in the tale and thus also involves the listener. The accompaniment is equally spirited, with excellent orchestral playing, and the recording is splendidly clear, yet not lacking atmosphere. This makes an excellent super-bargain recommendation.

Christopher Lee must certainly be included among the more memorable narrators of Prokofiev's epic fairy tale. It is a very relaxed performance, with Menuhin and his orchestra following the narrative rather lazily, but Lee's resonant, richly coloured voice keeps the action going agreeably. With the resonant recording making everything sound somewhat larger than life, it is good that the slinky cat is well contrasted (by both narrator and clarinettist) with the sinisterly characterized villain of the piece. Even so, the wolf marches in to the sounds of boldly expansive horns, while the hunters make their entrance very explosively indeed. The whimsical pace of the narrative does not preclude excitement and, after the capture, Grandfather's dusty comment is illustrated by some appropriate grumbling from the bassoon. The final procession is grandly expansive, surely the slowest on record, but then Lee delivers the final twist in the story, about the duck's survival, rather neatly. The supporting programme is unimaginatively chosen. Menuhin's account of the *Classical Symphony* is again very relaxed until the sparkling finale (the *Gavotte* is heavy as well as slow) and Hu Kun's account of the *Violin concerto* – its lyrical warmth underlined by the flattering sound – is enjoyable rather than distinctive.

Although narrative and orchestral commentary were recorded separately on the Eminence recording, it is remarkable how well the two fit together. William Rushton was able to add his story-telling to a vividly colourful orchestral tapestry which had its momentum already established. He is a personable narrator, adding touches of his own like a 'vast' grey wolf and 'nothing to report' from the bird; and this remains a direct, sparkling presentation, brightly and realistically recorded, which cannot fail to entertain children of all ages.

Phillip Schofield's narration is bright and determinedly up front. He makes his introductions freshly (though the oboe's response is a little mannered) and enters into the story with enthusiastic, youthful aplomb. His pacing is a bit erratic, quickening at moments of excitement, and the effect will surely appeal to younger TV addicts. While the closing processional is less ambitious than with Menuhin, the oboe is ethereal in resurrecting the duck – almost as if he were a ghost. The orchestral accompaniment is stylish and brightly recorded; there is the unique advantage here that half a dozen internal cues are provided for youngsters who want to repeat part of the story. The couplings are both old analogue recordings. Sir Charles Groves's performance of Britten's *Variations and fugue on a theme of Purcell* (from 1977) is lively and genial; if it lacks the last degree of finesse, it has both high spirits and a fine sense of pace. The trumpet variation displays splendid bravura and the flute and clarinet variations, too, are engagingly extrovert. The analogue recording is first class, colourful and vivid, and younger listeners should certainly respond to it. (There is no narrative.)

Sneaky Pete and the wolf (new text by Peter Schickele).
☞ Telarc Dig. CD 80350 [id.]. Peter Schickele, Atlanta SO, Yoel Levi – SAINT-SAENS: *Carnival of the animals.* *

Peter Schickele's extraordinarily crass and tasteless rewriting replaces the charming original with a vulgar and – worse – incredibly boring Country-and-Western narrative. The principal characters are singularly unattractive humans, and the nearest the story comes to a wolf is to call the villain El Lobo. As Morecambe and Wise would undoubtedly have commented: Rubbish!
This record is our 'turkey' of all time!

Romeo and Juliet (ballet), *Op. 64* (complete).
*** Decca 417 510-2 (2) [id.]. Cleveland O, Maazel.
*** DG 423 268-2 (2) [id.]. Boston SO, Ozawa.

Maazel will please those who believe that this score should above all be bitingly incisive. The rhythms are more consciously metrical, the tempi generally faster, and the precision of ensemble of the Cleveland Orchestra is little short of miraculous. The recording is one of Decca's most spectacular, searingly detailed but atmospheric too.

Immediately at the opening, one notices Ozawa's special balletic feeling in the elegance of the string phrasing and the light, rhythmic felicity. Yet he can rise to the work's drama and in the love-music his ardour is compulsive, even if the element of pungency which Maazel brings to the score is almost entirely missing in Boston. But this music-making is very easy to enjoy and the actual playing is very fine indeed, while Ozawa has the advantage of outstanding modern digital recording, full of atmosphere.

Romeo and Juliet (ballet): extended excerpts.
☞ **(*) BMG/RCA Dig. 09026 61388-2 [id.]. Philh. O, Flor.

The new BMG/RCA selection (made from all three ballet suites) is intensely felt and the Philharmonia playing is of the highest calibre, exquisite in *Romeo and Juliet before parting* and the delightful *Aubade*. Claus Peter Flor is much more involved than Dutoit (on Decca 430 279-2) who offers beautiful playing, demonstration recording-quality and 75 minutes of music, but an altogether lower level of tension. Flor is often warmly attentive to lyrical detail, while the dramatic moments are histrionically arresting. But mostly it is the beauty of the orchestral playing one remembers and the full, expansive sound, deriving from EMI's No. 1 Studio at Abbey Road. This is very rewarding; however, what finally makes the disc uncompetitive is the measure: only 58 minutes.

Romeo and Juliet (ballet), *Op. 64:* highlights.
*** Sony Dig. MK 42662 [id.]. BPO, Salonen.
☞ *** Virgin/EMI Dig. VC7 59278-2 [id.]. RLPO, Libor Pešek.

With magnificent playing from the Berlin Philharmonic Orchestra, Esa-Pekka Salonen's set seems marginally a first choice for those wanting merely a full-priced single disc of excerpts from Prokofiev's masterly score. The Berlin Philharmonic playing has an enormous intensity and a refined felicity in the score's more delicate moments. One is touched and deeply moved by this music-making, while the selection admirably parallels the work's narrative. The recording, made in the Philharmonie, matches sumptuousness with a potent clarity of projection, and the dynamic range is dramatically wide.

Like Salonen, Pešek's selection follows the narrative line, and one feels that the conductor and his players are highly involved in the course of events. At first there is much delicacy (*Juliet the little girl* is the title for band four, and that is exactly the charming picture we are given here) but as the story proceeds the tragic feeling builds up, while the delights of Prokofiev's marvellous orchestration are always warmly detailed. There are bursts of sheer energy (*The people continue to make merry* – band 13) and in the closing numbers Pešek tightens the screws so that the *Death of Juliet* is devastating. The Royal Liverpool Philharmonic Orchestra play very well indeed and achieve great freshness and spontaneity; they are given a satisfying concert-hall balance. This Virgin CD offers 71 minutes from Prokofiev's inspired score, and every minute is stimulating and enjoyable; but it has to be said that the Berlin Philharmonic playing for Salonen is quite superb and the Sony recording is even more lavish. The Virgin issue must win a prize, however, for the most uninviting cover-design we have ever encountered!

Romeo and Juliet (ballet): suites Nos. 1–3.
☞ ** Erato/Warner Dig. 2292 45817-2 [id.]. SRO, Jordan.

A generous selection from Erato (76 minutes), but there are better recommendations for this much-recorded repertoire. The SRO orchestral playing is lively, dramatic and sympathetic, but lacks the very last degree of finesse if not of pungency, and at times the woodwind playing lacks individuality of character. The sound is good, but the Decca recording is in the demonstration bracket.

Romeo and Juliet (ballet): suites Nos. 1 & 2, *Op. 64.*
(M) *** Mercury 432 004-2 [id.]. Minneapolis SO, Skrowaczewski – MUSSORGSKY: *Night.* ***

Skrowaczewski's recording of the two ballet suites was made in 1962. The playing of the Minneapolis orchestra is on a virtuoso level. The crystal-clear acoustic of the hall in Edison High School, with its backing ambience, seems ideally suited to the angular melodic lines and pungent lyricism of this powerful score, to underline the sense of tragedy without losing the music's romantic sweep. The fidelity and spectacle of the Mercury engineering reach a zenith in the powerful closing sequence of *Romeo at Juliet's tomb*. At mid-price this is highly recommendable.

Romeo and Juliet: suites Nos. 1 and 2: excerpts.
*** Telarc Dig. CD 80089 [id.]. Cleveland O, Yoel Levi.
☞ (M) **(*) Sony SBK 48169 [id.]. NYPO, Mitropoulos – STRAVINSKY: *Rite of spring.* *

Levi seems to have a special affinity with Prokofiev's score, for pacing is unerringly apt and characterization is strong. There are some wonderfully serene moments, as in the ethereal introduction of the flute melody in the first piece (*Montagues and Capulets*). The quicker movements have an engaging feeling of the dance and the light, graceful articulation in *The child Juliet* is a delight; but the highlights of the performance are the *Romeo and Juliet love scene* and *Romeo at Juliet's before parting*, bringing playing of great intensity, with a ravishing response from the Cleveland strings. The rich Telarc recording is in the demonstration class, but this offers less music than several of its competitors.

Under Mitropoulos, the New York Philharmonic played with tremendous conviction and dramatic flair. His *Romeo*, though not in every respect representative of the great conductor, should be investigated by all who admire this score. It is handicapped by its coupling, a very ordinary *Rite* under Mehta.

Romeo and Juliet (ballet): suite.
(M) *** Decca 417 737-2 [id.]. Cleveland O, Maazel – KHACHATURIAN: *Gayaneh; Spartacus.* **(*)

An intelligently chosen selection of six pieces (including *Juliet as a young girl*, the *Balcony scene* and *The last farewell*) makes a generous coupling for Decca's Khachaturian ballet scores.

Russian overture, Op. 72; Summer night: suite from *The Duenna, Op. 123; War and Peace* (suite, arr. Christopher Palmer).
☞ *** Chan. Dig. CHAN 9096 [id.]. Philh. O, Järvi.

The *Russian overture* – more like a symphonic poem – dates from 1936, soon after Prokofiev had returned to the Soviet Union. It is determinedly popular in appeal and is perhaps not one of his very best pieces, but it teems with ideas, both lyrical and grotesque, and has plenty of vitality. It is played here in a slightly reduced scoring which the composer made a year later. *The Duenna* (an opera after the play by Sheridan) was the source for the *Summer night suite* and it is notable for its delicate *Serenade* and a charmingly romantic movement called *Dreams*. But the finest music here is Christopher Palmer's suite of interludes from *War and Peace*, full of splendid ideas. From the peacetime *Ball* (ironic yet joyful echoes of Tchaikovsky's *Eugene Onegin*) we move to the ferocious *Snowstorm* and *Battle* music of the French retreat from Moscow. In between comes a lovely intermezzo (*May night*) depicting a moonlit evening on the Rostov country estate. The suite ends triumphantly with the magnificent patriotic tune associated with Marshal Kutuzov, the architect of the Russian victory. Järvi and the Philharmonia Orchestra are thoroughly at home in these scores, and the Chandos recording is characteristically spectacular. This is well worth exploring.

Sinfonia concertante in E min., Op. 125 (see also above, under Concertos).
☞ ** Sony Dig. SK 48382 [id.]. Yo-Yo Ma, Pittsburgh SO, Maazel – TCHAIKOVSKY: *Andante cantabile* etc. **

Yo-Yo Ma favours reticence and understatement in Prokofiev's late masterpiece, and his withdrawn tone at times comes close to affectation. As always with this artist, there are innumerable felicities, but Lorin Maazel's accompaniment is curiously leaden and prosaic. The recording rather favours the orchestra too. This work is well served by the catalogue, not least by its 'onlie begetter', Rostropovich, and this newcomer does not displace existing recommendations.

Sinfonietta in A, Op. 48; Symphony No. 1 in D (Classical), Op. 25.
(BB) *** Virgin/EMI Dig. VC5 61104-2. Lausanne CO, Zedda – DEBUSSY: *Danse* etc.; MILHAUD: *Création du monde.* ***

Prokofiev could not understand why the early *Sinfonietta* failed to make an impression on the wider musical public, and neither can we. Alongside the *Classical Symphony* the *giocoso* outer movements have a more fragile geniality but they are highly delectable, as are the somewhat angular *Andante*, the brief *Intermezzo* and the witty *Scherzo*. The use of the orchestral palette is as subtle as it is engaging and, with Alberto Zedda's affectionately light touch and fine Lausanne playing, the piece emerges here with all colours flying. The account of the *Classical Symphony* is also highly persuasive, the violins exquisitely gentle at their poised entry in the *Larghetto* and the outer movements spirited, with the finale mercurial in its zestful progress. The fairly resonant sound, with the orchestra slightly recessed, adds to the feeling of warmth without blunting the orchestral articulation. A first-class bargain.

SYMPHONIES

Symphonies Nos. 1–7.
*** Chan. Dig. CHAN 8931/4 [id.]. SNO, Järvi.

Symphonies Nos. 1–7; Overture russe, Op. 72; Scythian suite, Op. 20.
(B) **(*) Decca 430 782-2 (4). LSO or LPO, Walter Weller.

These Chandos recordings from the mid-1980s are of the highest quality. They have been shorn of their couplings in this box, the only important loss being the delightful *Sinfonietta*. Both versions of the *Fourth Symphony* are included: the 1947 revision appears with the *Classical* on the first disc, while the 1930 original is coupled with the *Third*. Nos. 2 and 6 are on the third disc, and 5 and 7 on the last, so that no side-breaks are involved. As performances, these are the equal of the best.

Weller began his 1970s Kingsway Hall recordings with the LSO (Nos. 1, 5 and 7) then turned to the LPO. The performances are polished and very well played, though at times they are emotionally a little earthbound. Transfers are well managed, though there is some loss of naturalness in the upper range. The finest of the set is No. 2. Elsewhere, the bitter tang of Prokofiev's language is again toned down and the hard-etched lines smoothed over. The *Seventh* suits Weller's approach readily and he catches the atmosphere of its somewhat balletic second movement particularly well. The *Russian overture* has plenty of energy but the *Scythian suite*, too, needs more abrasiveness. However, those who normally find Prokofiev's orchestral writing too pungent could well be won over by these performances.

Symphony No. 1 in D (Classical), Op. 25.
*** DG Dig. 423 624-2 [id.]. Orpheus CO – BIZET: *Symphony;* BRITTEN: *Simple symphony.* ***

The Orpheus performance has freshness and wit – the droll bassoon solo in the first movement against sparkling string figurations is delightful. In the cantilena of the *Larghetto*, some ears might crave a greater body of violin tone; but the playing has a fine poise, and the minuet and finale have equal flair. Excellent, truthful recording to make this a highly desirable triptych.

Symphonies Nos. 1 in D (Classical), Op. 25; 3 in C min., Op. 44.
☞ *** Ph. Dig. 432 992-2 [id.]. Phd. O, Muti.

Riccardo Muti's account of the *Third Symphony* is the most atmospheric to have appeared for a very long time. It is certainly the most strongly characterized and atmospheric of recent performances, and it has the edge on Walter Weller (Decca) or Neeme Järvi (Chandos) in this respect. Indeed this is the most thrilling account since Abbado's Decca LP, also coupled with the *Classical Symphony* and unaccountably never reissued on CD. It casts a strong spell and is superbly recorded with rich, present and well-detailed sonority – real state-of-the-art sound. The Philadelphia Orchestra may not sound as special as they did in the days of Ormandy or Stokowski, but they remain a first-class ensemble. The *Classical Symphony* is one of the best around – and even offers the occasional reminder of Koussevitzky's pioneering recording from the 1930s – there is no higher praise!

Symphonies Nos. 1 in D (Classical); 4 in C, Op. 112 (revised 1947 version).
*** Chan. Dig. CHAN 8400; *ABTD 1137* [id.]. SNO, Järvi.

Järvi succeeds in making out a more eloquent case for the revision of the *Fourth Symphony* than many of his predecessors. He also gives an exhilarating account of the *Classical Symphony*, one of the best on record. The slow movement has real douceur and the finale is wonderfully high-spirited. On CD, the recording has fine range and immediacy, but in the *Fourth Symphony* the upper range is a little fierce in some of the more forceful climaxes.

Symphonies Nos. 1 in D (Classical), Op. 25; 5 in B flat, Op. 100.
☞ (M) *** DG 437 253-2 [id.]. BPO, Karajan.
*** Decca Dig. 421 813-2 [id.]. Montreal SO, Dutoit.
☞ *** Sony Dig. SK 48239 [id.]. LSO, Tilson Thomas.
☞ (M) *** BMG/RCA Dig. 09026 61350-2 [id.]. LPO, Slatkin.
☞ (M) **(*) Sony SBK 53260 [id.]. Phd. O, Ormandy.
☞ (M) *(**) Sony SMK 47602 [id.]. NYPO, Bernstein.

Karajan's 1979 recording of the *Fifth* is in a class of its own. The playing has wonderful tonal sophistication and Karajan judges tempi to perfection so that proportions seem quite ideal. The Berlin Philharmonic are at the height of their form; in their hands the Scherzo is a *tour de force*. The recording has an excellent perspective and allows all the subtleties of orchestral detail to register; however, the digital remastering has overtly brightened the upper range, while the bass response is drier. Nevertheless this remains among the most distinguished *Fifths* ever recorded, and it is coupled with Karajan's 1982 digital recording of the *Classical Symphony*, in which his performance is predictably brilliant and the playing beautifully polished, with grace and eloquence distinguishing the slow movement. The outer movements are wanting in charm alongside Marriner, but his outstanding Decca/Argo version is currently withdrawn. The recording is clearly detailed, though the balance is not quite natural: the upper strings are very brightly lit, with a touch of digital edge, but the ambience is attractive.

Though at a relatively expansive speed, the lyricism of the *Fifth* is given full expressive rein by Dutoit who, with his rhythmic sharpness, balances that against the right degree of spikiness, very necessary in Prokofiev. The finale, superbly articulated, is fresh and animated, making much of the rough, pawky humour. In the *Classical Symphony* too, Dutoit points the humour infectiously, helped by beautifully sprung rhythms and crisp ensemble. The sound is warm and atmospheric, as well as brilliant.

Tilson Thomas gives a very well-thought-out reading of the *Fifth* and enjoys the benefit of first-class Sony recording. There is a sense of scale and strong character here, though the tenderness that surfaces from time to time in the slow movement eludes him and there could be a more carefree virtuosity in the finale. But these are quibbles and there is no reason not to give this three stars. It is a very lively and intelligent performance, and the recording has much going for it. All the same it does not offer any real challenge to the Dutoit and Karajan, which remain first recommendations.

Ultimately the same holds for Slatkin's St Louis performance on RCA at mid-price. It is eminently well shaped, spacious and characterful, and there is no want of virtuosity or lyricism. Thoroughly recommendable, without being a first choice.

The Philadelphia Orchestra play superbly and with much wit (note the pointed violins in the second subject of the first movement) in the *Classical Symphony*, though there is a touch of treble harshness on the otherwise spacious (1961) sound. Ormandy's expansive warmth in the *Adagio* and the easy brilliance of the orchestral articulation in the second and fourth movements make for splendid results in the *Fifth*. With naturally expressive phrasing, the underlying emotion is brought out beautifully and most convincingly, with the jocularity of the *giocoso* finale joyously spirited. Although the early stereo recording could be more opulent and less brightly lit, it still conveys impressively the ample body of tone this great orchestra was creating in the late 1950s.

In the first two movements, Bernstein's homage to the *Classical Symphony*'s eighteenth-century ancestry produces a slightly self-conscious stiffness of manner, but even so the bassoonist manages a gentle smile in his solo and the poise of the strings in the slow movement's upper cantilena is superb. The finale is exhilarating, yet played with admirable precision. In No. 5 he draws more exciting and at times affectionate playing from the NYPO but, setting a leisurely tempo for the first movement, he indulges in numerous agogic distortions before the symphony has got very far underway. Most successful is the Scherzo which has all the requisite drive and astringency. Apart from a tendency to dwell lovingly on phrases as they approach a cadential resolution (as in the coda of the slow movement), there are many things to admire in this reading. Bernstein certainly has an ear for the kind of sonority that Prokofiev wanted, and the atmosphere is often well captured (the second subject of the first movement is presented very effectively). Yet, for all its excitement and undoubted commitment, this performance may be found too idiosyncratic for repeated listening, although there are no complaints about the vividness of the recording, made in the Avery Fisher Hall in the mid-1960s.

Symphonies Nos. 1 in D, (Classical) Op. 25; 6 in E flat min., Op. 111.
☞ * DG Dig. 435 026-2. BPO, Seiji Ozawa.

The *Classical Symphony* fares better than the *Sixth*, but neither is in the top flight as an interpretation. Anyone expecting the Berlin Philharmonic to sound as it did under Karajan will be grievously disappointed. Indeed, by their standards this is pretty routine, though they are not helped by the airless and congested recording. Detail is very clear and focused, but the balance sounds a bit synthetic. Ozawa's tempi are very measured and his reading never has the sense of purpose and movement that distinguishes Mravinsky and Järvi.

Symphonies Nos. 1 (Classical); 7, Op. 131; Love for 3 oranges (opera): suite.
(B) *** CfP CD-CFP 4523. Philh. O, Malko.

All the performances here are quite excellent, and the *Seventh Symphony*, of which Malko conducted the UK première, is freshly conceived and finely shaped. What is so striking is the range and refinement of the 1955 stereo recording: the excellence of the balance and the body of the sound are remarkable.

Symphony No. 2 in D min., Op. 40; Romeo and Juliet (ballet): suite No. 1, Op. 64.
**(*) Chan. Dig. CHAN 8368; ABTD 1134 [id.]. SNO, Järvi.

The *Second Symphony* reflects the iconoclastic temper of the early 1920s; the violence and dissonance of its first movement betray Prokofiev's avowed intention of writing a work 'made of iron and steel'. Neeme Järvi produces altogether excellent results from the Scottish National Orchestra and the Chandos recording is impressively detailed and vivid. The *Romeo and Juliet* suite comes off well; the SNO play with real character.

Symphonies Nos. 3 in C min., Op. 44; 4 in C, Op. 47 (original, 1930 version).
*** Chan. Dig. CHAN 8401; ABTD 1138 [id.]. SNO, Järvi.

Neeme Järvi's account of the *Third* is extremely successful. In many ways the original of the *Fourth Symphony* seems more like a ballet suite than a symphony: its insufficient tonal contrast tells – yet the Scherzo, drawn from the music for the Temptress in *The Prodigal Son* ballet, is particularly felicitous.

Symphony No. 5 in B flat, Op. 100.
*** Chan. Dig. CHAN 8576 [id.]. Leningrad PO, Jansons.
☞ (*) Russian Disc RD CD11 165 Leningrad PO, Yevgeni Mravinsky – GLAZUNOV: *Symphony No. 5.* *

Symphony No. 5 in B flat, Op. 100; Waltz suite, Op. 110.
*** Chan. Dig. CHAN 8450; *ABTD 1160* [id.]. SNO, Järvi.

Mariss Jansons's reading with the Leningrad Philharmonic was recorded at a live concert in Dublin. Needless to say, the playing is pretty high voltage, with firm, rich string-tone, particularly from the lower strings, and distinctive wind timbre. Jansons goes for brisk tempi – and in the slow movement he really is too fast. The Scherzo is dazzling and so, too, is the finale, which is again fast and overdriven. An exhilarating and exciting performance, eminently well recorded, recommended to those willing to accept the ungenerous measure.

Järvi's credentials in this repertoire are well established and his direction unhurried, fluent and authoritative. His feeling for the music is unfailingly natural. The three *Waltzes* which derive from various sources are all elegantly played. The Chandos recording is set just a shade further back than some of its companions in the series, yet at the same time every detail is clear.

Mravinsky's performance was recorded at a concert given in 1968 and is really not recommendable. Artistically, there is much to interest students of this conductor, but the recording is pretty rough and strains tolerance; the sound is unpleasant, with shrill strings and raucous climaxes. It is sonically inferior to other recordings of the period such as the Honegger *Liturgique*, Hindemith's *Die Harmonie der Welt* or the Sibelius *Seventh*.

Symphonies Nos. 5 in B flat, Op. 100; 7 in C sharp min., Op. 131.
☞ (M) *** EMI CDM5 65181-2 [id.]. LSO, Previn.

In No. 5 Previn takes a weighty view of a wide-spanning symphony. His first-movement tempo is spacious, and the contrasts are strongly underlined, with Prokofiev's characteristic use of heavy brass, notably the tuba, superbly brought out by the LSO players, not to mention the EMI engineers. The slow movement too is firmly placed in the grand tradition of Russian symphonies. The Scherzo and later the finale have fractionally less brilliance than one expects from this source but, with full recording, the effect is still formidably powerful. In the *Seventh*, too, Previn produces much inner vitality and warmth, and again the EMI engineers provide a realistic and integrated sound.

Symphony No. 6 in E flat min., Op. 111. Waltz suite, Op. 110, Nos. 1, 5 and 6.
*** Chan. Dig. CHAN 8359; *ABTD 1122* [id.]. SNO, Järvi.

Though it lags far behind the *Fifth* in popularity, the *Sixth Symphony* goes much deeper than any of its companions; indeed it is perhaps the greatest of the Prokofiev cycle. Neeme Järvi has an instinctive grasp and deep understanding of this symphony; he shapes its detail as skilfully as he does its architecture as a whole. These artists have the measure of the music's tragic poignancy more than almost any of their predecessors on record. The fill-up, as its title implies, is a set of waltzes, drawn and adapted from various stage works.

Symphony No. 7 in C sharp min., Op. 131; Sinfonietta in A, Op. 5/48.
*** Chan. Dig. CHAN 8442; *ABTD 1154* [id.]. SNO, Järvi.

Neeme Järvi's account of the *Seventh Symphony* is hardly less successful than the other issues in this cycle. He gets very good playing from the SNO and has the full measure of this repertoire. The early *Sinfonietta* is a highly attractive coupling (what a sunny and charming piece it is!). The digital recording has great range and is excellently balanced.

CHAMBER AND INSTRUMENTAL MUSIC

Cello sonata in C, Op. 119.
*** Chan. Dig. CHAN 8340 [id.]. Yuli Turovsky. Luba Edlina – SHOSTAKOVICH: *Sonata.* ***

Yuli Turovsky and Luba Edlina are eloquent advocates of this *Sonata*. A finely wrought and rewarding score, it deserves greater popularity, and this excellent performance and recording should make it new friends. The balance is particularly lifelike on CD.

String quartets Nos. 1 in B min., Op. 50; 2 in F, Op. 92.
*** Olympia Dig. OCD 340 [id.]. American Qt.

The American Quartet play the *First Quartet* far more persuasively than any earlier version and reveal it to be a work of some appeal as well as substance. The *Second* incorporates folk ideas from Kabarda in the Caucasus, to highly characteristic ends. Although the performance does not have quite the bite and zest of the unforgettable pioneering disc by the Hollywood Quartet, it does not fall far short of it, and the recording is absolutely first class. A rewarding issue.

Violin sonata (for solo violin), *Op. 115; Sonata for two violins.*
*** Chan. Dig. CHAN 8988; *ABTD 1570* [id.]. Mordkovitch, Young – SCHNITTKE: *Prelude;*
SHOSTAKOVICH: *Violin sonata.* ***

Sonata for 2 violins, Op. 56.
*** Hyp. Dig. CDA 66473 [id.]. Osostowicz, Kovacic – MARTINU: *Violin sonata;* MILHAUD: *Violin duo* etc. **(*)

The solo *Violin sonata in D*, Op. 115, is a crisply characteristic piece in three short movements. The *Sonata in C for two violins*, written much earlier, is just as effective, played – as here – by solo violins. The warmth of Lydia Mordkovitch is well matched by her partner, Emma Young.

The *Sonata for two violins* gives the impression of being vintage Prokofiev, as performed by Krysia Osostowicz and Ernst Kovacic. The slow movement is played with exceptional imagination and poetry.

(i) *Violin sonatas Nos. 1 in F min., Op. 80; 2 in D, Op. 94a;* (ii) *Violin concerto No. 2 in G min., Op. 63.*
☞ (M) *** BMG/RCA 09026 61454-2 [id.]. Itzhak Perlman; (i) Vladimir Ashkenazy; (ii) Boston SO, Leinsdorf.

Both of the *Violin sonatas* date from the years immediately after Prokofiev returned to the Soviet Union. The *F minor Sonata* is one of his very finest works, and the *D major*, originally written for the flute and sometimes heard in that form, has a winning charm and melodiousness. Both works are masterly and rewarding. Perlman and Ashkenazy play them superbly, and the 1969 recording is well balanced, slightly dry in timbre, but otherwise truthful.

The *Second Violin concerto* was recorded three years earlier and represented Perlman's début record with the Boston orchestra. An admirable performance revealing a high degree of accomplishment, it is enjoyably fresh and spontaneous even if it falls short of the standards set by Heifetz in this splendid concerto. Nevertheless it is well worth having as a bonus even if the Boston orchestra under Leinsdorf provide just an accomplished accompaniment rather than always contributing strongly in their own right. The exception is the finale, which comes off vividly, helped by the lively condiment of percussion; and elsewhere there is some very fine playing from both woodwind and strings. The forward balance of the soloist does not obscure too much detail, while the Symphony Hall ambience adds atmosphere and warmth.

Violin sonatas Nos. 1 in F min., Op. 80; 2 in D, Op. 94a; 5 Mélodies, Op. 35b.
☞ * DG Dig. 431 803-2 [id.]. Gidon Kremer, Martha Argerich.

Kremer and Argerich never penetrate far below the surface in either work. They are both formidable players and are concerned not to let the listener forget it. Subtle differences of dynamics or of characterization do not detain them more than cursorily, and Prokofiev's lyricism takes second place to considerations of virtuosic display. This is not a strong contender, despite decent recorded sound.

Violin sonata No. 2 in D.
** Ph. Dig. 426 254-2. Viktoria Mullova, Bruno Canino – RAVEL: *Sonata in G;* STRAVINSKY: *Divertimento.* ***

The *Second Sonata* is given a brilliant performance by Mullova and Canino, even if the lyrical charm and tenderness of the first movement elude them and the scherzo is rather rushed. This is musically not as impressive as the Stravinsky or the Ravel with which it is coupled. The recording is quite superb.

PIANO MUSIC

Choses en soi, Op. 45; Divertissement, Op. 43 bis; Sonata No. 9 in C, Op. 103; 4 Etudes, Op. 2.
☞ *** Chan. Dig. CHAN 9211 [id.]. Boris Berman.

The *Ninth Sonata* (1947) can often make a weak impression by comparison with its immediate predecessors, but such is not the case here. As is the case with earlier records in this series, Chandos provide lifelike quality of striking presence, and Berman plays with tremendous concentration and control. His finely articulated and vital rhythms are matched by a good command of keyboard colour; aided by the clean, well-balanced (though rather forward) recording, he presents this sonata in the most persuasive light. The *Choses en soi* ('Things in themselves') come from the period of the *Third Symphony*, though there is a momentary hint of *The Prodigal Son*. The *Divertissement* is a delightful piece in Prokofiev's most acerbic manner which derived from the ballet, *Trapeze* (1925), and its relative neglect no doubt prompted him to transcribe it for the keyboard in 1938, some time after his return to the then Soviet Union. Berman couples them with the brilliant Op. 2 *Etudes* of 1909 with which Prokofiev made his Moscow début. A very satisfying recital.

Piano sonatas 1–9 (complete); *Lieutenant Kijé* (suite, transcribed Chiu).
☞ **(*) HM Dig. HMU 907086/8 (3) [id.]. Frederic Chiu.

Frederic Chiu is a brilliant young Chinese-American pianist who has just turned thirty. His Wigmore Hall appearance in London in the autumn of 1993 received an ecstatic press and he has been winning golden opinions everywhere; listening to his account of the Prokofiev sonatas, one can see why. Not only is his technical address impressive but he has a keen musical intelligence and elegance. This is exciting playing and, though there may be a number of interpretative decisions which may not persuade all listeners, this is a set that should be heard. In the *Eighth Sonata* his opening is a little wayward (Ashkenazy, now restored to circulation on Decca, is the one to have here) and some may quarrel with certain things in the *Ninth*. His tempi can be a little extreme – in some ways his is a more strongly characterized performance than Berman's and there are greater extremes of dynamics and colours. The Scherzo is a bit too fast and he is certainly too fast in one of the movements of the *Lieutenant Kijé* music, his own arrangement of which is to be heard on the third disc, after the *Eighth* and *Ninth sonatas*. The *Seventh* is brilliant and can be ranked along with the best, and the *Sixth*, though not superior to either of the Kissin accounts (Sony and RCA), is pretty dazzling. Throughout the cycle he impresses with his marvellous fingers, abundant energy and good musical taste. Unfortunately the recording lets him down: the tone is shallow and the balance a bit too close. Otherwise this would have been a strong three-star recommendation.

Piano sonata No. 1 in F min., Op. 1; 4 Pieces, Op. 4; Prelude and Fugue in D min. (Buxtehude, arr. Prokofiev); *2 Sonatinas, Op. 54; Gavotte (Hamlet, Op. 77bis); 3 Pieces, Op. 96.*
*** Chan. Dig. CHAN 9017 [id.]. Boris Berman.

Boris Berman's survey of the complete Prokofiev piano music is proving the most satisfactory all-round set of the sonatas so far. This excellent CD brings some transcriptions. He does not play these with quite the same elegance and distinction that mark the *Sonatinas*, which are beautifully character-ized and splendidly recorded.

Piano sonatas Nos. 3 in A min., Op. 28; 7 in B flat, Cp. 83; 8 in B flat, Op. 84.
*** DG Dig. 435 439-2 [id.]. Andrei Gavrilov.

Gavrilov's account of the *Seventh Sonata* is exciting and exhilarating, and in this work totally devoid of any exaggeration. In the *Eighth* he is equally if not more successful, and can withstand the most exalted comparisons. He rushes his fences in the *Third*, though as virtuoso playing it is pretty dazzling. Moreover he is given impressive recorded sound.

Piano sonata No. 4, Op. 29; Music for children, Op. 65; 6 Pieces, Op. 52.
*** Chan. Dig. CHAN 8926; ABTD 1527 [id.]. Boris Berman.

The *Fourth Sonata*, like its predecessor, takes its inspiration from Prokofiev's earlier notebooks. The Op. 52 *Pieces* are transcriptions of movements from other works: the ballet *The Prodigal Son*, the *Andante* from the *First Quartet*, the Scherzo from the *Sinfonietta* and one of the *Songs without words*, Op. 35. Berman plays them incisively, with marvellous articulation and wit.

Piano sonata No. 5 in C, Op. 38/135; 4 Pieces, Op. 32; Love for three oranges: Scherzo and March; Romeo and Juliet: 10 Pieces, Op. 75.
*** Chan. Dig. CHAN 8851; ABTD 1468 [id.]. Boris Berman.

Boris Berman plays the post-war revision of the *Fifth Sonata*, and its crisp, brittle inner movement is heard to splendid advantage. The other works are presented with equal perception. State-of-the-art recording from Chandos, made at The Maltings, Snape.

Piano sonata No. 6 in A, Op. 82.
⊛ *** DG Dig. 413 363-2 [id.]. Pogorelich – RAVEL: *Gaspard de la nuit.* ***

Pogorelich's performance of the *Sixth Sonata* is quite simply dazzling; indeed, it is by far the best version of it ever put on record. It is certainly Pogorelich's most brilliant record so far and can be recommended with the utmost enthusiasm in its CD format.

Piano sonata No. 7 in B flat, Op. 83.
*** DG 419 202-2 [id.]. Maurizio Pollini – *Recital.* ***

This is a great performance, well in the Horowitz or Richter category. It is part of a generous CD of twentieth-century music.

Piano sonata No. 7; Sarcasms, Op. 17; Tales of an old grandmother, Op. 31; Visions fugitives, Op. 22.
*** Chan. CHAN 8881; *ABTD 1494* [id.]. Boris Berman.

Berman is completely inside the astringent idiom and subtle character of these pieces, and his playing in the *Sarcasms* could scarcely be bettered. He gives altogether outstanding performances of all four works, and the superbly vivid recording greatly enhances the sheer musical satisfaction this disc gives.

Piano sonata No. 7; Toccata in C, Op. 11.
☞ (M) (***) BMG/RCA mono GD 60377 [id.]. Vladimir Horowitz – BARBER; KABALEVSKY: *Sonatas* etc. (***)

Horowitz's account of the *Seventh Sonata* is justly legendary. When he had recorded it in 1945 he sent a copy of the disc to the composer, who returned an autographed score to express his admiration. The better-known *Toccata* is hardly less electrifying, and the somewhat confined mono sound is never distracting with playing of this degree of magnetism.

Piano sonatas Nos. 7 in B flat, Op. 83; 8 in B flat, Op. 84.
*** Sony Dig. MK 44680 [id.]. Yefim Bronfman.

Yefim Bronfman has a formidable technique and his clarity of articulation and tonal finesse are unfailingly impressive. The opening of No. 8 has a good sense of forward movement. Highly accomplished playing throughout, though it is distinctly short measure these days. All the same, it is very recommendable.

Piano sonatas Nos. 7 in B flat, Op. 83; 8 in B flat, Op. 84; Romeo and Juliet, Op. 75: Romeo and Juliet before parting; Masks.
☞ (M) *** Decca 425 046-2 [id.]. Vladimir Ashkenazy – LISZT: *Impromptu* etc. ***

Ashkenazy gives commanding readings of these two sonatas. He plays with great authority and conviction, and he makes much of the two excerpts from *Romeo and Juliet*, which come off extremely well on the piano when played like this. The 1968 recording has transferred well to CD: the piano-tone is very good and the sound brings a wide dynamic range.

Piano sonatas Nos. 7 in B flat, Op. 83; 8 in B flat, Op. 84; 9 in C, Op. 103.
*** ASV Dig. CDDCA 755 [id.]. John Lill.

This disc, coupling the last three *Sonatas*, offers exceptionally good value, and the excellent ASV recording was made in Henry Wood Hall. All three performances are of high quality, and John Lill is never less than a thoughtful and intelligent guide in this repertoire.

Piano sonata No. 8 in B flat, Op. 84; Cinderella: 10 Pieces, Op. 97; 4 Pieces, Op. 3.
*** Chan. Dig. CHAN 8976; *ABTD1565* [id.]. Boris Berman.

In the expansive *Eighth Sonata*, there is more pianistic refinement in Berman's account than in the Lill reviewed above, though it is in the ten numbers from *Cinderella* and the Op. 3 *Pieces* that Berman's command of atmosphere and character tells most. The quality of the recorded sound is excellent.

Romeo and Juliet (suite), *Op. 75; Prelude, Op. 12/7; Suggestion diabolique, Op. 4/4.*
☞ **(*) DG Dig. 437 532-2 [id.]. Andrei Gavrilov – RAVEL: *Gaspard* etc. **

Andrei Gavrilov has been here before, on the EMI label. And although there is abundant evidence of pianistic mastery, there is no real need to replace those earlier versions, particularly as – despite the intervening years – these are not better recorded.

VOCAL MUSIC
(i) *Alexander Nevsky* (cantata), *Op. 78;* (ii) *Ivan the Terrible, Op. 116* (film music, arr. Lankester).
☞ *** Sony Dig. S2K 48387 (2) [id.]. (i) Dolora Zajic; (ii) Christopher Plummer (nar.), Sinyavskaya, Leiferkus; L. Symphony Ch., LSO, Rostropovich.

Alexander Nevsky (cantata), Op. 78; Ivan the Terrible, Op. 116 (film music, arr. in oratorio form by Stasevich); *Lieutenant Kijé:* (suite), *Op. 60.*
(B) **(*) VoxBox 1155022 (2) [CDX 5021]. St Louis SO & Ch., Slatkin.

Rostropovich's set offers not the usual cantata version of Prokofiev's music for the Eisenstein film but one, more comprehensive, prepared by Michael Lankester, which tells the story of the Tsar by way of an elaborate narration, dotted with biblical quotations. Having snatches of music joined by spoken narration suits this subject well, though there are occasional bizarre echoes of *Peter and the wolf* and having so much speech means that the piece spreads to a second disc. Particularly moving is the humming chorus which starts the second of the two discs, a hushed and meditative version of the great surging melody which later became a central theme in Prokofiev's epic opera, *War and Peace*, representing General Kutuzov's patriotic defiance. Christopher Plummer is the oratorical narrator, with Sergei Leiferkus and the fruity-toned Tamara Sinyavskaya the excellent soloists, and the London Symphony Chorus both powerful and refined. As a fill-up on the second disc comes the ideal coupling, the *Alexander Nevsky* cantata, arranged by Prokofiev himself from the music he wrote for another great Eisenstein historical film. Dolora Zajic is the moving mezzo soloist in the great *Lament for the dead* after the *Battle on the ice*, with Rostropovich again drawing an inspired performance from the LSO and Chorus.

The two-disc bargain VoxBox offers excellent performances of all three of the concert works derived from Prokofiev's film-scores. No date is given for the analogue recordings but the sound is full, and the chorus too sings incisively and, except in the first two choruses of *Alexander Nevsky*, the balance is not too distant. Vocally, the greatest glory is the darkly expressive singing of Claudine Carlson in the *Lament for the dead* in *Nevsky*, with the chest register revealing a glorious contralto quality. She is the soloist in items from *Ivan the Terrible* too. Very good value.

Alexander Nevsky (cantata), Op. 78.
(M) *** EMI CDM7 63114-2. Anna Reynolds, London Symphony Ch., LSO, Previn – RACHMANINOV: *The Bells.* ***
☞ *(**) Sup. 11.1948-2 [id.]. Soukupová, Czech PO Ch., Czech PO, Ančerl – STRAVINSKY: *Rite of spring.* *(**)

(i) *Alexander Nevsky, Op. 78. Lieutenant Kijé (suite), Op. 60.*
*** DG 419 603-2 [id.]. (i) Elena Obraztsova, London Symphony Ch.; LSO, Abbado.
(M) *** BMG/RCA GD 60176 [60176-2-RG]. (i) Rosalind Elias, Chicago SO Ch.; Chicago SO, Reiner – GLINKA: *Russlan Overture.* ***

(i) *Alexander Nevsky, Op. 78. Scythian suite, Op. 20.*
*** Chan. Dig. CHAN 8584 [id.]. (i) Linda Finnie, SNO Ch.; SNO, Järvi.

Abbado's performance culminates in a deeply moving account of the tragic lament after the battle (here very beautifully sung by Obraztsova), made the more telling when the battle itself is so fine an example of orchestral virtuosity. The chorus is as incisive as the orchestra. The digital remastering of the 1980 recording has been all gain and the sound is very impressive indeed. *Lieutenant Kijé* also sounds splendid, and Abbado gets both warm and wonderfully clean playing from the Chicago orchestra.

The bitter chill of the Russian winter can be felt in the orchestra at the very opening of Järvi's reading and the melancholy of the choral entry has real Slavic feeling. His climactic point is the enormously spectacular *Battle on the ice*, with the recording giving great pungency to the bizarre orchestral effects and the choral shouts riveting in their force and fervour. Linda Finnie sings the final lament eloquently and Järvi's apotheosis is very affecting, but at the close Obraztsova and Abbado create an even graver valedictory feeling which is unforgettable. As coupling, Järvi chooses the ballet *Ala and Lolly*, which subsequently became the *Scythian suite*. Its motoric rhythms are characteristic of the composer at his most aggressive, but the lyrical music is even more rewarding.

All the weight, bite and colour of the score are captured by Previn, and though the timbre of the singers' voices may not suggest Russians, they cope very confidently with the Russian text; Previn's direct and dynamic manner ensures that the great *Battle on the ice* scene is powerfully effective. Anna Reynolds sings the lovely *Lament for the dead* most affectingly. The sound is sharply defined, with plenty of bite; just a little of the old analogue ambient fullness has gone.

Reiner's version, recorded in 1959, was another of the astonishingly vivid early achievements of the RCA stereo catalogue. The performance is gripping from the first bar to the last, with choral singing of great fervour and a movingly eloquent contribution from Rosalind Elias in the great

Lament. The *Lieutenant Kijé suite*, recorded two years earlier, is another colourful example of the Chicago orchestra at their peak, the sound again full and atmospheric.

The strength of the Supraphon performance lies in the choral singing, which is splendid. Vera Soukupová movingly pays her elegiac tribute to the dead on the field of battle, and many will like her restraint; if without the passion of a traditional Russian account, the singing is also without Slavonic wobbles. Ančerl conducts what is essentially a powerfully lyrical reading, sombre at the opening and rising to the joyous climax when the chorus celebrate Alexander's entry into Pskov with a heady mixture of joy and fervour. The work is sung in idiomatic Russian (the translation is set against Cyrillic script), which adds much to its character. The remastering has clarified the reverberant (1962) recording but has also added an artificial edge to the choral sound. This increases the bite and power of the *Battle on the ice* sequence, adding to the menace of those Teutonic knights in Eisenstein's great film, but it also tends to tire the ear. Moreover the record is unrealistically reissued at full price.

Cantata for the 20th anniversary of the October Revolution, Op. 74.
☞ *** Chan. Dig. CHAN 9095 [id.]. Rozhdestvensky (speaker), Philh. Ch. & O, Järvi – *Stone Flower suite.* ***

Even Prokofiev rarely wrote so wild and totally original a piece as this cantata, designed to celebrate the twentieth anniversary of the 1917 Revolution. The key movement, centrally placed and the longest, uses such exotic percussion as rattles and sirens, with shouting from the chorus, in a graphic description of the revolution in St Petersburg. In 1938 the music was regarded as far too avant-garde and the first performance was cancelled, while at a later period Prokofiev's use of the words of Stalin in two of the movements equally barred a complete performance. Neeme Järvi in Estonia managed to defy the ban, and here with his fellow-conductor, Gennadi Rozhdestvensky, as narrator, he has made a first complete recording with the Philharmonia Chorus and Orchestra. A performance by a Russian chorus might have been even more bitingly uninhibited, but it is good to have so sharply original and refreshingly dramatic a piece complete on disc at last, an occasional work that rises far above its first inspiration. As a valuable fill-up comes a suite of excerpts from the folk-tale ballet of 1948, *The Stone Flower*.

Eugene Onegin (incidental music), *Op. 71; Hamlet* (incidental music), *Op. 77; Lieutenant Kijé* (suite), *Op. 60.*
*** Chant du Monde Dig. LDC 288 027/8 (2) [id.]. Koroleva, Stetsenko, Blagovest Ch., Maly Moscow SO, Vladimir Ponkin.

Prokofiev's incidental music for *Eugene Onegin* proves to be a major find, with an inspiration comparable to *Romeo and Juliet* in lyric fervour and melodic sweep. *Hamlet* is less ambitious, offering ten vignettes, but including three engaging songs for Ophelia charmingly sung here by Ludmilla Koroleva. The orchestral playing in both scores is fresh and ardent, and the Russian wind and brass playing is suitably vibrant. The performance of *Lieutenant Kijé* brings out the music's laconic melancholy in a specially Russian way. Excellent, modern, digital recording throughout. This is an indispensable set for any true Prokofievian.

5 Poems of Anna Akhmatova, Op. 27; 2 Poems, Op. 9; 5 Poems of Konstantin Balmont, Op. 36; 3 Romances, Op. 73.
**(*) Chan. Dig. CHAN 8509; *ABTD 1219* [id.]. Carole Farley, Arkady Aronov.

Rare and valuable repertoire. The songs are powerful and full of resourceful and imaginative touches. The Akhmatova settings are quite beautiful. The *Three Romances*, Op. 73, to words of Pushkin, are full of the wry harmonic sleights of hand that are so characteristic of his musical speech. The American soprano, Carole Farley, responds to the different moods and character of the poems and encompasses a rather wide range of colour and tone, although at times her voice is rather edgy and uneven in timbre. The accompanying of Arkady Aronov is highly sensitive and perceptive. The recording is completely truthful.

OPERA

L'amour des trois oranges (The Love for 3 oranges): complete.
**(*) Virgin/EMI Dig. VCD7 59566-2 (2) [id.]. Bacquier, Bastin, Dubosc, Gautier, Viala, Lyon Opera Ch. & O, Kent Nagano.

French was the language used when the opera was given its first, lavish production in Chicago in December 1921. It inevitably brings a degree of softening in vocal texture, but the brilliant young conductor, Kent Nagano, and his Lyon Opera House team make up for any loss in knife-edged precision of ensemble. Gabriel Bacquier as the King and Jules Bastin as the monstrous Cook, guardian of the three oranges, are well matched by the others, including Jean-Luc Viala as an aptly petulant Prince and Catherine Dubosc as a sweetly girlish Princess Ninette. A snag with the recorded sound is that the commenting chorus – very much a part of the action in *commedia dell'arte* style – is focused too vaguely, a pity when the timing is so crisp. Happily, the focus for the solo voices is clearer. However, it is irritating that there are so few cueing points on the CDs (just one for each scene), even if this is very much an ensemble opera, with few set solos.

The Fiery Angel (complete).
*** DG Dig. 431 669-2 (2) [id.]. Secunde, Lorenz, Zednik, Moll, Gothenburg SO, Järvi.

Though the story is largely distasteful, the score of *The Fiery Angel* is masterly, containing passages as rich and warm as anything Prokofiev ever wrote before his return to Soviet Russia. Prokofiev's vivid orchestration adds colour and atmosphere, although the final scene with the Inquisitor (Kurt Moll ever sinister) and chattering nuns does not quite rise to the expected climax. Nadine Secunde sings passionately as Renata, well supported by Siegfried Lorenz as Ruprecht. With such warm advocacy one can fully appreciate the work's mastery, even if the reasons for its failure to get into the repertory remain very clear.

Maddalena (complete).
**(*) Olympia Dig. OCD 215 [id.]. Ivanova, Martynov, Yakovenko, Koptanova, Rumyantsev, male group of State Chamber Ch., MoC SO, Rozhdestvensky.

Maddalena is an opera which Prokofiev wrote in 1911, two years after graduating, but he then failed to finish the scoring. It was left to Sir Edward Downes to complete the orchestration over 60 years later, revealing a fascinating example of Russian Grand Guignol. Downes's contribution has a true Prokofiev ring, with distinctive colouring. Any disappointment with the work lies more in the relative lack of melodic distinction in the vocal writing which, for the most part, flows in an easy cantilena. Rozhdestvensky, with his fine orchestra of young players, directs a persuasive performance, even if some of the singing is indifferent. Ivanova is a bright, precise soprano, with Martynov singing splendidly in the tenor role of her wronged husband, Genaro. By contrast, Yakovenko in the baritone role of Maddalena's lover is disappointingly wobbly. Full, forward sound, not always refined. The disc comes with libretto, translation and notes.

War and peace (complete).
⊛ (M) *** Erato/Warner 2292 45331-2 (4) [id.]. Vishnevskaya, Miller, Ciesinski, Tumagian, Ochman, Ghiuselev, Smith, Paunova, Petkov, Toczyska, Zakai, Gedda, Fr. R. Ch. & Nat. O, Rostropovich.
☞ *** Ph. Dig. 434 097-2 (3) [id.]. Gargalov, Prokina, Gregoriam, Borodina, Gerelo, Bogachova, Okhotnikov, Morozov, Kirov Theatre Ch. & O, Gergiev.

That the Soviet Union over 70 years spawned so many musical masterpieces despite the frightening restrictions of the system is a tribute to the purest genius, above all to that of Prokofiev and Shostakovich. And no single work encompasses that triumph over restriction, the demand to create people's music, more completely than Prokofiev's opera *War and Peace*. That any composer could even think of capturing in an opera the essence of Tolstoi's vast novel is remarkable enough; all the more astonishing that Prokofiev, struggling against illness in his final years, achieved it to produce one of the very greatest modern operas. *War and Peace* is not just aptly epic in scale but warmly approachable, with a fund of melody rarely matched this century. In this opera more than anywhere, Prokofiev squared the impossible Soviet circle.

Moreover a really complete rendering of Prokofiev's text – never heard by the composer in its finished form – shows triumphantly how the components cohere into an opera of epic achievement. The English National Opera's stage production at the Coliseum proved that beyond doubt, and here Rostropovich's similarly complete account on record, flawed in some of the casting, nevertheless confirms equally that this is one of the great operatic masterpieces of the century. Prokofiev was never more prolific in his tune-writing than here: one melody follows another, almost as in a musical. However, no one should be deceived by the ease of listening into thinking that the writing lacks strength or intensity; rather, Prokofiev, in his game with the Soviet authorities, was submitting to the impossible restrictions of writing a 'people's opera' and succeeding masterfully, knowing that only he could have done it.

In Rostropovich's powerful reading one revels – thanks also to the lively Erato recording – in the vividness of the atmosphere, both in the evocative love scenes and ball scenes of the first half (Peace) and in the high tensions of the battle scenes in the second (War). The opera culminates in a great patriotic chorus, using the most haunting tune of all, earlier sung by General Kutuzov after the Council of Fili, and the emotional thrust is overwhelming. The French Radio Choir sings that chorus with real Russian fervour – though anyone remembering the ENO production will be disconcerted to find the opera starting, not with the shattering choral epigraph which hit so hard at the Coliseum, but with a pot-pourri overture airing some of the main themes. Prokofiev wrote it as an option, and what Rostropovich has done, with fair logic, is to reserve the choral epigraph – telling of the invasion of Russia – for the beginning of the second half and the scenes of war.

Even with a total playing time of over four hours, the opera yet seems compact and fits on the four CDs very neatly, with the scenes of peace on the first two, the scenes of war on the second pair, and without a single scene broken in the middle. It was natural that Rostropovich's wife, Galina Vishnevskaya, should sing the central role of Natasha, as she did in the earlier, much-cut, Bolshoi recording. It is extraordinary how convincingly this mature soprano in her early sixties characterizes a young girl; there may be raw moments, but she is completely inside the role. The Hungarian baritone, Lajos Miller, not flawless either, is a clear-voiced Andrei, and Wieslaw Ochman is a first-rate Pierre, with the veteran, Nicolai Gedda, brought in as Kuragin. Katherine Ciesinski is a warm-toned Sonya, but Dimiter Petkov is disappointingly unsteady as Natasha's father, Count Rostov. The small role of Napoleon is strongly taken by Eduard Tumagian, while Nicola Ghiuselev is a noble Kutuzov, in some ways the most impressive of all.

The bite, energy and warmth which run through the whole performance are owed above all to Rostropovich, who promised the composer not long before the latter died that he would do all he could to get this masterpiece – his own final favourite among Prokofiev's works – fully recognized in its definitive form. This recording could hardly provide a more vital contribution to that process. The libretto contains French and English translations, but no Russian transliteration, only the Cyrillic text in a separate section.

On Philips the company of the Kirov Theatre in St Petersburg offers a rival version, recorded at a sequence of live performances in the theatre, using the production that was also seen on television. The comparisons with Rostropovich are fascinating. Almost inevitably with such large projects, the corners show in both recordings. The Kirov sound is on the dry side, faithful no doubt to the theatre's acoustic, but hardly allowing as full an expansion as the Erato for the big, stirring climaxes, notably those using the great patriotic theme associated with General Kutuzov. The Kirov perform-ance under Valery Gergiev, at rather more urgent speeds than Rostropovich's, may be less warmly expressive and atmospheric, but it brings the advantage of having in the principal roles younger voices. Many will prefer the Kirov Natasha, Yelena Prokina, to the controversially cast Vishnevskaya on the Rostropovich set. The voice is fresher as well as younger-sounding, though the tone becomes hard under pressure, losing any sweetness. Alexandr Gergalov, Prince Andrei in the Kirov perform-ance, is attractively young-sounding too, lighter and more lyrical than Rostropovich's principal, also good, the Hungarian baritone, Lajos Miller. Otherwise the Kirov principals, including Nikolai Okhotnikov as Kutuzov, are almost all as characterful and assured as their generally starrier rivals on Erato, and the sense of purpose from a very large company, well drilled in the music, counterbalances in part, though not entirely, the unhelpful dryness of the sound. The economical layout on three CDs may seem to favour Philips, but there is no price-advantage, when Rostropovich's Erato comes at mid-price in the Libretto series. Not only that, there are far too few entry points on the Philips, with only one track per scene (some lasting over half an hour). The Erato version provides a generous number, and the four-disc format brings a positive advantage in neatly dividing the seven scenes of peace from the six scenes of war, two discs apiece. The three-disc format on Philips is made possible by Gergiev's faster speeds and a briefer text for the final patriotic chorus, though the breaks between discs come awkwardly in the middle of scenes.

Puccini, Giacomo (1858–1924)

Crisantemi for string quartet.
*** CRD CRD 3366; *CRDC 4066* [id.]. Alberni Qt – DONIZETTI: *Quartet No. 13;*
    VERDI: *Quartet.* ***

Puccini's brief essay in writing for string quartet dates from the late 1880s; three years later he used the main themes in his first fully successful opera, *Manon Lescaut*. The piece is given a warm, finely controlled performance by the Alberni Quartet and makes a valuable makeweight for the two full-scale quartets by fellow opera-composers. The sound is excellent.

(i) *Crisantemi; Minuets Nos. 1–3; Quartet in A min.: Allegro moderato; Scherzo in A min.;* (ii) *Foglio d'album; Piccolo tango;* (iii; ii) *Avanti Urania; E l'uccellino; Inno a Diana; Menti all'avviso; Morire?; Salve regina; Sole e amore; Storiella d'amore; Terra e mare.*
*** Etcetera KTC 1050. (i) Raphael Qt; (ii) Tan Crone; (iii) Roberta Alexander.

It is fascinating to find among early, rather untypical songs like *Storiella d'amore* and *Menti all'avviso* a charming little song, *Sole e amore*, written jokingly for a journal, 'Paganini', in 1888, which provided, bar for bar, the main idea of the Act III quartet in *La Bohème* of eight years later. The two piano pieces are simple album-leaves; among the six quartet pieces, *Crisantemi* is already well known; the rest are student pieces, including a delightful fragment of a Scherzo. Performances are good, though Roberta Alexander's soprano is not ideally Italianate. The recorded sound is vivid and immediate against a lively hall ambience.

Messa di Gloria.
☞ (M) *** Ph. 434 170-2 [id.]. Lövaas, Hollweg, McDaniel, West German R. Ch., Frankfurt RSO, Inbal (with MOZART: *Vesperae solennes, K.339: Laudate Dominum:* Te Kanawa, London Symphony Ch., LSO, C. Davis ***).
*** Erato/Warner Dig. 2292 45197-2 [id.]. Carreras, Prey, Amb. S., Philh. O, Scimone.

(i) *Messa di gloria;* (ii) *Capriccio sinfonico; Preludio sinfonico.*
☞ (B) **(*) Erato/Warner 2292 45942-2 [id.]. (i) Johns, Huttenlocher, Ch. & O of Gulbenkian Lisbon Foundation, Corboz; (ii) Monte-Carlo Opéra O, Scimone.

Puccini's *Messa di Gloria*, completed when he was twenty, rebuts any idea that this composer was a late developer. Very much under the influence of Verdi (hearing *Aida* was a profound formative experience), Puccini still showed his positive character as a composer, writing bold melodies with just a hint here and there of individual fingerprints and using the orchestra with astonishing maturity. The various parts were written at different times and even for different purposes; but with the exception of an over-sweet setting of *Agnus Dei* (later used in *Manon Lescaut*) the work stands well together. Best of all is the ambitious and strong setting of the *Gloria*, the longest section and the earliest written. It has a cheeky recurring march theme which may be doubtfully apt for church but which is richly enjoyable. The section ends with a formidable fugue, echoing Beethoven's *Missa solemnis*, no less. This 1975 Philips version, available as a limited edition, is excellent value at mid-price. It has stylish soloists, a fine choral contribution and clean, well-balanced recording. Kiri Te Kanawa's ravishing account of the *Laudate Dominum* from Mozart's *Solemn Vespers* is thrown in as an enticing encore.

Scimone and a fine team are brisker and lighter than their predecessors on record, yet effectively bring out the red-bloodedness of the writing. José Carreras turns the big solo in the *Gratias* into the first genuine Puccini aria. His sweetness and imagination are not quite matched by the baritone, Hermann Prey, who is given less to do than usual, when the choral baritones take on the yearning melody of *Crucifixus*. Excellent, atmospheric sound.

The alternative earlier performance from Scimone is more affectionate and has splendid choral singing. The reverberant recording has been made to sound firmer and cleaner on CD and the sound is impressively full. This has a price advantage and his coupling includes two fascinating early orchestral works, with the *Capriccio sinfonico* suddenly producing out of a hat the famous theme that was to become the Bohemian motif of *La Bohème*. The playing of the Monte Carlo orchestra is committed, if not very polished.

OPERA

La Bohème (complete).
(***) EMI mono CDS7 47235-8 (2) [Ang. CDCB 47235]. De los Angeles, Bjoerling, Merrill, Reardon, Tozzi, Amara, RCA Victor Ch. & O, Beecham.
*** Decca 421 049-2 (2) [id.]. Freni, Pavarotti, Harwood, Panerai, Ghiaurov, German Op. Ch., Berlin, BPO, Karajan.
☞ ⊛ (B) (***) Decca mono 440 233-2 (2) [id.]. Tebaldi, Prandelli, Gueden, Inghilleri, Corena, Arié, Luise, Santa Cecilia Ac., Rome, Ch. & O, Erede.
(M) *** Decca 425 534-2 (2). Tebaldi, Bergonzi, Bastianini, Siepi, Corena, D'Angelo, St Cecilia Ac. Ch. & O, Serafin.
(***) EMI mono CDS7 47475-8 (2) [Ang. CDCB 47475]. Callas, Di Stefano, Moffo, Panerai, Zaccaria, La Scala, Milan, Ch. & O, Votto.
☞ (B) * Discover Dig. DICD 920107 (2) [id.]. Gauci, Aragall, Sardinero, Rosca, M. Krause, BRTN PO & Ch., Rahbari.

Beecham's is a uniquely magical performance with two favourite singers, Victoria de los Angeles and Jussi Bjoerling, challenged to their utmost in loving, expansive singing. The voices are treated far better by the CD remastering than the orchestra, which is rather thinner-sounding than it was on LP, though as ever the benefits of silent background are very welcome in so warmly atmospheric a reading. With such a performance one hardly notices the recording, but those who want fine modern stereo can turn readily to Karajan.

Karajan too takes a characteristically spacious view of *Bohème*, but there is an electric intensity which holds the whole score together as in a live performance. Pavarotti is an inspired Rodolfo, with comic flair and expressive passion, while Freni is just as seductive as Mimì. Elizabeth Harwood is a charming Musetta. Fine singing throughout the set. The reverberant Berlin acoustic is glowing and brilliant in superb Decca recording, with the clean placing of voices enhancing the performance's dramatic warmth.

The very early Decca set, one of the very first complete operas to appear on LP. Recorded in 1951, it immediately won glowing praise, above all for Tebaldi's radiant and rich-voiced portrayal of Mimì. The effect is still extraordinarily atmospheric in its sense of stage perspective, with sound effects mostly adding to the realism and not overdone (the door-knocks come off splendidly in Act I, but the tearing up of Rodolfo's manuscript was less well caught by the microphones!). Like the companion early Decca *Die Fledermaus*, it demonstrated the huge advantages of LP over 78s for recording opera. Like *Die Fledermaus*, the one drawback was the whistly sound of the violins (something to do with the microphones in use at Decca at that time). I. M. remembers playing the whole recording to the Opera Class at the Royal Manchester College of Music; most of them were reduced to tears by the very affecting closing scene, but Frederic Cox, the professor in charge – later to become College Principal – without disparaging the impact of the records commented that the strings sounded as if they were always muted! The CD transfer has improved the violin focus, but the effect is still emaciated above the stave. Yet one soon adjusts to this, for the acoustic is basically warm and evocative; the sheer vibrancy of the male singing in Act I is exhilarating, while the first meeting of Mimì and Rodolfo is wonderfully fresh and tender. It is still a lovely performance, and there are no appreciable weaknesses in the rest of the cast: Gueden (if not always completely Italianate in style) an exceptionally characterful Musetta (a part that fitted her like a glove), Pradelli a most likeable Rodolfo, engagingly light-voiced yet stirring at climaxes, Inghilleri rather old-sounding but still interesting as Marcello. The orchestral woodwind adds many glowing comments, especially the flutes. Erede keeps the music flowing: he is not a great conductor but he controls the great love duet of Act I spaciously. If he sets a very fast speed for the opening of Act II at the Café Momus, the vivacity of the crowd scenes comes over with wonderful vividness, especially at the close. Similarly the atmospheric opening of Act III at the Paris toll-gate is remarkably evocative, with the kind of production values that were to lead on to the vintage Decca opera recordings of the stereo era already apparent. Indeed, at times here one could almost think stereo had already arrived.

Tebaldi's second Decca set with Bergonzi dominated the catalogue in the early days of stereo. Vocally the performance achieves a consistently high standard, with Tebaldi as Mimì the most affecting. Carlo Bergonzi is a fine Rodolfo; Bastianini and Siepi are both superb as Marcello and Colline, and even the small parts of Benoit and Alcindoro (as usual taken by a single artist) have the benefit of Corena's magnificent voice. The veteran Serafin was more vital here than on some of his records. The recording has its striking vividness and sense of stage perspective enhanced on CD.

Callas, flashing-eyed and formidable, may seem even less suited to the role of Mimì than to that of Butterfly, but characteristically her insights make for a vibrantly involving performance. Though Giuseppe di Stefano is not the subtlest of Rodolfos, he is in excellent voice here, and Moffo and Panerai make a strong partnership as the second pair of lovers. Votto occasionally coarsens Puccini's score but he directs with energy. The comparatively restricted dynamic range means that the singers appear to be 'front stage', but there is no lack of light and shade in Act II.

As in other Puccini recordings made by Rahbari in Belgium, the recorded sound on the bargain Discover set is distractingly reverberant. Though the voices are given a welcome bloom, they lack immediacy and the performance, lively and well sprung, loses its bite. Sadly, neither Miriam Gauci – too often unsteady – nor Giacomo Aragall – with his fine tenor worn on top – is on form, making this much less attractive than other mid-price or bargain versions.

La Bohème: highlights.
*** Decca 421 245-2; *421 245-4* [id.] (from above recording with Freni and Pavarotti; cond. Karajan).

It is a pity to cut anything from so taut an opera as *La Bohème*; but those who feel they can make do with a single CD instead of two will find this selection from the Karajan set ideal.

La Fanciulla del West (The Girl of the Golden West) complete.

⊕ (M) *** Decca 421 595-2 (2) [id.]. Tebaldi, Del Monaco, MacNeil, Tozzi, St Cecilia Ac., Rome, Ch. & O, Capuana.

**(*) DG 419 640-2 (2) [id.]. Neblett, Domingo, Milnes, Howell, ROHCG Ch. and O, Mehta.

☞ ** BMG/RCA Dig. 09026 60597-2 (2) [id.]. Marton, Fondary, O'Neill, Planté, Rootering, Ivaldi, Bav. R. Ch., Munich R. O, Slatkin.

The Decca set of *La Fanciulla del West* has been remastered for CD with spectacular success. Tebaldi gives one of her most warm-hearted and understanding performances on record, and Mario del Monaco displays the wonderfully heroic quality of his voice to great – if sometimes tiring – effect. Cornell MacNeil as the villain, Sheriff Rance, sings with great precision and attack, but unfortunately has not a villainous-sounding voice to convey the character fully. Jake Wallace's entry and the song *Che faranno i viecchi miei* is one of the high spots of the recording, with Tozzi singing beautifully. Capuana's expansive reading is matched by the imagination of the production, with the closing scene wonderfully effective.

On DG, Mehta's manner – as he makes clear at the very start – is on the brisk side, not just in the cakewalk rhythms but even in refusing to let the first great melody, the nostalgic *Che faranno i viecchi miei*, linger into sentimentality. Sherrill Milnes as Jack Rance makes that villain into far more than a small-town Scarpia, giving nobility and understanding to the first-Act arioso. Domingo, as in the theatre, sings heroically, disappointing only in his reluctance to produce soft tone in the great aria *Ch'ella mi creda*. The rest of the team is excellent, not least Gwynne Howell as the minstrel who sings *Che faranno i viecchi miei*; but the crowning glory of a masterly set is the singing of Carol Neblett as the Girl of the Golden West herself, gloriously rich and true and with formidable attack on the exposed high notes. Full, atmospheric recording to match, essential in an opera full of evocative offstage effects, but the slight drying-out process of the digital sound adds some stridency in tuttis, readily acceptable with so strong a performance.

Leonard Slatkin conducts a strong and well-paced performance of Puccini's wild-west opera, taking a spacious, sympathetic view. It is good to have Dennis O'Neill taking the principal tenor-role in a major international recording, bringing out the lyrical side of Dick Johnson's role very persuasively. He also rises well to the challenge of the final scene, with the aria, *Ch'ella mi creda*, and the hero's disappearance with Minnie into the sunset. Alain Fondary's firm, dark baritone makes Sheriff Rance less of a villain than usual, conveying wronged nobility. For much of the time Eva Marton manages to sing far more gently than she usually does on disc, and she copes well with the big dramatic moments, but it is still a voice that quickly grows raw, with too many loud, unpitched notes. For all its qualities, this is not among the most recommendable versions.

Gianni Schicchi (complete).

☞ (B) * Discover Dig. DICD 920119 [id.]. Tumagian, Gauci, Perelstein, Ramiro, Belgian R. & TV PO, Brussels, Rahbari.

The liveliness and wit of Rahbari's direction of this frothy one-Acter are seriously undermined by the washy sound. The lack of inner detail in ensembles is less damaging than the backward placing of the principal soloists even at key moments. So Schicchi's dramatic entrance among the mourning relatives goes for nothing, and even the big arias for Rinuccio – Yordi Ramiro an insecure tenor – and Lauretta – Miriam Gauci at less than her finest – are set at a distance. A pity, when a good bargain version of this masterpiece would be very welcome.

Madama Butterfly (complete).

*** DG Dig. 423 567-2 (3) [id.]. Freni, Carreras, Berganza, Pons, Amb. Op. Ch., Philh. O, Sinopoli.

**(*) Decca 417 577-2 (3) [id.]. Freni, Ludwig, Pavarotti, Kerns, V. State Op. Ch., VPO, Karajan.

(M) *** BMG/RCA GD 84145 (2) [4145-2-RG]. Moffo, Elias, Valletti, Cesari, Catalani, Rome Op. Ch. & O, Leinsdorf.

(M) *** EMI CMS7 69654-2 (2) [Ang. CDMB 69654]. Scotto, Bergonzi, Di Stasio, Panerai, De Palma, Rome Op. Ch. & O, Barbirolli.

(M) **(*) EMI CMS7 63634-2 (2) [Ang. CDMB 63634]; *TC-CFPD 4446*. De los Angeles, Bjoerling, Pirazzini, Sereni, Rome Op. Ch. & O, Santini.

(***) EMI mono CDS7 47959-8 (2) [id.]. Callas, Gedda, Borriello, Danieli, La Scala, Milan, Ch. & O, Karajan.

☞ (B) (**(*)) Decca mono 440 230-2 (2) [id.]. Tebaldi, Campora, Inghilleri, Rankin, Santa Cecilia Academy, Rome, Ch. & O, Alberto Erede.

However expansive his speeds, Sinopoli is never sentimental or self-indulgent. Puccini's honeyed moments are given, not sloppily, but with rapt intensity. They are then set the more movingly against the biting moments, from the opening fugato of Act I, sharply incisive, through to the final aria, tough and intense. As she was for Karajan in his classic Decca set, Freni is a model Butterfly; though the voice is no longer so girlish, she projects the tragedy even more weightily than before. José Carreras is similarly presented as a large-scale Pinkerton. Juan Pons is a virile Sharpless and Teresa Berganza an equally positive, unfruity Suzuki. This is a set which in its spacious but intensely concentrated way brings a unique and unforgettable experience. But it is on three CDs.

Karajan's set is also extravagantly laid out on three discs instead of two as for most of the rival sets – slow speeds partly responsible. However, he inspires singers and orchestra to a radiant performance which brings out all the beauty and intensity of Puccini's score, sweet but not sentimental, powerfully dramatic but not vulgar. Freni is an enchanting Butterfly, consistently growing in stature from the young girl to the victim of tragedy, sweeter of voice than any rival on record. Pavarotti is an intensely imaginative Pinkerton, actually inspiring understanding for this thoughtless character, while Christa Ludwig is a splendid Suzuki. The recording is one of Decca's most resplendent, with the Vienna strings producing glowing tone. Recommended, alongside Sinopoli.

Anna Moffo's Butterfly proves delightful, fresh and young-sounding, and the *Flower duet* with Rosalind Elias is enchanting. Valletti's Pinkerton has a clear-voiced, almost Gigli-like charm – preferable to most rivals – and with Corena as the Bonze the only blot on the set vocally is the unimaginative Sharpless of Renato Cesari. Leinsdorf is efficient and undistracting and, with vivid recording (balanced in favour of the voices), this makes a first-class mid-priced recommendation, costing less than half the price of the Decca Karajan set with Freni, Ludwig and Pavarotti.

Under Sir John Barbirolli, players and singers perform consistently with a dedication and intensity rare in opera recordings made in Italy, and the whole score glows more freshly than ever. There is hardly a weak link in the cast. Bergonzi's Pinkerton and Panerai's Sharpless are both sensitively and beautifully sung; Anna di Stasio's Suzuki is more than adequate, and Renata Scotto's Butterfly has a subtlety and perceptiveness in its characterization that more than make up for any shortcoming in the basic beauty of tone-colour.

Victoria de los Angeles' 1960 recording displays her art at its most endearing, her range of golden tone-colour lovingly exploited. Opposite her, Jussi Bjoerling produces a flow of rich tone to compare with that of the heroine. Mario Sereni is a full-voiced Sharpless, but Miriam Pirazzini is a disappointingly wobbly Suzuki; Santini is a reliable, generally rather square and unimaginative conductor who rarely gets in the way. With recording quality freshened, this fine set is most welcome either on a pair of mid-priced CDs or in its CfP cassette format.

Callas's view, aided by superbly imaginative and spacious conducting from Karajan, gives extra dimension to the Puccinian little woman, and with some keenly intelligent singing too from Gedda as Pinkerton this is a set which has a special compulsion. The performance projects the more vividly on CD, even though the lack of stereo in so atmospheric an opera is a serious disadvantage.

Astonishingly, this Decca mono set was made (in 1951) before Tebaldi ever sang the part in the opera house. In the last resort she lacks temperament – the schoolgirl giggles of Act I are too hearty by far – but there is much magnificent singing. Campora is a fine Pinkerton and the fresh young voices of the two lovers are particularly convincing in Act I. Erede's conducting is stong and dramatic, and there is much to relish, not least the amazingly atmospheric Decca recording, which is very kind to the voices. Whatever the reservations, this comes over as a real, vibrant performance and it shows Tebaldi at the peak of her vocal powers. The orchestra sounds thinner, but the violins have more body here than on those old Ace of Clubs LP pressings. The two CDs come in a single jewel-case with an independent plot summary unrelated to the 40 cues which provide the (admirable) internal access.

Madama Butterfly: highlights.
*** Decca 421 247-2; *421 247-4* [id.] (from above recording with Freni and Pavarotti; cond. Karajan).

Karajan's disc offers an obvious choice for a highlights CD from *Butterfly* if you are willing to pay full price.

Madame Butterfly: highlights (sung in English).
☞ (B) **(*) CfP CD-CFP 4600; *TC-CFP 4600*. Collier, Craig, Robson, Griffiths, Sadler's Wells O, Brian Balkwill.

This 1960 recording was the first of a series of Sadler's Wells highlights discs of opera in English. There are few better examples, for the clear recording lets the listener hear almost every word, and this is achieved without balancing things excessively in favour of the voices. Marie Collier got inside the part very well; she has a big, full voice and she sings most movingly. Charles Craig is a splendid Pinkerton: his singing achieves international standards and he was in particularly fresh voice when this record was made. As to the choice of extracts, the one omission which is at all serious is the entry of Butterfly. As it is, the duet of Pinkerton and Sharpless cuts off just as she is about to come in. The recording wears its years lightly; just occasionally the bright CD transfer brings a touch of peakiness in the vocal climaxes, but the performance remains very involving.

Manon Lescaut (complete).

☞ *** Decca Dig. 440 200-2 (2) [id.]. Freni, Pavarotti, Croft, Taddei, Vargas, Bartoli, NY Met. Op. Ch. & O, Levine.

*** DG Dig. 413 893-2 (2) [id.]. Freni, Domingo, Bruson, ROHCG Ch., Philh. O, Sinopoli.

*** Decca Dig. 421 426-2 (2) [id.]. Kiri Te Kanawa, Carreras, Paolo Coni, Ch. & O of Teatro Comunale di Bologna, Chailly.

☞ *** Naxos Dig. 8.660019/20 (2) [id.]. Gauci, Sardinero, Kaludov, BRT Philh. Ch. & O, Rahbari.

(M) (***) BMG/RCA mono GD 60573 (2) [60573-2-RG]. Albanese, Bjoerling, Merrill, Rome Op. Ch. & O, Perlea.

(M) (***) EMI mono CDS7 47393-8 (2) [Ang. CDCB 47392]. Callas, Di Stefano, Fioravanti, La Scala, Milan, Ch. and O, Serafin.

☞ * Sony S2K 48474 (2) [id.]. Rautio, Dvorský, Quilico, Rossi, La Scala, Milan, Ch. & O, Maazel.

With Luciano Pavarotti as a powerful Des Grieux, James Levine conducts a comparably big-boned performance of *Manon Lescaut*, bringing out the red-blooded drama of Puccini's first big success, while not ignoring its warmth and tender poetry. The impact is enhanced by exceptionally full, vivid sound, with the voices balanced close, well in front of the orchestra in a way one associates with opera recordings of the 1950s. It represents an opposite view to that taken by the DG engineers when in one of the last Kingsway Hall sessions they recorded the Sinopoli version. There too the title-role was taken by Mirella Freni and, though the closeness of balance on the newer set exposes some inevitable blemishes of age in the voice, its fullness and warmth are more faithfully captured in a performance even warmer and more relaxed. It culminates in an account of the big Act IV aria, *Sola, perduta, abbandonata*, more involving and passionate than any in recent years, with the voice showing no signs of wear. Consistently, Levine conveys the tensions and atmosphere of a stage performance in a way that plainly owes much to his experience at the Met., avoiding the feeling of a studio performance.

Pavarotti's contribution as Des Grieux is more controversial. He tackles his little opening aria challenging the girls to make him fall in love, *Tra voi belle*, with a beefy bravado that misses the subtlety and point of Domingo, for example. But then he characteristically points word-meaning with a bright-eyed intensity that compels attention. The closeness of balance means that in volume his singing rarely drops below mezzo-forte, and as a vocal demonstration Domingo's performance is consistently more refined, but there is little harm in having so passionate a portrait of Des Grieux as Pavarotti's. The rest of the cast is strong too, with Dwayne Croft a magnificent Lescaut who brings out the character's wry humour. The veteran Giuseppe Taddei is superbly cast as Geronte, very characterful and still full-throated, while Cecilia Bartoli makes the unnamed singer in the Act II entertainment into far more than a cipher. One incidental advantage over most rivals is that the break between discs comes after Act II, avoiding any break within an Act.

Plácido Domingo's portrait of Des Grieux on DG is far subtler and more detailed, with finer contrasts of tone and dynamic, than in his earlier, EMI recording opposite Caballé. Freni proves an outstanding choice: her girlish tones in Act I rebut any idea that she might be too mature. Of the others, a first-rate team, Renato Bruson nicely brings out the ironic side of Lescaut's character, and having Brigitte Fassbaender just to sing the *Madrigal* adds to the feeling of luxury, as does John Tomlinson's darkly intense moment of drama as the ship's captain. The voices are more recessed than is common, but they are recorded with fine bloom, and the brilliance of the orchestral sound comes out impressively.

Dame Kiri also gives an affecting characterization, at times rather heavily underlined but passionately convincing in the development from innocent girl to fallen woman. The playing from Chailly's Bologna orchestra cannot quite match that of the Philharmonia, yet Chailly is a degree more idiomatic in his pacing. Both tenors are good but Carreras sounds a little strained at times. The Decca sound, with voices further forward, is the more vivid.

On the bargain Naxos issue, Miriam Gauci gives one of the most sensitive performances of this role on any set. Her Act II aria, *In quelle trine morbide*, is beautifully poised and her monologue in the death scene, *Sola, perduta, abbandonata*, is the more moving for being restrained at the start, building from there in intensity without sacrificing musical values. The young Bulgarian, Kaludi

Kaludov, is a clean-cut, virile Des Grieux, opening up impressively in his big moments. Vincente Sardinero makes a powerful Lescaut, and Rahbari, as in his Bratislava recordings of *Cav.* and *Pag.*, is a red-blooded interpreter of Italian opera, generally pacing well, even if at the very start he is disconcertingly hectic. Though the Brussels orchestra plays with refinement – the strings in particular – the sound is thinner than in the Slovakian recordings, with the orchestra set slightly back. This is the least expensive *Manon Lescaut* in the catalogue but, even if it cost more, it would still be very recommendable.

In Perlea's 1954 recording, the mono sound may be limited, but no Puccinian should miss it, when Jussi Bjoerling gives the finest ever interpretation on record of the role of Des Grieux. Robert Merrill too is superb as Manon's brother, giving delightful irony to the closing scene of Act I, which has rarely sounded so effervescent. The Manon of Licia Albanese is sensitively sung, but the voice is not at all girlish.

It is typical of Callas that she turns the final scene into the most compelling part of the opera. Serafin, who could be a lethargic recording conductor, is here electrifying, and Di Stefano too is inspired to one of his finest complete opera recordings. The cast-list even includes the young Fiorenza Cossotto, impressive as the singer in the Act II *Madrigal*. The recording – still in mono, not a stereo transcription – minimizes the original boxiness and gives good detail.

In the latest Sony version with the company of La Scala, the title-role is taken by a newcomer, Nina Rautio, who sings with full, creamy tone but with perilously little expression, consistently underplaying the meaning and with words barely identifiable. When at their first meeting she tells Des Grieux her name, she might be answering a civil service questionnaire, and the tenor, Peter Dvorský, often excellent in Slavonic opera, proves coarse here in Puccini, too loud and with no roundness of tone. Lorin Maazel, always on the stiff side in Puccini, sounds particularly square in this exuberantly youthful score, not helped by the dry Milan acoustic.

La Rondine (complete).
*** Sony Dig. M2K 37852 [id.]. Te Kanawa, Domingo, Nicolesco, Rendall, Nucci, Watson, Knight, Amb. Op. Ch., LSO, Maazel.

La Rondine has never caught on, and a recording like this will almost certainly surprise anyone at the mastery of the piece, with a captivating string of catchy numbers. Maazel's is a strong, positive reading, crowned by a superb and radiant Magda in Dame Kiri Te Kanawa, mature yet glamorous. Domingo, by age too mature for the role of young hero, yet scales his voice down most effectively in the first two Acts, expanding in heroic warmth only in the final scene of dénouement. Sadly, the second pair are far less convincing, when the voices of both Mariana Nicolesco and David Rendall take ill to the microphone.

Suor Angelica (complete).
☞ (B) * Discover Dig. DICD 920120 [id.]. Gauci, Van Deyck, Jaak Gregor Ch., BRTN PO, Brussels, Rahbari.

It might seem apt to have an opera set in a monastery recorded in a reverberant, church-like acoustic, but, as demonstrated here, it works only in full choral passages. The solo sequences – with light exchanges set round a big dramatic moment of confrontation – are all diluted by the sound, and only the fruity contralto of Lucienne van Deyck as the formidable Zia Principessa comes over with the necessary power. Miriam Gauci, as in her other Puccini recordings made for Discover at the same period, seems to be out of voice, and *Senza mamma* brings unsteadiness instead of a pure legato line.

Il Tabarro (complete).
(M) **(*) BMG/RCA GD 60865 (2) [60865-2]. Leontyne Price, Domingo, Milnes, John Alldis Ch., New Philh. O, Leinsdorf – LEONCAVALLO: *I Pagliacci.* ***

Leontyne Price may not be ideally cast as the bargemaster's wife, but she is fully in character. Sherrill Milnes is rather young-sounding for the bargemaster, but he sings memorably in the climactic aria. Plácido Domingo makes a fresh-voiced and well-characterized young bargee, while Leinsdorf is at his most sympathetic.

Tosca (complete).
⊛ *** EMI CDS7 47175-8 (2) [Ang. CDCB 47174]. Callas, Di Stefano, Gobbi, Calabrese, La Scala, Milan, Ch. and O, De Sabata.
*** DG Dig. 431 775-2 (2). Freni, Domingo, Ramey, Terfel, ROHCG Ch., Philh. O, Sinopoli.
(M) *** Decca 421 670-2 (2) [id.]. Leontyne Price, Di Stefano, Taddei, V. State Op. Ch., VPO, Karajan.
*** DG 413 815-2 (2) [id.]. Ricciarelli, Carreras, Raimondi, Corena, German Op. Ch., BPO, Karajan.

☞ (B) (***) Decca mono 440 236-2 (2) [id.]. Tebaldi, Campora, Mascherini, Santa Cecilia Academy, Rome, Ch. & O, Alberto Erede.

**(*) Decca Dig. 414 597-2 (2) [id.]. Te Kanawa, Aragall, Nucci, Welsh Nat. Opera Ch., Nat. PO, Solti.

☞ *(*) BMG/RCA Dig. 09026 61806-2 (2) [id.]. Kabaivanska, Pavarotti, Wixell, Rome Op. Ch. & O, Oren.

☞ (M) * Decca 440 051-2 (2) [id.]. Nilsson, Corelli, Fischer-Dieskau, Santa Cecilia Academy, Rome, Ch. & O, Lorin Maazel.

☞ * Ph. Dig. 434 595-2 (2) [id.]. Vaness, Giacomini, Zancanaro, Phd. O, Muti.

There has never been a finer recorded performance of *Tosca* than Callas's first, with Victor de Sabata conducting and Tito Gobbi as Scarpia. Gobbi makes the unbelievably villainous police chief into a genuinely three-dimensional character, and Di Stefano as the hero, Cavaradossi, was at his finest. The conducting of De Sabata is spaciously lyrical as well as sharply dramatic, and the mono recording is superbly balanced in Walter Legge's fine production. Though there is inevitably less spaciousness than in a stereo recording, the voices are caught gloriously.

Even more than the Puccini operas he had previously recorded – always with spacious, finely moulded treatment – *Tosca* seems to match Sinopoli's musical personality, helped by DG recording of spectacular weight and range. Ramey's is not a conventional portrait of the evil police-chief, but the role has rarely been sung with more sheer beauty, with such a climax as the *Te Deum* at the end of Act I sounding thrilling in its firmness and power. Domingo's heroic power is formidable too, and unlike many of his opera recordings for DG this one presents him in close-up, not distanced. Freni's is not naturally a Tosca voice, but it is still a powerful, heartfelt performance.

On Decca, Karajan deserves equal credit with the principal singers for the vital, imaginative performance, recorded in Vienna. Taddei himself has a marvellously wide range of tone-colour, and though he cannot quite match the Gobbi snarl he has almost every other weapon in his armoury. Leontyne Price is at the peak of her form and Di Stefano sings most sensitively. The sound of the Vienna orchestra is enthralling – both more refined and richer than usual in a Puccini opera – and it sounds quite marvellous in its digitally remastered format, combining presence with atmosphere and making a superb bargain at mid-price.

On Karajan's DG version the police chief, Scarpia, seems to be the central character, and his unexpected choice of singer, a full bass, Raimondi, helps to show why, for this is no small-time villain but a man who in full confidence has a vein of nobility in him. Katia Ricciarelli is not the most individual of Toscas, but the beauty of singing is consistent. Carreras gives a powerful, stylish performance. The recording is rich and full, with the stage picture clearly established and the glorious orchestral textures beautifully caught.

Tosca was one of Tebaldi's finest parts, and her earlier Decca mono set showed her at her most moving. In addition, Campora and Ezo Mascherini gave far more satisfying support as Cavaradossi and Scarpia respectively than did del Monaco and George London in the later Decca stereo set. The 1951 recording too stands the test of time remarkably well, the orchestra a little distant but the whole effect satisfyingly atmospheric. The choral climax with Scarpia in the *Te Deum* at the end of Act I is remarkably effective, even without the advantage of stereo. Erede's conducting is fittingly full-blooded, and Tebaldi admirers should not hesitate at the very reasonable price, even if there is no libretto/translation, only a synopsis.

Rarely has Solti phrased Italian melody so consistently *con amore*, his fiercer side subdued but with plenty of power when required. Even so, the timing is not always quite spontaneous-sounding, with transitions occasionally rushed. But the principal *raison d'être* of the set must be the casting of Dame Kiri as the jealous opera-singer. Her admirers will relish the glorious sounds, but the jealous side of Tosca's character is rather muted.

There is little to commend the RCA set conducted limply by Daniel Oren. This brings all the disadvantages of live recording with extraneous noises, including hysterical applause on the arrival of the principal singers, and with no compensating advantages. Kabaivanska is in squally voice, and Ingvar Wixell with his dry voice makes a dull Scarpia. Pavarotti's magnetism does not desert him, but even he was finer in the flawed Decca set conducted by Nicola Rescigno.

The cast of Decca's 1966 Rome recording on paper is impressive, but the result is intensely disappointing. Not only is it a question of both Nilsson and Fischer-Dieskau sounding so completely un-Italianate that Puccini's phrases stiffen and die, but the conducting of Maazel seems to have little sympathy for the passion and warmth of Puccini's writing. No complaints about the Decca engineering, which is rich and vivid with plenty of atmosphere.

Muti's version for Philips, recorded live at concert performances, offers high-powered conducting and fine playing from the orchestra, but disappointing singing from the principals, often curiously uninvolved. Fine singer as she is, Carol Vaness is miscast as Tosca, and both Giuseppe Giacomini and Giorgio Zancanaro sing too consistently loud. The recorded sound is of little help, with less feeling of the theatre than in most studio recordings.

Tosca: highlights.
*** DG 423 113-2 [id.] (from above set with Ricciarelli and Carreras; cond. Karajan).
☞ (M) ** Decca 421 888-2; *421 888-4* [id.]. Freni, Pavarotti, Milnes, Wandsworth School Boys' Ch., L. Op. Ch., Nat. PO, Rescigno.

The selection from Karajan's powerful, closely recorded Berlin version is welcome. The breadth of Karajan's direction is well represented in the longer excerpts; there is also Tosca's *Vissi d'arte*, but Scarpia's music is under-represented, which is a pity when Raimondi made such a distinctive Scarpia with his dark bass timbre.

A not especially generous (63 minutes) selection from Rescigno's 1978 Decca set is mainly notable for offering a sampler of Pavarotti's assumption of the role of Cavaradossi; but it is only in Act III that the voice acquires its full magic, and *E lucevan le stelle* is undoubtedly the highlight. As Tosca, Freni sounds rather taxed so that even *Vissi d'arte* produces her stressed tone rather than even, lyrical sound. Milnes is quite well represented in the Act II excerpts: his Scarpia is fresh and direct, with words finely enunciated, a fine characterization. However Rescigno's conducting, for all his control of rubato, sounds forced and unspontaneous, strange from an Italian conductor. The Decca sound has characteristic brilliance and atmosphere.

Il Trittico: (i) *Il Tabarro;* (ii) *Suor Angelica;* (iii) *Gianni Schicchi.*
☞ (M) *** EMI mono/stereo CMS7 64165-2 (3). (i; iii) Gobbi; (i) Pradelli, Mas; (ii–iii) De los Angeles; (ii) Barbieri; (iii) Canali, Del Monte, Montarsolo; Rome Op. Ch. & O; (i) Bellezza; (ii) Serafin; (iii) Santini.
**(*) Sony CD 79312 (3) [M3K 35912]. (i; ii) Scotto; (i; iii) Domingo; (i) Wixell, Sénéchal; (ii) Horne; (ii; iii) Cotrubas; (iii) Gobbi, Amb. Op. Ch.; (ii) Desborough School Ch.; (i; ii) Nat. PO; (iii) LSO, Maazel.

The classic EMI set of *Il Trittico* has dominated the catalogue since the earliest days of LP. This vividly atmospheric and brilliantly contrasted group of one-Acters has never been more richly and characterfully presented on record, with Tito Gobbi giving two of his ripest characterizations. The central role of the cuckolded bargemaster, Michele, in *Il Tabarro* inspires him to one of his very finest performances on record. Though this version of Puccini's *grand guignol* opera, set on a barge on the Seine in Paris, is a mono recording, not stereo, it conveys the sense of horror far more keenly than any, with Gobbi's voice vividly caught on CD. The central leaf of the triptych, *Suor Angelica*, brings a glowing performance from Victoria de los Angeles, giving a most affecting portrayal of Angelica, the nun ill-treated by her noble family, with Fedora Barbieri formidable as her unfeeling aunt, the Zia Principessa. De los Angeles reappears, charmingly girlish as Lauretta, in *Gianni Schicchi*, where the high comedy has never fizzed so deliciously outside the opera house. She and Gobbi come together just as characterfully in this final opera. Though Gobbi's incomparable baritone is not by nature comic-sounding, he is unequalled as Schicchi, sardonically manipulating the mourning relatives of Buoso Donati, as he frames a new will for them. Puccini, the master of tragedy, here emerges a supreme master of comic timing too. Only *Gianni Schicchi*, recorded last in 1958, is in genuine and excellent stereo; *Il Tabarro* (1955) and *Suor Angelica* (1957) are mono, but all the transfers are expert, clear and convincingly balanced.

Il Tabarro may most seriously lack atmosphere in Maazel's version, but his directness is certainly refreshing, and in the other two operas it results in powerful readings; the opening of *Gianni Schicchi*, for example, has a sharp, almost Stravinskian bite. In the first two operas, Scotto's performances have a commanding dominance, presenting her at her finest. In *Gianni Schicchi* the veteran Tito Gobbi gives an amazing performance, in almost every way as fine as his EMI recording of twenty years earlier – and in some ways this is even more compelling. The only snag is the lack of cueing; CBS provide only one track for the whole of *Il Tabarro* and only two each for *Gianni Schicchi* and *Suor Angelica*, the second in each case being used to indicate the main soprano aria.

Turandot (complete).
*** Decca 414 274-2 (2) [id.]. Sutherland, Pavarotti, Caballé, Pears, Ghiaurov, Alldis Ch., Wandsworth School Boys' Ch., LPO, Mehta.
(M) *** EMI CMS7 69327-2 (2) [Ang. CDMB 69327]. Nilsson, Corelli, Scotto, Mercuriali, Giaiotti, Rome Op. Ch. & O, Molinari-Pradelli.

*** DG Dig. 423 855-2 (2) [id.]. Ricciarelli, Domingo, Hendricks, Raimondi, V. State Op. Ch., V. Boys' Ch., VPO, Karajan.

(***) EMI mono CDS7 47971-8 (2) [id.]. Callas, Fernandi, Schwarzkopf, Zaccaria, La Scala, Milan, Ch. & O, Serafin.

☞ ** BMG/RCA Dig. 09026 60898-2 (2) [id.]. Marton, Heppner, M. Price, Ahnsjö, Rootering, Bav. R. Ch., Augsburg Cathedral Boys' Ch., Munich R. O, Roberto Abbado.

Joan Sutherland gives an intensely revealing and appealing interpretation, making the the icy princess far more human and sympathetic than ever before, while Pavarotti gives a performance equally imaginative, beautiful in sound, strong on detail. To set Caballé against Sutherland was a daring idea, and it works superbly well; Pears as the Emperor is another imaginative choice. Mehta directs a gloriously rich and dramatic performance, superlatively recorded, still the best-sounding *Turandot* on CD, while the reading also remains supreme.

The EMI set brings Nilsson's second assumption on record of the role of Puccini's formidable princess. As an interpretation it is very similar to the earlier, RCA performance, but its impact is far more immediate, thanks to the conducting of Molinari-Pradelli. Corelli may not be the most sensitive prince in the world, but the voice is in glorious condition. Scotto's Liù is very beautiful and characterful too. With vividly remastered sound, this makes an excellent mid-priced recommendation, though the documentation, as yet, does not include an English translation.

In Karajan's set, Hendricks is almost a sex-kitten with her seductively golden tone, and one wonders how Calaf could ever have overlooked her. This is very different from the usual picture of a chaste slave-girl. Ricciarelli is a far more vulnerable figure than one expects of the icy princess, and the very fact that the part strains her beyond reasonable vocal limits adds to the dramatic point, even if it subtracts from the musical joys. By contrast, Plácido Domingo is vocally superb, a commanding prince; and the rest of the cast present star names even in small roles.

With Callas, the character seems so much more believably complex than with others, and this 1957 recording is one of her most thrillingly magnetic performances on disc. Schwarzkopf provides a comparably characterful and distinctive portrait as Liù, far more than a Puccinian 'little woman', sweet and wilting. Eugenio Fernandi sounds relatively uncharacterful as Calaf, but his timbre is pleasing enough. By contrast, Serafin's masterly conducting exactly matches the characterfulness of Callas and Schwarzkopf, with colour, atmosphere and dramatic point all commandingly presented. With such a vivid performance, the 1957 mono sound hardly seems to matter, although the choral passages tend to overload at climaxes.

In a performance which, thanks to the conductor, lacks urgency, regularly falling back into limpness, the RCA version, recorded in Munich, is notable only for several individual performances. It is a joy to hear such strong and beautiful singing as Margaret Price's in the role of Liù and, though his tenor is not Italianate, Ben Heppner, singing Calaf, produces thrillingly heroic tone. Eva Marton has already recorded the role of Turandot in Lorin Maazel's powerful live version for Sony, and the voice has certainly not improved in steadiness or warmth – rather the opposite. This is a very large voice, often uncomfortable to listen to, though she is at her best in the final scene, completed by Alfano. The recorded sound is warm and full.

Turandot: excerpts.

(M) (***) EMI mono CDH7 61074-2 [id.]. Dame Eva Turner, Martinelli, Albanese, Favero, Tomei, Dua, ROHCG Ch., LPO, Barbirolli.

The excerpts were recorded at two separate 1937 performances and fascinatingly duplicate most of the items, with the second performance in each pair marginally more spacious and helpful in sound, and generally warmer and more relaxed as a performance. Martinelli's heroic timbre may be an acquired taste, but he is stirringly convincing, and Dame Eva Turner gloriously confirms all the legends, even more commanding than in her earlier studio accounts of the big aria, *In questa reggia*. Keith Hardwick's excellent transfers, for all the obvious limitations of recording on stage at Covent Garden, give a superb sense of presence. (This is another important EMI reissue currently withdrawn.)

Turandot: highlights.

☞ (M) *** Decca 433 438-2 [id.] (from above recording, with Sutherland, Pavarotti; cond. Mehta).

(M) *** DG Dig. 435 409-2; *435 409-4* [id.] (from above set, with Ricciarelli, Domingo; cond. Karajan).

A generous and shrewdly chosen collection of excerpts from the glorious Decca set of *Turandot*. *Nessun dorma*, with Pavarotti at his finest, is here given a closing cadence for neatness. The vintage Decca sound is outstandingly full and vivid.

Domingo is at his very finest on the DG alternative CD, and he is exceptionally well represented in this 70-minute selection of highlights, as indeed is the chorus.

Le Villi: complete.
*** Sony MK 76890 [MK 36669]. Scotto, Domingo, Nucci, Gobbi, Amb. Op. Ch., Nat. PO, Maazel.

Maazel directs a performance so commanding, with singing of outstanding quality, that one can at last assess Puccini's first opera on quite a new level. Scotto's voice tends to spread a little at the top of the stave but, like Domingo, she gives a powerful performance, and Leo Nucci avoids false histrionics. A delightful bonus is Tito Gobbi's contribution reciting the verses which link the scenes; he is as characterful a reciter as he is a singer. The recording is one of CBS's best.

COLLECTIONS

'Puccini heroines'; La Bohème: Sì, mi chiamano Mimì; Donde lieta uscì; Musetta's waltz song.
Edgar: Addio, mio dolce amor. La Fanciulla del West: Laggiù nel Soledad. Gianni Schicchi: O mio
babbino caro. Madama Butterfly: Bimba, bimba non piangere (Love duet, with Plácido Domingo); Un
bel dì. Manon Lescaut: In quelle trine morbide; Sola, perduta, abbandonata. La Rondine: Ore dolci a
divine. Tosca: Vissi d'arte. Turandot: In questa reggia. Le Villi: Se come voi piccina.
*** BMG/RCA RD 85999 [RCA 5999-2-RC]. Leontyne Price, New Philh. O or LSO, Downes; Santi.

This collection is a formidable demonstration of the art of Leontyne Price at the very peak of her career, still marvellously subtle in control (the end of Tosca's *Vissi d'arte* for example), powerfully dramatic, yet able to point the *Rondine* aria with delicacy and charm. The *Love duet* from *Butterfly* in which she is joined by Domingo is particularly thrilling, and there is much else here to give pleasure. The remastering is extremely vivid and the voice is given fine bloom and presence. A Puccinian feast!

'The world of Puccini': excerpts from *La Bohème; La Fanciulla del West; Gianni Schicchi; Madama*
Butterfly; Manon Lescaut; La Rondine; Suor Angelica; Tosca; Turandot.
☞ (M) ** Decca 433 865-2; *433 865-4* [id.]. Freni, Pavarotti, Harwood, Leona Mitchell, Previdi, Tebaldi, Bergonzi, Cossotto, Chiara, Zeani, Sutherland, McCracken, Di Stefano.

After the inspired choice of Decca's 'World of Verdi', this is a disappointment, mainly because of the roster of artists. All the singing is sympathetic and often stirring, but easily the most distinctive section of the disc is the Love scene from Act I of *La Bohème*, with Freni and Pavarotti; here Elizabeth Harwood adds on *Musetta's waltz song*. There are also extended excerpts (24 minutes) from the Tebaldi/Bergonzi *Butterfly*, but the thin violins may prove a drawback to the novice seeking a fuller, more modern Puccini sound. Joan Sutherland's *Vissi d'arte* is a rare example of her as Tosca and Giuseppe di Stefano's *Nessun dorma* ends the programme excitingly.

'Ti amo': Arias and excerpts: *La Bohème:* (i; ii) *Che gelida manina; O soave fanciulla; In un coupé . . .*
O Mimì, tu più non torni. Fanciulla del West: Ch'ella mi creda. Madama Butterfly: (i; iii; iv) *Addio*
fiorito asil; Vienna la sera; Manon Lescaut: Ma se vi talenta . . . Tra voi, belle; Donna non vidi mai;
Ah! non v'avvicinate! . . . No! no! pazzo son! Tosca: Recondita armonia; (i) *Gente là dentro! . . . Mario!*
Mario!; E lucevan le stelle. Turandot: Nessun dorma; (v) *Non piangere, Liù . . . Ah! per l'ultima volta.*
☞ **(*) Decca Analogue/Dig. 425 909-2 [id.]. Pavarotti, with (i) Freni; (ii) Panerai; (iii) Kerns; (iv) Ludwig; (v) Caballé, Ghiaurov, Krause, Poli, de Palma, John Alldis Ch.

This CD offers 70 minutes of Pavarotti in Puccini purple patches, including the arias from *Tosca* and *Turandot* for which he is most famous with the wider musical public, and the great Act I love scene from *La Bohème*, in which he is admirably partnered by Mirella Freni. She joins him again with similar success in *Madama Butterfly*. Alas, the CD (which is impeccably transferred from various sources, mostly complete recordings) is provided with no information about the music except titles, just a dissertation on the tenor voice. This is a full-priced reissue and it deserves better documentation.

'Favourite Puccini': (i) *La Bohème: Mi chiamano Mimì; Donde lieta uscì;* (ii) *Musetta's waltz song.*
Gianni Schicchi: O mio babbino caro. Madama Butterfly: Un bel dì; (iii; iv) *Spira sul mare; Flower*
duet; Con onor muore . . . Tu, tu. (ii) *Manon Lescaut: In quelle trine morbide;* (iii) *Sola, perduta,*
abbandonata. (ii) *La Rondine: Chi il bel sogno di Doretta.* (iii) *Suor Angelica: Senza mamma, O bimbo,*
tu sei morto. (i) *Tosca: Vissi d'arte. Turandot: Tu, che di gel sei cinta;* (i; v) *In questa reggia. Le Villi:*
Se come voi.

☞ (M) *** Sony analogue/Dig. SMK 48094 [id.]. (i) Eva Marton; (ii) Kiri Te Kanawa; (iii) Renata
Scotto; (iv) with Wixell and Knight; (v) with Carreras.

Kiri Te Kanawa's six ravishing contributions are the highlight of this collection – there is currently no
more luscious Puccini singing than this – but the others are very characterful too, even if Eva
Marton's Mimì is a shade forceful; she is better suited to the role of Turandot. However, *In questa
reggia*, which ends the disc excitingly, delivers a damp squib by fading out. Before that there is much
to enjoy, not least Scotto's beautiful *Senza mamma* from *Suor Angelica* and the two moving excerpts
(Butterfly's entrance and the opera's climax) from Maazel's complete set of *Madama Butterfly*. The
sound is excellent throughout, although sometimes the vocal balance is very forward. There is no
back-up documentation, apart from a list of titles and performers.

Arias: *La Bohème: Quando m'en vo' soletta. Gianni Schicchi: O mio babbino caro. Madama Butterfly:
Un bel dì. Manon Lescaut: In quelle trine morbide. La Rondine: Chi il bel sogno di Doretta. Tosca:
Vissi d'arte. Le Villi: Se come voi piccina.*
*** Sony Dig. MK 37298 [id.]. Kiri Te Kanawa, LPO, Pritchard – VERDI: *Arias.* ***

The creamy beauty of Kiri Te Kanawa's voice is ideally suited to these seven lyrical arias, including
such rarities as the little waltz-like song from *Le Villi*, well recorded and sounding especially
believable on CD.

Arias: *La Bohème; Sì, mi chiamano Mimì; Donde lieta uscì. Gianni Schicchi: O mio babbino caro.
Madama Butterfly: Un bel dì; Tu, tu piccolo Iddio. Manon Lescaut: In quelle trine morbide; Sola,
perduta, abbandonata. La Rondine: Chi il bel sogno di Doretta. Tosca: Vissi d'arte. Turandot: Signore,
ascolta!; Tu che di gel sei cinta. Le Villi: Se come voi piccina.*
*** EMI CDC7 47841-2 [id.]. Montserrat Caballé, LSO, Mackerras.

Montserrat Caballé uses her rich, beautiful voice to glide over these great Puccinian melodies. The
effect is ravishing, with lovely recorded sound to match the approach. This is one of the loveliest of
all operatic recital discs and the comparative lack of sparkle is compensated for by the sheer beauty
of the voice. The CD transfer is extremely successful, vivid yet retaining the full vocal bloom.

Love duets from: *La Bohème,* Act I; *Madama Butterfly,* Act I; *Manon Lescaut,* Act II (with
Intermezzo); *Tosca,* Act III.
☞ (M) ** EMI CDM7 64195-2. Lenora Lafayette, Richard Lewis, Hallé O, Barbirolli (with VERDI:
La forza del destino: Overture; La Traviata: Preludes, Acts I & III. MASCAGNI: *Cavalleria
rusticana: Intermezzo **).*

It is unexpected casting to have Richard Lewis (recorded in 1958) singing the big Puccini roles. The
voice is in good condition and he sings warmly, intelligently and (especially in the *Bohème* excerpt)
touchingly. Perhaps this is no substitute for the Italian temperament of a Pavarotti, but the freshness
is in no doubt and Lenora Lafayette makes a good partner, an interesting soprano with an Albanese-
like quality. The four duets are more sizeable than might strictly be imagined: the *Manon Lescaut*
excerpt goes from Des Grieux's entry to the entry of Geronte; the *Bohème* excerpt starts well before
Che gelida manina and moves on to the end of the Act; the *Tosca* goes from *E lucevan le stelle* to just
after the outburst on *Trionfal*; the *Butterfly*, from *Viene la sera* to the end of the Act. The recording is
very good and Barbirolli is obviously relishing his day back in the opera pit. The programme opens
with a vibrant Verdi *Forza del destino overture*, and the Hallé strings are equally intense in the
Traviata Preludes; indeed they play impressively throughout.

'Great operatic duets': *La Bohème:* (i; ii) *Che gelida manina . . . Sì, mi chiamano Mimì . . . O soave
fanciulla;* (ii; iii) *In un coupé? . . . O Mimì, tu più non torni.* (i; ii; vi) *Madama Butterfly: Viene la sera
. . . Bimba, dagli occhi . . . Vogliatemi bene . . . Un po' di vero c'è.* (iv; v) *Manon Lescaut: Oh, sarò la
più bella . . . Tu, tu, amore? Tu?* (iv; vi) *Tosca: Mario! Mario! Mario!* (vii; ii) *Turandot: Principessa di
morte!*
☞ (M) *** Decca analogue/Dig. 421 896-2; *421 896-4.* (i) Freni; (ii) Pavarotti; (iii) Panerai; (iv) Te
Kanawa; (v) Carreras; (vi) Aragall; (vii) Sutherland.

Puccini duets don't come any better than this – a 70-minute recital to show the great strength of the
Decca catalogue in the music of Puccini. The opening love-scene from *Madama Butterfly* is fine
enough, but the meeting of Rodolfo and Mimì in Act I of *La Bohème* brings a glorious sequence of
three aria/duets that is surely unsurpassed in romantic opera. Freni and Pavarotti sing with great
ardour and beauty, and Kiri Te Kanawa does not disappoint in her scenes from *Tosca* and *Manon
Lescaut*. Finally Pavarotti forms an equally memorable partnership with Sutherland in *Turandot*. The
sound, mostly analogue, is well up to Decca's expected high standards.

Purcell, Henry (1659–95)

Sonnatas of 3 parts Nos. 1–7, Z.790–6; Pavans: in A min.; B flat; G min., Z.749, Z.750, Z.752.
*** Chan. Dig. CHAN 8591; *ABTD 1287* [id.]. Purcell Quartet.

Sonnatas of 3 Parts Nos. 8–12, Z.797–801; Sonnatas in 4 Parts Nos. 1–2, Z.802–3; Chacony in G min., Z.751; Fantasia on a Ground in D & F; Pavans in A, Z.748; G min., Z.751.
*** Chan. Dig. CHAN 8663; *ABTD 1349* [id.]. Purcell Quartet.

Sonnatas of 4 Parts Nos. 3–10, Z.804–811; Prelude for solo violin in G min., Z.773; Organ voluntaries Nos. 2 in D min.; 4 in G, Z.718 & 710.
*** Chan. Dig. CHAN 8763; *ABTD 1401* [id.]. Purcell Quartet.

Sonnatas of 4 Parts Nos. 1–10, Z.802–11.
*** O-L 433 190-2 [id.]. Mackintosh, Huggett, Coin, Hogwood (chamber organ or spinet).

In these *Sonnatas* Purcell turned to the new, concerted style which had been developed in Italy. Interspersed among the *Sonnatas* are three earlier and highly chromatic *Pavans*, composed before Purcell embraced the sonata discipline. If anything, the second volume is more attractive than the first, for it includes the indelible *Chacony in G minor*. The third leaves room for a solo violin *Prelude* and two organ *Voluntaries*, both admirably presented and, like the *Sonnatas*, offering very realistic sound. The Purcell Quartet give a first-class account of themselves: their playing is authoritative and idiomatic, and the artists are firmly focused in a warm but not excessively reverberant acoustic. Strongly recommended.

The Oiseau-Lyre recording has the advantage of including all the four-part works on a single CD, and the playing is authoritative in style and feeling and the recording exemplary.

Harpsichord music (complete): *Suites Nos. 1–8* (with alternative Prelude for *Suite No. 4*). Abdelazar: Jig. 4 Airs; Canary; Celebrate the festival: Gavotte. Dioclesian: Trumpet tune. The Double Dealer: Air. Hornpipe; The Indian Queen: Trumpet tune. 2 Marches; The Married Beau: March. The Old Bachelor: Hornpipe. Minuet; A New ground; New Irish tune; New minuet; New Scotch tune; Prelude in G min.; Round O; The Queen's dolour; Raise the voice: Minuet. Rigadoon; Saraband with division; Sefauchi's farewell; 2 Song tunes; Suite of 5 Lessons; Timon of Athens: Chaconne. Trumpet tune called The Cibell.*
(M) *** Saga SCD 9009/10. Robert Woolley (harpsichord).

Robert Woolley's playing is vital and imaginative. The selection offers much that is not otherwise available, and Purcell's arrangements include many cherishable miniatures. A good deal of the music, including the *Suites*, derives from *A Choice Collection of Lessons* (published posthumously in 1696); other items are from *A Banquet of Musick* (1688) and many of the transcriptions come from the Second Part of *Musick's-Handmaid*, published by Playford in 1689, and were 'carefully revised and corrected by the same Mr Henry Purcell'. An indispensable set for those interested in English keyboard music.

VOCAL MUSIC

Anthems & Services, Vol. 1: *It is a good thing to give thanks; Let mine eyes run down with tears; My beloved spake; O give thanks unto the Lord; O praise God in his holiness; O sing unto the Lord; Praise the Lord, O Jerusalem.*
☞ *** Hyp. Dig. CDA 66585 [id.]. Witcomb, Finnis, Hallchurch, Bowman, Daniels, George, Evans, King's Cons., Robert King.

Anthems & Services, Vol. 2: *Behold now praise the Lord; Blessed are they that fear the Lord; I will give thanks unto Thee, O Lord; My song shall be alway; Te Deum and Jubilate.*
☞ *** Hyp. Dig. CDA 66609 [id.]. Bowman, Covey-Crump, George, New College, Oxford, Ch., King's Cons., Robert King.

Anthems & Services, Vol. 3: *Begin the song, and strike the living lyre; Blessed Virgin's expostulation: Tell me, some pitying angel. Blow up the trumpet in Zion; Hear my prayer, O Lord; Hosanna to the highest; Lord, I can suffer thy rebukes; The Lord is King, be the people never so impatient; O God, Thou has cast us out; O Lord, our governor; Remember not Lord our offences; Thy word is a lantern unto my feet.*
☞ *** Hyp. Dig. CDA 66623 [id.]. Dawson, Bowman, Daniels, George, Evans, King's Cons. Ch., King's Cons., Robert King.

Anthems & Services, Vol. 4: *Awake ye dead; Behold I bring you glad tidings; Early, O Lord, my fainting soul; The earth trembled; Lord, not to us but to thy name; Lord, what is man?; My heart is inditing of a good matter; O all ye people, clap your hands; Since God so tender a regard; Sing unto God; Sleep, Adam and take thy rest; The way of God is an undefiled way.*

☞ *** Hyp. Dig. CDA 66644 [id.]. Witcomb, Finnis, Hallchurch, Kennedy, O'Dwyer, Gritton, Bowman, Covey-Crump, Daniels, George, Varcoe, R. Evans, New College, Oxford, Ch., King's Cons., Robert King.

Anthems & services, Vol. 5: *Awake, and with attention hear; How long, great God; Let the night perish (Job's Curse); O God, the king of glory; O God, Thou art my God; O, I'm sick of life; O Lord, rebuke me not; Praise the Lord, O my soul, and all that is within me; Rejoice in the Lord alway; We sing to him, whose wisdom form'd the ear; When on my sick bed I languish; With sick and famish'd eyes.*

☞ *** Hyp. Dig. CDA 66656 [id.]. Witcomb, Finnis, Hallchurch, Kennedy, Gritton, Bowman, Covey-Crump, Daniels, George, Evans, King's Cons. Ch., King's Cons., Robert King.

Anthems & Services, Vol. 6: *Great God and just; Hear me, O Lord, the great support; I will love Thee, O Lord; Lord, who can tell how oft he offendeth?; My heart is fixed, O God; O Lord, grant the King a long life; O praise the Lord, all ye heathen; Plung'd in the confines of despair; Thou wakeful shepherd that dost Israel keep; Who hath believed our report?; Why do the heathen so furiously rage together?*

☞ *** Hyp. Dig. CDA 66663 [id.]. Witcomb, Kennedy, O'Dwyer, Bowman, Covey-Crump, Daniels, Agnew, George, New College, Oxford, Ch., King's Cons., Robert King.

Anthems & Services, Vol. 7: *Beati omnes qui timent; In the black dismal dungeon of despair; I was glad* (2 settings: coronation anthem & verse anthem); *Jubilate in B flat; O consider my adversity; Music for the funeral of Queen Mary; Save me O God; Te Deum in B flat; Thy way O God is holy.*

☞ ⊕ *** Hyp. Dig. CDA 66677 [id.]. Kennedy, O'Dwyer, Goodman, Gritton, Bowman, Short, Covey-Crump, Daniels, Millhofer, George, R. Evans, King's Cons. Ch., King's Cons., Robert King.

Anthems & Services, Vol. 8: *Be merciful unto me; Benedicte in B flat; Blessed is the man that feareth the Lord; Bow down thine ear, O Lord; Full of wrath, his threatening breath; In Thee, O Lord, do I put my trust; Jehova, quam multi sunt hostes mei; Magnificat and Nunc Dimittis in G min.; They that go down to the sea in ships.*

☞ *** Hyp. Dig. CDA 66686 [id.]. O'Dwyer, Kennedy, Bowman, Covey-Crump, Daniels, Padmore, Milhofer, George, King's Cons. Ch., King's Cons., Robert King.

Robert King follows up the success of his collection of Purcell's Odes and Welcome songs (see below) with an equally illuminating collection of the church music. The different categories of work, Services, Verse Anthems, Motets (or Full Anthems) and devotional songs, cover the widest range of style and expression, with King's own helpful and scholarly notes setting each one in context. Generally the most adventurous in style are the Full Anthems, with elaborate counterpoint often bringing amazingly advanced harmonic progressions. Yet the Verse Anthems too include some which similarly demonstrate Purcell's extraordinary imagination in contrapuntal writing. So though Volume 6 is confined to Verse Anthems and devotional songs, they too offer passages of chromatic writing which defy the idea of these categories as plain and straightforward. As the title suggests, the devotional song, *Plung'd in the confines of despair*, is a particularly fine example. Although all the earlier volumes are full of of good things, Volume 7 (to which we award a token Rosette for the extraordinary achievement of this series) is the one to recommend first to anyone simply wanting to sample Purcell's church music. Not only does it contain the *Music for the Funeral of Queen Mary* in 1695, with drum processionals, the solemn *March* and *Canzona for brass* and *Funeral sentences*, it has the *B flat Morning service*, two settings of the Coronation anthem, *I was glad*, (one of them previously unrecorded), a magnificent Full Anthem, three Verse Anthems and two splendid devotional songs. Robert King's meticulous notes include a detailed account of Queen Mary's funeral, providing evidence for his view that the *March* was not played with drums accompanying, but on its own. Volume 8, too, is full of fine music. The opening Verse Anthem, *In Thee, O Lord, do I put my trust*, opens with a very striking, slightly melancholy *Sinfonia*, with a six-note figure rising up from a ground bass, which sets the expressive mood. The closing anthem, so appropriate from an island composer, *They that go down to the sea in ships*, is characteristically diverse, with Purcell helping the Lord 'maketh the storm to cease' and at the end providing a joyful chorus of praise. It is astonishing how many of the pieces have never appeared on record before, and that includes some of the finest. King's notes and documentation closely identify each item, adding to one's illumination. An outstanding series, full of treasures, with King varying the scale of forces he uses for each item. Often he uses one voice per part, but he regularly expands the ensemble with the King's Consort Choir or turns to the full New College Choir, which includes trebles.

Anthems: *O sing unto the Lord; Praise the Lord, O Jerusalem; They that go down to the sea in ships.* Ode: *My heart is inditing; Te Deum and Jubilate Deo in D.*
(M) *** DG 427 124-2. Ch. of Christ Church Cathedral, Oxford, E. Concert, Preston.

The performances in this mid-priced collection are full of character, vigorous yet with the widest range of colour and feeling. The recording, made in London's Henry Wood Hall, is both spacious and well detailed.

Ayres, Theatre music and Sacred songs: *Awake awake, ye dead (Hymn for the Day of Judgement); Birthday ode for Queen Mary: Strike the viol. Dioclesian: O how happy's he; Chaconne. The earth trembled (A hymn on our Saviour's Passion). The Fairy Queen: One charming night. How plaisant is this flow'ry plain and grove (ode). The Indian Queen: Ye twice ten hundred deities; Wake Quivera. Ode for St Cecilia: Raise, raise the voice; Oedipus: Hear, ye sullen pow'rs below; Come away, do not stay. The Old Bachelor: Thus to a ripe consenting maid. Olinda: There ne'er was so wretched a lover as I* (duet). *Timon of Athens: Hark how the songsters. Pavane and Trio.*
(B) **(*) HM HMA 90214 [id.]. Deller Cons. & Ens., Deller.

Deller has put together what one might regard as a sampler of Purcell's vocal music, a varied collection which includes some of his finest inspirations. Always fresh and often lovely performances, given good if not outstanding recording.

Benedicte: O all ye works of the Lord. Coronation music for King James II: I was glad. Funeral music for Queen Mary: Man that is born of woman; In the midst of life; Thou knowest, Lord, the secrets of our hearts. Anthems: Blow up the trumpet in Sion; Hear my prayer, O Lord; I will sing unto the Lord; Jubilate; Lord, how long wilt Thou be angry; O God, Thou art my God; O God, Thou hast cast us out; O Lord God of Hosts; Remember not, Lord, our offences; Save me, O God.
*** Conifer Dig. CDCF 152; MCFC 152 [id.]. Trinity College Ch., Cambridge, Marlow; Matthews; G. Jackson (organ).

Richard Marlow gets good results from his singers; such expressive anthems as *Remember not, Lord, our offences* and *Hear my prayer, O Lord* are eloquently done and beautifully recorded. Excellent performances from all concerned – not least the Conifer recording team.

(i) *Come ye sons of art (Ode on the birthday of Queen Mary, 1694);* Anthems: (ii) *My beloved spake;* (iii) *Rejoice in the Lord alway (Bell anthem);* (iv) *Welcome to all the pleasures (Ode on St Cecilia's Day, 1683).*
(M) **(*) Van. 08.8027.71 [OVC 8027]. Alfred Deller, Deller Cons.; (i) Mark Deller, Mary Thomas, Bevan, Oriana Concert Ch. & O; (ii) Cantelo, English, Bevan; (iii; iv) Kalmar O; (iii) Thomas, Sheppard, Tear, Worthley; Oriana Concert O. (iv) Cantelo, McLoughlin, English, Grundy, Bevan.

An enjoyable anthology showing Deller at his finest. The other soloists are good too, especially the tenor, Gerald English. The two anthems make a fine centrepiece, responding to the demand of Charles II for composers 'not to be too solemn' and to 'add symphonies, etc., with instruments' to their sacred vocal music. The *Bell anthem* is so called because of the repeated descending scales in the introduction. The recording is closely balanced, though pleasingly full.

Come, ye sons of art away; Funeral music for Queen Mary (1695).
*** Erato/Warner 2292 45123-2 [id.]. Lott, Brett, Williams, Allen, Monteverdi Ch. and O, Equale Brass Ens., Gardiner.

Come, ye sons of art away; Ode on St Cecilia's Day: Welcome to all the pleasures; Of old when heroes thought it base (Yorkshire Feast song).
*** DG Dig. 427 663-2 [id.]. J. Smith, Priday, Amps, Chance, Wilson, Ainsley, George, Richardson, E. Concert Ch., E. Concert, Pinnock.

Come, ye sons of art, the most celebrated of Purcell's birthday odes for Queen Mary, is splendidly coupled on Erato with the unforgettable funeral music he wrote on the death of the same monarch. With the Monteverdi Choir at its most incisive and understanding, the performances are exemplary and the recording, though balanced in favour of the instruments, is clear and refined.

Pinnock directs comparably exuberant performances. The weight and brightness of the choral sound go with infectiously lifted rhythms, making the music dance. The soloists are all outstanding, with the counter-tenor duetting of Michael Chance and Timothy Wilson in *Sound the trumpet* delectably pointed. The coupling, the neglected *Yorkshire Feast song*, is full of wonderful inspirations, like the tenor and counter-tenor duet, *And now when the renown'd Nassau* – a reference to the new king, William III.

In guilty night (Saul and the Witch of Endor); Man that is born of woman (Funeral sentences); Te Deum and Jubilate Deo in D.
(B) **(*) HM HMA 90207 [id.]. Deller Cons., Stour Music Festival Ch. & O, Deller.

In guilty night is a remarkable dramatic scene depicting Saul's meeting with the Witch of Endor. The florid writing is admirably and often excitingly sung by Alfred Deller himself as the King and Honor Sheppard as the Witch. The *Te Deum and Jubilate* are among Purcell's last and most ambitious choral works; the *Funeral sentences* from early in his career are in some ways even finer in their polyphonic richness. The chorus here is not the most refined on record but, with sensitive direction, this attractive collection is well worth hearing. The recording is good.

Music for the funeral of Queen Mary: March & canzona in C min.; Funeral sentences; Anthems: Give sentence with me, O Lord; Hear my prayer, O Lord; Jehova, quam multi sunt hostes mei; My beloved spake; O God, Thou art my God; O, I'm sick of life; Rejoice in the Lord alway (Bell anthem); Remember not, Lord, our offences; Organ voluntaries: in C; in G.
☞ **(*) Argo Dig. 436 833-2 [id.]. Winchester Cathedral Ch., David Dunnett (organ), L. Bar. Brass, Brandenburg Cons., Hill.

David Hill and the Winchester Choir plus instrumentalists provide an interesting alternative to Robert King in the *Queen Mary funeral music*, opting – like most previous interpreters, but unlike King – to have the drum recessionals simultaneously with the *March*. Though the boy-trebles are attractively fresh-toned, the Winchester ensemble is markedly less polished than King's. The choice of other items includes a number of Purcell's most celebrated anthems, as well as the *Organ Voluntary in C*. Good, atmospheric sound.

Odes and Welcome songs Vols. 1–8 (complete).
☞ *** Hyp. Dig. CDS 44031/8 [id.]. Soloists, New College, Oxford, Ch., King's Cons., Robert King.

Odes & Welcome songs, Vol. 1: *Arise my muse (1690); Now does the glorious day appear (1689) (Odes for Queen Mary's birthday); Ode for St Cecilia's Day: Welcome to all pleasures (1683).*
*** Hyp. Dig. CDA 66314; *KA 66314* [id.]. Fisher, Bonner, Bowman, Chance, Daniels, Ainsley, George, Potts, King's Cons., Robert King.

Odes & Welcome songs, Vol. 2: *Ode on St Cecilia's Day (Hail! bright Cecilia!) (1692). Ode for the birthday of the Duke of Gloucester: Who can from joy refrain (1695).*
☞ *** Hyp. Dig. CDA 66349; *KA 66349* [id.]. Fisher, Bonner, Bowman, Covey-Crump, Ainsley, George, Keenlyside, New College, Oxford, Ch., King's Cons., King.

Odes & Welcome songs, Vol. 3: *Ode for Queen Mary's birthday: Celebrate this festival (1693). Welcome song for Charles II (1683): Fly, bold rebellion (1683). Welcome song for James II: Sound the trumpet, beat the drum (1687).*
☞ *** Hyp. Dig. CDA 66412; *KA 66412* [id.]. Fisher, Bonner, Bowman, Kenny, Covey-Crump, Müller, George, Pott, King's Cons., King.

Odes & Welcome songs, Vol. 4: *Ode for Mr Maidwell's School: Celestial music did the gods inspire (1689). Ode for the wedding of Prince George of Denmark and Princess Anne: From hardy climes and dangerous toils of war (1683). Welcome song for James II: Ye tuneful muses (1686).*
☞ *** Hyp. Dig. CDA 66456; *KA 66456* [id.]. Fisher, Bonner, Bowman, Kenny, Covey-Crump, Daniels, George, Pott, King's Cons., Robert King.

Odes & welcome songs, Vol. 5: *Ode for the birthday of Queen Mary: Welcome, welcome, glorious morn (1691). Ode for the Centenary of Trinity College, Dublin: Great parent, hail to thee (1694). Welcome song for King Charles II: The Summer's absence unconcerned we bear (1682).*
☞ *** Hyp. CDA 66476; *KA 66476* [id.]. Fisher, Tubb, Bowman, Short, Covey-Crump, Ainsley, George, Pott, King's Cons., Robert King.

Odes & Welcome songs, Vol. 6: *Ode for Queen Mary's birthday: Love's goddess sure was blind (1692). Ode for St Cecilia's Day: Laudate Ceciliam (1683). Ode for St Cecilia's Day: Raise, raise the voice (c. 1685). Welcome song for Charles II: From those serene and rapturous joys (1684).*
☞ *** Hyp. Dig. CDA 66494 [id.]. Fisher, Seers, Bowman, Short, Padmore, Tusa, George, Evans, King's Cons., King.

Odes & Welcome songs, Vol. 7: *Welcome song for Charles II: Swifter Isis, swifter flow* (1681). *Welcome song for the Duke of York: What shall be done in behalf of the man?* (1682). *Yorkshire feast song: Of old, when heroes thought it base* (1690).

☞ *** Hyp. Dig. CDA 66587 [id.]. Fisher, Hamilton,, Bowman, Short, Covey-Crump, Daniels, George, Evans, King's Cons., King.

Odes & welcome songs, Vol. 8: *Ode for the birthday of Queen Mary: Come ye sons of Art, away* (1694). *Welcome song for Charles II: Welcome, viceregent of the mighty king* (1680). *Welcome song for King James: Why, why are all the Muses mute?*

☞ *** Hyp. Dig. CDA 66598 [id.]. Fisher, Bonner, Bowman, Chance, Padmore, Ainsley, George, Evans, Ch. of New College, Oxford, King's Cons., King.

Just what a wealth of inspiration Purcell brought to the occasional music he wrote for his royal and noble masters comes out again and again in Robert King's splendid collection of the Odes and Welcome songs. It is sad that for three centuries this fine music has been largely buried, with just a few of the Odes achieving popularity. In those, King's performances do not always outshine the finest of previous versions, but with an outstanding team of soloists as well as his King's Consort the performances achieve a consistently high standard, with nothing falling seriously short. Being able to hear previously unrecorded rarities alongside the well-known works sets Purcell's achievement vividly in context, helped by informative notes in each volume, written by King himself. Volume 1 includes the shorter of the two *St Cecilia odes* and immediately – among the fine team of soloists – it is a delight to hear such superb artists as the counter-tenors James Bowman and Michael Chance in duet. Volume 3 with the 1693 *Birthday ode* and Volume 7 with the fascinating *Yorkshire feast song* are two more CDs that would make good samplers. Those who want to dive in at the deep end should invest in the complete set, where all eight CDs are offered in a slip-case. First-rate sound throughout.

Ode on St Cecilia's Day (Hail! bright Cecilia).
*** Erato/Warner Dig. 2292 45187-2 [id.]. Jennifer Smith, Stafford, Gordon, Elliott, Varcoe, David Thomas, Monteverdi Ch., E. Bar. Soloists, Gardiner.
(M) *** DG 427 159-2 [id.]. Woolf, Esswood, Tatnell, Young, Rippon, Shirley-Quirk, Tiffin Ch., Amb. S., ECO, Mackerras.

Gardiner's characteristic vigour and alertness in Purcell come out superbly in this delightful record of the 1692 *St Cecilia Ode* – not as well known as some of the other odes he wrote, but a masterpiece. Soloists and chorus are outstanding even by Gardiner's high standards, and the recording excellent.

A splendid all-male performance of Purcell's joyous *Ode* on DG, with an exceptionally incisive and vigorous choral contribution matched by fine solo singing. Simon Woolf is ideally cast here and the recording is excellent, although the balance between soloists and tutti does not make much distinction in volume between the smaller and the larger groups.

(i) *Odes for Queen Mary's birthday: Come ye sons of art; Love's Goddess sure.* (ii) *Funeral music for Queen Mary (March; Canzone;* Funeral sentences: *Man that is born of woman; In the midst of life; Thou knowest, Lord; March;* Anthems: *Hear my prayer, O Lord; Remember not, Lord, our offences).* Anthems: *Blessed are they that fear the Lord; My beloved spake; Rejoice in the Lord alway.* (iii) (Organ) *The Queen's doleur; Trumpet minuet in C* (including *March* from *The Married Beau); Trumpet tunes in C & D; Voluntary in A.*

☞ (B) *** EMI CZS7 67524-2 (2) [id.]. (i) Burrowes, Bowman, Lloyd, Brett; Ch.; York Skinner, Hill, Shaw, Lloyd; L. Early Music Cons., Munrow; (ii) Cockerhan, King, Hayes, Chilcott, Morell, Castle, Byram-Wigfield, Robarts, Grier, King's College Ch., ASMF, Philip Jones Brass Ens., Ledger; (iii) Jean-Patrice Brosse (organ of Cathedral of Sainte Marie de Saint Bertrand de Comminges).

Purcell wrote a series of ceremonial odes for the birthdays of Queen Mary, and rarely has a courtier writing occasional pieces been so deeply and genuinely inspired. *Come ye sons of art* is the richest of the sequence, with its magnificent overture or symphony (no doubt intended to outdo those French at Versailles), and such memorable pieces as the duet, *Sound the trumpet. Love's goddess sure*, though not quite so grand, brings more Purcellian delights. The late David Munrow inspires fine playing and singing from his excellent forces and gives sensitive, intelligent performances of both works, which deliberately opt for an intimate scale, using old instruments and an authentic style of string playing; the results are entirely congenial to the ear. The intimacy clearly detracts from the sense of grandeur and panoply which are apt for this music but, with refined yet full sound to match, this alternative approach is equally satisfying. The coupling, made around the same time (1976/7), at King's is hardly less stimulating. As can be seen from the listing above, *Queen Mary's funeral music* consists of far more than the unforgettable *March* for lugubrious trombones (sackbuts) with punctuating timpani (later repeated without timpani), which still sounds so modern to our ears. Philip Ledger has the advantage of spacious sound (the original LP was issued in quadraphony) and his account of the *March* is darkly memorable. The anthems are well sung too, if slightly less alertly. The organ pieces, very well played, are particularly characterful heard on a comparatively pungent French organ. They are used as a postlude for the two birthday odes, while the voluntary (on disc 2) becomes an overture to introduce the three great verse anthems. The trumpet ayres are jolly, with a hurdy-gurdy effect in the Minuet framing a march from *The Married Beau*; the *Voluntary in C* is dark in timbre to match the dolorous piece specifically dedicated to the Queen.

Duets and solos for counter-tenor: *Bonduca: Sing, sing ye Druids. Come, ye sons of art: Sound the trumpet. Elegy on the death of Queen Mary: O dive custos Auriacae domus. The Maid's last prayer: No, resistance is but vain. Ode on St Cecilia's Day: In vain the am'rous flute. O solitude, my sweetest choice. The Queen's epicedium: Incassum, Lesbia rogas. Timon of Athens: Hark how the songsters.*
*** Hyp. Dig. CDA 66253; *KA 66253* [id.]. James Bowman, Michael Chance, King's Cons., King –
   BLOW: *Ode* etc. ***

A sparkling collection of solos and duets which show both the composer and these fine artists in inspirational form. The performances are joyous, witty and ravishing in their Purcellian melancholy, with often subtle response to word meanings, and King's accompaniments have plenty of character in their own right. Excellent recording.

Songs and airs: *Bess of Bedlam; Evening hymn; If music be the food of love; Lovely, lovely Albina; Not all my torments; Olinda in the shades unseen; The Plaint; O, urge me no more; When first Amintas sued for a kiss.* Arias: *Birthday ode for Queen Mary: Crown the altar. The Fairy Queen: Hark! hark!; O, O let me weep; Ye gentle spirits of the air. The Indian Queen: I attempt from love's sickness to fly. Pausanias: Sweeter than roses. The Tempest: Dear pritty youths. Timon of Athens: The cares of lovers.*
*** O-L Dig. 417 123-2 [id.]. Emma Kirkby, Rooley, Hogwood.

The purity of Emma Kirkby's soprano suits this wide-ranging collection of Purcell songs splendidly, though you might argue for a bigger, warmer voice in the *Bess of Bedlam* song. The *Evening hymn* is radiantly done, and so are many of the less well-known airs which regularly bring new revelation. Excellent recording.

Songs: *Come, let us drink; A health to the nut brown lass; If ever I more riches; I gave her cakes and I gave her ale; Laudate Ceciliam; The miller's daughter; Of all the instruments; Once, twice, thrice I Julia tried; Prithee ben't so sad and serious; Since time so kind to us does prove; Sir Walter enjoying his damsel; 'Tis women makes us love; Under this stone; Young John the gard'ner.*
*** HM HMC 90242 [id.]. Deller Cons., Deller.

One section of this charming and stylish collection has a selection of Purcell's catches, some of them as lewd as rugby-club songs of today, others as refined as *Under this stone* – all of which the Deller Consort take in their stride. The final two pieces are extended items; *If ever I more riches*, a setting of Cowley, has some striking passages. The remastering for CD has greatly improved the sound, with voices fresh and first-rate recording of the instruments.

Songs: *Cupid, the slyest rogue alive; Dear pretty youth; From silent shades; The fatal hour comes on apace; If music be the food of love; Incassum Lesbia; Not all my torments; Now that the sun hath veil'd his light; O solitude* (2 versions); *Stripp'd of their green; Tell me, some pitying angel.* Theatre songs: *Dioclesian: Let us dance; Don Quixote: From rosy bow'rs. The Indian Queen: I attempt from love's sickness to fly. King Arthur: Fairest isle. The Massacre of Paris: Beneath a poplar's shadow. Pausanias: Sweeter than roses. Tyrannic Love: Ah! how sweet it is to love.*
☞ *** Virgin/EMI Dig. VC7 59324-2 [id.]. Nancy Argenta, Nigel North, Richard Boothby, Paul Nicholson.

All but two of these songs were published in Henry Playford's celebratory Purcell collection, *Orpheus Britannicus*, and every one is inspired, offering a remarkable variety of mood and expression. Nancy Argenta's voice seems exactly suited to the repertoire, her tone consistently beautiful but never bland, her feeling for the words matched by her skill at not-too-elaborate ornamentation. The opening and closing soliloquy, *O solitude*, readily shows the beauty of her line, and the poignant melancholy of *Now that the sun hath veil'd his light* and the ravishing account of the familiar *Fairest isle* help to make this a distinctive recital. She can sparkle delightfully in a coloratura number like *Hark! hark! the echoing air* with its reminder of *Nymphs and Shepherds*, or essay the capricious mood of *Cupid, the slyest rogue alive.* The infinite variety of the remarkable *From rosy bow'rs* shows her at her most imaginative, and she is fully equal to the range of the extended *Tell me, some pitying angel* (the Virgin's heartfelt and very human expostulation after the young Jesus has left home and she is fearful for his safety). The accompaniments are most beautifully managed, judiciously using archlute, viola da gamba and harpsichord and, in *Now that the sun hath veil'd his light*, a chamber organ. The recording is most natural and realistic.

Songs: *The fatal hour comes on apace; Lord, what is man?; Love's power in my heart; More love or more disdain I crave; Now that the sun hath veiled his light; The Queen's epicedium; Sleep, Adam, sleep; Thou wakeful shepherd; Who can behold Florella's charms.* Arias: *History of Dioclesian: Since from my dear Astrea's sight. Indian Queen: I attempt from love's sickness to fly. King Arthur: Fairest isle. Oedipus: Music for a while. Pausanias: Sweeter than roses. The Rival Sisters: Take not a woman's anger ill. Rule a wife and have a wife: There's not a swain.*
*** Etcetera Dig. KTC 1013 [id.]. Andrew Dalton; Uittenbosch; Borstlap.

Andrew Dalton has an exceptionally beautiful counter-tenor voice, creamy even in its upper register to make the extended 'Hallelujahs' of *Lord, what is man?* and *Now that the sun* even more heavenly than usual. A delightful disc, well recorded.

Songs and dialogues: *Go tell Amynta; Hence fond deceiver; In all our Cinthia's shining sphere; In some kind dream; Lost is my quiet; Stript of their green; What a sad fate is mine; What can we poor females do; Why my poor Daphne, why complaining.* Theatre music: *Amphitryon: Fair Iris and her swain. Dioclesian: Tell me why. King Arthur: You say 'tis love; For love every creature is formed by his nature. The Old Bachelor: As Amoret and Thyrsis lay.*
*** Hyp. CDA 66056 [id.]. Kirkby, Thomas, Rooley.

This nicely planned Hyperion collection has one solo apiece for each of the singers, but otherwise consists of duets, five of them from dramatic works. These near-ideal performances, beautifully sung and sensitively accompanied on the lute, make a delightful record, helped by excellent sound.

STAGE WORKS AND THEATRE MUSIC

Abdelazar: Overture and suite.
☞ *** O-L 433 191-2 [id.]. Joy Roberts, AAM, Hogwood – LOCKE: *The Tempest* etc. ***

Purcell's music for *Abdelazar* (which includes the tune Britten made famous in his *Young person's guide to the orchestra*) makes a worthwhile bonus for Matthew Locke's memorable incidental music for *The Tempest.* The performance here is stylish and carefully prepared, with Joy Roberts giving an attractive account of the song, *Lucinda is bewitching fair.* Excellent, clearly focused sound.

Chacony; Abdelazar: Overture and dance suite. Circe: incidental music *(suite). Don Quixote: From rosie bow'rs. The Libertine*: incidental music *(suite). Oedipus: Music for a while. Pausanias: Sweeter than roses.* Songs: *Bess of Bedlam; If music be the food of love; An Evening hymn.*
☞ (M) *** O-L 443 195-2 [id.]. Emma Kirkby, Elizabeth Lane, James Bowman, Martyn Hill, Christopher Keyte, Catherine Bott, Judith Nelson, David Thomas, Taverner Ch., Instrumental Ens., AAM, Hogwood.

Purcell wrote some of his most attractive theatre music for plays now long forgotten, and the pieces revived here come up with wonderful freshness in these performances using original instruments. Alongside the new discoveries there are familiar favourites: *Nymphs and Shepherds* (from *The Libertine*) and *Music for a while*, finely sung by James Bowman, from *Oedipus.* This collection has remarkable variety and makes a first-class entertainment (71 minutes in all). The recording is newly minted.

Dido and Aeneas (complete).
🏵 (M) *** Decca 425 720-2. Dame Janet Baker, Herincx, Clark, Sinclair, St Anthony Singers, ECO, Anthony Lewis.
☞ *** Teldec/Warner Dig. 4509 91191-2 [id.]. Della Jones, Harvey, Donna Dean, Bickley, Murgatroyd, St James's Singers & Baroque Players, Ivor Bolton.
*** Ph. Dig. 416 299-2 [id.]. Jessye Norman, McLaughlin, Kern, Allen, Power, ECO and Ch., Leppard.
*** Chan. Dig. CHAN 0521; *EBTD 0521* [id.]. Kirkby, Thomas, Nelson, Noorman, Rees, Taverner Ch. & Players, Parrott.
(M) (***) EMI mono CDH7 61006-2 [id.]. Flagstad, Schwarzkopf, Hemsley, Mermaid Theatre Singers & O, Geraint Jones.

☞ (M) *(*) Teldec/Warner Dig. 4509 93686-2 [id.]. Murray, Scharinger, Yakar, Schmidt, Schoenberg Ch., VCM, Harnoncourt.

☞ (M) *(*) Van. 08.2032.71 [id.]. Mary Thomas, Bevan, Sheppard, Watts, Oriana Concert Ch. & O, Alfred Deller.

Janet Baker's 1962 recording of *Dido* is a truly great performance. The radiant beauty of the voice is obvious enough, but the emotion is implied, as it should be in this music, not injected in great uncontrolled gusts. Listen to the contrast between the opening phrase of *When I am laid in earth* and its repeat a few bars later: it is a model of graduated mezza voce. Then with the words *Remember me!*, delivered in a monotone, she subdues the natural vibrato to produce a white tone of hushed, aching intensity. Anthony Lewis and the ECO (Thurston Dart a model continuo player) produce the crispest and lightest of playing, which never sounds rushed. The other soloists and chorus give very good support. Herincx is a rather gruff Aeneas, but the only serious blemish is Monica Sinclair's Sorceress. She overcharacterizes in a way that is quite out of keeping with the rest of the production. Like most vintage Oiseau-Lyre recordings, this was beautifully engineered.

Ivor Bolton and the St James's Singers and Players present a period performance, intimately scaled, which avoids the snags of earlier versions, with Della Jones as Dido giving her finest recorded performance yet. She has a weightier mezzo than her rivals in other period performances, yet her flexibility over ornamentation is greater, and *Dido's Lament* is the more moving when, unlike Von Otter on DG Archiv, she is restrained over expressive gestures, keeping a tender simplicity. She shades her voice tonally very much as Dame Janet Baker did in her classic recording with Sir Anthony Lewis and the ECO, made in 1961, long before period manners were adopted. Ivor Bolton's team, recorded with bright immediacy, has no weak link, with Peter Harvey as Aeneas, Susan Bickley as a clear-toned Sorceress, Donna Dean as a characterful Belinda, and Andrew Murgatroyd as the Sailor, a tenor who plays no stylistic tricks. Setting the seal on the performance's success, the choir is among the freshest and liveliest, and the use of a guitar continuo as well as brief guitar interludes (suggested by the original libretto) enhances the happy intimacy of the presentation.

Authenticists should keep away, but the security and dark intensity of Jessye Norman's singing make for a memorable performance, heightened in the recitatives by the equally commanding singing of Thomas Allen as Aeneas. The range of expression is very wide – with Norman producing an agonized whisper in the recitative just before *Dido's Lament*. Marie McLaughlin is a pure-toned Belinda, Patrick Power a heady-toned Sailor, singing his song in a West Country accent, while Patricia Kern's performance as the Sorceress uses conventionally sinister expression. Leppard's direction is relatively plain and direct, with some slow speeds for choruses. Excellent recording.

Andrew Parrott's concept of a performance on original instruments has one immediately thinking back to the atmosphere of Josias Priest's school for young ladies where Purcell's masterpiece was first given. The voices enhance that impression, not least Emma Kirkby's fresh, bright soprano, here recorded without too much edge but still very young-sounding. It is more questionable to have a soprano singing the tenor role of the Sailor in Act III; but anyone who fancies the idea of an authentic performance need not hesitate. The CD is exceptionally refined, the sound well focused, with analogue atmosphere yet with detail enhanced.

Though Flagstad's magnificent voice may in principle be too weighty for this music, she scales it down superbly in her noble reading, which brings beautiful shading and masterly control of breath and tone. Schwarzkopf is brightly characterful as Belinda, and though Thomas Hemsley is not ideally sweet-toned as Aeneas, he sings very intelligently; even in this age of period performance, this traditional account under Geraint Jones sounds fresh and lively still, not at all heavy. The mono sound, obviously limited, yet captures the voices vividly, and this above all is Flagstad's set.

Harnoncourt's idiosyncratic rhythmic style in Purcell, often in exaggerated marcato – as well as his extreme speeds in both directions – undermines the effectiveness of the whole performance, presenting the authentic view far less imaginatively than his direct rivals. Ann Murray sings beautifully as Dido but has to struggle against the funereal speed for the *Lament*. The chorus is excellent and the other soloists consistently good, well trained in English but still distractingly foreign-sounding, even the heady-toned Sailor of Josef Köstlinger. Rachel Yakar is an agile Belinda, but she does not always blend well with Dido, and Trudeliese Schmidt makes a resonant, fire-eating Sorceress.

Deller is a masterly Purcellian; but here, with a cast that often falls short of the standards set on rival versions, he does not do himself justice. Helen Watts' Sorceress is superb and the cackling response of her fellow witches (Honor Sheppard and Ellen Dales) is the most memorable thing in the performance. Maurice Bevan is a strong but colourless Aeneas and Mary Thomas is very variable, rarely achieving the necessary emotional weight. She begins well but her closing Lament is a disappointment. Good, vivid (1964) sound.

Dido and Aeneas (complete); *Ode for St Cecilia's Day: Welcome to all pleasures* (1683).
☞ **(*) Ph. Dig. 432 114-2 [id.]. C. Watkinson, Moseley, Monteverdi Ch., E. Bar. Soloists,
   Gardiner.

Gardiner's version of *Dido* generously couples the opera with the celebrated *St Cecilia's Day ode*
of 1683. Characteristically he often chooses brisk speeds for the ensembles, springing rhythms
infectiously; like Ivor Bolton, he includes guitar interludes in Acts I and II. His scale is a little larger
than Bolton's, generally with more than one instrument per part, but that highlights the fact
that the string sound comes near to the abrasive style of early period performances. Carolyn
Watkinson is a sensitive Dido, but not as involving as the finest (as for example Della Jones for
Ivor Bolton or Dame Janet Baker) with the voice at times suggesting a counter-tenor. Good
as Gardiner's team is, it does not quite match Bolton's, singer for singer. Recording is good,
though not always ideally balanced, as when the Sailor (Paul Tindall) sings his rollicking song as
though off-stage.

Dioclesian; Timon of Athens.
*** Erato/Warner 2292 45327-2 (2) [id.]. Dawson, Fisher, Covey-Crump, Elliot, George, Varcoe,
   Monteverdi Ch., E. Bar. Soloists, Gardiner.

The martial music, shining with trumpets, is what stands out from *Dioclesian*, adapted from a
Jacobean play first given in 1622. Gardiner is such a lively conductor, regularly drawing out the
effervescence in Purcell's inspiration, that the result is delightfully refreshing, helped by an outstanding
team of soloists. The incidental music for *Timon of Athens* offers more buried treasure, including such
enchanting inventions as *Hark! how the songsters of the grove*, with its 'Symphony of pipes imitating
the chirping of birds', and a fine *Masque for Cupid and Bacchus*, beautifully sung by Lynne Dawson,
Gillian Fisher and Stephen Varcoe. Excellent Erato sound.

The Fairy Queen (complete).
*** DG Dig. 419 221-2 (2) [id.]. Harrhy, Jennifer Smith, Nelson, Priday, Penrose, Stafford, Evans,
   Hill, Varcoe, Thomas, Monteverdi Ch., E. Bar. Soloists, Gardiner.
*** HM Dig. HMC 901308/9; *HMC 401308/9* [id.]. Argenta, Dawson, Daniels, Loonen, Correas,
   Les Arts Florissants, William Christie.
(M) *** Decca 433 163-2 (2) [id.]. Vyvyan, Bowman, Pears, Wells, Partridge, Shirley-Quirk,
   Brannigan, Norma Burrowes, Amb. Op. Ch., ECO, Britten.
☞ (BB) **(*) HM HMP 390257/8 [id.]. Sheppard, Knibbs, Bevan, Platt, Alfred Deller, Jenkins,
   Mark Deller, Buttrey, Clarke, Stour Music Ch. & O, A. Deller.

Purcell's setting of Shakespeare's *Midsummer Night's Dream*, written in 1692, followed in the wake of
the great success of *Dido and Aeneas*. The music takes the form of five masques, each symbolizing one
aspect of the play. Gardiner's performance is a delight from beginning to end, for, though authenticity
and completeness reign, scholarship is worn lightly and the result is consistently exhilarating, with no
longueurs whatever. The fresh-toned soloists are first rate, while Gardiner's regular choir and
orchestra excel themselves, with Purcell's sense of fantasy brought out in each succeeding number.
Beautifully clear and well-balanced recording.

William Christie uses a far bigger team of both singers and instrumentalists than John Eliot
Gardiner on the rival, DG Archiv set, allowing a wider range of colours. The bite of the performance
is increased by the relative dryness of the recorded sound. Among Christie's soloists, Nancy Argenta
and Lynne Dawson are outstanding, and the whole team is a strong one. The number of singers in
solo roles allows them to be used together as chorus too – an authentic seventeenth-century practice.
This makes a vigorous and refreshing alternative to the fine Gardiner set; but the Harmonia Mundi
booklet is inadequate.

William Christie uses a far bigger team of both singers and instrumentalists than John Eliot
Britten's version from the early 1970s used a newly reshaped arrangement of the music made by
Britten himself in collaboration with Imogen Holst and Peter Pears. The original collection of
individual pieces is here grouped into four satisfying sections: *Oberon's birthday*, *Night and silence*,
the *Sweet passion* and the *Epithalamium*. The cast is consistently satisfying.

Deller's set was recorded – very well too – at the Stour Music Festival in 1972 and, although the
balance is rather forward, the acoustic is pleasingly warm and the voices and orchestra combine
effectively. All the solo singing is of a high standard, with Honor Sheppard particularly memorable as
Night in Act II, well matched by Jean Knibbs's Mystery in some of Purcell's most evocative writing.
Norman Platt is a suitably bucolic Drunken Poet in Act I and becomes one of a pair of West Country
haymakers (Alfred Deller obviously enjoying himself as his companion, Mopsa) in Act III. The many
ensembles are eloquently sung and, although this has not quite the sophistication of Gardiner's set, its

robust warmth and Deller's considerable concern for detail make for an enjoyable entertainment, well worth its modest price when so smoothly and vividly transferred to CD.

The Indian Queen (incidental music; complete).
*** HM HMC 90243; *HMC 40243* [id.]. Knibbs, Sheppard, Mark and Alfred Deller, Elliot, Bevan, Deller Singers, King's Musick, Deller.
**(*) Erato/Warner 2292 45556-2 [id.]. Hardy, Fischer, Harris, Smith, Stafford, Hill, Elwes, Varcoe, Thomas, Monteverdi Ch., E. Bar. Soloists, Eliot Gardiner.

Deller's group is at its liveliest and most characterful in *The Indian Queen*. *Ye twice ten hundred deities* is sung splendidly by Maurice Bevan; and the duet for male alto and tenor, *How happy are we* (with Deller himself joined by Paul Elliot), as well as the best-known item, the soprano's *I attempt from love's sickness to fly* (Honor Sheppard), are equally enjoyable.

The reissued Erato version is fully cast and uses an authentic accompanying baroque instrumental group. The choral singing is especially fine, with the close of the work movingly expressive. John Eliot Gardiner's choice of tempi is apt and the soloists are all good, although the men are more strongly characterful than the ladies; nevertheless the lyical music comes off well. The recording is spacious and well balanced.

(i) *The Indian Queen* (incidental music); (ii) *King Arthur* (complete).
⊛ (M) *** Decca 433 166-2 (2) [id.]. (i) Cantelo, Wilfred Brown, Tear, Partridge, Keyte, St Anthony Singers, ECO, Mackerras; (ii) Morison, Harper, Mary Thomas, Whitworth, Wilfred Brown, Galliver, Cameron, Anthony, Alan, St Anthony Singers, Philomusica of L., Lewis.

This Decca Serenata (originally Oiseau-Lyre) version of *The Indian Queen* dates from 1966 and the recording, from a vintage era, remains first rate. With stylish singing and superb direction and accompaniment (Raymond Leppard's harpsichord continuo playing must be singled out), this is an invaluable reissue. Charles Mackerras shows himself a strong and vivid as well as scholarly Purcellian. The Rosette, however, is for the pioneering 1959 set (also Oiseau-Lyre) of *King Arthur*, fully worthy to stand alongside the companion recording of *Dido and Aeneas*, made three years later – see above. Here the success of the interpretation does not centre on the contribution of one inspired artist, but rather on teamwork among a number of excellent singers and on the stylish and sensitive overall direction of Anthony Lewis. Oiseau-Lyre's excellent stereo also plays a big part. A very happy example is the chorus *This way, that way*, when the opposing spirits (good and evil) make a joint attempt to entice the King, while the famous freezing aria will surely send a shiver through the most warm-blooded listener.

King Arthur (complete).
*** Erato/Warner 2292 45211-2 (2) [id.]. Jennifer Smith, Gillian Fischer, Priday, Ross, Stafford, Elliott, Varcoe, E. Bar. Soloists, Gardiner.
*** DG Dig. 435 490-2 (2) [id.]. Argenta, Gooding, Perillo, MacDougal, Tucker, Bannatyne-Scott, Finley, Ch. & E. Concert, Pinnock.

Gardiner's solutions to the textual problems carry complete conviction, as for example his placing of the superb *Chaconne in F* at the end instead of the start. Solo singing for the most part is excellent, with Stephen Varcoe outstanding among the men. *Fairest isle* is treated very gently, with Gill Ross, boyish of tone, reserved just for that number. Throughout, the chorus is characteristically fresh and vigorous, and the instrumentalists beautifully marry authentic technique to pure, unabrasive sounds.

Pinnock opens with the *Chaconne*, which is placed before the *Overture*. His performance is consistently refreshing and can be recommended alongside, though not in preference to Gardiner's. Linda Perillo makes a charming Philidel. Brian Bannatyne-Scott is superb in Aeolus's *Ye blust'ring brethren*, and in his *Frost aria* he achieves an unusual if controversial effect by beginning his series of shakes from slightly under the note. Not surprisingly, Nancy Argenta sings beautifully in the double roles of Cupid and Venus and her *Fairest isle* will not disappoint; both chorus and orchestra sing and play throughout with consistent vitality. The DG recording is first class, but why no coupling? The second CD plays for only 39 minutes.

King Arthur: highlights.
☞ (M) *** Erato/Warner Dig. 2292 45919-2 (from above complete set; cond. Gardiner).

A well-chosen 64-minute selection from John Eliot Gardiner's complete version, this can be strongly recommended for it contains a great deal of the music, including the famous stereophonic chorus, 'Hither this way'.

The Tempest (incidental music; complete).

*** Erato/Warner 2292 45555-2; *2292 45555-4* [id.]. Jennifer Smith, Hardy, Hall, Elwes, Varcoe, David Thomas, Earle, Monteverdi Ch. & O, Gardiner.

Whether or not Purcell himself wrote this music for Shakespeare's last play (the scholarly arguments are still unresolved), John Eliot Gardiner demonstrates how delightful it is, a masterly collection, in performances both polished and stylish and with excellent solo and choral singing. The recording, full and atmospheric, has transferred vividly to CD.

Theatre music (collection).
Disc 1: *Abdelazar: Overture and suite. Distressed Innocence: Overture and suite. The Gordian Knot Untied: Overture and suite; The Married Beau: Overture and suite. Sir Anthony Love: Overture and suite.*

Disc 2: *Bonduca: Overture and suite. Circe: suite. The Old Bachelor: Overture and suite. The Virtuous Wife: Overture and suite.*

Disc 3: *Amphitrion: Overture and suite; Overture in G min.; Don Quixote: suite.*
Disc 4: *Overture in G min. The Double Dealer: Overture and suite. Henry II, King of England: In vain, 'gainst love, in vain I strove. The Richmond Heiress: Behold the man. The Rival Sisters: Overture; 3 songs. Tyrannic Love: Hark my Damilcar!* (duet); *Ah! how sweet it is to love. Theodosius: excerpts. The Wives' Excuse: excerpts.*

Disc 5: *Overture in D min.; Cleomenes, the Spartan Hero: No, no, poor suff'ring heart. A Dialogue between Thirsis and Daphne: Why, my Daphne, why complaining?. The English Lawyer: My wife has a tongue: excerpts. A Fool's Preferment: excerpts. The History of King Richard II: Retir'd from any mortal's sight. The Indian Emperor: I look'd and saw within. The Knight of Malta: At the close of the ev'ning. The Libertine: excerpts. The Marriage-hater Match'd: As soon as the chaos . . . How vile are the sordid intregues. The Massacre of Paris: The genius lo* (2 settings). *Oedipus: excerpts. Regulus: Ah me! to many deaths. Sir Barnaby Whigg: Blow, blow, Boreas, blow. Sophonisba: Beneath the poplar's shadow. The Wives' Excuse: excerpts.*

Disc 6: *Chacony; Pavans Nos. 1–5; Trio sonata for violin, viola de gamba & organ. Aureng-Zebe: I see, she flies me. The Canterbury Guests: Good neighbours why?. Epsom Wells: Leave these useless arts. The Fatal Marriage: 2 songs. The Female Virtuosos: Love, thou art best. Love Triumphant: How happy's the husband. The Maid's Last Prayer: excerpts. The Mock Marriage: Oh! how you protest; Man is for the woman made. Oroonoko: Celemene, pray tell me. Pausanius: Song (Sweeter than roses) and duet. Rule a Wife and Have a Wife: There's not a swain. The Spanish Friar: Whilst I with grief.*

(M) *** O-L 425 893-2 (6). Kirkby, Nelson, Lane, Roberts, Lloyd, Bowman, Hill, Covey-Crump, Elliott, Byers, Bamber, Pike, David Thomas, Keyte, Shaw, George, Taverner Ch., AAM, Hogwood.

Most of the music Purcell wrote for the theatre is relatively little heard and much of the music comes up with striking freshness in these performances using authentic instruments. As well as the charming dances and more ambitious overtures, as the series proceeds we are offered more extended scenas with soloists and chorus, of which the nine excerpts from *Theodosius*, an early score (1680), are a particularly entertaining example. Before that, on Disc 3 we have already had the highly inventive *Overture and incidental music* for *Don Quixote*, with much enchanting singing from both the soprano soloists, Emma Kirkby and Judith Nelson. Disc 4 also includes a delightful duet from *The Richmond Heiress*, representing a flirtation in music. There are other attractive duets elsewhere, for instance the nautical *Blow, blow, Boreas, blow* from *Sir Barnaby Whigg*, which could fit admirably into *HMS Pinafore* (Rogers Covey-Crump and David Thomas) and the jovial *As soon as the chaos* from *The Marriage-hater Match'd*. In *Ah me! to many deaths* from *Regulus*, Judith Nelson is at her most eloquent while, earlier on Disc 5, she sings charmingly the familiar *Nymphs and shepherds*, which comes from *The Libertine*, a particularly fine score with imaginative use of the brass. The equally famous *Music for a while*, beautifully sung by James Bowman, derives from *Oedipus*. The last disc also includes a splendidly boisterous *Quartet* from *The Canterbury Guests*. The collection is appropriately rounded off by members of the Academy giving first-class performances of some of Purcell's instrumental music, ending with the famous *Chacony*. The discs are comprehensively documented and with full texts included.

Quantz, Joseph Joachim (1697–1773)

Flute concertos: in C; in D (For Potsdam); G; G min.

*** BMG/RCA Dig. RD 60247; *RK 60247* [60247-2-RC; *60247-4-RC*]. James Galway, Württemberg CO, Heilbron, Faerber.

Quantz was a skilled musician and all four concertos here are pleasing, while their slow movements show a genuine flair for melody. The *Arioso mesto* of the *G major* is particularly charming but the *Amoroso* of the *C major* is appealing too. Quantz also wrote well-organized allegros, and the opening *Allegro assai* of the *G major* shows him at his most vigorous, even if perhaps the *Potsdam concerto* is overall the best of the four works here. The thoroughly musical James Galway is most winning in the lyrical cantilenas, and the Württemberg group accompany with polish and much vitality. Excellent sound.

Quilter, Roger (1877–1953)

A Children's overture; Country pieces; 3 English dances; As you like it: suite; The Rake: suite; Where the Rainbow ends: suite.

☞ **(*) Marco Polo Dig. 8.223444. Slovak RSO (Bratislava), Adrian Leaper.

At long last a modern recording of Roger Quilter's enchanting *Children's overture*, so felicitously based on nursery rhymes. Adrian Leaper plays it with the lightest touch and the transparency of the recording ensures that all the woodwind detail comes through nicely, and the little fugato on 'A frog he would a-wooing go' is delightfully handled, even if his performance could ideally have had a shade more momentum. One might also have wished for a bigger band with a more opulent string sheen, but the texture here well suits the suites of incidental music, an agreeable mixture of the styles of Edward German (especially the *Country dance* from *As you like it*), Eric Coates and sub-Elgar of the *Nursery suites*. All this nicely scored and amiably tuneful music is freshly and spontaneously presented and the recording is nicely resonant.

Rachmaninov, Sergei (1873–1943)

Piano concertos Nos. (i) *1;* (ii) *2* (2 versions); (i) *3–4;* (ii) *Rhapsody on a theme of Paganini;* (iii) *The Isle of the Dead; Symphony No. 3; Vocalise.* (piano, 4 hands): (iv) *Polka italienne.* (Solo piano): *Barcarolle, Op. 10/3; Daisies* (song transcription); *Etudes-tableaux, Op. 33/2 & 7 & Op. 39/6; Humoresque, Op. 10/5; Lilacs* (song transcription; 2 versions); *Mélodie, Op. 3/3; Moment musical, Op. 16/2; Oriental sketch; Polichinelle, Op. 3/4; Polka de W. R.* (3 versions). *Preludes: in C sharp min., Op. 3/2* (3 versions); *in G min.; in G flat, Op. 23/5 & 10; in E, G, F min., F, G sharp, Op. 32/3, 5–7, 12; Serenade, Op. 3/5* (2 versions); (v) BEETHOVEN: *Violin sonata No. 8 in G, Op. 30/3.* SCHUBERT: *Violin sonata in A, D.574.* GRIEG: *Violin sonata in C min., Op. 45.* BACH: *Partita No. 4, BWV 828: Sarabande.* HANDEL: *Suite No. 5: Air and variations (The Harmonious blacksmith).* MOZART: *Piano sonata in A, K.331: Theme and variations; Rondo alla Turca.* BEETHOVEN: *32 Variations in C min. WoO 80.* LISZT: *Concert paraphrase of Chopin: Polish songs (Return home; The maiden's wish). Concert paraphrases of Schubert: Das Wandern; Serenade. Polonaise No. 2; Concert study: Gnomenreigen; Hungarian rhapsody No. 2.* MENDELSSOHN: *Song without words: Spinning song, Op. 67* (2 versions). *Etudes, Op. 104b/2–3.* SCHUBERT: *Impromptu in A flat, Op. 90/4.* GLUCK: *Orfeo ed Euridice: Mélodie.* SCHUMANN: *Der Kontrabandiste* (arr. Tausig); *Carnaval, Op. 9.* PADEREWSKI: *Minuet, Op. 14/1.* CHOPIN: *Sonata No. 2 (Funeral march); Nocturnes, Op. 9/2; Op. 15/2; Waltzes: Op. 18 (Grand valse brillante), Op. 34/3; Op. 42; Op. 64/1* (2 versions); *Op. 64/2; Op. 64/3* (2 versions); *Op. 69/2; Op. 70/1; in E min., Op. posth.; Ballade No. 3; Mazurkas, Op. 63/3, Op. 68/2; Scherzo No. 3.* BORODIN: *Scherzo in A flat.* TCHAIKOVSKY: *The Seasons: November (Troika;* 2 versions). *Humoresque, Op. 10/2; Waltz, Op. 40/8.* SCRIABIN: *Prelude, Op. 11/8.* Johann STRAUSS Jnr: *Man lebt nur einmal (One lives but once;* arr. Tausig). DAQUIN: *Le coucou.* SAINT-SAËNS: *Le Cygne* (arr. Siloti). GRIEG: *Lyric pieces: Waltz; Elfin dance.* DOHNÁNYI: *Etude, Op. 28/6.* HELSELT: *Etude, Op. 2/6 (Si oiseau j'étais).* MOSZKOWSKI: *Etude, Op. 52/4 (La jongleuse).* DEBUSSY: *Children's corner: Dr Gradus ad Parnassum; Golliwog's cakewalk.* Domenico SCARLATTI: *Pastorale* (arr. Tausig). Transcriptions: KREISLER: *Liebesfreud* (3 versions). BACH: (Unaccompanied) *Violin Partita No. 3, BWV 1003: Preludio; Gavotte & Gigue.* MENDELSSOHN: *A Midsummer Night's Dream: Scherzo.* SCHUBERT: *Wohin?.* MUSSORGSKY: *Gopak.* TCHAIKOVSKY: *Lullaby, Op. 16/1.* RIMSKY-KORSAKOV: *Flight of the bumble bee.* BEETHOVEN: *Ruins of Athens: Turkish march.* BIZET: *L'Arlésienne: Minuet.* TRAD.: (vi) *Powder and Paint.*

☞ ⊛ (M) (***) BMG/RCA mono 09026 61265-2 (10) [id.]. Sergei Rachmaninov (piano); with Phd. O, (i) Ormandy; (ii) Stokowski; (iii) cond. composer; (iv) with Natalie Rachmaninov; (v) Fritz Kreisler; (vi) Nadejda Plevitskaya.

(i) *Piano concerto No. 2; Rhapsody on a theme of Paganini;* (ii) *Vocalise.*
☞ (B) (***) Pickwick mono GLRS 104 [id.]. Rachmaninov, Phd. O, Stokowski; (ii) composer, Phd.
O.

It is good that RCA is at last unearthing some of the historic recordings in its unique archive that have lain buried for years. Spurred by the 50th anniversary of Rachmaninov's death, the company has issued a ten-disc box at mid-price collecting all the recordings the composer made from 1919, the time he arrived in America, until 1942, the year before his death. These include all four of his *Piano concertos* (No. 3 irritatingly cut) as well as the *Paganini rhapsody,* the *Third Symphony* and the tone-poem, *The Isle of the Dead* (also with cuts). Among Rachmaninov's many solo piano recordings it is fascinating to compare his different readings of the most celebrated piece of all, the *Prelude in C sharp minor.* The stiff performance of 1919 (made for Edison) leads to a much freer and subtler reading in 1921, while the 1928 version, using the new electrical process, remains free and subtle but is emotionally less charged. The acoustic recordings, made between 1920 and 1925, are on balance the most cherishable of all, with the sound astonishingly full and the readings sparkling and spontaneous. That is true even of his 1924 recording of the *Piano Concerto No. 2,* now for the very first time issued complete. As in his classic electrical recording of five years later, he is partnered by Stokowski and the Philadelphia Orchestra, but the earlier one has a more volatile quality, with the fingerwork even clearer. Interpreting Chopin, Rachmaninov was also at his freshest and most imaginative in the early recordings, yet dozens of items here bear witness to the claim often made that he was the greatest golden-age pianist of all, bar none. The delicacy of his playing in Daquin's little piece, *Le coucou,* shows how he was able to scale down his block-busting virtuosity and, though in Beethoven's *32 Variations in C minor* he omitted half-a-dozen variations so as to fit the piece on two 78 sides, it is full of flair. There is magic too in his collaborations with Fritz Kreisler, not just in Beethoven but also in the Grieg and Schubert sonatas, and in the private recordings, when he accompanies a gypsy singer in a traditional Russian song or plays a piano duet, the *Polka italienne,* with his wife, Natalie. Transfers are commendably clean but with high background hiss. The ten discs come in a box at mid-price.

For those who want just the two electrical concertante recordings made with Stokowski, the Pickwick CD serves admirably. The transfers are slightly less sharp in detail but agreeably full. Both here and in the RCA version of the second recording of the *C minor Concerto* the woodwind triplets which accompany the reprise of the main theme of the slow movement come out vividly as in no other recording. Even in a live performance these very effective decorations tend to become buried.

Piano concertos Nos. 1–4.
(B) *** EMI CZS7 67419-2 (2) [id.]. Collard, Capitole Toulouse O, Plasson.

Piano concertos Nos. 1–4; Rhapsody on a theme of Paganini.
☞ (B) ** Ph. Duo 438 326-2 (2) [id.]. Rafael Orozco, RPO, Edo de Waart.

Piano concertos Nos. 1 in F sharp min., Op. 1.; 4 in G min., Op. 40; Rhapsody on a theme of Paganini, Op. 43.
☞ **(*) Chan. Dig. CHAN 9192 [id.]. Howard Shelley, RSNO, Thomson.

Piano concertos Nos. 2 in C min., Op. 18; 3 in D min., Op. 30.
☞ **(*) Chan. Dig. CHAN 9192 [id.]. Howard Shelley, RSNO, Thomson.

Jean-Philippe Collard's recordings of the four Rachmaninov concertos date from the late 1970s. Collard is completely at home in this repertoire; his account of the *First* has splendid fire and can hold its own with all comers (even Pletnev and Ashkenazy, though the former is incomparable in the slow movement); and much the same goes for its companions. Perhaps the *Third Piano concerto* is the least incandescent in his hands, but readers wanting an inexpensive set (all four concertos for the price of one CD) need look no further, for this is playing of quality, and the recording, though not outstanding, is fully acceptable, and avoids the artificial edginess of the Decca transfers.

Howard Shelley's recordings, previously available only in a box, are now issued on two separate CDs – still at full price. The recording, made in Caird Hall, Dundee, is certainly sumptuous, almost overwhelmingly so at climaxes, with rich strings and powerfully resonant brass and a bold, truthful piano-image projected way out in front. The performances do not lack adrenalin either, although their ebb and flow of tension is not consistent, and at times the music-making almost tends to run away with itself, notably in the *Third Concerto.* The first-movement climax of the *Second Concerto* is very powerful, and there is some lovely playing from the orchestra at the end of the slow movement. The finales have great dash and much charisma from Shelley, but Bryden Thomson at times seems less assured in the idiom. Just after the opening of the *Rhapsody on a theme of Paganini* he produces a curious echo effect (in which his soloist joins), while his *Eighteenth variation* could have more unbuttoned fervour. In the finale of the *First Concerto* his caressing of the lyrical string-tune is too cosy. Moreover he fails to match exactly his soloist's ardour in the big statement of the great melody at the climax of the finale of the *Second Concerto*. The *Fourth Concerto* has some spectacular moments but lacks a really firm profile. Even so, there is much to enjoy here, and Howard Shelley's contribution is consistently distinguished.

Rafael Orozco – a Leeds prizewinner just over a decade ago – is a powerful and often impressive player, but his set of the Rachmaninov concertos cannot really be counted in any way memorable, in spite of some brilliant playing. Though in many ways creditable, his readings are in no way special; both soloist and conductor could be more responsive to the poetry and atmosphere of the music. There are undoubtedly good things in this set but, given the competition – particularly in the *Second* and *Third Concertos* and the *Paganini Rhapsody* – this is not a strong contender, despite good sound and a very economical price.

Piano concertos Nos. 1 in F sharp min., Op. 1; 2 in C min., Op. 18.
(***) Olympia mono OCD 190 [id.]. Moura Lympany, Philh. O, Nicolai Malko – PROKOFIEV: *Piano concerto No. 1.* **(*)

Piano concerto No. 3 in D min., Op. 30.
(***) Olympia mono OCD 191 [id.]. Moura Lympany, New SO, Anthony Collins – PROKOFIEV: *Piano concerto No. 3.* **(*)

Moura Lympany's recording of the *Third* comes from a 1952 Decca LP; it sounds simply amazing for its age. Her EMI account of the *First* yields nothing in terms of virtuosity or panache to many bigger names on the international circuit, and the mono sound is very good, though it is not quite as impressive as in the Decca *Third*. In No. 3, as was the custom in the 1950s, she plays Rachmaninov's later cadenza. These are very fine performances which will give pleasure, and Olympia must be congratulated on restoring them to circulation in such excellent transfers.

Piano concerto No. 1 in F sharp min., Op. 1.
☞ (M) *** Mercury 434 333-2 [id.]. Byron Janis, Moscow PO, Kondrashin – PROKOFIEV: *Piano concerto No. 3.* ***

As in the Prokofiev coupling, on the occasion of the first Western-engineered recordings made in the USSR, soloist and orchestra plainly challenged each other to the limit, and the American technical team brilliantly captured the warmly romantic and chimerical interpretation which resulted. The solo playing stands alongside that of Horowitz in this repertoire, scintillating in the finale, yet never offering virtuosity simply for its own sake. Even now the recording is impressive for its clarity of texture and subtle detail within a warm acoustic. The CD represents one of Wilma Cozart Fine's most successful transfers.

(i) *Piano concerto No. 1 in F sharp min., Op. 1;* (ii) *Rhapsody on a theme of Paganini, Op. 43.*
*** Virgin/EMI Dig. VC7 59506-2 [id.]. Pletnev, Philh. O, Pešek.
*** Decca Dig. 417 613-2; *417 613-4* [id.]. Ashkenazy, (i) Concg. O; (ii) Philh. O, Haitink.

Mikhail Pletnev's accounts of the *F sharp minor Concerto* and the *Rhapsody on a theme of Paganini* with the Philharmonia Orchestra under Libor Pešek are very fine indeed. The *Paganini rhapsody* is distinguished not only by quite stunning virtuosity and unobtrusive refinement but also by great feeling. This is playing of classic status, strong in personality and musicianship. The CD sounds especially vivid.

This coupling also finds Ashkenazy in excellent form. The *Paganini variations* are, if anything, even better than his earlier LP with Previn. Haitink gets splendid sound from the Philharmonia in the *Variations* and Decca provides excellent recording. The *First Concerto* is no less impressive, and the Concertgebouw Orchestra under Haitink offer luxurious support.

Piano concerto No. 2 in C min., Op. 18.
☞ (M) *** BMG/RCA 09026 61961-2 [id.]. Van Cliburn, Chicago SO, Reiner – BEETHOVEN: *Concerto No. 5.* ***
*** DG 415 119-2 [id.]. Sviatoslav Richter, Warsaw PO, Wislocki – PROKOFIEV: *Concerto No. 5.* ***
☞ (B) **(*) Erato/Warner Dig. 4509 92872-2 [id.]. Duchâble, Strasbourg PO, Guschlbauer – GRIEG: *Concerto.* *(*)
☞ *(*) Denon Dig. CO 75368 [id.]. Hélène Grimaud, RPO, López-Cobos – RAVEL: *Piano concerto in G.* *(*)

With Reiner making a splendid partner, Van Cliburn's 1958 account of the Rachmaninov *C minor Concerto* is second to none. The pacing of the first movement is comparatively measured, but the climax is unerringly placed, remaining relaxed yet enormously telling. The finale too does not seek to demonstrate runaway bravura but has sparkle and excitement, with the lyrical element heart-warming to match the very beautiful account of the central *Adagio*, full of poetry and romantic feeling. The recording is wonderfully rich, with the Chicago acoustic adding a glorious ambient glow, while the piano, though forwardly placed, has an unexpected body and fullness of timbre. In the finale the cymbals demonstrate an excellent upper range, and the enhancement of the digital remastering almost makes this seem as if it were made yesterday. The coupling with Beethoven's *Emperor* is unusual but stimulating, with Reiner again participating impressively.

With Richter the long opening melody of the first movement is taken abnormally slowly, and it is only the sense of mastery that Richter conveys in every note which prevents one from complaining. The slow movement too is spacious – with complete justification this time – and the opening of the finale lets the floodgates open the other way, for Richter chooses a hair-raisingly fast allegro. He does not, however, let himself be rushed in the great secondary melody, so this is a reading of vivid contrasts. The coupling is Richter's classic account of Prokofiev's *Fifth Concerto*, so this CD combines two of Richter's very finest performances for the gramophone. The sound is very good.

A fine, bold, romantic performance from François-René Duchâble, well paced and involving. Guschlbauer provides good support, and the modern, digital sound is full-blooded and well balanced. Not a subtle account but an enjoyable one. Unfortunately, it is coupled with a barnstorming account which is inappropriate for the more elusive Grieg *Concerto*.

Hélène Grimaud has earned golden opinions, but her account of the Rachmaninov *C minor Concerto* with the RPO and Jesús López-Cobos does not topple existing recommendations past or present. This is just a little wanting in the fire and panache this piece calls for, and the recording, though acceptable, is not overwhelming.

Piano concertos Nos. 2 in C min., Op. 18; 3 in D min., Op. 30.
(M) *** Chan. CHAN 6507; *MBTD 6507* [id.]. Earl Wild, RPO, Horenstein.
☞ (M) **(*) Decca 425 047-2 [id.]. Ashkenazy, (i) Moscow PO, Kondrashin; (ii) LSO, Fistoulari.

Piano concertos Nos. (i) *2 in C min, Op. 18;* (ii) *3 in D min., Op. 30. Preludes: in C sharp min., Op. 3/2; in E flat, Op. 23/6.*
⊛ (M) *** Mercury 432 759-2 [id.]. Byron Janis; (i) Minneapolis SO; (ii) LSO, Antal Dorati.

We have long admired these Mercury performances; coupled together, they represent Byron Janis's very finest record. Janis has the full measure of this music: his shapely lyrical phrasing and natural response to the ebb and flow of the melodic lines is a constant source of pleasure. In the finale there is all the sparkling bravura one could ask for, but the great lyrical tune is made beguilingly poetic. Although the 1960 recording has plenty of ambience, the Minneapolis violins lack the richness of the LSO strings, recorded at Watford in 1961. The simple opening of the *Third Concerto* benefits from the extra warmth, and Janis lets the theme unwind with appealing spontaneity, and in the great closing climax of the finale the passion is built up – not too hurriedly – to the greatest possible tension. Janis makes two cuts (following the composer's own practice), one of about ten bars in the second movement and a rather longer one in the finale. Two favourite *Preludes*, with the *E flat* coming first, most persuasively played, make some compensation.

Earl Wild's performances derive from a complete set produced by Charles Gerhardt for RCA and recorded at the Kingsway Hall in 1965. The first movement of the *C minor Concerto* is faster than usual, but the expressive fervour is in no doubt; the *Adagio*, too, blossoms readily. The *Third Concerto* is among the very finest versions of this work on record and, in terms of bravura, is in the Horowitz class. The digital remastering is a great success, the overall balance is truthful and the hall ambience brings a rich orchestral image and plenty of brilliance. However, unfortunately there are three cuts, one in the second movement and two in the third, a total of 55 bars.

Ashkenazy's first (1963) recording of the *C minor Concerto* is more successful than his much later, digital account with Haitink, but less compelling than his second version with Previn, which remains uniquely beautiful. But the performance with Kondrashin offers superb Walthamstow sound and, though Kondrashin does not hold the first movement at a consistent level of tension and its climax is almost over-stated in its accented emphasis, the close of the *Andante* is ravishing (if not quite as fine as with Previn) and no one should be disappointed with the passionate climax of the finale. The *Third Concerto* is another matter. Anatole Fistoulari proved a splendid partner, and this reading is the freshest and most spontaneous of his four recordings of this elusive work. Fistoulari is fully up to the the subtle changes of mood in the first movement; the *Adagio* has a Russian ardour, its nostalgic lyrical feeling beautifully caught, and the finale makes a splendid culmination. Both CD transfers are outstandingly successful and the vintage (again Walthamstow) sound-balance is very satisfying, present, full-bodied and vivid.

Piano concerto No. 2 in C min.; Rhapsody on a theme of Paganini, Op. 43.
(M) *** Decca 417 702-2 [id.]. Ashkenazy, LSO, Previn.
(BB) *** Naxos Dig. 8.550117; *4550117* [id.]. Jandó, Budapest SO, Lehel.
(B) *** CfP Dig. CD-CFP 9017; *TC-CFP 4383*. Tirimo, Philh. O, Levi.

For those not investing in the two-disc set, above, which includes the *Third Concerto* played by the same artists, Decca's recoupling of Ashkenazy's earlier recordings with Previn is a very desirable CD indeed. At mid-price it makes a first choice. In the *Concerto*, the gentle, introspective mood of the *Adagio* is among the most beautiful on record. The finale is broad and spacious rather than electrically exciting, but the scintillating, unforced bravura provides all the sparkle necessary. The *Rhapsody* too is outstandingly successful. The Kingsway Hall sound is rich and full-bodied in the best analogue sense. Detail is somewhat sharper in the *Rhapsody*; in the *Concerto*, however, atmosphere rather than clarity is the predominating factor.

Jenö Jandó's performances of both works are strongly recommendable. Jandó has the full measure of the ebb and flow of the Rachmaninovian phraseology, and the slow movement is romantically expansive, the reprise particularly beautiful, while the finale has plenty of dash and ripe, lyrical feeling. The *Rhapsody* is played brilliantly, as fine as any performance in the catalogue. The digital recording is satisfyingly balanced, with a bold piano image and a full, resonant orchestral tapestry.

Concentrated and thoughtful, deeply expressive yet never self-indulgent, Tirimo is outstanding in both the *Concerto* and the *Rhapsody*, making this another of the most desirable bargain versions of this favourite coupling, irrespective of price. Speeds for the outer movements of the *Concerto* are on the fast side, yet Tirimo's feeling for natural rubato makes them sound natural, never breathless, while the sweetness and repose of the middle movement are exemplary. The digital recording is full, clear and well balanced.

(i) *Piano concertos Nos. 2–3; Rhapsody on a theme of Paganini. Preludes: in C sharp min., Op. 3/2; in B flat & G min., Op. 23/2 & 5; in B min. & D flat, Op. 32/10 & 13; Etudes-tableaux, Op. 39/1, 2 & 5.*
☞ (B) *** Double Decca 436 386-2 (2) [id.]. Ashkenazy, (i) LSO, Previn.

This pair of Decca CDs – offered for the cost of a single premium-price disc – tends to sweep the board in including outstanding performances of Rachmaninov's three greatest concertante works for piano and orchestra, plus five favourite *Preludes* and three of the Op. 39 *Etudes-tableaux*. Unlike the previous complete set (425 576-2), the digital remastering offers first-class transfers, full and well-balanced, with the Kingsway Hall ambience casting a pleasing glow over the proceedings. This is very highly recommendable, including as it does Ashkenazy's outstanding version of the *C minor Piano concerto*, where the slow movement is memorably beautiful.

Piano concertos Nos. 2 in C min, Op. 18; 4 in G min., Op. 40.
☞ (*) Pickwick/RPO CDRPO 7022 [id.]. Sequeira Costa, RPO, Seaman.

The distinguished Portuguese pianist, Sequeira Costa, on the Pickwick label with the RPO and Christopher Seaman does not present a serious challenge.

(i; ii; iii) *Piano concerto No. 2; Rhapsody on a theme of Paganini;* (iv; iii) *Symphony No. 2 in E min.; The Isle of the dead;* (i) *(Piano) Preludes: in C sharp min., Op. 3/2; in G min., Op. 23/5;* (v) *Vocalise, Op. 34/14;* (i) arr. of KREISLER: *Liebesleid.*
☞ (B) ** Ph. Duo 438 383-2 [id.]. (i) Orozco; (ii) RPO; (iii) Edo de Waart; (iv) Rotterdam PO; (v) Zoltán Kocsis.

Philips have called their alternative bargain Duo offering: 'The best of Rachmaninov', and it is an enticing programme. But Orozco's performances of the concertante works are not particularly distinctive (see above), and Edo de Waart's reading of the *E minor Symphony*, with rather fast tempi, is somewhat lightweight. The slow movement is very beautiful and the refined orchestral playing is naturally expressive throughout, but the sense of melancholy rapture that lies at the core of Rachmaninov's sensibility is not strongly projected in any of the performances included here.

(i) *Piano concerto No. 2 in C min., Op. 18; Etudes-tableaux, Op. 39/1–2, 4–6 & 9.*
*** BMG/RCA Dig. RD 87982 [7982-2-RC]. Evgeny Kissin, (i) LSO, Valentin Gergiev.

Evgeny Kissin phrases intelligently and resists the temptation to play to the gallery in any way. He produces a beautiful sound throughout and it is a compliment to him that any comparisons that spring to mind are with great pianists. The LSO under Valentin Gergiev give him every support. The six *Etudes tableaux* are imaginatively played and impressively characterized. The recording is well balanced and truthful.

(i) *Piano concerto No. 2 in C min., Op. 18;* (ii) *Preludes: in C sharp min., Op. 3/2; in G sharp min., Op. 32/12.*

☞ (M) *** EMI Dig. CDU5 65057-2 [id.]; *EU 565057-4.* (i) Cécile Ousset, CBSO, Rattle; (ii) John Ogdon – GRIEG: *Piano concerto.* ***

Cécile Ousset gives a powerful, red-blooded performance in the grand manner, warmly supported by Simon Rattle and the CBSO. Her rubato may often be extreme but it never sounds studied, always convincingly spontaneous; and the EMI recording copes well with the range of the playing. Those wanting a coupling with the Grieg *Concerto* will find Ousset's account similarly strong. Two favourite *Preludes* (including the most famous of all in *C sharp minor*) are added for the reissue, admirably played by John Ogdon.

Piano concerto No. 3 in D min., Op. 30.
☞ *** Chesky CD 76. Earl Wild, RPO, Horenstein – MACDOWELL: *Piano concerto No. 2.* *** ⊛
**(*) Decca Dig. 417 239-2 [id.]. Ashkenazy, Concg. O, Haitink.
☞ (***) Testament mono SBT 1029 [id.]. Gilels, Paris Cons. O., Cluytens – SAINT-SAENS: *Piano concerto No. 2;* SHOSTAKOVICH: *Prelude and fugue in D.* (***)
*(**) BMG/RCA 09026 61564 [id.]. Horowitz, NYPO, Ormandy.

(i) *Piano concerto No. 3. Prelude in B flat, Op. 23/2; Vocalise, Op. 34/14.*
☞ ** BMG/RCA Dig. 09026 61548-2 [id.]. Kissin; (i) Boston SO, Ozawa.

(i) *Piano concerto No. 3. Sonata No. 2 in B flat min., Op. 36; Moment musical in E flat min., Op. 16/2; Polka; Prelude in C, Op. 32/5.*
(M) (***) BMG/RCA (mono) GD 87754 [7754-2-RC-]. Vladimir Horowitz; (i) with RCA SO, Reiner.

Earl Wild's performance was recorded at the Kingsway Hall in 1965. His *Third Concerto* is among the very finest versions of this work on record. Wild favours the less elaborate version of the first-movement cadenza and plays it with compelling bravura. Horenstein proves a most understanding partner. The digital remastering is a great success. However, unfortunately there are three cuts, one in the second movement and two in the third, a total of 55 bars. This alternative coupling on Chesky of the *Third Concerto* with the MacDowell *Second Concerto* is very attractive, but it is a full-priced CD, whereas the Chandos Rachmaninov pairing of the *Second* and *Third Concertos* (see above) is at mid-price.

Horowitz's RCA account with Reiner dates from 1951. As a performance it is full of poetry, yet electrifying in its excitement. In spite of its dated sound and a less than ideal balance, its magic comes over and it is to be preferred to his later performance with Ormandy. The *Sonata* comes from live concerts in 1980 and is also pretty electrifying. He plays the conflation he made (and which Rachmaninov approved) of the 1913 original and the 1931 revision plus a few further retouchings he subsequently added. An indispensable part of any Rachmaninov collection which, in its digitally remastered form, sounds better than it has before.

Horowitz's legendary association with Rachmaninov's *D minor Concerto* daunted even the composer; Horowitz made it virtually his own property over half a century. In January 1978 he was persuaded to re-record the work in stereo, this time at a live concert, with Ormandy drawing a committed and romantically expansive accompaniment from the New York Philharmonic Orchestra. Perhaps just a little of the old magic is missing in the solo playing, but it remains prodigious and Horowitz's insights are countless. Not all the playing is immaculate and there is some rhythmic eccentricity in the finale; but the communicative force of the reading is unquestionable. The snag is the recording, which was originally very dry and clinical, the piano timbre lacking bloom. For CD, the remastering has altered the sound-picture radically, considerably softening the focus to bring a more romantic aura to the music-making. The result is that at lower dynamic levels the image appears to recede. The effect is disconcerting - but one can adjust to it, and certainly the effect is more agreeable than the 'bare bones' of the original LP sound-quality.

Gilels's classic account of the *Concerto* with André Cluytens and the Paris Conservatoire Orchestra comes from 1955 and belongs among the 'greats'. The piano-sound is a bit shallow and at times the balance favours the soloist unduly – but what lovely playing. Rachmaninov's own account cannot be displaced, nor, for that matter, the Horowitz/Coates and Horowitz/Reiner versions, but this should still be in the collections of all who have an interest in Rachmaninov and piano playing.

Ashkenazy has recorded this concerto four times; as a work, it seems to prove elusive for him. On his Decca digital disc he is beautifully recorded and there is unfailing sensitivity and musicianship, but one needs a greater sense of impact and focus – his very first recording with Fistoulari had more ardour and spontaneity.

Yevgeni Kissin's opening is very measured and low-voltage. The pianism is supremely elegant and one can easily feel that it is curiously judicious, given the incandescence this artist can command. Yet there are a number of poetic insights which almost persuade the listener that the slow tempo is justified. The record is assembled from live performances and the piano is at times discoloured. Ozawa gets decent rather than distinguished results from the orchestra. The CD is copied at a low level and the recording is curiously veiled and badly wanting in transparency at the top. Nothing this remarkable pianist does is without interest, but this cannot be a first recommendation.

Piano concerto No. 4 in G min., Op. 40 (see also below, under *Monna Vanna*).
⚝ *** EMI CDC7 49326-2 [id.]. Michelangeli, Philh. O, Gracis – RAVEL: *Piano concerto in G.* *** ⚝

This is one of the most brilliant piano records ever made. It puts the composer's own recorded performance quite in the shade, and the Ravel coupling is equally illuminating. The recording does not quite match the superlative quality of the playing but still sounds pretty good.

Etudes-tableaux (orch. Respighi).
*** Collins Dig. 1175-2; *1175-4* [id.]. LPO, Rozhdestvensky – BRAHMS: *Piano quartet.* ***

Respighi was a master of the orchestra and his celebrated version of Rachmaninov's *Etudes-tableaux* sounds splendidly idiomatic. Rozhdestvensky gets excellent results from the LPO, and the Collins recording is absolutely first class.

The Isle of the dead, Op. 29.
☞ (M) *** BMG/RCA 09026 61250-2. Chicago SO, Reiner – Concert: *'The Reiner sound'.* ***

Arnold Böcklin's painting which inspired this unusual work shows a small boat travelling towards the harbour of an island. In the boat, by the side of the ferryman, is a single figure, and they are accompanied by a coffin. This macabre evocation inspired one of Rachmaninov's very finest and most powerful works. The idiom shares something with Sibelius, and the opening and closing pages are among the most hauntingly original that he ever wrote. Reiner builds the arch-like span of the music to an impassioned climax and manages the return to the sombre opening mood with equal distinction. The recording, made in 1957, is fairly closely balanced and, although the Chicago ambience remains, the upper strings lose some of their tonal weight at the climax and the range of dynamic is slightly reduced. Nevertheless this shows Reiner at his finest and there are other good things in this compilation.

The Isle of the dead, Op. 29; Symphonic dances, Op. 45.
(M) *** Decca Dig. 430 733-2. Concg. O, Ashkenazy.
(BB) **(*) Naxos Dig. 8.550583 [id.]. RPO, Enrique Bátiz.

Ashkenazy's is a superb coupling, rich and powerful in playing and interpretation, *The Isle of the dead* relentless in its ominous build-up, while the *Symphonic dances* have extra darkness and intensity too. The splendid digital recording highlights both the passion and the fine precision of the playing.

Bátiz gives the *Symphonic dances* an attractively spontaneous performance, full of lyrical intensity, with some splendid playing from the RPO strings. The vivid recording helps give the feeling that Bátiz almost goes over the top in his extremely passionate climax for *The Isle of the dead*. The performance certainly does not lack darker feelings, and at super-bargain price this remains well worth considering.

Rhapsody on a theme of Paganini, Op. 43.
☞ **(*) Decca Dig. 436 239-2 [id.]. Jablonski, RPO, Ashkenazy – SHOSTAKOVICH: *Piano concerto No. 1;* LUTOSLAWSKI: *Paganini variations.* ***

The twenty-year-old Swedish pianist Peter Jablonski gives a thoroughly recommendable account of the *Paganini rhapsody* with Ashkenazy and the RPO. There is sparkle and virtuosity, though not perhaps the high-voltage lyricism and authority of Pletnev and Ashkenazy himself, and the contrasting coupling (the near-contemporaneous Shostakovich *Concerto for piano, trumpet and strings*) is an intelligent one. The Decca recording is exemplary in balance and presence.

SYMPHONIES

Symphonies Nos. 1–3; The Isle of the dead; Symphonic dances; Vocalise.
☞ (M) *** Virgin/EMI Dig. VMT 759279-2 (3) [id.]. Bournemouth SO, Litton.

Symphonies Nos. 1–3; The Isle of the dead, Op. 29; Symphonic dances, Op. 45; Vocalise, Op. 34/14;
Aleko: Intermezzo & Women's dance.
☞ (M) *** EMI CMS7 64530-2 (3) [id.]. LSO, André Previn.

Symphonies Nos. 1–3; The Rock, Op. 7.
☞ (B) ** Ph. Duo 438 724-2 (2) [id.]. Rotterdam PO, De Waart.

Andrew Litton's mid-priced box is highly competitive alongside the Previn set. It offers first-class, modern, digital sound with a beauty of orchestral texture ideal for Rachmaninov, and in this respect is superior to Previn, although the Ashkenazy Decca series (available separately), if not quite so rich in its violin textures, remains very competitive sonically, with the Concertgebouw acoustic providing full and atmospheric ambience. Litton's performances combine power and ripeness of romantic feeling with tenderness, bringing out the refinement of Rachmaninov's scoring. *The Isle of the dead* and *Symphonic dances* are similarly distinguished.

While Ashkenazy's digital Decca mid-priced separate CDs of the three Rachmaninov symphonies with the Concertgebouw Orchestra will probably remain first choice for many collectors, Previn's LSO set at the same price offers some alternative couplings. His 1973 account of the *Second Symphony* – the most passionately committed performance on record, with a glorious response from the LSO strings – has been remastered for CD a second time, with improvement in the body of the string timbre. This remains a classic account, unlikely to be surpassed. No. 1 is a forthright, clean-cut performance, beautifully played and very well recorded. It may lack some of the vitality that one recognizes in Russian performances (Ashkenazy is more volatile and remains first choice in this work) but is still very enjoyable. Previn's account of the *Third*, however, is outstanding and the LSO's playing again has enormous bravura and ardour. This, like *The Isle of the dead* and *Symphonic dances*, has been remastered very successfully and the performances of the two shorter works have plenty of atmosphere and grip. With the *Aleko* excerpts and the *Vocalise* also included, this EMI box remains very competitive.

Edo de Waart secures excellent results from the Rotterdam Philharmonic; these performances are all well shaped and proportioned, fresh in conception and refined in phrasing and sonority. What they lack is the all-pervasive Slavic melancholy and the sense of rapture that lie at the core of Rachmaninov's sensibility. No complaints about the quality of the orchestral response at any point in the set; nor could one fault the excellence and truthfulness of the 1977/8 Philips recordings or the naturalness of the CD transfers. These records are attractively inexpensive, but readers will find the reissued Ashkenazy set on Decca or Andrew Litton on Virgin well worth their extra cost.

Symphony No. 1 in D min.; The Isle of the dead, Op. 29.
☞ (M) *** Decca Dig. 436 479-2 [id.]. Concg. O, Ashkenazy.
*** Virgin/EMI Dig. VC7 59547-2 [id.]. RPO, Andrew Litton.

Symphony No. 1 in D min.; The Rock (fantasy), Op. 13; Vocalise, Op. 34/14; Aleko: Intermezzo.
(M) *** DG Dig. 435 594-2 [id.]. BPO, Maazel.

Ashkenazy's 1982 recording now reappears at mid-price. His remains an outstanding version, volatile and extreme in its tempi, with the Concertgebouw players responding with total conviction. The digital recording is most impressive, for the sound is full, atmospheric and brilliant. Though the weight of the opening of the finale is magnificent, the relentless hammering rhythms are presented vividly in scale, where they can easily seem oppressive. The Scherzo at a very fast speed has Mendelssohnian lightness and the flowing *Larghetto* is presented as a lyrical interlude. The reissue is made even more competitive by its inclusion of *The Isle of the dead*, which one here recognizes as being among the very finest of Rachmaninov's orchestral works, relentless in its ominous build-up. The digital recording, made a year after the symphony, is out of Decca's very top drawer.

With a darkly intense account of *The Isle of the dead* as a generous fill-up, Litton's version of the *Symphony* brings exceptionally beautiful sound which captures the RPO strings in luminous form. This is a powerful performance, as the very opening indicates, but it is just as remarkable for its refinement and gentler qualities, with Litton persuasive in his free use of rubato.

Maazel's is a superb performance, beautifully transparent and consistently clarifying detail. He may lack something in Slavonic passion but, with generous fill-ups, the positive strength of the reading stands well against any rival. The 1984 recording is drier than Ashkenazy's Decca.

Symphony No. 2 in E min., Op. 27.

(B) *** Pickwick Dig. PCD 904; *CIMPC 904* [id.]. LSO, Rozhdestvensky.

☞ (BB) *** ASV CDQS 6107 [id.]. Philh. O, Ling Tung.

☞ **(*) Ph. Dig. 438 864-2 [id.]. Kirov O, Gergiev.

☞ **(*) Ph. Dig. 432 101-2 [id.]. O de Paris, Bychkov.

Symphony No. 2 in E min., Op. 27; The Rock, Op. 7.

☞ *(**) DG Dig. 439 888-2 [id.]. Russian Nat. O, Pletnev.

Symphony No. 2 in E min., Op. 27; Scherzo in D min.; Vocalise, Op. 34/14.

☞ *** EMI Dig. CDC5 55140-2 [id.]. St Petersburg PO, Jansons.

Symphony No. 2; 'Youth' Symphony in D min. (1891).

☞ (M) *** Decca Dig. 436 480-2 [id.]. Concg. O, Ashkenazy.

Symphony No. 2; (i) Vocalise, Op. 34/14.

*** Virgin/EMI Dig. VC7 59548-2 [id.]. RPO, Andrew Litton.

☞ **(*) Telarc Dig. CD 80312 [id.]. (i) Sylvia McNair; Baltimore SO, David Zinman.

☞ ** BMG/RCA Dig. 09026 61281-2 [id.]. St Petersburg PO, Temirkanov.

Rozhdestvensky gives a very Tchaikovskian reading of Rachmaninov's *E minor Symphony*. There is plenty of vitality but, with the big string melodies blossoming voluptuously, the slow movement, after a beguiling opening clarinet solo, has a climax of spacious intensity, its power almost overwhelming. The finale is flamboyantly broadened at the end, and the feeling of apotheosis is very much in the Tchaikovsky mould. With the LSO responding superbly, this is a most satisfying account, and the richness, brilliance and weight of the recording add to the compulsion of the music-making.

Refinement is the mark of Litton's well-paced reading, with the RPO caught in glowing form by the engineers as in the rest of the cycle. There is power in plenty, and Litton readily sustains his observance of the exposition repeat in the first movement, making it a very long movement indeed at over 23 minutes. But the moments of special magic are those where, as in his lightly pointed account of the Scherzo or, most of all, the lovely clarinet melody of the slow movement, subtlety of expression gives Rachmaninov's romanticism an extra poignancy.

Jansons's newest St Petersburg version offers a strong, warm reading in which climaxes are thrust home powerfully, with full dramatic impact. Phrasing is warmly idiomatic, even if occasionally over-moulded, and the recording gives fine body and immediacy to the sound, outshining most latter-day rivals. In Russian fashion the clarinet in the slow movement sounds like an organ stop. A warm, exciting reading which stands among the best modern versions. The coupling is generous, when in addition to *Vocalise*, beautifully done, it offers the early orchestral *Scherzo* of 1887. Jansons's much earlier version for Chandos with the Philharmonia (CHAN 8520) cannot match this later account in precision of ensemble, but in some ways it sounds more spontaneous and natural. It is a characteristically warm, expressive reading, with idiomatic pacing, even if the fine clarinettist in the slow movement is not allowed full expressive freedom and the overall effect is less sumptuously intense than with either Previn or Rozhdestvensky. Warm, atmospheric sound.

Ashkenazy's reading has a romantic urgency and drive that are missing from Previn's Telarc version, with the climaxes of the outer movements far more gripping. In the Scherzo too, the Amsterdam strings are tauter in ensemble; there is a vibrant impulse about the performance as a whole which is very Russian in its intensity. The Decca recording is full-bodied but with a degree of edge on the strings, and this extra bite suits Ashkenazy's approach. The mid-priced reissue now also includes the fragment of a projected symphony – with its first subject plainly indebted to Tchaikovsky's *Fourth* – which was written when Rachmaninov was only nineteen. It makes an enjoyable and unusual makeweight.

Ling Tung's reading is refined but he knows just how to mould the sweeping lines necessary to bring out the rapture inherent in this lovely symphony, notably at the climax of the slow movement and at the very satisfying close. This is a case where the CD transfer brings a striking improvement in the vividness of a 1978 recording which is backwardly balanced. One needs to play back at a fairly high level, then the Philharmonia strings emerge with a warmly natural, radiant sheen of tone. At super-bargain price this is well worth considering.

There is a distinct divergence of opinion about the new version from Pletnev. For R. L., the conductor/pianist brings a fresh mind to this symphony, with his approach very much controlled, giving a strong sense of onward current and producing none of the heart-on-sleeve emotion that can often afflict the slow movement, which seems to be conceived in one long paragraph. The clarity and lightness of articulation that distinguish his piano playing seem to be in ample evidence and, throughout the work, feeling is held in perfect control. It is a performance of quality, though the recording, while good, could be cleaner-detailed in the lower end of the range. For E. G., conversely, Pletnev's version is a disappointment, especially after his first recording with this orchestra, the Virgin version of Tchaikovsky's *Pathétique*. There is a similar attempt to whip up excitement, but ensemble is markedly less secure, endangered by some frenetically fast speeds – as in the finale. To E. G.'s ears, the Moscow-made recording brings edgy string-sound and lack of weight. However, the early fantasy, *The Rock*, inspired by Lermontov, makes a generous coupling.

As in his opera recordings, Gergiev gives a strong and well-paced reading, if lacking a little in individuality. Although he takes what one might think of as a more traditional approach, he brings an appropriate warmth and also possesses considerable command of the architecture. His first movement (with repeat) is very spacious (22½ minutes). The playing of the Kirov orchestra readily matches that of its symphonic rivals in virtuosity, though the otherwise admirable Philips recording does not quite convey its full body. Like Litton, Temirkanov and Zinman, Gergiev observes the exposition repeat in the first movement.

Bychkov, too, in the last resort fails to produce a reading that is either very individual or overwhelmingly compulsive, and without the first-movement exposition repeat this Philips CD seems short measure. But there is ardour here, a sparkling Scherzo and a fine clarinet solo in the slow movement, where there is nostalgia as well as passion. The finale has plenty of power and the Philips recording is expansive and full. Enjoyable, but not a first choice.

After a slack start Zinman builds the symphony persuasively, if with less character than some, helped by first-rate playing from the Baltimore orchestra. Good, clean sound. The coupling is an attraction when, unlike most rivals, Zinman has *Vocalise* with soprano soloist, the radiant Sylvia McNair. Even with that extra, Zinman manages to observe the exposition repeat in the first movement of the symphony.

Temirkanov characteristically gives a reading of extremes, with basic speeds on the fast side, notably in the finale, but with the big Rachmaninov melodies lovingly drawn out, marked by tenutos that most will find excessive. He adds to the heavenly length by observing the exposition repeat, and he adds *Vocalise*, taken very slowly indeed, not in Rachmaninov's own instrumental version but in the string arrangement of Kurt Sanderling. The recording, made in London, offers refined, if rather distanced, sound.

Symphony No. 3 in A min., Op. 44.
(M) *** EMI CDM7 69564-2. LSO, Previn – SHOSTAKOVICH: *Symphony No. 6.* ***
*** Chan. Dig. CHAN 8614; *ABT 1303* [id.]. LSO, Järvi – KALLINIKOV: *Intermezzos.* ***

Symphony No. 3 in A min.; Isle of the dead, Op. 29.
☞ *** Nimbus Dig. NI 5344 [id.]. BBC Welsh SO, Tadaaki Otaka.

Symphony No. 3 in A min.; Symphonic dances, Op. 45.
☞ (M) *** Decca Dig. 436 481-2 [id.]. Concg. O, Ashkenazy.
*** Virgin/EMI Dig. VC7 59549-2 [id.]. RPO, Andrew Litton.
☞ (B) *(*) CfP Dig. CD-CFP 4649; *TC-CFP 4649.* RLPO, Mackerras.

Previn's EMI CD brings an outstanding performance; the digital remastering brings plenty of body alongside the sharpened detail. Previn conveys the purposefulness of the writing at every point, revelling in the richness, but clarifying textures. The LSO has rarely displayed its virtuosity more brilliantly in the recording studio, and, with its generous Shostakovich coupling, this is first choice for this symphony.

Ashkenazy's is a performance of extremes, volatile and passionate in a very Russian way. In the first movement the varying speeds are contrasted far more than usual, the allegros faster, the slow, lyrical passages (notably the great melody of the second subject) slower with copious rubato. The finale is fast and hectic to the point of wildness, but the Concertgebouw players respond superbly and the digital recording is full, rich and brilliant. In Ashkenazy's hands the *Symphonic dances* – added for the reissue – have extra darkness and intensity, suggesting no relaxation whatever at the end of Rachmaninov's career. The splendid digital recording highlights both the passion and the fine precision of the playing.

The gentleness of Litton's treatment of the great second-subject melody in the *Third Symphony* means that the transparent beauty of Rachmaninov's scoring is brought out superbly. The slow movement has rarely been done so tenderly and, though the opening of the finale may sound not urgent enough, it is crisply pointed and leads on to a superbly brisk, tense conclusion. In the *Symphonic dances* the refinement and beauty go with sharp, clean attack, making an ideal and generous coupling for the *Symphony*.

Those with memories of their broadcasts from the 1960s and '70s may not have realized even now that the BBC Welsh Symphony Orchestra is transformed beyond recognition, and no better evidence is required than this highly impressive performance of the *Third Symphony* under Tadaaki Otaka. No attempt is made in any way to dress up or glamorize the work with glossy expressive emphases or agogic distortions. The symphony unfolds with complete naturalness and unfailing musical instinct that reflect great credit on their gifted Japanese conductor. There is no trace of unwelcome showmanship, but no lack of panache either. Tempi in all three movements are eminently well judged and phrases are well shaped. Apart from excellent orchestral playing, the technical side of the recording is also handled expertly. A natural concert-hall perspective with plenty of warmth from the acoustic but no lack of detail. The *Isle of the dead* is no less well served and, save for collectors dazzled by glossy names and sensation-seeking sonics, this can be recommended along with the very best on the market.

Järvi in his weighty, purposeful way misses some of the subtleties of this symphony, but with superb playing from the LSO – linking back to André Previn's unsurpassed reading with them – the intensity is magnetic, with even a very slow *Adagio* for the outer sections of the middle movement made to sound convincing, and with the finale thrusting on at an equivalently extreme tempo.

With recording that sets the orchestra at a distance and undermines clarity of detail, the Mackerras disc of this ideal coupling, welcome at bargain price, can be given only a modified recommendation. The performances too often sound studied and unspontaneous in their detailed expression, lacking necessary bite and focus.

CHAMBER AND INSTRUMENTAL MUSIC

Cello sonata in G min., Op. 19.
☞ ** EMI Dig. CDC7 54819-2 [id.]. Gary Hoffman, Jean-Philippe Collard – CHOPIN: *Cello sonata.*
*(*)

Cello sonata, Op. 19; Ne pol Krasavitsa, Op. 4/4.
☞ *(*) Pickwick Dig. MCD 72; *MCC 72* [id.]. Tim Hugh, Yonty Solomon – GRIEG: *Cello sonata* etc. *(*)

As in the case of the Grieg *Sonata*, with which it is coupled, the Rachmaninov receives a highly charged performance from Timothy Hugh and Yonty Solomon. They emote rather too freely and their reading would undoubtedly have gained from greater restraint. Those who like their Rachmaninov at a very high emotional temperature will perhaps warm to it; others will find it all too intense.

Gary Hoffman and Jean-Philippe Collard are a totally different proposition. Collard's credentials in this repertoire are well established since his remarkable cycle of the concertos with Plasson in the days of LP, and he approaches the work with impeccable taste. The playing of his partner, Gary Hoffman, is however not well balanced, and this underlines the reticent view he takes of the *Sonata*. He is an aristocratic and refined player. A disappointment, given the high hopes any recording containing Collard's name excites.

Trios élégiaques Nos. 1 in G min., Op. 8; 2 in D min., Op. 9.
*** Chan. Dig. CHAN 8431; *ABTD 1101* [id.]. Borodin Trio.

The *Trios* are both imbued with lyrical fervour and draw from the rich vein of melancholy so characteristic of Rachmaninov. The performances by the Borodin Trio are eloquent and masterly, and the recording is admirably balanced.

PIANO MUSIC

Suites Nos. 1–2, Opp. 5 & 17; Symphonic dances, Op. 45.
*** Hyp. Dig. CDA 66375 [id.]. Howard Shelley, Hilary Macnamara.

Howard Shelley and Hilary Macnamara give strong performances of both the *Suites* and the *Symphonic dances*. In the *Suites* their responses are not quite as imaginative as those of Ashkenazy and Previn, but there is plenty of dramatic fire in the *Symphonic dances* in this generously filled disc.

(i) *Suites for 2 pianos, Nos. 1 (Fantasy), Op. 5; 2, Op. 17.*
Etudes-tableaux, Op. 33.
(M) *** Decca 425 029-2 [id.]. Vladimir Ashkenazy, (i) with André Previn.

Ashkenazy's 1981 account of the Op. 33 *Etudes-tableaux* is very impressive indeed, but it is for the *Suites* that this reissue is especially valuable, reflecting a live performance by Ashkenazy and Previn in London in the summer of 1974. The sound is bold and has striking presence.

Suite No. 2, Op. 17; Russian rhapsody, Op. posth.; Symphonic dances, Op. 45.

☞ *** Hyp. Dig. CDA 66654 [id.]. Nikolai Demidenko, Dmitri Alexeev – MEDTNER: *Russian round dance* etc. **(*)

There are some beautiful things on the Alexeev–Demidenko disc. They shape the second group of the first of the *Symphonic dances* with exquisite sensitivity and colour, and there are many other felicities elsewhere. However, even allowing for the hazards of two pianos, there is some ugly fortissimo tone, which one never finds in a Kissin or a Pletnev recording. There is much to delight the listener all the same, even though Previn and Ashkenazy are to be preferred in this repertoire.

Barcarolle in G min., Op. 10/3; Etudes-tableaux, Op. 39/4 & 6; Humoresque in G, Op. 10/5; Lilacs, Op. 21/5; 5 Morceaux de fantaisie, Op. 3: (Elégie in E flat min.; Prelude in C sharp min.; Mélodie in E; Polichinelle in F sharp min.; Sérénade in B flat min.); Polka de W. R.; Prelude in G min., Op. 23/5. Transcriptions: MUSSORGSKY: *Hopak.* SCHUBERT: *Wohin?.* RIMSKY-KORSAKOV: *Flight of the bumble-bee.* KREISLER: *Liebeslied; Liebesfreud. The Star-spangled banner.*

(M) *** Decca 425 964-2 [id.]. Sergei Rachmaninov (Ampico Roll recordings, 1919–29).

Daisies, Op. 38/3; Etudes-tableaux, Op. 33/2 & 7; Op. 39/6; Humoresque, Op. 10/5; Lilacs, Op. 21/5; Mélodie, Op. 3/5; Moment musical, Op. 16/2; Oriental sketch; Polka de W. R.; Preludes: in C sharp min., Op. 3/2; in G flat, Op. 23/10; in E, F min. & F, Op. 32/3, 6 & 7; Serenade, Op. 3/5. Transcriptions: BACH: *Violin partita No. 2: Prelude; Gavotte; Rondo; Gigue.* MENDELSSOHN: *Midsummer Night's Dream: Scherzo.* KREISLER: *Liebesfreud.* SCHUBERT: *Wohin?.* MUSSORGSKY: *Gopak.* TCHAIKOVSKY: *Lullaby, Op. 16/11.* RIMSKY-KORSAKOV: *The Flight of the bumble-bee.*

(M) (***) BMG/RCA mono GD 87766 [7766-2-RG]. Sergei Rachmaninov.

These two records make a fascinating comparison. The RCA collection includes virtually all Rachmaninov's solo electric 78-r.p.m. recordings, made between 1925 and 1942, with most dating from 1940. The second offers the composer's Ampico piano-roll recordings, made during a shorter time-span, between 1919 and 1929, when Rachmaninov was at his technical peak. The Ampico recordings were reproduced on a specially adapted Estonia concert grand in the Kingsway Hall and recorded in stereo in 1978/9. On CD the sound is outstandingly real and the impression on the listener is quite uncanny when the recital opens with the *Elégie in E flat minor*, which was put on roll in October 1928 yet has all the spontaneity and presence of live music-making. A number of items are common to both discs, so it is possible to make direct comparisons. The Ampico system at that time could accurately reflect what was played, including note duration and pedalling, but the *strength* at which the notes were struck had to be edited on to the roll afterwards by a skilled musician/ technician. It can only be said that listening to these Ampico recordings never brings a feeling of any mechanical tone graduation, and in pieces like the *Humoresque in G major* or the *Polka de W. R.* not only does Rachmaninov's scintillating bravura sound absolutely natural, but also his chimerical use of rubato is more convincing on the earlier recordings. *The Flight of the bumble-bee*, a *tour de force* of exuberant articulation, brings only one second's difference in playing time between the two versions.

Andante semplice (fragments); Etudes-tableaux, Opp. 33 & 39; 2 Fantasy pieces; Moments musicaux, Op. 16; Morceaux de fantaisie, Op. 3; Morceaux de salon, Op. 10; Oriental sketch; Polka de W. R; 10 Preludes, Op. 23; 13 Preludes, Op. 32; Prelude, Op. posth.; Sonatas Nos. 1–2, Opp. 28 & 36; Variations on a theme of Chopin, Op. 22; Variations on a theme of Corelli, Op. 42. Transcriptions: Songs: *Daisies, Op. 38/3; Lilacs, Op. 21/5.* BACH: *Violin partita in E: Prelude, gavotte & gigue.* BIZET: *L'Arlésienne: Minuet.* KREISLER: *Liebesleid; Liebesfreud.* MENDELSSOHN: *Midsummer Night's Dream: Scherzo.* MUSSORGSKY: *Sorochinsky Fair: Gopak.* RIMSKY-KORSAKOV: *Flight of the bumble bee.* SCHUBERT: *Wohin?;* TCHAIKOVSKY: *Lullaby.*

☞ (M) *(*) Sony SM5K 48467 (5) [id.]. Ruth Laredo.

Ruth Laredo's Rachmaninov anthology is not of recent provenance, coming from the 1970s. She is a good pianist but is a good deal less distinguished than Shelley, whose world of feeling carries the more idiomatic and authoritative stamp. The recordings are acceptable but not top-drawer.

Etudes-tableaux, Opp. 33 & 39; Fragments; Fughetta in F; Mélodie in E; Moments musicaux; Morceaux de fantaisie; Morceaux de salon; 3 Nocturnes; Oriental sketch; 4 Pieces; Piece in D min.; 25 Preludes (complete); Sonatas 1–3 (including original & revised versions of No. 2); Song without words; Transcriptions (complete); Variations: on a theme of Chopin ; on a theme of Corelli.

☞ (M) *** Hyp. Dig. CDS 44041/8 (8). Howard Shelley.

Hyperion have collected Howard Shelley's exemplary survey of Rachmaninov into a mid-price, eight-CD set, and very good it is, too. Shelley can hold his own against most rivals not only in terms of poetic feeling (as you would expect from a distant descendant of the great poet) but in keyboard authority and virtuosity. The recordings are variable in quality but are mostly excellent.

Etudes-tableaux, Opp. 33 & 39.
*** Hyp. CDA 66091 [id.]. Howard Shelley.
*** EMI Dig. CDC7 54077-2 [id.]. Vladimir Ovchinikov.

The conviction and thoughtfulness of Shelley's playing, coupled with excellent modern sound, make this convenient coupling a formidable rival to Ashkenazy's classic versions, which in any case are not coupled together on CD.

Impressive and authoritative performances of all the *Etudes-tableaux* from Vladimir Ovchinikov, whose playing can hardly be faulted at any level and who has the advantage of excellent recorded sound.

Etudes-tableaux, Op. 39, Nos. 1–9; Variations on a theme of Corelli, Op. 42.
*** Decca Dig. 417 671-2 [id.]. Vladimir Ashkenazy.

Superb performances from Ashkenazy make this the most desirable of Rachmaninov issues. The *Corelli variations* is a rarity and a very fine work. The recording is first class.

Moments musicaux, Op. 16; Morceaux de salon, Op. 10.
*** Hyp. Dig. CDA 66184 [id.]. Howard Shelley.

Howard Shelley has a highly developed feeling for Rachmaninov and distinguishes himself here both by masterly pianism and by a refined awareness of Rachmaninov's sound-world. The recording is eminently realistic and natural.

Moments musicaux, Op. 16; Variations on a theme of Corelli, Op. 42. Transcriptions: *Daisies, Op. 38/ 3; Lilacs, Op. 21/5;* arr. of KREISLER: *Liebesleid; Liebesfreud.*
☞ ** Nimbus Dig. NI 5292 [id.]. Martin Jones.

Exemplary playing from this underrated artist, marred by less than satisfactory recording. The *Variations on a theme of Corelli* and the *Moments musicaux* are analogue recordings dating from 1977, while the four transcriptions are recorded digitally in 1991. The latter are more distantly balanced and the excessive reverberance does not flatter the piano tone. The pianist is still recorded from afar in the bigger works, but the results are nevertheless far more acceptable. The *Corelli variations* are particularly sensitive and idiomatic.

24 Preludes (complete).
☞ **(*) Erato/Warner Dig. 4509 91714-2 (2) [id.]. Dame Moura Lympany.

24 Preludes; Preludes in D min. and F; Morceaux de fantaisie, Op. 3.
*** Hyp. CDA 66081/2 (available separately) [id.]. Howard Shelley.

24 Preludes (complete); *Piano sonata No. 2 in B flat min., Op. 36.*
*** Decca 414 417-2 (2). Vladimir Ashkenazy.

There is superb flair and panache about Ashkenazy's playing. As a bonus, the compact discs offer the *Second Piano sonata*, with Ashkenazy generally following the 1913 original score but with some variants. He plays with great virtuosity and feeling, and the result is a *tour de force*.

Shelley is a compellingly individual interpreter of Rachmaninov. Each one of the *Preludes* strikes an original chord in him. These are very different readings from those of Ashkenazy but their intensity is well caught in full if reverberant recording.

Moura Lympany's new Erato recording of the Rachmaninov *Preludes* repeats an early success. While the pieces that need bravura seem to offer her no problems, she is at her finest in the lyrical pieces, which truly blossom in her hands, and the famous *G minor* and *A flat major* from Op. 23 are memorable. The whole set moves forward spontaneously, and this make a genuine alternative to the Decca Ashkenazy set, with fine, full and vivid recording of the piano. If you want the utmost bravura, then Ashkenazy would be first choice (and he isn't lacking in poetic feeling), but for romantic warmth the new set is hard to beat. The snag is that the two CDs play for barely 81 minutes: the whole set might have been squeezed on a single CD.

Preludes: Op. 3/2; Op. 23/1–2, 4–6; Mélodie, Op. 3/3; Polichinelle, Op. 3/4; Variations on a theme of Corelli, Op. 42.
*** Conifer Dig. CDCF 159; MCFC 159 [id.]. Kathryn Stott.

Kathryn Stott has a good feeling for Rachmaninov and gives well-considered accounts of all the pieces on this generously filled CD; there is a strong rhythmic grip and her phrasing is keenly articulate.

13 Preludes, Op. 32.
*** DG Dig. 427 766-2 [id.]. Lilya Zilberstein – SHOSTAKOVICH: *Sonata No. 1.* ***

Lilya Zilberstein faces rather more formidable competition in the Rachmaninov *Preludes* than in the Shostakovich *Sonata*, but she has technique, style and finesse, and the recording is excellent.

Piano sonatas Nos. 1 in D min., Op. 28; 2 in B flat min., Op. 36 (revised 1931).
*** Hyp. CDA 66047 [id.]. Howard Shelley.

Howard Shelley offers here the 1931 version of the *B flat Sonata*. He has plenty of sweep and grandeur and an appealing freshness, ardour and, when required, tenderness. He is accorded an excellent balance by the engineers.

Piano sonata No. 2 in B flat min., Op. 36 (original version); *Fragments in A flat; Fughetta in F; Gavotte in D; Mélodie in E; Morceau de fantaisie in G min.; Nocturnes Nos. 1–3; Oriental sketch in B flat; Piece in D min.; 4 Pieces; Prelude in E flat min.; Romance in F sharp min.; Song without words in D min.*
*** Hyp. CDA 66198 [id.]. Howard Shelley.

Howard Shelley now gives us the original version of Op. 36 and his performances here show unfailing sensitivity, intelligence and good taste. They have the merit of excellent recorded sound. A valuable issue.

Transcriptions: *Daisies; Lilacs; Polka de W. R.; Vocalise.* BACH: *Prelude; Gavotte; Gigue.* BIZET: *Minuet from L'Arlésienne.* KREISLER: *Liebesleid; Liebesfreud.* MENDELSSOHN: *Midsummer Night's Dream: Scherzo.* MUSSORGSKY: *Sorochinsky Fair: Gopak.* RIMSKY-KORSAKOV: *Flight of the bumble-bee.* SCHUBERT: *Wohin?.* TCHAIKOVSKY: *Lullaby.*
*** Hyp. Dig. CDA 66486 [id.]. Howard Shelley.

Shelley plays with an authority and sensitivity that is wholly persuasive and despatches the virtuoso transcriptions to the manner born. The transcription of the *Vocalise* is by Zoltán Kocsis, but otherwise all are Rachmaninov's own.

Song transcriptions: *Dreams; Floods of spring; In the silent night; The little island; Midsummer eve; The Muse; O, cease thy singing; On the death of a linnet; Sorrow in springtime; To the children; Vocalise; Where beauty dwells.*
**(*) Dell'Arte CD DBS 7001 [id.]. Earl Wild (piano).

Earl Wild is a pianist all too often taken for granted as a virtuoso pure and simple, rather than the great artist that he is. Of course his virtuosity is dazzling – but so too is his refinement of colour and his musicianship. The recording is not of comparable distinction but is acceptable enough.

Variations on a theme of Chopin, Op. 22; Variations on a theme of Corelli, Op. 42; Mélodie in E, Op. 3/3.
*** Hyp. CDA 66009 [id.]. Howard Shelley – MENDELSSOHN: *Scherzo.* ***

Howard Shelley gives dazzling, consistently compelling performances, full of virtuoso flair. The grouping of the more expansive *Chopin variations* brings a kind of sonata balance, with the climax of the final section built superbly by Shelley, helped by first-rate piano sound.

VOCAL MUSIC

The Bells, Op. 35.
(M) *** EMI CDM7 63114-2. Sheila Armstrong, Robert Tear, John Shirley-Quirk, London Symphony Ch., LSO, Previn – PROKOFIEV: *Alexander Nevsky.* ***

The Bells, Op. 35; 3 Russian songs, Op. 41.
☞ (M) *** Decca Dig. 436 482-2 [id.]. Natalia Troitskaya, Ryszard Karczykowski, Concg. Ch. & O, Ashkenazy.

The Bells, Op. 35; 3 Russian songs, Op. 41; Spring, Op. 20.
☞ *** Decca Dig. 440 355-2 [id.]. Alexandrina Pendachanska, Kaludi Kaludov, Sergei Leiferkus, Choral Arts Society, Phd. O, Dutoit.

Ashkenazy's volatile Russian style is eminently suitable for Rachmaninov's masterly cantata. His tenor soloist has just the right touch of temperament, and in the slow movement Natalia Troitskaya's contribution combines Slavonic feeling with freshness. The chorus respond readily to the black mood of the Scherzo and bring a melancholy intensity to the finale. The Decca recording is superb, wide in range, spacious and clear. At mid-price this is a clear first choice.

In *The Bells*, as in Previn's equally fresh and direct account of the other Russian choral work included on his CD, Prokofiev's *Alexander Nevsky*, the London Symphony Chorus sings convincingly in the original language. Previn's concentration on purely musical values as much as on evocation of atmosphere produces powerful results, even when the recording as transferred to CD has lost just a little of its ambient warmth in favour of added presence and choral brilliance.

Charles Dutoit's disc with the Philadelphia Orchestra conveniently couples all three of Rachmaninov's choral works with orchestra. The recording is one of the warmest and most refined to have come from Philadelphia in recent years, and with the composer's favourite orchestra Dutoit draws out comparable qualities in the music, with strings and woodwind solos sensuously beautiful. Compared with other versions, the performances are remarkable for subtle pianissimos and half-tones rather than for their dramatic bite. In *The Bells*, for example – much the longest work – Previn is more passionate and Ashkenazy more sparkling and volatile, and with both the recording gives greater sense of presence. The Ashkenazy – with the Concertgebouw – is also a Decca digital CD of the finest quality, but at mid-price the disc offers only the *3 Russian songs* as well as *The Bells*. *Spring*, the rarest work here, was written – like the *Second Symphony* and *Second Piano concerto* – as part of the composer's rehabilitation after his nervous breakdown. It is not as striking in its musical material as those works, but it builds up in Dutoit's fine performance to a magnificent climax. The Russian soloists sing with idiomatic bite and, though the chorus is backwardly placed, the dynamic range is impressive. Well worth having, alongside its competitors, if only at last to hear a great orchestra, so often ill-treated by the engineers, recorded properly by the Decca recording team.

6 Songs, Op. 4; 6 Songs, Op. 8; 12 Songs, Op. 14; 12 Songs, Op. 21; 15 Songs, Op. 26 (including (i) *Two partings*); *14 Songs, Op. 34; 6 Songs, Op. 38; Again you leapt, my heart; April! A festive spring day; By the gates of the holy dwelling; Did you hiccup?; Do you remember that evening?; A flower fell; From St John's Gospel; I shall tell you nothing; Letter to Konstantin Stanislavsky; Night; Powdered paint* (folksong); *Song of disappointment; Twilight has fallen.* (Piano solo): *Daisies; Lilacs.*
☞ (M) *** Decca 436 920-2 (3) [id.]. Elisabeth Söderstrom, Vladimir Ashkenazy, (i) with John Shirley-Quirk.

Recorded between 1974 and 1979, Elisabeth Söderström's set of the major Rachmaninov songs is a glittering jewel in the Decca catalogue. She is a fluent and radiant soloist, often inspired by her accompanist to performances of pure poetry, ranging over the wide span of Rachmaninov's career as well as his whole emotional range, so that you find, for instance, the highly characteristic *Brooding*, or the richly intense *O do not grieve*, alongside a comic skit on a drinking song, *Did you hiccup, Natasha?*. Sonia's final speech in Chekhov's *Uncle Vanya* becomes a song which nicely skirts sentimentality, and there is also a letter in music sent to Stanislavsky on the tenth anniversary of the Moscow Arts Theatre. John Shirley-Quirk joins the team for the wry dialogue, *Two partings*, and Ashkenazy allows himself two solo items in the composer's transcriptions of *Daisies* and *Lilacs*. The recording is vivid in its immediacy and presence. Full translations are provided.

Vespers, Op. 37.
☞ ⊛ (B) *** HM Chant du Monde Russian Season Dig. LDC 288 050 [id.]. St Petersburg Capella, Chernuchenko.
*** Hyp. Dig. CDA 66460 [id.]. Corydon Singers, Matthew Best.

Rachmaninov's *Vespers* – more correctly the 'All-night vigil' – rank not only among his most soulful and intensely powerful music but are also the finest of all Russian choral works. The St Petersburg Capella is in fact the Mikhail Glinka Choir and their lineage goes back to the fifteenth century. Their earlier recording of the piece was pretty impressive. Even so, this newcomer surpasses it and offers singing of an extraordinarily rapt intensity. The dynamic range is enormous, the perfection of ensemble and blend and the sheer beauty of tone such as to exhaust superlatives. Vladislav Chernuchenko gets performances of complete conviction from them, and it is hard to imagine that their singing can be surpassed. The recording does them justice and is made in a suitably atmospheric acoustic. It has now been reissued at bargain price in a handsome presentation – more like a slim hardback book – which also includes, besides documentation, a tempting catalogue of the Chant du Monde issues in their so-called 'Russian Season'.

Though Matthew Best's British choir, the Corydon Singers, lacks the dark timbres associated with Russian choruses and though the result could be weightier and more biting, this is a most beautiful performance, very well sung and recorded in an atmospheric, reverberant setting very apt for such church music.

Vocalise, Op. 34/14 (arr. Dubensky).
(M) *** BMG/RCA GD 87831 [7831-2-RG]. Anna Moffo, American SO, Stokowski –
   CANTELOUBE: *Songs of the Auvergne;* VILLA-LOBOS: *Bachianas Brasileiras No. 5.* ***

Rachmaninov's *Vocalise* was a favourite showpiece of Stokowski, usually in a purely orchestral
arrangement; but here with Moffo at her warmest it is good to have the vocal version so persuasively
matching the accompaniment.

OPERA

(i) *Monna Vanna* (incomplete opera: Act I, orch. Buketoff); (ii) *Piano concerto No. 4* (original
version).
**(*) Chan. Dig. CHAN 8987 [id.]. (i) Milnes, McCoy, Walker, Karoustos, Thorsteinsson, Blythe;
   (ii) William Black; Iceland SO, Buketoff.

Monna Vanna is the fragment of an opera based on Maeterlinck which Rachmaninov wrote around
the inspired period of his *Second Symphony*. He thought so well of the fragment that it was the one
score he brought away from Russia after the Revolution. Igor Buketoff, who knew the composer, has
rescued this Act I score and orchestrated it very sensitively to make an interesting curiosity. In its
ripely romantic manner the writing has lyrical warmth and flows freely, thrusting home climactic
moments with the same sureness as Rachmaninov's symphonies. Buketoff's performance with the
Iceland Symphony is warmly convincing, but the singing is flawed, with Sherrill Milnes, as Monna
Vanna's jealous husband, standing out from an indifferent team, otherwise thin-toned and often
wobbly. Buketoff's resurrection of the original score of the *Fourth Piano concerto* is rather more
expansive than the text we know. William Black is the powerful soloist, though the piano sound,
unlike that of the orchestra, lacks weight.

Raff, Joachim (1822–82)

Symphony No. 5 (Lenore).
(M) *** Unicorn UKCD 2031. LPO, Bernard Herrmann.

Raff's *Fifth Symphony*, with its colourful programmatic writing, is generally counted the finest of his
cycle. In some ways it is a very naïve work, based as it is on a high romantic ballad by the poet
Bürger. A dead soldier-lover calls upon the girl he has left behind, and on a devil's ride he
disconcertingly turns into a skeleton. The first two movements merely provide preparation for that
dramatic development, while the third depicts the lovers' parting, with the main march heard first in
crescendo then diminuendo to represent the arrival and departure of a troop of the lover's regiment –
a piece much beloved by the Victorians. A thoroughly enjoyable Mendelssohnian symphony,
colourfully performed with clean and vivid recording, given extra projection on CD, especially the
percussion. More of this composer's symphonies are now appearing on CD and we hope to include
these in our next edition.

Raid, Kaljo (born 1922)

Symphony No. 1 in C min.
*** Chan. Dig. CHAN 8525; *ABTD 1235* [id.]. SNO, Järvi – ELLER: *Dawn; Elegia* etc. ***

Raid's *First Symphony* shows a genuine feel for form and a fine sense of proportion, even though the
personality is not fully formed. Well worth hearing. Neeme Järvi gets very committed playing from
the Scottish National Orchestra and the recording is warm and well detailed.

Rameau, Jean Philippe (1683–1764)

Les Boréades: orchestral suite; Dardanus: orchestral suite.
*** Ph. Dig. 420 240-2 [id.]. O of 18th Century, Brüggen.

The orchestral suite from *Les Boréades* occupies the larger part of the disc. The invention is full of
resource and imagination, and the playing here of both this and *Dardanus* is spirited and sensitive and
will provide delight even to those normally unresponsive to authentic instruments.

Dardanus: suite; *Les Indes galantes*: suite.
☞ (M) **(*) HM/BMG 05472 77269-2 [id.]. Coll. Aur.

This early example of authentic performance dates from the 1960s. Any abrasiveness deriving from the use of original instruments is countered by the generous acoustics of the Cedernsaal in the Schloss Kirchheim. But the playing has both life and elegance and the sound, though warm and full, is by no means bland: the flutes and oboes (and trumpets in *Les Indes galantes*) bring plenty of added colour. The selection from *Les Indes galantes* is shorter than that provided by Herreweghe, but many will welcome the coupling with *Dardanus*, and the overall playing time is quite generous: 69 minutes.

Hippolyte et Aricie: orchestral suite.
(M) *** HM/BMG GD 77009 [77009-2-RG]. La Petite Bande, Kuijken.

This record collects virtually all the orchestral music from *Hippolyte et Aricie*; the melodic invention is fresh and its orchestral presentation ingenious. Sigiswald Kuijken gets delightful results from his ensemble. In every way an outstanding release – and not least in the quality of the sound.

Les Indes galantes: suites for orchestra.
(B) *** HM HMA 901130 [id.]. Chappelle Royale O, Philippe Herreweghe.

Besides the harpsichord arrangements listed below, Rameau also arranged his four 'concerts' of music from *Les Indes galantes* for orchestra. The result makes nearly three-quarters of an hour of agreeable listening, especially when played so elegantly – and painlessly – on original instruments, and very well recorded (in 1984).

Les Paladins (comédie-ballet): *orchestral suite.*
☞ *** Ph. Dig. 432 968-2 [id.]. O of Age of Enlightenment, Leonhardt.

Rameau's comédie-lyrique, *Les Paladins*, is a work of his last years and was produced in 1760, four years before his death. It met with scant success, however, thanks to its poor libretto. All too often, Gustav Leonhardt's instinct for scholarly rectitude can get in the way of musical imagination and flair, but here his recording of the ballet numbers with the Orchestra of the Age of Enlightenment is little short of a triumph. There is a liveliness, freshness and delight in the colours and rhythms of this inventive score that will captivate the listener and lay to rest any fears of scholarly caution. There is more than an hour's music here, all of it of quality and all played with a panache and style that will win many friends for this composer. The recording, made at St Giles', Cripplegate, is equally crisp and well detailed. Strongly recommended.

Le Temple de la Gloire: suites 1–2.
☞ (M) *** Decca 433 733-2 [id.]. ECO, Leppard – CAMPRA: *L'Europe galante.* ***

This is a most rewarding CD, and the spectacular (1966) Kingsway Hall recording – the opening, with its brass effects, is most impressive – is fully worthy of the attractive music and the spirited, stylish playing. Rameau's score has much character: the *Air for the demons* is a good example of his imaginative evocation. Raymond Leppard gives us an object lesson in how to perform music of this period on modern instruments; his springy rhythms and, especially, his use of the continuo to colour the texture are most imaginative.

Pièces de clavecin en concert Nos. 1–5.
☞ (M) *** Teldec/Warner 9031 77618-2. Brüggen, Sigiswald and Wieland Kuijken, Leonhardt.
☞ *** Virgin/EMI Dig. VC7 59154-2 [id.]. Trio Sonnerie.
☞ **(*) Denon Dig. CO-79045 [id.]. Masahiro Arita, Natsumi Wakamatsu, Wieland Kuijken, Chiyoko Arita.

The *Cinq pièces de clavecin en concert* are for harpsichord but are more familiar in ensemble versions: in addition to the harpsichord parts, Rameau included additional parts for violin or flute, second violin and bass viol. His models were the six sonatas of Mondonville (1734), though Rameau's obbligato instruments play a freer, more confident role. These pieces, published in 1741, are played on Teldec with a sure sense of style and a real understanding of the niceties of the period. They are recorded on period instruments – but, rest assured, this is no dull, pedantic performance full of musicological rectitude and little musical life. On the contrary, it is scholarly but has genuine liveliness and authenticity of feeling. The music, of course, is delightful, and very much helped by the admirably fresh, transparent recording.

The Trio Sonnerie are also perfectly attuned to the sensibility of the period and its requirements. Theirs is a performance which exhibits a sense of style and a quality of feeling that outweigh any shortcomings. The most notable of these is the fact that they choose to limit the instrumental colours available to them by confining themselves to string instruments and exclude the flute, usual in this repertoire. The Virgin recording is of great naturalness and presence, and the issue is a strong contender.

The Japanese players on Denon are all pupils of Wieland Kuijken, who plays the gamba here, and they are eminently expert; their flautist, Masahiro Arita, in addition to his expressive playing, provides informative notes. Their playing is generally vital and stylish (the *Tambourin* in the *Third Concert* is a particular delight) and they show a spirited lightness of touch in the *Fourth* which is not always in evidence elsewhere. The elegiac movement composed in memory of the Baron Livri is curiously awkward and wanting in elegance, and elsewhere the playing could also do with greater delicacy of feeling. The Trio Sonnerie have the better sense of style. The Denon recording is very natural and realistic, though the listener is never left in any doubt that he is in a studio.

KEYBOARD MUSIC

Les Indes galantes: excerpts (harpsichord transcriptions).
*** HM HMC 901028; *HMC 401028*. Kenneth Gilbert.

These transcriptions are Rameau's own, including not only dance numbers and orchestral pieces but arias as well. Kenneth Gilbert, playing a fine instrument in contemporary tuning, reveals these miniatures as the subtle and refined studies they are. He could not be better served by the recording engineers.

Music for harpsichord: *Book 1* (1706); *Pièces de clavecin* (1724); *Nouvelles suites de pièces de clavecin* (c. 1728); *5 Pièces* (1741); *La Dauphine* (1747).
*** O-L Dig. 425 886-2 (2) [id.]. Christophe Rousset (harpsichord).
(M) *** DG 427 176-2 (2). Kenneth Gilbert (harpischord).

Rousset's playing is marvellously persuasive and vital, authoritative and scholarly, yet fresh and completely free from the straitjacket of academic rectitude. He plays a Hemsch in a perfect state of preservation and a 1988 copy of a 1636 Ruckers harpsichord, modified by Hemsch. The sound is excellent.

Kenneth Gilbert, too, is not just a scholar but an artist of genuine insight and stature. He uses three harpsichords, all from the Paris Conservatoire and all from the period: a Goujon and a Hemsch and one by Dumont, restored by Pascal Taskin in 1789. They are superb instruments and are excellently recorded too (in 1977).

Pièces de clavecin: Suite (No. 1) in A min.; L'Agaçante; La Dauphine; L'Indiscrète; La Livri; La Pantomine: La Timide.
*** CRD CRD 3320; *CRDC 4020* [id.]. Trevor Pinnock.

Trevor Pinnock chose a mellow instrument here, making his stylish, crisply rhythmic performances even more attractive. The selection includes *La Dauphine*, the last keyboard piece which Rameau wrote, brilliantly performed. Excellent recording.

Harpsichord suites: in A min. (1728); *in E min.* (1724).
*** CRD CRD 3310; *CRDC 4010* [id.]. Trevor Pinnock.

Harpsichord suites: in D min./maj. (1724); *in G maj./min.* (1728).
*** CRD CRD 3330; *CRDC 4030* [id.]. Trevor Pinnock.

Trevor Pinnock is restrained in the matter of ornamentation, but his direct manner is both eloquent and stylish. The harpsichord is of the French type and is well recorded.

Grand motets: *In convertendo; Quam dilecta laboravi.*
*** HM HM 901078; *HM 401078* [id.]. Gari, Monnaliu, Ledroit, De Mey, Varcoe, Chapelle Royale Ch., Ghent Coll. Vocale, Herreweghe.

These two motets are among Rameau's finest works. The Ghent Collegium Vocale is stiffened by forces from La Chapelle Royale in Paris. They produce excellent results and the soloists are also very fine indeed. The instrumental ensemble includes several members of La Petite Bande and so its excellence can almost be taken for granted.

OPERA-BALLET AND OPERA

Anacréon (complete).
(B) *** HM HMA 90190 [id.]. Schirrer, Mellon, Feldman, Visse, Laplénie, Les Arts Florissants,
Christie.

The music here has charm; the performance is as authoritative and stylish as one would expect from
William Christie's group. It is not essential Rameau, but it has moments of great appeal. The
recording is admirable and this reissue is a genuine bargain.

Platée (complete).
** Erato/Warner Dig. 2292 45028-2 (2) [id.]. Ragon, Jennifer Smith, Guy de Mey, Le Texier, Gens,
Ens. Vocale Françoise Herr, Musiciens du Louvre, Minkowski.

Platée, written in 1745 and described as a *'ballet bouffon'*, is in fact a comic opera, based on a
classical theme. With such a send-up of classical tradition, the performers here understandably adopt
comic expressions and voices, which in a recording, as opposed to a stage performance, become
rather wearing on the listener. Also almost all the soloists aspirate heavily in florid passages. Within
that convention this is a lively, brisk performance, very well conducted by Marc Minkowski, but
marred by the dryness of the recording. As a work, *Platée* certainly provides a fascinating side-glance
at Rameau's mastery.

Pygmalion (complete).
(M) **(*) HM/BMG GD 77143 [77143-2-RG]. Elwes, Van der Sluis, Vanhecke, Yakar, Paris
Chapelle Royal Ch., La Petite Bande, Leonhardt.

Leonhardt's 1980 account with John Elwes as Pygmalion and Mieke van der Sluis as Céphise is
rather leisurely, but his soloists make a good team, while the use of period instruments brings
attractive transparency of texture. The documentation (including full translation) is first class.

Zoroastre (complete).
(M) **(*) HM/BMG GD 77144 (3) [77144-2-RG]. Elwes, De Reyghere, Van der Sluis, Nellon,
Reinhart, Bona, Ghent Coll. Vocale, La Petite Bande, Kuijken.

Though Kuijken's characteristically gentle style with his excellent authentic group, La Petite Bande,
fails to give the piece all the bite and urgency it needs, this is nevertheless a fine presentation of a
long-neglected masterpiece, with crisp and stylish singing from the soloists, notably John Elwes in the
name-part and Gregory Reinhart as Abramane. The Ghent Collegium Vocale, placed rather close,
sing with vigour in the choruses, but the individual voices fail to blend. The excellent documentation
(144 pages, including translations) puts the mid-priced issues of many of the large international
companies to shame.

Rautavaara, Einojuhani (born 1928)

Symphonies 1–3.
*** Ondine Dig. ODE 740-2 [id.]. Leipzig RSO, Max Pommer.

Einojuhani Rautavaara has been overshadowed outside Finland by Joonas Kokkonen and Aulis
Sallinen, but the present disc shows him to be a symphonist to reckon with. Ideas never outstay their
welcome and there is a sense of inevitability about their development. Those with a taste for
Shostakovich or Simpson should find these pieces congenial. Good performances by the Leipzig
Radio Orchestra under Max Pommer and very decent recorded sound too.

Ravel, Maurice (1875–1937)

Alborada del gracioso; Une barque sur l'océan; Boléro; (i) *Piano concerto in G; Piano concerto for the
left hand. Daphnis et Chloé* (complete ballet); *L'Eventail de Jeanne: Fanfare. Menuet antique; Ma
Mère l'Oye* (complete); *Pavane pour une infante défunte; Rapsodie espagnole; Le tombeau de Couperin;
La valse; Valses nobles et sentimentales.*
⊛ (M) *** Decca 421 458-2 (4). Montreal SO with Ch. and (i) Pascal Rogé; Dutoit.

(i) *Alborada del gracioso;* (ii) *Une barque sur l'océan; Boléro;* (i; iii) *Piano concerto for the left hand;*
(ii; iv) *Daphnis et Chloé* (complete ballet); (ii) *Fanfare pour L'Eventail de Jeanne; Menuet antique; Ma
Mère l'Oye* (complete ballet); (i) *Pavane pour une infante défunte; Rapsodie espagnole;* (ii)
Shéhérazade: Ouverture de féerie. Le tombeau de Couperin; La valse; Valses nobles et sentimentales.
(M) **(*) Sony SM3K 45842 (3) [id.]. (i) Cleveland O; (ii) NYPO; Boulez; (iii) with Entremont; (iv)
   Camerata Singers.

Anyone coming new to this repertoire will find Dutoit's four-disc mid-price box unbeatable value: the
orchestral playing is wonderfully sympathetic and the recording ideally combines atmospheric
evocation with vividness of detail. In the concertos, Pascal Rogé finds gracefulness and vitality for the
G major work and, if there is less dynamism in the *Left-hand concerto*, there is no lack of finesse. The
balance is very realistic and the recording throughout is in the demonstration class.

   Boulez's distinguished Sony set offers a glitteringly iridescent account of the *Ouverture de féerie*,
which is omitted by Dutoit. Entremont's account of the *Left-hand concerto* is strong and characterful
and not lacking in poetic colour; but the CBS sound is a little fierce and does not altogether flatter
the piano timbre. On the whole, however, the remastering makes the most of recordings which were
originally among the best of their period (1972–5). The *Alborada* is quite brilliant and, throughout,
Boulez allows all the music ample time to breathe; gentler textures have the translucence for which
this conductor is admired. *Une barque sur l'océan* has a genuine magic, while the complete *Daphnis et
Chloé* has a sense of ecstasy. Boulez is also at his very best in *Ma Mère l'Oye* with its luminous
textures, and his *Rapsodie espagnole* is equally distinctive: it is beautifully shaped and atmospheric in
an entirely different way from Karajan's; Boulez's Spain is brilliant, dry and well lit. Both *Boléro* and
La valse generate considerable tension and have powerful climaxes. There is no doubt that this music-
making with its cleanly etched sound is immensely strong in character, and many listeners will
respond to it very positively.

Alborada del gracioso; Une barque sur l'océan; Boléro; (i) *Daphnis et Chloé* (complete ballet). *Ma
Mère l'Oye* (complete); *Menuet antique; Pavane pour une infante défunte; Rapsodie espagnole; Le
tombeau de Couperin; La Valse; Valses nobles et sentimentales.*
☞ (M) ** DG 439 342-2 (3). Boston SO, Ozawa, (i) with Tanglewood Festival Ch.

It would be easy to underestimate this set, for the Boston orchestral playing is very fine and DG's
(mid-1970s) analogue recording is first class, making the most of the acoustics of Symphony Hall yet
giving excellent, natural definition. But Ozawa is, on this showing, not a deeply perceptive exponent
of Ravel. He is at his best in catching the atmosphere of *Une barque sur l'océan;* yet overall, in spite
of many felicitous touches (notably in *Le tombeau de Couperin*), he does not match Dutoit, Martinon
or Abbado either in atmosphere or in magic. *Boléro* moves to its climax steadily in a curiously
unmotivated way, and in the last resort the performances are wanting the final degree of character.
Daphnis and Chloé has not the radiance of the finest versions, while in *Ma Mère l'Oye* there is
something really quite cool about the music-making that limits its appeal.

Alborada del gracioso; Une barque sur l'océan; Boléro; Ma Mère l'Oye (complete ballet); *Menuet
antique; Pavane pour une infante défunte; Rapsodie espagnole; Le tombeau de Couperin; La valse;
Valses nobles et sentimentales.*
☞ (M) *** EMI CZS7 67897-2 [id.]. Paris Conservatoire O, Cluytens.

These 1961 performances, made in the Salle Wagram, Paris, are as good as any in the catalogue. They
have a strongly idiomatic and atmospheric feel; the *Rapsodie espagnole, La valse* and the *Valses nobles*
are exceptionally good, and so too is the complete *Ma Mère l'Oye*. The only snag is the wide vibrato
of the horn in *Pavane pour une infante défunte*. The recordings still sound remarkably realistic, and
not just for the period: they are very good by present-day standards. The two-disc set makes a
genuine bargain.

Alborada del gracioso; Boléro; Daphnis et Chloé (ballet): *Suite No. 2; Menuet antique; Ma Mère
l'Oye* (complete ballet); *Pavane pour une infante défunte; Rapsodie espagnole; Le tombeau de Couperin;
La valse; Valses nobles et sentimentales.*
☞ (B) **(*) Ph. Duo 438 745-2 [id.]. Concg. O, Bernard Haitink.

Although Haitink's Ravel collection, recorded in the early 1970s, is not as magnetic as the superb
companion Debussy set on Philips Duo, these are still fine performances, distinguished by instinctive
good judgement and taste. The playing of the Amsterdam orchestra is eminently polished and
civilized, even if the heady, intoxicating qualities of the music are missed. The *Rapsodie espagnole*
lacks the last ounce of dash in the *Feria*, but the *Habañera* is lazily appealing when the orchestral
playing is so sleek and refined. There is perhaps not quite enough atmosphere in *Le tombeau de*

Couperin, and Haitink's *La valse* fails to captivate or excite the listener as do the finest versions of this piece. Yet the orchestral playing seduces the ear with its refinement and finish, and the engineers produce a sound to match: the perspective is truthful and the overall effect on CD most pleasing, with the remastered recordings improved in firmness of outline without loss of atmosphere or bloom.

Alborada del gracioso; Boléro; Daphnis et Chloé: suite No. 2; La valse.
☞ * Teldec/Warner Dig. 2292 44945-2 [id.]. Cleveland O, Christoph von Dohnányi.

The Teldec recording for Dohnányi is in the demonstration bracket and the playing of the Cleveland Orchestra is virtuosity itself. But there is no magic here, no sense of mystery or atmosphere in *Daphnis*, and little sense of the intoxication one encounters in Karajan, Ormandy or in such Ravel conductors as Reiner or Munch. Nor does *La valse* fare better, and the *Alborada del gracioso* emerges as just a display piece. At full price – and, at 50 minutes, far from full measure – this is a non-starter, particularly in view of the great performances to be found elsewhere. As sound, this is worth a three-star rating, but as a musical experience Ravel-lovers will not want it.

Alborada del gracioso; Boléro; Rapsodie espagnole; La valse.
*** Decca 410 010-2 [id.]. Montreal SO, Dutoit.

The playing of the Montreal orchestra under Charles Dutoit is absolutely first class and thoroughly atmospheric, and the recorded sound defines the state of the art and, apart from the sumptuous music-making, has impressive refinement and a most musically judged and natural balance.

(i) *Alborada del gracioso;* (ii) *Boléro;* (i) *La valse.*
(M) *** EMI CDM7 64357-2 [id.]. (i) O de Paris; (ii) BPO; Karajan – DEBUSSY: *La Mer*. ***

Karajan's digitally remastered 1978 EMI Berlin Philharmonic *Boléro* has fine presence and a splendid forward impetus. The Paris *Alborada* and *La valse* have been tacked on for this reissue. They were recorded in 1974 as part of an outstanding French concert of Ravel's orchestral music (now withdrawn).

Alborada del gracioso; Fanfare for L'Eventail de Jeanne; Ma Mère l'Oye (complete ballet); *Miroirs: La vallée des cloches* (arr. Percy Grainger); *La valse;* (i) *Shéhérazade* (song-cycle).
*** EMI Dig. CDC7 54204-2 [id.]. (i) Maria Ewing; CBSO, Simon Rattle.

The recording of the CBSO, made in the Arts Centre of Warwick University, is extraordinarily spectacular, with a state-of-the-art sound-balance of the widest range and amplitude. The performances too have great magnetism and electricity, and the orchestral playing is superb. Rattle captures the lambent allure of Percy Grainger's orchestration of the last of the *Miroirs* and gives an equally glowing account of *Ma Mère l'Oye*; *La valse* sounds gorgeous too, climaxing with alarming power. At the beginning of the programme, Maria Ewing's *Shéhérazade* is matched in voluptuous intensity by Rattle and his players; in the aching yearning of *La flûte enchantée* the atmosphere becomes more impressionistic. But it is essentially a dramatic performance, and the shimmering *Alborada* is well placed to follow on afterwards.

Alborada del gracioso; Pavane pour une infante défunte; Rapsodie espagnole; Le tombeau de Couperin; La valse.
(M) *** Mercury 432 003-2 [id.]. Detroit SO, Paray – IBERT: *Escales*. **(*)

Paray's Ravel performances enjoyed a high reputation in the 1960s. His *Rapsodie espagnole* can be spoken of in the same breath as the Reiner/RCA and Karajan/EMI versions, with its languorous, shimmering textures and sparkling *Feria*. His *Alborada* glitters and the *Pavane* is glowingly elegiac. *La valse*, too, is impressively shaped and subtly controlled. *Le tombeau de Couperin* has great refinement and elegance: the solo oboist plays beautifully. All have been excellently remastered.

Alborada del gracioso; Pavane pour une infante défunte; Rapsodie espagnole; Valses nobles et sentimentales.
⊛ (M) *** BMG/RCA GD 60179 [60179-2-RG]. Chicago SO, Reiner – DEBUSSY: *Ibéria*. *** ⊛

These performances are in an altogether special class. In the *Rapsodie espagnole*, the *Prélude à la nuit* is heavy with fragrance and atmosphere; never have the colours in the *Feria* glowed more luminously, while the *Malagueña* glitters with iridescence. In the thirty years since it first appeared, this is the recording we have turned to whenever we wanted to hear this work for pleasure. No one captures its sensuous atmosphere as completely as did Reiner, and the recorded sound with its natural concert-hall balance is greatly improved in terms of clarity and definition.

Alborada del gracioso; Rapsodie espagnole.
*** Chan. Dig. CHAN 8850; *ABTD 1467* [id.]. Ulster O, Yan Pascal Tortelier – DEBUSSY: *Images.*
***

Yan Pascal Tortelier gives very good performances of both works and has the advantage of excellent Chandos sound. His *Rapsodie espagnole* is not quite as gripping as some celebrated accounts (Reiner, Karajan, Giulini and others) but it is highly atmospheric all the same, and some collectors may be swayed by the claims of the outstanding digital recording.

Boléro.
☞ (B) *** DG Double 437 404-2 (2) [id.]. BPO, Karajan – CHOPIN: *Les Sylphides* *** ⊛; DELIBES: *Coppélia: suite* ***; GOUNOD: *Faust* etc. **(*); OFFENBACH: *Gaîté parisienne:* excerpts; RAVEL: *Boléro* ***; TCHAIKOVSKY: *Sleeping Beauty* (suite). **(*)

Karajan's fine mid-1960s analogue *Boléro* comes here within a collection of ballet music, almost all of which shows Karajan in top form.

Boléro; Daphnis et Chloé: suite No. 2.
(M) *** DG 427 250-2. BPO, Karajan – DEBUSSY: *La mer; Prélude.* ***

Karajan's 1964 *Boléro* is a very characteristic performance, marvellously controlled, hypnotic and gripping, with the Berlin Philharmonic at the top of its form. The 1965 *Daphnis et Chloé* suite is outstanding, even among all the competition. He has the advantage of the Berlin Philharmonic at their finest and it would be difficult to imagine better or more atmospheric playing. The CD has opened up the sound spectacularly although now there is a touch of glare.

Boléro; (i) *Daphnis et Chloé: suite No. 2; Ma Mère l'Oye (suite); Valses nobles et sentimentales.*
(BB) *** Naxos Dig. 8.550173; *4550173* [id.]. (i) Slovak Philharmonic Ch.; Slovak RSO (Bratislava), Kenneth Jean.

The Slovak Radio Orchestra, which is a fine body and is superbly recorded, respond warmly to Kenneth Jean. At the price, this is very good value indeed; the *Ma Mère l'Oye* can hold its own alongside all but the most distinguished competition: indeed *Les entretiens de la belle et de la bête* is as keenly characterized as Dutoit at mid-price, and *Le jardin féerique* is enchanting. For those wanting these pieces this is a real bargain.

Boléro; (i) *Daphnis et Chloé: suite No. 2; Pavane pour une infante défunte; La valse.*
(M) *** Decca Dig. 430 714-2; *430 714-4* [id.]. Montreal SO, Dutoit; (i) with chorus.

A further permutation of Dutoit's beautifully made Montreal recordings, warmly and translucently recorded at St Eustache, now reissued at mid-price.

Boléro; Daphnis et Chloé: suite No. 2; La valse.
☞ (M) (***) BMG/RCA mono 09026 61392-2. Boston SO, Koussevitzky (with DEBUSSY: *Sarabande*) – MUSSORGSKY: *Pictures.* (***)

It was Koussevitzky who commissioned Ravel's orchestral transcriptions of the Mussorgsky *Pictures*, so that it is logical to couple them with two of his classic Ravel recordings. The *Boléro, La valse* and the transcription of the Debussy *Sarabande* all come from 1930 and were made at the same time as the *Pictures*. Oddly enough, the earlier recordings, certainly his marvellously atmospheric *La valse*, sound fresher and better focused. The second *Daphnis et Chloé* suite is much later (1944–5) and, though the performances could not be more vivid and vibrant, the sound-quality is not really good; there is some discoloration affecting climaxes. As with this conductor at his best, details of phrasing and texture feel just right, and the orchestral colours shine across the 50 years since they were first heard. His *Lever du jour* feels a shade faster than usual, and the remaining two movements have just the right sense of rapture. There is an inaccurate index-point for the stunning *Danse générale*. Intoxicating stuff despite the sonic limitations.

Boléro; L'Eventail de Jeanne: Fanfare; Ma Mère l'Oye (complete ballet); *Pièce en forme de habañera* (arr. Arthur Horérée); *Rapsodie espagnole.*
*** Sony Dig. MK 44800 [id.]. LSO, Tilson Thomas.

Tilson Thomas is wholly attuned to the sensibility of this magical music and Ravel's sumptuous orchestral colours are vividly reproduced. There is a beautifully sultry account of the *Prélude à la nuit* and plenty of atmosphere in the *Rapsodie espagnole*. Ravel's *Vocalise-étude en forme de habañera* has the remarkable John Harle as the saxophone soloist. These are seductive, delicious performances, beautifully recorded.

Boléro; Rapsodie espagnole.

☞ *** DG Gold Dig. 439 013-2 [id.]. BPO, Karajan – MUSSORGSKY: *Pictures.* ***

Karajan's later versions of *Boléro* and *Rapsodie espagnole* find the Berlin Philharmonic in characteristically brilliant form, recorded in very wide-ranging digital sound; the thrust of *Boléro* and the sensuousness of the *Rapsodie* are conveyed with unerring power and magnetism. The newly remastered transfer by Original-image-bit processing is very impressive in its realism – pianissimo detail is subtly delineated and the close of the *Feria* of the *Rapsodie espagnole* is spectacular indeed!

Boléro; Rapsodie espagnole; La valse.

☞ (M) (**) BMG/RCA mono 09026 61956-2 [id.]. Boston SO, Munch – DEBUSSY: *Images.* **

Munch's performances of *Boléro* and the *Rapsodie espagnole* date from 1956 and his *La valse* from the preceding year. The virtuosity of the Boston Symphony Orchestra is pretty dazzling and no one is likely to be disappointed by these idiomatic and masterly performances. All the same, Reiner's *Rapsodie espagnole* is headier and more atmospheric, and there are more seductive accounts of *La valse* (Koussevitzky, Cluytens, Karajan, etc.) – but no matter, this is still distinguished playing and is eminently recommendable.

Boléro; Le tombeau de Couperin; (i) *Tzigane;* (ii) *Shéhérazade* (song-cycle).

☞ (B) *** DG Classikon Dig. 439 414-2 [id.]. (i) Salvatore Accardo; (ii) Margaret Price; LSO,
   Abbado.

Highly sensitive, beautifully played performances. Abbado is on excellent form and brings out all the subtle colourings of Ravel's orchestration, in which he is greatly helped by the excellent DG recording. There is some lovely oboe playing in *Le tombeau de Couperin* and Accardo is superb in *Tzigane*. Margaret Price seems to come from within the orchestra instead of the voice floating effortlessly over the texture as does Crespin on Decca. Yet the singing itself is ravishingly ecstatic in both *Asie* and *La flûte enchantée*, even if she does not always seem to be quite inside the sensibility of the music. Only in *Boléro* is there any idiosyncrasy: near the climax Abbado makes a perceptible gear-change, pressing the tempo forward somewhat; his involvement is also conveyed in his vocal contributions to the closing pages. The recording here is spectacular, with fine focus and detail, yet with plenty of ambience and warmth. A genuine bargain.

Boléro; La valse.

*** Chan. Dig. CHAN 8903 [id.]. Ulster O, Yan Pascal Tortelier – DEBUSSY: *Jeux; Khamma.* ***

** Chan. Dig. CHAN 8996; *ABTD 1578* [id.]. Detroit SO, Järvi – ROUSSEL: *Bacchus; Symphony No. 3.* **(*)

Yan Pascal Tortelier's *Boléro* and *La valse* are recommendable performances and well recorded in the best traditions of the house.

Neeme Järvi's *La valse* is brisk and not without its moments of exaggeration – indeed affectation unusual in this conductor. Very natural recorded sound, though not a first choice for either Ravel piece.

Piano concerto in G.

⊛ *** EMI CDC7 49326-2 [id.]. Michelangeli, Philh. O, Gracis – RACHMANINOV: *Concerto No. 4.* *** ⊛

☞ *(*) Denon Dig. CO 75368 [id.]. Hélène Grimaud, RPO, López-Cobos – RACHMANINOV: *Piano concerto No. 2.* *(*)

Michelangeli plays with superlative brilliance which yet has great sympathy for the tender moments. The exquisite playing in the slow movement makes up for any deficiencies of dimensional balance. The recording has been remastered very successfully and is of high quality: clear, with bold piano timbre and excellent orchestral detail.

Hélène Grimaud's *G major Piano concerto* with the RPO and Jesús López-Cobos does not offer a serious challenge to the front runners. Moreover the coupling is not the most competitive when put alongside more logically partnered rivals. The outer movements have a certain sparkle, but this gifted young artist does not allow the middle movement to speak for itself. Nor, for that matter, is the recording top-drawer.

(i) *Piano concerto in G. Gaspard de la nuit; Sonatine.*

(M) *** DG 419 062-2 [id.]. Argerich, (i) BPO, Abbado.

Argerich's half-tones and clear fingerwork give the *G major Concerto* unusual delicacy, but its urgent virility – with jazz an important element – comes over the more forcefully by contrast. The compromise between coolness and expressiveness in the slow minuet of the middle movement is tantalizingly sensual. Her *Gaspard de la nuit* abounds in character and colour, and the *Sonatine* is a similarly telling performance. The *Concerto* balance is very successful.

Piano concerto in G; Piano concerto in D for the left hand.
(M) *** Erato/Warner 2292 45086-2 [id.]. Anne Queffélec, Strasbourg PO, Lombard – DEBUSSY: *Fantasy.* ***
(*) Chan. Dig. CHAN 8773 [id.]. Louis Lortie, LSO, Frühbeck de Burgos – FAURE: *Ballade.* *

(i) *Piano concerto in G; Piano concerto for the left hand. Une barque sur l'océan; L'Eventail de Jeanne: Fanfare; Menuet antique.*
**(*) Decca Dig. 410 230-2. (i) Rogé; Montreal SO, Dutoit.

Anne Queffélec's accounts of both *Concertos* are thoughtful and imaginative. She is a thorough musician with no mean sense of poetry. The excellent Strasbourg orchestra under Alain Lombard give her admirable support, and the well-balanced recording sounds fresher in its CD format.

Pascal Rogé brings both delicacy and sparkle to the *G major Concerto*, which he gives with his characteristic musical grace and fluency. He brings great poetry and tenderness to the slow movement; but in the *Left-hand concerto* he is a good deal less dynamic, even though there is much to admire in the way of pianistic finesse – and charm. The Decca recording offers excellent performances of three short orchestral pieces as a makeweight.

Louis Lortie's account of the two *Concertos* on Chandos has the advantage of altogether outstanding recording. In the *G major* he is often highly personal without becoming unduly idiosyncratic, with a fastidious sense of colour at his command. In the *Left-hand concerto* he really takes his time over the cadenzas and his agogic hesitations are sometimes over-indulgent. Immaculate playing as such, and superb recording.

(i) *Piano concerto in G; Piano concerto for the left hand in D. A la manière de Borodine; A la manière de Chabrier; Gaspard de la nuit; Jeux d'eau; Menuet antique; Menuet sur le nom de Haydn; Miroirs; Pavane pour une infante défunte; Prélude; Sonatine; Le tombeau de Couperin; Valses nobles et sentimentales.*
☞ (B) **(*) Ph. Duo 438 353-2 (2) [id.]. Werner Haas; (i) Monte-Carlo Opéra O, Galliera.

This well-recorded pair of CDs offers virtually all Ravel's piano music at a bargain price. Werner Haas has a genuine Ravel sensibility and he plays with delicacy and a fine feeling for the music's colour and its moments of gentle rapture. His tempi are consistently apt and he is fully equal to the technical demands of *Gaspard de la nuit*. His crisp articulation in the *Toccata* of *Le tombeau de Couperin* and the *Alborada* from *Miroirs* shows how a ready technical facility is always placed at the service of the composer. Faster passages are very slightly blurred by the resonant acoustic, but otherwise the recording is lifelike and very pleasing. The performances of the two *Concertos* match the rest, refined and satisfying. Perhaps the playing here is a little strait-laced (elsewhere Haas is often pleasingly flexible) but Galliera's fine accompaniments add to the authority of these performances, and the 1968 recording is well balanced. These are performances one could live with, and this set is excellent value.

(i) *Piano concerto in G; Piano concerto for the left hand in D;* (ii) *Tzigane;* (iii) *Shéhérazade* (song-cycle).
☞ (B) *(*) Erato/Warner Duo 4509 95358-2 (2) [id.]. (i) Duchâble; (ii) Amoyal; (iii) Yakar; SRO, Jordan – SAINT-SAENS: *Concertos Nos. 2 & 4.* *(*)

There is nothing special about Duchâble's accounts of the two piano concertos. The opening whipcrack of the *G major* could be more dramatic, while the slow movement is a little lacking in tension, although overall the performances are musical and well recorded. Rachel Yakar produces fine tone and a good line but is rather cool in *Schéhérazade* and she seems to have nothing especially individual to contribute; the most striking performance here is Amoyal's lively *Tzigane*, full of gypsy feeling. As usual with this Erato Bonsai Duo series, the documentation is sparse, with no text or translation for the song cycle.

Piano concerto for the left hand in D.
☞ (BB) *** ASV Dig. CDQS 6092. Osorio, RPO, Bátiz – FRANCK: *Symphonic variations* **(*); SAINT-SAENS: *Wedding-cake* ***; SCHUMANN: *Concerto.* ***
☞ *** Sony Dig. SK 47188 [id.]. Fleisher, Boston SO, Ozawa – BRITTEN: *Diversions;* PROKOFIEV: *Concerto No. 4.* ***

(i) *Piano concerto for the left hand. Miroirs: Alborada del gracioso.*
*** ASV Dig. CDDCA 555; *ZCDCA 555* [id.]. Osorio, RPO, Bátiz – PROKOFIEV: *Piano concerto No. 1 etc.* ***

Jorge Federico Osorio's account of the *Left-hand concerto* can hold its own with the best and it is very well recorded. With its tempting bargain couplings, about which there are only minor reservations, this disc is a genuine bargain. He also gives a crisp and colourful performance of the *Alborada* in an alternative, full-price coupling with Prokofiev.

Leon Fleisher's account of the Ravel *Concerto for the left hand* is strongly characterized and full of life and colour. Apart from its general artistic excellence, the strength of his CD also lies in the interest of the coupling. All three works share a common origin in that they were commissioned by the one-armed Austrian pianist, Paul Wittgenstein. Fleisher's account of the Ravel deserves to rank high among current recommendations, and choice will inevevitably depend upon couplings. Both the orchestral support and the Sony recording are very good indeed.

Daphnis et Chloé (ballet; complete).
☞ ⊛ (M) *** BMG/RCA 09026 61846-2 [id.]. New England Conservatory & Alumni Ch., Boston SO, Munch.
⊛ *** Decca Dig. 400 055-2. Montreal SO and Ch., Dutoit.
☞ (M) **(*) Decca 425 049-2 [id.]. Cleveland Ch. & O, Maazel – DEBUSSY: *Jeux.* *(*)
☞ * Ph. 438 281-2 [id.]. Netherlands Chamber Ch., Concg. O, Kondrashin – CASELLA: *Paganiniana.* **(*)

Daphnis et Chloé (complete); *Pavane pour une infante défunte.*
☞ ** Telarc Dig. CD 80352 [id.]. Atlanta Ch. & SO, Yoel Levi.

Daphnis et Chloé (complete); *Pavane pour une infante défunte; Rapsodie espagnole.*
(M) *** Decca 425 956-2 [id.]. ROHCG Ch., LSO, Pierre Monteux.

(i) *Daphnis et Chloé* (complete); *Valses nobles et sentimentales.*
☞ (M) * DG 437 648-2 [id.]. (i) Tanglewood Festival Ch.; Boston SO, Ozawa.

Charles Munch's Boston account is one of the great glories of the 1950s, superior in every way to his later version from the 1960s. The playing in all departments of the Boston orchestra is simply electrifying. The sound here may not be as sumptuous as the Monteux on Decca, but the richness of colour lies in the playing, and there is a heady sense of intoxication that at times sweeps you off your feet. A wonderful, glowing account, recorded before the virtuosity which Munch and his Bostonians commanded had become hard-driven. Spot-on intonation from the choir – the London Symphony Chorus did not hold their pitch so securely for Monteux. In John Pfeiffer's current remastering the sound is more open than in any previous issue. The strings have rather more body than before (this was one of the first RCA stereo recordings, made in Symphony Hall in 1955) and the integration of the chorus is impressively managed. Try the *Danse de supplication de Chloé* (track 15) and the ensuing scene in which the pirates are put to flight, and you will get a good idea of how dazzling this is. Then in Scene iii, beginning with *Daybreak* (track 17), there is an overwhelming sense of ecstasy, and the playing throughought tracks 18–21 is marvellous, with the ballet ending in tumultous orchestral virtuosity.

Dutoit adopts an idiomatic and flexible style, observing the minute indications of tempo change but making every slight variation sound totally spontaneous. The final *Danse générale* finds him adopting a dangerously fast tempo, but the Montreal players – combining French responsiveness with transatlantic polish – rise superbly to the challenge, with the choral punctuations at the end adding to the sense of frenzy. The digital recording is wonderfully luminous, with the chorus ideally balanced at an evocative half-distance.

Monteux conducted the first performance of *Daphnis et Chloé* in 1912; Decca's 1959 recording, a demonstration disc in its day, captured his poetic and subtly shaded reading in the most vivid colours within an agreeably warm ambience. The performance was one of the finest things Monteux did for the gramophone. Decca have added his 1962 recording of the *Pavane*, wonderfully poised and played most beautifully, and the highly spontaneous *Rapsodie espagnole*.

Maazel directs a finely moulded performance of Ravel's most magical score. His tempi in the brilliant numbers are fast, the precision of ensemble phenomenal; but elsewhere he indulges in a far more flexible style than is common with him. The result, helped by brilliant recording within the splendid Cleveland acoustics, is most impressive. *Daybreak*, with the chorus singing vividly, engulfs one just as it should. Unfortunately, the Debussy coupling is less recommendable.

Levi's Atlanta recording shows every evidence of careful preparation. Both playing and recording are refined and there is much that is beautiful in terms of orchestral playing and texture, but the feeling of ecstasy that lies within this score is only hinted at and, although the finale generates plenty of energy, overall the level of tension is too low. The sound is in the demonstration bracket.

Kondrashin's account of the complete *Daphnis* score was recorded at a public concert at the Concertgebouw in the late 1970s and though there are many good things, as one might expect from these splendid forces, there is little of the sense of magic that one encounters in rival versions. There is no lack of vitality, but the score does not captivate as it does in the hands of a Munch or Monteux. A pity that the attractive coupling should be encumbered by what is (in present-day terms) an uncompetitive disc.

Ozawa's account of *Daphnis* offers superior orchestral playing but nothing else. The interpretation is totally without personality or character; it brings Ravel's ecstatic landscape before one's eyes much as would an Ordnance Survey map. Cold and characterless – and the same goes for the *Valses nobles et sentimentales* on which DG lavish splendid recording. Artistically, this gets barely one star, even though as a recording it is eminently satisfying.

(i) *Daphnis et Chloé* (ballet; complete); (ii) *Shéhérazade.*
☞ (M) **(*) Sony SMK 47604 (i) Schola Cant., NYPO; (ii) Horne, Fr. Nat. R. O; Bernstein.

Bernstein's *Daphnis et Chloé* dates from 1964 and by itself is not a three-star recommendation, but it comes with an altogether seductive *Shéhérazade* with Marilyn Horne, one of the most sensuous accounts committed to disc. This is a desert-island version which does full justice to Ravel's sumptuous score; Bernstein is at his very best here and each movement is characterized to perfection. The sound, too, is very good. Horne's *Shéhérazade* weaves the most erotic tales, and while one is under its spell the claims of the incomparable Suzanne Danco and Régine Crespin are almost (though not quite) forgotten. By comparison, Bernstein's 1961 *Daphnis* is less successful; there are good things, of course – most notably the last part, which comprises the second suite, but there are moments of less-than-perfect intonation which diminish its appeal. The sound is a vast improvement on the CBS original – but then it needed to be. In spite of the *Daphnis*, this record is a must.

Daphnis et Chloé: suites 1 & 2; Pavane pour une infante défunte.
☞ ** DG Gold Dig. 439 008-2 [id.]. BPO, Karajan – DEBUSSY: *La Mer* etc. **

As in the case of *La Mer*, this digital Karajan performance does not have the magic and sense of rapture and intoxication that informed his earlier Berlin account of the second *Daphnis* suite – surely one of the greatest performances of this glorious score ever committed to disc (DG 427 250-2, including *Boléro* instead of the *Pavane* – see above). The remastered digital recording sounds very impressive, but is less atmospheric in effect.

Daphnis et Chloé: suite No. 2; Pavane pour une infante défunte.
☞ (***) Testament mono SBT1017 [id.]. Philh. O, Cantelli – CASELLA: *Paganiniana;* DUKAS:
    L'apprenti sorcier; FALLA: *Three-cornered hat.* (***)

Cantelli's account of *Daphnis* was among his last – and finest – records. It sounds remarkably good in this splendid transfer. Along with Koussevitzky, Ormandy and Karajan, this has classic status.

(i) *Introduction and allegro;* (ii) *Tzigane;* (iii) *Don Quichotte à Dulcineé.*
**(*) Chan. Dig. CHAN 8972 [id.]. (i) Masters; (ii) Yan Pascal Tortelier; (iii) Roberts; Ulster O,
    Y. P. Tortelier – DEBUSSY: *Danses sacrée* etc. ***

Whether or not Ravel approved the use of full strings, the *Introduction and allegro* loses something of its ethereal quality when given in this form, though the playing of the harpist Rachel Masters is impeccable. No grumbles at all about Stephen Roberts's fine singing in the *Don Quichotte* songs either.

Ma Mère l'Oye (complete ballet).
*** Ph. Dig. 400 016-2 [id.]. Pittsburgh SO, Previn – SAINT-SAENS: *Carnival of the Animals.* ***
*** Chan. Dig. CHAN 8711; *ABTD 1359* [id.]. Ulster O, Yan Pascal Tortelier – DEBUSSY: *Boîte à joujoux.* ***

Ma Mère l'Oye (complete); *Le tombeau de Couperin; Valses nobles et sentimentales.*
⊛ *** Decca Dig. 410 254-2 [id.]. Montreal SO, Dutoit.

Ma Mère l'Oye (complete); *Pavane pour une infante défunte.*
(BB) *** Virgin/EMI Dig. VJ7 59657-2 [id.]. SCO, Saraste – BIZET: *Symphony.* **(*)

Ma Mère l'Oye (complete); *Rapsodie espagnole.*
(M) *** DG 415 844-2 [id.]. LAPO, Giulini – MUSSORGSKY: *Pictures.* ***

A few bars of this Decca record leave no doubt as to its excellence. This offers demonstration quality, transparent and refined, with the textures beautifully balanced and expertly placed. The performances too are wonderfully refined and sympathetic. *Ma Mère l'Oye* is ravishingly beautiful, its special combination of sensuousness and innocence perfectly caught.

In Previn's version, played and recorded with consummate refinement, the quality of innocence shines out. The recording is superb, with the Philips engineers presenting a texture of luminous clarity.

More than usual, Tortelier's performance has a balletic feel to it, bringing out the affinities with *Daphnis et Chloé.* The exotic orchestration associated with *Laideronnette, Empress of the Pagodas* glitters vividly, yet the lovely closing *Jardin féerique,* opening serenely, moves to a joyous climax.

Saraste directs a most sensitive, beautifully scaled and well-paced reading, and the Scottish players produce lovely sounds in the gentler music. The *Pavane* is serenely spacious and with a very fine horn solo. Generously coupled with the youthful Bizet *Symphony* and given warmly atmospheric recording, this makes an excellent bargain issue.

The Giulini Los Angeles performance conveys much of the sultry atmosphere of the *Rapsodie espagnole.* Indeed some details, such as the sensuous string responses to the cor anglais tune in the *Feria,* have not been so tenderly caressed since the intoxicating Reiner version. The *Ma Mère l'Oye* suite is also sensitively done; though it is cooler, it is still beautiful.

Ma Mère l'Oye (ballet): *suite.*
(B) *** CfP CD-CFP 4086; *TC-CFP 40086.* SNO, Gibson – BIZET: *Jeux d'enfants;* SAINT-SAENS; *Carnival.* ***
(M) ** EMI Dig. CD-EMX 2165; *TC-EMX 2165.* LPO, Sian Edwards – BRITTEN: *Young person's guide* ***; PROKOFIEV: *Peter and the wolf.* **(*)

Ma Mère l'Oye (ballet): *suite; Pavane pour une infante défunte.*
☞ (M) *** Sony SMK 47545 [id.]. NYPO, Bernstein – DEBUSSY: *Images* etc. **(*)

The New York Philharmonic play Ravel's *Ma Mère l'Oye suite* with exquisite gentleness and much atmosphere. One can feel Bernstein's affection for the music in every bar, yet he is never mannered. The *Pavane,* too, is given a tender dignity and the horn solo is restrained and beautiful. The recording of the ballet suite was made in the Manhattan Center in 1965, and the sound is pleasing.

Gibson is highly persuasive, shaping the music with obvious affection and a feeling for both the innocent spirit and the radiant textures of Ravel's beautiful score. The orchestral playing is excellent and, with excellent couplings, this is very recommendable.

Warm and beautiful orchestral playing from the LPO under Sian Edwards, but Ravel's magical score does not yield all its secrets here; its sense of gentle, innocent ecstasy is missing.

Piano trio in A min. (orch. Tortelier).
☞ *(*) Chan. Dig. CHAN 9114 [id.]. Ulster O, Yan Pascal Tortelier – DEBUSSY: *La Mer* etc. *(*)

There is so much good orchestral music in the world still languishing in neglect, and yet musicians are still keen to transcribe chamber works including those as intimate and perfect as the Ravel *Trio.* Yan Pascal Tortelier's conviction, skilfully argued in his sleeve-note, that 'the best medium for its full expression is the symphony orchestra' begs the question that Ravel himself was surely rather good at orchestration and, had he thought otherwise, might have had a shot at it himself! Some of the orchestral effects are idiomatic, but others (particularly the climax in the finale) are more questionable. To most ears something quite essential is lost in the process; the soul as well as the scale of this music lies in the sonorities Ravel chose and, although Tortelier's skill and musicianship are not in question, this transcription is not one to which many will wish to return.

Le tombeau de Couperin; Valses nobles et sentimentales.
*** Chan. Dig. CHAN 8756; *ABTD 1395* [id.]. Ulster O, Yan Pascal Tortelier – DEBUSSY: *Children's corner* etc. ***

Yan Pascal Tortelier's accounts of *Le tombeau de Couperin* and the *Valses nobles* have plenty of appeal. The Ulster Orchestra certainly play very well for Tortelier and the recording is every bit as good as predecessors in this series.

Tzigane (for violin and orchestra).
☞ *** EMI Dig. CDC7 47725-2 [id.]. Perlman, O de Paris, Martinon – CHAUSSON: *Poème;* SAINT-
   SAENS: *Havanaise* etc. ***
*** DG Dig. 423 063-2 [id.]. Perlman, NYPO, Mehta – CHAUSSON: *Poème;* SAINT-SAENS: *Havanaise*
   etc.; SARASATE: *Carmen fantasy.* ***
☞ (M) *(*) Sony SMK 47548 [id.]. Francescatti, NYPO, Bernstein – CHAUSSON: *Poème* **; FAURÉ:
   Ballade *(*); FRANCK: *Symphony.* *(*)

Perlman's classic (1975) account of Ravel's *Tzigane* for EMI is marvellously played; the added
projection of the CD puts the soloist believably at the end of the living-room. The opulence of his
tone is undiminished by the remastering process and the orchestral sound retains its atmosphere,
while gaining in clarity.

Perlman's later, digital version is very fine and the recording is obviously modern. But the earlier
EMI performance has just that bit more charisma.

As in the Chausson coupling, Francescatti and the orchestra are not flattered by the close
microphones and, though he plays brilliantly, his close vibrato will not be to all tastes.

La valse.
☞ (M) ** Ph. Dig. 434 733-2; *434 733-4* [id.]. VPO, Previn – RIMSKY-KORSAKOV: *Scheherazade.*
   **(*)

Previn's performance is well played and recorded, though his rubato is not always absolutely
convincing. The record was made with an audience present.

Valses nobles et sentimentales.
(*) DG Dig. 429 785-2; *429 785-4* [id.]. NYPO, Sinopoli – MUSSORGSKY: *Night* etc. *

With Sinopoli Ravel's *Valses nobles et sentimentales* is perhaps a shade too idiosyncratic, even though
it is played superbly by the New York Philharmonic; in the last three sections he takes Ravel's
markings to an extreme, with the music almost coming to a halt in the middle of the *Moins vif.*

CHAMBER MUSIC

Introduction and allegro for harp, flute, clarinet and string quartet.
⊛ (M) *** Decca 421 154-2. Osian Ellis, Melos Ens. – DEBUSSY; FRANCK: *Sonatas.* *** ⊛

The beauty and subtlety of Ravel's sublime septet are marvellously realized by this 1962 Melos
account. The interpretation has great delicacy of feeling, and the recording hardly shows its age at all.

Piano trio in A min.
*** Ph. Dig. 411 141-2 [id.]. Beaux Arts Trio – CHAUSSON: *Piano trio.* ***
*** Decca Dig. 425 860-2 [id.]. Thibaudet, Bell, Isserlis – CHAUSSON: *Concert.* **(*)
*** Pickwick Dig. MCD 41; *MCC 41* [id.]. Solomon Trio – DEBUSSY; FAURÉ: *Piano trios.* ***
*** Chan. Dig. CHAN 8458; *ABTD 1170* [id.]. Borodin Trio – DEBUSSY: *Violin and Cello sonatas.*
   ***
**(*) Collins Dig. 1040-2 [id.]. Trio Zingara – SHOSTAKOVICH: *Piano trio No. 2.* **(*)

The most recent Beaux Arts account of the Ravel *Trio* is little short of inspired and is even finer than
their earlier record of the late 1960s. The recording, too, is of high quality, even if the piano is rather
forward.

Joshua Bell, Jean-Yves Thibaudet and Steven Isserlis are second to none in sensitivity, and both
Bell and Isserlis play with great tonal finesse and artistry. They are recorded with great clarity and
presence, and those wanting this particular coupling will find much to admire.

The Solomon Trio's account of the Ravel is very fine indeed and has the advantage of an
excellently balanced recording. It is thoroughly recommendable and has fine couplings, too, and a
price advantage.

The Borodin Trio are excellently recorded and their playing has great warmth and is full of
colour. Some may find them too hot-blooded by the side of the Beaux Arts.

A fine account of the *Piano trio* comes from the Trio Zingara. Their pianist, Annette Cole,
produces some beautiful *pianissimo* tone in the first movement, and the playing of all three is
sensitive. Theirs is a thoroughly enjoyable and impressive performance, and it is recorded with great
presence and clarity.

(i) *Piano trio in A min.;* (ii) *Sonatine: Menuet.*

(M) (**) BMG/RCA mono GD 87871; *GK 87871* [7871-2-RG; *7871-4-RG*]. Heifetz; (i) Rubinstein, Piatigorsky; (ii) Bay – DEBUSSY: *Sonata* etc. (**); RESPIGHI: *Sonata* (***); MARTINU: *Duo.* ***

It goes without saying that the million-dollar trio (Heifetz, Rubinstein and Piatigorsky), recorded in 1950, play the Ravel like a million dollars, yet its inspired opening is curiously lacking in magic and atmosphere. Peerless though the playing is, it is the couplings for which this CD is to be welcomed.

Piano trio in A min.; Sonata for violin and cello; (i) *Chansons madécasses; 3 Poèmes de Stéphane Mallarmé.*

☞ **(*) Virgin/EMI Dig. VC5 45016-2 [id.]. (i) Sarah Walker; Nash Ens.

The Virgin anthology offers a very good introduction to the less familiar Ravel, if you exclude the *Piano trio*. The *Sonata for violin and cello* is expertly played by Marcia Crayford and Christopher van Kampen – as good an account as any – and in the *Piano trio* Ian Brown joins them in what is a performance of real stature and eloquence. In the *Chansons madécasses* and the exquisite *Trois poèmes de Stéphane Mallarmé* Sarah Walker is *primus inter pares* rather than a soloist, though she is not balanced as reticently by the Andrew Keener team as their Debussy *Chansons de Bilitis* with Delphine Seyrig. A pity, since this spoils what would otherwise be an outstanding record.

String quartet in F.

☞ *** Denon Dig. CO 75164 [id.]. Carmina Qt – DEBUSSY: *Quartet.* ***

☞ *** DG Dig. 437 836-2 [id.]. Hagen Qt – DEBUSSY; WEBERN: *Quartets.* ***

☞ *** Sony Dig. SK 52554 [id.]. Juilliard Qt – DEBUSSY; DUTILLEUX: *Quartets.* ***

(M) *** Ph. 420 894-2. Italian Qt – DEBUSSY: *Quartet.* ***

(M) *** DG 435 589-2 [id.]. LaSalle Qt – DEBUSSY: *Quartet.* ***

☞ (B) *** CfP Dig. CD-CFP 4652; *TC-CFP 4652* [id.]. Chilingirian Qt – DEBUSSY: *Quartet.* ***

(B) **(*) Hung. White Label HRC 122 [id.]. Bartók Qt – DEBUSSY: *Quartet* **(*); DVORAK: *Quartet No. 12.* ***

☞ (BB) **(*) Discover Dig. DICD 920171 [id.]. Sharon Qt – BEETHOVEN: *Harp quartet* **(*); MOZART: *Quartet No. 1.* ***

(M) **(*) Pickwick Dig. MCD 17; *MCC 17* [id.]. New World Qt – DEBUSSY: *Quartet* **(*); DUTILLEUX: *Ainsi la nuit.* ***

String quartet in F; (i) *Introduction & allegro for harp, flute, clarinet and string quartet.*

(BB) *** Naxos Dig. 8.550249 [id.]. Kodály Qt; (i) with Maros, Gyöngyössy, Kovács – DEBUSSY: *Quartet.* **(*)

The Carmina Quartet give a splendid account of this elusive masterpiece; indeed theirs is among the very best versions to have appeared in the last year or two. The recording is fresh and wide-ranging (perhaps a trace fierce right at the very top) and the playing is of the highest quality. There is plenty of ardour when required, and some moments of impetuousness (the group moves the music along at each reappearance of the theme marked *bien chanté* at fig. A in the Scherzo), but these are small idiosyncrasies in a performance distinguished by good taste and impeccable ensemble. The slow movement has great refinement without being in the least self-conscious. Dynamic contrasts are strong without being excessive, and their playing has what one might call a narrative quality that holds the listener throughout, and the recording is very impressive. The one drawback to this issue is the absence of any additional work besides the usual Debussy coupling.

The equally impressive Hagen Quartet, by adding the Webern, are perhaps even more competitive They give a performance of great finesse and tonal refinement, and are beautifully recorded to boot, very well served by an excellent balance from one of DG's best engineers, Wolfgang Mitelehner. This can be considered alongside the Carmina and Britten versions and may even be preferred to those CDs by some collectors.

The Juilliard are very impressive too, not quite so youthful, elegant and fresh in their approach but eminently polished and sensitive. This Sony disc is to be recommended primarily to those attracted to the fine Dutilleux bonus. However, the earlier (and less expensive) versions remain very competitive.

For many years the Italian Quartet held pride of place in this coupling. Their playing is perfect in ensemble, attack and beauty of tone, and their performance remains highly recommendable, one of the most satisfying chamber-music records in the catalogue.

There is little to choose between the DG LaSalle performance and the Italian Quartet on Philips. If the latter have perhaps the greater immediacy and sense of vitality, the former create a superb feeling of atmosphere and bring great freshness and delicacy of feeling to this score.

The Chilingirian recording has plenty of body and presence, and also has the benefit of a warm acoustic. The players give a thoroughly committed account, with well-judged tempi and very musical phrasing. The Scherzo is vital and spirited, and there is no want of poetry in the slow movement. At mid-price this is fully competitive and the sound is preferable to that of the Italian Quartet on Philips.

The Naxos version can more than hold its own. Artistically and technically this is a satisfying performance which has the feel of real live music-making. The *Introduction and allegro* is not as magical or as atmospheric as that of the Melos Ensemble from the 1960s, nor is it as well balanced (the players, save for the harp, are a bit forward), but it is still thoroughly enjoyable.

The Bartók Quartet on Hungaroton's cheapest label also give a sympathetic and well-characterized reading, and they too are well recorded. Moreover they too offer an additional work. Those collectors looking for a bargain will not be disappointed here.

The Sharon Quartet are completely at home in this music and play with ardour and sensitivity. The resonant acoustic (a Cologne church) suits the work better than the Beethoven coupling. It certainly does not cloud the Scherzo or the energetic account of the finale (which also has much delicacy of feeling) and adds warmth and atmosphere to the *très lent*. Very good playing: if the couplings are suitable, this is a bargain.

The Harvard-based New World Quartet give an admirable account of the Ravel, a shade overprojected at times, and the leader's expressive rubato and that of the violist may not be to all tastes. Well recorded though it is, it does not displace existing recommendations though it offers the inducement of a Dutilleux rarity.

Violin sonata in G.
*** Collins Dig. 1112-2; *1112-4* [id.]. Lorraine McAslan, John Blakely – DEBUSSY; SAINT-SAENS: *Sonatas.* ***
*** Ph. Dig. 426 254-2. Viktoria Mullova, Bruno Canino – PROKOFIEV: *Sonata* **; STRAVINSKY: *Divertimento.* ***
*** DG Dig. 415 683-2 [id.]. Shlomo Mintz, Yefim Bronman – DEBUSSY; FRANCK: *Sonatas.* ***

Lorraine McAslan possesses a strong musical personality as well as excellent technique and a wide command of colour and dynamics. She is splendidly partnered by John Blakely, and their account of the *Sonata* is as characterful as any in the catalogue.

Mullova and Canino also give a beguiling performance. It is played with diamond-like precision and great character. The Philips recording is marvellous. However, the couplings are not as successful as McAslan's.

Shlomo Mintz and Yefim Bronman's account offers highly polished playing, even if it is not so completely inside Ravel's world in the slow movement. The glorious sounds both artists produce are a source of unfailing delight. They are beautifully recorded too.

PIANO MUSIC

Piano duet

Boléro; Introduction and allegro; Ma Mère l'Oye; Rapsodie espagnole; La valse.
*** Chan. Dig. CHAN 8905; *ABTD 1514* [id.]. Louis Lortie and Hélène Mercier.

Lortie's recital for piano (four hands and two pianos) with his Canadian partner, Hélène Mercier, is quite magical; these artists command an exceptionally wide range of colour and dynamic nuance. The acoustic is that of The Maltings, Snape, and the result is quite outstanding sonically: you feel that you have only to stretch out and you can touch the instruments. Ravel's transcriptions are stunningly effective in their hands, even, surprisingly, *Boléro*.

Entre cloches; Frontispiece (for 5 hands); Introduction and allegro; Rapsodie espagnol; Shéhérazade; La valse.
☞ ⊛ *** Gamut Dig. GAMCD 517 [id.]. Stephen Coombs, Christopher Scott.

Stephen Coombs and Christopher Scott are a young English duo partnership who have attracted much praise. This Ravel recital, which we were unable to squeeze into our last edition, is quite outstanding in every way – and is every bit as good as the Louis Lortie–Hélène Mercier (Chandos) in terms of imaginative vitality, sensibility and wit. The recording, too, is beautifully clear and atmospheric. We gave the Chandos a Rosette, but this is equally Rosette-worthy, so perhaps the one, having had that distinction for a couple of years, might now hand it on to this newcomer! Both records give much delight.

Ma Mère L'Oye.

*** Ph. Dig. 420 159-2 [id.]. Katia and Marielle Labèque – FAURE: *Dolly;* BIZET: *Jeux d'enfants.* ***

The Labèque sisters give an altogether delightful performance of Ravel's magical score, which he later orchestrated and expanded. The recording could not be more realistic and present.

Solo piano music

A la manière de Borodine; A la manière de Chabrier; Gaspard de la nuit; Jeux d'eau; Menuet antique; Menuet sur le nom de Haydn; Miroirs; Pavane pour une infante défunte; Prélude; Sérénade grotesque; Sonatine; Le tombeau de Couperin; Valses nobles et sentimentales.

☞ *** Decca Dig. 433 515-2 (2) [id.]. Jean-Yves Thibaudet.

*** CRD Dig. CRD 3383/4; *CRDC 4083/5* [id.]. Paul Crossley.

Jean-Yves Thibaudet's collected Ravel has won such golden opinions everywhere that one approaches it, like a much-hyped film, with a certain caution. Yet no one is likely to be disappointed, for this is quite outstanding playing on all counts; Thibaudet exhibits flawless technique, perfect control, refinement of touch and exemplary taste. He distils just the right atmosphere in *Oiseaux tristes* and *Une barque sur l'océan* – but then, one might as well choose any other piece from *Miroirs*, and his *Gaspard* can hold its own with any in the catalogue. This is playing of finesse and distinction, and the recording is of real distinction too.

Paul Crossley's accounts of all these works are beautifully fashioned. He is aristocratic, with an admirable feeling for tone-colour and line, and rarely mannered (the end of *Jeux d'eau* is an exception). His version of *Le tombeau de Couperin* has a classical refinement and delicacy that are refreshing. The CRD recording is very good indeed, and this fine set deserves the warmest welcome.

A la manière de Borodine; A la manière de Chabrier; Menuet antique; Menuet sur le nom de Haydn; Miroirs; Pavane pour une infante défunte; Prélude; Sérénade grotesque; Sonatine.

☞ *** ASV Dig. CDDCA 809 [id.]. Gordon Fergus-Thompson.

Gaspard de la nuit; Jeux d'eau; Le tombeau de Couperin; Valses nobles at sentimentales.

☞ *** ASV Dig. CDDCA 805 [id.]. Gordon Fergus-Thompson.

Turning to Gordon Fergus-Thompson's Ravel immediately after Thibaudet is to enter a different imaginative world. There is not quite the same concentration that distinguishes Thibaudet's set, nor quite the same keyboard control. Indeed he does not hold the listener in the same grip as the French pianist. However, this is still distinguished playing: there is an ample and rich colour-palette, and his presentation exhibits considerable personality and imagination, which is probably why it has attracted some adverse criticism. Not to be preferred to the Decca set, though readers considering it can be assured that he is very well recorded.

A la manière de Borodine; A la manière de Chabrier; Gaspard de la nuit; Jeux d'eau; Menuet antique; Menuet sur le nom d'Haydn; Miroirs; Pavane pour une infante défunte; Prélude; Sonatine; Le tombeau de Couperin; Valses nobles et sentimentales; (i) Ma mère l'Oye.

☞ (B) ** Double Decca 440 836-2 (2). Pascal Rogé, (i) with Denise Françoise.

Pascal Rogé made these recordings in 1973/4 at the beginning of his Decca contract. He is well recorded (though the effect is a little cool) and his playing is sensitive. His performances of the *Sonatine, Le tombeau* and the *Valses nobles et sentimentales* were widely praised on their first appearance, but we have heard more imaginative accounts of *Le tombeau*: the *Forlane* is not keenly delineated and characterized. He produces some finely coloured tone in *Miroirs*, but overall it is a shade pallid and under-characterized, and he does not match either Ashkenazy or Argerich – and certainly not Pogorlich in *Gaspard de la nuit* in terms of authority or panache. Yet there is much that is good here, and the set certainly indicated his natural gifts in this repertoire, which were to be realized more fully in later records.

A la manière de Borodine; A la manière de Chabrier; Gaspard de la nuit; Jeux d'eau; Menuet sur le nom de Haydn; Prélude; Sérénade grotesque; Sonatine; Valses nobles et sentimentales.

☞ **(*) Virgin/EMI Dig. VC7 59322-2 [id.]. Anne Queffélec.

Pavane pour une infante défunte; Menuet antique; Miroirs; Le tombeau de Couperin.

☞ **(*) Virgin/EMI Dig. VC7 59323-2 [id.]. Anne Queffélec.

No quarrels with Anne Queffélec's playing, which is alert, intelligent and vital, as one would expect from so excellent a stylist. There are some masterly and enjoyable interpretations here, but it is all far too closely observed, as if one were in the front row in the concert hall; as a result, not all the atmosphere registers to full effect once the dynamics rise above *mf*.

A la manière de Borodine; A la manière de Chabrier; Gaspard de la nuit; Menuet antique; Menuet sur le nom de Haydn; Miroirs; Prélude; Sonatine.
*** Chan. Dig. CHAN 8647; *ABTD 1333* [id.]. Louis Lortie.

The Canadian pianist, Louis Lortie, gives an impressive account of himself in *Gaspard de la nuit*. His account of *Le gibet* is chilling and atmospheric, and in the *Miroirs* he produces some ravishing pianism. His rhythmic articulation in the *Alborada* is marvellously clean, and throughout the whole set his playing is elegant, virile and sensitive. The recording is made in The Maltings, Snape. This is a distinguished and stimulating recital.

A la manière de Borodine; A la manière de Chabrier; Menuet antique; Prélude; Le tombeau de Couperin; Valses nobles et sentimentales.
**(*) Nimbus NI 5011 [id.]. Vlado Perlemuter.

Gaspard de la nuit; Jeux d'eau; Miroirs; Pavane.
**(*) Nimbus NI 5005 [id.]. Vlado Perlemuter.

Though Perlemuter's technical command is not as complete as it had been, he gives delightful, deeply sympathetic readings; the sense of spontaneity is a joy. There may be Ravel recordings which bring more dazzling virtuoso displays, but none more persuasive. Nimbus's ample room acoustic makes the result naturally atmospheric on CD.

Alborada del gracioso; Pavane pour une infante défunte; Valses nobles et sentimentales.
☞ ** Collins Dig. 14042 [id.]. Joanna MacGregor – BARTOK: *6 Dances* etc.; DEBUSSY: *Etudes*. **

Joanna MacGregor gives us three Ravel pieces to which she brings great tonal refinement. Her *Valses nobles* are horribly pulled about and cannot be recommended.

Gaspard de la nuit.
*** DG Dig. 413 363-2 [id.]. Pogorelich – PROKOFIEV: *Sonata No. 6.* *** ⊛

Pogorelich's *Gaspard* is out of the ordinary. In *Le gibet*, we are made conscious of the pianist's refinement of tone and colour first, and Ravel's poetic vision afterwards. But for all that, this is piano playing of astonishing quality. The control of colour and nuance in *Scarbo* is dazzling and its eruptive cascades of energy and dramatic fire have one sitting on the edge of one's seat.

Gaspard de la nuit; Pavane pour une infante défunte.
☞ ** DG Dig. 437 532-2 [id.]. Andrei Gavrilov – PROKOFIEV: *Romeo and Juliet suite* etc. **

There is no need to dwell at length on this issue. Andrei Gavrilov is revisiting this repertoire, but not quite as successfully as he did on the EMI label. There is an abundant pianistic finesse but, generally speaking, rather less atmosphere and poetry than first time around. Admittedly the comparison is between two performances of high quality, but the DG recording, though clearer, is not as pleasing as the EMI.

Gaspard de la nuit; Pavane pour une infante défunte; Valses nobles et sentimentales.
☞ (M) *** Decca Dig. 425 081-2 [id.]. Vladimir Ashkenazy (with DEBUSSY: *L'isle joyeuse* ***) –
   SCRIABIN: *Danses* etc. ***

Ashkenazy's earlier (1965) analogue version of *Gaspard* in its day was a yardstick by which others were judged. His new, digital account is hardly less impressive than the old and is in no way narcissistic. It remains a distinguished alternative to Pogorelich. His *Valses nobles* are splendidly refined and aristocratic. The recording has excellent range and is extremely vivid and open. Debussy's *L'isle joyeuse* was recorded at the time of the analogue *Gaspard* and is also a fine performance.

VOCAL MUSIC

(i) *Chansons madécasses;* (ii) *Don Quichotte à Dulcinée; 5 Mélodies populaires grecques;* (iii) *3 Poèmes de Stéphane Mallarmé;* (iv) *Shéhérazade.*
*** Sony Dig. MK 39023 [id.]. (i) Norman, Ens. InterContemporain; (ii) José van Dam; (iii) Jill
   Gomez; (iv) Heather Harper; BBC SO, Boulez.

Boulez's collection of Ravel's songs with orchestra (including arrangements) makes a delightful disc. The *Don Quichotte* and the *Greek popular songs* are rarely heard in this orchestral form. Van Dam may not be ideally relaxed, but the dark, firm voice is very impressive. Excellent sound, with translations provided.

Shéhérazade (song-cycle).
*** Decca 417 813-2 [id.]. Régine Crespin, SRO, Ansermet (with *Recital of French songs* ***).

Crespin is right inside these songs and Ravel's magically sensuous music emerges with striking spontaneity. She is superbly supported by Ansermet who, aided by the Decca engineers, weaves a fine tonal web round the voice. Her style has distinct echoes of the opera house; but the richness of the singer's tone does not detract from the delicate languor of *The enchanted flute*, in which the slave-girl listens to the distant sound of her lover's flute playing while her master sleeps.

OPERA

L'Enfant et les sortilèges (complete).
*** DG 423 718-2 [id.]. Ogéas, Collard, Berbié, Gilma, RTF Ch. & Boys' Ch., RTF Nat. O, Maazel.

L'Heure espagnole (complete).
*** DG 423 719-2 [id.]. Berbié, Sénéchal, Giraudeau, Bacquier, Van Dam, Paris Op. O, Maazel.

(i) *L'enfant et les sortilèges;* (ii) *L'heure espagnole* (complete).
☞ (M) **(*) Decca stereo/mono 433 400-2 (2) [id.]. (i) Wend, with Montmollin, Touraine, Migliette, Danco, Bise, Cuénod, Mollet, Lovano, Motet de Genève; (ii) Danco, Derenne, Hamel, Rehfuss, Vessières; (i; ii) SRO, Ansermet – DEBUSSY: *Le Martyre de Saint-Sébastien.* **(*)

Maazel's recordings of the two Ravel one-Act operas were made in the early 1960s and, though the solo voices in the former are balanced too close, the sound is vivid and the performances are splendidly stylish. Neo-classical crispness of articulation goes with refined textures that convey the tender poetry of the one piece, the ripe humour of the other. The CD remastering has been very successful and both performances are given striking presence, without loss of essential atmosphere. Full librettos are included. However, these records are surely now due for mid-price reissue.

Ansermet's vintage recordings, dating from the early 1950s, are among the most winning he ever made, with casts that add to the feeling of totally idiomatic performances. Ansermet is an objective interpreter of impressionist music, yet here there is no lack of either tenderness or incisiveness, with the charm of the pieces never underplayed. *L'enfant*, recorded in October 1954, brings an astonishingly vivid example of early stereo, with voices sharply focused, even if occasionally balances are odd – as with the most characterful soloist, Hugues Cuénod, whose voice is backwardly placed. The fresh, bright singing of Flore Wend as the Child contrasts strongly with some later interpreters. Recorded a year earlier, *L'heure espagnole* comes in mono sound that is not only less atmospheric but rather duller, with too little bloom on the voices. Yet Suzanne Danco is enchanting as the provocative wife who opts for the virile muleteer over her other inadequate suitors, with a slight flicker in the voice adding to its distinctively French timbre. Heinz Rehfuss sings with incisive clarity as the muleteer and, as in *L'enfant*, Hugues Cuénod gives a vivid character-study, this time as the old clockmaker-husband. Ansermet's recording of 50 minutes of Debussy's incidental music for *Le martyre de Saint-Sébastien* is a generous make-weight. The main omissions are the mélodrames with spoken narration. Like *L'enfant*, it is in early stereo, though the sound is duller.

Rawsthorne, Alan (1905–71)

Clarinet concerto.
*** Hyp. CDA 66031 [id.]. Thea King, NW CO of Seattle, Alun Francis – COOKE: *Concerto;* JACOB: *Mini-concerto.* ***

Though the *Clarinet concerto* is an early work of Rawsthorne's it already establishes the authentic flavour of his writing with a certain gritty and angular quality masking the obvious depth of feeling behind. That constraint makes for musical strength, the more obviously so in a performance as persuasive as this from soloist and orchestra alike. Excellent 1982 analogue recording, expertly transferred.

Piano concertos Nos. 1–2; (i) *Double piano concerto.*
☞ *** Chan. Dig. CHAN 9125 [id.]. Tozer, (i) with Cislowski; LPO, Bamert.

We badly need a new version of the *Symphonic studies*, surely Rawsthorne's masterpiece, and the *First Symphony* (or a reissue of the exemplary, 1977 performances by Sir John Pritchard and the LPO on Lyrita). Rawsthorne is a lively and intelligent as well as a highly individual composer. The *First Piano concerto* was a wartime work – vintage Rawsthorne, with its witty *Chaconne* – and the

Second (1951) was composed for the Festival of Britain and is also rewarding, though the finale with its cheap opening idea is a bit of a let-down. The *Concerto for two pianos* was written for John Ogdon and Brenda Lucas and is likewise stimulating. Tozer gives a good account of the concertos, not perhaps as compelling or understanding as the (now deleted) Malcolm Binns version on Lyrita or Moura Lympany's pioneering disc. The opening of No. 1 is a bit rushed; Tamara-Anna Cislowski is an excellent partner in the 1968 concerto. Matthias Bamert and the LPO are very supportive and the recording is in the best traditions of the house.

Madame Chrysanthème (ballet suite); *Street corner overture.*
☞ (M) *** EMI CDM7 64718-2 [id.]. Pro Arte O, composer – ADDISON: *Carte blanche;* ARNELL: *Great Detective;* BLISS: *Checkmate;* ARNOLD: *Grand grand overture.* (***)

The energetically pithy *Street corner overture* is deservedly one of Rawsthorne's more familiar short pieces: succinct, melodic, rumbustious. *Madame Chrysanthème* was composed for the Sadler's Wells ballet and takes place in nineteenth-century Nagasaki. The music is sharply characterized; the *Hornpipe* owes something to Lord Berners, but it is only the final, rather touching *Les Mousmès* that brings a hint of orientalism. The composer's direction is vivid, and musically these are among the most interesting pieces in this anthology of British music, very well played and brightly recorded in 1960.

Overture: Street corner.
(M) (***) EMI mono CDH7 63911-2 [id.]. Philh. O, Lambert – LAMBERT: *Horoscope* etc.; GORDON: *Rake's progress.* (***)

Street corner, following very much the mood of Walton's comedy overtures, is among Rawsthorne's most colourful and appealing works. It makes a welcome fill-up to the Lambert pieces in this première recording, made in 1946 and sounding astonishingly vivid.

Rebelo, João Lourenço (1610–61)

Lamentations for Maundy Thursday; Vesper Psalms.
☞ *** Sony Dig. SK 53115 [id.]. Huelgas Ens., Paul van Nevel.

One of the joys of the expanding CD catalogue is the discovery of composers previously unknown to the wider musical public; the present issue is one such release. João Lourenço Rebelo was court composer to John (João) IV of Portugal, and indeed fostered the King's interest in music and his gifts as a composer. (Unusually for this or any other period, the King dedicated his treatise, *Defensa de la Música Moderna contra la errada opinión del Obispo Cyrilo Franco*, to his friend and *Mestrado da Capela*.) The *música moderna* in question was Rebelo's, whose leaning was towards the polychoral Venetian style of Giovanni Gabrieli rather than the polyphony of Palestrina. Rebelo was one of the first to compose specific parts for instruments in his polyphonic works. The *Vesper Psalms* and the *Lamentations* recorded here are of striking expressive power and are both played and recorded marvellously with vivid realism. Those who admire Gabrieli and Schütz will find this a congenial yet distinctive voice.

Reger, Max (1873–1916)

Ballet suite; Variations on a theme of Hiller, Op. 100.
*** Orfeo C 090841 [id.]. Bav. RSO, C. Davis.

The *Hiller variations* (1907) is one of Reger's greatest works, full of wit, resource and, above all, delicacy. It culminates, as do so many Reger pieces, in a double fugue. The *Ballet suite* is a delightful piece, scored with great clarity and played, as is the *Hiller variations*, with charm and commitment. Sir Colin Davis emerges as a thoroughly *echt*-Reger conductor and the Bavarian orchestra is in excellent form.

(i) *Concerto in olden style, Op. 123;* (ii) *Sinfonietta, Op. 90.*
☞ **(*) Koch Dig. 31354-2 [id.]. (i) Harald Orlovsky; (i; ii) Peter Rosenberg; Bamberg SO, Horst Stein.

The *Concerto in olden style,* Reger's tribute to the great Baroque masters, dates from 1912 and was inspired by his work on Handel's Op. 3 *Concerti grossi,* though his Op. 123 is scored for somewhat larger forces! Earlier, Reger had spoken of his plans for a serenade for orchestra, but by 1905 this had turned into the *Sinfonietta in A major*, an ambitious work which lasts just over 50 minutes. It is generous in feeling, full of luxuriant invention, and is richly and at times thickly scored; at others, it is a model of delicacy. The Scherzo, which takes the best part of a quarter of an hour, overstays its welcome, but the *Largo* which follows, is absolutely inspired. Horst Stein gets very good playing from the Bamberg orchestra and the recording is very warm and sonorous, perhaps not transparent enough at the top end of the spectrum.

Piano concerto in F min., Op. 114.
(M) ** Sony MPK 46452 [id.]. Rudolf Serkin, Phd. O, Ormandy - PROKOFIEV: *Piano concerto No. 4.* (***)

Reger's *Piano concerto* is a remarkable and powerful composition. No one but Reger could have conceived the rugged, Brahmsian piano writing. The slow movement is a contemplative, rapt piece that touches genuine depths. Serkin gives a magisterial performance and is well supported by the Philadelphia Orchestra under Ormandy, even though the early-1960s sound is not very inviting.

Lyrisches Andante.
*** Claves Dig. D 8502 [id.]. Deutsche Kammerakademie Neuss, Goritzki – SCHOECK: *Cello concerto.* ***

Reger's *Lyrisches Andante* is a short, songful and gentle piece for strings; it should make many friends for this much misunderstood composer, particularly in this dedicated performance.

(i) *Symphonic prologue to a tragedy, Op. 108;* (ii) *2 Romances for violin and orchestra, Op. 50.*
**(*) Schwann CD311 076. (i) Berlin RSO, Albrecht; (ii) with Maile; cond. Lajovic.

The tragedy in question is Sophocles' *Oedipus Rex*, and Reger's *Symphonic prologue* is one of his very finest and most powerful works. Inspiration runs consistently high. The violin *Romances* are beautiful pieces and are very well played by Hans Maile and the Berlin Radio Orchestra. Strongly recommended, it must be said that the 1982 recording is serviceable rather than distinguished.

4 Tone poems after Böcklin, Op. 128; Variations on a theme by Hiller, Op. 100.
*** Chan. Dig. CHAN 8794; ABTD 1426 [id.]. Concg. O, Järvi.

Those who still think of Reger's music as densely contrapuntal and turgidly scored will be amazed by the delicacy and refinement of his orchestration. Of the four *Tone poems*, textures in *Der geigende Eremit* ('Hermit playing the violin') are wonderfully transparent, and *Im spiel der Wellen* has something of the sparkle of the *Jeu de vagues* movement of *La Mer* photographed in sepia; while the *Isle of the dead* is a lovely and often very touching piece. The *Hiller variations* are gloriously inventive. These works are beautifully recorded and Neeme Järvi's performances have the combination of sensitivity and virtuosity that this composer needs.

Variations and fugue on a theme by Mozart, Op. 132.
⊛ *** Ph. Dig. 422 347-2 [id.]. Bav. RSO, C. Davis – HINDEMITH: *Symphonic metamorphosis.* ***
☞ ** Teldec/Warner Dig. 9031 74007-2 [id.]. NYPO, Masur – BRAHMS: *Variations on a theme of Haydn;* IVES: *Variations on America.* **

Sir Colin Davis's account of Reger's *Variations and fugue on a theme by Mozart* has great subtlety and the strings produce a particularly cultured sound. The whole performance has a radiance and glow that does full justice to this masterpiece, which is not only scored with great delicacy but has wit and tenderness in equal measure. The Philips recording is state of the art. Recommended with enthusiasm.

Masur gives a sensible and persuasive account of the Mozart variations, and it is good to hear the New York Philharmonic producing a more refined and cultured sound than they have for some time. All the same, this does not offer a serious challenge to Sir Colin Davis's account with the Bayerisches Rundfunk Orchestra on Philips, which is altogether lighter in touch and rather better recorded.

ORGAN WORKS

Aus tiefer Not schrei ich zu dir, Op. 67/3; Intermezzo in F min., Op. 129/7; Introduction and Passacaglia in D min., Op. posth.; Prelude in D min., Op. 65/7.
☞ *** Chan. Dig. CHAN 9097 [id.]. Piet Kee – HINDEMITH: *Organ sonatas.* ***

Although he is a key figure in late-nineteenth- and early-twentieth-century organ music, Reger occupies a lower profile than he should in the catalogues. He was enormously prolific and there are times when inspiration is put on auto-pilot and his prodigious musical technique takes over. The four pieces Piet Kee offers on this CD are well chosen, well wrought and inventive. The Müller organ of

St Bavo in Haarlem seems ideally suited to this repertoire, as is the slightly reverberant acoustic which rather softens the textures and contours of the Hindemith. Piet Kee plays with his customary authority and distinction. A rewarding and satisfying issue.

Chorale fantasia on Straf' mich nicht in deinem Zorn, Op. 40/2; Chorale preludes, Op. 67/4, 13, 28, 40, 48; Introduction, passacaglia and fugue in E min., Op. 127.
*** Hyp. Dig. CDA 66223 [id.]. Graham Barber (Klais organ of Limburg Cathedral).

The *Introduction, passacaglia and fugue* is bold in conception and vision and is played superbly on this excellently engineered Hyperion disc by Graham Barber. The five *Chorale preludes* give him an admirable opportunity to show the variety and richness of tone-colours of this instrument.

PIANO MUSIC

Variations and fugue on a theme of Bach, Op. 81.
(BB) **(*) Naxos Dig. 8.550469 [id.]. Wolf Harden – SCHUMANN: *Humoreske.* **(*)

Wolf Harden's account of the Reger *Variations and fugue on a theme of Bach*, Op. 81, is very fine. Unfortunately there is far less air or sense of space round the piano here and the instrument sounds much drier than in the Schumann coupling. Yet such is the compelling quality of his playing that it would be curmudgeonly to withhold a recommendation on this count.

VOCAL MUSIC

8 Geistliche Gesänge, Op. 138.
*** Koch Bayer Dig. BR 100084. Frankfurt Vocal Ens., Ralf Otto – MARTIN: *Mass for double choir.* ***

These eight spiritual songs are simple homophonic settings of various sacred texts; all of them have a gravely expressive beauty that is conveyed well by this excellent Frankfurt choir. Excellent recording.

Reich, Steve (born 1936)

8 Lines.
☞ (M) *** Virgin/EMI Dig. CUV5 61121-2 [id.]. LCO, Warren-Green – ADAMS: *Shaker loops* ***
⊛; GLASS: *Company* etc. ***; HEATH: *Frontier.* ***

Steve Reich's *8 Lines* is minimalism in its most basic form, and, although the writing is full of good-humoured vitality, the listener without a score could be forgiven for sometimes thinking that the music was on an endless loop. The performance is expert.

(i) *Six Pianos;* (ii) *Music for mallet instruments;* (iii) *Variations for winds, strings and keyboards.*
☞ (B) *** DG Analogue/Dig. 439 431-2 [id.]. (i–ii) Chambers, Preiss, Hartenberger, Becker, Velez, composer; (ii) Ferchen, Harms, Jarrett, LaBarbara, Clayton; (iii) San Francisco SO, De Waart.

This collection – which might be entitled 'Stuck in a groove' – admirably charts the progress of Reich's minimalism. Both the first two pieces exploit the composer's technique of endlessly repeating a very brief fragment which gradually becomes transformed, almost imperceptibly, by different emphases being given to it. The result is mesmeric, though of limited expressive value. No doubt the drug culture provides parallels. *Six Pianos* (1973) is the longer piece (no less than 24 minutes) and, by its very texture, the more aggressive. With gentler, mellifluous marimbas the second piece is balmier and less wearing. Finally the *Variations*, written for the San Francisco orchestra in 1980, mark a new departure, using a large orchestra rather than one on a chamber scale. The repetitions and ostinatos, which gradually get out of phase, are used most skilfully to produce a hypnotic kind of poetry, soothing rather than compelling. The recording throughout is of high quality and the San Francisco (digital) sound is easy to wallow in. Here is an inexpensive way to sample the output of one of the leading minimalists – though, frankly, this is music that some listeners will not be able to take seriously.

Tehillim.
** ECM 827 411-2 [id.]. Steve Reich & musicians, George Manahan.

Steve Reich is listed among the percussion players in *Tehillim*, with Manahan conducting. The central focus, in this Hebrew setting of Psalms 19 and 18 (in that order), is on the vocal ensemble of four voices, a high soprano, two lyric sopranos and an alto. The minimalist technique is the same as in the purely instrumental works, but the result – with clapping and drumming punctuating the singing –

has an element of charm rare in minimalist music. With jazzy syncopations and Cuban rhythms, the first of the two movements sounds like Bernstein's *Chichester Psalms* caught in a groove. The second starts slowly but speeds up for the verses of praise to the Lord and the final *Hallelujahs*. Clear, forward, analogue recording.

Variations for winds, strings & keyboard.
*** Ph. 412 214-2 [id.]. San Francisco SO, De Waart – ADAMS: *Shaker loops.* ***

Reich's *Variations* uses a large orchestral rather than a small chamber scale. The repetitions and ostinatos, which gradually get out of phase, are again most skilfully used to produce a hypnotic kind of poetry, soothing rather than compelling.

Reicha, Antonín (1770–1836)

Oboe quintet in F, Op. 107.
*** Hyp. CDA 66143 [id.]. Sarah Francis, Allegri Qt – CRUSELL: *Divertimento;* R. KREUTZER:
Grand quintet. ***

Antonín Reicha's *F major Quintet* is spectacularly unmemorable but always amiable. The present performance is of high quality and very well recorded.

Wind quintets: in E flat, Op. 88/2; in F, Op. 91/3.
*** Hyp. Dig. CDA 66268 [id.]. Academia Wind Quintet of Prague.

Czech wind playing in Czech wind music has a deservedly high entertainment rating and the present performances are no exception. The music itself has great charm and geniality; it is ingenuous yet cultivated, with some delightful, smiling writing for the bassoon. The players are clearly enjoying themselves, yet they play and blend expertly. The sound too is admirable.

Reindl, Constantin (1738–99)

Sinfonia concertante in D for violin, two flutes, two oboes, bassoon, two horns and strings.
*** Novalis Dig. 150 031-2 [id.]. ECO, Griffiths – STALDER: *Symphony No. 5; Flute concerto.* ***

The *Sinfonia concertante* is fresh and inventive, and the finale has a most attractive (and obstinately memorable) main theme. A delightful performance by the ECO under Howard Griffiths and an excellent, natural and well-balanced recording.

Respighi, Ottorino (1879–1936)

(i) *Adagio con variazioni* (for cello and orchestra); *The Birds; 3 Botticelli pictures;* (ii) *Il tramonto.*
*** Chan. Dig. CHAN 8913; *ABTD 1517* [id.]. (i) Wallfisch; (ii) Linda Finnie; Bournemouth Sinf.,
Vásáry.

Respighi's *Adagio* is pleasant, but not distinctive, though Raphael Wallfisch is very persuasive. *The Birds* is an enchanting aviary of orchestral colour and the lovely playing and luminous recording give much pleasure. Dorati's Mercury version is not entirely upstaged, but the softer focus of the Chandos digital sound brings added warmth and atmosphere. The lambent Italianite evocation of the *Three Botticelli pictures* is also aurally bewitching. But what caps the success of this Chandos Respighi anthology is Linda Finnie's ravishing account of *Il tramonto*, even finer than Carol Madalin's on Hyperion – see below. Her vocal timbre is fresh yet has an element of gentle voluptuousness just right for this ecstatic setting of Shelley. Again very responsive orchestral playing and the recording is in the demonstration class throughout this CD.

Ancient airs and dances: suites Nos. 1–3; The Birds (suite).
☯ *** Van./Omega Dig. 08.1007.71. Australian CO, Gee.

Ancient airs and dances: suites 1–3; 3 Botticelli pictures (Trittico Botticelliano).
*** Telarc Dig. CD 80309 [id.]. Lausanne CO, Jesús López-Cobos.

Christopher Gee's performance of *The Birds* is a complete delight, opening and closing vigorously, yet providing the most refined portraits of the dove, nightingale and cuckoo, with particularly lovely oboe playing in *The dove*. The opening of the *First suite* of *Ancient airs and dances* has a comparable grace and delicacy of feeling; throughout, Lyndon Gee's response to Respighi's imaginative orchestration is wonderfully fresh. The strings produce lovely translucent textures at the beginning of the *Third suite*; yet when a robust approach is called for, the players provide it admirably. The recording, made at the ABC Studio at Chatsworth, Sydney, is in the demonstration class.

Opening brightly and comparatively robustly, the Lausanne performance yet has both warmth and finesse. The rhythmic pulse is lively without being heavy, and there is much engaging woodwind detail; at the graceful beginning of the *Third suite* textures are agreeably light and transparent. The Telarc recording is first rate and even more impressive in the *Botticelli pictures*, with *La primavera* burgeoning with the extravagantly exotic spring blossoming, and *The birth of Venus* rapt in its radiantly expansive ecstasy. The wind playing really is outstanding in this triptych, and the warm ambience of the Musica Theatre of La Chaux-de-Fonds gives the sound a lovely bloom.

Ancient airs and dances: suite No. 3; The Fountains of Rome; The Pines of Rome.
*** DG 413 822-2 [id.]. BPO, Karajan.

Karajan's highly polished, totally committed performances of the two most popular Roman pieces are well supplemented by the *Third suite* of *Ancient airs and dances*, brilliantly played and just as beautifully transferred, more impressive in sound than many more recent Karajan recordings. In the symphonic poems Karajan is in his element, and the playing of the Berlin Philharmonic is wonderfully refined.

Le astuzie di Colombina; La pentola magica; Sèvres de la vieille France.
*** Marco Polo Dig. 8.223346 [id.]. Slovak RSO (Bratislava), Adriano.

Sèvres de la vieille France is based on seventeenth- and eighteenth-century airs, scored with great elegance and charm; *La pentola magica* makes use of Russian models. *Le astuzie di Colombina*, described as a 'Scherzo Veneziano', uses popular Venetian melodies among other things. The scores are not the equal of *Belkis* but do contain some winning and delightful numbers. Not top-drawer by any manner of means but second-class Respighi is better than many other composers at their best. Decent performances and good recording.

Ballata delle Gnomidi; (i) *Concerto gregoriano; Poema autunnale.*
☞ *** Chan. Dig. CHAN 9232 [id.]. (i) Lydia Mordkovitch; BBC PO, Downes.

The *Concerto gregoriano* (1922) is not a display piece in the conventional sense of the word, more a meditative, lyrical outpouring making free use of Gregorian modes. Respighi thought of the soloist as the cantor and the orchestra as the congregation, so there is little of the dramatic tension between them that is an essential ingredient in concerto writing. The work meant a great deal to Respighi, and its failure to gain more than a foothold in the repertory disappointed him. Lydia Mordkovitch is a committed advocate and has the measure of its restrained, expressive eloquence. Apart from some moments of brilliant display, the slightly later *Poema autunnale* for violin and orchestra is also predominantly lyrical and has moments of a Delius-like mysticism. Again Lydia Mordkovitch gives a most affecting account of the piece and is very well supported by Downes and the BBC Philharmonic. The *Ballata delle Gnomidi* (1920) finds Respighi in his most exotic *Roman trilogy* mode: it is a dazzling exercise in colour and orchestration. This issue is one of the high points in the current Chandos survey of the composer.

Belkis, Queen of Sheba: suite. Metamorphoseon modi XII.
*** Chan. Dig. CHAN 8405; *ABTD 1142* [id.]. Philh. O, Simon.

The ballet-suite *Belkis, Queen of Sheba*, is a score that set the pattern for later Hollywood biblical film music; but *Metamorphoseon* is a taut and sympathetic set of variations. It has been ingeniously based on a medieval theme, and though a group of cadenza variations relaxes the tension of argument in the middle, the brilliance and variety of the writing have much in common with Elgar's *Enigma*. Superb playing from the Philharmonia, treated to one of the finest recordings that even Chandos has produced, outstanding in every way.

(i) *The Birds* (suite); *Brazilian impressions;* (ii) *The Fountains of Rome; The Pines of Rome.*
(M) **(*) Mercury 432 007-2 [id.]. (i) LSO; (ii) Minneapolis SO, Antal Dorati.

The Minneapolis Northrop Auditorium – for all the skill of the Mercury engineers – never produced a web of sound with quite the magical glow which Orchestral Hall, Chicago, could provide in the late 1950s. Nevertheless, in Dorati's hands the opening and closing evocations of the *Fountains of Rome* have a unique, shimmering brightness which certainly suggests a sun-drenched landscape, although the turning-on of the Triton fountain brings a shrill burst of sound that almost assaults the ears. The tingling detail in the companion *Pines of Rome* is again matched by Dorati's powerful sense of atmosphere, while the finale has an overwhelming juggernaut forcefulness. The coupling of *The Birds* and *Brazilian impressions* was made in the smoother, warmer acoustics of Watford Town Hall in 1957, and here the vividness of detail particularly suits Dorati's spirited account of *The Birds*, bringing pictorial piquancy of great charm and strongly projected dance-rhythms. *Brazilian impressions* recalls Debussy's *Ibéria*, though it is much less subtle. The finale, *Canzone e danza*, certainly glitters in Dorati's hands even if overall this work does not represent Respighi at his finest.

The Birds (suite); *The Fountains of Rome; The Pines of Rome.*
☞ (BB) *** Belart 450 110-2; *450 110-4* [id.]. LSO, István Kertész.

It is good to have Kertész's vintage (1969) triptych back in the catalogue on Polygram's Belart bargain label. It still sounds pretty spectacular and makes a fine bargain. *The Birds* is very engaging in its spirited elegance; seldom before has the entry of the nightingale's song been so beautifully prepared in the central section of *The Pines of Rome*, where Kertész creates a magical, atmospheric frisson. The iridescent brilliance of the turning-on of the Triton Fountain in the companion-piece is matched by the grandeur of the Trevi processional, when Neptune's chariot is imagined to be seen crossing the heavens. In sharpening detail the remastering loses only a little of the original ambient warmth and depth.

3 Botticelli pictures; (i) *Aretusa;* (ii) *Lauda per la Nativita del Signore;* (i) *Il tramonto.*
⊛ *** Collins Dig. 1349-2 [id.]. (i) Dame Janet Baker; (ii) Patricia Rosario, Louise Winter, Lynton Atkinson, Hickox Singers; City of L. Sinfonia, Hickox.

This collection is crowned by the contributions of Dame Janet Baker. As on the Virgin recording of *La sensitiva*, Dame Janet gives ravishing performances of two more of Respighi's warm and sensitive settings of Shelley poems, written at the same period. *Aretusa* was the first work in which Respighi established his mature style, with lightly surging fountain music that anticipates the *Fountains* and *Pines of Rome. Il tramonto* ('The sunset') evokes a mood remarkably similar to *Beim Schlafengehen* from Strauss's *Four Last Songs* and, with Dame Janet Baker as soloist, is just as beautiful. *Lauda* is a nativity cantata which touchingly presents the story as a simple pastoral sequence, with the tenderly expressive woodwind accompaniment suggesting rustic pipe music. The *Trittico Botticelliana* establishes its seductiveness in the shimmering sounds at the very opening of the first movement, *Primavera*. Refined playing and recording.

Brazilian impressions; Church windows (Vetrate di chiesa).
*** Chan. Dig. CHAN 8317; *ABTD 1098* [id.]. Philh. O, Simon.

Respighi's set of musical illustrations of church windows is not among his finest works but is well worth having when the recording is impressively spacious and colourful. Geoffrey Simon is sympathetic and he secures very fine playing from the Philharmonia. On CD, the wide dynamic range and a striking depth of perspective create the most spectacular effects.

Burlesca; Overture Carnevalesca; Prelude, chorale & fugue; Suite in E; Symphonic variations.
**(*) Marco Polo Dig. 8.223348 [id.]. Slovak RSO (Bratislava), Adriano.

The *Symphonic variations*, an early work, is very well crafted, with a lot of Brahms and Franck – though the scoring already betrays Respighi's future expertise. In the *Suite in E major* the influences are mainly Slavonic; primarily Dvořák and Rimsky-Korsakov, but in the *Burlesca* of 1906 with its whole-tone scale one can discern a whiff of Debussy. The release discovers no masterpieces but does afford a valuable insight into Respighi's creative development. Good performances from Adriano and the Slovak Radio Orchestra and decent recording.

Concerto Gregoriano; Poema autunnale.
**(*) Marco Polo Dig. 8.220152 [id.]. Nishizaki, Singapore SO, Choo Hoey.

The *Concerto Gregoriano* (for violin) is strongly modal in character, though its scoring is fully characteristic and at times lush. The first two movements are linked together and are both slow and ruminative in feeling, while there is a longer and more vigorous finale. Takako Nishizaki and the Singapore orchestra under Choo Hoey give a thoroughly committed account of both this work and the slightly later *Poema autunnale*, though the rather subfusc recording inhibits a totally unqualified welcome.

Piano concerto in A min.; Concerto in modo misolidio (for piano and orchestra).
☞ *** Chan. Dig. CHAN 9285 [id.]. Geoffrey Tozer, BBC PO, Downes.

Although the composer thought highly of the *Concerto in modo misolidio*, neither of Respighi's two piano concertos is likely to enter the repertoire, which makes this first-rate coupling doubly valuable. These are both first recordings. The *A minor Concerto* comes from Respighi's time in Russia and was composed in 1902, when he was still in his twenties. It is derivative (in his note, Jeremy Siepmann calls it 'a veritable festival of eclecticism'), but it is a highly spontaneous piece, the piano writing often very Rachmaninovian, especially its brilliantly chimerical scherzando roulades, but also its ready flow of ardent romantic lyricism. The writing bursts with striking ideas and even produces a grand final statement that recalls Grieg's concerto in the same key. It is splendidly played, and one can sense both soloist and orchestra relishing its effective keyboard writing, colourful orchestration and ready tunefulness.

The *Concerto in modo misolidio* (suggesting the use of the Mixolydian Mode) is a much later piece, dating from 1925, but in spite of the composer's belief in it, it has never made any headway in either the concert hall or the record catalogues. It is much the better of the two pieces, though its inspiration does not consistently match that of his more celebrated works: at 41 minutes it is nearly twice as long as its predecessor and is undoubtedly inflated. But the long first movement is thoughtful as well as flamboyant and certainly offers the soloist plenty of opportunity to be poetic as well as to display his bravura. The slow movement opens with a folk-like chorale on the strings (reminding one of the Vaughan Williams of *Dives and Lazarus*) which later sounds effectively sombre on the brass. The finale is a long passacaglia, introduced rather gruffly by the piano and based on a more elaborate development of the same idea. Respighi can't help being inventive even when he is prolix, and some of the variants (especially a deliciously delicate interlude featuring the solo oboe) are most engaging. Once more the soloist's artistic and technical resources are fully challenged, and in both works here Geoffrey Tozer rises to the occasion. He receives splendid support from Sir Edward Downes and the BBC Philharmonic throughout the disc. With a realistic balance and a full-bodied piano image the Chandos recording is in the demonstration bracket.

(i) *Piano concerto in modo misolidio. 3 Preludes on Gregorian themes.*
** Marco Polo Dig. 8.220176 [id.]. Sonya Hanke, (i) with Sydney SO, Myer Fredman.

Respighi's *Piano concerto in modo misolidio* is a far from ineffective piece, but the present recording falls short of the ideal: the piano is a bit close and the instrument does not sound in absolutely first-class condition. The *Three Preludes on Gregorian themes* for piano were written in 1919 and dedicated to Casella. They were subsequently scored and another movement added to become the more familiar *Vetrate di chiesa*. Good, but not particularly outstanding, playing from the Australian pianist, Sonya Hanke, with the Sydney orchestra.

Feste romane; The Fountains of Rome; The Pines of Rome (symphonic poems).
*** Ph. Dig. 432 133-2; *432 133-4* [id.]. ASMF, Marriner.
(BB) *** Naxos Dig. 8.550539 [id.]. RPO, Bátiz.
☞ (M) *** Decca Dig. 430 729-2 [id.]. Montreal SO, Dutoit.
*** EMI Dig. CDC7 47316-2 [id.]. Phd. O, Muti.
☞ (B) **(*) Sony SBK 48267 [id.]. Phd. O, Ormandy.
(M) (**(*)) BMG/RCA mono GD 60262; *GK 60262* [60262-2-RG; *60262-4-RG*]. NBC SO, Toscanini.

Marriner's set of Respighi's trilogy is the finest modern version by a tiny margin. The ASMF playing is wonderfully alluring, and if the climactic heavenly processional of the Triton fountain could have more weight, it remains pretty impressive, as does the Roman military juggernaut in *The Pines of the Appian Way*. In *Feste romane* Marriner achieves a splendid balance between exultant jubilation (in the Twelfth Night celebrations of Epiphany) and wildness, with the popular clamour made riotous without over-the-top vulgarity. The ASMF playing is polished, warm and intense, and the Philips recording is in the demonstration bracket.

But then so is the Naxos recording, engineered by Brian Culverhouse in St Barnabas, Mitcham. The climax of *The Fountain of Trevi at mid-day*, when Neptune parades across the heavens, is enormously spectacular, and here a computer organ was used to provide the underlying sustained pedal (the church organ was out of pitch), and effectively clean and weighty it is. The *Pines* and *Fountains* bring extremely fine playing with much warmth and finesse from the RPO, while the cascading waters of the *Triton fountain* become a positive torrent. The focus of the Naxos recording is slightly sharper than the Philips, and this brings an extra degree of brazen splendour to the tumultuous popular crowd sequences in the *Circus* and *Jubilee* scenes of the *Feste romane*, while at the close of the *October festival* the mandolin serenade emerges more tangibly.

Dutoit, as in other brilliant and colourful pieces, draws committed playing from his fine Montreal orchestra. Where many interpreters concentrate entirely on brilliance, Dutoit finds a vein of expressiveness too, which – for example in the opening sequence of *The Pines of Rome* – conveys the fun of children playing at the Villa Borghese. The recorded sound is superlative on CD, where the organ pedal sound is stunning. At mid-price, this is now very competitive, especially for those who enjoy the Montreal ambience.

Muti gives warmly red-blooded performances of Respighi's Roman trilogy, captivatingly Italianate in their inflexions. With brilliant playing from the Philadelphia Orchestra and warmly atmospheric recording, far better than EMI engineers have generally been producing in Philadelphia, these are exceptional for their strength of characterization.

No recording date is given for the Ormandy performances but *Feste romane* dates from the early days of stereo. The performance has great electricity and enormous surface excitement, and it is a pity that the sound-quality is fiercely brilliant. In the other two works the effect is more opulent, and the Philadelphia playing is fabulous, while the recording has come up astonishingly well. *The Pines* and *Fountains* were recorded in the Broadwood Hotel, Philadelphia, which has a warm resonance to support the brilliant lighting. The atmospheric central movements of the *Pines* are ravishing (as is the *Villa Medici Fountain*) and the final evocation of the Roman troops on the Appian Way is overtly sinister. It is a pity that such electrifying performances need some technical indulgence because of the microphone balance, but this is still a very exciting example of the Ormandy/Philadelphia regime at its most spectacularly compelling.

Toscanini's recordings of the Roman trilogy are in a class of their own; they (and Reiner in the *Pines* and the *Fountains*) are the yardstick by which all others are measured. This is electrifying playing, which comes over well in this transfer – though, to be fair, the old LPs had a rounder, fuller (less acidulated) tone on the strings above the stave.

Feste romane; The Pines of Rome.
☞ (M) *** Decca 425 052-2 [id.]. Cleveland O, Maazel – VERDI: *Le quattro stagioni.* ***

Maazel's 1976 account of *Feste romane* (musically the least interesting of Respighi's three symphonic poems inspired by the capital city) is a remarkable example of vintage Decca recording, with the most vivid detail. Respighi's gaudily evocative sound-pictures are brought glitteringly to life. The orchestral playing shows matching virtuosity, and the final festival scene ('The night before Epiphany in the Piazza Navona'), with its riotous clamour of trumpets and snatches of melody from the local organ-grinder, is projected with a kaleidoscopic imagery which fascinates the ear. *The Pines of Rome* has comparable electricity and plenty of glamour, and again the sound has a breathtaking sense of presence in the sharply defined CD transfer. The Verdi coupling (the *Four seasons ballet music* from *I vespri siciliani*) is also very successful.

Sinfonia drammatica.
☞ *** Chan. Dig. CHAN 9213 [id.]. BBC PO, Downes.

Respighi's *Sinfonia drammatica* (1914) is a work of ambitious proportions: epic in scale, it lasts just over an hour, the first movement alone taking 25 minutes. During his years as an orchestral player in St Petersburg he studied with Rimsky-Korsakov, to whose orchestral virtuosity he certainly responded. Mahler, Strauss and even early Schoenberg are obvious models and, on first hearing, the work might give the impression of being inflated and overblown. Yet it proves rich in incident and lavish in its orchestral colours and virtuosity. As a symphony it does not wholly convince; as Jeremy Siepmann's excellent notes say, it 'just fails to cohere at the highest level'. But even if it is not organic in conception or symphonic in the classical sense, it is an immensely worthwhile addition to the catalogue. If you enjoy the *Alpine Symphony*, you should try this. An excellent performance and outstanding recording.

Violin sonata in B min.
*** DG Dig. 427 617-2 [id.]. Kyung Wha Chung, Krystian Zimerman – R. STRAUSS: *Sonata.* ***
(M) (***) BMG/RCA mono GD 87871; *GK 87871* [*7871-2-RG*; *7871-4-RG*]. Heifetz, Bay –
    DEBUSSY: *Sonata* (**); RAVEL: *Trio* etc. (**); MARTINU: *Duo.* ***

Kyung Wha Chung is at her best and Krystian Zimerman brings an enormous range of colour and dynamics to the piano part – the clarity of his articulation in the *Passacaglia* is exceptional. This is undoubtedly the finest performance to appear on record since the Heifetz version. Their performance has never been surpassed. The latter remain the obvious recommendation, for it is difficult to summon up great enthusiasm for the Heifetz–Rubinstein–Piatigorsky Ravel *Trio*. All these Heifetz performances, save the Martinů, are in mono.

La sensitiva.
☞ (M) *** Virgin/EMI CUV5 61118-2 [id.]. J. Baker, City of L. Sinf., Hickox – BERLIOZ: Mélodies
(including *Nuits d'été*). ***

Tautly structured over its span of more than half an hour, Respighi's setting of Shelley's poem is a
most beautiful piece, which Dame Janet and Richard Hickox treat to a glowing first recording. An
unexpected but very enjoyable and generous coupling for the Berlioz items.

Il tramonto.
*** Hyp. Dig. CDA 66290; *KA 66290* [id.]. Carol Madalin, ECO, Bonavera – MARTUCCI: *Le
canzone dei ricordi; Notturno.* ***

Respighi's *Il tramonto* (*The sunset*) is a glorious work which at times calls to mind the world of late
Strauss. A most lovely record. Recommended with all possible enthusiasm.

OPERA

La Fiamma (complete).
*** Hung. Dig. HCD 12591/3 [id.]. Tokody, Kelen, Takács, Sólyom-Nagy, Hungarian R. and TV
Ch., Hungarian State O, Gardelli.

La Fiamma makes a fine impact in this excellent first recording, idiomatically conducted by Lamberto
Gardelli. The Hungarian cast is impressive, with Ilona Tokody producing Callas-like inflexions in the
central role of Silvana, the young wife of the exarch, Basilio. Sándor Sólyom-Nagy is impressive as
Basilio, Peter Kelen is aptly light-toned as the son-in-law, but it is the formidable Klára Takács as the
interfering Eudossia who personifies the grit in the oyster, providing high melodrama. The playing is
warmly committed and, apart from some distancing of the chorus, the sound is first rate, atmospheric
but also precisely focused.

Semirama (complete).
☞ *** Hung. Dig. HCD 31197/98 (2) [id.]. Marton, Bartolini, Kincses, Miller, Polgar, Hungarian
State O, Gardelli.

Imagine a cross between *The Pines of Rome* and Puccini's *Turandot* and you have a fair idea of
Respighi's *Semirama*. In this, his first opera, the daring young Italian composer saw no reason to
hold back. The year was 1910, and in the atmosphere of abandon after the operatic scandals of
Strauss's *Salome* and *Elektra*, the score goes over the top. Very differently from Rossini in *Semiramide*,
Respighi treats the story as a sort of reverse Oedipus: the lascivious Queen Semirama seduces the
young Babylonian general, Merodach, and then finds that he is her son. The opera was an instant
success with the first Bologna audience, and no wonder when Respighi offers such consistently
sumptuous sounds, along with an almost endless flow of melody. At that time Puccini was still the
reigning monarch of Italian opera, but after *Butterfly* in 1904 he faltered, wondering where to go
next, and it is surprising that the claims of Respighi in this formidable first opera did not bring it into
the repertory. With the outbreak of the First World War, the climate turned against lavish operas
about exotic figures of antiquity.

This first recording of *Semirama*, made in Budapest with Lamberto Gardelli pacing the score
masterfully, should help to bring the opera back from oblivion, perhaps even encourage stage
productions. The surprise is that this highly accomplished score dates from well before any of the
works for which Respighi is usually known, including *The Pines of Rome* (1924). He also anticipates
Puccini. One passage, when the Queen questions her victim with an imperiously repeated '*Rispondi!*',
is so like the riddle scene in *Turandot* that plainly Puccini was the one who copied, not the young
Respighi. This recording, like so many previous opera sets from Budapest, offers splendid playing
from the Hungarian State Orchestra, with fine singing from the Radio and Television Chorus and a
strong cast of soloists. Eva Marton makes a powerful Queen, and the voice, so often unsteady and ill-
focused in recordings, is here firmer than usual in the soaring melodies. Lando Bartolini produces
clear, heroic tone as Merodach, though he is reluctant to scale the voice down. Veronika Kincses as
the Chaldaean princess, Susiana, caresses the Respighi melodies with her sweet, pure tone, but then
grows rather edgy for the more dramatic moments. The booklet looks skimpy, but efficiently
provides libretto, translation and the necessary background.

Reubke, Julius (1834–58)

Sonata in C min. on Psalm 94.
*** Argo Dig. 430 244-2 [id.]. Thomas Trotter (organ of Ingolstadt Minster) – LISZT: *Ave Maria; Prelude & fugue on B-A-C-H* etc. ***

Julius Reubke's monothematic piece is powerfully conceived and ingeniously wrought; its three sections can be regarded either as separate movements or as different facets of a single structure. Trotter's performance is strongly controlled and the Argo recording makes an exciting spectacle of the work's fugal climax.

Revueltas, Silvestre (1899–1940)

Caminos; Musica para charlar; Ventanas.
*** ASV Dig. CDDCA 653 [id.]. Mexico City PO, Bátiz – CHAVEZ: *Sinfonia de Antigona; Symphony No. 4.* ***

The music on this record is highly colourful, with moments of considerable vulgarity rubbing shoulders with very evocative and imaginative episodes, such as the depiction of *Twilight* in the second *Musica para charlar*. Excellent playing from the Mexican orchestra under Bátiz and sound of demonstration quality, with great impact, detail and presence.

Rheinberger, Joseph (1839–1901)

Organ concerto No. 1 in F, Op. 137.
*** Telarc Dig. CD 80136 [id.]. Michael Murray, RPO, Ling – DUPRE: *Symphony.* ***

Rheinberger's *Concerto* is well made, its invention is attractive and it has suitable moments of spectacle that render it admirable for a coupling with the Dupré *Symphony*, with its use of the massive Albert Hall organ. The performance here is first rate. A fine demonstration disc.

Rihm, Wolfgang (born 1952)

Gesungene Zeit (Time chant).
☞ *** DG Dig. 437 093-2 [id.]. Mutter, Chicago SO, Levine – BERG: *Violin concerto.* ***

As a striking and unusual coupling for the Berg *Concerto*, Mutter offers a violin concerto which she commissioned from the 40-year-old German composer, Wolfgang Rihm. Under the title *Gesungene Zeit* ('Time Chant'), Rihm has written what in effect is an extended lyrical meditation for the soloist, heightened and illustrated by the orchestra in the most discreet way. As he says, 'In essence this is monophonic music. And it is always song, even where beat and pulse shorten the breath and press it hard.' As in the Berg, Mutter is inspired, playing with an inner hush that used only rarely to mark her recordings.

Rimsky-Korsakov, Nikolay (1844–1908)

Capriccio espagnol, Op. 34; Le coq d'or: suite; Russian Easter festival overture, Op. 34.
(M) *** Mercury 434 308-2 [id.]. LSO, Antal Dorati – BORODIN: *Prince Igor: Polovstian dances.* **(*)

Dorati's 1959 *Capriccio espagnole* brings glittering bravura and excitement from the LSO players, and the *Russian Easter festival overture*, recorded at Walthamstow at the same sessions, is equally dynamic and colourful. Even more remarkably, the rich-hued and vibrant *Le coq d'or* dates from as early as 1956, yet hardly sounds dated. The playing has plenty of allure in its evocation of Queen Shemakha, yet has drama and well defined detail.

Capriccio espagnol, Op. 34; May night overture; Russian Easter festival overture, Op. 36; Sadko, Op. 5.
☞ (BB) ** ASV Dig. CDQS 6089. Mexico City PO, Bátiz.

A spirited super-bargain collection from Bátiz. The snag is that the Mexico City violins do not produce a rich enough body of string tone to do justice to their expansive tune in the *Capriccio*, although the horns and woodwind are good. *Sadko* comes off best, *A May night* is enjoyable (with the same proviso as in the *Capriccio*) and the *Russian Easter festival overture*, with a fine trombone solo, has plenty of vitality, although the percussion-laced climaxes are a bit brassy and fierce. However, the sound has plenty of ambience, and this is fair value at the modest price asked.

Christmas eve (suite); Le Coq d'or: suite; *Legend of the invisible city of Kitezh:* suite; *May night:* overture; *Mlada:* suite; *The Snow Maiden:* suite; *The Tale of the Tsar Saltan:* suite.
*** Chan. Dig. CHAN 8327/9; *DBTD 3004* (3) [id.]. SNO, Järvi.

The *Prelude* to *The invisible city of Kitezh* is described as a hymn to nature, while the delights of the *Christmas eve suite* include a magical evocation of the glittering stars against a snow-covered landscape and, later, a flight of comets. Apart from the feast of good tunes, the composer's skilful and subtle deployment of the orchestral palette continually titillates the ear. Neeme Järvi draws the most seductive response from the SNO; he consistently creates orchestral textures which are diaphanously sinuous. Yet the robust moments, when the brass blazes or the horns ring out sumptuously, are caught just as strikingly and the listener is assured that here is music which survives repetition uncommonly well.

Christmas eve: suite; Le coq d'or: suite; The Tale of Tsar Saltan: suite; Flight of the bumble bee.
*** ASV Dig. CDDCA 772 [id.]. Armenian PO, Tjeknavorian.

Tjeknavorian and his fine Armenian Orchestra are completely at home in Rimsky's sinuous orientalism. There is a first-rate trumpeter to play the arresting fanfares which open each movement of the *Tsar Saltan suite* and articulate the pungently bizarre warnings of *The Golden cockerel*, matched elsewhere by glittering, iridescent wind-colouring. The racy vigour and sparkle of the playing brings a jet-setting bumble bee and the carolling horns and bold brass add to the vividness. The Tchaikovskian *Polonaise* music from *Christmas eve* exudes similar sparkling vitality within a glowing palette. In short this is one of the most desirable and generous Rimsky-Korsakov collections in the current catalogue, and only a degree of thinness in the violin timbre above the stave prevents the use of the adjective, sumptuous. In all other respects this is in the demonstration bracket.

Piano concerto in C sharp min., Op. 30.
☞ *** Hyp. Dig. CDA 66640 [id.]. Malcolm Binns, E. N. Philh. O, Lloyd-Jones – BALAKIREV: *Concertos Nos. 1–2.* ***
☞ ** Russian Disc MK 417087 [id.]. Igor Zhukov, USSR R. & TV Large SO, Alexander Dmitriev – BALAKIREV; MEDTNER: *Piano concertos.* **

If Malcolm Binns had a more glamorous name he might have won the reputation to which his artistry entitles him. As might be expected, he proves a sensitive and intelligent exponent in the Rimsky-Korsakov concerto, which comes coupled with Balakirev's two essays in the form. The Northern Philharmonia under David Lloyd-Jones give excellent support and the Hyperion recording is altogether superior to its Melodiya rival. Moreover the Hyperion disc has the advantage of a Balakirev rarity, the *Second Piano concerto*, which is not otherwise available.

Igor Zhukov is generally a big-boned, gutsy virtuoso but, as his account of the Medtner and Balakirev concertos with which this is coupled shows, he also has imagination and finesse. He makes out an excellent case for this piece and, although the orchestral playing is not as highly polished as the Northern Philharmonia's, the horns and brass tending to bray somewhat, the performance is still thoroughly recommendable. Some readers may recall this in its original, LP incarnation and they can be assured that the transfer is an improvement.

Legend of the invisible city of Kitezh: suite.
☞ ** Koch Schwann Dig. 311 202 [id.]. Saarbrücken RSO, Myung-Wha Chung – SHOSTAKOVICH: *Symphony No. 6.* **

Myung-Whun Chung's performance of this colourful and attractive score is satisfying and well prepared, and decently recorded too. But at full-price and at less than 50 minutes, it hardly represents good value for money.

Scheherazade (symphonic suite), *Op. 35.*
*** EMI CDC7 47717-2 [id.]. RPO, Beecham – BORODIN: *Polovtsian dances.* ***
☞ *** DG Dig. 437 818-2 [id.]. O de l'Opéra Bastille, Chung – STRAVINSKY: *Firebird suite.* ***
☞ (M) *** EMI CD-EMX 2214; *TC-EMX 2214.* LPO, Takuo Yuasa – PROKOFIEV: *Lieutenant Kijé.* ***
(M) *** BMG/RCA GD 60875 [60875-2-RG]. Chicago SO, Fritz Reiner – DEBUSSY: *La Mer.* ***
(B) *** CfP CD-CFP 4341; *TC-CFP 4341.* Philh. O, Kletzki – TCHAIKOVSKY: *Capriccio italien.* ***
(M) *** DG 419 063-2; *419 063-4* [id.]. BPO, Karajan – BORODIN: *Polovtsian dances.* ***
☞ (M) **(*) Ph. Dig. 434 733-2; *434 733-4* [id.]. VPO, Previn – RAVEL: *La valse.* **

Scheherazade; Capriccio espagnol, Op. 34.
⊛ *** Telarc Dig. CD 80208 [id.]. LSO, Sir Charles Mackerras.
☞ (BB) **(*) Tring Dig. TRP 003 [id.]. RPO, Barry Wordsworth.

Scheherazade; Fairy tale (Skazka), Op. 29; Sadko, Op. 5; Song of India, from Sadko (arr. Tjeknavorian).
*** ASV Dig. CDDCA 771; *ZCDCA 771* [id.]. Armenian PO, Tjeknavorian.

(i) *Scheherazade;* (ii) *May night overture; Sadko, Op. 5.*
☞ (BB) *** Belart 450 132-2. (i) LSO, Monteux; (ii) SRO, Ansermet.

Scheherazade; Russian Easter festival overture, Op. 36.
☞ **(*) BMG/RCA Dig. 09026 61173-2. NYPO, Yuri Temirkanov.
☞ **(*) Ph. Dig. 438 941-2 [id.]. VPO, Seiji Ozawa.

Scheherazade; Russian Easter festival overture; The Maid of Pskov: Hunt and storm.
☞ (M) (***) Biddulph mono WHL 010 [id.]. Phd. O, Stokowski.

Mackerras is a dynamic interpreter of this vividly Russian score and he has the advantage of a superb Telarc digital recording which is very much in the demonstration class. Mackerras's reading combines gripping drama with romantic ardour, subtlety of colour with voluptuousness; he is helped, as is Yuasa, by a wonderfully beguiling portrait of Scheherazade herself, provided by his orchestral leader, in this case Kees Hulsmann. Scheherazade's presence is felt at the very opening through the vivid kaleidoscoping colours of the second movement, blossoming in the ravishing slow movement, which recalls Beecham in its elegant sumptuousness. The charming closing reverie, with the Sultan lying peacefully satiated in the arms of his young wife, their themes blissfully intermingled, is unforgettable. After an appropriate pause, Mackerras then delivers a thrilling bravura account of *Capriccio espagnol*, lushly opulent in the variations, glittering in the exotic *Scena e canta gitano*, and carrying all before it in the impetus of the closing *Fandango asturiano*.

Beecham's 1957 *Scheherazade* is a performance of extraordinary drama and charisma. Alongside the violin contribution of Stephen Staryk, all the solo playing has great distinction; in the second movement Beecham gives the woodwind complete metrical freedom. The sumptuousness and glamour of the slow movement are very apparent and the finale has an explosive excitement, rising to an electrifying climax. However, this is surely due for a mid-price reissue.

On ASV a refreshing and totally gripping new-look recording of *Scheherazade* from Eastern Russia. Yuri Boghosian immediately presents a seductively slight and sinuous image for the heroine-narrator and the first movement brings the strongest attack and thrust from the strings. Throughout the central movements one is made aware of the lustrous oriental character of Rimsky's melodies. The finale, with its spectacular storm and shipwreck, has exhilarating animation and bite. Tjeknavorian shows great imaginative flair in realizing the vivid orchestral effects in the two shorter folk tales and also offers his own gently luscious arrangement of Rimsky's most famous melody, better known as the *Chant hindue*, which caresses the ear beguilingly. The brilliant recording has great vividness and projection, but relatively little sumptuousness. But it suits the performances admirably.

On EMI's mid-priced label, Eminence, comes another romantically compulsive account of *Scheherazade*, very responsively played by the same orchestra which was so successful in the earlier, Haitink version. Again there is a freshness and an absence of routine in the music-making, and the sinuously supple contribution of the orchestral leader, Stephen Bryant, in the role of the heroine is believably placed in the orchestral texture. Takuo Yuasa's reading is more spacious, less urgent than Mackerras's, but his evocation of the sea in the first movement is very compelling, and the central movements are full of colour and warmth, with a burst of passion to climax the idyllic rapture of the slow movement. The finale brings grippingly animated orchestral virtuosity and a powerful climax, with the tam-tam flashing out at the moment of the shipwreck. The poetic close has a lustrous rapture, even if it is not quite as enchanting as on the Mackerras disc. At mid-price, with a splendid Prokofiev coupling, no one will be disappointed with this, for the sound is full-bodied and brilliant, with an attractive ambient glow.

There is a certain freshness about the newest Paris account under Myung-Whun Chung; nothing is routine and the playing has a certain enthusiasm. Very fast and effective tempo in the finale. The sound has warmth and perspective, thanks to Wolfgang Mitlehner, one of DG's best *Tonmeister*, though the timpani resonate perhaps a bit too much. All the same, a very enjoyable newcomer.

Reiner's first movement opens richly and dramatically and has a strong forward impulse. The unnamed orchestral leader, naturally balanced, plays most seductively. Reiner's affectionate individual touches have much in common with Beecham's (full-price) version and sound comparably spontaneous and the finale, brilliant and very exciting, has a climax of resounding power and amplitude. The Chicago Hall ambience makes up in body and spaciousness for any lack of internal clarity.

With highly distinguished violin solos from Hugh Bean, Kletzki's reading is broad in the first movement (with less bite and thrust than with Tjeknavorian), but he makes the second glow and sparkle (the famous brass interchanges having the most vivid projection). The elegantly sinuous finesse of the Philharmonia string playing in the third movement is matched by the exhilaration of the finale. The admirably balanced recording has been enhanced by the CD transfer, and at bargain price this remains very competitive.

The recordings from Monteux and Ansermet on the Polygram Belart CD come from the earliest days of stereo. Monteux's version of *Scheherazade* still sounds vividly spontaneous and the recording remains brilliant and sparkling, the performance sensuous and exciting, full of charisma. Ansermet finds all the colour in the *May night overture* and *Sadko*, an exotic Rimskian fairy-tale with a colourful storm for a climax; while the Decca engineers, working in stereo for the very first time in Geneva, provided both atmosphere and the fullest orchestral palette. In the finale of *Scheherazade* Monteux holds back the climax until the last minute, then unleashes his forces to devastating effect. The orchestral playing lacks a little in ultimate polish but has tremendous zest and spontaneity, and this makes a fine bargain recommendation.

Karajan's 1967 recording is greatly enhanced in its CD format. The added presence increases the feeling of ardour from the glorious Berlin strings in the *Andante*. The outer movements have great vitality and thrust, and the bright percussion transients add to the feeling of zest. Yet Michel Schwalbé's sinuously luxuriant violin solos are still allowed to participate in the narrative. The fill-up is a sizzling account of the Borodin *Polovtsian dances*, with no chorus, but managing perfectly well without.

The highlight of the Temirkanov account lies in the richly languorous slow movement, with the warmest, most sensuous string playing at the opening and a delightfully wistful, almost elegiac close. The work opens boldly, with the brass heavily enunciating the Sultan's powerful theme; and the leader, Glenn Dicterow, portrays Scheherazade sinuously, helped by a lifelike balance. But the spacious opening movement lacks real tension, and the colourful events of the second movement are also very relaxed. The finale brings alert playing and vivid detail and an explosive climax at the shipwreck, where the bold tam-tam stroke is followed by a hammering nemesis from the timpani. But overall this cannot compete with current top recommendations, and the *Russian Easter festival overture*, too, takes a while to warm up properly, though again the climax is impressive. The recording was made in New York's Manhattan Center and is spacious and wide-ranging, if not quite as spectacular as Mackerras's Telarc CD, which remains first choice.

Barry Wordsworth's RPO version is also offered in the lowest price-range and is almost equally recommendable. As the dramatic opening shows, the digital recording is spectacularly full and wide-ranging and, while the solo violin (Jonathan Carney) is rather forwardly balanced, it means that 'Scheherazade' immediately takes a dominating role both at the opening and particularly in the closing section of the finale, where one feels she is very much in command of her situation. Yet the violin solos are well integrated with the woodwind in the colourful central episodes. The first movement has a fine, spacious sweep yet displays a less compulsive thrust than with Bátiz and, if the wind solos in the second movement are made to seem rather less spontaneous, the slow movement has an agreeable allure at the opening, with the RPO strings rather more lustrous than their Philharmonia colleagues. The movement does not languish at the close and the finale brings plenty of orchestral bravura and excitement. What makes this disc particularly attractive is the outstanding coupling. *Capriccio espagnol* is an elusive work on disc but here vitality is the keynote. The variations are sumptuous but provide plenty of glitter when the orchestral soloists so obviously relish their opportunities to take the limelight. Then with stabbing brass the *Scena e canto gitano* prepares the way for a vibrant close. The Tring recording was made in All Saints' Church, Petersham, and to counter the resonance the microphones are fairly close, which adds to the brilliance and produces a vivid orchestral presence.

After this, Ozawa's new full-price version, good as it is, cannot really compete. This VPO *Scheherazade* was recorded 'live' in the Musikvereinsaal, which certainly brings sentient richness to the VPO strings. Ozawa's tempi are relatively relaxed, but the concentration of music-making in front of an audience prevents any lapse of tension and climaxes make a powerful impact. Rainer Honeck has no lack of personality in his projection of the heroine, but the VPO wind solos in the second movement sound more calculated than with either Bátiz or Wordsworth. The *Russian Easter festival overture* is a studio recording and is enjoyable enough but not distinctive.

This collection of Leopold Stokowski's recordings of Rimsky-Korsakov centres on the first of his five versions of *Scheherazade*. Made in 1927, it is wilder and more passionate than later ones; fascinatingly, an alternative version of the first movement, never issued before, is included as a supplement. At a slightly broader speed, spreading to an extra 78-r.p.m. side, it is even more persuasive, and Stokowski's Philadelphia Orchestra, unlike British ones of the time, plays with high polish as well as passion. Equally impressive is Stokowski's intense, volatile account of the *Russian Easter festival overture*, dating from 1929, while the *Hunt and storm* sequence from the *The Maid of Pskov* comes from ten years later, with the sound drier and marginally less full. The Biddulph transfers are excellent with plenty of body.

Previn in his 1981 Vienna version opts for spacious speeds and a direct, unsentimental view. With his characteristic rhythmic flair and with sumptuous playing from the Vienna Philharmonic the result is certainly enjoyable, if more restrained than usual. Excellent, finely balanced sound, but there are more impressive mid-priced versions for those not insisting on digital sound. The Insignia reissue omits any notes about the music.

Scheherazade; Tsar Saltan: orchestral suite.
☞ (BB) *** Naxos Dig. 8.550726. Philh. O, Bátiz.
☞ ** Erato/Warner Dig. 4509 91717-2 [id.]. Chicago SO, Barenboim.

Naxos's use of the Philharmonia Orchestra certainly pays dividends when Enrique Bátiz is there to galvanize the players throughout a work that must be so familiar to them as to be in danger of bringing a routine response. But never for a moment does that happen here. Bátiz's reputation for spontaneity in the recording studio is demonstrated at its most telling. His performance is impulsive, full of momentum and seductively volatile. David Nolan's picture of Scheherazade is rhapsodically evanescent and in the key second movement the lilting Philharmonia wind solos are a constant pleasure. The slow movement combines refinement with its sensuous patina, and the finale has fine zest and excitement. The colourful *Tsar Saltan suite* is comparably dramatic and vivid. In short, with first-class recording, both clear in detail and full-bodied, at super-bargain price this is hard to beat.

Especially by the side of Bátiz, with his inherent vitality, Barenboim's overall approach is overtly sensuous (an approach shared by the orchestra leader, Samuel Magad, in his languorous assumption of the solo role representing the storyteller). The opening movement lacks real vitality and, immediately at the opening of the second movement, the bassoon solo sounds indulgent and unspontaneous, while in the central section of the *Andantino* (after an opulent opening from the strings) the clarinet solo is even more self-conscious. The finale is exciting; but overall this account is too mannered to give repeated satisfaction. The *Tsar Saltan suite* is sumptuously evocative and much more enjoyable, but this Erato *Scheherazade* cannot be seriously recommended in a very competitive field.

Symphonies Nos. 1 in E min., Op. 1; 2 (Antar), Op. 9; 3 in C, Op. 32; Capriccio espagnol, Op. 35; Russian Easter festival overture, Op. 36.
*** DG Dig. 423 604-2 (2). Gothenburg SO, Järvi.

Whatever Rimsky-Korsakov's symphonies may lack in symphonic coherence they make up for in colour and charm. Some of the material is a little thin but there is some highly attractive invention as well. *Antar* is not quite as strong as some of its protagonists would have us believe, but it should surely have a stronger presence in the concert and recorded repertoire than it has. The performances under Neeme Järvi have considerable merit and the Gothenburg orchestra is excellently recorded; moreover the addition of the *Capriccio espagnol* and the *Russian Easter festival overture* makes the Chandos set a very attractive proposition.

Symphonies Nos. 1 in E min., Op. 1; 2 (Antar), Op. 9; Capriccio espagnol, Op. 34.
☞ *** Chan. Dig CHAN 9178 [id.]. Bergen PO, Dmitri Kitaienko.

The *First Symphony*, composed while Rimsky-Korsakov was still in the navy, is not great music but, like much of his mature output, is full of colour. Kitaienko makes the most of it, as he does of *Antar*, more suite than symphony as its composer freely conceded. Indeed he draws very good playing from the Bergen Philharmonic and the exoticism of the latter is very well conveyed. Kitaienko holds the piece together well and gets very lively results in *Capriccio espagnol*. The recording is very good without being quite in the demonstration class. In any event this is a useful alternative to both Neeme Järvi on DG (for those who don't want to invest in his two CDs) and Svetlanov's less generously filled (though that bit better played) Hyperion disc with the Philharmonia.

Symphony No. 2 (Antar), Op. 9.
☞ (M) *** Telarc Dig. CD 82011 [id.]. Pittsburgh SO, Maazel – TCHAIKOVSKY: *Symphony No. 2.* ***

Symphony No. 2 (Antar), Op. 9; Russian Easter festival overture, Op. 36.
☞ **(*) Hyp. Dig. CDA 66399 [id.]. Philh. O, Svetlanov.

On Telerc's new mid-price label, Bravo!, *Antar* makes a particularly attractive coupling with Tchaikovsky's *Little Russian Symphony*. Maazel's taut yet sympathetic reading holds together a work which, structurally at least, might more aptly be counted as a suite (as *Scheherazade* is) but which, with strong and colourful yet refined treatment like this, is fittingly regarded as belonging to Rimsky's symphonic canon. Excellent playing – notably in the finale, where the Pittsburgh woodwind excel themselves in delicacy – and brilliant, finely balanced recording. The richness of the strings and bloom on the woodwind add lustre to Rimsky's sinuous oriental colouring.

It goes without saying that the Philharmonia Orchestra and Svetlanov produce an excellent account of Rimsky-Korsakov's colourful score and there is no want of atmosphere or spirit in their playing. Moreover they are given excellent recorded sound by the Hyperion team. However, even with a fill-up, the playing time is still a mite under 50 minutes, which is short measure for a full-price record these days, even one as good as this. The performances in themselves are not superior to those on the two-CD set on DG from the Gothenburg Orchestra under Neeme Järvi: indeed, if anything, the latter are more atmospheric. Were Hyperion to reissue this, either more competitively priced or with an additional work, it would warrant an unreserved recommendation.

Tsar Saltan, Op. 57: March.
*** Telarc Dig. CD 80107 [id.]. RPO, Previn – TCHAIKOVSKY: *Symphony No. 5.* ***

The crisp, stylized *March* from *Tsar Saltan* makes a delightful *bonne-bouche*, a welcome fill-up for Previn's fine account of the Tchaikovsky *Fifth Symphony*.

Piano and wind quintet in B flat.
*** Hyp. CDA 66163 [id.]. Capricorn – GLINKA: *Grand Sextet.* ***
*** CRD CRD 3409; *CRDC 4109* [id.]. Ian Brown, Nash Ens. – ARENSKY: *Piano trio No. 1.* ***

Rimsky-Korsakov's youthful *Quintet for piano, flute, clarinet, horn and bassoon* is a thoroughly diverting piece. It is like a garrulous but endearing friend whose loquacity is readily borne for the sake of his charm and good nature. The main theme of the finale is pretty brainless but singularly engaging, and the work as a whole leaves a festive impression. Capricorn's account has great vivacity and is very well recorded.

The Nash Ensemble give a spirited and delightful account of it on CRD that can be warmly recommended for its dash and sparkle and full, naturally balanced sound. The CD transfer retains all the analogue warmth but is not made at a high level; though those used to digital records might like sharper inner definition, the effect is very pleasing with no lack of presence.

The Tsar's Bride (complete).
☞ ** Chant du Monde Dig. LDC 288 056/7 [id.]. Glouboky, Kudriavchenko, Nizienko, Michenkine, Terentieva, Sveshnikov Russian Ac. Ch., Bolshoi Theatre O, Chistiakov.

One by one, the 15 operas of Rimsky-Korsakov are emerging from obscurity. The Chant du Monde set of Rimsky's ninth opera, *The Tsar's Bride*, first given in St Petersburg in 1899, provides a fair stop-gap, an unhelpfully dry recording of a performance by a Bolshoi cast. Rimsky, ever attentive to musical fashion, was in part reflecting the then recent arrival of Puccini and others, for his heroine, Marfa, is as vulnerable as Mimì or Butterfly. Yet Rimsky's easy, colourful music hardly reflects the darkness of this story of conspiracy, betrayal and poison set in the days of Ivan the Terrible. For him, it seems, writing operas was all too easy, and he here showed little or none of Puccini's power to involve. The Bolshoi performance under Andrei Chistiakov is amiable to match, conveying few stage tensions. As Marfa, Ekaterina Kudriavchenko is firmer than most Russian sopranos but has moments of rawness, and is rather upstaged by the fine mezzo, Nina Terentieva, in the villainous role of Lubacha. Unlike most of the others, she produces beautiful tone despite the dryness. The four Acts are squeezed on to two very well-filled CDs.

Robles, Marisa (born 1937)

Narnia suite.
(M) *** ASV CDWHL 2068. Composer, Christopher Hyde-Smith, Marisa Robles Harp Ens.

This incidental music was commissioned for ASV's integral recording of the C. S. Lewis *Narnia Chronicles*, as read (quite admirably) by Michael Hordern. Even though it consists entirely of a series of miniatures for harp, with the flute of Christopher Hyde-Smith used sparingly but to great effect, the music stands up well away from the narrative. Its freshness and innocence are entirely in keeping with the special atmosphere of C. S. Lewis's narrative. With the composer so admirably partnered, the music cannot fail to charm the listener, particularly as the digital recording is clear and lustrous. *The Chronicles of Narnia* are available on tape only (including the incidental music) as follows: *The*

Magician's Nephew (ASV *ZCSWD 351*); *The Lion, The Witch and The Wardrobe* (*ZCSWD 352*); *The Horse and His Boy* (*ZCSWD 353*); *Prince Caspian* (*ZCSWD 354*); *The Voyage of the Dawn Treader* (*ZCSWD 355*); *The Silver Chair* (*ZCSWD 356*); *The Last Battle* (*ZCSWD 357*).

Rodrigo, Joaquín (born 1902)

A la busca del más allá; (i) *Concierto Andaluz* (for 4 guitars); (ii) *Concierto de Aranjuez* (for guitar); (iii) *Concierto de estío* (for violin); (iv) *Concierto en modo galante* (for cello); (v) *Concierto heroico* (for piano); (vi) *Concierto madrigal* (for 2 guitars); (vii) *Concierto pastoral* (for flute); (viii) *Concierto serenata* (for harp). (ii) *Fantasia para un gentilhombre. Música para un jardin; Per la flor del Iliri blau; 5 Piezas infantiles; Soleriana; Zarabanda lejana y villancico.*

(M) *** EMI Dig. CDZ7 67435-2 (4) [id.]. (i) Moreno, Garibay, López, Ruiz; (ii) Alfonso Moreno;
  (iii) Augustín Léo Ara; (iv) Robert Cohen; (v) Jorge Osorio; (vi) Moreno, Mariotti; (vii) Lisa
  Hansen; (viii) Nancy Allen; LSO; Mexico State PO; RPO, Enrique Bátiz.

The only missing concertos are the second *Guitar concerto* (*Concierto para una Fiesta*) and the later *Cello concerto* (*Concierto como un divertimento*) commissioned by Julian Lloyd Webber. The present EMI recordings were made between 1980 and 1985, many of them in Watford Town Hall, and are of excellent quality, although the early digital technique often brings an overlit sound to the treble, perhaps appropriate for music drenched in Spanish sunshine. The *Summer concerto* for violin ('conceived in the manner of Vivaldi') is the composer's own favourite, and Augustin Léo Ara catches its neo-classical vitality admirably. The *Cello concerto* is given a masterly performance by Robert Cohen; he combines elegance of phrasing with warm beauty of timbre. His spirited articulation of the opening ostinato ideas and the lively Zapateado rondo finale is matched by Bátiz, who secures playing of fire and temperament from the LSO. The *Concierto serenata* for harp, a favourite of ours, has an unforgettable piquancy and charm. Nancy Allen consistently beguiles the ear with her gentleness (the very opening with its cascade of trickling notes is wonderfully inviting). The *Concierto pastoral* is a spikier piece than usual from this composer and its brilliant introduction is far from pastoral in feeling, but Rodrigo's fragmented melodies soon insinuate themselves into the consciousness. Rodrigo's *Piano concerto* has a programmatic content, with the four movements written 'under the sign of the Sword, the Spur, the Cross and the Laurel'. But heroism is not a quality one associates with Rodrigo's art, and the best part is the *Largo* which, seeking a medieval ambience, is attractively atmospheric. The performers give a strong, extrovert account of the piece.

The *Concierto Andaluz* has its weaknesses but remains engaging if a trifle inflated. A similar comment might be made about the effect of the duo *Concierto madrigal*, with its set of twelve delightful vignettes, many with a medieval flavour, but the four guitar soloists here do not achieve the strongest profile, and this is also one reason why Alfonso Moreno's account of the famous *Concierto de Aranjuez*, though bright and sympathetic, is in no way outstanding. The symphonic poem, *A la busca del más allá*, is evocative and powerfully scored; *Música para un jardin* is a quartet of cradle songs, originally conceived for the piano and scored with all the piquancy at the composer's command. The *Five Children's pieces* are delightful, while the two neo-classical evocations of eighteenth-century Spain (*Soleriana*) are also unostentatiously appealing. *Per la flor del Iliri blau* is based on a Valencian legend and has something in common with Smetana's famous cycle about his homeland, though Rodrigo is more impressive in moments of gently atmospheric detail than in the melodrama. The *Zarabanda lejana* was Rodrigo's first work for guitar. He later orchestrated it and added the *Villancico* to make a binary structure, the first part nobly elegiac, the second a gay dance movement.

(i) *Concierto Andaluz* (for 4 guitars); (ii) *Concierto de Aranjuez;* (ii; iii) *Concierto madrigal* (for 2 guitars); (ii) *Concierto para una fiesta; Fantasia para un gentilhombre.* Solo guitar pieces: *Bajando de la Meseta; En los trigales; Fandango; Junto al Generalife; 3 Little Pieces; Romance de Durandarte; Sonata a la española; Tiento antiquo.*

(M) *** Ph. 432 581-2 (3) [id.]. (i) Los Romeros; (ii) Pepe Romero; (iii) Angel Romero; ASMF,
  Marriner.

This distinguished set gathers together all Rodrigo's major concertante guitar works in first-class performances and adds a rewarding recital of solo works as a postlude, all played with natural spontaneity and complete authority by an artist who feels this music from his innermost being. The *Sonata* is no less strongly Spanish in character and the genre pieces are comparably picturesque in evoking Mediterranean atmosphere and local dance-rhythms. If the *Concierto para una fiesta* does not quite repeat the success of the *Concierto de Aranjuez*, it still has plenty of Andalusian colour, and

Pepe Romero's performance has all the freshness of new discovery. He is equally magnetic in the solo items. Throughout, Marriner and the Academy provide accompaniments which are thoroughly polished and have much warmth, and the Philips sound is most natural and beautifully balanced.

Concierto de Aranjuez (for guitar and orchestra).

⊛ (M) *** Decca Dig. 430 703-2; *430 703-4* [id.]. Carlos Bonell, Montreal SO, Dutoit – FALLA: *El amor brujo* etc. *** ⊛

☞ (BB) *** Naxos Dig. 8.550729 [id.]. Norbert Kraft, N. CO, Nicholas Ward – CASTELNUOVO-TEDESCO: *Concerto* ***; VILLA-LOBOS: *Concerto.* **(*)

Concierto de Aranjuez; (i) *Concierto madrigal* (for 2 guitars); *Fantasia para un gentilhombre.*

(M) *** Ph. 432 828-2; *432 828-4* [id.]. Pepe Romero; (i) Angel Romero; ASMF, Marriner.

Concierto de Aranjuez; Fantasia para un gentilhombre.

(M) *** Decca Dig. 417 748-2 [id.]. Carlos Bonell, Montreal SO, Dutoit (with FALLA: *Three-cornered hat* ***).

*** Sony Dig. CD 37848. John Williams, Philh. O, Frémaux.

(i) *Concierto de Aranjuez; Fantasia para un gentilhombre. En los trigales; Pastoral; Sonata a la española.*

☞ (B) *** CfP Dig. CD-CFP 4614; *TC-CFP 4614* [id.]. Ernesto Bitetti, (i) Philh. O, Antoni Ros-Marba.

Decca have reissued the much-praised Bonell/Dutoit recording of the *Concierto* a second time, now re-coupled with Alicia de Larrocha's splendid digital recording of Falla's *Nights in the gardens of Spain* plus Dutoit's outstanding complete *El amor brujo*. This is a very attractive pairing and the reasons for the success of the Rodrigo performance remain unaltered: an exceptionally clear, atmospheric and well-balanced digital recording plus Bonell's imaginative account of the solo part, and the strong characterization of the orchestral accompaniments by Charles Dutoit and his excellent Montreal orchestra.

The Bonell/Dutoit *Concierto* was originally paired with the *Fantasia para un gentilhombre*. Decca then made this issue even more attractive by adding a bonus of three dances from Falla's *Three-cornered hat* (taken from Dutoit's complete set). In the *Fantasia*, the balance between warmly gracious lyricism and sprightly rhythmic resilience is no less engaging.

Pepe Romero's performance of the *Concierto de Aranjuez* has plenty of Spanish colour, the musing poetry of the slow movement beautifully caught. The account of the *Fantasia* is warm and gracious, with the Academy contributing quite as much as the soloist to the appeal of the performance. Angel joins Pepe for the Renaissance-inspired duet, *Concierto madrigal*, which is very attractive indeed, making this a very viable alternative to the Decca couplings.

Norbert Kraft is a soloist of personality and he receives spirited, sensitive accompaniments from the Northern Chamber Orchestra under Nicholas Ward. Indeed the work sounds remarkably fresh using a smaller-sized orchestral group, which can bring a degree of intimacy yet produce sufficient body of violin-tone for the rapturous tutti near the end of the *Adagio*. Indeed the slow movement has plenty of atmosphere, and this Naxos CD deserves a place near the very top of the list. It is also a first-class bargain, especially for the Castelnuovo-Tedesco work, among the two enjoyably vivid couplings. The recording is very well balanced, with the guitar given a most convincing relationship with the orchestra and the sound itself vividly realistic.

An excellent bargain anthology from CfP, vividly recorded. Rodrigo's two favourite concertante guitar works are combined with some worthwhile solo items which are very well played by Ernesto Bitetti; indeed the *Sonata a la española*, which ends the programme, is dedicated to him. He gives a rather introspective performance of it, but the *Concierto* is bright-eyed while still finding a languorous intimacy in the slow movement. The performance of the *Fantasia*, too, is especially successful, with Ros-Marba and the Philharmonia providing a brilliantly coloured orchestral backing, full of bracing rhythmic vitality. They are helped by the lively yet atmospheric digital sound.

John Williams's newest version of the *Concierto* (his third) also has the advantage of first-class digital recording. The acoustic, however, is a little dry compared with the Decca issue, while the woodwind is a shade too forward. Nevertheless, this is technically superior to Williams's previous, analogue partnership with Barenboim and the performance is even finer.

The Julian Bream Edition

Concierto de Aranjuez.

☞ (M) *** BMG/RCA 09026 61598-2. Julian Bream, Melos Ens., Colin Davis – ARNOLD: *Concerto;*
BENNETT: *Concerto* ***.

☞ (M) *** BMG/RCA Dig. 09026 61605-2 [id.]. Julian Bream, COE, Gardiner – BERKELEY;
BROUWER: *Concertos.* ***

☞ *** EMI Dig. CDC7 54661-2 [id.]. Julian Bream, CBSO, Rattle – ARNOLD: *Concerto;*
TAKEMITSU: *To the edge of dream.* ***

(i) *Concierto de Aranjuez;* (ii) *Fantasia para un gentilhombre. Invocation and dance (Hommage à
Manuel de Falla); 3 Piezas españolas.*

☞ (M) *** BMG/RCA Dig. 09026 61611-2. Julian Bream, (i) COE, Gardiner; (ii) RCA Victor CO,
Leo Brouwer.

The differences between Bream's two earlier RCA readings of the *Concierto*, the first (analogue) with
Colin Davis in 1963, the second (digital) with Gardiner in 1982, are almost too subtle to analyse and
perhaps depend as much on the personalities of the two conductors as on that of the soloist.
Certainly neither account is upstaged by the most recent version with Rattle. Colin Davis's direction
is at its best in the opening movement, as crisply rhythmic as you could like, and in the slow
movement Bream is raptly inspirational, particularly at the close, while the analogue sound is full and
atmospheric. This is offered, coupled with concertos by Malcolm Arnold and Richard Rodney
Bennett.

Maybe the Gardiner version has a little extra dash and, for those who prefer an all-Rodrigo
programme, this could be a good choice. With outer movements offering strong dynamic contrasts
and some pungent accents, especially in the orchestra – emphasized by the bright, digital sound – the
music's flamenco associations are underlined and the famous *Adagio* is played in a very free,
improvisatory way, with some highly atmospheric wind solos in the orchestra. The whole presentation
is immensely vivid, and Gardiner's dynamism ensures that the wind solos in the outer movements are
made to sparkle. The finale is especially crisp rhythmically. The balance is natural, with the guitar
heard in a convincing perspective with the orchestra, although there is a hint of harshness on
orchestral tuttis. The *Fantasia para un gentilhombre* is mellower at its noble opening, but Leo
Brouwer, himself a guitarist, brings plenty of orchestral vitality to the later sections of the score. The
Tres Piezas españolas add to the value of the disc: the second piece, a Passacaglia, is one of Rodrigo's
finest shorter works, and both this and the *Homage to Falla* show Bream at his most inspirationally
spontaneous. The alternative coupling is with concertos by Berkeley and Brouwer.

The later, EMI recording of the *Concierto* with Rattle is also hugely enjoyable in a slightly more
relaxed way. This is not to suggest a lack of point and alertness but, with warmer, somewhat more
modern digital sound, the effect is more opulent. The glorious cor anglais solo by Peter Walden at the
opening of the *Adagio* immediately creates a more romantic atmosphere, although Bream maintains
his ruminative, improvisatory style convincingly. The finale is engagingly spirited and lighthearted. In
the end choice will depend on couplings.

(i) *Concierto de Aranjuez;* (ii) *Concierto madrigal* for two guitars.

☞ (M) ** DG 439 526-2 [id.]. Narciso Yepes; (i) Spanish R. & TV O, Alonso; (ii) with Godelieve
Monden, Philh. O, Navarro – BACARISSE: *Concertino.* **

Yepes is hauntingly improvisational in the famous *Adagio* of the *Concierto de Aranjuez*, but Alonso's
is a routine accompaniment, especially in the finale, which is rhythmically stiff. The 1969 sound is
also dated. The *Concierto madrigal* (with Monden the excellent second guitarist) is a different matter.
Each of the twelve delightful miniatures which make up this work springs vividly to life, and the 1979
recording is first class.

(i; ii) *Concierto de Aranjuez; Fantasia para un gentilhombre;* (iii; ii) *Cançoneta for violin and strings;* (i)
Invocación y danza; 3 Pieces.

☞ (M) *(*) Ph. Dig. 438 016-2; *438 016-4* [id.]. (i) Pepe Romero; (ii) ASMF, Marriner; (iii) Augustin
Léo Ara.

These performances rarely rise above the routine and sound as if the performers had played the music
one time too many; even the solo guitar items are lacking in electricity. The exception is the novelty,
the charming trifle for violin and strings, but this lasts for barely three minutes.

PIANO MUSIC

Music for 2 pianos: (i) *5 Piezas infantiles* (piano, 4 hands): *Atardecer; Gran marcha de los subsecretarios; Sonatina para dos Muñecas;* (solo piano): *Air de ballet sur le nom d'une jeune fille; Album de Cecilia; A l'ombre de Torre Bermeja; Bagatela; Berceuse d'automne; Berceuse de printemps; Danza de la Amapola; 3 Danzas de españa; 4 Estampas andaluzas; 3 Evocaciones; Pastorale; 4 Piezas (Caleseras: Homenaje a Chueca; Fandango del Ventorrillo; Plegaria de la Infanta de Castilla; Danza Valenciana); Preludio de Añoranza; Preludio al Gallo mañanero; Serenata española; Sonada de adiós (Hommage à Paul Dukas); 5 Sonatas de Castilla, con Toccata a modo de Pregón: Nos. 1–2 in F sharp min.; 3 in D; 4 in B min. (como un tiento); 5 in A. Suite: Zarabanda lejana.*
🏵 *** Bridge BCD 9027 A/B [id.]. Gregory Allen (i) with Anton Nel.

Rodrigo's keyboard music is all but unknown and, as this first-class and comprehensive survey shows, for all its eclecticism it is well worth exploring. In his earliest piano work, the *Suite* of 1923, with its sprightly *Prelude,* cool *Sicilienne* and Satie-ish minuet, the link with the French idiom is obvious, while the glittering brilliance of the *Preludio al Gallo mañanero* is unmistakably Debussian. If here the influences are unassimilated, later Rodrigo's use of French impressionism is entirely conscious. The soft melancholy of the last piano piece Rodrigo wrote, in 1987, *Preludio de Añoranza* poignantly recalls the refined delicacy of atmosphere one finds in Ravel. There are other influences too. The *Cinq Sonatas de Castilla* look back further in time and draw continually on the keyboard writing of Scarlatti. But they are spiced with piquant dissonances which the Italian composer would have disowned. The *Serenata española* marks Rodrigo's positive adoption of an overtly Andalusian style, while the *Cuatro Piezas* and the *Cuatro estampas andaluzas* are as sharply Spanish in character as any of the similarly picaresque miniatures of Granados or Albéniz. Rodrigo's children's pieces have especial charm. The delectable *Sonatina para dos Muñecas* (two puppets) was designed for four very small hands, those of his grandchildren, Cecilita and Patty, who gave the première at the tender ages of nine and twelve respectively! The darker side of Rodrigo's nature, sometimes brooding, sometimes nostalgic, is at its most expressive in the nocturne, *Atardecer,* an ambitious piece for two players; but it also colours some of the miniatures, not least the austere yet deeply felt *Plegaria de la Infanta de Castilla* from the *Cuatro Piezas.* The recording is uncommonly real and has great presence. In the duo works Allen is admirably partnered by Anton Nel.

Roman, Johan Helmich (1694–1758)

(i) *Violin concertos: in D min.; E flat; F min.; Sinfonias: in A; D and F.*
*** BIS Dig. CD 284 [id.]. (i) Nils-Erik Sparf; Orpheus Chamber Ens.

None of the *Sinfonias* have appeared on disc before. Of the five *Violin concertos,* the three recorded here are certainly attractive pieces, particularly in such persuasive hands as those of Nils-Erik Sparf and the Orpheus Chamber Ensemble, drawn from the Stockholm Philharmonic. Very stylish and accomplished performances that are scholarly in approach.

The Golovin music.
*** Cap. Dig. CAP 1325. Drottningholm Bar. Ens.

Count Golovin was the Russian Ambassador to the Swedish Court at the time of the coronation of the twelve-year-old tsar, Peter II, in 1728; for the festivities at his residence Roman provided what has been described as 'a generous bouquet of orchestral pieces', 45 movements in all, of which the Drottningholm Baroque Ensemble have recorded two dozen. The music has a good deal of charm; here it is recorded not only on period instruments but in the original acoustic in which the music was first heard. An attractive disc.

Suites: in D (Lilla Drottningsholmsmusiquen); G min. (Sjukmans-musiquen); (i) Piante amiche.
☞ *** Musica Sveciae Dig. MSCD 417 [id.]. (i) Pia-Maria Nilsson; Stockholm Nat. Museum CO, Claude Génetay.

In the seventeenth century Sweden imported talent, as did the Tsarist Court in the eighteenth. Roman is the first major native composer: hence the appellation he acquired as 'the Father of Swedish music'. The *Drottningholm Music* (1744) which Roman composed for the wedding festivities of the Crown Prince, Adolf Frederick, is familiar from various earlier recordings, but the D major suite of dances known as the *Little Drottningholm Music* consists of 17 dances, all from the same year, none of which appear in the larger collection. They have all the grace and charm we associate with this genial and attractive composer, and the somewhat earlier *Sjukmans-musiquen,* written for the opening of a hospital in the late 1720s, has no less appeal. The performances by the Stockholm National Museum Orchestra under one of the pioneers of the early-music revival in the 1950s, the late Claude Génetay, convey real pleasure in the music-making. The orchestra use modern instruments and play with an animation and sensitivity that is quite captivating. The disc includes a short cantata probably (but not certainly) by Roman, *Piante amiche*, which is attractive whatever its authenticity, and nicely sung too by Pia-Maria Nilsson. The recorded sound is well balanced and truthful.

(i) *Assaggi for violin in A, in C min. and in G min., Be RI 301, 310 & 320;* (i; ii) *Violin and harpsichord sonata No. 12 in D, Be RI 212;* (ii) *Harpsichord sonata No. 9 in D min., Be RI 233.*
*** Cap. CAP 21344 [id.]. (i) Jaap Schröder; (ii) Johann Sönnleitner.

The *Assaggi* (essays) recorded here often take one by surprise, particularly when played with such imagination as they are by Jaap Schröder. The harpsichord sonata is also more inward-looking than many others of Roman's pieces, and the only work that one could possibly describe as fairly predictable is the opening *Sonata for violin and continuo*. Excellent performances and recording, as well as exemplary presentation.

Ropartz, Joseph Guy (1864–1955)

Symphony No. 3 (for soloists, chorus and orchestra).
☞ (M) *** EMI Dig. CDM7 64689-2 [id.]. Pollet, Stutzman, Dran, Vassar, Orféon Donostiarra Ch., Toulouse Capitole O, Plasson.

Like the Magnard symphonies, the *Third Symphony* of Ropartz has much nobility and there is a sense of scale and grandeur. It takes over 55 minutes and the composer himself apparently retained a lifelong affection for it. It dates from 1905; half a century later, Honegger had planned to put it on LP; alas, both musicians died that same year. There is much in the pantheistic vision of its opening pages that one cannot fail to respond to, and some felicitous harmonic invention. The fugato in the second movement is a little reminiscent of d'Indy, and it is with this sensibility rather than that of Debussy that this work has greatest affinity. There is a certain unrelieved thickness of texture, particularly in the finale; for a work of these dimensions, one feels the need for stronger dramatic contrast and variety of pace. However, there is a personality here, and all lovers of French music will find it rewarding. Even if the recording (and some of the solo singing) is not of the very highest order, the orchestral playing under Michel Plasson is thoroughly committed.

Rore, Cipriano da (c. 1515–65)

Missa Praeter rerum seriem. Motets: *Ave regina; Descendit in hortum meum; Infelix ego; Parce mihi.*
☞ *** Gimell Dig. CDGIM 29; *1585T-29* [id.]. Tallis Scholars, Peter Phillips (with JOSQUIN DES PRES: Motet: *Praeter rerum seriem* ***).

The latest find of the Tallis Scholars is Cipriano da Rore, Josquin's successor at the Italian Court d'Este at Ferrara. His *Missa Praeter rerum seriem* is appropriately preceded by the richly textured six-part Josquin motet based on the same melodic sequence. There is no doubt that the two works are connected, so perhaps Rore's piece was intended as a tribute to his illustrious predecessor. It is a worthy accolade, lyrically powerful, contrapuntally fascinating, spiritually serene and beautifully sung by these highly experienced singers, whose director knows just how to pace and inflect its linear detail and shape its overall structure. The four motets are hardly less impressive, and Gimell's recording, as ever, is virtually flawless.

Rosenberg, Hilding (1892–1985)

Orfeus i sta'n (Orpheus in town): ballet suite; (i) *Sinfonia concertante for violin, viola, oboe, bassoon and orchestra;* (ii) *Violin concerto No. 1. Symphony Nos. 3 (The Four Ages of Man;* 1939 version); (iii) *4 (Johannes Uppenbarelse: The Revelation of St John the Divine):* excerpts; (iv) *5 (Ortagårdsmästaren); (v) Den heliga natten (The Holy Night); (vi) Suite in D: Pastorale.*
☞ (***) Caprice mono CAP 21510 (3) [id.]. Swedish RO or Stockholm PO, composer; with (i) Barter, Berglund, Lännerholm, Lavér; (ii) Charles Barkel; (iii) Anders de Wahl, Swedish R. Ch.; (iv) Lorri Lail, Swedish R. Ch.; (v) Björker, Lail, Lindberg-Torlind, Nilsson, Ohlson, Saedén, Widgren, Chamber Ch.; (vi) Lotte Andriesson.

The majority of these Archive recordings come from Swedish Radio steel tapes (each reel weighing something like 15 kilos!) made between 1940 and 1947. Two (the suite from the ballet, *Orpheus in Town*, and Rosenberg's Christmas oratorio, *The Holy Night*) come from the late 1940s and were originally issued on 78-r.p.m. shellac discs. The ballet shows the sophisticated man-about-town side of the composer and is inventive and witty, while his inspiration in the oratorio is spread rather thin – despite some memorable singing from the baritone, Erik Saedén. There is nothing thin about the *Third Symphony* (1939), another powerful score, heard here in its original form. Originally it was based on Romain Rolland's *The Four Ages of Man* and was interspersed with narration before each of the four movements. (On this CD, which the composer himself recorded in the 1970s, he reads the narrative.) Its Scherzo also included an elaborate fugal section. In the late 1940s Rosenberg dropped the programme and cut the fugue, and it was in this form that Tor Mann (Decca) and later Herbert Blomstedt (Swedish EMI) recorded it. The composer's own pacing, particularly in the first movement, is more expansive and leisurely (and, above all, convincing) than either of his compatriots, and the same measured style emerges in the excerpts from the *Fourth Symphony* (*The Revelation of St John the Divine*), recorded in 1940 with narrator rather than baritone. (Incidentally, if you imagine that an off-air radio recording from 1940 will be primitive, you will be quite taken aback by the immediacy of the sound.) The revelation for most collectors will not be *St John the Divine* but the *Fifth Symphony* (1944) for soprano, chorus and orchestra, whose subtitle is prosaically translated as *The Gardener*. Like the *Fourth*, it is based on a mixture of biblical texts and Hjalmar Gullberg, but it has a serenity, eloquence and strength which are very striking. There are the occasional resonances of Nielsen at his most pensive, but for the most part it finds Rosenberg at his most deeply characteristic best; it is an amazing reflection on the judgement of the Swedish musical establishment that nearly half a century after its première in 1944 it still awaits a commercial recording. The *Sinfonia concertante* is a good piece in neo-classical idiom (sounding like a Swedish Martinů) but the *Violin concerto No. 1* is of lesser interest and finds the composer in manufactured mode. It is good to hear him as pianist, accompanying Lotte Andriesson in 1935 in the *Pastorale* movement from his *Suite in D* for violin and piano. The documentation could not be more comprehensive or researched more scrupulously, and there is an excellent article by Carl-Gunnar Ahlen. A valuable issue of great documentary interest.

Symphony No. 4 (Johannes Uppenbarelse: The Revelation of St John the Divine).
☞ *** Caprice Dig. CAP 21429. Håkan Hagegård, Swedish R. Ch., Pro Musica Ch., Rilke Ens., Gothenburg SO, Ehrling.

Rosenberg is the leading Swedish composer of his generation and the most important after Stenhammar, with whom he studied briefly in the 1920s. His remarkable 80-minute symphony-oratorio to texts from the Bible and by the Swedish poet, Hjalmar Gullberg, is for large forces and is a powerful work of real vision. It was written in 1940 at the time of the Nazi invasion of Denmark and Norway and the fall of France. Its opening fourths recall the world of Walton's *Belshazzar's feast* or of Hindemith, and one's thoughts occasionally turn to Honegger's *King David*. There are purely orchestral movements, orchestral movements interspersed with choral interjections, chorales for unaccompanied choir and recitatives for baritone and brass. The biblical text inspires the most vividly expressive music, while the Gullberg poems are in an archaic and often serene style. Despite occasional longueurs, the overall impact of this score is very powerful. A splendid performance, very well recorded, though it needs to be played at a slightly higher level setting than usual.

Rossi, Luigi (1597–1663)

Oratorio per la Settimana Santa; Un peccator pentito (Spargete sospiri).
*** HM Dig. HMC 901297; *HMC 401297* [id.]. Soloists, Les Arts Florissants, William Christie.

William Christie and his talented period-performance group here revive one of the earliest examples of an oratorio. Complete with demons, singing solo and in chorus, it graphically tells the story of Christ's judgment before Pontius Pilate and His Crucifixion, including a magnificent lament for the Virgin Mary, a vigorous last chorus of demons and a superb final madrigal. The extra item is an equally moving motet setting a poem by Giovanni Lotti. The full and bright recording gives an edge to string tone.

Orfeo (opera; complete).
**(*) HM Dig. HMC 901358/60 (3); *HMC 401358/60* (3) [id.]. Mellon, Zanetti, Piau, Favat, Fouchécourt, Salzmann, Corréas, Deletré, Les Arts Florissants, Christie.

Luigi Rossi's *Orfeo* has a much more complex classical story than the Monteverdi, yet in its artificial way it is less effectively dramatic. Even so, it offers such incidental delights as a slanging match between Venus (enemy of Orfeo, when he represents marital fidelity) and Juno. That hint of a classical send-up adds sparkle, contrasting with the tragic emotions conveyed both in Orfeo's deeply expressive solos and in magnificent Monteverdi-like choruses. William Christie draws characteristically lively and alert playing from Les Arts Florissants, but his cast is not as consistent as those he usually has in his Harmonia Mundi recordings. Too many of the singers sound fluttery or shallow, and even Agnes Mellon as Orfeo is less even and sweet of tone than usual. Nevertheless this makes a most welcome recording of an important rarity.

Rossini, Gioacchino (1792–1868)

La boutique fantasque (ballet, arr. Respighi) complete.
⊛ (M) *** Sony Dig. MDK 46508 [id.]. Toronto SO, Andrew Davis – BIZET: *L'Arlésienne: suite No. 2 etc.* **(*)
(M) **(*) Decca Dig. 430 723-2; *430 723-4* [id.]. National PO, Bonynge – CHOPIN: *Les Sylphides.* **(*)

At last comes a really outstanding complete CD of *La boutique fantasque*. The Toronto orchestra is on peak form, playing with glittering bravura and warmth; the gentler second half of the ballet is particularly enticing. The digital recording has a spectacularly wide dynamic range; the magical opening (here taken faster than usual) with gentle pizzicato strings evoking gleaming horn chords, at first a mere whisper, then expands gloriously.

Bonynge goes for sparkle and momentum above all in Respighi's brilliant arrangement of Rossini. The Decca recording has great brilliance and the orchestral colours glitter within the Kingsway Hall ambience. But compare the very opening with Andrew Davis, and here there is much less magic and – more surprisingly – less atmosphere, while the dynamic range of the Toronto recording is much more dramatic.

La boutique fantasque: extended suite.
☞ (M) *** BMG/RCA 09026 61847-2 [id.]. Boston Pops O, Arthur Fiedler – OFFENBACH: *Gaîté parisienne.* *** ⊛

Fiedler offers nearly half an hour of the ballet, not missing out much of importance. The performance sparkles, the playing has warmth and finesse and the Boston acoustics add the necessary atmosphere at the magically evocative opening. John Pfeiffer's remastering of this 1956 recording leaves little to be desired and the coupling is indispensable.

La boutique fantasque (ballet, arr. Respighi): *suite.*
(M) **(*) Chan. CHAN 6503; *MBTD 6503* [id.]. SNO, Gibson – DUKAS: *L'apprenti sorcier;* SAINT-SAENS: *Danse macabre.* **(*)
(M) **(*) Sony SBK 46340 [id.]. Phd. O, Ormandy – TCHAIKOVSKY: *Sleeping Beauty:* highlights. **

Gibson's version of the suite is strikingly atmospheric. Helped by the glowing acoustics of Glasgow's City Hall, the opening has much evocation. The orchestra is on its toes and plays with warmth and zest, and the 1973 recording has transferred vividly to CD.

Ormandy presents Respighi's glittering orchestration with much brilliance and dash, and the Philadelphia Orchestra has all the sumptuousness one could ask for. This is more extrovert music-making than Gibson's and it is undoubtedly exhilarating, even if the effect of the recording is less refined.

Introduction, theme and variations in C min. for clarinet and orchestra.
*** ASV Dig. CDDCA 559; *ZCDCA 559* [id.]. Emma Johnson, ECO, Groves – CRUSELL: *Concerto No. 2* *** ⊛; BAERMANN: *Adagio* ***; WEBER: *Concertino.* ***

As in all her recordings, Emma Johnson's lilting timbre and sensitive control of dynamic bring imaginative light and shade to the melodic line. Brilliance for its own sake is not the keynote, but her relaxed pacing is made to sound exactly right. Vivid recording.

Overtures: *Armida; Il barbiere di Siviglia; Bianca e Faliero; La cambiale di matrimonio; La Cenerentola; Demetrio e Poblibio; Edipo a Colono; Edoardo e Cristina;* (i) *Ermione. La gazza ladra; L'inganno felice; L'Italiana in Algeri; Maometto II; Otello.* (i) *Ricciardo e Zoraide. La scala di seta; Semiramide; Le siège de Corinthe; Il Signor Bruschino; Tancredi; Il Turco in Italia; Torvaldo e Dorliska; Il viaggio a Reims; William Tell. Sinfonia al Conventello; Sinfonia di Bologna.*
(M) *** Ph. 434 016-2 (3) [id.]. ASMF, Marriner; (i) with Amb. S.

Marriner's three discs span all Rossini's overtures, but one must remember that the early Neapolitan operas, with the exception of *Ricciardo e Zoraide* and *Ermione*, make do with a simple Prelude, leading into the opening chorus. *Ricciardo e Zoraide*, however, is an extended piece (12 minutes 25 seconds), with the choral entry indicating that the introduction is at an end. *Maometto II* is on a comparable scale, while the more succinct *Armida* is an example of Rossini's picturesque evocation, almost like a miniature tone-poem. Twenty-four overtures plus two sinfonias make a delightful package in such sparkling performances, which eruditely use original orchestrations. Full, bright and atmospheric recording, spaciously reverberant, admirably transferred to CD, with no artificial brilliance.

Overtures: *Il barbiere di Siviglia; La cambiale di matrimonio; L'inganno felice; L'Italiana in Algeri; La scala di seta; Il Signor Bruschino; Tancredi; Il Turco in Italia.*
*** DG Dig. 415 363-2 [id.]. Orpheus CO.

The Orpheus Chamber Orchestra displays astonishing unanimity of style and ensemble in this splendid collection of Rossini overtures, played without a conductor. Not only is the crispness of string phrasing a joy, but the many stylish wind solos have an attractive degree of freedom. These are performances that in their refinement and apt chamber scale give increasing pleasure with familiarity. The DG recording is marvellously real with the perspective perfectly judged.

Overtures: *Il barbiere di Siviglia; La Cenerentola; La gazza ladra; L'Italiana in Algeri; La scala di seta; Semiramide; Il Signor Bruschino; William Tell.*
☞ (M) (***) EMI CDM7 67804-2 [id.]. Philh. O, Carlo Maria Giulini.

Giulini's performances derive from two LP sources, recorded in 1961 and 1965. The performances offer characteristically refined Philharmonia playing, with Giulini's careful attention to detail balanced by a strong sense of drama; although these are not the most genial performances on record, they are strong in personality. The performance of *William Tell* is outstanding for the beauty of the cello playing at the opening and the affectionate detail of the pastoral section. There is generous measure here (nearly 71 minutes) – it is a great pity that there must be the strongest reservations about the effect of the digital remastering, which brings the most aggressively fierce glare on the violins in fortissimo: the opening of *La scala di seta* is quite spoilt by the sound, which robs the music of all its elegance.

Overtures: *Il barbiere di Siviglia; La Cenerentola; La gazza ladra; L'Italiana in Algeri; Le siège de Corinthe; Il Signor Bruschino.*
(M) *** DG 419 869-2 [id.]. LSO, Abbado.

Brilliant, sparkling playing, with splendid discipline, vibrant rhythms and finely articulated phrasing – altogether invigorating and bracing. There is perhaps an absence of outright geniality here, but these are superb performances and this remains one of the very finest collections of Rossini overtures ever, for the wit is spiced with a touch of acerbity, and the flavour is of a vintage dry champagne which retains its bloom, yet has a subtlety all its own.

Overtures: *Il barbiere di Siviglia; La Cenerentola; La gazza ladra; La scala di seta; Il Signor Bruschino; William Tell.*
⊛ (M) *** BMG/RCA GD 60387 [60387-2-RG]. Chicago SO, Fritz Reiner.

As with the others in RCA's remastered Reiner/Chicago series, the 1958 sound-quality has been improved phenomenally; they are preferable to most digital collections. The blaze of brass tone, supported by a rich orchestral backcloth and resonant bass drum, at the gallop in the *William Tell* overture, is all-engulfing, a thrilling moment indeed; at the same time the scurrying violins display the utmost virtuosity. But it is the sparkle and vivacity of these performances that one remembers above all – and, in *La Cenerentola*, the wit, as well as fizzing orchestral bravura. One would have liked the opening flourish of *La scala di seta* to be neater – it is presented too lavishly here – but this is the solitary reservation over a magnificent achievement.

Overtures: *Il barbiere di Siviglia; La gazza ladra; L'Italiana in Algeri; La scala di seta; Semiramide; William Tell.*
☞ (B) **(*) DG 439 415-2 [id.]. BPO, Karajan.

This 1971 collection has been in and out of the catalogue regularly over the past two decades. Now it returns on DG's latest Classikon bargain label. Karajan's virtuoso performances are polished like fine silver. The main allegro of *La scala di seta* abandons all decorum when played as fast as this, and elsewhere bravura often takes precedence over poise. However, with the Berlin Philharmonic on sparkling form, there is wit as well as excitement. The recording was made (like so many other vintage Karajan recordings) in the Berlin Jesus-Christus-Kirche, but the remastering casts very bright lighting on the upper range, which makes sonic brilliance approach aggressiveness in some climaxes.

Overtures: *Il barbiere di Siviglia; La gazza ladra; L'Italiana in Algeri; La scala di seta; Il Signor Bruschino; Semiramide; William Tell.*
⊛ *** EMI Dig. CDC7 54091-2 [id.]. L. Classical Players, Norrington.

It is the drums that take a star role in Norrington's Rossini collection. They make their presence felt at the beginning and end of an otherwise persuasively styled reading of *Il barbiere*; at the introduction of *La gazza ladra*, where the snares rattle spectacularly and antiphonally; creating tension more distinctly than usual at the beginning of *Semiramide*, and bringing tumultuous thunder to the Storm sequence in *William Tell*. Of course the early wind instruments are very characterful too, with plenty of piquant touches: the oboe colouring is nicely spun in *L'Italiana in Algeri* and properly nimble in *La scala di seta*, a particularly engaging performance, mainly because of the woodwind chirpings. The brass also make their mark, with the stopped notes on the hand horns adding character to the solo quartet in *Semiramide*, and both horns and trumpets giving a brilliant edge to the announcement of the galop in *William Tell*. The strings play with relative amiability and a proper sense of line and are obviously determined to please the ear as well as to stimulate; altogether these performances offer a very refreshing new look over familiar repertoire. The recording is first class.

Overtures: *Il barbiere di Siviglia; La gazza ladra; La scala di seta; Semiramide; William Tell.*
☞ (B) **(*) Decca 433 606-2. LSO, Gamba.

Pierino Gamba's 1961 bargain collection wears its years lightly. His performances are taut and involving, the orchestral playing alive and polished. A strong disciplining force is felt in every piece, and care in phrasing is noticeable at every turn. The only quality missing is a touch of geniality – but, even so, *La scala di seta* is not overdriven. The very good recording re-emerges vividly and with plenty of ambient atmosphere, but the brightly lit violins, although not edgy, have a slightly artificial timbre.

Semiramide: Overture.
☞ (***) Testament mono SBT 1015 [id.]. BBC SO, Toscanini – BRAHMS: *Symphony No. 2* (***); MENDELSSOHN: *Midsummer Night's Dream* excerpt. (**)

Toscanini's famous concerts with the BBC Symphony Orchestra were obviously very special. This overture from a 1935 concert has one on the edge of one's seat. Quite electrifying. The sound calls for tolerance – but what playing!

String sonatas Nos. 1–6 (complete).
*** ASV CDDCA 767 [id.]. Serenata of London (members).
*** Hyp. Dig. CDA 66595 [id.]. O of Age of Enlightenment (members).
☞ (B) *** Ph. Duo 434 734-2. I Musici.

String sonatas Nos. 1 in G; 4 in B flat; 5 in E flat; 6 in D.
(M) *** Teldec/Warner 9031 74788-2 [id.]. Liszt CO, János Rolla – M. HAYDN: *Symphony, P.12.* ***

Almost simultaneously, Serenata of London, working as a string quartet, and a comparably sized group from the Orchestra of the Age of Enlightenment, playing period instruments, each manage to include all six of the *String sonatas* – the astonishingly assured work of the twelve-year-old Rossini – on one CD. As might be expected, the Serenata, playing modern instruments and led by the easily brilliant Barry Wilde, give the warmer, more sunny bouquet to Rossini's string textures; their competitors, led by the dazzling Elizabeth Wallfisch, offer a slightly drier vintage, though their approach is by no means unsmiling. Indeed their bass player, ChiChi Nwanoku, brings added sharpness of attack to his moments of bravura, where Michael Brittain, with comparable virtuosity, at times sounds rather deadpan. On both discs the recording is truthful and naturally balanced.

Philips have solved the problem of presenting all six of the *Sonatas*, which in many performances offer too long a playing time to fit on a single CD (in this instance 83 minutes), by placing them on a pair of discs in a slimline jewel-case, offered at the cost of one disc. I Musici play all six works spiritedly and with plenty of Italian sunshine warming the phrasing, which is already pleasingly elegant. There is not the degree of wit that is present in the ASMF/Marriner set, but there is no lack of genial vitality, and the refined naturalness of the early 1970s sound is considerable compensation.

The merits of the Liszt Chamber Orchestra and János Rolla, who directs from the first desk, are by now well known. They are virtuosic and polished, and they have the advantage of very natural digital sound. Moreover the attractive Michael Haydn coupling is considerable compensation for the two missing sonatas, and the disc comes at mid-price.

Cantata: *Giovanna d'Arco*. Songs: *L'âme délaissée; Ariette à l'ancienne; Beltà crudele; Canzonetta spagnuola (En medio a mis colores); La grande coquette (Ariette pompadour); La légende de Marguerite; Mi lagnerò tacendo* (5 settings including *Sorzico* and *Stabat Mater*); *Nizza; L'Orpheline du Tyrol (Ballade élégie); La pastorella; La regata veneziana* (3 songs in Venetian dialect); *Il risentimento; Il trovatore.*
*** Decca Dig. 430 518-2 [id.]. Cecilia Bartoli, Charles Spencer.

The songs of Rossini's old age were not all trivial, and this brilliantly characterized selection – with the pianist as imaginative as the singer – gives a delightful cross-section. Bartoli's artistry readily encompasses such a challenge, a singer who, even at this early stage of her career, is totally in command both technically and artistically. The recording, too, has splendid presence.

Stabat Mater.
⊛ *** Chan. Dig. CHAN 8780; *ABTD 1416* [id.]. Field, Della Jones, A. Davies, Earle, London Symphony Ch., City of L. Sinfonia, Hickox.

In his setting of *Stabat Mater* Rossini may upset the squeamish by having rip-roaring tunes, like the tenor's rumbustious march-setting of *Cujus animam* or the jaunty quartet setting of *Sancta Mater* with its persistent oom-pah rhythms. Richard Hickox rightly presents it warmly with gutsy strength. This is a most winning account which has one marvelling that a work written piecemeal should have such consistently memorable invention, much of it anticipating – or reflecting – early Verdi. All four soloists here are first rate, not Italianate of tone but full and warm, and the London Symphony Chorus sings with fine attack as well as producing the most refined pianissimos in the unaccompanied quartet, here as usual given to the full chorus rather than to the soloists. Full-bodied and atmospheric sound.

OPERA

Armida (complete).
*** Koch Europa Dig. 350211 [id.]. Gasdia, Merritt, Matteuzzi, Ford, Furlanetto, Workman, Amb. Op. Ch., I Sol. Ven., Scimone.

Armida is one of the most distinctive of the serious operas that Rossini wrote for Naples in the years after the *Barber of Seville*. Armida has some marvellous fire-eating moments of display, particularly in the last act, when the knight, Rinaldo, finally manages to resist her magic and escape. Her realization of defeat, dramatically conveyed on a repeated monotone, is intensely human. As Armida, Cecilia Gasdia may not be strikingly characterful (Maria Callas knew the role) but her singing is both powerful and agile, firm and bold in Rossini's brilliant coloratura. As for the problem of finding three high *bel canto* tenors capable of tackling elaborate ornamentation, William Matteuzzi and Bruce Ford more than match Chris Merritt as Rinaldo. Though the principal, he is the least gainly of the three, but still impressive, notably in the love duets with Armida. Ferruccio Furlanetto is excellent in two bass roles, and a fourth tenor, Charles Workman, might well have stood in for any of the others. The booklet includes an introduction in English, but no translation of the Italian libretto.

L'assedio di Corinto (The siege of Corinth; complete).
☞ (M) **(*) EMI CMS7 64335-2 (3). Sills, Verrett, Diaz, Theyard, Howell, Lloyd, Amb. Op. Ch., LSO, Schippers.

The siege of Corinth, like other Rossini operas, had a chequered history. In its final form (*Le siège de Corinthe,* in French) it was produced in Paris in 1826, a reworking of an earlier *opera seria, Maometto II,* given in Naples six years earlier. Thomas Schippers, the conductor here, first edited the score for a revival at La Scala, Milan, in 1969, and he then made this recording in London in 1974 in preparation for another production at the Met. in New York with virtually the same cast. The pity is that he has encouraged the coloratura prowess of the prima donna, Beverly Sills, at the expense of Rossini's final thoughts, with display material from the earlier version. Many Rossinians will no doubt remain untroubled by academic points, in gratitude that so much inspired music has been brought to the gramophone. Some of the most striking passages are the patriotic choruses, recognizably Rossinian but not at all in the usual vein. Sills, as so often on record, is variable, brilliant in coloratura but rarely sweet of tone, and she is completely upstaged by Shirley Verrett, singing magnificently as Neocle. Some strong singing too among the others, though not all the men are very deft with ornamentation. The recording, made at All Saints', Tooting, has plenty of atmosphere and has achieved a very satisfactory CD transfer.

Il barbiere di Siviglia (complete).

*** Decca Dig. 425 520-2 (3) [id.]. Cecilia Bartoli, Nucci, Matteuzzi, Fissore, Burchuladze, Ch. & O of Teatro Comunale di Bologna, Patanè.

☞ *** Teldec/Warner Dig. 9031 74885-2 (2) [id.]. Hagegård, Larmore, Giménez, Corbelli, Ramey, Lausanne CO, López-Cobos.

(м) *** EMI CMS7 64162-2 (2) [id.]; (в) CfP *TC-CFPD 4704*. De los Angeles, Alva, Cava, Wallace, Bruscantini, Glyndebourne Festival Ch., RPO, Gui.

*** EMI CDS7 47634-8 (2) [Ang. CDCB 47634]. Callas, Gobbi, Alva, Ollendorff, Philh. Ch. & O, Galliera.

☞ (в) *** Naxos Dig. 8.660027/29 [id.]. Ganassi, Serville, Vargas, Romero, De Grandis, Hungaria R. Ch., Failoni CO, Budapest, Will Humburg.

(м) *** BMG/RCA GD 86505 (3) [RCA 6505-2-RG]. Roberta Peters, Valletti, Merrill, Corena, Tozzi, Met. Op. Ch. & O, Leinsdorf.

☞ **(*) DG Dig. 435 763-2 (3) [id.]. Domingo, Battle, Lopardo, Raimondi, Ch. & COE, Abbado.

☞ *(*) EMI Dig. CDS7 54863-2 (3) [id.]. Hadley, Hampson, Ramey, Pratico, Mentzer, O della Toscana, Gelmetti.

Cecilia Bartoli made this recording when she was still in her early twenties, a mezzo with a rich, vibrant voice who not only copes brilliantly with the technical demands but who also gives a sparkling, provocative characterization. In her big Act I aria, *Una voce poco fa*, she even outshines the memorable Agnes Baltsa on the excellent Marriner set. Like the conductor, Bartoli is wonderful at bringing out the fun. So is Leo Nucci, and he gives a beautifully rounded portrait of the wily barber. Burchuladze, unidiomatic next to the others, still gives a monumentally lugubrious portrait of Basilio, and the Bartolo of Enrico Fissore is outstanding, with the patter song wonderfully articulated at Patanè's sensible speed.

López-Cobos conducts a scintillating performance, helped by brilliant ensembles, generally taken at high speed, with rhythms sprung delectably. Though Håkan Hagegård is a dry-toned Figaro, the recording sets him in a helpful ambience, which equally helps to enhance the comic atmosphere, with the interplay of characters well managed. There are few more stylish Rossini tenors today than Raúl Giménez and, though his voice is not as youthful as some, his musical imagination goes with fine flexibility and point. As for Jennifer Larmore, she is an enchanting Rosina, both firm and rich of tone and wonderfully agile. Crisply consistent, it makes a strong contender among modern digital versions, even next to the delectable Decca version featuring Cecilia Bartoli, particularly when it comes (with a minimal cut) on two discs instead of three.

Victoria de los Angeles is as charming a Rosina as you will ever find: no viper this one, as she claims in *Una voce poco fa*, and that matches the gently rib-nudging humour of what is otherwise a 1962 recording of the Glyndebourne production. It does not fizz as much as other Glyndebourne Rossini on record but, with a characterful line-up of soloists, it is an endearing performance which in its line is unmatched. The recording still sounds well. Tape collectors should be very well satisfied with the CfP equivalent, issued at bargain price on two cassettes in a chunky box, with synopsis instead of libretto.

Gobbi and Callas were here at their most inspired and, with the recording quality nicely refurbished, the EMI is an outstanding set, not absolutely complete in its text, but so crisp and sparkling it can be confidently recommended. Callas remains supreme as a minx-like Rosina, summing up the character superbly in *Una voce poco fa*. The early stereo sound comes up very acceptably on a pair of CDs, clarified to a degree, presenting a uniquely characterful performance with new freshness and immediacy.

With the comic interplay vividly conveyed, with some excellent singing and with first-rate playing from the Failoni Chamber Orchestra of Budapest, the Naxos set makes a first-rate bargain, very well recorded in good, modern, digital sound. Though the cast is not as starry as with most full-price rivals, the singing is hardly less stylish, with Sonia Ganassi a rich-toned Rosina, controlling vibrato well, and with Ramon Vargas an agile and attractively youthful-sounding Almaviva. Roberto Serville as Figaro may not have as distinctive a voice as many rivals but, helped by the conductor, he conveys the fun of the role brilliantly. The *buffo* characters are strongly cast too, with Basilio's *La calunnia* (Franco de Grandis) delightfully enlivened by comments from Bartolo (Angelo Romero), both very much involved in their roles. Will Humburg's often brisk speeds, with crisp recitative matched by dazzling ensembles, never prevent the music (and the singers) from breathing. The only reservation is that the glowing Glyndebourne version under Gui with Victoria de los Angeles as Rosina comes (on only two discs) at an even more reasonable price, though with a text not quite so complete.

Roberta Peters is a sparkling Rosina, a singer too little known in Europe, who here lives up to her high reputation at the Met., dazzling in coloratura elaborations *in alt*. Robert Merrill may not be a specially comic Figaro, but the vocal characterization is strong, with the glorious voice consistently firm and well focused. Valletti, Corena and Tozzi make up a formidable team, and Leinsdorf conducts with a lightness and relaxation rare for him on record. Good, clear sound of the period, set against a reverberant, helpful acoustic.

The casting of Plácido Domingo as Figaro in Rossini's *Barber of Seville* suggests some mistake. But no, Domingo, the superstar tenor – who started out as a baritone many years ago, and whose Otello has grown weightier with the years – has here recorded the role of Rossini's barber. On the cover of the DG set, guitar in hand, he is pictured cheerily wearing the regulation costume, heading a cast that would be hard to beat today, including Kathleen Battle, Frank Lopardo and Ruggero Raimondi, with Claudio Abbado conducting the Chamber Orchestra of Europe, as he did in his prize-winning set of Rossini's *Il viaggio a Reims*. So far from being just a gimmick, the irony is that Domingo is the set's biggest success. Compared with his earlier self, Abbado is freer and more spontaneous-sounding, but his touch, as conveyed in dry, close-up sound, is much heavier-handed, missing much of the sparkle of his earlier DG set, with ensemble-work surprisingly rough. Even Raimondi as Basilio in his big aria, *La calunnia*, is relatively undisciplined, if spontaneous-sounding, and the big bangs at the climax are completely miscalculated. Kathleen Battle makes a minx of a Rosina, coy but full of flair, and Frank Lopardo is a stylish Almaviva, though not well contrasted with Domingo.

The wayward conducting of Gianluigi Gelmetti – with speeds on the slow side and rhythms often too square – undermines the fine singing on the EMI set, recorded in Florence. Thomas Hampson makes a superb Figaro but, as recorded in a relatively unhelpful acoustic (surprisingly, a church), the voice lacks some of its usual bloom. Similarly Jerry Hadley is not quite as sweet-toned as usual, though he makes a strong, virile Almaviva. Susanne Mentzer is a characterful Rosina, though the recording tends to exaggerate her rapidly flickering vibrato, not unlike Conchita Supervia's. Even Samuel Ramey as Basilio is not as full-toned as on the Teldec set, recorded at the same period, though in character he is just as effective.

Il barbiere di Siviglia: highlights.
☞ *** Ph. Dig. 438 498-2 [id.] Allen, Baltsa, Araiza, Trimarchi, Lloyd, Amb. Op. Ch., ASMF, Marriner.
(M) *** EMI CDM7 63076-2; *EG 763076-4* (from complete set with Callas; cond. Galliera).
☞ (M) *** EMI CD-EMX 2219 (from above recording with Los Angeles, Bruscantini, Alva; cond. Gui).
☞ **(*) DG Dig. 437 841-2 [id.] (from above recording, with Domingo, Battle, Lopardo; cond. Abbado).

The Philips highlights are well chosen and admirably reflect the qualities of Marriner's deleted complete set, the sound particularly sparkling in the delightful Act II finale. The selection omits the Overture and is not particularly generous (57 minutes).

On EMI, Callas remains supreme as a minx-like Rosina. The highlights disc offers most of the key solo numbers from Act I, while in Act II it concentrates on Rossini's witty ensembles, including the extended Second Act *Quintet*. The *Overture* is included and, while it is stylishly played, it would have been better to have offered more of the vocal music.

An excellent 76 minutes, including the Overture, from Gui's 1962 Glyndebourne set, full of sparkle and fun and without a weak link in the cast and vivaciously conducted by Gui.

Abbado's DG selection is most generous (73 minutes) and will be especially valuable for those wanting to sample Domingo's highly successful assumption of the title-role.

La cambiale di matrimonio ; L'inganno felice; L'occasione fa il ladro; La scala di seta; Il Signor Bruschino (all complete).
☞ (M) ** Claves Dig. CD 50-9200 (8). Soloists (see below), ECO or I Filarmonico di Torini, Marcello Viotti.

The Claves versions of all five of Rossini's one-Act operas, discussed below, here come in a useful package, with the eight discs selling for the price of five. That offer is not specially generous when the performances are so variable and, of the works taking two discs instead of one, each lasts only just over 80 minutes. Like the individual issues, they come with Italian librettos but only summaries of the plots in English.

La cambiale di matrimonio (complete).
☞ * Claves Dig. CD 50-9101 [id.]. Praticò, Rossi, Comencini, De Simone, Facini, Baiano, ECO,
    Viotti.

This was the first of the Claves series to be recorded in London, and unfortunately the venue chosen
was the reverberant All Saints', Tooting. The voices have fair bloom on them, but the orchestra,
rather recessed, sounds washy, a significant flaw in such intimately jolly music, with ensembles
suffering in particular. Viotti is a relaxedly stylish Rossinian, drawing pointed playing from the ECO,
but the singing is poor. The tenor Maurizio Comencini sounds unsteady and strained, while
Alessandra Rossi as the heroine, agile enough, is too shrill for comfort. The best singing comes from
the buffo baritone, Bruno Praticò, as the heroine's father.

La Cenerentola (complete).
☞ *** Decca Dig. 436 902-2 (2) [id.]. Bartoli, Matteuzzi, Corbelli, Dara, Costa, Banditelli, Pertusi,
    Teatro Comunale (Bologna) Ch. & O, Chailly.
*** Ph. Dig. 420 468-2 (2) [id.]. Baltsa, Araiza, Alaimo, Raimondi, Amb. Op. Ch., ASMF,
    Marriner.
(M) (***) EMI mono CMS7 64183-2 (2) [Ang. CDMB 64183]. Gabarain, Oncina, Bruscantini,
    Noni, Glyndebourne Festival Ch. & O, Gui.

Cenerentola has been lucky on record, but Chailly's version sparkles even more brightly than any
predecessor. That is largely thanks to a team of Italian-speaking soloists who recorded the piece in
well-spaced sessions immediately after performing it on the Bologna stage, where the recording took
place. The result has the effervescence of a live performance, with none of the disadvantages of a live
recording. Cecilia Bartoli, one of the most vibrantly exciting singers of the younger generation, makes
an inspired Cenerentola. Her tone-colours are not just more sensuous than those of her rivals: her
imagination and feeling for detail add enormously to her vivid characterization, culminating in a
stunning account of the final rondo, *Non più mesta*. The rest of the cast has been just as carefully
chosen, with William Matteuzzi as an engaging prince, sweeter of tone and more stylish than his
direct rivals, while the contrasting of the bass and baritone roles is ideal between Alessandro Corbelli
as Dandini, Michele Pertusi as the tutor, Alidoro (substitute for the fairy godmother in the Cinderella
story), and Enzo Dara as Don Magnifico. Few Rossini opera-sets have such fizz as this, and the
recording is one of Decca's most vivid.

    Marriner's set of *Cenerentola* conveys Rossinian fun to the full. As in *Il barbiere*, the role of
heroine is taken by the formidable Agnes Baltsa – not so aptly cast this time in a vulnerable
Cinderella role – and that of the hero by Francisco Araiza, sweet and fresh of tone, though still
allowing too many aspirants in passage-work. Ruggero Raimondi's commanding and resonant
singing as Don Magnifico is very satisfying, and there is no weak link in the rest of the cast. The
sound is first class in all respects, nicely resonant with plenty of atmosphere.

    Gui's 1953 recording of *Cenerentola* has mono sound of amazing clarity and immediacy. Sadly the
text is seriously cut, but the effervescence of Gui's live performances at Glyndebourne has been
infectiously caught. Juan Oncina produces the most sweet-toned singing as the Prince, with the
vintage baritone, Sesto Bruscantini, a vividly characterful Dandini, almost another Figaro. The title
role is sung by the Spanish mezzo, Marina de Gabarain, a strikingly positive singer with a sensuous
flicker in the voice, very much in the style of the legendary Conchita Supervia.

Le Comte Ory (complete).
❀ (M) (***) EMI mono CMS7 64180-2 (2) [Ang. CDMB 64180]. Oncina, Roux, Jeannette and
    Monica Sinclair, Glyndebourne Festival Ch. & O, Gui.
❀ *** Ph. Dig. 422 406-2 (2) [id.]. Sumi Jo, Aler, Montague, Cachemaille, Quilico, Pierotti, Lyon Op.
    Ch. & O, Gardiner.

Gui's classic recording of *Le Comte d'Ory*, with the same Glyndebourne forces who gave this
sparkling opera on stage, brings pure delight. In limited but clearly focused mono sound, Gui conveys
an extra sparkle and resilience, even over Gardiner's brilliant Philips version. There is a natural sense
of timing here that regularly has you laughing in joy, as in the dazzling finale of Act I, one of the
most infectiously witty of all recordings of a Rossini ensemble. Juan Oncina in his prime as the
Count, the Hungarian Sari Barabas as the Countess Adèle and Michel Roux as the Count's friend are
superbly matched by Monica Sinclair as the Countess's housekeeper and Ian Wallace as the Count's
tutor. Some 10 minutes of text have been cut, but that allows the complete opera to be fitted on two
CDs, each containing a complete act.

    On Philips, with musical argument more sustained than in other comic pieces of the period,
Rossini's mastery is matched by the performance here, beautifully and sparklingly sung and with

ensembles finely balanced, as in the delectable Act II trio. Gardiner tends to be rather more tense than Gui was, with speeds on the fast side, and he allows too short a dramatic pause for the interruption to the Nuns' drinking choruses. But the precision and point are a delight. Though John Aler hardly sounds predatory enough as the Count, the lightness of his tenor is ideal, and Sumi Jo as Adèle and Diana Montague as the page, Isolier, are both stylish and characterful. So is the clear-toned Gino Quilico as the tutor, Raimbaud. With the cuts of the old Glyndebourne set opened out and with good and warm, if not ideally crystal-clear, recording, this set takes its place as a jewel of a Rossini issue.

La Donna del Lago (complete).
*** Sony Dig. M2K 39311 (2) [id.]. Ricciarelli, Valentini Terrani, Gonzalez, Raffanti, Ramey, Prague Philharmonic Ch., COE, Pollini.

Maurizio Pollini, forsaking the keyboard for the baton, draws a fizzing performance from the Chamber Orchestra of Europe. Katia Ricciarelli in the title-role of Elena, Lady of the Lake, has rarely sung so stylishly on record, the voice creamy and very agile in coloratura. Lucia Valentini Terrani is no less impressive in the travesti role of Elena's beloved, Malcolm; while Samuel Ramey as Elena's father, Douglas, with his darkly incisive singing makes you wish the role was far longer. Of the two principal tenors, Dalmacio Gonzalez, attractively light-toned, is the more stylish; but Dano Raffanti as Rodrigo Dhu copes with equal assurance with the often impossibly high tessitura. The recording is clear and generally well balanced and given added immediacy in the new format.

Elisabetta Regina d'Inghilterra (complete).
(M) *** Ph. 432 453-2 (2) [id.]. Caballé, Carreras, Masterson, Creffield, Benelli, Jenkins, Amb. S., New Philh. O, Masini.

The first surprise in this lively operatic setting of the Elizabeth and Leicester story comes in the overture, which turns out to be the one which we know as belonging to *Il barbiere di Siviglia*. It is one of a whole sequence of self-borrowings which add zest to a generally delightful score. In a well-sprung performance like this, with beautiful playing from the LSO and some very fine singing, it is a set for any Rossinian to investigate. Of the two tenors, José Carreras proves much the more stylish as Leicester, with Ugo Benelli, in the more unusual role of a tenor-villain, singing less elegantly than he once did. Caballé produces some ravishing sounds, though she is not always electrifying. Lively conducting and splendid recording.

Ermione (complete).
(M) *** Erato/Warner Dig. 2292 45790-2 (2) [id.]. Gasdia, Zimmermann, Palacio, Merritt, Matteuzzi, Alaimo, Prague Philharmonic Ch., Monte Carlo PO, Scimone.

Ermione begins very strikingly with an off-stage chorus, introduced in the slow section of the overture, singing a lament on the fall of Troy. The use of dramatic declamation, notably in the final scene of Act II, also gives due weight to the tragedy; however, not surprisingly, Rossini's natural sparkle keeps bursting through, often a little incongruously. Though the three tenors in this Monte Carlo set from Erato are good by modern standards – Ernesto Palacio (Pirro), Chris Merritt (Oreste) and William Matteuzzi (Pilade) – they are uncomfortably strained by the high tessitura and the occasional stratospheric top notes. Cecilia Gasdia makes a powerful Ermione, not always even enough in her production but strong and agile; while Margarita Zimmermann makes a firm, rich Andromaca. Scimone, not always imaginative, yet directs a strong, well-paced performance. The recording is rather dry on the voices, but the hint of boxiness is generally undistracting and this set is a must for true Rossinians.

Guglielmo Tell (*William Tell:* complete, in Italian).
*** Decca 417 154-2 (4) [id.]. Pavarotti, Freni, Milnes, Ghiaurov, Amb. Op. Ch., Nat. PO, Chailly.

Rossini wrote his massive opera about William Tell in French, but Chailly and his team here put forward a strong case for preferring Italian, with its open vowels, in music which glows with Italianate lyricism. Chailly's is a forceful reading, particularly strong in the many ensembles, and superbly recorded. Milnes makes a heroic Tell, always firm, and though Pavarotti has his moments of coarseness he sings the role of Arnoldo with glowing tone. Ghiaurov too is in splendid voice, while subsidiary characters are almost all well taken, with such a fine singer as John Tomlinson, for example, ripely resonant as Melchthal. The women singers too are impressive, with Mirella Freni as the heroine Matilde providing dramatic strength as well as sweetness. The recording, made in 1978 and 1979, comes out spectacularly on CD. The *Pas de six* is here banded into its proper place in Act I.

Guillaume Tell (William Tell) (sung in French).
(M) **(*) EMI CMS7 69951-2 (4). Bacquier, Caballé, Gedda, Mesplé, Amb. Op. Ch., RPO, Gardelli.

The interest of the 1973 EMI set is that it is sung in the original French. Gardelli proves an imaginative Rossini interpreter, allying his formidable team to vigorous and sensitive performances. Bacquier makes an impressive Tell, developing the character as the story progresses; Gedda is a model of taste, and Montserrat Caballé copes ravishingly with the coloratura problems of Mathilde's role. While Chailly's full-price Decca set puts forward a strong case for using Italian with its open vowels, this remains a fully worthwhile alternative, with excellent CD sound. The one considerable snag is that no English translation is provided.

L'inganno felice (complete).
☞ *(*) Claves Dig. CD 50-9211 [id.]. De Carolis, Felle, Zennaro, Previato, Serraiocco, ECO, Viotti.

Among the one-Act *farse* that Rossini wrote between 1810 and 1813 for the Teatro San Moise in Venice this is in many ways the most attractive of all. It badly needed a recording, but unfortunately this one is only a stop-gap. The plot is melodramatic, and it does not seem the stuff of farce, but is surprisingly effective when filled out with Rossini's music. The opera is stylishly and energetically conducted by Viotti with sprung rhythms and polished playing, but with a flawed cast. As the heroine, Amelia Felle is agile but too often raw-toned, even if on occasion she can crown an ensemble with well-phrased cantilena. As the hero, Bertrando, Iorio Zennaro has an agreeable natural timbre, but his tenor is not steady enough and strains easily. The buffo, Fabio Previato, is the soloist who comes closest to meeting the full challenge. The recorded sound has a pleasant bloom on it, but the orchestra is too recessed, and though the recitatives are briskly done, with crisp exchanges between the characters, the degree of reverberation is a serious drawback.

L'Italiana in Algeri (complete).
⊛ *** DG 427 331-2 (2) [id.]. Baltsa, Raimondi, Dara, Lopardo, V. State Op. Konzertvereinigung, VPO, Abbado.
*** Sony Dig. M2K 39048 (2) [id.]. Valentini Terrani, Ganzarolli, Araiza, Cologne R. Ch., Capella Coloniensis, Ferro.
(M) *** Erato/Warner 2292 45404-2 (2) [id.]. Horne, Palacio, Ramey, Trimarchi, Battle, Zaccaria, Prague Ch., Sol. Ven., Scimone.

Abbado's brilliant version was recorded in conjunction with a new staging by the Vienna State Opera, with timing and pointing all geared for wit on stage to make this the most captivating of all recordings of the opera. Agnes Baltsa is a real fire-eater in the title-role, and Ruggero Raimondi with his massively sepulchral bass gives weight to his part without undermining the comedy. The American tenor, Frank Lopardo, proves the most stylish Rossinian, singing with heady clarity in superbly articulated divisions, while both buffo baritones are excellent too. Like the CBS set, this uses the authentic score, published by the Fondazione Rossini in Pesaro.

The fine CBS version not only uses the critical edition of the score, it goes further towards authenticity in using period instruments, including a fortepiano instead of harpsichord for the recitatives (well played by Georg Fischer). Lucia Valentini Terrani here gives her finest performance on record to date, with her seductively rich, firm voice superbly agile in coloratura. Francisco Araiza as Lindoro peppers the rapid passage-work with intrusive aitches – but not too distractingly – and the strength of the voice makes the performance heroic with no suspicion of the twittering of a tenorino. Ganzarolli treats the role of the Bey, Mustafa, as a conventional buffo role, with a voice not ideally steady but full of character; the rest of the cast is strong, too.

Scimone's highly enjoyable version is beautifully played and recorded with as stylish a team of soloists as one can expect nowadays. The text is complete and alternative versions of certain arias are given as an appendix. Marilyn Horne makes a dazzling, positive Isabella, and Samuel Ramey is splendidly firm as Mustafa. Domenico Trimarchi is a delightful Taddeo and Ernesto Palacio an agile Lindoro, not coarse, though the recording does not always catch his tenor timbre well. Nevertheless the sound is generally very good indeed.

L'Italiana in Algeri: highlights.
*** DG Dig. 429 414-2 [id.] (from above set, with Baltsa and Raimondi; cond. Abbado).

This 67-minute selection of highlights from Abbado's complete set on DG provides an admirable and sparkling sampler.

Maometto II (complete).
*** Ph. Dig. 412 148-2 (3) [id.]. Anderson, Zimmermann, Palacio, Ramey, Dale, Amb. Op. Ch.,
  Philh. O, Scimone.

Claudio Scimone's account of *Maometto II* has Samuel Ramey magnificently focusing the whole
story in his portrait of the Muslim invader in love with the heroine. The other singing is less sharply
characterized but is generally stylish, with Margarita Zimmermann in the travesti role of Calbo and
June Anderson singing sweetly as Anna. Laurence Dale is excellent in two smaller roles, while
Ernesto Palacio mars some fresh-toned singing with his intrusive aitches. Excellent recording.

Mosè in Egitto (complete).
☞ (M) *** Ph. 420 109-2 (2) [id.]. Raimondi, Anderson, Nimsgern, Palacio, Gal, Fisichella, Amb.
  Op. Ch., Philh. O, Scimone.

For a century and more it was assumed that Rossini's later thoughts on the subject of a Moses opera
– his expanded version for Paris – were the ones to be preferred. It is good that Scimone took
scholarly advice and, in a direct and understanding reading, presents the second and far preferable of
the two Italian versions. So here the last and briefest of the three Acts is strongly expanded with a big
ensemble based on Moses' prayer, to make it almost a forerunner of another great chorus for the
Children of Israel, *Va pensiero* from Verdi's *Nabucco*. Other Verdian parallels come out, for some of
the ceremonial writing suggests a much later Egyptian opera, *Aida*, as well as a masterpiece written at
the same period, the *Requiem*. Clearly Scimone justifies his claim that the 1819 version is dramatically
more effective than both the earlier Italian one and the later Paris one. Rossini's score brings much
fine music and, among the soloists, Raimondi relishes not only the solemn moments like the great
invocation in Act I and the soaring prayer of Act III, but also the rage aria in Act II, almost like
Handel updated if with disconcerting foretastes of Dr Malatesta in Donizetti's *Don Pasquale*. The
writing for the soprano and tenor lovers (the latter the son of Pharaoh and in effect the villain of the
piece) is relatively conventional, though the military flavour of their Act I cabaletta is refreshingly
different. Ernesto Palacio and June Anderson make a strong pair, and the mezzo, Zehava Gal, is
another welcome newcomer as Pharaoh's wife. Siegmund Nimsgern makes a fine Pharaoh, Salvatore
Fisichella an adequate Arone (Aaron). The well-balanced recording emerges most vividly on CD.

L'occasione fa il ladro (complete).
☞ **(*) Claves Dig. CD 50-9208/9 [id.]. Bayo, De Carolis, Zennaro, Provvisionato, Previati, Massa,
  ECO, Viotti.

On two discs, this is one of the longer one-Acters in the Claves series, bringing one of the more
recommendable performances, with Viotti at his most relaxed. Maria Bayo as the heroine sings
warmly and sweetly, with no intrusive aspirates in the coloratura. The soubrette role of Ernestina is
also charmingly done, and the buffo characters sing effectively, though the tenor, Iorio Zennaro, is
hardly steady enough for Rossinian cantilena. This is a piece that the Buxton Festival presented with
success and, as the only available recording, the Claves set can be recommended. The two discs come
in a single hinged jewel-box at upper mid-price.

Otello (complete).
(M) *** Ph. 432 456-2 (2) [id.]. Carreras, Von Stade, Condò, Pastine, Fisichella, Ramey, Amb. S.,
  Philh. O, López-Cobos.

The libretto of Rossini's *Otello* bears remarkably little resemblance to Shakespeare – virtually none at
all until the last Act. It is some tribute to this performance, superbly recorded, and brightly and
stylishly conducted by López-Cobos, that the line-up of tenors is turned into an asset, with three
nicely contrasted soloists. Carreras is here at his finest – most affecting in his recitative before the
murder, while Fisichella copes splendidly with the high tessitura of Rodrigo's role, and Pastine has a
distinct timbre to identify him as the villain. Frederica von Stade pours forth a glorious flow of
beautiful tone, well-matched by Nucci Condò as Emilia. Samuel Ramey is excellent too in the bass
role of Elmiro.

La pietra del paragone (complete).
☞ (M) **(*) Van. 08 9031 73 (3) [id.]. Carreras, Wolff, Bonazzi, Elgar, Reardon, Foldi, Diaz,
  Murcell, Clarion Concerts Ch. & O, Jenkins.

This recording of the *opera buffa*, *La pietra del paragone*, made by Vanguard in New York in 1972,
presents the young José Carreras in an incidental role, just one in an attractively fresh-voiced cast of
soloists. It is given a vigorous, if occasionally hard-pressed performance under Newell Jenkins with
what is called the Clarion Concerts Orchestra and Chorus. This was an early piece, written when

Rossini was only twenty. Glyndebourne presented it as long ago as 1964 but scandalized that company's great Rossinian, Vittorio Gui, when they used 'a Germanized travesty'. Not so this recording. The plot of disguises and deceit is a throwback to artificial eighteenth-century conventions, involving a house-party with a couple of poets and a venal critic brought in. For modern performance the problem is the length, though on disc that evaporates when Rossini's invention is at its peak in number after number.

La scala di seta (complete).

☞ *** Claves Dig. 50-9219/20 [id.]. Corbelli, Ringholz, Vargas, De Carolis, Provvisionato, Massa, ECO, Viotti.

The overture is among the best known of all that Rossini wrote, and here Viotti establishes his individuality with an unusually expansive slow introduction leading to a brisk and well-sprung allegro, scintillatingly played by the ECO. The cast here is stronger vocally than those in the rest of the Claves series, with Teresa Ringholz delightful as the heroine, Giulia, warm and agile, shading her voice seductively. She and the buffo, sung by Alessandro Corbelli, have the biggest share of the solo work, and he is also first rate. The tenor Ramon Vargas sings without strain – rare in this series – and the mezzo, Francesca Provvisionato, sings vivaciously as the heroine's cousin, with a little aria in military rhythm a special delight. Warm sound with good bloom on the voices.

Semiramide (complete).

☞ *** DG Dig. 437 797-2 (3). Studer, Larmore, Ramey, Lopardo, Amb. Op. Ch., LSO, Ion Marin.

Semiramide (complete, but with traditional cuts).

(M) *** Decca 425 481-2 (3) [id.]. Sutherland, Horne, Rouleau, Malas, Serge, Amb. Op. Ch., LSO, Bonynge.

Rossini concentrates on the love of Queen Semiramide for Prince Arsace (a mezzo-soprano), and musically the result is a series of fine duets, superbly performed here by Sutherland and Horne (in the mid-1960s when they were both at the top of their form). In Sutherland's interpretation, Semiramide is not so much a Lady Macbeth as a passionate, sympathetic woman and, with dramatic music predominating over languorous cantilena, one has her best, bright manner. Horne is well contrasted, direct and masculine in style, and Spiro Malas makes a firm, clear contribution in a minor role. Rouleau and Serge are variable but more than adequate, and Bonynge keeps the whole opera together with his alert, rhythmic control of tension and pacing. The vintage Decca recording has transferred brilliantly to CD.

Even after the classic Decca set, conducted by Richard Bonynge, with Joan Sutherland and Marilyn Horne, there is room for a set as well cast as this DG version, particularly when Marin opens out many traditional cuts, notably in the role of the tenor, Idreno. Lopardo sings Idreno's splendid Act I aria magnificently, a scene omitted on Decca; and the newer performance, even at speeds generally faster, altogether lasts almost 40 minutes longer, though most of the extra material – recitative, repeats, introductions – is not of major importance. Though Cheryl Studer cannot match Sutherland in command or panache as the Babylonian queen, with the voice less firm and beautiful, it is still a strong, aptly agile performance. Jennifer Larmore sings superbly in the breeches role of Arsace, less powerful than Marilyn Horne but even more convincing in character, with the voice more youthfully fresh. What above all prevents Semiramide and Arsace's great duet, *Serbami ognor*, from sounding so seductively idiomatic is the conducting of Ion Marin, strong and purposeful but often too mechanical, generally missing the helpful rubatos that mark the Bonynge reading. The role of Assur is strongly sung by Samuel Ramey, but he gives little idea of the character's villainous side, which is far more tellingly conveyed on Decca by Joseph Rouleau, if with more variable vocalization. The mid-'60s sound of the Decca, transferred to CD at mid-price, is still very vivid, but the digital DG recording provides extra brilliance and range.

Il Signor Bruschino (complete).

☞ Claves Dig. CD 50-8904/5 [id.]. De Carolis, Orciani, Praticò, Canonici, Spagnoli, Lytting, I Filarmonico di Torino, Viotti.

This was recorded first in the Claves series, and acoustically the Turin sound provides an extreme contrast with the rest, dry to the point of rasping. It gives no help to the singers and exaggerates the flaws in the playing of the Turin orchestra. Viotti springs rhythms very persuasively, but the fun of the piece still fails to come over. The tenor, Luca Canonici, sounds strained, and the rapid patter-numbers bring a storm of aspirated singing from all concerned.

Tancredi (complete).

☞ ** Sony S3K 39073 (3) [id.]. M. Horne, Cuberli, Palacio, Zaccaria, Di Nissa, Schuman, Ch. and
O of Teatro la Fenice, Weikert.

Tancredi, first heard in the Teatro la Fenice in 1813, was enormously popular in its day, so famous
that Wagner many years later quoted from it in *Die Meistersinger*, knowing his audience would
appreciate the source. The chief glory of this live recording from Venice is the enchanting singing of
Lella Cuberli as the heroine, Amenaide. The purity and beauty of her tone, coupled with immaculate
coloratura and tender expressiveness, make it a memorable performance, confirming the high
opinions she won from the DG set of *Il viaggio a Reims*. Marilyn Horne, though not quite as fresh-
sounding as earlier in her career, gives a formidable performance in the breeches role of Tancredi,
relishing the resonance of her chest register, but finding delicacy too in her big aria, *Di tanti palpiti*.
Ernesto Palacio is an accomplished Rossini tenor, commendably agile in the role of Argirio, but the
tone tends to grow tight; and Zaccaria as Orbazzano sings with fuzzy, sepulchral tone. The
conducting is efficient rather than inspired, failing to make the music sparkle or to bring the drama to
life. The recording gives a realistic idea of a dryish theatre acoustic.

Il Turco in Italia (complete).

☞ *** Ph. Dig. 434 128-2 (2) [id.]. Sumi Jo, Alaimo, Fissore, Giménez, Mentzer, Corbelli, Bronder,
Amb. Op. Ch., ASMF, Marriner.

On Philips Sumi Jo, as Fiorilla, the sharp-tongued heroine, unhappily married to old Don Geronio, is
no fire-eater, as Callas was in her vintage recording, but she sparkles delightfully, a more believable
young wife than her other rival on disc; that is the heavyweight Montserrat Caballé on the CBS/Sony
set conducted by Riccardo Chailly. What seals the success of the Philips version is the playing of the
St Martin's Academy under Sir Neville Marriner, consistently crisper and lighter than their predecessors, wittily bringing out the light and shade in Rossini's score and offering an even fuller text than
Chailly. The big snag with the old Callas set was that it was severely cut by half an hour and more of
music. As for the rest of the Philips cast, Simone Alaimo as the visiting Turkish prince, Selim, may
lack the sardonic weight of Samuel Ramey on Sony, but it is a fine voice, and the buffo role of
Geronio finds Enrico Fissore agile and characterful in his patter numbers. Raúl Giménez is the stylish
tenor in the relatively small role of Narciso, which happily acquires an extra aria. Altogether a most
welcome follow-up to Marriner's excellent set of the *Barber*.

Il Turco in Italia (highlights).

☞ *** Ph. Dig. 438 505-2 [id.] (from above complete set, with Alaimo, Jo; cond. Marriner).

There will be many who will want just a highlights CD from *Il Turco in Italia*, and this Philips CD
will serve excellently, offering 72 minutes from a recording that is notable for its consistent casting
(led by the vivacious Sumi Jo) and Marriner's sparkling direction.

Il viaggio a Reims (complete).

❀ *** DG Dig. 415 498-2 (2) [id.]. Ricciarelli, Valentini Terrani, Cuberli, Gasdia, Araiza, Giménez,
Nucci, Raimondi, Ramey, Dara, Prague Philharmonic Ch., COE, Abbado.

☞ **(*) Sony Dig. S2K 53336 (2) [id.]. McNair, Valentini Terrani, Serra, Studer, Giménez, Matteuzzi,
Ramey, Raimondi, Berlin R. Ch., BPO, Abbado.

This DG set is one of the most sparkling and totally successful live opera recordings available, with
Claudio Abbado in particular freer and more spontaneous-sounding than he generally is on disc,
relishing the sparkle of the comedy, and the line-up of soloists here could hardly be more impressive,
with no weak link. Apart from the established stars the set introduced two formidable newcomers in
principal roles, Cecilia Gasdia as a self-important poetess and, even finer, Lella Cuberli as a young
fashion-crazed widow. Abbado's brilliance and sympathy draw the musical threads compellingly
together with the help of superb, totally committed playing from the young members of the Chamber
Orchestra of Europe.

It seems strange that Sony should so soon make a new recording of so rare – if delightful – an
opera as this in competition with DG's prize-winning version, particularly when Claudio Abbado is
again the conductor and the cast features many of the same singers. Again it is a live recording but,
with more distanced sound and voices less clear, it sparkles less. The Berlin Philharmonic is less
attuned to Rossini than the Chamber Orchestra of Europe. Though the Sony cast is strong, no
individual singer significantly outshines any predecessor, and most are less impressive.

Zelmira (complete).

*** Erato/Warner Dig. 2292 45419-2 (2) [id.]. Gasdia, Fink, Matteuzzi, Merritt, Amb. S., Sol. Ven., Scimone.

Zelmira has always had a bad press, but this recording, well sung (with one notable exception) and very well recorded, lets us appreciate that Rossinian inspiration had certainly not dried up. Scimone takes a generally brisk view of both the arias and the ensembles but never seems to race his singers. In this performance the choice of singers underlines the contrast between the two principal tenor-roles. Chris Merritt combines necessary agility with an almost baritonal quality as the scheming Antenore, straining only occasionally, and William Matteuzzi sings with heady beauty and fine flexibility in florid writing as Ilo. Star of the performance is Cecilia Gasdia in the name-part, projecting words and emotions very intensely in warmly expressive singing. She is well matched by the mezzo, Barbara Fink, as her friend, Emma, and only the wobbly bass of José Garcia as the deposed Polidoro mars the cast.

COLLECTIONS

L'assedio de Corinto: Avanziam' . . . Non temer d'un basso affetto! . . . I destini tradir ogni speme . . . Signormche tutto puio . . . Sei tu, che stendi; L'ora fatal s'appressa . . . Giusto ciel. La Donna del lago: Mura Felici; Tanti affetti. Otello: Assisa a pie d'un salice. Tancredi: Di tanti palpiti.

⊛ (M) *** Decca 421 306-2 [id.]. Marilyn Horne, Amb. Op. Ch., RPO, Henry Lewis.

Marilyn Horne's generously filled recital disc brings one of the most cherishable among all Rossini aria records ever issued. The voice is in glorious condition, rich and firm throughout its spectacular range, and is consistently used with artistry and imagination, as well as brilliant virtuosity in coloratura. By any reckoning this is thrilling singing, and the sound is full and brilliant, showing its age hardly at all.

Arias: La Cenerentola: Non piu mesta. La Donna del Lago: Mura felici . . . Elena! O tu, che chiamo. L'Italiana in Algeri: Cruda sorte! Amor tiranno! Pronti abbiamo . . . Pensa all patria. Otello: Deh! calma, o ciel. La Pietra del Paragone: Se l'Italie contrade . . . Se per voi lo care io torno. Tancredi: Di tanti palpiti. Stabat Mater: Fac ut portem.

*** Decca Dig. 425 430-2; *425 430-4* [id.]. Cecilia Bartoli, A. Schoenberg Ch., V. Volksoper O, Patanè.

Cecilia Bartoli's first recital of Rossini showpieces brings a formidable demonstration not only of Bartoli's remarkable voice but of her personality and artistry, bringing natural warmth and imagination to each item without ever quite making you smile with delight. Yet there are not many Rossini recitals of any vintage to match this. Vocally, the one controversial point to note is the way that Bartoli articulates her coloratura with a half-aspirate, closer to the Supervia 'rattle' than anything else, but rather obtrusive. Accompaniments are exemplary, and Decca provided the luxury of a chorus in some of the items, with hints of staging. Full, vivid recording. Recommended.

'Rossini heroines': Arias from: *La donna de lago; Elisabetta, Regina d'Inghilterra; Maometto II; Le nozze di Teti e Peleo; Semiramide; Zelmira.*

*** Decca Dig. 436 075-2; *435 075-4* [id.]. Cecilia Bartoli, Ch. & O of Teatro la Fenice, Marin.

Cecilia Bartoli follows up the success of her earlier Rossini recital-disc with this second brilliant collection of arias, mostly rarities. The tangy, distinctive timbre of her mezzo goes with a magnetic projection of personality to bring to life even formal passage-work, with all the elaborate coloratura bright and sparkling. The rarest item of all is an aria for the goddess Ceres from the classically based entertainment, *Le nozze di Teti e Peleo*, making a splendid showpiece. The collection is crowned by a formidably high-powered reading of *Bel raggio* from *Semiramide*, with Bartoli excitingly braving every danger.

Authentic Rossini Cookbook.

☞ *** Ph. 434 958-2. Various artists.

As well as a lively and imaginative CD compilation of Rossini items from the Philips catalogue, mostly from lesser-known operas, this boxed disc contains a booklet of 26 recipes 'à la Rossini'. The most elaborate is the well-known *filet de bœuf* (or *Tournedos*) dish, but the list also includes – some recipes more practical than others – *Thrush and chestnut soup à la Rossini, Ham and chicken mousse à la Rossini* and *Torta à la William Tell*. In keeping with such a mixture, the musical items include a high proportion of ensembles, such as the delicious Act I finale from *Count Ory*. A jolly gift for the culinary music-lover.

Rott, Hans (1858–84)

Symphony in E.
*** Hyp. Dig. CDA 66366 [id.]. Cincinnati Philh. O, Gerhard Samuel.

Although Hans Rott's *Symphony* owes much to Wagner as well as to Brahms, to whom allusion is made in the finale, it struck strong resonances in his fellow student, Gustav Mahler. It is astonishing to encounter in their pristine form ideas that took root in Mahler's *First* and *Fifth Symphonies*. Structurally the work is original, each movement getting progressively longer, the finale occupying nearly 25 minutes. But the music is full of good ideas and, anticipations of Mahler apart, has a profile of its own. The Cincinnati Philharmonia is a student orchestra who produce extraordinarily good results under Gerhard Samuel. The recording is good. Readers should investigate this issue without delay.

Roussel, Albert (1869–1937)

Bacchus et Ariane (complete ballet), *Op. 43; Le festin de l'araignée (The spider's feast): symphonic fragments.*
☞ (M) *** EMI Dig. CDM7 64690-2 [id.]. O Nat. de France, Prêtre.

This is a particularly valuable mid-priced reissue from 1986. *Bacchus et Ariane* is a relatively late score, composed in 1931 immediately after the *Third Symphony*. The ballet was originally choreographed by Lifar and had designs by Chirico, but it never captured the public imagination in quite the same way as *Le festin de l'araignée*. The music teems with life and is full of rhythmic vitality and richness of detail. It has perhaps less of the poetic feeling of *Le festin* but is nevertheless an exhilarating score. The recording, made in the generous acoustic of the Salle Wagram, is a shade too reverberant at times, but no essential detail is masked. Georges Prêtre obtains an excellent response from the Orchestre National de France in both scores. This supersedes Martinon's albeit excellently balanced earlier version on Erato which contained merely the two suites (or Acts) of the ballet and had no fill-up. The CD freshens detail a little, although the resonance means that the improvement is relatively limited. However, the background silence is certainly an asset in *The spider's feast*.

Le festin de l'araignée (ballet): *suite, Op. 17; (i) 5 mélodies: Amoureux séparés; Invocation; Le jardin mouillé; Light; Sarabande.*
☞ (M) (***) EMI mono CDC7 54840-2 [id.]. (i) O, composer; (ii) Claire Croïza, composer –
SCHMITT: *La tragédie de Salomé* etc. (***)

The composer's own account of the suite from the ballet *Le festin de l'araignée* ('The Spider's feast') has plenty of atmosphere and the benefit of very good recorded sound for its period. The orchestra is uncredited, but the performance evokes a sense of theatre and a strong, imaginative atmosphere. Roussel's recording has already appeared before, together with the songs he recorded with Croïza on Philips and also including some rather less special (relatively modern) performances of the piano music (see our 1990 edition). But this new EMI disc offers by far the more economical and better-transferred version, and it comes with a splendid coupling, Florent Schmitt's *La tragédie de Salomé*.

Sinfonietta; Symphony No. 4, Op. 53.
☞ ** Chan. Dig. CHAN 9072 [id.]. Detroit SO, Järvi – DEBUSSY: *La Mer;* MILHAUD: *Suite provençale.* **

Recordings of Roussel symphonies are not thick on the ground, though the best, Karajan's pioneering set with the Philharmonia, having made a brief reappearance on EMI, has now been deleted. Neeme Järvi gives a spirited and generally idiomatic account of the *Fourth Symphony*, though, as is occasionally his wont, he is far too fast in the slow movement. Roussel's textures can easily sound too dense and the contrapuntal detail is not always as clearly delineated as it is in Dutoit's Erato recording, which remains a first choice. An attractive enough programme in all conscience, but, despite its strong artistic merits and musically balanced recording, not a front-runner in any of the four works.

Suite in F, Op. 33.
(M) **(*) Mercury 434 303-2 [id.]. Detroit SO, Paul Paray – CHABRIER: *Bourrée fantasque* etc. ***

The outer movements of Roussel's *Suite in F* have a compulsive drive which also infects the harmonically complex, bittersweet central *Sarabande*. The scoring is rich (some might say thick), and the resonance of the Detroit Ford Auditorium makes it congeal a little. It is well played and alive, with Paray at his best in the closing *Gigue*.

Symphonies Nos. 1 in D min. (Le Poème de la forêt), Op. 7; 3 in G min., Op. 42.
*** Erato/Warner Dig. 2292 45253-2 [id.]. O Nat. de France, Dutoit.

The *First Symphony* is subtitled *Le Poème de la forêt*. The first movement, *Forêt d'hiver*, is a kind of prelude, and the closing bars have some of the balminess of a Mediterranean night. The *Third* is both Roussel's most concentrated and his best-known symphony. Dutoit gets first-class playing from the Orchestre National and the recording is excellent.

Symphonies Nos. 2 in B flat, Op. 23; 4 in A, Op. 53.
*** Erato/Warner Dig. 2292 45254-2 [id.]. O Nat. de France, Dutoit.

The *Second Symphony* has some of the opulence of the first two Bax symphonies, particularly in the lower wind, and in some of the work's brooding, atmospheric slow sections. The *Fourth Symphony* is a delightful score and has Roussel's most infectiously engaging Scherzo. In this and the captivating finale, Dutoit and the French National Orchestra are in excellent form. CD does particular justice to the richness of Roussel's scoring and is particularly imposing in the definition of the bottom end of the register.

Symphony No. 3 in G min., Op. 42; Bacchus et Ariane (ballet): *suite No. 2, Op. 43.*
**(*) Chan. Dig. CHAN 8996; *ABTD 1578* [id.]. Detroit SO, Järvi – RAVEL: *Boléro; La valse.* **

Neeme Järvi's account of the *Third Symphony* has an engaging vitality and character, and the playing of the Detroit orchestra is highly responsive. In the slow movement he indulges in a rather steep *accelerando* after the fugal section. Likewise his finale feels too fast. But it is a committed performance. His account of the second suite from *Bacchus et Ariane* is both vivid and atmospheric. Some may find the acoustic a shade too resonant, given the complexity of Roussel's textures, but the overall balance is very natural and pleasing.

Doute; 3 Pièces; Prélude & fugue, Op. 46; Rustiques, Op. 5; Segovia, Op. 29; Sonatine; Suite in F sharp min., Op. 14.
*** Chan Dig. CHAN 8887; *ABTD 1498* [id.]. Eric Parkin.

Eric Parkin is a sensitive and sympathetic advocate, and he is excellently recorded at The Maltings, Snape. Roussel's keyboard textures are sometimes thick, as in the *Retour de fête* movement from the early *Rustiques*, written at the time of the *First Symphony*. The *Prélude et Fugue* and the *Trois Pièces* are both late and speak with the same accents as the *Fourth Symphony* and *Bacchus et Ariane*.

Songs: *Jazz dans la nuit; Mélodie, Op. 19/1: Light; 2 Mélodies, Op. 20; 2 Poèmes chinois, Op. 35.*
**(*) Unicorn DKPCD 9035; *DKPC 9035* [id.]. Sarah Walker, Roger Vignoles – DEBUSSY;
  ENESCU: *Songs.* ***

Sarah Walker may not plumb the full emotions of some of the deceptively deep songs in her Roussel group – *Light* for example – but the point and charm of *Jazz dans la nuit* are superbly caught, and the group makes an attractive and generous coupling for the Debussy and Enescu songs, all superbly recorded, with Vignoles a most sensitive accompanist.

Padmâvatî (opera; complete).
☞ *** EMI Dig. CDS7 47891-8 (2) [id.]. M. Horne, Gedda, Van Dam, Berbié, Burles, Dran, Dale,
  Orféon Donostiarra, Toulouse Capitole O, Plasson.

Padmâvatî, rich and exotic in its Indian setting, was inspired by Roussel's visit to the ruins of Chitoor in Rajputana. Padmâvatî was the wife of the Prince of Chitoor who, rather than submit to being given to the soft-speaking but predatory Mogul sultan, Alla-uddin, stabs her beloved and commits *suttee*. That simple plot gives Roussel the opportunity to write colourful, richly atmospheric music, not just in the symbolic preludes to each of the two Acts but also in sequences which seek to combine full-scale ballet with opera – an entertainment for the Sultan in Act I and the rites of Siva's daughters in Act II. It is a heady mixture, with Plasson drawing warmly sympathetic playing from the Toulouse orchestra. In an excellent cast, José van Dam is superb as the evil, deceptive Sultan and, though Marilyn Horne sounds rather too mature for the name-part, hers is a powerful, convincing performance. One remarkable feature of the opera is the profusion of principal tenors required, and here Gedda as the Prince is splendidly matched with contrasted soloists in smaller roles, Charles Burles, Thierry Dran and Laurence Dale. Warm, convincingly balanced sound. This is well worth exploring.

Royer, Pancrace (1705–55)

Pièces de clavecin (1746): *La majestueuse; La Zaïde; Les matelots; Tambourins 1–2; L'incertaine; L'aimable; La bagatelle; Suite de la bagatelle; La remouleuse; Les tendres sentiments; Le vertigo; Allemande; La sensible; La marche des Scythes. La chasse de Zaïde.*
☞ ⊛ *** O-L Dig. 436 127-2 [id.]. Christophe Rousset (harpsichord).

In his own lifetime Royer was held in high regard, second only to Rameau. He was music teacher to Louis XV's daughters, composer of the Académie Royale de Musique and director of the Concert-Spirituel; the 1746 *Pièces de clavecin*, his only collection to appear in print, was dedicated to his royal charges. These pieces had their origins in his stage works but, unlike Rameau, who transcribed instrumental dances for the keyboard, Royer drew on arias and choral pieces as well. Similarly, *La chasse de Zaïde* comes from his *ballet-héroïque*, *Zaïde* (1739). All these pieces show flashes of real imagination and a refined and developed sensibility. Rousset plays a harpsichord from 1751 by Henri Hemsch which has been expertly restored and is tuned to Werckmeister III, a system closely approaching equal temperament. The instrument once belonged to Rameau's patron *fermier general*, La Poupelinière, and was in all probability played by Rameau himself. Rousset plays with great flair and poetic imagination and he is impeccably recorded; he also provides the useful and scholarly notes.

Rózsa, Miklós (born 1907)

Symphony in 3 movements, Op. 6a (ed. Palmer); *The Vintner's daughter, Op. 23a.*
☞ *** Koch Dig. 37244-2 [id.]. New Zealand SO, James Sedares.

Rózsa's early attempt in 1930 to write a large-scale symphony proved abortive, and the present structure, minus a Scherzo and heavily edited by Christopher Palmer, relies on an incomplete manuscript. However, as we know from his film scores, Rózsa had no difficulty finding memorable musical ideas and in the first movement uses them cogently and with intensity. The second-movement *Andante* is highly evocative and the finale does not lack fire and energy, even if structurally it remains the least convincing part of the work. *The Vintner's daughter*, a picturesque set of variations, again shows the composer's melodic appeal, and again he uses the orchestral palette as seductively as in his film music. James Sedares and his New Zealand players are obviously caught up in the music and present it persuasively, with the conductor showing a notably firm grip on the first movement of the symphony. The recording has plenty of body and colour.

Rubbra, Edmund (1901–86)

Violin concerto, Op. 103.
*** Unicorn Dig. DKPCD 9056; *DKPC 9056* [id.]. Carl Pini, Melbourne SO, Measham – IRELAND: *Piano concerto.* ***

As always with this composer, the music unfolds with a seeming inevitability and naturalness and a strong sense of purpose. Carl Pini is the capable soloist; the Melbourne orchestra under David Measham play with a conviction that more than compensates for the somewhat unventilated recording, which makes textures sound thicker than they in fact are.

Symphonies Nos. (i) *2 in D, Op. 45;* (ii) *7 in C, Op. 88;* (i) *Festival overture, Op. 62.*
☞ *** Lyrita SRCD 235 [id.]. (i) New Philh. O., Handley; (ii) LPO, Boult.

The *Second Symphony* dates from 1937 and, like its predecessor, showed Rubbra to be a symphonist of a rather special order, an artist able to think on a large scale and in long-breathed paragraphs, yet at the same time apparently indifferent to the orchestral medium. He subsequently thinned out the scoring and in 1950 made a cut in the middle of the first movement, not long after the composition of the *Fifth Symphony*. Rubbra's symphonies do not offer the cut-and-thrust of dramatic contrast but rather unfold in an overall organic flow whose incidental beauties are subservient to the general structural plan. His music lays stress on matter rather than manner and attaches scant importance to surface appeal. It is the slow movement that offers the deepest musical experience here. We have writing of a deep originality which has evolved from Holst and Sibelius, which inhabits a northern (but not a Scandinavian) landscape, and which is unlike anything else in the British music of its time. This and the finale are the most successful movements; the latter is inventive and original and has overtones of the *Perigourdine* movement of the *First Symphony*, though its accents are very English.

Not the most flawless of Rubbra's symphonies, perhaps, for the score is undoubtedly overladen with contrapuntal detail, and the orchestration is still thick in the first movement. Good performances from Handley of both symphony and the overture which bears an adjacent opus number to the *Fifth*.

The *Seventh Symphony* is a very considerable piece. The longest and most ambitious of its three movements – perhaps the most enigmatic, too – is the finale, an extended passacaglia and fugue displaying the composer's naturally contrapuntal mode of thought at its most typical. The first movement brings a cogent argument based on a simple four-note motif, and the second a rhythmic Scherzo that leads to a more lyrical, noble climax. Boult's performance is outstandingly successful and the 1970 recording, like that of the *Second* (made eight years later), is up to the high standards of realism one expects from this label. A thoroughly worthwhile and generous coupling (78 minutes).

Symphonies Nos. 3, Op. 49; 4, Op. 53; Resurgam overture, Op. 149; A Tribute, Op. 56.
*** Lyrita Dig. SRCD 202 [id.]. Philh O, Norman Del Mar.

The opening of the *Fourth Symphony* is of quite exceptional beauty and has a serenity and quietude that silence criticism; there is a consistent elevation of feeling and continuity of musical thought. Rubbra's music is steeped in English polyphony and it could not come from any time other than our own. Unquestionably both symphonies have a nobility and spirituality that is rare in any age. The fine *Resurgam overture* is a late work.

Symphony No. 5 in B flat, Op. 63.
(M) *** Chan. CHAN 6576 [id.]. Melbourne SO, Schönzeler – BLISS: *Checkmate* ***; TIPPETT: *Little music.* **(*)

Rubbra's *Fifth Symphony* is a noble work which grows naturally from the symphonic soil of Elgar and Sibelius. Although the Melbourne orchestra is not in the very top division, they play this music for all they are worth, and the strings have a genuine intensity and lyrical fervour that compensate for the opaque effect of the octave doublings. Altogether, though, this is an imposing performance which reflects credit on all concerned. The recording is well balanced and lifelike; but the ear perceives that the upper range is rather restricted.

(i) *Symphonies Nos. 6, Op. 80; 8 (Hommage à Teilhard de Chardin), Op. 132;* (ii) *Soliloquy for cello and orchestra, Op. 57.*
☞ *** Lyrita SRCD 234 [id.]. (i) Philh. O, Norman Del Mar; (ii) Rohan de Saram, LSO, Handley.

The *Sixth* is one of the most admired of Rubbra's symphonies and dates from 1953–4. It has much the same purity of spirit and directness of utterance that distinguish his finest work, and its slow movement is arguably the most beautiful single movement in all of Rubbra's output: in tranquillity of spirit and serenity it almost recalls the *Missa in honorem Sancti Dominici*, written five years earlier. As always in Rubbra there is a strong sense of linear continuity, of a melodic line that is supple yet unbroken. The *Eighth* (1968) pays tribute to Teilhard de Chardin, a Jesuit and palaeontologist (1881–1955) who fell out with the Church over his approach to evolution. It has something of the mystical intensity that finds its most visionary outlet in the *Ninth Symphony*. The clarity of its scoring reminds one that Rubbra was at one time a pupil of Holst. In Norman Del Mar's hands Rubbra's music speaks here with directness and without artifice; the Philharmonia play marvellously and the composer's sound-world is very well served by the recording balance. The *Soliloquy* has been described by Ronald Stevenson as 'a saraband, symphonically developed in flexible tempo . . . a meditation with flashes of interior drama', and its grave beauty exerts a strong appeal. Rohan de Saram plays with a restrained eloquence that is impressive and he has excellent support from the LSO under Vernon Handley.

Symphony No. 10 (Sinfonia da camera), Op. 145; Improvisations on virginal pieces by Giles Farnaby, Op. 50; A tribute to Vaughan Williams on his 70th birthday (Introduction and danza alla fuga), Op. 56.
☞ (M) *** Chan. CHAN 6599. Bournemouth Sinf., Schönzeler.

Rubbra's *Tenth Symphony* is for chamber orchestra; it is a short, one-movement work, whose opening has a Sibelian seriousness and a strong atmosphere that grip one immediately. Schönzeler is scrupulously attentive to dynamic nuance and internal balance, while keeping a firm grip on the architecture as a whole. The 1977 recording has been impressively remastered. It has a warm acoustic and reproduces natural, well-placed orchestral tone. The upper range is crisply defined. The *Farnaby variations* is a pre-war work whose charm Schönzeler uncovers effectively, revealing its textures to best advantage. *Loath to depart*, the best-known movement, has gentleness and vision in this performance. Strongly recommended. Even though this CD plays for only 40 minutes, it remains indispensable.

(i) *Violin sonata No. 2, Op. 31;* (ii) *Piano trio in one movement, Op. 68; Piano trio No. 2, Op. 138;*
Prelude and fugue on a theme of Cyril Scott, Op. 69; Fantasy fugue, Op. 161.
☞ Devorguilla DRVCD 104 [id.]. (i) Fletcher; (ii) Bailey, Wilson, Hill.

The *Second Violin sonata* and the *Piano trio in one movement* (1950) were both recorded in the early
days of mono LP, but the *Second Piano trio* and the *Fantasy fugue* are premières. The *First Piano trio*
is a work of some depth which ought to be more widely represented in the repertoire. Michael Hill
was the dedicatee of the *Fantasy fugue*, and his contribution in the solo pieces and accompanying Lyn
Fletcher in the sonata is accomplished. The performance of the two trios, however, leaves much to be
desired; and not the least of one's disappointments is the impoverished sound-quality with an
unusually constricted frequency range. This is the kind of repertoire to which the exploratory
collector will (and should) turn, but this issue is not recommendable and we must wait until
something better comes along.

(i) *Magnificat and Nunc dimittis in A flat, Op. 65. Missa in honorem Sancti Dominici, Op. 66; 3 Hymn
tunes, Op. 114; 3 Motets, Op. 78.*
☞ *** ASV Dig. CDDCA 881 [id.]. Gonville & Caius College, Cambridge, Ch., Geoffrey Webber;
     (i) Phillips (organ) – HADLEY: *Lenten cantata* etc. ***

The most important work here is the *Missa in honorem Sancti Dominici* (1948), written at about the
time of the *Fifth Symphony* and one of the most beautiful of twentieth-century *a cappella* choral
pieces written in this or any other country. None of the other works on the disc is its equal. The
performance by the Choir of Gonville & Caius College, Cambridge, under Geoffrey Webber is
dedicated and sensitive, though it does not altogether banish memories of Richard Hickox's RCA
version from the 1970s. Excellent balance, though the organ is obtrusive, particularly so in the first of
the Op. 78 *Motets*.

Rubinstein, Anton (1829–94)

Piano concertos Nos. 3 in G, Op. 45; 4 in D min., Op. 70.
☞ ** Marco Polo Dig. 8.223382 [id.]. Banowetz, Slovak State PO (Košice), Stankovsky.

The concertos are on the whole more rewarding than the symphonies but they need the advocacy of a
very great pianist to be wholly persuasive. Anyone who has heard the 1937 recording of Josef
Hofmann playing the *Fourth Concerto* with Reiner conducting is persuaded – at least while the music
is in progress – but these performances, though musicianly, are not in that category.

Symphony No. 6 in A min., Op. 111.
☞ ** Marco Polo Dig. 8.220489 [id.]. Philh. Hungarica, Varga.

All six symphonies of Anton Rubinstein are now on record. As David Brown put it in the *Companion
to the Symphony*, 'Insofar as a Rubinstein style may be identified, it is a compound of Mendelssohn
and Schumann, the more radical of the mid-century composers like Liszt and Berlioz being firmly
excluded.' Much of his music is pretty thin stuff and most outstays its welcome. The *Second
Symphony* (*Ocean*) (1851) is now available in its complete, seven-movement (1880) form in which it
runs to 72 minutes 39 seconds (Marco Polo 8.223449) and the inflated and garrulous *Fourth
Symphony* (*Dramatic*) (1874) is only a few minutes shorter and the musical ideas no less over-
extended. *No. 5 in G minor*, Op 107, (1880) (Marco Polo 8.223320) is more distinctively national and
better proportioned, but readers wanting to represent this composer's symphonies in their collections
might try *No. 6 in A minor*, composed in 1886. Its first three movements hold the attention and,
although the finale is weak, this is probably the best place to start if you are interested in this
undoubtedly important figure.

Piano sonatas Nos. 1 in F min., Op. 12; 3 in F, Op. 41.
*** Hyp. Dig. CDA 66017 [id.]. Leslie Howard.

Piano sonatas Nos. 2 in C min., Op. 20; 4 in A min., Op. 100.
*** Hyp. Dig. CDA 66105 [id.]. Leslie Howard.

Leslie Howard copes with the formidable technical demands of these *Sonatas* manfully. He proves
highly persuasive in all four works, though the actual invention is scarcely distinguished enough to
sustain interest over such ambitious time-spans. Rubinstein wrote these pieces for himself to play, and
doubtless his artistic powers and strong personality helped to persuade contemporary audiences. The
1981 recordings sound excellent.

Ruders, Poul (born 1949)

(i) *Concerto for clarinet and twin orchestra;* (ii) *Violin concerto No. 1;* (iii) *Drama trilogy No. 3 for cello and orchestra 'Polydrama'.*
*** Unicorn Dig. DKPCD 9114 [id.]. (i) Thomsen; (ii) Hirsch; (iii) Zeuten; Odense SO, Tamás Vetö.

Poul Ruders is one of the most naturally talented of the younger Danish composers. His *Violin concerto* is a tribute to the sunny atmosphere of Italian baroque music in general and Vivaldi's *Four Seasons* in particular. Apart from its neo-classicism there is a whiff of minimalism about much of it. The *Clarinet concerto* is strong stuff; to quote Ruders himself, the soloist is a 'Pierrot-like *vox humana* caught in a vice of orchestral onslaught', and the effect is often disturbing and almost surrealistic. He is an imaginative composer with a vein of lyrical feeling and melancholy that surfaces in the *Cello concerto.* A rewarding and interesting figure.

Rutter, John (born 1943)

(i; ii) *The Falcon;* (ii) *2 Festival anthems: O praise the Lord in heaven; Behold, the tabernacle of God;* (ii; iii) *Magnificat.*
*** Coll. Dig. COLCD 114; *COLC 114* [id.]. (i) St Paul's Cathedral Choristers; (ii) Cambridge Singers, City of L. Sinfonia; (iii) with Patricia Forbes; all cond. composer.

The Falcon was Rutter's first large-scale choral work. Its inspiration was a medieval poem, which is linked to the Crucifixion story, but the core of the piece is the mystical central *Lento.* The *Magnificat* has the usual Rutter stylistic touches, with a syncopated treatment of the opening *Magnificat anima mea,* and a joyous closing *Gloria Patri.* The two anthems are characteristically expansive and resplendent with brass. Fine performances and recording in the best Collegium tradition.

(i) *Gloria;* (ii) Anthems: *All things bright and beautiful; For the beauty of the earth; A Gaelic blessing; God be in my head; The Lord bless you and keep you; The Lord is my Shepherd; O clap your hands; Open thou my eyes; Praise ye the Lord; A prayer of St Patrick.*
*** Collegium Dig. COLCD 100; *COLC 100* [id.]. Cambridge Singers, (i) Philip Jones Brass Ens.; (ii) City of L. Sinfonia, composer.

John Rutter has a genuine gift of melody and his use of tonal harmony is individual and never bland. The resplendent *Gloria* is a three-part piece, and Rutter uses his brass to splendid and often spectacular effect. The anthems are diverse in style and feeling and, like the *Gloria,* have strong melodic appeal – the setting of *All things bright and beautiful* is delightfully spontaneous. It is difficult to imagine the music receiving more persuasive advocacy than under the composer, and the recording is first class in every respect.

3 Musical fables: (i) *Brother Heinrich's Christmas;* (ii) *The Reluctant Dragon; The Wind in the Willows.*
**(*) Coll. COLCD 115; *COLC 115* [id.]. City of L. Sinf.; with (i) Brian Kay, Cambridge Singers, composer; (ii) Richard Baker, King's Singers, Hickox.

John Rutter's name is readily associated with carols, and *Brother Heinrich's Christmas* is a musical narrative with choir, telling the story of how one of the most famous of all carols was introduced late at night by the angels to Brother Heinrich, just in time for it be included in the monks' Christmas Day service. It is all highly ingenuous but engagingly presented, and should appeal to young listeners who have enjoyed Howard Blake's *The Snowman.* The settings of the two famous Kenneth Grahame stories are no less tunefully communicative and include simulations of pop music of the 1940s (among other derivations), notably a Rodgers-style ballad which sentimentalizes the end of *The Wind in the Willows* episode, after Toad's escape from prison. All the music is expertly sung and played and blends well with the warmly involving narrative, splendidly done by Richard Baker.

(i) *Requiem; I will lift up mine eyes.*
*** Collegium Dig. COLCD 103; *COLC 103* [id.]. (i) Ashton, Dean; Cambridge Singers, City of L. Sinfonia, composer.

John Rutter's melodic gift, so well illustrated in his carols, is here used in the simplest and most direct way to create a small-scale *Requiem* that is as beautiful and satisfying in its English way as the works of Fauré and Duruflé. The penultimate movement, a ripe setting of *The Lord is my Shepherd* with a lovely oboe obbligato, sounds almost like an anglicized Song of the Auvergne; while Caroline Ashton's performance of the delightful *Pié Jesu* is wonderfully warm and spontaneous, most beautifully recorded on CD, and *I will lift up mine eyes* makes a highly effective encore piece.

Sainte-Colombe (died c. 1700)

Concerts à deux violes: Bourrasque; La dubois; La raporté; Le retour; Tombeau les regrets.
☞ *** Astrée Audivis Dig. E 7729 [id.]. Jordi Savall, Wieland Kuijken.

Concerts à deux violes: La conférence; Dalain; Le figuré; La rougeville; Le tendre.
☞ *** Astrée Audivis Dig. E 8743 [id.]. Jordi Savall, Wieland Kuijken.

Le Retour; Tombeau les Regrets.
☞ *** Naxos Dig. 8.550750 [id.]. Spectre de la Rose – MARAIS: *Tombeau pour M. de Sainte-Colombe*
    etc. ***

The extraordinary popular success of the fascinating conjectural film (*Tous les matins du monde*) about this mysterious, reclusive composer and his relationship with his brilliantly talented young pupil, Marin Marais, has led to the soundtrack album becoming a bestseller. However, this enterprising and inexpensive Naxos recital includes the 'hits' from the film. The two Saint-Colombe works included are austerely but certainly touchingly played by a fresh-sounding 'authentic' group led by Alison Crum (viola da gamba) and Marie Knight (baroque violin). The Naxos recording is vivid, but its forward balance means that for a realistic effect a modest setting of the volume control should be chosen.

Those who are then tempted to explore the music of Saint-Colombe further might invest in the pair of excellent Audivis CDs featuring Jordi Savall, who was associated with the film soundtrack. They are performed by artists who have this music in their bones, and the playing is more subtle and has even greater emotional depth. The two CDs are excellently recorded and are available separately; the second duplicates nothing on the Naxos CD.

Saint-Saëns, Camille (1835–1921)

(i) *Africa fantasy for piano and orchestra, Op. 89. Ascanio: Valse-finale; Parysatis: Airs de ballet. Sarabande et Rigaudon, Op. 93; Suite algérienne, Op. 60: Marche militaire française.* (ii) *Tarantelle for flute, clarinet and orchestra, Op. 6;* (iii) *Messe de Requiem, Op. 54.*
☞ **(*) Cala Dig. CACD 1015; *CAMC 1015* [id.]. LPO, Geoffrey Simon, with (i) Gwendolyn
    Mok; (ii) Susan Milan, James Campbell; (iii) Olafimihan, Wyn-Rogers, Roden, Kirkbride,
    Hertfordshire Ch., Harlow Ch., East London Ch.

La jota aragonesa, Op. 64; (i) *La muse et le poète. La princesse jaune: Overture;* (ii) *Symphony No. 3 in C min.;* (iii) *Danse macabre* (original vocal version). *Grande fantaisie on themes from Samson et Dalila* (arr. Luigini).
☞ ** Cala Dig. CACD 1016; *CAMC 1016* [id.]. LPO, Geoffrey Simon, with (i) Stephanie Chase,
    Robert Truman; (ii) James O'Donnell; (iii) Anthony Roden.

Geoffrey Simon is an amiably persuasive advocate of these Saint-Saëns novelties, even if his affectionate approach emphasizes the music's surface elegance. The resonant acoustics of All Hallows Church, Gospel Oak, cast a warm glow over the proceedings, and detail could be sharper. However, the nicely scored *Airs de Ballet*, which come from the incidental music for *Parysatis*, are certainly enticing. After the second number, which opens with a gentle woodwind chorale, the swirling energy of the third recalls Borodin's *Polovtsian dances*, and here the brass is very telling. The gracious *Sarabande* and genial *Rigaudon* certainly tickle the ear, as does the tuneful *Valse-finale* from *Ascanio*. But it is the lively and charming *Tarantelle* for flute, clarinet and orchestra which is the vivacious highlight of the first CD. It is winningly played by Susan Milan and James Campbell. The rich sonority of the sound suits the melodically catchy *Marche militaire française*, with its resplendent brass, but the exotically oriental *Africa fantasy for piano and orchestra* loses some of its point and glitter when the acoustic is so resonant. Even so, the performance is full of charm, and Gwendolyn Mok plays with affectionate flair. The *Messe de Requiem* is a real find, even if here the focus of the choral sound needs to be sharper.

The *Kyrie* opens dramatically, but the composer's richly seductive harmonic style immediately asserts itself. The *Dies Irae* introduces that famous semi-liturgical sequence in the brass, then the chorus dances along like skeletons fresh from the *Danse macabre*. Four unison trombones dominate the *Tuba mirum* and the organ enters equally dramatically. The choral and brass writing is powerfully sombre and, after the energetic *Rex Tremendae*, the *Oro supplex* leads movingly to a sustained *Hostias*, a dramatically concise *Sanctus* (only 1½ minutes) and a warmly romantic *Benedictus*, surrounded by flowing woodwind. The closing pages recall the searching question/answer passage that opened the work, with the *Agnus Dei* making a genuinely heartfelt postlude, which is well conveyed in Geoffrey Simon's committed performance. In its unpretentious, expressive style this work is a kind of French equivalent of Rossini's *Petite messe solennelle*. Pretty good choral singing, a well-matched team of soloists, and the recording gives the work a fine, sonorous impact, even if more bite is needed.

The undoubted highlight of the second disc is the fascinating original vocal version of *Danse macabre*, very much shorter than the familiar tone-poem. It lasts for only 2 minutes 52 seconds; indeed it seems almost to be cut off, but the result is a chrysalis for the orchestral piece. The words are from the poem by Henri Cazalis and make one understand the genial atmosphere of the orchestral work: 'Zig-a-zig-a-zig, Death is tapping at the tomb with his heel at midnight, playing an air on his out-of-tune fiddle – zig-a-zig-a-zag.' Geoffrey Simon opens rather imposingly, then follows the singer quite strongly as he enunciates the words clearly, presenting the repeated 'Zig-a-zig' with a Gallic sense of melodrama. The effect is semi-operatic, interrupted by the cock-crow. All the ideas are there, but one can understand why the composer wanted to expand his material and finally decided that the words were unnecessary. *La muse et le poète* is an extended (15 minutes 19 seconds) salon duo for violin and cello with orchestra. It opens dreamily, but as it becomes more passionate it also becomes technically demanding. Stephanie Chase and, especially, the cellist Robert Truman are good if not distinctive soloists. The CD opens with the *Jota aragonesa*, which is very like the Glinka fantasy and needs a recording with more glitter. The *Grande fantaisie on Samson et Dalila* arranged by Luigini is rather inflated but is not helped by Geoffrey Simon's very leisurely tempo for *Softly awakes my heart*, even though there is some lovely warm Philharmonia string-playing. The *Overture La princesse jaune* with its oriental flavour and pretty scoring is presented with real charm. But Geoffrey Simon then chooses to end his second CD with the *Organ Symphony* – an agreeable account, but no more than that. The lively playing (especially the wind articulation) in the first movement is clouded by the recording and, although the *Adagio* then creates a sumptuously warm and rich combination of organ and strings, Simon's indulgently relaxed tempo approaches lethargy. The Scherzo with its piano filigree is poorly focused, and in the finale the massive organ entry is without quite enough edge. The close is exciting but not compulsive.

Carnival of the animals.
(M) *** Virgin/EMI Dig. CU7 61137-2 [id.]. Anton Nel, Keith Snell, Ac. of L., Richard Stamp –
  PROKOFIEV: *Peter*. *** ⊛
*** Ph. Dig. 400 016-2 [id.]. Villa, Jennings, Pittsburgh SO, Previn – RAVEL: *Ma Mère l'Oye*. ***
(B) *** CfP CD-CFP 4086; *TC-CFP 40086*. Katin, Fowke, SNO, Gibson – BIZET: *Jeux d'enfants;*
  RAVEL: *Ma Mère l'Oye*. ***
(BB) *** ASV CDQS 6017. Goldstone, Brown, RPO, Hughes – PROKOFIEV: *Peter*. ***
☞ ** EMI CDC7 54730-2 [id.]. John Ogdon and Brenda Lucas, CBSO, Frémaux – PROKOFIEV:
  Peter and the wolf. **(*)

Richard Stamp directs an outstanding version of Saint-Saëns's witty zoology, full of affectionate humour. After Robert Bailey's gentle, slightly recessed image of *The Swan*, the finale bursts on the listener with infectious vigour, the two pianists producing flourishes of great bravura. Throughout, one responds to the polished overall presentation and sense of fun; although some may feel that the recording is rather resonant, it adds a genial warmth to the vitality of the proceedings.

Previn's version makes a ready alternative. The music is played with infectious rhythmic spring and great refinement. It is a mark of the finesse of this performance – which has plenty of bite and vigour, as well as polish – that the great cello solo of *Le Cygne* is so naturally presented. Fine contributions too from the two pianists, although their image is rather bass-orientated, within a warmly atmospheric recording.

On CfP the solo pianists, Peter Katin and Philip Fowke, enter fully into the spirit of the occasion, with Gibson directing his Scottish players with affectionate, unforced geniality. The couplings are attractive and the CD transfer confirms the vivid colourfulness and presence of the mid-1970s recording.

The two pianists on ASV also play with point and style, and the accompaniment has both spirit and spontaneity. *The Swan* is perhaps a trifle self-effacing, but otherwise this is very enjoyable, the humour appreciated without being underlined. The recording is excellent, and this makes a good super-bargain CD recommendation.

The Ogdon Duo gives a characteristically sturdy performance, with competent support from Frémaux. The 1971 recording is full and vivid, but the poker-faced approach offers neither humour nor a gracious touch. Even *The Swan* seems comparatively stoical. This won't do at full price.

Carnival of the animals (with poems by Peter Schickele).

☞ * Telarc Dig. CD 80350 [id.]. Peter Schickele, Ralph Markham and Kenneth Broadway, Atlanta SO, Yoel Levi – PROKOFIEV: *Sneaky Pete and the wolf.*

Peter Schickele, having tastelessly rewritten the story of Prokofiev's *Peter and the wolf*, now provides superfluous poems to introduce Saint-Saëns's zoological fantasy, which is otherwise well enough played. The coupling is execrable.

(i) *Carnival of the animals;* (ii) *Danse macabre, Op. 40; Suite algérienne, Op. 60: Marche militaire française. Samson et Dalila: Bacchanale.* (ii; iii) *Symphony No. 3 in C min., Op. 78.*

(M) *** Sony SBY 47655 [id.]. (i) Entremont, Gaby Casadesus, Régis Pasquier, Yan Pascal Tortelier, Caussé, Yo-Yo Ma, Lauridon, Marion, Arrignon, Cals, Cerutti; (ii) Phd. O, Ormandy; (iii) with E. Power Biggs.

(i) *Carnival of the animals;* (ii) *Danse macabre;* (iii) *Symphony No. 3;* (iv) *Wedding-cake* (caprice-valse for piano and orchestra), *Op. 76.*

☞ **(*) ASV Dig CDDCA 665 [id.]. (i) Guillermo Salvador Snr & Jnr, Mexico City PO; (ii) Mexicana State SO; (iii) Noel Rawsthorne, LPO; (iv) Osorio, RPO; Bátiz.

It would be churlish to bracket the third star for this very generous Sony collection (75 minutes 35 seconds) because the *Carnival of the animals* – performed in its original chamber version – strikes the listener as somewhat lacking in lustre at the opening. The ear adjusts to the rather dry effect. It is a starry cast: Yo-Yo Ma personifies *The Swan* gently and gracefully, and the finale is extremely spirited. Ormandy and his splendid orchestra play the other orchestral lollipops with fine panache – the exuberance at the end of the *Samson et Dalila Bacchanale* is overwhelming, with thundering drums. The catchy *French military march* also goes with a swing. No complaint about the 1962 sound in the *Symphony*. The performance is fresh and vigorous, with the conductor's affection fully conveyed. The alert, polished Philadelphia playing brings incisive articulation to the first movement and Scherzo. E. Power Biggs has the full measure of the hall's Aeolian-Skinner organ, and he makes a spectacular contribution to the finale, which Ormandy structures most excitingly.

A very generous anthology from ASV. The *Carnival of the animals* and *Danse macabre* have plenty of genial vitality but are less strong on finesse, and the forwardly balanced recording adds to the robust feeling. Jorge Federico Osorio, however, despatches the charming *Wedding-cake caprice-valse* with a winning sparkle. Bátiz's version of the spectacular *Organ symphony* was the first digital success for this work. The orchestral playing is exhilarating in its energy, while the *Poco Adagio* balances a noble, elegiac feeling with romantic warmth. The organ entry is an impressive moment and the sense of spectacle persists in the closing pages. Overall, with a playing time of 72 minutes, many will count this excellent value.

Cello concerto No. 1 in A min., Op. 33.

☞ *** ASV Dig. CDDCA 867 [id.]. Sophie Rolland, BBC PO, Gilbert Varga – LALO: *Cello concerto in D min.;* MASSENET: *Fantaisie.* ***

*** DG Dig. 427 323-2 [id.]. Matt Haimovitz, Chicago SO, Levine – LALO: *Concerto;* BRUCH: *Kol Nidrei.* ***

*** BMG/RCA Dig. RD 71003. Harnoy, Cincinnati SO, Kunzel – OFFENBACH: *Concerto;* TCHAIKOVSKY: *Rococo variations.* ***

(M) *** Mercury 432 010-2 [id.]. Janos Starker, LSO, Dorati – LALO: *Concerto* **(*); SCHUMANN: *Concerto.* ***

(B) *** DG 431 166-2. Heinrich Schiff, New Philh. O, Mackerras – FAURE: *Elégie;* LALO: *Cello concerto.* ***

**(*) Ph. Dig. 432 084-2 [id.]. Julian Lloyd Webber, ECO, Yan Pascal Tortelier – FAURE: *Elégie* **; D'INDY: *Lied* **(*); HONEGGER: *Concerto.* **(*)

The young Canadian cellist, Sophie Rolland, has been hailed in extravagant terms by Charles Dutoit and William Pleeth, with whom she studied, and, if this performance of the *A minor Cello concerto* is anything to go by, hers is indeed a formidable talent. She takes its technical hurdles in her effortless stride and is very well supported by the BBC Philharmonic under Gilbert Varga. Perhaps their opening is marginally too fast for an *Allegro non troppo*, but the performance is in every respect a highly enjoyable one. The excellence of the BBC/ASV recording makes for a strong recommendation.

Haimovitz and Levine also open the *Concerto* with a vigorous surge of passionate feeling, and the second subject is tenderly contrasted, with lovely warm timbre from Haimovitz. This strongly characterized account, full of spontaneity, is extremely realistically recorded.

Ofra Harnoy's is also a first-rate account, the opening full of fervour and impulse, played with full tone, while later the timbre is beautifully fined down for the *Adagietto* minuet. The orchestral response is equally refined here; and this well-recorded account is in every way recommendable for its unexpected and attractive Offenbach coupling.

Starker plays the Saint-Saëns *A minor* with charm and grace, and Dorati provides first-class support. The 1964 recording comes up amazingly well and is excellently (and naturally) balanced.

Schiff gives as eloquent an account of this concerto as any on record. He sparks off an enthusiastic response from Mackerras, and the recorded sound and balance are excellent. At bargain price, this deserves the strongest recommendation.

Julian Lloyd Webber plays both Saint-Saëns pieces with considerable virtuosity, though he does not command the range of sonority or colour possessed by some of his rivals. He has the advantage of first-class accompaniment, impressively natural recorded sound and couplings of special interest.

(i) *Cello concerto No. 1 in A min., Op. 33;* (ii) *Piano concerto No. 2 in G min., Op. 22;* (iii) *Violin concerto No. 3, Op. 61.*
⊛ (M) *** Sony Dig. MDK 46506 [id.]. (i) Yo-Yo Ma, O Nat. de France, Maazel; (ii) Cécile Licad,
  LPO, Previn; (iii) Cho-Liang Lin, Philh. O, Tilson Thomas.

Three outstanding performances from the early 1980s are admirably linked together in this highly desirable CBS mid-price reissue. Yo-Yo Ma's performance of the *Cello concerto* is distinguished by fine sensitivity and beautiful tone, while Cécile Licad and the LPO under Previn turn in an eminently satisfactory reading of the *G minor Piano concerto* that has the requisite delicacy in the Scherzo and seriousness elsewhere. Cho-Liang Lin's account of the *B minor Violin concerto* with the Philharmonia Orchestra and Michael Tilson Thomas is exhilarating and thrilling; indeed, this is the kind of performance that prompts one to burst into applause; his version is certainly second to none and is arguably the finest yet to have appeared.

(i; iii) *Cello concerto No. 1 in A min., Op. 33;* (ii; iii) *Piano concertos Nos. 2 in G min., Op. 22; 4 in C min., Op. 44;* (iv) *Introduction and Rondo capriccioso, Op. 28.*
☞ (B) *(*) Sony SBK 48276 [id.]. (i) Leonard Rose; (ii) Philippe Entremont; (iii) Phd. O, Ormandy;
  (iv) Zukerman, LSO, Mackerras.

Leonard Rose's account of the *Cello concerto* is first class, and Zukerman is brilliant in the *Introduction and Rondo capriccioso*, although the recording here is forwardly balanced and two-dimensional. The Entremont performances, however, lack elegance and charm and their brilliance is made to sound aggressive by the recording, especially in No. 4, which needs more warmth of sonority. The CD sounds fuller than the original LP, but is still unsatisfactory by present-day standards.

Piano concertos Nos. 1–5.
*** Decca 417 351-2 (2) [id.]. Rogé, Philh. O, LPO or RPO, Dutoit.

Played as they are here, these *Concertos* can exert a strong appeal: Pascal Rogé brings delicacy, virtuosity and sparkle to the piano part and he receives expert support from the various London orchestras under Dutoit. Altogether delicious playing and excellent piano sound from Decca, who secure a most realistic balance.

Piano concerto No. 2 in G min., Op. 22.
☞ (M) *** BMG/RCA 09026 61863-2 [id.]. Rubinstein, Phd. O, Ormandy – FALLA: *Nights in the gardens of Spain* etc. **(*); FRANCK: *Symphonic variations for piano and orchestra.* ***
☞ (***) Testament mono SBT 1029 [id.]. Gilels, Paris Cons. O, Cluytens – RACHMANINOV: *Piano concerto No. 3;* SHOSTAKOVICH: *Prelude and fugue in D.* (***)
(**(*)) Olympia mono OCD 236 [id.]. Moura Lympany, LPO, Jean Martinon – KHACHATURIAN: *Piano concerto.* (***)
☞ *(*) Pickwick Dig. MCD 71 [id.]. Valerie Traficante, RPO, Serebrier – FAURE: *Ballade for piano and orchestra;* D'INDY: *Symphonie.* *(*)

Rubinstein's version was made in 1969, and he is partnered by that most understanding of accompanists, Eugene Ormandy. Rubinstein's secret is that, though he appears sometimes to be attacking the music, his phrasing is full of little fluctuations so that his playing never sounds stilted. The recording of the piano is rather dry, even hard at times, but the glitter seems just right for the centrepiece.

Gilels's celebrated account of the Saint-Saëns *G minor concerto* comes from 1954 and is masterly in every respect. Its delicacy and refinement still come across in spite of the limitations of the recording. The slightly shallow piano-sound is soon forgotten when there is nothing shallow about the playing, and Gilels gets marvellous support from the Paris Orchestra under André Cluytens. Excellent transfers.

Moura Lympany's 1951 account of the *Second Piano concerto* is a delight. She is very well accompanied by Martinon, and it is a pity that the transfer of the (originally Decca) mono recording is so cavernous. Moreover there is a serious pitch fluctuation in the first movement (7 minutes 49 seconds).

Valerie Traficante plays this French triptych well enough, but there are better versions of all three works and the recording is rather resonant.

Piano concertos Nos. 2 in G min., Op. 22; 4 in C min., Op. 44.
☞ (B) *(*) Erato/Warner Duo Dig. 4509 95358-2 (2) [id.]. Duchable, Strasbourg PO, Lombard –
    RAVEL: *Concertos* etc. *(*)

The Erato coupling is much less winning than Rogé and the recording lacks the luminous colouring of the Decca alternative. The piano is forwardly balanced and Duchable's bold assertiveness in outer movements brings character of the wrong sort to music-making which at times sounds aggressive. There is little charm and, while the first movement of No. 2 is stronger than usual and the playing is never thoughtless or slipshod, this cannot compare with Licad or Rogé. Moreover the Erato Bonsai Duo reissue is inadequately documented.

Violin concertos Nos. 1 in A, Op. 20; 2 in C, Op. 58; 3 in B min., Op. 61; Caprice andalou, Op. 122; Le Déluge, Op. 45: Prélude. Havanaise, Op. 83; Introduction and rondo capriccioso, Op. 28; Morceau de concert, Op. 62; Romances: in D, Op. 37; in C, Op. 48; (i) La Muse et le Poète, Op. 132. (Also includes: YSAYE: *Caprice d'après l'Etude en forme de valse, Op. 52/6.)*
☞ (M) **(*) EMI CMS7 64790-2 (2) [id.]. Ulf Hoelscher, New Philh. O, Pierre Dervaux; (i) with
    Ralph Kirshbaum.

This two-CD box collects all Saint-Saëns's music for violin and orchestra (with a short bonus from Ysaÿe) in performances of excellent quality. Ulf Hoelscher is an extremely accomplished soloist who plays with artistry as well as virtuosity, and he uncovers music of genuine worth and much charm which is not as well-known as the *Third Violin concerto*. The *Second*, incidentally, has a most attractive *Andante* and a catchy *Allegro scherzando* finale, while the first of the two *Romances* deserves to be much better known. The aptly named *Morceau de concert* is most engaging, and the relatively ambitious extended duo concertante piece, *La Muse et le Poète*, in which Hoelscher is admirably partnered by Ralph Kirshbaum, seems much more substantial here than it does in Geoffrey Simon's anthology on Cala (see above). In this EMI set Pierre Dervaux directs excellent accompaniments, and the recording (made at Abbey Road in 1977) is basically of excellent quality. The slight snag is the forward balance of the solo violin, which means that, with the CD remastering, Hoelscher's timbre in the upper range is made to sound just a bit thin. This is also noticeable in the orchestral violins in the closing *Le Déluge Prélude*.

Violin concerto No. 1 in A, Op. 20.
☞ (M) *** Decca Dig. 436 483-2 [id.]. Kyung Wha Chung, Montreal SO, Dutoit – LALO: *Cello
    concerto No. 1* etc. ***

Saint-Saëns's *First violin concerto* is a miniature – in three sections, but playing altogether for only 11½ minutes. Kyung Wha Chung plays it delightfully, equally at home in its persuasively simple lyricism and in the energetic bravura of the outer sections. She is admirably accompanied, and the Decca recording is first class. This comes merely as a bonus, nicely sandwiched between Lalo's *D minor Cello concerto* and the *Symphonie espagnole*.

Violin concerto No. 3 in B min., Op. 61.
(M) *** DG Dig. 429 977-2 [id.]. Perlman, O de Paris, Barenboim – LALO: *Symphonie espagnole*. ***
*** DG Dig. 429 786-2 [id.]. Gil Shaham, NYPO, Sinopoli – PAGANINI: *Concerto No. 1*. ***
*** ASV Dig. CDDCA 680 [id.]. Xue Wei, Philh. O, Bakels – BRUCH: *Concerto No. 1*. ***

On DG, Perlman achieves a fine partnership with his friend, Barenboim, in a performance that is both tender and strong, while Perlman's verve and dash in the finale are dazzling. The forward balance is understandable in this work, but orchestral detail could at times be sharper.

One only has to sample the delectable way Gil Shaham presents the enchanting *Barcarolle*, which forms the principal theme of Saint-Saëns's *Andante*, to discover the distinction of this performance.

This is a performance which balances elegant *espressivo* with great dash and fire: neither the soloist nor the conductor lets even the slightest suspicion of routine into a performance which dazzles and charms in equal measure. The recording is first class.

Xue Wei's account is full of flair from the very first entry onwards. The orchestral accompaniment is strongly characterized as well, while the soloist creates an ideal mixture of ruminative lyricism and dash, especially in the slow movement. The sound is vivid, even if the balance, within a church acoustic, seems artificially contrived.

Danse macabre, Op. 40.
*** Denon Dig. DC 8097 [id.]. Tokyo Metropolitan SO, Jean Fournet – BERLIOZ: *Symphonie fantastique.* ***
(M) **(*) Chan. CHAN 6503; *MBTD 6503* [id.]. SNO, Gibson – DUKAS: *L'apprenti sorcier;*
ROSSINI/RESPIGHI: *La boutique fantasque.* **(*)

Jean Fournet's 1987 performance of *Danse macabre* is a very persuasive reading, well recorded. Gibson's performance is also well played and vividly recorded, but this CD offers rather short measure (37 minutes), even at mid-price.

Danse macabre, Op. 40; (i) *Havanaise, Op. 83; Introduction and rondo capriccioso, Op. 28. Le jeunesse d'Hercule, Op. 50; Marche héroïque, Op. 34; Phaéton, Op. 39; Le rouet d'Omphale, Op. 31.*
(M) *** Decca 425 021-2 [id.]. (i) Kyung Wha Chung, RPO; Philh. O; Charles Dutoit.

A splendidly conceived anthology. The symphonic poems are beautifully played, and the 1979 Kingsway Hall recording lends the appropriate atmosphere. Charles Dutoit shows himself an admirably sensitive exponent, revelling in the composer's craftsmanship and revealing much delightful orchestral detail in the manner of a Beecham. Decca have now added Kyung Wha Chung's equally charismatic and individual 1977 accounts of what are perhaps the two most inspired short display-pieces for violin and orchestra in the repertoire.

Havanaise, Op. 83; Introduction and rondo capriccioso, Op. 28.
☞ *** EMI Dig. CDC7 47725-2 [id.]. Perlman, O de Paris, Martinon – CHAUSSON: *Poème;* RAVEL: *Tzigane.* ***
*** DG Dig. 423 063-2 [id.]. Perlman, NYPO, Mehta – CHAUSSON: *Poème;* RAVEL: *Tzigane;*
SARASATE: *Carmen fantasy.* ***

Perlman plays these Saint-Saëns warhorses with splendid panache and virtuosity on EMI; his tone and control of colour in the *Havanaise* are ravishing. The digital remastering brings Perlman's gorgeous fiddling right into the room, at the expense of a touch of aggressiveness when the orchestra lets rip; but the concert-hall ambience prevents this from being a problem.

Perlman's DG recordings have the advantage of an excellent digital sound-balance and the closing pages of the *Havanaise* are particularly felicitous.

Introduction and Rondo capriccioso.
*** DG Dig. 427 676-2 [id.]. Mintz, Israel PO, Mehta – LALO: *Symphonie espagnole;* VIEUXTEMPS: *Concerto No. 5.* ***

Minz dazzles the ear with Saint-Saëns's fireworks, yet playing with elegance and finesse.

Symphonies in A; in F (Urbs Roma); Symphonies Nos. 1–3.
(B) *** EMI CZS7 62643-2 (2) [Ang. CDMB 62643]. French Nat. R. O, Martinon (with Bernard Gavoty, organ de l'église Saint-Louis des Invalides in *No. 3*).

The A and F major works were totally unknown and unpublished at the time of their recording and have never been dignified with numbers. Yet the A major, written when the composer was only fifteen, is a delight and may reasonably be compared with Bizet's youthful work in the same genre. Scored for strings with flute and oboe, the charming Scherzo is matched by the *moto perpetuo* finale, and the whole work makes delightful gramophone listening. More obviously mature, the *Urbs Roma Symphony* is perhaps a shade more self-conscious, but more ambitious too, showing striking imagination in such movements as the darkly vigorous scherzo and the variation movement at the end.

The first of the numbered symphonies is a well-fashioned and genial piece, again much indebted to Mendelssohn, and to Schumann too, but with much delightfully fresh invention. The *Second* is full of excellent ideas. Martinon directs splendid performances of the whole set, well prepared and lively. The account of the *Third* ranks with the best: freshly spontaneous in the opening movement, and the threads knitted powerfully together at the end of the finale. Here the recording could do with rather more sumptuousness. Elsewhere the quality is bright and fresh, with no lack of body, and it suits the Saint-Saëns textures very well.

Symphony No. 2 in A min., Op. 55; Phaéton, Op. 39; Suite algérienne, Op. 60.
*** ASV Dig. CDDCA 599 [id.]. LSO, Butt.

The *Second Symphony* is very well played here with the freshness of an orchestra discovering something unfamiliar and enjoying themselves; Yondani Butt's tempi are apt and he shapes the whole piece convincingly. He is equally persuasive in the picaresque *Suite algérienne*, the source of the justly famous *Marche militaire française*, and indeed in *Phaéton*. Warmly atmospheric recording

Symphonies Nos. 2 in A min., Op. 55; (i) 3 in C min., Op. 78.
*** Chan. Dig. CHAN 8822; *ABTD 1447* [id.]. Ulster O, Yan Pascal Tortelier; (i) with Gillian Weir.

Yan Pascal Tortelier's performances are very enjoyable and very well recorded. But in the *Second Symphony* Yondani Butt's account has greater freshness, and the slightly less reverberant ASV recording contributes to this. If your interest is primarily in this work, Butt's version is first choice, but if you need both *Symphonies* on one CD, then the Chandos issue has much in its favour. Certainly the hall resonance suits the *Organ symphony* and the work moves to an impressive dénouement.

Symphony No. 3 in C min., Op. 78.
☞ ⊛ (M) *** BMG/RCA 09026 61500-2. Berj Zamkochian, Boston SO, Munch – DEBUSSY: *La Mer* **(*); IBERT: *Escales.* ***
*** DG Dig. 419 617-2 [id.]. Simon Preston, BPO, Levine – DUKAS: *L'apprenti sorcier.* ***
(B) *** Pickwick Dig. PCD 847; *CIMPC 847* [id.]. Chorzempa, Berne SO, Maag.
(M) *** Mercury 432 719-2 [id.]. Marcel Dupré, Detroit SO, Paray – PARAY: *Mass.* **(*)
☞ ** DG Dig. 435 854-2 [id.]. Michael Matthes, Bastillle Opéra O, Myung-Whun Chung – MESSIAEN: *L'Ascension.* ***
☞ * DG Gold Dig. 439 014-2 [id.]. Pierre Cochereau (organ of Notre-Dame Cathedral, Paris), BPO, Karajan.

(i; ii) *Symphony No. 3;* (ii) *Danse macabre, Op. 40; Samson et Dalila: Bacchanale;* (i) *3 Rhapsodies sur des cantiques bretons, Op. 7.*
☞ *** BIS Dig. CD 555 [id.]. (i) Hans Fagius; (ii) Royal Stockholm PO, James de Preist.

(i) *Symphony No. 3;* (ii) *Danse macabre; Le Déluge: Prélude, Op. 45; Samson et Dalila: Bacchanale.*
(M) *** DG 415 847-2 [id.]. (i) Litaize, Chicago SO, Barenboim; (ii) O de Paris, Barenboim.

(i) *Symphony No. 3. Danse macabre; Le rouet d'Omphale.*
☞ (B) *(**) Erato/Warner 2292 45943-2 [id.]. (i) Alain; French Nat. R. O, Martinon – POULENC: *Organ concerto.* (**)

Munch's Boston recording dates from 1960 (three years after Paray's Detroit version), yet in its currently remastered form it sounds as overwhelmingly spectacular as many versions of three decades later. Indeed, anyone who has heard this work 'live' in Symphony Hall will realize that the RCA engineers have captured that overwhelming experience with remarkable accuracy. While the resonance enhances the blend of organ and strings in the *Poco adagio*, which has an enveloping warmth, and projects the huge and thrilling organ entry in the finale, the balance allows sparkling detail and represents one of the most successful and most believable recordings ever made in this difficult venue. It was achieved by taking the seats out of the front half of the auditorium and boldly spreading the orchestra out over the whole area, while the organ, situated at the back of the stage, was given its own three-channel microphone. The result is hugely successful and the listener really experiences the hall itself. The performance is stunning, full of lyrical ardour and moving forward in a single sweep of great intensity. The couplings, showing Munch and his Bostonians at their peak, are equally valuable, if not quite so outstandingly recorded.

With the Berlin Philharmonic in cracking form, Levine's is a grippingly dramatic reading, full of imaginative detail. The great thrust of the performance does not stem from fast pacing: rather it is the result of incisive articulation, while the clarity of the digital recording allows the pianistic detail to register crisply. The thunderous organ entry in the finale makes a magnificent effect, and the tension is held at white heat throughout the movement. The Dukas coupling is equally memorable.

From Stockholm comes an outstanding performance of the *Third Symphony* that is competitive even in a well-stocked market. De Preist is straight and unmannered, completely at the service of the music, and proves very persuasive in this repertoire. Hans Fagius plays the Stockholm Concert Hall organ so that, unlike some performances in which the organist is tacked on afterwards, this is a genuine performance. He plays the *Trois Rhapsodies sur des cantiques bretons* on the splendid Marcussen instrument of St Jakobs Kyrka in Stockholm to striking effect. What a fine player he is, too! The recording of all these items is full-blooded and has plenty of impact yet it is beautifully and naturally balanced and makes no attempt to be a 'sonic spectacular'. A very satisfying record.

Barenboim's inspirational 1976 version has long dominated the catalogue. Among the reissue's three attractive bonuses is an exciting account of the *Bacchanale* from *Samson et Dalila*. The performance of the *Symphony* glows with warmth from beginning to end. A brilliant account of the Scherzo leads into a magnificently energetic conclusion, with the Chicago orchestra excelling itself with radiant playing in every section. The digital remastering is not wholly advantageous: while detail is sharper, the massed violins sound thinner and the bass is drier. In the finale, some of the bloom has gone, and the organ entry has a touch of hardness.

Maag's extremely well-recorded Berne performance has a Mendelssohnian freshness and the sprightly playing in the Scherzo draws an obvious affinity with that composer. The closing pages have a convincing feeling of apotheosis and, although this is not the weightiest reading available, it is an uncommonly enjoyable one in which the sound is bright, full and suitably resonant.

The fine Paray/Mercury recording dates, astonishingly, from 1957. The early date brings just a hint of shrillness to the violins in the first movement; otherwise the sound remains bold, full and remarkably well detailed. Marcel Dupré's weighty organ entry introduces a finale which is powerfully co-ordinated, building to an impressive climax. However, not everyone may want the coupling, enjoyable as it is.

Martinon's account of the *Symphony* is, not surprisingly, distinguished, the first movement alert and sparkling, the *Poco adagio* warmly romantic, yet with a touch of nobility at the close. Marie-Claire Alain's organ entry at the end will disappoint no one. Unfortunately the CD transfer has an artificially brightened upper range, which brings shrillness to the violins and affects also the two orchestra encores, which are very well played, although *Le rouet d'Omphale* is taken rather fast.

Myung-Whun Chung's performance is lightweight, fresh but not encompassing the work's spectacular nature, while the *Poco adagio* is curiously slow and heavy. The recording is excellent, but there are far more compelling versions available.

It is extraordinary that DG should have chosen the 1981 recording of the *Third Symphony* for inclusion in the Karajan Gold series, for it proves the one dud! The performance goes well enough until the finale, although the *Poco adagio* is rather slow and heavy. Then, in an attempt to add spectacle, the orchestra is brought forward and the laminated Notre-Dame organ, very closely observed indeed, produces an unattractively harsh sound which even the most flexible controls cannot mitigate. The remastering has been unable to improve matters – but in any case to offer the work on its own (38 minutes) at full price is not very enticing.

Wedding-cake (Caprice-valse), Op. 76.
☞ (BB) *** ASV Dig. CDQS 6092. Osorio, RPO, Bátiz – FRANCK: *Symphonic variations* **(*);
   RAVEL: *Left-hand concerto* ***; SCHUMANN: *Concerto.* **(*)

A delightfully lightweight performance of Saint-Saëns's frothy but engaging *morceau de concert*, infectious and sparkling. Nicely recorded, too.

CHAMBER MUSIC

Carnival of the animals (chamber version); *Piano trio in F, Op. 18; Septet in E flat, for trumpet, strings & piano, Op. 65.*
*** Virgin/EMI Dig. VC7 59514-2 [id.]. Nash Ens.

This is a highly persuasive account of the first of Saint-Saëns's two *Piano trios*, while the Nash Ensemble capture the humour of the *Septet* and the *Grand fantaisie zoölogique* excellently. The acoustic has warmth and the balance between the instruments, particularly in the *Carnival of the animals*, is admirably judged.

Piano trio No. 1 in F, Op. 18.
☞ *** Ph. Dig. 434 071-2 [id.]. Beaux Arts Trio – FAURE: *Piano quartet No. 2.* ***

The *Piano Trio No. 1 in F major* comes from 1863 and is a delightful piece, Mendelssohnian in its lightness of touch and fleetness of invention. There are other versions, notably an excellent one from the Nash (Virgin), coupled with the *Septet* and the *Carnival of the animals*, but the present issue is second to none.

Romance for horn and piano, Op. 67.
(M) *** Decca 433 695-2 [id.]. Barry Tuckwell, Vladimir Ashkenazy – BRAHMS: *Horn trio;* FRANCK: *Violin sonata;* SCHUMANN: *Adagio & allegro.* ***

Saint-Saëns's unexpectedly sombre *Romance* is beautifully played by Tuckwell and Ashkenazy, who find exactly the right element of restraint. Excellent 1974 Kingsway Hall recording.

Violin sonata No. 1 in D min., Op. 75.
*** Essex CDS 6044 [id.]. Accardo, Canio – CHAUSSON: *Concert.* ***
*** Collins Dig. 1112-2 [id.]. Lorraine McAslan, John Blakely – DEBUSSY; RAVEL: *Sonatas.* ***

The performance by Accardo and Canio is marvellously played, selfless and dedicated. The recording too is very good, and this can be recommended strongly, if the coupling is suitable.

Lorraine McAslan and her fine pianist also give a good account of themselves, and their reading can hold its head high in the current catalogue with a wide range of colour. The recording is very good indeed, well balanced and truthful.

Mélodies: *Clair de lune; Les cloches de la mer; Danse macabre; Extase; Le lever de la lune; Le pas d'armes du Roi Jean; Rêverie; Si vous n'avez rien à me dire; Sonnet.*
☞ **(*) EMI Dig. CDC7 54818-2 [id.]. José van Dam, Jean-Philippe Collard – GOUNOD; MASSENET: *Mélodies.* **(*)

The velvet legato of José van Dam, with his firm, dark tone, is very satisfying in all but two of this group of Saint-Saëns songs, gentle inspirations which he transforms. The exceptions are the two livelier songs – *Danse macabre* (which prompted the orchestral piece of that name) and *Le pas d'armes du Roi Jean* – which are coarser and rather heavy-handed, not helped by Collard's accompaniments. A valuable recital nevertheless, coupled with Massenet and Gounod songs.

Messe à quatre voix, Op. 4.
☞ (M) **(*) Decca 425 077-2 [id.]. Simon Colston, Anthony deRivaz, John Vickers, Trevor Owen, Brian Harvey, Worcester Cathedral Ch., Roy Massey & Paul Trepte (grand et petit organs) – POULENC: *Gloria.* ***

Donald Hunt directs an enjoyable performance of an early rarity of Saint-Saëns. Written when he was only twenty-one, this *Mass* shows how well he had learnt his academic lessons for, at various points, he uses with total freshness what at the time were archaic techniques, as in the beautiful *Agnus Dei* at the end. The organ writing is characteristically fresh, and though one finds few signs of deep feeling the piece is well worth hearing. The soloists here are variable, but the choir is excellent and the recording suitably atmospheric.

OPERA

Samson et Dalila (opera): complete.
☞ *** EMI CDS7 54470-2 (2) [Ang. CDCB 54470]. Domingo, Meier, Fondary, Courtis, L'Opéra-Bastille Ch. & O, Myung-Whun Chung.
(M) **(*) DG 413 297-2 (2). Obraztsova, Domingo, Bruson, Lloyd, Thau, Ch. & O de Paris, Barenboim.

When the vintage DG set with Plácido Domingo as Samson offers Daniel Barenboim as conductor, it was a neat move by EMI to present the opera again with Domingo as the hero, but with Barenboim's successor at the Bastille Opéra in Paris, Myung-Whun Chung. Chung's view is altogether more volatile, more idiomatic, which helps Domingo to give a more imaginative and varied interpretation, even more detailed than before, with the voice still in glorious condition. So in the big Act III aria, when the blind Samson is turning the millstone, Domingo with Chung gives a deeper, more thoughtful performance, broader, with greater repose and a sense of power in reserve. When the big melody appears in Dalila's seduction aria, *Mon coeur s'ouvre*, Chung's conducting encourages a tender restraint, where others produce a full-throated roar. Meier may not have an ideally sensuous voice for the role, with some unwanted harshness in her expressive account of Dalila's first monologue, but her feeling for words is strong and the characterization vivid. Generally Chung's speeds are on the fast side, yet the performance does not lack weight, with some first-rate singing in the incidental roles from Alain Fondary, Samuel Ramey and Jean-Philippe Courtis. Apart from backwardly placed choral sound, the recording is warm and well focused.

Barenboim proves as passionately dedicated an interpreter of Saint-Saëns here as he did in the *Third Symphony*, sweeping away any Victorian cobwebs. It is important, too, that the choral passages, so vital in this work, be sung with this sort of freshness, and Domingo has rarely sounded happier in French music, the bite as well as the heroic richness of the voice well caught. Renato Bruson and Robert Lloyd are both admirable too; sadly, however, the key role of Dalila is given an unpersuasive, unsensuous performance by Obraztsova, with her vibrato often verging on a wobble. The recording is as ripe as the music deserves.

Salieri, Antonio (1750–1825)

Falstaff (opera): complete.
*** Hung. Dig. HCD 21789/91 [id.]. Gregor, Zempléni, Gulyás, Gáti, Pánczél, Csura, Vámossy, Salieri Chamber Ch. & O, Tamás Pál.

Like Verdi, Salieri and his librettist ignore the Falstaff of the histories. They tell the story within the framework of the conventional two-Act opera of the period. None of the ideas, however charming or sparkling, is developed in the way one would expect in Mozart, but it is all great fun, particularly in a performance as lively and well sung as this. Jószef Gregor is splendid in the name-part, with Dénes Gulyás equally stylish in the tenor role of Ford. Maria Zempléni as Mistress Ford and Eva Pánczél in the mezzo role of Mistress Slender (not Page) are both bright and lively. The eponymous chorus and orchestra also perform with vigour under Tamás Pál; the recording is brilliant, with a fine sense of presence.

Sallinen, Aulis (born 1935)

(i) *Cello concerto, Op. 44; Shadows (Prelude for Orchestra), Op. 52; Symphony No. 4, Op. 49.*
*** Finlandia Dig. FACD 346 [id.]. (i) Arto Noras; Helsinki PO, Kamu.

The *Cello concerto* of 1977 is the most commanding piece here. Sallinen's ideas and his sound-world resonate in the mind. Arto Noras has its measure and plays with masterly eloquence. The middle movement of the *Fourth Symphony* is marked *Dona nobis pacem*; throughout the finale, bells colour the texture, as is often the case in his orchestral writing. *Shadows* is an effective short piece which reflects or 'shadows' the content of the opera, *The King goes forth to France*. The performances under Okko Kamu are very impressive and the recording quite exemplary.

(i) *Violin concerto, Op. 18;* (ii) *Nocturnal dances of Don Juan Quixote, Op. 58; Some aspects of Peltoniemi Hintrik's funeral march, Op. 19; Variations for orchestra (Juventas variations), Op. 8.*
☞ *** BIS Dig. CD 560 [id.]. (i) Koskinen; (ii) Thedéen; Tapiola Sinf., Vänskä.

Both the *Variations for orchestra* and the *Violin concerto* come from the 1960s, after Sallinen had made his mark outside Finland with *Mauermusik*, composed to commemorate victims of the Berlin Wall. The *Variations for orchestra*, written when he was in his late twenties for a youth orchestra, is an imaginative and inventive piece which shows remarkable command of the orchestra. It is tonally ambiguous without being serial; indeed at one point there is a reminder of Britten. The *Violin concerto* comes from 1968 and is also rewarding and in the slow movement often beautiful; one can see that its lyrical impulse is not quite strong enough for it to become part of the standard repertoire, but it is nevertheless an arresting piece and finds a powerful advocate in Eeva Koskinen. *Some aspects of Peltoniemi Hintrik's funeral march* is a transcription for full strings of his *Third Quartet* (1969), a one-movement work in five variations that never lose sight of the basic folk-inspired idea; not one of his strongest works. Nor are *The Nocturnal Dances of Don Juanquixote*, which date from the mid-1980s, Sallinen at his most inventive. They sound pretty thin, though they enjoy excellent advocacy from Torleif Thedéen and the Tapiola Sinfonietta under Osmo Vänskä and a vivid, well-lit but not overbright BIS recording.

(i) *Symphonies Nos. 1; 3;* (ii) *Chorali;* (iii) *Cadenze for solo violin;* (iv) *Elegy for Sebastian Knight;* (v) *String quartet No. 3.*
*** BIS CD 41 [id.]. (i) Finnish RSO, Kamu; (ii) Helsinki PO, Berglund; (iii) Paavo Pohjola; (iv) Frans Helmerson; (v) Voces Intimae Qt.

The *First Symphony*, in one movement, is diatonic and full of atmosphere, as indeed is the *Third*, a powerful, imaginative piece which appears to be haunted by the sounds and smells of nature. The performances under Okko Kamu are excellent. *Chorali* is a shorter piece, persuasively done by Paavo Berglund; and there are three chamber works, albeit of lesser substance. The recordings are from the 1970s and are all very well balanced. Highly recommended.

(i) *Symphony No. 5 (Washington mosaics), Op. 57;* (ii; iii) *Chamber music III: The Nocturnal Dances of Don Juanquixote* (for cello & orchestra), *Op. 58;* (iii) (Solo) *Cello sonata, Op. 26.*
**(*) Finlandia Dig. FACD 370 [id.]. (i) Helsinki PO, or (ii) Finlandia Sinfonietta, Kamu; (iii) Arto Noras.

Washington mosaics is a five-movement work in which the outer movements form the framework for three less substantial but highly imaginative intermezzi. There are Stravinskian overtones in the first movement and the three intermezzi cast a strong spell; those who respond to the *First* and *Third Symphonies* will find comparable feeling for nature and a keen sense of its power. The performance is dedicated. *The Nocturnal Dances of Don Juanquixote* is pretty thin stuff; it incorporates nostalgic recollections of Sallinen's days working in a restaurant band. It is impeccably played by Arto Noras, but not even his art can persuade one of its merits. The solo *Cello sonata* of 1971 is hardly a substantial makeweight, even though Noras is a masterly advocate.

Kullervo (opera).
☞ *** Ondine Dig. ODE 780-3T. Hynninen, Sallinen, Jakobsson, Silvasti, Vihavainen, Finnish Nat. Op. Ch. & O, Ulf Söderblom.

Sallinen's fourth opera occupied him between 1986 and 1988, and was written for the Los Angeles Opera, who premièred it in 1992. The action is set in primitive times against a background of clan feuds and violence. Although the theme will be familiar from Sibelius's early symphony of the same name, Sallinen has based his *Kullervo* on the play by Aleksis Kivi and he wrote the libretto himself. The plot emerges from a mixture of narration, in which the chorus plays a central role, and dreams. Put crudely, the feud between two brothers, Kalervo and Unto, culminates in the burning of Kalervo's house. Kullervo, Kalervo's son, is abducted and sold into slavery; he destroys the smith's cattle and kills his young wife. Now a fugitive, Kullervo comes upon his parents, who have survived the fire, but they reject him when it emerges that he has unwittingly slept with his sister. Kullervo determines to exact vengeance on Unto, but on his way there Kimmo, his childhood friend and for a time a fellow-slave, intercepts him and reveals that his parents and sister have been killed. Kullervo decides to kill all Unto's family, and the opera ends with him going in search of Kimmo; finding that as a result of his experiences he has lost his sanity, he commits suicide.

The opera is a compelling musical drama, far more atmospheric and musically effective than its immediate predecessor, *The King goes forth to France.* Sallinen's musical language has debts to composers as diverse as Britten (shadows of the 'Sunday morning' interlude in *Peter Grimes* briefly cross the score in Kullervo's Dream at the beginning of Act II), Puccini, Debussy even, though they are synthesized into an effective vehicle for a vivid theatrical imagination. There is impressive variety of pace and atmosphere, and the black voices of the Finnish Opera Chorus resonate in the memory. So, too, do the impressive performances of Jorma Hynninen as Kullervo and Anna-Lisa Jakobsson as the smith's young wife and, indeed, the remainder of the cast and the Finnish National Opera Orchestra under Ulf Söderblom. While *Kullervo* may not be a great opera, it is gripping and effective musical theatre, and the Ondine recording has excellent presence and detail.

Sammartini, Giovanni Battista (1700–75)

Symphonies in D; G; String quintet in E.
(B) *** HM HMA 901245; *HMA 431245* [id.]. Ens. 145, Banchini – Giuseppe SAMMARTINI: *Concerti grossi* etc. ***

Giovanni Battista was the younger of the two Sammartini brothers; he spent his whole life in Milan. On this record, the Ensemble 145, led by Chiara Banchini, offer two of his symphonies; although neither attains greatness, they have genuine appeal. Good recording.

Sammartini, Giuseppe (c. 1693–1750)

Concerti grossi Nos. 6 & 8; (i) *Recorder concerto in F.*
(B) *** HM HMA 901245; *HMA 431245* [id.]. (i) Conrad Steinmann; Ens. 145, Banchini – Giovanni SAMMARTINI: *Symphonies* etc. ***

Giuseppe settled in England in the 1720s and he was a refined and inventive composer. The Ensemble 145 is a period-instrument group; they produce a firmly focused sound, even though the textures are light and the articulation lively. Excellent playing from Conrad Steinmann in the *Recorder concerto.*

Sarasate, Pablo (1844–1908)

Carmen fantasy, Op. 25.
⊛ *** EMI CDC7 47101-2 [id.]. Itzhak Perlman, RPO, Foster – PAGANINI: *Concerto No. 1.*** ⊛
*** DG Dig. 423 063-2 [id.]. Itzhak Perlman, NYPO, Mehta – CHAUSSON: *Poème;* RAVEL:
Tzigane; SAINT-SAENS: *Havanaise* etc. ***

Played like this on EMI, with superb panache, luscious tone and glorious recording, Sarasate's
Fantasy almost upstages the concerto with which it is coupled. The recording balance is admirable,
with the quality greatly to be preferred to many of Perlman's more recent digital records.

Perlman has re-recorded this work for DG in a fine new digital version, and it is generously
coupled with other famous showpieces. The new performance is beyond criticism – but the earlier one
was just that bit riper and more beguiling.

Zigeunerweisen, Op. 20.
*** DG Dig. 431 815-2 [id.]. Gil Shaham, LSO, Lawrence Foster – WIENIAWSKI: *Violin concertos
Nos. 1 & 2* etc. ***

Gil Shaham plays Sarasate's sultry and dashing gypsy confection with rich timbre, languorous ardour
and a dazzling display of fireworks at the close.

Sarum Chant

*Missa in gallicantu; Hymns: A solis ortus cardine; Christe Redemptor omnium; Salvator mundi,
Domine; Veni Redemptor omnium.*
*** Gimell Dig. CDGIM 017; *1585T-17* [id.]. Tallis Scholars, Peter Phillips.

Filling in our knowledge of early church music, the Tallis Scholars under Peter Phillips here present a
whole disc of chant according to the Salisbury rite – in other words *Sarum chant* – which, rather than
the regular Gregorian style, was what churchgoers of the Tudor period and earlier in England heard
at their devotions. The greater part of the record is given over to the setting of the First Mass of
Christmas, intriguingly entitled *Missa in gallicantu* or *Mass at cock-crow*. Though this is simply
monophonic (the men's voices alone are used), it is surprising what antiphonal variety there is. The
record is completed with four hymns from the Divine Offices of Christmas Day. The record is warmly
atmospheric in the characteristic Gimell manner.

Satie, Erik (1866–1925)

Les aventures de Mercure (ballet); *La belle excentrique: Grand ritournelle. 5 Grimaces pour 'Un songe
d'une nuit d'été'; Gymnopédies Nos. 1 & 3; Jack-in-the-box* (orch. Milhaud); *3 Morceaux en forme de
poire; Parade* (ballet); *Relâche* (ballet).
(M) **(*) Van. 8.4030.71 [OVC 4030]. Utah SO, Maurice Abravanel.

A generous budget collection of Satie's orchestral music, well played and given full, vivid recording
from the beginning of the 1970s; if Abravanel fails to throw off some of the more pointed music with
a fully idiomatic lightness of touch, these are still enjoyable performances; the ballet scores have
plenty of colour and rhythmic life.

Parade.
☞ (M) *** Mercury 434 335-2 [id.]. LSO, Dorati – AURIC: *Overture;* FETLER: *Contrasts;* FRANCAIX:
Piano concertino; MILHAUD: *Le bœuf sur le toit.* ***

Satie's *Parade* is the most audacious piece in an excellent Mercury compilation of (mostly) twentieth-
century French music, its scoring including several extra-musical effects, including a typewriter (very
nicely balanced here), a siren and gunshots. Dorati makes it all fit together wittily and entertainingly,
and the LSO make the most of the vivid scoring, with the brass obviously relishing their slightly
vulgar theme which is somewhat reminiscent of Kurt Weill. The necessary atmosphere and colour are
given to the more restrained sections of the score, and the Mercury recording team excel themselves
in presenting Satie's kaleidoscopic circus colours with the utmost vividness.

PIANO MUSIC

Aperçus désagréables; La belle excentrique (fantaisie sérieuse) (both for 4 hands); *Croquis et agaceries d'un gros bonhomme en bois; Descriptions automatiques; Embryons desséchés; En habit de cheval* (for 4 hands); *Le fils des étoiles, wagnerie kaldéenne du Sar Peladan; 6 Gnossiennes; 3 Gymnopédies; Jack-in-the-box; 3 Mouvements en forme de poire* (for 4 hands); *3 Nocturnes; Peccadilles importunes; 3 Petites pièces montées* (for 4 hands); *Pièces froides; Préludes flasques (pour un chien); Première pensée et sonneries de la Rose Croix; 3 Sarabandes; Sonatine bureaucratique; Sports et divertissements; 3 Valses distinguées du précieux dégoût.*

(B) **(*) EMI CZS7 67282-2 (2). Aldo Ciccolini.

Although Satie's achievement is sometimes overrated by his admirers, about much of this music there is a desperate melancholy and a rich poetic feeling which are altogether unique. The *Gymnopédies, Gnossiennes, Sarabandes* and *Pièces froides* show such flashes of innocence and purity of inspiration that criticism is disarmed, while the wit of the sharper vignettes is most engaging. Aldo Ciccolini is widely praised as a Satie interpreter and he plays here with unaffected sympathy. He certainly understands the *douloureux* feeling of the famous *Gymnopédies*, with which his recital opens, and he also finds the '*conviction et tristesse rigoureuse*' of the *Gnossiennes*. There is a noble, aristocratic dignity expressed in the *Première pensée et sonneries de la Rose Croix*, yet *La belle excentrique* is thrown off with great dash and élan. In the works where (by electronic means) Ciccolini provides all four hands, the percussive edge of the pianism seems somewhat accentuated by the recording (and this occasionally happens with the bolder articulation in some of the solo pieces too), but generally the piano recording is most realistic, and the CD transfer has plenty of colour and sonority. Altogether this 158-minute collection forms an excellent introduction to Satie's world.

Avant-dernières pensées; Chapitres tournés en tous sens; Croquis et agaceries d'un gros bonhomme en bois; Danses gothiques; Descriptions automatiques; Embryons desséchés; Enfantillages pittoresques; 3 Gnossiennes; 3 Gymnopédies; Heures séculaires et instantanées; Menus propos enfantins; 5 Nocturnes; Ogives; Les pantins dansent; Passacaille; Peccadilles importunes; Pièces froides; 4 Préludes; Prélude en tapisserie; Prélude de la porte héroïque du ciel; Premier menuet; Rêverie de l'enfance de Pantagruel; 3 Sarabandes; Sonatine bureaucratique; Sports et divertissements; 3 Valses distinguées du précieux dégoût; Véritables préludes flasques; Vieux séquins et vieilles cuirasses.

(B) **(*) VoxBox 1154862 [CDX 5011]. Frank Glazer.

Vox offers a great deal of Satie's solo piano music on two CDs in excellent performances by Frank Glazer, and this VoxBox scores over the competition by offering the widest range of music (though, curiously, not the last three *Gnossiennes*). Glazer seems to penetrate the character of each of these aphoristic and haunting miniatures with genuine flair and insight. In some ways his are more searching and sympathetic performances than those of Aldo Ciccolini, and the recording, although rather reverberant and a little veiled in the treble, is full-bodied and faithful. The Vox CD transfer slightly enhances the original piano-sound.

Avant-dernières pensées; Chapitres tournés en tous sens; Croquis et agaceries d'un gros bonhomme en bois; Descriptions automatiques; Deux rêveries nocturnes; Heures séculaires et instantanées; Nocturnes Nos. 1–3, 5; Nouvelles pièces froides; Pièces froides; Prélude de la porte héroïque du ciel; Les trois valses distinguées du précieux dégoût; Véritables préludes flasques.

*** Decca Dig. 421 713-2 [id.]. Pascal Rogé.

Pascal Rogé's choice of repertoire on this well-filled disc ranges from the Rose-Croix pieces through to the *Nocturnes*. As with the earlier recital, his playing has an eloquence and charm that are altogether rather special, and the recorded sound is very good indeed.

Avant-dernières pensées; Chapitres tournés en tous sens; Le fils des étoiles; Gnossiennes Nos. 2–3; 5 Grimaces pour 'Un songe d'une nuit d'été'; Je te veux (valse); Nocturnes Nos. 2–3 & 5; Les Pantins dansent; Pièces froids (Airs à faire fuir 1–3); Le Piège de Méduse; Première pensée rose + croix; Prélude de la porte héroïque du ciel; Rêverie du pauvre; 2 Rêveries nocturnes; 3 Valses distinguées du précieux dégoût; Valse-ballet.

☞ (M) *** Saga EC 3393-2 [id.]. John McCabe.

This entertaining and attractive anthology gets better and better as it proceeds. John McCabe has the full measure of Satie's understated melancholy and cool, lyrical nostalgia. The programme ranges from neglected early works like the simple, almost Chopinesque *Valse-ballet*, Satie's first published piano piece dating from 1885, to the quietly nostalgic elegy of the *Rêverie du pauvre* and the thoughtfully ambivalent *Deux Rêveries nocturnes*. The hauntingly simple *Je te veux* and the two sets of pieces, *Le Piège de Méduse* and *Le fils des Etoiles*, are particularly memorable, while the *Cinq Grimaces* end the recital with quirky good humour. The intelligent planning of this 62-minute recital and the penetrating response of the pianism places this CD among the finest Satie collections, and the recording, though not vividly present, is natural within a highly suitable ambience.

(i) *Avant-dernières pensées; Embryons desséchés; Gnossiennes Nos. 1–5; Gymnopédies Nos. 1–3; Nocturne No. 1; Sarabandes Nos. 1–3; Sonatine bureaucratique; 3 Valses distinguées du précieux dégoûté;* (ii) *Croquis et agaceries d'un gros bonhomme en bois; Descriptions automatiques; Je te veux; Poudre d'or.*

☞ (B) **(*) Sony SBK 48283 [id.]. (i) Daniel Varviso; (ii) Philippe Entremont.

Both recitals here were recorded in 1979. Daniel Varviso has the measure of these pieces and plays admirably. Perhaps the first of the *Embryons desséchés* could have greater delicacy and wit, and there could be greater melancholy in the second of the *Gymnopédies*. But there are many good things here and one's main reservation concerns the closely balanced recording of the piano and the slightly dry sound. Entremont, too, is placed forwardly, but he brings charm to the two waltzes, *Je te veux* and *Poudre d'or*, while the *Descriptions automatiques* are engagingly crisp and witty. The collection is generous (71 minutes).

Avant-dernières pensées; Embryons desséchés; 6 Gnossiennes; 3 Gymnopédies; Pièces froides; Sarabande No. 3; Sonatine bureaucratique; 3 Valses distinguées du précieux dégoûté; 3 Véritables préludes flasques (pour un chien).
*** BIS Dig. CD 317 [id.]. Roland Pöntinen.

Roland Pöntinen is a young Swedish pianist, still in his early twenties when this recording was made. He seems perfectly in tune with the Satiean world, and his playing is distinguished by great sensibility and tonal finesse. He is very well recorded too.

Caresse; Danse de travers No. 1; Musiques intimes et secrètes; 3 Nouvelles pièces enfantines; 3 Nouvelles pièces froides; Pages mystiques; Les pantins dansent; 12 Petits chorals; Pièces froides Nos. 1–2; Prélude en tapisserie; Préludes flasques.
☞ (BB) *(*) Naxos Dig. 8.550697 [id.]. Klára Körmendi.

5 Nocturnes; Ogives; Pensée rose + croix No. 1; Prélude de la porte héroïque du ciel; Rêverie de l'enfance de Pantagruel; 2 Rêveries nocturnes; Rêverie du pauvre; 3 Sarabandes; Sonneries de la rose + croix.
☞ (BB) ** Naxos Dig. 8.550696 [id.]. Klára Körmendi.

Klára Körmendi's Naxos survey is proving to be rather variable. She is acceptably if closely recorded in the Unitarian Church, Budapest, and the piano has a full sonority, so essential with this composer. The playing is sympathetic but tends to minimize the Satiesque fantasy. The twelve *Petits Chorals*, for instance, are played very sombrely, and elsewhere on 8.550697 there is too much deliberation. However, on the second CD listed (actually Volume I of the series) her calm deliberation rather suits the *Prélude de la porte héroïque du ciel*, the ceremonial *Sonneries* and the thoughtful *Rêveries*, while the four *Ogives* (inspired by Gothic and medieval architecture and in particular Notre Dame Cathedral) are rather imposing.

Embryons desséchés; 6 Gnossiennes; 3 Gymnopédies; Heures séculaires et instantanées; Nocturnes Nos. 1–5; Sonatine bureaucratique; Sports et divertissements.
*** Hyp. Dig. CDA 66344 [id.]. Yitkin Seow.

The Singapore-born pianist Yitkin Seow is a good stylist; his approach is fresh and his playing crisp and marked by consistent beauty of sound. Seow captures the melancholy of the *Gymnopédies* very well and the playing, though not superior to Rogé or Queffélec in character or charm, has a quiet reticence that is well suited to this repertoire. The recording is eminently truthful.

Embryons desséchés; 6 Gnossiennes; 3 Gymnopédies; Je te veux; Nocturne No. 4; Le Picadilly; 4 Préludes flasques; Prélude en tapisserie; Sonatine bureaucratique; Vieux séquins et vieilles cuirasses.
*** Decca Dig. 410 220-2; *410 220-4*. Pascal Rogé.

Rogé has real feeling for this music and conveys its bitter-sweet quality and its grave melancholy as well as he does its lighter qualities. He produces, as usual, consistent beauty of tone, and this is well projected by the recording. Very well recorded, this remains the primary recommendation on CD for this repertoire, together with its companion above.

Gnossiennes Nos. 1–5; 3 Gymnopédies; 3 Pièces froides; Sarabandes Nos. 1–3; Sonatine bureaucratique; Sports et divertissements; Véritable préludes flasques (pour un chien); Vieux séquins et vieilles cuirasses; 6 Pieces published posthumously: Désespoir agréable; Effronterie; Poésie; Prélude canin; Profondeur; Songe creux.
☞ (M) *** Saga EC 3970-2[id.]. John McCabe.

This is a very attractive anthology and is especially interesting in including six brief but highly characteristic pieces (not necessarily left in complete form) found in Satie's notebooks and not previously published. John McCabe is an intelligent and sympathetic exponent of this repertoire, catching its gently disconsolate atmosphere, and in this he is helped by the intimate quality of the recording. The *Sonatine bureaucratique* is played affectionately, its wit purveyed gently rather than projected audaciously, and in the quirky *Sports et divertissements* atmosphere takes precedence over percussive overstatement. The current reissue offers 63 minutes and this, alongside its companion above, is among the best Satie collections at less than premium price. It is a pity that no internal cues are provided for each group of pieces, and the back-up notes are also rather sparse. However, the Corneille painting used as the frontispiece was an inspired choice.

Sauguet, Henri (1901–89)

Mélodie concertante for cello and orchestra.
☞ *** Russian Disc RDCD 11108 [id.]. Rostropovich, USSR SO, composer – BRITTEN: *Cello Symphony.* **(*)

Rostropovich's account of Henri Sauguet's *Mélodie concertante*, a one-movement cello concerto, was recorded at its Moscow première with the composer conducting in 1964. (It first appeared in the UK in the early 1970s on the HMV Melodiya label, coupled with Tischenko's *Cello concerto*.) Best known for his ballet, *Les Forains*, Sauguet belongs at the heart of the Gallic tradition, and the opening of his *Mélodie concertante* has a dream-like, pastoral quality that is reminiscent of the Honegger *Cello concerto*. Its source of inspiration was an old, persistent memory of a young cellist from Bordeaux, and the 'warm, urgent sonorities with which she sought to interpret Debussy's music'. It is an extended improvisation, based on a haunting, introspective theme heard at the beginning of the piece. The performance is, of course, authoritative in every way, and the analogue recording sounds every bit as good as it did in its fine LP format.

Saxton, Robert (born 1953)

Chamber symphony (Circles of light); Concerto for orchestra; The Ring of eternity; The Sentinel of the rainbow.
*** EMI Dig. CDC7 49915-2. BBC SO or L. Sinf., Knussen.

The four linked sections of the *Concerto for orchestra* broadly follow a symphonic shape, as do those of the *Chamber symphony* of 1986, which uses smaller forces, with solo strings. That later work has the title *Circles of light* and was inspired by a quotation from Dante, when in the *Divine Comedy* he looks into the eyes of his beloved, Beatrice, and links what he sees to the movement of the heavens. The other two works also have evocative titles and are linked in the composer's mind to the *Concerto for orchestra* to form a sort of trilogy. Oliver Knussen draws intense, committed playing both from the BBC Symphony Orchestra and from the London Sinfonietta in the chamber-scale works. Full, warm recording.

(i) *In the Beginning;* (ii) *Music to celebrate the resurrection of Christ.*
*** Collins Dig. Single 2003-2. (i) BBC SO, Bamert; (ii) ECO, Bedford.

In the Beginning offers three compact movements, ending with an exhilarating *Dance of joy*. It is well coupled with another deeply felt, religiously inspired work, both very well recorded, in Collins's enterprising 20th-century Plus series.

Music to celebrate the resurrection of Christ.
*** Collins Dig. 1102-2; *1102-4* [id.]. ECO, Bedford – BRITTEN: *Piano concerto etc.* ***

Positive and colourful, to reflect wonder in the subject, Saxton's piece makes an unusual but valuable fill-up to Bedford's disc of Britten rarities.

Caritas (opera; complete).
*** Collins 1350-2 (id.]. Eirian Davies, Jonathan Best, Christopher Ventris, Linda Hibberd, Roger
    Bryson, David Gwynne, E. N. Philh. O, Diego Masson.

Caritas tells the story of Christine, the daughter of a carpenter, who became an anchoress. The
opening scene with its monastic choruses shows her as she is walled up in her cell. Only then does she
find out too late that she has no vocation. Amid incidental developments of stomach-turning
brutality, her pleas to be freed from her confinement are rejected, and madness finally takes over. It is
as disagreeable a plot as could be imagined, yet, thanks to Saxton's approachable, evocative and
generally well-paced score, it is a highly involving piece. Saxton subtly differentiates his echoes of
early church music to heighten individual characterization. The recording was made live at the 1991
Huddersfield Festival, with Diego Masson directing the English Northern Philharmonia and an
excellent cast, movingly headed by Eirian Davies as Christine, the anchoress. The stereo sound is of
spectacular range and spread, adding greatly to the work's impact.

Scarlatti, Alessandro (1660–1725)

*Concerti grossi Nos. 1 in F min.; 2 in C min.; 3 in F; (i) Sinfonie di concerti grossi for flute and strings
Nos. 7 in G min.; 8 in G; 9 in G min.; 10 in A min.; 11 in C; 12 in C min.*
(M) *** Ph. Dig./Analogue 434 160-2 [id.]. (i) William Bennett; I Musici.

These noble and elevated works, though not radical in style, have invention of real quality to
commend them. I Musici give performances of much eloquence and warmth and great transparency;
the latter is welcome in the fugal movements, especially as the 1979 analogue recording is of the very
first rank. The *Sinfonie di concerti grossi* feature a flute soloist, in this instance the excellent William
Bennett, who plays fluently and in fine style. The performances are lively and attractive, and
eminently freshly recorded in Philips's best digital sound.

Dixit Dominus.
*** DG Dig. 423 386-2 [id.]. Argenta, Attrot, Denley, Ashley Stafford, Varcoe, Ch. & E. Concert,
    Pinnock – VIVALDI: *Gloria.* ***

Pinnock, as so often, inspires his performers to sing and play as though at a live event. This Scarlatti
Psalm-setting, very well recorded, makes an attractive coupling for the better known of Vivaldi's
settings of the *Gloria.*

La Giuditta (oratorio).
*** Hung. Dig. HCD 12910 [id.]. Zadori, Gemes, Gregor, Minter, De Mey, Capella Savaria,
    McGegan.

La Giuditta, telling the biblical story of Judith, is a fascinating example of pre-Handelian oratorio as
it was developing in Italy at the end of the seventeenth century. Nicholas McGegan, who has made
several successful period-performance recordings for Hungaroton, here directs a fresh and stylish
account, with three Hungarian principals joined by the soft-grained but agile American counter-
tenor, Drew Minter, as Holofernes, and the excellent French tenor, Guy de Mey, as the Captain. The
two main principals, Maria Zadori as Judith and Katalin Gemes as Prince Ozias, both have
attractively bright, clear voices. Very well recorded in clean, immediate sound and with libretto and
notes included in the package, it makes a most attractive disc, generously filled.

(i) *St Cecilia Mass;* (ii) *Motets: Domine, refugium factus et nobis; O magnum mysterium.*
(M) *** Decca 430 631-2 [id.]. (i) Harwood, Eathorne, Cable, Eans, Keyte, St John's College Ch.,
    Wren O, Guest; (ii) Schütz Ch. of L., Norrington.

This is far more florid in style than Scarlatti's other Masses and it receives from Guest a vigorous and
fresh performance. The soloists cope with their difficult fioriture very confidently and they match one
another well. The two motets are noble in conception and are beautifully performed under Roger
Norrington.

Scarlatti, Domenico (1685–1757)

Keyboard sonatas (complete).
*** Erato/Warner 2292 45309-2 (34) [id.]. Scott Ross, Huggett, Coin, Henry, Vallon.

The tercentenary of Domenico Scarlatti's birth prompted the production of an integral recording of

Scarlatti's 555 *Keyboard sonatas*, including the three intended for organ, others for violin and continuo, and two for the unlikely combination of violin and oboe in unison. Scott Ross, who, with the participation of Monica Huggett (violin), Christophe Coin (cello), Michel Henry (oboe) and Marc Vallon (bassoon), is primarily responsible, plays five different harpsichords plus the organ, and he is very well recorded throughout in varying acoustics. Scarlatti's invention shows an inexhaustible resourcefulness, and Ross's playing is fully worthy: he is lively, technically assured, rhythmically resilient and, above all, he conveys his enjoyment of the music, without eccentricity. We cannot claim to have heard all thirty-four CDs, but all the evidence of sampling suggests that for the Scarlatti addict they will prove an endless source of satisfaction. The documentation is ample, providing a 200-page booklet about the composer, his music and the performers. The overall cost of this set is somewhere in the region of £200.

Keyboard sonatas, Kk. 1, 8, 9, 11, 13, 20, 87, 98, 119, 135, 159, 380, 450, 487 & 529.
☞ *** DG Dig. 435 855-2 [id.]. Ivo Pogorelich (piano).

Pogorelich, who can be exasperatingly wilful, here plays with captivating simplicity and convinces the listener that this is music which sounds far more enjoyable on the piano than on the harpsichord. His dazzling execution, using the lightest touch, consistently enchants the ear with its subtle tonal colouring, and the music emerges ever sparkling and fresh. These performances can be measured against those of Horowitz and not found wanting. Moreover Pogorelich is beautifully recorded in an ideal acoustic, and the hour-long programme is admirably chosen to provide maximum variety.

Keyboard sonatas: Kk. 1, 9, 30, 69, 113, 127, 132–3, 141, 159, 175, 215, 380, 430, 481, 492 & 502.
☞ *** Collins Dig. 1322-2 [id.]. Joanna MacGregor (piano).

Joanna MacGregor has a lively intelligence and exemplary taste; she plays all these sonatas with flawless technical address and flair. Pianistic narcissism seems foreign to her nature and her interpretations are quite properly conceived in pianistic terms and do not strive to imitate the terrace dynamics of the harpsichord. Moreover she is very well recorded.

Keyboard sonatas: Kk. 7, 33, 49, 54, 87, 96, 105–7, 159, 175, 206–7, 240–41, 347–8, 380–81, 441–4, 518–19, 524–5.
*** HM HMC90 1164/5 [id.]. Rafael Puyana (harpsichord).

Rafael Puyana gives eminently red-blooded performances of these *Sonatas*, which are refreshing and invigorating. He uses a three-manual harpsichord from 1740 by Hass of Hamburg, restored by Andrea Goble, which makes a splendidly rich sound, present and lively. Authoritative playing, though he tends, with some exceptions, to concentrate on the more outgoing and brilliant rather than the inward-looking *Sonatas*.

Keyboard sonatas, Kk. 8, 11, 52, 87, 159, 169, 202, 206, 208–9, 215, 337, 380, 415, 430 & 446.
☞ *** EMI Dig. CDC7 54483-2 [id.]. Bob van Asperen (harpsichord).

Bob van Asperen long ago established an enviable reputation in Bach's keyboard music, but he proves himself every bit as well suited to the fiery Latin temperament. This Scarlatti recital is exhilarating and dashing; its high spirits delight and invigorate, even when Van Asperen is inclined to opt for too dizzy a tempo. His instrument is a copy of a Dulcken and it is heard to excellent effect in this EMI recording. But it is not only in the dazzling virtuoso pieces that he is so impressive; he is equally persuasive in the more inward-looking and searching pieces which are included here. In short, this is one of the best Scarlatti recitals on the harpsichord to have appeared for some years and is warmly recommended. It has, alas, been withdrawn as we go to press.

Keyboard sonatas, Kk. 8, 20, 32, 107, 109, 124, 141, 159, 234, 247, 256, 259, 328, 380, 397, 423, 430, 440, 447, 481, 490, 492, 515 & 519.
☞ ⊛ (M) (***) EMI mono CHS7 64934-2 [id.]. Wanda Landowska (harpsichord).

No Scarlatti collection should be without this Landowska recital, which is truly one of the classics of the gramophone. Landowska led the revival of interest in the harpsichord at a time when it was a relative rarity both in the recital room and in the recording studio. (Both Falla and Poulenc, among others, were inspired to compose concertos for her.) She used a thunderous Pleyel that was specially built to withstand the rigours of 1920s and '30s travel; but her playing has more character than most modern players put together; it is electrifying in its sheer vitality and imagination. Lionel Salter's excellent notes quote her as saying she was 'sensitive to Scarlatti's bucolic mind, his rustic jauntiness . . . the elemental strength, the richness of his rhythmical power, as well as all that is Moorish in them. He has the genuine nobility, the heroism and the audacity of Don Quixote.' The first batch of sonatas was recorded in 1934 and the others in 1939 and 1940. Indispensable.

Keyboard sonatas: Kk. 18, 27, 30, 69, 87, 113, 119–20, 187, 299, 461, 463, 474 & 545.
☞ * Teldec/Warner Dig. 2292 46419 [id.]. Glen Wilson (harpsichord).

Glen Wilson plays a copy of an instrument by Gregorio (1726) whose sonority is not heard to best advantage on this disc, even when it is reproduced at a flattering level. But quite apart from this, his playing is far too strait-laced and wanting in abandon. It is all too judicious, without the flair, colour and rhythmic freedom Scarlatti's muse calls for.

Keyboard sonatas, Kk. 32, 95, 99, 107, 158, 162–4, 193, 208, 210, 213, 215, 246–7, 262, 304, 318, 378–80, 394, 443, 461, 474, 481, 484, 500, 513, 531, 540, 550.
(M) **(*) Collins Dig. 3016-2 [id.]. Fou Ts'ong (piano).

Fou Ts'ong is not the first name to spring to mind in connection with this repertoire and, not unexpectedly, his approach is at times rather wayward, though stopping short of being overtly romantic. But in those numbers in which keen articulation is called for (Kk. 484 in D and Kk. 378 in F, for instance) the playing is agreeably fresh, the ornamentation crisp and not fussy. The recording was produced by Fou Ts'ong himself and recorded at St John's Polish Roman Catholic Church, London, in 1984. The ambience is attractive, but the microphones are perhaps a shade too close to the piano.

Keyboard sonatas, Kk. 46, 87, 99, 124, 201, 204a, 490–92, 513, 520–21.
*** CRD CRD 3368; *CRDC 4068* [id.]. Trevor Pinnock (harpsichord).

No need to say much about this: the playing is first rate and the recording outstanding in its presence and clarity. There are few better anthologies of Scarlatti in the catalogue, although the measure is not particularly generous.

Keyboard sonatas: Kk. 98, 123–4, 147, 198, 326–7, 428–9, 454, 466–7.
☞ (M) ** O-L 433 179-2 [id.]. Colin Tilney (harpsichord).

Colin Tilney's 1981 recital is not an unqualified success, though the harpsichord on which he records is undoubtedly of interest: it is a Sodi of 1782 which is warm in the bass. Some of these pieces come off well but others have a somewhat pedantic air and a stiffness out of key with Scarlatti's mercurial temperament. The sound is truthful.

Keyboard sonatas, Kk. 108, 118–19, 141, 198, 203, 454–5, 490–92, 501–2, 516–19.
*** HM/BMG Dig. RD 77224 [77224-2]. Andreas Staier (harpsichord).

Andreas Staier characterizes each of these Scarlatti sonatas vividly and with real imagination. Playing (and recording) of this quality has no need to fear even the most exalted comparisons. A strongly recommended issue.

Keyboard sonatas: Kk. 115–16, 144, 175, 402–3, 449–50, 474–5, 513, 516–17, 544–5.
**(*) Decca Dig. 421 422-2 [id.]. András Schiff (piano).

Exquisite and sensitive playing, full of colour and delicacy. As always, András Schiff is highly responsive to the mood and character of each piece. At times one wonders whether he is not a little too refined: in some, one would have welcomed more abandon and fire. However, for the most part this is a delightful recital, and the Decca recording is exemplary in its truthfulness.

Stabat Mater.
*** Erato/Warner Dig. 2292 45219-2 [id.]. Monteverdi Ch., E. Bar. Soloists, Gardiner – Concert:
    'Sacred choral music'. ***

The *Stabat Mater* shows Scarlatti to be a considerable master of polyphony; though it falls off in interest towards the end, it still possesses eloquence and nobility – and it is far less bland than Pergolesi's setting. Gardiner's fine performance couples three motets of interest, by Cavalli, Gesualdo and Clément, which are also splendidly done. The recording is very good indeed, notably fresh in its CD format.

Schillings, Max von (1868–1933)

(i) *Violin concerto, Op. 23. King Oedipus* (tone-poem), *Op. 11; Moloch: Harvest festival scene.*
☞ *** Marco Polo Dig. 8.223324 [id.]. (i) Ernö Rozsa; Czecho-Slovak RSO (Bratislava), Alfred Walter.

Older collectors may recall Max von Schillings' name on the Parlophone label as conductor of the Berlin Staatsoper, where he directed performances of Pfitzner's *Palestrina*, Schreker's *Die Gezeichnich-*

ten and works by Strauss and Busoni. His music belongs to an earlier period in his career before he became so closely involved in conducting and opera administration. He was virulently anti-semitic, which temporarily furthered his reputation during the Nazi period but not in post-war Germany. His *Violin concerto* (1910) is a beautifully crafted and highly accomplished score in the post-Romantic idiom with echoes of Wagner, Richard Strauss, Reger and Pfitzner. It is a long work whose first movement alone runs to 23 minutes. Although it reveals no strong individuality, it has a certain rhetorical command and lyrical warmth to commend it, and its masterly handling of the orchestra will make a strong appeal to those with a taste for turn-of-the-century music. Its attractions are considerable and they are well conveyed in this passionate and committed performance. The eloquent soloist is the twenty-year-old Romanian-born Hungarian, Ernö Rozsa, who plays marvellously and inspires the Kosice Orchestra under Alfred Walter to great heights. Neither the excerpt from the opera *Moloch* (1906) nor the *Symphonic Prologue to the Oedipus Tyrannus of Sophocles* (1900) makes anywhere near as strong an impression. The Marco Polo recording is very well detailed and has plenty of warmth and presence.

Schmelzer, Johann (c. 1620–80)

Balletto di centauri, ninfe e salvatici; Balletto di spiritelli; Sonata I à 8; Sonata à 7 flauti; Sonata con arie zu der kaiserlichen Serenada.
*** O-L Dig. 425 834-2 [id.]. New L. Cons., Pickett – BIBER: *Sonatas.* ***

The *Balletto di spiritelli* is scored for recorders and curtal (an ancestor of the bassoon), violins and viols, and the *Balletto di centauri* uses cornetts and sackbuts, as well as recorders, strings and continuo. The even more robust *Sonata con arie zu der kaiserlichen Serenada* (with three trumpets, timpani plus a string ensemble and continuo) has six movements, including two *Arias* and a *Canario*, but lasts only seven minutes. Philip Pickett himself leads the consort of recorders in the *Sonata à 7*, which is a fairly ambitious continuous piece, longer than either of the ballets, and the *Sonata à 8* highlights a trumpet duo against a group of violins and viols. This is agreeably inventive music, which is brought refreshingly to life by Pickett's instrumental ensemble, using original instruments to persuasive effect. The recording is both clear and spacious.

Schmidt, Franz (1874–1939)

Symphony No. 2 in E flat.
*** Chan. Dig. CHAN 8779; *ABTD 1415* [id.]. Chicago SO, Järvi.

The *Second Symphony* owes much to Strauss and Reger and, if it is not as individual as his later works, like the noble *Fourth Symphony*, it shows the fertility of his invention and his command of the orchestra. The Chicago orchestra play magnificently for Järvi and are very well recorded.

Symphony No. 4 in C.
☞ (B) *** Decca 440 615-2 (2) [id.]. VPO, Zubin Mehta – MAHLER: *Symphony No. 2 (Resurrection).* ***

Schmidt's noble *Fourth Symphony* is much loved in Vienna, as the playing of the VPO on this Decca recording readily testifies. The work is given the intensity of Mahler, without the hint of hysteria, and the breadth and spaciousness of Bruckner – though it is very different from either; Mehta also finds a dignity that reminds one a little of Elgar. The brightened recording gains in vividness in its CD transfer but loses a little of its fullness, though the Vienna ambience remains very telling. The new coupling with Mahler makes up one of the best of the Double Decca series.

(i) *Clarinet quintet in B flat (for clarinet, piano and strings); (Quintet No. 1); (ii) 3 Phantasiestücke on Hungarian national themes; (iii) (Piano) Romance in A; Toccata in D min.*
☞ ** Marco Polo Dig. 8.223415 [id.]. (i) Aladár Jánoska, Frantisek Török, Alexander Lakatos; (i; ii) Ján Slávik; (i–iii) Daniela Ruso.

The *B flat Quintet* for clarinet, piano, violin, viola and cello of 1932, like so much of Schmidt's music with piano, was composed with the left-handed pianist, Paul Wittgenstein, brother of the philosopher, in mind. The piano part was subsequently rearranged for two hands by Friedrich Wührer. Despite the advantage of its relative brevity, it is as neglected in the recital room as its successor. Its character is predominantly elegiac; it was composed after the death of his daughter and can best be described as having something of the autumnal feeling of late Brahms, the subtlety of Reger and the dignity and nobility of Elgar or Suk. The players sound pretty tentative at the very start but soon settle down, though their tempo could with advantage have been slower. All the same, this is a thoroughly sympathetic, recommendable account. The *Drei Phantasiestücke* and the two piano pieces, the *Romance* and the *D minor Toccata*, are early and less interesting, though they are well enough played.

Piano quintet in G (arr. Wührer).
(M) *** Decca 430 296-2 [id.]. Eduard Mrasek, VPO Qt – BRUCKNER: *String quintet.* ***

This is rewarding music, full of unexpected touches; it also possesses a vein of genuine nobility, as one would expect from the composer of the *Fourth Symphony*. The performance is elegant and was beautifully recorded in the Sofiensaal in 1974. The CD retains the fullness and the natural, well-judged balance.

Quintet in A for clarinet, piano and strings.
*** Marco Polo Dig. 8.223414 [id.]. Jánoska, Mucha, Lakatos, Slávik, Ruso.

The *Quintet in A major for clarinet, piano and strings* is unusual: it begins like some mysterious other-worldly scherzo which immediately introduces a pastoral idea of beguiling charm. The second movement is a piano piece in ternary form; there is a longish scherzo, full of fantasy and wit, and there is an affecting trio, tinged with the melancholy of late Brahms. The fourth movement sets out as if it, too, is going to be a long, meditative piano piece, but its nobility and depth almost put one in mind of the Elgar *Quintet*. The fifth is a set of variations on a theme of Josef Labor, and is sometimes played on its own. In all, the piece takes an hour and, of the two performances now before the public, the Slovak account on Marco Polo is the one to go for. The recording has freshness and bloom, though it could benefit from a bigger recording venue. This is a glorious work.

Das Buch mit sieben Siegeln (The Book with 7 seals): oratorio.
**(*) Orpheus Dig. C 143862H (2). Schreier, Holl, Greenberg, Watkinson, Moser, Rydl, V. State
    Op. Ch., Austrian RSO, Zagrosek.

Das Buch mit sieben Siegeln has much music of substance and many moments of real inspiration. Peter Schreier's St John is one of the glories of this set, and there are fine contributions from some of the other soloists. This performance was recorded in the somewhat unappealing acoustic of the ORF studios and is wanting in the transparency that the score deserves; however, the sound is more than acceptable.

Schmitt, Florent (1870–1958)

Etude pour Le palais hanté (The haunted palace) after Edgar Allan Poe.
☞ (M) *** EMI Dig. CDM7 64687-2 [id.]. Monte Carlo PO, Prêtre – CAPLET: *Masque* **(*);
    DEBUSSY: *Chute de la maison Usher.* ***

Five years older than Ravel, Florent Schmitt also studied at the Paris Conservatoire with Fauré, Dubois, Massenet and André Gédalge, with whom Milhaud also studied (and of whom he spoke so warmly). Like Dukas, he occupies a rather solitary place in French music, standing aside from any special group or school. Like Debussy and Caplet in the works used for coupling in this well-planned CD, Schmitt found the inspiration for his *Etude* in Edgar Allan Poe. It is young man's music (written in 1904, shortly before the Caplet *Masque of the Red Death*), for though Schmitt was in his mid-thirties when he completed it, he used his years in Rome as a student-winner of the Prix de Rome for the composition. It is a richly evocative piece, some 12 minutes in length, and is given an enthusiastic performance under Prêtre. The recording is excellent; the work undoubtedly adds to the interest of an issue which is an indispensable acquisition for all Debussians.

La tragédie de Salomé (ballet; complete).
☞ *** Marco Polo Dig. 8.223448 [id.]. Fayt, Rheinland-Pfalz PO, Davin.

The full score of the original hour-long ballet now emerges from its long slumber to make its first appearance since 1907. Although the scoring is for fewer players, Schmitt's skill as an orchestrator is such that the heady, exotic draft he prepared is hardly less potent than the more sumptuously scored, 1908 version. The piece is as long again as the more familiar ballet, and much of the music that was lost in the process is every bit as atmospheric and colourful. Patrick Davin and the Rheinland-Pfalz Philharmonic Orchestra cast a strong spell, and Marie-Paule Fayt is the off-stage nymphet. The Marco Polo recording has a good, spacious acoustic and plenty of detail. This is a valuable addition to the catalogue, almost worthy of a Rosette insofar as the music really deserves to be heard and appreciated, and these performers do it justice. The documentation is of unusual interest and gives a detailed account of the action of the ballet.

(i) *La tragédie de Salomé, Op. 50;* (ii) *Piano quintet in B min., Op. 51: Lent.*
☞ (***) EMI mono CDC7 54840-2 [id.]. Composer (cond./piano), with (i) O des Concerts Straram; (i) Calvet Qt – ROUSSEL: *Le festin de l'araignée* etc. (***)

Florent Schmitt was only eight years younger than Debussy, whose influence he keenly absorbed, though he outlived the older man by 40 years. Like Dukas's *Poème dansé – La Péri*, whose exoticism it shares, *La tragédie de Salomé* comes from 1908 and it enjoyed a great success in pre-First World War Paris; even Stravinsky spoke enthusiastically of it. It has been neglected on record (Martinon recorded it in the 1970s and, more recently, Janowski) but none makes so strong an effect in terms of sheer atmosphere as this old (1930) account which, with its more leisurely tempi, allows the heady, exotic atmosphere to register far more effectively than do later records. The engineers have done wonders with the sound, which is making its first appearance since the original 78s. The account of the slow movement of the contemporaneous *Piano quintet* (1908) has appeared on LP and, though it is less memorable, at least it gives an opportunity for hearing the composer as pianist as well as conductor.

La tragédie de Salomé, Op. 50; (i) *Psalm 47, Op. 38.*
☞ *** Erato/Warner Dig. 2292 45029-2 [id.]. (i) Sharon Sweet, French R. Ch.; Gil; New PO, Janowski.

Perhaps Schmitt's best-known work is his colourful and atmospheric ballet, *La tragédie de Salomé*, composed in 1907, two years after Strauss's opera on the same theme, which has been out of the catalogue since the deletion of Jean Martinon's EMI 1973 recording. The work, like Dukas's *La Péri*, is full of *art nouveau* exoticism and heady atmosphere. Schmitt's setting of *Psalm 47* dates from his last year as a Prix de Rome scholar at the Villa Medici and is a stirring and imposing piece which contrasts two aspects of the great books of exaltation and jubilation: the tenderness and voluptuousness of the *Song of Songs*. Good performances from the Orchestre Philharmonique de Radio France under Marek Janowski are eminently recommendable – save for Sharon Sweet's wide and ugly vibrato.

Schnittke, Alfred (born 1934)

Concerto grosso No. 1.
☞ (B) *** DG Dig. 439 152-2 [id.]. Kremer, Grindenko, Smirnov, COE, Schiff – LIGETI: *Chamber concerto;* LUTOSLAWSKI: *Chain 3* etc. ***

With his semi-baroque pastiche, the *Concerto grosso No. 1*, Schnittke has provided the nearest he can get to a popular hit, so it will be interesting to see whether this budget Classikon reissue provides it with a large market; certainly the *Toccata* second movement and the *Rondo* are very striking. The soloists are balanced very forwardly in relation to the ripieno, but they can certainly stand up to the aural scrutiny, and the performance overall makes a strong impact.

(i) *Cello concerto No. 2. In memoriam . . .*
*** Sony Dig. SK 48241 [id.]. (i) Rostropovich; LSO, Ozawa.

Schnittke has a strong feeling for the cello, and his *Second Cello concerto* is a recent work and a strong and powerful one. It is conceived on a large scale, the main emotional weight residing in the fifth and last movement, a passacaglia lasting a quarter of an hour. Its powerful, concentrated atmosphere resonates long in the mind and leaves what one could describe as a strong aftertaste. So, for that matter, does *In memoriam . . .*, a transcription and re-working of the *Piano quintet*, written on the death of his mother. Something of the very private grief and spare, hollow textures of the quintet is lost but there are gains in colour in the highly imaginative use of the orchestra. The recording has exceptional richness, detail and depth and the performance of the concerto has all the authority and panache one might expect.

Violin concertos Nos. 1–2.
*** BIS Dig. CD 487 [id.]. Mark Lubotsky, Malmö SO, Eri Klas.

The *First Violin concerto* inhabits a post-romantic era. Its lyricism is profoundly at variance with its successor of 1966, commissioned by Mark Lubotsky, the soloist on this record. Here the central concept is what Schnittke calls 'a certain drama of tone colours', and there is no doubt that much of it is vividly imagined and strongly individual. The double-bass is assigned a special role of a caricatured 'anti-soloist'. There is recourse to the once fashionable aleatoric technique, but this is all within carefully controlled parameters. The Malmö orchestra under Eri Klas play with evident feeling in both works and are very well recorded. This is an altogether highly satisfactory coupling.

(i) *Gogol suite* (compiled Rozhdestvensky); *Labyrinths.*
*** BIS Dig. CD 557 [id.]. Malmö SO, Lev Markiz; (i) with Anton Kontra.

The *Gogol suite* was compiled by Rozhdestvensky from the music Schnittke composed to a commission for an unusual Gogol spectacle by Yuri Lyubimow. There is a surrealistic quality to it, reminiscent of Gogol's own words quoted in Jürgen Köchel's note, 'The world hears my laughter; my tears it does not see nor recognise.' *Labyrinths* is a ballet score composed in 1971, thin in development and musical ideas but sufficiently strong in atmosphere to survive the transition from stage to concert hall. The Malmö Orchestra under Lev Markiz play very well and the recording is in the demonstration class.

Cello sonata.
*** BIS Dig. CD 336 [id.]. Torleif Thedéen, Roland Pöntinen – STRAVINSKY: *Suite italienne;*
SHOSTAKOVICH: *Sonata.* ***

The *Cello sonata* is a powerfully expressive piece, its avant-garde surface enshrining a neo-romantic soul. Torleif Thedéen is a refined and intelligent player who gives a thoroughly committed account of this piece with his countryman, Roland Pöntinen.

Prelude in memoriam Shostakovich (for 2 solo violins).
*** Chan Dig. CHAN 8988; *ABTD 1570* [id.]. Mordkovitch, Young – PROKOFIEV; SHOSTAKOVICH:
Violin sonatas. ***

The Schnittke *Prelude* for two solo violins is the shortest of the works on Lydia Mordkovitch's excellent disc of Soviet violin music, but it is among the most moving in its intense, elegiac way. She is well matched by her partner, Emma Young.

Violin sonata No. 1; Sonata in the olden style.
*** Chan. Dig. CHAN 8343; *ABTD 1089* [id.]. Dubinsky, Edlina – SHOSTAKOVICH: *Violin sonata.*
***

Schnittke's *First sonata* dates from 1963 when he was still in his late twenties; it is a well-argued piece that seems to unify his awareness of the post-serial musical world with the tradition of Shostakovich. On this version it is linked with a pastiche of less interest, dating from 1977. Excellent playing from both artists, and very good recording too.

OPERA

Leben mit einem Idioten (Life with an idiot): complete.
☞ *** Sony Dig. S2K 52495 (2) [id.]. Duesing / Bischoff, Ringholz, Haskin, Zimnenko, Leggatte,
Vocal Ens. & Rotterdam PO, Rostropovich.

This is a live recording, with Mstislav Rostropovich conducting, of the world première production of Schnittke's first opera, *Life with an idiot*, staged by Netherlands Opera in Amsterdam in the spring of 1992. Predictably, the piece defies operatic convention, which means that it is at least as effective on disc as when seen in the theatre. This is an adaptation not of Dostoevsky but of a story by a fellow dissident, Victor Erofeyev, who like Schnittke spent some of his youth in the West. It is an allegory of Soviet oppression. As punishment for poor performance at work the central character, unnamed, with his wife, also unnamed, has to take an idiot, Vova, into his home. The first act tells how 'Vova becomes me', and the second how 'I become him'. The Russian text is down-to-earth and full of banal domestic detail, often expressed in profanities and off-colour slang; but basically this is a Kafka-esque nightmare, with descriptions of Vova's impossible behaviour generally taking the place of action. As an opera it hardly works, but Schnittke's often violent, always energetic score characteristically heightens nerve-jangling situations in the home to make it an involving personal cantata, with incidental musical echoes of Stravinsky's comparably stylized domestic cantata, *The Wedding*. Rostropovich draws a vigorous performance from the Rotterdam Philharmonic, with Dale Duesing and Teresa Ringholz as the central character and his wife, both excellent, and with Howard Haskin providing peremptory interjections as Vova. One hardly expected Schnittke's first opera to be in any way conventional in its approach to the genre, but with a composer whose music is so naturally dramatic one hopes he will before long apply himself to a less surreal story with stage action in it, not just a nightmare fantasy.

Schoeck, Othmar (1886–1957)

Cello concerto, Op. 61.
*** Claves Dig. D 8502 [id.]. Goritzki, Deutsche Kammerakademie Neuss – REGER: *Lyrisches Andante.* ***

The chamber-like scoring of the *Cello concerto* gives it a rather special, private quality and, although it has its longueurs, its atmosphere is at times strong and haunting. The performance is sensitive and totally dedicated, and the recording is very natural.

(i) *Violin concerto, Op. 21; Penthesilea:* suite (arr. Delfs).
☞ *** Claves Dig. CD 50-9201. Bettina Boller, Swiss Youth SO, Andreas Delfs.

Schoeck's *Violin concerto* or, to give it its formal title, *Concerto quasi una fantasia* is a glorious piece, full of warmth and lyricism. It was written for Stefi Geyer, who must have been a great beauty for she was also the dedicatee of Bartók's so-called *First Concerto* of 1907. She recorded the Schoeck in 1944 when time had taken its toll of both her beauty and her tone – not to mention her vibrato. The concerto breathes much the same air as Brahms, Strauss and perhaps Elgar, though, as one gets closer to it, it reveals a distinctive personality all its own. Its melodic ideas are of a striking and haunting quality. The young Swiss violinist, Bettina Boller, shows a rare and deep insight into this music; she plays with great sensitivity, impeccable technique and an evident love of the music. Her conductor is highly supportive and has a complete understanding of and feeling for Schoeck, and this also emerges in the suite he has compiled from the opera, *Penthesilea*. He inspires his youthful players to great heights in both pieces, and the natural sympathy that both performances evince outweighs sonic limitations. Unfortunately the engineers balance the solo violin in such a way as to accentuate a certain hardness (even wiriness) of tone, particularly above the stave. The wind are also a bit too close, particularly at the beginning of the concerto. But this is a performance of such quality that reservations must be set aside.

(i) *Violin concerto, Op. 21; Serenade, Op. 1; Suite in A flat, Op. 59.*
*** Novalis Dig. 150070-2; *150070-4.* (i) Ulf Hoelscher, ECO, Howard Griffiths.

Schoeck's *Violin concerto* has great warmth and enormous appeal and would doubtless enjoy wide popularity if only the public could find a way to it. Ulf Hoelscher and the English Chamber Orchestra under Howard Griffiths play the whole work as if they were in love with it (as indeed they should be). The *Serenade* of 1907 has some of the charm of late Strauss, and the *Suite for strings* (1945) is a work of strong character: it has the same luminous quality and sad, gentle ambience as the pastoral intermezzo, *Summer night*. The performance is dedicated and the recording is well balanced and has both clarity and warmth. Strongly recommended.

Notturno for voice and string quartet, Op. 47.
☞ *(*) EMI Dig. CDC7 54520-2 [id.]. Fischer-Dieskau, Cherubini Qt – MATTHUS: *Nachtlieder.* *(*)

Fischer-Dieskau made a memorable and authoritative recording of Schoeck's wonderful song-cycle with the Juilliard Quartet in the 1960s, which Sony should reissue. This new version, made in 1991, exhibits all the finesse, artistry and intelligence with which this great singer is endowed – but, alas, time takes its toll and sadly his voice no longer possesses the qualities we associate with it. There is no timbre or bloom and, for all the excellence of the recording and accomplishment of the players, regretfully we must recommend waiting until his classic account returns. This is the greater pity since the coupling, the *Nachtlieder* of Siegfried Matthus, is of great interest.

Die Entschwundene; Der Gott und die Bajadere, Op. 34; 12 Hafis-Lieder, Op. 33: Sommerabend; Wanderung im Gebirge.
☞ (*) Jecklin Dig. JD673-2 [id.]. Niklaus Tüller, Christoph Keller.

This is part of an ambitious Jecklin project to record all of the Swiss master's 300-plus songs. The present disc gives us his longest single song for voice and piano, *Der Gott und die Bajadere* ('The god and the dancing girl'), the recently discovered *Sommerabend* and *Die Entschwundene*, all of which are the product of the early 1920s and the artistic fruit of an affair with the Genovese pianist, Mary de Senger. The main work is the *Hafis-Lieder* – not the same poems (or even translator) as in Szymanowski's *Hafiz Songs*. Niklaus Tüller's earlier LP of the cycle, *Das stille Leuchten*, showed him to be a committed exponent of the composer, but the present issue finds him at less than his best. The voice now gives less pleasure: it has lost its bloom and has little in the way of tonal beauty. The microphone favours the piano somewhat. These songs are beautiful and this is likely to be the only means of coming to grips with them, but they deserve more persuasive advocacy.

Das Holde Bescheiden (song-cycle).

☞ *(*) Claves Dig. CD 50 9038/9 [id.]. Mitsuko Shirai, Dietrich Fischer-Dieskau, Hartmut Höll.

Das Holde Bescheiden is Schoeck's very last song-cycle, to poems by Mörike. It comprises 40 songs in all, and this performance represents its début on CD. Its neglect in the concert hall (it would require a complete, two-part recital) is perhaps understandable as it does not show his inspiration in full flow. Fischer-Dieskau has lost none of his artistry and intelligence but much of his vocal bloom and timbre. Nor is Shirai on best form.

3 Lieder, Op. 35; 6 Lieder, Op. 51; Das Wandsbecker Liederbuch, Op. 52; Im Nebel; Wiegenlied.

☞ ** Jecklin Dig. JD677-2 [id.]. Juliane Banse, Dieter Henschel, Wolfram Rieger.

Das Wandsbecker Liederbuch, written in the 1930s, is a latterday equivalent of the Hugo Wolf Songbooks; they offer a portrait of a poet (in this case Mathius Claudius) rather than a thematically connected cycle. Kurt von Fischer calls it 'a synthesis of the features of his lyric art', and the songs, though highly conservative in idiom, are full of subtleties and depth, as indeed are the remaining songs on this CD. They are decently sung and recorded, and admirers of Schoeck's art need not hesitate.

Das stille Leuchten, Op. 60.

**(*) Claves Dig. CD 50-8910 [id.]. Dietrich Fischer-Dieskau, Hartmut Höll.

Das stille Leuchten (The Silent Light or Illumination) is an altogether magnificent work. Many of the 24 songs which make up the cycle are touching and some are really inspired. Like late Strauss, they often convey a feeling of regret at life's evanescence and are full of a resigned but poignant melancholy. Dietrich Fischer-Dieskau sings with all his old artistry and imagination, although the voice has now lost some of its bloom and colour. Hartmut Höll is an inspired pianist.

Schoenberg, Arnold (1874–1951)

(i) *Accompaniment to a cinematograph scene, Op. 34;* (ii) *Chamber symphony No. 1, Op. 9;* (i; iii) *Die Jakobsleiter* (oratorio fragments, completed Zillig).

☞ (M) *** Sony SMK 48462 [id.]. (i) BBC SO; (ii) Ens. InterContemporain (members); (iii) Nimsgern, Bowen, Partridge, Hudson, Shirley-Quirk, Rolfe Johnson, Wenkel, Mesplé, BBC Singers; Boulez.

It is good to see the reappearance of Boulez's first Schoenberg survey on Sony at mid-price, even if, as seems likely, he re-records the repertory. The performance of the film scene is as atmospheric as one would expect, if not as emotionally involved as the *Chamber Symphony*, given a strong, warmly enjoyable account. (The second *Chamber Symphony* is coupled with *Moses und Aron* – see below.) *Die Jakobsleiter*, the composition of which was interrupted by the composer's army service in the First World War, is an ambitious oratorio, which he left fully sketched out. It was completed and orchestrated by Winifried Zillig, revealing an exceptionally powerful piece. Strongly cast, the perform-ance has passion and commitment and the recording projects it vividly.

Chamber symphony No. 1, Op. 9.

*** DG Dig. 423 307-2 [id.]. BPO, Sinopoli – MANZONI: *Mass.* ***

*** Teldec/Warner Dig. 2292 46019 [id.]. COE, Holliger – BERG: *Chamber concerto.* ***

☞ **(*) Decca Dig. 436 466-2 [id.]. Concg. O, Chailly – BRAHMS: *Symphony No. 3.* **(*)

A fine performance of Schoenberg's Op. 9 from Sinopoli. He links it positively back to the high romanticism of Richard Strauss, with the Berlin Philharmonic producing glorious sounds. Full recording to match.

Schoenberg's *Chamber Symphony No. 1* makes an apt coupling for the fine COE version of the Berg, played with equal warmth and thrust, with complex textural problems masterfully solved.

Though the solo violins emerge rather edgily, this is a strong, committed reading of a Schoenberg work that was one of his first to show him at full stretch. It makes an unusual, stimulating coupling for Chailly's Brahms.

Chamber symphonies Nos. 1, Op. 9; 2, Op. 38; Verklaerte Nacht.

*** DG Dig. 429 233-2 [id.]. Orpheus CO.

The Orpheus Chamber Orchestra couple their fine account of *Verklaerte Nacht* with the two *Chamber symphonies* of 1906 and 1939 respectively. Their *Verklaerte Nacht* is swift-moving and a bit overheated; it does not have the subtle range of colouring and dynamics that marks the classic Karajan version.

Both the *Chamber symphonies* come off well and the disc is worth acquiring solely for their sake. A rather brightly lit but very good recording.

(i) Piano concerto in C, Op. 42; (ii) Violin concerto, Op. 36.
(M) **(*) DG 431 740-2. (i) Brendel; (ii) Zeitlin; Bav. RSO, Kubelik – BERG: *Violin concerto.* ***

Brendel, who made a recording for Vox very early in his career, remains a committed Schoenbergian, and Zeitlin is impressive too. Though even the CD transfer does not manage to clarify the thorny textures completely, the sound, as transferred, is very good.

5 Orchestral pieces, Op. 16.
☞ *** Decca Dig. 433 151-2 [id.]. Concg. O, Chailly – BRAHMS: *Symphony No. 4.* **(*)

Chailly conducts a full-blooded reading of Schoenberg's mould-breaking masterpiece, characterizing each of the pieces very strongly, bringing out their ancestry in the romantic movement. That is apt, when this makes an unusual but refreshing coupling for Chailly's Brahms performance.

Pelleas und Melisande (symphonic poem), *Op. 5.*
☞ (M) **(*) EMI CDM7 65078-2 [id.]. New Philh. O, Barbirolli – R. STRAUSS: *Metamorphosen.*
**(*)

It was Richard Strauss who suggested to Schoenberg the subject of Maeterlinck's drama as an opera. Schoenberg opted for a Straussian symphonic poem, and this he completed before he ever knew that Debussy had turned the same subject into an opera. The score is rich and inventive, obviously indebted to Strauss (in 1902–3 Schoenberg had still to develop his own individual style) and with echoes, too, of Wagner's *Tristan und Isolde*. What Barbirolli underlines is the red-bloodedness of the emotions portrayed, and his account is full of passion. The recording is expansive to match, though the tuttis are vibrant rather than refined.

Pelleas und Melisande, Op. 5; Variations for orchestra, Op. 31; Verklaerte Nacht (orchestral version), *Op. 4.*
(M) *** DG 427 424-2 (3) [id.]. BPO, Karajan – BERG: *Lyric suite; 3 Pieces;* WEBERN: *Collection.*
***

The Straussian opulence of Schoenberg's early symphonic poem has never been as ravishingly presented as by Karajan and the Berlin Philharmonic in this splendidly recorded version. The gorgeous tapestry of sound is both rich and full of refinement and detail, while the thrust of argument is powerfully conveyed. These are superb performances which present the emotional element at full power but give unequalled precision and refinement. The Op. 31 *Variations*, the most challenging of Schoenberg's orchestral works, here receives a reading which vividly conveys the ebb and flow of tension within the phrase and over the whole plan. Superb recording, excellently remastered.

3 Pieces for chamber orchestra (1910); *Suite, Op. 29; Verklaerte Nacht* (string sextet version), *Op. 4.*
☞ (M) *** Sony Analogue/Dig. SMK 48465 [id.]. Ens. InterContemporain (members), Boulez.

Boulez first recorded *Verklaerte Nacht* in the version for full strings – see below – but this beautifully played account for solo strings is even more impressive. Here he supervises rather than directs the performance, as he does for Op. 29. Yet the precision of ensemble and refinement of balance suggest a strong but deeply sympathetic guiding hand. The neo-classical *Suite* – with Boulez this time conducting a mere seven players – reveals a totally different side of the composer, never so light as he himself must have intended in its very Germanic humour, but a spiky piece presented at its sharpest in this reading. There is no lack of intimacy and expressive feeling, and the CBS recording is first class. The *Three Pieces for chamber orchestra* were found after Schoenberg had died and date from 1910. They are atonal and the third piece was unfinished. This is an earlier analogue recording but of good quality.

5 Pieces for orchestra, Op. 16.
*** EMI Dig. CDC7 49857-2 [id.]. CBSO, Rattle – BERG: *Lulu: suite;* WEBERN: *6 Pieces.* ***
*** DG Dig. 419 781-2 [id.]. BPO, Levine – BERG: *3 Pieces;* WEBERN: *5 Pieces.* ***
(M) *** Mercury 432 006-2 [id.]. LSO, Dorati – BERG: *3 Pieces; Lulu suite;* WEBERN: *5 Pieces.* ***

Rattle and the CBSO give an outstanding reading of this Schoenberg masterpiece, bringing out its red-blooded strength, neither too austere nor too plushy. With sound of demonstration quality and an ideal coupling, it makes an outstanding recommendation.

The colour and power of Schoenberg's Opus 16 *Pieces* also come over superbly in Levine's purposeful, concentrated reading. This is an interpretation designed to relate Schoenberg to his predecessors rather than to the future. Warm, full-toned recording, with some spotlighting.

Dorati, in his pioneering coupling with other works written at the same period by Schoenberg's emergent pupils, used the version the composer made in 1949, with a slightly reduced orchestra. The performance is strong; the 1962 sound is admirably vivid and clear.

(i) *5 Pieces for orchestra, Op. 16;* (ii) *Ode to Napoleon Buonaparte, Op. 41* (for string quartet, piano and reciter); (iii) *Serenade, Op. 24* (for clarinet, bass clarinet, mandolin, guitar, violin, viola, cello and bass voice).
☞ *** Sony SMK 48463 [id.]. (i) BBC SO; (ii) David Wilson-Johnson; (iii) John Shirley-Quirk; (ii; iii) Ens. InterContemporain (members), Boulez.

The *Five Pieces for orchestra*, once regarded as difficult, now emerge as colourfully expressive, hardly more elusive than Debussy when played as strongly as this. The Abbey Road recording has plenty of body and atmosphere. The *Serenade* finds Schoenberg in rather crustily neo-classical mood, and even Boulez with his team (including Shirley-Quirk) cannot bring out all the lightness the composer seems to have intended. With David Wilson-Johnson a characterfully ironic narrator, the Byron setting of the *Ode to Napoleon* is more warmly memorable. Both are very clearly recorded and, if the balance is close, there is plenty of ambient warmth.

Variations for orchestra, Op. 31; Verklaerte Nacht, Op. 4.
❀ *** DG 415 326-2 [id.]. BPO, Karajan.

(i) *Variations for orchestra, Op. 31;* (ii) *Verklaerte Nacht, Op. 4;* (i; iii) *Die glückliche Hande, Op. 18.*
☞ (M) **(*) Sony SMK 48464 [id.]. (i) BBC SO; (ii) NYPO; (iii) Siegmund Nimsgern, BBC Singers; Boulez.

Karajan's version of *Verklaerte Nacht* is altogether magical and very much in a class of its own. There is a tremendous intensity and variety of tone and colour: the palette that the strings of the Berlin Philharmonic have at their command is altogether extraordinarily wide-ranging. Moreover on CD the sound is firmer and more cleanly defined.

Boulez's account of the thornily immediate *Variations* and the coupled New York Philharmonic performance of *Verklaerte Nacht* may lack the warmth, final polish and subtlety of Karajan's celebrated versions, but Boulez's earthiness, unrelentingly forceful, is compelling in the former, while in the latter he has the full measure of Schoenberg's poetry and secures responsive playing from the New York Philharmonic. The Sony recording is vivid but not as richly beautiful as the Berlin sound. There is also a bonus here in the 'psychological pantomime', *Die glückliche Hande*, which is sharply observed, with Nimsgern a fine soloist.

Verklaerte Nacht.
☞ *** Denon Dig. CO 79442 [id.]. Sinfonia Varsovia, Krivine – R. STRAUSS: *Metamorphosen;* WAGNER: *Siegfried idyll.* ***
☞ (M) *** EMI CDM5 65079-2 [id.]. ECO, Daniel Barenboim – BARTOK: *Divertimento for strings;* HINDEMITH: *Trauermusik.* ***
☞ *(*) DG Dig. 435 883-2 [id.]. BPO, Levine – R. STRAUSS: *Metamorphosen;* WAGNER: *Siegfried idyll.* *(*)

Emmanuel Krivine draws playing of refined sonority from his excellent Polish string ensemble, who play as if their lives are at stake. It is a performance of strong contrast both in dynamic range and in dramatic character, and is of a high emotional temperature. This is one of the most powerful and convincing of recent recordings and, though it does not displace Karajan's celebrated account, it is as deeply felt and in its way almost as subtle. It has the merit of excellent digital recorded sound.

Barenboim is a most persuasive advocate of this score and receives a warmly immediate response from his players. He is given very good (1967) Abbey Road sound, lacking only a very little in refinement in the extreme upper range, and with plenty of body. This is highly involving, and interestingly coupled.

Levine's *Verklaerte Nacht* with the Berlin Philharmonic is pretty ordinary and characterless and, given the competition, is unlikely to find much favour with collectors.

Verklaerte Nacht, Op. 4 (string sextet version).
☞ ❀ (***) Testament mono SABT 1031 Hollywood Qt, with Alvin Dinkin, Kurt Reher – SCHUBERT: *String quintet.* (***) ❀
*** Hyp. Dig. CDA 66425 [id.]. Raphael Ens. – KORNGOLD: *Sextet.* ***

The 1950 Hollywood account was the first version of *Verklaerte Nacht* in its original sextet form ever to appear on records, and arguably it remains unsurpassed and possibly unequalled. The Hollywood Quartet made music for the sheer love of it and as a relaxation from their daily work in the film studios, for which they were conspicuously over-qualified. They possessed a consummate artistry alongside impeccable technical address; there is a complete absence of glamour or overprojection. This almost flawless performance enjoyed the imprimatur of Schoenberg himself, who supplied the sleeve-note for it (reproduced in the excellent booklet), the only time he ever did so. The sound is remarkably good and very musical. Recommended with enthusiasm.

The Raphael Ensemble have the advantage of very good recorded sound and give a fine account of Schoenberg's score. They also have the advantage of a rarity in their coupling, the youthful *Sextet* of Korngold.

String quartets Nos. 1 in D min., Op. 7; (i) *2 in F sharp min., Op. 10. 3, Op. 30; 4, Op. 37.*
☞ (***) Archiphon ARC mono 103/4 [id.]. Kolisch Qt, (i) with C. Gifford.

Schoenberg's *First Quartet* comes from the earliest years of the century (1904–5) and the *Fourth* comes from 1936. No quartet has ever been more closely associated with these pieces than the Kolisch, and the present recordings were made at the turn of 1936–7, during the performing of the complete set, mounted by the great patroness of modern music, Elizabeth Sprague Coolidge, at the University of California in Los Angeles. The Hollywood composer, Alfred Newman, who was studying with Schoenberg at the time, brought the quartet into the film studio and recorded the whole cycle as a present for the composer. They were straight performances with no re-takes, though the Kolisch always played these works (and other repertoire) by heart – with the exception of the *Fourth*, which was new. They recorded this work just before giving its première. The recordings were briefly issued in the early 1950s as a limited edition on LP. Those who normally find Schoenberg's music rebarbative should try to hear these readings, which bring one closer to this repertoire than any other. It is well worth putting up with surface noise (which one soon barely notices anyway) for the sake of *real* music-making. Even Sir William Glock once asked, 'Why does Schoenberg's music sound so ugly?' Well, these performances make it sound – not beautiful – but at least both meaningful and humane. Indeed, given phrasing of this quality, one is tempted to say that even the sceptic will be persuaded that there is more to the rigorously disciplined *Third* and *Fourth Quartets* than later ensembles have found; and never have the two earlier *Quartets* sounded so eloquent. The set contains a short speech of thanks by Schoenberg and words by the quartet and also by Alfred Newman. An interesting and illuminating issue.

Suite (for E flat clarinet, clarinet, bass clarinet, violin, viola, cello & piano), *Op. 29; Wind quintet, Op. 26.*
(M) *** Decca 433 083-2 [id.]. L. Sinf. (members), David Atherton.

In his *Suite,* Op. 29, Schoenberg deliberately found inspiration in Viennese dance-rhythms. These recordings by the London Sinfonietta were made in 1973/4 in conjunction with a series of centenary concerts at London's Queen Elizabeth Hall. Happily the recording venue was All Saints' Church, Petersham, and the uncompromising and massive *Wind quintet*, though forwardly balanced, is given plenty of space. It is played with great commitment and bravura, and if not even these players can make the humour of the *Suite* anything but Germanic, the combination of fine playing and lively sound makes this generous 74-minute coupling highly recommendable.

Piano music: 3 Pieces, Op. 11; 6 Small Pieces, Op. 19; 5 Pieces, Op. 23; 3 Pieces, Op. 33a & b; Suite, Op. 25.
(M) *** DG 423 249-2 [id.]. Maurizio Pollini.
☞ * Symposium Dig. 1107. Katharina Wolpe.

This CD encompasses Schoenberg's complete piano music. Pollini plays with enormous authority and refinement of dynamic nuance and colour, making one perceive this music in a totally different light from other performers. He is accorded excellent sound (very slightly on the dry side), extremely clear and well defined.

A much-admired artist, Katharina Wolpe has made few records though she has been a tireless champion of contemporary music. Her Schoenberg collection is however something of a disappointment. The playing itself is not always responsive to dynamic nuance, and there is a certain want of both immediacy and intensity in the aphoristic Op. 19 pieces. Artistic considerations apart, the disc falls short in the all-important respect of sound: the acoustic is very dry and unappealing, and Schoenberg needs the most refined sound if his music is to be remotely persuasive.

VOCAL MUSIC

(i) *The Book of the Hanging Gardens, Op. 15;* (ii) *Pierrot lunaire, Op. 21.*
*** Nonesuch/Warner 7559 79237-2 [id.]. Jan DeGaetani; (i) Gilbert Kalish; (ii) Contemporary
   Chamber Ens., Arthur Weisberg.

The Nonesuch New York performance of *Pierrot lunaire* has long been admired for steering a
splendidly confident course among all the many problematic interpretative points. Now it comes
coupled with another equally impressive recording of *The Book of the Hanging Gardens.* Jan
DeGaetani is a superbly precise soloist, but there is no feeling whatever of pedantry in her
performances which, more than most, allow a welcome degree of expressiveness, while keeping a
sharp focus and projecting a strong sense of drama.

Erwartung, Op. 17.
*** Decca Dig. 417 348-2 (2) [id.]. Anja Silja, VPO, Dohnányi – BERG: *Wozzeck.* ***

Schoenberg's searingly intense monodrama makes an apt and generous coupling for Dohnányi's
excellent version of Berg's *Wozzeck.* As in the Berg, Silja is at her most passionately committed, and
the digital sound is exceptionally vivid.

(i) *Erwartung.* (ii) Cabaret songs: *Arie aus dem Spiegel von Arcadien; Einfältiges Lied; Galathea; Der
genügsame Liebhaber; Jedem das Seine; Mahnung; Nachtwandler* (with trumpet, piccolo & snare
drum).
☞ *** Ph. Dig. 426 261-2 [id.]. Jessye Norman; (i) Met. Op. O, Levine; (ii) James Levine (piano).

The monodrama, *Erwartung* – 'Expectation' – may be among the least appealing of Schoenberg's
formidable *œuvre,* but Jessye Norman and James Levine present it on a disc which could well win the
composer more friends than any ever issued before. The neurotic tensions behind this dramatic
monologue have never been in doubt, involving a woman who, lost in a forest, finds the dead body of
her lover.
   The libretto of Marie Pappenheim, a young doctor drawn into Schoenberg's Viennese circle, could
easily have come from a Freudian case-history. We have heard many performances that have
presented the piece powerfully, but always so as to leave an unpleasant taste afterwards. With Jessye
Norman it is quite different. She herself has said that Erwartung is 'technically the most difficult
thing I have ever sung' but that, having learnt it, she found it 'immensely singable'. That clearly
accounts for the warmth, intensity, range of expression and sheer beauty that she and Levine bring to
this score. Levine draws ravishing sounds from the Metropolitan Opera Orchestra, to relate this not
just to Schoenberg's early romantic string-piece, *Verklaerte Nacht,* but also to the closing scenes of
Berg's *Wozzeck* and even to Debussy's *Pelléas et Mélisande.* Jessye Norman's singing, beautiful and
totally secure over the widest range of expression and dynamic, is a revelation too. So far from
leaving a nasty aftertaste, this brings a fulfilment. Compare this with Anja Silja, accompanied by
Christoph von Dohnányi on their fine Decca issue, and the extra depth, range of emotion and
refinement of the New York performance come out at every point.
   The impact of this *Erwartung* is brilliantly heightened by the total contrast of the Schoenberg
coupling. Accompanied by Levine at the piano – a sparkily individual partner – Jessye Norman sings
all eight of the cabaret songs, the Brettl-Lieder, that Schoenberg wrote when he was working in
Berlin. In these witty, pointed, tuneful songs Schoenberg was letting his hair down in a way that to
his detractors must be almost unimaginable. These are art-songs that yet completely belong to the
half-world of cabaret.
   Jessye Norman projects her personality as masterfully as a latterday Marlene Dietrich. And it is
astonishing how she can colour her voice, slinkily inflecting it, scaling it down, so as as to capture the
authentic style. The swagger with which she sings the comic song about the heart beating faster
(boom, boom, boom!) is irresistible and, unlike any rival on record, she includes the final military
song, *Nachtwandler* ('Night Wanderer'), with extra accompaniment of piccolo, trumpet and drum.

(i) *Erwartung, Op. 17;* (ii) *Gurrelieder: Song of the Wood-dove;* (iii) *Pierrot lunaire, Op. 21.*
☞ (M) **(*) Sony SMK 48466 [id.]. (i) Janis Martin, BBC SO; (ii) Jessye Norman, Ens.
   InterContemporain (members); (iii) Minton, Barenboim, Debost, Pay, Zukerman, Harrell.

The monodrama *Ewartung* contrasts well with the lovely *Lied der Waldtaube* in its chamber scoring
with Jessye Norman a radiant soloist, crowning her performance with a thrilling top B flat. Boulez
brings passionate feeling to both, and the recording is full and immediate. As can be seen from the
cast list, the performance of *Pierrot lunaire* gathers together a distinguished group of instrumentalists,
but here the result lacks the expressive intensity one expects of Boulez in this music. With Yvonne
Minton eschewing sing-speech, the vocal line is precisely pitched, with frequent recourse to half-tones.

It is a most musical result but hardly conveys the cabaret associations which are important in this highly coloured, melodramatic work. However, Boulez's approach places Schoenberg's score within the mainstream of vocal writing, and many listeners will relish the comparative lack of difficulty in coming to terms with its highly original musical language.

Gurrelieder.
*** Decca Dig. 430 321-2 (2) [id.]. Jerusalem, Dunn, Fassbaender, Brecht, Haage, Hotter, St Hedwig's Cathedral Ch., Berlin, Düsseldorf State Musikverein, Berlin RSO, Chailly.

(i) *Gurrelieder;* (ii) *4 Orchestral songs.*
☞ (M) *** Sony SM2K 48459 (2) [id.]. (i) Jess Thomas, Napier, Nimsgern, Bowen, Reich, BBC Singers & Ch. Soc., Goldsmith's Ch. Union, Men's voices of LPO Ch.; (i; ii) Yvonne Minton, BBC SO; Boulez.

Chailly's magnificent recording of Schoenberg's massive *Gurrelieder* effectively supplants all existing versions, even Ozawa's impressive Boston set (Philips 412 511-2), recorded live. This Berlin recording not only brings richer, fuller, more detailed and better-balanced sound, but it conveys a natural dramatic tension not easy to find in studio conditions. Siegfried Jerusalem as Waldemar is not only warmer and firmer of tone than his rivals but more imaginative too. Susan Dunn makes a sweet, touchingly vulnerable Tove, while Brigitte Fassbaender gives darkly baleful intensity to the message of the Wood-dove. Hans Hotter is a characterful Speaker in the final section. The impact of the performance is the more telling with sound both atmospheric and immediate, bringing a fine sense of presence, not least in the final choral outburst.

Boulez's warm, expressive style using slow, luxuriating tempi brings out the operatic quality behind Schoenberg's massive score. With Boulez, the Wagnerian overtones are richly expressive and, though Marita Napier and Jess Thomas are not especially sweet on the ear, they show the big, heroic qualities which this score ideally demands, while Yvonne Minton is magnificent in the *Song of the Wood-dove.* Boulez builds that beautiful section to an ominous climax, which far outshines earlier versions, though not Chailly's account. But at mid-price Boulez remains competitive, for the CBS/ Sony recording has attractively vivid and atmospheric sound, and this set also offers a generous coupling of Yvonne Minton's fine account of the *Orchestral songs.*

Music for chorus: *2 Canons; 3 Canons, Op. 28; Dreimal Tausend Jähre, Op. 50a; Friede auf Erden, Op. 13; 3 Folksongs, Op. 49; 3 German folksongs; Kol Nidre, Op. 39; 4 Pieces, Op. 27; 6 Pieces, Op. 35; Psalm 130, Op. 50b; Modern Psalm No. 1, Op. 50 C; A Survivor from Warsaw, Op. 46.*
(M) *** Sony S2K 44571 (2) [id.]. John Shirley-Quirk, Günther Reich, BBC Singers, BBC SO, Pierre Boulez.

With passionately committed performances from the BBC Singers, this superb collection of choral music explodes any idea that Schoenberg was a cold composer. His adoption of an idiom far removed from abrasive atonality in most of these pieces makes this one of the most approachable of Schoenberg sets, with the use of a narrator in three of the works adding spice to the mixture. The later works, written in America, use twelve-note technique with astonishingly warm, rich results. First-rate recording. Translations are given of the full texts.

Pierrot lunaire, Op. 21 (see also above, under *The Book of the Hanging Gardens).*
(M) *** Chan. CHAN 6534; *MBTD 6534* [id.]. Jane Manning, Nash Ens., Rattle – WEBERN: *Concerto.* ***

Jane Manning is outstanding among singers who have tackled this most taxing of works, steering a masterful course between the twin perils of, on the one hand, actually singing and, on the other, simply speaking; her sing-speech brings out the element of irony and darkly pointed wit that is an essential. Rattle draws strong, committed performances from the members of the Nash Ensemble and, apart from some intermittently odd balances, the sound is excellent.

(i) *Pierrot lunaire, Op. 21;* (ii) *Serenade, Op. 24* (for clarinet, bass clarinet, mandolin, guitar, violin, viola, cello and bass voice); *Die eiserne Brigade* (march for string quartet and piano).
(M) *** Decca 425 626-2. (i) Mary Thomas; (ii) Shirley-Quirk; L. Sinf., Atherton.

These performances derive from David Atherton's distinguished 1973 survey of Schoenberg's chamber music, including vocal works. *Pierrot lunaire* is among the most incisive and dramatic yet recorded and, although not even these performers can make the humour of the *Serenade* anything but Teutonic, the performance remains compelling.

OPERA

Moses und Aron.

*** Decca Dig. 414 264-2 (2) [id.]. Mazura, Langridge, Bonney, Haugland, Chicago Ch. and SO, Solti.

☞ (M) ** Ph. 438 667-2 (2) [id.]. Reich, Devos, Mann, Austrian R. Ch. & O, Gielen.

(i) *Moses und Aron* (complete); (ii) *Chamber Symphony No. 2, Op. 38.*

☞ (M) *** Sony SM2K 48456 (2). (i) Reich, Cassilly, Palmer, Knight, BBC Singers, Orpheus Boys' Ch., BBC SO; (ii) Ens. InterContemporain; Boulez.

Solti gives Schoenberg's masterly score a dynamism and warmth which set it firmly – if perhaps surprisingly – in the grand romantic tradition, yet finds an element of fantasy and, in places – as in the *Golden Calf* episode – a sparkle such as you would never expect from Schoenberg. The Moses of Franz Mazura may not be as specific in his sing-speech as was Gunter Reich in the two previous versions – far less sing than speech – but the characterization of an Old Testament patriarch is the more convincing. As Aaron, Philip Langridge is lighter and more lyrical, as well as more accurate, than his predecessor with Boulez, Richard Cassilly. Aage Haugland with his firm, dark bass makes his mark in the small role of the Priest; Barbara Bonney too is excellent as the Young Girl. Above all, the brilliant singing of the Chicago Symphony Chorus matches the playing of the orchestra in virtuosity. More than ever the question-mark concluding Act II makes a pointful close, with no feeling of a work unfinished. The brilliant recording has an even sharper focus on CD.

So far from making this most formidable of operas just a tough intellectual exercise, Pierre Boulez presents it as a clear successor to the great tradition of romantic operas, as sensually involving as Wagner. The conductor is helped not just by the passionately committed singing and playing (with Günter Reich expansive in his fully rounded characterization of Moses) but also by the rich, atmospheric recording, which allows the operatic qualities are allowed to blossom. It is typical of Boulez that in the final scene Moses' mounting frustration in the face of the glib, articulate Aron is superbly built up, so that the final words – *O Wort, du Wort das mir fehlt* – come with a compelling sense of tragedy. Though the composer planned a third Act, such a moment makes a far more telling conclusion, explaining why Schoenberg in the last years of his life never went further with this, a project to which he was more deeply committed than to any other. Richard Cassilly makes a big-scaled Aron, a worthy brother-adversary to the central tragic figure. The *Second Chamber Symphony*, given an equally committed performance, follows the end of the opera to make a good bonus on the second CD.

Compared with Boulez, Michael Gielen presents a small-scale, drier reading. The opening scene of the burning bush is underpowered, but after that soloists, chorus and orchestra all sing confidently and incisively. However, with rather close recorded sound – although the acoustic is not without atmosphere – the result is a little like a performance of an extended chamber cantata.

Schreker, Franz (1878–1934)

(i) *Chamber symphony for 23 solo instruments;* (ii) *Nachtstück;* (i) *Prelude to a drama;* (ii) *Valse lente.*
**(*) Koch Int. Dig. CD 311 078. Berlin RSO, (i) Gielen, (ii) Rickenbacher.

Schreker's *Chamber symphony* is quite magical, scored with great delicacy and feeling for colour. The other works are not quite so seductive but they, too, have a heady art-nouveau atmosphere. A most rewarding disc, with good performances and very acceptable, though not out of the ordinary, recording. But don't miss this issue.

Der Schatzgräber (opera): complete.
**(*) Capriccio Dig. 60010-2 (2) [id.]. Protschka, Schnaut, Stamm, Haage, Hamburg State O, Gerd Albrecht.

The attractions of Schreker's sweet-sour treatment of a curious morality fairy-story are fairly well conveyed in this first recording, made live at the Hamburg State Opera in 1989, though there are very few signs of the audience's presence, with no applause, even at the end. Josef Protschka sings powerfully as Elis, hardly ever over-strenuous, but Gabriele Schnaut finds it hard to scale down her very bright and powerful soprano and seems happiest when she is scything your ears with loud and often unsteady top notes; yet she is certainly dramatic in this equivocal role. Outstanding among the others is Peter Haage as the court jester. *Der Schatzgräber* may be hokum, but it is enjoyable hokum, and, with Albrecht drawing committed performances from the whole company, this well-made recording is most welcome.

Schröter, Johann (1752–88)

Piano concerto in C, Op. 3/3.
*** Sony Dig. MK 39222 [id.]. Murray Perahia, ECO – MOZART: *Piano concertos Nos. 1–3, K.107.*
***

Johann Samuel Schröter was a highly accomplished pianist, and this sparkling little *Concerto* explains why he was so successful. Murray Perahia gives it all his care and attention without overloading it with sophistication. His account is delightful in every way, and beautifully recorded.

Schubert, Franz (1797–1828)

Rondo in A for violin and strings, D.438.
(B) *** Ph. 426 977-2. Grumiaux, New Philh. O, Leppard – HAYDN: *Violin concertos;* MOZART: *Adagio; Rondo.* ***
*** EMI Dig. CDC7 49663-2 [id.]. Nigel Kennedy, ECO, Tate – BRUCH; MENDELSSOHN: *Concertos.*
***

Schubert's *Rondo* has never danced more engagingly than on Grumiaux's bow, and Leppard captures the music's rhythmic lilt equally pleasingly. Excellent 1967 sound. A bargain.

The ideas in Schubert's *Rondo* also flow very sweetly with Kennedy, making this an attractive bonus to the usual Bruch–Mendelssohn coupling.

Symphonies Nos. 1–6; 8–9.
☞ **(*) Teldec/Warner Dig. 4509 91184-2 (4) [id.]. Concg. O, Harnoncourt.
☞ (B) **(*) Nimbus Dig. NI 5270/3 [id.]. Hanover Band, Roy Goodman.

Symphonies Nos. 1–6; 8 (Unfinished); 9 (Great); Overtures: Fierabras; In the Italian style in C; Des Teufels Lustschloss.
(B) **(*) Decca 430 773-2 (4). VPO, István Kertész.

Symphonies Nos. 1–6; 8–9; Grand Duo in C, D.812 (orch. Joachim); *Rosamunde overture (Die Zauberharfe), D.644.*
*** DG Dig. 423 651-2 (5) [id.]. COE, Abbado.

Symphonies Nos. 1–6; 8–9; Rosamunde: Overture (Die Zauberharfe) and incidental music.
☞ *(*) Sony Dig. M5K 45661 (5) [id.]. BPO, Barenboim.

Symphonies Nos. 1–6; 8–9; Rosamunde: Overture (Die Zauberharfe); Ballet music 1–2.
☞ (M) ** EMI Dig. CMS7 64873-2 (4) [id.]. VPO, Muti.

Abbado's is an outstanding set. Rarely has he made recordings of the central Viennese classics which find him so naturally sunny and warm in his expression. Speeds are often on the fast side but never feel breathless, and the recording is refined, with fine bloom on the string-sound. Textually too, the Abbado set takes precedence over its rivals and there are certain fascinating differences from what we are used to. The five CDs are now also available separately – see below.

Kertész began with Nos. 8 and 9 and the overtures (which are well worth having), and these two symphonies are the finest performances in the cycle. The *Ninth* is fresh, dramatic and often very exciting, the *Unfinished* highly imaginative and comparably dramatic in its wide dynamic contrasts. In the two early symphonies Kertész scores with the spirited VPO playing and a light touch, and this also applies to Nos. 3 and 6, even if they are without the last ounce of character and distinction. The playing of the VPO is beyond reproach throughout, and it has a pervading freshness, helped by the transparent yet full Decca sound.

It is a pity that Harnoncourt in his Schubert cycle did not turn to the Chamber Orchestra of Europe instead of to the Concertgebouw. His Beethoven cycle with that young orchestra has a freshness and intensity not quite matched in these weightier, bigger-scale performances. Had he done so, it would have been even more fascinating to compare Harnoncourt's Schubert with Abbado's, also featuring the COE. As it is, Harnoncourt takes a relatively severe view, and significantly he is at his finest in the darkness of the *Tragic Symphony*. There is little of Schubertian charm here, with his eccentrically slow tempo for the finale of No. 6 in its lumbering gait missing the pure sunlight of the piece. Echoing period practice, Harnoncourt's preference for short phrasing also tends to make slow movements less songful, though equally it adds to the bite and intensity of other movements, notably Scherzos with their sharp cross-rhythms. Not that any reservations detract seriously from a most refreshing cycle, direct and unmannered. Though the reverberance of the Amsterdam Concertgebouw hall obscures detail in tuttis, as well as reinforcing the weight of sound, the recording is warm and otherwise helpful. Harnoncourt, like Abbado, has used specially prepared texts, but they avoid the radical changes that spice the Abbado set.

As in his Beethoven cycle, also recorded for Nimbus, Goodman draws lively, beautifully sprung performances of the Schubert symphonies from the players of the Hanover Band. For anyone wanting period performances of these works, they can be warmly recommended as a mid-priced set, with the reservation that the characteristic Nimbus balance is more damaging here than it is in Beethoven. The strings are attractively caught in a warm acoustic, but the reverberation tends to obscure detail in tuttis, with the woodwind set so far backwards that it is often barely audible, and even the rasp of the natural horns is underplayed. Nos. 1 and 4 (*Tragic*) have also been issued separately on NI 5158, and the *Unfinished* is available coupled with the *Overture and incidental music from Rosamunde* (NI 5274), both at full price.

Muti's set is a disappointment: his robust approach is not endearingly Schubertian, even though he has the VPO at his disposal. With the playing relatively routine, despite the conductor's natural electricity and preference for urgent speeds there is little here to set the blood tingling or to charm the ear. With a relatively mannered if spacious account of the *Ninth*, this cannot compare with Abbado in either natural zest or warmth. The dull recording is no help.

Though Barenboim chooses generally sensible speeds and springs rhythms well, he is not well served by the Sony engineers. The sound is not as clean on detail as one wants and, surprisingly, the Berlin violins are often made to seem scrawny, the opposite of their sound under Karajan. With other rival sets offering more imaginative and more electrifying performances, better recorded, this is hardly competitive.

Symphonies Nos. 1–3; 4 (Tragic); 5–7; 8 (Unfinished); 9 in C (Great); 10 in D, D.936a; Symphonic fragments in D, D.615 and D.708a (completed and orch. Newbould).
*** Ph. Dig. 412 176-2 (6) [id.]. ASMF, Marriner.

Marriner's excellent set gathers together not only the eight symphonies of the regular canon but two more symphonies now 'realized', thanks to the work of Professor Brian Newbould of Hull University. For full measure, half a dozen fragments of other symphonic movements are also included, orchestrated by Professor Newbould. The set brings sparkling examples of the Academy's work at its finest, while the bigger challenges of the *Unfinished* (here completed with Schubert's Scherzo filled out and the *Rosamunde B minor Entr'acte* used as finale) and the *Great C major* are splendidly taken. These are fresh, direct readings, making up in rhythmic vitality for any lack of weight. The recordings, all digital, present consistent refinement and undistractingly good balance. But this set now seems expensive.

Symphonies Nos. 1 in D, D.82; 2 in B flat, D.125.
*** DG Dig. 423 652-2 [id.]. COE, Abbado.

The coupling of the two earliest *Symphonies* brings bright and sparkling performances, reflecting the youthful joy of both composer and players. Abbado brings out the sunny relaxation of the writing, most exhilaratingly of all in the light-hearted finales. The recording of both captures the refined playing of the COE very vividly.

Symphony No. 2 in B flat, D.125.
☞ (B) **(*) Pickwick Dig. PCD 1052; *PK 515* [id.]. West German Sinfonia, Dirk Joeres – VORISEK: *Symphony in D.* **(*)

The Westdeutsche Sinfonia give a spirited and thoroughly enjoyable account of the eighteen-year-old Schubert's *Second Symphony*, catching its youthful charm. Outer movements are brisk but never pressed on too hard, and the *Andante* is refreshing. The recording is forward and resonant and without ultimate crispness of focus, but it certainly does not lack body or colour. The Voříšek *Symphony* is equally lively and valuable.

Symphony No. 3 in D, D.200.
☞ *** BMG/RCA Dig. 09026 61876-2. N. German RSO, Wand – SCHUMANN: *Symphony No. 3.*
***

Günter Wand's Schubert *D major* is eminently acceptable: very well played and vital. Those who are collecting their Schubert in harness with the Schumann symphonies might consider it, though 56 minutes for a full-price CD is not particularly generous these days. The recording, made at the Musikhalle in Hamburg, has warmth and presence. Not a first recommendation, perhaps, but worth three stars.

Symphonies Nos. 3 in D, D.200; 4 in C min. (Tragic), D.417.
*** DG Dig. 423 653-2 [id.]. COE, Abbado.

Crisp, fast and light, No. 3 is given a delectable performance by Abbado. In No. 4, the *Tragic*, Abbado makes the slow C minor introduction bitingly mysterious before a clean, elegant *Allegro*, and with this conductor the other movements are also elegant and polished as well as strong. Textually, No. 4 eliminates the extra bars in the slow movement which had been inserted originally by Brahms. The slow movement is outstandingly beautiful, with the oboe solo – presumably COE's Douglas Boyd – most tenderly expressive.

Symphonies Nos. 3 in D, D.200; 5 in B flat, D.485; 6 in C, D.589.
✿ (M) *** EMI CDM7 69750-2. RPO, Beecham.

Beecham's are magical performances in which every phrase breathes. There is no substitute for imaginative phrasing and each line is shaped with affection and spirit. The *Allegretto* of the *Third Symphony* is an absolute delight. The delicacy of the opening of the *Fifth* is matched by the simple lyrical beauty of the *Andante*, while few conductors have been as persuasive as Beecham in the *Sixth* 'little' *C major Symphony*. The sound is now just a shade drier in Nos. 3 and 6 than in their last LP incarnation but is generally faithful and spacious. This is an indispensable record or tape for all collections and a supreme bargain in the Schubert discography.

Symphonies Nos. 3 in D, D.200; 8 in B min. (Unfinished), D.759.
(B) *** Pickwick Dig. PCD 848; *CIMPC 848* [id.]. City of L. Sinfonia, Hickox.

Hickox's coupling makes a first-rate bargain recommendation on the Pickwick label. These are fresh and direct readings, never putting a foot wrong, very well recorded, with a chamber orchestra sounding full and substantial. Others may find more individuality and charm, but the crisp resilience of the playing is consistently winning.

Symphony No. 5 in B flat, D.485.
✿ (M) **(*) Sony SMK 46246 [id.]. Marlboro Festival O, Casals – BEETHOVEN: *Symphony No. 4.* **

The Casals account is a concert performance, recorded at the Marlboro Festival in Vermont in 1970, and it is very special indeed. The reading is spacious and unhurried, eminently straightforward and unaffected, yet unfailingly illuminating. The recording inhibits an unreserved recommendation; the string-tone needs more bloom and tutti are a bit rough-grained – but never mind, the performance is full of insight.

Symphonies Nos. 5 in B flat, D.485; 6 in C, D.589.
*** DG Dig. 423 654-2 [id.]. COE, Abbado.

Abbado brings out the happy songfulness of the slow movements in these works, as well as the rhythmic resilience of the *Allegros*. As in No. 4, so also in No. 6 Abbado eliminates the extra bars added by Brahms in his original Schubert Edition. Excellent recording, with fine bloom and good, natural contrasts.

Symphonies Nos. 5 in B flat, D.485; 8 in B min. (Unfinished), D.759.
☞ (B) ** Decca 433 630-2 [id.]. Israel PO, Mehta.

The bargain CD is another coupling from Mehta's productive period with Decca in the late 1970s and well demonstrates the conductor's Viennese sympathies. Yet here his account of the *Fifth*, though no doubt freshly played, is notably less persuasive rhythmically than that of Beecham, except perhaps in the Minuet. Sensitive as Mehta unfailingly is, the underlying tensions of the *Unfinished* are not realized in the way they are with Karajan, for instance, nor is there the degree of imagination of the very finest accounts on record, even though there is some fine playing from the Israeli orchestra. They are convincingly balanced by the Decca engineers, however, and the bright vividness of the recording adds to the appeal of the music-making.

Symphonies Nos. 5 in B flat, D.485; 9 in C, D.944 (The Great).
(M) (**) BMG/RCA mono GD 60291 [60291-2-RG]. NBC SO, Toscanini.

In his 1947 performance of No. 9, Toscanini is tauter and faster than either his earlier or later recording. A useful antidote for it serves to remind one that Schubert was still a young man when this was composed with what was a bright future ahead and that the valedictory halo which came to surround it was a nineteenth-century phenomenon.

Symphony No. 8 in B min. (Unfinished), D.759.
(M) *** DG 415 848-2; *415 848-4* [id.]. BPO, Karajan – MENDELSSOHN: *Symphony No. 4.* ***

Karajan's 1965 DG recording of the *Unfinished* sounds fresher still in remastered form. Its merits of simplicity and directness are enhanced by the extraordinary polish of the orchestra playing, lighting up much that is often obscured. The first movement is extremely compelling in its atmosphere; the slow movement too brings tinglingly precise attack and a wonderful sense of drama.

Symphony No. 8 in B min. (Unfinished); Grand Duo in C, D.812 (orch. Joachim).
*** DG Dig. 423 655-2 [id.]. COE, Abbado.

Abbado's outstandingly refined and sensitive version comes with an unusual and valuable coupling, the orchestral arrangement of the piano-duet *Grand Duo* made by Joachim, once erroneously thought to be the missing *Symphony No. 7*. The second subject in the *Unfinished* brings some slightly obtrusive agogic hesitations at the beginning of each phrase; but with such responsive playing they quickly sound fresh and natural.

Symphonies Nos. 8 (Unfinished); 9 in C (Great).
☞ (M) **(*) Sony SBK 48268 [id.]. Cleveland O, Szell.
☞ (M) **(*) EMI CDM7 64628-2 [id.]. BPO, Karajan.
☞ (B) ** Erato/Warner Dig./Analogue 4509 94582-2 [id.]. (i) Basle SO, Jordan; (ii) New Philh. O, Guschlbauer.
☞ (M) ** Teldec/Warner CD 82008 [id.]. Cleveland O, Christoph von Dohnányi.

Szell's is a splendid performance of the *Unfinished*, strong yet sensitive. Phrasing and general discipline are so immaculate, one would expect the result to seem cold but, on the contrary, Szell never lacks warmth here, and drama and beauty walk hand in hand in the second movement. Apart from the lack of a real pianissimo, the 1960 recording is very good for its time. The *Ninth* dates from the previous year, and Szell's powerful reading brings a reminder that the parallels between him and another great disciplinarian conductor, Toscanini, were sometimes significant. Szell's control of tempo in the first movement brings a convincing onward flow, and the performance is notable for the alertness and rhythmic energy of the playing, yet there is no lack of resilience in the *Andante*. The interpretation is certainly dramatic: the Scherzo has great brio and leads naturally to the brilliant finale, where few rivals can match the precision of the hectic triplet rhythms. The sound is fuller in this remastered form than it was originally on LP, although the finale is a little lacking in weight, especially in the closing pages.

Karajan recorded a complete set of Schubert *Symphonies* for EMI towards the end of the 1970s and its culmination came, not in No. 9, but in the *Unfinished*, which, with Berlin refinement at its most ethereal, has an other-worldly quality, rapt and concentrated. The *Great C major* is compelling too, but here some may find that the reverberant acoustic gives the impression of too much weightiness. But this is not a superficial reading like Karajan's earlier, DG version, and it has plenty of impetus and power, while the *Andante* has freshness too. The finale has undoubted thrust, although tuttis bring a degree of heaviness, caused as much by the sound itself as by the playing.

Jordan's digitally recorded *Unfinished* is strong and direct, yet does not lack atmosphere. After beginning the work rather deliberately, Guschlbauer falls short in the drama of the climax of the slow movement of the *Great C major*, but the Philharmonia playing is first class, especially in the exciting and well-sustained finale; overall it is an enjoyably straightforward performance. Again very good sound, so this is a fair bargain coupling.

Dohnányi's *Unfinished* lacks a little in poetry and magic but it presents a fresh, direct view, beautifully played. The exposition repeat in the first movement is omitted. In the *Ninth* he paces the first movement briskly and is not subtle enough to accommodate the second subject flexibly within his conception. The slow movement is beautifully played. In the Scherzo Dohnányi is less generous with repeats than usual (which is why the two symphonies fit easily on a 78-minute CD) and the effect of the reading is lightweight. In both works the Telarc sound is warm and spacious but not brightly lit; in No. 9 the woodwind solos, though placed in a believable perspective, lack vividness. An enjoyable coupling, but not a distinctive one.

Symphony No. 9 in C (Great), D.944.
*** Virgin/EMI Dig. VC7 59669-2 [id.]. O of Age of Enlightenment, Mackerras.
(M) *** Decca 430 747-2 [id.]. VPO, Solti.
**(*) EMI Dig. CDC7 49949-2. L. Classical Players, Norrington.

Symphony No. 9 in C (Great); Overture in C in the Italian style.
☞ ** Decca Dig. 436 598-2 [id.]. San Francisco SO, Blomstedt.

Symphony No. 9 in C (Great); Rosamunde: Overture (Die Zauberharfe), D.644.
*** DG Dig. 423 656-2 [id.]. COE, Abbado.

Symphony No. 9 in C (Great); Symphonic fragments in D, D.615.
(M) *** Ph. Dig. 434 218-2; *434 218-4* [id.]. ASMF, Sir Neville Marriner.

Though the COE is by definition an orchestra of chamber scale, the weight of Abbado's version, taken from his complete cycle, is ample, while allowing extra detail to be heard, thanks also to the orchestra's outstandingly crisp ensemble. Speeds are very well chosen, and the expressive detail is consistently made to sound natural. This version is important too for including textual amendments, and the Scherzo has four extra bars that were originally cut by Brahms in his early edition. The sound is beautifully refined, to match the point and polish of the playing. The *Rosamunde* (*Zauberharfe*) *overture* makes a valuable and generous fill-up.

In the first recording to use period instruments, Sir Charles Mackerras and the Orchestra of the Age of Enlightenment on the Virgin Classics label give a winning performance, one that will delight both those who prefer conventional performance and devotees of the new authenticity. The character-ful rasp and bite of period brass instruments and the crisp attack of timpani are much more striking than any thinness of string tone. It is a performance of outstanding freshness and resilience. With every single repeat observed, the heavenly length is joyfully as well as powerfully sustained, and the warm, atmospheric recording gives a fine sense of presence.

Sir George Solti is not the first conductor one thinks of as a Schubertian, but the *Great C major symphony* prompted him to one of the happiest and most glowing of all his many records, an outstanding version, beautifully paced and sprung in all four movements and superbly played and recorded. Now reissued at mid-price, this is an unbeatable bargain and would be first choice, irrespective of cost, for I.M.

Taken from his collected edition of Schubert symphonies, Sir Neville Marriner's account of the *Great C major* makes up for any lack of weight with the fresh resilience of the playing, consistently well sprung. Though all repeats are observed, bringing the timing of the *Symphony* to over an hour, an attractive fill-up is provided in the little two-movement fragment, D.615, orchestrated by Brian Newbould. Written just after the *Sixth Symphony*, it consists of a slow introduction and first-movement exposition, plus a fragment of a sonata-rondo finale, which similarly breaks off. First-rate recording.

Roger Norrington's version is by far the most provocative of the period-performance versions of the *Great C major*. The first movement brings splendid snap and swagger, exhilaratingly presented with Mendelssohnian lightness. But it will take most listeners some time to adjust to the total absence of the usual slowings in the final coda, which here sounds perfunctory. Yet in his crisp, brisk reading of the slow movement Norrington does allow himself a relaxation in the cello melody after the big climax, rightly so. Only in the finale is the speed relatively conventional, with triplets clarified. All repeats are observed, even those in the da capo return of the Scherzo.

After Blomstedt's recent Mendelssohn coupling, this is a disappointment. It is a well-played and very well-recorded performance that obstinately refuses to take off. Blomstedt is generous with repeats, and one is certainly aware of the 'heavenly length', especially in the Scherzo. The first movement is purposeful but without incandescence, the *Andante* pleasing but unmemorable, while the finale generates plenty of energy without a really compulsive forward thrust. The *Overture* is stylishly played, but one is never persuaded here that Schubert's Rossini imitation comes off in its own right.

CHAMBER AND INSTRUMENTAL MUSIC

Arpeggione sonata, D.821 (arr. for cello).
*** Ph. Dig. 412 230-2 [id.]. Maisky, Argerich – SCHUMANN: *Fantasiestücke etc.* ***
(M) *** BMG/RCA GD 86531 [RCA 6531-2-RG]. Lynn Harrell, James Levine – DVORAK: *Cello concerto.* ***
(*) Decca 417 833-2 [id.]. Rostropovich, Britten – DEBUSSY: *Sonata;* SCHUMANN: *5 Stücke.* *

Mischa Maisky and Martha Argerich make much more of the *Arpeggione sonata* than any of their rivals. Their approach may be relaxed, but they bring much pleasure through their variety of colour and sensitivity. The Philips recording is in the very best traditions of the house.

Lynn Harrell's account of the *Arpeggione* with James Levine makes an excellent medium-price choice. Vital, sensitive playing excellently recorded, though the digitally remastered sound is rather light in bass.

Rostropovich gives a curiously self-indulgent interpretation of Schubert's slight but amiable *Arpeggione sonata*. However, the record is particularly valuable for the sake of the couplings.

Arpeggione sonata, D.821 (arr. in G min. for clarinet & piano).
*** Chan. Dig. CHAN 8506; *ABTD 1216* [id.]. Gervase de Peyer, Gwenneth Pryor – SCHUMANN: *Fantasiestücke; 3 Romances;* WEBER: *Silvana variations.* ***

So persuasive is the performance of Gervase de Peyer and Gwenneth Pryor that the listener is all but persuaded that the work was actually written for this combination.

Arpeggione sonata in A min. (arr. for flute); *Introduction and variations on Trock'ne Blumen* from *Die schöne Müllerin; Schwanengesang: Ständchen, D.957/4.*
**(*) BMG/RCA Dig. RD 70421. James Galway, Phillip Moll.

The *Arpeggione sonata* also transcribes surprisingly well for the flute and is played with skill and some charm by this partnership. The *Introduction and variations on Trock'ne Blumen* are as neatly played. Not distinctive, but a pleasing and well-recorded recital.

Octet in F, D.803.
⊛ *** EMI Dig. CDC7 54118-2. Hausmusik.
*** Chan. Dig. CHAN 8585; *ABTD 1276* [id.]. ASMF Chamber Ens.
☞ (M) *** Teldec/Warner 4509 91448-2 [id.]. Berlin Soloists.
*** O-L Dig. 425 519-2 [id.]. AAM Chamber Ens.
☞ (M) *** DG 437 318-2 [id.]. V. Chamber Ens.
*** ASV Dig. CDDCA 694; *ZCDCA 694* [id.]. Gaudier Ens.
☞ ** Virgin/EMI Dig. VC5 45017-2 [id.]. Nash Ens.
☞ (BB) *(*) ASV CDQS 6098 [id.]. Music Group of London.

Hausmusik's performance of Schubert's *Octet* on period instruments is so winning that it can be recommended warmly even to those who do not normally follow the authenticity cult. Speeds are rarely extreme, allowing full, open expressiveness, as in the *Adagio*; and allegros are generally easy enough to allow a delectable rhythmic spring. The pointing is the more infectious when period string-playing allows textures to be so transparent. There are few Schubert records that so consistently convey the joys of spring.

The new Chandos version brings a performance just as delightful as the earlier one by the ASMF, less classical in style, a degree freer in expression, with Viennese overtones brought out in Schubert's sunny invention. It has the benefit of excellent modern digital sound, cleaner on detail than before.

The Berlin Soloists give a strong and stylish performance which, on a bigger scale than most, designedly brings out the symphonic power of a piece lasting over an hour. Every single repeat is observed, and with such distinguished playing that length is readily sustained. This is very well characterized, not just in the big, symphonic movements but in the charming *Andante variations* too. Though the sound is not always ideally sweet on string-tone, the recording is full and clear, and at mid-price this is now very competitive.

The Academy's Chamber Ensemble using period instruments brings out the open joyfulness of Schubert's inspiration, with excellent matching and vivid recording. The reading is not at all stiff or pedantic, but personal and relaxed. Lightness is the keynote, with speeds never eccentrically fast.

The Vienna Chamber Ensemble do not overlap in personnel with the New Vienna Octet, who have recorded this work for Decca, though their performance has a similar polish and urbane Viennese warmth. This is mellifluous Schubert, and very engaging it is: fresh and elegant. The group produce a beautifully balanced sound and are accorded natural recording without edge on top. This dates from 1980, and the CD transfer maintains the smoothness and realism of the LP. Very enjoyable.

The Gaudier Ensemble give an entirely winning account of the *Octet*, essentially spontaneous yet very relaxed and catching all the ingenuous Schubertian charm. Excellent sound, vivid yet well balanced within a pleasing acoustic which gives a feeling of intimacy. An ideal record for a warm summer evening.

The Nash Ensemble's version on Virgin Classics returns to the catalogue, still at full price. It brings a refined performance, recorded in a warm church acoustic that gives the impression of a full concert hall, on the large side for this music. There is much beautiful solo playing – not least from the clarinettist, Michael Collins – but with underlying rhythms often on the square side the result is more studied, less spontaneous than in the very finest versions.

On ASV, the Music Group of London get off to a rather sluggish start. There is some musical phrasing and some warmth in this performance but it remains untouched by real distinction, and even in the lowest price-range it cannot be recommended with much enthusiasm.

Piano quintet in A (Trout), D.667.
*** Decca Dig. 411 975-2 [id.]. András Schiff, Hagen Qt.
*** Ph. 400 078-2 [id.]. Brendel, Cleveland Qt.
(M) ** Ph. 434 146-2 [id.]. Beaux Arts Trio (augmented) – BEETHOVEN: *Piano trio No. 5.* ***

(i) *Piano quintet in A (Trout);* (ii) *String quartet No. 14 (Death and the Maiden).*
(M) **(*) Decca 417 459-2 [id.]. (i) Curzon, Vienna Octet (members); (ii) VPO Qt.
(M) **(*) Sony SBK 46343 [id.]; *40-46343.* (i) Horszowski, Budapest Qt (members), Julius Levine; (ii) Juilliard Qt.
☞ (B) ** DG 439 416-2 [id.]. (i) Demus, Schubert Qt; (ii) Amadeus Qt.

(i) *Piano quintet in A (Trout);* (ii) *String trios, D.471 & D.581.*
(M) *** Ph. 422 838-2. (i) Haebler, Grumiaux, Janzer, Czako, Cazauran; (ii) Grumiaux String Trio.

(i) *Piano quintet in A (Trout);* (ii) *Die Forelle;* (iii) *Der Hirt auf dem Felsen.*
**(*) ASV Dig. CDDCA 684 [id.]. (i) Yitkin Seow, Prometheus Ens.; (ii; iii) Ann Mackay; (iii) Christopher Craker.

(i) *Piano quintet in A (Trout);* (ii) *Der Hirt auf dem Felsen.*
(B) **(*) Pickwick PCD 868; *CIMPC 868* [id.]. (i) Nash Ens.; (ii) Lott, Collins, Brown.

András Schiff and the Hagen Quartet give a delectably fresh and youthful reading of the *Trout quintet,* full of the joys of spring, but one which is also remarkable for hushed concentration, as in the exceptionally dark and intense account of the opening of the first movement. The Scherzo brings a light, quick and bouncing performance, and there is extra lightness too in the other middle movements. Unlike current rivals, this version observes the exposition repeat in the finale, and with such a joyful, brightly pointed performance one welcomes that.

The Brendel/Cleveland performance may lack something in traditional Viennese charm, but it has a compensating vigour and impetus, and the work's many changes of mood are encompassed with freshness and subtlety, with Brendel at his most persuasive. The recording is well balanced and truthful.

Clifford Curzon's 1958 recording of the *Trout* sounds its age in the thin violin timbre, although the piano tone has plenty of colour and it has a warm ambience. It remains a classic performance, with a distinguished account of the piano part and splendidly stylish support from the Vienna players. Schubert's warm lyricism is caught with remarkable freshness. The Vienna Philharmonic performance treats *Death and the Maiden* with comparable affection; the playing is peerless, Boskovsky, the leader, showing all his skill and musicianship in the variations. Both recordings have a pleasingly warm ambience and, in the *Trout,* the piano timbre is appealingly full in colour, but here the upper range is noticeably thin; in the string quartet the upper range is fuller.

There is some admirably unassertive and deeply musical playing from Miss Haebler and from the incomparable Grumiaux. These artists do not try to make 'interpretative points' but are content to let the music speak for itself. The quality of the recorded sound is good. Philips have added a pair of *String trios,* given characteristically refined performances by Grumiaux and his companions, delightful music superbly played.

Horszowski's contribution to the *Trout* is undoubtedly distinguished and his clean, clear playing dominates the performance which, although full of imaginative detail, is a little on the cool side – though refreshingly so, for all that. The Juilliard Quartet are far from cool in the *Death and the Maiden quartet,* the unanimity of ensemble consistently impressive. In both works the sound is a little dry, but not confined.

A very agreeable if not distinctive performance on DG Classikon, aptly coupled. Demus dominates, partly because the piano recording and balance are bold and forward, and the string timbre is thinner. Nevertheless the transfer brings very acceptable sound and there is – as befits the eponymous quartet – a real feeling for Schubertian lyricism here, and the performance has spontaneity. The first movement is especially arresting and the *Theme and variations* are well shaped. The earlier of the Amadeus's two stereo versions of the *Death and the Maiden quartet* gives a wonderful impression of unity as regards the finer points of phrasing, for example at the very beginning of the variations, even if this account has not the depth of the very finest versions. The DG transfer is well managed, although the sound is a little dated.

The Prometheus Ensemble turn in a very enjoyable and fresh account of the *Trout* on ASV. There are two bonuses in the shape of the equivalent song, charmingly done by Ann Mackay, and *The Shepherd on the rock.* The playing in the *Quintet* is alert and well shaped, and well recorded, too.

The account by the Nash Ensemble on Pickwick also brings a fill-up in the shape of *The Shepherd on the rock*. They are rather forwardly recorded here and their account is just a little wanting in the spontaneity that distinguishes the finest of the current versions. Ian Brown is, as always, a sensitive artist.

The Beaux Arts *Trout* is a delightfully fresh performance. Every phrase is splendidly alive, there is no want of vitality or sensitivity, and the recording is basically well balanced. The snag is the digital remastering, which gives undue prominence to Isidore Cohen's violin, lighting it up brightly and thinning down the timbre.

(i; ii) *Piano quintet in A (Trout); (i; iii) Piano trios Nos. 1 in B flat, D.898; 2 in E flat, D.929; Notturno in E flat, D.897; Sonata in B flat, D.28* (both arr. for piano trio).
(B) **(*) EMI CZS7 62742-2 (2) [id.]. (i) Hephzibah Menuhin; (ii) Amadeus Qt, J. Edward Merrett;
  (iii) Sir Yehudi Menuhin & Maurice Gendron.

The 1958 Hephzibah Menuhin/Amadeus *Trout* has a pleasingly domestic sense of scale and considerable charm, even though the bright recording creates a balance in favour of the upper register of the piano and the upper strings. The Amadeus Quartet play with nicely judged feeling. Intimacy is also the keynote of the works for piano trio, and in the *Trios* Menuhin relaxes with his pianist sister and cellist friend to produce delightfully spontaneous-sounding performances. The atmosphere of the *Second Trio* is caught perceptively and the unassertive music-making captures the music's spirit very appealingly. These recordings are cleanly remastered; the sound lacks something in fullness but the focus is natural and the balance realistic.

(i) *Piano trios Nos. 1–2; Adagio in E flat ('Notturno')* (for piano trio), *D. 897; Sonata in B flat* (for piano trio), *D. 28; (ii) String trios: in B flat* (in one movement), *D. 471; in B flat, D. 581.*
☞ (B) *** Ph. Duo 438 700-2 (2) [id.]. (i) Beaux Arts Trio; (ii) Grumiaux Trio.

The Beaux Arts set of the Schubert *Piano trios* from the late 1960s is another of the extraordinary bargains now offered on the Philips Duo label. The performances provide impeccable ensemble with the pianist, Menahem Pressler, always sharply imaginative and the cellist, Bernard Greenhouse, bringing simple dedication to such key passages as the great slow-movement melody of the *Trio No. 2 in E flat*. Written during Schubert's student days, the attractive early *Sonata in B flat* has the same kind of fluency as Beethoven's *First Piano trio*, though the lyrical flow has the unmistakable ring of Schubert. The *Notturno*, played here with great eloquence, recalls the rapt, hushed intensity of the glorious slow movement of the *String quintet*. The recording is naturally balanced, a little dry in the treble, which means that Daniel Guilet's violin timbre is sometimes a little ungenerous; but the CD transfer never makes it sound edgy. What makes the set doubly attractive is the inclusion of the two much rarer *String trios*, also early works from 1816/17. The four-movement *B flat Trio* is a sheer delight with that quality of innocence which lets Schubert's music stand apart, obviously post-Mozartian yet with a simplicity all its own. Given such persuasive advocacy, both pieces cannot fail to make a strong impression. The Grumiaux performances are deeply musical, unforced and well shaped, while the 1969 recording has vividness and presence as well as a natural, lifelike sound-quality.

Piano trio No. 1 in B flat, D.898.
☞ (M) *** Ph. Dig. 438 308-2 [id.]. Beaux Arts Trio – BEETHOVEN: *Archduke trio*. **

Piano trio No. 1 in B flat; Sonata movement in B flat.
(BB) **(*) Naxos Dig. 8.550131; 4550131 [id.]. Stuttgart Piano Trio.

The pairing of Beethoven's *Archduke* with Schubert's great *B flat Trio* is a happy idea, and it is a pity that one cannot be entirely enthusiastic about this Beaux Arts coupling, very well recorded though it is. The (1984) Schubert performance is a good deal more lively than the Beethoven and is undoubtedly enjoyable and certainly immaculate in ensemble. But their earlier, analogue account had greater freshness and spontaneity.

The Stuttgart Piano Trio may be at budget price but this is not a bargain-basement performance; the playing is musicianly and intelligent and there are many sensitive touches. Although the sound is somewhat less than ideal, there is a reasonable amount of air round the three instruments.

Piano trio No. 2 in E flat D. 929; Notturno in E flat, D. 897; Duo in A for violin and piano.
☞ (M) **(*) EMI Dig. CDM7 67806-2 [id.]. Jean-Philippe Collard, Augustin Dumay, Frédéric
  Lodéon.

The Collard/Dumay/Lodéon account of the *E flat Trio* is certainly fresh and spontaneous. The first movement is taken briskly, an effect emphasized by the clear, bright, digital stereo which gives the violin timbre an incisive edge. The *Andante* has a gentle eloquence that is appealing, and the finale sparkles with the players' light rhythmic articulation. The *Duo* is also attractively done. An enjoyable disc, but the brightly lit upper range is a drawback.

String quartets Nos. 1–15.
(M) ** DG 419 879-2 (6) [id.]. Melos Qt of Stuttgart.

The early quartets have an altogether disarming grace and innocence, and some of their ideas are most touching. The Melos are an impressive body whose accounts of this repertoire are unmannered and on the whole sympathetic. They are let down by recording quality that is less than distinguished, but the remastering has brought added presence.

String quartets Nos. 4 in C, D.46; 14 in D min. (Death and the Maiden), D.810.
☞ *** BMG/RCA Dig. RD 67990 [id.]. Tokyo Qt.

Among newer recordings, the Tokyo give a keenly felt and beautifully phrased account of *Death and the Maiden*, and they are persuasive advocates of the charming, early *C major Quartet*; moreover the RCA recording is first class. They make a very beautiful sound (which some might find too sweet) and in this respect are to be preferred to the Lindsays, though the latter go deeper into the music. But this is undoubtedly worth ranking among the top recommendations, for those looking for a modern version.

String quartets Nos. 8 in B flat, D.112; 13 in A min., D.804.
*** ASV Dig. CDDCA 593 [id.]. Lindsay Qt.

In the glorious *A minor* the Lindsays lead the field. It would be difficult to fault their judgement in both these works so far as tempi and expression are concerned, and dynamics are always the result of musical thinking. The recording team has done them much credit.

String quartets Nos. 9 in G min., D.173; 13 in A min., D.804.
**(*) Teldec/Warner 2292 43205-2 [id.]. Alban Berg Qt.

The Alban Berg recorded this account of the *A minor* in 1975, and this is to be preferred to their more recent, EMI version. It matches the latter in tonal finesse and perfection of ensemble and surpasses it in terms of spontaneity. The *G minor Quartet* is also very fine.

String quartets Nos. 10 in E flat, D.87; 14 in D min. (Death and the Maiden), D.810.
☞ *(*) EMI Dig. CDC7 54345-2 [id.]. Britten Qt.

Technically the coupling by the Britten Quartet is impressive, but musically it is a good deal less satisfying. These players do not penetrate far below the surface of the music or succeed in conveying much sense of pathos or depth. The rather well-lit recording does not help them project the feeling of a real performance: this is a very studio performance, flawed by its own technical precision.

String quartets Nos. 11 in E, D.353; 15 in G, D.887.
(M) *** Decca 433 693-2 [id.]. Allegri Qt.

The Allegri are recorded in a somewhat reverberant acoustic (the Church of St George the Martyr, London) but their account of the *G major Quartet* is most rewarding. The E major, composed a decade earlier, is if anything even finer, fresh and spontaneous and with excellent judgement in the matter of tempi. The analogue recordings date from the late 1970s and have been most realisically transferred to CD.

String quartets Nos. 12 in C min. (Quartettsatz), D.703; 14 in D min. (Death and the Maiden), D.810.
*** ASV Dig. CDDCA 560 [id.]. Lindsay Qt.
(BB) **(*) Naxos Dig. 8.550221; *4550221* [id.]. Mandelring Qt.

String quartet No. 14 in D min. (Death and the Maiden), D.810.
(M) *** Ph. 420 876-2. Italian Qt – DVORAK: *Quartet No. 12* *** (with BORODIN: *Nocturne* *).

The Lindsays' intense, volatile account of the *Death and the Maiden quartet* is played with considerable metrical freedom and the widest range of dynamic, and the *Quartettsatz*, which acts as the usual filler, is unusually poetic and spontaneous in feeling. The recording is excellent.

The Italian Quartet offer a fine coupling with Dvořák, and the Borodin *Nocturne* is thrown in for good measure. They bring great concentration and poetic feeling to this wonderful score. The sound of the reissue is vivid and clear.

The Mandelring Quartet are very good indeed. The performances are sensitively and sensibly played and very decently recorded, and anyone tempted by this Naxos disc will not be disappointed for so modest an outlay.

String quartets Nos. 13 in A min., D.804; 14 in D min. (Death and the Maiden), D.810.
(M) *** Ph. 426 383-2 [id.]. Italian Qt.

The Italians' version of the *A minor Quartet* has an impressive command of feeling. Their account of *Death and the Maiden* is also very fine. Here the slow movement is particularly telling, showing a notable grip in the closing pages. Technically the playing throughout is quite remarkable. The recordings are well balanced and truthful.

String quartets Nos. 13 in A min.; 14 in D min. (Death and the Maiden); 15 in G, D.887.
*** Nimbus NI 5048/9 [id.]. Chilingirian Qt.

In their two-disc set of the last three *Quartets*, the Chilingirians give strongly committed, characterful and spontaneous-sounding readings, warmly recorded and full of presence. On the upper-mid-priced Nimbus label, they make a most attractive recommendation.

String quartets Nos. 14 in D min. (Death and the Maiden); 15 in G.
(M) (***) EMI (mono) CDH7 69795-2 [id.]. Busch Qt.

The Busch Quartet's account is more than fifty years old, but it brings us closer to the heart of this music than any other. The slow movement of the *Death and the Maiden quartet* is a revelation, and the same must be said of the *G major*, which has enormous depth and humanity. For its age, the sound is still amazing.

String quintet in C, D.956.
*** ASV Dig. CDDCA 537; *ZCDCA 537* [id.]. Lindsay Qt with Douglas Cummings.
☞ ⊛ (M) *** Saga EC 3368-2. Aeolian Qt with Bruno Schreker.
☞ ⊛ (***) Testament mono SABT 1031 Hollywood Qt, Kurt Reher – SCHOENBERG: *Verklaerte Nacht.* (***) ⊛

(i) *String quintet in C; String quartet No. 12 (Quartettsatz), D.703.*
☞ *** Decca Dig. 436 324-2 [id.]. Takács Qt, (i) with Miklós Perényi.

String quintet in C; String trio in B flat, D.581.
(BB) *** Naxos Dig. 8.550388 [id.]. Villa Musica Ens.
☞ * Ph. Dig. 432 108-2 [id.]. Guarneri Qt.

The Lindsay version gives the impression that one is eavesdropping on music-making in the intimacy of a private concert. They observe the first-movement exposition repeat and the effortlessness of their approach does not preclude intellectual strength. In the ethereal *Adagio* they effectively convey the sense of it appearing motionless, suspended, as it were, between reality and dream, yet at the same time never allowing it to become static. Their reading must rank at the top of the list; it is very well recorded.

The augmented Aeolian Quartet give a strong, virile performance. It might seem bald, were it not for the depth of concentration that the players convey in every bar. In the slow movement the Aeolians daringly adopt the slowest possible *Adagio*, and the result might have seemed static but for the inner tension which holds one breathless through hushed pianissimos of the most intense beauty. The analogue recording, though not of the clearest in terms of individual definition of instruments, has been transferred to CD with remarkable presence and the body of tone has not been lost. This is a clear first bargain choice, and there are few premium-priced issues which approach, let alone match, its intensity.

The Hollywood Quartet's 1951 version of the *Quintet* with Kurt Reher as second cello stands apart. It is in a class of its own, and for those who were fortunate enough to encounter it in the early 1950s it remains a desert island disc. Writing at the time, the authors of *The Record Guide* rated it as 'one of the best in the discography of chamber music' and spoke of 'the sustained eloquence' of the players' bowing in the slow movement. Over 40 years on, its qualities of freshness and poetry, as well as an impeccably confident technical address, still impress as deeply as ever. The Hollywood Quartet made music for the sheer love of it rather than for money; they earned the latter in the Hollywood studios during the day and, although they did tour, their playing has none of the overprojection and glamour of present-day professional quartets, though it is more than their equal in mastery and finesse. Very different from the Casals and Amadeus accounts that appeared in its immediate wake, both of them impressive enough, this is the product of consummate artistry and remains very special indeed.

The Villa Musica players tackle the great *C major Quintet* with a freshness and concentration that are consistently compelling, even if the finale is neat and clean rather than urgently dramatic. The little *String trio* makes an attractive and generous fill-up, another assured and stylish performance.

With clear, well-balanced recording this super-budget issue makes an outstanding bargain and offers an excellent alternative to the Saga version for those wanting digital sound.

The Takács Quartet with Miklós Perényi on Decca (very well recorded), taking a freely expressive view and sounding spontaneous, regularly find Schubertian magic, as when the leader plays with the most withdrawn half-tone at the start of the *Adagio* slow movement. Also freer are the players of the Brandis Quartet on Nimbus, another fine Central European group. With beautiful matching, they too convey spontaneous expressiveness, not afraid to linger a little over the lovely second-subject melody. Yet particularly when the Takács disc also offers the *Quartettsatz* as a bonus, that Decca issue is the one to opt for among the newcomers, with the jollity of the Scherzo and finale set against the spacious strength of the first two massive movements.

The Guarneri Quartet attack the first movement of Schubert's *Quintet* as if it were Beethoven; indeed their powerful articulation and big sound are almost orchestral. The slow movement has none of the rapt pianissimo magic that distinguishes the finest versions of this work. The playing itself is assured and undoubtedly committed, and the recording is faithful, but as a reading of a great and very special masterpiece this is simply unacceptable.

Duo in A, D.574; Violin sonatina, D.385; Fantaisie in C, D.934.
(M) **(*) Decca 425 539-2. Szymon Goldberg, Radu Lupu.

There is an unaffected, Schubertian feeling in the Goldberg/Lupu performances that is most appealing. At times one could do with a greater variety of dynamic nuance and tonal colour, yet Radu Lupu's playing has a vitality and inner life that are consistently rewarding. The remastered recording also sounds full and natural, and is very realistically balanced.

Violin sonatinas Nos. 1–3, D.384/5 & D.408.
☞ (M) *** O-L 443 196-2 [id.]. Jaap Schröder, Christopher Hogwood (fortepiano) – MENDELSSOHN: *Violin sonata.* ***

This makes a clear choice for those wanting these works on original instruments. However, the inclusion of repeats (bringing a total playing time of 55 minutes) means that there was not room for the *Duo*, D.574, and an early Mendelssohn sonata has been added instead. Jaap Schröder uses a Stradivarius and Christopher Hogwood a piano from about 1825 by Georg Haschka. It does not produce the range of nuance and tonal subtlety of which the modern piano is capable, but its lightness of colour has its own special charm. Jaap Schröder plays with fine artistry, and both artists are truthfully recorded. Modern performances will enjoy a wider appeal – probably rightly – but this is undoubtedly a set to hear.

PIANO MUSIC FOR FOUR HANDS

Divertissement à l'hongroise in G min., D.818; Fantaisie in F min., D.940; Introduction and 4 variations on an original theme and finale in B flat, D.603; 3 Marches héroïques, D.602; Overture in F, D.675; 6 Polonaises, D.824; 8 Variations on a theme from Hérold's opera Marie in C, D.908.
☞ ** Sony S2K 58955 [id.]. Duo Tal and Groethuysen.

This is interesting and rare repertoire, and the Duo Tal and Groethuysen play it with lively vigour. They are at their best in the glorious *Fantaisie in F minor*, and they find charm in the *Introduction and four variations on an original theme*. But elsewhere they often seem too loud, in the *Overture* for instance and in the *Divertissement* (and the recording is not entirely flattering to their fortissimos).

Fantasia in D min., D.940.
*** Sony Dig. MK 39511 [id.]. Murray Perahia, Radu Lupu – MOZART: *Double piano sonata.* ***

Recorded live at The Maltings, the performance of Lupu and Perahia is full of haunting poetry, with each of these highly individual artists challenging the other in imagination. Warmly atmospheric recording.

PIANO MUSIC

Allegretto in C min., D.915; Moments musicaux Nos. 1–6, D.780; 2 Scherzi, D.593; 12 Valse nobles, D.969.
(M) **(*) DG 435 072-2. Daniel Barenboim.

Some of the finest playing here comes in the two *Scherzi*. The *Allegretto in C minor* is given an effective, improvisatory quality, but the twelve *Valses nobles* are played too forcefully for their full charm to be revealed. In the *Moments musicaux* there is much to admire, yet there is an element of calculation that robs the impact of freshness. The piano-tone on DG has presence and weight.

Fantasia in C (Wanderer), D.760.
*** Sony Dig. MK 42124 [id.]. Murray Perahia – SCHUMANN: *Fantasia in C.* ***
*** EMI CDC7 47967-2. Sviatoslav Richter – DVORAK: *Piano concerto.* ***
(M) *** Ph. 420 644-2. Alfred Brendel – *Sonata No. 21.* ***
*** DG 419 672-2 [id.]. Maurizio Pollini – *Sonata No. 16.* ***

Murray Perahia's account of the *Wanderer* stands alongside the finest. In his hands it sounds as fresh as the day it was conceived, and its melodic lines speak with an ardour and subtlety that breathe new life into the score. The recording is more than acceptable.

Richter's 1963 performance is masterly in every way. The piano timbre is real and the remastering gives the great pianist a compelling presence; the coupling is hardly less outstanding.

Brendel's playing is of a high order, and he is truthfully recorded and coupled with what is perhaps Schubert's greatest *Sonata*, so this is excellent value at mid-price.

Pollini's account is outstanding and, though he is not ideally recorded and the piano timbre is shallow, the playing still shows remarkable insights. Moreover the coupling is equally fine.

Fantasia in C (Wanderer), D.760; Impromptus, D.899/3 & 4; Piano sonata No. 21 in B flat, D.960.
⊛ *** BMG/RCA RD 86257 [RCA 6257-2-RC]. Artur Rubinstein.

Rubinstein plays the *Wanderer fantasia* with sure magnificence and, particularly in the variations section, he is electrifying. The two *Impromptus* are played with the most subtle shading of colour and delectable control of rubato, and the superb account of the *Sonata* shows Rubinstein as a magically persuasive Schubertian. The 1965 sound is remarkably real, with fine presence and little shallowness.

Impromptus Nos. 1–4, D.899; 5–8, D.935.
*** Sony Dig. MK 37291 [id.]. Murray Perahia.
☞ *** DG Dig. 435 788-2 [id.]. Andrei Gavrilov.
*** Ph. 411 040-2 [id.]. Alfred Brendel.
☞ *** Virgin/EMI Dig. VC7 59600-2 [id.]. Lambert Orkis (fortepiano).
*** Decca Dig. 411 711-2 [id.]. Radu Lupu.

Perahia's account of the *Impromptus* is very special indeed and falls barely short of greatness. Directness of utterance and purity of spirit are of the essence here. The CBS recording is very good, truthful in timbre.

One associates Andrei Gavrilov with Rachmaninov, Prokofiev and *Gaspard*, rather than with this quiet, sublime repertoire. But any fears can be put to one side. This playing has something of the divine simplicity for which this music calls. No expressive excesses and a wide dynamic range. Surprisingly, perhaps, this is quite selfless playing which serves Schubert well. So, too, does the admirably balanced DG recording. One of the best, even in a strongly competitive field, and recommendable alongside Perahia.

Brendel's analogue set of *Impromptus* is also magical. It is difficult to imagine finer Schubert playing than this; to find more eloquence, more profound musical insights, one has to go back to Edwin Fischer – and even here comparison is not always to Brendel's disadvantage. The piano image is warm and full but slightly diffuse.

Those who think they are allergic to the fortepiano in this repertoire above all should try this set from Lambert Orkis. It is vital, sensitive and fully attuned to the Schubertian sensibility. His is exceptional playing in every way – living and responsive to every nuance – and, although it will probably not be a sole recommendation for the *Impromptus*, it is certainly a disc that all Schubert lovers should consider as an alternative to a modern grand piano version.

Lupu's account of the *Impromptus* is of the same calibre as the Perahia and Brendel analogue versions, and he is most beautifully recorded on CD. Indeed, in terms of natural sound this is the most believable image of the three.

Impromptus Nos. 1–4, D.899; Piano sonata No. 21 in B flat, D.960.
*** Calliope Dig. CAL 9689 [id.]. Inger Södergren.

Inger Södergren's account of the first four *Impromptus* belongs in exalted company, and the *B flat Sonata* is hardly less fine. Her playing is marked throughout by sensitivity and a selfless and unostentatious dedication to Schubert. The recording is acceptable rather than outstanding.

4 Impromptus, D.899; Impromptu in B flat, D.935/3; Moments musicaux, D.780/1, 2 & 6.
(B) *** LaserLight Dig. 15609 [id.]. Jenö Jandó.

At last Jenö Jandó is heard, recorded in an acoustic that does justice to his talent. The sound, at least in the opening *B flat major Impromptu* of D.935, is fresh and truthful, the ambience is warm, and the playing is very good. The balance is not as good in the three *Moments musicaux* or in the D.899 *Impromptus*: it is closer and marginally drier.

Impromptus: Nos. 6 in A flat; 7 in B flat, D.935/2–3; 6 Moments musicaux, D.780; Valses nobles, D.969; SCHUBERT/LISZT: *Soirée de Vienne No. 6.*
☞ (M) **(*) Decca stereo/mono 433 902-2 [id.]. Wilhelm Backhaus – MENDELSSOHN: *Rondo capriccioso* etc. *** (with SCHUMANN: *Fantasiestück, Op. 12: Warum?* **(*)).

Backhaus's almost peremptory manner in Schubert, strongly classical in feeling, is quite different from the style of players like Perahia and Lupu, yet this remains magnetic music-making. Even if it is not the most subtle Schubert interpretation, there is much character, and considerable brilliance too, in the *B flat major Impromptu*. There is, however, less sweetness than usual in the equally famous *A flat Impromptu*, taken fairly briskly. This, like Schumann's *Warum?*, derives from a mono recording of an unidentified live recital. The recordings from 1955/6 are good.

Moments musicaux, D.780; 2 Scherzi, D.593; Piano sonata No. 14 in A min., D.784.
*** DG Dig. 427 769-2 [id.]. Maria João Pires.

Maria João Pires gives masterly accounts of the *Moments musicaux* and the *A minor Sonata*, distinguished throughout by thoughtful and refined musicianship, and she is fully aware of the depth of feeling that inhabits the *Moments musicaux*, without ever indulging in the slightest expressive exaggeration. The digital recording is exceptionally present and clear.

Piano sonatas Nos. 1 in E, D.157; 2 in C, D.279; 3 in E, D.459; 4 in A min., D.537; 5 in A flat, D.557; 6 in E min., D.566; 7 in E flat, D.568; 9 in B, D.575; 11 in F min., D.625; 13 in A, D.664; 14 in A min., D.784; 15 in C, D.840 (Relique); 16 in A min., D.845; 17 in D, D.850; 18 in G, D.894; 19 in C min., D.958; 20 in A, D.959; 21 in B flat, D.960.
(M) *** DG 423 496-2 (7) [id.]. Wilhelm Kempff.

Wilhelm Kempff's cycle was recorded over a four-year period (1965–9) and elicited much admiration in our earlier editions. DG has now collected the sonatas into a seven-CD box and those wanting a comprehensive survey of this repertoire need look no further at present. There have been performances of comparable stature: Gilels in the *A minor*, D.784, and *D major*, D.850, Lupu (*G major*, D.894), Perahia (*A major*, D.960) and Richter, but there is no individual overview of the whole cycle that has been musically as consistently satisfying as Kempff's. The recordings are not state of the art (there is an occasional hint of shallowness) but they are very acceptable indeed and there is a wisdom about his playing which puts it in a special category.

Piano sonatas Nos. 1 in E, D.157; 14 in A min., D.784; 20 in A, D.959.
(M) *** Decca 425 033-2 [id.]. Radu Lupu.

Lupu is sensitive and poetic throughout. In the *A major* work he strikes the perfect balance between Schubert's classicism and the spontaneity of his musical thought, and at the same time he leaves one with the impression that the achievement is perfectly effortless, with an inner repose and depth of feeling that remain memorable long after the record has ended. Excellent vintage Decca recording, made in the Kingsway Hall in the late 1970s.

Piano sonata No. 4 in A min., D.537.
** DG Dig. 400 043-2 [id.]. Michelangeli – BRAHMS: *Ballades.* ***

Michelangeli's Schubert is less convincing than the Brahms coupling. His playing, though aristocratic and marvellously poised, is not free from artifice, and the natural eloquence of Schubert eludes him. Splendid recording.

Piano sonatas Nos. 5 in A flat, D.557; 9 in B, D.575; 18 in G, D.894.
☞ *** Decca Dig 440 307-2 [id.]. András Schiff.

Piano sonatas Nos. 6 in E min., D.566; 14 in A min., D.784; 17 in D, D.850.
☞ *** Decca Dig. 440 306-2 [id.]. András Schiff.

Piano sonatas Nos. 8 in F sharp min., D.571; 15 in C (Relique), D.840; 16 in A min., D.845.
☞ *** Decca Dig. 440 305-2 [id.]. András Schiff.

András Schiff is now embarked on a seven-CD survey of the Schubert sonatas for Decca which has excited golden opinions. There are some distinguished rivals, including Imogen Cooper, but mostly in individual sonatas: Brendel, Perahia in the *A major*, Lupu, Ashkenazy, Richter and others; and the complete set from Wilhelm Kempff is still in currency. Schiff's promises to be a survey that blends pianistic finesse with keen human insights, and readers considering adding a new cycle to their collection need have no serious qualms about starting here. He has a good feeling for the architecture of these pieces, so often looked down upon as discursive, and he invests detail with just the right amount of feeling. The recordings, made in the Brahms-Saal of the Musikverein in Vienna, are eminently satisfying.

Piano sonatas Nos. 14–21; German dances; Impromptus; Moments musicaux; Wanderer fantasia.
*** Ph. Dig. 426 128-2 (7) [id.]. Alfred Brendel.

Piano sonatas Nos. 14 in A min., D.784; 17 in D, D.850.
*** Ph. Dig. 422 063-2 [id.] Alfred Brendel.

Piano sonatas Nos 15 in C (Relique), D.840; 18 in G, D.894.
*** Ph. Dig. 422 340-2 [id.]. Alfred Brendel.

Piano sonata No. 16 in A min., D.845; 3 Impromptus, D.946.
*** Ph. Dig. 422 075-2 [id.]. Alfred Brendel.

Piano sonata No. 19 in C min., D.958; Moments musicaux Nos. 1–6, D.780.
*** Ph. Dig. 422 076-2 [id.]. Alfred Brendel.

Piano sonata No. 20 in A, D.959; Allegretto in C min., D.915; 16 German dances, D.783; Hungarian melody in B min., D.817.
**(*) Ph. Dig. 422 229-2 [id.]. Alfred Brendel.

Piano sonata No. 21 in B flat, D.960; Wanderer fantasia, D.760.
*** Ph. Dig. 422 062-2 [id.]. Alfred Brendel.

Brendel's new digital set is perhaps more intense than his last cycle of recordings for Philips, though there was a touching freshness in the earlier set, and he has the benefit of clean, well-focused sound. Generally speaking, these are warm performances, strongly delineated and powerfully characterized, which occupy a commanding place in the catalogue. Their separate availability is also noted, and all of them can be confidently recommended to Brendel's admirers.

'The last six years, 1823–1828', Vol. 1: Piano sonatas Nos. 14 in A min., D.784; 18 in G, D.894; 12 German dances (Ländler), D.790.
☞ *** Priory/Ottavo Dig. OTR C68608 [id.]. Imogen Cooper.

Vol. 2: Piano sonatas Nos. 15 in C, D.840; 20 in C, D.959; 11 Ecossaises, D.781.
☞ *** Priory/Ottavo Dig. OTR C58714 [id.]. Imogen Cooper.

Vol. 3: Piano sonata No. 16 in A min., D.845; 4 Impromptus, D.935.
☞ *** Priory/Ottavo Dig. OTR C88817 [id.]. Imogen Cooper.

Vol. 4: Piano sonata No. 17 in D, D.850; 6 Moments musicaux, D.780.
☞ *** Priory/Ottavo Dig. OTR C128715 [id.]. Imogen Cooper.

Vol. 5: Piano sonata No. 21 in B flat, D.960; Allegretto in C min., D.915; 3 Impromptus (Klavierstücke), D.946.
☞ *** Priory/Ottavo Dig. OTR C88821 [id.]. Imogen Cooper.

Vol. 6: Piano sonata No. 19 in C min., D. 958; 4 Impromptus, D.899.
☞ *** Priory/Ottavo Dig. OTR C78923 [id.]. Imogen Cooper.

We are indebted to a reader for drawing our attention to Imogen Cooper's outstanding set of the late Schubert sonatas on the Dutch Ottavo label. Miss Cooper has a true Schubertian sensibility; her feeling for this composer's special lyricism is second to none, yet her playing has both strength and a complete understanding of the music's architecture. The recordings were made in the London Henry Wood Hall over a period of three years, between June 1986 and July 1989, using a Steinway for the first three volumes and a fine-sounding Yamaha for the later records. The balance is admirable and the sound full, with a convincing natural resonance. The playing has the spontaneity of live music-making, and the warm colouring and fine shading of timbre are as pleasing to the ear as the many subtle nuances of phrasing, which are essentially based on a strong melodic line.

Miss Cooper's playing immediately commands the attention with the rocking opening phrase of the *G major Sonata*, which comes first on Volume 1, while in the *Allegretto* finale of the same work the glorious secondary theme is treated with much imagination, using a wide dynamic range. The coupled *A minor Sonata* again brings a deceptively simple opening, while the *Andante* moves between repose and great lyrical fervour, and the finale has remarkable impetus. In Volume 2 the ear is drawn to the tenderness of the second subject of the first movement of the *A major Sonata*, while the *Andantino* with its gentle profundity is thoughtfully improvisatory. The use of light and shade in the closing Rondo is a joy.

With Volume 3 comes the *D major Sonata* with its delicious lilting finale, joyously articulated and sparkling, with the two episodes introduced with seeming inevitability. The strength and powerful sonority of the first movement of the A minor work which comes in Volume 4 is balanced by the charm and variety of colour in the following theme and variation, while the Scherzo erupts with much energy and Beethovenian sforzandos. Volume 5 brings the glorious *B flat Sonata*, generating real drama after its deceptively limpid opening, and with the *Andante* bringing a melting sense of repose.

There is comparable dramatic intensity in the C minor work on the final disc. The *Moments musicaux* and *Impromptus*, played with improvisational freedom, yet never narcissistically, are used to fill out this outstanding series of records and the *German dances* provide lighter interludes and much charm. These performances can be recommended alongside those by artists with the most illustrious names, and they do not fall short. With their fine, modern, digital recording these CDs will give much delight and refreshment.

Piano sonatas Nos. 14 in A min., D.784; 18 in G, D.894; 12 Waltzes, D.145.
(M) *** Decca 425 017-2 [id.]. Vladimir Ashkenazy.

Ashkenazy's account of the *A minor Sonata* surpasses the pianist's own high standards. On the other hand, the *G major Sonata* (which comes first on the disc) is altogether more controversial. The first movement is very slow indeed: he robs it of its normal sense of momentum. If further hearings prove more convincing, this is largely because Ashkenazy's reading is so totally felt and, equally, perceptive. This is a most searching and poetic account, and both sonatas are given highly realistic recording. The *Waltzes* make an attractive and generous encore.

Piano sonatas Nos. 15 in C (Unfinished), D.840; 19 in C min., D.958; 16 German Dances, D.783.
(M) *** Van. 08.4026.71 [OVC 4026]. Alfred Brendel.

Brendel was at his finest and most spontaneous in the 1960s. The *C minor Sonata* is particularly fine, with a thoughtful, improvisatory feeling in the slow movement which is consistently illuminating. The two-movement *C major Sonata* also has a memorable *Andante*, and the *German Dances* are an endless delight. The recording is full and bold.

Piano sonata No. 16 in A min., D.845.
*** DG 419 672-2 [id.]. Maurizio Pollini – *Fantasia in C (Wanderer)*. ***

Pollini's account of the *A minor Sonata* is searching and profound. The piano sound as such could do with slightly more body, but the recording is musically balanced.

Piano sonatas Nos. 16 in A min., D.845; 17 in D, D.850.
☞ ** Mer. Dig. CDE 84202; *KE 77202* [id.]. Paul Berkowitz.

The Canadian-born Paul Berkowitz is a pianist of fine musicianship and sensitivity. His readings are unaffected and direct and there are many felicitous touches, including a lovely slow movement of the *A minor*, D.845. Yet he makes surprisingly heavy weather of its first movement. He is not ideally served by the recording-balance or the unglamorous acoustic.

Piano sonatas Nos. 16 in A min., D.845; 18 in G, D.894.
⊛ *** Decca 417 640-2 [id.]. Radu Lupu.

Radu Lupu is searching and poetic throughout. He brings tenderness and classical discipline to bear on both sonatas, and his playing is musically satisfying in a very Schubertian way, full of glowing perception on points of detail. The analogue recordings date from 1975 and 1979 respectively and are of Decca's finest.

Piano sonata No. 17 in D, D.850.
☞ (M) *** BMG/RCA 09026 61614-2 [id.]. Emil Gilels – LISZT: *Sonata*. ***

Like the Liszt *Sonata* with which it is coupled, Gilels's highly perceptive account captures the music's Schubertian spirit in a somewhat similar way to Curzon's very persuasive account (currently missing from the CD catalogue). If in his own way Gilels is authoritative and commanding, like Curzon he finds a special magic to engage the ear in the delightful finale.

Piano sonatas Nos. 17 in D, D.850; 20 in A, D.959; 21 in B flat, D.960; March in E, D.606; Moments musicaux, D.780.
(M) (***) EMI mono CHS 764259-2 (2). Artur Schnabel.

It was thanks to Schnabel's championship that the *Piano sonatas* re-entered the repertory for they were rarities in the recital rooms of the 1920s and early 1930s. Both the *A major* and *B flat Sonatas* sound as well they are ever likely to, for neither was state-of-the-art piano-sound. The *Moments musicaux* sound remarkably full-bodied. The playing is full of characteristic insights, though it must be admitted that later recordings of the *B flat* from Kempff and Curzon surpassed Schnabel technically. But as always with this artist there is imagination of a remarkable order. These recordings are now fifty years old, but some of the playing Schnabel offers – at the opening of the *B flat* and in the slow movements of all three *Sonatas* – will never be less than special.

Piano sonata No. 18 in G, D.894.
☞ (*) Denon Dig. CO-75446 [id.]. Valery Afanassiev.

Highly self-conscious playing from Valery Afanassiev, who plays with the solemnity of a Trappist monk. Short measure, too, at less than 50 minutes. Very good recorded sound, but not recommendable all the same.

Piano sonata No. 19 in C min., D.958; Moments musicaux Nos. 1–6, D.780.
(M) *** Decca Dig. 417 785-2 [id.]. Radu Lupu.

Lupu's performance has a simple eloquence that is most moving. His *Moments musicaux* are very fine indeed. The Decca recording is very natural and, at mid-price, this is extremely competitive.

Piano sonatas Nos. 19 in C min., D.958; 20 in A, D.959.
*** DG Dig. 427 327-2 [id.]. Maurizio Pollini.

Piano sonata No. 21 in B flat, D.960; Allegretto in C min., D.915; Klavierstücke, D.946.
*** DG Dig. 427 326-2 [id.]. Maurizio Pollini.

In Pollini's hands these emerge as strongly structured and powerful sonatas, yet he is far from unresponsive to the voices from the other world with which these pieces resonate. Perhaps with his perfect pianism he does not always convey a sense of human vulnerability, as have some of the greatest Schubert interpreters.

Piano sonatas Nos. 19 in C min., D.958; 20 in A, D.959.
☞ **(*) Sony Dig. SK 46690 [id.]. Mark Swatzentruber.

Mark Swatzentruber makes a generally positive impression in his début record in the UK. He is a good player and allows the music to unfold without too much interpretative intrusion. Although they have some impressive moments, these are essentially decent rather than distinguished accounts, and the recorded sound is really not of three-star standard.

Piano sonatas Nos. 19 in C min., D. 958; 20 in A, D. 959; 21 in B flat, D. 960; 3 Impromptus (Klavierstücke), D. 946/1–3.
☞ (B) **(*) Ph. Duo 438 703-2 [id.]. Alfred Brendel.

Brendel's analogue recordings of the Schubert late *Sonatas* were among the finest of his records made in the early 1970s and would seem an obvious recommendation on Philips's Duo bargain label. But the *A major* suffers from rather more agogic changes than is desirable. Some listeners may find these interferences with the flow of the musical argument a little too personal. The *C minor Sonata* is not free from this charge but it remains an impressive performance. Brendel's account of the *B flat Sonata* is characteristically imposing and full of insight, as one would expect. Here his mood is both serious and introspective, and he is not unduly wayward; moreover he is at his very finest in the *Klavierstücke*. This is eloquent and profoundly musical playing. Throughout, the recording is well up to Philips's high standard of realism and the CD transfers are impeccable, with the background hiss a problem only for eagle ears.

Piano sonata No. 20 in A, D.959.
*** Sony Dig. MK 44569 [id.]. Murray Perahia – SCHUMANN: *Piano sonata No. 2.* ***

Perahia's combination of intellectual vigour and poetic insight shows that awareness of proportion and feeling for expressive detail which distinguish the greatest interpreters. As always with this artist, every phrase speaks and each paragraph breathes naturally.

Piano sonata No. 21 in B flat, D.960.
(M) *** Ph. 420 644-2. Alfred Brendel – *Wanderer fantasia.* ***

Brendel's earlier analogue performance is as impressive and full of insight as one would expect. He is not unduly wayward, for his recording has room for the *Wanderer fantasy* as well, and he is supported by excellent Philips sound.

VOCAL MUSIC

Lieder, Volume 1 (1811–17); Volume 2 (1817–28); Song cycles: *Die schöne Müllerin; Schwanengesang; Die Winterreise.*
☞ (B) *** DG 437 214-2 (21). Fischer-Dieskau, Gerald Moore (as below).

Fischer-Dieskau's monumental survey of all the Schubert songs suitable for a man's voice (some of the longer ones excepted) makes a welcome appearance on CD. The recordings were made over a relatively brief span, with the last 300 songs concentrated on a period of only two months in 1969, yet there is not a hint of routine. The two big boxes of nine discs come at bargain price, working out at around £50 each, whereas the smaller box, containing the song-cycles, comes at mid-price, around £25 for the three discs. Instead of a shelf-full of discs in conventional format, DG offer three small boxes containing over 600 songs, with paper inner-sleeves instead of jewel-cases, each one numbered, so that the three discs containing the three great song-cycles are in a package no bigger than you would expect for a single CD. Even more neatly, the rest of the songs are contained in two boxes of nine discs each, Volume 1 covering 1811–17 and Volume 2 1817–28. Nor has the background information been skimped. Each box contains complete German texts and English translations (plus summaries in French) as well as introductory essays. The one serious omission is an alphabetical list of titles. It makes it unnecessarily hard to find a particular song – much the most likely way of using so compendious a collection. Happily, most of the songs have been put in chronological order on the discs. Then, if you can find the Deutsch number of a particular song (easy enough for the specialist but not always for others), you can as a rule track it down.

  This collection of 21 CDs is offered at bargain price, as are the two separate 9-disc collections of Lieder listed below. The three great song-cycles – also included here – cost more if purchased separately.

Lieder, Volume I (1811–17): *Ein Leichenfantasie; Der Vatermörder* (1811); *Der Jüngling am Bache* (1812); *Totengräberlied; Die Schatten; Sehnsucht; Verklärung; Pensa, che questo istante* (1813); *Der Taucher* (1813–15); *Andenken; Geisternähe; Erinnerung; Trost, An Elisa; Die Betende; Lied aus der Ferne; Der Abend; Lied der Liebe; Erinnerungen; Adelaide; An Emma; Romanze: Ein Fräulein klagt' im finstern Turm; An Laura, als sie Klopstocks Auferstehungslied sang; Der Geistertanz; Das Mädchen aus der Fremde; Nachtgesang; Trost in Tränen; Schäfers Klagelied; Sehnsucht; Am See* (1814); *Auf einen Kirchhof; Als ich sie erröten sah; Das Bild; Der Mondabend* (1815); *Lodas Gespenst* (1816); *Der Sänger* (1815); *Die Erwartung* (1816); *Am Flusse; An Mignon; Nähe des Geliebten; Sängers Morgenlied; Amphiaraos; Das war ich; Die Sterne; Vergebliche Liebe; Liebesrausch; Sehnsucht der Liebe; Die erste Liebe; Trinklied; Stimme der Liebe; Naturgenuss; An die Freude; Der Jüngling am Bache; An den Mond; Die Mainacht; An die Nachtigall; An die Apfelbäume; Seufzer; Liebeständelei; Der Liebende; Der Traum; Die Laube; Meeres Stille; Grablied; Das Finden; Wandrers Nachtlied; Der Fischer; Erster Verlust; Die Erscheinung; Die Täuschung; Der Abend; Geist der Liebe; Tischlied; Der Liedler; Ballade; Abends unter der Linde; Die Mondnacht; Huldigung; Alles um Liebe; Das Geheimnis; An den Frühling; Die Bürgschaft; Der Rattenfänger; Der Schatzgräber; Heidenröslein; Bundeslied; An den Mond; Wonne der Wehmut; Wer kauft Liebesgötter?* (1815); *Der Goldschmiedsgesell* (1817); *Der Morgenkuss; Abendständchen: An Lina; Morgenlied: Willkommen, rotes Morgenlicht; Der Weiberfreund; An die Sonne; Tischlerlied; Totenkranz für ein Kind; Abendlied; Die Fröhlichkeit; Lob des Tokayers; Furcht der Geliebten; Das Rosenband; An Sie; Die Sommernacht; Die frühen Gräber; Dem Unendlichen; Ossians Lied nach dem Falle Nathos; Das Mädchen von Inistore; Labetrank der Liebe; An die Geliebte; Mein Gruss an den Mai; Skolie – Lasst im Morgenstrahl des Mai'n; Die Sternenwelten; Die Macht der Liebe; Das gestörte Glück; Die Sterne; Nachtgesang; An Rosa I: Warum bist du nicht hier?; An Rosa II: Rosa, denkst du an mich?; Schwanengesang; Der Zufriedene; Liane; Augenlied; Geistes-Gruss; Hoffnung; An den Mond; Rastlose Liebe; Erlkönig* (1815); *Der Schmetterling; Die Berge* (1819); *Genügsamkeit; An die Natur* (1815); *Klage; Morgenlied; Abendlied; Der Flüchtling; Laura am Klavier; Entzückung an Laura; Die vier Weltalter; Pflügerlied; Die Einsiedelei; An die Harmonie; Die Herbstnacht; Lied: Ins stille Land; Der Herbstabend; Der Entfernten; Fischerlied; Sprache der Liebe; Abschied von der Harfe; Stimme der Liebe; Entzückung; Geist der Liebe; Klage: Der Sonne steigt; Julius an Theone; Klage: Dein Silber schien durch Eichengrün;*

Frühlingslied; Auf den Tod einer Nachtigall; Die Knabenzeit; Winterlied; Minnelied; Die frühe Liebe; Blumenlied; Der Leidende; Seligkeit; Erntelied; Das grosse Halleluja; Die Gestirne; Die Liebesgötter; An den Schlaf; Gott im Frühling; Der gute Hirt; Die Nacht; Fragment aus dem Aeschylus (1816); *An die untergehende Sonne* (1816/17); *An mein Klavier; Freude der Kinderjahre; Das Heimweh; An den Mond; An Chloen; Hochzeitlied; In der Mitternacht; Trauer der Liebe; Die Perle; Liedesend; Orpheus; Abschied; Rückweg; Alte Liebe rostet nie; Gesänge des Harfners aus Goethes Wilhelm Meister: Harfenspieler I: Wer sich der Einsamkeit ergibt; Harfenspieler II: An die Türen will ich schleichen; Harfenspieler III: Wer nie sein Brot mit Tränen ass. Der König in Thule; Jägers Abendlied; An Schwager Kronos; Der Sänger am Felsen; Lied: Ferne von der grossen Stadt; Der Wanderer; Der Hirt; Lied eines Schiffers an die Dioskuren; Geheimnis; Zum Punsche; Am Bach im Frühling* (1816); *An eine Quelle* (1817); *Bei dem Grabe, meines Vaters; Am Grabe Anselmos; Abendlied; Zufriedenheit; Herbstlied; Skolie: Mädchen entsiegelten; Lebenslied; Lieden der Trennung* (1816); *Alinde; An die Laute* (1827); *Frohsinn; Die Liebe; Trost; Der Schäfer und der Reiter* (1817); *Lob der Tränen* (1821); *Der Alpenjäger; Wie Ulfru fischt; Fahrt zum Hades; Schlaflied; Die Blumensprache; Die abgeblühte Linde; Der Flug der Zeit; Der Tod und das Mädchen; Das Lied vom Reifen; Täglich zu singen; Am Strome; Philoktet; Memnon; Auf dem See; Ganymed; Der Jüngling und der Tod; Trost im Liede* (1817).

☞ (B) *** DG 437 215-2 (9). Dietrich Fischer-Dieskau, Gerald Moore.

This remarkable project, with Volume 1 recorded between 1966 and 1968 and Volume 2 over two months of intensive sessions in 1969, is an astonishing achievement in bringing together the greatest Schubertian of our time and the finest accompanist in a wide survey of the Lieder for solo voice. Already in 1811, as a boy in his early teens, Schubert was writing with astonishing originality, as is shown in the long (19 minutes) opening Schiller setting, a *Funeral Fantasy* with its rough, clashing intervals of a second and amazing harmonic pointers to the future. Drama comes very much to the fore in the second song here, *Der Vatermörder* ('A father died by his son's hand'), while the composer's endearing, flowing lyricism makes both *Der Jüngling am Bache* and *Die Schatten* sound remarkably mature. *Totengräberlied* ('Dig, spade, dig on!') brings a characteristically light touch to a gravedigger's soliloquy as he reflects that rich and poor alike, handsome and noble, are all in the end reduced to bones. Throughout these nine well-filled CDs the diversity of Schubert's imagination holds the listener, and his melodic gift almost never disappoints, especially when the performances are so completely at home with the music. The songs are presented in broadly chronological order and the arrangement of items ensures that each disc of the nine makes a satisfying recital in its own right. The CD transfers are impeccable, adding a little in presence to what were originally very well-balanced recordings.

Lieder, Volume II (1817–28): *An die Musik; Pax vobiscum; Hänflings Liebeswerbung; Auf der Donau; Der Schiffer; Nach einem Gewitter; Fischerlied; Das Grab; Der Strom; An den Tod; Abschied; Die Forelle; Gruppe aus dem Tartarus; Elysium; Atys; Erlafsee; Der Alpenjäger; Der Kampf; Der Knabe in der Wiege* (1817); *Auf der Riesenkoppe; An den Mond in einer Herbstnacht; Grablied für die Mutter; Einsamkeit; Der Blumenbrief; Das Marienbild* (1818); *Litanei auf das Fest Allerseelen* (1816); *Blondel zu Marien; Das Abendrot; Sonett I: Apollo, lebet noch dein Hold verlangen; Sonett II: Allein, nachdenken wie gelähmt vom Krampfe; Sonett III: Nunmehr, da Himmel, Erde schweigt; Vom Mitleiden Mariä* (1818) ; *Die Gebüsche; Der Wanderer; Abendbilder; Himmelsfunken; An die Freunde; Sehnsucht; Hoffnung; Der Jüngling am Bache; Hymne I: Wenige wissen das Geheimnis der Liebe; Hymne II: Wenn ich ihn nur hab; Hymne III: Wenn alle untreu werden; Hymne IV: Ich sag es jedem; Marie; Beim Winde; Die Sternennächte; Trost; Nachtstück; Prometheus; Strophe aus Die Götter Griechenlands* (1819); *Nachthymne; Die Vögel; Der Knabe; Der Fluss; Abendröte; Der Schiffer; Die Sterne; Morgenlied* (1820); *Frühlingsglaube* (1822); *Des Fräuleins Liebeslauschen* (1820); *Orest auf Tauris* (1817); *Der entsühnte Orest; Freiwilliges Versinken; Der Jüngling auf dem Hügel* (1820); *Sehnsucht* (1817); *Der zürnenden Diana; Im Walde* (1820); *Die gefangenen Sänger; Der Unglückliche; Versunken; Geheimes; Grenzen der Menschheit* (1821); *Der Jüngling an der Quelle* (1815); *Der Blumen Schmerz* (1821); *Sei mir gegrüsst; Herr Josef Spaun, Assessor in Linz; Der Wachtelschlag Ihr Grab; Nachtviolen; Heliopolis I: Im kalten, rauhen Norden; Heliopolis II: Fels auf Felsen hingewälzet; Selige Welt; Schwanengesang: Wie klage ich's aus; Du liebst mich nicht; Die Liebe hat gelogen; Todesmusik; Schatzgräbers Begehr; An die Leier; Im Haine; Der Musensohn; An die Entfernte; Am Flusse; Willkommen und Abschied* (1822); *Wandrers Nachtlied: Ein Gleiches; Der zürnende Barde* (1823); *Am See* (1822/3); *Viola; Drang in die Ferne; Der Zwerg; Wehmut; Lied: Die Mutter Erde; Auf dem Wasser zu singen; Pilgerweise; Das Geheimnis; Der Pilgrim; Dass sie hier gewesen; Du bist die Ruh; Lachen und Weinen; Greisengesang* (1823); *Dithyrambe; Der Sieg; Abendstern; Auflösung; Gondelfahrer* (1824); *Glaube, Hoffnung und Liebe* (1828); *Im Abendrot; Der Einsame* (1824); *Des*

Sängers Habe; Totengräbers Heimwehe; Der blinde Knabe; Nacht und Träume; Normans Gesang; Lied des gefangenen Jägers; Im Walde; Auf der Bruck; Das Heimweh; Die Allmacht; Fülle der Liebe; Wiedersehn; Abendlied für die Entfernte; Szene I aus dem Schauspiel Lacrimas; Am mein Herz; Der liebliche Stern (1825); *Im Jänner 1817 (Tiefes Leid); Am Fenster; Sehnsucht; Im Freien; Fischerweise; Totengräberweise; Im Frühling; Lebensmut; Um Mitternacht; Über Wildemann* (1826); *Romanze des Richard Löwenherz* (1827); *Trinklied; Ständchen; Hippolits Lied; Gesang (An Silvia); Der Wanderer an den Mond; Das Zügenglöcklein; Bei dir allein; Irdisches Glück; Wiegenlied* (1826); *Der Vater mit dem Kind; Jägers Liebeslied; Schiffers Scheidelied; L'incanto degli occhi; Il traditor deluso; Il modo di prender moglie; Das Lied im Grünen; Das Weinen; Vor meiner Wiege; Der Wallensteiner Lanznecht beim Trunk; Der Kreuzzug; Das Fischers Liebesglück* (1827); *Der Winterabend; Die Sterne; Herbst; Widerschein* (1828); *Abschied von der Erde* (1825/6).

☞ (B) *** DG 437 225-2 (9) [id.]. Dietrich Fischer-Dieskau, Gerald Moore.

Volume II of this great project brings the mature songs; performances and recording are just as compelling as in Volume 1. In their Berlin sessions Fischer-Dieskau and Moore adopted a special technique of study, rehearsal and recording most apt for the project. The sense of spontaneity and new discovery is unfailing, since each take was in fact a performance. On a later occasion, both artists might have taken a different view but, using the ease of access possible with CD, this collection is a unique way of sampling the many different aspects of Schubert's genius. The collection opens appropriately with *An die Musik* of 1817 and, as before, the songs in this volume are laid out chronologically with certain obvious exceptions – on disc 4, for instance, *Orest auf Tauris* (1817) is placed alongside the highly contrasted *Der entsühnte Orest* – 'Orestes purified' (1820), and the closing recital on disc 9 is suitably concluded with *Abschied von der Erde* ('Farewell to the Earth'), dating from 1825/6. Once again there is much unfamiliar repertory to discover, the four *Hymnes* grouped together on the second disc are little-known but show the composer's imaginative diversity in a specifically religious connotation, while the unexpected song dedicated to *Herr Josef Spaun, Assessor in Linz*, which closes the fourth CD, is strikingly operatic. Both booklets offer full translations and each includes also brief essays by Fischer-Dieskau and Walther Dürr on the composer.

Lieder, Volume III: Song-cycles: *Die schöne Müllerin; Schwanengesang; Die Winterreise.*

☞ (M) *** DG 437 235-2 (3) [id.]. Dietrich Fischer-Dieskau, Gerald Moore.

Fischer-Dieskau and Moore had each recorded these great cycles of Schubert several times already before they embarked on this set in 1971/2 as part of DG's Schubert song series. It was no mere repeat of earlier triumphs. If anything, these performances – notably that of the darkest and greatest of the cycles, *Winterreise* – are even more searching than before, with Moore matching the hushed concentration of the singer in some of the most remarkable playing that even he has put on record. As in the extensive recitals listed above, Fischer-Dieskau is in wonderfully fresh voice, and the transfers to CD have been managed very naturally.

Elly Ameling collection ('The early years'): Disc 1: *An die Laute; An die Nachtigall* (2 settings); *An Sylvia; Der Blumenbrief; Du bist die Ruh'; Du Liebst mich nicht; Das Lied im Grünen; Der Einsame; Fischerweise; Die Gebüsche; Im Abendrot; Im Freien; Im Haine; Die Liebe hat gelogen; Der liebliche Stern; Das Mädchen; Die Männer sind méchant; Minnelied; Nacht und Träume; Nachtviolen; Rosamunde: Romanze. Schlummerlied; Der Schmetterling; Seligkeit; Die Sterne; Die Vögel; Der Wachtelschlag.* Disc 2: *Ave Maria; Gretchen am Spinnrade; Gretchens Bitte; Heidenröslein; Jäger, ruhe von der Jagd; Der König in Thule; Die junge Nonnne; Die Liebende schreibt; Liebhabner in allen Gestalten; 4 Mignon Lieder (Kennst du das Land; Nur wer die Sehnsucht kennt; Heiss mich nicht reden; So lass mich scheinen); Nähe des Gelibten; Raste, Krieger!; Scene aus Faust; Suleika I & II.* Disc 3: *Abendbilder; An die Musik; An den Mond; Bertas Lied in der Nacht; Die Blumensprache; Erster Verlust; Frülingssehnsucht; Der Knabe; Nachthymne; Schwestergruss; Sei mir gegrüsst; Die Sterne; Wiegenlied.* Disc 4: *Am Bach im Frühling; An den Tod; An die Entfernte; An die untergehende Sonne; Auf dem Wasser zu singen; Die Forelle; Fülle der Liebe; Ganymed; Die Götter Griechenlands; Im Abendrot; Im Frühling; Der Musensohn; Der Schiffer; Schwanengesang: Sehnsucht; Sprach der Liebe.*

☞ (M) *** Ph. Analogue/Dig. 438 528-2 (4) [id.]. Elly Ameling, Dalton Baldwin (CDs 1–3); Rudolf Jansen (CD 4).

Elly Ameling appeared on the international scene in the mid-1960s. These records cover her period of maturity from 1972 until 1984. Her lovely voice with its diamond purity is consistently appealing and she is a persuasive interpreter, whether in the engaging *Mignon* songs or in the most familiar favourites: the poised freshness of *Nacht und Träume*, the innocence of *Nachtviolen* or the more emotionally fraught *Die Liebe hat gelogen*. These, like so much else, are most affecting; the analogue recordings on the first two discs show her at the peak of her form, with Dalton Baldwin most sensitive in support. The third disc, digitally recorded in 1982, had the distinction of being the first Lieder recital to appear on compact disc and readily deserved its accolade. It is a typically characterful and enchanting collection, starting with *An die Musik* and including other favourites like the *Cradle song* as well as lesser-known songs that admirably suit the lightness and sparkle of Ameling's voice. The fourth CD offers a 1984 digital recital with Rudolf Janson accompanying. It brings more delights, even if the voice is not quite as fresh and agile as in the earlier collections, notably the 1972 recordings included on the second disc. Yet she is able to bring new depths to such a song as *An die Entfernte* and her breath control remains immaculate – as in the opening *Ganymed* – while she still brings delightful bounce to the ever-popular *Der Musensohn*. Her voice is caught naturally by the engineers and the balance is excellent. A treasurable collection, marred only by the absence of translations: only the German texts are given.

The Graham Johnson Schubert Lieder Edition

When it comes to background information, the rival project to record all Schubert's songs – Graham Johnson's for Hyperion using some of the greatest singers of the day – sets standards it would be hard for anyone to match in whatever field. With each disc devoted to a group of songs on a particular theme, Johnson provides notes that add enormously to the enjoyment, heightening the experience of hearing even the most familiar songs.

Lieder Vol. 1: *Der Alpenjäger; Amalia; An den Frühling; An den Mond; Erster Verlust; Die Ewartung; Der Fischer; Der Flüchtling; Das Geheimnis; Der Jüngling am Bache; Lied; Meeres Stille; Nähe des Geliebten; Der Pilgrim; Schäfers Klagelied; Sehnsucht; Thekla; Wanderers Nachtlied; Wonne der Wehmut.*
*** Hyp. Dig. CDJ 33001 [id.]. Dame Janet Baker, Graham Johnson.

Hyperion's complete Schubert song edition, master-minded by the accompanist, Graham Johnson, is planned to mix well-known songs with rarities. Dame Janet's whole collection is devoted to Schiller and Goethe settings, above all those he wrote in 1815, an exceptionally rich year for the 18-year-old; one marvels that, after writing his dedicated, concentrated setting of *Wanderers Nachtlied*, he could on that same day in July write two other equally memorable songs, *Der Fischer* and *Erster Verlust* (*First loss*). Dame Janet is in glorious voice, her golden tone ravishing in a song such as *An den Mond* and her hushed tone caressing the ear in *Meeres Stille* and *Wanderers Nachtlied*. Presented like this, the project becomes a voyage of discovery.

Lieder Vol. 2: *Am Bach im Frühling; Am Flusse; Auf der Donau; Fahrt zum Hades; Fischerlied* (two settings); *Fischerweise; Der Schiffer; Selige Welt; Der Strom; Der Taucher; Widerschein; Wie Ulfru fischt.*
*** Hyp. Dig. CDJ 33002; *KJ 33002* [id.]. Stephen Varcoe, Graham Johnson.

Graham Johnson with the baritone, Stephen Varcoe, devises a delightful collection of men's songs, culminating in the rousing strophic song, *Der Schiffer*, one of the most catchily memorable that Schubert ever wrote, here exhilaratingly done. Otherwise the moods of water and wave, sea and river, are richly exploited. The last 28 minutes of the collection are devoted to the extended narrative, *Der Taucher* (*The Diver*), setting a long poem of Schiller which is based on an early version of the Beowulf saga. Varcoe and Johnson completely explode the long-accepted idea that this is overextended and cumbersome, giving it a thrilling dramatic intensity.

Lieder Vol. 3: *Abschied; An die Freunde; Augenlied; Iphigenia; Der Jüngling und der Tod; Lieb Minna; Liedesend; Nacht und Träume; Namenstagslied; Pax vobiscum; Rückweg; Trost im Liede; Viola; Der Zwerg.*
*** Hyp. Dig. CDJ 33003; *KJ 33003* [id.]. Ann Murray, Graham Johnson.

This is one of Ann Murray's finest records with the intimate beauty of the voice consistently well caught and with none of the stress that the microphone exaggerates on record. Like the songs that Johnson chose for Ann Murray's husband, Philip Langridge, these too represent Schubert in his circle of friends, with their poems his inspiration, including a long flower ballad, *Viola*, by his close friend, Franz von Schober, which Murray and Johnson sustain beautifully.

Lieder Vol. 4: *Alte Liebe rostet nie; Am See; Am Strome; An Herrn Josef von Spaun (Epistel); Auf der Riesenkoppe; Das war ich; Das gestörte Glück; Liebeslauschen; Liebesrausch; Liebeständelei; Der Liedler; Nachtstück; Sängers Morgenlied* (2 versions); *Sehnsucht der Liebe.*
*** Hyp. Dig. CDJ 33004; *KJ 33004* [id.]. Philip Langridge, Graham Johnson.

Philip Langridge brings a collection to illustrate Schubert's setting of words by poets in his immediate circle, ending with *Epistel*, a tongue-in-cheek parody song addressed to a friend who had left Vienna to become a tax collector, extravagantly lamenting his absence. It is Johnson's presentation of such rarities that makes the series such a delight. Langridge has rarely sounded so fresh and sparkling on record.

Lieder Vol. 5: *Die Allmacht; An die Natur; Die Erde; Erinnerung; Ferne von der grossen Stadt; Ganymed; Klage der Ceres; Das Lied im Grünen; Morgenlied; Die Mutter Erde; Die Sternenwelten; Täglich zu singen; Dem Unendlichen; Wehmut.*
*** Hyp. Dig. CDJ 33005; *KJ 33005* [id.]. Elizabeth Connell, Graham Johnson.

Thanks in part to Johnson's choice of songs and to his sensitive support at the piano, Connell has rarely sounded so sweet and composed on record, yet with plenty of temperament. The collection centres round a theme – this one, Schubert and the countryside, suggested by the most popular song of the group, *Das Lied im Grünen*. As ever, the joy of the record is enhanced by Johnson's brilliant, illuminating notes.

Lieder Vol. 6: *Abendlied für die Entfernte; Abends unter der Linde* (two versions); *Abendstern; Alinde; An die Laute; Des Fischers Liebesglück; Jagdlied; Der Knabe in der Wiege (Wiegenlied); Lass Wolken an Hügeln ruh'n; Die Nacht; Die Sterne; Der Vater mit dem Kind; Vor meiner Wiege; Wilkommen und Abschied; Zur guten Nacht.*
*** Hyp. Dig. CDJ 33006; *KJ 33006* [id.]. Anthony Rolfe Johnson, Graham Johnson (with chorus).

The theme of Anthony Rolfe Johnson's contribution is 'Schubert and the Nocturne'. Two items include a small male chorus, a group of individually named singers. *Jagdlied* is entirely choral, and the final *Zur guten Nacht*, a late song of 1827, has the 'Spokesman' answered by the chorus, ending on a gentle *Gute Nacht*. Rolfe Johnson's voice has never sounded more beautiful on record, and the partnership of singer and accompanist makes light even of a long strophic song (i.e. using essentially the same music for each verse) like *Des Fischers Liebesglück*, beautiful and intense.

Lieder Vol. 7: *An die Nachtigall; An den Frühling; An den Mond; Idens Nachtgesang; Idens Schwanenlied; Der Jüngling am Bache; Kennst du das Land?; Liane; Die Liebe; Luisens Antwort; Des Mädchens Klage; Meeres Stille; Mein Gruss an den Mai; Minona oder die Kunde der Dogge; Naturgenuss; Das Rosenband; Das Sehnen; Sehnsucht* (2 versions); *Die Spinnerin; Die Sterbende; Stimme der Liebe; Von Ida; Wer kauft Liebesgötter?.*
*** Hyp. Dig. CDJ 33007 [id.]. Elly Ameling, Graham Johnson.

An extraordinarily rewarding sequence of 24 songs, all written in the composer's *annus mirabilis*, 1815. With Ameling both charming and intense, Johnson's robust defence in his ever-illuminating notes of the first and longest of the songs, *Minona*, is amply confirmed, a richly varied ballad. Here too is a preliminary setting of *Meeres Stille*, less well-known than the regular version, written a day later, but just as clearly a masterpiece, sung by Ameling in a lovely intimate half-tone at a sustained pianissimo. It is fascinating too to compare the two contrasted settings of Mignon's song, *Sehnsucht*, the first of five he ultimately attempted.

Lieder Vol. 8: *Abendlied der Fürstin; An Chloen; An den Mond; An den Mond in einer Herbstnacht; Berthas Lied in der Nacht; Erlkönig; Die frühen Gräber; Hochzeitslied; In der Mitternacht; Die Mondnacht; Die Nonne; Die Perle; Romanze; Die Sommernacht; Ständchen; Stimme der Liebe; Trauer der Liebe; Wiegenlied.*
*** Hyp. Dig. CDJ 33008; *KJ 33008* [id.]. Sarah Walker, Graham Johnson.

For Sarah Walker, with her perfectly controlled mezzo at its most sensuous, the theme is 'Schubert and the Nocturne', leading from the first, lesser-known version of the Goethe poem, *An den Mond*, to two of the best-loved of all Schubert's songs, the delectable *Wiegenlied*, 'Cradle-song', and the great drama of *Erlkönig*, normally sung by a man, but here at least as vividly characterized by a woman's voice.

Lieder Vol. 9: *Blanka; 4 Canzonen, D.688; Daphne am Bach; Delphine; Didone abbandonata; Gott! höre meine Stimme; Der gute Hirte; Hin und wieder Fliegen Pfeile;* (i) *Der Hirt auf dem Felsen. Ich schleiche bang und still (Romanze). Lambertine; Liebe Schwärmt auf allen Wegen; Lilla an die Morgenröte; Misero pargoletto; La pastorella al prato; Der Sänger am Felsen; Thekla; Der Vollmond strahlt (Romanze).*
*** Hyp. Dig. CDJ 33009; *KJ 33009* [id.]. Arleen Augér, Graham Johnson; (i) with Thea King.

'Schubert and the theatre' is the theme of Arleen Augér's contribution, leading up to the glories of his very last song, the headily beautiful *Shepherd on the rock*, with its clarinet obbligato. The *Romanze, Ich schleiche bang* – adapted from an opera aria – also has a clarinet obbligato. Notable too are the lightweight Italian songs that the young Schubert wrote for his master, Salieri, and a lovely setting, *Der gute Hirt*, ('The good shepherd') in which the religious subject prompts a melody which anticipates the great staircase theme in Strauss's *Arabella*.

Lieder Vol. 10: *Adelwold und Emma; Am Flusse; An die Apfelbäume, wo ich Julien erblickte; An die Geliebte; An Mignon; Auf den Tod einer Nachtigall; Auf einen Kirchhof; Harfenspieler I; Labetrank der Liebe; Die Laube; Der Liebende; Der Sänger; Seufzer; Der Traum; Vergebliche Liebe; Der Weiberfreund.*
*** Hyp. Dig. CDJ 33010; *KJ 33010* [id.]. Martyn Hill, Graham Johnson.

Graham Johnson here correlates the year 1815 with what has been documented of his life over those twelve months, which is remarkably little. So the songs here form a kind of diary. The big item, overtopping everything else, is the astonishing 38-stanza narrative song, *Adalwold and Emma*, with Hill ranging wide in his expression. It is almost half an hour long, from the bold march-like opening to the final happy resolution.

Lieder Vol. 11: *An den Tod; Auf dem Wasser zu singen; Auflösung; Aus 'Heliopolis' I & II; Dithyrambe; Elysium; Der Geistertanz; Der König in Thule; Lied des Orpheus; Nachtstück; Schwanengesang; Seligkeit; So lasst mich scheinen; Der Tod und das Mädchen; Verklärung; Vollendung; Das Zügenglöcklein.*
*** Hyp. Dig. CDJ 33011; *KJ 33011* [id.]. Brigitte Fassbaender, Graham Johnson.

Starting with a chilling account of *Death and the maiden*, the theme of Brigitte Fassbaender's disc is 'Death and the composer'. Fassbaender's ability precisely to control her vibrato brings baleful tone-colours, made the more ominous by the rather reverberant, almost churchy, acoustic. So in *Auf dem Wasser zu singen* the lightly fanciful rippling-water motif presents the soul gliding gently 'like a boat' up to heaven, and the selection ends astonishingly with what generally seems one of the lightest of Schubert songs, *Seligkeit*. This, as Johnson suggests, returns the listener from heaven back to earth. In this, as elsewhere, Fassbaender sings with thrilling intensity, with Johnson's accompaniment comparably inspired.

Lieder, Vol. 12: *Adelaide; An Elise; An Laura, als sie Klopstocks Auferstehungslied sang; Andenken; Auf den Sieg der Deutschen; Ballade; Die Betende; Don Gayseros I, II, III; Der Geistertanz; Lied an der Ferne; Lied der Liebe; Nachtgesang; Die Schatten; Sehnsucht; Trost; Trost in Tränem; Der Vatermörder.*
** Hyp. Dig. CDJ 33012 [id.]. Adrian Thompson, Graham Johnson.

Adrian Thompson's disc brings the only disappointment so far in Graham Johnson's outstanding Schubert series. As recorded, the voice sounds gritty and unsteady, with the tone growing tight and ugly under pressure, yet this collection of early songs, all teenage inspirations, still illuminates the genius of Schubert at this earliest period of his career. But it is a pity a sweeter voice was not used.

Lieder, Vol. 13: (i) *Eine altschottische Ballade. Ellens Gesang I, II & III (Ave Maria); Gesang der Norna; Gretchen am Spinnrade; Gretchens Bitte; Lied der Anna Lyle; Die Männer sind mechant; Marie; Das Marienbild;* (i) *Norman's Gesang; Szene aus Faust. Shilrik und Vinvela; Die Unterscheidung.*
*** Hyp. Dig. CDJ 33013 [id.]. Marie McLaughlin, Graham Johnson; (i) with Thomas Hampson.

The theme for Marie McLaughlin's contribution to the Hyperion Schubert edition is broadly a survey of Schubert's inner conflicts and contradictions. The Goethe settings are crowned by one of the most celebrated of all Schubert songs, *Gretchen am Spinnrade*. McLaughlin gives a fresh and girlish portrait, tenderly pathetic rather than tragic. Fascinatingly the selection also includes *Gretchens Bitte*, an extended song that Schubert left unfinished and for which Benjamin Britten in 1943 provided a completion of the final stanzas. The translations of Scottish ballads cover a wide range. *Eine altschottische Liede* is one of the three dramatic items involving the baritone, Thomas Hampson, which also include a sinister dialogue for Gretchen and an evil spirit, *Szene aus Faust*. McLaughlin's voice comes over sweetly, with brightness and much charm.

Lieder, Vol. 14: *Amphiaraos; An die Leier;* (i) *Antigone und Oedip. Der entsühnte Orest; Freiwilliges Versinken; Die Götter Griechenlands; Gruppe aus dem Tartarus; Fragment aus dem Aeschylus;* (i) *Hektors Abschied. Hippolits Lied; Lied eines Schiffers an die Dioskuren; Memnon; Orest auf Tauris; Philoktet; Uraniens Flucht; Der Zürnenden Diana.*
*** Hyp Dig. CDJ 33014 [id.]. Thomas Hampson, Graham Johnson; (i) with Marie McLaughlin.

Thomas Hampson's theme here is 'Schubert and the classics', mainly Ancient Greece. Matching the hushed intensity of the opening song, *Die Götter Griechenlands*, singer and accompanist give a rapt performance, and Hampson's ecstatically sweet tone, with flawless legato, contrasts with the darkly dramatic timbre – satisfyingly firm and steady – that he finds for later songs and dialogues, including the finale *Hektors Abschied*. In that dialogue Marie McLaughlin sings the part of Andromache to Hampson's Hector.

Lieder, Vol. 15: *Am Fenster; An die Sonne; An die untergehende Sonne; Der blinde Knabe; Gondelfahrer; Im Frieien; Ins stille Land; Die junge Nonne; Klage an den Mond; Kolmas Klage; Die Mainacht; Der Mondabend; Der Morgenkuss; Sehnsucht; Der Unglückliche; Der Wanderer an den Mond; Der Winterabend.*
☞ ⊛ *** Hyp. Dig. CDJ 33015 [id.]. Dame Margaret Price, Graham Johnson.

In the fifteenth disc of his Hyperion series, Graham Johnson, accompanying Dame Margaret Price in songs on the theme of 'Night', achieves a new peak. It is fascinating to compare Dame Margaret and Graham Johnson with Fischer-Dieskau and Gerald Moore. One song that was new to us, *Klage an den Mond* ('Lament to the Moon'), gloriously fresh and lyrical, is expressive enough with Fischer-Dieskau and Moore but, next to their rivals, they sound generalized. Price and Johnson find here a distinctive magic – even in such an early song – so that its simple melody rings through the memory for hours. Johnson's notes commenting on this song point out that *Seligkeit*, one of Schubert's most joyfully tuneful inspirations similar to *Klage*, was written to a text by the same poet, Holty. The other Holty setting on Margaret Price's disc is of *Die Mainacht*, much better known in Brahms's raptly beautiful setting. The young Schubert, less gentle and with a strophic form and strongly rhythmic accompaniment, is not nearly so evocative of a May night but simply lets his lyricism flower as no one else could. Johnson and Dame Margaret match that with folk-like freshness, concealing art. In the best-known song, *Der Wanderer an den Mond*, Price is light and crisp, but she finds extra mystery in the moonlight scene of *Am Fenster*, poignantly reflecting the lover's sadness.

Lieder, Vol. 16: *An die Freude; An Emma; Die Bürgschaft; Die Entzückung an Laura I & II; Das Geheimnis; Der Jüngling am Bache; Laura am Clavier; Leichenfantasie; Das Mädchen aus der Fremde; Die vier Weltalter; Sehnsucht; Der Pilgrim.*
☞ *** Hyp. Dig. CDJ 33016 [id.]. Thomas Allen, Graham Johnson.

Following the pattern of Graham Johnson's unique Schubert series, Thomas Allen in Schiller settings is challenged to some of his most sensitive singing, using the widest tonal range. They include two extended narrative songs that are a revelation, one of them, *Leichenfantasie* ('Funereal fantasy'), written when Schubert was only fourteen. As before, Johnson's notes and commentaries greatly heighten one's understanding both of particular songs and of Schubert generally.

Lieder, Vol. 17: *Am Grabe Anselmos; An den Mond; An die Nachtigall; An mein Klavier; Aus 'Diego Manazares' (Ilmerine); Die Einsiedelei; Frühlingslied; Geheimnis; Der Herbstabend; Herbstlied; Die Herbstnacht; Klage; Klage um Ali Bey; Lebenslied; Leiden der Trennung; Lied; Lied in der Absehenheit; Litanei; Lodas Gespenst; Lorma; Minnelied; Pflicht und Liebe; Phidile; Winterlied.*
☞ *** Hyp. Dig. CDJ 33017 [id.]. Lucia Popp, Graham Johnson.

It was fitting that one of the last recordings which Lucia Popp made, only months before her tragic death in the autumn of 1993, was her contribution to Graham Johnson's Schubert series. These songs, written in 1816 and almost all of them little-known, inspire all her characteristic sweetness and charm. They include an extended narrative song to a text from Ossian, *Lodas gespent*, which, like others resurrected by the indefatigable Johnson, defies the idea that long equals boring. She also relishes two of Schubert's rare comic songs, pointing them deliciously. As ever, Johnson's notes are a model of fascinating scholarship.

Lieder, Vol. 18: *Abendlied; An den Schlaf; An die Erntfernte; An die Harmonie; An mein Herz; Auf den Tod einer Nachtigall; Auf der Bruck; 'Die Blume und der Quell'; Blumenlied; Drang in die Ferne; Erntelied; Das Finden; Das Heimweh (2 versions); Im Frühling; Im Jänner 1817 (Tiefes Lied); Im Walde; Lebensmut; Der Liebliche Stern; Die Nacht; Uber Wildemann; Um Mitternacht.*
☞ *** Hyp. Dig. CDJ 33018 [id.]. Peter Schreier, Graham Johnson.

This eighteenth disc in Graham Johnson's masterly series represents the halfway point, with Peter Schreier providing a keenly illuminating supplement to his prize-winning recordings with András Schiff of the great Schubert song-cycles for Decca. The challenge is just as great here, when this particular group centres on strophic songs. It is a mark of Schreier's mastery that with his shading of tone and word-meaning he avoids any hint of monotony. The first nine songs are all early ones, dating from 1816, leading to just one extended non-strophic song, *Das Heimweh*, D.851, of 1825. Its weight and complexity come over the more powerfully after such a preparation, particularly when a simple, carefree song of the same name, earlier in the selection, provides the sharpest contrast of all. Johnson then delivers a master-stroke by devising for Schreier what amounts to a new Schubert song-cycle, presenting in sequence ten settings of poems from the *Poetisches Tagebuch* ('Poetic Diary'), by the obsessive, unstable poet, Ernst Schulze, all written in 1825 and 1826. Quoting the first song, Johnson calls the cycle *Auf den wilden Wegen* ('On the wild paths'), with the sequence following the poet's madly fanciful love-affair with a beloved who in real life rejected him as a mere stranger. Schreier and Johnson in their imaginative treatment present clear parallels with *Winterreise*, offering one momentary haven of happiness, instantly shattered. That comes in the best-known song, *Im Frühling*, among the most haunting that even Schubert ever wrote. Johnson's very detailed notes, as in previous discs of the series, intensify enjoyment enormously.

Lieder, Vol. 19: *Abendlied; Am See; Auf dem See; Auf dem Wasser zu singen; Beim Winde; Der Blumen Schmerz; Die Blumensprache; Gott im Frühling; Im Haine; Der liebliche Stern; Nach einem Gewitter; Nachtviolen; Die Rose; Die Sterne; Suleika I & II; Die Sternennächte; Vergissmeinicht.*
☞ *** Hyp. Dig. CDJ 33019 [id.]. Felicity Lott, Graham Johnson.

Graham Johnson's theme for Felicity Lott's disc is 'Schubert and flowers', prompting a sequence of charming, ever-lyrical songs, mostly neglected but including such a favourite as *Nachtviolen* (raptly sung) and – less predictably – *Auf dem Wasser zu singen*, all enchantingly done. Lott's soprano is not caught quite at its purest, but the charm and tender imagination of the singer consistently match the inspired accompaniments. In his detailed notes Johnson manages to include a 'Schubertian florilegium', listing several hundred of the songs inspired by particular flowers.

Lieder, Vol. 20: *'Schubertiad'* (1815) Songs and part-songs: *Abendständchen (An Lina); Alles um Liebe; Als ich sie errötten sah; Begräbnislied; Bergknappenlied; Der erste Liebe; Die Frölichkeit; Geist der Liebe; Grablied; Heidenröslein; Hoffnung; Huldigung; Klage um Ali Bey; Liebesrausch; Die Macht der Liebe; Das Mädchen von Inistore; Der Morgenstern; Nachtgesang; Ossians Lied nach dem Falle Nathos; Osterlied; Punschlied (Im Norden su singen); Schwertlied; Schwangesang; Die Tauschung; Tischerlied; Totenkranz für ein Kind; Trinklied (2 versions); Trinklied vor der Schlacht; Wiegenlied; Winterlied; Der Zufriedene.*
☞ *** Hyp. Dig. CDJ 33020 [id.]. Patricia Rozario, John Mark Ainsley, Ian Bostridge, Michael George, Graham Johnson; L. Schubert Chorale, Stephen Layton.

The twentieth volume of the Hyperion Schubert series brings a different kind of recital disc, with a range of singers performing no fewer than 32 brief songs and ensemble numbers, all written in 1815. Johnson conceives that this might well have been the sort of Schubertiad to take place towards the end of that year and, aptly for the opening and closing numbers, chooses drinking songs. In between, the vigorous and jolly songs are effectively contrasted with a few darker ones, such as a burial song. The team of singers has the flair one expects of Johnson as founder of the Songmakers' Almanac, with the young tenor, Ian Bostridge, making a welcome first appearance, potentially an outstanding singer. More Schubertiads are planned for later on in the Hyperion series.

Miscellaneous vocal recitals

Lieder: *Die schöne Mullerin: Wohin?; Des Baches Wiegenlied. Schwanengesang: Liebesbotschaft. Winterreise: Die Post; Frühlingstraum. An die Geliebte; An die Musik; An die Nachtigall; An mein Klavier; Auf dem Wasser zu singen; Ave Maria; Das sie hier gewesen; Du bist die Ruh'; Der Einsame; Des Fischers Liebesglück; Fischerweise; Die Forelle (2 versions); Frühlingsglaube; Geheimes; Gretchen am Spinnrade; Heidenröslein; Das Heimweh; (i) Der Hirt auf dem Felsen; Im Abendrot; Die junge Nonne; Der Jüngling an der Quelle; Der Jüngling und der Tod; Lachen und Weinen; Liebhabner in allen Gestalten; Das Lied im Grünen; Litanei; Das Mädchen; Der Musensohn; Nacht und Träume; Nachtviolen; Nahe des Geliebten; Nur wer die Sehnsucht kennt; Der Schmetterling; Seligkeit; So lasst mich scheinen; Ständchen; Schweizerlied; Die Vögel; Wiegenlied. Claudine von Villa Bella, D.239: Hin und wieder fliegen Pfeile (2 versions); Liebe schwärmt. Rosamunde, D.797: Der Vollmond strahlt.*
(M) (***) EMI mono CHS7 63040-2 (2) [Ang. CDHB 63040]. Elisabeth Schumann (various pianists); (i) Reginald Kell.

The irresistible charm and pure, silvery tones of Elisabeth Schumann make this collection of Schubert songs a delight from first to last. On the two CDs are collected 49 songs, with *Der Hirt auf dem Felsen* (*The Shepherd on the rock*) given separate billing on the cover. The recordings were made between 1927 and 1949, but mostly come from Schumann's vintage period in the 1930s. Transfers capture the voice well but, with a brighter top than on LP, the piano sound has less body. What matters is the vivid personality of the singer.

Lieder: *Alinde; Am Tage aller Seelen; An die Entfernte; An die Laute; Auf dem Wasser zu singen; Auf der Riesenkoppe; Die Bürgschaft; Du bist die Ruh'; Der Fischer; Der Fischers Liebesglück; Fischerweise; Die Forelle; Die Götter Griechenlands; Greisengesang; Heidenröslein; Das Heimweh; Im Walde; Der Jüngling an der Quelle; Der Jüngling und der Tod; Lachen und Weinen; Lied des gefangenen Jägers; Das Lied im Grünen; Nachtgesang; Nachtstück; Nähe des Geliebten; Normans Gesang; Der Schiffer; Sei mir gegrüsst; Seligkeit; Das sie hier gewesen; Ständchen; Strophe aus Die Götter; Der Strom; Der Tod und das Mädchen; Der Wanderer; Der Winterabend; Das Zügenglöcklein; Der zürnende Barde.*

(M) *** EMI CMS7 63566-2 (2) [Ang. CDMB 63566]. Dietrich Fischer-Dieskau, Gerald Moore; Karl Engel.

Dating from 1965, most of the items in this collection of Schubert songs superbly represent the second generation of Fischer-Dieskau recordings with Gerald Moore, deeper and more perceptive than his mono recordings, yet with voice and manner still youthfully fresh. The contrast is fascinating, if subtle, between that main collection and the last nine songs on the second disc: they were recorded six years earlier, with three of them accompanied by Karl Engel, and with the voice still younger but presented in drier sound. (Alas, this set has just been withdrawn.)

Lieder: *Die Allmacht; An die Natur; Auf dem See; Auflösung; Erlkönig; Ganymed; Gretchen am Spinnrade; Der Musensohn; Rastlose Liebe; Suleika I; Der Tod und das Mädchen; Der Zwerg.*
*** Ph. Dig. 412 623-2 [id.]. Jessye Norman, Philip Moll.

Jessye Norman's characterization of the four contrasting voices in *Erlkönig* is powerfully effective, and the reticence which once marked her Lieder singing has completely disappeared. The poignancy of *Gretchen am Spinnrade* is exquisitely touched in, building to a powerful climax; throughout, the breath control is a thing of wonder, not least in a surpassing account of *Ganymed*. Fine, sympathetic accompaniment from Philip Moll, and first-rate recording.

Lieder: *Am Flusse; An den Mond; Der Fischer; Erster Verlust; Erlkönig; Ganymed; Geheimes; Gesänge des Harfners I, II & III; Heidenröslein; Hoffnung; Liebhaber in alten Gestalten; Meeres Stille; Mignon; Lied der Mignon I, II & III; Der Musensohn; Rastlose Liebe; Der Sänger; Schäfers Klagenlied; Wanderers Nachtlied I & II.*
☞ ** Sony Dig. SK 53104 [id.]. Brigitte Fassbaender, Cord Garben.

Fassbaender's Sony disc of Schubert songs, including many favourites, is marred by the ham-fisted playing of Cord Garben. Rich as her mezzo is, it comes near to being drowned under the busy piano-parts of *Erlkönig* and *Musensohn* when played and recorded so heavily. Yet the characterfulness of Fassbaender in everything she does transforms each song, making even the best-known of them fresh and individual.

Goethe Lieder: *An die Entfernte; An Schwager Kronos; Erlkönig; Erster Verlust; Heidenröslein; Rastlose Liebe; Schäfers Klagelied; Wilkommen und Abschied.* Lieder: *An Silvia; Im Abendrot; Der Wanderer an den Mond.*
☞ (M) *** Decca 436 203-2 [id.]. Herman Prey, Karl Engel – SCHUMANN: *Lieder.* ***

The Goethe Lieder, apart from the subtly dramatic *Erlkönig*, were recorded (together with most of the coupled Schumann songs) in 1964. Here Prey is at times very careful in his approach, perhaps too consciously meaningful for basically simple songs; while in the other four Lieder, recorded two years earlier, he is somewhat more free. *An Silvia* has the lightest touch and *Im Abendrot* is most touching. But any minor reservations are balanced by this singer's ability to match his lovely vocal timbre sensitively with the mood of each song and also use a wide range of dynamic to maximum effect (as indeed in *Erlkönig*). The closing lines both of *An die Entfernte*: *O komm, Geliebte, mir zurück!* ('Oh my beloved, come back to me!') and of *Erster Verlust*: *jene holde Zeit zurück!* ('Who will return those blissful hours to me?') bring a ravishing thread of tone. The accompaniments are also very good, and so is the recording, which is extraordinarily realistic and beautifully balanced.

Lieder: *An die Laute; An Silvia; An die Musik; Der Einsame; Im Abendrot; Liebhaber in allen Gestalten; Lied eines Schiffers an die Dioskuren; Der Musensohn; Ständchen.*
(M) *** DG 429 933-2 [id.]. Fritz Wunderlich, Hubert Giesen – BEETHOVEN: *Lieder* **(*); SCHUMANN: *Dichterliebe.* ***

Few tenors have matched the young Wunderlich in the freshness and golden bloom of the voice. The open manner could not be more appealing here in glowing performances well coupled with other fine examples of this sadly short-lived artist's work.

Lieder: *An die Musik; An Sylvia; Auf dem Wasser zu singen; Ave Maria; Du bist die Ruh'; Die Forelle; Ganymed; Gretchen am Spinnrade; Heidenröslein; Im Frühling; Die junge Nonne; Litanei; Mignon und der Harfner; Der Musensohn; Nacht und Träume; Sei mir gegrüsst; Seligkeit.*
(B) *** Pickwick Dig. PCD 898; *CIMPC 898* [id.]. Felicity Lott, Graham Johnson.

At bargain price, Felicity Lott's collection brings an ideal choice of songs for the general collector. With Graham Johnson the most imaginative accompanist, even the best-known songs emerge fresh and new, and gentle songs like *Litanei* are raptly beautiful.

Lieder: *An die Musik; An Sylvia; Auf dem Wasser zu singen; Ganymed; Gretchen am Spinnrade; Im Frühling; Die junge Nonne; Das Lied im Grünen; Der Musensohn; Nachtviolen; Nähe des Geliebten; Wehmut.*
(M) (***) EMI mono CDH7 64026-2 [id.]. Elisabeth Schwarzkopf, Edwin Fischer.

Schwarzkopf at the beginning of her recording career and Fischer at the end of his make a magical partnership, with even the simplest of songs inspiring intensely subtle expression from singer and pianist alike. Though Fischer's playing is not immaculate, he left few records more endearing than this, and Schwarzkopf's colouring of word and tone is masterly.

Lieder: *An die Nachtigall; An mein Klavier; Auf dem Wasser zu singen; Geheimnis;* (i) *Der Hirt auf dem Felsen; Im Abendrot; Ins stille Land; Liebhaben in allen Gestalten; Das Lied im Grünen; Die Mutter Erde; Romanze; Der Winterabend.*
*** HM Orfeo C 001811 A [id.]. Margaret Price, Sawallisch; (i) with H. Schöneberger.

Consistent beauty of tone, coupled with immaculately controlled line and admirably clear diction, makes Margaret Price's Schubert collection a fresh and rewarding experience. Sawallisch as ever shows himself one of the outstanding accompanists of the time, readily translating from his usual role of conductor.

(i; ii) Duets: *Antigone und Oedip; Cronnan; Hektors Abschied; Hermann und Thusnelda; Licht und Liebe (Nachtgesang); Mignon und der Harfner; Selma und Selmar; Sing-Ubungen;* (vi) *Szene aus Goethes Faust.* (ii; iii; iv; v) Trios: *Die Advokaten; Gütigster, Bester, Weisester; Die Hochzeitsbraten; Kantata zum Geburtstag des Sängers Johann Michael Vogl; Punschlied; Trinklied; Verschwunden sind die Schmerzen (a cappella).* (i–iv) Quartets: *An die Sonne; Gebet; Die Geselligkeit (Lebenslust); Gott der Weltschöpfer; Gott im Ungewitter; Hymne an den Undenlichen; Nun lasst uns den Leib begraben (Begräbnislied); Des Tages Weihe; Der Tanz.*
(M) *** DG 435 596-2 (2) [id.]. (i) Dame Janet Baker; (ii) Fischer-Dieskau; (iii) Ameling; (iv) Schreier; (v) Laubenthal; Gerald Moore; (vi) with Berlin RIAS Chamber Ch.

Not all these duets are vintage Schubert – some of the narrative pieces go on too long – but the artistry of Baker and Fischer-Dieskau makes for magical results. Gerald Moore, who is at his finest throughout the set, relishes the magic too. The trios are domestic music in the best sense. Specially delightful are the two contrasted drinking songs, but *The wedding feast (Die Hochzeitsbraten)* is even more remarkable, a 10½-minute scena in the style of *opera buffa*. The quartets, like the trios, were written for various domestic occasions, but the use of four voices seems to have led the composer regularly to serious or religious subjects. These are sweet and gentle rather than intense inspirations, but one could hardly ask for more polished and inspired performances than these. Fine recording from 1973/4, giving the singers a vivid presence on CD.

6 Antiphons for the Blessings of the Branches on Psalm Sunday; Auguste jam coelestium in G, D.488; Deutsche Messe, D.872 (with Epilogue, The Lord's Prayer); Graduale in C, D.184; Hymn to the Holy Ghost, D.964; Kyries: in D min., D.31; F, D.66; Lazarus, D.689; Magnificat in C, D.486; Offertorium (Totus in corde) in C, D.136; Offertorium (Tres sunt) in A min., D.181; 2 Offertoriums (Salve Regina) in F, D.223 & A, D.676; Psalm 23, D.706; Psalm 92, D.953; Salve Reginas: in B flat, D.106; in C, D.811; Stabat Mater in G min., D.175; Tantum ergo (3 settings) in C, D.460/1 & D.739; Tantum ergo in D, D.750.
☞ (M) *** EMI Dig./Analogue CMS7 64783-2 (3) [id.]. Popp, Donath, Rüggerberg, Venuti, Hautermann, Falk, Fassbaender, Greindl-Rosner, Dallapozza, Araiza, Protschka, Tear, Lika, Fischer-Dieskau, Capella Bavariae, Bav. R. Ch. & SO, Sawallisch.

Volume two of Sawallisch's great and rewarding Schubertian survey has much glorious music, sung with eloquence and richly recorded in the Munich Hercules Hall. Much of the content is rare and none of it is inconsequential. Even some of the shortest items – such as the six tiny *Antiphons*, allegedly written in half an hour – have magic and originality in them. Plainer, but still glowing with Schubertian joy, is the so-called *Deutsche Messe*. The *Magnificat*, too, is a strongly characterized setting, and even the three settings of St Thomas Aquinas's *Tantum ergo* (all in C) have their charm. There are other surprises. The lovely setting of the *Offertorium in C (Totus in corde)* is for soprano, clarinet and orchestra, with the vocal and instrumental lines intertwining delectably, while the no less appealing *Auguste jam coelestium* is a soprano–tenor duet. The *Salve Regina in C*, D.811, is written for four male voices, *a cappella*, and they again contribute to the performance of *Psalm 23*, where Sawallisch provides a piano accompaniment. The religious drama, *Lazarus*, nearly 80 minutes in length, has the third CD to itself. Schubert left it unfinished and, though no more dramatic than his operas, it contains much delightful music. Some of it is as touching as the finest Schubert, while other sections are little short of inspired; there are some thoroughly characteristic harmonic colourings and some powerful writing for the trombones. With Robert Tear in the name-role, Helen Donath as Maria, Lucia Popp as Jemima, Maria Venuti as Martha, Josef Protschka as Nathanael and Fischer-Dieskau as Simon, it is very strongly cast and the performance is splendid; indeed the singing is outstanding from chorus and soloists alike throughout this set, and the warm, well-balanced recording adds to one's pleasure.

Kyries: in B flat, D.45; D min., D.49; Masses Nos. 1 in F, D.105; 2 in G, D.167; 3 in B flat, D.324; 4 in C, D.452; 5 in A flat, D.678; 6 in E flat, D.950; Offertorium in B flat, D.963; Salve Reginas: in F, D.379; in B flat, D.386; Stabat Mater in F min., D.383; Tantum ergo in E flat, D.962.
☞ (M) *** EMI Dig./Analogue CMS7 64778-2 (4) [id.]. Popp, Donath, Fassbaender, Dallapozza, Schreier, Araiza, Protschka, Fischer-Dieskau, Bav. R. Ch. & SO, Sawallisch.

Sawallisch's highly distinguished survey of Schubert's church music – one of his most impressive gramophone achievements – was recorded in the early 1980s but is only now appearing on CD. This first volume is centred on his major Mass settings, especially his masterpiece in this form, the *E flat Mass*. Though the chorus is not flawless here, the performances are warm and understanding. The earlier Mass settings bring superb, lively inspirations, not to mention the separate *Kyries* and *Salve Reginas*. Excellent, cleanly focused sound, for the most part digital, with the benefit of the ambience of the Munich Herkulessall.

Mass No. 6 in E flat, D.950.
☞ (B) *** Erato/Warner Duo Dig. 4509 95307-2 (2) [id.]. Michael, Balleys, Baldin, Homberger, Brodard, Swiss R. Chamber Ch., Lausanne Pro Arte Ch., SRO, Jordan – SCHUMANN: *Mass*. ***

In every way this *Mass* is a richly rewarding work, product of the last year of Schubert's short life. The chorus is far more important than the soloists; nevertheless they are a good team, well led by the soprano, Audrey Michael. The Swiss and Lausanne choirs blend well together and sing with ardour and discipline. The digital sound is well focused and the acoustic expansive, and the results are powerful and satisfying. Coupled with a rare Mass of Schumann, this is a valuable reissue, the more attractive for being reissued in Erato's Bonsai series (two CDs for the price of one) and it is a great pity that there is no proper documentation offering information about the music itself.

Rosamunde Overture (Die Zauberharfe, D.644) and incidental music, D.797 (complete).
*** DG Dig. 431 655-2 (id.). Anne Sofie von Otter, Ernst Senff Ch., COE, Abbado.

Abbado and COE give joyful performances of this magical incidental music. It is a revelation to hear the most popular of the entr'actes played so gently: it is like a whispered meditation. Even with a slow speed and affectionate phrasing, it yet avoids any feeling of being mannered. Glowing recording to match. Anne Sofie von Otter is an ideal soloist.

Song-cycles

Song-cycles: Die schöne Müllerin, D.795; Schwanengesang, D.957; Winterreise, D.911. Lieder: *Du bist die Ruh'; Erlkönig; Nacht und Träume.*
(M) (***) EMI mono CMS7 63559-2 (3) [Ang. CDMC 63559]. Dietrich Fischer-Dieskau, Gerald Moore.

Fischer-Dieskau's early mono versions may not match his later recordings in depth of insight, but already the young singer was a searching interpreter of these supreme cycles. Gerald Moore was, as ever, the most sympathetic partner.

Die schöne Müllerin (song cycle), D.795.
*** DG 415 186-2 [id.]. Dietrich Fischer-Dieskau, Gerald Moore.
*** Decca Dig. 430 414-2 [id.]. Peter Schreier, András Schiff.
*** Capriccio Dig. 10 082 [id.]. Josef Protschka, Helmut Deutsch.

Die schöne Müllerin (complete); *An die Laute; Der Einsame; Die Taubenpost.*
☞ (M) **(*) Decca 436 201-2. Peter Pears, Benjamin Britten.

Fischer-Dieskau's classic 1972 version on DG remains among the very finest ever recorded, combining as it does his developed sense of drama and story-telling, his mature feeling for detail and yet spontaneity too, helped by the searching accompaniment of Gerald Moore. It is a performance with premonitions of *Winterreise.*

András Schiff brings new illumination in almost every phrase, to match the brightly detailed singing of Schreier, here challenged to produce his most glowing tone. Schreier, matching his partner as he did in their earlier, prize-winning recording of *Schwanengesang* (see below), transcends even his earlier versions of this favourite cycle, always conveying his response so vividly that one clearly registers his changes of facial expression from line to line. Outstandingly warm and well-balanced recording.

Josef Protschka gives an intensely virile, almost operatic reading, which is made the more youthful-sounding in the original keys for high voice. As recorded, the voice, often beautiful with heroic timbres, sometimes acquires a hint of stridency, but the positive power and individuality of the performance make it consistently compelling, with all the anguish behind these songs caught intensely. The timbre of the Bösendorfer piano adds to the performance's distinctiveness, well if rather reverberantly recorded.

Fischer-Dieskau may find more drama in the poems, and Gerald Moore matches his subtlety of inflexion at every point; but Pears is imaginative too, if for once in rather gritty voice, and Britten brings a composer's insight to the accompaniments so that, while Fischer-Dieskau provides more charm in this most sunny of song-cycles, the Pears/Britten partnership remains uniquely valuable.

Song-cycles: *Die schöne Müllerin, D.795* (complete); *Schwanengesang* (excerpts): *Liebesbotschaft; Kriegers Ahnung; Frühlingssehnsucht; Abschied; Der Atlas; Ihr Bild; Das Fischermädchen; Die Taubenpost* (only). *Winterreise, D.911* (complete). Lieder: *An die Laute; An die Musik; An Sylvia; Auf der Bruck; Dithyrambe; Der Doppelgänger; Erlkönig; Erster Verlust; Des Fischers Liebesglück; Die Forelle; Frühlingsglaube; Ganymed; Heidenröslein; Im Abendrot; Der Jüngling an der Quelle; Die Liebe hat gelogen; Lied eines Schiffers an die Dioskuren; Meeres Stille; Der Musensohn; Nacht und Träume; Normans Gesang; Rastlose Liebe; Der Schiffer; Ständchen; Der Tod und das Mädchen; Dem Unendlichen; Der Wanderer; Wandrers Nachtlied; Der Zwerg.*
☞ (M) *** Ph. 438 511-2 [id.]. Gérard Souzay, Dalton Baldwin.

Souzay's sunny style is particularly suited to *Die schöne Müllerin*, the most sunny of song-cycles. Fischer-Dieskau may find more drama in the poems, but Souzay's concentration on purely musical values makes for one of the most consistently attractive versions ever recorded, with the words never neglected and Dalton Baldwin giving one of his most imaginative performances on record. This dates from 1964; *Wintereisse* is earlier (1961/2), when Souzay also recorded his incomplete selection from *Schwanengesange* (one or two of the missing songs are included in the two recitals which follow). Once again the singing is intense and the cycle is firmly held together, with musical values paramount. But in *Winterreise* Souzay hardly outshines Peter Pears or Fischer-Dieskau.

The 29 miscellaneous Lieder combine the contents of two recitals, recorded in 1961 and 1967. The earlier collection, which includes many top favourites, is ideal in all respects. Souzay's style is wonderfully sympathetic, superbly dramatic in the *Erlkönig*, for instance – one of the finest performances of this song on record – and he spins his tone exquisitely in the quieter songs; *Wandrers Nachtlied* is a particularly fine example. In the later recordings, by skilful covering and the widening of his vibrato at points of pressure, Souzay provides consistent freshness of tone, and the consummate artistry in matters of inflexion and phrasing is always apparent. At times one feels that his mood is too unvaryingly introspective. Of course, many of Schubert's greatest songs are melancholy and inward-looking, but on a record the careful placing of a happy song can lighten the mood. Here, even though Souzay's contrasts between *An die Laute* and the following *Der Tod und das Mädchen* are beautifully made and the ear delights in *Der Musensohn*, there is some lack of variety overall. Dalton Baldwin's accompaniments are often superb, the ripples of the lute, or the brook in *Der Jüngling an der Quelle*, are delightfully characterized, while the strong, rhythmic mood of *Normans Gesang* (one of Schubert's most dramatic ballad songs) is an artistic highlight. But Baldwin participates actively in every song and he is helped by the excellent recording balance.

Schwanengesang (Lieder collection), *D.957;* Lieder: *An die Musik; An Sylvia; Die Forelle; Heidenröslein; Im Abendrot; Der Musensohn; Der Tod und das Mädchen.*
*** DG 415 188-2 [id.]. Dietrich Fischer-Dieskau, Gerald Moore.

Schwanengesang. Am Fenster; Bei dir allein; Herbst; Der Wanderer an den Mond.
*** Decca Dig. 425 612-2. Peter Schreier, András Schiff.

Schwanengesang; 5 Lieder: *Am Fenster; Herbst; Sehnsucht; Der Wanderer an den Mond; Wiegenlied, D.867.*
⊛ *** DG Dig. 429 766-2 [id.]. Brigitte Fassbaender, Aribert Reimann.

Schwanengesang. Im Freien; Der Wanderer an den Mond; Das Zügenglücklein.
*** EMI Dig. CDC 749997-2. Olaf Bär, Geoffrey Parsons.

Brigitte Fassbaender gives a totally distinctive and compelling account of *Schwanengesang*, defying the convention that this is a cycle for male singers and proving stronger and more forceful than almost any rival. She turns what was originally a relatively random group of late songs into a genuine cycle, by presenting them in a carefully rearranged order and adding five other late songs. Her magnetic power of compelling attention, bringing home every word, is intensified by her sharply rhythmic manner, heightened in turn by the equally positive accompaniment of Aribert Reimann. The celebrated Schubert *Serenade* to words by Rellstab is far more than just a pretty tune, rather a passionate declaration of love; and Fassbaender builds her climax to the cycle round the final Heine settings, heightening their dramatic impact by the new ordering. This is a unique recording which may well upset traditionalist lovers of Lieder but which brings home the power of the genre to communicate with new intensity.

Fischer-Dieskau's DG version with Moore, though recorded ten years before his CD with Brendel (currently withdrawn), brings excellent sound in the digital transfer, plus the positive advantages, first that the voice is fresher, and then that the disc also contains seven additional songs, all of them favourites.

Schreier's voice may no longer be beautiful under pressure, but the bloom on this Decca recording and the range of tone and the intensity of inflexion over word-meaning make this one of the most compelling recordings ever of *Schwanengesang*. Enhancing that are the discreet but highly individual and responsive accompaniments of András Schiff. Like Bär on his fine EMI version, Schreier makes up a generous CD-length by including not just the 14 late songs published together as *Schwanengesang*, but four more, also from the last three years of Schubert's life. The recording is vividly real.

Olaf Bär also amplifies the collection of late songs posthumously published as *Schwanengesang* with well-chosen extra items from the same period, notably (like Schreier) *Der Wanderer an den Mond*. Where Schreier is confidential in that song at a brisk speed, Bär brings out the agony and weariness of the traveller addressing the moon. In *Ständchen*, where Schreier is light and charming, Bär is strong and passionate.

Winterreise (song cycle), *D.911.*
*** DG 415 187-2 [id.]. Dietrich Fischer-Dieskau, Gerald Moore.
*** Ph. Dig. 411 463-2 [id.]. Dietrich Fischer-Dieskau, Alfred Brendel.
☞ (B) *** DG 439 432-2 [id.]. Fischer-Dieskau, Barenboim.
⊛ (M) *** Decca 417 473-2 [id.]. Peter Pears, Benjamin Britten.
*** EMI Dig. CDC7 49334-2 [id.]. Olaf Bär, Geoffrey Parsons.
*** EMI Dig. CDC7 49846-2 [id.]. Brigitte Fassbaender, Aribert Reimann.
☞ (BB) ** ASV CDQS 6085 [id.]. Robert Tear, Philip Ledger.

What is so striking about the Pears performance is its intensity. One continually has the sense of a live occasion and, next to it, even Fischer-Dieskau's beautifully wrought singing sounds too easy. As for Britten, he re-creates the music, sometimes with a fair freedom from Schubert's markings, but always with scrupulous concern for the overall musical shaping and sense of atmosphere. The sprung rhythm of *Gefror'ne Tränen* is magical in creating the impression of frozen teardrops falling, and almost every song brings similar magic. The recording and the CD transfer are exceptionally successful in bringing a sense of presence and realism.

In the early 1970s Dietrich Fischer-Dieskau's voice was still at its freshest, yet the singer had deepened and intensified his understanding of this greatest of song-cycles to a degree where his finely detailed and thoughtful interpretation sounded totally spontaneous, and this DG version is now freshened on CD. However, the collaboration of Fischer-Dieskau with one of today's great Schubert pianists, Alfred Brendel, brings endless illumination in the interplay and challenge between singer and pianist, magnetic from first to last. With incidental flaws, this may not be the definitive Fischer-

Dieskau reading, but in many ways it is the deepest and most moving he has ever given. The recording is excellent.

Fischer-Dieskau's fifth recording of Schubert's greatest cycle, made in 1979, has now appeared on DG's Classikon bargain label, with the voice still in superb condition. Prompted by Barenboim's spontaneous-sounding, almost improvisatory accompaniments, it is highly inspirational. In expression this is freer than the earlier versions, and though some idiosyncratic details will not please everyone the sense of concentrated development is irresistible. The recording is very natural and beautifully balanced, and full translations are included.

Bär, with Geoffrey Parsons a masterly accompanist, is both intensely dramatic and deeply reflective, while finding a beauty of line and tone to outshine almost anyone. The darkness of the close is given the intensity of live communication, and the sound is outstanding, with voice and piano given intimacy in a helpful atmosphere.

Brigitte Fassbaender gives a fresh, boyishly eager reading of *Winterreise*, marked by a vivid and wide range of expression; she demonstrates triumphantly why a woman's voice can bring special illumination to this cycle, sympathetically underlining the drama behind the tragic poet's journey rather than the more meditative qualities. Reimann, at times a wilful accompanist, is nevertheless spontaneous-sounding like the singer. Excellent sound.

It is good to have a super-bargain version of *Die Winterreise*, but the account by Robert Tear and Philip Ledger is disappointing from two artists who might have been expected to follow in the inspired tradition of Pears and Britten. It is partly the dryness and lack of bloom on the voice in the studio recording – with the piano sounding too close – which underlines a degree of squareness in the slower songs. The vigorous songs go much better, and the CD transfer has undoubtedly improved the sound, but the basic reservations remain.

OPERA

Fierrabras (complete).
*** DG Dig. 427 341-2 (2) [id.]. Protschka, Mattila, Studer, Gambill, Hampson, Holl, Polgár, Schoenberg Ch., COE, Abbado.

Few operas by a great composer have ever had quite so devastatingly bad a press as *Fierrabras*. Schubert may often let his musical imagination blossom without considering the dramatic effect, but there are jewels in plenty in this score. Many solos and duets develop into delightful ensembles, and the influence of Beethoven's *Fidelio* is very striking, with spoken melodrama and offstage fanfares bringing obvious echoes. A recording is the ideal medium for such buried treasure, and Abbado directs an electrifying performance. Both tenors, Robert Gambill and Josef Protschka, are on the strenuous side, but have a fine feeling for Schubertian melody. Cheryl Studer and Karita Mattila sing ravishingly, and Thomas Hampson gives a noble performance as the knight, Roland. Only Robert Holl as King Karl (Charlemagne) is unsteady at times. The sound is comfortably atmospheric, outstanding for a live recording.

Schuman, William (1910–92)

Judith; New England triptych; Symphony for strings; Variations on America.
*** Delos Dig. DE 3115 [id.]. Seattle SO, Gerard Schwarz.

The composer himself heard these performances and spoke of their combination of 'intellectual depth, technical superiority and emotional involvement' – and who are we to dissent! The *Symphony for strings*, his Fifth, is one of his strongest and most beautiful works. This Seattle account has the advantage of fresh recorded sound. The ballet, *Judith*, was written for Martha Graham. Powerful and atmospheric music, here given a performance with both these qualities. The *New England triptych* makes use of New England themes by the Bostonian, William Billings (1746–1800), whose music served to fuel the cause of the American Revolution. This present account is superior to the version by Howard Hanson on Mercury.

New England triptych.
(M) *** Mercury 432 755-2 [id.]. Eastman-Rochester O, Howard Hanson – IVES: *Symphony No. 3* etc. ***; MENNIN: *Symphony No. 5.* **(*)

A powerful and appropriate coupling for Ives's masterly *Three places in New England* and *Third Symphony*. William Schuman is not as outrageously original as Ives, but his sound-world is individual and wholly American. Each of the three pieces is an orchestral anthem, the first a thrustingly vibrant

Hallelujah; the second is in the form of a round, and the finale features a marching song. Splendidly alive playing and excellent (1963) Mercury recording, admirably transferred to CD.

Symphony No. 3.
*** DG Dig. 419 780-2 [id.]. NYPO, Bernstein – HARRIS: *Symphony No. 3.* ***

The *Third* of William Schuman's ten symphonies has an authentic American feel to it: it certainly creates a sound-world all its own, but the world it evokes is urban. The chorale movement is particularly evocative, full of nocturnal introspection and wholly original. Schuman is also one of the few modern composers to use fugue both individually and effectively. An impressive performance. The New York Philharmonic play with excellent discipline and are well recorded. Strongly recommended.

Schumann, Clara (1819–96)

Piano trio in G min., Op. 17.
*** Hyp. Dig. CDA 66331 [id.]. Dartington Piano Trio – Fanny MENDELSSOHN: *Trio.* ***

Clara's *Piano trio* moves within the Mendelssohn–Schumann tradition with apparently effortless ease and, when played as persuasively as it is here, makes a pleasing impression. If it does not command the depth of Robert, it has a great deal of charm to commend it. Excellent recording.

Schumann, Robert (1810–56)

Cello concerto in A min., Op. 129.
(M) *** Mercury 432 010-2 [id.]. Janos Starker, LSO, Skrowaczewski – LALO: *Concerto* **(*); SAINT-SAENS: *Concerto.* ***
(M) *** Decca Dig. 430 743-2 [id.]. Lynn Harrell, Cleveland O, Marriner – DVORAK: *Cello concerto.* **

The Schumann *Cello concerto* is not generously represented at the mid-price or bargain end of the catalogue; Janos Starker gives a persuasive account of it that is thoroughly sensitive to the letter and spirit of the score. Skrowaczewski accompanies with spirit and without the rather explosive, clipped tutti chords that rather disfigure the Lalo with which it is coupled. The 1962 recording is amazing for its age: people make great claims for these early Mercury recordings and, judging from this expertly engineered disc, rightly so!

Harrell's is a big-scale reading, strong and sympathetic, made the more powerful by the superb accompaniment from the Cleveland Orchestra. Its controversial point is that he expands the usual cadenza with a substantial sequence of his own. The digital recording is outstandingly fine.

(i) *Cello concerto in A min., Op. 129;* (ii) *Piano concerto in A min., Op. 54; Introduction and allegro appassionato, Op. 92.*
☞ (M) ** EMI CDM7 64626-2 [id.]. (i) Jacqueline du Pré, New Philh. O, Barenboim; (ii) Barenboim, LPO, Dietrich Fischer-Dieskau.

The most attractive performance here is Jacqueline du Pré's 1968 recording of the *Cello concerto*. Her spontaneous style is strikingly suited to this most recalcitrant of concertos and the slow moverment is particularly beautiful. She is ably assisted by Daniel Barenboim, and the only snag is the rather faded orchestral sound, unflattered by the present transfer, though the cello timbre is realistically focused. The coupling was recorded in the mid-1970s; the sound is somewhat firmer and the balance lets the piano dominate but, with the LPO below its best under Fischer-Dieskau (a good but not outstanding conductor), this is probably just as well. Barenboim is brisk and not particularly poetic, and these performances lack what he usually achieves on record: a sense of spontaneity, a simulation of a live performance.

(i) *Cello concerto;* (ii) *Piano concerto in A min.;* (iii) *Violin concerto in D min.;* (ii) *Introduction and allegro appassionata;* (iv) *Konzertstück in F for four horns and orchestra, Op. 86.*
☞ (B) **(*) EMI Analogue/Dig. CZS7 67521-2 (2) [id.]. (i) Paul Tortelier, RPO, Yan Pascal Tortelier; (ii) Barenboim, LPO, Fischer-Dieskau; (iii) Kremer, Philh. O, Muti; (iv) Hauptmann, Klier, Kohler, Seifert, BPO, Tennstedt.

This is a useful collection of Schumann's concertante works and it is a pity that it is let down somewhat by Barenboim's rather too direct account of the works for piano (see above). Tortelier's is a characteristically inspirational performance of the *Cello concerto*, at its most concentrated in the hushed rendering of the slow movement. The soloist's son matches the warmth of his father's playing in the accompaniment and both are suitably spirited in the finale. This is a less individual account than Jacqueline du Pré's, but the (1978) orchestral sound is a marked improvement on her version. The *Violin concerto* comes off pretty well in the hands of Gidon Kremer. Its vein of introspection seems to suit him and he gives a generally sympathetic account of it and has very good support from the Philharmonia under Riccardo Muti. It is not Schumann at his most consistently inspired but there are good things in it, including a memorable second subject and a characteristic slow movement, which Kremer plays very touchingly. The (digital) recording was made in the Kingsway Hall in 1982 and is full-bodied, vivid and convincingly balanced. What makes this two-disc set well worth considering in EMI's Rouge et Noir series (offering two CDs for the price of one) is the inclusion of the exuberant *Konzertstück* with its brilliant horn playing. The four soloists from the Berlin Philharmonic play with superbly ripe virtuosity and Tennstedt's direction is both urgent and expansive. The 1978 recording is admirably full-blooded.

(i) *Cello concerto in A min., Op. 129;* (ii) *Adagio and allegro in A flat, Op. 70; 5 Stücke im Volkston, Op. 102; Fantasiestücke, Op. 73.*
*** Sony Dig. MK 42663 [id.]. Yo-Yo Ma, (i) Bav. RSO, C. Davis; (ii) Emanuel Ax.

Yo-Yo Ma includes the whole of Schumann's music for the cello and piano. As always, Ma's playing is distinguished by great refinement of expression and his account of the *Concerto* is keenly affectionate, although at times he carries tonal sophistication to excess and drops suddenly into *sotto voce* tone and near-inaudibility. Both he and Sir Colin Davis are thoroughly attuned to the sensibility of this composer. The balance, both between soloist and orchestra and within the various departments of the orchestra, blends perfectly. The three pieces for cello and piano are well projected and full of feeling, with sensitive and well-characterized playing from Emanuel Ax.

Piano concerto in A min., Op. 54.
*** Ph. 412 923-2 [id.]. Kovacevich, BBC SO, C. Davis – GRIEG: *Concerto.* ***
☞ *** EMI Dig. CDC7 54746-2 [id.]. Lars Vogt, CBSO, Rattle – GRIEG: *Concerto.* ***
*** Sony Dig. MK 44899 [id.]. Perahia, Bav. RSO, C. Davis – GRIEG: *Concerto.* ***
*** CfP Dig. CD-CFP 4574. Pascal Devoyon, LPO, Maksymiuk – GRIEG: *Concerto.* ***
*** Ph. 412 251-2 [id.]. Brendel, LSO, Abbado – WEBER: *Konzertstück.* ***
(M) (***) EMI mono CDH7 69792-2. Lipatti, Philh. O, Karajan – MOZART: *Piano concerto No. 21.* (*(**))
(M) **(*) Decca 417 728-2 [id.]. Radu Lupu, LSO, Previn – GRIEG: *Concerto.* **(*)
(M) **(*) BMG/RCA GD 60420 [60420-2-RG]. Van Cliburn, Chicago SO, Reiner – MACDOWELL: *Concerto No. 2.* **(*)
(B) **(*) Decca 433 628-2 [id.]. Gulda, VPO, Andrae – FRANCK: *Symphonic variations* *** ⊛ ; GRIEG: *Concerto.* ***
(M) **(*) Sony/CBS CD 44849 [id.]. Fleisher, Cleveland O, Szell – GRIEG: *Concerto.* **(*)
☞ (BB) **(*) ASV Dig. CDQS 6092. Osorio, RPO, Bátiz – FRANCK: *Symphonic variations* **(*); RAVEL: *Left-hand concerto* ***; SAINT-SAENS: *Wedding-cake.* ***
☞ **(*) DG Gold Dig. 439 015-2 [id.]. Krystian Zimerman, BPO, Karajan – GRIEG: *Concerto.* **

(i) *Piano concerto in A min. Arabeske in C, Op. 18.*
(M) *** Mercury 432 011-2 [id.]. Byron Janis, Minneapolis SO, Skrowaczewski – TCHAIKOVSKY: *Piano concerto No. 1.* **(*)

(i) *Piano concerto in A min. Arabeske, Op. 18; Etudes symphoniques, Op. 13.*
☞ (M) *** BMG/RCA 09026 61444-2 [id.]. Rubinstein; (i) RCA Victor SO, Krips.

(i) *Piano concerto in A min.; Carnaval, Op. 9.*
☞ (M) (***) Dutton Lab. mono CDLX 7005 [id.]. Dame Myra Hess; (i) O, Walter Goehr – BACH: *Jesu, joy of man's desiring;* FRANCK: *Symphonic variations.* (***)

Our primary recommendation for this favourite Romantic concerto remains with the successful symbiosis of Stephen Kovacevich and Sir Colin Davis, who give an interpretation which is both fresh and poetic, unexaggerated but powerful in its directness and clarity, and the spring-like element of the outer movements is finely presented by orchestra and soloist alike. The sound has been admirably freshened.

Lars Vogt was the Second Prize winner at the 1990 Leeds International Piano Competition when he impressed by his sensitivity and innate sense of style. Both these attributes, and a keen imagination, are strongly in evidence in this account of the Schumann, in which he is well supported by Simon Rattle and the CBSO. There is stiff competition, of course, from Lipatti, Curzon, Kovacevich and Lupu, but among modern recordings Vogt acquits himself with honour. The Grieg coupling is very fine indeed.

Perahia's version also benefits from having the guiding hand of Sir Colin Davis directing the orchestra. The recording is live. The confident bravura in the performances presents Perahia in a rather different light from usual. He is never merely showy, but here he enjoys displaying his ardour and virtuosity as well as his ability to invest a phrase magically with poetry. With its full and spacious sound, the Perahia is among the finest recent versions of this favourite coupling.

It is good to have Rubinstein's early (1958) New York (Manhattan Center) recording of the *A minor Piano concerto* restored to the catalogue as it is clearly preferable to his later, Chicago version, which suffered from a more restricted dynamic range. As usual, John Pfeiffer has done wonders with the original master, and few apologies have to be made for the sound. Rubinstein takes the allegros of these two inter-connected movements (separated by the charming *Intermezzo*) at comparatively modest speeds. This leaves him room to space the romantic paragraphs with none of the tautness which afflicts too many performances by younger pianists. Of course, Rubinstein himself is not guiltless of riding roughshod over romantic works on occasion, but here he achieves the ideal compromise between an impression of spontaneous poetry in quieter passages (his rubato is marked but most natural) and a firm overall control. Listen to the way he plays the grace-notes at the opening of the finale. The work constantly sounds – as it should – gentle and poetic without losing stature as a bravura concerto. It is interesting that the conductor here, Josef Krips, was also the conductor on Kempff's old mono recording, which was also notable for its relaxed allegros, and one wonders what influence he had in the matter. The recording of the piano is just a little hard, but the stereo, by putting it into a realistic ambience, makes one forget the hardness, for the orchestral texture is full and pleasing. As couplings, we are offered Rubinstein's 1969 recording of the *Arabeske*, aristocratic in feeling and with nuances of rubato to remind us of his Chopin. The *Etudes symphoniques* were recorded at a live recital in Carnegie Hall in 1961, which means that the piano image is close (to minimize audience noises). But it is firm and full, and the commanding playing is made the more gripping by the communication with the audience – witness the burst of adrenalin at the *Allegro marcato* (*Etude No. 4*) and the variations which follow.

Even among the many fine transfers made by Michael Dutton from original 78-r.p.m. shellac pressings, this one stands out. Dame Myra Hess's treasurable performance of the Schumann *Piano concerto* (warmly feminine and poetic in the first and second movements yet with plenty of extrovert vigour and sparkle in the finale) was recorded at Abbey Road in 1937 and was the yardstick for judging other later versions of this lovely concerto. The transfer miraculously captures the original quality, the orchestral strings a little opaque but catching the woodwind dialogues with the piano in the first movement freshly and naturally. The name of the original balance engineer is unknown, but Walter Legge was the producer for *Carnaval*, an individual, very volatile performance, particularly commanding in the last three sections. Again, the piano timbre is remarkably full and truthful.

Pascal Devoyon is aristocratic without being aloof, pensive without being self-conscious, and brilliant without being flashy. Natural musicianship and artistry are always in evidence, and at bargain price this is very competitive, with excellent playing from the LPO under Jerzy Maksymiuk.

Byron Janis's Schumann *Concerto* is a lovely performance, and the 1962 recording sounds amazingly improved over its previous incarnations, especially in regard to the orchestra. Janis's reading finds an almost perfect balance between the need for romantic ardour and intimacy in the *Concerto* – the exchanges between the piano and the woodwind soloists in the first movement are most engagingly done. Skrowaczewski provides admirable support throughout, and this is highly recommendable too.

Brendel's is a thoroughly considered, yet fresh-sounding performance, with meticulous regard to detail. There is some measure of coolness, perhaps, in the slow movement, but on the whole this is a most distinguished reading.

Dinu Lipatti's celebrated EMI recording has acquired classic status and will more than repay study. The transfer is excellent. A splendidly aristocratic account in very acceptable sound.

Lupu's clean boldness of approach to the first movement is appealingly fresh, but the fusing together of the work's disparate masculine and feminine Romantic elements has not been solved entirely. The digital CD transfer is especially telling in the quieter moments, but tuttis are less transparent than with a digital recording.

Van Cliburn's performance is very persuasive, the first movement rhapsodical in feeling, certainly poetic but exciting too. The *Intermezzo* is pleasingly fresh and the finale admirably buoyant and spirited. Altogether this is most attractive, and so is the unusual MacDowell coupling.

Gulda's account is refreshingly direct yet, with light, crisp playing, never sounds rushed. The *Intermezzo* remains delicate in feeling, with nicely pointed pianism. The finale is just right, with an enjoyable rhythmic lift, and the early stereo (1956), though a little dated, is fully acceptable.

Fleischer's 1960 account with Szell is also distinguished, the reading combining strength and poetry in a most satisfying way, yet with a finale that sparkles, in spite of a very bold, upfront orchestral recording, which tends to sound a little fierce.

Jorge Federico Osorio's account of the Schumann *Concerto* is boldly romantic yet in no way lacking in poetry. The central *Intermezzo* is beautifully in scale, but in the first movement, with Bátiz bringing strong support in the tuttis, he presses on impulsively, and the finale has similar urgency. Some may prefer a more relaxed romanticism, but there is no lack of spontaneity here and the result is undoubtedly fresh and involving. Excellent recording and recommendable couplings make this disc a genuine bargain.

Zimerman gives a big-boned performance, bold rather than delicate, at the opposite pole from Kempff's. There is consummate pianism from this most aristocratic of younger artists, and Karajan draws fine playing from the Berlin orchestra. However, although the music-making is vivid, one expects rather more natural romantic spontaneity in this work. The remastered recording is very impressive, and the forward balance of the piano is not really troublesome when the orchestra sounds so full and brilliant.

Violin concerto in D min.
☞ (M) *** Teldec/Warner Dig. 4509 91444-2 [id.]. Zehetmair, Philh. O, Eschenbach – DVORAK: *Concerto* etc. **(*)

Thomas Zehetmair is perfectly cast for the Schumann *Concerto*. He understands the central European tradition and makes the very most of the comparatively weak first movement. The *Langsam* slow movement is glorious (Schumann seemingly at his most inspired) and even the erratic finale is made to sound jolly and not too disjointed. Eschenbach accompanies sympathetically and the recording is excellent. This is the finest version of this work currently available.

Fantasy in C for violin and orchestra, Op. 131.
☞ (M) *** Teldec/Warner Dig. 4509 91443-2 [id.]. Zehetmair, Philh. O, Eschenbach – BRAHMS: *Concerto.* **(*)

Having given us a splendid account of the *Violin concerto*, Zehetmair and Eschenbach turn to the even rarer *Fantasy*, written as a birthday present for Clara when she reached 34. It is not a masterpiece, but its lyrical inspiration is strong and its structure convincing. Excellent playing and fine recording.

Introduction and allegro appassionato in G, Op. 92.
*** Decca Dig. 417 802-2 [id.]. András Schiff, VPO, Dohnányi – DVORAK: *Piano concerto.* **(*)

The *Introduction and allegro appassionato in G major* brings the full flowering of Schumann's romanticism. Schiff and Dohnányi play it with dedication and commitment, and the recording, while favouring the soloist, is more realistic in balance than for the Dvořák coupling.

Overture, Genoveva.
☞ ** (M) mono BMG/RCA GD 60682. Boston SO, Munch – BRAHMS: *Symphony No. 2* etc. **

The *Genoveva overture* was recorded in mono in 1951, not long after Munch took over from Koussevitzky. Something of the Koussevitzky sonority remains, particularly in the quality and refinement of the strings. A good performance, coupled with an impressive account in early stereo of the Brahms *Second Symphony*.

Overture, scherzo and finale in E, Op. 52.
(B) *** DG 431 161-2. BPO, Karajan – BRAHMS: *Symphony No. 1.* ***

This serves merely as a bonus for Karajan's fine 1964 recording of the Brahms *First Symphony* and this performance is second to none.

Symphonies Nos. 1–4.
(M) *** DG 429 672-2 (2) [id.]. BPO, Karajan.
☞ (B) ** Ph. Duo 438 341-2 (2) [id.]. New Philh. O, Inbal.
☞ (B) ** Erato/Warner Duo Dig. 4509 95357-2 (2) [id.]. SRO, Jordan.

Symphonies Nos. 1–4; Overtures: Genoveva; Manfred.
☞ (B) *** DG Double 437 395-2 (2). BPO, Kubelik.

Symphonies Nos. 1 in B flat (Spring), Op. 38; 2 in C, Op. 61.
☞ (B) *** Sony SBK 48269 [id.]. Bav. RSO, Kubelik.

Symphonies Nos. 3 in E flat (Rhenish), Op. 97; 4 in D min., Op. 120; Overture Manfred, Op. 115.
☞ (B) *** Sony SBK 48270 [id.]. Bav. RSO, Kubelik.

Symphonies Nos. 1–4; Overture, scherzo and finale, Op. 52.
☞ (M) *** EMI CMS7 64815-2 (2) [id.]. Dresden State O, Sawallisch.

Symphonies Nos. 1–4; Scenes from Goethe's Faust: Overture.
☞ (M) ** EMI CMS7 63613-2 (2) [id.]. New Philh. O or Philh. O, Klemperer.

The Dresden CDs of the Schumann *Symphonies* under Sawallisch are as deeply musical as they are carefully considered; the orchestral playing combines superb discipline with refreshing naturalness and spontaneity. Sawallisch catches all Schumann's varying moods, and his direction has splendid vigour. These recordings have dominated the catalogue, alongside Karajan's, for some years and they are most welcome on CD. Although the reverberant acoustic brought a degree of edge to the upper strings, the sound-picture has the essential fullness which the Karajan transfers lack, and the remastering has cleaned up the upper range to a considerable extent. The set now appears in a mid-priced box and the individual CDs have been restored: CDM7 69471-2 (*Symphonies Nos. 1 & 4; Overture, scherzo and finale*) and CDM7 69472-2 (*Symphonies Nos. 2–3*).

Karajan's interpretations of the Schumann *Symphonies* stand above all other modern recordings. No. 1 is a beautifully shaped performance, with orchestral playing of the highest distinction; No. 2 is among the most powerful ever recorded, combining poetic intensity and intellectual strength in equal proportions; and No. 3 is also among the most impressive versions ever commited to disc: its famous fourth-movement evocation of Cologne Cathedral is superbly spacious and eloquent, with quite magnificent brass playing. No. 4 can be classed alongside Furtwängler's famous record, with Karajan similarly inspirational, yet a shade more self-disciplined than his illustrious predecessor. However, the reissued complete set brings digital remastering which – as with the Brahms symphonies – has leaner textures than before, while in tuttis the violins above the stave may approach shrillness.

Kubelik's earlier set on DG is beautifully played and well recorded. The readings have not the drive of Karajan, notably in No. 4, but have both eloquence and warmth. They are straightforward, unmannered and recorded in a spacious acoustic with good CD transfers. With the two overtures also very well played as a bonus, this is a real bargain on the Double DG label.

At bargain price, Kubelik's fine Sony set remains fully competitive. The recording was made in the Hercules-Saal, Munich, in 1979, and the advantages of that glowing acoustic can be felt in the great cathedral evocation of the fourth movement and the famous link to the finale of the *Fourth*, where the Bavarian brass is very impressive. The orchestral playing is generally very fine (if not quite as polished as the Berlin Philharmonic) and is especially eloquent in the spacious slow movements. Tempi are particularly apt (witness the pacing of the *Allegro animato e grazioso* finale of the *Spring Symphony*). These are strongly characterized readings with plenty of life and vitality which display the same bright and alert sensitivity to Schumann's style as did his earlier set for DG (which we have always admired). But the Sony recording is obviously more modern, and the latest CD transfer brings plenty of body to the sound and a better focus to the violins than in the Sawallisch set. That more logically includes the *Overture, scherzo and finale*, but many will count the *Manfred overture* an equally desirable alternative.

Inbal's Philips set comes from the early 1970s and the sound is slightly more refined than with Kubelik, but not more vivid. Originally it was on three CDs and included both the *Overture, scherzo and finale* and the fascinating early *Zwickau Symphony*, which has been abandoned for this bargain reissue. The performances are what one might call eminently serviceable but ultimately wanting the last ounce of distinction.

There is not much that is springlike about Klemperer's reading of No. 1. The opening is tremendously spacious and unsmiling, though the allegro itself has plenty of affectionate touches and a lightish rhythm. Needless to say, the orchestral playing is of high quality with the woodwind particularly distinguished. The lack of geniality is a drawback but it would be wrong to give the impression that the performance is merely heavy-handed. There are many touches that underline the strength of Schumann's thinking in a way that other conductors fail to do. It certainly emerges as a weightier document than it does in either the Kubelik or Jordan versions, even though they both display greater fire and urgency. Klemperer's determinedly measured approach is much less effective in No. 2 and the slow movement refuses to take off, while the *Rhenish* is again massively individual. Here the music is great enough to stand the conductor's heavy treatment, but the performance misses far too much of the exhilaration of Schumann's inspiration. The *Fourth Symphony* is a different matter and needs a separate reissue. It is a masterly performance, giving the symphony a special stature. Klemperer's slow introduction has a weight and consequence that immediately command attention, and the slow tempo for the allegro is equally weighty and compelling, even if initially one disagrees with it. The Scherzo with its striking main theme packs enormous punch, and the brief slow movement is exquisitely played. For the finale Klemperer's speed is faster than many and he makes the conclusion most exciting. Plainly the Philharmonia players were on their toes throughout: the intensity of Klemperer's conviction comes over in shaping of phrases that is often quite breathtaking. The transfers are generally well managed: the quality in the *Second* and *Third Symphonies* is less open and transparent.

No one can say that Jordan's performances lack zest; indeed at times, and especially in Nos. 1 and 4, he presses on with an urgency that is almost out of character. These readings lack the very gravitas that becomes an exaggerated feature with Klemperer. Jordan secures excellent, fresh playing from the Suisse Romande Orchestra and he has the advantage of well-balanced, modern, digital sound which makes orchestral textures sound airy, yet with fair weight, when required, from the brass. In the last resort the *Spring symphony* sounds a little anonymous, for all its vitality, although the *Larghetto* has a certain restrained eloquence. In the *Second* the slow movement passionately develops a full head of romantic steam. But Jordan is most impressive of all in the surging current of the opening movement of the *Rhenish Symphony*, and the cathedral-arched slow movement has genuine ardour, even if the Swiss brass cannot match the sonority which Karajan finds in Berlin or Sawallisch in Dresden. The *Fourth*, too, is vibrantly done (especially the energetic Scherzo), while the *Romanze* makes a charming interlude. But in preparing for the finale, the slow crescendo as the brass take over seems over-subtle and without the kind of tension that made Furtwängler's performance so riveting. These discs are inexpensive and undoubtedly good value, and it is to be regretted that, as usual with these Erato Bonsai Duo reissues, the ship is spoilt by the lack of a ha'porth of documentation about the music.

Symphony No. 1 in B flat (Spring), Op. 38.
(B) *** DG 429 158-2 [id.]. BPO, Karajan – MENDELSSOHN: *Symphony No. 4.* ***

Karajan's splendid bargain version of No. 1 is clean and clear and has weight too.

Symphonies Nos. 1; 3 in E flat (Rhenish), Op. 97.
(BB) *** ASV Dig. CDQS 6073 [id.]. RLPO, Janowski.

Janowski's pairing of the *Spring* and *Rhenish symphonies* is particularly successful. The pacing throughout both symphonies is most convincing, with a good deal of the inspirational pull that makes the Karajan readings so telling. In the Cologne Cathedral evocation of the *Rhenish*, the Liverpool brass rise sonorously to the occasion and the recording is altogether first class, bright, clear and full, with a concert hall ambience. At super-bargain price, this is strongly competitive.

Symphony No. 2 in C, Op. 61.
(M) *** DG 435 067-2 [id.]. BPO, Karajan – BRAHMS: *Symphony No. 2.* ***

Karajan's powerful account of Schumann's *C major Symphony* has great eloquence and is marvellously played. The recording here sounds rather more expansive than in the boxed set.

Symphony Nos. 2; 3 in E flat (Rhenish), Op. 97.
*** DG Dig. 423 625-2 [id.]. BPO, Levine.
(B) *** DG 429 520-2 [id.]. BPO, Kubelik.

Levine conducts warm and positive readings of both *Symphonies*, drawing superb playing from the Berlin Philharmonic. Though the Berlin recording is warm and full to match – allowing thrilling crescendos in the Cologne Cathedral movement of the *Rhenish* – the inner textures are not ideally clear. The compensation is that the modern digital recording gives a satisfyingly full body to the sound.

An excellent bargain coupling from Kubelik. No. 2 is beautifully played and eloquently shaped, and in the *Rhenish* Kubelik's straightforward, unmannered approach, coupled to a natural warmth, provides a musical and thoroughly enjoyable account.

Symphonies Nos. 2; 4 in D min., Op. 120.
☞ (BB) ** ASV CDQS 6084 [id.]. RLPO, Janowski.

This is a less successful coupling than Janowski's companion recordings of Nos. 1 and 3. No. 2 comes off better than No. 4, with some fine, expressive playing from the Liverpool strings in the *Adagio* and an exciting finale. There is no lack of freshness elsewhere. No. 4 is fast. Janowski does not relax enough to let the first movement's lyrical blossoming take the fullest effect. There is more poise in the *Romanze* (and some fine wind playing too), but the finale is pushed forward rather aggressively and the accelerandos at the end of both outer movements sound unspontaneous.

Symphony No. 3 in E flat (Rhenish), Op. 97.
(M) *** DG Dig. 427 818-2 [id.]. LAPO, Giulini – SCHUBERT: *Symphony No. 8 (Unfinished).* *** ✪
☞ *** BMG/RCA Dig. 09026 61876-2. N. German RSO, Wand – SCHUBERT: *Symphony No. 3.*
***

Giulini's *Rhenish* is completely free of interpretative exaggeration and its sheer musical vitality and nobility of spirit are beautifully conveyed. The Los Angeles players produce a very well-blended, warm and cultured sound that is a joy to listen to in itself. The recording is extremely fine, too.

Günter Wand's account of the *Rhenish* has integrity; it is straightforward and direct and in the Cologne Cathedral movement has no want of dignity. A cult figure in London in recent years, Wand is never pedestrian or *kapellmeister*ish, but at the same time he does not often rise to the heights of inspiration as his admirers tell us. Here he is in excellent form, and the recordings are both spacious and present. A firm recommendation if you want this particular coupling, but he does not displace Karajan, Sawallisch or Kubelik in Schumann.

Symphonies Nos. 3 in E flat (Rhenish); 4 in D min., Op. 120.
*** EMI CDC7 54025-2 [id.]. L. Classical Players, Norrington.

Norrington not only clarifies textures, with natural horns in particular standing out dramatically, but, at unexaggerated speeds for the outer movements – even a little too slow for the first movement of No. 3 – the results are often almost Mendelssohnian. Middle movements in both symphonies are unusually brisk, turning slow movements into lyrical interludes. Warm, atmospheric recording.

CHAMBER MUSIC

Abendlied, Op. 85/2; Adagio and allegro in A flat, Op. 70; Fantasiestücke, Op. 73; 3 Romances, Op. 94; 3 Pieces in Folk style, Op. 102/2–4.
(M) *** Ph. 426 386-2. Heinz Holliger, Alfred Brendel.

The three *Romances* are specifically for oboe, but Holliger suggests that the others too are suitable for oboe, since the composer himself gave different options. One misses something by not having a horn in the *Adagio and allegro*, a cello in the folk-style pieces, or a clarinet in the *Fantasiestücke* (the oboe d'amore is used here); but Holliger has never sounded more magical on record and, with superbly real recording and deeply imaginative accompaniment, the result is an unexpected revelation.

Adagio and allegro for horn and piano, Op. 70.
(M) *** Decca 433 695-2 [id.]. Barry Tuckwell, Vladimir Ashkenazy – BRAHMS: *Horn trio;* FRANCK: *Violin sonata;* SAINT-SAENS: *Romance.* ***

Adagio and allegro for horn and piano, Op. 70; (i) Andante and variations, Op. 46.
☞ **(*) Decca 433 850-2 [id.]. Radovan Vlatković, Vladimir Ashkenazy; (i) with Georg & Mathias Donderer, Vovka Ashkenazy – BRAHMS: *Horn trio.* **

Schumann's *Adagio and allegro* requires ripe romantic feeling and considerable virtuosity from the horn soloist. Needless to say, both these requirements are readily met by Barry Tuckwell and Vladimir Ashkenazy, and these artists create a fine artistic partnership. The 1974 Kingsway Hall recording cannot be faulted.

The *Adagio and allegro* is warmly played by Radovan Vlatkovic and Ashkenazy and is an effective enough piece, but the *Andante and variations*, Op. 46, for horn, two cellos and two pianos, although agreeable enough, tends to outlast its welcome although it receives persuasive advocacy. The recording is warm and atmospheric.

Fantasiestücke, Op. 73; 3 Romances, Op. 94.
*** Chan. Dig. CHAN 8506; ABTD 1216 [id.]. Gervase de Peyer, Gwenneth Pryor – SCHUBERT: *Arpeggione sonata;* WEBER: *Silvana variations.* ***

With warmth of tone and much subtlety of colour, Gervase de Peyer gives first-class performances and is well supported by Gwenneth Pryor. The recording is most realistic.

Fantasiestücke, Op. 73; 5 Stücke in Volkston, Op. 102.
*** Ph. Dig. 412 230-2 [id.]. Maisky, Argerich – SCHUBERT: *Arpeggione sonata.* ***

Mischa Maisky and Martha Argerich give relaxed, leisurely accounts of these pieces that some collectors may find almost self-indulgent. Others will luxuriate in the refinement and sensitivity of this playing.

Märchenbilder, Op. 113.
☞ *** Virgin/EMI Dig. VC7 59309-2 [id.]. Lars Anders Tomter, Leif Ove Andsnes – BRAHMS: *Viola sonatas.* *** ⊛
**(*) Chan. Dig. CHAN 8550; *ABTD 1256* [id.]. Imai, Vignoles – BRAHMS: *Viola sonatas.* **(*)

The young Norwegian duo bring great sensitivity and freshness to bear on the *Märchenbilder*, and their playing gives great pleasure, as does the Brahms coupling.

The *Märchenbilder* are pleasing miniatures, persuasively played here by Nobuko Imai and Roger Vignoles. The recording acoustic is not ideal, but this does not seriously detract from the value of this coupling.

Piano quartets: in C min.; in E flat, Op. 47.
☞ **(*) BMG/RCA Dig. 09026 61384-2 [id.]. André Previn, Young Uck Kim, Heichiro Ohyama, Gary Hoffman.

The *E flat Piano quartet* has never captured the public imagination to anything like the same extent as the *Piano quintet*, but it has still enjoyed fair exposure in the LP and CD catalogues. The present issue, however, enjoys a special claim on Schumann lovers in that it unearths a rarity in the form of the *C minor Quartet*, written in 1829 when Schumann was still in his teens. Schumann did not think sufficiently well of it to allot an opus number to the piece, and it languished unpublished for 150 years until 1979 when Wolfgang Boetticher prepared an edition. It is not the strongest Schumann and, given the fact that at 47 minutes this CD represents short measure, any recommendation is inevitably qualified. It is a pity that the accomplished team could not have found time to fit an additional work into their sessions.

Piano quartet in E flat, Op. 47; (i) Piano quintet in E flat, Op. 44.
*** Ph. 420 791-2 [id.]. Beaux Arts Trio, Rhodes, (i) with Bettelheim.
**(*) CRD CRD 3324; *CRDC 4024* [id.]. Rajna, members of the Alberni Qt.

The Beaux Arts Trio (with associates) give splendid performances of both these fine chamber works. The vitality of inspiration is consistently brought out, and with that goes the Beaux Arts' characteristic concern for fine ensemble and refined textures. The recording is beautifully clear and clean.

Though not quite so flawlessly polished in their playing, Rajna and the Alberni give performances that in their way are as urgent and enjoyable as those on the Philips disc. The recording is brighter and crisper, which gives an extra (and not unlikeable) edge to the performances.

Piano quintet in E flat, Op. 44.
(BB) *** Naxos Dig. 8.550406; *4550406* [id.]. Jenö Jandó, Kodály Qt – BRAHMS: *Piano quintet.* ***

A strongly characterized performance of Schumann's fine *Quintet* from Jenö Jandó and the Kodály Quartet. This is robust music-making, romantic in spirit, and its spontaneity is well projected by a vivid recording, made in an attractively resonant acoustic. With its comparable Brahms coupling, this makes an excellent bargain.

Piano trios Nos. 1 in D min., Op. 63; 2 in F, Op. 80; 3 in G min., Op. 110; Fantasiestücke in A min., Op. 88.
**(*) Chan. Dig. CHAN 8832/3; *DBTD 2020* (2) [id.]. Borodin Trio.

These are full-hearted performances that give undoubted pleasure – and would give more, were it not for some swoons from Rostislav Dubinsky who, at the opening of the *D minor Trio*, phrases with a rather ugly scoop. While too much should not be made of this, greater reticence would have been more telling throughout. The Chandos recording is vivid and faithful.

Piano trio No. 1 in D min., Op. 63.
**(*) CRD CRD 3433; *CRDC 4133* [id.]. Israel Piano Trio – BRAHMS: *Piano trio No. 2.* **(*)

The Israel Piano Trio give a powerfully projected account of the *D minor Trio*; the pianist is at times rather carried away, as if he were playing a Brahms concerto. There are, however, some sensitive and intelligent touches, and the recording is first class.

Funf Stücke (5 Pieces) im Volkston (for cello and piano).
(M) *** Decca 417 833-2 [id.]. Rostropovich, Britten – SCHUBERT: *Sonata* **(*); DEBUSSY: *Sonata.*
***

In the hands of masters, these *Five Pieces in folk style* have a rare charm, particularly the last, with its irregular rhythm. Excellent recording.

String quartets Nos. 1–3.
**(*) DG Dig. 423 670-2 (3). Melos Qt – BRAHMS: *String quartets 1–3* **(*).

The Melos performances, for all their ardour, do not seem completely at one with Schumann's world: there is a certain want of tenderness and introspection. Perhaps the brightly lit and forward recording militates against them, and at present they come linked only with Brahms.

String quartets Nos. 1 in A min.; 2 in F, Op. 41/1–2.
*** CRD CRD 3333; *CRDC 4033* [id.]. Alberni Qt.

The *String quartets* are not Schumann at his greatest, but they still offer many rewards. These well-recorded and sympathetic performances by the Alberni Quartet have plenty of finesse and charm and are guided throughout by sound musical instinct. Recommended.

Violin sonatas Nos. 1 in A min., Op. 105; 2 in D min., Op. 121.
*** DG Dig. 419 235-2 [id.]. Gidon Kremer, Martha Argerich.

The *Violin sonatas* both date from 1851 and are 'an oasis of freshness' in his last creative period. Kremer and Argerich are splendidly reflective and mercurial by turn and have the benefit of an excellent recording.

PIANO MUSIC

Abegg variations, Op. 1; Davidsbündlertänze, Op. 6.
☞ *** Ottavio Dig. OTRC 39027 [id.]. Imogen Cooper – BRAHMS: *Fantasias, Op. 116.* ***

This is among the most delectable of recent Schumann recitals. Imogen Cooper plays the *Abegg variations* with a rare combination of iridescent brilliance and poetic feeling, and she characterizes the *Davidsbündlertänze* with consistent imagination and colour. She is gently ravishing in the gentler numbers like *Innig* and the lovely closing *Nicht Schnell*, yet catches the robust geniality of *Mit Humour* without a hint of heaviness. The playing is spontaneous from first to last, and the recording most realistic.

Abegg variations, Op. 1; Fantasiestücke, Op. 12; March in G min., Op. 76/2; Novellette in F, Op. 21/1; Toccata in C, Op. 7; Waldszenen, Op. 82.
☞ (M) *** DG mono 435 751-2 [id.]. Sviatoslav Richter.

It was his 1956 DG mono LP of the *Waldszenen*, six of the *Fantasiestücken* and the *G minor March*, Op. 76, which served as Richter's visiting card in the West. Alec Robertson hailed his triumphant entry on the scene in the *Gramophone* magazine, and other great discs soon followed including the *Toccata* (1959) and the *Abegg variations* (1962). His supreme pianism shines through the years and, although the sound shows its age, it is an improvement over the original LP. The three stars are for the performances; some allowance must be made for the sound-quality.

Albumblätter, Op. 99; Arabeske, Op. 18; Etudes symphoniques, Op. 13.
(BB) *** Naxos Dig. 8.550144 [id.]. Stefan Vladar.

Stefan Vladar intersperses the additional studies that Schumann published as an appendix into the *Etudes symphoniques*. His account is quite simply superb in every respect and deserves recording of comparable excellence. His account of the *Albumblätter* is hardly less masterly. Artistically this rates three stars, with the compelling quality of the playing transcending the sonic limitations of the recording.

Allegro, Op. 8; Gesänge der Frühe, Op. 133; Novelletten, Op. 21; 3 Fantasiestücke, Op. 111.
☞ **(*) Olympia Dig. OCD 436 [id.]. Ronald Brautigam.

As the opening *Allegro* shows, this is strong, spontaneously impulsive playing and in the *Novelletten* some might wish for less passion and more poise. However, there is poetry too, the second and, especially, the third of the *Fantasiestücke* are very appealing. The *Gesänge der Frühe* ('Morning songs') – Schumann's last completed piano work, written in 1853 only months before his attempted suicide – brings the most responsive playing of all and is most touchingly done. Clear, bold piano recording.

Arabesque in C, Op. 18; Blumenstück, Op. 19; Carnaval, Op. 9; Davidsbündlertänze, Op. 6; Fantasia in C, Op. 17; 8 Fantasiestücke, Op. 12; 3 Fantasiestücke, Op. 111; Faschingsschwank aus Wien, Op. 26; Humoresque in B flat, Op. 20; Kinderszenen, Op. 15; 4 Nachtstücke, Op. 23; Novelletten, Op. 21; Papillons, Op. 2; 3 Romances, Op. 28; Piano sonatas Nos. 1 in F sharp min., Op. 11; 2 in G min., Op. 22; Waldszenen, Op. 82.
(M) **(*) Ph. 402 308-2 (7) [id.]. Claudio Arrau.

Claudio Arrau's playing has warmth, poise and the distinctive, aristocratic finesse that graced everything this artist touched. Arrau has the measure of Schumann's impulsive temperament and is almost always perfectly attuned to his sensibility. Not all the rubati ring true and there are moments that seem a little self-conscious. But there is a very great deal to admire in this compilation, and few collectors will be greatly disappointed.

Arabeske in C, Op. 18; Faschingsschwank aus Wien, Op. 26; Kreisleriana, Op. 16.
☞ (BB) *(*) Naxos Dig. 8.550783 [id.]. Jenö Jandó.

Carnaval, Op. 9; Kinderszenen, Op. 15; Papillons, Op. 2.
☞ (BB) ** Naxos Dig. 8.550784 [id.]. Jenö Jandó.

After his successful Beethoven and Haydn recordings, Jandó's Schumann is disappointing. He is inclined to fast tempi and is too impulsive by half, and the result – not helped by the bold, bright piano-sound – often becomes aggressive. *Kinderszenen* and *Carnaval* both have moments of poetry and display considerable virtuosity, but the former hardly ever seems to inhabit the innocent world of children. The opening of *Kreisleriana* and the *Finale* of *Faschingsschwank aus Wien* bring much dash but not nearly enough poise, and *Papillons*, too, needs a less forthright approach.

Arabeske in C, Op. 18; Etudes symphoniques, Op. 13.
*** DG Dig. 410 916-2 [id.]. Maurizio Pollini.

Pollini's account has a symphonic gravitas and concentration: it also has the benefit of excellent recorded sound. Pollini includes the five additional variations that Schumann omitted from both the editions published during his lifetime, placing them as a group between the fifth and sixth variations.

Arabeske, Op. 18; Etudes symphoniques, Op. 13; Papillons, Op. 2.
*** Decca Dig. 414 474-2 [id.]. Vladimir Ashkenazy.

Impressive playing, and well recorded too – yet Ashkenazy's *Etudes symphoniques* have a breadth and splendour that are not entirely in tune with Schumann's sensibility. The *Arabeske* and *Papillons*, however, must be numbered among Ashkenazy's most impressive contributions to this repertoire.

Blumenstück, Op. 19; 4 Fugues, Op. 72; March No. 2, Op. 76/2; Nachtstücke, Op. 23; Toccata, Op. 7.
☞ *** Decca Dig. 436 456-2 [id.]. Sviatoslav Richter.
A superb recital, recorded, with great fidelity, in Mantua in 1986. The programme makes a particularly satisfying whole, opening with the four diverse *Fugues* (not a bit pedagogic), on through the ebullient *March*, to the exhilaratingly joyful *Toccata*, and the meltingly characteristic *Blumenstück* – where Richter is at his most magically poetic. The recital ends with the comparatively rare *Nachtstücke*, in four sections ranging over the widest range of mood. It opens with another, essentially unassertive, little march that is played with the most subtle range of colour. This is Schumann playing of the highest distinction.

Blumenstück, Op. 19; Kreisleriana, Op. 16; Waldszenen, Op. 82.
☞ (BB) * Naxos Dig. 8.550401 [id.]. Paul Gulda.

Naxos have enriched the catalogue with many bargains which combine both artistic and decent technical quality. Paul Gulda's recital is not one of them. He is short on charm and (at least in *Kreisleriana*) long on rubato. Of course, he is an accomplished player and there are good things in the course of his recital, but both the performances and the recording fall well short of distinction.

Carnaval; Faschingsschwank aus Wien, Op. 26; Kinderszenen, Op. 15.
(B) *** DG 431 167-2. Daniel Barenboim.
Barenboim's 1979 reading of *Carnaval* is one of his finest recording achievements in his role as pianist rather than as conductor. His lively imagination lights on the fantasy in this quirkily spontaneous sequence of pieces and makes them sparkle anew. *Carnival jest from Vienna* is more problematic, but the challenge inspires Barenboim, and here too he is at his most imaginative and persuasive, bringing out the warmth and tenderness as well as the brilliance. The recital opens with a tender and

charismatic reading of *Kinderszenen*. The 1979 recording is bold and truthful, but the CD transfer has lost a little of the fullness in the bass.

Carnaval, Op. 9; Nachtstücke, Op. 23; Waldszenen, Op. 82.
☞ * BMG/RCA Dig. 09026 60977-2. Gerhard Oppitz.

Much admired in Germany, Gerhard Oppitz has enviable representation in the catalogue, though his complete Brahms on this label did not enjoy universal acclaim and was certainly not well received in our last volume. His Schumann recital is curiously anonymous – indeed, much of it is prosaic to the point of being purely matter-of-fact. Curiously unidiomatic and unimaginative performances – surprisingly so, given the respect in which he is held.

Davidsbündlertänze, Op. 6; Sonata No. 2 in G min., Op. 22; Toccata, Op. 7.
☞ *** Teldec/Warner Dig. 9031 77476 [id.]. Boris Berezovsky.

Boris Berezovsky was the First Prizewinner of the last Moscow Tchaikovsky Prize (he also did very well at Leeds a year or so earlier) and is a keyboard lion of the first order. Everything we have so far heard of his has been of exceptional artistry and great finesse. His formidable musicianship is allied to a technique of magisterial calibre (he is arguably second only to Pletnev among young Tchaikovsky Prizewinners) and this coupling is very impressive indeed.

5 Etudes, Op. posth.; Etudes symphoniques, Op. 13; Papillons, Op. 2.
**(*) Sony CD 76635 [MK 34539]. Murray Perahia.

Murray Perahia has a special feeling for the *Symphonic studies*. He also plays the additional five studies, which Schumann omitted from the published score, as an addendum. The *Papillons* are unlikely to be surpassed but the engineers give Perahia too close a balance to be ideal.

Etudes symphoniques.
*** Ph. Dig. 432 093-2; *432 093-4* [id.]. Alfred Brendel – BEETHOVEN: *Variations.* ***
☞ ** Olympia OCD 339 [id.]. Richter – BEETHOVEN: *6 Variations in D & F* etc. (*)

Brendel's new account of the *Etudes symphoniques* is one of his best records for a long time. This is ardent, beautifully controlled playing which is also given first-class sound.

Richter's performance dates from 1971 and is distinguished. The recording is not as poor as in some of the Beethoven variation sets with which the *Studies* are coupled, but it is far from first class. Three stars for Richter, and one for the recording makes two altogether.

Etudes symphoniques, Op. 13; Intermezzi, Op. 4; Sonata No. 2 in G min., Op. 22; Toccata, Op. 7.
☞ *** Conifer Dig. CDCF 227 [id.]. Mikhail Kazakevich.

Born in 1959, Mikhail Kazakevich is a young Russian pianist of the generation of Pletnev and Demidenko. This Schumann recital, his first recording for a Western label, bodes well. He has a natural feeling for both the virtuosic pianism and fervour of Schumann together with inwardness and poetic insight. Indeed his is one of the finest accounts of the *G minor Sonata* and the *Etudes symphoniques* to have appeared in recent years, perhaps even since Perahia's classic recordings. In terms of technical address and subtlety of colouring, Kazakevivh is the equal of Demidenko and refrains from interposing his considerable personality between the composer and the listener. The recording is good though just a trifle shallow at times. As this is his CD début, there is a sampler disc included, offering Brahms, Bach and his own piano transcription of the Scherzo of Mahler's *First Symphony*, all presumably on the way.

Fantasia in C, Op. 17.
*** Sony Dig. MK 42124 [id.]. Murray Perahia – SCHUBERT: *Wanderer fantasia.* ***

Murray Perahia's account of the *C major Fantasy* is a performance of vision and breadth, immaculate in its attention to detail and refinement of nuance. The recording is good, even if it does not wholly convey the fullest range of sonority and dynamics.

Fantasia in C, Op. 17; Fantasiestücke, Op. 12.
*** Ph. Dig. 411 049-2 [id.]. Alfred Brendel.

As the very opening of the *Fantasiestücke* demonstrates, this is magically spontaneous playing, full of imaginative touches of colour. The sound truthfully conveys the depth of timbre.

Fantasia in C, Op. 17; Faschingsschwank aus Wien (Carnival jest from Vienna), Op. 26; Papillons, Op. 2.
☞ (M) *** EMI CDM7 64625-2 [id.]; *EG 764625-4*. Sviatoslav Richter.

Richter's account of the *Fantasia in C* was recorded at Abbey Road in 1961. It is a wonderfully poetic performance of a great masterpiece of the piano repertoire. Richter's phrasing, his magnificent control of dynamics (especially in those typically Schumannesque accompanimental arpeggios), his gift for seeing a large-scale work as a whole – all these contribute towards the impression of unmatchable strength and vision. The recording is faithful, with genuine presence. The other two works included on this CD were recorded live during Richter's Italian concert tour a year later. The piano sound inevitably is somewhat less sonorous, shallower at fortissimo level, but fully acceptable, when the playing is so masterly and spontaneous. The account of *Papillons* is beguilingly subtle in control of colour.

Fantasiestücke, Op. 12; Kinderszenen, Op. 15; Kreisleriana, Op. 16.
☞ (M) *** Ph. Dig. 434 732-2 [id.]. Alfred Brendel.

Fantasiestücke is strong as well as poetic. The *Kinderszenen* is also one of the finest performances of the 1980s and is touched with real distinction. Brendel's *Kreisleriana* is intelligent and finely characterized. He is better recorded (in 1981/2) than most of his rivals and, though certain details may strike listeners as less spontaneous, the overall impression is highly persuasive.

Fantasia in C, Op. 17; Kreisleriana, Op. 16.
☞ (M) *** BMG/RCA 09026 61264-2 [id.]. Artur Rubinstein.

Rubinstein's account of the *Fantasia in C* is wonderfully subtle in its control of tempo and colour, and the poetry of the outer sections is quite magical. In spite of the close balance, Rubinstein achieves exquisite gradations of tone; the recording, made in 1965, is among the best he received during this period. *Kreisleriana* is hardly less compelling, with the great pianist at his most aristocratic, although the impetuous opening is recorded rather shallowly.

Fantasia in C, Op. 17; Piano sonata No. 1 in F sharp min., Op. 11.
*** DG 423 134-2 [id.]. Maurizio Pollini.

This is among the most distinguished Schumann records in the catalogue. Pollini's playing throughout has a command and authority on the one hand and deep poetic feeling on the other that hold the listener spellbound. The recording is good but not outstanding.

Humoreske in B flat, Op. 20.
(BB) **(*) Naxos Dig. 8.550469 [id.]. Wolf Harden – REGER: *Variations.* **(*)

Wolf Harden's performance of the Schumann *Humoreske* is highly imaginative, idiomatic and full of sensitive touches. There is plenty of air round the aural image.

Kinderszenen, Op. 15; Sonata No. 1 in F sharp min., Op. 11; Waldszenen, Op. 82.
*** Decca Dig. 421 290-2 [id.]. Vladimir Ashkenazy.

Ashkenazy has his finger(s) on the pulse of Schumann's inspiration. The playing is very natural and all the more impressive for that. He proves a sound guide in the *Waldszenen*, and his *Kinderszenen* is one of the most appealing in the catalogue, again with a naturalness and directness that are attractive. The Decca recording is excellent.

Kreisleriana, Op. 16; Novelette, Op. 21/8; Piano sonata No. 2 in G min., Op. 22.
**(*) Decca Dig. 425 940-2 [id.]. Vladimir Ashkenazy.

Vladimir Ashkenazy turns in a very fervent account of *Kreisleriana*, which is probably the best thing on this CD. In the *G minor Sonata, Op. 22* he is also highly charged, though he does not plumb its poetic depths and richness of fantasy to the same extent as does Perahia (see below). Decca's sound is of very good quality.

Piano sonata No. 2 in G min., Op. 22.
*** Sony Dig. MK 44569 [id.]. Murray Perahia – SCHUBERT: *Piano sonata No. 20.* ***
☞ (M) *(*) DG 437 252-2 [id.]. Martha Argerich – BRAHMS: *Rhapsodies* **(*); LISZT: *Sonata.* **

Perahia's account of the Schumann *G minor Sonata* is fresh, ardent and vital; every phrase is beautifully moulded yet somehow seems spontaneous in feeling – and spontaneity was the essence of Schumann's youthful genius. The recording places the listener fairly near the piano but is eminently truthful.

Argerich's impetuosity of approach is less suitable to Schumann than in the Liszt and Brahms couplings. Certainly here she keeps the music alive – something not all pianists are able to do in Schumann's piano repertoire – but the wide dynamic contrasts are sometimes inappropriate. There is no lack of impulse, but this degree of urgency (in the central section of the slow movement, for instance) seems out of style. The piano recording, too, lacks richness of sonority, though it does not lack presence.

ORGAN MUSIC

4 Sketches, Op. 58 (ed. Bate).
☞ (BB) *** ASV CDQS 6127 [id.]. Jennifer Bate (Royal Albert Hall organ) – LISZT: *Organ music.*
***

The *Four Sketches* were originally written for a piano with pedal attachment and are here arranged for organ by E. Power Biggs. Each of the pieces is in 3/4 time, but the writing is attractively diverse; they are pleasant trifles. Rich, atmospheric recording with fair detail, impressively transferred to CD. Generously coupled with Liszt's three major organ warhorses, this makes a very tempting super-bargain reissue.

VOCAL MUSIC

Lieder from *Album für die Jugend, Op. 79; Gedichte der Königen Maria Stuart, Op. 135; Myrthen Lieder, Op. 25:* excerpts. *Abends am Strand; Die Kartenlegerin; Ständchen; Stille Tränen; Veratine Liebe.*
*** CRD CRD 3401; *CRDC 4051* [id.]. Sarah Walker, Roger Vignoles.

Sarah Walker's 1982 Schumann collection is most cherishable, notably the five Mary Stuart songs which, in their brooding darkness, are among Schumann's most memorable. With superb accompaniment and splendid recording, this is an outstanding issue.

Dichterliebe, Op. 48.
(M) *** DG 429 933-2 [id.]. Fritz Wunderlich, Hubert Giesen – BEETHOVEN: *Lieder* **(*); SCHUBERT: *Lieder.* ***

Even with an often unimaginative accompanist, Wunderlich's freshness here is most endearing, irresistible with so golden a voice.

(i) *Dichterliebe, Op. 48;* (ii) *Frauenliebe und Leben, Op. 42.*
☞ (B) ** Analogue/Dig. DG 439 417-2 [id.]. (i) Dietrich Fischer-Dieskau, Christophe Eschenbach; (ii) Brigitte Fassbaender, Irwin Gage.

There are few enough bargain records of Lieder, and it is perhaps a pity that DG have chosen to couple two utterly different approaches to word-meanings. Fischer-Dieskau's earlier DG *Dichterliebe* (recorded between 1973 and 1977) is not quite as emotionally plangent as his later, digital version on Philips, but the contrasts between expressive warmth and a darker irony are still apparent. Eschenbach's accompaniment is always imaginative and the recording has fine presence. Fassbaender's account of the deeply moving female cycle is certainly strongly characterized, with a wide range of expression and fine detail, but she conveys little sense of vulnerability. She is undoubtedly involved, but clear exposition of the words seems to be this singer's prime aim and there is little attempt to beautify the voice – though it is a fine and consistent instrument. If the underlying sentimentality of the poems is here concealed, so is much else. Irwin Gage is an excellent accompanist and the digital recording is very vivid.

Dichterliebe, Op. 48; Liederkreis, Op. 39.
*** Ph. Dig. 416 352-2 [id.]. Dietrich Fischer-Dieskau, Alfred Brendel.
☞ (B) *** CfP CD-CFP 4651; *TC-CFP 4651.* Ian Partridge, Jennifer Partridge.
*** EMI CDC7 47397-2 [id.]. Olaf Bär, Geoffrey Parsons.

Fischer-Dieskau, in inspired collaboration with Alfred Brendel, brings an angry, inconsolable reading, reflecting the absence of fulfilment in the poet's love. The Op. 39 *Liederkreis* also brings inspired, spontaneous-sounding performances, with the voice here notably fresher.

Ian and Jennifer Partridge recorded this coupling in 1974. Blessed with a radiantly beautiful light voice, Ian's thoughtfulness illuminates every line, helped by superbly matched accompaniments. The recording is well balanced and truthful and is transferred most naturally to CD. A real bargain.

Olaf Bär's performances are not as strongly characterized readings as those of Fischer-Dieskau; but in their fresher, more youthful manner they are outstandingly successful. Excellent recording.

Dichterliebe (song-cycle), *Op. 48; Liederkreis* (song-cycle), *Op. 39; Myrthen Lieder, Op. 25.*
*** DG 415 190-2 [id.]. Dietrich Fischer-Dieskau, Christoph Eschenbach.

An outstandingly fine *Dichterliebe* plus the magnificent Op. 39 *Liederkreis*, made the more attractive on CD by the generous addition of seven of the *Myrthen* songs. Eschenbach is imaginative on detail without ever intruding distractingly. Very good sound for the period.

Frauenliebe und Leben (song-cycle), *Op. 42.*

⊛ (M) *** Saga SCD 9001 [id.]. Dame Janet Baker, Martin Isepp (with Lieder recital ***).

Janet Baker's range of expression in her earlier, Saga recording of the Schumann cycle runs the whole gamut from a joyful golden tone-colour in the exhilaration of *Ich kann's nicht fassen* through an ecstatic half-tone in *Süsser Freund* (the fulfilment of the line *Du geliebter Mann* wonderfully conveyed) to the dead, vibrato-less tone of agony at the bereavement in the final song. Martin Isepp proves a highly sensitive and supportive partner, and the recording balance – originally curiously artificial – has been immeasurably improved by the CD transfer.

Liederkreis, Op. 39; 12 Kerner-Lieder, Op. 35.

☞ *** Hyp. Dig. CDA 66596 [id.]. Margaret Price, Graham Johnson.

As a spin-off from Graham Johnson's Schubert recording with Margaret Price (No. 15 in the series) Johnson partners her here in a superb Schumann disc, coupling the sequence of 12 settings of Justinus Kerner, Op. 35, with the Eichendorff *Liederkreis*, Op. 39. The singer's presence, magnetism and weight of expression are superbly caught, and the tonal beauty and immaculate sense of line go with detailed imagination in word-pointing. So Price may underplay the horror of such a song from Opus 39 as *Waldesgesprach* about meeting the Lorelei, but the moment of confrontation is sharply pointed when legato is suddenly abandoned. The lesser-known *Kerner-Lieder* also contain many treasures. First-rate sound.

Lieder: *Der Hidalgo; Meine Rose; Der Spielmann.* Goethe Lieder: *An die Türen will ich schleichen; Lied Lynceus des Türmers; Der Sänger; Die wandelnde Glocke; Wer nie sein Brot mit Tränen; Wer sich der Einsamkeit ergibt.*

☞ (M) *** Decca 436 203-2 [id.]. Hermann Prey, Karl Engel – SCHUBERT: *Lieder.* ***

Like the coupled Schubert songs, these recordings are taken from two recitals, the Goethe Lieder dating from 1964 and the other three songs from two years earlier. Prey's thoughtful, conscientious style lends itself perfectly to these very varied and detailed songs which show Schumann's genius at its most intense. This is very fine singing indeed, and the recording is outstandingly real and vivid.

Mass in C min., Op. 147; Requiem für Mignon, Op. 98b.

☞ (B) *** Erato/Warner Dig. Duo 4509 95307-2 [id.]. Michael, Bizimeche-Elsinger, Silveira, Teiseira, Schoeffler, Brodard, Lisbon Gulbenkian Foundation Ch. & O, Corboz – SCHUBERT: *Mass No. 6.* ***

In 1852 Schumann had been proselytizing the music of Bach, including the *B minor Mass*, and perhaps that prompted the composition of his own *Mass in C minor*. It is a powerful work in which the chorus is all-important. The Lisbon singers rise to the challenge eloquently under Corboz, who is a persuasive exponent. He has good soloists, and Audrey Michael is particularly touching in the *Offertorium*, where she sings with a treble-like purity. The *Sanctus* which follows is also very fine. The less ambitious *Requiem für Mignon* is also very attractively done, with the matching of the female solo voices particularly pleasing. Excellent digital recording gives a natural projection and focus to the performers, and the only drawback to this excellent Erato Bonsai Duo set is the absence of documentation about the music, so necessary with rare repertoire of this kind.

Das Paradies und das Peri, Op. 50 (oratorio; complete).

**(*) Erato/Warner Dig. 2292 45456-2 (2). Edith Wiens, Sylvia Herman, Ann Gjevang, Robert Gambill, Christophe Prégardien, SRO Ch. & O, Armin Jordan.

Schumann described this oratorio as 'my greatest and, I hope, my best work'. Based on a quest poem by Thomas Moore, it centres on the heroine's search for gifts as a passport to heaven. The richness and the fluency of the writing carry you on with no let-up, strongly argued, but the melodic invention is less striking than in Schumann's songs, with themes plain rather than memorable. Armin Jordan draws first-rate singing and playing from his Suisse Romande forces, helped by warmly atmospheric recording. The soloists are reliable but not very distinctive.

(i) *Requiem in D flat, Op. 148;* (ii) *Requiem für Mignon, Op. 98b.*

☞ (B) *** EMI Dig. CZS7 67819-2 (2) [id.]. (i) Helen Donath, Doris Soffel, Nicolai Gedda; (i; ii) Dietrich Fischer-Dieskau; (ii) Brigitte Lindner, Andrea Andonian, Mechthild George, Monika Weichhold; Düsseldorf Musical Soc. Ch., Düsseldorf SO, Klee – BRAHMS: *German Requiem.* **(*)

Like Mozart, Schumann was unable to shake off the conviction that the *Requiem* was for himself. The opening *Requiem aeternam* is affecting and dignified, and the final *Benedictus* has a haunting eloquence. Bernhard Klee extracts a very sympathetic response from his distinguished team of soloists and the fine Düsseldorf chorus and orchestra. They also give an attentive and committed account of the 1849 *Requiem for Mignon*, Op. 98b. The EMI recording is natural and well balanced. This now comes in harness with Tennstedt's impressively spacious account of the Brahms *Requiem*.

Scenes from Goethe's Faust.
⊛ (M) *** Decca 425 705-2 (2). Harwood, Pears, Shirley-Quirk, Fischer-Dieskau, Vyvyan, Palmer, Aldeburgh Fest. Singers, ECO, Britten.

Though the episodic sequence of scenes is neither opera nor cantata, the power and imagination of much of the music, not least the delightful garden scene and the energetic setting of the final part, are immensely satisfying. In 1973, soon after a live performance at the Aldeburgh Festival, Britten inspired his orchestra and his fine cast of singers to vivid performances, which are outstandingly recorded against the warm Maltings acoustic. This is magnificent music, and readers are urged to explore it – the rewards are considerable.

Schurmann, Gerard (born 1928)

6 Studies of Francis Bacon for large orchestra; Variants for small orchestra.
☞ *** Chan. CHAN 9167 [id.]. BBC SO, composer.

Inspired by the fantastic, often violent or painful paintings of Francis Bacon, Schurmann here writes a virtuoso orchestral showpiece, full of colourful effects. The vigour of the writing is admirably caught in this performance under the composer, as it is too in the often spiky writing of the *Variants* for a rather smaller orchestra, set against passages of hushed beauty. First-rate 1979 recording, made in the warm acoustics of All-Saints', Tooting, and admirably transferred to CD.

Schütz, Heinrich (1585–1672)

Christmas oratorio (Weihnachtshistorie).
*** EMI Dig. CDC7 47633-2 [id.]. Kirkby, Rogers, Thomas, Taverner Cons., Taverner Ch., Taverner Players, Parrott – PRAETORIUS: *Christmas motets.* ***

There is no sense of austerity here, merely a sense of purity, with the atmosphere of the music beautifully captured by these forces under Andrew Parrott. One is soon gripped by the narrative and by the beauty and simplicity of the line.

(i) *Christmas oratorio;* (ii) *Deutsche Magnificat;* Motets for double choir: *Ach, Herr, straf mich nicht* (Psalm 6); *Cantate Domino* (Psalm 96); *Herr unser Herrscher* (Psalm 8); *Ich freu mich des* (Psalm 122); *Unser Herr Jesus; Wie lieblich* (Psalm 84).
(M) **(*) Decca 430 632-2 [id.]. (i) Partridge, soloists, Schütz Ch., Instrumental Ens., Philip Jones Brass Ens.; (ii) Schütz Ch., Symphoniae Sacrae Chamber Ens.; Norrington.

Norrington's Argo recording of the *Christmas oratorio* was made before he espoused the cause of original instruments. It offers some extremely fine singing from Ian Partridge as the Evangelist, while the Heinrich Schütz Choir phrases with great feeling and subtlety; indeed, some may feel that their singing is a little too self-consciously beautiful for music that is so pure in style. A similar comment might be made about the Motets. For all that, however, this offers much to admire, and the 1970 recording has great detail and sonority. The *Deutsche Magnificat* is given with admirable authority and is one of the best things in a very generous (75 minutes) and rewarding collection.

Christmas oratorio; Easter oratorio (Historia der Auferstehung Jesus Christi).
☞ *** Sony Dig. SK 45943 [id.]. Prégardien, Van der Sluis, Egeler, Kendall, Müller, Robson, Spägele, Stuttgart Chamber Ch., Cologne Musici Fiata, Stuttgart Bar. O, Bernius.

Bernius's fine account of the *Christmas oratorio* on Sony is certainly as good as any available, if not better, and enjoys the advantage of another major Schütz coupling, the *Historia der Auferstehung Jesus Christi*, a performance of exceptionally gripping quality. Schütz's second liturgical work after *The Psalms of David*, this *Easter oratorio* dates from 1623 and draws on both the text and the musical procedures of the *Easter Historia* by Antonio Scandello, one of Schütz's predecessors at Dresden. The work is one of grave, expressive beauty and a moving purity of utterance, and the performance here is excellent. It is more strongly projected than the inward and reposeful performance by René Jacobs and the Concerto Vocale on Harmonia Mundi (HMC 90 1311). On Sony Christopher Prégardien is an excellent Evangelist and Frieder Bernius has the advantage of first-rate soloists in Mieke van der Sluis, Andrea Egeler and Mona Spägele. Christoph Robson's Jesus is also moving. Bernius maintains an excellent sense of pace through both works and the instrumentalists are excellently balanced and recorded. Artistically and as a recording, this is among the finest of Schütz issues.

Italian Madrigals (complete).

(B) *** HM HMA 901162; *HMA 431162* [id.]. Concerto Vocale, René Jacobs.

(M) **(*) HM/BMG Dig. GD 77118 [77118-2-RG]. Consort of Musicke, Rooley.

Schütz's first and only *Book of Italian Madrigals* reflects his encounter with the music of Giovanni Gabrieli and Monteverdi. The Concerto Vocale, led by the counter-tenor, René Jacobs, employ a theorbo which provides added variety of colour, and at times they offer great expressive and tonal range. They omit the very last of the madrigals, the eight-part *Vasto mar.*

Anthony Rooley and the Consort of Musicke are perhaps less varied (no instruments are used) but style and intonation are impeccable, though there are occasional discrepancies of pitch between some madrigals.

Motets: *Auf dem Gebirge; Der Engel sprach; Exultavit cor meum; Fili mi Absolon; Heu mihi Domine; Hodie Christus natus est; Ich danke Dir, Herr; O quam tu pulchra es; Die Seele Christi, helige mich; Selig sind die Todten.*

☞ (BB) *** ASV CDQS 6105 [id.]. Pro Cantione Antiqua, L. Cornett & Sackbut Ens., Restoration Ac., Edgar Fleet.

An eminently useful and well-recorded super-bargain anthology of Schütz motets that offers such masterpieces as *Fili mi Absolon* (for bass voice, five sackbuts, organ and violone continuo) and the glorious *Selig sind die Todten* in well-thought-out and carefully prepared performances under Edgar Fleet. These accounts have a dignity and warmth that make them well worth considering. Moreover the CD transfer is excellently managed, the sound rich and clear.

Motets for double choir: *Die mit Tränen säen; List nicht Ephraim mein teurer Sohn.* Canzon: *Nun lob, meine Seel, den Herren.* Concertos: *Jauchzet dem Herren, alle Welt; Lobe den Herren, meine Seele; Zion spricht.* Psalms: *115: Nicht uns, Herr; 128: Wohl dem, der den Herren fürchtet; 136: Danket dem Herren; 150: Alleluja! Lobet den Herren.*

☞ (M) ** DG 437 078-2. Regensburger Domspätzen, Hamburg Wind Ens., Ulsamer Coll., Hans Martin Schneidt.

One needs a firmer focus here and a clearer definition of both the choral and accompanying brass and string groups. The cathedral acoustic is spaciously conveyed, but the composer's antiphonal effects are only partly realized. The choral focus is unclean in the opening setting of *Psalm 150* and, though it greatly improves in *Lobe den Herren* and the motet, *List nicht Ephraim mein teurer Sohn,* which are eloquently sung, the dominance of the Regensburger trebles makes the sound rather lightweight in effect.

Musicalische Exequien. Motets: *Auf dem Gebirge; Freue dich des Weibes Jugend; Ist nicht Ephraim mein teurer Sohn; Saul, Saul, was verfolgst du mich.*

*** DG Dig. 423 405-2 [id.]. Monteverdi Ch., E. Bar. Soloists, His Majesties Sackbutts & Cornetts, Gardiner.

Schütz's *Musical Exequien* contains music that is amazing for its period. The Monteverdi Choir responds with fiery intensity, making light of the complex eight-part writing in the second of the three *Exequies.* Four more superb motets by Schütz make an ideal coupling, with first-rate recorded sound.

O bone Jesu, fili Mariae.

☞ *** DG Dig. 427 660-2 [id.]. Monteverdi Ch., E. Bar. Soloists, Gardiner – BUXTEHUDE: *Membra Jesu nostri.* ***

A wonderfully eloquent performance of this *Spiritual concerto* by one of the greatest of baroque masters. Schütz juxtaposes stanzas of a poem ascribed to St Bernard of Clairvaux with prose passages of Latin devotional literature, treating the latter as recitative and the former set homophonically, and ending the cantata in *concertato* style. Beautifully recorded.

The Psalms of David (Psalmen Davids).

☞ *** Sony Dig. S2K 48042 (2) [id.]. Stuttgart Chamber Ch. & Soloists, Cologne Musica Fiata, Wilson & Bernius.

The Psalms of David Nos. 1, 2, 5–6, 8, 12, 14–17, 22–24.
☞ **(*) Conifer Dig. CDCF 190 [id.]. Trinity College, Cambridge, Ch., His Majesty's Sackbutts &
Cornetts, Marlow.

The Psalms of David (1619) was the first work Schütz composed on his return to northern Europe
after his years in Venice with Giovanni Gabrieli. It comprises 26 pieces and fuses the polychoral
Italian tradition of the Venetian master with his native German tradition. The Sony version, recorded
in 1991, is complete and the Stuttgart Chamber Choir and the Musica Fiata Köln under Frieder
Bernius give both lively and expressive accounts; all the pieces were recorded in the course of a few
days and the performances in some cases are a little routine. For the most part, however, this is a very
fine and recommendable set, very thoroughly annotated and a considerable advance over the Archiv
set made in 1971–2 by the Regensburger Domspätzen and the Hamburger Bläserkreis under Hans
Martin Schneidt.

The Conifer set offers a baker's dozen of the *Psalms* in very good performances under Richard
Marlow. Generally speaking, the choral sound is not as fine or as keenly focused as in the Stuttgart
set, but both the choir and the orchestra are attentive and intelligent, and the sound is more than
acceptable. Those who don't want the complete *Psalms* might reasonably consider this disc.

Sacred choral music (1648).
☞ (M) **(*) HM/BMG Dig. GD 77171 (2) [id.]. Knabenchor Hannover, Heinz Hennig.

The Hanover recording of the Schütz *Geistliche Chormusik* comes from the early 1980s and was made
in collaboration with Westdeutsche Rundfunk. It is of particular value in that it offers not only all 29
motets of the collection but also alternative versions of seven of them, two in more than one form.
The notes are scholarly and helpful, and at mid-price it remains an attractive proposition. On the
whole the singing is very good, though the tone of the Knabenchor of Hanover is not always perfectly
focused. It is impressive but not quite distinguished enough to earn a full three-star grading; the
recording, while generally acceptable, is at times a little opaque. However, there is at the time of
writing no alternative version, and the set is to be recommended. Readers will derive much
satisfaction from it.

St Matthew Passion.
☞ (M) *** Decca 436 221-2 [id.]. Pears, Shirley-Quirk, Luxon, Schütz Ch., Roger Norrington.

Schütz's setting of the *St Matthew Passion* is an austere one. The story is told, for the most part, in a
series of unaccompanied recitatives, eloquent but restrained in style. The drama is suddenly heightened
at the choral entries, but these are comparatively few, and the work relies on the artistry of the
soloists to project itself on the listener. The solo singing here is of a high order and the choral
contribution fine enough to make one wish there were more of it. The closing chorus, *Glory be to
Thee*, is more familiar than the rest of the work, for it is sometimes extracted to be sung on its own.
The 1971 (originally Argo) recording, made in St John's, Smith Square, is excellent, and it is
understandable that the original language is used. Even so, and although a full translation is
provided, one feels the work would communicate more readily when sung in English. The CD
transfer is splendidly done.

Scriabin, Alexander (1872–1915)

(i) *Piano concerto in F sharp min., Op. 20;* (ii) *Poème de l'extase, Op. 54;* (i) *Prometheus – The poem
of fire, Op. 60.*
*** Decca 417 252-2 [id.]. (i) Ashkenazy, LPO; (ii) Cleveland O; Maazel.

Ashkenazy plays the *Piano concerto* with great feeling and authority. *Prometheus* too, powerfully
atmospheric and curiously hypnotic, is given a thoroughly poetic and committed reading and
Ashkenazy copes with the virtuoso obbligato part with predictable distinction. Maazel's 1979
Cleveland recording of *Le Poème de l'extase* is a shade too efficient to be really convincing. The
playing is often brilliant and the recording is very clear but the trumpets are rather forced and
strident. However, it can be regarded as a bonus for the other two works.

Symphonies Nos. 1–3; Poème de l'extase; (i) Prometheus.
*** EMI CDS7 54251-2 (3) [id.]. Toczyska, Myers, Westminster Ch. (in *No. 1*), Phd. O, Muti, (i)
with Alexeev.

Muti's complete set of the Scriabin *Symphonies* can be recommended almost without reservation.
True, in No. 3 the recording could be more refined, but overall the sound is as vivid and richly

coloured as the performances. With the two additional symphonic poems (*Le Poème de l'extase* white-hot with passionate intensity, yet masterfully controlled) now added, in the place of the original, less appropriate Tchaikovsky couplings, this is an impressive achievement.

Symphony No. 1 in E, Op. 26.
*** Olympia Dig. OCD 159 [id.]. Gorokhovskaya, Pluzhnikov, Glinka State Ac. Ch. of Leningrad,
    USSR RSO, Fedoseyev.

The digital recording from the Soviet Union is relaxed and unforced and the two soloists, Yevgenia Gorokhovskaya and Konstantin Pluzhnikov, are every bit as fine as their EMI rivals, Stefania Toczyska and Michael Myers. This can be recommended with confidence.

(i) *Symphony No. 1 in E, Op. 26; Le Poème de l'extase, Op. 54.*
☞ *(*) Russian Disc Dig. RDCD 11056 [id.]. (i) Nina Gaponova, Andrei Salnynikov, USSR R.
    Ch.; USSR SO, Svetlanov.

Svetlanov's account of the discursive, rambling *First Symphony* was recorded at a live concert in 1990 in the ample acoustic of the Large Hall of the Moscow Conservatoire. In the finale, both his soloists and the USSR Radio Chorus are first rate but, judged by this conductor's own standards, the remainder of the performance is curiously lacklustre and under-powered. *Le Poème de l'extase* is one of his showpieces and his earlier LP account from the late 1960s was much (and rightly) prized during its day. This is no less highly ecstatic and powerful – indeed arguably more so. This is a three-star performance against the symphony's one but, alas, the 1990 recording does not do this once magnificent orchestra with its voluptuous string-tone anything like justice.

Symphony No. 2 in C min., Op. 29.
*** Chan. Dig. CHAN 8462; *ABTD 1176* [id.]. SNO, Järvi.

Although it is less amorphous than its predecessor, the *Second Symphony* needs the most fervent advocacy if the listener is to be persuaded. This splendid account from Järvi, with its richly detailed Chandos recording, can be recommended strongly.

Symphony No. 2 in C min., Op. 29; Le Poème de l'extase, Op. 54; Rêverie, Op. 24.
☞ *(*) BIS Dig. CD 535 [id.]. R. Stockholm PO, Leif Segerstam.

Leif Segerstam has a natural feeling for Scriabin's sound-world, and both the *Second Symphony* and *Le Poème de l'extase* are idiomatic, though Segerstam lingers at times so that tension sags. The Royal Stockholm Orchestra are highly responsive and give him excellent support, but the recording is backwardly balanced and is insufficiently transparent. We were critical of the sound of an earlier release in this series, coupling the *Piano concerto* and the *Third Symphony*, but this is if anything less detailed and present.

Symphony No. 3 in C min. (Le divin poème), Op. 43.
*** Chan. Dig. CHAN 8898; *ABTD 1509* [id.]. Danish Nat. RSO, Järvi – ARENSKY: *Silhouettes.*
    ***

Symphony No. 3 (Le divin poème); Le Poeme de l'extase, Op. 54; Rêverie, Op. 24.
*** Decca Dig. 430 843-2 [id.]. Berlin RSO, Ashkenazy.

Scriabin's mammoth *Third Symphony* calls for vast forces, but there is no doubt that it is original, both in layout and in substance. There is something refreshingly unforced and natural about Järvi's version which puts this score in a far better light than those conductors who play it for all they are worth. One of the special attractions of the Chandos issue is its rather endearing coupling, Arensky's *Silhouettes*, which are not otherwise available.

Vladimir Ashkenazy has the advantage of the more logical coupling, an all-Scriabin programme, and good engineering from the Decca team. The Berlin Radio forces are very good and there is a highly charged feel to the performances, particularly that of *Le Poème de l'extase*.

PIANO MUSIC

2 Danses, Op. 73; 4 Morceaux, Op. 51; 4 Morceaux, Op. 56; 2 Poèmes, Op. 32.
☞ (M) *** Decca Analogue/Dig. 425 081-2 [id.]. Vladimir Ashkenazy – RAVEL: *Gaspard* etc. ***

Ashkenazy is as thoroughly at home in these miniatures as he is in the *Sonatas*, readily finding their special atmosphere and colour, and the recording is first class. The recordings were made in 1977, with the exception of the Op. 51 *Morceaux*, which are later (1982) and digital.

Etudes (complete): *in C sharp min., Op. 2/1; 12 Etudes, Op. 8; 8 Etudes, Op. 42 (1903); in E flat, Op. 49/1; Op. 56/4 (1908); 3 Etudes, Op. 65.*
☞ **(*) Hyp. Dig. CDA 66607 [id.]. Piers Lane.

The Scriabin *Etudes* traverse a wide stylistic spectrum, beginning with the Chopinesque Opp. 2 and 8 through to the exploratory, visionary world of Op. 65. These pieces have been well served over the years by such artists as Richter, Sofronitzky and others. Piers Lane makes light of the various technical problems in which these pieces abound and he plays with an admirable sense of style. Yet he does not give us the whole picture. He has sensibility and produces a good sonority, aided in no small measure by an excellently balanced recording; but one misses the nervous intensity, the imaginative flair and the feverish emotional temperature that the later pieces call for. At the time of writing there is no alternative view of the complete *Etudes* to be had on CD, so that this fills an important gap in the catalogue.

12 Etudes, Op. 8; Piano sonatas Nos. 3–5, Opp. 23; 30; 53.
☞ *** Pianissimo Dig. PP 10394 [id.]. Yuki Matsuzawa.

Yuki Matsuzawa is a gifted young Japanese player with a remarkable feel for Scriabin. Whether in the Chopinesque *Etudes* or the bigger-boned *Third Sonata* she seems wholly attuned to the Scriabin sensibility; the opening of the *Third* is perhaps not as commanding or dramatic as Horowitz, but hers is a thoughtful and powerful reading too, and she is very persuasive in the *Fourth* and *Fifth Sonatas*, too.

Etudes, Op. 8/7 & 12; Op. 42/5. Preludes, Op. 11/1, 3, 9, 10, 13, 14, 16; Op. 13/6; Op. 15/2; Op. 16/1 & 4; Op. 27/1; Op. 48/3; Op. 51/2; Op. 59/2; Op. 67/1. Sonatas Nos. 3, Op. 23; 5, Op. 53.
(M) (***) BMG/RCA mono/stereo GD 86215 [6215-2-RC]. Vladimir Horowitz.

The RCA engineers have done wonders to these recordings from the 1950s though some of the original shallowness and clatter remains. The *Preludes* and the legendary account of the *Third Sonata* come from 1956. The *Fifth* is much later, coming from the mid-1970s, and has more bloom. The performances form an essential part of any good Horowitz collection.

Mazurkas, Op. 3/1–10; Op. 25/1–9; Op. 40/1–2.
☞ *** Collins Dig. 1394-2 [id.]. Artur Pizarro.

Apart from Chopin, Scriabin is the only composer to have raised the mazurka to an art-form. These are often exquisite miniature tone-poems, and they are splendidly played and recorded. Artur Pizarro is a Leeds Competition Prizewinner, and listening to this record one sees why his artistry was so much admired.

Piano sonatas Nos. 1–10.
(M) *** Decca 425 579-2 (2) [id.]. Vladimir Ashkenazy.

Piano sonatas Nos. 1–10; Piano sonata in E flat min. (1887–9); Sonata fantaisie in G sharp min.
(M) **(*) DG 431 747-2 (3). Roberto Szidon.

Ashkenazy is clearly attuned to this repertoire, though he is at his finest in the earlier sonatas. The last three are given with brilliance and vision, and there is no lack of awareness of the demonic side of Scriabin's musical personality. These are fine performances and are well recorded.

   Roberto Szidon's DG reissue offers the whole set. Szidon seems especially at home in the later works. His version of the *Black Mass sonata* (No. 9) conveys real excitement. At medium price this is an attractive reissue and can be considered alongside Ashkenazy's series. The DG recording is good but not ideal and the tone tends to harden at climaxes.

Piano sonata No. 3 in F sharp min., Op. 23; 2 Poems, Op. 32; Vers la flamme, Op. 72.
**(*) Kingdom Dig. KCLCD 2001; CKCL 2001. Gordon Fergus-Thompson – BALAKIREV: *Piano sonata.* **(*)

Gordon Fergus-Thompson gives a splendid account of Scriabin's overheated *F sharp minor Sonata* and sensitive, atmospheric performances of the other pieces here. A reverberant but good recording.

Piano sonatas Nos. 4, Op. 30; 5, Op. 53; 9 (Black Mass), Op. 68; 10, Op. 70. Etude in C sharp min., Op. 2/1; 8 Etudes, Op. 42.
**(*) ASV Dig. CDDCA 776 [id.]. Gordon Fergus-Thomson.

Fergus-Thomson is thoroughly inside this idiom. At the same time it must be conceded that his performances are not as manic or high-voltage as those of Richter and Horowitz and in the cruelly competitive world of the recorded music would not be a first choice. Nevertheless there is much musical nourishment here to satisfy the collector.

Piano sonatas Nos. 8, Op. 66; 9, Op. 68; 10, Op. 70; 2 Danses, Op. 73; 2 Poèmes, Op. 69; 2 Poèmes, Op. 71; 2 Preludes, Op. 67; 5 Preludes, Op. 74; Vers la flamme, Op. 72.
*(**) Altarus Dig. AIR-CD 9020 [id.]. Donna Amato.

Donna Amato seems wholly attuned to Scriabin's sensibility and plays all his late music (Opp. 66–74), including the last three *Sonatas*, to the manner born. Scriabin's world is claustrophobic – but unfortunately so is the recording, which sounds as if it was made in a small acoustic environment but with some echo added. The sound-quality diminishes the pleasure this CD gives but not of course Amato's artistry.

Segerstam, Leif (born 1942)

Symphonies Nos. (i) *11;* (ii) *14.*
☞ ** BIS Dig. CD 483 [id.]. (i) Swedish RSO, Leif Segerstam; (ii) Finnish RSO, Mikael Samuelson.

This gifted Finnish conductor is a prolific composer. His output includes no fewer than 17 symphonies and 27 quartets. He has also composed what he calls *Orchestral diary sheets*, and the symphonies recorded here comprise diary sheets Nos. 5 and 44. They exhibit something of the same mixture of flair and self-indulgence that is to be found in his conducting. There are flashes of imagination alongside long stretches of seemingly random activity. Those who are looking for symphonic writing in any real sense of the term will be disappointed, as will those expecting to encounter any strong or significant creative personality. Two stars for the recording and the expertise of the fine orchestras involved; for the composer none!

Seiber, Mátyás (1905–60)

Clarinet concertino.
*** Hyp. Dig. CDA 66215 [id.]. Thea King, ECO, Litton – BLAKE: *Concerto;* LUTOSLAWSKI: *Dance preludes.* ***

Mátyás Seiber's highly engaging *Concertino* was sketched during a train journey (in 1926, before the days of seamless rails) and certainly the opening *Toccata* has the jumpy, rhythmic feeling of railway line joints and points. Yet the haunting slow movement has a touch of the ethereal, while the Scherzo has a witty jazz element. Thea King has the measure of the piece; she is accompanied well by Litton, and very well recorded. Recommended.

Four French folk songs: Réveillez-vous; J'ai descendu; Le Rossignol; Marguerite, elle est malade.
☞ (M) *** BMG/RCA 09026 61601-2. Peter Pears, Julian Bream (guitar) – BRITTEN: *Songs from the Chinese* etc; WALTON: *Anon in love.* ***

Mátyás Seiber's arrangements of four French folksongs are enchantingly simple and, as Bream says, the accompaniments 'use the guitar adroitly'. The gentle, melancholy charm of *Réveillez-vous* and *Le Rossignol* brings ravishing tone and line from Pears, while the lighter *J'ai descendu* and the vibrant account of poor sick Marguerite make a deliciously spirited contrast. Vivid recording, made by a Decca team, but it was unconscionable of BMG/RCA not to provide translations, even if one can enjoy the songs without them.

Servais, Adrien-François (1807–66)

Caprice sur des motifs de l'opéra, Le Comte Ory; Caprices, Op. 11/2 & 4; Grand duo de concert sur deux airs nationaux anglais; Grand fantaisie, Op. 20; Souvenir de Bade; Souvenir de Spa, Op. 2.
*** HM/BMG Dig. GD 77108; [77108-2-RG]. Bylsma, Smithsonian Chamber Players.

Servais's music is entertaining stuff, particularly the *Grand duo de concert sur deux airs nationaux anglais*, written in collaboration with his colleague, Hubert Léonard. Somewhat unexpectedly the second 'air anglais' turns out to be *Yankee doodle dandy*! The Servais cello is currently in use at the Smithsonian Institute, and so it is appropriate that six expert string-players of the Smithsonian group, plus harmonium, perform this music for us, providing a delightful entertainment, and very well recorded too.

Sessions, Roger (born 1896)

Concerto for orchestra.
*** Hyp. Dig. CDA 66050 [id.]. Boston SO, Ozawa – PANUFNIK: *Symphony No. 8.* ***

Sessions's *Concerto for orchestra* finds him at his thorniest and most uncompromising, with lyricism limited to fleeting fragments of melody; but the playful opening leads one on finally to a valedictory close, sharply defined. Ozawa makes a powerful advocate, helped by superb playing from the Boston orchestra.

Symphony No. 4; Symphony No. 5; Rhapsody for orchestra.
*** New World Dig. NWCD 345 [id.]. Columbus SO, Badea.

Roger Sessions shares with Walter Piston, his tonal contemporary, a highly developed sense of structure and an integrity that remained unshaken by changes of fashion. His musical language is dense and his logic is easier to sense than to follow. The performances by the Columbus Symphony Orchestra under Christian Badea appear well prepared, and there is no doubt as to their commitment and expertise. The sound ideally needs a larger acoustic, but every strand in the texture is well placed and there is no feeling of discomfort.

Shapero, Harold (born 1920)

Symphony for classical orchestra; Nine-minute overture.
☞ **(*) New World Dig NW 373-2 [id.]. LAPO, Previn.

Harold Shapero's *Symphony for classical orchestra* dates from 1947 and is a very striking piece. It has a propulsive energy and moves with complete assurance. Here is a composer who, like the young Peter Mennin, seemed to know exactly where he was going and offered (like Mennin) real hope for the American symphony after Piston, Harris and Diamond. (Alas, neither promise was fulfilled.) This *Symphony for classical orchestra* seems to derive its inspiration from Beethoven and Stravinsky's *Symphony in C* and is a highly stimulating piece. Previn gets good results from the Los Angeles orchestra but does not bring the sheer vitality that distinguished Bernstein's pioneering record. Let's hope that this, along with Bernstein's recordings of William Schuman's *Third*, *Fifth* and *Eighth Symphonies*, will be restored to circulation within the lifetime of this volume.

Shchedrin, Rodion (born 1933)

(i) *Carmen* (ballet; arr. from Bizet): *suite; Humoresque. In imitation of Albéniz; Stalin cocktail.*
☞ *** Chan. Dig. CHAN 9288 [id.]. I Musici de Montréal, Yuli Turovski; (i) with Ens. Répercussion
– TURINA: *La oración del torero.* ***

Rodion Shchedrin's free adaptation of Bizet's *Carmen* music uses Bizet's tunes, complete with harmony, and reworks them into a new tapestry using only strings and percussion (including vibraphone). There is a degree of fragmentation and alteration of timing (not time-signatures) to effect some dramatic surprises. The whole thing is brilliantly done and wears surprisingly well. Shchedrin's answer to the obvious question is disarming. 'The image of Carmen has become so well known,' he writes. 'I think that a Carmen without Bizet will always tend to disappoint people. Our memory is too firmly attached to the musical images of the opera. That's why I decided to write a transcription.' There have been previous recordings of Shchedrin's score but this new Chandos version by I Musici de Montréal sweeps the board. Recorded in the richly resonant acoustic of the Eglise de la Nativité de la Sainte-Vierge, La Prairie, Quebec, the sound is very much in the demonstration bracket, with glittering percussion effects (marimba and vibraphone particularly well caught) and dramatic use of side drum snares. Yuli Turovski's performance opens evocatively and is highly dramatic, winningly expressive and subtle in its use of the wide range of string colour and dynamic. The ear hardly misses Bizet's famous woodwind writing. The pastiche, *In imitation of Albéniz*, and the grotesque, Shostakovich-like *Humoresque* are offset by a malignant parody-evocation of Stalin, full of creepy special effects and with a shout of horror at the end. They are very well presented here, but one would not want to return to them very often.

(i) *The Lady and the lapdog* (ballet); (ii) *Music for the city of Köthen.*
☞ *** Olympia OCD 262 [id.]. (i) Bolshoi Theatre O, Lazarev; (ii) Moscow Virtuosi Chamber O,
Spivakov.

Shchedrin's 50-minute ballet after Chekhov's *The Lady and the lapdog* comes from 1985. It is a haunting and atmospheric score that casts a powerful spell. As in his celebrated *Carmen ballet*, Shchedrin shows great imagination in the use of the orchestra: he uses strings, two oboes (one doubling the cor anglais), two horns and glockenspiel, but with such resource and finesse that one often feels that larger forces are involved. The invention is strong and, although its balletic origins are obvious, the music itself has a discernible narrative thread that makes for compelling listening. The fill-up, *Music for the city of Köthen*, comes from the same year and was commissioned by the then East German Radio to mark the tercentenary of Bach's birth. Again there is something of the same orchestral flair and resourcefulness; its scoring is for strings, two oboes, two bassoons and tambourine. A three-movement score, it makes inventive use of baroque forms and conventions. The analogue recordings were made not long after the works received their premières and have admirable body, clarity and warmth. The Bolshoi Orchestra under Alexander Lazarev produce excellent and responsive playing in the ballet, and the Moscow Virtuosi are hardly less impressive in the companion-piece. Unlike his younger contemporaries, Schnittke and Gubaidulina, Shchedrin has never enjoyed a fashionable vogue among Western critics or, the *Carmen ballet* excepted, found more than a modest following among the wider musical public; but he is a composer of real imagination and talent.

Sheppard, John *(c. 1515–c. 1559)*

Christe Redemptor omnium; In manus tuas; Media vita; Reges Tharsis; Sacris solemniis; Verbum caro.
*** Gimell Dig. CDGIM 016; *1585T-16* [id.]. Tallis Scholars, Peter Phillips.

All the music here is based on chant, and much of it is for the six-part choir, which produces a particularly striking sonority. The *Media vita* ('In the midst of life we are in death') is a piece of astonishing beauty, and it is sung with remarkable purity of tone by the Tallis Scholars under Peter Phillips. Glorious and little-known music: the recording could hardly be improved on.

Gaude virgo Christiphera; In manus tuas; Libera nos, salva 1–2; Reges Tharsis.
*** Proudsound Dig. PROUCD 126; *PROU 126* [id.]. Clerkes of Oxenford, David Wulstan – TYE:
    Mass Euge bone. ***

The Clerkes of Oxenford under David Wulstan produce a very different sonority from the Tallis group, wonderfully blended and balanced, with a tonal sophistication that is remarkable. They overlap only minimally with the Gimell disc, so both can be recommended to the enthusiast. They are placed rather more distantly than the Tallis Scholars but are splendidly recorded in a spacious but not over-reverberant acoustic.

Motets: *Filiae Hierusalem venite; Haec dies; In manus tuas Domine I; In pacem in idipsum; Justi in perpetuum vivent; Lauden dicite Deo; Libera nos, salva nos I; Paschal Kyrie; Regis Tharsis et insulae; Spiritus sanctus procedens I; Verbo caro factum est.*
⊛ *** Hyp. Dig. CDA 66259 [id.]. The Sixteen, Christophers.

Here in eleven superb responsories The Sixteen consistently convey the rapturous beauty of Sheppard's writing, above all in ethereal passages in the highest register, very characteristic of him. Even there The Sixteen's sopranos seem quite unstressed by the tessitura. There are not many more beautiful records of Tudor polyphony than this.

Motets: *Gaude, gaude, gaude Maria; In manus tuas* (1st setting); *Laudem dicite Deo; In pace; Verbum caro.*
☞ (B) **(*) CfP CD-CFP 4638; *TC-CFP 4638* [id.]. Clerkes of Oxenford, David Wulstan – TALLIS:
    Motets. **(*)

It was a bright idea to juxtapose a selection of motets by the lesser-known Sheppard alongside more famous examples by his great contemporary, Thomas Tallis. The performances by the Clerkes of Oxenford under Davis Wulstan are full of fervour, particularly in the inspired *Gaude, gaude, gaude Maria* and the closing *Verbum caro*. Wulstan presses on very strongly, and some might feel there is a lack of contrasting repose and not enough subtlety in the sheer thrust of his direction. But the commitment of the singing will surely convince anyone who buys this CD on impulse that this is great music and that its composer's name should be more familiar. The 1978 analogue recording, made in Merton College Chapel, is not absolutely refined in focus, but the sound has plenty of body and atmosphere.

Shostakovich, Dmitri (1906–75)

(i; ii; iii) *The Adventures of Korzinkina* (film music): *suite, Op. 59;* (iv; ii) *Alone* (film music): *suite, Op. 26;* (v) *La Comédie Humaine* (incidental music to Balzac), *Op. 37;* (i; ii) *Scherzos: in F sharp min., Op. 1; in E flat, Op. 7; Theme & variations in B flat, Op. 3;* (vi) *Spanish songs, Op. 100.*
**(*) Olympia OCD 194 [id.]. (i) USSR MoC SO, (ii) Rozhdestvensky; (iii) with Ch.; (iv) Soloists, Ens. of USSR Ac. SO; (v) Leningrad CO, Gurdzhi; (vi) Artur Eisen, A. Bogdanova.

None of the music on this record is without interest to admirers of this composer. The Op. 7 *Scherzo* is characteristic – there is a prominent part for the piano and there is already evidence of Shostakovich's special kind of wit. The *Spanish songs* come from 1956 and are more substantial; they are splendidly sung by Artur Eisen. The film scores are from the 1930s and uncover no masterpieces. Though the recordings were made during the 1980s and are not top-drawer, this disc is still well worth investigating.

The Age of gold: suite, *Op. 22.*
(M) *** Decca Dig. 430 727-2 [id.]. LPO, Haitink – JANACEK: *Sinfonietta* etc. ***

The joky *Age of gold* performance combines wit and feeling and is brilliantly recorded.

Chamber symphony in C min. Op. 110a (arr. Barshai from *String quartet No. 8); Symphony for strings, Op. 118a* (arr. Barshai from *String quartet No. 10).*
*** DG Dig. 429 229-2. COE, Rudolf Barshai.

The *Chamber symphony* is an arrangement for full strings of the *Eighth Quartet*, and the *Symphony for strings* is a similar transcription of the *Tenth*. Both were made by Rudolf Barshai and he directs them with the authority of the composer and bears his imprimatur. The young players of the Chamber Orchestra of Europe excel themselves in the tonal beauty, refinement and responsiveness of their playing, here recorded in the smaller Philharmonie Hall in Berlin. These are strong performances of real eloquence and power, which are excellently recorded and can be confidently recommended to those who prefer the dark, brooding transcriptions to the inward-looking originals.

Cello concerto No. 1 in E flat, Op. 107.
*** Sony Dig. MK 37840 [id.]. Yo-Yo Ma, Phd. O, Ormandy – KABALEVSKY: *Cello concerto No. 1.*
***

*** Chan. Dig. CHAN 8322 [id.]. Raphael Wallfisch, ECO, Geoffrey Simon – BARBER: *Cello concerto.* ***

(i) *Cello concerto No. 1, Op. 107;* (ii) *Symphony No. 5.*
(M) *** Sony Dig. MYK 44903 [id.]. (i) Ma, Phd. O, Ormandy; (ii) NYPO, Bernstein.

Yo-Yo Ma plays with an intensity that compels the listener and the Philadelphia Orchestra give eloquent support. This has now also been reissued at mid-price, generously coupled with Bernstein's exciting 1979 account of the *Fifth Symphony*, recorded in Tokyo when Bernstein and the New York Philharmonic were on tour there. Unashamedly Bernstein treats the work as a Romantic symphony. The slow movement is raptly beautiful, and the finale is brilliant and extrovert, with no hint of irony. On CD, the bass is made to sound full and rich, and the slight distancing of the sound places the orchestra within a believable ambience.

Wallfisch handles the first movement splendidly, though there is not quite the same sense of momentum as in Yo-Yo Ma's account. However, he gives a sensitive account of the slow movement and has thoughtful and responsive support from the ECO. The Chandos recording is outstandingly fine.

Cello concertos Nos. 1 in E flat, Op. 107; 2, Op. 126.
*** Ph. Dig. 412 526-2 [id.]. Heinrich Schiff, Bav. RSO, Maxim Shostakovich.
☞ **(*) BIS Dig. CD 626 [id.]. Torleif Thedéen, Malmö SO, James DePreist.

Schiff's superbly recorded account does not displace Yo-Yo Ma in the *First*, but it can hold its own. The *Second Concerto* is a haunting piece, essentially lyrical; it is gently discursive, sadly whimsical at times and tinged with a smiling melancholy that hides deeper troubles. The recording is enormously impressive.

With their 'onlie begetter' (Rostropovich) still dominating the catalogue, new recordings of the two *Cello concertos* face an unequal struggle. The gifted young Swedish cellist, Torleif Thedéen, has a lot going for him, however, and his passionately committed performances would honour any collection. He has the advantage of excellent engineering, which gives a very alive sound, plus good orchestral support from the Malmö Orchestra under James DePreist. If you have, say, Rostropovich's pioneering account with Ormandy and want a new recording, choice resides between this and Heinrich Schiff's equally eloquent account on Philips.

(i) *Cello concerto No. 1 in E flat, Op. 107; Piano concertos Nos.* (ii) *1 in C min., Op. 35;* (iii) *2 in F, Op. 102.*
(M) *** Sony MPK 44850 [id.]. (i) Rostropovich, Phd. O, Ormandy; (ii) Previn; (iii) Bernstein; NYPO, Bernstein.

Rostropovich made this recording of the *Cello concerto No. 1* within a few months of the first performance in Russia. Shostakovich himself attended the recording session in Philadelphia and gave his approval to what is a uniquely authoritative reading. Sony have now shrewdly made an attractive triptych for CD by including Bernstein's radiant account of the *Second Piano concerto*, along with Previn's equally striking account of No. 1. Though these New York performances bring somewhat dated recording, both pianists have a way of turning a phrase to catch the imagination, and a fine balance is struck between Shostakovich's warmth and his rhythmic alertness.

Cello concerto No. 2, Op. 126.
☞ (B) *** DG Double 437 952-2 (2) [id.]. Rostropovich, Boston SO, Ozawa – BERNSTEIN: *3 Meditations* etc.; BOCCHERINI: *Cello concerto No. 2;* GLAZUNOV: *Chant du Ménestrel;* TARTINI: *Cello concerto;* TCHAIKOVSKY: *Andante cantabile* etc.; VIVALDI: *Cello concertos.* ***

Rostropovich plays with beautifully controlled feeling, and Seiji Ozawa brings sympathy and fine discipline to the accompaniment, securing admirably expressive playing from the Boston orchestra. The analogue recording is first class. As can be seen, this is part of a remarkably generous Double DG anthology showing Rostropovich's art over the widest range.

Piano concerto No. 1 in C min., for piano, trumpet and strings, Op. 35.
☞ *** Decca Dig. 436 239-2 [id.]. Jablonski, RPO, Ashkenazy – LUTOSLAWSKI: *Paganini variations* ***; RACHMANINOV: *Rhapsody on a theme of Paganini.* **(*)

Despite his Polish name, Jablonski is Swedish and all of twenty years old. He proves a characterful and intelligent exponent of the Shostakovich concerto, and in Raymond Simmons has an excellent trumpet soloist. This is as good a performance and recording as any in the catalogue.

Piano concertos Nos. (i) *1 in C min. for piano, trumpet and strings, Op. 35;* (ii) *2 in F, Op. 102.*
☞ (M) *** SMK 47618-2. [id.]. (i) André Previn, William Vacciano; (ii) Leonard Bernstein; NYPO, Bernstein (with: POULENC: *Double piano concerto*: Arthur Gold & Robert Fizdale (pianos) ***).

This shrewd pairing of Bernstein's radiant account of the *Second Concerto* with Previn's equally striking reading of No. 1 makes an attractive disc, especially when coupled with a spiky yet genial version of the Poulenc *Double concerto*. The Shostakovich recordings are far from recent but sound most vivid. The Poulenc concerto, too, is both witty and abrasive, with an excellent contribution from the piano duo, Arthur Gold and Robert Fizdale. It was recorded at about the same time (1961) and the CD transfer of a not particularly smooth original was thoroughly satisfactory. This is one of the most winning discs in the Bernstein Royal Edition.

(i) *Piano concertos Nos. 1–2. 3 Fantastic dances, Op. 5; 24 Preludes & fugues, Op. 87/1, 4–5, 23–24.*
☞ **(*) EMI mono CDC7 54606-2 [id.]. Composer; (i) L. Vaillant, Fr. Nat. RSO, Cluytens.

In his youth Shostakovich was an accomplished pianist, sufficiently so to participate in the first Warsaw Chopin Piano Competition in 1929, where he did well enough to receive a placing in the Finals. He made a number of records of his own music, including the *Piano quintet* with the Beethoven Quartet (for whom most of the quartets were composed), and an old Melodiya version of the *First Piano concerto*. The two piano concertos were recorded, albeit in mono only, with the French Radio Orchestra under André Cluytens in 1958 for French Columbia (and were slow to reach the UK catalogues). Shostakovich's technical address and rhythmic vitality are not in question, though by this time he was just beginning to lose some of the finesse in matters of keyboard colour and dynamic nuance which he must obviously have commanded in his youthful days. However, both concertos are very well supported by Cluytens, and the trumpeter Ludovic Vaillant proves a high-spirited fellow-soloist. In addition to the early *Fantastic dances*, we have some of the Op. 87 *Preludes and fugues* that he recorded in the late 1950s. They admirably convey his intentions and have a special sense of concentration, even if they do not possess subtlety of colouring. An indispensable document for all admirers of the great composer. However, this should have been issued at mid-price.

Piano concertos Nos. 1–2; The Unforgettable year 1919, Op. 89; The Assault on beautiful Gorky (for piano and orchestra).
(B) *** CfP Dig. CD-CFP 4547; *TC-CFP 4547*. Alexeev, Philip Jones, ECO, Maksymiuk.

Alexeev is a clear first choice in both *Concertos*, and his record would sweep the board even at full price. The digital recording is excellent in every way and scores over its rivals in clarity and presence. There is a fill-up in the form of a miniature one-movement *Concerto* from a film-score called *The Unforgettable year 1919*.

(i) *Piano concerto No. 2 in F, Op. 102;* (ii) *Violin concerto No. 1 in A min., Op. 99.*
*** Decca Dig. 425 793-2 [id.]. (i) Ortiz; (ii) Belkin; RPO, Ashkenazy.

Cristina Ortiz gives a sparkling account of the jaunty first movement of the *Piano concerto No. 2*, and she also brings out the fun and wit of the finale with fluent, finely pointed playing, not least in the delicious interpolated bars of 7/8. Boris Belkin in the first and more popular of the violin concertos plays immaculately and with consistently sweet, pure tone, but he misses some of the work's darker, deeper undertones. Decca sound is full and well balanced, not as distanced as other recordings in Ashkenazy's series. A satisfying coupling.

Violin concertos Nos. 1 in A min., Op. 77; 2 in C sharp min., Op. 129.
*** Virgin/EMI Dig. VC7 59601-2 [id.]. Sitkovetsky, BBC SO, Andrew Davis.
*** Chan. Dig. CHAN 8820; *ABTD 1445*. Lydia Mordkovitch, SNO, Järvi.

Virgin's coupling by Sitkovetsky and the BBC Symphony Orchestra under Andrew Davis is impressive and intense; there is no doubt as to its excellence, it has tremendous bite. It is also splendidly recorded, and takes its place at the top of the list.
   Mordkovitch's concentrated reading of No. 2 is matched by Järvi and the orchestra in their total commitment. She even outshines the work's dedicatee and first interpreter, David Oistrakh, in the dark reflectiveness of her playing, even if she cannot quite match him in bravura passages. In the better-known concerto (No. 1) the meditative intensity is magnetic, with a fullness and warmth of tone that have not always marked her playing on record before.

Violin concerto No. 1 in A min., Op. 99.
*** EMI Dig. CDC7 49814-2 [id.]. Perlman, Israel PO, Mehta – GLAZUNOV: *Violin concerto.* ***
☞ ** EMI Dig. CD7 54314-2 [id.]. Salerno-Sonnenberg, LSO, M. Shostakovich – BARBER: *Violin concerto.* **

Perlman's version of the Shostakovich *First Violin concerto* was recorded live in the Mann Auditorium in Tel Aviv. There is no violinist in the world who in sheer bravura can quite match Perlman, particularly live, and the ovation which greets his dazzling performance of the finale is richly deserved. Yet some of the mystery and the fantasy which Russian interpreters have found – from David Oistrakh onwards – is missing, and the close balance of the solo instrument, characteristic of Perlman's concerto recordings, undermines hushed intensity.
   A new account of one of Shostakovich's most inward-looking and poignant utterances is inevitably a cause for rejoicing. Composed some years before the *Tenth Symphony*, the concerto is the product of comparable anguish and suffering but, unlike the symphony, it has not captured quite the same representation either on record or in the concert hall. Nadja Salerno-Sonnenberg does not believe in understatement, and the powerful first movement would have been better served by less feverish vibrato and expressive underlining. For all her expertise and despite many moments of artistry, she conveys the impression that she is trying to 'sell' this concerto to you rather than allowing it to speak for itself. She is well supported by the composer's son and the LSO, and very well recorded indeed. Those wanting this particular coupling might consider it, though in the long run there is the risk that it will prove cloying. On balance, however, it does not represent a strong challenge to Sitkovetsky on Virgin. It certainly does not encompass the emotional and spiritual depths that the pioneering Oistrakh–Mitropoulos or Oistrakh–Mravinsky accounts achieved.

Five days, five nights (suite), Op. 111a; Hamlet (suite), Op. 116a (film music); *King Lear (suite), Op. 137.*
*** BMG/RCA RD 87763 [7763-2-RC]. Belgian R. O, Serebrier.

Hamlet obviously generates powerful resonances in Shostakovich's psyche and prompts responsive and committed playing from the Belgian Radio Orchestra, while much of the score for *Five days, five nights* inhabits the bleak world of the *Eleventh Symphony*.

The Gadfly (film music): *suite, Op. 97a.*
(B) **(*) CfP CD-CFP 4463; *TC-CFP 4463.* USSR Cinema SO, Emin Khachaturian.

The score for *The Gadfly* is quite pleasing but at times is wholly uncharacteristic. On CfP, a musically committed and well-recorded issue, although the brightening of the sound in the digital remastering has lost some of the smoothness of the original LP.

The Golden Age (ballet; complete).
☞ **(*) Chan. Dig. CHAN 9251/2 [id.]. Royal Stockholm PO, Rozhdestvensky.

It is remarkable that we have had to wait so long for a complete recording of Shostakovich's first ballet, with its extraordinary plot of Soviet and capitalist sportsmen and women, complete with the attempted Western seduction of the Soviet hero and a final dance of solidarity and reconciliation in which Western workers eagerly participate. The famous *Polka* is meant to satirize a disarmament meeting in Geneva. The music as a whole is remarkably potent and full of succulent ideas (even *Tea for two* arrives during Act II) and with the big set-pieces expansively and sometimes darkly symphonic. The score is well played in Stockholm, but the warm orchestral style does not always readily bring out the music's plangent character and moments of barbed wit. Rozhdestvensky directs idiomatically as far as possible, but at times his tempi suggest that he is not directing a virtuoso group or one composed of musicians who can take naturally to the abrasive Slavonic idiom. But, with very good recording, this is fascinatingly more than a stop-gap.

Hamlet (incidental music), *Op. 116a.*
☞ (M) **(*) Unicorn UKCD 2066 [id.]. Nat. PO, Herrmann – KABALEVSKY: *Symphony No. 2* **(*);
    MIASKOVSKY: *Symphony No. 22.* ***

Shostakovich's music for a Soviet film of *Hamlet* (in a translation by Boris Pasternak) dates from 1963. Six of the eight movements of the suite are included here, ending with the *Duel and Death of Hamlet.* Bernard Herrmann, himself a distinguished composer of film music, here directs a strongly dramatic, atmospheric performance. The remarkable poisoning sequence is especially telling. The recording (originally made by Decca in Phase 4) is bright and plangent.

Symphonies Nos. 1 in F min., Op. 10; 3 (The First of May), Op. 20.
☞ (M) *** Decca Dig. 425 063-2 [id.]. LPO Ch., LPO, Haitink.

Haitink's complete set of the symphonies has now been reissued at mid-price. Both as performances and certainly as recordings these CDs stand up well against most of the current competition, for the few that were analogue offered Decca's vintage sound-quality. No. 1 may lack something in youthful high spirits but it is none the less a strong, well-played performance. It is now recoupled with No. 3, not one of Shostakovich's finest works but still worth hearing when played as committedly as it is here. The recording is outstandingly clean and brilliant.

Symphonies Nos. 1 in F min., Op. 10; 5 in D min., Op. 47; (i) *7 in C, Op. 60; Prelude No. 14 in E flat min., Op. 34* (arr. Stokowski).
☞ (***) Pearl GEMM CDS9044 [id.]. Phd. O; (i) NBC SO, Stokowski.

There is always something special about pioneering records – particularly those conducted by Stokowski (see our review of his *Petrushka*). The *First Symphony* was recorded in 1934, less than a decade after its première under Malko. The sound was dryish and, among the perfect ensemble and attack, the playing has one or two slight blemishes. But there is tremendous atmosphere and concentration, and the transfers are excellent. The 78-r.p.m. discs faded out each side, but this has been splendidly overcome; those who do not know the originals will scarcely notice the joins. Stokowski's (1939) pioneering *Fifth* was never transferred to LP in the 1950s or '60s (its first appearance since the war years was on a Stokowski Society LP in 1991). It is an electrifying performance, impeccably played and splendidly transferred. The slow movement has a gripping intensity that is quite exceptional, and readers who do not know it will find it as revealing as his 1940 *Sixth* (Dell Arte DA 9023). The famous transcription of the *E flat minor Prelude*, Op. 34, originally coupled with his 1937 *Firebird Suite*, has a brooding, Mussorgskian menace all its own. Stokowski, Toscanini and Koussevitzky all competed for the privilege of the first performance of the *Leningrad Symphony.* Toscanini's highly concentrated account has recently reappeared on RCA and this performance, given only four months later with Toscanini's orchestra, is hardly less gripping. This *Leningrad* for all its sonic defects makes for exciting listening.

Symphonies Nos. 1 in F min.; 6 in B min., Op. 54.
*** Chan. Dig. CHAN 8411; *ABTD 1148* [id.]. SNO, Järvi.

Järvi's account of the *First Symphony* is strikingly more volatile than Haitink's in the outer movements – there is no lack of quirkiness in the finale, while the *Largo* is intense and passionate. The *Sixth* has comparable intensity, with an element of starkness in the austerity of the first movement. The Scherzo is skittish at first but, like the finale, has no lack of pungent force.

Symphonies Nos. 1 in F min., Op. 10; 9 in E flat, Op. 70.
☞ *** Teldec/Warner Dig. 4509 90849-2 [id.]. Nat. SO of Washington, Rostropovich.

In Rostropovich's hands the youthful *First Symphony* begins very promisingly indeed and continues well. Indeed there is plenty of fulfilment. This *First* is a very good account, free from exaggeration, even if he rushes the Scherzo off its feet. Rostropovich is also given a decently balanced recording. The *Ninth*, too, is well served; fears that the slow movement might be pulled out of shape prove generally groundless, though there is one moment of agogic exaggeration. Generally, this can be recommended to those looking for this particular coupling.

Symphonies Nos. 2 (October Revolution), Op. 14; 10 in E min., Op. 93.
☞ (M) **(*) Dig./Analogue 425 064-2 [id.]. LPO Ch., LPO, Haitink.

Shostakovich was still in his early twenties when he composed the *Second* and *Third Symphonies*. They were originally coupled together but, as neither work shows him at his most inspired, it was sensible to pair each off with other symphonies. Certainly the performance of No. 2 is admirable, and it is given excellently balanced sound with great presence and body. No. 10 is a masterpiece, and Haitink really has the measure of the first movement, whose climaxes he paces with an admirable sense of architecture. He secures sensitive and enthusiastic playing from the LPO, both here and in the malignant Scherzo. In the third movement he adopts a slower tempo than usual, which would be acceptable if there were greater tension or concentration of mood; but here and in the slow introduction to the finale the sense of concentration falters. The 1977 analogue recording (like the digital *Second*, made in the Kingsway Hall) is outstandingly realistic.

Symphony No. 4 in C min., Op. 43.
*** Chan. Dig. CHAN 8640; *ABTD 1328* [id.]. SNO, Järvi.
☞ (M) **(*) Decca 425 065-2 [id.]. LPO, Haitink.

Järvi draws from the SNO playing which is both rugged and expressive, consistently conveying the emotional thrust of the piece and making the enigmatic ending, with its ticking rhythm, warmer than usual, as though bitterness is finally evaporating. He is helped by exceptionally rich, full recording.

Haitink brings out an unexpected refinement in the *Symphony*, a rare transparency of texture. He is helped by recording of Decca's finest quality, vividly remastered. Detail is caught superbly; yet the earthiness and power, the demonic quality which can make this work so compelling, are underplayed.

Symphony No. 5 in D min., Op. 47 (see also under Cello concerto No. 1).
(M) *** BMG/RCA GD 86801 [6801-2-RG]. LSO, Previn (with RACHMANINOV: *The Rock* ***).
☞ (M) *** Telarc Dig. CD 82001 [id.]. Cleveland O, Maazel – STRAVINSKY: *Rite of spring.* **(*)
*** EMI Dig. CDC7 49181-2 [id.]. Oslo PO, Jansons.
(M) *** Erato/Warner 2292 45752-2 [id.]. Leningrad PO, Mravinsky.
☞ (M) **(*) Mercury 434 323-2 [id.]. Minneapolis SO, Skrowaczewski – KHACHATURIAN: *Gayaneh ballet suite.* **(*)

Symphony No. 5; Age of gold: Polka.
☞ (B) **(*) Sony SBK 53261 [id.]. Phd. O, Ormandy – PROKOFIEV: *Love for 3 oranges: suite.* **

Symphony No. 5, Op. 47; Festive overture, Op. 96.
☞ ** EMI Dig. CDC7 54803-2 [id.]. Phd. O, Muti.

Symphony No. 5; 5 Fragments, Op. 42.
*** Decca Dig. 421 120-2 [id.]. RPO, Ashkenazy.

Ashkenazy's account of Shostakovich's most popular symphony is an exceptionally searching and intense reading, bitingly dramatic, yet finding an element of wry humour in the second and fourth movements to outshine any rival. Ashkenazy conveys in the slow movement's spareness a rare sense of desolation, hushed and refined, with the woodwind solos adding to the chill. The Decca fill-up, the very rare *Five Fragments*, sharp little inventions, like the main work are given demonstration sound quality.

Previn's RCA version, dating from early in his recording career (1965), remains at the top of the list of bargain recommendations. This is one of the most concentrated and intense readings ever, superbly played by the LSO at its peak. In the third movement he sustains a slower speed than anyone else, making it deeply meditative in its dark intensity, while his build-up in the central development section brings playing of white heat. The bite and urgency of the second and fourth movements are also irresistible. Only in the hint of analogue tape-hiss does the sound fall short of the finest modern digital recordings – and it is more vividly immediate than most.

Now reissued on Telarc's mid-price Bravo! label, generously coupled with spectacular Stravinsky, Maazel's version is well worth considering. Brilliant in performance, spectacular in recorded sound, like all of Maazel's Cleveland recordings for Telarc, this Shostakovich reading is also warm, with the Cleveland violins sweet and pure in the long-legged melody of the second subject in the first movement. Though Maazel is faster than is common in the exposition section, he allows himself less stringendo than usual in the build-up of the development. The other three movements are also on the fast side, with little feeling of Ländler rhythm in the Scherzo and a sweet rather than rarefied reading of the *Largo* slow movement. This fits neatly between the spacious but rather severe reading of Haitink and the boldly expressive Bernstein.

Jansons' EMI version with the Oslo orchestra on top form brings a tautly incisive, electrically intense reading, marked by speeds notably faster than usual that yet have the ring of authenticity. The development section in the first movement for example builds up bitingly into a thrilling climax, with the accelerando powerfully controlled. Not a first choice, but an exciting one.

Mravinsky conducted the première of the *Fifth Symphony* in 1937, and so brings a special authority to this work. The present version is not free from the odd untidiness but there is still evidence of a commanding personality, and even though the recording itself is not in the luxury bracket, this CD must figure high on any list.

The Philadelphia Orchestra made the very first recording of the *Fifth Symphony* (under Stokowski), and they play it marvellously here: the strings produce the most opulent tone and generate considerable eloquence in the slow movement; the solo flute, too, makes a highly distinguished contribution. Ormandy has always shown a special feeling for Shostakovich and he is direct and straightforward, but neither here (in 1965) nor in his later, RCA disc does one sense the degree of commitment that marked his earlier recording of the *First Symphony*. *The Age of gold polka* makes a witty encore after the Prokofiev coupling.

Skrowaczewski's Minneapolis account of Shostakovich's *Fifth* was one of the first really successful stereo recordings, with great concentration in the pianissimo string-playing in the *Largo* and a finale which, after an exhilarating *Allegro*, brings a trenchant, ponderous coda, anticipating much later performances, after the composer had revealed that his closing section was not intended to be an ingenuous triumphant celebration. The first movement has a fast opening speed, but the conductor understands Shostakovich's melodic line and, although this is a wilful reading, it is also an exciting one. The two climaxes of the slow movement are brought off powerfully, and the tension in the closing pages is considerable. The recording was made in the Northrop Auditorium in 1961 and is full yet astonishingly clear, but the upper strings have that curious thinness which was characteristic of Mercury's Minneapolis ventures at that time. However, the ear soon adjusts, and this performance is very compelling.

Gone are the days when the Philadelphia Orchestra sounded quite different from any other. Now it sounds like any first-class body and has lost that special individuality it had under Ormandy (and, before him, Stokowski). It goes without saying that Riccardo Muti's version offers excellent orchestral playing, but the virtuosity is routine rather than inspired. It is very well recorded, but we are not brought close to this music as we were by Stokowski. No challenge to the three-star recommendations.

Symphonies Nos. 5 in D min.; 9 in E flat, Op. 70.
☞ (M) *** Decca Dig. 425 066-2 [id.]. (i) Concg. O; (ii) LPO, Haitink.
(BB) *** Naxos Dig. 8.550427 [id.]. Belgian R. & TV O, Alexander Rahbari.
*** Olympia Dig. OCD 113 [id.]. USSR MoC SO, Rozhdestvensky.
☞ (M) **(*) Sony SMK 47615-2. NYPO, Bernstein.

This generous Decca reissue, splendidly recorded, is certainly value for money, playing for 76 minutes. In No. 5 Haitink is eminently straightforward, there are no disruptive changes in tempo, and the playing of the Concertgebouw Orchestra and the contribution of the Decca engineers are beyond praise. There could perhaps be greater intensity of feeling in the slow movement but, whatever small reservations one might have, it is most impressive both artistically and sonically. The coupled No. 9 is superb. Without inflation Haitink gives it a serious purpose, both in the poignancy of the waltz-like second movement and in the equivocal emotions of the outer movements. The recording is outstanding in every way.

Both in the hushed intensity of the lyrical passages and in the vigour and bite of Shostakovich's violent allegros Rahbari's reading is most convincing, with dramatic tensions finely controlled in a spontaneous-sounding way. In No. 9 Rahbari opts for a controversially slow *Moderato* second movement but sustains it well, and the outer movements are deliciously witty in their pointing. The playing of all sections is first rate, and the sound is full and brilliant. An outstandingly generous coupling makes this a most attractive issue, even with no allowance made for the very low price.

The *Ninth* in particular suits Rozhdestvensky's personality ideally, with the element of wit and humour brilliantly presented, and with the darker, more emotional elements emerging strongly and committedly. The Ministry of Culture Orchestra demonstrates in that work that it is second to none in Moscow, though the playing is less polished in No. 5, where violin-tone in the exposed passages is sometimes lacking fullness. Warm, vivid recording, with the players set fairly close against a reverberant acoustic.

This was Bernstein's first recording of the *Fifth*, made in 1959; he re-recorded it later digitally. His view of the work was admired by the composer, perhaps because the finale opens so ferociously. Overall the performance is more full-blooded than with Kertész but is no match for Previn's RCA version. However, Bernstein revels in the high spirits of the *Ninth*, and he also manages the alternation of moods very successfully. The sound has been greatly improved in both symphonies.

Symphony No. 6 in B min., Op. 54.
(M) *** EMI CDM7 69564-2. LSO, Previn – RACHMANINOV: *Symphony No. 3.* ***
(***) Dell'Arte mono DA 9023 [id.]. Phd. O, Stokowski – SIBELIUS: *Symphony No. 4* etc. (**)
☞ ** Koch Schwann Dig. 311 202 [id.]. Saarbrücken RSO, Myung-Whun Chung – RIMSKY-
KORSAKOV: *Legend of the invisible city of Kitezh.* **
☞ * (M) Ph. 438 283-2 [id.]. Concg. O, Kondrashin – NIELSEN: *Symphony No. 5.* *

Here Previn shows his deep understanding of Shostakovich in a powerfully drawn, unrelenting account of the opening movement, his slow tempo adding to the overall impact. After that the offhand wit of the central Scherzo comes over the more delicately at a slower tempo than usual, leaving the hectic finale to hammer home the deceptively joyful conclusion to the argument. Excellent recording, impressively remastered.

Stokowski's *Sixth* was made in 1940, only a few months after the work was premièred, and it brings one face to face not only with this symphony but also with the bleak, harsh times during which it came into being. It is powerfully atmospheric, the lines wonderfully sustained and the playing at times frighteningly intense. This performance has a special ring of authenticity.

Myung-Whun Chung's performance, strangely enough, has a more idiomatic feel to it than Kondrashin's, and is well enough played by the Saarbrücken Radio Orchestra. But at full price and given such short playing time (49 minutes), it is an uneconomic investment.

As in his earlier, EMI/Melodiya LP, Kirill Kondrashin takes the opening movement rather too fast and in so doing diminishes its impact. His version, though well played, is not a front runner, nor is his account of the Nielsen symphony with which it is coupled.

Symphonies Nos. 6 in B min., Op. 54; 12 in D min. (The Year 1917), Op. 112.
☞ (M) *** Decca Dig. 425 067-2 [id.]. Concg. O, Haitink.
*** Olympia Dig. OCD 111 [id.]. USSR MoC SO, Rozhdestvensky.

This is another generous recoupling. Haitink's performances of both symphonies are characteristically refined and powerful and, with superb playing from the Concertgebouw Orchestra, particularly the strings, and brilliant and atmospheric Decca recording, the textures are given an extra transparency. Haitink's structural control, coupled with his calm, taut manner, is particularly impressive in the slow movement of No. 6. As a work, No. 12 is more problematic. There is much of the composer's vision and grandeur here but also his crudeness. However, the sheer quality of the sound and the superb responsiveness and body of the Concertgebouw Orchestra might well seduce many listeners. As with the *Sixth* the slow movement has a marvellous sense of atmosphere, which is well conveyed in this Decca performance – as it is, to be fair, in Mravinsky's Erato account with the Leningrad Philharmonic. That has playing of electrifying intensity and remains preferable, even if the mid-priced Erato CD has no coupling (2292 45754-2). But the Amsterdam orchestra also play as if they believe every crotchet and, though not even their eloquence can rescue the finale, overall the performance is very successful, if not as thrilling as Mravinsky's account.

No. 6 is a work that Rozhdestvensky responds to with exceptional warmth, giving weight and intensity to the magnificent opening slow movement and bringing out the spark of dark humour in the Scherzo and finale while giving them necessary bite and power. He is also most persuasive in the programmatic No. 12, bringing out the atmosphere and drama. First-rate playing from the Ministry of Culture Orchestra and full-bodied, warm recording.

Symphony No. 7 in C (Leningrad), Op. 60.
*** Chan. Dig. CHAN 8623; *ABTD 1312* [id.]. SNO, Järvi.
☞ (M) **(*) Decca Dig. 425 068-2 [id.]. LPO, Haitink.
**(*) Olympia Dig. OCD 118 [id.]. USSR MoC SO, Rozhdestvensky.
☞ (M) **(*) Sony SMK 47616-2. NYPO, Bernstein.
(M) (***) BMG/RCA mono GD60293 [60293-2-RG]. NBC SO, Toscanini.

Järvi's is a strong, intense reading, beautifully played and recorded, which brings out the full drama of this symphony in a performance that consistently gives the illusion of spontaneity in a live performance, as in the hushed tension of the slow, expansive passages. There have been more polished versions than this, but, with its spectacular Chandos sound, it makes an excellent choice as a single-disc version.

Although he does not wear his heart on his sleeve, Haitink is here eminently straightforward and there are no disruptive changes in tempo. There could perhaps be greater intensity of feeling in the slow movement, and the long first-movement *ostinato* – now revealed as having quite different implications from the descriptive programme suggested by the Soviet propaganda machine in the war years – is not presented histrionically; but the deep seriousness which Haitink finds in the rest of the work challenges comparisons with the other wartime symphony, the epic *Eighth*. The playing of the Concertgebouw Orchestra is beyond praise, and the splendid contribution of the Decca engineers ensures the success of this CD.

Rozhdestvensky's view of the *Leningrad Symphony*'s controversial first movement is unusually broad. It is undeniably powerful but runs the risk of overplaying the element of banality in the notorious *ostinato*. Many will prefer a brisker and more polished reading, but the ruggedness here is certainly authentic; the other movements too bring warmly expressive, spontaneous-sounding performances, which lack only the last degree of subtlety. The sound is full and satisfying but grows coarse at the biggest climaxes.

Bernstein made his recording in 1962 when appreciation of the work was at its lowest ebb. He brings a certain panache and fervour to his reading, particularly in the inspired slow movement, so that one is tempted to look indulgently at its occasional overstatements (and the fact that the – originally CBS – recording does not compare with its Decca competitor).

Toscanini and the NBC Orchestra bring an urgency and fervour that is altogether special and an intensity that shines through the primitive recorded sound. There is a special feeling of authenticity that conveys the flavour of the period and the vividness of the experience more effectively than many modern recordings. Be warned, however, the 1942 sound does call for some tolerance.

Symphony No. 8 in C min., Op. 65.
*** Ph. Dig. 422 442-2 [id.]. Leningrad PO, Mravinsky.
☞ (M) *** Decca Dig. 425 071-2 [id.]. Concg. O, Haitink.
☞ *** Teldec/Warner Dig. 9031 74719-2 [id.]. Nat. SO of Washington, Rostropovich.

Symphony No. 8 in C min.; Funeral and triumphal prelude; Novorossisk chimes.
☞ **(*) Decca Dig. 436 763-2 [id.]. RPO, Ashkenazy.

Symphony No. 8 in C min.; Overture on Russian and Kirghiz folk tunes, Op. 115.
☞ (*) Praga mono 250 040 [id.]. Moscow PO, Kondrashin.

Symphony No. 8 in C min.; (i) 3 Satires from Op. 109.
*** Olympia Dig. OCD 143 [id.]. USSR MoC SO, Rozhdestvensky; (i) with Bogacheva.

Mravinsky's live recording in full, clear, digital sound gives a superb idea of the magnetism of his reading, demonstrating the firm structural strength while plumbing the deep personal emotions in this stressed wartime inspiration. Most significantly, Mravinsky's flowing speed for the elusive *Allegretto* finale makes the close of the work less equivocal than usual. It is a great performance and, though ensemble is inevitably not always quite as polished as in the finest studio recordings, discrepancies are minimal.

Rozhdestvensky conducts a thrustful and incisive reading of the *Eighth* with electrically intense playing that both holds the enormous structure together and brings out the element of fantasy which literal performances underplay. The digital recording is full-bodied and wide-ranging, growing a little coarse only in the biggest climaxes. The *Three Satires* are orchestral arrangements of songs from a cycle of poems by Sasha Cherny. Irina Bogacheva, a strong, very Slavonic mezzo, gives characterful performances, though her voice is balanced far too close.

Haitink characteristically presents a strongly architectural reading of this war-inspired symphony, at times direct to the point of severity. After the massive and sustained slow movement which opens the work, Haitink allows no lightness or relief in the Scherzo movements, and in his seriousness in the strangely lightweight finale (neither fast nor slow) he provides an unusually satisfying account of an equivocal, seemingly uncommitted movement.

The trouble with so many performances conducted by Rostropovich is that the great Russian musician tends diligently to cross every 't', dot every 'i' and underline everything else. But in his account of the *Eighth Symphony* his intensity and that of his players does not spill over into excess. This is a gripping account that can rank alongside the best performances one has heard on or off record – Mravinsky, Rozhdestvensky, Kondrashin and the excellent Haitink – and it is very well recorded too.

Ashkenazy is an eminently sound and reliable guide in this repertoire and gives a thoroughly committed, felt account of the symphony. He gets good playing from the RPO too, though they do not match Mravinsky's Leningrad or Haitink's mid-1980s Concertgebouw. The sound is not top-drawer Decca but very good. The fill-ups are worth hearing – once!

For all his authority and distinction, Kondrashin is far from persuasive in his 1969 mono account of the *Eighth Symphony*, recorded in Prague only a year after Soviet tanks crushed the Prague Spring. The recording is raw and shallow and, although the playing in the Scherzos is pretty amazing, his all-too-brisk tempi do not allow the breadth and tragedy to register. His pioneering recording of the *Fourth* was too fast and so was the first movement of his *Sixth*. The dark and moving *Passacaglia* is quite breathless, even faster than in his Melodiya LP. The *Overture on Russian and Kirghiz folk tunes*, not Shostakovich at his best, is of earlier provenance but sounds better. A write-off.

Symphony No. 9 in E flat, Op. 70; Festive overture, Op. 96; Katerina Ismailova (Lady Macbeth of Mtsensk): 5 Entr'actes. Tahiti trot (arr. of Youmans's *Tea for two*), *Op. 16.*
*** Chan. Dig. CHAN 8567; *ABTD 1279* [id.]. SNO, Järvi.

Järvi's version of the *Ninth* brings a warmly expressive, strongly characterized reading in superb, wide-ranging sound. The point and wit of the first movement go with bluff good humour, leading on to an account of the second-movement *Moderato* that is yearningly lyrical yet not at all sentimental, contrasted with the fun and jokiness of the final *Allegretto*. The mixed bag of fill-up items is both illuminating and characterful, ending with the jolly little chamber arrangement that Shostakovich did in the 1920s of Vincent Youmans's *Tea for two*, the *Tahiti trot*.

Symphonies Nos. (i) *9 in E flat;* (ii) *10 in E min.*
(M) (***) Sony mono MPK 45698 [id.]. NYPO, (i) Efrem Kurtz; (ii) Dmitri Mitropoulos.

Dmitri Mitropoulos's pioneering account of the *Tenth Symphony* with the New York Philharmonic penetrates more deeply into the heart of this score than any of the recent newcomers; only Karajan's mid-1960s version can be put alongside it. It comes with Efrem Kurtz's 1949 version of the *Ninth* with the same orchestra, playing with great virtuosity. The sound is remarkably good for its period (an edit has removed one note from the opening phrase of the scherzo), but apart from that hiccup this is a stunning performance.

Symphony No. 10 in E min., Op. 93.
*** DG Dig. 413 361-2 [id.]. BPO, Karajan.
(B) *** Pickwick Dig. PCD 955; *IMPC 955* [id.]. Hallé O, Skrowaczewski.
(M) (***) Saga mono EC 3366-2. Leningrad PO, Mravinsky.
☞ (M) ** EMI Dig. CDM7 64870-2 [id.]. Philh. O, Simon Rattle – BRITTEN: *Sinfonia da Requiem.*
***

Symphony No. 10 in E min., Op. 93; Ballet suite No. 4.
*** Chan. Dig. CHAN 8630; *ABTD 1319* [id.]. SNO, Järvi.

Already in his 1967 recording Karajan had shown that he had the measure of this symphony; this newer version is, if anything, even finer. In the first movement he distils an atmosphere as concentrated as before, bleak and unremitting, while in the *Allegro* the Berlin Philharmonic leave no doubts as to their peerless virtuosity. Everything is marvellously shaped and proportioned, and the digital sound is altogether excellent.

Järvi, too, conducts an outstandingly strong and purposeful reading in superb sound, full and atmospheric. In the great span of the long *Moderato* first movement he chooses an ideal speed, which allows for moments of hushed repose but still builds up relentlessly. The curious little *Ballet suite No.*

4, with its sombre *Prelude* leading to a bouncy *Waltz* and a jolly *Scherzo tarantella*, makes a delightful bonus.

Recorded in full, brilliant and weighty sound, Skrowaczewski's version of the *Tenth* is also a top recommendation. Above all, the spacious *moderato* of the long first movement has a natural power and concentration which put it among the finest versions, with the Hallé brass superbly focused at the great climaxes.

Mravinsky conducted the work's première, but his mono LP was originally let down by dim recording. The sound has been improved on CD. In the long first movement Mravinsky captures the doleful melancholy of the opening and he moves to the bitter desperation of the climax with great eloquence. The Leningrad Philharmonic plays the scherzo with staggering virtuosity and the work is satisfyingly resolved in the finale.

Rattle's Philharmonia version is curiously wayward in the two big slow movements, first and third in the scheme. In the first, Rattle is exceptionally slow, and though in principle such a view might yield revelatory results tension slips too readily. So too in the third movement. The Scherzo and energetic finale are much more successful. The recording does not help, with the strings sounding thin and lacking body.

Symphony No. 11 (The Year 1905), Op. 103.
☞ (M) *** EMI CDM7 65206-2 [id.]. Houston SO, Stokowski.
☞ (M) *** Decca Dig. 425 072-2 [id.]. Concg. O, Haitink.
**(*) DG Dig. 429 405-2 [id.]. Gothenburg SO, Järvi.
☞ *** Delos Dig. D/CD 3080 [id.]. Helsinki PO, James DePreist.
☞ ** Teldec/Warner Dig. 9031 76262-2 [id.]. Nat. SO of Washington, Rostropovich.
☞ Russian Disc mono RDCD1 1157 [id.]. Leningrad PO, Mravinsky.

1905 was the year of the first Russian uprising which foreshadowed the revolution to come rather more than a decade later. The result is a programme symphony conceived on a fairly large scale and, as in the *Leningrad Symphony*, its style is sometimes repetitive. But, as the powerful atmosphere of the opening immediately shows, Stokowski's characteristic intensity holds the structure together and the *Adagio* (*Eternal memory*) has great expressive feeling. He gave its first performance in the USA in April 1958 and the recording was made a few days later, only a year after Mravinsky's pioneering version; like so many recordings close to the date of composition, it has a very special feeling of authenticity. It has tremendous atmosphere and fire and, now that it has been so strikingly transferred – it has been remastered from the original session tapes – succeeds completely in bringing the whole feeling of the period back. Tremendous playing from all concerned and an interpretation of real vision. It has still not been surpassed and the early stereo, with rich strings, is vividly opulent if forwardly balanced and not very transparent.

Haitink's sense of architecture is as impressive as always, even if at times he seems almost detached, lacking the last degree of tension which both Stokowski and Mravinsky brought to this music. However, the Concertgebouw Orchestra plays superbly, and the Decca sound is as brilliant and realistic as ever.

The DePreist version came out some time ago and won golden opinions: it certainly has the benefit of magnificent recording. The Helsinki orchestra may lack the weight and richness of sonority of the greatest orchestras but it plays with great intensity and feeling. A performance that has great atmosphere and expressive power.

Neeme Järvi's account of the *Eleventh Symphony* has much to recommend it, including good orchestral playing and very fine recorded sound. Good though it is, the performance misses the last ounce of intensity that made the old LP accounts of Mravinsky and Stokowski so extraordinarily powerful.

There is atmosphere in Rostropovich's account with the Washington orchestra but, as can so easily happen in this score, the listener can soon wool-gather if the conductor does not have tremendous grip. Much has been made in the musical press of the out-of-tune timpani note, but for many this will not be as disturbing as its lack of narrative drive. No challenge to the other versions here.

Watch out! Readers who recall the spellbinding, powerfully concentrated and atmospheric Melodiya LPs of Mravinsky's Leningrad Philharmonic performance of the *Eleventh Symphony* will eagerly seize the Russian Disc performance recorded on 3 November 1957, turn down the lights and wait to be put under this conductor's spell. Alas, this is not the same performance. The restless audience and the incessant and intrusive barrage of coughing are so disruptive that we were forced to give up after about eight minutes, and a spot check later in the work showed little improvement! The recording also misses the beginning of the opening chord. A great disappointment.

Symphony No. 12 in D min. (The Year 1917), Op. 112.
(M) *** Erato/Warner 2292 45754-2 [id.]. Leningrad PO, Mravinsky.

(i) *Symphony No. 12 in D min. (The Year 1917), Op. 112;* (ii) *The Execution of Stepan Razin, Op. 119.*
☞ (M) *** Ph. 434 172-2 [id.]. (i) Leipzig GO, Durjan; (ii) Siegfried Vogel, Leipzig R. Ch. & RSO, Kegel.

The *Twelfth Symphony* is one of Shostakovich's more problematic essays in the genre. However, when a conductor of Mravinsky's quality is at the helm and drawing playing of electrifying intensity from the Leningrad Philharmonic, that impression is almost dispelled. Mravinsky's first version appeared in the early 1960s and long reigned supreme, but this Erato account, taken from a concert performance in 1984, is even higher in voltage, and the recording does ample justice to their playing.

More than in his other mature symphonies, Shostakovich apparently gave way in this evocation of the Revolution year to overtly propagandist aims, though he may have been writing satirically, tongue in cheek. However, in this work the dangers of falling over the cliff-edge into banality are considerable. Ogan Durjan avoids them most effectively, fearless in attack in even the bombastic passages, for the precision of the playing and the control of texture and weight reveal a far wider range of emotion than usual. There have been other fine recordings since (notably Mravinsky's – also at medium price) but none with a more generous coupling. *The Execution of Stepan Razin*, like the *Thirteenth Symphony*, is based on a Yevtushenko poem and is a vigorous and full-blooded cantata with some highly characteristic Shostakovich in it. Kegel's performance is a dramatic one, with an impressive contribution from the bass soloist, Siegfried Vogel, and excellent choral and orchestral response. Both recordings date from 1967 and have been remastered very successfully for CD. This reissue, however, is a limited edition, not likely to be available beyond the lifetime of this book.

Symphony No. 13 in B flat min. (Babi-Yar), Op. 113.
☞ (M) *** Decca Dig. 425 073-2 [id.]. Marius Rintzler, Concg. Male Ch. & O, Haitink.
☞ *** Teldec/Warner Dig. 4509-90848-2 [id.]. Yevtushenko, Leiferkus, New York Ch. Arts, NYPO, Masur.

The often brutal directness of Haitink's way with Shostakovich works well in the *Thirteenth Symphony*, particularly in the long *Adagio* first movement, whose title, *Babi-Yar*, gives its name to the whole work. That first of five Yevtushenko settings, boldly attacking anti-semitism in Russia, sets the pattern for Haitink's severe view of the whole. Rintzler with his magnificent, resonant bass is musically superb but, matching Haitink, remains objective rather than dashingly characterful. The resolution of the final movement, with its pretty flutings surrounding a wry poem about Galileo and greatness, then works beautifully. Outstandingly brilliant and full sound, remarkable even for this series.

Kurt Masur's reading of the *Babi Yar Symphony* is very powerful indeed, full of atmosphere and intensity. It has the benefit of Sergei Leiferkus and the Men of the New York Choral Artists and very clean and well focused recording. Another point of interest is Yevtushenko's readings which flank the performance. It does not sweep the board, but it is certainly among the best versions we have had to date.

Symphony No. 14 in G min., Op. 135.
☞ (M) **(*) Sony SMK 47617-2. Teresa Kubiak, Isser Bushkin, NYPO, Bernstein.

(i) *Symphony No. 14, Op. 135;* (ii) *King Lear (musical fragments), Op. 58a.*
*** Olympia Dig. OCD 182 [id.]. (i) Kasrashubili, Safiulin, USSR MoC SO, Rozhdestvensky; (ii) Romanova, Leningrad CO, Serov.

(i) *Symphony No. 14, Op. 135;* (ii) *6 Poems of Marina Tsvetaeva, Op. 143a.*
☞ (M) *** Decca Dig. 425 074-2 [id.]. (i) Varady, Fischer-Dieskau; (ii) Wenkel; Concg. O, Haitink.

The *Fourteenth* is Shostakovich's most sombre and dark score, a setting of poems by Lorca, Apollinaire, Rilke, Brentano and Küchelbecker, all on the theme of death; Haitink's version gives each poem in its original language. It is a most powerful performance, and the outstanding recording is well up to the standard of this fine Decca series. The song-cycle, splendidly sung by Ortrun Wenkel, makes a fine bonus.

The Ministry of Culture Orchestra's performance is magnetic in drawing the sequence together; sadly, however, the booklet does not include texts, only a summary of each poem. The full, bright, digital sound is more atmospheric than some in the Olympia series. The colourful but lightweight *King Lear* pieces, recorded in warm, full, analogue sound, make a useful coupling.

Bernstein's version with Teresa Kubiak and Isser Bushkin, recorded in 1976, does not have the benefit of such excellent sound as the Haitink, yet, taken in its own right, it is perfectly acceptable and the performance is both powerful and deeply felt without underlining expressive points to excess. Shostakovich's bleak ruminations on the theme of death exercise a compelling fascination even in those songs in which the quality of invention seems a little strained (as in *On watch*, the third of the Apollinaire settings). It casts its spell, for Bernstein gets good playing from the New Yorkers and there is a Mussorgskian atmosphere here which eludes the Decca performance. A pity there is no coupling: this plays for only 51 minutes.

(i) *Symphony No. 15 in A, Op. 141;* (ii) *From Jewish folk poetry* (song-cycle), *Op. 79.*
☞ ⊛ (M) *** Decca Analogue/Dig. 425 069-2 [id.]. (i) LPO; (ii) Söderström, Wenkel, Karczykowski, Concg. O; Haitink.

Early readings of the composer's last symphony seemed to underline the quirky unpredictability of the work, with the collage of strange quotations – above all the *William Tell* gallop, which keeps recurring in the first movement – seemingly joky rather than profound. Haitink by contrast makes the first movement sound genuinely symphonic, bitingly urgent. He underlines the purity of the bare lines of the second movement; after the Wagner quotations which open the finale, his slow tempo for the main lyrical theme gives it heartaching tenderness, not the usual easy triviality. The playing of the LPO is excellent, with refined tone and superb attack, and the recording is both analytical and atmospheric. The CD includes a splendidly sung version of *From Jewish folk poetry*, settings which cover a wide range of emotions including tenderness, humour and even happiness as in the final song. Ryszard Karczykowski brings vibrant Slavonic feeling to the work which, with its wide variety of mood and colour, has a scale to match the shorter symphonies.

CHAMBER AND INSTRUMENTAL MUSIC

Cello sonata in D min., Op. 40.
*** Chan. Dig. CHAN 8340; *ABTD 1372* [id.]. Turovsky, Edlina – PROKOFIEV: *Sonata.* ***
*** BIS Dig. CD 336 [id.]. Thedéen, Pöntinen – SCHNITTKE: *Sonata;* STRAVINSKY: *Suite italienne.*
***

Yuli Turovsky and Luba Edlina play the *Cello sonata* with great panache and eloquence, if in the finale they almost succumb at times to exaggeration in their handling of its humour – no understatement here.

The Swedish cellist, Torleif Thedéen, has a real feeling for its structure and the vein of bitter melancholy under its ironic surface. Roland Pöntinen gives him excellent support and the BIS recording does justice to this partnership.

Cello sonata in D min., Op. 40; (i) *Piano trio No. 2 in E min., Op. 67.*
**(*) Sony Dig. MK 44664 [id.]. Yo-Yo Ma, Emanuel Ax; (i) with Isaac Stern.

The *Trio* receives a deeply felt performance, one which can hold its own with any issue, past or present. The *Sonata* is another matter; the playing is as beautiful as one would expect, but here Ma's self-communing propensity for reducing his tone is becoming a tiresome affectation. Ax plays splendidly and the CBS recording is very truthful.

Piano quintet in G min., Op. 57.
**(*) CRD CRD 3351; *CRDC 4051* [id.]. Clifford Benson, Alberni Qt – BRITTEN: *Quartet No. 1.*
***
☞ *(*) Nimbus Dig. NI 5156 [id.]. John Bingham, Medici Qt – MENDELSSOHN: *Quartet, Op. 13.*

Piano quintet, Op. 57; Piano trio No. 2 in E min., Op. 67.
**(*) Chan. Dig. CHAN 8342; *ABTD 1088* [id.]. Borodin Trio, Zweig, Horner.
**(*) ASV ZCALH 929 [id.]. Music Group of London.
☞ ** Ph. Dig. 432 079-2 [id.]. Beaux Arts Trio, (i) with Drucker, Dutton.

The *Piano trio* is a particularly painful and anguished work, dedicated to the memory of a close friend, Ivan Sollertinsky, who died in the year of its composition. The Chandos version is bolder in character and more concentrated in feeling than its main rival. The Music Group of London show rather less panache but are still impressive, and in their hands the *Trio* is played affectingly.

Alternatively, there is a vigorous and finely conceived account from Clifford Benson and the Alberni Quartet, vividly recorded; if the Britten coupling is wanted, this will be found fully satisfactory. All three accounts of the *Quintet* are very satisfactory.

A decent performance of the *Piano quintet* from John Bingham and the Medici Quartet, but the recording is not entirely satisfactory. The quartet is rather forwardly placed in the aural picture; the piano is well behind them and is troubled with unwelcome reverberation.

The Beaux Arts Trio (with Eugene Drucker and Lawrence Dutton as violin and viola respectively) do not seriously challenge the Borodin–Richter account on EMI (see below), though they are far more beautifully recorded. Menahem Pressler is less dark and commanding in the opening measures of the *Prelude*, and one comes away from the performance feeling that there are layers of feeling that remain unexplored. There are very good things – the Scherzo of the *Quintet* and the finale of the *Trio* are examples – but they offer cultured performances rather than the dark and powerfully characterized readings you find elsewhere.

Piano trio No. 2 in E min., Op. 67.
**(*) Collins Dig. 1040-2 [id.]. Trio Zingara – RAVEL: *Piano trio in A min.* **(*)

The *E minor Piano trio* by the Trio Zingara is an assured and accomplished account, extremely well recorded and sensitively phrased. One quarrel: they take the slow movement slower than marked and, as a result, do not fully sustain its atmosphere and concentration. However, those who want this particular coupling will derive much musical satisfaction from it.

2 Pieces for string octet, Op. 11.
☞ *** Chan. Dig. CHAN 9131 [id.]. ASMF Chamber Ens. – ENESCU: *Octet in C;* R. STRAUSS: *Capriccio: Sextet.* ***

2 Pieces for string octet, Op. 11; (i) *Elegy, Polka.*
☞ *(*) Nimbus Dig. NI 5140 [id.]. Alberni Qt, (i) & Medici Qt – MENDELSSOHN: *Octet.* *(*)

The *Two Pieces for string octet* come from the period of the *First Symphony*, and the *Elegy and Polka* for quartet were written in 1931. The Academy of St Martin-in-the-Fields Chamber Ensemble play splendidly and with conviction; they are beautifully recorded and also offer a highly recommendable version of the Enescu *Octet*. The Nimbus disc with the Alberni and Medici gives very acceptable accounts, decently recorded, and there are relatively few current alternatives of either the Op. 11 pieces or the *Elegy and Polka* with which they couple it. All the same, at 47 minutes 44 seconds their disc is not good value for money.

String quartets

String quartets Nos. 1–15.
(M) *** Decca 433 078-2 (6). Fitzwilliam Qt.

The Shostakovich *Quartets* thread through his creative life like some inner odyssey and inhabit terrain of increasing spiritual desolation. The Fitzwilliam Quartet played to Shostakovich himself and gave the UK premières of his last three quartets, and they bring to the whole cycle complete and total dedication. One has only to sample the first two quartets to discover the sustained and often hushed intensity of this playing, which so consistently has the spontaneity of live music-making. They are given first-class recording too, with great presence and natural body. The recordings were made in All Saints Church, Petersham, Surrey between 1955 and 1957; a rather forward balance was chosen, perhaps because of the ecclesiastical acoustic, and this is slightly emphasized by the CD transfer, yet there is a natural transparency and a firm focus throughout. There are minor criticisms, but they are too trivial to weigh in the balance, for this set is by any standards a formidable achievement.

String quartets Nos. 1–15; (i) *Piano quintet in G min.*
☞ (M) *** EMI CMS5 65032-2 (6) [id.]. Borodin Qt, (i) with Sviatoslav Richter.

String quartets Nos. 1 in C, Op. 49; 9 in E flat, Op. 117; 12 in D flat, Op. 133.
*** EMI CDC7 49266-2 [id.]. Borodin Qt.

String quartets Nos. 2 in A, Op. 68; 3 in F, Op. 73.
☞ *** EMI CDC7 49267-2 [id.]. Borodin Qt.

String quartets Nos. 4 in D, Op. 83; 6 in G, Op. 101; 11 in F min., Op. 122.
*** EMI CDC7 49268-2 [id.]. Borodin Qt.

String quartets Nos. 5 in B flat, Op. 92; 15 in E flat min., Op. 144.
*** EMI CDC7 49270-2 [id.]. Borodin Qt.

String quartets Nos. 7 in F sharp min., Op. 108; 8 in C min., Op. 110; (i) *Piano quintet, Op. 57.*
☞ *** EMI Dig. CDC7 47507-2 [id.]. Borodin Qt, (i) with Sviatoslav Richter.

String quartets Nos. 10 in A flat, Op. 118; 13 in B flat min., Op. 138; 14 in F sharp, Op. 142.
*** EMI CDC7 49269-2 [id.]. Borodin Qt.

EMI offer the Borodin Quartet's second complete cycle. They are available separately, at full price, and regular readers will note that two CDs have been restored to the catalogue since our last edition. We hope they remain available in this individual format, but the complete set is a more economical investment. The present recordings are made in a generally drier acoustic than their predecessors, and Nos. 3 and 5 suffer noticeably in this respect. However, the ears quickly adjust and the performances can only be described as masterly. The Borodins possess enormous refinement, an altogether sumptuous tone and a perfection of technical address that is almost in a class of its own – and what wonderful intonation! These and the Bartók six are the greatest quartet cycles produced in the present century and are mandatory listening. The *Piano quintet* was recorded at a public concert at the Moscow Conservatoire, and it goes without saying that with Richter at the helm the account is a powerful one, although the quality of the sound here is noticeably dry and forward.

String quartets Nos. 1–15.
☞ *(**) Teldec/Warner Dig. 90311 71702-2 (6). Brodsky Qt.

String quartets Nos. 1 in C, Op. 49; 3 in F, Op. 73; 4 in D, Op. 83.
*** Teldec/Warner Dig. 2292 46009-2 [id.]. Brodsky Qt.

String quartets Nos. 2 in A, Op. 68; 5 in B flat, Op. 92.
☞ **(*) Teldec/Warner Dig. 9031 73110-2 [id.]. Brodsky Qt.

String quartets Nos. 6 in G, Op. 101; 10 in A flat, Op. 118; 14 in F sharp, Op. 142.
☞ **(*) Teldec/Warner Dig. 9031 73108-2 [id.]. Brodsky Qt.

String quartets Nos. 7 in F sharp min., Op. 108; 8 in C min., Op. 110; 9 in E flat, Op. 117.
☞ **(*) Teldec/Warner Dig. 2292 44919-2 [id.]. Brodsky Qt.

String quartets Nos. 11 in F min., Op. 122; 12 in D flat, Op. 133; 13 in B flat min., Op. 138.
☞ **(*) Teldec/Warner Dig. 9031 73109-2 [id.]. Brodsky Qt.

The Brodskys are recorded in good, well-detailed, digital sound, and they give well-prepared and intelligent performances of these *Quartets*. They are very attentive to detail but their playing is generally less searching than the Borodins. However, while their complete set (still offered at full price) is uncompetitive alongside those of the Borodin and Fitzwilliam groups, individual performances are still rewarding; while the recordings are rather close, if any of these particular groupings are required, the above comparisons need not inhibit quite a strong recommendation.

String quartets Nos. 2 in A, Op. 68; 12 in D flat, Op. 133.
☞ *** Virgin/EMI Dig. VC7 59281-2 [id.]. Borodin Qt.

String quartets Nos. 3 in F, Op. 73; 7 in F sharp min., Op. 108; 8 in C min., Op. 110.
☞ *** Virgin/EMI Dig. VC7 59041-2 [id.]. Borodin Qt.

The new Borodin accounts of the *Second* and *Twelfth Quartets* have the benefit of far better and more refined recording than their earlier, Melodiya account, now available on EMI at mid-price. The sound is richer and cleaner and has a pleasing bloom, as one would expect from the Snape Maltings. As far as the performances are concerned, some things come off better than others so that on balance there is little to choose between the earlier and newer sets; those who have the former need not make a change. This is one of the greatest quartets now before the public and they are completely inside this music. Those coming new to these works will probably opt for the newer, Virgin, digital versions.

String quartets Nos. 2 in A, Op. 68; 5 in B flat, Op. 92; 7 in F sharp min., Op. 108.
☞ **(*) Olympia OCD 532 [id.]. Shostakovich Qt.

String quartets Nos. 6 in G, Op. 101; 8 in C min., Op. 110; 9 in E flat, Op. 117.
☞ **(*) Olympia OCD 533 [id.]. Shostakovich Qt.

String quartets Nos. 12 in D flat, Op. 133; 13 in B flat min., Op. 138; 14 in F sharp, Op. 142.
☞ **(*) Olympia OCD 535 [id.]. Shostakovich Qt.

The Shostakovich Quartet recordings emanate from the 1970s and from Moscow Radio tapes; they offer eminently serviceable performances in decent, analogue sound. We have responded to their cycle with appreciation; theirs are the kind of performances one would be perfectly happy with if they were the only ones available; and the recordings are very satisfactory indeed.

String quartets Nos. 4 in D, Op. 83; 8 in C min., Op. 110; 11 in F min., Op. 122.
*** ASV Dig. CDDCA 631 [id.]. Coull Qt.

The *Fourth quartet* is a work of exceptional beauty and lucidity, one of the most haunting of the cycle; the *Eleventh Quartet* is a puzzling, almost cryptic work in seven short movements. The Coull are one of the most gifted of the younger British quartets and give eminently creditable accounts of all three pieces. A very good (if slightly overlit) recording on CD.

String quartet No. 8, Op. 110.
(M) **(*) Decca 425 541-2 [id.]. Borodin Qt – BORODIN; TCHAIKOVSKY: *Quartets.* **(*)
☞ *(*) Nimbus Dig. NI 5077 [id.]. Medici Qt – DEBUSSY: *String quartet.* *(*)

The Borodins' Decca performance is outstanding and the recording real and vivid, although the balance means that in the CD transfer the effect is very forward, almost too boldly immediate.

The Medici offer an unusual coupling but very short measure at 46 minutes 6 seconds (not, incidentally, 52 minutes 10 seconds as stated on the sleeve) and the performances and recording would need to be very special indeed – which they are not – for this to be seriously competitive.

String quartets Nos. 11 in F min., Op. 122; 12 in D flat, Op. 133; 13 in B flat min., Op. 138.
☞ **(*) Koch Dig. 3-1070-2 [id.]. Manhattan Qt.

A very good performance of No. 11 which perhaps falls short of distinction and certainly doesn't hold up against competition from the Borodins, who also make a far more beautiful sound. Even so, the Manhattan group play with intentness and gravity in the opening of the dark *Thirteenth* and bring both feeling and understanding to this music. The acoustic, though it enables every detail to be heard, is just a little dryish in all three quartets.

String quartets Nos. (i) 14, Op. 142; (ii) 15, Op. 144.
☞ *** HM/Praga PR 254043 [id.]. (i) Glinka String Qt; (ii) Beethoven Qt.

The Praga recordings date from 1976–7 and come from the Czech Radio archives. The Glinka Quartet is a first-rate ensemble and their intense account of the *Fourteenth Quartet*, recorded only a year after the composer's death, is deeply felt. The Beethoven Quartet was, of course, closely associated with Shostakovich throughout his life, and it was their sound that he had in his mind in composing these works. Their account of the *Fifteenth* (they also recorded it commercially for Melodiya) penetrates deeply into this death-haunted music and this can be recommended.

Viola sonata, Op. 147.
*** EMI Dig. CDC7 54394-2 [id.]. Tabea Zimmermann, Hartmut Höll – BRITTEN: *Lachrymae;*
  STRAVINSKY: *Elégie.* ***
☞ *** Gamut Dig. GAMCD 537 [id.]. Philip Dukes, Sophia Rahman – CLARKE: *Sonata;*
  MACONCHY: *5 Sketches.* ***

Shostakovich's *Viola sonata* is perhaps his most bleak and comfortless work, a true song of sorrow, ruminating on the imminence of death. Tabea Zimmermann and her partner, Hartmut Höll, give as powerful and chilling an account of it as one could imagine. The recording is of striking clarity and presence.

The performance by Philip Dukes and Sophia Rahman is also very powerful; the closing *Adagio* is particularly gripping. The recording is first class and the couplings include a splendid sonata by Rebecca Clarke. A very worthwhile disc.

Violin sonata, Op. 134.
*** Chan. Dig. CHAN 8988; *ABTD 1570* [id.]. Mordkovitch, Benson – PROKOFIEV: *Sonatas;*
  SCHNITTKE: *In memoriam.* ***
*** Chan. Dig. CHAN 8343; *ABTD 1089* [id.]. Dubinsky, Edlina – SCHNITTKE: *Sonata No. 1* etc.
  ***

The *Violin sonata* can seem a dry piece, but Mordkovitch's natural intensity, her ability to convey depth of feeling without sentimentality, transforms it. Clifford Benson is the understanding pianist. In first-rate sound it makes a fine central offering for Mordkovitch's well-planned disc of Soviet violin music.

Rostislav Dubinsky's account is undoubtedly eloquent, and Luba Edlina makes a fine partner. The recording is excellent too, although it is balanced a shade closely.

PIANO MUSIC

24 Preludes, Op. 34.
*** Decca Dig. 433 055-2 [id.]. Olli Mustonen – ALKAN: *25 Preludes.* ***

Of the recordings of the Shostakovich *Preludes*, Op. 34, currently listed in the catalogue the Decca version by the young Finnish pianist, Olli Mustonen, is the strongest contender both artistically and technically. This is the best record of the *Preludes* since Menahem Pressler's old LP from the 1950s.

24 Preludes, Op. 34; Piano sonata No. 2, Op. 61; 3 Fantastic dances, Op. 5.
☞ *** Hyp. Dig. CDA 66620 [id.]. Tatiana Nikolayeva.

Here are the most important Shostakovich piano works *not* inspired by Tatiana Nikolayeva, played by one of the composer's most trusted exponents and very well recorded indeed. Her account of the enigmatic *Second Piano sonata* does not eclipse memories of Gilels's magical account once available on RCA. But Nikolayeva is one of the authentic advocates of Shostakovich, and her CD will be a must for most collectors. Recommended alongside Mustonen.

24 Preludes and fugues, Op. 87.
⊛ *** Hyp. Dig. CDA 66441/3 [id.]. Tatiana Nikolayeva.

In this repertoire, the first choice must inevitably be Tatiana Nikolayeva, 'the onlie begetter', as it were, of the *Preludes and fugues*. It was when he heard her playing Bach in Leipzig in 1950 that Shostakovich conceived the idea of composing his cycle and, during the process of gestation, he telephoned Nikolayeva almost every day to discuss its progress. Her reading has enormous concentration and a natural authority that is majestic. There is wisdom and humanity here, and she finds depths in this music that have eluded most other pianists who have offered samples. No grumbles about the Hyperion recording, which is very natural.

Piano sonata No. 1.
*** DG Dig. 427 766-2 [id.]. Lilya Zilberstein – RACHMANINOV: *Preludes.* ***

The early *Sonata* is a radical piece, with something of the manic, possessed quality of Scriabin and the harmonic adventurousness of Berg. Lilya Zilberstein rises triumphantly to its formidable demands, and she makes a strong case for it; she is recorded with striking immediacy and impact. As piano sound, this is state of the art.

Lady Macbeth of Mtsensk (opera; complete).
⊛ *** EMI CDS7 49955-2 (2) [Ang. CDCB 49955]. Vishnevskaya, Gedda, Petkov, Krenn, Tear,
Amb. Op. Ch., LPO, Rostropovich.
☞ *** DG Dig. 437 511-2 (2) [id.]. Ewing, Haugland, Larin, Langridge, Kristine Ciesinski, Moll,
Kotcherga, Zednik, Paris Bastille Op. Ch. & O, Myung-Whun Chung.

Rostropovich, in his finest recording ever, proves with thrilling conviction that this first version of Shostakovich's greatest work for the stage is among the most original operas of the century. Vishnevskaya is inspired to give an outstanding performance and provides moments of great beauty alongside aptly coarser singing; and Gedda matches her well, totally idiomatic. As the sadistic father-in-law, Petkov is magnificent, particularly in his ghostly return, and there are fine contributions from Robert Tear, Werner Krenn, Birgit Finnilä and Alexander Malta.

If ever Rostropovich's classic EMI recording of this opera is unavailable, then Chung's provides an alternative not quite so violent or powerful, but even more moving. The contrasts are partly the result of the different recording balance on the newer set, recorded in the Bastille Opéra by a cast evidently experienced in singing the work on stage. The sound is more atmospheric, not quite so immediate, which enhances the gentler, lyrical approach that Chung takes in many passages from the very start. The biggest contrast comes in the portrayal of the heroine. Where Vishnevskaya makes her a ravening fire-eater, with the voice abrasive and aggressive, Maria Ewing's portrait is much more vulnerable, with moods and responses subtly varied. As a heroine she is insinuatingly seductive and by the last Act one comes to pity her far more than with Vishnevskaya; with a younger voice too, the heroine's feminine charms are more vividly conveyed in singing far more sensuous, with the beauty of hushed pianissimos most tenderly affecting. The vocal challenge stretches the voice to the very limit and beyond, but that itself adds to the vulnerability. Sergei Larin as Katerina's labourer-lover equally gains over his EMI rival, Nicolai Gedda, by sounding more aptly youthful, with his tenor both firm and clear yet Slavonic-sounding. His touch is lighter than Gedda's, with a nice vein of irony. Aage Haugland is magnificent as Boris, Katerina's father-in-law, and Philip Langridge sings sensitively as her husband, Zinovi, while Kurt Moll as the Old Convict provides an extra emotional focus in his important solo at the start of the last Act. The recording relies less on sound-effects than the EMI, but the balance more clearly mirrors that of a theatre performance.

Sibelius, Jean (1865–1957)

Academic march; Finlandia (arr. composer); *Har du mod? Op. 31/2; March of the Finnish Jaeger Battalion, Op. 91/1;* (i) *The origin of fire, Op. 32; Sandels, Op. 28; Song of the Athenians, Op. 31/3.*
** BIS CD 314 [id.]. (i) Sauli Tilikainen, Laulun Ystävät Male Ch., Gothenburg SO, Järvi.

The origin of fire is by far the most important work on this record. Sauli Tilikainen is very impressive indeed, and the playing of the Gothenburg Symphony Orchestra under Neeme Järvi has plenty of feeling and atmosphere. None of the other pieces is essential Sibelius. The singing of the Laulun Ystävät is good rather than outstanding, and the Gothenburg orchestra play with enthusiasm. Fine recording in the best BIS traditions.

Autrefois (Scène pastorale), Op. 96b; The Bard, Op. 64; Presto in D for strings; Spring song, Op. 16; Suite caractéristique, Op. 100; Suite champêtre, Op. 98b; Suite mignonne, Op. 98a; Valse chevaleresque, Op. 96c; Valse lyrique, Op. 96a.
*** BIS Dig. CD 384 [id.]. Gothenburg SO, Järvi.

A mixed bag. *The Bard* is Sibelius at his greatest and most powerful, and it finds Järvi at his best. The remaining pieces are all light: some of the movements of the *Suite mignonne* and *Suite champêtre* could come straight out of a Tchaikovsky ballet, and Järvi does them with great charm. The last thing that the *Suite*, Op. 100, can be called is *caractéristique*, while the three pieces, Op. 96, find Sibelius in Viennese waltz mood. The rarity is *Autrefois*, which has a beguiling charm and is by far the most haunting of these pastiches. Sibelius introduces two sopranos and their *vocalise* is altogether captivating. The *Presto in D major for strings* is a transcription – and a highly effective one – of the third movement of the *B flat Quartet*, Op. 4. Excellent recording, as one has come to expect from BIS.

Belshazzar's Feast (suite), Op. 54; Dance intermezzo, Op. 45/2; The Dryad, Op. 45/1; Pan and Echo, Op. 53; Swanwhite, Op. 54.
*** BIS Dig. CD 359 [id.]. Gothenburg SO, Neeme Järvi.

Belshazzar's Feast, a beautifully atmospheric piece of orientalism, and the incidental music for Strindberg's *Swanwhite* may not be Sibelius at his most powerful but both include many characteristic touches and some haunting moments. Neeme Järvi's collection with the Gothenburg orchestra is first class in every way.

Cassazione, Op. 6; Preludio; The Tempest: Prelude & suites 1–2, Op. 109; Tiera.
*** BIS Dig. CD 448 [id.]. Gothenburg SO, Järvi.

Järvi's recording of Sibelius's incidental music to *The Tempest* is the finest and most atmospheric since Beecham and, though it does not surpass the latter in pieces like *The Oak-tree* or the *Chorus of the winds*, it is still impressive and offers first-class modern recording. Järvi also includes the *Prelude*, omitted on Beecham's disc. The *Cassazione* in character resembles the *King Christian II* music, but it is well worth having on disc. Neither *Tiera* nor the *Preludio*, both from the 1890s, is of great interest or particularly characteristic.

Violin concerto in D min. (1903–4 version); *Violin concerto in D min., Op. 47* (1905; published version).
*** BIS Dig. CD 500 [id.]. Leonidas Kavakos, Lahti SO, Osmo Vänskä.

The first performance of the *Violin concerto* left Sibelius dissatisfied and he immediately withdrew it for revision. This CD presents Sibelius's initial thoughts so that for the first time we can see the familiar final version struggling to emerge from the chrysalis. Comparison of the two concertos makes a fascinating study: the middle movement is the least affected by change, but the outer movements are both longer in the original score, and the whole piece takes almost 40 minutes. Sibelius purified the concerto's form, deleting unnecessary ornament: the ability to sacrifice good ideas in the interests of structural coherence is one of the hallmarks of a great composer. But though there is some regret at the losses, the overall gain leaves one in no doubt as to the correctness of Sibelius's judgement. The Greek violinist, Leonidis Kavakos, proves more than capable of handling the hair-raising difficulties of the 1904 version and is an idiomatic exponent of the definitive concerto. The Lahti orchestra under Osmo Vänskä give excellent support and the balance is natural and realistic. An issue of exceptional interest and value.

Violin concerto in D min., Op. 47.

🏵 *** Sony Dig. MK 44548 [id.]. Cho-Liang Lin, Philh. O, Salonen – NIELSEN: *Violin concerto.* *** 🏵

*** BMG/RCA RD 87019 [RCD1 7019]. Heifetz, Chicago SO, Hendl – GLAZUNOV: *Concerto;* PROKOFIEV: *Concerto No. 2.* ***

(M) *** Ph. 420 895-2. Accardo, LSO, C. Davis – DVORAK: *Violin concerto.* ***

☞ (M) *** EMI Dig. CD-EMX 2203; *TC-EMX 2203* [id.]. Little, RLPO, Handley – BRAHMS: *Violin concerto.* ***

*** EMI CDC7 47167-2 [id.]. Perlman, Pittsburgh SO, Previn – SINDING: *Suite.* ***

*** EMI Dig. CDC7 54127-2 [id.]; *EL 7754127-4.* Nigel Kennedy, CBSO, Rattle – TCHAIKOVSKY: *Concerto.* **(*)

(M) (***) EMI mono CDH7 61011-2. Ginette Neveu, Philh. O, Susskind – BRAHMS: *Concerto.* (***)

(M) **(*) Sony SMK 47540 [id.]. Francescatti, NYPO, Bernstein – BRAHMS: *Concerto.* **(*)

(BB) *** Naxos Dig. 8.550329; *4550329* [id.]. Dong-Suk Kang, Slovak (Bratislava) RSO, Adrian Leaper – HALVORSEN: *Air Norvégien* etc.; SINDING: *Légende;* SVENDSEN: *Romance.* ***

(M) (**) EMI mono CDH7 64030-2 [id.]. Heifetz, LPO, Beecham – GLAZUNOV *Violin concerto* (***) 🏵; TCHAIKOVSKY: *Violin concerto.* (***)

☞ *(*) DG Dig. 437 540-2 [id.]. Gil Shaham, Philh. O, Sinopoli – TCHAIKOVSKY: *Violin concerto.* *(*)

Violin concerto in D min.; 6 Humoresques, Opp. 87 & 89; 2 Serenades, Op. 69.

☞ *** BMG/RCA Dig. 09026 60444-2. Joseph Swensen, Finnish RSO, Saraste.

(i) *Violin concerto in D min.; Serenade No. 2 in G min., Op. 69. En Saga, Op. 9.*

☞ *** Sony Classical SK 53272 [id.]. (i) Julian Rachlin; Pittsburgh SO, Lorin Maazel.

Cho-Liang Lin's playing is distinguished not only by flawless intonation and an apparently effortless virtuosity but also by great artistry. He produces a glorious sonority at the opening, which must have been exactly what Sibelius wanted, wonderfully clean and silvery, and the slow movement has tenderness, warmth and yet restraint with not a hint of over-heated emotions. Lin encompasses the extrovert brilliance of the finale and the bravura of the cadenza with real mastery. The Philharmonia Orchestra rise to the occasion under Esa-Pekka Salonen, and the recording is first class.

Joseph Swensen was a pupil of Dorothy DeLay at the Juilliard – like so many of the virtuosi now before the public – and he made a very positive impression with his recent Beethoven concerto on the same label. With the Sibelius he enters a highly competitive market and holds his own among the best. This is possibly the finest account of the concerto since Cho-Liang Lin and is certainly among the most intelligently planned for, in addition to an eloquent reading of the concerto, he offers the *Six Humoresques,* written in 1917 at the time of the *Fifth Symphony.* Despite their qualities of light (they convey the magic of the white summer nights to perfection), they have an all-pervasive sadness and a poignant, wistful melancholy all their own. Accardo also recorded them with the concerto in the 1970s but his set was not reissued along with the concerto. Nor did he include the two *Serenades.* Swensen and the Finnish Radio Orchestra under Saraste give an eloquent account of these and, though he does not displace Lin in the concerto or Dong-Suk Kang in the *Humoresques,* readers wanting this particular repertoire on one disc need not hesitate. The RCA sound is well balanced and the aural image is very natural.

Heifetz's stereo performance of the Sibelius *Concerto* with the Chicago Symphony Orchestra under Walter Hendl set the standard by which all other versions have come to be judged. It is also one of his finest recordings; in remastered form the sound is vivid, with the Chicago ambience making an apt setting for the finely focused violin line.

Some readers may recall Julian Rachlin as the winner of the Young European Musician of the Year in 1988; he is still only twenty. His account of the Sibelius *Concerto* is pretty stunning; indeed it is quite simply the finest to have appeared since Cho-Liang Lin's account with Salonen and the Philharmonia; you can forget most of the other recent rivals. It has a purity of tone and intonation which is remarkable and a silvery, aristocratic quality that is entirely in harmony with Sibelius's conception. There are one or two idiosyncratic touches in the first cadenza, and the music almost comes to a standstill at one point but, given his other qualities, who cares? His slow movement is strikingly fine and without any *zigeuner-*like sentiment. He understands the poignancy of the beautiful *G minor Serenade,* and it is a pity that he did not find room for its companion. Maazel gives excellent support throughout, and his *En Saga* is atmospheric but a bit brisk. The Sony engineers strike an excellent balance between soloist and orchestra, and the recording has great warmth, even if the upper strings could have greater transparency.

Of the mid-price versions, Salvatore Accardo and Sir Colin Davis would be a first choice. There is no playing to the gallery, and no schmaltz – and in the slow movement there is a sense of repose and nobility. The finale is exhilarating, and there is an aristocratic feeling to the whole which is just right.

The raptness of Tasmin Little's playing is even more striking in the Sibelius than in the Brahms with which it is generously coupled. Her hushed and mysterious account of the opening theme leads to a performance that is both poised and purposeful, magnetic in her combination of power and poetry. Kyung Wha Chung's reading with André Previn (Decca, currently withdrawn), one of her very first recordings, may be more overtly passionate, but Little's is just as deeply felt, with an even wider tonal range, and her virtuosity culminates in an account of the finale in which, as in the Brahms, she finds an element of wit in the pointing of insistent dance rhythms. Throughout she is splendidly matched by the colourful playing of the RLPO under Vernon Handley. With this disc Tasmin Little emerges on to a new plane as a recording artist.

Itzhak Perlman plays the work as a full-blooded virtuoso showpiece and the Pittsburgh orchestra under André Previn support him to the last man and woman. He makes light of all the fiendish difficulties in which the solo part abounds and takes a conventional view of the slow movement, underlining its passion, and he gives us an exhilarating finale. The sound is marvellously alive and thrilling, though the forward balance is very apparent.

Throughout, Nigel Kennedy's intonation is true and he takes the considerable technical hurdles of this concerto in his stride. There is a touch of the *zigeuner* throb in the slow movement, but on the whole he plays with real spirit and panache. This can be confidently recommended if the coupling with the Tchaikovsky, a rather more indulgent performance, is suitable. The playing of the Birmingham orchestra is excellent throughout as, indeed, is the EMI recording.

The magnetism of Neveu in this, her first concerto recording, is inescapable from her opening phrase onwards, warmly expressive and dedicated, yet with no hint of mannerism. The finale is taken at a speed which is comfortable rather than exciting, but the extra spring of the thrumming dance-rhythms, superbly lifted, is ample compensation, providing a splendid culmination.

Francescatti's account is stunning in its immediacy and impact. With Bernstein fully matching the intensity of his soloist this is a performance impossible to forget. Francescatti's richness of tone is immediately evident in the opening theme and dominates the impassioned reading of the slow movement. The snag is the brightly lit recording, made in the Avery Fisher Hall in 1963, which the remastering serves only to emphasize, with the solo violin artificially balanced well out in front, in a spotlight.

Dong-Suk Kang chooses some popular Scandinavian repertoire pieces, such as the charming Svendsen *Romance in G*, as makeweights. Although this version of the concerto is very fine, he is perhaps a little wanting – albeit only a little – in tenderness as opposed to passion in the slow movement, but there is splendid virtuosity in the outer movements. The orchestral playing is decent rather than distinguished. In the bargain basement, this enjoys a strong competitive advantage, but even if it were at full price it would feature quite high in the current lists.

Although many first recordings have something special that stands out, the Heifetz/Beecham Sibelius *Violin concerto*, marvellous though it is, excites admiration rather than affection. And despite Sir Thomas's direction, Heifetz gave the more powerful account of it in his later, Chicago recording with Walter Hendl in the early days of stereo. (The reverse was the case with the Glazunov.) A good transfer nevertheless, and well worth having.

Gil Shaham offers brilliant, Manhattan razzle-dazzle with plenty of *zigeuner*-like warmth (not that there is no room for this) and none of the silvery aristocratic quality which Sibelius wanted. Ultimately a shallow reading, which sees the concerto as a vehicle for display – which in a sense it is – but denies it the degree of expressive refinement and subtlety it possesses. Sinopoli appears a willing accomplice in turning this into a showpiece and making sure that no opportunity for expressive italics is unmissed. Good recording. Fortunately there is an abundance of first-class alternatives.

(i) *Violin concerto, Op. 47;* (ii) *Finlandia, Op. 26; Karelia suite, Op. 11; Kuolema: Valse trise, Op. 44; Legend: Lemminkäinen's return, Op. 22/4.*

☞ (M) **(*) EMI CDU5 65056-2 [id.]; *EU 565056-4.* (i) Ida Haendel, Bournemouth SO, Berglund; (ii) Hallé O, Barbirolli.

It is good to welcome back to the catalogue Ida Haendel's fine account of the *Violin concerto* from the mid-1970s. She brings virtuosity and attack to this score, and there is a refreshing lack of egocentricity to her interpretation. She plays with dash and authority, and Berglund accompanies sympathetically, though the finale could go with greater panache. The recording is impressive in detail and body. Had Berglund greater atmosphere, this would compete alongside Tasmin Little; even so, the performance is richly enjoyable, for Miss Haendel's tone and phrasing have memorable warmth and eloquence. Barbirolli directs the rest of the programme, opening with an arresting

Finlandia, and *Lemminkäinen's return* is also very exciting. Although the orchestral playing is not as polished as that from a virtuoso orchestra, it is enthusiastic and has the advantage of excellent recording from the 1960s.

(i) *Violin concerto in D min., Op. 47;* (ii) *Symphony No. 7 in C, Op. 105; Tapiola, Op. 112.*

☞ (***) Ondine mono ODE 809-2 [id.]. (i) David Oistrakh, Finnish RSO, Nils-Eric Fougstedt; (ii) Helsinki PO, Beecham.

These performances, recorded during the 1954 Sibelius Festival, come from Finnish Radio archives. David Oistrakh's account of the *Violin concerto* has a marvellous strength and nobility, as well as an effortless virtuosity that carries all before it. His artistry inspires a warm response from the Finnish Radio Orchestra under Nils-Eric Fougstedt, who give magnificent support. Not a great orchestra, and the Finnish Radio recording shows its age, but a performance that clamours to be heard. There was always a special sense of occasion, too, at any Beecham concert and this is no exception. As Erik Tawaststjerna put it, Beecham 'electrified the orchestra and public alike', and the opening of the *Seventh Symphony* is more dramatically intense and highly charged than his EMI commercial recording with the RPO. *Tapiola* also has great intensity, though the orchestral playing does not have the finesse, magic and tonal subtlety of the RPO recording. Subfusc recording, but a set well worth investigating all the same.

En Saga, Op. 9; Finlandia, Op. 26; Karelia suite, Op. 11; Legend: The Swan of Tuonela, Op. 22/2; Tapiola, Op. 112.
(M) **(*) EMI Analogue/Dig. EMI CDM7 64331-2 [id.]; *EG 764331-4.* BPO, Karajan.

Karajan's *En Saga* is more concerned with narrative than with atmosphere at the beginning; but the climax is very exciting and the *lento assai* section and the coda are quite magical. *Tapiola* is broader and more expansive than the first DG version; at the storm section, the more spacious tempo is vindicated and again the climax is electrifying. *The Swan of Tuonela* is most persuasively done. These recordings date from 1977. The later, digital recording of *Karelia* has been added for the current reissue. Here, in the outer movements, which Karajan paces deliberately, the rather weighty bass detracts somewhat from the freshness of the presentation.

En Saga, Op. 9; Finlandia, Op. 26; Karelia suite, Op. 11; (i) *Luonnotar, Op. 70; Tapiola, Op. 112.*
☞ (M) *** Decca Dig. 430 757-2 [id.]. Philh. O, Ashkenazy, (i) with Elisabeth Söderström.

These are all digital recordings of the first order: Decca sound at its very best. The performances are among the finest available, especially *En Saga,* which is thrillingly atmospheric, while the *Karelia suite* is freshly appealing in its directness. The climax of *Tapiola* is almost frenzied in its impetus – some may feel that Ashkenazy goes over the top here; but this is the only real criticism of a distinguished collection and a very real bargain. *Finlandia* is made fresh again in a performance of passion and precision, and Elisabeth Söderström is on top form in *Luonnotar,* a symphonic poem with a voice (although some ears may find her wide vibrato and hard-edged tone not entirely sympathetic).

En Saga, Op. 9; Scènes historiques, Opp. 25, 66.
*** BIS Dig. CD 295 [id.]. Gothenburg SO, Järvi.

Järvi has the advantage of modern digital sound and the Gothenburg orchestra is fully inside the idiom of this music and plays very well indeed. Järvi's *En Saga* is exciting and well paced.

Finlandia; Karelia suite, Op. 11. Kuolema: Valse triste. Legends: Lemminkäinen's return, Op. 22/4; Pohjola's daughter, Op. 49.
(M) **(*) EMI CDM7 69205-2 [id.]. Hallé O, Barbirolli.

Pohjola's daughter is extremely impressive, spacious but no less exciting for all the slower tempi. *Lemminkäinen's return* is also a thrilling performance. Overall, a desirable introduction to Sibelius's smaller orchestral pieces, with admirable stereo definition.

Finlandia, Op. 26; Karelia suite, Op. 11; Scènes historiques: Festivo, Op. 25/3; The Chase; Love song; At the drawbridge, Op. 66/1–3; The Tempest (incidental music): suites Nos. 1–2, Op. 109.
🏵 (M) (***) EMI mono CDM7 63397-2 [id.]. RPO, Beecham.

Beecham's mono performance of the incidental music for *The Tempest* is magical – no one has captured its spirit with such insight. A pity that he omits the *Prelude,* which he had done so evocatively on 78s, though the last number of the second suite covers much of the same ground. The four *Scènes historiques* are beautifully done, with the most vivid orchestral colouring: *The Chase* is particularly delectable. No apologies whatsoever need be made about the sound here, though in the *Intermezzo* from *Karelia* (which has a 78-r.p.m. source) the quality is curiously crumbly at the opening and close: surely a better original could have been found. The *Alla marcia* is better, although no one would buy this record for *Finlandia*.

Finlandia, Op. 26; Kuolema: Valse triste, Op. 44; Legend: The Swan of Tuonela, Op. 22/2.
☞ *** DG Gold Dig. 439 010-2 [id.]. BPO, Karajan – GRIEG: *Holberg suite* etc. ***
☞ (M) ** Sony SMK 47549 [id.]. NYPO, Bernstein – GRIEG: *Peer Gynt suites* etc. **

Coupled with Grieg, this is Karajan at his very finest in the early 1980s, and the remastered digital recording (reissued in the Karajan Gold series) is impressively real and present, particularly in the languorous *Valse triste* and in *The Swan*, Karajan's third and final account on record, powerful in its brooding atmosphere. There is a touch of brashness in the brass in *Finlandia*, but generally this Berlin/Karajan partnership has never been surpassed.

   Bernstein is an impressive Sibelian, and both *The Swan of Tuonela* and *Valse triste* have finesse and atmosphere, with a fine cor anglais solo from Thomas Stacy in the former. The CD transfer has added sonority to the brass in *Finlandia*; though the forward balance remains, the sound is quite spacious and the performance exciting.

Finlandia, Op. 26; Legends: The Swan of Tuonela, Op. 22/2; The Oceanides, Op. 73; Pohjola's daughter, Op. 49; Tapiola, Op. 112.
(M) **(*) Chan. CHAN 6508; *MBTD 6508* [id.]. SNO, Gibson.

The Oceanides is particularly successful and, if Karajan finds even greater intensity in *Tapiola*, Gibson's account certainly captures the icy desolation of the northern forests. He is at his most persuasive in an elusive piece like *The Dryad*, although *En Saga* is also evocative, showing an impressive overall grasp. The SNO are at the peak of their form throughout these performances.

(i) *6 Humoresques, Opp. 87 & 89; 2 Serenades, Op. 69; 2 Serious melodies, Op. 79; Ballet scene* (1891); *Overture in E* (1891).
*** BIS Dig. CD 472 (i) Dong-Suk Kang, Gothenburg SO, Neeme Järvi.

The *Humoresques* are among Sibelius's most inspired smaller pieces. They are poignant as well as virtuosic and have a lightness of touch, a freshness and a sparkle. The two *Serenades* have great poetic feeling and a keen Nordic melancholy. They are wonderfully played by this distinguished Korean artist, who is beautifully accompanied. The two orchestral works are juvenilia which predate the *Kullervo Symphony*. There are some characteristic touches, but Sibelius himself did not think well enough of them to permit their publication. All the violin pieces, however, are to be treasured, and the recording is top class.

King Christian II (suite), *Op. 27; Pelléas et Mélisande* (suite), *Op. 46; Swanwhite* (suite: excerpts), *Op. 54.*
☞ *** Chan. Dig. CHAN 9158 [id.]. Iceland SO, Petri Sakari.

Completely unaffected and totally dedicated playing from the Iceland Symphony Orchestra under Petri Sakari. The *King Christian II* music is a winner, by far the best on record, and full of the most musical touches. It also includes the *Fool's song*, excellently sung by Sauli Tiilikainen, and a previously unrecorded *Minuet*. Although the *Pelléas et Mélisande* suite does not displace either Beecham or Karajan, it makes a useful alternative to either – and that is praise indeed. It has plenty of atmosphere and, though tempi are on the slow side, there is always plenty of inner life. The *Swanwhite* (five movements only) is beautifully natural too, attentive to refinements of phrasing and dynamics and at the same time free from the slightest trace of narcissism. Beautifully natural recording, warm and well balanced.

4 Legends, Op. 22 (Lemminkäinen and the maidens of Saari; The Swan of Tuonela; Lemminkäinen in Tuonela; Lemminkäinen's return).
*** BIS Dig. CD 294 [id.]. Gothenburg SO, Järvi.

4 Legends, Op. 22; The Bard, Op. 64; (i) *Luonnatar, Op. 70.*
(M) *** Chan. CHAN 6586 [id.]. SNO, Gibson, (i) with Phyllis Bryn-Johnson.

(i) *4 Legends from the Kalevela, Op. 22;* (ii) *Tapiola, Op. 112.*
☞ (M) *** CDM5 65176-2 [id.]. (i) Phd. O, Ormandy; (ii) Helsinki PO, Berglund.

A choice for the *Four Legends* is not simple. Ormandy's 1978 set is very distinguished, with the great Philadelphia Orchestra playing superbly in every department. When the violins rise above the stave, the recording (made at the Old Met.) is not as full as Järvi's and in the first *Legend* the wind are more closely observed than is ideal. But the remastering has added somewhat more depth to the sound-picture and Ormandy's account of this opening piece is marvellously passionate (these Maidens of

Saari must have given Lemminkäinen quite a wild time!). This *Swan of Tuonela*, too, is among the very finest, darkly intense and full of atmosphere and poetry, while *Lemminkäinen in Tuonela* is brooding and menacing. In *Lemminkäinen's return* Ormandy comes close to the famous hell-for-leather excitement generated in Beecham's old 78 set. Among CD versions, Ormandy's is by far the fleetest horse. On the other hand, Berglund's *Tapiola*, recorded digitally in Helsinki a decade later, is given its impact by a spacious ruggedness. If the build-up of the storm sequence is less chillingly awesome than with Karajan, the very close of the work has a moving intensity. The recording is excellent.

Järvi has the advantage of fine, modern digital sound and a wonderfully truthful balance. Järvi gives a passionate and atmospheric reading of the first *Legend* and his account of *The Swan of Tuonela* is altogether magical, one of the best in the catalogue. He takes a broader view of *Lemminkäinen in Tuonela* than many of his rivals and builds up an appropriately black and powerful atmosphere. The slight disappointment is *Lemminkäinen's homeward journey* which, though exciting, hasn't the possessed, manic quality of Beecham's very first record, which sounded as if a thousand demons were in pursuit.

Gibson, however, is at mid-price; he also offers sensitive performances of *The Bard*, which has fine atmosphere and delicate textures, and *Luonnatar*, where the soprano voice is made to seem like another orchestral instrument. The Scottish orchestra play freshly and with much commitment. *The Swan of Tuonela* has a darkly brooding primeval quality, and there is an electric degree of tension in the third piece, *Lemminkäinen in Tuonela*. The two outer *Legends* have ardent rhythmic feeling, and altogether this is highly successful. The recorded sound is excellent.

The Oceanides, Op. 73; Pelléas et Mélisande: suite, Op. 46; Symphony No. 7 in C, Op. 105; Tapiola, Op. 112.
(M) *** EMI CDM7 63400-2 [id.]. RPO, Beecham.

The Oceanides is Sibelius's most poetic evocation of the sea, and this marvellous playing captures every nuance of the score. The *Pelléas et Mélisande suite* was a yardstick by which all others have been measured ever since. Only Karajan matches it, and even the Berlin Philharmonic textures do not sound more luminous and magical than here, for the CD transfer is wonderfully refined. However, Beecham omits the *By the sea* movement. *Tapiola* is also very impressive: it has all the requisite brooding power and must be numbered among the very finest accounts committed to disc. Only the *Seventh Symphony* disappoints – and that only relatively speaking.

Rakastava (suite), *Op. 14; Scènes historiques, Opp. 25, 66; Valse lyrique, Op. 96/1.*
☞ (M) *** Chan. CHAN 6591 [id.]. RSNO, Gibson.

Written for a patriotic pageant, the *Scènes historiques* are vintage Sibelius. In the *Love song* Gibson strikes the right blend of depth and reticence, while elsewhere he conveys a fine sense of controlled power. Convincing and eloquent performances that have a natural feeling for the music. Gibson's *Rakastava* is beautifully unforced and natural, save for the last movement which is a shade too slow. The *Valse lyrique* is not good Sibelius, but everything else certainly is. Gibson plays this repertoire with real commitment, and the recorded sound is excellent, with the orchestral layout, slightly distanced, most believable. At mid-price this is a specially desirable collection.

Scaramouche, Op. 71; The Language of the birds: Wedding march.
*** BIS Dig. CD 502 [id.]. Gothenburg SO, Neeme Järvi.

Scaramouche is scored for relatively small forces, including piano (not unlike Strauss's music for *Le bourgeois gentilhomme* of which one is perhaps reminded); at its best it reminds one of the luminous colourings of the *Humoresques* of five years later. A wistful, gentle and haunting score, slightly let down by its uneventful second Act. Sibelius did not think highly enough of the *Wedding march* to Adolf Paul's play, *The Language of the birds*, to give it an opus number but it is in fact quite an attractive miniature. The playing of the Gothenburg orchestra under Neeme Järvi is altogether excellent and so, too, is the BIS recording.

SYMPHONIES

Symphonies Nos. 1–7.
(M) *** Decca Dig. 421 069-2 (4). Philh. O, Ashkenazy.
(B) **(*) Decca 430 778-2 (3). VPO, Maazel.
(M) **(*) Chan. Dig. CHAN 6559 (3). SNO, Sir Alexander Gibson.

(i) *Symphonies Nos. 1–7;* (ii) *Night ride and sunrise;* (i) *The Oceanides; Scene with cranes.*
(M) **(*) EMI CMS7 64118-2 [Ang. CDMD 64118]; *EX 764118-4* (4). (i) CBSO, (ii) Philh. O,
    Simon Rattle.

Ashkenazy's Sibelius series makes a rich and strong, consistently enjoyable cycle. Ashkenazy by temperament brings out the expressive warmth, colour and drama of the composer rather than his Scandinavian chill, reflecting perhaps his Slavonic background. The recordings are full and rich as well as brilliant, most of them of demonstration quality, even though they date from the early digital period. On four CDs at mid-price, the set makes a most attractive first recommendation.

Simon Rattle's performances with the City of Birmingham Symphony Orchestra are available both as a four-CD boxed set and as individual discs. The best advice is probably to opt for the individual disc for the *Fourth* and *Sixth*, coupled together. They are both impressive, as is his *Seventh*, coupled with the *Fifth* and the highly atmospheric *Scene with cranes.* As a set the box is worth considering, but it would not be first choice.

By far the best of Maazel's performances are the *First* and *Fourth Symphonies* which are, of course, available on a separate disc. The *Seventh Symphony*, too, is another landmark in the Sibelius discography and has great majesty and breadth. The *Second* is also successful, but the *Fifth* and, more particularly, the *Sixth* do not come off as well. He sounds uninvolved in both works: the *Third* has a very good first movement but a faster-than-ideal second. The Decca analogue sound is excellent and is vividly transferred, and readers need not hesitate on that score.

Sir Alexander Gibson's Sibelius cycle is impressive, both musically and from an engineering point of view; there are no weak spots anywhere. (Indeed, one respected critic chose Gibson's version of No. 1 as his first choice on a BBC 'Record Review' some years ago.) At the same time it must be conceded that the peaks do not dwarf, say, the Maazel *Fourth* or *Seventh*. The performances are eminently sane, sound and reliable, and no one investing in the set is likely to be at all disappointed. Taken individually, none would be an absolute first choice.

Symphonies Nos. 1 in E min., Op. 39; 2 in D, Op. 43; 3 in C, Op. 52; (i) *Luonnotar; Pohjola's daughter.*
☞ (M) **(*) Sony SM2K 47619 (2) [id.]. (i) Phyllis Curtin; NYPO, Bernstein.

Bernstein recorded his New York cycle between 1961 and 1967. His *Second Symphony* is marvellously full-blooded and has even been compared with that of his mentor, Koussevitzky. The *First* is also impassioned and powerful. The *Third* is well paced (far superior to Maazel's, also made in the mid-1960s) and his *Pohjola's daughter* one of the very best accounts of this masterpiece. The only let-down is *Luonnotar*, which is very fast and needs just a little more sense of mystery. Phyllis Curtin is not perhaps the most alluring soloist either. The recordings show a great improvement over their LP originals in terms of spaciousness and tonal warmth.

Symphonies Nos. 1–3; 5; Belshazzar's Feast (incidental music), *Op. 51; Karelia suite; Pohjola's Daughter, Op. 49; Tapiola, Op. 112.*
(M) (***) Finlandia mono FACD 81234 (3). LSO, Robert Kajanus.

When the Finnish government sponsored recordings of the first two symphonies in 1930, Sibelius insisted on having Kajanus as the most authentic interpreter. These performances were all made in 1930 and 1932 and sound amazingly good for the period. The celebrated storm in *Tapiola*, taken at a much slower and more effective tempo than is now usual, still has the power to terrify despite the inevitable sonic limitations, and no conductor has ever given a more spell-binding and atmospheric account of the suite from *Belshazzar's Feast*. The broader, more leisurely view Kajanus takes of the *Third Symphony* comes as a refreshing corrective to the later, more hurried accounts by Anthony Collins and Lorin Maazel. No performer, save Beecham in the *Fourth* and *Sixth* symphonies, came closer to Sibelius's intentions. Essential listening for all Sibelians.

Symphony No. 1 in E min., Op. 39.
**(*) DG Dig. 435 351-2 [id.]. VPO, Bernstein.

Symphony No. 1 in E min.; En Saga, Op. 9.
*** Collins Dig. 1093-2 [id.]. RPO, Sir Alexander Gibson.

Symphony No. 1 in E min.; Finlandia, Op. 26; Karelia suite, Op. 11.
⊛ *** EMI Dig. CDC7 542732 [id.]. Oslo PO, Mariss Jansons.

Symphony No. 1 in E min.; In memoriam, Op. 59.
☞ Chan. Dig. CHAN 9107. Danish Nat. RSO, Leif Segerstam.

Symphony No. 1 in E min.; The Oceanides.
(M) **(*) EMI Dig. CDM7 64119-2 [id.]; *EG 764119-4.* CBSO, Simon Rattle.

Mariss Jansons's account of the *First Symphony* is the finest to have appeared since Maazel's in the 1960s. The Oslo Philharmonic is on peak form, playing with thrilling virtuosity both in the *Symphony* and *Finlandia* and in the *Karelia suite.* Tempi are well judged, the players are responsive to every dynamic nuance, phrasing is beautifully shaped and the overall architecture of the piece is splendidly realized. A very exciting performance, which has you on the edge of your seat, and very vividly recorded too.

Sir Alexander Gibson has recorded the symphony twice before, but this new Collins version is undeniably the best. He gets very good playing from the RPO, not quite as high-voltage or virtuosic as the Oslo Philharmonic for Jansons but still very committed. The recording is excellent. Gibson's account of *En saga* is a bit fast, but there is no want of atmosphere.

If the whole symphony was as fine as the first movement in Rattle's hands, this would be a clear first recommendation. He has a powerful grasp of both its structure and character. The slow movement is for the most part superb, but he makes too much of the commas at the end of the movement, which are so exaggerated as to be disruptive. The Scherzo has splendid character but is a good deal slower than the marking. *The Oceanides* has an atmosphere that is altogether ethereal. Simon Rattle has its measure and conveys all its mystery and poetry.

Another outstanding version from DG joins a catalogue already well stocked with three-star recordings. Leonard Bernstein gets some electrifying playing from the Vienna Philharmonic and he is superbly recorded at live concerts in the Grosser Saal of the Musikverein in February 1990. Of course there is some expressive self-indulgence, but this is by far the best of Bernstein's recent Sibelius cycle with the Vienna orchestra. However, uncoupled and at full price with only 40 minutes of playing time, it is uncompetitive, particularly when Karajan's excellent 1982 account (coupled with his superb reading of the *Sixth*) and Maazel's Vienna account (coupled with the *Fourth*) are both available at mid-price. All the same, Bernstein's is a version to hear.

Segerstam pulls the *First Symphony* mercilessly out of shape. He is more intrusive than almost any rival maestro, and his posturing in the finale is simply insupportable. He inflates *In memoriam* to almost twice its normal length. The excellent Chandos/Danish Radio recording cannot redeem this issue.

Symphonies Nos. 1 in E min.; 4 in A min., Op. 63.
(M) *** Decca 417 789-2. VPO, Maazel.

Maazel's VPO performance of the *First Symphony* has freshness of vision to commend it, along with careful attention to both the letter and the spirit of the score. The Vienna Philharmonic responds with enthusiasm and brilliance and the Decca engineers produce splendid detail (except for the important timpani part in the first movement echoing the main theme, which might have been more sharply defined). The *Fourth* is equally impressive. The players make the closest contact with the music, and Maazel's reading brings great concentration and power: the first movement is as cold and unremitting as one could wish. A fine bargain.

Symphonies Nos. 1 in E min.; 6 in D min., Op. 104.
(M) *** EMI Dig. CDD7 63896-2 [id.]. BPO, Karajan.

In the *First Symphony* Karajan, a great Tchaikovsky interpreter, identifies with the work's inheritance. But there is a sense of grandeur and vision here, and the opulence and virtuosity of the Berliners helps to project the heroic dimensions of Karajan's performance. The early digital recording (1981) is not top-drawer: the bass is overweighted, but the full upper strings sing out gloriously with the richest amplitude in the finale, which has an electrifying climax; the brass is comparably rich and resonant. Karajan's version of the *Sixth* was made in 1981 and it brings to life the other-worldly quality of this score. In short, this is Karajan at his finest: not even Beecham made the closing pages sound more magical. This recording is better than its predecessor, and the EMI team have achieved a more spacious acoustic ambience. (Unfortunately this has been withdrawn as we go to press.)

Symphonies Nos. 1 in E min., Op. 39; 7 in C, Op. 105.
☞ (M) *** Decca Dig. 436 473-2 [id.]. Philh. O, Ashkenazy.
☞ ⊛ (***) Beulah mono IPD 8 [id.]. LSO, Anthony Collins.
☞ * Sony Dig. SK 52566 [id.]. Pittsburgh SO, Maazel.

Ashkenazy's digital coupling of the *First* and *Seventh Symphonies*, recorded in 1982 and 1984 respectively, is outstandingly successful; at mid-price, it will become a ready first choice for most collectors. The performance of the *First* is held together well and is finely shaped. Ashkenazy is exactly on target in the Scherzo. The resultant sense of momentum is exhilarating; here, as when echoing the main theme of the first movement, the timpani make a riveting effect. Throughout, the sheer physical excitement that this score engenders is tempered by admirable control. Only at the end of the slow movement does one feel that Ashkenazy could perhaps have afforded greater emotional restraint, but the big tune of the finale is superbly handled. The recording has splendid detail and clarity of texture, and there is all the presence and body one could ask for, with the bass-drum rolls particularly realistic. The *Seventh Symphony* is also very fine. Ashkenazy does not build up this work quite as powerfully as some others do, but he has the measure of its nobility and there is much to admire – indeed, much that is thrilling in his interpretation. As in the *First Symphony*, the playing of the Philharmonia Orchestra, like the recording, is of the very first order.

Many collectors have been long awaiting the appearance on CD of Anthony Collins's set of the Sibelius symphonies. Engineered by Kenneth Wilkinson and recorded in Kingsway Hall, these famous mono recordings from the early 1950s were a landmark in the Sibelius discography of their day. They reappear now on the Beulah label, but have been transferred to CD by Tony Hawkins at Decca from the master tapes. There are those who (justly) count Collins's magnificent account of the *First Symphony* of 1952, with its haunting, other-worldly opening clarinet solo, as the finest ever put on disc, for the tension throughout the performance is held at the highest level. The electrifying climax of the first movement with the timpani thundering out the main theme is matched by the linear power of the apotheosis of the heart-warming tune of the finale. In between, the powerfully atmospheric *Andante* and the gripping Scherzo are perfectly placed in the overall scheme. The closely integrated *Seventh* is also well understood by Collins, and once again the closing moments of the symphony are drawn together very impressively. The Decca recording remains remarkably vivid and, if the fortissimos are more one-dimensional than we expect today and the massed violins could ideally be fuller, the brass certainly makes a fine impact. There is no lack of underlying fullness, and a little paring of the upper range works wonders. The comparatively rare *Karelia overture*, which was recorded later (1955), makes a brief bonus. The Rosette is from I. M., who first encountered No. 1 under Kajanus (on 78s) and then moved on to Collins in the mono LP era.

Maazel's Sony coupling is very different from his recordings with the Vienna Philharmonic in the 1960s – and in every respect inferior. Both symphonies are overblown and inflated, the *Seventh* drawn out to 26 minutes. The Scherzo-like theme at the *Allegro molto moderato* section is pulled grotesquely out of shape. A non-starter, despite some good playing from the Pittsburgh orchestra, and decent though not first-class recording.

Symphony No. 2 in D, Op. 43.
**(*) Chesky/New Note CD-3 [id.]. RPO, Barbirolli.
☞ (M) ** Mercury 434 317-2 [id.]. Detroit SO, Paray – DVORAK: *Symphony No. 9 (From the New World)*. ***

Symphony No. 2 in D, Op. 43; Andante festivo; Kuolema: Valse triste, Op. 44/1; Legend: The Swan of Tuonela, Op. 22/2.
☞ *** EMI Dig. CDC7 54804-2 [id.]. Oslo PO, Jansons.

(i) *Symphony No. 2 in D;* (ii) *En Saga; Legend: The Swan of Tuonela;* (i) *The Oceanides.*
☞ (M) *** EMI CDM7 67807-2 [id.]. (i) Helsinki PO, Berglund; (ii) VPO, Sargent.

Symphony No. 2 in D; Finlandia, Op. 26; Karelia suite, Op. 11.
(M) *** Decca Dig. 430 737-2; *430 737-4* [id.]. Philh. O, Ashkenazy.

Symphony No. 2 in D; Finlandia, Op. 26; The Swan of Tuonela, Op. 22/2; Kuolema: Valse trise, Op. 44/1.
☞ (M) *** Ph. 422 389-2 [id.]. Boston SO, Sir Colin Davis.

Symphony No. 2 in D; Finlandia, Op. 26; Kuolema: Valse triste, Op. 44/1.
☞ ** DG Dig. 437 828-2 [id.]. BPO, Levine.

Symphony No. 2 in D; Finlandia, Op. 26; Kuolema: Valse triste, Op. 44/1; Romance in C, Op. 42.
☞ *** EMI Dig. CDC7 54804-2 [id.]. Boston SO, Ashkenazy.

Symphony No. 2 in D; Finlandia, Op. 26; Pohjola's daughter, Op. 49; The Swan of Tuonela, Op. 22/2.
(M) (**(*)) BMG/RCA mono GD 60294 [09026 60294]. NBC SO, Toscanini.

Symphony No. 2 in D; Kuolema, Op. 44: Scene with cranes; Valse triste; Nightride and sunrise, Op. 55.
*** BMG/RCA Dig. RD 87919 [7919-2-RC]. Finnish RSO, Saraste.

Symphony No. 2 in D; Kuolema: Valse triste, Op. 44/1; Tapiola, Op. 112.
☞ ** Decca Dig. 433 810-2 [id.]. San Francisco SO, Blomstedt.

Symphony No. 2 in D; Romance for strings in C, Op. 42.
*** BIS Dig. CD 252 [id.]. Gothenburg SO, Järvi.

A very well shaped performance from Ashkenazy in Boston, and one of the most enjoyable accounts of Sibelius's most popular symphony to have appeared for some time. There is an impressive sense of line throughout and yet no feeling that Sibelius's muse is held on too taut a rein. On the contrary, the first and second movements succeed in conveying a real sense of relaxation as well as excitement. The Boston orchestra play very well for Ashkenazy and sound in better form than they have shown in recent years. Like Karajan, Blomstedt, Jansons and other Sibelians, Ashkenazy's approach to the first movement is more measured than earlier maestros (Kajanus, Beecham – and, in more recent times, Järvi). It is interesting to note that when Sibelius himself conducted a performance in Helsinki in 1916, his first biographer, Erik Furuhjelm, noted that his tempo was faster even than Kajanus's – then considered to be on the fast side. However, many paths lead to the truth and Ashkenazy's performance is even finer than his earlier account for Decca. It is musically very satisfying – and recorded in a very natural concert-hall perspective. The Boston strings respond very ardently but with aristocratic poise in the *Romance in C* and in the remaining works in the programme. Strongly recommended.

Järvi is very brisk in the opening *Allegretto*: this Gothenburg version has more sinew and fire than its rivals, and the orchestral playing is more responsive and disciplined than that of the SNO on Chandos (see below). Throughout, Järvi has an unerring sense of purpose and direction and the momentum never slackens. Of course, there is not the same opulence as with the Philharmonia under Ashkenazy on Decca, but the BIS performance is concentrated in feeling and thoroughly convincing. The *Romance for strings* is attractively done.

Even in a highly competitive field the Oslo Philharmonic account of the *Second Symphony* under Mariss Jansons is a force to be reckoned with. If it lacks something of the high voltage that charged his reading of the *First Symphony*, it has no lack of excitement; it is superbly controlled and tautly held together, with no playing to the gallery in the finale. There is an aristocratic feel to it, and this extends to *The Swan* and the *Andante festivo*, which is distinguished by string playing of great intensity. Jansons whips *Valse triste* into something of a frenzy towards the climax, but elsewhere these performances are totally free from exaggeration. Excellent recording.

Davis's 1976 account still impresses. He has an innate feel for Sibelius, harmonizing the nationalist-romantic rhetoric and the essential classicism of Sibelius's nature to striking effect. The orchestra play with eloquence and the sound is very good indeed. No quarrels either with the fill-ups, all familiar from the earlier, four-CD, full-price box of the seven symphonies.

Although Saraste's account of the *Second Symphony* is not a first choice, it is still highly recommendable. He has the measure of this symphony's breadth. He can also handle a Sibelian climax, and there is no lack of power here. Although Rattle casts a stronger spell in the *Scene with cranes*, Saraste gets very good results both here and in *Nightride and sunrise*. The recording is well detailed and the whole disc remains strongly competitive.

On Decca, Ashkenazy's control of tension and atmosphere makes for the illusion of live performance in the building of each climax, and the rich digital sound adds powerfully to that impression. Yet some listeners may find it more difficult to respond positively to this reading; like R.L., they may feel the performance is wanting in firmness of grip, especially in the slow movement, with the dramatic pauses lacking spontaneity and unanimity of response. Ashkenazy's performances of *Finlandia* and the *Karelia suite* are as fine as any and, like the symphony, are afforded first-class Decca sound. The *Symphony* and *Finlandia* were recorded at the Kingsway Hall (1979/80) and *Karelia* at Walthamstow (1985).

Barbirolli's version with the RPO is a performance of stature and is by far the finest of the four versions he committed to disc. There is a thrilling sense of live music-making here and a powerful sense of momentum. A high-voltage account, then, and very well recorded, though the upper strings are slightly drier than they were in the LP version on RCA. It retails at full price, which reduces its competitiveness, particularly as it comes without a fill-up.

Berglund is scrupulously faithful to the letter of the score as well as to its spirit. The build-up to the climax just before the restatement is magnificently handled. The slow movement also comes off well and its contrasting moods are effectively characterized. The scherzo and finale are of lower voltage than the finest versions. The Helsinki Philharmonic respond with no mean virtuosity and panache, but the last degree of intensity eludes them. Berglund's account of *The Oceanides* is splendidly atmospheric and can be put alongside Rattle's, which is praise indeed! The recording is well detailed and truthful, and the perspective natural. For the reissue, two of Sir Malcolm Sargent's excellent VPO performances of favourite tone-poems have been added, both offering playing of much character. The recording from the early days of stereo stands up remarkably well when heard alongside the modern digital sound given to Berglund.

Three recordings of the *Second Symphony* survive from Toscanini's baton: one from his BBC season in 1938, a second from 1939 and the present issue from 1940. All offer some superb playing but are a shade hard-driven. The account of *Pohjola's daughter* is arguably the most powerful and exciting ever committed to disc and in its elemental power even surpasses Kajanus and Koussevitzky.

Paray's account has plenty of tension – indeed one is immediately gripped by the excitement of the opening movement. The *Andante*, however, does not bring enough contrast and its histrionics seem episodic. The Scherzo has great energy and the finale develops a full head of steam, but overall, in spite of excellent early (1959) Mercury stereo, this reading with its impulsiveness fails to create the feeling of an organic whole.

Blomstedt's first Sibelius CD coupling the *Fourth* and *Fifth Symphonies* was an unqualified success. The *Second Symphony* is far more successful than some recent issues, but it is just a trifle cool. He gets cultured playing from the San Francisco orchestra and at no point – not even in the finale – does he play to the gallery as do so many conductors on and off record. Blomstedt's first movement is fairly measured. In the Scherzo he draws playing of great character from the orchestra, whose ensemble is marvellous. There is a very good account of *Tapiola*, though it is not as intense as Karajan's – let alone the classic recordings from the 1930s by Koussevitzky and Kajanus. Very clean and well-detailed Decca recording helps (though the oboe is a bit reticent at the opening of the development section of the first movement) but does not place this among first recommendations.

Levine gets some pretty gutsy and committed playing from the Berlin Philharmonic and his account of the symphony is well paced throughout. There is that sense of the music being borne along on a vital current so essential in good Sibelius playing, and the *Allegretto* tempo of the first movement is really idiomatic – brisk but not hurried. All the same, comparison with Karajan's account with the same orchestra, made in 1981, is not to the advantage of the newcomer. There is none of the tonal bloom and homogeneity Karajan could command, nor the refinement of sonority. Although it is not available at the time of writing, this should reappear during the lifetime of this book. There are sensitive touches in the Levine reading: the F sharp major theme of the slow movement comes off beautifully. But generally Levine tends to drive things along at full throttle, with little power being held in reserve for the final climax. *Finlandia* is uncontroversial, but many will find the *Valse triste* very self-conscious: Levine takes 6 minutes 36 seconds as opposed to Jansons' 5 minutes 11 seconds. Both the recent Jansons and Ashkenazy performances have greater personality and nobility.

Symphonies Nos. 2 in D; 3 in C, Op. 52.
(M) *** EMI CDM7 64120-2 [id.]; *EG 7644120-4*. CBSO, Simon Rattle.

In No. 2 the CBSO play with fervour and enthusiasm except, perhaps, in the first movement where the voltage is lower – particularly in the development, which is not easy to bring off; however, the transition to the finale is magnificent and Rattle finds the *tempo giusto* in this movement. The Birmingham strings produce a splendidly fervent unison both here and elsewhere. Rattle's account of the *Third* is vastly superior to his *First* and *Second*. The slow movement is particularly fine; few have penetrated its landscape more completely, and the movement throughout is magical. The way in which he gradually builds up the finale is masterly and sure of instinct. The recording, made in the Warwick Arts Centre, sounds very well balanced, natural in perspective and finely detailed.

Symphonies Nos. 2 in D; 5 in E flat, Op. 82.
(M) *** Chan. Dig. CHAN 6556; *MBTD 6556* [id.]. SNO, Sir Alexander Gibson.

The *Second* is among the best of Gibson's cycle and scores highly, thanks to the impressive clarity, fullness and impact of the 1982 digital recording. Gibson's reading is honest and straightforward, free of bombast in the finale. Tempos are well judged: the first movement is neither too taut nor too relaxed: it is well shaped and feels right. Overall this is most satisfying, as is the *Fifth*, which has similar virtues: at no time is there any attempt to interpose the personality of the interpreter, and the finale has genuine weight and power.

Symphonies Nos. 2 in D; 6 in D min., Op. 104.
☞ (***) Beulah mono 2PD 8 [id.]. LSO, Anthony Collins.

The Decca sound in Collins's 1953 recording of the *Second Symphony* is fuller than in the *First Symphony*, the strings have more body, and few apologies have to be made for the quality offered by the excellent CD transfer. The performance is superb, held together with a tension that carries the listener through from the first bar to the last. The closing pages of the finale, with the timpani again making a telling contribution, are particularly satisfying. The *Sixth* was recorded in 1955, and again the ear notices a further improvement in the sound, particularly at the radiant pastoral opening. Supporting the reticence of Collins's style there is a rapt intensity of feeling. The LSO play with much sensitivity, and woodwind and string detail is ever luminous; the conductor's special feeling for Sibelian colour and atmosphere is especially apparent in this work, with the beautiful final coda sustained with moving simplicity. Altogther a lovely performance.

Symphonies Nos. 2 in D; 7 in C, Op. 105.
☞ (B) *** Sony SBTK 53509; *SBT 53509* (id.]. Phd. O, Ormandy.

Ormandy was not so much underrated as taken for granted in an age which had the good fortune to have so many great conductors. The 1957 sound is far better than you might expect and the strings (and practically every other department) are much more sumptuous and responsive than they seem to be in Philadelphia nowadays. The *Second* gets a powerful (and, in the finale, rousing) performance, and the architecture is held together well throughout. The *Seventh*, recorded in 1960, is very impressive indeed: marvellously paced, intense and felt. To be perfectly truthful, it is stronger than the 1957 Beecham or either of the Karajan accounts. Ormandy was a considerable Sibelian and we have memories of a fine mono LP coupling of the *Fourth* and *Fifth* from this period which, should it appear in the lifetime of this book, should be snapped up – particularly if the transfer is as acceptable as it is here.

Symphony No. 3 in C, Op. 52; Belshazzar's feast (suite), *Op. 54; King Christian II (suite), Op. 27.*
☞ ** BMG/RCA Dig. 09026 60434-2 [id.]. Finnish RSO, Saraste.

The *Third Symphony* is the last to appear in Saraste's cycle with the Finnish Radio Orchestra. Although not every performance has been an unqualified success, Saraste has proved a reliable guide in this repertoire. His readings are free from exaggeration and over-emphasis, and he has proved himself to be a more selfless Sibelian than his compatriot, Leif Segerstam. Saraste has given us among other things a very fine *Fourth* and a magnificent account of *The Oceanides*: the *Sixth* was the sole disappointment. The first movement of the *Third* is not well paced: it is far too fast to be wholly convincing. Kajanus, who had the imprimatur of the composer, took a far steadier pace. The other movements are better, though the orchestral playing, good though it is, falls short of the last ounce of finesse. Saraste gives a very colourful account of the *King Christian* music, comparable with, if not superior to, its rivals. *Belshazzar's feast*, one of Sibelius's most evocative and atmospheric scores, is not wholly successful either. There is more poetry in *Solitude* than Saraste finds, and he seems anxious to move things on both here and in the *Night* movement. The recording is vivid and generally well balanced, though there is not really enough room for climaxes to expand with comfort.

Symphony No. 3 in C; King Kristian II (suite), Op. 27.
*** BIS Dig. CD 228 [id.]. Gothenburg SO, Järvi.

With the *Third Symphony* there is a sense of the epic in Järvi's hands and it can hold its own with any in the catalogue. In Gothenburg, the slow movement is first class and the leisurely tempo adopted here by the Estonian conductor is just right. Järvi's coupling is the incidental music to *King Christian II*. This is very beautifully played and recorded.

Symphony No. 3 in C; Kuolema: Scene with cranes, Op. 44/2; Tapiola, Op. 112.
☞ * Chan. Dig. CHAN 9083 [id.]. Danish Nat. RSO, Leif Segerstam.

Leif Segerstam sets out at exactly the right pace in the symphony, but it is not long before the brakes are abruptly applied. The natural flow of the first movement is impeded by similarly disruptive tempo changes. Despite some imaginative touches in the slow movement and good orchestral playing, this is not a reading with which it would be easy to live. The *Scene with cranes* is drawn out to almost twice its normal length, and in Segerstam's hands *Tapiola* lasts longer than most performances of the *Seventh Symphony*. All the same, *Tapiola* is the most impressive thing on the disc, though the great performances achieve every bit as much intensity and power without inflating the proceedings. The Chandos/Danish Radio engineering is of high quality.

Symphony No. 3 in C; Nightride and sunrise, Op. 55; Pelléas et Mélisande: suite, Op. 46; Pohjola's daughter, Op. 49.
☞ (***) Beulah mono 3PD8 [id.]. LSO, Anthony Collins.

More outstanding performances from Anthony Collins: only *Nightride and sunrise*, although dramatically effective, is slightly less memorable than the other works here. The other minor reservation concerns the chosen tempo for the second movement, *Andantino con moto, quasi allegretto*, of the *Third Symphony*. Some listeners, including R.L., find it rather too fast but the playing has much delicacy of feeling and texture; for I.M., Collins's approach matches the whole reading, which has a strong momentum overall. Certainly after the chimerical scherzando opening of the finale the introduction and transformation of the theme from the central movement is highly compelling, and the build-up of tension to the work's climax is satisfyingly controlled. The account of *Pohjola's daughter* is among the most imaginative and colourful available, and the excerpts from the incidental music to *Pelléas et Mélisande* (including *Mélisande: Pastorale*, the charmingly delicate *Mélisande and the spinning wheel* and the *Entr'acte*) are beautifully played: the final *Death of Mélisande* is especially moving. All the recordings, except *Nightride* (1955), were made in the Kingsway Hall in 1954 and absolutely no apologies need be made for the mono sound, which in this admirable CD transfer is remarkable for its vivid immediacy and fullness.

Symphonies Nos. 3 in C; 5 in E flat, Op. 82; March of the Finnish Jaeger Battalion, Op. 91/1.
☞ (**) Koch mono 37127-2 [id.]. LSO, Kajanus.

Kajanus's magnificent performances of both symphonies are a must. The transfers are not as good as the *Finlandia* (reviewed above), which were made from the masters; these are done from good commercial pressings, but there is inevitably a more obtrusive surface. The *March*, composed for the Finnish volunteers who fought in the First World War against the Russians, has scant artistic merit.

Symphonies Nos. 3 in C; 6 in D min., Op. 104.
☞ (M) *** Decca Dig. 436 478-2 [id.]. Philh. O, Ashkenazy.

Vladimir Ashkenazy and the Philharmonia Orchestra give a first-class account of both the *Third* and *Sixth Symphonies*. In the first movement of the *Third*, Ashkenazy is a shade faster than the metronome marking, so there is no want of forward momentum and thrust, either here or in the finale. The tempi and spirit of the *Andantino* are well judged, though the withdrawn passage in the slow movement (at fig. 6) could perhaps have more inwardness of feeling; however, Ashkenazy is not helped by the balance, closer than ideal, which casts too bright a light on a landscape that should be shrouded in mystery. It is clear that Ashkenazy has great feeling for the *Sixth* and its architecture. There is no lack of that sense of communion with nature which lies at the heart of the slow movement or the sense of its power which emerges in the finale. He is a good deal broader than Karajan – though that performance has an altogether special atmosphere – and Ashkenazy lets every detail tell in the *Poco vivace* third movement. Indeed this is possibly the most successful and technically impressive in the current Decca cycle, with the *Seventh* as a close runner-up. Early in the present century Sibelius enjoyed the championship of another great Russian pianist-conductor, Alexander Siloti, in whose concerts the *Third Symphony* was heard as early as 1909. In Ashkenazy he has found a natural heir and a worthy successor.

Symphonies Nos. 3 in C; 6 in D min.; 7 in C, Op. 105.
(M) *** Chan. CHAN 6557; MBTD 6557 [id.]. SNO, Sir Alexander Gibson.

With three symphonies offered, some 74 minutes overall, this is a fine bargain and an excellent way to experience Gibson's special feeling for this composer. The SNO is in very good form. The first movement of the *Third* has real momentum. The *Andantino* is fast, faster than the composer's marking. Such a tempo, while it gives the music-making fine thrust, means that Gibson, like Collins before him, loses some of the fantasy of this enigmatic movement. But there is more here to admire than to cavil at. The *Sixth* is impressive too, with plenty of atmosphere and some radiant playing from the Scottish violin section; the *Seventh* has a rather relaxed feeling throughout, but it does not lack warmth and, as in No. 1, Gibson draws the threads together at the close with satisfying breadth.

Symphony No. 4 in A min.; The Bard, Op. 64; The Oceanides, Op. 73; Pohjola's daughter, Op. 49.
*** RCA Dig. RD 60401 [60401-2-RC]. Finnish RSO, Saraste.

Symphony No. 4 in A min.; Kuolema: Valse triste. The Tempest, Op. 109: Berceuse.
(**) Dell'Arte mono DA 9023 [id.]. Phd. O, Stokowski – SHOSTAKOVICH: *Symphony No. 6.* (***)

Saraste's *Fourth* is well played and has plenty of atmosphere and power; though not all details are perfect, his is basically a convincingly shaped reading which penetrates well inside this dark, elusive world. *The Oceanides* is very fine indeed, and there is nothing much wrong with *The Bard* or *Pohjola's daughter* either – and a lot that is right. The Finnish Radio Orchestra plays well for him and the recording is both present and full-bodied.

Stokowski's 1932 account of the *Fourth Symphony* was the first ever made. It is a good performance, even if the finale is a bit too measured, but it does not have the same bleak concentration that distinguishes the Beecham. The *Berceuse* from *The Tempest* has a wonderful allure, but the principal interest of this record is the coupling.

Symphonies Nos. 4 in A min., Op. 63; 5 in E flat, Op. 82; 6 in D min., Op. 104; 7 in C, Op. 111.
☞ (M) **(*) Sony SM2K 4722 (2) [id.]. NYPO, Bernstein.

Whatever their failings, Bernstein's Sibelius are performances of stature. His *Fifth* is marvellously paced and has a sense of exhilaration and majesty, and his *Seventh* is also powerful. In his masterly survey of the symphonies on record, Guy Thomas speaks of them (and the *Second*) as being worthy of Koussevitzky, on whose Sibelius Bernstein would have been brought up. His *Fourth* has much to commend it too, though he uses some bizarre-sounding tubular bells in the finale. Bernstein aspired to a 'juicy, fat' tone (his own words) in Sibelius, which is perhaps less suited to the *Sixth*. None of these performances is negligible: Nos. 5 and 7 are marvellous, and the Sony engineers have done wonders in improving the sound.

Symphonies Nos. 4 in A min.; 5 in E flat, Op. 82.
*** Decca Dig. 425 858-2; *425 858-4* [id.]. San Francisco SO, Herbert Blomstedt.
☞ (M) *** Decca Dig. 430 749-2; *430 749-4* [id.]. Philh. O, Ashkenazy.
☞ (***) Beulah mono 4PD 8 [id.]. LSO, Anthony Collins.

Blomstedt allows the music to unfold naturally and conveys a real sense of space. The *Fourth Symphony* has the intimacy of chamber music and yet communicates a strong feeling of the Nordic landscape. Blomstedt is particularly attentive to dynamic shading and gets playing of great tonal refinement from the San Francisco orchestra; no one makes the closing bars of the finale sound more affecting. The *Fifth Symphony* is also wonderfully spacious. Some may find the accelerando between the two sections of the first movement a shade steep, but there is a powerful sense of mystery in the development section.

The reissue of Ashkenazy's digital cycle from the early 1980s continues with this highly recommendable coupling of the *Fourth* and *Fifth Symphonies*. Ashkenazy achieves great concentration of feeling in the *Fourth*. The brightness of the Philharmonia violins and the cleanness of attack add to the impact of this baldest of the Sibelius symphonies, and Ashkenazy's terracing of dynamic contrasts is superbly caught here. Like his other Sibelius readings, this one has something of a dark Russian passion in it, but freshness always dominates over mere sensuousness; as ever, Ashkenazy conveys the spontaneity of live performance. There is splendid drama and intensity throughout, and altogether this is most impressive. The *Fifth*, too, offers Decca's finest Kingsway Hall recording, spacious and well detailed. The reading is a thoroughly idiomatic one and disappoints only in terms of the balance of tempi between the two sections of the first movement.

Collins's opening to the *Fourth Symphony* with its desolate, Nordic atmosphere is remarkably restrained, yet the work as a whole has extraordinary underlying intensity. With Collins, every phrase breathes naturally and the lightening of mood in the Scherzo, with wind and string playing of great delicacy, is merely an interlude, before the powerfully sombre feeling of the *Il tempo largo* gives birth to a climax of compulsive power. In the finale the flux of mood and feeling that comes with its surge of animation is handled with great subtlety. The glockenspiel is used tellingly, and at the work's simple close Collins suggests that finally the composer has come to terms with his despondency. The performance of the *Fifth Symphony* carries all before it, with the reading moving forward in a single sweep. The control of tempos, tension and mood could hardly be better judged, with the gentle melancholy of the *Andante* triumphantly resolved in the exuberant finale. In both symphonies the LSO is marvellously responsive, both woodwind and strings bringing exceptional freshness to bear on every phrase and paragraph. The 1954/5 Kingsway Hall mono recordings were among the finest in terms of balance and truthfulness that Decca made throughout the mono LP era, and this CD reproduces superbly.

Symphonies Nos. 4 in A min.; 6 in D min.
(M) *** EMI CDM7 64121-2 [id.]. CBSO, Simon Rattle.

Simon Rattle's account of the *Fourth* invokes a powerful atmosphere in its opening pages: one is completely transported to its dark landscape with its seemingly limitless horizons. The string-tone is splendidly lean without being undernourished and achieves a sinisterly whispering pianissimo in the development. The slow movement is magical and the finale is hardly less masterly. Rattle's account of the *Sixth* is almost equally fine. It is still a *Sixth* to reckon with and its closing bars are memorably eloquent.

Symphonies Nos. (i) 4 in A min.; (ii) 6 in D min., Op. 104; (i) The Bard, Op. 64; Lemminkäinen's return, Op. 22/4; The Tempest: Prelude.
⊛ (M) (***) EMI mono CDM7 64027-2 [id.]. (i) LPO, (ii) RPO, Sir Thomas Beecham.

In its colour Beecham's account of the *Fourth Symphony* reflects his feeling that, far from being an austere work, as is often claimed, it is ripely romantic. No performance brings one closer to the music, while the recording, made over fifty years ago, sounds astonishingly fresh and bleak in this excellent transfer, and there is a concentration, darkness and poetry that few rivalled. Beecham's 1947 account of the *Sixth Symphony* was said to be Sibelius's favourite recording of all his symphonies. Its eloquence is no less impressive. In the three shorter works on the disc – also taken from the old Beecham Society volumes on 78-r.p.m. discs – Beecham's rhythmic sharpness and feeling for colour vividly convey the high voltage of Sibelius's strikingly original writing. *Lemminkäinen's homeward journey* is positively electrifying, while the *Prelude* to *The Tempest* is every bit as awesome an evocation of a storm as we had remembered. All these performances except the *Sixth Symphony* come from the late 1930s, but few allowances need be made, for they spring vividly to life in these remarkable transfers. Indispensable for all Sibelians.

Symphonies Nos. 4 in A min.; 7 in C; Kuolema: Valse triste.
☞ ⊛ (M) *** DG 439 527-2 [id.]. BPO, Karajan.

Karajan's celebrated 1965 account of the *Fourth Symphony* wears well. For many it remains the finest version of the *Fourth* on record, and it certainly ranks along with the Beecham as among the most insightful. The plush sonority of the Berlin Philharmonic at first deceives one into thinking that Karajan has beautified the symphony's landscape, but he comes closer to the spirit of the score than most others. (The symphony meant a great deal to him: he insisted on playing it alongside Beethoven in 1960 at his inaugural concert as the life-conductor of the orchestra at a time when Sibelius was held in the lowest esteem in Germany.) It is a performance of great concentration, deep thought and feeling. Although the new DG transfer of the recording does not have quite the body of violin-tone of the finest digital recordings, the acoustics of the Jesus-Christus-Kirche give weight and depth and a fine resonance to the bass. The performance is undoubtedly a great one. The *Seventh Symphony* is perhaps less successful though it comes off better than in Karajan's Philharmonia version, and the *Valse triste* is seductive. An indispensable record.

Symphony No. 5 in E flat, Op. 82.
☞ (M) *** EMI CDM7 64737-2 [id.]. Philh. O, Rattle – NIELSEN: *Symphony No. 4* etc. ***

Symphony No. 5; Finlandia; Kuolema: Valse triste. Tapiola, Op. 112.
☞ (B) *** DG Classikon 439 418-2 [id.]. BPO, Karajan.

Such is the excellence of the classic Karajan DG *Fifth* that few listeners would guess its age. It is a great performance, and this 1964 version is indisputably the finest of the four he made (two with the Philharmonia for Walter Legge's Columbia label, and the (1977) Berlin account for HMV). The fillers are familiar performances, also from the mid-1960s. *Tapiola* is a performance of great intensity and offers superlative playing; *Finlandia* is also one of the finest accounts available, but *Valse triste* is played very slowly and in a somewhat mannered fashion.

Simon Rattle's account of the *Fifth Symphony* with the Philharmonia was to the 1980s what Karajan's Berlin account was to the 1960s. It collected numerous prizes, even the *Deutscheschallplattenpreis* – and rightly! Everything about it feels right: the control of pace and texture and the balance of energy and repose. The development of the first movement has a compelling sense of mystery and the transition to the Scherzo section is beautifully judged. The Philharmonia Orchestra play splendidly and the EMI recording is very good indeed.

Symphonies Nos. 5 in E flat; 7 in C; Kuolema: Scene with cranes. Night ride and sunrise.
(M) *** EMI CDM7 64122-2 [id.]; *EG 764122-4*. CBSO, Simon Rattle.

In the *Fifth Symphony* Rattle is scrupulous in observing every dynamic nuance to the letter and, one might add, spirit. What is particularly impressive is the control of the transition between the first section and the Scherzo element of the first movement. There is a splendid sense of atmosphere in the development and a power unmatched in recent versions, save for the Karajan. The playing is superb, with recording to match. The *Seventh* is hardly less powerful and impressive: its opening is slow to unfold and has real vision. With the addition of an imaginative and poetic account of the *Scene with cranes* from the incidental music to *Kuolema*, this is the finest single disc in Rattle's Birmingham cycle.

Symphony No. 7 in C, Op. 105; Canzonetta, Op. 62a; Kuolema: Valse triste; Scene with cranes, Op. 44; Night ride and sunrise, Op. 55; Valse romantique, Op. 62b.
*** BIS Dig. CD 311 [id.]. Gothenburg SO, Järvi.

Neeme Järvi and the Gothenburg orchestra bring great energy and concentration to the *Seventh Symphony*. The only disappointment is the final climax, which is perhaps less intense than the best versions. However, it is a fine performance, and the music to *Kuolema* is splendidly atmospheric; *Night ride* is strongly characterized. The recording exhibits the usual characteristics of the Gothenburg Concert Hall and has plenty of body and presence.

The Tempest (incidental music), *Op. 109* (complete).
☞ *** BIS Dig. CD 581 [id.]. Tiihonen, Passikivi, Hirvonen, Kerola, Heinonen, Lahti Opera Ch. & SO, Osmo Vänskä.
☞ **(*) Ondine Dig. ODE 813-2 [id.]. Groop, Viljakainen, Hynninen, Silvasti, Tiilikainen, Op. Festival Ch., Finnish RSO, Saraste.

The familiar two suites from *The Tempest* plus the *Prelude* have been recorded many times (most notably and magically by Sir Thomas Beecham) but Sibelius's original score for the 1926 Copenhagen production of Shakespeare's play is extensive: it runs to some 34 numbers in all for soloists, mixed chorus, harmonium and orchestra, and takes about 65 minutes. For the Helsinki production the following year, the composer replaced the closing *Cortège* with an Epilogue drawing on material he had used in the *Cassazione*, Op. 6. There are some unfamiliar effects here: the muted strings with which we are familiar in the *Berceuse* were an afterthought. In the original, their music is allotted to the harmonium; and although this is at first startling, the effect is other-worldly in a completely unexpected way. There are other master-strokes that are missing (the insinuating bass clarinet in *The Oak-tree*) but much else that will be new. The *Chorus of the winds* with a real chorus is also quite magical – in fact the vocal writing is often highly imaginative – and the singers on the BIS CD are all good. The numbers are all presented in the order in which they appear in the play and, even though some sections would not survive translation to the concert hall, the level of inspiration is for the most part consistently high. At its best it is visionary. The atmosphere is very strong and puts one completely under its spell. The BIS recording, though good, needs to be reproduced at a higher than usual level setting: some may find it too recessed and there is at the bottom end of the spectrum a certain want of transparency.

If clarity and definition are a first priority, the Ondine version under Saraste is the one to go for. There is good singing here, too, from Monica Groop, Jorma Hynninen and the rest of the cast. The performance is given in Danish (as it would have been in the 1926 version, rather than the Finnish text used by BIS). However, Saraste is nowhere near as sensitive as Vänskä and does not have his sense of mystery or atmosphere. His *Prospero* is too fast, almost routine by comparison with Vänskä, who draws the listener more completely into Sibelius's and Shakespeare's world. Both accounts are recommendable and either is to be acquired rather than none. But the BIS makes a clear first choice.

CHAMBER MUSIC

(i) *Piano quintet in G min.; Piano trio in C (Lovisa); String quartet in E flat.*
*** Finlandia FACD 375 [id.]. Sibelius Ac. Qt, (i) with Tawaststjerna.

(i) *Piano quintet in G min.; String quartet in D min. (Voces intimae), Op. 56.*
*** Chan. Dig. CHAN 8742; *ABTD 1381* [id.]. (i) Anthony Goldstone; Gabrieli Qt.

The *Piano quintet* is a long and far from characteristic piece in five movements. Anthony Goldstone and the Gabrielis reverse the order of the second and third movements so as to maximize contrast. The first movement is probably the finest and Anthony Goldstone, an impressive player by any standards, makes the most of Sibelius's piano writing to produce a very committed performance. The *Voces intimae Quartet* is given a reflective, intelligent reading, perhaps at times wanting in momentum but finely shaped. Good recording.

The early *Quartet* is Haydnesque and insignificant, and the *Lovisa trio*, so called because it was written in that small town in the summer of 1888, offers only sporadic glimpses of things to come. The *Piano quintet* is given a fine performance on Finlandia, and there is little to choose between it and the more expansive Goldstone/Gabrieli account on Chandos.

String quartets: in E flat (1885); A min. (1889); B flat, Op. 4 (1890); D min. (Voces intimae), Op. 56.
(M) *** Finlandia Dig. FACD 522092 (2). Sibelius Ac. Qt.

The *E flat Quartet* is a student piece of little personality, very much influenced by the Viennese classics, above all Haydn. The *A minor Quartet* proves a delightful surprise with something of the freshness of Dvořák and Schubert. Sibelius obviously had ambivalent feelings towards the *B flat Quartet* and discouraged its performance. Its second movement bears a slight resemblance to a theme from *Rakastava*. Both are well worth resurrecting even if they do not, of course, match the mature *Voces intimae quartet* in artistry. The playing of the Sibelius Academy Quartet is exemplary and the recordings good: three are digital; *Voces intimae* dates from 1980 and is analogue.

PIANO MUSIC

10 Bagatelles, Op. 34; 6 Impromptus, Op. 5; 10 Pieces, Op. 24.
☞ *** Continuum Dig. CCD 1058 [id.]. Annette Servadei.

6 Finnish folksongs; Kavaljeren; Mandolinato; Morceau romantique; Pensées lyriques, Op. 40; 10 Pieces, Op. 58; Spagnuolo; Till trånaden; Valse triste, Op. 44/1.
☞ *** Continuum Dig. CCD 1059 [id.]. Annette Servadei.

Kyllikki, Op. 41; 4 Lyric Pieces, Op. 74; 2 Rondinos, Op. 68; Sonata in F, Op. 12; Sonatinas Nos. 1 in F sharp min., 2 in E; 3 in B flat min., Op. 67/1–3.
☞ *** Continuum Dig. CCD 1060 [id.]. Annette Servadei.

Although he composed for the piano throughout his life, Sibelius never had any great feeling for the medium. He once told Walter Legge it was 'an unsatisfying, ungrateful instrument which only one composer, Chopin, has fully succeeded in mastering and two others, Debussy and Schumann, have come on intimate terms'. While many of his keyboard miniatures are characteristic in the sense that they reveal the composer's fingerprints, few give any indication of his real potential as a composer. If only they survived, we would have as much idea of his stature as, say, one of Jupiter's moons reveal about the size of the giant planet. The sonatinas attracted the admiration of both Kempff, who never recorded them, and Glenn Gould who did (see below). Annette Servadei is a sympathetic and sensitive guide to this repertoire, and on the whole she is well recorded. She produces a wide range of keyboard colour and a good dynamic range. At times she is rather too closely observed by the microphone with a result that *forte* or *fortissimo* passages are insufficiently transparent. Erik T. Tawaststjerna's survey on the BIS label is still available but was recorded in less persuasive sound. On the whole the Continuum set makes a clear first choice.

Kyllikki (3 lyric pieces), Op. 41; Sonatinas Nos. 1–3, 0p. 67/1–3.
☞ (M) *(*) Sony SM2K 52654 (2). Glenn Gould – BIZET: *Nocturne* etc.; GRIEG: *Sonata.* *(*)

Glenn Gould's performances spring from conviction and the sound of this 1977 recording is much improved, but it comes in a two-CD box which is really rather poor value (the Grieg–Bizet disc runs to 45 minutes 5 seconds and the Sibelius sonatinas and *Kyllikki* combined take a mere 38 minutes 35 seconds). Erik Tawaststjerna *fils* (BIS) or Annette Servadei are perfectly satisfactory alternatives.

VOCAL MUSIC

Songs with orchestra: *Arioso; Autumn evening (Höstkväll); Come away, Death! (Kom nu hit Död); The diamond on the March snow (Diamanten på marssnön); The fool's song of the spider (Sången om korsspindeln); Luonnotar, Op. 70; On a balcony by the sea (På verandan vid havet); The Rapids-rider's brides (Koskenlaskian morsiammet); Serenade; Since then I have questioned no further (Se'n har jag ej frågat mera); Spring flies hastily (Våren flyktar hastigt); Sunrise (Soluppgång).*
*** BIS CD 270 [id.]. Jorma Hynninen, Mari Anne Häggander, Gothenburg SO, Panula.

Jorma Hynninen is a fine interpreter of this repertoire: his singing can only be called glorious. Mari-Anne Häggander manages the demanding tessitura of *Arioso* and *Luonnotar* with much artistry, and her *Luonnotar* is certainly to be preferred to Söderström's. Jorma Panula proves a sensitive accompanist and secures fine playing from the Gothenburg orchestra. In any event, this is indispensable.

Arioso, Op. 3; Narcissus; Pelléas et Mélisande: The three blind sisters. 7 Songs, Op. 17; 6 Songs, Op. 36; 5 Songs, Op. 37; 6 Songs, Op. 88. Souda, souda, sinisorsa.
*** BIS Dig. CD 457 [id.]. Anne Sofie von Otter, Bengt Forsberg.

This lovely recital by Anne Sofie von Otter marks the start of a BIS project to record all the songs; if the remaining issues are as good as this, the set will be a distinguished addition to the Sibelius discography. Miss von Otter always makes a beautiful sound, but she has a highly developed sense of line and brings great interpretative insight to such songs as *My bird is long in homing* and *Tennis at Trianon* which has even greater finesse than Söderström's. And what a good accompanist Bengt Forsberg is. The recording is good if a bit reverberant.

Finlandia (version for orchestra and mixed chorus), *Op. 26; Homeland (Oma maa), Op. 92; Impromptu, Op. 19;* (i) *Snöfrid, Op. 29. Song to the earth (Maan virsi), Op. 95; Song to Lemminkäinen, Op. 31; Väinö's song, Op. 110.*
** Ondine Dig. ODE 754-2 [id.]. (i) Stina Rautelin (reciter), Finnish Nat. Op. Ch. & O, Eri Klas.

While most of Sibelius's songs are to Swedish texts, the choral music is predominantly Finnish. *Oma maa* ('Homeland') is a dignified and euphonious work and includes a magical evocation of the wintry nights with Aurora borealis and the white nights of midsummer. *Väinö's song* is an appealing piece which bears an opus number between *The Tempest* and *Tapiola* – though it is not really fit to keep them company. The performances and the recording are decent rather than distinguished.

Kullervo Symphony, Op. 7.
☞ *** Sony Dig. SK 52563 [id.]. Marianna Rørholm, Jorma Hynninen, Helsinki University Ch., LAPO, Salonen.
☞ (M) *** EMI Dig. CDM5 65080-2 [id.]. Eeva-Liisa Saarinen, Jorma Hynninen, Estonian State Ac. Male Ch., Helsinki University Male Ch., Helsinki PO, Berglund.

Esa-Pekka Salonen's account of Sibelius's early *Kullervo Symphony* is gripping and held together tautly. The symphony put the composer firmly on the map in his native Finland and is an astonishing achievement, given the musically isolated world in which Sibelius grew up. It is amazing to think that it preceded the *Resurrection Symphony* of Mahler. Sibelius never allowed the work to be heard again after its first performances in 1892, but fortunately it escaped the fate of the *Eighth Symphony* and the score survives. Salonen's is its fourth commercial recording and the fourth in which Jorma Hynninen appears. It is arguably the best so far; it has a sweep and momentum that eluded Salonen's less-than-overwhelming Nielsen cycle. The Los Angeles orchestra, to whom this score must have been new, play with the enthusiasm of fresh discovery and Marianna Rørholm proves a worthy companion to the ubiquitous Hynninen. The first movement is taut, brisk and dramatic – very much as Sibelius's son-in-law took it at its first performance in recent times; the fifth is very imaginatively done, and only the fourth is perhaps a bit too fast, almost headlong.

On the mid-price EMI Matrix label there is a thoroughly recommendable alternative in the form of Paavo Berglund's 1985 recording with Eeva-Liisa Saarinen, Hynninen, the combined Estonian Academic and Helsinki University Male Choirs and the Helsinki Philharmonic. We thought well of this version when it first appeared, even though the digital recording did not have quite the warmth and ambience of Berglund's pioneering analogue set from the early 1970s with the Bournemouth orchestra. All the same, the performance is very fine indeed, with every point tellingly made and every phrase sounding splendidly fresh. He scores over Salonen in the fourth movement, which is steadier in tempo and no less effective for that. The sound is very good indeed – not quite the equal of the Sony but very truthful and present.

(i) *Luonnotar, Op. 70. Night ride and sunrise, Op. 55; The Oceanides, Op. 73.*
☞ (M) **(*) EMI CDM5 65182 [id.]. (i) Gwyneth Jones; LSO, Dorati – NIELSEN: *Symphony No. 5.*
**(*)

Gwyneth Jones's version of *Luonnotar* is powerful, though in no respect superior to the somewhat later Valjakka-Berglund. Dorati gives respectable, well-prepared accounts of all three scores, though neither his *Night ride* nor his *Oceanides* is a patch on Rattle's (or, in the case of the latter, Beecham's). All the same, the 1969 recording sounds very good; the coupling, Kubelik's version of Nielsen's *Fifth*, is a performance of some stature.

The Maiden in the tower (opera). *Karelia suite, Op. 11.*
*** BIS Dig. CD 250 [id.]. Häggander, Hynninen, Hagegård, Kruse, Gothenburg Ch. and SO, Järvi.

The Maiden in the tower falls into eight short scenes. The orchestral interlude between the first two scenes brings us the real Sibelius, and the second scene is undoubtedly impressive; there are echoes of Wagner, such as we find in some of the great orchestral songs of the following decade. All the same, it lacks something we find in all his most characteristic music: quite simply, a sense of mastery. Yet there are telling performances here from Mari-Anne Häggander and Jorma Hynninen and the

Gothenburg orchestra. Neeme Järvi's account of the *Karelia suite* is certainly original, with its *Intermezzo* too broad to make an effective contrast with the ensuing *Ballade*.

Simpson, Robert (born 1921)

Energy; Introduction & allegro on a theme by Max Reger; The Four Temperaments; Volcano; Vortex.
*** Hyp. Dig. CDA 66449 [id.]. Desford Colliery Caterpillar Band, James Watson.

The Four Temperaments is a four-movement, 22-minute symphony of great imaginative power, and ingeniously laid out for the band. Simpson played in brass bands as a boy and this is doubtless where he acquired some of his expertise in writing for them. *Energy* came in response to a commission from the World Brass Band Championships. The *Introduction and allegro on a theme by Max Reger* is awesome and impressive. Together with *Volcano* and his most recent piece, *Vortex*, this makes up his entire output in this medium. The Desford Colliery Caterpillar Band under James Watson play with all the expertise and virtuosity one expects, and the recording has admirable clarity and body, though the acoustic is on the dry side.

Symphonies Nos. 2; 4.
☞ *** Hyp. Dig. CDA 66505 [id.]. Bournemouth SO, Vernon Handley.

Robert Simpson's symphonies are at last coming into their own. The *Second*, composed in 1956 for Anthony Bernard's London Chamber Orchestra, is one of the very best; its opening is one of Simpson's most mysterious and inspired ideas, lean and sinuous but full of poetic vision. The variation slow movement, one of the most virtuosic and remarkable exercises in the palindrome (each variation is the same when played backwards as it is forward – as is the case with his *Ninth Quartet* and the early *Variations and Fugue on a theme of Haydn* for piano), yet such is the quality of Simpson's artistry in concealing his ingenuity that no one coming to it innocently would be aware of this. The *Second* is a work of enduring quality, music that is both accessible yet of substance. The *Fourth Symphony* is the more extended piece, which would appear to have given the composer some trouble. After its first performance by the Hallé Orchestra under James Loughran, Simpson revised the slow movement, quickening the pulse from *Adagio* to *Andante*, layering the contours of the cello solo near the beginning and directing the final climax to be hushed. Powerful and inspiriting music in totally dedicated performances by Vernon Handley, and excellent recording quality. Those coming to explore Simpson's symphonic world should start here, for both pieces show him at his most fully characteristic best.

(i) *Symphony No. 3;* (ii) *Clarinet quintet.*
(M) *** Unicorn UKCD 2028. (i) LSO, Jascha Horenstein; (ii) Bernard Walton (clarinet), Aeolian
 Qt.

The *Third Symphony* is in two long movements. There is something Sibelian about the way that, in the first movement, Simpson gradually brings together fragments of musical ideas; but generally this is a work which (within its frankly tonal idiom) asks to be considered in Simpson's own individual terms. The *Clarinet quintet* is a thoughtful, searching piece, dating from 1968 and among Simpson's profoundest utterances. It is played with total commitment here. Both works are given extremely vivid sound.

Symphonies Nos. 6; 7.
*** Hyp. Dig. CDA 66280 [id.]. RLPO, Handley.

The *Sixth* is inspired by the idea of growth: the development of a musical structure from initial melodic cells in much the same way as life emerges from a single fertilized cell in nature. The *Seventh*, scored for chamber orchestral forces, is hardly less powerful in its imaginative vision and sense of purpose. Both scores are bracingly Nordic in their inner landscape and exhilarating in aural experience. The playing of the Liverpool orchestra under Vernon Handley could hardly be bettered, and the recording is altogether first class.

Symphony No. 9.
🏵 *** Hyp. Dig. CDA 66299 [id.]. Bournemouth SO, Vernon Handley (with talk by the composer).

What can one say about the *Ninth* of Robert Simpson – except that its gestures are confident, its control of pace and its material are masterly; it is a one-movement work, but at no time in its 45 minutes does it falter – nor does the attention of the listener. The CD also includes a spoken introduction to the piece that many listeners will probably find helpful. It is played superbly by the Bournemouth Symphony Orchestra under Vernon Handley, and is no less superbly recorded.

String quartets Nos. 1; 4.
*** Hyp. Dig. CDA 66419 [id.]. Delmé Qt.

The *First Quartet* opens in as innocent a fashion as the Haydn *Lark Quartet* or Nielsen's *E flat* but, the better one comes to know it, the more it is obvious that Simpson is already his own man. The second movement is a palindrome (most modern composers do not know how to write forwards, let alone backwards as well) but its ingenuity is worn lightly. The *Fourth* is part of the trilogy which Simpson conceived as a kind of commentary on Beethoven's *Rasumovsky quartets*. Yet they live very much in their own right. Excellent performances from the Delmé, and fine recording too.

String quartets Nos. 3 and 6; String trio (Prelude, Adagio & fugue).
*** Hyp. Dig. CDA 66376 [id.]. Delmé Qt.

The *Third Quartet* is a two-movement piece. Its finale is a veritable power-house with its unrelenting sense of onward movement which almost strains the medium. Its first movement is a deeply felt piece that has a powerful and haunting eloquence. The *Sixth* is further evidence of Simpson's remarkable musical mind. The *String trio* is a marvellously stimulating and thoughtful piece. Dedicated performances and excellent recording.

String quartets Nos. 7 and 8.
*** Hyp. Dig. CDA 66117 [id.]. Delmé Qt.

The *Seventh Quartet* has a real sense of vision and something of the stillness of the remote worlds it evokes, 'quiet and mysterious yet pulsating with energy'. The *Eighth* turns from the vastness of space to the microcosmic world of insect-life, but, as with so much of Simpson's music, there is a concern for musical continuity rather than beauty of incident. Excellent playing from the Delmé Quartet, and very good recorded sound too.

String quartet No. 9 (32 Variations & fugue on a theme of Haydn).
*** Hyp. Dig. CDA 66127 [id.]. Delmé Qt.

What an original and, in its way, masterly conception the *Ninth Quartet* is! It is a set of thirty-two variations and a fugue on the minuet of Haydn's *Symphony No. 47*. Like the minuet itself, all the variations are in the form of a palindrome. It is a mighty and serious work, argued with all the resource and ingenuity one expects from this composer. A formidable achievement in any age, and a rarity in ours. The Delmé Quartet cope with its difficulties splendidly, and the performance carries the imprimatur of the composer. The recording sounds very good in its CD format.

String quartets Nos. 10 (For Peace); 11.
*** Hyp. Dig. CDA 66225 [id.]. Coull Qt.

The subtitle, *For Peace*, of No. 10 refers to 'its generally pacific character' and aspires to define 'the condition of peace which excludes aggression but not strong feeling'. Listening to this *Quartet* is like hearing a quiet, cool voice of sanity that refreshes the troubled spirit after a long period in an alien, hostile world. The one-movement *Eleventh* draws on some of the inspiration of its predecessor. It is a work of enormous power and momentum. Excellent performances and recording.

String quartet No. 12 (1987); (i) String quintet (1987).
*** Hyp. Dig. CDA 66503. Coull Qt, (i) with Roger Bigley.

Robert Simpson's *Twelfth Quartet* is a masterly and absorbing score. His *String quintet* is another work of sustained inventive power. We are unlikely to get another recording, so this is self-recommending; but it must be noted that the heroic demands this score makes on the players keep them fully stretched. The intonation and tone of the leader is not always impeccable, but the playing has commitment and intelligence.

Sinding, Christian (1856–1941)

Légende, Op. 46.
(BB) *** Naxos Dig. 8.550329 [id.]. Dong-Suk Kang, Slovak (Bratislava) RSO, Adrian Leaper –
  HALVORSEN: *Air Norvégien* etc.; SIBELIUS: *Violin concerto;* SVENDSEN: *Romance.* ***

Dong-Suk Kang plays Sinding's *Légende* with great conviction and an effortless, songful virtuosity. It is by no means as appealing as the Halvorsen and Svendsen pieces but makes a good makeweight for an excellent collection in the lowest price range.

Suite, Op. 10.
*** EMI CDC7 47167-2 [id.]. Perlman, Pittsburgh SO, Previn – SIBELIUS: *Concerto.* ***

Heifetz recorded this dazzling piece in the 1950s, and it need only be said that Perlman's version is not inferior. Such is the velocity of Perlman's first movement that one wonders whether the disc is playing at the right speed.

Smetana, Bedřich (1824–84)

Håkon Jarl, Op. 16; Prague carnival; Richard III, Op. 11; Wallenstein's Camp, Op. 14 (symphonic poems).
☞ (M) *** DG 437 254-2 [id.]. Bav. RSO, Kubelik – JANACEK: *Sinfonietta.* ***

These symphonic poems can be recommended to those who are attracted to the *Má Vlast* cycle. The jolly *Carnival in Prague*, the composer's last work, was written in 1883; the others are more melodramatic, dating from around 1860. The music has a flavour of Dvořák, if without that master's melodic and imaginative flair. The most spectacular is *Wallenstein's Camp* with its opportunities for offstage brass fanfares – very like Liszt's *Mazeppa* – well managed here. This is very enjoyable in its ingenuous way; but perhaps the most distinguished piece here is *Håkon Jarl*, which has a strong vein of full-blooded romanticism. The playing is first class throughout, the conductor's approach is fresh and committed, and the recording has good body and atmosphere, even if the CD transfer underlines a slight dryness in the bass, characteristic of this source.

Má Vlast (complete).
*** Sup. Dig. 11 1208-2 [id.]. Czech PO, Kubelik.
(M) *** Ph. Dig. 432 196-2 [id.]. Concg. O, Dorati.
*** Telarc CD 80265 [id.]. Milwaukee SO, Macal.
*** DG Dig. 431 652-2 [id.]. VPO, Levine.
*** Virgin/EMI Dig. VC7 59576-2 [id.]. RLPO, Pešek.
☞ ** Sup. Dig. 11 0957-2 [id.]. Czech PO, Bělohlávek.

In 1990 Rafael Kubelik returned to his homeland after an enforced absence of 41 years to open the Prague Spring Festival with this vibrant performance of *Má Vlast*. He had recorded the work twice before in stereo, but this Czech version is special, imbued with passionate national feeling, yet never letting the emotions boil over. At the bold opening of *Vyšehrad*, with the harp strongly profiled, the intensity of the music-making is immediately projected, and the trickling streams which are the source of *Vltava* have a delicacy almost of fantasy but, after the relaxation for the moonlit sequence, one realizes that the return of the chorale as the river flows past Vyšehrad is a key point in Kubelik's reading. *Sárka*, with its bloodthirsty tale of revenge and slaughter, is immensely dramatic, contrasting with the pastoral evocations of the following piece; the Slavonic lilt of the music's lighter moments brings the necessary contrast and release. The recording is vivid and full but not sumptuous, yet this suits the powerful impulse of Kubelik's overall view, with the build-up to the exultant close of *Blaník* producing a dénouement of great majesty.

Dorati's is also an extremely fine account of Smetana's cycle, avoiding most of the pitfalls with a reading which brings both vivid drama and orchestral playing of the finest quality. For those who put quality of recording as of prime importance, this could be first choice, particularly considering its cost. The music-making has a high adrenalin level throughout, yet points of detail are not missed. The accents of *Vyšehrad* may seem too highly stressed to ears used to a more mellow approach to this highly romantic opening piece, and *Vltava* similarly moves forward strongly. In the closing *Blaník*, Dorati finds dignity rather than bombast and the pastoral episode is delightfully relaxed, with a fine rhythmic bounce to the march theme which then leads to the final peroration. The Philips sound is splendid, with a wide amplitude and a thrilling concert-hall presence.

Macal's new Telarc version offers the finest recording of all; indeed it approaches the demonstration bracket. As with his version of Dvořák's *New World Symphony*, he provides a highly spontaneous and enjoyable performance, imaginatively conceived and convincingly paced. The very opening of *Vyšehrad*, with its relatively gentle harp roulades, sets the atmospheric mood of the reading; other accounts, notably Kubelik's, have greater slavic fire and find a more red-bloodedly patriotic feeling, but the excellent orchestral playing is responsive to his less histrionic view. *Sárka* has a folksy flavour, the melodrama good-humoured, while in *From Bohemia's woods and fields*, after the radiant high string passage, the horns steal in magically with their chorale. Throughout the brass are full and sonorous, mitigating any rhetorical bombast in the last two symphonic poems; and Macal's Czech nationality ensures that the performance has idiomatic feeling.

Levine is now upstaged by Dorati on Philips, who has a considerable price advantage plus the glorious acoustic of the Concertgebouw. Levine's performance is full of momentum and thrust, with much imaginative detail and most beautifully played. In *Tábor* and *Blaník* the VPO play with great vigour and commitment, and these patriotic pieces have both fervour and plenty of colour. The sound is full-bodied, with a wide amplitude and range, but it is less sumptuous and slightly less atmospheric than the Philips version.

Pešek's reading does not miss the music's epic patriotic feeling, yet never becomes bombastic. There is plenty of evocation, from the richly romantic opening of *Vyšehrad* to the more mysterious scene-setting in *Tábor*, while the climax of *Šárka*, with its potent anticipatory horn-call, is a gripping piece of melodrama. The two key sections of the work, *Vltava* and *From Bohemia's woods and fields*, are especially enjoyable for their vivid characterization, while at the very end of *Blaník* Pešek draws together the two key themes – the *Vyšehrad* motif and the Hussite chorale – very satisfyingly.

There is nothing special about Bělohlávek's recording of *Má Vlast*. Although it is well played, there is an element of routine here until the final *Blaník*, which is both gripping and expansive. The recording, made in Prague Castle, is rather closely balanced and lacks opulence. Those wanting the Czech Philharmonic in this work should turn to Kubelik, whose 1990 recording has all the fervour, excitement and passionate Czech lyric feeling which are missing here.

Má Vlast: Vltava.
☞ (M) *** Sony SBK 48264 [id.]. Cleveland O, Szell – BIZET: *Symphony;* MENDELSSOHN: *Midsummer Night's Dream.* ***
☞ **(*) DG Gold Dig. 439 009-2 [id.]. VPO, Karajan – DVORAK: *Symphony No. 9 (New World).* **(*)
(M) (**) BMG/RCA GD 60279 [60279-2-RG]. NBC SO, Toscanini – DVORAK: *Symphony No. 9;* KODALY: *Háry János suite.* (***)

Má Vlast: Vltava. The Bartered Bride: Overture; Polka; Furiant.
☞ (M) ** Decca 425 087-2 [id.]. Israel PO, Kertész – DVORAK: *Slavonic dances & rhapsody* **; ENESCU: *Roumanian rhapsody No. 1.* ***

The Clevelanders play *Vltava* superbly, from the opening trickle, through the village wedding and the moonlight sequence, to the climax at St John's rapids. The effect is both vivid and dramatic and the dynamic range not too restricted to spoil the element of contrast.

Karajan's VPO performance is characteristically well structured, and the recorded sound sounds quite expansive in this remastered format, even if the balance is not quite natural.

With Kertész these pieces are exceptionally vivid. *Vltava* opens delicately and atmospherically but develops brisk tempi (especially in the riverside wedding sequence), yet not losing its picturesque qualities. The *Bartered Bride overture and dances* are as brilliant as you like. The snag is that the very bright Israeli recording is not flattering to the violins above the stave, although the sound does not lack ambience.

Recorded several years earlier than the other two items on Toscanini's disc, *Vltava* has painfully dry and close sound; but the intensity of Toscanini's performance still makes it a valuable document.

Má Vlast: Vltava; Vyšehrad.
☞ *** Chan. Dig. CHAN 9230 [id.]. Detroit SO, Neeme Järvi – FIBICH: *Symphony No. 1.* ***

Järvi's are excellent performances of both pieces, vivid in pictorialism and colour, and they are very well played and recorded. But it is for the Fibich *Symphony* that this Chandos issue is most valuable.

Piano trio in G min., Op. 15.
*** Chan. Dig. CHAN 8445; *ABTD 1157* [id.]. Borodin Trio – DVORAK: *Dumky trio.* ***
** Teldec/Warner Dig. 2292 43715-2 [id.]. Trio Fontenay – CHOPIN: *Piano trio.* ***

Writing the *Trio* was a cathartic act, following the death of the composer's four-year-old daughter, so it is not surprising that it is a powerfully emotional work. The writing gives fine expressive opportunities for both the violin and cello, which are taken up eloquently by Rostislav Dubinsky and Yuli Turovsky, and the pianist, Luba Edlina, is also wonderfully sympathetic. In short, a superb account, given a most realistic recording balance. Highly recommended.

The Trio Fontenay take a more extrovert view of the *G minor Trio* than do earlier rivals and tend rather to dramatize its emotions. It is good to hear it played as if they believe every note, but they protest too much and do not allow this dignified, elegiac quality to speak as naturally as it might. Good recording.

String quartet No. 1 in E min. (From my life).

☞ *** Sony Dig. SK 53282 [id.]. Artis Qt – DVORAK: *String quartet No. 14.* ***

*** Ph. Dig. 420 803-2 [id.]. Guarneri Qt – DVORAK: *String quartet No. 12.* ***

☞ *** EMI Dig. CDC7 54215-2 [id.]. Alban Berg Qt – DVORAK: *String quartet No. 12.* ***

(M) *** Decca 430 295-2 [id.]. Gabrieli Qt – JANACEK: *String quartets Nos. 1–2.* ***

☞ (M) **(*) DG 437 251-2 [id.]. Amadeus Qt – DVORAK: *String quartet No. 12.* **(*)

The Artis Quartet give one of the finest accounts of the *First Quartet* for many years: imaginative, dramatic, ardent and sensitive. It is what one might call a narrative performance in that it holds one completely throughout without ever indulging in expressive overstatement. The Sony recording is in every way first class.

The Guarneri performance of the slow movement is wonderfully warm, romantic without a trace of sentimentality, with rich playing from the cellist, David Soyer. The happiness of the second-movement *Polka* ('Reminiscences of youth') is nicely caught and the finale is contrasted dramatically, with the catastrophic onset of deafness heralded by a high-pitched whistle on the first violin; the performance ends in a mood of touching elegiac reverie. The Philips recording is full-textured and most naturally balanced, with unexaggerated presence.

By the side of the Artis and Guarneri accounts, the Alban Berg Quartet sound just a shade polished and professional. There is not quite enough spontaneity by comparison with the Artis, who carry one onwards with greater freshness and impulsiveness. All the same, there is much more to admire in the Alban Berg's reading than to cavil at: the first movement comes off well, and the EMI recording is very truthful and present. There is no cause to withhold a third star, particularly as their Dvořák is very successful.

Artistically, the Gabrieli performance of Smetana's autobiographical *First Quartet* is first class; technically, it offers vivid and well-balanced 1977 recorded sound, although the upper range of the violin timbre is marginally less smooth than in the Janáček coupling, even though it was recorded at the same time in the warm acoustics of Rosslyn Hill Chapel.

A strongly felt and purposeful account of Smetana's autobiographical *Quartet* from the Amadeus on top form: their ensemble, matching of timbre and unanimous of attack, is peerless. At times one feels that Norbert Brainin's lyrical vibrato is not entirely suitable for this very personal utterance: he wears his heart too openly on his sleeve; but there is no doubt that the performance overall is gripping, and the 1977 recording is vividly realistic.

String quartet No. 1 (From my life) – orchestral version by George Szell. *The Bartered Bride: Overture and dances.*

*** Chan. Dig. CHAN 8412; *ABTD 1149* [id.]. LSO, Geoffrey Simon.

The Czech feeling of Szell's scoring is especially noticeable in the *Polka*, but overall there is no doubt that the fuller textures add a dimension to the music, though inevitably there are losses as well as gains. The powerful advocacy of Simon and the excellent LSO playing, both here and in the sparkling excerpts from *The Bartered Bride*, provide a most rewarding coupling. The recording is well up to the usual high Chandos standards.

String quartets Nos. 1 in E min. (From my life); 2 in D min.

☞ *** ASV Dig. CDDCA 777 [id.]. Lindsay Qt (with DVORAK: *Romance; Waltzes Nos. 1–2* ***).

☞ *** Collins Dig. 1323-2 [id.]. Talich Qt (with SUK: *Meditations on the St Wenceslas chorale* ***).

☞ *(*) Nimbus Dig. NI 5131 [id.]. Medici Qt.

(i) *String quartets Nos. 1 in E min. (From my life); 2 in D min.* (ii) *From the homeland.*

☞ (BB) ** Naxos Dig. 8.550379 [id.]. (i) Moyzes Qt; (ii) Takako Nishizaki, Tatiana Fránova.

The Lindsay Quartet bring dramatic intensity to the *E minor Quartet* and play with great fire and vitality. Their (perhaps slightly forward) recording is very good indeed, and readers wanting both the Smetana *Quartets* together need look no further than them or the Talich Quartet on Collins.

The Talich Quartet take their name from their violist, Jan Talich, once their leader – and they have no want of drama or fire either. This is cultured playing, and moreover they are better served by their recording engineers than they were in their earlier, Calliope version. There is not a great deal to choose between the Talich and the Lindsays, and readers can invest in either with confidence. In each case there are attractive bonuses.

The Moyzes Quartet, composed of members of the Slovak Philharmonic, turn in very respectable accounts of both *Quartets*. Like the Medicis, they do not match the fervour or polish of the Artis or Lindsays in the *E minor* or of the Lindsay and Talich Quartets in the *D minor*. The recording has less warmth and ambience than its top-price rivals. All the same this is to be preferred to some of the high-powered, jet-set ensembles, and is value for money.

The Medici give a robust and straightforward performance of both *Quartets* and are well recorded, though there is a slight edge to the sound. In the *E minor Quartet* they do not match the Alban Berg in terms of polish or the Artis in refinement or insight.

Czech dances I & II; 8 Bagatelles and impromptus.
☞ ** Unicorn Dig. DKPCD 9139 [id.]. Radoslav Kvapil.

Radoslav Kvapil is entirely inside this repertoire, even if his account of the *F major Polka* from the first book of *Czech dances* does not eclipse memories of Firkušný's celebrated Capitol LP from the days of mono, which had great exuberance and dash! All the same, he is a highly sensitive exponent of this repertoire. The recording is wanting in distinction; it lacks brightness and perspective. It is adequate, while the playing is much more than that.

OPERA

The Bartered Bride (complete in Czech).
*** Sup. Dig. 10 3511-2 (3) [id.]. Beňačková, Dvorský, Novák, Kopp, Jonášová, Czech Philharmonic Ch. and O, Košler.

The digital Supraphon set under Košler admirably supplies the need for a first-rate Czech version of this delightful comic opera. The performance sparkles from beginning to end, with folk rhythms crisply enunciated in an infectiously idiomatic way. The cast is strong, headed by the characterful Gabriela Beňačková as Mařenka and one of the finest of today's Czech tenors, Peter Dvorský, as Jeník. Miroslav Kopp in the role of the ineffective Vašek sings powerfully too. As Kecal the marriage-broker, Richard Novák is not always steady, but his swaggering characterization is most persuasive. The CDs offer some of the best sound we have yet had from Supraphon, fresh and lively. The discs are fairly generously banded, but this could now be fitted on a pair of CDs, so the set is unnecessarily expensive. The libretto, however, has been improved and is clear and easy to use.

Libuše.
☞ **(*) Sup. Dig. 11 1276-2 633 (3) [id.]. Beňačková, Zítek, Svorc, Vodička, Děpoltová, Prague Nat. Theatre Ch. & O, Košler.

Recorded live at the Prague National Theatre in 1983, this performance vividly communicates the fervour of nationalist aspirations, more intense when shared with an audience. Yet this opera, written for the opening of the National Theatre of Prague in 1881, inevitably has a limited appeal for the non-Czech listener, with a plot concerning the Czech royal dynasty. The cast here is even stronger than that of the previous recording under Krombholc, with Gabriela Beňačková-Cápová as Libuše memorable in her prophetic aria in Act III, while Václav Zítek as Přemysi, her consort, provides an attractive lyrical interlude in Act II which, with its chorus of harvesters, has affinities with *The Bartered Bride*. In Act I there is some Slavonic wobbling, notably from Eva Děpoltová as Krasava, but generally the singing is as dramatic as the plot-line will allow. Košler directs committedly; with the stage perspectives well caught, an unintrusive audience and no disturbing stage-noises with such a static plot, the recording is very satisfactory. Now reissued on three discs and with a clearly printed new libretto/translation, this is made more attractive, although the cues still provide poor internal access for an opera playing for not far short of three hours. Twelve extra index points have been added to the 14 bands – not nearly enough for a work of this kind.

Smyth, Ethel (1858–1944)

The Wreckers: Overture.
☞ (B) *** CfP CD-CFP 4635; TC-CFP 4635. RSNO, Gibson – GERMAN: *Welsh rhapsody;* HARTY: *With the wild geese;* MACCUNN: *Land of the Mountain and Flood.* ***

Ethel Smyth's *Overture* for her opera, *The Wreckers* (first performed in England in 1909), is a strong, meaty piece which shows the calibre of this remarkable woman's personality for, while the material itself is not memorable, it is put together most compellingly and orchestrated with real flair. The recording is full and the CD has refined detail. This CD makes a genuine bargain.

Mass in D; March of the Women; Boatswain's mate: Mrs Water's aria.
*** Virgin/EMI Dig. VC7 59022-2 [id.]. Harrhy, Hardy, Dressen, Bohn, Ch. & O of Plymouth Music Series, Minnesota, Philip Brunelle.

Ethel Smyth's *Mass in D* is one of her most ambitious works, a piece that boldly seeks to echo Beethoven's great *Missa solemnis* in its moods and idiom. Though Smyth's invention is less memorable than Beethoven's, the drive and the vehemence of her writing make this a warmly rewarding piece, with Brahms's *Requiem* another, if less marked, influence. The composer herself counted the *Gloria*, the longest and most energetic movement, as the finest and prescribed that it should be performed, not in the usual liturgical sequence, but last, as a happy ending, as is done here. Brunelle draws fine playing and singing from the members of the Plymouth Music Series. Smyth's once-celebrated suffragette march is done with polish rather than feminist fervour, and Eiddwen Harrhy makes a characterful soloist in the extended aria from Smyth's best-known opera. First-rate sound. We look forward to the complete recording of *The Wreckers*, currently promised by Conifer.

Soler, Antonio (1729–83)

KEYBOARD WORKS

Keyboard works: *Sonatas Nos. 1 in A; 3 in B flat; 24–5 in D min.; 28–9 in C; 30–31 in G; 96 in E flat; 118 in A min. Prelude No. 1 in D min.*
** Astrée Dig. E 8768 [id.]. Bob van Asperen (harpsichord).

Keyboard works: *Sonatas Nos. 7–9 in C; 20–21 in C sharp min.; 95 in A. Prelude No. 3 in C.*
** Astrée Dig. E 8769 [id.]. Bob van Asperen (harpsichord).

Keyboard works: *Sonatas Nos. 10 in B min.; 11 in B; 12–14 in G; 52 in E min.; 73–4 in D; 92 in D (Sonata des clarines); 106 in E min.; Allegro pastoril; Prelude No. 6 in G.*
** Astrée Dig. E 8770 [id.]. Bob van Asperen (harpsichord).

Keyboard works: *Sonatas Nos. 37 in D; 46 in D; 56 in F; 98 in B flat min.; 100 in C min.; 103 in C min.; 108 in C; 109 in F; 112 in D; Fandango No. 146; Prelude No. 5 in D.*
** Astrée Dig. E 8771 [id.]. Bob van Asperen (harpsichord).

An ambitious venture to record the complete keyboard output of Antonio Soler with Bob van Asperen is let down by insensitive engineering. He plays with plenty of vitality but the value of the enterprise is diminished by the oppressively close balance of the recording – admittedly not quite so bottom-heavy as Ton Koopman's Forqueray record for Erato. However ingenious and varied in colour the registration of the distinguished Dutch harpsichordist, the effect is reduced to an unrelieved and uniform dynamic level which produces aural fatigue. The music is so characterful and the playing so fresh that these discs must be recommended, but readers will want to listen at low level and only to one or two pieces at a time. Moreover the documentation is too generalized for such an important project, with essays about the composer, the performer, the project research, and a cursory discussion of the music, repeated with each CD. Information is not given about individual works and no attempt is made to differentiate between the single movement sonatas and the occasional more ambitious three- and four-movement combinations, like Nos. 92 and 98, in which Soler created composite works from movements of the same tonality but diverse character. The spectacular thirteen-minute *Fandango* which opens the fourth disc is presented without comment.

Sonatas Nos. 2 in E flat; 65 in A min.; 105 in E flat; 111 in D; 117 in D min.; 124 in C; 125 in C; 126a and 126b in C min.; 127 in D; 128 in E min.; 130 in G min.; 131 in A.
☞ ** Astrée Dig. E 8779 [id.]. Bob van Asperen (harpsichord).

Sonatas Nos. 4 in G; 5 in F; 6 in F; 49 in D min.; 55 in F; 69 in F; 72 in F min.; 99 in C; 101 in F; 110 in D flat; 114 in D min.; 115 in D min.; 120 in D min.; Prelude No. 4 in F min.
☞ ** Astree Dig. E 8777 [id.]. Bob van Asperen (harpsichord).

Sonatas Nos. 8 in C; 35 in G; 38 in C; 70; 71 in A min.; 77 in F sharp min.; 78 in F sharp min.; 79 in F sharp min.; 82 in G; 83 in F; 113 in E min.; 116 in G; Prelude No. 8 in F.
☞ ** Astrée Dig. E 8776 [id.]. Bob van Asperen (harpsichord).

Sonatas Nos. 15 in D min.; 22 in D flat; 23 in D flat; 54 in D min.; 61 in C; 75 in F; 76 in F; 80 in G min.; 81 in G min.; 84 in D; 86 in D.
☞ *(*) Astrée Dig. E 8772 [id.]. Bob van Asperen (harpsichord).

Sonatas Nos. 16 in E flat; 17 in E flat; 32 in G min.; 33 in G; 39 in D min.; 41 in F; 53 in A; 57 in G min.; 60a in C min.; 60b in C min.; 89 in F; Prelude No. 7 in C min.
☞ ** Astrée Dig. E 8775 [id.]. Bob van Asperen (harpsichord).

Sonatas Nos. 18 in C min.; 19 in C min.; 26 in E min.; 27 in E min.; 36 in C min.; 85 in F sharp min.; 90 in F sharp min.; 91 in D; 94 in G.
☞ ** Astrée Dig. E 8773 [id.]. Bob van Asperen (harpsichord).

Sonatas Nos. 35 in G; 38 in C; 70 in A min.; 71 in A min.; 77 in F sharp min.; 78 in F sharp min.; 79a & 79b in F sharp min.; 82 in G; 83 in F; 113 in E min.; 116 in G; Prelude No. 8 in F.
☞ ** Astrée Dig. E 8776 [id.]. Bob van Asperen (harpsichord).

Sonatas Nos. 42 in G min.; 43 in G; 47 in C min; 48 in C min.; 50 in C; 58 in G; 59 in F; 62 in E flat; 87 in G min.; 102 in D min.; 104 in D min.; 107 in F; 149 in F; Prelude No. 2 in G min.
☞ ** Astrée Dig. E 8778 [id.]. Bob van Asperen (harpsichord).

Sonatas Nos. 45 in C (por la Princesa de Asturias); 51 in C; 88 in D sharp; 93 in F; 97 in A; 119 in B flat; 132 in B flat; 154 in D sharp.
☞ ** Astrée Dig. E 8774 [id.]. Bob van Asperen (harpsichord).

There is some remarkable music in the second batch of the Astrée Soler series and it is marvellously played by Bob van Asperen. Throughout, he uses either a copy of a 1764 Taskin (made by Michael Johnson two centuries later) or a copy of a 1745 Dülcken, made by Rainer Schülze in Heidelberg in 1969. The recording remains very resonant, but if one plays back at a low level the effect can be acceptable, provided one does not try to take on too many sonatas in a single sitting. The music is so consistently inventive that it seems sensible to single out especially striking works. Volume 5 (E 8772) is, however, rather disappointing and Bob van Asperen seems to make heavy weather of some of these sonatas. The four-movement piece (No. 61 in C) is most notable for its elegant Minuet. Volume 6 (E 8773) is much more attractive; it opens with two very spontaneous works in F sharp minor (Nos. 85 and 90) and the two four-movement sonatas (Nos. 91 and 94) show Soler at his most striking, each opening with an *Andantino*, with a fast movement to follow, then an imposing *Maestoso* Minuet before the finale. All three *C minor Sonatas* on this CD are worth singling out. Volume 7 (E 8774) brings a *Sonata in C major* (No. 45) dedicated to the Princesa de Asturias, and for her Soler writes a very gracious single-movement work. The four-part *Sonata No. 97 in A* also has an elegant opening *Allegretto*, a strongly rhythmic Minuet for its second movement, then a winning lollipop *Rondo* marked *Andantino con moto* (which is played with great character) before its florid, flowing finale. But the most brilliant movement here is the finale of No. *93 in F*, a display piece which glitters with bravura in Van Asperen's hands.

Volume 8 (E 8775) is full of good things: the opening *Sonate des clarins in A major* (No. 53) is particularly characterful, and the following *D Minor* (No. 39) is distinctly catchy. At the close of this recital the thoughtful *Prelude No. 7 in C minor* is followed by an engaging *Cantabile* and *Allegro* of the two-part Sonata No. 60 (a and b). Volume 9 (E 8776) offers a remarkable linking of four sonatas in *F sharp minor* (Nos. 77, 78 and 79a and b). The first is a long, melancholy *Andante largo* which Bob van Asperen sustains impressively; the other three movements use the same basic theme, transforming it with remarkable facility. The *Andante/Cantabile* of No. 113 is an eloquently grave soliloquy, and the *F major Sonata* (No. 83) is another jolly, extrovert piece well sprinkled with trills.

The *Sonata in G minor* (No. 4) with its regal fanfares, which opens Volume 10 (E 8777), is very commanding, and the ambitious C major four-movement Sonata which follows (No. 99) offers a charming *Allegretto* (*Rondó pastoril*), matched by the gavotte-like *Sonata in D minor* (No. 49) and the freely flowing *Sonata in F* (No. 101) with its imitation of a drone bass. Volume 11 (E 8778) includes *Sonata No. 62*, another large-scale work, again bringing four movements of strikingly diverse character and including a memorable *Allegretto espressivo*. There are winning individual sonatas here too, notably *No. 59 in F* with its skipping *Rondón*.

Volume 12 (E 8779) includes a three-part *Sonata in A minor* (No. 65), with the *Allegro* the centrepiece between two outer slow movements, and the finale marked *Intent con movimiento contrario* somewhat improvisational in feeling. There are also the linked *Sonatas Nos. 126 a* and *b*, using the same material, at first introduced contrapuntally in the manner of a two-part invention, and then much more integrated. Some of these works have no indication of tempo, but Bob van Asperen's judgement in this matter seems impeccable. In spite of the recording balance, overall this is a remarkable achievement.

Keyboard sonatas, S.R. 15, 21, 42, 84–7, 89.
(M) *** Decca 433 920-2 (2) [id.]. Alicia de Larrocha – ALBENIZ: *Sonata* ***; GRANADOS: *Goyescas* etc. *** ⊛

Vital performances of eight sonatas by Soler, who, although not the equal of Domenico Scarlatti, is still a rewarding enough composer to warrant attention. Like Scarlatti's music, with an advocate of this calibre, these works are quite as pleasing heard on the piano rather than the harpsichord. Excellent, truthful 1981 recording.

Keyboard sonatas Nos. 18 in C min.; 19 in C min.; 41 in E flat; 72 in F min.; 78 in F sharp min.; 84 in D; 85 in F sharp min.; 86 in D; 87 in G min.; 88 in D flat; 90 in F sharp; Fandango.
*** Virgin/EMI Dig. VC7 59624-2 [id.]. Maggie Cole (harpsichord or fortepiano).

Maggie Cole plays a dozen Soler pieces, eleven *Sonatas* and the celebrated *Fandango*, half of them on the harpsichord and the remainder on the fortepiano; she gives altogether dashing performances on both. Good pieces to sample are *No. 87 in G minor* (track 5) and, on the harpsichord, *No. 86 in D major* (track 9) or the *Fandango* itself. The playing is all very exhilarating and inspiriting. Played at a normal level-setting, both instruments sound a bit thunderous but, played at a lower level, the results are very satisfactory.

Sondheim, Stephen (born 1930)

'Sondheim Songbook': excerpts from: *Anyone can whistle; Company; A Little Night Music.* BERNSTEIN: *West Side Story.* STYNE: *Gypsy.* Richard RODGERS: *Do I hear a waltz?*; Mary RODGERS: *The boy from . . .*
☞ (M) *** Sony SK 48201 [id.]. Lee Remick, Angela Lansbury, Harry Guardino, Elaine Stritch, Glynis Johns, Len Cariou, Hermione Gingold, Larry Kert, Ethel Merman, Linda Lavin and others.

Stephen Sondheim was just as importantly a lyricist as a song-writer. Leonard Bernstein, with whom he worked on *West Side Story*, said: 'His contribution was just enormous. What made him so valuable was that he was also a composer and so I could explain musical problems to him and he'd understand immediately.' Here is a selection of some of Sondheim's best songs, not only from his own shows, but also from those with music by others. The programme opens with two from *West Side Story* and carries on through to his own early musicals, notably four superb numbers from *Company*, dominated by the gravelly-voiced Elaine Stritch, and five from *A Little Night Music. You must meet my wife* shows him at his wittiest and the swinging *Weekend in the country* demonstrates equally his ready facility for ensemble writing. Hermione Gingold is unforgettable in *Liaisons*, and the disc ends with the haunting *Send in the clowns*, sung with memorable nostalgia by Glynis Johns. Before that there are many individual highlights from other shows, notably the two Richard Rodgers numbers from *Do I hear a waltz?*, the delightful ballad *Moon in my window* and the catchy *We're gonna be alright*. Sondheim's musicals are covered in much greater detail in our companion *Penguin Guide to Opera on CD*.

Sor, Fernando (1778–1839)

Fantasia, Op. 30; Fantasia, Op. 7; Variations on a theme of Mozart, Op. 9.
☞ (M) **(*) BMG/RCA Dig. 09026 61607-2. Julian Bream (guitar) – AGUADO: Collection. **(*)

Both Sor *Fantasias* are ambitious and each has a central set of variations. Bream's approach is spacious and his deliberation – for all the variety and skill of the colouring – means that the listener is conscious of the music's length, although it is all agreeable enough. The more concise Mozartian *Variations* remain Sor's most famous piece, and the variety and flair of the playing demonstrate why. The studio recording, made in New York, is eminently truthful.

'Classic guitar': Grand solo (Introduction and allegro), Op. 14. Sonata in C, Op. 25.
☞ (M) **(*) BMG/RCA 09026 61593-2. Julian Bream (guitar) – GIULIANI: *Grand overture, Op. 61* etc.; DIABELLI: *Sonata in A.* **(*)

Sor's *Grand solo* is quite an attractive piece, with an *Andante largo* introduction instead of a slow movement, and it includes the theme and variations seemingly obligatory to this composer. The *Sonata in C*, however, is extremely inconsequential and easily forgettable. But all the music is beautifully played and immaculately recorded.

Sousa, John Philip (1854–1932)

Marches: *The Ancient and Honorable Artillery Company; The Black Horse Troop; Bullets and bayonets; The Gallant Seventh; Golden jubilee; The Glory of the Yankee Navy; The Gridiron Club; High school cadets; The Invincible eagle; The Kansas Wildcats; The Liberty Bell; Manhattan Beach; The National game; New Mexico; Nobles of the mystic shrine; Our flirtation; The Piccadore; The Pride of the Wolverines; Riders for the flag; The Rifle Regiment; Sabre and spurs; Sesqui-centennial exposition; Solid men to the front; Sound off.*

(M) *** Mercury 434 300-2 [id.]. Eastman Wind Ens., Frederick Fennell.

Fennell's collection of 24 Sousa marches (73 minutes) derives from vintage Mercury recordings of the early 1960s. The performances have characteristic American pep and natural exuberance; the zest of the playing always carries the day. One of the more striking items is *The Ancient and Honorable Artillery Company*, which incorporates *Auld lang syne* as its middle section. The sound, is, of course, first class.

Spohr, Ludwig (1784–1859)

Clarinet concertos Nos. 1 in C min., Op. 26; 4 in E min.

**(*) Orfeo C 088101A [id.]. Leister, Stuttgart RSO, Frühbeck de Burgos.

Clarinet concertos Nos. 2 in E flat, Op. 57; 3 in F min.

**(*) Orfeo C 088201A [id.]. Leister, Stuttgart RSO, Frühbeck de Burgos.

The four *Clarinet concertos* of Spohr – the *Fourth* much grander than the other three – make up an attractive pair of discs, particularly when they are as beautifully played as by the long-time principal of the Berlin Philharmonic, Karl Leister. His smooth tone, the ease and agility with which he tackles virtuoso passage-work and his ability to bring out the smiling quality of much of the inspiration make for delightful performances. The radio recording has relatively little stereo spread, but is undistractingly natural.

Clarinet concerto No. 1 in C min., Op. 26.

☞ (M) *** Decca 433 727-2 [id.]. Gervase de Peyer, LSO, C. Davis – MOZART; WEBER: *Concertos.* ***

Clearly modelled on Mozart's masterpiece, Spohr's *Concerto* primarily exploits the lyrical side of the clarinet. The main theme of the first movement is perfectly conceived for the instrument, and the *Adagio* – very much Mozart-patterned – is charming too. The finale is a captivating Spanish rondo. It chuckles along in sparkling fashion and then surprises the listener by ending gently. Gervase de Peyer is just the man for these suave melodic lines and he receives excellent support from Davis. The recording – made by Oiseau-Lyre at Decca's West Hampstead studios – is faithful and sounds hardly dated.

(i) *Violin concerto No. 8 in A min. (In modo d'una scena cantate), Op. 47;* (ii) *Double quartet in D min., Op. 65.*

(M) (***) BMG/RCA mono GD 87870 [7870-2-RG]. Heifetz, with (i) RCA Victor O, Izler Solomon; (ii) Baker, Thomas, Piatigorsky, Amoyal, Rosenthal, Harshman, Lesser (with BEETHOVEN: *Serenade* **).

Spohr's *Gesangszenekonsert* is in mono and dates from 1954. A dazzling performance which, in sheer beauty and refinement of tone, remains unsurpassed. The first violin dominates the texture in the dryish (1968) stereo recording of the *D minor Double quartet*, Op. 65, a reminder both of Spohr's prowess as a violinist and – certainly – of Heifetz's. His distinctive timbre and glorious tone shine through.

Symphonies Nos. 1 in E flat, Op. 20; 5 in C min., Op. 102.

☞ **(*) Marco Polo Dig. 8.223363 [id.]. Slovak State PO (Košice), Alfred Walter.

Spohr wrote ten symphonies in all: the *First* when he was in his mid-twenties and still in thrall to Mozart; the *Fifth* comes from the late 1830s and was much admired by Schumann. The latter is certainly a better piece, but there is always a certain blandness about Spohr's invention even when he is at his best. His melodic inspiration is not quite strong enough even in the slow movement, by far the finest and most thoughtful. Although he is no great symphonist, Spohr is an eminently civilized composer, and the case for him is well put by Alfred Walther and the Košice orchestra, who are decently served by the engineers.

Symphonies Nos. 3 in C min., Op. 78; 6 in G, Op. 116.
☞ ** Marco Polo Dig. 8.223439 [id.]. Slovak State PO (Košice), Alfred Walter.

Spohr was held in such high esteem in his lifetime that his total absence from concert programmes (apart from occasional performances of the *Gesangszene* concerto) inevitably invites curiosity. His symphonies are now represented in the catalogue, and libraries should acquire them. This is the kind of repertoire to be investigated by all with exploratory tastes for, while its mastery is not in dispute, the personality that emerges is not quite strong enough to hold its own alongside Mendelssohn, Weber and Schumann. The *Third Symphony* makes as good an entry-point as any into the Ten, and is arguably the best of them. Mendelssohn was one of its early champions, but if the symphony suggests his neo-classical romanticism, its invention falls short of either Mendelssohn or Schumann in freshness and character. All the same, the *Third* is well crafted and thoroughly enjoyable, and is far more rewarding than its companion, the *Historical Symphony*, which parodies the styles of various masters to make an unconvincing whole. Alfred Walter draws very good playing from his Slovak forces, who do their best to persuade us as to this music's merits.

Nonet in F, Op. 31; Octet in E, Op. 32.
☞ *** Hyp. Dig. CDA 66699 [id.]. Gaudier Ens.
*** CRD CRD 3354; *CRDC 4054* [id.]. Nash Ens.

Spohr's *Octet* is a work of great charm; the variations on Handel's *Harmonious blacksmith* which form the third movement offer that kind of naïveté which, when played stylishly, makes for delicious listening. Here the Gaudier Ensemble (who have already given us an outstanding account of Beethoven's *Septet*) open the variations slowly and gently with the theme immediately echoed on the strings. The range of dynamic used here and, even more strikingly, after the florid horn variation is typical of a performance as imaginative as it is spontaneous, and the work's finale with its lolloping main theme is joyously spirited. The *Nonet* is also very attractive. Spohr's invention is again at its freshest and his propensity for chromaticism is held reasonably in check. Here there is another vivacious finale, but perhaps one remembers most the *Adagio*, where the expressive mood of the Gaudier performance has a gentle gravitas. The Hyperion recording is fresh and warm, clearly detailed against a resonant acoustic, although this means that the first violin is given a fractional hint of wiriness by the fairly close microphones.

The sound on the competing CRD disc is that bit more mellifluous, yet it remains natural and lifelike; some may prefer the greater suavity of the analogue tonal blend in this urbane music. The Nash Ensemble play both works with much elegance and style, and these performances are very civilized and hardly less spontaneous. They are well worth considering alongside their Hyperion competitors.

Piano and wind quintet in C min., Op. 52; Septet in A min. for flute, clarinet, horn, bassoon, violin, cello and piano, Op. 147.
*** CRD CRD 3399; *CRDC 4099* [id.]. Ian Brown, Nash Ens.

These two pieces are among Spohr's most delightful, both the sparkling *Quintet* and the more substantial but still charmingly lighthearted *Septet*. Ian Brown at the piano leads the ensemble with flair and vigour, and the recording quality is outstandingly vivid.

String quartets Nos. 3 in D min., Op. 11; 4 in E flat, Op. 15/1; 6 in G min., Op. 27.
** Marco Polo Dig. 8.223254 [id.]. New Budapest Qt.

These three quartets, dating from 1804, 1808 and 1812 respectively, do not show any marked development, rather a difference in adopted styles. The *D minor* is a 'Quatuor brillant' with the focus permanently on the first violin, and the other three players taking very subsidiary roles. The *E flat Quartet*, although still requiring a great deal of virtuosity from the leader, especially in the first movement, is written very much in the spirit of Haydn. *Quartet No. 6 in G minor* is the most ambitious work here and its long first movement (12 minutes 37 seconds) has a very characteristic main theme. It needs rather more grip than these players achieve, and greater polish too. Good recording.

String quartets Nos. 7 in E flat; 8 in C, Op. 29/1–2.
**(*) Marco Polo Dig. 8.22355 [id.]. New Budapest Qt.

The Op. 29 *Quartets* are associated with Johann Tost (dedicatee of Haydn's Opp. 54/5 and 65). Both are written in his friendly, accomplished style; the first ingeniously bases its opening movement on a two-note motto theme and has an outstanding set of variations for its slow movement, surely worthy of Haydn. The tender *Adagio* of the *C major* is even finer, daring in its expressive chromaticism. Both performances are spontaneous and the players seem inside the music. If the very last ounce of finesse is missing, this is still vibrant, felt quartet-playing, without artifice, and the recording is lively and present.

String quartets Nos. 27 in D min.; 28 in A flat, Op. 84/1–2.
**(*) Marco Polo Dig. 8.223251 [id.]. New Budapest Qt.

These two works, written in 1831–2, exemplify Spohr's smooth, finely integrated quartet-writing at its most characteristic. The slow movement, sustaining a mood of serene simplicity, is the most memorable in each case, although the lyrical finale of the *A flat major Quartet* is also rather appealing. Good performances, lively enough, but capturing the suaveness of the idiom. The recording is truthful.

String quartets Nos. 29 in B min., Op. 84/3; 30 (Quatuor brillant) in A, Op. 93.
**(*) Marco Polo Dig. 8.223252 [id.]. New Budapest Qt.

In many ways *No. 29 in B minor* is the finest of the Op. 84 set, with its touch of melancholy in the first movement, a lively minuet and a pensive slow movement. Op. 93, written in 1835, is more extrovert in atmosphere in the first movement (after a sombre introduction), but it offers another thoughtfully intense slow movement and a very jolly finale. It brings out the best in these players – and there is plenty of bravura for the first violin – and, again, good tonal matching plus a smooth, warm recording combine effectively for this slightly suave music.

VOCAL MUSIC

Lieder: *An Mignon; 6 German Lieder, Op. 103; 6 Lieder, Op. 154; Lied beim Runetanz; Schlaflied; Scottische Lied; Vanitas!; Zigeuner Lied.*
*** Orfeo Dig. C 103841A [id.]. Julia Varady, Dietrich Fischer-Dieskau, Sitkovetsky, Schoneberger, Hartmut Holl.

The amiable inspiration of Spohr in his songs is delightfully presented in this collection from Dietrich Fischer-Dieskau and Julia Varady. It is characteristic of the composer that, even in his setting of *Erlkönig*, he jogs along rather than gallops, and fails to use the violin dramatically, just giving it an ordinary obbligato. The most attractive songs are the set sung by Varady with clarinet obbligato, but those sung by Fischer-Dieskau are also all highly enjoyable, as long as you do not compare them with the finest of the genre. Excellent recording.

Spontini, Gasparo (1774–1851)

Olympie (opera): complete.
**(*) Orfeo Dig. C 137862H (3) [id.]. Varady, Toczyska, Tagliavini, Fischer-Dieskau, Fortune, Berlin RIAS Chamber Ch., German Op. Male Ch., Berlin RSO, Albrecht.

In Spontini's *Olympie*, based on an historical play by Voltaire about the daughter of Alexander the Great, the writing is lively and committed and, despite flawed singing, so is this performance. Julia Varady is outstanding in the name-part, giving an almost ideal account of the role of heroine, but Stefania Toczyska is disappointingly unsteady as Statire and Franco Tagliavini is totally out of style as Cassandre. Even Dietrich Fischer-Dieskau is less consistent than usual, but his melodramatic presentation is nevertheless most effective. The text is slightly cut.

Stainer, John (1840–1901)

The Crucifixion.
(B) *** CD-CFP 4519; *TC-CFP 4519*. David Hughes, John Lawrenson, Guildford Cathedral Ch., Barry Rose; Gavin Williams.
☞ (BB) ** ASV CDQS 6100. James Griffet, Michael George, Peterborough Cathedral Ch., Stanley Vann; Andrew Newberry.

(i) *The Crucifixion. Come thou long-expected Jesus* (hymn); *I saw the Lord* (anthem).
(B) *** Decca 436 146-2 [id.]. (i) Richard Lewis, Owen Brannigan, St John's College, Cambridge, Ch., Guest.

All five hymns in which the congregation is invited to join are included on the Decca (originally Argo) record. Owen Brannigan is splendidly dramatic and his voice makes a good foil for Richard

Lewis in the duets. The choral singing is first class and the 1961 recording is of Argo's best vintage, even finer than its CfP competitor. Moreover the Decca disc includes two bonuses: a hymn set to the words of Charles Wesley and a fine eight-part anthem, *I saw the Lord*, both of which are equally well sung.

The Classics for Pleasure version (from the late 1960s) is of high quality and, although one of the congregational hymns is omitted, in every other respect this can be recommended. John Lawrenson makes a movingly eloquent solo contribution and the choral singing is excellent. The remastered recording sounds first class, but the Decca version is finer still.

A super-bargain version is welcome, and the ASV performance (originally issued on the defunct Enigma label) is sincere and eloquent in a modestly restrained way. In his efforts not to overdramatize the narrative, Stanley Vann falls into the opposite trap of understatement, and at times there is a lack of vitality. The two soloists make a stronger contribution, and the tenor, James Griffet, is pleasingly lyrical. However, the style of presentation does not wholly avoid hints of the sentimentality that hovers dangerously near all performances of this work. The recording is atmospheric and the choral sounds warm rather than incisive, but the soloists are naturally projected and Andrew Newberry's fine organ accompaniment is well balanced.

Stalder, Joseph Franz Xaver (1725–65)

(i) *Flute concerto in B flat; Symphony No. 5 in G.*
*** Novalis Dig. 150 031-2 [id.]. (i) William Bennett; ECO, Griffiths – REINDL: *Sinfonia concertante in D.* ***

Though Joseph Stalder is not quite as interesting a composer as his younger compatriot, Reindl, both the short *G major Symphony* and the *Flute concerto* have freshness and charm and well repay investigation, particularly in such excellent performances and recording.

Stamitz, Johann (1717–57)

Trumpet concerto in D (arr. Boustead).
*** Ph. Dig. 420 203-2; *420 203-4* [id.]. Hardenberger, ASMF, Marriner – HAYDN; HUMMEL: *Concertos* *** ⊛; HERTEL: *Concerto.* ***

This recently discovered concerto was written either by Stamitz or by a composer called J. G. Holzbogen. The writing lies consistently up in the instrument's stratosphere and includes some awkward leaps. It is quite inventive, however, notably the finale, which is exhilarating on the lips of Håkan Hardenberger. There is no lack of panache here and Marriner accompanies expertly. Good if reverberant recording, with the trumpet given great presence.

Stanford, Charles (1852–1924)

Clarinet concerto in A min., Op. 80.
*** Hyp. CDA 66001 [id.]. King, Philh. O, Francis – FINZI: *Concerto.* ***

(i) *Clarinet concerto in A min.* (for clarinet and strings) *Op. 80;* (ii) *3 Intermezzi* (for clarinet and piano).
*** ASV Dig. CDDCA 787; *ZCDCA 787* [id.]. Emma Johnson; (i) RPO, Groves; (ii) Martineau – FINZI: *Clarinet concerto etc.* ***

The Stanford *Clarinet concerto*, less ambitious in scale than the Finzi with which it is coupled, finds Emma Johnson similarly inspired, again even freer and more fluent than Thea King on the rival Hyperion disc. It is a delight how Johnson can edge into a theme with extreme gentleness. So her first entry in the slow movement, taxingly high, seems to emerge ethereally from nowhere, while Thea King's firmer, sharper attack is less poetic. In the finale too King is strong and forthright, but Johnson is warmer and more personal with her cheekily witty treatment of the first solo. As in the Finzi, Sir Charles Groves and the RPO are warmly sympathetic accompanists, very well recorded, though the solo instrument is rather too close. It is an obvious advantage too that ASV provide substantial fill-ups in shorter pieces by the same composers.

(i) *Piano concerto No. 2 in C min., Op. 126;* (ii) *Becket, Op. 48: The Martyrdom (Funeral march);* (iii) *The Fisherman of Lough Neagh and what he saw (Irish rhapsody No. 4), Op. 141.*
*** Lyrita SRCD 219 [id.]. (i) Malcolm Binns, LSO; (ii–iii) LPO; (i; iii) Nicholas Braithwaite; (ii) Sir Adrian Boult.

Stanford's *Second Piano concerto,* although in three rather than four movements, is a work on the largest scale, recalling the Brahms *B flat Concerto.* Yet Stanford asserts his own melodic individuality and provides a really memorable secondary theme for the first movement. The piece is enjoyable and uninflated, especially when played with such spontaneous freshness. The recording is surely a demonstration of just how a piano concerto should be balanced: it is well nigh perfect, and the ambience is just right. The *Funeral march* comes from incidental music commissioned at the request of Tennyson for Irving's production of his tragedy, *Becket.* It has an arresting opening but otherwise is a fairly straightforward piece, strongly melodic in a Stanfordian manner. Like the more familiar *Irish rhapsody,* it is splendidly played and recorded.

Symphonies Nos. 1–7.
☞ *** Chan. Dig. CHAN 9279/82 (4) [id.]. Ulster O, Handley.

Now available in a box of four CDs, with the fill-ups which accompanied the original CDs now put aside for separate reissue, this is obviously the most attractive way to approach this generally impressive if uneven British symphonic canon. Handley and his Ulster Orchestra are completely at home in this repertoire, and the Chandos recording is consistently of this company's best quality.

Symphonies Nos. 1 in B flat., Op. 78; Irish rhapsody No. 2: The Lament for the Son, Ossian, Op. 84.
☞ *** Chan. Dig. CHAN 9049; ABTD 1590 [id.]. Ulster O, Handley.

Stanford's mature musical studies had been in Berlin and Hamburg (between 1875 and 1876) and he came back to England profoundly influenced by the German symphonic style (the Scherzo of the *First Symphony* (1876) even has the character of a Laendler). His work was duly performed and then, like the *Second,* put in a cupboard. Now we can discover for ourselves that, although he could assemble a convincing structure, his melodic invention was not yet strong enough to achieve real memorability. Handley and the Ulster Orchestra do their persuasive best for a piece which is certainly not a silk purse. The *Irish rhapsody* has distinctly more melodramatic flair. Excellent recording.

Symphony No. 2 in D min. (Elegiac); (i) *Clarinet concerto in A min., Op. 80.*
☞ *** Chan. Dig. CHAN 8991; ABTD 1573 [id.]. Ulster O, Handley; (i) with Janet Hilton.

The penultimate issue in Handley's fine series, the *Second Symphony* has until now lain neglected for over a century. The influences of German masters are strong but the work still has its own individuality, for the most part in the scoring. The delightful *Clarinet concerto* makes a splendid coupling, with Janet Hilton at her most seductive, both in timbre and in warmth, and articulating with nimble expertise. A delightful performance.

Symphony No. 3 in F min. (Irish), Op. 28.
☞ (M) *** EMI CDM5 65129-2 [id.]. Bournemouth Sinf., Norman Del Mar – ELGAR: *Scenes from the Bavarian highlands.* ***

Symphony No. 3 in F min. (Irish), Op. 28; Irish rhapsody No. 5, Op. 147.
*** Chan. Dig. CHAN 8545; ABTD 1253 [id.]. Ulster O, Handley.

This *Third* and most celebrated of the seven symphonies of Stanford is a rich and attractive work, none the worse for its obvious debts to Brahms. The ideas are best when directly echoing Irish folk music, as in the middle two movements, a skippity jig of a Scherzo and a glowing slow movement framed by harp cadenzas. The *Irish rhapsody No. 5* dates from 1917, reflecting perhaps in its martial vigour that wartime date. Even more characteristic are the warmly lyrical passages, performed passionately by Handley and his Ulster Orchestra, matching the thrust and commitment they bring also to the *Symphony.*

Norman Del Mar directs an equally ripe performance, noting that the finale gives an attractive forward glance to Stanford's pupils, Holst and Vaughan Williams. The EMI recording is warm and well defined.

Symphony No. 4 in F, Op. 31; Irish rhapsody No. 6 for violin and orchestra, Op. 191; Oedipus Rex Prelude, Op. 29.
☞ *** Chan. Dig. CHAN 8884; ABTD 1495 [id.]. Ulster O, Vernon, (i) with Lydia Mordkovitch.

The *Fourth Symphony,* like the *Third,* is a highly confident piece, commissioned and given its première in Berlin in 1889. Not for nothing had its composer thoroughly absorbed the manners of the late-nineteenth-century German symphonic style. It is an effective symphony, even if it runs out of steam before the close of the finale despite attractive invention. The *Irish* concertante *rhapsody* is a much later work (1922), its nostagia nicely caught by the soloist here, Lydia Mordkovitch, who is obviously involved. Handley, as ever, takes the helm throughout with ardent commitment and makes the most of the many nice touches of orchestral colour. Excellent recording.

Symphony No. 5 in D (L'Allegro ed il Penseroso), Op. 56; Irish rhapsody No. 4 in A min. (The Fisherman of Lough Neagh and what he saw), Op. 141.
*** Chan. Dig. CHAN 8581; *ABTD 1277* [id.]. Ulster O, Handley.

Stanford's *Fifth Symphony* is colourfully orchestrated and full of easy tunes, illustrating passages from Milton's *L'Allegro* and *Il Penseroso*. The essentially jolly first movement leads to a charming, gentle pastoral movement in an easy Laendler rhythm. The last two movements more readily live up to Stanford's reputation as a Brahmsian, representing the *Penseroso* half of the work, and the slow epilogue brings reminders of Brahms's *Third*. The *Irish rhapsody* is more distinctive of the composer, bringing together sharply contrasted, colourful and atmospheric Irish ideas under the title *The Fisherman of Lough Neagh and what he saw*. Excellent recording of the finest Chandos quality.

Symphony No. 6 in E flat (In memoriam G. F. Watts), Op. 94; Irish rhapsody No. 1 in D min., Op. 78.
*** Chan. Dig. CHAN 8627; *ABTD 1316* [id.]. Ulster O, Vernon Handley.

Stanford's *Sixth Symphony* is not the strongest of the set, but it has a rather lovely slow movement, with a pervading air of gentle melancholy. The first movement has some good ideas but the finale is too long, in the way finales of Glazunov symphonies tend to overuse their material. Nevertheless Vernon Handley makes quite a persuasive case for the work and an even better one for the enjoyable *Irish rhapsody No. 1*, which features and makes rather effective use of one of the loveliest of all Irish tunes, the *Londonderry air*. Excellent sound.

Symphony No. 7 in D min., Op. 124; (i) Concert pieces for organ and orchestra, Op. 181; (ii) Irish rhapsody No. 3 for cello and orchestra, Op. 137.
☞ *** Chan. Dig. CHAN 8861; *ABTD 1476* [id.]. Ulster O, Handley; with (i) Gillian Weir; (ii) Raphael Wallfisch.

The *Seventh Symphony* was commissioned for a centenary celebration in 1912 by the Philharmonic Society in London. It sums up its composer as a symphonist – structurally sound, yet not now so heavily indebted to Germany, and with the orchestration often ear-catching. It is not a masterpiece, but it could surely not be presented with more conviction than here by Handley and his excellent orchestra. The *Irish rhapsody* is very Irish indeed and makes the use of several good tunes. It is most sensitively played by Wallfisch, and Gillian Weir makes a strong impression in the *Organ 'concertino'*, where the composer uses only brass, strings and percussion in the accompaniment. The music has a touch of the epic about it.

Serenade (Nonet) in F, Op. 95.
*** Hyp. CDA 66291 [id.]. Capricorn – PARRY: *Nonet.* ***

Like the Parry *Nonet*, with which it is coupled, the *Serenade* is an inventive and delightful piece, its discourse civilized and the scherzo full of charm. Capricorn play this piece with evident pleasure and convey this to the listener. The recording is very natural and truthfully balanced.

Magnificat in B flat, Op. 164; 3 Motets, Op. 38; Motet: Eternal Father, Op. 135.
*** Conifer Dig. CDCF 155 [id.]. Trinity College, Cambridge, Ch., Marlow – PARRY: *Songs of farewell.* ***

The *Three Motets*, early works, are settings of Latin hymns; *Eternal Father* is an elaborate setting of Robert Bridges; while the big-scale unaccompanied *Magnificat* for double choir makes a magnificent culmination. Immaculate performances and beautifully balanced, atmospheric recording.

Stanley, John (1712–86)

6 Organ concertos, Op. 10.
*** CRD CRD 3365; *CRDC 4065* [id.]. Gifford, N. Sinfonia.

These bouncing, vigorous performances, well recorded as they are on the splendid organ of Hexham Abbey, present these *Concertos* most persuasively. No. 4, with its darkly energetic C minor, is particularly fine. The recording is natural in timbre and very well balanced.

Steffani, Agostino (1654–1728)

*Duetti da camera: E perché non m'uccidete; Già tu parti; Io voglio provar; Libertà! Libertà!; M'hai
da piangere un dì; No, no, no, non voglio se devo amare; Placidissime catene; Tu m'aspettasi al mare.*
☞ (M) *** DG Dig. 437 083-2. Mazzucato, Watkinson, Esswood, Elwes; Curtis.

Steffani was one of the leading Italian composers of the latter half of the seventeenth century and
served various courts as both composer and diplomat; his output includes several operas and a
quantity of sacred music (he was made a nominal bishop in 1708 but continued with his diplomatic
career). He composed over 80 duets, most of which are relatively late. Five can be shown as having
been composed in Brussels (1698–1700), where he was Hanoverian Ambassador. The eight duets
recorded here are delightfully inventive and fresh and make a strong impression, thanks to the charm
and expertise of these performances which are very persuasive indeed. They are well recorded too,
and will repay with much pleasure the curiosity of readers who investigate them.

Steiner, Max (1888–1971)

Film scores: *The Adventures of Don Juan; Dodge City; They Died With Their Boots On* (suites).
(M) *** BMG/RCA GD 80912; *GK 80912* [0912-2-RG; *0912-4-RG*]. Nat. SO, Charles Gerhardt
   (with WAXMAN: *Objective Burma!: Parachute Drop.* FRIEDHOFER: *The Sun Also Rises: Prologue;
   The Lights of Paris* ***) – KORNGOLD: Film scores. ***

Max Steiner's style is unashamedly eclectic, but his writing never sounds thin in ideas. The first disc,
which Steiner shares with Korngold and others, concentrates on swashbuckling Errol Flynn movies.
Sumptuous and exuberant orchestration and attractive lyrical themes bring the use of orchestral
colour in the most spectacular Hollywood tradition. The brief Waxman item is as dramatic as its title
suggests, and Friedhofer's bitter-sweet waltz theme for *The Sun Also Rises* makes a gentle interlude
after the strongly motivated action-sequences of the other contributors.

Film scores: *All This and Heaven too; Beyond the Forest; Dark Victory; In This Our Life; Jezebel;
The Letter; Now Voyager; A Stolen Life.*
(M) **(*) BMG/RCA GD 80183; *GK 80183* [0183-2-RG; *0183-4-RG*]. Nat. PO, Charles Gerhardt
   (with KORNGOLD: *The Private Lives of Elizabeth and Essex: Elizabeth. Juarez: Carlotta.* WAXMAN:
   Mr Skeffington: Forsaken. NEWMAN: *All About Eve: Main title.* ***)

This collection concentrates on the highly charged Bette Davis dramas for which Steiner appropriately
wrote emotionally drenched string themes, and the prevailing mood is mostly melodramatic. The two
vignettes from Korngold have more subtlety (his portrait of Queen Elizabeth I is most winning),
while Alfred Newman's introduction to *All About Eve* has characteristic vitality. Many of the excerpts
here are brief, and the overall selection at around 40 minutes could have been more generous.

Film scores: *The Big Sleep* (suite); *The Charge of the Light Brigade: The charge; The Fountainhead*
(suite). (i) *Four Wives: Symphonie moderne.* (ii) *The Informer* (excerpts). *Johnny Belinda* (suite); *King
Kong* (excerpts); *Now Voyager* (excerpts); *Saratoga Trunk: As long as I live. Since you went away:*
Title sequence.
(M) *** BMG/RCA GD 80136; *GK 80136* [0136-2-RG; *0136-4-RG*]. National PO, Charles
   Gerhardt, with (i) Earl Wild; (ii) Amb. S.

Steiner could always produce a good tune on demand, with the luscious themes for *Now Voyager* and
As long as I live from *Saratoga Trunk* almost approaching the famous *Gone with the Wind* melody in
memorability; and a dulcet touch was available for the wistful portrayal of the deaf-mute heroine in
Johnny Belinda. For *The Informer* the Ambrosian Singers provide a characteristic outpouring of
Hollywood religiosity at the final climax. Charles Gerhardt is a master of the grand orchestral gesture
and presents all this music with enormous conviction and with care for atmospheric detail.

Gone with the Wind (film score).
(M) *** BMG/RCA GD 80452; *GK 80452* [0452-2-RG; *0452-4-RG*]. National PO, Charles
   Gerhardt.

It was sensible of Steiner to associate his most potent musical idea in *Gone with the Wind* with Tara,
the home of the heroine. It says something for the quality of Steiner's tune that its ability to haunt the
memory is not diminished by its many reappearances. The rest of the music is professionally tailored
to the narrative and makes agreeable listening. As ever, Charles Gerhardt is a splendid advocate. The
recording, too, is both full and brilliant.

Stenhammar, Wilhelm (1871–1927)

(i) *Piano concerto No. 1 in B flat min., Op. 1. Symphony No. 3* (fragment).
☞ *** Chan. Dig. CHAN 9074 [id.]. (i) Widlund; Royal Stockholm PO, Rozhdestvensky.

(i) *Piano concerto No. 1 in B flat min., Op. 1;* (ii) *Florez och Blanzeflor, Op. 3;* (iii) *Two Sentimental Romances, Op. 28.*
*** BIS Dig. CD 550 [id.]. (i) Love Derwinger; (ii) Peter Mattei; (iii) Ulf Wallin, Malmö SO, Paavo Järvi.

Stenhammar's *First Piano concerto* is full of beautiful ideas and the invention is fresh; even if it is too long (at nearly 50 minutes), admirers of the composer will find much to reward them. Love Derwinger proves an impressive and sympathetic intepreter and gets good support from Järvi *fils*. Stenhammar's ballad, *Florez och Blanzeflor* ('Flower and Whiteflower'), Op. 3, is a beautiful piece despite its somewhat Wagnerian overtones, and is sensitively sung by the young Swedish baritone Peter Mattei, of whom we shall surely hear more.

Chandos offer the less substantial coupling, a three-minute fragment from the *Third Symphony*, on which Stenhammar embarked in 1918–19. In itself it is too insignificant a makeweight to affect choice. But in the *Concerto* Mats Widlund proves the more imaginative soloist and brings just that little bit more finesse to the solo part. Rozhdestvensky gives excellent support and the Stockholm orchestra (and in particular their strings) have greater richness of sonority. The Chandos recording also has the edge on its BIS competitor in terms of depth and warmth.

(i; ii) *Piano concerto No. 2 in D min., Op. 23.* (iii) *Serenade for orchestra, Op. 31.* (iii; iv) *Florez och Blanzeflor* (ballad).
☞ (M) *** EMI CDM5 65081-2. (i) Janos Solyom; (ii) Munich PO; (iii) Swedish RSO, Stig Westerberg; (iv) with Ingvar Wixell.

This generously filled mid-price disc could serve as an admirable introduction to this fine Swedish composer. The *Serenade for orchestra* here comes in its finished form, as opposed to Neeme Järvi's Gothenburg recording, which adds the *Reverenza* movement that Stenhammar had excised but which brings no fill-up. Westerberg's 1974 performance is glorious and very well recorded, though the Swedish Radio Orchestra's strings do not have quite the same freshness and bloom as the Järvi set. However, this remains the most recommendable account of the work to date and is to be preferred to the old Kubelik set. Similarly Janos Solyom's dazzling account of the *Second Piano concerto* remains unsurpassed and, like the *Serenade*, still sounds very good indeed. There is a Saint-Saëns-like exuberance and effervescence about this work, and the improvisatory character of the piece is beautifully captured. The early *Florez och Blanzeflor* ('Flower and Whiteflower'), a ballad by Oscar Levertin, brings a certain Wagnerian flavour but has a charm that is conveyed well by Ingvar Wixell and Westerberg.

Serenade in F, Op. 31 (with the *Reverenza* movement).
*** BIS Dig. CD 310 [id.]. Gothenburg SO, Järvi.

The *Serenade for orchestra* is Stenhammar's masterpiece, his most magical work, and this version restores the second movement, *Reverenza*, which the composer had removed, to its original place. It is thoroughly characteristic, yet it has some of the melancholy charm of Elgar. Glorious music, sensitively played and finely recorded. However, this record offers no couplings.

Symphony No. 1 in F.
*** BIS Dig. CD 219 [id.]. Gothenburg SO, Järvi.

The *First Symphony* displays sympathies with such composers as Brahms, Bruckner, Berwald and, in the slow movement, even an affinity with Elgar. Nevertheless there is plenty of originality in it. The recording has complete naturalness, and on CD there is additional presence and range, particularly at the bottom end of the register.

Symphony No. 2 in G min., Op. 34.
*** Cap. CAP 21151 [id.]. Stockholm PO, Westerberg.

Symphony No. 2; Overture, Excelsior!, Op. 13.
*** BIS CD 251 [id.]. Gothenburg SO, Järvi.

This is a marvellous symphony. It is direct in utterance; the melodic invention is fresh and abundant, and the generosity of spirit it radiates is heart-warming. The Stockholm Philharmonic under Stig Westerberg play with conviction and eloquence; the strings have warmth and body, and the wind are very fine too. The recording is vivid and full-bodied even by the digital standards of today: as sound, this record is absolutely first class.

Neeme Järvi takes an altogether brisker view of the first movement than Westerberg, but the playing is spirited and the recording very good indeed, though not quite as distinguished as on the Caprice rival. The special attraction of this issue, however, is the *Overture, Excelsior!* It is an opulent but inventive score in the spirit of Strauss and Elgar and is played with enormous zest. *Excelsior!* improves enormously on acquaintance and deserves to become a repertoire work.

String quartets Nos. 1 in C, Op. 2; 2 in C min., Op. 14; 3 in F, Op. 18; 4 in A min., Op. 25; 5 in C (Serenade), Op. 29; 6 in D min., Op. 35.
*** Cap. CAP 21337/9 [id.]. Fresk Qt; Copenhagen Qt; Gotland Qt.

The *First Quartet* shows Stenhammar steeped in the chamber music of Beethoven and Brahms, though there is a brief reminder of the shadow of Grieg; the *Second* is far more individual. By the *Third* and *Fourth*, arguably the greatest of the six, the influence of Brahms and Dvořák is fully assimilated and the *Fourth* reflects that gentle melancholy which lies at the heart of Stenhammar's sensibility. The *Fifth* is the shortest; the *Sixth* comes from the war years when the composer was feeling worn out and depressed, though there is little evidence of this in the music. The Copenhagen Quartet play this marvellously. Performances are generally excellent, as indeed is the recording.

Allegro con moto ed appassionato; 3 Fantasies, Op. 11; Impromptu; Impromptu-Waltz; Late summer nights, Op. 33; 3 Small piano pieces.
☞ *** BIS Dig. CD-554 [id.]. Lucia Negro.

It is strange that as fine a pianist as Stenhammar left so little music for his own instrument. In his day he was a notable accompanist, chamber musician and soloist (one of his solo recitals included Beethoven Opp. 109 and 110 with the *Diabelli variations* in the second half) and, apart from his own concertos, he toured Europe at the turn of the century playing the Brahms *D minor Concerto*. Brahms in fact is a dominant influence in the early *Allegro con moto ed appassionato* and in the Op. 11 *Fantasies*, but there is a strong individual personality at work too, and the *Sensommarnätter* ('Late summer nights'), which come from the period when Stenhammar was working on the *Serenade for orchestra*, are wonderfully thoughtful and atmospheric pieces that inhabit a wholly personal world. The *Late summer nights* are not new to the CD catalogue; they form a fill-up to the Sterling account of the *First Piano concerto* (in Kurt Atterberg's reconstruction), where they were well played by Irene Mannheimer. Lucia Negro is thoroughly at home in this repertoire and plays with an effortless assurance and elegance that is very persuasive, and the BIS recording is altogether first rate.

Lodolezzi sings: suite, Op. 39; (i) Midwinter, Op. 24; (ii) Snöfrid, Op. 5; The Song (interlude).
*** BIS Dig. CD 438 [id.]. (i; ii) Gothenburg Concert Hall Ch., (ii) with Ahlén, Nilsson, Zackrisson, Enoksson; Gothenburg SO, Järvi.

Snöfrid is an early cantata. The young composer was completely under the spell of Wagner at this time and it offers only occasional glimpses of the mature Stenhammar. *Midwinter* is a kind of folk-music fantasy or pot-pourri on the lines of Alfvén's *Midsummer vigil*, though not quite so appealing. *Lodolezzi sings* has much innocent charm. None of this is great Stenhammar but it is well worth hearing; the performances under Neeme Järvi are very sympathetic, and the recording is natural and present.

(i) The Song (Sången), Op. 44; (ii) Two sentimental romances, Op. 28; (iii) Ithaca, Op. 21.
*** Cap. CAP 21358 [id.]. (i) Sörenson, von Otter, Dahlberg, Wahlgren, State Ac. Ch., Adolf Fredrik Music School Children's Ch., (ii) Arve Tellefsen, (iii) Håkan Hagegård, Swedish RSO; (i) Blomstedt; (ii) Westerberg; (iii) Ingelbretsen.

The first half of *The Song* has been described as 'a great fantasy' and is Stenhammar at his best and most individual: the choral writing is imaginatively laid out and the contrapuntal ingenuity is always at the service of poetic ends. The second half is less individual, masterly in its way, a lively choral allegro in the style of Handel. The solo and choral singing is superb and the whole performance has the total commitment one might expect from these forces. The superbly engineered recording does them full justice. The *Two sentimental romances* have great charm and are very well played, and Hagegård is in fine voice in another rarity, *Ithaca*.

30 Songs.
*** Caprice MSCD 623. Von Otter, Hagegård, Forsberg, Schuback.

These songs cover the whole of Stenhammar's career: the earliest, *In the forest*, was composed when he was sixteen, while the last, *Minnesang*, was written three years before his death. The songs are unpretentious and charming, fresh and idyllic, and nearly all are strophic. Hagegård sings the majority of them with his usual intelligence and artistry, though there is an occasional hardening of timbre. Anne Sofie von Otter is in wonderful voice and sings with great sensitivity and charm. Bengt Forsberg and Thomas Schuback accompany with great taste, and the recording is of the highest quality.

Sterndale Bennett, William (1816–75)

Piano concertos Nos. 1 in D min., Op. 1; 3 in C min., Op. 9.
⊛ *** Lyrita Dig. SRCD 204 [id.]. Malcolm Binns, LPO, Nicholas Braithwaite.

Sterndale Bennett earned the admiration of both Mendelssohn and Schumann and was briefly the white hope of English music. Perhaps it was hearing Mendelssohn play his *G minor Concerto* in 1832 that prompted the young sixteen-year-old to write his Opus 1, a concerto in D minor and a work of extraordinary fluency and accomplishment. David Byers, who has edited the concertos, speaks of Bennett's 'gentle lyricism, the strength and energy of the orchestral tuttis'; and they are in ample evidence, both here and in the *Third Piano concerto*, composed when he was eighteen. No praise can be too high for the playing of Malcolm Binns whose fleetness of finger and poetic sensibility are a constant source of delight, and for the admirable support he receives from Nicholas Braithwaite and the LPO. The engineers produce sound of the highest quality. A most enjoyable disc.

Piano concertos Nos. 2 in E flat, Op. 4; 5 in F min.; Adagio.
*** Lyrita Dig. SRCD 205 [id.]. Malcolm Binns, Philh. O, Nicholas Braithwaite.

This coupling is hardly less successful than its companion, reviewed above. The *Second concerto* proves to be a work of great facility and charm. It takes as its model the concertos of Mozart and Mendelssohn, and the brilliance and delicacy of the keyboard writing make one understand why the composer was so highly regarded by his contemporaries. The *F minor concerto* of 1836 is eminently civilized music with lots of charm; the *Adagio*, which completes the disc, is thought to be an alternative slow movement for Bennett's *Third Concerto* (1837). Whether or not this is the case, it is certainly a lovely piece. Malcolm Binns plays with great artistry, and the accompaniment by the Philharmonia Orchestra and Nicholas Braithwaite is equally sensitive. First-class recording.

(i) *Piano concerto No. 4 in F min.; Symphony in G. min.;* (i) *Fantasia in A, Op. 16.*
(M) *** Unicorn Dig. UKCD 2032; *UKC 2032*. (i) Binns; Milton Keynes CO, Hilary Wetton.

William Sterndale Bennett's eclectical *Fourth Piano concerto* reflects Chopin rather more than Mendelssohn and is agreeable and well structured. Its lollipop slow movement is a winner, an engaging *Barcarolle*. The *Symphony* is amiable, not unlike the Mendelssohn string symphonies. Overall it is very slight, but enjoyable enough. Both performances are uncommonly good ones. Malcolm Binns is a persuasive advocate of the *Concerto*, while Hilary Wetton paces both works admirably and clearly has much sympathy for them. The solo *Fantasia* has been added for the CD issue, which offers excellent sound and a good balance.

Stevens, Bernard (1916–83)

(i) *Cello concerto; Symphony of liberation.*
*** Mer. CDE 84124. (i) Baillie, BBC PO, Downes.

Bernard Stevens came to wider notice at the end of the war when his *Symphony of liberation* won a *Daily Express* competition. What a fine work it proves to be, though the somewhat later *Cello concerto* is even stronger. Dedicated performances from Alexander Baillie and the BBC Philharmonic. Good recording.

(i) *Violin concerto; Symphony No. 2.*
*** Mer. CDE 84174 [id.]. (i) Ernst Kovacic; BBC PO, Downes.

The *Violin concerto* is a good piece and well worth investigating. Stevens is a composer of real substance, and the *Second Symphony* (1964) is impressive in its sustained power and resource. Ernst Kovacic is persuasive in the *Concerto* and Downes and the BBC Philharmonic play well. Good (but not spectacular) recording.

Still, William Grant (1895–1978)

Symphony No. 2 (Song of a new race) in G min.

☞ *** Chan. Dig. CHAN 9226 [id.]. Detroit SO, Neeme Järvi – DAWSON: *Negro Folk Symphony;* ELLINGTON: *Harlem.* ***

Stokowski conducted the première of this attractive piece in 1937, seven years after the composer's *First Symphony* had been the first work by an African-American composer to be played by a major orchestra (the NYPO). Still worked as an arranger, so he knew how to score (the opening has a particularly fresh colouring) and he had a fund of tunes: the slow movement is haunting, the high-spirited Scherzo whistles along like someone out walking on a spring morning. The idiom is totally American and, if the score is more a suite than a symphony, it remains very personable and rather more coherently structured than the Dawson coupling, although the finale is not its strongest movement. It is played most persuasively here and is given a richly expansive recording.

Stockhausen, Karlheinz (born 1928)

(i) *Mikrophonie 1; Mikrophonie 2;* (ii) *Klavierstücke 1–11.*

☞ (M) *** Sony S2K 53346 (2). (i) Members of W. German R. Ch. & Studio Ch. for New Music, Cologne, Kontarsky, Alings, Fritsch, Bojé, cond. Herbert Schernus; supervised by composer; (ii) Aloys Kontarsky (piano).

This reissue combines two important Stockhausen recordings from the mid-1960s. *Mikrophonie 1* is electronic music proper; *Mikrophonie 2* attempts a synthesis of electronic music and choral sounds. Fascinating as the purely electronic invention is from a composer as obviously imaginative as Stockhausen, it is the vocal work that is the more immediately intriguing. The main point of the writing, as the composer sees it, lies in the mixture of natural and 'transformed' sound, achieved with great subtlety by controlling speaker inputs with potentiometers. It may be in dispute just how valid performances like these are when the composer's score allows many variables, but at least it is the composer himself who is supervising the production. Outstanding recording-quality for its time – as of course it should be with so many musician-engineers around in the Cologne studios.

The *Klavierstücke* provide a stimulating coupling. Aloys Kontarsky plays these eleven pieces – arguably the purest expression yet of Stockhausen's musical imagination – with a dedication that can readily convince even the unconverted listener. Seven of the pieces are very brief epigrammatic utterances, each sharply defined. The sixth and tenth pieces (the latter placed separately on the second disc) are more extended, each taking over 20 minutes. The effect at the begining of the ninth piece provides a clear indication of Stockhausen's aural imagination. The pianist repeats the same, not very interesting discord no fewer than 228 times, and one might dismiss that as merely pointless. What emerges from sympathetic listening is that the repetitions go nagging on so that the sound of the discord seems to vary, like a visual image shimmering in heat-haze. The other pieces, too, bring similar extensions of musical experience, and all this music is certainly communicative. Excellent if forward recording and extensive back-up notes. A good set for sharpening avant-garde teeth on.

Stimmung (1968).

*** Hyp. CDA 66115 [id.]. Singcircle, Gregory Rose.

Gregory Rose with his talented vocal group directs an intensely beautiful account of Stockhausen's 70-minute minimalist meditation on six notes. Though the unsympathetic listener might still find the result boring, this explains admirably how Stockhausen's musical personality can magnetize, with his variety of effect and response, even with the simplest of formulae. Excellent recording.

Stradella, Alessandro (1644–82)

San Giovanni Battista (oratorio).

⊛ *** Erato/Warner Dig. 2292 45739-2 [id.]. Bott, Batty, Lesne, Edgar-Wilson, Huttenlocher, Musiciens du Louvre, Minkowski.

Stradella's oratorio on the Biblical subject of John the Baptist and Salome is an amazing masterpiece and offers unashamedly sensuous treatment of the story. Insinuatingly chromatic melodic lines for Salome (here described simply as Herodias' daughter) are set against plainer, more forthright writing for the castrato role of the saint, showing the composer as a seventeenth-century equivalent of Richard Strauss. There is one amazing phrase for Salome, gloriously sung here by Catherine Bott, which starts well above the stave and ends after much twisting nearly two octaves below with a glorious chest-note, a hair-raising moment. Herod's anger arias bring reminders of both Purcell and Handel, and at the end Stradella ingeniously superimposes Salome's gloating music and Herod's expressions of regret, finally cutting off the duet in mid-air as Charles Ives might have done, bringing the whole work to an indeterminate close. Quite apart from Catherine Bott's magnificent performance, at once pure and sensuous in tone and astonishingly agile, the other singers are most impressive, with Gerard Lesne a firm-toned counter-tenor in the title-role and Philippe Huttenlocher a clear if sometimes gruff Herod. Marc Minkowski reinforces his claims as an outstanding exponent of period performance, drawing electrifying playing from Les Musiciens du Louvre, heightening the drama. Excellent sound. Not to be missed!

The Strauss family

Strauss, Johann Snr (1804–49)   **Strauss, Johann Jnr** (1825–99)
Strauss, Josef (1827–70)   **Strauss, Eduard** (1835–1916)

(all music listed is by Johann Strauss Jnr unless otherwise stated)

Johann Strauss Jnr: The Complete Edition.
Volume 1: Mazurka: *Veilchen, Mazur nach russischen motiven.* Polkas: *Fledermaus; Herzenslust; Zehner.* Quadrilles: *Debut; Nocturne.* Waltzes: *Bei uns z'Haus; Freuet euch des Lebens; Gunstwerber; Klangfiguren; Maskenzug française; Phönix-Schwingen.*
☞ **(*) Marco Polo Dig. 8.223201-2. CSSR State PO (Košice), Alfred Walter.

Volume 2: *Kaiser Franz Josef 1, Rettungs-Jubel-Marsch.* Polkas: *Czechen; Neue Pizzicato; Satanella; Tik-Tak.* Polka-Mazurka: *Fantasieblümchen.* Quadrilles: *Cytheren; Indra.* Waltzes: *Die jungen Wiener; Solonsprüche; Vermälungs-Toaste; Wo die Zitronen blüh'n.*
☞ ** Marco Polo Dig. 8.223202-2. CSSR State PO (Košice), Alfred Walter.

Volume 3: Polkas: *Aesculap; Amazonen; Freuden-Gruss; Jux; Vergnügungszug.* Quadrilles: *Dämonen; Satanella.* Waltzes: *Berglieder; Liebeslieder; Lind-gesänge; Die Osterreicher; Wiener Punsch-lieder.*
☞ **(*) Marco Polo Dig. 8.223203-2. CSSR State PO (Košice), Alfred Walter.

Volume 4: Polkas: *Bürger-Ball; Hopser; Im Krapfenwald'l (polka française); Knall-Kügerin; Veilchen.* Marches: *Austria; Verbruederungs.* Quadrille: *Motor.* Waltzes: *Dividenden; O schoener Mai!; Serail-taenze.*
☞ **(*) Marco Polo Dig. 8.223204-2. CSSR State PO (Košice), Richard Edlinger.

Volume 5: *Russischer Marsch Fantasie.* Polkas: *Elisen (polka française); Heiligenstadt rendezvous; Hesperus; Musen; Pariser.* Quadrille: *Sur des airs français.* Waltzes: *Italienischer; Kennst du mich?; Nachtfalter; Wiener Chronik.*
☞ *** Marco Polo Dig. 8.223205-2. CSSR State PO (Košice), Oliver Dohnányi.

Volume 6: *Caroussel Marsch.* Polkas: *Bluette (polka française); Camelien; Warschauer.* Quadrilles: *Nach themen französischer Romanzen; Nordstern.* Waltzes: *Concurrenzen; Kuss; Myrthen-Kränze; Wellen und wogen.*
☞ ** Marco Polo Dig. 8.223206-2. CSSR State PO (Košice), Oliver Dohnányi.

Volume 7: *Deutscher krieger Marsch; Kron marsch.* Polkas: *Bacchus; Furioso; Neuhauser.* Polka-Mazurka: *Kriegers liebchen.* Quadrille: *Odeon.* Waltzes: *Ballg'schichten; Colonnen; Nordseebilder; Schnee-Glöckchen; Zeitgeister.*
☞ **(*) Marco Polo Dig. 8.223207-2. Polish State PO, Oliver Dohnányi.

Volume 8: *Banditen-Galopp; Erzherzog Wilhelm genesungs marsch.* Polkas: *Leichtes blut; Wiedersehen; Pepita.* Quadrilles: *Nach motiven aus Verdi's 'Un ballo in maschera'; Saison.* Waltzes: *Cagliostro; Carnevals-Botschafter; Lagunen; Die Sanguiniker; Schallwellen.*
☞ **(*) Marco Polo Dig. 8.223208-2. Polish State PO, Oliver Dohnányi.

This extraordinary Marco Polo enterprise – to record the entire output of the Strauss family – began in 1988, although the first issues did not arrive in the UK until the beginning of 1990. All these initial volumes centre on the music of Johann Junior. Apparently, when the output of the son is fully covered, his father, Johann Senior, will come next, then, after him, Josef. Enormous background research went into the project and Europe was scoured for the orchestral parts. The snag was that Johann and his orchestra were constantly on the move and, wherever they travelled to play, he was expected to come up with some new pieces. While obvious 'hits' and favourites stayed in the repertoire, often the novelties were treated as ephemeral, for it was simply not possible, under travelling conditions of the mid-nineteenth century, to take all the music around with them. Moreover this was a commercial enterprise and there was no scholarly librarian on hand to catalogue and look after the orchestral parts; in many instances, only the short piano-score has survived. It was then necessary – for the purpose of the recording – to hire professional arrangers to make suitable orchestrations; from these, new orchestral parts could be copied. Such is the perversity of human experience that quite regularly the original orchestral parts would suddenly appear for some of the pieces – after the recording had been made! It is therefore planned to have an appendix and to re-record those items later, from the autographs. However, the remarkable thing is that comparison of the new arrangements with the originals often reveals only minor differences. Johann wrote his music quickly and his orchestration, delightful as it is, formed a definite pattern, so it was not difficult for an expert professional to simulate the real thing.

The music is not being recorded in any special order, but simply as it comes to hand, when for each CD a reasonably varied selection of about a dozen pieces (or an hour of music) is assembled. So far the recordings have been made in Eastern Europe. Apart from cutting the costs, the Slovak Bohemian tradition provides a relaxed ambience, highly suitable for this repertoire. Much of the music is here being put on disc for the first time and indeed the excellent back-up documentation tells us that three items on the first CD were part of the young Johann's first concert programme: the *Gunstwerber* ('Wooer of favour') *Waltz*, *Herzenslust* ('Heart's desire') polka and, even more appropriately, the *Debut-Quadrille*, so that makes Volume 1 of the series something of a collector's item, while Volume 3 also seems to have above-average interest in the selection of its programme.

Evaluation of these recordings has not been easy. The first three CDs were made by the Slovak State Philharmonic under Alfred Walter. The mood is amiable and the playing quite polished. With the arrival of Richard Edlinger and Oliver Dohnányi on the scene, the tension seems to increase, and there is much to relish. Of this second batch we would pick out Volumes 5, 7 and 8, all representing the nice touch of Oliver Dohnányi, with Volume 5 perhaps a primary choice, although there are many good things included in Volume 8.

Volume 9: *Habsburg Hoch! Marsch; Indigo marsch.* Polkas: *Albion; Anen; Lucifer.* Polka-Mazurka: *Nachtveilchen.* Quadrille: *Festival quadrille nach englischen motiven.* Waltzes: *Carnevalsbilder; Gedanken auf den Alpen; Kaiser.*
☞ ** Marco Polo Dig. 8.223209-2. Polish State PO, Johannes Wildner.

Volume 10: *Pesther csárdás.* Polkas: *Bauern; Blumenfest; Diabolin; Juriston Ball.* Quadrille: *Nach beliebten motiven.* Waltzes: *Feuilleton; Morgenblätter; Myrthenblüthen; Panacea-klänge.*
☞ ** Marco Polo Dig. 8.223210-2. Polish State PO (Katowice), Johannes Wildner.

Volume 11: *Revolutions Marsch.* Polkas: *Frisch heran!; Haute-volée; Herrmann; Patrioten.* Polka-Mazurka: *Waldine.* Quadrilles: *Die Afrikanerin; Handels-élite.* Waltzes: *Aus den bergen; Donauweibchen; Glossen; Klänge aus der Walachei.*
☞ **(*) Marco Polo Dig. 8.223211-2. CSSR State PO (Košice), Alfred Walter.

Volume 12: *Krönungs Marsch.* Polkas: *Aurora; Ella; Harmonie; Meues leben (polka française); Souvenir; Stürmisch in lieb' und tanz.* Quadrille: *Fest.* Waltzes: *Die Gemüthlichen; Hofballtänze; Man lebt nur einmal!; Wiener frauen.*
☞ ** Marco Polo Dig. 8.223212-2. CSSR State PO (Košice), Alfred Walter.

Volume 13: *Egyptischer Marsch; Patrioten marsch.* Polkas: *Demolirer; Fidelen; Nur fort!; Tanzi-bäri; Was sich liebt, neckt sich (polka française).* Quadrilles: *Nach motiven aus der oper 'Die Belagerung von Rochelle'; Neue melodien.* Waltzes: *Sirenen; Thermen; Die Zillerthaler.*
☞ **(*) Marco Polo Dig. 8.223213-2. CSSR State PO (Košice), Alfred Walter.

Volume 14: *Romance No. 1 for cello and orchestra.* Polkas: *Champagne; Geisselhiebe; Kinderspiele (polka française); Vöslauer.* Quadrilles: *Bal champêtre; St Petersburg (quadrille nach russischen motiven).* Waltzes: *Du and du; Ernte-tänze; Frohsinns-spenden; Grillenbanner; Phänomene.*
☞ **(*) Marco Polo Dig. 8.223214-2. CSSR State PO (Košice), Alfred Walter.

Volume 15: *Jubelfest-Marsch.* Polkas: *Bijoux; Scherz.* Polka-Mazurkas: *Lob der frauen; La Viennoise.* Quadrilles: *Alexander; Bijouterie.* Waltzes: *Die Jovialen; Kaiser-Jubiläum; Libellen; Wahlstimmen.*
☞ ** Marco Polo Dig. 8.223215-2. CSR SO (Bratislava), Johannes Wildner.

Volume 16: *Fürst Bariatinsky-Marsch*. Polkas: *Brautschau* (on themes from *Zigeunerbaron*); *Eljen a Magyar!; Ligourianer Seufzer; Schnellpost; Studenten. La berceuse quadrille; Zigeuner-Quadrille* (on themes from Balfe's *Bohemian Girl*). Waltzes: *Bürgerweisen; Freuden-Salven; Motoren; Sangerfährten.*
☞ **(*) Marco Polo Dig. 8.223216 [id.]. CSSR State PO (Košice), Alfred Walter.

With Volume 9, we move to Poland and a new name, Johannes Wildner. He has his moments, but his approach seems fairly conventional. He does not make a great deal of the famous *Emperor Waltz* which closes Volume 9, although he does better with *Gedanken auf den Alpen*, another unknown but charming waltz. Alfred Walter – who began it all – then returns for Volumes 11–14. Of this batch, Volume 11 might be singled out, opening with the jolly *Herrmann-Polka*, while the *Klänge aus der Walachei*, *Aus den Bergen* ('From the Mountains') and *Donauweibchen* ('Nymph of the Danube') are three more winning waltzes; but the standard seems pretty reliable here, and these are all enjoyable discs. Volume 16 has another attractive batch of waltzes, at least two winning polkas and a quadrille vivaciously drawing on Balfe's *Bohemian Girl*. It also includes the extraordinary *Ligourian Seufzer polka*, in which the orchestra vocally mocks the Ligourians, a despised Jesuitical order led by Alfonso Maria di Ligouri. Another good disc.

Volume 17: *Kaiser Franz Joseph Marsch*. Polkas: *Armen-ball; 'S gibt nur a Kaiserstadt! 'S gibt nur a Wien; Violetta (polka française)*. Quadrille: *Melodien*. Waltzes: *Adelen; Bürgersinn; Freiheits-lieder; Windsor-klänge.*
☞ *** Marco Polo Dig. 8.223217-2. CSR SO (Bratislava), Alfred Eschwé.

Volume 18: *Alliance-Marsche; Studenten-Marsch*. Polkas: *Edtweder-oder!; Invitation à la polka mazur; Leopoldstädter; Stadt und Land; Cagliostro-Quadrille*. Waltzes: *Grossfürstin Alexandra; Lava-Ströme; Patronessen; Die Pulizisten; Rathausball-Tänz.*
☞ **(*) Marco Polo Dig. 8.223218-2. CSSR State PO, Alfred Walter.

Volume 19: *Hoch Osterreich! Marsch*. Polkas: *Burschenwanderung (polka française), Electro-magnetische; Episode (polka française)*. Quadrilles: *Le premier jour de bonheur, Opéra de Auber; Seladon*. Waltzes: *Dorfgeschichten (im Ländlerstyle); Novellen; Rosen aus dem Süden; Seid umschlungen, Millionen; Studentenlust.*
☞ **(*) Marco Polo Dig. 8-223219-2. Czecho-Slovak State PO (Košice), Alfred Walter.

Volume 20: *Dinorah-quadrille nach motiven der oper, 'Die Wallfahrt' nach Meyerbeer. Kaiser-Jäger Marsch. Slovianka-quadrille, nach russischen melodien*. Polkas: *Auf zum tänze; Herzel*. Polka-Mazurkas: *Ein herz, ein sinn; Fata Morgana*. Waltzes: *Aurora-ball-tänze; Erhöhte pulse; Flugschriften; Märchen aus dem Orient; Schwärmereien* (concert waltz).
☞ ** Marco Polo Dig. 8.223220-2. Czecho-Slovak State PO (Košice), Alfred Walter.

Volume 21: *Ottinger Reiter Marsch*. Polkas: *Figaro (polka française); Patronessen (polka française); Sans-souci*. Polka-Mazurka: *Tändelei*. Quadrilles: *Orpheus; Rotunde*. Waltzes: *Cycloiden; G'schichten aus dem Wienerwald; Johannis-Käferin.*
☞ ** Marco Polo Dig. 8.223221-2. Czecho-Slovak State PO (Košice), Johannes Wildner.

Volume 22: *Klipp-Klapp Galopp. Persischer Marsch*. Polkas: *L'Inconnue (polka française); Nachtigall*. Polka-Mazurka: *Aus der Heimat*. Quadrilles: *Carnevals-spektakel; Der lustige Krieg*. Waltzes: *Controversen; Immer heiterer (im Ländlerstyle); Maxing-tänze; Ninetta.*
☞ ** Marco Polo Dig. 8.223222-2. Czecho-Slovak State PO (Košice), Johannes Wildner.

Volume 23: *Deutschmeister-Jubiläumsmarsch*. Polkas: *Maria Taglioni; Die Pariserin (polka française); Rasch in der tat!*. Polka-Mazurka: *Glücklich ist, wer vergisst*. Quadrilles: *Le beau monde; Indigo*. Waltzes: *Gross-Wien; Rhadamantus-klänge; Telegramme; Vibrationen; Wien, mein Sinn!.*
☞ ** Marco Polo Dig. 8.223223-2. Czecho-Slovak State PO (Košice), Johannes Wildner.

Volume 24: *Gavotte der Königin. Viribus unitis, Marsch*. Polkas: *Demi-fortune (polka française); Heski-Holki; Rokonhangok (sympathieklänge); So ängstlich sind wir nicht!*. Polka-Mazurka: *Licht und Schatten*. Quadrille: *Streina-terrassen*. Waltzes: *Idyllen; Jux-brüder; Lockvögel; Sinnen und Minnen.*
☞ ** Marco Polo Dig. 8.223224-2. Czecho-Slovak State PO (Košice), Alfred Walter.

Volume 17 introduces another new name, Alfred Eschwé, and a particularly good collection, one of the highlights of the set. Try to identify all the good tunes (by Verdi) in the *Melodien-Quadrille*, while the *Bürgersinn* ('Public spirit') waltz has a charming introduction. But the opening to *Feenmärchen*, with its oboe and horn solos, is quite magical, and it is beautifully played. Volume 18 brings back

Alfred Walter and another very good mix of waltzes and polkas. Johannes Wildner then directs Volumes 21–23, and it must be said that the middle volume shows him in better light than the other two, and with a well-chosen programme.

Volume 25: *Grossfürsten Marsch*. Polkas: *Bonbon (polka française); Explosions; Lustger Rath (polka française); Mutig voran!*. Polka-Mazurka: *Le Papillon*. Quadrilles: *Künstler; Promenade*. Waltzes: *Frauen-Käferin; Krönungslieder; Spiralen; Ins Zentrum!*.
☞ ** Marco Polo Dig. 8.223225-2. Czecho-Slovak State PO (Košice), Johannes Wildner.

Volume 26: *Es war so wunderschön Marsch*. Polkas: *Elektrophor; L'Enfantillage (polka française); Gut bürgerlich (polka française); Louischen (polka française); Pasman*. Quadrilles: *Industrie; Sofien*. Waltzes: *Juristen-ball-tänze; Künstlerleben; Pasman; Sinngedichte*.
☞ *** Marco Polo Dig. 8.223226-2. Austrian RSO, Vienna, Guth.

Volume 27: *Spanischer Marsch*. Polkas: *Drollerie; Durch's telephon; Express; Gruss an Wien (polka française)*. Polka-Mazurka. *Annina*. Quadrilles: *Künstler; Sans-souci*. Waltzes: *Aeolstöne; Souvenir de Nizza; Wein, Weib und Gesang; Frühlingsstimmen*.
☞ ⊛ *** Marco Polo Dig 8.223227-2. Austrian RSO, Vienna, Guth.

Volume 28: *Freiwillige vor! Marsch (1887). Frisch in's feld! Marsch*. Polkas: *Unter Donner und Blitz; Pappacoda (polka française)*. Polka-Mazurkas: *Concordia; Spleen*. Quadrille: *Tête-à-tête*. Waltzes: *Einheitsklänge: Illustrationen; Lebenswecker; Telegraphische depeschen*.
☞ ** Marco Polo Dig. 8.223228-2. Czecho-Slovak State PO (Košice), Johannes Wildner.

Volume 29: *Brünner-Nationalgarde-Marsch. Der lustige Krieg, Marsch*. Polkas: *Die Bajadere; Hellenen; Secunden (polka française)*. Polka-Mazurka: *Une Bagatelle*. Quadrille: *Waldmeister*. Waltzes: *Deutsche; Orakel-Sprüche; Schatz; Tausend und eine Macht; Volkssänger*.
☞ ** Marco Polo Dig. 8.223229-2. Czecho-Slovak State PO (Košice), Alfred Walter.

Volume 30: *Fest-Marsch. Perpetuum mobile*. Polkas: *Alexandrinen; Kammerball; Kriegsabenteuer; Par force!*. Quadrille: *Attaque*. Waltzes: *Erinnerung an Covent Garden; Kluh Gretelein; Luisen-sympathie-Klänge; Paroxysmen; Reiseabenteuer*.
☞ ** Marco Polo Dig. 8.223230-2. Czecho-Slovak State PO (Košice), Alfred Walter.

Volume 31: *Napoleon-Marsch*. Polkas: *Husaren; Taubenpost (polka française); Vom Donaustrande*. Polka-Mazurka: *Nord und Süd*. Quadrilles: *Bonvivant; Nocturne*. Waltzes: *Gambrinus-tänze; Die ersten Curen; Hochzeitsreigen; Die Unzertrennlichen; Wiener bonbons*.
☞ ** Marco Polo Dig. 8.223231-2. Czecho-Slovak State PO (Košice), Alfred Walter.

Volume 32: *Wiener Jubel-Gruss-Marsch*. Polkas: *Auf der Jagd; Olge; Tritsch-tratsch*. Polka-Mazurka: *An der Wolga*. Quadrilles: *Methusalem; Hofball*. Waltzes: *Fantasiebilder; Ich bin dir gut!; Promotionen. Wiener Blut*.
☞ ** Marco Polo Dig. 8.223232-2. Czecho-Slovak State PO (Košice), Johannes Wildner.

Volume 26 brings another fresh name, and fresh is the right word to describe this attractive programme. From the bright-eyed opening *Elektrophor Polka schnell* this is winningly vivacious music-making and the waltz that follows, *Sinngedichte*, makes one realizes that there is something special about Viennese string-playing, for this is the Orchestra of Austrian Radio. The introduction of *Künstlerleben* with its lovely oboe solo and then the solo horn behind the strings (a favourite Strauss device) leads to the most delectable opening for the waltz itself. Volume 27 features the same orchestra and conductor and opens with the delectable *Künster-Quadrille*. After the aptly named *Drollerie* polka comes the *Aeolstöne* waltz with its portentous introduction, and the waltz itself is heart-warming. The *Souvenir de Nizza* waltz is hardly less beguiling and *Wine, women and song* and, to end the disc, *Frühlingsstimmen* – two top favourites – simply could not be better played. These two Peter Guth CDs are the finest of the series so far, and we award a token Rosette to the second of the two, although it could equally apply to its companion. After those two marvellous collections have shown us what potential there is in this repertoire with a first-rate Viennese orchestra and conductor, it is an anticlimax to return to the following volumes. There is much interesting music here, but the performances often have an element of routine.

Volume 33: *Saschen-Kürassier-Marsch*. Polkas: *Etwas kleines (polka française); Freikugeln*. Polka-Mazurka: *Champêtre*. Quadrilles: *Bouquet; Opern-Maskenball*. Waltzes: *Abschieds-Rufe; Sträusschen; An der schönen blauen Donau; Trau, schau, wem!*.
☞ ** Marco Polo Dig. 8.223233-2. Czecho-Slovak State PO (Košice), Wildner.

Volume 34: (i) *Dolci pianti* (Romance for cello and orchestra). *Im russischen Dorfe, Fantasie* (orch. Max Schönherr). *Russischer Marsch. Slaven-potpourri.* Polkas: *La Favourite (polka française); Niko.* Polka-Mazurka: *Der Kobold.* Quadrille: *Nikolai.* Waltzes: *Abschied von St Petersburg; Fünf paragraphen.*
☞ *** Marco Polo Dig. 8.223234-2. Slovak RSO (Bratislava), Dittrich, (i) with Jozef Sikora.

Volume 35: *Zivio! Marsch.* Polkas: *Jäger (polka française); Im Sturmschritt!; Die Zeitlose (polka française).* Polka-Mazurka: *Die Wahrsagerin.* Quadrilles: *Der blits; Der liebesbrunnen.* Waltzes: *Accelerationen; Architecten-ball-tänze; Heut' ist heut' Königslieder.*
☞ ** Marco Polo Dig. 8.223235-2. Slovak State PO (Košice), Wildner.

Volume 36: *Matador-Marsch.* Polkas: *Bitte schön! (polka française); Diplomaten; Kreuzfidel (polka française); Process.* Polka-Mazurka: *Der Klügere gibt nach.* Quadrilles: *Elfen; Fledermaus.* Waltzes: *D'Woaldbuama (im Ländlerstil)* (orch. Ludwig Babinski); *Extravaganten; Mephistos Höllenrufe; Neu-Wien.*
☞ ** Marco Polo Dig. 8.223236-2. Slovak State PO (Košice), Alfred Walter.

Among the last four volumes received (with quite a few more to come), again the one that stands out features another new name, Michael Dittrich; working with the Slovak Radio Symphony Orchestra, he produces a splendid collection to make up Volume 34. The flexible handling of the *Slav Potpourri* shows his persuasive sympathy for Strauss, while the *Fünf Paragraphen* waltz has an equally delectable lilt. There is great charm in the elegant *La Favourite* polka and the *Abschied von St Petersburg* waltz has a nicely beguiling opening theme.

'The Best of Johann Strauss'
Volume 1: (i) Overture: *Die Fledermaus.* Polkas: (ii) *Annen;* (iii) *Auf der Jagd;* (iv) *Unter donner und blitz;* (v) *Tick-Tack.* Waltzes: (iv) *Künstlerleben; Lagunen; Rosen aus dem Süden; Wein, Weib und Gesang.*
☞ (BB) **(*) Naxos Dig. 8.550336; 4.550336. (i) Czecho-Slovak R. O, Sieghart; (ii) Polish State PO, Dohnányi; (iii) Czecho-Slovak State PO, Alfred Walter; (v) Polish State PO, Wildner; (iv) Czecho-Slovak RSO, Lenárd.

Volume 2: (i) Overture: *Indigo und die 40 Räuber.* Polkas: (ii) *Pizzicato; Tritsch-Tratsch.* Quadrille: (i) *Die Fledermaus;* Waltzes: (ii) *An der schönen blauen Donau; Frühlingsstimmen;* (iii) *Morgenblätter;* (ii) *Tausend und eine Nacht;* (i) *Wo die Citronen blüh'n.*
☞ (BB) **(*) Naxos Dig. 8.550337; 4.550337. (i) CSSR State PO, Alfred Walter; (ii) Czecho-Slovak RSO, Lenárd; (iii) Polish State PO, Wildner.

Volume 3: (i) *Egyptischer Marsch.* Overture: (ii) *Zigeunerbaron.* Polkas: (iii) *Bitte schön;* (iv) *Im Krapfenwaldl';* (v) *Leichtes blut.* Waltzes: (i) *Accelerationen;* (i) *Du und du;* (iii) *Neu-Wien;* (i) *Wiener blut.*
☞ (BB) **(*) Naxos Dig. 8.550338; 4.550338. (i) Czecho-Slovak RSO, Lenárd; (ii) Czecho-Slovak RSO, Siegart; (iii) Czecho-Slovak State PO, Alfred Walter; (iv) Czecho-Slovak State PO, Edlinger; (v) Polish State PO, Dohnányi.

Volume 4: (i) *Perpetuum mobile.* (ii) Overture: *Karneval in Rom.* Polkas: *Eljen a Magyar!; Vergnügungszug.* Waltzes: (i) *Kaiser;* (iii) *Karnevalsbotschafter;* (ii) *Mephistos Höllenrufe; Seid Umschlungen, Millionen; Wiener bonbons.*
☞ (BB) **(*) Naxos Dig. 8.550339; 4.550339. (i) Czecho-Slovak RSO, Lenárd; (ii) CSSR State PO, Alfred Walter; (iii) Polish State PO, Dohnányi.

Volume 5: (i) *Persischer Marsch.* Overture: (ii) *Das Spitzentuch der Königin.* Polkas: *Kreuzfidel; Neue Pizzicato; Vom donaustrande.* Waltzes: *Freut euch des Lebens;* (i) *G'schichten aus dem Wienerwald;* (ii) *Liebeslieder;* (i) *Schatz.*
☞ (BB) **(*) Naxos Dig. 8.550340; 4.550340. (i) Czecho-Slovak RSO, Lenárd; (ii) CSSR State PO, Alfred Walter.

These discs make inexpensive samplers for the Johann Strauss Edition, although not quite all the repertoire is drawn from it, notably the recordings under Lenárd which are often very well done. Good value.

'Vienna Dance Gala, 3: Fledermaus Quadrille': Johann STRAUSS Jnr: *Fledermaus quadrille; Orpheus quadrille;* Waltzes: *Bei uns z'haus; Nordseebilder; Mephistos Höllenrufe; Erinnerung an Covent-Garden. Freikugeln polka; Aufs Korn marsch.* Josef STRAUSS: Polkas: *Ohne Sorgen; Im Fluge; Extempore; Rudolfsheimer.* Waltz: *Mein Lebenslauf ist Lieb und Lust.*

☞ (M) *** Decca *436 783-2* [id.]. VPO, Willi Boskovsky.

A splendid 75-minute anthology from Boskovsky's vintage years with the VPO, recorded between 1958 and 1973, issued (separately) as part of the five-CD Decca 'Dance Gala' series – see Concerts, below. It would be difficult to discover a collection with a gayer atmosphere, full as it is of colourful Strauss confectionery, sparklingly played with plenty of Viennese lilt and finesse. The opening *Fledermaus quadrille* gets the programme off to a vivacious start and later we hear a comparable selection from Offenbach's *Orpheus in the Underworld*. This is the Viennese strict-tempo version, presented relatively formally, and it is a pity that the disc did not also include the more unbuttoned concert version which Boskovsky recorded at the same time. The other pot-pourri here is of English music-hall songs, written for a series of promenade concerts that Johann II conducted at Covent Garden during the summer and autumn of 1867. The piece – full title: *Erinnerung an Covent Garden, Waltzer nach englischen Volksmelodien* – is dominated by *Champagne Charlie is my name* but also includes the ditty about 'The man on the flying trapeze', both sounding exotic in the context of a Strauss waltz. Among the other novelties is the jolly *Aufs Korn march* in which the Vienna State Opera Chorus are infectiously featured, even though not credited on the disc.

Overtures: *Die Fledermaus; Indigo und die vierzig Räuber. Egyptischer Marsch; Der Zigeunerbaron: March.* Polkas: *Eljen a Magyar!; Freikugeln; Pizzicato* (with Josef); *Unter Donner und Blitz.* Waltzes: *An der schönen blauen Donau; Frühlingsstimmen; Kaiser; Rosen aus dem Süden.*
☞ (B) ** DG Dig. 439 439-2 [id.]. VPO, Lorin Maazel.

This collection draws on Maazel's Vienna New Year concerts from 1980–83. He did not take on Boskovsky's mantle very readily; for all the brilliance of the playing, the impression is one of energy rather than of charm. He can certainly shape the beginnings and ends of waltzes elegantly, and the performances of the *Blue Danube* and the *Emperor* are not without lilt; but elsewhere the feeling of the music-making can seem too high-powered. The digital recording gives good presence – especially in the *Pizzicato polka* – but less atmosphere; and when the applause comes, one almost registers surprise.

(i) *Overtures: Die Fledermaus;* (ii) *Waldmeister.* (iii) *Perpetuum mobile.* Polkas: (iv) *Annen;* (v) *Auf der Jagd;* (vi) *Leichtes Blut;* (iv) *Pizzicato* (with Josef); (vii) *Tritsch-Tratsch;* (iv) *Vergnügungszug.* (viii) *Quadrille on themes from Verdi's 'Un ballo in maschera'.* Waltzes: (ix) *Accelerationen;* (x) *An der schönen blauen Donau;* (xi) *Du und Du;* (iv) *Frühlingsstimmen;* (vi) *G'schichten aus dem Wienerwald;* (xii) & (xiii) & (v) *Kaiser;* (iii) *Rosen aus dem Süden;* (ii) *Wein, Weib und Gesang.* Josef STRAUSS: (iv) *Dorfschwalben aus Osterreich;* (v) *Sphärenklänge.* (iv) Johann STRAUSS, Snr: *Radetzky march.*
(M) *** DG mono/stereo 435 335-2 (2). VPO, (i) Maazel; (ii) Boskovsky; (iii) Boehm; (iv) Clemens Krauss; (v) Karajan; (vi) Knappertsbusch; (vii) Mehta; (viii) Abbado; (ix) Josef Krips; (x) Szell; (xi) Erich Kleiber; (xii) Bruno Walter; (xiii) Furtwängler.

This delectable compilation for the 150th anniversary of the Vienna Philharmonic brings recordings of Strauss made between 1929 and 1990, notably from EMI, whose recordings of Erich Kleiber, Clemens Krauss and George Szell (made in the late 1920s and early 1930s) are particularly atmospheric, very well transferred. Other Clemens Krauss performances, plus more by Boskovsky and Knappertsbusch, come from the Decca label, justly famous in this repertoire. It is fascinating to compare Bruno Walter (1937), Wilhelm Furtwängler (1950) and Karajan (1987), all playing the *Emperor waltz*, and the many well-known favourites are well spiced with a few charming rarities.

'The world of Johann Strauss': Egyptischer Marsch; Perpetuum mobile; Polkas: *Auf der Jagd; Pizzicato* (with Josef); Waltzes: *An der schönen blauen Donau; Frühlingsstimmen; G'schichten aus dem Wienerwald; Rosen aus dem Süden; 1001 Nacht; Wiener Blut.*
(M) *** Decca 430 501-2; *430 501-4.* VPO, Boskovsky.

A generous and inexpensive Decca permutation of the justly famous Boskovsky/VPO recordings, which still dominate the Strauss family listings. If the programme suits, this is excellent value.

Napoleon-Marsch. Polkas: *Annen; Explosionen; Tritsch-Tratsch.* Waltzes: *An der schönen blauen Donau; Morgenblätter; 1001 Nights; Wein, Weib und Gesang; Wiener Bonbons.* Josef STRAUSS: *Dorfschwalben aus Osterreich.* Johann STRAUSS Snr: *Radetzky march.*
(B) *** Decca 433 609-2; *433 609-4.* VPO, Willi Boskovsky.

A particularly enjoyable concert of Boskovsky repertoire, chosen and ordered with skill, opening with the *Blue Danube* and closing with the rousing *Radetzky march.* The VPO are on their toes throughout. The recording dates range from 1958 to 1976; some are spikier than others in the upper range, but the warm Sofiensaal ambience is always flattering.

'1987 New Year Concert in Vienna': Overture: *Die Fledermaus.* Polkas: *Annen; Pizzicato* (with Josef);
Unter Donner und Blitz; Vergnügungszug. Waltzes: *An der schönen blauen Donau;* (i)
Frühlingsstimmen. J. STRAUSS Snr: *Beliebte Annen* (polka); *Radetzky march.* Josef STRAUSS: *Ohne
Sorgen polka;* Waltzes: *Delirien; Sphärenklänge.*
⊛ *** DG Dig. 419 616-2 [id.]. VPO, Karajan; (i) with Kathleen Battle.

In preparation for this outstanding concert, which was both recorded and televised, Karajan re-
studied the scores of his favourite Strauss pieces; the result, he said afterwards, was to bring an
overall renewal to his musical life beyond the scope of this particular repertoire. The concert itself
produced music-making of the utmost magic; familiar pieces sounded almost as if they were being
played for the first time. Kathleen Battle's contribution to *Voices of spring* brought wonderfully easy,
smiling coloratura and much charm. *The Blue Danube* was, of course, an encore, and what an encore!
Never before has it been played so seductively on record. In the closing *Radetzky march,* wonderfully
crisp yet relaxed, Karajan kept the audience contribution completely in control merely by the slightest
glance over his shoulder. This indispensable collection makes an easy first choice among any Strauss
compilations ever issued.

'New Year in Vienna': Banditen galop (from *Prinz Methusalem*); *Perpetuum mobile.* Polkas: *Auf der
Jagd; Freut euch des Lebens; Neue pizzicato Polka; Stürmische in Lieb' und Tanz.* Waltzes: *An der
schönen blauen Donau; Kaiser; Seid umschlungen, Millionen; Wo die Zitronen blüh'n.* Josef STRAUSS:
Polkas: *Auf Ferienreisen; Brennende Liebe; Im Fluge; Die tanzende Muse.* Johann STRAUSS Snr:
Radetzky march.
☞ *** DG Dig. 437 687-2 [id.]. VPO, Claudio Abbado.

These recordings are taken from Abbado's 1988, 1991 and 1993 New Year VPO concerts, recorded
live. Apart from Boskovsky (and Karajan's magical 1987 Concert – DG 419 616-2), the VPO took to
Abbado's coaxing direction more naturally than they did to other conductors like Carlos Kleiber and
Zubin Mehta, and the result is wholly sympathetic. There is much that is agreeably unfamiliar here,
but the two great waltzes sound gloriously fresh. The close of the *Emperor* is wonderfully subtle, and
the *Blue Danube* is pretty marvellous too. Elsewhere the playing is as sophisticated in detail as it is
joyous in execution, and the audience participation is not intrusive – except, understandably, in
Radetzky, where Abbado keeps everything well in hand. With 78 minutes of music, this is one of the
very finest of modern Strauss anthologies.

'1989 & 1992 New Year concerts' (complete).
☞ (M) *** Sony Dig. SX3K 53385 (3) [id.]. VPO, Carlos Kleiber.

At the beginning of 1994 Kleiber's New Year concerts were paired together as a limited-edition
promotional offer at lower-mid-price; the set may still be available in some shops when we are in
print. The earlier concert returns here to its two-CD format with the missing item, *Bei uns zu Haus,*
restored. The separate issues remain in the catalogue.

'1989 New Year Concert in Vienna': Overture: *Die Fledermaus.* Csárdás: *Ritter Pásmán.* Polkas:
Bauern; Eljen a Magyar!; Im Krapfenwald'l; Pizzicato (with Josef). Waltzes: *Accelerationen; An der
schönen blauen Donau; Frühlingsstimmen; Künstlerleben.* Josef STRAUSS: Polkas: *Jockey; Die Libelle;
Moulinet; Plappermäulchen.* Johann STRAUSS, Snr: *Radetzky march.*
**(*) Sony/CBS CD 45938 [id.]. VPO, Carlos Kleiber.

In style this is very similar to Kleiber's controversial complete recording of *Fledermaus,* for though he
allows all the rhythmic flexibility a traditionalist could want – and sometimes more – his pursuit of
knife-edged precision prevents the results from sounding quite relaxed enough, with the Viennese lilt
in the waltzes analysed to the last micro-second instead of just being played as a dance. In the
delicious polka, *Im Krapfenwald'l,* the cheeky cuckoo-calls which comically punctuate the main theme
are made to sound beautiful rather than rustic, and fun is muted elsewhere too. But in one or two
numbers Kleiber really lets rip, as in the Hungarian polka, *Eljen a Magyar!* ('Hail to Hungary!'), and
in the *Ritter Pásmán Csárdás.* This concert now reappears on a single full-price disc, playing for 76
minutes and omitting just one waltz, *Bei uns zu Haus.* Not everyone responds positively to Kleiber's
rather precise style with Viennese rhythms, but this is still an enjoyably spontaneous concert, made
the more attractive by the warm, full recording, with the presence of the audience nicely implied
without getting in the way.

'1990 New Year Concert': Einzugsmarsch (from *Der Zigeunerbaron*). Polkas: *Explosionen; Im Sturmschritt; Tritsch-tratsch*. Waltzes: *An der schönen blauen Donau; Donauweibchen; G'schichten aus dem Wienerwald; Wiener Blut*. Josef STRAUSS: Polkas: *Eingesendet; Die Emancipitre; Sport; Sympathie*. Johann STRAUSS Snr: *Indianer galop. Radetzky march.*
*** Sony Dig. SK 45808. [id.]. VPO, Zubin Mehta.

A worthy successor to Karajan's wonderful 1987 concert, not *quite* its equal but offering a programme of mainly novelties. This is Mehta's finest record for years; he conjures a magical response from the VPO and is just as persuasive in the famous waltzes. In the *Blue Danube* he hardly needs forgiveness for indulging himself (as Karajan sometimes did, only slightly more so) with a gentle, rather mannered reprise of one of the subsidiary melodies. But elsewhere his easy warmth and relaxed rhythmic style are beyond criticism. The recording is superb.

'1992 New Year Concert': Overture: *Der Zigeunerbaron*. Polkas: *Neue pizzicato; Stadt und Land; Tritsch-Tratsch; Unter Donner und Blitz; Vergnügungszug*. Waltzes: *An der schönen blauen Donau; Tausend und eine Nacht. Persischer march.* J. STRAUSS Snr: *Radetsky march.* JOSEPH STRAUSS: Waltzes: *Dorfschwalben aus Österreich; Sphärenklänge* (with NICOLAI: Overture: *The Merry Wives of Windsor*).
☞ **(*) Sony Dig. SK 48376 [id.]. VPO, Carlos Kleiber.

As with his earlier (1989) concert, Kleiber is very precise, and occasionally one wishes for a degree more relaxation. He opens his programme with a beautifully played account of Nicolai's *Merry Wives of Windsor overture*, and the introductions for *1001 Nights* and Josef's so-called *'Village swallows'* and *'Music of the spheres'* are nicely managed and attractively atmospheric. There is plenty of dash in the polkas; but at times elsewhere rubato seems just a trifle calculated, especially so in the *Blue Danube*. The playing and recording are well up to standard, and admirers of the Kleiber Strauss style, which certainly does not lack vitality, will be well pleased. All Straussians will find much to enjoy here.

'1994 New Year's Day Concert': *Caroussel-Marsch; Lieder-Quadrille, nach beliebten Motiven*. Polkas: *Ein Herr und ein Sinn; Enfantillage; Luzifer*. Waltzes: *Accelerationen; An der schönen blauen Donau; G'schichten aus dem Wienerwald; Die Fledermaus: Csárdás*. Johann STRAUSS Snr: *Radetzky march.* Josef STRAUSS: Polkas: *Aus der Ferne; Feuerfest!; Ohne Sorgen*. Eduard STRAUSS: *Mit Chic polka.* with LANNER: *Die Schönbrunner* (waltz).
☞ *** Sony Dig. SK 46694 [id.]. VPO, Lorin Maazel.

Lorin Maazel is not a conductor who by nature radiates fun, but here he makes the 1994 New Year concert one of the most effervescent ever, relaxing in a jovial way that one would hardly have expected, even remembering his earlier appearances at New Year concerts. His triumph is crowned when in *Tales from the Vienna Woods* he takes up the violin and with Werner Hink from the orchestra plays the slinky duet sections at the beginning and end in an *echt*-Viennese manner. Curiously, the disc fails to mention Maazel's other extra contribution: in the quick polka by Josef Strauss, *Ohne Sorgen* ('Without a care'), Maazel – using an instrument at his elbow, as the television relay revealed – provides decorations on the glockenspiel. Aptly the recording highlights the glockenspiel notes. That polka is just one of the sparkling rarities in the collection – ten of them out of a total of 15 items. The *Schönbrunner waltz* of Joseph Lanner is a first-ever recording, light and charming if not specially characterful, but other rare delights include the French polka *Feuerfest* by Josef Strauss with its clanging hammers and anvils, the *Lucifer polka* with bangs on the drum, and the galumphing *Caroussel march*, both by Johann Strauss Junior. Applause has been tactfully edited, but some may find there is still too much.

Overture: *Die Fledermaus*. Polkas: *Annen; Auf der Jagd; Explosionen*. Waltzes: *Frühlingsstimmen; Rosen aus dem Süden; Wein, Weib und Gesang; Windsor echoes*. Josef STRAUSS: *Feuerfest polka* (with ZIEHRER: *Kissing polka*).
(B) *** Pickwick PCD 902; *CIMPC 902* [id.]. LSO, Georgiadis.

Entitled *'An Evening in Vienna'*, the performances have nevertheless a British flavour – which is not to say that there is any lack of lilt or beguiling warmth in the waltzes; they are beautifully done, while the polkas all go with an infectious swing. This is very enjoyable and is John Georgiadis's best record to date.

Pappacoda polka; Der lustige Kreig (quadrille); *Klug Gretelein* (waltz). Josef STRAUSS: *Defilir marsch;* Polkas: *Farewell; For ever.* Eduard STRAUSS: *Weyprecht-Payer marsch;* Polkas: *Mädchenlaune; Saat und Ernte;* Waltzes: *Die Abonnenten; Blüthenkranz Johann Strauss'scher.* J. STRAUSS III (son of Eduard): *Schlau-Schlau polka.*
*** Chan. Dig. CHAN 8527; *LBTD 016*. Johann Strauss O of V., Rothstein, with M. Hill-Smith.

This programme is admirably chosen to include unfamiliar music which deserves recording; indeed, both the *Klug Gretelein waltz*, which opens with some delectable scoring for woodwind and harp and has an idiomatic vocal contribution from Marilyn Hill-Smith, and *Die Abonnenten* (by Eduard) are very attractive waltzes. *Blüthenkranz Johann Strauss'scher*, as its title suggests, makes a pot-pourri of some of Johann's most famous melodies. The polkas are a consistent delight, played wonderfully infectiously; indeed, above all this is a cheerful concert, designed to raise the spirits; the CD sound sparkles.

Perpetuum mobile. Polkas: *Annen; Auf der Jagd; Pizzicato* (with Josef); *Tritsch-Tratsch; Unter Donner und Blitz.* Waltzes: *An der schönen blauen Donau; G'schichten aus dem Wienerwald; Kaiser; Wiener Blut.* Josef STRAUSS: *Delirien waltz.*
☞ (M) **(*) DG 437 255-2 [id.]. BPO, Karajan.

The Karajan Strauss collections come and go. Here is a selection taken from two analogue LPs, made in 1966 and 1969 respectively. The performances have characteristic flair and the playing of the Berlin Philharmonic has much ardour as well as subtlety, with the four great waltzes of Johann II all finely done (the *Emperor* has a particularly engaging closing section) and the polkas wonderfully vivacious. The current remastering is satisfactory, brightly lit, but with the Jesus-Christus Kirche providing ambient fullness.

Polka: *Unter Donner und Blitz.* Waltzes: *An der schönen blauen Donau; Kaiser; Künstlerleben; Morgenblätter; Rosen aus dem Süden; Schatz; Wiener Blut.* Josef STRAUSS: Waltzes: *Dorfschwalben aus Osterreich; Mein Lebenslauf ist Lieb' und Lust.*
(M) *** BMG/RCA GD 60177 [60177-2-RG]. Chicago SO, Reiner.

Reiner's collection was recorded in 1957 and 1960, and the sound is voluptuous with the warmth of the Chicago Hall ambience. The performances are memorable for their lilting zest and the sumptuous richness of the Chicago strings, although the *Thunder and lightning polka* has an unforgettably explosive exuberance.

VOCAL MUSIC

Vocal waltzes

(i) *Auf's Korn! Bundesschützen-Marsch.* (ii) *Hoch Osterreich! Marsch.* Polkas: (i) *Burschenwanderung (polka française); 's gibt nur a Kaiserstadt! 's gibt nur ein Wien!;* (ii) *Sängerslust.* Waltzes: *An der schönen blauen Donau;* (i) *Bei uns z'Haus;* (ii) *Gross-Wien;* (i) *Myrthenblüthen;* (ii) *Neu-Wien; Wein, weib und gesang!.*
☞ **(*) Marco Polo Dig. 8.223250-2. Wiener Männergesangverein, Czecho-Slovak RSO (Bratislava), (i) Gerhard Track; (ii) Johannes Wildner.

A most enjoyable collection. Wildner is occasionally a bit strong with the beat, but the *Blue Danube* with chorus is much more enjoyable than his performance with orchestra alone. The singers are Viennese, so they have a natural lilt, and the recording has an ideal ambience.

OPERA

Die Fledermaus (complete).
*** Ph. Dig. 432 157-2 (2) [id.]. Kiri Te Kanawa, Gruberová, Leech, Wolfgang Brendel, Bär, Fassbaender, Göttling, Krause, Wendler, Schenk, V. State Op. Ch., VPO, Previn.
(M) (***) EMI mono CHS7 69531-2 (2) [Ang. CDHB 69531]. Schwarzkopf, Streich, Gedda, Krebs, Kunz, Christ, Philh. Ch. & O, Karajan.

André Previn here produces an enjoyably idiomatic account of Strauss's masterpiece, one which consistently conveys the work's exuberant high spirits. Dame Kiri Te Kanawa's portrait of Rosalinde brings not only gloriously firm, golden sound but also vocal acting with star quality. Brigitte Fassbaender is the most dominant Prince Orlofsky on disc. Singing with a tangy richness and firmness, she emerges as the genuine focus of the party scene. Edita Gruberová is a sparkling, characterful and full-voiced Adèle; Wolfgang Brendel as Eisenstein and Olaf Bär as Dr Falke both sing very well indeed, though their voices sound too alike. Richard Leech as Alfred provides heady tone and a hint of parody. Tom Krause makes a splendid Frank, the more characterful for no longer sounding young. Anton Wendler as Dr Blind and Otto Schenk as Frosch the jailer give vintage Viennese performances, with Frosch's cavortings well tailored and not too extended.

This now goes to the top of the list of latterday *Fledermaus* recordings, though with one serious reservation. The Philips production in Act II adds a layer of crowd noise as background throughout the Party scene, even during Orlofsky's solos. Strauss's gentler moments are then seriously undermined by the sludge of distant chatter and laughter, as in the lovely chorus *Bruderlein und Schwesterlein*, yearningly done. Otherwise the recorded sound is superb, with brilliance and bite alongside warmth and bloom, both immediate and well balanced. Like Kleiber on DG, Previn opts for the *Thunder and lightning polka* instead of the ballet.

The mono recording of Karajan's 1955 version has great freshness and clarity, along with the polish which for many will make it a first favourite. Schwarzkopf makes an enchanting Rosalinde, not just in the imagination and sparkle of her singing but also in the snatches of spoken dialogue (never too long) which leaven the entertainment. As Adèle, Rita Streich produces her most dazzling coloratura; Gedda and Krebs are beautifully contrasted in their tenor tone, and Erich Kunz gives a vintage performance as Falke. The original recording, crisply focused, has been given a brighter edge but otherwise left unmolested.

Die Fledermaus: highlights.
☞ *** Ph. Dig. 438 503-2 [id.] (from above recording, with Te Kanawa, Gruberová; cond. Previn).

The 62-minute selection from the exuberantly idiomatic Previn is the only choice for those wanting a highlights disc, even if it is considerably less generous than some highlights discs.

Strauss, Richard (1864–1949)

An Alpine Symphony, Op. 64.
☞ *** DG Gold Dig. 439 017-2 [id.]. BPO, Karajan.
*** Ph. Dig. 416 156-2 [id.]. Concg. O, Haitink.

An Alpine Symphony; Die Frau ohne Schatten: symphonic fantasy.
☞ *(*) Erato/Warner Dig. 2292 45997-2 [id.]. Chicago SO, Barenboim.

An Alpine Symphony; Don Juan, Op. 20.
*** Decca Dig. 421 815-2. San Francisco SO, Blomstedt.

Blomstedt's *Alpine Symphony* is superbly shaped and has that rare quality of relating part to whole in a way that totally convinces. He gets scrupulously attentive playing from the San Francisco orchestra and a rich, well-detailed Decca recording.

This DG reissue in the Karajan Gold series is one of the most remarkable in its improvement of the sound over the original CD issue. The acoustic boundaries of the sound seem to have expanded, and the huge dynamic expansion in the description of *Sunrise* is as thrilling as the echoing horns which follow *The Ascent*. Detail is not analytically clear, but the sumptuous body of tone created by the orchestra is glorious, with the violins glowing and soaring as they enter the forest. Undoubtedly this performance is in the highest flight, wonderfully spacious and beautifully shaped – the closing *Night* sequence is very touching – and played with the utmost virtuosity. There is no finer version.

Haitink's account on Philips is a splendid affair, a very natural-sounding recording and strongly characterized throughout. The perspective is excellent, and there is plenty of atmosphere, particularly in the episode of the calm before the storm. Above all, the architecture of the work as a whole is impressively laid out and the orchestral playing is magnificent. This can hold its own with the best.

These days when an abundance of alternatives is on offer, the view from the Alpine heights has to be pretty spectacular to command attention. Karajan, Kempe, Haitink, Solti and Previn have all made the ascent with very distinguished companions, and by their side Barenboim and his Chicago forces have little new to report. Indeed he does not even get the kind of high orchestral voltage or sense of atmosphere which he can often be counted on to command. By the side of Karajan, his grip is loose, and in comparison with Kempe there is little of the *echt*-Straussian atmosphere. Not even the inducement of a bonus in the form of the orchestral fantasy on themes from *Die Frau ohne Schatten* greatly enhances this disc's claims for a high star rating among the best.

(i) *Alpine Symphony, Op. 64;* (ii) *Der Rosenkavalier* (orchestral suite for silent film).
☞ (***) EMI mono CDC7 54610-2 [id.]. (i) Bav. State O; (ii) augmented L. Tivoli O; composer.

Strauss's 1941 account of the *Alpine Symphony* has been available in various LP formats, but it has never sounded better than it does in this excellent transfer. For all its sonic limitations, the performance still conveys lots of atmosphere, and although one needs the benefit of modern stereo sound to do this sumptuous score full justice Strauss's own reading still has special claims.

An Alpine Symphony, Op. 64; Aus Italien, Op. 16; Dance suite from pieces by François Couperin; (i) *Don Quixote, Op. 35. Macbeth, Op. 23; Metamorphosen for 23 solo strings.*
☞ (M) *** CMS7 64350-2 (3). (i) Paul Tortelier; Dresden State O, Kempe.

This is the third of the three boxes of Richard Strauss's orchestral and concertante music, recorded during the first half of the 1970s and previously issued, similarly grouped, in the LP era, although with the works laid out differently. The CD transfers retain the opulence and warmth of those original LPs; inner detail is not always absolutely clean, but this is a richly satisfying sound for the music of Strauss. The Dresden orchestra is a magnificent body and the strings produce gloriously sumptuous tone, which is strikingly in evidence in *Metamorphosen*. Rudolf Kempe had recorded the *Alpine Symphony* before with the RPO, and there is little to choose between the two so far as interpretation is concerned: he brings a glowing warmth to this score. His *Aus Italien* is more convincing than any previous version: the sound with its finely judged perspective is again a decisive factor here. He gives a most musical account of the delightful *Dance suite* based on Couperin keyboard pieces, although here some might wish for more transparent textures. Perhaps one could also quarrel with the balance in *Don Quixote*, which gives Tortelier exaggerated prominence and obscures some detail. The performance, however, is another matter and must rank with the best available. *Macbeth* also is convincing, and well paced.

(i) *An Alpine Symphony, Op. 64;* (ii) *Also sprach Zarathustra, Op. 30; Don Juan, Op. 20;* (iii) *Ein Heldenleben, Op. 40;* (ii) *Till Eulenspiegel, Op. 28.*
☞ (B) *** Double Decca 440 618-2 (2) [id.]. (i) Bav. RSO; (ii) Chicago SO; (iii) VPO; Solti.

The Bavarian Radio Orchestra recorded in the Herculessal in Munich could hardly sound more opulent in the *Alpine Symphony*, with brass of striking richness. That warmth of sound and the superb quality of the 1979 analogue recording tend to counterbalance Solti's generally fast tempi. Many of them are in principle too fast, but with such sympathetic and committed playing in such a setting the results are warm rather than frenetic. The performances of *Also sprach Zarathustra, Don Juan* and *Till Eulenspiegel* come from analogue originals, made in Chicago a few years earlier. Solti is ripely expansive in *Zarathustra*, and throughout all three symphonic poems there is the most glorious playing from the Chicago orchestra in peak form. This is Solti at his strongest, with the most Germanic of American orchestras responding as to the manner born. The transfer to CD is impressive, even if the finest digital versions aerate the textures more. For *Ein Heldenleben* Solti went (in 1977–8) to Vienna, and this is another fast-moving performance, tense to the point of fierceness in the opening tutti and elsewhere. It underlines the urgency rather than the opulence of the writing and, though many Straussians will prefer a warmer, more relaxed view, Solti finds justification in a superb account of the final coda after the fulfilment theme, where in touching simplicity he finds complete relaxation at last, helped by the exquisite playing of the Vienna Philharmonic concertmaster, Rainer Küchl. The Decca recording is formidably wide-ranging to match this high-powered performance and, as with the rest of the programme, the transfers to CD are full-bodied and vividly detailed.

Also sprach Zarathustra, Op. 30; Le bourgeois gentilhomme (suite of incidental music for Molière's play), *Op. 60;* (i) *Violin concerto in D min., Op. 8. Death and transfiguration, Op. 24; Josephslegende, Op. 63; Schlagobers* (waltz), *Op. 70; Sinfonia domestica, Op. 53; Der Rosenkavalier: Waltz sequence; Salome: Dance of the 7 veils.*
☞ (M) *** EMI CMS7 64346-2 (3). (i) Ulf Hoelscher; Dresden State O, Kempe.

The first record in Volume 2 of the Kempe/Strauss series contains the *Violin concerto* and the *Sinfonia domestica*, and we must hope that EMI will consider issuing it separately. Ulf Hoelscher's eloquent account of this attractive early concerto is more than welcome, as is the *Sinfonia domestica*. Kempe's version of this work is no less desirable than Karajan's, a little more relaxed without being in any way less masterly. Indeed Kempe's stature as a Strauss conductor is challenged only by Karajan. His *Also sprach Zarathustra* is completely free of the sensationalism that marks so many newer performances. *Josephslegende*, however, will call for tolerance even in this committed version; Strauss's inspiration is thin here and his craftsmanship runs away with him. The rest of the programme is well worth having, particularly *Le bourgeoise gentilhomme*. Recording and CD transfers are well up to standard.

Also sprach Zarathustra, Op. 30; Le bourgeois gentilhomme: Suite, Op. 60. Der Rosenkavalier: Waltzes.
(M) *** BMG/RCA 09026 60930-2 [60930-2]. Chicago SO, Reiner.

Reiner's 1954 account of *Also sprach Zarathustra* with its impressive feeling of space is a wonderful performance that ranks alongside the very best ever committed to disc. The same goes for the suite from *Le bourgeois gentilhomme* – possibly the finest ever, and sounding marvellously fresh considering its date (1956). Incandescent music-making, transferred to CD with stunning success.

(i) *Also sprach Zarathustra, Op. 30;* (ii) *Aus Italien: excerpt: On the shores of Sorrento;* (iii) *Death and transfiguration;* (iv) *Don Quixote;* (v) *Ein Heldenleben.*
(M) (***) BMG/RCA mono 09026 60929-2 (2) [60929-2]. (i) Boston SO, Koussevitzky; (ii) Chicago SO, Stock; (iii) Phd. O, Stokowski; (iv) Wallenstein, NYPO, Beecham; (v) NYPO, Mengelberg.

To have *Ein Heldenleben* conducted by its dedicatee seems almost miraculous, recorded in 1928 – only 30 years after its composition – in what was exceptionally good quality for the period. And what a performance it is, and what playing the New York Orchestra could produce in those days! Koussevitzky's superb (1935) Boston account of *Also sprach Zarathustra* was for long the only version in the catalogue. Beecham's New York account of *Don Quixote* with Alfred Wallenstein as soloist, made in 1932 (the year before Strauss's own with Mainardi), is another reading of enormous character (though the transfer has a slightly more strident top than we remember from the LP reissue). Stokowski's *Death and transfiguration* shows the Philadelphia Orchestra with similar opulence of tone and virtuosity.

Also sprach Zarathustra; Death and transfiguration, Op. 24; Don Juan, Op. 20.
☞ *** DG Gold Dig. 439 016-2 [id.]. BPO, Karajan.
*** Telarc Dig. CD 80167 [id.]. VPO, Previn.

Also sprach Zarathustra; Don Juan.
*** Denon Dig. CO 2259 [id.]. Dresden State O, Blomstedt.

As a performance the 1983 Karajan *Also sprach Zarathustra* (coupled with an exciting account of *Don Juan*) will be hard to beat and could very well be first choice. The playing of the Berlin Philharmonic is as glorious as ever; its virtuosity can be taken for granted, along with its sumptuous tonal refinement. And the newly remastered CD in the Karajan Gold series offers an improvement to sound that was already approaching the demonstration class. It has great dynamic range and presence, particularly at the extreme bass and treble, and the massed violins produce wonderfully radiant textures, as in the section marked *Von der grossen Sehnsucht* ('of the great longing'). The soaring main theme of *Don Juan* is hardly less sumptuous and the playing is electrifying in its energy. In Strauss, Karajan has no peer and this is one of his finest records from the early 1980s.

As a recording, the Denon CD could hardly be more impressive. The sound is rich, the acoustic is resonant but never clouds detail, and the range and presence are really quite stunning. The performance has all the sense of architecture and authority we have come to expect from Blomstedt, whose Strauss is always distinctive. The Denon disc also contains a very good *Don Juan*.

Previn draws magnificent playing from the Vienna Philharmonic in powerful, red-blooded readings of both symphonic poems, and the recording is among Telarc's finest. Strongly recommended for anyone wanting this particular coupling, and enjoying voluptuous sound-quality.

(i) *Also sprach Zarathustra; Death and transfiguration; Don Juan; Ein Heldenleben; Till Eulenspiegel;* (ii) *Der Rosenkavalier: Waltz sequence.*
☞ (B) *** Ph. Duo Dig./Analogue 442 281-2 (2) [id.]. Concg. O, (i) Haitink; (ii) Jochum.

We have long praised the Haitink/Concertgebouw triptych of *Death and transfiguration, Don Juan* and *Till Eulenspiegel*, which still takes the palm among current recordings of this most popular coupling. The Philips digital recording is not analytical, but the ambient bloom of the Concertgebouw is admirably suited to Strauss's rich orchestral tapestries and detail is naturally defined. Haitink's performances are undoubtedly distinguished, superbly played, persuasively and subtly characterized. He finds added nobility in *Death and transfiguration*, while there is no lack of swagger in the accounts of both the *Don* and *Till*. The easy brilliance of the orchestral playing is complemented by the natural spontaneity of Haitink's readings, seamless in the transition between narrative events, without loss of the music's picaresque or robust qualities. Haitink's (1974) *Also sprach Zarathustra* was often spoken of in the same breath as Karajan's analogue alternative, issued in the same year. There is no lack of ardour from the Concertgebouw players and the reading has breadth and nobility. The (1970) *Ein*

Heldenleben is also one of Haitink's finest records. He gives just the sort of performance, brilliant and swaggering but utterly without bombast, which will delight those who normally resist this rich and expansive work. With a direct and fresh manner that yet conveys consistent urgency, he makes even such fine rival versions as Karajan's 1959 recording sound just a little lightweight. In the culminating fulfilment theme, a gently lyrical 6/8, Haitink finds a raptness in restraint, a hint of agony within joy, that links the passage directly to the great Trio from *Der Rosenkavalier*. The Philips sound here is admirably faithful and skilfully remastered. For good measure Jochum's *Waltz sequence* from that very opera has been added, though here the recording, though good for its age (the early 1960s), has not quite the opulence of the Haitink recordings. An indispensable set nevertheless, and one of the finest of all the Duo bargains.

(i) *Also sprach Zarathustra;* (ii) *Don Juan; Till Eulenspiegel.*
(M) *** Collins Dig. 3002-2 [id.]. LSO, Jacek Kaspszyk.
(M) *** EMI Dig. CDD7 64106-2 [id.]. (i) Phd. O, Ormandy; (ii) VPO, André Previn.
☞ (B) *(**) DG 439 419-2 [id.]. BPO, Karl Boehm.

The Collins disc has the advantage of the very finest modern digital recording, with the orchestra set back naturally in a concert-hall acoustic. Kaspszyk's LSO account has fine breadth and momentum, with the LSO consistently on their toes, and with a memorable contribution from the leader, John Georgiadis, in the violin solos. The strings play with affecting sensuality, and this applies to *Don Juan* too, a performance which combines tenderness and passion with the excitement of the chase. *Till* is portrayed with an enjoyably genial vitality.

Ormandy's 1979 *Also sprach Zarathustra* is one of his very finest records. The performance unleashes enormous ardour and the superb playing of the Philadelphia Orchestra, especially the strings, is consistently gripping in its extrovert passion. This can be spoken of in the same breath as the Karajan versions, although its emotional feeling is more unbridled. The early recording was made in the Old Met., Philadelphia; on the original LP it was excessively brightly lit, but the balance has been improved vastly and there is now no want of opulence. Previn's *Don Juan* and *Till Eulenspiegel* were made a year later in the Musikverein; they are relatively direct, strong and urgent, rather than affectionate, refreshing rather than idiomatic. The sound is full and bright but not as open and brilliant as the Philadelphia recording. This has just been withdrawn as we go to press.

Boehm was a fine Straussian, but *Also sprach Zarathustra* is very early stereo (1958) and, for all the ardour of the Berlin Philharmonic, the violins are made to sound thin above the stave, although the Jesus-Christus-Kirche provides plenty of ambient warmth. Boehm's *Don Juan* and *Till* were recorded five years later; the sound is fuller and the orchestral playing is marvellous. *Don Juan* brings glorious leaping strings and rich thrusting horns, and Boehm provides an attractive German peasant-based characterization of *Till*.

Also sprach Zarathustra, Op. 30; (i) *Don Quixote, Op. 35.*
(M) **(*) Sony SBK 47656 [id.]. Phd. O, Ormandy; (i) with Lorne Munroe.

Ormandy's 1963 Sony *Also sprach Zarathustra*, if not as overwhelming as the later, EMI version (see above), has much virtuoso orchestral playing to commend it and many felicities of characterization. His (1961) *Don Quixote* will also give considerable pleasure. There is some marvellous orchestral playing and the two soloists play splendidly with plenty of character but without the 'star soloist' approach favoured by so many record companies. A very competitive coupling.

Also sprach Zarathustra, Op. 30; Ein Heldenleben.
☞ ❀ (M) *** BMG/RCA 09026 61494-2 [id.]. Chicago SO, Fritz Reiner.

These were the first stereo sessions the RCA engineers arranged with Fritz Reiner, after the company had taken over the Chicago orchestra's recording contract from Mercury. Legend has it that the RCA staff asked orchestral members where the Mercury team had placed their microphones, and it is surely no accident that RCA coined the logo, 'Living stereo', to match the 'Living presence' trademark of the smaller company. It must be said – to their enormous credit – that the RCA recording team 'got it right' from the very beginning and the series of records they made with Reiner and his players in Orchestra Hall remain a technical peak in the history of stereo recording.

For some collectors (certainly for R. L.) Reiner's 1954 account of *Also sprach Zarathustra* was their introduction to stereo and the impressive feeling of space it conveyed. Later reissues have improved on its definition but none has done so with the stunning success of the present transfer. Indeed, although modern digital techniques eradicate background hiss, they rarely have music-making as incandescent as this to convey. A wonderful performance that ranks alongside the very best ever committed to disc. *Ein Heldenleben* shows Reiner in equally splendid form. There have been more incisive, more spectacular and more romantic performances, and Ormandy's thrilling Philadelphia version, made six years later, should not be forgotten (see below). But Reiner achieves an admirable balance and whatever he does is convincing. Another conductor might sound mannered if (as Reiner does) he changed speed so uninhibitedly just after the beginning of the recapitulation. If anything, the recording sounds even better than *Also sprach* and the warm acoustics of Orchestra Hall help convey Reiner's humanity in the closing pages of the work.

Also sprach Zarathustra; Till Eulenspiegel; Salome: Salome's dance.
(M) *** DG 415 853-2; *415 853-4* [id.]. BPO, Karajan.

Karajan's 1974 DG analogue version of *Also sprach Zarathustra* is coupled with his vividly characterized performance of *Till Eulenspiegel* plus his powerfully voluptuous account of *Salome's dance*. The Berlin Philharmonic plays with great fervour (the timpani strokes at the very opening are quite riveting) and creates characteristic body of tone in the strings, although the digital remastering has thrown a much brighter light on the violins.

Also sprach Zarathustra, Op. 30; Der Rosenkavalier: Waltz sequence. Salome: Salome's dance of the 7 veils.
☞ (BB) ** Naxos Dig. 8.550182; *4.550182* [id.]. Slovak PO, Košler.

Košler's disc of *Also sprach Zarathustra* is no challenge to Karajan or Kempe; nor is the Slovak Philharmonic as responsive an instrument as the Berlin or Dresden orchestras. But at so modest an outlay it fills a gap at the bargain end of the spectrum and, given the more than adequate recorded sound, will find its welcome among collectors with modest means. All the same it is not a great performance.

Aus Italien, Op. 16; Die Liebe der Danae (symphonic fragment); *Der Rosenkavalier: waltz sequence No. 2.*
(BB) *** Naxos Dig. 8.550342 [id.]. Slovak PO, Zdenék Košler.

Aus Italien, Op. 16; (i) Songs: *Befreit; Meine Auge; Das Rosenband; Winterweihe.*
*** Chan. Dig. CHAN 8744; *ABTD 1383* [id.]. SNO, Järvi; (i) with Felicity Lott.

Aus Italien is early Strauss, but it does have marvellous moments, including the beautiful slow movement. Järvi takes a spacious view of the work and his recorded sound is full-bodied, with a natural perspective, and there is plenty of warmth. The Scottish orchestra seems at home in the score, giving the finale a certain Celtic lilt. The four songs, sung simply and eloquently by Felicity Lott, make an agreeable postlude.

On Naxos, a very well-recorded and vividly detailed account of *Aus Italien* with an excellent sense of presence. The orchestra plays very well for Zdenék Košler both here and in the ten-minute symphonic fragment Clemens Krauss made from *Die Liebe der Danae* and in the *Rosenkavalier* waltz sequence. The Slovak Philharmonic is a highly responsive body, with cultured strings and wind departments and, given the quality of the recorded sound, this represents a real bargain.

Le bourgeois gentilhomme (incidental music); *Divertimento* (after Couperin), *Op. 86.*
☞ *** DG Dig. 435 871-2 [id.]. Orpheus CO.

The Orpheus Chamber Orchestra continue to add to their laurels and enhance their already high reputation in these superbly vital and sensitive accounts. Straussians will have (or want) the Clemens Krauss, Beecham and Reiner old records of *Le bourgeois gentilhomme*, but of modern accounts this version is arguably unsurpassed – and all without the ministrations of a maestro. The performance of the *Divertimento* after Couperin delights, and the recordings do full justice to them.

Le bourgeois gentilhomme (suite), *Op. 60:* excerpts; (i) *Don Quixote, Op. 35.*
(M) (***) EMI mono CDH7 63106-2. (i) Tortelier; RPO, Beecham.

Tortelier and Beecham recorded their *Don Quixote* in 1947. The playing is pretty electrifying, with the newly formed RPO on their best form. Tortelier here plays for all the world as if his life depended on it. There is great delicacy in *Le bourgeois gentilhomme* and some delicious playing from the RPO's then leader, Oscar Lampe. Alas, this has just been withdrawn by EMI.

(i) *Burleske in D min. for piano and orchestra.* (ii) *Duet-concertino for clarinet, bassoon and strings.* (iii) *Horn concertos Nos. 1–2.* (iv) *Oboe concerto in D. Don Juan, Op. 20; Ein Heldenleben, Op. 40.* (v) *Panathenäenzug for piano (left hand) and orchestra; Parergon to Sinfonia domestica for piano (left hand) and orchestra. Till Eulenspiegel, Op. 28.*
☞ (M) *** EMI CMS7 64342-2 (3). (i) Malcolm Frager; (ii) Manfred Weise, Wolfgang Liebscher; (iii) Peter Damm; (iv) Manfred Clement; (v) Peter Rösel; Dresden State O, Kempe.

Volume 1 of the Kempe/EMI Strauss series includes all the major concertante works except, irritatingly, the *Violin concerto*. This box would have had an even stronger appeal to collectors if the CD including the latter work plus the *Sinfonia domestica* (in Volume 2) had been included here instead of the tone-poems. Most collectors will already have a *Don Juan*, which is perhaps the least electrifying of Kempe's symphonic poems, and the same surely applies to *Till Eulenspiegel*, although it is an excellent performance. The *Burleske* is well worth having (it is beautifully recorded) and there are no satisfactory alternative versions of the *Parergon* to the *Sinfonia domestica* or the *Panathenäen-zug*, both written for the one-armed pianist, Paul Wittgenstein, and played impressively here. Peter Damm's performances of the *Horn concertos* are second to none and although his use of a (judicious) degree of vibrato may be a drawback for some ears, his tone is gloriously rich. Similarly, while Manfred Clement's *Oboe concerto* is a sensitive reading, his creamily full timbre may not appeal to those brought up on Goossens. There can be no reservations whatsoever about the *Duet concertino*, where the sounds from bassoon and clarinet are beguilingly succulent, while the intertwining of both wind soloists with the dancing orchestral violins of the finale has an irresistible, genial finesse. Throughout, the superb playing of the Dresden orchestra under Kempe adds an extra dimension to the music-making.

Burleske for piano and orchestra.
☞ (M) *(**) Sony SBK 53262 [id.]. Rudolf Serkin, Phd. O, Ormandy – BRAHMS: *Piano concerto No. 2.* **(*)

Burleske, Op. 11; Parergon, Op. 73; Stimmungsbilder, Op. 9.
**(*) Ara. Dig. Z 6567 [id.]. Ian Hobson, Philh. O, Del Mar.

Ian Hobson's account of the *D minor Burleske*, on its own terms, is eminently satisfactory, and he is well supported by Norman Del Mar and the Philharmonia, and is well recorded. The *Parergon* for left hand is again very well played. The *Stimmungsbilder* are early, rather Schumannesque pieces, written in 1884: Hobson gives a rather touching account of *Träumerei*, and though one can imagine a performance of the *Intermezzo* with greater charm, there is still much to admire here. Decent recording.

The Sony alternative is a generally excellent performance of what is still a comparative rarity on disc. Serkin plays with great brilliance, and the music's lyrical side – uncharacteristic but winning – is well understood. The current remastering is an improvement on the original, but the piano timbre is bright and somewhat clattery and the orchestral textures are made somewhat two-dimensional by the close microphones. Nevertheless this is an arresting performance.

(i) *Burleske for piano and orchestra;* (ii) *Don Quixote, Op. 35.*
☞ (M) *** BMG/RCA 09026 61796-2 [id.]. (i) Byron Janis; (ii) Janigro; Chicago SO, Fritz Reiner.

Even at full price Reiner's *Don Quixote* was a top recommendation. Reiner was a masterly Straussian and this 1959 version was one of the very finest of RCA's Chicago Hall recordings, offering a wide-spread and rich tapestry of sound, now with more refined detail in this remarkable new transfer (for instance, in Variation IX: *The ride through the air*). Antonio Janigro plays stylishly and with assurance; if he brings less intensity than Fournier to the ecstatic solo cadenza in Variation V, his contribution to the close of the work is distinguished. The *Burleske* makes a good encore, a product of the composer's early twenties, when his brilliance almost outshone his inventiveness. The brilliance is brought out well by Byron Janis, who also does not miss the music's witty or lyrical side. The recording is somewhat shallower than the tone-poem (though a considerable improvement on the original LP), but this helps to ensure that Strauss's youthful writing does not sound too sweet.

(i) *Burleske in D min.; Sinfonia domestica, Op. 53.*
*** Sony MK 42322 [id.]. (i) Barenboim; BPO, Mehta.

Mehta's version of the *Sinfonia domestica* is humane and relaxed and has great warmth; he certainly gets pretty sumptuous playing from the Berlin Philharmonic and has the advantage of very good sound. As its fill-up, it has the *Burleske* for piano and orchestra, given with great brilliance and panache by Daniel Barenboim in a beautifully balanced recording. A highly recommendable disc.

Horn concerto No. 1 in E flat, Op. 11.
☞ (M) *** EMI Dig. CDM7 64851-2 [id.]. Radovan Vlatković, ECO, Tate – MOZART: *Horn concertos Nos. 1–4 etc.* ***

Radovan Vlatković gives a superb account of the *First Concerto* which, although ripely romantic, has so much in common with the spirit of the Mozart concertos with which it is coupled. He is particularly good in the bold central episode of the *Andante* and caps his performance with an exhilaratingly nimble account of the finale. Tate accompanies admirably and the rich, natural, Abbey Road recording could hardly be better balanced.

Oboe concerto.
*** Nimbus Dig. NI 5330 [id.]. John Anderson, Philh. O, Simon Wright – FRANCAIX: *L'horloge de flore;* MARTINU: *Concerto.* ***
(M) *** BMG/RCA Dig. GD 87989 [7989-2-RG]. John de Lancie, CO, Max Wilcox – FRANCAIX: *L'horloge de flore* *** ⊛; IBERT: *Symphonie concertante.* ***
*** ASV Dig. CDCOE 808 [id.]. Douglas Boyd, COE, Berglund – MOZART: *Oboe concerto.* ***
☞ (BB) *(*) Virgin/EMI Dig. VJ7 59686-2 [id.]. Ray Still, Ac. of L., Stamp – BACH: *Oboe d'amore concerto* etc.; MARCELLO: *Concerto.* *(*)

In the summer of 1945 a young American musician/GI (who before the war had been an oboist with the Pittsburgh Symphony Orchestra) suggested to Strauss that he write an oboe concerto, and only months later the eighty-one-year-old composer produced his famous work. That same oboist, John de Lancie, recorded it in 1987, playing persuasively and with much finesse. The chamber accompaniment could ideally sound riper, but the balance is realistic and the sound real.

John Anderson, principal oboe of the Philharmonia, gives a ravishing acount of Strauss's delectable concerto, his timbre slightly riper than that of the concerto's dedicatee, and the Nimbus digital recording that bit more modern. But John de Lancie's account is very enjoyable too, so choice can rest with the coupling.

Douglas Boyd winningly brings out the happy glow of Strauss's inspiration of old age, and his warm oboe tone, less reedy than some, brings out the *Rosenkavalier* element in this lovely concerto. With warm, well-balanced recording, the gentle contrast of romantic and classical in this work is conveyed delectably.

Ray Still will be remembered by many collectors for his recording of the Mozart *C major Concerto* with Abbado and the Chicago Symphony of which he was (and presumably still is) a principal. He possesses a pure, chaste tone and impeccable technical address, but the autumnal qualities of the Strauss concerto elude him. The performance is just a little wanting in charm and warmth, though perhaps the rather stiff orchestral support does not help. Very good if slightly clinical recorded sound (the Bach and Marcello couplings have more bloom), but this is not a strong recommendation.

Oboe concerto (with alternative endings).
☞ (M) **(*) Pickwick MCD 59; *MCC 59* [id.]. Robin Canter, LSO, James Judd – VAUGHAN WILLIAMS: *Concerto* etc. ***

The great interest of Robin Carter's Pickwick recording is that it offers the finale with alternative endings. If the disc is played straightforwardly, it produces the familiar (revised) close to the work, but the listener can choose instead to programme the CD player to offer Strauss's first thoughts which were very slightly more succinct. The performance itself is enjoyable, although the very opening phrase is almost thrown away: a little more poise here would have been welcome. Otherwise both soloist and accompanists acquit themselves impressively, and the recording is bright and clear.

(i) *Oboe concerto in D.* (ii) *Serenade for wind, Op. 7; Sonatine No. 1 in F for wind (From an invalid's workshop); Suite in B flat for 13 wind instruments, Op. 4; Symphony for wind (The happy workshop).*
☞ (B) *** Ph. Duo 438 733-2 (2) [id.]. (i) Heinz Holliger, New Philh. O; (ii) Netherlands Wind Ens.; Edo de Waart.

The *Serenade* is beautifully played, warm and mellifluous, and so is the *Sonatina*, a late work, written while Strauss was recovering from an illness and appropriately subtitled. It is a richly scored piece, as thoroughly effective as one would expect from this master of wind writing. (The scoring is for double wind, a C clarinet, a corno di bassetto, bass clarinet and double bassoon – and marvellously sonorous it is.) The *B flat Suite* was written in 1884 but not published until 1911. Both these delightful pieces are given beautifully characterized accounts here, while the performance of the *Symphony for wind instruments* is crisp and alert. Throughout this music-making, the ear is struck by the Netherlanders' beautifully homogeneous tone, and their phrasing is splendidly alive. The recordings (made between 1970 and 1972) are full, well-detailed and truthful. As if this were not bounty enough, Holliger's earlier (1970) version of the *Oboe concerto* is thrown in for good measure. The playing is masterly and, if at times there is a hint of efficiency at the expense of ripeness in one of Strauss's most glowing 'Indian summer' works, it is still an assured, styish account and Edo de Waart accompanies persuasively. Again very good recording.

Violin concerto in D min., Op. 8.
*** ASV Dig. CDDCA 780 [id.]. Xue Wei, LPO, Glover – HEADINGTON: *Violin concerto.* *** ⊛

With Jane Glover and the LPO warmly sympathetic accompanists, Xue Wei makes a very persuasive case for this very early work of Strauss, with its echoes of Mendelssohn and Bruch.

Death and transfiguration, Op. 24.
(M) (***) BMG/RCA mono GD 60312. Phd. O, Toscanini – TCHAIKOVSKY: *Symphony No. 6.* (***)

Toscanini's characteristically taut control of tension goes with what was for him a more warmly expressive style than usual, thanks to the influence of the Philadelphia Orchestra. With the transfer giving good body to the limited sound, it is comparable with his equally intense reading of Tchaikovsky's *Pathétique* from the same period.

Death and transfiguration, Op. 24; Don Quixote, Op. 35.
☞ (M) (**(*)) BMG/RCA mono GD 60295 [60295-2-RG]. NBC SO, Toscanini.

By the side of Munch (see below), Toscanini's account of *Don Quixote*, also from 1953 and equally electrifying and masterly, with a superb soloist in Frank Miller, sounds a shade overdriven. It does not have quite the humanity or expressive flexibility of the Piatigorsky–Munch reading. However, his 1952 *Tod und Verklärung* is quite simply stunning.

Death and transfiguration; Metamorphosen for 23 solo strings.
⊛ *** DG Dig. 410 892-2 [id.]. BPO, Karajan.

Death and transfiguration; Metamorphosen for 23 solo strings; Till Eulenspiegel.
☞ *** Denon Dig. CO 73801 [id.]. Dresden State O, Blomstedt.

Death and transfiguration; Metamorphosen for 23 solo strings; (i) Drei Hymnen, Op. 71.
☞ *** Chan. Dig. CHAN 8734; *ABTD 1374* [id.]. SNO, Järvi; (i) with Felicity Lott.

Karajan's digital account of *Metamorphosen* has even greater emotional urgency than the 1971 record he made with the Berlin Philharmonic and there is a marginally quicker pulse. The sound is fractionally more forward and cleaner but still sounds sumptuous, and the account of *Death and transfiguration* is quite electrifying. It would be difficult to improve on this coupling by the greatest Strauss conductor of his day.

The cultured richness of the Dresden string-playing and Blomstedt's spaciously noble interpretation combine to place his performance of the *Metamorphosen* alongside Karajan's in distinction. *Death and transfiguration* is hardly less impressive; perhaps Karajan has the edge in sheer tension, but Blomstedt and his players give the work a special dignified ardour. *Till* is as captivatingly witty as you like, and the Denon sound is first class, gloriously full.

Järvi's coupling is also splendidly played and the body of Scottish orchestral tone and ensemble stands up remarkably well in comparison with its Berlin and Dresden competitors. Järvi brings a vibrant feeling to the *Metamorphosen*, and the Chandos recording without lacking sumptuousness allows slightly more detail to emerge than in Dresden. Certainly *Death and transfiguration* does not lack excitement and its apotheosis is deeply felt. The special attraction here is the inclusion of Felicity Lott's radiant account of the *Drei Hymnen* with their rapturous operatic feeling and, appropriately, including a reference to *Death and transfiguration*. However, this performance is also now available in a separate collection of Strauss orchestral songs (see below).

(i) Death and transfiguration; Sinfonia domestica, Op. 53; (ii) Salome's dance of the seven veils.
☞ ⊛ (B) *** Sony SBK 53511 [id.]. (i) Cleveland O, Szell; (ii) Phd. O, Ormandy.

All these performances have tremendous electricity and display a gripping orchestral bravura of a kind we seldom hear from these two great American orchestras in the present era. Szell's *Death and transfiguration* dates from 1957 and it is still unsurpassed. The opening has the most compelling atmosphere and the triumphant closing pages are the more effective for Szell's complete lack of indulgence. The recording has been vastly improved in the present transfer, with Cleveland's Masonic Temple providing a richly expansive ambience. The *Sinfonia domestica*, recorded in 1964, is less naturally balanced: the engineers seem more concerned with making every detail tell, but the performance brings such powerful orchestral playing, with glorious strings especially in the passionate *Adagio*, that criticism is disarmed: there is certainly no lack of body here. The widely expressed view that it is inconceivable to build a huge orchestral canvas, rich in a typically Straussian way, to describe putting the baby to bed and making the early-morning tea, as well as moments of human passion, is countered by the composer's characteristic comment: 'I do not understand why I should not write an autobiographical symphony – I find myself just as interesting as Napoleon or Alexander.'

The programme ends with an extraordinarily voluptuous Philadelphia performance of *Salome's dance*, which conjures up a whole frieze of naked female torsos. Ormandy directs with licentious abandon, and the orchestra responds with tremendous virtuosity and ardour, unashamedly going over the top at the climax. Here the sound is a bit glossy but, with playing like this, one can certainly adjust.

Don Juan; (i) *Don Quixote. Till Eulenspiegel.*
☞ *** Virgin/EMI Dig. VC7 59234-2 [id.]. (i) Isserlis; Minnesota O, De Waart.

The chief attraction on this issue is Steven Isserlis's firmly characterized account of *Don Quixote*. His is a strongly narrative yet poetic reading of the solo part and, although Edo de Waart and the Minnesota Orchestra may not succeed in producing the same refinement of texture as such Straussians as Reiner, Karajan and Kempe, the orchestral playing is generally very good indeed, both here and in the two other tone-poems. Although this may not displace old favourites in these oft-recorded works, it is recommendable, and the sound has reasonable depth and clarity.

Don Juan; Ein Heldenleben, Op. 40.
☞ (M) (*) Decca mono 425 993-2 [id.]. VPO, Clemens Krauss.

Clemens Krauss was a great Straussian, and these performances from the early 1950s have considerable stature. The Decca transfers are not, however, very successful. No doubt memory deceives, but surely these performances did not sound so scrawny or the strings quite so undernourished on LP. The performances are three-star all right, but the sound is not pleasant.

(i) *Don Juan, Op. 20;* (ii) *Ein Heldenleben, Op. 40;* (i) *Till Eulenspiegel, Op. 28.*
☞ (M) *** Sony SBK 48272 [id.]. (i) Cleveland O, Szell; (ii) Phd. O, Ormandy.

This is an exhilarating record, demonstrating the greatness of both Szell and Ormandy, and offering some astonishing orchestral bravura. Szell's *Don Juan*, sounding really impetuous yet never rushed, delights ear and senses by its forward surge of passionate lyricism, the whole interpretation founded on a bedrock of virtuosity from the remarkable Cleveland players. *Till* is irrepressibly cheeky (the characterization again created from the most polished orchestral response) and here the recording acoustic is almost perfect, with a warm glow on the tone of the players and every detail – and Szell makes sure one can hear every detail – crystal clear, without any loss of momentum or drama.

Ormandy's *Ein Heldenleben* is a really big conception. It is an engulfing performance, and the composite richness of tone and the fervour of the playing, from the Battle section onwards, bring the highest possible level of orchestral tension, finally relaxing most touchingly for the fulfilment sequence and closing with a sonorous brass cadence that is made to sound inevitable. The 1960 recording is more two-dimensional, less full, than the Cleveland recordings (which, surprisingly, were made as early as 1957) but still appropriately spacious.

Don Quixote.
☞ (M) (***) BMG/RCA mono 09026 61485-2 [id.]. Piatigorsky, de Pasquale, Boston SO, Munch –
BRAHMS: *Double concerto.* (***)

Piatigorsky's account of *Don Quixote* is something special even now after the passage of over 40 years. Recorded in 1953 with a Boston Symphony Orchestra which still produced the sound it made for Koussevitzky, this has tremendous electricity. Apart from Piatigorsky's beauty of tone, still discernible for all the sonic limitations, there is Munch's masterly support and excellent contribution from his Sancho Panza, Joseph de Pasquale (who made so signally successful a contribution to Ormandy's *Harold in Italy* a decade or so later). The sound is pretty good for its age and any deficiencies are soon forgotten. This is a great performance.

(i) *Don Quixote, Op. 35; Death and transfiguration.*
(M) *** DG 429 184-2 [id.]. (i) Fournier; BPO, Karajan.

Fournier's partnership with Karajan is outstanding. He brings great subtlety and (when required) repose to the part. The finale and Don Quixote's death are very moving, while Karajan's handling of orchestral detail is quite splendid. The 1966 recording is of DG's very finest quality and (given its price) this can be strongly recommended, more particularly since the disc includes Karajan's superlative 1973 analogue version of *Death and transfiguration*.

Ein Heldenleben, Op. 40.
*** Denon Dig. C37 7561 [id.]. Dresden State O, Blomstedt.

Ein Heldenleben; Don Juan, Op. 20.
(M) *** DG 429 717-2 [id.]. BPO, Karajan.

Ein Heldenleben; Till Eulenspiegel.
*** Sony Dig. MK 44817 [id.]. LSO, Tilson Thomas.
☞ ** Decca Dig. 436 444-2 [id.]. Cleveland O, Dohnányi.

Blomstedt shapes his performance with both authority and poetry. There is a genuine heroic stride and a sense of dramatic excitement here, while the Dresden orchestra creates glorious Straussian textures and the whole edifice is held together in a way that commands admiration. In these respects, Blomstedt's account is the most completely satisfying CD.

Karajan's 1959 *Heldenleben* is a superb performance. Playing of great power and distinction emanates from the Berlin Philharmonic and, in the closing section, an altogether becoming sensuousness and warmth. The remastering has plenty of ambient atmosphere; *Don Juan*, made over a decade later, brings only a marginal difference in body and none in breadth.

Michael Tilson Thomas's account is also a performance of genuine authority and no less well laid out than other outstanding versions. His interpretation has an epic breadth and humanity that are impressive. If it does not displace its rivals, it can be recommended with complete confidence alongside them, and moreover it has the additional attraction of *Till Eulenspiegel*.

The Cleveland performances offer some superb orchestral playing and fine Decca recording. But neither the musical characterization nor Dohnányi's overall grip yield the kind of performance of *Ein Heldenleben* that resonates in the memory, while *Till* is a genial fellow, but his portrayal lacks any kind of peasant quirkiness. If one turns to Karajan in both works, the musical experience is altogether more compulsive.

Josephslegende (ballet): *suite, Op. 63; Sinfonia domestica, Op. 53.*
**(*) Delos Dig. DE 3082 [id.]. Seattle SO, Gerard Schwarz.

Strauss composed the *Josephslegende* for Diaghilev on the grandest scale for a large orchestra. There are many felicities, the *Dance of the Turkish Boxers* being a good example, while there are delicious touches in the fourth scene, *Joseph's dance*. Gerard Schwarz gives us the suite from the ballet in addition to a very idiomatic account of the *Sinfonia domestica*. There is very good playing from the Seattle orchestra: cultured, thoroughly idiomatic and with splendid sweep; the recording, too, is splendidly detailed, if perhaps just a bit too brightly lit to be ideal.

Metamorphosen for 23 solo strings.
☞ *** Denon Dig. CO 79442 [id.]. Sinfonia Varsovia, Emmanuel Krivine – SCHOENBERG: *Verklaerte Nacht;* WAGNER: *Siegfried idyll.* ***
☞ *** Delos Dig. DE 3121 [id.]. Seattle SO, Gerard Schwarz – HONEGGER: *Symphony No. 2;* WEBERN arr. Schwarz: *Langsamer satz.* ***
☞ (M) **(*) EMI CDM7 65078-2 [id.]. New Philh. O, Barbirolli – SCHOENBERG: *Pelleas und Melisande.* **(*)
☞ *(*) DG Dig. 435 883-2 [id.]. BPO, Levine – SCHOENBERG: *Verklaerte Nacht;* WAGNER: *Siegfried idyll.* *(*)

Emmanuel Krivine and the Sinfonia Varsovia give as eloquent an account of Strauss's elegiac masterpiece as any in the catalogue. It is the first which can be mentioned in the same breath as the celebrated Karajan accounts from the early 1980s (and his pioneering version with the Vienna Philharmonic). The Polish ensemble produce a sonority of great beauty and flexibility, and they have great expressive and dynamic range; they bring great feeling to this performance, and Krivine characterizes the work with masterly confidence. In addition, the digital sound is very natural and atmospheric.

Gerard Schwarz's account of Strauss's elegiac threnody is sumptuously recorded (it is even more successful in terms of realism than the Honegger with which it is coupled). The performance itself takes 7 minutes longer than Kempe's and 5–6 longer than Karajan – though, to be fair, at no point does it feel too slow. Indeed this *Metamorphosen* is as deeply felt and dignified as it is unhurried, and it should be heard. The listener is completely drawn into its world and, although it does not supersede the Kempe or any of the the Karajan accounts except perhaps in terms of recorded realism, it deserves to be recommended alongside them. At 32 minutes it may be the slowest *Metamorphosen* on disc, but it is certainly one of the best.

Barbirolli's 1967 recording exudes a warm glow and an intense, valedictory feeling. The playing of the NPO strings is most eloquent, and this deeply felt performance has a very powerful ambience. The Abbey Road recording is full and well focused.

Levine's account of *Metamorphosen* with the Berlin Philharmonic puts him firmly in his place when one recalls the accounts Karajan gave with this great orchestra. The Berlin strings can't help making a rich sound, but in every other respect this is pretty ordinary.

Schlagobers (ballet), *Op. 70:* complete.
** Denon Dig. CO 73414 [id.]. Tokyo Met. SO, Wakasugi.

Schlagobers comes from the early 1920s, but it is held in low esteem by most Strauss scholars. There are some delights, such as the *March and military exercises of marzipan*, *Plum soldiers and honey cakes* and the *Dance of the tea cakes* in Act I; but elsewhere his inspiration lapses into routine, as in the *Whipped cream waltz*. Hiroshi Wakasugi gets good results from the Tokyo Metropolitan Orchestra and the recording is more than acceptable, though insufficiently transparent in climaxes.

Sinfonia domestica; (i) *Death and transfiguration.*
(M) **(*) BMG/RCA stereo/mono GD 60388 [60388-2-RG]. Chicago SO; (i) (mono) RCA Victor O; Fritz Reiner.

Sinfonia domestica, Op. 53; Till Eulenspiegel. (i) Songs: *Die heiligen drei Könige aus Morgenland; Zueignung.*
**(*) Chan. Dig. CHAN 8572; *ABTD 1267* [id.]. SNO, Järvi; (i) with Felicity Lott.

Reiner's account of the *Sinfonia domestica* comes from 1956, the earliest days of stereo, and is a wonderful performance, a reading of stature, worthy to rank alongside the best. *Death and transfiguration* is a 1950 mono recording, and it was perverse of RCA not to include his marvellous 1957 Vienna Philharmonic version (in surprisingly good stereo even now).

Järvi's is a strongly characterized, good-natured account, not as refined in ensemble as some past rivals but gutsy and committed to remove any coy self-consciousness from this extraordinarily inflated but delightful musical portrait of Strauss's family life. The performance of *Till* brings out the joy of the work, too; and Felicity Lott's performance of two of Strauss's most delightful songs makes a generous coupling.

Symphony in F min., Op. 12; (i) *6 Lieder, Op. 68.*
☞ **(*) Chan. Dig. CHAN 9166 [id.]. (i) Eileen Hulse, SNO, Järvi.

The *F minor* is neither a good symphony nor good Strauss, though Järvi makes out a better case for it than any previous recording. The work is cunningly crafted and the young master puts his ideas through their paces with skill and proficiency. But the ideas themselves are not really very distinguished – or indeed characteristic. Järvi paces the score with real mastery and gets very good playing from the Royal Scottish National Orchestra. The glorious Brentano *Lieder*, Op. 68, date from 1918 and Strauss transcribed them for orchestra in 1941. Eileen Hulse produces some beautiful tone and is sensitively supported throughout. Not core repertory this, but a disc for Straussians.

CHAMBER MUSIC

Capriccio, Op. 85: String sextet.
☞ *** Chan. Dig. CHAN 9131 [id.]. ASMF Chamber Ens. – ENESCU: *Octet in C;* SHOSTAKOVICH: *2 Pieces for string octet.* ***

The autumnal preface to *Capriccio* is the expertly played fill-up to Enescu's remarkable *Octet;* very well recorded it is, too.

Cello sonata in F, Op. 6.
**(*) Sony Dig. MK 44980 [id.]. Yo-Yo Ma, Emanuel Ax – BRITTEN: *Sonata.* **(*)

Yo-Yo Ma and Emanuel Ax give a generally fine account of the *Cello sonata*, although there are moments when Ax's fortissimos overpower the cellist and Ma is not wholly free from self-consciousness. The recording is reasonably truthful, though the constraints of the CBS acoustic produce a very slightly synthetic character.

String quartet in A, Op. 2.
**(*) Hyp. Dig. CDA 66317 [id.]. Delmé Qt – VERDI: *Quartet.* **(*)

The Strauss *Quartet* is early and derivative, as one might expect from a sixteen-year-old, but it is amazingly assured and fluent. The Delmé version is well played; however, although the basic acoustic is pleasing, the sound-balance remains a little on the dry side.

Violin sonata in E flat, Op. 18.
*** DG Dig. 427 617-2 [id.]. Kyung Wha Chung, Krystian Zimerman – RESPIGHI: *Sonata.* ***
*** Virgin/EMI Dig. VC5 45002-2 [id.]. Dmitry Sitkovetsky, Pavel Gililov – DEBUSSY: *Sonata* **;
JANACEK: *Sonata.* ***

Among modern versions Kyung Wha Chung is *primus inter pares*, and her version of the Strauss scores over rivals also in the power and sensitivity of Krystian Zimerman's contribution and the excellence of the DG recording. There is, however, a cut of 42 bars in the coda of the first movement (Universal Edition) which appears to be sanctioned, as Heifetz also observed it in his recording.

Dmitry Sitkovetsky is also a passionate and characterful player, who gives a powerful account of the Strauss. Musically, his coupling is more rewarding in that the Debussy and Janáček *Sonatas* are of greater substance than the Respighi which Chung and Zimerman offer.

VOCAL MUSIC

Choral music: (i) *An den Baum Daphne;* (ii) *Der Abend; Hymne, Op. 34/1–2;* (iii) *Deutsche Motette, Op. 62;* (iv) *Die Göttin im Putzzimer.*
☞ *** Chan. Dig. CHAN 9223 [id.]. (i) Marianne Lund, Christian Lisdorf, Copenhagen Boys' Ch.;
(iii) Tina Kiberg, Randi Stene, Gert Henning-Jensen, Ulrik Cold; (i–iv) Danish Nat. R. Ch.,
Stefan Parkman.

Although Stefan Parkman's account of the *Deutsche Motette* does not eclipse memories of the magical singing of the Swedish Radio Choir under Eric Ericson, this disc brings very good performances of some very beautiful and curiously little-known music. The engineers produce a realistic sound too.

Drei Hymnen, Op. 71. Orchestral songs: *Des Dichters Abendgang; Frühlingsfeier; Gesang der Apollopriesterin; Liebeshymnus; Das Rosenband; Verführung; Winterliebe; Winterweihe; Zueignung.*
☞ *** Chan. Dig. CHAN 9159 [id.]. Felicity Lott, SNO, Järvi.

Four Last songs; Lieder: *Das Bächlein; Befreit; Cäcilie; Freundliche Vision; Die heiligen drei Könige aus Morgenland; Mein Auge; Meinem Kinde; Morgen; Muttertändelei; Ruhe, meine Seele!; Waldseligkeit; Wiegenlied.*
☞ **(*) Chan. Dig. CHAN 9054 [id.]. Felicity Lott, SNO, Järvi.

Felicity Lott's two discs bring together a whole series of recordings of Strauss songs in their orchestral versions which originally appeared as couplings for Järvi's discs of the Strauss symphonic poems. She sings them beautifully, though the voice is not always caught at its most golden, notably in the *Four Last songs* which yet are movingly done. The second CD includes the first recording of *Drei Hymnen*, Holderlin settings composed in 1921, pantheistic poems about love of nature which are full of ardour and are provided with the most opulent accompaniments. Lott's voice, for the most part well focused, rides over the rich orchestral textures impressively, and throughout both discs there is agreeably warm, full, orchestral sound.

8 Lieder, Op. 10; 5 Lieder, Op. 15; 6 Lieder, Op. 17; 6 Lieder, Op. 19; Schlichte Weisen, Op. 21; Mädchenblumen, Op. 22; 2 Lieder, Op. 26; 4 Lieder, Op. 27; Lieder, Op. 29/1 & 3; 3 Lieder, Op. 31; Stiller Gang, Op. 31/4; 5 Lieder, Op. 32; Lieder, Op. 36/1–4; Lieder, Op. 37/1–3 & 5–6; 5 Lieder, Op. 39; Lieder, Op. 41/2–5; Gesänge älterer deutscher Dichter, Op. 43/1 & 3; 5 Gedichte, Op. 46; 5 Lieder, Op. 47; 5 Lieder, Op. 48; Lieder, Op. 49/1 & 2; 4–6; 6 Lieder, Op. 56; Krämerspiegel, Op. 66; Lieder, Op. 67/4–6; Lieder, Op. 68/1 & 4; 5 kleine Lieder, Op. 69; Gesänge des Orients, Op. 77; Lieder, Op. 88/1–2; Lieder ohne Opuszahl.
(M) *** EMI CMS7 63995-2 (6). Dietrich Fischer-Dieskau, Gerald Moore.

Fischer-Dieskau and Moore made these recordings of the 134 Strauss songs suitable for a man's voice between 1967 and 1970, tackling them in roughly chronological order. With both artists at their very peak, the results are endlessly imaginative, and the transfers are full and immediate, giving fine presence to the voice.

Lieder: *Allerseelen; Ach Lieb ich muss nun Scheiden; Befreit; Du meines Herzens Krönelein; Einerlei; Heimliche Aufforderung; Ich trage meine Minne; Kling!; Lob des Leidens; Malven; Mit deinen blauen Augen; Die Nacht; Schlechtes Wetter; Seitdem dein Aug; Ständchen; Stiller Gang; Traume durch die Dämmerung; Wie sollten wir geheim; Wir beide wollen springen; Zeltlose.*
*** Ph. Dig. 416 298-2 [id.]. Jessye Norman, Geoffrey Parsons.

Jessye Norman's recital of Strauss brings heartfelt, deeply committed performances, at times larger than life, which satisfyingly exploit the unique glory of the voice. The magnetism of the singer generally silences any reservations, and Geoffrey Parsons is the most understanding of accompanists, brilliant too. Good, natural recording.

Lieder: *Befreit; Hat gesagt, bleibt's nicht dabei; Ich trage meine Minne; Meinem Kinde; Der Rosenband; Die sieben Siegel; Wie sollten wir geheim sie halten.*
☞ *** DG 437 515-2 [id.]. Anne Sofie von Otter, Bengt Forsberg – BERG: *Early Lieder.* KORNGOLD: *Lieder.* ***

Anne Sofie von Otter and Bengt Forsberg follow up their prize-winning disc of Grieg songs with another inspired set of performances. Though they are even more illuminating in Berg and Korngold, the imaginative selection of seven Strauss songs brings warm, intense singing and sensitive accompaniments.

Four Last songs; Orchestral Lieder: *An die Nacht; Der Arbeitsmann; Mein Auge; Das Bächlein; Befreit; Des Dichters Abendgang; Die heil'gen drei Könige aus Morgenland; Ich liebe dich; Morgen!; Das Rosenband; Traum durch die Dämmerung; Zueignung.*
☞ (B) **(*) EMI CD-EMX 2191; *TC-EMX 2191.* Heather Harper, LSO, Hickox.

Heather Harper gives sensitive, sharply characterized readings of the *Four Last songs*, marked by much beautiful singing, but the closeness of the recording exposes the fact that her gorgeous soprano is a degree less pure than it once was. These are performances very much in the light of day, lacking mystery even in *Beim Schlafengehen*. Hickox directs a relatively plain, unmoulded reading of the orchestral accompaniment, fresh and sympathetic but lacking the evocative overtones of the finest versions, again not helped by the closeness of recording. The majority of the twelve songs with orchestral accompaniment work better, when Harper's consistently perceptive characterization distinguishes each one so sharply. It is good to have included *Der Arbeitsmann*, which has never been recorded in orchestral form before; at mid-price, this recital is worth investigating, for there is much to enjoy here.

Four Last songs; Lieder: *Befreit; Morgen; Muttertändelei; Ruhe, meine Seele; Wiegenlied; Zueignung.*
**(*) Sony MK 76794 [id.]. Kiri Te Kanawa, LSO, Andrew Davis.

Four Last songs; Lieder: *Cäcilie; Meinem Kinde; Morgen; Ruhe, meine Seele; Wiegenlied; Zueignung.*
⊛ *** Ph. Dig. 411 052-2 [id.]. Jessye Norman, Leipzig GO, Masur.

(i) *Four Last songs.* (ii) *Arabella* (opera): excerpts. (i) *Capriccio* (opera): Closing scene.
(M) (***) EMI mono CDH7 61001-2 [id.]. Elisabeth Schwarzkopf, (i) Philh. O, Ackermann; (ii) Metternich, Gedda, Philh. O, Von Matačić.

Strauss's publisher Ernest Roth says in the score of the *Four Last songs* that this was a farewell of 'serene confidence', which is exactly the mood Jessye Norman conveys. The start of the second stanza of the third song, *Beim Schlafengehen*, brings one of the most thrilling vocal crescendos on record, expanding from a half-tone to a gloriously rich and rounded forte. In concern for word-detail Norman is outshone only by Schwarzkopf, but both in the *Four Last songs* and in the orchestral songs the stylistic as well as the vocal command is irresistible, with *Cäcilie* given operatic strength. The radiance of the recording matches the interpretations.

Schwarzkopf's 1953 version of the *Four Last songs* comes with both its original coupling, the closing scene from *Capriccio*, also recorded in 1953, and the four major excerpts from *Arabella* which she recorded two years later. The *Four Last songs* are here less reflective, less sensuous, than in Schwarzkopf's later version with Szell, but the more flowing speeds and the extra tautness and freshness of voice bring equally illuminating performances. Fascinatingly, this separate account of the *Capriccio* scene is even more ravishing than the one in the complete set, and the sound is even fuller, astonishing for its period.

Dame Kiri Te Kanawa gives an open-hearted, warmly expressive reading of the *Four Last songs*. If she misses the sort of detail that Schwarzkopf uniquely brought, her commitment is never in doubt. Her tone is consistently beautiful, but might have seemed even more so if the voice had not been placed rather too close in relation to the orchestra. The orchestral arrangements of other songs make an excellent coupling and Andrew Davis directs most sympathetically.

OPERA

Die Agyptische Helena (complete).
(M) **(*) Decca 430 381-2 (2) [id.]. Dame Gwyneth Jones, Hendricks, Kastu, Detroit SO, Dorati.

Dorati, using the original Dresden version of the score, draws magnificent sounds from the Detroit orchestra, richly and forwardly recorded. The vocal sounds are less consistently pleasing. Gwyneth Jones has her squally moments as Helen, though it is a commanding performance. Matti Kastu manages as well as any Heldentenor today in the role of Menelaus, strained at times but with a pleasing and distinctive timbre.

Arabella (complete).
*** Orfeo Dig. C 169882H (2). Varady, Fischer-Dieskau, Donath, Dallapozza, Schmidt, Berry, Bav. State Op. Ch. & O, Sawallisch.
*** Decca Dig. 417 623-2 (3) [id.]. Te Kanawa, Fontana, Grundheber, Seiffert, Dernesch, Guttstein, ROHCG Ch. & O, Tate.
(M) **(*) Decca 430 387-2 (2) [id.]. Della Casa, Gueden, London, Edelmann, Dermota, V. State Op. Ch.,???
VPO, Solti.

This Orfeo set of *Arabella* has an immediate advantage over the Decca version with Kiri Te Kanawa in being a digital recording on two CDs against the three for the Decca. Moreover the recording is splendid in every way, not just in sound but in the warmth and understanding of Sawallisch, the characterful tenderness of Julia Varady as the heroine, and Fischer-Dieskau's fine-detailed characterization of the gruff Mandryka, *der Richtige* (Mr Right) according to the heroine's romantic view. Helen Donath too is charming as the younger sister, Zdenka, though the voice might be more sharply contrasted. Highly recommended.

Dame Kiri Te Kanawa, in the name-part, gives one of her very finest opera performances on record. It is a radiant portrait, languorously beautiful, and it is a pity that so unsuited a soprano as Gabriele Fontana should have been chosen as Zdenka next to her, sounding all the more shrill by contrast. Franz Grundheber makes a firm, virile Mandryka, Peter Seiffert a first-rate Matteo, while Helga Dernesch is outstandingly characterful as Arabella's mother. Tate's conducting is richly sympathetic and the Decca recording is first class.

Della Casa soars above the stave with the creamiest, most beautiful sounds and constantly charms one with her swiftly alternating moods of seriousness and gaiety. Perhaps Solti does not linger as he might over the waltz rhythms, and it may be Solti too who prevents Edelmann from making his first scene with Mandryka as genuinely humorous as it can be. Edelmann otherwise is superb, as fine a Count as he was an Ochs in the Karajan *Rosenkavalier*. Gueden, too, is ideally cast as Zdenka and, if anything, in Act I manages to steal our sympathies from Arabella, as a good Zdenka can. George London is on the ungainly side, but then Mandryka is a boorish fellow anyway. Dermota is a fine Matteo, and Mimi Coertse makes as much sense as anyone could of the ridiculously difficult part of Fiakermilli, the female yodeller. The sound is brilliant.

Ariadne auf Naxos (complete).
⊛ (M) (***) EMI mono CMS7 69296-2 (2) [Ang. CDMB 69296]. Schwarzkopf, Schock, Rita Streich, Dönch, Seefried, Cuenod, Philh. O, Karajan.
*** Ph. Dig. 422 084-2 (2) [id.]. Jessye Norman, Varady, Gruberová, Asmus, Bär, Leipzig GO, Masur.
(M) **(*) Decca 430 384-2 (2) [id.]. Leontyne Price, Troyanos, Gruberová, Kollo, Berry, Kunz, LPO, Solti.
☞ (M) **(*) EMI CMS7 64159-2 (2) [Ang. CDMB 61459]. Janowitz, Geszty, Zylis-Gara, King, Schreier, Prey, Dresden State Op. O, Kempe.

Elisabeth Schwarzkopf makes a radiant, deeply moving Ariadne, giving as bonus a delicious little portrait of the Prima Donna in the Prologue. Rita Streich was at her most dazzling in the coloratura of Zerbinetta's aria and, in partnership with the harlequinade characters, sparkles engagingly. But it is Irmgard Seefried who gives perhaps the supreme performance of all as the Composer, exceptionally beautiful of tone, conveying a depth and intensity rarely if ever matched. Rudolf Schock is a fine Bacchus, strained less than most, and the team of theatrical characters includes such stars as Hugues Cuenod as the Dancing Master. The fine pacing and delectably pointed ensemble add to the impact of a uniquely perceptive Karajan interpretation. Though in mono and with the orchestral sound a little dry, the voices come out superbly.

Jessye Norman's is a commanding, noble, deeply felt performance, ranging extraordinarily wide; she provides the perfect focus for a cast as near ideal as anyone could assemble today. Julia Varady as the Composer brings out the vulnerability of the character, as well as the ardour, in radiant singing. The Zerbinetta of Edita Gruberová is a thrilling performance and, even if the voice is not always ideally sweet, the range of emotions Gruberová conveys, as in her duet with the Composer, is enchanting. Paul Frey is the sweetest-sounding Bacchus on record yet, while Olaf Bär as Harlekin and Dietrich Fischer-Dieskau in the vignette role of the Music-Master are typical of the fine team of artists here in the smaller character parts. Masur proves a masterly Straussian and he is helped by the typically warm Leipzig recording.

Brilliance is the keynote of Solti's set of *Ariadne*. What the performance is short of is charm and warmth. Everything is so brightly lit that much of the delicacy and tenderness of the writing tends to disappear. Nevertheless the concentration of Solti in Strauss is never in doubt, and Leontyne Price makes a strong central figure, memorably characterful. Tatiana Troyanos is affecting as the composer, and Edita Gruberová establishes herself as the unrivalled Zerbinetta of her generation, though here she is less delicate than on stage. René Kollo similarly is an impressive Bacchus. The Decca CD transfer is characteristically vivid.

Kempe's relaxed, languishing performance of this most atmospheric of Strauss operas is matched by opulent recording, warmly transferred to CD. Gundula Janowitz sings with heavenly tone-colour (marred only when hard-pressed at the climax of the Lament), and Teresa Zylis-Gara makes an ardent and understanding Composer. Sylvia Geszty's voice is a little heavy for the fantastic coloratura of Zerbinetta's part, but she sings with charm and assurance. James King presents the part of Bacchus with forthright tone and more taste than do most tenors. Compared with Karajan's mono set with Schwarzkopf, this is less than ideal, but that has rather dry mono sound and here there is warmth and atmosphere in plenty, and there is a price advantage over the Philips digital stero set with Jesseye Norman.

(i) *Ariadne auf Naxos* (excerpts). Lieder: (ii) *Befreit; Einerlei; Hat gesagt; Morgen!; Schlechtes Wetter; Seit dem dein Aug'; Waldseligkeit.*
☞ *** Testament SBT 1036 [id.]. Lisa della Casa, with (i) Rudolf Schock, BPO, Erede; (ii) Sebastian Peschko.

Lisa della Casa recorded these excerpts from *Ariadne* in June 1959 for Electrola, the German branch of EMI; but with EMI's complete Karajan recording also available, the LP's currency was limited. The stereo recording is full and immediate, bringing out the glories of Della Casa's creamy soprano but failing to convey the full, atmospheric beauty of the music, notably in the echo chorus of Naiads. Della Casa had earlier recorded *Ariadne's Lament* for Decca, but this is even more powerful. The first excerpt is of the opening of the entertainment from the overture through to Ariadne's first solo. There follow her second solo, *Ein Schönes war*, and the *Lament*, while the last extended excerpt has the whole of the final scene from the entry of Bacchus. Rudolf Schock, as in the Karajan version, sings nobly, and Erede brings out the lyrical warmth of the writing. Della Casa is less imaginative in the Strauss Lieder but still sings very beautifully and persuasively. The faithful and full Testament transfers bring out the wide range of the recording, tending to emphasize sibilants in the singing.

Capriccio (complete).
(***) EMI mono CDS7 49014-8 (2) [Ang. CDCB 49014]. Schwarzkopf, Waechter, Gedda, Fischer-Dieskau, Hotter, Ludwig, Moffo, Philh. O, Sawallisch.

In the role of the Countess in Strauss's last opera, Elisabeth Schwarzkopf has had no equals. This recording, made in 1957 and 1958, brings a peerless performance from her, full of magical detail both in the pointing of words and in the presentation of the character in all its variety. Not only are the other singers ideal choices in each instance, they form a wonderfully co-ordinated team, beautifully held together by Sawallisch's sensitive conducting. As a performance this is never likely to be superseded. The mono sound presents the voices with fine bloom and presence, but the digital transfer makes the orchestra a little dry and relatively backward by comparison.

Elektra (complete).
*** Decca 417 345-2 (2) [id.]. Nilsson, Collier, Resnik, Stolze, Krause, V. State Op. Ch., VPO, Solti.

Nilsson is almost incomparable in the name-part, with the hard side of Elektra's character brutally dominant. Only when – as in the Recognition scene with Orestes – she tries to soften the naturally bright tone does she let out a suspect flat note or two. As a rule she is searingly accurate in approaching even the most formidable exposed top notes. One might draw a parallel with Solti's direction – sharply focused and brilliant in the savage music which predominates, but lacking the languorous warmth one really needs in the Recognition scene, if only for contrast. The brilliance of the 1967 Decca recording is brought out the more in the digital transfer on CD, aptly so in this work. The fullness and clarity are amazing for the period.

(i) *Elektra: Soliloquy; Recognition scene; Finale. Salome: Dance of the seven veils; Finale.*
(M) *** BMG/RCA GD 60874 [60874-2-RG]. Inge Borkh, Chicago SO, Fritz Reiner; (i) with
   Schoeffler, Yeend, Chicago Lyric Theatre Ch.

With Borkh singing superbly in the title-role alongside Paul Schoeffler and Francis Yeend, this is a
real collectors' piece. Reiner provides a superbly telling accompaniment; the performance of the
Recognition scene and final duet are as ripely passionate as Beecham's old 78-r.p.m. excerpts and
outstrip the complete versions. The orchestral sound is thrillingly rich, the brass superbly expansive.
For the reissue, Reiner's full-blooded account of *Salome's dance* has been added, and Borkh is
comparably memorable in the finale scene. No Straussian should miss this disc.

Die Frau ohne Schatten (complete).
⊛ *** Decca Dig. 436 243-2 (3) [id.]. Behrens, Varady, Domingo, Van Dam, Runkel, Jo, VPO, Solti.

Solti and his Decca colleagues waited patiently until they could assemble what was felt to be the ideal
cast. So the Heldentenor role of the Emperor is taken by Plácido Domingo and, as in Solti's
recording of Wagner's *Lohengrin*, the superstar tenor gives a performance that is not only beautiful to
the ear beyond previous recordings but which has an extra feeling for expressive detail, deeper than
that which was previously recorded. Similarly, Solti was willing to delay the recording sessions so as
to secure Hildegard Behrens as the Dyer's wife. Vocally that choice is a huge success. What has at
times limited her as Brünnhilde in Wagner's *Ring* cycle, her very feminine vulnerability, is here a
positive strength, and the voice has rarely sounded so beautiful on record. Julia Varady as the
Empress is equally imaginative, with a beautiful voice, and José van Dam with his clean, dark voice
brings a warmth and depth of expression to the role of Barak, the Dyer, which goes with a
satisfyingly firm focus. Reinhild Runkel in the key role of the Nurse is well in character, with her
mature, fruity sound. Eva Lind is shrill in the tiny role of the Guardian of the Threshold, but there is
compensation in having Sumi Jo as the Voice of the Falcon. With the players of the Vienna
Philharmonic, 120-strong, surpassing themselves, and the big choral ensembles both well disciplined
and warmly expressive, this superb recording is unlikely to be matched, let alone surpassed, for many
years. Solti himself is inspired throughout.

Intermezzo (complete).
*** EMI CDS7 49337-2 (2) [Ang. CDCB 49337]. Popp, Brammer, Fischer-Dieskau, Bav. RSO,
   Sawallisch.

The central role of *Intermezzo* was originally designed for the dominant and enchanting Lotte
Lehmann; but it is doubtful whether even she can have outshone the radiant Lucia Popp, who brings
out the charm of a character who, for all his incidental trials, must have consistently captivated
Strauss and provoked this strange piece of self-revelation. The piece inevitably is very wordy, but
with this scintillating and emotionally powerful performance under Sawallisch, with fine recording
and an excellent supporting cast, this set is as near ideal as could be, a superb achievement. The CD
transfer is well managed but – unforgivably in this of all Strauss operas – no translation is given with
the libretto, a very serious omission.

Der Liebe der Danae (complete).
☞ (***) Orfeo mono C 292923 A (3) [id.]. Kupper, Felbermeyer, Schoeffler, Gostic, VPO, Krauss.

One may very well argue that Strauss reserved for his last years his very greatest music, as with the
Four Last songs, *Metamorphosen* and the final opera, *Capriccio*. Yet unfairly the opera immediately
preceding *Capriccio*, not given its first performance until long after the composer's death, *Der Liebe
der Danae* ('The love of Danae'), has been more neglected than any. This belated first recording was
not made in the spectacular stereo which this sumptuous score cries out for, but in limited mono
sound in an Austrian Radio recording from the very first Salzburg Festival performance in August
1952. As transferred to CD it has a vivid sense of presence, with the voices full-bodied. Despite the
limitations and the intrusive stage noises, *Der Liebe der Danae*, here under Clemens Krauss,
establishes itself as one of Strauss's richest scores. Completed in 1940, it in effect marked the
beginning of the last period, warm and mellow like the works which followed but, unlike them,
attempting a scale and complexity that Strauss had left behind in his epic opera, *Die Frau ohne
Schatten*, written during the First World War.

Like *Ariadne auf Naxos*, *Daphne* and *Die Agyptische Helena*, *Der Liebe der Danae* presents Greek
myth in light-hearted post-romantic guise. The idea, originally put forward by Hofmannsthal and
taken up by Strauss's later librettist, Joseph Gregor, was to superimpose two well-known myths, that
of Jupiter appearing to Danaë in a shower of golden rain and of Midas with his curse of turning
everything to gold. They described it as a 'cheerful mythology in three Acts', but that gives no idea of

the breadth of treatment. It is not just lyrical in Strauss's *Daphne* manner but a genuinely tuneful score, in places harking back to the diatonic Wagner of *Meistersinger*, and bringing ensembles that were directly influenced by Strauss's favourite Mozart opera, *Così fan tutte*. Midas is reduced from king to donkey-driver, initially the catspaw for Jupiter in his philandering. In the last of the three Acts Strauss lets himself go expansively in a sequence of duets, first between Danaë and Midas, and finally between Danaë and Jupiter, who, rather like Hans Sachs in *Meistersinger* (or the Marschallin in *Rosenkavalier*), nobly cedes any rights in the young lover, a situation that plainly touched the aged Strauss. With the Vienna Philharmonic already restored after the war, Krauss's affectionate reading is backed by some splendid singing, notably from Paul Schoeffler, Sachs-like as Jupiter, and the full-toned heroic tenor, Josef Gostic, as Midas. Annelies Kupper in the title-role has a few raw moments, but she produces pure, creamy tone for the many passages of ravishing cantilena above the stave. With important sequences for Danaë's servant, Xanthe (the resonant Anny Felbermeyer), and four mythical queens, Semele, Europa, Alkmene and Leda, the writing for women's voices brings grateful echoes of the *Rosenkavalier* Trio. Sadly, the three full-price discs come without a libretto, merely providing a note by Strauss's biographer, Willi Schuh, plus a synopsis in fractured English.

Der Rosenkavalier (complete).

⊛ *** EMI CDS7 49354-8 (3) [Ang. CDCC 49354]. Schwarzkopf, Ludwig, Stich-Randall, Edelmann,
    Waechter, Philh. Ch. & O, Karajan.

*** EMI Dig. CDS7 54259-2 (3) [Ang. CDCC 54259]. Kiri Te Kanawa, Anne Sofie von Otter,
    Rydl, Grundheber, Hendricks, Dresden Op. Ch., Dresden Boys' Ch., Dresden State O, Haitink.

**(*) DG Dig. 423 850-2 (3) [id.]. Tomowa-Sintow, Baltsa, Moll, Perry, Hornik, VPO Ch. & O,
    Karajan.

(M) (**(*)) Decca mono 425 950-2 (3) [id.]. Reining, Weber, Jurinac, Gueden, V. State Op. Ch.,
    VPO, Erich Kleiber.

The glory of Karajan's 1956 version, one of the greatest of all opera recordings, shines out the more delectably on CD. Though the transfer in its very clarity exposes some flaws in the original sound, the sense of presence and the overall bloom are if anything more compelling than ever. As to the performance, it is in a class of its own, with the patrician refinement of Karajan's spacious reading combining with an emotional intensity that he has rarely equalled, even in Strauss, of whose music he remains a supreme interpreter. Matching that achievement is the incomparable portrait of the Marschallin from Schwarzkopf, bringing out detail as no one else can, yet equally presenting the breadth and richness of the character, a woman still young and attractive. Christa Ludwig with her firm, clear mezzo tone makes an ideal, ardent Octavian and Teresa Stich-Randall a radiant Sophie, with Otto Edelmann a winningly characterful Ochs, who yet sings every note clearly.

Haitink's EMI set, recorded in Dresden, brings a satisfyingly rich Strauss sound. That matches the conductor's beautifully paced reading, dramatic without a hint of vulgarity, bringing out the nobility of the music. Vocally the biggest triumph is the Octavian of Anne Sofie von Otter, not only beautifully sung but acted with a boyish animation to make most rivals sound very feminine by comparison. If the first great – and predictable – glory of Dame Kiri's assumption of the role of the Marschallin is the sheer beauty of the sound, the portrait she paints is an intense and individual one, totally convincing. The portrait of Sophie from Barbara Hendricks is a warm and moving one, but less completely satisfying, if only because her voice is not quite so pure as one needs for this young, innocent girl. Kurt Rydl with his warm and resonant bass makes a splendid Baron Ochs, not always ideally steady, but giving the character a magnificent scale and breadth. Other portraits are presented just as colourfully. Whatever the detailed reservations over the singing, it is mainly due to Bernard Haitink, and his long experience conducting this opera at Covent Garden and elsewhere, which makes this the most totally convincing and heartwarming recording of *Rosenkavalier* since Karajan's 1956 set. This recording, unlike the Karajan, opens out the small stage cuts sanctioned by the composer.

Karajan's digital set brings few positive advantages, not even in recorded sound: for all the extra range of the modern recording, the focus is surprisingly vague, with the orchestra balanced too far behind the soloists. For the principal role Karajan chose Anna Tomowa-Sintow; the refinement and detail in her performance present an intimate view of the Marschallin, often very beautiful indeed, but both the darker and more sensuous sides of the character are muted. The Baron Ochs of Kurt Moll, firm, dark and incisive, is outstanding, and Agnes Baltsa as Octavian makes the lad tough and determined, if not always sympathetic. Janet Perry's Sophie, charming and pretty on stage, is too white and twittery of tone to give much pleasure.

Decca's set with Erich Kleiber was the first ever complete recording of *Rosenkavalier*, and it has long enjoyed cult status. Sena Jurinac is a charming Octavian, strong and sympathetic, and Hilde

Gueden a sweetly characterful Sophie, not just a wilting innocent. Ludwig Weber characterizes deliciously in a very Viennese way as Ochs; but the disappointment is the Marschallin of Maria Reining, very plain and lacking intensity. She is not helped by Kleiber's refusal to linger; with the singers recorded close, the effect of age on what was once a fine voice is very clear, even in the opening solo of the culminating trio. And ensemble is not good, with even the prelude to Act I a muddle. On the prelude more than anywhere, the CD transfer brings out a shrillness and lack of body in the orchestral sound, though voices are well caught.

(i) *Der Rosenkavalier* (abridged version); Lieder: (ii) *All' mein Gedanken; Freundliche Vision; Die Heiligen drei Könige; Heimkehr; Ich schwebe; Des Knaben Wunderhorn: Hat gesagt . . .; Morgen; Muttertändelei; Schlechtes Wetter; Ständchen* (2 versions); *Traum durch die Dämmerung;* (iii) *Mit deinen blauen Augen; Morgen; Ständchen; Traum durch die Dämmerung.*

☞ (M) (***) EMI mono CHS7 64487-2 (2) [Ang. CDHB 64487]. (i) Lehmann, Schumann, Mayr, Olszewska, Madin, V. State Op. Ch., VPO, Robert Heger; (ii) Elisabeth Schumann; (iii) Lotte Lehmann (with var. accompanists).

It is good to have a fresh CD transfer, immaculate in quality, of this classic, abridged, early recording of *Der Rosenkavalier*, containing some 100 minutes of music, made in 1933 in Vienna by the famous EMI pioneer of opera recording, Fred Gaisberg. Subsequent LP versions have told us that this is not definitive (as we once may have thought); but Lotte Lehmann as the Marschallin and Elisabeth Schumann as Sophie remain uniquely characterful and, though 78-r.p.m. side-lengths brought some hastening from Heger, notably in the great trio of Act III, the passion of the performance still conveys a sense of new discovery, a rare Straussian magic. There is no libretto, but a synopsis is cued with each excerpt. As a bonus we are offered a glorious Lieder recital, featuring both the principal sopranos, and demonstrating Lehmann's darker timbre, the richness immediately noticeable at her first song, the lovely *Mit deinen blauen Augen.* Versions of *Traume durch die Dämmerung* and the soaring *Ständchen are* sung by both artists, and two different Schumann performances are included of the latter: one (from 1927) fresh and lilting, the other (from 1930) faster and with much clearer sound. *Heimkehr* (1938) is ravishing, and *Die Heiligen drei Könige,* from ten years earlier, with a remarkably well-recorded orchestral accompaniment, is also memorable. No song translations are included, but again the CD transfers are well managed.

Der Rosenkavalier: highlights.
(M) *** EMI CDM7 63452-2 (from above complete set, with Schwarzkopf, Ludwig; cond. Karajan).

On EMI we are offered the Marschallin's monologue to the end of Act I (25 minutes); the Presentation of the silver rose and finale from Act II; and the Duet and Closing scene, with the Trio from Act III, flawlessly and gloriously sung and transferred most beautifully to CD.

Salome (complete).
*** DG. Dig. 431 810-2 (2) [id.]. Studer, Rysanek, Terfel, Hiestermann, German Opera, Berlin, Ch. & O, Sinopoli.
*** Decca 414 414-2 (2) [id.]. Nilsson, Hoffman, Stolze, Kmentt, Waechter, VPO, Solti.
*** EMI CDS7 49358-8 (2) [Ang. CDCB 49358]. Behrens, Bohme, Baltsa, Van Dam, VPO, Karajan.
(M) *** BMG/RCA GD 86644 (2) [6644-2-RG]. Caballé, Richard Lewis, Resnik, Milnes, LSO, Leinsdorf.

The glory of Sinopoli's DG version is the singing of Cheryl Studer as Salome, producing glorious sounds throughout. Her voice is both rich and finely controlled, with delicately spun pianissimos that chill you the more for their beauty, not least in Salome's attempted seduction of John the Baptist. Sinopoli's reading is often unconventional in its speeds, but it is always positive, thrusting and full of passion, the most opulent account on disc, matched by full, forward recording. As Jokanaan, Bryn Terfel makes a compelling recording debut, strong and noble, though the prophet's voice as heard from the cistern sounds far too distant. Among modern sets this makes a clear first choice, though Solti's vintage Decca recording remains the most firmly focused, with the keenest sense of presence.

Birgit Nilsson is splendid throughout; she is hard-edged as usual but, on that account, more convincingly wicked: the determination and depravity are latent in the girl's character from the start. Of this score Solti is a master. He has rarely sounded so abandoned in a recorded performance. Waechter makes a clear, young-sounding Jokanaan. Gerhardt Stolze portrays the unbalance of Herod with frightening conviction, and Grace Hoffman does all she can in the comparatively ungrateful part of Herodias. The vivid CD projection makes the final scene, where Salome kisses the head of John the Baptist in delighted horror (*I have kissed thy mouth, Jokanaan!*), all the more spine-tingling, with a close-up effect of the voice whispering almost in one's ear.

Hildegard Behrens is also a triumphantly successful Salome. The sensuous beauty of tone is conveyed ravishingly, but the recording is not always fair to her fine projection of sound, occasionally masking the voice. All the same, the feeling of a live performance has been captured well, and the rest of the cast is of the finest Salzburg standard. In particular José van Dam makes a gloriously noble Jokanaan, and in the early scenes his offstage voice from the cistern at once commands attention. Karajan – as so often in Strauss – is at his most commanding and sympathetic, with the orchestra, more forward than some will like, playing rapturously. This is a performance which, so far from making one recoil from perverted horrors, has one revelling in sensuousness.

Montserrat Caballé's formidable account of the role of Salome was recorded in 1968, utterly different from that of Birgit Nilsson on Decca and much closer to the personification of Behrens on the Karajan set on EMI (both at full price). For some listeners Caballé might seem too gentle, but in fact the range of her emotions is even wider than that of Nilsson. There are even one or two moments of fantasy, where for an instant one has the girlish skittishness of Salome revealed like an evil inverted picture of Sophie. As for the vocalization, it is superb, with glorious golden tone up to the highest register and never the slightest hesitation in attack. Lewis, Resnik and Milnes make a supporting team that matches the achievement of the Decca rivals, while Leinsdorf is inspired to some of his warmest and most sympathetic conducting on record.

Salome (complete; sung in French).
**(*) Virgin/EMI Dig. VCD7 59054-2 (2) [id.]. Huffstodt, Van Dam, Viala, Dupouy, Jossoud, Lyon Opera Ch. & O, Kent Nagano.

Nagano's version is unique. Adventurously, he has revived the adaptation of the vocal line which Strauss himself made to accommodate the original Oscar Wilde text in French. Karen Huffstodt is the sensuous soprano who sings Salome, occasionally over-strained. In the final scene the phrase, *Ah! j'ai baisé ta bouche, Jokanaan*, seems all the more dissolute in French. The drawback of the adaptation is that it makes the whole drama seem smaller-scale than in the original German, and that is heightened by the closeness of the voices in the relatively intimate Lyon acoustic. Even in the biting drama of the final scene Nagano brings out the lilting dance rhythms. Yet at the end the big moments of climax are shattering, notably when the head of John the Baptist is held high by the executioner. José van Dam sings with characteristic nobility as Jokanaan, though sounding a little old for the role. Jean Dupouy with rather throttled tenor tone sounds aptly decadent as Herod.

Arias from: *Die Agyptische Helena; Ariadne auf Naxos; Die Frau ohne Schatten; Guntram; Der Rosenkavalier; Salome.*
(M) *** RCA GD 60398 [60398-2-RG]. Leontyne Price, Boston SO or New Philh. O, Leinsdorf; LSO, Cleva.

Leontyne Price gives generous performances of an unusually rich collection of Strauss scenes and solos, strongly accompanied by Leinsdorf (or Cleva in *Ariadne*), always at his finest in Strauss. Recorded between 1965 and 1973, Price was still at her peak, even if occasionally the voice grows raw under stress in Strauss's heavier passages. It is particularly good to have rarities as well as such regular favourites as the Empress's awakening from *Die Frau ohne Schatten*, one of the finest of all the performances here.

Stravinsky, Igor (1882–1971)

The Stravinsky Edition: Volume 1, Ballets, etc.: (i) *The Firebird;* (i) *Fireworks;* (iii) *Histoire du soldat;* (i) *Pétrushka;* (iv, iii) *Renard the fox;* (i) *The Rite of spring;* (i) *Scherzo à la russe;* (ii) *Scherzo fantastique;* (v) *The Wedding (Les Noces).*

Volume 2, Ballets etc.: (vi) *Agon;* (i) *Apollo;* (i) *Le baiser de la fée;* (i) *Bluebird (pas de deux);* (vii) *Jeux de cartes;* (viii) *Orphée;* (ix, i) *Pulcinella;* (ii) *Scènes de ballet.*

Volume 3, Ballet suites: (i) *Firebird; Pétrouchka; Pulcinella.*
Volume 4, Symphonies: (i) *Symphony in E;* (ii) *Symphony in C;* (i) *Symphony in 3 movements;* (x, ii) *Symphony of Psalms;* (i) Stravinsky in rehearsal: *Apollo; Piano concerto; Pulcinella; Sleeping beauty; Symphony in C; 3 Souvenirs.*

Volume 5, Concertos: (xi, i) *Capriccio for piano and orchestra* (with Robert Craft); *Concerto for piano and wind;* (xii, i) *Movements for piano and orchestra;* (xiii, i) *Violin concerto in D.*

Volume 6, Miniatures: (i) *Circus polka; Concerto in D for string orchestra; Concerto in E flat for chamber orchestra;* (ii) *4 Etudes for orchestra;* (i) *Greeting prelude;* (ii) *8 Instrumental miniatures; 4 Norwegian moods; Suites Nos. 1–2 for small orchestra.*

Volume 7, Chamber music and historical recordings: (iii) *Concertino for 12 instruments;* (xiv, xv) *Concerto for 2 solo pianos;* (xv, xvi) *Duo concertant for violin and piano;* (xvii, xviii) *Ebony Concerto (for clarinet and big band);* (iii) *Octet for wind;* (xix, iii) *Pastorale for violin and wind quartet;* (xv) *Piano rag music;* (xviii) *Preludium;* (xx, iii) *Ragtime* (for 11 instruments); (xv) *Serenade in A;* (iii) *Septet;* (xii) *Sonata for piano;* (xxi) *Sonata for 2 pianos;* (xviii) *Tango;* (xxii) *Wind symphonies.*

Volume 8, Operas and songs: (xxiii, iii) *Cat's cradle songs;* (xxiii, xxiv) *Elegy for J. F. K.;* (xxv, ii) *Faun and shepherdess;* (xxvi,iii) *In memoriam Dylan Thomas;* (xxvii, iii) *3 Japanese Lyrics* (with Robert Craft); (xxvii, xxix) *The owl and the pussycat;* (xxvii, iii) *2 poems by K. Bal'mont;* (xxx, i) *2 poems of Paul Verlaine;* (xxiii,i) *Pribaoutki (peasant songs);* (xxiii, i) *Recollections of my childhood;* (xxviii, xxxi) *4 Russian songs;* (xxxvii) *4 Russian peasant songs;* (xxiii, iii) *3 songs from William Shakespeare;* (xxvii, i) *Tilim-Bom (3 stories for children);* (xxxii) *Mavra;* (xxxiii) *The Nightingale.*

Volume 9: (xxxiv) *The Rake's progress.*
Volume 10, Oratorio and melodrama: (xxxv, i) *The Flood* (with Robert Craft); (i) *Monumentum pro Gesualdo di Venosa (3 madrigals recomposed for instruments);* (vii) *Ode;* (xxxvi) *Oedipus Rex;* (xxxvii, xxxviii, i) *Perséphone.*

Volume 11, Sacred works: (x) *Anthem (the dove descending breaks the air);* (x) *Ave Maria;* (xxxix, x, i) *Babel;* (xxviii, xxvi, x, iii) *Cantata;* (xl) *Canticum sacrum;* (x, ii) *Credo;* (x, iii) *Introitus (T. S. Eliot in Memoriam);* (xli) *Mass;* (x, i) *Pater noster;* (xlii, i) *A Sermon, a narrative & a prayer;* (xliii, i) *Threni;* (x, i) *Chorale: Variations on: Vom Himmel hoch, da komm ich her* (arr.); *Zvezdoliki.*

Volume 12, Robert Craft conducts: (xliv, i) *Abraham and Isaac;* (iii) *Danses concertantes;* (xlv) *Double canon: Raoul Dufy in memoriam;* (xlvi) *Epitaphium;* (i) *Le chant du rossignol* (symphonic poem); (i) *Orchestral variations: Aldous Huxley in memoriam;* (xlvii) *Requiem canticles;* (i) *Song of the nightingale (symphonic poem).*

(M) *** Sony SX 22K 46290 (22) [id.]. (i) Columbia SO; (ii) CBC SO; (iii) Columbia CO; (iv) Shirley, Driscoll, Gramm, Koves; (v) Allen, Sarfaty, Driscoll, Samuel Barber, Aaron Copland, Lukas Foss, Roger Sessions, American Chamber Ch., Hills, Columbia Percussion Ens.; (vi) Los Angeles Festival SO; (vii) Cleveland O; (viii) Chicago SO; (ix) Jordan, Shirley, Gramm; (x) Festival Singers of Toronto, Iseler; (xi) Philippe Entremont; (xii) Charles Rosen; (xiii) Isaac Stern; (xiv) Soulima Stravinsky; (xv) Igor Stravinsky; (xvi) Szigeti; (xvii) Benny Goodman; (xviii) Columbia Jazz Ens.; (xix) Israel Baker; (xx) Tony Koves; (xxi) Arthur Gold, Robert Fizdale; (xxii) N. W. German RSO; (xxiii) Cathy Berberian; (xxiv) Howland, Kreiselman, Russo; (xxv) Mary Simmons; (xxvi) Alexander Young; (xxvii) Evelyn Lear; (xxviii) Adrienne Albert; (xxix) Robert Craft; (xxx) Donald Gramm; (xxxi) Di Tullio, Remsen, Almeida; (xxxii) Belinck, Simmons, Rideout, Kolk; (xxxiii) Driscoll, Grist, Picassi, Smith, Beattie, Gramm, Kolk, Murphy, Kaiser, Bonazzi, Washington, D. C., Op. Society Ch. & O; (xxxiv) Young, Raskin, Reardon, Sarfaty, Miller, Manning, Garrard, Tracey, Colin Tilney, Sadler's Wells Op. Ch., John Baker, RPO; (xxxv) Laurence Harvey, Sebastian Cabot, Elsa Lanchester, John Reardon, Robert Oliver, Paul Tripp, Richard Robinson, Columbia SO Ch., Gregg Smith; (xxxvi) Westbrook (nar.), Shirley, Verrett, Gramm, Reardon, Driscoll, Chester Watson Ch., Washington, D. C., Op. Society O; (xxxvii) Gregg Smith Singers, Gregg Smith; (xxxviii) Zorina, Molese, Ithaca College Concert Ch., Fort Worth Texas Boys' Ch.; (xxxix) John Calicos (nar.); (xl) Robinson, Chitjian, Los Angeles Festival Ch. & SO; (xli) Baxter, Albert, Gregg Smith Singers, Columbia Symphony Winds & Brass; (xlii) Verrett, Driscoll, Hornton (nar.); (xliii) Beardslee, Krebs, Lewis, Wainner, Morgan, Oliver, Schola Cantorum, Ross; all cond. composer. (xliv) Richard Frisch; (xlv) Baker, Igleman, Schonbach, Neikrug; (xlvi) Anderson, Bonazzi, Bressler, Gramm, Ithaca College Concert Ch., Gregg Smith; cond. Robert Craft.

On these 22 discs you have the unique archive of recordings which Stravinsky left of his own music. Presented in a sturdy plastic display box that enhances the desirability of the set, almost all the performances are conducted by the composer, with a few at the very end of his career – like the magnificent *Requiem canticles* – left to Robert Craft to conduct, with the composer supervising. In addition there is a handful of recordings of works otherwise not covered, mainly chamber pieces. With some recordings of Stravinsky talking and in rehearsal (included in the box devoted to the symphonies) it makes a vivid portrait.

Stravinsky may not have been a brilliant conductor, but in the recording studio he knew how to draw out alert, vigorous performances of his own music, and every one of these items illuminates facets of his inspiration which other interpreters often fail to notice. There are few if any rival versions of the *Rite of spring* – nowadays, astonishingly, his most frequently recorded work – to match his own recording of 1960 in its compelling intensity and inexorable sense of line.

The two volumes containing the major ballets are now also available separately, and are discussed below, also the *Symphonies* (Volume 4) and *The Rake's Progress* (Volume 9). In *Le rossignol* the singing is not always on a par with the conducting, but it is always perfectly adequate and the recording is brilliant and immediate. *Mavra* is sung in Russian and, as usual, the soloists – who are good – are too closely balanced, but the performance has punch and authority and on the whole the CD quality is fully acceptable.

The iron-fingered touch of Philippe Entremont has something to be said for it in the *Capriccio for piano and wind*, but this performance conveys too little of the music's charm. The *Movements for piano and orchestra* with the composer conducting could hardly be more compelling. Stern's account of the *Violin concerto in D* adds a romantic perspective to the framework, and at one time, no doubt, Stravinsky would have objected. But an expressive approach to Stravinsky is permissible in a soloist, when the composer is there to provide the bedrock under the expressive cantilena. Plainly this has the forthright spontaneity of a live performance.

The *Dumbarton Oaks concerto* with its obvious echoes of Bach's *Brandenburgs* is one of the most warmly attractive of Stravinsky's neo-classical works, all beautifully played and acceptably recorded. The *Octet for wind* of 1924 comes out with surprising freshness and, throughout, the unexpected combination of neo-Bach and neo-Pop is most refreshing. The *Ragtime* could be more lighthearted, but Stravinsky gives the impression of knowing what he wants. The *Ebony concerto*, in this version conducted by the composer, may have little of 'swung' rhythm, but it is completely faithful to Stravinsky's deadpan approach to jazz.

The songs represent a fascinating collection of trifles, chips from the master's workbench dating from the earliest years. There are many incidental delights, not least those in which the magnetic Cathy Berberian is featured.

The *Mass* is a work of the greatest concentration, a quality that comes out strongly if one plays this performance immediately after *The Flood*, with its inevitably slack passages. As directed in the score, trebles are used here, and it is a pity that the engineers have not brought them further forward: their sweet, clear tone is sometimes lost among the lower strands. In *The Flood*, originally written for television, it is difficult to take the bald narrations seriously, particularly when Laurence Harvey sanctimoniously keeps talking of the will of 'Gud'. *Perséphone* is full of that cool lyricism that marks much of Stravinsky's music inspired by classical myths. As with many of these vocal recordings, the balance is too close, and various orchestral solos are highlighted.

The *Cantata* of 1952 is a transitional piece between Stravinsky's tonal and serial periods. However, of the two soloists, Alexander Young is much more impressive than Adrienne Albert, for her voice is entirely unsuitable, with an unformed choirboy sound somehow married to wide vibrato. For the sake of Stravinsky one endures her. The *Canticum sacrum* includes music that some listeners might find tough (the strictly serial choral section). But the performance is a fine one and the tenor solo from Richard Robinson is very moving. The Bach *Chorale variations* has a synthetic modernity that recalls the espresso bar, though one which still reveals underlying mastery. The *Epitaphium* and the *Double canon* are miniatures, dating from the composer's serial period, but the *Canon* is deliberately euphonious.

Of the items recorded by Robert Craft, the *Requiem canticles* stands out, the one incontrovertible masterpiece among the composer's very last serial works and one of the most deeply moving works ever written in the serial idiom. Even more strikingly than in the *Mass* of 1948, Stravinsky conveys his religious feelings with a searing intensity. The *Aldous Huxley variations* are more difficult to comprehend but have similar intensity. Valuable, too, are the ballad *Abraham and Isaac* and the brief *Introitus for T. S. Eliot*.

Stravinsky Edition, Volume 2: Ballets etc.: *Agon; Apollo; Le baiser de la fée; Jeux de cartes; Orpheus;* (i) *Pulcinella. Scènes de ballet;* arr. of Tchaikovsky: *Bluebird pas de deux.*
(M) *** Sony SM3K 46292 [id.]. Columbia SO, LASO, Cleveland O, CBC SO, Chicago SO, composer; (i) with Jordan, Shirley, Gramm.

Stravinsky Edition, Volume 1: Ballets, etc.: *The Firebird; Fireworks; Histoire du soldat (The soldier's tale):* suite; *Les Noces (The Wedding); Petrushka* (original 1911 score); *Renard the fox; The Rite of spring; Scherzo à la russe; Scherzo fantastique.*
(M) *** Sony SM3K 46291 (3) [id.]. American Concert Ch., Columbia SO, CBC SO, Columbia Chamber Ens., Columbia Percussion Ens., composer.

Of the major ballets, *Petrushka* and *The Firebird* are valuable, but *The Rite* is required listening: it has real savagery and astonishing electricity. The link between *Jeu de cartes* from the mid-1930s and Stravinsky's post-war opera, *The Rake's Progress*, is striking and Stravinsky's sharp-edged conducting style underlines it, while the curiously anonymous-sounding *Scènes de ballet* certainly have their attractive moments. *Orpheus* has a powerful atmosphere, although one of Stravinsky's most classically restrained works. A good performance, with the composer's own authority lending it special interest. However, its invention is less memorable and distinguished than *Apollo*, one of Stravinsky's most gravely beautiful scores. *Agon* is one of the most stimulating of Stravinsky's later works. The orchestra respond with tremendous alertness and enthusiasm to Stravinsky's direction. The recording of *Le baiser de la fée* is a typical CBS balance with forward woodwind. However, if the recorded quality does not inspire too much enthusiasm, the performance certainly does. Stravinsky's recording of *Pulcinella* includes the vocal numbers, which, when well sung, add to the variety and sparkle of the piece, while in the orchestra the clowning of the trombone and the humour generally is strikingly vivid and never too broad. Similarly with the chamber scoring of the suite from *The Soldier's tale*, the crisp, clear reading brings out the underlying emotion of the music with the nagging, insistent little themes given an intensity that is almost tear-laden. There is a ruthlessness in the composer's own reading of *Les Noces* which exactly matches the primitive robustness in this last flowering of Russian nationalism in Stravinsky. The earlier parts are perhaps too rigid, but as the performance goes on so one senses the added alertness and enthusiasm of the performers. *Renard* is a curious work, a sophisticated fable which here receives too unrelenting a performance. The voices are very forward and tend to drown the instrumentalists.

Apollo (Apollon Musagète): ballet (complete).
*** DG 415 979-2 [id.]. BPO, Karajan – *Rite of spring.* ***
☞ (B) ** Virgin/EMI Dig. VJ5 61106-2 [id.]. SCO, Saraste – BARTOK: *Miraculous Mandarin.* **(*)

(i) *Apollo;* (ii) *The Firebird; Petrushka* (1911 score); *The Rite of spring* (complete ballets).
☞ ⑧ (B) *** Ph. Duo 438 350-2 [id.]. (i) LSO, Markevitch; (ii) LPO, Haitink.

An extraordinary bargain is offered by this highly recommendable Philips Duo reissue in combining the complete scores of Stravinsky's three popular, early, Diaghilev ballets with the later, sublime masterpiece, scored for strings alone. *Apollon Musagète* was written in 1927 and made famous a year later with choreography by Balanchine. Markevitch gives a gravely beautiful reading, and the slightly distanced balance is surely ideal, for the focus is excellent. The great *Pas de deux* is ravishing. No more refined account of *The Firebird* has ever been put on record than Haitink's. The sheer savagery of *Kashchei's dance* may be a little muted, but the sharpness of attack and clarity of detail make for a thrilling result, while the magic and poetry of the whole score are given a hypnotic beauty, with the LPO at its very finest. The 1973 recording has been remastered with great success, as it has in the other two Haitink ballets, made at the same time. In *Petrushka* the rhythmic feeling is strong, especially in the Second Tableau and the finale, where the fairground bustle is vivid. The LPO wind playing is especially fine; the recording's firm definition and the well-proportioned and truthful aural perspective make it a joy to listen to. The natural, unforced quality of Haitink's *Rite* also brings real compulsion. Other versions may hammer the listener more powerfully, thrust him or her along more forcefully; but the bite and precision of the playing here are most impressive.

Though Stravinsky tended to disparage Karajan's approach to his music as not being rugged enough, *Apollo* is a work where Karajan's moulding of phrase and care for richness of string texture make for wonderful results, and the writing is consistently enhanced by the magnificent playing of the Berlin Philharmonic Orchestra. The recording dates from 1973 and sounds excellent.

By the side of Markevitch, Saraste's version of *Apollo*, though very well played and spaciously recorded, sounds a much more routine affair, and the *Pas de deux* lacks magic. But if the coupling is suitable, this inexpensive Virgo disc might be considered.

Apollo; (i) *Capriccio for piano and orchestra. Le chant du rossignol; Circus polka;* (ii) *Concerto for piano and wind;* (iii) *Violin concerto. Petrushka* (complete; original (1911) ballet); *Symphony in E flat, Op. 1; Symphony in C; Symphony in 3 movements;* (iv) *Symphony of Psalms;* (iv; v) *Oedipus Rex.*
☞ ** Chan. Dig. CHAN 9240 (5) [id.]. SRO, Järvi, with (i) Geoffrey Tozer; (ii) Boris Berman; (iii) Lydia Mordkovitch; (iv) Chamber Ch., Lausanne Pro Arte Ch., Société Ch. de Brassus; (v) Gabriele Schnaut, Peter Svensson, Ruben Amoretti, Franz Grundheber, Günther von Kannen, Rudolf Rosen, Jean Plat.

Neeme Järvi offers typically red-blooded readings of this big five-disc collection of symphonies, concertos and ballets – plus *Oedipus Rex* – which firmly counters the idea that Stravinsky is a cold composer. These performances do not as a rule have the refinement and sharpness of focus that one ideally wants, but the thrust of the music comes over very convincingly, except in some of the slow movements, which – as in the *Symphony in three movements* – grow curiously stodgy rhythmically at relatively slow speeds. One exception to that is the *Violin concerto*, which is beautifully played by the richly warm-toned Lydia Mordkovitch, with the romantic expressiveness of the two central *Arias* an apt counterpart to the vigour and panache of the outer movements. Particularly winning is Järvi's performance of *Petrushka*, in which – using the 1911 score – he finds a sense of fun in the Shrovetide Fair, with the *Russian dance* given a superb bounce and with the ballerina's trumpet in the third tableau sounding genuinely jolly. Some of the work's subtlety may be missing, but such beefy treatment is most attractive, as it is in the *Circus polka* on the same disc. Even in *Apollo*, warmth is a quality to welcome. Otherwise the symphonies and concertos are all very successful in their outer movements and disappointing in their slow ones, with Geoffrey Tozer and Boris Berman both convincingly muscular soloists in the two concertante works with piano. The performance of the youthful *Symphony*, Op. 1, is particularly convincing in its warmth and thrust. Recording is warm and full, with less distracting reverberation than some Chandos offerings, though the chorus in the *Symphony of Psalms* is rather backwardly placed. *Oedipus Rex* is dealt with separately under opera.

Apollo; Orpheus (ballets).
*** ASV CDDCA 618 [id.]. O of St John's, Lubbock.

The ASV issue offers an ideal and generous coupling, with refined performances and excellent recording. The delicacy of the rhythmic pointing in *Apollo* gives special pleasure, and there is a first-rate solo violin contribution from Richard Deakin. This is one of Stravinsky's most appealing later scores, as readily accessible as the more famous ballets of his early years.

Le baiser de la fée (ballet; complete). TCHAIKOVSKY, arr. STRAVINSKY: *Sleeping Beauty: Bluebird pas de deux*.
*** Chan. CHAN 8360; *ABTD 1123* [id.]. SNO, Järvi.

The scoring here is a constant delight, much of it on a chamber-music scale; and its delicacy, wit and occasional pungency are fully appreciated by Järvi, who secures a wholly admirable response from his Scottish orchestra. The ambience seems exactly right, bringing out wind and brass colours vividly. The condensation of the scoring of the *Sleeping Beauty Pas de deux*, made for a wartime performance when only limited forces were available, also shows Stravinsky's orchestral individuality – he even introduces a piano.

Le baiser de la fée (Divertimento); The Firebird: suite (1919 version); *Pulcinella: suite*.
**(*) BMG/RCA Dig. RD 60394 [60394-2-RC]. RPO, Yuri Temirkanov.

Yuri Temirkanov has a feel for balletic nuance and a fine ear for orchestral detail. The performance of *Le baiser de la fée* is particularly attractive, with the lightest touch in the *Scherzo* and *Pas de deux*. The Rimskian colours in the *Firebird* emerge vividly, yet King Kastchei and his entourage are as malignantly pungent as anyone could wish, and the finale expands gloriously. Perhaps in *Pulcinella* the warm acoustics of Watford Town Hall are a little too amiable for the dances of Pergolesi focused through Stravinsky's harmonic and rhythmic distorting lens, but otherwise the recording is first class.

Le baiser de la fée (Divertimento); The Soldier's tale: suite; Suites for orchestra Nos. 1–2; Octet.
(M) *** Decca Dig. 433 079-2 [id.]. L. Sinf., Chailly.

Chailly's version of the *Le baiser de la fée* divertimento, admirably fresh, is superbly played and Decca's recording is in the finest traditions of the house. The pointing of the lighter rhythmic patterns is especially effective – and the espressivo playing is at once responsive and slightly cool, a most engaging combination. The two *Orchestral suites*, vivid orchestrations of *'Easy' pieces* for piano, provide a kaleidoscopic series of colourful vignettes. The 1922 *Octet* is a considerable piece for flute, clarinet, two bassoons, two trumpets, trombone and bass trombone. It is given a performance of infectious virtuosity, with individual bravura matched by polished ensemble and fine tonal blending. The surprisingly little-recorded concert suite from *The Soldier's tale*, added for this reissue, makes an impressive finale. The performance has great flair and finds sardonic humour in the combination of *Tango, Waltz* and *Ragtime* in the sparkling sixth movement. Throughout the programme, the CD is very much in the demonstration class.

(i) *Capriccio for piano and orchestra;* (ii) *Le chant du rossignol: Marche chinoise;* (iii) *Concerto for 2 solo pianos;* (ii) *Duo concertant; The Firebird: Berceuse; Scherzo. Petrushka: Danse russe;* (ii; iv) *Pastorale;* (ii) *Suite italienne: Serenata II; Scherzino. Piano-rag-music.* (v) *Ragtime. Serenade in A;* (vi) *Octet for wind;* (vii) *Les Noces;* (viii) *Symphony of Psalms.*

☞ (***) EMI mono CDS7 54607-2 (2) [Ang. ZCDB 54607]. Composer (piano or conductor), with (i) Walther Straram Concerts O, Ansermet; (ii) Samuel Dushkin; (iii) Soulima Stravinsky; (iv) Gromer, Durand, Vacellier, Grandmaison; (v) Lavaillotte, Godeau, Devemy, Foveau, Tudesq, Charmy, Volant, Ginot, Juste, Racz, Morel; (vi) Moyse, Godeau, Dhérin, Piard, Foveau, Vignal, Lafosse, Delbos; (vii) Mason, Heward, Lush, Benbow (pianos), Winter, Seymour, Parry Jones, Henderson, BBC Ch.; (viii) Vlassov Ch., Walther Straram Concerts O.

In the 1930s Stravinsky made a whole series of recordings on short-playing 78s which as performances are marvellously alert and refreshing. Aptly, as one of the first issues in EMI's 'Composers in Person' series, they have been collected into this two-disc box. They provide the most revealing of all Stravinsky's own recordings of his music, more intense and less mechanical than his American recordings. So in Paris in 1931 he recorded the *Symphony of Psalms* within a year of its première in Boston and the performance, though flawed, has a warmth and energy missing from his later LP recording, made with Canadian forces in 1963. Similarly in 1930 he had recorded another of his newer works of the time, the *Capriccio for piano and orchestra*, taking the solo part himself, with Ernest Ansermet conducting. He was not the greatest pianist, but there is a rhythmic point in the playing which allows a winning flexibility in the jazzy syncopations, while slily bringing out the echoes of Bach. In the last movement of the *Octet* too, which Stravinsky recorded with splendid French wind-players in 1932, the Cuban rhythms have a wit that is missing in his stricter, less expressive American recordings. In London in 1934 he also recorded the ballet, *Les Noces* (The Wedding), using an English translation and excellent British singers, led by the wonderfully firm and true soprano, Kate Winter. The other soloists were Linda Seymour, Parry Jones and Roy Henderson, with the professional BBC Chorus already beginning to establish a new British choral tradition. The four pianists too were all closely associated with the BBC's pioneering on radio at the time, and the result in what was then a difficult, avant-garde work is still electrifying, despite the limitations of the sound.

Much of the second of the two discs is taken up with violin and piano works and transcriptions, in which Stravinsky is joined by Samuel Dushkin; but even more enjoyable are the two jazz inspirations, *Ragtime for eleven instruments* and *Piano-Rag-Music*. It is understandable that Stravinsky's early recordings of the *Rite of spring* and *Petrushka* are left out here – the one poorly played, the other much cut – but, irritatingly, other 78 recordings of Stravinsky conducting have also been omitted, such as some movements from *Pulcinella*.

Le chant du rossignol (symphonic poem).
*** Erato/Warner 2292 45382-2 [id.]. Fr. Nat. O, Boulez – *Pulcinella.* **(*)
*** Decca Dig. 417 619-2 [id.]. Montreal SO, Dutoit – *Petrushka* etc. ***

The symphonic poem that Stravinsky made from the material of his opera, *Le Rossignol*, with its extraordinarily rich fantasy and vividness of colouring, deserves a more established place in the concert repertoire. The Boulez performance is masterly; the French National Orchestra on Erato capture detail vividly and have the advantage of a first-class 1982 recording.

Dutoit's account is full of colour and atmosphere and has the advantage of marvellous Montreal sound. The couplings too are particularly apt, and this is a very desirable disc in all respects.

Ebony concerto.
☞ *** BMG/RCA Dig. 09026 61350-2 [id.]. Stoltzman, Woody Herman's Thundering Herd –
   BERNSTEIN: *Prelude, fugue and riffs;* COPLAND; CORIGLIANO: *Concertos.* ***
*** Sony MK 42227 [id.]. Benny Goodman, Columbia Jazz Ens., composer – COPLAND: *Concerto;*
   BARTOK: *Contrasts;* BERNSTEIN: *Prelude, fugue and riffs;* GOULD: *Derivations.* (***)

Richard Stoltzman follows Benny Goodman before him in offering a suitably cool, yet lively and entirely idiomatic account of Stravinsky's *Ebony concerto*, coupled with Bernstein's *Prelude, fugue and riffs* and Copland's *Concerto*. Stolzman has the advantage of modern digital sound, and he also includes a fine account of John Corigliano's *Concerto*.

The *Ebony concerto* also sounds strikingly vivid in an apt compilation centred on Benny Goodman's other comparable recordings.

Violin concerto in D.
(M) *** Decca 425 003-2 [id.]. Kyung Wha Chung, LSO, Previn – PROKOFIEV: *Concertos 1–2.* ***
*** DG Dig. 423 696-2 [id.]. Mutter, Philh. O, Sacher – LUTOSLAWSKI: *Chain II; Partita.* ***
*** DG 413 725-2 [id.]. Perlman, Boston SO, Ozawa – BERG: *Concerto.* ***
☞ (M) *** Ph. 434 167-2 [id.]. David Oistrakh, LOP, Haitink – MOZART: *Violin concerto No. 1.* ***
☞ *** Decca Dig. 436 837-2 [id.]. Chantal Juillet, Montreal SO, Dutoit – SZYMANOWSKI: *Violin concertos.* **(*)

Kyung Wha Chung is at her most incisive in the spikily swaggering outer movements, which with Previn's help are presented here in all their distinctiveness, tough and witty at the same time. In the two movements labelled *Aria*, Chung brings fantasy as well as lyricism, less overtly expressive than Perlman (at full price) but conveying instead an inner, brooding quality. Brilliant Decca recording, the soloist diamond-bright in presence, but with plenty of orchestral atmosphere.

Mutter gives a strikingly characterful reading, neither brittle nor over-romanticized, with playing and recording of the very finest. There is no more recommendable version, and the coupling – an invigorating rather than a popular choice – is equally fine.

Perlman's precision, remarkable in both concertos on this disc, underlines the neo-classical element in the outer movements of the Stravinsky. The two *Aria* movements are more deeply felt and expressive, presenting the work as a major twentieth-century concerto. The balance favours the soloist, but no one will miss the commitment of the Boston orchestra's playing, vividly recorded.

Oistrakh's is a stunning performance of the Stravinsky *Concerto*, even stronger and more penetrating than Isaac Stern's under the composer. It is also better recorded. Both violinists were among the first to scotch the old idea of this work as something cold and arid, and Oistrakh brings out unexpected Russian qualities behind the neo-classical façade. The 1963 recording is reverberant, but the CD is much better focused than the old LP was. This limited edition is not likely to be available beyond the lifetime of this book.

A wiry and truthfully balanced performance by Juillet of the original and entertaining concerto Stravinsky composed for Samuel Dushkin in the early 1930s. No attempt is made to glamorize the soloist's sound, which is small-sounding in relation to the orchestra, as indeed it would be in the concert hall. By comparison with the tone produced by such artists as Perlman and Mutter, Chantal Juillet's is of minuscule size, but the performance as a whole has great character and orchestral detail is beautifully observed. A thoroughly enjoyable performance, with opulent Decca rcording.

(i) *Violin concerto in D; Symphony in E flat.*
☞ *** Chan. Dig. CHAN 9236 [id.]. (i) Mordkovitch; SRO, Neeme Järvi.

A highly recommendable account of the early *Symphony in E flat* from Neeme Järvi, coupled with a very characterful reading of the *Violin concerto*. This is very different from the clean, immaculate reading given by Chantal Juillet – this is gutsy and very Russian with a few rough edges (including an out-of-tune first entry). It has bags of character and is highly enjoyable. The Chandos recording is well balanced and finely detailed.

Danses concertantes; Pulcinella (ballet): *suite.*
*** Chan. Dig. CHAN 8325; *ABTD 1065* [id.]. ECO, Gibson.

Gibson and the ECO are very well recorded on Chandos and give highly enjoyable accounts of both works. The *Pulcinella* suite does not quite eclipse the Marriner (see below), but it is still very lively, and the *Danses concertantes* scores even over the composer's own in terms of charm and geniality. The CD is especially impressive in its firmness of detail.

The Firebird (ballet): complete.
☞ (M) *** Ph. 434 731-2; *434 731-4*. Concg. O, C. Davis – MUSSORGSKY: *Night.* **

The Firebird (complete); *Le chant du rossignol; Fireworks; Scherzo à la russe.*
⊛ (M) *** Mercury 432 012-2 [id.]. LSO, Dorati.

The Firebird (ballet; complete); *Fireworks, Op. 4; Scherzo fantastique, Op. 3.*
*** Decca Dig. 414 409-2 [id.]. Montreal SO, Dutoit.

The CD transfer of Dorati's electrifying, 1960 Mercury version of *The Firebird* with the LSO makes the recording sound as fresh and vivid as the day it was made; the brilliantly transparent detail and enormous impact suggest a modern digital source rather than an analogue master made over 30 years ago. The performance sounds completely spontaneous and the LSO wind playing is especially sensitive. Only the sound of the massed upper strings reveals the age of the original master, although this does not spoil the ravishing final climax; the bite of the brass and the transient edge of the percussion are thrilling. The recording of Stravinsky's glittering symphonic poem, *The song of the nightingale*, is hardly less compelling. Dorati's reading is urgent and finely pointed, yet is strong, too, on atmosphere. The other, shorter pieces also come up vividly.

Dutoit's version brings a characteristically colourful and atmospheric reading of Stravinsky's brilliant ballet score, ideally and generously coupled with the two early orchestral pieces which led Diaghilev to spot the young composer's talent. Thanks in part to Decca's sensuously beautiful

Montreal recording, this is a reading that brings out the light and shade of the writing, so that even *Kashchei's dance* is not just a brilliant showpiece but part of the poetic and dramatic scheme. The pianissimos are of breathtaking delicacy – very vital in this work: the hushed introduction to the final scene with its lovely horn solo brings a sense of wonder. The fill-ups are sparklingly done, making this a fine alternative choice.

With superb 1978 analogue sound, Sir Colin Davis directs a magically evocative account of the complete *Firebird* ballet, helped not just by the playing of the Concertgebouw Orchestra (the strings outstandingly fine) but also by the ambience of the hall, which allows inner clarity yet gives a bloom to the sound, open and spacious, superbly co-ordinated. The CD, digitally remastered, has sharpened up detail somewhat, at the expense of the magical analogue atmosphere. While there is more depth and bite, it is not all gain: although the brass has greater presence, the high violins sound less natural. Background noise has been virtually eliminated. The reissue on the Philips Insignia label omits any information about the music, concentrating instead on the conductor.

The Firebird: suite (1919 version).
☞ *** DG Dig. 437 818-2 [id.]. O de l'Opéra Bastille, Chung – RIMSKY-KORSAKOV: *Scheherazade*.
***

(*) Sony SK 45935 [id.]. Concg. O, Giulini – MUSSORGSKY: *Pictures*. *

Myung-Whun Chung gets very musical results from his players and there are many imaginative touches. The sound has great warmth and richness (perhaps too much for some tastes) but the perspective is absolutely right and benefits from the technical expertise of Wolfgang Mitelehner and Lennart Dehn, who was Chung's Gothenburg producer.

The Concertgebouw acoustic – as anyone who has experienced live music-making there will know – is less than ideal for fast-moving, sharply dissonant twentieth-century music. Its wide reverberation tends to blur the transients, as here in *Kashchei's dance* which, however, does not lack malignancy. It also brings a voluptuous weight to the richly scored finale, perhaps unmatched on record. Giulini secures wonderfully refined playing in the gentler music, but the lack of rhythmic bite minimizes the balletic feeling and makes the suite seem more symphonic than usual.

Jeu de cartes.
☞ (*) Teldec/Warner mono 9031 76440-2 [id.]. BPO, composer – HINDEMITH: *Mathis der Maler*. (*)

Although the Nazis had at first been cool towards Stravinsky, the composer's admiration for Mussolini and his 'negative attitude' – to use no stronger expression – towards communism and jewry resulted in no obstacles being placed in the way of his 1938 visit when this pioneering account of *Jeu de cartes* was recorded. The recording was apparently squeezed between a Mengelberg concert on the previous day and a repeat performance for the 'Strength through Joy' movement that evening, so it is not the last word in polish. There is plenty of vitality though, and the recording was excellent for its period, even if the present transfer does not do it full justice. The disc offers short measure at 45 minutes 53 seconds.

Petrushka (ballet; 1911 score) complete.
*** DG Dig. 423 901-2 [id.]. LSO, Abbado – MUSSORGSKY: *Pictures*. ***

Petrushka (1911 score); *4 Etudes*.
*** Decca Dig. 417 619-2 [id.]. Montreal SO, Dutoit – *Chant du rossignol*. ***

Dutoit in his Montreal version, benefiting from superb, atmospheric but well-detailed sound, gives a sparkling performance that brings out the light and shade of *Petrushka*, its poetry and its rhythmic effervescence. As in other brilliant showpieces, the refinement of Montreal pianissimos adds to the atmospheric thrill, but there is no lack of either power or bite in this subtle telling of the story. The coupling of *Le Chant du rossignol* and the *Four Studies* is apt.

Abbado combines refinement and a powerful sense of dramatic atmosphere (he is especially sympathetic in the central tableaux) with a kaleidoscopic brilliance. The recording has impressive range and colour, but there is a degree of digital edge on the upper strings which is certainly not entirely natural.

Petrushka (1911 version; complete). *The Firebird: suite* (1919). *Fireworks; Pastoral* (arr. Stokowski).
☞ ⊛ (***) Dutton Lab. mono CDAX 8002 [id.]. Phd. O, Stokowski (with: SHOSTAKOVICH: *Prelude in E flat min., Op. 34/14*, arr. Stokowski (***)).

Strangely enough, the present version of *Petrushka* has not been reissued in any form (at least in the UK) since the days of 78s. It is very special indeed. Those who have the 78s will know that the sound is tremendously present and amazingly detailed for its period (1937) – high fidelity even by today's standards – and that the performance is marvellously characterized and full of atmosphere: indeed it is difficult to think of a portrayal of Petrushka himself that is more poignant, keenly felt or brilliantly coloured. (Perhaps Bernstein's CBS account from the 1960s comes closest.) The playing of the Philadelphia Orchestra is quite stunning, and the Dutton transfer gets far more detail on to CD than the RCA rival; it is also smoother on top. The 1935 *Firebird suite* (its ending cut, to fit on a 78-r.p.m. side) takes wing too – equally strongly characterized and full of atmosphere. The shorter pieces are rarities: the Shostakovich *Prelude*, a brand-new piece at this time, was the fill-up to *Firebird*, and the *Pastoral* and *Fireworks* were issued only in the USA. A marvellous collection – indeed, a desert island disc.

Petrushka (1911 version); *The Rite of spring*.
☞ (M) (***) BMG/RCA mono 09026 61394-2. Phd. O, Stokowski.

Leopold Stokowski's pioneering recordings of *Petrushka* and the *Rite of spring* make an ideal CD coupling in RCA's Legendary Performers series at mid-price. It is an astonishing tribute to the standards that Stokowski was achieving, that the Philadelphia Orchestra in 1929 was able to play *The Rite* with such flair, and *Petrushka* similarly in 1937. The transfers are bright and vivid but rather shallow, with *Petrushka* no match for the Dutton issue, and the *Rite* less full-bodied than in the Pearl issue of works that Stokowski included in the Disney film *Fantasia* (GEMM CD 9488).

Petrushka (1947 version); *The Rite of spring*.
(M) *** Collins Dig. 3033-2 [id.]. LSO, Frühbeck de Burgos.

(i) *Petrushka* (1947 score); *The Rite of spring;* (ii) *4 Etudes for orchestra*.
☞ (M) **(*) Mercury 434 331-2 [id.]. (i) Minneapolis SO; (ii) LSO; Dorati.

Frühbeck de Burgos's *Rite of spring* may go over the top a bit in its high-flying histrionics but, if the reading has less firmness of grip than Haitink's, the result is much more thrilling, with the forward balance of the drums bringing a thundering impact to an already spectacular recording. The LSO are clearly on their toes and their playing in *Petrushka* is even more impressive. The bite of the strings and edge on the brass gives the piece great rhythmic vitality; the pathos of Petrushka's predicament in his cell is the more striking, contrasted with the animated jollity of the *Danse russe*, and there is a galaxy of colour in the vibrant Shrovetide fair sequences. The digital recording, made at Walthamstow Town Hall, approaches the demonstration bracket.

Dorati's famous (1959) Mercury recording of *Petrushka* is exceptionally clean and vivid, with the semi-clinical Minneapolis recording bringing stereoscopic detail in the two central tableaux. There is plenty of drama too, and the final scene is touchingly done. Inevitably the sound is dated, with the bright upper range as caught by the Telefunken microphones not quite natural, but this adds a sharp cutting edge and impact to Dorati's extremely violent performance of *The Rite of spring*. His speeds are fast – sometimes considerably faster than is indicated in the score – but the LSO players carry complete conviction, the tautness of the work the more clearly revealed. Salient details shine out aginst the overall texture like flashes of lightning even in the middle of the loudest, most complex tuttis. The effect is very powerful and the classic status of this performance is confirmed. The orchestral *Etudes* were recorded later (1964) in Watford, and have a fuller ambience but no less vividness.

Petrushka (1947 version); *Symphony in 3 movements*.
*** EMI Dig. CDC7 49053-2 [id.]. CBSO, Rattle.

Using the revised, 1947 scoring, Rattle gives a reading which brings out powerfully the sturdy jollity of the ballet, contrasting it with the poignancy of the puppet's own feelings. The full and brilliant recording is beefy in the middle and bass, but Rattle and his players benefit in clarity from the 1947 scoring, finely detailed to bring out many points that are normally obscured. The *Symphony in three movements*, done with comparable power, colour and robustness, makes an unusual but attractive coupling. With his jazz training, Rattle brings out the syncopations and pop references with great panache.

Pulcinella (ballet) complete.
☞ (M) *** EMI CDM7 64739-2 [id.]. Jennifer Smith, John Fryatt, Malcolm King, N. Sinfonia,
    Rattle – WEILL: *Die sieben Todsünden*. ***
**(*) Erato/Warner 2292 45382-2 [id.]. Murray, Rolfe Johnson, Estes, Ens. InterContemporain,
    Boulez – *Le Chant du rossignol*. ***

(i) *Pulcinella* (complete); *Danses concertantes.*

☞ (M) *** Virgin/EMI Dig. VJ5 61107-2 [id.]. (i) Murray, Hill, D. Thomas; City of L. Sinfonia, Richard Hickox.

(i) *Pulcinella* (complete); *Dumbarton Oaks concerto.*

*** Decca Dig. 425 614-2 [id.]. Bernadette Manca di Nissa, Gordon, Ostendorf, Howard, St Paul CO, Hogwood – GALLO: *Trio sonata movements;* PERGOLESI: *Sinfonia.* ***

(i) *Pulcinella* (complete); *Renard. Ragtime; Octet.*

*** Sony Dig. SK 45965 [id.]. (i) Kenny, Aler, Tomlinson, Robson, Wilson-Johnson; L. Sinf., Esa-Pekka Salonen.

Richard Hickox emphasizes the colour in *Pulcinella*, to bring this neo-classical work, rooted in the eighteenth century, into the full light of the twentieth. So with sound that gives weight and body as well as plenty of detail he relishes the joke behind the *Vivo*, for example, with its trombone raspberries and lumbering double-bass. Equally he gives plenty of balletic bounce to the allegro movements and expressive warmth to the vocal numbers, phrasing in a romantic rather than a classical way. Among the soloists the tenor, Martyn Hill, stands out, though all are good. Hickox similarly gives a strong reminder that the *Danses concertantes* are, above all, ballet music, colourful and vigorous. Warm, full sound. Now reissued on the bargain Virgo label, this version of *Pulcinella* makes a clear first choice.

Christopher Hogwood has here investigated Stravinsky's own sources. The composer used material from 21 different sources, all of them attributed to Pergolesi at the time, but in fact written by five different composers. As a delightful appendix, Hogwood adds some of the originals. The Pergolesi *Sinfonia* provides in its finale the idea for the *Vivo*, while the four movements from *Trio sonatas* by Domenico Gallo provide the themes for the opening overture, among other things. In keeping with this approach, Hogwood directs refined, deliberately lightweight performances of the two Stravinsky works, as much classical as neo-classical. Yet comparison with the eighteenth-century originals consistently makes you understand how Stravinsky's additions transform rather plain ideas. Of the three vocal soloists in *Pulcinella* the most striking is the firm-toned mezzo-soprano, Bernadette Manca di Nissa.

Simon Rattle, within a somewhat dry recording acoustic, conveys far more than usual the links between this score and the much later neo-classical opera, *The Rake's Progress.* With lively and colourful playing from the Northern Sinfonia (the solos strong and positive) and with first-rate contributions from the three soloists, the high spirits of this score come over superbly. The current CD transfer adds vividness and presence without loss of bloom, and the new coupling is very generous indeed.

The complete *Pulcinella* is generously coupled on Sony with three other characteristic works from the years following the First World War, with Salonen taking every opportunity to point the music with wit. He may be less objective than some rivals, but not only is the fun behind much of this music delightfully brought out, he moulds it sufficiently to suggest a warmth behind neo-classical forms and, frequently, a debt to jazz. That is so not just in *Ragtime* but also in such a work as the delightful *Octet* of 1922–3. When *Pulcinella* is here given with voices, it is good to have another early example of music-theatre in *Renard*, necessarily a rarity in concert, with the Russian folk-tale presented with bluff good humour. Warm recording to match.

Boulez secures superb playing from the Ensemble InterContemporain, and his singers are first class in every way. His is a fine performance, but his pacing is more extreme than some versions, with contrasts between movements almost overcharacterized. However, some may like the periodic added edge, and the Erato recording has been excellently transferred to CD.

(i) *Pulcinella* (ballet; complete); *The Rite of spring.*

☞ (B) *** DG 439 433-2 [id.]. (i) Berganza, Ryland Davies, Shirley-Quirk; LSO, Abbado.

Abbado gives a vividly high-powered reading of the neo-classical score of *Pulcinella*. If he is in danger of over-colouring, the bite and flair are entirely and convincingly Stravinskian, with rhythms sharply incisive. Not just the playing but the singers too are outstandingly fine. The LSO plays with superb virtuosity and Abbado's feeling for atmosphere and colour is everywhere in evidence, heard against an excellently judged perspective. There is a degree of detachment in *The Rite of spring*; but on points of detail it is meticulous. There is a hypnotically atmospheric feeling at the opening of Part Two, emphasizing the contrast with the brutal music which follows. The drama is heightened by the wide dynamic range of the recording, and the effect is forceful without ever becoming ugly. An excellent Classikon bargain coupling.

The Rite of spring (complete ballet) (see also above, under *Petrushka*).

*** DG 415 979-2 [id.]. BPO, Karajan – *Apollo*. ***

(M) *** EMI Dig. CDM7 64516-2 [id.]. Phd. O, Muti – MUSSORGSKY: *Pictures*. ***

☞ (M) **(*) Telarc Dig. CD 82001 [id.]. Cleveland O, Maazel – SHOSTAKOVICH: *Symphony No. 5*. ***

☞ *(**) Sup. 11 1948-2 [id.]. Czech PO, Karel Ančerl – PROKOFIEV: *Alexander Nevsky*. **(*)

☞ (M) (*) Sony SBK 48169 [id.]. NYPO, Mehta – PROKOFIEV: *Romeo & Juliet*. **(*)

The Rite of spring; Circus Polka; Fireworks, Op. 4; Greeting prelude (Happy birthday).

(M) **(*) EMI Dig. CD-EMX 2188. LPO, Mackerras.

The Rite of spring (complete); *4 Etudes for orchestra; Scherzo à la russe*.

☞ (M) **(*) Teldec/Warner Dig. 4509 91449-2 [id.]. Philh. O, Inbal.

Karajan's earlier (1966) version (currently not available) came in for criticism from the composer, who doubted whether Berlin Philharmonic traditions could encompass music from so different a discipline. Nevertheless, in his 1977 version (coupled with *Apollo*), tougher, more urgent, less mannered, Karajan goes a long way towards rebutting Stravinsky's complaints, and the result is superb, above all powerfully dramatic.

Muti's *Rite of spring* offers a performance which is aggressively brutal yet presents the violence with red-blooded conviction. Muti generally favours speeds a shade faster than usual, and arguably the opening bassoon solo is not quite flexible enough, for metrical precision is a key element all through. The recording, not always as analytically clear as some rivals, is strikingly bold and dramatic, with brass and percussion caught exceptionally vividly. At mid-price, coupled with an equally outstanding version of Mussorgsky's *Pictures*, this is very competitive indeed.

Mackerras's version is at mid-price on the Eminence label and brings a powerful, often spacious performance, recorded in opulent and finely textured, if slightly distanced sound. The weight of the recording adds powerfully to the dramatic impact, though it is a pity that timpani are backward and less sharply focused than they might be. Though short measure, the three little orchestral trifles are done by Mackerras with delectable point and wit.

The sound on the Cleveland Orchestra version conducted by Lorin Maazel is also pretty spectacular. However, there are a number of sensation-seeking effects, such as excessive ritardandi in the *Rondes printanières* so as to exaggerate the trombone glissandi, which are vulgar. Compare, too, the opening of Part Two in this version with that of Karajan, and one is in a totally different world.

Many collectors regard Karel Ančerl's 1963 recording of *The Rite of spring* very highly. The Czech Philharmonic was playing extremely well in the early 1960s and there is much power and virtuosity in this performance and a very high level of adrenalin, particularly in the *Adoration* and *Danse de la terre* in Part One and in the final *Danse sacrale*. The dark melancholy of the *Cercles mystérieux des adolescentes* is poignantly conveyed. The recording was originally very reverberant, and the Czech remastering brings that pinched effect in the treble which gives added bite and clarity and increases the impact, but which also adds an artificial edge to the sound. However, to reissue this at full price, even with an outstanding Prokofiev coupling, seems unrealistic.

Inbal's version was placed among the top three of all available recordings of Stravinsky's ballet in a survey by Michael Stewart in *Gramophone* magazine in September 1992. He admired its 'earthiness', violence and sense of mystery. We find Inbal rather metrical, making the music sound too safe, though the effect is clean and pungent. The couplings are ungenerous but very well played, especially the *Scherzo à la russe* with its flavour of *Petrushka*. The recording is full, smooth and vivid.

Mehta's account of *The Rite* is pretty characterless – activity without any real excitement. The New York orchestra play efficiently and the disc is to be acquired for the coupling: Mitropoulos's *Romeo and Juliet*.

The Rite of spring (orchestral & pianola versions).

(M) *** Pickwick Dig. MCD 25; *MCC 25*. Boston PO, Zander.

The most fascinating of the recent recordings of Stravinsky's *Rite of spring* is Benjamin Zander's live recording with the Boston Philharmonic, full and vivid if slightly confined in sound. It brings a hard-hitting, colourful performance, directly related to the pianola version with which it is coupled. Stravinsky himself in the 1920s supervised the original Pleyela piano roll recording, which Rex Lawson 'plays' very effectively on a resonant Bösendorfer Imperial. The speeds at which everything is presented remain predetermined and unalterable; and here the most striking point on speed is the very fast tempo for the opening of the final *Sacrificial dance*, markedly faster even than Stravinsky's own on the last – and finest – of his three recordings. Zander suggests (and he offers additional documentary evidence) that Stravinsky intended a faster pacing for the ballet's finale and that he modified the tempo only when he discovered that orchestras could not cope with the music at his intended speed (even his own 1960 recording contains inaccuracies). There is no doubt that, played up to this faster tempo, the *Danse sacrale* is electrifying and, once experienced, the slower speed to which we are all accustomed seems comparatively restrained.

The Soldier's tale (complete).
*** Nimbus Dig. NI 5063 [id.]. Christopher Lee, SCO, Lionel Friend.

With the actor Christopher Lee both narrating and taking the individual parts, the Nimbus issue brings an attractively strong and robust reading, lacking the last degree of refinement but with some superb solo playing – from the violinist, for example. The recording is vivid and full of presence, with the speaking voice related to instruments far better than is usual. For a version in English, it makes an excellent investment.

The Soldier's tale (suite).
(M) *** Van. 08.8013.71 [OVC 8013]. Instrumental Ens., Leopold Stokowski – THOMSON: *Film scores.* ***

Stokowski works his magic upon this surprisingly neglected score, making the most of its lyrical warmth as well as the more abrasive Devil's music, which has plenty of rhythmic bite. The septet of expert instrumentalists is naturally recorded in a studio acoustic, but one which has plenty of ambience.

Stravinsky Edition, Volume 4: *Symphony in E flat; Symphony in C; Symphony in 3 movements;* (i) *Symphony of Psalms.* Stravinsky in rehearsal; Stravinsky in his own words.
(M) *** Sony SM2K 46294 (2) [id.]. Columbia SO or CBC SO; (i) Toronto Festival Singers, composer.

In the early *Symphony in E flat*, Op. 1, the young Stravinsky's material may be comparatively conventional and the treatment much too bound to the academic procedures taught him by his master, Rimsky-Korsakov, but at least in this performance the music springs to life. Each movement has its special delights to outweigh any shortcomings. The performance is obviously as near definitive as it could be. The composer's account of the *Symphony in three movements* is an object lesson for every conductor who has tried to perform this work. Stravinsky shows how, by vigorous, forthright treatment of the notes, the emotion implicit is made all the more compelling. The Columbia Symphony plays superbly and the recording is full and brilliant. Stravinsky never quite equalled the intensity of the pre-war 78-r.p.m. performance of the *Symphony of Psalms.* That had many more technical faults than his later, stereo version, and it is only fair to say that this new account is still impressive. It is just that, with so vivid a work, it is a shade disappointing to find Stravinsky as interpreter at less than maximum voltage. Even so, the closing section of the work is very beautiful and compelling. The CD transfers of the American recordings are somewhat monochrome by modern standards but fully acceptable.

Symphony in C; Symphony in 3 movements.
(M) *** Chan. Dig. CHAN 6577 [id.]. Royal Scottish O, Sir Alexander Gibson.

Even when compared with the composer's own versions, these performances by the Royal Scottish Orchestra – in excellent form – stand up well. The vivid naturalness of the splendid 1982 digital recording compensates for any slight lack of bite, and the inner movements of both works are beautifully played. The cool, almost whimsical beauty of the *Andante* of the *Symphony in three movements* is most subtly conveyed, and altogether this is very enjoyable.

(i) *Symphony in C; Symphony in 3 movements;* (ii) *Symphonies of wind instruments; Scherzo fantastique, Op. 3.*
☞ (M) *** Decca Dig. 436 474-2 [id.]. (i) SRO; (ii) Montreal SO; Dutoit.

Although the Suisse Romande Orchestra is not in the very first rank, the brilliant recording it now receives from the Decca team and the alert direction of Charles Dutoit make this a very winning coupling. The *Symphony in C* and *Symphony in three movements* are both exhilarating pieces and Dutoit punches home their virile high spirits and clean-limbed athleticism. The *Symphonies of wind instruments*, the work Stravinsky composed in 1920 in memory of Debussy, is given a very effective and crisp performance, and the sparkling *Scherzo fantastique* also demonstrates the greater polish of the Montreal players.

CHAMBER AND INSTRUMENTAL MUSIC

Concerto for two solo pianos; Scherzo à la russe (arr. Stravinsky); *Sonata for two pianos; Le sacre du printemps* (arr. Stravinsky).
☞ *** Decca Dig. 433 829-2 [id.]. Vladimir Ashkenazy, Andrei Gavrilov.

Recording two pianos is no easy task, but the Decca engineers rise to the occasion. So, it must be said, do the two distinguished pianists, who give a breath-taking exhibition of unanimity, rhythmic projection and keyboard colour. Their account of Stravinsky's own arrangement of *Le sacre du printemps* can only be described as dazzling, and the *Scherzo à la russe*, a rarity in this transcription, is a delight. The *Concerto for two solo pianos*, Stravinsky at his most neo-classical, comes from the 1930s and was written for him and his son Soulima to play on tour. Both this and the 1943 *Sonata* are given marvellously exhilarating performances by Ashkenazy and Gavrilov, whose virtuosity is matched by a sense of spontaneity and delight in their music-making.

Divertimento.
*** Ph. Dig. 426 254-2 [id.]. Viktoria Mullova, Bruno Canino – PROKOFIEV: *Sonata No. 2 in D* **;
    RAVEL: *Sonata in G.* ***

The *Divertimento* is an arrangement Stravinsky made in 1933 of his orchestral score, *Le Baiser de la fée*. Quite simply, it is played marvellously by Viktoria Mullova and Bruno Canino and most vividly and naturally recorded.

Elégie, for solo viola.
*** EMI CDC7 54394-2 [id.]. Tabea Zimmermann – BRITTEN: *Lachrymae;* SHOSTAKOVICH: *Viola sonata.* ***

Stravinsky's solo *Elégie* is finely played and recorded here and comes with moving accounts of the Britten *Lachrymae* and Shostakovich's deeply felt *Sonata*.

Suite italienne.
*** BIS Dig. CD 336 [id.]. Torleif Thedéen, Roland Pöntinen – SCHNITTKE: *Sonata;*
    SHOSTAKOVICH: *Sonata.* ***

Stravinsky made several transcriptions of movements from *Pulcinella*, including the *Suite italienne* for violin and piano. The performances by Torleif Thedéen and Roland Pöntinen, Swedish artists both in their mid-twenties, are felicitous and spontaneous, and they are afforded strikingly natural recording.

*Circus polka; 4 Etudes, Op. 7; Piano-rag-music; Scherzo; Serenade in A; Sonata in F sharp min.;
Sonata (1924); Tango.*
☞ *** Collins Dig. 1374-2 [id.]. Victor Sangiorgio.

Victor Sangiorgo plays with great character and virtuosity, and in some pieces is more successful and more thoughtful than his previous rivals. He also benefits from vivid and present recording. Thoroughly recommendable.

Circus polka; Piano-rag-music; Serenade in A; Sonata; 4 Studies; Tango.
☞ (M) **(*) Saga EC 3391-2 [id.]. Thomas Rajna.

Some may feel that in Thomas Rajna's hands Stravinsky's piano music is made to sound too soft-centred and without enough rhythmic toughness – even the *Tango* and *Circus polka* have charm. But the *Sonata* is taken seriously and there is an imaginative variety of colour in the *Serenade*: its unexpectedly tranquil closing *Cadenza finala* is played with lucid imperturbability. This is always intelligent as well as sympathetic playing, and many may respond to it who would reject a more percussive approach. The recording is natural but is projected not very forwardly.

3 Movements from Petrushka.
*** DG 419 202-2 [id.]. Maurizio Pollini – *Recital.* ***

Staggering, electrifying playing from Pollini, creating the highest degree of excitement. This is part of an outstandingly generous recital of twentieth-century piano music.

VOCAL MUSIC

*4 Cat's cradle songs; 4 Chants; Elegy for JFK; In memoriam Dylan Thomas; 3 Japanese lyrics;
Pastorale; 2 Poems by Konstantin Bal'mont; 2 Poems by Paul Verlaine; Pribaoutki* (4 songs);
Recollections of childhood (3 songs); *2 Sacred songs* (from WOLF: *Spanish Lieder Book*); *3 Shakespeare songs; 4 Songs; Tilim-bom; Mavra: Parasha's aria.*

(M) *** DG 431 751-2 [id.]. Bryn-Julson, Murray, Tear, Shirley-Quirk, Ens. InterContemporain,
   Boulez.

Anyone who thinks a Stravinsky song could not be utterly charming should try the first item of this
recital, the *Pastorale*, a song without words for voice and four wind instruments: Phyllis Bryn-
Julson's performance is captivating. Practically all of Stravinsky's songs are accommodated on this
useful CD. All the singing here is very persuasive and well characterized. The Verlaine songs are,
oddly enough, given in Russian (Stravinsky originally set them in French), but Shirley-Quirk makes
them sound very appealing nevertheless. The record also includes a 1968 transcription of two of
Wolf's Spanish songs, his very last opus. The CD transfer is immaculate, with natural, well-focused
sound, and translations are provided where necessary.

(i) *Mass;* (ii) *Les Noces.*
(M) *** DG 423 251-2 [id.]. (i) Trinity Boys' Ch., E. Bach Festival O; (i, ii) E. Bach Festival Ch.; (ii)
   Mory, Parker, Mitchinson, Hudson; Argerich, Zimerman, Katsaris, Francesch (pianos),
   percussion; cond. Bernstein.

In the *Mass* the style is overtly expressive, with the boys of Trinity Choir responding freshly, but it is
in *Les Noces* that Bernstein conveys an electricity and a dramatic urgency which give the work its
rightful stature as one of Stravinsky's supreme masterpieces, totally original and – even today –
unexpected, not least in its black-and-white instrumentation for four pianos and percussion. The star
pianists here make a superb, imaginative team.

(i) *Perséphone. The Rite of spring.*
(M) *** Virgin/EMI Dig. VCK7 91511-2 (2) [id.]. (i) Anne Fournet, Rolfe Johnson, Tiffin Boys'
   School Ch., LPO Ch.; LPO, Kent Nagano.

Stravinsky's two great evocations of spring make fascinating partners. Where Stravinsky himself – at
speeds consistently more measured than Nagano's – takes a rugged, square-cut view of *Perséphone*,
Nagano, much lighter as well as more fleet, makes the work a far more atmospheric evocation of
spring. The playing and singing are consistently more refined, and the modern digital recording gives
a warm bloom, while the sung French sounds far more idiomatic from everyone. The narration of
Anne Fournet brings out all the beauty of Gide's words, with Anthony Rolfe Johnson free-toned in
the taxing tenor solos. Nagano's reading of *The Rite of spring* has similar qualities. If it is less
weightily barbaric than many, the springing of rhythm and the clarity and refinement of instrumental
textures make it very compelling, with only the final *Danse sacrale* lacking something in dramatic
bite. The two separate discs are offered at mid-price in a single slim jewel-case.

(i) *Renard. The Soldier's tale;* (ii) *3 Pieces for clarinet solo; Ragtime;* (iii) *3 Japanese lyrics.*
(B) *** Hung. White Label HRC 078. Budapest Chamber Ens., András Mihály, (i) Gulyás, Keonch,
   Polgar, Bordas; (ii) Berkes; (iii) Adrienne Csengery.

Mihály's well-planned Stravinsky collection, colourfully performed and recorded, makes an outstanding bargain in Hungaroton's White Label series. The oddity is that *The Soldier's tale* has the full text
of the entertainment, over half an hour long, but without any dramatic dialogue. Both in the
dramatic scena, *Renard* – with four excellent soloists – and in *Ragtime*, the cimbalom plays a
prominent part and, aptly in Budapest performances, Marta Fabian's brilliant, idiomatic playing of
that Hungarian instrument is put well to the fore. The clear, silvery soprano, Adrienne Csengery,
gives delightful performances of the *Japanese lyrics* and Kálmán Berkes is an agile clarinettist in the
unaccompanied pieces.

OPERA

Oedipus Rex (opera-oratorio).
*** Sony Dig. SK 48057 [id.]. Cole, Von Otter, Estes, Sotin, Gedda, Chéreau, Eric Ericson Chamber
   Ch., Swedish RSO & Ch., Salonen.
☞ *** EMI Dig. CDC7 54445-2 [id.]. Rolfe Johnson, Lipovšek, Tomlinson, Miles, LPO Ch., LPO,
   Welser-Möst.
☞ ** Ph. Dig. 438 865-2 [id.]. Schreier, Norman, Terfel, Peters, Wilson, Shinyukai Male Ch., Saito
   Kinen O, Ozawa.
☞ ** Chan. CHAN 9235 [id.]. Svensson, Schnaut, Von Kannen, Grundheber, Amoretti, Piat (nar.),
   Suisse Romande R. Ch., SRO, Järvi.

Salonen with his Swedish forces and an outstanding cast, more consistent than any previous one,
conducts the strongest performance yet on disc of this landmark of modern opera. He offers an ideal
combination of rugged power and warmth, delivered expressively but without sentimentality. The

pinpoint precision of ensemble of the choruses, substantial but not so big as to impair sharpness of focus, does more than anything else to punch home the impact of this so-called opera-oratorio, with its powerful commentary, Greek-style. The singing of the two principals, Vinson Cole as Oedipus and Anne Sofie von Otter as Jocasta, then conveys the full depth of emotion behind the piece. Simon Estes as Creon and Hans Sotin as Tiresias are both firm and resonant, with Nicolai Gedda still strong as the Shepherd. With recorded sound both dramatically immediate and warm, and with splendid narration in French from Patrice Chéreau, this displaces all rivals, even the composer's own American version.

As the years go by, the depth of emotion in Stravinsky's baldly stylized opera-oratorio hits the listener, despite the detached treatment and abrasive idiom. Following that, Franz Welser-Möst and the London Philharmonic take an expressive rather than a severe, neo-classical view. The singing of the men of the London Philharmonic Choir is less incisive than that of the principal rivals but is satisfyingly weighty, and the soloists are on balance the most involvingly characterful of any, led by Anthony Rolfe Johnson, magnificent as Oedipus. Sir Colin Davis's fine Bavarian Radio version for Orfeo was marred by the unsteady Oedipus of Thomas Moser, and Esa-Pekka Salonen's Swedish performance for Sony had an exceptionally light and lyrical Oedipus in Vinson Cole, where Rolfe Johnson is not only weightily heroic but inflects words more meaningfully than any. Marjana Lipovšek brings mature warmth and weight to the role of Jocasta, easily to rival Anne Sofie von Otter on Sony, while John Tomlinson as Creon and John Mark Ainsley as the Shepherd are outstanding too. Only the brisk, prosaic French narration of Lambert Wilson sells the listener short.

Where the prize-winning stage production of *Oedipus Rex* from Japan (available on video) has Philip Langridge in the title-role, the CD offers a very similar cast but with Peter Schreier as Oedipus. Ozawa's conducting is just as warmly dramatic and powerful, and Jessye Norman's Jocasta has a commanding intensity never surpassed, with a relatively short role assuming key importance. Yet Schreier sounds too old and strained to be convincing, robbing the rest of the impact it should have. Only in his final hushed *Lux facta est* does Schreier convey full intensity, but that is hardly enough.

As in the rest of his boxed set of Stravinsky recordings with the Suisse Romande Orchestra, Järvi offers a full-blooded reading of *Oedipus Rex*, but the casting is uneven, with Gabriele Schnaut wobbly and shrill as Jocasta and with pianissimos sadly lacking from anyone, partly a question of recording-balance. The result in its roughness conveys power, with a good narrator in Jean Piat, but this masterpiece requires more refinement of detail.

Stravinsky Edition, Volume 9: *The Rake's progress* (complete).
(M) *** Sony SM2K 46299 (2) [id.]. Young, Raskin, Reardon, Sarfaty, Miller, Manning, Sadler's Wells Op. Ch., RPO, composer.

The Rake's progress (complete).
**(*) Decca Dig. 411 644-2 (2) [id.]. Langridge, Pope, Walker, Ramey, Dean, Dobson, L. Sinf. Ch. & O, Chailly.

The Rake of Alexander Young is a marvellous achievement, sweet-toned and accurate and well characterized. In the choice of other principals, too, it is noticeable what store Stravinsky set by vocal precision. Judith Raskin makes an appealing Anne Trulove, sweetly sung if not particularly well projected dramatically. John Reardon too is remarkable more for vocal accuracy than for striking characterization, but Regina Sarfaty's Baba is marvellous on both counts. The Sadler's Wells Chorus sings with even greater drive under the composer than in the theatre, and the Royal Philharmonic play with a warmth and a fittingly Mozartian sense of style to match Stravinsky's surprisingly lyrical approach to his score. The CDs offer excellent sound.

Riccardo Chailly draws from the London Sinfonietta playing of a clarity and brightness to set the piece aptly on a chamber scale without reducing the power of this elaborately neo-classical piece. Philip Langridge is excellent as the Rake himself, very moving when Tom is afflicted with madness. Samuel Ramey as Nick, Stafford Dean as Trulove and Sarah Walker as Baba the Turk are all first rate, but Cathryn Pope's soprano as recorded is too soft-grained for Anne. Charming as the idea is of getting the veteran Astrid Varnay to sing Mother Goose, the result is out of style. The recording is exceptionally full and vivid but the balances are sometimes odd: the orchestra recedes behind the singers and the chorus sounds congested, with little air round the sound.

Suk, Josef (1874–1935)

Asrael Symphony, Op. 27.
⊛ *** Chan. Dig. CHAN 9042; *ABTD 1593* [id.]. Czech PO, Bělohlávek.

*** Virgin/EMI VC7 59638-2 [id.]. RLPO, Pešek.

☞ (***) Sup. mono 11 1902-2 (2) [id.]. Czech PO, Talich (with DVORAK: *Stabat mater* (*)).

☞ *** Panton 81 1101-2 [id.]. Bav. RSO, Kubelik.

Jiří Bělohlávek, the principal conductor of the Czech Philharmonic, draws powerfully expressive playing from the orchestra in a work which in its five large-scale movements is predominantly slow. Next to Pešek's fine Liverpool performance, the speeds flow a degree faster and more persuasively, and the ensemble, notably of the woodwind, is even crisper, phenomenally so. It helps too that the sound is warmer, closer and more involving than the refined but more distant Virgin recording.

Pešek's Liverpool version has altogether greater sensitivity and imagination than the earlier Supraphon account from Vaclav Neumann, and the sympathy of the Liverpool players is very apparent, but there is no doubt that Bělohlávek's gutsier Czech performance has a greater sense of thrust and power, and for those coming new to this fine work it will be a revelation. Our previous Rosette, which was as much for the music as the earlier Virgin Classics performance, now passes on naturally to the splendid new Chandos disc.

Vaclav Talich's pioneering mono account from the early 1950s has great intensity of utterance and poignancy and provides a link with the composer himself. Talich knew him well and conducted many Suk premières. The sound is very acceptable for the period, and it is a pity that it comes harnessed to a less successful *Stabat Mater*.

Kubelik's performance has all the fervour and pain of the Talich version but has much better sound, emanating from a 1981 studio recording with the Bavarian Radio Symphony Orchestra. It has great expressive refinement and a subtlety of colouring that are quite special. It is as powerful as any *Asrael* on or off record.

A Fairy-tale, Op. 16; Praga (symphonic poem), Op. 26.
*** Sup. Dig. 10 3389-2 [id.]. Czech PO, Libor Pešek.

Suk's *A Fairy-tale* is full of charm and originality, and it is persuasively played here. On this compact disc it is coupled with *Praga*, a patriotic tone-poem reflecting a more public, out-going figure than *Asrael*, which was to follow it. Libor Pešek secures an excellent response from the Czech Philharmonic; the recordings, which date from 1981–2, are reverberant but good.

A Fairy-tale, Op. 16; Serenade for strings in E flat, Op. 6.
☞ *** Chan. Dig. CHAN 9063 [id.]. Czech PO, Jiří Bělohlávek.

This new Chandos account of the unfailingly fresh *Serenade for strings* is probably the most captivating since the days of Talich, and the Czech Philharmonic strings play with their customary warmth and eloquence. *A Fairy tale* (*Pohádka*), a somewhat earlier piece which has a lot of Strauss and Mahler in its pedigree, is beautifully played and certainly better recorded than in the earlier version Bělohlávek made with the Prague Symphony for Supraphon.

Fantasy in G min. (for violin and orchestra), Op. 24.
(B) *** Sup. 110601-2. Josef Suk, Czech PO, Ančerl – DVORAK: *Violin concerto*. ***

Suk's *Fantasy* is a brilliant piece which relates to the traditional essays in violin wizardry as well as to the Czech nationalist tradition. The work has music of characteristic fantasy, though the rhetorical brilliance is equally strong. Suk's playing is refreshing and the orchestral accompaniment under Ančerl is no less impressive. Good remastered 1960s sound.

Fantastic Scherzo, Op. 25.
*** Chan. Dig. CHAN 8897; *ABTD 1508* [id.]. Czech PO, Bělohlávek – MARTINU: *Symphony No. 6; JANACEK: Sinfonietta*. ***

This captivating piece brings playing from the Czech Philharmonic under Bělohlávek which is even finer than any of the earlier performances and it cannot be too strongly recommended, particularly in view of the excellence of the coupling.

Praga, Op. 28; (i) Ripening, Op. 34 (symphonic poems).
☞ *** Virgin/EMI Dig. VC7 59318-2 [id.]. (i) RLPO Ch.; RLPO, Pešek.

Another first-class score, *Ripening* came after the *Asrael Symphony* and *A Summer tale* and occupied Suk for the best part of five years (1913–17). Many commentators see it as his finest orchestral score after *Asrael*, and there is no doubt as to its imaginative resource and richness of invention. Libor Pešek and his Liverpool forces give as dedicated an account of this as one could possibly wish. *Prague*, an earlier piece from 1904, is not quite in the same league but it is still an admirable makeweight and is played with exemplary commitment. Very good recorded sound too.

Serenade for strings in E flat, Op. 6.

☞ (BB) *** ASV CDQS 6094. Polish R. CO, Duczmal – TCHAIKOVSKY: *Serenade* ***; GRIEG: *Holberg suite.* **(*)

(BB) *** Naxos 8.550419 [id.]. Capella Istropolitana, Kr(e)chek – DVORAK: *String serenade.* **(*)

Suk's *Serenade* is a gorgeous work and it receives a lovely performance from the Polish Radio Chamber Orchestra under Agnieszka Duczmal. The opening is immediately winning, light and gracious, yet the orchestra can produce a rich body of timbre when needed. The *Adagio* is very beautifully played indeed; it follows Suk's unusual *Allegro ma non troppo e grazioso*, which is nearly a waltz but not quite. The orchestra's sparkling articulation and subtle rhythmic feeling here are most distinctive. This is altogether first rate, and the recording is full-textured and well balanced, bringing out Duczmal's many fine shadings of colour.

On Naxos another entirely delightful account of Suk's *Serenade*, which ought to be far better known. The innocent delicacy of the opening is perfectly caught and the charm of the dance movement which follows is just as winning. The *Adagio* is played most beautifully and then, with a burst of high spirits (and excellent ensemble), the finale bustles to its conclusion with exhilarating zest. The recording is first class, fresh yet full-textured, naturally balanced and transparent.

PIANO MUSIC

About Mother, Op. 28; Lullabies, Op. 33; 4 Piano pieces, Op. 7; Spring, Op. 22a; Summer, Op. 22b; Things lived and dreamed, Op. 30.
*** Chan. Dig. CHAN 9026/7 [id.]. Margaret Fingerhut.

It is striking how the earliest works here have a carefree, sweetly lyrical character, gentler than Dvořák but typically Czech. Then, after the death in 1904 and 1905 of his mentor, Dvořák, and his wife (Dvořák's daughter), even these fragmentary inspirations, like the massive *Asrael Symphony*, become sharp, sometimes even abrasive. The second disc brings the finest and most ambitious of the suites in which Suk generally collected his genre pieces, *Things lived and dreamed*. Margaret Fingerhut proves a devoted advocate, playing with point and concentration, helped by full-ranging Chandos sound.

Sullivan, Arthur (1842–1900)

The Merchant of Venice (suite); *The Tempest* (incidental music).
(M) *** EMI CMS7 64412-2 (2). CBSO, Sir Vivian Dunn – *Ruddigore.* ***

The longer orchestral work, the suite of incidental music for *The Tempest*, dates from 1861, when the student composer was only nineteen. Not surprisingly it made him an overnight reputation, for it displays an astonishing flair and orchestral confidence. The shorter *Merchant of Venice* suite was composed five years later, and almost immediately the writing begins to anticipate the lively style which was so soon to find a happy marriage with Gilbert's words. The performance here is highly infectious, and the sound is first class.

(i) *Overtures: Cox and Box; Princess Ida; The Sorcerer;* (ii) *Overture in C (In Memoriam).*
(M) **(*) EMI CMS7 764409-2 (2) [Ang. CDMB 64409]. (i) Pro Arte O, Sargent; (ii) RLPO, Groves – *The Pirates of Penzance.* ***

This collects together the overtures from the operas not recorded by Sargent in his EMI series. The performances are characteristically bright and polished. *In Memoriam* is a somewhat inflated religious piece written for the 1866 Norwich Festival.

Overture Di Ballo.
(M) ** EMI CMS7 64400-2 (2). BBC SO, Sargent – *Iolanthe.* ***

Sullivan's gay, Italianate overture, felicitously scored, makes a good bonus for Sargent's *Iolanthe*. However, we are indebted to a reader for pointing out that EMI have mistakenly used Sargent's recording (which is truncated) instead of the much superior Groves/RLPO version.

Overtures: *Di Ballo; The Gondoliers; HMS Pinafore; Iolanthe; Patience; The Pirates of Penzance; Princess Ida; Ruddigore; The Sorcerer; The Yeomen of the Guard* (all arr. Geoffrey Toye).
*** Nimbus Dig. NI 5066 [id.]. SCO, Alexander Faris.

A well-played and well-recorded collection of Sullivan overtures. Mostly they are little more than pot-pourris, but *The Yeomen of the Guard* is an exception, and the gay *Di Ballo* is vivacious and tuneful and shows Sullivan's scoring at its most felicitous.

Pineapple Poll (ballet; arr. Mackerras).
(M) *** Decca Dig. 436 810-2 (2). Philh. O, Mackerras – *Princess Ida.* ***
☞ (B) *** CfP CD-CFP 4618. LPO, Mackerras – VERDI: *Lady and the fool.* ***

(i) *Pineapple Poll: ballet music* (arr. Mackerras); (ii) *Savoy dances* (arr. Robinson); (i) *Overtures: Iolanthe; Mikado.*
(M) **(*) EMI CDM7 63961-2. Pro Arte O, (i) John Hollingsworth; (ii) Stanford Robinson.

On Decca Mackerras conducts with warmth as well as vivacity, and the elegantly polished playing of the Philharmonia Orchestra gives much pleasure. The record was made in the Kingsway Hall with its glowing ambience, and the CD transfer, though brightly vivid, has a pleasing bloom. Indeed the quality is in the demonstration bracket, with particularly natural string textures.

Mackerras has recorded his vivacious Sullivan arrangement several times, but this LPO version of the suite on CfP, made in the London Henry Wood Hall in 1977, is striking for its brio and warmth. With an apt Verdi coupling, this is excellent value, very well transferred to CD.

Hollingsworth offers a lively reading of *Pineapple Poll*, supported by good orchestral playing, and the slightly brash recorded quality quite suits the ebullience of the score. The upper register is over-bright but can be smoothed out. With its tuneful bonuses more smoothly done, this is enjoyable and quite good value for money. However, Mackerras's own recording of *Pineapple Poll* is even finer.

Symphony in E (Irish).
(M) *** EMI CMS7 64406-2 (2) [Ang. CDMB 64406]. RLPO, Groves – *Patience.* ***

Sullivan's *Irish Symphony* is a pleasing work, lyrical, with echoes of Schumann as much as the more predictable Mendelssohn and Schubert. The jaunty *Allegretto* of the third movement with its 'Irish' tune on the oboe is nothing less than haunting. Groves and the Royal Liverpool Philharmonic give a fresh and affectionate performance, and the CD transfer of the 1968 recording is generally well managed.

Songs: *The absent-minded beggar; The Dove song; Gone!; Let me dream again; The lost chord; The Marquis de Mincepie; Mary Morison; The moon in silent brightness; Shakespeare songs: O mistress mine; Orpheus with his lute; Willow song; St Agnes' Eve; Sweethearts; What does the little birdie say?; Winter.*
*** Conifer Dig. CDCFC 156 [id.]. Jeanne Ommerle, Sanford Sylvan, Gary Wedow.

It has taken a pair of American singers (with a pianist who is also chorus master of the Sante Fe Opera) to discover the delights of these Sullivan songs and bring them to our attention in an admirably planned recital which offers singing to catch their style superbly. The ballads have all the melodic resource of the Savoy Operas and the duet *Sweethearts* could almost have come from *Patience*, although it has an appropriate link with Victor Herbert in its added sentimentality. The Shakespeare settings are memorable, particularly the unexpected soaring line of *Orpheus with his lute*, though the gentle *Willow song* is equally lovely. *What does the little birdie say?* is a children's lullaby, while the splendid Kipling narrative of *The absent-minded beggar* reminds one of the repertoire Peter Dawson made famous. A most involving and entertaining collection without one dull number.

OPERAS

Early recordings

(i) *HMS Pinafore* (complete; without dialogue); (ii) *The Mikado* (complete; without dialogue).
(M) (***) Conifer mono CDHD 253/4 [id.]. (i) Sir Henry Litton, George Baker, Charles Goulding, Elsie Griffin, Nellie Briercliffe, Ch., SO, Dr Malcolm Sargent (i; ii) Darrell Fancourt; Sydney Granville; (ii) Martyn Green, Derek Oldham, Leslie Rands, Josephine Curtis, Brenda Bennett, Marjorie Eyre, Elizabeth Nickel-Lean, Ch., SO, Isidore Godfrey.

This coupling, clearly transferred and with background noise minimized by the Cedar process, makes a remarkable historical introduction to the world of the Savoy Operas. Surprisingly, of the two performances Godfrey's 1936 *Mikado* is far more polished than Sargent's *Pinafore* of six years earlier, where ensembles seem at times under-rehearsed and orchestral playing is occasionally not very precise, presumably because of a limited budget. The soloists were mainly drawn from the D'Oyly Carte companies of the period. The voices of the lead singers in the earlier *Pinafore* sound fruitier than we would expect today, with the dilemma of hero and heroine conveyed with ripe, expressive feeling; the later *Mikado* gives a fresher effect, much more like a D'Oyly Carte recording of a few decades later, with Derek Oldham a full-voiced Nanki-Poo, Brenda Bennett a pert Yum-Yum and the three little maids charmingly precocious. Godfrey, at his inimitable best, keeps everything crisp and alive, and the madrigal, *Brightly dawns*, is very nicely sung. The great Darrell Fancourt is common to both sets, and if – without the dialogue – he has not enough to do as Dick Deadeye, as the Mikado he produces his usual scrumptious laugh. It is fascinating to hear Sir Henry Lytton giving an almost geriatric portrayal of Sir Joseph Porter, dry-voiced and very much in character, well contrasted with George Baker's resounding Captain Corcoran. In *The Mikado* Martyn Green's characterization of Koko is straighter than it was later to become. But both performances are enjoyably spontaneous, and virtually every word is clear; as to the recordings: *Pinafore*, with all but two numbers made in Kingsway Hall, and *The Mikado*, done at Abbey Road, have a pleasant ambient atmosphere. The voices are forwardly balanced but not unnaturally so. The documentation is sparse.

The major Decca and EMI sets

(i) *Cox and Box* (libretto by F. C. Burnand) complete; (ii) *Ruddigore* (complete; without dialogue).
☞ (M) *** Decca *417 355-4* (2). (i) Styler, Riordan, Adams; New SO of L.; (ii) Reed, Round, Sandford, Riley, Adams, Hindmarsh, Knight, Sansom, Allister, D'Oyly Carte Op. Ch., ROHCG O, Godfrey.

The Gondoliers (complete; with dialogue).
(M) *** Decca 425 177-2 (2). Reed, Skitch, Sandford, Round, Styler, Knight, Toye, Sansom, Wright, D'Oyly Carte Op. Ch., New SO of L., Godfrey.

The Gondoliers (complete; without dialogue).
(M) **(*) EMI CMS7 64394-2 (2) [Ang. CDMB 64394]. Evans, Young, Brannigan, Lewis, Cameron, Milligan, Monica Sinclair, Graham, Morison, Thomas, Watts, Glyndebourne Festival Ch., Pro Arte O, Sargent.

(i; ii) *The Grand Duke*. (ii) *Henry VIII: March & Graceful dance*. (iii) *Overture Di Ballo*.
☞ *** Decca 436 813-2 (2) [id.]. (i) John Reed, Meston Reid, Sandford, Rayner, Ayldon, Ellison, Conroy-Ward, Lilley, Holland, Goss, Metcalfe, D'Oyly Carte Op. Ch.; (ii) RPO, Nash; (iii) Philh. O, Mackerras.

HMS Pinafore (complete; with dialogue).
⊛ (M) *** Decca 414 283-2; *414 283-4*. Reed, Skitch, Round, Adams, Hindmarsh, Wright, Knight, D'Oyly Carte Op. Ch., New SO of L., Godfrey.

HMS Pinafore (complete; without dialogue); *Trial by Jury*.
(M) *** EMI CMS7 64397-2 (2) [Ang. CDMB 64397]. George Baker, Cameron, Lewis, Brannigan, Milligan, Morison, Thomas, M. Sinclair, Glyndebourne Festival Ch., Pro Arte O, Sargent.

HMS Pinafore: highlights.
☞ (B) *** Decca 436 145-2; *436 145-4* (from above D'Oyly Carte Opera recording; cond. Godfrey).

Iolanthe (complete; with dialogue).
(M) *** Decca 414 145-2; *414 145-4* (2). Sansom, Reed, Adams, Round, Sandford, Styler, Knight, Newman, D'Oyly Carte Op. Ch., Grenadier Guards Band, New SO, Godfrey.

Iolanthe (complete; without dialogue).
(M) *** EMI CMS7 64400-2 (2). George Baker, Wallace, Young, Brannigan, Cameron, M. Sinclair, Thomas, Cantelo, Harper, Morison, Glyndebourne Festival Ch., Pro Arte O, Sargent – *Di Ballo overture*. **

The Mikado (complete; without dialogue).
(M) *** Decca 425 190-2 (2). Ayldon, Wright, Reed, Sandford, Masterson, Holland, D'Oyly Carte Op. Ch., RPO, Nash.
(M) **(*) EMI CMS7 644403-2 (2) [Ang. CDMB 64403]. Brannigan, Lewis, Evans, Wallace, Cameron, Morison, Thomas, J. Sinclair, M. Sinclair, Glyndebourne Festival Ch., Pro Arte O, Sargent.

The Mikado: highlights.
(B) *** Decca 433 618-2; *433 618-4* [id.] (from above D'Oyly Carte Opera recording; cond. Nash).

Patience (complete; with dialogue).

(M) *** Decca 425 193-2 (2). Sansom, Adams, Cartier, Potter, Reed, Sandford, Newman, Lloyd-Jones, Toye, Knight, D'Oyly Carte Op. Ch. & O, Godfrey.

Patience (complete; without dialogue).

(M) *** EMI CMS7 64406-2 (2) [Ang. CDMB 64406]. Morison, Young, George Baker, Cameron, Thomas, M. Sinclair, Harper, Harwood, Glydebourne Festival Ch., Pro Arte O, Sargent – *Symphony.* ***

The Pirates of Penzance (complete; with dialogue).

(M) *** Decca 425 196-2; *414 286-4.* Reed, Adams, Potter, Masterson, Palmer, Brannigan, D'Oyly Carte Op. Ch., RPO, Godfrey.

The Pirates of Penzance: highlights.

☞ (B) *** Decca 436 148-2; *436 148-4* [id.]. Reed, Adams, Brannigan, Masterson, Potter, Palmer, D'Oyly Carte Op. Co. Ch., RPO, Godfrey.

The Pirates of Penzance (complete; without dialogue).

(M) *** EMI CMS7 64409-2 (2) [Ang. CDMB 64409]. George Baker, Milligan, Cameron, Lewis, Brannigan, Morison, Harper, Thomas, Sinclair, Glyndebourne Festival Ch., Pro Arte O, Sargent – *Overtures.* **(*)

(i) *Princess Ida* (complete; without dialogue); (ii) *Pineapple Poll* (ballet; arr. Mackerras)

☞ (M) *** Decca 436 810-2 (2) [id.]. (i) Sandford, Potter, Palmer, Skitch, Reed, Adams, Raffell, Cook, Harwood, Palmer, Hood, Masterson, D'Oyly Carte Op. Ch., RPO, Sargent; (ii) Philh. O, Mackerras.

Ruddigore (complete; without dialogue).

(M) *** EMI CMS7 64412-2 (2). Lewis, George Baker, Brannigan, Blackburn, Morison, Bowden, M. Sinclair, Harwood, Rouleau, Glyndebourne Festival Ch., Pro Arte O, Sargent – *Merchant of Venice; Tempest:* incidental music. ***

(i) *The Sorcerer* (complete, without dialogue); (ii) *The Zoo* (libretto by Bolton Rowe).

☞ *** Decca 436 807-2 (2) [id.]. (i) Adams, David Palmer, Styler, Reed, Christene Palmer, Masterson; (ii) Reid, Sandford, Ayldon, Goss, Metcalfe; nar. Geoffrey Shovelton; (i; ii) D'Oyly Carte Op. Ch., RPO; (i) Godfrey; (ii) Nash.

(i) *Utopia Ltd* (complete). Overtures: *Macbeth; Marmion. Victoria and Merrie England.*

☞ **(*) Decca 436 816-2 (2) [id.]. (i) Sandford, Reed, Ayldon, Ellison, Buchan, Conroy-Ward, Reid, Broad, Rayner, Wright, Porter, Field, Goss, Merri, Holland, Griffiths, D'Oyly Carte Op. Ch.; RPO, Nash.

The Yeomen of the Guard (complete; without dialogue).

(M) *** EMI CMS7 64415-2 (2) [Ang. CDMB 64415]. Dowling, Lewis, Evans, Brannigan, Morison, M. Sinclair, Glyndebourne Festival Ch., Pro Arte O, Sargent.

(i) *The Yeomen of the Guard* (complete; without dialogue); (ii) *Trial by Jury.*

(M) *** Decca 417 358-2; *417 358-4.* Hood, J. Reed, Sandford, Adams, Raffell; (i) Harwood, Knight; (ii) Round; D'Oyly Carte Op. Ch.; (i) RPO, Sargent; (ii) ROHCG O, Godfrey.

As can be seen, the two basic sets of recordings of the major Savoy Operas, nearly all from Godfrey (on Decca) and Sargent (on EMI), are now back in the catalogue at mid-price. The Decca series usually has the advantage (or disadvantage, according to taste) of including the dialogue. Certain of the operas are available only in D'Oyly Carte versions, and of these the most fascinating is *Cox and Box.* This pre-Gilbertian one-Acter is based on a play (called *Box and Cox*) with the story of two men sharing the same rooms – one is a hatter, the other works on a newspaper at night – without knowing it, so that Bouncer, the unscrupulous landlord, can collect a double rent. The problems begin when they both have the same day off. It was written in 1867 and thus pre-dates the first G&S success, *Trial by Jury,* by eight years. One must notice the lively military song, *Rataplan* – projected with great gusto by Donald Adams, an ideal Bouncer – which was to set the style for many similar and later pieces with words by Gilbert, and also the captivating *Bacon 'Lullaby',* so ravishingly sung by Joseph Riordan. Later on, in Box's recitative telling how he 'committed suicide', Sullivan makes one of his first and most impressive parodies of grand opera, which succeeds also in being effective in its own right. The D'Oyly Carte performance is splendid in every way. It is given a recording which, without sacrificing clarity, conveys with perfect balance the stage atmosphere.

The Grand Duke, on the other hand, was the fourteenth and last of the Savoy operas. In spite of a spectacular production and a brilliant first night on 7 March 1896, the work played for only 123 performances then lapsed into relative oblivion, although it has been revived by amateur societies. The present recording, the only complete version, came after a successful concert presentation in 1975, and the recorded performance has both polish and vigour, although the chorus does not display the crispness of articulation of ready familiarity. Act I brings a whole stream of lyrically attractive numbers. The quintet, *Strange the views some people hold*, is in the best Sullivan glee tradition, and the inimitable John Reed (as the Grand Duke) has two memorable songs, more melancholy than usual: *A pattern to professors of monarchical autonomy* and the candid *When you find you're a broken-down critter*. In Act II Julia Goss is first rate in her eloquent lament, *So ends my dream . . . Broken ev'ry promise plighted*. The recording is characteristically brilliant. The bonuses are well worth having, with Mackerras's account of the *Overture Di Ballo* showing more delicacy of approach than usual, though certainly not lacking sparkle. Here the recording is digital. The other items are somewhat more inconsequential but are vivid enough to give pleasure.

Turning now to the major G&S successes, it seems sensible to consider the Decca and EMI alternatives together. EMI usually offer some orchestral bonuses and, in the case of *HMS Pinafore*, add *Trial by Jury* as well (as was the practice in the theatre in the heyday of the D'Oyly Carte Opera Company). Godfrey's Decca *Trial by Jury* is saved for inclusion with their outstanding *Yeomen of the Guard*. The Sargent version of *Trial by Jury* (with George Baker as the Judge) is by general consent the best there is, if only by a small margin, and the EMI version of *Pinafore* is wonderfully fresh too, beautifully sung throughout, while the whole of the final scene is musically quite ravishing.

But the 1960 Godfrey set of this opera is very special indeed, and *HMS Pinafore* is in our view the finest of all the D'Oyly Carte stereo recordings. While Owen Brannigan, on EMI, without the benefit of dialogue conveys the force of Dick Deadeye's personality remarkably strongly, Donald Adams's assumption of the role on Decca (which does have the dialogue) is little short of inspired, and his larger-than-life characterization underpins the whole piece. The rest of the cast make a splendid team: Jean Hindmarsh is a totally convincing Josephine – she sings with great charm – and John Reed's Sir Joseph Porter is a delight.

The D'Oyly Carte set of *The Gondoliers* has now been remastered and the quality brought up to Decca's usual high standard. The solo singing throughout is consistently good, the ensembles have plenty of spirit and the dialogue is for the most part well spoken. As a performance this is on the whole preferable to the Sargent account, if only because of the curiously slow tempo Sargent chooses for the *Cachucha*. However, on EMI there is still much to captivate the ear, and Owen Brannigan, a perfectly cast Don Alhambra, sings a masterly *No possible doubt whatever*. The age of the 1957 recording shows in the orchestra but the voices sound fresh and there is a pleasing overall bloom.

With *Iolanthe*, choice between the two alternatives is a case of swings and roundabouts. The 1960 Decca set was given added panache by the introduction of the Grenadier Guards Band into the *March of the Peers*. Mary Sansom is quite a convincing Phyllis, and if her singing has not the sense of style that Elsie Morison brings to the part, she is completely at home with the dialogue. Also Alan Styler makes a vivid and charming personal identification with the role of Strephon, an Arcadian shepherd, whereas John Cameron's dark timbre on EMI seems much less suitable for this role, even though he sings handsomely. However, on EMI the climax of Act I, the scene in which the Queen of the Fairies lays a curse on members of both Houses of Parliament, shows most excitingly what can be achieved with the 'full operatic treatment': this is a dramatic moment indeed. George Baker, too, is very good as the Lord Chancellor: the voice is fuller, more baritonal than John Reed's dryly whimsical delivery, yet he provides an equally individual characterization. Godfrey's conducting is lighter and more infectious than Sargent's in the Act I finale, but both performances offer much to delight the ear in the famous Trio of Act II with the Lord Chancellor and the two Earls.

The 1973 stereo remake of *The Mikado* by the D'Oyly Carte Company directed by Royston Nash is a complete success in every way and shows the Savoy tradition at its most attractive. It is a pity no dialogue is included, but the choral singing is first rate, and the glees are refreshingly done, polished and refined, yet with plenty of vitality. John Reed is a splendid Ko-Ko, Kenneth Sandford a vintage Pooh-Bah and Valerie Masterson a charming Yum-Yum. John Ayldon as the Mikado provides a laugh of terrifying bravura, and Lyndsie Holland is a formidable and commanding Katisha. The Sargent set, with its grand operatic style, brings some fine moments, especially in the finales to both Acts. Owen Brannigan is an inimitable Mikado and Richard Lewis sings most engagingly throughout as Nanki-Poo, while Elsie Morison is freshly persuasive as his young bride-to-be. All in all, there is much to enjoy here, but this remains very much a second choice.

Owen Brannigan was surely born to play the Sergeant of Police in *The Pirates of Penzance*, and he does so unforgettably in both the Decca and EMI sets. On Decca there is a considerable advantage in the inclusion of the dialogue, and here theatrical spontaneity is well maintained. Donald Adams is a splendid Pirate King. John Reed's portrayal of the Major General is one of his strongest roles, while Valerie Masterson is an excellent Mabel. Godfrey's conducting is as affectionate as ever, and one can hear him revelling in the many added touches of colour that are made possible when he has the RPO to play for him. Sargent's version is great fun, too. Its star is George Baker, giving a new and individual portrayal of the Major General. The opera takes a little while to warm up, but there is much to enjoy here. On balance, the Decca set is to be preferred, for Brannigan is especially vivid, and the dialogue undoubtedly adds an extra sense of the theatre.

A 62-minute selection from the vintage 1968 Decca set is self-recommending. The CD transfer is bright and lively, to the point of a degree of sibilance on the solo voices, but there is plenty of theatrical atmosphere.

Patience and *Ruddigore* were the two greatest successes of the Sargent series. Although there is no dialogue in *Patience*, there is more business than is usual in these EMI productions and a convincing theatrical atmosphere. Elsie Morison's Patience, George Baker's Bunthorne and John Cameron's Grosvenor are all admirably characterized, and the many concerted numbers beguile the ear. The extra card in the D'Oyly Carte hand is the dialogue, so important in this opera above all, with its spoken poetry; if Mary Sansom does not quite match her EMI counterpart, both Bunthorne and Grosvenor are well played, while the military numbers, led by Donald Adams in glorious voice, have an unforgettable vigour and presence. The EMI *Ruddigore* is musically superior. The whole performance is beautifully sung and Sargent's essentially lyrical approach emphasizes the associations of this delightful score with the music of Schubert. Pamela Bowden is a first-class Mad Margaret and her duet – after she has reformed – with Owen Brannigan has an irresistible gentility. The drama of the score is well managed too, and the CD transfer is first class. There is even an interesting bonus in Sullivan's Shakespearean incidental music. But here there is competition from the That's Entertainment set, which includes the original finale – see below.

The D'Oyly Carte *Ruddigore*, too, comes up surprisingly freshly, in fact better than we had remembered it, though it was a pity the dialogue was omitted. The performance includes *The battle's roar is over*, which is (for whatever reason) traditionally omitted. There is much to enjoy here (especially Gillian Knight and Donald Adams, whose *Ghosts' high noon* song is a marvellous highlight). Isidore Godfrey is his inimitable sprightly self and the chorus and orchestra are excellent. A fine traditional D'Oyly Carte set, then, brightly recorded, even if in this instance the Sargent version is generally even finer.

Princess Ida was recently revived in London and, although the Ken Russell production brought a too heavily underlined jokiness, Gilbert's own humour proved to remain fresh, and Sullivan's score itself certainly has no lack of vitality. This is fake feminism with a vengeance, but it makes for a very entertaining opera. Sir Malcolm Sargent is completely at home here, and his broadly lyrical approach has much to offer in this 'grandest' of the Savoy operas. Elizabeth Harwood in the name-part sings splendidly, and John Reed's irritably gruff portrayal of the irascible King Gama is memorable; he certainly is a properly 'disagreeable man'. The rest of the cast is no less strong and, with excellent teamwork from the company as a whole and a splendid recording, spacious and immediate, this has much to offer, even if Sullivan's invention is somewhat variable in quality. The CD transfer is outstanding and the 1965 recording has splendid depth and presence. As a bonus we are offered Mackerras's 1982 digital recording of his scintillating ballet score, *Pineapple Poll*. Mackerras conducts with warmth as well as vivacity, and the elegantly polished playing of the Philharmonia Orchestra gives much pleasure. The record was made in the Kingsway Hall with its glowing ambience, and the CD transfer, though brightly vivid, has a pleasing bloom. Indeed the quality is in the demonstration bracket, with particularly natural string textures.

The Sorcerer is the Gilbert and Sullivan equivalent of *L'elisir d'amore*, only here a whole English village is affected, with hilarious results. John Reed's portrayal of the sorcerer himself is one of the finest of all his characterizations. The plot drew from Sullivan a great deal of music in his fey, pastoral vein. Returning to this freshly remastered recording, however, one discovers how many good and little-known numbers it contains. By 1966, when the set was made, Decca had stretched the recording budget to embrace the RPO, and the orchestral playing is especially fine, as is the singing of the D'Oyly Carte chorus, at their peak. The entrance of John Wellington Wells is an arresting moment; John Reed gives a truly virtuoso performance of his famous introductory song, while the spell-casting scene is equally compelling. The final sequence in Act II is also memorable. While the score is undoubtedly uneven in invention, the best numbers are not to be dismissed, especially in so dedicated a performance. The sound is well up to Decca's usual high standard and the CD transfer is first rate, full, atmospheric and with a natural presence for the voices.

Both recordings of *The Yeomen of the Guard*, Decca's and EMI's, are conducted by Sir Malcolm

Sargent. Each has many merits. On EMI all the solo singing is very persuasive indeed, and the presence of Owen Brannigan as Wilfred is very much a plus point, while Monica Sinclair is a memorable Dame Carruthers. In both versions the trios and quartets with which this score abounds are most beautifully warm and polished. But the later Decca account has marginally the finer recording and Sir Malcolm's breadth of approach is immediately apparent in the *Overture*. Both chorus and orchestra (the RPO) are superbly expansive and there is again consistently fine singing from all the principals (and especially from Elizabeth Harwood as Elsie). This Decca *Yeomen* is unreservedly a success, with its brilliant and atmospheric recording. In any case, the trump card is the inclusion of Godfrey's immaculately stylish and affectionate *Trial by Jury* with John Reed as the Judge.

Utopia Ltd was first performed in 1893, ran for 245 performances and then remained unheard (except for amateur productions) until it was revived for the D'Oyly Carte centenary London season in 1974, which led to this recording. Its complete neglect is unaccountable; the piece stages well and, if the music is not as consistently fine as the best of the Savoy Operas, it contains much that is memorable. Moreover Gilbert's libretto shows him at his most wittily ingenious, and the idea of a utopian society *inevitably* modelled on British constitutional practice suggests Victorian self-confidence at its most engaging. Also the score offers a certain nostalgic quality in recalling earlier successes.

Apart from a direct quote from *Pinafore* in the Act I finale, the military number of the First Light Guards has a strong flavour of *Patience*, and elsewhere *Iolanthe* is evoked. *Make way for the Wise Men*, near the opening, immediately wins the listener's attention, and the whole opera is well worth having in such a lively and vigorous account. Royston Nash shows plenty of skill in the matter of musical characterization, and the solo singing is consistently assured. When Meston Reid as Captain FitzBattleaxe sings 'You see I can't do myself justice' in *Oh, Zara*, he is far from speaking the truth – this is a performance of considerable bravura. The ensembles are not always as immaculately disciplined as one is used to from the D'Oyly Carte, and *Eagle high* is disappointingly focused: the intonation here is less than secure. However, the sparkle and spontaneity of the performance as a whole are irresistible. The CD transfer shows the 1975 recording as being of Decca's best vintage quality, full, atmospheric and capturing the orchestra splendidly in an admirable balance with the voices. Of the fillers, the *Macbeth overture* is dramatic and brightly coloured but not inspired, and the *Marmion Overture*, too, is not really memorable. The short ballet, *Victoria and Merry England*, includes some pleasing ideas but again is not top-drawer Sullivan. All are vividly played and brightly recorded.

The Zoo (with a libretto by Bolton Rowe, a pseudonym of B. C. Stevenson) dates from June 1875, only three months after the success of *Trial by Jury* – which it obviously seeks to imitate, as the music more than once reminds us. The piece was restaged with some initial success in 1879 but, after eighteen performances, was withdrawn. Unpublished, the score lay neglected for nearly a century in the vaults of a London bank. Although the libretto lacks the finesse and whimsicality of Gilbert, it is not without humour, and many of the situations presented by the plot (and indeed the actual combinations of words and music) are typical of the later Savoy Operas. The plot contains reminders of Offenbach's *La Périchole*, which at the time of the first production of *The Zoo* was playing at another theatre in London, in harness with *Trial by Jury*. As the piece has no spoken dialogue it is provided here with a stylized narration, well enough presented by Geoffrey Shovelton. The performance is first class, splendidly sung, fresh as paint and admirably recorded, and it fits very well alongside *The Sorcerer*. The CD transfer is more brightly lit than its companion, and the opera has animal noises to set the scene and close the opera.

Other complete recordings

The Gondoliers (complete; without dialogue); *Overture Di Ballo*.
☞ *** That's Entertainment CD-TER2 1187; *ZCTED 1187* (2) [id.]. Suart, Rath, Fieldsend, Oke, Ross, Hanley, Woollett, Pert, Creasy, D'Oyly Carte Op. Ch. & O, John Pryce-Jones.

This splendid new set of *The Gondoliers* is considered here separately because it essentially represents a new generation of D'Oyly Carte recordings, It was recorded at Abbey Road studios in 1991, offers the best sound the Savoy operas have ever received on disc and speaks very well indeed for the standards of the resuscitated D'Oyly Carte company. The men are very good indeed: Marco's *Take a pair of sparkling eyes* (David Fieldsend) is fresh and stylish; Richard Suart's Duke of Plaza-Toro is as dry as you could wish, while the voice itself is resonant, and his duet in Act II with the equally excellent Duchess (Jill Pert), in which they dispense honours to the undeserving, is in the best Gilbertian tradition. The Duchess too shows her mettle in *On the day when I was wedded*, taken with brisk aplomb. Perhaps Gianetta (Lesley Echo Ross) and Casilda (Elizabeth Woollett) are less individually distinctive and slightly less vocally secure than their counterparts on the Godfrey and Sargent versions, but they always sing with charm. The chorus is first class – the men are especially virile at the opening of Act II. The orchestral playing is polished (noticeably elegant in *I am a courtier grave and serious*) and the ensembles are good too: the Luiz/Casilda duet, *There was a time*, is most affecting, while *In a contemplative fashion* has a relaxed charm, though the spurt at the end could have brought more fire. This apart, John Pryce-Jones conducts with vigour and an impressive sense of theatrical pacing. The finale opens with a burst of energy from the horns and brings an exhilarating closing *Cachucha* to round the opera off nicely. The acoustic of the recording has both warmth and atmosphere, the vocal balance is not too forward, yet words are remarkably clear, a great credit to the company's vocal coach. It was a great pity that the dialogue was not included (on CD, providing it is separately cued, the listener who wants just the music can make his or her own choice). However, this particular opera stands up well without it.

Iolanthe (complete; without dialogue). *Thespis* (orchestral suite).
☞ **(*) That's Entertainment Dig. CD-TER2 1188; *ZCTED2 1188* (2) [id.]. Suart, Woollett, Blake Jones, Richard, Creasy, Pert, Rath, Hanley, D'Oyly Carte Opera Ch. & O, Pryce-Jones.

After the great success of the new D'Oyly Carte *Gondoliers*, this fresh look at *Iolanthe* is something of a disappointment. John Pryce-Jones obviously sees it as a very dramatic opera indeed, and he ensures that the big scenes have plenty of impact (the *March of the Peers*, resplendent with brass, quite upstages the Decca version incorporating a Guards band). But his strong forward pressure means that the music feels almost always fast-paced, and the humour is completely upstaged by the drama, especially in the long Act I Finale, which is certainly zestful. The Lord Chancellor's two patter songs in Act I, *The law is the true embodiment* and *When I went to the bar*, are very brisk in feeling, and Richard Suart, an excellent Lord Chancellor, is robbed of the necessary relaxed delivery so that the words can be relished for themselves. Jill Pert is certainly a formidable Queen of the Fairies, but elsewhere the lack of charm is a distinct drawback. And the dialogue, particularly between Phyllis and the two Earls, is sadly missed. Clearly Pryce-Jones was seeking a grand-operatic presentation, but, if you want that, Sargent is a far better bet, for he does not lose the sense of Gilbertian fun, which emerges only sporadically here, even in the delightful trio, *If you go in*. The sound is splendid and, if that is of paramount importance, this set dwarfs all previous recordings.

(i) *Iolanthe:* highlights; (ii) *The Mikado* (complete, without dialogue).
☞ (B) *** CfP CD-CDPD 4730; *TC-CFPD 4730* (2). (i) Shilling, Harwood, Moyle, Dowling, Begg, Bevan, Greene, Kern; (ii) Holmes, Revill, Wakefield, Studholme, Dowling, Allister, John Heddle Nash; Sadler's Wells Op. Ch. & O, Alexander Faris.

The new generation of Gilbert and Sullivan recordings is fast expanding, but these two from an earlier era can stand up against all the competition, representing excellent examples of early forays into this repertoire by the Sadler's Wells company in the early 1960s, which produced the freshest results.

It is perhaps a shame that only highlights are available from the 1962 *Iolanthe*, making a rather piecemeal selection; but this means they will fit handily on to a pair of CDs together with the excellent complete *Mikado* from the same year. The Sadler's Wells *Iolanthe* is stylistically superior to Sargent's earlier EMI recording and is often musically superior to the Decca/D'Oyly Carte versions. Alexander Faris often chooses untraditional tempi. *When I went to the bar* is very much faster than usual, with less dignity but with a compensating lightness of touch. Eric Shilling is excellent here, as he is also in the *Nightmare song*, which is really *sung*, much being made of the ham operatic recitative at the beginning. The lovers, Elizabeth Harwood as Phyllis and Julian Moyle as Strephon, make a charming duo, and the Peers are splendid. Their entry chorus is thrilling and their reaction to the Fairy Queen's curse is delightfully, emphatically horrified, while the whole Act I finale (the finest in any of the operas) goes with infectious stylishness. All the solo singing is of a high standard and Leon Greene sings the Sentry song well. But one has to single out special praise for Patricia Kern's really lovely singing of Iolanthe's aria at the end of the opera. This beautiful tune – introduced in the Overture – has never been sung better on record, and the whole scene is very moving. The recording has splendid presence and realism.

The Sadler's Wells *Mikado* is traditional in the best sense, bringing a humorous sparkle to the proceedings, which gives great delight. Clive Revill is a splendid Ko-Ko; his performance of *Tit willow* and his verse of *The flowers that bloom in the spring* (aided by a momentary touch of stereo gimmickry) have a charming individuality. John Heddle Nash is an outstanding Pish-Tush, and it is partly because of him that the *Chippy chopper* trio is so effective. The madrigal, *Brightly dawns*, is beautifully sung (more refined than in the D'Oyly Carte version) and the tale of the mythical execution of Nanki-Poo (*The criminal cried*) is a delight, so humorously is the story told by each of the three 'guilty' parties. Denis Dowling is a superb Pooh-Bah, and Marion Studholme a charming Yum-Yum. She sings *The sun, whose rays* with a delectable lightness of style. Jean Allister's Katisha is first rate in every way. The part is taken very seriously and she is often very dramatic; listen to the venom she puts into the word '*bravado*' in the Act I finale. Even the chorus scores a new point by their stylized singing of *Mi-ya-sa-ma*, which sounds engagingly mock-Japanese. The one disappointment is John Holmes in the name-part. He sings well but conveys little of the mock-satanic quality. But this is a small point in an otherwise magnificent set, which has a vivacious new overture arranged by Charles Mackerras. The CD transfer of both sets is admirable. The words are clear everywhere, even in the choruses (Gilbert would have been delighted), and there is a nice combination of presence and stage atmosphere. A marvellous bargain, with excellent track-by-track synopses provided by an expert in the field, Arthur Jacobs.

The Mikado (complete, but without Overture).
⚈ *** Telarc Dig. CD 80284 [id.]. Donald Adams, Rolfe Johnson, Suart, McLaughlin, Palmer, Van Allan, Folwell, Welsh Nat. Op. Ch. and O, Mackerras.

With the overture omitted (not Sullivan's work) and one of the stanzas in Ko-Ko's 'little list' song (with words unpalatable today), the whole fizzing Mackerras performance is fitted on to a single, very well-filled disc. The full and immediate sound is a credit to Telarc's American engineers. The cast, with no weak link, is as starry as those in EMI's 'Glyndebourne' series of G&S recordings of thirty years ago, yet far more than Sir Malcolm Sargent on those earlier recordings, Mackerras is electrically sharp at brisk speeds, sounding totally idiomatic and giving this most popular of the G&S operettas an irresistible freshness at high voltage. The tingling vigour of Sullivan's invention is constantly brought out, with performances from the WNO Chorus and Orchestra at once powerful and refined. With that sharpness of focus Sullivan's parodies of grand opera become more than just witty imitations. So Katisha's aria at the end of Act II, with Felicity Palmer the delectable soloist, has a Verdian depth of feeling. It is good too to hear the veteran Savoyard, Donald Adams, as firm and resonant as he was in his D'Oyly Carte recording made no less than 33 years earlier.

Ruddigore (complete recording of original score; without dialogue).
*** That's Entertainment CDTER2 1128; *ZCTED 1128* [MCA MCAD2 11010]. Hill Smith, Sandison, Davies, Ayldon, Hillman, Innocent, Hann, Ormiston, Lawlor, New Sadler's Wells Op. Ch. & O, Simon Phipps.

What is exciting about the New Sadler's Wells production of *Ruddigore* is that it includes the original finale, created by the logic of Gilbert's plot which brought *all* the ghosts back to life, rather than just the key figure. The opera is strongly cast, with Marilyn Hill Smith and David Hillman in the principal roles and Joan Davies a splendid Dame Hannah, while Harold Innocent as Sir Despard and Linda Ormiston as Mad Margaret almost steal the show. Simon Phipps conducts brightly and keeps everything moving forward, even if his pacing is not always as assured as in the classic Sargent version. The recording is first class, with fine theatrical atmosphere.

'*Gilbert and Sullivan classics*': Arias, duets and trios from: *The Gondoliers; The Grand Duke; Haddon Hall; HMS Pinafore; Iolanthe; The Mikado; Patience; The Pirates of Penzance; Ruddigore; The Sorcerer; the Yeomen of the Guard.*
☛ (M) *** EMI CDM7 64393-2 [id.]. Valerie Masterson, Sheila Armstrong, Robert Tear, Benjamin Luxon, Bournemouth Sinf., Alwyn; or N. Sinfonia, Hickox.

This superb collection combines the best part of two recitals of G&S, the first made by Valerie Masterson and Robert Tear with Kenneth Alwyn in 1982 and recorded at the Guildhall, Southampton, and the second, in which the balance is even more realistic, in EMI's No. 1 Studio at Abbey Road, with Sheila Armstrong, Tear and Benjamin Luxon under the direction of Richard Hickox in 1984. The result is one of the most successful (and generous – nearly 73 minutes) anthologies of this repertoire ever put on disc. Quite apart from the excellence of the singing and the sparkling accompaniments, the programme is notable for the clever choice of material, with items from different operas engagingly juxtaposed instead of being just gathered together in sequence. The singing from the first group is particularly fine. Valerie Masterson's upper range is ravishingly fresh and free. It is a pity her *Pinafore* number had to be omitted, but the final cadence of *Leave me not to pine alone* (*Pirates*) is very touching, and she sings Yum-Yum's famous song from *The Mikado*, *The sun, whose rays*, with a captivating, ingenuous charm. Robert Tear too is in excellent form and his *A wandering minstrel* is wonderfully stylish, while *A magnet hung in a hardware shop* has fine sparkle. The *Prithee, pretty maiden* duet (also from *Patience*) is hardly less endearing. In the second recital it is the ensemble items that score, notably the duets from *Ruddigore, The Gondoliers* and the vivacious *Hereupon we're both agreed* from *The Yeomen of the Guard*; the star here is Benjamin Luxon. He is splendid in the principal novelty, *I've heard it said*, from *Haddon Hall* – a vintage Sullivan number even if the words are not by Gilbert – and he is left to end the concert superbly with a bravura account of *My name is John Wellington Wells* from *The Sorcerer* and a splendidly timed, beguilingly relaxed account of *When you find you're a broken-down critter* from *The Grand Duke*, in which Richard Hickox and the Northern Sinfonia make the very most of Sullivan's witty orchestral comments. The current CD transfer seems at times to add a bit of edge to the voices but this is not too serious.

Highlights from: *The Gondoliers; HMS Pinafore; Iolanthe; The Mikado; The Pirates of Penzance; The Yeomen of the Guard.*
(B) **(*) CfP CD-CFP 4238; *TC-CFP 40238* [id.]. Soloists, Glyndebourne Festival Ch., Pro Arte O, Sargent.

Another attractive selection of highlights offering samples of six of Sargent's vintage EMI recordings. There is some distinguished solo singing and, if the atmosphere is sometimes a little cosy, there is a great deal to enjoy. The recordings have transferred well.

'The world of Gilbert and Sullivan': excerpts from: (i) *The Gondoliers; HMS Pinafore; Iolanthe;* (ii) *The Mikado;* (i) *The Pirates of Penzance;* (iii) *The Yeomen of the Guard.*
(M) *** Decca 430 095-2; *430 095-4.* Soloists, D'Oyly Carte Op. Co., New SO or RPO, (i) Godfrey; (ii) Nash; (iii) Sargent.

A quite admirable selection from the vintage series of Decca D'Oyly Carte recordings, with John Reed shining brightly as Koko and Sir Joseph Porter, KCB, in *Pinafore.* Owen Brannigan's unforgettable portrayal of the Sergeant of Police is demonstrated in the excerpts from *The Pirates of Penzance* (as is Valerie Masterson's charming Mabel), and two of the most delectable items are the Second Act trios from *Pinafore* and *Iolanthe,* both liltingly infectious.

'The world of Gilbert and Sullivan' Vol. 2: excerpts from: (i) *The Gondoliers; HMS Pinafore; Iolanthe;* (ii) *The Mikado;* (i) *Patience; The Pirates of Penzance;* (iii) *Princess Ida;* (i) *Ruddigore; The Sorcerer;* (iii) *The Yeomen of the Guard.*
☞ (M) *** Decca 433 868-2; *433 868-4* [id.]. Soloists, D'Oyly Carte Op. Co. Ch., New SO, RPO or ROHCG O, (i) Godfrey; (ii) Nash; (iii) Sargent.

Volume 2 covers the ten most popular operas and includes ensembles as well as solo items. As ever, John Reed's contribution is outstanding in *Patience, Ruddigore* (where his role is more lyrical) and especially in *The Sorcerer* (a virtuoso *My name is John Wellington Wells*) and the delicious *If you give me your attention* from *Princess Ida.* But there is plenty to enjoy here, and Donald Adams's *Ghosts' high noon* song from *Ruddigore* is unforgettable. Lively recording with plenty of theatrical atmosphere.

Suppé, Franz von (1819–95)

Overtures: *Beautiful Galathea; Boccaccio; Light cavalry; Morning, noon and night in Vienna; Pique dame; Poet and peasant.*
(M) *** Mercury 434 309-2 [id.]. Detroit SO, Paul Paray – AUBER: *Overtures.* *** ⊛

Listening to Paray, one discovers a verve and exhilaration that are wholly Gallic in spirit. His chimerical approach to *Beautiful Galathea* (with a wonderfully luminous passage from the Detroit strings near the very opening) is captivating, and the bravura violin playing in *Light Cavalry* is remarkably deft. With its splendid Auber coupling this is one of Mercury's most desirable reissues.

Overtures: *Beautiful Galathea; Fatinitza; Flotte Bursche; Jolly robbers; Light Cavalry; Morning, noon and night in Vienna; Pique dame; Poet and peasant. March: O du mein Osterreich.*
(BB) **(*) LaserLight Dig. 15 611 [id.]. Hungarian State Op. O, János Sándor.

Sándor's LaserLight collection is very generous and the Hungarian State Opera Orchestra know just how to play this repertoire: the *zigeuner* section in the middle of *Light Cavalry* is most winning, while the cello solo in *Morning, noon and night* has an attractive, romantic simplicity. Sándor offers two extra novelties in *Flotte Bursche* (which brings an amiable quotation of *Gaudeamus igitur*) and a vivid Viennese-style march. The digital recording is basically full-bodied but has brilliance too, and this is a real bargain.

Overtures: *Beautiful Galathea; Fatinitza; Jolly robbers; Light cavalry; Morning, noon and night in Vienna; Pique dame; Poet and peasant.*
*** Decca Dig. 414 408-2 [id.]. Montreal SO, Dutoit.

Dutoit's pacing is splendid, combining warmth and geniality with brilliance and wit, as in the closing *galop* of *Fatinitza*. The orchestral playing is admirably polished, the violins sounding comfortable even in the virtuoso passages of *Light cavalry*, one of the most infectious of the performances here. It is difficult to imagine these being bettered, while the Decca sound is superb, well up to the usual Montreal standards.

Overtures: *Beautiful Galathea; Jolly robbers; Light cavalry; Morning, noon and night in Vienna; Pique dame; Poet and peasant.*
*** BMG/Eurodisc RD 69037. RPO, Gustav Kuhn.

Kuhn takes this music very seriously indeed, lavishing care over every detail. Tempi are spacious, consistently slower than normal, but the effect is not to rob the music of vitality, merely to add to its stature. In the lyrical sections he conjures the most beautiful, expansive playing from the RPO, yet he can be racy in the galops, while not rushing the music off its feet. The richly upholstered recording, made in St Barnabas' Church, London, seems exactly right for the music-making.

Overtures: *Fatinitza; Die Frau Meisterin; Der Gascogner; Die Irrfahrt um's Glück; Juanita; Das Modell; Wiener-Jubel.*
*** BMG/RCA Dig. RD 69226. RPO, Gustav Kuhn.

Gustav Kuhn's second collection of Suppé overtures is as distinctive as the first. It is also made more attractive by its concentration on novelties, with three items entirely new to the CD catalogue. As before Kuhn seeks to remove any suggestion of cheapness from the music, and these are performances of breadth and stature. While they do not have the unbuttoned gusto of some, there is no lack of vitality and much delicacy of detail. He is in his element in the powerfully solemn opening of *Die Irrfahrt um's Glück*, with its magical/mystical portents. Full, resonant sound, made at Abbey Road, but so strong is the influence of the conductor that this is very like a German recording, made, say, in the Leipzig Gewandhaus.

Overtures: *Die Frau Meisterin; Die Irrfahrt um's Glück; Light cavalry; Morning, noon and night in Vienna; Pique Dame; Poet and Peasant; Tantalusqualen; Wiener-Jubel (Viennese Jubilee).*
ⓦ *** EMI Dig. CDC7 54056-2 [id.]. ASMF, Marriner.

Marriner's new collection of Suppé *Overtures* goes straight to the top of the list. It is expansively recorded in EMI's No. 1 Studio and, played up to concert volume on big speakers, it produces the most spectacular demonstration quality. The sound has bloom, a wide amplitude, plenty of sparkle and a natural presence. The performances have tremendous exuberance and style: this is one of Marriner's very best records. The novelties are delightful. *Die Irrfahrt um's Glück* – concerned with magical goings-on – has a massively portentous opening, superbly realized here; *Die Frau Meisterin* produces a deliciously jiggy waltz tune, and *Wiener-Jubel*, after opening with resplendent fanfares, is as racy as you could wish. Not to be missed.

Svendsen, Johan Severin (1840–1911)

Romance in G, Op. 26.
(BB) *** Naxos Dig. 8.550329 [id.]. Dong-Suk Kang, Slovak (Bratislava) RSO, Adrian Leaper –
   HALVORSEN: *Air Norvégien* etc.; SIBELIUS: *Violin concerto;* SINDING: *Légende.* ***

Dong-Suk Kang plays Svendsen's once-popular *Romance in G* without sentimentality but with full-hearted lyricism. The balance places him a little too forward, but the recording is very satisfactory.

Symphonies Nos. 1–2; 2 Swedish folk-melodies, Op. 27.
*** BIS Dig. CD 347 [id.]. Gothenburg SO, Neeme Järvi.

Svendsen excelled (where Grieg did not) in the larger forms and, as befits a conductor, was a master of the orchestra. The *D major Symphony* is a student work of astonishing assurance and freshness, in some ways even more remarkable than the *B flat*. Neeme Järvi is a splendid guide to this terrain; these are first-class performances, sensitive and vital, and the excellent recordings earn them a strong recommendation.

Symphony No. 2 in B flat, Op. 15; Carnival in Paris, Op. 9; Norwegian Artists Carnival, Op. 14; Norwegian Rhapsody No. 2, Op. 19; (i) *Romance in G, for violin and orchestra, Op. 26.*
☞ **(*) Chatsworth Dig. FCM1002 [id.]. (i) Marianne Thorsen; Stavanger SO, Grant Llewelyn.

This Stavanger account of the *Second Symphony* and other popular Svendsen pieces under the Welsh conductor, Grant Llewelyn, is certainly worth considering. The orchestra plays with all the freshness and enthusiasm this captivating music calls for and, though the strings do not have the depth of sonority of their Gothenburg rivals, they produce a very decent sound. The 21-year-old Marianne Thorsen, a pupil of György Pauk, plays with an unaffected simplicity and purity that is most appealing. The recording has the advantage of clean, well-balanced sound with good perspective and presence.

Octet in A, Op. 3; (i) *Romance in G for violin and strings, Op. 26.*
☞ *** Chan. Dig. CHAN 9258 [id.]. (i) Sillito; ASMF Ens. – NIELSEN: *String quintet in G.* ***

Svendsen's youthful *Octet*, Op. 3, is a product of his student years at Leipzig and was obviously inspired by Mendelssohn. Unlike much of Gade's music, it has a strong personality of its own and is full of lively and attractive invention. The Scherzo is particularly delightful. It is beautifully played by the Academy of St Martin-in-the-Fields Chamber Ensemble, whose leader, Kenneth Sillito, is the soloist in the *G major Romance*, composed not long before Svendsen abandoned composition to become what nowadays we would call a 'star' conductor. It is coupled with Nielsen's early *String quintet in G major* – appropriately enough, since Svendsen first played under and then succeeded him; not a really characteristic piece but eminently well fashioned, and equally well played. Three-star performances and recording.

Sweelinck, Jan (1562–1621)

Ballo del Granduca; Echo fantasia; Engelsche Fortuyn; Puer nobis nascitur.
*** Chan. Dig. CHAN 0514; *EBTD 0514* [id.]. Piet Klee (organ of St Laurens Church, Alkmaar) – BUXTEHUDE: *Collection.* ***

Sweelinck lived during the Dutch Golden Age and was a contemporary of Rembrandt. His music is colourful and appealing, and it could hardly be better represented than in this engaging 'suite' of four contrasted pieces, three of which are based on melodies by others. Piet Klee is a very sympathetic advocate and he is given a recording of demonstration standard.

Szymanowski, Karol (1882–1937)

Violin concertos Nos. 1, Op. 35; 2, Op. 62.
☞ **(*) Decca Dig. 436 837-2 [id.]. Chantal Juillet, Montreal SO, Dutoit – STRAVINSKY: *Violin concerto.* ***

Neither of the Szymanowski concertos is generously represented in the catalogue and the appearance of this dedicated performance from Chantal Juillet and the Montreal orchestra under Charles Dutoit is a welcome addition. The good news is that the orchestral sound is quite sumptuous and beautifully detailed, though there are some oddities of perspective: for example, the orchestral piano looms much larger than the soloist in the opening pages. Juillet is a selfless and dedicated interpreter and is truthfully balanced: at no time does she play to the gallery. In fact, the engineers might have helped her a little, for her small tone does not always sing through Szymanowski's opulently coloured textures. There could be greater lyrical fervour, and not all the heady, intoxicating radiance of this extraordinary work comes across in her hands. The orchestral detail emerges with much great fidelity in the Decca recording and Dutoit's conducting is unfailingly sympathetic.

Symphonies Nos. 1 in F min., Op. 15; 2 in B flat, Op. 19.
** Marco Polo Dig. 8.223249 [id.]. Polish State PO, Stryja.

Neither of Szymanowski's early symphonies is characteristic. The incomplete *First* is undoubtedly a congested and derivative score – as, for that matter, is the more familiar *Symphony No. 2*, which leaves no doubt as to the composer's interest in Strauss and Reger. The Dorati recording (Decca) does greater justice to the complex textures of this score, but nevertheless this is well balanced and well played.

Symphonies Nos. (i) *2;* (ii) *3;* (i) *Concert overture in E, Op. 12.*
☞ (M) *** EMI CDM7 65082-2 [id.]. Polish R. Nat. SO; (i) cond. Jacek Kasprzyk; (ii) Wieslaw Ochman, Polish R. Ch. of Krakow, cond. Jerzy Semkow.

The *Second* is not as rewarding a score as the *Third*, but it is unusual in form: there are only two movements, the second being a set of variations culminating in a fugue. The influences of Strauss and Scriabin are clearly audible and not altogether assimilated. *The Song of the night* is one of the composer's most beautiful scores with its heady, intoxicated – and intoxicating – atmosphere. The Polish Radio recordings on EMI date from 1982 and the performances are the most atmospheric and sensitive currently available. The recording is not quite as detailed and analytical as the sound the Decca engineers gave Dorati (on a record that has just been deleted), but it is expansive and has impressive atmosphere. The EMI disc also includes a gripping account of the ambitious *Concert overture*, for all the world like an undiscovered symphonic poem by Richard Strauss.

(i) *Symphony No. 3 (Song of the Night);* (ii) *Symphony No. 4 (Sinfonia concertante); Concert overture.*
**(*) Marco Polo Dig. 8.223290 [id.]. (i) Ochman, Polish State Philharmonic Ch.; (ii) Taduesz Zmudzinski, Katowice Polish State PO, Karol Stryja.

The Marco Polo version of the *Third Symphony* (but not the *Fourth*) has the advantage of good, well-detailed sound in a resonant hall and Karol Stryja succeeds in getting plenty of atmosphere in No. 3. He uses a tenor rather than a soprano, but his choir is not first class. The *Sinfonia concertante* is not ideally balanced, but the pianist, Taduesz Zmudzinski, plays with refinement and sensitivity, as witness the opening of the *Andante*, which is quite magical. This is the best stereo *Sinfonia concertante* to date. The Straussian *Concert overture* makes a useful makeweight, though the recording is over-resonant and the balance synthetic.

String quartets Nos. 1 in C, Op. 37; 2, Op. 56.
⊛ *** Denon Dig. CO 79462 [id.]. Carmina Qt – WEBERN: *Slow movement for string quartet.* *** ⊛
*** Olympia OCD 328 [id.]. Varsovia Qt – LUTOSLAWSKI: *Quartet;* PENDERECKI: *Quartet No. 2.*
***

The Carmina Quartet provides outstanding music-making and is recorded with the utmost realism and fidelity. The opening of the *Second* has always seemed like being in a magical moonlit landscape listening to the Ravel quartet in the distance, and the Carmina succeed in evoking this whispered dreamlike quality to perfection.

The Varsovia Quartet have impeccable intonation and splendid sonority. Theirs are subtle and deeply felt performances. There are glorious things in both works, and the Varsovia play marvellously throughout.

Mythes, Op. 30; Kurpian folk song; King Roger: Roxana's aria (both arr. Kochanski).
⊛ (M) *** DG 431 469-2. Kaja Danczowska, Krystian Zimerman – FRANCK: *Violin sonata.* ***

Kaja Danczowska brings vision and poetry to the ecstatic, soaring lines of the opening movement of *Mythes, The Fountains of Arethusa.* Her intonation is impeccable, and she has the measure of these other-worldly, intoxicating scores. There is a sense of rapture here that is totally persuasive, and Krystian Zimerman plays with a virtuosity and imagination that silence criticism. An indispensable issue.

Violin sonata in D min., Op. 9; Berceuse, Op. 52; Mythes, Op. 30; Nocturne and tarantella, Op. 28; 3 Paganini caprices, Op. 40.
☞ *(*) Ondine Dig. ODE 759-2 [id.]. Eeva Koskinen, Juhani Lagerspetz.

Violin sonata in D min., Op. 9; Mythes, Op. 30; Nocturne and tarantella, Op. 28.
*** Chan. Dig. CHAN 8747; *ABTD 1386* [id.]. Lydia Mordkovitch, Marina Gusk-Grin.

The *Violin sonata in D minor* is an early work, very much in the received tradition; but with the *Mythes* and the *Nocturne and tarantella* the influence of Brahms and Franck has completely gone and we are in a totally different and wholly individual sound-world. Lydia Mordkovitch is ideally attuned to this sensibility and plays both the *Sonata* and the later works beautifully, and she is sensitively partnered by Marina Gusk-Grin. This can be recommended, though this account of the *Mythes* does not displace Danczowska and Zimerman.

The rather unappealing sound on the Ondine recital diminishes its appeal. If the acoustic constraints produce sound that is neither magical nor other-worldly, much of the battle is already lost. Eeva Koskinen and Juhani Lagerspetz are no match for existing rivals, particularly in the *Mythes.*

PIANO MUSIC

4 Etudes, Op. 4; 12 Etudes, Op. 33; 2 Mazurkas, Op. 62; Shéhérezade (Masques), Op. 34; Variations on a Polish theme, Op. 10.
☞ (M) ** Channel Classics Dig. CDG 9110 [id.]. Arielle Vernède.

In the repertoire that overlaps Dennis Lee's masterly Hyperion anthology, Arielle Vernède offers little real challenge, though her playing is far from wanting in distinction and character. His recital does not include the Op. 10 *Variations* or the demanding but (it must be admitted) unrewarding Op. 33 *Etudes*, and this mid-price CD can be thought of as a useful supplement but not an alternative to the Hyperion CD.

4 Etudes, Op. 4; Fantasy, Op. 14; Masques, Op. 34; Métopes, Op. 29.
*** Hyp. Dig. CDA 66409 [id.]. Dennis Lee.

Dennis Lee not only encompasses the technical hurdles of *Masques* and *Métopes* with dazzling virtuosity but also provides the keenest artistic insights. His Hyperion CD is quite simply the finest record of Szymanowski's piano music to have appeared to date; he conveys the exoticism and hothouse atmosphere of these pieces; moreover he handles the early Chopinesque *Etudes* and the *Fantasy* with much the same feeling for characterization and artistry. The Hyperion sound is very good indeed.

VOCAL MUSIC

(i) Demeter, Op. 37b; Litany to the Virgin Mary, Op. 59; (ii) Penthesilea, Op. 18; (iii) Stabat Mater; (iv) Veni Creator, Op. 57.
*** Marco Polo Dig. 8.223293 [id.]. (i) Roma Owsinska; (ii) Anna Malewicz-Madej; (iii) Jadwiga Gadulanka, Krystyna Szostek-Radkova, Andrzej Hiolski; (iv) Barbara Zagórzanka; Polish State PO & Ch., Katowice, Karol Stryja.

Szymanowski's *Stabat Mater* is not only one of his greatest achievements but one of the greatest choral works of the present century. This welcome account has the advantage of highly sensitive conducting and an excellent response from the orchestra, but some of the solo singing is less distinguished, and Jadwiga Gadulanka's intonation is less than perfect. The *Litany to the Virgin Mary* is another late work of great poignancy; but *Demeter*, composed not long after the *Violin concerto* and the *Third Symphony*, has the same exotic, almost hallucinatory textures that distinguish these works. It is all heady and intoxicating stuff, and not to be missed by those with a taste for this wonderful composer.

(i) 3 Fragments of the poems by Jan Kasprowicz, Op. 5; (ii) Love songs of Hafiz, Op. 24; (iii) Songs of the fairy-tale princess, Op. 31; (iv) Songs of the infatuated muezzin, Op. 42.
*** Schwann Dig. CD 314 001 [id.]. (i) Krystyna Szostek-Radkova; (ii) Krystyna Rorbach; (iii) Izabella Klosińska; (iv) Barbara Zagórzanka, Polish Nat. Op. O, Satanowski.

In the *Songs of the fairy-tale princess*, one feels that Szymanowski must have known Stravinsky's *Le Rossignol* – Izabella Klosińska certainly sings like one. All the singing is very good, but Barbara Zagórzanka in the imaginative *Songs of the infatuated muezzin* deserves special mention. Satanowski achieves marvellously exotic and heady atmosphere throughout, and the recording is excellent.

(i) 3 Fragments of the poems by Jan Kasprowicz, Op. 5; (ii) Love songs of Hafiz, Op. 24; (iii) Songs of the fairy-tale princess, Op. 31; (iv) Songs of the infatuated muezzin, Op. 42; (v) King Roger: Roxana's Song.
**(*) Marco Polo Dig. 8.223294. (i) Anna Malewicz-Madej; (ii & iv) Ryszard Minkiewicz; (iii) Jadwiga Gadulanka; (v) Barbara Zagórzanka; Katowice Polish State PO, Karol Stryja.

On Marco Polo, both the *Songs of the infatuated muezzin* and the *Love songs of Hafiz* are sung by a tenor (Ryszard Minkiewicz) with impressive insight, but the 1989 recording is more resonant and does not flatter him. Jadwiga Gadulanka is hardly less impressive than Klosińska in the extraordinary *Songs of the fairy-tale princess* and Barbara Zagórzanka sings the famous *Chant de Roxane* beautifully, and both she and Anna Malewicz-Madej in the Kasprowicz songs are very well balanced.

STAGE WORKS

(i) *Harnasie, Op. 55;* (ii) *Mandragora, Op. 43.*
*** Schwann Musica Mundi/Koch Dig. 311064. (i) Jozef Stépień; (ii) Paulus Raptus; (i) Polish Nat. Op. Ch.; Polish Nat. Op. O, Robert Satanowski.

Robert Satanowski's version of Szymanowski's choral ballet, *Harnasie*, is the best so far. It is an opulent score and, like the Op. 50 *Mazurkas*, is the product of the composer's encounter with the folk music of the Gorá mountains. It is richly coloured and luxuriant in texture and has a powerfully heady atmosphere. Full justice is done to its opulence and character in this excellent performance. *Mandragora* is a harlequinade for chamber forces, and the performance is persuasive. Both works are very well served by the engineers. A most valuable addition to the catalogue.

Taffanel, Paul (1844–1908)

Wind quintet in G min.
*** Sony Dig. CD 45996. Ens. Wien-Berlin – NIELSEN: *Wind quintet.* ***

This quintet is an urbane, expertly fashioned piece by a musician of obvious culture who knows how to pace the flow of his ideas. The Ensemble Wien-Berlin play it with the utmost persuasion and charm, but this is a very lightweight companion to the Nielsen masterpiece.

Takemitsu, Toru (born 1930)

Guitar concerto.
☞ *** EMI Dig. CDC7 54661-2 [id.]. Julian Bream, CBSO, Rattle – RODRIGO: *Concierto de Aranjuez;* TAKEMITSU: *To the edge of dream.* ***

A highly sympathetic account of Takemitsu's hypnotically evocative concertante work, using a large orchestra with great economy so as never to overwhelm the soloist. The music is very atmospheric, texturally beautiful but essentially static. It could hardly be better recorded.

A Way A Lone.
☞ *** BMG/RCA Dig. 09026 61387-2 [id.]. Tokyo Qt – BARBER: *Quartet;* BRITTEN: *Quartet No. 2.* ***

Takemitsu's *Quartet* was written in response to a commission from the Tokyo Quartet to mark its tenth anniversary in 1981. *A Way A Lone*, as it is subtitled, is rather Bergian but, like so much of Takemitsu's music, shows a refined ear for sonority. Marvellous playing and recording.

Tallis, Thomas (c. 1505–85)

Absterge Domine; Candidi facti sunt; Nazareri; Derelinquat impius; Dum transisset sabbatum; Gaude gloriosa Dei Mater; Magnificat and Nunc dimittis; Salvator mundi.
*** CRD CRD 3429; *CRDC 4129* [id.]. New College, Oxford, Ch., Higginbottom.

The performances by the Choir of New College, Oxford – recorded in the splendid acoustic of the College Chapel – are eminently well prepared, with good internal balance, excellent intonation, ensemble and phrasing. The *Gaude gloriosa* is one of Tallis's most powerful and eloquent works.

Audivi vocem de celo a 4; Candidi facti sunt Nazarei eius a 5; Dum transisset sabbatum a 5; Hodie nobis celorum rex a 4; Homo quidam fecit cenam magnam a 6; Honor, virtus et potestas a 5; In pace in idipsum a 4; Loquebantur variis linguis a 7; Spem in alium a 40; Videte miraculum a 6.
*** EMI Dig. CDC7 49555-2 [id.]. Taverner Ch. and Cons., Andrew Parrott.

Gaude gloriosa Dei Mater a 6; In jejunio et fletu a 5; Lamentations of Jeremiah I and II a 5; Miserere nostri a 7; O nata lux de lumine a 5; O sacrum convivium a 5; Salvator mundi I and II a 5; Suscipe, quaeso Domine a 7; Te lucis ante terminum (Procol recedant somnia) I a 5.
*** EMI Dig. CDC7 49563-2 [id.]. Taverner Ch. and Cons., Andrew Parrott.

The Taverner style is brighter and more abrasive than we are used to in this often ethereal music, but, quite apart from the scholarly justification, the polyphonic cohesion of the writing comes out the more tellingly. The first of the two discs is the obvious one to investigate initially, containing as it does the 40-part motet, *Spem in alium*, as well as *Videte miraculum* and *Dum transisset sabbatum* –

almost as extended in argument. The second of the two discs has the two magnificent *Lamentations of Jeremiah*, as well as an even more expansive motet which Tallis wrote early in his career, *Gaude gloriosa Dei Mater*.

Anthems: *Blessed are those that be undefiled; Christ, rising again; Hear the voice and prayer; If ye love me; A new commandment; O Lord, in Thee is all my trust; O Lord, give thy holy spirit; Out from the deep; Purge me; Remember not, O Lord God; Verily, verily I say: 9 Psalm Tunes for Archbishop Parker's Psalter.*
*** Gimell Dig. CDGIM 007; *1585T-07* [id.]. Tallis Scholars, Phillips.

This disc collects the complete English anthems of Tallis and is thus a valuable complement to the discs listed above. Here, of course, women's voices are used instead of boys', but the purity of the sound they produce is not in question, and the performances could hardly be more committed or more totally inside this repertoire. Strongly recommended.

Derelinquat impius; Ecce tempus idoneum; In jejunio et fletu; In manus tuas; O nata lux; Salvator mundi; (ii) *Sancte Deus;* (i) *Spem in alium* (40-part motet); *Te lucis ante terminum I & II; Veni Redemptor gentium;* (ii) *Videte miraculum; Organ lesson.*
(M) **(*) Decca 433 676-2 [id.]. King's College, Cambridge, Ch., Willcocks; (i) with Cambridge University Musical Society; Langdon; (ii) Andrew Davis.

The highlight of the programme is the magnificent forty-part motet, *Spem in alium*, in which the Cambridge University Musical Society joins forces with Kings. But the simpler hymn settings are no less impressive. The two other motets, *Sanctus Deus* and *Videte miraculum*, like *Spem in alium*, organ accompanied, are less well balanced, giving over prominence to the trebles, but the young Andrew Davis provides an excellent performance of the *Lesson* for organ.

Motets: *Ecce tempus idoneum; Gaude gloriosa Dei Mater; Loquebantur variis linguis; O nata lux de lumine; Spem in alium.*
☞ (B) **(*) CfP CD-CFP 4638; *TC-CFP 4638* [id.]. Clerkes of Oxenford, David Wulstan –
SHEPPARD: *Motets.* **(*)

A useful issue, since it not only juxtaposes motets by Tallis against those of his great (but less familiar) contemporary, John Sheppard, but also gives us a strongly sung bargain version of the famous forty-part motet, *Spem in alium*. Here the resonance of Merton College Chapel means that definition could be more refined, and throughout the programme David Wulstan's tempi are somewhat brisk, while at times there is also some sense of strain among the women. (Interestingly, Wulstan's timing for *Loquebantur variis linguis* is almost identical with that of Jeremy Summerly on Naxos, which yet feels slightly less tense.) Reservations notwithstanding, there are fine things on this inexpensive EMI CD, and it can be recommended.

Gaude gloriosa; Loquebantur variis linguis; Miserere nostri; Salvator mundi, salva nos, I and II; Sancte Deus; Spem in alium (40-part motet).
⊛ *** Gimell CDGIM 006; *1585T-06* [id.]. Tallis Scholars, Phillips.

Within the admirably suitable acoustics of Merton College Chapel, Oxford, the Tallis Scholars give a thrilling account of the famous 40-part motet, *Spem in alium*, in which the astonishingly complex polyphony is spaciously separated over a number of point sources, yet blending as a satisfying whole to reach a massive climax. The *Gaude gloriosa* is another much recorded piece, while the soaring *Sancte Deus* and the two very contrasted settings of the *Salvator mundi* are hardly less beautiful. The vocal line is beautifully shaped throughout, the singing combines ardour with serenity, and the breadth and depth of the sound is spectacular.

The Lamentations of Jeremiah.
☞ (M) *(*) DG 437 077-2. Pro Cantione Antiqua, Bruno Turner – BYRD: *Mass for 3 voices.* *(*)

Lamentations of Jeremiah. Motets: Absterge domine; Derelinquat impius; In jejunio et fletu; In manus tuas; Mihi autem nimis; O sacrum convivium; O nata lux de lumine; O salutaris hostia; Salve intemerata virgo.
*** Gimell Dig. CDGIM 025; *1385T-25* [id.]. Tallis Scholars, Peter Phillips.

This, the third of the Tallis Scholars' discs devoted to their eponymous composer, is centred on the two great settings of the *Lamentations*. They have often been recorded before, but never more beautifully than here, performances that give total security. As well as the eight fine motets, the collection also has a rare Marian antiphon, *Salve intemerata*, that is among Tallis's most sustained inspirations. Clear, atmospheric recording of striking tangibility.

Bruno Turner's account of the *Lamentations* is perhaps a little too expressive and with too wide a dynamic range for some tastes. Moreover the voices are closely balanced instead of being distanced against a convincing ambience.

Mass for four voices; Motets: *Audivi vocem; In manus tuas Domine; Loquebantur variis linguis; O sacrum convivium; Salvator mundi; Sancte Deus; Te lucis ante terminum; Videte miraculum.*
☞ (B) **(*) Naxos Dig. 8.550576 [id.]. Oxford Camerata, Jeremy Summerly.

The Oxford Camerata with their beautifully blended timbre have their own way with Tallis. Lines are firm, the singing has serenity but also a firm pulse. In the *Mass* (and particularly in the *Sanctus*) the expressive strength is quite strongly communicated, while the *Benedictus* moves on spontaneously at the close. The motets respond particularly well to Jeremy Summerly's degree of intensity. The opening *Loquebantur variis linguis* has much passionate feeling, and this (together with the *Audivi vocem*, and especially the lovely *Sante Deus*) shows this choir of a dozen singers at their most eloquent. The recording, made in the Chapel of Wellington College, is very fine indeed, and there is a brief musical note provided by the conductor. Excellent value.

Missa Salve intemerata Virgo.
☞ (B) *** CfP Dig. CD-CFP 4654; *TC-CFP 4654* [id.]. St John's College, Cambridge, Ch., George Guest – TAVERNER: *Western Wynde mass & song.* ***

Taverner's Mass, *The Western wynde*, with which this is coupled, is based on the celebrated popular tune of the day, while the Tallis derives from an earlier motet of the same name. But the *Missa Salve intemerata Virgo* does in fact rework more of the original than is customary in parody Masses; only about a quarter is completely new. The Choir of St John's College, Cambridge, under George Guest is very well recorded and give a very spirited account of themselves, very different from the small, chamber-like performances which are prevalent nowadays, but musically no less satisfying. At this price, a splendid bargain.

Taneyev, Sergei (1856–1915)

Symphony Nos. (i) *2 in B flat* (ed. Blok); (ii) *4 in C min., Op. 12.*
☞ ** Russian Disc RD CD11008. (i) USSR R. & TV Large SO, Fedoseyev; (ii) Novosibirsk PO, Katz.

In the *Fourth Symphony* Arnold Katz gets very good results from the Novosibirsk orchestra; his is a spirited reading and in terms of character and imagination his performance can hold its own against Neeme Järvi's excellent account on Chandos without necessarily displacing it as a first recommendation. The recording, though not quite in the three-star bracket, is more than acceptable. While dates of the artwork are clearly given, those of the recordings are not. This recording of the *Second Symphony in B flat* would seem to be identical with Fedoseyev's 1969 LP; climaxes are a bit raw and raucous. The performance itself is satisfactory, and there is at present no alternative. The *C minor Symphony* deserves 2½ stars and the B flat 1½, hence the compromise rating.

Symphony No. 4 in C min., Op. 12; Overture The Oresteia, Op. 6.
*** Chan. Dig. CHAN 8953 [id.]. Philh. O, Järvi.

The *Fourth Symphony*, sometimes known as the *First* as it was the first to be published in Taneyev's lifetime, is a long piece of 42 minutes; some of its gestures are predictable, to say the least! Its best movement is the delightful scherzo which betrays his keenness of wit. Elsewhere neither his ideas nor their working out are quite as fresh or as individual as in such pieces as, say, the *Piano quintet*. Neeme Järvi gets very good playing from the Philharmonia and his performance supersedes earlier versions.

Piano quartet in E, Op. 20.
**(*) Pro Arte Dig. CDD 301 [id.]. Cantilena Chamber Players.

The *Piano quartet* is a finely wrought and often subtle work. With a superbly sensitive contribution from Frank Glazer, the performance is altogether first rate, though the acoustic in which it is recorded is not quite big enough.

Piano quintet in G min., Op. 30.
*** Ara. Dig. Z 6539 [id.]. Jerome Lowenthal, Rosenthal, Kamei, Thompson, Kates.

Not only is the *Piano quintet* well structured and its motivic organization subtle, its melodic ideas are strong and individual. It is arguably the greatest Russian chamber work between Tchaikovsky and Shostakovich. The recording is not in the demonstration bracket, but it is very good; and the playing, particularly of the pianist Jerome Lowenthal, is excellent. Strongly recommended.

Piano trio in D, Op. 22.
*** Chan. Dig. CHAN 8592; *ABTD 1262* [id.]. Borodin Trio.

This *Trio* is a big, four-movement work. The invention is attractive – and so, too, is the excellent performance and recording. Strongly recommended.

String quartets Nos. 8 in C; 9 in A.
**(*) Olympia OCD 128 [id.]. Leningrad Taneyev Qt.

Both these *Quartets* are large-scale works in the classical mould, and both are beautifully crafted, though they are not strongly personal. The minuet of No. 8 and the scherzo of No. 9 are highly attractive. They are well played, though the violin tone above the stave has a tendency to harden.

Tansman, Alexandre (1897–1986)

Symphony No. 5 in D min.; 4 Movements for orchestra; Stèle in memoriam d'Igor Stravinsky.
☞ **(*) Marco Polo Dig. 8.223379 [id.]. Slovak PO (Kosice), Meir Minsky.

The Polish-born Alexandre Tansman was a prolific composer, well-known for his music for guitar which Segovia popularized. He was the author of a biography of Stravinsky, whose neighbour he was in Hollywood and whose memory his *Stèle* celebrates. After the Second World War he returned to Paris where he received several commissions from the French Radio, including a highly imaginative and dramatic opera, *Le serment* ('The solemn oath'), which would be well worth recording. Readers will recognize a certain affinity with his countryman Szymanowski; his craftsmanship is fastidious and his command of the orchestra impressive. His music is highly atmospheric, with shimmering textures enhanced by celeste, piano and vibraphones and sensitively spaced pianissimo string chords, plus poignant wind writing. The slightly earlier *Quatre mouvements pour orchestre*, composed in the late 1960s, is hardly less impressive and resourceful. The *Fifth Symphony*, which dates from his Hollywood years, is less successful, though it is well laid out for the orchestra and many of the ideas are pleasing without being as memorable or as individual as the two companion works. The performances are eminently serviceable and the recordings are decent, though there is an ugly edit at the first-time repeat bar in the second movement of *Stèle*. Let us hope that this will lead to more recordings of Tansman's music.

Tarp, Svend Eric (born 1908)

(i) *Piano concerto in C, Op. 39;* (ii) *Symphony No. 7 in C min, Op. 81;* (iii) *The Battle of Jericho, Op. 51;* (iv) *Te Deum, Op. 33.*
☞ **(*) Marco Polo Dacapo Dig. DCCD 9005 [id.]. Danish Nat. RSO, with (i) Per Solo; (i; iii) Schønwandt; (ii) Schmidt; (iv) Danish Nat. R. Ch., Nelson.

The only familiar work here is the neo-classical, Françaix-like *Piano concerto* (1944), which was recorded way back in the late 1940s. This Danish composer – who belongs to the same generation as Vagn Holmboe – has succeeded in eluding the attention of the major record companies; indeed all these works derive from Danish Radio performances. The *Concerto* is a light, attractive piece whose acquaintance is well worth making. There is a distinctively Danish feel to the *Te Deum* (1938), though the piece is eclectic and owes a lot to Stravinsky and may even at times remind English listeners of Walton. The *Seventh Symphony* is much later (1977), still neo-classical in feeling, very intelligent music, and only occasionally bombastic; though not the equal of Bentzon or Holmboe in terms of imagination or depth, it is certainly worth hearing. The performances, which come from 1986–90, are enthusiastic and committed, and the recordings are serviceable without being top-drawer.

Tartini, Giuseppe (1692–1770)

Cello concerto in A.
☞ (B) *** DG Double 437 952-2 (2) [id.]. Rostropovich, Zurich Coll. Mus., Sacher – BERNSTEIN: *3 Meditations;* BOCCHERINI: *Cello concerto No. 2;* GLAZUNOV: *Chant du Ménestrel;* SHOSTAKOVICH: *Cello concerto No. 2;* TCHAIKOVSKY: *Andante cantabile* etc.; VIVALDI: *Cello concertos.* ***

As with the other works in this fine 1978 collection, Rostropovich's view of Tartini's *A major Concerto* is larger than life; but the eloquence of the playing disarms criticism, even when the cellist plays cadenzas of his own that are not exactly in period. This is part of a first-class Double DG anthology which can be recommended almost without reservation.

Violin concertos: in E min., D.56; in D, D.96; in A min., D.113.
☞ (M) *** Erato/Warner 4509 92188-2 [id.]. Uto Ughi, Sol. Ven.

Tartini is a composer of unfailing originality, and the three violin concertos on this record are all very rewarding. The *Concerto in A major*, which comes last on the disc, has an additional (probably) alternative slow movement, a *Largo Andante* which is particularly beautiful. Uto Ughi's performances are distinguished by excellent taste and refinement of tone, and I Solisti Veneti are hardly less polished. The harpsichord continuo is somewhat reticent, but otherwise the recording is exemplary. Highly recommended.

Concertino for clarinet (arr. Jacob).
*** ASV Dig. CDDCA 585; *ZCDCA 585* [id.]. Emma Johnson, ECO, Yan Pascal Tortelier –
CRUSELL: *Introduction, theme and variations;* DEBUSSY: *Rapsodie;* WEBER: *Concerto No. 1.* ***

Gordon Jacob's arrangement of sonata movements by Tartini as a brief, four-movement *Clarinet concerto* is a delightful oddity; but, with sprightly, characterful playing, it is an attractive and unusual makeweight in Emma Johnson's mixed collection of concertante pieces, well recorded.

Tavener, John (born 1944)

Eternal memory.
☞ *** BMG/RCA Single 09026 61966-2 [id.]. Steven Isserlis, Moscow Virtuosi, Spivakov – BLOCH:
From Jewish life. ***

Those who have responded to Tavener's *Protecting veil* (from which the composer actually quotes in this shorter, more succinct evocation) will readily be drawn to this mystical, three-part structure which, unexpectedly, begins with a chant-like whiff of the opening of Tchaikovsky's *1812*, moves on to a motoric central section, then ends in mysticism, a suggestion of the end of mortal existence. Isserlis reaffirms his total identification with Tavener's muse, here bringing an alternation of life's disquieting alarms and its final serenity. The recording is suitably atmospheric and the documentation excellent. The choice of presentation – a CD single – and an apt coupling should also make this a good sampler for those collectors who have not yet ventured beneath *The Protecting veil.*

(i) *The Protecting veil* (for cello and orchestra); *Thrinos.*
☞ *** Virgin/EMI Dig. VC7 59052-2; *VC 759052-4* [id.]. Steven Isserlis, (i) LSO, Rozhdestvensky –
BRITTEN: *Cello suite No. 3.* ***

In the inspired performance of Steven Isserlis, dedicatedly accompanied by Rozhdestvensky and the LSO, *The Protecting veil* has an instant magnetism, at once gentle and compelling. Tavener's simplicity of idiom is of quite a different order from the easy-pleasing of minimalism. He has you escaping at once into a spiritual world, sharing his visions. The 'protecting veil' of the title refers to the Orthodox Church's celebration of a tenth-century vision, when in Constantinople the Virgin Mary appeared and cast her protecting veil over the Christians who were being attacked by the Saracen armies. Tavener, himself a Russian Orthodox convert, echoes the cadences of Orthodox chant, ending each section with passages of heightened lyricism for the soloist. Each time that guides the ear persuasively on into the next section, leading at the end to the work's one sharply dramatic moment, when a sudden surge represents Christ's Resurrection. It is as dramatic as the sudden eruption of *Et resurrexit* in Bach's *B minor Mass*, after the darkness of *Et crucifixus*. Much is owed to the performance, with Isserlis a commanding soloist. He is just as compelling in the other two works on the disc, not just the Britten but also the simple lyrical lament, *Thrinos*, which Tavener wrote especially for him. Excellent recording.

The Repentant thief.
*** Collins Dig. Single 2005-2. Andrew Marriner, LSO, Tilson Thomas.

In this memorable work for clarinet and orchestra (Andrew Marriner the keenly responsive soloist) Tavener creates a sharply defined structure, contrasting visionary intensity with rhythmic urgency in alternating *Dances, Laments* and *Refrains*.

String quartets: *The Hidden Treasure;* (i) *The Last sleep of the Virgin.*

☞ *** Virgin/EMI Dig. VC5 45023-2; *VC 545023-4* [id.]. Chilingirian Qt, (i) with Iain Simcock (handbells) – PART: *Fratres; Summa.* ***

'Quiet and intensely fragile' is Tavener's guide to performances of *The Last sleep of the Virgin,* a work which might be described as an ethereal suggestion, using the simplest means (string quartet and tolling bell) to convey both the reality and the implications of the death and burial of 'the Mother of God'. *The Hidden Treasure* in its seeking for Paradise offers more violent contrasts (a brief cello cadenza-soliloquy a key factor) with cries of anguish interrupting the flow of the spiritual journey. Tavener's world is all his own and listeners must enter into it without any expectation of traditional musical development of ideas; instead, the artists have to create the music's logic with a hypnotic concentration which is certainly achieved here, using a suitable resonance of acoustic. The mystical close of *The Hidden Treasure* brings a shimmering *pianissimo-diminuendo* of remarkable intensity.

The Akathist of Thanksgiving.
☞ ⊛ *** Sony Dig. SK 64446 [id.]. Bowman, Wilson, Westminster Abbey Ch., BBC SO & Singers, Martin Neary.

Even among Tavener's many works inspired by his Russian Orthodox faith, *The Akathist of Thanksgiving* stands out for its concentrated intensity. In its ten substantial sections, each between five and ten minutes long, this hymn of thanksgiving is just as dedicated as – and even more sustained than – *The Protecting veil.* Russian chant lies behind the writing, linking this with Rachmaninov's magnificent *Vespers.* The composer's personal response to the text by a monk in the Stalin era inspires striking atmospheric contrasts of motif and texture, with the main choir set against a phalanx of 16 soloists, mainly counter-tenors and basses, led by James Bowman and Timothy Wilson. The recording was taken live from the performance given in January 1994 at Westminster Abbey. The result on disc is both warmly atmospheric and well defined, with high dynamic contrasts involving not just choral forces but strings, heavy brass and percussion. Martin Neary proves an inspiring conductor, drawing incandescent tone from the choirs, thrillingly reinforced by the underlying weight of instrumental sound.

Angels; Annunciation; God is with us; Hymns of Paradise; Lament of the Mother of God; Thunder entered her.
☞ *** Virgin/EMI Dig. VC5 45035-2 [id.]. Kringelborn, Kendall, Sweeney, Winchester Cathedral Ch., Hill; Dunnett (organ).

'*Thunder entered her*' is the sobriquet given to a choral collection named after the longest and most striking piece of the six recorded here, which, with distant choirs set against the main body and weighty organ accompaniment, relates closely to the *Akathist.* David Hill conducts the Winchester Cathedral Choir with David Dunnett at the organ, all very atmospherically recorded. Though some of the longer and more meditative pieces rather outstay their welcome with Tavener resorting too readily to formulae like scalic ostinati and oriental augmented intervals, each one presents a sharply distinctive vision, culminating in a magnificent Christmas proclamation, *God is with us.*

Funeral Ikos; (i) Ikon of Light. Carol: The Lamb.
*** Gimell CDGIM 005; *1585T-05* [id.]. Tallis Scholars, (i) Chilingirian Qt (members), Phillips.

Ikon of Light is a setting of Greek mystical texts, with chant-like phrases repeated hypnotically. The string trio provides the necessary textural variety. More concentrated is *Funeral Ikos,* an English setting of the Greek funeral sentences, often yearningly beautiful. Both in these and in the brief setting of Blake's *The Lamb,* the Tallis Scholars give immaculate performances, atmospherically recorded in the chapel of Merton College, Oxford.

We shall see Him as He is.
☞ *** Chan. Dig. CHAN 9128 [id.]. Rosario, Ainsley, Murgatroyd, Britten Singers, Chester Festival Ch., Hickox.

Like the opera, *Mary of Egypt,* written at the same period, this large-scale choral work has a bareness which initially can seem daunting. *We shall see Him as He is,* first heard in July 1992 in Chester Cathedral and, later, at the Proms, is inspired (like all Tavener's mature works) by his Orthodox faith. It is a sequence of what Tavener describes as musical ikons, setting brief, poetic texts based on the Epistle of St John, each inspired by a salient event in the life of Christ: His baptism, the Wedding Feast at Cana, the cleansing of the Temple, and on to the Last Supper, the Crucifixion and the Resurrection. Each ikon is punctuated by a choral Refrain, setting the words of the work's title in Greek. Though at first the inspiration may seem painfully thin, the simple ritual becomes magnetic, with its structured, highly atmospheric use of large-scale choral forces. Long before the end, Tavener, as in the hugely popular *The Protecting veil*, makes one share the full devotional intensity of his own emotions, as he progresses towards rapt contemplation of the Resurrection, the ultimate ikon. The recording, with Richard Hickox conducting the BBC Welsh Symphony Orchestra, the Britten Singers and Chester Festival Chorus, was made live at the Prom performance, with the dedication totally cancelling out any detailed flaw. The tenor, John Mark Ainsley, in the central solo role of St John sings immaculately with deep feeling, while Patricia Rozario makes her brief, wide-ranging solo a soaring climax. Not just the work's dedication, but the radiance of the massed choral sound, and the violence of incidental sequences, add to the physical compulsion, with each simple motif sharply memorable.

The Whale.
☞ *** Apple/EMI CDP7 98947-2; *SAPCOR 15* [id.]. Anna Reynolds, Raimund Herincx, Alvar Lidell, London Sinf. and Ch., David Atherton; composer (organ & Hammond organ).

The Whale was the piece which set the seal on an unforgettable occasion: the very first concert given by David Atherton and the London Sinfonietta in January 1968. It was written well before Tavener turned to the Russian Orthodox Church for inspiration but, with its roots in the biblical story of Jonah, the anticipations of Tavener's later devotional manner are plain, despite the surreal reading from the Encyclopedia Britannica (by Alvar Lidell) with which it starts. Thanks to its dramatic timing as well as Tavener's ear for striking effect, it wears well, though at 31 minutes it makes very short measure for a full-price CD. The new disc is a reissue of the original recording in spectacular sound, made for the Beatles' Apple label by the original performers.

Mary of Egypt (complete).
☞ *** Collins Dig. 7023-2 (2) [id.]. Rozario, Varcoe, Goodchild, Ely Cathedral Ch., Britten-Pears Chamber Ch., Aldeburgh Festival Ens., Lionel Friend.

Tavener, inspired as he is by his Greek Orthodox faith, says that 'Music is a form of prayer, a mystery', and that applies to this stylized opera. *Mary of Egypt* was recorded live at the Aldeburgh Festival first performances in June 1992 and, characteristically, Tavener compels you to accept his slow pacing and paring down of texture. The idiom brings points in common with the minimalists, but one can hardly miss the dedication behind the writing, giving it something of the magnetic quality which has brought Tavener's concertante cello piece, *The Protecting veil*, such wide success. In many ways the disc works better than the live staging, when with the help of the libretto the developments in the bald, stylized plot can be more readily followed. The five brief Acts of what Tavener describes as an 'Icon of Music and Dance' tell the story of Mary, the harlot who finds salvation as a hermit in the desert, giving comfort to the pious, ascetic monk, Zossima, teaching him the need for love. The musical landmarks are sharply defined in clear-cut, memorable motifs, with moments of violence set sharply against the predominant mood of meditation. What is disconcerting is Tavener's use as a frame for each Act of a disembodied voice to represent the Mother of God. It sounds like a very raw baritone, but in fact is the voice of Chloe Goodchild, using weird oriental techniques. Her message of salvation, strange as it sounds, comes to be magnetic too. Under Lionel Friend the performance has a natural concentration, with Patricia Rozario as Mary and the baritone, Stephen Varcoe, as Zossima both outstanding. Their confrontation in Act III brings a radiant duet that acts as a climactic centrepiece to the whole work. After that Act IV – a voiceless pageant on Mary's life up to her death – and the equally brief Act V – her burial by Zossima – come almost as epilogue, with the 100 minutes treated as a single span. A synopsis and libretto are provided, but instead of notes there is a 15-minute interview with the composer, informative but disconcertingly overamplified.

Taverner, John *(c.* 1495–1545)

Missa gloria tibi Trinitas; Audivi vocem (responsory); ANON.: *Gloria tibi Trinitas.*
*** Hyp. CDA 66134 [id.]. The Sixteen, Harry Christophers.

Missa gloria tibi Trinitas; Dum transisset sabbatum; Kyrie a 4 (Leroy).
*** Gimell Dig. CDGIM 004; *1585T-04* [id.]. Tallis Scholars, Phillips.

This six-voice setting of the Mass is richly varied in its invention (not least in rhythm) and expressive in a deeply personal way very rare for its period. Harry Christophers and The Sixteen underline the beauty with an exceptionally pure and clear account, superbly recorded and made the more brilliant by having the pitch a minor third higher than modern concert pitch.

Peter Phillips and the Tallis Scholars give an intensely involving performance of this glorious example of Tudor music. The recording may not be as clear as on the rival Hyperion version, but

Phillips rejects all idea of reserve or cautiousness of expression; the result reflects the emotional basis of the inspiration the more compellingly. The motet, *Dum transisset sabbatum*, is then presented more reflectively, another rich inspiration.

Missa Mater Christi; Motets: *Mater Christi; O Wilhelme, pastor bone.*
*** Nimbus Dig. NI 5218 [id.]. Christ Church Cathedral Ch., Stephen Darlington.

This is a liturgical reconstruction by Andrew Carwood for the Feast of the Annunciation of Our Lady, at Eastertide, which intersperses Taverner's *Missa Mater Christi* with the appropriate chant. The disc also includes the Motet *Mater Christi*, on which the Mass itself is built, and the antiphon, *O Wilhelme, pastor bone.* The singing under Stephen Darlington is first class, and the recording made, not at Christ Church, but at Dorchester Abbey, Oxfordshire, is difficult to fault: it is well focused and excellently balanced with a firm image.

Mass, O Michael; Dum transisset sabbatum; Kyrie a 4 (Leroy).
*** Hyp. Dig. CDA 66315 [id.]. The Sixteen, Harry Christophers.

The *Missa O Michael* is an ambitious six-part Mass lasting nearly 40 minutes which derives its name from the respond, *Archangeli Michaelis interventione*, which prefaces the performance. The chant on which the Mass is built appears no fewer than seven times during its course. The so-called Leroy *Kyrie* (the name thought to be a reference to *le roi* Henry) fittingly precedes it: the *Missa O Michael* has no Kyrie. The Easter motet, *Dum transisset sabbatum*, completes an impressive disc.

Missa Sancti Wilhelmi; Dum transisset Sabbatum; Ex eius tumba; O Wilhelme, pastor bone.
*** Hyp. Dig. CDA 66427 [id.]. The Sixteen, Harry Christophers.

The *Missa Sancti Wilhelmi* (known as 'Small Devotion' in two sources and possibly a corruption of *S. Will devotio*) is prefaced by the antiphon, *O Wilhelme, pastor bone*, written in a largely syllabic, note-against-note texture, and the second of his two five-part settings of the Easter respond, *Dum transisset Sabbatum*, and washed down, as it were, by the Matin responds for the Feast of St Nicholas, *Ex eius tumba*, and believed to be the only sixteenth-century setting of this text. The singing of The Sixteen under Harry Christophers is expressive and ethereal, and the recording impressively truthful. Recommended with confidence.

Mass: The Western wynde; Song: The Western wynde.
☞ (B) *** CfP Dig. CD-CFP 4654; *TC-CFP 4654* [id.]. St John's Coll., Cambridge, Ch., George
    Guest – TALLIS: *Missa Salve intemerata Virgo.* ***

This St John's performance of John Taverner's mass, *The Western wynd*, is prefaced by the song on which both it and the motet of the same name are based. It also attracted both Tye and Sheppard. The Mass is basically a sequence of 36 variations of much subtlety and ingenuity on the theme and is one of the key works of the period. This spirited and robust performance by the Choir of St John's College, Cambridge, under George Guest is very well recorded; it is very different in style from the small, chamber-like, vibrato-free performances to which we are becoming accustomed (and beguiled), but is every bit as valid. An admirable and, at this price, very economical introduction to the composer.

Tchaikovsky, André (1935–82)

String quartet No. 2, Op. 5.
☞ *** ASV Dig. CDDCA 825 [id.]. Lindsay Qt – BARBER: *String quartet;* WIREN: *String quartet No. 3;* WOOD: *String quartet No. 3.* ***

The Polish-born pianist André Tchaikovsky, who died in his forties, made few commercial records though he was a frequent contributor to BBC programmes. His *Second Quartet* was composed for the Lindsays, who had given the first performance of his *First* in 1971. The *Second*, recorded at its first performance in 1978, is a highly concentrated and substantial piece in three interlinked movements, including a central passacaglia. Its musical language is complex and chromatic, of indeterminate tonality rather than twelve-note. It is not 'listener-friendly' but leaves one with the feeling that it is worth taking trouble over.

Tchaikovsky, Peter (1840–93)

Andante cantabile for cello and orchestra, Op. posth; (i) *Variations on a rococo theme, Op. 33.*

☞ (B) *** DG Double 437 952-2 (2) [id.]. Rostropovich, BPO; (i) cond. Karajan – BERNSTEIN: *3 Meditations;* BOCCHERINI: *Cello concerto No. 2;* GLAZUNOV: *Chant du Ménestrel;* SHOSTAKOVICH: *Cello concerto No. 2;* TARTINI: *Cello concerto;* VIVALDI: *Cello concertos.* ***

☞ ** Sony Dig. SK 48382 [id.]. Yo-Yo Ma, Pittsburgh SO, Maazel – PROKOFIEV: *Sinfonia concertante.* **

Rostropovich indulges himself affectionately in the composer's arrangement, and the balance – all cello with a discreet orchestral backing – reflects his approach. Rostropovich's famous and much-praised account of the *Rococo variations* with Karajan (see below) has been added as part of a highly desirable anthology – a real bargain in DG's Double-CD series with two discs offered for the price of one.

There is no lack of refinement from Yo-Yo Ma in the *Andante cantabile* and the *Rococo variations* and, although his playing is at times just a little mannered, he always engages the listener's sympathy. Maazel's less than inspired accompaniment does, however, diminish the appeal of this CD; and their account of the Prokofiev *Sinfonia concertante*, which is the main work on the disc, is not the complete success one would have hoped.

(i) *Andante cantabile* (from *String quartet No. 1,* arr. Marriner); (ii; iii) *Capriccio italien;* (iv) *Piano concerto No. 1 in B flat min.;* (v) *Violin concerto in D;* (vi) *1812 Overture;* (vii; viii) *Marche slave; Nutcracker* (extended suite); (ii; ix) *Romeo and Juliet* (fantasy overture); (vii; x) *Serenade for strings;* (vii; viii) *Sleeping Beauty; Swan Lake* (extended suites); (ii; ix) *Symphonies Nos. 4–6 (Pathétique);* (xi) *Waltz* from *Eugene Onegin;* (xii) (Song): *None but the lonely heart* (sung in Russian).

☞ (M) *** EMI Analogue/Dig. CZS 767700-2 (5) [id.]. (i) ASMF, Marriner; (ii) Philh. O; (iii) Ozawa; (iv) Gavrilov, BPO, Ashkenazy; (v) Perlman, Phd. O, Ormandy; (vi) Oslo PO, Jansons; (vii) LSO; (viii) Previn; (ix) Muti; (x) Barbirolli; (xi) RPO, Beecham; (xii) Boris Christoff, Labinsky.

Among all the back-catalogue collections designed to commemorate the centenary of Tchaikovsky's death, this five-CD 'Tchaikovsky Box' from EMI readily takes first place. It includes much of the composer's most inspired music in consistently distinguished performances and vintage recordings, almost all admirably transferred to CD. The only possible technical reservation concerns the CD remastering of the *String serenade.* Barbirolli (following the composer's wish for 'as many players as possible') uses the full string section of the LSO. They were recorded (in 1964) within the resonant Kingsway Hall acoustic to give a rich, broad sonority. Barbirolli's account has characteristic vigour and ardour, especially in the *Elegy,* and it is a pity that, although the recording had plenty of body and warmth, the violins playing full out above the stave are made to sound slightly fierce and unrefined. This is the more noticeable as the *Serenade* directly follows Marriner's lovely performance of the *Andante cantabile* (on the first disc), where the Academy strings, digitally recorded, sound warm and natural. However, adjusting the controls works wonders, and this is a small blemish when Muti's accounts of the three greatest *Symphonies,* strong, direct and spontaneous, are as fine as almost any in the catalogue. The two *Concertos* are both highly successful in most respects (although Perlman is too closely balanced), and the shorter pieces are all very enjoyable. Muti (not Jansons as originally indicated in the documentation) directs an exciting and imaginative *Romeo and Juliet,* and Previn is in his element in the *Marche slave* and the three splendid ballet selections. It was good, too, that room was found for Beecham's *Eugene Onegin Waltz* and Boris Christoff's performance of Tchaikovsky's most famous song. The documentation, including some interesting photographs, is first class.

Andante cantabile, Op. 11; Chant d'automne, Op. 37/10; Nocturne, Op. 19/4 (all arr. for cello & orchestra); *Pezzo capriccioso, for cello & orchestra, Op. 62; Sérénade mélancolique, Op. 26; Valse sentimentale, Op. 51/6* (both arr. for cello & orchestra); *Variations on a rococo theme for cello & orchestra, Op. 33; Eugene Onegin: Lensky's aria* (arr. for cello & orchestra).

**(*) BMG/RCA Dig. RD 60758 [09026 60758-2]. Ofra Harnoy, LPO, Mackerras.

Ofra Harnoy plays with much lightness and grace in this Tchaikovsky programme, managing to embrace almost every conceivable item which might be transcribed for cello and orchestra. As it so happens, the most successful performance here is *Lenski's aria* from *Eugene Onegin* which Harnoy plays with gentle lamenting ardour, with the orchestral wind soloists decorating the vocal line with affectionate sensibility. The famous *Variations on a rococo theme* are presented in a similar way – using the published score – and though at times Harnoy fines the melodic line down seductively to just a thread of tone, at others one craves a slightly more robust effect. But in the rest of the programme this delicacy and refinement work well enough. Mackerras accompanies very sensitively and the LPO playing is quite lovely, while the recording balance is ideal, within a pleasingly warm ambience.

Andante cantabile, Op. 11; Nocturne, Op. 19/4; Pezzo capriccioso, Op. 62 (1887 version); *2 Songs: Legend; Was I not a little blade of grass; Variations on a rococo theme, Op. 33* (1876 version).
*** Chan. Dig. CHAN 8347; *ABTD 1080* [id.]. Wallfisch, ECO, Simon.

This delightful record gathers together all of Tchaikovsky's music for cello and orchestra – including his arrangements of such items as the famous *Andante cantabile* and two songs. The major item is the original version of the *Rococo variations* with an extra variation and the earlier variations put in a more effective order, as Tchaikovsky wanted. Geoffrey Simon draws lively and sympathetic playing from the ECO, with Wallfisch a vital if not quite flawless soloist. Excellent recording, with the CD providing fine presence and an excellent perspective.

Andante cantabile for strings; Souvenir de Florence (version for string orchestra), *Op. 70.*
☞ **(*) Unicorn Dig. DKPCD 9134 [id.]. Primevera CO, Paul Manley – ARENSKY: *Variations.* ***

A warmly affectionate account of the famous *Andante cantabile*, bringing out all its charming nostalgia, to match the coupled Arensky variations with which it has much in common. The athletic account of the exuberant *Souvenir de Florence*, however, tends to fall between two stools. It has not the individual textural clarity of a performance by six players, yet it is not ideally sumptuous as an orchestral version: in the finale the glowing Tchaikovskian melody swings along zestfully, but the effect could be riper. The sound is clear and truthfully conveys the effect of a modest-sized chamber group. Enjoyable but not distinctive. Entremont's account of the *Souvenir* on Naxos (coupled with the *Serenade*) is not only cheaper but even more rewarding (8.550404).

Capriccio italien, Op. 45.
(BB) *** BMG/RCA Dig. VD 87727 [7727-2-RV]. Dallas SO, Mata (with *Concert* ***).
(B) *** CfP CD-CFP 4341; *TC-CFP 4341* [id.]. Philh. O, Kletzki – RIMSKY-KORSAKOV: *Scheherazade.* ***

On Mata's Dallas disc the concert-hall effect of the recording is very impressive indeed. The performance is colourful and exciting, and the piece is issued within an attractive compilation of favourite orchestral showpieces (see Concerts section, below).

Kletzki's performance is very enjoyable. It offers superb Philharmonia playing (the opening bugle call is most arresting) and is very well recorded indeed for its period (late 1950s).

(i; ii) *Capriccio italien, Op. 45;* (iii) *Piano concerto No. 1 in B flat min., Op. 23;* (iv; v; vi) *Violin concerto in D, Op. 35;* (v; vii) *Overture 1812, Op. 49;* (i; ii) *The Nutcracker* (ballet): *Waltz of the flowers;* (viii; ii) *Serenade for strings in C, Op. 48;* (ix; viii; x) *Valse-scherzo* (for violin and orchestra), *Op. 34;* (v; xi) *The Sleeping Beauty* (ballet): *Rose adagio;* (viii; xii) *Swan Lake* (ballet): Act II: *Pas d'action.*
☞ (B) ** Ph. Duo 438 386-2 (2) [id.]. (i) LPO; (ii) Stokowski; (iii) Haas, Monte-Carlo Opéra O,
Inbal; (iv) Szeryng; (v) Concg. O; (vi) Haitink; (vii) Markevitch; (viii) LSO; (ix) Midori; (x)
Slatkin; (xi) Dorati; (xii) Monteux.

Described somewhat optimistically as 'The best of Tchaikovsky', this Duo bargain double-album nevertheless offers a generous and enjoyable programme. Stokowski's contribution derives from a series of recordings he made in London for Philips in the mid-1970s, preceding the conductor's Indian summer in the CBS recording studios just before he died. *Capriccio italien* has exuberant panache, especially at the close, and many characteristic touches of detail before that, but the *Serenade for strings* is surprisingly straight, as if Stokowski were seeking to acknowledge the music's Mozartian ancestry, with unsumptuous sound to match. There is some very neat playing from the LSO violins, the *Waltz* has elegance and the *Elegy* unexaggerated fervour. The finale is lively enough but does not unleash the degree of bustle one might have expected. The *Waltz of the flowers* is more characteristic, with a sudden dramatic fortissimo towards the end. Haas's account of the *B flat minor Concerto* has plenty of excitement; he is let down by a less than outstanding orchestral accompaniment (see below), but these players rise to the adrenalin of the soloist in the finale, and throughout Haas's own contribution is first rate. Szeryng is luckier in having the Royal Concertgebouw Orchestra in the *Violin concerto*, but Haitink is rather slack in directing the accompaniment in the outer movements. Szeryng is sweetly lyrical and the relaxed manner of the performance may appeal to some listeners but, while the solo playing in the finale is spirited, the end-result fails to catch fire. The recording is excellent. Midori plays the *Valse-scherzo* with a delightfully light touch, and there are no complaints about the other performances. Markevitch's *1812* is lively enough, but it has a resonantly boomy bass drum instead of cannon in the final climax.

Capriccio italien, Op. 45; 1812 Overture, Op. 49; Fatum, Op. 77; Festive overture on the Danish National Anthem, Op. 15; Francesca da Rimini, Op. 32; Hamlet (fantasy overture), *Op. 67a; Romeo and Juliet* (fantasy overture); *The Tempest* (symphonic fantasy), *Op. 18.*
☞ *** Olympia Dig. OCD 512 A/B [id.]. SO of Russia, Dudarova.

This is the most exciting Tchaikovsky compilation to have come from Russia for some years. It includes the finest performance of *The Tempest* ever recorded, structurally convincing, full of atmosphere and with the great leaping love-theme for Ferdinand and Miranda wonderfully ecstatic. Veronika Dudarova cannot do quite so much for *Fatum*, which remains an obstinately clumsy structure (Tchaikovsky destroyed his score but forgot about the orchestral parts!). However, she makes the most of it – and it has one really good tune and some impressive scoring – as she does the patriotically pompous *Festive overture on the Danish National Anthem*, providing a resplendent ceremonial climax. *Romeo and Juliet* has passion, excitement and a certain Slavonic reserve at the presentation of the love theme, which make for a very satisfying whole; and a certain spacious gravitas informs *1812*, although it does not lack impetus, with the climax (using drums rather than cannon) bringing a gloriously expansive treatment of the Russian hymn – banned for so long – which the players clearly relish. *Capriccio italien* is very Russian too, especially the nostalgic treatment of the broad string melody, but there is plenty of energy and spectacle, and the end is almost alcoholically rumbustious, with a not quite convincing sudden accelerando at the coda. *Francesca da Rimini* and *Hamlet* here can almost be spoken of in the same breath as the famous Stokowski versions. The former is not as uninhibited at the climax representing the lovers' passion as with Stokowski, but it has some glorious playing in the middle section, full of rich woodwind colouring, and a ferociously demonic portrayal of the inferno and the lovers' final, cataclysmic punishment; the latter has a uniquely touching portrayal of Ophelia's onset of madness (a poignant oboe solo) and a passionately sombre close. The Symphony Orchestra of Russia is apparently a permanent pick-up group, formed from members of other Russian orchestras, who play with great ardour and virtuosity; its conductor, Veronika Dudarova, is a very experienced musician who is clearly a natural Tchaikovskian. The 1992 digital recording, engineered by another lady, Margarita Kozhukhova, is red-bloodedly spectacular to suit the music-making, yet not blatant; and Studio No. 5 of Moscow Radio and TV clearly has the proper spacious acoustics to bring out the resonant weight of Tchaikovsky's most brilliant fortissimos. There are excellent notes, written in highly readable English. Not to be missed by any true Tchaikovskian – there are many new insights here.

Capriccio italien, Op. 45; 1812 Overture; Marche slave, Op. 31; Romeo and Juliet (fantasy overture).
(BB) *** Naxos Dig. 8.550500; *4550500* [id.]. RPO, Adrian Leaper.

Like Sian Edwards, Adrian Leaper is a natural Tchaikovskian; whether in the colourful extravagance of the composer's memento of his Italian holiday, the romantic ardour and passionate conflict of *Romeo and Juliet*, the sombre expansiveness of *Marche slave* with its surge of adrenalin at the close, or in the extrovert celebration of *1812*, he produces playing from the RPO that is spontaneously committed and exciting. The brilliantly spectacular recording, with plenty of weight for the brass, was made in Watford Town Hall, with realistic cannon and an impressively resonant imported carillon to add to the very exciting climax of *1812*. A splendid disc that would still be recommendable if it cost far more.

Capriccio italien, Op. 45; 1812 Overture, Op. 49; Marche slave, Op. 31; Swan Lake (ballet): *suite.*
☞ **(*) Teldec/Warner Dig. 4509 90201-2 [id.]. Israel PO, Mehta.

This is a quite generously conceived popular Tchaikovsky collection, very well played and given full-bodied, resonant sound, much more flattering than we are used to from the Mann Auditorium in Tel Aviv. With the Israel brass sonorously robust, the concert opens with a lively and warmly conceived *Capriccio italien*, a Slavonically solemn yet exciting *Marche slave* and an exuberant *1812* with a properly spectacular fusillade at the end. The highlight is the suite from *Swan Lake*, played with style and affection and with good solo contributions from woodwind and violin and cello soloists and producing a thrilling *scène finale*. Overall this is an enjoyable concert; if these performances in the last resort are not the finest available, they stand up quite well against the competition if you want this particular programme.

(i) *Capriccio italien; 1812 overture; Romeo and Juliet* (fantasy overture); (ii) Song: *None but the lonely heart; Eugene Onegin: Onegin's aria.*
☞ **(*) Dig. EMI CDC5 55018-2 [id.]; *EL 555018-4*. (i) Philh. O, Domingo; (ii) Domingo, Philh. O, Behr.

Here we have Domingo in his newest role as conductor giving heartfelt, somewhat idiosyncratic and quite individual readings of three popular orchestral favourites, with plenty of drama and the passion worn on the sleeve. *1812* is ceremonially measured, with the organ adding breadth and spectacle at the close. The recording is appropriately spacious and resonant. Any lack of sharp co-ordination of ensemble is surely compensated for by the impact throughout. The vocal items show that Domingo can still tug at the emotions in his more familiar role. The recording, made in All Saints', Tooting, provides an expansively resonant panoply of Tchaikovskian hyperbole.

Capriccio italien, Op. 45; Elégie for strings; Francesca da Rimini, Op. 32; Romeo and Juliet (fantasy overture).
*** Decca Dig. 421 715-2 [id.]. RPO, Ashkenazy.

Capriccio italien is superb, spectacular, elegant and possessed of exhilarating impetus. *Romeo and Juliet* takes a little while to generate its fullest excitement with the love-theme introduced a little coolly, but its climax has great ardour. *Francesca da Rimini* is very exciting too, with much fine wind-playing from the RPO in the lyrical central section. Then the programme ends with Tchaikovsky's haunting *Elégie*, a lovely, wistful string melody played with a wonderful feeling of nostalgia. What makes this concert especially successful is the superb recording.

(i) *Capriccio italien, Op. 45; 1812, Op. 49;* (ii) *Fatum, Op. 77; Francesca da Rimini, Op. 32 ; Hamlet, Op. 67;* (i) *Marche slave;* (ii) *Romeo and Juliet* (fantasy overture); *The Tempest, Op. 18; The Voyevoda, Op. 78.*
☞ (B) **(*) Double Decca 443 003-2 (2) [id.]. (i) National SO of Washington, DC; (ii) Detroit SO; Antal Dorati.

Dorati made his recordings of the symphonic poems in Washington in the early 1970s, while the triptych of *Capriccio italien, 1812* and *Marche slave* marked the return of the Detroit orchestra to the recording scene at the beginning of 1979. The recording has the benefit of the splendid Detroit acoustics, although *1812*, rather endearingly, has a spectacular laminated eruption of American Civil War cannon and bells – including Philadelphia's Liberty Bell! – at the end. The result is unbelievable but certainly spectacular, and clearly was aimed at the hi-fi demonstration market of the time. The performance of the *Capriccio* is not without elegance, but *Marche slave* seems almost excessively sombre until the change of mood at the coda, which is taken briskly. The symphonic poems are vividly done, if without the degree of ardour one finds in the competing Russian performances (see above/below).

Fatum ('Fate'), though published as Op. 77, is one of Tchaikovsky's earliest works, dating from 1868. Many of the Tchaikovskian fingerprints are already apparent in the orchestral treatment, and the piece opens imaginatively and almost immediately produces a rather good tune. It ought to be better known. Dorati's accounts of *Francesca da Rimini* and *Hamlet* are rather underpowered compared with Stokowski, but they are spacious readings, not without individuality, and the central section of *Francesca* is sensitively done. *Romeo and Juliet* takes a while to warm up. When it does, Dorati gives the love theme a distinctive sweep, and the closing pages are very convincing. *The Tempest* obviously excited the conductor's imagination and is vividly done, particularly the opening horn sequence, while the rapturous love theme is played with tingling ardour. *The Voyevoda,* a late work dating from 1890–91, is hardly one of the composer's more inspired pieces, although its scoring is sophisticated. It is unconnected with the opera of the same name (they are based on different subjects). The plot is very melodramatic, having something in common with *Francesca da Rimini* – husband returning to slay wife's lover – yet it is the husband (the *Voyevoda*) who receives the bullet in error, in a brief coda. Dorati makes the most of its melancholy and dark wind colouring which matches the sombre lower strings.

Capriccio italien, Op. 45; Nutcracker suite, Op. 71a; Sleeping Beauty (ballet): *suite, Op. 66a.*
(M) *** DG 431 610-2 [id.]. BPO, Rostropovich.

We have given the highest praise (and a Rosette) to the Rostropovich triptych combining the three Tchaikovsky ballet suites, which added *Swan Lake* to the two listed here (see below) and that still seems the most appropriate coupling; but anyone whose collection has room for *Capriccio italien* rather than *Swan Lake* will find the present reissue hardly less rewarding. These were among the finest recordings the DG engineers made in the Philharmonie in the late 1970s.

Capriccio italien, Op. 45; Nutcracker suite, Op. 71a; Eugene Onegin: Waltz and Polonaise.
☞ ** Erato/Warner Dig. 2292 45964-2 [id.]. Bolshoi SO, Lazarev.

There is nothing special here. Fine, polished orchestral playing (except for a degree of vulgarity from the trumpets in the *Capriccio*), but Alexander Lazarev's tempi are affectionately lazy in the *Nutcracker suite*, which needs more sparkle. The two *Eugene Onegin* dances come off well enough, but the *Capriccio italien*, though lively, is not wholly spontaneous – there is a sudden lurching accelerando in the coda which is unconvincing, and the resonant Bolshoi acoustics make the heavy brass fortissimos sound blatant. Otherwise the sumptuous digital sound is agreeable enough.

(i) *Concert fantasy, Op. 56; Piano concertos Nos. 1–3;* (ii) *Violin concerto in D;* (iii) *Variations on a rococo theme for cello and orchestra, Op. 33.*

☞ (M) **(*) EMI Dig./Analogue CMS7 64887-2 [id.]. (i) Peter Donahoe, Bournemouth SO, Rudolph Barshai; (ii) Nigel Kennedy, LPO, Okko Kamu; (iii) Paul Tortelier, N. Sinfonia, Yan Pascal Tortelier.

If only Peter Donohoe could have repeated the success of his recording of the *Second Piano concerto* (which won the *Gramophone* magazine's Concerto Award in 1988 and a Rosette from us) when he returned to the Poole Arts Centre to record these other Tchaikovsky works, this mid-priced box would have been a very attractive proposition. But the account of the *B flat minor Concerto*, although thoroughly sympathetic and spaciously conceived, lacks the thrust and indeed the electricity of the finest versions. The *Third Piano concerto* is altogether more successful, dramatic and lyrically persuasive, and held together well by Barshai; this is now available at full price, sensibly coupled with the *Second*, and is a better buy than the present box. The *Concert fantasia* is even more in need of interpretative cohesion. It is laid out in two balancing movements, lasting about half an hour. The first opens with charming *Nutcracker* overtones yet develops a powerful central cadenza, which Donohoe plays grandly and rumbustiously. The second movement brings a series of chimerical changes of mood and tempo, which both pianist and conductor negotiate with zestful, spontaneous abandon. The lyrical interludes have a pleasing Russian folksiness, and the rhetoric of the allegros brings an exhilarating dash which almost carries the performers away with it. A little more poise would have been welcome, but there is no denying the spontaneous combustion of the music-making; the recording – but for a little too much resonance for the solo cadenza in the opening movement – is effectively spectacular.

Nigel Kennedy gives a warmly romantic reading of the Tchaikovsky *Violin concerto*, full of temperament, with one of the most expansive readings of the first movement ever put on disc. Though the sound is ample, his idiosyncrasies will not please everyone. For all his many *tenutos* and *rallentandos*, however, Kennedy is not sentimental, and his range of tone is exceptionally rich and wide, so that the big moments are powerfully sensual. Okku Kamu and the LPO do not always match their soloist; the accompaniment sometimes sounds a little stiff in tuttis, though the final coda is thrilling. The collection is completed by the Torteliers' enjoyably polished account of the *Rococo variations*, not a first choice, perhaps, but a recommendable one and given excellent analogue sound.

Piano concertos Nos. 1–3; Andante and finale, Op. 79 (orch. Tanayev); *Concert fantasia.*

☞ (B) ** Ph. Duo 438 329-2 (2) [id.]. Werner Haas, Monte-Carlo Opéra O, Inbal.

Piano concertos Nos. 1–3; Concert fantasia.

☞ (M) *** BMG/RCA 09026 61631-2 (3). Barry Douglas, LSO or Philh. O, Leonard Slatkin.

A first-class set in every way from Barry Douglas, giving a splendid survey of Tchaikovsky's major concertante works for piano. The *First Concerto* was recorded before the others in 1986 and did not receive too enthusiastic a welcome from us at the time, as it was issued at full price without a coupling! Barry Douglas – outright winner of the Moscow Tchaikovsky competition that same year – proved an admirable soloist, his bravura always at the service of the music, and he provided many imaginative touches, especially in the first-movement cadenzas and the *Andante*, beautifully done. If Slatkin and the LSO made a more routine response, with a rather heavy reprise of the big tune in the finale, this still proved an impressive and enjoyable account. The other works in this box were all recorded together in June 1992. The *Second Concerto* immediately proves a great success, a perform-ance to rank alongside the Donohoe version in its vigour and romantic sweep, with plenty of sparkle in the finale. The slow movement is beautifully played, with Douglas creating a warmly intimate relationship with the orchestral string soloists. They do not project such strong solo profiles as the starry names on the EMI CD, but the friendly integration of the three artists is most enjoyable. The spaciously opulent Watford Town Hall recording suits the style of the playing.

The remaining two works were recorded at EMI's No. 1 Studio at Abbey Road, so yet again a resonant, concert-hall balance creates an expansive effect. Some might feel that in the *Concert fantasy* a more intimate acoustic would be preferable, but soloist and conductor both find plenty of delicacy for the composer's very winning balletic orchestral effects which provide the contrast for the more rhetorical pages. The *Third Concerto* is splendidly done, and here Slatkin's broadly passionate treatment of the main theme immediately reminds us that this work was originally planned as a symphony. The vigorous articulation of the jiggy *Allegro* is most infectious, and a highlight of the performance is Slatkin's handling of the recapitulation and especially the reprise of Tchaikovsky's lyrical secondary material.

This Philips Duo issue, for all its inadequacies, offers a remarkable bargain in putting together all Tchaikovsky's music for piano and orchestra at the cost of a single premium-priced CD! As we know from his complete Ravel survey on the same label, Werner Haas is an intelligent and masterly player, and moreover he is a true Tchaikovskian. His enviable technical command means that the many passages of pianistic rhetoric can be thrown off powerfully. He is very impressive in the *B flat minor* (the central section of the *Andante* scintillates), and the finale of the *Second concerto* – which is presented, uncut, in its original version – brings a burst of exhilarating bravura to compare with Donahue's famous recording. The solo passages for violin and cello in the *Andante* of that work are played with fair competence and a modest degree of ardour by Franco Ferrari and Jean-Max Clement, but no more than that. Poetry is consistently at Haas's fingertips, however; and Inbal, though not always the most imaginative accompanist, directs all the music with enthusiastic vigour and often with real passion. The *Third Concerto* and *Concert fantasia* have no lack of excitement. The nub is the orchestral playing. The fullest sonority which the Monte-Carlo Orchestra possessed in 1970/71, when these recordings were made, lacks the body of the major European orchestras and, although Inbal often shows a fine ear for detail (the opening of the *Concert fantasia*, with its charming *Nutcracker* overtones, sparkles as it should), the accompaniments here are no more than adequate. Fortunately these players can sometimes rise to the occasion, and the gentle opening of the rare *Andante*, Op. 79 (completed by Tanayev), is affectionately done, until the entry of the lacklustre cello and violin solos. This is a rather repetitive movement and the *Allegro maestoso* finale is laboured (not entirely the fault of the players), but this rare example of Tchaikovsky's concertante style is still worth having on disc. The recording balance allows Haas to dominate easily, and the orchestral sound itself has a truthful amount of body. The resonance occasionally clouds the more complex orchestral tuttis, notably in the *Third Concerto*, but that is not necessarily disadvantageous in hiding some of the sins of ensemble. But with Haas's contribution so consistently musical and technically reliable, there is more here to enjoy than to cavil at, and these discs are incredibly cheap.

Piano concerto No. 1 in B flat min., Op. 23.
☞ ⊛ (M) (***) BMG/RCA mono GD 60321. Horowitz, NBC SO, Toscanini – MUSSORGSKY: *Pictures.* (***)
(M) *** BMG/RCA 09026 61961-2. Van Cliburn, RCA SO, Kondrashin – BEETHOVEN: *Piano concerto No. 5.* ***
*** Chesky CD-13 [id.]. Earl Wild, RPO, Fistoulari – DOHNANYI: *Variations on a nursery tune* etc. ***
(M) *** Decca 417 750-2 [id.]. Ashkenazy, LSO, Maazel – CHOPIN: *Concerto No. 2.* ***
☞ (M) *** BMG/RCA 09026 61262-2 [id.]. Artur Rubinstein, Boston SO, Leinsdorf – GRIEG: *Concerto.* **(*)
(M) **(*) Mercury 432 011-2 [id.]. Byron Janis, LSO Menges – SCHUMANN: *Concerto.* ***
(M) (***) BMG/RCA mono GD 60449 [60449-2-RG]. Horowitz, NBC SO, Toscanini – MUSSORGSKY: *Pictures* etc. (***)
☞ (M) *(*) Telarc Dig. CD 82009 [id.]. Jon Kimura Parker, RPO, Previn – PROKOFIEV: *Concerto No. 3.* **

(i) *Piano concerto No. 1. Theme and variations, Op. 19/6.*
(M) *** EMI CDM7 64329-2 [id.]. Gavrilov, (i) Philh. O, Muti – BALAKIREV: *Islamey*; PROKOFIEV: *Concerto No. 1.* ***

Horowitz's famous record of the *B flat minor Concerto*, recorded at a concert in Carnegie Hall in 1943 with his father-in-law conducting, has achieved legendary status and has dwarfed almost every record of the work made since. The sheer power of the playing means that within seconds the ear makes allowances for the sonic limitations. This performance has now been reissued as part of the Toscanini Edition with a more attractive coupling than in its last incarnation. A record not to be missed on any account. (Readers should note that this live concert version of the Tchaikovsky *Concerto* is still also available coupled with Horowitz's 1952 recording, conducted by Reiner, of Beethoven's *Emperor Piano concerto*, on BMG/RCA GD 87992.)

Van Cliburn and the Soviet conductor Kondrashin in short give an inspired performance with as much warmth as glitter. The 1958 recording is forward and could do with more atmosphere, but the digital remastering has brought a firmer orchestral image, and the piano timbre is also improved. Coupled with an outstanding version of the *Emperor concerto*, this is a very distinguished reissue indeed, even if the piano timbre here is shallower than in the coupling.

Even in the shadow of Horowitz, the spectacular reissue by Earl Wild with the RPO under Fistoulari stands as one of the finest accounts ever of this much-recorded work and needs no apology for its sound, which is vintage quality of the early 1960s, although the violins have become a little drier with the digital remastering for CD. From the first sweep of the opening the reading is distinguished by its feeling of directness and power, yet the lyrical side of the music (the first movement's second subject, the outer sections of the *Andantino*) brings a comparable sensitivity. In the first movement there are some wholly spontaneous bursts of bravura from the soloist which are quite electrifying; and in the big cadenza one is equally reminded of Horowitz when Wild, by impetuous tempo changes in the imitative passages, makes himself sound almost like a piano duo. The finale too, taken with crackling bravura, again recalls the famous Horowitz/Toscanini live Carnegie Hall recording and Fistoulari makes a superb final climax.

Ashkenazy refuses to be stampeded by Tchaikovsky's rhetoric, and the biggest climaxes of the first movement are made to grow naturally out of the music. In the *Andantino* too, Ashkenazy refuses to play flashily. The finale is very fast and brilliant, yet the big tune is broadened at the end in the most convincing way. The remastering is highly successful: the piano sounds splendidly bold and clear while the orchestral balance is realistic.

Older readers who, like us, remember the Horowitz recording on 78s will also recall Rubinstein's similarly famous recording of the same era. He re-recorded the work for RCA in stereo in 1963 and is hardly less dashing than Horowitz. Yet, as before, there is a mercurial quality here, not only in the central section of the slow movement but also in the finale. The result, if perhaps not as overwhelming as with Horowitz, is hardly less magnetic, with fine bravura in the outer movements and a poetic *Andante*. Leinsdorf is obviously caught up in the music-making and the Boston Symphony opens the work splendidly and provides plenty of excitement throughout. The sound is remarkably good in its new CD incarnation; the strings are obviously close-microphoned but the piano image is impressively bold and clear. The result is very compelling and enjoyable.

Byron Janis's account is in many ways as dazzling as his Rachmaninov recordings. Menges is not as strong an accompanist as Dorati, most noticeably so in the finale. But this remains a memorable performance, with much dash and power from the soloist in the outer movements and the *Andantino* agreeably delicate. The Mercury sound is excellent, full and resonant, with a big piano image up front.

Horowitz's earlier version, coupled with the Mussorgsky, was made in Carnegie Hall, in 1941, under studio conditions. The recording is altogether better balanced than the live performance by the same artists, and the orchestral sound is much fuller; indeed the quality brooks no real criticism. But throughout one feels that Toscanini – with his soloist responding readily – is forcing the pace, creating enormous urgency. This is an exhilarating listening experience; but the sense of occasion of the live performance created a really great performance which is undoubtedly more satisfying despite its sonic limitations.

Gavrilov is stunning in the finale of the *Concerto*; however, the final statement of the big tune is broadened so positively that one is not entirely convinced. Similarly in the first movement, contrasts of dynamic and tempo are extreme, and the element of self-consciousness is apparent. The *Andante* is full of tenderness and the *prestissimo* middle section goes like quicksilver, displaying the vein of spontaneous imagination that we recognize in Gavrilov's other records. The recording is full and sumptuous. In the *Variations*, Op. 19, Tchaikovsky's invention has great felicity. Gavrilov's playing is stylishly sympathetic here, and the Balakirev and Prokofiev couplings are dazzling.

Jon Kimura Parker and Previn give a spaciously relaxed reading, with no lack of poetry in the lyrical moments of the first movement and an agreeably intimate *Andantino*. The finale is effective, but the adrenalin does not run very high and the rich Telarc recording, somewhat opaque and with a resonant bass, helps to make the closing sections of both outer movements sound somewhat ponderous.

Piano concerto No. 1 in B flat min., Op. 23; Concert fantasy, Op. 56.
☞ *** Virgin/EMI Dig. VC7 59612-2 [id.]. Pletnev, Philh. O, Fedoseyev.

Mikhail Pletnev's masterful account of the *First Concerto* has all the qualities we associate with his remarkable pianism. This high-voltage account, together with that of the *Concert fantasy*, is among the very finest modern recordings in the catalogue. Vladimir Fedoseyev and the Philharmonia Orchestra give excellent support and the production by Andrew Keener is exemplary.

(i) *Piano concerto No. 1;* (ii) *Violin concerto in D, Op. 35.*
☞ (B) *** DG 439 420-2 [id.]. (i) Martha Argerich, RPO, Dutoit; (ii) Milstein, VPO, Abbado.
(BB) *** BMG/RCA VD 60491 [60491-2-RV]. (i) John Browning; (ii) Erick Friedman, LSO,
    Ozawa.
☞ (B) *** Erato/Warner 4509 92685-2 [id.]. (i) Devoyon; (ii) Amoyal; Philh. O, Dutoit.
(M) **(*) Sony Dig. MDK 44643 [id.]. (i) Gilels, NYPO; (ii) Zukerman, Israel PO; Mehta.

This reissue in DG's Classikon series makes an almost unbeatable bargain. Argerich's 1971 version of
the *First Piano concerto* with Dutoit has long been among the top recommendations. The sound is
firm, with excellent presence, and its ambience is more attractive than the later version. The weight of
the opening immediately sets the mood for a big, broad performance, with the kind of music-making
in which the personalities of both artists are complementary. Argerich's conception encompasses the
widest range of tonal shading. In the finale she often produces a scherzando-like effect; then the
orchestra thunders in with the Russian dance-theme to create a real contrast. The tempo of the first
movement is comparatively measured, but satisfyingly so; the slow movement is strikingly atmospheric, yet delicate, its romanticism light-hearted. Milstein's 1973 performance of the *Violin concerto*
is equally impressive, undoubtedly one of the finest available, while Abbado secures playing of
genuine sensitivity and scale from the Vienna Philharmonic, with a recording that is also well
balanced.

Browning's mid-1960s interpretation of the solo role in the *Piano concerto* is remarkable, not only
for power and bravura but for wit and point in the many *scherzando* passages, and in the finale he
adopts a fast and furious tempo to compare with Horowitz. Erick Friedman, Heifetz's pupil, is a
thoughtful violinist who gives a keenly intelligent performance of the companion work, imbued with
a glowing lyricism and with a particularly poetic and beautiful account of the slow movement. There
is plenty of dash and fire in the finale, and Ozawa gives first-rate support to both soloists. The
recording is excellent. Two performances to match those of almost any rival; moreover this disc is in
the lowest price-range.

Devoyon's performance of the *Piano concerto* is the very opposite of barnstorming. It opens and
closes spaciously and, even in the big final statement of the finale, the participants hold back from
unleashing a torrent of rhetoric. The result is refreshing. There is no lack of spontaneity and the first
movement unfolds grandly, its lyrical impulse fully realized. With Dutoit in charge, the Philharmonia
playing is predictably polished and committed, and the soloist is persuasive too, refusing to be
stampeded at any point. While there are fewer switchback thrills here than usual, there is much that is
satisfying. About Amoyal's account of the *Violin concerto* there can be no reservations. He plays with
passionate commitment, his slow movement is particularly beautiful, and he is accompanied very
sensitively. Dutoit gets exciting results from the Philharmonia, and the analogue recording from the
early 1980s is first class.

On CBS there are more reservations about the Gilels performance than the Zukerman. The
former offers less than first-class orchestral playing and not very distinguished sound, but Gilels's
own playing is masterly. In Israel, the sound is much better, and Mehta secures generally good results
from the Israel orchestra. The soloist is balanced closely and is made very tangible; Zukerman's
warmth is most attractive, and the performance overall has both excitement and spontaneity.

Piano concerto No. 2 in G (complete); *Piano sonata No. 1 in G (Grande sonate), Op. 37.*
*** Teldec/Warner Dig. 9031 72296-2 [id.]. Elisabeth Leonskaja; (i) Leipzig GO, Kurt Masur.

A splendid new version of Tchaikovsky's *G minor Piano concerto*, weightier and more expansive
(more German!) than the famous Donohoe version and certainly compelling. The red-blooded
orchestral tuttis are matched by Leonskaja's (forwardly balanced) bold pianism, and if the slow
movement misses some of the delicacy of feeling that Donohoe finds, and the extended solos for
violin and cello have rather less individuality than with Kennedy and Isserlis, there is much lyrical
ardour. The finale, too, is not chimerical but forceful in its exuberance, powerful and exciting, and
the rich Leipzig recording matches the style of the performance. The coupling of Tchaikovsky's
Grand Sonata in the same key is surely an ideal one. Leonskaja has the full measure of its rhetoric
and she plays the *Andante* with an appealing spontaneity and freshness.

Piano concertos Nos. 2 in G, Op. 44; 3 in E flat, Op. 75.
⊛ *** EMI Dig. CDC7 49940-2 [id.]. Donohoe, Bournemouth SO, Barshai.
*** Ara. Dig. Z 6583 [id.]. Jerome Lowenthal, LSO, Comissiona.
☞ (M) *(*) Decca Dig. 436 485-2 [id.]. Victoria Postnikova, VPO, Rozhdestvensky.

Donohoe's much-praised recording of Tchaikovsky's *Second Piano concerto* is coupled with his
excellent account of the *Third*. This superb recording of the full, original score of the *Second* in every

way justifies the work's length and the unusual format of the slow movement, with its extended solos for violin and cello; these are played with beguiling warmth by Nigel Kennedy and Steven Isserlis. Barshai's pacing is perfectly calculated. The first movement goes with a splendid impetus, and the performance of the slow movement is a delight from beginning to end. Peter Donohoe plays marvellously and in the finale he is inspired to bravura which recalls Horowitz in the *B flat minor Concerto*. The main theme, shooting off with the velocity of the ball in a pinball machine, is exhilarating, and the orchestral response has a matching excitement. The recording has a fine, spacious ambience and is admirably realistic and very well balanced.

In an obviously attractive coupling of two unjustly neglected works, the energy and flair of Lowenthal and Comissiona combine to give highly spontaneous performances, well balanced and recorded. If the *G major Concerto* has not quite the distinction of the EMI version, it is still satisfyingly alive; the soloist brings an individual, poetic response as well as bravura. With very good sound, this is well worth investigating, as the account of the *Third Concerto* is comparably spontaneous.

Postnikova and Rozhdestvensky use the complete original score of the *Second*, but with slow speeds the performance hangs fire. The long single movement of the *Third concerto* also needs more consistently persuasive treatment, though the dactylic dance-theme is delectably pointed. Close balance for the piano in a firm, vivid recording. But this is not really competitive.

(i) *Piano concerto No. 2 in G, Op.44* (arr. Siloti); (ii) *Concert fantasia in G, Op. 56.*
*** Olympia OCD 229 [id.]. (i) Gilels, USSR Ac. SO, Svetlanov; (ii) Zhukov, USSR Ac. SO, Kitaenko.

The Russian recording of the abridged Siloti version, made at a public concert in the Moscow Conservatoire in 1972, is hugely exciting and, taken on its own merits, is a great success. Gilels's playing is masterly and Svetlanov brings plenty of vigour to the occasion. The orchestral soloists make the most of the section of concertante music which is left to them, and in the finale the glittering brilliance of Gilels's articulation is matched by his witty restraint in the treatment of the secondary material. The coupling is a splendid account of the *Concert fantasia*, an engaging and much underrated piece, demanding comparable technical virtuosity from its soloist, which Igor Zhukov provides in full measure.

Piano concerto No. 3.
☞ **(*) Chan. Dig. CHAN 9130 [id.]. Geoffrey Tozer, LPO, Järvi – *Symphony No. 7.* ***

It was a very good idea to record the *Third Piano concerto* alongside the *Seventh Symphony*, on whose first movement it is based (see below). Geoffrey Tozer is an excellent soloist and, as in his Medtner performances for Chandos, plays with sympathy as well as powerful bravura. The playing of the London Philharmonic is not so consistent, with violin tone as recorded often thin, not opulent enough for big Tchaikovsky melodies.

Violin concerto in D, Op. 35.
☞ *** EMI Dig. CDC7 54753-2 [id.]. Sarah Chang, LSO, Sir Colin Davis – BRAHMS: *Hungarian dances.* ***
(BB) *** Naxos Dig. 8.550153; *4550153* [id.]. Takako Nishizaki, Slovak PO, Kenneth Jean – MENDELSSOHN: *Concerto.* ***
(M) *** DG 419 067-2 [id.]. Milstein, VPO, Abbado – MENDELSSOHN: *Concerto.* ***
*** Decca Dig. 421 716-2 [id.]. Joshua Bell, Cleveland O, Ashkenazy – WIENIAWSKI: *Violin concerto No. 2.* ***
☞ (***) Testament mono SBT 1038 [id.]. Ida Haendel, RPO, Goossens – BRAHMS: *Violin concerto.* (***)
(M) (***) EMI mono CDH7 64030-2 [id.]. Heifetz, LPO, Barbirolli – GLAZUNOV: *Violin concerto* (***) ⊛; SIBELIUS: *Violin concerto.* (**)
☞ (M) *** BMG/RCA 09026 61495-2. Heifetz, Chicago SO, Reiner – BRAHMS: *Concerto.* ***
☞ **(*) Trittico Dig. 27103 [id.]. Vanessa-Mae, LSO, Bakels – BEETHOVEN: *Violin concerto.* **(*)
☞ ** Discover Dig. DICD 920122 [id.]. Evgeny Bushkov, Slovak R. New PO, Rahbari – MENDELSSOHN: *Concerto.* **(*)
☞ ** BMG/RCA Dig. 09026 60759-2. Kyoko Takezawa, Moscow RSO, Fedoseyev – PROKOFIEV: *Violin concerto No. 2.* **
☞ ** DG Dig. 437 540-2 [id.]. Gil Shaham, Philh. O, Sinopoli – SIBELIUS: *Violin concerto.* *(*)
☞ *(*) BMG/RCA 09026 60990-2. Vladimir Spivakov, RPO, Temirkanov – PROKOFIEV: *Violin concerto No. 1.* *(*)

Violin concerto in D; Sérénade mélancholique, Op. 26; Souvenir d'un lieu cher, Op. 42/3: Mélodie.
Valse-scherzo, Op. 34.
*** ASV Dig. CDDCA 713 [id.]. Xue-Wei, Philh. O, Accardo.

Violin concerto in D; Sérénade mélancolique, Op. 26; Valse-scherzo, Op. 34.
☞ (M) *** Erato/Warner 2292 45971-2 [id.]. Pierre Amoyal, Philh. O, Dutoit.

Sarah Chang's version establishes itself in a category apart. Here is a very young artist who really does live up to the claims of the publicists, for from her first note onwards she compels attention with her poetic and imaginative treatment of each phrase, always sounding spontaneous. What immediately strikes one is the dynamic range of her playing. She is helped there by the natural balance, allowing genuine pianissimos. Not only does Chang play with exceptionally pure tone, avoiding heavy coloration, her individual artistry does not demand the wayward pulling-about often found in this work. In that she is enormously helped by the fresh, bright and dramatic accompaniment provided by the LSO under Sir Colin Davis, always a sensitive and helpful concerto conductor, and here encouraging generally steady speeds. Even Chang's relatively slow tempo for the central Canzonetta is acceptable, when the tone is so true and sweet and the shading so refined. In the outer movements Chang conveys wit along with the power and poetry, and the intonation is immaculate. Like Takezawa, but unlike Spivakov and Kennedy, she observes the tiny cuts in the passage-work, which until recently were always traditional in the finale. The snag is the ungenerous coupling, but Chang's performances of the four Brahms *Hungarian dances* are delectable.

Xue-Wei gives a warmly expressive reading of this lovely concerto, lacking some of the fantasy and mystery, but, with rich, full tone, he brings out the sensuousness of the work, while displaying commanding virtuosity. The central *Canzonetta* is turned into a simple song without words, not over-romanticized. The coupling will be ideal for many, consisting of violin concertante pieces by Tchaikovsky, not just the *Sérénade mélancolique*, but the *Valse-scherzo* in a dazzling performance, and *Mélodie*, the third of the three pieces that Tchaikovsky grouped as *Souvenir d'un lieu cher*, freely and expressively done. The orchestral playing under another great violin virtuoso is warmly sympathetic but could be crisper, not helped for detail in tuttis by the lively acoustic of St Barnabas Church, Mitcham. However, this makes a very enjoyable collection.

Like Xue-Wei, Pierre Amoyal offers Tchaikovsky's other music for violin and orchestra as coupling, although (unlike the ASV disc) the *Souvenir d'un lieu cher* is not included. However, the Erato collection has a considerable price advantage and the remastered 1981 analogue recording is very beautiful. Even in a strongly competitive field the Amoyal performance of the *Concerto* is strongly recommendable. His is a warmly lyrical performance, yet there is no lack of passionate commitment, and the slow movement is particularly beautiful when the sound is so lovely, warm and natural, and much better balanced than with Heifetz. While Dutoit does not press the first movement on as fiercely as Reiner, he still gets exciting results from the Philharmonia, and the two shorter pieces, equally sympathetic, make a perfect foil for the major work.

Takako Nishizaki gives a warm and colourful reading, tender but purposeful and full of temperament. As in the Mendelssohn with which this is coupled, the central slow movement is on the measured side but flows sweetly, while the finale has all the necessary bravura, even at a speed that avoids breathlessness. Unlike many, Nishizaki opens out the little cuts which had become traditional. With excellent playing and recording, this makes a first-rate recommendation in the super-bargain bracket.

Milstein's fine 1973 version with Abbado is here coupled with the Mendelssohn *Concerto* and remains one of the best mid-price reissues.

Bell may not have quite the fantasy of a version like Chung's deleted Decca performance, but it is an outstanding account nevertheless, very recommendable if you fancy the unusual coupling of Wieniawski. In the finale of the Tchaikovsky, Bell does not open out the tiny cuts in the passage-work that until recently have been traditional. Full, brilliant recording, with the soloist well balanced.

Recorded in mono in 1953, Ida Haendel's red-bloodedly romantic reading of the Tchaikovsky was not issued for five years, and then it had limited currency. When it is such a distinctive, positive and powerful reading, one is grateful to Testament for bringing back so unjustly neglected a recording, and in such a vivid transfer. With speeds on the broad side in the first two movements, and generally kept steady, Haendel's warmly expressive style is the more compelling, leading to a fast and muscular account of the finale. It is generously and ideally coupled with Haendel's masterly reading of the Brahms, similarly neglected.

Heifetz's first (mono) recording of the Tchaikovsky *Violin concerto*, made in 1937, has tremendous virtuosity and warmth. The sound is opaque by modern standards but the ear quickly adjusts, and the performance is special even by Heifetz's own standards. The transfer, too, is very good and, coming as it does with a classic account of the Glazunov and a fascinating Sibelius, is a real bargain.

There can be no real reservations about the sound of the present remastering of Heifetz's 1957 recording, with the Chicago acoustics ensuring a full ambience to support the brilliance of the orchestra. Heifetz is closely balanced, but the magic of his playing can be fully enjoyed. There is some gorgeous lyrical phrasing, and the slow movement marries deep feeling and tenderness in an ideal performance. The finale is dazzling but is never driven too hard. Reiner always accompanies understandingly, producing fierily positive tuttis. The Brahms coupling is equally desirable and much more generous than the offerings with the older, full-priced CD.

Vanessa-Mae recorded the Tchaikovsky *Concerto* when she was only twelve, and the free expressiveness rarely fails to be persuasive and spontaneously convincing. In the middle section of the central *Canzonetta* her phrasing is a little perfunctory, and one or two rhythms get rushed in the finale but, all told, this is an amazing demonstration from so young an artist, if hardly to be compared with Sarah Chang's achievement at a similar age. The recording is full and bright, making this a formidable, generous coupling.

Surprisingly, the young Russian soloist Evgeny Bushkov is less successful in the Tchaikovsky concerto than in the coupled Mendelssohn. He and Rahbari take the first movement in a fairly relaxed manner, with bursts of energy, but towards the end the spontaneity slips, although the playing of both soloist and orchestra is of a high standard and the recording is full and well balanced.

Kyoko Takezawa is yet another of the brilliant young Japanese violinists now dazzling the public. It is no surprise to learn that, like Kyung Wha Chung, Cho-Liang Lin, Joseph Swensen and practically every other virtuoso of the present day, Takezawa was a student of Dorothy DeLay at the Juilliard School. Her performance of the *Violin concerto* was recorded at the Alte Oper in Frankfurt while the Moscow Radio Orchestra was on tour in 1990. Her account has much to recommend it, and if the coupling is what you want it has its rewards, though it must in fairness be said that in neither concerto would it be a first choice. The quality of the recorded sound is very good: the soloist is rather (but not too) forwardly balanced, and orchestral detail is clearly defined. Her playing is eloquent and has appropriate feeling and, when required, restraint. In this she is much to be preferred to Gil Shaham on DG.

Gil Shaham's heart is worn firmly on his sleeve – in fact it is almost up to his fingertips which, it goes without saying, are uncommonly sure! There is no want of dazzling virtuosity, but nobility is not in strong supply. There is nothing routine about the playing, but there are other versions which have greater refinement of feeling. Neither Shaham nor Sinopoli leaves any expressive stone unturned in music that can speak for itself with great eloquence.

The Spivakov coupling is less recommendable, even though in the central movement of the Tchaikovsky he adopts a more appropriately flowing speed than the others. It may not worry everyone but, particularly in the outer movements, his heavy vibrato quickly becomes obtrusive. It makes the big melodies seem too soupy, when his use of rubato and portamento are also extreme. Unfortunately, a heavily romantic style is much less appropriate in the Prokofiev. The accompaniment of Temirkanov and the RPO is warmly sympathetic though, thanks to the recording, the orchestra is not well defined.

(i) *Violin concerto;* (ii) *Variations on a Rococo theme, Op. 33.*
☞ **(*) EMI Dig. CDC7 54890-2 [id.]; *EL 754890-4.* (i) Nigel Kennedy, LPO, Kamu; (ii) Paul Tortelier, N. Sinfonia, Yan-Pascal Tortelier.

Nigel Kennedy gives a warmly romantic reading of the *Concerto*, full of temperament, with one of the most expansive readings of the first movement ever put on disc. Though the sound is ample, his idiosyncrasies will not please everyone. For all his many *tenutos* and *rallentandos*, however, Kennedy is not sentimental, and his range of tone is exceptionally rich and wide, so that the big moments are powerfully sensual. Okku Kamu and the LPO do not always match their soloist; the accompaniment sometimes sounds a little stiff in tuttis, though the final coda is thrilling. This performance is available coupled to an outstanding version of the Sibelius *Concerto* with Simon Rattle (EMI CDC7 54 127-2; *EL 754 127-4*) or in the above pairing with Tortelier's finely wrought account of the *Rococo variations*, which is very enjoyable if of less generous measure. Here the recording is analogue and of excellent quality.

1812 Overture; Francesca da Rimini; Marche slave; Romeo and Juliet (fantasy overture).
(M) *** EMI Dig. CD-EMX 2152; *TC-EMX 2152.* RLPO, Sian Edwards.

1812 Overture; Hamlet (fantasy overture), *Op. 67; The Tempest, Op. 18.*
*** Delos Dig. D/CD 3081 [id.]. Oregon SO, James DePreist.

The control of the emotional ebb and flow of *Francesca da Rimini* shows Sian Edwards as an instinctive Tchaikovskian. Francesca's clarinet entry is melting and the work's middle section has a Beechamesque sense of colour. The passionate climax, representing the discovery of the lovers, falls only just short of the vehement force of the Stokowski version, while the spectacular recording gives great impact to the closing whirlwind sequence and the despair-laden final chords, where the tam-tam makes its presence felt very pungently. *1812* is also very enjoyable indeed, full of vigour and flair, a majestic final sequence with superbly resounding cannon. In *Romeo and Juliet*, the love-theme is ushered in very naturally and blossoms with the fullest ardour, while the feud music combined with the Friar Lawrence theme reaches a very dramatic climax. *Marche slave*, resplendently high-spirited and exhilarating, makes a perfect foil. The full-bodied recording is well balanced and thrilling in the proper Tchaikovskian way.

The Oregon orchestra show their paces in this vividly colourful triptych, and James DePreist is a highly sympathetic Tchaikovskian. In *1812*, the cannon are perfectly placed and their spectacular entry is as precise as it is commanding. The performance overall is highly enjoyable, energetic but with the pacing unforced, though the ritenuto before the final peroration is not quite convincing. The performances of both *Hamlet* and *The Tempest* are passionately dramatic, the latter generating comparable intensity (but more melodrama) than Dorati's Decca version, the former approaching yet not quite equalling Stokowski's account in imaginative vividness. But overall this is an impressive CD début.

Festival coronation march in D; (i) *Romeo and Juliet:* duet (orch. Taneyev).
*** Chan. Dig. CHAN 8476; *ABTD 1187* [id.]. (i) Murphy, Lewis, Wilson-Johnson; SNO, Järvi –
RACHMANINOV: *The Bells* etc. **(*)

Tchaikovsky's *Festival coronation march* is suitably grandiloquent but has a rather engaging trio, plus a whiff of the Tsarist hymn we recognize from *1812*. It is very well played here and superbly recorded. The vocalization of *Romeo and Juliet*, with the music drawn from the famous fantasy overture, was left in the form of posthumous sketches, which Taneyev completed and scored. The effect is more like a symphonic poem with vocal obbligatos, rather than operatic. It is well sung here but is mainly of curiosity value.

Festival overture on the Danish national anthem, Op. 15; (i) *Hamlet: Overture and incidental music, Op. 67 bis. Mazeppa: Battle of Poltava and Cossack dance; Romeo and Juliet* (fantasy overture; 1869 version); *Serenade for Nikolai Rubinstein's saint's day.*
⊛ *** Chan. Dig. CHAN 8310/11; *DBTD 2003* (2) [id.]. LSO, Simon, (i) with Janis Kelly,
    Hammond-Stroud.

Tchaikovsky himself thought his *Danish Festival overture* superior to *1812*, and though one cannot agree with his judgement it is well worth hearing. The *Hamlet* incidental music is another matter. The overture is a shortened version of the *Hamlet fantasy overture*, but much of the rest of the incidental music is unknown, and the engaging *Funeral march* and the two poignant string elegies show the composer's inspiration at its most memorable. The music from *Mazeppa* and the tribute to Rubinstein make engaging bonuses, but the highlight of the set is the 1869 version of *Romeo and Juliet*, very different from the final, 1880 version we know so well. It is fascinating to hear the composer's early thoughts before he finalized a piece which was to become one of the most successful of all his works. The performances here under Geoffrey Simon are excitingly committed and spontaneous; the orchestral playing is nearly always first rate, and the digital recording has spectacular resonance and depth to balance its brilliance. Edward Johnson, who provided the initial impetus for the recordings, writes the excellent notes and a translation of the vocal music, which is sung (as the original production of *Hamlet* was performed) in French.

Francesca da Rimini; Romeo and Juliet (fantasy overture); *Serenade for strings, Op. 48; Symphony No. 4 in F min., Op. 36.*
☞ (B) *(*) Erato/Warner Dig. Duo 4509 95360-2 (2) [id.]. USSR MoC SO, Rozhdestvensky.

An Erato Bonsai Tchaikovsky programme which obstinately refuses to become the sum of its component parts. A disappointment. One can hardly believe this is a Russian orchestra in *Francesca da Rimini*. Rozhdestvensky pushes on hard after the opening, but there is a lack of underlying fervour, the middle section of the piece is bland and the climax brings no feeling of despairing, unbridled passions and the stark punishment of Hell. The *Serenade for strings* is also a very low-key performance; the first movement is far too slack, and the rhythms of the finale are heavy rather than buoyant. The best thing here by far is the ebullient *Marche slave*. The *Symphony* is more convincing – far from a routine performance but one which, like *Romeo and Juliet*, takes a while to warm up and is never really gripping in the way that, for instance, Monteux's RCA version is so compulsive. It is well recorded and certainly enjoyable in its more relaxed way, even if the central section of the slow movement (which, according to the composer, represents 'active life') has its dotted rhythms treated rather too romantically. As usual with these Duo reissues, the documentation consists merely of titles and cues.

(i) *Hamlet: Overture and incidental music, Op. 67 bis. Romeo and Juliet* (fantasy overture: original (1869) version).

☞ ⊛ *** Chan. Dig. CHAN 9191 [id.]. (i) Janis Kelly, Derek Hammond-Stroud; LSO, Geoffrey Simon.

An admirable recoupling. The (1869) original version of *Romeo and Juliet* is very different from the 1879 revision we all know so well: it has a completely different opening section and, after a less well-organized development of the feud and love music, ends sombrely but rather less tellingly than Tchaikovsky's final masterpiece. The composer's second thoughts were undoubtedly superior but, even so, the earlier version is a most enjoyable work in its own right with at least two unfamiliar tunes, and it remains a very Russian response to Shakespeare's tragedy. As the orchestral parts are readily available in Moscow, it ought to be heard at concerts, perhaps alongside the revision. Geoffrey Simon is a committed advocate and the performances here are exciting and spontaneous. The *Hamlet incidental music* is hardly less valuable. The overture is a shortened version of the *Hamlet fantasy overture*, but much of the rest of the incidental music is unknown, and the engaging *Funeral march* and the two poignant string elegies show the composer's inspiration at its most memorable. *Ophelia's mad scene* is partly sung and partly spoken, and Janis Kelly's performance is most sympathetic, while Derek Hammond-Stroud is suitably robust in the *Gravedigger's song*. A translation of the vocal music is provided. It is sung here in French (as the original production of *Hamlet* was performed in St Petersburg), using a translation of the play. The digital recording has spectacular resonance and depth to balance its brilliance, and there are excellent new notes by Noël Goodwin, though why Edward Johnson's commentary (which accompanied the original issue) has been replaced is difficult to understand, particularly as he provided the initial impetus for these recordings.

Manfred Symphony, Op. 58.
⊛ *** Chan. Dig. CHAN 8535; *ABTD 1245* [id.]. Oslo PO, Jansons.
☞ *** Virgin/EMI Dig. VC7 59230-2 [id.]. Bournemouth SO, Litton.
☞ (M) *** EMI Dig. CDM7 64872-2 [id.]. Philh. O, Muti.
☞ **(*) Teldec/Warner Dig. 9031 73130-2 [id.]. Leipzig GO, Kurt Masur.

Manfred Symphony; Hamlet (fantasy overture).
☞ (M) **(*) Decca 425 051-2 [id.]. VPO, Maazel.

Except in a relatively relaxed view of the *vivace* second movement, Jansons favours speeds flowing faster than usual, bringing out the drama but subtly varying the tensions to press each climax home to the full and always showing his mastery of Tchaikovskian rubato: his warmly expressive phrasing never sounds self-conscious when it is regularly given the freshness of folksong. The performance culminates in a thrilling account of the finale, leading up to the entry of the organ, gloriously resonant and supported by luxuriant string sound. The Chandos recording is among the finest in the Oslo series, atmospheric but with fine inner detail.

Litton and the Bournemouth orchestra are particularly successful in the delicate, poetic moments of *Manfred*. The Astarte theme in the first movement has rarely been moulded so affectionately, and Litton, after a relatively lightweight start, controls tension to bring out the narrative sequence of this programme work, the dramatic cohesion. Characteristically, his warmly affectionate treatment never falls into sentimentality or vulgarity. The string-tone may be less resonant than with some rivals, but there is an equivalent gain in the extra clarity of texture, and in clean articulation the Bournemouth players of all sections readily match all rivals. Litton points the chattering semiquavers of the 'Alpine Fairy' Scherzo with engaging wit and fantasy, and his broad speed for the third-movement *Andante* allows the oboist to play his opening solo with a tender expressiveness to make most others seem prosaic. The sound is clean-cut and well balanced, with the organ entry at the end of the finale among the most dramatic of all.

Muti's 1981 digital *Manfred* is welcome back in the catalogue at mid-price and as such is very competitive. Muti's reading is forceful and boldly dramatic throughout. His Scherzo has a quality of exhilarating bravura, rather than concentrating on delicacy; the lovely central melody is given a sense of joyous vigour. The *Andante*, after a refined opening, soon develops a passionate forward sweep; in the finale the amplitude and brilliant detail of the recording, combined with magnificent playing from the Philharmonia Orchestra, brings a massively compulsive projection of Tchaikovsky's bacchanale and a richly satisfying dénouement. The CD adds to the weight and definition of the recording and, if the effect is slightly less sumptuous than Jansons's Chandos version, the Kingsway Hall ambience adds plenty of warmth and colour.

Maazel recorded *Manfred* in 1971, some time after his complete symphony cycle. It is a keenly alert, fresh performance, direct and often exciting, and by no means to be dismissed. The slow movement has plenty of ardour to balance its pastoralism, and the entry of the organ in the finale is impressively managed by the Decca engineers. Indeed the Sofiensaal recording is of vintage Decca quality. If other versions are more individual, the generous *Hamlet* coupling may well tempt some collectors. It does not match Stokowski's famous account but is both excitingly dramatic and strong on atmosphere, with the opening and closing pages given a sombre colouring to catch the essence of Shakespeare's tragedy. Again the CD transfer brings a vividly believable orchestral balance.

Masur conducts a powerful performance of Tchaikovsky's unconventionally constructed programme symphony. In his characteristically straight manner, as unhysterical in his approach to the composer as is possible, he is less concerned with illustrating the Byronic programme than with building symphonic strength into the music. With a structure that can seem loosely held together, his approach here generally works better than with the numbered symphonies in his Tchaikovsky series for Teldec. In the outbursts of the first movement of *Manfred* there may be little passion but plenty of power. The Leipzig orchestra plays brilliantly, and the very forward recorded sound makes the results bitingly dramatic to the point of fierceness. The second–movement Scherzo is brilliant but lacking in charm, and there is too little affection or tenderness in the third-movement *Andante*. Warm Leipzig sound.

Manfred Symphony; Symphonies Nos. 5–6 (Pathétique); Romeo and Juliet (fantasy overture); *The Tempest* (symphonic fantasy).
☞ (M) *** Virgin/EMI Dig. VMT7 59701-2 (3) [id.]. Bournemouth SO, Andrew Litton.

With Litton's accounts of *Manfred* and the *Pathétique* both among the finest available and the performances of Tchaikovsky's two greatest Shakespearean fantasies equally recommendable, this makes a very attractive mid-priced package. Litton's account of the *Fifth* is also rewarding, although the first movement lacks the high voltage so striking in those other works. The other three movements are first rate. The slow movement brings a beautiful horn solo, with the sound exquisitely distanced and with Litton sustaining his slow *Andante* well. At a well-judged speed, the Waltz third movement is then delightfully fresh and delicate in a simple way and the finale, again on the broad side, is warm rather than ominously histrionic, with very clean articulation in the playing and fine detail. Atmospherically recorded, with slightly distanced sound, this performance certainly has many attractions despite that squarely symphonic view of the first movement.

Complete ballets: (i; ii) The Nutcracker, Op. 71; (iii; ii) The Sleeping Beauty, Op. 66; Swan Lake, Op. 20; (i; iv) Serenade for strings, Op. 48.
☞ (B) *** EMI Dig./Analogue CZS7 67743-2 (6) [id.]. (i) RPO; (ii) André Previn; (iii) LSO; (iv) Barbirolli.

Anyone wanting a bargain package of the major Tchaikovsky ballets will find Previn an admirable guide through three of the composer's greatest scores, bursting at the seams with melody and inspired orchestral colouring. Without neglecting the narrative flow or underplaying the drama, Previn is at his finest in the *Divertissements* with their vividly hued characteristic dances, showing the composer endlessly imaginative and never at a loss for indelible ideas. Both the RPO and LSO solo playing is of a consistently high calibre, and the recordings are all out of EMI's top drawer. *The Nutcracker* (1986) is digital and *The Sleeping Beauty* (1974) analogue and not as brilliant as its companions, though with a compensating opulence. Both were made at Abbey Road, while *Swan Lake* (1976), also analogue, offers the Kingsway Hall ambience. The CD transfers are excellently managed, though there are two small cuts in the *Sleeping Beauty* – see below. Each set is separately packaged in its own box (within the slipcase containing all three), and *The Nutcracker* packaging also includes Barbirolli's 1964 LSO recording of the *Serenade for strings*, characteristically ripe and romantic – especially in the *Elégie*, with its expressive *Waltz* and bustling finale. Here the sound of the violins above the stave has a degree of thinness, but the Kingsway Hall acoustic ensures overall warmth. The back-up documentation for the ballets includes a cued analysis of the narrative related to each number.

The Nutcracker (ballet), *Op. 71* (complete).
*** Decca Dig. 433 000-2 (2) [id.]. Finchley Children's Music Group. RPO, Ashkenazy – GLAZUNOV: *Seasons*.
*** Telarc Dig. CD 8137 (2) [id.]. London Symphony Ch., LSO, Mackerras.
☞ (M) *** CfP CD-CFPD 4706; *TC-CFPD 4706* (2) [Ang.CDCB 47267]. Amb. S., LSO, Previn.
☞ **(*) BMG/RCA 09026 61704-2 (2). St Louis Ch. & SO, Leonard Slatkin.
(M) **(*) Decca 425 450-2 (2) [id.]. Nat. PO, Richard Bonynge – OFFENBACH: *Le Papillon*. ***
☞ **(*) EMI Dig. CDS7 54600-2 (2) [Ang. CDQB 54649-2]. New L. Children's Ch., LPO, Jansons.
(*) ROH Dig. ROH 304/5 [id.]. ROHCG O, Mark Ermler – ARENSKY: *Variations*. *
☞ (M) ** Melodiya/BMG 7432 117081-2 (2) [id.]. Russian State SO, Svetlanov.

(i) *The Nutcracker* (complete); (ii) *Serenade for strings in C, Op. 48*.
(M) *** Mercury 432 750-2 (2). (i) LSO; (ii) Philharmonia Hungarica, Antal Dorati.

The Nutcracker (complete); *The Sleeping Beauty: Aurora's Wedding*.
☞ *** Decca Dig. 440 477-2 (2) [id.]. Face School Children's Ch., Montreal SO, Charles Dutoit.

(i) *The Nutcracker* (complete); (ii) *Swan Lake* (ballet): highlights.
(B) **(*) Pickwick DUET 20 CD [MCAD2 9801]. (i) LPO, Artur Rodzinski; (ii) Utah SO, Abravanel.

The Nutcracker (complete); *Eugene Onegin: Introduction; Waltz; Polonaise*.
*** Ph. Dig. 420 237-2 (2) [id.]. BPO, Bychkov.

Although Dorati's justly famous Mercury set remains highly competitive at mid-price, Ashkenazy's digital *Nutcracker* now takes its place fairly easily at the top of the list. It is ideally coupled with Glazunov's *Seasons*, a no less enticing performance, and has the benefit of Walthamstow acoustics and state-of-the-art Decca digital sound, glowingly warm, with much colour and bloom for the woodwind. The *Snowflakes* choral *waltz* has warmth as well as charm and the famous characteristic dances of the Act II Divertissement match elegance and character with a multi-hued palette of colour. Ideally the recording could be more generously cued in the accompanying documentation, and the narrative needs to be better related to the music in the notes, but for the music-making and recording there can only be the highest praise.

Dutoit's newest Decca recording obviously comes into immediate competition with the Ashkenazy set. It is beautifully played, with much sophisticated detail, and the Montreal acoustic provides brilliance, vivid colouring and striking transparency of detail. The party scene has great zest and character and the famous characteristic dances of the Act II *Divertissement* are made to sound wonderfully fresh, as is the *Waltz of the Snowflakes*, with its charming chorus of children. The sound is less sumptuous than with Ashkenazy (noticeable in the Pine forest journey), but both recordings are out of Decca's top drawer and each of the two sets has its own felicities. For a coupling Dutoit offers *Aurora's Wedding*, a truncated version of *The Sleeping Beauty* which swiftly encapsulates the storyline, then moves on to the last-Act *Divertissement*. Diaghilev conceived this and put it into the repertory of the Ballets Russes when his 1921 London production of the complete ballet proved disastrously expensive. It makes an agreeable set of highlights, especially when played as spiritedly and elegantly as it is here, and the Decca recording is particularly successful. But Ashkenazy's coupling of Glazunov's *Seasons* is even more enticing.

The Telarc set was recorded in Watford Town Hall, which adds a little glamour to the violins and a glowing warmth in the middle and lower range. When the magic spell begins, the spectacularly wide dynamic range and the extra amplitude make for a physical frisson in the climaxes, while the glorious climbing melody, as Clara and the Prince travel through the pine forest, sounds richly expansive. Before that, the battle has some real cannon-shots interpolated but is done good-humouredly, for this is a toy battle. The great *Pas de deux* brings the most sumptuous climax, with superb sonority from the brass on the Telarc version. The Telarc presentation, too, with a detailed synopsis, is superior to the Decca documentation.

Undoubtedly Dorati's LSO version is the finest of the mid- and bargain-priced analogue *Nutcrackers*. The engineering is sophisticated, with a natural balance; the hall ambience provides warmth and bloom, yet detail is characteristically refined. Dorati relishes every detail, his characterization is strong, and the playing is full of life and elegance. The *Journey through the pine forest* expands magnificently while the choral delicacy of the *Waltz of the snowflakes* is full of charm. In Act II the characteristic dances have much colour and vitality. Altogether a great success. The *Serenade for strings* is less compelling. The slightly dry effect does not capture quite enough of the hall ambience and turns a close scrutiny on ensemble from the Philharmonia Hungarica, who could at times be more polished. It is an affectionate performance, but not an especially vital one.

Previn's earlier (1972) analogue set with the LSO has been freshly remastered. As in his later, digital version (only available, combined with the other two ballets), the famous dances in Act II are played with much sophistication, and indeed the orchestral playing throughout is of very high quality. With Act I sounding brighter and more dramatic than in its original LP format, this CfP reissue makes a fine bargain alternative to Dorati's mid-priced Mercury set with the LSO.

Semyon Bychkov has the services of the Berlin Philharmonic (an orchestra that always identifies readily with Tchaikovsky) and they offer superlative playing, of striking flair and character. Although a concert-hall ambience is favoured, the strings seem more forward, inner detail is very clear and the cymbals have a thrilling metallic clash. There is some superbly stylish playing in the *Divertissement*, and there are many moments when the extra vividness of the Berlin recording is especially compelling; and, of course, Bychkov offers a modest bonus, and the *Eugene Onegin* excerpts are brilliantly done. The Philips notes are extensive but not so conveniently matched to the CD cues.

Rodzinski's *Nutcracker* derives from the old Westminster label and dates from the earliest days of stereo. The tingling vitality of the playing brings infectious zest to the party scene of Act I – and a smile to the face of the listener, when the clock striking midnight to herald the beginning of the magic is recognized, incongruously, as none other than Big Ben! The studio recording has a glowing richness of string texture, so effective in the lilting *Waltz of the flowers*. The rather robust contribution of the chorus robs the *Waltz of the snowflakes* of some of its essential delicacy; yet the whole performance is so grippingly involving that reservations are of less moment, with the set in the bargain range. Fortunately the coupling has comparable vividness and excitement; the selection from *Swan Lake* produces often electrifying playing from Abravanel's splendid Utah orchestra.

Slatkin's 1985 recording has been reissued, sumptuously packaged in a gift box which happily recalls the more lavish days of LP presentation. It is obviously aimed at the younger generation. There are cardboard press-outs of the main characters and robust, free-standing card backgrounds of the principal sets. The quality of the artwork is high and these bonus artefacts will surely delight any young fan of the ballet, the more so as the beautifully illustrated accompanying booklet offers an excellent, user-friendly narrative and in addition relates the story to the music, track by track, describing the orchestration with silhouettes of the orchestral instruments. Charming coloured drawings of Clara, the heroine, and the Nutcracker himself are also beautifully printed on the silver discs. Slatkin's brightly paced reading always keeps the action moving in Act I, and the orchestral playing has plenty of character throughout. Other versions have more charm but are not more vivid. The lively St Louis recording, though spacious, is a little lacking in sumptuousness and richness of woodwind colour, but its vitality is a plus point, especially for younger listeners at whom the set is clearly aimed. With such high production values, it would certainly make a good present.

Bonynge's set is made the more attractive by its rare and substantial Offenbach coupling. His approach is sympathetic and the orchestral playing is polished, even if in the opening scene he misses some of the atmosphere. With the beginning of the magic, as the Christmas tree expands, the performance becomes more dramatically involving, and in the latter part of the ballet Bonynge is at his best, with fine passion in the Act II *Pas de deux* and plenty of colour in the characteristic dances. The Decca recording is brilliant and vivid.

Jansons's new EMI version is highly dramatic, the histrionic effect emphasized by spectacular recording, especially of the brass which sounds almost Wagnerian at times in its amplitude. This is certainly lively and exciting, and it is stylishly played, but it has less warmth and magic than the Decca Ashkenazy digital recording. Moreover there is no coupling.

Mark Ermler's version was recorded as one of the first issues on the new Royal Opera House label. As in the companion recording of *Swan Lake*, the players respond warmly and idiomatically to Tchaikovsky's ballet music, but the orchestral ensemble is not quite so crisp here, and the warmly reverberant recording tends to inflate the performance, undermining the piece's delicacy, its fairy-tale atmosphere. It is an enjoyable version nevertheless, recommendable to those who expressly want the engaging Arensky coupling.

The Russian State Symphony Orchestra under Svetlanov certainly give a vital performance. Svetlanov moves the music onward strongly. The Battle is fiercely fought (in spite of a curiously muffled opening gun-shot). But after that the Pine Forest journey with its great climbing melody is vulgarized at its climax by an abrasive brass entry. Similarly the charming choral *Waltz of the snowflakes* is made brazen at the end by the brass. The Act II *Divertissement* brings vivid solo wind-playing throughout and offers much to enjoy. But while the overall sound is warm and the woodwind are naturally balanced, the violins, when they go loudly above the stave, can be fierce; overall, this is not among the most enticing, currently available complete sets of a score that above all needs sonic elegance.

The Nutcracker (ballet): excerpts, *Op. 71.*
(M) *** Sony Dig. MDK 44656 [id.]. Amb. S., Philh. O, Tilson Thomas.
*** Telarc Dig. CD 80140 [id.]. Tiffin School Boys' Ch., LSO, Mackerras.

On the face of it, the Tilson Thomas CD would seem to be the strongest recommendation: it offers considerably more music (70 minutes) than the Telarc disc; the bright-eyed Philharmonia playing is always alive and zestful; and the CBS recording is brilliant and well balanced. Moreover the selection is offered at mid-price.

But when one turns to the Telarc disc, which plays for some 55 minutes only, one enters a different, more expansive Tchaikovskian sound-world: the flair of the Battle sequence between the Nutcracker and the Mouse King immediately captures the imagination. Mackerras misses out much of Act I, but not the famous *Marche* nor the sequence called *The Magic Spell begins,* which is superbly expansive. Similarly, the *Scene in the Pine Forest* with Tchaikovsky's great climbing, scaling melody has a frisson-creating tension, and the *Waltz of the snowflakes* sets the mood for the famous characteristic dances of Act II, all splendidly done, and recorded in Telarc's most spectacular manner. Nevertheless the CBS disc is undoubtedly a bargain in its own way.

The Nutcracker: extended suite; Swan Lake: suite.
☞ (BB) *(*) Tring TRP 006 [id.]. RPO, Yuri Simonov.

Simonov gives a surprisingly routine account of the *Nutcracker suite,* and even the *Waltz of the flowers* fails to sparkle. Extra items from the ballet are included and the music-making does manage to expand with a degree of passion for the *Pas de deux.* The *Swan Lake suite* is more successful, with a pert *Dance of the Little Swans* and a fine violin/cello duet. But even with full, modern, digital recording (made at Walthamstow) this is hardly recommendable, even at its super-budget price.

Nutcracker suite, Op. 71a.
(M) **(*) Sony SBK 46550 [id.]. Phd. O, Ormandy – CHOPIN: *Les Sylphides;* DELIBES: *Coppélia; Sylvia: Suites.* ***

The Philadelphia Orchestra made this wonderful music universally famous in Walt Disney's *Fantasia* and they know how to play it just as well under Ormandy in 1963 as they did under Stokowski. Perhaps there is less individuality in the characteristic dances, but the music-making has suitable moments of reticence (as in the neat *Ouverture miniature*) as well as plenty of flair. In the *Waltz of the flowers* Ormandy blots his copybook by taking the soaring violin tune an octave up on its second appearance.

(i) *The Nutcracker; Sleeping Beauty; Swan Lake:* excerpts.
(B) **(*) EMI CZS7 62816-2 (2) [id.]. LSO, André Previn, (i) with Amb. S.

By the use of two CDs, offering some 148 minutes of music, this EMI box (issued in the 'two for the price of one' series) covers a substantial proportion of the key numbers from all three ballets. *The Nutcracker* selection is particularly generous in including, besides virtually all the most famous characteristic dances, the 13-minute episode in Act I starting with the Battle sequence, continuing with the magical Pine forest journey and finishing with the delightful choral *Waltz of the snowflakes.* Previn and the LSO provide vivacious, charismatic playing and the recording is full, bright and vivid. The remastering, however, loses some of the smoothness and refinement of focus of the original, analogue recordings in the interest of a lively upper range. But this remains very enjoyable and excellent value.

The Nutcracker; Sleeping Beauty; Swan Lake: highlights.
(M) *** EMI Dig. CDU5 65046-2; *EU* 565046-4. Philh. O, Lanchbery.

Those wanting a single disc of highlights from Tchaikovsky's three major ballets will surely find Lanchbery's selection fits the bill readily enough. Although it is perhaps a pity that the whole *Nutcracker suite* was not included, the favourite items are here, and there are eight popular excerpts from *Swan Lake* and seven from the *Sleeping Beauty* score. There are 79 minutes of music in all, played with great flair, warmth and polish, and given EMI's top-drawer digital sound.

Nutcracker suite; Sleeping Beauty: suite; Swan Lake: suite.
⊛ (M) *** DG 429 097-2; *429 097-4* [id.]. BPO, Rostropovich.
(M) *** EMI CDM7 64332-2. LSO, Previn.

Rostropovich's triptych of Tchaikovsky ballet suites is very special. His account of the *Nutcracker suite* is enchanting: the *Sugar plum fairy* is introduced with ethereal gentleness, the *Russian dance* has marvellous zest and the *Waltz of the flowers* combines warmth and elegance with an exhilarating vigour. The *Sleeping Beauty* and *Swan Lake* selections are hardly less distinguished. The CD remastering is entirely beneficial, combining bloom with enhanced detail. 69 minutes of sheer joy, and at mid-price too.

The digital remastering has been very successful on the EMI disc, freshening the sound of the excellent recordings, taken from Previn's analogue complete sets (which means that the *Dance of the sugar plum fairy* in *The Nutcracker* has the longer coda rather than the ending Tchaikovsky devised for the *Suite*). The performances are at once vivid and elegant, warm and exciting. Previn's panorama from *Sleeping Beauty* is hardly less beguiling than Rostropovich's and the recording has comparable warmth. There is nearly 73 minutes of music here, and this version can be strongly recommended alongside the DG disc; it is a most enjoyable record.

Nutcracker suite, Op. 71a; Symphony No. 4 in F min., Op. 36.
(M) (***) EMI mono CDM7 63380-2 [id.]. RPO, Sir Thomas Beecham.

Beecham himself praised the balance in the *Nutcracker suite*, one of his own favourite records. Endearingly, the tambourine player in the characteristically zestful account of the *Trépak* almost gets left behind at the end. The performance overall has a Mozartian elegance; the *Dance of the flutes*, seductively slow, is ravishing and so is the closing *Waltz of the flowers*. Sir Thomas allowed his performance of the *Fourth Symphony* to be recorded in mono, though it was made as late as 1957/8. Even so, the sound is outstandingly vivid, and the ear could easily be fooled into thinking it was stereo, so full are the strings and so rich the brass, with their glorious depth of sonority. The performance is unforgettably full of charisma.

Serenade for strings in C, Op. 48.
☞ (BB) *** ASV CDQS 6094 [id.]. Polish R. CO, Duczmal – SUK: *Serenade* ***; GRIEG: *Holberg suite* etc. **(*)
☞ (M) **(*) BMG/RCA 09026 61424-2 [id.]. Boston SO, Munch – BARBER: *Adagio* etc. ***;
    ELGAR: *Introduction and allegro.* **

The Polish Radio Chamber Orchestra is a first-class body of players, and they give a highly individual reading, full of subtlety and grace. The conductor's imaginative nuancing of dynamic shading is most winning, and this account often finds a rare quality of tenderness alongside its vigour and expansiveness. The very opening leads to a hint of nostalgia before the main theme of the allegro is gently ushered in, while later the orchestra's lightness of articulation in the busy second subject is delightfully intimate. The Waltz is relaxed and gentle, very refined, even thoughtful, with radiant violin timbre; later there is a wistful delicacy in the *Elégie* as Tchaikovsky's lovely cantilena is floated over gentle pizzicatos. Yet there is no lack of temperament or romantic ardour. The finale is exquisitely prepared, then the allegro is off with the wind, very fast, light and balletic, again with engagingly crisp articulation. Altogether this is the kind of performance that makes one appreciate this as one of the composer's greatest works, with its Mozartian elegance and perfection of form. The recording is excellent, full, transparent, yet with a fine overall bloom.

A strong, full-blooded reading from Munch, lacking in charm, but with an elegant *Waltz*, an *Elegy* which climaxes with great ardour and a well-prepared finale which generates comparable vigour. The playing of the Boston strings displays considerable bravura and virtuosity, and the 1957 recording sounds remarkably well, robust, well-detailed and with plenty of ambient atmosphere.

Serenade for strings; Souvenir de Florence, Op. 70.
(BB) **(*) Naxos Dig. 8.550404 [id.]. Vienna CO, Philippe Entremont.

Entremont's performances of Tchaikovsky's two major string works communicate above all a feeling of passionate thrust and energy. The *Waltz*, with its neatly managed tenutos, has a nice touch of romantic feeling and, after the ardour of the *Elégie*, the finale steals in persuasively, again producing an unflagging impetus, with dance-rhythms bracing and strong. The unaccountably neglected *Souvenir de Florence* has comparable momentum and eagerness. The dashing main theme of the first movement swings along infectiously, while the wistful secondary idea also takes wing. Entremont brings out the charm and responds easily to the variety of mood, both here and in the *Allegretto*, permeated with a flavour of Russian folksong. Throughout, the commitment and ensemble of the VCO bring the most persuasive advocacy and make one wonder why the *Souvenir* does not have a more central place in the string repertoire.

The Sleeping Beauty (ballet), *Op. 66* (complete).

☞ (BB) *** Naxos Dig. 8.550490/2 [id.]. Slovak State PO (Košice), Andrew Mogrelia.

☞ *** BMG/RCA Dig. 09026 61682-2 (2) [id.]. St Louis SO, Leonard Slatkin.

☞ **(*) EMI CDS7 54814-2 (2) [Ang. CDQB 54814]; *EX 764814-4*. LSO, Previn.

☞ **(*) Ph. Dig. 434 922-2 (3). Kirov O (St Petersburg), Gergiev.

(M) **(*) Decca 425 468-2 (3). Nat. PO, Richard Bonynge – MEYERBEER: *Les Patineurs.* ***

☞ (M) ** Melodiya/BMG 7432 117080-2 (3) [id.]. Russian State SO, Svetlanov.

Andrew Mongrelia spent part of his early career in the ballet pit, and he conducts Tchaikovsky's score with an ideal combination of warmth, grace and vitality. Moreover the Slovak State Philharmonic prove to be an excellent orchestra for this repertoire, with fine wind-players and equally impressive string principals for the important violin and cello solos. Mogrelia relishes the orchestral detail – and there is much inspired Tchaikovskian scoring here – and he moves the music on with a natural sense of pacing and generates plenty of excitement in the big set-pieces: the climaxes which come at the ends of Acts I and II are splendidly expansive. The Naxos digital recording is full and brilliant without being overlit, and the acoustics of the House of Arts in Košice bring a spacious ambience so that the spectacular moments have sufficient room to expand, and the orchestral colours are vivid. The set is generously banded and the documentation provides the narrative detail for each of the 65 separate cues. The result is both enjoyable and stimulating, and the three discs come for little more than the cost of a single, full-priced CD. A clear first choice among all available recordings, irrespective of cost.

Slatkin's version was recorded in 1990/91 but has not appeared before in the UK. Like the complete *Nutcracker*, above, it is impressively packaged with an eye on the younger balletomane. There are cardboard push-out pictures of the Prince and Princess and the Lilac Fairy which are charmingly conceived in a gracious traditional style, while the wicked fairy (Carabosse) looks appropriately like a witch, although she also is given wings. The cardboard set backdrops are handsome and, as with the companion *Nutcracker* set, there is a pleasing and detailed plot summary, plus a cued narrative linked to silhouettes of the orchestral instruments featured in each track. The performance has consistent vitality and plenty of drama and colour, and the Act III *Divertissement* brings both sparkle and grace. The recording is somewhat fuller than the earlier *Nutcracker*, with the hall ambience well conveyed, yet detail is clear and the strings have a realistic sheen. There is not the degree of glowing warmth or expansiveness in the bass one would expect from, say, a Decca recording made at St Eustache, but the sound is very well balanced.

Previn's 1974 complete set has also been reissued at full price, lavishly packaged, obviously intended to compete with Slatkin on RCA. The EMI booklet is illustrated with many pictures, somewhat Disneyesque in their vivid colouring. As with the competing version, each track relates the narrative to the orchestration, but there are no cardboard cut-outs, and generally the presentation is less extravagant than with Slatkin, and the artwork is not so appealing. The analogue EMI recording too is less brilliant, the balance slightly recessed so that the sound is sumptuous with a richly resonant bass. But there is a distinct absence of glitter. With warm, polished orchestral playing, Previn conveys his affection throughout, but too often – in the famous *Waltz*, for instance – there is a lack of vitality, and in the *Entr'acte* between Scenes i and ii of Act II, with its elegant violin solo from John Brown, the atmosphere is so cosy that the style hovers perilously near that of the salon. On the other hand, the *Panorama* which comes immediately before this shows Previn and his orchestra at their very best, the tune floating over its rocking bass in the most magical way. With Previn's tempi sometimes indulgently relaxed, it has been impossible to get the complete recording on to a pair of CDs, and the *Pas berrichon* and *Sarabande* included in the original (three-disc) LP issue have been cut.

The Kirov recording of Tchaikovsky's complete ballet is in every way satisfying. The playing – from an orchestra completely inside the music – is warmly sympathetic and vital, with no suggestion that familiarity has bred any sense of routine. Indeed the opening of each of the three Acts readily demonstrates the zestful vitality of the playing and, throughout, Gergiev's rhythms have plenty of take-off. Yet there is gracious warmth too, especially whenever the lovely theme representing the Lilac Fairy appears, where the tender string-playing is very affecting. The woodwind solos, too, are elegant and bring out the full colour of Tchaikovsky's glowing orchestral palette. Gergiev can often be subtle, and his performance of the beautiful *Panorama* floats gently and radiantly over its rocking base. The Act III *Pas de quatre* for all four fairies is a highlight of the sparkling Act III *Divertissement*, while *Puss-in-Boots and the White Cat* are tangible in their feline altercation. The Philips recording is sumptuous without being cloudy and it expands magnificently for Tchaikovksy's rhetorically exciting climaxes without assaulting the ears. All in all, this is first class; however, although it takes precedence over the Naxos set by a small margin, it costs about 2½ times as much, and the use of three CDs makes it uncompetitive alongside Slatkin, whose presentation is so much more elaborate. Bonynge secures brilliant and often elegant playing from the National Philharmonic Orchestra and his rhythmic pointing is always characterful. As recorded, however, the upper strings lack sumptuousness; otherwise, the sound is excellent and there is much to give pleasure, notably the drama of the awakening scene and the Act III *Divertissement*. The Decca sound has a fine sparkle here, and the solo violin (Mincho Minchev) and cello (Francisco Gabarro) provide most appealing solo contributions.

Svetlanov's opening tempo for the introduction to the *Prologue* must be the fastest on record; otherwise, although there is plenty of vitality, tempi are not over-driven. There is much fine wind and string playing, but the famous *Waltz* brings coarse brass playing at the climax, and this happens elsewhere at fortissimo levels, notably in the Act I finale. In Act II the lovely *Panorama* is played slowly and seductively, and the orchestra comes into its own in the celebratory dances of the third Act; but the 1980 recording brings a distinct lack of bloom on the violins when they are high up. The set is on three CDs, which minimizes its economy.

Sleeping Beauty (ballet): highlights.
**(*) ROH Dig. ROH 003; *ROHMC 003* [id.]. ROHCG O, Ermler.
(M) ** Sony SBK 46340 [id.]. Phd. O, Ormandy – ROSSINI: *Boutique fantasque.* **(*)

Those wishing to sample the Ermler set will find this disc contains 72 minutes of well-chosen key items. One can certainly appreciate the polish and grace of the orchestral playing here, when the recording – made in St Jude-on-the-Hill, Hampstead – is so flattering.

Ormandy provides a sumptuously glossy selection, with nearly an hour's music (the CD plays for 76 minutes overall). Superbly polished and often exciting playing but, with a forward balance, the effect is somewhat overwhelming. The sound is opulently brilliant rather than refined.

Sleeping Beauty (ballet): *Suite.*
☞ (B) **(*) DG Double 437 404-2 (2) [id.]. BPO, Karajan – CHOPIN: *Les Sylphides* *** ⊛; DELIBES: *Coppélia: suite* ***; GOUNOD: *Faust* etc. **(*); OFFENBACH: *Gaîté parisienne:* excerpts; RAVEL: *Boléro.* ***
(BB) ** Naxos Dig. 8.550079; *4550079* [id.]. Czech RSO (Bratislava), Ondrej Lenárd – GLAZUNOV: *The Seasons.* **(*)

Karajan's *Sleeping Beauty* suite generates an equal measure of elegance, warmth and adrenalin and is very well played indeed. But the recording, though quite full-bodied, is very brightly lit in the CD transfer and may need a degree of cutting back on top. It comes as part of a distinctive collection of ballet music, almost all showing the conductor and his orchestra on top form.

The Czech Radio Orchestra under Ondrej Lenárd play Tchaikovsky's ballet suite with spirit and colour, and the recording has plenty of weight and ambience and no lack of brilliance but the *Panorama* is disappointing, taken fast and with a lack of subtlety in the rocking bass rhythm.

Sleeping Beauty (ballet): *suite; Swan Lake* (ballet): *suite.*
☞ ** Erato/Warner Dig. 2292 45963-2 [id.]. Bolshoi SO, Lazarev.

This is no more distinctive than Lazarev's companion disc including the *Nutcracker suite*. It is sumptuously recorded and the orchestral playing is sympathetic and polished, with a creamy *Swan Lake* oboist and fine violin and cello solos in the *Danse des cygnes*. But Lazarev's tempi are sometimes unconvincing, often too relaxed, almost lethargic (as in the *Adagio* and *Panorama* from *Sleeping Beauty*), or brilliantly hard-driven (as in the *Czardas* and *Spanish dance* from *Swan Lake*), although no one could complain about a lack of vitality here. The trumpet soloist in the *Neapolitan dance* brings a style reminiscent of the bandstand. The CD offers only 54 minutes; there are far more generous selections elsewhere.

Suites Nos. 1 in D min., Op. 43; 2 in C (Caractéristique) Op. 53.
☞ (M) *** Melodiya/BMG Dig. 7432 117099-2 [id.]. USSR SO, Svetlanov.
☞ (BB) *** Naxos Dig. 8.550644. [id.]. Nat. SO of Ireland, Stefan Sanderling.

Tchaikovsky's *Orchestral suites* are directly descended from the dance suites of the Baroque era; Svetlanov brings to them an appropriately light touch. The highlight of the *First Suite* is the deliciously orchestrated *Marche miniature* which tends to dwarf everything else in sheer memorability – except perhaps the *Introduction*, where Tchaikovsky's innate melancholy at the opening is effectively dispersed by the following fugato. But the other movements are also immediately attractive, especially the closing *Gavotte*. Svetlanov's inspirational reading of the *Second Suite* is doubly distinctive for making the listener realize that this is a far more substantial and attractive work than was previously thought. The *Scherzo burlesque* has a part for accordions in its central section, but here they are mixed in with folksy woodwind sounds and the effect is highly piquant. In the final *Danse baroque* the Russian energy of the performance bubbles right over. With such sympathetic playing and first-class digital recording this is a prime recommendation at mid-price.

Stefan Sanderling (son of Kurt) also shows how well he understands the music's baroque ancestry in nicely turned performances of works which are neglected on record and almost never heard in the concert hall. The playing of the excellent National Symphony Orchestra of Ireland – another Naxos discovery – is polished and sympathetic to the Tchaikovskian ardour that wells up every now and then. Each of the movements (six in No. 1; five in No. 2) is neatly characterized, and there is much charm and colour. In the *Scherzo burlesque* of No. 2 the four interpolated accordions come through well in the middle section, and the suite's closing *Danse baroque* is very spirited indeed. The recording, made in Dublin's National Concert Hall, is spacious yet allows the intimate detail of the orchestration to emerge vividly. A fine, super-bargain alternative to Svetlanov.

(i) Suites Nos. 2 in C, Op. 53; 4 in G (Mozartiana), Op. 61; (ii) Sérénade mélancolique, Op. 26; Mélodie, Op. 42/3.
(M) **(*) Sony/CBS Dig. MDK 46503 [id.]. (i) Philh. O, Tilson Thomas; (ii) Zukerman, Israel PO, Mehta.

Michael Tilson Thomas makes a very good case for Tchaikovsky's *Mozartiana suite*. The Philharmonia's response is first class, and the *Second Suite* is also played with great vitality. The bright, slightly dry, early digital recording (made in EMI's No. 1 Studio at Abbey Road), which suits *Mozartiana* rather well, makes the more extrovert, fully scored first movement of the *Second, Jeu de sons*, seem a little aggressive in its brilliance, although the sharp focus is just right for the *Scherzo burlesque*, bustling with its accordions. The fill-ups, if brief, are scarcely apt but are tenderly played and very appealing.

Suite No. 3; Festival coronation march.
☞ **(*) Erato/Warner Dig. 2292 45970-2 [id.]. USSR MoC SO, Rozhdestvensky.

This is the most impressive of Rozhdestvensky's Tchaikovsky discs for Erato so far, although it offers short measure (46 minutes). In spite of a spirited performance, the *Festival coronation march* is not one of Tchaikovsky's more memorable occasional pieces, and there would easily have been room for another *Suite* instead. The *Third*, with its marvellous closing set of variations – Tchaikovsky at his most inspired – is by common consensus the best of the four *Suites*, even if its finale tends to dwarf the rest of the work. The nostalgic Russian lyricism of the opening *Élégie* and the slighter *Valse mélancolique* are well caught here in a performance which has ardour and finesse and is without hyperbole. The Scherzo is as crisp as fresh-fallen snow, with nicely pointed brass playing in the Trio. But it is the *Theme and variations* finale, with its infinite variety and melodic resource, which recommends this disc, and Rozhdestvensky gives a lively, sympathetic and colourful account for the most part, with a vivid closing *Polacca*. The orchestral playing is first class, and the recording, if lacking something in sumptuousness of string-tone, is well balanced and quite full-bodied.

Suites Nos. 3 in G, Op. 55; 4 in G (Mozartiana), Op. 61.
☞ (M) *** Melodiya/BMG Dig. 7432 117100-2 [id.]. USSR SO, Svetlanov.
☞ (BB) **(*) Naxos Dig. 8.550728 [id.]. Nat. SO of Ireland, Stefan Sanderling.

Svetlanov treats Tchaikovsky's finest suite, the *Third*, very freely, supported by the most eloquent response from one of the premier Soviet orchestras. In the *Theme and variations*, some of Svetlanov's tempi are unexpected, and the finale *Polacca* is less overwhelming than in some previous versions, Svetlanov emphasizing its dance rhythms rather than seeking to be grandiose. Svetlanov is hardly less successful in the *Fourth Suite* (*Mozartiana*), where Tchaikovsky's neat scoring is always respectful of the original music. Even so, the *Preghiera*, based on Mozart's *Ave verum*, can sometimes sound too opulent, but not here. The closing *Variations* (where Mozart used Gluck's '*Unser dummer Pöbel meint*' suite) are a delight. With excellent digital recording in both works and an attractive concert-hall ambience this is very recommendable, particularly at mid-price.

Sanderling's splendidly recorded Naxos disc also offers very enjoyable performances. He shows much delicacy of feeling both in the opening *Gigue* of *Mozartiana* and in the *Elégie*, the first movement of the *Third suite*, where he is warm without being carried away; in No. 4, the *Preghiera* is touching without the climax becoming too lavish. The orchestral playing is of the highest quality in terms of sensitivity and polish, and it is a pity that one has reservations about the performances of the sets of variations which Tchaikovsky uses for each finale. In *Mozartiana* Sanderling is very romantic and, although orchestral detail is nicely observed, his affectionate rubato affects the directness of manner with which Mozart's original piano variations would have been presented. The masterly *Theme and variations* which end the *Third suite* are superbly done until the finale. The lovely transformation of the tune played by the cor anglais over shimmering violins and the great blossoming on the full orchestra is most affecting, then in the final *Polacca* Sanderling is just that bit too grandiloquent and measured. With such richly expansive recording it cannot fail to make its effect but, with a little more pace and a touch more rhythmic lift, it could have been the overwhelming culmination the composer intended.

Swan Lake (ballet), *Op. 20* (complete).
☞ *** Decca Dig. 436 212-2 (2) Montreal SO, Dutoit.
☞ *** ROH Dig. 301/2 [id.]. ROHCG O, Mark Ermler.
(B) *** CfP Dig. CD-CFPD 4727; *TC-CFPD 4727* (2). Philh. O, John Lanchbery.
(M) **(*) Decca 425 413-2 (3) [id.]. Nat. PO, Richard Bonynge – MASSENET: *Cigale*. ***
☞ (M) **(*) Melodiya/BMG 7432 117082-2 (3) [id.]. Russian State SO, Svetlanov.

Dutoit offers the complete original score, as Tchaikovsky conceived it – a kind of dramatic symphony in four movements, with a distinct narrative line and a clearly mapped-out key structure, as much as a ballet. Into it he poured some of his finest melodic inspiration and colouristic orchestral skill, to provide just over two and a half hours of consistently appealing music in which there is not a single dull bar. The Montreal orchestra play it beautifully, rising to the plot's histrionic moments and (with the help of St Eustache acoustics and the Decca engineers) the final apotheosis, when the great Swan melody achieves its transformation into an exultant B major climax, is gloriously expansive. Dutoit's reading, without lack of drama, emphasizes the warmth and grace of the music, its infinite variety (particularly in the *Pas de deux*, *trois* and *six*, where the separate dances are so engagingly diverse). The Montreal solo violinist, Chantas Juillet, is not a sumptuous-timbred player but plays the *Danse russe* interpolation in Act III with exquisite charm. This was added by the composer after the first performance, as was an extra *Pas de deux* for Siegfried and Odile which follows the *Pas de six* slightly earlier in the same Act, depicting the visiting princesses offered for the Prince's approval. With wind solos of much character, and warm, nicely turned string phrasing and pacing which alternates bursts of liveliness within a romantically mellow basic conception, Dutoit's reading is easy to enjoy. Lanchbery's digital EMI set (not absolutely complete, but marvellous value on Classics for Pleasure) has a more exhilarating theatrical vitality, but the EMI sound is less glamorously full than the Decca recording. Decca's documentation is excellent, with John Warrack's splendid synopsis relating the narrative line closely to the music itself. Each number is cued, but not the individual sections of the *pas de deux*, *trois* etc.; and not even the famous seven-movement *Danses de cygnes* of Act II is banded separately.

Released from the Covent Garden pit to record in the warm acoustic of All Saints', Tooting, the players have responded to Ermler's deeply sympathetic direction with both refinement and red-blooded commitment, and one is constantly aware of the idiomatic feeling born of long acquaintance. The sound is exceptionally full and open, with the brass in particular giving satisfying weight to the ensemble without hazing over the detail. The set has now been reissued complete on a pair of CDs with the break coming in Act II after the *Dance of the little swans*. Ermler's broad speeds consistently convey, more than most rivals', the feeling of an accompaniment for dancing, as in the great andante of the Act I *Pas de deux*. This is a set to have you sitting back in new enjoyment of a gorgeous score.

Lanchbery's 1982 *Swan Lake* makes a superb bargain. The CfP reissue on a pair of CDs, which play for 79 minutes and 75 minutes respectively, accommodates Acts I and II on the first disc and Acts III and IV on the second. Though two numbers are cut, the set includes the extra music (a *Pas de deux*) which Tchaikovsky wrote to follow the *Pas de six* in Act III, when Siegfried dances with Odile, mistakenly believing her to be Odette. The EMI recording, made at Abbey Road, is very fine indeed: spacious, vividly coloured and full, with natural perspective and a wide (but not uncomfortably wide) dynamic range. The orchestral playing is first class, with polished, elegant string phrasing matched by felicitous wind solos. Lanchbery's rhythmic spring is a constant pleasure; everything is alert, and there is plenty of excitement at climaxes.

Bonynge's approach is essentially strong and vigorous, bringing out all the drama of the score, if less of its charm. The forward impulse of the music-making is immediately striking. As in the other sets of his Decca Tchaikovsky series, the string timbre is somewhat leonine; overall there is fullness without sumptuousness. The brass sounds are open and vibrant and the upper range is brightly lit. The balance is managed well although the (very well-played) violin solos sound rather larger than life. While this lack of ripeness may not appeal to all ears, there is a consistent freshness here, and the moments of spectacle often make a thrilling impact.

Swan Lake is easily the most successful of Svetlanov's recordings of the three great Tchaikovsky ballets and, were it on two discs instead of three, it would be very competitive. Svetlanov is often exhilarating in his lively pacing, very Slavonic in impetus. Yet all the famous numbers relax glowingly and emerge with flying colours. The opening of Act II with its famous oboe swan theme is ideally paced and the climax is unspoiled by brass blatancy, though they certainly are given their head. Later, the *Danses des cygnes* are very persuasive (with excellent violin and cello soloists) and the Act III *Divertissement* brings vivid solo wind playing. At the end, the spectacular finale has great excitement and passion. The digital recording is admirably full-blooded and the strings have plenty of amplitude.

Swan Lake (ballet), *Op. 20:* highlights.
(B) *** CfP CD-CFP 4296 [Ang. CDB 62713]. Sir Yehudi Menuhin, Philh. O, Efrem Kurtz.

A fine bargain selection on CfP with Menuhin present for the violin solos. He finds a surprising amount to play here. The 1960 recording matches the exuberance which Kurtz brings to the music's climaxes with an expansive dynamic range, and it has atmosphere as well as brilliance. The Philharmonia are on top form and the woodwind acquit themselves with plenty of style, while the string playing is characteristically elegant.

SYMPHONIES

Symphonies Nos. 1–6.
(M) *** DG 429 675-2 (4) [id.]. BPO, Karajan.
☞ ** Teldec/Warner Dig. 9031 74389-2 (4) (id.]. Leipzig GO, Masur.

Symphonies Nos. 1–6; Andante cantabile; Capriccio italien; Fatum; Francesca da Rimini, Op. 22; Romeo and Juliet (fantasy overture); *Serenade for strings, Op. 48; The Tempest; Voyevoda.*
☞ (B) **(*) BMG/Melodiya 74321 17101-2 (6) [id.]. USSR SO, Svetlanov.

Symphonies Nos. 1–6; Capriccio italien; Fatum; Francesca da Rimini; Marche slave; Romeo and Juliet (fantasy overture); *Swan Lake (suite).*
☞ (M) ** BMG/RCA Dig. 09026 61821-2 (6) [id.]. RPO, Temirkanov.

Symphonies Nos. 1–6; Capriccio italien; Manfred Symphony.
☸ (M) *** Chan. Dig. CHAN 8672/8; *DBTD 7001* (7) [id.]. Oslo PO, Jansons.

Symphonies Nos. 1–6; Manfred Symphony, Op. 58; or Romeo and Juliet (fantasy overture).
☞ (B) *** EMI CZS7 67742-2 (5) [Ang. CDZE 67742]. Philh. O or New Philh. O, Riccardo Muti (with *Manfred*).
☞ (B) *** EMI CZS7 67314-2 (4). Philh. O, Riccardo Muti (with *Romeo and Juliet*).

Symphonies Nos. 1–6; Romeo and Juliet (fantasy overture).
(B) *** Decca 430 787-2 (4) [id.]. VPO, Lorin Maazel.

Jansons' outstanding Tchaikovsky series, which includes *Manfred*, is self-recommending. The full romantic power of the music is consistently conveyed and, above all, the music-making is urgently spontaneous throughout, with the Oslo Philharmonic Orchestra always committed and fresh, helped by the richly atmospheric Chandos sound. The seven separate CDs offered here are packaged in a box priced as for five premium discs, with cassette equivalents.

Muti's outstanding set of the Tchaikovsky symphonies is made the more attractive by the addition of *Manfred*, which he recorded digitally in the Kingsway Hall in 1981. This is also available separately at mid-price (see above). He recorded his cycle of the numbered symphonies over a period of six years in the late 1970s. It represented not only the high point of his recording partnership with the Philharmonia Orchestra but also the peak of his interpretative career. It is a measure of Muti's success that even the first of the series to be recorded, No. 1, brings a performance as refined and persuasive as it is exciting, and the three early symphonies all bring orchestral playing which is both sophisticated and colourful. Throughout the cycle, and especially in the strong and urgent No. 4, Muti's view is brisk and dramatically direct, yet never lacking in feeling or imagination. In No. 5 he underlines the symphonic strength of the first movement rather than the immediate excitement. The finale then presents a sharp contrast, with its fast tempo and controlled excitement. In the *Pathétique* tempi are again characteristically fast, yet the result is fresh and youthful, with the flowing first-movement second subject given an easy expressiveness. The March, for all its urgency, never sounds brutal and the finale has satisfying depth and power. The sound generally is well up to EMI's best analogue standard of this period, and it has been transferred to CD very impressively, with the focus firm and no lack of body and weight. Choice lies between *Manfred* (involving five CDs) and Muti's superb analogue *Romeo and Juliet*, one of the finest available and full of imaginative touches, offered on four CDs.

Karajan's set, however, offers a quite outstanding bargain. Without *Manfred* (a work he never recorded), the six symphonies are fitted on to four mid-priced CDs, the only drawback being that Nos. 2 and 5 are split between discs. From both a performance and a technical point of view, the accounts of the last three symphonies are in every way preferable to his later, VPO digital versions; all offer peerless playing from the Berlin Philharmonic which the Oslo Philharmonic cannot always quite match, for all their excellence.

Maazel's performances from the mid-1960s have been remastered and reissued on four CDs, necessitating a break only at the centre of No. 4. The recordings come from a vintage Decca period and are remarkably full and vivid. In the early symphonies the hint of edge in the digital remastering (and it is very minimal) increases the bite and sense of urgency at the expense of charm (this is not a strong feature of Nos. 2 and 3 anyway). But in Nos. 4–6 (and especially in No. 4) the performances, always grippingly spontaneous, sound newly minted, helped by the freshness of the VPO playing. Perhaps No. 5 lacks the fullest expansive qualities, but there are few more effective accounts of the March/Scherzo from the *Pathétique. Romeo and Juliet* is exciting too, with plenty of romantic flair.

Evgeny Svetlanov's Tchaikovsky cycle of the symphonies comes from 1967 and they were available on LP; most of the additional orchestral items date from 1970. *Voyedova*, the *Andante cantabile* and the *Capriccio italien* are later: the late 1980s. The merits of these performances are well known: full-blooded, intense and thoroughly idiomatic, without being in the aristocratic, Mravinsky class. However, they are well worth considering at this price. The boxed package of six CDs is offered at bargain price.

Masur's cycle can be recommended to those who want a degree of detachment in this music. His readings underplay the romanticism and rely on solid symphonic strength, which is admirable, though in his severely Germanic approach he misses the charm in these works. Good Leipzig sound.

Temirkanov is a wilful Tchaikovskian. In concert his free approach on questions of tempo, exaggerating speed-changes, can result in exciting performances. In the studio it is harder to get the necessary adrenalin working and, even with the RPO in first-rate form, the wilfulness quickly comes to sound mannered or contrived, not spontaneous. Recommended for devotees. The six discs are offered for the price of four.

Symphonies Nos. 1–4.
☞ (M) *** Virgin/EMI VMT7 59699-2 (3) [id.]. Bournemouth SO, Litton.

Litton's box containing Nos. 1–4 is highly recommendable, with only No. 4 marginally less successful than the other three. First-class, modern, digital sound.

Symphony No. 1 in G min. (Winter daydreams), Op. 13.
*** Chan. Dig. CHAN 8402; *ABTD 1139* [id.]. Oslo PO, Jansons.

Symphony No. 1 (Winter Daydreams); Hamlet (fantasy overture), *Op. 67.*
☞ (BB) *** Naxos Dig. 8.550517 [id.]. Polish Nat. RSO, Adrian Leaper.

Refreshingly direct in style, Jansons with his brilliant orchestra gives an electrically compelling performance of this earliest of the symphonies. Structurally strong, the result tingles with excitement, most of all in the finale, faster than usual, with the challenge of the complex fugato passages taken superbly. The recording is highly successful.

Leaper conducts a taut and sympathetic reading of *Winter Daydreams*, with excellent playing from the Polish orchestra enhanced by vivid recording, fresh and clear, with plenty of body and with refined pianissimo playing from the strings in the slow movement. This is among the finest Tchaikovsky recordings on the Naxos list, with all four movements sharply characterized. The overture too comes in a tautly dramatic reading. An outstanding bargain.

Symphonies Nos. 1 (Winter Daydreams); 2 (Little Russian).
*** Virgin/EMI Dig. VC7 59588-2 [id.]. Bournemouth SO, Andrew Litton.

In their Tchaikovsky series for Virgin, Litton and the Bournemouth orchestra here come up with a clear winner, giving urgently spontaneous performances of both symphonies. Not only is this ideal coupling of the first two symphonies exceptionally generous (a few seconds under 80 minutes), but the performances in every way rival any in the catalogue. With warm and full recording, less distanced than many on this label, the disc earns the strongest recommendation. Litton reveals himself as a volatile Tchaikovskian, free with accelerandos and slowings, yet never sounding self-conscious or too free. The hushed pianissimos of the Bournemouth strings in the slow movement of No. 1 are ravishing, and the *Second Symphony* too brings a beautifully sprung reading which allows plenty of rhythmic elbow-room in the jaunty account of the syncopated second subject in the finale.

Symphony No. 2 in C min. (Little Russian), Op. 17 (original (1872) score); *Festive overture on the Danish national anthem, Op. 15; Serenade for Nikolai Rubinstein's saint's day; Mazeppa: Battle of Poltava; Cossack dance.*
☞ *** Chan. Dig. CHAN 9190 [id.]. LSO, Geoffrey Simon.

This is the first recording of Tchaikovsky's original score of the *Little Russian symphony* and probably the first performance outside Russia, prompted by the enterprising enthusiasm of Edward Johnson, whose admirably exhaustive original sleeve-note has now unaccountably been replaced by a new (if perfectly satisfactory) commentary by Noël Goodwin. Although the original format gained considerable success at its early performances, it gave the composer immediate and serious doubts, and so in 1879 Tchaikovsky retrieved the score and immediately set to work to rewrite the first movement. He left the *Andante* virtually unaltered, touched up the scoring of the Scherzo, made minor excisions and added repeats, and made a huge cut of 150 bars (some two minutes of music) in the finale. He then destroyed the original. (The present performance has been possible because of the surviving orchestral parts.) There can be no question that he was right. The reworked first movement is immensely superior to the first attempt, and the finale – delightful though it is – seems quite long enough, shorn of the extra bars. However, to hear the composer's first thoughts (as with the original version of *Romeo and Juliet*) is fascinating, and this is an indispensable recording for all Tchaikovski-ans. Geoffrey Simon secures a committed response from the LSO, and the recording is striking in its inner orchestral detail and freshness, although the lower range is without the resonant richness of some CDs. For the reissue other music has been added. The music from *Mazeppa*, the *Danish Festival overture* and the tribute to Rubinstein make engaging bonuses.

Symphony No. 2 in C min. (Little Russian), Op. 17.
☞ (M) *** Telarc Dig. CD 82011 [id.]. Pittsburgh SO, Lorin Maazel – RIMSKY-KORSAKOV: *Symphony No. 2 (Antar).* ***

Symphony No. 2 (Little Russian); Capriccio italien, Op. 45.
*** Chan. Dig. CHAN 8460; *ABTD 1173* [id.]. Oslo PO, Jansons.

Like other conductors who learned their craft in the Soviet Union, Jansons prefers a fastish speed for the *Andantino* second movement, but what above all distinguishes this version is the joyful exuberance both of the bouncy Scherzo – fresh and folk-like in the Trio – and of the finale, and the final coda brings a surge of excitement, making most others seem stiff. The coupling is a fizzing performance of the *Capriccio italien*, bringing a gloriously uninhibited account of the coda with its deliberately vulgar reprise of the Neapolitan tune. With some edge on violin tone, this is not the finest of the Chandos Oslo recordings, but is still fresh and atmospheric.

Maazel's slow introduction is weightier and much more measured than with his competitors. From then on, he believes in treating Tchaikovsky directly and without sentimentality, incisive of attack, refined of texture. The undistracting freshness of his view – never too tense – is enhanced by excellent, well-balanced recording. If the fine *Antar* coupling is suitable, this is thoroughly worthwhile.

Symphonies Nos. (i) 2 (Little Russian), Op. 17; (ii) 4 in F min.
❀ (B) *** DG 429 527-2; *429 527-4.* (i) New Philh. O; (ii) VPO, Claudio Abbado.
❀ (M) *** DG 431 604-2; *431 604-4.* (i) New Philh. O; (ii) VPO, Abbado.

Abbado's coupling of Tchaikovsky's *Second* and *Fourth Symphonies* is one of the supreme bargains of the current catalogue. His account of the *Little Russian Symphony* is very enjoyable, although the first movement concentrates on refinement of detail. The *Andantino* is very nicely done and the Scherzo is admirably crisp and sparkling. The finale is superb, with fine colour and thrust and a memorably spectacular stroke on the tam-tam before the exhilarating coda. The 1967 recording still sounds excellent. But this is merely a bonus for an unforgettable account of the *Fourth Symphony*, unsurpassed on record. Abbado's control of the structure of the first movement is masterly. The *Andantino*, with its gentle oboe solo, really takes wing in its central section, followed by a wittily crisp Scherzo, while the finale has sparkle as well as power, epitomizing the Russian dance spirit which was Tchaikovsky's inspiration. It was recorded in 1975 in the Musikverein and still sounds very good indeed. At the time of going to press, the bargain Privilege issue is still available. Should it disappear, however, the second listing above is more than worth its slightly higher price, although the insert leaflet still includes nothing about the music!

Symphony No. 3 in D (Polish), Op. 29.
*** Chan. Dig. CHAN 8463; *ABTD 1179* [id.]. Oslo PO, Jansons.

Symphony No. 3 in D (Polish); Capriccio italien; Eugene Onegin: Polonaise.
*** Virgin/EMI Dig. VC 790761-2 [id.]. Bournemouth SO, Litton.

Symphony No. 3 (Polish); Coronation march; Gopak.
☞ ** Teldec/Warner Dig. 2292 46322-2 [id.]. Leipzig GO, Masur.

Symphony No. 3 (Polish); 1812 Overture.
☞ ** Sony Dig. SK 45939 [id.]. Chicago SO, Abbado.

Symphony No. 3 (Polish); Hamlet overture; Romeo and Juliet (fantasy overture).
☞ (M) (**) Biddulph mono WHL 014 [id.]. LSO, Albert Coates.

Symphony No. 3 (Polish); The Tempest, Op. 18.
☞ (BB) **(*) Naxos Dig. 8.550518 [id.]. Polish Nat. RSO, Antoni Wit.

Tchaikovsky's *Third* is given a clear, refreshingly direct reading by Jansons, but it is the irresistible sweep of urgency with which Jansons builds the development section of the first movement that sets his performance apart, with the basic tempo varied less than usual. The second movement is beautifully relaxed, the *Andante elegiaco* heartwarmingly expressive, tender and refined, and the Scherzo has a Mendelssohnian elfin quality; but it is the swaggering reading of the finale, always in danger of sounding bombastic, which sets the seal on the whole performance. Though the recording does not convey a genuinely hushed pianissimo for the strings, it brings full, rich and brilliant sound.

In the outer movements Andrew Litton challenges the players to the limit in his fast speeds, but the clean, purposeful manner is very satisfying, weighty without coarseness, even if some other versions spring rhythms more infectiously. Litton's finesse comes out impressively in the *Andante elegiaco*, where he chooses a flowing speed which needs no basic modification for the broad melody which follows. He then moulds that with satisfyingly Elgar-like nobility. In the *Capriccio italien*, the playing and recording display to the full the dramatic contrasts of texture and dynamic, while the *Eugene Onegin Polonaise* brings an even more infectiously rhythmic performance. As we go to press, Litton's individual CD has been withdrawn, but his performance of No. 3 is still available in a mid-priced box containing the first four symphonies on three discs (see above).

Though Wit cannot match Leaper with the same orchestra in the *Symphony No. 1*, with playing a degree less alert and the recording not so full and forward, his *Little Russian Symphony* is still an attractive reading. The first and last movements both have a fine swagger, and if the ensemble could be crisper in the middle movements, Wit characterizes them well. *The Tempest*, an extended fantasia based on Shakespeare, not to be confused with *The Storm*, makes an attractive and unusual coupling and is again given a fine if not distinctive performance.

Abbado gives sympathetic readings of both the symphony and the overture, but there is a hint of reticence, an avoidance of vulgarity, which, particularly in the overture, prevent the merits from adding up. The slow movement of the symphony does not avoid stodginess and, though there is no lack of power in the playing, the sound lacks something in inner detail.

Masur's reading is characteristically crisp and well disciplined, with emotions underplayed, and very well recorded. His preference for fast speeds leads him in the central slow *Andante elegiaco* to one that comes near to being eccentric, undermining the elegiac quality. The *Gopak* brings another rushed performance, and Masur does little to put magic into the banal march.

Made in 1932 and sadly cut, Albert Coates's recording of the *Polish Symphony* was the first ever issued. It compensates for the cuts in a performance that is both urgent and persuasive, with rhythms beautifully sprung. Coates's account of the *Romeo and Juliet overture* is characteristically wilful, but the fire and urgency in his conducting are hard to resist in any of these items.

Symphonies Nos. 4–6.
☞ (M) *** BMG/RCA stereo/mono 09026 61901-2 (2) [id.]. Boston SO, Monteux.
☞ (B) **(*) Ph. Duo 438 335-2 (2) [id.]. LSO, Markevitch.
☞ (**) BMG/RCA Dig. 09026 61377-2 (2) [id.]. St Petersburg PO, Yuri Temirkanov.

Symphonies Nos. 4–6; The Nutcracker; Sleeping Beauty; Swan Lake: ballet suites.
(M) (***) EMI mono/stereo CMS7 63460-2 (3) [Ang. CDMC 63460]. Philh. O, Karajan.

Monteux's Boston recordings, part of BMG/RCA's Monteux Edition, were made between 1955 and 1958 and are among the finest versions of these works ever committed to disc. We understand that by the time we are in print they will be available as a separate package (two CDs in a single jewel-case).

Alongside them, many more modern versions sound unimaginative, even perfunctory in observing detail, and none has a more natural spontaneity and excitement. Monteux draws a clear distinction between Nos. 4–5 and No. 6. The former are played with a passionate forward romantic sweep and, although there are some interpretative eccentricities in No. 5, notably the finale, the panache of the music-making carries the listener readily through them. The *Pathétique* has rather more reserve and dignity (curiously, the 5/4 movement is pressed on very hard indeed). But although there is no lack of electricity in the first movement, and the Scherzo/March is indeed both a Scherzo and a march, with a broadening at the climax, the finale brings both nobility and great depth of feeling, with the restrained epilogue of the coda especially moving. This is a mono recording, but the full, spacious Boston sound all but covers this up. In Nos. 4 and 5 the recording – unbelievably improved over previous LP incarnations – is satisfyingly full-blooded and with hardly a hint of the harshness that used to disfigure the equivalent LPs.

The Philharmonia in the early 1950s was an extraordinary body, and these early records are worth having even if you already possess Karajan's later accounts with the Berlin Philharmonic. Nos. 4 and 5 are mono, but the 1959 *Pathétique* is stereo. Exhilarating performances that still sound amazing for their period.

There are many collectors who count Markevitch's Philips recordings from the 1960s as having a similar distinction, and again the remastered sound here gives a much more vivid and realistic presence to the orchestra than the original LPs. Certainly Markevitch's *Fourth* is as exciting as almost any available. It has a superb thrusting first-movement Allegro and throughout Markevitch allows himself a lilting degree of rubato in the rocking crescendo passage; as with Monteux, it is the forward momentum of the performance that captures the listener. The close of the movement, like the coda of the finale, brings the highest degree of tension and a real sense of triumph. The central movements are no less striking, with – again like Monteux – a vigorous climax to the *Andantino* contrasting with the repose of the outer sections and a fast Scherzo where the duple rhythms of the woodwind trio are emphasized to bring out the peasant imagery. After a less evocative opening than Monteux, Markevitch applies to the first movement of the *Fifth* the forthright, highly charged approach which was so effective in the *Fourth*. He makes no concessions to the second-subject group, which is presented with no let-up on the fast pace at which he takes the main *Allegro*. Tchaikovsky's romanticism is turned into energy and the intended contrast is lost. The slow movement is undoubtedly powerful but the Waltz lacks charm, and in the vigorous finale the final statement of the big tune is slow and rather stolid. In the *Pathétique* Markevitch provides great intensity in his account of the first movement. The result is undoubtedly powerful, but some might feel that he is too aggressive, even though the performance is always under emotional control. The second movement has both warmth and elegance – more so than with Monteux – and the march is treated broadly, providing suitable contrast before a deeply felt performance of the finale, where the second subject is introduced with great tenderness. With three symphonies offered for the cost of one premium-priced CD, this is certainly worth considering, for all the reservations about the *Fifth*.

Whatever their merits, Yuri Temirkanov's accounts of the last three symphonies cannot be recommended. The star rating is to acknowledge the naturalness of the recording quality, but there is nothing natural about the readings, which are full of agogic affectations. Intolerably mannered and difficult to sit through.

Symphony No. 4 in F min., Op. 36.
*** Chan Dig. CHAN 8361; *ABTD 1124* [id.]. Oslo PO, Jansons.
☞ **(*) DG Gold Dig. 439 018-2 [id.]. VPO, Karajan.

Symphony No. 4; Capriccio italien.
(M) *** DG 419 872-2 [id.]. BPO, Karajan.

Symphony No. 4; Francesca da Rimini.
*** DG Dig. 429 778-2 [id.]. NYPO, Bernstein.

(i) *Symphony No. 4;* (ii) *Romeo and Juliet* (fantasy overture).
☞ (M) *** Telarc Dig. CD 82002 [id.]. Cleveland O, Lorin Maazel.
☞ (M) ** Ph. Dig. 438 303-2 [id.]. (i) Pittsburgh SO; (ii) LAPO; Previn (with GLINKA: (ii) *Russlan and Ludmilla overture* **).

Jansons conducts a dazzling performance of the *Fourth*, unusually fresh and natural in its expressiveness, yet with countless subtleties of expression, as in the balletic account of the second-subject group of the first movement. The *Andantino* flows lightly and persuasively, the Scherzo is very fast and lightly sprung, while the finale reinforces the impact of the whole performance: fast and exciting, but with no synthetic whipping-up of tempo. That is so until the very end of the coda, which finds Jansons pressing ahead just fractionally as he would in a concert, a thrilling conclusion made the more so by the wide-ranging, brilliant and realistic recording.

Karajan's 1977 version is undoubtedly more compelling than his previous recordings and is in most respects preferable to the newer, digital, Vienna version too. It is the vitality and drive of the performance as a whole that one remembers, although the beauty of the wind playing at the opening and close of the slow movement can give nothing but pleasure. The CD transfer is extremely vivid. The ubiquitous *Capriccio italien* is offered as a filler.

Bernstein's is not a performance to compare with any other: it is one that came from an interpreter of genius at a particular moment, white-hot and compelling. Most surprisingly, in a live recording from Avery Fisher Hall in New York, one of the most difficult for engineers, the sound is aptly big and fruity. The last two movements are taken at speeds that no one would regard as unconventional. The pizzicato scherzo is not ideally precise of ensemble but it is infectiously sprung and, in Bernstein's big, bold account of the finale, his slowing for the second subject (the *Birch tree* theme) is extreme but persuasive. The close is predictably exciting, with an unashamed accelerando in the closing bars, though without applause and obviously recorded at an editing session. The fill-up, *Francesca da Rimini*, brings a comparably spacious and big-scale performance.

Maazel's 1979 Telarc Cleveland recording, now reissued at mid-price, established a reputation for sound of spectacular depth and brilliance within natural concert-hall acoustics. Maazel's reading is very similar to his very successful 1965 Decca record, and only in the finale does the new version differ markedly from the old, by seeking amplitude and breadth in preference to uninhibited, extrovert excitement. Maazel's approach generates a strong forward momentum in the first movement and is consistently involving in its directness. Yet he lightens the tension effectively (like Jansons) by his balletic approach to the second-subject group. The slow movement, with a plaintive oboe solo, is distinctly appealing, and at the *Più mosso* Maazel makes a swift, bold tempo change. In the finale the Cleveland Orchestra produces a thrillingly rich body of timbre in the upper strings and the fullest resonance from the lower strings and brass. *Romeo and Juliet*, recorded two years later, is given a spaciously romantic performance, reaching a climax of considerable passion.

The *Fourth* is the most successful of the last three Tchaikovsky symphony recordings which Karajan made in 1985 in connection with the Telemodial video project. Although the playing of the Vienna orchestra does not match that of the Berlin Philharmonic in earlier versions, the performance itself has greater flexibility and more spontaneity. The freer control of tempo in the first movement brings a more relaxed second-subject group, while in the *Andantino* the Vienna oboist is fresher (though the timbre is edgier) than his Berlin counterpart, the phrasing less calculated. The Scherzo is attractively bright, if less precise, and the finale has splendid urgency and excitement. The remastered CD, in the Karajan Gold series, brings a slightly firmer bass, but the difference is less marked than in some others of the series. The warmly resonant acoustic is attractive; even if detail is not absolutely clear, there is no lack of fullness, and Karajan admirers should not be disappointed.

Previn's *Fourth* was recorded in 1980. His preference in Tchaikovsky is for directness and no mannerisms. Here there are unusually slow speeds for the first three movements, which produces limited excitement and very little charm. The finale makes up for that with a very fast tempo which is a formidable challenge for the Pittsburgh orchestra, here distinguishing itself with fine playing. The sound is fresh and full-bodied, and it is even more sumptuous in *Romeo and Juliet*, recorded six years later in UCLA's Royce Hall, Los Angeles. However, this cannot be counted among the more memorable versions of the piece, and the same could be said of the Glinka encore, which lacks the infectious zest of the Solti Decca version.

Symphony No. 5 in E min., Op. 64.
*** Chan. Dig. CHAN 8351; *ABTD 1111* [id.]. Oslo PO, Jansons.
*** Telarc Dig. CD 80107 [id.]. RPO, Previn – RIMSKY-KORSAKOV: *Tsar Saltan: March.* ***
*** Olympia OCD 221 [id.]. Leningrad PO, Mravinsky (with LIADOV: *Baba Yaga, Op. 56.*
    MUSSORGSKY: *Khovanshchina: Prelude.* WAGNER: *Tristan: Prelude and Liebstod****).
☞ **(*) DG Gold Dig. 439 019-2 [id.]. VPO, Karajan.

Symphony No. 5; Francesca da Rimini.
☞ **(*) EMI Dig. CDC7 54338-2 [id.]. Phd. O, Muti

Symphony No. 5; Marche slave.
(M) *** DG 419 066-2 [id.]. BPO, Karajan.
☞ **(*) Pickwick/RPO Dig. CDRPO 7017 [id.]. RPO, Koizumi.

(i) *Symphony No. 5 in E min., Op. 64;* (ii) *Nutcracker suite, Op. 71a.*
☞ (B) *** DG 439 434-2 [id.]. (i) Leningrad PO, Mravinsky; (ii) BPO, Karajan.

Symphony No. 5; (i) *Eugene Onegin: Tatiana's letter scene.*
❀ (M) *** EMI Dig. CD-EMX 2187. LPO, Sian Edwards; (i) with Eilene Hannan.

Sian Edwards conducts an electrifying and warm-hearted reading of Tchaikovsky's *Fifth*, which matches any version in the catalogue, particularly when it comes with an unusual and exceptionally attractive fill-up, Tchaikovsky's greatest inspiration for soprano, *Tatiana's letter scene*. That is freshly and dramatically sung, in a convincingly girlish impersonation, by the Australian, Eilene Hannan. Sian Edwards's control of rubato is exceptionally persuasive, notably so in moulding the different sections of the first movement of the symphony, while the great horn solo of the slow movement is played with exquisite delicacy by Richard Bissell. The Waltz third movement is most tenderly done, while the finale brings a very fast and exciting allegro, challenging the orchestra to brilliant, incisive playing.

In the first movement, Jansons' refusal to linger never sounds anything but warmly idiomatic, lacking only a little in charm. The slow movement again brings a steady tempo, with climaxes built strongly and patiently but with enormous power, the final culmination topping everything. In the finale, taken very fast, Jansons tightens the screw of the excitement without ever making it a scramble, following Tchaikovsky's notated slowings rather than allowing extra rallentandos. The sound is excellent, specific and well focused within a warmly reverberant acoustic, with digital recording on CD reinforcing any lightness of bass.

Previn's fine concern for detail is well illustrated by the way that the great horn melody in the slow movement (superbly played by Jeff Bryant) contains the implication of a quaver rest before each three-quarter group, where normally it sounds like a straight triplet. In the first movement, rhythms are light and well sprung, and the third movement is sweet and lyrical yet with no hint of mannerism, for Previn adopts a naturally expressive style within speeds generally kept steady, even in the great climax of the slow movement which then subsides into a coda of breathtaking delicacy. The finale, taken very fast indeed, crowns an outstandingly satisfying reading. The Telarc recording is full and wide-ranging, not as detailed as some, but very naturally balanced.

Mravinsky's Olympia recording of Tchaikovsky's *Fifth* was recorded in Leningrad in 1973; the remaining pieces come from a concert at the Moscow Conservatoire. If anything, the *Symphony* is even more electrifying than either of the earlier DG versions. Climaxes are still somewhat rough on this version – but this is easily overlooked, given the excitement of the playing. Another factor prompting a strong recommendation is the other material on the disc. Liadov's *Baba Yaga* is given a virtuoso performance and is also well recorded; the Mussorgsky is predictably atmospheric, and the Wagner leaves no doubt that Mravinsky must have been a great interpreter of this composer.

Mravinsky's exciting and very Russian account of the *Fifth* with the Leningrad Philharmonic on DG would occupy a distinguished place in any collection. The performance is full of Slavonic vitality and the reading is romantic as well as red-blooded (the second subject of the first movement is both warm and graceful). The solo horn has a faint wobble in the famous solo in the slow movement, and the trumpets in the final peroration of an exhilaratingly fast finale also have a vibrato, but these details are unimportant when the reading has such fire and individuality. The recording, made in Watford Town Hall in 1960, is resonant and full, if not always absolutely clean in focus. By comparison Karajan's 1966 *Nutcracker suite* sounds a little cool, but it is marvellously polished and vivid, and the *Waltz of the flowers* has the most agreeable elegance.

Karajan's 1976 recording stands out from his other recordings of the *Fifth*. The first movement is unerringly paced and has great romantic flair; in Karajan's hands the climax of the slow movement is grippingly intense, though with a touchingly elegiac preparation for the horn solo at the opening. The Waltz has character and charm too – the Berlin Philharmonic string playing is peerless – and in the finale Karajan drives hard, creating a riveting forward thrust. The remastered recording brings a remarkable improvement.

Karajan's latest VPO version of the *Fifth* brings a characteristically strong and expressive performance; however, neither in the playing of the Vienna Philharmonic nor even in the recorded sound can it quite match his earlier, Berlin Philharmonic version for DG. Like Karajan's most recent recordings of the Beethoven symphonies, this was done with video as part of the project; though the long takes have brought extra spontaneity, the recording of the strings in the Musikvereinsaal (a difficult venue for the engineers) is inconsistent, with front-desk players sharply focused but not the whole body of strings behind them, and with woodwind set at a distance. The slack ensemble and control of rhythm in the waltz movement is specially disappointing. The finale, however, goes especially well, with the Vienna brass biting superbly in the first reprise of the movement's main theme. The remastered recording improves the body and definition of the sound, and the strings are rather more convincing in effect.

The oddity of Muti's Philadelphia version is that, though the first two movements have the disappointingly over-relaxed manners that marked his *Pathétique* earlier, often with surprisingly slack ensemble, the last two movements are played with the high voltage one expects of this conductor and orchestra at their finest. Maybe change of tension reflects the atmosphere of two separate sessions, the second much sharper than the first. The fill-up too is played at white heat, a powerful performance. It makes a rare and generous coupling. The sound, not as clear as it might be, has warmth and weight beyond most new Philadelphia issues.

Koizumi's warmly expressive, spontaneous-sounding reading of the symphony has many sympathetic qualities, offering an account of the great horn melody of the slow movement from the RPO principal that is among the gentlest and most beautiful of all. Yet at upper mid-price, with only *Marche Slave* for coupling in a routine performance, it is no match for Sian Edwards's outstanding version on the rather cheaper EMI Eminence label.

Symphony No. 6 in B min. (Pathétique), Op. 74.
*** Chan. Dig. CHAN 8446; *ABTD 1158* [id.]. Oslo PO, Jansons.
(M) (***) BMG/RCA mono GD 60312 [60312-2-RG]. Phd. O, Toscanini – R. STRAUSS: *Death and transfiguration.* (***)
☞ **(*) DG Gold Dig. 429 020 [id.]. VPO, Karajan.
☞ **(*) Sony Dig. SK 45836 [id.]. Nat. SO of Washington, Rostropovich (with J. STRAUSS Jnr: *Vergnügungszug polka;* GRIEG: *Peer Gynt: Death of Aase;* PAGANINI: *Moto perpetuo;* PROKOFIEV: *Romeo & Juliet: Death of Tybalt;* GERSHWIN: *Walking the dog;* SOUSA: *Stars & Stripes forever*).

Symphony No. 6 (Pathétique); Capriccio italien; Eugene Onegin: Waltz & Polonaise.
(M) **(*) Sony SBK 47657 [id.]. Phd O, Ormandy.

Symphony No. 6 (Pathétique); Marche slave, Op. 31.
⊛ *** Virgin/EMI VC7 59661-2 [id.]. Russian Nat. O, Mikhail Pletnev.

Symphony No. 6 (Pathétique); Nutcracker suite, Op. 71a.
☞ (M) (**) BMG/RCA mono GD 60297. NBC SO, Toscanini.

Symphony No. 6 (Pathétique); Romeo and Juliet (fantasy overture).
☞ *** Virgin/EMI Dig. VC7 59239-2 [id.]. Bournemouth SO, Andrew Litton.
(M) (***) BMG/RCA mono GD 60920 [09026 60920-2]. Boston SO, Koussevitzky.
☞ ** Decca Dig. 430 507-2 [id.]. Montreal SO, Charles Dutoit.

(i) *Symphony No. 6 (Pathétique);* (ii) *Swan Lake (ballet): suite.*
☞ (BB) **(*) ASV Dig. CDQS 6091 [id.]. (i) LPO; (ii) RPO, Bátiz.

The *Pathétique* is Mikhail Pletnev's début on record as a conductor with the Russian National Orchestra that has been formed for him. There is no doubt that this is among the most vividly dramatic accounts of this symphony to have appeared for some years. The way in which Pletnev launches us into the development of the first movement still takes one aback, even when one knows what to expect. His hand-picked orchestra is as virtuosic as Pletnev himself can be on the keyboard. The Scherzo may seem too fast for some people but it is marked *Allegro molto vivace* and Koussevitzky (see below) is not much slower. There is a stirring account of *Marche slave* too, and a very fine recording, perfectly balanced, although the effect is a little recessed.

Litton's is an outstanding performance, full of temperament, not just fiery but tender too, arguably the finest of the whole Litton cycle. The Bournemouth playing has never been neater, with the sound bringing out the fine clarity of articulation. The only idiosyncrasy is that in the big second-subject melodies of the outer movements Litton prefers speeds broader than usual, but with no hint of self-indulgence in the finely moulded phrasing. With an account of *Romeo and Juliet* that builds up powerfully from a restrained start, the disc makes a splendid culmination, a match even for the earlier, Virgin version with Pletnev, and more fully and cleanly recorded. It also gains in practical terms even over the Pletnev issue when the coupling is so much more generous.

Mariss Jansons and the Oslo Philharmonic crown their magnetically compelling Tchaikovsky series with a superbly concentrated account of the last and greatest of the symphonies. It is characteristic of Jansons that the great second-subject melody is at once warm and passionate yet totally unsentimental, with rubato barely noticeable. The very fast speed for the third-movement *March* stretches the players to the very limit, but the exhilaration is infectious, leading to the simple dedication of the slow finale, unexaggerated but deeply felt. Fine, warm recording as in the rest of the series.

Ormandy's fine 1960 performance is a reading of impressive breadth, dignity and power, with no suggestion of routine in a single bar. The orchestra makes much of the first-movement climax and plays with considerable passion and impressive body of tone in both outer movements; yet there is an element of restraint in the finale which prevents any feeling of hysteria. In short, this is most satisfying, a performance to live with; the CD transfer, while brightly lit, avoids glare in the upper range. Ormandy's panache and gusto give the *Capriccio italien* plenty of life without driving too hard, and the dances are rhythmically infectious.

Quite apart from the attractions of the lively sequence of encores on this disc, celebrating Rostropovich's return to Russia in February 1990 – with the audience clapping joyfully to Sousa's *Stars and Stripes forever* – the reading of the main work is intense and passionate, yet not self-indulgent or even expansive, as Rostropovich was in his very distinctive LP cycle of the Tchaikovsky symphonies for EMI. Speeds are on the fast side, and in the great broad melodies of the first and last movements Rostropovich's approach is urgent, with *espressivo* interpreted as a cue for pressing ahead, not drawing back. The string ensemble throughout is excellent, with exceptionally clean articulation, and the principal reservation must be over the recorded sound, very good considering the problems of recording live in Moscow, but with a vagueness of focus in the bass. Among the encores, the Strauss *Excursion train polka* comes not in its usual form but in an extraordinary orchestration by Shostakovich, with witty commentary from percussion and brass. The Grieg then brings ravishing pianissimos from the Washington strings, and Rostropovich reinforces his achievement with the players when the violins *en masse* then play the Paganini showpiece with amazingly precise ensemble.

Koussevitzky's account of the *Pathétique* comes from 1930 but though the sound may lack the vivid colouring of present day recording, the performance certainly doesn't. This is another version of outsize personality that will have you on the edge of your chair for it is tremendously high voltage. Not that it is free from the odd mannerism: he italicizes the passage immediately after the explosive fortissimo that opens the development in the first movement. The 1936 *Romeo and Juliet* was issued in an RCA Boston Symphony compilation in the 1970s, and ranks as one of the most impassioned accounts of the piece made in that era. The RCA engineers have done their best with the sound, which in spite of some discoloration in climaxes, is more than acceptable.

Toscanini's Philadelphia version of the *Pathétique* glows with the special magic that developed between him and the orchestra over the winter season of 1941–2. Though far more disciplined than most readings, it is altogether warmer than his NBC recording, with the great second-subject melody of the first movement tender in its emotions, not rigid in its easy rubato. He even eases the tempo sympathetically for the fortissimo entries of the march in the third movement. Alongside a magnificent account of the Strauss – an apt link, with death the theme – it makes a superb historical document.

Recorded, like the VPO *Fourth* and *Fifth*, with video as part of the project, Karajan's last digital recording of the *Pathétique* has many characteristic strong points, and the reading has both intensity and spontaneity. If it lacks the supreme grip of the earlier, Berlin Philharmonic recordings, it is still an exciting performance, even if the Vienna ensemble is noticeably slacker than that of the Berliners and the finale in consequence is less powerful. The 5/4 movement is slower than before and rather heavy in style; though the speed of the march movement remains as fast as previously, the result is less tense than before. Even so, the close has plenty of free-flowing adrenalin. The sound is greatly improved in this remastering for the Karajan Gold series: the violins are fuller and the brass more firmly focused. But this is not a first choice.

Bátiz's (1982) reading of the *Pathétique* is distinctly enjoyable, attractively fresh and direct, with the great second-subject melody the more telling for being understated and with transitions just a little perfunctory. The Scherzo/march comes off especially well. The brass are set rather forward, but this makes for a very exciting climax. Otherwise the balance is good and the sound is generally excellent. It is even better in the *Swan Lake suite*, recorded five years later. The RPO playing is very good indeed, polished, warm and alert. Barry Griffiths and Françoise Rive are sensitive string soloists in the *Danse des cygnes*. The suite ends with the great tune near the end of the ballet where the violins are echoed powerfully by the four horns in unison. An excellent super-bargain coupling.

The Montreal sound for Dutoit is gloriously rich and resonant but, rather as in his earlier version of the Tchaikovsky *Fifth*, Dutoit's reading, warmly expressive, yet lacks the final bite of tension which in Tchaikovsky is such an essential ingredient. He leaves you feeling that the performance is too well controlled, not daring enough. It is the same with the overture.

The 1947 recording for Toscanini, dry and unhelpful, also has high 78 surface hiss, which detracts from a characteristically powerful and intense performance. Speeds are all on the fast side, but only in the first movement do the results ever sound perfunctory, and the middle movements are delectably pointed in rhythm, while the slow finale at a flowing speed is both noble and passionate. The sound for the *Nutcracker* is far clearer, a crisp, bright interpretation, even if the Sugar-Plum Fairy is heavy-footed.

Symphony No. 7 (arr. Bogatyryev).
☞ *** Chan. Dig. CHAN 9130 [id.]. LPO, Neeme Järvi – *Piano concerto No. 3.* **(*)

Symphony No. 7 in E flat (reconstructed Bogatyryev); (i) *Variations on a rococo theme for cello and orchestra, Op. 33.*
(M) ** Sony MPK 46453 [id.]. Phd. O, Ormandy; (i) with Leonard Rose.

In 1892 Tchaikovsky began a new symphony, but he was not satisfied with the way his ideas were working out and decided that the material was more suitable for a piano concerto. The sketches for the symphony as originally planned were not destroyed and it was to these that the Soviet musicologist, Bogatyryev, turned. As there was no Scherzo, one was provided from a set of piano pieces written in 1893. The finale, however, is bizarre and in Ormandy's version sounds rumbustious, blatant, even vulgar, with the reprise of the main theme against a side-drum in no way characteristic of Tchaikovsky's symphonic writing.

Just over 30 years after Eugene Ormandy and the Philadelphia Orchestra first recorded Boga-tyryev's completion of Tchaikovsky's *Symphony No. 7*, Neeme Järvi provided this valuable alternative, helpfully coupled with the one-movement *Piano concerto No. 3* which Tchaikovsky drew from the symphony's first movement. This reconstructed symphony, abandoned not long before Tchaikovsky wrote his culminating masterpiece in the *Pathétique Symphony*, may be no match for the regular canon, but it brings many Tchaikovskian delights. Having symphony and concerto side by side makes it very easy to compare Bogatyryev's reconstruction of the original version, in structure identical except for the central solo cadenza which Tchaikovsky inserted in the concerto. Having the piano set against the orchestra predictably brings sharper contrasts of texture, but the version for orchestra alone regularly sounds more Tchaikovskian, with the big opening theme far more effective on violins than in hollow octaves on the piano. In the *Symphony* Jarvi, with speeds a degree more expansive than Ormandy in all four movements, finds more poetry, more fantasy, and the modern digital recording allows far more light and shade over a much wider dynamic range. With Jarvi, the Scherzo, drawn from the tenth of Tchaikovsky's Opus 72 piano pieces, is lighter and more resilient and, though in the finale the opening is less exciting, the march theme of the second subject, which with Ormandy is square and banal, is made to sound delightfully jaunty. Apart from the thinness on the upper strings, the recorded sound is satisfyingly full and warm. Geoffrey Tozer – see above – gives a fine performance of the *Concerto* but there are more reservations here – see above – notably about the orchestral string timbre.

Ormandy's performance has great fervour and is superbly played; but the recording, although spectacular, also has the harshness one associates with this source. Leonard Rose's warm and elegant account of the *Rococo variations* comes like balm to the ears after the noisy finale of the symphony.

Variations on a rococo theme for cello and orchestra (original version).
*** Ph. Dig. 434 106-2 [id.]. Julian Lloyd Webber, LSO, Maxim Shostakovich – MIASKOVSKY: *Cello concerto.* ***

At last the composer's own version of the *Variations on a rococo theme* is coming into its own. A scholarly edition appeared as long ago as 1941, but the corrupt edition retained its hold on the repertory. Lloyd Webber's approach is both leisurely and, aided no doubt by the exemplary Philips recording, he produces a pleasingly cultured sound. Not as virtuosic in outlook or as strongly profiled as Rostropovich's version of the corrupt score, but very musical and refreshingly enjoyable.

Variations on a rococo theme for cello and orchestra, Op. 33.
*** DG 413 819-2 [id.]. Rostropovich, BPO, Karajan – DVORAK: *Concerto.* ***
(M) *** Decca 425 020-2; *425 020-4* [id.]. Harrell, Cleveland O, Maazel – BRUCH: *Kol Nidrei* ***;
   DVORAK: *Cello concerto.* ***
*** BMG/RCA Dig. RD 71003. Ofra Harnoy, Victoria SO, Freeman – OFFENBACH: *Concerto;*
   SAINT-SAENS: *Concerto No. 1.* ***
☞ (M) *** Sony SBK 48278 [id.]. Leonard Rose, Phd. O, Ormandy – BLOCH: *Schelomo* ***; FAURÉ:
   Élégie ***; LALO: *Concerto.* **(*)
☞ **(*) Virgin/EMI Dig. VC7 59325-2 [id.]. Truls Mørk, Oslo PO, Jansons – DVORÁK: *Cello concerto.* **(*)

No grumbles about Rostropovich's performance in partnership with Karajan. He plays as if this were one of the greatest works for the cello, and he receives glowing support from Karajan and the Berlin

Philharmonic. Rostropovich (in common with all his competitors here) uses the published score, not Tchaikovsky's quite different, original version as played by Wallfisch and Julian Lloyd Webber. The recording is rich and refined and sounds fresh in its digitally remastered form.

An assured, vividly characterized set of *Variations* from Lynn Harrell, with plenty of matching colour from the Cleveland woodwind. The analogue recording is bright and colourful.

Ofra Harnoy's scale is smaller, the style essentially elegant, not missing its colour or ardour but never forgetting the word 'rococo' in the title. It is a considerable performance, stylish yet emotionally responsive, and Paul Freeman's accompaniment is first class, too.

Leonard Rose's warm and elegant – yet at times quite ardent – account of these splendid variations is balm to the senses, and Ormandy provides admirable support. The recording is forwardly balanced but the dynamic range remains reasonably wide, and the cello is firmly and realistically focused.

A fine performance from Truls Mørk, with plenty of energy and finesse, and the *Andante* of Variation 11 played with an appealingly Slavonic, plaintive feeling. Very good recording too, but in sheer elegance and panache this is no match for Rostropovich.

CHAMBER AND INSTRUMENTAL MUSIC

Album for the young, Op. 39: (i) original piano version; (ii) trans. for string quartet by Dubinsky.
*** Chan. CHAN 8365; *ABTD 1129* [id.]. (i) Luba Edlina; (ii) augmented Borodin Trio.

These 24 pieces are all miniatures, but they have great charm; their invention is often memorable, with quotations from Russian folksongs and one French, plus a brief reminder of *Swan Lake*. Here they are presented twice, in their original piano versions, sympathetically played by Luba Edlina, and in effective string quartet transcriptions arranged by her husband, Rostislav Dubinsky. The Borodin group play them with both affection and finesse. The CD has plenty of presence.

Piano trio in A min., Op. 50.
☞ (M) *** Erato/Warner Dig. 2292 45972-2 [id.]. Pascal Rogé, Pierre Amoyal, Frédéric Lodéon.
☞ ** Pickwick/RPO Dig. MCD 52; *MCC 52* [id.]. Solomon Trio – ARENSKY: *Piano trio No. 1.* **
☞ ** Sony Dig. MK 417001 [id.]. Timofeyeva, Fedotov, Rodin.
☞ (BB) * Naxos Dig. 8.550467 [id.]. Stamper, Jackson, Vovka Ashkenazy – ARENSKY: *Piano trio.* *
☞ (M) * BMG/Melodia 74321 17087-2 [id.]. Natalia Zertsalova, Igor Oistrakh, Evgeny Altman.
☞ (*) Victoria Dig. VCD 19079 [id.]. Nilsson, Kvalbein, Bratlie – GRIEG: *Andante con moto;*
  MARTIN: *Trio sur des mélodies populaires irlandaises.* (*)

The reissue of this excellent Erato disc brings a fully recommendable mid-priced version of Tchaikovsky's masterly *Piano trio* to the catalogue. The French team give the *Trio* in its entirety. Theirs is a warmly eloquent performance and finds Pierre Amoyal, who has already given us a splendid account of Tchaikovsky's *Violin concerto*, in impressive form. The same must be said of Pascal Rogé, whose account of the piano part is hardly less brilliant than that of Ashkenazy on EMI's alternative version (see below). The EMI recording has a larger acoustic and the performance is on a bigger scale, perhaps more orchestral in feeling. But although the balance is a shade close, the more intimate effect of the French acoustic minimizes the sense of rhetoric in the first movement, without diminishing the warmth of feeling. Artistically, the French team are in no way inferior and many will count their performance equally rewarding and certainly just as involving. The variations which form the second movement are splendidly realized, with much diversity of character.

Rodney Friend, Yonty Solomon and Timothy Hugh give a highly intelligent and well-thought-out performance of the *Trio*. There are times when Yonty Solomon treats it as if it is a concerto – understandably enough in some of the variation movements of the second movement. There is a good rapport between him and his colleagues and the only reservation one may have is that the admittedly thorny problems of balance are not wholly overcome in this acoustic. The piano can sound thick and bottom-heavy.

Lyubov Timofeyeva, Maxim Fedotov and Kirill Rodin have impressive credentials as prize-winners and their account of the *Trio* is as far removed from some of their rivals as can be imagined. One feels that this is the sort of playing one might have encountered in a highly cultured Russian home at the turn of the century, communicating a sensitivity and reticence that make a refreshing change in these days of glamourized, packaged sentiment. But having said this, the fact remains that the tempo in the first movement is expansive, almost sluggish (they take the best part of 20 minutes over it), thus minimizing any contrast between the two movements. Many of the variations are beautifully done but, despite their refined musicianship, one ends up feeling the need for just a bit more projection – without going to the extreme of heart-on-sleeve eloquence that one so often encounters. Decent recording, but short measure in that there is no coupling.

Despite its highly competitive price, the Naxos is not really a strong recommendation. The acoustic is far from ideal and the playing of Richard Stamper, Christine Jackson and Vovka Ashkenazy, though often felicitous, is not quite distinguished enough to reward repeated listening.

Igor Oistrakh dominates the aural picture in the BMG/Melodiya account of the *Piano trio*. It dates from 1984 and is all highly accomplished but rather unmoving, good but ultimately unmemorable playing, and no challenge to the front recommendations.

The claims of the Oslo Trio are stronger in the Grieg rarity than they are here. Not that they do not play with character and feeling, but they are not well served by the recording. They are so closely observed by the microphones that there is a danger of discoloration in the louder passages (try the sixth variation of the second movement and you will see for yourself). The players make the usual cuts, omitting the fugue and pages 86–102 in the Eulenberg score.

(i) *Piano trio in A min., Op. 50;* (ii) *String quartets Nos. 1–3; String sextet (Souvenir de Florence), Op. 70.*

☞ (M) **(*) EMI CMS7 64879-2 (3) [id.]. (i) Ashkenazy, Perlman, Harrell; (ii) Borodin Qt.

This set assembles all Tchaikovsky's major chamber works and, given performances of this distinction and music of this quality of inspiration, the set is self-recommending, with the proviso that the CD transfer of analogue recordings made between 1979 and 1981 is very brightly lit and will need some smoothing in the upper range if the violin timbre is not to seem slightly aggressive. The balance in the *Piano trio* is the least attractive. This was recorded in the CBS studios in New York and the sound is on the dry side for such an expansive work. The remastering emphasizes the dryness, sharpness of focus and lack of ambience, and undoubtedly the Erato alternative is preferable sonically. But the EMI performance is unforgettable. The dominating keyboard role of the first movement can so easily sound rhetorical, as well as gripping and commanding – and that element is not entirely avoided here. But the *Variations* which form the second part of the work are very successful, with engaging characterization and a great deal of electricity in the closing pages. Indeed, generally this group carry all before them with their sense of artistic purpose and through their warmth and ardour.

Souvenir de Florence, Op. 70.
** Mer. Dig. CDE 84211; *KE 77211* [id.]. Arienski Ens. – ARENSKY: *String quartet No. 2* ***;
    BORODIN: *Sextet movements.* **

A very good rather than a distinguished performance of Tchaikovsky's eloquent *Souvenir de Florence*, very decently recorded. The strength of the issue lies in the interest of its coupling, an Arensky rarity, the *A minor Quartet*, from which the well-known *Variations on a theme of Tchaikovsky* derive, and two Mendelssohnian movements from the Borodin *Sextet*.

String quartets Nos. 1 in D, Op. 11; 2 in F, Op. 22; 3 in E flat min., Op. 30; (i) *Souvenir de Florence* (string sextet), *Op. 70.*
*** EMI Dig. CDS7 49775-2 (2). Borodin Qt, (i) with Y. Bashmet, N. Gutman.

String quartet in B flat; String quartets Nos. 1–3; (i) *Souvenir de Florence.*
☞ (M) *** BMG/Melodiya 74321 18290-2 (2) [id.]. Borodin Qt, (i) with Rostropovich, Talalyan.
☞ *** Teldec/Warner Dig. 4509 90422-2 (2) [id.]. Borodin Qt, (i) with Yurov, Milman.

String quartets Nos. 1 in D, Op. 11; 3 in E flat, Op. 30.
☞ **(*) Nimbus Dig. NI 5380 [id.]. Franz Schubert Qt.

String quartet No. 2 in F, Op. 22; (i) *Souvenir de Florence.*
☞ **(*) Nimbus Dig. NI 5399 [id.]. Franz Schubert Qt, (i) with Flieder, Schultz.

Long gone are the days when the only Tchaikovsky *Quartet* in the catalogue was No. 1 in D. Now there are three versions of all of them, plus the *Souvenir de Florence*, all by the same quartet: the Borodin, and all of them superb. The EMI set with the three *Quartets*, dating from 1978–9 plus the *Souvenir de Florence* with Bashmet and Natalia Gutman of 1980, was reissued and repackaged in 1993 as part of the centenary celebrations. Given performances of this distinction and music of this quality of inspiration, the set is self-recommending. The digital recording is very nearly as outstanding as the performances, and there is no reason to qualify the strength and warmth of our recommendation. The mid-priced BMG/Melodiya set is of earlier provenance in the case of the *Souvenir de Florence* with Rostropovich and Talalyan; it comes from 1965, while the three *Quartets* plus the student *Quartet movement* that Tchaikovsky wrote in 1865 are roughly the same (1979–80). The Teldec set, made in 1993 in the Berlin Teldec studios, is digital and the sound is a shade drier: it also includes the early (and, to be frank, not wildly interesting) *B flat movement*. All the same, all three are superb and are without peer, and either the EMI/Melodiya or BMG/Melodiya are unassailable recommendations; the Teldec is hardly less impressive. One need look no further.

The two Nimbus discs have the same advantage as the Shostakovich on Olympia (see below) of being available separately. The two couplings, of *No. 1 in D major* and *No. 3 in E flat*, and the *F major quartet* and the *Souvenir de Florence*, offer good playing and the sound-balance offers one of the best chamber-music recordings Nimbus have given us. The Franz Schubert Quartet possess smooth, beautifully produced sound and good ensemble. All the same, as a performance the playing is not in the same league as the Borodins.

String quartets Nos. 1 in D, Op. 11; 2 in F, Op. 22; 5 early pieces for string quartet.
☞ ** Olympia OCD 521 [id.]. Shostakovich Qt.

String quartet No. 3 in E flat, Op. 30; (i) Adagio molto in E flat for string quartet & harp.
☞ **(*) Olympia OCD 522 [id.]. (i) Moskvitina; Shostakovich Qt – GRECHANINOV: *String quartet.*
**(*)

The versions by the Shostakovich Quartet are also masterly but not in the Borodins' league. The performances emanate from Moscow Radio broadcasts from 1976 (*No. 1*) and 1978 (*No. 2*) and 1973 in the case of the early pieces dating from the composer's student years at the St Petersburg Conservatoire (not masterpieces, though they are of interest, as is almost anything that the master penned, to Tchaikovsky lovers). Coming to them immediately after any of the Borodins, they sound just a shade strident at the upper end of the spectrum, though this is easily tamed. Indeed in the *Third Quartet*, recorded in 1976, this is barely noticeable; the sound has warmth and presence. The *Adagio* for string quartet and harp is one of the few Tchaikovksy rarities that are not of real interest. The coupling is unusual – a pleasing if unmemorable quartet by Grechaninov, better known for his vocal and choral music.

String quartet No. 1 in D, Op. 11.
(M) **(*) Decca 425 541-2 [id.]. Gabrieli Qt – BORODIN; SHOSTAKOVICH: *Quartets.* **(*)
☞ *(*) DG Dig. 427 618-2 [id.]. Emerson Qt – BORODIN: *Quartet No. 2.* *(*)

The Gabrielis give a finely conceived performance, producing well-blended tone-quality, and the 1977 recording is clean and alive; but ideally the upper range could be less forcefully projected.

The Emerson Quartet are immaculate in terms of technical address, but they do not allow the music to speak for itself. We are rarely unaware of their virtuosity. The DG recording is very clean and present.

PIANO MUSIC

Album for the young, Op. 39; Aveu passioné in E min.; Capriccio in G flat, Op. 8; Dumka, Op. 59; Impromptu in A flat; Impromptu-caprice in G; Military march in B flat; Momento Lyrico in A flat; 6 Morceaux composés sur un seul thème, Op. 21; 2 Morceaux, Op. 10; 3 Morceaux, Op. 9; 6 Morceaux, Op. 19; 6 Morceaux, Op. 51; 12 Morceaux, Op. 40; 18 Morceaux, Op. 72; 2 Pieces, Op. 1; Potpourri on themes from the opera 'Voyevoda'; Romance in F min., Op. 5; 3 Romances; (i) arr: 50 Russian folksongs. The Seasons, Op. 37b; Sonata No. 1 in C sharp min., Op. 80; (Grand) Sonata (No. 2 in G), Op. 37a; 3 Souvenirs de Hapsal, Op. 2; Theme and variations in A min.; Valse caprice in D, Op. 4; Valse-scherzo in A; Valse-scherzo in A, Op. 7.
☞ **(*) Erato/Warner Dig. 2292 45969-2 (7) [id.]. Viktoria Postnikova, (i) Gennady Rozdestvensky.

Piano sonata No. 1 in C sharp min.; The Seasons, Op. 37b.
☞ **(*) Erato/Warner Dig. 2292 45512-2 [id.] (from above). Viktoria Postnikova.

It is no secret that Tchaikovsky was a remarkable melodist and almost every one of these pieces is attractive in this respect; each is also well crafted and needs care, polish and real style in presentation. Viktoria Postnikova has obviously lived with this music and her imagination is patently caught by even the simplest inspirations. In her hands nothing sounds trivial. The *Grand sonata* has a comparable rhetoric to the first movements of the *Second Piano concerto* and the *Piano trio*, yet the result here is never hectoring and the slow movement is most sensitively played. The two most famous sets of genre pieces, *The Seasons* and the Op. 39 collection for young people, are affectionately and perceptively characterized. Pletnyev has said that, in order to bring out the full potential of these apparently inconsequential works, one needs to read Russian poetry; all the evidence here is that Postnikova has steeped herself in such literature. Rostrapovich, no less, joins her for Tchaikovsky's four-handed arrangements of the 50 Russian folksongs. Many of them are very brief, but one can see how they became part of the composer's musical consciousness, for the sixth is instantly familiar from its use in the second movement of the *Little Russian Symphony*. Similarly, the Scherzo of the *C sharp minor Sonata* which (in spite of its high opus number) is a student work, brings a reminder of the *Winter Daydreams Symphony*. This somewhat Schumannesque sonata is available separately, coupled to *The Seasons*. The *Theme and variations in A minor* is an engaging piece and the *Pot-pourri on themes from The Voyevoda* offers a fascinating sampler of ideas from a virtually unknown opera. In short, everything here is well worth having, and the last item on the very first disc of early pieces brings a *Humoresque* (Op. 10/2) which Stravinsky appropriated and scored for horns to produce one of the most memorable themes in his *Baiser de la fée* pastiche ballet score. Postnikova in her notes makes the point that it was apt for some of these recordings to be made in France, where the composer's piano music was recognized and performed during his own lifetime. The only snag is that the recording quality, while live and present, is sometimes a bit hard on top.

Capriccioso in B flat, Op. 19/5; Chanson triste, Op. 40/2; L'espiègle, Op. 72/12; Humoresque in G, Op. 10/2; Méditation, Op. 72/5; Menuetto-scherzoso, Op. 51/3; Nocturne in F, Op. 10/1; Rêverie du soir, Op. 19/1; Romances: in F min., Op. 5; in F, Op. 51/5; The Seasons: May (White nights), June (Barcarolle), November (Troika); January (By the fireplace). Un poco di Chopin, Op. 72/15; Valse de salon, Op. 51/2; Waltz in A flat, Op. 40/8; Waltz-scherzo in A min., Op. 7.
☞ *** Olympia Dig. OCD 334 [id.]. Sviatoslav Richter.

It is good to hear Richter (recorded in 1993 by Ariola-Eurodisc) given first-class, modern, digital sound and on top technical form, showing that he has lost none of his flair. These miniatures are invested with enormous character in playing of consistent poetry; there is never a whiff of the salon. The opening *Nocturne in F major*, the charming neo-pastiche called *Un poco di Chopin* and the haunting *Rêverie du soir* readily demonstrate Richter's imaginative thoughtfulness, while the apparently simple *Capriccioso in B flat* produces a thrilling burst of bravura at its centrepiece. They are all captivating, and the bolder *Menuetto-scherzoso* also shows Tchaikovsky at his most attractively inventive, as of course does the *Humoresque* which Stravinsky used so indelibly (scored for horns) in his *Baiser de la fée* ballet music. In Richter's hands the famous *Barcarolle* (*June*) from *The Seasons* is full of charming nostalgia, while the more quirky *Troika* (*November*) is hardly less winning. With its very truthful sound-picture, this is a first recommendation for anyone wanting a single CD of Tchaikovsky's piano music.

The Seasons, Op. 37a.
**(*) Chan. Dig. CHAN 8349; ABTD 1070 [id.]. Lydia Artymiw.

The Seasons, Op. 37b; Dumka, Op. 59; Romance in F min., Op. 5; Valse-scherzo in A, Op. 7.
☞ (B) **(*) Pickwick Dig. PCD 976; CIMPC 976. James Lisney.

Tchaikovsky's twelve *Seasons* (they would better have been called 'months') were written to a regular deadline for publication in the St Petersburg music magazine, *Nuvellist*. They are lightweight but attractively varied in character and style. It is the gentler, lyrical pieces that are most effective in the hands of Lydia Artymiw, and she plays them thoughtfully and poetically. Elsewhere, she sometimes has a tendency marginally to over-characterize the music. The digital recording is truthful.

James Lisney provides a fine, stylish set of these pieces which Tchaikovsky wrote to order, monthly, for the journal *Nuvellist*. His playing is perhaps not as perceptive as that of Postnikova and his style is not very Slavonic in its expressive feeling. Yet if there is a touch of Mendelssohn's *Songs without words*, they are warmly presented, along with the other genre pieces, and are well recorded. But let us hope Pletynev decides to record them.

Sleeping Beauty (excerpts) arr. Pletnev.
⊛ *** Virgin/EMI Dig. VC7 59611-2 [id.]. Mikhail Pletnev – MUSSORGSKY: *Pictures at an exhibition.*
*** ⊛

In the present transcription Pletnev gives us about 30 minutes of *The Sleeping Beauty* in a dazzling performance. In sheer clarity of articulation and virtuosity this is pretty remarkable – also in poetry and depth of feeling. An altogether outstanding issue and in every way a *tour de force*.

VOCAL MUSIC

Songs: *Amid the noise of the ball; As over burning ashes; The cuckoo; Cradle song; Deception; Do not believe it, my friend; Evening; The fearful minute; If I'd only known; It was in the early spring; Les larmes; Last night; Mezza notte; My guiding spirit, my angel, my friend; The nightingale; None but the lonely heart; O do sing that song; Poème d'octobre; Serenade (Aurore); Simple words; Spring; The sun has never set; Take my heart away; To forget so soon; Whether day reigns; Why?; Why did I dream of you?; Zemfira's song.*
☞ (M) *** Decca Analogue/Dig. 436 204-2 [id.]. Elisabeth Söderström, Vladimir Ashkenazy.

This song collection brings many delights, including *Zemfira's song* – in which a young girl repulses the attentions of an old man – and the spoken exchanges briefly present Ashkenazy as an actor. This and *Amid the noise of the ball* (which surely has an affinity with Tatiana in *Eugene Onegin*), plus the famous *None but the lonely heart*, are among Tchaikovsky's finest inspirations, but even the lighter numbers are enchanting as sung by this artist, with Ashkenazy an ever-imaginative partner. Fine Decca recording from 1982/3, with the artists given a natural presence. (Generous measure, too: 74 minutes.)

Songs: *Amid the noise of the ball; Behind the window; The canary; Cradle song; The cuckoo; Does the day reign; Do not believe; The fearful minute; If only I had known; It was in the early spring; Last night; Lullaby in a storm; The nightingale; None but the lonely heart; Not a word, O my friend; Serenade; Spring; To forget so soon; Was I not a little blade of grass?; Why?; Why did I dream of you?*.
☞ *** Hyp. Dig. CDA 66617 [id.]. Joan Rodgers, Roger Vignoles.

The warmly distinctive timbre of Joan Rodgers' lovely soprano has been heard mainly in opera but she is equally compelling in this glowing first solo disc of songs. Her fluency with Russian texts as well as the golden colourings of her voice make this wide-ranging collection a delight from first to last. Though the voice is not quite at its richest in the most celebrated song of all, *None but the lonely heart*, the singer's subtle varying of mood and tone completely refutes the idea that Tchaikovsky as a song-composer was limited. One of the finest discs issued to mark the Tchaikovsky centenary in 1993.

The Snow Maiden (Snegourotchka): complete incidental music.
**(*) Chant du Monde LDC 278 904 [id.]. Simonova, Martinov, Elnikov, Lomonossov, USSR R. & TV Ch. & O, Provatorov.

This single disc conveniently and generously includes all the 80 minutes of incidental music Tchaikovsky wrote for *The Snow Maiden*, and much of it is vintage material, very delightful, bringing reminders of *Eugene Onegin* in the peasant choruses and some of the folk-based songs, and of the later Tchaikovskian world of *The Nutcracker* in some of the dances. With fine, idiomatic performances, this work is a most cherishable rarity. The soloists are characterfully Slavonic, better caught in the recording than the chorus, which is not helped by backward balance; the bite of their fine singing does not come over fully. Though the digital recording is bright and full-bodied, there is occasional coarseness in the orchestral sound too.

OPERA

Eugene Onegin (complete).
*** Decca 417 413-2 (2) [id.]. Kubiak, Weikl, Burrows, Reynolds, Ghiaurov, Hamari, Sénéchal, Alldis Ch., ROHCG O, Solti.
**(*) DG Dig. 423 959-2 (2) [id.]. Freni, Allen, Von Otter, Schicoff, Burchuladze, Sénéchal, Leipzig R. Ch., Dresden State O, Levine.
☞ **(*) Ph. Dig. 438 235-2 (2) [id.]. Hvorostovsky, Focile, Shicoff, Borodina, Anisimov, St Petersburg Chamber Ch., O de Paris, Bychkov.
☞ (M) (**(*)) BMG/Melodiya mono 743211 70902 (2) [id.]. Belov, Vishnevskaya, Lemeshev, Avdeyeva, Bolshoi Theatre Ch. & O, Khaikin.

Solti, characteristically crisp in attack, has plainly warmed to the score of Tchaikovsky's colourful opera, allowing his singers full rein in rallentando and rubato to a degree one might not have expected of him. The Tatiana of Teresa Kubiak is most moving – rather mature-sounding for the *ingénue* of Act I, but with her golden, vibrant voice rising most impressively to the final confrontation of Act III. The Onegin of Bernd Weikl may have too little variety of tone, but again this is firm singing that yet has authentic Slavonic tinges. Onegin becomes something like a first-person storyteller. The rest of the cast is excellent, with Stuart Burrows as Lensky giving one of his finest performances on record yet. Here, for the first time, the full range of musical expression in this most atmospheric of operas is superbly caught, with the Decca CDs capturing every subtlety – including the wonderful off-stage effects.

The DG version brings a magnificent Onegin in Thomas Allen, the most satisfying account of the title-role yet recorded. It is matched by the Tatiana of Mirella Freni, even at a late stage in her career readily conveying girlish freshness in her voice. The other parts are also strongly taken. The tautened-nerves quality in the character of Lensky comes out vividly in the portrayal by Neil Schicoff, and Anne Sofie von Otter with her firm, clear mezzo believably makes Olga a younger sister, not the usual over-ripe character. Paata Burchuladze is a satisfyingly resonant Gremin and Michel Sénéchal, as on the Solti set, is an incomparable Monsieur Triquet. What welds all these fine components into a rich and exciting whole is the conducting of James Levine with the Dresden Staatskapelle: passionate, at times even wild in Slavonic excitement, yet giving full expressive rein to Tchaikovskian melody, allowing the singers to breathe. The Leipzig Radio Choir sings superbly as well. The snag is that the DG recording is unevocative and studio-bound, with sound close and congested enough to undermine the bloom on both voices and instruments. In every way the more spacious acoustic in the Solti set is preferable.

Dmitri Hvorostovsky makes a strong, heroic Onegin in the Philips set, though Bychkov's conducting does not always encourage him to be as animated as one wants, and the voice at times comes near to straining. Nuccia Focile also emerges at her most convincing only in the final scene of confrontation with Onegin. Earlier, her voice is too fluttery to convey the full pathos of the young Tatiana in the *Letter scene*, edgy at the top. The digital recording may well exaggerate unevenness of production, for Neil Shicoff as Lensky also suffers, though he sings with passionate commitment, conveying the neurotic element in the poet's character. As Gremin, Alexander Anisimov also has a grainy voice. Olga Borodina sings impressively as Olga, but on balance the other characters are better cast in Solti's earlier, Decca set. When the Philips sound has less presence than that Decca analogue recording and Bychkov is less adept at lifting rhythms, not least in the great dance sequences, finding less light and shade, the older set is clearly to be preferred.

The BMG transfer of the 1955 Bolshoi recording clarifies the sound, with voices focused well forward, even though big ensembles bring serious distortion. With Boris Khaikin a deeply sympathetic conductor, this is a powerfully idiomatic performance which captures the authentic Russian tradition more persuasively than most recordings from the Soviet period, with the genre numbers crisply sprung and with some first-rate playing from some of the Bolshoi instrumentalists, even if the horn adopts a typical howling tone. Though the mono sound is limited, the voices are not constricted, and the off-stage choruses, so important in this work, are well balanced to make them as atmospheric as possible. As Onegin, Evgeni Belov is clear and forthright, while Galina Vishnevskaya, near the beginning of her Bolshoi career, is firm and bright, if rarely able to convey subtler half-tones, partly thanks to the close-up recording. Also very Russian-sounding, but clear and not whining, is the Lensky of Sergei Lemeshev. A historic set, worth investigating. Only brief notes are provided, with no libretto or translation.

Eugene Onegin (complete; in English).
☞ **(*) EMI Dig. CDS5 55004-2 (2) [id.]. Hampson, Te Kanawa, Rosenshein, Bardon, Connell, Gedda, Welsh Nat. Op. Ch. and O, Mackerras.

Thanks to the Peter Moores Foundation, who earlier sponsored the Goodall *Ring* cycle in English, EMI presents this greatest of Tchaikovsky operas with a star cast in David Lloyd-Jones's English translation. Partly through a recording balance which favours the voices, words are exceptionally clear, which makes it a first-rate recommendation for anyone who prefers opera in English, an extreme rarity on disc. Thomas Hampson is a superb Onegin, presenting a dashing, volatile character, singing magnificently. Kiri Te Kanawa matches him in her bitingly intense singing in the final scene of confrontation, but the character of Tatiana as a girl eludes her, with the voice inevitably sounding too mature. The Olga of Patricia Bardon, too, does not sound girlish enough, and the Lensky of Neil Rosenshein is disappointingly uneven in production, with a pronounced judder. The others are first rate, with Nicolai Gedda providing a delightful vignette at the Larins' ball as the aged M. Triquet. Sir Charles Mackerras paces the opera beautifully, but the impact of the WNO Orchestra's playing is blunted, thanks to the backward balance.

The Queen of Spades (Pique Dame) (complete).
☞ *** Ph. Dig. 438 141-2 (3) [id.]. Grigorian, Putilin, Chernov, Solodovnikov, Arkhipova, Gulegina, Borodina, Kirov Op. Ch. & O, Gergiev.
**(*) Sony Dig. S3K 45720 [id.]. Dilova, Evstatieva, Toczyska, Konsulov, Ochman, Masurok, Bulgarian Nat. Ch., Sofia Festival O, Tchakarov.
☞ ** BMG/RCA Dig. 09060 60992-2 (3) [id.]. Freni, Atlantov, Hvorostovsky, Forrester, Leiferkus, Katherine Ciesinski, Tanglewood Festival Ch., Boston SO, Seiji Ozawa.

When each new recording of this opera for many years has been flawed, it is good that Gergiev and his talented team from the Kirov Opera in St Petersburg have produced a winner. The very opening, refined and purposeful, sets the pattern, with Gergiev controlling this episodic work with fine concern for atmosphere and dramatic impact, unafraid of extreme speeds and telling pauses. Though the engineers fail to give a supernatural aura to the voice of the Countess when she returns as a ghost, the recorded sound is consistently warm and clear. It is good to have the veteran Irina Arkhipova singing powerfully and bitingly in that key role, while the other international star, Olga Borodina, is unforgettable as Pauline, singing gloriously with keen temperament. Otherwise Gergiev's chosen team offers characterful Slavonic voices that are yet well focused and unstrained, specially important with the tenor hero, Herman, here dashingly sung by Gegam Grigorian. As the heroine, Lisa, Maria Gulegina sings with warm tone and well-controlled vibrato, slightly edgy under pressure.

Tchakarov in his Sony series of Russian operas conducts a fresh, expressive and alert account of *Queen of Spades*, very well recorded. Wieslaw Ochman makes an impressive Herman, amply powerful and only occasionally rough. Yuri Masurok is a superb Yeletsky, and the duet of Lisa and her companion, Pauline, is beautifully done by Stefka Evstatieva and Stefania Toczyska, one of Tchaikovsky's most magical inspirations. As the old Countess, Penka Dilova has a characteristically fruity Slavonic mezzo, very much in character, if with a heavy vibrato. The Countess's famous solo is taken very slowly indeed but is superbly sustained. Ensembles and chorus work are excellent, timed with theatrical point.

Looking at the starry cast-list, you would assume that the RCA version conducted by Ozawa would be a clear winner. Not so when, as a live recording spliced together from performances in Boston and New York, the acoustic is unhelpfully dry, allowing little bloom on the voices, and with the orchestra consigned to the background. The rich contralto of Maureen Forrester fares best in the role of the Countess, and even then the distancing of the voice when she reappears as a ghost adds more bloom. Ozawa moulds the music most persuasively and draws keenly polished playing from the orchestra, but this is not as volatile or naturally dramatic a performance as that on the Sony set from Bulgaria. Both in the conducting and in the singing one registers that this is a concert performance rather than one linked to stage experience. The chorus, for example, sing with knife-edged precision but sound far less idiomatic than their Bulgarian counterparts. Vocally what is disappointing in the set is the contributions of the two principals, Vladimir Atlantov and Mirella Freni, who are no longer young enough to be fully convincing in the roles of Herman and Lisa. Freni in particular sounds strained and unsteady in the big scene with Herman in Act III, and Atlantov, though warmly expressive and still strong and heroic when not under pressure, was fresher in his earlier, Bolshoi recording of 1974, previously available on Philips. The advantage of having star names in the rest of the cast, notably Dmitri Hvorostovsky and Sergei Leiferkus, need not weigh too heavily when their roles are so incidental.

Yolanta (complete).
☞ (M) **(*) Erato/Warner Dig. 2292 45973-2 (2) [id.]. Vishnevskaya, Nicolai Gedda, Groenroos, Petkov, Krause, Cortez, Tania Gedda, Anderson, Dumont, Groupe Vocale de France, O de Paris, Rostropovich.

Tchaikovsky's one-Act opera *Yolanta* (*Iolanthe*) is a much later (1892) work than *Eugene Onegin*. Tchaikovsky's imagination was obviously touched by the fairy-tale story of a blind princess in medieval Provence who is finally cured by the arrival of the knight who falls in love with her. The libretto may be flawed but the lyrical invention is a delight. The performance offered here was recorded at a live concert performance in the Salle Pleyel in December 1984, with excellent, spacious sound. Rostropovich's performance has a natural expressive warmth to make one tolerant of vocal shortcomings. Though Vishnevskaya's voice is not naturally suited to the role of a sweet young princess, she does wonders in softening her hardness of tone, bringing fine detail of characterization. Gedda equally by nature sounds too old for his role, but again the artistry is compelling and ugly sounds are few. More questionable is the casting of Dimiter Petkov as the King, far too wobbly as recorded. However, now reissued on a pair of mid-priced CDs, this is well worth exploring.

Arias from: *The Enchantress; Eugene Onegin; Iolantha; Mazeppa; The Queen of Spades*.
*** Ph. Dig. 426 740-2 [id.]. Dmitri Hvorostovsky, Rotterdam PO, Gergiev – VERDI: *Arias*. ***

Hvorostovsky presents an eager, volatile Onegin, a passionate Yeletski in *Queen of Spades* and an exuberant Robert in *Iolantha*. One can only hope that he will be guided well, to develop such a glorious instrument naturally, without strain.

Tcherepnin, Alexander (1899–1977)

Symphony No. 4, Op. 91; Romantic overture, Op. 67; Russian dances, Op. 50; Suite for orchestra, Op. 87.
☞ *** Marco Polo Dig. 8.223380 [id.]. Czech-Slovak State PO (Košice), Wing-Sie Yip.

Alexander Tcherepnin was the only son of Nikolai, the conductor who directed the first season of the Diaghilev Ballet in Paris in 1909. The *Fourth Symphony* is probably Tcherepnin's best work, and its appearance in the catalogue is greatly to be welcomed. Written in the mid-1950s to a commission from Charles Munch and the Boston Symphony Orchestra, it is a colourful, tautly compact work, neo-classical in idiom, very well organized and full of lively and imaginative musical invention. The *Suite*, Op. 67, written for the Louisville Orchestra in 1953, is less individual and in places recalls the Stravinsky of *Petrushka* and *Le chant du rossignol*. Like the much earlier *Russian dances* (1933), it is uneven in quality but far from unattractive. The *Romantic overture* was composed in wartime Paris when taxis and private cars were forbidden and there was a return to horse-drawn traffic, which reminded Tcherepnin of his childhood in St Petersburg. Generally good performances, decently recorded too under the young Chinese conductor, Wing-Sie Yip, who draws a lively response from her players.

Telemann, Georg Philipp (1681–1767)

Concertos: for 2 chalumeaux in D min.; for flute in D; for 3 oboes, 3 violins in B flat; for recorder & flute in E min.; for trumpet in D; for trumpet & violin in D.
*** DG Dig. 419 633-2 [id.]. Soloists, Col. Mus. Ant., Goebel.

As Reinhard Goebel points out, Telemann 'displayed immense audacity in the imaginative and ingenious mixing of the colours from the palette of the baroque orchestra', and these are heard to excellent effect here. Those who know the vital *B flat Concerto* – or, rather, A major, for that is how it actually sounds – for three oboes and violins, from earlier versions, will find the allegro very fast indeed and the slow movement quite thought-provoking. The chalumeau is the precursor of the clarinet, and the concerto for two chalumeaux recorded here is full of unexpected delights. Marvellously alive and accomplished playing, even if one occasionally tires of the bulges and nudges on the first beats of bars.

Concerto for flute, oboe d'amore and viola d'amore in E; Concerto polonois; Double concerto for recorder and flute in E min.; Triple trumpet concerto in D; Quadro in B flat.
*** O-L Dig. 411 949-2 [id.]. AAM with soloists, Hogwood.

'An attentive observer could gather from these folk musicians enough ideas in eight days to last a lifetime,' wrote Telemann after spending a summer in Pless in Upper Silesia. Polish ideas are to be found in three of the concertos recorded here – indeed, one of the pieces is called *Concerto polonois*. As always, Telemann has a refined ear for sonority, and the musical discourse with which he diverts us is unfailingly intelligent and delightful. The performances are excellent and readers will not find cause for disappointment in either the recording or presentation.

(i) *Concerto for 2 flutes, 2 oboes and strings in B flat;* (ii) *Triple concerto for flute, oboe d'amore, violin and strings in E; Oboe d'amore concerto in D; Trumpet concerto in D;* (iii) *Concerto for trumpet, 2 oboes in D;* (ii) *Double viola concerto in G;* (i) *Concerto for 3 trumpets, 2 oboes, timpani and strings in D;* (iv) *Double concerto for violin, trumpet and strings in D;* (i) *Suite in G (La Putain); Tafelmusik, Part I: Conclusion in E min. for 2 flutes and strings.*
☞ (M) *** Van. 08.9138.72 (2) [id.]. (i) Soloists, Esterhazy O, David Blum; (ii) Soloists, I Solisti di Zagreb, Antonio Janigro; (iii) Peter Masseurs, Amsterdam Bach Soloists; (iv) Mincho Minchev, Nikolai Chochev, Sofia Soloists, Vasil Kazandiev.

The sheer interest of the repertoire here outweighs any minor reservations about the recording, which comes from the 1960s rather than three decades later, as suggested by the copyright date on the box. However, the sound, particularly in the Esterhazy recordings, is warm and full and the performances are expert. The diversity of Telemann's inexhaustible invention is well demonstrated. In the *Concerto for two violas* the soloists interweave inseparably from the orchestral texture, a device borrowed from Vivaldi who named it 'violette all'inglese'. The four movements are appropriately described as *Avec douceur, Gay, Largo* and *Vivement*. The solo *Oboe d'amore concerto* and *Trumpet concerto* are both fine, four-movement works, but it is the collective concertos that offer the greatest interest. The *Concerto for two flutes, two oboes and strings* begins elegantly with richly mellifluous blending; then, after a busy *Presto*, the two oboes open the *Cantabile* unaccompanied in a gravely Handelian melody. The flutes enter later and blend in engagingly; the finale then sparkles, with paired oboes and flutes echoing each other. This is a wonderfully inventive movement, like an amalgam of Bach and Mozart. The *Triple concerto for flute, oboe d'amore and violin in E major* opens with an imposingly spacious

Andante, very like an introduction to an aria or a chorus from an oratorio; then, after a lively allegro, comes a particularly fine *Siciliano*. The *Concerto for three trumpets, two oboes and timpani* begins with an imposing *Intrada*, then follows a sprightly Handelian fugue, including trumpets and oboes within the part-writing. The oboes gently dominate the gravely expressive *Largo* arietta, and the piece ends with more rollicking interplay between all concerned. The result is an irresistible masterpiece. The suite, *La Putain* ('The Prostitute'), is very colourful. The overture in itself contains considerable tempo variations and an invitation by way of a folksong (*Ich bin so lang nicht bei dir g'west*) to 'Come up and see me sometime'. The suite of strongly characterized dances which follow reminds one not a little of the incidental music of Lully and Rameau in its feeling for colour. One can sense Telemann's eyes twinkling, especially in the *Sarabande* which momentarily becomes skittish then reverts to gracious dignity, while the closing *Bourrée* and *Hornpipe* end the piece cheerfully. The *Concerto for trumpet and two oboes in D* is added on to the end of the first CD, and the performance by the Amsterdam Bach Soloists (with Peter Masseurs a splendid soloist) appears to use original instruments, nowhere to better effect than in the third-movement *Aria* where the oboes play together against a strong bassoon continuo. The jolly finale completes a fine five-movement piece which comes off splendidly. The second CD closes the programme with a brief contribution from Sofia, the *Concerto for violin, trumpet and strings in D*, vividly played but rather thinly recorded. But overall this highly stimulating set must receive the warmest possible welcome.

Horn concerto in D; Double horn concerto in D; Triple horn concerto in D; Suite in F for 2 horns and strings; Tafelmusik, Book 3: *Double horn concerto in E flat.*
*** Ph. Dig. 412 226-2 [id.]. Baumann, Timothy Brown, Hill, ASMF, Iona Brown.

The *E flat Concerto* comes from the third set of *Tafelmusik* (1733) and is the best-known of the four recorded here. The playing here and in the other concertos is pretty dazzling, not only from Hermann Baumann but also from his colleagues, Timothy Brown and Nicholas Hill. Mention should also be made of the concertante contributions from the two violinists. Telemann's invention rarely fails to hold the listener, and the recording has warm ambience and excellent clarity.

Oboe concertos: in C min.; D (Concerto gratioso); E; E flat; F; Oboe d'amore concerto in G.
☞ *** Unicorn Dig. DKPCD 9128 [id.]. Sarah Francis, L. Harpsichord Ens.

Oboe concertos in C min.; D min.; F min.; Oboe d'amore concertos in E; E min.; (i) Triple concerto for oboe d'amore, flute and viola d'amore.
☞ *** Unicorn Dig. DKPCD 9131 [id.]. Sarah Francis; (i) Graham Mayer, Elizabeth Watson; L. Harpsichord Ens.

Sarah Francis is beginning a survey of Telemann's *Oboe* and *Oboe d'amore* concertos for Unicorn and, though these are modern-instrument performances, they are a model of style. The *G major Oboe d'amore concerto* on the first disc is particularly gracious (the first movement marked *soave* and the colouring dark-timbred like a cor anglais). The *Concerto gratioso*, too, is aptly named, although that sobriquet is centred on the first movement, which is immediately followed by a jaunty *Vivace*, a lovely arioso *Adagio* and a scherzando finale. But all the works here show Telemann's invention at its freshest.

If anything, the second collection is even more inviting than the first. The *C minor Oboe concerto* begins with a *Grave*, then the main Allegro brings a witty dialogue between soloist and violins, with the theme tossed backwards and forwards like a shuttlecock. But it is the works for oboe d'amore that are again so striking. the *A major* immediately introduces a lovely *Siciliano*, while the *E minor* brings a sombre, beautiful central *Adagio*, with the vivacious outer movements giving lightweight contrast using an linking idea, somewhat tailored in the finale. Most imaginative of all is the *Triple concerto* with its sustained opening *Andante* (a bit like a Handel aria) and *Siciliano* third movement with the melody alternating between oboe d'amore and viola d'amore, and nicely decorated by flute triplets. The finale is even more inventively original in its interplay of colour. The performances are full of joy and sparkle and are equally impressive for their nicely judged expressive feeling. They are beautifully recorded and make a very good case for playing this repertoire on modern instruments.

Oboe concertos: in C min.; D; D min.; E min.; F min.
*** Ph. Dig. 412 879-2 [id.]. Holliger, ASMF, Iona Brown.

The *C minor Concerto* with its astringent opening dissonance is the most familiar of the concertos on Holliger's record, and the *E minor* has also been recorded before, but the remaining three were all new to the catalogue. Telemann was himself proficient on the oboe and wrote with particular imagination and poignancy for this instrument. The performances are all vital and sensitively shaped and a valuable addition to the Telemann discography. Well worth investigation.

Recorder concerto in C; (i) Double concerto in A min., for recorder, viola da gamba and strings. Suite in A min. for recorder and strings.
☞ ** O-L Dig. 433 043-2 [id.]. Philip Pickett, New L. Consort; (i) with Mark Levy.

Pickett's concert opens with the famous *A minor Suite*, and for once the *Overture* seems a little on the long side. Throughout, the playing is alive and polished and not too abrasive, yet Pickett (who directs as well as taking the solo recorder role) is very serious in his approach, almost dour. The music survives such a relatively long-faced approach and the recording is first class, but Telemann can be made to sound sunnier than this.

Recorder concertos in C; in F; Suite in A min; (i) Sinfonia in F.
**(*) Hyp. Dig. CDA 66413 [id.]. Peter Holtslag, Parley of Instruments, Peter Holman or (i) Roy Goodman.

The three solo concertos here are a delight. Just try the *Affettuoso* opening of the *F major concerto* and you will surely be seduced. Both this and the *C major* are quite substantial pieces, too, with four movements apiece. Peter Holtslag's piping treble recorder is truthfully balanced, in proper scale with the authentic accompaniments, which are neat, polished, sympathetic and animated. The *Sinfonia* is curiously scored, for recorder, oboe, solo bass viol, strings, cornett, three trombones and an organ, with doubling of wind and string parts. Even with Roy Goodman balancing everything expertly the effect is slightly bizarre, if stimulating. About the great *Suite in A minor* we have some reservations: it is played with much nimble bravura and sympathy on the part of the soloist, but the orchestral texture brings a degree of anorexia; after hearing how grand this piece can sound on a modern string group, the results here are faintly dispiriting.

Recorder concerto in C; (i) Double concerto for recorder and bassoon.
*** BIS Dig. CD 271 [id.]. Pehrsson, (i) McGraw; Drottningholm Bar. Ens. – VIVALDI: *Concertos.* ***

Clas Pehrsson and Michael McGraw are most expert players, as indeed are their colleagues of the Drottningholm Baroque Ensemble; the recordings are well balanced and fresh.

Recorder concerto in G min.; Double concerto in A min. for recorder, viola da gamba and strings; Double concerto in A for 2 violins in scordatura; Concertos for 4 violins: in C and D.
☞ (B) *** DG 439 444-2 [id.]. Soloists, Col. Mus. Ant., Goebel.

These are chamber concertos rather than solo concertos such as we associate with Vivaldi. They are diverting and inventive, without at any point reaching any great depths: like so much of Telemann, they are pleasing without being memorable. Nevertheless they are eminently well served by these artists and well recorded, and any reservations are forgotten when one looks at the price of this CD.

Double concerto in F, for recorder, bassoon & strings; Double concerto in E min., for recorder, flute & strings; Suite in A min., for recorder & strings.
*** Ph. Dig. 410 041-2 [id.]. Petri, Bennett, Thunemann, ASMF, Iona Brown.

The *E minor Concerto* for recorder, flute and strings is a delightful piece and is beautifully managed, even though period-instrument addicts will doubtless find William Bennett's tone a little fruity. The playing throughout is highly accomplished and the *Suite in A minor*, Telemann's only suite for treble recorder, comes off beautifully. The orchestral focus is not absolutely clean, though quite agreeable.

(i–iii) Double concerto in E min. for recorder and transverse flute; (iv) Viola concerto in G; (i; v) Suite in A min. for flute and strings; (iii) Overture des Nations anciens et modernes in G.
☞ ⊛ (M) *** Teldec/Warner 9031 77620-2 [id.]. (i) Frans Brüggen, (ii) Franz Vester, (iii) Amsterdam CO, André Rieu; (iv) Paul Doctor, Concerto Amsterdam, Brüggen; (v) SW German CO, Friedrich.

This Das Alte Werk reissue must now be regarded as the most attractive single Telemann collection in the catalogue, finer even than the Naxos disc. Two works are duplicated, but these Teldec performances are so refreshing that readers shouldn't let that put them off acquiring both CDs. All these works show Telemann as an original and often inspired craftsman. His use of contrasting timbres in the *Double concerto* has considerable charm; the *Overture des Nations anciens et modernes* is slighter but is consistently and agreeably inventive, and the *Suite in A minor*, one of his best-known works, is worthy of Handel or Bach. Frans Brüggen and Franz Vester are expert soloists and Brüggen shows himself equally impressive on the conductor's podium accompanying Paul Doctor, the rich-timbred soloist in the engaging *Viola concerto*. The sound, splendidly remastered, is unbelievably good, with fine body and presence: it is difficult to believe that these recordings are now three decades old.

Trumpet concerto in D; (i) Double trumpet concerto in E flat; (ii) 2 Concertos in D for trumpet, 2 oboes & strings; (i; iii) Concerto in D for 3 trumpets & strings.

☞ *** Ph. Dig. 420 954-2 [id.]. Hardenberger, with (i) Laird; (ii) Nicklin, Miller; (iii) Houghton; ASMF, Iona Brown.

The effortless higher tessitura of Hardenberger and his admirable sense of style dominate a concert where all the soloists are expert and well blended by the engineers. The concertos with oboes offer considerable variety of timbre and have fine slow movements; there is for instance an engaging *Poco andante* where the oboes are given an *Aria* to sing over a simple but effective continuo, given here to the bassoon (Graham Sheen). That same work is structured unusually in five movements, with two short *Grave* sections to provide pivots of repose. Telemann is always inventive and, with such excellent playing and recording, this can be recommended to anyone who enjoys regal trumpet timbre.

Concerto in D for 3 trumpets, 2 oboes and strings; Suite in G min. for 3 oboes, bassoon and strings; Tafelmusik, Production II: Suite (Overture) in D.

☞ *** DG Dig. 439 893-2 [id.]. E. Concert, Pinnock.

As usual, Pinnock lifts rhythms engagingly and keeps everything fresh and vital. The *Suite in G minor*, using regal trumpets but never upstaging the oboes, is a particularly felicitous example of the composer's own special semi-*concerto grosso* style, with the soloists and ripieno in a colourful interplay; yet in some ways the *G minor Suite*, using three oboes, is even more ear-tickling. Here two of the inner movements have sobriquets: *Les Irresoluts* and *Les Capricieuses*, while there is also a French *Loure* and a robust *Gasconnade* for good measure. The closing excerpt from the *Tafelmusik* has a single trumpet to brighten the texture and the invention is remarkably consistent. Excellent recording and splendid music.

(i) Viola concerto in G; (ii) Suite in A min. for recorder and strings; Tafelmusik, Part 2: (iii) Triple violin concerto in F; Part 3: (iv) Double horn concerto in E flat.

⊛ (BB) *** Naxos Dig. 8.550156; 4550156 [id.]. (i) Kyselak; (ii) Stivín; (iii) Hoelblingova, Hoelbling, Jablokov; (iv) Z. & B. Tylšar, Capella Istropolitana, Richard Edlinger.

Our Rosette is awarded for enterprise and good planning – to say nothing of good music-making. It is difficult to conceive of a better Telemann programme for anyone encountering this versatile composer for the first time and coming fresh to this repertoire, having bought the inexpensive Naxos CD on impulse. Ladislav Kyselak is a fine violist and is thoroughly at home in Telemann's splendid four-movement concerto; Jiři Stivín is an equally personable recorder soloist in the masterly *Suite in A minor*; his decoration is a special joy. The *Triple violin concerto* with its memorable *Vivace* finale and the *Double horn concerto* also show the finesse which these musicians readily display. Richard Edlinger provides polished and alert accompaniments throughout. The digital sound is first class.

Darmstadt overtures (suites), TWV 55/C6 (complete).

☞ (M) *** Teldec/Warner 4509 93772-2 (2) [id.]. VCM, Harnoncourt.

What strikes one with renewed force while listening to these once again is the sheer fertility and quality of invention that these works exhibit. This is music of unfailing intelligence and wit and, although Telemann rarely touches the depths of Bach, there is no lack of expressive eloquence either. The performances are light in touch and can be recommended with real enthusiasm. This would make an excellent start to any Telemann collection.

Suites: in B flat, TW 55/B 10; in C, TWV 55/C6; in D, TWV 55/D 19.

☞ *** DG Dig. 437 558-2 [id.]. E. Concert, Trevor Pinnock.

There is some marvellous music here, and each suite has its own lollipops, the *Hornpipe* and charming *Plainte* in the *B flat major Suite*, the sensuous *Someille* in the C major work (although one can imagine this would sound even creamier on modern wind instruments) while the D major work has a most fetching *Bourée*, fully worthy of Handel. It brings a feather-light *moto perpetuo* for strings at its centre, and the *Ecossaise* with its witty Scottish snap has a similar contrast, bringing the neatest possible articulation from the English Concert players. There is lots of vitality here and crisp, clean rhythms. Just occasionally one feels the need for more of a smile and greater textural warmth – the rasping, integrated hunting horns don't add a great deal to the *D major Suite* – but this is still a very worthwhile and generous collection (76 minutes), realistically recorded.

(i) *Suites: in E flat (La Lyra);* (i; ii) *in F* (for violin and orchestra). (iii) *Paris quartets Nos. 1–6* (complete).

☞ ⊛ (M) *** Teldec/Warner 4509 92177-2 (2) [id.]. (i) Concerto Amsterdam, Brüggen, (ii) with Jaap Schröder; (iii) Amsterdam Qt (Frans Brüggen, Schröder, Anner Bylsma, Gustav Leonhardt).

The Telefunken recording of the *Paris Quartets* was one of the jewels of the LP Das Alte Werk catalogue, and it received a Rosette from us on its original issue. We see no reason to withhold it from these admirably transferred CDs. These are most inventive works and the level of inspiration is extraordinarily even. The performances are of such an order of virtuosity that they silence criticism, and Frans Brüggen in particular dazzles the listener. The recording is of the very top class, beautifully balanced and tremendously alive (like the performances themselves), and this is surely a set that will convert the most doubtful to Telemann's cause. The two orchestral suites which have been added for the CD issue are almost equally distinguished. The *Lyra suite* is also highly inventive and colourful, with a marvellously apt imitation of a hurdy-gurdy. The *Suite in F major* features the solo violin as a concertante instrument rather than a dominating soloist. The scoring with its use of woodwind and horns is felicitous. Brüggen directs throughout with plenty of spirit, though he is inclined to overdo the accents in the *Minuet* which closes the *F major Suite*. Again the recording is excellent, though not perhaps in the demonstration class of the *Quartets*.

Tafelmusik (Productions 1–3) complete.
*** Teldec/Warner Dig. 2292 44688-2 (4). VCM, Harnoncourt.
*** DG Dig. 427 619-2 (4) [id.]. Col. Mus. Ant., Reinhard Goebel.

The playing of the Musiqua Antiqua is distinguished by the highest order of virtuosity and unanimity of ensemble and musical thinking. They also have the advantage of very vivid and fresh recording quality; the balance is close and present without being too forward and there is a pleasing acoustic ambience.

Harnoncourt has a slightly more distant, less analytical balance, and his recording has the added poignancy of offering the last performances by the oboists, Jürg Schaeftlein and David Reichenberg (the set bears a dedication to their memory). It also offers distinguished playing, perhaps less virtuosic than the Cologne ensemble but no less sensitive. However, the greater breadth of the Harnoncourt set tells in its favour: Reinhard Goebel and his Cologne players opt for breathlessly quick tempi in which liveliness becomes headlong and there are some self-conscious dynamic exaggerations and expressive bulges.

Tafelmusik: Overtures (suites): in E min. (from Part 1); *in D* (from Part 2); *in B flat* (from Part 3).
(M) *** Teldec/Warner 2292 43546-2 [id.]. Concerto Amsterdam, Brüggen.

Essentially, these works are made up of French dance-movements of considerable diversity, and the *E minor Suite* is engagingly scored for a pair of recorders with strings; although it has no *Badinerie*, its sound is not unlike Bach's B minor work; while Telemann's *D major*, with its forthright use of a trumpet, similarly reminds one of the Bach *Third Suite*, even though its invention has nothing in it as memorable as Bach's famous *Air*. The third suite here is perhaps the most agreeable of all, using two oboes with considerable flair. All this music is expertly played by the Concerto Amsterdam under Frans Brüggen, and the remastered 1970 recording is fresh and full, so that the disc sounds hardly dated at all.

Tafelmusik, Part 2: *Overture (Suite) in D; Triple violin concerto in F; Conclusion in D.*
☞ (B) *** Erato/Warner Dig. 4509 92868-2 [id.]. Paillard CO, Jean-François Paillard.

Although the measure is fairly short (46 minutes) these are bright and alert performances of some very attractive music. The *D major Overture (Suite)* with its brilliant trumpet writing recalls the Bach *Suite* in the same key, and the trumpeter here, Bernard Gabel, is a fine player. The digital recording is truthful and well balanced.

Tafelmusik, Production 3: *Overture in B flat; Quartet in E min.;* Production 2: *Concerto in F; Trio sonata in E flat; Solo (Violin) sonata in A; Conclusion in B flat.*
*** DG Dig. 429 774-2 [id.] (from above set, directed Goebel).

For those not wanting a complete set, this arbitrary but well-chosen 75-minute selection may prove useful. The recording is faithful, though the edginess of Goebel's violin timbre will not suit all tastes.

Water Music (Hamburg Ebb and Flow); Concertos in A min.; B flat; F.
**(*) DG Dig. 413 788-2 [id.]. Col. Mus. Ant., Goebel.

Telemann's *Water Music* is one of his best-known works and, save for the opening *overture*, is given a very lively performance, with sprightly rhythms and vital articulation. The eccentric opening is less than half the speed of Marriner's (deleted) version on Argo or Wenzinger's famous old Archiv account. Of particular interest are the three *Concertos* which form the coupling, two of which (in F major and A minor) are new to records. The invention is of unfailing interest, as is the diversity of instrumental colouring. The balance is admirably judged and the recording excellent.

CHAMBER MUSIC

Fantasias for (solo) *treble recorder: in C, TWV 40/2; in D min., TWV 40/4; in F, TWV 40/8; in G min., TWV 40/9; in A min., TWV 40/11; in B flat, TWV 40/12.* (i) *Essercizii musici: Sonatas in C, TWV 41/C5; in D min., TWV 41/D4; Der getreue Music-Meister: Canonic sonata in B flat, TWV 41/B3; in C, TWV 41/C2; Sonatas: in F min., TWV 41/F1; in F TWV 41/F2.*
☞ (M) *** Teldec/Warner 4509 93688-2 [id.]. Frans Brüggen, (i) with Anner Bysma, Gustav Leonhardt.

This 75-minute anthology, taken from recordings made between 1963 and 1971, is most welcome. Frans Brüggen is unsurpassed in this repertory and he plays with his usual mastery. The *Fantasias* for solo recorder, though inventive, are best taken one at a time, but the rest of the programme shows the composer at his most winningly felicitous. Brüggen's virtuosity is breathtaking (sample the finale of the *D minor Sonata* from *Essercizii musici* or the *Vivace* close to the *C major* of *Der getreue Music-Meister* which is captivating) and he shows a marvellous sense of style. As one would expect from Anner Bylsma and Gustav Leonhardt's continuo partnership, all these performances have polish and authority as well as charm. As so often in the reissues from the Telefunken Das Alte Werk series, the immaculately balanced recording is transferred to CD with the utmost truthfulness.

Der getreue Music-Meister: Nos. 4, 7, 13, 20, 28, 31, 35, 50, 53, 59, 62.
*** Denon Dig. C37 7052 [id.]. Holliger, Thunemann, Jaccottet.

This CD offers three of the most important works from *Der getreue Musik-Meister* for oboe and continuo, two *Sonatas* and a *Suite*, as well as the *F minor Sonata*, designated for recorder or bassoon and played here by Klaus Thunemann. They are interspersed with various miniatures, all well played and recorded. Holliger's playing is unusually expressive and his eloquence alone makes this selection worth having.

Sonatas for two recorders Nos. 1–6.
*** BMG/RCA Dig. RD 87903. Michala Petri and Elisabeth Selin.

Sonatas for two recorders Nos. 1–6; Duetto in B flat.
*** BIS Dig. CD 334 [id.]. Clas Pehrsson, Dan Laurin.

Canon sonatas Nos. 1–6; Duettos Nos. 1–6.
*** BIS Dig. CD 335 [id.]. Clas Pehrsson, Dan Laurin.

All the *Duet sonatas* are in four movements, the second being a fugue; the *Canon sonatas* are for two flutes, violins or bass viols. Needless to say, listening to two recorders for longer than one piece at a time imposes a strain on one's powers of endurance, however expert the playing – and expert it certainly is.

The RCA and BIS versions can be recommended alongside each other, although the BIS disc does contain one extra work. The playing of Michala Petri and Elisabeth Selin is particularly felicitous and the recording first class. However, although it is good to have the two treble recorders blending so well together, a clearer degree of separation would have been advantageous in the imitative writing.

VOCAL MUSIC

(i) *St Matthew Passion;* (ii) *Magnificat in C.*
(M) ** Ph. 432 500-2 (2) [id.]. (i) Jurinac, Altmeyer, Günter, Crass, Lucerne Festival Ch., Swiss Festival O; (ii) Giebel, Malaniuk, Altmeyer, Rehfuss, Reuter-Wolf, Choeur des Jeunes, Lausanne, Munich Pro Arte O, Redel.

Telemann was even more prolific than Bach, and this *Passion* does not always show him at his most inspired. The memorable feature, which is also interesting historically, is the series of interpolations in the gospel story. The first of these comes from the bass, Franz Crass, who comments powerfully on the 'Foolish knavery' and 'scheming guile' of Judas; but the highlight of the whole work is the series of poignant soliloquies from the soprano – Sena Jurinac in glorious voice – on the pathos of Christ's predicament, climaxed by an unexpectedly cheerful affirmation at the moment of crucifixion: 'Rejoice deeply for his most lamentable passing brings delight . . . with the joys of heaven . . . and destroys the torment of Hell'. Then at the very close of the story she sings a radiant postlude to Jesus, 'Sleep softly in Thy chamber'. The performance overall, directed by Kurt Redel, is hardly vibrant, but the 1964 recording is musically balanced, if not exactly vivid. The *C major Magnificat* is impressively scored for soloists, chorus and a fairly large orchestra, including trumpets. The piece is adequately performed so far as chorus and orchestra are concerned, though Kurt Redel is still essentially *kapellmeister*ish, and the soloists are uneven. The recording, as in the *St Matthew Passion*, is spacious and resonant.

Die Tageszeiten.
*** HM/BMG RD 77092 [77092-RC-2]. Bach, Georg, Blochwitz, Mannov, Freiburg Vocal Ens. & Coll. Mus., Wolfgang Schäfer.

Telemann's cantata, *Die Tageszeiten* (1759), is a work of great freshness and inventive resource. Its four sections portray the various times of day (*Morning, Midday, Evening* and *Night*) and are full of imaginative ideas. This new version, recorded with period instruments and four excellent soloists, makes a strong impression. The strings prompt a fleeting nostalgia for the more robust timbre of modern forces, and the playing under Wolfgang Schäfer could afford to be more full-bodied. But there is some excellent singing, and the recording is clean and well balanced. An enjoyable disc.

Thomas, Ambroise (1811–96)

Overtures: *Mignon; Raymond.*
☞ (M) *** Mercury 434 321-2 [id.]. Detroit SO, Paray – BIZET: *L'Arlésienne; Carmen: suites.* **(*)

These justly famous overtures are almost never heard in the concert hall nowadays. *Mignon*, opening with a delightful series of lyrical ideas on flute, clarinet and then horn, is matched by the ebullience of *Raymond*, perhaps more of a bandstand piece. The Detroit orchestra play both with wonderful finesse and Gallic spirit: this is repertoire which Paray directs as to the manner born, like his Auber overtures on the same label. The excellent (1960) recording was made in the Cass Technical High School Auditorium.

Hamlet (complete).
☞ *** EMI Dig. CDS7 54820-2 (3) [Ang. CDCC 54820]. Hampson, Anderson, Ramey, Graves, Kunde, Garino, Le Roux, Trempont, Amb. S., LPO, Antonio de Almeida.
☞ (M) *** Decca Dig. 433 857-2 (3) [id.]. Milnes, Sutherland, Morris, Winbergh, Conrad, Tomlinson, WNO Ch. & O, Bonynge.

The weight of Shakespeare is missing in Ambroise Thomas's setting of *Hamlet*, but this is more faithful to the author than Gounod's *Faust* is to Goethe. Moreover Bonynge here provides a far better answer to the problems of Act V. He has devised a composite of Thomas's original happy ending ('*Vive Hamlet, notre roi!*' cry the chorus) and the suicide alternative which Thomas wrote for Covent Garden. The plot now follows Shakespeare reasonably closely – if with far too many survivors – and the opera is revealed as a surprisingly deft if inevitably superficial compression of the play, full of splendid theatrical effects. It has colour, atmosphere, soaring tunes and jolly dances, presented in subtle and often original orchestration, with even a saxophone used to striking effect. 'To be or not to be' (*Être ou ne pas être*) as a soliloquy may not be as dramatically compelling as the original speech, but Hamlet's swaggering drinking song greeting the players is most effective, quoted later in mad, Berlioz-like bursts at the climax of the Play scene, when Hamlet's ruse with Claudius has worked. Musically, Ophélie has priority vocally in brilliant and beautiful numbers, with Sutherland taking all the challenges commandingly. Ophelia's famous Mad scene was one of the finest of her early recordings, and here, 24 years later, she still gives a triumphant display, tender and gentle as well as brilliant in coloratura. The heroine's primacy is reinforced when the role of Hamlet is for baritone, here taken strongly if with some roughness by Sherrill Milnes. Outstanding among the others is Gösta Winbergh as Laërte (in French without the final 's'), heady and clear in the only major tenor role. John Tomlinson as Le Spectre sings the necessary monotones resonantly, James Morris is a gruff Claudius and Barbara Conrad a fruity Gertrude. The compelling success of the whole performance of a long, complex opera is sealed by Bonynge's vigorous and sympathetic conducting of first-rate Welsh National Opera forces, brilliantly and atmospherically recorded. The layout, with Act I on the first CD and the other four Acts, two apiece, on the other two, is surely ideal, and the documentation is good.

Thomas's *Hamlet* may be an unashamed travesty of Shakespeare – complete with happy ending (in its original form) – but it remains a strong and enjoyable example of French opera of its period. So much was evident from Richard Bonynge's 1983 Decca set with his wife, Joan Sutherland, as Ophelia and Sherrill Milnes as Hamlet. If the EMI set is even more strikingly successful, it is not just that it provides an unusually full text – with the tragic, so-called Covent Garden ending and the ballet music in an appendix – but that Thomas Hampson gives such a commanding performance in the title-role. Milnes sang well, but hardly made the character sound any different from dozens of baritones in opera, where Hampson's superb, finely shaded singing goes with truly Shakespearean power in the acting, and the character emerges as a young hero, ardent but vulnerable, endlessly self-questioning. One no longer finds the aria, *Être ou ne pas être*, sounding conventional or trivial, and consistently Hampson magnetizes the attention the moment he begins to sing. June Anderson is not so happily cast as Ophelia. The voice is inclined to sound too edgy, and she is hardly more successful at sounding girlish than Sutherland at the end of her career, hardly matching her older rival in the Act III ballad, but the singing is felt and expressive. The rest of the cast may not be as starry as that in the Decca version, but there is no serious weakness. The Decca digital sound is rather cleaner and more vivid than the EMI, giving more bite to Bonynge's strong and sympathetic performance. Almeida is understanding too, and the presentation of the full text, conveniently, with trivia consigned to the appendix, and with a recently discovered duet for Claudius and Gertrude a valuable extra, makes it a highly enjoyable set.

Thomson, Virgil (1896–1989)

Film scores: *The Plow that broke the Plains; The River* (suites).
(M) *** Van. 08.8013.71 [OVC 8013]. Symphony of the Air, Leopold Stokowski – STRAVINSKY: *Soldier's Tale.* ***

Virgil Thomson's orchestral music may be sub-Copland (he too uses cowboy tunes like *Old paint*), but in Stokowski's charismatic hands these two film scores emerge with colours glowing and their rhythmic, folksy geniality readily communicating. The recording is resonantly atmospheric, but vivid too. Most enjoyable, and with a worthwhile coupling. This is at upper mid-price in the USA.

Lord Byron (complete).
☞ ** Koch Dig. 3-7124-2Y6 (2) [id.]. Lord, Zeller, Johnson, Mercer, Woodman, Owen, Ommerlé, Fortunato, Csengery, Jonason, Vanderlinde, Dry, Monadnock Music, Bolle.

Lord Byron is the third and last opera of Virgil Thomson, who died in 1989 aged 92. It is a weird piece, set mainly in Poet's Corner in Westminster Abbey after Byron's death, with his heirs and friends in dispute and his ghost periodically commenting. The settings of Byron's own words are fluent but do not avoid blandness, and the lyrical if shortwinded invention takes you effectively through the offbeat plot. The main trouble is that under James Bolle the playing of the Monadnock Festival Orchestra is limp. Soloists are efficient enough. Only periodically does Thomson let you know what he could have done as an opera-composer when, Puccini-like, he tellingly points the opening of a big number, as with Byron's solo at the end of Act I or in a splendid duet for Byron and his sister in Act II.

Tiomkin, Dimitri (1894–1979)

Film music: *The Fall of the Roman Empire: Overture; Pax Romana. The Guns of Navarone: Prologue-Prelude; Epilogue. A President's country. Rhapsody of steel. Wild is the wind.*
**(*) Unicorn DKPCD 9047; *DKPC 9047* [id.]. Royal College of Music O, Willcocks; D. King (organ).

Dimitri Tiomkin contributed scores to some of the most famous movies of all time, for Hitchcock and Frank Capra among others. But it was Carl Foreman's *High noon* that produced his most memorable idea, and he quotes its famous theme, among others, in *A President's country*, a well-crafted medley used as background music for a documentary about President Johnson's Texas. *Wild is the wind* is another familiar melody; Christopher Palmer's arrangement makes a tastefully scored showcase. The latter has arranged and orchestrated all the music here except *Rhapsody of steel*, a complex pseudo-symphonic score written for another documentary, which lasts some 22 minutes. The music of *Pax Romana* has the robust character of a typical Hollywood epic costume spectacular, featuring a bold contribution from the organ. All the music is played with obvious enjoyment by the Orchestra of the Royal College of Music; no apologies need be made for their technique, which is fully professional. Sir David Willcocks conducts with understanding of the idiom and great personal conviction. The recording is very impressive too, though the balance gives brass and percussion rather too much prominence.

Tippett, Michael (born 1905)

(i) *Concerto for double string orchestra;* (ii) *Fantasia concertante on a theme of Corelli;* (iii; iv) *Piano concerto;* (v) *String quartet No. 1;* (iii) *Piano sonatas Nos. 1–2.*
(M) *(**) EMI CMS7 63522-2 (2). (i) Moscow CO & Bath Festival O, Barshai; (ii) Y. Menuhin, Masters, Simpson, Bath Festival O, composer; (iii) John Ogdon; (iv) Philh. O, Sir Colin Davis; (v) Edinburgh Qt.

Tippett's eloquent *Concerto for double string orchestra* is well served by Barshai's performance, which has both warmth and vitality. The recording is lively but a shade dry in the upper range. The string textures are clear but not ideally expansive. The *Fantasia concertante* is not as immediately striking as its predecessor but, with the composer in charge and Menuhin as principal soloist, its inventiveness and expressive feeling are never in doubt. Again, the sound is clear and vivid but could be more sumptuous. The *Piano concerto* also represents Tippett's complex-textured and starkly conceived earlier style. Ogdon gives it a fine performance, although he does not rescue it from waywardness, while the recording, if not ideal, now sounds clearer than originally. The *First String quartet* is played rather slackly here; the sound is on the thin side. Ogdon plays the two *Piano sonatas* well and is especially convincing in the *First*. The work has a vitality of invention that it is easy to admire, even if as piano writing it is not as effective in the traditional sense as Tippett's later essay in this form. This is much more compressed in its argument, and though a more uninhibited approach can bring out the point of Tippett's scheme better, Ogdon displays his usual integrity, as well as virtuosity. The recording is faithful but a shade hard.

Concerto for double string orchestra; Fantasia concertante on a theme of Corelli. (i) *Songs for Dov.*
*** Virgin/EMI Dig. VC7 90701-2 [id.]. SCO, composer; (i) Nigel Robson.

The octogenarian Tippett gives delightfully pointed readings of the outer movements of the *Concerto*, bringing out the jazzy implications of the cross-rhythms, not taking them too literally, while the lovely melody of the slow movement has never sounded more warmly expressive. The Scottish Chamber Orchestra plays with comparable passion in the *Fantasia concertante*, a related work from Tippett's middle period, while Nigel Robson is a wonderfully idiomatic and convincing tenor soloist in the difficult vocal lines of the three *Songs for Dov*. Warm, full recording. (Alas, as we go to press, this has been withdrawn.)

Little music for string orchestra.
(M) **(*) Chan. Dig. CHAN 6576 [id.]. Soloists of Australia, Ronald Thomas – BLISS: *Checkmate*; RUBBRA: *Symphony No. 5*. ***

Tippett's *Little music* was written in 1946 for the Jacques Orchestra. Its contrapuntal style is stimulating but the music is more inconsequential than the *Concerto for double string orchestra*. It receives a good if not distinctive performance here, truthfully recorded.

Praeludium for brass, bells & percussion; Suite for the birthday of Prince Charles; The Midsummer marriage: (i) *Ritual dances;* (ii) *Sosostris's aria.*
**(*) Nimbus Dig. NI 5217 [id.]. (i; ii) Alfreda Hodgson, (i) Ch. of Opera North; E. N. Philh. O, Tippett.

Tippett draws a committed performance, not the most brilliant account but, quite apart from the composer's insight, it brings an obvious advantage in including the vocal parts in the fourth dance. *Sosostris's aria* makes another good concert item, but the soloist, Alfreda Hodgson, like the chorus, is balanced much too far behind the orchestra. The *Praeludium* is a sustained ceremonial piece, marked by sharp contrasts of dynamic and texture, wayward and distinctive. The *Prince Charles suite* offers another example of Tippett's occasional music, idiosyncratically bringing together echoes of Elgar, Vaughan Williams and Holst in a very Tippett-like way. With warm, atmospheric recording this is more than just an invaluable document.

Symphonies Nos. (i) *1–2;* (ii; iii) *3; 4; Suite for the birthday of Prince Charles.*
(M) *** Decca 425 646-2 (3) [id.]. (i) LSO, C. Davis; (ii) Chicago SO, Solti; (iii) Heather Harper.

All the symphonies have previously been available separately, the *First* and *Third* on Philips, the

Second on Argo and the *Fourth* on Decca. The Polygram merger permits all four to be accommodated in a box of three CDs. The transfers are splendidly vivid.

Symphony No. 4; (i) *Byzantium.*
☞ *** Decca Dig. 433 668-2 [id.]. (i) Faye Robinson; Chicago SO, Solti.

Byzantium, written to celebrate Sir Georg Solti's 30-year association with the Chicago orchestra, is an extended setting for soprano of the Yeats poem of that name. This is Tippett at his most exotic, responding vividly to the words; and the live recording (made in Carnegie Hall, New York, at one of the first performances) can hardly be faulted. Faye Robinson, taking over from Jessye Norman at the last minute, gives a radiant performance, triumphantly breasting the problems of the often stratospheric and angular vocal-line; equally, Solti draws brilliant, responsive playing from the orchestra. It is apt to have Tippett's *Symphony No. 4* as coupling, another work written for, and played by, Solti and the Chicago orchestra, though most Tippett devotees will already have this 1981 recording.

String quartet No. 4.
*** ASV Dig. CDDCA 608; *ZCDCA 608* [id.]. Lindsay Qt – BRITTEN: *Quartet No. 3.* ***

Tippett's *Fourth Quartet* develops even more rigorously the birth-to-death theme of his *Fourth Symphony,* written at about the same time. The emotional core lies in the slow and still abrasive movement which comes third, bringing no easy solution. The Lindsay Quartet give a powerful, deeply committed reading of music far thornier than the late Britten *Quartet* with which it is coupled. Fine, vivid recording, with the players presented rather close, so that playing noises sometimes intrude.

String quartet No. 5.
☞ *** ASV Dig. CDDCA 879 [id.]. Lindsay Qt (with BROWN: *Fanfare to welcome Sir Michael Tippett;* MORRIS: *Canzoni ricertati;* PURCELL: *3 Fantasias;* WOOD: *String quartet ***).

Tippett's *Fifth Quartet,* first heard in 1992, marks a return to a less dense, more lyrical style after the earlier eruptions of his vigorous, creative Indian summer during his seventies and early eighties. It is in two large-scale movements, the first fantasia-like in its rapid changes of mood, but with sonata-form overtones; the second consciously echoing the great *Heilige Dankgesang* of Beethoven's *Quartet* Op. 132, a visionary, meditative movement which leads to a strong, affirmative close. The Lindsay Quartet, for whom the piece was written, give a passionately committed performance. The other varied items are designed as a pendant to the Tippett, music by composers with whom he is associated, from Purcell, always a strong influence, to Christopher Brown from a young generation, paying tribute in a vigorous fanfare. R. O. Morris and Charles Wood were Tippett's teachers, both represented in beautifully crafted quartet pieces, the one a pair of contrasted fugal movements, the other a crisp, four-movement work with echoes of Irish folksong and dance-rhythms, a most attractive piece. Excellent, full-bodied sound.

Piano sonatas Nos. 1 (Fantasy sonata); 2–4.
*** CRD Dig. CRD 34301; *CRDC 4130/1* (2) [id.]. Paul Crossley.

Paul Crossley has been strongly identified with the Tippett sonatas; he recorded the first three for Philips in the mid-1970s: indeed, No. 3 was written for him. The *Fourth* and most recent (1983–4) started life as a set of five bagatelles. Crossley contributes an informative and illuminating note on the sonata and its relationship with, among other things, Ravel's *Miroirs;* his performance has all the lucidity and subtlety one would expect from him. These masterly accounts are matched by truthful and immediate sound-quality on CD, with chrome cassettes of high quality.

VOCAL MUSIC

A Child of our time (oratorio).
*** Collins Dig. 1339-2. Robinson, Walker, Garrison, Cheek, CBSO Ch. & SO, composer.
☞ *** Chan. Dig. CHAN 9123 [id.]. Haymon, Clarey, Evans, White, L. Symphony Ch., LSO, Hickox.
**(*) Ph. 420 075-2 [id.]. Norman, J. Baker, Cassilly, Shirley-Quirk, BBC Singers, BBC Ch. Soc., BBC SO, C. Davis.

Sir Michael Tippett in his mid-eighties may not secure the best-disciplined performance on record of this earliest of his oratorios, but it is generally the most moving. The spirituals which punctuate the story like chorales in a Bach Passion have a heart-easing expressiveness, warmly idiomatic, while the lightness and resilience of *Nobody knows* allows the syncopations to be pointed with winning jazziness. Next to Sir Colin Davis's taut, tough reading on Philips this may be relatively slack, taking a full five minutes longer overall, but the Collins sound is fuller and warmer than that of rival versions. The soloists are placed well forward, an outstandingly characterful team of singers specially associated with Tippett's music. On the whole this must be counted first choice.

Hickox's version of Tippett's oratorio, *A Child of our time*, establishes its place against severe competition largely through the exceptionally rich recording and its distinctive choice of soloists, a quartet of black singers. Not only do Cynthia Haymon, Cynthia Clarey, Damon Evans and Willard White make the transitions into the spirituals (used in the way Bach used chorales) seem all the more natural, their timbres all have a very sensuous quality. The London Symphony Chorus, though not at its most incisive, sings well, responding to Hickox's warmly expressive style, often even more expansive than the composer himself on his recent recording.

Sir Colin Davis on Philips, though more detached in style with a much older recording, offers a more sharply focused performance with by far the finest quartet of soloists. Davis's speeds tend to be on the fast side, both in the spirituals (taking the place which Bach gave to chorales) and in the other numbers. He may miss some of the tenderness; by avoiding all suspicion of sentimentality, however, the result is incisive and very powerful, helped by excellent solo and choral singing. The CD transfer of 1975 analogue sound is full and atmospheric.

The Ice-break.
*** Virgin/EMI Dig. VC7 59048-2 [id.]. Sylvan, Harper, Wilson-Johnson, Page, Tear, Clarey, Randle, L. Sinf., Atherton.

The Ice-break is presented here more as a modern dramatic oratorio than as an opera. Characteristically full of ideas, it is a work for which the listener can readily provide the imaginary settings. The music has the physical impact characteristic of later Tippett, but with less of the wildness that developed in his works of the 1980s. Centrally in Act II comes a lament for one of the principal black characters, the nurse Hannah (beautifully sung by Cynthia Clarey). In its bald simplicity that solo provides a vital, touching moment of repose, warmly emotional, to contrast with the tensions of a plot that centres on the Cold War period, with violence, racial conflict and student demonstrations part of the scheme. David Atherton directs an electrically tense performance, with the American baritone, Sanford Sylvan, singing superbly in the central role of Yuri, a second-generation immigrant, set against Heather Harper as his mother, Nadia, full-voiced and characterful, and David Wilson-Johnson as Lev, the father who in the first scene arrives after 20 years of prison and exile. The single disc comes boxed with libretto and excellent notes by Meirion Bowen.

The Mask of Time.
☞ (M) *** EMI Dig. CMS7 64711-2 (2) [id.]. Robinson, Walker, Tear, Cheek, BBC Singers, BBC Ch., BBC SO, Andrew Davis.

The Mask of Time is a piece bursting with exuberant invention. There is richness, generosity and overwhelming vigour in this 'Seven Days of Creation for a Nuclear Age', astounding in a composer who was nearing eighty when he wrote it. With his BBC forces, Andrew Davis brilliantly clarifies and sharpens the ever-busy score, and the fine discipline brings out a creative, purposeful control behind the wildness, while the poetry of the piece emerges the more intensely, culminating in the lovely setting for soprano and humming chorus of lines by Anna Akhmatova in *Hiroshima, mon amour*. The final wordless chorus then projects the role of music into eternity, under the title, *The singing will never be done*. Davis draws incandescent singing from the BBC Symphony Chorus and attendant professionals. The quartet of soloists is also outstanding, three of them in the original Boston performance. No finer recording has ever been made in the difficult acoustics of the Royal Festival Hall. This is most welcome, back in the catalogue at mid-price.

King Priam (complete).
*** Decca 414 241-2 (2) [id.]. Tear, Allen, Bailey, Palmer, Minton, Langridge, Robert, Harper, L. Sinf. Ch., L. Sinf., Atherton.

In this superb performance under David Atherton, with an outstanding cast and vivid, immediate recording, the power of Tippett's opera, offbeat as the treatment often is, both musical and dramatic, comes over from first to last. Norman Bailey, thanks to his long association with Wagner, sounds agedly noble to perfection. Robert Tear is a shiningly heroic Achilles and Thomas Allen a commanding Hector, vocally immaculate, illuminating every word.

Tishchenko, Boris (born 1939)

Symphony No. 5.
*** Olympia OCD 213 [id.]. USSR MoC SO, Rozhdestvensky.

Boris Tishchenko's *Fifth Symphony* was composed in 1976, the year of Shostakovich's death; and it pays tribute to Shostakovich not only in the various quotations but at a deeper level; throughout these strong resonances Tishchenko still speaks his own language. A powerful document, this is played with enormous conviction by the Ministry of Culture Symphony Orchestra under Gennady Rozhdestvensky, and is vividly recorded.

Tomasi, André (1901–71)

Trumpet concerto.
(*) Sony MK 42096 [id.]. Wynton Marsalis, Philh. O, Salonen – JOLIVET: *Concertos.* *

Like the Jolivet couplings, this is essentially crossover music, if with a neo-classical flavour. The structure is chimerical, but not without spontaneity and, with Wynton Marsalis offering scintillating bravura throughout and an easy affinity with the swiftly changing moods, the result is quite attractive. In playing time, however, this issue is singularly ungenerous.

Tomkins, Thomas (1572–1656)

The Great service (No. 3); Anthems: Know you not; Oh, that the salvation; O Lord, let me know mine end; Organ voluntaries: in A; in C; in G.
☞ *** CRD Dig. CRD 3467; *CRDC 4167* [id.]. New College, Oxford, Ch., Edward Higginbottom; David Burchell.

The Great service (No. 3); When David heard; Then David mourned; Almighty God, the fountain of all wisdom; Woe is me; Be strong and of a good courage; O sing unto the Lord a new song; O God, the proud are then risen against me.
*** Gimell Dig. CDGIM 024; *1585T-24* [id.]. Tallis Scholars, Phillips.

Tomkins is a madrigalist and fluent contrapuntist in the Elizabethan manner who found his highest fulfilment in church music like the magnificent examples contained on this Gimell disc. The *Great Service*, in no fewer than ten parts, sets the four canticles – *Te Deum, Jubilate, Magnificat* and *Nunc dimittis* – with a grandeur rarely matched, using the most complex polyphony. The following motets bring comparable examples of his mastery. *When David heard*, the best known, is beautifully contrasted with the more agonizing lament, *Then David mourned*, with its clashing dissonances. These complex pieces bring the flawless matching and even tone for which the Tallis Scholars are celebrated, and with recording to match. Admirers of previous Gimell issues will enjoy these, but it is a pity that the choir's manner remains constant and the pulse generally even through settings of some of the most glorious texts in the English language. Surely *O sing unto the Lord a new song* should bring some clearer expression of joy.

Many will prefer the more direct and throatier style of the Choir of New College, Oxford; even if the choral sound (recorded in the chapel of New College) is less sharply defined, the effect is very satisfying and real. The service is given added variety by the inclusion of three organ voluntaries, well if not strikingly played by David Burchall. What makes this record especially attractive is the inclusion of three of Tomkins' most beautiful anthems. The treble solos in *Know you not* and *Oh, that the salvation* are ravishingly done, and the alto soloist in *O Lord, let me know mine end* is hardly less impressive.

Tomlinson, Ernest (born 1924)

An English overture; 3 Gaelic sketches: Gaelic lullaby. Kielder Water; Little serenade; Lyrical suite: Nocturne. Nautical interlude; 3 Pastoral dances: Hornpipe. Silverthorne suite; 2nd Suite of English folk dances; Sweet and dainty. arr. of Coates: *The fairy coach; Cinderella waltz.*
*** Marco Polo Dig. 8.223413 [id.]. Slovak RSO (Bratislava), the composer.

Ernest Tomlinson's orchestral pieces charm by the very lightness of their being, with scoring as frothy as lace. The delicately winning *Little serenade*, which opens the disc, is the most famous, but the gentle, evocative *Kielder Water*, the captivating *Canzonet* from the *Silverthorn suite* and the *Nocturne* are hardly less appealing. *Love-in-a-mist* is as intangible as it sounds, with the most fragile of oboe solos, and it is not surprising that *Sweet and dainty* has been used for a TV commercial. Of course there is robust writing too, in the *Folk song suite* – but not too robust, although the jolly *English*

Overture begins with *Here's a health unto His Majesty* and certainly does not lack vitality. The arrangements of music from Eric Coates's *Cinderella phantasy*, commissioned for a BBC Christmas radio play, even brought forth a Leroy Anderson-style galop called *The fairy coach*. The music is played with much grace and the lightest possible touch by the remarkably versatile Slovak Radio Orchestra under the composer, and the vivid recording has delightfully transparent textures, so vital in this repertoire.

Tosti, Francesco (1846–1916)

Songs: *L'alba separa della luce l'ombra; Aprile; 'A vucchella; Chanson de L'adieu; Goodbye; Ideale; Malia; Marechiare; Non t'amo; Segreto; La serenata; Sogno; L'ultima canzone; Vorrei morire.*
(M) *** Ph. 426 372-2. José Carreras, ECO, Muller.

Tosti (knighted by Queen Victoria for his services to music) had a gently charming lyric gift in songs like these, and it is good to have a tenor with such musical intelligence – not to mention such a fine, pure voice – tackling once-popular trifles like *Marechiare* and *Goodbye*. The arrangements are sweetly done, and the recording is excellent.

Tubin, Eduard (1905–82)

(i) *Balalaika concerto; Music for strings; Symphony No. 1.*
*** BIS Dig. CD 351 [id.]. (i) Sheynkman; Swedish RSO, Järvi.

The opening of the *First Symphony* almost puts one in mind of Bax, and there is a Sibelian breadth; but for the most part it is a symphony apart from its fellows. The quality of the musical substance is high; its presentation is astonishingly assured for a young man still in his twenties; indeed, the scoring is quite masterly. Emanuil Sheynkman's account of the *Balalaika concerto* with Neeme Järvi is first class, both taut and concentrated. Excellent recording.

(i) *Ballade for violin and orchestra;* (ii) *Double-bass concerto;* (i) *Violin concerto No. 2; Estonian dance suite; Valse triste.*
*** BIS Dig. CD 337 [id.]. (i) Garcia; (ii) Ehren; Gothenburg SO, Järvi.

Tubin's highly imaginative *Double-bass concerto* has an unflagging sense of momentum and is ideally proportioned; the ideas never outstay their welcome and one's attention is always held. The *Second Violin concerto* has an appealing lyricism, is well proportioned and has a strong sense of forward movement. The *Ballade* is a work of gravity and eloquence. *Valse triste* is a short and rather charming piece, while the *Dance suite* is the Estonian equivalent of the *Dances of Galánta*. Splendid performances from both soloists in the *Concertos* and from the orchestra under Järvi throughout, and excellent recording.

Symphonies Nos. 2 (The Legendary); 6.
*** BIS CD 304 [id.]. Swedish RSO, Järvi.

The opening of the *Second Symphony* is quite magical: there are soft, luminous string chords that evoke a strong atmosphere of wide vistas and white summer nights, but the music soon gathers power and reveals a genuine feeling for proportion and of organic growth. If there is a Sibelian strength in the *Second Symphony*, the *Sixth*, written after Tubin had settled in Sweden, has obvious resonances of Prokofiev – even down to instrumentation – and yet Tubin's rhythmic vitality and melodic invention are quietly distinctive. The Swedish Radio Symphony Orchestra play with great commitment under Neeme Järvi, and the engineers have done a magnificent job.

Symphonies Nos. 3; 8.
*** BIS Dig. CD 342 [id.]. Swedish RSO, Järvi.

The first two movements of the wartime *Third Symphony* are vintage Tubin, but the heroic finale approaches bombast. The *Eighth* is his masterpiece; its opening movement has a sense of vision and mystery, and the atmosphere stays with you. This is the darkest of the symphonies and the most intense in feeling, music of real substance and importance. Järvi and the Swedish orchestra play it marvellously and the recording is in the demonstration bracket.

Symphonies Nos. (i) *4 (Sinfonia lirica);* (ii) *9 (Sinfonia semplice); Toccata.*
⊛ *** BIS Dig. CD 227 [id.]. (i) Bergen SO, (ii) Gothenburg SO, Järvi.

The *Fourth* is a highly attractive piece, immediately accessible, the music well argued and expertly crafted. The opening has a Sibelian feel to it but, the closer one comes to it, the more individual it seems. The recording comes from a concert performance and has an exceptionally well-behaved audience. The *Ninth Symphony* is in two movements: its mood is elegiac and a restrained melancholy permeates the slower sections. Its musical language is direct, tonal and, once one gets to grips with it, quite personal. If its spiritual world is clearly Nordic, the textures are transparent and luminous, and its argument unfolds naturally and cogently. The playing of the Gothenburgers under Järvi is totally committed in all sections of the orchestra. The performances are authoritative and the recording altogether excellent.

Symphony No. 5 in B min.; Kratt (ballet suite).
*** BIS Dig. CD 306 [id.]. Bamberg SO, Järvi.

The *Fifth* makes as good a starting point as any to investigate the Tubin canon. Written after he had settled in Sweden, it finds him at his most neo-classical; the music is finely paced and full of energy and invention. The ballet suite is a work of much character, tinged with folk-inspired ideas and some echoes of Prokofiev.

Symphony No. 7; (i) Concertino for piano and orchestra; Sinfonietta on Estonian motifs.
*** BIS Dig. CD 401 [id.]. (i) Roland Pöntinen; Gothenburg SO, Järvi.

The *Seventh* is a marvellous work and it receives a concentrated and impressive reading. As always with Tubin, you are never in doubt that this is a real symphony which sets out purposefully and reaches its goal. The ideas could not be by anyone else and the music unfolds with a powerful logic and inevitability. Neeme Järvi inspires the Gothenburg orchestra with his own evident enthusiasm. The *Concertino for piano and orchestra* has some of the neo-classicism of the *Fifth Symphony*. Roland Pöntinen gives a dashing account of the solo part. The *Sinfonietta* is a fresh and resourceful piece, a Baltic equivalent of, say, Prokofiev's *Sinfonietta*, with much the same lightness of touch and inventive resource. Superb recording – a quite indispensable disc.

Symphony No. 10; (i) Requiem for fallen soldiers.
*** BIS Dig. CD 297 [id.]. Gothenburg SO, Järvi; (i) with Lundin, Rydell, Hardenberger, Lund Students' Ch., Järvi.

Tubin's *Requiem*, austere in character, is for two soloists (a contralto and baritone) and male chorus. The instrumental forces are merely an organ, piano, drums, timpani and trumpet. The simplicity and directness of the language are affecting and the sense of melancholy is finely controlled. The final movement is prefaced by a long trumpet solo, played here with stunning control and a masterly sense of line by the young Håkan Hardenberger. It is an impressive and dignified work, even if the quality of the choral singing is less than first rate. The *Tenth Symphony* is a one-movement piece that begins with a sombre string idea, which is soon interrupted by a periodically recurring horn call – and which resonates in the mind long afterwards. The recordings are absolutely first class and in the best traditions of the house.

(i; iii) *Ballade; Capricci Nos. 1 & 2; The Cock's dance; Meditation; 3 Pieces; Prelude.* (i) *Sonata for unaccompanied violin.* (i; iii) *Violin sonatas Nos. 1 & 2; Suite of Estonian dance tunes; Suite on Estonian dances.* (ii; iii) *Viola sonata; Viola sonata* (arr. of *Alto saxophone sonata*).
☞ *** BIS Dig. CD 541/542 (2) [id.]. (i) Leibur; (ii) Vahle; (iii) Rumessen.

Nearly 2½ hours of music here, much of it well worth investigating. The early music, the *Three Pieces* and the *Meditation*, show Gallic sympathies, perhaps inherited from Tubin's master, Heino Eller, and the two suites, one from 1944 and the much later second, for solo violin, are closer to the world of Bartók and Kodály. Although the smaller pieces are finely wrought, Tubin seems to come into his own on a larger canvas. Particularly impressive are the *Second Violin sonata* (*In the Phrygian mode*), which comes from the period of the *Fifth Symphony*, the visionary *Second Piano sonata*, and the two sonatas for viola, one a transcription of the alto-saxophone sonata with its foretaste of the *Sixth Symphony* (1954) in which that instrument plays a prominent, almost soloistic role, and the later *Viola sonata* (1965). There is a sense of momentum and organic continuity, and traces of Prokofiev's influence are still faintly discernible. As so often with Tubin's non-symphonic music, there is much of interest to reward the listener. Highly accomplished and cultured performances from Arvo Leibur and Petra Vahle, and exceptionally thorough documentation from the pianist Vardo Rumessen, with over 40 music-type examples. The recording is truthful, but the acoustic lends a shade too much resonance to the piano, which is often bottom-heavy. Admirers of this important composer will want this set and should acquire it, though newcomers to Tubin's music should start with one of the symphonies – Nos. 4 or 5.

Complete piano music: *Album leaf; Ballad on a theme by Maat Saar; 3 Estonian folk-dances; 4 Folksongs from my country; A little march for Rana; Lullaby; 3 Pieces for children; Prelude No. 1; 7 Preludes; Sonatas Nos. 1–2; Sonatina in D min.; Suite on Estonian shepherd melodies; Variations on an Estonian folk-tune.*
*** BIS Dig. CD 414/6 [id.]. Vardo Rumessen.

Tubin's first works for piano inhabit a world in which Scriabin, Ravel and Eller were clearly dominant influences but in which an individual sensibility is also to be discerned. The resourceful *Variations on an Estonian folk-tune* is a lovely work that deserves a place in the repertoire, as does the *Sonatina in D minor*, where the ideas and sense of momentum are on a larger scale than one would expect in a sonatina. The *Second Sonata* is a key work in Tubin's development. It opens with a shimmering figure in free rhythm, inspired by the play of the aurora borealis, and is much more concentrated than his earlier piano works. Vardo Rumessen makes an excellent case for it and it is impressive stuff. The performances are consistently fine, full of understanding and flair, and the recording is very natural.

OPERA

Barbara von Tisenhusen.
☞ *** Ondine Dig. ODE776-2 (2). Raamat, Sild, Kuusk, Puurabar, Ants Kollo, Estonian Op.
    Company & O, Peeter Lilje.

Tubin served his musical apprenticeship in the 1930s and early '40s in the Vanemuine Theatre in Tallinn, and it is quite clear that he has a real feeling for theatre. He left his native Estonia in 1944 and spent the rest of his life in exile in Sweden. He was however invited back to Tallinn in the mid-1960s for a production of his ballet, *Kratt* ('The Goblin'), and it was during this visit that the Estonian company commissioned *Barbara von Tisenhusen*. His libretto, adapted by Jaan Kross from a short story by the Finnish-born writer, Aino Kallas, concerns illicit passion. The opera is not long, consisting of three Acts of roughly 30 minutes each. It has pace and variety of dramatic incident and musical textures, and the main roles in the action are vividly characterized. The musical substance of the opera is largely based on a chaconne-like figure of nine notes heard at the very outset, yet the theme changes subtly and skilfully to meet the constantly shifting dramatic environment so that the casual listener will probably not be consciously aware of the musical means Tubin is employing. All the singers are dedicated and serve the composer well and, though the orchestra is not first class, it too plays with spirit and enthusiasm under Peeter Lilje. The recording produces a sound comparable to that of a broadcast relay rather than the opulent sound one can expect from a commercial studio recording. A strong recommendation.

The Parson of Reigi; (i) *Requiem for fallen soldiers.*
☞ *** Ondine Dig. ODE783-2 (2). Maiste, Eensalu, Tônuri, Kuusk, Estonian Op. Company & O,
    Paul Mägi; (i) Urve Tauts; Talevaldis Deksnis, Urmas Leiten; Rein Tiido, Rein Roos, Estonian
    Nat. Male Ch., Eri Klas.

After the success of *Barbara von Tisenhusen* in 1968, the Estonian Opera immediately commissioned Tubin to compose another. The result was *The Parson of Reigi*, which was composed in 1971, between the *Ninth* and *Tenth Symphonies*. Like *Barbara von Tisenhusen*, *The Parson of Reigi* is relatively short (82 minutes) and it, too, turns for its inspiration to Aino Kallas. It also concerns an illicit relationship. Tubin's music powerfully evokes the claustrophobic milieu of a small, closely knit fishing community and is particularly successful in conveying atmosphere. The dawn scene where the parson, Lampelius, blesses the departing fishermen is particularly imaginative, as is the evocation of the white summer nights in the Garden scene, where the heroine confesses her illicit passion. As in the case of *Barbara von Tisenhusen*, Tubin's powers of characterization of both the major and supporting roles are striking, and there is a compelling sense of dramatic narrative as well as variety of pace. The performance of the three principal singers is very good – especially the parson, splendidly sung by the baritone, Teo Maiste – and the only let-down is in the quality of the orchestral playing, which is little more than passable. For all its simplicity of plot, *The Parson* makes effective musical theatre and, though the invention is not quite of the same quality as its predecessor, its acquaintance is well worth making.

The *Requiem for Fallen Soldiers* has a strange history: it was begun in 1950, but Tubin encountered one of those creative blockages that affect many artists and put it to one side after completing the first section. He returned to it only in the late 1970s, almost 30 years later, conducting its first performance in 1981. This is its second recording and it is generally to be preferred to the rival account on BIS coupled with the *Tenth Symphony* (see above). The Estonian singers produce better focused and darker tone than their Swedish colleagues, though the BIS recording has some amazingly lyrical playing by Håkan Hardenberger. The Estonian player, Urmas Leiten, is very eloquent too. Strongly recommended.

Turina, Joaquin (1882–1949)

Danzas fantásticas, Op. 22; La procesión del Rocio, Op. 9; Ritmos, Op. 43; Sinfonia sevillana, Op. 23.
*** BMG/RCA Dig. RD 60895 [09026 60895-2]. Bamberg SO, Antonio de Almeida.

La procesión del Rocio (1913) was Turina's first great success in picaresque Spanish tone-painting, corruscating with *seguidilla* and *garrotín* dance-rhythms. We are more than familiar with the three equally exotic *Danzas fantásticas* (1918), with the opening shaft of bright sunlight of *Exaltación* leading to chimerical mood-changes, and evening bells in *Ensueño*. The closing *Orgía*, for all its flamenco vigour, later also brings dreamlike imagery of floral perfumes drifting on the night air. The three-movement *Sinfonia sevillana* is no less descriptive, beginning with a *Panorama*, then suggesting the river which runs through the centre of Seville and ending with an exuberant *Fiesta*. *Ritmos* (1928), subtitled '*Fantasia coreografica*', is a series of sharply characterful vignettes, ear-tickling in their tunefulness and the diversity of their orchestral palette. The Bambergers clearly relish the southern sunshine, balmy nocturnal breezes and glittering flamenco dances and, with Almeida directing persuasively, they respond with distinction to this evocative repertoire. The recording too is spacious, with the necessary resonance hardly clouding the more garish tuttis and bringing lustrously transluscent strings and glowing wind.

La Oración del Torero (version for string orchestra).
☞ *** Chan. Dig. CHAN 9288 [id.]. I Musici di Montréal, Yuli Turovsky – SHCHEDRIN: *Carmen ballet suite* etc. ***

The composer's string-orchestral version of the haunting *Oración del Torero* is warmly and sensitively played and very well recorded here, and if the quartet version is even more subtle (see below) this makes an enjoyable foil for Shchedrin's brilliant arrangement of music from Bizet's *Carmen*.

CHAMBER MUSIC

La Oración del Torero.
*** Collins Dig. 1267-2 [id.]. Britten Qt – CHERUBINI; VERDI: *Quartets.* ***

Turina's seductively gentle evocation was conceived with lutes in mind, but quartet playing of this calibre makes the string medium seem exactly right for the music, and brings a refined ravishing of the senses. The performance is full of lush Andalusian atmosphere, yet has an element of restraint and never becomes over-ripe, helped by superb recording and a most sympathetic acoustic. The '*delicadisimo*' close is quite magical.

Piano trios Nos. 1, Op. 35; 2, Op. 76; Circulo, Fantasia for piano trio, Op. 91.
*** Calig. Dig. CAL 50902 [id.]. Munich Piano Trio.

Turina's *First Piano trio* comes from the mid-1920s and maintains a delicate balance between national Spanish elements and classical forms: prelude and fugue, theme and variations and so on. The Munich Piano Trio have plenty of temperament and make the most of character contrasts without ever exaggerating them. Although neither the *Second Piano trio* (1933) nor the later *Circulo* (1936) is a masterpiece, both are well wrought and the latter has some very appealing ideas. Both works are persuasively presented by this ensemble.

Turnage, Mark-Anthony (born 1960)

Greek (opera; complete).
☞ *** Argo Dig. 440 368-2. Quentin Hayes, Richard Suart, Fiona Kimm, Helen Charnock, Greek Ens., Bernas.

Based on Steven Berkoff's play of the same name, Turnage's opera, *Greek*, is out to shock at all costs, beginning with a spoken introduction from the central character, Eddy, rich in vulgarities. This is the Oedipus myth freely adapted to the East End of London ('Eddy-pus' you might deduce), and Turnage says of his first contact with Berkoff's work, 'Nothing prepared me for the exhilarating shock I felt on seeing this amazingly original playwright/director/actor. His combination of poetry, humour and physical theatre is incendiary.' The opera aims to reflect that, and it scored an immediate success at the Munich Biennale of 1988, where it won the opera prize. Later, at the Coliseum in London its impact was a little blunted by the size of the theatre, but here on disc one can both identify the words more clearly and follow more exactly the plan of the two crisply structured Acts, each lasting just under 40 minutes. The colour and energy of Turnage's writing, violently dissonant with copious percussion, is brilliantly caught. The unprepared listener may resist at first, but Turnage with his echoes of popular music and his element of lyricism is a powerful communicator. What comes out less well than on stage is the humour, which seems heavy-handed, though the parody of a music-hall duet for Mum and Dad at the end of Act I has plenty of wit. Quentin Hayes has all the impact needed as the central rough diamond, with Richard Suart as Dad, Fiona Kimm as Wife and Helen Charnock as Mum all singing with bite and conviction, tackling not just those roles but incidentals too. On a single disc with libretto and notes, it can be strongly recommended to the adventurous.

Tye, Christopher (c. 1505–c. 1572)

Mass: Euge bone; Peccavimus patribus nostris.
*** Proudsound Dig. PROUCD 126; *PROU 126* [id.]. Clerkes of Oxenford, David Wulstan –
    SHEPPARD: *Collection.* ***

Christopher Tye was a clerk at King's College, Cambridge, before moving on to Ely Cathedral in the 1540s. Mass settings of the period were often based on a setting of a votive antiphon, using the opening to provide a motto for each Mass section. Tye's *Euge bone* belongs to this genre. It is a work of great beauty; it is sung here with characteristic tonal sophistication by the Clerkes of Oxenford under David Wulstan, and splendidly recorded in a spacious but not over-reverberant acoustic.

Vals, Francisco (1665–1747)

Missa Scala Aretina.
☞ **(*) HM/BMG Dig. 05472 77277-2 [id.]. Mieke van der Sluis, David Cordier, John Elwes,
    Netherlands Bach Festival Bar. Ch. & O, Leonhardt – BIBER: *Requiem in F min.* **(*)

Francisco Vals, another name to spring suddenly out of the past, was choirmaster at Barcelona Cathedral, and the *Missa Scala Aretina* (1702) is the only one of his ten Masses to have gained any kind of fame outside Spain. It is a powerfully expressive piece, with its harmony not always conventional, and is laid out for four separate groups of performers, containing, respectively, the soloists, instrumentalists (including harp in the continuo) and two choral ensembles. Leonhardt delivers a committedly spontaneous performance, but the choral singing does not convey the impression that the Netherlanders are thoroughly at home in the Spanish idiom, nor is it always ideally crisp in ensemble. Nevertheless, with rich recording, this is by no means unimpressive and it certainly is not dull.

Vaňhal, Jan (1739–1813)

(i) *Double bassoon concerto in F; Sinfonias: in A min.; F.*
**(*) BIS CD 288 [id.]. (i) Wallin, Nilsson; Umeå Sinf., Saraste.

The best thing here is the *Concerto*, which is an arresting and inventive piece. The slow movement has real distinction, touching a deeper vein of feeling than anything else on this record. It is not too fanciful to detect in some of the harmonic suspensions the influence of Gluck, with whose music Vaňhal came into contact in the late 1760s. The two *Sinfonias* are less musically developed but far from uninteresting: the minuet of the *F major* has a distinctly 'Sturm und Drang' feel to it: Vaňhal's symphonies may well have paved the way for Haydn at this period; they were certainly given by Haydn while Kapellmeister at the Esterhazy palace. The recording is good, as one has come to expect from this source, even if the acoustic is on the dry side. The playing of the Umeå ensemble is eminently respectable.

Varèse, Edgar (1883–1965)

Ameriques; Arcana; Density 21.5; Intégrales; Ionisation; Octandre; Offrandes.
(M) *** Sony Analogue/Dig. SK 45844 [id.]. Yakar, NYPO, Ens. InterContemporain, Boulez.

In the inter-war period Varèse was regarded as a wild man of the avant-garde in writing a work like *Ionisation* for percussion alone and abandoning conventional argument in favour of presenting blocks of sound. Yet performances like these show what a genius he had – not for assaulting but for tickling the ear with novelty. Boulez brings out the purposefulness of his writing, not least in the two big works for full orchestra, the early *Ameriques* and *Arcana*, written for an enormous orchestra in the late 1920s. Those two works are here played by the New York Philharmonic and are not digitally recorded. The selection recorded more recently in digital sound covers his smaller but just as striking works for chamber ensembles of various kinds, with Rachel Yakar the excellent soprano soloist in *Offrandes*.

Amériques; (i; ii) *Ecuatorial;* (ii) *Nocturnal* (ed. & completed Chou Wen-Chung).
☞ (M) **(*) Van. 08 4031-71 [OVC 4031]. (i) Ariel Bybee; (ii) University Civic Choral Bass Ens.;
 Utah SO, Abravanel (with HONEGGER: *Pacific 231* **).

Varèse is one of the great avant-garde figures of the 1920s. His early scores were remarkably prophetic and they have a phantasmagorical exuberance which puts him well ahead of his many imitators and successors. *Amériques* was written when the composer was still under the spell of his first impressions of New York. Its rhythms are unpredictable and its cross-currents and dissonant colourings suggest the organized chaos of the metropolitan civilization of the twentieth century. The *Nocturnal* was commissioned by the Koussevitzky Foundation, and the composer began it in 1961. But Varèse did not live to finish his music, and it was first performed in an incomplete state. However, the composer also left notes about intended changes, although these are sometimes ambiguous. Chou Wen-Chung has bravely edited the completed portion of the piece and added closing material from the composer's sketches. The result is surprisingly convincing and, although we know where Chou Wen-Chung's section begins, the ear does not detect any sudden drop in intensity or quality. The montage as a whole is much less taut than either of the other works here, but that was to be expected. Like the account of *Amériques*, the performance is not lacking in exuberance and even humour (even if perhaps this is not all intentional). The exotic sounds mix well together from the opening bass chorus: *Wa ya you you*, which is very jungle-like. There are vocal pitch glissandi, moans, and even a direction to the soprano to 'puff'! *Ecuatorial* is a stronger and more directly emotional work, mystical, and based on a high-flown but poetic text by Miguel Asturias. The music in some ways recalls Milhaud's *L'homme et son désir* in creating a background atmosphere suggestive of a tropical jungle. The voices are used with great colouristic imagination. All these performances are most convincing, with the orchestra plainly enjoying themselves, and the characteristically atmospheric Utah acoustic seems ideal for these scores; even if Honegger's picture of a railway engine, which is added as a fill-up, is less well-focused, the sound is never ugly. An important reissue, with texts included.

Vaughan Williams, Ralph (1872–1958)

(i) *Concerto accademico in D min. Fantasia on a theme of Thomas Tallis.*
☞ (M) (***) Dutton mono CDAX 8007 [id.]. (i) Frederick Grinke; Boyd Neel O, Neel – BRITTEN:
 Simple Symphony etc. (***)

The Boyd Neel String Orchestra was formed in the early 1930s and soon established itself as the premier ensemble of its kind in England. In 1936 they made what were the first recordings of the *Tallis fantasia* (in the presence of the composer) and, three years later, the *Concerto accademico* with Frederick Grinke as soloist. Sir Adrian Boult's version with the BBC Symphony Orchestra rather stole its thunder at the time and was better recorded. The *Concerto accademico* has hardly been surpassed and is splendidly fresh and down-to-earth. The *Variations on a theme of Frank Bridge*, with which these works are coupled, is also indispensable. There is nearly always something very special about pioneering recordings in terms of imaginative freshness and communicative intenstiy. Michael Dutton has done a splendid job in restoring these discs, and those who are acquainted with or possess the originals will be astonished at his results. The same applies to the *Simple Symphony*, which they recorded some months later; but it is the hauntingly atmospheric *Tallis fantasia* that resonates in the memory.

Concerto grosso for strings; (i) *Concerto accademico for violin;* (ii) *Oboe concerto;* (iii) *Piano concerto in C;* (iv) *Tuba concerto. Two Hymn-tune Preludes;* (v) *The Lark ascending. Partita for double string orchestra;* (vi) *Towards the unknown region.*
☞ *** Chan. Dig. CHAN 9262/3 [id.]. (i) Sillito; (ii) Theodore; (iii) Shelley; (iv) Patrick Harrild; (v) Michael Davis; (vi) LSO Ch.; LSO, Bryden Thomson.

Chandos offer here as a separate compendium the series of mostly concertante works that were used as fillers for Bryden Thomson's set of the *Symphonies,* and with generous measure and characteristically fine recording this pair of CDs is very attractive. With immaculate LSO string ensemble, the *Concerto grosso* under Thomson's persuasive direction shows how in glowing sound its easy, unforced inspiration can transcend its utilitarian background and bring it close to the world of the *Tallis fantasia.* While many performances of the *Concerto Accademico* make the composer's neo-classical manner sound like Stravinsky with an English accent, Thomson and Sillito find a rustic jollity in the outer movements that is very characteristic of Vaughan Williams and a gentle, withdrawn quality in the slow movement. David Theodore's plangent tones in the *Oboe concerto* effectively bring out the equivocal character of this highly original work, making it far more than just another pastoral piece, sharply emphasizing the contrasts of mood and manner. Howard Shelley addresses the neglected *Piano concerto* with flair and brilliance, making light of the disconcerting cragginess of the piano writing and consistently bringing out both the wit and the underlying emotional power. The bluff good humour of the *Tuba concerto* is beautifully caught in Patrick Harrild's rumbustious account and this outstanding tuba soloist plays with wit and panache, even if the instrument as recorded sounds rather muffled by the resonance. Michael Davis makes a rich-toned soloist in *The Lark ascending,* presenting it as more than a pastoral evocation.The *Hymn-tune Preludes* are unashamedly pastoral in tone; then the *Partita* finds the composer in more abrasive mood, less easily sympathetic. This curiously angular work sounds more convincing in a more purposeful performance than this, but in the *Fantasia* finale – a replacement movement that Vaughan Williams wrote after the rest – Thomson effectively brings out the foretastes of the dark first movement of the *Sixth Symphony,* helped by string timbre with more edge on it than is usual with Chandos. *Towards the unknown region* is the only relative disappointment – a setting of Whitman that antedates the *Sea Symphony.* The choral sound is beautiful, but this early work really needs tauter treatment than Thomson provides.

Concerto grosso; (i) *Oboe concerto. English folksongs suite; Fantasia on Greensleeves; Fantasia on a theme by Thomas Tallis;* (ii) *Romance for harmonica and strings.*
☞ (M) **(*) Decca 440 320-2 [id.]. (i) Celia Nicklin; (ii) Tommy Reilly; ASMF, Marriner.

With the addition of the *Tallis fantasia* to the original collection, this fairly lightweight programme is given added ballast. Celia Nicklin gives a most persuasive account of the elusive *Oboe concerto,* while the *Concerto grosso* is lively and polished. The atmospheric *Romance* is not one of the composer's most inspired works but is still worth having, and the *Folksongs* could hardly be presented more breezily. The *Tallis fantasia* is given a performance at once vital and refined. Here the sound might ideally have had an even greater resonance in the acoustic (though it is by no means studio-ish), but the performance has considerable intensity.

Oboe concerto in A min.; 6 Studies in English folk songs (arr. Carter, for oboe d'amore and strings).
☞ (M) *** Pickwick Dig. MCD 59; *MCC 59* [id.]. Robin Canter, LSO, Judd – R. STRAUSS: *Concerto.* **(*)

Robin Canter gives a first-rate account of Vaughan Williams's elusive *Oboe concerto,* holding its florid cantilena together most convincingly. This is not one of the composer's finest pieces, but Canter makes its gentle pastoral evocation seem more firmly focused than usual. He has arranged the *Folk songs* (originally scored for cello and piano) most persuasively for this new combination, and the performance is equally winning. These settings are most appealing. Excellent recording.

(i) *Oboe concerto. Fantasia on Greensleeves;* (ii) *The Lark ascending.*
☞ (M) *** DG 439 529-2 [id.]. (i) Neil Black; (ii) Zukerman, ECO, Barenboim – DELIUS: *Aquarelles* etc.; WALTON: *Henry V.* ***

Neil Black's creamy tone is particularly suited to Vaughan Williams's *Oboe concerto* and he gives a wholly persuasive performance. Zukerman's account of *The Lark ascending* is full of pastoral rapture – even if perhaps not totally idiomatic, the effect is ravishing. The recordings from the late 1970s have not lost their allure or atmospheric warmth in the digital remastering.

(i) *Oboe concerto. Fantasia on Greensleeves; Fantasia on a theme of Thomas Tallis; Five variants of Dives and Lazarus; The Lark ascending; The Wasps: Overture.*

☞ (M) *** Nimbus Dig. NI 7013 [id.]. (i) Maurice Bourgue; English String O or SO, William Boughton.

Opening with an exuberant account of *The Wasps overture*, this is a very attractive and generous 70-minute collection of favourite Vaughan Williams orchestral pieces, most sympathetically played under William Boughton and presented amply and atmospherically. The spacious acoustic of the Great Hall of Birmingham University ensures that the lyrical string-tune in the overture is properly expansive without robbing the piece of bite, and that both the deeply felt *Tallis fantasia*, with its passionate climax, and *Dives and Lazarus* have a rich amplitude of string-sound. For the former the distanced solo quartet echoes ethereally, as if in a cathedral, and in the *Greensleeves fantasia* the flute solo is nicely distanced. Michael Bochmann, the sympathetic soloist in *The Lark ascending*, playing simply yet with persuasive lyrical freedom is nicely integrated with the warm orchestral backing. More questionable is the *Oboe concerto*, with the superb French soloist, Maurice Bourgue, balanced too close. Nevertheless Bourgue's playing, sharply rhythmical and with a rich, pastoral timbre, makes a good case for a comparatively neglected piece.

(i) *Concerto for 2 pianos in C; Symphony No. 5 in D.*

☞ (B) *** Virgin/EMI Dig. VC5 61105-2 [id.]. (i) Ralph Markham, Kenneth Broadway; RPO, Sir Yehudi Menuhin.

Vaughan Williams's arrangement of his thornily inspired *Piano concerto* of 1931 for two pianos and orchestra has never sounded so convincing as here, thanks to the inspired duo of Ralph Markham and Kenneth Broadway, making light of the technical problems of piano writing that rarely fits under the fingers and gives few lyrical rewards. In the *Fifth Symphony* Sir Yehudi Menuhin, rather than dwelling on pastoral Englishry, takes a thrustful, purposefully symphonic view, with little lingering yet with warm expressiveness in each movement and with climaxes pressed home with satisfying power. It is an individual version, superbly recorded. Now reissued on the Virgo bargain label, this CD becomes even more attractive.

Piano concerto in C.

☞ *** Lyrita SRCD 211 [id.]. Howard Shelley, RPO, Handley – FOULDS: *Dynamic triptych.* ***

The heavyweight piano textures and thorny counterpoint (whether Bach-like or Hindemithian) led the composer to revise his *Piano concerto* of 1931 as a two-piano concerto, in which form it has been recorded (see above). This was the first recording of the *Concerto* in solo form, not quite as originally written, because the definitive score, published not too long before this Lyrita record was made and giving the alternatives of one or two pianos, opts for ending with a serene coda instead of the original brief dispatching coda of ten bars. That is certainly an improvement, and the wonder is that, though the solo piano writing is hardly pianistic, the very challenge to as fine an exponent as Shelley brings out an extra intensity to a highly individual work, written when Vaughan Williams was at the peak of his powers, at the time of *Job* and just before the *Fourth Symphony*. Despite the thick textures, there is lightheartedness in much of the writing, whether the urgently chattering *Toccata* or the *Alla tedesca* which emerges out of the toughly chromatic fugue of the finale. Since this record was made, Shelley has re-recorded the piece digitally for Chandos (see below), but that is coupled with the *Ninth Symphony*, and many may find the stimulating Foulds coupling on Lyrita even more enticing. Certainly the 1984 recording is very impressive in its remastered form, well up to this label's usual high standard.

(i) *Piano concerto; Symphony No. 9 in E min.*

*** Chan. Dig. CHAN 8941; *ABTD 1537* [id.]. (i) Howard Shelley, LPO, Bryden Thomson.

Perhaps the most strikingly original of the three movements of the *Piano concerto* is the imaginative and inward-looking *Romanza*, which has some of the angularity of line one finds in *Flos campi*, while the finale presages the *Fourth Symphony*. The piece abounds in difficulties of the most demanding nature, which Howard Shelley addresses with flair and brilliance. He makes light of the disconcerting cragginess of the piano writing and consistently brings out both the wit and the underlying emotional power. Bryden Thomson conducts a powerful performance of the last of Vaughan Williams's symphonies. Though the playing may not be as crisply incisive as that on Previn's 1971 version with the LSO, it brings out an extra warmth of expression. Both performances are greatly helped by the richness and weight of the Chandos sound, warmly atmospheric but with ample detail and a fine sense of presence.

(i) *Violin concerto in D min.;* (ii) *Flos campi.*

(M) (***) EMI mono CDH7 63828-2. (i) Yehudi Menuhin, LPO; (ii) William Primrose (viola), Philh. O; Boult – WALTON: *Viola concerto* etc. (***)

Though the 1946 mono sound inevitably limits the atmospheric beauty of *Flos campi*, this première recording of a masterpiece brings revelatory playing from Primrose, as well as deeply understanding conducting from Boult. The recording, made in 1952 but never issued at the time, is limited; but with excellent CD transfers and equally valuable Walton works as a generous coupling, this is a historic CD to cherish.

English folksongs suite; Fantasia on Greensleeves; In the Fen Country; (i) *The Lark ascending; Norfolk rhapsody No. 1;* (ii) *Serenade to music.*

(M) *** EMI CDM7 64022-2 [id.]. LPO, LSO or New Philh. O, Sir Adrian Boult; (i) with Hugh Bean; (ii) 16 soloists.

All the music here is beautifully performed and recorded. Hugh Bean understands the spirit of *The Lark ascending* perfectly and his performance is wonderfully serene. The transfers are fresh and pleasing; in the lovely *Serenade* (which Boult does in the original version for 16 soloists) the voices are given greater presence.

English folksongs suite; Toccata marziale.

(BB) *** ASV CDQS 6021. London Wind O, Denis Wick – HOLST: *Military band suites* etc. ***

As in the Holst suites, the pace of these performances of the original scores is attractively zestful, and if the slow movement of the *English folksongs suite* could have been played more reflectively, the bounce of *Seventeen come Sunday* is irresistible.

English folksongs suite; Sea songs (march).

☞ (M) *** EMI Dig. CDM5 65122-2. Central Band of the RAF, Wing Commander Eric Banks – HOLST: *Suites;* GRAINGER: *Lincolnshire posy* etc.

Both these works were written for military band – and how well they sound here! The solo playing in the darkly atmospheric central movement of the suite, *Intermezzo* (*My bonny boy*), is specially sensitive. This movement is quite haunting in its original scoring, conjuring up an impression of mist drifting over the lowland Fen country. The marches have great spirit and ebullience, and the recording is first class in every way.

Fantasia on Greensleeves; Fantasia on a theme of Thomas Tallis.

(B) **(*) Pickwick Dig. PCD 930; *CIMPC 930* [id.]. LSO, Frühbeck de Burgos – ELGAR: *Cello concerto.* ***

Though Frühbeck is rather heavy-handed in his treatment of these Vaughan Williams favourites, the playing of the LSO is refined and the recording first rate.

Fantasia on Greensleeves; Fantasia on a theme by Thomas Tallis; Five variants on 'Dives and Lazarus'; In the Fen Country; (i) *The Lark ascending. Norfolk rhapsody No. 1.*

☞ **(*) Argo Dig. 440 116-2 [id.]. New Queen's Hall O, Barry Wordsworth; (i) with Hagai Shaham.

The re-formed New Queen's Hall Orchestra (the original title is associated with Sir Henry Wood and his early Promenade Concerts) is an authentic group with a difference. They concentrate on late-nineteenth-century and early-twentieth-century repertoire, playing instruments in use at the turn of the century. The stringed instruments use gut rather than steel strings, brass instruments have a narrow bore, reedy French bassoons are favoured rather than the mellower, fatter-timbred German instrument, and wooden flutes are preferred to metal ones. The horns are genuine French *cors* and not the more elaborate (and more reliable) German double horns. *Portamento* is featured in the string style but here it is applied very judiciously, and for the most part the ear notices the fuller, warmer sonority of the violins, the treble less brilliant in attack. In works like the *Tallis fantasia* and *Dives and Lazarus* one can readily wallow in the richly refined textures, but Wordsworth's performance of *Tallis* misses the final degree of intensity at the climax, and the opening of *Dives and Lazarus* is also rather relaxed, even indulgent, in relishing the sheer breadth of sonority achieved, though the closing pages are ethereally lovely. For *The Lark ascending*, Hagai Shaham is placed within the orchestra and she plays very gently, displaying a rather recessive personality. Although the effect has a simple, serene beauty, the rapt intensity of the closing solo passage (which both Christopher Warren-Green and Iona Brown capture radiantly) is here rather subdued. The performers are at their finest in the evocative opening of the *Norfolk rhapsody*, while *In the Fen Country* has a fine idyllic ardour, with some very sensitive playing from wind and brass in the coda. The Argo recording, made in the

Walthamstow Assembly Hall, is splendidly expansive and natural, and we await other CDs from this source with great interest.

Fantasia on Greensleeves; Fantasia on a theme by Thomas Tallis; (i) The Lark ascending.
☞ ⊛ (M) *** Virgin/EMI Dig. CUV5 61126-2 [id.]. (i) Christopher Warren-Green; LCO, Warren-Green – ELGAR: *Introduction and allegro* etc. *** ⊛

Fantasia on Greensleeves; Fantasia on a theme of Thomas Tallis; Five variants of Dives and Lazarus; (i) Flos Campi.
(M) *** Van. 08.4053.71 [OVC 4071]. (i) Sally Peck, Utah University Ch.; Utah SO, Maurice Abravanel.

Christopher Warren-Green and his London Chamber Orchestra give a radiant account of *The Lark ascending*, in which Warren-Green makes a charismatic solo contribution, very free and soaring in its flight and with beautifully sustained true pianissimo playing at the opening and close. For the *Tallis fantasia*, the second orchestra (2.2.2.2.1) contrasts with the main group (5.4.2.2.1) and here, though the effect is beautifully serene, Warren-Green does not quite match the ethereal, other-worldly pianissimo that made Barbirolli's reading unforgettable. But that is a minor quibble; the performance overall has great ardour and breadth, almost to match the coupled *Introduction and allegro* of Elgar in its intensity. The recording, made at All Saints' Church, Petersham, is quite ideal in its resonant warmth and atmosphere, yet has good definition. This is an altogether superb disc.

On Vanguard *Greensleeves* is slow and gracious, and there are more passionate versions of the *Tallis fantasia* available; but the noteworthy point is the way Abravanel catches the inner feeling of the music. Both here and in *Dives and Lazarus* the full strings create a gloriously rich sonority. Sally Peck, the violist, is placed with her colleagues rather than as a soloist in *Flos Campi* (following the composer's expressed intention), yet her personality still emerges well. Abravanel, always a warm, energetic conductor, displays real understanding, allowing the music to relax as it should in this evocation of the Song of Solomon, but never letting it drag either. The CD transfer is excellent, retaining the naturalness of the original recording.

Fantasia on a theme by Thomas Tallis.
☞ (M) **(*) EMI Dig. CDM7 54407-2 [id.]. City of L. Sinfonia, Hickox – ELGAR: *Introduction and allegro* **(*); WALTON: *Sonata for strings.* ***

Although recorded in a church (St Augustine's, Kilburn), the comparatively close microphones bring a sound-picture less than ideally atmospheric for Richard Hickox's new version of the *Tallis Fantasia*. Fine playing and no lack of ardour, but the Barbirolli and Warren-Green versions are more evocative.

Fantasia on a theme of Thomas Tallis; Five variants of Dives and Lazarus; In the Fen Country; Norfolk rhapsody.
*** Chan. Dig. CHAN 8502; *ABTD 1212* [id.]. LPO, Bryden Thomson.

Boult recorded *In the Fen Country* and the *Norfolk rhapsody* successfully, but neither is otherwise available in modern digital sound. Bryden Thomson is a thoroughly persuasive guide in all this repertoire, and in the other two pieces more than holds his own with most of the opposition.

(i) *Fantasia on a theme by Thomas Tallis; Five variants of Dives and Lazarus; Norfolk rhapsody No. 1;*
(ii) *In Windsor Forest;* (i; iii) *Towards the Unknown Region.*
☞ (M) *** EMI CDM5 65131-2 [id.]. (i) CBSO; (ii) Bournemouth Symphony Ch. & Sinf.; (iii) with CBSO Ch.; Norman Del Mar.

Norman Del Mar's strong and deeply felt account of the *Tallis fantasia* is given a splendid digital recording, with the second orchestral group creating radiant textures. The direct approach, however, lacks something in mystery, and not all of the ethereal resonance of this haunting work is conveyed. The early (1907) cantata, *Towards the Unknown Region*, set to words of Walt Whitman, and *In Windsor Forest*, which the composer adapted from his Falstaff opera, *Sir John in love*, makes a perfect coupling. The movements are not always exact transcriptions from the opera, for the composer rethought and amplified certain passages. Norman Del Mar directs warmly sympathetic performances, given excellent sound.

Fantasia on Sussex folk tunes for cello and orchestra.
*** BMG/RCA Dig. RD 70800. Lloyd Webber, Philh. O, Handley – DELIUS: *Cello concerto;* HOLST: *Invocation.* ***

The *Fantasia on Sussex folk tunes* has lain neglected since its first performance by Casals, and it proves something of a discovery. This is a highly appealing work, most persuasively performed too. The recording is first class.

Five variants of Dives and Lazarus; (i) The Lark ascending.
☞ (M) *** Decca 440 325-2 [id.]. (i) Iona Brown, ASMF, Marriner – BUTTERWORTH: *Banks of green willow* etc.; WARLOCK: *Capriol suite* etc. ***

Iona Brown is second to none in her beautiful (1972) account of *The Lark ascending*, and the account of *Dives and Lazarus* has comparable intensity and refinement. With excellent transfers, this generous collection in Decca's 'British Classics' series readily reflects the excellence of the (originally Argo) recordings.

Five variants of Dives and Lazarus; (i) The Lark ascending; The Wasps: Overture and suite.
(M) *** EMI Dig. CD-EMX 9508; *TC-EMX 2082*. (i) David Nolan; LPO, Handley.

The immediacy of the recording allows no mistiness in *The Lark ascending*, but it is still a warm, understanding performance. The overture is spaciously conceived and it leads to charming, colourful accounts of the other, less well-known pieces in the suite, tuneful and lively. The *Five Variants of Dives and Lazarus* is superbly played and recorded. The sound is fresh and clear, if rather brightly lit.

Job (A masque for dancing)
*** Collins Dig. 1124-2 [id.]. Philh. O, Wordsworth – HOLST: *The Perfect Fool*. ***

Job (A masque for dancing); Variations for orchestra (orch. Jacob).
*** EMI Dig. CDC7 54421-2 [id.]. Bournemouth SO, Richard Hickox.

The claims of Barry Wordsworth's version are strong, even in competition with the excellent accounts of Richard Hickox and Vernon Handley (the latter currently withdrawn but to be reissued shortly, with extra music added). The Collins recording is the brightest and fullest of all, spectacularly vivid and with tremendous impact in some of the great brass passages. Though, relatively speaking, Wordsworth misses some of the music's hushed intensity, his is the most warmly expressive reading, with excellent playing from the Philharmonia. Typically he characterizes Job's comforters more positively than his rivals, making the saxophone solo whine and sneer. With a comparably colourful Holst coupling, this will for many be a first choice.

Richard Hickox conducts a strong and spacious account of Vaughan Williams's biblical ballet-score, warmly recorded. In its fine pacing it brings out the spiritual intensity of the music, while presenting dramatic contrasts at full power. The coupling is a welcome rarity. The composer scored it for brass band, but here it is given in the fine orchestral arrangement by Gordon Jacob, a fresh and colourful little work, sharply structured.

The Lark ascending.
☞ *** BMG/RCA 09026 61700-2 [id.]. Anne Akiko Meyers, Philh. O, Andrew Litton –
MENDELSSOHN: *Violin concerto*. ***

Meyers' opening brings a pianissimo of breathtaking intensity, instantly established by the Philharmonia strings under Andrew Litton and matched by the soloist. Even next to a sensitive, if small-scale reading of the Mendelssohn *Concerto*, the Vaughan Williams takes priority, for the raptness of Miss Meyers' playing is magnetic, and Andrew Litton – who from the start of his career has shown what sympathy he has for British music – makes the most understanding accompanist. The atmospheric intensity of the performance is enhanced by the vividly full-bodied recording, built on a very solid bass; and the refinement of sound, with the violin set naturally rather than spotlit, is equally impressive in the other items, all most sympathetically done.

(i) *Suite for viola and orchestra;* (ii) *Flos campi;* (iii) *Hymn-tune preludes Nos. 1 & 2; Overture: The poisoned kiss; The running set.*
(M) **(*) Chan. CHAN 6545 [id.]. Bournemouth Sinf., (i) with Riddle, cond. Del Mar, (ii) with Ch.;
(iii) cond. Hurst.

The *Suite* is lightweight but engaging, unpretentious music to be enjoyed, with its charming *Carol* and quirky *Polka mélancolique*. Frederick Riddle is an eloquent soloist, even if the playing is not always technically immaculate, and Norman Del Mar directs sympathetically. The overture to the opera *The poisoned kiss* is merely a pot-pourri, but it is presented most persuasively here. *The running set* is an exhilarating fantasy on jig rhythms. Fine performances under George Hurst.

SYMPHONIES

Symphonies Nos. 1–9.
☞ **(*) Chan. Dig. CHAN 9087/91 [id.]. LSO, Thomson (with Yvonne Kenny, Brian Rayner Cook
in *No. 1*; Kenny in *No. 3*; Catherine Bott in *No. 7*; London Symphony Ch. in *Nos. 1 & 7*).

Symphonies Nos. 1–9 (complete); *Fantasia on Greensleeves; Fantasia on a theme of Tallis; Norfolk
rhapsody No. 1; 5 Variants of Dives and Lazarus.*
☞ (M) **(*) BMG/RCA 09026 61460-2 (6) [id.]. Philh. O, Slatkin.

By omitting the various fillers, Chandos have fitted the nine Vaughan Williams symphonies on to five
CDs; each work is offered without a break. However, Bryden Thomson's achievement is somewhat
uneven through the cycle. In the *Sea Symphony* the chorus lacks the sharpest focus and the
microphone is not kind to Brian Rayner Cook, the baritone soloist. In the *Pastoral Symphony* the
orchestral sound is almost too tangible, losing some of the more gentle atmospheric feeling, and this
applies also to the *Sinfonia Antartica*. Generally there is no lack of power, and the readings certainly
have both individuality and warmth and, of course, the advantage of modern, digital recording. But
in the last resort both Previn and Boult have more to say and greater insights to express in this music.
    Leonard Slatkin, following in the footsteps of André Previn in the earlier VW cycle for RCA,
shows consistent sympathy for the idiom. Like the composer himself in his surviving recordings,
Slatkin prefers speeds faster than usual, and that makes the central symphonies of the cycle less
warmly expressive and less atmospheric than some rivals, but the earliest and, notably, the last
symphonies find Slatkin at his finest. His achievement in this cycle is above all to demonstrate that
the last three symphonies make a worthy conclusion, unconventionally but tellingly symphonic. Fine
playing and generally full, atmospheric recording. The six CDs are offered for the price of four.

A Sea Symphony (No. 1).
(M) **(*) EMI Dig. CD-EMX 2142. Rodgers, Shimell, Liverpool PO Ch., RLPO, Handley.
(BB) *** Virgin/EMI Dig. VJ7 59687-2. Margaret Marshall, Stephen Roberts, London Symphony
    Ch., Philh. O, Richard Hickox.
☞ (BB) (***) Belart mono 450 144-2. Baillie, Cameron, LPO Ch. & O, Boult.
*** EMI Dig. CDC7 49911-2 [id.]. Lott, Summers, LPO Ch. LPO, Haitink.
(M) *** BMG/RCA GD 90500 [60580-2-RG]. Harper, Shirley-Quirk, London Symphony Ch.,
    LSO, Previn.
(M) *** EMI CDM7 64016-2 [id.]. Armstrong, Carol Case, LPO Ch., LPO, Boult.
☞ *** BMG/RCA Dig. 09026 61197-2 [id.]. Benita Valente, Thomas Allen, Philh. Ch. & O,
    Leonard Slatkin.

Vernon Handley conducts a warmly idiomatic performance, which sustains relatively slow speeds
masterfully. The reading is crowned by Handley's rapt account of the slow movement, *On the beach
at night alone*, as well as by the long duet in the finale, leading on through the exciting final ensemble,
Sail forth, to a deeply satisfying culmination in *O my brave Soul!*. Joan Rodgers makes an
outstandingly beautiful soprano soloist, with William Shimell drier-toned but expressive. The recording, full and warm, presents problems in its extreme dynamic range, while placing the two soloists
rather distantly. Yet to have such a performance in modern digital sound on a mid-price issue is self-
recommending.
    Richard Hickox directs a strong, warmly expressive reading. His relatively brisk speeds and his
ability to mould melodic lines with an affectionate rubato – notably with the bright-toned, finely
drilled London Symphony Chorus – never sounds breathless, and he relishes the sea-sounds that
Vaughan Williams gives to the orchestra. Margaret Marshall is a bright, fresh soprano soloist, but
Stephen Roberts lacks some of the weight needed for the baritone solos, thoughtful and well detailed
as his singing is. Nevertheless this is a genuine bargain.
    As a performance, Boult's (early 1952) Decca mono recording with outstanding soloists and
incisive and sympathetic singing from the LPO Choir has never been surpassed. However diffuse the
argument may be, conveyed here is the kind of urgency one normally gets only at a live performance.
The realistic presence of the dramatic opening has not lost its power to astonish. Boult was at his
most inspired. This newly transferred Belart CD makes the very most of the master tape, and only
the lack of body of the massed upper strings betrays the age of the original. The choral sound is full
and well focused and the Kingsway Hall acoustic spacious and warm; the closing section, *Away O
soul*, is particularly beautiful.
    As in the rest of his Vaughan Williams series, Bernard Haitink takes what to traditional English
ears may seem a very literal view, not at all idiomatic but strong and forthright. Speeds are almost all

unusually spacious, making this (at well over 70 minutes) the slowest version on record; but Haitink sustains that expansive manner superbly. It is the nobility of the writing, rather than its emotional warmth, that is paramount. The recording is the fullest and weightiest yet given to this work, with the orchestra well defined in front of the chorus. Felicity Lott and Jonathan Summers are both excellent.

Previn does not always relax, even where, as in the slow movement, he takes a rather measured tempo. The finale similarly is built up over a longer span, with less deliberate expressiveness. The *Epilogue* may not be so deliberately expressive, but it is purer in its tenderness and exact control of dynamics. Previn has clear advantages in his baritone soloist and his choir. The rich ambience remains, with the performers set slightly back.

Boult's stereo version demonstrates his affectionate style, drawing consistently expressive but never sentimental phrasing from his singers and players. John Carol Case's baritone does not sound well on disc with his rather plaintive tone-colour, but his style is right, and Sheila Armstrong sings most beautifully. The set has been remastered with outstanding success.

With Slatkin drawing passionate playing and singing from his Philharmonia performers and with Thomas Allen outstanding among the baritones who have tackled this role, the RCA version is a strong contender. This is a work in which Slatkin's ability to lift the folk-like rhythms of the early Vaughan Williams makes for idiomatically expressive results, though he cannot match Handley, for example, in conveying the mystery behind some of these Whitman settings. The bright, clear tones of the soprano soloist, Benita Valente, are marred by an intrusive vibrato, robbing the sound of purity. The recording of the chorus is full and bright, with soloists balanced relatively close.

A London Symphony (No. 2; original score).
☞ (***) Biddulph mono WHL 016 [id.]. Cincinnati SO, Eugene Goossens – WALTON: *Violin concerto* (***) (with Concert (***)).

This is the only recording ever made of the 1920 version of Vaughan Williams's *London Symphony*. That involves three minutes of intensely poetic music, later excised in RVW's definitive 1936 edition. The sessions immediately followed the first recording of the *Violin concerto* with Heifetz in 1941 in which Goossens and the Cincinnati orchestra provided the accompaniment. The coupling (together with other British music) is among the most valuable of all the reissues in the Biddulph catalogue, for the CD transfers are of high quality.

A London Symphony (No. 2).
☞ (M) **(*) EMI CDM5 65109-2 [id.]. Hallé O, Barbirolli – IRELAND: *London overture.* ***

A London Symphony (No. 2); (i) Concerto accademico; The Wasps: Overture.
(M) *** BMG/RCA GD 90501 [60581-2-RG]. LSO, Previn; (i) with James Buswell.

A London Symphony; Fantasia on a theme of Thomas Tallis.
(M) *** EMI CDM7 64017-2. LPO, Boult.
*** EMI CDC7 49394-2 [id.]. LPO, Haitink.

A London Symphony; (i) The Lark ascending.
*** Telarc Dig. CD 80158 [id.]. RPO, Previn; (i) with Barry Griffiths.

A London symphony; The Wasps: Overture.
☞ (BB) *** Naxos Dig. 8.550734. Bournemouth SO, Kees Bakels.

Previn's Telarc version brings an exceptionally spacious reading, marked by a vivid and refined sound-balance, and the slow movement in particular brings a radiant, deeply poetic performance, caressing the ear. The faster movements consistently bring out the conductor's natural idiomatic feeling for this music, with rhythms nicely sprung – not least the sharp syncopations – and with melodies warmly moulded, though without sentimentality. Barry Griffiths' account of *The Lark ascending* is a welcome bonus, but it is not as instinctively rapturous a performance as those by Iona Brown or Warren-Green.

On RCA, though the actual sonorities are subtly and beautifully realized by Previn, the architecture is presented equally convincingly, with the great climaxes of the first and last movements powerful and incisive. Most remarkable of all are the pianissimos which here have great intensity, a quality of frisson as in a live performance. The LSO play superbly and the digitally remastered recording, made in Kingsway Hall, still sounds well with its wide range of dynamic. The fill-ups are welcome, especially James Buswell's fine account of the *Concerto*.

The sound remains spacious on Boult's splendid 1970 version and the orchestral playing is outstandingly fine. The orchestra produces lovely sounds, the playing deeply committed; and criticism is disarmed. With Boult's noble, gravely intense account of the *Tallis fantasia* offered as a coupling, this remains an attractive alternative to Previn. The new CD transfer is remarkably successful.

In jaunty themes Haitink's straight manner at times brings an unexpected Stravinskian quality, and the expansively serene handling of the lovely melodies of the slow movement brings elegiac nobility rather than romantic warmth. In the *Tallis fantasia* the straight rhythmic manners make the result sound somewhat unidiomatic too, but very powerful in its monumental directness. The recording has spectacular range, though it is not quite as transparent or as atmospheric as Previn on Telarc.

The Naxos version of Vaughan Williams's *London Symphony*, coupled with the *Wasps Overture*, is powerful and dedicated. Kees Bakels draws ravishing sounds from the Bournemouth Symphony Orchestra, notably the strings, with the slow movement both warm-hearted and refined, and with pianissimos that have you catching the breath. The problem is the extraordinary range of dynamic in the recording. If you adjust the volume-level for the pianissimo at the start, you are quickly blasted out of your seat by the first fortissimo. A thrilling experience none the less, and throughout this is a performance to stimulate the ear, not least the Scherzo, which is full of atmosphere with VW's clever scoring very nicely realized.

In his 1968 EMI recording of the *London Symphony*, Barbirolli did not quite achieve the intensity of his earlier, Pye version, choosing a more relaxed and spacious approach. In many places this brings a feeling of added authority, as at the end of the first movement where the threads are drawn together with striking breadth. The slow movement gains from the fuller recording but has less passion, while the Scherzo, taken relatively slowly, is more controversial. The powerful finale and finely graduated pages of the Epilogue make considerable amends, and this remains an impressive account.

(i) *A London Symphony (No. 2); Fantasia on Greensleeves; The Wasps Overture;* (ii) *Serenade to music.*

☞ (M) (***) Dutton Laboratories mono CDAX 8004 [id.]. (i) Queen's Hall O; (ii) Isobel Baillie, Stiles Allen, Elsie Suddaby, Eva Turner, Margaret Balfour, Astra Desmond, Muriel Brunskill, Mary Jarred, Heddle Nash, Walter Widdop, Parry Jones, Frank Titterton, Roy Henderson, Robert Easton, Harold Williams, Norman Allin, BBC SO; Sir Henry Wood.

The historic Decca recording of Vaughan Williams's *London Symphony*, with the specially assembled group of musicians designated as the 'Queen's Hall Orchestra', conducted by Sir Henry Wood, brings a most striking discrepancy of pace with modern performances. The first movement alone takes over three minutes less than in most latterday recordings. The not-so-slow introduction may lack mystery but there has never been a more passionate account of the work than this on record, and even with limited dynamic range – no true pianissimo is caught – the hushed intensity of the slow movement is tellingly conveyed in a way that only Barbirolli has since matched in his early stereo recording for Pye. The *Symphony* comes coupled with shorter Vaughan Williams works, *The Wasps Overture, Greensleeves* and, best of all, the original (1938) Columbia recording of the *Serenade to music*, with the 16 soloists specified in the score, a stellar group of quite remarkable distinction. The gently soaring phrase 'of sweet harmony' has never sounded so sweetly angelic as when sung here by Isobel Baillie. The Dutton Laboratory transfers are outstandingly true to the originals.

A London Symphony (No. 2); Fantasia on a theme of Thomas Tallis; Norfolk rhapsody.

☞ **(*) BMG/RCA Dig. 09026 61193-2 [id.]. Philh. O, Slatkin.

Characteristically, Slatkin takes a brisk view of many of the themes of the *London Symphony*, opting for a direct rather than a warmly expressive style. The result is less atmospheric than with many rivals but, more than most, he keeps the work tautly symphonic. The sound is refined but not as immediate as it might be, except with the opulent Philharmonia brass. The coupling is unusual and generous, offering a refined rather than weighty account of the *Tallis Fantasia*, as well as the rare and attractive *Norfolk rhapsody*.

A London Symphony (No. 2); Symphony No. 8 in G min.

☞ (M) *** EMI Dig. CD-EMX 2209; *TC-EMX 2209*. RLPO, Handley.

Vernon Handley gives a beautifully paced and well-sprung reading of the *London Symphony*, not as crisp in ensemble as some and with the sound diffused rather than sharply focused. The result is warmly sympathetic and can be strongly recommended, if the generous coupling of the *Eighth Symphony*, an underestimated work, is preferred.

(i) *A Pastoral Symphony (No. 3); Symphony No. 4 in F min.*

(M) *** BMG/RCA GD 90503 [60583-2-RG]. (i) Heather Harper; LSO, Previn.

(M) *** EMI Dig. CD-EMX 2192. (i) Barlow; RLPO, Vernon Handley.

(i) *A Pastoral Symphony (No. 3); Symphony No. 4 in F min.; Fantasia on Greensleeves.*
☞ **(*) BMG/RCA Dig. 09026 61194-2 [id.]. (i) Linda Hohenfield; Philh. O, Slatkin.

Previn draws an outstandingly beautiful and refined performance from the LSO, the bare textures sounding austere but never thin, the few climaxes emerging at full force with purity undiminished. In the *F minor Symphony* only the somewhat ponderous tempo Previn adopts for the first movement lets it down. But on the whole this is a powerful reading, and it is vividly recorded.

Although Vernon Handley's speeds are relatively fast – as those of his mentor, Boult, tended to be – he has the benefit of refined modern digital recording to help bring out the element of mystery in the *Pastoral Symphony*. The extra bite and warmth of expressiveness in Previn's view brings even greater dividends in the *Fourth Symphony*, when he sustains generally slower speeds. Handley's approach is lighter and less violent. But in a symphony that is less brutal than was originally thought, there is a case for this sympathetic alternative approach.

Taking his cue from the composer's own recording of the *Fourth Symphony*, Slatkin's speeds not just for that violent work but for the elusive *Pastoral Symphony* are consistently on the fast side. In the *Pastoral* it tends to mean – as it did even with Boult – that mystery is lacking and, though the *Fourth* gains in power and urgency, the rhythms are sprung less infectiously. The recording is atmospheric but clearly focused, which helps the *Fourth* more than its predecessor. In this coupling the older, RCA version from Previn and the LSO offers even more powerful, dramatic and evocative performances, with 1960s sound still giving a vivid illusion of presence.

(i) *A Pastoral Symphony (No. 3);* (ii) *Symphony No. 5 in D.*
(M) *** EMI CDM7 64018-2. (i) Margaret Price, New Philh. O; (ii) LPO, Boult.

On EMI, in the *Pastoral Symphony* Boult is not entirely successful in controlling the tension of the short but elusive first movement, although it is beautifully played. The opening of the *Lento moderato*, however, is very fine, and its close is sustained with a perfect blend of restraint and intensity. Boult gives a loving and gentle performance of No. 5, easier and more flowing than most rivals', and some may prefer it for that reason, but the emotional involvement is a degree less intense, particularly in the slow movement. Both recordings have been very successfully remastered.

Symphony No. 4 in F min.
(**) Koch mono 3-7018-2 [id.]. BBC SO, composer – HOLST: *Planets.* (**)

Vaughan Williams made his recording of the *Fourth Symphony* in 1937, not long after the ink had dried on the score. It is a performance of blazing intensity in which he made no attempt to smooth over any rough edges, while the BBC Symphony Orchestra played as if their very lives depended on it. The transfer is less full-bodied than the LP version which appeared in the 1970s (the upper strings are lacking in timbre), but this should not deter collectors from acquiring it, particularly in view of the interest of the coupling.

Symphonies Nos. 4 in F min.; 6 in E min.
(M) **(*) EMI CDM7 64019-2 [id.]. New Philh. O, Sir Adrian Boult.

Symphony Nos. (i) *4 in F min.;* (ii) *6 in E min.;* (i) *Fantasia on a theme by Thomas Tallis.*
☞ (M) (***) Sony mono SMT 58933 [id.]. NYPO, (i) Mitropoulos; (ii) Stokowski.

The recordings of Vaughan Williams's two apocalyptic symphonies made by the New York Philharmonic – No. 4 conducted in 1956 by Dmitri Mitropoulos (in a reading approved by the composer himself) and No. 6 in 1949 by Stokowski (directing with unsentimental thrust) – make a fascinating coupling. As transferred to CD in Sony's mid-price British Heritage series, they sound far better than they ever did on LP. Both demonstrate what idiomatic power and brilliance American players could bring to the composer's two most abrasive symphonies. Stokowski's reading is the more controversial, disconcertingly fast in the slow movement and unpointed in the slow visionary finale. Mitropoulos in a generous fill-up shows equal understanding of the rarefied *Tallis Fantasia.*

In the *Fourth Symphony* Sir Adrian procures orchestral playing of the highest quality from the New Philharmonia, and the slow movement is particularly successful. The recording, too, is first class, and this increases the sense of attack in the first movement of the powerful *Sixth Symphony*. Here, the strange finale is played beautifully, and the atmosphere is not without a sense of mystery, but a greater degree of underlying tension is needed.

Symphony No. 5 in D; The England of Elizabeth: 3 Portraits (arr. Mathieson).
(M) *** BMG/RCA GD 90506 [60586-2-RG]. LSO, Previn.

Symphony No. 5 in D; (i) *Flos campi* (suite).

⊛ (M) *** EMI Dig. CD-EMX 9512; TC-EMX 2112 [Ang. CDM 62029]. RLPO, Handley; (i) with Christopher Balmer & Liverpool Philharmonic Ch.

Vernon Handley's disc is outstanding in every way, a spacious yet concentrated reading, superbly played and recorded, which masterfully holds the broad structure of this symphony together, building to massive climaxes. The warmth and poetry of the work are also beautifully caught. The rare and evocative *Flos campi*, inspired by the Song of Solomon, makes a generous and attractive coupling, equally well played, though the viola solo is rather closely balanced. The sound is outstandingly full, giving fine clarity of texture.

Previn refuses to be lured into pastoral byways. His tempi may be consistently on the slow side, but the purity of tone he draws from the LSO, the precise shading of dynamic and phrasing, and the sustaining of tension through the longest, most hushed passages produce an outstanding performance, very well transferred to CD. Previn's later, Telarc version with the RPO does not match this in raptness and emotional thrust. The *England of Elizabeth suite* is a film score of no great musical interest but is undoubtedly pleasant to listen to.

Symphonies Nos. 5 in D; 6 in E min.
**(*) BMG/RCA Dig. RD 60556 [60556-2-RD]. Philh. O, Leonard Slatkin.

Except in the third movement *Romanza* of No. 5 and the pianissimo finale of No. 6 Slatkin opts for speeds on the fast side, yet with his preference for keeping a very steady beat, he remains a restrained interpreter of RVW. The big climaxes of the *Preludio* in No. 5 and of the *Romanza* lack the emotional weight they can have, and the second movement of No. 6 with its insistent anapaestic interruptions lacks menace. Yet there is still much to enjoy in these performances, with refined and intensely beautiful string playing from the Philharmonia.

Symphony No. 6 in E min.; Fantasia on a theme of Thomas Tallis; (i) *The Lark ascending.*
*** Teldec/Warner Dig. 9031 73127-2 [id.]. (i) Tasmin Little; BBC SO, Andrew Davis.

Andrew Davis's reading of the *Sixth* is taut and urgent, with emotions kept under firm control. The two shorter works which come as supplement are given more warmly expressive, exceptionally beautiful performances, with Tasmin Little an immaculate soloist in *The Lark ascending*. Teldec's wide-ranging sound, setting the orchestra at a slight distance, slightly blunts the impact of the symphony in the first three movements, but then works beautifully in the chill of the hushed pianissimo meditation of the finale, as it does too in the fill-ups.

Symphonies Nos. 6 in E min.; 9 in E min.
(M) *** BMG/RCA GD 90508 [60588-2-RG]. LSO, Previn.

In the first three movements Previn's performance is superbly dramatic, clear-headed and direct, with natural understanding. His account of the mystical final movement with its endless pianissimo is not, however, on the same level, for the playing is not quite hushed enough, and the tempo is a little too fast. The *Ninth* stimulates Previn to show a freshness and sense of poetry which prove particularly thought-provoking and rewarding. The RCA recording is highly successful.

Sinfonia Antartica (No. 7).
*** EMI Dig. CDC7 47516-2 [id.]. Sheila Armstrong, LPO Ch., LPO, Haitink.

(i) *Sinfonia Antartica (No. 7); Five Variations of Dives and Lazarus; Sea songs* (Quick march).
☞ **(*) BMG/RCA Dig. 09026 61195-2 [id.]. (i) Linda Hohenfield; Women of Philh. Ch.; Philh. O, Slatkin.

(i) *Sinfonia Antartica (No. 7); Serenade to music.*
(M) *** EMI Dig. CD-EMX 2173; *TC-EMX 2173.* (i) Alison Hargan; RLPO and Ch., Vernon Handley.

(i) *Sinfonia Antartica (No. 7); The Wasps* (incidental music): *Overture and suite.*
(M) **(*) EMI CDM7 64020-2 [id.]. (i) Sheila Armstrong; LPO, Sir Adrian Boult.

With stunningly full and realistic recording, Haitink directs a revelatory performance of what has long been thought of as merely a programmatic symphony. Based on material from VW's film music for *Scott of the Antarctic*, the symphony is in fact a work which, as Haitink demonstrates, stands powerfully as an original inspiration in absolute terms. Only in the second movement does the 'penguin' music seem heavier than it should be, but even that acquires new and positive qualities, thanks to Haitink.

As in his other Vaughan Williams recordings, Handley shows a natural feeling for expressive rubato and draws refined playing from the Liverpool orchestra. At the end of the epilogue Alison

Hargan makes a notable first appearance on disc, a soprano with an exceptionally sweet and pure voice. In well-balanced digital sound it makes an outstanding bargain, particularly when it offers an excellent fill-up, the *Serenade to music*, though in this lovely score a chorus never sounds as characterful as a group of well-chosen soloists. This can be recommended alongside Haitink but costs much less.

Sir Adrian gives a stirring account and is well served by the EMI engineers. The inclusion of Vaughan Williams's Aristophanic suite, *The Wasps*, with its endearing participation of the kitchen utensils plus its indelibly tuneful *Overture*, is a bonus, although in the *Overture* the upper strings sound a bit thin.

The Slatkin version offers an exceptionally strong and dramatic account of the *Sinfonia Antartica* which, thanks to speeds brisker than usual, notably in the first movement, is presented as a symphonic structure rather than a programme work, just a series of atmospheric sound-pictures. The slow movement may not convey the same chill as other versions, with the cleanly focused recording dispelling mistiness, but the originality of instrumentation adds to a feeling of tautness in the argument, not usually conveyed in this work. The soprano soloist could also sound more mysterious, but she sings with bright, clear tone. The couplings, idiomatically done, are unusual and attractive.

(i) *Sinfonia Antartica (No. 7); Symphony No. 8 in D min.*
(M) *** BMG/RCA GD 90510 [60590-2-RG]. (i) Heather Harper, Ralph Richardson, London Symphony Ch.; LSO, Previn.

In the *Sinfonia Antartica* Previn's interpretation concentrates on atmosphere rather than drama in a performance that is sensitive and literal. Because of the recessed effect of the sound, the portrayal of the ice-fall (represented by the sudden entry of the organ) has a good deal less impact than on Vernon Handley's version. Before each movement Sir Ralph Richardson speaks the superscription written by the composer on his score. Previn's account of the *Eighth* brings no reservations, with finely pointed playing, the most precise control of dynamic shading, and a delightfully Stravinskian account of the bouncing Scherzo for woodwind alone. Excellent recording, which has been opened up by the digital remastering and made to sound more expansive.

Symphonies Nos. 8 in D min.; 9 in E min.
(M) *** EMI CDM7 64021-2 [id.]. LPO, Sir Adrian Boult.

Symphonies Nos. 8 in D min.; 9 in E min.; Flourish for Glorious John.
☞ *** BMG/RCA Dig. 09026 61196 [id.]. Philh. O, Slatkin.

The concluding disc brings a deeply satisfying culmination to Slatkin's Vaughan Williams cycle, arguably the finest of all, brilliantly played and recorded. The *Flourish*, never previously recorded, is a 90-second work that says much more than its brevity might suggest, a tribute to Sir John Barbirolli that seems almost to present the composer's work in microcosm. Both the last two symphonies are seriously underestimated, and Slatkin's bitingly intense performances, adopting speeds faster than usual, give them a tautness that has rarely been appreciated. So the finales of both symphonies prove exceptionally satisfying, not just the bell-like ostinatos of No. 8 but the elusive string-writing of No. 9, which here emerges as a close relation to the visionary slow finale of No. 6. Bright, immediate recording, with more presence than in most of the series, and splendid playing.

Boult's account of the *Eighth* may not be as sharply pointed as Previn's version, but some will prefer the extra warmth of the Boult interpretation with its rather more lyrical approach. The *Ninth* contains much noble and arresting invention, and Boult's performance is fully worthy of it. He draws most committed playing from the LPO, and the recording is splendidly firm in tone. The digital remastering is well up to the high standard EMI have set with these reissues of Boult's recordings.

CHAMBER MUSIC

(i) *Phantasy quintet (for 2 violins, 2 violas & cello); String quartet No. 2 in A min. (For Jean on her birthday);* (ii; iii) *6 Studies in English folk-song for cello and piano;* (iii; iv) *Violin sonata in A.*
☞ (M) *** EMI CDM5 65100-2 [id.]. (i) Music Group of London; (ii) Eileen Croxford; (iii) David Parkhouse; (iv) Hugh Bean.

This collection of relatively little-known chamber works, very well performed and recorded at Abbey Road in 1972/3, can be recommended strongly – and not only to devotees of Vaughan Williams. The *Phantasy quintet* dates from the composer's full maturity in 1912. It is conceived in a compressed one-movement form but falls into four distinct sections: these to be played (attacca) without a break, as advocated by W. W. Cobbett. The ethereal opening is Vaughan Williams at his most ecstatically pastoral in feeling, and the *Alla Sarabanda* third section is also very beautiful. The *Six studies in English folk-song* are highly characteristic, while the *Violin sonata* (1954) is a relatively gawky work but one which, like much later Vaughan Williams, has a tangily distinctive flavour, especially in a performance as fine as this. The *Second quartet*, written between the *Fifth* and *Sixth Symphonies*, was offered as a birthday present to a viola player friend of the composer, Jean Stewart. It contains some strikingly original ideas, notably in the purposefully sombre but bleakly haunting *Largo* with its harmonium-like textures and, in the plangent Scherzo, with its *tremolandos* and *sul ponticello* devices. The performances by the Music Group of London bring out the deeper qualities of both this and the richly scored *Quintet*.

6 Studies in English folksong for clarinet and piano.
*** Chan. Dig. CHAN 8683; *ABTD 1078* [id.]. Hilton, Swallow – BAX: *Sonata* **(*); BLISS: *Quintet*. ***

These *Folksong studies*, which Vaughan Williams published in arrangements for the viola and cello, come from the mid-1920s and are really very beautiful; they are played with the utmost sensitivity by Janet Hilton and Keith Swallow.

VOCAL MUSIC

(i) *10 Blake songs* (for voice and oboe); (ii) *Songs of travel*. Songs: *Linden Lea; Orpheus with his lute; The water mill; Silent noon*.
(M) *** Decca 430 368-2. Robert Tear; (i) Neil Black; (ii) Philip Ledger – BUTTERWORTH: *Shropshire lad*. ***

Robert Tear, recorded in 1972, cannot match Ian Partridge in his wonderfully sensitive account (currently withdrawn) of the *Blake songs*, but his rougher-grained voice brings out a different kind of expressiveness, helped by Neil Black's fine oboe playing. The *Songs of travel*, here presented complete with the five extra songs published later, are also most welcome, as are the other four songs, notably *Silent noon*, added for this reissue. Ledger is a most perceptive accompanist.

(i) *3 Choral hymns (Easter hymn; Christmas hymn; Whitsunday hymn); *(ii) *Communion service in G min.: Sanctus.* (i) *Come down, O love divine.* (ii) *Festival Te deum.* (i) *For all the Saints; O taste and see; Prayer to the Father; Te deum in G; Valiant for truth; We've been awhile a-wandering; Wither's Rocking hymn.*
☞ (M) ** Chan. CHAN 6550 [id.]. (i) Worcester Cathedral Ch., Christopher Robinson; H. Bramma; (ii) Westminster Abbey Ch., Douglas Guest.

A useful if not distinctive collection of Vaughan Williams's shorter choral works. Besides the short *Te Deum* and the *Festival Te Deum*, among the more striking settings is *Valiant for truth*, a much subtler piece than its Salvation Army-like title would suggest. The three *Choral hymns* are spaciously conceived but would have benefited from a recording with more bite. As it is, the sound is atmospheric but not very clear in detail. The performances generally are of a good standard. The documentation provides all the words but no comments about the settings.

Dona nobis pacem; (i) *5 mystical songs.*
*** Chan. Dig. CHAN 8590; *ABTD 1297* [id.]. Wiens, (i) Rayner-Cook, LPO Ch., LPO, Bryden Thomson.

The *Dona nobis pacem* is well performed on this Chandos disc by Edith Wiens and Bryan Rayner-Cook. The latter gives an eloquent account of the much earlier *Five mystical songs*. Bryden Thomson gets playing of total commitment from the London Philharmonic Orchestra. The recording is made in an appropriately resonant acoustic and the orchestral detail registers well.

(i) *Epithalamion;* (ii) *Merciless Beauty.*
☞ (M) *** EMI Dig./Analogue CDM7 64730-2 [id.]. (i) Roberts, Shelley, Bach Ch., LPO, Willcocks; (ii) Langridge, Endellion Qt – *Riders to the sea*. ***

There are no rivals here: none of the three pieces is otherwise available and all are rarities. Vaughan Williams's setting of *Epithalamion* began life as a masque in the late 1930s and, only a year before he died, he expanded it into the coolly lyrical cantata recorded here. Scored for baritone and small orchestra with piano (Howard Shelley quite superb) and solo parts for flute and viola, it is an eloquent and thoroughly characteristic piece. Stephen Roberts gives a beautiful account of it, and Philip Langridge is hardly less impressive in *Merciless beauty*, three much earlier settings for voice and string trio. *Riders to the sea* is also indispensable – see below. This reissue makes a most valuable addition to the Vaughan Williams discography. The first two works were recorded digitally; *Riders to the Sea* is analogue (1970) but sounds equally vivid and well focused. Splendid performances throughout.

(i) *Fantasia on Christmas carols;* (ii) *Flos Campi;* (i) *5 Mystical songs;* (iii) *Serenade to music.*
*** Hyp. Dig. CDA 66420 [id.]. (i) Thomas Allen, (ii) Imai & Corydon Singers; (iii) 16 soloists;
    ECO, Best.

This radiant record centres round the *Serenade to music,* one of the great celebratory works of the
century, specially composed for the jubilee of Sir Henry Wood in 1938. As in the original performance,
sixteen star soloists are here lined up and, though the team of women does not quite match the stars
of 1938 – who included Dame Eva Turner and Dame Isobel Baillie – the men are generally fresher
and clearer. Above all, thanks largely to fuller, modern recording, the result is much more sensuous
than the original, with ensemble better matched and with Matthew Best drawing glowing sounds
from the English Chamber Orchestra. The other items are superbly done too, with Nobuko Imai a
powerful viola soloist in the mystical cantata, *Flos campi,* another Vaughan Williams masterpiece.
Thomas Allen is the characterful soloist in the five *Mystical songs.* Warmly atmospheric sound to
match the performances.

Fantasia on Christmas carols; Hodie.
**(*) EMI Dig. CDC7 54128-2 [id.]. Gale, Tear, Roberts, London Symphony Ch., LSO, Hickox.

Though the three soloists cannot match the original trio in Sir David Willcocks's pioneering version
(on EMI, now withdrawn), Hickox directs a more urgent and more freely expressive reading of the
big Christmas cantata, *Hodie,* helped by more refined and incisive choral singing. As on the earlier
disc, the *Christmas carol fantasia* proves an ideal coupling, also warmly done.

Lord Thou hast been our refuge; Prayer to the Father of Heaven; A vision of aeroplanes.
*** Chan. Dig. CHAN 9019 [id.]. Finzi Singers, Spicer – HOWELLS: *Requiem* etc. ***

These three choral pieces make an apt coupling for the Howells choral works on the Finzi Singers'
disc. *A vision of aeroplanes* improbably but most imaginatively uses a text from Ezekiel.

Mass in G min.; Te Deum in C.
*** Hyp. CDA 66076 [id.]. Corydon Singers, Best – HOWELLS: *Requiem.* ***

Matthew Best and the Corydon Singers give as committed an account of the *Mass* as King's College
Choir and, despite the spacious acoustic, there is admirable clarity of texture.

On Wenlock Edge (song-cycle): orchestral version.
☞ (M) *** Unicorn UKCD 2062 [id.]. Gerald English, W. Australian SO, David Measham –
    IRELAND: *Epic march* etc. ***

(i) *On Wenlock Edge;* (ii) *Songs of Travel* (song-cycles).
☞ (M) *** EMI Dig. CDM7 64731-2 [id.]. (i) Robert Tear; (ii) Thomas Allen, CBSO, Rattle –
    BUTTERWORTH; ELGAR: *Songs.* ***

Vaughan Williams's own orchestration of his famous song-cycle, made in the early 1920s, has been
curiously neglected. It lacks something of the apt, ghostly quality of the version for piano and string
quartet, but some will prefer the bigger scale. Gerald English is very persuasive and the relatively
close recorded balance helps him to project great intensity and ardour. Yet the sound, though
forward, is never unacceptably so and the orchestral texture is full, vivid and very realistically defined
by the CD transfer.
    Orchestral arrangements of two song-cycles originally written for lighter accompaniment make an
attractive and apt coupling on EMI. The more revelatory is the collection of *Songs of travel,* to words
by Robert Louis Stevenson, originally written with piano accompaniment and here discreetly
orchestrated. The orchestral version brings home the aptness of treating the nine songs as a cycle,
particularly when the soloist is as characterful and understanding a singer as Thomas Allen. Only in
1960 was the epilogue song finally published (after the composer's death), drawing together the two
sets of four songs that had previously been published separately. The Housman settings in the other
cycle are far better-known, and Robert Tear – who earlier recorded this same orchestral version with
Vernon Handley and the Birmingham orchestra – again proves a deeply perceptive soloist, with his
sense of atmosphere, feeling for detailed word-meaning and flawless breath control. Warm, understanding conducting and playing, and excellent sound. For the mid-priced reissue the Butterworth and
Elgar songs have been added.

*The Shepherds of the Delectable Mountains; 3 Choral hymns; Magnificat; A Song of thanksgiving;
Psalm 100.*
*** Hyp. Dig. CDA 66569 [id.]. Gielgud, Dawson, Kitchen, Wyn-Rogers, Ainsley, Bowen,
    Thompson, Opie, Terfel, Best, Corydon Singers, L. Oratory Jun. Ch., City of L. Sinf., Best.

With Sir John Gielgud as narrator and Lynne Dawson as the sweet-toned soprano soloist, Best gives *A Song of thanksgiving* a tautness and sense of drama, bringing out the originality of the writing, simple and stirring in its grandeur, not for a moment pompous. The *Magnificat* brings more buried treasure, a massive setting designed not for liturgical but for concert use. With its haunting ostinatos it is closer to Holst's choral music than most Vaughan Williams. The *Three Hymns* and the setting of *Psalm 100* are comparably distinctive in their contrasted ways, and it is good to have a recording of the Bunyan setting, *The Shepherds of the Delectable Mountains*. Most of the solo singing is excellent, and the chorus is superb, helped by warmly atmospheric recording.

Songs of travel; The House of Life (6 sonnets); *4 Poems by Fredegond Shove; 4 Last songs: No. 2, Tired;* Songs: *In the spring; Linden Lea.*
**(*) Chan. Dig. CHAN 8475; *ABTD 1186* [id.]. Benjamin Luxon, David Williams.

Though Benjamin Luxon's vibrato is distractingly wide, the warmth and clarity of the recording help to make his well-chosen collection of Vaughan Williams songs very attractive, including as it does not only the well-known Stevenson travel cycle but the Rossetti cycle, *The House of Life* (including *The Water mill*), as well as the most famous song of all, *Linden Lea.*

The Pilgrim's progress (incidental music, ed. Palmer).
*** Hyp. CDA 66511; *KA 66511* [id.]. Sir John Gielgud, Richard Pasco, Ursula Howells, Corydon Singers, City of L. Sinfonia, Best.

Vaughan Williams had a lifelong devotion to Bunyan's great allegory, which fired his inspiration to write incidental music for a BBC radio adaptation of the complete *Pilgrim's Progress*. Much of the material, but not all, then found a place in the opera. Christopher Palmer has here devised a sequence of twelve movements, which – overlapping with the opera and the *Fifth Symphony* – throws up long-buried treasure. Matthew Best draws warmly sympathetic performances from his singers and players, in support of the masterly contributions of Sir John Gielgud, taking the role of Pilgrim as he did on radio in 1942, and Richard Pasco as the Evangelist.

(i) *5 Tudor Portraits;* (ii) *Benedicte;* (iii) *5 variants of Dives and Lazarus.*
☞ (M) *** EMI CDM7 64722-2 [id.]. (i) Bainbridge, Carol Case, Bach Ch., New Philh. O; (ii) Harper, Bach Ch., LSO; (iii) Jacques O; Willcocks.

Another of EMI's generous reassemblies of fine performances of British music from the analogue era, dating from 1968/9 and playing for 71 minutes. Ursula Vaughan Williams reports in her biography of the composer that the first performance of the *Five Tudor portraits* – in Norwich in 1936 – was remarkable for shocking many of the audience. ('The elderly Countess of Albemarle sat in the front row getting pinker and pinker in the face,' Mrs Vaughan Williams reports; after the old lady had departed, the composer complimented the chorus on its diction.) The composer deliberately chose bawdy words by the early Tudor poet, John Skelton, and set them in his most rumbustious style. This is a good, strong performance, but the soloists are not earthy enough for such music. It is a pity that the humour was not underlined more strongly, but the musical invention is still more than enough to sustain compelling interest, and the digital remastering has brought splendid bite and projection to the chorus without losing too much of the original ambience. The *Benedicte* is another strong work, compressed in its intensity, too brief to be accepted easily into the choral repertory, but a fine addition to the RVW discography. The *Five Variants of Dives and Lazarus* is beautifully played and warmly recorded and adds a touch of serenity and balm after the vigour of the vocal works.

OPERA

Hugh the Drover (complete).
☞ *** Hyp. Dig. CDSA 66901/2 [id.]. Bonaventura Bottone, Rebecca Evans, Sarah Walker, Richard Van Allan, Alan Opie, Corydon Singers & O, Matthew Best.
☞ (M) *** CMS5 65224-2 (2) [id.]. Robert Tear, Sheila Armstrong, Helen Watts, Robert Lloyd, Michael Rippon, Amb. Op. Ch., RLPO, Groves.

Described as a ballad opera, *Hugh the Drover* uses folk-themes with full-throated Puccinian warmth. The Hyperion version in atmospheric digital sound offers the fresher, lighter view, resilient and urgent in the first Act, hauntingly tender in the second. Rebecca Evans is superb as the heroine, Mary, with Bonaventura Bottone an amiable Hugh, only occasionally strained, well supported by a cast of generally fresh young singers. Groves's 1978 version, also very well recorded and well sung by a rather starrier cast led by Sheila Armstrong and Robert Tear, is beefier at more measured speeds – at mid-price an excellent bargain.

The Pilgrim's Progress.
(M) *** EMI CMS7 64212-2 (2). Noble, Burrowes, Armstrong, Herincx, Carol Case, Shirley-Quirk, Keyte, LPO Ch., LPO, Boult.
☞ **(*) RNCM PP1/2 (2) [id.]. Richard Whitehouse, Wyn Griffiths & soloists, Ch. & O of Royal N. Coll. of Music, Igor Kennaway.

What comes out in a recorded performance is that, so far from being slow and undramatic, *The Pilgrim's Progress* is crammed full of delectable ideas one after the other, and the drama of the mind – as in the book – supplements more conventional dramatic incident. John Noble gives a dedicated performance in the central role of Pilgrim, and the large supporting cast is consistently strong. Vanity Fair may not sound evil here, but Vaughan Williams's own recoil is vividly expressed, and the jaunty passage of Mr and Mrs By-Ends brings the most delightful light relief. Boult underlines the virility of his performance with a fascinating and revealing half-hour collection of rehearsal excerpts, placed at the end of the second CD. The outstanding recording quality is confirmed by the CD transfer, which shows few signs of the passing of two decades.

Enterprisingly, in 1992 the Royal Northern College of Music in Manchester presented a staging which effectively brought out the operatic qualities of a work too often dismissed as an oratorio. Happily, they had sound engineers on hand, and the result is this very vigorous and colourful complete recording. The stage-producer at the College, Joseph Ward, was the tenor who sang the role of Lord Lechery in the earlier recording conducted by Sir Adrian Boult.

Obviously student voices cannot match those of the front-rank singers of the 1970s who appear on the earlier recording, now reissued by EMI. There are some odd balances in the sound too, but the vitality is what matters. Richard Whitehouse as the Pilgrim boldly shoulders the weightiest individual burden, but this is an opera in which good teamwork is more important than individual performances, and under Igor Kennaway the young singers and players perform with a dedication that could hardly be more compelling. The two CDs can be obtained direct from the College and are in the mid-price range.

Riders to the sea (opera) complete.
☞ (M) *** EMI CDM7 64730-2 [id.]. Burrowes, M. Price, Watts, Luxon, Amb. S., L. O Nova, Meredith Davies – *Epithalamion; Merciless Beauty*. ***

Riders to the sea is a moving one-Act opera which tells of an Irish woman, Maurya, who has already lost her husband and five sons to the sea. As the narrative begins she foresees the death of her only remaining son, Bartley, who is about to leave on his boat for Galway Fair with his mare and her pony. She is left behind with her two daughters, Cathleen and Nora, and finally comes to terms with the power of the sea and the destiny of her family. The opera is Vaughan Williams's most dramatically effective stage work with a consistently high level of inspiration. It is beautifully performed and recorded, though there is too much wind-machine. All who care about this composer should investigate this record with its equally rare couplings. The analogue recording, clear yet wonderfully atmospheric, approaches the demonstration bracket in its CD format.

Verdi, Giuseppe (1813–1901)

Ballet music, Overtures and Preludes: *Aida* (prelude and ballet); *Un ballo in maschera* (prelude); *La forza del destino* (overture); *Macbeth* (ballet); *Nabucco* (overture); *La Traviata* (Preludes to Acts I & III); *I vespri siciliani* (overture).
*** Collins Dig. 1072-2 [id.]. Philh. O, Jacek Kaspszyk.

All the performances here are first class and have an exhilarating spontaneity. There is drama – *Nabucco* is particularly successful in this respect – and the ballet music has an engaging rhythmic sparkle. What makes this Collins disc especially enjoyable is the full, resonant sound and the realistic balance within the pleasing acoustics of London's Henry Wood Hall.

The Lady and the fool (ballet suite; arr. Mackerras).
☞ (B) *** CfP CD-CFP 4618. LPO, Mackerras – SULLIVAN: *Pineapple Poll*. ***

Mackerras's arrangement of Verdi has not caught the public fancy in quite the way of the coupled *Pineapple Poll*, but the scoring is witty and the music vivacious, and it is very well played and recorded here.

Overtures and Preludes: *Un ballo in maschera* (prelude); *La Battaglia di Legnano; Il Corsaro* (sinfonias); *Ernani* (prelude); *La Forza del destino; Luisa Miller* (overtures); *Macbeth; I Masnadieri* (preludes); *Nabucco* (overture); *Rigoletto; La Traviata* (preludes); *I vespri siciliani* (sinfonia).
(M) *** DG 419 622-2 [id.]. BPO, Karajan.

Make no mistake, this playing is in a class of its own and has an electricity, refinement and authority that sweep all before it. Some of the overtures are little known (*Il Corsaro* and *La Battaglia di Legnano*) and are given with tremendous panache and virtuosity. These are performances of real spirit and are vividly recorded, even if the climaxes could expand more.

Le quattro stagioni (*The four seasons:* ballet from *I vespri siciliani*).
☞ (M) *** Decca 425 052-2 [id.]. Cleveland O, Maazel – RESPIGHI: *Feste romane* etc. ***

Verdi's *Seasons* ballet, written for the Paris Opéra production of *I vespri siciliani*, is a slight but extensive score playing for nearly half an hour. It is not great Verdi but is tuneful and nicely scored. Maazel, who obviously enjoys the music, succeeds in securing first-class playing from the Cleveland Orchestra (listen, for instance, to the oboe at the beginning of *L'estate*) and he is given admirable recorded quality which, though bright, is not clinical and combines detail with atmosphere. A good bonus for some outstanding Respighi performances.

String quartet in E min.
*** Collins Dig. 1267-2 [id.]. Britten Qt – CHERUBINI: *Quartet No. 1;* TURINA: *La Oración del Torero.* ***
*** CRD CRD 3366; *CRDC 4066* [id.]. Alberni Qt – DONIZETTI: *Quartet No. 13;* PUCCINI: *Crisantemi.* ***
**(*) Hyp. Dig. CDA 66317 [id.]. Delmé Qt – R. STRAUSS: *Quartet.* **(*)

A quite outstanding performance of Verdi's only *String quartet* from the Britten group. They match polished energy in the outer movements with much warmth and elegance in the inner ones, particularly the charming Neapolitan serenade theme at the centre of the miniature scherzo. With full, immediate, yet transparent sound this is very impressive indeed.

The Alberni Quartet's performance is also strong and compelling, and it is most imaginatively and attractively coupled with the Puccini and Donizetti pieces.

The Delmé are not a 'high-powered', jet-setting ensemble and they give a very natural performance of the Verdi which will give much pleasure: there is the sense of music-making in the home among intimate friends, and it is refreshingly unforced, even if the sound is just a shade on the dry side.

Requiem Mass.
**(*) Decca 411 944-2 (2) [id.]. Sutherland, Horne, Pavarotti, Talvela, V. State Op. Ch., VPO, Solti.
☞ (M) **(*) BMG/RCA 09026 61403-2 (2) [id.]. L. Price, J. Baker, V. Luchetti, Van Dam, Chicago Symphony Ch. & SO, Solti.
☞ (B) **(*) DG Double 437 473-2 (2) [id.]. Freni, Ludwig, Cossutta, Ghiaurov, V. Singverein, VPO, Karajan.
☞ (M) **(*) Sony SM2K 47639 (2) [id.]. Arroyo, Veasey, Domingo, Raimondi, L. Symphony Ch., LSO, Bernstein.

(i) *Requiem Mass;* (ii) *4 Sacred pieces.*
☞ *** DG Dig. 435 884-2 (2) [id.]. Studer, Lipovšek, Carreras, Raimondi, V. State Op. Ch., VPO, Abbado.
**(*) EMI CDS7 47257-8 (2) [Ang. CDCB 47257]. (i) Schwarzkopf, Ludwig, Gedda, Ghiaurov; (ii) J. Baker; Philh. Ch. & O, Giulini.
(M) (***) DG mono 429 076-2 (2). Stader, Dominguez, Carelli, Sardi, St Hedwig's Cathedral Ch., Berlin RIAS Chamber Ch. & RSO, Fricsay.

(i) *Requiem Mass.* Choruses from: *Aida; Don Carlo; Macbeth; Nabucco; Otello.*
*** Telarc Dig. CD 80152 (2) [id.]. (i) Dunn, Curry, Hadley, Plishka; Atlanta Ch. & SO, Shaw.

The benefits of live recording are tellingly illustrated in Claudio Abbado's Vienna version of the Verdi *Requiem*. Only seven years earlier Abbado had made a studio recording in Milan with forces from La Scala and a starry but variable quartet of soloists. The DG live recording was taken from performances at the Vienna Musikverein with the Vienna Philharmonic and Vienna choirs, as well as an even starrier solo quartet: Cheryl Studer, Marjana Lipovšek, José Carreras and Ruggero Raimondi, all in superb voice and finely matched, even if Carreras has to husband his resources. In detail Abbado's reading is little different, but the sense of presence, of the tension of a live occasion, makes the later account far more magnetic from the hushed murmurings of the opening onwards. The Vienna forces are not only more expressive but more polished too. Abbado maintains fine control even in the great outburst of the *Dies irae*, but with the Vienna recording vividly conveying the massive power and bite of the performance this now must count as the finest of modern digital versions, generously coupled with the *Four Sacred Pieces*, also superbly done in another live recording.

Robert Shaw, in the finest of his Atlanta recordings, may not have quite the same searing electricity as Toscanini's rough old NBC recording, but it regularly echoes it in power and the well-calculated pacing. In the *Dies irae* for example, like Toscanini he gains in thrust and power from a speed marginally slower than usual. With sound of spectacular quality, beautifully balanced and clear, the many felicities of the performance, not least the electricity of the choral singing and the consistency of the solo singing, add up to an exceptionally satisfying reading, more recommendable than those of even the most eminent conductors. Though none of the singers are international stars, their clear, fresh, well-focused voices are beautifully suited to recording, and they make a fine team. The fill-up of five Verdi opera choruses is more colourful, and again brings superb choral singing. An outstanding issue.

What Giulini proves is that refinement added to power can provide an even more intense experience than the traditional Italian approach. In this concept a fine English chorus and orchestra prove exactly right. The array of soloists could hardly be bettered. Schwarzkopf caresses each phrase, and the exactness of her voice matches the firm mezzo of Christa Ludwig in their difficult octave passages. Gedda is at his most reliable, and Ghiaurov with his really dark bass actually manages to sing the almost impossible *Mors stupebit* in tune without a suspicion of wobble. Giulini's set also finds space to include the *Four Sacred pieces* and there is no doubt that in a performance as polished and dramatic as this the element of greatness in these somewhat uneven works is magnified. The CD is successful enough in the *Sacred pieces*; but it tends to emphasize the occasional roughness of the heavy climaxes in the *Requiem*, even though generally the quality is fully acceptable.

Fricsay's live performance, given in 1960, is a commanding account, often at measured speeds but with a biting sense of drama and a gravity that plainly reflect the conductor's own emotions during his last illness. Like him, the two male soloists are Hungarian, and both are first rate, with the tenor, Gabor Carelli, pleasingly Italianate of tone. Maria Stader sings with a pure, clear tone, very occasionally suffering intonation problems. Oralia Dominguez is the fruity mezzo, and the chorus is superbly disciplined, with the mono recording remarkably full and spacious. The *Four Sacred pieces* were also recorded live, but ten years earlier. Fricsay gives another dedicated performance.

There is little or nothing reflective about Solti's Decca account, and those who criticize the work for being too operatic will find plenty of ammunition here. The team of soloists is a very strong one, though the matching of voices is not always ideal. It is a pity that the chorus is not nearly as incisive as the Philharmonia on the EMI set – a performance which conveys far more of the work's profundity than this. But if you want an extrovert performance, the firmness of focus and precise placing of forces in the Decca engineering of 1967 make for exceptionally vivid results on CD.

On RCA, with an unusually sensitive and pure-toned quartet of soloists – Luchetti perhaps not as characterful as the others, Leontyne Price occasionally showing strain – and with superb choral singing and orchestral playing, Solti's 1977 Chicago version has all the ingredients for success. The set is well worth having for Janet Baker's deeply sensitive singing, but the remastered recording – less than ideally balanced – tends to be fierce on climaxes and in sound; and in other ways too, Solti's earlier, Decca/Vienna set is preferable.

Karajan's earlier recording of the *Requiem* has been greatly enhanced in its CD transfer, with the whole effect given greater presence and immediacy. He has a fine team of soloists, too. However, Karajan's reading still smooths over the lines of Verdi's masterpiece. The result is often beautiful, but, apart from the obvious climaxes, such as the *Dies irae*, there is a lack of dramatic bite. However, with two discs offered for the price of one, many collectors may be tempted to try this.

Bernstein's 1970 *Requiem* was recorded in the Royal Albert Hall. By rights, the daring of that decision should have paid off; but with close balancing of microphones the result is not as full and free as one would have expected. Bernstein's interpretation remains marvellously persuasive in its drama, exaggerated at times, maybe, but red-blooded in a way that is hard to resist. The quartet of soloists is particularly strong.

(i; ii) *Requiem Mass;* (iii; iv) *Inno delle nazione;* (ii) *Te Deum;* (iii) *Luisa Miller: Quando le sere al placido.* (iv) *Nabucco: Va pensiero.*

(M) (***) BMG/RCA mono GD 60299; *GK 60299* (2) [60299-RG-2; *60299-RG-4*]. (i) Nelli, Barbieri, Di Stefano, Siepi; (ii) Robert Shaw Ch.; (iii) Jan Peerce; (iv) Westminster Ch.; NBC SO, Toscanini.

Toscanini's account of the *Requiem* brings a supreme performance, searingly intense. The opening of the *Dies irae* has never sounded more hair-raising, with the bass-drum thrillingly caught, despite the limitation of dry mono recording. And rarely has the chorus shone so brightly in this work on record, while the soloists are near-ideal, a vintage team. The other works make fascinating listening, too. The *Te Deum* was one of Toscanini's very last recordings, a performance more intense than usual with this work, and it is good to have the extraordinary wartime recording of the potboiling *Hymn of the Nations*. The *Internationale* is added to Verdi's original catalogue of national anthems, to represent the ally, the USSR.

OPERA

Aida (complete).
(M) *** EMI CMS7 69300-2 (3) [Ang. CDMC 69300]. Freni, Carreras, Baltsa, Cappuccilli, Raimondi, Van Dam, V. State Op. Ch., VPO, Karajan.
*** Decca 417 416-2 (3) [id.]. Leontyne Price, Gorr, Vickers, Merrill, Tozzi, Rome Op. Ch. & O, Solti.
(M) *** Decca 414 087-2 (3) [id.]. Tebaldi, Simionato, Bergonzi, MacNeil, Van Mill, Corena, V. Singverein, VPO, Karajan.
(M) (***) BMG/RCA mono GD 86652 (3) [6652-2-RG]. Milanov, Bjoerling, Barbieri, Warren, Christoff, Rome Op. Ch. & O, Perlea.
(**) EMI mono CDS7 49030-8 (3) [Ang. CDCC 49030]. Callas, Tucker, Barbieri, Gobbi, La Scala, Milan, Ch. & O, Serafin.
☞ (B) (**) Decca mono 440 239-2 (2) [id.]. Tebaldi, Stignani, Del Monaco, Protti, Caselli, Corena, Santa Cecilia Ac., Rome, Ch. & O, Erede.
(M) (**) BMG/RCA mono GD 60300 (3) [60300-RG-2]. Nelli, Gustavson, Tucker, Valdengo, Robert Shaw Ch., NBC SO, Toscanini.

On EMI, Karajan's is a performance of *Aida* that carries splendour and pageantry to the point of exaltation. Yet Karajan's fundamental approach is lyrical. On record at least, there can be little question of Freni lacking power in a role normally given to a larger voice, and there is ample gain in the tender beauty of her singing. Carreras makes a fresh, sensitive Radames, Raimondi a darkly intense Ramphis and Van Dam a cleanly focused King, his relative lightness no drawback. Cappuccilli here gives a more detailed performance than he did for Muti on EMI, while Baltsa as Amneris crowns the whole performance with her fine, incisive singing. Despite some overbrightness on cymbals and trumpet, the Berlin sound for Karajan, as transferred to CD, is richly and involvingly atmospheric, both in the intimate scenes and, most strikingly, in the scenes of pageant, which have rarely been presented on record in greater splendour.

Leontyne Price is an outstandingly assured Aida on Decca, rich, accurate and imaginative, while Solti's direction is superbly dramatic, notably in the Nile Scene. Merrill is a richly secure Amonasro, Rita Gorr a characterful Amneris, and Jon Vickers is splendidly heroic as Radames. Though the digital transfer betrays the age of the recording (1962), making the result fierce at times to match the reading, Solti's version otherwise brings full, spacious sound, finer, more open and with greater sense of presence than most versions since.

On Decca, as on EMI, Karajan was helped by having a Viennese orchestra and chorus; but most important of all is the musicianship and musical teamwork of his soloists. Bergonzi in particular emerges here as a model among tenors, with a rare feeling for the shaping of phrases and attention to detail. Cornell MacNeil too is splendid. Tebaldi's creamy tone-colour rides beautifully over the phrases and she too acquires a new depth of imagination. Among the other soloists Arnold van Mill and Fernando Corena are both superb, and Simionato provides one of the very finest portrayals of Amneris we have ever had in a complete *Aida*. The recording has long been famous for its technical bravura and flair. CD enhances the overall projection, but the brightness on top at times strikes the ear rather too forcibly. Nevertheless this remains a remarkable technical achievement.

All four principals on the historic RCA set are at their very finest, notably Milanov, whose poise and control in *O patria mia* are a marvel. Barbieri as Amneris is even finer here than in the Callas set, and it is good to hear the young Christoff resonant as Ramfis. Perlea conducts with great panache.

The Nile Scene has never been performed more powerfully and characterfully on record than in this vintage La Scala set. Though Callas is hardly as sweet-toned as some will think essential for an Aida, her detailed imagination is irresistible, and she is matched by Tito Gobbi at the very height of his powers. Tucker gives one of his very finest performances on record, and Barbieri is a commanding Amneris. The mono sound is more than acceptable, but this remains at full price.

Decca's 1952 mono *Aida* was one of their earliest Italian opera recordings and it does not show the polish that the Decca producers later developed, although the recording has plenty of stage atmosphere. Tebaldi is solid and reliable, Mario del Monaco is trumpet-like (especially in the ringing *Celeste Aida*) but often coarse. Aldo Protti is an uninspiring Amonasro. That may not sound very tempting but, at its modest reissue price, it is still worth getting – if only for Tebaldi, then at the peak of her vocal form. Just how satisfying her rich reliability can be is clear in *Ritorna vincitor*, where against less than riveting orchestral playing she established a commanding strength, while her radiant *O patria mia* was more secure than in the later, stereo set with Karajan. It is good to have Stignani's Amneris on record. She was past her best and one has to make allowances, but in her big scenes there is still the grand dramatic sweep of a great artist. The Nile scene (once issued separately on a Decca ten-inch mono 'medium-play' LP) has plenty of red-blooded drama and, despite its failure to convey the full brilliance of the Triumphal scene, where Erede could drive harder, the recording comes up remarkably well – there is no thinness of texture and plenty of warmth and atmosphere with the voices vividly and naturally projected.

Toscanini's 1949 performance of *Aida* is the least satisfying of his New York opera recordings. Richard Tucker sings well but makes a relatively colourless Radames, and Herva Nelli lacks weight as Aida, neatly though she sings and with some touching moments. Nancy Gustavson's Amneris lacks all menace, and Valdengo as Amonasro is the only fully satisfying principal. Yet Toscanini is so electrifying from first to last that his admirers will accept the limited, painfully dry recording.

Aida: highlights (scenes & arias).
(M) *** Decca 417 763-2 [id.] (from above set, with Tebaldi, Bergonzi, cond. Karajan).

Aida: highlights.
(M) (***) BMG/RCA mono GD 60201 [60201-2-RG] (from above recording with Milanov, Bjoerling; cond. Perlea).
(M) *** Decca 433 444-2 [id.] (from above recording, with Leontyne Price, Gorr, Vickers, Merrill, Tozzi; cond. Solti).
☞ (M) *(*) EMI CD-EMX 2174. Nilsson, Corelli, Bumbry, Sereni, Giaiotti, Mazzolini, Rome Op. Ch. & O, Mehta.

The selection from the Solti recording is very generous (71 minutes) and would seem an obvious first choice for those wanting a highlights CD from this opera. Nevertheless the alternative Decca compilation called 'Scenes and arias' from John Culshaw's Karajan recording, made during the early stereo era, remains particularly enticing. The RCA highlights disc is valuable above all for providing a sample of one of Milanov's most compelling performances on record, poised and commanding. The EMI highlights come from Mehta's very first opera recording, dating from 1967. Nilsson's Aida is undeniably powerful, but her contribution is one of the only points in favour of the performance. Corelli and Bumbry are both below their best form and Sereni is an unimpressive Amonasro. The selection plays for 65 minutes, and the CD transfer is bright and vivid, but there are better selections of this favourite opera.

Alzira (complete).
*** Orfeo CO 57832 (2) [id.]. Cotrubas, Araiza, Bruson, George, Bonilla, Bav. R. Ch., Munich R. O, Gardelli.

Alzira is the shortest of the Verdi operas, but its concision is on balance an advantage on record. In musical inspiration it is indistinguishable from other typical early operas, with Verdian melodies less distinctive than they became later, but consistently pleasing. Gardelli is a master with early Verdi, and the cast is strong, helped by warm and well-balanced recording supervised by Munich Radio engineers.

Aroldo (complete).
** Sony CD 79328 [M2K 39506] (2). Caballé, Cecchele, Lebherz, Pons, NY Oratorio Soc., Westminster Ch. Soc., NY Op. O, Queler.

Aroldo is Verdi's radical revision of his earlier unsuccessful opera, *Stiffelio*: he translated the story of a Protestant pastor with an unfaithful wife into this tale of a crusader returning from the Holy Land. Less compact than the original, it contains some splendid new material such as the superb aria for the heroine, beautifully sung by Caballé. The final scene too is quite new, for the dénouement is totally different. The storm chorus (with echoes of *Rigoletto*) is most memorable – but so are the rum-ti-tum choruses common to both versions. This recording of a concert performance in New York is lively, though the tenor is depressingly coarse.

Attila (complete).
(M) *** Ph. 426 115-2 (2). Raimondi, Deutekom, Bergonzi, Milnes, Amb. S., Finchley Children's
   Music Group, RPO, Gardelli.

With its dramatic anticipations of *Macbeth*, the musical anticipations of *Rigoletto* and the compression
which (on record if not on the stage) becomes a positive merit – all these qualities, helped by a fine
performance under Gardelli, make this Philips version of *Attila* an intensely enjoyable set. Deutekom,
not the most sweet-toned of sopranos, has never sung better on record, and the rest of the cast is
outstandingly good. The 1973 recording is well balanced and atmospheric.

Un ballo in maschera (complete).
*** Decca Dig. 410 210-2 (2) [id.]. Margaret Price, Pavarotti, Bruson, Ludwig, Battle, L. Op. Ch.,
   Royal College of Music Junior Dept Ch., Nat. PO, Solti.
*** DG Dig. 427 635-2 (2) [id.]. Domingo, Barstow, Nucci, Quivar, Sumi Jo, V. State Op.
   Konzertvereinigung, VPO, Karajan.
*** DG 415 685-2 (2) [id.]. Ricciarelli, Domingo, Bruson, Obraztsova, Gruberová, Raimondi, La
   Scala, Milan, Ch. & O, Abbado.
(M) *** BMG/RCA GD 86645 (2) [6645-2-RG]. L. Price, Bergonzi, Merrill, Grist, Verrett, Flagello,
   RCA Italiana Op. Ch. & O, Leinsdorf.
(M) *** EMI CMS7 69576-2 (2) [Ang. CDMB 69576]. Arroyo, Domingo, Cappuccilli, Grist,
   Cossotto, Howell, ROHCG Ch., New Philh. O, Muti.
☞ (M) **(*) Decca 440 042-2 (2). Tebaldi, Pavarotti, Milnes, Donath, Regina Resnik, Santa Cecilia
   Academy, Rome, Ch. & O, Bartoletti.
☞ (M) (***) BMG/RCA mono GD 60301 (2) [60301-2-RG]. Herva Nelli, Jan Peerce, Robert
   Merrill, Virginia Haskins, Claramae Turner, Nicola Moscona, NBC Ch. & SO, Toscanini.

Shining out from the cast of Solti's set of *Ballo* is the gloriously sung Amelia of Margaret Price in one
of her richest and most commanding performances on record, ravishingly beautiful, flawlessly
controlled and full of unforced emotion. The role of Riccardo, pushy and truculent, is well suited to
the extrovert Pavarotti, who swaggers through the part, characteristically clear of diction, challenged
periodically by Price to produce some of his subtlest tone-colours. Bruson makes a noble Renato,
Christa Ludwig an unexpected but intense and perceptive Ulrica, while Kathleen Battle is an Oscar
whose coloratura is not just brilliant but sweet too. Solti is far more relaxed than he often is on
record, presenting a warm and understanding view of the score. The recording is extremely vivid
within a reverberant acoustic.

Recorded in Vienna early in 1989, *Un ballo in maschera* was Karajan's last opera recording and it
makes a fitting memorial, characteristically rich and spacious, with a cast – if not ideal – which still
makes a fine team, responding to the conductor's single-minded vision. Standing out vocally is the
Gustavo of Plácido Domingo, strong and imaginative, dominating the whole cast. He may not have
the sparkle of Pavarotti in this role, but the singing is richer, more refined and more thoughtful.
Amelia is Josephine Barstow's finest achievement on record, and dramatically she is most compelling.
Leo Nucci, though not as rough in tone as in some of his other recent recordings, is over-emphatic,
with poor legato in his great solo, *Eri tu*. Sumi Jo, a Karajan discovery, gives a delicious performance
as Oscar, the page, coping splendidly with Karajan's slow speed for her Act I solo. Florence Quivar
produces satisfyingly rich tone as Ulrica. Though the sound is not as cleanly focused as in the Decca
recording for Solti, it is warm and full.

Abbado's powerful reading, admirably paced and with a splendid feeling for the sparkle of the
comedy, remains highly recommendable. The cast is very strong, with Ricciarelli at her very finest
and Domingo sweeter of tone and more deft of characterization than on the Muti set of five years
earlier. Bruson as the wronged husband Renato (a role he also takes for Solti) sings magnificently,
and only Obraztsova as Ulrica and Gruberová as Oscar are less consistently convincing. The
analogue recording clearly separates the voices and instruments in different acoustics, which on CD
is distracting only initially and after that brings the drama closer.

The reissued RCA set makes a fine bargain. Leontyne Price is a natural for the part of Amelia,
spontaneous-sounding and full of dramatic temperament. Only in the two big arias does Price for a
moment grow self-conscious. Robert Merrill here seems to have acquired all sorts of dramatic,
Gobbi-like overtones to add to the flow of firm, satisfying tone. Bergonzi is a model of sensitivity,
while Reri Grist makes a light, bright Oscar, and the Ulrica of Shirley Verrett has a range of power,
richness and delicacy coupled with unparalleled firmness that makes this one of her most memorable
recorded performances. Excellent recording, hardly showing its age, with the voices rather forward.

On EMI the quintet of principals is also unusually strong, but it is the conductor who takes first
honours in a warmly dramatic reading. Muti's rhythmic resilience and consideration for the singers

go with keen concentration, holding each Act together in a way he did not quite achieve in his earlier recording for EMI of *Aida*. Arroyo, rich of voice, is not always imaginative in her big solos, and Domingo rarely produces a half-tone, though the recording balance may be partly to blame. The sound is vivid, but no translation is provided for this mid-price reissue.

The main interest in the earlier Decca set rests in the pairing of Tebaldi and Pavarotti. The latter was in young, vibrant voice, but Tebaldi made her recording in the full maturity of her career. Much of her singing is very fine indeed, but there is no mistaking that her voice here is nowhere near as even as it once was. For the command of her performance this is a version well worth hearing and the supporting cast is strong, not only Milnes as Renato and Donath as Oscar, but Resnik a dark-voiced Ulrica. Bartoletti directs the proceedings dramatically, and the (1970) Decca recording remains strikingly vivid and atmospheric.

Un ballo was the very last of the complete operas that Toscanini conducted in New York in concert performance. It was given in Carnegie Hall in January 1954, just three months before the maestro finally retired. Though the performance cannot match in exhilaration his unique reading of *Falstaff*, it stands as one of the most cherishable mementoes of his conducting of Verdi. Speeds are often fast and the control characteristically taut, but it is wrong to think of the performance as rigid, when rubato is often so freely expressive. Fascinatingly, in the quintet, *E scherzo od è follia*, Toscanini encourages Jan Peerce to adopt the extra 'ha-has' that had become traditional, defying the idea that he invariably followed the text strictly.

Peerce misses some of the lightness of the role, clear in diction but not very characterful, yet Toscanini's pointing of rhythm regularly brings out the sharp wit of much of the writing. Herva Nelli, one of Toscanini's favourite sopranos in his last years, here gives one of her finest performances, with a beautiful, finely moulded line in her big numbers, including the two arias. Robert Merrill is superb as Renato, singing magnificently in *Eri tu*, while Claramae Turner is firm as a rock as Ulrica. The sound is typically dry, not at all atmospheric, but clean and well detailed with a good sense of presence.

Un ballo in maschera: highlights.
*** DG Dig. 429 415-2 [id.] (from above complete recording, with Domingo, Barstow; cond. Karajan).

This highlights selection from Karajan's version is generous (71 minutes), following through the opera's narrative with both Acts well represented.

La Battaglia di Legnano (complete).
(M) *** Ph. 422 435-2 (2). Ricciarelli, Carreras, Manuguerra, Ghiuselev, Austrian R. Ch. & O, Gardelli.

La Battaglia di Legnano is a compact, sharply conceived piece, made the more intense by the subject's obvious relationship with the situation in Verdi's own time. One weakness is that the villainy is not effectively personalized, but the juxtaposition of the individual drama of supposed infidelity against a patriotic theme brings most effective musical contrasts. Gardelli directs a fine performance, helped by a strong cast of principals, with Carreras, Ricciarelli and Manuguerra all at their finest. Excellent recording, with the depth of perspective enhanced on CD.

Il Corsaro (complete).
(M) *** Ph. 426 118-2 (2). Norman, Caballé, Carreras, Grant, Mastromei, Noble, Amb. S., New Philh. O, Gardelli.

In *Il Corsaro*, though the characterization is rudimentary, the contrast between the two heroines is effective, with Gulnara, the Pasha's slave, carrying conviction in the *coup de foudre* which has her promptly worshipping the Corsair, an early example of the Rudolph Valentino figure. The rival heroines are taken splendidly here, with Jessye Norman as the faithful wife, Medora, actually upstaging Montserrat Caballé as Gulnara. Gardelli directs a vivid performance, with fine singing from the hero, portrayed by José Carreras. Gian-Piero Mastromei, not rich in tone, still rises to the challenge of the Pasha's music. Excellent, firmly focused and well-balanced Philips sound.

Don Carlos (complete).
(M) *** EMI CMS7 69304-2 (3) [Ang. CDMC 69304]. Carreras, Freni, Ghiaurov, Baltsa, Cappuccilli, Raimondi, German Op. Ch., Berlin, BPO, Karajan.
*** EMI CDS7 47701-8 (3) [Ang. CDCC 47701]. Domingo, Caballé, Raimondi, Verrett, Milnes, Amb. Op. Ch., ROHCG O, Giulini.
**(*) DG Dig. 415 316-2 (4) [id.]. Ricciarelli, Domingo, Valentini Terrani, Nucci, Raimondi, Ghiaurov, La Scala, Milan, Ch. & O, Abbado.

☞ **(*) Sony Dig. S3K 52500 (3) [id.]. Furlanatto, Millo, Zajick, Sylvester, Chernov, Ramey, Battle, NY Met. Ch. & O, James Levine.

☞ (M) (**(*)) EMI mono CMS7 64642-2 [CDMC 64642] (3). Christoff, Stella, Nicolai, Mario Filippeschi, Gobbi, Neri, Rome Op. Ch. & O, Santini.

☞ (M) **(*) DG 437 730-2 (3) [id.]. Christoff, Stella, Cossotto, Labò, Bastianini, La Scala, Milan, Ch. & O, Santini.

☞ **(*) EMI Dig. CDS7 54867-2 (3) [Ang. CDMB 54867-2]. Pavarotti, Dessì, D'Intino, Coni, Ramey, Anisimov, La Scala, Milan, Ch. & O, Muti.

Karajan opts firmly for the later, four-Act version of the opera, merely opening out the cuts he adopted on stage. The *Auto da fé* scene is here superb, while Karajan's characteristic choice of singers for refinement of voice rather than sheer size consistently pays off. Both Carreras and Freni are most moving, even if *Tu che le vanità* has its raw moments. Baltsa is a superlative Eboli and Cappuccilli an affecting Rodrigo, though neither Carreras nor Cappuccilli is at his finest in the famous oath duet. Raimondi and Ghiaurov as the Grand Inquisitor and Philip II provide the most powerful confrontation. The sound is both rich and atmospheric, giving great power to Karajan's uniquely taut account of the four-Act version.

There is extra joy in the *Auto da fé* scene as it is pointed by Giulini, who uses the full, five-Act text. Generally the cast is strong; the only major vocal disappointment among the principals lies in Caballé's account of the big aria *Tu che le vanità* in the final Act. The CD transfer of the 1971 analogue recording brings astonishing vividness and realism, a tribute to the original engineering of Christopher Parker. Even in the big ensembles the focus is very precise, yet atmospheric too, not just analytic.

Abbado's set was the first recording to use the language which Verdi originally set, French; in addition to the full five-Act text in its composite 1886 form including the Fontainebleau scene (recorded twice before), there are half a dozen appendices from the original 1867 score, later cut or recomposed. By rights, this should be the definitive recording of the opera, for Abbado is a masterly interpreter of Verdi. The first disappointment lies in the variable quality of the sound, with odd balances, so that although the Fontainebleau opening, with its echoing horns, is arrestingly atmospheric, the *Auto da fé* scene lacks bite, brilliance and clarity. In addition, large-scale flair and urgency are missing; once that is said, however, the cast of singers is a strong one. Domingo easily outshines his earlier recording with Giulini (in Italian), while Katia Ricciarelli as the Queen gives a tenderly moving performance, if not quite commanding enough in the Act V aria. Ruggero Raimondi is a finely focused Philip II, nicely contrasted with Nicolai Ghiaurov as the Grand Inquisitor in the other black-toned bass role. Lucia Valentini Terrani as Eboli is warm-toned if not very characterful, and Leo Nucci makes a noble Posa.

Recorded in the Manhattan Center, New York, James Levine's version with the company of the Metropolitan has full, forward sound, more faithful than most from this source, making it the best digital recommendation for the full, five-Act score. The heavy-handedness of Levine as a Verdian is exaggerated by the sound, but far better that than the tepid results from La Scala in Abbado's recording for DG. With Levine the *Auto da fé* ensemble may lack refinement, taken fast, but it is certainly dramatic, and the whole performance has a thrust and bite that reflect opera-house experience. The cast is very acceptable, if not ideally distinguished. In the title-role the American tenor, Michael Sylvester, produces fine, clear, heroic tone and, unlike most rivals, he is not afraid to shade his voice down to a pianissimo. Aprile Millo's ripe soprano is very apt for the role of Elisabetta and, though her vibrato tends to become obtrusive, she controls her line well, not least in the perilous phrases of her big Act V aria, *Tu che le vanità*. As Eboli, Dolora Zajic's fruity mezzo is not well caught by the close-up recording, again with unevenness exaggerated, but this is a rich characterization. As King Philip, Ferruccio Furlanetto is not as firm as he usually is, while Vladimir Chernev as Rodrigo is not flattered either, with fluttery timbre exaggerated. He makes little of the character, the key to the whole opera, leaving a disappointing blank where one wants the keenest intensity.

The vintage EMI mono recording offers a seriously cut version of the four-Act score, indifferently conducted by Gabriele Santini, but it is still an indispensable set, with performances from Tito Gobbi as Rodrigo and Boris Christoff as Philip which have never been remotely matched. Gobbi's singing in the Death scene is arguably the finest recorded performance that even this glorious artist ever made, with a wonderful range of tone and feeling for words. The bitingly dark tone of Christoff as the King also goes with intense feeling for the dramatic situation, making his big monologue one of the peaks of the performance. It may be a sign of declining standards today that the flaws in the other solo singing do not seem as serious as they did when the set was issued in the 1950s. Antonietta Stella, never a very distinctive artist, gives one of her finest recorded performances as Elisabetta, only occasionally squally. As Eboli, Elena Nicolai controls her fruity mezzo well, even if the vibrato becomes obtrusive; and the most serious blot is the singing of the tenor, Mario Filippeschi, and even that is not as coarse or strained as we have often had latterly.

Two of the principal soloists on the analogue DG set – Christoff and Stella – as well as the conductor are the same as in the old HMV mono recording but, quite apart from the advantages of the stereo, this newer set has the advantage of including the Fontainebleau forest scene, whereas the EMI stuck to the heavily cut Paris version. Christoff is again superb. No other bass in the world today comes anywhere near him in this part either in vocal strength, musicianship or power of characterization. The tragic dilemma of the ageing King Philip II has an intense nobility when in Act IV he faces the grim demands of the Inquisitor. Antonietta Stella is no more successful here than she was on EMI: she still has poor discipline, and in her big aria, *Tu che le vanità*, this makes for some squally sounds. Fiorenza Cossotto proves a warm-voiced Eboli who copes strongly with the difficulties of *O don fatale*. Labò is a surprisingly good Don Carlos. Unlike Filippeschi on the old mono set, he sings expressively and intelligently.

The real loss, of course, in comparing the two versions, is the replacement of Tito Gobbi by Bastianini. Rodrigo's death in the earlier set was vocally one of the high peaks of modern recorded opera. Firm and rich as Bastianini unfailingly is, he does not begin to plumb the character in that way. The DG recording-balance favours the voices, while the orchestra is comparatively distant; but the lively CD transfer makes everything sound more vivid, even if the orchestra is masked in the moments of spectacle. The tingling excitement of the *Auto da fé* scene is inevitably diluted. But this is such a wonderful opera that even these flaws cannot prevent this recording from proving a most moving experience.

The EMI set with Muti was recorded live at La Scala in the run of performances in 1992 which followed Pavarotti's first appearance as Don Carlo. The recording shows how unfair the much-publicized adverse response to his singing was on the first night. Though Carlo is only one of the central characters in this epic opera, and arguably not the most important, Pavarotti's magnetism and sensitive control of word-meaning provide a fine focus, even though he is inclined to rush his fences, rarely singing gently. Even so, in the final duet he makes amends; Muti, uncomfortably taut for much of the opera and pressing ahead with fast, unsprung tempi, finds more relaxation and a more lyrical style by the close. Daniela Dessì is a positive, characterful Elisabetta, though often gusty in production. Ramey is a sympathetic Philip II, though the voice is not quite dark or firm enough, and Paolo Coni is a strong if not very imaginative Rodrigo. Luciana D'Intino as a fine Eboli makes one hope that she will be used more on disc. The sound is dry in the La Scala manner, with voices placed forward, though some bloom remains. For a recording of Verdi's four-Act version of this opera, this hardly compares with Karajan's still-magnificent account for EMI, which has a far more consistent cast and more refined playing, as well as more atmospheric recording.

Don Carlos: highlights.
(M) *** EMI CDM7 63089-2 (from above recording with Domingo, Caballé; cond. Giulini).

Giulini's disc of highlights can be highly recommended. In selecting from such a long opera, serious omissions are inevitable; nothing is included here from Act III, to make room for the *Auto da fé* scene from Act IV – some 37 minutes of the disc is given to this Act. With vivid sound this is most stimulating; the only reservation concerns Caballé's *Tu che le vanità*, which ends the selection disappointingly.

I due Foscari (complete).
(M) *** Ph. 422 426-2 (2). Ricciarelli, Carreras, Cappuccilli, Ramey, Austrian R. Ch. & SO, Gardelli.

I due Foscari brings Verdian high spirits in plenty, erupting in swinging cabalettas and much writing that anticipates operas as late as *Simon Boccanegra* and *La forza del destino*. The cast here is first rate, with Ricciarelli giving one of her finest performances in the recording studio to date and with Carreras singing tastefully as well as powerfully. The crispness of discipline among the Austrian Radio forces is admirable, but there is less sense of atmosphere here than in the earlier, London-made recordings in the series.

Ernani (complete).
(M) *** BMG/RCA GD 86503 (2) [6503-2-RG]. Leontyne Price, Bergonzi, Sereni, Flagello, RCA Italiana Op. Ch. & O, Schippers.
**(*) EMI Dig. CDS7 47083-2 (3) [Ang. CDC 47082]. Domingo, Freni, Bruson, Ghiaurov, La Scala, Milan, Ch. & O, Muti.

At mid-price, Schippers' set, recorded in Rome in 1967, is an outstanding bargain. Leontyne Price may take the most celebrated aria, *Ernani involami*, rather cautiously, but the voice is gloriously firm and rich, and Bergonzi is comparably strong and vivid, though Mario Sereni, vocally reliable, is dull, and Ezio Flagello gritty-toned. Nevertheless, with Schippers drawing the team powerfully together, it is a highly enjoyable set, with the digital transfer making voices and orchestra sound full and vivid.

The great merit of Muti's set, recorded live at a series of performances at La Scala, is that the ensembles have an electricity rarely achieved in the studio, even if the results may not always be so precise and stage noises are often obtrusive. The singing, generally strong and characterful, is yet flawed. The strain of the role of Elvira for Mirella Freni is plain from the big opening aria, *Ernani involami*, onwards. Even in that aria there are cautious moments. Bruson is a superb Carlo and Ghiaurov a characterful Silva, but his voice now betrays signs of wear. As Ernani himself, Plácido Domingo gives a commandingly heroic performance, but under pressure there are hints of tight tone such as he rarely produces in the studio. The CD version gives greater immediacy and presence, but also brings out the inevitable flaws of live recording the more clearly.

Falstaff (complete).

*** DG Dig. 410 503-2 (2) [id.]. Bruson, Ricciarelli, Nucci, Hendricks, Egerton, Valentini Terrani, Boozer, LA Master Ch., LAPO, Giulini.

*(**) EMI CDS7 49668-2 (2) [Ang. CDCB 49668]. Gobbi, Schwarzkopf, Zaccaria, Moffo, Panerai, Philh. Ch. & O, Karajan.

(M) (***) BMG/RCA mono GD 60251 (2) [60251-RG-2]. Valdengo, Nelli, Merriman, Elmo, Guarrera, Stich-Randall, Robert Shaw Ch., NBC SO, Toscanini.

☞ ** BMG/RCA Dig. 09026 60705-2 (2) [60705-2]. Panerai, M. Horne, Titus, Sweet, Lopardo, Bav. R. Ch. and RSO, Sir Colin Davis.

☞ ** Decca Dig. 440 650-2 (2) [id.]. Van Dam, Serra, Coni, Canonici, Norberg-Schulz, Lipovšek, Graham, Begley, Lefebvre, Luperi, Berlin R. Ch., BPO, Solti.

This was Giulini's first essay in live opera-conducting in fourteen years, and he treated the piece with a care for musical values which at times undermined the knockabout comic element. On record that is all to the good, for the clarity and beauty of the playing are caught superbly on CD. Bruson, hardly a comic actor, is impressive on record for his fine incisive singing, giving tragic implications to the monologue at the start of Act III after Falstaff's dunking. The Ford of Leo Nucci, impressive in the theatre, is thinly caught, where the heavyweight quality of Ricciarelli as Alice comes over well, though in places one would wish for a purer sound. Barbara Hendricks is a charmer as Nannetta, but she hardly sounds fairy-like in her Act III aria. The full women's ensemble, though precise, is not always quite steady in tone, though the conviction of the whole performance puts it among the most desirable of modern readings.

This earlier (1956) Karajan recording presents not only the most pointed account orchestrally of Verdi's comic masterpiece (the Philharmonia Orchestra at its very peak) but the most sharply characterful cast ever gathered for a recording. If you relish the idea of Tito Gobbi as Falstaff (his many-coloured voice, not quite fat-sounding in humour, presents a sharper character than usual), then this is clearly the best choice, for the rest of the cast is a delight, with Schwarzkopf a tinglingly masterful Mistress Ford, Anna Moffo sweet as Nannetta and Rolando Panerai a formidable Ford. Unfortunately the digital remastering has been mismanaged. While the precision and placing of voices on the stereo stage, a model even today, comes out the more clearly on CD, the transfer itself, at a low level and with high hiss, has lost the bloom and warmth of the original analogue master which was outstanding for its time.

Toscanini's fizzing account of Verdi's last masterpiece has never been matched on record, the most high-spirited performance ever, beautifully paced for comedy. Even without stereo, and recorded with typical dryness, the clarity and sense of presence in this live concert performance set the story in relief. The cast is excellent, led by the ripe, firm baritone, Giuseppe Valdengo. Such singers as Nan Merriman as Mistress Page, Cloe Elmo as a wonderfully fruity Mistress Quickly and Frank Guarrera as Ford match or outshine any more recent interpreters. Toscanini's favourite soprano in his last years, Herva Nelli, is less characterful as Mistress Ford, rather over-parted but still fresh and reliable.

Where so many digital recordings of opera offer coarse, close-up sound, RCA's set of Verdi's *Falstaff* conducted by Sir Colin Davis suffers from the opposite problem. Soloists and the Bavarian Radio Orchestra are set in a reverberant acoustic which not only confuses detail (with even the semiquaver figure of the opening barely identifiable) but also makes it hard for the fun of the piece to come across. Davis, as he has shown many times at Covent Garden, is masterly in his Verdian timing, but the result fails to sparkle. It is all serious and Germanic. The cast is a good one, including two veterans: Rolando Panerai still strong and resonant in the title-role and Marilyn Horne producing stentorian tones as Mistress Quickly. Sharon Sweet is a forceful Alice, with Julie Kaufmann as Nannetta well-matched against Frank Lopardo, stylish in Verdi as he was in Rossini. Yet with such sound it is not a set to recommend with enthusiasm.

Solti's second recording of *Falstaff* was made, live, in the Philharmonie in Berlin just before the same performers gave it on stage at the Salzburg Easter Festival. Characteristically he points rhythms and textures with fine concern for detail, but the fun of the piece is muted. With José van Dam not a natural Falstaff – his beautifully shaded voice too often sounding serious – and with the sound of the Berlin Philharmonic on the weighty side for the piece, this cannot compare with Solti's earlier version with Geraint Evans in the title-role conveying far more sparkle. There is some good singing, but Luciana Serra makes a shrill Alice and Paolo Coni a dull Ford. Applause intrudes only at the beginning and end of the performance. New or not, this is hardly a serious contender.

La forza del destino (complete).
*** BMG/RCA RD 81864 (3) [RCD3-1864]. Leontyne Price, Domingo, Milnes, Cossotto, Giaiotti, Bacquier, Alldis Ch., LSO, Levine.
*** DG Dig. 419 203-2 (3) [id.]. Plowright, Carreras, Bruson, Burchuladze, Baltsa, Amb. Op. Ch., Philh. O, Sinopoli.
(M) *** BMG/RCA GD 87971 (3) [4515-2-RG]. Leontyne Price, Tucker, Merrill, Tozzi, Verrett, Flagello, Foiani, RCA Italiana Op. Ch. & O, Schippers.

James Levine directs a superb performance. The results are electrifying. Leontyne Price recorded the role of Leonora in an earlier RCA version made in Rome in 1956, but the years have hardly touched her voice, and details of the reading have been refined. The roles of Don Alvaro and Don Carlo are ideally suited to the regular team of Plácido Domingo and Sherrill Milnes so that their confrontations are the cornerstones of the dramatic structure. Fiorenza Cossotto makes a formidable rather than a jolly Preziosilla, while on the male side the line-up of Bonaldo Giaiotti, Gabriel Bacquier, Kurt Moll and Michel Sénéchal is far stronger than on rival sets. In a good, vivid transfer of the mid-1970s sound, this is a strong, well-paced version with an exceptionally good and consistent cast.

Sinopoli draws out phrases lovingly, sustaining pauses to the limit, putting extra strain on the singers. Happily, the whole cast seems to thrive on the challenge, and the spaciousness of the recording acoustic not only makes the dramatic interchanges the more realistic, it brings out the bloom on all the voices, above all the creamy soprano of Rosalind Plowright. Though José Carreras is sometimes too conventionally histrionic, even strained, it is a strong, involved performance. Renato Bruson is a thoughtful Carlo, while some of the finest singing of all comes from Agnes Baltsa as Preziosilla and Paata Burchuladze as the Padre Guardiano, uniquely resonant.

On RCA, Leontyne Price's voice (in 1964) was fresher and more open; on balance this is a more tender and delicate performance than the weightier one she recorded with Levine. Richard Tucker as Alvaro is here far less lachrymose and more stylish than he was earlier in the Callas set, producing ample, heroic tone, if not with the finesse of a Domingo. Robert Merrill as Carlo also sings with heroic strength, consistently firm and dark of tone; while Shirley Verrett, Giorgio Tozzi and Ezio Flagello stand up well against any rivalry. The sound is remarkably full and vivid.

La forza del destino (slightly abridged).
(***) EMI mono CDS7 47581-8 (3) [Ang. CDCC 47581]. Callas, Tucker, Tagliabue, Clabassi, Nicolai, Rossi-Lemeni, Capecchi, La Scala, Milan, Ch. & O, Serafin.

Though there are classic examples of Callas's raw tone on top notes, they are insignificant next to the wealth of phrasing which sets a totally new and individual stamp on even the most familiar passages. Apart from his tendency to disturb his phrasing with sobs, Richard Tucker sings superbly; but not even he – and certainly none of the others (including the baritone Carlo Tagliabue, well past his prime) – begin to rival the dominance of Callas. Serafin's direction is crisp, dramatic and well paced, again drawing the threads together. The 1955 mono sound is less aggressive than many La Scala recordings of this vintage and has been freshened on CD.

La forza del destino: highlights.
☞ ** EMI Dig. CDC7 54326-2 [id.]. Freni, Domingo, Zancanaro, Zajic, Pliskhka, La Scala, Milan, Ch. & O, Muti.

Few are likely to choose Muti's complete set of *La forza del destino*, because of its indifferent digital sound, but those wanting to sample Domingo's arresting Don Alvaro might consider this highlights disc. He is included in two excerpts from Act III and three from Act IV. The CD includes 67 minutes of music and is well documented, but it comes at full price.

Un giorno di regno (complete).

(M) *** Ph. 422 429-2 (2). Cossotto, Norman, Carreras, Wixell, Sardinero, Ganzarolli, Amb. S., RPO, Gardelli.

Un giorno di regno may not be the greatest comic opera of the period, but this scintillating performance under Gardelli clearly reveals the young Verdi as more than an imitator of Rossini and Donizetti, and there are striking passages which clearly give a foretaste of such numbers as the duet *Si vendetta* from *Rigoletto*. Despite the absurd plot, this is as light and frothy an entertainment as anyone could want. Excellent singing from a fine team, with Jessye Norman and José Carreras outstanding. The recorded sound is even more vivid on CD.

I Lombardi (complete).

(M) *** Ph. 422 420-2 (2). Deutekom, Domingo, Raimondi, Amb. S., RPO, Gardelli.

I Lombardi reaches its apotheosis in the famous *Trio*, well known from the days of 78-r.p.m. recordings. By those standards, Cristina Deutekom is not an ideal Verdi singer: her tone is sometimes hard and her voice is not always perfectly under control, yet there are also some glorious moments and the phrasing is often impressive. Domingo as Oronte is in superb voice, and the villain Pagano is well characterized by Raimondi. Among the supporting cast Stafford Dean and Clifford Grant must be mentioned. Gardelli conducts dramatically and the action projects vividly.

(i) *I Lombardi, Act III: Trio.* (ii) *Rigoletto, Act IV* (complete).

(M) (**) BMG/RCA mono GD 60276 (2); [60276-2-RG]. (i) Della Chiesa, Peerce, Moscona; (ii) Warren, Milanov, Peerce, Moscona, Merriman, All City Highschool Ch. & Glee Clubs, NBC SO, Toscanini – BOITO: *Mefistofele: Prologue.* (***)

It is interesting to find a little-known singer, Vivian della Chiesa, emerging strongly alongside Jan Peerce and Nicola Moscona. The last Act of *Rigoletto* was given in a wartime fund-raising concert in Madison Square Garden and, though the brittleness of sound is at times almost comic and the tautness of Toscanini's control was unrelenting, the performances of the principals are formidable, with Zinka Milanov at her most radiant. With Toscanini's searing account of the *Mefistofele Prologue*, this makes a generous compilation.

Luisa Miller (complete).

*** Sony Dig. S2K 48073 (2) [id.]. Domingo, Millo, Chernev, Rootering, Quivar, Plishka, Met. Op. O and Ch., Levine.

*** Decca 417 420-2 (2) [id.]. Caballé, Pavarotti, Milnes, Reynolds, L. Op. Ch., Nat. PO, Maag.

*** DG 423 144-2 (2) [id.]. Ricciarelli, Obraztsova, Domingo, Bruson, ROHCG Ch. & O, Maazel.

(M) *** BMG/RCA GD 86646 (2) [6646-2-RG]. Moffo, Bergonzi, Verrett, MacNeil, Tozzi, Flagello, RCA Italiana Op. Ch. & O, Cleva.

Levine conducts his forces from the Met. in a red-blooded, exceptionally high-powered reading of this elusive opera. In the role of Miller, the heroine's father, Chernev is even more characterful and musically more individual than either of his main rivals on the other sets, with the power of his singing brought home by the close balance of the voice. Though the sound tends to make Levine's direction seem less subtle than it is, less elegant than Maag on Decca, less refined in texture than Maazel on DG, the impact of the score is brought home formidably. It is significant how Plácido Domingo, who takes the role of the hero Rodolfo both for Maazel and for Levine, sings with much greater animation in the New York recording. Among the others Jan-Henrik Rootering, Florence Quivar and Paul Plishka all sing powerfully, even if all three suffer from occasional unsteadiness. The snag is the variable quality of Aprile Millo's singing in the title role. She has the right Verdian timbre, more girlish-sounding than her rivals, but in Act I the coloratura taxes her severely; however, by the final Act she produces some lovely singing with some beautifully floated high pianissimos. It is in that final act that the extra dramatic bite of Levine's reading tells most in its impact.

On Decca, Caballé, though not as flawless vocally as one would expect, gives a splendidly dramatic portrait of the heroine and Pavarotti's performance is full of creative, detailed imagination. As Federica, Anna Reynolds is distinctly preferable to Obraztsova, and Maag's sympathetic reading, by underlining the light and shade, consistently brings out the atmospheric qualities of Verdi's conception. Vividly transferred, this Decca recording has the balance of advantage over the DG set.

Though taut in his control, Maazel uses his stage experience of working with these soloists to draw them out to their finest, most sympathetic form. Ricciarelli gives one of her tenderest and most beautiful performances on record, Domingo is in glorious voice and Bruson as Luisa's father sings with velvet tone. Gwynne Howell is impressive as the Conte di Walter and Wladimiro Ganzarolli's vocal roughness is apt for the character of Wurm. The snag is the abrasive Countess Federica of Elena Obraztsova.

In many ways the RCA set provides a performance to compete with the full-price versions and is just as stylish, with Moffo at her very peak, singing superbly, Carlo Bergonzi unfailingly intelligent and stylish, and Verrett nothing less than magnificent in her role as a quasi-Amneris. MacNeil and Tozzi are also satisfyingly resonant, and Fausto Cleva tellingly reveals his experience directing the opera at the Met. Good recording.

Macbeth (complete).
*** Ph. Dig. 412 133-2 (3) [id.]. Bruson, Zampieri, Shicoff, Lloyd, German Op. Ch. & O, Berlin, Sinopoli.
*** DG 415 688-2 (3) [id.]. Cappuccilli, Verrett, Ghiaurov, Domingo, La Scala, Milan, Ch. & O, Abbado.
☞ (M) *** EMI CMS7 64339-2 (2) [Ang. CDMB 64339]. Milnes, Cossotto, Raimondi, Carreras, Amb. Op. Ch., New Philh. O, Muti.
☞ (M) **(*) Decca 440 048-2 (2) [id.]. Fischer-Dieskau, Suliotis, Ghiaurov, Pavarotti, Amb. Op. Ch., LPO, Gardelli.
(M) **(*) BMG/RCA GD 84516 (2) [4516-2-RG]. Warren, Rysanek, Bergonzi, Hines, Met. Op. Ch. & O, Leinsdorf.

Even more than his finest rivals, Sinopoli presents this opera as a searing Shakespearean inspiration, scarcely more uneven than much of the work of the Bard himself. In the Banqueting scene, for example, Sinopoli creates extra dramatic intensity by his concern for detail and his preference for extreme dynamics, and Renato Bruson and Mara Zampieri respond vividly. Zampieri's voice may be biting rather than beautiful, occasionally threatening to come off the rails, but, with musical precision an asset, she matches exactly Verdi's request for the voice of a she-devil. Neil Schicoff as Macduff and Robert Lloyd as Banquo make up the excellent quartet of principals, while the high voltage of the whole performance clearly reflects Sinopoli's experience with the same chorus and orchestra at the Deutsche Oper in Berlin. CD adds vividly to the realism of a recording that is well balanced and focused but atmospheric.

At times Abbado's tempi are unconventional, but with slow speeds he springs the rhythm so infectiously that the results are the more compelling. The whole performance gains from superb teamwork, for each of the principals – far more than is common – is meticulous about observing Verdi's detailed markings, above all those for *pianissimo* and *sotto voce*. Verrett, hardly powerful above the stave, yet makes a virtue out of necessity in floating glorious half-tones, and with so firm and characterful a voice she makes a highly individual, not at all conventional Lady Macbeth. As for Cappuccilli, he has never sung with such fine range of tone and imagination on record as here, and Plácido Domingo makes a real, sensitive Macduff. Excellent, clean recording.

Muti's 1976 version of *Macbeth*, made at Abbey Road, appeared within weeks of Abbado's, confirming that, in this opera, new standards were being set on record. Though Muti and his team do not quite match the supreme distinction of Abbado and, later, Sinopoli, they provide a valid alternative. Both Milnes and Cossotto sing warmly and are richly convincing in their relatively conventional views of their roles, while the comfortable reverberation and warmth of the EMI recording conceal any slight shortcomings of ensemble. The reissue therefore provides a firm mid-priced recommendation for this opera, and it fits neatly on to a pair of CDs.

It is now a matter of recording history that when in the summer of 1971 Gobbi was prevented – at the very last minute – from attending the London recording sessions in the Kingsway Hall, Decca had the great good fortune to persuade Fischer-Dieskau to take the name-role instead. The German baritone does not give a traditional performance in this great tragic role, for characteristically he points the words in full Lieder-style. Nor is he in his freshest voice, growing gritty in some climaxes; but it is still a marvellous, compelling performance which stands repeated hearing. Suliotis is – to put it kindly – a variable Lady Macbeth. In the first aria there are moments when her voice runs completely out of control, but she still has imagination, and her 'voice of a she-devil' (Verdi's words) is arguably the precise sound needed. Certainly she settles down into giving a striking and individual performance, while Ghiaurov as Banquo and Pavarotti as MacDuff sing with admirable poise. Gardelli and the LPO are treated to specially vivid recording which has transferred vibrantly to CD.

On two mid-price discs in the Victor Opera series, the Leinsdorf version makes a good bargain, bringing a large-scale performance featuring three favourite principals from the Met. Leonie Rysanek here gives one of her finest performances on record, producing her firmest, creamiest sound for the Sleepwalking scene, even though the coloratura taxes her severely. Leonard Warren, much admired in this part before his untimely death (on stage, singing Don Carlo in *La forza del destino*), gives a strong, thoughtful reading, marred by the way the microphone exaggerates his vibrato. Carlo Bergonzi is a stylish, clear-toned Macduff. Good sound for its period.

Macbeth: highlights.
(M) *** Decca 421 889-2 [id.]. Fischer-Dieskau, Suliotis, Pavarotti, Ghiaurov, Ambrosian Op. Ch., LPO, Gardelli.

On Decca a generous selection (75 minutes) from a finely dramatic set, splendidly recorded in the Kingsway Hall in 1971 and flawed only by the variable singing of Suliotis. This is arguably Fischer-Dieskau's finest Verdi performance on record and the cast includes a young Pavarotti as Macduff.

I Masnadieri (complete).
(M) *** Ph. 422 423-2 (2). Caballé, Bergonzi, Raimondi, Cappuccilli, Amb. S., New Philh. O, Gardelli.
☞ (M) **(*) Decca Dig. 433 854-2 (2) [id.]. Sutherland, Bonisolli, Manuguerra, Ramey, WNO Ch. & O, Bonynge.

Few will seriously identify with the hero-turned-brigand of *I Masnadieri* who stabs his beloved rather than lead her into a life of shame; but, on record, flaws of motivation are of far less moment than on stage. The melodies may only fitfully be out of Verdi's top drawer, but the musical structure and argument often look forward to a much later period with hints of *Forza*, *Don Carlo* and even *Otello*. With Gardelli as ever an urgently sympathetic Verdian, and a team of four excellent principals, splendidly recorded, the set can be warmly welcomed.

I Masnadieri, with four principal roles of equal importance, is not a prima donna's opera, but with Sutherland cast as Amalia it tends to become one. This is a weightier view than Caballé took in the earlier, Philips recording, conveying more light and shade. The cabaletta for her great Act II aria brings a coloratura display, with Sutherland still at her very peak. Though Bonisolli sings with less refinement than Bergonzi on the rival set, he has great flair, as in his extra flourishes in the final ensemble of Act II. Manuguerra sings strongly too. He may not be as refined as his rival, Cappuccilli, but he sounds more darkly villainous. Ramey as Massimiliano sings with fine clarity, but the voice does not sound old enough for a father. The Welsh National Opera Chorus projects with the lustiness of stage experience, even if the Kingsway Hall acoustic clouds some choral detail slightly. Even so, the digital sound is very impressive in its fullness and depth, and at mid-price this is certainly worth considering, especially by Sutherland fans.

Nabucco (complete).
*** DG Dig. 410 512-2 (2) [id.]. Cappuccilli, Dimitrova, Nesterenko, Domingo, Ch. & O of German Op., Berlin, Sinopoli.
*** Decca 417 407-2 (2) [id.]. Gobbi, Suliotis, Cava, Previdi, V. State Op. Ch. & O, Gardelli.

With Sinopoli one keeps hearing details normally obscured. Even the thrill of the great chorus *Va, pensiero* is the greater when the melody first emerges at a hushed pianissimo, as marked, sound almost offstage. Dimitrova is superb in Abigaille's big Act II aria, noble in her evil, as is Cappuccilli as Nabucco, less intense than Gobbi was on Gardelli's classic set for Decca, but stylistically pure. The rest of the cast is strong too, including Domingo in a relatively small role and Nesterenko superb as the High Priest, Zaccaria. Bright and forward digital sound, less atmospheric than the 1965 Decca set with Gobbi and Suliotis, conducted by Gardelli.

On Decca, the Viennese choral contribution was less committed than one would ideally like in a work which contains a chorus unique in Verdi's output, *Va, pensiero*; but in every other way this is a masterly performance, with dramatically intense and deeply imaginative contributions from Tito Gobbi as Nabucco and Elena Suliotis as the evil Abigaille. Suliotis made this the one totally satisfying performance of an all-too-brief recording career, wild in places but no more than is dramatically necessary. Though Carlo Cava as Zaccaria is not ideally rich of tone, it is a strong performance, and Gardelli, as in his later Verdi recordings for both Decca and Philips, showed what a master he is at pointing Verdian inspiration, whether in the individual phrase or over a whole scene, simply and naturally, without ever forcing. Vividly real and atmospheric 1965 Decca recording.

Nabucco: highlights.
(M) *** Decca 421 867-2; *421 867-4* (from above recording with Gobbi; cond. Gardelli).

Suliotis's impressive contribution is well represented on the Decca highlights disc, and there are fine contributions too from Gobbi. Needless to say, the chorus *Va, pensiero* is given its place of honour and the selection runs for 58 minutes. The 1965 recording sounds splendid.

Oberto (complete).
*** Orfeo C 105843 F (3) [id.]. Dimitrova, Bergonzi, Panerai, Baldani, Bav. R. Ch., Munich R. O,
  Gardelli.

In every way this issue matches the success of Gardelli's earlier, Philips recordings, despite the change
of venue to Munich. Gardelli successfully papers over the less convincing moments, helped by fine
playing from the orchestra, an outstanding chorus and first-rate principals. Ghena Dimitrova makes
a very positive heroine, powerful in attack in her moment of fury in the Act I finale, but also gently
expressive when necessary. Only in cabalettas is she sometimes ungainly. The veterans, Carlo
Bergonzi and Rolando Panerai, more than make up in stylishness and technical finesse for any
unevenness of voice, and Ruza Baldani is a warm-toned Cuniza, the mezzo role. First-rate recording.

Otello (complete).
*** BMG/RCA RD 82951 (2) [RCD2-2951]. Domingo, Scotto, Milnes, Amb. Op. Ch., Nat. PO,
  Levine.
*** Decca Dig. 433 669-2 (2) [id.]. Pavarotti, Te Kanawa, Nucci, Rolfe Johnson, Chicago SO & Ch.,
  Solti.
(M) *** BMG/RCA GD 81969 (2) [1969-2-RG]. Vickers, Rysanek, Gobbi, Rome Op. Ch. & O,
  Serafin.
(M) *** EMI CMS7 69308-2 (2) [Ang. CDMB 69308]. Vickers, Freni, Glossop, Ch. of German Op.,
  Berlin, BPO, Karajan.
☞ (M) **(*) Decca 440 045-2 (2) [id.]. Cossutta, M. Price, Bacquier, V. Boys' Ch., V. State Op. Ch.,
  VPO, Solti.
(M) (**(*)) BMG/RCA mono GD 60302 (2) [60302-2-RG]. Vinay, Valdengo, Nelli, Merriman,
  Assandri, NBC Ch. & SO, Toscanini.
☞ (B) ** Decca 440 245-2 (2) [id.]. Del Monaco, Tebaldi, Protti, Santa Cecilia Academy, Rome, Ch.
  & O, Erede.

Levine's is the most consistently involving *Otello*; on balance, it has the best cast and is superbly
conducted as well as magnificently sung. Domingo as Otello combines glorious heroic tone with
lyrical tenderness. Scotto is not always sweet-toned in the upper register, and the big ensemble at the
end of Act III brings obvious strain; nevertheless, it is a deeply felt performance which culminates in
a most beautiful account of the all-important Act IV solos, the *Willow song* and *Ave Maria*, most
affecting. Milnes too is challenged by his role: this Iago is a handsome, virile creature beset by the
biggest of chips on the shoulder. In the transfer of the 1977 analogue original the voices are caught
vividly and immediately, and the orchestral sound too is fuller and cleaner than in many more recent
versions.

Solti has never sounded more warmly communicative in Verdi. The fast speeds never seem too
taut or breathless, but simply add to the high voltage of the drama. Leo Nucci, taking the role of
Iago for the first time, is sound rather than inspired, warmly Italianate in timbre but lacking in
menace. Dame Kiri Te Kanawa produces consistently sumptuous tone; the *Willow song* is glorious.
The key element is the singing of Pavarotti as Otello, like Nucci new to his role. Following the
pattern of the whole performance, he often adopts faster speeds than usual. Whatever the detailed
reservations this is a memorable reading heightened by Pavarotti's detailed feeling for the words and
consistently golden tone. With close microphone balance, he like the others is prevented from
achieving genuine pianissimos, but above all he offers a vital, animated Otello, not a replacement for
Domingo but a magnificent alternative. The impact of the whole is greatly enhanced by the splendid
singing of the Chicago Symphony Chorus, helped by digital sound fuller and more vivid than on any
rival set.

No conductor is more understanding of Verdian pacing than Serafin and, with sound that hardly
begins to show its age (1960), it presents two of the finest solo performances on any *Otello* recording
of whatever period: the Iago of Tito Gobbi has never been surpassed for vividness of characterization
and tonal subtlety; while the young Jon Vickers, with a voice naturally suited to this role, was in his
prime as the Moor. Leonie Rysanek is a warm and sympathetic Desdemona, not always ideally pure-
toned but tender and touching in one of her very finest recorded performances. The sense of presence
in the open, well-balanced recording is the more vivid on CD, thanks to a first-rate transfer.

Karajan directs a big, bold and brilliant account, for the most part splendidly sung and with all
the dramatic contrasts strongly underlined. There are several tiny, but irritating, statutory cuts, but
otherwise on two mid-price CDs this is well worth considering. Freni's Desdemona is delightful,
delicate and beautiful, while Vickers and Glossop are both positive and characterful, only occasionally
forcing their tone and losing focus. The recording is clarified on CD.

Although Solti recorded outstanding versions of *Aida* and *Falstaff* in the 1960s, in later years he neglected Verdi in his recording programme, so that the warmth and tenderness of his reading of *Otello* as well as its incisive sense of drama take one freshly by surprise. The recording is bright and atmospheric to match, which leaves the vocal contributions as a third and more debatable deciding point. Of the very finest quality is the singing of Margaret Price as Desdemona, a ravishing performance, with the most beautiful and varied tonal quality allied to deep imagination. Carlo Cossutta as Otello is not so characterful a singer but, more than most rivals, he sings with clear, incisive tone and obvious concern for musical qualities. Gabriel Bacquier gives a thoughtful, highly intelligent performance as Iago, but his relative weakness in the upper register brings obvious disappointment. The Decca recording, however, has a sense of spectacle (notably in the opening scene) and perspective which is particularly appealing, the whole production managed with Ray Minshull's characteristic flair.

Toscanini's historic 1947 reading suffers more than usual from dry, limited sound but in magnetic intensity it is irresistible, bringing home the biting power of Verdi's score as few other recorded performances ever have. Ramon Vinay makes a commanding Otello, baritonal in vocal colouring but firm and clear, with a fine feeling for words. Giuseppe Valdengo had few rivals among baritones of the time in this role, strong, animated and clean in attack, though the vocal differentiation between hero and villain is less marked than usual. Herva Nelli is sweet and pure if a little colourless as Desdemona. The recording prevents her from achieving a really gentle pianissimo, and Toscanini, for all his flowing lines fails to allow the full repose needed.

The earliest Decca Rome set conducted with some flair by Alberto Erede dates from 1954, yet the effect of the stereo in the opening scene is little short of astonishing; with the brightening of the CD transfer entirely beneficial, the atmospheric spread of the stage perspective is remarkable. Later the close balance of the voices is less sophisticated, but the sound is always impressive for its time. *Otello* was in many ways Mario del Monaco's most successful role and, while his later set under Karajan is clearly preferable, he sings strongly enough here and Tebaldi's fresh-voiced and touching early portrait of Desdemona is always worth hearing. However, this set is best recommended to bargain-hunters. It is offered in a single jewel-case with a synopsis in the place of a libretto/translation.

Rigoletto (complete).
*** Ph. Dig. 412 592-2 (2) [id.]. Bruson, Gruberová, Shicoff, Fassbaender, Lloyd, St Cecilia Ac., Rome, Ch. & O, Sinopoli.
*** Decca 414 269-2 (2) [id.]. Milnes, Sutherland, Pavarotti, Talvela, Tourangeau, Amb. Op. Ch., LSO, Bonynge.
(***) EMI mono CDS7 47469-8 (2) [Ang. CDCB 47469]. Gobbi, Callas, Di Stefano, Zaccaria, La Scala, Milan, Ch. & O, Serafin.
(M) **(*) BMG/RCA GD 86506 (2) [6506-2-RG]. Merrill, Moffo, Kraus, Elias, Flagello, RCA Italiana Op. Ch. & O, Solti.
☞ ** Teldec/Warner Dig. 4509 90851-2 (2) [id.]. Leech, Agache, Vaduva, Ramey, Larmore, Welsh Nat. Op. Ch. & O, Rizzi.
☞ (B) (*) Decca mono 440 242-2 (2) [id.]. Protti, Gueden, Del Monaco, Siepi, Simionato, Santa Cecilia Academy, Rome, Ch. & O, Erede.

Edita Gruberová might have been considered an unexpected choice for Gilda, remarkable for her brilliant coloratura rather than for deeper expression, yet here she makes the heroine a tender, feeling creature, emotionally vulnerable yet vocally immaculate. Similarly, Renato Bruson as Rigoletto does far more than produce a stream of velvety tone, detailed and intense, responding to the conductor and combining beauty with dramatic bite. Even more remarkable is the brilliant success of Neil Shicoff as the Duke, more than a match for his most distinguished rivals. Here the *Quartet* becomes a genuine climax. Brigitte Fassbaender as Maddalena is sharply unconventional but vocally most satisfying. Sinopoli's speeds, too, are unconventional at times, but the fresh look he provides makes this one of the most exciting Verdi operas on disc, helped by full and vivid recording, consistently well balanced.

Just over ten years after her first recording of this opera, Sutherland appeared in it again, this time with Pavarotti who is an intensely characterful Duke: an unmistakable rogue but an unmistakable charmer, too. Thanks to him and to Bonynge above all, the *Quartet*, as on the Sinopoli set, becomes a genuine musical climax. Sutherland's voice has acquired a hint of a beat, but there is little of the mooning manner which disfigured her earlier assumption, and the result is glowingly beautiful as well as being technically supremely assured. Milnes makes a strong Rigoletto, vocally masterful and with good if hardly searching presentation of character. The digital transfer is exceptionally vivid and atmospheric.

There has never been a more compelling performance of the title-role in *Rigoletto* than that of

Gobbi on his classic Scala set of the 1950s. At every point, in almost every single phrase, Gobbi finds extra meaning in Verdi's vocal lines, with the widest range of tone-colour employed for expressive effect. Callas, though not naturally suited to the role of the wilting Gilda, is compellingly imaginative throughout, and Di Stefano gives one of his finer performances. The transfer of the original mono recording is astonishingly vivid in capturing the voices, but this remains at full price.

Anna Moffo makes a charming Gilda in the Solti set of 1963. Solti at times presses too hard, but this is a strong and dramatic reading, with Robert Merrill producing a glorious flow of dark, firm tone in the name-part. Alfredo Kraus is as stylish as ever as the Duke, and this rare example of his voice at its freshest should not be missed. A good bargain, though there are statutory cuts in the text.

Carlo Rizzi as music director of Welsh National Opera made an immediate impact both in the theatre and on record, but this account of *Rigoletto*, recorded in 1993, brings an underpowered performance. In the title-role Agache has the benefit of a glorious voice, but his characterization of the hunchback is sketchy, lacking bite and conviction. Richard Leech sings strongly as the Duke, but there is no charm in a performance that lacks finer shading, with no suspicion of Italianate timbres. As Gilda, Leontina Vaduva uses her light, sweet, pretty voice very capably, poised as well as agile, but she is not helped by the general slackness. Having such fine singers as Samuel Ramey and Jennifer Larmore in subsidiary roles hardly compensates.

Erede's (1954) mono recording has come up fairly well for its age, although it does not compare with the stereo *Otello* made in the same year, and there is some microphone edge on Del Monaco's voice. The orchestral playing and the singing of the minor soloists are enjoyable, but Protti is a characterless Rigoletto, as he was a characterless Iago, and the whole story loses much of its point if you cannot quite believe in the conflicting emotions of the malicious court jester. Hilde Gueden makes Gilda into an attractive, pouting miss, a girl more knowing than the general run of Gildas, but some of the singing is extremely unidiomatic; for all Gueden's coloratura powers, the tessitura is on the high side for her. Mario del Monaco is very loud indeed: this was one of his most uninhibited and least attractive performances.

Rigoletto: highlights.
(M) *** DG 435 416-2 [id.] (from above complete set, with Cappuccilli, Cotrubas, Domingo; cond. Giulini).

A useful and generous set of highlights for those who do not want to go to the expense of a complete set. The 61-minute DG collection is now reissued at mid-price as part of the 'Domingo Edition' and makes a clear first choice.

Simon Boccanegra (complete).
⊛ *** DG 415 692-2 (2) [id.]. Cappuccilli, Freni, Ghiaurov, Van Dam, Carreras, La Scala, Milan, Ch. & O, Abbado.
(M) (***) EMI mono CMS7 63513-2 (2) [Ang. CDMB 63513]. Gobbi, Christoff, De los Angeles, Campora, Monachesi, Dari, Rome Op. Chor & O, Santini.

Abbado's 1977 recording of *Simon Boccanegra* is one of the most beautiful Verdi sets ever made. Under Abbado the playing of the orchestra is brilliantly incisive as well as refined, so that the drama is underlined by extra sharpness of focus. The cursing of Paolo after the great Council Chamber scene makes the scalp prickle, with the chorus muttering in horror and the bass clarinet adding a sinister comment, here beautifully moulded. Cappuccilli, always intelligent, gives a far more intense and illuminating performance than the one he recorded for RCA earlier in his career. He may not match Gobbi in range of colour and detail, but he too gives focus to the performance; and Ghiaurov as Fiesco sings beautifully too. Freni as Maria Boccanegra sings with freshness and clarity, while Van Dam is an impressive Paolo. With electrically intense choral singing as well, this is a set to outshine even Abbado's superb *Macbeth* with the same company, superbly transferred to CD.

Tito Gobbi's portrait of the tragic Doge of Genoa is one of his greatest on record, and it emerges all the more impressively when it is set against equally memorable performances by Boris Christoff as Fiesco and Victoria de los Angeles as Amelia. The Recognition scene between father and daughter has never been done more movingly on record; nor has the great ensemble, which crowns the Council Chamber scene, been so powerfully and movingly presented, and that without the help of stereo recording. The transfer is full and immediate, giving a vivid sense of presence to the voices, though tape-hiss is on the high side.

Stiffelio (complete).
(M) *** Ph. 422 432-2 (2). Carreras, Sass, Manuguerra, Ganzarolli, V. ORF Ch. & SO, Gardelli.

Coming just before the great trio of masterpieces, *Rigoletto, Il Trovatore* and *La Traviata, Stiffelio* is still a sharply telling work, largely because of the originality of the relationships and the superb final scene in which Stiffelio reads from the pulpit the parable of the woman taken in adultery. Gardelli directs a fresh performance, at times less lively than Queler's of *Aroldo* but with more consistent singing, notably from Carreras and Manuguerra. First-rate recording from Philips, typical of this fine series.

La Traviata (complete).

*** Decca Dig. 430 491-2; *430 491-4* (2) [id.]. Sutherland, Pavarotti, Manuguerra, L. Op. Ch., Nat. PO, Bonynge.

☞ *** Teldec/Warner Dig. 9031 76348-2 (2) [id.]. Gruberová, Shicoff, Zancanaro, Amb. S., LSO, Rizzi.

☞ (B) **(*) CfP CD-CFPD 4450; *TC-CFPD 4450* (2). De los Angeles, Del Monte, Sereni, Rome Op. Ch. & O, Serafin.

☞ (B) **(*) Double Decca 443 002-2 (2) [id.]. Lorengar, Aragall, Fischer-Dieskau, Ch. & O of German Op., Berlin, Maazel.

(M) **(*) Decca 411 877-2 (2) [id.]. Sutherland, Bergonzi, Merrill, Ch. & O of Maggio Musicale Fiorentino, Pritchard.

☞ **(*) Ph. Dig. 438 238-2 (2) [id.]. Te Kanawa, Kraus, Hvorostovsky, Maggio Musicale (Florence) Ch. & O, Mehta.

(M) (*(**)) EMI mono CMS7 63628-2 (2) [Ang. CDMB 63628]. Callas, Di Stefano, Bastianini, La Scala Ch. & O, Giulini.

☞ ** DG Dig. 435 797-2 (2) [id.]. Studer, Pavarotti, Pons, Met. Op. Ch. & O, Levine.

☞ (M) (**) BMG/RCA mono GD 60303 (2) [id.]. Albanese, Peerce, Merrill, NBC Ch. & SO, Toscanini.

☞ *(*) Sony Dig. S2K 52486 (2) [id.]. Fabbricini, Alagna, Conti, La Scala, Milan, Ch. & O, Muti.

Sutherland's second recording of the role of Violetta has a breadth and exuberance beyond her achievement in the earlier version of 1963, conducted by John Pritchard, and the richness and command of the singing put this among the very finest of her later recordings. Pavarotti too, though he overemphasizes *Di miei bollenti spiriti*, sings with splendid panache as Alfredo. Manuguerra as Germont lacks something in authority, but the firmness and clarity are splendid. Bonynge's conducting is finely sprung, the style direct, the speeds often spacious in lyrical music, generally undistracting. The digital recording is outstandingly vivid and beautifully balanced but the CD booklet is not ideal.

The big success of the Teldec set, consistently refined in its treatment of Verdian rhythms and textures, is the conducting of Carlo Rizzi in his first major opera recording, confirming Welsh National Opera's wisdom in appointing him music director. He draws subtle, refined playing from the LSO, which in turn brings refined singing from a well-matched cast. Giorgio Zancanaro is a characterful Germont, giving depth of feeling to the first scene of Act II up to *Di Provenza il mar*. Though Edita Gruberová's bright soprano acquires an unevenness under pressure, she is freshly expressive and increasingly through the opera, up to the great challenge of the death scene, produces the most delicate pianissimos, with phrasing and tone exquisitely shaded. She may not match the finest Violettas of the past, and the tenor, Neil Shicoff, sings with markedly less finesse than the other principals, but among the current versions of this opera there is no modern digital version to rival it.

Even when Victoria de los Angeles made this EMI recording in the late 1950s, the role of Violetta lay rather high for her voice. Nevertheless it drew from her much beautiful singing, not least in the coloratura display at the end of Act I which, though it may lack easily ringing top notes, has delightful sparkle and flexibility. As to the characterization, De los Angeles was a far more sympathetically tender heroine than is common; though neither the tenor nor the baritone begins to match her in artistry, their performances are both sympathetic and feeling, thanks in part to the masterly conducting of Serafin. All the traditional cuts are made, not just the second stanzas. The CD transfer is vivid and clear, with plenty of atmosphere; only the sound of violins betrays the age of the recording and not that seriously; the choral focus is remarkably good. Reissued at bargain price, this is worth any collector's money, though only a synopsis is provided.

The 1968 Maazel set was more complete in its text than some earlier three-disc versions. Though second verses of arias are excluded (always the practice in opera houses), Alfredo's cabaletta after *Di miei bollenti spiriti* and Germont's after *Di provenza* are both included at least once around, which is rare enough. As to the performance, much will depend on the listener's reaction to Lorengar's voice. Her interpretation is most affecting, deeply felt and expressively presented, but the vibrato is often intrusive to the point where the tone-colour is seriously marred. That will not worry all ears – and in any case with Fischer-Dieskau a searchingly intense Germont (if hardly an elderly-sounding one) and Aragall making impressive trumpet-sounds as Alfredo, this is a strong cast. Maazel's conducting is characteristically forceful. At first he may seem over-forceful – the opening of Act I begins at a very brisk pace indeed, as though attempting to out-Toscanini Toscanini – but once he settles down after the first party music, his reading is both intelligent and sensitive. The recording quality is excellent and, as usual with Decca, the CD transfer belies its age.

In Sutherland's 1963 recording of *La Traviata*, it is true that her diction is poor, but it is also true that she has rarely sung on record with such deep feeling as in the final scene. The *Addio del passato* (both stanzas included and sung with an unexpected lilt) merely provides a beginning, for the duet with Bergonzi is most winning, and the final death scene, *Se una pudica vergine*, is overwhelmingly beautiful. This is not a sparkling Violetta, true, but it is vocally closer to perfection than almost any other in a complete set. Bergonzi is an attractive Alfredo and Merrill an efficient Germont. Pritchard sometimes tends to hustle things along with too little regard for shaping Verdian phrases, but the recording quality is outstandingly good in its CD format.

Though the casting is starry, the snag of the Mehta set on Philips is that the tenor hero sounds so old and his father so young. Though both Alfredo Kraus as Alfredo and Dmitri Hvorostovsky as Germont sing well, they offer an unconvincing partnership. Kraus's musical imagination is masked by dry tone and strain on top, with a very gusty entry for example in the duet *Parigi o cara*. Equally the rich-toned Hvorostovsky hardly sounds fatherly, though he does his best in a firm, spacious account of the aria, *Di Provenza*. Dame Kiri Te Kanawa is tenderly beautiful as Violetta, finely poised in *Ah fors'è lui* and the Farewell, as well as in a hushed, intense account of the Act II duet with Germont. This is one of Mehta's more convincing Verdi performances, generally well recorded, though there are better choices even among modern digital sets.

Callas's version with Giulini was recorded in 1955, three years before the Ghione Lisbon set, when the voice was fresher. There is no more vividly dramatic a performance on record than this, unmatchable in conveying Violetta's agony; sadly, the sound, always limited, grows crumbly towards the end. It is sad too that Bastianini sings so lumpishly as Germont père, even in the great duet of Act II, while di Stefano also fails to match his partner in the supreme test of the final scene. The transfer is fair.

DG, relying on a superstar, Luciano Pavarotti, offers a set recorded in New York, with James Levine conducting a cast based on the Metropolitan Opera production, with Cheryl Studer as Violetta and Juan Pons as Germont. There is much to be said for the beefy energy of Levine in this score, but the recorded sound is relatively coarse, and Pavarotti, for all his detailed feeling for words, does not match his previous recording for Decca opposite Joan Sutherland. Studer too is more exaggerated in expression than she usually is, and Pons is ill-cast as Germont, singing with none of the paternal weight needed.

Toscanini's live recording, made in December 1946, was one of the first he made of complete operas in his final years in New York, following after *La Bohème* in the previous February. Here, even more than in the Puccini and certainly more than in his later Verdi recordings, his speeds are not just fast but relentless. Even so, the high tension of the drama is hair-raising, and both Licia Albanese and Jan Peerce respond impressively, not letting the strict discipline mar their vocal production. The sound, as always with Toscanini recordings of this period, is painfully dry but very clear and forward.

Response to Muti's Sony version will depend greatly on the ear's response to the voice of Tiziana Fabbricini as Violetta. Its Callas-like tang goes with many of the same vocal flaws that afflicted that supreme diva, but Fabbricini has nothing like the same musical imagination or charisma. The effort is hardly worth it for, though she produces one or two impressive top notes in *Sempre libera* at the end of Act I, the edge on the voice is generally unattractive. Muti, always a taut Verdian, does not pace the opera any more sympathetically than in his earlier, EMI set, and in a live performance the flaws of ensemble are distracting, with the dry La Scala acoustic generally unhelpful despite clever balancing by the Sony engineers. Paolo Coni is a strong, smooth-toned Germont but not very imaginative, and the main enjoyment from the set comes from the fresh, virile singing of the tenor, Roberto Alagna, as Alfredo, an excellent recruit to the ranks of leading Italian tenors.

La Traviata: highlights.

(M) *** EMI CDM7 63088-2. Scotto, Kraus, Bruson, Amb. Op. Ch., Philh. O, Muti.

☞ (B) **(*) DG 439 421-2 [id.]. Cotrubas, Domingo, Milnes, Bav. State Op. Ch. & State O, Carlos Kleiber.

☞ ** DG Dig. 437 726-2 [id.] (from above complete set, with Studer, Pavarotti; cond. Levine).

Muti's complete set is at full price and it isn't a first choice, so many will be glad to have this fairly generous (61 minutes) mid-price disc of highlights, including both the Act I and Act III *Preludes* and a well-balanced selection from each of the three Acts, with most of the key numbers included.

For many, Cotrubas makes an ideal star in *Traviata*, but unfortunately the microphone-placing in

Carlos Kleiber's complete set (DG 415 132-2) exaggerates technical flaws and the vibrato becomes too obvious at times. Such is her magic that some will forgive the faults, for her characterization combines strength with vulnerability, but Kleiber's direction is equally controversial with more than a hint of Toscanini-like rigidity in the party music and an occasionally uncomfortable insistence on discipline. However, the strong contributions of Domingo and Milnes make this bargain-priced Classikon highlights CD very worthwhile, as it contains 71 minutes of music, including the two *Preludes*. The documentation is well thought out, except that it omits a track-by track synopsis of the narrative.

The other DG highlights, based on a Metropolitan Opera production in New York, is at premium price yet offers less music (65 minutes)! It relies for its appeal on a superstar, Luciano Pavarotti. There is much to be said for the beefy energy of Levine in this score, but Pavarotti does not match his previous recording (for Decca, opposite Joan Sutherland); Studer too is more exaggerated in expression than she usually is and Juan Pons lacks paternal weight as Germont.

La Traviata (complete, in English).
(M) **(*) EMI CMS7 63072-2 (2). Masterson, Brecknock, Du Plessis, E. Nat. Op. Ch. & O, Mackerras.

Mackerras directs a vigorous, colourful reading which brings out the drama, and Valerie Masterson is at last given the chance on record she has so long deserved. The voice is caught beautifully, if not always very characterfully, and John Brecknock makes a fine Alfredo, most effective in the final scene. Christian Du Plessis' baritone is less suitable for recording. The conviction of the whole enterprise is infectious – but be warned, Verdi in English has a way of sounding on record rather like Gilbert and Sullivan.

La Traviata (sung in English): highlights.
(M) **(*) EMI CDM7 63725-2 [id.] (from above complete recording; cond. Mackerras).

Those wanting to sample this excellent performance in English will find that the 63-minute selection is fairly evenly divided over the three Acts and it is vividly transferred.

Il Trovatore (complete).
⊛ *** BMG/RCA RD 86194 (2) [6194-2-RC]. Leontyne Price, Domingo, Milnes, Cossotto, Amb. Op. Ch., New Philh. O, Mehta.
*** DG Dig. 423 858-2 (2) [id.]. Plowright, Domingo, Fassbaender, Zancanaro, Nesterenko, Ch. & O of St Cecilia Academy, Rome, Giulini.
☞ *** Sony Dig. S2K 48070 (2) [id.]. Millo, Domingo, Chernov, Zajick, Morris, Kelly, Met. Op. Ch. & O, Levine.
(***) EMI CDS7 49347-2 (2) [Ang. CDCB 49347]. Callas, Barbieri, Di Stefano, Panerai, La Scala, Milan, Ch. & O, Karajan.
(M) (***) BMG/RCA mono GD 86643 (2) [6643-2-RG]. Milanov, Bjoerling, Warren, Barbieri, Robert Shaw Ch., RCA Victor O, Cellini.
☞ ** ASV Dig. CDDCS 225 [id.]. (2) [id.]. Wilson, Bisatt, Quinn, Grevelle, Parfitt, Tallis Chamber Ch. (members), European Chamber Op. Ch. & O, Duncan Hinnells.

The soaring curve of Leontyne Price's rich vocal line (almost too ample for some ears) is immediately thrilling in her famous Act I aria, and it sets the style of the RCA performance, full-bodied and with the tension consistently held at the highest levels. The choral contribution is superb; the famous *Soldiers'* and *Anvil choruses* are marvellously fresh and dramatic. When *Di quella pira* comes, the orchestra opens with tremendous gusto and Domingo sings with a ringing, heroic quality worthy of Caruso himself. There are many dramatic felicities, and Sherrill Milnes is in fine voice throughout; but perhaps the highlight of the set is the opening section of Act III, when Azucena finds her way to Conte di Luna's camp. The ensuing scene with Fiorenza Cossotto is vocally and dramatically quite electrifying. The CDs are transferred vibrantly to make one of the most thrilling of all early Verdi operas on record.

Giulini flouts convention at every point. The opera's white-hot inspiration comes out in the intensity of the playing and singing, but the often slow tempi and refined textures present the whole work in new and deeper detail. Rosalind Plowright, sensuous yet ethereal in *Tacea la notte*, masterfully brings together the seemingly incompatible qualities demanded, not just sweetness and purity but brilliant coloratura, flexibility and richly dramatic bite and power. Plácido Domingo sings Manrico as powerfully as he did in the richly satisfying Mehta set on RCA, but the voice is even more heroic in an Otello-like way, only very occasionally showing strain. Giorgio Zancanaro proves a gloriously firm and rounded Count di Luna and Evgeny Nesterenko a dark, powerful Ferrando, while Brigitte Fassbaender, singing her first Azucena, finds great intensity and detail, matching Giulini's freshness. The recording is warm and atmospheric with a pleasant bloom on the voices, naturally balanced and not spotlit.

James Levine conducts his Met. cast in a performance that with full, forward sound brings out the blood-and-thunder of the piece, not least in ensembles. Plácido Domingo as Manrico shows few if any signs of wear in the voice, even in relation to his singing on two of the very finest earlier sets – with both Mehta on RCA and Giulini on DG. Aprile Millo as Leonora has never been more impressive on record, disciplining a voice that can often sound unruly. Vladimir Chernov is a magnificent Count di Luna, with James Morris formidably cast as Ferrando. Dolora Zajick is aptly fruity-toned as Azucena, but heavy vibrato in the voice disturbs her legato singing. Strong as the performance is, it yields before both the vintage Mehta with Leontyne Price at her finest and the inspired Giulini, in which Rosalind Plowright sings far more beautifully and movingly than Millo.

The combination of Karajan and Callas is formidably impressive. There is toughness and dramatic determination in Callas's singing, whether in the coloratura or in the dramatic passages, and this gives the heroine an unsuspected depth of character which culminates in Callas's fine singing of an aria which used often to be cut entirely – *Tu vedrai che amore in terra*, here with its first stanza alone included. Barbieri is a magnificent Azucena, Panerai a strong, incisive Count, and Di Stefano at his finest as Manrico. On CD the 1957 mono sound, though dry and unatmospheric, is one of the more vivid from La Scala at that period.

Though dating from 1952, using a cut text as in the Met. production, the Cellini version brings a vivid reminder of that great opera house at a key period. Milanov, though at times a little raw in Leonora's coloratura, gives a glorious, commanding performance, never surpassed on record, with the voice at its fullest. Bjoerling and Warren too are in ringing voice, and Barbieri is a superb Azucena, with Cellini – rarely heard on record – proving an outstanding Verdian.

European Chamber Opera is an enterprising group that aims to promote talented young singers. Here their efforts are effectively translated on to disc and, though it is a tall order to expect purchasers to pay premium price for an opera-recording featuring little-known singers, the results are refreshing and more than just promising. In particular Susan Bisatt with a very sweet and pure soprano sings most beautifully, coping splendidly, if with a hint of caution, with the problems of *Tacea la notte* and other vocal tests. The other voices are not quite so distinguished, though all are fresh and clear, and the well-balanced recording gives a good idea of a performance no less effective for being on the plain side.

Il Trovatore: highlights.

(M) *** DG Dig. 435 418-2 [id.] (from above recording, with Plowright, Domingo, Fassbaender; cond. Giulini).

(M) (***) RCA mono GD 60191 [60191-2-RG] (from above recording; cond. Cellini).

(M) **(*) Decca 421 310-2; *421 310-4*. Sutherland, Pavarotti, Horne, Wixell, Ghiaurov, L. Op. Ch. & Nat. PO, Bonynge.

Those who have the earlier RCA set in which Domingo participated should consider these highlights from Giulini's unconventional but highly compelling performance, especially as the CD is offered at mid-price.

For many, a highlights CD will be the ideal way to approach this outstanding 1952 RCA recording, much admired in its day. Two dozen excerpts (68 minutes) span the opera very effectively.

The selection from Bonynge's Decca set is especially valuable as a reminder of Sutherland's Leonora. Pavarotti may be stretched by the role of Manrico, but he is nearly always magnificent. Horne is represented by her powerful *Stride la vampa*, Wixell by an undernourished *Il Balen*.

Il Trovatore: highlights (sung in English).

☞ (B) ** CfP CD-CFP 4604; *TC-CFP 4604*. Fretwell, Johnson, Craig, Glossop, McIntyre, Hunter, Sadler's Wells Op. Ch. & O, Moores.

This potted version of *Il Trovatore* in English dates from 1962. It is vividly recorded, the words are admirably clear and there is plenty of drama in the presentation. However, this is not as successful as the companion selection from Puccini's *Madame Butterfly*. Away from the stage some of the singing does not stand up too well, although Elizabeth Fretwell (as Leonora) is undoubtedly both strong and stylish, even if *Tacea la notte* is rather shaky. Charles Craig once again is as ringing and well controlled a tenor as you will find anywhere. Patricia Johnson and Peter Glossop are not quite up to their stage form, but their singing has plenty of conviction and, in scenes like the *Miserere* and the finale to the Convent scene, the presence and depth of the recording are persuasive.

I vespri siciliani (complete).
**(*) BMG/RCA RD 80370 (3) [0370-2-RC]. Arroyo, Domingo, Milnes, Raimondi, Ewing, Alldis
  Ch., New Philh. O, Levine.
**(*) EMI CDS7 54043-2 (3) [Ang. CDCC 54043]; *EX 754043-4*. Merritt, Studer, Zancanaro,
  Furlanetto, Ch. & O of La Scala, Milan, Muti.

This opera has been sadly neglected on record; Levine's 1974 RCA set, made in London, remains a
first choice, dominated by the partnership of Plácido Domingo and Sherrill Milnes. Their Act II duet,
using a melody well known from the *Overture*, is nothing short of magnificent, with both singers at
their very peak. Though Martina Arroyo is less responsive than Studer on Muti's EMI alternative
version, Domingo, Milnes and the young Ruggero Raimondi are all preferable to the La Scala
singers, and the sharpness of focus in both performance and recording exposes the relative fuzziness
of Muti's live account. The rest of the singing in the RCA cast is good if rarely inspired, and James
Levine's direction is colourful and urgent. Good recording, vividly remastered.

The EMI set is the most successful yet of the live recordings made by Muti at La Scala, Milan,
plagued by a difficult acoustic which is dispiritingly dry for the engineers. The atmosphere is well
caught and, though Muti can be too tautly urgent a Verdian, his pacing here is well geared to bring
out the high drama. Outstanding in the cast is Cheryl Studer as the heroine, Elena, singing radiantly;
while the tenor Chris Merritt as Arrigo sounds less coarse and strained than he has in the past.
Giorgio Zancanaro also responds to the role of Monforte – the governor of Sicily, discovered to be
Arrigo's father – with new sensitivity, and though Ferruccio Furlanetto as Procida lacks the full
weight to bring out the beauty of line in the great aria, *O tu Palermo*, his is a warm performance too.

COLLECTIONS

Arias & excerpts (recorded 1906–16, with Gadski, Hempel, Scotti, Alda, Ruffo, Tetrazzini, Jacoby,
Amato, Gluck, Schumann-Heink) from: *Requiem; Aida; Un ballo in maschera; Don Carlo; La forza
del destino; I Lombardi; Macbeth; Otello; Rigoletto; La Traviata; Il Trovatore.*
☞ (M) (***) BMG/RCA mono 09026 61242-2 [id.].

Like the miscellaneous Caruso collections included in the Recitals sections (see below), these
recordings were restored by Thomas Stockham using the Soundstream digital process which removes
unwanted horn resonances; the improvement in sound is phenomenal. The voice often sounds
pristine, and only the heavily scored accompaniments serve to remind the listener of the early
recording dates. There are many famous recordings here and it is good that other singers are featured
too, Gadski in *La fatal pietra* from *Aida*, Hemel in *La rivedrà nell'estasi* from *Un ballo in maschera*,
Scotti in the excerpts from Act I of *Don Carlo* and Act III of *La forza del destino*, and so on. The
version of the *Quartet* from *Rigoletto* (*Bella figlia*) includes Tetrazzini, Josephine Jacoby and Amato.
The programme is well chosen and the sound revelatory. Sample the superbly stylish *Questa o quella*
or *La donna è mobile* (from *Rigoletto*), or the soaring *Ah sì, ben mio* (*Il Trovatore*), all recorded in
1908, which sound amazingly free from the mechanical problems of the early recording process.
Surface noise is reduced, but still present; yet the ear soon programmes it out.

Arias: *Aida: Ritorna vincitor. Un ballo in maschera: Ecco l'orrido campo. Don Carlos: Tu che le
vanità. Ernani: Ernani involami. I Lombardi: O Madre dal cielo. Macbeth: Nel dì della vittoria; La
luce langue una macchia. Nabucco: Anch'io dischiuso un giorno. I vespri siciliani: Arrigo! Oh parli.*
*** EMI CDC7 47730-2 [id.]. Maria Callas, Philh. O, Rescigno.

In this first of two Verdi recital records issued to commemorate the tenth anniversary of Callas's
death, the great soprano is at her most commanding, not flawless but thrilling, both in her creative
musicianship and in her characterizations. Generally good transfers and clean sound.

'Famous arias' from: (i; ii; iii) *Aida;* (iv) *Un ballo in maschera;* (v) *Luisa Miller;* (vi; vii) *Rigoletto;*
(viii) *Otello;* (ix) *La Traviata;* (x; xi) *Il Trovatore.*
☞ (M) ** Decca 433 442-2 [id.]. (i) Vickers; (ii) L .Price; (iii) Cerquetti; (iv) Tebaldi; (v) Bergonzi; (vi)
  Pavarotti; (vii) Sutherland; (viii) Crespin; (ix) Fischer-Dieskau; (x) Simionato; (xi) Del Monaco.

This Decca anthology is enjoyable, if not really distinctive. Highlights include Pavarotti's opening
(1972) *La donna è mobile* and Sutherland's ravishing 1960 *Caro nome* from the same opera (exquisite
trills), while both Vickers' and Leontyne Price's key arias from Solti's *Aida* are very commanding
indeed. Mario del Monaco rounds off the recital rousingly with a *Di quella pira* which could surely
raise the roof of the Met. Characteristically vivid sound throughout.

Arias from: *Un ballo in maschera; I due Foscari; Ernani; La forza del destino; Luisa Miller; Macbeth; Rigoletto; La Traviata; Il Trovatore.*
☞ (M) ** Decca Dig. 421 893-2 [id.]. Leo Nucci, Nat. PO, Armstrong.

This was Leo Nucci's début recital for Decca in 1982. It demonstrates a fine voice and good control of colour and line (as in *Di Provenza il mar* from *Traviata*). But there is nothing here to make the blood tingle, although the digital sound is excellent and Richard Armstrong is a strong and sympathetic accompanist.

Arias: *Don Carlo: Son io, mio Carlo . . . Per me giunto . . . O Carlo, ascolta. Luisa Miller: Sacra la scelta. Macbeth: Perfidi! All'anglo contra me v'unite . . . Pietà, rispetto, amore. La Traviata: Di Provenza il mar. Il Trovatore: Tutto è deserto . . . Il balen.*
*** Ph. Dig. 426 740-2 [id.]. Dmitri Hvorostovsky, Rotterdam PO, Gergiev – TCHAIKOVSKY: *Arias.* ***

With a glorious voice, dark and characterful, and with natural musical imagination, Dmitri Hvorostovsky on this disc made his recording début in the West not just in Tchaikovsky arias, but here in Verdi, stylishly sung. With a voice of such youthful virility, he hardly sounds like the father-figure of the *Traviata* and *Luisa Miller* items, but the legato in Macbeth's Act IV aria is most beautiful. He also brings the keenest intensity to Posa's death-scene aria from *Don Carlo.*

Arias: *Don Carlos: Tu che le vanità. La Traviata: Ah fors'è lui. Il Trovatore: Timor di me.*
*** Sony Dig. M K 37298 [id.]. Kiri Te Kanwa, LPO, Pritchard – PUCCINI: *Arias.* ***

The Verdi part of Kiri Te Kanawa's Verdi–Puccini recital brings three substantial items, less obviously apt for the singer, but in each the singing is felt as well as beautiful. The coloratura of the *Traviata* and *Trovatore* items is admirably clean, and it is a special joy to hear Elisabetta's big aria from *Don Carlos* sung with such truth and precision. Good recording, enhanced on CD.

Arias & duets: *Un ballo in maschera: Teco io sto. Il Corsaro: Egli non riede ancora! Don Carlos: Non pianger, mia compagna. Giovanna d'Arco: Qui! Qui! Dove più s'apre libero il ciela; O fatidica foresta. Jérusalem: Ave Maria. I Masnadieri: Dall'infame banchetto io m'involai; Tu del mio; Carlo vive. Otello: Già nella notte densa; Ave Maria. Il Trovatore: Timor di me; D'amor sull'ali rosee; Tu vedrai che amor in terr. I vespri siciliani: Arrigo! Ah, parli a un cor.*
(M) *** BMG/RCA GD 86534 [6534-2-RG]. Katia Ricciarelli, Plácido Domingo, Rome PO or St Cecilia Ac. O, Gavazzeni.

At mid-price this collection of Verdi arias and duets from two star singers, both in fresh voice, makes a good bargain. The inclusion of rarities adds to the attractions, and though the sound is not the most modern, it is more than acceptable in the bright digital transfer.

Choruses from: *Aida; Un ballo in maschera; Don Carlo; I Lombardi; Macbeth; I Masnadieri; Nabucco; Otello; Rigoletto; La Traviata; Il Trovatore. Requiem Mass: Sanctus.*
*** Decca Dig. 430 226-2 [id.]. Chicago Symphony Ch. & SO, Solti.

The Solti collection is not drawn from the maestro's previous complete opera sets but is a first-class studio production, recorded in Orchestra Hall, Chicago, with Decca's most resplendent digital sound. The choral balance is forward, but there is also plenty of depth and a wide dynamic range. Solti is on top form. Besides the many exciting histrionic moments there are many refined touches too, notably in the stylish *La Traviata* excerpt, with soloists from the chorus, and the flashing fantasy of *Fuoco di gioia* from *Otello*. Full translations are included.

Choruses from: *Aida; La Battaglia di Legnano; Don Carlo; Ernani; La forza del destino; Macbeth; Nabucco; Otello; La Traviata; Il Trovatore.*
(BB) *** Naxos Dig. 8.550241; 4.550241 [id.]. Slovak Philharmonic Ch. & RSO, Oliver Dohnányi.

The super-bargain Naxos collection by the excellent Slovak Philharmonic Choir brings very realistic sound and the slightly recessed choral balance in the Bratislava Radio Concert Hall is very natural: it certainly does not lack impact and, in the *Fire chorus* from Otello, detail registers admirably. Under Oliver Dohnányi's lively direction the chorus sings with admirable fervour. The collection ends resplendently with the Triumphal scene from *Aida*, omitting the ballet but with the fanfare trumpets blazing out on either side most tellingly. With a playing time of 56 minutes this is excellent value in every respect.

'The world of Verdi': (i) *Aida: Celeste Aida;* (ii) *Grand march and ballet.* (iii) *La forza del destino: Pace, pace mio Dio.* (iv) *Luisa Miller: O! Fede negar potessi . . . Quando le sere al placido.* (v) *Nabucco: Va pensiero.* (vi) *Otello: Credo. Rigoletto:* (vii) *Caro nome;* (viii) *La donna è mobile;* (vii; viii; ix) Quartet: *Belle figlia dell'amore.* (x) *La Traviata: Prelude, Act I;* (vii; xi) *Brindisi: Libiamo ne'lieti calici. Il Trovatore:* (xii) *Anvil chorus;* (xiii) *Strida la vampa;* (viii) *Di quella pira. I vespri siciliani:* (xiv) *Mercè, diletti amiche.*

☞ (M) *** Decca 433 221-1; *433 221-4.* (i) Vickers; (ii) Rome Op. Ch. & O, Solti; (iii) G. Jones; (iv) Bergonzi; (v) Amb. S., LSO, Abbado; (vi) Evans; (vii) Sutherland; (viii) Pavarotti; (ix) Tourangeau, Milnes; (x) Maggiò Musicale O, Fiorentino, Pritchard; (xi) Bergonzi; (xii) L. Op. Ch., Bonynge; (xiii) Horne; (xiv) Chiara.

Opening with the *Chorus of the Hebrew Slaves* from *Nabucco* and closing with Pavarotti's *Di quella pira* from *Il Trovatore*, this quite outstandingly red-blooded Verdi compilation should surely tempt any novice to explore further into Verdi's world, yet at the same time it provides a superbly arranged 74-minute concert in its own right. The choice of items and performances demonstrates a shrewd knowledge of both popular Verdi and the Decca catalogue, for not a single performance disappoints. Joan Sutherland's melting 1971 *Caro nome* with its exquisite trills is the first of three splendid excerpts from *Rigoletto*, ending with the famous Quartet, and other highlights include Dame Gwyneth Jones's glorious *Pace, pace, mio Dio*, introduced of course by the sinisterly scurrying *Forza del destino* motif, Sir Geraint Evans's superb account of Iago's evil *Credo* from *Otello* – here the Decca sound adds to the riveting impact – and Marilyn Horne's dark-timbred *Strida la vampa* from *Trovatore*. Solti, too, is at his most electric in the great March scene from *Aida*. The stereo throughout is splendidly vivid, and this mid-priced collection is worth every penny of its modest cost.

Victoria, Tomás Luis de *(c. 1548–1611)*

(i) Motets: *Ascendit Christus in altem; Ave Maria; Gaudent in coelis; O magnum mysterium; Missa de Requiem in 6 parts;* (ii) Mass & motet: *O quam gloriosum;* (iii) *Responsories de Tenebrae.*

☞ (M) **(*) Decca 433 914-2 (2) [id.]. (i) St John's College Ch., Cambridge, Guest; (ii) King's College Ch., Cambridge, Cleobury; (iii) Westminster Cathedral Ch., Malcolm.

Easily the most impressive of these recordings is George Malcolm's complete set of the 18 *Tenebrae responses* for Maundy Thursday, Good Friday and Holy Saturday. Victoria's magnificent music, austere but with underlying passionate feeling, finds the Westminster Cathedral Choir at their finest, catching the Latin fervour of the music. The recording has a finely judged acoustic and atmosphere. However, Malcolm's set of *Responsories* is also available on a very attractive single-disc collection (see below), including the Motets (but not the *Requiem*) and offering instead the beautiful *Litaniae de Beata Virgine.* The St John's Choir under George Guest also sing well in tune and with an impressive sense of line, but their whole approach is rather Anglican for this passionate Spanish music. The motets fare much better than the *Requiem*. The King's coupling of Mass and motet, *O quam gloriosum,* offers modern digital sound, the voices finely blended to produce an impressive range of sonority. The recording is admirably faithful and, while there is an element of introspection here, the singing also offers moments of affecting serenity.

Ascendens Christus (motet); *Missa Ascendis Christus in altum; O Magnum mysterium* (motet); *Missa O Magnum mysterium.*

*** Hyp. Dig. CDA 66190; *KA 66190* [id.]. Westminster Cathedral Ch., David Hill.

Missa Ave maris stella; O quam gloriosum est regnum (motet); *Missa O quam gloriosum.*

⊕ *** Hyp. CDA 66114; *KA 66114* [id.]. Westminster Cathedral Ch., David Hill.

The Latin fervour of the singing is very involving; some listeners may initially be surprised at the volatile way David Hill moves the music on, with the trebles eloquently soaring aloft on the line of the music. The spontaneous ebb and flow of the pacing is at the heart of David Hill's understanding of this superb music. The recording balance is perfectly judged, with the Westminster acoustic adding resonance (in both senses of the word) to singing of the highest calibre, combining a sense of timelessness and mystery with real expressive power.

Ave Maria; Ave Maris stella (hymn). *Missa Vidi speciosam. Ne timeas, Maria; Sancta Maria, succurre miseris; Vidi speciosam* (motets).

*** Hyp. Dig. CDA 66129; *KA 66129* [id.]. Westminster Cathedral Ch., David Hill.

An outstanding collection of some of Victoria's most beautiful music celebrating the Virgin Mary.

The four-part *Ave Maria* may not be authentic, but the composer would surely not be reluctant to own it. The Westminster Choir again show their flexibly volatile response to this music with that special amalgam of fervour and serenity that Victoria's writing demands. The acoustics of Westminster Cathedral add the right degree of resonance to the sound without clouding.

Officium defunctorum.
*** Gimell Dig. CDGIM 012; *1585T-12* [id.]. Tallis Scholars, Phillips (with LOBO: Motet: *Versa est in luctum* ***).
*** Hyp. Dig. CDA 66250; *KA 66250* [id.]. Westminster Cathedral Ch., David Hill.

The *Officium defunctorum* was Victoria's swan-song – he died only six years later. It is a work of great serenity and beauty. Honours are fairly evenly divided between the Westminster Cathedral Choir on Hyperion and the Tallis Scholars under Peter Phillips. The Westminster Choir has the advantage of boys' voices and larger forces; they are recorded in a warmer, more spacious acoustic. By comparison with the Gimell recording, the sound seems a little less well focused, but on its own terms it is thoroughly convincing. They permit themselves greater expressiveness, too. Moreover the *Requiem* is set in the wider liturgical context by the use of some chants. The Tallis Scholars achieve great clarity of texture; they are twelve in number and, as a result, the polyphony is clearer, and so too are their words. They offer also a short and deeply felt motet by Alonso Lobo (*c.* 1555–1617). The recording has a warm, glowing sound which almost persuades you that you are in the imperial chapel.

Missa Surge propera; Stabat Mater.
(B) *** Pickwick Dig. PCD 970; *CIMPC 970* [id.]. Mixolydian, Piers Schmidt – PADILLA: *Missa Ego flos campi* etc. ***

The *Missa Surge propera* is a five-voiced parody Mass, published in 1583, the only one of Victoria's works to be based on Palestrina. It is a beautiful work and, like the *Stabat Mater*, is very well sung by Mixolydian under Piers Schmidt and is recorded with exemplary skill.

Responsories for Tenebrae.
*** Hyp. Dig. CDA 66304; *KA 66304* [id.]. Westminster Cathedral Ch., David Hill.
** Gimell Dig CDGIM 022; *1385T-22* [id.]. Tallis Scholars, Peter Phillips.

The *Tenebrae Responses* are an essential element in any collection of Renaissance polyphony and they have been well represented on record over the years. Memories of George Malcolm's famous recording from the late 1950s – see below – are not dislodged by either of these newcomers. The Tallis Scholars sound absolutely perfect in both blend and intonation but are curiously uninvolving. They are beautifully recorded and technically immaculate but convey little real intensity of feeling. The Westminster Cathedral Choir under David Hill on Hyperion find far more atmosphere in this music and bring a sense of spontaneous feeling to their performance. Of recent versions, this can be welcomed without reservation.

(i) *Responsories for Tenebrae;* (ii) *Litaniae de Beata Virgine. Motets: Ascendens Christus in altum; Ave Maria; Gaudent in coelis; O magnum mysterium.*
☞ (M) *** Decca 425 078-2 [id.]. (i) Westminster Cathedral Ch., George Malcolm; (ii) St John's College, Cambridge, Ch., George Guest.

The *Tenebrae responsories* are so called because of the tradition of performing them in the evening in increasing darkness as the candles were extinguished one by one. The music here offers Victoria's settings for Maundy Thursday, Good Friday and Holy Saturday. The three sections between them tell the story of the Crucifixion from Judas's betrayal through to the burial of Jesus. This (originally Argo) recording dates from 1959, a period when the Westminster Cathedral Choir under George Malcolm was at its peak. The performance has great vigour and eloquence, and the recording is very fine. The coupled motets from the St John's Choir must be numbered among the finest Victoria gave us. The performances are admirably done and, if one accepts the fact that English choirs lack the harsh lines drawn by the firmer-toned Spanish bodies, there is little at which one can cavil. Indeed one would place this record high on the list of CDs of the music of Victoria for the collector who wants to sample this composer or this period, and it would be a useful starting-point for any library. The transfers are clear and well focused.

Vierne, Louis (1870–1937)

Suite No. 3, Op. 54: Carillon de Westminster.
*** DG Dig. 413 438-2 [id.]. Simon Preston (organ of Westminster Abbey) – WIDOR: *Symphony No. 5.* ***

The Vierne *Carillon de Westminster* is splendidly played by Simon Preston and sounds appropriately atmospheric in this spacious acoustic and well-judged recording. It makes an attractive makeweight to the Widor *Fifth Symphony*.

Symphonies Nos. 1–4.
*** Erato Dig. 2292 45485-2 (2). Marie-Claire Alain (Cavaillé-Coll organ of the Abbey of St-Etienne de Caen).

Marie-Claire Alain is here in her element. In terms of registration, pacing and overall grip these performances are very authoritative indeed, and the Cavaillé-Coll organ at St-Etienne de Caen is perfectly suited to this repertoire. Its reedy colouring combined with plenty of underlying sonority in the pedals is especially effective in the *Final* movements, notably that for No. 1, although curiously the sound on the second CD (containing *Symphonies Nos. 1* and *3*) is slightly smoother and better balanced than on its companion.

Symphonies Nos. 1 in D min., Op. 14; 2 in E min., Op. 20.
*** Mer. CDE 84192 [id.]. David Sanger (organ of La Chiesa Italiana di San Pietro, London).

Symphonies Nos. 3 in F sharp min., Op. 28; 4 in G min., Op. 32.
*** Mer. CDE 84176; *KE 77176* [id.]. David Sanger (organ of La Chiesa Italiana di San Pietro, London).

Symphonies Nos. 5 in A min., Op. 47; 6 in B min., Op. 59.
*** Mer. CDE 84171; *KE 77171* [id.]. David Sanger (organ of La Chiesa Italiana di San Pietro, London).

David Sanger's recordings of the Vierne *Organ symphonies* are highly rewarding and can be strongly recommended alongside those of Marie-Claire Alain on Erato. Indeed some listeners are likely to prefer the very appealing patina of the San Pietro organ. There is no cause to complain of the sound quality, which maintains the high standards Meridian have set themselves: the resonance of the pedals is very telling without muddying the overall sound-picture.

Symphonies Nos. 1 in D min., Op. 14; 3 in F sharp min., Op. 28.
☞ **(*) Telarc Dig. CD 80329 [id.]. Michael Murray (organ of St Ouen Abbey, Rouen).

Strong, direct performances from Michael Murray, attractively registered. The Telarc engineers also create a spectacularly full-blooded sound-picture of the Cavaillé-Coll organ at Rouen. But in the last resort Murray seems less naturally at home in this repertoire than his competitors.

Vieuxtemps, Henri (1820–81)

Violin concerto No. 5 in A min., Op. 37.
*** DG Dig. 427 676-2 [id.]. Mintz, Israel PO, Mehta – LALO: *Symphonie espagnole;* SAINT-SAENS: *Intro & Rondo capriccioso.* ***
*** Ph. Dig. 422 332-2 [id.]. Mullova, ASMF, Marriner – PAGANINI: *Concerto No. 1.* ***
*** BMG/RCA RD 86214 [RCA 6214-2-RC]. Heifetz, New SO of L., Sargent – BRUCH: *Concerto No. 1; Scottish fantasia.* ***
☞ (M) **(*) Sony SBK 48274 [id.]. Zukerman, LSO, Mackerras – BRUCH: *Concerto No. 1;* LALO: *Symphonie espagnole.* **(*)

Minz's performance has enormous dash, and real lyrical magic too. Mehta, obviously caught up in the inspiration of the solo playing, provides an excellent accompaniment; this is another example of a memorable live performance recorded 'on the wing', and if the acoustic is not especially flattering the sound is obviously truthful and well balanced.

Like her Paganini No. 1, Viktoria Mullova's account of the *A minor Concerto* is remarkable for its breathtaking virtuosity and its great fire and style. Sir Neville Marriner and the Academy are supportive and the Philips recording, though a bit bass-resonant, is first class and very vivid and present.

The quicksilver of Heifetz is well suited to the modest but attractive *Fifth Concerto* of Vieuxtemps, and Sir Malcolm provides a musical and well-recorded accompaniment. The balance of the soloist is rather close, but the digital remastering is successful and the couplings are both attractive and generous.

Zukerman provides here an enjoyable bonus to his dazzling accounts of the Bruch and Lalo works. There is comparable dash for Vieuxtemps, yet he coaxes the *Adagio* tenderly. Again a very forward balance, but the ear adjusts.

Villa-Lobos, Heitor (1887–1959)

Amazonas; Dawn in a tropical forest; Erosão; Gênesis.
☞ *** Marco Polo Dig. 8.223357 [id.]. Czecho-Slovak RSO (Bratislava), Roberto Duarte.

These are imaginative scores with lots of tropical colouring and exotic textures, all sounding rather similar in their luxuriance – but who cares! *Erosão* or *The Origin of the Amazon* and *Dawn in a tropical forest* were both composed for the Louisville Orchestra (in 1950 and 1953 respectively); *Gênesis* is a ballet commissioned by the American dancer, Janet Collins, and comes from 1954; *Amazonas* is the earliest and most astonishing score, dating from before the First World War, and in its vivid sonorities affirms Villa-Lobos's contention that his first harmony book was the map of Brazil. The Bratislava strings could perhaps be more opulent, but the performances under a Brazilian conductor are really very good indeed and so is the recording.

Bachianas brasileiras Nos. 1–9; Chôros Nos. 2 (for flute & orchestra); 5 (for piano, Alma Brasileira); 10 (for chorus & orchestra); (i) 11 (for piano & orchestra). 2 Chôros (bis) (for violin & cello); (i) Piano concerto No. 5; Descobrimento do Brasil; Invocação em defesa da Patria; (i) Momoprecoce (fantasy for piano & orchestra); Symphony No. 4. Qu'est-ce qu'un Chôros? (Villa-Lobos speaking).
(M) (**(*)) EMI mono CZS7 67229-2 (6). De los Angeles, Kareska, Basrentzen, Braune, Tagliaferro, Du Frene, Plessier, Cliquennois, Bronschwak, Neilz, Benedetti; (i) Blumental; Chorale des Jeunesses Musicales de France, Fr. Nat. R. & TV Ch. & O, cond. composer.

This six-CD box is a colourful, warm-hearted collection, not helped by dull mono recordings and ill-disciplined performances, but full of a passionately surging intensity that plainly reflects the personality of a composer of obvious charisma, if of limited ability as a conductor. Endearingly, there is a 10-minute track spoken in French by Villa-Lobos himself, 'What is a *Chôros*?' – one of the musical forms he invented for himself. The personal genre for which Villa-Lobos will obviously be remembered is the *Bachianas brasileiras*, relating his love for native Brazilian music to neo-classical Bachian forms, if often rather distantly. All nine of them are recorded here, including the celebrated No. 5 for soprano and eight cellos, with Victoria de los Angeles a radiant soloist. That recording is already well known, but most of the others have had very limited circulation. They make an enjoyable collection for, despite the dull sound, the warmth of the writing never fails to come over. Unfortunately, this set has been withdrawn as we go to press.

Bachianas Brasileiras Nos. (iii) 1; (i; iii) 5; (i; ii) Suite for voice and violin. (iii) arr. of BACH: The Well-tempered clavier: Prelude in D min., BWV 583; Fugue in B flat, BWV 846; Prelude in G min., BWV 867; Fugue in D, BWV 874.
*** Hyp. Dig. CDA 66257 [id.]. (i) Jill Gomez, (ii) Peter Manning, (iii) Pleeth Cello Octet.

Jill Gomez is outstanding in the popular *Fifth Bachianas Brasileiras* and with the violinist, Peter Manning, in the *Suite* (1923). Villa-Lobos' favourite 'orchestra of cellos' produce sumptuous sounds in both the *Bachianas Brasileiras*, and an added point of interest is the effective transcriptions for cellos of unrelated Bach preludes and fugues. An eminently attractive introduction to this most colourful of composers.

Guitar concerto.
☞ (BB) *** Naxos Dig. 8.550729 [id.]. Norbert Kraft, Northern CO, Nicholas Ward –
CASTELNUOVO-TEDESCO: *Concerto ***; RODRIGO: Concierto de Aranjuez. ***

An excellent account comes also from Norbert Kraft, spontaneous and catching well the music's colour and atmosphere. If it is not quite as individual as Bream's version, it has the advantage of vivid, well-balanced, modern, digital recording and excellent couplings. Another genuine Naxos bargain.

(i) *Guitar concerto. 12 Etudes; 5 Preludes.*
☞ (M) *** BMG/RCA 09026 61604-2. Julian Bream, (i) LSO, André Previn.

A highly distinguished account of the *Guitar concerto* from Bream, magnetic and full of atmosphere in the slow movement and finale. Previn accompanies sympathetically and with spirit. The rest of the programme also shows Bream in inspirational form. He engages the listener's attention from the opening of the first study and holds it to the last. The vigour and energy of the playing are matched by its spontaneity, and there is considerable subtlety of colour: several of the *Preludes* are hauntingly memorable when the concentration of the music-making is so readily communicated. The recording has a nice intimacy in the concerto and the solo items have fine presence against an attractive ambience.

Piano concertos Nos. 1–5.
*** Decca Dig. 430 628-2 (2) [id.]. Cristina Ortiz, RPO, Gómes-Martínez.

What emerges from the series of concertos, as played by Cristina Ortiz here, is that the first two are the most immediately identifiable as Brazilian in their warm colouring and sense of atmosphere, even though the eclectic borrowings are often more unashamed than later, with many passages suggesting Rachmaninov with a Brazilian accent. No. 3, the work Villa-Lobos found it hard to complete, tends to sound bitty in its changes of direction. No. 4, more crisply conceived, has one or two splendid tunes, but it is in No. 5 that Villa-Lobos becomes most warmly convincing again, returning unashamedly to more echoes of Rachmaninov. With Ortiz articulating crisply, there is much to enjoy from such colourful, undemanding music, brilliantly recorded and sympathetically performed.

Discovery of Brazil: suites Nos. 1–3; (i) 4.
☞ **(*) Marco Polo Dig. 8.223551 [id.]. Slovak RSO (Bratislava), Roberto Duarte; (i) with Adam Blazo, Slovak Philharmonic. Ch.

The *Discovery of Brazil* dates from 1936 when an ambitious film project on this theme was undertaken and Villa-Lobos was commissioned for the music. Subsequently Villa-Lobos fashioned three orchestral suites from it, plus a fourth which employs a soloist and choir. (As Pierre Vidal points out in his excellent note, not all the music was newly composed; four episodes derive from earlier works.) Villa-Lobos himself recorded all four suites in Paris in a two-LP deluxe box in the late 1950s, and they have reappeared in France in a six-CD set of all his recordings. To be frank, although there are good things in this music and some exotic orchestral effects, the colours are not quite as vivid and dazzling as one would have expected from this prolific Brazilian master. Not three-star music exactly, but the performances are really rather good, and so is the recording.

Berceuse, Op. 50; Divigačao; O canto do capadócio; O canto do cisne negro; O canto do nossa terra; Sonhar, Op. 14.
** Marco Polo Dig. 8.223298 [id.]. Rebecca Rust, David Apter – ENESCU: *Cello sonata.* **

These pieces are all new to the catalogue and are well played and recorded, but they are a bonus for the Enescu *First Cello sonata*, some 37 minutes long, which may not hold the attention of all listeners to the last bar!

String quartets Nos. 4 (1917); 6 (Quarteto Brasileiro) (1938); 14 (1953).
☞ *** Marco Polo Dig. 8.223391 [id.]. Danubius Qt.

Not long before his death, Villa-Lobos told the French critic, Pierre Vidal, that the string quartet was his favourite medium (he spoke of it as a mania) and, given the repertoire explosion with which Marco Polo (and many others) are confronting us, we have a chance of discovering all 17. The first dates from 1915 and the last from 1957; he was engaged on an eighteenth at the time of his death. The three recorded here are all well crafted and their ideas are of quality. The *Fourth* is perhaps the most Gallic; the *Sixth* (*Quarteto Brasileiro*) was one of the first to reach the gramophone (in the hands of the incomparable Hollywood Quartet) and is one of the most individual and rewarding. It makes intelligent use of Brazilian folk-material. The *Fourteenth*, like so much of Villa-Lobos, is not entirely free from note-spinning. The Danubius Quartet are an accomplished ensemble and play with evident commitment. The recording places them rather forward in the aural picture.

Suite populaire brésilienne; Etudes Nos. 5 in C; 7 in E.
☞ (M) *** BMG/RCA 09026 61596-2. Julian Bream – Recital: *'Twentieth-century guitar II'.* ***

The *Suite populaire brésilienne* is deservedly among Villa-Lobos's most popular music. The composer disclaims the idea that these four chôros (pieces in the style of Brazilian street-bands) were intended as a suite, but they fit together remarkably well. Bream plays them with his usual flair and brings out all their vivid colouring. The two contrasted *Etudes* are also fine pieces. Excellent late-1970s recording.

PIANO MUSIC

Alma brasileira, Bachiana brasileira No. 4; Ciclo brasileiro; Chôros No. 5; Valsa da dor (Waltz of sorrows).
*** ASV Dig. CDDCA 607 [id.]. Alma Petchersky.

Alma Petchersky's style is romantic, and some might find her thoughtful deliberation in the *Preludio* of the *Bachianas Brasileira No. 4* overdone. Her very free rubato is immediately apparent in the *Valsa da dor* which opens the recital. Yet she clearly feels all this music deeply, and the playing is strong in personality and her timbre is often richly coloured. She is at her finest in the *Brazilian cycle*. The recording is first class.

VOCAL MUSIC

Bachianas Brasileiras No. 5 for soprano and cellos.
*** Decca Dig. 411 730-2 [id.]. Te Kanawa, Harrell and instrumental ens. – CANTELOUBE: *Songs of the Auvergne.* **(*)
(M) *** BMG/RCA GD 87831 [7831-2-RG]. Anna Moffo, American SO, Stokowski –CANTELOUBE: *Chants d'Auvergne;* RACHMANINOV: *Vocalise.* ***

The Villa-Lobos piece makes an apt fill-up for the Canteloube songs completing Kiri Te Kanawa's recording of all five books. It is, if anything, even more sensuously done, well sustained at a speed far slower than one would normally expect. Rich recording to match.

Anna Moffo gives a seductive performance of the most famous of the *Bachianas Brasileiras*, adopting a highly romantic style (matching the conductor) and warm tone-colour.

Magdalena.
*** Sony Dig. SK 44945 [id.]. Kaye, Rose, Esham, Gray, Hadley, O, Evans Haile.

Magdalena is a colourful, vigorous piece, alas lacking the big tunes you really need in a musical, but full of delightful ideas. It tells the sort of story that Lehár might have chosen, only translated to South America. Sadly, in spite of an enthusiastic response from everyone, it closed on Broadway in 1948 after only eleven weeks. The present recording was prompted by a concert performance to celebrate the Villa-Lobos centenary, a splendid, well-sung account of what is aptly described as 'a musical adventure'.

Viotti, Giovanni Battista (1755–1824)

Violin concerto No. 13 in A.
*** Hyp. Dig. CDA 66210 [id.]. Oprean, European Community CO, Faerber – FIORILLO: *Violin concerto No. 1.* ***

Viotti wrote a great many violin concertos in much the same mould, but this is one of his best. Adelina Oprean's quicksilver style and light lyrical touch give much pleasure – she has the exact measure of this repertoire and she is splendidly accompanied and well recorded. The measure, though, is short.

Vivaldi, Antonio (1675–1741)

L'Estro armonico (12 Concertos), Op. 3.
*** DG Dig. 423 094-2 (2) [id.]. Standage & soloists, E. Concert, Trevor Pinnock.
*** O-L 414 554-2 (2) [id.]. Holloway, Huggett, Mackintosh, Wilcock, AAM, Hogwood.

Vivaldi's *L'Estro armonico* was published in 1711. The set includes some of his finest music and had great influence. This new chamber version from Pinnock (with one instrument to a part) seems instinctively to summarize and amalgamate the best features from past versions: there is as much sparkle and liveliness as with Hogwood, for rhythms are consistently resilient, ensemble crisp and vigorous. Yet in slow movements there is that expressive radiance and sense of enjoyment of beauty without unstylish indulgence that one expects from the ASMF. The recording was made in EMI's Abbey Road studios and the balance and ambient effect are judged perfectly.

There is no question about the sparkle of Christopher Hogwood's performance with the Academy of Ancient Music. The captivating lightness of the solo playing and the crispness of articulation of the accompanying group bring music-making that combines joyful vitality with the authority of scholarship. Hogwood's continuo is first class, varying between harpsichord and organ, the latter used to add colour as well as substance. The balance is excellent, and the whole effect is exhilarating.

L'Estro armonico (12 Concertos), Op. 3.
(M) *** Ph. 426 932-2 (2) [id.]. Michelucci, Gallozzi, Cotogni, Vicari, Colandrea, Altobelli, Garatti, I Musici.

La Stravaganza (12 Concertos), Op. 4.
(M) *** Ph. 426 935-2 (2) [id.]. Ayo, Gallozzi, Altobelli, Garatti, I Musici.

These Philips reissues draw on recordings made (mostly in the highly suitable acoustics of La Chaux-de-Fonds, Switzerland) in 1962/3. The transfers to CD are admirable. These are refreshing and lively performances; melodies are finely drawn and there is little hint of the routine which occasionally surfaces in I Musici – and, for that matter, in Vivaldi himself. Maria Teresa Garatti's continuo features a chamber organ as well as harpsichord in Op. 4, to excellent effect.

La Stravaganza, Op. 4 (complete).
⊛ (M) *** Decca 430 566-2 (2) [id.]. ASMF, Sir Neville Marriner.
*** O-L Dig. 417 502-2 (2) [id.]. Huggett, AAM, Hogwood.
☞ (M) ** Erato/Warner 2292 45450-2 (2) [id.]. Toso, Rybin, Sol. Ven., Scimone.

Marriner's performances make the music irresistible. The solo playing of Carmel Kaine and Alan Loveday is superb and, when the Academy's rhythms have such splendid buoyancy and lift, it is easy enough to accept Marriner's preference for a relatively sweet style in the often heavenly slow movements. As usual, the contribution of an imaginatively varied continuo (which includes cello and bassoon, in addition to harpsichord, theorbo and organ) adds much to the colour of Vivaldi's score. The recording, made in St John's, Smith Square, in 1973/4, is of the very highest quality and the CD transfers are in the demonstration class.

Monica Huggett brings not only virtuosity but also considerable warmth to the solo concertos, and the Academy of Ancient Music are both spirited and sensitive. Those who think of Vivaldi's music as predictable will find much to surprise them in *La Stravaganza*; his invention is unflagging and of high quality. Strongly recommended to those preferring period instruments.

Scimone directs direct, energetic readings of the twelve concertos, enjoyable in their way, with recording well balanced, except for backward continuo. But Marriner's outstanding set in the same price-range is altogether more imaginative, and the Erato recording sounds very plain alongside the glowing ASMF textures.

6 Violin concertos, Op. 6.
(M) **(*) Ph. 426 939-2 [id.]. Pina Carmirelli, I Musici.

These concertos are not otherwise available and, while their invention is more uneven than in the named sets, their rarity will undoubtedly tempt keen Vivaldians. The 1977 performances, with Pina Carmirelli a stylish and responsive soloist, are polished and with well-judged tempi, if with no special imaginative flair. Excellent sound.

12 Concertos (for violin or oboe), Op. 7.
(M) *** Ph. 426 940-2 (2) [id.]. Accardo or Holliger (Opp. 7/1 & 7), I Musici.

The Op. 7 set is relatively unfamiliar and is certainly rewarding. The playing of Accardo and Holliger is altogether masterly, and they have fine rapport with their fellow musicians in I Musici. The acoustically sympathetic venue is La Chaux-de-Fonds, Switzerland, and the two CDs are economically priced. This is among the most desirable of the boxes in the Philips Vivaldi Edition.

The Trial between harmony and invention (12 Concertos), Op. 8.
☞ (M) *** Sony M2YK 46462 (2) [id.]. Pinchas Zukerman, ECO.
☞ (B) **(*) Ph. Duo 438 344-2 (2). Felix Ayo, I Musici.
**(*) O-L Dig. 417 515-2 (2) [id.]. Bury, Hirons, Holloway, Huggett, Mackintosh, Piguet, AAM, Hogwood.

The Trial between harmony and invention, Op. 8: Concertos Nos. 5–12.
☞ (B) *** Sony SBK 53513 [id.]. Pinchas Zukerman, Neil Black, ECO, Philip Ledger.

Zukerman's solo playing is distinguished throughout, and the ECO provide unfailingly alert and resilient accompaniments. In *Concerto No. 9 in D min.* oboist Neil Black takes the solo position and provides a welcome contrast of timbre – Vivaldi designed this concerto as optionally for violin or oboe, but it probably sounds more effective on the wind instrument. The recording is lively, with a close balance for the soloists. The sound is attractive on CD and does not lack fullness. The alternative 77-minute CD generously encapsulates all the concertos from Op. 8 except the first four and includes such favourites as *La tempesta di mare* (RV 253), *Il piacere* (RV 180) and *La Caccia* (RV 362).

Felix Ayo recorded the first four concertos (*The Four Seasons*) in 1959 and his was one of the finest of the early versions, although the recording was rather resonant. The remaining concertos in the set – full of typically Vivaldian touches which stamp these works as among the best of their time – date from 1961/2 and the recording, though still full-bodied, is less reverberant. The solo playing is very good and an undoubted freshness pervades the music-making here, although Maria Teresa Garatti's continuo fails to come through adequately. Good value.

There is no want of zest in the Academy of Ancient Music's accounts of Op. 8. These are likeable and, generally speaking, well-prepared versions and differ from some rivals in choosing the oboe in two of the concertos, where Vivaldi has indicated an option. There are moments where more polish would not have come amiss, and intonation is not above reproach either. The recordings are well up to standard and are given fine presence.

The Four Seasons, Op. 8/1–4.
(M) *** Virgin/EMI CUV5 61145-2. Christopher Warren-Green with LCO – ALBINONI: *Adagio;* PACHELBEL: *Canon.* ***
*** ASV Dig. CDDCA 579 [id.]. José Luis Garcia, ECO (with HANDEL: *Water music: suite No. 1 in F ****).
**(*) Argo 414 486-2 [id.]. Alan Loveday, ASMF, Marriner.
**(*) DG Dig. 400 045-2 [id.]. Simon Standage, E. Concert, Pinnock.
**(*) BIS Dig. CD 275 [id.]. Nils-Erik Sparf, Drottningholm Bar. Ens.
**(*) EMI Dig. CDC7 49557-2 [id.]. Nigel Kennedy, ECO.
(B) *** DG 427 221-2. Schneiderhan, Lucerne Festival Strings, Baumgartner (with ALBINONI: *Adagio;* PACHELBEL: *Canon & Gigue;* PURCELL: *Chacony;* BACH: *Suite No. 3, BWV 1068: Air ****).
☞ (BB) * Tring Dig. TRP 009 [id.]. Jonathan Carney, RPO (with: BACH: *Brandenburg concerto No. 3;* PACHELBEL: *Canon **).

The Four Seasons, Op. 8/1–4 (with sonnets in Italian and English).
*** Helios/Hyp. CDH 88012; *KH 88012* [id.]. Bruni, Edwards (readers), Adelina Oprean, European Community CO, Faeber.

The Four Seasons, Op. 8/1–4; Violin concertos: in E flat (La tempesta di mare), RV 253; in C (Il piacere), RV 180, Op. 8/5–6.
☞ *** Teldec/Warner Dig. 4509 91683-2 [id.]. Marieke Blanestijn, COE.
☞ (M) **(*) Teldec/Warner 4509 91851-2 [id.]. Alice Harnoncourt, VCM, Harnoncourt.

(i) *The Four Seasons, Op. 8/1–4;* (ii) *Violin concertos: L'Estro armonico: in A min., Op. 3/6. La Stravaganza: in A, Op. 4/5. Concerto in C min. (Il sospetto), RV 199.*
(M) *** EMI CDM7 64333-2; *EG 764333-4.* Perlman, (i) LPO; (ii) Israel PO.

(i) *The Four Seasons, Op. 8/1–4;* (ii) *L'Estro armonico: Double violin concerto in A min., Op. 3/8;* (iii) *Double trumpet concerto in C, RV 537.*
(BB) *** Virgin/EMI Dig. VJ7 91463-2; *VJ7 91463-4* [id.]. (i) Andrew Watkinson, (ii) with Nicholas Ward; (iii) Crispian Steele-Perkins, Michael Meeks; City of L. Sinfonia, Watkinson.

The Four Seasons; (i) *L'Estro armonico: Quadruple violin concerto in B min., RV 580, Op. 3/10.*
☞ (BB) *** Discover Dig. DICD 920202 [id.]. Oldřich Vlček; (i) with Hessová, Kaudersová, Nováková; Virtuosi di Praga.

The Four Seasons; (i) *L'Estro armonico: Quadruple violin concerto in B min., RV 580, Op. 3/10. Sinfonia in B min. (Al Santo Sepolcro), RV 169.*
☞ ⊛ *** Sony Dig. SK 48251 [id.]. Jeanne Lamon, Tafelmusik.

The Four Seasons, Op. 8/1–4; La Stravaganza: Concerto in A min., Op. 4/4; Concerto in E min., RV 278.
*** BMG/RCA Dig. RD 60369; *RK 60369* [60369-2-RC; *60369-4-RC*]. Vladimir Spivakov, Moscow Virtuosi.

(i) *The Four Seasons; Concerto for strings in G (Alla rustica), RV 151;* (ii) *Violin concerto in E (L'amoroso), RV 271; Sinfonia in B flat, (Al Santo Sepolcro), RV 169.*
☞ (B) *** DG 439 422-2 [id.]. (i) Michel Schwalbé; (ii) Thomas Brandis; BPO, Karajan.

The Four Seasons, Op. 8/1–4; Triple violin concerto in F, RV 551; Quadruple violin concerto in B min., RV 580.
*** Ph. Dig. 422 065-2 [id.]. Accardo and soloists with CO.

(i) *The Four Seasons;* (ii) *Flute concertos, Op. 10/1–3.*
(M) *** BMG/RCA GD 86553. (i) La Petite Bande, Kuijken; (ii) Brüggen, O of 18th Century.

Tafelmusik have already given us some highly recommendable CDs of Haydn symphonies. Now they offer a superbly imaginative new version of Vivaldi's *Four Seasons* on original instruments, which is for the 1990s what Marriner's famous ASMF version was for the '70s. The playing is at once full of fantasy and yet has a robust gusto that is irresistible. The opening of *Spring,* with its chirruping bird calls, sets the scene and the second movement brings a lovely cantilena from Jeanne Lamon, while the barking dog is as musical as he is gruff. The performances throughout are full of dramatic contrasts. The same shimmering delicacy in *Summer* alternates with invigoratingly robust tutti from the lower strings in the finale so that the soloist, bowing away for dear life, is nearly blown away. The sleepy *Adagio* of *Autumn* brings a gentle, musing commentary from the archlute, followed by the gutsy hunting music over which the soloist soars with dazzling bravura. The weird frozen landscape of *Winter* is introduced in a half-light, but the solo entry is soon dramatically dominant. After *Winter's* roisterous finale comes the hauntingly austere texture of the opening of the highly original *Sinfonia al Sepulcro;* and the famous *Concerto for four violins* makes a fitting finale. The Sony recording is first class, absolutely clean in focus, with plenty of body and the most refined detail.

For those still preferring the fuller texture of modern instruments, the new Teldec version provides the perfect alternative. The chimerical solo playing of Marieke Blankestijn is a delight and her clean style shows that she has learned from authentic manners. There is more imaginative delicacy here, particularly in the improvisatory central movement of *Summer* and the gentle haze of *Autumn,* where the gutsy finale has splendid bite and energy; and the opening of *Winter* mirrors the impressionism of the Tafelmusik version. However, the cheerful COE approach to the *Largo* central movement is even more attractive than with Tafelmusik, to make the finale the more distinctive. With two extra concertos from Opus 8 also included, this is now also a strong primary recommendation. The Teldec recording is superb.

Salvatore Accardo's version is of particular interest in that Accardo uses a different Stradivarius for each of the four concertos – period instruments with a difference! Thanks to this aristocrat of violinists, the sounds are of exceptional beauty, both here and also in the two multiple concertos which are added as a bonus. The performances are much enhanced, too, by the imaginative continuo playing of Bruno Canino. The recording itself is a model of fidelity and has plenty of warmth; it must rank very high in the Vivaldi discography and probably first choice for those preferring modern instruments.

As a top mid-priced recommendation Christopher Warren-Green makes a brilliantly charismatic soloist, with the London Chamber Orchestra providing delectably pointed bird-imitations in *Spring* and *Summer.* Tempi of allegros are very brisk, but the effect is tinglingly exhilarating when the soloist's bravura is so readily matched by the accompanying ensemble. Slow movements offer the widest contrast, with delicate textures and subtle use of the continuo, as in *Winter* where Leslie Pearson makes a delightful surprise contribution to the finale, having already embroidered the opening allegro and prevented it from being too chilly. The recording, made in All Saints' Church, Wallington, has plenty of ambient fullness but remains bright and fresh. With its equally attractive couplings, this can be recommended to those who like their Vivaldi to be dashing and vital, and yet imaginatively pictorial at the same time.

An excellent super-bargain version from the Virtuosi di Praga, fresh, bright and clean, with a strong, highly responsive soloist in Oldřich Vlček. *Spring* is immediately vivacious and the viola produces a nice little rasp for the shepherd's dog. *Autumn* is delicately somnambulant, and the opening of *Winter* is well below zero and is decorated with a clink from the continuo. The *Concerto for four violins* makes for a popular encore. Excellent sound and very good value indeed.

On the bargain Virgin Virgo label Andrew Watkinson directs the City of London Sinfonia from the solo violin in one of the very finest available versions, superbly played and beautifully recorded with clean, forward sound. Anyone wanting a version on modern instruments cannot do better than this, with fresh, resilient playing in allegros, reflecting lessons learnt from period performance, and with sweet, unsentimental expressiveness in slow movements. The two double concertos provide a valuable makeweight, though the orchestra is more backwardly balanced in the *Concerto for two trumpets.* The documentation is poor.

The ASV version of *The Four Seasons,* with José Luis Garcia as soloist and musical director, is particularly pleasing, with the violins of the accompanying group sweetly fresh and the soloist nicely balanced. The overall pacing is beautifully judged, and each movement takes its place naturally and spontaneously in relation to its companions. The effects are well made, but there are no histrionics and, although the continuo does not always come through strongly, the unnamed player makes a useful contribution to a performance that is very easy to live with. The one drawback to this issue is that there is only one track for each of the *Four Seasons*. However, there is an attractive Handel bonus.

There are innumerable recordings of Vivaldi's *Four Seasons* and it seems to us that those versions offered without fill-ups in a crowded marketplace have become uncompetitive. However, Marriner's 1970 Academy of St Martin-in-the-Fields version with Alan Loveday is an exception and still remains near the top of the list of recommended CDs. The performance is as satisfying as any and will surely delight all but those who are ruled by the creed of authenticity. It has an element of fantasy that makes the music sound utterly new; it is full of imaginative touches, with Simon Preston subtly varying the continuo between harpsichord and organ. The opulence of string tone may have a romantic connotation, but there is no self-indulgence in the interpretation, no sentimentality, for the contrasts are made sharper and fresher, not smoothed over. But without any coupling this now calls for reissue on a lower-priced label.

Karajan here indulges himself in repertoire which he clearly loves but for which he does not have the stylistic credentials. Yet his 1972 recording of *The Four Seasons* was an undoubted success and remains very enjoyable. Its tonal beauty is not achieved at the expense of vitality and, although the harpsichord hardly ever comes through, the overall scale is acceptable. Michel Schwalbé is a memorable soloist; his playing is neat, precise and very musical, with a touch of Italian sunshine in the tone. The current remastering for DG's bargain label, Classikon, has restored the body and breadth of the original, and in the additional works (recorded in the St Moritz Französische Kirche in Switzerland two years earlier) the string-sound is glorious. The sheer charisma of the BPO playing, notably in the *Sinfonia al Santa Sepolcro*, where the first movement is presented with great expressive depth, is difficult to resist, and the *Concerto alla rustica* sounds wonderfully sumptuous. (Vivaldi would surely have been amazed!) The refinement of execution is remarkable, and if this music comes to life in an inflated way it makes for a unique listening experience, a Vivaldi record like no other.

The Archiv version by Simon Standage with the English Concert, directed from the harpsichord by Trevor Pinnock, has the advantage of using a newly discovered set of parts, which have brought the correction of minor textual errors in the Le Cène text in normal use. The Archiv performance also (minimally) introduces a second soloist and is played on period instruments. The players create a relatively intimate sound, though their approach is certainly not without drama, while the solo contribution has impressive flair and bravura. The overall effect is essentially refined, treating the pictorial imagery with subtlety. The result finds a natural balance between vivid projection and atmospheric feeling. The digital recording is first class. Authenticists should be well satisfied.

The BIS recording by Nils-Erik Sparf and the Drottningholm Baroque Ensemble has astonishing clarity and presence; and as playing, it is hardly less remarkable in its imaginative vitality. These Swedish players make the most of all the pictorial characterization without ever overdoing anything: they achieve the feat of making one hear this eminently familiar repertoire as if for the very first time.

Perlman's imagination holds the sequence together superbly, and there are many passages of pure magic, as in the central *Adagio* of *Summer*. The digital remastering of the 1976 recording is managed admirably, the sound firm, clear and well balanced, with plenty of detail. Now this record has been made much more competitive by the addition of three extra violin concertos, all fine works. Although the acoustic is somewhat dryish, this does not prevent these extra works from sounding very good.

Vladimir Spivakov's highly enjoyable account of Vivaldi's *Four seasons* is made the more attractive by opening with two of Vivaldi's most imaginative concertos. Both are very well played indeed by soloist and orchestra alike, as is the more famous main work, given an essentially chamber-style account, yet one not lacking its robust moments. Characterization is strong. There is plenty of vigour for the summer storms and *Spring* is tinglingly fresh, with its central movement played with contrasting gentle delicacy. Altogether this is highly successful, with the vivid, well-balanced recording achieving excellent presence against the background ambience of L'Eglise du Liban, Paris.

The novelty of the Helios issue is the inclusion of the sonnets which Vivaldi placed on his score to give his listeners a guide to the illustrative detail suggested by the music. Before each of the four concertos, the appropriate poem is read, first in a romantically effusive Italian manner and then in BBC English (the contrast quite striking). On CD, of course, one can programme out these introductions; one would hardly want to hear them as often as the concertos. The performances are first class. Adelina Oprean is an excellent soloist, her reading full of youthful energy and expressive freshness; her timbre is clean and pure, her technique assured. Faeber matches her vitality, and the score's pictorial effects are boldly characterized in a vividly projected sound-picture.

On RCA, La Petite Bande (soloist unnamed, but presumably Kuijken) offer an authentic version of considerable appeal. Although the accompanying group can generate plenty of energy when Vivaldi's winds are blowing, this is essentially a small-scale reading, notable for its delicacy. But this issue offers not just the four concertos of Op. 8 but also three favourite *Flute concertos* from Op. 10: *Tempesta di mare*, *La notte* and *Il gardinello*. With the master-instrumentalist, Frans Brüggen, playing a period instrument and directing the Orchestra of the 18th Century, the excellence of these performances, vividly recorded, can be taken for granted.

Kennedy's account is certainly among the more spectacular in conveying its picaresque imagery; only *Autumn* brings a degree of real controversy, however, with weird special effects, including glissando harmonics in the slow movement and percussive applications of the wooden part of the bow to add rhythmic pungency to the hunting finale. There is plenty of vivid detail elsewhere. The ECO's playing is always responsive, to match the often very exciting bravura of its soloist, and allegros have an agreeable vitality. However, at 41 minutes, with no fillers, this is not generous and it would not be our first choice for repeated listening.

Schneiderhan's 1959 version of *The Four Seasons* re-emerges, as fresh as paint, now well buttressed by Pachelbel's *Canon*, Purcell's *Chacony* and the famous Bach *Air* all sounding serenely spacious, while the Albinoni/Giazotto *Adagio* also has a certain refined dignity. Schneiderhan's timbre, pure and sweetly classical, suits Vivaldi very well indeed. The aptly chamber-scaled performance, with brisk tempi and alert orchestral playing, is full of life, with the pictorial detail emerging naturally but without being overcharacterized.

There is an element of eccentricity in Harnoncourt's approach to Vivaldi's Op. 8, and his control of dynamics and tempi, with allegros often aggressively fast and chimerical changes of mood, will not convince all listeners. Alice Harnoncourt's timbre is leonine and her tone-production somewhat astringent in the 'authentic' baroque manner. The dramatic style of her solo playing is certainly at one with the vivid pictorialism of Vivaldi's imagery, even if it is somewhat overcharacterized. The shepherd's dog in *Spring* barks vociferously, and the dance rhythms in the finale of the same concerto are extremely invigorating. The interpretative approach throughout emphasizes such strong contrasts: the languorous opening of *Summer* makes a splendid foil for the storm and buzzing insects, yet the zephyr breezes are wistfully gentle. The continuo uses a chamber organ to great effect, and picaresque touches of colour are added to the string texture. The CD includes two other colourful works from the set and the sound is extremely lively to match the playing.

Jonathan Carey's version in the Tring RPO collection is a non-starter. The solo playing is lively enough and often lyrically sympathetic, but the old-fashioned orchestral accompaniment is lustreless, not helped by the close, unexpansive sound-balance. Characterization is minimal, and *Winter* completely fails to convey an icy impression at its opening. The lethargic account of Pachelbel's *Canon* and routine Bach *Brandenburg* are no incentive either.

'The world of Vivaldi': (i) *The Four Seasons, Op. 8/1–4;* (ii) *Guitar concerto in D, RV 43;* (iii) *Piccolo concerto in C, RV 443;* (iv) *Concerto for strings in G (alla rustica), RV 151;* (v) *Double trumpet concerto in C, RV 537.*

☞ (M) **(*) Decca 433 866-2; *433 866-4.* (i) Kulka, Stuttgart CO, Münchinger; (ii) Fernández, ECO, Malcolm; (iii) Bennett, ASMF, Marriner; (iv) Lucerne Festival Strings, Baumgartner; (v) Wilbraham, Jones, ASMF, Marriner.

Konstanty Kulka's performance of *The Four Seasons* from the early 1970s has stood the test of time. The solo playing is first class and Münchinger's accompaniment is stylish and lively. It was Münchinger who, with a different soloist, put this famous concertante work on the map with his first mono LP recording in the 1950s (the first in the UK – though Scherchen pioneered the work in the USA in the late 1940s) and so it is good to have the present reminder of his Vivaldi sympathies. The sound is a little astringent on top but does not lack body, and its brightness adds to the freshness. The quartet of concertos now offered as ballast certainly give a good cross-section of Vivaldi's world, all played with expertise and well recorded. The *Concerto for guitar* is digital; the *Double trumpet concerto* sounds a shade over-bright.

The Four Seasons, Op. 8/1–4 (arr. for flute and strings).

(M) *** BMG/RCA GD 60748 [60748-2-RG]. James Galway, Zagreb Soloists.

James Galway's transcription is thoroughly musical and so convincing that at times one is tempted to believe that the work was conceived in this form. The playing itself is marvellous, full of detail and imagination, and the recording is excellent, even if the flute is given a forward balance, the more striking on CD.

La Cetra (12 Violin concertos), Op. 9.

☞ ⊛ (M) *** Decca 433 734-2 (2) [id.]. Iona Brown, ASMF.

*** O-L Dig. 421 366-2 (2) [id.]. Standage, AAM, Hogwood.

(M) **(*) Ph. 426 946-2 (2) [id.]. Ayo, Cotogni (in Op. 9/9), Altobelli, Garatti, I Musici.

La Cetra (The Lyre) was the last set of violin concertos Vivaldi published. Iona Brown, for some years the leader of St Martin's Academy, here acts as director in the place of Sir Neville Marriner. So resilient and imaginative are the results that one hardly detects any difference from the immaculate and stylish Vivaldi playing in earlier Academy Vivaldi sets. There is some wonderful music here; the later concertos are every bit the equal of anything in *The Trial between harmony and invention*, and it is played gloriously. The recording too is outstandingly rich and vivid, even by earlier Argo standards with this group, and the Decca transfer to CD retains the demonstration excellence of the original analogue LPs, with a yet greater sense of body and presence.

Simon Standage gives an attractive and fluent account of the set, and the recording is excellent, slightly dry but very clean.

I Musici's *La Cetra* dates from 1964 and is again recorded at La Chaux-de-Fonds, which ensures a realistic and pleasing sound-balance. With Felix Ayo the principal soloist, the playing is spirited, characterful and expressively rich, though the overall effect is less individual than in the finest versions from the past. One drawback is that solo passages are given no continuo support, though Maria Teresa Garatti provides an organ continuo for the ripieno. Overall this is fair value at mid-price.

6 Flute concertos, Op. 10.
☞ *** DG Dig. 437 839-2 [id.]. Patrick Gallois, Orpheus CO.
*** DG Dig. 423 702-2 [id.]. Liza Beznosiuk, E. Concert, Pinnock.
*** O-L 414 685-2 [id.]. Stephen Preston, AAM.
*** Ph. 412 874-2 [id.]. Michala Petri, ASMF, Marriner.
(M) *** Ph. 422 260-2; *422 260-4*. Gazzelloni, I Musici.
(M) *** Ph. 426 949-2 [id.]. Gazzelloni, I Musici.
(B) *** Pickwick Dig. PCD 961; *CIMPC 961* [id.]. Judith Hall, Divertimenti of L., Paul Barritt.
☞ (M) **(*) BMG/RCA 09026 61351-2. James Galway, New Irish CO.

These works are extremely well served on CD, and it is almost impossible to suggest a clear first choice. However, among recent issues this Gallois/Orpheus set is arguably the lightest and most spirited of any, be they on period instruments or not. Collectors who recall Gallois' dazzling account of the Nielsen *Concerto* will know what to expect: effortless virtuosity, refined musicianship, intelligence and taste. He has an excellent rapport with the splendid Orpheus Chamber Orchestra and is very well served too by the engineers. A most distinguished issue.

There is some expressive as well as brilliant playing on the DG Archiv CD, which should delight listeners. Try track 8 (the *Largo* movement of *Concerto No. 2 in G minor, La Notte*) for an example of the beautifully refined and cool pianissimo tone that Liza Beznosiuk can produce – and almost any of the fast movements for an example of her virtuosity. Her playing in *Il gardellino* is a delight, and Trevor Pinnock and the English Concert provide unfailingly vital and, above all, imaginative support. The DG recording is exemplary in its clarity. Recommended with enthusiasm.

Stephen Preston also plays a period instrument, a Schuchart, and the Academy of Ancient Music likewise play old instruments. Their playing is eminently stylish, but also spirited and expressive, and they are admirably recorded, with the analogue sound enhanced further in the CD format.

Michala Petri uses a modern recorder and plays with breathtaking virtuosity and impeccable control, and she has the advantage of superb recording. In the slow movements – and occasionally elsewhere – there is more in the music than she finds, but the sheer virtuosity of this gifted artist is most infectious. She uses a sopranino recorder in three of the concertos.

Severino Gazzelloni's version of the six *Concertos*, Op. 10, has been in circulation throughout the 1970s and its merits are well established; it is a safer recommendation for the general collector than the authentic rivals, good though the best of these is.

Judith Hall's record of the Op. 10 *Flute concertos* is fresh and brightly recorded. She plays with considerable virtuosity and a great deal of taste. The Divertimento of London is a modern-instrument group and the players are both sensitive and alert.

James Galway directs the New Irish Chamber Orchestra from the flute – and to generally good effect. The playing is predictably brilliant and the goldfinch imitations in *Il Cardellino* (which comes first on the disc) are enticing. Slow movements demonstrate Galway's beauty of timbre and sense of line to consistently good effect, although some may find the sweet vibrato a bit too much for baroque repertoire. But this record is directed towards the broader public and, if it attracts newcomers to Op. 10, well and good. No complaints about the recording quality of the orchestral contribution, but those who do invest in this mid-priced CD are warned that the pauses between movements are very short.

6 Violin concertos, Op. 11.
(M) *** Ph. 426 950-2 [id.]. Salvatore Accardo, I Musici.
☞ *** O-L Dig. 436 172-2 [id.]. Stanley Ritchie, Frank de Bruine, AAM, Hogwood.

6 Violin concertos, Op. 12.
(M) *** Ph. 426 951-2 [id.]. Salvatore Accardo, I Musici.

More rare repertoire here. The Opp. 11 and 12 concertos are perhaps of uneven quality, but the best of them are very rewarding indeed and, played so superlatively by Salvatore Accardo, they are likely to beguile the most unwilling listener. Recorded in 1974/5, these two individual CDs are among the most desirable of the Philips Vivaldi Edition, and their CD transfers are among the best in the series.

The Vivaldi repertoire convincingly using original instruments continues to expand. The last of the Op. 11 set is given an accomplished performance by Frank de Bruine (oboe), and Stanley Ritchie is a vital and suitably expressive soloist in the others (which include the familiar *Il Favorito*). Accompaniments are fresh and bracing in the way of the Academy of Ancient Music, and Hogwood's continuo uses organ as well as harpsichord, besides featuring the theorbo. If you like the 'authentic' approach as presented by these artists, the recording projects them with a vivid presence.

Concertos for strings: in C, RV 117; in C min., RV 118; in D, RV 123; in D min., RV 128; in F, RV 136; in F min., RV 143; in G, RV 146; in A, RV 159; in A, RV 160; in B flat (Conca), RV 163.
☞ *** Ph. 438 876-2 [id.]. I Musici.

Here are ten (about a quarter) of the ripieno concertos Vivaldi wrote for strings, and once again we are offered a remarkably varied glimpse into the extraordinarily wide range of invention this composer could achieve, without the extra colour of specific soloists. The textural advantages of modern instruments show up in the more expansive moments, with the expansive lower range underpinning a rich tonal blend. But there is no lack of brightness on top, while the fugal writing is cleanly detailed and held in a positive grip. I Musici convey readily that they have spent much time with this music over the years, yet still enjoy playing it.

37 Bassoon concertos (complete).
(M) *** ASV Dig. CDDCX 625 (6). Daniel Smith, ECO, Ledger; Zagreb Solists, Ninić.

Bassoon concertos: in C, RV 466; in C, RV 467; in F, RV 486; in F, RV 491; in A min., RV 499; in A min., RV 500.
**(*) ASV Dig. CDDCA 565 [id.]. Daniel Smith, ECO, Ledger.

Bassoon concertos in C, RV 469; in C, RV 470; in C, RV 474; in C, RV 476; in F, RV 487; in G, RV 494.
**(*) ASV Dig. CDDCA 571 [id.]. Daniel Smith, ECO, Ledger.

Bassoon concertos: in C, RV 472; in C, RV 477; in C, RV 479; in D min., RV 481; in F, RV 488; in B flat (La notte), RV 501.
**(*) ASV Dig. CDDCA 662 [id.]. Daniel Smith, ECO, Ledger.

The bassoon seems to have uncovered a particularly generous fund of inspiration in Vivaldi, for few of his 37 concertos for that instrument are in any way routine. Daniel Smith's achievement in recording them all is considerable, for he plays with constant freshness and enthusiasm. His woody tone is very attractive and he is very well caught by the engineers. This set can be welcomed almost without reservation and, dipped into, the various recordings will always give pleasure. We have listened to every one of these concertos and have come up smiling. Daniel Smith is a genial and personable player and he has considerable facility; even if some of the more complicated roulades are not executed with exact precision, his playing has undoubted flair. He is balanced well forward, but the orchestral accompaniment has plenty of personality and registers well enough.

Bassoon concertos: in C, RV 471; in C, RV 475; in F, RV 490; in G, RV 492; in G min., RV 495; in G min., RV 496.
*** ASV CDDCA 734 [id.]. Daniel Smith, Zagreb Soloists, Tonko Ninić.

Bassoon concertos: in C, RV 473; in C, RV 478; in E flat, RV 483; in F, RV 485; in A min., RV 497; in A min., RV 498; in B flat, RV 502.
**(*) ASV CDDCA 752 [id.]. Daniel Smith, Zagreb Soloists, Tonko Ninić.

For the last three CDs of the series the Zagreb Soloists take over the accompaniments and offer alert, vivacious playing that adds to the pleasure of the performances. Daniel Smith too, responds with more vigour and polish and overall there is plenty of affectionate warmth.

Bassoon concertos: in C min., RV 480; in E min., RV 484; in F, RV 489; in G, RV 493; in B flat, RV 503; in B flat, RV 504.
*** ASV Dig. CDDCA 751 [id.]. Daniel Smith, Zagreb Soloists, Tonko Ninić.

This is the record to begin with if you intend sampling this enterprising ASV series. Almost all the works here show Vivaldi at his most inventively spontaneous. Smith and the Zagreb group rise to the occasion and the recording is pleasingly vivid.

Bassoon concerto in F, RV 485; (i) *Double concerto in G min., for recorder and bassoon (La Notte), RV 104.*
*** BIS Dig. CD 271 [id.]. McGraw, (i) Pehrsson, Drottningholm Bar. Ens. – TELEMANN: *Concertos.* ***

The concerto subtitled *La Notte* exists in three versions: one for flute (the most familiar), RV 439; another for bassoon, RV 501; and the present version, RV 104. Clas Pehrsson, Michael McGraw and the Drottningholm Baroque Ensemble give a thoroughly splendid account of it, and the *Bassoon concerto in F major* also fares well. Excellent recording.

Cello concertos: in C, RV 398; in G, RV 413.
☞ (B) *** DG Double 437 952-2 (2) [id.]. Rostropovich, Zurich Coll. Mus., Sacher – BEERNSTEIN: *3 Meditations;* BOCCHERINI: *Cello concerto No. 2;* GLAZUNOV: *Chant du Ménestrel;* SHOSTAKOVICH: *Cello concerto No. 2;* TARTINI: *Cello concerto;* TCHAIKOVSKY: *Andante cantabile* etc. ***

Performances of great vigour and projection from Rostropovich; every bar comes fully to life. Spendidly lively accompaniments and excellent CD transfers, bright and clean with no lack of depth. Rostropovich's performances come as part of a very generous Double DG compilation, with the two discs offered for the price of one.

Cello concertos: in C, RV 399; in C min., RV 401; in D min., RV 405; in B flat, RV 423; in F, RV 538; Largo. (i) *Concerto in E min. for cello and bassoon, RV 409.*
*** BMG/RCA Dig. RD 87774 [7774-2-RC]. Harnoy, (i) McKay, Toronto CO, Robinson.

Ofra Harnoy's are traditional performances with modern instruments, and none the worse for that; she plays with style, impeccable technique and eloquence: in short, she is a first-class artist with a good lyrical sense. She is given good support from the Toronto Chamber Orchestra under Paul Robinson, and very well recorded.

Cello concertos: in C min., RV 402; in D, RV 403; in D min., RV 406; in F, RV 412; in G, RV 414; in A min., RV 422; in B min., RV 424.
*** BMG/RCA Dig. RD 60155 [60155-2-RC]. Ofra Harnoy, Toronto CO, Paul Robinson.

Ofra Harnoy's strength lies not so much in her tone, which is not big, but in her selfless approach to this repertoire. She does not regard this music as a vehicle for her own personality but plays it with an agreeable dedication and a delight in its considerable felicities.

Cello concertos: in D, RV 404; D min., RV 407; F, RV 411; G min., RV 417; A min., RV 420; (i) *Double concerto for violin, cello and strings in F (Il Proteo o sia il mondo), RV 544.*
☞ *** BMG/RCA Dig. 09026 61578-2 [id.]. Ofra Harnoy, (i) with Igor Oistrakh; Toronto CO, Paul Robinson.

Ofra Harnoy's latest grouping is just as attractive as the previous collections in her Vivaldi series. The *Double concerto* brings an excellent partnership with Igor Oistrakh and here the *Adagio* is particularly touching. Excellent recording.

Cello concertos: in G, RV 413; in G min., RV 417.
☞ (M) **(*) EMI CDM7 64326-2 [id.]. Lynn Harrell, ECO, Zukerman – HAYDN: *Concertos.* **(*)

Though Lynn Harrell is hardly a classical stylist among cellists (as he shows in the Haydn coupling), he gives lively, imaginative performances of two fine Vivaldi concertos (the *G major* particularly attractive) and is well accompanied by Zukerman. The sound is lively and full, if not as smooth as on the Haydn concertos, which are interspersed with Vivaldi on the generous (74-minute) CD.

Flute concertos: in A min., RV 108; in F, RV 434; Double flute concerto in C, RV 533; Sopranino recorder concertos: in C, RV 443 & RV 444; in A min., RV 445.
(BB) *** Naxos Dig. 8.550385; *4550385* [id.]. Jálek, Novotny, Stivin, Capella Istropolitana, Oliver Dohnányi.

The Capella Istropolitana, who are drawn from the excellent Slovak Philharmonic, play with vitality and sensitivity for Oliver Dohnányi and the soloists show appropriate virtuosity and flair. As always, there are rewards and surprises in this music, revealed by Jiři Stivin's undoubted artistry. The sound is very good indeed, and so is the balance.

Flute concertos in D, RV 427; in D (Il gardellino), RV 428; in D, RV 429; in G, RV 436; in G, RV 438; in A min., RV 440; (i) in C, for 2 flutes, RV 533.
*** HM Dig. HMC 905193; *HMC 405193* [id.]. Janet See, (i) S. Schultz; Philh. Bar. O, McGegan.

Janet See is not only a first-class player but also a real artist whose phrasing is alive and imaginative. Moreover the Philharmonia Baroque Orchestra, a West Coast American group, give her excellent support. Vivaldi also deserves some of the credit for all this, too. The diversity and range of these pieces is astonishing. Highly enjoyable.

Concertos for flute, oboe, violin, bassoon and continuo: in C, RV 88; in D (Il gardellino), RV 90; in D, RV 94; in F, RV 99; in G min., RV 107; Concerto for flute, violin, bassoon and continuo, RV 106.
*** Unicorn Dig. DKPCD 9071; *DKPC 9071* [id.]. Magyer, Francis, Stevens, Jordan, London Harpsichord Ens., Sarah Francis.

A highly engaging group of chamber concertos, suitable for the late evening. Vivaldi's felicitous interplay of wind-colours is ever imaginative. The players persuasively work together as a team, creating a most attractive intimacy, and the truthful and well-balanced recording adds to the listener's pleasure in nearly an hour of music in which the composer's invention never flags.

Guitar concertos in D, RV 93; in B flat, RV 524; in G min., RV 531; in G, RV 532. Trios: in C, RV 82; in G min., RV 85.
*** DG Dig. 415 487-2 [id.]. Söllscher, Bern Camerata, Füri.

Göran Söllscher further enhances his reputation both as a master-guitarist and as an artist on this excellently recorded issue, in which he has first-class support from the Camerata Bern under Thomas Füri. In RV 532, Söllscher resorts to technology and plays both parts. The DG balance is admirably judged.

(i) *Lute concerto in F, RV 93; Double concerto in G, RV 532;* (ii) *Sonatas for lute and harpsichord: in C; in G, RV. 82 & 85* (arr. from *Trio sonatas*).
☞ (M) **(*) BMG/RCA 09026 61588-2 [id.]. Julian Bream, Monteverdi O, Gardiner – HANDEL; KOHAUT: *Concertos.* **(*)

The *Lute concerto* receives a first-class performance from Bream, and he is well accompanied. The slow movement with its delicate embroidery over sustained strings is particularly fine. In the arrangement of the *Double mandolin concerto* Bream is able by electronic means to assume both solo roles. This too is a highly effective performance, though the forward balance makes the solo instruments sound larger than life and negates much of the dynamic contrast with Gardiner's excellent accompanying group. The two chamber works were originally *Trio sonatas for lute, violin and continuo*, but as the violin part doubles much of what the lute has to contribute it can be omitted without problems arising. The music is pleasingly lightweight and the performances are fresh and imaginative. Once again, however, the balance is unnaturally forward.

Mandolin concerto in C, RV 425; Double mandolin concerto in G, RV 532; (Soprano) Lute concerto in D, RV 93; Double concerto in D min. for viola d'amore and lute, RV 540. Trios: in C, RV 82; in G min., RV 85.
*** Hyp. CDA 66160; *KA 66160* [id.]. Jeffrey, O'Dette, Parley of Instruments, Goodman and Holman.

These are chamber performances, with one instrument to each part, and this obviously provides an ideal balance for the *Mandolin concertos*. There are other innovations, too. An organ continuo replaces the usual harpsichord, and very effective it is; in the *Trios* and the *Lute concerto* (but not in the *Double concerto,* RV 540) Paul O'Dette uses a gut-strung soprano lute. The delightful sounds here, with all players using original instruments or copies, are very convincing. The recording is realistically balanced within an attractively spacious acoustic.

Oboe concertos: in C, Op. 8/12, RV 64; in C, RV 447 & RV 452; in D, RV 453; in D min., RV 454; in F, RV 456; in A min., RV 461; in B flat, RV 464.
☞ (B) *** Erato/Warner 2292 45944-2 [id.]. Pierre Pierlot, Sol. Ven., Scimone.

As in his companion collection of Albinoni *Concertos* on the same Erato Bonsai label, Pierre Pierlot proves an ideal soloist, his small, sweet timbre expressive without being overly romantic, and there is pleasingly nimble articulation in allegros. Scimone accompanies sympathetically and the playing of I

Solisti Veneti is alert and stylish. Excellent sound, too, from the late 1960s. These eight performances have the kind of charm which is missing from Boyd's Archiv set, below, and the disc makes a generous (70 minutes) bargain. Alas, no information is provided about the music itself.

Oboe concertos: in C, RV 447 & RV 451; in F, RV 455 & RV 457; in A min., RV 461 & RV 463.
☞ (BB) *** Naxos Dig. 8.550860 [id.]. Stefan Schilli, Budapest Failoni CO, Béla Nagy.

Oboe concertos: in C, RV 450 & RV 452; in D, RV 453; in D min., RV 454; (i) *Double oboe concertos: in C, RV 534; D min., RV 535; A min., RV 536.*
☞ (BB) *** Naxos Dig. 8.550859 [id.]. Stefan Schilli; (i) with Diethelm Jonas; Budapest Failoni CO, Béla Nagy.

Excellent playing from these Budapest musicians who seem set to provide us with a survey of Vivaldi's concertante works for oboe. The second of these two discs offers the three *Double concertos*, and the two CDs between them include half the solo works. They are often surprisingly florid, requiring considerable bravura from the soloist. A good example is the Minuet finale of RV 447, which is a cross between a Rondo and a theme and variations. Vivaldi is never entirely predictable, except that his invention never seems to flag, and many of the simple *Grave, Larghetto* and *Largo* slow movements are very pleasing indeed.

Oboe concertos: in C, RV 447 & 450; in D, RV 453; in A min., RV 461 & 463; (i) *Double concerto in B flat for oboe & violin, RV 548.*
☞ **(*) DG Dig. 435 873-2 [id.]. Douglas Boyd, (i) with Marieke Blanestijn; COE.

These performances have plenty of vitality, with Douglas Boyd an expert soloist, whose embellishments are nicely managed. He is given alert accompaniments and is very well balanced and recorded. Yet in the last resort there is a lack of charm here which prevents the fullest enjoyment.

Viola d'amore concertos: in D, RV 392; in D min., RV 393, 394 & 395; in A, RV 396 & 397.
☞ (M) **(*) Erato/Warner 4509 92190-2 [id.]. Nane Calabrese, Sol. Ven., Scimone.

Nane Calabrese is an excellent player with a full timbre and excellent intonation. If the viola d'amore does have its limitations, the quality of Vivaldi's invention is surprisingly high; although the orchestra, using modern instruments, makes an ample sound, the balance is cleverly contrived so that the continuo detail comes through well. Well worth exploring.

L'Estro armonico: Violin concerto in A min.; (i) *Double violin concertos in A min. & D min., Op. 3/6, 8 & 11. Violin concerto in C min. (Il sospetto), RV 199.*
☞ (M) **(*) Sony SBK 48273 [id.]. Zukerman; (i) Sillito, LAPO – BACH: *Violin concertos 1–2.* **(*)

With Zukerman directing as well as leading, these are delightful performances of two memorable *Double concertos* from Op. 3, the slow movements especially beautiful, with fine contributions from Philip Ledger – what you can hear of him. The recording, conceived with quadrophony in mind, is warmly resonant. For the reissue two solo concertos are added, also very enjoyable.

L'Estro armonico: Quadruple violin concerto in D; Triple concerto for 2 violins and cello in D min., Op. 3/10–11; Double violin concerto in C min., RV 510.
☞ (M) ** EMI Dig. CD-EMX 2205; *TC-EMX 2205.* Y. Menuhin, Hu Kun, Mi-Kyung Li, Vassallo, Camerata Lysy, Gstaad – BACH: *Double concerto etc.* **

Three multiple-string concertos by Vivaldi make an attractive coupling for the Bach *Concertos*. With Menuhin the most persuasive leader, the performances are fresh and understanding, if not immaculate, but they suffer from a dryness of sound, unflattering to all.

Violin concertos, Op. 8, Nos. 5 in E flat (La Tempesta di mare), RV 253; 6 in C (Il Piacere), RV 180; 10 in B flat (La Caccia), RV 362; 11 in D, RV 210; in C min. (Il Sospetto), RV 199.
(B) *** CfP Dig. CD-CFP 4522. Sir Yehudi Menuhin, Polish CO, Jerzy Maksymiuk.

Menuhin's collection of five concertos – four of them with nicknames and particularly delightful – brings some of his freshest, most intense playing in recent years. Particularly in slow movements – notably that of *Il Piacere* ('Pleasure') – he shows afresh his unique insight in shaping a phrase. Fresh, alert accompaniment and full digital recording.

MISCELLANEOUS CONCERTO COLLECTIONS

(i) *Concerto in B flat in due cori con violino discordato;* (i; ii) *Concerto in A con violino principale con altro violino per eco in lontana, RV 522;* (i) *Violin concerto in D, RV 581;* (iii) *Mandolin concerto in C, RV 425;* (iii; iv) *Double mandolin concerto in G, RV 532; Concerto for 2 mandolins, 2 theorbos, 2 flutes, 2 salmo, 2 violins in tromba marina & cello, RV 558.*

☞ (B) **(*) Erato/Warner 2292 45946-2 [id.]. (i) Piero Toso; (ii) Giuliano Carmignola; (iii) Bonifacio Bianchi; (iv) Alessando Pitrelli; Sol. Ven., Scimone.

A fascinating collection. The *Concertos in due cori* were probably written for performance in St Mark's, Venice, where antiphonal and echo effects (especially tangible in RV 522) were all the rage. The *Mandolin concertos*, RV 425 and 532, both have fine, expressive slow movements, and the balance with the small-timbred solo instruments is expertly managed; RV 558, with its galaxy of instrumental colour, also shows Vivaldi imaginatively exploring textural possibilities. Excellent performances and good recording from the 1970s; the reservation concerns the works for violin, where the upper range of the strings is not as sweet and smooth as elsewhere. But this is of no great consequence when the programme is so interestingly varied and generous (73 minutes) and the disc reasonably priced. There is, however, no back-up documentation, and identification of the contents is incomplete.

Bassoon concerto in A min., RV 498; Cello concerto in C min., RV 401; Oboe concerto in F, RV 455; Concerto for strings in A, RV 158; Violin concerto in E min., RV 278; Concerto for 2 violins and 2 cellos, RV 575.
*** Novalis Dig. 150016-2; *150016-4* [id.]. Camerata Bern.

The Camerata Bern is an excellent ensemble, playing on modern instruments with great expertise and a sure sense of style. There is some particularly good playing from the bassoon soloist in the *A minor Concerto*, RV 498; but throughout the disc there is much to divert and delight the listener, and there is no cause for complaint so far as the recording is concerned.

Bassoon concerto in B flat, RV 502; Cello concerto in C min., RV 401; Oboe concerto in C, RV 447; Double trumpet concerto in C, RV 537. L'Estro armonico: Double violin concerto in A min., RV 522; Quadruple violin concerto in B min., RV 580; Op. 3/8 & 10. Triple violin concerto in F, RV 551.
*** Virgin/EMI Dig. VC7 59609-2 [id.]. Soloists, LCO, Christopher Warren-Green.

Christopher Warren-Green and his LCO seldom disappoint and this generous (75 minutes) collection, offering seven of Vivaldi's most appealing concertos, is another fine example of their vividly spontaneous music-making. For some reason a continuo is used only in the two woodwind concertos. The harpsichord swirls are rather effective in the first movement of the *Oboe concerto* and in the *Largo* of the *Bassoon concerto* a chamber organ piquantly introduces the solo entry. Excellent recording, made in All Saints', Petersham, yet with the resonance never becoming oppressive.

Bassoon concerto in E min., RV 484; Flute concerto in G, RV 436; Concerto for oboe and bassoon in G, RV 545; Concerto for strings in A, RV 159; Concerto for viola d'amore and lute in D min., RV 540; Violin concerto in E (L'Amoroso), RV 271.
*** DG Dig. 419 615-2 [id.]. Soloists, E. Concert, Pinnock.

Entitled '*L'Amoroso*' after the fine *E major Violin concerto* which is one of the six varied concertos on the disc, this collection brings lively, refreshing performances with fine solo playing from wind and string players alike, using period instruments in the most enticing way.

Bassoon concerto in A min., RV 498; Flute concerto in C min., RV 441; Oboe concerto in F, RV 456; Concerto for 2 oboes in D min., RV 535; Concerto for 2 oboes, bassoon, 2 horns and violin in F, RV 574; Piccolo concerto in C, RV 444.
(M) *** Decca 417 777-2; *417 777-4*. ASMF, Marriner.

The playing here is splendidly alive and characterful, with crisp, clean articulation and well-pointed phrasing, free from overemphasis. The *A minor Bassoon concerto* has a delightful sense of humour. Well-balanced and vivid recording.

Bassoon concerto in G min.; Flute concerto in D (Il Gardellino); Double concerto for flute, bassoon and strings (La Notte); Guitar concertos: in A; C; Double mandolin concerto in G; Concerto for strings; Piccolo concertos: in A min.; C; Double trumpet concerto in C; Violin concerto in G min., Op. 12/1; Concerto 'per La Ss. Asunzione di Maria Vergine' for violin, double string orchestra & 2 harpsichords in C; Sinfonia in G.
☞ (M) ** Van. 08.9132.72 (2) [id.]. Rudolf Klepack, Julius Baker, Alirio Diaz, Anton Ganocki &

Ferdo Pavlinek, Mark Bennett & Andrew Crowley, Jelka Stanic, Jan Tomasov, I Solisti di
Zagreb, Janigro; V. State Op. O, Prohaska; Camerata of St Andrew, Fiedman; V. State Op. CO,
Leonhardt.

Vanguard have here assembled a clutch of Vivaldi recordings from the 1960s and give the impression
with the new copyright of the CDs that they are much more current than this. They have not
bothered to identify them with their catalogue numbers, so nor have we, as most of the repertoire is
much more familiar now than when it first appeared. The wind soloists are virtuosi with taste,
technique and style, and they are well matched by Jelka Stanic in the great C major work with its two
separate string groups. *La Notte* comes off well, too, as does the *G minor Bassoon concerto* (Rudolf
Klepack). The mandolin soloists (Anton Ganocki and Ferdo Pavlinek) give a lively and presentable
account of their attractive *Double concerto*, and Diaz is both thoughtful and spirited in the concertos
for guitar. The two trumpet soloists, Mark Bennett and Andrew Crowley, are nimble and well
balanced. The unidentified little *Sinfonia in G* has an engaging 'lollipop' central movement: it is nicely
played by the Camerata of St Andrew, directed by Leonard Friedman. Otherwise most of the
accompaniments come from I Solisti di Zagreb under Antonio de Janigro, and they play with verve
and feeling. The recording, however, is a bit dry and lustreless, though truthfully remastered. It
sounds somewhat dated now but is acceptable enough.

*Double cello concerto in G min., RV 531; Flute concerto in C min., RV 441; Concerto in G min., for
flute and bassoon (La notte), RV 104; Concerto in F for flute, oboe and bassoon (La Tempesta di
mare), RV 570; Guitar concerto in D, RV 93; Concerto in F for 2 horns, RV 539; Concerto in B flat
for violin and cello, RV 547.*
*** ASV Dig. CDDCA 645 [id.]. Soloists, ECO, Malcolm.

With George Malcolm in charge it is not surprising that this 65-minute collection of seven diverse
concertos is as entertaining as any in the catalogue. Perhaps most striking of all is the *Double cello
concerto*, vigorously energetic in outer movements, but with a short, serene central *Largo*, with
overlapping phrases at the beginning, to remind one of the slow movement of Bach's *Double violin
concerto*. The concert ends with the duet version of *La notte*, which has much to charm the ear.
Accompaniments are sympathetic and stylish, and the whole programme beams with vitality and
conveyed enjoyment. The digital sound is vivid and realistic.

*Double concertos: for 2 cellos in G min., RV 531; 2 flutes in C, RV 533; 2 oboes in D min., RV 535; 2
mandolins in G, RV 532; 2 trumpets in C, RV 537; 2 violins, RV 523.*
(M) *** Ph. 426 086-2. I Musici.

This makes an attractively diverse collection. Most of these concertos are admirably inventive and the
performances show I Musici at their very best, on sparkling form. The sound is good too.

*Double cello concerto in G min., RV 531; Lute (Guitar) concerto in D, RV 93; Oboe concerto in F,
F.VII, No. 2 (R.455); Double concerto for oboe and violin; Trumpet concerto in D (trans. Jean
Thilde); Violin concerto in G min., Op. 12/1; RV 317.*
(BB) *** Naxos Dig. 8.550384; 4550384 [id.]. Capella Istropolitana, Jaroslav Kr(e)chek.

This is a recommendable disc from which to set out to explore the Vivaldi concertos, especially if you
are beginning a collection. Gabriela Krcková makes a sensitive contribution to the delightful *Oboe
concerto in F major*, F.VII, No. 2 (R.455), and the other soloists are pretty good too. Should this
programme meet your particular needs, there is no need for hesitation.

*L'Estro armonico: Quadruple violin concerto in D; Double violin concerto in D min., Op. 3/1 & 11;
Bassoon concerto in E min., RV 484; Flute concerto in G min. (La notte), Op. 10/2; Double mandolin
concerto in G, RV 532; Oboe concerto in B flat, RV 548; Orchestral concerto (con molti stromenti) in
C, RV 558; Concerto for strings in G (Alla rustica), RV 151.*
(M) *** DG Dig. 431 710-2; 431 710-4 [id.]. Soloists, E. Concert, Trevor Pinnock.

This collection of very varied works shows Pinnock and the English Concert at their liveliest and
most refreshing, although not always so strong on charm. The *Concerto for four violins* is very lithe,
and throughout the concert the solo playing is predictably expert. The *Orchestral concerto* involves an
astonishing array of instruments; authenticists will enjoy the timbres displayed here.

*L'Estro armonico: Double violin concertos in A and A min., Op. 3/5 & 8, RV 519 & 522. Cello
concerto in B min., RV 424; Violin concerto in C min. (Il Sospetto), RV 199; Double concerto for
violin and cello in B flat, RV 547; Concertos for strings in D; in G (Alla rustica), RV 151.*
☞ (B) **(*) Virgin/EMI Dig. VJ5 61103-2 [id.]. Rees, Murdoch, Niall Brown, Scottish Ens., Rees.

An enjoyably fresh collection of Vivaldi string concertos, using modern instruments with brisk, unsentimental and certainly stylish musicianship. The soloists do not have larger-than-life personalities, but they play very sympathetically and match timbres beautifully in the double concertos, especially in the *Andante* of RV 547, with its closely overlapping parts for violin and cello, and the tender *Larghetto* of RV 522. The alert allegros are particularly stimulating in the concertos for strings. Fresh, clean, natural sound, giving an authentic effect without the astringencies of original instruments.

L'Estro armonico: Quadruple violin concerto in B min., Op. 3/10; La Stravaganza: Violin concerto in B flat, Op. 4/1; Cello concerto in C min., RV 401; Double horn concerto in F, RV 539; Concerto in F for 2 oboes, bassoon, 2 horns and violin, RV 569; Double trumpet concerto in C, RV 537.
(M) *** Decca 425 721-2. ASMF, Marriner.

Another excellent collection from the considerable array of Vivaldi concertos recorded by Marriner and his ASMF (on modern instruments) between 1965 and 1977. The soloists are all distinguished, offering playing that is constantly alert, finely articulated and full of life and imagination.

(i) *Flute concertos: in D, RV 429; in G, RV 435, Op. 10/4; Recorder concerto in F, RV 434, Op. 10/5;*
(ii) *Concertos for strings: in D, RV 121; in G min., RV 156;* (iii) *Double concerto for viola d'amore, lute and strings in D min., RV 540; Concerto for lute, 2 violins and continuo in D, RV 93;* (ii) *Sonata in E flat (Al santo sepolcro), RV 130.*
☞ (B) *** CfP CD-CFP 4655; *TC-CFP 4655.* (i) Hans-Martin Linde, Prague CO; (ii) ECO, Leppard; (iii) Win Ten Have, Anthony Bailes, Danske Strings (members).

By combining first-rate analogue recordings from three separate sources, Classics for Pleasure have assembled a representative and first-rate collection to show almost every aspect of Vivaldi's unique contribution to the baroque concerto. The German flautist, Hans-Martin Linde, has an attractively fresh tone on both flute and recorder. Two of the regular Op. 10 works are included – No. 4 expressly written for transverse flute and No. 5 intended for treble recorder, as it is played here. Rhythmically lively, Linde is splendidly accompanied by the excellent strings of the Prague Chamber Orchestra, and the 1979 recording is firm and full. Leppard's string concertos are equally attractive, with the playing polished and committed. They date from 1970 and the remastering is highly successful and strikingly fresh, yet again there is a pleasing fullness. The standard of invention is high and, although *Al Santo sepolcro* has only two brief movements, they are strongly contrasted. These performances all use modern instruments, but now we are offered a stimulating contrast as the concerto pairing viola d'amore and lute is heard on original instruments and makes the most piquant contrast. To create a fragile effect, Vivaldi has all the instruments muted. The companion work for lute is equally delicate, a chamber concerto with the accompaniment scored for two violins and continuo. This stimulating group of concertos should find a useful niche in any collection.

Double flute concerto in C, RV 533; Double horn concerto in F, RV 539; Double mandolin concerto in G, RV 536; Double oboe concerto in A min., RV 536; Concerto for oboe and bassoon in G, RV 545; Double trumpet concerto in D, RV 563.
*** Ph. Dig. 412 892-2 [id.]. Soloists, ASMF, Marriner.

Apart from the work for two horns, where the focus of the soloists lacks a degree of sharpness, the recording often reaches demonstration standard. On CD, the concerto featuring a pair of mandolins is particularly tangible, with the balance near perfect, the solo instruments in proper scale yet registering admirable detail. The concertos for flutes and oboes are played with engaging finesse, conveying a sense of joy in the felicity of the writing. Once again Marriner makes a very good case for the use of modern wind instruments in this repertoire.

Double concerto for oboe and violin in B flat, RV 548; Triple concerto in C for violin, oboe and organ, RV 554; Double concertos for violin and organ: in D min., RV 541; in C min. & F, RV 766–7.
*** Unicorn Dig. DKPCD 9050; *DKPC 9050* [id.]. Francis, Studt, Bate, Tate Music Group, Studt.

An engaging clutch of concertos, two of which (RV 766–7) are first recordings. The works featuring the organ in a concertante role are in the concerto grosso tradition and are notable for their imaginative juxtaposition of colours – which is not to say that they lack vitality of invention. The recording is very attractive in ambience and the balance is admirable, with the sound first class.

(i) *Concertos for strings in D, RV 121; in G min., RV 156; Sonata al Santo Sepulcro, RV 130;* (ii) *Flute concertos: in D, RV 429; in G, Op. 10/4; Treble recorder concerto in F, Op. 10/5;* (iii) *Oboe concerto in A min., RV 461;* (iii) *Concerto for lute and 2 violins, in D, RV 93; Concerto for viola d'amore and lute in D min., RV 540.*

☞ (M) *** EMI CDM7 67809-2 [id.]. (i) ECO, Leppard; (ii) Hans-Martin Linde, Prague CO; (iii) Hans de Vries, I Solisti di Zagreb.

A sensibly compiled, 72-minute Vivaldi anthology that can be cordially recommended. The disc opens with Raymond Leppard, freshly creative in some fine string concertos with the ECO, and continues with Hans-Martin Linde, not quite so free as an interpreter, but an expert Vivaldian; then come some authentic performances of music for lute with the small original string-sound exactly right to balance (on either side of the stereo spectrum) with its small-scale soloist; finally, Hans de Vries gives a warmly elegant account of the lovely *A minor Oboe concerto*. The sound is fresh, with bright lighting on Leppard's violins to increase the feeling of liveliness. This collection readily shows that Vivaldi did *not* write the same concerto 500 times!

Concertos for strings: in D min. (Concerto madrigalesco), RV 129; in G (Alla rustica), RV 151; in G min., RV 157. (i) Motet: *In turbato mare irato, RV 627;* Cantata: *Lungi dal vago volto, RV 680. Magnificat, RV 610.*
*** Hyp. Dig. CDA 66247 [id.]. (i) Kirkby, Leblanc, Forget, Cunningham, Ingram, Tafelmusik Ch. & Bar. O, Lamon.

Mingling vocal and instrumental items, and works both well-known and unfamiliar, Jean Lamon provides a delightful collection, with Emma Kirkby a sparkling, pure-toned soloist in two items never recorded before: the motet, *In turbato mare irato*, and the chamber cantata, *Lungi dal vago volto*. The performance is lively, with fresh choral sound. The Tafelmusik performers come from Canada, and though the use of period instruments has some roughness, their vigour and alertness amply make up for that. Good, clear recorded sound.

CHAMBER MUSIC

Cello sonatas Nos. 1–9, RV 39/47.
*** CRD Dig. CRD 3440; *CRDC 4140* [id.] (*Nos. 1–4*); CRD 3441; *CRDC 4141* [id.] (*Nos. 5–9*). L'Ecole d'Orphée.

Cello sonatas Nos. 1–6, RV 40–41, 43, 45–7.
*** O-L Dig. 421 060-2 [id.]. Christophe Coin, Hogwood, Zweistra, Ferre, Finucane.
☞ (B) **(*) Erato/Warner Duo 4509 95359-2 (2) [id.]. Paul Tortelier, Robert Veyron-Lacroix –BACH: *Cello (Viola da gamba) sonatas.* **(*)

All nine *Sonatas* are given highly musical performances on CRD; they do not set out to impress by grand gestures but succeed in doing so by their dedication and sensitivity. Susan Sheppard is a thoughtful player and is well supported by her continuo team, Lucy Carolan and Jane Coe. The CRD recording is well focused and very present.

On Oiseau-Lyre, Coin and Hogwood offer only six of the nine *Sonatas*: the half-dozen that were collected together and published in 1740, towards the end of Vivaldi's life, as Op. 14. Compared to the CRD version, Coin is the more authoritative player, whose technique is effortless, and the continuo support is more varied in colour. In addition to Christopher Hogwood's harpsichord, there is baroque guitar and an archlute to lend a diversity of colour and texture that is most welcome. The Oiseau-Lyre sound is excellent.

Like Coin and Hogwood, Tortelier and Veyron-Lacroix chose the six best-known sonatas and, with the great cellist at his most persuasive, they provide a genuine alternative, with the full-timbred modern cello well forward, yet – with the sound fresh and well ventilated – only occasionally and marginally masking detail. Tortelier's playing has predictable warmth and a strong sense of line. The opening *Largo* of RV 43 readily demonstrates its strength and the rapport between the two players, while the slow movements of RV 40 and 45 are hardly less eloquent, with the genial finale of the latter work nicely elegant in its pointing. The documentation is inadequate, but in all other respects this Bonsai Duo bargain coupling is recommendable.

12 Sonatas for 2 violins & continuo, Op. 1.
(M) *** Ph. 426 926-2 (2) [id.]. Accardo, Gulli, Canino, De Saram.

12 Violin sonatas, Op. 2.
(M) *** Ph. 426 929-2 (2) [id.]. Accardo, Canino, De Saram.

It is unlikely that Salvatore Accardo's performances, so ably supported by Bruno Canino and Rohan de Saram (and in Op. 1 by Franco Gulli), could be surpassed in terms of sympathetic fluency, musicianship and sheer beauty of tone. The shadow of Corelli still hangs over the earlier set, yet slow movements often have those specially memorable Vivaldian harmonic inflexions. The dance movements are genially vigorous and the invention is remarkably pleasing and fresh. Collectors will find unexpected rewards in both sets, and the CD transfer of recordings made in 1977 are completely natural yet vivid in Philips's best manner.

6 Violin sonatas, Op. 5.
(M) **(*) Ph. 426 938-2 [id.]. Accardo, Gazeau (in Op. 5/5–6), Canino, De Saram.

Warm, mellifluous playing from Salvatore Accardo in the Op. 5 *Sonatas* of 1716–17, four being solo works with continuo and the remainder *Trio sonatas*. The music is not quite as interesting or inventive as Opp. 1 and 2, but those collecting this Edition will still find much that is rewarding. The 1977 sound is well up to the excellent standard of this series.

VOCAL MUSIC

Beatus vir, RV 597; Credo, RV 592; Magnificat, RV 610.
(M) *** Ph. 420 651-2. Soloists, Alldis Ch., ECO, Negri.

Beatus vir, RV 598; Dixit Dominus in D, RV 594; Introduzione al Dixit: Canta in prato in G, RV 636 (ed. Geigling); *Magnificat in G min., RV 611* (ed. Negri).
(M) *** Ph. 420 649-2. Lott, Burgess, Murray, Daniels, Finnie, Collins, Rolfe Johnson, Holl, Alldis Ch., ECO, Negri.

Crediti propter quod, RV 105; Credo, RV 591; Introduction to Gloria, RV 639; Gloria, RV 588; Kyrie, RV 587; Laetatus sum, RV 607.
(M) *** Ph. 420 650-2. M. Marshall, Lott, Finnie, Rolfe Johnson, Alldis Ch., ECO, Negri.

Dixit dominus, RV 595; In exitu Israel, RV 604; Sacrum, RV 586.
(M) *** Ph. 420 652-2. Alldis Ch., ECO, Negri.

Introduction to Gloria, RV 642; Gloria in D, RV 589; Lauda Jerusalem in E min., RV 609; Laudate Dominum in D min., RV 606; Laudati pueri Dominum in A, RV 602.
(M) *** Ph. 420 648-2. Marshall, Lott, Collins, Finnilä, Alldis Ch., ECO, Negri.

These Philips recordings come from the late 1970s. Vittorio Negri does not make use of period instruments, but he penetrates as deeply into the spirit of this music as many who do, and they come up splendidly in their new format, digitally refurbished. Any lover of Vivaldi is likely to be astonished that not only the well-known works but the rarities show him writing with the keenest originality and intensity. There is nothing routine about any of this music, or any of the performances either.

Beatus vir, RV 597; Dixit dominus, RV 594.
*** Argo Dig. 414 495-2 [id.]. Buchanan, Jennifer Smith, Watts, Partridge, Shirley-Quirk, King's College Ch., ECO, Cleobury.

Dixit dominus cannot fail to attract those who have enjoyed the better-known *Gloria*. Both works are powerfully inspired and are here given vigorous and sparkling performances with King's College Choir in excellent form under its latest choirmaster. The soloists are a fine team, fresh, stylish and nimble, nicely projected in the CD format with its extra sharpness of definition.

Beatus vir, RV 597; Dixit Dominus, RV 595; Gloria, RV 588; Magnificat, RV 610; Nisi Dominus, RV 608; Stabat Mater, RV 621.
☞ (B) **(*) Erato/Warner 4509 91936-2 (2) [id.]. Soloists; Lausanne Vocal Ens. & CO; Lisbon Gulbenkian Foundation Ch. & O; E. Bach Festival Ch. & Baroque O; Corboz.

The recordings on Corboz's Duo-Bonsai issue derive from three different sources. Those from the English Bach Festival, which include the *Gloria*, RV 588 (shorn of its three-movement *Introduction* on a non-liturgical text), and *Nisi Dominus* (beautifully sung by Helen Watts), offer baroque orchestral playing on authentic instruments. The *Beatus vir, Dixit Dominus*, RV 595, and *Magnificat* come from Lausanne, and modern instruments are used to produce a warm, well-focused sound; the acoustic is spacious and the performances vital and musical. The professional singers of the Lausanne Choir are generally admirable and the soloists are sweet-toned. The *Magnificat* is given in its simpler first version on a relatively small scale, with the chorus singing the alto solo, *Fecit potentiam*. The *Stabat Mater* (a most affecting piece, thought to have been composed at great speed) was recorded in Lisbon, and here the performance is pleasingly old-fashioned with robust tone and modern instruments. There is much to enjoy on this pair of CDs and this is a recommendably inexpensive way to get to know some of Vivaldi's finest choral music.

Beatus vir, RV 598; Gloria in D, RV 589.

☞ (M) *(*) Sony SBK 48280 [id.]. Burgess, Chamonin, Watkinson, Passaquet Vocal Ens., Grande
Écurie et la Chambre du Roy, Malgoire – BACH: *Magnificat.* **

Malgoire has the virtues of commitment and spirit and, were the singing and the orchestral playing a
little more polished, this would be recommendable. The two sopranos, Mary Burgess and Jocelyne
Chamonin, are just about adequate in the concise *Beatus vir* and, like the double choir, they are
effectively focused separately and vividly. Period instruments are used, but wind intonation in the
Gloria surely did not need to be as awry as it is here. For all their vitality and robustness, these
performances are not really satisfying enough to suffer repeated hearing, and the acoustic is not quite
expansive enough for comfort.

Dixit dominus, RV 594; Gloria in D, RV 589.

*** DG Dig. 423 386-2 [id.]. Argenta, Attrot, Denley, Stafford, Varcoe, E. Concert & Ch., Pinnock.

Pinnock's versions of the better-known of Vivaldi's two settings of the *Gloria* and the grander of his
two settings of the psalm, *Dixit dominus* (the one for double chorus), make an attractive and strong
coupling. His fresh, vigorous performances, beautifully recorded, add impressively to his developing
reputation as a choral conductor on record, with first-rate playing and singing.

Gloria in D, RV 589.

(M) *** Decca 421 146-2. Vaughan, J. Baker, King's College, Cambridge, Ch., ASMF, Willcocks –
HAYDN: *Nelson Mass.* ***

☞ *** EMI Dig. CDC7 54283-2 [id.]. Hendricks, Murray, Rigby, Heilmann, Hynninen, ASMF Ch.
& O, Marriner – BACH: *Magnificat.* ***

☞ (M) *** O-L 443 178-2 [id.]. Nelson, Kirkby, Watkinson, Ch. of Christ Church Cathedral, Oxford,
AAM, Simon Preston – HANDEL: *Utrecht Te Deum and Jubilate.* ***

*** DG Dig. 423 386-2 [id.]. Argenta, Attrot, Denley, Ch. & E. Concert, Pinnock – A. SCARLATTI:
Dixit Dominus. ***

Gloria, RV 589; Ostro picta, armata spina, RV 642.

☞ *** Chan. Dig. CHAN 0518; *EBTD 0518* [id.]. Kirkby, Bonner, Chance, Coll. Mus. 90, Hickox
– BACH: *Magnificat.* ***

The CD remastering of the stylish 1962 Willcocks recording of Vivaldi's *Gloria* is strikingly vivid and,
with excellent choral and solo singing, this makes a fine and generous bonus for the Haydn *Nelson
Mass.*

Both Richard Hickox and Neville Marriner couple the more popular of the two *D major Glorias*
with the Bach *Magnificat* and offer a pretty clear choice between period and modern instruments.
Honours are fairly evenly divided between them: Hickox directs a strong musical account and has the
benefit of a fine team of soloists and good Chandos recording; Marriner's performance with the
Academy on modern instruments is well paced, as is the Bach *Magnificat*. His soloists are also very
fine, and the recording has warmth and immediacy. Both can be recommended with confidence.

The freshness and point of the Christ Church performance of the *Gloria* are irresistible; anyone
who normally doubts the attractiveness of authentic string technique should sample this, for the
absence of vibrato adds a tang exactly in keeping with the performance. The soloists too keep vibrato
to the minimum, adding to the freshness, yet Carolyn Watkinson rivals even Dame Janet Baker in the
dark intensity of the Bach-like central aria for contralto, *Domine Deus, Agnus Dei*. The choristers of
Christ Church Cathedral excel themselves, and the recording is outstandingly fine. This now comes
generously coupled with Handel, making a total playing time of 74 minutes.

Trevor Pinnock directs a bright, refreshing account of the grander and better known of Vivaldi's
Gloria settings, with excellent playing and singing from the members of the English Concert.
Unusually but attractively coupled with the rare Scarlatti setting of *Dixit Dominus*, and very well
recorded, it makes a first-rate alternative recommendation.

Gloria in D, RV 588; Gloria in D, RV 589.

*** Argo Dig. 410 018-2 [id.]. Russell, Kwella, Wilkens, Bowen, St John's College, Cambridge, Ch.,
Wren O, Guest.

The two settings of the *Gloria* make an apt and illuminating coupling. Both in D major, they have
many points in common, presenting fascinating comparisons, when R V 588 is as inspired as its
better-known companion. Guest directs strong and well-paced readings, with R V 588 the more lively.
Good, warm recording to match the performances.

Gloria in D, RV 589; Kyrie in G min., RV 587.

☞ (B) *** Erato/Warner 2292 45923-2 [id.]. J. Smith, Staempfli, Rossier, Schaer, Lausanne Vocal &
Instrumental Ens., Corboz – BACH: *Magnificat.* ***

(M) *** DG 427 142-2. Regensburg Cathedral Ch., V. Capella Academica, Schneidt – BACH: *Motets.*
***

Michel Corboz, a fine choral conductor, gives a lively performance of Vivaldi's famous *Gloria*, and
his bargain version is aptly coupled with an equally spontaneous account of Bach's *Magnificat* and
another richly rewarding liturgical work of Vivaldi. The *Kyrie* is magnificent with its four soloists,
double chorus and double string orchestra spread spaciously across the sound stage. The CD transfer
of an excellent (1974) analogue recording is very well managed.

In the superb setting of the *Kyrie*, and the well-known *Gloria*, Schneidt with his fresh-toned
Regensburg Choir (the celebrated Domspatzen, 'cathedral sparrows') brings out what may seem a
surprising weight for an 'authentic' performance. The use of semi-chorus for solo numbers is
questionable, but no one hearing these performances is likely to dismiss the music as trivial.

(i) *Gloria in D, RV 589;* (ii) *Magnificat, RV 610.*

(M) **(*) Decca 425 724-2; *425 724-4.* (i) Vaughan, J. Baker; (ii) Castle, Cockerham, King; King's
College Ch., ASMF; (i) Willcocks; (ii) Ledger – PERGOLESI: *Magnificat.* **(*)

The Willcocks version of the *Gloria* uses comparatively small forces and, save for the occasional trace
of preciosity, it is very stylish. It has excellent soloists and is very well recorded. Ledger offers the
small-scale setting of the *Magnificat* and opts for boys' voices in the solos such as the beautiful duet,
Esurientes; though the singers are taxed by ornamentation, the result has all the accustomed beauty of
this choir's recordings. Excellent transfers.

(i; ii) *Gloria in D, RV 589; Magnificat in G min., RV 610/611;* (ii) *Salve Regina in C min., RV 616*
(with ANON.: (i; ii) *Te Deum in D, RV App. 38*).

(M) **(*) Ph. 426 952-2 (2). (i) Giebel; (ii) Höffgen; La Fenice di Venezia Ch. & O, Negri.

This acts as a pendant to Negri's fine choral series with the John Alldis Choir and the ECO (see
above), although the recordings were made a decade earlier in 1964/5. They have been effectively
remastered, however, and though not as cleanly focused as the later set, they have an agreeable
spaciousness and atmosphere. The choral singing in Venice is less refined than the London group, but
Negri secures performances that are vigorously committed and always alive. The recordings were
made in San Marco, where traditionally the performers were dispersed in separate groups, thus
achieving both a polychoral and polyinstrumental effect. Throughout the acoustics bring the richest
orchestral textures (no suspicion of original instruments here) and the choral sound is comparably
full. Even though inner detail is not sharp, the antiphony is highly effective and the results sonically
sumptuous. The *Te Deum in D* is spurious, a lighter piece, but one can understand its mistaken
attribution to Vivaldi.

Juditha triumphans (oratorio) complete.

(M) *** Ph. 426 955-2 (2). Finnilä, Springer, Hamari, Ameling, Burmeister, Berlin R. Soloists Ch. &
CO, Negri.

Described as a 'military' oratorio, *Juditha triumphans* demonstrates its martial bravado at the very
start, as exhilarating a passage as you will find in the whole of Vivaldi. The vigorous choruses stand
as cornerstones of commentary in a structure which, following convention, comes close to operatic
form, with recitatives providing the narrative between formal *da capo* arias. It is a pity that the role of
Judith is taken by one of the less interesting singers, Birgit Finnilä, and that Elly Ameling takes only
a servant's role, though that is one which demands more brilliant technique than any. Overall,
however, this is a considerable success.

Laudate pueri dominum, RV 601; Nisi Dominus, RV 608.

*** Mer. Dig. CDE 84129; *KE 77129* [id.]. Lynne Dawson, Christopher Robson, King's Consort,
Robert King.

The present setting of Psalm 113, RV 601, is a strong work whose inspiration runs at a consistently
high level; Lynne Dawson sings with an excellent sense of style and is given splendid support. The
coupling, the *Nisi Dominus*, a setting of Psalm 126, is much better known but makes an attractive
makeweight. It is also given an excellent performance by Christopher Robson. Good recording.

OPERA

L'Olimpiade: highlights.
(B) **(*) Hung. White Label HRC 078 [id.]. Kováts, Takács, Zempleni, Miller, Horvath, Kaplan, Gati, Budapest Madrigal Ch., Hungarian State O, Szekeres.

In the inexpensive White Label series of Hungaroton recordings, a generous collection of highlights from Vivaldi's opera, *L'Olimpiade*, is well worth investigating. An early delight in this selection is the work's most attention-grabbing number, a choral version of what we know as *Spring* from *The Four Seasons*. Ferenc Szekeres' conducting of the Hungarian State Orchestra is too heavy by today's standards, now that we are attuned to period performance, but the singing of soloists and choir is good, and the recording is brightly focused, with clean directional effects.

Orlando Furioso (complete).
*** Erato/Warner 2292 45147-2 (3) [id.]. Horne, De los Angeles, Valentini Terrani, Gonzales, Kozma, Bruscantini, Zaccaria, Sol. Ven., Scimone.

Outstanding in a surprisingly star-studded cast is Marilyn Horne in the title-role, rich and firm of tone, articulating superbly in divisions, notably in the hero's two fiery arias. In the role of Angelica, Victoria de los Angeles has many sweetly lyrical moments, and though Lucia Valentini Terrani is less strong as Alcina, she gives an aptly clean, precise performance. The remastering has somewhat freshened a recording which was not outstanding in its analogue LP form.

Vořišek, Jan Vaclav (1791–1825)

Symphony in D, Op. 24.
☞ (B) **(*) Pickwick Dig. PCD 1052; *PK 515* [id.]. W. German Sinfonia, Joeres – SCHUBERT: *Symphony No. 2.* **(*)

Vořišek is the nearest the Czechs got to producing a Beethoven, and this remarkably powerful work has fingerprints of the German master everywhere yet manages to retain a certain individuality. The slow movement is impressive and after an attractive Scherzo the finale has something in common with that of Beethoven's *Fourth*. The Westdeutsche Sinfonia give a boldly committed performance and Dirk Joeres does not miss the music's energy or gravitas. The sound adds to the weight of the music-making, although the resonant acoustic prevents the sharpest focus. Very enjoyable just the same and, with an attractive Schubert coupling, well worth its modest cost.

Fantasia, Op. 12; Impromptus Nos. 1–6, Op. 7; Sonata in B flat min., Op. 19; Variations in B flat, Op. 19.
☞ *** Unicorn Dig. DKPCD 9145 [id.]. Radoslav Kvapil.

Vořišek's *Sonata in B flat minor* (1920), like his *D major Symphony*, is one of his most representative and well-argued works and is the centrepiece of this beautifully played recital. Radoslav Kvapil is a highly sensitive and imaginative artist, deeply committed to this repertoire. The slightly later *B flat variations* will be a welcome discovery for those who do not know them, and Kvapil's accounts of the *Impromptus* are as good as, if not better than, any predecessor's. The recording, though not outstanding, serves him well, certainly more faithfully than in the Fibich's diary pieces in the same series.

Wagenseil, George (1715–77)

Harp concerto in G.
(B) *** DG 427 206-2. Zabaleta, Paul Kuentz CO – HANDEL: *Harp concerto;* MOZART: *Flute and harp concerto.* ***

Wagenseil's *Harp concerto* is a pleasant example of the *galant* style; the felicity of the writing in the first two movements is capped by a very jolly finale. Both performance and recording here can be commended and the remastering is fresh and clear.

Wagner, Richard (1813–83)

Siegfried idyll.

☞ *** Denon Dig. CO 79442 [id.]. Sinfonia Varsovia, Krivine – SCHOENBERG: *Verklärte Nacht;* R. STRAUSS: *Metamorphosen.* ***

(B) *** Pickwick Dig. PCD 928; *CIMPC 108.* SCO, Jaime Laredo – DVORAK: *String serenade* etc. ***

(M) **(*) EMI CMS7 63277-2 (2) [Ang. CDMB 63277]. Philh. O, Klemperer – MAHLER: *Symphony No. 9.* ***

Siegfried Idyll is the additional item (and placed first) in what is nowadays a not unusual coupling (Strauss's *Metamorphosen* and Schoenberg's *Verklärte Nacht*) and, though this would not in itself be a reason for buying it, it does offer an additional inducement, given the quality of these performances. Emmanuel Krivine gives a strongly characterized and obviously well-thought-out view of the piece and gets a very sensitive and totally committed response from his Warsaw orchestra. Both the wind and the strings give us playing of the utmost warmth, and they are beautifully recorded. In such oft-recorded repertoire one cannot speak of first choices, but this disc comes very high on the list.

A beautiful performance from Jaime Laredo and the Scottish Chamber Orchestra, warm and poised and ending serenely, yet moving to a strong central climax. The recording, made in Glasgow City Hall, has a pleasingly expansive ambience, yet textures are clear.

Klemperer favours the original chamber-orchestra scoring and the Philharmonia players are very persuasive, especially in the score's gentler moments. However, the balance is forward and, although the sound is warm, the ear craves a greater breadth of string tone at the climax.

(i; ii) *Siegfried idyll.* (iii; iv) *Overture: Der fliegende Holländer.* (i; v) *Götterdämmerung: Siegfried's Rhine journey. Lohengrin:* (i; ii) *Prelude to Act I;* (vi; iv) *Prelude to Act III. Die Meistersinger:* (vi; iv) *Overture;* (vii; viii) *Prelude to Act III.* (ix; viii) *Parsifal: Prelude & Good Friday music. Overtures:* (vi; iv) *Rienzi;* (vii; x) *Tannhäuser. Tristan:* (iii; iv) *Preludes to Acts I & III;* (vi; iv) *Death of Isolde.* (i; v) *Die Walküre: Ride of the Valkyries.*

☞ (B) *** DG Double 439 687-2 (2) [id.]. (i) BPO; (ii) Kubelik; (iii) Bayreuth Festival O; (iv) Karl Boehm; (v) Karajan; (vi) VPO; (vii) Deutsche Op., Berlin, O; (viii) Jochum; (ix) Bav. RSO; (x) Otto Gerdes.

This Double DG collection (146 minutes) will be very difficult to beat for those collectors wanting an analogue collection of Wagnerian overtures and orchestral preludes, including the *Siegfried idyll.* It is beautifully shaped by Kubelik and equally beautifully played by the Berlin Philharmonic. He also conducts an impressive *Lohengrin Act I Prelude,* again with the BPO, who have played it under everyone who matters, including, of course, Furtwängler. He placed those two central cymbal clashes with unique prescience, but Kubelik does not do too badly! Boehm not only provides a richly sustained opening for *Rienzi* but is pretty exciting in *Der fliegende Holländer* and at his finest in the *Tristan Preludes* – taken from his 1966 Bayreuth complete set – which glow with intensity. Surprisingly, Karajan contributes only two items, but both bring plenty of adrenalin. It is good that the anthology includes the fine account of the *Tannhäuser overture* conducted by Otto Gerdes, a DG recording producer whose talents ranged much further than balancing an orchestra. But the highlight of the set comes last, Jochum's electrifying and Rosette-worthy performance of the *Prelude and Good Friday* music from *Parsifal.* Recorded in the Munich Herculessaal, it is not only a demonstration record from the earliest days of stereo, but the playing has a spiritual intensity that has never been surpassed. Elsewhere the recordings, dating from the late 1950s to the early 1980s, have all been transferred vividly, with some sounding fuller and more refined than others. The documentation, as with the rest of this series, is totally inadequate.

Siegfried idyll. Der fliegende Holländer: Overture. Lohengrin: Preludes to Acts I and III. Die Meistersinger: Overture.

*** DG Dig. 419 169-2 [id.]. NYPO, Sinopoli.

Superbly spacious performances from Sinopoli, with *Der fliegende Holländer* seeming less melodramatic than usual, yet played with free rubato in the most effective way. The emotional arch of the *Lohengrin* Act I *Prelude* is superbly graduated, with the New York violins finding radiant tone for the closing pianissimo. *Die Meistersinger* is massively stately. Sinopoli opens and closes the *Siegfried idyll* with the greatest delicacy, and the end is wonderfully serene and romantic; the middle section is fast and volatile, moving to its climax with passionate thrust.

Siegfried idyll. Die fliegende Holländer: Overture. Lohengrin: Prelude to Act III. Rienzi: Overture.
Tannhäuser: Overture.
☞ (BB) *** Tring Dig. TRP 008 [id.]. RPO, Vernon Handley.

A splendid super-bargain collection, given spectacular sound. The *Siegfried idyll* is beautifully played and radiantly recorded, but the highlight is Handley's excitingly rumbustious account of the *Rienzi overture* with thrilling brass and an exuberant contribution from the side-drum, snares a-rattling. This is a demonstration item. The heavy brass also makes a splendidly weighty contribution to the famous *Lohengrin Act III Prelude* and is hardly less effective at the climax of the *Ride of the Valkyries.* Handley uses the concert ending in both these pieces, and his spacious treatment of the reprise of the Pilgrim's chorale at the close of the *Tannhäuser overture* makes a satisfying close to a programme which is played as well as it is recorded (in the suitable resonance of St Augustine's Church, Kilburn).

Siegfried idyll. Lohengrin: Preludes to Acts I & III. Die Meistersinger: Prelude to Act I. Parsifal:
Prelude to Act I. Tristan und Isolde: Prelude and Liebestod.
(M) *** Ph. 420 886-2. Concg. O, Haitink.

The addition of Haitink's simple, unaffected reading of the *Siegfried idyll* to his 1975 collection of *Preludes* enhances the appeal of a particularly attractive concert. The rich acoustics of the Concertge-bouw are surely ideal for *Die Meistersinger,* given a memorably spacious performance, and Haitink's restraint adds to the noble dignity of *Parsifal.* The *Lohengrin* excerpts are splendidly played. The digital remastering is almost entirely beneficial.

Siegfried idyll. Lohengrin: Prelude to Acts I & III. Die Meistersinger: Overture. Die Walküre: Ride of
the Valkyries; (i) Wotan's farewell and Magic fire music.
*** ASV Dig. CDDCA 666 [id.]. Philh. O, Francesco d'Avalos, (i) with John Tomlinson.

The opening *Siegfried idyll* has all the requisite serenity and atmosphere; here, as elsewhere, the Philharmonia play most beautifully. The boldly sumptuous recording brings a thrilling resonance and amplitude to the brass, especially trombones and tuba, and in the expansive *Meistersinger overture,* and again in *Wotan's farewell* the brass entries bring a physical frisson. John Tomlinson's noble assumption of the role of Wotan, as he bids a loving farewell to his errant daughter, is very moving here, and the response of the Philharmonia strings matches the depth of feeling he conveys. With the Valkyries also given a splendid sense of spectacle, this collection should have a wide appeal.

Siegfried idyll. Tannhäuser: overture. (i) Tristan: Prelude and Liebestod.
*** DG Dig. 423 613-2 [id.]. (i) Jessye Norman; VPO, Karajan.

This superb Wagner record was taken live from a unique concert conducted by Karajan at the Salzburg Festival in August 1987. The *Tannhäuser overture* has never sounded so noble, and the *Siegfried idyll* has rarely seemed so intense and dedicated behind its sweet lyricism; while the *Prelude and Liebestod,* with Jessye Norman as soloist, bring the richest culmination, sensuous and passionate, but remarkable as much for the hushed, inward moments as for the ineluctable building of climaxes.

ORCHESTRAL EXCERPTS FROM THE OPERAS

Der fliegende Holländer: Overture. Lohengrin: Prelude to Act I. Die Meistersinger: Overture. (i)
Tannhäuser: Overture and Venusberg music. Tristan: Prelude and Liebestod.
(M) *** EMI CDM7 64334-2 [id.]. BPO, Karajan; (i) with German Op. Ch.

All the music here is played excellently, but the *Overture and Venusberg music* from *Tannhäuser* (Paris version, using chorus) and the *Prelude and Liebestod* from *Tristan* are superb. In the *Liebestod* the climactic culmination is overwhelming in its sentient power, while *Tannhäuser* has comparable spaciousness and grip. There is an urgency and edge to the *Flying Dutchman overture,* and *Die Meistersinger* has weight and dignity, but the last degree of tension is missing.

Götterdämmerung: (a) Siegfried's Rhine journey and Funeral music; (b) Lohengrin: Prelude to Act III;
(a) Die Meistersinger: Overture; Prelude to Act III; Dance of the apprentices; Procession of the
Masters. (b) Tannhäuser: Grand march.
☞ (M) ** BMG/RCA (a) stereo / (b) mono 09026 61792-2 [id.]. (a) Chicago SO; (b) RCA Victor O;
    Fritz Reiner.

It is rare that one has to complain about the stereo sound achieved by the RCA engineers in Chicago's Orchestral Hall in the late 1950s, but in the stereo Wagner sessions included here the sound is too sumptuously inflated: all amplitude, with no sparkle in the treble. It makes Reiner's spacious account of the *Die Meistersinger overture* seem too weighty and overblown, although the close of the

Procession of the Masters is more effective. However, there is some glorious playing from the horns in the great *Prelude to Act III* from the same opera, and the opening of *Siegfried's Rhine journey* has plenty of tension and atmosphere. The other three items use an East Coast pick-up orchestra and were recorded in mono in New York's Manhattan Center in 1950.

Götterdämmerung: Dawn and Siegfried's Rhine journey; Funeral march. Lohengrin: Preludes to Acts I & III. Die Meistersinger: Overture; Dance of the apprentices. Die Walküre: Ride of the Valkyries.
(B) *** CfP Dig. CD-CFP 9008. LPO, Rickenbacher.

Karl Anton Rickenbacher secures first-class playing from the LPO with the strings at their peak in the radiant opening of the *Lohengrin Prelude*. Some might feel that his pacing of the *Die Meistersinger overture* is fractionally fast. The CD sound is firm and full; indeed the *Prelude to Act III* of *Lohengrin* makes a splendid demonstration recording; an exciting performance, particularly vividly projected.

Götterdämmerung: Dawn and Siegfried's Rhine journey; Siegfried's death and funeral march. Lohengrin: Prelude to Act I. Tannhäuser: Overture and Venusberg music. Tristan und Isolde: Liebestod. Die Walküre: Ride of the Valkyries.
☞ (M) (***) BMG/RCA mono GD 60306 [09026 60306-2]. NBC SO, Toscanini.

Götterdämmerung: Dawn; (i; ii) Zu neuen Taten; Willst du mir Minne schenken; O heilige Götter; Siegfried's Rhine journey; Brünnhilde's immolation: (i) Starke Scheite schichtet mir dort; Wie Sonne lauter strahlt mir sein Licht; Mein Erbe nun nehm'ich zu eigen; Fliegt heim ihr Raben!; Grane, Mein Ross, sei mir gegrüsst. Siegfried: Forest murmurs.
☞ (M) (***) BMG/RCA mono GD 60304 [09026 60304-2]. (i) Helen Traubel; (ii) Lauritz Melchior; NBC SO, Toscanini.

Toscanini's special brand of electricity comes over vividly in these characteristic Wagner performances. The *Lohengrin Prelude* and the soaring *Tristan Liebestod* have typical intensity and, although the dynamic range is compressed, the sound is surprisingly good, as it is in the tenderly sensuous *Venusberg* sequence in *Tannhäuser*. One is offered a choice here of the *Götterdämmerung Dawn* sequence with or without the vocal contribution in which both Helen Traubel and Melchior are strong enough musical personalities to stand up against Toscanini. The recordings date from the 1940s and 1950s and, as transferred, are surprisingly full, with something of a concert-hall effect in the Carnegie Hall *Immolation* sequence of 1941. Traubel rides over the orchestra with considerable dominance.

Götterdämmerung: Dawn and Siegfried's Rhine journey; Siegfried's death and funeral march; (i) Brünnhilde's immolation. Siegfried: Forest murmurs. Die Walküre: Ride of the Valkyries.
*** Erato/Warner Dig. 2292 45786-2 [id.]. (i) Deborah Polaski; Chicago SO, Barenboim.

Here Barenboim dons his Furtwänglerian mantle to splendidly spacious effect. Even with tempi measured, he secures playing of great concentration and excitement from the Chicago orchestra, and the recording is one of the finest made in Chicago's Orchestra Hall for many years. Deborah Polaski makes a bold, passionate Brünnhilde, and if her voice is not flattered by the microphones, and under pressure her vibrato widens and there is a loss of focus at the climax of the *Immolation scene*, this is still histrionically thrilling, and Barenboim and the orchestra provide an overwhelming final apotheosis.

Götterdämmerung: Dawn and Siegfried's Rhine journey; Siegfried's death and funeral music. Die Meistersinger: Prelude. Das Rheingold: Entry of the Gods into Valhalla. Siegfried: Forest murmurs. Tristan und Isolde: Prelude & Liebestod. Die Walküre: Wotan's farewell and Magic fire music.
⊛ (M) *** SBK 48175 [id.]. Cleveland O, Szell.

The orchestral playing here is in a very special class. Its virtuosity is breathtaking. Szell generates the greatest tension, particularly in the two scenes from *Götterdämmerung*, while the *Liebestod* from *Tristan* has never been played on record with more passion and fire. The *Tristan* and *Meistersinger* excerpts (from 1962) have been added to the contents of the original LP, which contained the *Ring* sequences made later (in 1968), and the improvement in quality with the latest remastering for CD is little short of miraculous. Like the similarly remastered Dvořák *Slavonic dances*, this is reasonably worthy of Szell's extraordinary achievement in Cleveland in the 1960s, even if the forward balance of the recording places a limit on the dynamic range.

Götterdämmerung: Siegfried's Rhine journey & Funeral music. Parsifal: Prelude to Act I. Siegfried: Forest murmurs. Tristan und Isolde: Prelude & Liebestod. Die Walküre: Ride of the Valkyries.
*** Collins Dig. 1207-2 [id.]. Philh. O, Yuri Simonov.

If you want a spectacular, modern, digital recording of Wagnerian orchestral excerpts, this one is hard to beat. The magnificent account of *Siegfried's Rhine journey* (with a splendid horn solo) is followed by a performance of the *Funeral music* which has blazing drama and enormously expansive sound, with the brass biting venomously at Siegfried's betrayal. The *Prelude and Liebestod* from *Tristan* brings playing of great ardour from the Philharmonia strings, while – at a very spacious tempo – they find considerable intensity in the *Parsifal Prelude*. The *Valkyries* come in at a fine canter, nostrils flaring yet not driven too hard.

VOCAL MUSIC

Das Liebesmal der Apostel (cantata).
☞ (B) **(*) Pickwick PCD 1042; *PK 515* [id.]. Ambrosian Male Voice Ch., L. Symphonica, Wyn Morris – BRUCKNER: *Helgoland.* ***

While eagerly welcoming this CD and the fine performance it contains, one must register disappointment at the size of the chorus. Wagner's strange Pentecostal cantata was written originally for massed choirs in Dresden at a time when he was composing *Tannhäuser* (so very obvious from the music). Some 1,200 singers from all over Saxony gathered for the première in 1843 – even so, the composer was disappointed with the lack of impact! There is no lack of impact here, and the balance with the large orchestra is expertly managed when it finally appears – two-thirds of the way through the piece. But its spectacular framework tends to underline the relative smallness of the choral group. Yet the Ambrosians sing incisively and with much fervour, and the thrills remain when the direction is so strong. If the climax is not as monumental as the composer undoubtedly envisaged, it is still most compelling. The unaccompanied opening sections (unfortunately not individually banded, when the work overall runs for 33 minutes) are splendidly vivid and immediate, again helped by the recording with its remarkable presence and wide dynamic range.

Lieder: Les deux Grenadiers; Lied des Mephistopheles (Es waar einmal ein König; Was machst du mir); Mignonne; Der Tannenbaum; Tout n'est qu'images fugitives.
☞ ⊛ *** EMI Dig. CDC5 55047-2 [id.]. Thomas Hampson, Geoffrey Parsons – BERLIOZ: *Irlande;* LISZT: *Lieder.* *** ⊛

Thomas Hampson's unforgettable collection of romantic songs – for which he himself has written highly perceptive notes – is crowned by the rarest items of all, six songs which Wagner wrote between 1831 and 1839. Starting with a charming French salon piece, *Mignonne*, to words by Ronsard, the collection presents a virtually unknown side of the composer. As well as another French love-song, there is a setting in French of the Goethe poem about the two grenadiers, not as subtle as Schumann's version but building to a tremendous climax with a reference to the *Marseillaise*. Two of Mephistopheles' songs from *Faust* (in German) date from earlier, including a jaunty setting of the *Song of the flea*. With Hampson in magnificent voice, powerfully accompanied by Geoffrey Parsons, this makes up a winning disc, very well recorded.

Wesendonk Lieder.
☞ (M) *(*) Decca 436 200-2 [id.]. Marilyn Horne, RPO, Henry Lewis – MAHLER: *Kindertotenlieder* etc. *(*)

Marilyn Horne's singing is tonally beautiful but lacking in emotional warmth. There is much to admire, but in these lovely songs that is not enough.

Wesendonk Lieder: Der Engel; Stehe still; Im Treibhaus; Schmerzen; Träume. Götterdämmerung: Starke Scheite schichet mir dort. Siegfried: Ewig war ich. Tristan: Doch nun von Tristan?; Mild und leise.
(M) (***) EMI mono CDH7 63030-2 [id.]. Kirsten Flagstad, Philh. O, Furtwängler, Dobrowen.

Recorded in the late 1940s and early '50s, a year or so before Flagstad did *Tristan* complete with Furtwängler, these performances show her at her very peak, with the voice magnificent in power as well as beautiful and distinctive in every register. The *Liebestod* (with rather heavy surface noise) may be less rapt and intense in this version with Dobrowen than with Furtwängler but is just as expansive. For the *Wesendonk Lieder* she shades the voice down very beautifully, but this is still monumental and noble rather than intimate Lieder-singing. (Alas, this has been withdrawn as we go to press.)

OPERA

Die Feen (complete).
*** Orfeo Dig. C062833 (3) [id.]. Gray, Lovaas, Laki, Studer, Alexander, Hermann, Moll, Rootering, Bracht, Bav. R. Ch. & SO, Sawallisch.

Wagner was barely twenty when he wrote *Die Feen*, yet even when he has a *buffo* duet between the second pair of principals, the result is distinctive and fresh, delightfully sung here by Cheryl Studer and Jan-Hendrik Rootering. Sawallisch gives a strong and dramatic performance, finely paced; central to the total success is the singing of Linda Esther Gray as Ada, the fairy-heroine, powerful and firmly controlled. John Alexander as the tenor hero, King Arindal, sings cleanly and capably; the impressive cast-list boasts such excellent singers as Kurt Moll, Kari Lovaas and Krisztina Laki in small but vital roles. Ensembles and choruses – with the Bavarian Radio Chorus finely disciplined – are particularly impressive, and the recording is generally first rate.

Der fliegende Holländer (complete).
(M) *** Ph. Dig. 434 599-2 (2) [id.]. Estes, Balslev, Salminen, Schunk, Bayreuth Festival (1985) Ch. & O, Nelsson.
☞ (B) *** Naxos Dig. 8.660025/6 [id.]. Muff, Haubold, Knodt, Seiffert, Budapest R. Ch., Vienna ORF SO, Steinberg.
☞ (M) **(*) EMI Dig. CMS7 64650-2 (2) [Ang. CDMB 64650]. Van Dam, Vejzovic, Moll, Hofmann, Moser, Borris, V. State Op. Ch., BPO, Karajan.
**(*) Decca 414 551-2 (3) [id.]. Bailey, Martin, Talvela, Kollo, Krenn, Isola Jones, Chicago SO Ch. & O, Solti.
(M) **(*) Decca 417 319-2 (2) [id.]. London, Rysanek, Tozzi, ROHCG Ch. & O, Dorati.
☞ ** Decca Dig. 436 418-2. (2). Hale, Behrens, Rydl, Protschka, Vermillion, Heilmann, V State Op. Konzertvereinigung VPO, Dohnányi.

Woldemar Nelsson, with the team he had worked with intensively through the season, conducts a performance even more glowing and responsively paced than those of his starrier rivals. The cast is more consistent than any, with Lisbeth Balslev as Senta firmer, sweeter and more secure than any current rival, raw only occasionally, and Simon Estes a strong, ringing Dutchman, clear and noble of tone. Matti Salminen is a dark and equally secure Daland and Robert Schunk an ardent, idiomatic Erik. The veteran, Anny Schlemm, as Mary, though vocally overstressed, adds pointful character, and the chorus is superb, wonderfully drilled and passionate with it. Though inevitably stage noises are obtrusive at times, the recording is exceptionally vivid and atmospheric. On two mid-priced discs only, it makes an admirable first choice.

Recorded in collaboration with Austrian Radio, the bargain version on Naxos is in every way a strong contender against even the finest of the full-price versions. Pinchas Steinberg, who has been outstandingly successful as music director of the ORF Orchestra and who was responsible for RCA's brilliant recording of Massenet's *Cherubin*, here proves a warmly sympathetic Wagnerian. More than most rivals, he brings out the light and shade of this earliest of the regular Wagner canon, helped by the refined, well-balanced recording, and by brilliant, sharply dramatic playing from the orchestra. His speeds are more urgent than most, with rhythms well sprung and melodic lines understandingly moulded. The chorus too sings with a bite and precision to match any rival. The cast of soloists may not be in that league, but they sing clearly and on the whole freshly, avoiding most of the cardinal faults of Wagner singers today. Alfred Muff as the Dutchman focuses far better than in the EMI recording of Strauss's *Die Frau ohne Schatten*. Though the voice is not beautiful, he attacks the notes cleanly, with vibrato only occasionally intrusive. The vibrato of Ingrid Haubold is more of a problem but, except under pressure, it is well controlled, and she begins *Senta's Ballad* with a meditative pianissimo, a rare achievement. Both tenors are excellent, Peter Seiffert as Erik and Joerg Hering as the Steersman, and though Erich Knodt with rather a gritty baritone is an uncharacterful Daland, his Act II aria is light and refreshing, thanks to Steinberg's fine rhythmic pointing. The recording is both atmospheric and clear, and the set comes with libretto, translation, notes and very detailed synopsis, an outstanding bargain.

The extreme range of dynamics in EMI's recording for Karajan, not ideally clear but rich, matches the larger-than-life quality of the conductor's reading. He firmly and convincingly relates this early work to later Wagner, *Tristan* above all. His choice of José van Dam as the Dutchman, thoughtful, finely detailed and lyrical, strong but not at all blustering, goes well with this. Van Dam is superbly matched and contrasted with the finest Daland on record, Kurt Moll, gloriously biting and dark in tone, yet detailed in his characterization. Neither the Erik of Peter Hofmann, nor – more seriously – the Senta of Dunja Vejzovic matches this standard; nevertheless, for all her variability,

Vejzovic is wonderfully intense in *Senta's Ballad* and she matches even Van Dam's fine legato in the Act II duet. The CD transfer underlines the heavyweight quality of the recording, with the *Sailors' chorus* for example made massive, but effectively so, when Karajan conducts it with such fine spring. The banding is not generous, making the issue less convenient to use than most Wagner CD sets, and the break between the two CDs is not ideally placed. But there is a full libretto/translation.

What will disappoint some who admire Solti's earlier Wagner sets is that this most atmospheric of the Wagner operas is presented with no Culshaw-style production whatever. Characters halloo to one another when evidently standing elbow to elbow, and even the Dutchman's ghostly chorus sounds very close and earthbound. But with Norman Bailey a deeply impressive Dutchman, Janis Martin a generally sweet-toned Senta, Martti Talvela a splendid Daland, and Kollo, for all his occasional coarseness, an illuminating Erik, it remains well worth hearing.

Dorati, with rhythms well sprung, draws strong and alert playing and singing from his Covent Garden forces in a consistently purposeful performance, helped by Culshaw-style sound-effects. The well-spread recording is full and atmospheric and, like the Philips set, the reissue is offered on two mid-price CDs. George London's Dutchman brings one of his most powerful performances on disc, occasionally rough-toned but positive. Leonie Rysanek may sound too mature for Senta, but as a great Wagnerian she brings a commanding presence and the most persuasive sense of line. There is no weak link in the rest of the cast, well set up at the start by the characterful Richard Lewis as the Steersman.

Issued around the same time as the Naxos version, Dohnányi's Decca set, also made in Vienna but with starrier forces, is disappointing. The sound is rich and full, if not as clear on detail as the Naxos, but Dohnányi's relatively sluggish speeds go with rhythms too often square and unsprung. In all he takes over 10 minutes longer than Nelsson in his Bayreuth set on Philips – on balance still the finest – and almost as many more than Steinberg. Nor does his cast fulfil expectations. Robert Hale is a powerful, intense Dutchman but, as recorded, the voice is ill-focused, lacking necessary firmness. Hildegard Behrens too has trouble with vibrato, which is intrusive except when her voice opens out richly at the top, a far less satisfying performance than those she gives as Brünnhilde in the Levine *Ring* cycle. The others are more satisfying, though in varying degrees they also have voice-production problems, even Kurt Rydl whose ripely characterful Daland is not as steady as it might be. Not surprisingly for the first of its new, post-Solti generation of Wagner recordings, Decca chose the opera that was the least successful with Solti, but this is hardly a replacement even for that flawed set.

Götterdämmerung (complete).
*** Decca 414 115-2 (4) [id.]. Nilsson, Windgassen, Fischer-Dieskau, Frick, Neidlinger, Watson,
    Ludwig, V. State Op. Ch., VPO, Solti.
*** DG 415 155-2 (4) [id.]. Dernesch, Janowitz, Brilioth, Stewart, Kelemen, Ludwig, Ridderbusch,
    German Op. Ch., BPO, Karajan.
*** Ph. 412 488-2 (4) [id.]. Nilsson, Windgassen, Greindl, Mödl, Stewart, Neidlinger, Dvořáková,
    Bayreuth Festival (1967) Ch. & O, Boehm.
☞ *** EMI Dig. CD7 54485-2 (4) [Ang. CDCD 54485]. Marton, Jerusalem, Tomlinson, Adam,
    Hampson, Bundschuh, Lipovšek, Bav. R. Ch., RSO, Haitink.
☞ (M) *** Ph. 434 424-2 (4) [id.]. G. Jones, Jung, Hübner, Becht, Mazura, Altmeyer, Killebrew,
    (1979) Bayreuth Festival Ch. & O, Boulez.

Solti's *Götterdämmerung* represented the peak of his achievement in recording the *Ring* cycle. His reading had matured before the recording was made. He presses on still, but no longer is there any feeling of over-driving, and even the *Funeral march* is made into a natural, not a forced, climax. There is not a single weak link in the cast. Nilsson surpasses herself in the magnificence of her singing: even Flagstad in her prime would not have been more masterful as Brünnhilde. As in *Siegfried*, Windgassen is in superb voice; Frick is a vivid Hagen, and Fischer-Dieskau achieves the near impossible in making Gunther an interesting and even sympathetic character. As for the recording quality, it surpasses even Decca's earlier achievement, and the CDs bring added weight to balance the brilliant upper range.

Karajan's singing cast is marginally even finer than Solti's, and his performance conveys the steady flow of recording sessions prepared in relation to live performances. But ultimately he falls short of Solti's achievement in the orgasmic quality of the music. Karajan is a degree less committed, beautifully as the players respond, and warm as his overall approach is. Dernesch's Brünnhilde is warmer than Nilsson's, with a glorious range of tone. Brilioth as Siegfried is fresh and young-sounding, while the Gutrune of Gundula Janowitz is far preferable to that of Claire Watson on Decca. The matching is otherwise very even.

Boehm's urgently involving reading of *Götterdämmerung*, very well cast, is crowned by an incandescent performance of the final Immolation scene from Birgit Nilsson as Brünnhilde. It is an astonishing achievement that she could sing with such biting power and accuracy in a live performance, coming to it at the very end of a long evening. The excitement of that is matched by much else in the performance, so that incidental stage noises and the occasional inaccuracy, almost inevitable in live music-making, matter hardly at all. Josef Greindl is rather unpleasantly nasal in tone as Hagen, and Martha Mödl as Waltraute is unsteady; but both are dramatically involving. Thomas Stewart is a gruff but convincing Gunther and Dvořáková, as Gutrune, strong if not ideally pure-toned. Neidlinger as ever is a superb Alberich.

Haitink's reading is magnificent. In its strength, nobility and thrustfulness it crowns all his previous Wagner, culminating in a forceful and warmly expressive account of the final Immolation scene. Siegfried Jerusalem clearly establishes himself as the finest latterday Siegfried, both heroic and sweet of tone. Thomas Hampson is a sensitive and virile Gunther, John Tomlinson a sinister but human Hagen, Marjana Lipovšek a warmly intense Waltraute and Eva-Maria Bundschuh a rich, rather fruity Gutrune. The obvious reservation to make is with the singing of Eva Marton as Brünnhilde, when the unevenness of the vocal production is exaggerated by the microphone in a way that at times comes close to pitchless yelping. However, that drawback is clearly outweighed by the set's positive qualities, and the scale of her singing is in no doubt, an archetypal Brünnhilde voice in timbre if not in firmness.

Boulez's 1979 analogue recording is warm and urgent. The passion of the performance is established in the Dawn music before the second scene of the Prologue and, with a strong if not ideal cast, it has a clear place as a first-rate mid-price recommendation. Manfred Jung as Siegfried gives a fresh, clean-cut performance. Jeannine Altmeyer sings Gutrune, sweet but not always ideally clean of attack; Fritz Hübner is a weighty Hagen, Franz Mazura a powerful Gunther and Gwendoline Killebrew a rich, firm Waltraute. Dame Gwyneth Jones as Brünnhilde, always very variable, has some splendid moments, notably at the close of the Immolation scene. The sound is aptly atmospheric but lacks something in weight in the brass, though there is no lack of excitement at the end of Act II.

The Twilight of the Gods (Götterdämmerung: complete; in English).
(M) *** EMI CMS7 64244-2 (5) [id.]. Hunter, Remedios, Welsby, Haugland, Hammond-Stroud,
   Curphey, Pring, E. Nat. Op. Ch. & O, Goodall.

Goodall's account heightens the epic scale. The few slight imprecisions and the occasional rawness of wind tone actually seem to enhance the earthiness of Goodall's view. Both Rita Hunter and Alberto Remedios give performances which are magnificent in every way. In particular the golden beauty of Remedios's tenor is consistently superb, with no Heldentenor barking at all, while Aage Haugland's Hagen is giant-sounding to focus the evil, with Gunther and Gutrune mere pawns. The voices on stage are in a different, drier acoustic from that for the orchestra, but considering the problems the sound is impressive. As for Goodall, with his consistently expansive tempi he carries total concentration – except, curiously, in the scene with the Rhinemaidens, whose music (as in Goodall's *Rhinegold* too) lumbers along heavily.

The Twilight of the Gods (Götterdämmerung): Act III: excerpts (in English).
☞ (M) *** Chan. CHAN 6593 [id.]. Rita Hunter, Alberto Remedios, Norman Bailey, Clifford
   Grant, Margaret Curphey, Sadler's Wells Opera Ch. & O, Goodall.

Originally recorded by Unicorn in the early 1970s, even before the Sadler's Wells company had changed its name to the English National Opera, this single Chandos CD brings an invaluable reminder of Reginald Goodall's performance of the *Ring* cycle when it was in its first flush of success. The two-LP set is here transferred on to a single CD, lasting 66 minutes and covering the closing two scenes. In many ways it possesses an advantage over even the complete live recording of the opera, made at the Coliseum five years later, when Rita Hunter and Alberto Remedios are here obviously fresher and less stressed than at the end of a full evening's performance. It is good too to have this sample, however brief, of Clifford Grant's Hagen and Norman Bailey's Gunther, fine performances both. Fresh, clear recording, not as full as it might be. But at mid-price this CD is well worth investigating.

Lohengrin (complete).
⊛ *** Decca Dig. 421 053-2 (4) [id.]. Domingo, Norman, Nimsgern, Randová, Sotin, Fischer-
   Dieskau, V. State Op. Concert Ch., VPO, Solti.
*** EMI CDS7 49017-2 (3) [Ang. CDCC 49017]. Jess Thomas, Grümmer, Fischer-Dieskau,
   Ludwig, Frick, Wiener, V. State Op. Ch., VPO, Kempe.

It is Plácido Domingo's achievement singing Lohengrin that the lyrical element blossoms so consistently, with no hint of Heldentenor barking; at whatever dynamic level, Domingo's voice is firm and unstrained. Jessye Norman, not naturally suited to the role of Elsa, yet gives a warm, commanding performance, always intense, full of detailed insights into words and character. Eva Randová's grainy mezzo does not take so readily to recording, but as Ortrud she provides a pointful contrast, even if she never matches the firm, biting malevolence of Christa Ludwig on the Kempe set. Siegmund Nimsgern, Telramund for Solti, equally falls short of Fischer-Dieskau, his rival on the Kempe set; but it is still a strong, cleanly focused performance. Fischer-Dieskau here sings the small but vital role of the Herald, while Hans Sotin makes a comparably distinctive King Henry. Radiant playing from the Vienna Philharmonic, and committed chorus work too. This is one of the crowning glories of Solti's long recording career.

Kempe's is a rapt account of *Lohengrin* which has been surpassed on record only by Solti's Decca set and which remains one of his finest monuments in sound. The singers seem uplifted, Jess Thomas singing more clearly and richly than usual, Elisabeth Grümmer unrivalled as Elsa in her delicacy and sweetness, Gottlob Frick gloriously resonant as the king. But it is the partnership of Christa Ludwig and Fischer-Dieskau as Ortrud and Telramund that sets the seal on this superb performance, giving the darkest intensity to their machinations in Act II, their evil heightening the beauty and serenity of so much in this opera. Though the digital transfer on CD reveals roughness (even occasional distortion) in the original recording, the glow and intensity of Kempe's reading come out all the more involvingly in the new format. The set is also very economically contained on three CDs instead of the four for all rivals, though inevitably breaks between discs come in the middle of Acts.

Lohengrin: highlights.
☞ **(*) Ph. Dig. 438 500-2 [id.]. Frey, Studer, Schnaut, Wlaschiha, Schenk, Bayreuth (1990) Festival Ch. and O, Peter Schneider.

Elsa was one of the roles which won Cheryl Studer international fame, and she tangibly brings out the equivocal development of the character. Paul Frey is a strong, noble Lohengrin, though with a slow vibrato occasionally obtruding on the sweetness of his tone. Wlaschiha is a dark, sinister Telramund and Schenk a powerful King Heinrich. Although this 1990 Bayreuth recording (434 602-2) is not a top choice among available versions of this opera, the 78-minutes highlights disc might be worth considering for admirers of Studer. The digital sound is atmospheric with good detail, though the chorus is placed rather backwardly – but why is it offered at full price?

Die Meistersinger von Nürnberg (complete).
*** DG 415 278-2 (4) [id.]. Fischer-Dieskau, Ligendza, Lagger, Hermann, Domingo, Laubenthal, Ludwig, German Op. Ch. & O, Berlin, Jochum.
**(*) Decca 417 497-2 (4) [id.]. Bailey, Bode, Moll, Weikl, Kollo, Dallapozza, Hamari, Gumpoldskirchner Spatzen, V. State Op. Ch., VPO, Solti.

Jochum's is a performance which, more than any, captures the light and shade of Wagner's most warmly approachable score, its humour and tenderness as well as its strength. Above all, Jochum is unerring in building long Wagnerian climaxes and resolving them – more so than his recorded rivals. The cast is the most consistent yet assembled on record. Though Caterina Ligendza's big soprano is a little ungainly for Eva, it is an appealing performance, and the choice of Domingo for Walther is inspired. The key to the set is of course the searching and highly individual Sachs of Fischer-Dieskau, and Horst Laubenthal's finely tuned David matches this Sachs in applying Lieder style. The recording balance favours the voices, but on CD they are made to sound slightly ahead of the orchestra. There is a lovely bloom on the whole sound and, with a recording which is basically wide-ranging and refined, the ambience brings an attractively natural projection of the singers.

The great glory of Solti's set is the mature and involving portrayal of Sachs by Norman Bailey. Kurt Moll as Pogner, Bernd Weikl as Beckmesser and Julia Hamari as Magdalene are all excellent, but the shortcomings are comparably serious. Both Hannelore Bode and René Kollo fall short of their far-from-perfect contributions to earlier sets, and Solti for all his energy gives a surprisingly square reading of this most appealing of Wagner scores, pointing his expressive lines too heavily and failing to convey real spontaneity. It remains an impressive achievement for Bailey's marvellous Sachs, and the Decca sound comes up very vividly on CD.

Parsifal (complete).
⊛ *** DG Dig. 413 347-2 (4) [id.]. Hofmann, Vejzovic, Moll, Van Dam, Nimsgern, Von Halem, German Op. Ch., BPO, Karajan.
*** Decca 417 143-2 (4) [id.]. Kollo, Ludwig, Fischer-Dieskau, Hotter, Kelemen, Frick, V. Boys' Ch., V. State Op. Ch., VPO, Solti.

☞ (M) (***) Teldec/Warner mono 9031 76047-2 (4)˙(id˙). Windgassen, London, Weber, Mödl, Uhde, Van Mill, (1951) Bayreuth Festival Ch. & O, Knappertsbusch.

**(*) DG 435 718-2 (3) [id.]. James King, Gwyneth Jones, Stewart, Ridderbusch, McIntyre, Crass, Bayreuth Festival Ch. & O (1970), Boulez.

**(*) Ph. 416 390-2 (4) [id.]. Jess Thomas, Dalis, London, Talvela, Neidlinger, Hotter, Bayreuth Festival (1962) Ch. & O, Knappertsbusch.

Communion, musical and spiritual, is what this intensely beautiful Karajan set provides. The playing of the Berlin orchestra is consistently beautiful; but the clarity and refinement of sound prevent this from emerging as a lengthy serving of Karajan soup. Kurt Moll as Gurnemanz is the singer who, more than any other, anchors the work vocally, projecting his voice with firmness and subtlety. José van Dam as Amfortas is also splendid. The Klingsor of Siegmund Nimsgern could be more sinister, but the singing is admirable. Dunja Vejzovic makes a vibrant, sensuous Kundry who rises superbly to the moment in Act II when she bemoans her laughter in the face of Christ. Only Peter Hofmann as Parsifal leaves any disappointment; at times he develops a gritty edge on the voice, but his natural tone is admirably suited to the part and he is never less than dramatically effective. He is not helped by the relative closeness of the solo voices, but otherwise the recording is near the atmospheric ideal, a superb achievement. The four CDs are still among DG's finest so far.

Solti's singing cast could hardly be stronger, every one of them pointing words with fine, illuminating care for detail; and the complex balances of sound, not least in the *Good Friday music*, are beautifully caught; throughout, Solti shows his sustained intensity in Wagner. There remains just one doubt, but that rather serious: the lack of a rapt, spiritual quality. The remastering for CD, as with Solti's other Wagner recordings, opens up the sound, and the choral climaxes are superb.

Hans Knappertsbusch was the inspired choice of conductor made by Wagner's grandsons for the first revivals of *Parsifal* after the war. The Teldec historic reissue is taken from the first season in 1951 and makes a striking contrast with the later Knappertsbusch recording, made in stereo for Philips 11 years later. The 1951 performance is no less than 20 minutes longer overall, with Knappertsbusch even more dedicated than in his later reading. The cast is even finer, with Wolfgang Windgassen making other Heldentenors seem rough by comparison, singing with warmth as well as power. Ludwig Weber is magnificently dark-toned as Gurnemanz, much more an understanding human being than his successor, Hans Hotter, less of a conventionally noble figure. Martha Mödl is both wild and abrasive in her first scenes and sensuously seductive in the long Act II duet with Parsifal; and Hermann Uhde is bitingly firm as Klingsor. Though the limited mono sound is not nearly as immediate or atmospheric as the later stereo, with much thinner orchestral texture, the voices come over well, and the chorus is well caught.

Boulez's speeds are so consistently fast that in the age of CD it has brought an obvious benefit in being fitted – easily – on three discs instead of four, yet Boulez's approach, with the line beautifully controlled, conveys a dramatic urgency rarely found in this opera, and never sounds breathless, with textures clarified in a way characteristic of Boulez. Even the flower-maidens sing like young apprentices in *Meistersinger* rather than seductive beauties. James King is a firm, strong, rather baritonal hero, Thomas Stewart a fine tense Amfortas, and Gwyneth Jones as Kundry is in strong voice, only occasionally shrill, though Franz Crass is disappointingly unsteady as Gurnemanz. The live Bayreuth recording is most impressively transferred to CD.

Knappertsbusch's expansive and dedicated 1962 reading is caught superbly in the Philips set, arguably the finest live recording ever made in the Festspielhaus at Bayreuth, with outstanding singing from Jess Thomas as Parsifal and Hans Hotter as Gurnemanz. Though Knappertsbusch chooses consistently slow tempi, there is no sense of excessive squareness or length, so intense is the concentration of the performance, its spiritual quality; and the sound has undoubtedly been further enhanced in the remastering for CD. The snag is that the stage noises and coughs are also emphasized, with the bronchial afflictions particularly disturbing in the *Prelude*.

Das Rheingold (complete).

*** Decca 414 101-2 (3). London, Flagstad, Svanholm, Neidlinger, VPO, Solti.

☞ *** Teldec/Warner Dig. 4509 91185-2 (2) [id.]. Tomlinson, Brinkmann, Schreibmayer, Clark, Finnie, Johansson, Svendén, Von Kannen, Pampuch, Hölle, Kang, Liedland, Küttenbaum, Turner, Bayreuth Festival (1991) O, Barenboim.

☞ (M) *** Ph. 434 421-2 (2) [id.]. McIntyre, Schwarz, Zednik, Pampuch, Becht, (1980) Bayreuth Festival O, Boulez.

**(*) DG 415 141-2 (3) [id.]. Fischer-Dieskau, Veasey, Stolze, Kelemen, BPO, Karajan.

**(*) Ph. 412 475-2 (2) [id.]. Adam, Nienstedt, Windgassen, Neidlinger, Talvela, Böhme, Silja, Soukupová, Bayreuth Festival (1967) Ch. & O, Boehm.

The first of Solti's cycle, recorded in 1958, *Rheingold* remains in terms of engineering the most spectacular on CD. The immediacy and precise placing are thrilling, while the sound-effects of the final scenes, including Donner's hammer-blow and the Rainbow bridge, have never been matched since. Solti gives a magnificent reading of the score, crisp, dramatic and direct. Vocally, the set is held together by the unforgettable singing of Neidlinger as Alberich. He vocalizes with wonderful precision and makes the character of the dwarf develop from the comic creature of the opening scene to the demented monster of the last. Flagstad learned the part of Fricka specially for this recording, and her singing makes one regret that she never took the role on the stage. George London is sometimes a little rough, but this is a dramatic portrayal of the young Wotan. Svanholm could be more characterful as Loge, but again it is a relief to hear the part really sung. An outstanding achievement.

Barenboim's recording of the *Ring* cycle for Teldec was made during the 1992 Bayreuth Festival and, more than most live recordings of opera, it is clearly the product of a staged event. Though this first instalment may not outshine the finest of previous versions, it is most welcome as easily the most involving of modern versions. By 1992, the last year of the Harry Kupfer production at Bayreuth, the impact of Daniel Barenboim's reading was intensified by an orchestra and a cast totally in tune with his reading. When Barenboim as Wagnerian has at times seemed lethargic, what is particularly surprising is the dramatic tension of the performance. Even with slow speeds, the sense of flow carries the ear on, where neither of the two most recent rival recordings, Haitink's for EMI and Levine's for DG, ever quite lets you forget the atmosphere of the studio. Even with often-thunderous stage noises, the Barenboim performances magnetize you much more consistently, with the atmosphere of the Festspielhaus well caught by the engineers. It is very satisfying too to have on disc John Tomlinson's magnificent performance as Wotan, cleaner in attack and more searching with his bass resonances than James Morris on both the EMI and DG sets. British singers stand out, with Graham Clark an electrifying, dominant Loge, Linda Finnie a thoughtful, intense Fricka.

Like the Boehm set, also recorded live by Philips at Bayreuth, the Boulez version, taken from the 1980 Festival, the last year of the Patrice Chéreau production, comes on only two discs and has the advantage of a more modest medium price. The early digital sound has plenty of air round it, giving a fine impression of a performance in the Festspielhaus with all its excitement, though voices are not caught as immediately as on the Boehm set. Sir Donald McIntyre here gives a memorable and noble performance, far firmer than his rival for Boehm, Theo Adam. Heinz Zednik is splendid as Loge and Hanna Schwarz is a powerful Fricka, while Siegfried Jerusalem brings beauty of tone as well as distinction to the small role of Froh. Hermann Becht is a weighty rather than incisive Alberich, and the only weak link is Martin Egel's unsteady Donner. Though not as bitingly intense as Boehm, Boulez, with speeds almost as fast, shatters the old idea of him as a chilly conductor.

Karajan's very reflectiveness has its less welcome side, for the tension rarely varies. One finds such incidents as Alberich's stealing of the gold or Donner's hammer-blow passing by without one's pulse quickening as it should. On the credit side, however, the singing cast has hardly any flaw at all, and Fischer-Dieskau's Wotan is a brilliant and memorable creation, virile and expressive. Among the others, Veasey is excellent, though obviously she cannot efface memories of Flagstad; Gerhard Stolze with his flickering, almost *Sprechstimme* as Loge gives an intensely vivid if, for some, controversial interpretation. The 1968 sound has been clarified in the digital transfer, but generally the lack of bass brings some thinness.

Boehm's preference for fast speeds here brings the benefit that the whole of the *Vorabend* is contained on two CDs. The pity is that the performance is marred by the casting of Theo Adam as Wotan, keenly intelligent but rarely agreeable on the ear, at times here far too wobbly. On the other hand, Gustav Neidlinger as Alberich is superb, even more involving here than he is for Solti, with the curse made spine-chilling. It is also good to have Wolfgang Windgassen as Loge; among the others, Anja Silja makes an attractively urgent Freia.

The Rheingold (complete, in English).

(M) **(*) EMI CMS7 64110-2 (3). Bailey, Hammond-Stroud, Pring, Belcourt, Attfield, Collins, McDonnall, Lloyd, Grant, English Nat. Op. O, Goodall.

Goodall's slow tempi in *Rheingold* bring an opening section where the temperature is low, reflecting hardly at all the tensions of a live performance, even though this was taken from a series of Coliseum presentations. Nevertheless the momentum of Wagner gradually builds up so that, by the final scenes, both the overall teamwork and the individual contributions of such singers as Norman Bailey, Derek Hammond-Stroud and Clifford Grant come together impressively. Hammond-Stroud's powerful representation of Alberich culminates in a superb account of the curse. The spectacular orchestral effects (with the horns sounding glorious) are vividly caught by the engineers and impressively transferred to CD, even if balances (inevitably) are sometimes less than ideal.

Rienzi (complete).

(M) ** EMI CMS7 63980-2 (3) [Ang. CDMB 63980]. Kollo, Wennberg, Martin, Adam, Hillebrand, Vogel, Schreier, Leipzig R. Ch., Dresden State Op. Ch., Dresden State O, Hollreiser.

It is sad that the flaws in this ambitious opera prevent the unwieldy piece from having its full dramatic impact. This recording is not quite complete, but the cuts are unimportant and most of the set numbers make plain the youthful, uncritical exuberance of the ambitious composer. Except in the recitative, Heinrich Hollreiser's direction is strong and purposeful, but much of the singing is disappointing. René Kollo at least sounds heroic, but the two women principals are poor. Janis Martin in the breeches role of Adriano produces tone that does not record very sweetly, while Siv Wennberg as the heroine, Rienzi's sister, slides most unpleasantly between notes in the florid passages. Despite good recording, this can only be regarded as a stop-gap.

Der Ring des Nibelungen (complete).

⊛ (M) *** Decca 414 100-2 (15) [id.]. Nilsson, Windgassen, Flagstad, Fischer-Dieskau, Hotter, London, Ludwig, Neidlinger, Frick, Svanholm, Stoltze, Böhme, Hoffgen, Sutherland, Crespin, King, Watson, Ch. & VPO, Solti.

(M) *** Ph. 420 325-2 (14) [id.]. Nilsson, Windgassen, Neidlinger, Adam, Rysanek, King, Nienstedt, Esser, Talvela, Böhme, Silja, Dernesch, Stewart, Hoeffgen, Bayreuth Festival (1967) Ch. & O, Boehm.

(M) *** DG 435 211-2 (15) [id.]. Veasey, Fischer-Dieskau, Stolze, Kelemen, Dernesch, Dominguez, Jess Thomas, Stewart, Crespin, Janowitz, Vickers, Talvela, Brilioth, Ludwig, Ridderbusch, BPO, Karajan.

(M) (***) EMI mono CZS7 67123-2 (13) [Ang. CDZM 67123]. Suthaus, Mödl, Frantz, Patzak, Neidlinger, Windgassen, Konetzni, Streich, Jurinac, Frick, RAI Ch. & Rome SO, Furtwängler.

Solti's was the first recorded *Ring* cycle to be issued. Whether in performance or in vividness of sound, Solti's remains the most electrifying account of the tetralogy on disc, sharply focused if not always as warmly expressive as some. Solti himself developed in the process of making the recording, and *Götterdämmerung* represents a peak of achievement for him, commanding and magnificent. Though CD occasionally reveals bumps and bangs inaudible on the original LPs, this is a historic set that remains as central today as when it first appeared.

Anyone who prefers the idea of a live recording of the *Ring* cycle can be warmly recommended to Boehm's fine set, more immediately involving than any. Recorded at the 1967 Bayreuth Festival, it captures the unique atmosphere and acoustic of the Festspielhaus very vividly. Birgit Nilsson as Brünnhilde and Wolfgang Windgassen as Siegfried are both a degree more volatile and passionate than they were in the Solti cycle. Gustav Neidlinger as Alberich is also superb, as he was too in the Solti set; and the only major reservation concerns the Wotan of Theo Adam, in a performance searchingly intense and finely detailed but often unsteady of tone even at that period. The sound, only occasionally constricted, has been vividly transferred.

Karajan's recording of *The Ring* followed close on the heels of Solti's for Decca, providing a good alternative studio version which equally stands the test of time. The manner is smoother, the speeds generally broader, yet the tension and concentration of the performances are maintained more consistently than in most modern studio recordings. Casting is not quite consistent between the operas, with Régine Crespin as Brünnhilde in *Walküre*, but Helga Dernesch at her very peak in the last two operas. The casting of Siegfried is changed between *Siegfried* and *Götterdämmerung*, from Jess Thomas, clear and reliable, to Helge Brilioth, just as strong but sweeter of tone. The original CD transfers are used without change for this mid-price compilation.

When in 1972 EMI first transferred the Italian Radio tapes of Furtwängler's studio performances of 1953, the sound was disagreeably harsh, making sustained listening unpleasant. In this digital transfer, the boxiness of the studio sound and the closeness of the voices still take away some of the unique Furtwängler glow in Wagner, but the sound is acceptable and actually benefits in some ways from extra clarity. Furtwängler gives each opera a commanding sense of unity, musically and dramatically, with hand-picked casts including Martha Mödl as a formidable Brünnhilde, Ferdinand Frantz a firm-voiced Wotan and Ludwig Suthaus (Tristan in Furtwängler's recording) a reliable Siegfried. In smaller roles you have stars like Wolfgang Windgassen, Julius Patzak, Rita Streich, Sena Jurinac and Gottlob Frick.

The Ring 'Great scenes': Das Rheingold: Entry of the Gods into Valhalla. Die Walküre: Ride of the Valkyries; Magic fire music. Siegfried: Forging scene; Forest murmurs. Götterdämmerung: Siegfried's funeral march; Brünnhilde's immolation scene.

(M) *** Decca 421 313-2. Nilsson, Windgassen, Hotter, Stolzel, VPO, Solti.

These excerpts are often quite extended – the *Entry of the Gods into Valhalla* offers some 10 minutes of music, and the *Forest murmurs* from *Siegfried* starts well before the orchestral interlude. Only *Siegfried's funeral march* is in any sense a 'bleeding chunk' which has to be faded at the end; and the disc closes with 20 minutes of Brünnhilde's Immolation scene.

The Ring: highlights: *Das Rheingold: Lugt, Schwestern! Die Wenken lacht in den Grund; Zur Burg führt die Brücke. Die Walküre: Der Männer Sippe sass hier im Saal; Ride of the Valkyries; Wotan's farewell and Magic fire music. Siegfried: Forest murmurs; Aber, wie sah meine Mutter wohl aus?; Nun sing! Ich lausche dem Gesang; Heil dir, Sonne! Heil dir, Licht!. Götterdämmerung: Funeral music; Fliegt heim, ihr Raben!.*
☞ (B) *** DG 439 423-2 [id.] (from above complete recording; cond. Karajan).

The task of selecting highlights to fit on a single disc, taken from the whole of the *Ring* cycle, is daunting. But the DG producer of this Classikon super-bargain issue has extended the previous selection to 77 minutes and managed to assemble many key items, either very well tailored or ending satisfactorily. The whole of Wotan's great *Farewell* scene with the *Magic Fire music* is included, and much else besides. Moreover the *Funeral music* from *Götterdämmerung* (where the previous CD ended) is now followed by *Brünnhilde's Immolation* and continues to the end of the opera. The transfers are extremely brilliant (the *Ride of the Valkyries* is given an edge of excitement) and this makes a magnificent bargain reissue. It seems carping to complain that the notes do not find space to detail what happens in each excerpt. But sonically this should surely tempt any novice in this repertoire to want to go on and explore Wagner's masterly cycle still further.

Siegfried (complete).
*** Decca 414 110-2 (4). Windgassen, Nilsson, Hotter, Stolze, Neidlinger, Böhme, Hoffgen,
    Sutherland, VPO, Solti.
*** Ph. 412 483-2 (4) [id.]. Windgassen, Nilsson, Adam, Neidlinger, Soukupová, Köth, Böhme,
    Bayreuth Festival (1967) Ch. & O, Boehm.
☞ (M) *** Ph. Dig. 434 423-2 (3). Jung, G. Jones, McIntyre, Zednik, Becht, Wenkel, Hübner, Sharp,
    (1980) Bayreuth Festival O, Boulez.
** DG 415 150-2 (4) [id.]. Dernesch, Dominguez, Jess Thomas, Stolze, Stewart, Kelemen, BPO,
    Karajan.
** DG Dig. 429 407-2 (4) [id.]. Goldberg, Behrens, Morris, Zednik, Wlaschiha, Moll, Battle, NY
    Met. O, Levine.

Siegfried has too long been thought of as the grimmest of the *Ring* cycle, but a performance as buoyant as Solti's reveals that, more than in most Wagner, the message is one of optimism. Each of the three Acts ends with a scene of triumphant optimism. Solti's array of singers could hardly be bettered. Windgassen is at the very peak of his form, lyrical as well as heroic. Hotter has never been more impressive on record, his Wotan at last captured adequately. Stolze, Neidlinger and Böhme are all exemplary, and predictably Joan Sutherland makes the most seductive of woodbirds. With singing finer than any opera house could normally provide, with masterly playing from the Vienna Philharmonic and with Decca's most vivid recording, this is a set likely to stand comparison with anything the rest of the century may provide.

The natural-sounding quality of Boehm's live recording from Bayreuth, coupled with his determination not to let the music lag, makes his account of *Siegfried* as satisfying as the rest of his cycle, vividly capturing the atmosphere of the Festspielhaus, with voices well ahead of the orchestra. Windgassen is at his peak here, if anything more poetic in Acts II and III than he is in Solti's studio recording, and vocally just as fine. Nilsson, as in *Götterdämmerung*, gains over her studio recording from the extra flow of adrenalin in a live performance; and Gustav Neidlinger is unmatchable as Alberich. Erika Köth is disappointing as the woodbird, not sweet enough, and Soukupová is a positive, characterful Erda. Theo Adam is at his finest as the Wanderer, less wobbly than usual, clean and incisive.

Like the first two music-dramas in his Bayreuth *Ring* cycle, Boulez's version takes a disc less than usual and comes at mid-price in the Philips Bayreuth series. Here the advantage is even greater when each Act is complete on a single disc. It was recorded in 1980, the last year of the controversial Patrice Chéreau production, when, after teething troubles, Boulez had won the warm regard of the orchestra. If anything, Boulez is even more warmly expressive than in *Rheingold* or *Walküre*, directing a most poetic account of the *Forest murmurs* episode and leading in each Act to thrillingly intense conclusions. Manfred Jung is an underrated Siegfried, forthright and, by latterday standards, unusually clean-focused, and Heinz Zednik is a characterful Mime. As in the rest of the cycle, Sir Donald McIntyre is a noble Wotan, though Hermann Becht's weighty Alberich is not as strongly contrasted as it might be. Norma Sharp as the Woodbird enunciates her words with exceptional clarity and, though Gwyneth Jones as Brünnhilde has a few squally moments, she sings with honeyed beauty when the Idyll theme emerges, towards the end of the love duet. The digital sound is full and atmospheric, though it is a pity that the brass is not caught as weightily as it might be.

When Siegfried is outsung by Mime, it is time to complain, and though the DG set has many fine qualities – not least the Brünnhilde of Helga Dernesch – it hardly rivals the Solti or Boehm versions. Windgassen on Decca gave a classic performance, and any comparison highlights the serious shortcomings of Jess Thomas. Even when voices are balanced forward, the digital transfer helps little to make Thomas's singing as Siegfried any more acceptable. Otherwise, the vocal cast is strong, and Karajan provides the seamless playing which characterizes his cycle. Recommended only to those irrevocably committed to the Karajan cycle.

Levine is markedly less successful than any of his competitors in conveying the feeling of a live, dramatic performance. Behrens sings steadily but is over-stressed as Brünnhilde, and Reiner Goldberg's Siegfried is seriously flawed. James Morris is impressive as the Wanderer.

Siegfried (complete, in English).
(M) *** EMI CMS7 63595-2 (4). Remedios, Hunter, Bailey, Dempsey, Hammond-Stroud, Grant, Collins, London, Sadler's Wells Op. O, Goodall.

More tellingly than in almost any other Wagner opera recording, Goodall's spacious direction here conveys the genuine dramatic crunch that gives the experience of hearing Wagner in the opera house its unique power, its overwhelming force; this is unmistakably a great interpretation caught on the wing. Remedios, more than any rival on record, conveys not only heroic strength but clear-ringing youthfulness, caressing the ear as well as exciting it. Norman Bailey makes a magnificently noble Wanderer, steady of tone, and Gregory Dempsey is a characterful Mime, even if his deliberate whining tone is not well caught on record. The sound is superbly realistic, even making no allowances for the conditions. Lovers of opera in English should grasp the opportunity of hearing this unique set.

Tannhäuser (Paris version; complete).
*** DG. Dig. 427 625-2 (3) [id.]. Domingo, Studer, Baltsa, Salminen, Schmidt, Ch. & Philh. O, Sinopoli.
*** Decca 414 581-2 (3) [id.]. Kollo, Dernesch, Ludwig, Sotin, Braun, Hollweg, V. State Op. Ch., VPO, Solti.

Plácido Domingo here makes another Wagnerian sortie, bringing balm to ears wounded by the general run of German heroic tenors, producing sounds of much power as well as beauty. Giuseppe Sinopoli here makes his most passionately committed opera recording yet, warmer and more flexible than Solti's Decca version, always individual, with fine detail brought out, always persuasively, and never wilful. Agnes Baltsa is not ideally opulent of tone as Venus, but she is the complete seductress. Cheryl Studer – who sang the role of Elisabeth for Sinopoli at Bayreuth – gives a most sensitive performance, not always ideally even of tone but creating a movingly intense portrait of the heroine, vulnerable and very feminine. Matti Salminen in one of his last recordings makes a superb Landgrave and Andreas Schmidt a noble Wolfram, even though the legato could be smoother in *O star of Eve*.

Solti gives one of his very finest Wagner performances to date, helped by superb playing from the Vienna Philharmonic and an outstanding cast, superlatively recorded. Dernesch as Elisabeth and Ludwig as Venus outshine all rivals; and Kollo, though not ideal, makes as fine a Heldentenor as we are currently likely to hear. The compact disc transfer reinforces the brilliance and richness of the performance. The sound is outstanding for its period (1971), and Ray Minshull's production adds to the atmospheric quality.

Tannhäuser (Dresden version; complete).
**(*) Ph. 420 122-2 (3) [id.]. Windgassen, Waechter, Silja, Stolze, Bumbry, Bayreuth Festival (1962) Ch. & O, Sawallisch.

Though CD brings out all the more clearly the thuds, creaks and audience noises of a live performance (most distracting at the very start), the dedication of Sawallisch's version is very persuasive, notably in the Venusberg scene where Grace Bumbry is a superb, sensuous Venus and Windgassen – not quite in his sweetest voice, often balanced rather close – is a fine, heroic Tannhäuser. Anja Silja controls the abrasiveness of her soprano well, to make this her finest performance on record, not ideally sweet but very sympathetic. Voices are set well forward of the orchestra, in which strings have far more bloom than brass; but the atmosphere of the Festspielhaus is vivid and compelling throughout.

Tristan und Isolde (complete).
(M) *** EMI CMS7 69319-2 (4) [Ang. CDMD 69319]. Vickers, Dernesch, Ludwig, Berry,
    Ridderbusch, German Op. Ch., Berlin, BPO, Karajan.
*** DG 419 889-2 (3) [id.]. Windgassen, Nilsson, Ludwig, Talvela, Waechter, Bayreuth Festival
    (1966) Ch. & O, Boehm.
(M) *** Decca 430 234-2 (4) [id.]. Uhl, Nilsson, Resnik, Van Mill, Krause, VPO, Solti.
(***) EMI mono CDS7 47322-8 (4) [Ang. CDC47321]. Suthaus, Flagstad, Thebom, Greindl,
    Fischer-Dieskau, ROHCG Ch., Philh. O, Furtwängler.

Karajan's is a sensual performance of Wagner's masterpiece, caressingly beautiful and with superbly refined playing from the Berlin Philharmonic. Dernesch as Isolde is seductively feminine, not as noble as Flagstad, not as tough and unflinching as Nilsson; but the human quality makes this account if anything more moving still, helped by glorious tone-colour through every range. Jon Vickers matches her, in what is arguably his finest performance on record, allowing himself true pianissimo shading. The rest of the cast is excellent too. The 1972 sound has plenty of body, making this an excellent first choice, with inspired conducting and the most satisfactory cast of all.

The benefit is enormous with Boehm's Bayreuth performance in presenting one of the big Wagner operas for the first time on disc without any breaks at all, with each Act uninterrupted. Boehm is on the urgent side in this opera and the orchestral ensemble is not always immaculate; but the performance glows with intensity from beginning to end, carried through in the longest spans. Birgit Nilsson sings the *Liebestod* at the end of the long evening as though she was starting out afresh, radiant and with not a hint of tiredness, rising to an orgasmic climax and bringing a heavenly pianissimo on the final rising octave to F sharp. Opposite Nilsson is Wolfgang Windgassen, the most mellifluous of Heldentenoren; though the microphone balance sometimes puts him at a disadvantage to his Isolde, the realism and sense of presence of the whole set have you bathing in the authentic atmosphere of Bayreuth. Making up an almost unmatchable cast are Christa Ludwig as Brangaene, Eberhard Waechter as Kurwenal and Martii Talvela as King Mark, with the young Peter Schreier as the Young Sailor.

Solti's performance is less flexible and sensuous than Karajan's, but he shows himself ready to relax in Wagner's more expansive periods. On the other hand the end of Act I and the opening of the Love duet have a knife-edged dramatic tension. Nilsson is masterly in her conviction and – it cannot be emphasized too strongly – she never attacks below the note as Flagstad did, so that miraculously, at the end of the Love duet the impossibly difficult top Cs come out and hit the listener crisply and cleanly, dead on the note; and the *Liebestod* is all the more moving for having no soupy swerves at the climax. Fritz Uhl is a really musical Heldentenor. Dramatically he leaves the centre of the stage to Isolde, but his long solo passages in Act III are superb and make that sometimes tedious Act into something genuinely gripping. The Kurwenal of Tom Krause and the King Mark of Arnold van Mill are both excellent and it is only Regina Resnik as Brangaene who gives any disappointment. The production has the usual Decca/Culshaw imaginative touch, and the recording matches brilliance and clarity with satisfying co-ordination and richness.

Wilhelm Furtwängler's concept is spacious from the opening *Prelude* onwards, but equally the bite and colour of the drama are vividly conveyed, matching the nobility of Flagstad's portrait of Isolde. The richly commanding power of her singing and her always distinctive timbre make it a uniquely compelling performance. Suthaus is not of the same calibre as Heldentenor, but he avoids ugliness and strain, which is rare in Tristan. Among the others, the only remarkable performance comes from the young Fischer-Dieskau as Kurwenal, not ideally cast but keenly imaginative. One endearing oddity is that – on Flagstad's insistence – the top Cs at the opening of the love-duet were sung by Elisabeth Schwarzkopf. The Kingsway Hall recording was admirably balanced, catching the beauty of the Philharmonia Orchestra at its peak. The CDs have opened up the original mono sound and it is remarkable how little constriction there is in the biggest climaxes, mostly shown in the *fortissimo* violins above the stave.

Tristan und Isolde (slightly abridged).
(M) (***) EMI mono CHS7 64037-2 (3) [Ang. CDHC 64037]. Melchior, Flagstad, Herbert Janssen,
    Margarete Klose/Sabine Kalter, Sven Nilsson/Emanuel List, ROHCG Ch., LPO, Beecham/
    Reiner.

In both recordings used here, Melchior and Flagstad take the title-roles, with Herbert Janssen as Kurwenal, three legendary singers in those roles, but the parts of King Mark and Brangane were sung by different singers – and, above all, Fritz Reiner was the conductor in the 1936 recordings. It is astonishing to find that the warmly expansive account of Act I is the work of Reiner, while it is Beecham who is responsible for the urgent view of Act II with its great love duet – part of it cut following the manner of the day. Act III is divided between Beecham in the first part, Reiner in the second. Whatever the inconsistencies, the result is a thrilling experience, with Flagstad fresher and even more incisive than in her studio recording with Furtwängler of 15 years later, and with Melchior a passionate vocal actor, not just the possessor of the most freely ringing of all Heldentenor voices.

Die Walküre (complete).

*** Ph. 412 478-2 (4) [id.]. King, Rysanek, Nienstedt, Nilsson, Adam, Burmeister, Bayreuth Festival (1967) Ch. & O, Boehm.

*** Decca 414 105-2 (4) [id.]. Nilsson, Crespin, Ludwig, King, Hotter, Frick, VPO, Solti.

☞ *** Teldec/Warner Dig. 4509 91186-2 (4) [id.]. Elming, Hölle, Tomlinson, Secunde, A. Evans, Finnie, Johansson, Floeren, Close, Bayreuth Festival (1992) O, Barenboim.

(M) (***) EMI mono CHS7 63045-2 (3) [Ang. CHS 63045]. Mödl, Rysanek, Frantz, Suthaus, Klose, Frick, VPO, Furtwängler.

☞ (M) *** Ph. 434 422-2 (3) [id.]. Hofmann, Altmeyer, G. Jones, McIntyre, Schwarz, Salminen, (1980) Bayreuth Festival O, Boulez.

**(*) DG 415 145-2 (4) [id.]. Crespin, Janowitz, Veasey, Vickers, Stewart, Talvela, BPO, Karajan.

Rarely if ever does Boehm's preference for fast speeds undermine the music; on the contrary, it adds to the involvement of the performance, which never loses its concentration. Theo Adam is in firmer voice here as Wotan than he is in *Rheingold*, hardly sweet of tone but always singing with keen intelligence. As ever, Nilsson is in superb voice as Brünnhilde. Though the inevitable noises of a live performance occasionally intrude, this presents a more involving experience than any rival complete recording. The CD transfer transforms what on LP seemed a rough recording, even if passages of heavy orchestration still bring some constriction of sound.

Solti sees Act II as the kernel of the work, perhaps even of the whole cycle, with the conflict of wills between Wotan and Fricka making for one of Wagner's most deeply searching scenes. That is the more apparent when the greatest of latterday Wotans, Hans Hotter, takes the role, and Christa Ludwig sings with searing dramatic sense as his wife. Before that, Act I seems a little underplayed. This is partly because of Solti's deliberate lyricism – apt enough when love and spring greetings are in the air – but also (on the debit side) because James King fails both to project the character of Siegmund and to delve into the word-meanings as all the other members of the cast consistently do. Crespin has never sung more beautifully on record, but even that cannot cancel out the shortcoming. As for Nilsson's Brünnhilde, it has grown mellower, the emotions are clearer, and under-the-note attack is almost eliminated.

Like his account of *Das Rheingold*, also recorded live at the 1992 Bayreuth Festival, Barenboim's reading of *Die Walküre* is by a fair margin the most involving of modern versions, with orchestra and soloists after four years of the same production totally in sympathy. Even more strikingly than in *Rheingold*, Barenboim's control of dramatic tension is masterly. Even with characteristically slow speeds, the results are magnetic. Consistently there is a natural sense of flow so that, despite intrusive stage noises, Barenboim compels attention from first to last. It could not be more welcome to have on disc John Tomlinson's magnificent performance as Wotan, even more demanding in *Walküre* than in *Rheingold*. Again he is cleaner in attack and more searching with his bass resonances than James Morris on both the EMI and DG sets. The other British singer who stands out in this opera is Anne Evans, at last showing her paces on disc as a radiant Brünnhilde. Maybe she is not as powerful as such rival loud ladies, Eva Marton and Hildegard Behrens, but she is far truer and clearer in focusing notes, singing with more expressive variety. With Barenboim conveying the full emotional thrust, the final duet between Brünnhilde and Wotan has rarely been so moving on disc. Also outstanding is the Danish tenor, Poul Elming, as Siegmund. Again the Bayreuth atmosphere is very well caught.

Furtwängler, an excellent cast and the Vienna Philharmonic in radiant form match any of their successors. Ludwig Suthaus proves a satisfyingly clear-toned Heldentenor, never strained, with the lyricism of *Wintersturme* superbly sustained. Neither Léonie Rysanek as Sieglinde nor Martha Mödl as Brünnhilde is ideally steady, but the intensity and involvement of each is irresistible, classic performances both. Similarly, the mezzo of Margarete Klose may not be very beautiful, but the projection of words and the fire-eating character match the conductor's intensity. Gottlob Frick is as near an ideal Hunding as one will find, sinister but with the right streak of arrogant sexuality; while the Wotan of Ferdinand Frantz may not be as deeply perceptive as some, but to hear the sweep of Wagner's melodic lines so gloriously sung is a rare joy. The 1954 sound is amazingly full and vivid, with voices cleanly balanced against the inspired orchestra. The only snag of the set is that, to fit the whole piece on to only three CDs, breaks between discs come in mid-Act.

The major advantage of the Boulez Bayreuth version of 1980 is that it comes at mid-price on only three discs, with atmospheric digital sound and a strong, if flawed, cast. Jeannine Altmeyer is a generally reliable Sieglinde, but Peter Hofmann's tenor had already grown rather gritty for Siegmund and in Act I is not as melliflous as he should be. Donald McIntyre makes a commanding Wotan, Hanna Schwarz a firm, biting Fricka and Gwyneth Jones is at her least abrasive, producing beautiful, gentle tone in lyrical passages. Boulez's fervour will surprise many, even if he does not match Boehm's passionate urgency in this second instalment of the tetralogy.

The great merits of Karajan's version are the refinement of the orchestral playing and the heroic strength of Jon Vickers as Siegmund. With that underlined, one cannot help but note that the vocal shortcomings here are generally more marked, and the total result does not add up to quite so compelling a dramatic experience: one is less involved. Thomas Stewart may have a younger, firmer voice than Hotter, but the character of Wotan emerges only partially; it is not just that he misses some of the word-meaning, but that on occasion – as in the kissing away of Brünnhilde's godhead – he underlines too crudely. Josephine Veasey as Fricka conveys the biting intensity of the part. Gundula Janowitz's Sieglinde has its beautiful moments, but the singing is ultimately a little static. Crespin's Brünnhilde is impressive, but nothing like as satisfying as her study of Sieglinde on the Decca set. The DG recording is good, but not quite in the same class as the Decca and the bass is relatively light.

The Valkyrie (complete; in English).

(M) *** EMI CMS7 63918-2 (4). Hunter, Remedios, Curphey, Bailey, Grant, Howard, E. Nat. Op. Ch. & O, Goodall.

The glory of the ENO performance lies not just in Goodall's spacious direction but in the magnificent Wotan of Norman Bailey, noble in the broadest span but very human in his illumination of detail. Rita Hunter sings nobly too, and though she is not as commanding as Nilsson in the Solti cycle she is often more lyrically tender. Alberto Remedios as Siegmund is more taxed than he was as Siegfried in the later opera (lower tessituras are not quite so comfortable for him) but his sweetly ringing top register is superb. If others, such as Ann Howard as Fricka, are not always treated kindly by the microphone, the total dramatic compulsion is irresistible. The CD transfer increases the sense of presence and at the same time confirms the relative lack of sumptuousness.

Die Walküre, Act I (complete).

(M) (***) EMI mono CDH7 61020-2 [id.]. Lehmann, Melchior, List, VPO, Bruno Walter.

(M) **(*) Decca 425 963-2 [id.]. Flagstad, Svanholm, Van Mill, VPO, Knappertsbusch.

One is consistently gripped by the continuity and sustained lines of Walter's reading, and by the intensity and beauty of the playing of the Vienna Philharmonic. Lotte Lehmann's portrait of Sieglinde, arguably her finest role, has a depth and beauty never surpassed since, and Lauritz Melchior's heroic Siegmund brings singing of a scale and variety – not to mention beauty – that no Heldentenor today begins to match. Emanuel List as Hunding is satisfactory enough, but his achievement at least has latterly been surpassed.

Flagstad may not have been ideally cast as Sieglinde, but the command of her singing with its unfailing richness, even after her official retirement, crowns a strong and dramatic performance, with Svanholm and Van Mill singing cleanly. The early stereo still sounds vivid.

Die Walküre: highlights.

(M) *** Decca 421 887-2 [id.] (from above complete set with Nilsson, King, Crespin, Hotter; cond. Solti).

☞ *** EMI Dig. CDC7 54328-2 [id.]. Goldberg, Marton, Studer, Morris, Bav. RSO, Haitink.

The mid-priced Solti highlights disc is not as generous as some (54 minutes) but is spectacularly well recorded. The items chosen, opening with Siegmund's (James King) *Winterstürme wichen dem Wonnemond*, ravishingly lyrical, and including the *Ride of the Valkyries*, make a particularly satisfying reminder of some of the finest moments in the set. Recommendable to those who cannot stretch to the full opera.

Those who have chosen another complete set will surely want a reminder of Haitink's glowingly spacious EMI set. The selection here is generous (76 minutes), and it includes Cheryl Studer's *Du bist der Lenz* within the 21 minutes from Act I, while the excerpts from Act III include the *Ride of the Valkyries* and end with the *Magic fire music* sequence at the end of the opera. Splendidly rich recording.

VOCAL COLLECTIONS

'Wagner singing on record': Excerpts from: (i) *Der fliegende Holländer;* (ii) *Götterdämmerung;* (iii) *Lohengrin;* (iv) *Die Meistersinger von Nürnberg;* (v) *Parsifal;* (vi) *Das Rheingold;* (vii) *Siegfried;* (viii) *Tannhäuser;* (ix) *Tristan und Isolde;* (x) *Die Walküre.*

(M) (***) EMI mono/stereo CMS7 640082 (4) [id.]. (i) Hermann, Nissen, Endrèze, Fuchs, Beckmann, Rethberg, Nilsson, Hotter; (ii) Austral, Widdop, List, Weber, Janssen, Lawrence; (iii) Rethberg, Pertil, Singher, Lawrence, Spani, Lehmann, Lemnitz, Klose, Wittrisch, Rosavaenge; (iv) Schorr, Thill, Martinelli, Bockelmann, Parr, Williams, Ralf, Lemnitz; (v) Leider, Kipnitz, Wolff; (vi) Schorr; (vii) Nissen, Olszewska, Schipper, Leider, Laubenthal, Lubin; (viii) Müller, Lorenz, Janssen, Hüsch, Flagstad; (ix) Leider, Marherr, Larsen-Todsen, Helm, Melchior, Seinemeyer, Lorenz; (x) Lawrence, Journet, Bockelmann.

This collection, compiled in Paris as *'Les Introuvables du Chant Wagnerien'*, contains an amazing array of recordings made in the later years of 78-r.p.m. recording, mostly between 1927 and 1940. In 49 items, many of them substantial, the collection consistently demonstrates the reliability of the Wagner singing at that period, the ability of singers in every register to produce firm, well-focused tone of a kind too rare today. Some of the most interesting items are those in translation from French sources, with Germaine Lubin as Isolde and Brünnhilde and with Marcel Journet as Wotan, both lyrical and clean-cut. The ill-starred Marjorie Lawrence, a great favourite in France, is also represented by recordings in French, including Brünnhilde's Immolation scene from *Götterdämmerung*. Not only are such celebrated Wagnerians as Lauritz Melchior, Friedrich Schorr, Frida Leider, Lotte Lehmann and Max Lorenz very well represented, but also singers one might not expect, including the Lieder specialist, Gerhard Husch, as Wolfram in *Tannhäuser* and Aureliano Pertile singing in Italian as *Lohengrin*. Significantly, Meta Seinemeyer, an enchanting soprano who died tragically young, here gives lyric sweetness to the dramatic roles of Brünnhilde and Isolde; and among the baritones and basses there is none of the roughness or ill-focus that marks so much latter-day Wagner singing. It is a pity that British-based singers are poorly represented, but the Prologue duet from *Götterdämmerung* brings one of the most impressive items, sung by Florence Austral and Walter Widdop. First-rate transfers and good documentation.

Arias: *Götterdämmerung:* (i) *Zu neuen Taten; Starke Scheite schichter mire dort. Lohengrin: Euch Lüften mein Klagen. Parsifal:* (i) *Ich sah' das King. Tristan: Mild und leise. Die Walküre: Du bist der Lenz; Ho-jo-ho!.*

(M) (***) RCA mono GD 87915 [87915-2-RG]. Flagstad, (i) with Melchior, San Francisco Op. O, or Victor SO (both cond. Edwin McArthur); Phd. O, Ormandy

Recorded for RCA in America between 1935 and 1940, this first generation of Wagner recordings by Flagstad reveals the voice at its noblest and freshest, the more exposed in consistently close balance on the 78s of the period. It is a pity that only two of the shortest items – from *Lohengrin* and *Walküre* – have Ormandy conducting. Most of the rest are conducted by Flagstad's protégé, Edwin McArthur, including the two longest, the big duet for Parsifal and Kundry and Brünnhilde's Immolation scene. Yet the grandeur of Flagstad's singing is never in doubt, the commanding sureness, and, though the orchestral sound is unflatteringly dry, the voice is gloriously caught in clean transfers.

Choruses from: *Der fliegende Holländer; Lohengrin; Die Meistersinger; Parsifal; Tannhäuser.*
(M) *** Decca 421 865-2 (from complete sets, cond. Solti).

Solti's choral collection is superb, with an added sophistication in both performance and recording. The collection opens with a blazing account of the *Lohengrin* Act III *Prelude*, since of course the *Bridal chorus* grows naturally out of it. But the *Pilgrims' chorus*, which comes next, creates an electrifying pianissimo and expands gloriously, while the excerpts from *Die Meistersinger* and *Parsifal* show Solti's characteristic intensity at its most potent.

Waldteufel, Emile (1837–1915)

Polkas: *Les Bohémiens; Retour des champs; Tout ou rien.* Waltzes: *Ange d'amour; Dans des nuages; España; Fontaine lumineuse; Je t'aime; Tout-Paris.*
☞ ** Marco Polo Dig. 8.223438 [id.]. Slovak State PO (Košler), Alfred Walter.

Polkas: *Camarade; Dans les bois; Jeu d'esprit.* Waltzes: *Bien aimés; Chantilly; Dans tes yeux; Estudiantina; Hommage aux dames; Les Patineurs.*
☞ ** Marco Polo Dig. 8.223433 [id.]. Slovak State PO (Košice), Walter.

Polkas: *L'esprit français; Par-ci, par-là; Zig-zag.* Waltzes: *Hébé; Les Fleurs; Fleurs et baisers; Solitude; Toujours ou jamais; Toujours fidèle.*
☞ **(*) Marco Polo Dig. 8.223450 [id.]. Slovak State PO (Košice), Walter.

Invitation à la gavotte; Polkas: *Joyeux Paris; Ma Voisine.* Waltzes: *Pluie de diamants; Les Sirènes; Les Sourires; Soirée d'été; Très jolie; Tout en rose.*
☞ ** Marco Polo Dig. 8.223441 [id.]. Slovak State PO (Košice), Alfred Walter.

Like Johann Strauss, Emile Waldteufel, born in Strasbourg, was a member of a family of musicians whose speciality was to provide dance music for society balls, but his output quickly had a much more democratic parlance. His orchestra played for Napoleon III and his waltzes soon also became familiar at the English court and were popular with Queen Victoria. Waldteufel's music, if not matching that of the Strauss family in range and expressive depth, has grace and charm and is prettily scored in the way of French ballet music. Moreover its lilt is undeniably infectious. The most famous waltz, *Les Patineurs,* is mirrored in style here by many of the others (*Dans les nuages,* for instance), and there are plenty of good tunes. *Plus de diamants,* with lots of vitality, is among the more familiar items, as is the sparkling *Très jolie,* but many of the unknown pieces are equally engaging. Like Strauss, Waldteufel usually introduces his waltzes with a section not in waltz-time, and he is ever resourceful in his ideas and in his orchestration. The polkas are robust, but the scoring has plenty of character. The third disc listed (Volume 3 in the overall Marco Polo series) is a good starting point for the collector wanting to explore. It begins with *Zig-zag,* a lively polka featuring a solo cornet; then the horns open *Les Fleurs,* which produces yet another of the composer's best singing melodies. Both *Solitude* and *Fleurs et baisirs* have much charm. Yet another cornet solo appears in *Toujours fidèle,* but the strings join him when the main waltz begins. *L'Esprit français,* a very gay French polka with a whiff of Offenbach, then makes a good foil for the two final waltzes, *Toujours ou jamais* and *Hébé,* which is Straussian in its melodic contour and worthy of the Viennese master. The performances are direct and have fresh, unmannered rubato. They are played with warmth and a good deal of finesse and, if Alfred Walter emerges as a sympathetic rather than an individual exponent, better this than exaggerated presentation, pulling the rhythms out of shape. The French style is understood as being more *galant,* less languorously indulgent, than the Viennese manner.

Walton, William (1902–83)

Anniversary fanfare; Crown imperial; March for the history of the English-speaking peoples; Orb and sceptre; A Queen's fanfare; (i) *Antiphon; 4 Christmas carols: All this time; King Herod and his cock; Make we now this feast; What cheer?. In honour of the City of London; Jubilate Deo; Where does the uttered music go?.*
*** Chan. Dig. CHAN 8998; *ABTD 1580* [id.]. (i) Bach Ch.; Philh. O, Willcocks.

Sir David Willcocks conducts performances of the two *Coronation marches* full of panache, with the brass superbly articulated and inner detail well caught. Also the *March for the history of the English-speaking peoples.* The *a cappella* choral items are very well done too, if less intimately than on the Conifer disc of Walton choral music from Trinity College Choir. With the original organ parts orchestrated, the *Jubilate* and *Antiphon* gain greatly from having full instrumental accompaniment. The brief fanfares, never previously recorded, are a welcome makeweight, with the *Anniversary fanfare* (written for EMI's 75th anniversary in 1973) designed to lead directly into *Orb and sceptre,* which is what it does here.

Capriccio burlesco; The First shoot (orch. Palmer); *Granada* (Prelude for orchestra); *Johannesburg festival overture; Music for children. Galop finale* (orch. Palmer); *Portsmouth Point: overture; Prologo e fantasia; Scapino.*
*** Chan. Dig. CHAN 8968; *ABTD 1560* [id.]. LPO, Bryden Thomson.

With Walton's three brilliant comedy overtures providing the cornerstones, this makes a delightful collection of miscellaneous orchestral pieces, another welcome addition to Chandos's Walton series. You might even count the *Capriccio burlesco* as a fourth comedy overture. It is ravishingly orchestrated, with some apt echoes of Gershwin, and the *Prologo e Fantasia* completes an American group. The *Granada* Prelude, written for the television company, taps Walton's patriotic march vein in a jaunty way. *The First shoot* comes in Christopher Palmer's brilliant orchestration of the brass band suite. The opening *Giocoso* is a re-run of *Old Sir Faulk,* and the other movements bring more echoes of *Façade.* As for the other novelty, the ten brief movements of *Music for children,* crisply orchestrated versions of pieces for piano-duet, are here supplemented by a *Galop final*. Palmer has here orchestrated the piano score. Though the opulent Chandos recording tends to take some of the bite away from Walton's jazzily accented writing, the richness of the orchestral sound is consistently satisfying.

(i) *Capriccio burlesco*; (ii) *Music for children; Portsmouth Point overture*; (i) *The Quest* (ballet suite); *Scapino overture*; (ii) *Siesta*; (i; iii) *Sinfonia concertante*.
*** Lyrita SRCD 224 [id.]. (i) LSO or (ii) LPO, composer; (iii) with Peter Katin.

When Walton made these recordings, he was in his late sixties, and his speeds had grown a degree slower and safer. *Portsmouth Point* loses some of its fizz at so moderate a speed. In *Scapino* Walton also adopts a relatively slow speed, taking a full minute longer than on his own earlier 78-r.p.m. version (see below). By contrast with the earlier comedy overture it suffers hardly at all from the slower speed, rather the opposite, with the opening if anything even jauntier and the big cello melody drawn out more expressively. *Siesta* too takes a full minute longer than it does in its 78 counterpart, bringing out the piece's romantically lyrical side, rather than making it a relatively cool intermezzo. The *Capriccio burlesco* is delightfully done. The ten little pieces of the *Music for children* are delightful too, with the subtleties of the instrumentation beautifully brought out. Much the biggest work here is the *Sinfonia concertante*, and in the outer movements the performance lacks the thrust that Walton himself gave it in his very first wartime recording, in which Phyllis Sellick was a scintillating soloist. Yet Peter Katin is a very responsive soloist too, and the central slow movement is much warmer and more passionate than on Conifer, with orchestral detail rather clearer. It is good too to have the first stereo recording of the suite from Walton's wartime ballet based on Spenser's 'Faerie Queene', *The Quest*, only a fraction of the whole but bright and colourful.

Cello concerto.
☞ (M) *** Sony Dig. SMK 53333 [id.]. Yo-Yo Ma, LSO, Previn – ELGAR: *Cello concerto.* ***
☞ *** EMI Dig. CDC7 54572-2 [id.]. (i) Lyn Harrell, Birmingham SO, Rattle – *Symphony No. 1.* ***
☞ (M) *** BMG/RCA 09026 61498-2. Piatigorsky, Boston SO, Munch – DVORAK: *Concerto.* **(*)

Yo-Yo Ma and Previn give a sensuously beautiful performance. With speeds markedly slower than usual in the outer movements, the meditation is intensified to bring a mood of ecstasy, quite distinct from other Walton, with the central allegro becoming the symphonic kernel of the work, far more than just a scherzo. In the excellent CBS recording, the soloist is less forwardly and more faithfully balanced than is common. The CD is one of CBS's most impressive.

Lynn Harrell's reading of the *Cello concerto*, with Rattle an ever-sympathetic partner, is outstanding in every way. In the lovely opening theme Harrell is both noble and deeply reflective, and in the second-movement *Allegro appassionato* he is at once mercurial while establishing the movement's symphonic power. With Harrell more than his rivals there is no feeling of the slow music in this largely lyrical work overbalancing the fast, and his most remarkable achievement comes in the variation finale. There he plays the two cadenzas with such power and concentration that, far more than usual, they take the argument forward instead of emerging as unaccompanied interludes for the cellist. The solo instrument is placed well forward, but not aggressively so. Coupled with an equally compelling account of the *Symphony*, this is highly recommendable.

There is always something special about first recordings, notably when the performance is by the work's dedicatee. The *Cello concerto* – the last of Walton's three concertos – was written for Piatigorsky and he plays it with a gripping combination of full-blooded eloquence and subtlety of feeling, readily capturing the bitter-sweet melancholy of its flowing lyrical lines. The closing pages of the final variations are particularly haunting. Munch provides a totally understanding accompaniment, with the strings of the Boston Symphony finding that special quality of lyrical ecstasy which is such a distinctive part of this concerto. The 1957 recording is a bit close, but the improvement of the CD over the old LP is enormous, and the ambience of Symphony Hall is much more apparent than before.

(i; ii) *Cello concerto*; (ii) *Improvisations on an impromptu of Benjamin Britten; Partita for orchestra*; (i) *Passacaglia for solo cello.*
*** Chan. Dig. CHAN 8959; *ABTD 1551* [id.]. (i) Rafael Wallfisch; (ii) LPO, Bryden Thomson.

With its all-Walton coupling, this is plainly the version to recommend to those primarily concerned with the composer rather than with the cello. With his rich, even tone, Wallfisch is just as warm and purposeful in the solo *Passacaglia* Walton wrote at the end of his life for Rostropovich, while Thomson relishes the vivid orchestral colours in both the *Improvisations*, here wider-ranging in expression than usual, and the brilliant *Partita*. Excellent Chandos sound.

Viola concerto; Violin concerto.
*** EMI Dig. CDC7 49628-2 [id.]. Nigel Kennedy, RPO, Previn.

Kennedy's achievement in giving equally rich and expressive performances of both works makes for an ideal coupling, helped by the unique insight of André Previn as Waltonian. Kennedy on the viola produces tone as rich and firm as on his usual violin. The Scherzo has never been recorded with more panache than here, and the finale brings a magic moment in the return of the main theme from the opening, hushed and intense. In the *Violin concerto* too, Kennedy gives a warmly relaxed reading, in which he dashes off the bravura passages with great flair. He may miss some of the more searchingly introspective manner of Chung in her 1971 version, but there are few Walton records as richly rewarding as this, helped by warm, atmospheric sound.

(i) *Viola concerto;* (ii) *Sinfonia concertante.*
(M) (***) EMI mono CDH7 63828-2. (i) William Primrose, Philh. O; (ii) Phyllis Sellick, CBSO; composer – VAUGHAN WILLIAMS: *Violin concerto* etc. (***)

William Primrose here gives a formidable account of the greatest of viola concertos, with the composer conducting. Recorded in 1946, the mono sound fails to capture a genuine pianissimo, but otherwise the combination of romantic warmth tempered by classical restraint provides a lesson to some more recent interpreters. Unlike them, Primrose adopts an aptly flowing speed for the opening *Andante comodo*, refusing to sentimentalize it. The scherzo is phenomenally fast, sometimes sounding breathless, but the virtuosity is astonishing; and the spiky humour of the finale is delightfully pointed, leading to a yearning account of the epilogue. The *Sinfonia concertante* is another historic recording well deserving study, made in 1945, the first ever of this work. Phyllis Sellick readily matches the composer-conductor in the thrusting urgency and romantic power of the performance. Excellent transfers of both concertos, generously coupled with the two Vaughan Williams works.

(i) *Viola concerto; Sonata for string orchestra; Variations on a theme of Hindemith.*
☞ *** Chan. Dig. CHAN 9106 [id.]. (i) Nobuko Imai; LPO, Jan Latham-Koenig.

When for many Waltonians the *Viola concerto* is a special favourite among his works, it is surprising that it has not been recorded more often. Though latterly the *Violin concerto* has appeared in multiple versions, the only significant modern rival to this account of the *Viola concerto* in Chandos's Walton series is Nigel Kennedy's on EMI, with André Previn conducting. There is little direct rivalry, when the couplings are so different, and both can be warmly recommended. Imai is satisfyingly firm and true in all her playing, keenly confident in the virtuoso passages, with the central Scherzo not at all breathless-sounding. Like Kennedy and other latterday interpreters, Imai – ignoring the evidence of early recordings with Walton conducting – uses a very broad *Andante* to bring out the full lyrical warmth, but it means that the following bravura section enters with a jolt rather than developing naturally. The movement is not helped either by the forward balance of the soloist. Though the recording also obscures some orchestral detail, not just a question of balance, Jan Latham-Koenig secures crisply rhythmic playing from the orchestra in all three movements. The main theme of the finale is even jauntier than usual, again at a speed fractionally slower than normal.

The warmth of the LPO string-tone comes over impressively in the *Sonata for strings*. This is a bigger-scale reading than the rival ones from the Guildhall String Ensemble on RCA or from the Australian Chamber Orchestra on Sony, both of them excellent too. Yet the bigger scale is not all gain. Though the extra weight and tonal warmth are often very satisfying, as in the opening of the slow movement, the contrast between the passages for solo string quartet (echoing the original quartet version) and the full string ensemble is too extreme. Latham-Koenig is also warmly expressive in the *Hindemith variations*, another work that has tended to be neglected on disc. Latham-Koenig provides a first-rate modern account, not as lightly pointed or cleanly detailed as it might be, partly a question of the recording, but with extra weight and thrust to make it richly satisfying. Any reservations are peripheral when the three works on the disc not only make an exceptionally generous triptych, but one which reflects Walton's mastery over the full range of his career.

(i) *Viola concerto;* (ii) *Symphony No. 1;* (iii) *3 Songs from Façade.*
☞ ❀ (M) (***) Dutton Laboratories mono CDAX 8003 [id.]. (i) Riddle, LSO, composer; (ii) LSO, Harty; (iii) Dora Stevens, Foss.

This first ever recording of the *Viola concerto*, made for Decca in December 1937 with Walton conducting the LSO and with Frederick Riddle as soloist, puts a totally different complexion on the piece from usual. Riddle's performance has never been surpassed by even the starriest viola-players since for, unlike almost every rival today, he takes the first movement, *Andante comodo*, at a flowing speed that avoids over-romanticizing the yearning melody at the start. Yet, unlike William Primrose, who also made an early recording of the concerto at fast speeds, again with the composer conducting (1946), Riddle finds a poignant tenderness in the concerto, using far subtler half-tones than Primrose. Riddle in the central Scherzo is more relaxed, with wittily sprung rhythms, while after a fast, spiky account of the finale the epilogue is wistful rather than tragic, again far subtler than in Primrose's reading. Amazingly, this historic recording was never transferred to LP, making the superb transfer from Dutton Laboratories doubly welcome. It is coupled ideally with the very first recording of Walton's *First Symphony*, made in 1935 – also for Decca – soon after the first complete performance by the LSO under Sir Hamilton Harty. Though the playing is not always as polished as in modern versions, the emotional thrust under Harty has never been surpassed, not even by André Previn in his classic 1966 recording, which otherwise remains the finest version of all. Again the sound is beefy and full, amazingly so when you think that Decca's improvised studio was in a warehouse building near Cannon Street station. The songs, with Dora Stevens accompanied by her husband, Hubert Foss, Walton's publisher from OUP, are a charming makeweight.

Violin concerto.
☞ (M) *** Decca 440 324-2 [id.]. Kyung Wha Chung, LSO, Previn – *Belshazzar's Feast* etc. ***
☞ (M) *** EMI CDM7 64202-2 [id.]. Ida Haendel, Bournemouth SO, Berglund – BRITTEN: *Violin concerto.* ***
(M) (***) BMG/RCA mono GD 87966 [7966-2-RG]. Heifetz, Philh. O, composer – ELGAR: *Concerto.* (***)
☞ (***) Biddulph mono WHL 016 [id.]. Heifetz, Cincinnati SO, Goossens – VAUGHAN WILLIAMS: *A London Symphony (No. 2)* (***) (with Concert (***)).

In the brooding intensity of the opening evocation, Kyung Wha Chung presents the first melody with a depth of expression, tender and hushed, that has never been matched on record, not even by Heifetz. With Previn as guide and with the composer himself a sympathetic observer at the recording sessions, Chung then builds up a performance which must remain a classic, showing the *Concerto* as one of the greatest of the century in this genre. Outstandingly fine recording, sounding the more vivid in its CD format. This now comes, coupled with Solti's *Belshazzar's Feast* and the *Coronation anthem*, at 78 minutes a generous CD if ever there was one.

A sunny, glowing, Mediterranean-like view of the concerto from Ida Haendel, with brilliant playing from the soloist and eloquent orchestral support from the Bournemouth orchestra under Paavo Berglund. Kyung Wa Chung's Decca version is wirier and in some ways more in character, but many collectors will respond just as positively, or even more, to Miss Haendel's warmth. The CD transfer of the fine (1977) recording, made in the Guildhall, Southampton, brings a brilliant orchestral tapestry to provide the necessary contrast and, given the quality of the playing (as well as the interest of the equally successful Britten coupling), this is an eminently desirable reissue.

It was Heifetz who commissioned the Walton *Concerto* and who gave the first performances, as well as making a wartime recording in America. This is the later version on BMG/RCA, first issued in 1951, which Heifetz made with Walton conducting, using the revised score. Speeds are often hair-raisingly fast, but few Heifetz records convey as much passion as this. The mono recording is dry, with a distracting hum in the transfer, but the high-voltage electricity has never been matched in this radiant music.

Jascha Heifetz made the very first recording in 1941 with Eugene Goossens and the Cincinnati orchestra, and it has never quite been matched since for its passionate urgency as well as its brilliance. Speeds are much faster than has latterly become the norm, but the romantic warmth of the work has never been more richly conveyed. Here in an excellent CD transfer it is coupled with the only existing recording of the original score of Vaughan Williams's *London Symphony*, plus other British music.

(i) *Violin concerto;* (ii; iii) *Capriccio burlesco;* (iv; iii) *Façade suite No. 1; Johannesburg festival overture.*
☞ (M) *** Sony SMK 58931 [id.]. (i) Francescatti, Phd. O, Ormandy; (ii) orchestra; (iii) André Kostelanetz; (iv) NYPO.

Zino Francescatti's 1959 recording of the Walton *Violin concerto* with Eugene Ormandy and the Philadelphia Orchestra comes close to matching the power and thrust of both the Heifetz versions that preceded it. Francescatti may not always convey the finer shadings of the music, but the assurance of his playing is consistently compelling. In a first-rate transfer to CD in Sony's British Heritage series, it is very well coupled with the Walton recordings made in New York by André Kostelanetz, far more than a light-music specialist. These include the characteristically bustling showpiece that Walton dedicated to him, the *Capriccio burlesco*, given a performance of tremendous brio, the ever-delectable *Façade* pieces as well as the most lovable and exuberant of Walton's three witty overtures, the *Johannesburg Festival*, stunningly done. Forward, larger-than-life recording.

(i) *Violin concerto. Capriccio burlesco; Henry V: Suite; Spitfire prelude & fugue.*
☞ **(*) HM Dig. HMU 907070 [id.]. (i) Aaron Rosand; Florida PO, Judd.

In this first international recording made by the Florida Philharmonic under its British music director, James Judd, it is good to welcome an unusual coupling of Walton works. One can hardly imagine a comparable British orchestra setting off on a recording career with American music. Judd – whose work training international orchestras, mainly of young players, has resulted in some impressive recordings – draws warmly idiomatic playing from the orchestra in the colourful pieces based on wartime film music, for *The First of the Few* and *Henry V*, with the oboe solo in the *Bailero* theme after the Agincourt music achingly beautiful, and with the brass consistently ripe and resonant. The *Capriccio burlesco* is aptly witty and spiky. It is good to have Aaron Rosand returning to the recording studio in the *Violin concerto*. He made a number of recordings for Vox in the early days of LP, and in this formidable concerto written for Heifetz he shows that his virtuosity is as impressive as ever. Against the latterday trend, Rosand comes near to matching the formidable drive and agility of Heifetz himself in the work, without sounding over-stressed. The snag is that the recording balances the soloist so close that orchestral detail is dim, and tuttis lack the bite and thrust they need. The contrast in the orchestral sound between the concerto and the other items is made the more extreme, when all but the *Capriccio burlesco* have a more helpful, more atmospheric acoustic. Despite the dryness of sound in the concerto and a lightness in bass, the bite and thrust of Rosand's performance are most refreshing, while the *Henry V* and *Spitfire music* are treated with great warmth.

Violin concerto; 2 Pieces for violin and orchestra; Sonata for violin and orchestra (both orch. Palmer).
☞ *** Chan. Dig. CHAN 9073; *ABTD 1595* [id.]. Mordkovitch, LPO, Jan Latham-Koenig.

Lydia Mordkovitch gives the most expansive account of the Walton *Violin concerto* on disc, sustaining spacious speeds warmly and persuasively. The very opening finds her deeply meditative in the soaring melody of the first theme, yet her double-stopping in the bravura passages designed for Heifetz is irresistibly purposeful, never sounding too slow or laboured. Latham-Koenig may not have quite the spark that Previn brings to the orchestral writing in both the Chung and Kennedy versions but he is keenly idiomatic, both in his feeling for sharply syncopated rhythms and in flexible rubato for Walton's romantic melodies. In the central *Presto* Scherzo, a virtuoso display piece, the speed is no slower than that chosen by most rivals, while the Spanish dance-rhythm of the first contrasting interlude is seductively slinky, whether from soloist or orchestra. The characteristically warm Chandos recording is also a help, allowing plenty of detail to be heard, but helping to give extra cohesion to such a passage as the final march coda.

The unique coupling makes this version particularly attractive to Walton devotees. Christopher Palmer's arrangements of the *Sonata* and the two short pieces are full of Waltonian fingerprints in the instrumentation. So, his scoring of the *Sonata* offers a sensuousness of sound comparable with that in the opera *Troilus and Cressida*. That dates from very much the same period when, after the death of his long-time friend, Lady Wimborne, Walton married his young wife, Susana, and settled in Italy. Palmer's perceptive note suggests that the new sensuousness had first appeared in the scoring of the *Violin concerto* of 1939, a reflection of his love-affair then not just with Alice Wimborne but with Italy. Fairly enough, he asks to what degree the *Violin sonata* of 1948 is an elegy and how much celebration of new-found happiness. Certainly the effect of his orchestration is to emphasize the latter element. Though his use of the harp or pizzicato strings for arpeggio accompaniments is not always comfortable, Palmer is right in seeing much of the piano part as already implying orchestration. With Mordkovitch just as powerful and rich-toned as in the regular concerto, the work makes a far bigger impact than in its original chamber form, a valuable addition to the Walton repertory. The two shorter pieces make an agreeable supplement, with Palmer's lush orchestration removing them even further from their medieval source-material. Walton came upon this when writing the French court sequence of his music for the film *Henry V*, but the ideas have been totally Waltonized.

Coronation marches: Crown imperial; Orb and Sceptre; Façade suites Nos. 1 & 2; (i; ii) *Gloria;* (ii) *Te Deum.*
☞ (M) *** EMI CDM7 64201-2 [id.]. (i) Robothom, Rolfe Johnson, Rayner Cook, CBSO Ch.; (ii)
    Choristers of Worcester Cathedral; CBSO, Frémaux.

'Shatteringly apt displays of pomp and circumstance' is Frank Howes's delightful description of the three Walton works inspired by coronations, and here they are splendidly coupled with the grand setting of the *Gloria* which Walton wrote in 1961 for a double celebration at Huddersfield: the 125th anniversary of the Choral Society and the 30th anniversary of its association with Sir Malcolm Sargent. That last work, the longest of the four, has not quite the same concentration as the others, for it represents Walton tending to repeat himself in his jagged Alleluia rhythms and jazzy fugatos. Frémaux directs a highly enjoyable performance nevertheless; but it rather pales before the Coronation *Te Deum*, which may use some of the same formulas but has Walton electrically inspired. It is a grand setting which yet has a superb formal balance (almost a sonata form) while exploiting every tonal and atmospheric effect imaginable between double choirs and semi-choruses. The two splendid marches are marvellously done too. The rich, resonant recording is apt for the music, spacious and with excellent perspectives, and it has transferred splendidly to CD, with the brass both sonorous and biting and the choral sound fresh as well as with plenty of weight. The *Façade suites* have been added for the CD (total playing time: 67 minutes) and here the remastering is even more telling, adding point to playing which is already affectionately witty. Frémaux's rhythmic control gives a fresh, new look to familiar music: his jaunty jazz inflexions in *Old Sir Faulk* are deliciously whimsical.

Crown Imperial (concert band version).
⊛ (M) *** Mercury 432 009-2 [id.]. Eastman Wind Ens., Fennell – BENNETT: *Symphonic songs;*
    HOLST: *Hammersmith;* JACOB: *William Byrd suite.* ***

Paced with dignity, yet with joyously crisp articulation, Fennell's splendidly spacious performance is part of a highly recommendable collection of music for concert band; the entry of the organ at the climax brings a frisson-creating dynamic expansion which is unforgettably exciting. The coda, too, is quite superb. The Mercury sound, from the late 1950s, remains in the demonstration bracket.

Façade (complete, including *Façade 2*).
**(*) ASV Dig. CDDCA 679 [id.]. Prunella Scales, Timothy West, L. Mozart Players (members),
    Jane Glover.
**(*) Chan. Dig. CHAN 8869; *ABTD 1484* [id.]. Lady Susana Walton, Richard Baker, City of L.
    Sinfonia (members), Richard Hickox.

Scales and West as a husband-and-wife team are inventive in their shared roles, and generally it works well. *Scotch rhapsody* is hilariously done as a duet, with West intervening at appropriate moments, and with sharply precise Scots accents. Regional accents may defy Edith Sitwell's original prescription – and her own example – but here, with one exception, they add an appropriate flavour. The exception is *Popular song*, where Prunella Scales's cockney accent clashes horribly with the allusive words, with their 'cupolas, gables in the lakes, Georgian stables'. For fill-up the reciters have recorded more Sitwell poems, but unaccompanied.

Susana Walton, widow of the composer, makes a bitingly characterful reciter, matching with her distinctive accent – she was born in Argentina – the exoticry of many numbers. Richard Baker, phenomenally precise and agile in enunciating the Sitwell poems, makes the perfect foil, and Hickox secures colourful and lively playing from members of the City of London Sinfonia, who relish in particular the jazzy inflexions. *Façade 2* consists of a number of poems, beyond the definitive series of 21. All of them are fun and make an apt if not very generous coupling for the regular sequence. Warm sound, rather too reverberant for so intimate a work.

(i) *Façade* (complete); (ii) *Siesta; Overtures: Portsmouth Point; Scapino.*
⊛ (M) *** Decca mono 425 661-2 [id.]. (i) Sitwell, Pears, E. Op. Group Ens., Collins; (ii) LPO, Boult
    – ARNOLD: *English dances.* (***)

Anthony Collins's 1954 recording of *Façade* is a gramophone classic, sounding miraculously vivid and atmospheric in a CD transfer that seems almost like modern stereo. Dame Edith Sitwell had one of the richest and most characterful of speaking voices, and here she recites her early poems to the masterly, witty music of the youthful Walton with glorious relish. Peter Pears is splendid too in the fast poems, rattling off the lines like the *grande dame* herself, to demonstrate how near-nonsense can be pure poetry. The Boult mono versions of *Scapino* and *Siesta* make a valuable coupling, although *Portsmouth Point* misses some of the rhythmic bite of his first 78-r.p.m. disc. Malcolm Arnold's own première recording of his masterly *English dances*, full of exuberance and colour, completes a fascinating programme that no lover of English music should miss.

Façade: suites Nos. 1–3; Overture Portsmouth Point (arr. Lambert); *Siesta;* (i) *Sinfonia concertante.*
WALTON/ARNOLD: *Popular birthday.*
☞ *** Chan. Dig. CHAN 9148 [id.]. (i) Eric Parkin; LPO, Latham-Koenig or Thomson.

Adapted from a ballet score written for Diaghilev (but then rejected), the *Sinfonia concertante*, with its sharply memorable ideas in each movement and characteristically high voltage, has never had the attention it deserves. That is the more regrettable when there is such a dearth of attractive British piano concertos. To try and get it better known, Walton in 1943 reduced the orchestration and made other amendments, but to little avail. Towards the end of his life Walton told Stewart Craggs, his bibliographer, that he found the earlier version 'better and more interesting'. Like the Conifer issue with Kathryn Stott as soloist, the Chandos recording restores the original version, though the differences are hardly noticeable without close study of the score. Eric Parkin as soloist is perfectly attuned to the idiom, warmly melodic as well as jazzily syncopated, making this the most sympathetic account on disc since the original version of 1945 with Phyllis Sellick as soloist and Walton himself conducting, even if the *Maestoso* introduction is hardly grand enough. The recording sets the piano a little more backwardly, no doubt to reflect the idea that this is not a full concerto.

Jan Latham-Koenig is most understanding of Walton's 1920s idiom, giving the witty *Façade* movements just the degree of jazzy freedom they need. The third suite, devised and arranged by Christopher Palmer, draws on three apt movements from the *Façade* entertainment, ending riotously with the rag-music of *Something lies beyond the scene*. That is a first recording, and so is Constant Lambert's arrangement for small orchestra of the *Overture Portsmouth Point*, clearer than the original. *Siesta* is given an aptly cool performance under Bryden Thomson, and the *Popular birthday* is Malcolm Arnold's fragmentary linking of 'Happy birthday to you' with the *Popular song* from *Façade*, originally written for Walton's seventieth birthday. The impact of some of the pieces, notably in *Façade*, would have been even sharper had the warmly atmospheric Chandos recording placed the orchestra a little closer.

Façade: suites 1 & 2.
*** Hyp. Dig. CDA 66436 [id.]. E. N. Philh. O, Lloyd-Jones – BLISS: *Checkmate* ***; LAMBERT: *Horoscope.* *** ⊛

Brilliantly witty and humorous performances of the two orchestral suites which Walton himself fashioned from his 'Entertainment'. This is music which, with its outrageous quotations, can make one chuckle out loud. Moreover it offers, to quote Constant Lambert, 'one good tune after another', all scored with wonderful felicity. The playing here could hardly be bettered, and the recording is in the demonstration bracket with its natural presence and bloom.

(i) *Façade: suites 1 & 2;* (ii) *Henry V: 2 pieces for strings;* (iii) *Scapino* (comedy overture); (i) *Siesta;* (iv) *Spitfire prelude and fugue* (film music); (v) *Belshazzar's feast.*
(M) (***) EMI mono CDH7 63381-2 [id.]. (i) LPO; (ii) Philh. String O; (iii) Philh. O; (iv) Hallé O; (v) Dennis Noble, Huddersfield Choral Soc., Liverpool Philh. O; all cond. composer.

The composer's recording of *Belshazzar's feast*, made at the height of the Second World War, was an astonishing achievement: it still sounds amazingly full and clear, very well transferred, though inevitably with some surface noise. The percussion comes out most vividly, and here even more compellingly than in his later stereo recording Walton establishes the claims of speeds far faster than have latterly become common in this work. The chorus, *Babylon was a great city*, goes at an astonishing pace, but the incisiveness of playing and singing makes it intensely exciting and not merely breathless. Ensemble is not always perfect, and the final chorus brings some untidiness at the end, but the magnetic building of tension over the whole work makes this more compelling than almost any version since. It will be a revelation to all who love the work, with Dennis Noble living up to his surname. The other items bring vintage performances too, and in the transfer the most remarkable example of sound well in advance of its time is in the *Façade suites*. It is scarcely credible that the recordings were made as early as 1936. However, this CD is another current withdrawal from the EMI catalogue.

Film scores

As you like it; Hamlet.
*** Chan. Dig. CHAN 8842; *ABTD 1461* [id.]. Catherine Bott, Sir John Gielgud, ASMF, Marriner.

Walton's score for *Hamlet*, thanks to the diligence of Christopher Palmer, offers some 40 minutes of music, a rich and colourful suite, superbly played and recorded, and much enhanced by the contribution of Sir John Gielgud in two of Hamlet's soliloquies, 'O that this too, too solid flesh' and 'To be or not to be'. The selection of music from the pre-war film of *As you like it* makes a valuable fill-up. It adds the splendid setting of *Under the greenwood tree* in a radiant performance by Catherine Bott. Marriner and the Academy draw out all the romantic warmth of both scores, and the sound is richly atmospheric to match.

The Battle of Britain (suite); Escape me never (suite); The First of the Few: Spitfire prelude and fugue; Three Sisters; A Wartime sketchbook.
*** Chan. Dig. CHAN 8870; *ABTD 1485* [id.]. ASMF, Marriner.

This heartwarming record gathers together many of the fragments of film music that constituted what Walton regarded as his 'war work'. *The Spitfire prelude and fugue*, from *The First of the Few*, was immediately turned into a highly successful concert-piece, but we owe it to Christopher Palmer that there is the 'Wartime Sketchbook', drawing material from three of the wartime films, plus scraps that Colin Matthews did not use in the suite from the much later *Battle of Britain* film music and not least in the stirring theme from the credits of the film, *Went the day well*. The brief suite from the music for Olivier's film of Chekhov's *The Three Sisters*, from much later, brings more than one setting of the *Tsar's Hymn* and a charming imitation of *Swan Lake*. Earliest on the disc is *Escape me never*, the first of Walton's film-scores, written in 1935 in a more popular idiom; but the war-inspired music is what this delightful disc is really about. Marriner and the Academy give richly idiomatic performances, full of panache. Aptly opulent recording.

Henry V: A Shakespeare scenario (arr. Christopher Palmer).
*** Chan. Dig. CHAN 8892; *ABTD 1503* [id.]. Christopher Plummer (nar.), Westminster Cathedral
   Ch., ASMF, Marriner.

Few film-scores can match Walton's for the Olivier film of *Henry V* in its range and imagination, the whole lasting just over an hour. The most controversial change is to 'borrow' the first section of the march which Walton wrote much later for a projected television series on Churchill's *History of the English-speaking Peoples*; otherwise, the chorus's call to arms, *Now all the youth of England is on fire*, would have had no music to introduce it. As an appendix, three short pieces are included which Walton quoted in his score. Sir Neville Marriner caps even his previous recordings in this series, with the Academy and Westminster Choir producing heartfelt playing and singing in sumptuous sound. As narrator, Christopher Plummer makes an excellent substitute for Olivier, unselfconsciously adopting a comparably grand style.

Henry V: Passacaglia; The Death of Falstaff; Touch her soft lips and part.
☞ (M) *** DG 439 529-2 [id.]. ECO, Barenboim – DELIUS: *Aquarelles* etc.; VAUGHAN WILLIAMS:
   Oboe concerto etc. ***

These two fine Walton string pieces make an admirable complement to a sensuously beautiful collection of English music, with Barenboim at his most affectionately inspirational and the ECO very responsive, and with the 1975 recording retaining its warmth and bloom.

Macbeth: Fanfare & march. Major Barbara (suite); Richard III (Shakespeare scenario).
*** Chan. Dig. CHAN 8841; *ABTD 1460* [id.]. Sir John Gielgud (nar.), ASMF, Marriner.

Disappointingly, Sir John Gielgud underplays Richard III's great 'Now is the winter of our discontent' speech, but working to the underlying music – much of it eliminated in the film – may have cramped his style. The performance generally has all the panache one could wish for, leading up to the return of the grand Henry Tudor theme at the end. The six-minute piece, based on Walton's music for Gielgud's wartime production of *Macbeth*, is much rarer and very valuable too, anticipating in its Elizabethan dance-music the *Henry V* film-score. *Major Barbara* also brings vintage Walton material. Marriner and the Academy give performances just as ripely committed as in their previous discs in the series, helped by sonorous Chandos sound.

The Quest (ballet): complete; *The Wise Virgins* (ballet): suite.
*** Chan. Dig. CHAN 8871; *ABTD 1486* [id.]. LPO, Bryden Thomson.

Walton's two wartime ballet-scores make an attractive coupling, particularly when the greater part of *The Quest*, based on Spenser's *Faerie Queene*, remained unheard for almost half a century. Walton, even in a hurry, could not help creating memorable ideas and, with the help of Constant Lambert – not to mention Christopher Palmer, who has expanded the instrumentation in line with the suite – the orchestral writing is often dazzling. Quite apart from the dramatic power of the performance, the recording is superb, among the fullest and clearest from Chandos. The sound for *The Wise Virgins* is more reverberant and the performance has less electricity, though Walton's distinctive arrangements of Bach cantata movements – including *Sheep may safely graze* – remain as fresh as ever.

Sinfonia concertante for piano & orchestra (original version).
*** Conifer Dig. CDCF 175; *MCFC 175* [id.]. Kathryn Stott, RPO, Handley – BRIDGE: *Phantasm;*
   IRELAND: *Piano concerto.* ***

Kathryn Stott, warmly and strongly accompanied by Vernon Handley and the RPO, gives an outstanding reading, the more interesting for being the first ever recording of the work's original version. It was in 1943, just before making the very first recording with Phyllis Sellick as soloist – also a superb performance – that Walton revised the score, simplifying the solo part and thinning the orchestration. Stott and Handley opted to go back to the original, and the result seems to strengthen what is a consistently memorable work, built from vintage Walton material. First-rate recorded sound, and a coupling both generous and apt.

Sonata for strings.
☞ (M) *** EMI Dig. CDM7 54407-2 [id.]. City of L. Sinfonia, Hickox – ELGAR: *Introduction and allegro.* VAUGHAN WILLIAMS: *Fantasia on a theme by Tallis.* **(*)

Walton's *Sonata for strings* (an arrangement of the 1947 *String quartet*) is made to sound highly effective in this outstanding performance under Hickox. The passionate account of the third-movement *Lento* is a highlight of a reading which is full of intensity, and Hickox's athletic style and the bright, clearly focused, digital sound suit this work better than either the Elgar or Vaughan Williams couplings.

Symphonies Nos. 1–2.
☞ *** Decca Dig. 433 703-2 [id.]. RPO, Ashkenazy.
☞ (M) *** EMI Dig. CD-EMX 2206. (i) LPO; (ii) LSO; Sir Charles Mackerras.

Vladimir Ashkenazy showed his natural sympathy for the Walton idiom in his live recording of the *Second Symphony* on the RPO's own label, giving Walton's nagging syncopations a degree of jazzy freedom and the great romantic melodies an expressive warmth such as he might adopt for Rachmaninov. This studio recording of the *Second Symphony* on Decca, also with the RPO, offers ensemble predictably more precise, more richly recorded and ideally coupled with an account of the *First Symphony* which confirms Ashkenazy's Waltonian credentials even more impressively. It even comes near to matching Previn's classic version, recorded with the LSO for RCA in 1966, and the coupling is both more generous and more apt.

Sir Charles Mackerras in coupling Walton's two symphonies makes a particularly strong case for No. 2, with the LSO sharply incisive, helping to bring out both its consistency with No. 1 and a new sensuousness of expression. Where too often No. 2 has been dismissed as Walton imitating himself, saying nothing new, Mackerras firmly establishes the work's distinction, above all in its control of argument and its brilliant use of a very large orchestra. The thematic material may not be as striking as in the high-voltage *First Symphony*, with its eruption of youthful inspiration, but there is consistent lyrical warmth. Mackerras's reading of No. 1, using the LPO, adopts broader speeds than usual. It may not be as bitingly dramatic as the very finest versions, but the richness and strength of the symphony, one of the key British works of its period, come over powerfully. Warm, full recording in both symphonies. An outstanding bargain.

Symphony No. 1 in B flat min.
☞ *** EMI Dig. CDC7 54572-2 [id.]. CBSO, Rattle – *Cello concerto* ***.
(M) *** BMG/RCA GD 87830 [7830-2-RG]. LSO, Previn (with VAUGHAN WILLIAMS: *Wasps overture* ***).
☞ (M) ** Chan. Dig. CHAN 6570 [id.]. SNO, Gibson (with ELGAR: *Cockaigne* ***).

(i) *Symphony No. 1;* (ii) *Spitfire Prelude and fugue.*
☞ (BB) ** ASV CDQS 6093. (i) RLPO, Handley; (ii) ECO, Bedford.

Symphony No. 1; Varii Capricci.
*** Chan. Dig. CHAN 8862; *ABTD 1477* [id.]. LPO, Bryden Thomson.

Simon Rattle's disc with the CBSO is outstanding, not just because of the electrifying account of the *First Symphony*, but because it has as the most generous coupling the most powerful version of the *Cello concerto* yet. Repeatedly when reviewing new versions of this symphony we have underlined the importance of Waltonian rubato, of treating the jazzy syncopations with a degree of freedom, not absolutely literally. Previn in his 1966 version with the LSO provides the classic instance, and it is a quality that also marks out the Bryden Thomson version in the Chandos Walton Edition, while Leonard Slatkin seems to grow into it, treating the finale more sharply and idiomatically than the rest. Where Rattle scores very strongly in the *Symphony* is that, like Previn in his classic 1966 version (RCA), he combines idiomatic rhythmic freedom in jazzy syncopations with keen precision of ensemble.

Though the EMI sound could have more beef in it, it has an exceptionally wide dynamic range, and Rattle exploits it powerfully to intensify the drama. When in the first movement Walton piles one ostinato on another, screwing the tension ever tighter, Rattle may not be as biting or relentless as some, but his control of tension is unerring in its contrasts of light and shade. After pressing home the marking *con malizia* in the Scherzo, Rattle finds a poignancy as well as power in the slow movement, with the recording again heightening the contrasts of light and shade. In the finale he touchingly brings out the Last Post overtones in the hushed trumpet-theme of the epilogue, again finding natural poignancy. With its brilliant, wide-ranging digital sound it will be a clear first choice for many, particularly when the coupling proves so commanding (see above). In every way an outstanding issue.

On RCA Previn gives a marvellously biting account of the magnificent *First Symphony*. His fast tempi may initially make one feel that he is pressing too hard, but his ability to screw the dramatic tension tighter and tighter until the final resolution is most assured. '*Presto con malizia*' says the score for the Scherzo, and malice is exactly what Previn conveys, with the hints of vulgarity and humour securely placed. In the slow movement Previn finds real warmth, giving some of the melodies an Elgarian richness; and the finale's electricity here helps to overcome any feeling that it is too facile, too easily happy a conclusion. The bright recording – made by Decca engineers in the vintage 1960s – has splendid focus in its CD remastering, yet does not lack body.

Thomson's is a warmly committed, understandingly idiomatic account of the work, weighty and rhythmically persuasive, which brings out the full emotional thrust. In the slow movement his tender expressiveness goes with a flowing speed, well judged to avoid exaggeration. If the Scherzo is a degree less demonic than it might be, at a speed fractionally slower than usual, it is infectiously sprung. Previn's famous RCA version of the *Symphony* has a unique, biting intensity, but Thomson's performance, helped by the splendid modern sound, is very satisfying in its own right and is among the best of the modern digital recordings. The Chandos coupling is not as generous as some but is very welcome when it brings the first recording of *Varii capricci*, the orchestral suite in five compact movements which Walton developed from his set of guitar *Bagatelles*, written for Julian Bream. With a brilliant performance and sumptuous sound, it makes a fine supplement.

Vernon Handley's interpretation of Walton's *First Symphony* matured when he conducted a number of performances with the Liverpool orchestra during Walton's seventieth birthday celebrations. It is essentially a broad view and tends to play down the work's cutting edge: there is very little suggestion of *malizia* in the Scherzo and the slow movement is lyrically rich in the overall English symphonic tradition. But Handley's spontaneity ensures that the reading hangs together: the first-movement climax is impressively shaped to a considerable peak of excitement, although it is the orchestral brass that makes the most striking effect; the string playing lacks bite and incisiveness both here and in the finale. The recording is resonant and spacious and this is certainly enjoyable, if no match for the biting intensity of Previn's famous RCA record. The bonus is brief but well played and digitally recorded.

Gibson's is a convincingly idiomatic view, well paced but with ensemble not always bitingly precise enough for this darkly intense music (malice prescribed for the Scherzo, melancholy for the slow movement). Recording is first rate, but with less body than usual from Chandos and with timpani resonantly obtrusive. The compact disc is somewhat disappointing, bringing out the thinness on top. Gibson's fine performance of *Cockaigne* has been added for the reissue, but this disc is not really competitive.

Symphony No. 2.
*** RPO Dig. CDRPO 8023; *ZCRPO 8023* [id.]. RPO, Ashkenazy – BRITTEN: *Serenade;* KNUSSEN: *Symphony No. 3.* ***

Symphony No. 2; Partita for orchestra; Variations on a theme by Hindemith.
⊛ (M) *** Sony MPK 46732 [id.]. Cleveland O, Szell.

In a letter to the conductor, Walton expressed himself greatly pleased with Szell's performance of the *Second Symphony*: 'It is a quite fantastic and stupendous performance from every point of view. Firstly it is absolutely right musically speaking, and the virtuosity is quite staggering, especially the Fugato; but everything is phrased and balanced in an unbelievable way.' Listening to the splendidly remastered CD of this 1961 recording, one cannot but join the composer in responding to the wonderfully luminous detail in the orchestra. Szell's performance of the *Hindemith variations* is no less praiseworthy. Again the music-making is technically immaculate, and under Szell there is not only a pervading warmth, but each fragment is perfectly set in place. Finally comes the *Partita*, which was commissioned by the Cleveland Orchestra and given its première a year before the recording was made. The recordings are bright, in the CBS manner, but the ambience of Severance Hall brings a backing warmth and depth, and these are technically among the finest of Szell's recordings in this venue.

In this live recording, ensemble is inevitably less crisp than in most studio performances – as in the fugato of the finale – but the power and passion of Ashkenazy's reading amply compensate. He is somewhat brisker and more urgent than either Previn or Mackerras in the outer movements, bringing out the scherzando element in the finale even more effectively. He then most tellingly draws out the lyrical warmth of the central slow movement at a marginally slower speed. It could hardly be more sensuous, helped by sound that is amazingly good, considering the problems of live recording, atmospheric with plenty of detail and, on the whole, a natural balance.

CHAMBER MUSIC

Passacaglia for solo cello.
*** Chan. Dig. CHAN 8499; *ABTD 1209* [id.]. Raphael Wallfisch – BAX: *Rhapsodic ballad;*
    BRIDGE: *Cello sonata;* DELIUS: *Cello sonata.* ***

William Walton's *Passacaglia* for solo cello was composed in the last year of his life. It has restraint and eloquence, and Raphael Wallfisch gives a thoroughly sympathetic account of it. Excellent recording.

(i) *Piano quartet; String quartet in A min.*
**(*) Mer. Dig. CDE 84139; *KE 77139* [id.]. John McCabe, English Qt.

The *Piano quartet* is a work of Walton's immaturity, though there are many indications of what is to come. It is coupled with the mature *String quartet;* this is a substantial piece with stronger claims on the repertoire. McCabe and the English Quartet give a convincing enough account of the early piece, but the latter's account of the *String quartet* does not present a strong challenge to that of the Gabrielis on Chandos. If you want this particular coupling rather than the Elgar, however, this is certainly worth investigating.

Piano quartet; Violin sonata.
*** Chan. Dig. CHAN 8999 [id.]. Sillito, Smissen, Orton, Milne.

This performance of the *Piano quartet* with Hamish Milne as pianist makes one marvel that such music could have been the inspiration of a 16-year-old. Admittedly Walton revised the piece, but here is music which instantly grabs the ear, with striking ideas attractively and dramatically presented in each movement. This is a more sharply focused reading than the rival Meridian one, both in the performance and in the recorded sound, with speeds generally flowing more freely and strongly and the string sound more satisfyingly resonant. The two principal performers from the quartet make a warmly sympathetic rather than high-powered duo for the *Violin sonata* of 1949. Yet the combination of Sillito's ripely persuasive style and Milne's incisive power, clarifying textures and giving magic to the phrasing, keeps tensions sharp. The satisfyingly full sound helps too.

String quartet No. 1 (ed. Christopher Palmer); *String quartet in A min.*
*** Chan. Dig. CHAN 8944; *ABTD 1540* [id.]. Gabrieli Qt.

Coupled ideally with the mature *String Quartet in A minor*, completed in 1946, is the atonal quartet, long thought to be lost, which Walton wrote when an undergraduate at Oxford. Discovered in the Walton archive and edited by Christopher Palmer, it proves an astonishing work not just for a 21-year-old but for any British composer writing in the early 1920s. The result is hardly recognizable as Walton at all but is full of fire and imagination. The first movement is 'pastoral-atonal', lyrical in its counterpoint, but the Scherzo, built on vigorously rhythmic motifs and jagged ostinatos, has much more of Bartók in it than of Schoenberg, while the fugue of the finale seeks to emulate Beethoven's *Grosse Fuge* in its complexity and massive scale, alone lasting almost 16 minutes. The performance, recorded in 1991 by the reconstituted Gabrieli Quartet (leader John Georgiadis), brings out all the latent power and lyrical warmth, often implying an underlying anger. It provides a fascinating contrast with the highly civilized *A minor* work of 25 years later. That comes in a red-blooded Gabrieli recording of 1986 (leader Kenneth Sillito) earlier available in coupling with the Elgar *Quartet*. Both recordings were made in the warm, rich acoustic of The Maltings, Snape, with little discrepancy between them.

String quartet in A min.
*** Collins Dig. 1280-2 [id.]. Britten Qt – ELGAR: *Quartet.* ***
*** Virgin/EMI Dig. VC7 59026-2 [id.]. Endellion Qt – BRIDGE: *String quartet No. 3.* ***

Walton's *Quartet in A minor* was written at a time when he knew that his then-partner of many years, Lady Wimborne, was dying of cancer. The Britten Quartet bring out the emotional intensity, playing with refinement and sharp focus, finding a repose and poise in the slow movement that brings it close to late Beethoven. The contrasts of wistful lyricism and scherzando bite in the first movement make most other versions seem clumsy by comparison, and the incisiveness of Walton's jaggedly rhythmic writing is a delight. Warmly expressive as the Gabrieli Quartet are in the Chandos coupling of these same works, the Brittens are even more searching.

The contrast between haunting melancholy and spiky wit exactly suits the Endellion players. The warmth of their understanding culminates in an outstanding performance of the *Lento* slow movement, superbly sustained at a very measured speed. The marked difference of style and mood here between this work and the other fine quartet on the disc is beautifully brought out, the Walton resigned, the Bridge angry in a way that Walton had rather left behind in his pre-war work. Excellent, warm sound.

Violin sonata.
**(*) ASV Dig. CDDCA 548 [id.]. Lorraine McAslan, John Blakely – ELGAR: *Sonata.* **(*)

Lorraine McAslan gives a warmly committed performance of Walton's often wayward *Sonata.* The romantic melancholy of the piece suits her well, and though the recording does not make her tone as rounded as it should be, she produces some exquisite pianissimo playing. John Blakely is a most sympathetic partner, particularly impressive in crisply articulated scherzando passages.

CHORAL MUSIC

All this time; Antiphon; Chichester service: Magnificat; Nunc dimittis. Jubilate Deo; King Herod and the cock; A Litany (Drop drop slow tears); Make we now joy in this fest; Missa brevis; Set me as a seal upon thine heart; The Twelve; What cheer?; Where does the uttered music go?.
☞ **(*) Nimbus Dig. NI 5364 [id.]. Christ Church Cathedral Ch., Oxford, Stephen Darlington.

There are special reasons for welcoming performances from Christ Church Cathedral Choir. It was this choir which Walton joined as a boy of ten, the foundation of his whole career, and he was still a member when at the age of fifteen he wrote the beautiful *a capella* setting of Phineas Fletcher's *A Litany*, the first item on this disc. Later, towards the end of his life, he wrote two major items for Christ Church, both the powerful setting of the *Jubilate* and the longest piece here, *The Twelve*, setting words specially written by another Christ Church man, W. H. Auden. The clear distinction between the Christ Church performances and those of the two other choirs, giving a strikingly different timbre as well as a different scale, is that you have boy trebles singing instead of sopranos. The vigour and freshness of these performances, so important with Walton's jaggedly rhythmic invention, would have delighted the composer himself and, though the Nimbus recording has the sound of the organ much more recessed than on the Conifer and Chandos discs, the voices are bright and clear, with plenty of bite and presence. The trebles on their own even manage the tricky opening of the *Kyrie* of the *Missa brevis* with confidence at a flowing speed.

Predictably one gets the impression of liturgical performances far more than with the other versions, and in the *Missa brevis* Christ Church observes the revised order of the Mass in the Church of England, returning to Roman practice with the *Gloria* after the *Kyrie*, instead of following the old English Prayerbook order with the *Gloria* at the end. Unfortunately, that reordering makes nonsense of Walton's intended musical scheme, which is that after the three *a capella* sections the organ should enter dramatically for the *Gloria*. What works superbly is the Christ Church performance of *Where does the uttered music go?*, the setting of John Masefield written as a memorial tribute to Sir Henry Wood. At a much faster speed than usual, it has new freshness and a winning flexibility, bringing out the word-meaning. The snag about the Nimbus version is that it omits a major item included by both rivals, the *Cantico del sole* of 1974, setting words of St Francis of Assisi in the original Italian.

All this time; Cantico del sole; Jubilate Deo; King Herod and the cock; A Litany; Magnificat and Nunc dimittis; Make we joy now in this feast; Missa brevis; Set me as a seal (antiphon); The Twelve; What cheer?; Where does the uttered music go?.
*** Conifer Dig. CDCF 164; MCFC 164 [id.]. Trinity College Ch., Richard Marlow.

Richard Marlow conducts his Cambridge choir of mixed voices in a delectable collection of Walton's sacred choral music, both unaccompanied and with organ. The *Missa brevis* for Coventry Cathedral in its spareness strikes a darker, deeper note. The *Cantico del sole*, idiomatically setting Italian words of St Francis, is warmly distinctive, and the longest piece, *The Twelve*, to words specially written by W. H. Auden, is far more than an occasional piece. Marlow draws phenomenally responsive singing from his talented choir, with matching and ensemble that approach the ideal. The recording is just as alive and immaculate.

Anon in love (song-cycle).

☞ (M) *** BMG/RCA 09026 61601-2. Peter Pears, Julian Bream (guitar) – BRITTEN: *Songs from the Chinese* etc; SEIBER: *Four French folk songs.* ***

Walton wrote his cycle, *Anon in love*, for Pears and Bream, and the melisma of the opening song, *Fain would I change that note*, soars aloft in a way that Pears made his own. The other songs progress from nostalgia and romantic feeling to jolly revelry (*I gave her cakes and ale*) and consummation (*To couple is a custom*), with the closing number in the form of a brilliantly earthy scherzando. With attractive couplings this (Volume 18) is one of the most attractive and valuable reissues in the Julian Bream Edition, providing an entire programme played and sung by the artists who inspired the music.

Antiphon; Cantico del sole; 4 Christmas carols; Coronation Te Deum; Jubilate Deo; A Litany; Magnificat & Nunc dimittis; Missa brevis; Set me as a seal upon thine heart; The Twelve; Where does the uttered music go?.

☞ **(*) Chan. Dig. CHAN 9222 [id.]. Finzi Singers, Paul Spicer; Andrew Lumsden.

The significant advantage of the Chandos collection of shorter choral works over the Conifer version from Trinity College Choir is that it offers an additional item, the setting of the *Te Deum* which Walton wrote for the coronation of Queen Elizabeth II in 1953. That comes, not in the version as originally performed and previously recorded, with orchestra, but in the version with organ, suitable for use on rather less grand occasions. The loss of weight makes it less stirring, but the clarity of Walton's structure, a simplified sonata-form, and the ingenuity with which he fits it to the long and complex text of the *Te Deum* comes over all the more clearly.

Otherwise, the Conifer issue offers even finer performances, with phenomenal precision of ensemble and extra expressiveness. Much of the difference lies in the much closer balance of the Chandos sound, which at times allows you to identify individual voices. What matters is that the Finzi Singers' freshness and liveliness is equally winning in bringing out the rich variety of Walton's inspiration in this field. As ever in this series, Christopher Palmer's vividly written notes whet one's appetite to hear and enjoy the music, setting the pieces against the portrait of the man.

(i) *Belshazzar's Feast. Henry V* (film score): *suite.*
*** ASV Dig. CDRPO 8001 [id.]. (i) Luxon, Brighton Festival Ch., L. Coll. Mus., RPO, Previn.

(i) *Belshazzar's Feast. Henry V: 2 Pieces for strings. Partita for orchestra.*
(M) **(*) BMG/RCA Dig. RD 60813 [60813-2-RC]. (i) Allen, LPO Ch.; LPO, Slatkin.

(i) *Belshazzar's Feast. Improvisations on an impromptu of Benjamin Britten; Overtures: Portsmouth Point; Scapino.*
☞ (M) *** EMI CDM7 64723-2 [id.]. LSO, Previn, (i) with John Shirley-Quirk, L. Symphony Ch.

(i) *Belshazzar's Feast. In honour of the City of London.*
☞ (M) *** EMI Dig. CD-EMX 2225; *TC-EMX 2225* [id.]. (i) David Wilson-Johnson; L. Symphony Ch., LSO, Hickox.

Richard Hickox not only conducts the most sharply dramatic account of *Belshazzar's Feast* currently available, even crisper and keener (if less jazzy) than Previn's superb (1971) EMI version; but he couples it with the one major work of Walton left unrecorded: his cantata, *In honour of the City of London.* With forces almost as lavish as those in the oratorio, its vitality and atmospheric colour come over on this record to a degree generally impossible in live performance. As for *Belshazzar* under Hickox, its voltage has never seemed higher on record, thanks not just to the LSO and Chorus – in far sharper form than for Previn, 17 years earlier – but also to the full and brilliant digital recording. The dramatic soloist is David Wilson-Johnson, colouring his voice with chilling menace in the writing-on-the-wall sequence. Now reissued on EMI's mid-priced Eminence label, this makes a strong primary recommendation.

Previn's EMI version of *Belshazzar's Feast* remains among the most spectacular yet recorded. The digital remastering has not lost the body and atmosphere of the sound but has increased its impact. This fine performance was recorded with Walton present on his seventieth birthday and, though Previn's tempi are occasionally slower than those set by Walton himself in his two recordings, the authenticity is clear, with consistently sharp attack and with dynamic markings meticulously observed down to the tiniest hairpin markings. Chorus and orchestra are challenged to their finest standards, and John Shirley-Quirk proves a searching and imaginative soloist. The *Improvisations*, given a first recording, make a generous fill-up alongside the two overtures in which Previn, the shrewdest and most perceptive of Waltonians, finds more light and shade than usual. Again the remastered sound is excellent.

André Previn's RPO digital version of Walton's oratorio brings a performance in some ways even sharper and more urgent than his fine earlier version for EMI with the LSO. The recording is very clear, revealing details of Walton's brilliant orchestration as never before. The chorus, singing with biting intensity, is set realistically behind the orchestra, and though that gives the impression of a smaller group than is ideal, clarity and definition are enhanced. Benjamin Luxon – who earlier sang in Solti's Decca version – is a characterful soloist, but his heavy vibrato is exaggerated by too close a balance. The five-movement suite from Walton's film-music for *Henry V* makes an attractive coupling. Previn was the first conductor on record since Walton himself to capture the full dramatic bite and colour of this music, with the cavalry charge at Agincourt particularly vivid.

Leonard Slatkin conducts the briskest of all modern versions of *Belshazzar*. In the final chorus, *Then sing, sing aloud,* Slatkin is even fractionally faster than Walton, but the syncopated jollity of the music is then diminished. Despite some questionable intonation, the choral ensemble is first rate, and the singing of the baritone soloist, Thomas Allen, is superb, covering the broadest tonal and expressive range. Sadly, the recording places him, like the chorus, rather at a distance, with too little feeling of presence. It lacks the biting impact the work needs. The distancing of sound affects the *Partita*, even if this account hardly replaces the original Szell version. In the two little string-pieces from the *Henry V* music Slatkin sustains very slow speeds well.

(i) *Belshazzar's Feast;* (ii) *Coronation Te Deum.*
☞ (M) *** Decca 440 324-2 [id.]. (i) Benjamin Luxon, LPO Ch.; (ii) Choirs of Salisbury, Winchester & Chichester Cathedrals; LPO, Solti – *Violin concerto.* ***

Belshazzar's Feast; Coronation Te Deum; Gloria.
**(*) Chan. Dig. CHAN 8760 [id.]. Howell, Gunson, Mackie, Roberts, Bach Ch., Philh. O, Willcocks.

Whether or not prompted by the composer's latterday dictum that *Belshazzar's Feast* is more a choral symphony than an oratorio, Sir Georg Solti directs a sharply incisive performance which brings out the symphonic basis rather than the atmospheric story. Fresh, scintillating and spiky, it is a performance that gives off electric sparks, not always quite idiomatic, but very invigorating. Solti observes Walton's syncopations very literally, with little or none of the flexibility that the jazz overtones suggest, and his slow tempo for the lovely chorus, *By the waters of Babylon,* remains very steady, with little of the customary rubato. But with generally excellent singing from the chorus and a sympathetic contribution from Luxon (marred only slightly by vibrato) this is a big-scale reading which overall is most convincing. Moreover from the very opening with its dramatic trombone solo, one is aware that this is to be a Decca spectacular, with superbly incisive and clear choral sound, slightly sparer in texture in *Belshazzar's Feast* than in the *Te Deum,* written for Queen Elizabeth's coronation in 1953, a splendid occasional piece which makes the ideal coupling. And for this reissue in the 'British Classics' series, Decca have added Chung's classic account of the *Violin concerto.*

Willcocks scores over some rivals in his pacing which, far more than is common, follows the example set by the composer himself in his two recordings. Speeds tend to be a degree faster, as in *By the waters of Babylon* which flows evenly yet without haste. The soloist, Gwynne Howell, firm and dark of tone, is among the finest of all exponents but, with the Bach Choir placed rather more distantly than in most versions, this is not as incisive as its finest rivals. The *Coronation Te Deum* receives a richly idiomatic performance, and Willcocks also gives weight and thrust to the *Gloria,* with the tenor, Neil Mackie, outstanding among the soloists. The microphone unfortunately catches an unevenness in Ameral Gunson's mezzo. The recording is warmly reverberant, not ideally clear on choral detail but easy to listen to.

(i) *Christopher Columbus (suite of incidental music);* (ii) *Anon in love;* (iii) *4 Songs after Edith Sitwell: Daphne; Through gilded trellises; Long steel grass; Old Sir Faulk. A Song for the Lord Mayor's table; The Twelve (an anthem for the Feast of any Apostle).*
*** Chan. Dig. CHAN 8824; *ABTD 1449* [id.]. (i) Linda Finnie, Arthur Davies; (ii) Martyn Hill; (iii) Jill Gomez; Westminster Singers, City of L. Sinfonia, Hickox.

The composer's own orchestral versions of his song-cycles *Anon in love* (for tenor) and *A Song for the Lord Mayor's table* (for soprano) are so beautifully judged that they transcend the originals, which had, respectively, guitar and piano accompaniments. The strength and beauty of these strongly characterized songs is enormously enhanced, particularly in performances as positive as these by Martyn Hill and Jill Gomez. The anthem, *The Twelve*, which Walton wrote for his old college, Christ Church, Oxford, to words by W. H. Auden, also emerges far more powerfully with orchestral instead of organ accompaniment. The four Sitwell songs were orchestrated by Christopher Palmer, who also devised the suite from Walton's incidental music to Louis MacNeice's wartime radio play, *Christopher Columbus*, buried for half a century. It is a rich score which brings more happy anticipations of the *Henry V* film-music in the choral writing, and even of the opera *Troilus and Cressida*, as well as overtones of *Belshazzar's Feast*. Warmly committed performances, opulently recorded.

OPERA

The Bear (complete).
☞ *** Chan. Dig. CHAN 9245 [id.]. Della Jones, Opie, Shirley-Quirk, Northern Sinfonia, Hickox.

When Sir William Walton rather surprisingly agreed to write an opera for Benjamin Britten's Aldeburgh Festival, he took it as a challenge. In its way the one-Acter *The Bear*, based on Chekhov, matches in its point and flair any of Britten's own chamber operas written for Aldeburgh. Walton used to suggest that only Britten would have opted in his chamber operas for an orchestral lay-out so awkward for the composer, using single instead of the usual double woodwind, thus limiting options. In following that formula for *The Bear*, Walton betrayed no signs of struggle whatever, producing textures that are sumptuous rather than spare. It is a masterly score, with the farcical element in the Chekhov reflected in dozens of parodies and tongue-in-cheek musical references, starting cheekily with echoes of Britten's own *Midsummer Night's Dream*.

Just how rich the piece is comes out in this very welcome recording, the first on CD, in almost every way outshining the old LP version of 1967, long unavailable. Already in Chandos's Walton series Richard Hickox has shown what an understanding interpreter he is. Here with members of the Northern Sinfonia he paces the music superbly, flexibly heightening the moments of mock-melodrama that punctuate this tale of a mourning widow who faces the demands of one of her dead husband's creditors. The casting of the three characters is ideal, with Della Jones even more commanding as the affronted widow than Monica Sinclair was before, with words much clearer. Alan Opie far outshines his predecessor, clean-cut and incisive as the creditor or 'Bear' of the title, and with John Shirley-Quirk as the old retainer. In many ways this is a piece – with its climactic duel scene leading to an amorous *coup-de-foudre* – which comes off even better on disc than on stage.

Troilus and Cressida: Scenes: (i) Act I: *Is Cressida a slave?; Slowly it all comes back;* Act II: *How can I sleep if one last doubt remain;* (ii) *Is anyone there?;* (i) *If one last doubt; Now close your arms; Interlude; From isle to isle chill waters;* Act III: *All's well!; Diomede! Father!.*
☞ (M) *** EMI (i) mono; (ii) stereo CDM7 64199-2. (i) Lewis, Schwarzkopf, M. Sinclair, Philh. O; (ii) Collier, Pears, ROHCG O; composer.

Walton wrote this superbly lyrical and atmospheric opera with Schwarzkopf in mind to play the heroine. She never sang the part on stage, but these highlights are more than enough to show what we missed. The melodies may not be as immediately striking as Puccini's but they grow more haunting on repetition, and it would be hard to find a more directly appealing modern romantic opera. The selections are well chosen, and for the reissue a reminder of Sir Peter Pears's Pandarus is now included. As a Decca artist he was not included in the original EMI recording, but now his brief duet with Maria Collier (the Cressida of the 1963 Covent Garden revival) can happily be included. It was recorded in stereo in 1968, again using the Kingsway Hall, the venue for the original sessions 13 years earlier. With Walter Legge then producing, it is not surprising that the mono quality is almost as impressive as the later stereo, particularly the scene in Act III (*All's well*) with Cressida, Evadne and the Watchman which has a magical sense of perspective. A most valuable and rewarding reissue.

Ward, John (1571–1638)

Madrigals: *Come sable night; Cruel unkind; Die not, fond man; Hope of my heart; If heaven's just wrath; If the deep sighs; I have retreated; My breast I'll set; Oft have I tender'd; Out from the vale; Retire, my troubled soul; Sweet Philomel.*
*** Hyp. Dig. CDA 66256 [id.]. Consort of Musicke, Anthony Rooley.

Ward's music speaks with a distinctive voice, free from the self-conscious melancholy that afflicts some of his contemporaries. He chooses poetry of high quality and his music is always finely proportioned and organic in conception. These settings represent the madrigal tradition at its finest; such is the quality of this music and the accomplishment with which it is presented that collectors who respond to this repertoire should not hesitate.

Ward, Robert (born 1917)

(i) *Symphony No. 6;* (ii) *Appalachian ditties and dances;* (iii) *Dialogues;* (iv) *Lamentation and Scherzo.*
** Bay Cities BCD 1015 [id.]. (i) St Stephen's CO, Lorenzo Muti; (ii) Stephen Shipps; (ii; iv) Eric Larsen; (iii) Amadeus Trio.

Robert Ward's idiom is tonal and unproblematic and his music is impeccably crafted. However, this disc is a disappointment: the *Symphony* is pretty anonymous, with none of the freshness one recalls from his earlier music, and there are few strong or individual ideas in the remaining pieces. Generally goodish performances and recording.

Warlock, Peter (1894–1930)

Capriol suite (for strings); *Serenade for strings (for the sixtieth birthday of Delius).*
☞ (M) *** Decca 440 325-2 [id.]. ASMF, Marriner – BUTTERWORTH: *Banks of green willow* etc.; VAUGHAN WILLIAMS: *Lark ascending* etc. ***

Capriol suite (orchestral version); *Serenade for strings (for the sixtieth birthday of Delius).*
*** Chan. Dig. CHAN 8808; *ABTD 1436* [id.]. Ulster O, Vernon Handley – MOERAN: *Serenade* etc. ***

The *Capriol suite* exists in piano-duet form, a very familiar version for strings (both from 1926), and the present full orchestral score, which followed in 1928. The effect is to rob the music of some of its astringency. A dryish wine is replaced with one with the fullest bouquet, for the wind instruments make the textures more rococo in feeling as well as increasing the colour. There are losses as well as gains, but it is good to have Handley's fine performance, made to sound opulent by the acoustics of Ulster Hall, Belfast. The lovely *Serenade*, for strings alone, is also played and recorded very beautifully.

Warlock's gentle *Serenade*, written for Delius, is beautifully played and recorded here by Marriner, an unjustly neglected work receiving its due. The *Capriol suite*, based on Elizabethan dances, is given a comparably lively, polished and stylish account which readily reveals the freshness of Warlock's invention. The recording is first rate.

'Centenary collection': (i) *Capriol suite;* (ii) *Serenade to Frederick Delius on his 60th birthday.* Songs: (iii) *Adam lay ybounden;* (iv) *Autumn twilight;* (v) *Balulalow;* (vi) *Bethlehem Down;* (vii) *Captain Stratton's fancy;* (viii) *The Curlew* (song-cycle); (ix) *I saw a fair maiden;* (x) *The Lady's birthday* (arrangement); (v) *Pretty ring time;* (x) *The shrouding of the Duchess of Malfi;* (xi) *Where riches is everlasting;* (xii) *Yarmouth Fair.*
☞ (M) *** EMI CDM5 65101-2 [id.]. (i) E. Sinf., Neville Dilkes; (ii) Bournemouth Sinf., Norman Del Mar; (iii) Robert Hammersley, Gavin Williams; (iv) Frederick Harvey, Gerald Moore; (v) Janet Baker, Philip Ledger; (vi) Guildford Cathedral Ch., Barry Rose; (vii) Robert Lloyd, Nina Walker; (viii) Ian Partridge, Music Group of London; (ix) Westminster Abbey Ch., Douglas Guest; (x) Baccholian Singers, Jennifer Partridge; (xi) King's College, Cambridge, Ch., Willcocks; (xii) Owen Brannigan, Ernest Lush.

A splendid anthology of Warlock – less well-known as the music critic, Peter Heseltine – showing some of the riches that lie hidden in the EMI back-catalogue. Opening with one of our favourite versions of the *Capriol suite* from the English Sinfonia under Neville Dilkes, brightly coloured and full of vigour, followed by Warlock's touchingly tender tribute to Delius, the selection ranges over a well-chosen selection of favourite songs, solo and choral. The other key item is *The Curlew*, Warlock's most striking and ambitious work, a continuous setting of a sequence of poems by Yeats which reflect the darker side of his complex personality. Ian Partridge, with the subtlest shading of tone-colour and the most sensitive response to word-meanings, gives an intensely poetic performance, beautifully recorded. Among other performances those of Dame Janet Baker stand out, but many of the songs here are persuasively beautiful. At the very close of the recital Owen Brannigan restores our high spirits with his characteristically ebullient delivery of *Yarmouth Fair*. The transfers are consistently well managed.

Songs: *As ever I saw; Autumn twilight; The bachelor; The bayly berith the bell away; Captain Stratton's fancy; First mercy; The fox; Hey, trolly, loly lo; Ha'nacker Mill; I held love's head; The jolly shepherd; Late summer; Lullaby; Milkmaids; Mourne no more; Mr Belloc's fancy; My gostly fader; My own country; The night; Passing by; Piggesnie; Play-acting; Rest, sweet nymphs; Sleep; Sweet content; Take, o take those lips away; There is a lady sweet and fair; Thou gav'st me leave to kiss; Walking the woods; When as the rye; The wind from the west; Yarmouth Fair.*
*** Chan. Dig. CHAN 8643 [id.]. Benjamin Luxon, David Willison.

A remarkably generous recital of 32 Warlock songs, ranging wide, from the melancholy and drama to 'hey-nonny-nonny' Elizabethan pastiche. Songs like *Autumn twilight*, the powerfully expressive *Late summer* and *Captain Stratton's fancy* are appealing in utterly different ways, and there is not a single number in the programme that does not show the composer either in full imaginative flow or simply enjoying himself, as in *Yarmouth Fair*. Luxon's performances are first class and David Willison provides sensitive and sparkling accompaniments. The recording is first class.

Wassenaer, Unico Wilhelm (1692–1766)

Concerti armonici Nos. 1–6.
☞ *** Hyp. Dig. CDA 66670 [id.]. Brandenburg Cons., Goodman.

These splendid concertos have long been attributed to Pergolesi, but finally (in 1979) their true source was discovered, one Unico Wilhelm, Graf von Wassenaer, a Dutch part-time composer of remarkable accomplishment. Their invention, vigorous and expressive, is sustained by a remarkably harmonic individuality: in short they are first-class works, almost on a par with the *concerti grossi* of Handel. These fine new performances restore them to the catalogue in the most presentable manner and Hyperion's recording is very good indeed, to eclipse previous issues of this rewarding repertoire.

Waxman, Franz (1906–67)

Film scores: *Bride of Frankenstein: Creation of the female monster; Old Aquaintance: Elegy for strings. Philadelphia Story: Fanfare; Main title; True love. A Place in the Sun: suite. Prince Valiant: suite. Rebecca: suite. Sunset Boulevard: suite. Taras Bulba: suite.*
🏵 (M) *** BMG/RCA GD 80708; *GK 80708* [0708-2-RG; *0708-4-RG*]. Nat. PO, Charles Gerhardt.

Of the many European musicians who crossed the Atlantic to make careers in Hollywood, Franz Waxman was among the most distinguished. His first important score was for James Whale's *Bride of Frankenstein*, a horror movie to which many film buffs give classic status. His marvellously evocative music for *The creation of the female monster* was restored by the conductor, mainly from listening to the film sound-track, as the orchestral parts are lost. Waxman stayed on to write for 188 films over 32 years. The opening of the first item on this CD and tape, the *Suite* from *Prince Valiant*, immediately shows the vigour of Waxman's invention and the brilliance of his Richard Straussian orchestration, and this score includes one of those sweeping string tunes which are the very epitome of Hollywood film music. Perhaps the finest of these comes in *A Place in the Sun*, and in the *Suite* it is used to preface an imaginative rhapsodical movement for solo alto sax (brilliantly played here by Ronnie Chamberlain). The collection ends with *The ride to Dubno* from *Taras Bulba* (Waxman's last film-score), which has thrilling impetus and energy and is scored with great flair. The orchestral playing throughout is marvellously eloquent, and the conductor's dedication is obvious. The recording is rich and full, with no lack of brilliance in this very successful transfer to compact disc.

Weber, Carl Maria von (1786–1826)

Bassoon concerto in F, Op. 75.
*** Denon Dig. CO 79281 [id.]. Werba, V. String Soloists, Honeck – HUMMEL; MOZART: *Concertos.*
***

Michael Werba's performance of the Weber concerto completes an attractive triptych. Both he and the accompanying group under Rainer Honeck capture the grand operatic flourishes of the first movement and the geniality of the finale. The recording is well balanced and vivid.

Clarinet concertino in C min., Op. 26.
*** ASV Dig. CDDCA 559; *ZCDCA 559* [id.]. Emma Johnson, ECO, Groves – CRUSELL:
    Concerto No. 2 *** ⊛; BAERMANN: *Adagio* ***; ROSSINI: *Introduction, theme and variations.* ***

Emma Johnson is in her element in Weber's delightful *Concertino.* Her phrasing is wonderfully
beguiling and her use of light and shade agreeably subtle, while she finds a superb lilt in the final
section, pacing the music to bring out its charm rather than achieve breathless bravura. Sir Charles
Groves provides an admirable accompaniment, and the recording is eminently realistic and naturally
balanced.

Clarinet concerto No. 1 in F min., J.114.
*** ASV Dig. CDDCA 585; *ZCDCA 585* [id.]. Emma Johnson, ECO, Yan Pascal Tortelier –
    DEBUSSY: *Rapsodie;* CRUSELL: *Introduction, theme and variations;* TARTINI: *Concertino.* ***

In this fine, inspired version of the Weber *First Concerto* the subtlety of Emma Johnson's expression,
even in relation to most of her older rivals is astonishing, with pianissimos more daringly extreme and
with distinctively persuasive phrasing in the slow movement, treated warmly and spaciously. In the
sparkling finale she is wittier than almost any, plainly enjoying herself to the full, and is given natural
sound, set in a helpful acoustic.

Clarinet concertos Nos. 1 in F min., Op. 73; 2 in E flat, Op. 74; Clarinet concertino in E flat, Op. 26.
⊛ *** Denon Dig. CO 79551 [id.]. Paul Meyer, RPO, Günther Herbig.
*** Virgin/EMI Dig. VC7 59002-2 [id.]. Antony Pay, O of Age of Enlightenment.
(BB) *** Naxos Dig. 8.550378 [id.]. Ernst Ottensamer, Slovak State PO (Košice), Johannes Wildner.

The brilliant twenty-year-old Paul Meyer shows his prowess here in scintillating accounts of these
three Weberian showpieces. He takes every risk in the book, using the widest possible dynamic range,
at one moment using a robust cutting edge to his tone, at another fining it down to a magical *sotto
voce.* In the slow movement of the *F minor Concerto* he blends delicately with the horn chorale and
then, after a beautifully controlled diminuendo, dashes off, chortling through the finale with great
glee. He is fortunate in having an excellent accompanist in Günther Herbig, and the RPO provides
admirable support: the opening tutti of the *E flat Concerto* is particularly impressive. The *Concertino*
is sheer delight from beginning to end. With fine recording this record is in a class of its own.

Antony Pay and the Orchestra of the Age of Enlightenment offer period-instrument performances.
Pay uses a copy of a seven-keyed clarinet by Simiot of Lyons from 1800. The sonority is cleaner and
less bland than can be the case in modern performances, and the solo playing is both expert and
sensitive. A further gesture to authenticity is the absence of a conductor; however, the ensemble might
have been even better and the texture more finely judged and balanced had there been one. The
recording is vivid and truthful.

Neither the soloist nor the conductor on Naxos is a household name. Ernst Ottensamer is a highly
sensitive clarinettist, who has played with the major Viennese orchestras and is a member of the
Vienna Wind Ensemble. His account of the two *Clarinet concertos* can hold its own against nearly all
the competition in the current catalogue in any price category. The Košice orchestra also responds
well to Johannes Wildner's direction, and the recorded sound is very natural and well balanced. A
real bargain.

Clarinet concerto No. 2 in E flat, Op. 74.
☞ (M) *** Decca 433 727-2 [id.]. Gervase de Peyer, LSO, C. Davis – MOZART; SPOHR: *Concertos.*
    ***

This first appeared in 1961, coupled with Spohr. For the reissue, the Mozart has been added to make
an entertaining triptych, well recorded. With its operatic *Andante* and witty finale, the work invites
and receives masterly playing from Gervase de Peyer – he is quite captivating in the closing *Rondo,*
with some hair-raising roulades towards the end. The studio recording is a little dryish, but not
excessively so. Excellent value.

Horn concertino in E min., Op. 45.
*** Ph. Dig. 412 237-2 [id.]. Baumann, Leipzig GO, Masur – R. STRAUSS: *Horn concertos.* **(*)

Baumann plays Weber's opening lyrical melody so graciously that the listener is led to believe that
this is a more substantial work than it is. At the end of the *Andante* Baumann produces an undulating
series of chords (by gently singing the top note as he plays) and the effect is spine-tingling, while the
easy virtuosity of the closing *Polacca* is hardly less breathtaking. Masur's accompaniment has
matching warmth, while the Leipzig Hall adds its usual flattering ambience.

Konzertstück in F min., Op. 79.
*** Ph. 412 251-2 [id.]. Brendel, LSO, Abbado – SCHUMANN: *Piano concerto.* ***

This Philips version of Weber's programmatic *Konzertstück* is very brilliant indeed, and finds the distinguished soloist in his very best form: Brendel is wonderfully light and invariably imaginative. In every respect, including the recording quality, this is unlikely to be surpassed for a long time.

Overtures: *Abu Hassan; Der Beherrscher der Geister; Euryanthe; Der Freischütz; Oberon; Peter Schmoll; Invitation to the dance* (orch. Berlioz), *Op. 65.*
⊛ *** Nimbus Dig. NI 5154 [id.]. Hanover Band, Roy Goodman.

Goodman and the Hanover Band give delectable performances of the six Weber overtures plus *Invitation to the dance* in Berlioz's arrangement. This is among the most persuasive records of period performance, likely to convert even those who resist new-style authenticity. The rasp of trombones at the start of *Euryanthe* has a thrilling tang, and the warm acoustic ensures that the authentic string-players sound neither scrawny nor abrasive, yet present rapid passage-work with crystal clarity. Of feathery lightness, the scurrying of violins in the *Abu Hassan overture* is a delight, and each item – including a rarity in *Der Beherrscher der Geister* – brings its moments of magic, with Goodman, both fresh and sympathetic, securing consistently lively and alert playing from his team.

Overtures: *Der Freischütz; Oberon.*
(M) *** DG 415 840-2 [id.]. Bav. RSO, Kubelik – MENDELSSOHN: *Midsummer Night's Dream.* ***

Kubelik offers Weber's two greatest overtures as a fine bonus for his extended selection from Mendelssohn's *Midsummer Night's Dream* incidental music. The playing is first class and compares favourably with the Karajan versions.

Symphonies Nos. 1 in C; 2 in C.
*** ASV Dig. CDDCA 515; *ZCDCA 515* [id.]. ASMF, Marriner.

Curiously, both Weber's *Symphonies* are in C major, yet each has its own individuality and neither lacks vitality or invention. Sir Neville Marriner has their full measure; these performances combine vigour and high spirits with the right degree of gravitas (not too much) in the slow movements. The recording is clear and full in the bass, but the bright upper range brings a touch of digital edge to the upper strings.

CHAMBER AND INSTRUMENTAL MUSIC

Clarinet quintet in B flat, Op. 34.
(M) *** Decca 430 297-2 [id.]. Gervase de Peyer, Melos Ens. – HUMMEL: *Piano quintet etc.* ***
☞ *** O-L Dig. 433 044-2 [id.]. Antony Pay, AAM Chamber Ens. – BEETHOVEN: *Septet.* **(*)

Clarinet quintet; Flute trio in G min., Op. 63 (for flute, cello and piano).
*** CRD CRD 3398; *CRDC 4098* [id.]. Nash Ens.

(i) *Clarinet quintet;* (ii) *Grand Duo concertante, Op. 48; 7 Variations on a theme from Silvana, Op. 33.*
**(*) Chan. Dig. CHAN 8366; *ABTD 1131* [id.]. Hilton, (i) Lindsay Qt; (ii) Keith Swallow.

Weber's *Quintet* is delightful music as well as being a willing vehicle for the soloist's immaculate display of pyrotechnics. Gervase de Peyer is in his element here and the strings give him admirable support. The 1959 (originally Oiseau-Lyre) recording is first class; it is vivid, with plenty of atmosphere, and does not sound at all dated.

On the CRD version, Antony Pay makes the very most of the work's bravura, catching the exuberance of the *Capriccio* third movement and the breezy gaiety of the finale. The Nash players provide an admirable partnership and then adapt themselves readily to the different mood of the *Trio*, another highly engaging work with a picturesque slow movement, described as a *Shepherd's lament.* The recording is first class, vivid yet well balanced.

For his second Oiseau-Lyre recording, Antony Pay uses a reconstruction of an 1810 clarinet and he has completely tamed it. This is another fresh and pleasing performance, with a finely sensitive *Adagio*, a brilliant third movement and some splendid giocoso roulades in the bravura finale. Those wanting an authentic account will find this hard to beat.

Janet Hilton plays with considerable authority and spirit though she is not always as mellifluous as her rivals. However, her account of the *Grand Duo concertante* is a model of fine ensemble, as are the *Variations on a theme from Silvana* of 1811, in both of which Keith Swallow is an equally expert partner. At times the acoustic seems almost too reverberant in the two pieces for clarinet and piano, but the sound in the *Quintet* is eminently satisfactory.

7 Variations on a theme from Silvana in B flat, Op. 33.
*** Chan. Dig. CHAN 8506; *ABTD 1216* [id.]. Gervase de Peyer, Gwenneth Pryor – SCHUBERT: *Arpeggione sonata;* SCHUMANN: *Fantasiestücke* etc. ***

These engaging Weber *Variations* act as a kind of encore to Schubert's *Arpeggione sonata* and with their innocent charm they follow on naturally. They are most winningly played by Gervase de Peyer; Gwenneth Pryor accompanies admirably. The recording is first class.

Piano sonatas Nos. 1 in C, Op. 24; 2 in A flat, Op. 39.
(M) *** Pianissimo Dig. PP 20792 [id.]. Martin Jones.

Piano sonatas Nos. 1–2; Rondo brillante in E flat (La Gaîté), Op. 52; Invitation to the dance, Op. 65.
*** CRD Dig. CRD 3485; *CRDC 4185* [id.]. Hamish Milne.

These two Weber *Sonatas* are not easy to bring off, with their classical heritage and operatic freedom of line. Martin Jones is clearly at home in both works, pacing the music so that it never sounds brittle, revealing an unexpected depth where some pianists would find only opportunities for surface display. He is particularly impressive in the *A flat major* work, concluding the Rondo finale with a fine balance between virtuosity and grazioso feeling. The recording, made in the resonant but not too-resonant acoustic of the Concert Hall of Cardiff University, is admirable and seems just right for his relatively grand manner.

Hamish Milne's style is less overtly expansive, more chimerical, his performances have a lightness of touch that is most appealing, without ever being superficial, and his playing in the slow movements has attractive lyrical feeling. If you want added gravitas, turn to Jones, but Milne's readings are equally truthful to the composer's intentions. Moreover he also provides a sparkling account of the *Rondo brillante* and, as a final encore, a totally captivating account of the charming *Invitation to the dance*, making it sound every bit as appealing on the piano as in Berlioz's orchestration. He is realistically recorded in the BBC Studios at Pebble Mill in Birmingham.

Piano sonata No. 2 in A flat, Op. 39.
*** Ph. Dig. 426 439-2 [id.]. Alfred Brendel – BRAHMS: *4 Ballades.* ***

Masterly playing from Alfred Brendel, who makes out a strong case for the Weber *Sonata* which in his hands has seriousness and strength as well as charm. Everything is thoroughly thought out, and one feels that the slightest hesitation is carefully calculated. If there is a certain want of spontaneity, there is no want of mastery. Brendel is recorded in sound of marvellous presence and clarity.

Piano sonata Nos. 3 in D min., Op. 49; 4 in E min., Op. 70; Polacca brillante in E (L'Hilarité) (with LISZT: *Introduzione (Adagio)).*
*** CRD Dig. CRD 3486; *CRDC 4186* [id.]. Hamish Milne.

Hamish Milne here completes his admirable survey of the Weber *Piano sonatas* with a sterner approach to the opening *Allegro feroce* of *No. 3 in D minor,* cast in an almost Beethovenian mould. But Weber was always himself, and operatic feeling inevitably creeps into the lyrical material as well as the passage-work. The last sonata is more introspective in its colouring and feeling, and the work concludes with a ruthless Tarantella, driven on by its own restless energy. The *Polacca brillante* returns to the world of dazzling articulation and sparkling display. It is heard here with a slow introduction which Liszt arranged from the *Grande Polonaise* of 1808. Hamish Milne's playing is thoroughly inside Weber's world and technically equal to the composer's prodigious demands. He is very well recorded.

OPERA

Der Freischütz (complete).
(M) *** EMI CMS7 69342-2 (2). Grümmer, Otto, Schock, Prey, Wiemann, Kohn, Frick, German Op. Ch., Berlin, BPO, Keilberth.
*** DG 415 432-2 (2) [id.]. Janowitz, Mathis, Schreier, Adam, Vogel, Crass, Leipzig R. Ch., Dresden State O, Carlos Kleiber.
☞ (B) ** DG Double 439 717-2 (2) [id.]. Seefried, Holm, Streich, Böhme, Waechter, Bav. R. Ch. & O, Jochum.
☞ ** Ph. Dig. 426 319-2 (2) [id.]. Karita Mattila, Francisco Araiza, Eva Lind, Ekkehard Wlaschiha, Kurt Moll, Dresden Op. Ch. & State O, Sir Colin Davis.

Keilberth's is a warm, exciting account of Weber's masterpiece which makes all the dated conventions of the work seem fresh and new. In particular the *Wolf's glen* scene on CD acquires something of the genuine terror that must have struck the earliest audiences and which is far more impressive than any mere scene-setting with wood and cardboard in the opera house. The casting of the magic bullets with each one numbered in turn, at first in eerie quiet and then in crescendo amid the howling of demons, is superbly conveyed. The bite of the orchestra and the proper balance of the voices in relation to it, with the effect of space and distance, helps also to create the illusion. Elisabeth Grümmer sings more sweetly and sensitively than one ever remembers before, with Agathe's prayer exquisitely done. Lisa Otto is really in character, with genuine coquettishness. Schock is not an ideal tenor, but he sings ably enough. The Kaspar of Karl Kohn is generally well focused, and the playing of the Berlin Philharmonic has plenty of polish. The overall effect is immensely atmospheric and enjoyable.

The DG set marked Carlos Kleiber's first major recording venture and this fine, incisive account of Weber's atmospheric and adventurous score fulfilled all expectations. With the help of an outstanding cast, excellent work by the recording producer, and transparently clear recording, this is a most compelling version of an opera which transfers well to the gramophone. Only occasionally does Kleiber betray a fractional lack of warmth, but the full drama of the work is splendidly projected in the enhanced CD format.

On the face of it, Jochum's cast is as impressive as that on the EMI version, but there are too many disappointments here for the DG set to measure up. To begin with, Seefried is decidedly off-colour. She seems quite incapable of producing anything like a *mezza voce*, and that is perhaps the first essential of a good Agathe. There is nothing 'inner'; it is all too matter-of-fact, with the usual creamy tone sounding beautiful but hardly ever moving or in character. Streich sings her charming coquettish song, *Kommt ein schlanker Bursch gegangen*, with delicious lightness, but again the characterization is not very well conveyed and what dialogue remains here is not done as dramatically as on the HMV set. The recording weighs heavily in favour of the voices at the expense of the orchestra, and in the Wolf's Glen scene this detracts from the sense of excitement. Jochum, too, is below form in this scene and there is none of the biting tension of Keilberth's interpretation. However, overall the performance is lively enough and the CD transfer of a set first published on LP in 1960 is remarkably vivid. This is very reasonably priced, but the reservations remain while the inadequate documentation offers a very brief synopsis, although some judicious cutting was needed in order to fit the opera originally on to a pair of LPs.

After his years of experience at Covent Garden, Sir Colin Davis paces this magic score very well indeed, and the Dresden forces respond with some fine playing and singing. To add to the drama there are plenty of production sounds, even including the barking of hounds, with shots that have you jumping out of your seat. Even so, this is a set that fails to convey the full power of this high-romantic horror story, most strikingly of all in the Wolf's Glen scene, where the casting of the magic bullets sounds tame, not frightening at all. The singing is flawed too. Karita Mattila's warm, vibrant soprano is apt enough for Agathe, and she controls the soaring lines of her two big arias very beautifully, but *Und ob die Wolke* brings under-the-note coloration which may distress some ears. As Max, Francisco Araiza is seriously stressed, with the basically beautiful voice sounding throaty, and Eva Lind is unpleasantly fluttery and shallow as Aennchen. Ekkehard Wlaschiha, best known as Alberich in the *Ring*, is darkly sinister as Kaspar, and it is good too to have Kurt Moll as the Hermit. The impact of the performance is blunted by the heavy reverberation, more than usual in recordings from the Lukaskirche in Dresden.

Der Freischütz: highlights.

☞ *(*) Ph. 438 497-2 [id.]. Mattila, Araiza, Lind, Wlaschiha, Liepzig R. Ch., Dresden State O, Sir Colin Davis.

With flawed singing the Philips highlights CD comes from a disappointing complete set. The CD brings a playing time of 67 minutes, including the *Overture*.

Oberon (complete).

(M) *** DG 419 038-2 (2) [id.]. Grobe, Nilsson, Domingo, Prey, Hamari, Schiml, Bav. R. Ch. & SO, Kubelik.

☞ *(*) EMI Dig. CDS7 54739-2 (2) [Ang. CDCB 54739]. Gary Lakes, Deborah Voigt, Ben Heppner, Dwayne Croft, Delores Ziegler, Victoria Livengood, Machiko Obata, Cologne Concert Soc., Conlon.

Weber's delicately conceived score is a sequence of illogical arias, scenas and ensembles strung together by an absurd pantomime plot. Although, even on record, the result is slacker because of that loose construction, one can appreciate the contribution of Weber, in a performance as stylish and refined as on DG. The original issue included dialogue and a narrative spoken by one of Oberon's fairy characters. In the reissue this is omitted, cutting the number of discs from three to two, yet leaving the music untouched. With Birgit Nilsson commanding in *Ocean, thou mighty monster*, and excellent singing from the other principals, helped by Kubelik's ethereally light handling of the orchestra, the set can be recommended without reservation, for the recording remains of excellent quality.

Conlon's EMI version presents the Mahler edition of this ragbag of a work, re-ordering the items and presenting them in German translation with a linking narration, often as melodrama, over orchestral links drawn from material in the *Overture*. Sadly, the performance is not only indifferently cast, Conlon's direction is prosaic, lacking the fairytale fantasy which this often magical score requires. Ben Heppner has an attractive tenor, with both lyric and heroic qualities apt for the role of Hüon, but he is strained by the impossibly high tessitura. Gary Lakes' heroic tenor is far rougher in the surprisingly less prominent role of Oberon, and Deborah Voigt, though fresh of tone, is rather over-parted as Rezia, particularly in face of the formidable demands of *Ocean, thou mighty monster*. Delores Ziegler as Fatima is more aptly cast, though even she grows unsteady under pressure. The low-level sound with edgy violins and over-close dialogue undermines the magic still further.

Webern, Anton (1883–1945)

(i) *Concerto for nine instruments, Op. 24; 5 Movements for string quartet* (orchestral version), *Op. 5; Passacaglia, Op. 1; 6 Pieces for large orchestra, Op. 6; 5 Pieces for orchestra, Op. 10; Symphony, Op. 21; Variations for orchestra, Op. 30*. Arrangements of: BACH: *Musical offering: Fugue* (1935). (ii) SCHUBERT: *German dances* (for small orchestra), *Op. posth*. Chamber music: (iii) *6 Bagatelles for string quartet, Op. 9; 5 Movements for string quartet, Op. 5;* (iv; v) *4 Pieces for violin and piano, Op. 7;* (v; vi) *3 Small pieces for cello and piano, Op. 11;* (v; vii) *Quartet, Op. 22* (for piano, violin, clarinet & saxophone); (iii) *String quartet, Op. 28; String trio, Op. 20;* (v) *Variations for piano, Op. 27*. (Vocal) (viii; i) *Das Augenlicht, Op. 26;* (ix; x) *5 Canons on Latin texts, Op. 16;* (viii; ix; i) *Cantata No. 1, Op. 29;* (viii; ix; xi; i) *Cantata No. 2, Op. 31;* (viii) *Entflieht auf leichten Kähnen, Op. 2;* (ix; x) *5 Sacred songs, Op. 15;* (xii; v) *5 Songs, Op. 3; 5 Songs, Op. 4;* (xii; x) *2 Songs, Op. 8;* (xii; v) *4 Songs, Op. 12;* (xii; x) *4 Songs, Op. 13; 6 Songs, Op. 14;* (ix; x; xiii) *3 Songs, Op. 18;* (viii; i) *2 Songs, Op. 19;* (xii; v) *3 Songs, Op. 23;* (ix; v) *3 Songs, Op. 25;* (ix; x) *3 Traditional rhymes, Op. 17*.

(M) *** Sony SM3K 45845 (3) [id.]. (i) LSO (or members), Pierre Boulez; (ii) Frankfurt R. O, composer (recorded December 1932); (iii) Juilliard Qt (or members); (iv) Stern; (v) Rosen; (vi) Piatigorsky; (vii) Majeske, Marcellus, Weinstein; (viii) John Alldis Ch.; (ix) Lukomska; (x) with Ens., Boulez; (xi) McDaniel; (xii) Harper; (xiii) with John Williams. Overall musical direction: Boulez.

These three CDs contain all Webern's works with opus numbers, as well as the string orchestra arrangements of Op. 5 and the orchestration of the *Fugue* from Bach's *Musical offering*. A rare recording of Webern himself conducting his arrangement of Schubert dances is also included. What Pierre Boulez above all demonstrates in the orchestral works (including those with chorus) is that, for all his seeming asceticism, Webern was working on human emotions. The Juilliard Quartet and the John Alldis Choir convey comparable commitment; though neither Heather Harper nor Halina Lukomska is ideally cast in the solo vocal music, Boulez brings out the best in both of them in the works with orchestra. Rarely can a major composer's whole *oeuvre* be appreciated in so compact a span. There are excellent notes, every item is cued, and perhaps it is carping to regret that the *Passacaglia* and *Variations for orchestra* were not indexed.

Concerto for 9 instruments, Op. 24.
(M) *** Chan. CHAN 6534; *MBTD 6534* [id.]. Nash Ens., Simon Rattle – SCHOENBERG: *Pierrot Lunaire*. ***

This late Webern piece, tough, spare and uncompromising, makes a valuable fill-up for Jane Manning's outstanding version of Schoenberg's *Pierrot Lunaire*, a 1977 recording originally made for the Open University. First-rate sound and a beautifully clean CD transfer.

Langsamer satz (arr. Schwarz).
☞ *** Delos Dig. DE 3121 [id.]. Seattle SO, Gerard Schwarz – HONEGGER: *Symphony No. 2 ;* R. STRAUSS: *Metamorphosen*. ***

The slow movement Webern composed in 1905 for string quartet sounds even more Mahlerian in Gerard Schwarz's transcription for full strings, which is eloquently played and sumptuously recorded.

5 Movements, Op. 5; Passacaglia, Op. 1; 6 Pieces for orchestra, Op. 6; Symphony, Op. 21.
(M) *** DG 427 424-2 (3) [id.]. BPO, Karajan – BERG: *Lyric suite; 3 Pieces;* SCHOENBERG: *Pelleas und Melisande; Variations; Verklaerte Nacht.* ***
(M) *** DG 423 254-2 [id.]. BPO, Karajan.

Available either separately or within Karajan's three-CD compilation, this collection, devoted to four compact and chiselled Webern works, is in many ways the most remarkable of all. Karajan's expressive refinement reveals the emotional undertones behind this seemingly austere music, and the results are riveting. Karajan secures a highly sensitive response from the Berlin Philharmonic, who produce sonorities as seductive as Debussy. Incidentally, he plays the 1928 version of Op. 6. A strong recommendation, with excellent sound.

5 Pieces for orchestra, Op. 10.
(M) *** Mercury 432 006-2 [id.]. LSO, Dorati – BERG: *3 Pieces; Lulu suite;* SCHOENBERG: *5 Pieces.* ***

Webern's *Five pieces*, Op. 10, written between 1911 and 1913, mark a radical point in his early development. Their compression is extreme. The couplings could hardly be more fitting, and the whole record can be strongly recommended to anyone wanting to explore the early work of Schoenberg and his followers before they formalized their ideas in twelve-note technique. Bright, clear, 1962 recording to match the precision of the writing.

6 Pieces for orchestra, Op. 6.
*** EMI Dig. CDC7 49857-2 [id.]. CBSO, Rattle – SCHOENBERG: *5 Pieces;* BERG: *Lulu: suite.* ***
*** DG Dig. 419 781-2 [id.]. BPO, Levine – BERG: *3 Pieces;* SCHOENBERG: *5 Pieces.* ***

Rattle and the CBSO bring out the microcosmic strength of the six Webern *Pieces*, giving them weight and intensity without inflation. Warmth is rightly implied here, but no Mahlerian underlining. A superb performance, given sound of demonstration quality.

Levine brings out the expressive warmth of Webern's writing, with no chill in the spare fragmentation of argument and with much tender poetry. With the longest of the six tiny movements, the *Funeral march*, particularly powerful, it complements the other works on the disc perfectly. Ripe recording, with some spotlighting of individual lines.

Slow movement for string quartet (1905).
⊛ *** Denon Dig. CO 79462 [id.]. Carmina Qt – SZYMANOWSKI: *String quartets Nos. 1 & 2.* *** ⊛
☞ *** DG Dig. 437 836-2. Hagen Qt – DEBUSSY; RAVEL: *Quartets.* ***

The single-movement Webern *Quartet* was composed in Carinthia in the summer of 1905 and was first heard in the 1960s. It has an intense and chromatic study, and is played with great refinement by the Hagen Quartet and beautifully recorded. An excellent *bonne bouche*, if that term is appropriate, for a superb Debussy and Ravel coupling.

On Denon, Webern's early quartet movement is equally beautifully played and comes as a pendant to an altogether outstanding performance and recording of the two Szymanowski quartets.

Weill, Kurt (1900–1950)

(i) *Violin concerto; Kleine Dreigroschenmusik* (suite for wind orchestra from *The Threepenny Opera*).
(M) *** DG 423 255-2 [id.]. (i) Lidell; L. Sinf., Atherton.

Weill's *Concerto* for violin and wind instruments is an early work, resourceful and inventive, the product of a fine intelligence and a good craftsman. The style is somewhat angular (as was that of the young Hindemith) but the textures are always clear and the invention holds the listener's attention throughout. It is splendidly played by Nona Lidell and the wind of the London Sinfonietta, and well recorded too. The *Suite* from *The Threepenny Opera* is given with good spirit and élan.

Symphonies Nos. 1–2.
☞ (M) ** Ph. 434 171-2 [id.]. Leipzig GO, De Waart.

Kurt Weill's pair of symphonies won't be to all tastes, but they are fascinating works, the first amazingly assured for a 'prentice piece, the second masterly and original. The performances here lack something in the bite and intensity which Weill demands but, with fine ensemble and first-rate solo playing presented in warm (1973) sound, this is rather more than a stop-gap. The disc is offered for a limited time-period only.

Theatre songs: *Aufstieg und Fall der Stadt Mahagonny: Alabama song; Wie man sich bettet. Das Berliner Requiem: Zu Potsdam unter den Eichen. Die Dreigroschenoper: Die Moritat von Mackie Messer; Salomon song; Die Ballade von der sexuellen Hörigkeit. One Touch of Venus: I'm a stranger here myself. Der Silbersee: Ich bin eine arme Verwandte; Rom war eine Stadt; Lied des Lotterieagenten.* Songs: *Je ne t'aime pas; Nannas-Lied; Speak low; Westwind.*
*** Decca Dig. 425 204-2 [id.]. Ute Lemper, Berlin R. Ens., John Mauceri.

Ute Lemper is nothing if not a charismatic singer, bringing a powerful combination of qualities to Weill: an ability to put over numbers with cabaret-style punch as toughly and characterfully as Lotte Lenya herself, as well as a technical security that rarely lets her down. Lemper is not the least troubled with singing in English as well as in German, and the recording vividly captures the distinctive timbre of her voice. Many will find her singing more seductive than that of Lotte Lenya, and the accompaniments are a pleasure in themselves, most atmospherically recorded.

The Ballad of Magna Carta; Der Lindberghflug.
*** Capriccio Dig. 60012-l [id.]. Henschel, Tyl, Calaminus, Clemens, Cologne Pro Musica Ch. & RSO, Latham-König; Wirl, Schmidt, Feckler, Minth, Scheeben, Berlin R. Ch. & O, Scherchen.

Der Lindberghflug ('The Lindbergh Flight') is a curiosity, a radio entertainment on the subject which was then (in 1927) hitting the headlines: the first solo flight across the Atlantic by Charles Lindbergh. Brecht wrote the text, and Weill started on the music, but for the Baden-Baden Festival it was diplomatic to ask Hindemith to set some of the numbers, and that is how it first appeared. Only later did Weill set the complete work, and that is how it is given in this excellent Cologne recording. As a curiosity, a historic 1930 performance of the original Weill–Hindemith version, conducted by Hermann Scherchen, is given as an appendix, recorded with a heavy background roar but with astonishingly vivid voices. One can understand why Weill was so enthusiastic about the fine, very German tenor who sang Lindbergh in 1930, Erik Wirl. The tenor in the new recording is not nearly so sweet-toned, and the German narrator delivers his commentary in a casual, matter-of-fact way. Otherwise the performance under Jan Latham-König maintains the high standards of Capriccio's Weill series; and the other, shorter item, *The Ballad of Magna Carta*, another radio feature, written in America in 1940 to fanciful doggerel by Maxwell Anderson, is most enjoyable too, a piece never recorded before. Clear, if rather dry, recording with voices vivid and immediate.

Die Dreigroschenoper (The Threepenny Opera): complete.
*** Decca Dig. 430 075-2 [id.]. Kollo, Lemper, Milva, Adorf, Dernesch, Berlin RIAS Chamber Ch. & Sinf., Mauceri.
*** Sony MK 42637 [id.]. Lenya, Neuss, Trenk-Trebisch, Hesterberg, Schellow, Koczian, Grunert, Ch. & Dance O of Radio Free Berlin, Brückner-Rüggeberg.

By cutting the dialogue down to brief spoken links between numbers and omitting instrumental interludes which merely repeat songs already heard, Decca's all-star production is fitted on to a single, generously filled CD. The opening is not promising, with the Ballad-singer's singing voice – as opposed to his tangy spoken narration – sounding very old and tremulous. There are obvious discrepancies too between the opera-singers, René Kollo and Helga Dernesch, and those in the cabaret tradition, notably the vibrant and provocative Ute Lemper (Polly Peachum) and the gloriously dark-voiced and characterful Milva (Jenny). That entails downward modulation in various numbers, as it did with Lotte Lenya, but the changes from the original are far less extreme. Kollo is good, but Dernesch is even more compelling. The co-ordination of music and presentation makes for a vividly enjoyable experience, even if committed Weill enthusiasts will inevitably disagree with some of the controversial textual and interpretative decisions.

The CBS alternative offers a vividly authentic abridged recording, darkly incisive and atmospheric, with Lotte Lenya giving an incomparable performance as Jenny. All the wrong associations, built up round the music from indifferent performances, melt away in the face of a reading as sharp and intense as this. Bright, immediate, real stereo recording, made the more vivid on CD.

Happy End (play by Brecht with songs); *Die sieben Todsünden (The Seven deadly sins).*
(M) *** Sony mono/stereo MPK 45886 [id.]. Lotte Lenya, male quartet & O, Ch. & O, Brückner-Rüggeberg.

The Sony/CBS performance of *The Seven deadly sins*, with the composer's widow as principal singer, underlines the status of this distinctive mixture of ballet and song-cycle as one of Weill's most concentrated inspirations. The rhythmic verve is irresistible and, though Lenya had to have the music transposed down, her understanding of the idiom is unique. The recording is forward and slightly harsh, though Lenya's voice is not hardened, and the effect is undoubtedly vivid. *Happy end* was made in Hamburg-Harburg in 1960. Lenya turned the songs into a kind of cycle (following a hint from her husband), again transposing where necessary, and her renderings in her individual brand of vocalizing are so compelling they make the scalp tingle.

The Rise and fall of Mahagonny (complete).
**(*) Sony MK 77341 (2) [M2K 37874]. Lenya, Litz, Gunter, Mund, Gollnitz, Markworth, Saverbaum, Roth, Murch (speaker), NW German R. Ch. and O, Brückner-Rüggeberg.

Though Lotte Lenya, with her metallic rasping voice, was more a characterful *diseuse* than a singer, and this bitterly inspired score had to be adapted to suit her limited range, it remains a most memorable performance. The recording lacks atmosphere, with voices (Lenya's in particular) close balanced. Yet even now one can understand how this cynical piece caused public outrage when it was first performed in Leipzig in 1930.

Der Silbersee (complete).
*** Capriccio Dig. 60011-2 (2) [id.]. Heichele, Tamassy, Holdorf, Schmidt, Mayer, Korte, Thomas, Cologne Pro Musica Ch., Cologne RSO, Latham-König.

This restoration of the original score of *Der Silbersee*, written just before Weill left Nazi Germany, aims to cope with the basic problem presented by having his music as adjunct, not to a regular music-theatre piece, but to a full-length play by Georg Kaiser. Between Weill's numbers a smattering of the original dialogue is here included to provide a dramatic thread and the speed of delivery adds to the effectiveness. Led by Hildegard Heichele, bright and full-toned as the central character, Fennimore, the cast is an outstanding one, with each voice satisfyingly clean-focused, while the 1989 recording is rather better-balanced and kinder to the instrumental accompaniment than some from this source, with the voices exceptionally vivid.

Die sieben Todsünden (The seven deadly sins) complete.
☞ (M) *** EMI Dig. CDM7 64739-2 [id.]. Ross, Rolfe Johnson, Caley, Rippon, Tomlinson, CBSO, Rattle – STRAVINSKY: *Pulcinella.* ***

(i) *Die sieben Todsünden (The seven deadly sins); Kleine Dreigroschenmusik.*
☞ *** Sony Dig. SK 44529 [id.]. (i) Migenes, Tear, Kale, Opie, Kennedy; LSO, Tilson Thomas.

(i) *Die sieben Todsünden (The seven deadly sins);* (ii) *Mahagonny Singspiel.*
☞ *** Decca Dig. 430 168-2 [id.]. Lemper, Wildhaber, Haage, Mohr, Jungwirth, Berlin RIAS Chamber Ens., Mauceri, (ii) with J. Cohen.

(i; ii) *Die sieben Todsünden (The seven deadly sins);* (i) Songs: *Berlin im Licht; Complainte de la Seine; Es regnet; Youkali; Nannas Lied (Meine Herren, mit Siebzehn); Wie lange noch?.*
☞ **(*) HM Dig. HMC 90 1420 [id.]. (i) Fassbaender; (ii) Brandt, Sojer, Komatsu, Urbas; Hanover R. PO, Garben.

Rattle's moving account of this Brecht–Weill collaboration gives it a tender but refreshing new look. The key point is the casting of Elsie Ross as the two Annas, the one idealistic, the other practical, who in this sharply drawn sequence visit various American cities and their respective deadly sins. It was the first version to use the original soprano pitch (as does the newer account with Fassbaender on Harmonia Mundi). The higher pitch makes it easier for Elsie to contrast the singing of Anna I with the speaking of Anna II. The final epilogue brings them back to where they started, beside the Mississippi in Louisiana; and the agony of disillusion is presented with total heartache, thanks to Miss Ross's acting. Her singing is sweet and tender, rather than a more abrasive cabaret style: she is far less aggressive than Lotte Lenya's version (see above, under *Happy end*), and though Rattle's direction is sharp and analytical the spring in the rhythm and nicely judged expressiveness of phrase give a warmth which is very attractive and also brings out the work's often Mahlerian intensity. Rattle's speeds – nearer to Tilson Thomas's fast ones than to Mauceri's slow – have the dramatic bite of the one and the poignancy of the other, and the vocal quartet has the best voices of all, but loses some impact from being balanced (like the soprano) relatively distantly. But with such a generous coupling and at mid-price, it must be our primary recommendation. The digital recording has plenty of theatrical atmosphere.

Using the lower-pitch version of *The Seven deadly sins* originally designed for Lotte Lenya, but with Weill's original instrumentation, the Decca issue presents Ute Lemper in one of her finest performances on record. Her sensuous, tough voice, in the tradition of Lenya but very distinct from her in its characterfulness, exactly suits the role of the first Anna, who does all the singing. Mauceri's speeds, consistently slower than those of Rattle or Tilson Thomas, also enhance the sensuous element while bringing out the strange poignancy of the Prologue and Epilogue. The chattering ensemble of four male singers – closely balanced in a slightly different acoustic from the orchestra – is well cast with voices apt for German cabaret style, and John Mauceri equally brings out the tang of the instrumental writing. He is rather less successful in the Singspiel, perhaps reflecting the fact that Lemper's role – mainly in duet with a singer of similar timbre – is less distinctive. Yet with similar forces required, it makes the ideal coupling. Full, bright sound to bring out the bite of the music.

In Tilson Thomas's performance with the LSO, Julia Migenes also uses the lower version of the score, colouring the voice even more boldly than Ute Lemper, echoing, even imitating, Lenya closely. With voices and instruments forwardly focused in the same consistent acoustic, the bite of the writing and its tangy beauty are put over powerfully, with Tilson Thomas's relatively brisk speeds adding to the power rather than to the poignancy. This makes a formidable alternative to the Rattle and Mauceri versions, in some ways more forceful than either, but with a coupling, apt as it is, rather less generous.

The Harmonia Mundi version stars Brigitte Fassbaender who, using the original pitch, brings a Lieder-singer's feeling for word-detail and a comparable sense of style. Her account is obviously less street-wise than Lemper's but there is a plangent feeling that is highly appropriate. The songs are equally impressive, mostly connected in some way or another with the main piece. The vocal quartet make an impressive team but, especially alongside Rattle, the conductor, Cord Garben, at times seems on the leisurely side in his choice of tempi. Excellent, vivid recording.

Street scene (opera): complete.
*** TER Dig. CDTER2 1185 (2) [id.]. Kristine Ciesinski, Janis Kelly, Bonaventura Bottone,
    Richard Van Allan, ENO Ch. and O, Carl Davis.

Street scene was Kurt Weill's attempt, late in his Broadway career, to write an American opera as distinct from a musical. The TER set was made with the cast of the ENO production at the Coliseum, and the idiomatic feeling and sense of flow consistently reflect that. Some of the solo singing in the large cast is flawed, but never seriously, and the principals are all very well cast – Kristine Ciesinski as the much-put-upon Anna Maurrant, Richard van Allan as her sorehead husband, Janis Kelly sweet and tender as the vulnerable daughter, and Bonaventura Bottone as the diffident young Jewish neighbour who loves her. Those are only a few of the sharply drawn characters, and the performance on the discs, with dialogue briskly paced, reflects the speed of the original ENO production. Warm, slightly distanced sound.

Der Zar lässt sich Photographieren (complete).
**(*) Capriccio Dig. 60 007-1 [id.]. McDaniel, Pohl, Napier, Cologne R. O, Latham-König.

This curious one-act *opera buffa* is a wry little parable about assassins planning to kill the Tsar when he has his photograph taken. Angèle, the photographer, is replaced by the False Angèle, but the Tsar proves to be a young man who simply wants friendship, and the would-be assassin, instead of killing him, plays a tango on the gramophone, before the Tsar's official duties summon him again. Jan Latham-König in this 1984 recording directs a strong performance, though the dryly recorded orchestra is consigned to the background. The voices fare better, though Barry McDaniel is not ideally steady as the Tsar.

Weiss, Silvius (1686–1750)

Overture in B flat; Suite in D min.; Suite No. 17 in F min.
(M) *** BMG/RCA GD 77217 [77217-2-RG]. Konrad Junghänel (lute).

The Silesian composer Silvius Leopold Weiss was an almost exact contemporary of J. S. Bach and was regarded in his day as the greatest lutenist of the Baroque. Konrad Junghänel plays a Baroque 13-string lute by Nico van der Waals with splendid authority and musicianship, though, as so often with recordings of soft-spoken instruments like the lute or the clavichord, the level is too high and best results are obtained by playing this at a lower volume setting.

Widor, Charles-Marie (1844–1937)

Salve regina; Symphony No. 6: 1st movt.
(M) *** Mercury 434 311-2 [id.]. Marcel Dupré (organ of St Thomas's Church, NY City) – FRANCK:
    3 Chorales etc. ***

These are each movements from symphonies, as the composer later interpolated his *Salve regina* into his *Second*. In both Marcel Dupré displays those qualities of musicianly fervour for which the older generation of French organists was noted, and this recording, made on an exceptionally fine instrument, cannot fail to impress even the most casual listener.

Organ symphony No. 5 in F min., Op. 42/1. ·
*** DG Dig. 413 438-2 [id.]. Simon Preston (organ of Westminster Abbey) – VIERNE: *Carillon de Westminster.* ***
☞ *** Chan. Dig. CHAN 9271 [id.]. Ian Tracey (organ of Liverpool Cathedral), BBC PO, Yan Pascal Tortelier – GUILMANT: *Symphony No. 1 for organ and orchestra* ***; POULENC: *Concerto.* **(*)

Organ symphonies No. 5 in F min., Op. 42/1 (complete); *6 in B. Op. 42/2: 1st movt; 8 in B, Op. 42/4: 4th movt (Prelude).*
(M) *** Saga SCD 9048 [id.]. David Sanger (organ of St Peter's Italian Church, Clerkenwell, London).

David Sanger's account of the Widor *Symphony No. 5* is first class in every respect and is recorded with fine bloom and clarity. His restraint in registering the central movements prevents Widor's cosy melodic inspiration from sounding sentimental, and the finale is exciting without being overblown. The other symphonic movements are well done but serve to confirm the conclusion that the famous *Toccata* from No. 5 was Widor's masterpiece.

Simon Preston also gives a masterly account of the Widor *Fifth Symphony*, with a fine sense of pace and command of colour; there is a marvellous sense of space in this DG recording.

The long reverberation-period of Liverpool Cathedral gives a special character to Widor's *Fifth Symphony*, especially the mellow central movements. Ian Tracey makes the most of the colouristic possibilities of his fine instrument and also uses the widest possible range of dynamics, with the tone at times shaded down to a distant whisper. Yet the famous *Toccata* expands gloriously if without the plangent bite of a French instrument.

Symphonies Nos. 5, Op. 42/1: Adagio & Toccata; 6, Op. 42/2: 1st movt: Allegro; 8, Op. 42/4: Moderato cantabile; Allegro; 9 (Symphonie gothique), Op. 70 (complete); *3 Nouvelles pièces, Op. 87.*
*** Argo Dig. 433 152-2; *433 152-4* [id.]. Thomas Trotter (Cavaillé-Coll organ of Saint-François-de-Sales, Lyon).

The inner movements of the *Symphonie gothique* are attractive and the finale undoubtedly inventive – it is essentially in variation form with an extended coda. The excerpts from the *Eighth Symphony* are also very agreeable. Thomas Trotter is an impressive advocate and he is splendidly recorded on an organ highly suited to this repertoire.

Wieniawski, Henryk (1835–80)

Violin concertos Nos. 1 in F sharp min., Op. 14; 2 in D min., Op. 22; Légende, Op. 17.
*** DG Dig. 431 815-2 [id.]. Gil Shaham, LSO, Lawrence Foster – SARASATE: *Zigeunerweisen.* ***

Listening to Gil Shaham's new DG record, it becomes even more mystifying that Wieniawski's *First Violin concerto* should always be upstaged by the *Second*, which is so often recorded. The Paganinian pyrotechnics in the first movement can be made to dazzle, as Shaham readily demonstrates and Lawrence Foster makes a good deal of the orchestral part. Both soloist and orchestra are equally dashing and lyrically persuasive in the better known *D minor Concerto*, and make an engaging encore out of the delightful *Légende*. With first-class DG recording this record is very recommendable.

Violin concerto No. 2 in D min., Op. 22.
*** Decca Dig. 421 716-2 [id.]. Joshua Bell, Cleveland O, Ashkenazy – TCHAIKOVSKY: *Violin concerto.* ***

Joshua Bell gives a masterly performance, full of flair, even if he does not find quite the same individual poetry in the big second-subject melody or in the central *Romance* as Shaham. Excellent recording, brilliant and full.

Wikmanson, Johan (1753–1800)

String quartet No. 2 in E min., Op. 1/2.

☞ *** CRD CRD 3361; *CRD C 4061* [id.]. Chilingirian Qt – BERWALD: *Quartet.* ***

*** CRD CRD 33123 (2) [id.]. Chilingirian Qt – ARRIAGA: *String quartets Nos. 1–3.* ***

Wikmanson was a cultured musician, but little of his music survives and two of his five *Quartets* are lost. The overriding influence here is that of Haydn and the finale of the present quartet even makes a direct allusion to Haydn's *E flat Quartet,* Op. 33, No. 2. The Chilingirian make out a persuasive case for this piece and are very well recorded. As can be seen, this work is available coupled with either Arriaga or Berwald.

Wirén, Dag (1905–86)

(i) *Violin concerto, Op. 23;* (ii) *String quartet No. 5, Op. 41;* (iii) *Triptych, Op. 33;* (iv) *Wind quintet, Op. 42.*

** Cap. Dig./Analogue CAP 21326. (i) Nils-Erik Sparf, Stockholm PO, Comissiona; (ii) Saulesco Qt; (iii) Stockholm Sinf., Wedin; (iv) Stockholm Wind Quintet.

Wirén is a 'one-work composer', and little of his music is widely known or shares the celebrity of the *Serenade for strings.* The best piece here is probably the post-war *Violin concerto* whose first two movements are often imaginative and inventive; it is very well played by Nils-Erik Sparf and the Stockholm Philharmonic under Sergiu Comissiona. Only the finale is a let-down. The other three pieces, the *Triptych,* the *Fifth String quartet* and the *Wind quintet,* are all disappointingly thin and scrappy. Excellent performances and recordings all the same.

Serenade for strings, Op. 11.

☞ *** BIS Dig. CD 285 [id.]. Stockholm Sinf., Salonen (with *Concert* **(*)).

Wirén's famous *Serenade* is very freshly played here and excellently recorded.

String quartet No. 3 in D min.

☞ *** ASV Dig. CDDCA 825 [id.]. Lindsay Qt – BARBER: *String quartet;* A. TCHAIKOVSKY: *String quartet No. 2;* WOOD: *String quartet No. 3.* ***

Dag Wirén's is a small-scale talent, even if he speaks with a distinctive voice. His was one of the most natural and instinctive of musical gifts, and the *Sinfonietta* for orchestra, the *Cello Concerto* and the neglected *Divertimento* for orchestra all betray a vein of poetic feeling that is quite haunting. The *Third* of his five quartets speaks with his familiar and engaging accents, but the thematic substance is short-breathed and deficient in contrast. A very good live performance and recording from the (1987) BBC's Lunchtime Concerts at St John's, Smith Square.

Wolf, Hugo (1860–1903)

String quartet in D min.

☞ (M) ** DG 437 128-2 (2) LaSalle Qt – BRAHMS: *Quartets Nos. 1–2.* *(*)

The *String quartet* was written when Wolf was only twenty. The finale was added later. It is an ambitious work (41 minutes long), original in its metric flow, and the music has all the direct passion of youth. It suits the LaSalle Quartet better than the Brahms coupling. Though they press hard at times, the long slow movement is eloquent and often beautifully played and the finale has plenty of impetus. Bright, immediate, 1967 sound.

Lieder: Frage nicht; Frühling übers Jahr; Gesang Weylas; Kennst du das Land? (Mignon); Heiss mich nicht reden (Mignon I); Nur wer die Sehnsucht kennt (Mignon II); So lasst mich scheinen (Mignon III); Der Schäfer; Die Spröde.

*** DG Dig. 423 666-2 [id.]. Anne Sofie von Otter, Rolf Gothoni – MAHLER: *Das Knaben Wunderhorn* etc. ***

It is astonishing that so young a singer can tackle even the most formidable of Wolf's *Mignon* songs, *Kennst du das Land?,* a culminating peak of Lieder for women, with such firm, persuasive lines. The gravity of such a song is then delightfully contrasted against the delicacy of *Frühling übers Jahr* or *Die Spröde.* The sensitivity and imagination of Rolf Gothoni's accompaniment add enormously to the performances in a genuine two-way partnership. Well-balanced recording.

6 Lieder für eine Frauenstimme. Goethe-Lieder: Die Bekehrte; Ganymed; Kennst du das Land?;
Mignon I, II & III; Philine; Die Spröde. Lieder: *An eine Aeolsharfe; Auf einer Wanderung; Begegnung;*
Denk es, o Seele; Elfenlied; Im Frühling; Sonne der Schlummerlosen; Wenn du zu den Blumen gehst;
Wie glänzt der helle Mond; Die Zigeunerin.
(M) **(*) EMI CDM7 63653-2. Elisabeth Schwarzkopf, Gerald Moore or Geoffrey Parsons.

This is a superb collection, representing the peak of Schwarzkopf's achievement as a Lieder singer. It
is disgraceful that no texts or translations are provided as this will seriously reduce its appeal for
some collectors; but the selection of items could hardly be better, including many songs inseparably
associated with Schwarzkopf's voice, like *Mausfallen spruchlein* and, above all, *Kennst du das Land?*.

Mörike Lieder: An den Schlaf; Auf ein altes Bild; Auf einer Wanderung; Begegnung; Bei einer
Trauung; Denk'es, o Seele!; Der Feuerreiter; Fussreise; Der Gärtner; Gebet; Gesang Weylas; Im
Frühling; In der Frühe; Jägerlied; Der Knabe und das Immlein; Lebe wohl; Nimmersatte Liebe;
Peregrina 1 & 2; Schlafendes Jesuskind; Selbstgeständnis; Storchenbotschaft; Das verlassene Mägdlein;
Verborgenheit; Zum neuen Jahr.
☞ *** Decca Dig. 440 208-2 [id.]. Brigitte Fassbaender, Thibaudet.

Not since Elisabeth Schwarzkopf has a woman singer tackled Hugo Wolf lieder as characterfully as
Brigitte Fassbaender on her disc of 25 of the Mörike-Lieder with the pianist, Jean-Yves Thibaudet.
Here is a dangerous, even violent singer who, with light in the eye, heightens the character of each
song, bringing out the good humour in such a song as *Fussreise*, rambling, drawing out the beauty of
line in *Verborgenheit*, but often positively taking an individual approach. So there is passionate
intensity as much as rapt concentration behind *Schlafendes Jesuskind*, and the loss of a lover in *Der
verlassene Mägdlein* is treated not as tragedy but as something to be shrugged off by the servant-girl.
Characteristically, Fassbaender concludes with a shattering account of the most violent of Wolf
songs, normally reserved for men, *Der Feuerreiter* ('The fire-rider').

Spanisches Liederbuch (complete).
(M) *** DG 423 934-2 (2) [id.]. Schwarzkopf, Fischer-Dieskau, Moore.

In this superb CD reissue the sacred songs provide a dark, intense prelude, with Fischer-Dieskau at
his very finest, sustaining slow tempi impeccably. Schwarzkopf's dedication comes out in the three
songs suitable for a woman's voice; but it is in the secular songs, particularly those which contain
laughter in the music, where she is at her most memorable. Gerald Moore is balanced rather too
backwardly – something the transfer cannot correct – but gives superb support. In all other respects
the 1968 recording sounds first rate, the voices beautifully caught. A classic set.

Wolf-Ferrari, Ermanno (1876–1948)

L'amore medico: Overture; (i) *Intermezzo. Il Campiello: Intermezzo; Ritornello. La Dama Bomba:*
Overture. I gioielli della Madonna (suite). I 4 rusteghi: Prelude & Intermezzo. Il segreto di Susanna:
Overture & Intermezzo.
☞ *** EMI CDC7 54585-2 [id.]. ASMF, Marriner, (i) with Stephen Orton.
☞ *** ASV Dig. CDDCA 861 [id.] (without *Il segreto* & *L'amore medico Intermezzi*). RPO, José
Serebrier.

In spite of the considerable attractions of his opera, *Susanna's secret*, Wolf-Ferrari holds a permanent
place in the catalogue only with recordings of his operatic *intermezzi* – not surprising, perhaps, when
they are so readily tuneful and charmingly scored. Marriner and the Academy are only marginally
short of their finest form here, and this concert makes a delightful entertainment, with everything
elegantly played and warmly (if a little resonantly) recorded at Abbey Road.
Serebrier's performances are by no means upstaged. He conjured at times exquisite playing from the
RPO (especially the strings) and, even though he takes Susanna's sparkling overture slightly slower
than Marriner, it is hardly less successful. What is specially memorable is his delicate treatment of the
gossamer string-pieces from *I quattro rusteghi* and the *Ritornello* from *Il Campiello* which almost have
a Beecham touch. The ASV recording, made in the Henry Wood Hall, is slightly more open (the
brass in *La Dama Bomba* is splendidly biting and resonant) and indeed marginally more transparent
and fresh. But the snag is that the ASV collection omits three of the more delectable pieces included
by Marriner (and even the latter gives us only 54 minutes), including the concertante *Intermezzo* from
L'amore medico in which Stephen Orton takes the solo cello role most winningly.

Wood, Haydn (1882–1959)

Apollo overture; A Brown bird singing (paraphrase for orchestra); *London cameos:* suite (*Miniature overture: The City; St James's Park in the spring; A State ball at Buckingham Palace); Mannin Veen* (Manx tone-poem); *Moods* (suite): *Joyousness* (concert waltz). *Mylecharane* (rhapsody); *The Seafarer (A nautical rhapsody); Serenade to youth; Sketch of a Dandy.*
*** Marco Polo Dig. 8.22340-2. Slovak RSO (Bratislava), Adrian Leaper.

Haydn Wood was Christian-named after the great Austrian composer (although here it is pronounced 'Hayden'), as his Yorkshire father had been to a performance of *The Creation* not long before his son arrived. H. W. was an almost exact contemporary of Eric Coates and nearly as talented. Wood spent his childhood on the Isle of Man, and much of his best music is permeated with Manx folk-themes (original or simulated), which often bring a Celtic flavour to his invention. He wrote for the multitude of small orchestras which played on piers and in spas during the Edwardian era and up to the 1940s. Now most of his output is all but forgotten, although military bands in the parks stay faithful to him and *Mannin Veen* ('Dear Isle of Man') is a splendid piece, based on four Manx folksongs. The companion rhapsody, *Mylecharane*, also uses folk material if less memorably, and *The Seafarer* is a wittily scored selection of famous shanties, neatly stitched together. The only failure here is *Apollo*, which uses less interesting material and is over-ambitious and inflated. But the English waltzes are enchanting confections. This generous collection (69 minutes) opens with a most engaging miniature, *Sketch of a Dandy*, endearingly dated but deliciously frothy and elegant, and played here with an ideal lightness of touch. Adrian Leaper is obviously much in sympathy with this repertoire and knows just how to pace it; his Czech players obviously relish the easy tunefulness and the sheer craft of the writing (as do all orchestral musicians, anywhere). With excellent recording in what is surely an ideal acoustic, this is very highly recommendable.

Wood, Hugh (born 1932)

(i) *Cello concerto;* (ii) *Violin concerto.*
(M) *** Unicorn UKCD 2043. (i) Parikian; (ii) Welsh; RLPO, Atherton.

Wood is a composer of integrity who has steeped himself in the music of Schoenberg and Webern, yet emerged richer for the experience – in contrast to many post-serial composers. His music is beautifully crafted and far from inaccessible. Here he is given the benefit of good recording, and the performances are thoroughly committed. Those who like and respond to the Bartók concertos or even to the Walton should try this. Excellently balanced recording, well transferred to CD.

Piano concerto, Op. 31.
☞ *** Collins Single Dig. 2007-2 [id.]. Joanna MacGregor, BBC SO, Andrew Davis.

Hugh Wood's *Piano concerto*, written for Joanna MacGregor, who studied with him at Cambridge, is one of his most important new works – a three-movement piece whose central movement is a haunting set of variations on *Sweet Loraine*, the song popularized in the 1950s by Nat King Cole. Expert playing from both the soloist and the BBC Symphony Orchestra under Andrew Davis, and first-class recorded sound.

String quartet No. 3, Op. 20.
☞ *** ASV Dig. CDDCA 825 [id.]. Lindsay Qt – BARBER: *String quartet;* A. TCHAIKOVSKY: *String quartet No. 2;* WIREN: *String quartet No. 3.* ***

Wood has a highly sophisticated feeling for sonority and texture, and his *Third Quartet* (1978) is the product of skilled musicianship and a well-stocked imagination. His music shows that the example of Schoenberg and the Second Viennese School need not be inhibiting if it is intelligently absorbed. His *Third Quartet* is a one-movement work, musically dense and varied; not one to yield up its secrets on a casual hearing but worth perseverance and study. The Lindsay performance, recorded at St John's, Smith Square, in 1980 is admirably prepared and dedicated, and the BBC recording eminently well balanced.

Wordsworth, William (1908–88)

Symphonies Nos. 2 in D, Op. 34; 3 in C, Op. 48.
*** Lyrita Dig. SRCD 207 [id.]. LPO, Nicholas Braithwaite.

William Wordsworth was a direct descendant of the poet's brother, Christopher; on the evidence of this disc, he was a real symphonist. The *Second*, dedicated to Tovey, has a real sense of space; it is distinctly Nordic in atmosphere and there is an unhurried sense of growth. It is serious, thoughtful music, both well crafted and well laid out for the orchestra. At times it almost suggests Sibelius or Walter Piston in the way it moves, though not in its accents, and the writing is both powerful and imaginative. The *Third* is less concentrated and less personal in utterance, but all the same this is music of integrity, and readers who enjoy, say, the symphonies of Edmund Rubbra should sample the *Second Symphony*. Nicholas Braithwaite gives a carefully prepared and dedicated account of it, and the recording is up to the usual high standard one expects from this label.

Ysaÿe, Eugène (1858–1931)

6 Sonatas for solo violin, Op. 27.
*** Chan. Dig. CHAN 8599; *A B T D 1286* [id.]. Lydia Mordkovich.
☞ * Hung. Dig. HCD74176 [id.]. Vilmos Szabadi.

The six *Sonatas* were all written for the great virtuosi of the time (Szigeti, Thibaud, Enescu and so on). Lydia Mordkovich plays with great character and variety of colour and she characterizes No. 4 (the one dedicated to Kreisler, with its references to Bach and the *Dies Irae*) superbly. These *Sonatas* can seem like mere exercises, but in her hands they sound really interesting. Natural, warm recorded sound. Recommended.

Vilmos Szabadi is an accomplished young player with an attractive personality who enjoys much popularity in his native Hungary. He is at his very best in *zigeuner* showpieces and is perhaps intimidated by these Ysaÿe sonatas, in which he sounds a little inhibited. Of course there are good things: the *Sixth*, for example, is appropriately rhapsodic, but elsewhere he is a little strait-laced and sober-suited and does not bring these pieces alive in the same way as his more distinguished rival.

Zandonai, Riccardo (1883–1944)

Francesca da Rimini: excerpts from Acts II, III & IV.
(M) **(*) Decca 433 033-2 (2) [id.]. Olivero, Del Monaco, Monte Carlo Op. O, Rescigno –GIORDANO: *Fedora*. **(*)

Magda Olivero is a fine artist who has not been represented nearly enough on record, and this rare Zandonai selection, like the coupled set of Giordano's *Fedora*, does her some belated justice. Decca opted to have three substantial scenes recorded rather than snippets and, though Mario del Monaco as Paolo is predictably coarse in style, his tone is rich and strong and he does not detract from the achievement, unfailingly perceptive and musicianly, of Olivero as Francesca herself. Excellent, vintage 1969, Decca sound.

Zelenka, Jan (1679–1745)

Capriccios Nos. 1–5; Concerto in G; Hipocondrie in A; Overture in F; Sinfonia in A min.
⊛ (M) *** DG 423 703-2 (3) [id.]. Camerata Bern, Van Wijnkoop.

In this superb orchestral collection, as in the companion Archiv issue of Zelenka *Sonatas* (see below), this long-neglected composer begins to get his due, some 250 years late. On this showing he stands as one of the most distinctive voices among Bach's contemporaries, and Bach himself nominated him in that role, though at the time Zelenka was serving in a relatively humble capacity. As in the sonata collection, it is the artistry of Heinz Holliger that sets the seal on the performances, but the virtuosity of Barry Tuckwell on the horn is also a delight, and the music itself regularly astonishes. And in his bald expressiveness Zelenka often comes to sound amazingly modern, and often very beautiful, as in the slow *Aria No. 2* of the *Fourth Capriccio*. Superb recording, to match Van Wijnkoop's lively and colourful performances, makes these CDs very welcome indeed.

6 Sonatas for 2 oboes and bassoon with continuo.
⊛ (M) *** DG 423 937-2 (2) [id.]. Holliger, Bourgue, Gawriloff, Thunemann, Buccarella, Jaccottet.

In these *Trio sonatas* it is almost as though Zelenka had a touch of Ives in him, so unexpected are some of the developments and turns of argument. The tone of voice is often dark and intense, directly comparable to Bach at his finest; and all through these superb performances the electricity of the original inspiration comes over with exhilarating immediacy. Fine recording, admirably remastered.

Another set to recommend urgently to any lover of Baroque music.

Lamentationes Jeremiae Prophetae (Lamentations for Holy Week).
(M) *** HM/BMG GD 77112 [77112-2-RG]. Jacobs, De Mey, Widmer, Instrumentalists of the Schola Cantorum Basiliensis, Jacobs.

These solo settings of the six *Lamentations* for the days leading up to Easter reinforce Zelenka's claims as one of the most original composers of his time. The spacious melodic lines and chromatic twists in the harmonic progressions are often very Bachian, but the free-flowing alternation of arioso and recitative is totally distinctive. This mid-price issue of René Jacobs's 1983 recording for Deutsche Harmonia Mundi follows close on a very recommendable full-price version on the Hyperion label with the Chandos Baroque Players. Here, too, all three soloists are excellent, with the least-known, the baritone Kurt Widmer, easily matching the other two in his exceptionally sweet and fresh singing. But, quite apart from price, this BMG disc has the advantage of focusing the voices more cleanly and offering a rather less abrasive instrumental accompaniment, with speeds generally more flowing.

Missa dei Filii; Litaniae Laurentanae.
*** HM/BMG Dig. RD 77922 [7922-2-RC]. Argenta, Chance, Prégardien, Gordon Jones, Stuttgart Chamber Ch., Tafelmusik, Bernius.

This fine set offers not only one of Zelenka's late Masses, but also a splendid *Litany* too, confirming him – for all the obscurity he suffered in his lifetime – as one of the most inspired composers of his generation. The *Missa dei Filii* (Mass for the Son of God), is a 'short' mass, consisting of *Kyrie* and *Gloria* only. It seems that Zelenka never heard that Mass, but his *Litany*, another refreshing piece, was specifically written when the Electress of Saxony was ill. Zelenka, like Bach, happily mixes fugal writing with newer-fangled concertato movements. Bernius provides well-sprung support with his period-instrument group, Tafelmusik, and his excellent soloists and choir.

Requiem in C min.
**(*) Claves Dig. CD 50-8501 [id.]. Brigitte Fournier, Balleys, Ishii, Tüller, Berne Chamber Ch. and O, Dahler.

This record of the *Requiem in C minor* confirms Zelenka's originality. *The Last Trump*, for example, is a thoughtful soprano solo without any of the dramatic gestures one might expect; and the *Agnus Dei* is quite unlike any other setting of his period – or of any other – austere, intent and mystical. There is hardly a moment that is not of compelling interest here; the only minor qualification that needs to be made concerns the balance, which places the solo singers too forward. The performance is well prepared and thoroughly committed. On CD one might have expected the choral focus to be sharper, but in all other respects the sound is very good, with the ambience nicely judged.

Zemlinsky, Alexander von (1871–1942)

Symphony No. 2 in B flat; (i) *Psalm 23.*
*** Decca Dig. 421 644-2 [id.]. (i) Ernst Senff Chamber Ch.; Berlin RSO, Chailly.

Relatively conservative as the idiom is, this *Symphony* is a striking and warmly expressive work that richly deserves revival, particularly in a performance as strong, committed and brilliantly recorded as this. The piece inspires Chailly and the Berlin Radio Symphony Orchestra to one of their finest performances on record, helped by vivid sound, full of presence. The setting of *Psalm 23* is in a rather more advanced harmonic idiom but is just as warm in expression, airy and beautiful. But do not expect a religious atmosphere: this is sensuous music, beautifully played and sung, which uses the much-loved words of the Psalm as an excuse for musical argument, rather than illuminating them.

String quartets Nos. 1, Op. 4; 2, Op. 15; 3, Op. 19; 4, Op. 25.
(M) *** DG Dig. 427 421-2 (2). LaSalle Qt.

None of the four Zemlinsky *Quartets* is in the least atonal: the textures are full of contrapuntal interest and the musical argument always proceeds with lucidity. There is diversity of mood and a fastidious craftsmanship, and the listener is always held. The musical language is steeped in Mahler and, to a lesser extent, Reger, but the music is undoubtedly the product of a very fine musical mind and one of considerable individuality. Collectors will find this a rewarding set: the LaSalle play with polish and unanimity, and the recording is first class, as is the admirable documentation.

VOCAL MUSIC

Gesänge Op. 5, Books 1–2; Gesänge (Waltz songs on Tuscan folk-lyrics), Op. 6 ; Gesänge, Opp. 7–8, 10 & 13; Lieder, Op. 2, Books 1–2; Op. 22 & Op. 27.
*** DG Dig. 427 348-2 (2) [id.]. Barbara Bonney, Anne Sofie von Otter, Hans Peter Blochwitz, Andreas Schmidt, Cord Garben.

Thanks to recordings, the art of Alexander von Zemlinsky is coming to be ever more widely appreciated, and this two-disc DG collection of songs can be warmly recommended for the fresh tunefulness of dozens of miniatures. With Cord Garben accompanying four excellent soloists, the charm of these chips from the workbench comes over consistently. Best of all is von Otter, more sharply imaginative than the others, making the one consistent cycle that Zemlinsky ever wrote, the six Maeterlinck Songs, Opus 13, the high-point of the set.

Lyric symphony, Op. 18.
*** DG Dig. 419 261-2 [id.]. Varady, Fischer-Dieskau, BPO, Maazel.

Zemlinsky's *Lyric symphony* is essentially a symphonic song-cycle, modelled on *Das Lied von der Erde* and based on Eastern poetry; its lush textures and refined scoring make it immediately accessible. The idiom is that of early Schoenberg (*Verklaerte Nacht* and *Gurrelieder*), Mahler and Strauss. Yet it is not just derivative but has something quite distinctive to say. Its sound-world is imaginative, the vocal writing graceful and the orchestration masterly. Both soloists and the orchestra seem thoroughly convinced and convincing, Maazel's refined control of texture prevents the sound from cloying, as does his incisive manner, and the engineering is first class.

Eine florentinische Tragödie (opera; complete).
*** Schwann Dig. CD 11625 [id.]. Soffel, Riegel, Sarabia, Berlin RSO, Albrecht.

A Florentine Tragedy presents a simple love triangle: a Florentine merchant returns home to find his sluttish wife with the local prince. Zemlinsky in 1917 may have been seeking to repeat the shock tactics of Richard Strauss in *Salome* (another Oscar Wilde story) a decade earlier; but the musical syrup which flows over all the characters makes them far more repulsive, with motives only dimly defined. The score itself is most accomplished; it is compellingly performed here, more effective on disc than it is in the opera house. First-rate sound.

Der Gerburtstag der Infantin (opera; complete).
*** Schwann Dig. CD 11626 [id]. Nielsen, Riegel, Haldas, Weller, Berlin RSO, Albrecht.

The Birthday of the Infanta, like its companion one-Acter, was inspired by a story of Oscar Wilde, telling of a hideous dwarf caught in the forest and given to the Infanta as a birthday present. Even after recognizing his own hideousness, he declares his love to the princess and is casually rejected. He dies of a broken heart, with the Infanta untroubled: 'Oh dear, my present already broken.' Zemlinsky, dwarfish himself, gave his heart to the piece, reproducing his own rejection at the hands of Alma Mahler. In this performance, based on a much-praised stage production, Kenneth Riegel gives a heartrendingly passionate performance as the dwarf declaring his love. His genuine passion is intensified by being set against lightweight, courtly music to represent the Infanta and her attendants. With the conductor and others in the cast also experienced in the stage production, the result is a deeply involving performance, beautifully recorded.

Collections

Because of space limitations this is a very selective list. We hope to include many more collections in our next volume.

Concerts of Orchestral and Concertante Music

Academy of St Martin-in-the-Fields, Sir Neville Marriner

Italian concertos: GABRIELI: *Canzona noni toni.* CORELLI: *Concerti grossi in D; in G min., Op. 6/7, 8.*
GEMINIANI: *Concerto grosso in E min., Op. 3/3.* MANFREDINI: *Concerto grosso in G min., Op. 3/10.*
ALBINONI: *Concerto a 5 in A min., Op. 5/5.* TORELLI: *Concerto musicale in D min., Op. 6/10.*
LOCATELLI: *Concerto grosso in D min., Op. 1/9.*
☞ ⊕ (M) *** Decca 436 224-2.

Although it opens with the noble, antiphonally conceived Gabrieli *Canzona* – how strongly this composer's musical personality comes through, even in a short piece – which derives from a slightly later source, in essence this 72-minute CD combines much of the contents of the two LPs which at the beginning of the 1960s launched the Academy of St Martin-in-the-Fields. This particular field of small chamber ensembles specializing in performances of baroque music had previously been cornered by Italian groups like I Musici, often restricting themselves very much to the home product. From the very beginning, Marriner and the St Martin's group showed themselves willing to offer a repertoire covering the widest possible range; furthermore the standard of playing and care for style and detail were to set and maintain a new international standard of excellence which even now, three decades later, has not been surpassed. However, the collection assembled for the reissue omits the non-Italian repertoire (the Avison and the excerpts from Handel's Op. 6, for instance) and lets the Academy upstage the Italian groups on their own ground. The playing is wonderfully alive and spirited, and the works by Manfredini and Locatelli, instead of sounding anonymous, as they so often do, emerge with as strong an expressive individuality as those by their more celebrated compatriots, Corelli and Albinoni. The recording is admirably remastered; its slight touch of astringency in the violins seems properly authentic and there is plenty of body and warmth.

(i) American Symphony Orchestra Wind Group or (ii) Orchestra, Leopold Stokowski

(i) MOZART: *Serenade No. 10 for 13 wind instruments in B flat, K.361.* (ii) VIVALDI: *L'Estro armonico: Concerto grosso in D min., Op. 3/11.* BACH: *Jesu, joy of man's desiring* (arr. Schickele); *Sheep may safely graze* (arr. Stokowski). CORELLI: *Concerto grosso in G min.* [*Christmas*], *Op. 6/8.*
☞ (M) *** Van. 08 8009 71 [id.].

Stokowski's expressive exaggerations – inevitable even in Mozart – are never extreme, so that they do not get in the way of enjoyment of this highly characterful performance of the *Wind serenade*. The solo work in the lovely *Adagio* third movement is exceptionally sensitive in its flexibility, and the sprung rhythms of the fast movements are infectiously controlled. The Bach transcriptions, too, are warmly enjoyable, but it is the baroque *concerti grossi* that show the Stokowski magnetism at its most telling. In the Corelli, Igor Kipnis provides the continuo and he is nicely balanced. Allegros sparkle and the famous *Pastorale* is expressively beautiful. In the Vivaldi, the continuo is almost inaudible, but again the string playing is buoyant and joyful in allegros, while the third-movement *Largo* is quite ravishing. The 1966/7 recordings are excellent and the transfers first rate.

Amsterdam Loeki Stardust Quartet, Academy of Ancient Music, Christopher Hogwood

'Concerti di flauti': HEINICHEN: *Concerto a 8 in C.* SCHICKHARDT: *Concerto No. 2 in D min. for 4 recorders & continuo; Concerto No. 3 in G for 4 recorders & continuo.* TELEMANN: *Concertos for 2 recorders & strings: in A min.; in B flat.* MARCELLO: *Concerti di flauti in G.* VIVALDI: *Concerto in A in due cori, con flauti obbligati, RV 585.*

☞ *** O-L Dig. 436 905-2 [id.].

A recorder quartet, however expert, can easily suffer from over-exposure, but the Amsterdam group play with great style and match their timbres with extraordinary expertise so that, provided one does not try to take this all at one go, the ear is consistently tickled. The Heinichen *Concerto a 8* (which doesn't mean there are eight soloists!) is a charmer, with a barely scored drone effect in the *Pastorel* followed by a graceful minute-long *Adagio* to counter the chortling in the outer movements; the finale has such colour that one thinks of Mendelssohn and the *Scherzo* from *A Midsummer Night's Dream.* The Schickhardt D minor work opens equally invitingly (with the effect of a carol) and is elegantly tuneful throughout. In its companion in G major, the solo style is very chordal, with moments almost like a piquant harmonium. Both the Telemann works are predictably inventive and enjoyable; perhaps the first, in A minor, wins by a short head, while in the happy Marcello piece one can feel the Italian sunshine. But the most masterly concerto here is the splendid Vivadi antiphonal *Concerto in A major* which uses violin soloists as well as the recorders (used sparingly as an obbligato) and even brings in a brief solo organ contribution. The slow movement is dominated by the violin duo. Needless to say, the whole programme is expertly and authentically presented. The recording, made in London's Henry Wood Hall, has a nice ambience, though the balance is a trifle close (particularly in the Vivaldi). A very stimulating concert just the same.

André, Maurice (trumpet)

Trumpet concertos and arrangements: (with (i) Munich CO; (ii) Stadlmair; (iii) Richter. (iv) Hedwig Bilgram (organ); (v) ECO, Mackerras; (vi) Zurich Coll. Music O, Sacher). (i; ii) Joseph HAYDN: *Concerto in E flat.* (i; iii) TELEMANN: *Concertos in C min.; E min.* (fom *Oboe concerto*); *Sonata for trumpet and strings in D.* (i; ii) Franz Xaver RICHTER: *Concerto in D.* (i; iii) HANDEL: *Concertos Nos 1–3* (arr. from *Oboe concertos*). (iv) VIVIANI: *Sonata No. 1 for trumpet and organ in C.* (v) VIVALDI: *Double trumpet concerto in C, P. 75.* TORELLI: *Concerto in D.* Gottfried Heinrich STOELZEL: *Concerto in D.* (i; ii) Michael HAYDN: *Concerto in D.* (vi) A. SCARLATTI: *Sinfonia No. 2 in D for flute, trumpet and strings.*

☞ (B) **(*) DG Double DG 413 853-2 (2) [id.].

This pretty impressive 130-minute collection would seem to be a 'best buy' for trumpet fanciers who, rightly, admire Maurice André's expertise and musicianship and don't mind that some of the earlier recordings here sound a bit dated. He is a big star in France, which is why there are so many of his records around. There are quite a few transcriptions in the programme, notably the three fine *Oboe concertos* of Handel, which are quite effective on trumpet. But the concert opens with the greatest trumpet concerto of all, by Haydn, and here André takes the *Andante* in a rather leisurely fashion; but he is gracious and serene, and most listeners will respond to his elegance. Often the baroque concertos, too, temper the virtuosity in outer movements with very agreeable central *Andantes*, of which the Torelli is a fine example. The *Sonata for trumpet and organ* by Giovanni Bonaventura Viviani (1683–c. 1692) is a very attractive piece, comprising five brief but striking miniatures, each only a minute or so in length. Alessandro Scarlatti's engaging *Sinfonia* is also in five movements and incorporates a solo flute. The latter is all all but drowned out in the *Spiritoso* first movement but takes the solo role in the two brief *Adagios* (the second quite touching); the trumpet returns to echo the flute in the central *Allegro* and they share the *Presto* finale. Michael Haydn's concerto, a two-movement concertante section of a seven movement *Serenade*, has incredibly high tessitura but, characteristically, Maurice André reaches up for it with consummate ease. In the Vivaldi *Double concerto* he plays both solo parts. The three Telemann works are all characteristcally inventive, and one can understand why André wanted to play the transcribed oboe concerto which ends the concert. The solo trumpet is generally well caught, but the Munich recordings date from the late 1960s and the strings as recorded are a bit thin and husky, the focus not improved by the digital remastering. Not that there is any lack of warmth or ambience overall, but the later recordings with Mackerras and the ECO, made a decade later, are smoother and obviously more modern.

Backhaus, Wilhelm (piano)

'Wilhelm Backhaus Edition – 2': BEETHOVEN: *Piano concertos Nos. 1–5* (with VPO, Schmidt-Isserstedt); *Diabelli variations, Op. 120* (433 891-2 – 3 discs). BRAHMS: *Piano concertos Nos. 1;* (i) *2* (with VPO, Boehm); *Capriccio in B min., Op. 76/2; Rhapsody in B min., Op. 79/1; Intermezzi: in E, Op. 116/6; in E flat, Op. 117/1; in E & C, Op. 119/2–3.* 6 Pieces, Op. 118 (433 895-2 – 2 discs). MOZART: *Piano concerto No. 27 in B flat, K.595* (with VPO, Boehm); *Piano sonatas Nos. 11 in A, K.331; 14 in C min., K.457; Rondo in A min., K.511* (433 898-2). SCHUMANN: *Piano concerto in A min., Op. 54* (with VPO, Wand); *Waldszenen, Op. 82* (433 899-2). MOZART: *Piano sonatas Nos. 4 in E flat, K.282; 5 in G, K.283; 10 in C, K.330; 12 in F, K.332.* HAYDN: *Piano sonatas: in C, Hob XVI/48; in E flat, Hob XVI/52* (433 900-2); *Andante with variations in F min., Hob XVII/6; Fantasia in C, Hob XVII/4; Piano sonata in E min., Hob XVI/34.* BACH: *English suite No. 6 in D min., BWV 811; French suite No. 5 in G, BWV 816; Well-tempered Clavier: Preludes and fugues in G, BWV 860 & BWV 884* (433 901-2). SCHUBERT: *6 Moments musicaux, D.790; Impromptus in* (i) *A flat; B flat, D.935/2–3;* Valses nobles, D.969. SCHUBERT/LISZT: *Soirée de Vienne No. 6.* SCHUMANN: (i) *Fantasiestücke: Warum?, Op. 12/2.* MENDELSSOHN: *Rondo capriccioso, Op. 14; Songs without words in G, C & A, Op. 62/1, 4 & 6* (433 902-2).

☞ (M) **(*) Decca stereo/(i) mono 433 903-2 (10) [id.].

In the very earliest days of stereo, Decca put Wilhelm Backhaus under contract and made a number of recordings with him – mostly in the late 1950s and early '60s – of the German repertoire in which he specialized. The most important endeavour was a complete set of the Beethoven *Piano sonatas*, and this forms Volume 1 of the current reissued Backhaus Edition (see our Composer index, above). Volume II includes almost everything else and represents a considerable achievement for a pianist in his seventies and eighties nearing the end of a long and distinguished musical life. He was born in 1884, 13 years before the death of Brahms (towards whose music he has a special empathy) and his career thus spanned the end of the nineteenth and first half of the twentieth century. He was greatly gifted, an unflamboyant musical personality whose playing generated considerable power and continuing concentration, yet whose peremptory manner and lack of a coaxing style could be disconcerting. He made sparing use of the sustaining pedal, his use of colour was considered and reserved, and his strong, classical manner avoided the least suspicion of exaggerated romanticism. Backhaus never set out to charm his audiences. His Bach was crisply literal, his Beethoven was formidable and his Brahms powerfully authoritative. He was, perhaps, better suited to Haydn than to Mozart – although he played both with great character. With Schubert he was very direct, yet still individual, and he obviously enjoyed playing Mendelssohn. All the concerto performances here are very rewarding (with excellent orchestral support) and, throughout, his spontaneous imagination, completely untainted with any wish to superimpose his own personality over that of the composer, holds every performance together and projects it vividly to the listener. Fortunately the Decca sound is remarkably real and present – sometimes too present, at the expense of the widest dynamic range. All these performances are available separately, although sometimes grouped in two- or three-CD sets. They are discussed in more detail under their individual composer entries, but the complete set is well worth considering in its own right.

Baumann, Hermann (horn), Leipzig Gewandhaus Orchestra, Kurt Masur

Concertante works for horn: GLIÈRE: *Concerto in B flat, Op. 91.* SAINT-SAENS: *Morceau de concert, Op. 94.* CHABRIER: *Larghetto.* DUKAS: *Villanelle.*

☞ *** Ph. Dig. 416 380-2 [id.].

This collection makes up in quality for what it lacks in quantity. Apart from the splendid Glière concerto, which is a major discovery (see under its composer entry), the Saint-Saëns *Morceau* is also very personable, essentially a jolly set of variations on a dotted theme that receives a central transformation into an *Andante* before the brief, vigorous, closing section. Chabrier's operatic *Larghetto* has a rather fine tune with a passionately romantic climx, and the Dukas *Villanelle* – a favourite encore of Dennis Brain's – opens engagingly with a 6/8 villanella (an Italian folk dance) which later becomes more animated to produce an exciting coda. Baumann is in splendid form, playing with warmth and easy command. He uses a judicious degree of rubato (which is entirely in style in all this music), and Masur's accompaniments are committed and beautifully played. First-rate recording.

Boskovsky Ensemble, Willi Boskovsky

'*Viennese bonbons*': J. STRAUSS, Snr: *Chinese galop; Kettenbrücke Waltz; Eisele und Beisele Sprünge. Cachucha galop.* J. STRAUSS, Jnr: *Weine Gemüths waltz; Champagne galop; Salon polka.* LANNER: *Styrian dances; Die Werber & Marien waltzes; Bruder halt galop.* MOZART: *3 Contredanses, K.462; 4 German dances, K.600/1 & 3; K.605/1; K.611.* SCHUBERT: *8 Waltzes & Ländler.*
(M) *** Van. 8.8015.71 [OVC 8015].

This is a captivating selection of the most delightful musical confectionery imaginable. The ensemble is a small chamber group, similar to that led by the Strausses, and the playing has an appropriately intimate Viennese atmosphere. The transfer is impeccable and the recording from the early 1960s, made in the Baumgarten Hall, Vienna, is fresh, smooth and clear, with a nice bloom on sound which is never too inflated.

'*Rare old Vienna dances*, Vol. 2: *The charm of old Vienna*': Johann STRAUSS Snr: *Gitana galop; Annen polka; Hofball-Tänze; Seufzer galop.* MAYER: *Schnofler-Tanz'.* HAYDN: *Zingarese Nos. 1, 6 & 8; Katherinen Tänze Nos. 4, 6, 8 & 12.* SCHUBERT: *Tänze from Opp. 9, 18, 67, 77 & 127; Ecossaisen, Op. 49.* LANNER: *Abendsterner waltz; Cerrito polka; Neue Wiener Ländler, Op. 1.* STELZMÜLLER: *Stelzmüller Tanz'.*
☞ (M) **(*) Van. 08 8016.71 [OVC 8016].

Boskovsky's series of recordings of Viennese light music continues to intoxicate with their lightness of touch and transparency of texture. The style is not so far removed from a Schrammeln orchestra, and the recording is warm and lively throughout. However, the present disc is a little below the very high standard of Volumes 1 and 3, containing a certain amount of wallpaper music, while the CD transfers are not always too smooth, occasionally bringing a touch of edge to Boskovsky's violin, with textures not cleanly focused in the Schubert *Ecossaisen* and Haydn *Katherinen Tänze*. Even so, there are some delectable lollipops here, notably the opening *Gitana galop* of Johann Strauss Senior with its horn obbligato, and his very catchy *Annen polka* (not to be confused with his son's piece of the same name). Lanner's *Cerrito polka*, too, is most engaging, and Mayer's *Schnofler-Tanz'* have an almost decadant touch of schmalz.

'*Rare old Vienna dances*, Vol. 3: *Greetings from old Vienna*': SCHUBERT: *Gratzer galop; Ecossaisen; Galop.* LANNER: *2 Mazurkas; Malapou galop. Hansjörgel polka.* Johann STRAUSS Snr: *Badjaderen Waltz, Op. 53.* Johann STRAUSS Jnr: *Scherz polka, Op. 72.* Josef STRAUSS: *Marien-Klänge waltz, Op. 214.* PAYER: *Galanterie Waltz.* BEETHOVEN: *6 Contredanses. Four 'Dances of old vienna'* by STELZMULLER, GRUBER and ANON.
☞ (M) *** Van. 08.8017.71 [OVC 8017].

This is just as delightful as the first issue in Boskovsky's delectable series. The opening Schubert *Gratzer galop* will entice anyone, played as lightly as this, and Lanner's pieces are equally sparkling. Hieronymus Payer's *Galanterie waltz* is aptly named and quite charming, as are the four brief '*Dances of old Vienna*', with two included from the composer of the carol, *Silent night*. Even with this intimate group of strings, Boskovsky manages the authentically silky Viennese lilt, notably in the *Marien-Klänge waltz* of Josef Strauss, but father Johnann's *Badjaderen* is hardly less winning. Wonderfully natural and transparent sound, immaculately transferred to CD.

Boston Symphony Orchestra, Serge Koussevitzky

COPLAND: *El Salón México.* FOOTE: *Suite in E min., Op. 63.* HARRIS: *Symphony (1933); Symphony No. 3.* MCDONALD: *San Juan Capistrano – Two Evening Pictures.*
(M) (***) Pearl mono GEMMCD 9492.

Koussevitzky's performance of the Roy Harris *Third Symphony* has never been equalled in intensity and fire – even by Toscanini or Bernstein – and Copland himself never produced as exhilarating an *El Salón México*. The Arthur Foote *Suite* is unpretentious and has great charm. Sonic limitations are soon forgotten, for these performances have exceptional power and should not be missed.

Boston Symphony Orchestra, Chicago Symphony Orchestra or San Francisco Symphony Orchestra, Pierre Monteux

'Pierre Monteux Edition': BEETHOVEN: *Symphonies Nos. 4, Op. 60; 8, Op. 93; Overture: The Ruins of Athens.* BACH: *Passacaglia & fugue in C min.* (09026 61892-2). BERLIOZ: *Symphonie fantastique; Benevenuto Cellini overture; Les Troyens: Act II Prelude. La damnation de Faust: Rákóczy march* (09026 61894-2). BRAHMS: *Symphony No. 2, Op. 73; Schicksalslied, Op. 54.* MAHLER: *Kindertotenlieder* (with Gladys Swarthout) (09026 61891-2). CHAUSSON: *Symphony, Op. 20; Poème de l'amour et de la mer.* CHABRIER: *Le roi malgré lui: Fête-polonaise* (09026 61899-2). DEBUSSY: *Images; Sarabande; Nocturnes* (09026 61900-2). LISZT: *Les Préludes.* SCRIABIN: *Poème de l'extase, Op. 54.* SAINT-SAENS: *Havanaise, Op. 83.* DEBUSSY: *La mer* (09026 61890-2). DELIBES: *Coppélia: suite; Sylvia: suite.* GOUNOD: *Faust: ballet music* (09026 61975-2). FRANCK: *Symphony in D min; Pièce héroique.* D'INDY: *Istar* (symphonic variations), *Op. 42* (09026 61967-2). D'INDY: *Symphony on a French mountain air (cévenole), Op. 25; Fervaal, Op. 40; Symphony No. 2, Op. 57* (09026 61888-2). RIMSKY-KORSAKOV: *Scheherazade* (symphonic suite), *Op. 35; Sadko, Op. 5; Symphony No. 2 (Antar), Op. 9* (09026 61897-2). R. STRAUSS: *Ein Heldenleben, Op. 40; Death and transfiguration, Op. 24* (09026 61889-2). STRAVINSKY: *Petrushka; The Rite of spring* (09026 61898-2). TCHAIKOVSKY: *Symphonies Nos. 4, 5 & 6 (Pathétique)* (09026 61901-2).

☞ (M) (***) BMG/RCA 09026 61893-2 (15) [id.].

Monteux was born in 1875, thirteen years after Debussy and seven before Stravinsky, and the great French conductor's career was to co-exist and readily adapt to the enormous changes that came in music in the first half of the twentieth century. He made recordings from the 1920s onwards and, while he obviously brought special insights to French music, there is universal agreement that his repertoire had no geographical limitations and his interpretive versatility was extraordinary: everything was made to sound fresh. He loved the German repertoire and hated to be type-cast as a French specialist. His insights were as compelling in a Beethoven or Brahms symphony as in Stravinsky's *Rite of spring*, of which he conducted the 1913 world première in the city of his birth. (Noting the dismayed fury of the public at the *Rite of Spring*'s début, he confessed with great candour that 'At that time I did not understand one note!') Later, of course, he came to know every note and worked with the composer on the score before it entered his concert repertoire. He also directed the opening performances of *Petrushka*, *Daphnis et Chloé* and *Jeux* for Diaghilev's Ballets Russes. He was a guest with many of the world's major orchestras, sharing the Concertgebouw with Mengelberg for a decade from 1924 and also conducting the Orchestre Symphonique de Paris, with which in 1929 he made the first really convincing recording of the *Rite*.

For Americans, his name will always be associated with the San Francisco Symphony, whose musical director he became in 1936 and where he stayed for 16 years, until 1952. He was very happily married – his wife, Doris, came from Hancock, Maine, and he referred to her affectionately as 'the Eroica'. Many of the recordings in this Edition derive from that era. Monteux had the common touch and was a famous figure in the city and the trolley-car drivers would all bid him 'Good morning'.

From 1951, he also conducted regularly at Boston, where he recorded both French and Russian repertory. In the mid-1950s he also came regularly to London, where he made some of his finest later recordings with the LSO for Decca; these would surely make an excellent stereo Monteux Edition. A famous story about him at that period comes from the LSO players. He was rehearsing a performance of a Beethoven symphony and commented: 'Gentlemen, you may think this is too fast, but that is how the critics like it!' and that is the way he recorded it and made it seem exactly right. Indeed his San Francisco coupling of the Beethoven 4th and 8th symphonies has all the exuberant freshness one associates with his Beethoven. He told his students (at a famous American school for conductors which he set up in his wife's birthplace, where it remains to the present day) that the development section in a Beethoven symphony should always bring a fractional reduction in pace, but of course in a first-rate performance the ear seldom notices such a subtle change.

In his 1945 *Symphonie fantastique*, one of the finest ever recorded, the volatile manipulation of tempo in the first movement grows naturally out of the music and, with the sparkling waltz providing a pleasingly elegant interlude, the slow movement combines Byronic romanticism with intensity. The last two movements generate great excitement and the clipped rhythms of the *March to the scaffold* are full of Gallic charcter. The close balance of the mono recording also means that not only are the strings given plenty of body in their slow-movement cantilena but remarkable detail also registers in the finale.

Monteux had a very special place in his heart for Brahms and he recorded the *Second Symphony* four times. In many ways his later, VPO version is the finest and it includes the first-movement exposition repeat. But the present San Franciso performance is unerringly paced and has great warmth and energy. It is direct and powerful, and comparing it with Barenboim's recent self-indulgent Chicago recording for Erato makes one wonder if some of the present generation of conductors need to pay a visit to Monteux's conducting school in Maine. The Chausson *Symphony* is warm, fresh and subtly coloured in the first movement, the *très lent*, darker, more intense without neurosis, while the finale is certainly exuberantly *animé*. A refreshing reading, remarkably well recorded, In Debussy's *Images*, the *Gigues* has every bit as strong an atmosphere as one remembered; so, too, has the middle movement of *Ibéria* (*Parfums dans la nuit*), which never appeared in the UK (according to W.E.R.M., the complete set appeared on LP in France). The *Sarabande* (orchestrated by Ravel), recorded in 1946, is masterly and elegant. The 1955 *Nuages* is a great improvement in sound and is marvellously paced, with sumptuous string sonority – one of the best *Nuages* ever! It has the advantage of the ambience of Boston's Symphony Hall. So has *La Mer*, another performance showing Monteux's ear for detail and atmosphere, the *Dialogue du vent et de la mer* exciting without going over the top.

The performance of Liszt's *Les Préludes* has tremendous panache and gusto. Can today's performers, one wonders, believe in its melodarama as Monteux and his players did (in 1952)? Scriabin's *Poème de l'extase* has refined, translucent detail and a passionate climax, achieved in spite of the comparatively limited dynamic range of the recording. These performances were made in Carnegie Hall and are close-miked, but for Saint-Saëns's *Havanaise* we return to Boston and join Leonid Kogan, who gives a sparkling and deliciously sultry account (with the advantage of stereo). This piece, like many of the other orchestral works, has individual sections banded, so one can isolate the coda and enjoy Kogan's wonderfully chimerical closing bars.

Monteux's ballet experience was not confined to twentieth-century scores and he knew just how to bring a sparkle to the eyes and a bloom to the cheeks of *Coppélia*. He points the *Valse de la poupée* delightfully and there is plenty of vigour in the lively music for the corps de ballet. In *Sylvia* the *Intermezzo* and *Valse lente* are played gently and with tender warmth. The Boston acoustics add bloom and this 1953 recording sounds almost like stereo; Gounod's ballet suite from *Faust* was recorded in San Francisco six years earlier, and the Opera House acoustics are also pleasing.

The stereo César Franck *Symphony*, dating from 1961, is masterly – perhaps Monteux's very finest recording. The present remastering by John Pfeifer brings an astonishing improvement even over the earlier CD; indeed the quality reflects the acoustics of Chicago's Orchestra Hall in the same way as the Reiner recordings, with textures full-bodied and glowing without loss of detail. The addition of Charles O'Donnell's orchestration of the *Pièce héroïque* is a distinct bonus. Its chromatic links with the *Symphony* are the more obvious in its orchestral format: it sounds rather like a symphonic poem with a brassy denouement. The 1941 mono recording (like the *Faust* ballet music) shows the excellence of the acoustics of San Francisco's War Memorial Opera House. Vincent d'Indy's *Istar* (from 1945) completes Volume 8. It is a colourful and increasingly energetic piece. Although it opens *Très lent*, the other two movements are significantly labelled *Un peu plus animé* and *Le double plus vite*, although, because of the programme, the music broadens satisfyingly at the end. Although the sound is boxier, the strings have plenty of middle sonority and the performance is unlikely to be bettered, since Monteux was a friend of the composer and took special care with recordings of his music (as did Beecham with Delius).

Volume 9, devoted entirely to the music of d'Indy, is an especially valuable disc, since the *Second Symphony* held a special place in Monteux's affections. This was its first commercial recording and it remained the only one for the best part of 40 years. The 1941 recording of the *Symphonie sur un chant montagnard français* is splendidly paced and comes up sounding very fresh, even though there is some distortion in the lower end of the range and the piano tone calls for some tolerance. The Russian-born pianist, Maxim Schapiro, relatively little known nowadays, is very good indeed. The *Second Symphony* is a marvellous performance, though this transfer is a bit flat. Checked against the LP (RCA LCT 1125) and a tuning fork, we made it over half a semitone down!

Monteux made his complete recording of *Daphnis et Chloé* for Decca, but the *First suite* (initially described as 'symphonic fragments') has remarkable allure, even if the sound is not quite secure at the opening. It includes not only a chorus but also a wind-machine. The other Ravel pieces are distinctive (some of the *Valses nobles* have captivating delicacy), but Lalo's melodramatic overture and Ibert's translucent *Escales* suffer from the restricted mono sound. No such complaints about the 1942 *Scheherazade*, where once more the resonance of the San Francisco Opera House provides mono sound of unexpected warmth and allure. With the orchestra's concertmaster, Naoum Blinder, (very well balanced) taking the role of the heroine with panache this is a tremendously compelling performance. The orchestra produces sumptuous tone and in the finale the playing is so riveting that the ear hardly notices that there is any dynamic restriction: the final climax is truly magnificent. In many ways this is even finer than Monteux's later, stereo, Decca record. *Sadko* is hardly less intoxicating and *Antar* has plenty of exotic colour and impetus, but here the sound is two-dimensional.

As a recording, the 1947 *Ein Heldenleben* must be counted a virtual failure. In spite of the use of the San Francisco Opera House, the engineers obviously sought brilliance above all and the violins are made to sound paper-thin and shrill. Obviously the microphones were far too close, and the cellos and basses sound comparably dry and lustreless. However, there are few CDs in the whole catalogue which give a better demonstration of the advantages of stereo recording after a badly balanced mono, for Monteux's glorious 1960 *Death and transfiguration*, recorded in California Hall, ranks with the very finest, as gripping as – and even more sumptuous than – Szell's Cleveland version. Like his Brahms, it shows just how well this extraordinarily versatile conductur could handle main-line German repertioire, with the San Francisco brass sounding like Reiner's Chicago players and the transformation scene at the end both radiant and thrillingly voluptuous.

The Stravinsky coupling offers the finer of Monteux's two stereo *Petrushkas*, coupled with a remarkably fine mono *Rite of spring* from 1951. *Petrushka* is much better played here than the later, Decca version with the Paris Conservatoire Orchestra: vivid throughout, with the tension especially high in the final scene, and all the bustle of the Shrovetide Carnival brilliantly conveyed. The new transfer has brought an altogether more congenial sound than ever before and, though the focus is not sharp, the colouring of the Boston resonance does not blunt the transients unduly. *The Rite* is marvellously played and, because of the Boston ambience, sounds remarkably like stereo. There is plenty of rhythmic vehemence and the closing *Danse de la terre* of Part 1 brings thrillingly menacing articulation. Although the balance is close, the *Cercles mystérieux des adolescentes* is hauntingly evocative and the final *Sacrificial dance* with its snarling brass brings a powerful climax and a quickening of tension in the very last bars.

The three great Tchaikovsky *Symphonies* were recorded in Boston between 1955 and 1959 and are among Monteux's finest records. The *Fourth* is a most compulsive reading which sweeps through the score with its momentum sustained from first to last. The slow movement has a fine oboe solo and the central section really takes off: some might find this too wilful, but its spontaneous lift is exhilating; the coda of the finale, too, generates great excitement when the Boston sound has such spectacular breadth. The *Fifth* (1958) is direct, full-blooded and exciting, still among the finest versions available. The remastered recording is a revelation: strings and brass sound wonderfully rich and this is one of the best of all the RCA recordings made in Boston in the early stereo era. There are a few minor eccentricities of tempo, and in the finale Monteux makes a few agogic distortions, but the performance has such panache that he convinces the listener in all he does.

The *Pathétique* is a mono recording, but the ear would hardly guess when the Boston sound has such amplitude and depth. The reading is essentially dignified, except in the *Allegro con grazia*, which has a curious feeling of urgency, even of hurry. The first movement lacks neither power nor excitement, but Monteux does not wear his heart on his sleeve – he holds back for the finale. The Scherzo/March is both, with energetic detail and a slowing for the final bold presentation of the tune. The finale, the apex of the reading, is heartfelt and spontaneously passionate without ever gushing. The orchestra responds nobly, especially in the restrained, dignified coda.

All in all, the Monteux Edition is a considerable achievement.

(i) **British Symphony Orchestra,** (ii) **London Symphony Orchestra,** (iii) **Symphony Orchestra,** (iv) **Queen's Hall Orchestra,** (v) **London Philharmonic Orchestra; Sir Henry Wood**

'The Best of Sir Henry J. Wood': (i) BACH: *Brandenburg concerto No. 3.* (ii) HAYDN: *Symphony No. 45 in F sharp min. (Farewell).* (ii) SCHUBERT: *Symphony No. 8 in B min. (Unfinished).* (ii) LITOLFF: *Concerto No. 4: Scherzo* (with Irene Scharrer). (iii) RACHMANINOV (arr. Wood): *Prelude in C sharp min.* (iv) DVORAK: *Symphonic variations* (with rehearsal sequence). (iv) BRUCKNER: *Overture in C min.* (iv) BEETHOVEN: *Symphony No. 5 in C min., Op. 67.* (iv) BRAHMS: *Variations on a theme of Haydn.*

☞ (M) (***) Dutton Laboratories mono 2CDAX 2002 (2) [id.].

This collection is aptly named. During the great days of the Proms, this annual summer musical jamboree, so essentially British, was the source of a musical education for many devotees, long before the coming of LPs, tapes and CDs, and when a Beethoven symphony on four or five 78 shellac discs could cost a substantial part of a week's wages. During the war years it was possible to get a Promenade season ticket (covering also the first and last nights) for around £2.50 – about a shilling (5p) a concert. The concerts were far more generous in playing time in those days. The first half lasted about as long as the whole of a contemporary Proms programme; then the second half could last up to another hour and usually included a twentieth-century composition, though real music, not *avant-garde* 'barbed wire'. There were composer nights, so that the regular attender was able to hear live performances of an amazing amount of standard repertoire during a single season. Wood was a totally reliable interpreter. There were no frills (except perhaps in a Tchaikovsky symphony, where he was inclined to allow himself a fair amount of freedom), and he delivered strong, direct readings of uncommon freshness – as these recordings illustrate. The Bach *Third Brandenburg* is a joy. It uses a large group of strings but with plenty of light and shade and possesses an invigorating vitality. Haydn's *Farewell Symphony* – played here with remarkable finesse – was recorded at a time when only the late *London Symphonies* were heard at concerts – and that almost solely due to Sir Thomas Beecham. Beethoven's *Fifth* is without the histrionics of a Toscanini, a sound reading which is surprisingly satisfying even today. We also hear Wood rehearsing (the words remarkably clear) in his direct, no-nonsense manner (he had only limited rehearsal time at his disposal, but British musicians could always sight-read with incredible dexterity – even at a performance, if they had to!). The transfers are typical of Dutton expertise and are remarkably full and vivid. Everything here sounds alive; only the Dvořák *Symphonic variations* is disappointing, but that is at least partly because the Decca recording is so lacklustre – made in 1937, just before the arrival of Arthur Haddy who was to transform the company's technical prowess with the coming of wartime FFRR 78s. But that is another story.

'Proms favourites': (iv) COATES: *London suite; London Bridge march.* GRAINGER: (i) *Molly on the shore; Mock Morris.* (iv) *Handel in the Strand.* (iv) WAGNER: *The Ride of the Valkyries.* (v) BERLIOZ: *Roman carnival overture.* (v) GOUNOD: *Funeral march of a marionette.* ELGAR: (v) *Pomp and circumstance marches Nos. 1 in D (Land of hope and glory); 4 in G.* (ii) *Fantasia on British sea songs* (arr. Wood). (iii) JARNEFELT: *Praeludium.*

☞ (M) (**(*)) Dutton Laboratories mono CDAX 8008 [id.].

In the early days, the Proms were the exact opposite of what they have become under the BBC's current programming policy, and this collection of 'pops' is representative of the kind of music Wood introduced, especially on Saturday evenings, to draw in the widest audience. It includes the famous *Sea-songs* which became a staple of the 'Last night' celebrations, put together in 1905 to celebrate the centenary of the Battle of Trafalgar. It was recently used at London's Royal Tournament for a similar purpose and sounds incredibly vivid here, especially the famous *Sailor's hornpipe*, where one is immediately tempted to clap and which works up into such a zestful frenzy at the end that the listener is left breathless. Wood conducts everything with aplomb. The programme is slight and, for all the skill of the transfer engineers, one needs modern stereo for the shorter lollipops to sound their best; even so, the *Carnaval romain overture* (from 1940) has a strikingly convincing ambience. The early Decca recordings (both here and above) are available only because Wood bequeathed his own collection of test pressings to the Royal Academy of Music, where they lay, unplayed, for many years. Most of those included here sound rather dry and studio-ish, especially the unexpansive *Ride of the Valkyries* (not Wood's fault). But the lollipop which leaps off the original shellac is track 7, Wood's own re-orchestration of Grainger's *Handel in the Strand*, and this is surely the demonstration item. This record and its companion set above are issued to coincide with Arthur Jacobs' splendid new biography, *Henry J. Wood, Maker of the Proms.*

Brüggen, Frans (recorder)

Recorder concertos (with VCM, Harnoncourt): VIVALDI: *Concerto in C min., RV 441.* SAMMARTINI: *Concerto in F.* TELEMANN: *Concerto in C.* NAUDOT: *Concerto in G.*
(M) *** Teldec/Warner 2292 43547-2 [id.].

Frans Brüggen is an unsurpassed master of his instrument, and he gives the four assorted concertos his keen advocacy on this excellent record, reissued from 1968. There is spontaneity too and, with superb musicianship, good recording and a well-balanced orchestral contribution, this mid-priced CD can earn nothing but praise.

(i) Chicago Symphony Orchestra, Frederick Stock; (ii) Cincinnati SO, Eugene Goossens; (iii) with Jascha Heifetz (violin)

English music: (i) BENJAMIN: *Overture to an Italian comedy*. ELGAR: *Pomp and circumstance march No. 1*. (ii) VAUGHAN WILLIAMS: *A London Symphony* (*No. 2; original version*); (ii; iii) WALTON: *Violin concerto*.
☞ (***) Biddulph mono WHL 016 [id.].

This superbly transferred Biddulph issue celebrates the fact that some of the very finest recordings of British music have come from America. Heifetz's historic first recording of the Walton *Violin concerto* is imaginatively coupled with the only recording ever made (also by Goossens and the Cincinnati Orchestra immediately following the Walton sessions in 1941) of the 1920 version of Vaughan Williams's *London Symphony*. As welcome fill-ups come Elgar's *Pomp and Circumstance No. 1* and Arthur Benjamin's *Overture to an Italian comedy*, brilliantly played by the Chicago orchestra under Frederick Stock.

Cincinnati Pops Orchestra, Erich Kunzel

'Favourite overtures': SUPPE: *Light cavalry; Poet and peasant*. AUBER: *Fra Diavolo*. HEROLD: *Zampa*. REZNICEK: *Donna Diana*. OFFENBACH: *Orpheus in the Underworld*. ROSSINI: *William Tell*.
☞ *** Telarc Dig. CD 80116 [id.].

We are indebted to a reader for drawing our attention to the omission from previous editions of this spectacularly recorded (1985) collection of favourite bandstand overtures. The playing has fine exuberance and gusto (only the galop from *William Tell* could perhaps have had greater impetus) and the resonant ambience of Cincinnati's Music Hall lends itself to Telarc's wide-ranging engineering, with the bass drum nicely caught. Perhaps the opening of *Fra Diavolo* would have benefited from a more transparent sound, but for the most part the opulence suits the vigorous style of the music-making, with *Zampa* and the Suppé overtures particularly successful.

'The Fantastic Leopold Stokowski' (transcriptions for orchestra): BACH: *Toccata & fugue in D min., BWV 565; Little fugue in G min., BWV 578*. BOCCHERINI: *Quintet in E flat: Minuet*. BEETHOVEN: *Moonlight sonata: adagio sostenuto*. BRAHMS: *Hungarian dance No. 6*. DEBUSSY: *Suite bergamasque: Clair de lune; La cathédrale engloutie*. ALBENIZ: *Fête-Dieu à Seville*. RACHMANINOV: *Prelude in C sharp min., Op. 3/2*. MUSSORGSKY: *Night on the bare mountain; Pictures at an exhibition: The Great gate of Kiev*.
☞ ⊛ *** Telarc Dig. CD 80338 [id.].

Stokowski began his conducting career in Cincinnati in 1909, moving on to Philadelphia three years later; so a collection of his orchestral transcriptions from his first orchestra is appropriate, particularly when the playing is so committed and polished and the recording so sumptuous. Indeed, none of Stokowski's own recordings can match this Telarc disc in sheer glamour of sound. The arrangement of *La cathédrale engloutie* is very free and melodramatically telling. Most interesting is *Night on the bare mountain*, which has a grandiloquent brass chorale added as a coda. Any admirer of Stokowski should regard this superbly engineered CD as an essential purchase. It is now reissued with two extra items added, the Brahms *Hungarian dance No. 6* and Stokowski's extraordinary transcription of *The Great Gate of Kiev* from Mussorgsky's *Pictures at an exhibition*. Kunzel has the advantage of Telarc's bass-drum recording, and at the very close there is a highly imaginative added touch as the old magician introduces an evocation of Moscow cathedral bells.

Cleveland Symphonic Winds, Fennell

'Stars and stripes': ARNAUD: *3 Fanfares*. BARBER: *Commando march*. LEEMANS: *Belgian Paratroopers*. FUCIK: *Florentine march, Op. 214*. KING: Barnum and Bailey's favourite. ZIMMERMAN: *Anchors aweigh*. J. STRAUSS S: *Radetzky march*. VAUGHAN WILLIAMS: *Sea songs; Folk songs suite*. SOUSA: *The Stars and stripes forever*. GRAINGER: *Lincolnshire posy*.
*** Telarc Dig. CD 80099 [id.].

This vintage collection from Frederick Fennell and his superb Cleveland wind and brass group is one of the finest of its kind ever made. Severance Hall, Cleveland, has ideal acoustics for this programme and the playing has wonderful virtuosity and panache. Add to all this digital engineering of Telarc's highest calibre, and you have a very special issue.

Dallas Symphony Orchestra, Eduardo Mata

TCHAIKOVSKY: *Capriccio italien, Op. 45.* MUSSORGSKY: *Night on the bare mountain.* DUKAS: *L'apprenti sorcier.* ENESCU: *Rumanian rhapsody No. 1.*
(BB) *** BMG/RCA Dig. VD 87727 [7727-2-RV].

One of the outstanding early digital orchestral demonstration CDs. The acoustic of the Dallas Hall produces a thrilling resonance without too much clouding of detail. The Mussorgsky piece is rather lacking in menace when textures are so ample. *The Sorcerer's apprentice* is spirited and affectionately characterized, and the Tchaikovsky and Enescu are richly enjoyable.

Detroit Symphony Orchestra, Paul Paray

'*French opera highlights*': HEROLD: *Overture: Zampa.* AUBER: *Overture: The Crown diamonds.* GOUNOD: *Faust: ballet suite; Waltz* (from Act II). SAINT-SAENS: *Samson et Dalila: Bacchanale.* BIZET: *Carmen: Danse bohème.* BERLIOZ: *Les Troyens: Royal hunt and storm.* MASSENET: *Phèdre overture.* THOMAS: *Mignon: Gavotte.*
(M) *** Mercury 432 014-2 [id.].

Paul Paray's reign at Detroit tempted the Mercury producers to record a good deal of French music under his baton, and here is a good example of the Gallic verve and sparkle that were achieved. The only disappointment is the unslurred horn phrasing at the magical opening and close of the *Royal hunt and storm.*

'*Marches and overtures à la Française*': MEYERBEER: *Le Prophète: Coronation march.* GOUNOD: *Funeral march of a marionette.* SAINT-SAENS: *Marche militaire française; Marche héroïque.* DE LISLE: *La Marseillaise.* Overtures: ADAM: *Si j'étais roi.* BOIELDIEU: *La Dame blanche.* ROSSINI: *William Tell.* OFFENBACH: *La belle Hélène; Orpheus in the Underworld. Contes d'Hoffmann: Barcarolle* etc.
☞ (M) **(*) Mercury 434 332-2 [id.].

A generous and flavourful Gallic concert, recorded in three different Detroit venues, with acoustics not entirely flattering to the orchestra, who nevertheless always play splendidly. The Adam and Boieldieu overtures need the glow of Kingsway Hall: here the resonance of Cass Technical High School slightly clouds detail (as with the virtuoso bassoon accompaniment for the reprise of the secondary theme of the charming Boieldieu *Dame blanche*). The marches and the Offenbach items were recorded in 1959 in Old Orchestral Hall, and the sound is more expansive. The most memorable pieces are the wittily engaging Gounod (always to be remembered as Alfred Hitchcock's TV signature-tune) and the spirited *Belle Hélène overture*, not put together by the composer, but none the worse for that. Throughout, the élan of the playing always brings enjoyment, and the virtuosity of the fiddles in the *William Tell galop* is exhilarating.

Du Pré, Jacqueline (cello)

'*The Art of Jaqueline Du Pré*': (with (i) LSO, Sir John Barbirolli; (ii) RPO, Sir Malcolm Sargent; (iii) New Philh. O; (iv) Chicago SO, (v) ECO; (vi) Daniel Barenboim; (vii) Valda Aveling; (viii) Gerald Moore; (ix) Ernest Lush; (x) Steven Bishop). (i) ELGAR: *Cello concerto in E min., Op. 85.* (ii) DELIUS: *Cello concerto.* (iii; vi) SAINT-SAENS: *Cello concerto No. 1 in A min., Op. 33.* (iv; vi) DVORAK: *Cello concerto in B min., Op. 104; Waldesruhe, Op. 68.* (iii; vi) SCHUMANN: *Cello concerto in A min., Op. 129.* (i; vii) MANN: *Cello concerto in G min.* HAYDN: *Cello concertos in* (i) *C and* (v; vi) *D, Hob VIIb/1–2.* (vi) CHOPIN: *Cello sonata in G min., Op. 65.* (vi) FRANCK: *Cello sonata in A.* (viii) FAURE: *Elégie in C min., Op. 24.* (viii) BRUCH: *Kol nidrei, Op. 47.* BACH: *(Unaccompanied) Cello suites Nos. 1–2, BWV 1007/8.* (ix) HANDEL: *Cello sonata in G min.* BEETHOVEN: (vi) *Variations in G min, WoO 45; on Judas Maccabeus: See the conqu'ring hero comes;* (x) *Cello sonatas Nos. 3, in A, Op. 69; 5 in D, Op. 102/2.* (vi) *Variations on themes from 'The Magic Flute': 7 variations in D, WoO 46 (Bei Männern, welche Liebe fühlen); 12 variations in F, WoO 66 (Ein Mädchen oder Weibchen).*
☞ (B) *** EMI CZS5 68132-2 (6) [id.].

Admirers of this remarkably gifted artist, whose career ended so tragically, will welcome this survey of her major recordings, made over the incredibly brief period of a single decade. Her first recordings (1961) have a BBC source and her last (the Chopin and Franck *Sonatas*) were made at Abbey Road in 1971. But of course she made her real breakthrough in 1965 with the justly famous Kingsway Hall recording of the Elgar *Concerto* with Barbirolli. Some items included here are not otherwise currently available (including the *Concerto* by Matthias Georg Monn) and, with excellent transfers, this set is an admirable and economical way of exploring her art. There are good if brief notes and some heart-rending photographs showing this young prodigy playing with characteristic concentration and joyously in conversation with her equally young husband, Daniel Barenboim.

Eastman-Rochester Orchestra, Howard Hanson

American orchestral music: BARBER: *Capricorn concerto, Op. 21* (with Joseph Mariano (flute), Robert Sprenkle (oboe), Sidney Mear (trumpet)). PISTON: *The Incredible flutist* (ballet suite). GRIFFES: *Poem for flute and orchestra.* MCCAULEY: *5 Miniatures for flute and strings* (all with Jospeh Mariano (flute)). BERGSMA: *Gold and the Señor Commandante* (ballet suite).
(M) *** Mercury 434 307-2 [id.].

A first-rate concert of pioneering recordings, made between 1957 and 1963. The collection is worth having for Barber's *Capricorn concerto* alone, a less characteristic work than say any of the *Essays for orchestra*, or the solo concertos. Walter Piston's ballet *The Incredible flutist* comes from 1938 and the suite is one of the most refreshing and imaginative of all American scores. Griffes' *Poem* with its gentle, shimmering textures is French in feeling but is thoroughly worthwhile in its own right. Joseph Mariano is an excellent soloist as he is in the more simplistic but engaging *Miniatures* of the Canadian, William McCauley (born 1917). Kent Kennan's *Three Pieces* are clearly influenced by the ballet music of Stravinsky. Bergsma's ballet is rather noisy at times, and fails to be memorable, though brightly scored. Excellent performances throughout and typically vivid Eastman Rochester sound.

American orchestral music II: MCPHEE: *Tabuh-Tabuhan (Toccata for orchestra).* SESSIONS: *The Black maskers (suite).* V. THOMSON: *Symphony on a hymn tune; The Feast of love* (with David Clatworthy).
(M) *** Mercury 434 310-2 [id.].

McPhee's *Tabuh-Tabuhan*, written in 1936 uses Balinese music for its main colouring and rhythmic background. Roger Sessions' *Black maskers suite* was written as incidental music for a play by Andreyev about devil worship and the Black Mass, but it is not in the same class as, say, Prokofiev's *Scythian suite*. This is no fault of the performance or recording. The Virgil Thomson *Symphony*, although based on hymn-like material, is attractively quirky (reflecting the composer's Parisian years, the influence of Les Six, and Satie in particular). The cantata could hardly be more contrasted in its warmly flowing lyricism, a heady setting of an anonymous Latin love poem. The poet revels in the erotic joys of love, and the composer and his excellent soloist are obviously delighted by the voluptuous feeling of the words. As always the vintage Mercury sound is vivid with colour.

American music: MOORE: *Pageant of P. T. Barnum.* CARPENTER: *Adventures in a perambulator.* Bernard ROGERS: *Once upon a time (5 Fairy tales).* Burrill PHILLIPS: *Selection from McGuffey's Reader.*
☞ (M) *** Mercury 434 319-2 [id.].

This is a particularly happy and successful combination of early-twentieth-century American music which is the very opposite of the avant garde. John Alden Carpenter's suite was a favourite of American audiences before the Second World War and is diverting and often charming. The idiom is amiably innocuous but surprisingly seductive, not least the closing number, *Dreams.* Douglas Moore's *Pageant of P. T. Barnum* is hardly less accessible, with its engaging portraits of *Jenny Lind, General and Mrs Tom Thumb* and *Joice Heth,* a negress who was supposedly 160 years old! Bernard Rogers's set of *Five Fairy tales* is scored with whimsical charm and includes *The tinder box soldier, The song of Rapunzel, The story of a darning needle, The dance of the twelve princesses* (a Ravellian pavane) and the *Ride of Koschei the Deathless,* the least successful movement. William Holmes McGuffey's *Readers* formed the staple textbook diet of schoolchildren in mid-nineteenth-century America. Thus Burrill Phillips chose an apt title for a suite inspired by Americana. The gently nostalgic second movement pictures *John Alden and Priscilla* (who sailed on the *Mayflower*), and the noisy finale depicts *Paul Revere's midnight ride.* If this is perhaps the least memorable of the four works included here, its composer sums up rather succinctly the ethos of the whole programme. He tells us that he felt that Grant Wood's painting of the famous Revere ride 'contained all the elements of what I had felt to be at the center of the strong old American legends' and suggested the universal characteristics of the American nation: 'a certain naive strength of moral fiber, some sentiment verging on the sentimental, love of movement and grand gestures and attitudes'. The performances are affectionate and committed throughout and the early stereo (1956–8) remarkably truthful.

Eastman Wind Ensemble, Frederick Fennell

'Hands across the sea – Marches from around the world': SOUSA: *Hands across the sea; The US Field Artillery; The Thunderer; Washington Post; King Cotton; El Capitan; The Stars and Stripes forever.* GANNE: *Father of victory (Père de la victoire).* Mariano SAN MIGUEL: *The golden ear.* TIEKE: *Old comrades.* PROKOFIEV: *March, Op. 99.* HANSSEN: *Valdres march.* Davide DELLE CESE: *Inglesina.* COATES: *Knightsbridge.* MEACHAM: *American patrol.* GOLDMAN: *On the Mall.* MCCOY: *Lights out.* KING: *Barnum and Bailey's favourite.* ALFORD: *Colonel Bogey.* KLOHR: *The Billboard.*
☞ (M) *** Mercury 434 334-2 [id.].

March records don't come any better than this, and nor does military/concert-band recording. The sparkling transients at the opening of *Hands across the sea* and the peppy spirit of the playing (as with all the Sousa items, and especially *The Stars and Stripes forever*) give the listener a real lift, while the French *Father of victory* and German *Old comrades* are just as full of character. The Prokofiev is as witty as you like, and Fennell shows he understands the more relaxed swagger of the British way in *Colonel Bogey*. First rate – but, with a 65-minute programme, this needs to be taken a march or two at a time, unless you want to fall out with the neighbours – this is not a CD to reproduce gently!

English Chamber Orchestra, Daniel Barenboim

English music (with (i) Neil Black; (ii) Pinchas Zukerman): DELIUS: *On hearing the first cuckoo in spring; Summer night on the river; 2 Aquarelles; Fennimore and Gerda: Intermezzo.* VAUGHAN WILLIAMS: *Fantasia on Greensleeves;* (i) *Oboe concerto;* (ii) *The Lark ascending.* WALTON: *Henry V* (film incidental music): *Passacaglia: The death of Falstaff; Touch her soft lips and part.*
☞ (M) *** DG 439 529-2 [id.].

We have always had a soft spot for Barenboim's warmly evocative ECO collection of atmospheric English music. Even if the effect is not always totally idiomatic, the recordings have a warmth and allure that are wholly seductive (see under various composer entries).

English Chamber Orchestra, Donald Fraser

'World anthems': WILLIAMS: *Olympic theme.* National anthems of Spain, Australia, Poland, Brazil, Denmark, Kenya, Canada, Great Britain, China, Finland & Estonia, Hungary, Norway, Germany, Czechoslovakia, USA, Greece, The Netherlands, Japan, Israel, Egypt, France, Argentina, Sweden, Mexico, Ethiopia, Austria, Lithuania, Italy (all arr. Fraser).
☞ *(*) BMG/RCA Dig. 09026 61342-2.

Potentially this is a useful disc, but Donald Fraser's arrangements for a small orchestra are almost entirely without pomp and circumstance – *God save the queen* even ends with a diminuendo. The result often produces pleasing and at times piquant sounds but little or no gravitas. Not surprisingly, the rather jolly *Marseillaise* and *The Star-spangled banner* (which begins with a fife and tabour effect) come off best, but there are a surprising number of rather good tunes here. Both the Italian and Brazilian examples have an operatic flavour, the latter almost Rossinian; and both Ethiopia and Lithuania produce attractive brass chorales. Spain's *Marcha real* is quite frothy in its lighthearted scoring. Not surprisingly, Russia and Yugoslavia are notably absent. Only one verse is included of each anthem and the (full-priced) CD plays for only 38 minutes. Performances are lively and colourful and the recording excellent, but one wonders who would want to buy this.

English Chamber Orchestra, Raymond Leppard

ALBINONI: *Sonata a 5 in A, Op. 2/3; Sonata a 5 in G min., Op. 2/6.* VIVALDI: *Concertos: in D, P.175; in G min., P.392; Sonata in E flat (Al Santo sepolcro), P.441.* CORELLI: *Concerto grosso in F, Op. 6/9.*
(B) *** CfP CD-CFP 4371; *TC-CFP 4371.*

An outstanding collection of Italian string concertos, recorded in 1970 and sounding first class. The standard of invention throughout the concert is high and the playing is polished and committed. Except for those who can accept only original instruments, this is a fine concert for the late evening.

English String Orchestra or English Symphony Orchestra, William Boughton

'The spirit of England': ELGAR: Overture Cockaigne; Introduction and allegro, Op. 47; Sospiri, Op. 70. DELIUS: Summer evening. BUTTERWORTH: The banks of green willow; A Shropshire lad. FINZI: Suite from Love's Labour's Lost; Clarinet concerto (with Alan Hacker). VAUGHAN WILLIAMS: The lark ascending (with Michael Bochmann); Oboe concerto (with Maurice Bourgue); Fantasia on a theme of Thomas Tallis; Fantasia on Greensleeves. PARRY: Lady Radnor's suite. BRIDGE: Suite for string orchestra. HOLST: St Paul's suite. WARLOCK: Capriol suite. BRITTEN: Variations on a theme of Frank Bridge, Op. 10.

⊛ (B) *** Nimbus Dig. NI 5210/3 [id.].

The Birmingham-based English String and Symphony Orchestras under William Boughton is completely at home in this repertoire. One has only to sample the excitingly animated account of Holst's St Paul's suite (which also has much delicacy of feeling), the ideally paced Warlock Capriol suite, or the vibrant account of Britten's Frank Bridge variations, to discover the calibre of this music-making. The recordings were made in the Great Hall of Birmingham University which, with its warm reverberation, gives the strings a gloriously rich body of tone, supported by sumptuous cello and bass sonorities. The Elgar Introduction and allegro expands wonderfully at its climax (yet the fugue is not blurred) and in Vaughan Williams's Lark ascending, where the violin solo is exquisitely played with wonderful purity of tone by Michael Bochmann, the closing pianissimo seems to float in the still air. The work most suited to such an expansive acoustic is Vaughan Williams's Tallis fantasia, a deeply expressive performance which gives the listener the impression of sitting in a cathedral, with the solo string group, perfectly matched and blended in timbre, evoking a distant, ethereal organ. The lovely Butterworth pieces are tenderly sympathetic, and Alan Hacker's rhapsodically improvisatory account of Finzi's Clarinet concerto is full of colour and warmth. Perhaps Maurice Bourgue's oboe is balanced a little too closely in Vaughan Williams's Oboe concerto but the ear adjusts. On the other hand, the flutes melt magically into the strings in the famous Greensleeves fantasia. Delius's Summer evening, an early work, is quite memorable, and the suites of Parry and Finzi are full of colourful invention. The Bridge Suite for strings brings a lively response, with sumptuous textures. Only the opening Cockaigne overture of Elgar is a little lacking in profile and drama – and even here Boughton's relaxed, lyrical approach is enjoyable, for he broadens the final climax very satisfyingly. Very inexpensively priced indeed, this box makes an outstanding bargain.

Galway, James (flute)

'Pachelbel's Canon and other Baroque favourites' (with various orchestras & conductors): VIVALDI: Concerto in D (Il Cardinello), Op. 10/3: First and second movements. Four Seasons: Spring (arr. Galway). TELEMANN: Suite for strings in A min.: Réjouissance; Polonaise. PACHELBEL: Canon. HANDEL: Sonatas: in A min., Op. 1/4: Fourth movement; in F, Op. 1/11: Siciliana; Allegro (both with Sarah Cunningham, Philip Moll). Solomon: Arrival of the Queen of Sheba (arr. Gerhardt). Messiah: Pifa (Pastoral Symphony). Xerxes: Largo. BACH: Suite Nos. 2 in B min., BWV 1067: Minuet & Badinerie; 3 in D, BWV 1068: Air. Trio sonata Nos. 2 in G, BWV 1039: 4th movt (with Kyung Wha Chung, Moll, Welsh); Flute sonatas: Nos. 2 in E flat, BWV 1031: Siciliano (with Maria Graf, harp); 4 in C, BWV 1033: Second movement (arr. Gerhardt for flute & O). Concerto in E min., BWV 1059/35 (ed. Radeke): Third movement. ALBINONI: Adagio. QUANTZ: Concerto in C: Finale. MARAIS: Le Basque (arr. Galway/Gerhardt).

☞ *** BMG/RCA Dig./Analogue 09026 61928-2 [id.].

James Galway is completely at home in Baroque repertoire an area where a fair degree of stylistic freedom is to be expected. If the famous Bach Air from BWV 1068 is spun out somewhat romantically and the Siciliano from BWV 1031 (with harp accompaniment) is too solemn, Handel's famous Largo is gloriously managed, completely vocal in feeling. Galway certainly dominates Pachelbel's Canon in a way not intended by the composer, but his elegant line and simple divisions on the lovely theme are very agreeable. Any of the composers included here would surely have been amazed at the beauty of his tone and the amazing technical facility, always turned to musical effect. He is a wonderful goldfinch in Vivaldi's Op. 10/3, while Gerhardt's arrangement of Handel's Arrival of the Queen of Sheba, which exchanges oboes for flutes, is ear-tickling. The engaging Quantz concerto movement is as sprightly in the strings (of the Württemberg Chamber Orchestra) as it is in the felicitously decorated solo part. The Bach and Handel sonata excerpts are refreshing and the

(Handel) *Siciliana* from Op. 1/11 is matched in pastoral charm by the beautiful account of the *Pifa* from *Messiah*, played with much delicacy. The *moto perpetuo* second movement from Bach's BWV 1033 is breathtaking, but not more engaging than the lollipop of the whole concert: the delicious *La Basque* of Marais, one of Galway's most endearing arrangements. The recording naturally balances the soloist forward, but the sound is first class throughout. This is a full-price record but it includes 68 minutes of entertainment, perfect for a fine summer evening.

'*Dances for flute*' (with Nat. PO, Gerhardt or Mancini; I Solisti di Zagreb, Scimone; The Chieftains; RPO, Myung-Whun Chung; and other artists): GODARD: *Waltz.* CHOPIN: *Minute waltz in D flat, Op. 64/1.* DEBUSSY: *La plus que lente; Petite suite: Ballet.* J. S. BACH: *Suite No. 2, BWV 1067: Polonaise; Menuet; Badinerie.* TRAD.: *Crowley's reel; Brian Boru's march; Belfast hornpipe.* KHACHATURIAN: *Waltz; Sabre dance.* MERCADANTE: *Concerto in D: Polacca.* MANCINI: *Pie in the face polka; Pennywhistle jig.* RODRIGO: *Fantasia para un gentilhombre: Canario.* BENJAMIN: *Jamaican rhumba.* MOZART: *Divertimento in D, K.334: Menuetto.* VIVALDI: *Concerto in D (Il Cardellino): Cantabile.* DINICU: *Hora staccato.* GOSSEC: *Tambourin.* KREISLER: *Schöen Rosmarin.*
☞ *** BMG/RCA 09026 50917-2 [id.].

Galway can certainly make his flute dance – often in scintillating fashion. This collection is essentially for the sweet-toothed, but its consumate artistry is remarkable: just sample the delicious opening Godard *Waltz.* The traditional pieces are especially enjoyable, and two real lollipops are the Mercadante *Polacca* (from a virtually forgotten concerto) and the (Beechamesque) Gossec *Tambourin.* We also have a soft spot for Mancini's *Pennywhistle Jig.* Good sound and 64 minutes of music.

Glennie, Evelyn (percussion)

'*Light in darkness*': Music by GLENNIE; ABE; MCLEOD; EDWARDS; MIKI; TANAKA.
☞ **(*) RCA Dig. RD 60557.

'*Dancin*' (with Nat. PO, Barry Wordsworth): Music by RODGERS; HEROLD; SAINT-SAENS; J. STRAUSS Jnr; arr. by Gordon LANGFORD.
☞ *** RCA Dig. RD 60870; *RK 60870.*

Evelyn Glennie's remarkable artistic skills have caught the fancy of the wider public, fascinated with the idea of her apparently insuperable affliction – for a musician. But she tells us that, such is the ingenuity of nature, she can sense everything directly, through her body. Included on the first collection is her own imaginative piece, *Light in darkness*, using tuned percussion instruments and highlighting the exotic marimba. Here she explores music from a wide geographical range for which the percussion condiment is essential. However, for most listeners the more obviously popular alternative collection called '*Dancin*' will be an easy first choice. Here she receives splendid back-up from Barry Wordsworth and the National Philharmonic in the widest range of music for the dance, which surely does make one's feet tap, whether it be a clever arrangement by Gordon Jacob, pieces by Johann Strauss, a ballet by Richard Rodgers, a medley associated with the Broadway team of Ginger and Fred, or the irresistible *Clog dance* from *La fille mal gardée.* The recording is first rate and makes one recall the title of an early RCA stereo demonstration LP dominated by percussion, called '*Music for Band, Brrroom and harp*' (which RCA should dig out of their vaults and reissue).

'*Rebounds*' (with Scottish CO, Paul Daniel): MILHAUD: *Concerto pour batterie et petite orchestre.* Richard Rodney BENNETT: *Concerto for solo percussion and chamber orchestra.* ROSAURO: *Concierto para marimba e orquestra de cordas.* MIYOSHI: *Concerto for marimba and strings.*
☞ *** BMG/RCA Dig. 09026 61277-2; *09026 61277-4* [id.].

Here finally is a chance for Glennie to show what she can do with more ambitious concert music – although, of course, there are popular influences and jazz rhythms in the works by both Richard Rodney Bennett and Rosauro. Bennett even offers an aleatory element for the percussionist. But his concerto is imaginatively thought out and has plenty of atmosphere and colour. The Milhaud concerto (its title sounds so much more inviting in French) is a most spontaneous piece, without fireworks but very effectively written. Other than that, the most enjoyable work here is the tuneful four-movement concerto by the Brazilian, Ney Rosaurio, with a haunting *Lament* for slow movement, an engaging *Dança*, followed by an imaginative finale. The Miyoshi *Marimba concerto* is in a kaleidoscopic single movement. All these works are brilliantly played and the collection is much more diverse and entertaining than one might expect. The recording engineers have a field day yet they do not try to create exaggerated effects.

Grumiaux, Arthur (violin)

'Favourite violin concertos' (with (i) Concg. O, (ii) New Philh. O, (iii) Sir Colin Davis; (iv) Bernard Haitink; (v) Jan Krenz): BEETHOVEN: (i; iii) *Concerto in D;* (i; iv) *Romance No. 2 in F.* BRAHMS: (ii; iii) *Concerto in D.* (ii; v) MENDELSSOHN: *Concerto in E min.* TCHAIKOVSKY: *Concerto in D.*
☞ ⊛ (B) *** Ph. Duo 442 287-2 (2) [id.].

Another extraordinary Duo bargain set from Philips, containing some of the great Belgian violinist's very finest performances. He recorded the Beethoven twice for Philips, and this is the later account from the mid-1970s with Sir Colin Davis. Grumiaux imbues this glorious concerto with a spirit of classical serenity and receives outstanding support from Davis. If we remember correctly, the earlier account with Galliera had slightly more of a sense of repose and spontaneous magic in the slow movement, but the balance of advantage between the two versions is very difficult to resolve as the Concertgebouw recording is fuller and richer and (even if there is not absolute orchestral clarity) there is less background noise. The performance of the Brahms, it goes without saying, is full of insight and lyrical eloquence, and again Sir Colin Davis lends his soloist the most sympathetic support. The (1973) account of the Mendelssohn is characteristically polished and refined, and Grumiaux, even if he does not wear his heart on his sleeve, plays very beautifully throughout: the pure poetry of the playing not only lights up the *Andante* but is heard at its most magical in the key moment of the downward arpeggio which introduces the second subject of the first movement. In the Tchaikovsky his playing similarly – if less overtly emotional than some – has the usual aristocratic refinement and purity of tone to recommend it. His reading is beautifully paced and has a particularly fine slow movement; both here and in the brilliant finale he shows superb aplomb and taste. With excellent accompaniments in both works from Krenz, this adds to the attractions of the set, for the 1970s recording has a wide range and is firmly focused in its CD format.

Hardenberger, Håkan (trumpet)

Trumpet concertos (with LPO, Elgar Howarth): M. HAYDN: *Concerto No. 2 in C.* HERTEL: *Concerto No. 1 in E flat.* MOLTER: *Concerto No. 1 in D.* L. MOZART: *Concerto in D.* F. RICHTER: *Concerto in D.*
*** Ph. Dig. 426 311-2 [id.].

Håkan Hardenberger makes everything sound completely effortless and, although none of these pieces is an imperishable masterpiece, he plays them all as if they were. Hugely enjoyable and beautifully recorded, with just the right amount of resonance, presence and bloom. Strongly recommended.

Twentieth-century trumpet concertos (with BBC PO, Elgar Howarth): HARRISON BIRTWISTLE: *Endless parade.* MAXWELL DAVIES: *Trumpet concerto.* BLAKE WATKINS: *Trumpet concerto.*
*** Ph. 432 075-2 [id.].

All three works here offer considerable difficulties for the everyday music-lover to approach, but the performances are of a superlative standard, and a record of this calibre gives one the chance to explore their musical intricacies at leisure. In Harrison Birtwistle's aptly named *Endless parade*, textures and ideas, dynamics and colour all continually vary, as in a kaleidoscope. Maxwell Davies uses a plainsong, *Franciscus pauper et humilis*, as a basis, centrally evoking the idea of St Francis preaching to the birds. There is no question as to the evocative power of this work, in spite of its cryptic format. Michael Blake Watkins's *Concerto* may have an apparently more conventional layout, but its argument is complex; at one point the soloist has a heated dialogue with the three orchestral trumpets. The recording is outstandingly vivid.

Heifetz, Jascha (violin)

'The Acoustic Recordings 1917–1924' (with André Benoist; Samuel Chotzinoff; O, Pasternak): SCHUBERT: *Ave Maria.* DRIGO: *Valse bluette.* ELGAR: *La Capricieuse, Op. 17.* SARASATE: *Malagueña, Habanera, Op. 21/1 & 2; Introduction and tarantelle, Op. 43; Zapateado, Op. 23/2; Zigeunerweisen, Op. 20/1; Carmen fantasy, Op. 25.* BAZZINI: *La ronde des lutins.* BEETHOVEN: *Ruins of Athens: Chorus of Dervishes; Turkish march.* WIENIAWSKI: *Scherzo-Tarantelle, Op. 16; Concerto No. 2, Op. 22: Romance.* ACHRON: *Hebrew melody, Op. 33; Hebrew lullaby, Hebrew dance, Op. 35; Stimmung, Op. 32.* PAGANINI: *Moto perpetuo; Caprices, Nos. 13 & 20.* KREISLER: *Minuet; Sicilienne et Rigaudon.* GLAZUNOV: *Meditation; Valse.* MOSZKOWSKI: *Guitarre, Op. 45/2.* CHOPIN: *Nocturnes, Op. 9/2; Op. 27/2.* TCHAIKOVSKY: *Souvenir d'un lieu cher: Scherzo, Op. 42/2. Serenade: Valse, Op. 48/2. Concerto,*

Op. 35: Canzonetta. Sérénade mélancolique, Op. 26. MENDELSSOHN: *On wings of song, Op. 34/2; Concerto in E min.: finale.* DVORAK: *Slavonic dances, Op. 46/2; Op. 72/2 & 8.* SCHUMANN: *Myrthen: Widmung, Op. 25/1.* LALO: *Symphonie espagnole, Op. 21: Andante.* MOZART: *Divertimento No. 17, K.334: Minuet. Haffner Serenade, K.250: Rondo.* D'AMBROSIO: *Serenade, Op. 4.* JUON: *Berceuse, Op. 28/3.* GOLDMARK: *Concerto in A min., Op. 28: Andante.* GODOWSKY: *Waltz in D.* BRAHMS: *Hungarian dance No. 1 in G min.* HAYDN: *Quartet (Lark), Op. 64/5: Vivace.* GRANADOS: *Danzas españolas, Op. 37/5; Andaluza.* BOULANGER: *Nocturne in F; Cortège.* SCOTT: *The gentle maiden.* SAINT-SAENS: *Havanaise, Op. 83.*
(M) (***) BMG/RCA mono GD 80942 [0942-2-RG] (3).

A complete Heifitz Edition is due from RCA during the lifetime of this book. Meanwhile these recordings serve as a salutary reminder of his extraordinary powers. The earliest records come from the year of the Russian Revolution, when Heifetz was still sixteen and only five years after he had made his début in St Petersburg. As always with Heifetz, even the highest expectations are surpassed: his effortless technical mastery is dazzling, the golden tone strong and pure, the accuracy of his intonation almost beyond belief and his taste impeccable. The collector will also be agreeably surprised by the quality of sound; the earliest was made only two weeks after his Carnegie Hall début, when the art of recording was still relatively primitive, and the original 78-r.p.m. disc was single-sided. Seventy or more years later, his brilliance remains undimmed. The recordings are arranged in chronological order, though the differences during the period are relatively small. This set is a mandatory purchase for all who care about the art of violin playing.

Horowitz, Vladimir (piano)

The 'Horowitz Editions'

Obviously these expensive compilations are designed for libraries and ambitious private collectors. The BMG/RCA set includes concertos, so is listed here under Orchestral Collections. The smaller Sony (CBS) set consists entirely of solo piano music and is listed below in our Recitals section. In one sense, both sets are highly desirable and to choose between them is almost impossible. Yet as the Sony reissues are not available separately, most collectors will have to make a choice.

'The Vladimir Horowitz Edition': (complete RCA recordings with var. orchestras & conductors):
BEETHOVEN: *Sonatas Nos. 14 (Moonlight); 21 (Waldstein); 23 (Appassionata)* (GD 60375). CHOPIN: *Sonata No. 2; Nocturnes, Op. 9/2; 55/1; Impromptu No. 1, Op. 29; Etudes, Op. 10/3–4; Ballade No. 1, Op. 23; Mazurka, Op. 30/4; Scherzo No. 1, Op. 20* (GD 60376). PROKOFIEV: *Sonata No. 7, Op. 83; Toccata, Op. 11.* BARBER: *Sonata, Op. 26.* KABALEVSKY: *Sonata No. 3, Op. 46.* FAURE: *Nocturne No. 13.* POULENC: *Presto in B flat* (GD 60377). MUSSORGSKY: *Pictures at an exhibition; By the water.* TCHAIKOVSKY: *Concerto No. 1* (with NBC SO, Toscanini) (GD 60449). CZERNY: *La Ricordanza (Variations on a theme by Rode), Op. 33.* MOZART: *Sonata, K.332.* MENDELSSOHN: *Variations sérieuses, Op. 54.* SCHUBERT: *Sonata, D.960* (GD 60451). SCARLATTI: *Sonata, Kk.380.* BACH (arr. Busoni): *Nun komm' der Heiden Heiland (Come Redeemer).* HAYDN: *Sonata, Hob XVI/52.*
BEETHOVEN: *Sonata No. 14 (Moonlight).* BRAHMS: *Violin sonata No. 3* (with Nathan Milstein). SCHUMANN: *Träumerei* (GD 60461). SCHUMANN: *Kinderszenen; Clara Wieck variations.* LISZT: *Valse oublié No. 1; Hungarian rhapsody No. 6.* DEBUSSY: *Sérénade à la poupée.* FAURE: *Impromptu No. 5.* MENDELSSOHN: *Songs without words: May breezes.* BRAHMS: *Waltz in A flat.* CHOPIN: *Barcarole; Nocturne, Op. 15/2; Mazurkas Opp. 24/4; 30/4; Scherzo No. 3.* LISZT/BUSONI: *Etude No. 2* (GD 60463). BRAHMS: *Concerto No. 2, Op. 83* (with NBC SO, Toscanini); *Intermezzo, Op. 117/2.* SCHUBERT: *Impromptu, D.899.* LISZT: *Au bord d'une source; Sonetto No. 4 del Petrarca; Hungarian rhapsody No. 2* (GD 60523). MUSSORGSKY: *Pictures at an exhibition.* SCRIABIN: *Etude, Op. 2/1; Preludes Nos. 11/5; 22/1; Sonata No. 9.* HOROWITZ: *Danse excentrique.* TCHAIKOVSKY: *Dumka.* BIZET/HOROWITZ: *Carmen variations.* PROKOFIEV: *Sonata No. 7: III.* RACHMANINOV: *Humoresque; Barcarolle.* DEBUSSY: *Sérénade à la poupée.* SOUSA/HOROWITZ: *The Stars and stripes forever* (GD 60526). SCRIABIN: *Sonatas Nos. 3, Op. 23; 5, Op. 53; Preludes, Op. 11/1, 3, 9–10, 13–14, 16; 13/6; 15/2; 16/1, 4; 27/1; 48/3; 51/2; 59/2; 67/1; Etudes, Op. 8/7, 12; 42/5* (GD 86215). SCHUMANN: *Sonata No. 3 (Concerto without orchestra); Humoresque, Op. 20; Fantasiestücke, Op. 111; Nachtstücke, Op. 23* (GD 86680). CHOPIN: *Polonaise-Fantaisie, Op. 61; Ballades Nos. 1, Op. 23; 4, Op. 52; Barcarolle, Op. 60; Etudes, Opp. 10/5; 25/7; Waltz, Op. 69/1; Andante spinato & grande polonaise, Op. 22* (GD 87752). CLEMENTI: *Sonatas, Opp. 14/3; 26/2; 33/3 (Sonata quasi concerto); 34/2; 47/2 (rondo)* (GD 87753). RACHMANINOV: *Sonata No. 2, Op. 36; Moment musicale, Op. 16/2; Prelude, Op. 32/5; Polka V. R.; Concerto No. 3* (with RCA Victor SO, Fritz Reiner) (GD 87754). BIZET/HOROWITZ: *Carmen*

variations. SAINT-SAENS/LISZT/HOROWITZ: *Danse macabre.* MOZART: *Rondo alla turka.*
MENDELSSOHN/LISZT/HOROWITZ: *Wedding march & variations.* MENDELSSOHN: *Songs without words:*
Elégie; Spring song; The Shepherd's complaint. DEBUSSY: *Sérénade à la poupée.* MOSZKOWSKI:
Etudes in A flat; in F; Etincelles. CHOPIN: *Polonaise, Op. 53.* SCHUMANN: *Träumerei.* MENDELSSOHN:
Scherzo a capriccio. LISZT/HOROWITZ: *Rakóczy march.* RACHMANINOV: *Prelude in G min.* SOUSA/
HOROWITZ: *The Stars and stripes forever* (GD 87755). TCHAIKOVSKY: *Concerto No. 1* (with NBC
SO, Toscanini). BEETHOVEN: *Concerto No. 5 (Emperor)* (with RCA Victor SO, Fritz Reiner) (GD
87992). SCARLATTI: *Sonatas, Kk.46; 87; 322; 380; 455; 531.* SCARLATTI/TAUSIG: *Capriccio (Sonata,*
K.20/L.375). BEETHOVEN: *Sonata No. 7.* CHOPIN: *Mazurka, Op. 30/3; Nocturnes, Opp. 27/1; 72/1;*
Waltzes, Opp. 34/2; 64/2; Ballade No. 3, Op. 47. VON DOHNAANYI: *Concert etude, Op. 28/6*
(Capriccio) (09026 60986-2). CHOPIN: *Scherzos Nos. 1–2; Mazurkas, Opp. 7/3; 41/1; 50/3; 59/3; 63/*
2–3 (09026 60987-2). *God save the queen.* CHOPIN: *Polonaise-fantaisie, Op. 61; Ballade No. 1.*
SCHUMANN: *Kinderszenen, Op. 15.* SCRIABIN: *Etude, Op. 8/12* (09026 61414-2). LISZT: *Sonata in B*
min.; Ballade No. 2; Consolation No. 3; Funerailles; Mephisto waltz No. 1 (09026 61415-2).
SCARLATTI: *Sonatas, L.33; 118; 186; 189; 224; 494.* CHOPIN: *Ballade No. 4; Waltz (L'adieu), Op.*
69/1. LISZT: *Ballade No. 2.* RACHMANINOV: *Prelude, Op. 23/5* (09026 61416-2). RACHMANINOV:
Concerto No. 3 (with NYPO, Ormandy) (09026 61564-2).
☞ (M) (***) BMG/RCA Dig./analogue mono/stereo 09026 61655-2 (22) [id.].

The RCA set comprises 22 CDs, ranging from the 1940s through to the 1980s before he was lured to
DG – and omitting the period when he was out of the public eye or with the CBS label. Included in
the survey are the two accounts of the Rachmaninov *Third Piano concerto*, the 1951 account with
Reiner (which is to be preferred) and the 1978 account with Ormandy. There are two versions of the
Pictures at an exhibition, one from 1947 and the other from a Carnegie Hall recital in 1951. Not to be
missed in the RCA set are the epoch-making Barber *Sonata* and Prokofiev *Seventh*, his Clementi
sonata disc and his Scriabin *Third* and *Fifth sonatas*, as well as the electrifying Tchaikovsky *B flat*
minor Concerto with Toscanini. His 1951 *Emperor concerto* with Reiner has been consistently
underrated and has a splendid authority; his Brahms *Second* with Toscanini is less compelling and
lacks spontaneity and, in the slow movement, warmth. His Liszt *Sonata* is magnificent but not as
breathtaking as the 1933 version, included in the EMI set. The recordings vary greatly: many are an
improvement on the originals – though in many cases they needed to be. As suggested below, advice
for those considering the boxes in juxtaposition would be to buy the Sony set complete and choose
liberally from among the CDs singled out for special mention in the RCA set, most of which are
discussed indivdually in our composer section.

Hungarian State Orchestra, Mátyás Antal

'Hungarian festival': KODALY: *Háry János: suite.* LISZT: *Hungarian rhapsodies for orchestra Nos. 1, 2*
& 6 (arr. Doeppler). HUBAY: *Hejre Kati* (with Ferenc Balogh). BERLIOZ: *Damnation de Faust:*
Rákóczy march.
(BB) *** Naxos Dig. 8.550142; 4550142 [id.].

The Hungarian State Orchestra are in their element in this programme of colourful music for which
they have a natural affinity. There is no more characterful version of the *Háry János suite* (we have
already mentioned it in the Composer index) and Hubay's concertante violin piece, with its gypsy
flair, is similarly successful, even if the violin soloist is not a particularly strong personality. The
special interest of the Liszt *Hungarian rhapsodies* lies in the use of the Doeppler orchestrations, which
are comparatively earthy, with greater use of brass solos than the more sophisticated scoring most
often used in the West. The performances are suitably robust and certainly have plenty of charisma.
The brilliant digital recording is strong on primary colours but has atmosphere too, and produces
plenty of spectacle in the Berlioz *Rákóczy march.*

Kogan, Leonid (violin), (i) Philh. O, Kyril Kondrashin; (ii) Paris Conservatoire O, Constantin Silvestri

'Leonid Kogan Profile': BRAHMS: (i) *Concerto in D.* LALO: *Symphonie espagnole.* TCHAIKOVSKY:
Sérénade mélancholique; (ii) *Concerto in D.* BEETHOVEN: *Concerto in D.*
☞ (B) **(*) EMI CZS7 67732-2 (2) [id.].

Kogan made these recordings at either Abbey Road or the Salle Wagram, Paris, in 1959 and the stereo is of excellent quality. He was then at the peak of his performing career, and he went on later to become head of the violin faculty at Moscow Conservatoire. He died in a railway accident in 1982. Of the performances here the Tchaikovsky is, not surprisingly, the finest. Enjoyment, sincerity and spontaneity are written in every bar, and the finale is especially infectious. Kogan really makes it dance, to evoke something of the Russian festival atmosphere of *Petrushka*. In that movement he allows himself more lilt in the rhythm; but in the first two movements, where he is more concerned with architecture, he is steadier. His build-up of tension when the main theme is developed in the first movement is most exciting through his very refusal to slacken the speed. His tone is gloriously rich and, though he rarely achieves a true pianissimo, that may be the fault of the the recording, which is otherwise very good. The *Sérénade mélancholique* has much the same distinction. Kogan brings to it all the dark melancholy that is his to summon up, and the Philharmonia accompany beautifully. The Lalo *Symphonie espagnole* also brings tone which is round and warm, and musical sensibility of a high order. But the Spanish aspect of the score – its sense of Mediterranean colour and abandon – is somewhat minimized. Even so, it is a winning performance. Kogan gives a grand rather than a great performance of the Beethoven. He plays very beautifully but the first movement loses momentum, and in the *Larghetto*, which is already very measured, he slows down for the big cantilena and again sacrifices the flow. His account of the Brahms has more verve, although the finale is not quite up to the standard of the first two movements, and the CD transfer brings a touch of thinness to the solo timbre. Kondrashin accompanies with some distinction in the latter work, and if this is not a performance to place among the very finest versions it is still very enjoyable because of the calibre of the solo playing. The set is worth having for the Tchaikovsky works alone.

Koussevitzky, Serge (double-bass and conductor)

Collections (with (i) Pierre Luboshutz; (ii) Boston SO; (iii) Bernhard Zighera, Pierre Luboshutz):
BEETHOVEN: (i) *Minuet in G* (arr. Koussevitzky): (ii) *Symphony No. 6 in F, (Pastoral)*. (iii) ECCLES: *Largo*. (i) LASKA: *Wiegenlied*. KOUSSEVITZKY: *Concerto, Op. 3: Andante; Valse miniature*. (ii) Johann STRAUSS Snr: *Wiener Blut; Frühlingstimmen*.
☞ (M) (***) Biddulph mono WHL 019 [id.].

In his youth and before he was established as a conductor of international celebrity, Koussevitzky was regarded as the greatest double-bass virtuoso of the age. In 1928–9, in his mid-fifties, he was enticed into the New York Studios to record the above with the pianist, Bernard Zighera, but he then re-recorded everything with Pierre Luboshutz the following year. These performances confirm that he brought to the double-bass the same lyrical intensity and feeling for line and sonority that distinguished his conducting. Judging from the two concerto movements included here, he was no great composer, but the 1928 recording of the *Pastoral Symphony* with the Boston Symphony Orchestra is little short of a revelation. As an interpretation it feels just right; generally speaking, it is brisk but totally unhurried, each phrase wonderfully shaped. Given the fact that he never lingers, the paradox is that this performance seems strangely spacious. One young and knowledgeable collector to whom we played this thought it quite simply 'among the best *Pastorals* ever'; moreover the recorded sound is remarkable for its age and comes up very freshly.

Lipatti, Dinu (piano)

(with Nadia Boulanger; Philh. O, Zürich Tonhalle O, Lucerne Festival O; Galliera, Ackermann, Karajan): BACH: *Chorale, Jesu, joy of man's desiring* (arr. Hess, from BWV 147); *Chorale preludes, BWV 599 & 639* (both arr. Busoni); *Partita No. 1, BWV 825; Siciliana* (arr. Kempff, from BWV 1031). D. SCARLATTI: *Sonatas, Kk. 9 & 380*. MOZART: *Piano concerto No. 21 in C, K.467; Piano sonata No. 8 in A min., K.310*. SCHUBERT: *Impromptus Nos. 2–3, D.899/2 & 3*. SCHUMANN: *Piano concerto in A min., Op. 54*. GRIEG: *Piano concerto in A min., Op. 16*. CHOPIN: *Piano concerto No. 1 in E min., Op. 11; Barcarolle, Op. 60; Etudes, Op. 10/5 & 25/5; Mazurka No. 32, Op. 50/3; Nocturne No. 8, Op. 27/2; Piano sonata No. 3 in B min., Op. 58; Waltzes Nos. 1–14*. LISZT: *Années de pèlerinage, 2nd Year: Sonnetto 104 del Petrarca*. RAVEL: *Alborada del gracioso*. BRAHMS: *Waltzes* (4 hands), *Op. 39/1–2, 5–6, 10, 14–15*. ENESCU: *Piano sonata No. 3 in D, Op. 25*.
❀ (M) (***) EMI CZS7 67163-2 (5).

This set represents Lipatti's major recording achievements. Whether in Bach (*Jesu, joy of man's desiring* is unforgettable) or Chopin – his *Waltzes* seem to have grown in wisdom and subtlety over the years – Scarlatti or Mozart, these performances are very special indeed. The remastering is done well, and this is a must for anyone with an interest in the piano.

London Gabrieli Brass Ensemble

'The splendour of baroque brass': SUSATO: *La Danserye: suite.* G. GABRIELI: *Canzona per sonare a 4: La Spiritata.* SCHEIDT: *Suite.* PEZEL: *Ceremonial brass music.* BACH: *The Art of fugue: Contrapunctus IX.* CHARPENTIER: *Te Deum: Prelude in D.* arr. James: *An Elizabethan suite.* CLARKE: *The Prince of Denmark's march.* HOLBORNE: *5 Dances.* STANLEY: *Trumpet tune.* LOCKE: *Music for His Majesty's sackbutts and cornetts.* PURCELL: *Trumpet tune and ayre. Music for the funeral of Queen Mary* (with Chorus).
⊕ (BB) *** ASV CDQS 6013.

This is one of the really outstanding brass anthologies, and the digitally remastered analogue recording is very realistic. The brass group is comparatively small: two trumpets, two trombones, horn and tuba; and that brings internal clarity, while the ambience adds fine sonority. This makes a superb entertainment to be dipped into at will. The closing *Music for the funeral of Queen Mary* brings an eloquent choral contribution. Introduced by solemn drum-beats, it is one of Purcell's finest short works and the performance here is very moving. The arrangements throughout the concert (usually made by Crispian Steele-Perkins, who leads the group both sensitively and resplendently) are felicitous and the documentation is excellent. This is a very real bargain.

London Gabrieli Brass Ensemble, Christopher Larkin

Original 19th-century music for brass: BEETHOVEN: *3 Equales for 4 trombones.* CHERUBINI: *Trois pas redoublés et la première marche; Trois pas redoublés et la seconde marche.* DAVID: *Nonetto in C min.* DVORAK: *Fanfare.* LACHNER: *Nonet in F.* RIMSKY-KORSAKOV: *Notturno for 4 horns.* SIBELIUS: *Overture in F min; Allegro; Andantino; Menuetto; Praeludium.*
*** Hyp. Dig. CDA 66470 [id.].

'From the steeples and the mountains': IVES: *From the steeples and the mountains; Let there be light.* BARBER: *Mutations for brass.* HARRIS: *Chorale for organ and brass.* Virgil THOMSON: *Family portrait.* COWELL: *Grinnell fanfare; Tall tale; Hymn and fuguing tune No. 12.* GLASS: *Brass sextet.* RUGGLES: *Angels.* CARTER: *A Fantasy upon Purcell's Fantasia upon one note.*
*** Hyp. Dig. CDA 66517 [id.].

It is difficult to decide which of these two programmes is the more enterprising and the more rewarding. If you are responsive to brass sonorities and you acquire one of them, you will surely want its companion. Beethoven's *Equales* were used at the composer's funeral. They are brief, but noble and dignified. The Sibelius suite, is folksy, uncharacteristic writing, but has genuine charm.

The second concert opens and closes with the always stimulating music of Charles Ives. *From the steeples to the mountains* is scored for four sets of bells, trumpet and trombones, and its effect is clanguorously wild! Elliot Carter's Purcell arrangement also has tolling bells, and is quite haunting. Of the other pieces the most striking is the Barber *Mutations*, which draws on the chorale, *Christe du Lamm Gottes* with highly individual effect. Most passionate of all is Ruggles' pungently compressed, muted brass *Angels*, yet the piece is marked 'Serene'! The brass playing throughout the two discs is as communicative as it is expert and the recording is splendidly realistic and present.

London Philharmonic Orchestra, Sir Thomas Beecham

'Favourite overtures': MENDELSSOHN: *The Hebrides (Fingal's Cave). Ruy Blas.* SUPPE: *Morning noon and night in Vienna.* NICOLAI: *The Merry Wives of Windsor.* ROSSINI: *La scala di seta; William Tell; La gazza ladra; Semiramide.*
☞ (M) (**(*)) Michael Dutton Laboratories mono CDLX 7001 [id.].

These are all very famous performances, recorded at Abbey Road in the 1930s and admirably balanced by Walter Legge, and the Mendelssohn *Fingal's Cave overture* is uniquely evocative and poetic, one of the finest performances ever recorded. The transfers are expert (the brass in *Ruy Blas* sounds tangibly robust) with only one exception – but unfortunately that was one of Sir Thomas's most famous records. In May 1933 (originally issued on Columbia LX 255) he recorded a delectable but slightly cut version of Rossini's *La scala di seta* overture, making room on side two for an encore, Handel's *Arrival of the Queen of Sheba*. This piece instantly became a favourite lollipop and it has remained so until the present day. For some reason it is omitted here; also the transfer of the opening of the overture is fuzzy in focus, which certainly was not the case with the original 78 disc as we knew it. The other Rossini items are splendid. *La gazza ladra* was also slightly cut (to fit on two 78 sides) but has characteristic panache, and one can see Sir Thomas's whiskers bristling at the opening flourish of *Morning, noon and night*.

'The Beecham touch': DVORAK: *Slavonic rhapsody No. 3.* DEBUSSY: *Prélude à l'après-midi d'un faune.* ROSSINI (arr. Respighi): *Rossiniana.* BIZET: *La Jolie fille de Perth* (suite). BERLIOZ: *La damnation de Faust.*
☞ (M) (***) Dutton Laboratories mono CDLX 7002 [id.].

The Beecham touch was one of utter magic, especially in French music which he so loved. Bizet's *Fair maid of Perth* suite is uniquely cultivated and special, and what is so remarkable here is the warmth and fullness of the sound and the Abbey Road glow on the woodwind: the famous *Sérénade* is wonderfully refined. The Berlioz *Dance of the Sylphes* is sheer gossamer (only Stokowski among other conductors could create this kind of luminous delicacy), while the *Prélude à l'après-midi d'un faune*, both refined and sensuous, immediately casts a spell over the listener. (Incidentally, here as elsewhere the playing dates itself by occasional subtle portamenti in the string phrasing.) Dvořák's *Slavonic rhapsody* has great rhythmic flair. These are among the very finest of Michael Dutton's transfers, and no Beecham admirer should miss them.

'Vintage Beecham': HANDEL: *Solomon: Arrival of the Queen of Sheba.* DVORAK: *Legend, Op. 59/3.* BIZET: *Carmen suite.* DELIUS (arr. Fenby): *Koanga: La Calinda.* MENDELSSOHN: *A Midsummer Night's Dream: Incidental music, Op. 61.* J. STRAUSS Jnr: *Waltz: Voices of spring.* BORODIN: *Prince Igor* (excerpts).
☞ ⊛ (M) (***) Dutton Laboratories mono CDLX 7003 [id.].

The quality of Michael Dutton's transfers here is even more remarkable than on the companion disc, above. All the repertoire comes from the 1930s, yet for most of the time the ear has to make few concessions to enjoy this music-making, almost as if it had been put on disc yesterday. The opening *Arrival of the Queen of Sheba* (a demonstration item in the 78-r.p.m. era) has remarkably more tangibility and profile than on the VAI transfer (see under Handel, above) which is still very good, and no one ever 'magicked' the *Barcarolle* from the *Tales of Hoffmann* as did Beecham. But it is the *Carmen* excerpts which help to make this collection indispensable, played with such glowing, lyrical feeling and colour – the cultivated way Beecham builds up the climax of the *Danse bohème* is an object lesson in combining orchestral finish with a steadily increasing spontaneous surge of energy. The Borodin *Polovtsian dances* (a famous recording from the 1934 Leeds Festival) is a tribute to Walter Legge's skill with location recording – something much less easy to manage then than now – and the result is breathtaking. Even Beecham's later stereo version does not quite achieve the sheer abandon at the end, yet the Leeds performance was not recorded 'live'. Detail is less than perfect, but the full-bodied choral sound, topped by the percussion, yet with plenty of weight in the bass, makes a glorious impact, and the final accelerando is breathtaking. The 73-minute concert concludes with a bitingly Russian *Polovtsian march*.

London Symphony Orchestra, Albert Coates

'Russian favourites': GLINKA: *Russlan and Ludmilla: Overture; Kamarinskaya.* BORODIN: *In the Steppes of Central Asia; Prince Igor: Polovtsian march.* LIADOV: *8 Russian folksongs, Op. 58.* MUSSORGSKY: *Sorochinsky Fair: Gopak.* TCHAIKOVSKY: *Marche slave.* RIMSKY-KORSAKOV: *May night: Overture. Dubinushka; Maid of Pskov: Storm music; Mlada: Procession of the Nobles; Snow Maiden: Danse des bouffons.* STRAVINSKY: *The Firebird: The princesses' game; Infernal dance.*
☞ (***) Koch mono 37700-2 [id.].

On the Koch Historic label comes a collection of Coates's recordings with the LSO of Russian lollipops, vividly transferred by H. Ward Marston. Made between 1928 and 1930, they sound astonishingly fresh, with brass bright and forward. The *Procession of the Nobles* from Rimsky-Korsakov's *Mlada* has never been recorded with such flair and excitement, and consistently these performances reflect the natural understanding of a musician of British parentage born in Russia. As well as four other Rimsky items, the disc also has nine favourite pieces by Glinka, Borodin (a famous version of *In the Steppes of Central Asia*), Liadov, Mussorgsky, Tchaikovsky and Stravinsky.

London Symphony Orchestra, Bruno Walter

'The Classic 1938 HMV recordings': BEETHOVEN: Overture Coriolan, Op. 62. HAYDN: Symphony No. 86 in D. SCHUMANN: Symphony No. 4 in D min., Op. 120. SMETANA: The Bartered Bride overture. CORELLI: Concerto grosso in G min. (Christmas), Op. 6/8.

☞ ❀ (M) (***) Dutton Laboratories mono CDLX 7008 [id.].

How remarkably Beethoven encapsulated the spirit of Coriolan in his seven-minute overture, and how well Bruno Walter balances its lyrical and dramatic elements. The Haydn D major Paris Symphony bursts with energy, although there is an unashamed rallentando for the second subject. The Minuet and trio is most fetching. The Schumann Fourth has great lyrical warmth, the transition to the finale not as remarkable as with Furtwängler, but the close of the finale is very spirited indeed. The Bartered Bride overture isn't rushed but still has energy and the Corelli Concerto grosso shows that, even with a relatively large body of strings and a close balance Walter knew just how to preserve the element of contrast between solo group and ripieno. The performances all have total spontaneity, and it is impossible to believe that they were put on wax four minutes at a time! Dutton Labs have worked their usual magic with the transfers, and the sound itself is so full and believable that one forgets the 78-r.p.m. source within a minute or so of the music commencing.

Ma, Yo-Yo (cello)

'Great cello concertos': HAYDN: Concerto in D, Hob VIIb/2 (with ECO, Garcia). SAINT-SAENS: Concerto No. 1, Op. 33 (with O Nat. de France, Maazel). SCHUMANN: Concerto in A min., Op. 129 (with Bav. RSO, C. Davis). DVORAK: Concerto in B min., Op. 104 (with BPO, Maazel). ELGAR: Concerto in E min., Op. 85 (with LSO, Previn).

(M) *** Sony Dig./Analogue M2K 44562 (2) [id.].

An enticing mid-priced package, offering at least two of the greatest of all cello concertos, in Yo-Yo Ma's characteristic and imaginatively refined manner. Only the performance of the Haydn gives cause for reservations and these are slight; many will enjoy Ma's elegance here. He is also lucky in his accompanists, and the CBS sound gives no reasons for complaint.

(Eduard) Melkus Ensemble – see under Ulsamer Collegium

Milstein, Nathan (violin)

'The art of Nathan Milstein' (with (i) Pittsburgh SO, Steinberg; (ii) New Philh. O, Frühbeck de Burgos; (iii) Philh. O, Fistoulari, or (iv) Leinsdorf; (v) Erica Morini & CO; (vi) O, Robert Irving; (vii) Leon Pommers; (viii) Artur Balsam; (ix) Rudolf Firkušný): (i) GLAZUNOV: Violin concerto in A min., Op. 90. (ii) PROKOFIEV: Violin concerto No. 2, Op. 63. (iii) SAINT-SAËNS: Violin concerto No. 3, Op. 61. (i) TCHAIKOVSKY: Violin concerto in D, Op. 35. (iii) BRAHMS: Violin concerto in D, Op. 77. (iv) BEETHOVEN: Violin concerto in D, Op. 61. (i) DVORÁK: Violin concerto in A min., Op. 53. (v) VIVALDI: Double violin concerto in D min., Op. 3/11. (vi) RACHMANINOV: Vocalise, Op. 34/14. MUSSORGSKY: Sorochintsky Fair: Gopak. GLAZUNOV: Meditation, Op. 32. TCHAIKOVSKY: Waltz-scherzo, Op. 34; Souvenir d'un lieu cher, Op. 42. RIMSKY-KORSAKOV: Fantasia on Russian themes, Op. 33 (arr. Kreisler). (vii) VIVALDI: Violin sonata No. 2 in A. HANDEL (arr. Hubay): Larghetto. CORELLI: La Follia, Op. 5/12. TARTINI: Violin sonata in G min. (Devil's trill). BACH: Air from Suite No. 3, BWV 1068. MOZART: Violin sonatas: in C, K.296; in E min., K.304. RIMSKY-KORSAKOV: Tsar Sultan: Flight of the bumble bee. GLUCK: Orfeo: Dance of the Blessed spirits. BRAHMS: Hungarian dance No. 2. MASSENET: Thaïs: Méditation. CHOPIN: Nocturne No. 20 in C min. FALLA: Jota. WIENIAWSKI: Scherzo-Tarantelle, Op. 16. DEBUSSY: Minstrels. SARASATE: Introduction and tarantella, Op. 43. KREISLER: Prelude and allegro in the style of Pugnani. (viii) HANDEL: Violin sonata in D, Op. 1/4. VITALI: Chaconne. PROKOFIEV: Violin sonata No. 2 in D. (ix) BEETHOVEN: Violin sonata No. 5 in F (Spring).

☞ (M) **(*) EMI stereo/mono ZDMF7 64830-2 (6).

BACH: (Unaccompanied) Violin sonatas and partitas, BWV 1001/6 (complete).

☞ ❀ (M) (***) EMI mono ZDS7 64793-2 (2) [id.].

Milstein recorded for companies other than EMI, and his career went on long after the mid-1960s, when this survey ends. But certainly the recordings here often show him at his freshest and in fine technical form. In 1960 he played the Tchaikovsky Concerto with glitter and panache, with Steinberg absolutely on the ball with the matching accompaniment. He also found the warmth to do justice to the romanticism of the Glazunov and the scintillating technique to bring off the fireworks in the finale; he was pretty impressive, too, in the Saint-Saëns No. 3. His Dvořák, however, was efficient and clean rather than particularly beguiling, and the Prokofiev No. 2 does not find him at his best either. The Brahms *Concerto* was a straightforwardly lyrical reading, with the slow movement particularly beautiful. It is most satisfying; but he treated the Beethoven *Concerto* at that time as a relatively lightweight and intimate tonal edifice and played his own cadenzas to prove he had an individual view. The set also includes an impressive *Spring Sonata* with Firkušný, but why no Kreutzer? Many of the shorter pieces come off with the flair we associate with Perlman, and in the classical chamber works Milstein is always impressive. With generally excellent transfers, admirers of this artist should find much to relish here, even if he was to go on to record finer versions of some of the key works later.

As an appendix, EMI have reissued Milstein's superb early mono set of the Bach *Sonatas and partitas* for solo violin. With brisker tempi than in his later, DG, stereo recording (see under the composer), the result is exhilaratingly fresh and spontaneous, and the vivid recording has remarkable presence.

'Monteux Edition' – see under **Boston Symphony Orchestra** etc.
Montreal Symphony Orchestra, Charles Dutoit

'Fête à la française': CHABRIER: *Joyeuse marche; España* (rhapsody). DUKAS: *L'apprenti sorcier.* SATIE: *Gymnopédies 1 and 2.* SAINT-SAENS: *Samson et Dalila: Air and Danse bacchanale.* BIZET: *Jeux d'enfants.* THOMAS: *Overture: Raymond.* IBERT: *Divertissement.*
*** Decca Dig. 421 527-2 [id.].

A nicely organized programme, opening vivaciously with Chabrier's *Joyeuse marche* and closing with a gloriously uninhibited account of the finale of Ibert's *Divertissement*, police-whistle and all. The *Gymnopédies* have a wistfully gentle melancholy, and Bizet's *Jeux d'enfants* a fine sense of style; while Thomas's *Raymond Overture* has all the gusto of the bandstand. First-class Decca sound, brightly vivid to suit the music.

Musica ad Rheinum, Jed Wentz (flute)

'Baroque concerti from the Netherlands': SCHICKHARDT: *Concerto in G min. for flute, 2 oboes and strings.* SOLNITZ: *Sinfonia in A for strings, Op. 3/4.* DE FESCH: *Concerto in B flat for 2 violins and strings, Op. 10/2.* GRONNEMAN: *Concerto in G for flute, 2 violins and continuo.* HURLEBUSCH: *Concerto in A min. for 2 oboes, violin and strings.*
☞ ⊛ *** 8NM Classics Dig. 92037 [id.].

Music-making flourished in the Netherlands during the Baroque era, and itinerant composer/musicians were drawn by the magnet of wealth from all over Europe. Indeed the only Dutch-born composer represented in this programme is Willem de Fesch (1687–1757) who, perversely, after being Kapellmeister at Antwerp Cathedral for a few years, emigrated to England, which is why his is the only name which is at all familiar. His *Double violin concerto* is an attractive piece but it cannot be said that it exerts a strong individuality, and that applies to his colleagues here whose biographical details are uncertain but most of whom seem to have begun life in Bohemia or Germany. Their music, while not showing personal hallmarks, is wonderfully diverse and inventive, especially in the use of instrumental colour. As the leader of Musica ad Rhenum is a flautist, many of the concertos here are dominated by this instrument but, because of the delightfully graceful and spirited solo playing, none outstays its welcome. Gronneman's *Concerto for solo flute in G major* felicitously uses the two other flutes in the ripieno to play trios; on the other hand, Schickhardt's six-movement *Concerto in G minor* makes use of his oboes orchestrally in the outer movements, varying the textures internally: the second opens with the two solo oboes, the third and fourth are scored for flute and bass continuo alone. It is a beautifully conceived work, while the more robust *Concerto grosso in A minor* of Hurlebusch, with its sombre slow movement for strings alone, integrates the oboes and solo violin within the ripieno, although the oboes get a chance to shine in the finale. The performances here are wonderfully spirited and cultivated, authentic in texture yet captivatingly so. The recording is full, transparent and real. Well worth seeking out – it is distributed by Impetus in the UK.

Musica da Camera, Robert King

Baroque chamber works: BACH: *Cantata No. 42: Sinfonia.* CORELLI: *Concerto grosso in G min. (Christmas), Op. 6/8.* PACHELBEL: *Canon and Gigue.* HANDEL: *Concerto grosso in B flat, Op. 3/2.* VIVALDI: *L'Estro armonico: Concerto in D min., Op. 3/11.* ALBINONI, arr. Giazotto: *Adagio for organ and strings.*
☞ *** Linn Dig. CKD 012 [id.].

An exceptionally successful concert of baroque music, with a very well-chosen programme, presented on an authetic scale, with what appears to be one instrument to a part. Phrasing is thoroughly musical and the intimacy and transparency of sound are achieved without loss of sonority or disagreeable squeezing of phrases. The familiar *Largo* of the Corelli *Christmas concerto* is particularly fresh, and the opening of the famous Pachelbel *Canon* on a sombre solo bass-line is very telling. The colour of the lively Bach and Handel works (using wind as well as strings) is attractively realized. Excellent, realistic recording.

I Musici

ALBINONI: *Adagio in G min.* (arr. Giazotto). BEETHOVEN: *Minuet in G, WoO 10/2.* BOCCHERINI: *Quintet in E, Op. 11/5: Minuet.* HAYDN (attrib.): *Quartet, Op. 3/5; Serenade.* MOZART: *Serenade No. 13 in G (Eine kleine Nachtmusik), K.525.* PACHELBEL: *Canon.*
*** Ph. Dig. 410 606-2 [id.].

An exceptionally successful concert, recorded with remarkable naturalness and realism. The compact disc is very believable indeed. The playing combines warmth and freshness, and the oft-played Mozart *Night music* has no suggestion whatsoever of routine: it combines elegance, warmth and sparkle. The Boccherini *Minuet* and (especially) the Hofstetter (attrib. Haydn) *Serenade* have an engaging lightness of touch.

Mutter, Anne-Sophie (violin), Vienna Philharmonic Orchestra, James Levine

'Carmen-fantasie': SARASATE: *Zigeunerweisen; Carmen fantasy.* WIENIAWSKI: *Légende.* TARTINI: *Sonata in G min. (Devil's trill).* RAVEL: *Tzigane.* MASSENET: *Thaïs: Méditation.* FAURE: *Berceuse.*
☞ *** DG Dig. 437 544-2 [id.].

This is an unashamedly fun record, with Mutter playing with freedom and warmth and obviously enjoying herself. Comparing the *Carmen fantasy* of Sarasate with Perlman shows Mutter as equally sharp in characterization, yet Perlman's easy style is in the end the more beguiling. But Mutter's Ravel *Tzigane* is made stunningly Hungarian in its fiery accelerando at the end, while Tartini's famous *Devil's Trill Sonata* is played as a virtuoso piece, rather than placed back in the eighteenth century – no harm in that in the present context. The recording is vividly close.

National Philharmonic Orchestra, Leopold Stokowski

'Stokowski showcase': Overtures: BEETHOVEN: *Leonora No. 3.* MOZART: *Don Giovanni* (arr. Stokowski). SCHUBERT: *Rosamunde (Die Zauberharfe).* BERLIOZ: *Le carnaval romain.* ROSSINI: *William Tell.* TCHAIKOVSKY: *Solitude, Op. 73/6.* SOUSA: *The Stars and Stripes forever* (both arr. Stokowski). CHABRIER: *España.* SAINT-SAENS: *Danse macabre.* IPPOLITOV-IVANOV: *Caucasian sketches: Procession of the Sardar.*
(M) *** EMI CDM7 64140-2.

Stokowski's collection of overtures dates from just before his ninety-fourth birthday – yet the electricity crackles throughout and his charisma is apparent in every bar. The Beethoven is immensely dramatic – the distanced trumpet especially effective – while *Rosamunde* combines high romanticism with affectionate warmth. Dissatisfied with Mozart's ending to *Don Giovanni*, Stokowski extends this piece to include music from the opera's finale. The pacing in *William Tell* is fast but, here as elsewhere, the players obviously relish the experience, and the exhilarating *Stars and Stripes forever* was re-scored by the conductor to include xylophone glissandi. Full, resonant sound.

Osipov State Russian Folk Orchestra, Vitaly Gnutov

'Balalaika favourites': BUDASHIN: *Fantasy on two folk songs.* arr. GORODOVSKAYA: *At sunrise.*
KULIKOV: *The Linden tree.* OSIPOV: *Kamarinskaya.* MIKHAILOV/SHALAYEV: *Fantasy on Volga melodies.* ANDREYEV: *In the moonlight; Under the apple tree; Waltz of the faun.* SOLOVIEV/SEDOY: *Midnight in Moscow.* TCHAIKOVSKY: *Dance of the comedians.* SHISHAKOV: *The living room.* arr. MOSSOLOV: *Evening bells.* arr. POPONOV: *My dear friend, please visit me.* RIMSKY-KORSAKOV: *Flight of the bumble-bee.*
⊛ (M) *** Mercury 432 000-2 [id.].

The Mercury recording team visited Moscow in 1962 in order to make the first recordings produced in the Soviet Union by Western engineers since the Revolution. The spirit of that unique occasion is captured wonderfully here – analogue atmosphere at its best. The rippling waves of balalaika sound, the accordion solos, the exhilarating accelerandos and crescendos that mark the style of this music-making: all are recorded with wonderful immediacy. Whether in the shimmering web of sound of *The Linden tree* or *Evening bells*, the sparkle of the folksongs or the sheer bravura of items like *In the moonlight*, which gets steadily faster and louder, or in Rimsky's famous piece (sounding like a hive full of bumble-bees), this is irresistible, and the recording is superbly real in its CD format.

Perlman, Itzhak (violin)

'Great Romantic Violin Concertos' (with (i) Chicago SO or (ii) Philh. O, Giulini; (iii) Concg. O, Haitink; (iv) RPO, Lawrence Foster; (v) Phd. O, Ormandy): (i) BRAHMS: *Concerto in D, Op. 77.* (iii) BRUCH: *Concerto No. 1 in G min., Op. 26.* (ii) BEETHOVEN: *Concerto in D, Op. 61.* (iv) PAGANINI: *Concerto No. 1 in D, Op. 6.* (iii) MENDELSSOHN: *Concerto in E min., Op. 64.* (v) TCHAIKOVSKY: *Concerto in D, Op. 35.*
☞ (M) **(*) EMI Analogue/ Dig. CMS7 64922-2 (3).

These major Perlman recordings include his earlier (1980) studio recording of the Beethoven *Concerto*; it is among the most commanding of his readings and the element of slight understatement, the refusal to adopt too romantically expressive a style, makes for a compelling strength, perfectly matched by Giulini's thoughtful, direct accompaniment. Steadiness of pulse is a hallmark of this version, but there is never a feeling of rigidity. The beautiful slow movement has a quality of gentle rapture and the finale, joyfully and exuberantly fast, is charged with the fullest excitement. The recording is satisfyingly full and spacious. The Brahms is also a distinguished performance, again finely supported by Giulini, this time with the Chicago orchestra, a reading of darker hue than is customary, with a thoughtful and searching slow movement rather than the autumnal rhapsody which it so often becomes. Granted a certain want of impetus in the first movement, this is an impressive and convincing performance, and the full-bodied (1976) Chicago sound had been brightly transferred. The (1983) Bruch *G minor concerto*, must be counted a disappointment, however, not helped by the harsh, early digital recording which gives an edge to the solo timbre. The performance is heavily expressive and, like the Mendelssohn (recorded at the same time), is not nearly as spontaneous as Perlman's earlier, analogue recording with Previn. In Amsterdam the soloist is balanced far too close. The balance is righted by the Paganini and Tchaikovsky *Concertos*. The Paganini (1971) is one of Perlman's very finest records and, although the traditional cuts are observed, the performance has irresistible panache and has been transferred to CD very well. In the Tchaikovsky (1978) the soloist is placed less aggressively forward than is usual with this soloist, although the analogue recording cannot match the finest versions of this work on CD in transparency and openness. Perlman's expressive warmth goes with a very bold orchestral texture from Ormandy and the Philadelphia Orchestra. However, admirers of these artists are unlikely to be disappointed.

'The Art of Itzak Perlman' (with Israel PO, Mehta; Pittsburgh SO, Previn; LPO, Ozawa; RPO, Foster; also Ashkenazy, Bruno Canino, Samuel Sanders, Previn (piano) and other artists): BACH: *Concerto, BWV 1056; Partita No. 3, BWV 1006.* VIVALDI: *Concerto, RV 199.* MOZART: *Oboe quartet, K.370.* BRAHMS: *Sonata No. 3; Hungarian dances 1–2, 7 & 9.* SINDING: *Suite, Op. 10.* WIENIAWSKI: *Concerto No. 1.* SIBELIUS: *Concerto.* KHACHATURIAN: *Concerto.* KORNGOLD: *Concerto.* STRAVINSKY: *Suite italienne.* ANON.: *Doyna.* YELLEN/POLLACK: *My Yiddishe Momma.* FOSTER (arr. Heifetz): *The Old folks at home.* PONCE (arr. Heifetz): *Estrellita.* JOPLIN: *The Rag-time dance; Pineapple rag.* SMETANA: *Z domoviny.* KREISLER: *Liebesfreud; Liebeslied.* RACHMANINOV (arr. Press/Gingold): *Vocalise.* GRAINGER: *Molly on the shore.* PREVIN: *Look at him; Bowing and scraping.* TRAD. (arr. Kreisler): *Londonderry air.* SARASATE: *Carmen fantasy.*

☞ (M) *** EMI Analogue/Dig. CMS7 64617-2 (4) [id.].

This box contains a feast of this great violinist's recordings. He made the choice himself and, while the concertos, particularly the Wieniawski, Sibelius, Khachaturian, and Korngold (and not forgetting the dazzling concertante *Carmen fantasy* of Sarasate or the *Suite* of Sinding) are all indispensable, the shorter pieces on the last disc just as readily display the Perlman magic. They include the delectable jazz collaboration with Previn, the beautifully played Kreisler encores, and many popular items which are readily turned into lollipops. The stylish account of the Stravinsy *Suite italienne* which ends disc three is also one of the highlights of the set. For the most part the recordings have the violin very forwardly balanced, but that was Perlman's own choice; the sound is otherwise generally excellent.

Philadelphia Orchestra, Leopold Stokowski

'Fantasia': BACH, orch. Stokowski: *Toccata and Fugue in D min.* DUKAS: *L'apprenti sorcier.* MUSSORGSKY, arr. Stokowski: *A Night on the Bare Mountain.* STRAVINSKY: *The Rite of spring.* TCHAIKOVSKY: *Nutcracker Suite.*
(M) (***) Pearl mono GEMMCD 4988.

A self-recommending disc. *The Rite of spring* comes from 1929–30 and the *Nutcracker* from as early as 1926, though one would never believe it. Everything Stokowski did at this period was full of character, and the engineers obviously performed miracles. The latest recording is Stokowski's amazing arrangement of *A Night on the Bare Mountain*, which dates from 1940. Such is the colour and richness of sonority Stokowski evokes from the fabulous Philadelphians that surface noise and other limitations are completely forgotten. The transfers are very good.

(i) Philharmonia Orchestra, (ii) Royal Philharmonic Orchestra, Paul Kletzki

'Paul Kletzki profile': (i) GLINKA: *Jota aragonesa.* RIMSKY-KORSAKOV: *Tsar Saltan* (suite). TCHAIKOVSKY: *Andante cantabile.* SIBELIUS: *Symphony No. 2.* SCHUBERT: (ii) *Rosamunde overture.* MAHLER: (i) *Symphonies Nos. 4 in G; 5: Adagietto* (only).
☞ (B) *** EMI CZS7 67726-2 (2) [id.].

Kletzki made these recordings between 1955 and 1958, and they offer a characteristic profile of a musician who found it impossible to produce performances that were in any sense routine. He was the most sympathetic of Mahler conductors, evoking the underlying emotions with great sensitivity and showing them, not as neurotic self-searchings, but as full-blooded and warm. In the first movement of the *Fourth Symphony* his affectionately relaxed approach, full of warmly individual touches, means that the structure is loosely held. But there is little else to criticize in the reading; the slow movement is raptly spanned and, though its climax is broad rather than electrifying, Kletzki's simplicity of style in the finale, with Emmy Loose singing very beautifully, makes for a perfect conclusion. The Kingsway Hall recording was considered outstanding in its day for its lovely bloom, and so it is on CD. The *Adagietto* from the *Fifth Symphony* is slow and languorous but has a sudden surge of adrenalin at the climax. The Sibelius *Second Symphony* is finely conceived as a whole and generates considerable tension in the opening movement. But it had originally arrived not too long after Collins's famous Decca mono version, and by the side of that the closing pages are not as overwhelming as they might be. However, the spacious stereo adds to the impact of a performance which was certainly among the finest of the early stereo era. The Glinka and Rimsky-Korsakov pieces are also vividly played and brilliantly recorded and make the strongest impression.

Philharmonia Orchestra, Carlo Maria Giulini

'Carlo Maria Giulini Profile': RAVEL: *Aborado del gracioso; Daphnis et Chloé: suite No. 2.* BRITTEN: *Peter Grimes: 4 Sea interludes; The Young person's guide to the orchestra.* TCHAIKOVSKY: *Symphony No. 2 (Little Russian).* SCHUMANN: *Manfred* (overture). FRANCK: *Psyché et Eros.*
☞ (B) *** EMI CZS7 67723-2 (2) [id.].

Giulini's Ravel offers most refined Philharmonia playing and *Daybreak* has genuine ecstasy, with the most rapurous birdsong trilling at the first climax, but perhaps with a shade too much percussion at the second, while the *Danse générale* is also a bit noisy at the end, even if certainly exciting. The performance of the Britten works again brings outstandingly good playing and the recording is crystalline in its clarity, yet certainly does not lack atmosphere in the *Sea interludes*. The performances are scrupulously attentive to the composer's demands, but there is a curiously detached quality about the readings, even though they remain compelling for their lucidity. Tchaikovsky's *Little Russian Symphony* is full of energy, if rather less strong on charm, although the *Andantino marziale* brings the most refined orchestral response. Giulini sets a brisk pace in the finale, and the crisp articulation adds to the feeling of vitality. In the coda he goes faster still, and the final pages are dazzling. The first movement of the Franck *Symphony*, though not unspontaneous, takes a while to get properly underway, and this is one of those readings where the conductor never really establishes a firm tempo in the first movement. When the second subject finally emerges, it is presented quite broadly. The slow movement is most beautifully done and the finale, too, is a success – although Giulini's temptation to linger is again felt when the earlier themes are recalled. Nevertheless, with good sound, this is certainly not dull or predictable, and the Love scene from *Psyché* is also beautifully played, if rather lacking in eroticism.

Philharmonia Orchestra, Efrem Kurtz

'Efrem Kurtz Profile': RIMSKY-KORSAKOV: *The Snow maiden* (suite); *The Golden cockerel* (suite); *Dubinushka.* LIADOV: *Kikimora; Baba Yaga; The Enchanted lake; A Musical snuffbox.* SHOSTAKOVICH: *Symphony No. 1.* KHACHATURIAN: *Masquerade: Waltz and galop.* GLINKA: *A Life for the Tsar* (ballet music). KABALEVSKY: *The Comedians* (suite). PROKOFIEV: *Symphony No. 1 (Classical).*
☞ ❋ (B) *** EMI CZS7 67729-2 (2) [id.].

This is a superb set, the most obviously desirable of the four issues so far in EMI's Conductor Profile series. Kurtz's early stereo recordings of the Prokofiev *Classical* and Shostakovitch *First Symphonies* are bursting with wit and panache. In many ways they have never been surpassed, for the EMI recording was always first class. The Rimsky-Korsakov suites and the Glinka and Liadov miniatures are equally persuasive, revealing the most vivid orchestral palette, and Kabalevsky's *Comedians suite*, which can easily sound blatant, has both dash and the most cultivated orchestral response. Many of the brief movements here sound Beechamesque in their charm. In short, with marvellously polished Philharmonia playing and direction of great zest and refinement, this is one of the finest collections of Russian music currently on offer in any price range. Moreover it has been remastered to sound as fresh as the day the music was originally recorded.

Pierlot, Pierre (oboe)

'The magic of the oboe' (with Sol. Ven., Scimone; or Paillard CO, Jean-François Paillard): VIVALDI: *Concertos in C, RV 452; F, RV 455.* ALBINONI: *Concerto a cinque in D min., Op. 9/2.* CIMAROSA: *Concerto* (arr. Benjamin). ZIPOLI: *Adagio for oboe, cello, organ and strings* (arr. Giovannini). MARCELLO: *Concerto in C min.* BELLINI: *Concerto.*
☞ (M) *** Erato/Warner 4509 92130 [id.].

For once, a record company's sobriquet for a collection does not disappoint: this is indeed a magical and very generous (74 minutes) collection, well recorded. One might say the cream of baroque oboe concertos are included here, and Benjamin's arrangement of movements by Cimarosa with its delightful central *Siciliano* and spiccato finale is as engaging as any. The Albinoni and Marcello concertos have memorable slow movements, too, and the Bellini a catchy Polacca finale. The novelty is Zipoli's *Adagio*, sumptuously arranged by Francesco Giovannini after the manner of Giazotto's 'Albinoni *Adagio*'. It doesn't quite come off, but it is a very near miss. Throughout, Pierlot's sweet, finely focused timbre and graceful phrasing are a constant pleasure.

(i) RCA Victor Symphony Orchestra (ii) Symphony of the Air, Leopold Stokowski

'Rhapsodies': (i) LISZT: *Hungarian rhapsody No. 2.* ENESCU: *Rumanian rhapsody No. 1.* SMETANA: *Má Vlast: Vltava. The Bartered Bride overture.* (ii) WAGNER: *Tannhäuser: Overture and Venusberg music* (with chorus). *Tristan und Isolde: Prelude to Act III.*
☞ (M) *** BMG/RCA 09026 61503-2 [id.].

Recorded in 1960 and 1961, this collection shows the great orchestral magician at his most uninhibitedly voluptuous. The opening tutti of the Liszt *Hungarian rhapsody* with full-throated horns and richly sonorous double basses makes a huge impact, and the Enescu is comparably sumptuous in its glowing colours. *Vltava* is romanticized, with an expansive treatment of the main lyrical theme, but *The Bartered Bride Overture* is bursting with energy, with the stereo clearly defining the emphatic string entries of the opening fugato. The *Overture and Venusberg music* from *Tannhäuser* combines sensuousness with frenetic excitement, and then a sentient relaxation appears in the *Tristan Prelude* to Act III. This is over-the-top Stokowski at his most compulsive, but is not for musical puritans. The CD transfers encompass the breadth of amplitude of the forwardly balanced recordings without problems.

Reilly, Tommy (harmonica)

Harmonica concertos (with (i) Munich RSO, Gerhardt; (ii) Basel RSO, Dumont; (iii) SW German RO, Smola; (iv) Munich RSO, Farnon; (v) O, Farnon): (i) SPIVAKOVSKY: *Harmonica concerto;* (ii) ARNOLD: *Harmonica concerto, Op. 46;* (iii) VILLA-LOBOS: *Harmonica concerto;* (iv) MOODY: *Toledo (Spanish fantasy);* (v) FARNON: *Prelude and dance.*
☞ *** Chan. Dig. CHAN 9218 [id.].

This is definitely the most attractive of Tommy Reilly's three concertante collections. Moreover it is very well recorded; the harmonica has seldom been so well caught on disc, nicely focused with just the right degree of plangent bite. The Spivakovsky is a particularly winning piece, with a catchy tune in the first movement, rather like a Leroy Anderson encore, a popular, romantic central interlude, marked *Dolce*, and a delicious *moto perpetuo* finale. Not suprisingly, the Malcolm Arnold is very appealing too, one of this composer's best miniature concertos, written in 1954 for the BBC Proms. The *Grazioso* first movement is hauntingly melodic in the way of the *English dances*, with exuberant comments from an orchestra minus woodwind; the *Mesto* centrepiece is surprisingly dark in feeling, with the sonorous brass and percussion accompanying without strings; the mood lightens wittily and irrepressibly in the spirited *Con brio* finale, which has another unforgettable swinging tune floating over a rocking rhythm. The Villa-Lobos, written in 1955, should be much better known. Scored for a small orchestra of strings, single wind, harp, celesta and percussion, it has a neo-classical character with a rhythmically complex but expressively simple opening movement, pastoral in feeling. It then produces a quite lovely melody for the *Andante*; only the finale, which moves along at a genial pace, has piquant hints of the composer's usual Brazilian preoccupation. Here Tommy Reilly substitutes his own fairly long cadenza for the composer's suggestions, and very effective it is. James Moody's *Spanish fantasy* might be described as good cheap music, and it offers the soloist a glittering chance to demonstrate his bravura with infectious panache. Farnon's hauntingly nostalgic *Prelude and Dance* (a charmingly inconsequential little waltz) brings a felicitous interleaving of both themes. It is perhaps a shade long and, again, makes virtuoso demands on its soloist which are met with panache. The recording balance is surely as near perfect as one could wish.

Royal Philharmonic Orchestra, Sir Thomas Beecham

French music: BIZET: *Carmen suite No. 1.* FAURÉ: *Pavane, Op. 60; Dolly suite, Op. 56.* DEBUSSY: *Prélude à l'après-midi d'un faune.* SAINT-SAENS: *Le rouet d'Omphale.* DELIBES: *Le Roi s'amuse* (ballet suite).
⊛ (M) *** EMI CDM7 63379-2 [id.].

No one conducts the *Carmen Prelude* with quite the flair of Sir Thomas, while the last movement of the *Dolly suite, Le pas espagnole,* (in Rabaud's orchestration) has the kind of dash we associate with Beecham's Chabrier. But for the most part the ear is beguiled by the consistently imaginative and poetic phrasing that distinguished his very best performances. Delibes' pastiche ballet-score, *Le Roi s'amuse*, is given the special elegance that Sir Thomas reserved for music from the past unashamedly rescored to please the ear of later generations. The remastering is marvellously managed.

'French favourites' (with (ii) O Nat. de l'ORTF; (iii) LPO): (ii) CHABRIER: *Overture Gwendoline;* (iii) *España* (rhapsody). (i) GOUNOD: *Faust: ballet music.* GRETRY: *Zémir et Azor: ballet music.* (i) MASSENET: *Cendrillon: Waltz. La Vierge: The last sleep of the Virgin.* BIZET: *Roma: Carnaval à Roma. Patrie overture.*
(M) (***) EMI mono CDM7 63401-2 [id.].

A programme of French music which Sir Thomas loved so well and played incomparably, derives from a number of (mainly late-1950s) sources, with the supercharged *Gwendoline Overture* recorded in Paris, the seven numbers of the elegantly vivacious *Faust ballet music* in Walthamstow, along with most of the other pieces, except the two most famous items, the delectably fragile *Last sleep of the Virgin* of Massenet (Abbey Road) and the incomparably effervescent *España* in Kingsway Hall. These latter two items derive from 78s, and Michael Dutton's transfers have remarkable realism and brilliance; the upper range of *España* only slightly pinched and the percussive condiment glittering.

'Lollipops': TCHAIKOVSKY: *Eugene Onegin: Waltz.* SIBELIUS: *Kuolema: Valse triste.* BERLIOZ: *Damnation of Faust: Menuet des follets; Danses des sylphes. Les Troyens: Marche.* DVORAK: *Legend in G min., Op. 59/3.* DEBUSSY: *L'enfant prodigue: Cortège et Air de danse.* CHABRIER: *Marche joyeuse.* GOUNOD: *Roméo et Juliette: Le sommeil de Juliette.* VIDAL: *Zino-Zina: Gavotte.* GRIEG: *Symphonic dance No. 2 in A, Op. 64/2.* DELIUS: *Summer evening.* SAINT-SAENS: *Samson et Dalila: Danse des prêtresses de Dagon; Bacchanale.* MOZART: *Thamos, King of Egypt: Entr'acte. Divertimento in D, K.131: Minuet. March in D (Haffner), K.249.*
(M) **(*) EMI CDM7 63412-2 [id.]; *EG 763412-4.*

It was Beecham who first used the word 'lollipop' to describe his brand of succulent encore pieces. In this selection of 17 examples, Beecham's devotion to French music shines out, with over half of the items by French composers; but the account of the *Waltz* from Tchaikovsky's *Eugene Onegin* chosen to start the disc is totally untypical of Beecham, with its metrical, unlilting rhythms. The transfers generally convey a good sense of presence but tend to emphasize an edge on top, which is an unfortunate addition to previous incarnations of this music on disc.

Royal Philharmonic Orchestra, Sir Charles Groves

'An English celebration': ELGAR: *Serenade for strings, Op. 20.* BRITTEN: *Variations on a theme of Frank Bridge, Op. 10.* VAUGHAN WILLIAMS: *Fantasia on a theme by Thomas Tallis.* TIPPETT: *Fantasia concertante on a theme of Corelli.*
⊕ (B) *** Pickwick/RPO Dig. CDRPO 5005 [id.].

With gloriously full and real recording, providing the most beautiful string textures, this is one of Sir Charles Groves's very finest records and it makes a worthy memorial to the achievement of the closing decade of his long career. The RPO players give deeply felt, vibrant accounts of four great masterpieces of English string music.

Slovak Philharmonic Orchestra

'Russian Fireworks' (cond. (i) Richard Hayman; (ii) Kenneth Jean; (iii) Stephen Gunzenhauser; (iv) Michael Halász): (i) IPPOLITOV-IVANOV: *Caucasian sketches: Procession of the Sardar.* (ii) LIADOV: *8 Russian folksongs.* KABALEVSKY: *Comedian's galop.* MUSSORGSKY: *Sorochinski Fair: Gopak. Khovanshchina: Dance of the Persian slaves.* (iii) LIADOV: *Baba Yaga; The enchanted lake; Kikimora.* (iv) RUBINSTEIN: *Feramor: Dance of the Bayaderes; Bridal procession. The Demon: Lesginka.* (ii) HALVORSEN: *Entry of the Boyars.*
(BB) *** Naxos Dig. 8.550328 [id.].

A vividly sparkling concert with spectacular digital sound, more than making up in vigour and spontaneity for any lack of finesse. The Liadov tone-poems are especially attractive and, besides the very familiar pieces by Ippolitov-Ivanov, Halvorsen and Mussorgsky, it is good to have the Rubinstein items, especially the *Lesginka* which has a rather attractive tune.

Solomon (piano), Philharmonia Orchestra, Herbert Menges

'Solomon Profile': BEETHOVEN: *Concertos Nos. 1 in C, Op. 15; 3 in C min., Op. 37; Sonata No. 27 in E min., Op. 90.* GRIEG: *Concerto in A min., Op. 16.* SCHUMANN: *Concerto in A min., Op. 54.*
☞ (B) *** EMI CZS7 67735-2 (2) [id.].

This set cannot be recommended too highly, offered as two CDs for the price of one. Solomon is at his most inspired throughout. The Beethoven *Concertos* are particularly fresh and spontaneous, and his Grieg/Schumann coupling has been highly praised by us since the earliest days of stereo. The Op. 90 *Sonata* in unsurpassed in wisdom. The (1956) Abbey Road recordings have never sounded better, and Solomon's wide range of colour is faithfully caught.

Steele-Perkins, Crispian (trumpet), Tafelmusik, Jeanne Lamon

STRADELLA: *Sonata for 8 strings and trumpet.* BIBER: *Sonatas Nos. 1 & 4 for trumpet, strings & continuo; Trumpet duets Nos. 1, 5, 11 & 13.* VIVALDI: *Concerto for 2 trumpets.* ALBINONI: *Trumpet concerto.* TELEMANN: *Trumpet concerto.* HANDEL: Arias from: *Serse: Caro voi siete all'alma; Admeto: Se L'arco avessi.* Marches from: *Scipone; Judas Maccabaeus; Atalanta* (overture).
☞ *** Sony Dig. SK 53365 [id.].

Crispian Steele-Perkins has been heard to comment that the trouble with baroque trumpet concertos is that there are too many of them (each repeating most of the same period gestures). But here he has picked a winning batch. The Stradella and Biber *Sonatas* are in essence trumpet-led miniature suites, interspersing slow and fast movements appealingly; while Biber's four brief duets are also full of character. The Vivaldi *Double concerto* is comparatively well known, and the Albinoni work which combines solo trumpet with three oboes is divertingly colourful, especially with baroque oboes. The Telemann *Concerto* is a splendid piece, and in the *Aria* Steele-Perkins plays with exquisitely fined-down tone against the equally subtle continuo. He is a superb soloist and uses a natural baroque trumpet with almost unbelievable refinement, yet is appropriately robust when the music calls for it. In the works involving two instruments he has a fine partner in John Thiessen. What makes this collection special is the beauty of the accompaniments from the superb Tafelmusik, playing their original instruments under the direction of Jeanne Lamon – although in the Stradella and Biber *Sonatas* the partnership between trumpet and ripieno is more equal. The recording is of the highest quality.

Stinton, Jennifer (flute)

'*20th-century flute concertos*' ((i) with Geoffrey Browne; SCO, Steuart Bedford): HONEGGER: (i) *Concerto da camera for flute, cor anglais and strings.* IBERT: *Flute concerto.* NIELSEN: *Flute concerto.* POULENC, arr. Berkeley: *Flute sonata.*
*** Collins Dig. 1210-2; *1210-4.*

Honegger's *Concerto da camera for flute, cor anglais and strings* is a duo concertante piece, and the Poulenc is a transcription by Lennox Berkeley of the *Sonata for flute and piano* (1957). The Nielsen is a fine performance although its contrasts could be more strongly made. But Ibert's charming and effervescent piece comes off very well, though the orchestral playing is not particularly subtle. Honegger's *Concerto da camera* is very nicely played, as is the Poulenc, and beautifully recorded; though the orchestral contribution falls short of real distinction, this remains a very enjoyable recital, which deserves its third star.

Stockholm Sinfonietta, Esa-Pekka Salonen

'*A Swedish serenade*': WIREN: *Serenade for strings, Op. 11.* LARSSON: *Little serenade for strings, Op. 12.* SODERLUNDH: *Oboe concertino* (with A. Nilsson). LIDHOLM: *Music for strings.*
**(*) BIS Dig. CD 285 [id.].

The most familiar piece here is the Dag Wirén *Serenade for strings*. Söderlundh's *Concertino for oboe and orchestra* has a lovely *Andante* whose melancholy is winning and with a distinctly Gallic feel to it. It is certainly played with splendid artistry by Alf Nilsson and the Stockholm Sinfonietta. The Lidholm *Music for strings* is somewhat grey and anonymous though it is expertly wrought. Esa-Pekka Salonen gets good results from this ensemble and the recording lives up to the high standards of the BIS label. It is forwardly balanced but has splendid body and realism.

Stockholm Sinfonietta, Jan-Olav Wedin

'*Swedish pastorale*': ALFVEN: *The Mountain King, Op. 37: Dance of the Cow-girl.* ATTERBERG: *Suite No. 3 for violin, viola and string orchestra.* BLOMDAHL: *Theatre Music: Adagio.* LARSSON: *Pastoral suite, Op. 19; The Winter's Tale: Four vignettes.* ROMAN: *Concerto in D, for oboe d'amore, string orchestra and harpsichord, BeRI 53.* ROSENBERG: *Small piece for cello and string orchestra.*

*** BIS Dig. CD 165 [id.].

In addition to affectionate accounts of the *Pastoral suite* and the charming vignettes for *The Winter's Tale*, the Stockholm Sinfonietta include Atterberg's *Suite No. 3*, which has something of the modal dignity of the Vaughan Williams *Tallis fantasy*. It has real eloquence and an attractive melancholy, to which the two soloists, Nils-Erik Sparf and Jouko Mansnerus, do ample justice. The Blomdahl and Roman works are also given alert and sensitive performances; they make one think how delightful they are. Hilding Rosenberg's piece is very short but is rather beautiful. A delightful anthology and excellent (if a trifle closely balanced) recording. Confidently recommended.

Stuttgart Chamber Orchestra, Karl Münchinger

'Baroque favourites': PACHELBEL: *Canon.* ALBINONI: *Adagio in G min.* (arr. Giazotto). CORELLI: *Concerto grosso No. 8 (Christmas concerto).* BACH: *Suite No. 3 in D: Air; Suite No. 2 in B min.: Badinerie. Christmas oratorio: Sinfonia.* HANDEL: *Solomon: Arrival of the Queen of Sheba. Oboe concerto No. 3 in G min.* (with Lothar Koch); *Water music: Air.* GLUCK: *Paris and Helen: Chaconne.* MOZART: *Divertimento No. 17 in D, K.334: Minuet and Trio.*
☞ (B) **(*) Decca 433 631-2; *433 631-4.*

Most of the essential lollipops are here, played in a somewhat stately fashion. The stiffness of style that mars some of Münchinger's work surfaces occasionally, but those who like traditional performances will find the playing expert, the recording reliable, and the playing-time generous (70 minutes).

Suisse Romande Orchestra, Ernest Ansermet

RAVEL: *Boléro.* DUKAS: *The sorcerer's apprentice.* RAVEL: *Rapsodie espagnole.* CHABRIER: *España.* (with: SAINT-SAENS: *Carnival of the animals* – Katchen, Graffman, LSO, Skitch Henderson).
☞ (B) *** Decca 433 613-2; *433 613-4.*

Here is an attractive bargain reminder of Ansermet at his most magnetic. All the recordings were originally out of Decca's top drawer. The 1963 *Boléro* and *Sorcerer's apprentice* were much admired in their day and still approach the demonstration bracket; the 1957 *Rapsodie espagnole* has remarkable transparency and, like Chabrier's glittering *España*, shows the conductor's special feeling for French orchestral texture. The *Carnival of the animals*, from a different source, is a bright and breezy affair, with brilliant pianism from Katchen and Graffman, not subtle but very lively and entertaining.

'Overtures Françaises': LALO: *Le Roi d'Ys.* AUBER: *Le Domino noir; Fra Diavolo.* HEROLD: *Zampa.* THOMAS: *Raymond; Mignon.* BOIELDIEU: *La dame blanche.* OFFENBACH: *La Belle Hélène* (arr. Haensch); *Orpheus in the Underworld.*
☞ (M) **(*) Decca 425 083-2 [id.].

These vintage Ansermet performances, recorded in 1960, have never sounded better. The Suisse Romande Orchestra are good at French music, and Ansermet punctiliously points the opening of *Fra Diavolo* and prevents *Le Roy d'Ys* from becoming too melodramatic, yet he delivers an exhilaratingly rumbustious account of *Raymond*. The galop in *Zampa* is reined back a bit and the Can-can in *Orpheus in the Underworld* could be more unbuttoned; but for the most part the playing here, if lacking the last degree of finesse, brings all these bandstand overtures vividly to life. The collection is much more generous than the original LP, playing for 77 minutes; admirers of the Swiss maestro should be well satisfied.

Thames Chamber Orchestra, Michael Dobson

'The baroque concerto in England' (with Black, Bennett): ANON. (probably HANDEL): *Concerto grosso in F.* BOYCE: *Concerti grossi: in E min. for strings; in B min. for 2 solo violins, cello and strings.* WOODCOCK: *Oboe concerto in E flat; Flute concerto in D.*
*** CRD CRD 3331; *CRDC 4031* [id.].

A wholly desirable collection, beautifully played and recorded. Indeed the recording has splendid life and presence and often offers demonstration quality – try the opening of the Woodcock *Flute concerto*, for instance. The music is all highly rewarding. The opening concerto was included in Walsh's first edition of Handel's Op. 3 (as No. 4) but was subsequently replaced by another work. Whether or not it is by Handel, it is an uncommonly good piece, and it is given a superbly alert and sympathetic performance here. Neil Black and William Bennett are soloists of the highest calibre, and it is sufficient to say that they are on top form throughout this most enjoyable concert.

Udagawa, Hideko (violin)

Concertante works (with LPO, Klein): GLAZUNOV: *Violin concerto in A min., Op. 82.* TCHAIKOVSKY: *Souvenir d'un lieu cher, Op. 42.* CHAUSSON: *Poème, Op. 25.* SARASATE: *Romanze andaluza, Op. 22/1.* SAINT-SAENS: *Caprice, Op. 52.*
(B) *** Pickwick Dig. PCD 966; *IMPC 966* [id.].

With the violin balanced forward, the Glazunov receives a heartfelt performance which rivals almost any, even if the finale does not offer quite such bravura fireworks as Itzhak Perlman (at full price). It is valuable to have all three of the haunting pieces which Tchaikovsky called *Souvenirs d'un lieu cher* – the *Méditation* and *Mélodie*, much better known than the central *Scherzo*. They are here done in Glazunov's orchestral arrangements. The Chausson *Poème* is warmly convincing if a little heavy-handed, the Sarasate Andalusian *Romanze* dances delightfully, and only in the final Saint-Saëns *Caprice* does Udagawa's playing sound a little effortful in its virtuosity. Warm, full recording to match.

Ulsamer Collegium, Josef Ulsamer with Konrad Ragossnig (lute) and Eduard Melkus Ensemble

'Dance music through the ages': I: Renaissance dance music: ANON:. *Lamento di Tristano; Trotto; Istampita Ghaetta; Instampita Cominciamento di gioia; Saltarello; Bassa danza à 2; Bassa danza à 3.* GULIELMUS: *Bassa danza à 2.* DE LA TORRE: *Alta danza à 3.* ATTAIGNANT: *Basse danses: La brosse – Tripla – Tourdion; La gatta; La Magdelena.* DALZA: *Calata ala Spagnola.* NEUSIEDLER: *Der Judentanz; Welscher Tanz.* MILAN: *Pavana I/II.* MUDARRA: *Romanesca guarda me las vacas.* PHALESE: *Passamezzo – Saltarello; Passamezzo d'Italye – Reprise – Gallarde.* LE ROY: *Branle de Bourgogne.* B. SCHMIDT: *Englischer Tanz; Tanz: Du hast mich wollen nemmen.* PAIX: *Schiarazula Marazula; Ungaresca – Saltarello.* SUSATO: *Ronde.* GERVAISE: *Branle de Bourgogne; Branle de Champagne.*

II: Early Baroque dance music: MAINERIO: *Schiarazula Marazula; Tedesca – Saltarella; Ungaresca – Saltarella.* BESARDO: *Branle – Branle gay.* MOLINARO: *Saltarello; Ballo detto Il Conte Orlando: Saltarello.* GESUALDO: *Gagliarda del Principe di Venosa.* CAROSO: *Barriera (Balletto in lode della Serenissima D. Verginia Medici d'Este, Duchessa di Modena); Celeste Giglio (Balletto in lode delli Serenissimi Signori Don Ranuccio Farnese, e Donna Margarita Aldobrandina Duca, e Duchessa di Parma e idi Piacenza etc.).* CAROUBEL: *Pavana de Spaigne; 2 Courantes; 2 Voltes.* HOLBORNE: *Pavane: The Funerals; Noel's galliard; Coranto: Heigh ho holiday.* ANON.: *Kempe's jig.* DOWLAND: *Queen Elizabeth her galliard; Mrs Winter's jump.* SIMPSON: *Alman.* GIBBONS: *Galliard.* PRAETORIUS: *Galliarde de la guerre; Reprinse.* HAUSSMANN: *Tanz; Paduan; Galliard; Catkanei.*

III: High Baroque dance music: ANON.: *Country dances: Running footman; Greensleeves and Pudding eyes; Cobler's jigg; How can I keep my Maiden head.* SANZ: *Canarios.* CORRETTE: *Menuet I/II.* HOTTERTERRE: *Bourrée.* BOUIN: *La Montauban.* SANZ: *Pasacalle de la Cavalleria de Napoles; Españoletas; Gallarda y Villano.* CHEDEVILLE: *Musette.* REUSNER: *Suite Paduan (Allemande; Courantel Sarabande; Gavotte; Gigue).* POGLIETTI: *Balletto (Allemande; Amener; Gavotte; Sarabande; Gavotte).* DESMARETS: *Menuet; Passe-pied.* FISCHER: *Bourrée; Gigue.* ANON.: *Gavotte.* LOEILLET II DE GANT: *Corente; Sarabande; Gigue.* LULLY: *L'Amour malade* (opéra ballet): Conclusion; *Une Noce de Village* (dance suite).

IV Rococo Dance music (Eduard Melkus Ensemble): C. P. E. BACH: *5 Polonaises, Wq.190; 2 Menuets with 3 Trios, Wq.189.* RAMEAU: *Zoroastre: Dances (Air tendre en Rondeau; Loure; Tambourin en Rondeau; Sarabande; Gavotte gaye avec Trio; Premier Rigaudon; Air en Chaconne.* STARZER: *Contredanse; Gavotte mit Trio; Pas de deux; Menuet; Gavotte mit Trio; Moderato; Gavotte; Menuet mit Trio; Gavotte mit Trio; Passe-pied mit Trio.*

V: Viennese classical dance music: EYBLER: *Polonaise.* HAYDN: *2 Menuets, Hob IX/11:4 & IX/16:12.* GLUCK: *Orfeo ed Euridice: Ballet: Don Juan (Allegretto).* MOZART: *6 Landerische, K.606; 5 Kontretänze, K.609.* ZEHN: *Deutsche.* BEETHOVEN: *4 Kontretänze, WoO 14/4, 5, 7 & 12.* SALIERI: *Menuetto.* WRANITZKY: *Quodlibet.*

VI: Viennese dance music from the Biedermeier period (1815–48): PALMER: *Waltz in E*. BEETHOVEN: *Mödlinger Tänze Nos. 1–8, WoO 17*. MOSCHELES: *German dances with trios and coda*. SCHUBERT: *5 Minuets with Trios, D.89; 4 komische Ländler, D.354*. ANON.: *Linzer Tanz; Vienna polka*. LANNER: *Hungarian galop in F*.

☞ ⊛ (B) *** DG 439 964-2 (4) [id.].

This is a top-quality anthology showing the DG-Archiv tradition at its very finest – a happy amalgam of musical scholarship and musical delight. The collection, on four well-filled CDs (recorded between 1972 and 1974) explores the history of European dance music from the beginning of the fifteenth century right through to the first three decades of the nineteenth century, just about the time when Johann Strauss Senior was making his début. The very opening piece on disc one – the *Lamento di Tristano* – is downbeat, but this is immediately dispelled by the second part of the piece, a *Rotta* based on the same tune, and the mood perks up. The members of the Ulsamer Collegium play an extraordinary range of authentic period instruments. Keyboards, strings, wind and plucked vihuela, as well as guitar, lute and hurdy-gurdy, are used with the greatest imagination, always to seduce the ear with variety of colour. There is not a whiff of pedantry or of abrasiveness of the kind that too often accompanies 'authentic' performances, yet the documentation is characteristically and fascinatingly thorough. It shows the enormous amount of background research behind this undertaking, yet the feeling of scholarly rectitude is totally absent, both in the music-making and in the admirablly full documentation. The consistent tunefulness of the music is a constant source of pleasure and surprise, and one has space here to mention only a few key items. On the first disc the pieces by Attaignant, Neusiedler and Phalèse are particularly characterful, while the two *Branles* of Gervaise are given the most winning instrumentation. Among the composers of early baroque dance music, Piere Francisque Caroubel and Mario Fabrizio Caroso stand out: the suite of dances by the former, played variously on gambas and recorder consort, is most diverting. On the second CD, the keyboard, gamba and lute pieces from the English Elizabethan school hardly need advocacy, but they are beautifully played (the lute and guitar solos of Konrad Rogossnig are most distinguished throughout the set) as is the jolly suite of dances by Valentin Haussman – another unfamiliar name to turn up trumps. Among the high baroque composers Esaias Reusner (1636–79) provides another diverting dance suite which, like the ballet music of Alessandro Poglietti, proves as elegant and finished as the ballet suite of Lully with its *Sarabande pour le père et la mère du marié* and *Galliard pour les parents et amis*. In the Rococo era, Carl Philipp Emanuel Bach contributes five spirited *Polonaises*, and after a gracious interlude from Rameau there is a set of more robust and extrovert dances from Josef Starzer (1726–87). We enter the Viennese classical period with a clash of cymbals enlivening a *Polonaise* by Joseph Eybler (1764–1846), who sounds ahead of his time; but the two *Minuets* of Haydn stay well in period. As this stage of the proceedings the excellent Eduard Melkus Ensemble take over and their marvellously intimate style recalls the early Vanguard discs by the Boskovsky Ensemble – only the DG recording is more sophisticated, especially in its transparency of texture. The first of the Mozart *Contredances*, K.609, which opens the fourth CD makes reference to a famous tune from *Figaro*, and Paul Wranitzky quotes from the same opera in his *Quodlibet*. Beethoven in 1819, taking his summer holiday at Mödling near Vienna, was serenaded by a band of seven players in the local tavern and at once wrote a set of dances for them. Then at the end of his frustrating fallow period, he produced irresistible music. Moschelles and Schubert follow his example, the latter providing some deliciously flimsy *Ländler*, while the delicate *E major Waltz* of Michael Pamer (1782–1827), the two anonymous dances from Linz and Vienna and the *Hungarian galop* of Joseph Lanner (which ends the programme) point onwards to the heyday of Viennese dance music, when Johann Strauss Junior was to reign supreme. Overall, this is a most stimulating and rewarding survey. Each of the CDs lasts at least 70 minutes, and the whole collection is superbly played and recorded. However, readers are advised to ensure that the proper documentation is included with this set, as we have found some boxes contain totally inadequate notes.

Vienna Philharmonic Orchestra, Claudio Abbado

'New Year Concert 1988' (with Vienna Boys' Ch.): REZNICEK: *Donna Diana: overture*. Josef STRAUSS: *Brennende Liebe; Auf Ferienreisen; Im Fluge* (polkas). Johann STRAUSS, Jnr: *Die Fledermaus overture; Neue pizzicato polka; Freut euch des Lebens* (waltz); *Chit-chat polka; Un Ballo in maschera: Quadrille on themes from Verdi's opera. Liechtes Blut polka; Seid unschlungen Millionen* (waltz); *Perpetuum mobile; Banditen-Galopp; An der schönen blauen Donau*. Johann STRAUSS, Snr: *Radetzky march*.
*** DG Dig. 423 662-2; *423 662-4*.

If this record, which also includes the Vienna Boys' Choir, does not quite match Karajan's, it still has a real sense of occasion and offers some delectable performances. Obvious favourites like *The Blue Danube*, *Die Fledermaus overture* and, of course, the *Radetzky march* are duplicated, but most of the programme is new. With Rezniček's *Donna Diana* opening the proceedings vivaciously, the mixture is nicely varied to include the familiar and the unfamiliar, and both playing and recording are excellent.

Vienna Philharmonic Orchestra, Carlos Kleiber

'1992 New Year Concert': J. STRAUSS Jnr: Overture: *Der Zigeunerbaron*. Polkas: *Neue pizzicato; Stadt und Land; Tritch-Tratch; Unter Donner und Blitz; Vergnügungszug*. Waltzes: *An der schönen, blauen Donau; Tausend und eine Nacht. Persischer march*. J. STRAUSS Snr: *Radetsky march*. Joseph STRAUSS: Waltzes: *Dorfschwalben aus Osterreich; Sphärenklänge*. NICOLAI: Overture: *The Merry wives of Windsor*.
☞ *** Sony Dig. SK 48376 [id.].

When Carlos Kleiber conducted the 1989 event, he seemed at times a little stiff. But here he manages precision alongside lilt, discipline as well as verve. There is plenty of elegance and warmth too, in a programme entirely without novelties but where the waltzes nearly always go as spontaneously as the polkas, though the *Blue Danube* is no match for Karajan's version two years earlier. The recording is well up to standard, vivid yet spacious and full.

Vienna Philharmonic Orchestra, Riccardo Muti

'1993 New Year Concert': J. STRAUSS Snr: *Sperl-Galop; Radetzsky march*. J. STRAUSS Jnr: *Klipp Klapp galop; Egyptischer Marsch; Overture Indigo und die Vierzig Rauber; Perpetuum mobile;* Polkas: *Auf der Jagd; Diplomaten; Pizzicato polka; Veilchen;* Waltzes: *Die Publicisten; An der schönen blauen Donau*. Josef STRAUSS: *Transaktionen*. LANNER: *Steyrische-Tänz; Hans-Jörgel*.
☞ *** Ph. Dig. 438 493-2; *438 493-4* [id.].

Riccardo Muti seems an unlikely candidate for sweet-toothed Vienna *bon-bons*, but the atmosphere of this celebrated occasion has its usual effect and he clearly lets his hair down after a while. Once again (following Carlos Kleiber's intransigence the previous year, which no doubt the conservative Viennese audience relished) there are novelties and they sparkle readily when Muti can produce such unselfconscious Straussian manners. Lanner's *Steyrische-Tänz* provides the surprise of the CD by unexpectedly turning out to be the source of the barrel-organ waltz in Stravinsky's *Petrushka*. The tension is not quite consistent throughout the concert, with the second half (beginning with the overture) setting an even more compelling atmosphere; but overall this is such a happy occasion that one cannot but enjoy the experience. Applause is nicely edited and is not too much of a problem. The documentation reveals the history of the event, fascinating in itself. Excellent recording.

Vienna Philharmonic Orchestra, Mozart Ensemble or Boskovsky Ensemble, Willi Boskovsky

'Vienna Dance Gala, 1: 'Invitation to the Dance' (with VPO): Johann STRAUSS Jnr: Overtures: *Die Fledermaus; Der Zigeunerbaron*, with *March. Ritter Pásmán (csárdás)*. LEHÁR: *Gold and Silver waltz*. WEBER/BERLIOZ: *Invitation to the waltz. Graduation Ball* (complete ballet, arr. Dorati).
☞ (M) **(*) Decca 436 781-2 [id.].

'Vienna Dance Gala, 2: Romances and Dances' (with V. Mozart Ens.): BEETHOVEN: *12 Contretänze, WoO 14; 2 Romances for violin and orchestra, Opp. 40 & 50. Mödlinger Tänze, WoO 17*. MOZART: *Les Petits Riens: Overture and ballet music*.
☞ (M) **(*) Decca 436 782-2 [id.].

'Vienna Dance Gala, 3: Fledermaus Quadrille' (with VPO): Johann STRAUSS Jnr: *Fledermaus quadrille; Orpheus quadrille;* Waltzes: *Bei uns z'haus; Nordseebilder; Mephistos Höllenrufe; Erinnerung an Covent-Garden. Freikugeln polka; Aufs Korn Marsch*. Josef STRAUSS: Polkas: *Ohne Sorgen; Im Fluge; Extempore; Rudolfsheimer*. Waltz: *Mein Lebenslauf ist Lieb und Lust*. Johann, Josef and Eduard STRAUSS: *Schützen-Quadrille*.
☞ (M) *** Decca 436 783-2 [id.].

'*Vienna Dance Gala, 4: Dances of Old Vienna'* (with V. Mozart Ens. or Boskovsky Ens.): MOZART: *Kontretanz: La Bataile; 2 Minuets, K.604; 5 Kontretänze (Non più andrei), K.609; 6 Deutsche Tänze, K.567.* Johann STRAUSS Snr: *Jugendfeuer-Galopp; Indianer-Galopp; Tivoli-Rutsch waltz; Exeter polka.* Johann STRAUSS Jnr: *Liebeslieder waltz.* Josef STRAUSS: *Die guten alten Zeiten waltz.* SCHUBERT: *4 Waltzes & 4 Ecossaisen; 4 Waltzes & 2 Ecossaisen.* LANNER: *Pesther waltz; Jägers Lust-Galopp.*
☞ (M) *** Decca 436 784-2 [id.].

'*Vienna Dance Gala, 5: Overtures of Old Vienna'* (with VPO):
Johann STRAUSS Jnr: *Waldmeister; Cagliostro in Wien; Prinz Methusalem; Indigo und die vierzig Räuber; Das Spitzentuch der Königin; Carnaval in Rom.* REZNICEK: *Donna Diana.* SUPPE: *Die Schöne Galathée.* HEUBERGER: *Der Opernball.* NICOLAI: *The Merry wives of Windsor.*
☞ (M) *** Decca 436 785-2 [id.].

An enticing collection of Viennese confectionery, played with typical élan and sparkle and never a hint of routine under Boskovsky. The recordings all derive from his vintage recording period for Decca from the late 1950s until early 1970s. Each generously filled CD is available separately, and all offer zestful music-making and are consistently ear-tickling in content, with the possible exception of the two Beethoven *Romances* on the second disc, in which Boskovsky, rather misguidedly, takes the solo role and produces a lean, unromantic timbre. But the Mozart ballet music more than makes amends in this programme. It is appropriate that the first collection should include the Weber/Berlioz *Invitation to the dance*, with its opening cello solo so stylishly done, and also include the delightful Lehár masterpiece, *Gold and silver* – the finest Viennese waltz not by Johann junior. The collection of 'Dances from Old Vienna', with its bright Decca sound, is less intimate in effect than Boskovsky's Vanguard records, but is notable for showing us Johann Strauss senior at his most spontaneous plus the rustic charm of Lanner, and also including some utterly delectable morsels of Schubert. The collection of ten overtures is particularly generous: only five were included on the original LP of the same name. This was regarded as something of a demonstration disc in its day, particularly for *Prinz Methusalem* with its well-managed off-stage-band effect in the middle. One of the newcomers here, *Waldmeister*, is particularly welcome, brimming over with tunes and with some delightful writing for the flutes. The racy forward impulse of *Donna Diana* is nicely judged, and there is an infectious Viennese lilt in Heuberger's *Opernball*. This sounds thinner in the violins than it did on LP but, for the most part, the vivid CD transfers, brightly lit, give the music-making plenty of body and presence.

Williams, John (guitar)

Guitar concertos (with ECO, (i) Sir Charles Groves; (ii) Daniel Barenboim): (i) GIULIANI: *Concerto No. 1 in A, Op. 30.* VIVALDI: *Concertos in A and D.* RODRIGO: *Fantasia para un gentilhombre;* (ii) *Concierto de Aranjuez.* VILLA-LOBOS: *Concerto.* (i) CASTELNUOVO-TEDESCO: *Concerto No. 1 in D, Op. 99.*
(M) *** Sony M2YK 45610 (2) [id.].

This bouquet of seven concertante works for guitar from John Williams could hardly be better chosen, and the performances are most appealing. Moreover the transfers are very well managed and, if the guitar is very forward and larger than life, the playing is so expert and spontaneous that one hardly objects. All these performances are among the finest ever recorded, and Groves and Barenboim provide admirably polished accompaniments, matching the eager spontaneity of their soloist.

'*The Seville concert'* ((i) with Orquesta Sinfónica de Sevilla, José Buenagu): ALBENIZ: *Suite españolas: Sevilla; Asturias.* BACH: *Lute suite No. 4, BWV 1006a: Prelude.* D. SCARLATTI: *Keyboard sonata in D min., Kk 13* (arr. Williams). (i) VIVALDI: *Concerto in D, RV 93.* YOCUH: *Sakura variations.* KOSHKIN: *Usher waltz, Op. 29.* BARRIOS: *Sueño en la Floresta.* (i) RODRIGO: *Concierto de Aranjuez: Adagio.*
☞ *** Sony Dig. SK 53359 [id.].

With so much reappearing from the Juliam Bream archive, it is good to have a first-rate, modern recital from the estimable John Williams. It was recorded in Spain (in the Royal Alcázar Palace) as part of a TV programme, which accounts for its hour-long duration and the inclusion of the ubiquitous Rodrigo *Adagio* as the closing item. The recording is very realistic and present, yet the balance is natural and the effect not jumbo-sized. John Williams's intellectual concentration is as formidable as his extraordiany technique. This playing comes as much from the head as from the heart. He is first rate in Bach and brings a sense of keyboard articulation to the engaging *D minor*

Sonata of Scarlatti (who was Bach's almost exact contemporary). His strength is felt in the flamenco accents of Albéniz's *Asturias*, a sense of the darkly dramatic is powerfully conveyed in Koshkin's *Usher waltz* (after Edgar Allan Poe). Yet his playing can be charmingly poetic, as in the delicate account of the *Largo* of the Vivaldi concerto; touchingly gentle, as in Yocuh's charming pentatonic evocation of cherry blossoms; or thoughtfully improvisational, as in the Barrios *Sueño en la Floresta*.

Yepes, Narciso (guitar)

'*Guitarra española*' (with Spanish R. & TV O, Odón Alonso; LSO, Rafael Frübeck de Burgos): SANZ: *Suite española.* MUDARRA: *Fantasia que contrahaza la harpa en la manera de Ludovico.* NARVAEZ: *Diferencias sobre 'Guárdame las vacas'.* SOLER: *Sonata in E.* SOR: *10 Etudes; Theme and variations, Op. 9.* ALBENIZ: *Suite española: Asturias (Leyenda). Recuerdos de viaje: Rumores de la caleta. Malagueña. Piezas caracteristicas: Torre bermeja (Serenata). Malaguena, Op. 165.* GRANADOS: *Danza española No. 4 (Villanesca).* TARREGA: *Alborada (Capriccio); Danza mora; Sueño; Recuerdos de la Alhambra; Marieta (Mazurka); Capricho árabe (Serenata); Tango.* FALLA: *El amor brujo: El círculo mágico; Canción del fuego fatuo. Three-cornered hat: Danza del molinaro (Farruca). Homenaje: Le tombeau de Claude Debussy.* TURINA: *Sonata, Op. 61. Fandaguillo, Op. 36; Garrotín y soleares; Ráfaga.* BACARISSE: *Passapie; Concertino in A min. for guitar and orchestra Op. 72.* YEPES: *Catarina d'Alió.* RODRIGO: *En los trigales; Concierto de Aranjuez; Fantasia para un gentilhombre; Concierto madrigal for 2 guitars and orchestra* (with Godelieve Monden, Phil. O, Garcia Navarro). PUJOL: *El abejorro; Estudios.* TORROBA: *Madroños.* MONTSALVATGE: *Habañera.* OHANA: *Tiento; Concierto tres gráficos for guitar and orchestra.* RUIZ-PIPO: *Canción y danza No. 1; Tablas para guitarra y orquestra.* ANON:. *Jeux interdits (Romance); Canciones populares catalanes: La filla del marxant; La filadora; El mestre; La cançó del lladre.*
(M) *** DG 435 841-2 (5).

This collection celebrates Yepes' long-lived and distinguished recording achievement in music from his own country. It was inevitable that the three most famous concertante works of Rodrigo would be included, which will involve duplication for many collectors, but the other concertante works, by Barcarisse, Ruiz-Pipó and Ohana are less familiar and very welcome. Among the more ambitious solo pieces are the *Suite* of Sanz and Soler *Sonatas*, plus the *Studies* of Sor. But many of the miniatures are equally memorable in their atmospheric potency (not least the Falla transcriptions), when Yepes's performances – with their vivid palette and high level of concentration – constantly remind us of Beethoven's assertion that a guitar is an orchestra all by itself. Generally excellent sound.

Zabaleta, Nicanor (harp)

'*Great concertante works for harp*': MOZART: *Flute and harp concerto, K.299* (with Karlheinz Zöller, BPO). BOIELDIEU: *Harp concerto.* RODRIGO: *Concierto serenata* (with Berlin RSO, Märzendorfer). HANDEL: *Harp concerto, Op. 4/6.* ALBRECHTSBERGER: *Harp concerto in C.* DITTERSDORFF: *Harp concerto in A.* DEBUSSY: *Danses sacrée et profane.* RAVEL: *Introduction and allegro for harp, string quartet, flute and clarinet* (all with members of Paul Kuentz CO).
☞ (B) *** DG Double 439 693-2 (2) [id.].

Zabaleta was an absolute master of his instrument and all these performances are touched with distinction. Johann Albrechtsberger taught Hummel and Beethoven, and his lightweight concerto is very pleasing when played with such flair and delicacy. The same might be said of the charming Boieldieu and Dittersdorf works, both of which display invention of some character, while the Handel and Mozart concertos are acknowledged masterpieces. In the latter, Karlheinz Zöller makes a distinguished partner. When it was first issued on LP, we gave Zabaleta's version of Rodrigo's delectable *Concierto serenata* a Rosette. In the outer movements especially, the delicate yet colourful orchestration tickles the ear in contrast to the beautifully focused harp timbre. Zabaleta is marvellous too in Ravel's *Introduction and allegro*, with sensitive support from members of the Paul Kuenz Chamber Orchestra, and warmly atmospheric sound. The Mozart and Boieldieu works come from the early 1960s; the others are later and, with excellent transfers, this 145 minutes of concertante harp music will surely offer much refreshment, though these are obviously not CDs to be played all at once.

Instrumental Recitals

Amsterdam Loeki Stardust Quartet: Daniel Brüggen, Bertho Driever, Paul Leenhouts, Karel van Steenhoven (recorders)

'Capriccio di flauti': MERULA: Canzon: La Lusignuola. JOHNSON: The Temporiser. BYRD: Sermone blando. ANON.: Istampa: Tre fontane; Prince Edward's paven; The Queen of Ingland's pavan. J. S. BACH: Contrapunctus I. Fuge alla breve e staccato, BWV 550; Brandenburg concerto No. 3, BWV 1048: Finale. SWEELINCK: Mein juges Leben hat ein end. FRESCOBALDI: Capriccio V sopra la Bassa Fiamenga; Canzon prima. CONFORTI: Ricercar del quarto tono. PALESTRINA: Lamentationes Hieremiae. TRABACI: Canzon Franzesa terza. ASTON: Hugh Ashton's maske. TAVERNER: In nomine. SHOTT: Aan de Amsterdamse Grachten.

☞ (M) *** O-L 440 207-2 [id.].

The Amsterdam Loeki Stardust Quartet are superbly expert players: their blend is rich in colour and their ensemble wonderfully blended and polished. They can also be heard in an outstanding collection of concertos for recorders in consort with the Academy of Ancient Music – see below – but here they are in holiday mood, presenting an enticing series of lollipops. Not that everything is frivolous. There are moments of solemnity, and the pieces by Conforti and Palestrina (among others) bring an appropriate touch of gravitas, while the Sermone blande of Byrd is aptly named. But it is the piquant bravura one returns to most readily. The Temporiser of Johnson is a delicious tour de force and Bach's Fuga alla breve e staccato and the sparkling finale of the Third Brandenburg concerto are a joy. After a remarkable variety of mood and colour, the concert ends with the winningly florid Aan de Amsterdamse Grachten, which readily conjures up a picture of a Dutch carousel. The recording has striking presence and realism.

Barere, Simon (piano)

'The complete HMV recordings, 1934–6': LISZT: Etude de concert, G.144/2. Années de pèlerinage, 2nd Year (Italy): Sonnetto 104 del Petrarca, G.161/5. Gnomenreigen, G.145/2; Réminiscences de Don Juan, G.418 (2 versions); Rapsodie espagnole, G.254; Valse oubliée No. 1, G.215. CHOPIN: Scherzo No. 3 in C sharp min., Op. 39; Mazurka No. 38 in F sharp min., Op. 59/3; Waltz No. 5 in A flat, Op. 42. BALAKIREV: Islamey (2 versions). BLUMENFELD: Etude for the left hand. GLAZUNOV: Etude in C, Op. 31/1. SCRIABIN: Etudes: in C sharp min., Op. 2/1; in D sharp min., Op. 8/12 (2 versions). LULLY/ GODOWSKI: Gigue in E. RAMEAU/GODOWSKI: Tambourin in E min. SCHUMANN: Toccata in C, Op. 7 (2 versions).

⊛ (***) Appian mono CDAPR 7001 (2) [id.].

This two-CD set offers all of Barere's HMV recordings, made in the mid-1930s, including the alternative takes he made in the studio. What can one say of his playing without exhausting one's stock of superlatives? His fingerwork is quite astonishing and his virtuosity almost in a class on its own. The set contains an absolutely stunning account of the Réminiscences de Don Juan, and his Islamey knocks spots off any successor in sheer virtuosity and excitement; it is altogether breathtaking, and much the same might be said of his Rapsodie espagnole. Nor is there any want of poetry – witness the delicacy of the Scriabin C sharp minor Etude or Liszt's La leggierezza. Readers wanting to investigate this legendary artist should start here. One of the most important functions of the gramophone is to chart performance traditions that would otherwise disappear from view, and this set is one to celebrate.

Bate, Jennifer (various organ)

Eighteenth-century organ music on period instruments from Adlington Hall, the Dolmetsch Collection, St Michael's Mount, Kenwood House, Killerton House, Everingham chapel.

Vol. 1: John READING: *Airs for French horns & flutes.* STANLEY: *Voluntaries, Op. 5/7 & 10; Op. 6/5; Op. 7/3.* HANDEL: *Fugue in B flat.* ROSEINGRAVE: *Voluntary in G min.* TRAVERS: *Voluntary in D min. & major.* WALOND: *Voluntary in A min.* RUSSELL: *Voluntary in E min.* Samuel WESLEY: *Short pieces Nos. 7 & 12; Voluntary, Op.6/1.*
☞ *** Unicorn Dig. DKPCD 9096 [id.].

Vol. 2: GREENE: *Voluntary in C min.* STANLEY: *Voluntaries, Op. 5/6 & 9; Op. 6/7; Op. 7/2.* HANDEL: *Fugue in A min.* LONG: *Voluntary in D min.* WALOND: *Voluntary in B min.* NARES: *Introduction and fugue in F.* RUSSELL: *Voluntary in A min.* Samuel WESLEY: *Short piece No. 9; Voluntary, Op. 6/3.*
☞ **(*) Unicorn Dig. DKPCD 9099 [id.].

Vol. 3: GREENE: *Voluntary in B min.* STANLEY: *Voluntaries, Op. 6/1 & 10; Op. 7/1 & 6.* WALOND: *Voluntary in G.* HANDEL: *Fugue in B min.; Voluntary in C.* BURNEY: *Cornet piece in E min.* RUSSELL: *Voluntary in A.* WESLEY: *Short pieces Nos 6 & 8. Voluntary, Op. 6/6.*
☞ *** Unicorn Dig. DKPCD 9101 [id.].

Vol. 4: GREENE: *Voluntary in E flat.* STANLEY: *Voluntaries, Op. 5/8; Op. 6/6, 8 & 9; Op. 7/7.* HANDEL: *Voluntary in C; Fugue in G min.* ROSEINGRAVE: *Fugue No. 13.* DUPUIS: *Voluntary in B flat.* WESLEY: *Voluntary, Op. 6/9.*
☞ **(*) Unicorn Dig. DKPCD 9104 [id.].

Jennifer Bate is making a survey of eighteenth-century English organ music, using five different English organs from stately homes to secure maximum variety of presentation. But these instruments are all relatively light-textured and sound bright and sweet. Each programme is made up in the same way: opening with an agreeable *Voluntary* of Maurice Greene, then offering a clutch of *Voluntaries* by John Stanley, followed by music of Walond and Handel, and usually ending with *Short pieces* by Samuel Wesley. None of these are great composers, save Handel, and his chosen examples are relatively minor works. Jennifer Bate plays all this music in impeccable style and she is beautifully recorded; so the attractions of each disc depend on the items included. Easily the most engaging are the works which use cornet or trumpet stops, which are colourful and jolly, while the Vox humana stop, as in the finale of Stanley's Op. 6/5 on the first disc, is also ear-tickling. Indeed the first volume is a good place to start, with Op. 5/7 by the same composer also quite engaging. The voluntaries are usually in two sections, and William Russell's E minor piece is in three with an imposing opening and the fugue used as a centrepiece. Samuel Wesley's *Short piece No. 12* is a contrapuntal moto perpetuo. The second disc also offers more examples of Stanley's ready facility, notably Op. 7/2 and Op. 5/6, but on the whole this is a less interesting programme than Volume 3 which again shows Stanley at his more inventive in Op. 7/1; Op. 6/1 begins with a pleasing *Siciliano*. Handel's *Voluntary in C* brings some attractive interplay of parts in its second movement and it is followed by Burney's *Cornet piece*, which has a whiff of the *Halleluia chorus*. In Volume 4 Jennifer Bate registers Stanley's Op. 5/8 with piquant skill: this is a three-part work, while the trumpet theme in Op. 6/6 might almost have been written by Purcell. Volume 1, however, is the disc to try first, then, if you enjoy this, go on to Volume 3. But only the real enthusiast will want all four CDs, for much of the writing here is fairly conventional.

Bergen Wind Quintet

BARBER: *Summer music, Op. 31.* SAEVERUD: *Tunes and dances from Siljustøl, Op. 21a.* JOLIVET: *Serenade for wind quintet with principal oboe.* HINDEMITH: *Kleine Kammermusik, Op. 24/2.*
*** BIS CD 291 [id.].

Barber's *Summer music* is a glorious piece dating from the mid-1950s; it is in a single movement. Saeverud's *Tunes and dances from Siljustøl* derive from piano pieces of great charm and sound refreshing in their transcribed format. Jolivet's *Serenade* is hardly less engaging, while Hindemith's *Kleine Kammermusik*, when played with such character and finesse, is no less welcome. Throughout, the fine blend and vivacious ensemble give consistent pleasure.

Bream, Julian

※ *'The Julian Bream Edition'*

The Julian Bream Edition runs to some 30 CDs (available as a boxed set in the USA: 09026 61583-2), representing three decades of a remarkably distinguished recording career. Bream has now moved over to EMI, so this edition is essentially retrospective. The miscellaneous recitals are considered below, although the concertante collections are in the Concerts section or as composer entries above, and the Elizabethan lute songs are listed under Peter Pears among Vocal Recitals. The whole is an astonishing achievement overall, but we especially recommend Volumes 1–2 and 26–27.

Julian Bream (lute)

Volume 1. *'The golden age of English lute music'*: Robert JOHNSON: *2 Almaines; Carman's whistle.* John JOHNSON: *Fantasia.* CUTTING: *Walsingham; Almaine; Greensleeves.* DOWLAND: *Mignarda; Galliard upon a galliard of Daniel Bachelar; Batell galliard; Captain Piper's galliard; Queen Elizabeth's galliard; Sir John Langton's pavan; Tarleton's resurrection; Lady Clifton's spirit.* ROSSETER: *Galliard.* MORLEY: *Pavan.* BULMAN: *Pavan.* BACHELAR: *Monsieur's almaine.* HOLBORNE: *Pavan; Galliard.* BYRD: *Pavana Bray; Galliard; Pavan; My Lord Willoughby's welcome home.*
☞ (M) *** BMG/RCA 09026 61584-2 [id.].

Bream is a natural lutenist and a marvellously sensitive artist in this repertoire, and here he conjures up a wide range of colour, matched by expressive feeling. Here Dowland is shown in more extrovert mood than in many of his lute songs, and overall the programme has plenty of variety. The CD combines two recitals, the first 15 items recorded by Decca in London in September 1963, and the rest of the programme in New York City 2½ years later. The recording is exemplary and hiss is minimal.

Volume 2. *'Lute music from the Royal Courts of Europe'*: LANDGRAVE OF HESSE: *Pavan.* MOLINARO: *2 Saltarelli; Ballet detto Il Conte Orlando; Fantasia.* PHILLIPS: *Chromatic pavan and galliard.* DOWLAND: *Fantasia; Queen Elizabeth's galliard.* HOWLETT: *Fantasia.* DLUGORAJ: *Fantasia; Finale; Villanellas Nos. 1–2; Finale.* FERRABOSCO II: *Pavan.* NEUSIDLER: *Mein Herz hat sich mit Lieb' verpflicht; Hie' folget ein welscher Tanz; Ich klag' den Tag; Der Juden Tanz.* BAKFARK: *Fantasia.* BESARD: *Air de cour; Branle; Guillemette; Volte.* DOWLAND: *Forlorn hope fancy; My Lord Willougby's welcome home* (for 2 lutes).
☞ (M) *** BMG/RCA 09026 61585-2.

The lute has much in common with the guitar, but its slightly plangent tang gives this early music a special colour. Bream here achieves miracles in creating diversity of timbre and dynamic, and the programme itself makes a remarkably varied and entertaining recital. Molinaro's music has a disconsolate, nostalgic quality: its atmosphere attracted Respighi, who included *Il Conte Orlando* when he orchestrated his suite of *Ancient airs and dances*. Wojciech Dlugoraj's two *Villanella* are equally touching and his busy *Finale* (which we hear in two versions) gives Bream a chance to display some crisply articulated bravura. Hans Neusidler, a leading German lutenist of the period, offers an equally varied group, with each piece curiously titled, ending with an exotic so-called 'Jewish dance'. The Burgundian Jean-Baptiste Besard's music is hardly less characterful, again bringing contrast between the doleful *Air de cour* and *Guillemette* and the two lively dances. Phillips's *Chromatic fantasia and pavane* is strongly written, and both the Dowland *Fantasia* included here and his splendidly regal *Galliard* for Queen Elizabeth are much more positive in feeling than much of his writing. However, at the end of the programme he returns to form with *Forlorn hope fancy*, before Lord Willoughby rides in vigorously in an arrangement for two lutes, both, of course, played by Bream.

Volume 4. *'The Woods so wild'*: BYRD/CUTTING: *The Woods so wild.* DA MILANO: *Fantasias Nos. 1 in C min.; 2 in F; 3 in G min.; 4 (La Campagna); 5 in C; 6 in F; 7 in F; 8 in G.* CUTTING: *Packington's Pound; Greensleeves.* DOWLAND: *Walsingham; Go from my window; Bonny sweet Robin; Loth to depart; 2 Fancies; Farewell.* HOLBORNE: *The Fairy round; Heigh ho holiday; Heart's ease.*
☞ (M) *** BMG/RCA 09026 61587-2.

A cleverly planned recital. The title-piece in Byrd's setting with variations, arranged by Cutting, is immensely striking and the eight Milano *Fantasias* are distinctive in character, both in quality of invention and in argument. (Try No. 4 – *La Campagna* – most fetching and exciting.) They are interspersed with the pieces by Cutting, Holborne and Dowland, who is almost always his doleful self, especially in the two closing *Fancies* and the Farewell – an extended piece with a very poignant closing section. Holborne's works are winningly lightweight except for *Heart's ease*, which sounds very like Dowland in its pervading despondency. It has a connection with Shakespeare's *Romeo and Juliet*, and John Duarte in the excellent accompanying note suggests it is in fact by Dowland. Characteristically alive and sympathetic performances from Bream and immaculately real recording.

Bream, Julian (guitar)

Volume 8. *'Popular classics for the Spanish guitar'*: VILLA-LOBOS: *Chôros No. 1; Études in E min. & C sharp min.; Prelude in E min.; Suite popolar brasileira: Schottische-chôro.* TORROBA: *Madraños.* FALLA: *Homenaje pour le tombeau de Debussy. Three-cornered Hat: Miller's dance* (arr. Bream). TURINA: *Fandaguilla.* arr. LLOBET: *El testament d'Amelia.* SANZ: *Canarios.* M. ALBENIZ: *Sonata* (arr. Pujol). RODRIGO: *En los trigales.* MOZART: *Larghetto and Allegro, K.229.* GIULIANI: *Sonata in C, Op. 15: Allegro. Rossiniana No. 1, Op. 119* (both ed. Bream).
☞ (M) *** BMG/RCA Analogue/Dig. 09026 61591-2.

This collection in itself admirably scans Bream's RCA recording career, opening with material from an outstanding early recital made at Kenwood House in 1962, to which other items have been judiciously added from as early as 1959, and from 1965–8 and 1971, plus the two digital Falla pieces which are as late as 1983. Not surprisingly, the tension is a little variable, though the recital makes a very satisfactory whole. The highest voltage comes in the Villa-Lobos pieces which, though often thoughtful and ruminative, sound wonderfully spontaneous, and the Turina *Fandanguillo* is also very fine. The Mozart and Giuliani excerpts are appropriately mellow. Very real recording, with the various acoustics always well managed.

Volume 9. *'Baroque guitar'*: SANZ: *Pavanas; Galliardas; Passacalles; Canarios.* GUERAU: *Villano; Canario.* J. S. BACH: *Prelude in D min., BWV 999; Fugue in A min., BWV 1000.* WEISS: *Passacaille; Fantasie; Tombeau sur la mort de M. Comte de Logy.* VISÉE: *Suite in D min.* FRESCOBALDI: *Aria con variazione detta la Frescobalda* (arr. Segovia). D. SCARLATTI: *Sonata in E min., K.11* (arr. Bream); *Sonata in E min., K.87* (arr. Segovia). CIMAROSA: *Sonata in C min., Sonata in A* (both arr. Bream).
☞ (M) *** BMG/RCA 09026 61592-2.

The four Sanz pieces are strong in colour and atmosphere, and Bream makes a clear distinction between this repertoire and that of Bach, which is presented directly and is very cleanly detailed. Sylvius Weiss, who played for the Dresden court in the mid-eighteenth century, also emerges with an individual voice and his eloquent *Tombeau* inspires playing of elegiac nobility. The eight-movement *Suite* by Robert Visée, a French court lutenist who lived from about 1650 until 1725, has the most attractive invention. The famous 'La Folia' emerges seductively as the *Sarabande* (it is beautifully played); and the *Gavotte*, two *Minuets*, *Bourrée* and *Gigue* which follow are all loosely based on its melodic contour. Frescobaldi's *Aria con variazione* is another memorable work. Scarlatti's keyboard sonatas transcribe well enough for guitar (though perhaps a lute would have been even more effective) and the two sonatas of Cimarosa, though not strictly baroque music, are very personable. Again excellent recordings coming from three different periods (three of the Sanz pieces and those by Guerau are digital), but convincingly reassembled.

Volume 10. *'Classic guitar'*: GIULIANI: *Grand overture, Op. 61; Rossiniana No. 3, Op. 121; Rossiniana No. 3.* SOR: *Grand solo (Introduction and allegro), Op. 14. Sonata in C, Op. 25.* DIABELLI: *Sonata in A* (ed. Bream).
☞ (M) **(*) BMG/RCA 09026 61593-2.

No complaints about the playing here, or the recording. Giuliani's *Grand overture* is justly named, but Sor's *Grand solo* opens more coaxingly and is rather enjoyable. The rest of the music is relatively inconsequential, although very well played and recorded. It is discussed under each composer entry.

Volume 11. *'Romantic guitar'*: PAGANINI: *Grand sonata in A.* SCHUBERT: *Sonata in G, D.894: Menuetto.* MENDELSSOHN: *Venetian boating song; Canzonetta* (all 3 ed. Bream). FALLA: *Homenaje pour le tombeau de Debussy.* RAVEL: *Pavane pour une infante défunte.* ALBENIZ: *Suite española: Granada; Leyenda (Asturias)* (arr. Bream). TARREGA: *Lagrima (Prelude); 3 Mazurkas.*
☞ (M) ** BMG/RCA 09026 61594-2.

A pleasant but uneven recital. The opening Paganini *Grand sonata* (21 minutes) is a trifle inflated and the Schubert arrangement is not a great success, while the Mendelssohn *Song without words* comes off much better than the *Canzonetta* (arranged from the *String quartet*, Op. 72). Of the other items, the

Tarrega pieces have the greatest memorability. The recordings come from three different sources and there is an uncomfortably awkward tape-join between the very relaxed account of the Ravel *Pavane* and the first of the Albéniz pieces.

Volume 12. *'Twentieth-century guitar I':* BERKELEY: *Sonatina, Op. 52/1; Theme and variations.* ROUSSEL: *Segovia, Op. 29.* SMITH BRINDLE: *El polifemo de oro (4 Fragments).* MARTIN: *4 Pièces brèves.* HENZE: *Kammermusik: 3 Tentos.* RAWSTHORNE: *Elegy.* WALTON: *5 Bagatelles.*
☞ (M) *** BMG/RCA 09026 61595-2.

The finest works here are the Walton *Bagatelles* – dedicated to Bream – which (to quote John Duarte) 'represent the composer at his most winsome', and Henze's *Drei Tentos*, interludes from a larger work, which are very attractive in their picturesque impressionism. Lennox Berkeley's *Sonatina*, too, is an enjoyably amiable piece; the *Theme and variations* is more ambiguous thematically and harmonically. Roussel's *Segovia* has a characteristic touch of acerbity. The other pieces are beautifully written for the instrument but are of varying degrees of appeal. Reginald Smith Brindle's *Fragments* provides four musical invocations of the poetry of Lorca, while in his *Four Pièces* Frank Martin recreates for the guitar with characteristic finesse the world of the eighteenth-century lute suite. Segovia rejected the work and the composer rearranged his music for piano and orchestra and never again wrote for the guitar. Bream makes the most of all his opportunities and where the music can charm the ear he does not miss a trick. He concludes the Rawsthorne *Elegy*, which the composer did not live to complete, by reprising the restrained opening section. Overall, however, the work remains emotionally uncompromising. Excellent recording.

Volume 13. *'Twentieth-century guitar II':* MOMPOU: *Suite compostellana.* OHANA: *Tiento.* TORROBA: *Sonatina.* GERHARD: *Fantasía.* VILLA-LOBOS: *Suite populaire brésilienne; Etudes Nos. 5 in C; 7 in E.*
☞ (M) *** Dig./Analogue BMG/RCA 09026 61596-2.

This is an exceptionally rewarding recital of one of the very finest of the many reissues in the Julian Bream Edition. Mompou's six-movement *Suite compostellana* is sheer delight with its muted flamenco feeling and air of wistful melancholy. Ohana's *Tiento*, a considerable piece which looks back to the sixteenth century, opens by musing over the famous *La Folia*, and Gerhard's almost equally striking *Fantasía* is similarly improvisational in feeling. Bream plays both pieces marvellously and is quite melting in the *Andante* of Torroba's *Sonatina* – a more ambitious piece than the name would suggest and the composer's finest work for guitar. To this digital collection the attractive, lighter Villa-Lobos suite is added, recorded two decades earlier, but impressively real and present.

'Volume 14: *Dedication':* BENNETT: *5 Impromptus.* WALTON: *5 Bagatelles.* MAXWELL DAVIES: *Hill Runes.* HENZE: *Royal Winter music.*
☞ (M) *** BMG/RCA 09026 61597-2 [id.].

Julian Bream here recorded (in 1981/2) four of the many works of which he is dedicatee. For most listeners the engaging Walton *Bagatelles* will prove the most rewarding music, although Henze's atonal suite of miniature portraits of Shakespearean characters is texturally highly imaginative. Maxwell Davies's *Hill Runes* are certainly atmospheric and the Bennett *Impromtus* ingenious in construction. As usual with these reissues in the Julian Bream Edition, the recording is excellent and immaculately transferred to CD.

Volume 16: 'Julian Beam and Friends'(with (i) Cremona Qt; (ii) George Malcolm (harpsichord); (iii) Melos Ens.): (i) BOCCHERINI: *Guitar quintet in E min., G.451;* (ii) *Guitar quintet in D, G.448: Introduction and Fandango.* (i) HAYDN: *Quartet in E, Op. 2/2.* (iii) GIULIANI: *Concerto No. 1 in A, Op. 30.*
☞ (M) *** BMG/RCA 09026 61599-2 [id.].

This rearrangement of Bream repertoire makes a most agreeable lightweight compilation. The Boccherini *Quintet* is an attractive work with an appealing slow movement; the colourful *Introduction and fandango* comes from another quintet and is effectively arranged for guitar and harpsichord, with both Bream and Malcolm relishing the fireworks of the *Fandango*. The Haydn work is the usual arrangement from an early string quartet, and the Giuliani concerto (slight but amiable) also has the atmosphere of 'the music of friends' – it was originally coupled with the Malcolm Arnold concerto. The recording is good, if a little dated in the concerto, but the performances are delightfully intimate and spontaneous.

Volume 26. Music of Spain: *'La guitarra romántica'*: TARREGA: *Mazurka in G; Etude in A; Marieta; Capricho árabe; Prelude in A min.; Recuerdos de la Alhambra.* MALATS: *Serenata.* PUJOL: *Tango Español; Guajira.* LLOBET: *Canciones populares catalanas.* TURINA: *Fandanguillo, Op. 36; Sevillana, Op. 29; Homenaje a Tárrega.*

☞ (M) *** BMG/RCA Dig./Analogue 09026 61609-2.

A mainly digital recital of Spanish music opens with an attractive, lightweight Tárrega group including the *Capricho árabe* and his most famous evocation, the *Recuerdos de la Alhambra*, which in Bream's hands is curiously muted and withdrawn. Then after works by Malats and Pujol (his *Guajira* has some fine special effects) there follows the delightful Llobet suite of nine *Canciones populares catalanas*, of which *El testament d'Amelia*, in which Bream – helped by the digital background silence – creates a magnetically delicate pianissimo, is unforgettable. The programme ends with vibrant flamenco-inspired music of Turina, including the composer's last (two-part) guitar work, the *Homenaje a Tárrega*. Bream's dynamism in these performances makes one almost believe he was Spanish-born. The final work (consisting of a *Garrotín* and *Soleares*) was recorded at Kenwood House in 1962 and is exceptional in that here the resonance inflates the guitar image; for the rest of the recital the recording is ideal in all respects.

Volume 27. *'Guitarra'* (Music of Spain): MUDARRA: *Fantasias X & XIV.* Luis DE MILAN: *Fantasia XXII.* Luis DE NARVÁEZ: *La canción del Emperador; Conde claros.* Santiago DE MURCIA: *Prelude & Allegro.* BOCCHERINI: *Guitar quintet in D, G. 448* (arr. for 2 guitars): *Fandango.* SOR: *Grand solo, Op. 14; Variations on a theme of Mozart, Op. 9; Fantasie, Op. 7; Sonata, Op. 25: Minuet.* AGUADO: *Rondo in A min., Op. 2/3.* TARREGA: *Study in A; Prelude in A min.; Recuerdos de la Alhambra.*

☞ (M) *** BMG/RCA Dig./Analogue 09026 61610-2 [id.].

An admirable survey covering 400 years and featuring several different instruments, all especially built by José Ramanillos and including a Renaissance guitar and a modern classical guitar. Bream's natural dexterity is matched by a remarkable control of colour and unerring sense of style. Many of the earlier pieces are quite simple but have considerable magnetism. The basic recital was recorded digitally in 1983 at Bream's favourite venue, Wardour Chapel, Windsor, and is laid out chronologically. Two additional Sor items, the *Fantasie*, Op. 7, and the *Minuet* from Op. 25, were made 18 years earlier in New York and, as they are analogue, have sensibly been added at the end.

'Homage to Segovia': TURINA: *Fandanguillo, Op. 36; Sevillana, Op. 29.* MOMPOU: *Suite compostelana.* TORROBA: *Sonatina.* GERHARD: *Fantasia.* FALLA: *Homenaje pour le tombeau de Claude Debussy; Three cornered hat* (ballet): *3 Dances.* OHANA: *Tiento.*

☞ (M) *** BMG/RCA Dig. 09026 61353-2 [id.].

Readers who have already acquired Bream's earlier digital recital concentrating on the music of Albéniz and Granados will find this hardly less impressive, both musically and technically. The programme here is even more diverse, with the Gerhard *Fantasia* adding a twentieth-century dimension, while Ohana's *Tiento* has a comparable imaginative approach to texture. Throughout, Bream plays with his usual flair and spontaneity, constantly imaginative in his use of a wide dynamic range and every possible colouristic effect. The set of six miniatures by Federico Mompou is particularly diverting. The recording has the most tangible realism and presence. This fine recital is particularly welcome at mid-price.

'Nocturnal': MARTIN: *4 pièces brèves.* BRITTEN: *Nocturnal after John Dowland.* BROUWER: *Sonata.* TAKEMITSU: *All in Twilight.* LUTOSLAWSKI: *Folk melodies* (trans. Bream).

☞ *** EMI Dig. CDC7 54901-2 [id.].

After his remarkable achievement on the RCA label, Julian Bream has now changed recording companies and seems to be starting all over again. However, this recital of twentieth-century guitar music is – in parts at least – a tough nut to crack. This is not a CD to play all at once. The Martin *Pièces* and the ingenious extended *Nocturne* of Britten, concentrated as the playing is, need to be taken one at a time, and the Brouwer *Sonata* (for all its quotations – notably from Beethoven's *Pastoral Symphony*) does not make friends immediately. The Takemitsu is shameless guitar impressionism and not especially tangible. Finally we have some readily inviting folk tunes, aptly harmonized by Lutoslawski, and charm makes its entry for the first time in a 72-minute programme. Vividly immediate recording, but don't set the volume level too high.

Bream, Julian and John Williams (guitar duo)

'Together': LAWES: *Suite for 2 guitars* (arr. Bream). CARULLI: *Duo in G, Op. 34.* SOR: *L'encouragement, Op. 34.* ALBENIZ: *Cantos de España: Córdoba, Op. 232/4.* GRANADOS: *Goyescas: Intermezzo* (arr. Pujol). *Danzas españolas: Oriental, Op. 37/2.* FALLA: *La vida breve: Spanish dance No. 1.* RAVEL: *Pavane pour une infante défunte.* FAURE: *Dolly* (suite), *Op. 56* (both arr. Bream).
☞ (M) *** BMG/RCA 09026 61450-2 [id.].

CARULLI: *Serenade in A, Op. 96.* GRANADOS: *Danzas españolas: Rodella aragonesa; Zambra, Op. 37/ 6 & 11.* ALBENIZ: *Cantos de España: Bajo la palmera, Op. 232/3. Ibéria: Evocación.* GIULIANI: *Variazioni concertanti, Op. 130.* JOHNSON: *Pavan & Galliard* (arr. Bream). TELEMANN: *Partie polonaise.* DEBUSSY: *Rêverie; Children's corner: Golliwog's cakewalk. Suite bergamasque: Clair de lune.*
☞ (M) *** BMG/RCA 09026 61452-2 [id.].

The rare combination of Julian Bream and John Williams was achieved by RCA in the studio on two separate occasions, in 1971 and 1973, providing the basic contents of these two recitals. Further recordings were made live in Boston and New York in 1978, during a North American concert tour. Curiously, it is the studio programmes which seem the more spontaneous, and Fauré's *Dolly* suite, which sounds a little cosy, is the only disappointment (it also brings some audience noises). Highlights are the music of Albéniz and Granados (notably the former's haunting *Evocación* from *Iberia*, and *Cordoba*, which Bream also included on a very successful solo recital). The transcription of the *Goyescas Intermezzo* is also very successful, as is Debussy's *Golliwog's cakewalk* in a quite different way. Guiliani's *Variazioni concertanti*, actually written for guitar duo, brings some intimately gentle playing, as does the *Theme and variations* which forms the second movement of Sor's *L'encouragement*; while the *Cantabile* which begins this triptych is delightful in its simple lyricism. The Carulli *Serenade* opens the second recital very strikingly, while on the first disc the performance of Ravel's *Pavane*, very slow and stately, is memorable. The sound has good presence and is naturally balanced; analogue hiss is never a problem.

Brüggen, Frans (recorder), Anner Bylsma (cello), Gustav Leonhardt

(harpsichord)

Italian recorder sonatas: COREELLI: *Variations on La Follia, Op. 5/12; Sonata in F, Op. 5/4.* BARSANTI: *Sonata in C.* VERACINI: *Sonatas: in G; A min.* BIGAGLIA: *Sonata in A min.* VIVALDI: *Sonata in G min., Op. 13/6.* MARCELLO: *Sonata in D min., Op. 2/11.*
☞ (M) *** Teldec/Warner 4509 93669-2 [id.].

The king of recorder players here demonstrates his expertise and musicianship to maximum effect, admirably partnered by Anner Bylsma and Gustav Leonhardt. Perhaps the Corelli *Variations* need the violin to be fully in character, though the recorder version is authentic and aurally most engaging. Corelli puts the famous 'Follia' melody through all possible hoops and Brüggen obliges with nimble virtuosity. The Vivaldi comes from *Il Pastor Fido* and, alongside the other works by Corelli (written with the violin in mind) and the fine sonata of Marcello with its memorable slow movement, offers the most attractive music on the disc. The Veracini works are also primarily for violin, though for the *G major Sonata* the recorder is an optional alternative. All this music is played with exemplary skill, and no recorder enthusiast will want to be without this splendid example of Brüggen's art; even if some of the music by the minor composers has limited appeal, there is plenty to divert in this 73-minute programme, which is recorded with remarkable realism and immaculately transferred to CD.

Cann, Claire and Antoinette (piano duo)

'Romantic favourites on 2 pianos': SAINT-SAENS: *Danse macabre.* DEBUSSY: *Petite suite.* TCHAIKOVSKY (arr. Cann): *Nutcracker suite:* excerpts. BRAHMS: *Variations on a theme of Haydn (St Anthony chorale), Op. 56b; Waltzes, Op. 39/1–2, 5–6, 9–11 & 15.* MACDOWELL (arr. Niemann): *Hexentanz.* LISZT (arr. Bendel): *Hungarian rhapsody No. 2.*
☞ ⊛ (M) *** Pianissimo Dig. PP 10393 [id.].

It is difficult to imagine a more scintillating piano duet record than this. Saint-Saëns's skeletons – summoned by an evocative midnight bell – dance as vigorously as do MacDowell's witches in the brilliant *Hexameron*, while Debussy's delightful *Petite suite* – played here very effectively on two pianos, rather than with four hands on one – is full of charm. The Cann sisters then produce a rich-textured fullness of tone for the Brahms *Haydn variations*, which are every bit as enjoyable here as in their orchestral dress. Most remarkable of all are the excerpts from the *Nutcracker suite*, conceived entirely pianistically and glittering with colour. Indeed the *Sugar plum fairy* has a much stronger profile than usual and the *Chinese dance* an irresistible oriental glitter. The *Hungarian dances* bring beguiling variety of mood and texture and display an easy bravura, ending with a lovely performance of the famous *Cradle song* (*No. 15 in A flat*), while the dazzling Liszt *Hungarian rhapsody* ends the recital with great exuberance and much digital panache. The recording, made in Rosslyn Hill Chapel, is exceptionally real and vivid and is ideally balanced.

'Gemini': LUTOSLAWSKI: *Variations on a theme of Paganini* (for 2 pianos). HOROVITZ: *Concerto for dancers*. SHOSTAKOVICH: *Concertino* (for 2 pianos). POULENC: *Sonata for four hands*. BLINKO: *Gemini* (for 2 pianos). RAVEL: *Rapsodie espagnole* (for piano, four hands).
☞ **(*) Pianissimo Dig. PP 21192 [id.].

The Cann sisters present the famous Lutoslawski *Variations* with great dash: maybe just a shade more poise would have benefited this piece. They find the ironic wit and toccata-like energy of the Shostakovich *Concertino*, and the delightful Poulenc *Sonata à quatre mains* is just as keenly characterized. The Horovitz *Concerto* has a charming *Andantino* and a brilliant, lightweight finale, which again show the Duo in their best form. Timothy Blinko's *Gemini* gives the collection its title. An eclectic piece, it is exotically (even sensuously) tuneful and grateful to play, with its Ravelian roulades. The recital closes with Ravel and the shifting nocturnal colours of the *Prélude* and the glittering *Malagueña* are beautifully done, with the *Feria* certainly providing a spectacular close. The recording is first class.

Cherkassky, Shura (piano)

'Live at the Queen Elizabeth Hall': SCHUBERT: *Sonata No. 13 in A, D.664*. CHOPIN: *Nocturne in F min., Op. 55; Preludes, Op. 28/4, 6, 7, 10, 13, 17, 20 & 23; Ballade No. 3 in A flat; Etudes, Op. 25/7 & 10; Op. 10/4*. RACHMANINOV: *Polka de V. R.* SCRIABIN: *Prelude in D, Op. 11/5*. RUBINSTEIN: *Melody in F.* ALBENIZ/GODOWSKY: *Tango*. SCHUBERT/GODOWSKY: *Moment musical No. 3*.
☞ *** Decca Dig. 443 653-2 [id.].

This collection is taken from two different live recitals in 1975 and shows Cherskassky at once at his most discerning, certainly at his most unpredictable and spontaneous. He is not an artist who has made a reputation with genre series of major works, since he likes to play in recital and to an audience. His Schubert is as individual as his Chopin. He is very well recorded, and the CD runs for 72 minutes.

'Shura Cherkassky live' (80th birthday recital): BACH (arr Busoni): *Chaconne*. SCHUMANN: *Symphonic Etudes, Op. 13*. CHOPIN: *Nocturne in F min., Op. 55/1; Tarantelle, Op. 43*. IVES: *3-Page sonata*. HOFMANN: *Kaleidoscope, Op. 40/4*. PABST: *Paraphrase on Tchaikovsky's Eugene Onegin*. GOULD: *Boogie Woogie Etude*.
☞ *** Decca Dig. 433 654-2 [id.].

Cherkassky's eightieth-birthday recital won the *Gramophone* Instrumental Award for 1993. The programme has rather more range than the companion disc, above, and the Bach/Busoni *Chaconne* and Schumann *Symphonic studies* show him at his most commanding. There are few examples of a spontaneous live recital captured more successfully on disc than this, and the Decca recording is most real and vivid.

Clarion Ensemble

'Trumpet collection': FANTINI: *Sonata; Brando; Balletteo; Corrente*. MONTEVERDI: *Et e pur dunque vero*. FRESCOBALDI: *Canzona a canto solo*. PURCELL: *To arms, heroic prince*. A. SCARLATTI: *Si suoni la tromba*. BISHOP: *Arietta and Waltz; Thine forever*. DONIZETTI: *Lo L'udia*. KOENIG: *Post horn galop*. ARBAN: *Fantasia on Verdi's Rigoletto*. CLARKE: *Cousins*. ENESCU: *Legende*.
⊛ *** Amon Ra CD-SAR 30 [id.].

The simple title '*Trumpet collection*' covers a fascinating recital of music for trumpet written over three centuries and played with great skill and musicianship by Jonathan Impett, using a variety of original instruments, from a keyed bugle and clapper shake-key cornopean to an English slide trumpet and a posthorn. Impett is a complete master of all these instruments, never producing a throttled tone; indeed in the Purcell and Scarlatti arias he matches the soaring soprano line of Deborah Roberts with uncanny mirror-image precision. Accompaniments are provided by other members of the Clarion Ensemble. The Frescobaldi *Canzona* brings a duet for trumpet and trombone, with a background harpsichord filigree, which is most effective. With demonstration-worthy recording, this is as enjoyable as it is interesting, with the *Post horn galop* and Arban's *Rigoletto variations* producing exhilarating bravura.

Cohler, Jonathan (clarinet)

'*Cohler on clarinet*' (with Judith Gordon, piano): BRAHMS: *Sonata No. 1 in F min., Op. 120/1.*
WEBER: *Grand duo concertante, Op. 48.* BAERMANN: *Quintet No. 3, Op. 23: Adagio* (arr. for clarinet
& piano). SARGON: *Deep Ellum nights* (3 Sketches).
☞ *** Ongaku Dig. 024-101 [id.].

This fine collection marks the recording début of an outstanding, Boston-born, American clarinettist. He has a splendid technique and a lovely tone, and he is already master of an extraordinarily wide range of repertoire. The opening Brahms *F minor Sonata* is a supreme test, and he passes with distinction: the *Andante un poco adagio* is full of intimate feeling and the finale has a fine, rhapsodical flair. The Weber *Grand duo concertante* is suitably good-natured, with a songful central cantilena and plenty of wit in the finale. The Baermann *Adagio* shows how ravishingly Cohler can shape a melting legato line with a breath-catching pianissimo at its peak. He then throws his hat in the air in the three exuberant *Sketches* of Simon Sargon, where sultry melodic lines are interrupted by all kinds of jazzy glissandos and uninhibited syncopations, notably an explosive burst of energy intruding into the *Quiet and easy* central section. The finale is like a flashy cakewalk. Only an American musician could play this with such understanding spontaneity. The recording is truthful, but the piano is placed behind in a too resonant acoustic (the empty Paine Concert Hall at Harvard University), which is a tiresome misjudgement. Even so, Judith Gordon provides sympathetic support and the playing more than compensates. (The UK distributor at the time of going to press is Quantum Audio.)

'*More Cohler on clarinet*' (with Randall Hodkinson, piano): BRAHMS: *Sonata No. 2 in E flat, Op.*
120/2. POULENC: *Sonata.* SCHUMANN: *Fantaisiestücke, Op. 73.* MILHAUD: *Sonatina, Op. 100.*
STRAVINSKY: *3 Pieces* (for solo clarinet).
☞ *** Ongaku Dig. 024-102 [id.].

Cohler's second disc is much more satisfactorily balanced and recorded in an acoustic that has space but not too much of it. His excellent partner, Randall Hodgkinson, is fully in the picture. This is a wholly delectable recital. The opening of the Brahms *E flat Sonata* is agreeably warm and relaxed, and the theme-and-variations finale brings a pleasing interplay between the two artists. Poulenc's *Sonata* is beautifully done, the lovely *Romanza* (*Trè calme*) is cool in the way only a player who knows about jazz can manage, while the fizzing finale also brings a hint of rapture in its contrasting lyrical theme. The warmth of the Schumann pieces, for which Cohler imaginatively modifies his timbre, contrasts with the outrageous Milhaud sonatina, with both outer movements marked *Très rude* but the *Lent* centrepiece quite magical. The three dry Stravinsky fragments make a perfect close to a disc which is outstanding in every way.

Curley, Carlo

'*The Emperor's Fanfare*' (Organ of Girard College Chapel, Philadelphia): SOLER: *Emperor's fanfare*
(arr. Biggs). WAGNER: *Tristan und Isolde: Liebestod.* JONGEN: *Choral.* BACH: *Toccata and fugue in D
min., BWV 565.* ALBINONI: *Adagio* (arr. Giazotto). ALAIN: *Litanies.* SCHUBERT: *Ave Maria.* KARG-
ELERT: *Nun danket alle Gott, Op. 65/9.* GRIEG: *Sigurd Jorsalfar: Homage march.* GUILMANT: *March
upon Handel's 'Lift up your heads', Op. 15.*
*** Argo Dig. 430 200-2; *430 200-4* [id.].

The performances here are full of drama and temperament, unashamedly romantic yet very compelling. The title-piece by Soler is an anachronistic but irresistible arrangement by E. Power Biggs which provides an opportunity for great splashes of throaty timbre and uses – as does the Alain *Litanies* – the powerful *Tuba mirabilis* stop. 'Its pipes', Curley tells us, 'lie horizontally or *en chamade*, and this stop speaks with an unrivalled speed and clarity on twenty-five inches of wind pressure, a veritable hurricane when compared to the two to four inches common to modern instruments.' The sheer verve and panache of Curley's playing, matching the eloquence of his prose and the depth and spectacle of the reproduced sound – the pedals are stunningly caught – cannot fail to entertain any organ fancier.

Du Pré, Jacqueline (cello)

Early BBC recordings, Vol. 1 (with Stephen Kovacevich, Ernest Lush): BACH: (Unaccompanied) *Cello suites Nos. 1 in G; 2 in D min., BWV 1007/8.* BRITTEN: *Cello sonata in C, Op. 65; Scherzo; Marcia.* FALLA: *Suite populaire espagnole* (arr. Maréchal).
(M) (***) EMI mono CDM7 63165-2.

Early BBC recordings, Vol. 2 (with Ernest Lush, (i) William Pleeth): BRAHMS: *Cello sonata No. 2 in F, Op. 99.* F. COUPERIN: (i) *13th Concert a 2 instrumens (Les Goûts-réunis).* HANDEL: *Cello sonata in G min.* (arr. Slatter).
(M) (***) EMI mono CDM7 63166-2.

These two discs gather together some of the radio performances which Jacqueline du Pré gave in her inspired teens. Her 1962 recordings of the first two Bach *Cello suites* may not be immaculate, but her impulsive vitality makes phrase after phrase at once totally individual and seemingly inevitable. In two movements from Britten's *Cello sonata in C*, with Stephen Kovacevich as her partner, the sheer wit is deliciously infectious, fruit of youthful exuberance in both players. The first of the two discs is completed by Falla's *Suite populaire espagnole*, with the cello matching any singer in expressive range and rhythmic flair. The second has fascinating Couperin duets played with her teacher, William Pleeth; the Handel *Sonata* is equally warm and giving. Best of all is the Brahms *Cello sonata No. 2*, recorded at the 1962 Edinburgh Festival.

Eden, Bracha and Alexander Tamir (piano duet)

'Dances around the world': RACHMANINOV: *Polka italienne.* MOSZKOWSKI: *Spanish dances, Op. 65/1– 2.* GRIEG: *Norwegian dances Nos. 2–3.* BRAHMS: *Hungarian dances and Waltzes.* DVORAK: *Slavonic dances, Op. 46/6–7; Op. 72/8.* SCHUBERT: *Waltzes.* BARBER: *Souvenirs: Pas de deux.* DEBUSSY: *Petite suite: Menuet and ballet.*
(BB) *** Pickwick Dig. PWK 1134.

Eden and Tamir travel the world as a piano duo, and this record is exactly like going to one of their concerts: it is both exhilarating and beguiling, full of variety and spontaneity. They sound as if they are enjoying everything they play, and so do we. Very good sound too.

Fergus-Thompson, Gordon (piano)

'Reverie': DEBUSSY: *Rêverie; Arabesque No. 1; Suite bergamasque: Clair de lune.* SCRIABIN: *Etude, Op. 42/4.* BACH: *Chorales: Wachet auf* (trans. Busoni); *Jesu, joy of man's desiring* (trans. Hess). GLINKA: *The Lark* (trans. Balakirev). GODOWSKY: *Alt Wien.* SAINT-SAENS: *The Swan* (arr. Godowsky). SCHUMANN: *Arabeske in C, Op. 18; Kinderszenen: Träumerei.* BRAHMS: *Intermezzo in A, Op. 118.* GRIEG: *Lyric pieces: Butterfly, Op. 43/1; Nocturne, Op. 54/4.* RAVEL: *Le tombeau de Couperin: Forlane. Pavane pour une infante défunte.*
(M) *** ASV Dig. CDWHL 2066; ZCWHL 2066.

This 76-minute recital fills a real need for a high-quality recital of piano music for the late evening, where the mood of reverie is sustained without blandness. Gordon Fergus-Thomson's performances are of high sensibility throughout, from the atmospheric opening Debussy items to the closing Ravel *Pavane*. Perhaps his Bach is a little studied but the rest is admirably paced, and the two favourite Grieg *Lyric pieces* are particularly fresh. Excellent recording.

Fernández, Eduardo (guitar)

'The World of the Spanish guitar': ALBENIZ: *Sevilla; Tango; Asturias.* LLOBET: *6 Catalan folksongs.* GRANADOS: *Andaluza; Danza triste.* TARREGA: *Estudio brillante; 5 Preludes; Minuetto; 3 Mazurkas; Recuerdos de la Alhambra.* SEGOVIA: *Estudio sin luz; Neblina; Estudio.* TURINA: *Fandagillo; Ráfaga.*
(M) *** Decca Dig 433 820-2; *433 820-4* [id.].

Fernández is most naturally recorded in the Henry Wood Hall. His programme is essentially an intimate one and centres on the highly rewarding music of Tárrega, although opening colourfully with items from Albéniz's *Suite española*. The Llobet group of *Folksongs*, and Segovia's hauntingly atmospheric *Neblina* ('Mist') make further highlights. Later there is bravura from Turina, notably the spectacular *Ráfaga* ('Gust of wind') but even here, though the playing is vibrant, there is no flashiness. With an hour of music and digital sound, this well-chosen programme is excellent value.

'French Impressions'

'French impressions' (played by: Er'ella Talmi, flute; Avigail Amheim, clarinet; Gad Levertov, viola; Alice Giles, harpsichord; Kaminkovsky Quartet): RAVEL: *Introduction and allegro*. DEBUSSY: *Sonata for flute, viola & harp*. ROUSSEL: *Trio, Op. 58*. CAPLET: *Conte fantastique*.
(BB) *** Pickwick/CDI Dig. PWK 1141.

Excellent, highly sensitive playing throughout an interesting and rewarding programme. This is one of the finest modern versions of Ravel's magically atmospheric *Introduction and allegro*, and the improvisatory nature of the lovely Debussy *Sonata* is captured equally well. The Roussel is of a drier vintage, but the programme ends in high drama with André Caplet's imaginative story in music based on Edgar Allan Poe's *Masque of the Red Death*.

Fretwork

'In nomine': 16th-century English music for viols: TALLIS: *In nomine a 4, Nos. 1 & 2; Solfaing song a 5; Fantasia a 5; In nomine a 4, No. 2; Libera nos, salva nos a 5*. TYE: *In nomine a 5 (Crye); In nomine a 5 (Trust)*. CORNYSH: *Fa la sol a 3*. BALDWIN: *In nomine a 4*. BULL: *In nomine a 5*. BYRD: *In nomine a 4, No. 2. Fantasia a 3, No. 3*. TAVERNER: *In nomine; In nomine a 4*. PRESTON: *O lux beata Trinitas a 3*. JOHNSON: *In nomine a 4*. PARSONS: *In nomine a 5; Ut re mi fa sol la a 4*. FERRABOSCO: *In nomine a 5; Lute fantasia No. 5; Fantasia a 4*.
*** Amon Ra CD-SAR 29 [id.].

This was Fretwork's début CD. The collection is not so obviously of strong popular appeal as the later collection for Virgin but is nevertheless very rewarding and distinguished, and it includes the complete consort music of Thomas Tallis. The sound is naturally pleasing in a fairly rich acoustic and readers can be assured that there is no vinegar in the string-timbre here; indeed, the sound itself is quite lovely in its gentle, austere atmosphere.

'Heart's ease': HOLBORNE: *The Honiesuckle; Countess of Pembroke's paradise; The Fairie round*. BYRD: *Fantasia a 5 (Two in one); Fancy in C*. DOWLAND: *Mr Bucton, his galliard; Captaine Digorie Piper, his galliard; Lachrimae antiquae pavan; Mr Nicholas Gryffith, his galliard*. BULL: *Fantasia a 4*. FERRABOSCO: *In nomine a 5*. GIBBONS: *In nomine a 5; Fantasia a 4 for the great dooble base*. LAWES: *Airs for 2 division viols in C: Pavan of Alfonso; Almain of Alfonso. Consort sett a 5 in C: Fantasia; Pavan; Almain*.
*** Virgin Dig. VC7 59667-2 [id.].

An outstanding collection of viol consort music from the late Tudor and early Stuart periods; the playing is both stylish and vivacious, with a fine sense of the most suitable tempo for each piece. The more lyrical music is equally sensitive. This is a tuneful entertainment, not just for the specialist collector, and Fretwork convey their pleasure in all this music. The William Byrd *Fancy* (from *My Ladye Nevells Booke*) is played exuberantly on the organ by Paul Nicholson, to bring some contrast before the closing Lawes *Consort set*. The recording is agreeably warm, yet transparent too.

Gendron, Maurice (cello)

'The early years (1960–67)' (with (i) Jean Françaix; (ii) Peter Gallion, piano): (i) SCHUBERT: *Arpeggione sonata, D.821*. BEETHOVEN: *Variations: on Mozart's 'Ein Mädchen', Op. 66; 'Bei Männern', WoO 46* (both from *Die Zauberflöte*); *Variations on Handel's 'See the conqu'ring hero comes' from Judas Maccabaeus, WoO 45*. DEBUSSY: *Sonata in D min*. FAURE: *Sonata No. 2 in D min., Op. 117*. FRANCAIX: *Berceuse; Rondino staccato; Nocturne; Sérénade* (all arr. Gendron); *Mouvement perpétuel*. MESSIAEN: *Quatuor pour la fin du temps: Louange à l'éternité de Jésus*. (ii) POPPER: *Serenade, Op. 54/2*. HANDEL: *Xerxes: Largo* (arr. Gendron). SAINT-SAENS: *Carnival of the animals: Le cygne*. SCHUMANN: *Kinderszenen: Träumerei*. RIMSKY-KORSAKOV: *Flight of the bumble bee*.

PAGANINI: *Variations on a theme of Rossini* (*Moses fantasy*, arr. Gendron). MOSZKOWSKI: *Guitare, Op. 45/2* (arr. Gendron). KREISLER: *Liebesleid*. FALLA: *La vida breve: Spanish dance No. 1*. BACH: *Chorale: Ich ruf' zu dir, Herr Jesu Christ, BWV 639* (arr. Gendron). CHOPIN: *Introduction and Polonaise brillante in C, Op. 3*. FITZENHAGEN: *Moto perpetuo* (arr. Gendron). GRANADOS: *Andaluza, Op. 37/5*. DVORAK: *Humoresque, Op. 101/7*.

☞ (M) *** Ph. 438 960-2 (3) [id.].

The elegant French cellist, Maurice Gendron, has always been well served by the Philips recording engineers who consistently catch his urbane, polished timbre in perfect focus. He does not readily wear his heart on his sleeve, yet while he shows himself a naturally debonair Schubertian in the *Arpeggione sonata* he can also rise with ardour to the expressive feeling of the Debussy and Fauré sonatas which are played with discerning eloquence. His slightly recessive solo personality is surely ideal for the engaging Françaix miniatures, and it is this composer himself who provides a remarkably sympathetic partnership for the diverse programme on the first two CDs – just sample the cultivated way the pair of them introduce Handel's fine melody in Beethoven's *Judas Maccabaeus variations*. The second CD ends with a characteristically intimate account of the famous cello soliloquy from Messiaen's *Quartet for the end of time*. The immaculately played lollipops on the third disc are given a slightly more forward balance. Yet perhaps one needs a more extrovert approach to some of these items. Rimsky's bumble bee buzzes comparatively gently and the neat bravura of Fitzenhagen's *Moto perpetuo* is a more suitable example of Gendron's virtuosity, though he readily demonstrates his easy command in the high tessitura of the Paganini variations, where his timbre is always sweet. Perhaps overall this collection is a rather lightweight representation of a great artist, but the finish of Gendron's playing is always a pleasure in itself.

Gilels, Emil (piano)

MEDTNER: *Sonata reminincenza, Op. 38*. PROKOFIEV: *Sonata No. 3 in A min., Op. 28*. SCRIABIN: *Sonata No. 4 in F sharp, Op. 30*. STRAVINSKY: *Petrushka suite* (arr Gilels). VAINBERG: *Sonata No. 4 in B min.*

☞ *** Russian Disc. MK 417702.

This is piano playing in a class of its own. It communicates that special authority which only great pianists have, together with that sense of dash and élan given to very few. The recordings, made in the Grand Hall of the Moscow Conservatory in 1957 and (in the case of the Medtner) 1968, are emphatically not three-star but the artistry of this playing transcends all sonic limitations, and the *Petrushka*, one of his most celebrated performances, has a dazzling brilliance and extraordinary powers of characterization. Any very occasional slip is more musical than many a dry virtuoso's right notes.

Grumiaux, Arthur (violin), Riccdardo Castagnone (piano)

'*The early years*': DEBUSSY: *Sonata in G min*. LEKEU: *Sonata in G*. SCHUBERT: *3 Sonatinas; Duo sonata in A*. KREISLER: *Liebesleid; Liebesfreud; Schön Rosmarin; Capricce viennoise; Tambourin chinoise*. TARTINI: *Sonata in G min. (Devil's trill), Op. 1/4*. CORELLI: *Sonata in D min., Op. 5/12*. VITALI: *Ciaccona*. VERACINI: *Sonata in A, Op. 1/7*. PAGANINI: *I Palpiti, Op. 13; La Treghe, Op. 8*.

☞ (M) *** Ph. 438 516-2 (3) [id.].

Here are three CDs of beautifully natural and unaffected music-making. The Debussy and Lekeu sonatas occupy the first CD and come from 1956, as does the Tartini *Devil's Trill sonata* and its companions. The Schubert *Sonatinas* and *Duo* were made two years later but the sound is amazingly fresh. These performances have an aristocratic finesse that will delight all connoisseurs of violin playing. Not to be missed.

Headington, Christopher (piano)

British piano music of the twentieth century: BRITTEN: *Holiday Diary*. DELIUS: *3 Preludes*. ELGAR: *Adieu; In Smyrna; Serenade*. HEADINGTON: *Ballade-image; Cinquanta*. IRELAND: *The island spell*. MOERAN: *Summer valley*. PATTERSON: *A Tunnel of time, Op. 66*.

☞ *** Kingdom Dig. KCLD 2017; CKCL 2017 [id.].

The novelties here are fascinating. The Delius *Preludes* (1923) have much of the luminous atmosphere of the orchestral music, while Britten's *Holiday Diary* (what a happy idea for a suite!), written when he was just twenty, is most winning. The Elgar pieces are well worth having, and Headington again reveals himself as an appealing composer. Both his pieces were written for fiftieth-birthday celebrations and the *Ballad-image* expressly seeks to conjure up an atmosphere combining the influences of Chopin and Debussy. It is most engaging. John Ireland's *Island spell* is beautifully played. A 69-minute recital which is skilfully planned to be listened to in sequence. Good, if not outstanding, recording.

Horowitz, Vladimir (piano)

'*The Horowitz Edition*': CHOPIN: *Sonata No. 2; Etudes, Opp. 10/12; 25/7; Scherzo No. 1.* RACHMANINOV: *Etudes-tableaux, Opp. 33/2; 39/5.* SCHUMANN: *Arabesque, Op. 18; Kinderszenen, Op. 15; Toccata, Op. 7.* LISZT: *Hungarian rhapsody No. 19* (trans. Horowitz). D. SCARLATTI: *Sonatas, Kk. 322, 455, 531.* BEETHOVEN: *Sonata No. 8.* SCHUBERT: *Impromptu No. 3.* DEBUSSY: *3 Préludes, Book II.* SCRIABIN: *Poème, Op. 32/1; Etudes, Opp. 2/1; 8/12* (S2K 53457). SCARLATTI: *Sonatas, Kk. 25, 33, 39, 52, 54, 96, 146, 162, 197, 198, 201, 303, 466, 474, 481, 491, 525, 547* (SK 53460). BACH/BUSONI: *Toccata, Adagio & Fugue, BWV 564.* SCHUMANN: *Fantaisie, Op. 17; Träumerei, Op. 15/7; Blumenstück, Op. 19.* SCRIABIN: *Sonatas Nos. 9–10; Poème, Op. 32/1; Etude in C sharp min., Op. 2/ 1.* CHOPIN: *Mazurkas, Opp. 30/4; 33/4; Etude, Op. 10/8; Ballade No. 1; Polonaise-fantaisie, Op. 61; Nocturne, Op. 72/1.* DEBUSSY: *Serenade for the doll; L'Isle joyeuse.* MOSZKOWSKI: *Etude in A flat, Op. 72/11.* MOZART: *Sonata No. 11, K.331.* HAYDN: *Sonata, Hob XVI/23.* LISZT: *Vallée d'Obermann.* (S3K 53461). CHOPIN: *Ballade No. 1; Nocturne, Op. 55/1; Polonaise, Op. 44.* D. SCARLATTI: *Sonatas, Kk. 55; 380.* SCHUMANN: *Arabeske, Op. 18; Traümerei.* SCRIABIN: *Etude, Op. 8/12.* HOROWITZ: *Variations on a theme from Carmen.* (SK 53465). CLEMENTI: Excerpts from: *Sonatas, Opp. 12/2; 25/ 3; 50/1. Adagio sostennuto in F, from Gradis ad Parnassum, Book I/14.* J. S. BACH: *Chorale prelude: 'Ich ruf zu dir, Herr Jesu Christ'.* D. SCARLATTI: *Sonatas, Kk. 260; 319.* HAYDN: *Sonata, Hob XVI/ 48.* BEETHOVEN: *Sonata No. 28, Op. 101.* (SK 53466). BEETHOVEN: *Sonatas Nos. 14, Op. 27/2 (Moonlight); 21, Op. 53 (Waldstein); 23, Op. 57 (Appassionata).* (SK 53467). CHOPIN: *Mazurkas, Opp. 7/3; 17/4; 30/3; 33/2; 41/2; 50/3; 59/3; Etudes, Op. 10/3–6, 12; 3 Nouvelles études, No. 2; Introduction & rondo, Op. 16; Waltzes, Op. 34/2; 64/2; Polonaises, Opp. 40/1; 53; Prélude, Op. 28/6, 15.* SCHUMANN: *Variations on a theme by Clara Wieck; Kreisleriana, Op. 16.* (S2K 53468). SCHUBERT: *Impromptus, D.899/2, 4; D.935/1–2.* LISZT: *Consolation No. 2; Scherzo & Marsch.* DEBUSSY: *Pour les arpèges composées; La terrasse des audiences du clair de lune.* MENDELSSOHN: *Etude, Op. 104b/3.* (SK 53471). SCRIABIN: *Feuillets d'album Opp. 45/1; 58; Etudes, Opp. 8/2, 8, 10–11; 42, 3–5; 65/3; 2 Poèmes, Op. 69; Vers la flamme.* MEDTNER: *Fairy tale, Op. 51/3.* RACHMANINOV: *Sonata No. 2; Prélude, Op. 32/12; Moment musical, Op. 16/3; Etudes-tableaux, Opp. 33/2, 5; 39/9.*
☞ (M) (***) Sony mono SX13K 53456 (13) [id.].

The strength of the Sony box which runs to 13 CDs and includes all Horowitz's recordings from 1962–73 resides in the fact that nearly all these discs are essential repertory for Horowitz collectors but in any case are not now obtainable separately in the UK. Hardly any of these performances can be passed over, whether it be the Scarlatti sonatas or the stunning accounts of Scriabin's *Ninth* and *Tenth*. There is almost nothing that does not show him in top form – and the sound, though not ideal, is greatly improved. Advice for those considering the boxes rather than individual releases would be to buy the Sony and choose liberally from among the CDs singled out for special mention in the RCA set.

'*In London*': *God save the Queen* (arr. Horowitz). CHOPIN: *Ballade No. 1 in G min., Op. 23; Polonaise No. 7 in A flat (Polonaise-Fantaisie), Op. 61.* SCHUMANN: *Kinderszenen, Op. 15.* SCRIABIN: *Étude in D sharp min., Op. 8/12.*
☞ (M) *** BMG/RCA 09026 61414-2 [id.].

Horowitz's London and New York recitals were both recorded live by RCA and now reappear at mid-price. The highlights from the memorable 1982 London recital omit the elegant Scarlatti sonatas he played on that occasion, doubtless because it would duplicate 'Horowitz at the Met.' – see below. However, room could surely have been found for the Rachmaninov *Sonata* or for his encores, as the CD is not generously filled. As those who attended this electrifying recital will know, there were idiosyncratic touches, particularly in the *Kinderszenen* (and also in the Chopin *Ballade*), but this is remarkable testimony to his wide dynamic range and his refined *pianopianissimo*. There are many fascinating points of detail in both works (but notably in the Chopin) which give one the feeling of hearing the music for the first time.

'At the Met.': D. SCARLATTI: Sonatas: in A flat, Kk. 127; in F min., Kk. 184 & 466; in A, Kk. 101; in B min., Kk. 87; in E, Kk. 135. CHOPIN: Ballade No. 4 in F min., Op. 52; Waltz No. 9 in A flat, Op. 69/1. LISZT: Ballade No. 2 in B min., G. 171. RACHMANINOV: Prelude No. 6 in G min., Op. 23/5.
☞ (M) *** BMG/RCA 09026 61416-2 [id.].

The playing is in a class of its own, and all one needs to know is that this recording reproduces the highly distinctive tone-quality Horowitz commanded. This recital, given at the Metropolitan Opera House and issued here at the time of his London Festival Hall appearance in 1982, comes closer to the real thing than anything else on record, except his DG recitals. The quality of the playing is quite extraordinary.

Recital: BACH/BUSONI: Chorale prelude: Nun komm der Heiden Heiland. MOZART: Piano sonata No. 10 in C, K. 330. CHOPIN: Mazurka in A min., Op. 17/4; Scherzo No. 1 in B min., Op. 20; Polonaise No. 6 in A flat, Op. 53. LISZT: Consolation No. 3 in D flat. SCHUBERT: Impromptu in A flat, D. 899/4. SCHUMANN: Novellette in F, Op. 21/1. RACHMANINOV: Prelude in G sharp min., Op. 32/12. SCRIABIN: Etude in C sharp min., Op. 2/1. MOSZKOWSKI: Etude in F, Op. 72/6 (recording of performances featured in the film Vladimir Horowitz – The Last Romantic).
*** DG Dig. 419 045-2 [id.].

Recorded when he was over eighty, this playing betrays remarkably little sign of frailty. The Mozart is beautifully elegant and the Chopin A minor Mazurka, Op. 17, No. 4, could hardly be more delicate. The only sign of age comes in the B minor Scherzo, which does not have the leonine fire and tremendous body of his famous 1950 recording. However, it is pretty astonishing for all that.

'The studio recordings': SCHUMANN: Kreisleriana, Op. 16. D. SCARLATTI: Sonatas: in B min., Kk. 87; in E, Kk. 135. LISZT: Impromptu (Nocturne) in F sharp; Valse oubliée No. 1. SCRIABIN: Etude in D sharp min., Op. 8/2. SCHUBERT: Impromptu in B flat, D. 935/3. SCHUBERT/TAUSIG: Marche militaire, D. 733/1.
🅑 *** DG 419 217-2 [id.].

The subtle range of colour and articulation in the Schumann is matched in his Schubert Impromptu, and the Liszt Valse oubliée offers the most delicious, twinkling rubato. Hearing Scarlatti's E major Sonata played with such crispness, delicacy and grace must surely convert even the most dedicated authenticist to the view that this repertoire can be totally valid in terms of the modern instrument. The Schubert–Tausig Marche militaire makes a superb encore, played with the kind of panache that would be remarkable in a pianist half Horowitz's age. With the passionate Scriabin Etude as the central romantic pivot, this recital is uncommonly well balanced to show Horowitz's special range of sympathies.

'In Moscow': D. SCARLATTI: Sonata in E, Kk. 380. MOZART: Sonata No. 10 in C, K. 330. RACHMANINOV: Preludes: in G, Op. 32/5; in G sharp min. Op. 32/12. SCRIABIN: Etudes: in C sharp min., Op. 2/1; in D sharp min., Op. 8/12. LISZT/SCHUBERT: Soirées de Vienne; Petrarch Sonnet 104. CHOPIN: Mazurkas, Op. 30/4; Op. 7/3. SCHUMANN: Kinderszenen: Träumerei.
*** DG Dig. 419 499-2; 419 499-4 [id.].

This is familiar Horowitz repertoire, played with characteristic musical discernment and spontaneity. Technically the pianism may not quite match his finest records of the analogue era, but it is still both melting and dazzling. The sound too is really excellent, much better than he ever received from his American engineers in earlier days.

'Encores': BIZET/HOROWITZ: Variations on a theme from Carmen. SAINT-SAENS/LISZT/HOROWITZ: Danse macabre. MOZART: Sonata No. 11, K.331: Rondo alla turca. MENDELSSOHN/LISZT/HOROWITZ: Wedding march and variations. MENDELSSOHN: Elégie, Op. 85/4; Spring song, Op. 62/6; The shepherd's complaint, Op. 67/5; Scherzo a capriccio: Presto. DEBUSSY: Children's corner: Serenade of a doll. MOSZKOWSKI: Etudes, Op. 72/6 & 11; Etincelles, Op. 36/6. CHOPIN: Polonaise in A flat, Op. 53. SCHUMANN: Kinderszenen: Träumerei. LISZT: Hungarian rhapsody No. 15; Valse oubliée No. 1. RACHMANINOV: Prelude in G min., Op. 23/5. SOUSA/HOROWITZ: The Stars and stripes forever.
(M) (***) BMG/RCA mono GD 87755 [7755-2-RG].

These encore pieces have been around for some time and, apart from the Rachmaninov Prelude and the Mendelssohn, derive from the days of the 78-r.p.m. record and the mono LP. Allowances have to be made for the quality which, as one would expect in this kind of compilation, is variable. So in its different way is the playing, which varies from dazzling to stunning!

Hough, Stephen (piano)

'The Piano Album': MACDOWELL: *Hexentanz, Op. 12.* CHOPIN: *Chant polonaise No. 1.* QUILTER: *The crimson petal; The fuchsia tree.* DOHNANYI: *Capriccio in F min., Op. 28/8.* PADEREWSKI: *Minuet in G, Op. 14/1. Nocturne in B flat, Op. 16/4.* SCHLOZER: *Etude in A flat, Op. 1/2.* GABRILOWITSCH: *Mélodie in E; Caprice-burlesque.* RODGERS: *My favourite things.* WOODFORDE-FINDEN: *Kashmiri song.* FRIEDMAN: *Music box.* SAINT-SAENS: *Carnival: The Swan.* ROSENTHAL: *Papillons.* GODOWSKI: *The gardens of Buitenzorg.* LEVITZKI: *Waltz in A, Op. 2.* PALMGREN: *En route, Op. 9.* MOSZKOWSKI: *Siciliano, Op. 42/2; Caprice espagnole, Op. 3.*
⊛ *** Virgin Dig. VC7 59509-2 [id.].

There are few young pianists who can match Stephen Hough in communicating on record. This Virgin Classics collection captures more nearly than almost any other recent record the charm, sparkle and flair of legendary piano virtuosos from the golden age of Rosenthal, Godowski and Lhévinne. MacDowell's *Hexentanz (Witches' dance),* launches the listener into pure pianistic magic, with playing totally uninhibited and with articulation and timing that are the musical equivalent of being tickled up and down the spine. Hough's own arrangements of Roger Quilter and Amy Woodforde-Finden, in their tender expressiveness, are most affecting. In the grand tradition, Hough does a Valse-caprice arrangement he himself has made of *My favourite things* from *The Sound of Music,* as well as firework pieces by Rosenthal and Moszkowski, among others, along with old-fashioned favourites like Paderewski's *Minuet in G* and Godowski's arrangement of the Saint-Saëns *Swan.* It is a feast for piano-lovers, very well recorded in venues in both London and New York.

Hurford, Peter (organ)

Sydney Opera House organ: *'Great organ works':* BACH: *Toccata and fugue in D min., BWV 565; Jesu, joy of man's desiring.* ALBINONI: *Adagio* (arr. Giazotto). PURCELL: *Trumpet tune in D.* MENDELSSOHN: *A Midsummer Night's Dream: Wedding march.* FRANCK: *Chorale No. 2 in B min.* MURRILL: *Carillon.* WALFORD DAVIES: *Solemn melody.* WIDOR: *Organ symphony No. 5: Toccata.*
(M) **(*) Decca Dig. 425 013-2; 425 013-4 [id.].

Superb sound here, wonderfully free and never oppressive, even in the most spectacular moments. The Widor is spiritedly genial when played within the somewhat mellower registration of the magnificent Sydney instrument (as contrasted with the Ratzeburg Cathedral organ – see above), and the pedals have great sonority and power. The Murrill *Carillon* is equally engaging alongside the Purcell *Trumpet tune,* while Mendelssohn's wedding music has never sounded more resplendent. The Bach is less memorable, and the Albinoni *Adagio,* without the strings, is not an asset to the collection either.

Israeli Flute Ensemble

'Flute Serenade': BEETHOVEN: *Serenade in D, Op. 25* ⊛. MOZART: *Flute quartet No. 1 in D, K.285.* SCHUBERT: *String trio in B flat, D.471.* HOFFMEISTER: *Flute quartet in A.*
(BB) *** Pickwick/CDI Dig. PWK 1139.

We have already praised this delightful account of Beethoven's *D major Serenade* in our composer index. The rest of the concert is hardly less winning, including not only one of the more memorable of Mozart's *Flute quartets* but also Hoffmeister's ingenious transcription of a favourite Mozart piano sonata, with its *Rondo Alla turca* finale sounding very sprightly in the arrangement for flute, violin and piano. The Schubert *String trio* makes a graceful interlude and an attractive change of texture; and the recording adds to the listener's pleasure by its complete naturalness of timbre and balance: one can readily imagine the players sitting at the end of one's room.

(i) Jackson, Francis (organ of York Minster); (ii) Michael Austin (organ of Birmingham Town Hall)

'Pipes of splendour': (i) COCKER: *Tuba tune.* PURCELL: *Trumpet tune and almand.* JACKSON: *Division on 'Nun Danket'.* LEIGHTON: *Paean.* DUBOIS: *Toccata in G.* GUILMANT: *Allegretto in B min., Op. 19.* GIGOUT: *Scherzo in E.* MULET: *Carillon-Sortie.* (ii) REGER: *Toccata and fugue in D min./major, Op. 59/5-6.* DUPRE: *Prelude and fugue in B, Op. 7.* FRANCK: *Final in B flat.*

☞ (M) *** Chan. CHAN 6602 [id.].

This 68-minute collection is aptly titled! Collections of British cathedral organ music on CD don't come any better than this. It was Francis Jackson who made Cocker's *Tuba tune* (with its boisterous, brassy, principal tune) justly famous, and it makes a splendid opener. But the entire programme shows that it is possible to play and record an English organ without the result sounding flabby. The *Toccata* of Dubois is very winning and, in its quieter central section, detail is beautifully clear, as it is in the charming Guilmant *Allegretto* and the lightly articulated Gigout *Scherzo*. Mulet's *Carillon-Sortie* rings out gloriously and Leighton's *Paean* brings a blaze of tone. The items played in Birmingham by Michael Austin are no less stimulating, especially the two French pieces which have a fine piquant bite, while the Reger isn't in the least dull. Superb transfers of demonstration-standard analogue recording from the early 1970s.

John, Keith (organ)

'*Great European organs No. 10*': Tonhalle, Zurich: MUSSORGSKY (trans. John): *Pictures at an exhibition*. ALAIN: *3 Danses (Joies; Deuils; Luttes)*.
☞ *** Priory Dig. PRCD 262 [id.].

Keith John has made his own transcription of Mussorgsky's *Pictures* – and pretty remarkable it sounds. Only the pieces like *Tuileries* that require pointed articulation come off less well than on orchestra or piano. but *Gnomus* and *Bydlo* and, especially, the picture of the two Polish Jews are all remarkably powerful, while the closing sequence of *Catacombes*, *The Hut on fowl's legs* and *The Great gate of Kiev* are superb. The three Alain pieces make a substantial encore. This is as much a demonstration CD as an orchestral version of the Mussorgsky.

'*Great European organs No. 26*': Gloucester Cathedral: STANFORD: *Fantasia and toccata in D min.*, *Op. 57*. REGER: *Prelude and fugue in E, Op. 56/1*. SHOSTAKOVICH: *Lady Macbeth of Mstensk: Passacaglia*. SCHMIDT: *Chaconne in C min*. RAVANELLO: *Theme and variations in B min*.
☞ *** Priory Dig. PRCD 370 [id.].

Keith John, having shown what he can do with Mussorgsky, turns his attention here to little-known nineteenth- and twentieth-century organ pieces. The programme is imaginatively chosen and splendidly played – indeed the bravura is often thrilling – and most realistically recorded on the superb Gloucester organ. Both the Schmidt *Chaconne* and Ravenello *Theme and variations* are fine works. and the Shostakovich *Passacaglia*, an opera entr'acte, was originally conceived as a work for organ.

Johnson, Emma (clarinet)

'*A Clarinet celebration*' (with Gordon Back): WEBER: *Grand duo concertante; Variations concertantes*. BURGMULLER: *Duo*. GIAMPIERI: *Carnival of Venice*. SCHUMANN: *Fantasy pieces, Op. 73*. LOVREGLIO: *Fantasia de concerto, La Traviata*.
*** ASV Dig. CDDCA 732; ZCDCA 732 [id.].

These are party pieces rather than encores, all of them drawing electric sparks of inspiration from this winning young soloist. Even in such virtuoso nonsense as the Giampieri *Carnival of Venice* and the Lovreglio *Fantasia*, Johnson draws out musical magic, while the expressiveness of Weber and Schumann brings heartfelt playing, with phrasing creatively individual. Gordon Back accompanies brilliantly, and the sound is first rate.

'*British clarinet music*' (with Malcolm Martineau (piano); (i) Judith Howard (soprano)): IRELAND: *Fantasy sonata in E flat*. VAUGHAN WILLIAMS: *6 Studies in English folk song;* (i) *3 Vocalises for soprano voice and clarinet*. BAX: *Clarinet sonata*. BLISS: *Pastoral;* (i) *2 Nursery rhymes*. STANFORD: *Clarinet sonata*.
☞ *** ASV Dig. CDDCA 891 [id.].

A very generous recital, offering a wide range of British music written between 1912 and 1958. Stanford's *Sonata* has the usual Brahmsian flavour but uses an Irish lament for the expressive central *Adagio*; then the finale has the best of both worlds by combining both influences. Vaughan Williams's *Six Studies in English folksong* (1927) are beguilingly evocative, while the *Vocalises* for soprano voice and clarinet are brief but rather touching; they were written in the last year of the composer's life. Both the Bax two-movement *Sonata* and the Ireland *Fantasy Sonata* are fine works, and Bliss's *Pastoral* is wartime nostalgia written while the composer was in France during World War One.

Needless to say, Emma Johnson plays everything with her usual spontaneity and musicianship, and she has a fine partner in Malcolm Martineau, while Judith Howard's contribution is pleasingly melismatic. Excellent, atmospheric recording, made in the London Henry Wood Hall.

Kang, Dong-Suk (violin), Pascal Devoyon (piano)

French violin sonatas: DEBUSSY: *Sonata in G min.* RAVEL: *Sonata in G.* POULENC: *Violin sonata.* SAINT-SAENS: *Sonata No. 1 in D min.*
(BB) *** Naxos Dig. 8.550276; *4550276* [id.].

One of the jewels of the Naxos catalogue, this collection of four of the finest violin sonatas in the French repertoire is self-recommending. The stylistic range of this partnership is evident throughout: they seem equally attuned to all four composers. This is warm, freshly spontaneous playing, given vivid and realistic digital recording in a spacious acoustic. A very real bargain.

Kayath, Marcelo (guitar)

'Guitar classics from Latin America': PONCE: *Valse.* PIAZZOLA: *La muerte del angel.* BARRIOS: *Vals, Op. 8/3; Choro de saudade; Julia florida.* LAURO: *Vals venezolanos No. 2; El negrito; El marabino.* BROUWER: *Canción de cuna; Ojos brujos.* PERNAMBUCO: *Sons de carrilhes; Interrogando; Sono de maghia.* REIS: *Si ela perguntar.* VILLA-LOBOS: *5 Preludes.*
(B) *** Pickwick Dig. PCD 853; *CIMPC 853* [id.].

Marcelo Kayath's inspirational accounts of the Villa-Lobos *Preludes* can stand comparison with the finest performances on record. He plays everything here with consummate technical ease and the most appealing spontaneity. His rubato in the Barrios *Vals* is particularly effective, and he is a fine advocate too of the engaging Lauro pieces and the picaresque writing of João Pernambuco, a friend of Villa-Lobos. The recording, made in a warm but not too resonant acoustic, is first class.

Kempff, Wilhelm (piano)

'The music of BACH and Transcriptions': BACH: *English suite No. 3 in G min., BWV 808. Capriccio in B flat (on the departure of his most beloved brother), BWV 992.* Transcriptions (arr. Kempff): *Chorales: Nun komm' der Heiden heiland, BWV 569; Es ist gewisslich an der Zeit, BWV 307 & 734; Befiehl du deine Wege, BWV 727; Wohl mir, dass ich Jesum habe, BWV 147; In dulci jubilo, BWV 751; Zion hört die Wächter singen, BWV 140; Ich ruf zu dir, Herr Jesu Christ, BWV 639; Siciliano in G min. from BWV 1031; Sinfonia in D from cantata, BWV 29. Largo in A flat from clavier concerto in F min., BWV 1056.* HANDEL: *Minuet in G min. HWV 434/1.* GLUCK: *Orfeo ed Euridice: Orpheus's lament; Dance of the Blessed Spirits.*
☞ (M) *** DG 439 108-2 [id.].

The Kempff magic permeates this recital, mostly of transcriptions. His clear, precise style in the Bach *English suite* is a joy and the programmatic *Capriccio* is characterized with great imagination. The *Adagiosissimo* is wonderfully gentle and serene and the closing Fugue imitating the postilion's posthorn is captivating. The chorales are generally rather serious in mood, *Nun komm' der Heiden Heiland* nobly grave. But the Handel *Minuet* is delightfully luminous and the famous slow movement of the *F minor Harpischord concerto* is thoughtfully improvisational in feeling. The *Siciliano in G minor* arrangement is rightly famous and the closing Gluck transcriptions are very beautiful. Kempff is splendidly recorded (in the Hanover Beethovensaal, in 1975) and the CD sounds very realistic.

King, Thea (clarinet), Britten Quartet

Clarinet music: HOWELLS: *Rhapsodic quintet.* COOKE: *Clarinet quintet.* MACONCHY: *Clarinet quintet.* FRANKEL: *Clarinet quintet, Op. 28.* HOLBROOKE: *Eilean shona.*
*** Hyp. Dig. CDA 66428 [id.].

Five strongly characterized works for clarinet quintet by British composers make up a most attractive disc, beautifully played by Thea King and the outstanding Britten Quartet. The masterpiece which sets the pattern for the sequence is the beautiful *Rhapsodic quintet* of Howells, one of the finest of his early works, dating from 1917. The Holbrooke rounds the group off, a brief, song-like soliloquy for clarinet and strings inspired by a Celtic story. The recording is clear and forward with a fine bloom on all the instruments.

Kissin, Yevgeni (piano)

'*Carnegie Hall Début'* (30 September 1990) *Highlights*: LISZT: *Etude d'exécution transcendante No. 10; Liebestraum No. 3; Rhapsodie espagnole.* SCHUMANN: *Abegg Variations, Op. 1; Etudes symphoniques, Op. 13; Widmung* (arr. Liszt).
*** BMG/RCA Dig. 09026 61202-2 [61202-2].

Yevgeni Kissin has phenomenal pianistic powers; not only is this a *tour de force* in terms of technical prowess but also in sheer artistry. Both sets of Schumann *Variations* are remarkable. The Liszt *Rhapsodie espagnole* is played with superb bravura. Kissin's range of colour and keyboard command throughout is dazzling. The Carnegie Hall was packed and the recording balance, while a bit close, is perfectly acceptable. The excitement of the occasion is conveyed vividly.

'*In Tokyo'* (12 May 1987): CHOPIN: *Nocturne in A flat, Op. 32/2; Polonaise in F sharp min., Op. 44.* LISZT: *Concert studies Nos. 1 in D flat (Waldesrauschen); 2 in F min. (La Leggierezza).* PROKOFIEV: *Sonata No. 6 in A, Op. 82.* RACHMANINOV: *Etudes tableaux, Op. 39/1 & 5; Lilacs.* SCRIABIN: *Etude in C sharp min., Op. 42/5; Mazurka in E min., Op. 25/3.*
*** Sony Dig. SK 45931 [id.].

Kissin was only fifteen at the time of his Tokyo début, but he sounds fully mature throughout this recital. He plays Prokofiev's *Sixth Sonata* for all it is worth with no holds barred, and the effect is altogether electrifying – one finds oneself on the edge of one's chair. He is no less at home in the Rachmaninov *Etudes tableaux* and the Liszt *La Leggierezza*, which he delivers with marvellous assurance and poetic feeling. His Scriabin, too, is pretty impressive. The microphone placing is too close – but no matter, this is breathtaking piano playing.

Labèque, Katia and Marielle (piano duo)

'*Encore!':* Adolfo BERIO: *Polka; Maria Isabella (Waltz); La Primavera (Mazurka).* BACH: *Jesu, joy of man's desiring* (arr. Hess). GERSHWIN: *Preludes Nos. 1–3; Promenade (Walking the dog).* STRAVINSKY: *Tango; Waltz.* Luciano BERIO: *Wasserklavier.* BRAHMS: *Waltz in A flat.* TCHAIKOVSKY: *The Seasons: June.* BERNSTEIN: *West Side story: Jet song; America.* JOPLIN: *Bethena (Ragtime waltz); The Entertainer.* JAELL: *Valse.* BARTOK: *New Hungarian folksong.* SCHUMANN: *Abendlied.*
☞ *** Song Dig. SK 48381 [id.].

The Labèque sisters have never made a better record than this, and the recording – made at Abbey Road – is ideally balanced, with just the right degree of resonance. It is an unashamedly popular programme. The playing scintillates, especially the Bernstein and Stravinsky items, while the Labèques' Scott Joplin is admirably cool and the account of Myra Hess's arrangement of the famous Bach *Chorale* is gentle and quite beautiful. Luciano Berio's evocative *Wasserklavier* is a real lollipop, but the surprise is the selection of four catchy and often boisterous pieces by Berio's grandfather, Adolfo, a church organist 'of doubtful faith' (according to his grandson), who gives his imprimatur to the lively Labèque performances, even while he feels that their 'modern and uninhibited pianism' might not have suited his more conventional grandfather. But it is very entertaining, as is the whole 61-minute recital. Highly recommended.

Larrocha, Alicia de (piano)

'*Musica española':* FALLA: *Three-cornered hat: 3 dances. El amor brujo: suite.* TURINA: *Sacromonte, Op. 55/5. Zapateado, Op. 8/3.* HALFFTER: *Danza de la pastora; Danza de la gitana.* MONSALVATGE: *Sonatina para Yvette. Divertimento No. 2 (Habanera).* NIN-CULMELL: *6 Tonadas, Vol.2.* SURIÑACH: *3 Canciones y danzas españolas.* ⊛ MOMPOU: *Impresiones intimas; Preludio a Alicia de Larrocha. Música callada, IV; 7 cançons i dansas.*
(M) *** Decca 433 929-2 (2) [id.].

Alicia de Larrocha is ideally cast here. Much of the music is delightful. Joaquín Nin-Culmell's *6 Tonadas* are flashingly characterful in their folk feeling: the closing *Muñeira (Galicia)* has spectacular flamenco fireworks. Xavier Monsalvatge's *Sonata* in its finale quotes 'Twinkle twinkle, little star', yet its audaciously quirky satire has more in common with Poulenc and Satie than Debussy's *Children's corner*. Miss de Larrocha plays the whole sonata with breathtaking virtuosity. The Mompou pieces have much charm and an atmosphere all their own – they are discussed in more detail under their composer entry. They are digitally recorded; the rest of the recital is analogue but hardly less real.

LaSalle Quartet

Chamber music of the Second Viennese School: BERG: *Lyric suite; String quartet, Op. 3.* SCHOENBERG: *String quartets: in D; No. 1 in D min., Op. 7; No. 2 in F sharp min., Op. 10/3* (with Margaret Price); *No. 3, Op. 30; No. 4, Op. 37.* WEBERN: *5 Movements, Op. 5; String quartet* (1905); *6 Bagatelles, Op. 9; String quartet, Op. 28.*
(M) *** DG 419 994-2 (4) [id.].

DG have compressed their 1971 five-LP set on to four CDs, offering them at a reduced and competitive price. They have also retained the invaluable and excellent documentary study edited by Ursula Rauchhaupt – which runs to 340 pages! It is almost worth having this set for the documentation alone. The LaSalle Quartet give splendidly expert performances, even if at times their playing seems a little cool; and they are very well recorded. An invaluable issue for all who care about twentieth-century music.

Lawson, Peter (piano)

'The American piano sonata, Vol. 1': COPLAND: *Piano sonata.* IVES: *Three page sonata.* CARTER: *Piano sonata.* BARBER: *Piano sonata, Op. 26.*
*** Virgin Dig. VC7 59008-2 [id.].

Peter Lawson plays the Copland *Sonata* with an understanding that is persuasive and an enthusiasm that is refreshing. Elliott Carter's *Sonata* is thoroughly accessible as well as convincing. Lawson can hold his own with such earlier recordings as the Charles Rosen, and he certainly has the advantage of fresher recording quality. In the 1950s and 1960s, the Barber *Sonata*, Op. 26, like that of Ginastera, had a far stronger profile than any other American sonata, and the catalogue has recently been enriched by the return of Horowitz's and Van Cliburn's recordings. Lawson comfortably takes its various hurdles in his stride, and he also gives us the Charles Ives *Three page Sonata*. For what it is worth, in playing the Ives *Three page sonata* Lawson uses the Cowell edition, rather than the later Kirkpatrick. A generous and valuable recital.

'The American piano sonata, Vol. 2': GRIFFES: *Sonata.* SESSIONS: *Sonata No. 2.* IVES: *Sonata No. 1.*
☞ *** Virgin/EMI Dig. VC7 59316-2 [id.].

The Griffes and Sessions *Sonatas* are American classics and Peter Lawson has their measure. Ives is Ives, and that means a real original, even if some of his writing is little short of exasperating – but stimulating, too. The piano recording is nothing if not boldly vivid. An important disc and a generous one: 76 minutes.

Leach, Joanna (piano)

'Four square': SOLER: *Sonata No. 90 in F sharp.* HAYDN: *Sonata in C, Hob XVI/1.* J. S. BACH: *Partita No. 1 in B flat: Prelude; Minuets I & II; Gigue.* MOZART: *Fantasie in D min., K.397; Sonata No. 11 in A, K.331.* SCHUBERT: *Impromptu in A flat D.899/4.* MENDELSSOHN: *Songs without words, Op. 19/1.*
☞ *** Athene Dig. CD 3 [id.].

There is no more convincing fortepiano recital than this. Joanna Leach uses a 1823 Stodart with its effectively dark lower register for the Soler *Sonata*, then plays the same instrument later to show its attractive upper range in an almost romantic performance of Mozart's *Fantasia in D minor*; she ends the recital with the *A major Sonata*, K.331, with the introductory variations particularly inviting. For the Haydn, she chooses a 1789 Broadwood, a more brittle sound, and for the Bach a very effective 1787 instrument made by Longman & Broderip. In the Schubert and Mendelssohn pieces an 1835 D'Almaine brings us that bit nearer a modern piano. Fine performances throughout, and excellent recording. A fascinating way of discovering what the piano's ancestors could do best.

Lipatti, Dinu (piano)

CHOPIN: *Sonata No. 3 in B min., Op. 58.* LISZT: *Années de pèlerinage: Sonetto del Petrarca, No. 104.* RAVEL: *Miroirs: Alborada del gracioso.* BRAHMS: *Waltzes, Op. 39/1, 2, 5, 6, 10, 14 & 15* (with Nadia Boulanger). ENESCU: *Sonata No. 3 in D, Op. 25.*
(M) (***) EMI mono CDH7 63038-2.

The Chopin is one of the classics of the gramophone, and it is good to have it on CD in this excellent-sounding transfer. The Brahms *Waltzes* are played deliciously with tremendous sparkle and tenderness; they sound every bit as realistic as the post-war records. The Enescu *Sonata* is an accessible piece, with an exuberant first movement and a rather atmospheric *Andantino*, but the sound is not as fresh as the rest of the music on this valuable CD. A must for all with an interest in the piano.

'Last recital – Besançon, 16 November 1950': J. S. BACH: *Partita No. 1 in B flat min., BWV 825.* MOZART: *Sonata No. 8 in A min., K.310.* SCHUBERT: *Impromptus in E flat; in G flat, D.899/2–3.* CHOPIN: *Waltzes Nos. 1, 3–14.*
☞ (M) (***) EMI mono CDH5 65166-2 [id.].

No collector should overlook this excellent 73-minute recital, originally issued on a pair of LPs. Most of these performances have scarcely been out of circulation since their first appearance: the haunting account of the Mozart *A minor Sonata* and the Bach *B flat Partita* have had more than one incarnation: the collection of Chopin *Waltzes* is perhaps most famous of all, and its legendary reputation is well earned. The remastering is expertly done, and the ear notices that among his other subtleties Lipatti creates a different timbre for the music of each composer.

Lloyd Webber, Julian (cello)

'British cello music' (with (i) John McCabe, piano): (i) RAWSTHORNE: *Sonata for cello and piano.* ARNOLD: *Fantasy for cello.* (i) IRELAND: *The Holy Boy.* WALTON: *Passacaglia.* BRITTEN: *Teme (Sacher); Cello suite No. 3.*
*** ASV Dig. CDDCA 592; ZCDCA 592 [id.].

A splendid recital and a most valuable one. Julian Lloyd Webber has championed such rarities as the Bridge *Oration* at a time when it was unrecorded and now devotes this present issue to English music that needs strong advocacy; there is no alternative version of the Rawsthorne *Sonata*, in which he is most ably partnered by John McCabe. He gives this piece – and, for that matter, the remainder of the programme – with full-blooded commitment. Good recording.

British cello music, Vol. 2 (with John McCabe (piano)):
STANFORD: *Sonata No. 2, Op. 39.* BRIDGE: *Elegy; Scherzetto.* IRELAND: *Sonata in G min.*
☞ ⑱ *** ASV CDDCA 807 [id.].

The Stanford *Second Cello sonata* (1893 – written between the *Fourth* and *Fifth Symphonies*) is revealed here as an inspired work whose opening theme flowers into great lyrical warmth on Lloyd Webber's ardent bow. The movement is imaginatively worked out and is followed by a lovely *Andante* with sparkling scherzando interludes, then a high-spirited finale offering yet more memorable invention in a Rondo of a strong contrapuntal character. The focus of the recording is a little diffuse, but that serves to add to the atmosphere. Ireland's *Sonata*, too, is among his most richly inspired works, a broad-spanning piece in which ambitious, darkly intense, outer movements frame a most beautiful *Poco largamente*. Again Lloyd Webber, who has long been a passionate advocate of the work, conveys his full expressive power. The piano is placed at a distance, but perhaps that is apt for a piece in which the cello should be presented in full strength. The Bridge *Elegy* (written as early as 1911) is another darkly poignant evocation which points forward to the sparer, more austere style of the later Bridge and the *Scherzetto* (even earlier, 1902) and makes a winning encore: it should ideally have been placed at the end of the recital. John MacCabe is a sympathetic partner – in spite of the balance – but this collection offers what are perhaps Lloyd Webber's finest performances on disc.

Lympany, Moura (piano)

'Best-loved piano classics', Volume 1: CHOPIN: *Fantaisie-impromptu, Op. 66; Etudes, Op. 10/4 & 5.*
BRAHMS: *Waltz, Op. 39/15.* MOZART: *Sonata No. 11, 'Alla Turca', K.331.* BEETHOVEN: *Minuet in G;*
Für Elise. SCHUMANN: *Kinderszenen: Träumerei.* LISZT: *Concert study: Un sospiro.* DVORAK:
Humoresque. Op. 101/7. MACDOWELL: *To a wild rose.* CHAMINADE: *Autumn.* DEBUSSY: *Suite*
bergamasque: Clair de lune. Children's corner: Golliwog's cakewalk. RACHMANINOV: *Prelude in C*
sharp min., Op. 3/2. RUBINSTEIN: *Melody in F, Op. 3/1.* GRANADOS: *Goyescas: The Maiden and the*
nightingale. FALLA: *El amor brujo: Ritual fire dance.* ALBENIZ: *Tango, Op. 165/2.*
(M) *** EMI Dig. CDZ5 68252-2.

Miss Lympany has lost none of the flair and technical skill which earned her her reputation: the
whole programme has the spontaneity of a live recital. At times the playing has a masculine strength,
pieces like *Träumerei* and *Clair de lune* emerge the more freshly through a total absence of
sentimentality and even the more trivial items sound newly minted. At medium price this is very good
value, with the Spanish pieces ending the collection memorably. The piano timbre is faithful and
realistic, if a little dry.

'Best-loved piano classics, Volume 2': BACH, arr. Hess: *Jesu, joy of man's desiring.* DAQUIN: *Le*
Coucou. HANDEL: *Suite No. 5: Air and variations (The harmonious blacksmith).* BEETHOVEN: *Rondo*
a capriccio, Op. 129; Piano sonata No. 14 (Moonlight): lst movt. DEBUSSY: *Images: Reflets dans*
l'eau. Préludes, Book 1: *La fille aux cheveux de lin; La cathédrale engloutie.* CHOPIN: *Waltzes: in C*
sharp min., Op. 64/2; in G flat, Op. 70/1; Mazurka in A min., Op. 17/4. ALBENIZ: *Malagueña, Op.*
165/3. RAVEL: *Jeux d'eau.* PADEREWSKI: *Minuet in G, Op. 14/1.* SCHUMANN: *Waldszenen: Der Vogel*
als Prophet. SATIE: *Gymnopédie No. 1.* SCRIABIN: *Etude in D sharp min., Op. 8/12.*
(M) *** EMI Dig. CDZ5 68253-2.

Moura Lympany begins here with Myra Hess's famous arrangement of Bach's *Jesu, joy of man's*
desiring, presented with an innocent simplicity of line which is immediately appealing. She is equally
good in Handel's famous set of variations and in the French impressionism. There is sparkle in the
Chopin and Albéniz, and she is equally captivating in Daquin and Satie. As in her first recital, the
piano image is clear and vivid with plenty of presence, and at 71 minutes the programme is certainly
generous.

Marsalis, Wynton (trumpet), Judith Lynn Stillman (piano)

'On the 20th century': RAVEL: *Pièce en forme de Habanera.* HONEGGER: *Intrada.* TOMASI: *Triptyque.*
STEVENS: *Sonata.* POULENC: *Eiffel Tower polka.* ENESCU: *Légende.* BERNSTEIN: *Rondo for Lifey.*
BOZZA: *Rustiques.* HINDEMITH: *Sonata.*
☞ *** Sony Dig. SK 47193 [id.].

What a wonderful player Wynton Marsalis is! His instrumental profile is so strong and stylish, his
basic timbre unforgettably full of character, as at the very opening with the quiet, stately presentation
of Ravel's *Pièce en forme de Habanera.* The Enescu *Légende* is hardly less distinctive, while the
melodic line of Bozza's *Rustiques* (not in the Ravel class) yet sounds remarkably special, and the jolly
roulades of the finale bring the easy manner of true virtuosity. Yet for fizzing bravura turn to the
witty Poulenc polka (*Discours du général* from *Les Mariés de la Tour Eiffel* – like a silent movie
speeded up – transcribed by Don Stewart for two trumpets in which Wynton takes both parts, with a
little electronic help). The Halsey Stevens *Sonata* is a first-class piece and Marsalis makes the
Hindemith, which has an effectively dry slow movement and a *Trauermusik* finale, sound almost like
a masterpiece, helped by the fine piano contribution of Judith Stillman. The recording has an
uncanny presence and realism: it as if this superb artist was just out beyond the speakers.

McLachlan, Murray (piano)

Piano music from Scotland: SCOTT: *8 Songs* (trans. Stevenson): *Since all thy vows, false maid; Wha is*
that at my bower-door?; O were my love yon lilac fare; Wee Willie Gray; Milkwort and bog-cotton;
Crowdieknowe; Ay waukin, O; There's news, lasses, news. CENTER: *Piano sonata; 6 Bagatelles, Op. 3.;*
Children at play. STEVENSON: *Beltane bonfire. 2 Scottish ballads: The Dowie Dens O Yarrow;*
Newhaven fishwife's cry.
❀ *** Olympia Dig. OCD 264 [id.].

Francis George Scott (1880–1958) was a prolific and striking composer of songs and Ronald Stevenson's very free transcriptions, somewhat after the fashion of Liszt's concert paraphrases, are imaginatively creative in their own right. Ronald Center's *Piano sonata* is restless and mercurial, lacking much in the way of repose, but the joyous syncopations of the first movement are infectious and the work is a major contribution to the repertory and not in the least difficult to approach. The *Six Bagatelles* are even more strikingly diverse in mood. *Children at play* is an enchanting piece, with a musical-box miniaturism of texture at times, yet the writing is by no means inconsequential. All this music is played with commitment and considerable bravura by Murray McLachlan, who is clearly a sympathetic exponent, and the recording is extremely vivid and real. Our Rosette is awarded not just for enterprise, but equally from admiration and pleasure.

Moiseiwitsch, Benno (piano)

1938–1950 recordings: MUSSORGSKY: *Pictures at an exhibition.* BEETHOVEN: *Andanti favori, WoO 57; Rondo in C, Op. 51/1.* WEBER: *Sonata No. 1: Presto; Invitation to the dance* (arr. Tausig). MENDELSSOHN: *Scherzo in E min., Op. 16.* SCHUMANN: *Romanzen: No. 2, Op. 28/2.* CHOPIN: *Nocturne in E flat, Op. 9/2; Polonaise in B flat, Op. 71/2; Barcarolle, Op. 60.* LISZT: *Liebestraume No. 3; Etude de concert: La leggierezza. Hungarian rhapsody No. 2 in C sharp min. Concert paraphrase of Wagner's Tannhäuser overture.* DEBUSSY: *Pour le piano: Toccata. Suite bergamasque: Clair de lune. Estampes: Jardins sous la pluie.* RAVEL: *Le tombeau de Couperin: Toccata.*
(**(*)) APR mono CDAPR 7005 (2) [id.].

Moiseiwitsch never enjoyed quite the exposure on records to which his gifts entitled him, though in the earlier part of his career he made a great many. Later, in the electrical era he was a 'plum-label' artist and was not issued on the more prestigious and expensive 'red-label'. In this he was in pretty good company, for Solomon and Myra Hess were similarly relegated. This anthology gives a good picture of the great pianist in a wide variety of repertory: his *Pictures at an exhibition*, made in 1945, was for some time the only piano version; and those who identify him solely with the Russians will find his Chopin *Barcarolle* and Debussy *Jardins sous la pluie* totally idiomatic. The transfers are variable – all are made from commercial copies, some in better condition than others.

Nakarjakov, Sergei (trumpet), Alexander Markovich (piano)

'Trumpet works': GERSHWIN: *Rhapsody in blue* (arr. Dokshitser). ARENSKY: *Concert waltz.* ARBAN: *Carnival of Venice.* RAVEL: *Pavane pour une infante défunte.* BERNSTEIN: *Rondo for Lifey.* GLAZUNOV: *Albumblatt.* STOLTE: *Burleske.* HARTMANN: *Arbucklenian polka.* FIBICH: *Poème.* RIMSKY-KORSAKOV: *Flight of the bumble-bee.* DINICU: *Hora staccato.* GLIÈRE: *Valse.* RUEFF: *Sonatina.*
☞ *** Teldec/Warner Dig. 9031 77705-2 [id.].

An astonishing CD début by a brilliant Russian schoolboy virtuoso, barely fifteen at the time it was recorded. It is the more remarkable as (coming from a musical family) he began his career as a pianist, changing to trumpet at the tender age of nine, after a car accident. Nakarjakov's supreme command of the instrument is matched by instinctive musicality and taste. He manages to sound suitably transatlantic in an incredible full-length arrangement of Gershwin's *Rhapsody in blue*, and is even better in Bernstein's entertainingly ebullient *Rondo for Lifey*. Lovely tone and simplicity of line make Fibich's *Poème* sound appealingly restrained, and in the bandstand variations by Arban and Hartmann the playing is stylishly infectious. Highlights are Stolte's witty *Burlesque* and the very considerable *Sonatina* by Jeanine Rueff in which trumpeter and pianist, as elsewhere, make a genuine partnership. But for ear-tickling bravura try Dinicu's *Hora staccato*, which surely would have impressed Heifetz. Excellently balanced and realistic recording. We shall hear more of Sergei Nakarjakov, whose smiling sleeve picture shows him as disarmingly good-looking and modestly untarnished by success.

Nettle and Markham (two-piano duo)

'In England': CARMICHAEL: *Puppet overture.* GRAINGER: *Country gardens; Lisbon; The brisk young sailor; The lost lady found; Handel in the Strand; English waltz.* VAUGHAN WILLIAMS: *Fantasia on Greensleeves.* WALTON: *Façade: Popular song; Tango pasodoble; Old Sir Faulk; Swiss yodelling song; Polka.* NICHOLAS: *Quiet peace No. 1.* DRING: *Fantastic variations on Lillibulero.* BRIDGE: *Sally in our*

alley. COATES: *By the sleepy lagoon.* BLAKE: *Slow ragtime; Folk ballad.* GAY: *Lambeth Walk.* SCOTT: *Lotus Land.* LAMBERT: *3 Pièces négres: Siesta.* WARLOCK: *Capriol suite: Pavane.* BRITTEN: *Mazurka elegiaca, Op. 23/2.* HOLST: *The Planets: Jupiter.*
☞ *** Pickwick MCD 65; *MCC 65* [id.].

A recital of mostly brief lollipops lasting nearly 78 minutes might seem too much of a good thing, but Nettle and Markham play with such spirit that the result is almost always diverting. Perhaps they languish a bit in some of the slower pieces, *Greensleeves* and Warlock's *Pavane,* for instance; but for the most part the effect is highly spontaneous, and especially so in the Grainger items which are nicely sprinkled around the programme. *Lisbon, The brisk young sailor* and *The lost lady found* all come together, following neatly after Cyril Scott's *Lotus Land,* to make a winning triptych. The recording is excellent.

Paik, Kun Woo (piano)

POULENC: *Nocturnes Nos. 1, 5 & 6; Presto; Improvisations Nos. 10, 12 & 15. Intermezzo; Mouvements perpétuelles Nos. 1–3.* DEBUSSY: *Pour le piano; Suite bergamasque: Clair de lune.* SATIE: *Gnossiennes Nos. 4 & 5; Ogives Nos. 1–2: Vaisseaux; Casque. Celui qui parle trop; Españaña; Embryons desséchés; Gymnopédies Nos. 1–3.*
(BB) *** Virgin/EMI Dig. VJ7 59653-2 [id.].

The distinguished Korean pianist Kun Woo Paik has already given us a splendid Liszt recital on Virgo; if his collection of French music is slightly more idiosyncratic, there is still much to relish, notably Poulenc's *Mouvements perpétuelles* – and indeed the other pieces by this composer. But the outer movements of Debussy's *Pour le piano* bring some electrifying bravura, and his imagination is given full rein in the quirkier Satie miniatures. There is 75 minutes of music here and, even though the back-up documentation is disappointingly sparse, this is undoubtedly a bargain.

Parker-Smith, Jane (organ)

Organ of Coventry Cathedral: *'Popular French Romantics':* WIDOR: *Symphony No. 1: March pontifical. Symphony No 9 (Gothique), Op. 70: Andante sostenuto.* GUILMANT: *Sonata No. 5 in C min., Op. 80; Scherzo.* GIGOUT: *Toccata in B min.* BONNET: *Elfes, Op. 7.* LEFEBURE-WELY: *Sortie in B flat.* VIERNE: *Pièces de fantaisie: Clair de lune, Op. 53/5; Carillon de Westminster, Op. 54/6.*
*** ASV Dig. CDDCA 539; *ZCDCA 539* [id.].

The modern organ in Coventry Cathedral adds a nice bite to Jane Parker-Smith's very pontifical performance of the opening Widor *March* and creates a blaze of splendour at the close of the famous Vierne *Carillon de Westminster,* the finest performance on record. The detail of the fast, nimble articulation in the engagingly Mendelssohnian *Elfes* of Joseph Bonnet is not clouded; yet here, as in the splendid Guilmant *Scherzo* with its wider dynamic range, there is also a nice atmospheric effect. Overall, a most entertaining recital.

Organ of Beauvais Cathedral: *'Popular French Romantics' Vol. 2:* FRANCK: *Prélude, fugue et variation, Op. 18.* GUILMANT: *Grand choeur in D* (after Handel). MULET: *Carillon-sortie.* RENAUD: *Toccata in D min.* SAINT-SAENS: *Prelude and fugue.* VIERNE: *Symphony No. 1: Finale. Stèle pour un enfant défunt.* WIDOR: *Symphony No. 4: Andante and Scherzo.*
*** ASV Dig. CDDCA 610; *ZCDCA 610* [id.].

With his *Prélude and fugue,* Saint-Saëns is in more serious mood than usual but showing characteristic facility in fugal construction; Widor is first mellow and then quixotic – his *Scherzo* demands the lightest articulation and receives it. High drama and great bravura are provided by the Vierne *Finale* and later by Albert Renaud's *Toccata* and Henri Mulet's *Carillon-sortie,* while Franck's *Prélude, fugue et variation* and the poignant Vierne *Stèle pour un enfant défunt* bring attractive lyrical contrast: here Jane Parker-Smith's registration shows particular subtlety. The organ is splendidly recorded.

Perahia, Murray (piano)

'Aldeburgh Recital': BEETHOVEN: *32 Variations in C min., WoO 80.* SCHUMANN: *Carnival jest from Vienna, Op. 26.* LISZT: *Hungarian rhapsody No. 12.* RACHMANINOV: *Etudes-tableaux in C, Op. 33/2; in E flat min., A min., D, Op. 39/5, 6 & 9.*
*** Sony Dig. SK 46437 [id.].

Murray Perahia plays here with all the spontaneity and freshness that distinguish his concert appearances. Perahia produces an extraordinary range of colour and tone; though one knows him to be a great Schumann interpreter, it is good to hear him in such barnstorming repertoire as the *Hungarian rhapsody No. 12* and the *Etudes-tableaux*, with which we do not normally associate him.

Petri, Michala (recorder or flute)

'Greensleeves' (with Hanne Petri, harpsichord, David Petri, cello): ANON.: *Greensleeves to a grounde; Divisions on an Italian ground.* EYCK, Jacob van: *Prins Robberts Masco; Philis Schoon Herderinne; Wat Zal Men op den Avond Doen; Engels Nachtegaeltje.* CORELLI: *Sonata, Op. 15/5: La Folia.* HANDEL: *Andante.* LECLAIR: *Tambourin.* F. COUPERIN: *Le rossignol vainqueur; Le rossignol en amour.* J. S. BACH: *Siciliano.* TELEMANN: *Rondino.* GOSSEC: *Tambourin.* PAGANINI: *Moto perpetuo, Op. 11.* BRUGGEN: *2 Studies.* CHRISTIANSEN: *Satie auf hoher See.* HENRIQUES: *Dance of the midges.* SCHUBERT: *The Bee.* MONTI: *Czárdás.* HERBERLE: *Rondo presto.* RIMSKY-KORSAKOV: *Flight of the bumble-bee.*
(M) *** Ph. Dig. 420 897-2.

Marvellously nimble playing from Michala Petri, and 71 minutes, digitally recorded at mid-price, so one can afford to pick and choose. Some of the music opening the recital is less than distinctive, but the Couperin transcriptions are a delight and Paganini's *Moto perpetuo* vies with Henriques' *Dance of the midges* for sparkling bravura. There are some attractively familiar melodies by Bach and Handel, among others, to provide contrast, and Henning Christiansen's *Satie auf hoher See* is an unexpected treat. Monti's *Czárdás* ends the programme infectiously.

Petri, Michala (recorder), George Malcolm (harpsichord)

Recorder sonatas: VIVALDI: *Il Pastor fido: Sonata No. 6 in G min., RV 58.* CORELLI: *Sonata in C, Op. 5/9.* D. BIGAGLIA: *Sonata in A min.* BONONCINI: *Divertimento da camera No. 6 in C min.* SAMMARTINI: *Sonata in G, Op. 13/4.* B. MARCELLO: *Sonata in F, Op. 2/1.*
⊕ *** Ph. Dig. 412 632-2 [id.].

Six recorder sonatas in a row might seem too much of a good thing, but the playing is so felicitous and the music has such charm that the collection is a source of much delight. Throughout, Michala Petri's playing is wonderfully fresh: she has made many records for Philips, but none more enticing than this. George Malcolm proves an equally imaginative partner, and both artists embellish with admirable flair and taste, never overdoing it. The Philips recording is quite perfectly balanced and wonderfully tangible.

Peyer, Gervase de (clarinet), Gwenneth Pryor (piano)

French music for clarinet and piano: SAINT-SAENS: *Sonata, Op. 167.* DEBUSSY: *Première rhapsodie; Arabesque No. 2; Prélude: La fille aux cheveux de lin.* POULENC: *Sonata.* SCHMIDT: *Andantino, Op. 30/1.* RAVEL: *Pièce en forme de habañera.* PIERNE: *Canzonetta, Op. 19.*
⊕ *** Chan. Dig. CHAN 8526; *ABTD 1236.*

A gorgeous record. The Saint-Saëns *Sonata* is an attractively crafted piece, full of engaging invention. Poulenc's *Sonata* is characteristically witty, with contrast in its lovely central *Romanza* (*très calme*); and the other short pieces wind down the closing mood of the recital, with De Peyer's luscious timbre drawing a charming portrait of *The girl with the flaxen hair* before the nimbly tripping closing encore of Pierné. This is a quite perfect record of its kind, the programme like that of a live recital and played with comparable spontaneity. The recording is absolutely realistic; the balance could hardly be improved on.

Pollini, Maurizio (piano)

PROKOFIEV: *Piano sonata No. 7 in B flat, Op. 83*. STRAVINSKY: *Three movements from Petrushka.*
BOULEZ: *Piano sonata No. 2.* WEBERN: *Variations for piano, Op. 27.*
*** DG 419 202-2.

The Prokofiev is a great performance, one of the finest ever committed to disc; and the Stravinsky *Petrushka* is electrifying. Not all those responding to this music will do so quite so readily to the Boulez, fine though the playing is; but the Webern also makes a very strong impression. This is the equivalent of two LPs and is outstanding value.

Preston, Simon (organ)

'The world of the organ' (organ of Westminster Abbey): WIDOR: *Symphony No. 5: Toccata.* BACH: *Chorale prelude, Wachet auf, BWV 645.* MOZART: *Fantasia in F min., K.608.* WALTON: *Crown imperial* (arr. Murrill). CLARKE: *Prince of Denmark's march* (arr. Preston). HANDEL: *Saul: Dead march.* PURCELL: *Trumpet tune* (arr. Trevor). ELGAR: *Imperial march* (arr. Martin). VIERNE: *Symphony No. 1: Finale.* WAGNER: *Tannhäuser: Pilgrims' chorus.* GUILMANT: *March on a theme of Handel.* SCHUMANN: *Study No. 5* (arr. West). KARG-ELERT: *Marche triomphale (Now thank we all our God).*
(M) *** Decca 430 091-2; *430 091-4.*

A splendid compilation from the Argo catalogue of the early to mid-1960s, spectacularly recorded, which offers 69 minutes of music and is in every sense a resounding success. Simon Preston's account of the Widor *Toccata* is second to none, and both the Vierne *Finale* and the Karg-Elert *March triomphale* lend themselves admirably to Preston's unashamed flamboyance and the tonal splendour afforded by the Westminster acoustics. Walton's *Crown imperial*, too, brings a panoply of sound which compares very favourably with an orchestral recording. The organ has a splendid trumpet stop which makes both the Purcell piece and Clarke's *Prince of Denmark's march*, better known as the *'Trumpet voluntary'*, sound crisply regal.

Prometheus Ensemble

'French impressions': RAVEL: *Introduction & allegro for harp, flute, clarinet and string quartet.* DEBUSSY: *Danses sacrée et profane; Sonata for flute, viola and harp.* ROUSSEL: *Serenade.*
*** ASV Dig. CDDCA 664; *ZCDCA 664* [id.].

This young group gives eminently well-prepared and thoughtful accounts of all these pieces. The *Danses sacrée et profane* sound particularly atmospheric and the Debussy *Sonata* is played with great feeling and sounds appropriately ethereal. The Roussel, too, is done with great style and, even if the *Introduction and allegro* does not supersede the celebrated Melos account, the Prometheus do it well.

Rév, Lívia (piano)

'For children': BACH: *Preludes in E, BWV 939; in G min., BWV 930.* DAQUIN: *Le coucou.* MOZART: *Variations on Ah vous dirai-je maman, K.265.* BEETHOVEN: *Für Elise.* SCHUMANN: *Album for the young Op. 63:* excerpts. CHOPIN: *Nocturne in C min., Op. posth.* LISZT: *Etudes G. 136/1 & 2.* BIZET: *Jeux d'enfants: La Toupie.* FAURE: *Dolly: Berceuse.* TCHAIKOVSKY: *Album for the young, Op. 39: Maman; Waltz.* VILLA-LOBOS: *Prole do bebê:* excerpts. JOLIVET: *Chansons naïve 1 & 2.* PROKOFIEV: *Waltz, Op. 65.* BARTOK: *Evening in the country; For Children:* excerpts. DEBUSSY: *Children's corner:* excerpts. MAGIN: *3 Pieces.* MATACIC: *Miniature variations.*
*** Hyp. CDA 66185; *KA 66185.*

A wholly delectable recital, and not just for children either. The whole is more than the sum of its many parts, and the layout provides excellent variety, with the programme stimulating in mixing familiar with unfamiliar. The recording is first class. Highly recommended for late evening listening.

Richter, Sviatoslav (piano)

CHOPIN: *Préludes, Op. 28/2; 4–11; 13; 19; 21 & 23.* TCHAIKOVSKY: *Nocturne in F, Op. 10/1; Valse-scherzo in A, Op. 7.* RACHMANINOV: *Etudes-tableaux, Op. 33/3, 5 & 6; Op. 39 1–4; 7 & 9.*
*** Olympia OCD 112 [id.].

Some marvellous playing here from Richter. He plays an odd assortment of Chopin *Preludes*, Nos. 4 through to 10 in the published sequence, then 23, 19, 11, 2, 23 and 21! These obviously derive from a public concert, as there is applause. He is distinctly ruminative and wayward at times. The two Tchaikovsky pieces are done with extraordinary finesse and the Rachmaninov is masterly. The recordings are not top drawer and the disc gives no details of their provenance; but the sound is perfectly acceptable.

DEBUSSY: *Estampes; Préludes, Book I: Voiles; Le vent dans la plaine; Les collines d'Anacapri.*
PROKOFIEV: *Visions fugitives, Op. 22, Nos. 3, 6 & 9; Sonata No. 8 in B flat, Op. 84.* SCRIABIN: *Sonata No. 5 in F sharp, Op. 53.*
(M) *** DG 423 573-2.

The Debussy *Préludes* and the Prokofiev *Sonata* were recorded at concerts during an Italian tour in 1962, while the remainder were made the previous year in Wembley Town Hall. The former sound more open than the rather confined studio acoustic – but what playing! The Scriabin is demonic and the Debussy could not be more atmospheric. The performance of the Prokofiev *Sonata* is, like the legendary Gilels account, a classic of the gramophone.

Robles, Marisa (harp)

'The world of the harp': FALLA: *Three-cornered Hat: Danza del corregidor.* ALBÉNIZ: *Rumores de Caleta; Torre bermeja.* BIDAOLA: *Viejo zortzico.* EBERL (attrib. Mozart): *Theme, variations and rondo pastorale.* BEETHOVEN: *Variations on a Swiss song.* BRITTEN: *Ceremony of carols: Interlude.* FAURÉ: *Impromptu, Op. 86.* PIERNÉ: *Impromptu-caprice, Op. 9.* SALZEDO: *Chanson de la nuit.* BRAHMS: *Lullaby.* BACH: *Well-tempered Clavier: Prelude No. 1.* CHOPIN: *Mazurka, Op. 7/1; Prelude, Op. 28/15 (Raindrop).* HASSELMANS: *La source.*
☞ (M) *** Decca 433 869-2; 433 869-4 [id.].

The artistry of Marisa Robles ensures that this is a highly attractive anthology and the programme is as well chosen as it is beautifully played. As ex-Professor of the harp at the Madrid Conservatory, Miss Robles has a natural affinity for the Spanish music that opens her programme, and other highlights include a magnetic account of the Britten *Interlude* and the Salzedo *Chanson de la nuit* with its bell-like evocations. The Eberl *Variations* are highly engaging. The excellent recordings derive from the Argo catalogue of the 1960s and '70s, except for the Chopin, Brahms, Bach and Hasselmans pieces, which have been added to fill out the present reissue (75 minutes). The delicious Hasselmans roulades are the epitome of nineteenth-century harp writing. The CD has a most realistic presence.

Rogé, Pascal (piano) and Wind Ensemble

French chamber music: SAINT-SAENS: *Caprice sur des airs danois et russes.* D'INDY: *Sarabande et menuet.* ROUSSEL: *Divertissement.* TANSMAN: *Danse de la sorcière.* FRANCAIX: *L'heure du berger.* POULENC: *Elégie.* MILHAUD: *Sonata, Op. 47.*
*** Decca Dig. 425 861-2 [id.].

The Saint-Saëns *Caprice sur des airs danois et russes* is great fun, as is most of the music on the disc, notably the delightful minuet of Vincent d'Indy's *Sarabande et menuet*, the early Roussel *Divertissement* and Alexandre Tansman's *Danse de la sorcière*. Perhaps the humour of Françaix's *L'heure du berger* may strike some as a bit arch but, played with such flair, such thoughts are instantly banished. Poulenc's *Elégie* for horn and piano is eloquently played by André Cazalet. Catherine Cantin and those stalwarts of French wind music, Maurice Bourgue, Michel Portal and Amaury Wallez, are equally splendid. Milhaud's *Sonata, Op. 47*, for flute, oboe, clarinet and piano has the fresh, easy-going zest of this composer at his best. The recording is very well balanced and should give unqualified delight to all who are sensible enough to buy it.

Rubinstein, Artur (piano)

'Carnegie Hall highlights': DEBUSSY: Préludes, Book I: La cathédral engloutie; Book II: Ondine. Images, Book I: Hommage à Rameau; Book II: Poissons d'or. SZYMANOWSKI: Mazurkas, Op. 50/1– 4. PROKOFIEV: 12 Visions fugitives from Op 22. VILLA-LOBOS: Próle do Bébé. SCHUMANN: Arabesque, Op. 18. ALBENIZ: Navarra.
☞ (M) *** BMG/RCA 09026 61445-2 [id.].

Rubinstein was still at his technical peak when these recordings were made during a series of recitals at Carnegie Hall in October, November and December 1961. The microphones were perhaps a little close, but the recording is still realistic, if with a touch of hardness at times. The performances are wonderfully poised and spontaneous, and the technical accuracy is little short of amazing when one realizes there were no tape splices here. The Debussy pieces are musically outstanding (Rubinstein announces Ondine himself, so it must have been an encore, and he plays it beautifully). The Szymanowski Mazurkas have wonderful style and the Prokofiev miniatures show an amazing range of colour and sharp characterization. The titles (Con eleganza – Pittoresco; Ridicolosamente; Con vivacità; Con una dolce lentezza; Dolente; Feroce and the slightly misleading Allegretto tranquillo) all speak for themselves. The Villa-Lobos suite of dolls is delightful and the closing Clown doll (Polichinelle) brings fabulous articulation. After the Schumann Arabesque, Rubinstein finds a closing burst of passion for Albéniz's Navarra, and the audience's response confirms that this was a closing item. But apart from the applause, the audience is remarkably unobtrusive.

'The music of France': (a) RAVEL: Valses nobles et sentimentales; Le tombeau de couperin: Forlane. Miroirs: La vallée des cloches. POULENC: 3 Mouvements perpétuels; Intermezzi: in A flat; in D flat. FAURE: Nocturne in A flat, Op. 33/3. CHABRIER: Pièce pittoresque No. 10: Scherzo-valse. (b) DEBUSSY: Estampes: La soirée dans Grenade; Jardins sous la pluie; Images, Book I: Hommage à Rameau; Reflets dans l'eau; Book 2: Poissons d'or. La plus que lente; Préludes, Book I: Minstrels.
☞ (M) *** BMG/RCA (a) stereo / (b) mono 09026 61446-2 [id.].

The main part of this recital dates from 1963. The playing is eminently aristocratic and full of insights. The Ravel pieces and the Poulenc could hardly be bettered. The recording has been further enhanced in the present transfer and has both sonority and presence – it is finer than the Carnegie Hall recordings listed above. The Debussy programme derives from 78s made in 1945 and a 1952 mono LP (Minstrels is a very striking account). Indeed all the performances are well worth having, especially Reflets dans l'eau where the sound is remarkably open.

Schiller, Allan (piano)

'Für Elise': Popular piano pieces: BEETHOVEN: Für Elise. FIELD: Nocturne in E (Noontide). CHOPIN: Mazurka in B flat, Op. 7/1; Waltz in A, Op. 34/2. 3 Ecossaises, Op. 72/3; Fantaisie-impromptu, Op. 66. MENDELSSOHN: Songs without words: Venetian gondola song, Op. 19; Bees' wedding, Op. 67. LISZT: Consolation No. 3 in D flat. DE SEVERAC: The music box. DEBUSSY: Suite bergamasque: Clair de lune. Arabesques Nos. 1 and 2. Prélude: The girl with the flaxen hair. GRIEG: Wedding day at Trodhaugen; March of the dwarfs. ALBENIZ: Granada; Tango; Asturias.
(BB) *** ASV CDQS 6032; ZCQS 6032.

A particularly attractive recital, diverse in mood, spontaneous in feeling and very well recorded. The acoustic is resonant, but the effect is highly realistic. There are many favourites here, with Allan Schiller at his most personable in the engaging Field Nocturne, De Severac's piquant Music box and the closing Asturias of Albéniz, played with fine bravura. The Chopin group, too, is particularly successful, with the Scottish rhythmic snap of the Ecossaises neatly articulated and the famous B flat Mazurka presented most persuasively.

Scott Whiteley, John (organ)

Organ of York Minster: 'Great Romantic organ music': TOURNEMIRE: Improvisation on the Te Deum. JONGEN: Minuet-Scherzo, Op. 53. MULET: Tu es Petra. DUPRE: Prelude and fugue in G min., Op. 3/7. R. STRAUSS: Wedding prelude. KARG-ELERT: Pastel in B, Op. 92/1. BRAHMS: Chorale prelude: O Gott, du frommer Gott, Op. 122/7. LISZT: Prelude and fugue on BACH, G.260.
*** York CD 101.

A superb organ recital, with the huge dynamic range of the York Minster organ spectacularly captured on CD and pianissimo detail registering naturally. John Scott Whiteley's playing is full of flair: the attractively complex and sparklingly florid *Prelude and fugue* of Marcel Dupré is exhilarating and reaches a high climax, while the grand Liszt piece is hardly less overwhelming. The opening Tournemire *Improvisation* is very arresting indeed, while Jongen's *Minuet-Scherzo* displays Scott Whiteley's splendidly clear articulation.

Wild, Earl (piano)

'The virtuoso piano': HERZ: *Variations on 'Non più mesta' from Rossini's La Cenerentola.* THALBERG: *Don Pasquale fantasy, Op. 67.* GODOWSKY: *Symphonic metamorphosis on themes from Johann Strauss's Kunsterleben (Artist's life).* RUBINSTEIN: *Etude (Staccato), Op. 23/2.* HUMMEL: *Rondo in E flat, Op. 11.* PADEREWSKI: *Theme and variations, Op. 16/3.*
(M) *** Van. 08.4033.71 [OVC 4033].

Earl Wild's famous performances from the late 1960s re-emerge on CD with their scintillating brilliance given even greater projection by the digital remastering. Wild's technique is prodigious and his glittering bravura in the engaging Herz *Rossini variations* and Thalberg's equally entertaining *Don Pasquale fantasy* is among the finest modern examples of the grand tradition of virtuoso pianism. Godowsky's piece may have a heavy title, but in Earl Wild's hands, for all the decorative complexities, the lilting waltz-rhythms are still paramount.

Williams, John (guitar)

'Spanish guitar music': I. ALBENIZ: *Asturias; Tango; Cordoba; Sevilla.* SANZ: *Canarios.* TORROBA: *Nocturno; Madroños.* SAGRERAS: *El Colibri.* M. ALBENIZ: *Sonata in D.* FALLA: *Homenaje; Three-cornered hat: Corregidor's dance; Miller's dance. El amor brujo: Fisherman's song.* CATALAN FOLKSONGS: *La Nit de Nadal; El noy de la mare; El testamen de Amelia.* GRANADOS: *La maja de Goya. Spanish dance No. 5.* TARREGA: *Recuerdos de la Alhambra.* VILLA-LOBOS: *Prelude No. 4 in E min.* MUDARRA: *Fantasia.* TURINA: *Fandanguillo, Op. 36.*
(M) *** Sony SBK 46347 [id.].

John Williams has the full measure of this repertoire. He can show strong Latin feeling, as in the vibrant *Farruca* of the *Miller's dance* from Falla's *Three-cornered hat*, or create a magically atmospheric mood, as in the hauntingly registered transcription of the *Fisherman's song* from *El amor brujo*. He can play with thoughtful improvisatory freedom, as in the Villa-Lobos *Prelude*, with its pianissimo evocation, or be dramatically spontaneous, as in the memorable performance of Turina's *Fandanguillo*, which ends the recital magnetically. The instinctive control of atmosphere and dynamic is constantly rewarding throughout a varied programme, and the technique is phenomenal, yet never flashy, always at the service of the music. The remastering brings a clean and truthful, if very immediate, image. Background is minimal and never intrusive.

Zabaleta, Nicanor (harp)

'Arpa española': ALBENIZ: *Managueña, Op. 165/3; Suite española: Granada (Serenata); Zaragoza (Capricho); Asturias (Leyenda). Mallorca, Op. 202; Tango español.* FALLA: *Serenata andaluza.* TURINA: *Ciclo pianistico No. 1: Tocata y fuga.* GOMBAU: *Apunte bético.* GRANADOS: *Danza española No. 5.* HALFFTER: *Sonatina (ballet): Danza de la pastora.* LOPEZ-CHAVARRI: *El viejo castillo moro.*
⊛ (M) *** DG 435 847-2 [id.].

A good deal of the music here belongs to the guitar (or piano) rather than the harp, but Nicanor Zabaleta, with his superb artistry and sense of atmosphere makes it all his own. Throughout this delightful programme, Zabaleta gives each piece strong individuality of character. In the Granados *Spanish dance No. 5* he matches the magnetism of Julian Bream's famous recording, and Manuel de Falla's *Serenata andaluza* is hardly less captivating. DG's sound balance is near perfection, as is the choice of acoustic, and the magic distilled by Zabaleta's concentration, often at the gentlest levels of dynamic, is unforgettable.

Vocal Recitals and Choral Collections

Many operatic recitals are not included here; they can be found in our companion volume, *The Penguin Guide to Opera on Compact Disc*

Angeles, Victoria de los (soprano)

'The fabulous Victoria de Los Angeles':
Disc 1: RAVEL: *Shéhérazade; 5 Mélodies populaires grecques; 2 Mélodies hébraïques.* DUPARC: *L'invitation au voyage; Phidylé.* DEBUSSY: *L'Enfant prodigue: L'année en vain chasse l'année.* CHAUSSON: *Poème de l'amour et de la mer.*

Disc 2. MONTSALVATGE: *5 canciones negras.* GRANADOS: *Colección se canciones amatorias; Llorad corazón; Iban al pinar.* RODRIGO: *4 madrigales amatorios; Triptic de Mossèn Cinto.* ESPLÁ: *5 canciones playeras españolas.* TOLDRA: *4 cançons.* TRAD.: *La Dama d'Aragó; El cant dels ocells; Cançó de Sega.* MOMPOU: *El Combat del Somni.*

Disc 3. DEBUSSY: *Chansons de Bilitis; Fêtes galantes; Noël des enfants qui n'ont plus de maisons.* RAVEL: *Chants populaires.* HAHN: *3 jours de vendage; Le rossignol de lilas.* FAURE: *Tristesse; Au bord de l'eau; Les Roses d'Ispahan; Toujours.* FALLA: *7 canciones populares españolas. Psyché; Soneto a Córdoba.* TOLDRA: *12 canciones gallegas: As floriñas dos toxos.* TURINA: *Farruca.* RODRIGO: *Villancicos: Pastorcito santo.*

Disc 4. SACRATI: *Prosperina: E dove t'aggiri.* A. SCARLATTI: *Le violette.* HANDEL: *Joshua: Oh! had I Jubal's lyre.* SCHUBERT: *Der Tod und das Mädchen. Die schöne Müllerin: Wohin?; An die Musik; Mignon und der Harfner.* BRAHMS: *Dein blaue Auge; Vergebliches Ständchen; Sapphische Ode.* FAURE: *Chansons d'amour; Clair de lune; Pleurs d'or.* PURCELL: *Let us wander; Lost is my quiet.* HAYDN: *Schlaf in deiner engen Kammer.* J. C. BACH: *Ah! lamenta, oh bella Irene.* BEETHOVEN: *Irish songs: Oh! would I were but that sweet linnet; He promised me at parting; They bid me slight my Dermot dear. Welsh song: The dream.* BERLIOZ: *Les fleurs des landes: Le Trébuchet.* DVORAK: *Möglichkeit; Der Apfel.* TCHAIKOVSKY: *Scottish ballad.* SAINT-SAENS: *Pastorale.* MOZART: *La Pertenza.*
☞ (M) *** EMI CMS7 565061-2 (4) [id.].

A seventy-fifth-birthday celebration, this well-documented set subdivides into a pair of CDs of French and Spanish repertoire with orchestra, and two more with piano. While the French classics give special delight, it is good that room was made for the two separate Rodrigo song selections, as this composer prized his vocal music above all else and it is too little known. Apart from the mélodies, the third disc includes some especially delightful folk-inspired repertoire from both countries, where De los Angeles was in her element; on the fourth, a wide-ranging programme (in which she has the estimable support of Gerald Moore) shows her remarkable versatility. The recordings were made in the 1960s when the voice was at its freshest. If you are an admirer of this lovely voice, snap the set up quickly, for it is unlikely to be around for very long.

Argentea Collection

Argentea Collection.
☞ (M) **(*) DG 437 070-2 (20).

Disc 1: *Gregorian Chant: First Mass for Christmas* (Choir of Monks of Montserrat Abbey, Father Gregori Estrada). *Responsories for Christmas Matins* (Choir of Benedictine Abbey, Münsterschwarzach, Father Godehard Joppich).
☞ (M) *** DG 437 071-2.

Disc 2: PALESTRINA: *Missa Aeterna Christi munera;* Motets: *O bonne Jesu; Sicut cervus desiderat; Super flumina Babylonis.* LASSUS: Motets: *Ave Regina caelorum; O mors, quam amara est; Salve Regina. First Penetential Psalm: Domine, ne in furore tuo* (Pro Cantione Antiqua, Hamburg Wind Ens., Bruno Turner).
☞ (M) **(*) DG 437 072-2.

Disc 3: Giovanni GABRIELI: *Canzoni e Sonate: Canzon a 5; Canzon a 6; Canzon a 7; Canzon a 8; Sonata a 4; Sonata a 8; Sonata a 15. Sacrae symphoniae: 2 Canzoni septimi toni a 8; Canzon septimi e octavio toni a 12; Sonata octavi toni a 8; Sonata pian e forte a 8* (London Cornett and Sackbutt Ens., Andrew Parrott).
☞ (M) **(*) DG 437 073-2.

Disc 4: Marco DA GAGLIANO: *La Dafne* (Lerer, Schlick, Kollecker, Rogers, D. Thomas, Possemeyer, Hamburg Monteverdi Ch. & Camerata Accademia, Jürgen Jürgens).
☞ (M) *** DG 437 074-2.

Disc 5: *Canti amorosi:* MONTEVERDI: *Se vittorie si belle; Non voglio amare; Vaga su spina Ascosa; O mio bene; Zefiro torna* (Rogers, I. Partridge, Keyte, Tilney). CACCINI: *Perfidissimo volto; Belle rose porporine; Udite amanti; Amarilli mia bella. Sigismondo d'India: Crusa Amarilli; Intenerite voi, largrime mie.* Claudio SARACINI: *Io moro; Deh, come invan chiedete; Quest'amore, quest'arsura; Giovinetta vezzosetta; Da te perto.* Jacobo PERI: *O durezza di ferro; Tra le donne; Bellissima regina.* Marco DA GAGLIANO: *Valli profonde.* Francesco RASI: *Indarno Febo.* Giovanni DEL TURCO: *Occhi belli.* Vincenzo CALESTANI: *Damigella tutta bella* (Rogers, Tilney, Bailes, Savall, Ros).
☞ (M) *** DG 437 075-2.

Disc 6: 'The Triumphs of Oriana': Madrigals: EAST: *Hence stars! too dim of light.* NORCOMBE: *With angel's face.* MUNDY: *Lightly she whipped o'er the dales.* Ellis GIBBONS: *Long live fair Oriana; Round about her charret.* BENNETT: *All creatures now are merry.* HILTON: *Fair Oriana, beauty's queen.* MARSON: *The nymphs and shepherds danced.* CARLTON: *Calm was the air.* HOLMES: *Thus bonny-boots.* NICHOLSON: *Sing, shepherds all.* TOMKINS: *The fauns and satyrs tripping.* CAVENDISH: *Come, gentle swains.* COBBOLD: *With wreaths of rose and laurel.* MORLEY: *Arise, awake, awake; Hard by a crystal fountain.* FARMER: *Fair nymphs I heard one telling.* WILBYE: *The lady Oriana.* HUNT: *Hark! did ye ever hear.* WEELKES: *As Vesta was from Latmos.* MILTON: *Fair Orian, in the morn.* KIRBYE: *With angel's face.* JONES: *Fair Oriana, seeming to wink.* LISLEY: *Fair Cytherea presents her doves.* JOHNSON: *Come, blessed bird* (Pro Cantione Antiqua, I. Partridge).
☞ (M) *** DG 437 076-2.

Disc 7: TALLIS: *The Lamentations of Jeremiah.* BYRD: *Mass for 3 voices* (Pro Cantione Antiqua, Bruno Turner).
☞ (M) *(*) DG 437 077-2.

Disc 8: SCHUTZ: Motets for double choir: *Die mit Tränen säen; List nicht Ephraim mein teurer Sohn.* Canzon: *Nun lob, meine Seel, den Herren.* Concertos: *Jauchzet dem Herren, alle Welt; Lobet den Herren, meine Seele; Zion spricht.* Psalms: *115: Nicht uns, Herr; 128: Wohl dem, der den Herren fürchtet; 136: Danket dem Herren; 150: Alleluja! Lobet den Herren* (Regensburger Domspätzen, Hamburg Wind Ens., Ulsamer Coll., Hans-Martin Schneidt).
☞ (M) ** DG 437 078-2.

Disc 9: 'De Profundis' (German baroque cantatas): SCHUTZ: *Erbarm dich mein, O Herre Gott.* Franz TUNDER: *An Wasserflüssen Babylon; Ach Herr lass deine lieben Engelein.* BRUHNS: *De profundis clamavi.* Matthias WECKMANN: *Wie liegt die Stadt so wüste.* Nicolaus STRUNGT: *Ich ruf zu dir, Herr Jesu Christ* (Zedelius, Schopper, Col. Mus. Ant., Goebel).
☞ (M) **(*) DG Dig. 437 079-2.

Disc 10: FROBERGER: *Harpsichord suites Nos. 1 in E min.; 2 in A; 3 in G min.; 4 in A min.; 5 in D; 6 in C. Lamentation for the death of Ferdinand III* (Kenneth Gilbert (harpsichord)).
☞ (M) *** DG 437 080-2.

Disc 11: MUFFAT: *Concerto No. 1 in D min. (Bonna nova); Suite (Indissolubilis Amicitia).* BIBER: *Battalia a 10; Sonata in D min. for 2 violins, trombone and bass viola da gamba; Sonata a 6 in B flat (Peasants's church-going); Sonata No. 8 in B flat* (VCM, Harnoncourt).
☞ (M) *** DG 437 081-2.

Disc 12: VIVALDI: *Cantatas: Amor hai vinto, RV 683; Cessate, omai cessate, RV 684; O mie porpore più belle, RV 685* (Jacobs, Barocco, Curtis). BONONCINI: *Cantatas: Cara luci del mio bene; Siedi, Amarilli mia* (Jacobs, S. & W. Kuijken, Van Dael, Kohnen).
☞ (M) *** DG 437 082-2.

Disc 13: Agostini STEFFANI: *Duetti da camera: E perché non m'uccidete; Già tu parti; Io voglio provar; Libertà! Libertà!; M'hai da piangere un dì; No, no, vo, non voglio se devo amare; Placidissime catene; Tu m'aspettasi al mare* (Mazzucato, Watkinson, Esswood, Elwes, Curtis).
☞ (M) *** DG Dig. 437 083-2.

Disc 14: Louis COUPERIN: *Pièces de clavecin: Suites: in A min.; D; F; G min.* (Alan Curtis (harpsichord)).
☞ (M) *** DG 437 084-2.

Disc 15: Louis-Nicolas CLERAMBAULT: *Harpsichord suites Nos. 1 in C; 2 in C min.* (Kenneth Gilbert); *Cantatas: Orphée; Medée* (Yakar, Goebel, Hazelzet, Medlam, Curtis).
☞ (M) *** DG Dig./Analogue 437 085-2.

Disc 16: *'La parnasse français'*: MARAIS: *Le Sonnerie de Saint-Geneviève du Mont de Paris; Sonate à la Marienne.* Jean-Féry REBEL: *Le tombeau de Monsieur de Lully.* François COUPERIN: *Sonata (La Sultane).* LECLAIR: *Ouverture Op. 13/2; Ouverture du Trio in A, Op. 14* (Col. Mus. Ant., Goebel).
☞ (M) *** DG 437 086-2.

Disc 17: Jean GILLES: *Messe des morts (Requiem mass).* CORETTE: *Carillon des morts* (Rodde, Nirouët, Hill, U. Studer, Kooy, Ghent Coll. Voc., Col. Mus. Ant., Herreweghe).
☞ (M) *** DG 437 087-2.

Disc 18: *'English baroque concertos'*: STANLEY: *Concerto in G, Op. 2/2.* ARNE: *Harpsichord concerto in G min.* BOYCE: *Symphony in B flat.* GEMINIANI: *Concerto grosso in D min. after Corelli: La Follia variations, Op. 5/12.* Pieter HELLENDAL: *Concerto grosso in E flat, Op. 3/4.* AVISON: *Concerto grosso No. 9 in C/A min. after Domenico Scarlatti: Lessons for the harpsichord* (E. Concert, Pinnock).
☞ (M) *** DG 437 088-2.

Disc 19: *German chamber music before Bach*: Johann Adam REINCKEN: *Sonata in A min.* BUXTEHUDE: *Sonata in B flat, Bux WV 273.* Johann ROSENMULLER: *Sonata in E min.* Johann Paul VON WESTHOFF: *Sonata in A (La guerra).* PACHELBEL: *Partita (Suite) in G; Canon & Gigue in D* (Col. Mus. Ant., Goebel).
☞ (M) *** DG 437 089-2.

Disc 20: *'The Bach family before Johann Sebastian'*: Cantatas: Johann Michael BACH: *Ach, bleib be uns, Herr Jesu Christ; Ach, wie sehnlich wart'ich der Zeit. Liebster Jesu, hör mein Flehen.* Georg Christoph BACH: *Siehe, wie fein und lieblich; Herr, wende dich, und sei mir gnädig.* Johann Christoph BACH: *Meine Freundin, du bist schön* (Zedelius, Cordier, Elliott, Meens, Schopper, Varcoe, Rheinische Kantorei, Col. Mus. Ant., Goebel).
☞ (M) *** DG Dig. 437 090-2.

Using the title 'Collectio Argentea', Deutsche Grammophon have here dug deeply into their Archiv stereo back-catalogue. The sobriquet is chosen to reflect the silver label which is the identifying logo of the Archiv series. It provides the content for 20 mid-priced CDs offering music which ranges from Gregorian chant through to the eighteenth century. Much of this repertoire is not otherwise available and performances are generally distinguished. The CDs are available either separately or all together in a slip-case and priced somewhat more economically. Playing times vary a great deal and some discs seem much better value than others, but all are of interest. The more important composer collections have been given an additional entry in our composer index above.

The Gregorian chant CD offers a fascinating glimpse into the German tradition of plainsong, which combines dedication with careful preparation. It is different in style and timbre from the choirs of Italy and France but not less eloquent. The recordings (from 1973 and 1981) are spacious and beautifully balanced but are perhaps of interest to the specialist rather than to the ordinary collector. The offering is generous: 73 minutes.

Bruno Turner's coupling of Lassus and Palestrina also brings a comparatively restrained style and conjectural instrumental accompaniments for the former, which are the more successful of the two groups of performances. The Palestrina *Mass* lacks something in warmth and Latin ardour. There is an element of restraint too in Andrew Parrott's Gabrielli collection, but the use of authentic instruments and first-rate recording is a major plus point here.

The delightful early opera, *La Daphne*, by a little-known contemporary of Monteverdi is undoubtedly one of the finds of the collection. Marco da Gagliano's setting of the story of the nymph Daphne, who turns herself into a laurel tree to avoid the attentions of the god Apollo, is arranged in a series of recitatives (which at times almost become arias), interspersed with lively choruses. The recitative is full of expressive life and the choruses comment on the action. With a fine cast the performance could hardly be bettered.

The following collection of *Canti amorosi* opens with madrigals by Monteverdi, either for tenor duet or for a trio of two tenors and bass; a widely varied collection of accompanied solo songs follows, demonstrating the artistry of Nigel Rogers and his equally varied continuo support.

'*The Triumphs of Oriana*' celebrates the Elizabethan madrigal and, at the same time, Queen Elizabeth herself. There are 25 attractively different examples which form a collection, commissioned from a wide range of musicians – many of the names here are unfamiliar – which was published by Thomas Morley in praise of the Virgin Queen in 1601. Rather more than half are in five parts, the rest in six; with the performing group containing such names as James Bowman, Paul Esswood and Ian Partridge (who directs), it is not surprising that the performances are of high quality. So is the music; some of the lesser-known composers produce the most memorable items, not least the opening *Hence stars! too dim of light* by Michael East and Richard Carlton's *Calm was the air and clear the sky*, while John Holmes's *Thus bonny-boots* is most engaging. Immaculate recording.

Bruno Turner's Byrd/Tallis coupling is a disappointment, with the recording too closely miked to be convincing despite much fine singing. Similar problems affect the balance of the Schütz motets, with the trebles of the Regensburger Domspätzen dominating the sound-picture. The focus is rather variable (the opening *Alleluja!* is not clean) and the microphone placing, while it conveys the spaciousness of the acoustic, does not clearly define the antiphonal brass and choral groups. There is much to stimulate the listener here, but ideally one needs a firmer and at times weightier effect.

The collection called '*De Profundis*' offers authentically performed and very sensitively sung versions of some very fine music. But the pervasive doleful mood and sparse textures give the concert as a whole a specialist appeal. The three most striking works come last. Nicolaus Bruhns's setting for bass voice of *Psalm 130* opens dramatically and has considerable variety. This is followed by the dialogue cantata, *Wie liegt die Stadt so wüste* of Mattias Weckmann, a pupil of Schütz, in which the composer uses verses from *The Lamentations of Jeremiah*, divided between soprano and bass voice. The effect here is at times almost operatic, and both singers make the most of their opportunities. Maria Zadelius's contribution is beautifully sung: she is very touching in the expressive opening section of *Ich ruf zu dir* by Nicolaus Adam Strungk and is delightfully nimble as the tempo quickens. The closing florid *Amen* is charming, ending with surprising abruptness.

Kenneth Gilbert's collection of Froberger's harpsichord suites can be recommended without reservation. He finds the music's full character, especially its searching, expressive melancholy, and it is beautifully recorded.

Nikolaus Harnoncourt's programme of Austrian baroque court music is equally rewarding. Heinrich Biber's *Battle* scene is as spectacular as you could wish, with all kinds of bizarre orchestral effects, and his *Sonatas* for strings (in one instance incorporating a solo trombone) are equally inventive. Georg Muffat, too, is shown as a resourceful composer of imitation French ballet music and he is equally adept at writing an orchestral concerto in the Italian style, though still with a Telemann-like German overlay. Excellently vital performances and vivid sound here.

René Jacobs then gives us three lively and expressive cantatas by Vivaldi and demonstrates that Vivaldi's contemporary, Giovanni Bononcini, could turn an equally attractive Italianate phrase: *Care luce mio bene* is a particularly fine example of the genre, with an almost Handelian melodic line. Jacobs sings it most beautifully. The instrumental accompaniments are authentic, and pleasingly so.

The *Duetti di camera* by the ambassador/composer, Agostini Steffani, are freshly rewarding and admirably presented, while Alan Curtis is equally persuasive with the harpsichord suites of Louis Couperin, the uncle of François. Louis-Nicolas Clérambault is represented by his only surviving keyboard music (Kenneth Gilbert at his most spontaneous) and two fine cantatas in which Rachey Yakar sings gloriously.

If you are looking for an authentic CD of French viol music by Marin Marais and his contemporaries, it would be difficult to better the collection given the sobriquet '*La Parnasse Français*' (inspired by the French monument to the arts which was planned but never built), which offers two strikingly characterful pieces by the great viol virtuoso, Marin Marais: the indelible *La Sonnerie de Saint-Geneviève du Mont de Paris* and the colourful *Sonata à la Marésienne*. *Le Tombeau de Monsieur Lully*, a five-movement suite by Jean-Féry Rebel, is almost operatic in its *espressivo*, *lamento* character, and the *Ouvertures* of Jean-Marie Leclair make an extrovert finale. All are presented very impressively indeed by members of the Cologne Musica Antiqua, directed by Reinhard Goebel.

The Gilles *Requiem* was used at the composer's own funeral. It has long been admired in France and, on the evidence of Herrewege's fine performance, should be better known this side of the channel.

Trevor Pinnock and his English Consort then provide a stimulating programme of mainly English repertoire, including a symphony by William Boyce and a keyboard concerto by Thomas Arne, with works by Geminiani and Hellendaal to show the continental influences. Plenty of sparkle and vitality here and a characteristically bright and astringently bracing string-sound. The Avison *Concerto grosso* which ends the concert is particularly successful.

The penultimate CD moves us back to Germany for a programme of pre-Bach chamber music, including a fine *Sonata* by Buxtehude, a strikingly expressive work by Rosenmüller and another, less ambitious, war simulation, placed within a series of nine brief sonata movements, by Johann von Westhoff. The concert ends with chamber versions of Pachelbel's famous *Canon and Gigue* but precedes this pairing with a tuneful suite (*Partie*) by the same composer.

Finally comes a collection of cantatas by Bach's forefathers, which the great composer himself felt were worthy of preservation. The performances are of the highest quality and so is the digital sound.

Augér, Arleen (soprano)

'Love songs' (with Dalton Baldwin, piano): COPLAND: *Pastorale; Heart, we will forget him.* OBRADORS: *Del Cabello más sutil.* OVALLE: *Azulao.* R.STRAUSS: *Ständchen; Das Rosenband.* MARX: *Selige Nacht.* POULENC: *Fleurs.* CIMARA: *Stornello.* QUILTER: *Music, when soft voices die; Love's philosophy.* O.STRAUS: *Je t'aime.* SCHUMANN: *Widmung; Du bist wie eine Blume.* MAHLER: *Liebst du um Schönheit.* TURINA: *Cantares.* LIPPE: *How do I love thee?* COWARD: *Conversation Piece: I'll follow my secret heart.* GOUNOD: *Serenade.* SCHUBERT: *Liebe schwärmt auf allen Wegen.* BRIDGE: *Love went a-riding.* FOSTER: *Why, no one to love.* DONAUDY: *O del mio amato ben.* BRITTEN (arr.): *The Salley Gardens.* LOEWE: *Camelot: Before I gaze at you again.*
❀ *** Delos Dig. D/CD 3029 [id.].

This extraordinarily wide-ranging recital is a delight from the first song to the last. Arleen Augér opens with Copland and closes with *Camelot*, and she is equally at home in the music by Roger Quilter (*Love's philosophy* is superbly done), Noël Coward and the *Rückert* song of Mahler. Britten's arrangement of *The Salley Gardens*, ravishingly slow, is another highlight. The layout of the recital could hardly have been managed better: each song creates its new atmosphere readily, but seems to be enhanced by coming after the previous choice. Dalton Baldwin's accompaniments are very much a partnership with the singing, while the playing itself is spontaneously perceptive throughout. With a good balance and a very realistic recording, this projects vividly like a live recital.

'The art of Arleen Augér' (with (i) members of St Paul CO and Minnesota O; (ii) Joel Revzen (piano)): (i) LARSEN: *Sonnets from the Portuguese.* (ii) PURCELL: *3 Songs* (ed. Britten): *If music be the food of love; Nymphs and shepherds; Sweeter than roses.* SCHUMANN: *Widmung; Lied der Braut I & II* (Rückert). *Die Soldatenbraut; Der Nussbaum.* MOZART: *Das Veilchen; Dans un bois solitaire; Trennunghslied; Als Luis die Briefe; Abendemfindung.*
☞ **(*) Koch Dig. 3-7248-2 [id.].

These songs were all recorded at American music festivals, in St Paul, Minnesota, in 1991 and Aspen, Colorado, in 1986 and 1989. Arleen Augér was at her very best in Libby Larsen's delightful settings of Elizabeth Barrett-Browning's sonnets, especially the last, *How do I love thee?* The Purcell songs are uneven, *Nymphs and Shepherds* the most effective, and it is also the final Schumann song, *Der Nussbaum*, which she invests with the greatest charm. Her Mozartian line is impressive in *Trennungslied*, but there is a hint of strain; *Das Veilchen* and especially the final, touching *Abendempfindung* find her back on form. She is lucky in her accompaniments, especially in having Joel Revzen, who is so musical and supportive. The recording is tangibly vivid and kind to the voice.

Baker, Dame Janet (mezzo-soprano)

'Arie amarose' (with ASMF, Marriner): GIORDANO: *Caro mio ben.* CACCINI: *Amarilli mia bella.* STRADELLA: *Ragion sempra addita.* SARRI: *Sen corre l'agnelletta.* CESTI: *Intorno all'idol mio.* LOTTI: *Pur dicesti, o bocca bella.* Alessandro SCARLATTI: *Spesso vibra per suo gioco; Già il sole dal gange; Sento nel core.* CALDARA: *Come raggio del Sol; Sebben crudele me fai languir'; Selve amiche.* BONONCINI: *Deh più a me non v'ascondete.* DURANTE: *Danza fanciulla gentile.* PERGOLESI: *Ogni pena più spietata.* MARTINI: *Plaisir d'amour.* PICCINI: *O notte o dea del mistero.* PAISIELLO: *Nel cor più non mi sento.*
☞ (M) *** Ph. 434 173-2 [id.].

A delightful recital of classical arias, marred only by the absence of libretti. However, unlike the original (1978) LP, the CD has good supporting notes by Lionel Salter, which are essential for proper enjoyment of this repertoire. The programme is cleverly arranged to contrast expressive with sprightly music and the wide range of tonal graduation and beautiful phrasing is matched by an artless lightness of touch in the slighter numbers. The accompaniments are intimate and tasteful; there is no more fetching example than Pergolesi's *Ogni pena più spietata*, with its deft bassoon obbligato (which Stravinsky used for *Pulcinella*) or the short closing song with harpsichord, Paisiello's *Nel cor più non mi sento*. Caldara's *Come raggio del Sol* and *Selve amiche* are most touching, while Scarlatti is there to lighten the mood with *Già il sole dal gange*. The recording has a warm acoustic and the resonance is kind to the voice without loss of orchestral detail. The CD transfer is pleasingly vivid and natural.

Bartoli, Cecilia (soprano)

Italian songs (with András Schiff): BEETHOVEN: *Ecco quel fiero istante!; Che fa il mio bene?* (2 versions); *T'intendo, si, mio cor; Dimmi, ben mio; In questa tomba oscura.* MOZART: *Ridente la calma.* HAYDN: *Arianna a Naxos.* SCHUBERT: *Vedi quanto adoro ancora ingrato!; Io vuo'cantar di Cadmo; La pastorella; Non t'accostar all'urna; Guarda, che bianca luna; Se dall'Etra; Da quel sembiante appresi; Mio ben ricordati; Pensa, che questo istante; Mi batte'l cor!.*
☞ Decca Dig. 440 297-2; *440 297-4* [id.].

Bartoli and Schiff make a magic partnership, each challenging the other in imagination. These 17 Italian songs and one cantata by the great Viennese masters make a fascinating collection, not just Haydn and Mozart but Beethoven and Schubert as well. Beethoven's darkly intense *In questa tomba'* is well enough known but, as sung by Bartoli, with András Schiff adding sparkle, the lighter songs are just as magnetic, with Beethoven showing his versatility in two astonishingly contrasted settings of the same love-poem.

Berganza, Teresa (mezzo-soprano)

'*Canciones españolas*' (with Narciso Yepes, guitar, Félix Lavilla, piano): ALFONSO X. EL SABIO: *Rosa das rosas; Santa Maria.* MIGUEL DE FUENLLANA: *Pérdida de Antequera. ANON.: Dindirindin; Nuaves te traygo, carillo; Los hombres con gran plazer.* MUDARRA: *Triste estaua el rey David; Si me llaman a mí; Claros y frescos rios; Ysabel, perdiste la tu faxa.* FRANCISCO DE LA TORRE: *Dime, triste corazón; Pámpano verde.* ENRIQUE DE VALDERRÁBANO: *De dónde venis, amore?* LUIS DE MILÁN: *Toda mi vida os amé; Aquel caballero, madre.* JUAN DE TRIANA: *Dínos, madre del donsel.* JUAN DEL ENCINA: *Romerico.* VÁZQUEZ: *Vos me matastes; En la fuente del rosel.* NARVÁEZ: *Con qué la lavaré?* JUAN DE ANCHIETA: *Con amores, la mi madre.* ESTEVE: *Alma sintamos.* GRANADOS: *La maja dolorosa: ¡Oh, muerte cruel!; ¡Ay, majo de mi vida!; De aquel majo amante. El majo discreto; El tra la lá y el punteado; El majo timido.* GURIDI: *Canciones castellanas: Llámale con el pañuelo; No quiero tus avellanas; ¡Cómo quieres que adivine!* FALLA: *7 Canciones populares españolas.* LORCA: *13 Canciones españolas antiquas.* TURINA: *Saeta en forma de Salve a la Virgen de la Esperanza; Canto a Sevilla: El fantasma. Poema en forma de canciones: Cantares.* MONTSALVATGE: *5 Canciones negras.*
☞ (M) *** DG 435 848-2 (2).

This collection dates from the mid-1970s when Berganza was at her peak, the voice fresh, her artistry mature. In essence she provides here a history of Spanish song, opening with two pieces taken from the *Cantigas de Santa Maria*, dating from the thirteenth century, and moving on through Renaissance repertory and, with only one song from the eighteenth century, to the nineteenth and twentieth, traditional settings by Lorca, Falla's *7 Spanish popular songs* and the engaging *Canciones negras* of Montsalvatge. The collaboration with Narciso Yepes seems ideal, for he is an inspirational artist, while her husband, Félix Lavilla, provides the later piano accompaniments. This is not a specialist recital: the music communicates readily in the most direct way, and excellent notes and translations are provided. The balance is very natural and the CD transfers are immaculately managed. This is repertoire one first associates with Victoria de los Angeles, but Berganza makes it her own and there are not many more attractive Spanish song-recitals than this.

Bott, Catherine (soprano), New London Consort, Philip Pickett

'Music from the time of Columbus': VERARDI: *Viva El Gran Re Don Fernando.* ANON.: *A los Maytines era; Propinan de Melyor; Como no le andare yo; Nina y viña; Calabaza, no sé, buen amor; Perdí la mi rueca; Al alva venid buen amigo; Dale si la das.* URREDA: *Muy triste.* J. PONCE: *Como esta sola mi vida.* ANCHIETA: *Con amores mi madre.* ENCINA: *Triste españa; Mortal tristura; Mas vale trocar; Ay triste que vengo; Quedate carillo.* MEDINA: *No ay plazer en esta vida.* DE LA TORRE: *Danza alta.* DE MONDEJAR: *Un solo fin des mis males.*
*** Linn Dig. CKD 007 [id.].

Philip Pickett has drawn on the impressively extensive 'Palace Songbook' of Ferdinand and Isabella, held at the Biblioteca Real in Madrid, and the even earlier 'Cancionero Musical della Biblioteca Columbino', found in the Library of Columbus's illegitimate son, Fernando Colon. The songs offered here are broadly divided into two groups, the romantic ballads, usually of a melancholy disposition (the word 'triste' occurs frequently), and the usually jollier *villancio* form, which brings a repeated refrain. Catherine Bott is the most delightful soloist, singing freshly and simply, often with ravishing tone, and there is much to give pleasure. In the anonymous songs it is fascinating to discover just how international medieval folk music was, for more than once the listener is reminded of the Auvergne songs collected later in France by Canteloube. The two most delightful items are saved until the end, first a truly beautiful love song, *Al alva venid buen Amigo* ('Come at dawn my friend') in which a young woman reflects on her lover's visits, and then lets her thoughts change to consider the birth of 'him who made the world' from the Virgin Mary. In complete contrast is the robust and charmingly naughty villancio, *Dale si la das* ('Come on, wench of Carasa'). The recording is first class, naturally balanced in a pleasing acoustic, and full documentation is provided.

'Mad songs': PURCELL: *From silent shades; From rosy bow'rs; Not all my torments can your pity move. Don Quixote: Let the dreadful engines. A Fool's Preferment: I'll sail upon the dog star.* ECCLES: *The Mad Lover: Must them a faithful lover go?; Let all be gay; Cease of Cupid to complain; She ventures and He wins: Restless in thought. Don Quixote: I burn, my brain consumes to ashes. Cyrus the Great: Oh! take him gently from the pile. The Way of the World: Love's but the frailty of the mind.* WELDON: *Reason, what art thou?; While I with wounding grief.* D. PURCELL: *Achilles: Morpheus, thou gentle god.* BLOW: *Lysander I pursue in vain.* ANON.: Mad *Maudlin; Tom of Bedlam.*
☞ *** O-L Dig. 433 187-2 [id.].

Purcell and his contemporaries, including his brother Daniel, John Eccles, John Blow and others, in such mad-songs as these, devised a whole baroque genre. The best-known song here is Purcell's *I'll sail upon the dog-star*, but mostly these are miniature cantatas in contrasted sections of recitative and aria, displaying a refreshingly unclassical wildness, often set against pathos. They make a marvellous vehicle for the soprano Catherine Bott, who in this and other discs emerges as an outstanding star among early-music performers, with voice fresh, lively and sensuously beautiful.

'O primavera': DE ROREG/DELLA CASA: *Beato me direi.* DE'CAVALIERI: *Godi turba mortal.* ARCHILEI: *Dalle più alte sfere.* LUZZASCHI: *O primavera.* CACCINI: *Sfogava con le stelle; Filli, mirando il cielo; Al fonte, al prato; O che nuovo stupor.* RASI: *Indarno Febo; Ahi, fuggitivo ben.* GAGLIANO: *Pastor levate su.* MARINI: *Con le stele in ciel che mai; Invito all'allegressa.* FRESCOBALDI: *Aria di Romanesca; Sonnetto spirituale: Maddalena alla Croce; Se l'aura spira.* MONTEVERDI: *Exulta filia Sion; Laudate Dominum.* BERNARDI: *O dulcissima dilecta mea.* ROSSI: *La gelosia.* CARISSIMI: *Il lamento in morte di Maria Stuarda.*
☞ (M) *** O-L Dig. 443 184-2 [id.].

This collection is for those who like to explore, in this case Italian vocal music of the sixteenth and the first half of the seventeenth century. Catherine Bott is in her element in this repertoire and at her most inspired in the moving Carissimi *Lament*, when Mary Queen of Scots calls on cruel fate in a long extended monologue as she awaits execution. Then the singer dramatically becomes the narrator: 'Here she fell silent . . . Shortly afterwards an unworthy and wicked stroke divided her body and united her soul with God.' The other songs here explore all aspects of love, unrequited (the opening *Beato me direi*), ardent (*Sfogava con le stelle* and *O dulcissima dilecta mea*), jealous (*La gelosia*), a young girl's fear of losing her beauty to the ravages of age (*Filli, mirando il cielo*) and lost love at springtime (*O primavera*). To balance the programme there are also some fine sacred settings by Monteverdi and Frescobaldi. Good singing throughout by an artist with a lovely voice and line, and full understanding of the subtleties of ornamentation; while the New London Consort accompany with thoughtful and stylish use of a wide range of instrumental possibilities. Full documentation and translations and fine recording complete the overall excellence of this enterprising recital.

Bowman, James (counter-tenor)

'A portrait': LANDINI: *Giunta vaga biltà; Donna 'l tuo partimento.* ANON.: *Parti de mal.* VON VOGELWEIDE: *Palästinalied.* LE CHATELAIN DE COUCI: *Li nouviaus tens.* RICHARD CUR-DE-LION: *Ja nus hons pris.* PURCELL: *Music for a while; Sweeter than roses.* MONTEVERDI: *Ego flos campi.* SCHUTZ: *Was hast du Verwirket?; Bringt her dem Herrn.* PURCELL: *Sweeter than roses.* Excerpts from VIVALDI: *Stabat Mater;* PERGOLESI: *Stabat Mater;* HANDEL: *Orlando; Athalia; Israel in Egypt;* CAVALLI: *La Calisto.*
☞ (M) *** Decca Analogue/Dig. 436 799-2 [id.].

This 'Portrait' admirably demonstrates the artistic range of an artist of distinction, unsurpassed among British counter-tenors. The first six medieval items all come from recordings made with David Munrow's Early Music Consort, and the Landini songs are particularly beautiful, as are the motets of Monteverdi and Schütz with organ accompaniment by David Lumsden. But perhaps the highlights are the Purcell songs (*Sweeter than roses* accompanied by Benjamin Britten), the excerpts from Handel opera and oratorio (with the part of Orlando, intended for the alto castrato but admirably suited to Bowman's individual timbre, demanding and receiving great vocal bravura). Best of all is the gorgeous Cavalli aria, *Ludissima face*, from Raymond Leppard's seductive realization of *La Calisto*. The offering is generous (72 minutes) and the recordings, dating from between 1968 and 1989, are excellently transferred.

(Julian) Bream Consort

Volume 6: Consort music (with (i) Robert Spencer): BYRD: *Monsieur's alman; Pavin; My Lord of Oxenford's maske.* JOHNSON: *Flatt pavin.* ALLISON: *The Bachelar's delight.* ANON.: *Kempe's Jig; Le rosignol.* PHILLIPS: *Phillips pavin.* MORLEY: (i) *O mistress mine. Fantasie: La Rondinella; Frog galliard; Joyne hands.* DOWLAND: *Lachrimae pavin; Fantasie; Dowland's adew; Tarleton's resurrection; Can she excuse: galliard.* ALLISON: *De la tromba pavin.* CAMPION: (i) *It fell upon a summer's day.* BRITTEN: *Gloriana: Courtly dances.* VIVALDI: *Concerto in D, RV 93.*
☞ (M) *** BMG/RCA 09026 61589-2 [id.].

Volume 7: 'Fantasies, ayres and dances' (with (i) Robert Tear): MORLEY: (i) *Joyne hands.* PHILLIPS: *Phillips Pavin.* DOWLAND: *Frog galliard;* (i) *Go nightly cares.* NICHOLSON: *Jew's dance.* BYRD: *Fantasy.* ALISON: *The bachelar's delight.* MORLEY: *Sacred end pavin & Galliard;* (i) *Thirsis and Milla.* ALISON: *De la tromba pavin; Alison's knell; Go from my window.* ANON.: *Grimstock.* BACHELAR: *Daniel's almain.* STROGERS: *In nomine pavin.* DOWLAND-EYCK: *Come again.* DOWLAND: *Lachrimae pavin;* (i) *Can she excuse.*
☞ (M) **(*) BMG/RCA 09026 61590-2 [id.].

These two concerts were recorded some 15 years apart, so the make-up of the group is different. But each offers consort music with a bare sprinkling of songs. As they are so well sung it would have been a good idea to have been more generous with them, for they provide a welcome diversion, even if the consort itself provides varying textures. Bream's lute contribution (often embroidering with considerable bravura) is consistently imaginative. What adds piquancy to the first collection is the inclusion of the *Courtly dances* from Britten's *Gloriana*, and the Vivaldi concerto is also a welcome bonus.

Cambridge Singers, John Rutter

'Portrait': BYRD: *Sing joyfully; Non vos relinquam.* FAURE: *Cantique de Jean Racine; Requiem: Sanctus.* RUTTER: *O be joyful in the Lord; All things bright and beautiful; Shepherd's pipe carol; Open thou mine eyes; Requiem: Out of the deep.* PURCELL: *Hear my prayer, O Lord.* STANFORD: *Beati quorum via; The Bluebird.* TRAD.: *This joyful Eastertide; In dulci jubilo.* HANDEL: *Messiah: For unto us a child is born.* FARMER: *A pretty bonny lass.* MORLEY: *Now is the month of maying.* DELIUS: *To be sung of a summer night on the water.* VICTORIA: *O magnum mysterium.* TERRY: *Myn lyking.*
(M) *** Coll. Dig./Analogue CSCD 500; *CSCC 500* [id.].

John Rutter has arranged the items here with great skill so that serene music always makes a contrast with the many exuberant expressions of joy, his own engaging hymn-settings among them. Thus the bright-eyed hey-nonny songs of John Farmer and Thomas Morley are aptly followed by the lovely wordless *To be sung of a summer night on the water* of Delius, and Stanford's beautiful evocation of *The Bluebird* (one of Rutter's own special favourites). The sound, vivid and atmospheric, suits the colour and mood of the music quite admirably. Not to be missed!

'There is sweet music' (English choral songs): STANFORD: *The blue bird.* DELIUS: *To be sung of a summer night on the water I & II.* ELGAR: *There is sweet music; My love dwelt in a Northern land.* VAUGHAN WILLIAMS: *3 Shakespearean songs: Full fathom five; The cloud-capp'd towers; Over hill, over dale.* BRITTEN: *5 Flower songs, Op. 47.* Folksongs: arr. MOERAN: *The sailor and young Nancy.* Arr. GRAINGER: *Brigg Fair: Londonderry air.* Arr. CHAPMAN: *Three ravens.* Arr. HOLST: *My sweetheart's like Venus.* Arr. BAIRSTOW: *The oak and the ash.* Arr. STANFORD: *Quick! We have but a second.*
⊛ *** Coll. Dig. COLCD 104 [id.].

Opening with an enchanting performance of Stanford's *The blue bird* and followed by equally expressive accounts of Delius's two wordless summer evocations, this most attractive recital ranges from Elgar and Vaughan Williams, both offering splendid performances, to various arrangements of folksongs, less fashionable today than they once were, but giving much pleasure here. The recording, made in the Great Hall of University College, London, has an almost ideal ambience: words are clear, yet the vocal timbre is full and natural. A highly recommendable anthology, and if you enjoy this you will enjoy other fine compilations from this group: English madrigals on *'Flora gave me fairest flowers'* (COLCD 105) and English church music on *'Faire is the Heaven'* (COLCD 107) and *'Hail gladdening light'* (COLCD 113).

Christoff, Boris (bass)

'Russian songs' (with LAP, Tzipine; Pais Conservatoire O, Cluytens; Alexandre Labinsky, Alexandre Tcherepnine, Janine Reiss, Serge Zapolsky, or Nadia Gedda-Nova (piano); Gaston Marchesini, Maud-Martin Tortelier (cello)): GLINKA: *The Midnight review; Cradle song; What, young beauty; Where is our rose?; The Lark; Ah, you darling, lovely girl; Doubt; Grandpa, the girls once told me; How sweet to be with thee; Do not say the heart is sick; Hebrew song; Elegy; I remember the wonderful moment.* BORODIN: *Those folk; Song of the dark forest; From my tears; The Sea princess; The Pretty girl no longer loves me; The Magic garden; Arabian melody; The false note; The fishermaiden. Listen to my song, little friend; The Sleeping princess; Pride; For the shores of thy far native land; The sea; Why art thou so early, dawn?; My songs are poisoned.* CUI: *Songs, Op. 44: Le Hun; Berceuse; Le ciel est transi; Les songeants. Ici-bas; The tomb and the rose; The Love of a departed one; A Recent dream; Pardon!; Desire; Conspiracy; Song of Mary; The Imprisoned knight; Album leaf; The Prophet; The Statue of Tsarkoïe; In Memory of V. S. Stassov.* BALAKIREV: *Prologue; Song of Selim; Song: The Yellow leaf trembles; The Pine tree; Nocturne; Starless midnight, coldly breathed; The Putting-right; November the 7th; Dawn; Hebrew melody; The Wilderness; The Knight; The Dream; Look, my friend.* RIMSKY-KORSAKOV: *The Pine and the palm; On the hills of Georgia; The Messenger; Quietly evening falls; Hebrew song; Zuleika's song; Across the midnight sky; I waited for thee in the grotto at the appointed hour; The sea is tossing; The Upas tree; The Prophet; Quiet is the blue sea; Slowly drag my days; Withered flower; The rainy day has waned.* TCHAIKOVSKY: *Don Juan's serenade; The Mild stars shone for us; Child's song; Night; Cradle song; Night; Do not ask; As they kept on saying, 'Fool'; To sleep; Disappointment; the canary; None but the weary heart; Again, as before, alone; A Legend.* RACHMANINOV: *Fate; How fair is this spot; When yesterday we met; All once I gladly owned; Morning; All things depart; Thy pity I implore; Christ is risen; Loneliness; O never sing to me again; The dream; The soldier's wife; The Harvest of sorrow; Oh stay, my love; The world would see thee smile; Night is mournful.* Folksongs: arr. SEROV: *The Evil power.* TRAD.: *Doubinouchka: Song of the Volga; The Bandore; Down Peterskaya Street; Going down the Volga; Notchenka* (Folksongs with Russian Ch., Potorjinsky).
☞ (B) *** EMI mono CZS7 67496-2 (5) [id.].

This survey covers recordings by the great Bulgarian bass made between 1954 and 1969. The great majority come from the 1960s, the earliest are the Russian folksongs recorded in 1954 and the Rachmaninov and Rimsky-Korsakov (1959). But throughout this remarkably extensive programme, the magnificent voice is in perfect shape and the recordings are faithfully transferred. Some might think a big voice like Christoff's would be unsuitable for art songs, but his sensitivity is never in question and, whenever necessary, he scales it down, especially (for instance) in several of the Glinka songs where he has a cello obbligato. This repertoire is enormously rich in melody and, just as in the opera house, Christoff's art demonstrates the widest emotional range. Characterization is always strong and his feeling for words is just as striking here as in his performances of the stage repertory. Most of the songs are piano accompanied (with a whole range of excellent accompanists) but occasionally orchestral versions are used, as in Rimsky-Korsakov's *The prophet* or Balakirev's

Prologue, when the orchestra is vividly balanced. The collection ends with an exhilarating half-dozen traditional Russian folksongs in which Christoff is joined by an enthusiastic (if backwardly balanced) Russian chorus and balalaika ensemble. The result is irresistible, with melancholy and joy side by side in a wonderfully Slavonic way. These five well-filled discs not only demonstrate some of the riches hitherto hidden in EMI's international vaults; they also give us unique performances of repertoire most of which is otherwise totally inaccessible. The snag lies in the documentation. As this derives from EMI's French stable, even the song-titles are given in French. (It was a major task identifying and translating them!) No texts are provided, simply a 2½-page biographical note.

Clare College, Cambridge, Choir and Orchestra, John Rutter

'The Holly and the ivy' (Carols): RUTTER: *Donkey carol; Mary's lullaby.* TRAD., arr. RUTTER: *King Jesus hath a garden; Wexford carol;* (Flemish) *Cradle song; Child in a manger; In dulci jubilo; I saw three ships; The holly and the ivy.* TRAD., arr. WOODWARD: *Up! Good Christian folk.* TRAD., arr. WILLCOCKS: *Gabriel's message; Ding! dong! merrily on high; Quelle est cette odeur agréable.* TRAD., arr. PETTMAN: *I saw a maiden.* DARKE: *In the bleak mid-winter.* PRAETORIUS: *The noble stem of Jesse; Omnis mundus jocundetur.* TCHAIKOVSKY: *The crown of roses.* POSTON: *Jesus Christ the apple tree.* TRAD., arr. VAUGHAN WILLIAMS: *Wassail song.*
ⓑ (M) *** Decca 425 500-2.

This outstanding collection, recorded by Argo in the Lady Chapel at Ely Cathedral in 1979, is a model of its kind. Rutter's admirers, among whom we can be counted, will surely want this disc for the Christmas season. The opening arrangement of *King Jesus hath a garden*, using a traditional Dutch melody, immediately sets the mood with its pretty flute decorations. Moreover Rutter's own gentle syncopated *Donkey carol!*, which comes fourth, is indispensable to any Christmas celebration. The whole programme is a delight – not always especially ecclesiastical in feeling, but permeated throughout by the spirit of Christmas joy.

Columbus Consort

'Christmas in early America' (18th-century carols and anthems): BELCHER: *How beauteous are their feet.* HOLYOKE: *How beauteous are their feet. Th'Almighty spake and Gabriel sped; Comfort ye my people.* STEPHENSON: *If angel's sung a Saviour's birth.* HUSBAND: *Hark! The glad sound.* HEIGHINGTON: *While shepherds watched their flocks by night.* FRENCH: *While shepherd's watched their flocks by night.* BILLINGS: *While shepherds watched their flocks by night.* PETER: *Unto us a child is born.* ANTES: *Prince of Peace, Immanuel.* MICHAEL: *Hail Infant newborn.* HERBST: *To us a Child is born.* SCHULZ: *Thou Child divine.* DENCKE: *Meine Seele erhebet den Herrn.* GREGOR: *Hosanna! Blessed he that comes in the name of the Lord.* Charles PACHELBEL: *Magnificat anima mea Dominum.*
☞ *** Channel Classics Dig. CC 5693 [id.].

A fascinating look back to the celebration of Christmas in the New World in the late eighteenth century, both by the British colonial settlers in New England and by their Moravian counterparts in Pennsylvania and North Carolina, where the inheritance was essentially in the European tradition. The English style is usually fairly simple and hymn-like, but with overlapping part-writing and occasional solo dialogues (as in the rhythmically interesting *Th'Almighty spake*). Samuel Holyoke shows himself to be a strikingly fresh melodist while, of the three settings of *While Shepherds watched* to different tunes, William Billings emerges as the most striking and imaginative. Benjamin Carr's *Anthem for Christmas* is a musical pastiche (indeed a kind of 'musical switch' with brief quotations from Corelli's *Christmas concerto* and Handel's *Messiah* among other works). The Moravian/German music is usually more elaborate. Johann Peter's delightful motet-like carol, *Unto us a Child is born*, has characteristically resourceful accompanimental string-writing and those who follow him – David Moritz Michael, Johannes Herbst, J. A. P. Schulz and Jeremiah Dencke – all write in a tradition descended from the great German composers, capped by Charles Pachelbel (son of the Johann Pachelbel of *Canon* fame). He played the organ in Boston, New York and Charleston in the 1730s and 1740s, and his *Magnificat* for double chorus celebrates a much more florid style, utterly different from the music which opens this programme. The surprise is that this concert is performed not by American singers but by a Dutch group of expert vocal soloists, with a choral and string ensemble who sing and play with convincing authenticity and an agreeably stylish spontaneity. The recording is realistic and clear and made within a perfectly judged acoustic.

Consort of Musicke, Anthony Rooley

'Lamento d'Arianna': MONTEVERDI: *Lamento d'Arianna: a voce solo; a 5; Pianto della Madonna a voce solo.* BONINI: *Lamento d'Arianno in stile recitativo.* PARI: *Il Lamento d'Arianna a 5.* COSTA: *Pianto d'Arianna a voce solo.* IL VERSO: *Lasciatemi morire a 5.* RASCARINI: *Reciproco Amore: Lasciatemi morire a 3.* (M)

☞ (M) *** BMG/RCA GD 77115 (2) [id.].

It is difficult to appreciate today what an enormous influence Monteverdi's *Lamento d'Arianna* had both on his contemporaries and on the immediate course of musical history. Here was a profoundly moving female soliloquy which, in its poignant sorrow and desperation, was to recur again and again, as other musicians realized that its message made a profound impression on their audiences (the famous *Dido's Lament* of Purcell – 1689 – is but one later example of a very similar and equally inspired response of a great composer to a woman's suffering when facing betrayal and death). Here Anthony Rooley assembles some fine examples, and Emma Kirkby opens touchingly with the great Monteverdi orginal and concludes with its later transmutation into a religious context, *Pianto della Madonna.* Bonini and others can't match this level of inspiration but they try.

Deller, Alfred (counter-tenor)

'The three ravens' (with Desmond Dupré, guitar & lute): *The three ravens; Cuckoo; How should I your true love know; Sweet nightingale; I will give my love an apple; The oak and the ash;* (Lute): *Go from my window. King Henry; Coventry carol. Barbara Allen; Heigh ho, the wind and the rain; Waly, waly; Down in yon forest; Matthew, Mark, Luke and John.* (Lute): *A Toye. The tailor and the mouse; Greensleeves; The Wraggle Taggle gipsies; Lord Rendall; Sweet Jane; The frog and the mouse; The seeds of love; Near London town; Who's going to shoe your pretty little foot?; Blow away the morning dew; Searching for lambs; Sweet England; Dabbling in the dew; Just as the tide was a-flowing.*
(M) *** Vanguard 08.8026 71 [OVC 8026].

This CD represents the content of two LPs, and the recordings date from 1956 when Alfred Deller's voice was at its freshest and most winning. In songs which demand a simple line his sweet, pure timbre is ravishing and the performances of the title-song, *How should I your true love know, I will give my love an apple,* the *Coventry carol* and *The seeds of love* are all glorious examples. In one or two of the livelier numbers, *Heigh ho, the wind and the rain* for instance, some might wish for a more robust effect, but *The tailor and the mouse, The frog and the mouse* and the dainty *Who's going to shoe your pretty little foot?* have great charm. Deller is given intimate accompaniments by Desmond Dupré, who also provides two solo interludes. With a 73-minute programme this is not a disc to play all at once; but with the songs played in groups, Deller's lovely tone and natural artistry will give great pleasure. The recording is impeccable.

Early Music Consort of London, David Munrow

'Music of the Crusades': Anonymous thirteenth-century French music, and music by: MARCABRU; CUIOT DE DIJON; WALTER VON DER VOGEL-WEIDE; FAIDIT; CONON DE BETHUNE; RICHARD COEUR-DE-LION; THIBAUT DE CHAMPAGNE.
(M) *** Decca 430 264-2; *430 264-4.*

Of all the Early Music groups, the Early Music Consort under the late David Munrow can be relied on best to entertain and titillate the ear without ever descending into vulgarity. The characteristic combination of familiarity with their repertoire and imaginative flair which characterizes the work of this group informs the whole programme. Most of the accompaniments are purely speculative (only the melodic line survives in some cases) but the performances, like the realizations, are brilliantly effective and the presentation deserves the highest praise for its blend of scholarship and inventiveness. The 1970 (Argo) recording sounds as fresh here as the day it was made.

'Ecco la Primavera' (Florentine music of the fourteenth century, with James Bowman, Nigel Rogers, Martyn Hill): LANDINI: *Ecco la primavera; Giunta vaga biltà; Questa fanciull'amor; De! dinmi tu;Cara mie donna; La bionda treçça; Donna 'l tuo partimento.* PIERO: *Con dolce brama.* ZACHARA DA TERAMO: *Rosetta.* Giovanni DA FIRENZE: *Chon brachi assai.* Lorenzo DA FIRENZE: *Dà, dà, a chi avaregia.* Jacobo DI BOLOGNA: *Fenice fu'e visse.* ANON.: *Lamento di Tristano; Trotto; Due saltarelli; Quan ye voy le duç; La Manfredina; Istampita Ghaetta; Biance flour.*
☞ (M) *** Decca 436 219-2 [id.].

This collection of fourteenth-century Florentine music should have a wide general appeal. Landini has an immediate approachability, and this extends to much else on this fine disc. No one knows exactly how or on what instruments the accompaniment would have been performed, and the Early Music Consort solve the problem with their usual combination of scholarship and imagination. The singers include artists of the distinction of James Bowman, and the players are quite first rate. David Munrow's recorder playing is virtuosic. Attractive music, expertly transcribed and played, and well recorded in 1969. Full texts and translations are included.

'The Triumphs of Maximilian' (with James Bowman, Martyn Hill, Philip Langridge, Geoffrey Shaw): SENFL: *Mit Lust tritt ich an diesen Tanz; Ich stuend an einem Morgen; Das Gläut zu Speyer; Meniger stellt nach Geld; Gottes Namen fahren wir; Ach Elslein, liebes Elselein mein; Ich weiss nit, was er ihr verhhierss; Entlaubet ist der Walde; Was wird es doch;* (attrib. SENFL): *Quis dabit oculis nostris.* KOTTER: *Kochersperger Spanieler.* ISAAC: *Innsbruck, ich muss dich lassen; Helogierons nous; Maudit soyt; La Mora.* FINCK: *Sauff aus und machs nit lang.* KEUTZENHOFF: *Frisch und frölich wölln wir leben.* ANON.: *Welscher Tanz; Christ ist erstanden.*
☞ (M) *** Decca 436 998-2 [id.].

Maximilian I was inordinately vain. He was also shrewd enough to realize that lavish patronage of the arts would ensure that posterity would remember him. His dedicated support meant that the decade between 1486 and 1496 became a watershed for the medieval development of the German Lied. Clearly the turn of the century was dominated by the music of Ludwig Senfl (who died about 1542), and Senfl's music is rightly given the lion's share of this excellent collection. To sample the individuality of Senfl's musical personality, try track 4, the piquant bell-ringers' trio, *Das Gläut zu Speyer*. In variety of arrangement and sophistication of presentation this record represents the zenith of the achievement of Munrow and his Consort. The 1972 recording is both immediate and atmospheric and, as usual, texts and translations are provided.

'Dances from Terpsichore and Secular songs': PRAETORIUS: *Terpsichore: Suites de ballets; Suite de voltes.* Flemish Renaissance music: JOSQUIN DESPREZ: *Scaramella va alla guerra; Allegez moy, dolce plaisant brunette* (2 versions); *El grillo è buon cantore; Adieu mes amours* (2 versions). Hayne van GHIZEGHEM: *De tous biens plaine* (4 versions). BRUMEL: *Du tout plongiet / Fors seulement l'attente; Fortuna desperata.* BARBIREAU or OBRECHT: *Ein fröhlich wesen* (3 versions). OCKEGHEM: *Prenez sur moi; Ma bouche rit.*
☞ (M) **(*) EMI CDM7 67803-2 [id.]. Early Music Cons. of L., Munrow – PRAETORIUS: *Dances from Terpsichore.* **(*)

To David Munrow's admirably lively and re-creative set of Praetorius dances EMI have now added an equally stimulating collection of secular pieces from the Flemish Renaissance School, music which surely mirrors the paintings of Memling and Bruegel and their contemporaries. The performances are exceptionally vivid and often fascinate the ear by including several different settings of the same melody (both vocal and instrumental, set in different numbers of parts). Among the highlights is Josquin's *El grillo*, while the closing *Fortuna desperata* of Antoine Brumel is very touching. Excellent sound, but appalling documentation: there are no translations and the listings are printed in type so small as to need a magnifying glass in order to read them easily.

Ferrier, Kathleen (contralto)

'The world of Kathleen Ferrier': TRAD.: *Blow the wind southerly; The Keel Row; Ma bonny lad; Kitty my love.* arr. BRITTEN: *Come you not from Newcastle.* HANDEL: *Rodelinda: Art thou troubled? Serse: Ombra mai fu.* GLUCK: *Orfeo: What is life?* MENDELSSOHN: *Elijah: Woe unto them; O rest in the Lord.* BACH: *St Matthew Passion: Have mercy, Lord, on me.* SCHUBERT: *An die Musik; Gretchen am Spinnrade; Die junge Nonne; Der Musensohn.* BRAHMS: *Sapphische Ode; Botschaft.* MAHLER: *Rückert Lieder: Um Mitternacht.*
🏵 (B) (***) Decca mono 430 096-2; 430 096-4.

This selection, revised and expanded from the original LP issue, admirably displays Kathleen Ferrier's range, from the delightfully fresh folksongs to Mahler's *Um Mitternacht* in her celebrated recording with Bruno Walter and the VPO. The noble account of *O rest in the Lord* is one of the essential items now added, together with an expansion of the Schubert items (*Die junge Nonne* and *An die Musik* are especially moving). The CD transfers are remarkably trouble-free and the opening unaccompanied *Blow the wind southerly* has uncanny presence. The recital plays for 65 minutes and fortunately there are few if any technical reservations to be made here about the sound quality.

Fretwork, with Jeremy Budd (treble), Michael Chance (countertenor)

'*A Play of passion*': ANON.: *In paradise; The Dark is my delight; What meat eats the Spaniard; Come tread the paths; Allemand and galliard; Ah, silly poor Joas.* HOLBORNE: *Infernum and galliard; Pavanne and galliard* (3 versions). ALBARTI: *Pavanne and galliard.* FERRABOSCO: *Alman a 5; Pavanne and alman a 5.* JOHNSON: *Eliza is the fairest Queen; Come again.* COBBOLD: *Ye mortal weights.* BYRD: *Fair Britain Isle.* GIBBONS: *The Silver swan; Pavanne and galliard; What is our life?.*
☞ **(*) Virgin/EMI Dig. VCS5 45997-2 [id.].

The title of this new compilation from Fretwork may be confusing. The words are Sir Walter Raleigh's: 'What is our life? a play of passion', and Gibbons's setting of Raleigh's verse is the closing item here. Much of the repertoire here has a feeling of Elizabethan melancholy and, although there are some more robust songs, the mood of the instrumental interludes is also very restrained; although the atmosphere is sustained well, one would like the clouds to lift rather more often. The recording is very refined and true.

Gabrieli Consort & Players, Paul McCreesh

'*A Venetian coronation (1595)*': Giovanni GABRIELI: *Canzonas Nos. XIII a 12; IX a 10; XVI a 15; Deus qui beatum Marcum a 10 Intonazione ottavo toni; Intonazione terzo e quarto toni; Intonazioni quinto tono alla quarta bassa; Omnes gentes a 16; Sonata No. VI a 8 pian e forte.* Andrea GABRIELI: *Intonazione primo tono; Intonazione settino tono;* Mass excerpts: *Kyrie a 5-12; Gloria a 16; Sanctus a 12; Benedictus a 12; O sacrum convivium a 5; Benedictus dominus Deus sabbaoth.* BENDINELLI: *Sonata CCCXXXIII; Sarasinetta.* THOMSEN: *Toccata No. 1.*
☞ *** Virgin/EMI Dig. VC7 59006-2; *VC 759006-4* [id.].

This recording and its DG successor below won *Gramophone* Early Music Awards in two consecutive years. '*A Venetian coronation*' is a highly imaginative if conjectural reconstruction of the Mass and its accompanying music as performed at St Mark's for the ceremonial installation of Doge Marino Grimaldi in 1595. The evocation begins with sounding bells (Betjemann would have approved) and the choice of music is extraordinarily rich, using processional effects to simulate the actual scene, like a great Renaissance painting. The climax comes with the Mass itself; and the sounds here, choral and instrumental, are quite glorious. The spontaneity of the whole affair is remarkable and the recording superb.

'*Venetian Vespers*' including: MONTEVERDI: *Laudate pueri; Laudate dominum; Deus qui mundum; Laetatus sum.* Giovanni GABRIELI: *Intonazione* (for organ). RIGATTI: *Dixit dominus; Nisi dominus; Magnificat; Salve regina.* GRANDI: *O intemerata; O quam tu pulchra es.* FASALO: *Intonazione* (for organ). BANCHIERI: *Suonata prima; Dialogo secondo* (for organ). FINETTI: *O Maria, quae rapis corda hominum.* CAVALLI: *Lauda Jetrusalem.* MARINI: *Sonata con tre violini in eco.* ANON.: *Praeambulum.*
☞ *** DG Dig. 437 552-2 (2) [id.].

Sequels can sometimes fall flat (as Hollywood so often demonstrates), but this one certainly doesn't, for the musical intensity of the performance is no less vivid here, and the spatial effects and polychoral interplay are equally impressive in this hypothetical re-creation of a Vespers at St Mark's. Grandiose effects alternate with more intimate sonorities, but the feeling of drama which was part and parcel of the Venetian Renaissance tradition is fully conveyed. Once again all the participants are on their toes, and playing and singing (soloists as well as chorus) are transcendent with detail in the accompaniment always effective and stylish. The recording is splendidly opulent, yet never loses its definition.

Glyndebourne Opera

'*Glyndebourne Festival Opera*' (1934–1994): Excerpts from MOZART: *Le nozze di Figaro* (Audry Mildmay, Aulikki Rautawaara; Monica Sinclair; Sesto Bruscantini; Ian Wallace; Daniel McCoshan; Franco Calabrese; Graziella Sciutti; Claudio Desderi; Gianna Rolandi; Glyndebourne Festival Ch.); *Così fan tutte* (Heddle Nash; Erich Kunz; Delores Ziegler; Claudio Desderi; Carol Vaness); *Don Giovanni* (Luise Helletsgruber, Audrey Mildmay; Koloman von Pataky; Roy Henderson, Ina Souez; Salvatore Bassaloni; Thomas Allen; Elizabeth Gale); *Idomeneo* (Richard Lewis; Sena Jurinac; Léopold Simoneau); *Die Entführung aus dem Serail* (Margaret Price). GAY: *The Beggar's opera* (Constance Willis; Michael Redgrave; Audrey Mildmay). ROSSINI: *La Cenerentola* (Juan Oncina); *Le Comte Ory* (Cora Canne-Meijer; Juan Oncina; Sari Barabas); *Il barbiere di Siviglia* (Victoria de Los Angeles;

Lugi Alva; Sesto Bruscantini). MONTEVERDI: *L'Incoronazione di Poppea* (Magda László; Richard Lewis). GERSHWIN: *Porgy and Bess* ((Willard White; Cynthia Haymon).
☞ (M) (***) EMI stereo/mono; Analogue/Dig. CDH5 65072-2 [id.].

Issued to celebrate the opening of the new opera house at Glyndebourne in May 1994, exactly 50 years after the original theatre, this delightful compilation of 20 items ranges wide, starting with the original *Figaro* recording of 1934 conducted by Fritz Busch and concluding with Gershwin's *Porgy and Bess* conducted by Simon Rattle. In his choice of items Paul Campion has opted for some less predictable numbers, even from the obvious classic recordings, like the pre-war Busch sets or the Haitink recordings of recent years. Even more welcome are the rarities. The 1940 recording of *The Beggar's Opera* is a period piece, with Audrey Mildmay, wife of John Christie, the founder, opposite Michael Redgrave as singer. The recordings from the immediate post-war period were of excerpts only and have had very limited currency over the years. The samples here come out very freshly, with Busch conducting for Erich Kunz and Blanche Thebom in *Così fan tutte* and for Richard Lewis in *Idomeneo*. The Vittorio Gui period is well represented in Rossini as well as in Mozart, even if Victoria de los Angeles never actually sang Rosina at Glyndebourne but only recorded it with the company. It is good too to have the sensuously beautiful final duet from Monteverdi's *Poppea* in the Raymond Leppard version, and a rare CfP recording of *Entführung* with the young Margaret Price as Constanze. A treasury of singing to capture the unique flavour of opera at Glyndebourne.

Gomez, Jill (soprano), John Constable (piano)

'Cabaret classics' (with John Constable, piano): WEILL: *Marie Galante: 4 Songs. Lady in the Dark: My ship. Street scene: Lonely house. Knickerbocker holiday: It never was you.* ZEMLINSKY: *3 Songs from Op. 27.* SCHOENBERG: *4 Brettl Lieder.* SATIE: *3 Café-concert songs: La Diva de l'Empire; Allons-y, Chochotte; Je te veux.*
⊛ *** Unicorn Dig. DKPCD 9055; *DKPC 9055* [id.].

Jill Gomez's delicious Schoenberg performances make clear that writing these innocently diatonic numbers can have been no chore to the future ogre of the avant-garde. The same is true of the two Kurt Weill groups, strikingly contrasted at the beginning and end of the recital. The French-text songs from *Marie Galante* use material adapted from *Happy End*. Weill's mastery is even more strikingly illustrated in the three Broadway songs, ravishing numbers all three: *My ship*, *Lonely house* and *It never was you*. It is worth getting the record just for Gomez's ecstatic pianissimo top A at the end of that last item. The other groups, as delightful as they are revealing, are from Alexander von Zemlinsky (not quite so light-handed), and the Parisian joker, Satie, in three café-concert songs, including the famous celebration of English music-hall, *La Diva de l'Empire*. John Constable is the idiomatic accompanist. Gomez's sensuously lovely soprano is caught beautifully.

Gothic Voices, Christopher Page

'The Guardian of Zephirus' (Courtly songs of the 15th century, with Imogen Barford, medieval harp): DUFAY: *J'atendray tant qu'il vous playra; Adieu ces bons vins de Lannoys; Mon cuer me fait tous dis penser.* BRIQUET: *Ma seul amour et ma belle maistresse.* DE CASERTA: *Amour ma' le cuer mis.* LANDINI: *Nessun ponga speranza; Giunta vaga bilta.* REYNEAU: *Va t'en mon cuer, avent mes yeux.* MATHEUS DE SACTO JOHANNE: *Fortune, faulce, parverse.* DE INSULA: *Amours n'ont cure le tristesse.* BROLLO: *Qui le sien vuelt bien maintenir.* ANON.: *N'a pas long temps que trouvay Zephirus; Je la remire, la belle.*
*** Hyp. CDA 66144 [id.].

In 1986 The Gothic Voices began what was to become a large-scale survey of medieval music, secular and sacred – for the two are inevitably intermingled. This has now expanded to 10 CDs, all available separately. From the beginning, the project was an adventure in exploration, as much for the artists as for the listener, for comparatively little is known about how this music sounded on voices of the time. The songs of the troubadours and trouvères – outside the church – sometimes drew on ecclesiastical chant, but other such chansons had a modal character of their own. They were essentially monophonic, i.e. a single line of music, perhaps with an instrumental accompaniment, but the rhythmic patterns were unrecorded and, like much else in this repertoire, are inevitably conjectural in modern re-creative performance. Much of the repertoire on the first disc (and indeed elsewhere) is unfamiliar, with Dufay the only famous name; but everything here is of interest, and the listener inexperienced in medieval music will be surprised at the strength of its character. The performances are naturally eloquent and, although the range of colour is limited compared with later writing, it still has immediacy of appeal, especially if taken in short bursts. The recording balance is faultless and the sound first rate. With complete security of intonation and a chamber-music vocal blend, the presentation is wholly admirable. There is full back-up documentation.

'The Castle of Fair Welcome' ('Courtly songs of the latter 15th Century', with Christopher Wilson, lute): ANON.: *Las je ne puis; En amours n'a si non bien; Mi ut re ut.* MORTON: *Le souvenir de vous me tue; Que pourroit plus; Plus j'ay le monde regardé.* REGIS: *Puisque ma dame.* BEDYNGHAM: *Myn hertis lust.* BINCHOIS: *Deuil angoisseux.* VINCENET: *La pena sin ser sabida.* FRYE: *So ys emprinted.* ENRIQUE: *Pues servićio vos desplaze.* CHARLES THE BOLD: *Ma dame, trop vous mesprenés.* DUFAY: *Ne je ne dors.*
☞ *** Hyp. Dig. CDA 66194 [id.].

Christopher Page has by now established a basic procedure for his presentation of this early vocal repertoire: he has decided that it will be unaccompanied and usually performed by a modest-sized vocal group. So, in the present collection, further variety is provided with four instrumental pieces (played on harp and lute). Not surprisingly, the two most striking works here are by Dufay (remarkably compelling) and Binchois; but the programme overall has been carefully chosen and it is given a boldly spontaneous presentation which cannot but intrigue the ear. As always, the recording is first class.

'The Service of Venus and Mars': DE VITRY: *Gratissima virginis; Vos quie admiramini; Gaude gloriosa; Contratenor.* DES MOLINS: *De ce que fol pense.* PYCARD: *Gloria.* POWER: *Sanctus.* LEBERTOUL: *Las, que me demanderoye.* PYRAMOUR: *Quam pulchra es.* DUNSTABLE: *Speciosa facta es.* SOURSBY: *Sanctus.* LOQUEVILLE: *Je vous pri que j'aye un baysier.* ANON.: *Singularis laudis digna; De ce fol, pense. Lullay, lullay; There is no rose; Le gay playsir; Le grant pleyser; Agincourt carol.*
*** Hyp. Dig. CDA 66283 [id.].

The subtitle of this collection is '*Music for the Knights of the Garter, 1340–1440*'; few readers will recognize many of the names in the list of composers above. But the music itself is fascinating and the performances bring it to life with extraordinary projection and vitality. The recording too is first class, and this imaginatively chosen programme deservedly won the 1988 *Gramophone* award for Early Music. Readers interested in trying medieval repertoire could hardly do better than to start here.

'A song for Francesca': ANDREAS DE FLORENTINA: *Astio non mori mai. Per la ver'onesta.* JOHANNES DE FLORENTINA: *Quando la stella.* LANDINI: *Ochi dolenti mie. Per seguir la speranca.* ANON.: *Quando i oselli canta; Constantia; Amor mi fa cantar a la Francesca; Non na el so amante.* DUFAY: *Quel fronte signorille in paradiso.* RICHARD DE LOQUEVILLE: *Puisquie je suy amoureux; Pour mesdisans ne pour leur faulx parler; Qui ne veroit que vos deulx yeulx.* HUGO DE LATINS: *Plaindre m'estuet.* HAUCOURT: *Je demande ma bienvenue.* GROSSIN: *Va t'ent souspir.* ANON.: *O regina seculi; Reparatrix Maria; Confort d'amours.*
*** Hyp. Dig. CDA 66286 [id.].

The title, '*A Song for Francesca*', refers not only to the fourteenth-century French items here, but to the fact that the Italians too tended to be influenced by French style. More specifically, the collection is a well-deserved tribute to Francesca MacManus, selfless worker on behalf of many musicians, not least as manager of Gothic Voices. The variety of expression and mood in these songs, ballatas and madrigals is astonishing, some of them amazingly complex. The Hyperion recording is a model of its kind, presenting this long-neglected music most seductively in a warm but clear setting.

'The marriage of Heaven & Hell' (Anonymous motets, songs and polyphony from 13th-century France). Also: BLONDEL DE NESLE: *En tous tans que vente bise.* MUSET: *Trop volontiers chanteroie.* BERNART DE VENTADORN: *Can vei la lauzeta mover.* GAUTIER DE DARGIES: *Autre que je laureta mover.*
☞ *** Hyp. Dig. CDA 66423 [id.].

The title of this collection dramatically overstates the problem of the medieval Church with its conflicting secular influences. Music was universal and the repertoire of the *trouvère* had a considerable melodic influence on the polyphonic motets used by the Church, though actual quotation was very rare. Nevertheless, on occasion, vulgar associations in a vocal line could ensue and the clergy tore their hair. It all eventually led to the Council of Trent when, the story goes, the purity of Palestrina's contrapuntal serenity saved the day. Certainly medieval church music was robust and full of character, but here one is also struck by its complexity and intensity. The performances have a remarkable feeling of authenticity, and the background is admirably documented.

'*Music for the Lion-hearted King*' (Music to mark the 800th anniversary of the coronation of Richard I): ANON.: *Mundus vergens; Noves miles sequitur; Anglia planctus itera; In occasu sideris.* BRULE: *A la douçour de la bele saison; Etas auri reditu; Pange melos lacrimosum; Vetus abit littera; Hac in anni ianua.* LI CHASTELAIN DE COUCI: *Li nouviauz tanz; Soi sub nube latuit.* BLONDEL DE NESLE: *L'amours dont sui espris; Ma joie me semont; Purgator criminum; Ver pacis apperit; Latex silice.* ☞ *** Hyp. Dig. CDA 66336 [id.].

Partly because of the intensity, partly because of the imaginative variety of the choral response, all this twelfth-century music communicates readily, even though its comparatively primitive style could easily lead to boredom. The performances are polished but vital, and there is excellent documentation to lead the listener on. This may be a specialist record, but it could hardly be better presented.

'*The Medieval romantics*' (French songs and motets, 1340–1440): ANON: *Quiconques veut; Je languis d'amere mort; Quant voi le douz tanz; Plus bele que flors; Degentis vita; Mais qu'ilvous viegne.* SOLAGE: *Joieux de cuer.* DE PORTA: *Alma polis religio.* MACHAUT: *C'est force; Tant doucement; Comment qu'a moy lonteinne.* TENORISTA: *Sofrir m'estuet.* SENLECHES: *En ce gracieux temps.* DUFAY: *Je requier a tous; Las, que feray.* VELUT: *Je voel servir.* LYMBURGIA: *Tota pulchra es.* ☞ *** Hyp. Dig. CDA 66463 [id.].

Machaut (fourteenth century) and Dufay (fifteenth) are names which have now become individually established. Dufay was master of the secular song-form called the 'virelais' (opening with a refrain, which then followed each verse) and Machaut was one of the first (if not *the* first) composers to set the Ordinary of the Mass; he too wrote chansons and virelais. But of course there is also much music here by other (unknown) composers and our old friend, Anon. The virelais are sung unaccompanied. Sometimes there are vocal melismas (extra parts without words) set against the textual line. So this collection represents the medieval blossoming of songs and part-songs alongside the motets, for secular and sacred never really grew apart. As usual, the Gothic Voices perform this repertoire with skill and confidence and lots of character, and the splendid documentation puts the listener fully in the historical picture.

'*Lancaster and Valois*' (French and English music, 1350–1420): MACHAUT: *Donnez, signeurs; Quand je ne voy; Riches d'amour; Pas de tor en thies pais.* SOLAGE: *Tres gentil cuer.* PYCARD: *Credo.* STURGEON: *Salve mater domini.* FONTEYNS: *Regail ex progenie.* CESARIS: *Mon seul voloir; Se vous scaviez, ma tres douce maistresse.* BAUDE CORDIER: *Ce jour de l'an.* ANON.: *Sanctus; Soit tart, tempre, main ou soir; Je vueil vivre au plaisir d'amours; Puis qu'autrement ne puis avoir; Le ior; Avrai je ja de ma dame confort?.* ☞ *** Hyp. Dig. CDA 66588 [id.].

This stimulating series has always been essentially experimental, for we do not know just how unaccompanied medieval voices were balanced or how many were used. In the documentation with this record, Christopher Page suggests that on this disc he feels he has the internal balance just about right, and the vocal mix varies, sometimes led by a female voice, sometimes by a male. More Machaut here, some slightly later French settings, and the usual balance between sacred and secular. Everything sounds vital and alive.

'*The study of love*' (French songs and motets of the 14th century): ANON.: *Pour vous servir; Puis que l'aloe ne fine; Jour a jour la vie; Combien que j'aye; Marticius qui fu; Renouveler me feist; Fist on dame; Il me convient guerpir; Le ior; En la maison Dedalus; Combien que j'aye; Le grant biauté; En esperant; Ay las! quant je pans.* MACHAUT: *Dame, je suis cilz – Fin cuers; Trop plus – Biauté paree – Je ne suis; Tres bonne et belle; Se mesdisans; Dame, je vueil endurer.* SOLAGE: *Le basile.* PYCARD: *Gloria.* ☞ *** Hyp. Dig. CDA 66619 [id.].

The Gothic Voices' exploration is moving sideways rather than forward, for Machaut is still with us. The present collection of settings demonstrates the medieval literary and poetic understanding of 'love' – romantic and spiritual. The anonymous examples are often as stimulating as any of the songs and motets here, and the Pycard *Gloria* is obviously included to remind us again that church music is about the love of God. This and the previous three CDs should be approached with some caution, starting perhaps with '*The Medieval romantics*'.

'*The voice in the garden*' (Spanish songs and motets, 1480–1530): JUAN DEL ENCINA: *Mi libertad; Los sospiros no sosiegan; Triste España sin ventura.* LUIS DE NARVAEZ: *Fantasias;* (after) *Paseávase el rey Moro.* FRANCISCO DE PENALOSA: *Precor te, Domine; Ne reminiscaris, Domine; Por las sierras de*

Madrid; Sancta Maria. JULIUS DE MODENA: *Tiento.* PALERO (after): *Paseávase el rey Moro.*
ENRIQUE: *Mi querer tanto vos quiere.* LUIS MILAN: *Fantasias Nos. 10; 12; 18.* GABRIEL: *La Bella
Malmaridada; Yo creo que n'os dió Dios.* ANON.: *Dentro en el vergel; Harto de tanta porfía; Entra
Mayo y sale Abril; Dindirin; Ave, Virgo, gratia plena; A la villa voy; Pasa el agoa.*
☞ *** Hyp. Dig. CDA 66653 [id.].

Here the Gothic Voices travel to Spain and take with them Christopher Wilson (vihuela) and
Andrew-Lawrence King (harp). Their earlier concerts have included instrumental items (kept separate
from the vocal music) and here the same policy is followed, but the mix of sacred, secular and
instrumental is more exotic than usual. As throughout this series, the recording is of the highest
quality.

Hvorostovsky, Dmitri (bass)

'Songs and dances of death' (Russian songs and arias; with Kirov O, St Petersburg, Gergiev):
MUSSORGSKY: *Songs and dances of death.* Arias from: RIMSKY-KORSAKOV: *Sadko; Kashei the
Immortal; The Snow Maiden; The Tsar's Bride.* BORODIN: *Prince Igor.* RUBINSTEIN: *The Demon;
Nero.* RACHMANINOV: *Aleko.*
☞ *** Ph. Dig. 438 872-2; *438 872-4* [id.].

This magnificent collection, which displays the dark, tangy baritone of Hvorostovsky superbly, takes
its title from the culminating items, Mussorgsky's *Songs and dances of Death,* here given in their
orchestral form. Only occasionally is the firm projection of the beautiful voice marred by a
roughening under pressure. Otherwise this is among the finest recital discs of its kind, with fascinating
rarities like the Demon's arias from Rubinstein's opera, *The Demon,* and arias from four Rimsky-
Korsakov operas, as well as the Prince's magnificent aria from Borodin's *Prince Igor.* Excellent sound
and warm, intense accompaniments.

Kanawa, Dame Kiri Te (soprano)

'Classics': Arias from: MOZART: *Die Entführung aus dem Serail; Idomeneo; Don Giovanni; Vesperae
solennes de Confessore; Die Zauberflöte; Exsultate, jubilate.* HANDEL: *Samson.* GOUNOD: *Messe
solennelle de Saint Cécile; Faust.* SCHUBERT: *Ave Maria.* J. STRAUSS Jnr: *Die Fledermaus.*
☞ (M) *** Ph. Dig. 434 725-2 [id.].

Admirers of Dame Kiri will find this a pretty good sampler of her diverse talents, including as it does
Mozart's *Exsultate jubilate* with its famous *Alleluia* and the similarly beautiful *Laudate dominum* from
the *Solemn Vespers,* plus Handel's brilliant *Let the bright seraphim.* An excellent 74-minute selection
from recordings made over two decades from the early 1970s onwards. The notes, however,
concentrate on the singer rather than the music.

King's College, Cambridge, Choir, Philip Ledger

'Festival of lessons and carols' (1979) includes: TRAD.: *Once in Royal David's city; Sussex carol;
Joseph and Mary; A maiden most gentle; Chester carol; Angels, from the realms of glory.* HANDEL:
Resonet in laudibus. ORD: *Adam lay ybounden.* GRUBER: *Stille Nacht.* MATHIAS: *A babe is born.*
WADE: *O come all ye faithful.* MENDELSSOHN: *Hark! the herald angels sing.*
(M) *** EMI CDM7 63180-2 [id.]; *EG 763180-4.*

This most recent version on record of the annual King's College ceremony has the benefit of modern
recording, even more atmospheric than before. Under Philip Ledger the famous choir keeps its
beauty of tone and incisive attack. The opening processional, *Once in Royal David's city,* is even more
effective heard against the background quiet of CD, and this remains a unique blend of liturgy and
music.

King's College, Cambridge, Choir, Sir David Willcocks

'A Festival of Lessons and carols' (recorded live in the Chapel, Christmas Eve 1958, with Simon
Preston, organ): *Once in Royal David's City.* BACH: *Christmas Oratorio: Invitatory.* Lesson I. *Adam
lay ybounden.* Lesson II. *I saw three ships.* Lesson III. *Gabriel's message. God rest you merry,*

gentlemen; Sussex carol. Lesson IV. *In dulci jubilo.* Lesson V. *Away in a manger; While shepherd's watched.* Lesson. VI. *O come, all ye faithful.* Lesson VII. *Hark! the herald angels sing.*
☞ (B) *** Decca 436 646-2; *436 646-4.*

It was the early mono recording of the King's Christmas Eve service of lessons and carols which – together with the BBC recording of Dylan Thomas's *Under Milk Wood* – brought initial success to the Argo label before it became part of the Decca group. With the coming of stereo the Fesival was re-recorded to provide what only stereo can provide: an imaginary seat in the Chapel. The present CD offers that early stereo venture and shows the remarkable success with which the Argo engineers captured the magic of the chapel acoustic – the opening processional remains demonstration-worthy today. Seven of the nine lessons are interspersed with the favourite carols to remind us indelibly what Christmas is really about.

'Carols from King's': TRAD., arr. WILLCOCKS: *On Christmas night; Tomorrow shall be my dancing day; Cherry tree carol; The Lord at first; A Child is born in Bethlehem; While shepherds watched.* TRAD., arr. VAUGHAN WILLIAMS: *And all in the morning.* CORNELIUS: *Three Kings.* EBERLING: *All my heart this night rejoices.* GRUBER: *Silent night* (arr. Willcocks). Trad. Italian, arr. WOOD: *Hail, blessed Mary.* TRAD., arr. SULLIVAN: *It came upon the midnight clear.* Trad. French, arr. WILLCOCKS: *Ding dong! merrily.* Trad. Basque, arr. PETTMAN: *I saw a maiden.* DARKE: *In the bleak midwinter.* Trad. German: *Mary walked through a wood of thorn.* BAINTON: *A Babe is born I wys.* PRAETORIUS: *Psallite unigenito.*
(B) *** CfP CD-CFP 4586; *TC-CFP 4586* [CDB 67356].

This recital was planned and recorded as a whole in 1969. The programme has an attractive lyrical flavour, with plenty of delightful, unfamiliar carols to add spice to favourites like *Tomorrow shall be my dancing day* and *In the bleak midwinter*, which sound memorably fresh. The arrangements are for the most part straightforward, with added imaginative touches to charm the ear, like the decorative organ 'descant' which embroiders *Ding dong! merrily on high*. The King's intimacy gives much pleasure here, yet the disc ends with a fine, robust version of *While shepherds watched*. Most rewarding and a real bargain.

King's College, Cambridge, Choir, Willcocks or Philip Ledger

'Christmas carols from King's College': GAUNTLETT: *Once in Royal David's city.* TRAD., arr. VAUGHAN WILLIAMS: *O little town of Bethlehem.* TRAD., arr. STAINER: *The first nowell.* TRAD., arr. LEDGER: *I saw three ships.* TRAD. German, arr. HOLST: *Personent hodie.* TERRY: *Myn Lyking.* HOWELLS: *A spotless rose.* KIRKPATRICK: *Away in a manger.* HADLEY: *I sing of a maiden.* TRAD. French, arr. WILLCOCKS: *O come, o come Emmanuel.* TRAD. arr. WILLCOCKS: *While shepherds watched; On Christmas night.* arr. WOODWARD: *Up! Good Christian folk and listen.* DARKE: *In the bleak midwinter.* GRUBER: *Silent night.* TRAD. arr. WALFORD DAVIES: *The holly and the ivy.* TRAD., arr. SULLIVAN: *It came upon the midnight clear.* CORNELIUS: *Three kings.* SCHEIDT: *A Child is born in Bethlehem.* TRAD. German, arr. PEARSALL: *In dulci jubilo.* WADE: *O come, all ye faithful.* MENDELSSOHN: *Hark! the herald angels sing.*
(M) *** EMI CDM7 63179-2 [id.]; *EG 763179-4.*

With 71 minutes of music and 22 carols included, this collection, covering the regimes of both Sir David Willcocks and Philip Ledger, could hardly be bettered as a representative sampler of the King's tradition. Opening with the famous processional of *Once in Royal David's city*, to which Willcocks contributes a descant (as he also does in *While shepherds watched*), the programme is wide-ranging in its historical sources, from the fourteenth century to the present day, while the arrangements feature many famous musicians. The recordings were made between 1969 and 1976, and the CD transfers are first class. The two closing carols, featuring the Philip Jones Brass Ensemble, are made particularly resplendent.

Kirkby, Emma (soprano)

'Madrigals and wedding songs for Diana' (with David Thomas, bass, Consort of Musicke, Rooley): BENNET: *All creatures now are merry-minded.* CAMPION: *Now hath Flora robbed her bowers; Move now measured sound; Woo her and win her.* LUPO: *Shows and nightly revels; Time that leads the fatal round.* GILES: *Triumph now with joy and mirth.* CAVENDISH: *Come, gentle swains.* DOWLAND: *Welcome, black night . . . Cease these false sports.* WEELKES: *Hark! all ye lovely saints; As Vesta was.*

WILBYE: *Lady Oriana.* EAST: *Hence stars! too dim of light; You meaner beauties.* LANIER: *Bring away this sacred tree; The Marigold; Mark how the blushful morn.* COPERARIO: *Go, happy man; While dancing rests; Come ashore, merry mates.* E. GIBBONS: *Long live fair Oriana.*
*** Hyp. CDA 66019 [id.].

This wholly delightful anthology celebrates early royal occasions, aristocratic weddings, and in its choice of Elizabethan madrigals skilfully balances praise of the Virgin Queen with a less ambivalent attitude to nuptial delights. Emma Kirkby is at her freshest and most captivating, and David Thomas, if not quite her match, makes an admirable contribution. Accompaniments are stylish and well balanced, and the recording is altogether first rate.

'*O tuneful voice*' (with Rufus Müller, Timothy Roberts (fortepiano or harpsichord), Frances Kelley (harp)): HAYDN: *O tuneful voice; She never told her love; Sailor's song.* Samuel ARNOLD: *Elegy.* PINTO: *Invocation to Nature; A Shepherd lov'd a nymph so fair; From thee, Eliza, I must go; Eloisa to Abelard; Minuet in A.* STORACE: *The curfew.* LINLEY THE ELDER: *The lark sings high in the cornfield; Think not, my love.* JACKSON: *The day that saw thy beauty rise; Time has not thinn'd my flowing hair.* SHIELD: *Ye balmy breezes, gently blow; Hope and love;' 'Tis only no harm to know it, you know.* CARDON: *Variations on 'Ah vous dirai-je, maman'.* HOOK: *The emigrant.* SALOMON: *Go, lovely rose; Why still before these streaming eyes; O tuneful voice.*
☞ *** Hyp. Dig. CDA 66497.

This programme is centred in eighteenth-century England, although Haydn could be included because of his London visits. Indeed Salomon, his impresario, is featured here as a composer, and a very able one, too; but it is Haydn's comparatively rare song which gives the CD its title and shows Emma Kirkby on top form, just as charming but with greater depth of expression than in her companion Hyperion and Oiseau-Lyre collections, the latter having the same geographical basis but offering repertoire from an earlier period. Kirkby sings like a lark in the cornfield, and Rufus Müller joins her in some duets by William Jackson and also shares the solo numbers. There are innocently rustic songs from William Shield in which each artist participates, and much else besides: this 74-minute programme has a wide range of mood and style.

'*The Lady Musick*': (with Anthony Rooley, lute): EDWARDS: *Where gryping griefs.* CAMPION: *Come let us sound; When to her lute.* DOWLAND: *I saw my Lady weep; In this trembling shadow.* DANYEL: *Like as the lute delights.* PILKINGTON: *Come all ye; Musick deare sollace; Rest sweet Nimph.* MORLEY: *I saw my Ladye weeping.* JONES: *If in this flesh.* BARTLETT: *Sweete birdes deprive us never.*
☞ **(*) O-L 425 892-2 [id.].

This excellent compilation of Elizabethan repertoire first appeared on LP in 1979 when Emma Kirkby's voice and style was pristine. She sings with delightful freshness, and if you enjoy this kind of vocal purity the programme here is artfully chosen and this fine singer certainly does not lack artistic imagination in its presentation. But such a 53-minute collection should have been reissued at mid-price.

'*A Portrait*' (with AAM, Hogwood): HANDEL: *Disseratevi, o porte d'Averno; Gentle Morpheus, son of night.* PURCELL: *Bess of bedlam; From rosie bow'rs.* ARNE: *Where the bee sucks there lurk I; Rise, Glory, rise.* DOWLAND: *I saw the lady weepe.* D'INDIA: *Odi quel rosignuolo.* TROMBONCINO: *Se ben hor non scopro il foco.* VIVALDI: *Passo di pena in pena.* J. S. BACH: *Ei! wie schmeckt der Coffee süsse.* HAYDN: *With verdure clad.* MOZART: *Laudate Dominum; Exsultate, jubilate, K.165.*
☞ (M) *** O-L Dig. 443 200-2 [id.].

Emma Kirkby with her bright, boyish treble-like tone excites strong opinions both ways, but we are on the side of the angels. Certainly admirers of her style in early and baroque music will delight in this well-chosen 76-minute sampler of her work. L'Oiseau-Lyre have altered and expanded the orginal issue to make the programme more enticingly enterprising. There is now only one Vivaldi item, and the excerpt from Handel's *Messiah* has been replaced by the remarkable Angel's aria, *Disserratevi, o porte d'Averno*, from Part I of *La Resurrezione* (calling on the gates of the Underworld to be unbarred to yield to God's glory). It opens with joyous baroque trumpets and oboes, and Emma Kirby shows with her florid vocal line that anything they can do, she can do better. This is rather effectively followed by Purcell's melancholy mad song, *Bess of Bedlam*, and the equally touching *From rosie bow'rs*. Music by Arne lightens the mood and later there are excerpts from Bach's *Coffee cantata* and popular solos by Haydn and Mozart. This recital is as well planned as it is enjoyable, and Hogwood ensures that accompaniments are consistently fresh and stylish. First-class sound.

Kirkby, Emma and Judith Nelson (sopranos)

'Duetti da camera': NOTARI: Intenerite voi, lagrime mie. D'INDIA: Alla guerra d'amore; La Virtù; La mia Filli crudel. VALENTINI: Vanne, o carta amorosa. FRESCOBALDI: Maddelena alla Croce. GRANDI: Spine care e soavi. FONTEI: Fortunato cantore. ROVETTA: Chi vuol haver felice e lieto il core. MONTEVERDI: O come sei gentile. SABBATINI: Udite, o selve; Fulmina de la bocca.
☞ *** O-L 436 861-2 [id.].

The repertoire here is exceedingly rare and is expertly and appealingly presented. Whether in the touching Intenerte voi, lagrime mie of Notari, with its melting overlapping phrases, or in the more florid and diverse Fontunato cantore of Fontei, these two fine artists match their voices with extraordinary precision and skill, to say nothing of lyrical beauty. They sing as one, yet the subtle contrast of colour always tickles the ear. Almost every item is very rewarding, but one must single out D'India's Alla guerra d'amore, which makes a fine contrast with the Notari duet, Monteverdi's delightful O comme sei gentile (again needing real bravura as well as tonal beauty), Frescobaldi's Maddelena alla Croce and the two delightful closing Sabbatini songs. The accompaniments are discreetly and stylishly authentic, as one would expect with Anthony Rooley in charge, and the CD is admirably documented. The sound is wholly natural and the CD transfer immaculate.

Lott, Felicity (soprano), Graham Johnson (piano)

Mélodies on Victor Hugo poems: GOUNOD: Sérénade. BIZET: Feuilles d'album: Guitare. Adieux de l'hôtesse arabe. LALO: Guitare. DELIBES: Eclogue. FRANCK: S'il est un charmant gazon. FAURE: L'absent; Le papillon et la fleur; Puisqu'ici bas. WAGNER: L'attente. LISZT: O quand je dors; Comment, disaint-ils. SAINT-SAENS: Soirée en mer; La fiancée du timbalier. M. V. WHITE: Chantez, chantez jeune inspirée. HAHN: Si mes vers avaient des ailes; Rêverie.
(B) *** HM HMA 901138 [id.].

Felicity Lott's collection of Hugo settings relies mainly on sweet and charming songs, freshly and unsentimentally done, with Graham Johnson an ideally sympathetic accompanist. The recital is then given welcome stiffening with fine songs by Wagner and Liszt, as well as two by Saint-Saëns that have a bite worthy of Berlioz. It makes a headily enjoyable cocktail. Now reissued in the Musique d'Abord series, this is a bargain not to be missed.

Ludwig, Christa (mezzo-soprano)

'The Art of Christa Ludwig' (with Gerald Moore or Geoffrey Parsons (piano) & (i) Herbert Downes (viola); (ii) Philh. O, Klemperer; (iii) Berlin SO, Stein or Forster): BRAHMS: Sapphische Ode; Liebestreu; Der Schmied; Die Mainacht. 8 Zigeunerlieder. 4 Deutsche Volkslieder: Och mod'r ich well en Ding han!; We kumm ich dann de Pooz erenn?; In stiller Nacht; Schwesterlein. Lieder: Dein blaues Auge; Von ewiger Liebe; Das Mädchen spricht; O wüsst ich doch; Wie Melodien zieht es mir; Mädchenlied; Vergebliches Ständchen; Der Tod, das ist die kühle Nacht; Auf dem See; Deldeinsamkeit; Immer leiser word mein Schlummer; Ständchen; Gestillte Sehnsucht; (i) Geistliches Wiegenlied. MAHLER: Hans und Grete; Frühlingsmorgen; Des Knaben Wunderhorn: Ich ging mit Lust durch einen grünen Wald; Woe die schönen Trompeten blasen; Der Schildwache Nachtlied; Um schlimme Kinder; Das irdische Leben; Wer hat dies Liedlein erdacht; Lob des hohen Verstandes;Des Antonius von Padua Fischpredigt; Rheinlegendchen. Rückert Lieder: Ich atmet' einen linden Duft; Liebst du um Schönheit; Um Mitternacht; Ich bin der Welt abhanden gekommen. SCHUMANN: Frauenliebe und -Leben, Op. 42. REGER: Der Brief; Waldeinsamkeit. SCHUBERT: Die Allmacht; Fischerweise; An die Musik; Der Musensohn; Ganymed; Auf dem Wasser zu singen; Ave Maria; Die Forelle; Gretchen am Spinnrade; Frühlingsglaube; Der Tod und das Mädchen; Lachen und Weinen; Litanei auf das Fest Aller Seelen; Erlkönig; Der Hirt auf dem Felsen. WOLF: Gesang Weylas; Auf einer Wanderung. R. STRAUSS: Die Nacht; Allerseelen; Schlechtes Wetter. RAVEL: 3 Chansons madécasses. SAINT-SAENS: Une flûte invisible. RACHMANINOV: Chanson géorgienne; Moisson de tristesse. ROSSINI: La regata veneziana (3 canzonettas). (ii) WAGNER: Wesendonk Lieder. (iii) HANDEL: Giulio Cesare: Cleopatra's aria. BACH: St John Passion: Aria: Es ist vollbracht!. (ii) WAGNER: Tristan und Isolde: Mild und leise.
☞ (M) *** EMI CMS7 64074-2 (4).

Christa Ludwig is an extraordinarily versatile artist with a ravishing voice, readily matched by fine intelligence and natural musical sensitivity to place her among the special singers of our time, including De los Angeles and Schwarzkopf (to name two from the same EMI stable). She was as impressive in Schubert as she was in Strauss and Brahms, and her Mahler is very special indeed. This compensates for the below-par Schumann song-cycle. Her voice took naturally to the microphone, so this four-disc set is another source of infinite musical pleasure to be snapped up quickly before it disappears. The recordings come from the 1950s and 1960s and are very well transferred indeed.

McCormack, John (tenor)

'Songs of my heart': TRAD.: *The garden where the praties grow; Terence's farewell to Kathleen; Believe me if all those endearing young charms; The star of the County Down; Oft in the stilly night; The meeting of the waters; The Bard of Armagh; Down by the Salley Gardens; She moved thro' the fair; The green bushes.* BALFE: *The harp that once through Tara's halls.* ROECKEL: *The green isle of Erin.* SCHNEIDER: *O Mary dear.* LAMBERT: *She is far from the land.* HAYNES: *Off to Philadelphia.* MOLLOY: *The Kerry dance; Bantry Bay.* MARSHALL: *I hear you calling me.* E. PURCELL: *Passing by.* WOODFORD-FINDEN: *Kashmiri song.* CLUTSAM: *I know of two bright eyes.* FOSTER: *Jeannie with the light brown hair; Sweetly she sleeps, my Alice fair.*
☞ (M) (***) EMI mono CDM7 64654-2 [id.]; *EG 764654-4.*

In Irish repertoire like *The star of the County Down* McCormack is irresistible, but in lighter concert songs he could also spin the utmost magic. *Down by the Salley Gardens* and Stephen Foster's *Jeannie with the light brown hair* are superb examples, while in a ballad like *I hear you calling me* (an early pre-electric recording from 1908) the golden bloom of the vocal timbre combining with an artless line brings a ravishing frisson on the closing pianissimo. Many of the accompaniments are by Gerald Moore, who proves a splendid partner. Occasionally there is a hint of unsteadiness in the sustained *piano* tone, but otherwise no apology need be made for the recorded sound which is first class, while the lack of 78-r.p.m. background noise is remarkable.

Monteverdi Choir, English Baroque Soloists, Gardiner

'Sacred choral music': D. SCARLATTI: *Stabat Mater.* CAVALLI: *Salve regina.* GESUALDO: *Ave, dulcissima Maria.* CLEMENT: *O Maria vernana rosa.*
*** Erato/Warner Dig. 2292 45219-2 [id.].

This collection is centred round Domenico Scarlatti's *Stabat Mater*, which is praised in the Composer section. The shorter works which fill out this collection are no less worthwhile, notably the rewarding Gesualdo motet from the *Sacrae cantiones*, whose remarkably expressive opening has few precedents in its harmonic eloquence, and another Marian motet by Jacques Clément, better known as Clemens non Papa. The recording is very good indeed without being in the demonstration bracket.

'Christmas in Venice': Giovanni GABRIELI: *Canzona: Sol sol la sol; Audite principes; Angelus ad pastores; Quem vidistis, pastores?; Salvator noster; Sonata pian' e forte; O magnum mysterium.* BASSANO: *Hodie Christus natus est.* MONTEVERDI: *Exultent caeli. Vespers: Magnificat.*
☞ (M) *** Decca 436 285-2 [id.].

A welcome for the reissue of this famous collection, first published in 1972; on the CD, the *Magnificat* from Monteverdi's *Vespers* has been added. Although one could not imagine a more welcome Christmas present, it would be a pity if this concert were relegated to a purely seasonal category, for the record is one to be enjoyed the year through. The insert-note draws a picture of Christmas being celebrated in St Mark's in Venice at the beginning of the seventeenth century, with the church ablaze with the light of more than a thousand candles, plus sixty huge torches and silver lamps. The acoustic chosen for this recording has been beautifully managed. The rich, sonorous dignity of Gabrieli's *Sonata pian'e forte* sounds resplendent, and in the choral numbers the vocal and instrumental blend is expert. The most impressive work here (apart from the *Magnificat*) is Gabrieli's glorious *Quem vidistis pastores?*; Monteverdi's *Exultent caeli* is shorter, but one is again amazed by the range of expressive contrast, from the exultant opening *Let the heavens rejoice* to the magically simple setting of the phrase *O Maria*, a moment of great beauty each time it recurs. Then there is Gabrieli's fine *Salvator noster*, a motet for three five-part choirs, jubilantly rejoicing at the birth of Christ. One especially attractive feature of Gabrieli's writing is his setting of the word *Alleluia* used to close each of his pieces; the jauntiness of the style is fresh and exhilarating. The CD transfer is admirable.

'*Music of the Chapels Royal of England*': PURCELL: Motet: *Jehova, quam multi sunt hostes mei;* Verse anthem: *My beloved spake;* Full anthems: *O God, Thou has cast us out and scatter'd us abroad; Hear my prayer.* LOCKE: *How doth the city sit solitary.* BLOW: Motet: *Salvator Mundi.* Pelham HUMFREY: *Verse anthem: O Lord my God.*
☞ (M) *** Erato/Warner 2292 45987-2 [id.].

Pelham Humfrey (or Humphrey) studied abroad, and his complex and ambitious 13-minute verse anthem, *O Lord my God,* is the masterly highlight of this fine collection of music centred round the Chapel Royal. It is set in an expressive style very much like Italian opera. Thus a devotional text, using soloists most tellingly, is almost un-English in its passionate supplication for God's help which has the kind of pathos Purcell expressed in Dido's famous lament. The Purcell anthems are splendid, of course (notably the succinct *Hear my prayer,* which is wonderfully powerful and concentrated), but are comparatively well known. What is also valuable in this impressive collection is the glorious anthem of Matthew Locke, *How doth the city sit solitary* and John Blow's very moving motet, *Salvator Mundi,* in which he, too, married Italian and English expressive styles and conveyed great depth of feeling. John Eliot Gardiner paces all this music unerringly, and the singing of the English Baroque Soloists – whether as a choral group or individually – is well up to standard. The expansive recording, made in the London Henry Wood Hall, is spacious and full. Highly recommended: a splendid collection celebrating a very special period in the history of Englsih music.

New College, Oxford, Choir, Higginbottom

'*Carols from New College*': *O come all ye faithful; The angel Gabriel; Ding dong merrily on high; The holly and the ivy; I wonder as I wander; Sussex carol; This is the truth; A Virgin most pure; Rocking carol; Once in Royal David's city.* ORD: *Adam lay y-bounden.* BENNETT: *Out of your sleep.* HOWELLS: *A spotless rose; Here is the litle door.* DARKE: *In the bleak midwinter.* MATHIAS: *A babe is born; Wassail carol.* WISHART: *Alleluya, a new work is come on hand.* LEIGHTON: *Lully, lulla, thou little tiny child.* JOUBERT: *There is no rose of such virtue.*
*** CRD CRD 3443; *CRDC 4443* [id.].

A beautiful Christmas record, the mood essentially serene and reflective. Both the Mathias settings are memorable and spark a lively response from the choir; Howells' *Here is the little door* is matched by Wishart's *Alleluya* and Kenneth Leighton's *Lully, lulla, thou little tiny child* in memorability. Fifteen of the twenty-one items here are sung unaccompanied, to maximum effect. The recording acoustic seems ideal and the balance is first class. The documentation, however, consists of just a list of titles and sources – and the CD (using the unedited artwork from the LP) lists them as being divided on to side one and side two!

'*O Sing unto the Lord*' (with Instrumental Ens. led by Roy Goodman): VAUGHAN WILLIAMS: *O Clap your hands* (motet). STANFORD: *Magnificat and Nunc dimittis in G.* TAVERNER: *Mater Christi* (motet). PURCELL: *O Sing unto the Lord* (Verse anthem). BAINTON: *And I saw a new heaven.* BRITTEN: *Missa brevis.* MONTEVERDI: *Beatus vir.* HARVEY: *I love the Lord.*
⊛ *** Proudsound PROUCD 114 02; *PROU 114* [id.].

It is difficult to conceive of a better or more rewarding collection of (mainly British) church music than this, marvellously sung by this fine choir of 16 trebles and 12 men. The recording, made in New College Chapel, is ideally balanced, very real indeed, and offers the most beautiful choral textures, used over the widest range of dynamic. The programme opens quite spectacularly with Vaughan Williams's brief but ambitious setting of Psalm 47 for double chorus, brass, percussion and organ (a demonstration item if ever there was one) and continues with Stanford's inspired *Magnificat and Nunc dimittis in G.* Then the programme ranges from Taverner's fine motet, *Mater Christi,* written some 400 years earlier, to Harvey's rich modern setting of Psalm 16, with its satisfyingly pungent dissonances.

New London Consort, Philip Pickett

'*The Pilgrimage to Santiago*' (21 cantigas from the collection of King Alfonso el Sabio).
*** O-L Dig. 433 148-2 (2) [id.].

Philip Pickett and his brilliant team of singers and players present what is described as 'a musical journey along the medieval pilgrim road to the shrine of St James at Santiago de Compostela'. The 21 pieces, lasting over two hours, together provide a mosaic of astonishing richness and vigour, directly related to the four main pilgrim routes to the shrine, via Navarre, Castille, Leon and Galicia. Pickett argues the importance of the Islamic influence in Spain, with bells and percussion often added to the fiddles, lutes, tabors and other early instruments. So the long opening cantiga, *Quen a virgen ben servira*, begins with an instrumental introduction, where (echoing Islamic examples) the players attract attention with tuning-up and flourishes, before the singing begins. The main cantiga then punctuates the 12 narrative stanzas sung by the solo soprano with a catchy refrain, *Those who serve the virgin well will go to paradise*. Standing out among the singers is the soprano, Catherine Bott, the soloist in most of the big cantigas, warm as well as pure-toned, negotiating the weird sliding portamentos that, following Islamic examples, decorate some of the vocal lines. Vivid sound, though the stereo spread of the chorus is limited.

'The Feast of Fools': 1st Vespers; Music from the Office; The drinking bout in the cathedral porch; Mass of the asses, drunkards and gamblers; 2nd Vespers; Ceremony of the Baculus; The banquet; Processional.
☞ *** O-L Dig. 433 194-2 [id.].

Philip Pickett and the New London Consort, inspired in their treatment of early music, present an invigorating, ear-catching sequence drawn from the roistering parodies of church practice that in medieval times were celebrated between Christmas and Epiphany. In modern terms the jokes may be heavy-handed, whether involving vestry humour, drunken cavortings or animal-imitations (as in the *Kyrie* of the *Asses*, *'Hinhan Eleison'*), but the wildness of much of the music is infectious, performed here with uninhibited joy. Carl Orff's *Carmina Burana* (inspired from similar Latin sources) hardly outshines these originals.

Oxford Camerata, Jeremy Summerly

'Lamentations': WHITE: *Lamentations.* TALLIS: *Lamentations, Sets I & II.* PALESTRINA: *Lesson I for Maundy Thursday.* LASSUS: *Lessons I & III for Maundy Thursday.* Estâvão DE BRITO: *Lesson I for Good Friday.*
☞ ⊛ (BB) *** Naxos Dig. 8.550572 [id.].

On the bargain Naxos label come nearly 70 minutes of sublime polyphony, beautifully sung by the fresh-toned Oxford Camerata under Jeremy Summerly. All these *Lamentations* (*Lessons* simply means collection of verses) are settings from the Old Testament book, *The Lamentations of Jeremiah*. They were intended for nocturnal use and are usually darkly intense in feeling. The English and Italian *Lamentations* have their own individuality, but the most striking of all is the *Good Friday Lesson* by the Portuguese composer, Estâvão de Brito. This is very direct and strong in feeling for, as the anonymous insert-note writer points out, Portugal was under Spanish subjugation at the time and de Brito effectively uses dissonance at the words *non est lex* ('there is no law') to assert his nationalistic defiance. The recorded sound is vividly beautiful within an ideal ambience.

Oxford Pro Musica Singers, Michael Smedley

20th-century sacred choral music: TAVENER: *Annunciation; Ikon of the Nativity; The Lamb; A Nativity; Today the Virgin; The Lord's prayer; Many years; Wedding prayer; He hath entered heaven; The acclamation.* PART: *Magnificat; Summa.* GORECKI: *Euntes Ibant; Totus tuus; Amen.*
☞ ⊛ *** Proudsound Dig. PROUCD 136 [id.].

This moving and very beautiful collection of sacred choral music gives us the heart to believe that the twentieth century is still producing great cathedral motets as inspired as almost anything produced over the last four centuries. The ten pieces by John Tavener – although written at different times over the last decade and a half – make a remarkably cohesive whole when heard in the sequence presented here. They are framed by the *Annunciation* which opens gently and ethereally with a quartet of solo voices placed in the distance and answered immediately and powerfully by the full choir, and the *Acclamation* which reaches a climax of great splendour. Like much of Tavener's choral writing, this closing piece uses Byzantine chant as its basis and soon develops parallel, organum-like harmonies, which create an ageless, medieval atmosphere. We have experienced this style already in *Today the Virgin* and the *Wedding prayer*, which opens sombrely but soon brings a wonderful radiance from the female voices at the words 'Grant them of the fruit of their bodies, fair children, concord of body and soul.' The haunting carol, *The Lamb*, is the most familiar of these works, but it is not more beautiful than Tavener's peaceful first setting of *The Lord's Prayer*, using the Aeolian mode, or the touchingly serene wedding greeting, *Many years*. The most ambitious setting of all is *He that hath entered Heaven*, which brings within its stillness and beauty the tinkling sounds of a set of suspended handbells, used very discreetly, until the treble line, released, soars rapturously. Arvo Pärt's *Magnificat* is more mellifluously static but undoubtedly eloquent, and it makes a positive statement of faith, as does the *Summa* (a setting of the Creed) with its lines flowing like the waves of the ocean). Górecki's *Euntes Ibant et Flebant* is a 12-part Psalm setting with phrases mystically repeated over a sustained pedal note, bringing some scrumptious dissonance. *Totus tuus* is a characteristic affirmation ('I am entirely yours, Mary, Mother of our Redeemer') with a recurring melodic line building to a great climax on '*Maria*' the tension falling back later on the words '*Mater mundi*'. Finally comes a similarly elliptical *Amen* that has much in common with Barber's *Adagio for strings*. Those who have enjoyed Górecki's *Third Symphony* will be equally at home in this highly sympathetic choral writing which Michael Smedley paces so unerringly. The whole programme is gloriously sung, and this well-rehearsed group of 32 singers sustains tension as movingly at pianissimo level as they do in the great arching climaxes. The dynamic range is wide and the very generous resonance of St Barnabas' Church, Oxford, adds atmosphere and beauty to the sound without clouding the focus.

Pears, Sir Peter (tenor), Julian Bream (lute)

Julian Bream Edition, Volume 19. *Elizabethan lute songs*: MORLEY: *Absence; It was a lover and his lass; Who is is?*. ROSSETER: *What then is love?; If she forsake me; When Laura smiles*. DOWLAND: *I saw my lady weep; Dear, if you change; Stay, Time; Weep you no more; Shall I sue?; Sweet, stay awhile; Can she excuse?; Come, heavy sleep; Wilt thou unkind, thus leave me?; Sorrow stay; The lowest trees have tops; Time's eldest son, Old Age; In darkness let me dwell; Say, love, if ever thou didst find*. FORD: *Come Phyllis; Fair, sweet, cruel*.
☞ (M) *** BMG/RCA 09026 61609-2 [id.].

This vintage collection was recorded between 1963 and 1969 when Pears was at the peak of his form. The Dowland songs are particularly fine, sung with Pears's usual blend of intelligence and lyrical feeling, their nostalgic melancholy tenderly caught. Excellent, vivid, well-balanced recording, with Bream's expert accompaniments well in the picture. Most refreshing.

Pro Cantione Antiqua, Bruno Turner

'*Ars Britannica*': Old Hall Manuscript: COOKE: *Alma proles*. DUNSTABLE: *Crux fidelis; O crux gloriosa; Gaude virgo*. FOREST: *Qualis est dilectus; Albanus roseo rutilat*. PYCARD: *Gloria*. DAMETT: *Salve porta paradisi*. POWER: *Credo*. CHIRBURY: *Agnus dei*. Madrigals: WEELKES: *Those sweet delightful lillies; Some men desire spouses; Come sirrah Jack ho!; Come, let's begin to revel't*. WARD: *Retire, my troubled soul; O my thoughts surcease*. MORLEY: *Hark, jolly shepherds; Die now, my heart; You black bright stars*. BYRD: *Come, woeful Orpheus*. TOMKINS: *O let me dye for true love; O yes, has any found a lad?*. WILBYE: *Lady, when I behold; As matchless beauty; Weep, o mine eyes*. PILKINGTON: *Care for my soul*. Lute songs: PILKINGTON: *Down-a-down*. DOWLAND: *A shepherd in a shade; Fine knacks for ladies; Where sin sore wounding; Sweet, stay awhile; Mr Dowland's midnight; Now, oh now I needs must part*. CAMPION: *Never weather-beaten sail; Jack and Jone; A secret love*. FORD: *Since first I saw; There is a lady*.
☞ (M) *** Teldec/Warner 2292 46004-2 (2) [id.].

On two mid-price CDs Bruno Turner directs his superb all-male vocal team (with the tenor, Ian Partridge, prominent) in one of the richest and most enjoyable collections available of Elizabethan madrigals and lute songs. As a prelude comes church music from the fifteenth-century Old Hall manuscript, covering such remarkable pre-Tudor composers as Pycard and Lionel Powers, as well as John Dunstable. The Elizabethan collection also covers the widest range of composers, including Byrd, Wilbye, Weelkes, Pilkington and the still-underappreciated John Ward. Recorded between 1977 and 1979, the sound is exceptionally full and well focused.

Rolfe Johnson, Anthony (tenor), David Willison (piano)

English songs: VAUGHAN WILLIAMS: *Songs of travel.* BUTTERWORTH: *A Shropshire Lad.* IRELAND: *The land of lost content.* GURNEY: *Down by the Salley Gardens; An Epitaph; Desire in spring; Black Stitchel.* WARLOCK: *My own country; Passing by; Pretty ring time.*
☞ (B) *** Pickwick PCD 1065; *CIMPC 1065* [id.].

It would be hard to design a better programme of twentieth-century English songs than this, providing one accepts the omission of Britten, and it a surprise to discover that this nearly-70-minutes-long programme derives from two (Polygram) Polydor LPs from the mid-1970s. At that time this label was not exactly famous for this kind of repertoire but there is hidden treasure here. The performances of the Vaughan Williams and Butterworth cycles are full of life and colour (and are splendidly accompanied), and it is especially good to have the far lesser-known Gurney songs. The recordings have transferred well. A bargain.

St George's Canzona, John Sothcott

Medieval songs and dances: *Lamento di Tristano; L'autrier m'iere levaz. 4 Estampies real; Edi beo thu hevene quene; Eyns ne soy ke plente fu; Tre fontane.* PERRIN D'AGINCOURT: *Quant voi en la fin d'este.* Cantigas de Santa Maria: *Se ome fezer; Nas mentes semper teer; Como poden per sas culpas; Maravillosos et piadosos.*
*** CRD CRD 3421; *CRDC 4121* [id.].

As so often when early music is imaginatively re-created, one is astonished at the individuality of many of the ideas. This applies particularly to the second item in this collection, *Quant voi en la fin d'este*, attributed to the mid-thirteenth-century trouvère, Perrin d'Agincourt, but no less to the four Cantigas de Santa Maria. The instrumentation is at times suitably robust but does not eschew good intonation and subtle effects. The group is recorded vividly and the acoustics of St James, Clerkenwell, are never allowed to cloud detail. The sound is admirably firm and real in its CD format.

(Heinrich) Schütz Choir, Roger Norrington

'A Baroque Christmas' (with London String Players, Philip Jones Brass Ensemble; Camden Wind Ensemble; Charles Spinks): SCHUTZ: *Hodie Christus natus est; Ach Herr, du Schöpfer aller Ding.* PURCELL: *Behold I bring you glad tidings.* ANON.: *Soberana Maria.* HAMMERTSCHMIDT: *Alleluja! Freuet euch, ihr Christen alle.* BOUZIGNAC: *Noé! Pastores, cantate Dominum.* G. GABRIELI: *O magnum mysterium.* MONTEVERDI: *Christe Redemptor.* PRAETORIUS: *Singt, ihr lieben Christen all.* HASSLER: *Angeles ad pastores ait.*
🏵 (M) *** Decca 430 065-2; *430 065-4* [id.].

A superlative collection which celebrates the joyful Renaissance approach to Christmas. The glorious opening number is matched in memorability by the engaging lullaby, *Soberana Maria*, and *Noé! Pastores* has a delightful interplay between Gabriel (Hazel Holt) and the Shepherds. Giovanni Gabrieli's *O magnum mysterium* is justly famous and sounds superbly sonorous here, while the Michael Praetorius carol has a tune most will readily recognize. The performances are splendid and the 1968 analogue recording remains in the demonstration bracket. There are few more unusual or more rewarding Christmas celebrations than this.

Schwarzkopf, Dame Elisabeth (soprano)

'Encores' (with Gerald Moore or Geoffrey Parsons): BACH: *Bist du bei mir.* GLUCK: *Einem Bach der fliesst.* BEETHOVEN: *Wonne der Wehmut.* LOEWE: *Kleiner Haushalt.* WAGNER: *Träume.* BRAHMS: *Ständchen; 3 Deutsche Volkslieder.* MAHLER: *Um schlimme Kinder artig zu machen; Ich atmet' einen linden Duft; Des Antonius von Padua Fischpredigt.* TCHAIKOVSKY: *Pimpernella.* arr. WOLF-FERRARI: *7 Italian songs.* MARTINI: *Plaisir d'amour.* HAHN: *Si mes vers avaient des ailes.* DEBUSSY: *Mandoline.* arr. QUILTER: *Drink to me only with thine eyes.* ARNE: *When daisies pied; Where the bee sucks.* arr. GUND: *3 Swiss folk songs.* arr. WEATHERLY: *Danny Boy.* J. STRAUSS, Jnr: *Frühlingsstimmen* (with VPO, Joseph Krips).
(M) *** EMI stereo/mono CDM7 63654-2.

Schwarzkopf herself has on occasion nominated this charming account of *Danny Boy* as her own favourite recording of her singing, but it is only one of a whole sequence of lightweight songs which vividly capture the charm and intensity that made her recitals so memorable, particularly in the extra items at the end. As a rule she would announce and explain each beforehand, adding to the magic. The range here is wide, from Bach's heavenly *Bist du bei mir* to the innocent lilt of the Swiss folksong, *Gsätzli*, and Strauss's *Voices of spring*.

'Unpublished recordings' (with (i) Philh. O, Thurston Dart; (ii) Kathleen Ferrier, VPO, Karajan; (iii) Philh. O, Galliera; (iv) Walter Gieseking, Philh. O, Karajan): J. S. BACH: (i) *Cantata No. 199: Mein Herze schwimmt im Blut: Auf diese Schmerzens Reu; Doch Gott muss mir genädig sein; Mein Herze schwimmt im Blut.* (ii) *Mass in B min.: Christe eleison; Et in unum Dominum; Laudamus te.* (iii) MOZART: *Nehmt meinen Dank, K.383.* (iv) GIESEKING: *Kinderlieder.* R. STRAUSS: *4 Last songs.* (M) (**(*)) EMI CDM7 63655-2.

Long-buried treasure here includes Bach duets with Kathleen Ferrier conducted by Karajan, a collection of charming children's songs by Gieseking, recorded almost impromptu, and, best of all, a live performance of Strauss's *Four Last songs* given under Karajan at the Festival Hall in 1956, a vintage year for Schwarzkopf. Sound quality varies, but the voice is gloriously caught.

Seefried, Irmgard (soprano)

Lieder (with Erik Werba, piano): MOZART: *Das Veilchen; Die Verschweigung; Das Lied der Trennung; Das Kinderspiel; Die kleine Spinnerin; Als Luise die Briefe ihres ungetreuen Liebhabers verbrannte; Einsam ging ich jüngst im Haine; An Chloe; Abendempfindung; Sehnsucht nach dem Frühling.* SCHUBERT: *Auf dem Wasser zu singen; Lachen und Weinen.* BRAHMS: *Dein blaues Auge hält so still; Ständchen.* MUSSORGSKY: *The Nursery* (cycle). BARTOK: *Village scenes* (cycle). WOLF: *An eine Äolsharfe; Das verlassene Mägdlein; Begegnung.* R. STRAUSS: *Ständchen.* SCHUMANN: *Die Lotosblume; Mit Myrten und Rosen; Du bist wie eine Blume; Frauenliebe und Leben* (cycle). SCHUBERT: *Der König in Thule; Das Lied im Grünen; Die junge Nonne; Fischerweise; Seligkeit; Die Forelle; An die Musik.* R. STRAUSS: *Traum durch die Dämmerung; Meinem Kinde; Allerseelen; Morgen.*
☞ ⊛ (M) *** DG mono/stereo 437 348-2 (2).

This tribute to a much-loved singer of German Lieder in the 1950s and early '60s has been lovingly assembled to make a superb continuous recital which, taken in two sections, gives some two hours and fifteen minutes of sheer delight. After the Mozart group, which she sings with appealing freshness (the last two songs, *Abendempfindung* and *Sehnsucht nach dem Frühling*, are given a Schubertian lilt), comes an enchanting series of live recordings made in 1953, including the sparkling Bartók *Village scenes* and the hardly less engaging Mussorgsky group, ending with a rapturous account of Strauss's *Ständchen*. The songs in the second half are hardly less captivating. Schumann's *Die Lotosblume* and *Du bist wie eine Blume* are ravishing, and Seefried brings her own experience to the great *Frauenliebe und -leben* cycle. The last song may not have quite the passionate intensity of Dame Janet Baker's famous version, but the colourless tone and withdrawn emotion create a strong impression after the earlier songs have revelled in the young bride's happier experiences, with the song about the wedding ring (*Du Ring an meinem Finger*) particularly poignant. Erik Werba accompanies with complete understanding and the vivid sound is equally realistic throughout; the ear can hardly tell that only the closing Schubert and Strauss songs, recorded mainly in 1958, are in stereo. Full documentation makes this a very desirable set indeed.

The Sixteen, Harry Christophers

Music from the Eton Choirbook
Volume I, *'The Rose and the ostrich feather'*: FAYRFAX: *Magnificat (Regale).* HYGONS: *Salve regina.* TURGES: *From stormy wyndis.* BROWNE: *Stabat iuxta Christi Crucem.* ANON.: *This day dawes.* CORNYSH: *Salve regina.*
☞ *** Collins Dig. 1314-2 [id.].

Volume II, *'Crown of thorns'*: DAVY: *Stabat mater.* BROWNE: *Jesu, mercy, how may this be?; Stabat mater.* CORNYSH: *Stabat mater.* SHERYNGHAM: *Ah, gentle Jesus.*
☞ *** Collins Dig. 1316-2 [id.].

Volume III, 'The Pillars of Eternity': CORNYSH: *Ave Maria, mater Dei.* DAVY: *O Domine caeli terraeque; A myn hart remembir the well; A blessed Jheso.* LAMBE: *Stella caeli.* WILKINSON: *Credo in Deum – Jesus autem; Salve regina.*
☞ *** Collins Dig. 1342-2 [id.].

Volume IV: 'The Flower of all Virginity': Hugh KELLY: *Gaude flore Virginali.* ANON.: *Ah, my dear, ah, my dear Son!; Afraid, alas, and why so suddenly?* NESBETT: *Magnificat.* FAYRFAX: *Most clear of colour.* BROWNE: *Salve regina; O Maria salvatoris mater.*
☞ *** Collins Dig. 1395-2 [id.].

This is a glorious anthology, gloriously sung. The music in the Eton Choirbook was not restricted to local performance and the emblems which give the first volume its sobriquet demonstrate the link with the Chapel Royal. What the chosen music also demonstrates (as with other anthologies of early church music) is the close links between secular music and music for worship. Throughout the rich textures with soaring trebles are thrilling. The settings of Cornysh and John Browne are particularly memorable: the latter's *O Maria Salvatoris Mater* which closes the fourth volume is breathtakingly beautiful. Volume IV is devoted to Marian antiphons but includes also the Nesbett *Magnificat* and three songs which have associations with the Marian theme and which certainly do not lack intensity. The second volume, 'Crown of Thorns', centres on setting of the *Stabat Mater* and adds to the two composers mentioned the music of Richard Davy; the third explores Davy's output further in the ambitious and profound *O Domine caeli.* Two new names also appear in this tribute to musical eternity, Robert Wilkinson's complex canon, *Credo in Deum – Jesus autem*, and Lambe's impressive *Stella caeli.* But perhaps the best place to start exploring this remarkable series is Volume 4, 'The Flower of all Virginity', which opens with Hugh Kellyk's glowing appraisal of the Virgin: *Gaude flore virginali* ('Rejoice in the flower of your maidenhood, and in the special honour due to you, surpass all the shining hosts of angels'). Christophers seem to have an instinct for the right tempo for these tonally abundant works with their flowing lines, and the expansive beauty of the choral sound never interferes with one's ability to hear the detail. The Sixteen constantly produce radiant tone and their performances match warm, expressive feeling with commendable accuracy of intonation.

American choral music: BARBER: *Agnus Dei; Reincarnations, Op. 16.* FINE: *The hour glass.* REICH: *Clapping music.* BERNSTEIN: *The Lark* (choruses). COPLAND: *4 Motets.* DEL TREDICI: *Final Alice* (acrostic song).
☞ **(*) Collins Dig. 1287-2 [id.].

The Sixteen now make a big jump from the early sixteenth century to the mid-twentieth. They begin with our old friend, Barber's *Adagio*, but in choral form as an *Agnus Dei*, and here the choral climax compares well with the intensity of the better string versions. Reich's *Clapping* literally welcomes the Bernstein choruses (incidental music for a Hellman play) but Copland's *Four Motets* – a 1921 student work – is not typical, and the rest of the programme has a more limited appeal, though very well sung and recorded.

Souzay, Gérard (baritone)

Mélodies (with Jacqueline Bonneau): FAURE: *Tristesse; Au bord de l'eau; Après un rêve; Clair de lune; Arpège; En sourdine; L'Horizon chimérique; Spleen; C'est l'extase; Prison; Mandoline.* CHAUSSON: *Nanny; Le charme; Sérénade italienne; Le Colibri; Cantique à l'épouse; Les papillons; Le temps de lilas.* Airs: BOESSET: *Me veux-tu voir mourir?.* ANON.: *Tambourin.* BATAILLE: *Cachez, beaux yeux; Ma bergère non légère.* CANTELOUBE: *Brezairola; Malurous qu'o uno fenno.*
⊛ (M) (***) Decca mono 425 975-2.

The great French baritone made these recordings for Decca when he was at the very peak of his form. The Fauré were recorded in 1950 and the glorious Chausson songs in 1953. Souzay was endowed with the intelligence of Bernac as well as his powers of characterization, the vocal purity of Panzera and a wonderful feeling for line. The Decca transfer does complete justice to the original sound, and it is good to have these performances without the surface distractions of LP. Full texts and translations are provided. A marvellous record worth as many rosettes as stars!

Streich, Rita (soprano)

Lieder: (with (i) Erich Werba; (ii) Günther Weissenborn): (a) (i) MOZART: *An Chloe; Die kleine Spinnerin; Das Lied der Trennung; Das Veilchen; Der Zauberer; Sehnsucht nach dem Frühling; Un moto di gioia; Oiseaux, si tous les ans; Dans un bois solitaire; Das Kinderspiel; An die Einsamkeit; Die Verschweigung. Warnung.* SCHUBERT: *Die Forelle; Auf dem Wasser zu singen; Seligkeit.* WOLF:

Wohin mit der Freud?; Wiegenlied; Die Kleine; Nachtgruss. R. STRAUSS: *Der Stern; Einerlei; Schleschtes Wetter.* MILHAUD: *Au clair de la lune. 4 Chansons de Ronsard, Op. 223; Folksongs: Canto delle risaiole; Gsätzli; Z'Lauterbach.* (b) (i) SCHUBERT: *Heidenröslein; Arietta der Claudine; Lied der Mignon II; Nähe des Geliebten; Liebhabner in allen Gestalten; Der Hirt auf dem Felsen* (with Heinrich Geuser); *An den Mond; Die Vögel; Das Lied im Grünen.* (b) SCHUMANN: *Der Nussbaum; Die Stille; Schneeglöcken; Die Lotusblume; Intermezzo; Aufträge.* BRAHMS: *Ständchen; Mädchenlied; Vergebliches Ständchen; Wiegenlied.* (a) WOLF: *Verschwiegene Liebe; Die Spröde; Die Bekehrte; Der Gärtner.* (b) R. STRAUSS: *Schlagende Herzen; Wiegenlied; Amor; An die Nacht.*
☞ (M) ** DG (a) mono; (b) stereo 437 680-2 (2) [id.].

Rita Streich's voice was naturally suited to Mozart, and on the first of these two discs, recorded in mono, these simple songs cannot fail to touch the listener: *Das Veilchen* is gently ravishing and the line of *An Die Einsamkeit* is beautifully shaped, while *Warnung* is made to sound charmingly operatic. When it comes to the first group of Schubert Lieder, however, charm is not enough; one needs to feel more involvement with the words, and the same applies to Wolf, although the *Wiegenlied* suits her style admirably. The radiant vocalism cannot fail to add a rich colouring in a song like Richard Strauss's *Der Stern*, while *Schlechtes Wetter* has an attractive lightness of touch. But the outstanding highlight of the first of these two CDs is the songs of Milhaud. Her easy coloratura encompasses the leaps and vocal bravura of the *Chansons de Ronsard* quite spectacularly, especially the engaging *Tais-toi babillarde* ('Hush your chatter') and the delightful *Dieu vous gard'* ('God keep you faithful harbingers of Spring'). The three folksongs become delectable lollipops, especially the petite valse, *Gsätzli*, and the ravishing vocalise, *Canto delle risaiole*, while *Au clair de la lune* and *Z'Lauterbach* (with its lightly pointed upper tessitura) show her at her most enchanting. These songs need to be extracted for separate issue. On technical grounds there need be no qualms, so vivid is the sound-picture that this might almost be stereo.

The second disc offers stereo recordings made between 1959 and 1961 while the voice was still as fresh as ever, as the opening *Heidenröslein* of Schubert shows. She sings throughout with ease and purity of tone: the line of the *Ariette der Claudine* cannot be faulted. There is also much evidence of a keenly sensitive mind, not perhaps that of a born Lieder singer, but certainly that of a born musicisn. In her generation Fischer-Dieskau and Gérard Souzay set such a high standard for German Lied that it is perhaps too easy to criticize other artists whose approach is different. In the famous 'Shepherd on the rock' (*Der Hirt auf dem Felsen*) she forms an almost instrumental partnership with the fine clarinet soloist, Heinrich Geuser, and there is no doubt of the appeal of *Die Vögel* when the vocalism is without any kind of blemish. She is certainly sympathetic to the more withdrawn mood of many of the Schumann songs and finds an affinity with Brahms too, especially in *Vergebliches Ständchen* and the lovely *Wiegenlied*. Her directness of manner can be very effective in a song like Wolf's *Der Gärtner*, and she has her own way with the closing Richard Strauss group. Throughout, she is accompanied most sympathetically, and the recording is very real and natural.

Tallis Scholars, Peter Phillips

'*Christmas carols and motets*': *Ave Maria* settings by JOSQUIN DES PRES; VERDELOT; VICTORIA. *Coventry carol* (2 settings). BYRD: *Lullaby.* PRAETORIUS: *Es ist ein Ros'entsprungen; Joseph lieber, Joseph mein; In dulci jubilo; Wachet auf.* BACH: *Wachet auf.* Medieval carols: *Angelus ad virginem; There is no rose; Nowell sing we.*
*** Gimell Dig. CDGIM 010; *1585T-10* [id.].

There is something unique about a carol, and even the very early music here has that special intensity of inspiration which brings memorability. There are some familiar melodies too, notably those set by Praetorius; but much of this repertoire will come as refreshingly new to most ears. The singing has a purity of spirit. The CD is very much in the demonstration class for the clear choral image, heard against the ideal acoustics of St Pierre et St Paul, Salle, Norfolk.

'*Western Wind Masses*': SHEPPARD: *Mass, The Western wynde.* TAVERNER: *Mass, Western Wynde.* TYE: *Mass, Western wind.*
☞ *** Gimell Dig. CDGIM 027; *1585T-27* (cassette also includes ANON.: *Westron Wynde ***).

It was a splendid idea for Gimell to gather together the three key Mass settings which use the the well-known source theme, the Western (which, incidentally, is given a separate presentation on the cassette, but not on the CD, which already plays for 80 minutes). The performances are as eloquent as we can expect from this source and they are beautifully recorded. Taverner's setting emerges as the most imaginative, but Tye comes pretty close. A most enterprising issue which deserves support.

Taverner Consort, Choir and Players, Andrew Parrott

'Venetian church music': GABRIELI: *Intonazione del non tono; In ecclesiis; Canzon VIII; Fuga del nono tono; Magnificat.* MONTEVERDI: *Adoramus te, Christ; Currite populi; Christe, adoramus te.* GRANDI: *O quam tu pulchra es.* CASTELLO: *Sonata seconda.* LEGRENZI: *Sonata da chiesa.* LOTTI: *Crucifixus.*
☞ *** EMI Dig. CDC7 54117-2 [id.].

This superb collection brings home what inspired music was written for St Mark's, Venice, in addition to what we know by Monteverdi and the Gabrielis. The tradition persisted and developed over the century which followed, thanks to such composers as Giovanni Legrenzi and Antonio Lotti, a contemporary of Vivaldi. The choral items are aptly punctuated by such fine instrumental pieces as Dario Castello's *Sonata secunda* (with John Holloway the expressive violinist), heightening the impact of such magnificent motets as *In ecclesiis* by Giovanni Gabrieli, in Andrew Parrott's skilled hands expansive as well as brilliant.

'The Carol album': ANON.: *Veni, veni Emmanuel; Stille Nacht; Il est né, le divin enfant; Nova! Nova!; Marche des rois; The Babe of Bethlehem; Verbum caro; Y la Virgen; Glory to God on high; This endere nyghth; O Jesulein süss; God rest you merry, gentlemen; Swete was the song the Virgine soong; Quem pastores laudavere; Quanno nascete ninno; Riu, riu, chiu; Gabriel fram heven-king; Christum wir sollen loben schon; Coventry carol; Gaudete! Verbum caro; In hac anni circulo; Alleluya; A nywe werk is come on hondde; The old year now away is fled; Ding! dong! merrily on high (Branle de l'Officiel).*
☞ *** EMI Dig. CDC7 49809-2 [id.].

'The Carol album' 2: TYE: *While shepherds watched.* HOPKINS: *Three Kings of Orient.* NILES: *I wonder as I wander; Lullay, thou tiny little child; Procedenti Puero-Eya! novus annus est.* ANON.: *Qui crevit celum (Song of the Nunns of Chester); There is no rose of swych Vertu. Quelle est cette odeur agréable?* arr. JOUBERT: *There is no rose of such virtue.* BENDINELLI: *Sonata for 3 trumpets on Joseph, lieber, Joseph mein.* English TRAD.: *All hayle to the dayes; The Lord at first did Adam make.* French TRAD.: *O du fröhliche! O du selige!; Lullay, lullay: Als I lay on Yoolis Night.* Sarum Plainchant: *Letabundus.* THOMSEN: *Sonata for 5 trumpets based upon In dulci jubilo.* MENDELSSOHN: *Hark! the Herald Angels sing* (with WESLEY: organ interlude).
☞ *** EMI Dig. CDC7 54902-2 [id.].

The Taverner group's much-praised first Christmas record was initially missed by us. Now the balance is redressed and we include also the even more successful second collection, which has perhaps greater general appeal. In Volume I Andrew Parrott sought to go back to the originals of these Chrismas songs, from early medieval times through almost to the present day, and the result is unusually refreshing, with simplicity the keynote, yet with great variety inherent in the programme itself. The performances are sometimes robust, sometimes tenderly gentle, but always vivid and appealing, and the recording is first class.

The second disc is even more stimulating. It opens and closes with favourites, but in between comes the widest range of styles, with some delightful solo performances: *I wonder as I wander, Lullay, thou little tiny child* and *Lullay, lullay: Als I lay on Yoolis night. The Song of the Chester Nunns* is particularly beautiful, as is the fifteenth-century English version of the famous *Ther is no rose of swych vertu,* which makes a contrast with Joubert's adaptation of an even barer medieval setting of the same carol. The Sarum Plainchant, *Letabundus,* is made the more telling by a tolling bell, and the two traditional English carols are presented in a robust, colloquial manner. The recording is most realistically balanced, with the ecclesiastical acoustic perfectly managed. It need hardly be said that on both CDs documentation is excellent.

'The Christmas Album' (Festive music from Europe and America): BILLINGS: *Methinks I see an heav'nly host; A virgin unspotted.* FOSTER: *While shepherds watched their flocks.* CEREROLS: *Serafin, quin con dulce harmonia.* Francisco de VIDALES: *Los que fueren de buen gusto.* PRAETORIUS: *Magnificat super Angelus ad pastores.* Marc-Antoine CHARPENTIER: *In nativitatem Domini nostri Jesu Christi canticum.* PASCHA: *Gloria.* arr. GREATOREX: *Adeste fidelis.*
☞ (M) *** EMI Dig. CDC7 54529-2 [id.].

A refreshing new Christmas collection which treads much unfamiliar territory. Opening and closing with jolly carols that sound almost like rustic drinking songs, from the New England composer William Billings – with the chorus giving their pronunciation an appropriate transatlantic tang – the concert moves from a bright baroque setting of *While shepherds watched their flocks,* a new tune, with Bachian trumpets, by John Foster (1762–1822) to a haunting *Gloria* by Edmund Pascha. This represents Slovakia; from France there is a charming Christmas sequence by Marc-Antoine Charpentier. In between comes a gloriously sonorous *Magnificat* by Michael Praetorius and, at last something familiar, *Adeste fidelis*, arranged by Thomas Greatorex in a choral *concerto grosso* style. Best of all are the *Villancicos*, one by Joan Cererols from Catalonia, one even jollier by the seventeenth-century Mexican, Francisco de Vidales, which in their colour and vitality reflect the popular dance music of the time. Performances are as lively as they are stylish and the soloists are excellent. The recording has plenty of atmosphere and presence.

Walker, Sarah (mezzo-soprano), Roger Vignoles (piano)

'*Dreams and fancies*' (Favourite English songs): IRELAND: *If there were dreams to sell*. DELIUS: *Twilight fancies*. ARMSTRONG GIBBS: *Silver; Five eyes*. VAUGHAN WILLIAMS: *Silent noon; The water mill*. WARLOCK: *The fox; Jillian of Berry; The first mercy; The night*. SULLIVAN: *Orpheus with his lute*. HOWELLS: *King David; Gavotte; Come sing and dance. The little road to Bethlehem*. STANFORD: *The monkey's carol*. BRIDGE: *Isobel*. CLARKE: *The seal man; The aspidestra*. HAVELOCK NELSON: *Dirty work*. HOIBY: *Jabberwocky*. QUILTER: *Now sleeps the crimson petal*. GURNEY: *Sleep*. DUNHILL: *The cloths of heaven*.
☞ *** CRD Dig. CRD 3473; *CRDC 4173* [id.].

A well-designed and delightful programme, and it is good to see the Roger Quilter favourite, *Now sleeps the crimson petal*, back in favour alongside both the familiar and unfamilar items included here. Dunhill's *The cloths of heaven*, too, leaves the listener wanting more. The secret of a miscellaneous (72 minutes) recital like this is for each song to lead naturally into the next, and that is what happens here, while the listener relaxes and enjoys each contrasted setting as it flows by. Sarah Walker is in inspired form and is very well accompanied.

Walker, Sarah (mezzo-soprano), Thomas Allen (baritone)

'*The Sea*' (with Roger Vignoles, piano): IRELAND: *Sea fever*. HAYDN: *Mermaid's song; Sailor's song*. DIBDIN: *Tom Bowling*. WALTON: *Song for the Lord Mayor's table; Wapping Old Stairs*. WOLF: *Seemanns Abschied*. FAURE: *Les Berceaux; Au cimetière; L'horizon chimerique*. SCHUBERT: *Lied eines Schiffers an die Dioskuren*. BORODIN: *The Sea; The Sea Princess*. DEBUSSY: *Proses lyriques: De grève*. IVES: *Swimmers*. SCHUMANN: *Die Meerfee*. BERLIOZ: *Nuits d'été: L'ile inconnue*. MENDELSSOHN: *Wasserfahrt*. BRAHMS: *Die Meere*. TRAD.: *The Mermaid*. Arr. BRITTEN: *Sail on, sail on*.
✪ *** Hyp. CDA 66165 [id.].

With Roger Vignoles as master of ceremonies in a brilliantly devised programme, ranging wide, this twin-headed recital celebrating 'The Sea' is a delight from beginning to end. Two outstandingly characterful singers are mutually challenged to their very finest form, whether in solo songs or duets. As sample, try the setting of the sea-song, *The Mermaid*, brilliantly arranged by Vignoles, with hilarious key-switches on the comic quotations from *Rule Britannia*. Excellent recording.

Westminster Cathedral Choir, David Hill

'*Treasures of the Spanish Renaissance*': GUERRERO: *Surge propera amica mea; O altitudo divitiarum; O Domine Jesu Christe; O sacrum convivium; Ave, Virgo sanctissima; Regina coeli laetare*. LOBO: *Versa est in luctum; Ave Maria; O quam suavis es, Domine*. VIVANCO: *Magnificat octavi toni*.
*** Hyp. CDA 66168 [id.].

This immensely valuable collection reminds us vividly that Tomas Luis de Victoria was not the only master of church music in Renaissance Spain. Francisco Guerrero is generously represented here, and the spacious serenity of his polyphonic writing (for four, six and, in *Regina coeli laetare*, eight parts) creates the most beautiful sounds. A criticism might be made that tempi throughout this collection, which also includes fine music by Alonso Lobo and a superb eight-part *Magnificat* by Sebastian de Vivanco, are too measured, but the tension is held well, and David Hill is obviously concerned to convey the breadth of the writing. The singing is gloriously firm, with the long melismatic lines admirably controlled. Discreet accompaniments (using Renaissance double harp, bass dulcian and organ) do not affect the essentially a cappella nature of the performances. The Westminster Cathedral acoustic means the choral tone is richly upholstered, but the focus is always firm and clear.

Westminster Cathedral Choir, James O'Donnell

'Masterpieces of Mexican polyphony': FRANCO: *Salve regina.* PADILLA: *Deus in adiutorium; Mirabilia testimonium; Lamentation for Maundy Thursday; Salve regina.* CAPILLAS: *Dis nobis, Maria; Magnificat.* SALAZAR: *O sacrum convivium.*
☞ *** Hyp. Dig. CDA 66330 [id.].

The Westminster Choir under James O'Donnell are finding their way into hithero unexplored Latin vocal repertoire – and what vocal impact it has! These musicians were employed in the new cathedrals when Spain colonized Mexico; only Capillas was native-born (though of Spanish descent). Padilla shows he had brought over a powerful Renaissance inheritance with him and uses double choir interplay to spectacularly resonant effect. Not all the other music is as ambitious as this, but there is a devotional concentration of feeling which illuminates even the simpler settings. The singing has the body and fervour this music needs, and the choir is splendidly recorded.

'Masterpieces of Portuguese polyphony': CARDOSO: *Lamentations for Maundy Thursday; Non mortui; Sitvit anima mea; Mulier quae erat; Tulerunt lapides; Nos autem gloriosi.* REBELO: *Panis angelicus.* DE CRISTO: *3 Christmas responsories; Magnificat a 8; Ave Maria a 8; Alma redemptoris mater; Ave maris stella; O crux venerabilis; Sanctissima quinque martires; Lachrimans sitivit; De profundis.*
☞ *** Hyp. Dig. CDA 66512; *KA 66512* [id.].

With the help of the Tallis Scholars we have already discovered Manuel Cardoso and the unique character of Portuguese Renaissance music. The present collection duplicates four of the motets on the Tallis Scholars' CD, but the Westminster performances are slightly more robust and add to their character. The *Lamentations for Maundy Thursday* show the composer at his most imaginatively expressive, 'a resplendent example of his chromatic serenity', as Ivan Moody, the writer of the excellent notes on this CD, aptly puts it. The music of Cardoso's contemporary, Pedro de Cristo (*c.* 1550–1618) is hardly less individual. His *Magnificat a 8* for two choirs is particularly arresting, as is the much simpler *O magnum mysterium*, while the *Sanctissimi quinque martires* (celebrating five Franciscans who were killed in 1220 while attempting to convert Moroccan Moslems) has a radiant, flowing intensity. Rebelo's *Panis angelicus* is rich in its harmonic feeling, and Fernandez's *Alma redemptoris mater* ends the programme in a mood of quiet contemplation.